McKinley
Internet Directory
New Edition

Christine Maxwell
The McKinley Group, Inc.

New Riders Publishing, Indianapolis, Indiana

Published by:
New Riders Publishing
201 West 103rd Street
Indianapolis, IN 46290 USA

All rights reserved. No part of this book may be reproduced or transmitted in any form or by any means, electronic or mechanical, including photocopying, recording, or by any information storage and retrieval system, without written permission from the publisher, except for the inclusion of brief quotations in a review.

Copyright © 1995 by The McKinley Group, Inc.

Printed in the United States of America 1 2 3 4 5 6 7 8 9 0

CIP data available upon request

Warning and Disclaimer

This book is designed to provide information about the Internet and the World Wide Web. Every effort has been made to make this book as complete and as accurate as possible, but no warranty or fitness is implied.

The information is provided on an "as is" basis. The author and New Riders Publishing shall have neither liability nor responsibility to any person or entity with respect to any loss or damages arising from the information contained in this book or from the use of the disks or programs that may accompany it.

Trademark Acknowledgments

All terms mentioned in this book that are known to be trademarks or service marks have been appropriately capitalized. New Riders Publishing cannot attest to the accuracy of this information. Use of a term in this book should not be regarded as affecting the validity of any trademark or service mark.

New Riders Publishing

Publisher	Don Fowley
Marketing Manager	Ray Robinson
Acquisitions Manager	Jim LeValley
Managing Editor	Tad Ringo

About the Authors

Christine Maxwell is Senior Vice President and Publisher for The McKinley Group. She is also President and CEO, of Research On Demand (ROD), an information search and retrieval organization. Maxwell has been in the information brokering business for over 15 years.

Previously, she worked in senior positions in the international scientific and educational publishing industry. She was Director of Pergamon Press Publishers from 1982-1991. She is also a trained elementary school teacher and has taught for several years in British and American public schools.

She is the creator and co-author of New Riders Official Internet Yellow Pages . Maxwell particularly likes to focus her writing skills on books that deal with problems of information access. Her eclectic background has proven well-suited to exploring the Internet and helping its riches become more accessible to everyone.

The McKinley Group was founded in 1993 by a team of international publishers and information specialists, committed to delivering the best navigational and informational directory for the Internet.

The McKinley Internet Directory, the company's innovative online Internet directory, contains listings for hundreds-of-thousands of sites, many of which are fully described, reviewed and rated (with one to four stars) by the McKinley Group's in-house team of high-level subject matter specialists, in coordination with The McKinley Editorial Advisory Board, a panel of international experts.

About the Licensees

AT&T, IBM, NETCOM and Nynex have licensed the McKinley data for use in their own Internet environments. If you would like information about licensing McKinley data, please contact the McKinley Group directly at: license@mckinley.com

The McKinley Group, Inc.
85 Liberty Ship Way, Suite 201
Sausalito, CA 94965-1768, USA
Tel +1 (415) 331-1884
Fax +1 (415) 331-8609

Acknowledgments

Special thanks are due to:

Isabel Maxwell and David Hayden for their special support in the preparation of this new edition. Thanks are particularly due to Rick Wilson both for his excellent work and overall management assistance, Suresh Thakur for his excellent programming work and un-ending patience, and to Helen Yoon for her editorial management, very hard work on the directory taxonomy and driving the work to its final completion! To James A. Hammett for his writing and work on the Internet Highlights and newsgroups and all the other editors and support staff mentioned below.

Database Development
David Hayden
Isabel Maxwell
Alex Cohen

Programming
Suresh Thakur

Programming Support
Patrick Deharveng

Technical Support
Alex Cohen
Behram Anita
Reuben Antman
Mark Walsh

Managing Editor
Helen Yoon

Indexing Support
Elinor Lindheimer
Tony Lincoln

Editorial Staff
Paul Anderson
Penny Benda
Margaret de Santos
Alex Frankel
Monique Gross
James A. Hammett
Richard Howard
Cara Lee Kahn
Jennifer Lind
Michael Pederson
Barbara Lee Williams

Administrative Support
Hillary Hayden
Jeremy Bled

Public Relations
Helene Atkin

Design
Richard A. Wilson, Intelligent Tool & Eye, San Francisco, CA

Cover Illustration
Jack Kendrick, San Francisco, CA

Production
Becky Brockmann
I.Q. Technologies, Ltd., Clayton, MO

Contents at a Glance

Preface　　1
Introduction　　3

1
How to Use this Directory　　9

2
Internet Listings
Listed by Major Category and Sub Category

Arts & Music	15
Business & Economics	101
Communications	153
Computing & Mathematics	169
Education	233
Engineering & Technology	291
Government & Politics	313
Health & Medicine	367
Humanities & Social Sciences	413
Internet	453
Law & Criminal Justice	489
Popular Culture & Entertainment	509
Religion & Philosophy	557
Science	565
Sports & Recreation	619

3
Email and Mailing Lists　　673

4
Newsgroups　　705

5
Commercial Online Services　　741

6
A Whimsical Internet Tour　　757

Appendices

A Internet Highlights Index　　761

B International Internet Providers　　763

C Glossary of Terms and Acronyms　　775

D Keyword Index　　783

E Audience Index　　809

F How to Add or Update a Resource in this Directory　　819

Credits　　820

Contents

Preface   *1*
Introduction   *3*

1
How to Use this Directory   9

Organization of directory   *9*
What's in a rating?   *10*
What's in a listing?   *11*
What's on a page?   *12*

2
Internet Listings
Listed by Major Category and Sub Category

Arts & Music   15

Architecture   *15*
Art Galleries   *17*
Art History   *21*
Art Museums   *22*
Art Organizations   *27*
Art Resources   *28*
Artists   *31*
Arts Funding   *32*
Career & Employment   *33*
Decorative Arts   *33*
Design   *33*
Electronic Arts   *34*
Film & Video   *47*
Music Genres   *50*
Music History   *57*
Music Organizations   *58*
Music Resources   *62*
Musical Groups   *71*
Musicians   *82*
Performing Arts   *90*
Visual Arts   *97*

Business & Economics   101

Accounting   *101*
Advertising & Marketing   *102*
Banking   *104*
Benefits   *106*
Business Schools   *106*
Career & Employment   *109*
Commerce   *112*
Consumer Issues   *116*
Economics   *117*
Finance   *118*
Home Office   *119*
Industries   *120*
International Business   *125*
Investment   *128*
Management   *133*
Non Profits   *134*
Publishing   *136*
Real Estate   *140*
Reference   *142*
Retail   *145*
Services   *148*

Communications   153

Communications   *153*
Mass Communications   *154*
Networking   *158*
Organizations   *161*
Telecommunications   *163*

Contents

Computing & Mathematics 169

Analysis 169	Mathematical Formulae 194	Resources 215
Applications 169	Mathematics 195	Software 220
Artificial Intelligence 176	Networking 201	Standards 228
Career & Employment 179	Operating Systems 203	Statistics 228
Companies 179	Organizations 205	Systems 229
Computer Science 185	Programming 209	Theory 232
Hardware 193	Reference 213	

Education 233

Academic Libraries 233	Funding 249	Universities - Africa 264
Alternative Education 237	Government Libraries 250	Universities - Asia (including Middle East) 264
Career & Employment 237	International Education 250	Universities - Australia 266
Continuing Education 239	Language Acquisition 252	Universities - Canada 267
Curriculum & Instruction 240	Organizations 252	Universities - Europe (including Eastern Europe) 270
Distance Education 241	Primary & Secondary Education 255	Universities - South America 275
Educational Issues 242	Professional Education 260	Universities - United States 276
Educational Policy 243	Public Libraries 260	Vocational Education 288
Educational Projects 244	Resources 261	
Educational Technology 246	Special Libraries 263	

Engineering & Technology 291

Aeronautical Engineering 291	Electrical Engineering 294	Mechanical Engineering 303
Bioengineering 292	Engineering 296	Nuclear Engineering 304
Career & Employment 292	Environmental Engineering 300	Standards 305
Chemical Engineering 293	Industrial Engineering 301	Technology 305
Civil Engineering 294	Material Science 303	Transportation Engineering 311

Government & Politics 313

Agencies 313	History 339	Policies 349
Career & Employment 320	Individuals 340	Political Science 353
Cities 320	International 340	Reference 355
Countries 330	Issues 344	Regions 359
Doctrines 339	Military 346	States 362

Health & Medicine 367

Addictions 367	Family Health 381	Public Health 396
Aging 367	Health Conditions 383	Reference 400
Alternative Medicine 368	Medical Schools 385	Resources 404
Biomedicine 370	Medical Specialties 389	Services 407
Career & Employment 371	Medicine 391	Sexuality 407
Dental Health 372	Mental Health 392	Sexually Transmitted Diseases 408
Disabilities 372	Organizations 394	Veterinary Medicine 409
Diseases 374	Personal Care 395	Women's Health 409

Humanities & Social Sciences 413

Anthropology 413
Archaeology 414
Area & Cultural Studies 414
Classics 422
Geography 423
History 424
Languages 427
Library & Information Studies 429
Linguistics 431
Literature 433
Psychology 445
Sociology 446
Women's Studies 450

Internet 453

Career & Employment 453
Internet Access 453
Internet Business 455
Internet Communications 458
Internet Issues 461
Internet Protocols 462
Internet Resources 462
Internet Security 470
Internet Services 472
Internet Tools 476
Networking 480
Organizations 482
Virtual Communities 482

Law & Criminal Justice 489

Business Law 489
Career & Employment 490
Conferences & Events 490
Constitutional Law 490
Criminal Justice 492
Environmental Law 492
Ethics 493
Family Law 494
Intellectual Property 495
International & Comparative Law 496
Judicial Branch 497
Law Schools 498
Legal History & Theory 500
Legal Issues 500
Legal Resources 500
Litigation & Procedures 502
Reference 503
Statutes 505
Tax Law 506
Torts 506

Popular Culture & Entertainment 509

Automobiles 509
Books 511
Celebrities & Personalities 516
Family & Community 517
Fashion 522
Genealogy 522
General Reference 523
Humor 525
Lifestyles 530
Magazines & Newspapers 533
Movies 541
Multimedia 543
Museums & Theme Parks 544
Shopping 545
Television 550
Unexplained Phenomena 552
Weather & Traffic 554

Religion & Philosophy 557

Doctrines 557
Mythology 557
Philosophy 558
Religions 559
Religious Artifacts 562
Religious History 562
Resources 562

Science 565

Agriculture 565
Aquatic Sciences 568
Astronomy 571
Biology 574
Biosciences 579
Botany 582
Career & Employment 584
Chemistry 585
Earth Sciences 587
Environmental Sciences 591
Geosciences 597
Individuals 600
Neurosciences 600
Organizations 601
Paleontology 603
Physics 603
Space Science 609
Zoology 613

Contents **vii**

Sports & Recreation 619

Aquatic Sports *619*
Aviation *620*
Career & Employment *621*
Crafts & Hobbies *621*
Food & Dining *624*

Games *634*
Gardening *636*
Motor Sports *638*
Organizations *639*
Outdoor Recreation *640*

Personal Fitness *642*
Pets & Animals *643*
Recreation *648*
Sports *648*
Travel & Tourism *653*

3

Email and Mailing Lists 673

Arts & Music *675*
Business & Economics *678*
Communications *679*
Computing & Mathematics *679*
Education *684*
Engineering & Technology *686*

Government & Politics *687*
Health & Medicine *688*
Humanities & Social Sciences *690*
Internet *693*
Law & Criminal Justice *695*
Popular Culture & Entertainment *696*

Religion & Philosophy *698*
Science *699*
Sports & Recreation *701*

4

Newsgroups 705

Arts & Music *708*
Business & Economics *709*
Communications *711*
Computing & Mathematics *711*
Education *718*
Engineering & Technology *719*

Government & Politics *719*
Health & Medicine *720*
Humanities & Social Sciences *722*
Internet *724*
Law & Criminal Justice *726*
Popular Culture & Entertainment *726*

Religion & Philosophy *733*
Science *734*
Sports & Recreation *735*

5

Commercial Online Services 741

America Online *741*
AT&T WorldNet Services *741*
BIX *742*
CompuServe *742*
Delphi *747*

eWorld *747*
GEnie *748*
IBM's infoMarket *751*
Internet MCI *751*
MSN (Microsoft Network) *752*

NETCOM *752*
Prodigy *752*
The WELL *753*
Women's Wire *756*

6

A Whimsical Internet Tour 757

Appendices

A
Internet Highlights Index — *761*

B
International Internet Providers — *763*

C
Glossary of Terms and Acronyms — *775*

D
Keyword Index — *783*

E
Audience Index — *809*

F
How to Add or Update a Resource in this Directory — *819*

Credits *820*

Cyberspace, the New Information Frontier

PREFACE

This McKinley Internet Directory is an abridged version of the McKinley database from which the first and second editions of *New Riders Official Internet Yellow Pages* were also created. Now that *The McKinley* is available online, it is appropriate to change the title of the work to more accurately reflect the origins of the content.

More Targeted Browsing

Everyone who has searched the Internet has been frustrated by the high number of times that they waste time opening up a site that contains little or no information or relevance to their search. This directory points clearly in a new direction. The use of a well developed organizing scheme and enhanced subject indexes ensures that resources can be easily located.

The McKinley provides comprehensive coverage of Internet sites but also adds unique value-added information about those sites. Each resource is carefully described, evaluated and rated for its contents, up-to-dateness, organization and ease of access, and then assigned a McKinley Star Rating. The information provided allows the Internet user to have a much better idea of what is in a given resource before they have to visit the site. This allows for much more effective and targeted browsing while at the same time giving the user a rating regarding the content within.

Many industries, not the least publishing, are questioning their place in this new paradigm - a place where anyone can self-publish, where the transference of a publisher's 'stamp of approval' is getting lost in the vast forest of information that is growing exponentially on the Net. *The McKinley* helps to bring back that stamp of approval by careful selection and evaluation of Internet resources and a unique focus on quality and presentation of that information in an easy-to-read and instantly understandable way.

The World Wide Web is revolutionizing access to and dissemination of administrative, technical, scientific and cultural knowledge. It commands the fascination of all who are already fortunate enough to be able to sample its extraordinary power - a power that is able to link text with graphics, sound and multimedia. This Directory mirrors this interest by extensive coverage of World Wide Web sites. The authors continue however, to recognize that major information sources continue to be found in other areas of the Internet - namely mailing lists and newsgroups. Ftp sites are also included as they continue to be major archival places, rich in resources.

At the same time, the global reach of the Internet means that more and more resources from around the world are being placed on the Net. *The McKinley* continues to pay special attention to the international reach of the Internet and to including content from around the world.

The door to cyberspace is wide open. Everyone can and should have an interest in the enterprise of creating cyberspace, a contribution to make and a historical mark to place upon it.

We are indeed contemplating the forming of a new world, a world that starts at the least as an extension of the world as we know it, but also one where the architecture of Cyberspace is in ferment and disarray and open to whoever has the courage and the vision to create the new cyber architecture for an information-based planet.

The goal of *The McKinley* is to provide all users with the most useful and informative Internet directory to help their rite of passage into the Internet be as easy and as immediately fulfilling as it can be.

Christine Maxwell
September 1995
publisher@mckinley.com

Introduction

- Accessing the Internet Today — 3
- The World Wide Web — 3
- The Future of the Web — 4
- Who Uses the Web? — 5
- Practicing 'Safe Internet' for your Children — 5
- Commerce on the Internet — 6
- Conclusion — 7

The McKinley Internet Directory has been carefully structured to ensure maximum ease in finding information and resources pertinent to our users' changing interests. The directory's extensive indices help to ensure that fact, along with the addition of cross-referencing of resources throughout the directory. This attention to detail and ease of use will ensure that subsequent editions will continue to be responsive to the needs of users.

Accessing the Internet Today

Accessing the Internet is getting easier by the day — at least in terms of the number of access providers that people can choose from. The major commercial online services (Services that provide an environment of carefully formulated information areas that only subscribers can access.) now include AOL (America OnLine), Compuserve, Delphi, Genie, MCI, MSN (Microsoft Network), Netcom, and Prodigy. Smaller commercial services like The WELL and Women's Wire are also growing in number. The growth of such smaller services indicates a growing market for the establishment of unique electronic communities in addition to providing Internet access. (Choose the provider that offers the most focused content for your information needs.) There are also tens of thousands of Internet providers around the world who simply provide direct Internet access. An overview of the major online services can be found in Part 6, while Appendix B provides information on how to find some international Internet Providers.

The World Wide Web

A unique place on the Internet

One of the main differences in this new edition is the amount of space given to listing resources that can be found on the World Wide Web. The World Wide Web (known as WWW or simply the Web), is part of the vast network of computers around the world that form a part of the Internet. The Web consists of individual documents or pages which are linked by a computer language called Hyper Text Markup Language (HTML). This language is what makes the Web exciting as it allows sound, graphics, and text to coexist on the same page; in effect making the Web a multimedia paradise. These linked pages form a web of documents that is world-wide in scope and that is the fastest growing part of the Internet.

Where did the Web start?

The WWW project was started by CERN (the European Laboratory for Particle Physics) in Geneva, Switzerland. Its purpose was to build a hypermedia system encompassing text, sound, and graphics, that allowed physicists to exchange research with each other in many parts of the world.

Hypertext

The tremendous advantage of hypertext is that within a hypertext document, if you want more information about a particular subject mentioned, you just click on the pointer (usually high-lighted text or a graphic) and it automatically takes you to the appropriate document or even to another place on the Internet — the links are built in and let you deal with the pointers in a seamless way.

All you need to view what the WWW has to offer is a web browser. We have listed some of the major web browsers on the next page.

Internet Browsers

Mosaic
Mosaic was the first graphical browser, and in many ways is synonymous with the Web. Developed at the National Center for Super Computing Applications (NCSA), this application has become the 'mother' to a number of very good alternatives — in particular, Netscape which has leapt ahead as the browser of choice. The strength of Mosaic and its offspring is in their straightforward graphical interface and ease of use. There is no need to switch between different Internet applications (like anonymous FTP, WAIS, and Gopher) as they are included in the browsers and operate automatically.

To download a free copy of Mosaic, you can access the following URLs:

Macintosh

http://www.ncsa.uiuc.edu/SDG/Software/
Brochure/MacSoftDesc.
html#MacMosaic

Windows

http://www.ncsa.uiuc.edu/SDG/Software/
WinMosaic/General.htm#obtain

UNIX

http://www.ncsa.uiuc.edu/SDG/Software/
Brochure/UNIXsoftDesc.
htmll#XMosaic

Netscape
Netscape was developed by Netscape Communications, a company founded by the creator of Mosaic, Marc Andreessen and Dr. James H. Clark, founder of Silicon Graphics, Inc. Essentially, Netscape further refines the concepts behind Mosaic. It behaves in a multithreaded manner, enabling you to start moving through documents while images are being downloaded. You can also open two or more Netscape windows to work with different Web pages simultaneously and it has a feature called *Bookmarks*. This feature allow you to place a marker into Netscape memory which remembers how to access a particular web site. In essence, Netscape keeps a list of favorite sites which you can access simply by highlighting and choosing. Also included are threaded-newsreading capabilities, mailing functions, and a text-only function which greatly speeds up access time.

To download a free copy of Netscape, you can access the following URL:

http://home.mcom.com/comprod/mirror/
index.html

Netcruiser
Netcruiser is a product of Netcom, a full-service Internet access provider. It is similar to the other browsers and also offers mail, news and WWW capabilities. In addition, it includes IRC (Internet Relay Channel) which is an application that allows real-time chatting with other people. Note however, that Netcruiser can only be used if you subscribe to Netcom's Internet access service. Netcom and Netcruiser provide easy, Internet access for the new user. In a real sense, Netcom is a one-stop-shop for the Internet.

To download a free copy of Netcruiser, you can access the following URL:

http://www.ix.netcom.com/netcom/
software/cruiser.html

Cello
Cello is a PC browser developed by Thomas R. Bruce and the Legal Information Institute of Cornell Law School. It supports WWW, Gopher, ftp, CSO/ph/qi, and Usenet browsing, and can be used to view hypermedia documents. The one catch to this browser is that you need a 386SX processor or faster and more than 2mb of RAM in order to operate the current version of Cello. This is a very popular browser among the PC crowd.

To download a free copy of Cello, you can access the following URL:

http://www.law.cornell.edu/cello/
cellotop.html

winWeb
winWeb is Tradewave's Web browser. It is currently available for free, though Tradewave has plans to market it commercially. It fully supports WWW, ftp, Gopher, Usenet news, and mailing lists. Its basic operation is similar to that of the other browsers as it has a history of sites visited, an intuitive toolbar, and a hotlist of favorite sites. It operates with Windows 3.1, and does not require the Win32s subsystem.

To download a free copy of winWeb, you can access the following URL:

http://www.einet.net/EINet/WinWeb/
WinWebHome.html

The Future of the Web

What Lies Ahead: VRML (Virtual Reality Modeling Language)

Virtual Reality Modeling Language (VRML) is a method of navigating the World Wide Web that is more highly developed than the standard Hyper Text Markup Language (HTML). Though still in its early stages, VRML attempts to introduce a new level of interactivity to the Web enabling users to interact in real-time. (Real time means the user receives responses quickly enough so that there is no effective time delay in the activity he/she involved in while online.) A user browsing the Internet with VRML moves through virtual worlds that are linked on the World Wide Web. With VRML a user can access stored material that include three dimensional images and animation. VRML was conceived in the Spring of 1994 at the first annual WWW Conference in Geneva. Tim Berners-Lee (Developer of WWW) and Dave Raggett were instrumental in its inception

To view VRML files, a user must configure a browser to interpret VRML. There are several sites that provide shareware for browsing. Currently supported platforms include Windows, Sun, SGI, IBM AIX, DEC, LINUX, and HPUX, with the Macintosh platform currently in developmental stages.

To access a full array of browser links, go to the VRML repository at:

http://www.sdsc.edu/SDSC/Partners/vrml/
software/browsers.html

Additional information on VRML is found at VRML's primary WWW site:

http://www.vrml.wired.com

Who uses the Web?

The answer is millions of people world wide. Unlike today, when the Internet was first created, it was solely the domain of scientists and the military. Now, however, the number and diversity of people using the Internet is growing at an amazing rate with the most explosive area of growth occuring on the World Wide Web. While the rest of the world is catching up to the web revolution, usage and production of web sites remains the highest in the United States. With so many people using the Web, you may wonder just who these people are. The answer is just around the corner at your neighbor's house, in the computer lab of your child's school, or on your co-worker's desk at the office.

Teachers and Students

Educators and students are one of the largest user groups on the Web and for good reason. University students often have the Internet access (supplied by most institutions), resources, and time to spend on building Web sites quite easily and cheaply. As a result, their web creations add a unique spirit often found in university populations. The Web also gives schools the opportunity to create their own Web pages on a variety of topics as well as giving students the opportunity to research subjects for assignments. As a result, there are plenty of splendid education sites available on the Web. A good example of this is **Plugged In.**

In this project, out of Palo Alto, California, students use computer technology in creative ways to provide an enriched learning environment. This site can be found in this directory under the Category and Sub Category of Education/Educational Projects.

Parents and Children

Parents and children can also use the Web to find useful information. In addition to all of the education sites, there are easy to use sites made just for parents in which they will find helpful and interesting information on parenting today. One such site is the **Family World Features Page** (Health and Medicine/Family Health). It covers such topics as home health, family, babies, parenting and a column called Dad's Eye View.

Children also have their own sites such as the **Lion King Coloring Book** (Popular Culture and Entertainment/Family and Community) or **Newton** (Education/Educational Projects), a site where kids can ask a scientist or mathematician any question and receive an answer geared to their level of understanding. Sites such as these, make the Web a fascinating and useful place for parents and children to explore together.

Lately, there has been a lot of debate and news coverage about the safe use of the Internet by children. People are concerned that the unregulated nature of the Internet allows unsavory information and people to contact and impact children. As a result, companies are quickly creating software programs that allow parents to control exactly what their children are able to access. Please refer to 'Practicing Safe Internet with your Children' further on in this introduction.

Scientists and Researchers

The Internet has historically been a place for scientists and researchers to post their findings, collaborate on research projects, exchange information, and talk to others who are interested in the same topic. It is only natural that they are now finding ways to use the Web to continue this tradition. Almost every branch of science you could imagine is represented ranging from such sites as the renowned French national research institute for computer science and control - **Institut National de Recherche en Informatique et en Automatique** (Computer and Mathematics/Computer Science) to the **BDT Base de Dados Tropical Web** produced by the Brazilian organization Fundacao Tropical de Pesquisas e Tecnologia (Science/Biosciences), which maintains a database on biodiversity and the environment.

Business Professionals

Internet and Web usage among business professionals and businesses is experiencing the most phenomenal growth. Thousands of companies are going online with their product lines such as Maximov's Companion - A Who's Who to Who Governs the Russian Federation (Government & Politics/International) in search of new consumers. Much of the recent exponential growth can be attributed to companies who see the immense opportunities for exposure and advertising that the web environment has to offer. Where else can you reach millions of viewers at a fraction of the cost of traditional advertising? The answer is particularly apparent in the enormous opportunities for entrepreneurial or start-up companies to find a niche and global customer base from advertising and creating a web site on the Internet.

Politicians and Government Agencies

Likewise, politicians have jumped at the chance to go online. You can find the current press releases from the White House, or visit the Web site of the African National Congress (ANC) and access pictures of prominent political rights activists and numerous articles on a variety of topics. Governments and politicians have also recognized that the Internet is a quick, economical way to distribute information and even party platforms to a large number of people. In the 1995 French presidential elections the Web was used to disseminate information on the candidates and their political platforms as well as provide poll results before the final vote. The site can be reached at:

http://Mosaique.OLEANE.COM:80/elysee/fra/candidats/

The Web is truly a place for everyone to visit and leave their visiting card in the form of their own web page, or even a web site! No matter who you are, or what you are interested in, there is a place for you on the Web. Ultimately, the answer to who uses the Web, is you!

Practicing 'Safe Internet' For Your Children

Protecting children from the perceived "dangers" of the Internet is fast turning into a controversial subject. Where do you draw the line between free speech and protection of children from unsuitable material?

Many commercial online providers already offer ways to institute a screening process through the use of special screen names and passwords (which prevents the user from entering areas that might be considered too risqué). But software packages are now available and can be

Introduction

Commerce on the Internet

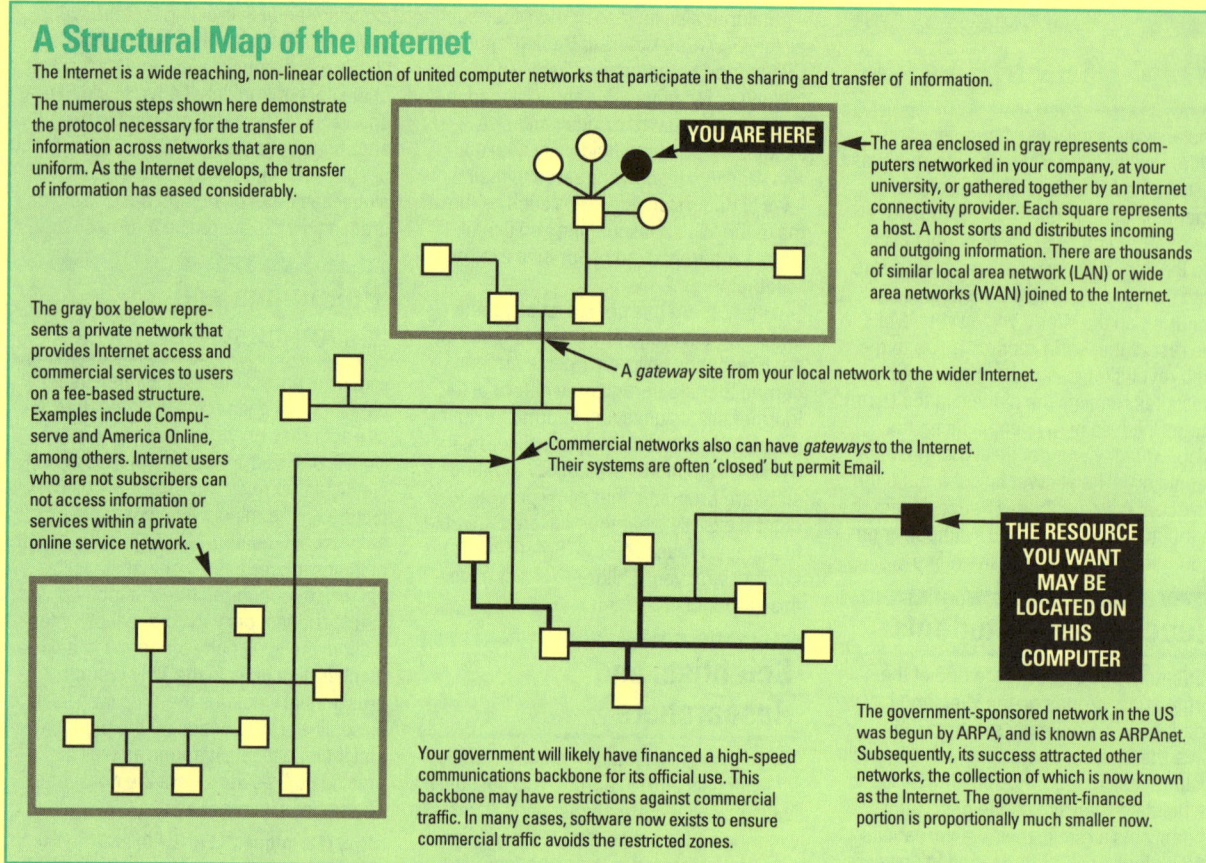

A Structural Map of the Internet
The Internet is a wide reaching, non-linear collection of united computer networks that participate in the sharing and transfer of information.

The numerous steps shown here demonstrate the protocol necessary for the transfer of information across networks that are non uniform. As the Internet develops, the transfer of information has eased considerably.

The area enclosed in gray represents computers networked in your company, at your university, or gathered together by an Internet connectivity provider. Each square represents a host. A host sorts and distributes incoming and outgoing information. There are thousands of similar local area network (LAN) or wide area networks (WAN) joined to the Internet.

The gray box below represents a private network that provides Internet access and commercial services to users on a fee-based structure. Examples include Compuserve and America Online, among others. Internet users who are not subscribers can not access information or services within a private online service network.

A *gateway* site from your local network to the wider Internet.

Commercial networks also can have *gateways* to the Internet. Their systems are often 'closed' but permit Email.

THE RESOURCE YOU WANT MAY BE LOCATED ON THIS COMPUTER

The government-sponsored network in the US was begun by ARPA, and is known as ARPAnet. Subsequently, its success attracted other networks, the collection of which is now known as the Internet. The government-financed portion is proportionally much smaller now.

Your government will likely have financed a high-speed communications backbone for its official use. This backbone may have restrictions against commercial traffic. In many cases, software now exists to ensure commercial traffic avoids the restricted zones.

---

loaded onto personal computers to keep a young person from wandering into an area on the Internet deemed "unsafe" because of strong language or sexually-explicit graphics.

Parental Guidance, from Providence Systems is one such very helpful product designed to assist families manage the time, cost and quality of their children's computer experience. The product is available for Windows 95. It enables parents to budget overall usage of online services, monitor or limit children's play of video games or other applications, and oversee electronic mail correspondence. The software product uses an easy to follow interview process so that parents can tailor the guidelines, including Internet Web site access. Information on Parental Guidance can be obtained by using their fax response system at 1-800-525-5763 or at:.

http://www.PGuidance.com

Net Nanny software from Trove Investment Corporation is another software package designed to block access to specified sites (by the user) on the Internet. This software package can be ordered via the Internet through Trove at:

http://www.netnanny.com/netnanny/product.html

CYBERsitter is a Windows program that will give the user the capability to block access to common types of graphics files, as well as specific files and programs on the Internet. It can be ordered through Solid Oak Software Inc. online at:

http://www.rain.org/~solidoak/announce.htm

The use of these Internet monitoring programs will allow parents to sit back and relax, not having to worry about or hover over their children at the computer. This software turns the reins of control over to the parent and yet, it still lets the child feel as if they have the freedom to surf the Internet.

Commerce on the Internet

Digital Transactions on the Net

The issue of protection does not exist solely in the domain of the family. Protection is also big business with commercial Internet sites. More and more companies are involved in selling products over the Internet. The use of a cash transaction system which flows over the Internet has yet to become a reality due to issues of security and implementation. But there are many firms working to make Internet cash transactions a reality in the near future.

Three such companies are Digicash, First Virtual and Cybercash. Each company offers a secure method of electronic transactions over the Internet.

Digicash and Cybercash use an encryption method so that data is coded and protected. More information can be found on their web sites.

Cybercash:

http://www.cybercash.com

Digicash:

http://www.digicash.com

First Virtual relies on a telephone verification system combined with regular email. More information can be found on the Internet as well.

First Virtual:

http://www.fv.com

In the meantime, Internet transactions are still credit card based with no sortage of security issues to solve there either!

No one wants to have their credit card stolen! As a result, companies are increasingly interested in secure transaction software. This software allows for the secure exchange of information via electronic means. If you do plan to purchase products over the Internet, be sure that the transaction uses some sort of security software.

One off-shoot of this precaution, is personal encryption software for email. It is possible to download a freeware program called PGP (Pretty Good Privacy). This program provides solid data encryption for email and file transfer procedures. It operates on MS-DOS, UNIX, VAX/VMS and Macintosh and is available at:

http://web.mit.edu/network/pgp

Once you have a secure means of purchasing products, a wide choice opens up before you. Small companies to multinational corporations are voraciously exploring the Internet (primarily the WWW) as a means of doing business. The McKinley Directory lists many of these sites and highlights them with a symbol next to the title indicating that it is a commercial site.

Conclusion

Whether you use the Internet for pleasure, research, or profit, the McKinley Internet Directory will provide a solution to information overload. Instead of being presented with a laundry list of hot links and left to guess at which of the links is most likely to give you what you are looking for. The McKinley Internet Directory has provided each titled resource with solid descriptions, keywords, audience fields, contact information and a Star rating (See 'What's In A Rating'). These fields of value-added information are all presented in a logical and easy to follow format not to be found in any other hard copy Internet directory.

What we are about at the McKinley Group, is the setting of a standard for the organization, description and evaluation of Internet resources. Our decades of experience in international publishing and information brokering is well adapted to this new hyper-linked computer oriented information world and has proven to be a strong base for our content driven approach. The McKinley brings the lawlessness of the Net under control, yet leaves plenty of browsing room for the roaming traveler and the curiosity bug that lies deep within us all.

How to Use this Directory

Organization of the Directory 9
Search Strategies for the Directory 10
What is the McKinley Rating System? 10

Organization of the Directory

Part 1
Preface and Introduction

Here you will find a general preface to the McKinley Internet Directory as well as an overview about the Internet, the World Wide Web and its users, and commerce and security on the Internet.

Part 2
Internet Listings

This chapter comprises the heart of the McKinley Internet Directory. There are 15 sections, one for each major subject category with over 250 accompanying sub categories. You will find thousands of evaluated, rated, and reviewed resources containing all types of Internet resources (such as http, gopher, telnet, and ftp). Mailing lists and newsgroups are covered in Parts 3 and 4.

Part 3
Email and Mailing Lists

This chapter introduces Email and mailing lists. A brief explanation of mailing lists, how to subscribe and unsubscribe to the different lists, as well as a compilation of mailing lists is provided here.

Each listing in this section is organized by category and sub category as in the main directory of Internet listings. Pertinent information such as the title of the mailing list, a brief description, and subscription address and instructions are provided.

Part 4
Newsgroups

This section gives an introduction to Usenet and contains a myriad collection of newsgroups that come under each of the 15 categories and over 250 sub categories. Information provided about the each newsgroup includes newsgroup name, a brief description, and whether it is moderated or not.

Part 5
Commercial Online Services

This section includes information about major online services such as America OnLine and Compuserve. Each service is described including features, sign up information, cost of service, points of presence, and contact information is provided whenever available. In addition, sample listings of discussion forums or chat groups available to the users of those services are provided.

Part 6
A Whimsical Internet Tour

This Internet Tour will take you on a fun, fascinating tour of specially chosen sites that offer something different, interesting or useful on the Internet. Plug in one of the many urls highlighted for you into your browser and take off into cyberspace!

Appendices

The appendices in the directory are provided as additional aids.

Appendix A - Internet Highlights Index
The Internet Highlights index is also arranged using McKinley's category and sub category organization scheme. Simply go to the page number indicated in the index to find the Internet Highlights of interest to you.

Appendix B - International Internet Providers
This section comprises a list of international Internet providers found in most countries around the world. Contact and general information about each service is provided in a chart alphabetized by country and company names.

Organization of the Directory – What is the McKinley Rating System?

How to Use This Directory

Appendix C - Glossary of Terms and Acronyms
The Internet has spawned many terms and acronyms that may be foreign to many of us. We have provided a glossary to many of the common technical terms that you will encounter as you roam the Internet.

Appendix D - Keyword Index
Alphabetically arranged list of all keywords assigned to each listing. Each keyword will reference all the categories (accompanied by page numbers) to every instance where that keyword appears throughout the main directory of listings.

Appendix E - Audience Index
Alphabetically arranged list of all audiences assigned to each listing. Similar to the keyword index, each audience will reference all categories (accompanied by page numbers) to every instance where that audience field appears throughout the main directory of listings. Looking up the resources by audience interest is another way to find the relevant information in many different categories

Appendix F - How to Add or Update an Internet Resource in "The McKinley"
There are many resources that the McKinley Internet Directory has yet to include or we may have a listing in our directory that needs a bit of updating.

Due to the constantly changing and ever-expanding nature of the Internet, we need your help in keeping our resources current. Help us make this directory even better by giving us your corrections/additions. Fill out the form provided for you in this appendix located in the back of the book.

Search Strategies for the Directory

Each Internet resource listing in the McKinley Internet Directory is organized under a two-level hierarchical subject organization scheme to help you find what you need. We have provided two basic search strategies to get you started.

Search Strategy I
Search by Category and Sub Category

Step 1
Start your search by going to one of the 15 major subject categories organized alphabetically in the directory. Two ways to do this are:
 a. Use the book's helpful green thumb tabs to flip to the topical category of choice.
 b. Find the exact page number by using our complete detailed list of major categories and sub categories in the **Contents** page in the front of the book.
Example:
Major Category
Arts & Music

Step 2
Then use one of the sub categories listed in the green vertical bar of the first page of each major category section to help you narrow your search. The Internet resources are then listed alphabetically by title under each sub category.
Example:
Major Category Arts & Music
Subcategory Architecture

Search Strategy II
Search by Using the Keyword or Audience Index

Step 1
Go to the keyword or audience index in the appendices in the back of the directory. Look for the keyword or audience that most interests you.

Step 2
Next to each keyword you will find a reference to categories with accompanying page references where you can find other listings with the same keyword.

Step 3
Go to the page number and view the listings by title. (Notice that most listings are assigned more than one keyword and audience. These additional keywords or audiences help you to easily locate additional related or relevant listings to extend your search to areas you might not have considered!)

What is the McKinley Star Rating System?

Not only does The McKinley describe Internet resources but it also assigns a star rating (like the Michelin Guide) based on content and value. The ratings have been developed in cooperation with the McKinley International Editorial Advisory Board. The tailored ratings help you save time, and focus on the most current resources with the most in-depth coverage on your topic of interest.

The McKinley ★ Star Rating System appears in the upper right hand of each listing in this directory. The (1-4) rating system is based on the following criteria:
- Completeness of content presented in the resource
- Organization of the resource
- Up-to-dateness of the information presented
- Ease of access to the resource

The Role of the International Editorial Advisory Board

The Board is composed of recognized international specialists in specific subject areas, formed to help evaluate the listings selected for publication in this directory.

Getting expert advice about the information you find is always a key element. In many instances you will have no idea whether the Internet information available is valid, biased, complete, or reliable. The McKinley rating helps you to make a more informed choice.

In the world of print, scholarly publishers developed mechanisms for "peer review", by which articles and manuscripts were subjected to a rigorous evaluation process by the author's peers. This process ensured objectivity, critical judgment and ultimately reliability.

Similar conventions can be applied to the evaluation of Internet resources. Members of the Editorial Advisory Boards are asked to help evaluate Internet resources which are found within their specific areas of expertise. The Star ★ Rating System will inform you about the relative merit of a resource as determined by a panel of experts in the field.

What's in a Listing?

Below you will find described each field of information provided in each McKinley listing.

Commercial
Presence of this icon immediately alerts you as to whether a resource is a commercial or non commercial site.

Title of Resource
The title of the resource is given. Sometimes Internet resources do not appear to have an 'official' title. In these cases, The McKinley has tried to assign an accurate title for these resources.

★★★★ **McKinley Star Rating**
Each resource includes a special McKinley rating. These ratings are based on a 1 to 4 star scale in which a resource is judged on completeness of content, presentation, organization, currency of information presented, as well as ease of access to the resource.

Description
This description gives you a good idea of what a resource contains before you actually visit the site online.

Keywords
Keywords are provided for you to focus quickly on the most relevant resources. Additional keywords are supplied to help you expand a search into other categories of the directory.

Audience
The audience field is intended to give you an idea of the type of users who will be most interested in the resource. Additional audience groups are supplied to help you expand a search into other areas of the directory.

Contact Name and Email Address
Contact and email address for the resource is provided whenever available.

 Cost
Each resource includes a cost/no cost rating that allows you to know beforehand if there is a cost to use the resource. Presence of the alerts you that the resource is free.

 CareerMosaic ★★★★

CareerMosaic™ is an online guide to companies and opportunities. Using CareerMosaic, individuals can research companies in a variety of businesses. Users can find out what they do, where they do it, and what their environments are like. All the information has been developed by the employers in cooperation with CareerMosaic. There is also a section for college internships and co-op opportunities, a forms-based search of all UseNet Job categories, and an extensive career library containing studies, articles, and tips related to the job market.

Keywords Employment, Internships, Online Databases, Companies

Audience Employment Counselors, Human Resources Departments, Job Recruiters, Job Seekers

Contact bmoore@pa.hodes.com

Free

http://www.careermosaic.com/

URLs
Each resource is accompanied by one or more Internet addresses (URLs - Uniform Resource Locators) for the site.

What's on a Page?

Each feature on the page is carefully described. (For complete details of what's in each resource, see 'What's in a Listing'.)

The McKinley Internet Directory gives you an alphabetical listing of Internet resources by title. Each listing is topically arranged under a major subject category and sub category. (For extra hints on searching the directory, see 'Search Strategies for the Directory' on page 10.)

Major Category Headings

These are the top level headings under which each sub category will be found. Each of the 15 carefully created major subject categories is meant to help users start a search by general topic.

Sub Category Headings

Sub categories help focus your search within each major category enabling you to turn quickly to the resources of most interest to you.

A list of sub categories with their relevant starting page numbers can be found in the green bar on the starting page of each major category heading.

All sub categories are easily locatable on the pages themselves. They are in *bold green italics* and have a solid green line above and below them.

See Also References

Nearly all sub categories have *See also* references. These are pointers (cross-references) to other relevant or related listings found under different categories throughout the directory. Each *See also* entry will include the category and sub category of a listing.

Health & Medicine

Addictions	375
Aging	375
Alternative Medicine	376
Biomedicine	378
Career & Employment	380
Dental Health	380
Disabilites	381
Diseases	383
Family Health	389
Health Conditions	392
Medical Schools	393
Medical Specialties	397
Medicine	399
Mental Health	401
Organizations	402
Personal Care	403
Public Health	404
Reference	407
Resources	411
Services	414
Sexuality	414
Sexually Transmitted Diseases	416
Sports Medicine	416
Veterinary Medicine	416
Women's Health	417

Addictions

See also
Health & Medicine · *Women's Health*

AL-ANON and ALATEEN ★★★

Al-Anon and Alateen for teenagers are self-help programs for partners and families of alcoholics. Their home page is designed to provide basic information about their programs, and includes the documents The 12 Steps of Alcoholics Anonymous and The 12 Traditions. A questionnaire to see if you need Al-Anon is also provided, as well as lists of phone numbers and addresses of Al-Anon addresses.
Keywords Alcoholism, Organizations, Teenage Issues
Audience Alcoholics, Families
Contact Don R.
odat@ccnet.com
Free
http://solar.rtd.utk.edu/~al-anon/

Drugs in the Workplace ★★★

This site is a monthly publication that provides news and analysis of drug use in the workplace. The issues contain practical news and help for company decision makers, human resource managers, and employee assistance professionals responsible for managing the impact of alcohol and drugs on the workplace. This site focuses on the effects of the federal government's rules and guidelines on the lawful prevention, detection and treatment of substance abuse on the job. Special areas of coverage focus on medical developments and breakthroughs, employee assistance programs, and cutting-edge solutions to common jobsite problems.
Keywords Business, Drugs, Human Resources, Management
Audience Business Owners, Employees, Managers, Medical Researchers
Free
gopher://gopher.enews.com:70/11/magazines/alphabetic/af/dIw

HabitSmart ★★★

HabitSmart is designed to provide a resource for people with destructive habits and addictions of all types, containing documents and links to other addiction-related links on the Web. Users will find the document Coping with Addiction, which addresses questions about risky substance use and offers options for change. There are also documents for parents of children with addictions. A guide to drinking alcohol and blood alcohol levels is also provided, along with tips for reducing smoking and coping with urges. The HabitSmart Archivist newsletter, published bimonthly, prints research information and breakthroughs.
Keywords Alcoholism, Drug Abuse, Smoking
Audience Alcoholics, Drug Users, Families, Smokers

Contact habtsmrt@cts.com
Free
http://www.cts.com/~habtsmrt/

Information about Alcoholics Anonymous ★★★

This web site is designed to provide information about the self-help alcohol recovery program Alcoholics Anonymous (AA). Users will find articles written by members of Alcoholics Anonymous about their lives, as well as several AA publications with personal recovery stories. Other online resources include information about upcoming conferences, addresses and phone numbers of centers worldwide, and AA pamphlets and brochures.
Keywords Alcoholism, Organizations
Audience Alcoholics, Families
Contact Phil W.
an184160@anon.penet.fi
Free
http://www.moscow.com/Resources/SelfHelp/AA/

NicNet ★★★

NicNet is The Arizona Nicotine and Tobacco Network web site, with resources and local information regarding tobacco and smoking research. Users will find numerous links to online resources, grouped into categories such as treatment and prevention, policy issues, commercial resources, government resources, journals and databases. Local information includes materials from the University of Arizona Program for Nicotine and Tobacco Research, and users will also find the home pages of several Arizona cancer and health related organizations.
Keywords Smoking
Audience Smokers, Smoking Researchers
Contact Jacqueline Shober
jshober@ccit.arizona.edu
Free
http://www.medlib.arizona.edu/~pubhlth/tobac.html

Aging

See also
Government & Politics · *States*
Health & Medicine · *Biomedicine*
Health & Medicine · *Mental Health*
Science · *Agriculture*

Aeiveos Corporation ★★★★

Aeiveos Corporation is a biotechnology research and education company dedicated to understanding the causes of aging. Aeiveos develops technologies which minimize the impact of age related diseases and

What's on a Page?

Headers
Each page has a running header showing you which sub categories can be found on each page. Headers help the reader keep track of which sub category they are in at any one time.

Page Numbers
All page numbers are clearly marked. The indexes in the back of the directory refer to these page numbers when supplying the location of each index reference.

Internet Highlights
This is an example of one of over 150 featured resources that can be found on pages throughout the directory. The resources are highlighted on a green tinted background and have been chosen for their usefulness, level of interest and often just plain fun! Many of them include an image from the site itself. (A full index of Internet Highlights can be found in Appendix A.)

Thumb Tabs
Browsing through the directory is made easy. Just use the green thumb tabs found on the margin for each of the 15 major categories.

Listings
Listings can be found alphabetically by title under each sub category. The reader can refer to 'What's in a Listing' on page 11.

Diseases   385

programs, and links to other gophers at Harvard and elsewhere.
KEYWORDS Cancer, Medical Administration, Medical Research, Organizations
AUDIENCE Cancer Specialists, Health Care Professionals, Medical Professionals, Medical Researchers
FREE
gopher://farber.dfci.harvard.edu/

Diabetes Dictionary ★★
This dictionary of diabetes terms defines words that are often used when talking or writing about diabetes. An alphabetical searchable index, along with facts and information on diabetes, are also available.
KEYWORDS Diabetes, Diseases, Glossaries, Medical Education
AUDIENCE Diabetics, Medical Researchers, Medical Students, Physicians
FREE
http://www.niddk.nih.gov/DiabetesDictionary/DiabDictIndex.html

Diabetes Knowledgebase ★★★★
The Diabetes Knowledgebase contains a variety of links to areas focusing on diabetes control and complications trials, diabetic eye disease, insulin-dependent diabetes, noninsulin dependent diabetes, and glycemic index.
KEYWORDS Diabetes, Diseases, Medical Research
AUDIENCE Diabetics, Health Care Professionals, Physicians
CONTACT Donald A. Lehn, Ph.D.
         dalehn@facstaff.wisc.edu
FREE
http://www.biostat.wisc.edu/diaknow/index.html

Do Power Lines Cause Cancer? ★★★
This Powerlines—Cancer FAQ is a document that offers scientific and medical discussion of the assertion that electromagnetic fields generated by high-tension power lines cause cancer.
KEYWORDS Cancer, Medicine
AUDIENCE Health Care Professionals, Researchers
FREE
ftp://rtfm.mit.edu/pub/usenet/sci.answers/powerlines-cancer-FAQ/

Fred Hutchinson Cancer Research Center Gopher ★★★
This gopher hole is an information resource about cancer. It is maintained by the Fred Hutchinson Cancer Research Center Gopher (FHCRC), a cancer research institute in Seattle, Washington. The resources include FHCRC news, seminar dates, grants and funding information, and research news.
KEYWORDS Cancer, Diseases, Health Care, Medical Research

Connections to Your Heart
Zing went the strings of my heart.

The Heart

From the moment it begins beating until the moment it stops, the human heart works tirelessly. In an average lifetime, the heart beats more than two and a half billion times, without ever pausing to rest. Like a pumping machine, the heart provides the power needed for life.

This life-sustaining power has, throughout time, caused an air of mystery to surround the heart. Modern technology has removed much of the mystery, but there is still an air of fascination and curiosity.

Explore the heart. Discover the complexities of its development and structure. Follow the blood through the blood vessels. Wander through the weblike body systems. Learn how to have a healthy heart and how to monitor your heart's health. Look back at the history of heart science.

Soon, the fascination and curiosity will lead to understanding and respect.

Hearts are broken, some are healed, and some rule the head. If you want to know anything about your heart, the Internet provides a way to check in on your "ticker."

Through "The Franklin Institute," you can get information—including heart history—as well as on the effects of fried foods, automobiles, elevators and vacuum cleaners on the heart. As a matter of fact, you will learn that before 1900, very few people died of heart disease. This site also provides opportunities for interactive play with a virtual heart, using visuals and sounds. You can even access information about medicine and treatment for heart disease.

(http://sln.fi.edu/biosci/heart.html)

AUDIENCE Health Care Professionals, Health Care Providers, Medical Researchers
CONTACT Michael Parker
         mparker@fhcrc.org
FREE
gopher://gopher.fhcrc.org/

German Cancer Research Center ★★★★
This site contains medical and biological information concerning cancer and cancer research. Projects like HELIOS-2 - the Advanced Informatics in Medicine project of the European Commission's research program can be accessed here. Additional resources include information on research in Cell Kinetics, collections of scientific images, papers and technical reports. The site also contains links to other medical servers including Medline and additional national research centers in Germany.
KEYWORDS Cancer, Germany, Medical Research
AUDIENCE Cancer Patients, Educators, Health Care Professionals, Medical Students, Oncologists, Researchers
CONTACT MBI@DKFZ-Heidelberg.de
FREE
http://mbi.dkfz-heidelberg.de/

Global Resources for Cancer Information ★★★★
Global Resources for Cancer Information provides numerous links to extensive cancer-related information. The subjects range from government sites, associations and support groups, to electronic references, hospitals, universities and institutes.
KEYWORDS Breast Cancer, Cancer, Cancer Research
AUDIENCE Cancer Patients, Health Care Professionals, Nurses, Physicians
FREE
http://cancer.med.upenn.edu/stuff/index.html

H. Lee Moffitt Cancer Center & Research Institute Home Page ★★★
This is the home page for the H. Lee Moffitt Cancer Center & Research Institute at the University of South Florida. It contains links to information on research, education, and links to other cancer related sites. The mission of Moffitt Cancer Center is to contribute to the prevention and cure of cancer. The Moffitt Cancer Center is supported by the teaching and research activities of the USF College of Medicine. The progressive university medical center environment offers patients and the community superior opportunities and

Arts & Music

Architecture	15
Art Galleries	17
Art History	21
Art Museums	22
Art Organizations	27
Art Resources	28
Artists	31
Arts Funding	32
Career & Employment	33
Decorative Arts	33
Design	33
Electronic Arts	34
Film & Video	47
Music Genres	50
Music History	57
Music Organizations	58
Music Resources	62
Musical Groups	71
Musicians	82
Performing Arts	90
Visual Arts	97

Architecture

See also
Arts & Music · *Art History*
Arts & Music · *Art Museums*
Arts & Music · *Design*

The Alvar Aalto Museum ★★★★

The Alvar Aalto Museum specializes in architecture. It preserves, researches, and maintains a permanent display of material related to Aalto's work as an architect and designer. The museum's architectural collection features over 1000 original models and artifacts designed by Aino and Alvar Aalto, together with an extensive picture archive and a steadily growing selection of reproductions of Aalto's original drawings. The museum also serves as Jyväskylä's art museum. It owns an extensive collection of art, and is involved in a wide variety of exhibition projects.

KEYWORDS Architectural History, Architecture, Design
AUDIENCE Architects, Architecture Historians, Art Historians, Artists, Finns
FREE

http://www.cs.jyu.fi/~jatahu/aalto/homepage.html

ArchiGopher ★★★

This site at the College of Architecture and Urban Planning at the University of Michigan offers access to a variety of architectural resources particularly images of architecture (Palladio, Greek, Turkish, Lunar). This site also offers links to other related servers.

KEYWORDS Architectural History, Architecture, Universities
AUDIENCE Architecture Students, Architects, Educators
CONTACT wjabi@libra.arch.umich.edu
FREE

gopher://libra.arch.umich.edu/

Architectural Visualization ★★★★

This is the University of Auckland interactive guide to the Architecture courses, services and institutions that students may encounter during their term of study. One feature of this site is a set of flythroughs of a three dimensional model of the Campus, put together by Matiu Carr of the School of Architecture, Property and Planning's (Auckland) The site also includes Architecture Resources, Galleries and access to ArchPropPlan in Web World and the Auckland University Students' Association. Computer reconstructions of architectural sites available include the Hadrian Baths at Leptis Magna; the reconstructions include comprehensive historical and bibliographic notes.

KEYWORDS Architecture, Computer Aided Instruction, New Zealand, Universities
AUDIENCE Architects, Architecture Historians, Art Historians, Classicists
CONTACT Matiu Carr or Bill Rattenbury
m.carr@auckland.ac.nz
FREE

http://archpropplan.auckland.ac.nz/People/Mat/Mat.html

Architecture ★★★

This document is a compilation of information resources focused on architecture. Topics included are architecture schools, architectural images, architectural libraries, government resources, etc. Resources may include Internet/Bitnet Mailing Lists, Gophers, World Wide Web Sites, Mail Servers, Usenet Newsgroups, FTP Archives, Commercial Online Services, and Bulletin Board Systems.

KEYWORDS Architectural History, Graduate Programs, Libraries, Meta-Index (Architecture)
AUDIENCE Architects, Builders, Civil Engineers, Management Information Specialists
FREE

ftp://una.hh.lib.umich.edu/inetdirsstacks/archi:brown

Bauhaus Archives ★★★

This site offers images of the Bauhaus Archives in Berlin, and also links to other images of other art museums worldwide and to information on architects.

KEYWORDS Architecture, Bauhaus, Germany
AUDIENCE Architects, Architecture Historians, Art Historians, Educators, Students
FREE

http://www.bwk.tue.nl/lava/galleries/museums/bauhaus1.jpg

Covered Bridges ★★

This site presents a guide to Old Covered Bridges of Southeastern Pennsylvania and nearby areas. Users will find images, directions on how to find these bridges, and more. The images are organized by season, location, and structural type. There are also pointers to other sites with information on bridges.

KEYWORDS Architectural Images, Bridges, Covered Bridges, Pennsylvania
AUDIENCE Architects, Architecture Enthisiasts
CONTACT Roger A. McCain
FREE

http://william-king.www.drexel.edu/top/bridge/CB1.html

Architecture

Curtin University of Technology - School of Architecture Construction and Planning

The Curtin University of Technology, School of Architecture Construction and Planning home page provides a comprehensive listing of courses of study including requirements and classes offered. A faculty listing is also provided including email addresses. A selection of faculty and student architecture-related projects are also available at this site.

KEYWORDS Architecture Education, Australia
AUDIENCE Architecture Faculty, Architecture Students, Technology Faculty, Technology Students
CONTACT Simon Crone
crones@puffin.curtin.edu.au
FREE

http://puffin.curtin.edu.au/

The English Shredder

This site contains several art- and architecture-related book reviews (e.g., Evolutionary Art and Computers, by Henri Achten; The Wright Space, Pattern and Meaning in Frank Lloyd Wright's Houses, by Grant Hildebrand, 1991; and Architecture in Europe—Memory and Invention Since 1968, by Henri Achten). The site also has links to other architectural resources.

KEYWORDS Architectural History, Architecture, Book Reviews, Europe
AUDIENCE Architects, Architecture Enthusiasts, Architecture Historians, Art Historians, Educators, Students
FREE

http://www.bwk.tue.nl/lava/forum/books/shred_e.html

I.M. Pei and Partners

This file contains JPEG images of the Louvre pyramids designed by I.M. Pei and Partners. The views include an exterior shot (from the courtyard) and four interior shots (central staircase and three views of the glass walls). The site also links to numerous other museums worldwide, organized by architect, country, project, location and year.

KEYWORDS Architects, Architectural Images, Architecture, Museums
AUDIENCE Architects, Architecture Historians, Art Historians, Educators, Students
FREE

http://www.bwk.tue.nl/lava/galleries/museums/louvre3.jpg

Index - Architecture - WWW Virtual Library

The architecture branch of the WWW Virtual Library offers users links to a wealth of architectural resources on the Internet. Regular users will appreciate the comprehensive and regularly-updated 'What's New' section. This site offers links to university departments, professional associations, image archives, and other useful resources related to the field of architecture.

KEYWORDS Architecture, Meta-Index (Architecture)
AUDIENCE Architects, Architecture Educators, Architecture Enthusiasts, Architecture Students

CONTACT Rodney Hoinkes
rodney@clr.toronto.edu
FREE

http://www.clr.toronto.edu:1080/VIRTUALLIB/arch.html

The Institute of Urban and Regional Development

This gopher server provides information about the Institute of Urban and Regional Development (IURD) at the University of California at Berkeley. This includes the IURD mission statement, newsletter and publications, and research projects.

KEYWORDS Environment, Urban Planning, Urban Studies
AUDIENCE Educators (University), Students (University), Urban Planners
CONTACT Martha Conway
iurd@uclink.berkeley.edu
FREE

gopher://uclink.berkeley.edu:1612/

Islamic Architecture in Isfahan

Isfahan is one of ten cities designated by UNESCO as a universal heritage. It contains a wide range of Islamic Architectural styles ranging from the 11th century (C.E.) to the 19th. This archive contains photographs and descriptions of some of the most interesting and unusual architectural examples including Mosques and Shrines (Masjed-e-Hakim — The Portal of Jorjir, Shahshahan, Masjed-e-'Ali — The Mosque of 'Ali), Palaces and Bridges (The Palace of Hasht Behesht), Minarets (Monar-e-Sareban — The Camel Drivers'Minaret), and other architectural sites of interest. Users can visit a section explaining the eight traditional forms of Persian architecture (garden, platform, porch, gateway, room, dome, four-arched chamber, minaret) and a bibliography. The site was nominated by GNN as one of the best on the net for 1995.

KEYWORDS Architecture, Iran, Islamic Architecture
AUDIENCE Architects, Architecture Historians, Architecture Students, Educators, Muslims
CONTACT trochford@bridge.anglia.ac.uk
FREE

http://www.anglia.ac.uk/~trochford/isfahan.html

Louis H. Sullivan, 1856-1924

This site contains information and select images related to the Chicago architect Louis Sullivan. Two images are featured—the Carrie Eliza Getty Tomb (Graceland Cemetary, Chicago) and a tracing from an original stencil used in the Schiller Theater (1890-92). The site also contains links to art and architecture resources.

KEYWORDS Architects, Architectural History, Architecture, Chicago
AUDIENCE Architecture Students, Educators, General Public, Students
FREE

http://www.artn.nwu.edu/sullivan.html

Mosques and Shrines

Mosques and Shrines provides information and pictures about a number of architectural styles used in Mosques and Shrines which were intended for use by Islamic congregations. Each photo is accompanied by details for the architectural style, and a history of the shrine or mosque. There are hotlinks to Minerets, Bridges and Palaces, and an explanation on the fundamental concepts of the architectural style.

KEYWORDS Islam, Mosques, Palaces
AUDIENCE Architecture Students, History Students, Tourists
CONTACT rochford@bridge.anglia.ac.uk
FREE

http://www.anglia.ac.uk/~trochford/masjed.html

Museum Architecture

This site contains images of architecture, specifically museum architecture, from around the world. The information is organized (and cross-referenced) by project, country, place, architect, and year. Institutions include the Bauhaus archive in Berlin, the Kunstsammlung Nord-Rhein in Westfalen, the Museum fuer Kunsthandwerk in Frankfurt, the Musee d'Orsay in Paris, the Guggenheim in New York, the Staatsgalerie in Stuttgart, etc. All images in the archive are JPEG. The site also offers links to essays on the application of modern technology to architectural study.

KEYWORDS Architects, Architectural Images, Museums
AUDIENCE Architects, Architecture Historians, Art Historians, Educators, Students
FREE

http://www.bwk.tue.nl/lava/galleries/museums/musea_ix.html

Radiance

Radiance is a lighting, graphic, rendering and analysis tool designed site, written chiefly at Lawrence Berkeley Laboratories in Berkeley, California. Users are presented with an extensive collection of images and information including a 3D representation of The American Bar by Adolf Loos. Also accessible is what can be accomplished using this software, a material and objects library. Users can procure textures and patterns for mapping and learn about the subject through a list of reports and articles. Available is the distribution site to obtain the software itself.

KEYWORDS Architectural Visualization, Electronic Arts, New Zealand, Software
AUDIENCE Computer Artists, Computer Graphic Designers, Graphic Designers, Virtual Reality Enthusiasts
CONTACT Matiu Carr
m.carr@auckland.ac.nz
FREE

http://archpropplan.auckland.ac.nz/Graphics/radiance/radiance.html

Syracuse Univeristy School of Architecture

This is the home page for the School of Architecture at Syracuse. Provided is information about the school (lectures and exhibitions, architectural images, faculty projects on the web, faculty lists), its academic pro-

Architecture – Art Galleries

Arts & Music

grams —including graduate programs and the architectural study at Florence (Italy) program. The Image Archives contains architectural images Anasazi architecture as well as other examples of American architecture, and work by Syracuse architecture students. The site also has a clickable image map and links to other architecture sites on the web.

KEYWORDS American Architecture, Anasazi Architecture, Graduate Programs
AUDIENCE Architects, Architecture Historians, Architecture Students, Art Historians, Educators
CONTACT Timothy Swischuk
tkswisch@mailbox.syr.edu
FREE

http://mirror.syr.edu/soa.html

University at Buffalo PAIRC (Planning and Architecture Internet Resource Center) ★★★★

This site hosts a large index of architectural and planning resources on the Internet. Users will find a well organized set of links to resources such as architecture and planning firms, university departments, building and construction engineering sites, CAD (Computer Aided Design) and GIS (Geographic Information Systems) sites, and much more.

KEYWORDS Architecture, Architecture Education, Meta-Index (Architecture), Urban Planning
AUDIENCE Architects, Architecture Educators, Architecture Enthusiasts, Architecture Students
CONTACT Dan Tasman
tasman@acsu.buffalo.edu
FREE

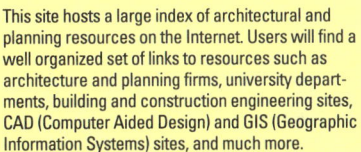

http://arch.buffalo.edu:8001/internet/h_pa_resources.html

University of Oregon School of Architecture and Allied Arts ★★★

The University of Oregon School of Architecture and Allied Arts home page gives a well-organized, in-depth look at programs in many disciplines ranging from Architecture to Public Planning and Management. The site offers an extensive listing of faculty in each department, many of them email accessible, as well as a subject index. Online registration is not available at this time.

KEYWORDS Architecture, Art Education, Art History, Oregon
AUDIENCE Architectuire Students, Architecture Faculty, Art Historians, Artists
CONTACT webmaster@aaa.uoregon.edu
FREE

http://laz.uoregon.edu/

Art Galleries

See also
Arts & Music · *Artists*
Arts & Music · *Visual Arts*
Humanities & Social Sciences · *Archaeology*
Popular Culture & Entertainment · *Museums & Theme Parks*

ANIMA (Arts Network for Integrated Media Applications) ★★★★

ANIMA (Arts Network for Integrated Media Applications) is an online art gallery providing global and cultural media arts information. Subjects include the exploration of the relationship between art and technology, new arts and media publications online, digital art spaces on the net, a resource and reference library, experimental programs, tools and applications, a discussion forum, and special events. Viewing ANIMA with Netscape reveals its full format.

KEYWORDS Art Exhibitions, Multimedia, Reference
AUDIENCE Art Enthusiasts, Computer Artists, Computer Graphic Designers, Multimedia Enthusiasts
CONTACT Derek Dowden
anima@artworld.com
FREE

http://www.wimsey.com/anima/ANIMAhome.html

The ARTA Gallery, Jerusalem ★★★

This site contains images from exhibitions at the Arta gallery in Jerusalem, including 'The Genius of Marc Chagall' (Chagall Lithographs, Chagall Kidush Cup, Chagall Candlesticks, and Chagall Mezuza Series). Each image is accompanied by a brief commentary. There is also information concerning purchase of the limited edition lithographs and select items by Chagall. The site is operated with the cooperation of the Chagall estate.

KEYWORDS Art Exhibitions, Artists, Israel, Jewish Art
AUDIENCE Art Enthusiasts, Arts Community
CONTACT info@macom.co.il
FREE

http://www.macom.co.il/arta/index.html

Aart Gallery ★★★

This site presents several exhibits related to traditional and photographic arts. Users will find images of artwork along with extensive commentary and information on how the artwork was created. There are also links to other online art galleries available here, as well as a link to Generality, the creator of the site.

KEYWORDS Online Art Galleries, Photography, Visual Arts
AUDIENCE Art Enthusiasts, Photography Enthusiasts
CONTACT Kent Barrett
kent@wimsey.com
FREE

http://www.wimsey.com/Generality/aart_Gallery.html

Aboriginal Art Gallery ★★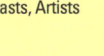

This site offers a small collection of art works created by aboriginal peoples. Users can view information about each artist, as well as view images in GIF format of each artist's work.

KEYWORDS Aboriginal Art, Anthropology, Online Art Galleries
AUDIENCE Aboriginal Peoples, Art Enthusiasts, Artists
CONTACT Peggy Jubinville
FREE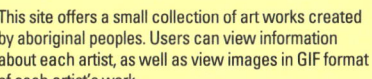

http://www.abinfohwy.ca/abinfohwy/aboartgl/

Absolut Access ★★

The Absolut Access site is a virtual gallery of art works by artists from around the world. Users can view and interact with some of the online exhibits, as well as obtain information about the artists whose work comprises the exhibit. There is also information here on visiting the actual site of the art exhibits, as well as information on the sponsors and galleries that are involved.

KEYWORDS Interactive Art, Online Art Galleries, Visual Arts
AUDIENCE Art Enthusiasts, Art Patrons
CONTACT Mark Dziecielewski
markdz@easynet.co.uk
FREE

http://www.bt.net/intervid/absolut/

Adventures on the Right Side of the Brain ★★★

Adventures on the Right Side of the Brain is a Web site devoted to the exploration of the creative potential in all of us. Users will find a collection of images from Elizabeth Reid Maruska, who encourages us to leave the analytical brain behind and learn to express our inherent creativity and imagination. Information on an exhibit of these artworks is also available at this site, as well as interpretations of the artworks found on this page.

KEYWORDS Art Education, Electronic Arts, Online Art Galleries
AUDIENCE Art Enthusiasts, Electronic Art Enthusiasts
CONTACT Elizabeth Reid Maruska
lmaruska@slonet.org
FREE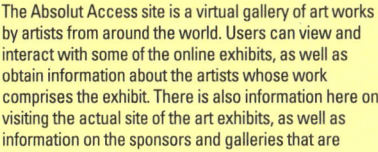

http://www-sloan.mit.edu/Gallery/Maruska/maruska.html

Alt.art - A Compendium of Bad Art Form ★★★

The Alt.art - A Compendium of Bad Art Form page offers a humorous look into the world of serious art. Users will find tongue-in-cheek commentary, and an offbeat look into some of the world's greatest artworks. In addition, this site offers images and commentary on what some consider 'bad' art, and a discussion of how Michelangelo's Sistine Chapel reflects some of the principles of 'bad' art.

KEYWORDS Art Criticism, Artists, Online Art Galleries
AUDIENCE Art Enthusiasts, Artists, Humor Enthusiasts

Art Galleries

CONTACT janet@power.net
FREE

http://www.power.net/users/janet/alt.art.html

Art Crimes - The Writing on the Wall ★★★★

This is a gallery of grafitti art from various cities. It's called 'Art Crimes' because in most places, painting grafitti is illegal. Many of these pieces no longer exist in the real world. The grafitti art works are from all over the world (Prague - Czech Republic, Munich - Germany, British Columbia - Canada, San Diego - California, Amsterdam - Netherlands) rendering this site truly international. The site also contains links to 'other cool pages on the Web.'

KEYWORDS Art Exhibitions, Contemporary Art, Grafitti Art, Visual Arts
AUDIENCE Art Historians, Artists, Arts Community, Educators, Grafitti Enthusiasts, Students
CONTACT Susan Farrell sf15@prism.gatech.edu sf15@prism.gatech.edu
FREE

http://www.gatech.edu/desoto/graf/Index.Art_Crimes.html

Art of Matsushita ★★★

The Art of Matsushita page offers a collection of information, images, and poetry from Matsushita Studios. Users will find several images, as well as a collection of poetry written by the artists in the studio. In addition, this site provides an essay on art and inspiration, as well as a guest book and a section for users to leave feedback.

KEYWORDS Artists, Commercial Art Studios, Poetry
AUDIENCE Art Enthusiasts, Artists, Poetry Enthusiasts
CONTACT info@matsushita.com
FREE

http://www.matsushita.com/matsushita/studio.html

Art Studio ★★★★

The works of conventional artists are presented in this online gallery with thumbnail images and enlarged views. Covering a wide range of media and subjects, the viewer can select subject or media indices. Media cover acrylics, metal assemblage, oils, photography and watercolors, among others. Traditional subjects predominate with abstracts, still lifes, sports art and wildlife images available. Information about each artist is presented, along with details of the art including the purchase price and ordering forms.

KEYWORDS Art Exhibitions, Fine Art, Painting
AUDIENCE Art Professionals, Artists, Arts Community, Photographers
CONTACT Jeannie Novak jeannie@kspace.com
FREE

http://kspace.com/cgi-bin/imagemap/wheel?302,24

ArtCity ★★★★

ArtCity is a Web site that allows users to browse through the work of many artists. Users will find a gallery and exhibit hall with images and information on those images. In addition, there is biographical information presented on each artist, as well as some general information about ArtCity itself. In addition, this site hosts information on purchasing the works of art that you see, as well as a collection of links to other art sites on the Net.

KEYWORDS Artists, Online Art Galleries, Web Art
AUDIENCE Art Consumers, Art Enthusiasts, Artists
CONTACT cardova@interport.net
FREE

http://www.artcity.com/

Artist Points ★★★

Artist Points is a Web site devoted exclusively to art created solely with pen and ink. This includes line art and pointillism, as well as other forms of art. Users will find a gallery of images, and a section with information on the artists whose work is displayed here. Information on ordering the artwork found here is also available.

KEYWORDS Online Art Galleries, Graphic Art
AUDIENCE Art Enthusiasts, Pen and Ink Art Enthusiasts
CONTACT Gerry Smith gsmith@peak.org
FREE

http://www.peak.org/~tacyb/

Between - A Collection of Digital Work ★★★★

The Between Web pages present an art design project to the Internet public. Users will find a collection of images under various headings. Most of the work is some form of digitally-retouched photographs. Users will find background information on the images and the site itself, as well as information on the author. In addition, this site presents several drawings composed with both electronic and traditional means.

KEYWORDS Art Projects, Electronic Arts, Online Art Galleries
AUDIENCE Art Enthusiasts, Artists
CONTACT Daniel J. Mulligan dmuligan@dworld.com
FREE

http://www.dworld.com/gallery/

Cesium133 Online Art Gallery ★★★★

The Cesium133 Online Art Gallery offers a collection of images and other graphic art. Users can browse through exhibitions of individual artists, or view artwork by the medium it is in. In addition, this site offers occasional featured exhibits, as well as a collection of links to other art sites on the Net. Information on ordering the artwork found on this site is also available.

KEYWORDS Art Galleries, Online Art Galleries
AUDIENCE Art Enthusiasts, Artists
CONTACT Sales@Cesium133.Com
FREE

http://www.cesium133.com/

Chinese Archaic Jades from the Kwan Collection ★★★

The Chinese Archaic Jades from the Kwan Collection page offers a virtual art gallery with striking images of jade carvings from ancient China. Users will find many images in the GIF format, as well as background information on each image.

KEYWORDS Chinese Art, Jade, Online Art Galleries, Stonework
AUDIENCE Art Enthusiasts, Asian Art Enthusiasts
CONTACT Chiu-yee Cheung
FREE

http://www.arts.cuhk.hk/KwansJade/Kwans.html

Digital Avatar ★★★★

The Digital Avatar Web site offers a collection of computer-composed images. Users will find a selection of images and text information on these images, as well as background material on the artist who created the images. The art on this page is strongly influenced by Indian mythology and tradition. Links to Buddhist spiritual resources are also provided at this site.

KEYWORDS Digital Imaging, Electronic Arts, Indian Art, Online Art Galleries
AUDIENCE Art Enthusiasts, Artists, Electronic Art Enthusiasts
CONTACT Vasant Nayak nayak@charm.net
FREE

http://www.charm.net/~nayak/avtar2.html

Edith Carter ★★★

The Edith Carter page offers images and information from this Canadian artist. Users will find a selection of abstract images, as well as written material on the artist's inspirations. Information is also provided on past and future exhibitions of her work. Images are available as large format GIF files.

KEYWORDS Artists, Electronic Arts, Online Art Galleries
AUDIENCE Art Enthusiasts, Artists, Canadians
CONTACT Edith Carter
FREE

http://www.inasec.ca/com/ecarter/ecarter.htm

Frida Kahlo Home Page ★★★★

The Frida Kahlo Home Page offers an extensive archive of information and images related to this renowned artist. Users will find a comprehensive collection of biographical information on the artist, as well as a selection of images of her artwork. Of particular interest is the collection of Kahlo's self-portraits. Links to a Kahlo FTP site, as well as other Web sites about her, are also provided.

KEYWORDS Art History, Artists, Online Art Galleries
AUDIENCE Art Educators, Art Enthusiasts, Art Students, Frida Kahlo Enthusiasts

Art Galleries

CONTACT carrie@cascade.net
FREE

http://www.cascade.net/kahlo.html

GEN ART Home Page ★★★★

The GEN ART Home Page is a non-profit arts organization in New York that is exclusively devoted to presenting art by new, undiscovered artists. Users will find a catalog of images, as well as information on ordering the artworks found online. Links to Gen Art's 'friends,' as well as to other art sites on the Net can be found here.

KEYWORDS Online Art Galleries, Artists
AUDIENCE Art Enthusiasts, Artists
CONTACT scott@emedia.net
FREE

http://www.emedia.net/genart/

Galleries & Artists ★★★★

The Galleries & Artists Web page offers an index listing of many artists whose work is on display for Internet users around the world. Visitors will find a selection of jewelry, traditional and electronic art work, as well as information on ordering the work that you see here.

KEYWORDS Artists, Online Art Galleries, Jewelry
AUDIENCE Art Consumers, Art Enthusiasts, Jewelry Enthusiasts
FREE

http://www.interart.net/galleries/artistlist.html

The Gallery of Fine Art ★★★

The Gallery of Fine Art presents a collection of artwork from Australian artists. Users will find a series of images, as well as background information on the artists and their work. In addition, this site provides a location map for those who wish to physically visit the site, as well as information on upcoming exhibits.

KEYWORDS Artists, Australia, Online Art Galleries
AUDIENCE Art Enthusiasts, Australians
CONTACT ausart@iinet.net.au
FREE

http://www.iinet.net.au/~ausart/

Gallery Walk ★★★★

Gallery Walk is a collection of images and background information from many art galleries from all over the world. Users will find commercial galleries, independent galleries, individual artist galleries, and more. This site provides background information on the individual galleries such as the owner name, details about the type of work shown, and images from current and past exhibitions.

KEYWORDS Art Galleries, Online Art Galleries
AUDIENCE Art Enthusiasts, Artists
CONTACT Joseph F. Gregory
mfjfg@uxa.ecn.bgu.edu
FREE

http://www.ecn.bgu.edu/users/mfjfg/galwalk.html

Connections to The Art Site on the World Wide Web

Is it worth a look?

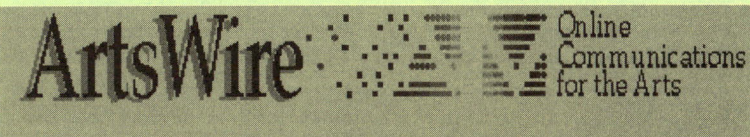

- About Arts Wire, a communications network for the arts community
- For more information about subscribing to Arts Wire
- See A Road Map to Arts Wire's Home Page
- See Home Pages by Arts Wire's Artists
- See Home Pages by Arts Wire's Arts Organizations
- Read HOTWIRE, a weekly summary of arts news and information
- Explore the Arts Wire WebBase
- Visit the Arts Wire Gopher
- Arts Wire WWW Tour Guide

If you're a student of the arts and want to find out about art in cyberspace, you need only turn to "The Art Site" on the World Wide Web. This site features an essay, including hypertext links, on some 40 electronic art galleries from around the Internet. Each gallery is reviewed and analyzed with the intention of producing a topology of the various art spaces and showcases on the Web.

(http://cwis.usc.edu/dept/annenberg/artfinal.html)

also, (http://www.tmn.com/Oh/Artswire/www/awfront.html)

Guild Exhibit ★★★★

This site is an online gallery of a photographic art display on at the Peoria Art Guild. The digitized photos are available for viewing as JPEG images.

KEYWORDS Art Exhibitions, Computer Art, Photography
AUDIENCE Artists, Arts Community, Photographers
CONTACT Howard Goldbaum
howard@bradley.bradley.edu
FREE

http://www.bradley.edu/exhibit/index.html

Image Dot Gallery ★★★★

Image Dot Gallery provides a forum and a place to exhibit works of art to the students and faculty of Arizona State University. Users will find a collection of images of art in several different media, including creative writing, painting, and digital photography. Information is also available on the students and staff whose contributions are found in this gallery.

KEYWORDS Art Education, Online Art Galleries
AUDIENCE Art Educators, Art Enthusiasts, Art Students
CONTACT John Colt, Jo Ann Briseno
john.colt@asu.edu, joann.briseno@asu.edu
FREE

http://www.asu.edu/asu-cwis/finearts/image.gallery

Internet Arts Museum For Free ★★★

This site provided by Artists for Revolution through Technology on the Internet (ARTnet), is an attempt to provide an online digital gallery of electronic art. Users will find visual art, as well as digital audio and video. There is also information on submitting your work to the collective, as well as a help section with information on helper applications which users need in order to play audio or video.

KEYWORDS Computer Art, Computer Graphics, Multimedia
AUDIENCE Art Enthusiasts, Artists, Computer Artists, Multimedia Enthusiasts
CONTACT info@artnet.org
FREE

http://www.artnet.org/iamfree/

Knoxville Museum of Art ★★★

The Knoxville Museum of Art Web page provides information on upcoming exhibitions. Users will find information such as how to get to the museum, exhibition schedules, and sample images from the current and past exhibit. There is also information on special museum activities, such as jazz music concerts, and a collection of links to other art sites on the Net.

KEYWORDS Art Museums, Online Art Galleries
AUDIENCE Art Enthusiasts, Artists, Knoxville Residents
CONTACT kma@esper.com
FREE

http://www.esper.com/kma/index.html

Marc Broadway, Southwestern Artist ★★★

The Marc Broadway, Southwestern Artist page offers information and images from this artist who chooses

Arts & Music — Art Galleries

Native American subjects as his focus. Users will find images in GIF and JPEG formats, as well as background information on the artist himself. In addition, the artist provides some material on the source of his inspiration, as well as links to other art resources on the Net.

- **KEYWORDS** Artists, Native American Art, Online Art Galleries, Southwestern Art
- **AUDIENCE** Art Enthusiasts, Southwestern Art Enthusiasts
- **CONTACT** Marc Broadway — marcb@frontier.net
- **FREE**

http://www.hwi.com/MB/MBHOME.html

Minnesota Online Art Gallery ★★★

The Southern Minnesota Online Art Gallery offers a collection of images and information on the gallery, its exhibits, and visitor information. Users will find images from several different artists, as well as background and historical material on the artists themselves. In addition, this site provides links to other art resources on the Net.

- **KEYWORDS** Minnesota, Online Art Galleries
- **AUDIENCE** Art Enthusiasts, Minnesota Residents
- **FREE**

http://www.ic.mankato.mn.us/ent/art/gallery.html

National Museum of the American Indian ★★★★

The National Museum of the American Indian page offers a collection of Native American artwork, images, and information. Users will find images culled from the museum's collection, as well as information of use to visitors. There is also material on upcoming events at the museum, and a collection of links to other Native American sites on the Net.

- **KEYWORDS** Native American Art, Online Art Galleries
- **AUDIENCE** Art Enthusiasts, Native Americans
- **CONTACT** logomanc@interport.net
- **FREE**

http://www.interport.net/~logomanc/heye.html

Net in Arcadia ★★★

Net In Arcadia is a Web site exploring Modernist Art and Western Figurative Tradition through the art of three humanists. Users will find the art linked by artist, with thumbnails and full screen images, as well as artists biographies and short descriptions of the art. A summary of the Arcadian theme and Utopia is also included.

- **KEYWORDS** Art Exhibitions, Modern Art, Paintings
- **AUDIENCE** Art Enthusiasts, Art Historians, Art Students, Artists
- **CONTACT** net.in.arcadia@parnasse.com
- **FREE**

http://www.parnasse.com/net.in.arcadia.html

Paintings of Vermeer ★★★★

The Paintings of Vermeer Web page offers a wealth of information on the Dutch artist Jan Vermeer. Users will find biographical information on the artist, as well as a collection of images of his paintings. The images span his entire career and are in small and large GIF and JPEG formats. Users will also find a handy guide to locating exhibits of his paintings in galleries all around the world. The site also includes information on upcoming exhibits and links to other Vermeer sites on the Net.

- **KEYWORDS** Art History, Artists, Online Art Galleries
- **AUDIENCE** Art Enthusiasts, Art Historians, Artists, Vermeer Enthusiasts
- **CONTACT** Roy Williams Clickery — roy@ccsf.caltech.edu
- **FREE**

http://www.ccsf.caltech.edu/~roy/vermeer/

Paper + Cathode ★★★★

Paper + Cathode is an online gallery of graphic design and electronic art by international artist P. Scott Makela. Users will find a collection of images in several categories, including artwork done for CD covers and other commercial projects. In addition, this site offers considerable background information on the artist and his work, as well as pointers to other art resources on the Net.

- **KEYWORDS** Electronic Arts, Graphic Design, Online Art Galleries
- **AUDIENCE** Art Enthusiasts, Artists, Electronic Art Enthusiasts, Graphic Art Enthusiasts
- **CONTACT** P. Scott Makela — makela-comments@grfn.org
- **FREE**

http://www.grfn.org/~makela/

Rossi & Rossi ★★★

Rossi & Rossi is a gallery of Oriental Art specializing in the the art of India, Nepal, Tibet and Southeast Asia. In one gallery you may view examples of Himlayan sculpture and paintings. In another gallery there are images of early Tibetan mandalas from the Early Tibetan Mandala exhibition. When you visit the virtual galleries you can click on thumbnail prints of the exhibit and download JPEG images. (The size of each JPEG is provided.) Catalogues published by Rossi & Rossi can be ordered by contacting Rossi & Rossi and the producer address listed herein.

- **KEYWORDS** Asian Arts, India, Southeast Asia
- **AUDIENCE** Art Historians, Artists, Asian Art Enthusiasts, Educators (University)
- **FREE**

http://www.ingress.com/~asianart/rossi/rossi.html

Strange Interactions ★★★

This site contains an archive of images by John Jacobsen including paintings, drawings, woodblocks, engravings and lithographs. The images are all black and white—most are realistic in style with fantastic or surreal elements. Works reproduced include Night Outside the Citadel, containing some of the artists favorite imagery (crosses, phallic symbols, buildings, masks, cables, fish), Toxic Beam Dump (inspired by Jurassic Park, high-energy physics, and the art of Gregory Gillespie), and Cybersex (an ode to those who use the Internet to conduct their sex lives).

- **KEYWORDS** Multimedia, Online Arts, Paintings
- **AUDIENCE** Art Educators, Art Enthusiasts, Art Students, Artists
- **CONTACT** jacobsen@amanda.physics.wisc.edu
- **FREE**

http://amanda.physics.wisc.edu/show.html

gopher://amanda.physics.wisc.edu:70/11/show

Tandanya Aboriginal Art ★★★★

The Tandanya Aboriginal Art page presents a large collection of images and information on art, and links to information on, the Australian Aborigines. Users will find many images in the GIF format. In addition, this site provides information on the artists whose work is exhibited here, as well as links and information on Australia itself.

- **KEYWORDS** Aboriginal Art, Australia, Cultural Art, Online Art Galleries
- **AUDIENCE** Aboriginal Art Enthusiasts, Australian Culture Enthusiasts
- **CONTACT** nanou@chopper.macmedia.com.au
- **FREE**

http://www.macmedia.com.au/homepage.html

A Transcendental Gallery ★★★★

A Transcendental Gallery offers a collection of Indian images, sculpture, and other forms of art. Users will find many images in the JPEG format, with title and size information. There is also information on contributing to the gallery, as well as information on joining a mailing list to receive updates when the Web page has new pictures. Links to other art-related sites are also available here.

- **KEYWORDS** Art History, Indian Art
- **AUDIENCE** Art Enthusiasts, Indian Art Enthusiasts
- **CONTACT** gallery@rayk.vip.best.com
- **FREE**

http://www.best.com/~rayk/html/picidx.html

Wentworth Gallery Home Page ★★★

The Wentworth Gallery provides a wide variety of original oil paintings, limited edition serigraphs, lithographs, and sculptures from artists around the world. Users can view images of artwork online, as well as read background information on the artists and their work. Users can browse by artist or style, and retrieve pricing information for each piece. This site also provides an online ordering facility, as well as sections with information on gift certificates and arranging a home showing of up to twenty works of art.

- **KEYWORDS** Arts, Online Art Galleries, Visual Arts
- **AUDIENCE** Art Buyers, Art Enthusiasts, Art Sellers, Artists
- **CONTACT** gallery@wentworth-art.com
- **FREE**

http://wentworth-art.com/

Art Galleries – Art History

Wingspread Collectors Guide to New Mexican and Southwest Art ★★★★

The Wingspread Collectors Guide to New Mexican and Southwest Art offers a number of resources related to this unique American art style. Users will find images and essays on Southwestern Art, as well as information on art galleries in the regions that display this type of art. A search facility is available here, as well as a collection of pointers to other related resources on the Net.

KEYWORDS Native American Art, New Mexico, Online Art Galleries, Southwestern Art
AUDIENCE Art Enthusiasts, Native American Art Enthusiasts, Southwest Art Enthusiasts
CONTACT artinfo@wingspread.com
FREE

http://www.wingspread.com/

The World Wide Web Virtual Library-Museums ★★★★

The World Wide Web Virtual Library-Museums page offers a large index of museums both on and off the Web. Users will find a well-organized hierarchy of links to many sites on the Net with museum information. Links to popular sites such as the Web Louvre are provided, along with a regionally organized list of physical museum sites.

KEYWORDS Art Museums, Museums
AUDIENCE Art Enthusiasts, Educators, Museum Enthusiasts, Students
CONTACT Jonathan Bowen
Jonathan.Bowen@comlab.ox.ac.uk
FREE

http://www.comlab.ox.ac.uk/archive/other/museums.html

Art History
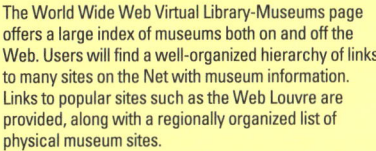

See also
Arts & Music · *Architecture*
Arts & Music · *Art Museums*
Arts & Music · *Artists*
Humanities & Social Sciences · *Area & Cultural Studies*

African Art - Aesthetics and Meaning ★★★★

The African Art - Aesthetics and Meaning site contains an online sculpture exhibition of art from Africa. This site was compiled by the Bayly Art Museum in Charlottesville, Virginia. The site contains information about the elements of the African aesthetic, the exhibition, a bibliography, about the Electronic Exhibition Catalog, and credits. There are images of totems, masks, Chi Wara headdresses, epa headdresses and other sculptures from Mali, Sierre Leone, Liberia, Nigeria, and Ghana. The exhibition was curated by Benjamin C. Ray and has detailed notes on each work and the tribe that created it.

KEYWORDS Africa, African Art, Art Exhibitions, Sculpture
AUDIENCE African Art Enthusiasts, Art Students, Artists, Arts Community, Educators
CONTACT Christie D. Stephenson
cds2e@virginia.edu
FREE

http://www.lib.virginia.edu/dic/exhib/93.ray.aa/African.html

The Age Of Enlightenment In The Paintings Of France's National Museums ★★★★

This site contains works of art painted during the Age of Enlightenment and owned by French National Museums. The site includes an historical background, a short genealogy, the collection of paintings, and an index of the artists. The collection contains works by Jean Simeon Chardin, Jean-Baptiste Boucher, Jean Honore Fragonard, Jean-Baptiste Perronneau, Elizabeth-Louise Vigee-Lebrun, and more. It also contains information on painting genres and French history, and brief explanations of significant figures in the Age of Englightenment. The site includes many links to related subjects including Napooleon Bonaparte, Louis XVI, The French Revolution, the Royal Academy of Painting and Sculpture, among others.

KEYWORDS Art Exhibitions, France
AUDIENCE Art Historians, Art Students, Educators, Students
CONTACT Laurent Manoeuvre
manoeuvre@culture.fr
FREE

http://dmf.culture.fr/files/imaginary_exhibition.html

ArtServ, The ANU Mosaic for the Humanities ★★★★

This site contains a collection of over 10,000 images and descriptions pertaining to world art history. There are some 2,500 images of classical architecture and architectural sculpture from around the Mediterranean. Additional images include classical, medieval and Renaissance architecture, sculpture and icons, the Pergamon Altar, Islamic architecture, contemporary Hong Kong architecture, and a tutorial on the Palace of Diocletian at Split. The book entitled 'The Greek and Roman Cities of Western Turkey' can also be searched at this site.

KEYWORDS Architectural History, Medieval Studies, Sculpture, Visual Arts
AUDIENCE Art Historians, Art Students, Arts Community, Researchers
CONTACT Michael Greenhalgh
gremarth@fac.anu.edu.au
FREE

http://rubens.anu.edu.au/

The City of Trier, Germany — Art and Architecture ★★★

This site contains information on the German city of Trier and its art, particularly that dating from ancient times (the city is believed to have been founded in 16 b.c. under Augustus) through the medieval period. The site includes a brief history of Trier, Germany's oldest city, laced with numerous links to images of artifacts and ruins of the city. There is also a portrait, and brief summary of the life, of Karl Marx who was born here.

KEYWORDS Architectural History, Germany, History (Ancient)
AUDIENCE Archaeologists, Educators, Germans, Historians
FREE

http://www.uni-trier.de/trier/trier_eng.html

Commentary on Art ★★★

This is the site for a college-level art history course taught by Jerrold Mattox of Penn State University (Pennsylvania) for the spring semester of 1995. The scope of the course is broad and includes Rodin, Jasper Johns, and Dutch landscape painting. The visual materials include an exhibition of etchings by Rembrandt taken from an exhibition at the Carnegie-Mellon Museum at the Palmer Museum of Art. The site includes a reading list (On Photography by Susan Sontag , Other Criteria by Leo Steinberg , Still Life with a Bridle by Zbignew Herbert) with weekly assignments, paper assignments, and schedule of field trips. The site also contains links to other arts-related resources.

KEYWORDS Contemporary Art, Distance Education, Universities
AUDIENCE Art Students, Educators, Students
CONTACT Jerrold Maddox
jxm22@psu.edu
FREE

http://salazar.aa.psu.edu/courses/art122w/122WHomepage.html

Demo On Mosaic - Rosen Sculpture Exhibition ★★★

This is the Web site for the Appalachian State University Department of Art and contains selections from the Rosen Outdoor Sculpture Exhibition and competition (with notes on artists and their works). The site also holds art historical information on several sculptors, including Michelangelo. There is also a limited set of links to other art resources available on the Net.

KEYWORDS Art Exhibitions, Contemporary Art, Fine Arts, Sculpture
AUDIENCE Art Educators, Art Enthusiasts, Art Students, Arts Community
CONTACT Douglas Brantz
Brantzdr@xx.acs.appstate.edu
FREE

http://www.acs.appstate.edu:80/art/

The Essential Escher Gallery ★★★★

The art and life of M.C. Escher is presented by displays of his art, biographical information, and discussion of the mathematical bases for his art. The viewer can browse the art based on an alphabetical listing, a chronological presentation, or a selection of some of his most popular pieces. A short biographical outline of the artist's life is available as is a chronology highlighting importants moments in Escher's life. Images of each thumbnail image lists the title, date, technique and size, while larger JPEG images can be viewed and downloaded.

KEYWORDS Art Galleries, Artists, Prints

Audience Art Educators, Art Historians, Artists, Graphic Artists
Contact Matt Ransford mransfrd@umich.edu
Free

http://www.umich.edu/~mransfrd/escher/

The Getty Art History Information Program (AHIP) ★★★

AHIP is part of the The J. Paul Getty Trust, which seeks to make a significant contribution to the visual arts and the humanities in the areas of conservation, scholarship, and education. AHIP provides publications and long-established resources in electronic form, including bibliographic databases (Bibliography of the History of Art and the Avery Index to Architectural Periodicals), historical inventory and catalogue information, and the Provenance Index, containing documents related to the history of collecting as well as an index of paintings sold in the British Isles. The site contains the resources such as the Art & Architecture Thesaurus for cataloging and indexing, and a census of antique art and architecture known in the Renaissance. This site also provides links to humanities and arts resources on the Net.

Keywords Architectural History, Art Conservation, Art Museums, Visual Arts
Audience Art Historians, Educators, Researchers, Students
Contact ahip@getty.edu.
Free

http://www.ahip.getty.edu/ahip/Text_home.html

The Palace of Diocletian at Split ★★★★

This site contains an art historical presentation on the Palace of Diocletian at Split (ex-Yugoslavia), compiled by art historian Michael Greenhalgh. The essay contains several historical reconstructions of the Palace, with historical commentary, and a comparison with the Palatine Hill in Rome. There are also separate mosaic pages on diverse aspects of the palace site—images of the colonnaded streets, a comparison with Split's architecture, the Emperor's apartments, the temple, the Emperor's mausoleum, the walls and gates, bibliography, and more.

Keywords Ancient Art, Architectural History, Historical Sites, Yugoslavia
Audience Architecture Historians, Art Historians, Art Students, Classicists, Educators
Contact Michael Greenhalgh gremarth@fac.anu.edu.au
Free

http://www.ncsa.uiuc.edu/SDG/Experimental/split/split1.html

Perseus Home Page ★★★★

This server is for the Perseus project sponsored by Tufts University. The site contains a description of the project and translations of several ancient texts including Aristotle, Aristophanes, Demosthenes, Demades, Euripides, Homer, Lysias, Plato, Sophocles, and more. The site also contains comprehensive notes on Antique art, especially vase painting. There are also links to other classics and archaeology sites on the web.

Keywords Ancient Art, Archaeology
Audience Art Students, Classicists, Educators
Contact Adam Lewis adam@perseus.tufts.edu
Free

http://www.perseus.tufts.edu/

Romarch — A Resource for Art and Archaeology in Ancient Italy and Rome ★★★★

The ROMARCH home page is a crossroads for Web resources on the art and archaeology of Italy and the Roman provinces, from 1000 B.C. to A.D. 600. The ROMARCH Internet discussion group is sponsored by the Interdepartmental Program in Classical Art and Archaeology (IPCAA) at the University of Michigan, currently with more than 350 subscribers world-wide. Topics are quite varied—bricks and tiles, an Archaeology course, gender in the roman house, houses, job announcements, and more. The site also contains links to many general resources.

Keywords Ancient Art, Archaeology, Classics, Italy
Audience Archaeologists, Art Students, Arts Community, Educators
Contact majordomo@rome.classics.lsa.umich.edu
Free

http://www.umich.edu/~pfoss/ROMARCH.html

Rome Reborn - The Vatican Libary & Renaissance Culture ★★

This site is sponsored by the University of Virginia. It includes access to the Vatican Library and Renaissance Culture Art Exhibition. The site contains nine parts with essays on diverse topics in the humanities including archaeology, theology, music, medicine and biology, nature, etc. It also contains JPEG images relating to the nine areas.

Keywords Art Exhibitions, Renaissance Art, Universities, Vatican (The)
Audience Art Activists, Art Educators, Art Enthusiasts, Art Historians
Free

gopher://gopher.lib.virginia.edu:70/11/alpha/vat

Zimbabwean Stone Sculpture ★★★

This site gives information on works of Zimbabwean sculptors, provides access to view photos of a few of the sculptures, and gives references to books providing more information. The site also gives some biographical information as well as information on relevant exhibitions. Sculptors include Edward Chiwawa, Joram Mariga, Bernard Matemera, Richard Mteki, Henri Munyaradzi, and the Takawira brothers. The site also contains lists of exhibitions of African/Shona Sculpture around the world.

Keywords African Art, African Studies, Sculpture, Zimbabwe
Audience Art Enthusiasts, Art Historians, Art Students, Arts Community
Contact Eelco Essenberg E.Essenberg@TWI.TUDelft.NL
Free

http://www.twi.tudelft.nl/Local/ShonaSculpture/ShonaSculpture.html

Art Museums

See also
Arts & Music · *Art Galleries*
Arts & Music · *Art History*
Arts & Music · *Film & Video*
Arts & Music · *Visual Arts*
Popular Culture & Entertainment · *Museums & Theme Parks*

Allen Memorial Art Museum ★★★

This is the site for the Allen Art Museum in Oberlin College (California). The building was designed in 1917 by New York architect Cass Gilbert and the site contains a brief description, image and architectural history of the museum. The collection is strong in several areas of world art and this site contains images from their Ancient, European, American, Asian, and African collections. There are also links to other Oberlin College pages.

Keywords African Art, American Art, Architectural History, Art Museums
Audience Art Students, Artists, Arts Community, Californians, Educators
Contact webmaster@www.oberlin.edu.
Free

http://www.oberlin.edu/wwwmap/allen_art.html

Andy Warhol Museum ★★★★

The Andy Warhol Museum considers itself 'essential to the understanding of the most influential American artist of the second half of the 20th century.' The museum is also a primary resource for anyone who wishes to study contemporary art and popular culture. The site contains a tour through the Museum, art samples from throughout Warhol's career (Self-portraits, Jackie O, Marilyn, Shoe, Electric Chair), exhibition schedules and descriptions, as well as film schedules and descriptions. The site also has general information about the museum and links to other art resources.

Keywords Artists, Contemporary Art, Film, Visual Arts
Audience Art Collectors, Art Enthusiasts, Artists, Curators
Contact www@warhol.org
Free

http://www.usaor.net/warhol/

The Art Museum at San Jose State University ★★

This site allows you to browse or initiate a word search of the museum image database. While browsing, one can choose from Africa, the Americas, Europe, Asia, the Near East, or Oceania. A sample pages of images and associated information with Islamic Images is included.

- KEYWORDS: African Art, Asian Arts, Islamic Art
- AUDIENCE: Artists, Arts Community, Educators, Students, Tourists
- FREE

http://gallery.sjsu.edu/ArtH/art-museum.html

Asian Arts ★★★

Asian Arts is 'the online forum for the study and exhibition of the arts of Asia'. The site features Exhibitions such as the Early Tibetan Mandalas-The Rossi Collection, Articles, Notes including Jane Casey Singer-A Taglung Lama, Galleries wiht Rossi and Rossi, London, England-Fine South Asian, Himalayan and Southeast Asian Art, and Auction Results at Christie's, King Street - London, England. Also included are links to a calendar of events and exhibitions as well as other Asian Art Sources.

- KEYWORDS: Asia, Asian Arts, Online Arts, Tibet
- AUDIENCE: Art Enthusiasts, Art Historians, Artists
- CONTACT: asianart@rt66.com
- FREE

http://www.ingress.com/~asianart/asianart.html

Christus Rex (Art from the Vatican) ★★★★

This site contains images of and information about the Vatican City collection. Images include exterior shots of Michelangelo's St. Peter's Cathedral, the Sistine Chapel, the Raphael Stanzas and Loggias and the Vatican Museum collection. The site contains descriptions and histories of the art and architecture and over 1100 images of works by Bernini, Michelangelo, Raphael, Arnolfo di Cambio and other artists, as well as images from the Apostolic Library collection and the treasury of St. Peter's.

- KEYWORDS: Rome, Vatican (The)
- AUDIENCE: Art Historians, Artists, Arts Community, Museum Enthusiasts, Tourists
- CONTACT: Michael Olteanu root@christusrex.org
- FREE

http://www.christusrex.org/www1/icons/index.html

Conservatoire National des Arts et Métiers (National Conservatory of Arts and Crafts) ★★★

This is the web site of the Conservatoire National des Arts et Métiers (National Conservatory of Arts and Crafts) in France. Information is available here on topics including Paris, the subway, the Museum of Arts and Crafts, the virtual museum of technology (which offers pictures, and texts in French), the Institut Informatique d'Entreprise, and the Centre d'Etude et de Recherche en Informatique du CNAM.

- KEYWORDS: Art Museums, France, Paris
- AUDIENCE: Computer Users, Educators, Internet Users, Researchers, Students
- CONTACT: webmaster@cnam.fr
- FREE

http://ftp.cnam.fr/index_english.html

Dallas Museum of Art Online ★★★

This archive contains approximately 200 digital images of artworks owned by the Dallas Museum of Art and includes images of contemporary art, European Art, Art of the Americas, Art of Africa, Asia, and the Pacific. The site also contains images of works from the museum sculpture garden and information about museum educational programs.

- KEYWORDS: Art Museums, Contemporary Art, Pre-Columbian Art, Sculpture
- AUDIENCE: African Art Enthusiasts, Art Historians, Artists, Arts Community, Students
- CONTACT: Kevin J. Comerford czbb020@access.texas.gov
- FREE

http://www.unt.edu/dfw/dma/www/dma.htm

The David and Alfred Smart Museum of Art ★★★★

The core of this site is 'The Collection,' a guide to a portion of the Smart Museum's impressive and diverse holdings. The collection catalogue offers an online selection of paintings, sculptures, drawings, prints, and decorative works, intended to extend and encourage use of the museum's resources to the greater academic community. This site contains SmartNews, an overview of upcoming events and exhibitions, lectures, recent acquisitions, and updates on recent gifts to the museum and related development topics as well as links to other art resources.

- KEYWORDS: Art Museums, Asian Arts, Contemporary Art
- AUDIENCE: Art Historians, Artists, Illinois Residents, Researchers
- CONTACT: John Casler casler@cs.uchicago.edu
- FREE

http://csmaclab-www.uchicago.edu/SmartMuseum/default.html

I Am Free — The Internet Arts User for Free ★★★

IAMfree has embarked on an ever-changing series of exhibits in modern art, 'bereft of the pitfalls and commercialization that is currently stifling art.' In this way they hope to create a new system for the creation, business and distribution of the arts. They also believe new technologies will offer possibilities for new directions in art. This site showcases the finest contemporary art in a variety of media - music, photography, video/film, computer art and literature. These arts are presented to the world complete, downloadable and free.

- KEYWORDS: Art Exhibitions, Video, Visual Arts
- AUDIENCE: Artists, Arts Community, Educators, Students
- CONTACT: info@artnet.org
- FREE

http://www.artnet.org/iamfree/index.html

The Krannert Art Museum and Kinkead Pavilion ★★★

The Krannert Art Museum and Kinkead Pavilion, located on the campus of the University of Illinois at Urbana-Champaign, houses a collection of more than eight thousand works of art, ranging in date from the fourth millennium, B.C., to the present. This site provides access to images and information about the museum collections (specialties include twentieth-century art, American and European art, Asian Art and Old World Antiquities) and traveling exhibitions (e.g., 'Concerned Theatre Japan—The Graphic Art of Japanese Theatre, 1960-1980'), as well as an online hypermedia display. The site also contains a museum calendar of events detailing educational programs and exhibition information.

- KEYWORDS: Art Museums, Asian Arts, Universities
- AUDIENCE: Art Historians, Artists, Illinois Residents, Students
- FREE

http://www.art.uiuc.edu/kam/Guide/Intro.html

La Trobe University Art Museum ★★★

The LaTrobe Art Museum at La Trobe University (Melbourne, Australia) provides images and information concerning the current exhibitions at the gallery. The site contains images from the Clifton Pugh Collection and links to the Glenn College home page.

- KEYWORDS: Art Galleries, Art Museums, Australia, Contemporary Art
- AUDIENCE: Art Historians, Artists, Arts Community, Australians
- CONTACT: Rhonda Noble M.Kosten@latrobe.edu.au
- FREE

http://www.latrobe.edu.au/Glenn/Museum/ArtMuseumHome.html

Los Angeles County Museum of Art ★★★★

The Los Angeles County Museum of Art (LACMA) web site features selected masterpieces from its permanent collection, current and future exhibition schedules, information on education programs, membership opportunities, the museum shop, and occasional feature projects. Clickable thumbnail sketches are provided for American Art, Ancient and Islamic Art, Costumes and Textiles, Decorative Arts, European Painting and Sculpture, Photography, Far Eastern Art, Prints and Drawings, Twentieth Century Art, and more.

- KEYWORDS: California, Paintings
- AUDIENCE: Artists, Public, Scholars, Students
- FREE

http://www.lacma.org/

Moscow Kremlin ★★★

This site contains images and brief descriptions of the following Russian sites, the Cathedral of Annunciation, Cathedral Square (Sobornaya Ploschad), Ivan the Great Bell-Tower, Lenin's Mausoleum, Our Saviour (Spasskaya) Tower, Red Square, the Residence of the President, the Senate Building, the Tsar-Bell and the

Art Museums

Tsar-Cannon. The site also contains a map of the Kremlin.

KEYWORDS Architecture, Art Museums, Russia
AUDIENCE Educators, Russian Culture Enthusiasts, Russians, Students, Tourists
CONTACT cdguide@cominf.msk.su
FREE

http://www.kiae.su/www/wtr/kremlin/begin.html

Musée de l'Orangerie ★★★

This site for the Musée de l'Orangerie contains information concerning current exhibits and admission to the museum. The site also has links to other French museums and to Metro information for Paris. The Musee de l'Orangerie is renown for its huge decorative panels by Claude Monet which are installed in the basement galleries of the museum.

KEYWORDS Art Exhibitions, Paris
AUDIENCE Artists, Arts Community, Educators, Students, Tourists
CONTACT nbarth@ucsd.edu
FREE

http://meteora.ucsd.edu:80/~norman/paris/Musees/Orange/

Musée d'Orsay ★★★★

This site contains images of many Impressionist and Post-Impressionist paintings from the collection including works by Monet, Manet, Degas, Seurat, Gauguin, and Cezanne. It also contains general information about current and forthcoming exhibitions [e.g. Les Oublies du Caire; Ingres, Coubet, Monet, Gauguin from the National Egyptian Collection of French Art, Whistler (1834 - 1903), etc.] as well as information about museum location and admission.

KEYWORDS Art Museums, Impressionism, Paris
AUDIENCE Artists, Arts Community, Educators, Francophiles, Students, Tourists
FREE

http://meteora.ucsd.edu:80/~norman/paris/Musees/Orsay/Collections/Paintings/

Musée du Louvre ★★★

This site contains images from and information about the Louvre Museum in Paris. Its 'Treasures of the Louvre' section contains images of famous, universally admired art works in the collection (Venus de Milo, Winged Victory, da Vinci's Mona Lisa, Théodore Géricault's Raft of the Medusa) and examples of Egyptian antiquities, Oriental antiquities, and decorative arts. It also has a section on the organization of the collections, a short history of the Louvre, images of the Louvre and Chateau Vincennes and links to other arts resources.

KEYWORDS Art Museums, Paris, Renaissance Art
AUDIENCE Architecture Students, Art Enthusiasts, Art Historians, Artists, Educators, Students
FREE

http://meteora.ucsd.edu:80/~norman/paris/Musees/Louvre/

Musee National d'Histoire et d'Art - Luxembourg's National Museum of Art and History ★★★★

This is the site for Luxembourg's National Museum. It contains images of the Roman mosaics found near Luxembourg, information on current exhibitions, (currently an exhibition of Modern Art), a history of the museum, a schedule of events for 1995 in the city of Luxembourg, and a section on the Luxembourg's National Commission for UNESCO. Art reproduced in JPEG images includes work by modern artists (Kandinsky, Paul Cauldfield), Renaissance Art (Rosso), Coins, Archaeology (Neolithic and Bronze Age artifacts) as well as images of the museum's architecture. The site also has links to additional servers in Luxembourg and other museum sites.

KEYWORDS Ancient Art, Archaeology, Luxembourg
AUDIENCE Armchair Travelers, Artists, Arts Community, Researchers, Tourists
CONTACT fumanti@men.l4
FREE

http://www.men.lu/~fumanti/LuxMusee.html

Musées de Paris ★★★★

This site contains information on, and images from, several important Paris museums including the Musée du Petit Palais, the Musée National d'Art Moderne - Centre Georges Pompidou, the Musée du Louvre, Musée d'Orsay, Galeries Nationales du Grand Palais, L'Institut du Monde Arabe, and Musée de l'Orangerie. The site also contains links to the Centre National d'Art et de Culture Georges Pompidou and the Musée des Arts et Metiers. The site also contains an interactive map of Paris with general information on each historic site (a brief history, description of the area, metro information) and images.

KEYWORDS Art Museums, Paris
AUDIENCE Art Historians, Artists, Arts Community, Tourists
CONTACT Centre national d'art et de culture Georges Pompidou
norman@ucsd.edu
FREE

http://meteora.ucsd.edu/~norman/paris/Musees/

The Museums and Historical Societies of Cayuga County ★★★

This site contains information concerning the museums and historical society of Cayuga County (New York) including the Cayuga Museum which houses objects representative of North American industry, domestic textiles and costumes, folk art, military and medical artifacts; Indian collections, and more. In addition, exhibitions highlighting regional fine art, contemporary crafts, photography, architecture and design, children's art and much more are located at The Schweinfurth Memorial Art Center. The site also contains information on Concerts, lectures, and workshops at the museums as well as information on the Cayuga County Agricultural Museum.

KEYWORDS Art Museums, Folk Art, New York
AUDIENCE Arts Community, Native Americans, Photography Enthusiasts
FREE

http://www.cnyric.org/museums.html

Museums in London ★★★

This page contains addresses for, and links to, museums in London, including the British Museum, the Imperial War Museum, the The Natural History Museum, the National Maritime Museum, the Royal Naval College Cabinet War Rooms, the Wellington Museum, the Victoria and Albert, the Museum of Mankind, and numerous other history and natural history museums.

KEYWORDS London, Museums
AUDIENCE Art Historians, Arts Community, Tourists, United Kingdom Residents
CONTACT M.Handley
M.Handley@cs.ucl.ac.uk
FREE

http://www.cs.ucl.ac.uk/misc/uk/london/museums.html

Museums in Stockholm ★★★★

This site contains decriptions and a map locating the museums in Stockholm, Sweden which calls itself the museum city. The museums included are the National Museum of Art (with examples fromthe permanent collection of paintings, sculpture, icons, etc., and special exhibitions), the Hallwyl Museum, a private home from the turn of the 19th century with collections of art and handicrafts), The Museum of National Antiquities (Swedish cultural artifacts), the Museum of Natural History, the Museum of Cultural History, the Music Museum, and others.

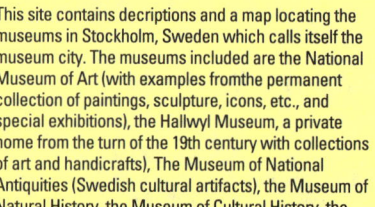

KEYWORDS Antiquities, Sweden
AUDIENCE Artists, Arts Community, Educators, Museum Enthusiasts, Students, Swedes, Tourists
CONTACT webmaster@nrm.se
FREE

http://www.sunet.se/stockholm/museums/museums.html

The National Gallery (London) ★★★

Founded in 1824, the National Gallery houses the National Collection of Western European painting, comprising more than 2,000 pictures dating from the late 13th to the early 20th century—in other words, from Giotto to Picasso. This site contains general information on the British Museum and its current exhibitions. It also contains links to other London museums and resources.

KEYWORDS Art Exhibitions, Visual Arts
AUDIENCE Tourists, United Kingdoms Residents
FREE

http://www.cs.ucl.ac.uk/local/museums/NationalGallery.html

The New Guinea Sculpture Garden at Stanford

This site, sponsored by Stanford University, contains images from the permanent exhibition of New Guinea Sculpture executed during the summer of 1994, by ten master carvers from Papua New Guinea. This page contains images of and information about the project, the outdoor site, the works (in wood and stone) and the individual artists who ranged in age from 27 to 73 and came from two different cultural groups, the Kwoma and the Latmul. Users will also find a link to a photograph of anthropologist Jim Mason, the project's director, and a link to the Stanford University home page.

KEYWORDS Anthropology, Exhibitions, Universities, Visual Arts
AUDIENCE Art Students, Artists, Arts Community, Californians
CONTACT Mike Peters
mjpeters@leland.stanford.edu
FREE

http://fuji.stanford.edu/icenter/png/ngp.html

The New Orleans Museum of Art

This site for the The New Orleans Museum of Art contains excerpts (images and information) from the Museum's current exhibitions and general information concerning the Museum itself (admission, location). The site also contains links to other Louisiana museums (Louisiana Children's Museum, Louisiana State Museum, etc.).

KEYWORDS Contemporary Art, Louisiana
AUDIENCE Arts Community, Louisiana Residents, Tourists
CONTACT vno@yatcom.com
FREE

http://yatcom.com/neworl/museum/noma2.html

North Carolina Museum of Art

This site contains information about the North Carolina Museum of Art including selections from the permanent collection (American art, European art, Egyptian art, African art, Judaica). Images in the site include works by the American artists Georgia O'Keeffe and Andrew Newell Wyeth, and the German Expressionist Karl Schmidt-Rottluff. Forthcoming exhibitions are listed and include both contemporary subjects and historical subjects. The site also contains general information and links to other art resources, as well as to the School of Library Science at the University of North Carolina at Chapel Hill.

KEYWORDS American Art, Contemporary Art, North Carolina
AUDIENCE Artists, Arts Community, North Carolina Residents, Tourists
FREE

http://ils.unc.edu/ncma/ncma.html

Connections to Museums
What can I see?

IMAGES FOR ART HISTORY AT THE AUSTRALIAN NATIONAL UNIVERSITY

There's hardly a museum in the world that isn't now on the Internet. Le Louvre in France, The Vatican in Rome, The Smithsonian in Washington, D.C., and the Bauhaus Archives in Berlin are just a handful of the exhibits you can visit in cyberspace. To get there, start your journey at "Museums and Expositions."

(http://www.rrz.uni-koeln.de:80/~a0055/expo.html)

If you want to trace the journey of Rome from the 14th century (when that great ancient city dwindled to a villa) to its rise from the ruins during the Renaissance Era, you can visit exhibit "rooms" devoted to different topics including the Vatican Library, Archaeology, Humanism, Mathematics, Music, and more. You can even view slides of music scores, as well as math books and more.

(http://www.nesa.uiuc.edu/SDG/Experimental/vatican.exhibit/vatican.exhibit.html)

Perhaps you would like to explore the varied exhibits at Museum Insel Hombroich in Neuss, Germany.

(http://www.bwk.tue.nl/lara/galleries/museums/hombroich/murr.gif)

How about the exhibits of Maori art at the Museum of New Zealand—TePapa Tongarewa? The site includes "Natural History in New Zealand," and decorative art collections. There are also sound files that go along with many of the images.

(http://hyperg.tu-graz.ac.at:80/76105FF2/CNew-Zealand)

Ohio State University at Newark Gallery

This site for the University Museum at Newark includes general museum information and exhibition information. Recent exhibitions include 'Ralph Rosenfield— First live arts performance on the WWW' and 'Licking County Artists.' The site also contains a movie of the gallery interior.

KEYWORDS Contemporary Art, Universities, Visual Arts
AUDIENCE Art Historians, Artists, Arts Community, Ohio Residents
CONTACT mkruse@cgrg.ohio-state.edu
FREE

http://www.cgrg.ohio-state.edu/~mkruse/osu.html

Online Museum of Singapore Art & History

This site provides access to numerous exhibits on the history and art of Singapore. Topics include Singapore Historical Postcards, 19th-Century Prints of Singapore, Ponts des Arts—Nanyang Artists in Paris, The Founding of Singapore and the Exploits of Her Founder, Sir

Thomas Stamford Raffles, and Paintings Inspired by Bali (at the Singapore Art Museum). The site also has links to other online arts resources.

KEYWORDS Art Exhibitions, Singapore
AUDIENCE Art Historians, Artists, Arts Community, Singapore Residents
FREE

http://king.ncb.gov.sg/nhb/museum.html

The Philbrook Museum of Art ★★★

Originally the home of oilman Waite Phillips and his family, Villa Philbrook was designed in the Italian Renaissance Revival style by architect Edward Buehler Delk during the mid-1920s. The Villa rests amid 23 acres of formal and informal Italian gardens designed by Herbert Hare. This site offers information about and images of the Philbrook Gardens, the Museum's forthcoming exhibitions (e.g., Durer and Rembrandt—The Felix Warburg Collection of German and Netherlandish Prints, 20th-Century American Art from the Williams Companies Collections), the Museum School and gift shop, and descriptions of tours available at the museum.

KEYWORDS American Art, Architecture, Oklahoma
AUDIENCE Arts Community, Oklahoma Residents, Tourists
FREE

http://www.wiltel.com/tulsa/phbrook.html

Portland Art Museum ★★★

This site contains information about the Portland Museum's forthcoming exhibitions including Breaking Barriers—Recent American Craft, Gauguin and the School of Pont-Aven, and Imperial Tombs of China. The site also contains general information, in addition to information about the Portland Museum's Rex Arragon Library, the Northwest Film Center, and the Rental Sales Gallery. It also offers a link to the home page for the Pacific Northwest College of Art.

KEYWORDS Asian Arts, Contemporary Art, Film, Museums
AUDIENCE Art Historians, Artists, Arts Community, Educators, Oregon Residents, Students
CONTACT Dan Lucas
danlucas@teleport.com
FREE

http://www.teleport.com/~danlucas/pam.html

The Royal Holloway Collection ★★★★

This site contains an introduction — in the form of images and commentary — to the The Royal Holloway Collection of paintings at Holloway College (University of London). Highlights of the world renown collection include works by Sir John Everett Millais, William Powell Frith, Luke Fildes, and other painters from the Royal Academy. The site also contains a brief history of Thomas Holloway and the founding of Holloway College for women. The site also contains links to other Holloway College sites (Physics, Geology, Library, home page).

KEYWORDS British Art, England
AUDIENCE Anglophiles, Art Historians, Artists, Arts Community

CONTACT www.@sun.rhbnc.ac.uk
FREE

http://www.rhbnc.ac.uk/ART/art1.html

Stuart Collection of Sculpture ★★★

This site contains selections from the Stuart Collection of Sculpture at the University of California, San Diego. The purpose of the collection is to enrich the cultural, intellectual, and scholarly life of the UCSD campus and of the San Diego community by building and maintaining a unique collection of site-specific works by leading artists of our time. The site includes a map of campus locating the works of art and two sound files discussing the collection. The artists include William Wegman, Niki de Saint Phalle, Nam June Paik, Jenny Holtzer, Robert Irwin and others. Each work is reproduced with a bibliography.

KEYWORDS California, Contemporary Art, Sculpture, Universities
AUDIENCE Arts Community, Californians, Sculptors
CONTACT Susan Jurist
sjurist@ucsd.edu
FREE

http://gort.ucsd.edu/sj/stHome.html

Tel Aviv Museum Of Art ★★★

This site supplies general museum information (hours, admissions, locations), a calendar of events, and information concerning new and continuing exhibitions ('Conrad Felixmuller—His Dresden Years,' 'Keith Harding'). The museum features European art of the 16th-19th Centuries, Impressionist collections, and Israeli art. It also plans to add online exhibitions. The calendar includes musical events, video, and cinema, as well as art exhibitions.

KEYWORDS Art Exhibitions, Israel, Jewish Art
AUDIENCE Tel Aviv Residents, Tourists
CONTACT info@macom.co.il
FREE

http://www.macom.co.il/ta-museum/index.html

Treasures of the Czars ★★★

This site provides you with a virtual tour of the treasures of the Czars at the Florida International Museum. You can learn about the royal family that once ruled in Russia. The museum tour presents some of the amazing treasures that have survived. In the playground of the Czars, you can read fun facts and play games.

KEYWORDS Art Exhibitions, Museums, Russia
AUDIENCE Children, History Buffs, Parents, Students (Primary/Secondary)
CONTACT Comments@Times.St-Pete.FL.US
FREE

http://www.times.st-pete.fl.us/treasures/TC.Lobby.html

Tromsø Museum ★★★

This is the site for the National Museum at the University of Tromso and contains information on the museum and its collections and publications (cultural history, archaeology, music, natural history, and more) mostly in Norwegian. The site contains a link to the home page for the University.

KEYWORDS Archaeology, Museums, Norway
AUDIENCE Educators, Museum Enthusiasts, Norwegian Speakers, Norwegians
FREE

http://beatles.imv.uit.no/homepage-imv.uit.no.html

University Art Museum/Pacific Film Archives ★★★

The University Art Museum and Pacific Film Archive (UAM/PFA) is the principal visual arts center of the University of California at Berkeley. The site includes information about the purpose and structure of the museum, current and permanent exhibitions (including images), and a calendar for the adjacent Pacific Film Archive. Exhibitions excerpted online include 'In a Different Light,' co-curated by Nayland Blake and Lawrence Rinder, which explores the resonance of gay and lesbian experience in twentieth-century American art. There are also descriptions of the film and video collections and programs of the PFA.

KEYWORDS Art Exhibitions, Film, Visual Arts
AUDIENCE Art Historians, Artists, Arts Community, Californians, Students
CONTACT Lawrence Rinder,
rinehart@uclink2.berkeley.edu
FREE

http://www.uampfa.berkeley.edu

WebMuseum! ★★★★

This is a virtual museum which aims to distribute its exhibits to a broad audience, and is dedicated to multimedia exhibitions (not only art exhibits). It includes pointers to famous paintings, and, although most efforts have been concentrated on developing materials related to Impressionism, other themes include Baroque Painting (1600-1790), Revolution and Restoration (1740-1860), and Cubism to Abstract Art (1900-1960). The medieval art exhibit includes 'Les Tres Riches Heures du Duc de Berry,' the medieval illustrated manuscript. There are also featured artists, such as Cézanne, whose art can be studied in its context. The featured artist site has links to additional (related) artists.

KEYWORDS Art Museums, Paintings, Paris
AUDIENCE Art Historians, Art Professionals, Art Students, Artists, Tourists
CONTACT Nicolas Pioch
els@emf.net
FREE

http://sunsite.unc.edu/louvre/

Whitney Museum of American Art ★★★

This site offers a virtual tour of the Whitney Museum of American Art in New York. Users can link to various artists' web projects made available here, as well as browse exhibitions of artwork. In addition, users can read feedback given from other users, as well as submit their own, and browse material from the museum stores. This site also provides a library with historical information on the museum, as well as material on the staff and site of the museum.

KEYWORDS American Art, Art Museums, Online Art Galleries, Visual Arts
AUDIENCE American Art Enthusiasts, Art Educators, Art Enthusiasts, Art Students
FREE

http://www.echonyc.com/~whitney/

World Art Treasures ★★★

This site contains online exhibitions of art from Egypt, China, Japan, India, Burma, Laos, Cambodia, and Thailand—compiled by Rene Berger and Jacques Edouard Berger. The art is arranged in two programs. The first has an interactive (world) map which allows the viewer to select the region preferred—these images can be enlarged and there are identifying captions, but no historical commentary. The second program contains an educational Pilgrimage to ABYDOS (Egypt) with diagrams and historical commentary, including a glossary and history of Egyptology.

KEYWORDS Art Exhibitions, Asian Arts, Egyptian Art, Indonesian Art
AUDIENCE Artists, Arts Community, Educators, Students
CONTACT   Professor René Berger or Jacques-Edouard Berger
          berger@uliis.unil.ch
FREE

http://sgwww.epfl.ch/BERGER/index.html

Art Organizations

See also
Arts & Music · *Art Galleries*
Arts & Music · *Art Museums*
Business & Economics · *Non Profits*

1995 Edinburgh Festival Fringe ★★★★

Billing itself as the 'largest arts festival in the world,' the Edinburgh Festival Fringe maintains this site to offer information on the programs, activites, and venues that will be available at the latest incarnation of the festival. Users can browse event schedules, find out about attending the festival, and read about future festival plans. There is also a section with various descriptions and reviews of the festival by Internet users, and a place to provide your own review or submit feedback.

KEYWORDS Arts Festivals, Events, Scotland, United Kingdom
AUDIENCE Edinburgh Residents, Festival Enthusiasts Tourists
CONTACT   Evan Welsh
          evan@quadstone.co.uk
FREE

http://www.presence.co.uk/~edfringe/

Academy of Media Arts Cologne ★★★

This site offered by the Academy of Media Arts, in Cologne, Germany provides information and resources related to the Academy's research in new and emerging forms of media. There is information on such cutting-edge projects as the 'WindDancer' project, an exploration into tactile sensation and computer communication. This site also provides information on the Academy itself, with links to material on the faculty and staff, academic programs, and more.

KEYWORDS Art Research, Germany, Media Research
AUDIENCE Art Enthusiasts, Media Enthusiasts, Media Professionals, Media Researchers
FREE

http://www.khm.uni-koeln.de/

American Arts Alliance ★★★

The mission of the American Arts Alliance is to be the principal advocate for America's professional nonprofit arts organizations and their publics in representing arts interests and advancing arts support before Congress and other branches of the Federal government. This page contains information about the federal government's support of the arts including recent advocacy, myths and facts about national support of the arts and statistics on the economic impact of the cultural Institutions on their communities. this page also has links to other arts pages on the net.

KEYWORDS Activism, Music, Performing Arts, Visual Arts
AUDIENCE Artists, Arts Community, Arts Educators
CONTACT   aaa@tmn.com
FREE

http://www.tmn.com/Oh/Artswire/www/aaa/aaahome.html

ArtFBI - Artists For A Better Image ★★★

The ArtFBI (Artists For A Better Image) gopher site provides access to publications and information produced by this arts advocacy organization. Users will find an online magazine called 'ArtFax,' which attempts to examine media stereotypes of artists, as well as a collection of bumperstickers that users can purchase. There is also a section called 'Stereotype of the Hour,' and a 'Cultural Working Class List' which is an index of artists who have contributed to their communities.

KEYWORDS Art Organizations, Non Profit Organizations
AUDIENCE Artists, Arts Advocates, Cultural Critics
CONTACT   Jeff Gates
          jgates@tmn.com
FREE

gopher://gopher.tmn.com/11/Artswire/artfbi/

CraftWEB ★★★

CraftWEB is a page devoted to the pursuit of professional craft arts. Information available includes material on joining the CraftWEB project, an article on selling your craft art, art festival schedules, and more. A gallery is provided to display members' craft artwork. This site also provides a collection of links to other art sites on the Net.

KEYWORDS Crafts, Art Festivals
AUDIENCE Artists, Crafts Artists
CONTACT   Kathleen McMahon
          kmcmahon@craftweb.com
FREE

http://www.craftweb.com/

CultureNet ★★★

CultureNet is a resources page dedicated to promoting and preserving culture in the face of new technology. Users will find a collection of information and research on the subject of culture, including material on using new technology to provide access to cultural resources. Links to founding members of CultureNet can be found here, as well as links to other Canadian cultural sites on the Net.

KEYWORDS Canada, Canadian Culture, Cultural Organizations
AUDIENCE Art Enthusiasts, Artists
CONTACT   Ken Hewitt
          culturenet@cnetmail.ffa.ucalgary.ca
FREE

http://www.culturenet.ucalgary.ca/

International Sculpture Center ★★★

The International Sculpture Center offers a directory of sculptors from around the world. Users will find information on the Center itself, including material on the benefits of being a member, information on conferences, raw materials sources, and more. In addition, users can browse through a directory of artists, and examine their work through the images available here.

KEYWORDS Artists, Sculpture
AUDIENCE Art Enthusiasts, Sculpture Enthusiasts, Educators
FREE

http://www.dgsys.com/~sculpt/

Kunsten Festival des Arts ★★★

The Kunsten Festival des Arts is an international multimedia arts festival. Users will find information on the festival, including images and a MPEG movie clip describing the experience. In addition, this site offers a collection of Web 'experiments,' which explore new and artistic uses of the Internet.

KEYWORDS Arts Festivals, International Art
AUDIENCE Artists, Arts Enthusiasts
CONTACT   kunstenfestivaldesarts@innet.be
FREE

http://www.innet.net/brussels-arts/

The Minneapolis College of Art and Design Gopher Server ★★★★

This site is a gopher server of the Minneapolis College of Art and Design. Information provided includes the design and media arts resources, computer resources, continuing studies programs, the graduate program in visual studies, and sample color images. As well, it offers information on network resources and other resources on the Internet.

KEYWORDS Art Education, Art Schools, Design, Media Arts
AUDIENCE Art Professionals, Artists, Educators, Students
CONTACT   andym@mcad.edu
FREE

gopher://gopher.mcad.edu/

Art Organizations – Art Resources

Mobius - Boston's Artist-Run Center For Experimental Work In All Media ★★★

This page contains excerpts of works by artists working in diverse media including performance art, installation pieces, dance, video, sound art, film, new music, and interdisciplinary media. the page also contains a brief history of Mobius, information on classes and events, as well as links to other art related sites on the net.

KEYWORDS Dance, Music, Performance Art, Video
AUDIENCE Artists, Arts Community, Dancers, Filmmakers, Massachusetts Residents, Musicians
CONTACT Joseph Wilson
jwilson@tiac.net
FREE

http://www.tmn.com/0h/Artswire/www/mobius/mobius.html

New York Foundation for the Arts ★★★

The New York Foundation for the Arts (NYFA) is a nonprofit arts service organization, one of the largest providers of grants and services to individual artists and their organizations in all artistic disciplines in the United States. The three areas covered by this page are — Artists' Programs and Services (serving individual artists and organizations by providing cash grants, sponsoring artists' projects and providing financial and administrative services to their organizations), Education and Information (incorporating Artists in Residence, FYI, the Common Ground conference and seminars), and Finance and Administration (which operates the Revolving Loan program, and provides administrative and financial support to the other programs of the Foundation). The page also contains links to other arts resources such as Arts Wire.

KEYWORDS Arts Education, Grants, New York, Visual Arts
AUDIENCE Artists, Arts Community, New York Residents
FREE

http://www.tmn.com/Artswire/www/nyfa.html

Portland State University, School of Fine and Performing Arts ★★★

The Portland State University, School of Fine and Performing Arts Web site offers information on the faculty, staff, students, and academic program available at the University. Users will find information such as course descriptions, faculty and staff bios, and more. Images of artwork by students and staff are also available here.

KEYWORDS Art Education, Art Schools, Fine Arts, Performing Arts
AUDIENCE Art Educators, Art Students, Artists
CONTACT fpa@pdx.edu
FREE

http://www.ee.pdx.edu/depts/fpa/

School of Visual Arts (SVA) ★★

This is the home page for the School of Visual Arts (SVA), located in New York City. The viewer can see admission information, special projects sponsored by the SVA such as the Third Annual New York Digital Salon 1995, and artistic endeavors created by the students of the school.

KEYWORDS Art Schools, Computer Art, Fine Arts, Photography
AUDIENCE Art Students, Photographers, Students
FREE

http://www.sva.edu/

Tasmanian School of Art at Hobart ★★★★

The Tasmanian School of Art at Hobart provides information on the school, its academic programs, facilities, and projects through this Web page. Users will find several art projects online, as well as a description of the degree programs and computing facilities available at the art school. In addition, users will find some information on the faculty and staff of this school.

KEYWORDS Art Education, Art Schools, Online Art Galleries
AUDIENCE Art Educators, Art Students, Artists
CONTACT Robin Petterd
petterd@toolshed.artschool.utas.edu.au
FREE

http://toolshed.artschool.utas.edu.au/home.html

Women's Studio Workshop ★★★

Women's Studio Workshop in Rosendale, New York, is a not for profit artists' space founded in 1974 to provide a supportive working environment for all persons interested in the arts. WSW staff artists coordinates grants, fellowships, internships, and exhibition opportunities for visual artists in state of the art printmaking, papermaking and photography studios. This page contains information on the organization, examples of work by members, funding information and links to other related arts and women's sites on the net. There is also an artists' journal available online.

KEYWORDS Funding, Photography, Visual Arts, Women's Issues
AUDIENCE Art Students, Artists, Arts Community, Women
FREE

http://www.webmark.com/wsw/wswhome.htm

Art Resources

See also
Arts & Music · Art Museums
Humanities & Social Sciences · Literature
Popular Culture & Entertainment · Books

Arc - The Interactive Media Festival ★★★★

Arc, The Interactive Media Festival, makes a pilgrimage once a year to Los Angeles where they assemble a gallery of interactive art and projects that best represents interactive media in its most advanced and newest forms. How they do it, why they do it, and where they do it are all posted in here as well. The festival is organized by Digital World and held in Los Angeles. This year, Digital World is expanding its program. The main conference, modeled after past Digital World conferences, brings together key leaders to discuss all the major industry issues. Two new tracks, the Multimedia Legal Symposium and Wiring America - Broadband Networking Strategies, will help to meet the demand for focused information about the digital revolution. Also, Digital Demo Days will preview cutting-edge works of interactive media.

KEYWORDS Art Galleries, Computer Art, Digital Photography, Interactive Media
AUDIENCE Arts Community, Computer Artists, Digital Photographers, Multimedia Enthusiasts
CONTACT webmaster@arc.org
FREE

http://www.arc.org/vrml/index.html

Art & Architecture ★★

This document is a compilation of information resources focused on art and architecture including art history, architecture and urban design, criticism, animation, ceramics and crafts, etc. Resources may include Internet/Bitnet Mailing Lists, Gophers, World Wide Web Sites, Mail Servers, Usenet Newsgroups, FTP Archives, Commercial Online Services, and Bulletin Board Systems.

KEYWORDS Architecture, Industrial Design, Visual Arts
AUDIENCE Architects, Art Historians, Artists, Educators, Researchers, Students
FREE

ftp://una.hh.lib.umich.edu/inetdirsstacks/acadlist.art

Art in the Public Interest ★★★

Art in the Public Interest is a nonprofit organization providing information about artists, organizations, projects and ideas that bring the arts together with community and social concerns. This dynamic page features images of artworks and projects by a variety of artists including Lily Yeh, Joseph Williams, Israel McCloud, Peggy Diggs and others. The page also contains High Performance, a quarterly arts magazine focusing on art and the community, as well as links to other arts pages on the net.

KEYWORDS Magazines, Non Profit Organizations, Public Interest
AUDIENCE Art Students, Artists, Arts Community

Art Resources

Arts & Music

CONTACT Steven Durland
highperf@tmn.com

FREE

http://artsedge.kennedy-center.org/

Art on the Net   ★★★★

Art on the Net is an art resource on the Web, created by a collective of artists working in diverse fields, in which individual artists and galleries can create their own home pages. Individual artists' studios are divided up by genre, such as performance art, visual art, sculpture, or poetry. The Gallery provides a virtual walk through several halls in which different galleries have sponsored art exhibits, with both online art and information about the physical gallery itself. Other features include sound bytes of quotes or music from artists, listings of current events in the art world, and links to other art and music reference Web sites.

KEYWORDS Art Exhibitions, Artists, Online Arts
AUDIENCE Art Enthusiasts, Art Organizations, Art Students, Artists
CONTACT   Lile Elam
          webmaster@art.net
FREE

http://www.art.net/

Arts and Entertainment at the Gate   ★★★★

This site contains articles and columns on the arts by contributors to the San Francisco Chronicle and the San Francisco Examiner. Subjects covered include the fine arts (exhibition and book reviews by David Bonetti and Kenneth Baker), theater (reviews by Robert Hurwitt), film (diverse reviews), music (jazz reviews by Philip Elwood, rock by Barry Walters), as well as dance and television (articles and reviews by John Carman). The site includes a weekend guide to arts in the Bay Area, including classical performances. There are also links to other arts resources and to the Gate, the Chronicle/Examiner home page.

KEYWORDS Art Criticism, Film, Visual Arts
AUDIENCE Art Critics, Arts Community, Californians, Music Enthusiasts, Theater Enthusiasts
CONTACT   George Shirk
          gshirk@sfgate.com
FREE

http://sfgate.com/ea/

Arts Wire   ★★★★

Arts Wire is a national communications network for the arts designed to enable artists, individuals, and arts organizations to better communicate and share information. This page provides access to news, information, and discussions of the conditions affecting the arts today. Contents of this page include 'Hotwire,' a timely summary of arts news with sources both on Arts Wire and in the field; 'Artistworlds,' commissioned texts by artists who also participate as online 'artists-in-residence'; and extensive grant information (NEA recipients, Macarthur Foundation information, Guggenheim Fellowship applications, etc.). There are also links to the American Arts Alliance, Dance/USA, and NewMusNet, a music forum.

KEYWORDS Employment, Funding, Jobs
AUDIENCE Artists, Arts Community, Musicians, Writers

CONTACT Judy Malloy
         artswire@tmn.com
COST

http://www.tmn.com/Oh/Artswire/www/awfront.html

ArtsEdge   ★★★

ARTSEDGE sponsored by the John F. Kennedy Center for the Performing Arts and the National Endowment for the Arts, with support from the U.S. Department of Education. The intention behind the page is to place and maintain the arts alongside science, math, and other subject areas among the vast resources and services comprising the new National Information Infrastructure. This page contains links to art news, educational resources in the arts, as well as an extensive guide to using the Internet.

KEYWORDS Arts Education, Performing Arts, Visual Arts
AUDIENCE Artists, Arts Educators, Musicians, Performing Artists
CONTACT   Scott D. Stoner
          stoner@artsedge.kennedy-center.org
FREE

http://artsedge.kennedy-center.org/ik-main.html

Connections to Leonardo (Online)
Where the arts and sciences meet

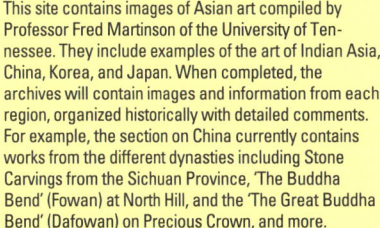

If you are interested in the latest information on technology in the arts, music, and science, "Leonardo OnLine" is the place to get the scoop.

Leonardo actually has three Internet sites affiliated with Leonardo's monthly electronic publication—a venture which covers the fusion of art, music, science and technology. "Welcome to Leonardo" is a good place to start your tour. There you'll get an overview of Leonardo's world and focus. You can also order books or subscribe to various publications on this new medium for the arts and sciences. Next, visit the "Leonardo Public Plaza" and either view material graphically or through a text-only browser.

The "Leonardo Internet: Home Page" provide users with a place to obtain Internet Access and information on computer graphics and programming. You can also check out "Leonardo's Digital Reviews," a resource bank of material created by a wide array of artists and musicians (you can also download sound files).

(http://www-mitpress.mit.edu/Leonardo/home.html)

also, (http://www-mitpress.mit.edu/LEA/home.html)

Asian Art Archive   ★★★

This site contains images of Asian art compiled by Professor Fred Martinson of the University of Tennessee. They include examples of the art of Indian Asia, China, Korea, and Japan. When completed, the archives will contain images and information from each region, organized historically with detailed comments. For example, the section on China currently contains works from the different dynasties including Stone Carvings from the Sichuan Province, 'The Buddha Bend' (Fowan) at North Hill, and the 'The Great Buddha Bend' (Dafowan) on Precious Crown, and more.

KEYWORDS Asian Arts, Japan, Korea, Universities
AUDIENCE Artists, Arts Community, Asian Art Enthusiasts, Educators, Students
FREE

http://solar.rtd.utk.edu/artwww/art.html

Atlantis   ★★★★

This online arts publication offers book and music reviews, art exhibits, and a link to a pop culture journal called 'millennium pop,' as well as art criticism and articles. The page links to areas like MOBA, the Museum of Bad Art, and works by better known contemporary artists. Artist reviews include images by

Art Resources

...the artist. The page also points out up-and-coming galleries and new books of note.

- **KEYWORDS** Art Criticism, Art Exhibitions
- **AUDIENCE** Art Enthusiasts, Museum Enthusiasts, Music Enthusiasts, Popular Culture Enthusiasts
- **FREE**

http://mirror.wwa.com/mirror/atlantis/

Envoy E-Zine ★★★★

Envoy is written by and for artists, writers, and booksellers in and around the state of Texas. Also provided are notices of meetings, conventions and shows as well as articles of interest to those working in the arts community in Texas.

- **KEYWORDS** Books, E-Zines, Texas
- **AUDIENCE** Artists, Arts Community, Texas Residents, Writers
- **CONTACT** Aaron Allston, allston@io.com
- **FREE**

http://io.com/user/shiva/allston/envoy/

ftp://io.com/pub/usr/envoy/

Free-Art for HTML ★★★

This site gives a collection of graphics which users may obtain for use in their HTML documents, provided they give appropriate recognition to the creator. The graphics are mostly unusual forms of bars, plaques, and bullets bases on natural formations such as marbles, metals, and vomitones.

- **KEYWORDS** Computer Graphics, Hypertext, Multimedia
- **AUDIENCE** Computer Graphic Designers, Computer Users, Internet Users, Multimedia Enthusiasts
- **CONTACT** Harlan Wallach, wallach@mcs.com
- **FREE**

http://www.mcs.net/~wallach/freeart/buttons.html

The Image Server ★★★

This image server for the City University (UK) contains JPEG pictures of animals, cars (race cars, road cars), countries (Germany, Italy , Japan , UK, USA, USSR), art by M.C. Escher, fantasy books, Boris Vallejo, films, fractals , insects , logos, cities (London), maps, molecules, Monet, planes, scenery, science fiction, space, trains, television, etc.

- **KEYWORDS** Artists, Images
- **AUDIENCE** Artists, Children, Educators (Primary/Secondary), Parents, Students (Primary/Secondary)
- **CONTACT** Alan Messer
- **FREE**

http://www.cs.city.ac.uk/archive/image/image.html

Internet Art Resources ★★★

The Internet Art Resources web site is designed as a forum for the introduction of art resources around the world. Users may look at the pages of individual artists, art galleries, museums, art shows and exhibitions, or magazine/booksellers who have registered with Internet Art Resources. These sites include online art, descriptions of the participants, and detailed information. Complimentary listings of galleries and museums across the United States are also included, with brief descriptions of their exhibitions and opening hour information. A search engine is also included for subject, artists, or area searches.

- **KEYWORDS** Art Galleries, Art Museums, Artists, Online Arts
- **AUDIENCE** Art Enthusiasts, Art Galleries, Artists, Museums
- **CONTACT** webmaster@ftgi.com
- **FREE**

http://www.ftgi.com

Photon - World Wide Web Photo Magazine ★★★★

PHOTON comes to you from the Celtic fringe of Europe courtesy of Icon Publications Limited. The site contains recent issues and an PHOTONet Index of photo sites which is regularly updated. The issues contain articles on photographers, professional news items (e.g., updates from photographic trade shows), question and answer problem pages and software information. This site also contains links to other photography-related sites.

- **KEYWORDS** Photography, Software, Visual Arts
- **AUDIENCE** Arts Community, Photographers
- **CONTACT** David Kilpatrick, DavidKilpatrick@photon.scotborders.co.uk
- **FREE**

http://www.scotborders.co.uk:80/photon/

Santa Cruz Visual Arts Index ★★★★

This site provides information about art and art resources in the Santa Cruz, California area. Listed are exhibitions at local museums and galleries, archives from past shows, art services, and an index to related Web sites. A registry of local artists include samples of the art and personal statements.

- **KEYWORDS** Art Exhibitions, California, Visual Arts
- **AUDIENCE** Art Enthusiasts, Artists, Californians
- **CONTACT** Rick Jacoby and Susan Anne Shannon, crows@netcom.com
- **FREE**

http://www.cruzio.com/arts/scva/scva.html

Scultura Arts Forum ★★★

This site is a fine arts forum with information and resources for artists. Their page includes information about artists and galleries, and provides resources and a place for art dialogue. Also included is a classified section, and information about interior design and handmade crafts.

- **KEYWORDS** Art Exhibitions, Art Galleries, Crafts, Visual Arts
- **AUDIENCE** Art Collectors, Art Organizations, Artists
- **CONTACT** scultura@rain.org
- **FREE**

http://www.rain.org/~scultura/art.html

Smithsonian Online ★★★★

This ftp server, located in the Smithsonian Institution's Office of Printing & Photographic Services in Washington, D.C., is designed to make a variety of Smithsonian photographs available as electronic image files. The images in these extensive archives include natural history photographs, science subjects, air and space images, fine art images, people and places, etc.

- **KEYWORDS** Archives, Images, Photography, Visual Arts
- **AUDIENCE** Educators, Researchers, Students
- **CONTACT** PSDMX@SIVM.SI.EDU
- **FREE**

ftp://photo1.si.edu/

Spydoor Web ★★

Spydoor Web is an online multimedia magazine concentrating on New York City. It deals with the people, events, art, and all else that make up the Big Apple. Although a majority of content on this 'zine is devoted to promoting NYC artists and their work, there are also sections centering on other regions of the country. Viewers will find links to areas like Music, including the NYC Bar & Club Index, news and reviews; Art, which features online galleries, as well as contact information for art exhibits, galleries, and museums in NYC; and Features, covering topics like finding an apartment in Manhattan and the Cabs of Manhattan County. A reader-sponsored page and a sports section complete the options available to the viewer.

- **KEYWORDS** Contemporary Art, New York, Zines
- **AUDIENCE** Artists, Musicians, New York Residents, Popular Culture Enthusiasts
- **CONTACT** Sean Riley, Editor in Chief, captfsr@pipeline.com
- **FREE**

http://anansi.panix.com:80/Spydoor/

Stereograms FTP Server ★★★

The Stereograms FTP Server offers a collection of 3D SIRDS (Single Image Random Dot Stereograms) images, as well as programs for several computing platforms which can generate these images. In addition, this site offers SIRDS images, as well as a FAQ file and other information on how these images are processed by the brain into 3D images.

- **KEYWORDS** 3D Images, stereograms
- **AUDIENCE** 3D Image Enthusiasts, Computer Users, Internet Users
- **CONTACT** michael@eccles.anu.edu.au
- **FREE**

ftp://katz.anu.edu.au/pub/stereograms/

World Arts Resources ★★★★

The World Arts Resources page offers a comprehensive index to arts resources, both on the Net and off. Users will find gallery directories and links, information on art museums all over the world, and links to many of the best art sites on the Net. Information on art publications and commercial arts organizations is also available here. Antiques, institutions, and governmental

Art Resources – Artists

agencies related to the art world can also be found here.

KEYWORDS Art Museums, Meta-Index (Art), Online Art Galleries, Web Art
AUDIENCE Art Educators, Art Enthusiasts, Art Students, Artists
CONTACT   Markus Kruse
          mkruse@cgrg.ohio-state.edu
FREE

http://www.cgrg.ohio-state.edu/Newark/artsres.html

Young Fine Arts Auctions, Inc. ★★★

Young Fine Arts Auctions provides a way to bid on works of art via email and telephone from this page. Users will find a catalog of works to be auctioned, with pictures, descriptions and opening bid information. Users can browse through a catalog of lots in upcoming auctions, as well as find out more information on participating in the auctions.

KEYWORDS Art Auctions, Online Art Galleries
AUDIENCE Art Buyers, Art Enthusiasts, Art Sellers, Artists
CONTACT   George and Patricia Young
          gyoung@maine.com
FREE

http://www.maine.com/yfa

Artists

See also
Arts & Music · *Art Galleries*
Arts & Music · *Art Museums*
Arts & Music · *Electronic Arts*
Arts & Music · *Performing Arts*

Bas Van Reek Art Building ★★★★

The Bas Van Reek Art Building is the title of this artist's home page, a metaphor for his location in cyberspace. Imaginatively drawn humanoids gather in anticipation near a partly opened door. The site will not disappoint—it's a small, happy, well-designed gallery of Van Reek's art, with links to news of his works in progress. In 1995 it was chosen Cool Site of the Day.

KEYWORDS Electronic Arts, Painting, Printmaking, Visual Arts
AUDIENCE Art Enthusiasts, Artists, Computer Artists, General Public
CONTACT   Bas Van Reek
          basvreek@xs4all.nl
FREE

http://www.xs4all.nl/~basvreek/

Belinda Di Leo MFA Project ★★★★

This site provides access to a collection of 24 paintings depicting the native culture of central Appalachia. They can be viewed as GIF images. Each painting comes with a brief description which includes the artist's interpretation.

KEYWORDS Appalachia, Art Exhibitions, Painting, Virginia

Connections to Hot Pictures
From Moscow, with . . . art

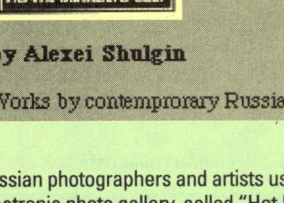

Electronic PhotoGallery

HOT PICTURES

by Alexei Shulgin

Works by contemporrary Russian artists using photography and photographers.

Russian photographers and artists using photography have opened the first Russian-based electronic photo gallery, called "Hot Pictures." This site presents the works of artists who in some manner use photography in their work. The spectrum of work ranges from direct, immediate photography to computer-processed images. The different works have been united in this collection with the intention of bringing greater fluidity to the artificial boundaries that remain between painting, photography, and computer graphics.

The gallery features a wide variety of artists; exploring it is as simple as clicking onto thumbnail icons for various works. Each artist is featured in a separate room so that his or her works can be viewed and studied separately.

(http://www.kiae.su/www/wtr/hotpictures/gallery.html)

AUDIENCE Art Educators, Art Students, Artists, General Public
CONTACT   mwaggoner@ucsd.edu
FREE

http://gort.ucsd.edu/mw/bdl.html

Diatribe Webzine ★★★

A new Webzine, Diatribe is a collaboration between a number of artists and writers. This graphics-intensive magazine can be downloaded in PDF or PostScript format from their index page.

KEYWORDS Graphics, Magazines, Poetry
AUDIENCE Artists, Poets, Reading Enthusiasts, Writers
FREE

http://sunsite.unc.edu/otis/MASS/Stastny_E/extra/diatribe.html

Dilbert ★★★★

This site is dedicated to the comic strip Dilbert. Here you'll find Dilbert strips and nearly 100 pages of never-before-seen and original Dilbert material (including early sketches, rejection letters, photographs, and more). The strips, which appear one week after their publication in newspapers, will be updated every day and be collected in a two-week archive. Recent additions include The 1994 Dilbert Gripe Index, The Dilbert Licensed Vendor List, Find a newspaper in your area with Dilbert, and The Dilbert Zone FAQ.

KEYWORDS Comedy, Comics, Humor
AUDIENCE Comics Enthusiasts, Dilbert Enthusiasts, Humor Enthusiasts
CONTACT   Scott Adams
          scottadams@aol.com
FREE

http://www.unitedmedia.com/comics/dilbert

Enrique Vega Metalsmith ★★★★

The Enrique Vega Metalsmith site offers information and images from this intriguing artist. Users can browse through information on commissioning a work, as well as view images of all types of art work. Those who wish a look into the artist's creative process can view the collection of CAD models of pieces the artist has created.

KEYWORDS Metalwork, Sculpture
AUDIENCE Art Consumers, Metalwork Enthusiasts
CONTACT   Enrique Vega
          evega@artmetal.pdial.interpath.net
FREE

http://wuarchive.wustl.edu/edu/arts/metal/Gallery/vega_e.html

Arts & Music

Artists – Art Funding

Homepage of the Brave - Laurie Anderson ★★★★

This site is dedicated to singer and multimedia performance artist Laurie Anderson. This site has a FAQ as well as a discography, bibliography and filmography. It also has listings of articles written by and about Laurie. It also has tour information, and lyrics with interpretations of her lyrics.

KEYWORDS Multimedia, Music, Performance Art
AUDIENCE Alternative Music Enthusiasts, Multimedia Enthusiasts, Musicians, New Media, Performance Artists
CONTACT Jim Davies
jimmyd@lanl.gov
FREE

http://www.c3.lanl.gov:8080/cgi/jimmyd/quoter?home

Kaleidospace ★★★★

Kaleidospace is a Web site dedicated to showcasing the work of independent Internet Artists working in diverse mediums such as electronic and traditional art, music and video. Their site includes showcases of artists' work with biographies and interviews, interactive art projects, information about electronic art resources, and a newstand and reading room for articles, reviews, and further art information. The art is organized according to medium, genre, subject and artist, and new artists include Clive Barker and Dr. Fiorello Terenzi.

KEYWORDS Art Exhibitions, Electronic Arts, Interactive Media, Music
AUDIENCE Art Enthusiasts, Artists, Electronic Artists, Musicians
CONTACT Jeannie Novak and Pete Markewicz
editors@kspace.com
FREE

http://kspace.com/

Kent Musgrave's Home Page ★★★

This site contains synthetic (fractal) images by Kent Musgrave and several other computer artists. Topics of the images include landscapes, planets, artistic renderings, and scientific visualization renderings. The site also provides information regarding purchase of the images.

KEYWORDS Art Galleries, Computer Art, Fractals, Mathematics
AUDIENCE Artists, Computer Artists, Scientists
CONTACT Kent Musgrove
musgrave@seas.gwu.edu
FREE

http://www.seas.gwu.edu:80/faculty/musgrave/art_gallery.html

Leonardo da Vinci ★★★

The current exhibit displays images and information relating to Leonardo da Vinci. Works reproduced (with commentary) include the Mona Lisa from the Louvre in Paris, the Last Supper from the Refectory of Santa Maria delle Grazie in Milan, the Baptism of Christ from the Uffizi in Florence, and The Benois Madonna from the Hermitage in St. Petersburg, Russia. The site also contains reproductions of Leonardo's engineering and futuristic designs (weapons, flying machines, devices) and a historical exhibition about the life and times of Leonardo.

KEYWORDS Art Exhibitions, Artists, Renaissance Art
AUDIENCE Art Educators, Artists, Renaissance Scholars, Students
CONTACT Jim Pickrell
robert@leonardo.net
FREE

http://www.leonardo.net/main.html

Magritte Home Page ★★★★

The Magritte home page contains 34 large, good quality, downloadable images of Rene Magritte's paintings, including less well known images. The accompanying text is in French, without English translation.

KEYWORDS Art History, French Painting, Modern Art, Surrealism
AUDIENCE Art Educators, Art Enthusiasts, Art Students, Artists
FREE

heiwww.unige.ch/art/magritte

Arts Funding

See also
Education · *Funding*
Government & Politics · *Agencies*
Popular Culture & Entertainment · *Family & Community*

American Arts Alliance Home Page ★★★

The American Arts Alliance, an advocacy organization for nonprofit arts in the US, offers a home page with current information on the state of arts funding in the Federal government and on what people can do about it. Sections cover arts advocacy in general, an action alert on proposed 1995 budget rescissions, 'Myths and Facts about National Support of Arts and Culture,' economic impact of arts institutions, and details of relevant upcoming Congressional hearings. There are also links to other arts and cultural information pages.

KEYWORDS Art Organizations, Non Profit Organizations, Visual Arts
AUDIENCE Art Enthusiasts, Artists, Arts Community, Political Advocates
CONTACT Scott Burns, Metasystems Design Group, Inc.
scott@tmn.com
FREE

http://www.tmn.com/Oh/Artswire/www/aaa/aaahome.html

Art DEADLINES List ★★★

The Art DEADLINES List is a list of competitions, contests, call for entries/papers, grants, scholarships, fellowships, jobs, internships, etc, in the arts or related areas (painting, drawing, animation, poetry, writing, music, multimedia, reporting/journalism, cartooning, dance, photography, video, film, sculpture, etc.), some of which have prizes worth thousands of dollars. It is international in scope. Contests and competitions for students, K-12 and college-aged, are included. The site also contains links to other interesting art resources including art galleries.

KEYWORDS Art Exhibitions, Art Galleries, Visual Arts
AUDIENCE Art Students, Artists, Arts Community, Arts Educators
CONTACT ptbast@cs.wpi.edu
FREE

http://cs.wpi.edu/~ptbast/rlg/r.html

Arts USA ★★★

Arts USA, supplies resources for 'discussing and exploring the nature of American Culture.' This site provides links on how to find and write for grants. Those who wish to become more active in the support of American Arts will find links to discussion groups and ecomonic reports on the impact of public policy on the arts. There also links to other arts resources such as books and fund management tools.

KEYWORDS Arts Advocacy, Arts Funding
AUDIENCE Arts Advocates, Grant Writers, Grantseekers
CONTACT webmaster@artsusa.org
FREE

http://www.artsusa.org/index.html

Grants, Fellowships and Contests ★★★★

Delta 9 hosts this list of Grants, Fellowships and Contests. Information includes dates, addresses and award amounts for some current arts competitions in the US. Also provided are rules, submission requirements and entry fees (where they apply).

KEYWORDS Arts Funding, Fellowships, Grants
AUDIENCE Artists, Filmmakers, Grantseekers, Grantwriters, Screen Writers
CONTACT Tommy Pallotta, Terrelita Price
gwynneth@eden.com
FREE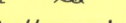

http://www.eden.com/~delta-9/grants.html

National Endowment for the Humanities ★★★★

The WWW site for the National Endowment for the Humanities, an American Federal Government agency devoted to funding projects and individuals in the arts, philosophy, literature, and history, offers a number of resources. Users will find information on submission guidelines, NEA history, review processes, and specific criteria for each discipline. The site also details specific NEA programs in the fields of media, education, and research, to name a few.

KEYWORDS Arts Agencies, Grants, Humanities Funding
AUDIENCE Artists, Educators, Scholars, Writers
FREE

http://www.neh.fed.us/

Career & Employment – Design   33

Career & Employment

See also
Arts & Music · *Arts Funding*
Business & Economics · *Career & Employment*
Education · *Resources*
Government & Politics · *Agencies*

ARTJOB ★★★

ARTJOB, a service of the Western States Arts Federation, an online resource for international and national current job listings in all areas of the arts and related information, including grants, competitions, and internships. Other job categories include agencies, presenting organizations, and academic positions. Issues of ARTJOB are published every two weeks.

KEYWORDS   Art Competitions, Arts Funding, Job Listings
AUDIENCE   Art Activists, Art Professionals, Artists, Job Seekers
CONTACT   Frank Burns of The Meta Network
           frank@tmn.com
COST

gopher://gopher.tmn.com:70/11/Artswire/artjob

Screenwriters and Playwright's Home Page ★★★★

The Screenwriters and Playwright's Home Page offers a wealth of resources for both screenwriters and playwrights, including a large archive of dramatic scripts from classics to new unpublished work, as well as many documents meant to help guide new writers. Much of the information is stored locally at this site, but some of it is linked to remote locations.

KEYWORDS   Acting, Drama, Screenwriting, Theater
AUDIENCE   Playwrights, Screenwriters, Theater Professionals, Writers
CONTACT   Charles Deemer
           cdeemer@teleport.com
FREE

http://www.teleport.com/~cdeemer/scrwriter.html

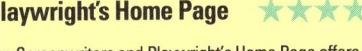

The Virtual Headbook ★★★

The Virtual Headbook is an electronic collection of headshots (black and white portraits of performing artists looking for employment in their field) and corresponding resumes. The index is searchable by name, area or keyword, and comprehensive instructions on the use of the service area available on the introductory page. The service is commercial, and charges those who wish to display their picture and resume on a monthly basis.

KEYWORDS   Acting, Employment, Entertainment, Performing Arts
AUDIENCE   Acting Students, Casting Agents, Job Seekers, Theater Professionals
CONTACT   Wintronix Inc. Webmaster
           wintrnx@xmission.com
FREE

http://www.xmission.com/~wintrnx/virtual.html

Decorative Arts

See also
Arts & Music · *Design*
Popular Culture & Entertainment · *Fashion*
Sports & Recreation · *Crafts & Hobbies*

Alaimo Ceramics ★★★

At the Alaimo Ceramics Web site users may view the work of potter, Cindy Alaimo, consisting primarily of highly decorative and functional ceramic ware. Users can access information about the artist and a schedule of current ceramic art exhibits and gallery displays of her work across the U.S. The site also includes price information for prospective purchasers of the artwork.

KEYWORDS   Ceramics, Crafts, Functional Art, Pottery
AUDIENCE   Ceramic Shoppers, Craft Shoppers, Gallery Owners, Potters
CONTACT   Cindy Alaimo
           alaimo@commerce.com
FREE

http://www.commerce.com/alaimo/top.html

College of Textile of the North Carolina State University ★★★

This gopher server provides information about the College of Textile of the North Carolina State University. It covers scholarship opportunities, textile curriculum, textile off-campus television education, the North Carolina Textile Foundation, the Alumni Society, and the library. It also contains information about the National Textile Center.

KEYWORDS   Education (College/University), Research & Development, Technology
AUDIENCE   Academics, Educators (University), Students
FREE

gopher://gopher.tx.ncsu.edu/

Conservatoire National des Arts et Metiers (CNAM) ★★★

The French National Conservatory of Arts and Crafts site offers a virtual museum of technology, some curiosities of the Web, some links to laboratories, institutes and departments, and contact links.

KEYWORDS   Art Exhibitions, Crafts, France, Museums
AUDIENCE   Art Enthusiasts, Tourists
CONTACT   webmaster@cnam.fr
FREE

http://web.cnam.fr/

WWW Virtual Library - Furniture & Interior Design ★★★

This section of the WWW Virtual Library is devoted to furniture and interior design and is maintained out of Sweden. There are links to academic sites such as The Architectural Association in London and Princeton University School of Architecture in New Jersey; miscellaneous and commercial sites such as designOnline and Encore Systems recycled furniture; reviews, journals and books such as architronic electronic journal of architecture; museums and exhibitions such as the Alvar Aalto Museum in Jyvaskyla, Finland; and other related subjects such as the O2W3 home page forum for the exploration of new possibilities in design, promoting respect for the environment.

KEYWORDS   Furniture, Home, Interior Design, Virtual Libraries
AUDIENCE   Architects, Furniture Buyers, Interior Designers, Students
CONTACT   erik@i3.se, jesper.weissglas@mikrolit.se
FREE

http://www.i3.se/furniture.html

Design

See also
Arts & Music · *Architecture*
Arts & Music · *Decorative Arts*
Arts & Music · *Electronic Arts*
Business & Economics · *Industries*
Business & Economics · *Publishing*
Business & Economics · *Services*

DesignOnline ★★★

Welcome to DesignOnline(tm), the Information Resource for Design. Here you will find information on design organizations, portfolios and resumes, design agencies, products, and services, FAQs (Frequently Asked Questions), dol. newsgroups, and more.

KEYWORDS   Architecture, Design Industry, Interior Design, Trade Shows
AUDIENCE   Architects, Furniture Dealers, Furniture Manufacturers, Interior Designers
CONTACT   Peter Fraterdeus
           peterf@dol.com
FREE

http://www.dol.com/

Scholes Library Art & Design ★★★★

The Scholes Library Art & Design page offers a compendium of links to Internet sites with art and design information. Users will find links to design schools, design studios, and design professionals that have a presence on the Internet. In addition, visitors to this site will find a wealth of artists' page links and pointers to design resources.

KEYWORDS   Art Resources, Interior Design
AUDIENCE   Artists, Designers, Graphic Designers
CONTACT   Mark Smith
FREE

http://scholes.alfred.edu/ArtDesign.html

Design – Electronic Arts

University of Art and Design Helsinki, UIAH gopher ★★

This site offers access to information about departments at the University of Art and Design in Finland. It covers Art Education, Visual Communication, Environmental Design, and more, and it also discusses administration, application, and budget data. This site provides links to other related servers.

KEYWORDS Art, Design, Education (College/University), Finland
AUDIENCE Art Educators, Art Students, Finns
FREE

gopher://uiah.fi/

Virtual Design Center ★★★

The Virtual Design Center provides links to information on the best product of the month, industry trade shows, industry publication, catalogues, furniture dealers, events, and a gallery. The Virtual Design Center World Wide Web (WWW) is a very large Internet-based corporate communication and marketing system serving the needs of contract manufacturers, service providers and interior designers worldwide.

KEYWORDS Design Industry, Interior Design, Trade Shows
AUDIENCE Architects, Furniture Dealers, Furniture Manufacturers, Interior Designers
CONTACT info@info.vdc.com
FREE

http://www.vdc.com/

WWW Virtual Library-Design ★★★★

The WWW (World Wide Web) Virtual Library-Design site presents a comprehensive index of design related sites on the Internet. Included are headings for architecture, art, computer graphics, furniture & interior design, and human-computer interface. Users will find links to many professional pages, design sites, and much more.

KEYWORDS Architecture, Design Arts, Graphic Arts, Visual Arts
AUDIENCE Architects, Designers, Graphic Artists
CONTACT webmaster@designum.umu.se
FREE

http://www.dh.umu.se/vlib.html

Electronic Arts

See also
Arts & Music · *Art Resources*
Arts & Music · *Design*
Computing & Mathematics · *Applications*
Computing & Mathematics · *Software*
Popular Culture & Entertainment · *Multimedia*

3D Graphic Engines ★★★★

If you are interested in 3D computer graphics you should make a visit to this Web site. What you will find is an overview of software 3D engines including 6DOF texture mapping engines, 6DOF gouraud shading engines, Doom/Wolfenstein engines, flat-shading engines, wireframe/no shading engines, non-realtime engines. Each section outlines the features of several software products which demonstrate the particular category. You are also provided links for further information which sometimes includes sites where you can obtain the software being described.

KEYWORDS 3D Webs, Computer Art, Electronic Arts
AUDIENCE Computer Artists, Computer Graphic Designers, Computer Programmers, Graphic Designers
CONTACT Karsten Isakovic
ki@cs.tu-berlin.de
FREE

http://www.cs.tu-berlin.de/~ki/engines.html

3D-Gray Icons ★★★★

As part of their support for inhouse development of Web pages, The U.S. Army Artificial Intelligence Center has developed an extensive array of 3D gray icons. These GIF format icons are presented along with the their URL addresses. The icons cover a wide range of subject areas and, contrary to the page title, some even contain some color.

KEYWORDS Computer Art, Electronic Arts, Icons
AUDIENCE Artists, Computer Artists, Computer Graphic Designers, Graphic Designers
CONTACT Paul Beda
beda@pentagon-ai.army.mil
FREE

http://www.pentagon-ai.army.mil/images/icons/3d-gray/3d-gray.html

3D Site ★★★★

This is a Web site for 3D computer graphics containing links to a wide range of 3D related topics. The choices offered include galleries of images, job listings, software packages and information related to VRML(Virtuality Reality Modeling Language).

KEYWORDS Computer Art, Electronic Arts
AUDIENCE Artists, Computer Artists, Computer Graphic Designers, Graphic Designers
CONTACT Daniele Colajacomo
daniele@netcom.com
FREE

http://www.lightside.com:80/3dsite/

3D Web - Stereoscopy Information and Resources ★★★

3D Web is a site filled with all sorts of 3D imagery, from stereograms to old-fashioned photography. Visitors will find a 3D Gallery of artwork and photography, a Yellow Pages of 3D resources, and archives from the Photo-3D Mail List as well as a list of 3D related web sites. Users can also see information about conferences, browse through a series of FAQs, or even read a newsletter from the National Stereoscopic Association.

KEYWORDS 3D Graphics, Computer Graphics, Stereoscopy, stereograms
AUDIENCE Artists, Computer Graphic Designers, Computer Graphics Enthusiasts
CONTACT Bob Mannle
FREE

http://www.tisco.com/3d-web

911 Gallery ★★★

The 911 Gallery site offers users an online electronic art gallery. The 911 Gallery Electronic Media Arts, Inc. is a non profit organization that promotes electronic media in fine arts. The gallery also provides users the opportunity to visit its constantly changing schedule of online shows and exhibits. Users will find works in several mediums, including digital audio and video. There is also a collection of past exhibits, as well as information on submitting your own work to the gallery for online exhibition.

KEYWORDS Digital Media, Multimedia, Video
AUDIENCE Artists, Computer Artists, Computer Musicians, Video Artists
CONTACT Mary Ann Kearns
artgal@iquest.net
FREE

http://www.iquest.net/911/iq_911.html

@art Gallery ★★

@art is an electronic art gallery affiliated with the School of Art and Design, the University of Illinois at Urbana-Champaign. Exhibits are curated by the founding members, with the intention of providing an electronic viewing space for talented and mature artists of outstanding merit.

KEYWORDS Art Exhibitions, Electronic Arts, Visual Arts
AUDIENCE Artists, Computer Artists
FREE

http://gertrude.art.uiuc.edu/@art/gallery.html

(Art)^n Laboratory ★★★★

Virtual Photography is the subject of this site. Images called PHSCologrograms are presented for viewing, along with documentation on this image format and how they are created. These artworks, created directly from 3D data, in reality are 3D digital transparencies meant to be displayed in lightboxes etc. The JPEG versions in this gallery will give you a 2D version of the PHSCologrograms.

KEYWORDS Computer Art, Electronic Arts
AUDIENCE Artists, Computer Artists, Computer Graphic Designers, Graphic Designers
CONTACT Janine Fron
janine@artn.nwu.edu
FREE

http://www.artn.nwu.edu/index.html

AI Center Image Libraries ★★★

The U.S. Army Artificial Intelligence Center is the source for the computer generated images presented on this page. The images provide a small gallery displaying 3D rendered imagery.

KEYWORDS Computer Art, Electronic Arts
AUDIENCE Artists, Computer Artists, Computer Graphic Designers, Graphic Designers

CONTACT Paul Beda
 beda@pentagon-ai.army.mil
FREE

http://www.pentagon-ai.army.mil/images/
related/related.html

ALOZOYA ★★★★

Graphic designer Albert Lozoya has created an attractive home page that could serve as a model for anyone wishing to design a home page. Cybert, as Lozoya calls his page, has links to a gallery of Lozoya's designs, his own hot list, Marilyn Monroe pictures, Formula One cars, and tips on home page creation. Following hypertext, the viewer is treated to a pen and ink portrait of the artist, who received his B.F.A. from the University of Texas, El Paso in 1987. He has created graphics for many of the home pages in his area, including the Rio Grand Freenet otherwise known as RGFN.

KEYWORDS Computer Art
AUDIENCE Computer Users, Graphic Designers
CONTACT ab169@rgfn.epcc.edu
FREE

http://www.hooked.net/users/alozoya

ART + COM e.V. ★★★★

ART+COM is an independent, interdisciplinary, non-profit research and development institute founded in 1988 and located in Berlin, Germany. The staff of 30 are working on projects related to technoculture in diverse media including film, multimedia, videos, computer art, performance art, etc.

KEYWORDS Art Exhibitions, Computer Art, Electronic Arts, Germany
AUDIENCE Artists, Computer Artists, Internet Users, Software Developers
FREE

http://www.artcom.de/

ASCII Art Sites Index ★★★

The ASCII Art Sites Index offers information on numerous areas of online information regarding ASCII computer art. The Index provides links to other sites developed by Scarecrow, in addition to other ASCII enthusiasts, including lists of Frequently Asked Questions, FTP and gopher files on graphic design using ASCII.

KEYWORDS ASCII Art, Computer Graphics, Graphic Design
AUDIENCE ASCII Artists, ASCII Enthusiasts, Graphic Designers
CONTACT Scarecrow
 boba@wwa.com
FREE

http://gagme.wwa.com/~boba/sites.html

ASCII Stereograms ★★

The ASCII Stereograms web page provides a downloadable example of a stereogram in addition to an example of one that has already been compiled. A short history of the stereogram is also provided in addition to an ASCII example of a 3-D image. There is a link provided to Seattle Pacific University.

KEYWORDS ASCII Art, Graphic Design, stereograms

Connections to The Smithsonian
The world, from the American perspective

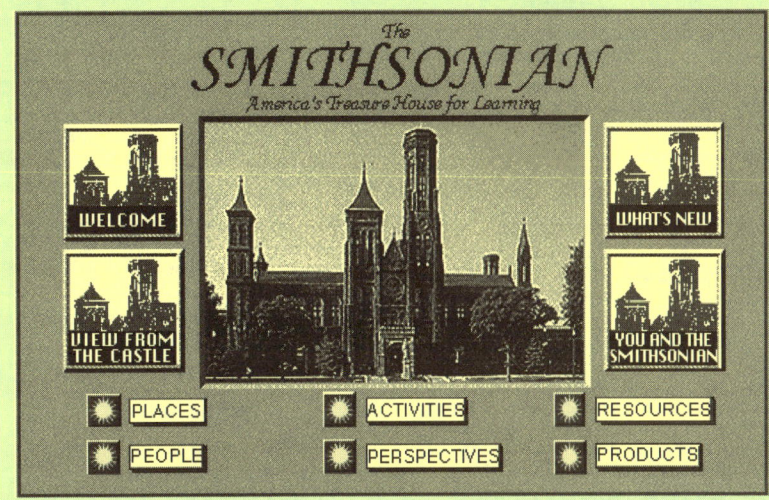

For many people, The Smithsonian is the national museum of America. The complex of 16 buildings house a wealth of information about the world, America, and Americans. But you don't have to go to Washington D.C. to visit the Smithsonian. You can peruse virtually the entire museum online.

Among the exhibits available through the "Smithsonian Home Page" are the museum's gem and mineral collection, the world of fish, and the National Aerospace Museum—where you can view the very first flying machines from the early 1900s on up to a lunar landing module from one of the Apollo missions. You'll also see moon rocks and space suits, along with explanations about many facets of space flight.

For the Smithsonian Home Page (which is a busy place to visit) try

(http://www.si.edu/)

To view the Gem and Mineral Collection, try

(http://galaxy.einet.net/images/gems/gems-icons.html)

If you want to find out more about Smithsonian fellowships and internships—what kinds are available and how to apply—try

(http://www.si.edu/youandsi/ofgfel.htm)

AUDIENCE ASCII Artists, Graphic Designers, Students
CONTACT pvenable@spu.edu
FREE

http://paul.spu.edu/~pvenable/
stereo.html

About Teichmuller
Navigator 2.0 ★★★

Part of an undergraduate research project at the Geometry Center at the University of Minnesota, this Web site presents an interactive glimpse into the geometry of Teichmuller Space. Learn more about this subject, or just try out the program by clicking near the blue points in the navigator.

KEYWORDS Art Exhibitions, Electronic Arts, Geometry
AUDIENCE Artists, Computer Artists, Computer Graphic Designers, Graphic Designers

CONTACT webmaster@geom.umn.edu
FREE

http://www.geom.umn.edu/apps/teich-nav/about.html

Agusti Torres ★★★

Agusti Torres creates digitally retouched classical paintings which explore themes of consumerism and voyeurism. The thumbnail previews can be selected to view the full size JPEG images.

KEYWORDS Computer Art, Electronic Arts, Visual Arts
AUDIENCE Artists, Computer Artists, Computer Graphic Designers, Graphic Designers
CONTACT Geoff Broadway
 G.Broadway@derby.ac.uk
FREE

http://dougal.derby.ac.uk/gallery/
agustitorresdoc.html

Alias Alian Nation

Alias Research, Inc. presents this site as an entry point to the 3D imaging software they produce. You can get information on several of their products and venture into an animation or image gallery to get an idea of the images that can be produced using Alias products.

KEYWORDS Computer Art, Electronic Arts
AUDIENCE Artists, Computer Artists, Computer Graphic Designers, Graphic Designers
CONTACT webmaster@alias.com
FREE

http://www.alias.com/

Alias Animations from Selected Projects

As part of their Industrial Design efforts, Teague Associates create 3D rendered animations. Presented on this page are two sample MPEG animations demonstrating the capabilities provided by the Alias software used in their creation.

KEYWORDS Art Exhibitions, Computer Art, Electronic Arts
AUDIENCE Computer Artists, Computer Graphic Designers, Graphic Designers
FREE

http://walter.wdta.com/Teagueanim.html

Alt.Binaries.Pictures Utilities Archive

Jim Howard maintains a picture utility archive that has an extensive collection of picture information and binaries. There are no images available, but just about any information related to graphics utilities resides at this FTP site.

KEYWORDS Art Exhibitions, Computer Art, Electronic Arts
AUDIENCE Computer Artists, Computer Graphic Designers, Graphic Designers
CONTACT Jim Howard
deej@cadence.com
FREE

ftp://infolane.com/pub/picutils/index.html

The American Indian Computer Art Project

The American Indian Computer Art Project offers information and images on Native American electronic art. Users will find images, event information, and Native American myths and legends. There is also a small collection of traditional song lyrics, as well as pointers to other Native American resources on the Net.

KEYWORDS Digital Imaging, Native American Art
AUDIENCE Electronic Art Enthusiasts, Native American Art Enthusiasts
CONTACT Turtle Heart
turtle@aicap.s21.com
FREE

http://www.mit.edu:8001/activities/aises/aicap/archive/aicap.html

Animania!

Animania! contains a collection of short 3-D animations made by students in the Graduate Computer Art Dept. of the School of Visual Arts, New York. Students in the Computer Art Program at SVA come from all over the world geographically and bring diverse cultural heritages and disparate artistic roots to their studies. The site also has information on a Digital Salon call for entries, hosted by the School of Visual Arts, and links to other animation sites.

KEYWORDS Animation, Art Schools, Computer Art, New York, Visual Arts
AUDIENCE Animation Enthusiasts, Animators, Computer Artists
CONTACT ken@sva.edu
FREE

http://www.sva.edu/animania/homepage.html

Animation Graphics 3RD Dimension Tech

Have you ever wished you could turn one of those great photographs of yours into a 3D model? Well now you can. This Web site is a mix between a commercial enterprise and a resource site. The company, 3RD Dimension Technologies,Inc., has developed a program that lets you define certain characteristics of a photograph and then transform the information into a 3D wire frame mesh of the image. You can then texture map the photo onto the wire frame and voila!, a 3D model. The information presented on this page gives you details on how the program works and how you can obtain it. It even offers an opportunity to contract with them to develop models for them. Along with all this there are some interesting 3D images and animations you can download.

KEYWORDS Computer Art, Electronic Arts
AUDIENCE Artists, Computer Artists, Computer Graphic Designers, Graphic Designers
CONTACT rmclaine@rain.org
FREE

http://www.webcom.com/~3d-art/welcome.html

Animation Master Hobbyist

This Web site is devoted to the fans and users of Animation Master or Playmation. A tremendous amount of information is presented. You can select links to the Animation Master Gallery, Animation Master Objects, Animation Master Textures, Utilities and Tips and Tricks. If animation is your passion you will find kindred spirits at this site.

KEYWORDS Animation, Electronic Arts
AUDIENCE Artists, Computer Artists, Computer Graphic Designers, Graphic Designers
CONTACT fogald@mcmail.cis.mcmaster.ca
FREE

http://www.xmission.com/~gastown/animation/index.html

Arrows - Graphic Element Samples

Arrows, pointers, and buttons are found in abundance on this page. Moreover, this large collection has a wide assortment of styles, content and sizes. Some have 3D elements, and some are black and white line drawings. Whatever your needs, you probably will find something here to meet them. Download the compressed file of the whole collection and select the ones you need.

KEYWORDS Computer Art, Electronic Arts
AUDIENCE Computer Artists, Computer Graphic Designers, Graphic Designers
CONTACT Toine Andernach
andernac@cs.utwente.nl
FREE

http://hydra.cs.utwente.nl/~andernac/icons/arrows.html

The ArtVark Gallery

This online gallery of art covers a broad range of techniques. Images of paintings, drawings, photographs, computer images and body sculptures can be found here. Each of the categories is set up as a separate room in the exhibit, with each room containing several artworks. If you would like to have your work exhibited here, you can find instructions on submissions, as well.

KEYWORDS Computer Art, Electronic Arts, Netherlands
AUDIENCE Artists, Computer Artists, Computer Graphic Designers, Graphic Designers
CONTACT Hylke Sprangers
artvark@fwi.uva.nl
FREE

http://www.fwi.uva.nl/~boncz/artvark/

Artist Magazine Home Page

If you are working in the area of 3D art, or are just interested, this site is a good place to visit. Run by 3D Artist Magazine, this page provides links to resources and information regarding 3D Art, and information on the magazine, including some of its past issues.

KEYWORDS Computer Art, Electronic Arts
AUDIENCE Artists, Computer Artists, Computer Graphic Designers, Graphic Designers
CONTACT info@3dartist.com
FREE

http://www.3dartist.com/

The Background Sampler

This site contains a large collection of GIF files available for use as backgrounds in HTML documents. The images can be downloaded to your disk, or their URLs at this site can be referred to in your document.

KEYWORDS Computer Art, Electronic Arts
AUDIENCE Computer Artists, Computer Graphic Designers, Graphic Designers, Internet Users

FREE

http://www.netscape.com/assist/
net_sites/bg/backgrounds.html

Bill Curr's Art Page ★★★

As described by the artist, this site demonstrates the 'printmaker gone digital.' The page leads to several others which index and display a wide variety of digital prints which are completely computer generated, or are computer manipulations of photographs and scanned images.

KEYWORDS Art Exhibitions, Computer Art, Electronic Arts
AUDIENCE Artists, Computer Artists, Graphic Artists, Photographers
CONTACT Bill Curr
         billcurr@cyberspace.com
FREE

http://www.cyberspace.com/billcurr/
home.html

 ## BrainBug Graphics Introduction Page ★★★

BrainBug Graphics is a commercial design firm that has created a Web site to serve as a showcase for its creations, and to offer Web design technique tips. In their workshop area tips are provided on topics such as interlacing, transparency, image maps, and page color. If you are new to Web page construction or want to get some different ideas, look here. For examples of what can be done on the Web go to the portfolio on Web graphics. Other portfolios are available for business cards, illustrations, logos and newsletters. Samples of the work done at BrainBug are also provided.

KEYWORDS Art Exhibitions, Electronic Arts, Web Design
AUDIENCE Artists, Computer Artists, Computer Graphic Designers, Graphic Designers
CONTACT brainbug@connix.com
FREE

http://ybi.com/brainbug/introd.html

Bug's Graphics & Raytracing Page ★★★

The artist-author of this Web page provides us with a gallery of photorealistic 3D raytraced images and fractals. Each GIF image can be viewed in it's preview size, or at 576 X 450 pixels, or even at 1152 X 900 pixels. Links are also provided to other Web sites related to computer graphics, raytracing and virtual reality.

KEYWORDS Computer Art, Electronic Arts, Fractals, Ray Tracing
AUDIENCE Artists, Computer Artists, Computer Graphic Designers, Graphic Designers
CONTACT James F Thomas
         bug@dcs.warwick.ac.uk
FREE

http://www.csv.warwick.ac.uk/~esued/
cg.html

Buttons Icons ★★★★

Buttons for all occasions is what you will find in this large collection of images provided by The U.S. Army Artificial Intelligence Center. Intended for use on in house Web pages, these button icons are provided for public use also. The icons provide numerous images of text, numerals, and assorted shapes. Several sizes are also made available. Use the filenames and locations provided to download the images you need.

KEYWORDS Computer Art, Electronic Arts
AUDIENCE Artists, Computer Artists, Computer Graphic Designers, Graphic Designers
CONTACT Paul Beda
         beda@pentagon-ai.army.mil
FREE

http://www.pentagon-ai.army.mil/images/
icons/buttons/buttons.html

CICA Project Rock.Slices ★★★

The Center for Innovative Computer Applications at Indiana University, working with geologists, is using Application Visualization System (AVS) software to construct three-dimensional representations of invertebrates which lived 450 - 500 million years ago. The geologists scan slices of an invertebrate-bearing rock, then align the sequential images, and view the volume in AVS. This site presents several JPEG images resulting from these visualizations.

KEYWORDS Archaeology, Computer Art, Electronic Arts, Invertebrates
AUDIENCE Computer Artists, Computer Graphic Designers, Graphic Designers
CONTACT Brian Kaplan
         brian@cica.indiana.edu
FREE

http://www.cica.indiana.edu/projects/
Rock.Slices/index.html

CICA Project Theatre ★★★

The Theatre Department at Indiana University is interested in photorealistic rendering of stage and lighting situations. Using radiosity rendering techniques, indirect lighting can be modeled in the computer, and lighting situations can be designed before expensive (and time-consuming) stage sets are built. Eventually, the lighting designer will be able to specify (in a designer's language) lighting situations and the computer will not only be able to produce a rendering of what the scene will look like, but will also be able to position and control lights before and during a performance. This site provides information and images related to this research.

KEYWORDS Computer Art, Electronic Arts, Stage Design, Theater
AUDIENCE Artists, Computer Artists, Computer Graphic Designers, Graphic Designers
CONTACT Brian Kaplan
         brian@cica.indiana.edu
FREE

http://www.cica.indiana.edu/projects/
Theatre/index.html

California Digitographers' Gallery ★★★

California Digitographers is a gallery that features a collection of digital artists who use digital tools to transform their traditional photographs into computer art. These artists are interested in breaking new ground, rather than working within the conventional art paradigms, and their images are not just digitized replications of the originals. Each of the contributing artists has a separate gallery room to display their JPEG images. There are also links to other Web pages that have interesting original visual art.

KEYWORDS California, Computer Art, Electronic Arts, Photography
AUDIENCE Computer Artists, Computer Graphic Designers, Graphic Designers, Photographers

---

Connections to The X-Files

On the trail of Scully and Mulder

Perhaps you're one of many people who believe that there have been government cover-ups of actual alien visits to earth. Or maybe you wonder whether spontaneous combustion of human beings is possible, or if possession and exorcism are authentic. This American television program is cultishly popular and takes its lead from a U.S. Government "blue book" (or so say those who believe such a thing exists) which documents recorded UFO sightings, as well as visits and abductions by aliens. The series is about two federal agents who investigate cases of highly classified unexplained phenomena.

If you missed an episode on television, or want to find out more about the show and get the inside scoop on the show's X-Files (the X-Files of "The X-Files"), you don't have to wait until Friday night (its current time slot in the U.S.). Any day and at any time, you can turn to the Internet to connect to many sites pertaining to the series, including "The X-Files Cyberspace Home Page."

From this site you can download loads of information about the series, as well as get the FTP archives containing X-Files of "The X-Files." You can also join a fan club and gain access to the Usenet group.

(http://www.public.iastate.edu/
~sbwright/xfiles.html)

Electronic Arts

CONTACT Roland Dumas
radumas@hooked.net
FREE

http://www.hooked.net/hooked/users/radumas/index.html

Center for Electronic Art

The Center for Electronic Art is a resource for media and production. The Center serves students of electronic media literacy and technology, and public interest organizations who use the media facilities. The Center accepts pro bono clients. This site provides links to information of the Center's mission, facilities, registration, financial aid, policies, schedule, and photos of the Center.

KEYWORDS Education, Multimedia, Non Profit Organizations
AUDIENCE Art Enthusiasts, Art Professionals, Computer Artists, Computer Graphic Designers, Nonprofit Organizations, Students
CONTACT nfo@cea.edu
FREE

http://www.cea.edu

Chez Skal ★★★★

The menu options presented on this page allow you to view single inline stereograms, 3D fractal art, a collection of raytraced images, and animations. Every page has something to come back for if you can't get through on a single surf.

KEYWORDS Computer Art, Electronic Arts, Fractals
AUDIENCE Artists, Computer Artists, Computer Graphic Designers, Graphic Designers
CONTACT Paul Massimino
Pascal.Massimino@ens.ens.fr
FREE

http://acacia.ens.fr:8080/home/massimin/index.ang.html

Color Fractals ★★★

This site presents a collection of colorful fractal images that were created by a program called Fractint, on a Macintosh. This freeware program is also available on the PC. The images are displayed in small preview versions that can be enlarged to show the full size GIF files by selecting any of the images.

KEYWORDS Computer Art, Electronic Arts
AUDIENCE Artists, Computer Artists, Computer Graphic Designers, Graphic Designers
CONTACT J. Guy Stalnaker
jstalnak@students.wisc.edu
FREE

http://why.doit.wisc.edu/~jstalnak/Fractals.html

Color Ramper

The Web provides a facility to use computer generated graphics to convey not only images, but emotion and a sense of interaction. If you use a browser that supports backgrounds you undoubtedly have noticed the cycling of background colors. This site provides a color ramper that helps you create a background that ramps from one color to another. You merely enter the starting color and the ending color value, and a number of steps. The results are immediately usable in your pages by cutting the resulting list and pasting it into your page.

KEYWORDS Computer Art, Electronic Arts
AUDIENCE Artists, Computer Artists, Computer Graphic Designers, Graphic Designers
CONTACT Ryan Scott
rscott@netcreations.com
FREE

http://www.netcreations.com/ramper/index.html

The Comic Book and Comic Strip Page ★★★★

This site contains literally hundreds of links to Internet sites related to or containing comics and cartoons, as well as a significant local collection of digitized comic and cartoon art. Contact information for various comic, cartoon and animation artists and producers is also available, as are other miscellaneous resources for fans of comics and cartoons, both in print, on television, and in the movies. The many links available here are updated on a weekly basis.

KEYWORDS Animation, Cartoons, Comics, Meta-Index (Cartoons)
AUDIENCE Animation Enthusiasts, Art Enthusiasts, Artists, Comics Enthusiasts, Humor Enthusiasts
CONTACT Martin Ward
860099w@dragon.acadiau.ca
FREE

http://dragon.acadiau.ca:1667/~860099w/comics/comics.html

Conny's Ray Tracing ★★★★

This modest appearing home page is merely the front end for a large array of photorealistic 3D raytraced imagery. Links are provided to images created by the page author, and there is an exhibition of images by other artists. For further information on this field of computer graphics, the author provides links to utilities, other home pages, other 3D WWW resources, and the site for the 6th Eurographics Workshop on rendering.

KEYWORDS Computer Art, Electronic Arts
AUDIENCE Artists, Computer Artists, Computer Graphic Designers, Graphic Designers
CONTACT Conny Jonsson
cjo@esrange.ssc.se
FREE

http://www.kiruna.se/is/cjo/raytrace.html

Copyright Protection of Digital Images ★★★★

The distribution of graphic images over the Web raises serious questions about copyright protection in this digital realm. This site offers an approach to providing both copyright protection and ownership recognition. A set of program files can be downloaded for various platforms. Once set up the program casts an id_number as an invisible signature on any digital image. At another time the owner can examine whether the image which is suspected of being copied has it's own signature id_number. Currently the platforms supported are Silicon Graphics, Sun Microsystems, Hewlett Packard, and MD-DOS.

KEYWORDS Arts, Computer Art, Copyright
AUDIENCE Artists, Computer Artists, Computer Graphic Designers, Graphic Designers
CONTACT Prof. Ioannis Pitas
pitas@zeus.csd.auth.gr
FREE

http://poseidon.csd.auth.gr/signatures/

Dave gives the brush-off... ★★★

This galley presents a series of digital paintings by David S. Hull. Working on a Macintosh with Fractal Design's Painter 3.0, the artist has created JPEG images that provide ample evidence of the natural media look available with today's computer graphics tools.

KEYWORDS Art Exhibitions, Computer Art, Electronic Arts
AUDIENCE Artists, Computer Artists, Computer Graphic Designers, Graphic Designers
CONTACT Koonkie Kungenyeriwallin
quark@apocalypse.org
FREE

http://apocalypse.org/pub/u/quark/art.html

Demo Page of Computer Graphics Research Group ★★★

On this page, created by the Computer Graphics Research Group at Sheffield University, UK, you will find links including — Modeling and Animation Control of Deformable Objects, Computer Animation using Implicit Surfaces, Physically Based Modeling of Humans for Computer Animation, Surface Reconstruction from Medical Data, Fluid Dynamics Visualization, and Modeling Imperfections. You can view a series of thumbnail previews or the full size JPEG images (the file sizes are listed for each image). The animation option leads to a page which uses MPEG animations to demonstrate the concept of Implicit Surfaces.

KEYWORDS Art Exhibitions, Electronic Arts, Modeling
AUDIENCE Artists, Computer Artists, Computer Graphic Designers, Graphic Designers
CONTACT Agata Opalach
a.opalach@dcs.shef.ac.uk
FREE

http://www.dcs.shef.ac.uk:80/research/groups/graphics/demo.html

Digital Gallery ★★★

Using a variety of digital tools such as Adobe photoshop, Adobe Illustrator, Pixar Typestry, Fractal Design's Painter, and HSC KPT Bryce, artist Hillary Rhodes has created the art presented in this online gallery. This sizable collection covers a wide range of styles and techniques. Each image is displayed in a thumbnail view that can be enlarged to the full size, full color JPEG version. The file size of the JPEG image is noted next to each title.

KEYWORDS Art Exhibitions, Computer Art, Electronic Arts
AUDIENCE Artists, Computer Artists, Computer Graphic Designers, Graphic Designers

CONTACT   Hilary Rhodes
          hilary@geko.com.au
FREE

http://www.geko.com.au/users/hillary/Gallery.html

Digital Illusions ★★★★

Digital Illusions is a computer graphics E-zine that covers a broad range of computer graphic information. You can select information on different platforms companies, production houses and services, among many others. Selections lead to the pages offered by these companies and providers. This E-zine is a good starting in exploring the realm of computer graphics.

KEYWORDS Art Exhibitions, E-Zines, Electronic Arts
AUDIENCE Artists, Computer Artists, Computer Graphic Designers, Graphic Designers
CONTACT   Brian Leach
          bcleach@mcs.com
FREE

http://www.mcs.com/~bcleach/illusions/

Digital Photography 1995 ★★★

The Digital Photography page contains images from an exhibition sponsored by the Peoria Art Guild and Bradley University. Users may do a walkthoughof of the gallery and browse walls containing digital photography, and look at thumbnails or full screen images of the art. Also provided is an artists index, with personal intent statements, and video from the gallery opening. Information about the city of Peoria and Bradley University is also provided, as well as art from the 1994 exhibition.

KEYWORDS Art Exhibitions, Digital Photography, Video
AUDIENCE Art Enthusiasts, Digital Photography Enthusiasts, Photographers
CONTACT   Howard Goldbaum
          howard@bradley.bradley.edu
FREE

http://www.bradley.edu/exhibit95/

Digital Picture Archive on the 17th Floor ★★★

The Digital Picture Archive contains thousands of pictures in GIF and JPEG format. Users can look at images in categories such as art, comics, cars, faces, nature, technology, or space (with no X-rated pictures), with numerous pictures of famous celebrities. Other features include lists of the top fifty images accessed daily, as well as the top fifty people who accessed them the most.

KEYWORDS Archives, Celebrities, Pictures
AUDIENCE Celebrity Enthusiasts, General Public, Home Page Developers, Internet Users
CONTACT   patrick@muresh.et.tudelft.nl
FREE

http://olt.et.tudelft.nl/fun/pictures/pictures.html

Dingbats - Graphic Element Samples ★★★★

Dingbats are bitmapped icons that have a wide range of appearances, content, sizes, and uses. This collection is truly enormous, but does not compromise on quality. If you can't find it here, it probably does not exist. The entire collection has been placed into a compressed file to make it easy to download.

KEYWORDS Computer Art, Electronic Arts
AUDIENCE Computer Artists, Computer Graphic Designers, Graphic Designers
CONTACT   Toine Andernach
          andernac@cs.utwente.nl
FREE

http://hydra.cs.utwente.nl/~andernac/icons/dingbats.html

Directory of Computer Images ★★★

Located on this anonymous FTP server running at the Department of Math, Trinity College, Dublin, Ireland, is a truly huge collection of GIF and JPEG files of computer generated art. What is lost by the lack of current contributions is more than made up for by the scope and size of this exhibit.

KEYWORDS Art Exhibitions, Computer Art, Electronic Arts, Ireland
AUDIENCE Artists, Computer Artists, Computer Graphic Designers, Graphic Designers
CONTACT   archive@maths.tcd.ie
FREE

ftp://ftp.maths.tcd.ie/pub/images/Computer/

Directory of Fractal Programs ★★★★

If you are looking for fractal programs that will start you on your way to becoming a fractal artist, begin your journey at this Web site. A comprehensive listing of executable programs related to fractal imagery is provided across a wide range of platforms, including Amiga, IBM PC, Macintosh and UNIX. This site may not have everything, but it seems to come close.

KEYWORDS Computer Art, Electronic Arts, Fractals
AUDIENCE Artists, Computer Artists, Computer Graphic Designers, Graphic Designers
CONTACT   Noel Giffin
          noel@triumf.ca
FREE

http://spanky.triumf.ca/pub/fractals/programs/

Directory of Graphics Textures ★★★★

This site contains a large collection of textures for use in texture mapping applications. The textures are grouped in sub-directories based on qualities such as — good textures that wrap, images that need only a little work to wrap, textures that wrap only horizontally, and simple textures like windows backgrounds.

KEYWORDS 3D Webs, Computer Art, Electronic Arts
AUDIENCE Computer Artists, Computer Graphic Designers, Graphic Designers
FREE

ftp://ftp.cs.tu-berlin.de/pub/sci/virtual-reality/graphics/texture/

Directory of Rendering ★★★

Located at this FTP site is a good collection of files relating to 3D rendering. Several TIFF texture files are available in their own subdirectory. A large collection of IPAS plug ins for 3D Studio are in the IPAS directory. You can get an overview of the files at this site by reading the All Files text file.

KEYWORDS Computer Art, Electronic Arts
AUDIENCE Artists, Computer Artists, Computer Graphic Designers, Graphic Designers
CONTACT   Ron Ohmer
          ftpadmin@athis.jkcg.com
FREE

ftp://athis.gttw.com/pub/

Electronic Art ★★★

The Design Research Centre Virtual Gallery contains new work produced by artists and students in the United Kingdom. The Electronic Wing consists of a wide variety of work produced using various technological methods ranging from computer aided image processing and computer generated imagery to a color photocopier.

KEYWORDS Art Exhibitions, Computer Art, Electronic Arts
AUDIENCE Artists, Computer Artists, Computer Graphic Designers, Graphic Designers
CONTACT   Geoff Broadway
          G.Broadway@derby.ac.uk
FREE

http://dougal.derby.ac.uk/gallery/electronic-wing.html

Elektra ★★★★

Elektra is the first dynamic online publication at Harvard. In addition to articles, Elektra also contains artwork (still images, animation, and sound). Contents include Technology News (the latest in technology news), Multimedia Studio (projects that involve graphics, audio, and video), Virtual Kiosk (upcoming events) and the Voter Booth (reader feedback). The page also contains links to an extensive list of other Harvard web sites.

KEYWORDS Computer Art, Electronic Arts, Multimedia
AUDIENCE Computer Artists, Computer Graphic Designers, Multimedia Designers, Multimedia Enthusiasts
CONTACT   elektra@digitas.org
FREE

http://www.digitas.org/

Favorite Wall Paper ★★★

This site contains a collection of ZIP files, some very large, which contain photographic images and photorealistic raytraced images. The subject matter includes scanned photographs of Stonehenge, a photograph of a brick wall, a photograph of a snow covered mountain, raytraced images of a room, and more. The images have been sized at 1024 X 768 pixels so they can be used as wallpaper in Windows, but some are also useful as background images for Web pages.

KEYWORDS Computer Art, Electronic Arts
AUDIENCE Computer Artists, Computer Graphic Designers, Computer Users, Graphic Designers

Electronic Arts

CONTACT Tim Hauser
         thauser@drwatson.com

FREE

http://drwatson.com/tim/wallpaper.htm

Fine Art Drawings and Paintings ★★★

This collection has a number of black and white fine art drawings. All have been saved in JPEG format making downloading easier. In this room your will find various figures studies and other imagery.

KEYWORDS Art Exhibitions, Computer Art, Electronic Arts
AUDIENCE Artists, Computer Artists, Computer Graphic Designers, Graphic Designers
CONTACT   Errol Lanier
          serpent@ssnet.com

FREE

http://www.art.net/Studios/Visual/Bianchi/fine.html

Fine Art Forum Online Edition ★★★

The Fine Art Forum Online Edition contains an online gallery with works by dozens of artists using the Internet as part of their medium, a large list of Internet services for artists (moderated by Jane Patterson, and a number of articles for artists and others using the Internet or other electronic networks as a part of their art.

KEYWORDS Design, Electronic Arts, Magazines
AUDIENCE Art Educators, Art Students, Artists
CONTACT   Paul Brown
          paul_brown@siggraph.org

FREE

http://www.msstate.edu/Fineart_Online/index.html

gopher://gopher.msstate.edu/11/Online_services/fineart_online/

Fractal Collections ★★★

The artist has created a Web site that presents two collections of fractal images in GIF format. The Planet Collection displays fractal creations resembling planets. The Sunflowers Collection presents a series of sunflower fractals that are accompanied by explanations of how the images reflect the underlying fractal structure.

KEYWORDS Art Exhibitions, Computer Art, Electronic Arts, Fractals
AUDIENCE Artists, Computer Artists, Computer Graphic Designers, Graphic Designers
CONTACT   Len Bruton
          bruton@enel.ucalgary.ca

FREE

http://www-mddsp.enel.ucalgary.ca/People/bruton/fractal.html

Fractal Design Painter 3 ★★★★

Computer artists who want the ability to produce digital art with techniques and tools that are familiar in traditional media have a powerful tool in 'Painter' by the Fractal Design Corp. This site provides an online brochure of the capabilities of this Natural-Media software. If you want to know what you can do with Painter this is the page to view.

KEYWORDS Computer Art, Electronic Arts
AUDIENCE Artists, Computer Artists, Computer Graphic Designers, Graphic Designers

FREE

http://www.fractal.com/p3.html

GIFs Directory ★★★★

As the name states, this site is a repository of GIF images. Categories cover everything from Ads to Xmas (Christmas, with a difference). The images are available from an alphabetized index in each subject's sub-directory.

KEYWORDS Art Exhibitions, Computer Art, Electronic Arts, Images
AUDIENCE Artists, Computer Artists, Computer Graphic Designers, Graphic Designers
CONTACT   Rob Malick
          rmalick@www.acm.uiuc.edu

FREE

http://www.acm.uiuc.edu/rml/Gifs/

GNN Digital Drive-In ★★★

Global Network Navigator Magazine presents 'The Digital Drive-In' which looks at digital movies on the Internet, and is brought to you via MPEG, QuickTime and other formats as appropriate. Topics include profiles of Internet movie producers, technical tips on viewing and making digital movies and current topics and trends in digital video hardware and software.

KEYWORDS Computer Art, Electronic Arts, Software, Video Hardware
AUDIENCE Computer Artists, Computer Graphic Designers, Graphic Designers, Video Artists
CONTACT   forum@gnn.com

FREE

http://gnn.com/gnn/special/drivein/index.html

Genetic Art from the Virtual World ★★★★

This online brochure contains excerpts from a talk by the artist William Latham, a Henry Moore Scholar at the Royal College of Art, London, showcasing three designs inspired by natural shapes. They were created by applying a selective mutation process, using a program call Mutator. If you know what a selective mutation process is, or just want to look at some interesting art, stop by this page.

KEYWORDS Art Exhibitions, Computer Art, Electronic Arts
AUDIENCE Artists, Computer Artists, Graphic Artists, Graphic Designers
CONTACT   jw@scitsc.wlv.ac.uk

FREE

http://www.scit.wlv.ac.uk/events/latham.html

Gopher-Based ASCII Clipart Collection ★★★★

This directory contains hundreds of ASCII art archives from different sources. Some collections included in this archive are Steven Sullivan's famous Small ASCII Pics collection, Bob Allison's Scarecrow Archives, Paul Fawcett's ASCII atlas 1.0. and a vt100 animation section mirrored from Chris Groom's collection.

KEYWORDS ASCII Art, Animation, Computer Art, Electronic Arts
AUDIENCE Computer Art Enthusiasts, Computer Artists, Computer Users, General Public
CONTACT   Texas Tech University Computer Sciences Gopher Server
          gripe@cs.ttu.edu

FREE

gopher://gopher.cs.ttu.edu:70/11/Art%20and%20Images/ClipArt%20%28ASCII%29

ftp://ftp.cs.ttu.edu:/pub/asciiar/

Graphic Element Samples ★★★★

This Web site has a large collection of bitmapped icons for all types of uses. Some are black and white, some are multicolor. If you just have to have a Bart Simpson icon, you can find it here. There are various sizes, and subjects, and all have been collected into compressed files making it relatively painless to download the whole collection.

KEYWORDS Computer Art, Electronic Arts
AUDIENCE Computer Artists, Computer Graphic Designers, Graphic Designers
CONTACT   Toine Andernach
          andernac@cs.utwente.nl

FREE

http://hydra.cs.utwente.nl/~andernac/icons/othericons.html

The Graphic Utilities' Site & Version FAQ ★★★★

This FAQ was created to answer questions about computer graphic utilities for DOS, Macintosh, OS/2, Windows, and X-Windows, such as What is the newest version of the utility? On what FTP site can this version be found? What types of files does it handle? Just follow the on screen directions and all these questions will be answered.

KEYWORDS Computer Art, Electronic Arts
AUDIENCE Artists, Computer Artists, Computer Graphic Designers, Graphic Designers
CONTACT   Brian D. Stark
          stark@iastate.edu

FREE

http://www.public.iastate.edu/~stark/gutil_sv.html

Graphics, Visualization, and Usability Center Animation ★★★★

The Graphics, Visualization, and Usability Center Animation Lab at Georgia Tech University is working on developing techniques to produce realistic computer animation of people, animals and robots. Examples of

Electronic Arts 41

several research projects covering such topics as the simulation of human runners, splashes created by a platform diver and gymnastic vault are provided. Each page discusses the background and approaches taken in the creation of the imagery. Still JPEG images and MPEG animations are available to illustrate the solutions discussed in the papers.

KEYWORDS   Computer Art, Electronic Arts
AUDIENCE   Artists, Computer Artists, Computer Graphic Designers, Graphic Designers
CONTACT   James F. O'Brien
           obrienj@cc.gatech.edu
FREE

http://www.cc.gatech.edu/gvu/animation/Animation.html

HMS - Research ★★★

The Center for Human Modeling and Simulation at the University of Pennsylvania has developed this Web site to present information regarding the work and education produced at the Center. Pages which demonstrate some of the approaches and techniques used in the study of computer graphic modeling, rendering and animation can be accessed here. Topics cover areas such as the modeling of human behavior in 3D virtual environments, animation control techniques, physics-based modeling, animation and control, and rendering techniques for complex environments.

KEYWORDS   Art Exhibitions, Computer Art, Electronic Arts
AUDIENCE   Computer Artists, Computer Graphic Designers, Graphic Designers
CONTACT   HMS@graphics.cis.upenn.edu
FREE

http://www.cis.upenn.edu/~hms/research.html

HTML Working with Images: LTP: Cornell ★★★★

The Learning Technologies Center at Cornell University has created this online tutorial to assist in Web page design. This section deals primarily with the use of graphics, and covers such topics as downloading an image from WWW to your hard disk, image file size, developing WWW images in Adobe Photoshop, cross-platform compatibility and image support applications. If you are putting a page on the Web you will be well served to read this page and the pages provided through its links.

KEYWORDS   Computer Art, Electronic Arts, WWW (World Wide Web)
AUDIENCE   Artists, Computer Artists, Computer Graphic Designers, Graphic Designers
CONTACT   Cynthia Frazier
           cf12@cornell.edu
FREE

http://frazier.cit.cornell.edu/style/images.html

Hiddi's Raytracing Page ★★★

Raytraced images and MPEG animations are the focus of this Web page. You are presented with still shots from five animations which can be selected to view or download. A short description accompanies the images providing background information on how the animations were created. Also displayed are five still JPEG previews which will be displayed in full size when selected. The size of all files is identified, so you can plan how much time you will need if you want to take a look.

KEYWORDS   Computer Art, Electronic Arts
AUDIENCE   Artists, Computer Artists, Computer Graphic Designers, Graphic Designers
CONTACT   Torsten Hiddessen
           math@sun.rz.tu-clausthal.de
FREE

http://www.rz.tu-clausthal.de/~math/Raytracing.html

HypArt - The Project ★★★★

This server provides the opportunity to view and create hyperpaintings, which are computer paintings created by different people on different computers. Anyone with the appropriate software is invited to contribute.

KEYWORDS   Art Exhibitions, Computer Art, Computer Graphics, Hypermedia
AUDIENCE   Art Educators, Art Enthusiasts, Art Professionals, Art Students, Artists
CONTACT   rosenfeld@rrz.uni-hamburg.de
FREE

http://rzsun01.rrz.uni-hamburg.de/cgi-bin/HypArt.sh

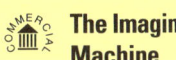

i3D: A High Speed 3D Scene Browser ★★★★

With Virtual Reality becoming increasingly present on the Web this site helps to provide the tools, and point the way to exploring this virtual realm. If you are operating an SGI workstation under IRIX 5.2 or can take advantage of the current version of i3D, a high speed 3D scene Web browser integrated with Mosaic or Netscape you can place and view hyperlinks to 3D data in your HTML documents.

KEYWORDS   Electronic Arts, Virtual Reality
AUDIENCE   Computer Artists, Computer Graphic Designers, Graphic Designers, Virtual Reality Enthusiasts
CONTACT   iadm@crs4.it
FREE

http://www.crs4.it/~3diadm/i3d-help.html

Images Index ★★★

Vern Hart's page displays an extensive gallery of clip art GIF images. The collection provides a good selection of non-commercial art which may be used for the design of Web pages, among other functions.

KEYWORDS   Art Exhibitions, Computer Art, Electronic Arts
AUDIENCE   Artists, Computer Artists, Graphic Artists, Graphic Designers
CONTACT   Vern Hart
           vern@cs.uidaho.edu
FREE

http://www.cs.uidaho.edu:80/~vern/images/

ImAgInE aMaTiOn WeB pAgE ★★★★

If you want to get an idea of the diversity of 3D photorealistic graphic images and animations being produced on the desktop, stop by this Web site. Individual pages are offered with GIF stills and MPEG animations. Links are also provided to areas where the authors offer their artistic talents for Web site creation and other graphic services.

KEYWORDS   Computer Art, Electronic Arts
AUDIENCE   Computer Artists, Computer Graphic Designers, Graphic Designers
CONTACT   imagine@kaiwan.com
FREE

http://www.kaiwan.com/~imagine/

The Imaging Machine ★★★★

The Imaging Machine is a service that downloads, installs and configures imaging software for image processors. Users may download their imaging software ImageMagick after having read a background description of its functions and uses. Also provided are links to their other services, including filters, indexing, image combining, transparent gifts, and cool imaging. Users choose the service they want and send in the URLs of the images they want the Imaging Machine to manipulate.

KEYWORDS   Computer Graphics, Graphics, Imaging
AUDIENCE   Computer Graphic Artists, Electronic Artists, Home Page Developers, Imaging Specialists
CONTACT   webmaster@vrl.com
FREE

http://www.vrl.com/Imaging/

Index of Animals ★★★★

From apes and otters to zacks and zebras; this is a site dedicated to images of animals. The pictures range in size from 320 X 200 pixels to 1236 X 768 pixels, and you have a good selection at all file sizes. As the title states, this is the place to come if you want pictures of animals, provided by the people who know animals, The American Association of Zookeepers.

KEYWORDS   Computer Art, Electronic Arts, Societies
AUDIENCE   Artists, Computer Artists, Computer Graphic Designers, Graphic Designers
CONTACT   hpear3@aazk.ind.net
FREE

http://aazk.ind.net/animal_gifs/

Insect Nest ★★★★

This site will give you a new outlook on the insect world. If you wonder whether insects such as scorpions, beetles and spiders should be considered beautiful, this page will help you decide. Renee Recker has taken photographs and applied her artistic skills to transform these creatures into undeniable works of art. Moreover, they 'speak' for themselves. (The site provides the software necessary to listen to the .aiff files if you need it.) What do these extraordinary insects have to say? You'll just have to surf to this site and listen for yourself.

KEYWORDS   Computer Art, Electronic Arts, Insects
AUDIENCE   Artists, Computer Artists, Computer Graphic Designers, Graphic Designers

Electronic Arts

CONTACT Renee Recker
HeyRenee@aol.com

FREE

http://www.interport.net:80/~rexalot/insectnest.html

Inspired Arts, Inc.

Inspired Arts develops Interactive CD-ROM titles, art and music, and does WWW publishing. Besides providing information about their business, their site includes an art gallery, sound bites from their recording artists, and information about CD-ROMs and CD+.

KEYWORDS CD-ROMs, Interactive Media, Visual Arts
AUDIENCE Art Enthusiasts, CD-ROM Publishers, Music Enthusiasts
CONTACT Karen Morgan
kymorgan@inspiredarts.com
FREE

http://www.cts.com/~inspired/virtualgallery.html

Joel's Ray Tracing Niche

Photorealistic 3D rendered graphics are a hallmark of what can be accomplished on the desktop computer. To get a good idea of what is being done come to this site. A collection of GIF images provides a very visual idea of the scope of the current state of the art. Several links are also provided which will lead you deeper into the world of raytracing by connecting to related sites on the Web.

KEYWORDS Computer Art, Electronic Arts
AUDIENCE Artists, Computer Artists, Computer Graphic Designers, Graphic Designers
CONTACT Joel Davis
davis@vsl.ist.ucf.edu
FREE

http://www.vsl.ist.ucf.edu/~davis/raytrace.html

JuliaSets

Twelve black and white fractal images of the Julia Set are presented at this Web site. The images were created using a program for the Macintosh called Julia's Dream. Each of the images, presented in small previews, can be seen in their full size by clicking on the image you want to see.

KEYWORDS Computer Art, Electronic Arts, Exhibits
AUDIENCE Artists, Computer Artists, Computer Graphic Designers, Graphic Designers
CONTACT J. Guy Stalnaker
jstalnak@students.wisc.edu
FREE

http://why.doit.wisc.edu:80/~jstalnak/JuliaSets.html

KODAK: Sample Digital Images

The Eastman Kodak Company is not typically a provider of images, but this site represents the company's effort to promote digital photography while demonstrating the value of their digital PhotoCD imaging format. What the user will find is a fairly sizable collection of images taken on traditional film and scanned to PhotoCD format. The quality is excellent, and the images are available for personal use.

KEYWORDS Computer Art, Digital Photography, Electronic Arts
AUDIENCE Computer Artists, Computer Graphic Designers, Graphic Designers, Photographers
CONTACT webmaster@www.kodak.com
FREE

http://www.kodak.com/digitalImages/samples/samples.shtml

Kai's Power Tips and Tricks for Photoshop

If you use Adobe's Photoshop then you owe it to yourself to check out Kai Krause's page. Here there are 23 in-depth articles showing how to take full advantage of the tools provided with Photoshop and by Kai's company, HSC. You can also venture into an archive of image tiles that can be used as backgrounds for Web pages, or you can find more information from this graphics expert.

KEYWORDS Art Exhibitions, Computer Art, Electronic Arts
AUDIENCE Artists, Computer Artists, Computer Graphic Designers, Graphic Designers
CONTACT Josh Hartmann
josh@the-tech.mit.edu
FREE

http://the-tech.mit.edu/KPT/KPT.html

Kali

Kali is an interactive geometry program that lets you draw Escher-like tilings, infinite knots and more. Users may begin by drawings patterns based on planar symmetry groups. What are they, you might wonder? This page provides the answer to that question and gives you the tools to begin creating.

KEYWORDS Electronic Arts, Geometry
AUDIENCE Artists, Computer Artists, Computer Graphic Designers, Graphic Designers
CONTACT Nina Amenta
nina@geom.umn.edu
FREE

http://www.geom.umn.edu/apps/kali/about.html

La Galleria — The 9th Floor BBS Art Gallery

This online gallery has a collection of GIF files which represent the current trends in computer generated graphics. Most of the images were created with the raytracing program POV-Ray. Each image title is followed by a short statement providing a little background on the picture. Clicking on the title link will display the full size image.

KEYWORDS Art Exhibitions, Art Galleries, Computer Art, Electronic Arts
AUDIENCE Artists, Computer Artists, Computer Graphic Designers, Graphic Designers
FREE

http://leccata.nmsu.edu/users/Techs-Misc/bbs.gallery.html

Leonardo Electronic Almanac

This is the Web site of Leonardo Electronic Almanac (LEA), the electronic journal of Leonardo/ISAST and MIT Press. It contains back issues of the journal and materials accompanying the articles and information found in the journal, such as sound samples and galleries. LEA is dedicated to providing a forum for those who are interested in the realm where art, science and technology converge. The contents of LEA's archives are described and pointers are provided for viewing the various documents stored there.

KEYWORDS Electronic Magazines, Electronic Media, Technology
AUDIENCE Artists, Electronic Media Professionals, Multimedia Enthusiasts, Scientists
CONTACT Craig Harris
harri067@maroon.tc.umn.edu
FREE

http://www-mitpress.mit.edu/LEA/home.html

Leonardo Electronic Members Forum

Leonardo Electronic Members Forum is the password-protected area of the Leonardo World Wide Web Site. The forum contains articles, galleries, sound samples, an artists' Words on Works section, and areas devoted to special projects guest-edited by artists in various parts of the world. In addition, the forum is dedicated to providing services to Leonardo Electronic Members and providing meeting places for collaborations among members.

KEYWORDS Computer Art, Electronic Media, Multimedia
AUDIENCE Artists, Multimedia Enthusiasts, Scientists, Sound Artists
CONTACT Pat Bentson
pbentson@mercury.sfsu.edu
FREE

http://www-mitpress.mit.edu/Leonardo/members.html

The Leonardo World Wide Web Site

The Leonardo World Wide Web Site is the latest entry in a long tradition of publications by the International Society for the Arts, Sciences and Technology (ISAST). The Leonardo WWW Site offers many of the same features as the print journal Leonardo and the electronic journal Leonardo Electronic Almanac, while taking advantage of the unique qualities of the Web. The site includes articles by artists and theorists, a gallery section presenting multimedia works by fine artists, sound samples, Words on Works (short pieces by artists about their work), bibliographies, documentation of special collaboratory projects with artists and art groups around the world, a directory of people and resources of interest, plus links to other Web sites. The site includes both a 'free' section and a 'members-only' password-protected section, which is available to subscribers of either the print journal or the electronic journal.

KEYWORDS Art Theory, Artists, Computer Music, Electronic Arts
AUDIENCE Artists, Arts Community, Musicians, Scientists

Electronic Arts

CONTACT Mason
isast@mercury.sfsu.edu
FREE

http://www-mitpress.mit.edu/Leonardo/home.html

Lines Icons ★★★★

Horizontal rules (lines) are commonly used in Web pages as paragraph or subject separators. Sooner or later you will need this kind of icon if you are making your own page. When you do need a line then come to this page. The U.S.Army Artificial Intelligence Center has developed an extensive collection of line icons for their in-house use, but has made them available for public use as well. Here you have a wide variety of sizes, colors, textures and images to meet your needs. Each image can be downloaded individually.

KEYWORDS Computer Art, Electronic Arts
AUDIENCE Artists, Computer Artists, Computer Graphic Designers, Graphic Designers
CONTACT Paul Beda
beda@pentagon-ai.army.mil
FREE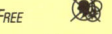

http://www.pentagon-ai.army.mil/images/icons/lines/lines.html

MOSAIC pgmcrater ★★★★

We know there are surfers who have those great visions of creating worlds of their own. The creator of this site decided to provide the once in a lifetime opportunity to specify of a world you want to create. Users start with world size and press the Submit button. After a brief pause a photorealistic image of your world, as seen from space, is returned to you. At the present time only random parameters are available, but it sounds like you may get more control in the future. Check back, or better yet email the author to find out what is in store.

KEYWORDS Computer Art, Electronic Arts, Fractals
AUDIENCE Artists, Computer Artists, Computer Graphic Designers, Graphic Designers
CONTACT Rene Eberhard
kelvin@Autodesk.com
FREE

http://www.itr.ch/~reberhar/forge/

MPEG Movie Archive ★★★★

If your predilection for computer graphics includes MPEG videos, this page will be of interest. Links on the page lead to separate archives which contain extensive selections of MPEG files. Archive categories include Supermodels, Animations, Movie and TV, Music, Space, and even R-rated. Links are also provided to take you to further MPEG information, or sites to obtain necessary viewer programs.

KEYWORDS Animation, Computer Art, Computer Graphics, Space
AUDIENCE Computer Artists, Computer Graphic Designers, Graphic Designers, Video Artists
CONTACT Heini Withagen
www@eeb.ele.tue.nl
FREE

http://www.eeb.ele.tue.nl/mpeg/index.html

Macromedia - Interactive Gallery ★★★★

One of the major forces in today's world of computer graphics is Macromedia, Inc. Here, at their home page they have installed an interactive gallery where you can see samples of the work being produced with Macromedia products. (The samples are available to download as QuickTime formatted files.) There is a wide range of categories in the gallery including Presentations, Consumer Titles, Kiosks, and Graphics and Animations. Naturally there are links taking you throughout the extensive Macromedia Home Page.

KEYWORDS Art Exhibitions, Computer Art, Electronic Arts
AUDIENCE Computer Artists, Computer Graphic Designers, Graphic Designers
CONTACT questions@macromedia.com
FREE

http://www.macromedia.com/Gallery/index.html

Martin Jopson ★★★

Martin Jopson presents QuickTime and MPEG animations of nine digitally constructed images exploring repetition of forms within artworks. Set aside the time to load the files, and enjoy the creativity of this artist.

KEYWORDS Art Exhibitions, Computer Art, Electronic Arts
AUDIENCE Artists, Computer Artists, Computer Graphic Designers, Graphic Designers
CONTACT Geoff Broadway
G.Broadway@derby.ac.uk
FREE

http://dougal.derby.ac.uk/gallery/martindoc.html

The Mercury Project ★★★★

This site is a participatory story of a research project. Users are able to remotely control a robot and log their findings. All data is collected in order to discover a 'secret'!

KEYWORDS Computer Art, Fiction, Robots
AUDIENCE Artists, Game Enthusiasts, General Public, Internet Users
CONTACT Eric Mankin
eric@skymir.usc.edu
FREE

http://www.usc.edu/dept/raiders/story/mercury-story.html

Mr. Potato Head Home Page ★★★★

What! You' no longer have your Mr. Potato Head game from when you were a kid? Well all is not lost. Here you can read the history of Mr. Potato Head, play Mr. Potato Head (the game), and see a Mr. Potato Head animation. If it is about Mr. Potato Head, this page has it, or links to the place that does. Definitely the final word on Mr. Potato Head!

KEYWORDS Computer Art, Electronic Arts
AUDIENCE Computer Artists, Cyberculture Enthusiasts

CONTACT potatoe@acsu.buffalo.edu
FREE

http://winnie.acsu.buffalo.edu/cgi-bin/potatoe

Multi-Scale Maps ★★★

One purpose of computer generated graphics is to allow visualization of subject matter in ways not previously available. The Multi-Scale Maps page is an excellent example of how computer generated graphics makes the unrealizable possible. Here you can select from a small group of maps that respond to your commands. You select the level of zoom (resolution), you select the region to view, you even select the manner in which the map is presented to you, but it won't help you find your way across town — yet!

KEYWORDS Art Exhibitions, Computer Art, Electronic Arts
AUDIENCE Computer Artists, Computer Graphic Designers, Graphic Designers
CONTACT Calvin J. Hamilton
cjhamil@lanl.gov
FREE

http://www.c3.lanl.gov/~cjhamil/Browse/main.html

NCSA Icons ★★★★

As part of their support for inhouse development of Web pages, The U.S. Army Artificial Intelligence Center has collected a series of icons from NCSA and has made them available to the public as well as their in house staff. The icons are a variety of sizes, and colors, and are useful across a broad range of subjects.

KEYWORDS Computer Art, Electronic Arts
AUDIENCE Artists, Computer Artists, Computer Graphic Designers, Graphic Designers
CONTACT Paul Beda
beda@pentagon-ai.army.mil
FREE

http://www.pentagon-ai.army.mil/images/icons/NCSA/NCSA.html

NYU Center for Digital Multimedia ★★★★

NYU's Center for Digital Multimedia works to integrate new information technologies into the spectrum of activities that have made New York state a world economic and cultural center. The center assists individuals and small multimedia developers by sharing information, providing access to laboratory and library resources, creating networking opportunities, offering semester-long and 'target' seminars, providing on-site and online job retraining, and a special affiliates program. This site contains information on education and research at the Center. Information is also available concerning the staff of the Center.

KEYWORDS Computer Art, Electronic Arts, Multimedia, Multimedia Education
AUDIENCE Artists, Computer Artists, Computer Graphic Designers, Multimedia Enthusiasts
CONTACT Elizabeth Fischer
nwhq@wimsey.com
FREE

http://found.cs.nyu.edu/CAT_new/CATdescription.html

Arts & Music

Nurse's Tile Archive ★★★

Tiles! Tiles! Tiles! This is a site for WWW page designers that want to use background images. Although the theme of the images is somewhat macabre — they include skeletons, reptiles, bones — it is surprising how they look when tiled as page backgrounds.

KEYWORDS   Art Exhibitions, Computer Art, Electronic Arts
AUDIENCE   Computer Artists, Computer Graphic Designers, Cybernauts, Internet surfers
CONTACT   Nurse@Tezcat.com
FREE

http://www.tezcat.com/~nurse/NURSETILE.html

Occi-Ori's Sample Work ★★★

Occi-Ori Enterprises is a creative services agency working closely with ShadowWorks Productions, to produce special effects, video, and multimedia products and services. This site serves as a gallery and promotional site to display some of the work being done by these groups. From cartoons hand-drawn on the computer, to 3D rendered images and digitally manipulated photographs, the art presented on this page will encourage you to learn more about this genre.

KEYWORDS   Art Exhibitions, Computer Art, Electronic Arts
AUDIENCE   Artists, Computer Artists, Computer Graphic Designers, Graphic Designers
CONTACT   occiori@oneworld.wa.com
FREE

http://oneworld.wa.com/occiori/sample.html

Omphalos- Works by Jon McCormack

Omphalos- Works by Jon McCormack is a Web page that offers a collection of electronic art. Users will find several computer animation sequences in the QuickTime movie format. In addition, there are several interactive works here, which are downloadable and playable on host machines. Users can also get a list of where this artist's work is showing. Links to other electronic art sites are available here.

KEYWORDS   Computer Animation, Online Art Galleries
AUDIENCE   Artists, Electronic Art Enthusiasts
CONTACT   Jon McCormack
               jonmc@indy04.cs.monash.edu.au
FREE

http://www.cs.monash.edu.au/~jonmc/art.html

Orbifold Pinball ★★★

Orbifold Pinball is an online interactive Pinball game with a difference. The game board features three bumpers, and the board is curved. Even if the ball closely misses the bumper it will still whip around it as if it hit.

KEYWORDS   Art Exhibitions, Electronic Arts, Pinball
AUDIENCE   Computer Artists, Computer Graphic Designers, Graphic Designers
CONTACT   webmaster@geom.umn.edu
FREE

http://www.geom.umn.edu/apps/pinball/about.html

Pattern Land! ★★★★

For Web designers constructing pages with backgrounds, this site provides over 150 pattern images. Just select one of the pages in the index and you are presented with up to 16 thumbnails of background patterns which you can download for your own pages.

KEYWORDS   Computer Art, Electronic Arts
AUDIENCE   Artists, Computer Artists, Computer Graphic Designers, Graphic Designers
CONTACT   Ryan Scott
               rscott@netcreations.com
FREE

http://www.netcreations.com/patternland/

PixelChrome Professional ★★★

Photographer, Jeremy Woodhouse has developed the PixelChrome Professional web site to market his CD-ROM of scenic and wildlife photography to online users. Visitors to the site can access a gallery of selected photos from the CD mostly shot in Africa. The site also outlines what computer equipment is required for desktop publishers to make use of the photos once purchased. The site provides links both to Durban, a city in South Africa, and to the Internet Mall.

KEYWORDS   CD-ROMs, Desktop Publishing, Multimedia, Photography
AUDIENCE   Desktop Publishers/Designers, Nature Buffs, Photography Enthusiasts
CONTACT   Jeremy Woodhouse
               pixlchrm @onramp.net
FREE

http://rampages.onramp.net/~pixlchrm

Projekte am WSI-GRIS ★★★

A project page from the University of Tuebingen, Germany, is presented at this Web site. This English language paper discusses creating computer generated images of cloth, and modeling of cloth-draping using particle systems and 3D rendering packages. A series of MPEG animations (with file sizes indicated) is available via a link to demonstrate some of information discussed in the paper.

KEYWORDS   Computer Art, Electronic Arts, Germany, Textiles
AUDIENCE   Artists, Computer Artists, Computer Graphic Designers, Graphic Designers
CONTACT   Bernd Eberhardt
               beberh@gris.informatik.uni-tuebingen.de
FREE

http://greco.gris.informatik.uni-tuebingen.de/gris/proj/hc.html

QuasiTiler ★★★★

This site presents a research project at the Geometry Center of the University of Minnesota. QuasiTiler draws Penrose tilings and their generalizations. Here you will find mathematical explanation of the complexities of Penrose tilings and discussion of how the QuasiTiler works. If you get the itch you can also just jump in and start creating. The images are fun, and the instructions will easily take you through the process.

KEYWORDS   Electronic Arts, Geometry
AUDIENCE   Artists, Computer Artists, Computer Graphic Designers, Graphic Designers
CONTACT   Eugenio Durand
               durand@geom.umn.edu
FREE

http://www.geom.umn.edu/apps/quasitiler/start.html

RMTop ★★★★

Created by Pixar, RenderMan provides a standard mechanism for modeling and animation software to send data to rendering systems in a device-independent way, with minimal regard to the actual rendering algorithms being used. Serving as a repository for all things RenderMan, this page provides information under the topics — What is RenderMan, RIBS, Shaders, and Texture Maps. Links to FTP sites with RenderMan related files and to the RenderMan FAQ are also found on this page.

KEYWORDS   Animation, Electronic Arts
AUDIENCE   ARtists, Computer Artists, Computer Graphic Designers, Graphic Designers
CONTACT   tal@cs.caltech.edu
FREE

http://pete.cs.caltech.edu/RMR/rmTop.htmld/rmTop.html

Rayshade Homepage ★★★★

Rayshade is a system for creating raytraced images, written in C. This site contains links on everything related to Rayshade, including the Rayshade FTP archives where the program itself can be located along with ports to various platforms, the Rayshade user's guide, the Rayshade quick-reference sheet, and sample rayshade images. There is much, much more, so set aside some time and get into the fast lane with raytracing online.

KEYWORDS   Computer Art, Electronic Arts, Ray Tracing
AUDIENCE   Artists, Computer Artists, Computer Graphic Designers, Graphic Designers
CONTACT   Craig Kolb
               cek@flux.stanford.edu
FREE

http://www-graphics.stanford.edu/~cek/rayshade/rayshade.html

Raytraced Images ★★★

This site provides access to several raytraced images done solely by Michael Mittelstadt (Meek) with the Povray raytracer. Other tools, such as the Moray Modelling System, were used to generate some of the images. Images are available in Compuserve Image Format and are readily accessible. The images available at this location include a mirrored skyscraper with a blimp overhead, a dark and foreboding fantastical castle, a futuristic office, a coffee mug, a gold pocketwatch, a splendid room, a lighthouse in the fog, a robot (designed with Moray), a sword, and finally, a cathedral/temple with fountains.

KEYWORDS   Computer Art, Images
AUDIENCE   Computer Artists, Computer Users

Electronic Arts   **45**

Arts & Music

CONTACT   Michael Mittelstadt
meek@alpha2.csd.uwm.edu
FREE

ftp://ftp.execpc.com/pub/meek/

Scarecrow's ASCII Art Archives ★★★

Users can check out Scarecrow's ASCII Art Archives for a wealth of sample designs collected from ASCII buffs Internet-wide. The collection includes ASCII rendered funnies, some pretty cool login screens, and a section of best pics. The site also provides links to lists of Frequently Asked Question about ASCII art.

KEYWORDS   ASCII Art, Computer Design, Computer Graphics
AUDIENCE   ASCII Buffs, Computer Hackers, Electronic Designers
FREE

http://gagme.wwa.com/~boba/ascii.html

Shaun Edwin Varney ★★★

Saun Varney combines fine art paintings with computer generated imagery which explore the complex relationship of art and technology. This series of JPEG images will foster thoughts about this relationship, as well as provide enjoyable viewing.

KEYWORDS   Art Exhibitions, Computer Art, Electronic Arts
AUDIENCE   Artists, Computer Artists, Computer Graphic Designers, Graphic Designers
CONTACT   Geoff Broadway
G.Broadway@derby.ac.uk
FREE

http://dougal.derby.ac.uk/gallery/shaundoc.html

Simon Crone's Radiance Home Page ★★★

Radiance is a popular raytracing program that generates photorealistic 3D images. Located on this page are many resources of interest to Radiance users, and raytracing enthusiasts in general. Radiance function files and scanned materials are located in a Material Library and there is an online gallery which contains Radiance generated images. There is also a Radiance Users Manual that can be downloaded in Word 5.0 or Postscript formats.

KEYWORDS   Computer Art, Electronic Arts
AUDIENCE   Artists, Computer Artists, Computer Graphic Designers, Graphic Designers
CONTACT   Simon Crone
crones@puffin.curtin.edu.au
FREE

http://puffin.curtin.edu.au/rad_home.html

Solar Images Received 95/06/20 ★★★

A feature of the Web that makes it so popular is the capability to display graphic images. As this Web site demonstrates, some of the images displayed through the use of computer graphics present scenes that are not easily seen in the real world, but are only accessible through digital imaging techniques. The solar images shown on this page provide a range of imaging techniques and formats. Some are in black and white, some in color, and all are offered in GIF or FITS format to view or download.

KEYWORDS   Computer Graphics, Solar Images
AUDIENCE   Scholars, Students(High School And Up)
CONTACT   Vern Raben
vraben@sel.noaa.gov
FREE

http://www.sel.bldrdoc.gov/current_images.html

Spanky Other Fractal Programs ★★★★

If you have seen gallery after gallery of fractal images, you may be ready to become a contributor, not just a browser. If so, then this site can help. On this page, you will find an extensive listing of fractal generating programs which can be downloaded. Whatever your platform of choice, there is something here for you. Thank you Spanky.

KEYWORDS   Computer Art, Electronic Arts, Fractals
AUDIENCE   Artists, Computer Artists, Computer Graphic Designers, Graphic Designers
CONTACT   Noel Giffin
noel@triumf.ca
FREE

http://spanky.triumf.ca/www/other_progs.html

Star Wars WWW ★★★★

Are you a Star Wars fan? Then this site is what your are looking for! Images of your favorite characters and scenes have been taken from all parts of the Trilogy and installed here for your enjoyment. There are selections of movie stills, production art, cover art, and promotional Star Wars artwork. All images are large format JPEG files. May the Force be with you.

KEYWORDS   Computer Art, Movies, Science Fiction, Star Wars
AUDIENCE   Graphics Game Players, Science Fiction Enthusiasts, Star Wars Enthusiasts
CONTACT   David Koran
jedi+@cmu.edu
FREE

http://bantha.pc.cc.cmu.edu:1138/StarWars/Pictures/SWPictures.html

Stoney's Page ★★★★

Included on this page is an extensive list of links to files related to viewing, manipulating or converting various graphic and video image formats. On the home page, the files listed are for DOS and Windows. (A separate page is provided for Macintosh related files.) Each file is in a compressed format, either a ZIP or sef-extracting ZIP (EXE). A short description of the function of the program is provided along with the actual file size. The files can be downloaded to your hard disk directly from this page.

KEYWORDS   Computer Art, Electronic Arts
AUDIENCE   Artists, Computer Artists, Computer Graphic Designers, Graphic Designers
CONTACT   D. Morgen
dmorgen@netaxs.com
FREE

http://www.netaxs.com/people/dmorgen/stoney.htm

Strawberry Jam's ASCII Art Collection & Links ★★★★

Strawberry Jam's Ascii Art Collection & Links page offers a large collection of text-based artworks. Users will find pictures of characters from movies, stories, and other sources, as well as pictures from popular science fiction works, all created using the ASCII character set. There are also many links to other pages with ASCII art works, as well as information on the artists who created the images.

KEYWORDS   ASCII Art
AUDIENCE   ASCII Art Enthusiasts, Electronic Art Enthusiasts
CONTACT   Jenni A. Mott
jmott@wimsey.com
FREE

http://www.wimsey.com/~jmott/AsciiArt/AsciiArt.html

Targa.format ★★★

Information is available at this gopher site that will be helpful to anyone who needs the technical description of the file format for Targa images. Excerpted from the Truevision Technical Guide, this document provides the data format for color-mapped images, unmapped RGB images, run length encoded color-mapped images, and run length encoded RGB images.

KEYWORDS   Computer Art, Electronic Arts
AUDIENCE   Computer Programmers, Graphic Designers
CONTACT   Chris Green
chrisg@cbmvax.commodore.com
FREE

gopher://ics.tj.chiba-u.ac.jp/00/graphics.formats/targa.format

Tightrope ★★★

The curent issue contains information on the 1995 German Multimedia Congress 1995 and past issues of the journal Tightrope which coontains commentary on arts, philosophy and science. This resource is accessible in both German and in English.

KEYWORDS   Germany, Journals, Multimedia, Visual Arts
AUDIENCE   Artists, Arts Community, Computer Artists, German Speakers
CONTACT   Jens Geelhaar (Editor)
jens@HBKS.saarlink.de
FREE

http://www.phil.uni-sb.de/tightrope.html

Tool User Comics ★★★

Tool User is an index and archive for both professional and non-professional comic artists. This page has links to two broad categories of online comics- public domain, and subscription.

KEYWORDS   Comedy, Comics
AUDIENCE   Comics Enthusiasts, Humor Enthusiasts

CONTACT zap@armory.com
FREE
http://www.armory.com/comics/

Unifweb — Hyperbolic Riemann Surfaces with Symmetry ★★★

One of the projects from the Geometry Center at the University of Minnesota is a package of programs and C libraries designed to help in the study of Riemann Surfaces. Here you can find out what Rieman surfaces are, and play an interactive Web game to modify and interact with the production of images representing that surface.

KEYWORDS Art Exhibitions, Electronic Arts, Symmetry
AUDIENCE Computer Artists, Computer Graphic Designers, Graphic Designers
CONTACT   Carlos O'Ryan Lira
          coryan@mat.puc.cl
FREE
http://www.geom.umn.edu/apps/unifweb/about.html

The University of Manchester CGU Movies ★★★

As part of the curriculum at the Computer Graphics Unit of the University of Manchester, students create MPEG movies of their computer generated animations. This site displays a collection of these animations and presents them along with a short description of the tools used and the area of graphics being studied.

KEYWORDS Art Exhibitions, Computer Art, Electronic Arts
AUDIENCE Artists, Computer Artists, Computer Graphic Designers, Graphic Designers
CONTACT   cgu-info@mcc.ac.uk
FREE
http://info.mcc.ac.uk:80/CGU/research/movies/

VMSD Projects - Virtual Studio ★★★★

This Web site presents work done to create a Virtual Studio. The author's goal is to eliminate the expensive and time consuming aspects of TV studio production by integrating authentic looking, computer generated environments with people (actors) in the studio. This paper describes the background and technical specifications for creating virtual backdrops and artificial lightning. The authors provide a good description of the needs for this kind of presentation as well as some of the difficulties.

KEYWORDS Art Exhibitions, Electronic Arts, Virtual Studios
AUDIENCE Artists, Computer Artists, Computer Graphic Designers, Graphic Designers
CONTACT   Simon.Gibbs
          Simon.Gibbs@gmd.de
FREE
http://viswiz.gmd.de:80/VMSD/PAGES.en/projects.vst.html

VRML from HELL ★★★★

This site will be particularly useful for those interested in the exploding field of Virtual Reality on the Web. This page provides numerous links which cover all aspects of this field. You can link to technical information systems, software information, sources for VRML files as well as sites with extensive lists of links.

KEYWORDS Computer Art, Electronic Arts
AUDIENCE Artists, Computer Artists, Computer Graphic Designers, Graphic Designers
CONTACT   Jim Race
          caferace@well.com
FREE
http://www.well.com/user/caferace/vrml.html

Vern's SIRDS Gallery ★★★

Get ready to cross your eyes! Presented on this page is a collection of Single Image Stereograms, some being Random Dot format. The images are organized by creator, but can also be viewed, with or without thumbnails versions, from alphabetical listing by image name. A set of links to other Stereogram Web sites is also provided.

KEYWORDS Computer Art, Electronic Arts
AUDIENCE Artists, Computer Artists, Computer Graphic Designers, Graphic Artists
CONTACT   Vern Hart
          vern@cs.uidaho.edu
FREE
http://www.cs.uidaho.edu:80/~vern/sirds/

The WWW Graphics Page — Computer Support ★★★★

This site provides lists of FTP sites for an extensive range of computer graphic programs. Separate listings are available for Macintosh, IBM PC, UNIX, and QuickTime files. If you can't get the information you are looking for here, there is even an online ARCHIE search.

KEYWORDS Computer Art, Electronic Arts
AUDIENCE Artists, Computer Artists, Computer Graphic Designers, Graphic Designers
CONTACT   bryanw@best.com
FREE
http://www.best.com/~bryanw/support.html

Welcome to Abekas ★★★
(COMMERCIAL)

Abekas is a company based in Redwood City, California and Reading, UK. They specialize in digital video hardware and applications. Users can browse through product information, read about the company, or find out about obtaining technical help on their products. There is also trade show information as well as research material and links to related servers on the net.

KEYWORDS Computer Hardware, Digital Video, Multimedia
AUDIENCE Broadcasting Professionals, Digital Video Engineers, Television Industry Professionals
CONTACT   info@abekas.com
FREE
http://www.abekas.com/

What is it? ★★★★

While there are many computer graphics artists who strive for photorealistic images, this page goes in the other direction. Here you will find a small preview image which should be viewed in its enlarged version. Your task, should you take on this mission impossible, is to identify 'What on Earth it is.' To give you some help, users are provided with the guesses others have made. Good luck!

KEYWORDS Art Exhibitions, Computer Art, Electronic Arts
AUDIENCE Computer Artists, Cyberculture enthusiasts, Internet Users
CONTACT   Eve A. Andersson
          eveander@cco.caltech.edu
FREE
http://mirsky.caltech.edu/~eveander/guess.html

What's New at the MCL (Multimedia Communications Lab) ★★★

Multimedia Communications Lab (MCL) is exploring the construction of general-purpose distributed multimedia information systems (DMISs), with emphasis on time-dependent data as typified by on-demand video applications. Its online lab contains MPEG-I video compression files and is a very good source of audio/visual experimentation and development.

KEYWORDS Animation, Computer Aided Instruction, Video
AUDIENCE Multimedia Enthusiasts, Video Artists
CONTACT   T.D.C. Little
          tdcl@bu.edu
FREE
http://spiderman.bu.edu/whatsnew.html

Xtoys Gallery ★★★
(COMMERCIAL)

Xtoys is a site that contains a set of cellular automata simulators written for Xwindows. The xtoys gallery shows lots of pictures produced by these programs (beware if you have a slow link). The collection covers titles such as Classical Life Cellular Automaton, Fires, Ants, Filmore, and more. Fortunately, there is a description of the theoretical bases for all the images.

KEYWORDS Computer Art, X-Windows
AUDIENCE Artists, Computer Artists, Computer Graphic Designers, Graphic Designers
CONTACT   Mike Creutz
          creutz@wind.phy.bnl.gov
FREE
http://penguin.phy.bnl.gov/www/xtoys/gallery/gallery.html

Yuval's Virtual Separator Bar Collection ★★★★

Everyone who builds their own Web page will need, sooner or later, a horizontal line separator. The collection offered here is an extensive group of a very varied

Electronic Arts – Film & Video

styles. With a collection that ranges from black and white or color gradients to textures and drawings, you are sure to find a line to your liking.

Keywords Computer Art, Electronic Arts
Audience Computer Artists, Computer Graphic Designers, Desktop Publishers, Graphic Designers
Contact Yuval Fisher
 yfisher@ucsd.edu
Free

http://inls.ucsd.edu/y/OhBoy/bars.html

Film & Video

See also
Communications · *Mass Communications*
Popular Culture & Entertainment · *Celebrities & Personalities*
Popular Culture & Entertainment · *Movies*
Popular Culture & Entertainment · *Television*

AMPAS - Academy of Motion Picture Arts and Sciences ★★★★

The website of the Academy of Motion Picture Arts and Sciences offers several kinds of information about the Academy, the Academy Awards, and the other programs and activities of the Academy and its affiliated organization, the Academy Foundation. There is access to press releases on celebrity photos, the Academy Foundation and silent serial heroines. The 67th Annual Academy Awards is reviewed with listings of nominees and winners.

Keywords Acting, Film History, Filmmakers, Movies
Audience Film Enthusiasts, Film Makers, Movie Enthusiasts
Contact ampas@ampas.org
Free

http://www.ampas.org/ampas/

Aboriginal Film and Video Arts Alliance ★★

The Aboriginal Film and Video Arts Alliance was set up in 1991 to promote Canadian Aborginal Film. The home page is designed to be a source of information for those making, or interested in aboriginal cinema. The page posts work opportunities and lists of relevant films by title and subject.

Keywords Aborigines, Canada, Foreign Film, Indigenous Studies
Audience Film Historians, Film Makers, Film Students, Film/Video Researchers, Indigenous People
Contact AFVAA@cpnetmail ffa ucalgary.ca
Free

http://www.culturenet.ucalgary.ca/afvaa/afvaa.html

Asian-American Filmography ★★★

Asian-American Filmography is a non-hyperlinked list of films by Asian Americans. Each film is listed by title, followed by the length of the film, the language, a brief description of the film, the producer, and what year it was produced. Subjects range from the internment policy of Japanese Americans during WWII to the role of Asian women in film and television.

Keywords Asian Americans, Film, World War II
Audience Asian Americans, Women, Film Historians
Free

gopher://english.hss.cmu.edu/OF-2%3A5662%3AAsian-American%20Filmography

Boston Film and Video Foundation ★★★

This is the home page for The Boston Film and Video Foundation (BF/VF), a regional arts center whose mission is to encourage and facilitate access to and understanding of film, video and electronic media as a means of creative expression. This page contains membership information, classes and workshops, examples of work by BF/VF members, instructors, and students, a list of Who's Who at BF/VF and local information about film listings in the Boston area.

Keywords Arts Education, Boston, Film History, Filmmaking
Audience Film Enthusiasts, Film Historians, Film Students, Massachusetts Residents
Contact bfvf@actwin.com
Free

http://www.actwin.com:80/BFVF/index.html

 Buena Vista MoviePlex ★★★★

The Buena Vista MoviePlex is where you can preview movies and see what's coming from Hollywood Pictures, Walt Disney Pictures, and Touchstone Pictures. Each movie title includes a brief description and is hyperlinked to a press kit with JPEGs, promotional clips with quicktime movies, promotional stills, interview sound bites, and quicktime movies of actors and actresses. The format—color or black and white—and size in bytes is included. You can use the text mode or the graphical mode to view this site depending on the speed of your Internet connection and your Web browser. To enjoy the graphics you will need a graphical browser that supports forms, a JPEG viewer and a QuickTime player. Locations for obtaining these browsers and players are linked here. You may also visit the frequently asked questions (FAQs) section.

Keywords Actors, Hollywood, Movies
Audience Film Makers, Film/Video Researchers, Movie Directors, Movie Enthusiasts
Free

http://www.wdp.com/BVPM/

Canadian Film Center ★★★★

As a national organization, the Centre's mission is to advance the artistic and technical skills of writers, directors and producers in support of a dynamic industry, and to increase the awareness and appreciation of Canadian film and television. This site has information on the Film Center's programme for resident filmmakers, their productions, famous players lecture series and the Warner Brothers Library and Resource Center. The site also contains information on the center's annual festival of dramatic television.

Keywords Canada, Film Archives, Film Reviews, Filmmaking
Audience Film Enthusiasts, Film Makers, Film Students
Free

http://www.hype.com/cfc/home.htm

Cinemedia Site ★★★★

This site is the Internet's largest Cinema and Media Directory. The directory provides comprehensive information on films, film production, film memorabilia, film databases, television programs and production as well as radio sites, discussion groups and multimedia sites. Some of the pages listed in the directory include cinema sites (information on film companies, scripts, organizations and related topics.) For users seeking information pertaining to media related publications, the directory provides a journals and magazine page. The movies, images and sound clips page lists sites which contain a variety of still images, movie clips, sound clips and theme songs. Also included for television and radio fans are the following pages - the television sites page (listings for television networks, station scripts, programs, episodes and regulations) and the radio sites page which offers a list of sites relating to radio. Finally, to join media related discussion groups check out the discussion group page.

Keywords Directories, Film, Multimedia, Television
Audience Film Enthusiasts, Film Historians, Media Enthusiasts, Television Enthusiasts
Contact Dan Harries
 d.harries@hum.gu.edu.au
Free

http://www.gu.edu.au/gwis/cinemedia/CineMedia.HOME.HTML

 Click 3x/MEDIA CIRCUS Home Page ★★★

The Click 3x/Media Circus Home Page offers access to both Click 3x and Media Circus company pages. Click 3x offers full animation and special effects services with information about their services and past productions. Media Circus is an interactive production company that is still developing their home page.

Keywords Animation, Companies, Multimedia, Special Effects
Audience Animators, Business Professionals, Multimedia Enthusiasts
Contact info@Click3x.com, click3x@aol.com
Free

http://www.click3x.com/

Doc Film - Documentary Film Group Page ★★★

The Documentary Film Group is on record with the Museum of Modern Art as the longest continuously running student film society in the nation. Founded in 1932, we have a sixty-two year history as an all volunteer, student run organization committed to the concept of providing a low cost, high quality venue for a wide variety of films, dedicated to the goal of providing the best possible, socially relevant movies to the University of Chicago community and the city of Chicago. This site contains a history and explanation of Doc Films, special

Film & Video

announcements, the schedule for Spring 1995, schedules from previous quarters, and the coming week's films. This site also has links to other film sites and to other University of Chicago sites.

KEYWORDS   Filmmakers, Filmmaking, Universities
AUDIENCE   Film Directors, Film Enthusiasts, Film Makers, Film Researchers, Illinois Residents
CONTACT   Anil Mudholkar
           a-mudholkar@uchicago.edu
FREE

http://rainbow.uchicago.edu/docfilms/index.html

Early Motion Pictures Home Page ★★★

The Early Motion Pictures Home Page contains a collection of actuality films which are about two to three minutes in length. The motion pictures may be downloaded and displayed locally on players which support the AVI format using the Indeo code. This codec is available from Intel for Microsoft Video for Windows, QuickTime for the Macintosh, and QuickTime for Windows (Link to site is available here). Collections on this site include Early Films of San Francisco and Early Films of New York. Background information includes information on Actuality Films, early 1900's in America, The Paper Print Film Collection at the Library of Congress, and a bibliography.

KEYWORDS   Film History, Film Technology
AUDIENCE   Film, Film Directors, Film Enthusiasts, Film Makers, Film/Video Researchers, Movie Enthusiasts
FREE

http://lcweb2.loc.gov/papr/mpixhome.html

Entertainment Technology Center (USC) ★★★

This is the home page for the University of Southern California's Entertainment Technology Center (ETC). The ETC is sponsored by a consortium of companies interested in developing the practical applications of emerging technologies for the entertainment industry. One such project is HollyNet, another is the Integrated Studio Project and a third is called the ATM/CalREN project. This site contains a link to a home page on each of these projects. The page also contains links to the ETC gopher, to the school of Cinema Television, and to other USC pages.

KEYWORDS   Cinema, Film History, Film Technology, Television
AUDIENCE   Film Historians, Film Makers, Film Students
CONTACT   Davis Belson
           belson@usc.edu
FREE

http://cwis.usc.edu/dept/etc/

Film and Video ★★★

This document is a compilation of information resources focused on film and video. Resources include movie reviews (by genre, Women's Studies, Science Fiction, Horror), scholarly discussions, film theory, filmmakers, experimental film, and fan clubs (Woody Allen, James Bond, Monty Python, etc.).

KEYWORDS   Film, Filmmaking, Video
AUDIENCE   Film Enthusiasts, Film Makers, Film Researchers, Film/Video Enthusiasts
FREE

ftp://una.hh.lib.umich.edu/inetdirsstacks/filmvideo:woodgarlock

GRAFICS ★★★

GRAFICS stands for Groupe de Recherche sur l'Avenement et la Formation des Institutions Cinematographique et Scenique (Research Group on the Beginnings and the Formation of the Cinema and Theatrical Institutions). GRAFICS is a research group about early cinema in Quebec, located at the University of Montreal. The site, which contains resources in French and English, provides facts about early cinema, a description of the project, member information, articles, indexes, documents, film and video resources on the Internet, and links to information on Montreal, as well as other film pages.

KEYWORDS   Canada, Film, Film History, Foreign Film
AUDIENCE   Film Enthusiasts, Film Historians, Film Students, Film/Video Researchers
CONTACT   Denis Simmard
           simmardde@ere.umontreal.ca
FREE

http://grafics.histart.umontreal.ca/default-eng.html

Hong Kong Movies ★★★

This site is dedicated to the Hong Kong movie industry and its movies. To introduce users, this site provides a 'new to Hong Kong Movies' page which lists favorite films made in Hong Kong. For more exstensive information you may click on 'locally stored information' which contains filmographies, film lists, interviews, movie reviews and a Frequently Asked Questions list. Users can also isolate and retrieve information on specific actors, films, and pictures in the site by using the searchable database. In addition, access to related sites can be found under 'Links to the Internet.'

KEYWORDS   Actors, Film, Hong Kong
AUDIENCE   Film Enthusiasts, Film Makers, Film Students, Hong Kong Residents
FREE

http://www.mdstud.chalmers.se/hkmovie/

Hype! Movies ★★★

Hype! Movies is a subsection of the Hype! Art, Entertainment & Tourism Guide to Toronto. This site contains the home pages for the Canadian Film Centre and the Toronto International Film Festival Group, Canadian film organizations which support film writers, directors and producers and promote Canadian cinema. These sites describe programs, local film festivals, and film screenings year-round, as well as job opportunities and a film reference library. Hype! Movies also includes a list all international film festivals, a summer movie guide, video releases, and includes a browser to find reviews for the films you want to see.

KEYWORDS   Canada, Film Festivals, Foreign Film, Movies
AUDIENCE   Film Directors, Film Enthusiasts, Film Makers, Students
FREE

http://www.hype.com/movies

Indian Films in the Library of Congress ★★

This gopher lists the films from India in the Library of Congress. Films descriptions are listed alphabetically with production information, cast and crew members, and language information, but no plot summaries.

KEYWORDS   Film History, Filmmaking, India, Library of Congress
AUDIENCE   Film Enthusiasts, Film Makers, Film Researchers, Film Students, India Residents
FREE

gopher://marvel.loc.gov/00/research/reading.rooms/motion.picture/mopic.tv/mpfind/india

Informedia Digital Video Library ★★★

This site describes the Informedia Digital Video Library project. The goal is to produce an online digital video library which will provide full-content and knowledge-based searches and retrieval via desktop computer and metropolitan area networks. The library will initially contain approximately 1000 hours of raw and edited video provided by various educational resources. This page gives information on the sponsors, a project description, the investigators, researchers, partners, press, etc.

KEYWORDS   Multimedia
AUDIENCE   Educators, Film/Video Researchers, Video Enthusiasts
CONTACT   fuzzy@cmu.edu
FREE

http://fuzine.mt.cs.cmu.edu/im/informedia.html

The Internet Film Commissioner ★★★

The Internet Film Commissioner provides resources for filmmakers and production companies in the United Kingdom. The site is divided into several sections—information about commercial and goverment financing for film, backgrounds on production companies, legal issues, and trade organizations. The 'Reading Room' allows you to read screenplays, online film magazines, relevant legislation across the world, and can link you to the pages of film institutions, colleges, and archives. This is part of the Screen Finance Web site, a newsletter discussing financial options for filmmakers.

KEYWORDS   Film Industry, Filmmaking, Foreign Film, Screenplays
AUDIENCE   Film Directors, Film Makers, Film Students
CONTACT   Nick Hobdell
           nick@nick-h.demon.co.uk
FREE

http://Penny.ibmPCUG.CO.UK:80/~scrfin/ifc/ifc.html

Keno-Eye - Chicago Filmmakers' Homepage ★★★★

This site is sponsored by Chicago Filmmakers and contains a current schedule of events including PerforMedia Events by Lisa Kotin, William Easton, METAMKINE and others, as well as dance and theater events. It also contains information on classes and workshops, and on the organization Chicago Filmmakers.

KEYWORDS   Chicago, Film, Filmmaking, Performance Art
AUDIENCE   Film Directors, Film Enthusiasts, Film Makers, Film Researchers, Illinois Residents
CONTACT   chifilm@tezcat.com
FREE

http://www.tezcat.com/~chifilm/homepage.html

Krzysztof Kieslowski and his Films

This site thoroughly examines Polish film director Krzysztof Kieslowski and his films. It includes pictures and a biography of Kieslowski and his collaborators, as well as interviews with them. The page has a filmography including plots of all of his films, links to reviews of his work all over the Web, and a reference list of outside sources which discuss Kieslowski.

KEYWORDS   Film, Filmmakers, Poland
AUDIENCE   Film Enthusiasts, Film Makers, Film Students, Polish
CONTACT   Zbigniew J. Pasek
           zbigniew@engin.umich.edu
FREE

http://www.engin.umich.edu/~zbigniew/Kieslowski/kieslowski.html

Kubrick Home Page

This page provides background information and a filmography of the popular film director Stanley Kubrick. Video and audio selections from various Kubrick films (i.e., Dr. Strangelove, 2001, Spartacus, Lolita, A Clockwork Orange, and Full Metal Jacket), and selections from interviews with various actors and staff who worked with Kubrick.

KEYWORDS   Cinema, Filmmakers, Filmmaking
AUDIENCE   Actors, Drama Enthusiasts, Film Directors, Film Enthusiasts, Film Makers
CONTACT   Partrick J. Larkin
FREE

http://www.lehigh.edu/~pjl2/kubrick.html

LUMO - The Finnish Film Foundation

The Finnish Film Foundation (FFF) finances, helps produce, and exports and promotes Finnish cinema across the world. Their Web site provides basic information about the activities of the FFF as well as opportunities through the European Union Media Programme. This page includes the publication Films from Finland, which gives extended summaries and information about current Finnish film releases. Also listed are film festivals, books and resources, film institutions, and the centenary of Finnish cinema.

KEYWORDS   Film, Filmmaking, Finland, Foreign Film
AUDIENCE   Film Enthusiasts, Film Makers, Finns
CONTACT   Paula Blafield
           lumo@kaapeli.fi
FREE

http://www.kaapeli.fi/~lumo/English/lumo.html

Connections to Movie Studios
I'm ready for my close-up Mr. DeMille...

What's coming to a theater near you from movie makers around the world? How 'bout the latest on English actor Hugh Grant? Why did the movie "Forrest Gump" flop in China, while "True Lies" was a smash? Where can you get the scoop on "Casper," a film based on the American television cartoon character? If there's anything about movies you want know, you can find it on the Internet. Not only do movie studios have Web sites, but there are previews, sound tracks, and movie trailers through other sources.

For the low-down on current movies including behind-the-scenes info, try the studios that distribute the film.

(http://www.digiplanet.com/MGM/)

The latest news on movie stars and press releases from studios, can be found at "Movie Studio Promotions Sites." There are also film listings and the latest scoop on films slated for release in the coming months.

(http://www.disney.com/)

also, (http://spe.Sony.com/Pictures/SonyMovies/index.html)

The Norwegian Film Institute

This site is the home of the Norwegian Film Institute, which supports and promotes film from Norway. The site provides information about the Norwegian Short Film Festival and gives descriptions of the films to be shown. It gives background on functions of the Norwegian Film Institute as well as articles, reviews and summaries covering all Norwegian film releases for 1994 and 1995.

KEYWORDS   Film Festivals, Film History, Foreign Film, Norway
AUDIENCE   Film Enthusiasts, Film Makers, Norwegians
CONTACT   Reider Bratsberg Foreign Film
           wwww@dnfi.no
FREE

http://www.dnfi.no/krtflmf/

Polish Cinema Database

The Polish Cinema Database allows browsers to search for information about Polish Cinema. By entering the title, director, year released, or keywords relating to a film, the Database will retrieve a list of relevant films. Film descriptions include production information and a plot summary.

KEYWORDS   Film, Film History, Foreign Film, Poland

Film & Video – Music Genres

AUDIENCE Film Enthusiasts, Film Students, Polish
CONTACT Wojtek Bogusz and Zbigniew J. Pasek
zbigniew@engin.umich.edu
FREE

http://info.fuw.edu.pl:80/Filmy/

Russian Films in the Library of Congress ★★★

This gopher lists films produced in Russia that are in the Library of Congress. Film descriptions are listed alphabetically and include a brief summary, cast and crew members, production information, and Library of Congress information.

KEYWORDS Film History, Filmmaking, Library of Congress, Russia
AUDIENCE Film Enthusiasts, Film Historians, Film Researchers, Film Students, Russians
FREE

gopher://marvel.loc.gov/00/research/
        reading.rooms/motion.picture/
        mopic.tv/mpfind/russian

Silent Movies ★★★

This site provides a glimpse into the world of silent movies, with pages focusing on the stars, the filmmakers, the films and the preservation of these films. If you wish to learn about the stars of the silent era, there are profiles on Charlie Chaplin, Lilian Gish, and Buster Keaton and links to information on many other silent film stars. There are also explanations of why many early films have been completely lost. The site also has links to other Silent Movies pages and to Silent Movie trivia.

KEYWORDS Film History, Film Preservation, Filmmakers, Silent Movies
AUDIENCE Comedy Fans, Film Historians, General Public, Silent Movie Enthusiasts
CONTACT Glen Pringle
pringle@cs.monash.edu.au
FREE

http://www.cs.monash.edu.au/~pringle/
        silent/

Sundance Institute ★★★

This is the site for the Sundance film Institute. It contains information on the institute itself including its mission, budget, artistic programs (such as the Sundance Film Festival and the Feature Film Program as well as children's programs), special programs, notable films, Sundance labs, awards, facilities, and more. There are also links to other film sites.

KEYWORDS Film, Film Festivals, Filmmakers, Filmmaking
AUDIENCE Film Directors, Film Enthusiasts, Film Makers, Film Researchers
FREE

http://cybermart.com/sundance/institute/
        institute.html

 ## Videomaker's Camcorder & Desktop Video Site ★★★

Videomaker's Camcorder & Desktop Video Site offers a place for people of various backgrounds to research and discuss the subject of videomaking. There is access to frequently asked questions, a forum, classified advertisements, search tools specific for this site, and upcoming events. There is also access to Videomaker's books, products and services, and the magazine itself.

KEYWORDS Camcorders, Magazines, Video, Videomaking
AUDIENCE Film/Video Enthusiasts, Magazine Readers, Video Amateurs, Video Professionals
CONTACT webmaster@www.videomaker.com
FREE

http://www.videomaker.com/

Music Genres

See also
Arts & Music · *Music History*
Arts & Music · *Music Resources*
Arts & Music · *Musical Groups*
Arts & Music · *Musicians*

ACM - Australian Christian Music ★★

The ACM Australian Christian Music page/zine is keeping an eye on what's happening with Australian Christian Music in Australia and abroad. It provides news, tour schedules and recording information. At this site one can give feedback, take a chance on a VIP trip to the 1995 Australian Gospel Music Awards or explore any other of the eight links. This is a good site to explore in text only mode as it has many large and unnessessary graphics that take an extremely long time to download.

KEYWORDS Australia, Christian Music
AUDIENCE Christians, Gospel Music Enthusiasts, Music Enthusiasts
CONTACT David Cook
cook@ozemail.com.au
FREE

http://www.ozemail.com.au/~cook/acm/

American Music Network ★★

This is the gopher server of the American Music Network which is offered by the Sonneck Society for American Music to stimulate the appreciation, creation, and study of American music in all its historical and contemporary styles and contexts. On this network, one can find information on American music such as American Music Week, Coming Events in American Music, an American Music Speakers Performance Bureau or Important Events in American Music History. The information page has not been updated since the end of 1994.

KEYWORDS Events, Folk Music
AUDIENCE American Music Enthusiasts, Music Enthusiasts
CONTACT Sonneck Society
sonneck@tmn.com
FREE

gopher://tmn.com/11/Artswire/amn

Aussie Music Online ★★★★

For the 'Best in Australian Music,' Aussie Music Online (AMO) invites you to stop in and surf. AMO aims to take Aussie Music to the world and to bring the world to Aussie music, providing music lovers with access to information, sound and graphic images from Australian musicians and news, views and contacts on the Australian music industry. At the same time AMO gives Australian musicians the chance to introduce their music to people who are interested in what is new, exciting and fresh. For those who want to see a perfectly organized, comprehensive site that is easy to use and up-to-date, this one is an excellent site to visit.

KEYWORDS Australia, Online Music
AUDIENCE Australian Culture Enthusiasts, Music Enthusiasts, Musicians
FREE

http://www.aussiemusic.com.au/

Australian Folk Songs ★★★

This collection of more than 100 Australian Folk Songs has words, music and information about each song. The plan is to build it up to be a comprehensive collection with Quicktime movies to help illustrate the variety of cultures that make up Australia.

KEYWORDS Australia, Folk Music
AUDIENCE Australian Culture Enthusiasts, Music Enthusiasts
CONTACT Mark Gregory
mark.gregory@mq.edu.au
FREE

http://www.wise.mq.edu.au/WWWise/
        MarkG/songNet/intro.html

Batish Institute of Indian Music and Fine Arts ★★

This is a Batish Family Music site which covers the music of North India. It was established by Pandit S.D. Batish in loving memory of his guru, Shri Chaandanraam 'Charan.' There are links to concerts, new releases, RagaNet Magazine and artist biographies.

KEYWORDS Folk Music, India, Indian Music
AUDIENCE Folk Music Enthusiasts
FREE

http://hypatia.ucsc.edu:70/1/RELATED/
        Batish

Birmingham Jam ★★★

Birmingham Jam, the major fall music event in Birmingham, Alabama is a festival that promotes the city as well as the Southern musical heritage in jazz, blues and gospel. The 1995 Festival is scheduled for October 6, 7 and 8 and this Web site provides a list of the performers, sponsors, and resources.

KEYWORDS Blues, Jazz, Music Festivals
AUDIENCE Blues Enthusiasts, Gospel Music Enthusiasts, Jazz Enthusiasts
FREE

http://www.the-matrix.com/bham/
        jam.html

Blars Filk Page ★★★

Filk music is a type of folk music loosely related to Science Fiction. This site, maintained from the University of Southern California, provide a couple of dozen

Music Genres 51

links to Folk and Filk music around the world including links to Austria and Germany.

KEYWORDS Folk Music
AUDIENCE Folk Music Enthusiasts, Music Enthusiasts
FREE

http://sundry.hsc.usc.edu/filk.html

The Blue Highway ★★★

The Blue Highway page offers a brief history of the blues with a multimedia accompaniment of images, sounds, and original text. Blues News presents current news related to the blues. A guestbook allows users to share comments and information with other visitors. There is also a page that offers dozens of links to other blues and related resources on the Net.

KEYWORDS Biographies, Blues, Music History, Musicians
AUDIENCE Blues Enthusiasts, Music Enthusiasts, Music Historians, Musicians
CONTACT Curtis Hewston
curtis@magicnet.net
FREE

http://www.magicnet.net/~curtis/

The Bluebird Cafe ★★★

The Bluebird Cafe in Nashville, Tennessee is a new country and acoustic music venue where original music can be heard seven days a week. Online information is thorough and includes schedules, information on the music business in general, the artists, the employees, etc. Address and phone information are given right up front which makes this listing very user friendly.

KEYWORDS Country Music, Folk Music
AUDIENCE Country Music Enthusiasts
CONTACT Hidwater
dmon@hidwater.com
shade@hidwater.com
FREE

http://www.hidwater.com/bluebird/

BluesNet Home Page ★★★

The BluesNet page is for lovers of blues music. It maintains a collection of artist summaries, an archive of blues-related pictures, and a collection of articles and documents related to this American art form. What makes this server particularly unique is that it includes an index of 'mentors,' (people who are extremely knowledgeable about certain types of blues music or particluar blues artists) who are willing to answer questions via email. In addition, this server archives several Net-documents such as various FAQ files on the blues.

KEYWORDS Blues, Folk Music, Music, Music Research
AUDIENCE Blues Enthusiasts, Folk Music Enthusiasts, Music Enthusiasts
CONTACT Rob Hutten
rob@acadiau.ca
FREE

http://dragon.acadiau.ca/~rob/blues/blues.html

Boris Sebastien Cournede ★★★

Boris Sebastian Cournede maintains an extremely interesting and eclectic homepage that covers many classical music sites including Richard Wagner, Johann Sebastian Bach and Wolfgang Amadeus Mozart. He also has mountain climbing links, dictionaries, a guide to HTML with a list of accented characters, a virtual tourist map and images of the Sistine Chapel.

KEYWORDS Classical Music, Composers, Opera
AUDIENCE Classical Music Enthusiasts, Internet Users, Mountain Climbing Enthusiasts
FREE

http://acacia.ens.fr:8080/home/cournede/index.html

Branson Online Music Show Index ★★★

This site makes excellent use of the Internet to link to all kinds of music shows in Branson, MO. The coverage is excellent and up-to-date and there are all the links a tourist or new resident might need such as lodging, real estate, attractions, etc.

KEYWORDS Country Music, Events
AUDIENCE Music Enthusiasts, Tourists
CONTACT marketing@branson.com
FREE

http://usa.net/branson/music.htm

Building a Library — A Collector's Guide ★★★

A comprehensive review of various recordings of Beethoven's nine symphonies is to be found here. It is a very informative site, though the author seems to have a preference for older recordings and the most recent listing is for 1989.

KEYWORDS Beethoven, Classical Music, Ludwig Van, Music, Reviews
AUDIENCE Classical Music Enthusiasts, Compact Disc Users, Music Enthusiasts, Music Librarians
CONTACT Deryk Barker
pubs@ncsa.uiuc.edu
FREE

http://www.ncsa.uiuc.edu/SDG/People/marca/barker-beethoven.html

Cajun/Zydeco in Baltimore & Washington ★★★★

This Web page serves as a guide to Cajun and Zydeco music in Baltimore and Washington, and all across the world. It includes lists of clubs and venues where users can find this type of music in different cities in the United States, and instructions for how to dance to Cajun/Zydeco music (or where to find an instructor). Links to Louisiana culture and music pages on the web are also included, as well as the web sites of records companies that produce Cajun/Zydeco music. Users will also find regional information for New Orleans.

KEYWORDS Cajun Music, Ethnic Music
AUDIENCE Ethnomusicologists, Music Enthusiasts, Tourists

CONTACT jrice@bme.jhu.edu
FREE

http://www.bme.jhu.edu/~jrice/cz.html

Casa Verdi ★★★

Casa Verdi is home to information about the life and music of Giuseppe Verdi. Research projects are published here and 'Tutto nel mondo...' interested in Verdi are welcome to browse. There are links to a Verdi Biography, Verdi Operas, and the Parma Citta della Musica in Italy.

KEYWORDS Composers, Music Education
AUDIENCE Music Historians, Opera Music Enthusiasts, Researchers, Students
CONTACT Tim Cordell
Cordell@vax.edinboro.edu
FREE

http://www.edinboro.edu/CWIS/Music/Cordell/00hpverdi.html

Christian Music Online Welcome Page ★★★

This page offers a database of information on Christian music. Users can browse through a database of Christian artists which includes song samples, information on Christian record labels, pictures, and biographical information for each artist. Users may query this database for particular artists or song titles. This server also offers concert information as well as material culled from several Christian and Christian music magazines.

KEYWORDS Christian Music, Music, Music Databases
AUDIENCE Christian Music Enthusiasts, Music Enthusiasts, Music Researchers
CONTACT Steven Lee
slee@cmo.com
FREE

http://www.cmo.com/cmo/

Classic Pop ★★★

This is the WWW page defines Classic Pop not as true jazz nor all big band music, but as what you heard on the radio years ago. It has links to two Usenet groups for big band music and jazz as well as several links to online discographies that give transcripts, music bits, and various information about classic pop musicians and singers. There is even a link to Frank Sinatra's own Home Page!

KEYWORDS Jazz, Music Archives
AUDIENCE Jazz Enthusiasts, Music Enthusiasts, Music Historians
CONTACT William Denton
buff@io.org
FREE

http://www.io.org/~buff/classic-pop.html

Classic World's Opera ★★

Opera/Vocal allows Web browsers to meet the greatest opera singers of yesterday and today and to read over 40 Opera Stories. There are also links to the origins of opera, and opera talk BBS and to the Opera Schedule Server.

KEYWORDS Classical Music, Opera

Music Genres

AUDIENCE Opera Music Enthusiasts
FREE

http://classicalmus.com/opera.html

The Classical Music Box ★★★★

This site contains numerous links to classical music pages on the Net. Subjects covered by the pages include a composers list, a classical music introduction, a list of music business corporations, and links to music reviews and other resources. This is a comprehensive source for learning what is available on the Net concerning classical music. The introduction to classical music includes sound files and competitions. The authors also recommend software.

KEYWORDS Classical Music, Composers, Music History, Music Reviews
AUDIENCE Arts Community, Music Historians, Music Librarians, Music Professionals, Musicians
FREE

http://rulgla.leidenuniv.nl:8080/zeger/clasmus.html

Classical Music Repertoire List ★★★★

This is a basic repertoire list for building a library of classical recordings. The listings are sorted into eras, Medieval/Renaissance, Baroque, Classical, Romantic, 20th Century. Each listing begins with a brief description of the era in question, followed by a surprisingly diverse set of recommendations for each era including symphonic, opera, chamber, solo, guitar music, and even Gilbert & Sullivan! The only weakness is that the 20th-century section is a bit too narrow in focus. (The list is also available as a text file at http://www.ncsa.uiuc.edu/SDG/People/marca/lampson/Repertor.txt)

KEYWORDS Classical Music, Contemporary Music, Music, Recordings, Symphonic Music
AUDIENCE Classical Music Enthusiasts, Compact Disc Users, Music Enthusiasts, Music Librarians
CONTACT L.D. Lampson
lampson@pulse.com
FREE

http://www.ugcs.caltech.edu/~werdna/repertoire.html

Classical Music Reviews ★★★

The Classical Music Reviews is an index of classical music organized by style. There are entries for Baroque, Classical, Romantic, and Modern music. There is also a section of recommended performances, as well as a 'basic repertoire' section with information on starting a collection of classical music.

KEYWORDS Classical Music, Events, Music Collectors, Music Reviews
AUDIENCE Classical Music Enthusiasts, Instrumental Music Enthusiasts, Music Enthusiasts, Music Researchers
CONTACT National Center for Supercomputing Applications (NCSA)
pubs@ncsa.uiuc.edu
FREE

http://www.ncsa.uiuc.edu/SDG/People/marca/music-reviews.html

Consumable ★★★

This twice-monthly newsletter contains tour dates, interviews, album reviews and other information of interest to fans of alternative music (and sometimes mainstream rock music as well).

KEYWORDS Alternative Music, Music Industry, Rock Music
AUDIENCE Alternative Music Enthusiasts, Rock Fans
CONTACT Bob Gajarsky
gajarsky@pilot.njin.net
FREE

ftp://quartz.rutgers.edu/pub/journals/Consumable/

Current Opera Home Page ★★★

The Current Opera Home Page offers links to the 'Current Opera Digest,' the goings on at the Portland and Seattle Operas, the Pacific Northwest opera schedule and also includes monographs on the life of Giovanni Bottesini, reviews, interesting Web sites to visit and an explanation of 'What this stuff is anyway.'

KEYWORDS Events, Opera, Washington State
AUDIENCE Musicians, Opera Enthusiasts
CONTACT Richard Edwards
redwards@webcom.com
FREE

http://www.webcom.com/~redwards/

Directory of/pub/MSB ★★★★

This home page is an archive of information about progressive rock. It contains discographies of various bands, FAQs, pictures, and much other information about progressive music. There's a section devoted to trading lists of fans who trade tapes. It also has links to home pages of various progressive bands.

KEYWORDS Contemporary Music, Progressive Music, Rock Music
AUDIENCE Music Historians, Music Researchers, Progressive Music Enthusiasts, Rock Fans
CONTACT Mike Borella
borella@cs.ucdavis.edu
FREE

ftp://ortega.cs.ucdavis.edu/pub/MSB/

Dreampop Magazine ★★★

A webzine aimed at listeners and creators of commercial 'hard pop' and rock music, Dreampop presents a number of band profiles, interviews and album reviews in its first (January 1995) issue. In this issue, artists such as Husker Du, Sonic Youth, Kitchens of Distinction and The Cure are highlighted.

KEYWORDS Online Magazines, Pop Music, Rock Music
AUDIENCE Pop Music Enthusiasts, Rock Fans
CONTACT Brendon Macaraeg
bqm1808@is.nyu.edu
FREE

http://www.itp.tsoa.nyu.edu/~student/brendonm/dream1.html

Early Music WWW page ★★★★

Yet another excellent resource on Early Music. Here you will find information relating to music which predates the year A.D. 1850. Topics include historical instruments and builders, composers, recommended music for listening/performing, Early Music organizations, upcoming events, concerts, and more. Also contains links to other Web sites of interest to lovers of Early Music a list of CD's of early keyboard music.

KEYWORDS Classical Music, Composers, Early Music, Musical Instruments
AUDIENCE Classical Music Enthusiasts, Early Music Enthusiasts, Music Enthusiasts
CONTACT Justin Renquist
justinr@sirius.com
FREE

http://www.catalog.com/virtual/jr/earlym.html

Electronic Bluegrass Magazine ★★★

Electronic Bluegrass Magazine is the first WWW page dedicated to Bluegrass music only. The magazine is maintained by Bob Cherry and sponsored by Infonet Services Corporation. There are ten subdivisions to the magazines that include libraries, files and archives, want-ads, Internet links, etc. This is a very comprehensive site.

KEYWORDS Country Music, Online Magazines
AUDIENCE Bluegrass Enthusiasts, Country Music Enthusiasts
CONTACT Bob Cherry
cherry@info.net
FREE

http://www.info.net/BG/bg_home.html

Exclaim Magazine ★★★★

Exclaim is a Toronto-based magazine dedicating itself to the independent and alternative music scene. It offers numerous special features and interviews with big-name performers as well as regular features including letters, an advice column, and a monthly music business rundown.

KEYWORDS Alternative Music, Canada, Magazines, Music Reviews
AUDIENCE Alternative Music Enthusiasts, Canadians, Music Industry Professionals, Musicians
CONTACT Editor
exclaim@io.org
FREE

http://www.inforamp.net/pwcasual/exclaim/index.html

Finland's Music Through American Ears ★★★

This is the launching point for a project known as Roots World that includes commercial and non-commercial links to African, jazz and folk music, especially international folk music. There are several other links to sites in Finland as well as to folk festivals. It is a cooperative effort of Cliff Furnald and Futuris Networks of Stamford, Connecticut.

KEYWORDS Finland, Folk Music, Jazz
AUDIENCE Folk Music Enthusiasts, Jazz Enthusiasts

CONTACT Cliff Furnald
cliff@rootsworld.com
FREE

http://www.rootsworld.com/rw/finland/finn.html

Folk Music Home Page ★★★

This is a popular site for accessing folk music on the web run by Jay Glicksman of EIT (Enterprise Integration Technologies), an R&D and consulting company specializing in information technology and online commerce. It includes dozens of links for concert schedules, commercial resources, artists, albums, etc. The site is often busy, but with patience, it can be accessed. In a pinch, access through 'www.eit.com' as an http address, then search on 'folk music.'

KEYWORDS Directories, Events, Folk Music
AUDIENCE Folk Music Enthusiasts, Music Educators
FREE

http://www.eit.com/web/folk/folkhome.html

Folk Roots Magazine ★★★

These are the Web Pages of Folk Roots magazines which advertises itself as the world's leading roots, folk and world music magazine. The site contains magazine and subscription information, a festival list, a music competition, album reviews, and a table of contents of this month's issue.

KEYWORDS Folk Music, Music Festivals, Online Music, World Music
AUDIENCE Folk Music Enthusiasts, World Music Enthusiasts
CONTACT mjau@henry.demon.co.uk
FREE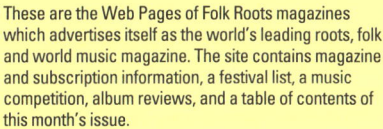

http://www.cityscape.co.uk/froots/

FolkBook - An Online Acoustic Music Establishment ★★★

FolkBook offers information about artists and venues, resources for musicians and lists pointers to other folk-related Web sites.

KEYWORDS Folk Music, Online Music
AUDIENCE Folk Music Enthusiasts, Musicians, Songwriters
CONTACT Stephen Spencer
spencer@cgrg.ohio-state.edu
FREE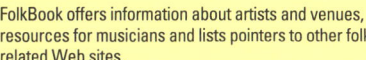

http://www.cgrg.ohio-state.edu/folkbook/folkbook.html

Forward Progress - Progressive Rock Show and Music Archives ★★★

This home page is a site dedicated to progressive music. It contains rock music archives and many links to other progressive rock resources.

KEYWORDS Contemporary Music, Music Archives, Progressive Music, Rock Music

Connections to Rock Groups
Give me some good old Rock and Roll

If you're into Aerosmith, the Rolling Stones, Blur Central, Kate Bush, U2, Zion Train, or Yello, you don't have to scour the latest issue of Rolling Stone to get information on your favorite group. The Internet has many sites for accessing the work of rock groups, including discographies, sound bites, fascinating facts about the groups, and behind-the-scenes information on the groups' recordings.

"The Beastie Boys" includes graphics and the latest updates on that group's tours.
(http://www.nando.net/music/gm/BeastieBoys/)

"Megadeath" provides information about band members, as well as lots of graphics on the group.
(http://bazaar.com/Megadeath/)

If REM is your kind of band, then check out lyrics and guitar chords on the FAQ, as well as other REM pages around the Internet.
(http://www.halcyon.com/rem/index.html)

For Brian Eno fans, provides up-to-date information on the man, his music, and links to other related sites, as well as to the Eno mailing list.
(http://www.acns.nwu.edu/eno-l/)

"Kraftwerk" provides fans with the usual band-type stuff, but you also get a selection of MIDI files of the band for those who play their own synthesizers.
(http://www.cs.umu.se/~dvlawm/kraftwerk/)

Rolling Stones fans can get the latest information on the band, its music, and tour information.
(http://stones.com/)

"Kate Bush" provides large sound samples of songs by the singer. However, you'll need 2MB of space or more for many of the songs.
(http://actor.cs.vt.edu/~wentz/index.html)

Music Genres

AUDIENCE   Music Historians, Music Researchers, Progressive Music Enthusiasts, Rock Fans
CONTACT   The Reverend
           mdb0213@tam2000.tamu.edu
FREE

http://tam2k.tamu.edu/~mdb0213/

FutureNet - Classic CD ★★★

This is a classical music site of Classic CD magazine run out of the UK and includes lots of links to anything from fan clubs to a Classic CD beginners guide, to top rated new CDs. It takes a long time to download on a low-end machine due to large photographs.

KEYWORDS   Classical Music, Online Magazines
AUDIENCE   Classical Music Enthusiasts, Musicians
FREE

http://www.futurenet.co.uk/music/classiccd.html

Genetically Generated Music ★★★★

This is an experiment in trying to evolve programs that write 'music.' It uses genetic programming to evolve expressions for note length, amplitude, frequency, duration and the spacing between notes. It plays music for users who can then vote for the different sounds produced.

KEYWORDS   Contemporary Music, Electronic Music, MIDI (Musical Instrument Digital Interface), Music
AUDIENCE   Contemporary Music Enthusiasts, Electronic Music Enthusiasts, MIDI Enthusiasts, Music Enthusiasts
CONTACT   jefu@nmt.edu
FREE

http://nmt.edu/~jefu/notes/notes.html

The Gilbraltar Encyclopedia of Progressive Rock ★★★★

This home page contains the Gilbraltar Encyclopedia of Progressive Rock—compiled by the readers of Gilbraltar, the Internet Progressive Rock mailing list. It is primarily designed for people to discover bands that they may not have been previously familiar with, and it contains information about hundreds of bands.

KEYWORDS   Contemporary Music, Music Archives, Progressive Music, Rock Music
AUDIENCE   Progressive Music Enthusiasts, Rock Fans, Rock Musicians
CONTACT   Phil Kime
           philkime@cogsci.ed.ac.uk
FREE

http://www.cogsci.ed.ac.uk/~philkime/gepr.html

ftp://ortega.cs.ucdavis.edu/pub/MSB/GEPR/

Giovanni Bottesini ★★

Giovanni Bottesini, an opera composer and Contrabass soloist as well as 'globe-straddling' conductor, has a home page here with 4 links and more to come.

KEYWORDS   Composers, Conductors, Opera
AUDIENCE   Musicians, Opera Enthusiasts
CONTACT   Richard Edwards
           redwards@netcom.com
FREE

http://www.webcom.com/~redwards/gbmain.html

Granger's Fiddle Tunes for Guitar ★★★

Adam Granger of Granger Publications has produced this page of fiddle tunes and information, including a short course in flatpicking, the basics of rhythm guitar, and sample tunes from his syndicated column, 'Granger's Fiddle Tunes for Guitar.' There is also ordering information and a couple of reviews.

KEYWORDS   Country Music
AUDIENCE   Bluegrass Musicians, Country Music Enthusiasts
FREE

http://www.msen.com/johng/ag/gft.html

Hampton Court Palace Festival ★★

The Hampton Court Palace Festival in London has featured such performers as José Carreras, Dame Kiri Te Kanawa, and James Galway. Performances take place outdoors and include drama, as well as concerts, ballet and opera. Information is available here on the current Artistic Programme as well as booking, special hospitality and additional information.

KEYWORDS   Ballet, Concerts, Drama, Opera
AUDIENCE   Musicians, Opera Enthusiasts
FREE

http://www.micromedia.co.uk/img/hampton.htm

Hard C.O.R.E. Magazine ★★★★

Hard C.O.R.E. contains a large volume of exceedingly detailed reviews of the latest rap and Hip-Hop recordings, authored by the members of Hard C.O.R.E.'s review board. Feature stories, articles, notices and reviews of live shows and, occasionally, interviews also appear in each issue.

KEYWORDS   E-Zines, Hip-Hop, Music Reviews, Rap Music
AUDIENCE   Hip-Hop Music Enthusiasts, Music Industry Professionals, Rap Music Enthusiasts
CONTACT   Steve 'Flash' Juon
           juonstevenja@bvc.edu
FREE

gopher://gopher.etext.org/Zines/HardCORE

ftp://ftp.etext.org/pub/Zines/HardCORE/

Industrial Music and Related Information ★★★★

This page offers a comprehensive index of industrial music resources on the Internet. Users will find extensive artist listings, information on record labels that have a page on the World Wide Web, and a collection of links to Web-based magazines with content about industrial music. In addition, this server provides a set of links to other information sources on industrial music, such as a page with information on creating/composing your own industrial music.

KEYWORDS   Composing, Industrial Music, Music, Record Labels
AUDIENCE   Industrial Music Enthusiasts, Music Enthusiasts, Techno/Ambient Music Enthusiasts
CONTACT   Sunil Mishra
           smishra@nwu.edu
FREE

http://www.eecs.nwu.edu:80/~smishra/Industrial/

J.S. Bach ★★★★

This home page is dedicated to the classical composer Johann Sebastian Bach. It has a biography, and listings of his complete works by number, category, instrument and title. It also has a listing of recordings by number, instrument, performer, record label and title.

KEYWORDS   Classical Music, Composers, Music History
AUDIENCE   Classical Music Enthusiasts, Music Historians, Musicians, Musicologists
CONTACT   Jan Hanford
           bach@shelby.com
FREE

http://www.tile.net/tile/bach/

Jazz at the Philharmonic ★★★

Jazz at the Philharmonic is a site introducing the CD, `Jazz At The Philharmonic- The First Concert' that is available to order at the University of California at Irvine's online Bookstore. The site includes a JPEG image file and one 837k Ulaw Sound sample for downloading.

KEYWORDS   Compact Discs (CDs), Events, Jazz
AUDIENCE   Jazz Enthusiasts, Jazz Historians, Jazz Students
CONTACT   James A. Harrod, Director
           jaharrod@uci.edu
FREE

http://bookweb.cwis.uci.edu:8042/Jazz/CDLists/JazzatthePhil_C DL.html

Jazz Improvisation ★★★

This site is designed as a resource for students of jazz improvisation and gives links to a series of articles that are part of the syllabus for Jazz Improvisation courses taught by Professor Joan Wildman at the University of Wisconsin at Madison. However, it is also a trove of information about Jazz and Jazz improvisation with 30 more links to sounds, articles, jazz sites, etc.

KEYWORDS   Jazz, Music Education
AUDIENCE   Jazz Enthusiasts, Jazz Improvisation Students

Music Genres

CONTACT	Dr. Joan Wildman
	jwildman@facstaff.wisc.edu
FREE	

http://www.wisc.edu/jazz

A Jazz Improvisation Primer by Marc Sabatella ★★★★

This is everything you want to know about jazz improvisation, the hypertext version of Marc Sabatella's jazz improvisation primer. Marc Sabatella is a jazz musician by calling, a Hewlett Packard computer programmer by day, who can also frequently be heard/read in the jazz/blues usenet group, rec.music.bluenote.

KEYWORDS	Jazz, Music Education
AUDIENCE	Jazz Enthusiasts, Jazz Historians, Jazz Improvisation Students
CONTACT	Ed Price
	edp@panix.com
FREE	

http://www.acns.nwu.edu/jazz/ms-primer/

KPIG Radio - CyberSwine World Headquarters ★★★

KPIG is a country-western station now available live online at 14.4k through RealAudio software which is downloadable on site for free. KPIG Radio's homebase is Freedom, California near Santa Cruz. They serve up what they call a format-defying blend of adult rock, acoustic music, blues, country, Hawaiian, cajun, bluegrass, and folk.

KEYWORDS	Country Music, Online Music
AUDIENCE	Country Music Enthusiasts, Music Enthusiasts
CONTACT	wildbill@kpig.com
FREE	

http://www.kpig.com

Le Nozze di Figaro (The Marriage of Figaro) ★★★

The 'Marriage of Figaro' lives at this site in Italian and English. There are links to the composer, Mozart, the music, the actors, and general information.

KEYWORDS	Composers, Opera
AUDIENCE	Musicians, Opera Enthusiasts
CONTACT	Matthew Ross Davis
	ross.davis@vt.edu
FREE	

http://www.music.vt.edu/lenozze/lenozzehome.html

 ### The Musical Offering ★★★

The Musical Offering is an independent record shop in the San Francisco Bay Area that specializes in early music, choral, chamber and keyboard music, as well as selected symphonic and operatic recordings. They intend to have the finest selection of early music on the planet and keep a stock of about 15,000 new CDs, plus a selection of used CDs. The site is basically for PR only and does not have an online ordering facility at this time. One can link to some of their selections through the Chapel Court and Countryside radio show site as well as take a look at their picks and recommendations, their inhouse cafe/bistro and their buying policy.

KEYWORDS	Chamber Music, Choral Music, Classical Music, Retail
AUDIENCE	Music Enthusiasts, Musicians
CONTACT	The Fractal Images Company
	tmo@fractals.fractals.com
FREE	

http://www.fractals.com/tmo/html/tmo_intro.html

Nashville Network ★★★

The Nashville Network is a collection of resources and information related to country music. Users will find a wide selection of pages for individual country music artists, with album information, pictures, and more. Users can also find fan club information for individual artists, as well as a comprehensive set of links to other country music information on the Net.

KEYWORDS	Country Music, Folk Music, Music, Tennessee
AUDIENCE	Country Music Enthusiasts, Folk Music Enthusiasts, Music Enthusiasts
CONTACT	Mike Blanche
	mab23@cam.ac.uk
FREE	

http://club.eng.cam.ac.uk/~94mab/country/

New Orleans Jazz and Heritage Festival ★★★

This site contains information on the New Orleans Jazz and Heritage Festival including its Background (What Jazz Fest is All About), a copy of the press releases, performance schedules, and accommodations. A highlight of this site is the collection of Jazz Fest Posters, which forms a pictorial history of the festival. At this site you can also read the legend of the Cajun cat, Pet de Kat Krewe....

KEYWORDS	Jazz, Louisiana, Music
AUDIENCE	Cajun Music Enthusiasts, Jazz Enthusiasts, Louisiana Residents, Musicians
CONTACT	vno@yatcom.com
FREE	

http://www.yatcom.com/neworl/jfest/jfesttop.html

New York City Opera ★★★

The New York City Opera Online provides general information, ticket and schedule facts, and links to the New York City Opera Online Library which is still under construction, but will offer biographical and historical profiles. One can also shop online at the New York City Opera Gift Shop, and make links to other opera sites.

KEYWORDS	New York, Opera
AUDIENCE	New York Residents, Opera Enthusiasts
CONTACT	Interport Communications
	nycopera@interport.net
FREE	

http://www.interport.net/nycopera/

Connections to Music Soundtracks to Movies and Television

Stop the violins!

Got a tune going on in your head, and you can't quite remember where you heard it? It might be the theme song from The Brady Bunch, or an instrumental from Chariots of Fire.

If you want to know more about the theme songs or soundtracks from your favorite shows and films, check out the soundtracks sites. Among other things, you'll hear the music for the American television show "Babylon 5" and find out who wrote it (Christopher Franke, formerly of the group Tangerine Dream).

(http://www.sonicimages.com/b5/b5home.html)

If you want to acquire the sound track from a movie like Legends of the Fall, you can find the record label and the title for the sound track by checking into such sites like "The Web Wide World of Film Music." And if you want to order a sound track online, there are several sites that let you do that too.

(http://www.sonicimages.com/cgi-bin/order.html)

also, **(http://web.syr.edu/~ebdgert/film_music_www.html)**

Oper der Stadt Koeln (Cologne Opera) ★★★

The Cologne Opera WWW Server is a site in German offering a schedule of events, a look behind the scenes, a history of the Opera House, FAQs, other music sites, and a chance to express your opinion (Schreiben Sie eine email!). It is run by Matthias Brixel, an art instructor at the University of Cologne who has his own home page link with a lifesize photo for downloading.

KEYWORDS	Germany, Opera
AUDIENCE	Musicians, Opera Enthusiasts
CONTACT	Matthias Brixel
	diplco@ora.de
FREE	

http://www.rrz.uni-koeln.de/koeln/oper/index.html

Music Genres

Opera ★★★

Opera is home page to an academic course at Edinboro University of Pennsylvania. Student and guest research projects are published here and those interested in opera are welcome to browse. There are dozens of links that are updated regularly and maintained by Professor Tim Cordell. The link to Professor Cordell's home page is also well worth exploring.

- **KEYWORDS** Music Education, Universities
- **AUDIENCE** Music Historians, Opera Enthusiasts, Researchers, Students
- **CONTACT** Tim Cordell
  Cordell@vax.edinboro.edu
- **FREE**

http://www.edinboro.edu/CWIS/Music/Cordell/00hpopera.html

Opera Glass ★★★

Opera Glass is an opera information server on the World Wide Web. Here one can get detailed information, including performance histories, synopses, libretti, and eventually sound bites, plus pointers to other opera servers.

- **KEYWORDS** Events, Opera
- **AUDIENCE** Musicians, Opera Enthusiasts
- **CONTACT** Rick Bogart
  rick@rick.Stanford.EDU
- **FREE**

http://rick.stanford.edu/opera/main.html

Opera Libretti and Other Vocal Texts ★★★

This site consists of pointers to a dozen or so Web sites where one can find opera libretti and other vocal texts.

- **KEYWORDS** Opera
- **AUDIENCE** Music Enthusiasts, Opera Enthusiasts
- **CONTACT** Lyle Neff
  lneff@ucs.indiana.edu
- **FREE**

http://copper.ucs.indiana.edu/~lneff/libretti.html

Opera-L Server ★★

The Opera-L Server, which is described as 'experimental,' is based in Australia and offers a good number of links to other opera servers as well as links to a guide of recorded opera, composers from A to Z, and operas from A to Z. Many of the services are under construction, and the page has not been updated since August of 1994. However, a good deal of the links are still intact.

- **KEYWORDS** Australia, Opera
- **AUDIENCE** Music Enthusiasts, Opera Enthusiasts
- **FREE**

http://www.physics.su.oz.au/~neilb/operah.html

Oz-Jazz Worldwide ★★★

Oz Jazz Worldwide contains information about the Australian jazz scene offered as a free service, compiled and maintained by George Howell for Right Words Pty.Ltd.

- **KEYWORDS** Australia, Jazz, Online Music
- **AUDIENCE** Australians, Jazz Enthusiasts
- **CONTACT** George Howell
  georgeh@magna.com.au
- **FREE**

http://magna.com.au/~georgeh/

Pacific Opera Victoria Home Page ★★★

The Pacific Opera in Victoria, Canada bills itself as a 'future site.' It is designed or will be designed to introduce the Opera Company, 'the Jewel of the Northwest,' and keep the world informed about productions, special events, fund-raisers, etc. Currently there are six operative links for the Pacific Opera Victoria Online and about eight other links to other related Web sites.

- **KEYWORDS** Canada, Opera
- **AUDIENCE** Canadian Culture Enthusiasts, Opera Enthusiasts
- **CONTACT** Pacific Opera Victoria
  opera@islandnet.com
- **FREE**

http://www.islandnet.com/~opera/povhome.html

Progressive Music ★★

This gopher site is dedicated to progressive music. It contins the alt.music.progressive FAQ, a couple of interview transcripts and a few sound files.

- **KEYWORDS** Contemporary Music, Progressive Music, Rock Music
- **AUDIENCE** Progressive Music Enthusiasts, Rock Fans
- **CONTACT** The Reverend
  mdb0213@tam2000.tamu.edu
- **FREE**

gopher://tam2k.tamu.edu/11/.dir/kanm.dir/top-dir/

Progressive Rock Home Page ★★★★

This home page is an archive of information about progressive rock. It contains discographies of various bands, FAQs, pictures, and tons of other information about progressive music, including back issues of Gibraltar, the Internet progressive rock magazine. There's a section devoted to trading lists of fans who trade tapes. It also has links to home pages of various progressive bands.

- **KEYWORDS** Gibraltar, Progressive Music, Rock Music
- **AUDIENCE** Progressive Music Enthusiasts, Rock Fans, Technocrats
- **CONTACT** Mike Borella
  borella@cs.ucdavis.edu
- **FREE**

http://ortega.cs.ucdavis.edu/Prog.html

Ragtime Home Page ★★★★

This ragtime site contains information on the three key ragtime artists — Scott Joplin (1868-1917), James Scott (1886-1938), Joseph Lamb (1887-1960) — as well as a collection of MIDI files and some of their sheet music covers. Users will also find ragtime events around the world, ragtime and related recordings on CD, amateur samples of ragtime music, a definition of New World piano music, listings of music books/sheet music, Louis Moreau Gottschalk Society, and a Ragtime FAQ. There are also links to other ragtime sites.

- **KEYWORDS** Events, Music History, Music Manuscripts, Ragtime
- **AUDIENCE** Music Educators, Music Students, Musicians, Ragtime Enthusiasts
- **FREE**

http://www.ragtimers.org/~ragtimers/

The Rat Pack Home Page ★★

Although the Rat Pack Home Page is dedicated more to a large number of huge photos, it is certainly worth a visit from serious fans of this group, the most famous of whom are Frank Sinatra, Dean Martin and Sammy Davis, Jr. Run by Dr. Bombay, there are links to Vegas and its neon splendor, sound links, the Big Casino Home Page, Women (Dolls), and to Dr. B's own prose, located on the site called, 'Real Stories of the Dark & Strange Page.' There is also a Kool Linx Index, and Previous Monthly Specials.

- **KEYWORDS** Jazz, Online Music
- **AUDIENCE** Classical Pop Enthusiasts, Jazz Enthusiasts
- **CONTACT** Dr. Bombay
  drbmbay@primenet.com
- **FREE**

http://www.primenet.com/~drbmbay/index.html

Seconds Magazine Online ★★★
(COMMERCIAL)

This is the electronic complement of the magazine Seconds, which covers punk, hardcore and alternative rock music. This monthly magazine contains numerous profiles and show reviews of a wide array of acts, including Helmet, Tad, Therapy?, Gary Panter and even poet/performance artist Allen Ginsberg.

- **KEYWORDS** Allen, Alternative Rock, Punk Music
- **AUDIENCE** Punks, Rock Fans
- **CONTACT** Seconds Editor
  root@iuma.com
- **FREE**

http://www.iuma.com

Sidmouth Festival ★★★

This site provides information on the Sidmouth Folk Arts Festival, the 'grandaddy' of all folk festivals, pioneering world music of all shapes and sizes. It contains a description and brief history and links to information on Sidmouth itself. The site contains information on several folk bands and dance troupes (The Old Swan and Bull, Dave Whetstone Band, Stomp, The Eelgrinders, The Woodpecker Band, The Kitchen Girls, Junction 24, The Rakes, Hillbillies from Mars and The Flatville Aces, Bayou Seco On Bouge), as well as links to information about folk arts.

- **KEYWORDS** Dance Music, Folk Music, Music
- **AUDIENCE** Dance Enthusiasts, Folk Dancers, Folk Music Enthusiasts
- **CONTACT** Martin Kiff
  mgk@csu.npl.co.uk
- **FREE**

http://www.npl.co.uk:80/~mgk/dance/festivals/sidmouth.html

Music Genres – Music History

Sleepbot - Ambience for the Masses ★★★★

This web site is a huge archive of ambient music resources and links. Dozens of descriptions and sound files of electronic music albums.
- KEYWORDS: Archives, Meta-Index (Ambiant Music)
- AUDIENCE: Ambient Music Enthusiasts, Electronic Music Enthusiasts, Experimental Music Enthusiasts, Techno Music Enthusiasts
- CONTACT: questions @skrclassical.schoolkids.com
- FREE

http://underground.internet.com/lookit/sleepbot/sleepbot.html

TLEM (The Lighthouse Electronic Magazine) ★★★

TLEM is aimed at fans of contemporary Christian music and others interested in the industry side of the genre. It features interviews, reviews, articles and songlists.
- KEYWORDS: Christian Music, Music Industry, Zines
- AUDIENCE: Christian Music Enthusiasts, Christians, Music Industry Professionals, Rock Fans
- CONTACT: J. Warner Soditus
  jws@sabine.acs.psu.edu
- FREE

gopher://gopher.etext.org/11/Zines/Lighthouse/

The World-Wide Web Virtual Library - Classical Music ★★★★

This is a catalogue of online information about classical music. The page offers resources about various artists, academic and commercial organizations, and online periodicals related to classical music. Users can also sample music reviews, and browse a list of computer software and related discussion forum groups.
- KEYWORDS: Classical Music, Music Resources, Music Archives
- AUDIENCE: Classical Music Enthusiasts, Music Enthusiasts, Musicians
- CONTACT: Sandy Nicholson
  S.Nicholson@ed.ac.uk
- FREE

http://www.maths.ed.ac.uk/classical/

Wotan's Hompage ★★

'Welcome to the Halls of Bayreuth'. Here you will find information on all facets of opera, biographies, discographies, etc. The site includes Verdi and Puccini biographies and a synopsis of Wagner's 'Ring.'
- KEYWORDS: Biographies, Classical Music, Opera
- AUDIENCE: Classical Music Enthusiasts, Music Enthusiasts, Opera Enthusiasts
- CONTACT: Andrew Higgins
  wotan@interport.net
- FREE

http://www.interport.net:80/~wotan/

Ziggy's Blues Home Page ★★★

This site stores interviews with notable Blues Performers, such as B.B. King and Jazz Pianist Sun Ra.
- KEYWORDS: Blues, Musicians
- AUDIENCE: Blues Enthusiasts, Jazz Enthusiasts
- FREE

http://ivory.lm.com/~davidsr/

Music History

See also
Arts & Music · *Music Genres*
Arts & Music · *Music Organizations*
Arts & Music · *Musicians*
Popular Culture & Entertainment · *Books*
Religion & Philosophy · *Religions*

The Chamber Music Page ★★★

This site is a comprehensive resource for information on chamber music. Topics include information on various conferences around the country and links to other Chamber Music related sites, Composers pages, Performers pages and arrangements.
- KEYWORDS: Chamber Music, Classical Music, Music
- AUDIENCE: Chamber Music Enthusiasts, Classical Music Enthusiasts, Music Enthusiasts
- CONTACT: cwholl@ultranet.com
- FREE

http://www.ultranet.com/~cwholl/cmc/cmc.html

Classical Composer Biographies ★★★

This is a site of composer biographies annotated and assembled by classical music enthusiast Michael Norrish. Missing are sample music clips for each composer. Content is basically light overviews and opinions, best for a quick glance or update on a particular composer.
- KEYWORDS: Biographies, Classical Music, Composers
- AUDIENCE: Classical Music Enthusiasts, Musicians
- CONTACT: Michael Norrish
  Michael.Norrish@cl.cam.ac.uk
- FREE

http://www.cl.cam.ac.uk/users/mn200/music/composers.html

Electronic Early Music ★★★★

This is a compilation of sound files of Early Music performed on a synthesizer, ready for downloading. This site is produced by Yasuhiko Higaki at Chiba University in Japan. The site also lists the equipment used and other details useful to fans and enthusiasts of Electronic Music.
- KEYWORDS: Early Music, Electronic Music, MIDI (Musical Instrument Digital Interface), Music
- AUDIENCE: Classical Music Enthusiasts, Early Music Enthusiasts, Electronic Music Enthusiasts
- CONTACT: higaki@hike.te.chiba-u.ac.jp
- FREE

http://www.hike.te.chiba-u.ac.jp/eem/

The Great Composers - By Period ★★★

For an education on the great composers by musical period, this is the place to be. The categories are early, renaissance, baroque, classical, romantic, early 20th century and contemporary. There are music clips and short biographies. This resource is useful for a brief overview, not much for detailed study.
- KEYWORDS: Classical Music, Composers
- AUDIENCE: Music Enthusiasts, Students
- FREE

http://classicalmus.com/composerperiod.html

Gregorian Chant Home Page ★★★★

The main purpose of this academically solid site, the Gregorian Chant Homepage, is to support advanced research on Gregorian chant, particularly in the graduate seminar 'Problems in Early Christian Music' (Music 511) taught at Princeton. The author notes 'In our time the Internet has become a significant repository of information relevant to chant scholarship. This page aims to make as much as possible of this information conveniently available to all of those with a serious interest in chant studies, but especially to those involved in the forthcoming Nassau Edition of Gregorian chant, which will utilize fully the new technologies for humanistic and scholarly computing.' The site also contains numerous links to other chant research sites on the Web.
- KEYWORDS: Christian Music, Classical Music, Gregorian Chant, Music
- AUDIENCE: Classical Music Enthusiasts, Early Music Enthusiasts, Music Enthusiasts, Religious Music Enthusiasts
- CONTACT: Peter Jeffery
  jeffery@phoenix.princeton.edu
- FREE

http://www.music.princeton.edu:80/chant_html/

Gustav Leonhardt ★★★★

(COMMERCIAL)

This page is dedicated to Gustav Leonhardt and includes a biography, discography, and access to the Sony Artists Tour Schedule. This Dutch music theorist is been one of the most respected specialists in both the theory and practice of early music, and one of those the most in demand. After studies in musicology Leonhardt became professor of harpsichord at the Vienna Academy of Music. Leonhardt holds the post of organist at Amsterdam's Nieuwe Kerk. This page also contains links to information on other classical musicians.
- KEYWORDS: Classical Music, Early Music, Musicology
- AUDIENCE: Classical Music Enthusiasts, Compact Disc Users, Early Music Enthusiasts, Music Enthusiasts
- CONTACT: Sony Music Online
  SonyMusicOnline@sonymusic.com
- FREE

http://www.music.sony.com/Music/ArtistInfo/GustavLeonhardt.html

Music History – Music Organizations

Measure For Measure Home Page

Measure for Measure, located in Upton, NY, is devoted to authentic performances of instrumental and vocal music of the period from about 1200 to 1600, the late Middle Ages and Renaissance. The repertoire features sacred and secular music, songs, and dances from the courts and countryside of Europe during one of the most musically innovative periods in European history. The seven musicians play amongst themselves 26 wind and string instruments plus a number of percussion instruments. This website includes information and ways to contact the group, plus an interesting set of descriptive essays on Early Music Instruments.

KEYWORDS	Chamber Music, Classical Music, Instrumental Music
AUDIENCE	Classical Music Enthusiasts, Early Music Enthusiasts, Music Enthusiasts, New York Residents
CONTACT	slug@siddons.dial.bnl.gov
FREE	

http://lspc6.nsls.bnl.gov/MFM/

New Albion's John Cage Page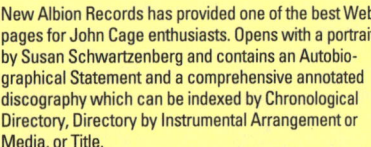

New Albion Records has provided one of the best Web pages for John Cage enthusiasts. Opens with a portrait by Susan Schwartzenberg and contains an Autobiographical Statement and a comprehensive annotated discography which can be indexed by Chronological Directory, Directory by Instrumental Arrangement or Media, or Title.

KEYWORDS	Alternative Music, Compact Discs (CDs), Composers, Music
AUDIENCE	Alternative Music Enthusiasts, Compact Disc Users, John Cage fans, Music Enthusiasts
CONTACT	ergo@newalbion.com
FREE	

http://newalbion.com:70/0h/artists/cagej/cagej.html

Renaissance Consort

If you need information on Early Music instruments from the Middle Ages and the Rennaissance, this is an excellent site with pictures and sound clip demonstrations of various instruments, including the Shawm, Bass Recorder, Glastonbury Pipe, Treble Viole, Tabor, Bass Viole, Tenor Crumhorn, and Bass Crumhorn. The sites are very educational and fun!

KEYWORDS	Classical Music, Early Music, Music, Musical Instruments
AUDIENCE	Classical Music Enthusiasts, Early Music Enthusiasts, Music Educators, Music Enthusiasts
FREE	

http://www.hike.te.chiba-u.ac.jp/cons1/

SILENCE - the John Cage Discussion List

SILENCE - the John Cage discussion list is for discussions of the music, philosophies, writings, art, life, and influence of the late John Cage. The list includes a wide range of members, ranging from those who have recently read or heard of him for the first time to experts on his work. It is not connected in any way with the John Cage estate. The homepage includes an index of Silence Digests, and links to other John Cage resources.

KEYWORDS	Alternative Music, Composers, Music, Music Publications
AUDIENCE	Alternative Music Enthusiasts, Contemporary Music Enthusiasts, Music Enthusiasts
CONTACT	jzitt@humansystems.com
FREE	

http://www.realtime.net/~jzitt/Cage/

The Symphonies of Gustav Mahler on Record

The Symphonies of Gustav Mahler on Record page provides detailed, text-based descriptions of currently available recordings of his work. Mahler's symphonies and other works are discussed, with information on the various conductors who have attempted them on record, quotes from the composer and others regarding each work, history and comments on each symphony. This document rates both the quality of the recording as well as the finesse of the conductors, and recommends those records which achieve admirable quality in both departments. There is also an incomplete discography of many of the better recordings at the end of this file.

KEYWORDS	Classical Music, Composers, Instrumental Music, Music Archives
AUDIENCE	Classical Music Enthusiasts, Instrumental Music Enthusiasts, Music Enthusiasts, Music Librarians, Music Students
CONTACT	National Center for Supercomputing Applications (NCSA) pubs@ncsa.uiuc.edu
FREE	

http://www.ncsa.uiuc.edu/SDG/People/marca/barker-mahler.html

Thesaurus Musicarum Latinarum

The Thesaurus Musicarum Latinarum at Indiana University, currently under construction, aims to be an evolving database that will eventually contain the entire corpus of Latin music theory written during the Middle Ages and the early Renaissance.

KEYWORDS	Classical Music, Music, Music Collections
AUDIENCE	Music Educators, Music Enthusiasts, Music Researchers, Musicologists
CONTACT	Mathiese@UCS.INDIANA.EDU
FREE	

Tom Morgan's Homepage

Tom Morgan's homepage is divided between promotion of his book, 'From Cakewalks to Concert Halls-An Illustrated History of African-American Popular Music 1895-1930,' the two radio shows he produces and hosts, his other musical activities, and some great links to WWW music sites, Web sites of the week, a hotlist and music companies.

KEYWORDS	African American Studies, Jazz
AUDIENCE	Jazz Enthusiasts, Musicians
CONTACT	Tom Morgan bartender@virginia.edu
FREE	

http://poe.acc.Virginia.EDU/~tm4q/

Music Organizations

See also
Arts & Music · *Film & Video*
Arts & Music · *Music Resources*
Arts & Music · *Musical Groups*

American Recordings Home Page

This site contains information and reviews on various American Recordings artists. It provides forms to send email to the bands and to sign up to their listserv. Audio and video samples are provided as well as links to other music sites.

KEYWORDS	Independent Music, Music Industry, Record Labels
AUDIENCE	Alternative Music Enthusiasts, Alternative Music Enthusiasts, Music Enthusiasts
CONTACT	american@american.recordings.com
FREE	

http://american.recordings.com/

ArrayMusic

The home page for ArrayMusic, an eight-member Toronto-based new music ensemble, recognized world-wide for its innovative programming and superb performance. Known for searching out composers with highly individual voices, the ArrayMusic Ensemble has developed a unique repertoire that reflects a postmodern sensibility and a distinctly North American eclecticism. Their home page includes CD listings, press quotes, and an extract from Michael Baker's 'Unfinished Business', performed by ArrayMusic.

KEYWORDS	Canada, Classical Music, Contemporary Music, Music
AUDIENCE	Canada Residents, Classical Music Enthusiasts, Contemporary Music Enthusiasts, Music Enthusiasts
CONTACT	Todd Harrop cott8334@mach1.wlu.ca
FREE	

http://www.io.org:80/~rixax/Array.html

Atlanta Symphony Orchestra

The Atlanta Symphony Orchestra is celebrating its 50th Anniversary Season in 1995 and takes us on a tour of their history, general information and two years of concert schedules. There is also ample information on the conductors, musicians, Atlanta Symphony Associates, their volunteer organization and associated arts centers and theater companies.

KEYWORDS	Classical Music, Symphony Orchestras
AUDIENCE	Classical Music Enthusiasts, Music Enthusiasts
CONTACT	Webmaster webmaster@isotropic.com
FREE	

http://isotropic.com/symphony/asohome.html

Music Organizations   59

Auricular ★★★★

The Auricular web site offers information about the Aricular Records label, and a collection of digital artwork. Users will find information on Nox Vomica, a group that has releases on Auricular, as well as read about other releases from this label. This site also maintains links to other sites with music information on the web.
- **KEYWORDS**: Companies, Music, Online Art Galleries, Record Labels
- **AUDIENCE**: Music Enthusiasts, Techno Music Fans
- **CONTACT**: Alan Herrick, Auricular@aol.com
- **FREE**

http://128.218.7.140/Auricular.html

The Austin Symphonic Band ★★★★

The Austin Symphonic Band is a collection of amateur musicians which perform a variety of concerts for the Austin-area community, and for their own enjoyment. The ASB currently has about 100 members. Their homepage includes reviews, news about the ASB, membership information, rehearsal schedules, board meetings, music selection, performance venues, the ASB Schedule, ASB Funding, an ASB Contact List, and an ASB Photo.
- **KEYWORDS**: Classical Music, Symphony Orchestras, Texas
- **AUDIENCE**: Classical Music Enthusiasts, Music Enthusiasts, Symphony Enthusiasts, Texas Residents
- **CONTACT**: rboerger@io.com
- **FREE**

http://www.io.com/~rboerger/ASB.html

The Boethius Server at UC Santa Barbara ★★★★

This server is the site for the Society for Music Theory and music at UC Santa Barbara. You may view the access statistics for this and other SMT Web pages with this link. With the Music Theory Online Home Page, where you can find out more about the SMT's electronic journal. The most-frequently-used MTO links are provided here. The SMT Home Page enables access to a large database of journal articles, the SMT email conference guide, and other information. The most frequently used links are provided here.
- **KEYWORDS**: Classical Music, Music Resources, Music Schools, Music Theory
- **AUDIENCE**: Classical Music Enthusiasts, Music Educators, Music Enthusiasts, Music Researchers
- **CONTACT**: rothfarb@boethius.music.uscb.edu
- **FREE**

http://boethius.music.ucsb.edu/boethius.html

Boston Chamber Ensemble Homepage ★★★

The Boston Chamber Ensemble home page at MIT includes concert schedules, facts about their nationwide composition competition, and other information.
- **KEYWORDS**: Chamber Music, Classical Music, Massachusetts
- **AUDIENCE**: Classical Music Enthusiasts, Massachusetts Residents, Music Enthusiasts
- **CONTACT**: Jeff Bigler, jcb@mit.edu
- **FREE**

http://www.mit.edu:8001/people/jcb/BCE/bce.html

Boulder Philharmonic Orchestra ★★

The Boulder Philharmonic Orchestra site contains the 1994-1995 concert guide with schedule, subscriber information, special programs and events, membership information, information on the Boulder Philharmonic Staff and the Boulder Philharmonic Academy. There is no obvious address or directions anywhere to be found, so one must call their box office number to get this information.
- **KEYWORDS**: Classical Music, Symphony Orchestras
- **AUDIENCE**: Classical Music Enthusiasts, Music Enthusiasts
- **FREE**

http://www.aescon.com/music/phil/index.htm

Colorado Springs Symphony ★★★

This site is currently under construction, and at the moment is a little clunky and hard to use. Currently contains a schedule for only one upcoming concert (Britten's War Requiem), information on Christopher Wilkins (Music Director and Conductor) and David Ball (Executive Director) as well as a group photo.
- **KEYWORDS**: Classical Music, Colorado, Music, Symphony Orchestras
- **AUDIENCE**: Classical Music Enthusiasts, Colorado Residents, Music Enthusiasts, Symphony Enthusiasts
- **CONTACT**: symphony@ceram.com
- **FREE**

http://www.mothra.com/symphony/index.html

IRCAM WWW Server (Institut de Recherche et Coordination Acoustique/Musique) ★★★★

IRCAM's (Institut de Recherche et Coordination Acoustique/Musique) WWW server offers users a look at the research programs and music production of this famous French music laboratory. Items to be found on this server include detailed descriptions of the facilities, descriptions of the software and hardware developed at IRCAM, and information on current research programs in psychoacoustics, synthesis, and other topics of interest to the scientific music community. Users can also read IRCAM publications, and search the catalog of the IRCAM library.
- **KEYWORDS**: Contemporary Music, Electronic Music, Music, Music Education
- **AUDIENCE**: Electronic Music Enthusiasts, Music Enthusiasts, Music Historians, Music Researchers, Musicians
- **CONTACT**: manager@ircam.fr
- **FREE**

http://www.ircam.fr/index-e.html

Imperial College Symphony Orchestra ★★★★

Recognized as one of the most adventurous and accomplished university orchestras in the UK, Imperial College Symphony Orchestra (ICSO) is an extremely large orchestra, which could, at one point, boast even four tuba players. The past few years have seen many impressive works, which have included Shostakovich's Fifth Symphony, Stravinsky's Petrushka and Rite Of Spring, and Mahler's IInd, IVth and Vth Symphonies. Their Web page includes information on music at ICSTM, Richard Dickins - Musician-In-Residence, background of ICSO, Ash Music Scholarships, the joint Physics with Musical Performance Degree, forthcoming events, a review of the last concert, and links to other classical music Web pages.
- **KEYWORDS**: Classical Music, Events
- **AUDIENCE**: Classical Music Enthusiasts, Music Enthusiasts, Music Students, United Kingdom Residents
- **CONTACT**: Alasdair Gill, a.gill@ic.ac.uk
- **FREE**

http://www.su.ic.ac.uk/clubs/societies/scab/ICSO/top.html

The Indianapolis Symphony Orchestra Homepage ★★★★

The Indianapolis Symphony Orchestra Homepage offers a brief history of the ISO, 'Meet the Orchestra,' 'Meet our Concertmaster,' schedules for the 1995-96 Classical, Pops, and Family Series, a monthly schedule, the ISO Administration, CD Library, a 47K JPG file of the Circle Theatre (the home of the ISO), and links to more music related Web sites.
- **KEYWORDS**: Classical Music, Indiana, Music, Symphony Orchestras
- **AUDIENCE**: Classical Music Enthusiasts, Indianapolis Residents, Music Enthusiasts, Symphony Enthusiasts
- **CONTACT**: cello@in.net
- **FREE**

http://www.in.net/iso/

KISS FM ★★★

This site is sponsored by WXKS Radio (also known as KISS FM), a top 40 radio station serving the greater Boston, Massachusetts area. Users will find playlists, radio station promotion information, local events, music news and concert information. This site also hosts information about the on-air personalities as well as

Music Organizations

providing a place for listeners to give feedback and request songs.
- **KEYWORDS** Boston, Radio Stations, Top 40 Radio
- **AUDIENCE** Popular Music Enthusiasts, Radio Enthusiasts, Top 40 Music Enthusiasts
- **CONTACT** request@kissfm.com
- **FREE**

http://www.kissfm.com/kiss/

KTRU 91.7 FM Jazz Page ★★★

KTRU 91.7 FM is an all-volunteer, student-run, non-commercial Jazz radio station at Rice University in Houston, Texas. Their general Web page links to several seasonal 'best-of' playlists, the KTRU Avant-Jazz Festival and to other radio stations on the Web.
- **KEYWORDS** Jazz, Radio
- **AUDIENCE** Jazz Enthusiasts, Students
- **FREE**

http://spacsun.rice.edu/~vek/ktru.html

The Keio University Ein Kleines Orchster Homepage ★★★

Keio University Ein Kleines Orchster was founded in April, 1990 at Keio University Shonan Fujisawa Campus. The University also has two other orchestras, the Wagner Society Orchestra and the Keio University Medical School Philharmonic Orchestra, in other campuses. Ein Kleines Orchester was a group of nine students when it was founded, and now, in its fifth year, it consists of 70 members. Not only undergraduate students but also those in the master's and doctoral degree programs are the members of this orchestra. The home page includes 'What is Ein Kleines Orchester?,' concert information, and the history of the orchestra.
- **KEYWORDS** Classical Music, Japan, Music, Symphony Orchestras
- **AUDIENCE** Classical Music Enthusiasts, Japan Residents, Music Enthusiasts, Symphony Enthusiasts
- **FREE**

http://www.sfc.keio.ac.jp/~t93414km/eko/katsudou.html

Longwood Symphony Orchestra ★★★★

Now in its eleventh season, the Longwood Symphony Orchestra (Francisco Noya, Music Director) is an orchestra composed primarily of health-care professionals that supports the medically underserved community of Boston through high-quality musical performances. Their webpage includes the Winter Spring 1995 Schedule and an audio file containing the Longwood Symphony playing Beethoven's 9th Symphony.
- **KEYWORDS** Classical Music, Music, Symphonic Music
- **AUDIENCE** Classical Music Enthusiasts, Massachusetts Residents, Music Enthusiasts
- **CONTACT** Rich Lethin
  lethin@ai.mit.edu
- **FREE**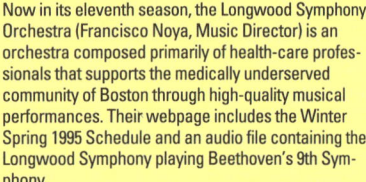

http://www.ai.mit.edu/people/lethin/longwood.html

New England Philharmonic Homepage ★★★★

This site contains the concert schedule for the New England Philharmonic, an orchestra of volunteer professionals dedicated to the performance of new and unusual music. Since its founding in 1976, the New England Philharmonic has dedicated itself to bringing first-rate performances of symphonic repertoire to Boston, Cambridge and Metro-West locations.
- **KEYWORDS** Classical Music, Music, Symphony Orchestras
- **AUDIENCE** Classical Music Enthusiasts, Music Enthusiasts, New England Residents
- **CONTACT** Jeff Bigler
  jcb@mit.edu
- **FREE**

http://www.mit.edu:8001/people/jcb/NEP/nep.html

New Zealand Symphony Orchestra ★★★

The New Zealand Symphony Orchestra claims to be the first orchestra in the world with a Web Site. Here you'll find their concert schedule and information about programs, featured artists and their recordings. There is very comprehensive links to all kinds of other music sites on the web and more information on New Zealand for future tourists.
- **KEYWORDS** Classical Music, Symphony Orchestras
- **AUDIENCE** Classical Music Enthusiasts
- **CONTACT** Actrix Communication Networks
  dgold@basso.actrix.gen.nz
- **FREE**

http://www.actrix.gen.nz/users/dgold/nzso.html

The Nittany Valley Symphony Homepage ★★★★

The Nittany Valley Symphony is a non-profit group that performs orchestral works from all periods. Their home page includes 'What's new on the NVS WWW pages,' the 1994-95 Concert Schedule, 1995-96 Concert Schedule, a biography of Michael Jinbo (Music Director and Conductor), and a brief history of the symphony. The site also contains links to other music-related sites.
- **KEYWORDS** Classical Music, Music, Music Resources, Symphony Orchestras
- **AUDIENCE** Classical Music Enthusiasts, Music Enthusiasts, Pennsylvania Residents, Symphony Enthusiasts
- **CONTACT** 3DJohnBalogh@psu.edu
- **FREE**

http://jdb.psu.edu/john.html

The Orchestra London Homepage ★★★

The Orchestra London Homepage from London Ontario, Canada, features 'What's New at Orchestra London,' featured events, the 1995-96 season calendar, ticket orders and subscriptions, information on donations, a list of Orchestra London musical recordings, and how to contact Orchestra London.
- **KEYWORDS** Canada, Classical Music, Music, Symphony Orchestras
- **AUDIENCE** Canada Residents, Classical Music Enthusiasts, Music Enthusiasts, Symphony Enthusiasts
- **CONTACT** orchestra.london@icis.on.ca
- **FREE**

http://www.icis.on.ca/orchestra/

Oregon Bach Festival ★★★★

Each summer the Oregon Bach Festival presents two weeks of concerts and events. Under conductor Helmuth Rilling musicians and music enthusiasts from around the world gather in Eugene, Oregon to participate in the Fesitval. This site contains information on Rilling, program notes and schedules and additional information about the history of the festival.
- **KEYWORDS** Classical Music, Music Festivals, Oregon
- **AUDIENCE** Classical Music Enthusiasts, Music Enthusiasts, Musicians, Oregon Residents
- **CONTACT** George Evano, Director of Communications
  gevano@oregon.uoregon.edu
- **FREE**

http://jrusby.uoregon.edu/obf/obfhome.html

Parma Cittadella Musica ★★

This site offers a visit to the great Italian Opera House, 'Parma Cittadella Musica.' The site is written in Italian and has links to Parma, the Opera Falstaff, and the singer Verdi, among others.
- **KEYWORDS** Italy, Opera
- **AUDIENCE** Italians, Opera Enthusiasts
- **FREE**

http://aida.eng.unipr.it/segno/gennaio-95/segnoint.html

Perihelion's Home Page ★★★★

The home page for Perihelion, the Ensemble in Residence at the University of Queensland. Comprising clarinet, viola, cello and piano, the quartet's repertoire includes music of all periods. Perihelion is particularly acclaimed for its championing of Australian music, which it regularly performs in concerts and broadcasts. This page includes information on the group, the latest edition of 'The Perihelion Rag,' member information, a 1995 concert schedule, and information on the subscription series.
- **KEYWORDS** Australia, Chamber Music, Classical Music, Music
- **AUDIENCE** Australia Residents, Chamber Music Enthusiasts, Classical Music Enthusiasts, Music Enthusiasts
- **CONTACT** Kim Kirkman
  angela@bach.music.uq.oz.au
- **FREE**

http://www.uq.oz.au/~mukkirkm/peri.html

Music Organizations   61

Polygram Home Page ★★★

This is the site for PolyGram Records' family of entertainment companies, including A&M, Def Jam, Deutsche Grammophon, Gramercy Pictures, Island, London, Mercury, Motown, Philips, Polydor, PolyGram Video, Verve, and more. Users can find out about new releases, get information on PolyGram artists, download interactive press kits for musicians and upcoming film releases. There is also information available on special promotions as well as downloadable music samples of new releases.

KEYWORDS   Films, Music, Record Labels
AUDIENCE   Film Enthusiasts, Music Enthusiasts, Musicians
CONTACT   polyinfo@polygram.com
FREE

http://spider.media.philips.com/polygram/PolyGram.html

The Redwood Symphony Homepage ★★★★

The Redwood Symphony (Eric Kujawsky, Music Director) performs at the Canada College theater in Redwood City, California. Their webpage includes 'A Message to our Audience,' bios on members of the orchestra, a listing of Compact Discs from the Redwood Symphony, soundclips, and a concert schedule.

KEYWORDS   Classical Music, Music, Symphonic Music
AUDIENCE   Californians, Classical Music Enthusiasts, Music Enthusiasts
CONTACT   Steve Auerbach
           sauerbac@netcom.com
FREE

http://www.globalcenter.net/~redwood/

The San Diego Young Artists Symphony Orchestra Homepage ★★★

The San Diego Young Artists Symphony Orchestra was established to provide orchestral training and performance for outstanding talented young musicians. The orchestra is led by Louis Campiglia, who recently announced his retirement as the Conductor of the San Diego Youth Symphony after an illustrious 28 year career with the orchestra. The orchestra is open to all young musicians of exceptional promise through the age of thirty.

KEYWORDS   Classical Music, Music, Symphony Orchestras
AUDIENCE   Californians, Classical Music Enthusiasts, Music Enthusiasts, Symphony Enthusiasts
CONTACT   jfrey@ucsd.edu
FREE

http://crayfish.ucsd.edu/home/sinuhe/www/sdyaso.html

Sinfonia Lahti ★★★

The Lahti Symphony Orchestra was founded in 1949 to maintain the traditions of the orchestra established in 1910 by the society Lahti Friends of Music. This is not a particularly thorough site so there are no schedules. However, there is a discography, links to its conductor and awards as well as to the 'Classical Music on the World Wide Web' site.

KEYWORDS   Classical Music, Finnish Music, Symphony Orchestras
AUDIENCE   Classical Music Enthusiasts
FREE

http://www.php.fi/lahti/eng/sinfonia.html

The Stanford Symphony Orchestra ★★★★

The Stanford Symphony Orchestra (SSO) is a a student-run organization under the Stanford University Music Department. The 80 members have backgrounds in many different fields and majors, and includes Stanford undergraduates, graduate students, postdoctoral fellows, and community members. The Web site includes general information, concert information, the Summer 1995 tour to China, hiring musical ensembles, a bio of the conductor, and access info on the SSO newsgroup.

KEYWORDS   Classical Music, Music
AUDIENCE   Californians, Classical Music Enthusiasts, Music Enthusiasts, Music Students
CONTACT   Rod Philander
FREE

http://www-leland.stanford.edu/group/sso

The Symphony Nova Scotia Homepage ★★★★

The Symphony Nova Scotia's mission is to enhance the quality of life of the people of Nova Scotia and beyond through the presentation of high quality professionally performed orchestral music. With the guidance of Artistic Advisor, Georg Tintner, the artistic committee has put together a season rich in artistry and variety, to satisfy a wide range of musical tastes. Features of the home page include information on subscription benefits, the Celebrity Series Concerts, the Pops Series, U-Pick Concert Series, Baroque Series, Romantics Series, Cole Harbour / Bedford Series, and Special Concerts.

KEYWORDS   Canada, Classical Music, Music, Symphony Orchestras
AUDIENCE   Canada Residents, Classical Music Enthusiasts, Music Enthusiasts, Symphony Enthusiasts
CONTACT   sns@fox.nstn.ca
FREE

http://www.nstn.ca/kiosks/sns/sns.html

The University of Edinburgh Faculty of Music ★★★

The Web site for the University of Edinburgh Faculty of Music takes us on a tour of the University Music Department, graduate and undergraduate study programs and faculty. There is a staff and postgraduate directory including an email database. There are quite a few photographs that take a long time to download as well.

KEYWORDS   Music Education
AUDIENCE   Music Historians, Music Teachers, Students
CONTACT   Webmaster
           webmasters@music.ed.ac.uk
FREE

http://www.music.ed.ac.uk/

The University of Oslo Symphony Orchestra ★★★

The University of Oslo Symphony Orchestra home page is a bilingual site in Norwegian and English, though the List of Concerts is only on the Norwegian page. The Orchestra is comprised of approximately 80 amateur musicians, and has a full symphony orchestra setting. There are usually three to four concerts a year, in addition to the Orchestra's regular participation in University events and Student-society events.

KEYWORDS   Classical Music, Events, Norway, Symphony Orchestras
AUDIENCE   Classical Music Enthusiasts, Music Enthusiasts, Oslo Residents, Symphony Enthusiasts
FREE

http://www.ifi.uio.no/~hph/uso/index-eng.html

WMUC Radio ★★★

WMUC is the radio station serving the University of Maryland at College Park. In operation since 1937, WMUC has for decades been the only source of the latest and greatest indiePop, electronic music, hardcore, experimental music, jazz and blues, and more in the Washington, DC area. Users will find programming information, schedules, events calendar, and advertising information. There is also a section with technical information about the radio station.

KEYWORDS   College Radio, Music, Radio
AUDIENCE   Maryland Residents, Radio Enthusiasts, Students
CONTACT   Mark Burdett
           sleven@wam.umd.edu
FREE

http://www.wam.umd.edu/~sleven/

West Bay Opera ★★★

West Bay Opera is the second oldest opera company in the San Francisco Bay Area and one of America's leading regional companies. Their Web site connects to information about the current and next season, their performance history, costume rentals, reviews, auditions and access to a brochure. There are ten additional links to other relevant sites.

KEYWORDS   California, Opera
AUDIENCE   Music Enthusiasts, Opera Enthusiasts
CONTACT   Rick Bogart
           rick@rick.stanford.edu
FREE

http://lucia.stanford.edu/wbo/wbo.html

Winham Computer Music Laboratory at Princeton ★★★

The Winham Laboratory, which grew from an early commitment to electro-acoustic music at the Columbia-Princeton Electronic Music Center, includes information on the Laboratory, links to such places as the

Princeton Sound Kitchen, and offers data about a CD of music from the Winham Lab.

KEYWORDS Electronic Music, Music, Music Schools, Synthesizers
AUDIENCE Electronic Music Enthusiasts, Music Enthusiasts, Music Students, Synthesizer Users
FREE

http://www.music.princeton.edu:80/winham/index.html

Winnipeg Symphony Orchestra ★★★★

The home page of the Winnipeg Symphony Orchestra includes 'A Message From The Maestro,' as well as schedules and information for the Fanfare Classics, Festival Classics, Bank of Montreal Mad About The Classics, The Real Canadian Superconcerts For Kids, MTS Pops, du Maurier Arts Ltd. New Music Festival, The Crown Royal Evening, and special concerts. The site also contains information on ticket pricing and seating plans, and a discography of recordings by the WSO.

KEYWORDS Canada, Classical Music, Events, Symphony Orchestras
AUDIENCE Canada Residents, Classical Music Enthusiasts, Music Enthusiasts, Symphony Enthusiasts
CONTACT www@ee.umanitoba.ca.
FREE

http://www.ee.umanitoba.ca/wpg/WSO.html

The Zamir Chorale of Boston ★★★★

The Zamir Chorale of Boston is a choral ensemble specializing in music that has evolved from various Jewish traditions. Since its formation by the music director Joshua Jacobson 25 years ago, the Chorale has remained committed to the highest quality performance of this literature, which spans thousands of years, four continents and a variety of styles. Their webpage includes information on upcoming and recent performances, recordings available, sheet music, membership information, and links to other Jewish resources on the Web.

KEYWORDS Boston, Choral Singing, Classical Music, Judaism
AUDIENCE Choral Singers, Classical Music Enthusiasts, Massachusetts Residents, Music Enthusiasts
CONTACT Andrew Greene amgreene@mit.edu
FREE

http://www.mit.edu:8001/people/amgreene/zamir.html

Music Resources

See also
Arts & Music · *Art Resources*
Arts & Music · *Music Resources*
Arts & Music · *Musicians*
Arts & Music · *Performing Arts*

AMO's Music Magazine ★★★★

Aussie Music Online's Music Magazine offers interesting news and information on Australian music, where to hear Aussie music around the world, a guide to the Australian music industry as a whole with contacts and sound clips for listening and ordering online.

KEYWORDS Australia, Online Magazines, Online Music
AUDIENCE Australian Culture Enthusiasts, Music Enthusiasts
FREE

http://www.aussiemusic.com.au/mag.html

AMP Magazine ★★★★

MCA Records' high-budget webzine, AMP, delivers numerous articles, interviews and features dealing with MCA artists (featured in a January 1995 article is Mary J. Blige). An image-mapped interface complements the substance of the magazine.

KEYWORDS E-Zines, Newsletters, Rap Music, Rock Music
AUDIENCE Musicians, Rap Music Enthusiasts, Rock Fans
CONTACT editor amp@mca.com
FREE

http://www.mca.com/mca_records/index.html

Addicted To Noise Webzine ★★★★

A large, graphics-intensive first issue (January, 1995) heralds this new Webzine to the Internet. Addicted To Noise (ATN) is sponsored by a number of mainstream and alternative record labels, bands such as Throwing Muses, and others. Editor Michael Goldberg says ATN's purpose is to document, critique and discuss all of rock 'culture,' regardless of genre. Numerous features, columns, interviews, letters and editorials fill the many pages of this exhaustive resource for any fan of rock music.

KEYWORDS Alternative Music, Rock Music, Zines
AUDIENCE Music Enthusiasts, Musicians, Rock Fans
CONTACT atn@addict.com
FREE

http://www.addict.com/ATN/

All-Music ★★★

The All-Music Guide is a comprehensive catalog of thousands of record reviews written by music journalists. As the title suggests, all kinds of music are represented from pop and rock to classical, country, and anything in between.

KEYWORDS Classical Music, Country Music, Music Reviews, Rock Music
AUDIENCE Music Enthusiasts, Music Researchers
CONTACT Michael Erlewine AMG@ALLMUSIC.FERRIS.EDU
FREE

gopher://allmusic.ferris.edu:70/

 Allegro ★★★★

Allegro is the largest distributor of independent classical music in America. Allegro also distributes Jazz, World music, Nostalgia, Special Effects, and Military Marching Band Music. The site contains sound files and extensive notes on the music included. The site also has an archive and catalogues of each genre from which music may be purchased.

KEYWORDS Classical Music, Jazz, Military Music, World Music
AUDIENCE Jazz Enthusiasts, Music Enthusiasts, Music Students, Musicians
CONTACT mailcs@allegro-music.com
FREE

http://www.teleport.com/~allegro/

American Music Center ★★★★

This is the page for the American Music Center, a music information and resource organization. The page contains a circulating collection of over 55,000 scores and recordings, repertoire selection assistance, lists of works for specific instrumentation, lists of composers by special categories (by gender, ethnic background, from specific geographic areas, etc.), information on specific composers and/or works for program notes, etc. It also has information on local composer organizations, on grants and competitions for composers and performers, as well as information on published and unpublished composers.

KEYWORDS Classical Music, Contemporary Music, Jazz
AUDIENCE Music Enthusiasts, Music Historians, Music Professionals, Musicians
CONTACT amc@dorsai.org
FREE

http://www.ingress.com/amc/

Artist Information ★★★

This is Sony Corporation Headquarters for all Artist Information. One can search by key letter or by genre. There is a complete list of artists to scan through as well.

KEYWORDS Classical Music, Country Music, Jazz, Music
AUDIENCE Artists, Music Enthusiasts, Musicians
CONTACT Sony Online SonyMusicOnline@sonymusic.com
FREE

http://www.music.sony.com/Music/ArtistInfo/ArtistInfo.html

Audio Online ★★★

Audio Online offers a collection of resources related to professional audio production. Users can browse through a sound-effects and music library which is available for purchase, as well as information on the Canadian recording studio market. In addition, this site offers information on professional audio products and computer software.

KEYWORDS Audio, Audio Technology, Digital Audio, Electronics

Music Resources

AUDIENCE Audio Enthusiasts, Audiophiles, Professional Audio Engineers
CONTACT Michael Farnsworth
audio-info@audio-online.com
FREE

http://www.audio-online.com/ao/

Audioweb Home Page ★★★

The Audioweb Home Page provides professional audio engineers and audio hobbyists with a collection of valuable resources. Users will find a library of files about all aspects of audio technology, as well as an international classified market where all types of audio equipment can be bought and sold. In addition, this site hosts a collection of information about audio equipment provided by manufacturers, as well as a section with critical reviews of audio components and recordings. There is also a professional journal, Sound Practices, that is archived here.

KEYWORDS Audio, Audio Technology, Consumer Audio, Electronics
AUDIENCE Audio Enthusiasts, Audiophiles, Music Industry Professionals, Professional Audio Engineers, Recording Industry Professionals
CONTACT Bob Clark
audioweb@crcgroup.com
FREE

http://www.audioweb.com/Audioweb/default.htm

Australian Music World Wide Web Site ★★★

The Australian Music Web Site is a series of links and pages that exist as a tribute to Australian music. The pages aim to become a useful reference of discographies, lyrics, and the latest news for as many Australian artists as possible. There are (at last count) 880 artists listed and 215 with a page or link. The site is maintained free of charge by Eva Zsigri of the University of Western Sydney-Nepean.

KEYWORDS Australia, Discographies, Meta-Index (Music)
AUDIENCE Australian Music Enthusiasts, Musicians
CONTACT Eva Zsigri
ezsigri@st.nepean.uws.edu.au
FREE

http://www.st.nepean.uws.edu.au/~ezsigri/ausmusic/

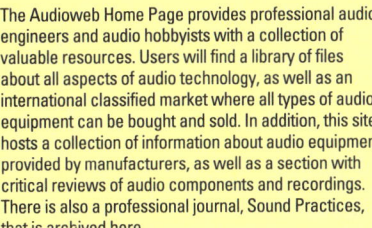

BMI Homepage ★★★

This site provides a valuable online reference of Broadcast Music Incorporated (BMI) publishers, song catalogs, and writers, as well as information about BMI and the services it provides. It will continue to add resources over time.

KEYWORDS Classical Music, Composers, Music Publishers
AUDIENCE Music Librarians, Music Publishers, Music Researchers, Musicians
FREE

http://bmi.com/

BigO Worldwide ★★★

This Singapore-based trendy culture zine does its best to combine the hippest of the hip in two separate categories - American indie-rock and Asian action films. BigO (short for Before I Get Old) is filled with ruminations on the latest comings and goings of bands like Green Day and The Stone Temple Pilots, with a smattering of local Singapore talent tossed into the mix. Top ten charts, interviews, and even downloadable sound files of the latest hits compete for space with features on top Asian filmmakers and new cinematic releases.

KEYWORDS E-Zines, Movies, Punk Rock
AUDIENCE Alternative Music Enthusiasts, Movie Enthusiasts, Popular Culture Enthusiasts
CONTACT S. H. Yong
shyong@singnet.com.sg.
FREE

http://www.asia-online.com/bigo/

The Bodhran Page ★★★

This is a great page to find out about Irish music and the bodhran, a dumlike instrument traditionally made with a wooden body and a goat-skin head.

KEYWORDS Celtic Music, Folk Music, Irish Music
AUDIENCE Folk Music Enthusiasts, Irish Music Enthusiasts
CONTACT Josh Mittleman
mittle@panix.com
FREE

http://www.panix.com/~mittle/bodhran.html

The Bottom Line ★★★★

The Bottom Line, an electronic newsletter for bassists and those interested in this instrument, contains numerous articles on musicians, music and instruments as well as photographs and the occasional interview.

KEYWORDS E-Zines, Music, Musical Instruments, Newsletters, String Instruments
AUDIENCE Bassists, Classical Musicians, Music Historians
CONTACT Janne Himanka
shem@syy.oulu.fi
FREE

http://www.oulu.fi/tbl.html

The Bregman Electro Acoustic Music Studio ★★★★

This is the home page for the Bregman Electro-Acoustic Music studios at Dartmouth College. It contains home pages for the faculty and graduate students in the Electro-Acoustic masters program, and has information regarding the program and research done in the studios.

KEYWORDS Classical Music, Electronic Music, Music Schools
AUDIENCE Classical Music Enthusiasts, Electronic Music Enthusiasts, Music Enthusiasts, Music Students
CONTACT dupras@dartmouth.edu
FREE

http://music.dartmouth.edu/

Chicago Concert Search ★★★★

This is a search tool for the Chicago area and allows one to search for concerts from today to next year and includes all of Chicago's orchestras. There is an optional search for a performer, composer or work available as well.

KEYWORDS Classical Music, Concerts, Symphony Orchestras
AUDIENCE Classical Music Enthusiasts, Music Enthusiasts
CONTACT Andrew Hatchell
a-hatchell@uchicago.edu
FREE

http://student-www.uchicago.edu/users/achatche/music/concerts.html

Classical MIDI Archives ★★★

The Classical MIDI Archives contain an archive of music (sound files) by modern and classical composers. The composers include Bach, Bartok, Beethoven, Chopin, Satie, Saint Saens, Mendelssohn, Mozart, Mussorgsky, Vivaldi, etc. The site also has links to other music pages.

KEYWORDS Classical Music, Composers, MIDI (Musical Instrument Digital Interface), Multimedia, Music Archives
AUDIENCE Educators, Music Students, Musicians
CONTACT Pierre R. Schwob
FREE

http://www.hk.net/~prs/midi.html

Classical Music in Italy ★★★★

This is a comprehensive database of musical events in Italy. It indexes festivals and concerts, theaters, orchestras, musical associations, musical competitions, music press, music education, and musical groups.

KEYWORDS Classical Music, Italy, Music
AUDIENCE Classical Music Enthusiasts, Italy Residents, Music Enthusiasts
CONTACT Deborah Vico
d.vico@fastnet.it
FREE

http://www.fastnet.it/cultura/music_en.htm

Classical Music Online ★★★★

Classical Music Online is a new online database that offers a variety of resources and event listings. The News category lists the latest and greatest classical music news; the Classical CD Titles category allows you to get information on CD's including labels, composers, and instruments. The Artists category describes a variety of classical musicians, the Conductors category describes a variety of classical conductors, and the Classified Ads category allows you to place an ad for a music event. Membership and submission information is available to those interested in adding their classical music related Web page to Classical Music Online.

KEYWORDS Classical Music, Compact Discs (CDs), Music
AUDIENCE Classical Music Enthusiasts, Compact Disc Users, Music Enthusiasts, Music Researchers

CONTACT 3Dvirtualv@crl.com
FREE

http://www.crl.com/~virtualv/cmo/

Classical Music Resources ★★★

Formerly a part of WWW Classical Music Resources, Classical Music Resources has instrument resources listed by instrument. It includes string instruments, flute and piccolo, single reed instruments, double reed instruments, brass players, percussionists, harpists, pianists, and organists. There are also links to other classical music sites on the Net.

KEYWORDS Classical Music, Musical Instruments, Online Directories
AUDIENCE Classical Music Enthusiasts, Music Historians, Music Researchers, Music Students, Musicians
CONTACT Sandy Nicholson
S.Nicholson@ed.ac.uk
FREE

http://www.maths.ed.ac.uk/classical/resources/instruments.html

Colorado Music Festival ★★★★

The Colorado Music Festival strives to fill the summer months with traditional symphonic literature, challenge audiences with contemporary compositions, and stimulate an intellectual experience through the presentation of an annual multi-cultural project. This homepage includes the 1995 Summer Concert Schedule, ticket information, the Statement of Purpose of the Colorado Music Festival, a profile of the Music Director, Giora Bernstein, some quotes about the Colorado Music Festival, and a background on the history of the Colorado Music Festival.

KEYWORDS Classical Music, Colorado, Events, Music Festivals
AUDIENCE Classical Music Enthusiasts, Colorado Residents, Music Enthusiasts, Symphony Enthusiasts
CONTACT aesmoot@aescon.com
FREE

http://www.aescon.com/music/cmf/index.htm

Composers' Desktop Project ★★

The Composers' Desktop Project is committed to making state of the art sound processing software available to those working with sound both in and outside of educational and research institutions. This page, which is under construction, offers no links of any kind.

KEYWORDS Electronic Music, Music, Software, Synthesizers
AUDIENCE Electronic Music Enthusiasts, Music Enthusiasts, Musicians, Synthesizer Users
CONTACT tendrich@cix.compulink.co.uk
FREE

http://www.bath.ac.uk/~masjpf/CDP.html

Computer Entertainment Ireland (C.ENT.I) ★★★

Dedicated to bringing Irish music (of all genres) and other forms of Irish-based entertainment to an international market, C.ENT.I's Web pages offer an online catalog of the items they sell, articles and features on various artists in Ireland and their activities, and a number of compressed sound files—a 'try before you buy' idea for those interested in sampling any of the pieces they read about here.

KEYWORDS Folk Music, Ireland, Irish Music, Music
AUDIENCE Irish, Irish Music Enthusiasts, Music listeners
CONTACT webmaster@centi.ie
FREE

http://starbase.ingress.com/cent/about.html

Computer Music Journal Home Page ★★★

This is the home page for the Computer Music Journal, a publication of the MIT Press dedicated to the exploration of electronic, computer-generated music. Topics include computer music hardware and software, electroacoustic and electronic music, audio reproduction, music representation and cognition, and much more. Users will find a complete table of contents and abstracts for all issues, author guidelines, sample documents and articles from the journal, the source code of music software, and contact information for the Journal's staff. There is also a set of links to other Internet music resources.

KEYWORDS Computer Music, Electronic Music, Music, Music Education
AUDIENCE Computer Musicians, Electronic Musicians, Music Enthusiasts, Music Researchers, Musicians
CONTACT CMJ@CNMAT.Berkeley.edu
FREE

ftp://mitpress.mit.edu/pub/Computer-Music-Journal/CMJ.html

The Concert Connection, Ltd. ★★★

The Concert Connection, Ltd. site provides listings of upcoming concerts in the New York metropolitan area, including venues such as Madison Square Garden, the Meadowlands, and Carnegie Hall. Users can browse a text-based listing, and then use the online order form to purchase tickets for the event of their choice.

KEYWORDS Concerts, Live Music, New York
AUDIENCE Concert Goers, Live Music Enthusiasts, Music Enthusiasts
CONTACT 102163.2234@compuserve.com
FREE

http://usa.net/cge/concerts.htm

Conductors Home Page ★★★★

This home page for conductors provides links to the Orchestralist mailing list, subscription information, a database of new works recommended by Orchestralist subscribers, the Orchestralist archives, and the Choralist mailing list information. It also includes a proposed model on how to incorporate elements of the Internet into music appreciation instruction, links to 'America's Funniest Classical Music Bloopers', Richard Strauss' 'Ten Golden Rules for Conductors', and other conducting resources.

KEYWORDS Classical Music, Conductors, Music
AUDIENCE Classical Music Enthusiasts, Music Enthusiasts, Music Researchers, Symphony Conductors
CONTACT Andrew Levin
alevin@hubcap.clemson.edu
FREE

http://www.clemson.edu/~alevin/Conductors.html

Contemporary Music Info-Junction ★★★★

This site contains an excellent set of links to sources around the world concerned with contemporary art music. Topics include contemporary composition and theory, orchestration and media, reviews, discussion, and information by genre or composer, institutes, organizations and academic programs, and a good music meta-index.

KEYWORDS Classical Music, Composers, Contemporary Music, Music Schools
AUDIENCE Classical Music Enthusiasts, Music Enthusiasts, Music Students
CONTACT bq Mackintosh
bq@Thoughtport.com
FREE

http://www.missouri.edu/~uc489745/music.html

Music Resources

DOS Orchestra ★★★

DOS Orchestra is a publication of the International Conference of Symphony and Opera Musicians (ICSOM) and is published weekly. Four months of issues are kept on the home page and 1994 issues may also be accessed. Free email subscriptions are also available.

- **KEYWORDS** Classical Music, Music Publications, Online Magazines, Opera
- **AUDIENCE** Music Enthusiasts, Musicians
- **CONTACT** dos@icsom.org
- **FREE**

http://www.actrix.gen.nz/users/dgold/do/

Digital Domain's Home Page ★★★

This page is presented by Digital Domain, a CD mastering studio located in New York City. This site offers a tutorial on the technical aspects of mastering a recording for CD format, as well as a collection of links to information of interest to the professional audio community. There is also information on the products and services offered by Digital Domain.

- **KEYWORDS** Audio, Audio Recording, Audio Technology, Digital Audio
- **AUDIENCE** Audiophiles, Digital Audio Engineers, Professional Audio Engineers, Recording Industry Professionals
- **CONTACT** bobkatz@panix.com
- **COST**

http://anansi.panix.com/userdirs/bobkatz/

Dizionario Elementare dell'Opera Registrata (Registered Opera Basic Dictionary) ★★★

Mario Biondi's Recorded Opera Basic (Italian/English) Dictionary reflects his own personal tastes, and comes out of his own collection of CDs, discs and tapes. Besides the dictionary, one can take a look at his last novel (in Italian), 'Un giorno e per tutta la vita.' (One day and for all your life)

- **KEYWORDS** Dictionaries, Opera
- **AUDIENCE** Literary Critics, Opera Enthusiasts, Students
- **CONTACT** Mario Biondi
  mbiondi@micronet.it
- **FREE**

http://joshua.micronet.it/italian/mariobiondi/opere/diz_opera_.html

Dreamtime - The Didjeridu W3 Server ★★★

This site connects you with everything you wanted to know about the Didjeridu, like just what is a Didjeridu anyway? An aboriginal musical instrument, it's a hollowed piece of bamboo four or five feet long which the player blows into trumpet fashion. The site includes some history of Australian aborigines and the instruments they play.

- **KEYWORDS** Folk Music, Musical Instruments, Traditional Music, World Music
- **AUDIENCE** Folk Music Enthusiasts, Music Educators
- **CONTACT** Sean Borman
  borman@nd.edu
- **FREE**

http://www.nd.edu/~sborman/didjeridu/

The Drums And Percussion Page ★★★

This server maintains a collection of information and resources on drums and percussion. Users will find information on different percussion instruments, a message board where users can leave feedback, comments, and information for other users, and a collection of drum grooves in MIDI and chart formats. There is also a directory of percussionists on the Net that users can add themselves to, and a selection of information related to drum instruction and maintenance. Finally, this site maintains a list of drum manufacturers with contact information, and a collection of how-to guides for budding percussionists.

- **KEYWORDS** Drums, Music, Music Education, Musical Instruments
- **AUDIENCE** Drummers, Music Enthusiasts, Music Instructors, Percussionists
- **CONTACT** jlewis@cse.ogi.edu
- **FREE**

http://www.cse.ogi.edu/Drum/

Ellisif's Music & Dance Page ★★★

This site is a good source of information on Early Music and Dance. One of the most impressive features of this site is the collection of Medieval & Renaissance music compositions and arrangements. The site also contains articles on Early Music and dance, as well as links to other resources.

- **KEYWORDS** Classical Music, Dance, Early Music, Music
- **AUDIENCE** Classical Music Enthusiasts, Early Music Enthusiasts, Music Enthusiasts
- **CONTACT** Monica Cellio
  mjc@cs.cmu.edu
- **FREE**

ftp://grand.central.org/afs/transarc.com/public/mjc/html/ef-music-dance.html

The Ensoniq VFX Home Page ★★★★

The Ensoniq VFX Home Page presents resources related to Ensoniq VFX/VFXsd/SD-1 synthesizers. The features of this site include a VFX Users Group Patch Archive, information on the VFX mailing list, info on 'The Transoniq Hacker' the newsletter for all Ensoniq owners, and a Frequently Asked Questions list about the VFX family.

- **KEYWORDS** Electronic Music, MIDI (Musical Instrument Digital Interface), Music
- **AUDIENCE** Computer Musicians, Electronic Music Enthusiasts, MIDI Enthusiasts, Music Enthusiasts
- **CONTACT** Sean McCreary
  mccreary@cs.colorado.edu
- **FREE**

http://www.cs.colorado.edu/~mccreary/vfx/

European Forum of Worldwide Music Festivals ★★★★

This site is for the European Forum of Worldwide Music Festivals (EFWMF), a network of twenty-six major European festivals in the area of world, ethnic, traditional and roots music in fifteen European countries.

- **KEYWORDS** Classical Music, Europe, Events, World Music
- **AUDIENCE** Educators, Music Enthusiasts, Musicians
- **CONTACT** pdegroote@sfinks.be
- **FREE**

http://www.eunet.fi/gmc/efwmf/efwmf.html

Finlandia ★★

The purpose of Finlandia is to offer a forum of discussion on Finnish classical and contemporary music. The list is in English and is open to everyone. A low-volume, but high-quality mailing list, this site includes repertoire lists for Sibelius and Kuula. Submit articles at FINLANDIA@phoenix.oulu.fi.

- **KEYWORDS** Classical Music, Finland, Music
- **AUDIENCE** Classical Music Enthusiasts, Music Enthusiasts, Music Researchers
- **CONTACT** Marko Hotti
  mhotti@paju.oulu.fi
- **FREE**

http://phoenix.oulu.fi/~mhotti/finlandia.html

Flava For Ya Screen! ★★★★

This page known as the Internet Ghetto Blaster, offers information on the latest hip-hop music. In addition to music reviews and samples, this page offers selected reviews of hip-hop classics, as well as offering information on hip-hop that hasn't even hit the streets yet. In addition, this server offers a place for users to leave comments, as well as a collection of links to other hip-hop sites on the Internet (which are few and hard to find).

- **KEYWORDS** Hip-Hop, Internet Ghetto Blaster, Music, Music Reviews
- **AUDIENCE** Hip-Hop Enthusiasts, Music Enthusaists, Music Enthusiasts
- **CONTACT** Clayton Wynter
  cswynter@eniac.seas.upenn.edu
- **FREE**

http://www.seas.upenn.edu/~cswynter/jams.html

Folk Music ★★★

This is a fairly rich resource of links to folk music pages that is accessed through the Time, Inc. server and maintained by the webmaster for the VIBE Magazine home page who carries almost any music-related URL in his database of linked resources.

- **KEYWORDS** Databases, Folk Music
- **AUDIENCE** Folk Music Enthusiasts, Music Educators

Music Resources

CONTACT Vibe Online
vibe@pathfinder.com

FREE

http://www.timeinc.com/vibe/mmm/music_folk.html

Folk Stuff ★★★

Folk Stuff is a Web site dedicated to providing 'how to' and 'where' information for folk musicians, and those designing and building folk and experimental musical instruments including dulcimers, kalimbas, theremins, didjeridus, autoharps and folk flutes.

KEYWORDS Folk Music, Musical Instruments
AUDIENCE Folk Music Enthusiasts, Folk Musicians
CONTACT dshu@telerama.lm.com

FREE

http://www.lm.com/~dshu/folkstuff.html

Fourth Annual Rocky Mountain Ragtime Festival ★★★

The page includes a schedule of events, and a list of performers and hotels. There are also links to additional ragtime sites on the web, and information about the Third Annual Rocky Mountain Ragtime Festival.

KEYWORDS Colorado, Events, Music Festivals, Ragtime
AUDIENCE Colorado Residents, Music Students, Ragtime Music Enthusiasts, Tourists

FREE

http://www.ragtimers.org/~ragtimers/rmrf/

FutureNet - Future Music January 95 ★★★★

This web site is home of the British electronic music magazine Future Music. It has features, reviews, interviews, back issues, and letters to the editor.

KEYWORDS Electronic Music, Future Music, Magazines
AUDIENCE Ambient Music Enthusiasts, Electronic Music Enthusiasts, Experimental Music Enthusiasts
CONTACT ajones@futurenet.co.uk

FREE

http://www.futurenet.co.uk/music/futuremusic.html

General Music Resources on the Internet ★★

This document is a general compilation of information resources focused on music. Topics covered include music history, criticism, genres, instruments, schools, etc. Resources may include Internet/Bitnet Mailing Lists, Gophers, World Wide Web Sites, Mail Servers, Usenet Newsgroups, FTP Archives, Commercial Online Services, and Bulletin Board Systems.

KEYWORDS Classical Music, Music, Music Archives, Recordings
AUDIENCE Music Enthusiasts, Music Historians, Music Librarians, Music Research, Musicians

FREE

ftp://una.hh.lib.umich.edu/inetdirsstacks/acadlist.music

Giant Electrazine ★★★

Each issue of Giant promotes a number of new house, alternative and DJ acts, and includes several short music samples from the profiled artist (in the form of .wav files), comics, a few regular features, and more.

KEYWORDS Alternative Music, Newsletters, Raves
AUDIENCE Alternative Music Enthusiasts, Musicians, Ravers, Rock Fans
CONTACT Editor
giant@phantom.com

FREE

http://www.phantom.com/~giant/hype.html

Global Electronic Music Marketplace Home Page ★★★★

This company purportedly offers a comprehensive search and retrieval mechanism to find out about the latest in music of all kinds. Users can search and 'subscribe' to the database through a simple HTML forms interface. This database will provide links to information on the Internet if it is available, as well as providing information on ordering the music in the database. The GEMM database will update users on new music that matches their interests via email. There is also a directory of music retailers available here, as well as information on telnetting directly into GEMM's database.

KEYWORDS Classical Music, Music, Rock Music
AUDIENCE Music Enthusiasts, Music Industry Professionals
CONTACT admin@gemm.com

FREE

http://gemm.com/

telnet://gemm.com

Grand Royal ★★★

Grand Royal records is the home of the hip-hop/punk group the Beastie Boys, as well as a number of other bands. Their Web page offers band information, audio samples, pictures, movies, and more. In addition, users will find the online version of Grand Royal magazine, a mail-order catalog of albums, t-shirts, and other Grand Royal merchandise, as well as artist tour itineraries.

KEYWORDS Hip-Hop, Music, Record Labels
AUDIENCE Hip-Hop Enthusiasts, Music Enthusiasts, Rock Fans
CONTACT FISTFULAYEN@nando.net

FREE

http://www.nando.net/music/gm/GrandRoyal/

HRRC (Home Recording Rights Coalition) Home Page ★★★

The Home Recording Rights Coalition home page offers users a collection of resources related to home recording and copyright issues. Information on current laws and pending legislation is available, as are profiles of the typical person who tapes audio and video at home. In addition, this site maintains a collection of links to other related resources, as well as information on the Coalition's activities in Washington and elsewhere.

KEYWORDS Consumer Audio, Consumer Electronics, Copyright Law, Digital Audio
AUDIENCE Consumers, Home Recording Enthusiasts
CONTACT hrrc@access.digex.net

FREE

http://now.org/hrrc/hrrc.html

Harmony Central ★★★

Harmony Central is a collection of resources geared toward the working musician and audio engineer. Users will find information on various instruments, both traditional and electronic, as well as specific information on MIDI and computers and music. In addition, this server maintains a collection of links to band pages on the Internet, user reviews of various effects processors available on the market, and files with music and recording techniques and tips.

KEYWORDS Audio, Audio Technology, Music Equipment, Musical Instruments
AUDIENCE Audio Enthusiasts, Music Enthusiasts, Musicians, Professional Audio Engineers
CONTACT Scott Lehman Professional Audio
slehman@mit.edu

FREE

http://harmony-central.mit.edu/

Helsinki University of Technology Acoustics Laboratory ★★★★

The Acoustics Laboratory of the Helsinki University of Technology in Finland offers university-level teaching and research primarily in acoustics and audio signal processing. Their home page includes information on personnel, teaching, research, publications, current activities, FINSIG'95, the Finnish Signal Processing Symposium, sound demos, and links to related topics.

KEYWORDS Acoustics, Electronic Music, Finland, Music Schools
AUDIENCE Audio Enthusiasts, Music Enthusiasts, Music Researchers, Sound Engineers
CONTACT Martti.Rahkila@hut.fi

FREE

http://www.hut.fi/English/HUT/Units/Faculties/S/Acoustics/index.html

Homr- Music Recommendation Service ★★

This is a music rating and selection service. You rate several artists on a scale from 1 to 7, and it tells you what you might like. Bands and musicians referenced include alternative rock group, heavy metal, pop, jazz,

Music Resources

country, classical, etc. It is a personalized system and rather imaginative—type in Tori Amos and the recommended artists include the Thompson Twins, Love and Rockets, Gary Moore, 13 Engines, Violent Femmes, Oscar Peterson, and Frederick Chopin.

KEYWORDS Music Reviews, Progressive Music, Recordings, Rock Music
AUDIENCE Music Enthusiasts, Music Students, Musicians
CONTACT ringo-sysop@media.mit.edu
FREE

http://jeeves.media.mit.edu:80/ringo/

Hype! Alphabetical List of Classical Music Reviews ★★★★

This site provides a small but growing set of classical CD reviews, and the opportunity to submit you own. The site contains reviews of Borodin's Symphony No 2 - Prince Igor (Excerpts), Berlioz's Symphonie Fantastique (Idil Biret, piano), Mozart's Bass Arias (Conal Coad, bass), Tchiakovsky's Early Piano Works, The Prima Voice Sampler (Various Opera Arias), and The Russian Chant for Vespers (Novospassky Monastery Choir), all reviewed by Rita Bogna. Contains links to the Hype! Music Home Page, and a submission form to submit your own reviews.

KEYWORDS Classical Music, Compact Discs (CDs), Music, Music Reviews
AUDIENCE Classical Music Enthusiasts, Compact Disc Users, Music Enthusiasts, Music Librarians
CONTACT joey@hype.com
FREE

http://www.hype.com/music/classic/classic.htm

The ICMA Software Library ★★★★

The ICMA Software Library is an attempt to centralize information concerning non-commercial software currently available for use by computer music researchers and composers. These software listings are maintained for the benefit of the computer music community and in no way should be taken as an endorsement of any kind. The ICMA does not make any warranty as to the accuracy of these listings, nor does it maintain any control over the listed software.

KEYWORDS Computer Music, Computer Software, ICMA
AUDIENCE Computer Music Researchers, Computer Musicians, Electronic Music Enthusiasts, Music Enthusiasts
CONTACT Peter J. Nix
         p.j.nix@leeds.ac.uk
FREE

http://www.leeds.ac.uk/music/NetInfo/ICMA/icma_cat.html

Index of/Bulgaria/sounds/ ★★★

This is an index of Bulgarian sounds with access to clips. It is offered by a Bulgarian student at Rockefeller University in New York, and his home page has tons of links to everything anyone may want to find out about Bulgaria on the Internet.

KEYWORDS Bulgaria, Folk Music, Meta-Index (Music)
AUDIENCE Bulgarians, Music Enthusiasts

CONTACT Penio Penev
         Penev@pisa.Rockefeller.edu
FREE

http://pisa.rockefeller.edu:8080/Bulgaria/sounds/

Institut de Recherche et Coordination Acoustique/Musique ★★★

This site offers a variety of computer music resources from the Institut de Recherche et Coordination Acoustique/Musique in Paris, France. It contains a list and brief description of IRCAM software (digital signal processing, voice and sound synthesis, music composition, wind instrument making, and other programs). There are also calendars of the IRCAM-EIC concerts and tours, information about academic programs, and links to various other music servers.

KEYWORDS Computer Music, Music Composition, Music Software
AUDIENCE Computer Music Researchers, Computer Musicians
CONTACT manager@ircam.fr
FREE

http://www.ircam.fr

Interactive Filter Design ★★★

This is an interactive filter design package, for designing digital filters by the bilinear transform method. Users can fill in the form and press the 'Submit' button, and a filter will be designed for them. The source code (in C) for the programs that do the work is available for browsing or down-loading. The graphs are produced with the help of the excellent gd GIF manipulation library from Quest Protein Database Center.

KEYWORDS Electronic Music, MIDI (Musical Instrument Digital Interface), Music, Synthesizers
AUDIENCE Electronic Music Enthusiasts, MIDI Enthusiasts, Music Enthusiasts, Synthesizer Users
CONTACT fisher@minster.york.ac.uk
FREE

http://Dcpu1.cs.york.ac.uk:6666/fisher/mkfilter/

The International Conference on New Music Notation ★★★★

A conference on New Music Notation was held at the State University of Ghent (Belgium) from October 22-25, 1974. Participation in the Conference was open to anyone professionally interested in new musical notation. This site represents an online version of the report from the conference. Well organized and easy-to-use.

KEYWORDS Classical Music, Contemporary Music, Music, Music Notation
AUDIENCE Contemporary Music Enthusiasts, Music Educators, Music Enthusiasts, Music Researchers
CONTACT Dirk.Moelants@rug.ac.be
FREE

http://next.rug.ac.be/Notatieindex.html

Internet Underground Music Archive ★★★★

One of the first original music archives on the Net, the Internet Underground Music Archive allows bands to upload their music and information for others to hear and read. There are links to labels, and online music-oriented publications, as well as live real time concerts. They've even made MTV.

KEYWORDS Events, Music Archives, Rock Music, Underground Music
AUDIENCE Alternative Music Enthusiasts, Musicians, Rock Fans
CONTACT support@iuma.com
FREE

http://www.iuma.com/

Knitting Factory ★★★
COMMERCIAL

The Knitting Factory Works is an internationally distributed independent record label with offices in New York and Amsterdam. There are links to a CD Catalog, new releases, jazz musicians and bands, as well as who's who at the Knitting Factory and what the future holds for the Web site. Connect also to a recording studio, emailing list, the Knitting Factory Cinema and WFMU 91.1 FM radio station's mail order catalog.

KEYWORDS Music Industry, Record Labels
AUDIENCE Jazz Enthusiasts
FREE

http://www.knittingfactory.com/

The Leo Archive WWW Charts ★★★★

The Leo Archive WWW Charts are an interactive system designed to let WWW users vote for their current favorite song and have it tallied with other users votes. Votes are updated hourly, and tallies reflect votes gathered over the past month.

KEYWORDS Music, Music Research, Recordings, Reference
AUDIENCE Internet Users, Music Enthusiasts, Music Librarians, Music Researchers
CONTACT Christoph Lorenz
         lorenzc@informatik.tu-muenchen.de
FREE

http://www.leo.org/archiv/music/charts/results.html

Leonardo Music Journal Home Page ★★★★

This is the home page of the print journal Leonardo Music Journal (LMJ) with CD, which publishes writings and sounds by artists from diverse areas of the world who are inventing media, implementing developing technologies and expanding the boundaries of experimental aesthetics. The home page includes tables of contents of the print journal, links to sound samples, abstracts of articles, descriptions of the LMJ CD Series, and more. LMJ is a companion volume to Leonardo, the journal of the International Society for the Arts, Sciences and Technology. LMJ is an extension of Leonardo's dedication to fostering connections between the contemporary arts and sciences. LMJ provides a scholarly, international, peer-reviewed forum for musicians, composers, sound artists, scien-

Music Resources

tists, researchers, theoreticians, technicians, and instrument builders to discuss and present their work in a context of mutual influence and exchange.

KEYWORDS Electronic Music, Music, Music Reviews
AUDIENCE Composers, Musicians, Scientists, Sound Artists
CONTACT Grace Sullivan
grace@mercury.sfsu.edu
FREE

http://www-mitpress.mit.edu/Leonardo/isast/journal/hplmj.html

Living Blues Description ★★

Living Blues is a Journal of the African-American Blues Tradition published bimonthly and now listed online and available for subscription through email.

KEYWORDS Blues, Journals
AUDIENCE Blues Enthusiasts, Musicians
FREE

http://imp.cssc.olemiss.edu/blues.html

MKB Music Harmony List ★★★★

This site has links to over 1100 (and growing) music-oriented resources. It is indexed by artists, classical, cultures, discographies, events, instruments, jazz, labels, lists, magazines, places, radio stations, research, resources, studios, and styles. Each of these areas are further broken down into subcategories.

KEYWORDS Classical Music, Events, Jazz, Meta-Index (Music)
AUDIENCE Music Enthusiasts, Music Historians, Music Researchers, Music Students, Musicians
CONTACT Michael K. Breen
webmaster@ucsd.edu
FREE

http://orpheus.ucsd.edu/webmaster/music.html

The Mammoth Music Meta-List ★★★★

The Mammoth Music Meta-List is a very broad and diverse set of links including information local to specific geographical areas, specific artists and some recording labels, lyrics and discographies, reviews and top-N charts, specific instruments, styles/genres of music, radio stations and shows, and performances. The site also includes sounds, MIDI and other computer music, information on and access to national and regional retail outlets, music festivals, music schools, libraries, and research archives, other music services and other (similar) collections of music resources.

KEYWORDS Classical Music
AUDIENCE Classical Music Enthusiasts, Music Enthusiasts, Music Researchers, Music Students
CONTACT vibe@pathfinder.com
FREE

http://www.pathfinder.com/@@3kjx7wAAAAAAAAjq/vibe/mmm/music.html

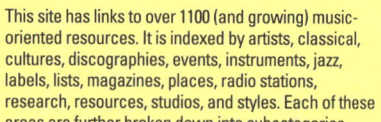

Musi-Cal ★★★★

This server allows users to find out about the latest musical events worldwide. Users can implement a search via HTML forms, specifying dates, musical genres, geographical areas and individual artists. The server will return with a list of known events that match these criteria. In addition, users can add information on events that the Musi-Cal database doesn't already know about. This server also allows geographic distance searching as well, so users are capable of searching for all musical events within 10 miles of New York, for example.

KEYWORDS Contemporary Music, Events, Music, New York
AUDIENCE Live Music Enthusiasts, Music Enthusiasts, Popular Music Enthusiasts
CONTACT Skip Montanaro
skip@automatrix.com
FREE

http://www.automatrix.com/concerts/

Music Instruction Software ★★★

Designed to provide teachers with access to music instruction software programs, most of the pointers here are to FTP sites and downloadable shareware. There are also several links to other Web sites of related interest.

KEYWORDS Music Education, Music Software
AUDIENCE Educators, Music Teachers
CONTACT Brent Hugh
BHugh@CSTP.UMKC.EDU
FREE

http://www.cstp.umkc.edu/users/bhugh/musici.html

The Music Library Gopher ★★

This gopher provides access to the resources of the Music Library of Indiana University. The resources online include the ability to browse through the library's bibliographies of recent acquisitions of books, scores, and recordings. The server also gives access to the Music Library Association Clearinghouse, a mechanism to distribute information related to music librarianship. Much of the information accessed by this gopher hole is being moved to a World Wide Web site.

KEYWORDS Libraries, Music Archives, Music Education
AUDIENCE Music Enthusiasts, Music Librarians, Music Researchers
CONTACT ml-tech@theme.music.indiana.edu
FREE

gopher://theme.music.indiana.edu/

Music Research Information System ★★★★

This gopher hole contains information on music education, music psychology, music therapy, and music medicine. The site is a project of Institute for Music Research at the University of Texas at San Antonio. The information includes information about the Institute for Music Research, connections to databases, archives of music software, and publications regarding musical research.

KEYWORDS Music, Music Education, Music Research, Music Software
AUDIENCE Health Care Professionals, Music Researchers, Music Students, Psychologists
CONTACT Kimberly Walls
kwalls@lonestar.utsa.edu
FREE

gopher://runner.utsa.edu:3000/

Music Resources on the Internet ★★★★

This meta-list has links to hundreds of music-oriented Web sites, gopher sites, FTP sites and telnet sites. The resources are listed according to several criteria such as geography, variety of music, and nature of the producing institution. The categories include academic and non-academic sites, artist-specific sites, and other indices.

KEYWORDS Classical Music, Meta-Index (Music), Music Research, Rock Music
AUDIENCE Music Enthusiasts, Music Researchers, Music Students, Musicians, Musicologists
CONTACT webmaster@www.music.indiana.edu
FREE

http://www.music.indiana.edu/misc/music_resources.html

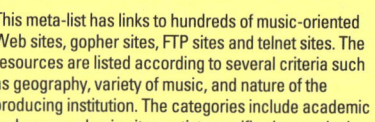

Music West ★★

Music West is the Home page for the Music West Conference, Festival and Music Show dedicated to the Convergence of Music and Technology. The conference schedule for '96 will be posted at this site. The site allows users to download MPEG soundbites from bands that played at the festival, links to music 'zines and other related spots on the Internet.

KEYWORDS Events, Internet
AUDIENCE Music Distributors, Musicians
CONTACT @musicwest.com
FREE

http://www.musicwest.com/

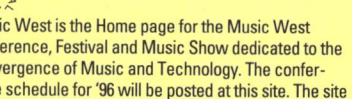

Music Sources ★★

This Music Sources Webpage contains information about the Berkeley, California organization's workshops and classes, collection of replicas of historic instruments, Music Sources library, and more. It offers one link to its concert and event schedules.

KEYWORDS Classical Music, Early Music, Events, Music History
AUDIENCE Californians, Classical Music Enthusiasts, Early Music Enthusiasts, Music Enthusiasts
FREE

http://www.catalog.com/virtual/jr/msrc.html

Pleasures And Wayward Distractions ★★★

Pleasures And Wayward Distractions is a home page for 89 Records, a Salt Lake City, Utah-based independent record label. You can check out their recording artists and visit sites with related music, music production, and other media. (The page also includes a warning about offensive language, nudity, violence, adult situations etc. that may be present at this site.)

KEYWORDS Alternative Music, Record Labels

Music Resources

AUDIENCE Adults, Artists, Consumers, Internet Users, Musicians
CONTACT Roger Weeks
smegma@xmission.com
FREE

http://www.xmission.com/~smegma

RISM-US ★★★★

This RISM (Répertoire International des Sources Musicales) Office collects information from libraries in the United States about music manuscripts, printed music, and libretti from the years 1580-1825. The Office makes available cataloguing for manuscripts and libretti through Internet-accessible databases in the United States free of charge. It also maintains several additional information files that may be of interest to librarians and scholars. Online resources include the RISM-US Music Manuscripts Database, RISM Libretto Project, RISM Names Authority File RISM-L, and the RISM news list maintained by the US RISM Office.

KEYWORDS Classical Music, Music History, Music Manuscripts, Opera
AUDIENCE Classical Music Enthusiasts, Music Enthusiasts, Music Librarians, Music Researchers, Music Students
CONTACT rismhelp@rism.harvard.edu
FREE

http://www.rism.harvard.edu/RISM/

Rare Groove ★★★

This site is an information center for rare music, independent artists and labels, and alternative music. Samples of recordings are available to listen to over the Net and it is possible to order recordings, read record reviews, post to a bulletin board, or connect to other music-related sites.

KEYWORDS Alternative Music, Music Reviews, Newsletters, Recordings
AUDIENCE Alternative Music Enthusiasts, Multimedia Enthusiasts, Pop Music Enthusiasts
CONTACT rgmag@media.mit.edu
FREE

http://rg.media.mit.edu/RG/RG.html

The Roland SoundCanvas Users Group ★★★

The SoundCanvas Users group was formed on the Internet in June of 1994 so composers and musicians who use the Roland SoundCanvas family of synthesizers could share their music with each other and those who are interested. The group's goal is to compile and release in one archive a collection of new and original music done on and for the SoundCanvas by as wide a variety of composers as possible, thus making available new and possibly interesting musical creations.

KEYWORDS Composing, Electronic Music, Music
AUDIENCE Computer Musicians, Electronic Music Enthusiasts, MIDI Enthusiasts, Music Enthusiasts
CONTACT Paul Stillwell
Paul_G._Stillwell@intacc.web.net
FREE

http://www.eeb.ele.tue.nl/midi/scgroup/index.html

SCA Music and Dance Homepage ★★★

This site is a good starting point for links and information on Early Music and Dance. Headings include Early Music, Renaissance Dance, Non-Western Music and Dance, Songs, Mailing Lists and Archives, SCA Dance, Lute, Middle-Eastern Music, Bardic, and Morris Dancing.

KEYWORDS Classical Music, Dance, Early Music, Music
AUDIENCE Classical Music Enthusiasts, Dance Enthusiasts, Early Music Enthusiasts, Music Enthusiasts
CONTACT Greg Lindahl
gl8f@virginia.edu
FREE

http://fermi.clas.virginia.edu/~gl8f/music_and_dance.html

A Short History of British Pop Music ★★★

This site covers in great detail an extensive history of British pop music. British pop music was quite different from the American. In the contents you will find groups and singers who entered and exited the pop charts of the UK from the fifties through the end of the sixties - the singers who influenced several generations of music listeners. You can read about what music the Beatles listened to and who they were influenced by.

KEYWORDS Britain, Music, Music Industry
AUDIENCE British Pop Music Enthusiasts, Music Enthusiasts, Music Researchers
CONTACT Saki
saki@evolution.bchs.uh.edu
FREE

ftp://bobcat.bbn.com/pub/beatles/welcome/britpop1

SKR Classical Homepage ★★★★

SKR Classical is located in Ann Arbor, Michigan, and offers a broad selection of study scores and a wide ranging, in-depth selection of compact discs, cassettes and videos comprising over 30,000 titles. The site also includes free in-store concerts, music appreciation lectures, laserdisc opera and concert viewings, and receptions for visiting artists. This site contains access to the online catalog and subscription information for the newsletter 'skrclassical.'

KEYWORDS Classical Music, Compact Discs (CDs), Events, Music
AUDIENCE Classical Music Enthusiasts, Compact Disc Users, Music Enthusiasts
CONTACT questions@skrclassical.schoolkids.com
COST

http://www.schoolkids.com/skr/classical/

The Somewhat Unofficial 'The Bottom Line' Home Page ★★★

This page maintains an archive of The Bottom Line, an electronic newsletter for electric and acoustic bassists. In addition to the complete archive of back issues found at this site, users will find a collection of bass-related FAQs. This site also hosts many instructional files designed to teach users different aspects of playing and maintaining both acoustic and electric basses. Users can also obtain the addresses to submit material for publication in The Bottom Line newsletter here.

KEYWORDS E-Zines, Music, Musical Instruments, Newsletters
AUDIENCE Acoustic Bass Players, Electric Bass Players, Music Enthusiasts, Musicians
CONTACT Brennan Underwood
elric@unm.edu
FREE

http://www.unm.edu/~elric/music/tbl.html

Sound Wire ★★★

The Sound Wire web server allows users to preview new music, find information about musicians, and purchase albums online for mail-order delivery. Each available album has a short description, and many have MPEG sound files and JPEG album covers available for download. Sound Wire allows users to purchase with credit cards (using PGP encryption and email or by calling a toll-free number), Netcash, or using the First Virtual Internet Payment System.

KEYWORDS Internet Shopping, Music, Recordings, Storefronts
AUDIENCE Internet Users, Music Enthusiasts, Musicians
CONTACT feedback@soundwire.com
FREE

http://soundwire.com/

System-X ★★★★

System-X is 'an Internet system aimed specifically at artists working in the electronic domain (i.e. electronic and computer music, video, computer graphics, interactive art, and so on).' This homepage includes System-X Information, artwork available on sysx, FTP directories on sysx, Sysx aims and objectives, and SoundSite, a WWW publication for sound artists, practitioners and theorists and links to other sites - not sorted or indexed.

KEYWORDS Electronic Music, MIDI (Musical Instrument Digital Interface), Music, Synthesizers
AUDIENCE Electronic Music Enthusiasts, MIDI Enthusiasts, Music Enthusiasts, Synthesizer Users
CONTACT admin@sysx.apana.org.au
FREE

http://sysx.apana.org.au/

Thora-Zine Online ★★★

The editors of Thora-zine recently put up these Web pages as an electronic complement to their magazine. While full issue contents are not available here, selected articles are offered, as are sample clips from the magazine's flexidisc. Some of the bands featured are L7, Santana, Beck, Joey Ramone, Man or Astroman, and Supersuckers.

KEYWORDS E-Zines, Newsletters, Punk Rock, Rock Music
AUDIENCE Musicians, Rock Fans
FREE

http://www.eden.com/zines/thorazine.html

Music Resources

The TuneWeb ★★★

This is an extensive list of connections to tunes/clips of folk music, traditional music and various ethnic music, including jigs, marches and waltzes among others.

Keywords Folk Music, Traditional Music
Audience Ethnic Music Enthusiasts, Folk Music Enthusiasts
Contact support@ece.ucdavis.edu
Free

http://www.ece.ucdavis.edu/~darsie/tunebook.html

The USA Used Electronic Music Gear Price List ★★★★

This list represents asking prices on used synthesizing and recording gear taken from rec.music.makers.synth and rec.music.makers.marketplace. It is meant as a guide for buyers and sellers. The equipment is listed alphabetically by manufacturer. Prices are organized by date. Commercial postings are allowed.

Keywords Electronic Music, Music
Audience Computer Musicians, Electronic Music Enthusiasts, MIDI Enthusiasts, Music Enthusiasts
Contact afo@an.hp.com
Free

http://www.pitt.edu/~cjp/usedgear.html

The Ultimate Band List— Main Page ★★★★

The Ultimate Band List is an interactive list of music links to hundreds of different groups. Visitors can peruse previous links or add new ones. It is indexed alphabetically, by musical genre, and by type of resource. Genres covered include jazz, blues, r & b, classical, new age, vocals, dance, techno, rap, pop, rock, alternative, country, hard rock, metal, and industrial.

Keywords Meta-Index (Music), Music, Music Research
Audience Internet Users, Music Enthusiasts, Music Librarians, Music Researchers
Contact ubl@american.recordings.com
Free

http://american.recordings.com/wwwofmusic/ubl.html

VIBEonline ★★★

This is the online version of VIBE magazine. VIBE chronicles and celebrates urban music and the American youth culture that inspires and consumes it. Key sections of VIBE focus on music, fashion, politics, media, technology and sports. The full text and some pictures from the print magazine are included here, as well as sound clips and video samples from some of the latest recording stars and movie soundtracks. Other features of VIBEonline are a best of the Web page, back issues from June of 1994, and a page of give-aways and promotions. There can be frequent delays when trying to connect with this page.

Keywords E-Zines, Movies, Music, Urban Music
Audience Generation X, Men, Rap Music Enthusiasts, Women
Contact Chan Suh, Webmaster suh@hand.timeinc.com
Free

http://www.vibe.com

Virtual Radio Home Page ★★★

A space for bands to advertise music by providing samples for browsers to download. Some samples are a part of the song, some have an entire song. Contains information on how to order music and contact various bands.

Keywords Pop Music, Radio, Recordings, Rock Music
Audience Alternative Music Enthusiasts, Music Enthusiasts
Contact vradio@ugly.microserve.net
Free

http://www.microserve.net/vradio/

Web Wide World Of Music ★★★

The Web Wide World of Music is a meta-index of many music-related Web sites. It contains links to information on over 500 bands, a music discussion forum, and a music trivia quiz. It also lets people post information about their band or concert dates.

Keywords Alternative Music, Classical Music, Meta-Index (Music), Rock Music
Audience Alternative Music Enthusiasts, Music Enthusiasts, Music Researchers
Contact ubl@american.recordings.com
Free

http://american.recordings.com/wwwofmusic

William Ransom Hogan Archive of New Orleans Jazz ★★★

The Hogan Jazz Archive at Tulane University is well-regarded resource for New Orleans Jazz research. The collection includes oral history interviews, recorded music, photographic collections and film, sheet music and orchestrations and numerous files containing manuscript materials, clippings, and bibliographic references. The online site has contact information, a list of holdings and a music exerpt.

Keywords Jazz, Music Archives
Audience Jazz Enthusiasts, Musicians
Contact Bruce Boyd Raeburn raeburn@mailhost.tcs.tulane.edu
Free

http://www.tulane.edu/~lmiller/JazzHome.html

Wood and Wire - Indie Music on the WWW ★★★★

This service is run by musicians for musicians, music industry professionals and music lovers. This site provides links to pages for bands like Ashtray Boy and Cuddlefish, as well as links to online fanzines and some record labels. They also provide links to other music sites. They run an online store to sell the music of some of the bands.

Keywords Music Reviews, Online Shopping, Record Labels, Rock Music
Audience Alternative Music Enthusiasts, Musicians, Rock Fans
Contact tallis@magna.com.au
Free

http://www.ether.com.au/woodwire/

World Of Audio ★★★★

This site is an excellent collection of resources of interest to the professional audio enthusiast. Users can search the site by keyword, or browse through the list of offerings, such as information on MIDI and digital audio equipment, material on audio file formats, a collection of tips, tricks, and techniques for recording quality sounds, and a directory of professional audio equipment manufacturers. There is also a searchable database of audio engineers and studios that can be added to by those working in the industry.

Keywords Audio, Audio Technology, Digital Audio, Electronics
Audience Audio Enthusiasts, Audiophiles, Professional Audio Engineers, Recording Industry Professionals
Contact Brian Clark, Tammy Kearns bclark@magicnet.net, tkearns@magicnet.net
Free

http://www.magicnet.net/rz/world_of_audio/woa.html

 Worldwide Internet Live Music Archive (WILMA) ★★★

This site contains information on concert venues and tour itineraries, and provides reviews of selected concerts. Users can select from the 1200+ available bands to see tour dates, or find out about venues in over 200 cities in the U.S., Canada, and Europe. Pop, classical and jazz music events are covered, but the primary focus is on rock groups.

Keywords Classical Music, Concerts, Music Reviews, Rock Music
Audience Concert Goers, Rock Fans
Contact Chris McBride mcbride@earthlink.net
Free

http://underground.net/Wilma/

The Yamaha TX-16w WWW Page ★★★

This is the HTML page for the Yamaha TX-16w Digital Wave Filtering Sampler. It was created by Steven Selick to allow easier access to the archives for the TX-16w mailing list, and the samples and programs available there.

Keywords Electronic Music, Music
Audience Computer Musicians, Electronic Music Enthusiasts, MIDI Enthusiasts, Music Enthusiasts

Music Resources – Musical Groups

Arts & Music

CONTACT Sven Schroter
schroeter@ls7.informatik.uni-dortmund.de

FREE

http://ls7-www.informatik.uni-dortmund.de/html/tx16w.html

Musical Groups

See also
Arts & Music · *Music Resources*
Arts & Music · *Musicians*

A Band & His Dog ★★

This is the home page for A Band and His Dog, a folk-rock band from Salt Lake City, Utah. It's still under construction, but it will have band information, contact information, and sound files.

KEYWORDS Contemporary Music, Rock Music, Utah
AUDIENCE Folk Music Enthusiasts, Rock Fans, Utah Residents

FREE

http://linex.com:80/~dylan/band/band.html

A Nirvana Home Page ★★★

This site is dedicated to the popular rock band Nirvana. It has an album list and lyrics, neither of which include UNPLUGGED. (However, it does have a history that includes the release of UNPLUGGED.) It also has a bootleg reference guide, and some transcripts of interviews, as well as guitar tabs and links to more resources, Nirvana and otherwise.

KEYWORDS Alternative Music, Discographies, Rock Music
AUDIENCE Alternative Music Enthusiasts, Complainers, Rock Fans
CONTACT Mr. Guy Smiley
smiley@seds.lpl.arizona.edu

FREE

http://seds.lpl.arizona.edu/~smiley/nirvana/home.html

Alan Braverman's Beatles Page ★★★

Alan Braverman's Beatles Page maintains a collection of information and resources related to the '60s supergroup. Users will find archives of images, lyrics, and music, as well as information on some of the many myths surrounding the group at the height of their poopularity. This server also offers links to other places on the Internet where users will find Beatles information.

KEYWORDS Beatles (The), Lyrics, Rock Music
AUDIENCE Beatles Fans, Music Enthusiasts, Popular Music Enthusiasts, Rock Fans
CONTACT Alan Braverman
alanb@ncsa.uiuc.edu

FREE

http://turtle.ncsa.uiuc.edu/alan/beatles.html

All Together Now - A Compendium of Beatles Books ★★★

This site contains a list of Beatles related publications and are listed in order of author name, then by title. In alphabetical listing by author you will find books such as The Beatles Film, published in 1964, which covers the making of Hard Day's Night produced by the Sun Newspaper group. In alphabetical title order you can find an in depth book titled 'All You Need is Love' - a moderately balanced view of the interwoven lives of our Fab Four from about the time of the Rooftop concert right up until John Lennon's murder. An acceptable starting point for more serious reading. There are over 100 titles on this list so be prepared to spend some time here.

KEYWORDS Beatles (The), Books, Pop Music, Rock Music
AUDIENCE Beatles Fans, Book Dealers, Book Readers
CONTACT Stephen Carter
S.Carter@central.sussex.ac.uk

FREE

ftp://bobcat.bbn.com/pub/beatles/welcome/allbooks

The Allman Brothers Band ★★★

This web site is dedicated to pioneering Southern rock band The Allman Brothers. It has current band news, fan resources, and an archive section.

KEYWORDS Contemporary Music, Musical Groups, Rock Music
AUDIENCE Blues Enthusiasts, Country Music Enthusiasts, Guitar Music Enthusiasts, Rock Fans
CONTACT abb-web@nwu.edu

FREE

http://pubweb.acns.nwu.edu/~slee/allman/abb.html

Altraworld - The Unofficial Orb Home Page ★★★★

This home page is dedicated to British techno act the Orb. It has a discography, bootleg discography, artwork, song samples, articles, and screen savers.

KEYWORDS Britain
AUDIENCE Ambient Music Enthusiasts, Electronic Music Enthusiasts, Experimental Music Enthusiasts, Techno Music Enthusiasts
CONTACT wally@hyperreal.com

FREE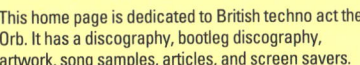

http://hyperreal.com/music/artists/orb/www/index.html

American Music Club Web Page ★★★

This site is dedicated to the Bay Area band American Music Club. This site has a discography, the official biography, some articles and interviews, and instructions on how to join the American Music Club mailing list.

KEYWORDS Alternative Music, Discographies, Music Organizations, Rock Music

AUDIENCE Alternative Music Enthusiasts, Californians, Rock Fans
CONTACT L. Jason Colton
ljason@wam.umd.edu

FREE

http://www.wam.umd.edu/~ljason/amc/

An Excess of INXS ★★★

This text-only page has a wealth of resources about the band INXS. In addition to information from the INXS mailing list, users will find discography and biography information, interviews and other articles on the band, and the latest news, information, and tour dates available. There is also a collection of lyrics, pictures, and guitar tablature, as well as a section with links to other Internet INXS resources.

KEYWORDS Alternative Music, Music, Rock Music
AUDIENCE Alternative Music Enthusiasts, Music Enthusiasts, Pop Music Enthusiasts, Rock Fans
CONTACT Neil Kothari
nak6@columbia.edu

FREE

http://www.columbia.edu/~nak6/inxs.html

Answers to Frequently Asked Questions about Camper Van Beethoven ★★★

This Web site is a FAQ for the defunct underground rock band Camper Van Beethoven. The FAQ also deals with some of Camper Van Beethoven's offshoot bands, such as the Monks of Doom and the increasingly popular Cracker. Some of the band members have contributed answers for this FAQ.

KEYWORDS Alternative Music, Rock Music
AUDIENCE Alternative Music Enthusiasts, Californians, Rock Fans
CONTACT John Relph
relph@presto.ig.com

FREE

http://www.bio.net/music/cbv-faq.html

The Atomic Underground ★★

This home page is dedicated to the funky alternative band Fishbone. It has a discography and some sound files.

KEYWORDS Alternative Music, Music, Rock Music
AUDIENCE Alternative Music Enthusiasts, Funk Music Enthusiasts, Punk Rock Enthusiasts, Rock Fans
CONTACT cschatz@gladstone.uoregon.edu

FREE

http://gladstone.uoregon.edu:80/~cschatz/fishbone.html

Austin Horn Ensemble ★★★

The Austin Horn Ensemble (AHE) is a group of French Horn players from all walks of life who play a variety of music, but with horns only - which means that you have horns playing bass, tenor, and alto parts. Current membership fluctuates between 10 and 15 players. The AHE performs several times a year, most often for the sponsoring organization, St. Martin's Lutheran Church in Austin, Texas. The AHE is a non-profit group and funds go to purchase new supplies such as music for the group, not to individual members. This website includes information on membership, rehearsals, a concert schedule and photo.

Keywords Classical Music, Musical Instruments
Audience Classical Music Enthusiasts, French Horn Enthusiasts, Music Enthusiasts, Texas Residents
Free

http://www.io.com/~rboerger/AHE.html

Budgie Homepage ★★★

This web site is dedicated to early British metal pioneers Budgie. It has a discography of their early recordings, reprints of reviews and a history of the band.

Keywords Music Reviews, Progressive Music, Rock Music
Audience Heavy Metal Fans, Rock Fans
Contact Brandon Whitcher
brandon@stat.washington.edu
Free

http://www.stat.washington.edu/brandon/music/budgie.html

Babes With Axes Home Page ★★★★

This home page is dedicated to Babes With Axes, a Eugene, Oregon folk music group. It has a band history, information about each of the members, tour dates, and sound files.

Keywords Contemporary Music, Folk Music, Musical Groups
Audience Alternative Music Enthusiasts, Folk Music Enthusiasts, Oregon Residents
Contact Gordon Kelley
gordon_k@efn.org
Free

http://www.efn.org/~gordon_k/babes.html

Bad Brains ★★★

This site is set up to provide information on the hardcore and reggae combination band Bad Brains. Users will find cover art, audio samples, and the latest news and information on the band. This site also provides links to other pages with Bad Brains information.

Keywords Hardcore Music, Punk Music, Reggae Music
Audience Bad Brains Enthusiasts, Hard Rock Fans, Reggae Enthusiasts
Contact Brains@ix.netcom.com
Free

http://www.computel.com/~whatsup/brains/

The Bad Examples ★★★

This Web site contains the home page of the Chicago rock band, The Bad Examples. It contains a discography, some lyrics and some sound files.

Keywords Contemporary Music, Musical Groups, Rock Music
Audience Illinois Residents, Rock Fans
Free

http://turtle.ncsa.uiuc.edu:80/bad-examples/

Bad Livers ★★★

This Web site is the home page of the Austin, Texas folk band, Bad Livers. It has a band history, discography, and tour information.

Keywords Texas, Folk Music, Musical Groups
Audience Texas Residents, Folk Music Enthusiasts
Contact info@southern.com
Free

http://www.southern.com/southern/band/BADLI/index.html

Bad Religion ★★★★

This Web site is devoted to the long-existing California punk rock band Bad Religion. It contains a discography with lyrics, guitar tabs, interviews, pictures, and a section on Epitaph records, the band's independent label. And the layout is simple and striking.

Keywords Contemporary Music, Musical Groups, Punk Rock, Rock Music
Audience Alternative Music Enthusiasts, Punk Rock Enthusiasts, Rock Fans
Contact Patrick LE POULTIER
lepoulti@enstb.enst-bretagne.fr
Free

http://nebuleuse.enst-bretagne.fr/~lepoulti/BAD.RELIGION/

Barefoot Serpents ★★★

This is the Web site of the Barefoot Serpents, a Pittsburgh, PA (USA) rock band. It has pictures, a list of upcoming shows and current band news.

Keywords Contemporary Music, Rock Music
Audience Pennsylvania Residents, Rock Fans
Contact barefoot-request@cs.pitt.edu
Free

http://www.pitt.edu/~infidel/barefoot/

Barenaked Heaven ★★★

This the official homepage of Canadian alternative band Barenaked Ladies. It has information on band members, an FAQ in progress, a discography, tour dates, some lyrics, guitar tabs and pictures. It also has information on how to contact the band and a place to contribute Barenaked Ladies concert stories.

Keywords Canada, Contemporary Music, Rock Music
Audience Alternative Music Enthusiasts, Canadians, Rock Fans
Contact Gnat Hammerstrom
gnat@yar.cs.wisc.edu
Free

http://yar.cs.wisc.edu:80/~gnat/bnl/

Bauhaus Discography ★★★

This is a Web site dedicated to the gothic pioneers Bauhaus. It contains a huge discography of Bauhaus and all of its spin-off groups.

Keywords Alternative Music, Rock Music
Audience Alternative Music Enthusiasts, Gothic Rock Enthusiasts, Rock Fans
Contact Greg Clow
ecurrent@sizone.pci.on.ca
Free

http://gothic.acs.csulb.edu:8080/Gothic/Text/bauhaus-discog.html

Be Happy or Die! ★★★

This web page is devoted to the techno-pop band Art of Noise. It has a discography, reprints of the band's album liner notes, and some pictures.

Keywords Music, Musical Groups, Rock Music
Audience Alternative Music Enthusiasts, Dance Music Enthusiasts, Pop Music Enthusiasts
Contact Jason Ross
jross@emba.uvm.edu
Free

http://www.emba.uvm.edu/~jross/aonhome.html

Beatles Covers List ★★★★

This Web site is dedicated to the Beatles. It is an extensive list attempting to name every artist who ever played or recorded a Beatles song. This august group includes Aerosmith, Wes Montgomery, Otis Redding, Ramsey Lewis Trio, Sting, Quincy Jones, Count Basie, Billy Preston, Keely Smith, Johnny Tedesco, Ten Tuff Guitars, David Bowie, Duke Ellington, Bob Marley, Chubby Checker, Chet Atkins, Xaviar Cugat, Dweezil Zappa, and Frank Sinatra.

Keywords Beatles (The), Contemporary Music, Recordings, Rock Music
Audience Beatles Fans, Pop Music Enthusiasts, Rock Fans
Contact Ross Clement
clemenr@westminster.ac.uk.
Free

http://www.wmin.ac.uk/~clemenr/covers/covers.html

Bel Canto ★★★

This web site is dedicated to Bel Canto, a Norwegian pop band. It has background information, reprints of articles and lyrics.

Keywords Contemporary Music, Norway, Pop Music
Audience Alternative Music Enthusiasts, Electronic Music Enthusiasts, Pop Music Enthusiasts, Technocrats
Contact Kjetil T. Homme
Free

http://math-www.uio.no/bel-canto/

Musical Groups

Believer info ★★★
This Web site contains the home page of Believer—a progressive-rock Christian metal band. It contains a brief description of the band, and a discography.
- KEYWORDS: Christian Music, Progressive Music, Rock Music
- AUDIENCE: Heavy Metal Fans, Progressive Music Enthusiasts, Rock Fans
- CONTACT: Brian "Mel" Meloon / bmeloon@geom.umn.edu
- FREE

http://www.geom.umn.edu/~bmeloon/music/bandinfo/believer.html

Best Beatles Bootleg CD's ★★★
This site contains a list of Beatles bootlegged CD's, chosen because of sound quality and/or historic performance. The list is categorized into early Beatles, live performances, BBC radio shows, studio outtakes and home demos, get back sessions and miscellaneous.
- KEYWORDS: Beatles (The), Musical Groups, Rock Music
- AUDIENCE: Beatles Fans, Music Enthusiasts, Rock Fans
- CONTACT: Mario Giannella / mg@cesr10.1ns.cornell.edu
- FREE

ftp://bobcat.bbn.com/pub/beatles/misc/gudboots

Big Ass Truck ★★★
The Big Ass Truck Homepage is the only place to get all the Big Ass Truck information you need. Tour information, full music listening section, merchandise, band member email, art gallery, and more! The busy graphics make it a bit difficult to read.
- KEYWORDS: Music Resources, Soul Music
- AUDIENCE: Consumers, Music Enthusiasts, Musicians, Students (High School/ College), Teenagers
- CONTACT: Robby Grant / Steve Selvidge / URDGRANT@MSUVX1.MEMPHIS.EDU /
- FREE

http://www.towery.com/BigAssTruck/

Big Home Orchestra Home Page ★★★
This home page is dedicated to the Australian band Big Home Orchestra. It has a discography, and a biography with links to associated bands.
- KEYWORDS: Australia, Contemporary Music, Rock Music
- AUDIENCE: Alternative Music Enthusiasts, Australians, Rock Fans
- CONTACT: Thomas Tallis / tallis@magna.com.au
- FREE

http://www.magna.com.au/woodwire/BHO.html

Black Crowes Home Page ★★★★
This Web site is dedicated to the rock and roll band, The Black Crowes. It has a FAQ, tour dates past and current, discography, articles, and a CD bootleg review section. It also has fan club and mailing list information.
- KEYWORDS: Contemporary Music, Musical Groups, Rock Music, Blues
- AUDIENCE: Rock Fans
- CONTACT: Doug Fierro / fierro@sv.legent.com
- FREE

http://www.sfm.com/rwi/listeners/black-crowes/

Blue House ★★
This is the Web site for songwriters Marlies de Veer and Amy Beasley who have collaborated both as a duo and with various bands for a year. They joined together with Don Dias to form the Blue House group. One can listen to Blue House music cuts, order merchandise and find general information about the group here.
- KEYWORDS: Folk Music
- AUDIENCE: Folk Music Enthusiasts, Music Educators
- FREE

http://www.ipac.net/HW/bluehouse/

Blues Traveler Home Page ★★★★
This page is a central location for information on the band Blues Traveler. It contains a large amount of material on the band, such as personal and crew information, articles, a discography of releases with bootlegs and 'official releases,' as well as some links to other Internet resources such as the Blues Traveler mailing list. There is also an archive of guitar tablature, lyrics, and band images for the diehard Blues Traveler fan.
- KEYWORDS: Blues, Guitar, Music
- AUDIENCE: Blues Enthusiasts, Music Enthusiasts, Rock Fans
- CONTACT: Misha Rutman / misha+@cmu.edu
- FREE

http://www.contrib.andrew.cmu.edu/usr/mr6d/blues.traveler.html

The Bobcat Archive ★★★★
This Web site contains direct links to a FTP site containing information culled from the rec.music.beatles newsgroup. It also contains general Beatles information, bootleg information, pictures of album covers, and related miscellaneous stuff.
- KEYWORDS: Beatles (The), Contemporary Music, Rock Music
- AUDIENCE: Beatles Fans, Pop Music Enthusiasts, Rock Fans
- CONTACT: jonas@cs.rochester.edu
- FREE

http://www.cs.rochester.edu/users/grads/jonas/beatles/bobcat.html

Bourbon Tabernacle Choir ★★★
The Bourbon Tabernacle Choir of Nova Scotia, Canada has a Web site through the University of King's College. There is not too much detail here, but one can listen to some sound clips, find out the tour dates, book the band, order albums and join some newsgroups as well as link to other networks and newsgroups.
- KEYWORDS: Choral Singing, Music Archives
- AUDIENCE: Canadians, Music Enthusiasts
- FREE

http://www.ukings.ns.ca/btc/BTC.HTML

Butt Trumpet Home Page ★★★
This is the home page of the punk band Butt Trumpet. It has a couple of sound files, tour dates, and Butt Trumpet comix.
- KEYWORDS: Contemporary Music, Punk Rock, Rock Music
- AUDIENCE: Alternative Music Enthusiasts, Punk Rock Enthusiasts, Rock Fans
- CONTACT: lkhort@paul.spu.edu
- FREE

http://paul.spu.edu/~lkohrt/btrumpet.html

Canadian Brass ★★★★
This is one of a series of classical artist pages sponsored by BMG Classics World. This page, dedicated to Canadian Brass, includes a portrait, biography, and list of recommended recordings. Since their first appearance on the music scene in 1970, The Canadian Brass have revolutionized brass music and established the brass quintet as a vital force in the music world. These classically trained virtuoso musicians have transformed a previously neglected group of instruments with a limited repertoire into an exciting and versatile ensemble which performs everything from Bach and Mozart to Gershwin and Dixieland. This site also includes a tour schedule for the group.
- KEYWORDS: Canadian Brass, Classical Music, Compact Discs (CDs), Music
- AUDIENCE: Classical Music Enthusiasts, Compact Disc Users, Music Enthusiasts, Performers
- CONTACT: rbourne@panix.com
- FREE

http://www.classicalmus.com/artists/canadian.html

The Capitol Steps ★★★★
This site contains sounds, hits and information about 'Capitol Steps,' a group composed of Congressional staffers turned songwriters and political satirists. President George Bush claims that 'The Capitol Steps make it easier to leave public office.' Some of the sample tunes are 'Let Me Go, F. Lee Bailey' to be sung to the jury by O.J. Simpson to the tune of 'Won't You Come Home, Bill Bailey?' and 'Gun Nuts Boasting They Can Open Fire,' to the tune of 'Chestnuts Roasting on An Open Fire.' Users should be forewarned that these are rather large music files up to 900K.
- KEYWORDS: Folk Music, Satire
- AUDIENCE: Folk Music Enthusiasts, Humorists, Politicians

CONTACT Mike Tilford
capsteps@aol.com

FREE

http://pfm.het.brown.edu/people/mende/steps/

The Catherine Wheel Home Page ★★★

The Web site is dedicated to the alternative band, Catherine Wheel. It has a brief FAQ, a discography with lyrics, and information on how to join the mailing list for the band.

KEYWORDS Alternative Music, Progressive Music, Rock Music
AUDIENCE Alternative Music Enthusiasts, Rock Fans
CONTACT Patty Haley
patty@gdb.org

FREE

http://gdbdoc.gdb.org/~patty/CW/CW_home_page.html

The Cause & Effect Homepage ★★★

This home page is dedicated to the synth-pop group Cause & Effect. It has band information, tour information, and a discography with lyrics.

KEYWORDS Chameleons, Contemporary Music, Pop Music, Rock Music
AUDIENCE Alternative Music Enthusiasts, Dance Music Enthusiasts, Pop Music Enthusiasts, Synth-pop Enthusiasts
CONTACT Dan Wellman
wellman@uiuc.edu

FREE

http://www.cen.uiuc.edu/~wellman/cause_effect/

Ceili's Muse ★★★

This page is dedicated to an Ceili's Muse, a Celtic Folk band from Texas. It has information on the band members, a discography, and former and upcoming shows. It also has booking information.

KEYWORDS Celtic Music, Contemporary Music, Folk Music
AUDIENCE Celtic Music Enthusiasts, Folk Music Enthusiasts, Texas Residents

FREE

http://starbase.neosoft.com/%7Ekaetron/Muse/

Chalkhills, The XTC Mailing List ★★★★

This is the home page for Chalkhills, the mailing list dedicated the the rock group XTC. Besides instructions on how to subscribe to the list, this resource contains answers to FAQs and back issues of the list. It also has the Chalkhills Archive, containing XTC lyrics, images, and discographies.

KEYWORDS Alternative Music, Music Archives, Rock Music
AUDIENCE Alternative Music Enthusiasts, Anglophiles, Pop Music Enthusiasts, Rock Fans

CONTACT John Relph
relph@presto.ig.com

FREE

http://www.bio.net/chalkhills/html/

Chicago- The Home Page ★★

This page offers fans of the '70s group Chicago a collection of resources and information about the band. Users will find information on the current activities of the band and some former members, as well as information on fan clubs, tour dates, image files, and more. This server also has a collection of song lyrics, guitar tablature, and general MIDI files available for download.

KEYWORDS Chicago, Music, Pop Music, Rock Music
AUDIENCE Music Enthusiasts, Popular Music Enthusiasts, Rock Fans
CONTACT James Alexander
adrock@cyberspace.com

FREE

http://www.cyberspace.com:80/adrock/

The Church ★★

This home page is dedicated to the ethereal Australian alternative group, The Church. It has a loosely organized lyrics section and information on how to join the mailing list with links to a discography.

KEYWORDS Alternative Music, Australia, Contemporary Music, Rock Music
AUDIENCE Alternative Music Enthusiasts, Rock Fans
CONTACT Vernon H Harmon II
vernon@cs.cmu.edu

FREE

http://www.cs.cmu.edu/afs/cs/user/vernon/www/church.html

The Circle of Dust Home Page ★★

This home page is dedicated to New York industrial band Circle of Dust. It has some information about the band, pictures, and a couple of images and soundfiles.

KEYWORDS Contemporary Music, New York, Rock Music
AUDIENCE Alternative Music Enthusiasts, Electronic Music Enthusiasts, Heavy Metal Fans, Industrial Music Enthusiasts
CONTACT Steve Wilder
wilder@virtu.sar.usf.edu

FREE

http://www.sar.usf.edu/~wilder/dust/

Coil Home Page ★★★

This home page is dedicated to the experimental band Coil. It has a discography with lyrics, many articles, and information on the band members other projects.

KEYWORDS Alternative Music, Music, Rock Music
AUDIENCE Alternative Music Enthusiasts, Electronic Music Enthusiasts, Experimental Music Enthusiasts

CONTACT Greg Clow
gclow@octrf.on.ca

FREE

http://iuma.southern.com/Coil/coil.html

Concrete Blonde Website ★★★★

This page is devoted to the defunct rock band Concrete Blonde. In addition to background material on the band, this server provides an archive of images and sound, a complete discography, lyrics, guitar tablature, and more. There is also directions on joining the Concrete Blonde mailing list, fan club information, a section about rumors and current projects of the band members, and an online survey for fans of the band.

KEYWORDS Alternative Music, Music, Rock Music
AUDIENCE Alternative Music Enthusiasts, Music Enthusiasts, Rock Fans
CONTACT Dean S. Mah
mah@cs.ualberta.ca

FREE

http://web.cs.ualberta.ca/~mah/CB/

The Crossing — Big Country ★★

This home page is dedicated to the Scottish alternative band, Big Country. It has discographies, lyrics to a couple of their albums, and information on how to subscribe to the Big Country mailing list.

KEYWORDS Big Country, Contemporary Music, Rock Music, Scotland
AUDIENCE Alternative Music Enthusiasts, Rock Fans
CONTACT John N. Underwood
junderw@cs.clemson.edu

FREE

http://www.cs.clemson.edu/~junderw/music/bc/

Curve WWW Page ★★★

This page is devoted to the defunct band Curve. It contains a wide variety of resources about the band, including lyrics, discography, and images, as well as interviews and images of the band. There is also an archive of digitized sound files of the band's songs in MPEG, and a section where fans can trade Curve merchandise and memorabilia. There is also a section which archives the Curve mailing list, and a section containing news about the band's members and their current projects.

KEYWORDS Alternative Music, Music, Rock Music
AUDIENCE Alternative Music Enthusiasts, Music Enthusiasts, Pop Music Enthusiasts, Rock Fans
CONTACT Conrad Sauerwald
conrad@stack.urc.tue.nl

FREE

http://www.stack.urc.tue.nl/~conrad/

Cynic Info ★★★

This Web site contains the home page of Cynic—a progressive rock band with metal overtones. It contains a history of the band, a discography, pictures, and a listing of bootlegs.

KEYWORDS Progressive Music, Rock Music

AUDIENCE   Heavy Metal Fans, Progressive Music Enthusiasts, Rock Fans
CONTACT   Brian "Mel" Meloon
           bmeloon@geom.umn.edu
FREE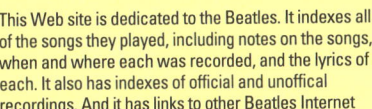

http://www.geom.umn.edu/~bmeloon/music/bandinfo/cynic.html

David Robinson's Beatles Index ★★★★

This Web site is dedicated to the Beatles. It indexes all of the songs they played, including notes on the songs, when and where each was recorded, and the lyrics of each. It also has indexes of official and unoffical recordings. And it has links to other Beatles Internet resources.

KEYWORDS   Beatles (The), Contemporary Music, Rock Music
AUDIENCE   Beatles Fans, Pop Music Enthusiasts, Rock Fans
CONTACT   David Robinson
           RobinsDJ@phymat.bham.ac.uk
FREE

http://sun1.bham.ac.uk/cca93054/beatles/index.html

Dead Can Dance ★★★

This page contains a wide variety of resources about the band Dead Can Dance, including a discography with lyrics, press release information, and digitized sound files from the individual albums. In addition, users will find current information on the band's activities, biographical information, the complete FAQ files, and a gallery of band images. Users will also find a collection of links to other Dead Can Dance information on the Internet.

KEYWORDS   Alternative Music, Rock Music
AUDIENCE   Alternative Music Enthusiasts, Music Enthusiasts, Rock Fans
CONTACT   Raven Zachary
           webmaster@nets.com
FREE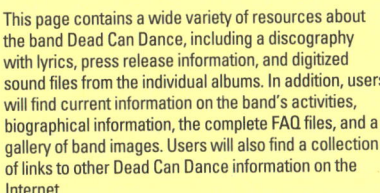

http://www.nets.com/dcd

Definitely Oasis — The Oasis Homepage ★★

This home page is dedicated to the one of the United Kingdom's recent phenomena, Oasis. It has current news, and lyrics. The page also has links to other Oasis and rock music sites on the net.

KEYWORDS   Alternative Music, Lyrics, Rock Music
AUDIENCE   Alternative Music Enthusiasts, Pop Music Enthusiasts, Rock Fans
CONTACT   Darren Lewis
           djl1@st-andrews.ac.uk
FREE

http://www.st-and.ac.uk:80/~www_sa/personal/djl1/Oasis/

Dire Straits Home Page ★★★

The Dire Straits Home Page is a collection of information and resources related to the band. Of interest at this site is the HTML version of the Dire Straits FAQ file, photos and cover art from the band's albums, and a collection of audio samples and full songs. There are also pointers to lyrics archives, as well as other Dire Straits resources on the Internet.

KEYWORDS   Music, Rock Music
AUDIENCE   Music Enthusiasts, Popular Music Enthusiasts, Rock Fans
CONTACT   Eugene Tyurin
           gene@insti.physics.sunysb.edu
FREE

http://www.physics.sunysb.edu/~gene/DS/DS.html

Directory of /Pub/Devo ★★★★

This is an FTP site for the band Devo. It has guitar tabs, lyrics, pictures, and musical samples. It has the archives for the newsgroup alt.fan.devo.

KEYWORDS   Alternative Music, Music Archives, Rock Music
AUDIENCE   Alternative Music Enthusiasts, Rock Fans
CONTACT   Devo
           optimus@nvg.unit.no
FREE

ftp://ftp.nvg.unit.no/pub/devo/

Connections to Music Listening
I heard it on the Internet

Tired of the same old "bells and whistles" on your PC? Through the Internet you can make that computer "sing." The World Wide Web offers users a vast collection (and it's growing still) of musical options—classical, Latin Beat, jazz, and good old rock 'n roll.

"Musicians On the Internet" is your virtual listening booth. There you'll gain access to music excerpts, interactive movies, photos, and artwork from your favorite artists.

(http://www.escape.com/~rpisen/MOIhome.html)

At "Musicians Across the Internet" you have access to World Wide Web Home Pages of many musicians who are active online. You can check out reviews of the latest recordings and get in touch with the fans and fan clubs of your favorite musicians.

(http://iris3.carb.nist.gov:8000/pub/ram/music/indie/indie.html)

The Doors ★★★

This site offers fans of the '60s supergroup, The Doors, a collection of resources and information about the classic band. Included are a complete set of song lyrics from 6 albums and Jim Morrison's book of poetry, the Doors FAQ file, a bootleg discography, and pictures of the band for users to download. In addition, there are links to the newsgroup devoted to discussion of the Doors, as well as links to the All Music Guide and Ultimate Band List entries for The Doors.

KEYWORDS   Pop Music, Rock Music
AUDIENCE   Music Enthusiasts, Popular Music Enthusiasts, Rock Fans, The Doors Enthusiasts
CONTACT   Neal Kettler
           kettler@cs.colostate.edu
FREE

http://www.vis.colostate.edu/~user1209/doors/

Drumbeats ★★

Drumbeats is the name of a gopher that provides information about the rock group Rush. The information includes images, lyrics, fan magazines, and concert dates. Drumbeats is maintained at the Univeristy of Maryland.

KEYWORDS   Rock Music

Musical Groups

AUDIENCE: Music Enthusiasts, Rock Fans
FREE

gopher://syrinx.umd.edu:2112/

Echo and the Bunnymen Page ★★★

This page is devoted to the alternative-pop band Echo and the Bunnymen. Fans of the now defunct band will find the latest information on what members are doing, an archive of the mailing list devoted to Echo and the Bunnymen, a discography, and an image gallery. There is also a section with a complete discography, as well an archive of lyrics.

KEYWORDS: Alternative Music, Pop Music
AUDIENCE: Alternative Music Enthusiasts, Music Enthusiasts, Musicians, Rock Fans
CONTACT: Jason and Jill
jgreshes@dfw.net
FREE

http://www.netaxs.com/~jgreshes/echo.html

Elan Home Page ★★

This site is the home page for the Iowa progressive rock group Elan. It has a short description of the band, lyrics, and sound files, as well as instructions on how to mail-order their CD. There is also a review section, with some bilingual reviews.

KEYWORDS: Music Reviews, Progressive Music, Rock Music
AUDIENCE: Heavy Metal Fans, Progressive Music Enthusiasts, Rock Fans
CONTACT: mist@netins.net
FREE

http://www.infonet.net:80/showcase/elan/

The Elastica Connection ★★★

This home page is dedicated to the British alternative band Elastica. It has an FAQ, discography, chronology, pictures, lyrics and information on each of the band memebers.

KEYWORDS: Alternative Music, Music, Rock Music
AUDIENCE: Alternative Music Enthusiasts, Punk Rock Enthusiasts, Rock Fans
CONTACT: Mark Longair
mark_longair@uk.ibm.com
FREE

http://www.wmin.ac.uk/~braziej/elastica/e_main.html

Enigma ★★★

The Enigma page is all about the ethereal alternative band Enigma. All kinds of information are available, including material on the individual members of Enigma (with information about previous and current outside projects). There is a HTML version of the Enigma FAQ here, as well as an archive of lyrics, articles, and interviews. Users will also find a complete discography, an image gallery, a listing of ads for Enigma rarities, and a selection of music samples.

KEYWORDS: Alternative Music
AUDIENCE: Alternative Music Enthusiasts, Music Enthusiasts, Rock Fans
CONTACT: Joar Grimstvedt
joarg@hsr.no
FREE

http://www.hsr.no/~joarg/Enigma.html

The Ergot Derivative ★★★★

This home page is for the Australian band The Ergot Derivative. It has information about the band, songs, reviews, pictures and a discography.

KEYWORDS: Alternative Music, Australia, Rock Music
AUDIENCE: Alternative Music Enthusiasts, Australians, Rock Fans
CONTACT: ergots@widget.maths.monash.edu.au
FREE

http://www.maths.monash.edu.au/people/ernie/ergot/

The Evolution Control Committee ★★★★

This home page is for the band Evolution Control Committee. It has a discography, some reviews and interviews, and their unusual Sub-Atomic Opera, which they describe as a serialized story that plays out something like an audio comic strip.

KEYWORDS: Alternative Music, Music, Rock Music
AUDIENCE: Alternative Music Enthusiasts, Rock Fans
CONTACT: George 'Spanky' Esoterica III
ecc@gnu.ai.mit.edu
FREE

http://www.infinet.com/~markg/ecc.html

Faith No More FTP Site ★★★

This FTP site is dedicated to the band Faith No More (and Mr. Bungle, lead singer Mike Patton's other band). It has pictures, sound files and a movie.

KEYWORDS: Alternative Music, Heavy Metal Music, Rock Music
AUDIENCE: Alternative Music Enthusiasts, Heavy Metal Fans, Pop Music Enthusiasts, Rock Fans
CONTACT: andy@preferred.com
FREE

ftp://ftp.preferred.com/pub/fnm/

The Fischer-Z Homepage ★★★★

This home page is for the popular European band Fischer-Z. It has a discography, reviews, pictures, lyrics, tour dates and current news.

KEYWORDS: Alternative Music, Europe, Rock Music
AUDIENCE: Alternative Music Enthusiasts, Europeans, Rock Fans
CONTACT: mepk@rbg.informatik.th-darmstadt.de
FREE

http://www.rbg.informatik.th-darmstadt.de/~mepk/fischer-z/home.html

Fonya - Electronic/Progressive Instrumental Band ★★★

This site is the home page for the progressive rock group Fonya. It has a short description of the band, and a track from one of their albums.

KEYWORDS: Progressive Music, Rock Music
AUDIENCE: Electronic Music Enthusiasts, Progressive Music Enthusiasts, Rock Fans
CONTACT: fournier@asic.sc.ti.com
FREE

http://tam2000.tamu.edu/~mdb0213/fonya.html

The Fruvous Page ★★★★

This is the home page of the Canadian alternative band Moxy Fruvous. It has band information, articles, pictures, a discography with lyrics, upcoming shows, and a preview of their new album including sound files and lyrics.

KEYWORDS: Alternative Music, Canada, Rock Music
AUDIENCE: Alternative Music Enthusiasts, Canadians, Rock Fans
CONTACT: Joshua Cragun
jcragun@csc.cornell-iowa.edu
FREE

http://wwwcsc.cornell-iowa.edu/~jcragun/fruvous.html

Future Sound of London ★★★★

This web site is dedicated to the British experimental electronic duo Future Sound of London. It has a discography, sound samples, pictures, and articles.

KEYWORDS: Britain, Techno/Ambient Music
AUDIENCE: Ambient Music Enthusiasts, Electronic Music Enthusiasts, Experimental Music Enthusiasts, Techno Music Enthusiasts
CONTACT: wally@hyperreal.com
FREE

http://www.hyperreal.com:80/music/artists/fsol/www/

Genesis World Wide Web Home Page ★★★★

This home page is devoted to the British progressive rock institution Genesis. It covers Genesis in all of its incarnations—from early Peter Gabriel musical theatre days to current status as a perennial hit machine. It contains an FAQ, lyrics to band and solo albums, a brief history, and other Genesis information.

KEYWORDS: Progressive Music, Rock Music
AUDIENCE: Pop Music Enthusiasts, Progressive Music Enthusiasts, Rock Fans
CONTACT: Adrian Catchpole
a.g.catchpole@bradford.ac.uk
FREE

http://www.brad.ac.uk/~agcatchp/gen_home.html

Musical Groups

Gentle Giant Home Page ★★★★

This Web site is for fans of Gentle Giant—one of the more influential progressive rock bands of the 1970s. It has information about the band, a discography with pictures and lyrics, ratings for various albums and ways to access the Gentle Giant fan club and also the Internet newsletter.

KEYWORDS Music Newsletters, Progressive Music, Rock Music
AUDIENCE Progressive Music Enthusiasts, Rock Fans, Technocrats
CONTACT Daniel Barrett
barrett@cs.umass.edu
FREE

http://zoo.cs.umass.edu/~barrett/gentlegiant.html

Get Crued ★★★★

This web site is dedicated to the popular 80's metal act Motley Crue. It has a discography with lyrics, pages for key members, the monthly newsletter, sound and video files, and information on the mailing list.

KEYWORDS Hard Rock Music, Musical Groups, Rock Music
AUDIENCE Hard Rock Fans, Heavy Metal Fans, Rock Fans
CONTACT motley.crue@aquila.com
FREE

http://www.aquila.com:80/motley.crue/

The Grateful Dead ★★★

This page is a collection of resources for fans of the veteran psychedelic rock group, the Grateful Dead. Dead-heads will find all of the latest news and information about the band here, including complete set lists from recent shows, information on recording shows and trading tapes, a graphic archive with images and popular graphics, and a section with digitized music from the band. In addition, this server sports a selection of written material by members of the band, as well as a collection of links to other Grateful Dead pages on the Net.

KEYWORDS Music Newsletters, Recordings, Rock Music
AUDIENCE Deadheads, Rock Fans
CONTACT Mark Leone
mleone@cs.cmu.edu
FREE

http://www.cs.cmu.edu:8001/afs/cs.cmu.edu/user/mleone/web/dead.html

 ### Hole Page ★★★

This is Geffen Record's Web page for the alternative rock band Hole. There are a couple of song excerpts, and a short biography. Hole's LIVE THROUGH THIS album is available here, too.

KEYWORDS Alternative Music, Feminist Music, Rock Music
AUDIENCE Alternative Music Enthusiasts, Musicians, Rock Fans, Women
FREE

http://geffen.com/hole.html

Home Page of Afterforever ★★★

This web site is the home page of the Canadian Heavy Metal band Afterforever. It has band information, album artwork, concert dates, reviews and sound files.

KEYWORDS Contemporary Music, Musical Groups, Rock Music
AUDIENCE Canadians, Heavy Metal Fans, Rock Fans
CONTACT bball@gill.ifmt.nf.ca
FREE

http://www.ifmt.nf.ca:80/bball/aft4ever.html/

Indigo Girls Main Page ★★★

This page is for fans of the acoustic folk-rock duo, the Indigo Girls. Users will find a FAQ file on the artists, the latest tour information, album cover images, and more. In addition, this server is home to an exhaustive annotated discography of the Indigo Girls' work, complete with song titles, recording information, personnel, and more. There is also information on the Indigo Girls mailing list, as well as links to other Indigo Girls information on the Net.

KEYWORDS Feminist Music, Folk Music, Rock Music
AUDIENCE Folk Music Enthusiasts, Indigo Girls Enthusiasts, Music Enthusiasts, Rock Fans
CONTACT Colin Reed
mtp@mtp.com, kidfears@tezcat.com
FREE

http://www.tezcat.com/~mtp/IG/HTML/ig-page.html

Info on Atheist ★★★

This web site contains the home page of Atheist—a progressive rock band combining elements of heavy metal and jazz. It contains a brief description of the band, a discography and some pictures.

KEYWORDS Jazz, Progressive Music, Rock Music
AUDIENCE Heavy Metal Fans, Progressive Music Enthusiasts, Rock Fans
CONTACT Brian "Mel" Meloon
bmeloon@geom.umn.edu
FREE

http://www.geom.umn.edu/~bmeloon/music/bandinfo/atheist.html

 ### Inka Inka ★★★

Inka Inka, a popular reggae band, offers stereo or mono exerpts of one of their songs and MPEG or audio only excerpts. There are links to comments and reviews and more songs, as well as to other locations on the Internet Underground Music Archive.

KEYWORDS Reggae Music
AUDIENCE Music Enthusiasts, Reggae Enthusiasts
FREE

http://www.iuma.com/IUMA/band_html/Inka_Inka.html

The Internet Beatles Album ★★★★

This Web site is dedicated to the Beatles. It has portfolios of each band member and information on unreleased or rare songs. It also has a section devoted to their 1968 The Beatles double album, including sound files of unreleased or mono takes of of many songs from that record. It also has tons of other stuff including screen savers, lists of Beatles covers, and a lot, lot more.

KEYWORDS Beatles (The), Contemporary Music, Rock Music
AUDIENCE Beatles Fans, Pop Music Enthusiasts, Rock Fans
CONTACT Dave Haber
dhaber@primenet.com
FREE

http://www.primenet.com/~dhaber/beatles.html

Into the Flood Again — The Alice in Chains Homepage ★★★

This home page is dedicated to the Seattle alternative band Alice in Chains. It has a chronological history of the band, pictures, a discography and lyrics.

KEYWORDS Alternative Music, Rock Music
AUDIENCE Alternative Music Enthusiasts, Heavy Metal Fans, Rock Fans
CONTACT Mike Coleman
mikec@csos.orst.edu
FREE

http://www.csos.orst.edu/~mikec/aic.html

Iron Maiden Page ★★★

This site is a repository of information on the heavy-metal band Iron Maiden. It contains reviews of many of the group's albums, as well as information on the current incarnation of the band. There are also some sound clips available for download, and a collection of pages with information on each individual album. Hardcore Iron Maiden fans will appreciate the links to other sites with Iron Maiden information.

KEYWORDS Hard Rock Music, Music, Rock Music
AUDIENCE Hard Rock Fans, Heavy Metal Fans, Music Enthusiasts, Rock Fans
CONTACT Allan Stratton
stratton@cs.tufts.edu
FREE

http://www.cs.tufts.edu/~stratton/maiden/maiden.html

Jan Hoiberg's WWW Page on The Band ★★

This home page is dedicated to the Band, Bob Dylan's most noted backing group, fine musicians in their own stead. It is mostly a series of links related artists and topics.

KEYWORDS Folk Music, Rock Music
AUDIENCE Canadians, Folk Rock Fans, Rock Fans

CONTACT Jan Hiberg
FREE

http://www-ia.hiof.no/~janh/TheBand.html

Jethro Tull Music Archive ★★★★

This home page is devoted to British progressive rock institution, Jethro Tull. It has a hypertext FAQ, an album list including pictures of covers and lyrics, and a link to the archives of the St. Cleve Chronicle, the Jethro Tull mailing list.

KEYWORDS Folk Music, Pop Music, Rock Music
AUDIENCE Folk Music Enthusiasts, Progressive Music Enthusiasts, Rock Fans
CONTACT JTull-Request@remus.rutgers.edu
FREE

http://remus.rutgers.edu:80/JethroTull/

ftp://remus.rutgers.edu/pub/JethroTull/

KISS Conventions ★★★★

This is the home page for the official, authorized KISS conventions. Perhaps you thought KISS was finished, but as you'll learn from this site, they're alive and well and just finished touring in Japan and Australia. Learn about the upcoming conventions, planned convention weddings, giveaways, appearances by the likes of Jay Leno, KISS memorabilia and much, much more.

KEYWORDS Conventions, Hard Rock Music, Rock Music
AUDIENCE Hard Rock Fans, Heavy Metal Fans, Pop Music Enthusiasts, Rock Fans
CONTACT Michael Brandvold
mikeb@interaccess.com
FREE

http://www.interaccess.com/users/mikeb/kissconventions.html

The KISS Network - Los Angeles, CA ★★★★

This web site is dedicated to KISS. It has album information, the FAQ, discography, bootlegraphy, sound files, and news clippings. It also looks really cool.

KEYWORDS Hard Rock Music, Rock Music
AUDIENCE Hard Rock Fans, Heavy Metal Fans, Pop Music Enthusiasts, Rock Fans
CONTACT Aurelius Prochazka
aure@galcit.caltech.edu
FREE

http://www.galcit.caltech.edu/~aure/strwys.html

King Crimson ★★★★

This Web site houses back issues of Elephant Talk, the Internet newsletter devoted to Robert Fripp and King Crimson. It has a nifty little mechanism to make the searching process simple and painless.

KEYWORDS Alternative Music, Music Newsletters, Rock Music
AUDIENCE Progressive Music Enthusiasts, Rock Fans
CONTACT Mike Stok
Mike.Stok@meiko.concord.ma.us.
FREE

http://www.meiko.com:80/crimson/

The Kinks ★★★★

This comprehensive web site is dedicated to the legendary British rock band The Kinks. It has current information, a discography with extensive lyrics, pictures, sound files, bootlegraphy, bibliography and mailing list information.

KEYWORDS Musical Groups, Pop Music, Rock Music
AUDIENCE 60's Music Enthusiasts, Hard Rock Fans, Pop Music Enthusiasts, Rock Fans
CONTACT dte@cs.rit.ed
FREE

http://hobbes.it.rit.edu/kinks/kinks.html

Kronos Quartet ★★★

These pages are devoted to the Kronos Quartet. Topics include the latest recordings, reviews, concert schedules, discussion pages, lists of composers whose music has been performed by the quartet, and works performed in concert but not yet recorded, etc. The site also contains a discography and GIF format images of the quartet. The site also contains links to other classical music sites.

KEYWORDS Chamber Music, Classical Music, Music
AUDIENCE Music Enthusiasts, Music Historians, Music Professionals, Musicians
CONTACT Gary Stephens
FREE

http://www.nwu.edu/music/kronos/

Lash Out Home Page ★★

This is the home page of Norwegian punk band Lash Out. It has current information about the band, pictures, and sound files.

KEYWORDS Musical Groups, Punk Music, Rock Music
AUDIENCE Alternative Music Enthusiasts, Punk Rock Enthusiasts, Rock Fans
CONTACT paalst@ifi.uio.no
FREE

http://www.ifi.uio.no/~paalst/music/lashout.html

Led Zeppelin Home Page ★★★

This page is home to the legendary '70s band Led Zeppelin. It contains a wealth of resources related to this classic band, such as a FAQ file, guitar tablature for budding guitarists, an archive of song lyrics, a discography, and a collection of digitized images. In addition, users will find a selection of sound clips of Led Zeppelin's music, information on the Led Zeppelin mailing list, and a set of links to other Internet sites with Led Zeppelin information. There are also some biographical, anecdotal, and historical files about Led Zeppelin on this server.

KEYWORDS Music, Rock Music
AUDIENCE Hard Rock Fans, Heavy Metal Fans, Music Enthusiasts, Rock Fans
CONTACT Jeff White
jeffw@virginia.edu
FREE

http://uvacs.cs.virginia.edu/~jsw2y/zeppelin/zeppelin.html

The Levellers Home Page ★★★

This home page is dedicated to British band, The Levellers. It has news, a discography, pictures, lyrics, some sound files, and comments from previous readers of the page.

KEYWORDS Alternative Music, Music, Rock Music
AUDIENCE Activists, Alternative Music Enthusiasts, Rock Fans
CONTACT pfleming@magnus.acs.ohio-state.edu
FREE

http://chem-www.mps.ohio-state.edu/~pfleming/lvlrs/

Little Feat ★★★

This web site is dedicated to the long-running bluesy band Little Feat. It has tour information, a blurb on its most recent album, an FAQ, pictures, set lists, and a little tribute to Feat founder Lowell George.

KEYWORDS Blues, Musical Groups, Rock Music
AUDIENCE Blues Enthusiasts, Rock Fans
CONTACT FMiller@IT.Berklee.EDU
FREE

http://www.ultranet.com/~amygoode/FEATS.HTML

Live ★★★★

This web site is dedicated to the very popular alternative band, Live. It has current news, a discography, lyrics, videography, an FAQ, biography, interviews, and pictures. It also has information about the Live mailing list.

KEYWORDS Alternative Music, Musical Groups, Rock Music
AUDIENCE Alternative Music Enthusiasts, Pop Music Enthusiasts, Rock Fans
CONTACT jlang@cerf.net
FREE

http://www.cerf.net/live.html

Marillion & Fish WWW Server ★★★★

This Web site is dedicated to British progressive outfit Marillion and their lead singer, Fish. It has a hypertext FAQ, lyrics, pictures, articles about the band, a list of bootlegs, and other Marillion-related stuff. It also has information on how to subscribe to the Marillion Internet mailing list.

KEYWORDS Progressive Music, Rock Music
AUDIENCE Progressive Music Enthusiasts, Rock Fans
CONTACT Pierre-Yves Lochou
lochou@cnam.fr
FREE

http://www.cnam.fr/Marillion/Marillion.html

Musical Groups

Marilyn Manson ★★★★
This is the home page of the alternative/industrial/metal band Marilyn Manson. It has a FAQ, discography, pictures, magazine articles, guitar tabs, and mailing list information.
- KEYWORDS: Alternative Music, Rock Music
- AUDIENCE: Alternative Music Enthusiasts, Heavy Metal Fans, Industrial Music Enthusiasts, Rock Fans
- CONTACT: ned kmaling@calumet.yorku.ca
- FREE

http://www-home.calumet.yorku.ca/kmaling/www/mm/MM.htm

Mastermind - The Progressive Rock Trio of the 90s ★★★
This site is the home page for the progressive rock group Mastermind, the self-proclaimed Progressive Rock Trio of the 90s. It has a short description of the band, images of album covers and the band, some lyrics, and some reviews. They also have a sound file.
- KEYWORDS: Musical Groups, Progressive Music, Rock Music
- AUDIENCE: Heavy Metal Fans, Progressive Music Enthusiasts, Rock Fans
- CONTACT: bberends@pipeline.com
- FREE

http://tam2000.tamu.edu/~mdb0213/mastermind.html

Mazzy Star Home Page ★★★
This home page is dedicated to the alternative band Mazzy Star. It has a discography, lyrics, pictures, and a video.
- KEYWORDS: Alternative Music, Musical Groups, Rock Music
- AUDIENCE: Alternative Music Enthusiasts, Pop Music Enthusiasts, Rock Fans
- CONTACT: kj7341@xx.acs.appstate.edu
- FREE

http://www.acs.appstate.edu/~kj7341/mazzy.html

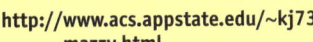 Megadeth Arizona ★★★★
This is Capitol Records home page dedicated to the popular metal band Megadeth. It's a brilliantly designed site built around a tour guide of the fictional city Megadeth, Arizona. The primary focus is to promote their 1994 Youthanasia album. It has giveaways, fan club information, tour dates, tour diaries, songs, current news, and tons and tons of other trivia, promotions, software and stuff although the site seems to be missing the usual discography and lyrics. If Bevis and Butthead had Netscape, they'd never leave this site.
- KEYWORDS: Hard Rock Music, Rock Music
- AUDIENCE: Hard Rock Fans, Heavy Metal Fans, Rock Fans
- CONTACT: robin@caprec.com
- FREE

http://underground.net/Megadeth/megadeth.html

Mike Markowski's Beatles Page ★★★★
This site is one of the more complete Beatles pages on the web. Aside from the obligatory links to other Beatles resources, this server has biographical pages for each member of the Beatles, a complete selection of discographies with LP, EP, singles, and bootlegs, and a virtual 'tour' of Liverpool, the town the Beatles came from. There is also a section on where to obtain Beatles memorabilia, information on the 'Paul is Dead' hoax, and much more.
- KEYWORDS: Beatles (The), Pop Music, Rock Music
- AUDIENCE: Beatles Fans, Music Enthusiasts, Popular Music Enthusiasts, Rock Fans
- CONTACT: Mike Markowski markowsk@cis.udel.edu
- FREE

http://www.eecis.udel.edu/~markowsk/beatles/

The Monkees Home Page ★★★★
This Web site is dedicated to 60's pop and TV phenomena, The Monkees. It has sections on the albums, the TV show, the individual Monkees, a history, a FAQ, guitar tabs, lyrics and pictures.
- KEYWORDS: Musical Groups, Pop Music, Rock Music
- AUDIENCE: 60's Music Enthusiasts, Pop Music Listeners, Rock Fans, TV Enthusiasts
- CONTACT: Brad Waddell flex@primenet.com
- FREE

http://www.primenet.com/~flex/monkees.html

The Mudkats ★★★
This web page is dedicated to the Bay Area alternative band Mudkats. It contains a biography, songs, reviews, upcoming shows, and mailing list information.
- KEYWORDS: Alternative Music, Rock Music
- AUDIENCE: Alternative Music Enthusiasts, Bay Area Residents., Hard Rock Fans, Rock Fans
- CONTACT: Eric Friedmann mudkats-info@klinzhai.iuma.com
- FREE

http://klinzhai.iuma.com/mudkats/index.html

NEU ★★★
This home page is for the pioneering Ambient/Techno band NEU! It contains a very long and well-written profile with a discography.
- KEYWORDS: Musical Groups, Techno/Ambient Music
- AUDIENCE: Ambient Music Enthusiasts, Electronic Music Enthusiasts, Experimental Music Enthusiasts, Techno Music Enthusiasts
- FREE

http://hyperreal.com:70/1/music/artists/neu

The New Early Sunrise Band ★★★
The New Early Sunrise Band is one of Baltimore's leading country and western bands, formed over 15 years ago by fiddler Dave Goodman. Their first recording, 'Telephone' which is introduced online has been recently released.
- KEYWORDS: Sound Clips
- AUDIENCE: Country Music Enthusiasts, Musicians
- CONTACT: Archie Warnock warnock@clark.net
- FREE

http://www.clark.net/pub/warnock/nesb.html

The Official Breeders Web Page ★★★★
The Breeders Home Page offers an assortment of information and material on this popular 'alternative' band. An extensive discography is available which includes singles and promotional-only releases, as well as an archive of images. Users will also find sound samples to download, an archive of song lyrics, and a section with an interview of the band.
- KEYWORDS: Alternative Music, Lyrics, Rock Music
- AUDIENCE: Alternative Music Enthusiasts, Breeders Enthusiasts, Music Enthusiasts, Rock Fans
- CONTACT: Patrick Asselman patrick@stack.urc.tue.nl
- FREE

http://www.nando.net:80/music/gm/Breeders/

The Official Duran Duran Home Page ★★★★
This page is all about the popular '80s glam-rock band that has managed to make a successful comeback in the '90s, Duran Duran. Users will find a wealth of resources about the band, such as information on the latest Duran Duran happenings, information on upcoming releases, and a section of images and art related to the band. In addition, there is a complete discography and fanzine index here, as well as information on Tiger, the Duran Duran mailing list.
- KEYWORDS: Music, Pop Music, Rock Music
- AUDIENCE: Music Enthusiasts, Pop Music Enthusiasts, Popular Music Enthusiasts, Rock Fans
- CONTACT: Troy Whitsett, Sarah March troyw@onramp.net, smarch@sal.cs.uiuc.edu
- FREE

http://hal.cs.uiuc.edu/~smarch/Duranduran.html

The Official Organum & David Jackman Page ★★★
This is the home page of the experimental band Organum (the nom de band of David Jackman). It contains a discography, and links to pages on various people who have performed on the Organum records. It also has links to an experimental music marketplace.
- KEYWORDS: Experimental Music, Industrial Music

Musical Groups

AUDIENCE Experimental Music Enthusiasts, Industrial Music Enthusiast, Techno/Ambient Music Enthusiasts
CONTACT jgreid@u.washington.edu
FREE

http://weber.u.washington.edu/~jgreid/org/org.html

The Official Unofficial Cranberries Home Page! ★★★

This page offers fans of the Irish band, The Cranberries, a collection of resources and information about the band. Aside from the complete discography, song lyric and guitar tablature archive, and image gallery, users will find a selection of digitized songs in the sun audio format, as well as a compilation of links to other Cranberries information on the Internet. There is also information on current tour dates, and a place for users to add information about the band.

KEYWORDS Alternative Music, Irish Music, Rock Music
AUDIENCE Alternative Music Enthusiasts, Cranberries Enthusiasts, Music Enthusiasts, Rock Fans
CONTACT Francois Gibello
d90-fgi@nada.kth.se
FREE

http://www.nada.kth.se/~d90-fgi/Cranberries/cranberries.html

Orbit Home Page ★★★

This is the home page of the Massachusetts alternative band Orbit. It has a biography, sound files, pictures, and upcoming shows. The page also has links to other alternative music sites on the net.

KEYWORDS Alternative Music, Massachusetts, Rock Music
AUDIENCE Alternative Music Enthusiasts, Massachusetts Residents, Pop Music Enthusiasts, Rock Fans
CONTACT orbit@breakfast.com
FREE

http://www.breakfast.com:2500/breakfast/orbit/orbit.html

Orphanage ★★★

This web site is dedicated to the Dutch death metal band Orphanage. It contains a biography, discography with lyrics and sound files, reviews, and tour dates. You will also find links to other rock music pages here.

KEYWORDS Hard Rock Music, Netherlands, Orphanages, Rock Music
AUDIENCE Dutch Residents, Hard Rock Fans, Heavy Metal Fans, Rock Fans
CONTACT Jules Vleugels
jules@cs.ruu.nl
FREE

http://www.cs.ruu.nl/~jules/Orphanage/

Pantera Home Page ★★★

This page is devoted to the heavy metal band Pantera. Users will find each of Pantera's album covers available as a GIF file, as well as the lyrics for all of the songs. There is also some anecdotal information available on the band, and a collection of other Pantera images. Fans have posted reviews of Pantera's live performances here for all to read. This page also has information on the Pantera mailing list and fan club, as well as a collection of guitar and bass tablature of Pantera's songs. Lastly, this site includes a link to the site where users can order Pantera merchandise.

KEYWORDS Heavy Metal Music, Music, Rock Music
AUDIENCE Hard Rock Fans, Music Enthusiasts, Rock Fans
CONTACT Jeff Garzik
jgarzik@cc.gatech.edu
FREE

http://www.wwwi.com/~jgarzik/pantera.html

Pearl Jam ★★★

The Pearl Jam site contains a collection of information and resoucres on this popular band. Fans will find Pearl Jam images, audio clips, and lyrics, as well as the latest news from the alt.music.pearl-jam newsgroup. This server is also home to a collection of articles about the band, as well as some MPEG movie clips and a bootleg disocography. Musicians will enjoy the guitar tablature archive on this server, and true fans can get information on joining the mailing list devoted to Pearl Jam.

KEYWORDS Alternative Music, Music, Rock Music
AUDIENCE Alternative Music Enthusiasts, Music Enthusiasts, Rock Fans
CONTACT Mike VanderPloeg
galvin@umich.edu
FREE

http://www.engin.umich.edu/~galvin/pearljam.html

The People of the South Wind ★★★

This Web site is dedicated to the progressive rock band Kansas. It has an FAQ, a discography, some lyrics, and transcripts of interviews. It also has information on how to subscribe to The People of the South Wind, the Kansas Internet mailing list.

KEYWORDS Progressive Music, Rock Music
AUDIENCE Progressive Music Enthusiasts, Rock Fans
CONTACT Ryan Waldron
rew@traveller.com
FREE

http://www.traveller.com/~rew/kansas.html

Phish.Net ★★★

This site is dedicated to the eclectic 'jazz-fusion-funk-blues-classic-rock' band Phish. It contains a wealth of information about the band, such as chord charts and song lyrics, an archive of the Phish mailing list, a section with the latest Phish information and updates, and the current tour schedule for this busy band. There is also a collection of Phish graphics, and information on joining one of the many taping trees that exist for this band.

KEYWORDS Jazz, Music, Rock Music
AUDIENCE Music Enthusiasts, Rock Fans
CONTACT Lee Silverman
Lee_Silverman@Brown.edu
FREE

http://www.netspace.org:80/phish/
gopher://archive.phish.net/11/phish

Planet Claire ★★★★

This Web page is dedicated to the Athens, Georgia, alternative music pioneers, The B-52's. It has a discography, some lyrics, pictures, and a sound file.

KEYWORDS Contemporary Music, Musical Groups, Rock Music
AUDIENCE Alternative Music Enthusiasts, Rock Fans
CONTACT Theo Payne
T.J.payne@durham.ac.uk
FREE

http://www.dur.ac.uk/~d43e4d/b-52s.html

The Pogues ★★★

This page is about the Irish folk/punk band The Pogues. In addition to the discography and personnel information, this site boasts a collection of Pogues lyrics, a few pictures of the band and their album covers, and information about the Pogues fan club. This site also provides a historical background to the Pogues, as well as a collection of links to other Pogues material on the Internet.

KEYWORDS Folk Music, Music, Rock Music
AUDIENCE Folk Music Enthusiasts, Music Enthusiasts, Rock Fans
CONTACT Chuck Jordan
torgo@mindspring.com
FREE

http://www.mindspring.com/~torgo/pogues.html

Police Home ★★★

This site is devoted to the talented '80s band, The Police. It contains detailed biographical information on the members of the band, as well as a collection of 'rare' pictures, music samples, and song lyrics. Users can vote for their favorite Police song, and fans will appreciate the links to other Police information on the Internet.

KEYWORDS Music, Rock Music
AUDIENCE Music Enthusiasts, Popular Music Enthusiasts, Rock Fans
CONTACT Daniel Gorelick
dang@violet.berkeley.edu
FREE

http://violet.berkeley.edu:8080/

The Posies (Dear 23) Home Page ★★★

This home page is dedicated to the alternative band, The Posies, and the Big Star reunion that two of the members participated in. It has an extensive discography, pictures, and a screed about moshing written by one of the band members. It also has information about Dear 23, the Posies mailing list.

KEYWORDS Contemporary Music, Musical Groups, Rock Music

Musical Groups

AUDIENCE Alternative Music Enthusiasts, Pop Music Enthusiasts, Rock Fans
CONTACT Wendi Dunlap
litlnemo@slumberland.com
FREE

http://www.seanet.com/litlnemo/dear23.html

The Queensryche Page ★★★★

This page is devoted to the progressive heavy-metal band Queensryche. It houses biographical information on each of the band's members, material on each of the albums that Queensryche has released, and a file with historical information on the band. This site also archives the Internet newsletter, 'Screaming in DIgital,' which is all about the band and its activities. Users will also find complete song lyrics for all of the band's songs, album reviews, sound clips in the .WAV format, and guitar tablature files.

KEYWORDS Heavy Metal Music, Music, Rock Music
AUDIENCE Hard Rock Fans, Music Enthusiasts, Rock Fans
CONTACT Nick Kramer
nk24+ryche@andrew.cmu.edu
FREE

http://www.cs.cmu.edu:8001/afs/cs.cmu.edu/user/nkramer/ryche/ryche.html

Rage Page ★★

This site is devoted to the group Rage Against The Machine. Users will find discographical information, an archive of pictures, and information on joining the Rage Against The Machine fan club. In addition, this server sports a list of all of the known songs that Rage Against The Machine has written, detailed bootleg information, and a FAQ file for the curious.

KEYWORDS Music, Rock Music
AUDIENCE Hard Rock Fans, Music Enthusiasts, Rock Fans
CONTACT Ben Harden
bharden@csugrad.cs.vt.edu
FREE

http://csugrad.cs.vt.edu/~bharden/ragepage.html

Rubriques de l'Ensemble InterContemporain ★★★

This is the homepage for the famous IRCAM in Paris. The contents include chamber music, a section on Pierre Boulez (Revendiquer l'aventure), the history and intention of l'Ensemble InterContemporain, and a discography. It is largely in French.

KEYWORDS Contemporary Music, Electronic Music, Music Schools, Paris
AUDIENCE Classical Music Enthusiasts, Electronic Music Enthusiasts, Music Enthusiasts
FREE

http://www.ircam.fr/eic/index.html

The Rutles Home Page ★★★★

This home page is dedicated to the Rutles, Liverpool's legendary Prefab Four. It has a biography, sound and picture files, a photo gallery, etc..

KEYWORDS Beatles (The), Comedy, Rock Music
AUDIENCE Beatles Fans, Monty Python Enthusiasts, Rock Fans
CONTACT Dave Haber
dhaber@primenet.com.
FREE

http://www.primenet.com/~dhaber/rutles.html

Severed Heads ★★★

This home page is for the Australian electronic band Severed Heads. It contains a profile and a discography.

KEYWORDS Alternative Music, Electronic Music
AUDIENCE Alternative Music Enthusiasts, Electronic Music Enthusiasts, Experimental Music Enthusiasts, Industrial Music Enthusiasts
FREE

http://hyperreal.com:70/1/music/artists/severed_heads

Side Saddle ★★

This is the Web Site for the Folk group, 'Side Saddle.' It is worthwhile to visit only for those who have computers capable of easily accessing large song clip files in Macintosh or X-Windows format. There is a huge graphic on the home page as well that delays downloading.

KEYWORDS Folk Music
AUDIENCE Folk Music Enthusiasts, Music Enthusiasts
CONTACT Benalia@eworld.com
FREE

http://www.microserve.net/vradio/sidesaddle/sidesadd.html

Skankin' Pickle Home Page ★★★

Skankin' Pickle is a mixture of ska, punk, metal, reggae, rap, funk, speed metal, hip-hop, polka and vaudeville. Claiming that 'six freaks have never had such a good time on stage,' the San Francisco-based band is now having fun on the Internet offering tour dates and venues, audio samples, a discography and lyrics as well as the 'Lifestyles of the Rich and Picklish,' band members bios.

KEYWORDS Ska Music
AUDIENCE Music Enthusiasts, Reggae Enthusiasts
CONTACT Dave DoBry
grue@xmission.com
FREE

http://www.xmission.com/~grue/pickle/index.html

Stutter Home Page ★★★

This home page is dedicated to the alternative act James. It has a discography, and back issues of the mailing list. It also has information on how to subscribe to the mailing list.

KEYWORDS Alternative Music, Music, Rock Music
AUDIENCE Alternative Music Enthusiasts, Rock Fans
CONTACT lrussink@drunivac.drew.edu
FREE

http://daniel.drew.edu/~lrussink/james/james.html

Sub Pop Home Page ★★★

The home page of the Seattle-based record label Sub Pop. It has a museum of sounds and images of Sub Pop bands, as well as a direct order facility.

KEYWORDS Record Labels, Rock Music, Washington State
AUDIENCE Alternative Music Enthusiasts, Punk Rock Enthusiasts, Rock Fans
CONTACT Webmaster@subpop.com
FREE

http://www.subpop.com/

The Sugar Bowl ★★★

This web site is dedicated to the pop-punk band Sugar. It has an extensive discography, lyrics, and links to Sugar graphics, including the Sugar screen saver.

KEYWORDS Alternative Music, Musical Groups, Rock Music
AUDIENCE Alternative Music Enthusiasts, Pop Music Enthusiasts, Punk Rock Enthusiasts
CONTACT Peter Demarest
pdemares@sparc2000.utsi.edu
FREE

http://sparc10_work1.utsi.edu:8000/~pdemares/sugar.html

Super-Connected ★★

This web page is dedicated to American Alternative band, Belly. It has pictures and lyrics.

KEYWORDS Contemporary Music, Musical Groups, Rock Music
AUDIENCE Alternative Music Enthusiasts, Rock Fans
CONTACT Patrick Asselman
patrick@blade.stack.urc.tue.nl
FREE

http://www.stack.urc.tue.nl/~patrick/belly/

TUU ★★★

This is the Beyond Records label home page for the band TUU. It has information about the band, their recordings, and tour dates.

KEYWORDS Electronic Music, Musical Groups
AUDIENCE Ambient Music Enthusiasts, Electronic Music Enthusiasts, Experimental Music Enthusiasts, Techno Music Enthusiasts
FREE

http://iuma.southern.com/beyond/tuu/

Talking Heads ★★★

The Talking Heads page offers a wealth of resources about the defunct but influential band. Users will find information on joining the Talking Heads mailing list, bootleg and official release discographies, pointers to FTP archives of lyrics and guitar tablature, digitized

Musical Groups – Musicians

songs, images, and more. In addition, this server provides links to pages detailing the current activities of Talking Heads members, as well as other information about the band.

- KEYWORDS: Alternative Music, Rock Music
- AUDIENCE: Alternative Music Enthusiasts, Music Enthusiasts, Rock Fans
- CONTACT: Cole D. Robison
  milo@ukanaix.cc.ukans.edu
- FREE

http://129.237.17.3/Heads/Talking_Heads.html

Too Posh to Mosh — Little Angels ★★★

This home page is for the British hard rock band Little Angels. It has an FAQ, a history of the band, discographies, a list of shows, and some pictures.

- KEYWORDS: Hard Rock Music, Rock Music
- AUDIENCE: Hard Rock Fans, Heavy Metal Fans
- CONTACT: eta@tardis.ed.ac.uk
- FREE

http://www.tardis.ed.ac.uk/~eta/angels.html

The Truth (About Clawfinger) ★★

This home page is all about Clawfinger, a heavy metal band from Sweden. It has lyrics, sound files and a little information about the band.

- KEYWORDS: Contemporary Music, Rock Music, Sweden
- AUDIENCE: Heavy Metal Fans, Rock Fans, Swedes
- CONTACT: g.i.west@bradford.ac.uk
- FREE

http://www.brad.ac.uk/~giwest/clawfinger.html

U2 Guess the Lyric of the Week ★★★★

This site has a fan-driven weekly contest based on the lyrics of the popular Irish rock band U2. Somebody has posted a lyric to a U2 song on the site, and the first person to guess the song gets to post the next week's lyric. This site also has links to the U2 newsgroups, the U2 mailing list, other U2 Web sites, the U2 Zoo TV screen saver program, and CDNOW.

- KEYWORDS: Alternative Music, Lyrics, Rock Music
- AUDIENCE: Alternative Music Enthusiasts, Pop Music Enthusiasts, Rock Fans
- CONTACT: Steve Theodorou
  STHEO@CRL.COM
- FREE

http://www.mps.ohio-state.edu/cgi-bin/hpp?hewson.html

The Unofficial Nine Inch Nails Home Page ★★★★

This home page is dedicated to the popular Industrial band Nine Inch Nails and songwriter/creator Trent Reznor. It has general information on the band, a complete discography, lyrics, tour information, reviews and guitar tabs. It also has the NIN FAQ links to other NIN resources.

- KEYWORDS: Discographies, Industrial Music, Rock Music
- AUDIENCE: Alternative Music Enthusiasts, Generation X, Industrial Music Enthusiasts
- CONTACT: Jason Patterson
  patters@dirac.scri.fsu.edu
- FREE

http://www.scri.fsu.edu/~patters/nin.html

The Unofficial Violent Femmes Home Page ★★★

This site is dedicated to the American rock band Violent Femmes. It contains information on band members, some lyrics and guitar tabs, as well as descriptions of the albums, and where to get more information on the band.

- KEYWORDS: Alternative Music, Feminist Music, Rock Music
- AUDIENCE: Alternative Music Enthusiasts, Feminists, Rock Fans
- CONTACT: Mike Merryman
  mmerry2@umbc8.umbc.edu
- FREE

http://umbc8.umbc.edu/~mmerry2/femmes.html

Urban Tapestry ★★

This site describes Urban Tapestry, a Canadian 'filk' group. What is filk? The site offers an article about the birth of filk music—apparently, it's a parody of folk music that arose at Science Fiction conventions when people started singing folk songs and changed the lyrics (!?) There are sound clips available for listening.

- KEYWORDS: Canada, Folk Music, Science Fiction
- AUDIENCE: Folk Music Enthusiasts, Science Fiction Enthusiasts
- CONTACT: Debbie Ridpath Ohi
  morgaine@utcc.utoronto.ca
- FREE

http://www.interlog.com/~ohi/ut_page/urbantap.html

Verse Chorus Verse - The Nirvana Homepage ★★★★

This site is dedicated to the popular rock band Nirvana. It has the FAQ, lyrics, a discography, and a list of covers and tributes. It also has a Kurt Cobain equipment FAQ, some selected articles from Usenet, images, and links to other Nirvana resources.

- KEYWORDS: Discographies, Rock Music
- AUDIENCE: Alternative Music Enthusiasts, Complainers, Rock Fans
- CONTACT: jedi@ecst.csuchico.edu
- FREE

http://www2.ecst.csuchico.edu/~jedi/nirvana.html

Welcome to Paradise, the Unofficial Green Day Page ★★

This page is devoted to the popular bubblegum-punk band Green Day. It offers some of the historical and biographical background of the band, as well as a selection of pictures and articles about the band. Fans will also find a complete discography with information on unofficial bootleg releases, song lyrics, and a collection of pointers to other Green Day sites on the Internet.

- KEYWORDS: Music, Punk Rock, Rock Music
- AUDIENCE: Alternative Music Enthusiasts, Music Enthusiasts, Punk Rock Enthusiasts, Rock Fans
- CONTACT: Adam Rifkin
  adam@vlsi.caltech.edu
- FREE

http://www.cs.caltech.edu/~adam/greenday.html

Yes Archive WWW Server ★★★★

This is the WWW server for the archive dedicated to the band Yes. It has a discography, lyrics, images, and the back issues of Notes From The Edge, the Internet Yes newsletter. It also has an extensive rarities and bootleg file.

- KEYWORDS: Progressive Music, Rock Music
- AUDIENCE: Progressive Music Enthusiasts, Rock Fans, Rock Musicians
- FREE

http://www.meiko.com/yes-archive/

Musicians

See also
Arts & Music · *Music Genres*
Arts & Music · *Musical Groups*
Arts & Music · *Performing Arts*
Popular Culture & Entertainment · *Celebrities & Personalities*

461 Ocean Boulevard ★★★

461 Ocean Boulevard is a page devoted to the works of guitar 'god' Eric Clapton. Fans will find a wide variety of material about this blues-rock guitarist, including pictures and animations, digitized songs, a thorough discography including bootleg releases, and an archive of lyrics. In addition, this server offers pointers to guitar tablature of Eric's songs, an Eric Clapton FAQ file, and a selection of pointers to other Eric Clapton resources on the Net.

- KEYWORDS: Blues, Music, Rock Music
- AUDIENCE: Blues Enthusiasts, Music Enthusiasts, Rock Fans
- CONTACT: Dave Hillman
  d-hillman@uchicago.edu
- FREE

http://http.bsd.uchicago.edu/~d-hillman/welcome.html

Musicians   83

The Alfred Schnittke Page ★★★★

This web page is dedicated to Twentieth-Century Russian composer Alfred Schnittke. It contains biographical information, a list of compositions, a photo, music sample, and links to other artists.

KEYWORDS Classical Music, Composers, Music
AUDIENCE Classical Music Enthusiasts, Contemporary Music Enthusiasts, Music Enthusiasts, Music Researchers
FREE

http://ccnet.com/~drolon/Schnitt.html

All of Kevin's Tori Pointers ★★★★

This web site is dedicated to Tori Amos. It is a comprehensive listing of links to all of the Tori Amos Internet resources.

KEYWORDS Contemporary Music, Rock Music, Songwriters
AUDIENCE Alternative Music Enthusiasts, Progressive Music Enthusiasts, Rock Fans
CONTACT Kevin Hawkins
khawkins@ncsa.uiuc.edu
FREE

http://gto.ncsa.uiuc.edu/khawkins/tori.html

Amy Grant Archive ★★★

This well-stocked fan archive is about the singer/songwriter Amy Grant. It maintains a large number of articles, press releases, interviews, and biographical material on the artist. There are also song lyrics, discographies and videographies, tour information and current news, and much more. This server also maintains an archive of the Amy Grant newsgroup, as well as an image gallery and pointers to other Amy Grant Internet resources.

KEYWORDS Pop Music, Rock Music, Songwriters
AUDIENCE Country Music Enthusiasts, Music Enthusiasts, Popular Music Enthusiasts, Rock Fans
CONTACT Andreas J. Haug
ajh@ipc.uni-tuebingen.de
FREE

http://www.ipc.uni-tuebingen.de/art

And Through The Wire-Peter Gabriel ★★★★

Fans of the musician Peter Gabriel will find a lot of good information and resources on this popular artist. Users will find complete discographies, including bootlegs, singles, and international releases, a 'classifieds' section with information and advertisements on Peter Gabriel memorabilia and merchandise, and much more. There are also links to sound and image archives, biographical material, and a wealth of links to other Internet resources on the man and his music.

KEYWORDS Music, Pop Music, Rock Music
AUDIENCE British Pop Music Fans, Music Enthusiasts, Popular Music Enthusiasts, Rock Fans

CONTACT John N. Underwood
junderw@cs.clemson.edu
FREE

http://www.cs.clemson.edu/~junderw/pg.html

The Ani DiFranco Home Page ★★★

The focus of this Web page is folksinger and songwriter Ani DiFranco. Tour dates, interviews, her biography and discography are all available, as are lyrics to some more popular songs.

KEYWORDS Folk Music, Music, Songwriters
AUDIENCE Folk Music Enthusiasts, Music Enthusiasts
CONTACT Margarita Suarez
marg@columbia.edu
FREE

http://www.cc.columbia.edu/~marg/ani/

Beck ★★

This is a homepage dedicated to Beck. It contains some lyrics, pictures, audio files and links to other Beck pages (Mike Paige's Beck Page, alt.music.beck, Amy Broski's Beck Home Page).

KEYWORDS Contemporary Music, Rock Music
AUDIENCE Alternative Music Enthusiasts, Folk Music Enthusiasts, Rap Music Enthusiasts, Rock Fans
CONTACT Matt Herbison
mxh160@psu.edu
FREE

http://mxh160.rh.psu.edu/Docs/Beck.html

The Bell - The Mike Oldfield Mailing List Home Page ★★★

This home page is dedicated to musician Mike Oldfield. It has a discography, biography, listing of song books, and fan club information. There are also links here to other Mike Oldfield sites and related music sites on the net. The author of this page claims, " In case you've never heard of him, Mike Oldfield is probably the best musician this side of Gershwin. His style of music varies greatly, and his new albums are always a surprise."

KEYWORDS Musicians, Progressive Music, Rock Music
AUDIENCE Film Enthusiasts, Guitar Music Enthusiasts, Progressive Music Enthusiasts, Rock Fans
CONTACT pettypi@csd.uwo.ca
FREE

http://www.csd.uwo.ca/~pettypi/mike_oldfield/the_bell.html

Björk Gumundsdóttir ★★★★

This home page is dedicated to Bjork, the Icelandic chanteuse and former lead singer of the Sugarcubes. It has a discography of her solo work, some articles and interviews, a history of the group, and links to her mailing lists.

KEYWORDS Iceland, Punk Rock, Rock Music
AUDIENCE Alternative Music Enthusiasts, Pop Music Enthusiasts, Progressive Music Enthusiasts, Rock Fans

CONTACT Stig R. Kristoffersen
srk@math.uio.no
FREE

http://math-www.uio.no/bjork/index.html

Cecilia Bartoli Homepage ★★★★

This Web page is dedicated to Grammy-winning Classical Music singer Cecilia Bartoli. It includes a discussion thread, links to related sites, a discography and live performances schedule. Users can also browse an archive of downloadable images of the opera star in both GIF and JPEG formats.

KEYWORDS Classical Music, Opera
AUDIENCE Classical Music Enthusiasts, Opera Enthusiasts
CONTACT Gary Stephens
stephens@sse.ie
FREE

http://www.nwu.edu/music/bartoli/

Chris Rea Home Page ★★★

This server offers users information and resources about the UK-based rock/blues guitarist and singer/songwriter Chris Rea. Users will find such things as UK and international discographies, album information, song lyrics, and biographical material. In addition, this server hosts a collection of audio files in the .WAV format, as well as a section with the latest news on the artist. Fans will appreciate the section with information on Chris Rea memorabilia. Finally, the Chris Rea home page has links to an FTP site with material on the artist, chart information, and links to other Chris Rea Web sites.

KEYWORDS Blues, Music, Rock Music
AUDIENCE Hard Rock Fans, Music Enthusiasts, Rock Fans
CONTACT Miro Wikgren
Miro.wikgren@helsinki.fi
FREE

http://www.helsinki.fi/~wikgren/chrisrea.html

Christine Lavin Home Page ★★★★

Christine Lavin, a songwriter known for such works as 'Sensitive New Age Guys' and albums such as 'Please Don't Make Me Too Happy,' has a home on the Web. This site is maintained by a long time fan, and offers new information directly from Lavin and the Four Bitchin' Babes. Users will find images of Lavin and her concert performances, concert reviews, biographical information, a discography, and links to other sites devoted to Lavin or selected musical pages (such as Windham Hill and Suzanne Vega). Plans in the works include a bulletin board page and other projects.

KEYWORDS Recording Artists, Songwriters
AUDIENCE Folk Music Enthusiasts, Music Enthusiasts
FREE

http://www.automatrix.com/~lavin/

Cyndi Lauper — WWW Home Page ★★★

This home page is dedicated to pop artist and film performer Cyndi Lauper. It contains a short biography,

Musicians

discographies, an extensive concert list, videography, and a listing of her appearances on other people's records.
- **KEYWORDS** Musicians, Pop Music, Rock Music
- **AUDIENCE** Alternative Music Enthusiasts, Film Buffs, Pop Music Enthusiasts, Rock Fans
- **CONTACT** jean-marc.piraprez@csl.sni.be
- **FREE**

http://www.sni.be/en/goodies/cyndi/welcome.htm

DI-1-9026 ★★★★

This home page is dedicated to alternative musician Jim 'Foetus' Thirlwell. It has a discography, lyrics, pictures, interviews, and an place where people can review the latest release.
- **KEYWORDS** Alternative Music, Music, Rock Music
- **AUDIENCE** Alternative Music Enthusiasts, Industrial Music Enthusiasts, Rock Fans
- **CONTACT** elnitsky@coos.dartmouth.edu
- **FREE**

http://coos.dartmouth.edu/~elnitsky/Foetus.html

Dark Horse - The George Harrison Home Page ★★

This page is devoted to George Harrison, a former member of the Beatles. It follows the artist throughout his career, from his time as a guitarist for the Beatles through his work with the Traveling Wilburys. Users will find guitar tablature, lyrics, biographical information, and material on the artist's many albums.
- **KEYWORDS** Pop Music, Rock Music
- **AUDIENCE** Beatles Fans, British Pop Music Fans, Music Enthusiasts, Rock Fans
- **CONTACT** Jeffrey C. Jacobs
  timelord@binkley.cs.mcgill.ca
- **FREE**

http://www.cs.mcgill.ca/~timelord/Harrison/George.html

The David Benoit Home Page ★★★★

These pages contain numerous articles and other materials relating to jazz composer and musician David Benoit. Audio samples from many of Benoit's recordings are available, as are digitized images of the covers of many of his albums.
- **KEYWORDS** Composers, Jazz, Music
- **AUDIENCE** Jazz Enthusiasts, Music Enthusiasts
- **CONTACT** Jean C. Wang
  csdismas@leland.Stanford.EDU
- **FREE**

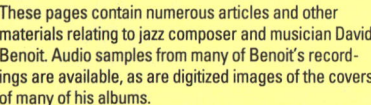

http://www-leland.stanford.edu/~csdismas/benoit.html

The David Bowie File ★★★★

The focus of this group of Web pages is the life and work of musician David Bowie. Many photographs of Bowie are available here, as is a discography, comprehensive biographical information, and a few audio clips.
- **KEYWORDS** Rock Music
- **AUDIENCE** Alternative Music Enthusiasts, Music Enthusiasts, Rock Fans
- **CONTACT** Evan Torrie
  torrie@cs.stanford.edu
- **FREE**

http://liber.stanford.edu/~torrie/Bowie/BowieFile.html

David Kikoski ★★★★

This artist page, dedicated to David Kikoski, includes a biography, discography, and access to the Sony Artists Tour Schedule. David Kikoski's first music lessons came from his father, a part-time musician who Count Basie and Duke Ellington as well as the basics of Chopin and Beethoven. But David Kikoski's compositions are not simply pianistic experiments out on the fringes of jazz. This artist draws on styles as diverse as Brazilian samba and English progressive rock. This Web page also includes David Kikoski Album information.
- **KEYWORDS** Classical Music, Compact Discs (CDs), Composers
- **AUDIENCE** Classical Music Enthusiasts, Compact Disc Users, Music Enthusiasts, Performers
- **CONTACT** SonyMusicOnline@sonymusic.com
- **FREE**

http://www.music.sony.com/Music/ArtistInfo/DavidKikoski.html

Dmitri Shostakovich Home Page ★★★

This page offers a selection of resources related to the classical composer Dmitri Shostakovich. Users will find a collection of Shostakovich sound samples in AIFC format, some pictures, biographical information, and a collection of links to other Shostakovich material on the Net.
- **KEYWORDS** Classical Music, Composers, Instrumental Music
- **AUDIENCE** Classical Music Enthusiasts, Instrumental Music Enthusiasts, Music Enthusiasts
- **CONTACT** Rob Hudson
  rhudson@uta.edu
- **FREE**

http://www.uta.edu/acs/microsys/mac/.HOME/rhudson/dsch1.html

Ed Alleyne-Johnson's Homepage ★★★★

The homepage for Ed Alleyne-Johnson, who plays electric violin, and has produced two albums to date - Purple Electric Violin Concerto, and Ultraviolet. The description on the page reads simply 'The sound Ed produces is difficult to describe. It is a kind of fusion of ambient, rock, and classical.'
- **KEYWORDS** Classical Music, Compact Discs (CDs), Contemporary Music, Music
- **AUDIENCE** Classical Music Enthusiasts, Contemporary Music Enthusiasts, Music Enthusiasts, Violinists
- **CONTACT** Graham Hick
  graham@cyberspace.org
- **FREE**

http://cyberspace.org/u/graham/www/eaj/home.html

Elvis Costello ★★★

Elvis Costello fans will find many interesting resources on the Elvis Costello home page. There is an archive of the Elvis Costello mailing list, as well as instructions on how to join, and information on concerts and other upcoming Elvis Costello events. In addition, there is a section of concert reviews, a discography, archives of song lyrics and guitar tablature, and a poll (as well as the results from past polls) of fans of the popular musician.
- **KEYWORDS** Alternative Music, Music, Rock Music
- **AUDIENCE** Alternative Music Enthusiasts, Music Enthusiasts, Pop Music Enthusiasts, Rock Fans
- **CONTACT** Mark Schnitzius
  schnitzi@east.isx.com
- **FREE**

http://east.isx.com/~schnitzi/elvis.html

Elvis Home Page ★★★

This site is dedicated to Elvis Presley. It's in a state of flux at this point due to a threatening letter sent by Elvis Presley Enterprises. The full text of the letter is at the site. This site still has The Adventures of Space Elvis, and some links to copyright law and other legal issues. There are also links to Elvis multimedia stuff and Elvis applications for Windows and Mac.
- **KEYWORDS** Contemporary Music, Music, Rock Music
- **AUDIENCE** Elvis Presley Fans, Popular Culture Enthusiasts, Rock Fans
- **CONTACT** Andrea Helene Berman
  andrea@sunsite.unc.edu
- **FREE**

http://sunsite.unc.edu/elvis/elvishom.html

Emanuel Ax ★★★★

Emanuel Ax is acclaimed throughout the world for his performances of the chamber music. He performs duo recitals every season with the cellist Yo-Yo Ma. In recent years they have both collaborated with Isaac Stern in various chamber music configurations specialising in the Romantic repertoire. This classical artist page, sponsored by Sony Music Entertainment, includes a biography, discography, and access to the Sony Artists Tour Schedule. This site also includes works on the Chopin Chamber Works Album and a soundclip from the album.
- **KEYWORDS** Classical Music, Compact Discs (CDs), Music
- **AUDIENCE** Classical Music Enthusiasts, Compact Disc Users, Music Enthusiasts, Performers
- **CONTACT** SonyMusicOnline@sonymusic.com
- **FREE**

http://www.music.sony.com/Music/ArtistInfo/EmanuelAx.html

Eno Home ★★★

The Eno home page is dedicated to the experimental/avant-garde/ambient musician Brian Eno. The page includes a biography and chronology of the artist, a bibliography of books and magazines, a list of video and television appearances, and information on Eno's record label. There is also a selection of liner notes from some of Eno's albums, and a section of links to other Eno Internet resources.

- KEYWORDS: Progressive Music, Rock Music
- AUDIENCE: Alternative Music Enthusiasts, Experimental Music Enthusiasts, Music Enthusiasts
- CONTACT: malcolm@wrs.com
- FREE

http://www.acns.nwu.edu/eno-l/

Enrico Caruso ★★★★

This page is dedicated to Enrico Caruso and includes a portrait, biography, and list of recommended recordings. For many music lovers, Enrico Caruso is the quintessential Italian tenor - headstrong, romantic, with a voice brimming with passion and a temperament to match. In truth, the short life of this musical legend contained many of these seemingly mythical components. Born in Naples in 1873, the 18th child born to a working class family - and the first to survive infancy. His musical breakthrough came in 1898, when he was selected to perform the lead role in the premiere of Giordano's Fedora in Milan. The engagement was an unqualified success, and led to more high-profile appearances culminating with a leading role in La Boheme at La Scala.

- KEYWORDS: Classical Music, Compact Discs (CDs), Opera Singers, Performing Artists
- AUDIENCE: Classical Music Enthusiasts, Compact Disc Users, Music Enthusiasts, Opera Enthusiasts
- CONTACT: rbourne@panix.com
- FREE

http://www.classicalmus.com/artists/caruso.html

Esa-Pekka Salonen ★★★★

Esa-Pekka Salonen is a renown composer, the principal conductor of the Swedish Radio Symphony Orchestra, and a principal guest conductor of the Philharmonic Orchestra in London. Born in Helsinki in 1958, he studied at the Sibelius Academy and went on to study composition with Niccolo Castiglioni in Italy. This site includes a biography, discography, and access to the Sony Artists Tour Schedule.

- KEYWORDS: Classical Music, Compact Discs (CDs), Music
- AUDIENCE: Classical Music Enthusiasts, Compact Disc Users, Music Enthusiasts, Symphony Conductors
- CONTACT: SonyMusicOnline@sonymusic.com
- FREE

http://www.music.sony.com/Music/ArtistInfo/EsaPekkaSalonen.html

Expecting Rain ★★★

Expecting Rain is a site dedicated to the venerable folk-rock singer/songwriter Bob Dylan. It houses a large collection of Dylan resources such as pictures, lyrics, video, discographies, and more. This server also maintains a list of 'who's who' in the world of Bob Dylan, an atlas with information on all of the places mentioned in Dylan songs, an archive of sound files, and much more.

- KEYWORDS: Folk Music, Rock Music, Songwriters
- AUDIENCE: Folk Music Enthusiasts, Folk Rock Fans, Music Enthusiasts, Rock Fans
- CONTACT: Karl Erik Andersen Karl.Erik.Andersen@nbr.no
- FREE

http://128.39.161.105/dok/keahome.html

Gilby Clarke Home Page ★★★

This page is dedicated to Pawnshop Guitars, the new solo recording by Guns And Roses guitarist Gilby Clarke. Biographical information, photographs and the complete lyrics to the album are all available here.

- KEYWORDS: Rock Music
- AUDIENCE: Heavy Metal Fans, Rock Fans
- CONTACT: Jeff Boerio boerio@ichips.intel.com
- FREE

http://www.teleport.com/~boerio/gnr/gilby.html

Gloria Estefan ★★

This is Sony Music's home page for popular singer Gloria Estefan. It has a partial discography, information on a couple of her records, and a few songs.

- KEYWORDS: Dance Music, Music, Urban Music
- AUDIENCE: Dance Music Enthusiasts, Latin Music Enthusiasts, Pop Music Enthusiasts
- CONTACT: Lawerence Wright skybird@shbbs.demon.co.uk
- FREE

http://www.music.sony.com/Music/ArtistInfo/GloriaEstefan.html

Harry Belafonte ★★

This site contains a short biography of Harry Belafonte and some music clips as well as access to a CD Catalog for purchasing his music as well as that of other artists.

- KEYWORDS: Caribbean Music, Compact Discs (CDs), Music Resources
- AUDIENCE: Music Enthusiasts
- FREE

http://www.classicalmus.com/artists/belafont.html

Husker Du/Bob Mould/Sugar ★★★★

This web site is devoted to the career of Bob Mould, the amazing songwriter and guitarist. It has information on his former band, Husker Du his solo career, and his current band, Sugar. This site has a discography, bootlegraphy, the Sugar FAQ, lyrics, articles, and guitar tabs. It also has fan club and mailing list information.

- KEYWORDS: Lyrics, Rock Music, Songwriters
- AUDIENCE: Alternative Music Enthusiasts, Guitar Music Enthusiasts, Punk Rock Enthusiasts, Rock Fans
- CONTACT: sanford@math.montana.edu
- FREE

http://math.montana.edu/~sanford/sugar.html

Hyper Idol — The Billy Idol Home Page ★★★

This is a homepage dedicated to professional punk poseur Billy Idol. It has a discography, some pictures, and links to places where you can purchase Billy's music.

- KEYWORDS: Punk Rock, Rock Music
- AUDIENCE: Alternative Music Enthusiasts, Pop Music Enthusiasts, Punk Rock Enthusiasts, Rock Fans
- CONTACT: Mark A. Lindner markl@zoo.cs.yale.edu
- FREE

http://minerva.cis.yale.edu/~markl/billy-idol/

Jan's Home Page ★★★★

This is the home page of Ambient musican Jan Hanford. It has information on Jan, her album in progress, and sound files.

- KEYWORDS: Feminist Music
- AUDIENCE: Ambient Music Enthusiasts, Electronic Music Enthusiasts, Experimental Music Enthusiasts, Techno Music Enthusiasts
- CONTACT: Jan Hanford jan@shelby.com
- FREE

http://www.shelby.com/pub/wsg/html/jan/home.html

Janet's Home Page ★★★

The Janet Jackson Home Page offers fans of the popular musician a collection of resources and information about this pop music artist. Users can browse an archive of images from magazines and album covers, get news and the latest tour dates, and listen to a selection of sound files, including some unavailable remixes and other hard-to-find pieces. There is also a collection of links to other Janet resources on the Internet.

- KEYWORDS: Dance Music, Music, Pop Music
- AUDIENCE: Dance Music Enthusiasts, Janet Jackson Enthusiasts, Music Enthusiasts, Popular Music Enthusiasts
- CONTACT: Acee Agoyo agoyo1@mit.edu
- FREE

http://www.mit.edu:8001/people/agoyo1/janet.html

Jimi Hendrix Server ★★★★

Another site devoted to this extraordinary guitarist, the Jimi Hendrix Server boasts a wealth of resources gathered together in one place. Many pictures and album cover images are made available in the picture gallery, and there is also a complete discography with bootlegs, singles, covers by other artists, and albums with Jimi as a guest. Jimi Hendrix fans can also get guitar tablature and lyrics here, as well as a list of books and videos about the guitarist.

Keywords   Guitar, Music, Rock Music
Audience   Guitar Music Enthusiasts, Music Enthusiasts, Rock Fans
Contact   Colin Reed
             Colin.Reed@parks.tas.gov.au
Free

http://www.parks.tas.gov.au/jimi/jimi.html

Jimmy Buffett Web Page ★★★

Fans of Jimmy Buffett need look no further than the Jimmy Buffett Web Page. This site offers users a complete selection of information and resources about this booze-rock artist. Users will find Jimmy Buffett FAQs, images, and sound samples, as well as the latest tour information, lyrics, and a complete discography. There are also links to electronic newsletters on Jimmy Buffett, FTP archives of Buffett material, and alcoholic beverage recipes from the artist.

Keywords   Music, Pop Music, Rock Music
Audience   Music Enthusiasts, Popular Music Enthusiasts, Rock Fans
Contact   Dave April
             april@ils.nwu.edu
Free

http://ameritech.ils.nwu.edu/buffett/buffett.html

The Joe Jackson Archive ★★

This home page is an archive of information about British singer/songwriter Joe Jackson. It has a discography, bootlegraphy, tour dates, magazine articles and mailing list information.

Keywords   Alternative Music, Rock Music, Songwriters
Audience   Alternative Music Enthusiasts, Jazz Enthusiasts, Pop Music Enthusiasts, Rock Fans
Contact   Andreas Wostrack
             a.wostrack@mail.cryst.bbk.ac.uk
Free

http://www.cryst.bbk.ac.uk/~ubcg5ab/JJ/joe.html

Johann Sebastian Bach ★★

For a short biography and music clips of Johann Sebastian Bach, this site is worth visiting. Returning to the main menu will allow one to select another composer or musician to study.

Keywords   Biographies, Classical Music, Composers
Audience   Music Enthusiasts, Students
Free

http://classicalmus.com/composers/bach.html

John Moran ★★★★

This is dedicated to composer John Moran. It includes a biography, discography, and access to the Sony Artists Tour Schedule. Often called "a protege of Philip Glass," the Nebraska-born John Moran has composed five operas in addition many other works. A recorded version of Moran's "The Manson Family" was the first classical disc to receive a "Parental Advisory" sticker. Moran and director Bob McGrath received an Obie (Off Broadway) Award last spring for Sustained Excellence in Collaborative Creation.

Keywords   Classical Music, Compact Discs (CDs), Music
Audience   Classical Music Enthusiasts, Compact Disc Users, Music Enthusiasts, Performers
Contact   SonyMusicOnline@sonymusic.com
Free

http://www.music.sony.com/Music/ArtistInfo/JohnMoran.html

John Taveneris ★★★★

Born in London in 1944, John Taveneris a renowned classical pianist and organist. He is also a composer with an originality of concept and an intensely personal idiom which renders his voice quite separate from those of his contemporaries. This page, one of a series of classical artist pages sponsored by Sony Music Entertainment, includes a biography, discography, and access to the Sony Artists Tour Schedule. This Web page also includes information on the 'Akathist Of Thanksgiving' Album and a soundclip from the album.

Keywords   Classical Music, Compact Discs (CDs), Pianists
Audience   Classical Music Enthusiasts, Compact Disc Users, Music Enthusiasts, Performers
Contact   SonyMusicOnline@sonymusic.com
Free

http://www.music.sony.com/Music/ArtistInfo/JohnTavener.html

Joni Mitchell ★★

This site is dedicated to influential folk/rock/jazz artist Joni Mitchell. It has a short biography, a small discography, and some sound files. This site also contains links to other music pages including the Ultimate Band List.

Keywords   Folk Music, Musicians, Rock Music
Audience   Folk Music Enthusiasts, Jazz Enthusiasts, Pop Music Enthusiasts, Rock Fans
Free

http://calvin.bu.edu/bios/Mitchell.html

Klaus Schulze ★★★

This home page is for ambient musician Klaus Schulze. It has a profile, some news, description of his music and a place where his albums are rated.

Keywords   Electronic Music, Experimental Music
Audience   Ambient Music Enthusiasts, Electronic Music Enthusiasts, Experimental Music Enthusiasts
Free

http://hyperreal.com:70/1/music/artists/klaus_schulze

Little Guyville ★★★

This site is dedicated to alternative singer/songwriter Liz Phair. This site has some pictures, lyrics, and links to other Liz Phair sites.

Keywords   Alternative Music, Rock Music, Songwriters
Audience   Alternative Music Enthusiasts, Musicians, Rock Fans
Contact   andras@is.co.za
Free

http://hermes.is.co.za/andras/music/lp/little-guyville.html

The Lloyd Cole Web Page ★★★★

This home page is dedicated to alternative singer/songwriter Lloyd Cole. It has a discography, an autobiography, most of his lyrics, pictures, and reviews. It also has mailing list information, and a letter Lloyd wrote to his fans in 1993.

Keywords   Cole, Lyrics, Rock Music, Songwriters
Audience   Alternative Music Enthusiasts, Pop Music Enthusiasts, Rock Fans
Contact   Ethan Straffin
             drumz@best.com
Free

http://www.best.com/~drumz/Cole/

Locust ★★★

This home page is for techno/ambient musician Locust. It has a profile, a discography, and some sound files.

Keywords   Alternative Music, Techno/Ambient Music
Audience   Ambient Music Enthusiasts, Electronic Music Enthusiasts, Experimental Music Enthusiasts, Techno Music Enthusiasts
Contact   Brian Hostetler
             brianh@hyperreal.com
Free

http://hyperreal.com/music/artists/locust/locust.html

Loreena McKennitt Home Page ★★★

This page is for fans of the folk singer/songwriter Loreena McKennitt. It houses a FAQ file, a gallery of pictures, and a section where users can provide feedback or news about the artist. In addition, this server offers a collection of Loreena McKennitt's song lyrics, a selection of audio files in .AU and AIFC formats, as well as some interview material culled from online forums and television appearances. Users will also find a complete discography and links to similar artists on the Internet.

Keywords   Folk Music, Songwriters
Audience   Country Music Enthusiasts, Folk Music Enthusiasts, Loreena McKennitt Enthusiasts, Music Enthusiasts
Contact   Aaron McMahon
             drcool@halcyon.com
Free

http://www.halcyon.com/coolweb/loreena.html

Lou Reed WWW Site ★★★

This site is devoted to both the Velvet Underground and Lou Reed. Users will find resources such as an interview with John Cale, articles about Lou Reed and other Velvet Underground members, and discography files for both Lou and the Underground. There is also information on the Lou Reed mailing list, as well as some of the

Musicians

latest news and information on the latest activities of both Lou Reed and the Velvet Underground.

KEYWORDS: Music, Rock Music
AUDIENCE: Alternative Music Enthusiasts, Music Enthusiasts, Rock Fans
CONTACT: Matt Carmichael
charm@nwu.edu
FREE

http://charlotte.acns.nwu.edu/charm/html/lou/discog.html

Mariah Carey ★★★

This page is dedicated to the popular vocalist Mariah Carrey. It includes an archive of pictures of Mariah, the Mariah Carey FAQ file, a complete set of song lyrics, and a discography. In addition, Marian fans will find information on the official Mariah Carey Fan Club, an archive of the Vision mailing list devoted to discussion of Mariah Carey, and links to her biography page at Sony Music.

KEYWORDS: Music, Pop Music, Rock Music
AUDIENCE: Music Enthusiasts, Popular Music Enthusiasts, Rock Fans
CONTACT: vision-dude@biogopher.wustl.edu
FREE

http://biogopher.wustl.edu:70/0h/audio/mariah_carey/mariah

 Mary Chapin-Carpenter ★★★

This is Sony Music's official web site for popular Country singer Mary Chapin-Carpenter. It has a couple of recent press releases, information about her Stones in the Road album, an extensive biography, tour information, and an interactive press kit.

KEYWORDS: Contemporary Music, Pop Music
AUDIENCE: Country Music Enthusiasts, Pop Music Enthusiasts, Rock Fans
FREE

http://www.sony.com/Music/ArtistInfo/MaryChapinCarpenter.html

 Michael Jackson Homepage ★★★

This home page is dedicated to King of Pop Michael Jackson. It has current news, magazine covers, pictures, books written by Michael and tour dates.

KEYWORDS: Pop Music, Urban Music
AUDIENCE: Dance Music Enthusiasts, Pop Music Enthusiasts, Rhythm & Blues Enthusiasts, Soul Music Enthusiasts
CONTACT: listen@primenet.com
FREE

http://www.primenet.com/~listen/

Michael Nesmith Home Page ★★★★

The Michael Nesmith Home Page is dedicated to the post-Monkee career of musician and TV producer Michael Nesmith. It has information on his music, and on his Elephant Parts videos, as well as reviews, interviews, sound files, pictures, and various Usenet posts from tNesmith. A lot of interesting information can be found here.

KEYWORDS: Musicians, Pop Music, Rock Music
AUDIENCE: 60's Music Enthusiasts, Pop Music Listeners, Rock Fans, TV Enthusiasts
CONTACT: Brad Waddell
flex@primenet.com
FREE

http://www.primenet.com/~flex/nesmith.htm

Michael Sterns ★★★

This home page is for electronic musician Michael Sterns. It has a biography, discographies, sound files, filmography and information on works in progress.

KEYWORDS: Electronic Music, Experimental Music
AUDIENCE: Ambient Music Enthusiasts, Electronic Music Enthusiasts, Experimental Music Enthusiasts, Film Buffs
CONTACT: Raven Zachary
raven@nets.com
FREE

http://www.nets.com/stearns

 Midori ★★★★

This classical music page is dedicated to Midori, the violinist, and includes a biography, discography, and access to the Sony Artists Tour Schedule. Midori, born in Osaka, Japan, in 1971, began studying the violin at the age of four. She has shared the great concert stages of the world with such eminent artists as Claudio Abbado, Vladimir Ashkenazy, Daniel Barenboim, Leonard Bernstein, Charles Dutoit, Yo-Yo Ma, Zubin Mehta, and many others. Midori is equally active as a recitalist, having made several highly-acclaimed tours of North America and Europe. This Web page includes information on the Sibelius Violin Concerto Album, and a soundclip from the album.

KEYWORDS: Classical Music, Compact Discs (CDs), Music
AUDIENCE: Classical Music Enthusiasts, Compact Disc Users, Music Enthusiasts, Performers
CONTACT: SonyMusicOnline@sonymusic.com
FREE

http://www.music.sony.com/Music/ArtistInfo/Midori.html

Mike Keneally Page ★★★★

This Web site is dedicated to progressive rock musician Mike Keneally. It has tons of information on Mike—from a comic he drew as a kid to an interview with musician Adrian Belew to information on his records. The site has great graphics as well.

KEYWORDS: Progressive Music, Rock Music
AUDIENCE: Guitarists, Progressive Music Enthusiasts, Rock Fans
CONTACT: Scott Chatfield
scott@psy.ucsd.edu
FREE

http://psy.ucsd.edu/~scott/keneally.html

Miles Davis HTML Discography ★★★

This site houses a complete and exhaustive discography of the lifework of Miles Davis, the acclaimed jazz trumpeter and major proponent of what is now known as improvisational modern jazz. Biographical material and a few images are also available.

KEYWORDS: Jazz, Music
AUDIENCE: Jazz Enthusiasts, Musicians
CONTACT: Peter Losin
losinp@wam.umd.edu
FREE

http://www.wam.umd.edu/~losinp/music/md-list.html

The Music of Jeff Harrington ★★★★

Composer Jeff Harrington has produced a web page to present and diffuse his music. He offers PostScript Score samples and MIDI file sound samples for perusal purposes only. Also included is a price list for the music of Jeff Harrington, and a biography of the composer/editor.

KEYWORDS: Classical Music, Contemporary Music, Harrington, Jeff, Music Resources
AUDIENCE: Classical Music Enthusiasts, Contemporary Music Enthusiasts, Music Enthusiasts
CONTACT: jeff@parnasse.com
FREE

http://www.parnasse.com/jeff.htm

Music ★★★

This page contains information on the music of Terre Thaemlitz, and is maintained by the artist himself. Users will find information on the artists' own record label, Comatose Recordings, as well as a discography file with detailed information on each album. This server also houses audio samples of Terre Thaemlitz' work in AIFF format, as well as a selection of articles and reviews of his work. Fans will appreciate the section with Terre Thaemlitz 'top ten' all-time greatest albums.

KEYWORDS: Music, Record Labels, Techno/Ambient Music
AUDIENCE: Instrumental Music Enthusiasts, Music Enthusiasts, Techno/Ambient Music Enthusiasts
CONTACT: Terre Thaemlitz
terremt@mail.med.cornell.edu
FREE

http://www2.med.cornell.edu/~terremt/subdir/music.html

Nanci Griffith ★★★

The Nanci Griffith page has information and resources related to the pop-folk singer/songwriter. Fans of the prolific artist will find album information, biographical information, and a FAQ file here. In addition, there are archives of guitar tablature, pictures, and sound samples that can be accessed through this page, as well as information on Nanci Griffith's projects with other musicians.

KEYWORDS: Folk Music, Rock Music
AUDIENCE: Folk Music Enthusiasts, Music Enthusiasts, Pop Music Enthusiasts, Rock Fans

Musicians

CONTACT Paul Roberts
paul@nvg.unit.no

FREE

http://www.nvg.unit.no/~paul/nanci/nanci1.html

Neftoon's Hair ★★★

This page is the creation of former 'Monkee' Michael Nesmith. It contains a serialized story — 'The Long Sandy Hair of Neftoon Zamora.'

KEYWORDS Musicians, Pop Music, Rock Music
AUDIENCE 60's Music Enthusiasts, Pop Music Listeners, Rock Fans, TV Enthusiasts
CONTACT Michael Nesmith
nez@videoranch.com

FREE

http://www3.primenet.com/~nez/

Nicholas Lens ★★★★

This page, dedicated to composer Nicholas Lens, includes a biography and discography. Lens was born near the French border in Belgium. While studying at the Royal Conservatory of Music in Brussels, he started composing professionally for theatrical projects, film and television. Mendi Rodan offered him a contract with the Israel Sinfonietta in Beersheva, Israel and, inspired by his traveling, Lens wrote a Requiem based on the primitive death rituals he witnessed, in which fire is considered as a positive energy. The page also offers access to the Sony Artists Tour Schedule.

KEYWORDS Classical Music, Compact Discs (CDs), Composers, Lens
AUDIENCE Classical Music Enthusiasts, Compact Disc Users, Contemporary Music Enthusiasts, Music Enthusiasts
CONTACT SonyMusicOnline@sonymusic.com

FREE

http://www.sony.com/Music/ArtistInfo/NicholasLens_Biography.html

Nick Cave Page ★★★

The Nick Cave page is a collection of resources and information related to the brooding alternative rock musician Nick Cave. Visitors of this site will find photos, video and audio clips, tour information, and much more. The server offers guitar tablature, biographical information and a section of reviews and interviews. In addition, the Nick Cave page has bootleg information, mailing list information, and links to other related resources on the Internet.

KEYWORDS Alternative Music, Music, Rock Music
AUDIENCE Alternative Music Enthusiasts, Gothic Rock Enthusiasts, Music Enthusiasts, Rock Fans
CONTACT bretth@lovelace.maths.monash.edu.au

FREE

http://www.maths.monash.edu.au/people/brett/nick/nick.html

Ozzy Osbourne ★★★

This is Sony Music's web site for Ozzy Osbourne. Besides a funny picture, and a discography, it has information on a of recent releases, and a day-to-day diary on the recording of his Ozmosis album. Unfortunately, the diary wasn't written by Ozzy himself. The page also has links to related music sites.

KEYWORDS Hard Rock Music, Rock Music
AUDIENCE Animal Rights Activists, Hard Rock Music Enthusiasts, Heavy Metal Fans, Rock Fans

FREE

http://www.music.sony.com/Music/ArtistInfo/OzzyOsbourne.html

P.J. Harvey - WWW Home Page ★★★★

This page is devoted to P.J. Harvey, the female musician who made a splash in 1993 with her 'Rid of Me' album on Island records. It maintains a complete discography of works by this artist, including singles as well as audio and video bootleg material. In addition, P.J. Harvey fans will find a comprehensive archive of P.J.'s song lyrics, a section of guitar chord and tablature transcriptions of her songs, and sound, image, and movie files for download.

KEYWORDS Alternative Music, Feminist Music, Rock Music
AUDIENCE Alternative Music Enthusiasts, Music Enthusiasts, Rock Fans
CONTACT Jason A. Dour
jadour01@homer.louisville.edu

FREE

http://www.louisville.edu/public/jadour01/pjh/

Patricia Barber Page ★★★

This page contains biographic information on and various audio samples from jazz musician Patricia Barber. A few photographs of her and her most recent album cover, and selected reviews of her work are also available here.

KEYWORDS Jazz, Music
AUDIENCE Blues Enthusiasts, Jazz Enthusiasts
CONTACT Webmaster
bliss@mcs.com

FREE

http://www.mcs.com/~bliss/starchild/jazz/barber.html

Ragged Clown Home Page ★★★

This page is devoted to the singer/songwriter Bob Dylan. Users will find detailed information on Dylan, including an extensive collection of interviews, an archive of the rec.music.dylan newsgroup, reviews of bootleged performances, and an index of articles and books related to the living legend. In addition, there are links to other Dylan resources on the Net, as well as information on tour dates and other current Bob Dylan news.

KEYWORDS Folk Music, Rock Music, Songwriters
AUDIENCE Folk Music Enthusiasts, Folk Rock Fans, Music Enthusiasts, Rock Fans
CONTACT Ben Taylor
b.p.taylor@ncl.ac.uk

FREE

http://www.ncl.ac.uk/~n246543/

Reba McEntire ★★★

This web site is dedicated to popular country artist Reba McEntire. It has a discography, videography, reviews of her work by fans, tour dates, special events, and mailing list information.

KEYWORDS Pop Music
AUDIENCE Country Music Enthusiasts, Pop Music Enthusiasts
CONTACT phillips@hagar.ph.utexas.edu

FREE

http://ruby.ph.utexas.edu/RebaWWW/Reba.html

Rodelius ★★

This home page is for electronic musician Rodelius. It has a profile and a discography.

KEYWORDS Alternative Music, Electronic Music
AUDIENCE Ambient Music Enthusiasts, Electronic Music Enthusiasts, Experimental Music Enthusiasts

FREE

http://hyperreal.com:70/0/music/artists/roedelius

Ryuichi Sakamoto Discography ★★★

This page contains a thorough discography of jazz saxophonist Ryuichi Sakamoto. Users will find detailed information on the artists' albums, including his collaborative work and guest appearances. There is also a brief biographical section on this page, as well as track listings, songwriter/arranger credits, liner notes, and record label information.

KEYWORDS Instrumental Music, Jazz, Music
AUDIENCE Instrumental Music Enthusiasts, Jazz Enthusiasts, Music Enthusiasts
CONTACT Kai Seidler
oswald@cs.tu-berlin.de

FREE

http://duplox.wz-berlin.de/people/oswald/sakamoto.ryuichi.html

SDP Artist - Phoebe Legere! ★★★

This home page is dedicated to alternative musician Phoebe Legere. It has information on her and her band, 4 Nurses of the Apocalypse, a video of her in China, sound files, pictures, a transcript of her AOL appearance, her paintings, and her New York Diary. In all it's a well done page.

KEYWORDS Alternative Music, Musicians, Rock Music
AUDIENCE Alternative Music Enthusiasts, Pop Music Enthusiasts, Rock Fans
CONTACT superbytch@aol.com

FREE

http://www.webcom.com/~sdp3/phoebe.html

Musicians

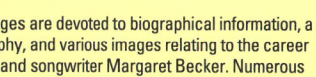

Sam Choukri's John Lennon Web Page ★★★★

This Web site is dedicated to the late John Lennon. It has a discography, pictures, QuickTime Movies, and sound files, including unreleased material.

Keywords Contemporary Music, Music, Rock Music
Audience Beatles Fans, Pop Culture Enthusiasts, Pop Music Enthusiasts, Rock Fans
Contact sam@biosci.mbp.missouri.edu
Free

http://www.missouri.edu/~c588349/john-page.html

Sheena Easton ★★★

This page contains lyrics, images from album sleeves, and other information relating to popular Irish-born singer and musician Sheena Easton. Separate linked pages for each solo album she has recorded (15 in all) are available.

Keywords Dance Music, Ireland, Pop Music
Audience Jazz Enthusiasts, Music Enthusiasts
Contact Jim Guloien
jguloien@edtel.alta.net
Free

http://www.edtel.alta.net/~jguloien/sheena.html

The Slowhand FTP Site (Eric Clapton) ★★★★

This is the FTP site for Slowhand, the Eric Clapton mailing list. It has an archive of over 450 back issues of the list, as well as guitar tabs, lyrics, pictures, and a lot of other Clapton information.

Keywords Blues, Contemporary Music, Rock Music
Audience Blues Enthusiasts, Guitar Music Enthusiasts, Rock Fans
Free

ftp://eosdev2.gsfc.nasa.gov/pub/slowhand/

Sound Bytes ★★★★

Sound Bytes is an electronic music site produced by Jim Hurley. The music is experimental, composed and performed on an 8-track Tascam 38 tape deck with a Tascam M308B mixer. The tracks are 8-bit quality, and identified as 'one of my complete compositions (1.2Mbytes),' 'a small fragment (150K) of another,' and 'a small soundfile for the WWW.' The page also contains a listing of gear and equipment for the technically oriented.

Keywords Contemporary Music, Electronic Music, MIDI (Musical Instrument Digital Interface)
Audience Contemporary Music Enthusiasts, Electronic Music Enthusiasts, MIDI Enthusiasts, Music Enthusiasts
Contact Jim Hurley
hurleyj@arachnaut.org
Free

http://www.webcom.com/~hurleyj/music.html

Steve Roach ★★★

This home page is for electronic musician Steve Roach. It has a profile, a discography, and information on his ARTIFACTS album.

Keywords Electronic Music, Experimental Music
Audience Ambient Music Enthusiasts, Electronic Music Enthusiasts, Experimental Music Enthusiasts
Free

http://hyperreal.com:70/1/music/artists/steve_roach

Stranglehold - Ted Nugent Page ★★★

Stranglehold is a page dedicated to the enduring guitarist Ted Nugent. Aside from information on Nugent's latest album release, this site maintains a discography, an archive of lyrics, and a collection of images. There is also information available on Ted Nugent fan clubs, as well as a FAQ file on the 'Nuge.' Fans will enjoy the collection of articles and interviews with the artist, as well as the section which contains the latest Ted Nugent tour dates and information.

Keywords Guitar, Music, Rock Music
Audience Hard Rock Fans, Music Enthusiasts, Rock Fans
Contact Joshua Nelson
ngonzo@thunder.indstate.edu
Free

http://thunder.indstate.edu/h5/jngonzo/.nuge.html

Thomas Dolby Home Page ★★★ (Commercial)

This page contains a few audio and video clips from recent Thomas Dolby albums and videos. This page is part of Kaleidoscope's 'Virtual Kiosk' system that allows visitors to buy albums online.

Keywords Alternative Music, Dolby, Music
Audience Alternative Music Enthusiasts, Music Enthusiasts
Contact Jeannie Novak
jeannie@kspace.com
Free

http://www.kspace.com/KM/spot.sys/Dolby/pages/home.html

Tony Banks Page ★★★

This page is devoted to Genesis keyboardist and founding member Tony Banks. A discography of his solo work is available, as is a photograph and some short biographical information.

Keywords Rock Music
Audience Musicians, Rock Fans
Contact Adrian Catchpole
a.g.catchpole@bradford.ac.uk
Free

http://www.brad.ac.uk/~agcatchp/tb/banks.html

The Unofficial Home Page For Margaret Becker ★★★

These pages are devoted to biographical information, a discography, and various images relating to the career of singer and songwriter Margaret Becker. Numerous articles about and by Becker are also available.

Keywords Christian Music, Folk Music, Songwriters
Audience Christians, Folk Music Enthusiasts
Contact Susan Anderson
anderson@cs.iastate.edu
Free

http://www.cs.iastate.edu/~anderson/mb.html

Van Morrison Home Page ★★★★

A web site dedicated to the unpredictable and brilliant Van Morrison. It has a discography with lyrics, a bootlegraphy, QuickTime videos, a listing of biographical sources, and a searchable database of songs and sidemen. It also has mailing list information.

Keywords Folk Music, Musicians, Rock Music
Audience Blues Enthusiasts, Celtic Music Enthusiasts, Folk Music Enthusiasts, Rock Fans
Contact Michael Hayward
hayward@sfu.edu
Free

http://www.harbour.sfu.ca/~hayward/van/van.html

Vanessa Paradis' Homepage ★★

This page is about the French pop vocalist Vanessa Paradis. Users will find a limited amount of news and information about the artist, as well as a selection of pictures of the artist in GIF format. Users will also find song lyrics, and a copy of the All Music Guide's entry for Vanessa. There is also a section with information on Vanessa's music videos.

Keywords France, Music, Pop Music
Audience Hard Rock Fans, Music Enthusiasts, Rock Fans
Contact Joshua Silverghost
joshua@ludd.luth.se
Free

http://www.ludd.luth.se/~joshua/vphome.html

The Very Official Charlie Peacock Internet Site ★★★★

This web site is dedicated to Christian rock artist Charlie Peacock. It has a discography of his music, music he's produced, information on his most recent album and a sound file of his latest single. It also contains an interactive interview and a place where you can buy Charlie Peacock products.

Keywords Christian Music, Contemporary Music, Rock Music
Audience Christians, Rock Fans

Musicians – Performing Arts

FREE

http://www.netcentral.net/sparrow/charlie/

Vladimir Horowitz ★★★★

This page, dedicated to the pianist Vladimir Horowitz, includes a biography, discography, and access to the Sony Artists Tour Schedule. Horowitz was born in the Ukraine and studied at the Kiev Conservatory. During his lifetime he gave the American premieres of Prokofiev's Sonatas Nos. 6, 7 and 8 and did much to champion the music of Samuel Barber and Dmitri Kabalevsky.

KEYWORDS   Classical Music, Compact Discs (CDs), Music
AUDIENCE   Classical Music Enthusiasts, Compact Disc Users, Music Enthusiasts, Performers
CONTACT   SonyMusicOnline@sonymusic.com
FREE

http://www.music.sony.com/Music/ArtistInfo/VladimirHorowitz.html

WWW Page of Rocky Mountain High ★★★

The WWW Page of Rocky Mountain High is the home of The John Denver Internet Fan Club, which is according to its authors, dedicated to his 'Rocky Mountain highness.' At this site, one can find information on all aspects of John Denver's career, subscribe to a monthly email newletter and check out back issues, find out about concerts, new CD releases or go to the 'alt.fan.john-denver' newsgroup.

KEYWORDS   Discographies
AUDIENCE   Country Music Enthusiasts, Music Enthusiasts
CONTACT   Emily Parris
           emily@sky.net
FREE

http://www.sky.net/~emily/

Welcome To The Motherpage! ★★★

The Motherpage is a collection of information on the various incarnations of George Clinton's musical projects—Parliament, P-Funk, and Funkadelic. Users will find a FAQ file which explains the many mutations of these funk masters, as well as information on many albums released by the funk posse. There is also a gallery of images available for download, biographical and historical information, and an attempt to list the samples taken from George Clinton's music.

KEYWORDS   Funk Music, Music
AUDIENCE   British Pop Music Fans, Funk Music Enthusiasts, Funkadelic Enthusiasts, Music Enthusiasts
FREE

http://www.acpub.duke.edu/~eja/pfunk.html

Welcome to Jimi Hendrix's Electric Ladyland ★★★★

Electric Ladyland is a site devoted to the legendary guitarist, Jimi Hendrix. Aside from links to other Jimi Hendrix Internet resources, this server hosts a collection of album covers and other images of Jimi, an archive of song lyrics, a collection of quotes about the extraordinary guitarist from people in the music industry, and a section with soundfiles of his music. There is also extensive information on many of the albums that Jimi recorded, including some of the records released after his death.

KEYWORDS   Guitar, Lyrics, Rock Music
AUDIENCE   Guitar Music Enthusiasts, Music Enthusiasts, Rock Fans
CONTACT   Olivier Grange-Labat
           minfo002@univ-pau.fr
FREE

http://www.univ-pau.fr/~minfo002/Jimi/

Willie Nelson Home Page ★★

This page contains a limited amount of resources about the legendary country music artist Willie Nelson. Users will find brief biographical information, as well as a small collection of sound samples in .AU format of the artist's work.

KEYWORDS   Folk Music, Music
AUDIENCE   Country Music Enthusiasts, Folk Music Enthusiasts, Music Enthusiasts
FREE

http://www.msu.edu/mfest94/willie.html

Yefim Bronfman ★★★★

This artist page is dedicated to Yefim Bronfman and includes a biography, discography, and access to the Sony Artists Tour Schedule. A dedicated chamber music performer, Yefim Bronfman has collaborated with the Guarneri, Juilliard and Cleveland Quartets. Bronfman's central role in the music life of Israel and United States was recognized when he was awarded the 1991 Avery Fisher Prize for outstanding achievement and excellence. This Web site also includes information on the 'Concertos No 2 and 4' album and a soundclip from the album.

KEYWORDS   Classical Music, Compact Discs (CDs), Music
AUDIENCE   Classical Music Enthusiasts, Compact Disc Users, Music Enthusiasts, Performers
CONTACT   SonyMusicOnline@sonymusic.com
FREE

http://www.music.sony.com/Music/ArtistInfo/YefimBronfman.html

Yevgeny Kissin ★★★★

This is one of a series of classical artist discographies sponsored by Sony Music Entertainment, dedicated to pianist Yevgeny Kissin. The discography includes recordings from 1988 through 1993 as well as access to the Sony Artists Tour Schedule.

KEYWORDS   Classical Music, Compact Discs (CDs), Music
AUDIENCE   Classical Music Enthusiasts, Compact Disc Users, Music Enthusiasts, Performers
CONTACT   SonyMusicOnline@sonymusic.com
FREE

http://www.music.sony.com/Music/ArtistInfo/YevgenyKissin.html

Yo-Yo Ma ★★★★

This page, dedicated to cellist Yo Yo Ma, is one of a series of classical artist pages sponsored by Sony Music Entertainment. Each artist page includes a biography, discography, and access to the Sony Artists Tour Schedule. In addition, this Web page also includes information on Ma's 'The New York Album' and the 'Chopin Polonaise Brillante' Album, as well as a sound clip of Albert's 'Cello Concerto' from The New York Album (SK 57961).

KEYWORDS   Classical Music, Compact Discs (CDs), Music
AUDIENCE   Classical Music Enthusiasts, Compact Disc Users, Music Enthusiasts, Performers
CONTACT   SonyMusicOnline@sonymusic.com
FREE

http://www.music.sony.com/Music/ArtistInfo/YoYoMa.html

Zubin Mehta ★★★

This is one of Sony Corporations excellent artist information sites for the conductor Zubin Mehta and includes his biography, disography, new releases, tour information, and miscellaneous information plus music clips.

KEYWORDS   Classical Music, Conductors, Discographies
AUDIENCE   Classical Music Enthusiasts, Music Enthusiasts
FREE

http://www.music.sony.com/Music/ArtistInfo/ZubinMehta.html

Performing Arts

See also
Arts & Music · *Film & Video*
Arts & Music · *Musicians*
Popular Culture & Entertainment · *Multimedia*

Arc - The Interactive Media Festival ★★★★

The Arc - Interactive Media Festival Web page provides users with well organized and visually interesting information on this annual festival of the arts scheduled to be held on June 4 - 8, 1995, at the Variety Arts Center in Los Angeles. The page provides background information on some of the performers at the event, including The Blue Man Group and the Merce Cunningham Dance Company as well as bios of the members of the 'Arc Jury 1995.' Users may access a gallery of interactive media projects recognized for their excellence at the festival.

KEYWORDS   Arts Festivals, California, Interactive Media, Multimedia
AUDIENCE   Artists, Concert Goers, Musicians, Web Users
CONTACT   webmaster@arc.org
FREE

http://spark.com/

Art and Music News Austria 1995 ★★★

This site offers detailed information and background on a very wide range of Austrian Cultural festivals and exhibitions. Exhibitions and music festivals can be browsed either by province or by date. Listings are accompanied by descriptions of each exhibition in German, French and English. Each festival notice also lists phone numbers and addresses of local tourist boards. This site lists exhibitions on history, culture, art, and technology, and has a section on commemorative exhibitions for the 50th Anniversary of the Second Republic of Austria.

Keywords Art, Art Exhibitions, Austria, Events
Audience Art Enthusiasts, Music Enthusiasts, Austrian Culture Enthusiasts
Contact Bernhard Nocker
bnocker@cosy.sbg.ac.at
Free

http://hirsch.cosy.sbg.ac.at/kultur/amusa95/

Autocad Lighting Diagrams ★★

This directory contains a few collections of theatrical lighting diagrams and symbols constructed using Autocad software. The files are all in autocad format and are compressed using the PC software package 'zip.'

Keywords Stagecraft, Theater, Theatrical Lighting
Audience Lighting Designers, Set Designers, Theater Professionals
Free

ftp://scorpion.cowan.edu.au/pub/lighting/

Autumn Leaf Performance - SONiC BOOM ★★★★

Autumn Leaf Performance's mandate is to focus on the training, development, and production of contemporary music-theater and opera. In conjunction with this mandate ALP presents an annual series of contemporary music performance, opera, and concert events from across Canada and around the world under the banner of SONiC BOOM. This Web site includes listings of new works, registration information, performance schedules, and biographical information. The site operates from Ontario, Canada.

Keywords Canada, Musicals, Opera, Theater
Audience Canadians, Classical Music Enthusiasts, Music Enthusiasts, Music Students
Contact boom@interlog.com
Free

http://www.interlog.com/~boom/alp.htm

Balanchine ★★★

George Balanchine (1904-1983) has a home page maintained by a Ballet enthusiast, Estelle Souche from Lyons, France. It is quite comprehensive with links to about half of his ballets as well as a short biography.

Keywords Ballet, Dance
Audience Ballet Enthusiasts, Dance Historians
Contact Estelle Souche
esouche@ens.ens-lyon.fr
Free

http://www.ens-lyon.fr/~esouche/danse/Balan.html

Ballet Austin ★★★

The Ballet in Austin, Texas, under the leadership of Artistic Director Lambros Lambrou, is a dynamic, classically-based company with 24 professional dancers and four apprentices. Their web site offers information on the 94-95 season, general information, and sponsorships and benefits.

Keywords Ballet, Classical Music
Audience Ballet Enthusiasts
Contact Pencom World Wide Web Services
webmaster@pencom.com
Free

http://www.pencom.com/arts/ballet/

Ballet Terms ★★

This site contains a dictionary of ballet terms that is not particularly comprehensive but may be worth visiting.

Keywords Ballet, Dictionaries
Audience Ballet Enthusiasts, Dance Students
Free

http://sleepless.acm.uiuc.edu/signet/JHSI/dance.html

The Belgium Dance Server ★★★

The Belgian Dance Server offers details about different styles of dance and a list of events in Belgium within the next weeks and months. There is also a query form available.

Keywords Belgium, Dance
Audience Dance Enthusiasts, Tourists
Free

http://www.net-shopper.co.uk/dance/belgium.htm

Broadway World-Wide ★★★★

Broadway World-Wide is an online magazine of news, schedules and gossip about shows currently running on Broadway. Information about specific actors, directors and producers is available in volume, as are job listings, current schedules, and information on various shows that are in rehearsal.

Keywords Broadway, Jobs, Musical Theater, Theater
Audience Musical Theater Enthusiasts, New York Residents, Theater Enthusiasts, Theater Professionals
Contact Playbill Webmaster
playbill@ix.netcom.com
Free

http://www.webcom.com/~broadway/

Cajun Dance ★★★

This site of Cajun Dance and Music highlights the exciting, passionate music of the Cajun French people of south Louisiana, which is intended for dancing and partying. There are links to 'Where to dance Cajun,' and a couple of cajun bands.

Keywords Cajun Music, Dancing
Audience Cajun Music Enthusiasts, Dance Enthusiasts
Contact Internet Shopper
DanceMaster@net-shopper.co.uk
Free

http://www.net-shopper.co.uk/dance/cajun/index.htm

Cal Performances ★★★

This is the gopher server for Cal Performances, located at the University of California at Berkeley. Cal Performances is a center for fine arts offering dance, theater, and music events throughout the year. The gopher offers information on current Cal performance events, event information archives, Berkeley Festival & Exhibition details, music in history, and more.

Keywords Dance, Drama, Music, Performing Arts
Audience Arts Community, Dance Enthusiasts, Drama Enthusiasts, Music Enthusiasts, Performing Arts Students, Theater Enthusiasts
Contact Daniel Orjuela
calprfrm@uclink.berkeley.edu
Free

gopher://uclink.berkeley.edu:1800/

Calliope Productions, Inc. ★

Calliope Productions is a nonprofit cultural institution that presents theatrical performances and provides performance opportunities and instruction in the central Massachusetts region. The page gives information about the theater and its past productions.

Keywords Educational Resources, Massachusetts, Non Profit Organizations, Theater
Audience Actors, Actresses, Theater Enthusiasts
Free

http://worcester.lm.com/calliope.html

Cantus Colln ★★★★

 COMMERCIAL

This page is dedicated to Cantus Colln and includes a portrait, biography, and list of recommended recordings. Cantus Colln, a soloist vocal ensemble, was formed in 1987 by the renowned lutanist Konrad Junghanel. In the span of a few short years, the group has become one of the most respected vocal ensembles in the world. The core of its musical activity includes the German and Italian vocal literature of the Renaissance and the Baroque. This site also includes a sound clip of Claudio Monteverdi's 'Sestina - Lagrime d'Amante al Sepulcro dell'Amate'.

Keywords Classical Music, Compact Discs (CDs), Music
Audience Classical Music Enthusiasts, Compact Disc Users, Music Enthusiasts, Performers
Contact rbourne@panix.com
Free

http://www.classicalmus.com/artists/colln.html

Carnegie Mellon University Ballroom Dance ★★★

The Ballroom Dance Club of Carnegie Mellon University in Pittsburgh, PA is one of the largest student organizations on this campus. It is dedicated to teaching people how to dance and providing them with opportunities to do so. The online site is divided into club information, activities, library, suggestions and contact information.

- **KEYWORDS** Dancing
- **AUDIENCE** Dance Students, Performing Arts Students
- **CONTACT** Samuel Kass
  sam@cs.cmu.edu
- **FREE**

http://www.contrib.andrew.cmu.edu/org/ballroom/home

Cecilia Bartoli ★★★

These unofficial Cecilia Bartoli Web pages are the devoted efforts of a fan, Gary Stephens. The site is very comprehensive about the famous mezzo soprano, and includes a tool to add links and make updates.

- **KEYWORDS** Opera, Opera Singers
- **AUDIENCE** Musicians, Opera Enthusiasts
- **CONTACT** Gary Stephens
  stephens@sse.ie
- **FREE**

http://www.nwu.edu/music/bartoli/

Dance Directory ★★★

This is an archive of dance sites and information on folk dancing (Austrian, German) with information about the dances themselves, festivals, music, and dance troupes. The list of events is extensive. It is in German and English, and the translations are rough but coherent. The site also contains links to courses (Dances from the Bretagne) and information about the International Festival of Folk Arts in Sidmouth, England.

- **KEYWORDS** Austria, Dance, Europe, Folk Dance
- **AUDIENCE** Austrians, Dancers, Folk Dance Enthusiasts, Folk Dancers, German Speakers
- **CONTACT** Roland Bauer
  bauer@afthp001.tuwien.ac.at
- **FREE**

ftp://ftp.ft.tuwien.ac.at/pub/dance/

(Dance) Listing By Group Name ★★★

This site is an Internet search tool to locate various dance sites on the Web. One can search by letter or scroll through the links that are listed alphabetically.

- **KEYWORDS** Ballet, Dance
- **AUDIENCE** Dance Enthusiasts
- **FREE**

http://bighorn.terra.net/menlo/dance/name.html

Dance Pages ★★★

The Dance pages on the Web are maintained by a French dance enthusiast, Estelle Souche, who has put tremendous time and energy into putting on the Web a comprehensive listing of dance sites, and a very thorough history of dance.

- **KEYWORDS** Ballet, Dance
- **AUDIENCE** Ballet Enthusiasts, Dancers
- **CONTACT** Estelle Souche
  esouche@ens.ens-lyon.fr
- **FREE**

http://www.ens-lyon.fr/~esouche/danse/dance.html

Danclink ★★★

Danclink contains basic diagrams of dance steps for the Fox Trot, Waltz, Tango, Swing, Rumba, and Cha Cha. The site includes voice instruction to make following the diagrams easier. Danclink is producing 'PC Video Disks' that will teach you the different dances and steps via your computer. (These are available for purchase.) The site also contains a brief history of modern dance and frequently asked questions. Eventually this site will also include a virtual ballroom.

- **KEYWORDS** Dance, Instructional Materials, Performing Arts, Video
- **AUDIENCE** Dance Instructors, Dancers, Performing Arts Enthusiasts
- **FREE**

http://www.cts.com/~danclink/

The Dramatic Exchange ★★★

The Dramatic Exchange is a directory on the Caltech FTP site dedicated to archiving and distributing scripts. The site intends to provide a place for playwrights to 'publish' and distribute their plays, a place for producers to find new plays they might want to produce, and a place for anyone who is interested in drama to browse. The site contains information about submitting plays and procedures for producers who wish to use any of the plays. The site also contains a history of the exchange, information on people active in the exchange and links to other drama or theater-related sites.

- **KEYWORDS** Drama, Stagecraft, Theater
- **AUDIENCE** Drama Educators, Drama Enthusiasts, Playwrights, Producers, Writers
- **CONTACT** Robert A. Knop Jr.
  rknop@cco.caltech.edu
- **FREE**

http://www.cco.caltech.edu/~rknop/dramex.html

ftp://ftp.cco.caltech.edu/pub/plays/incoming/

The European Dance Server ★★★

This site is the European Dance Server where you will find details about different styles of dance and a list of events in Europe. The Server lists dance pages according to countries (including Belgium, France, Hungary, Sweden, the USA), dance styles (Cajun, Swing Dance, Western Square Dancing, Tap Dancing, Ballroom), dance troupes and non-European dance servers and other dance resources. The site's intention is to provide three types of information (1) information about types of dancing so that people can read and see the differences between various styles; (2) information about the leaders of style for a particular dance (e.g. Frankie Manning in Lindy) and (3) an up-to-date list of events.

- **KEYWORDS** Dance, Europe, Performing Arts, Square Dancing
- **AUDIENCE** Arts Community, Dance Enthusiasts, Dancers
- **CONTACT** webmaster@net-shopper.co.uk
- **FREE**

http://www.net-shopper.co.uk/dance/index.htm

The Finnish Dance Server ★★★

The Finnish Dance Server has half a dozen local Finnish links and regional links to other countries' dance servers. It is offered in Finnish and English.

- **KEYWORDS** Dance, Finland
- **AUDIENCE** Dance Enthusiasts, Finns
- **FREE**

http://www.utu.fi/harrastus/tanssi/english/index.html

The Frank Sinatra WWW Page ★★★

The Frank Sinatra World Wide Web Page attempts to make a home on the Internet for 'the greatest singer of the century.' To that end, the producer of this site, an avid Sinatra fan, William Denton, has compiled an impressive database of links to 'old blue eyes.' The categories so far include What's New, The Frank Sinatra Mailing list, Reference Material, Concerts, Books/Newspaper/Magazine Articles, Pictures, Miscellaneous, and links to related Web sites.

- **KEYWORDS** Jazz, Online Music, Pop Music
- **AUDIENCE** Classical Pop Enthusiasts, Jazz Enthusiasts, Music Enthusiasts
- **CONTACT** William Denton
  buff@io.org
- **FREE**

http://www.io.org/~buff/sinatra.html

The French Dance Server ★★★

The French Dance Server offers details about different styles of dance and a list of events in and around Paris. There is a query form provided as well.

- **KEYWORDS** Dance, France
- **AUDIENCE** Dance Enthusiasts, French
- **FREE**

http://www.net-shopper.co.uk/dance/france.htm

Gilbert & Sullivan Archive ★★★★

This archive is dedicated to the works of William S. Gilbert and Arthur S. Sullivan, and is operated as a service to Gilbert & Sullivan fans by members of the SavoyNet distribution list. It includes a variety of G&S-related items, including clip art, librettos, song scores, and newsletter articles.

- **KEYWORDS** Classical Music, Music Newsletters, Opera
- **AUDIENCE** Classical Music Enthusiasts, Gilbert & Sullivan Enthusiasts, Opera Enthusiasts

CONTACT   Alex Feldman
          alex@math.idbsu.edu
FREE

http://math.idbsu.edu/gas/GaS.html

Hair - The Musical ★★★★

This is the 'unofficial' home page for the hit Broadway musical and film 'Hair,' the 'American Tribal Love-rock Musical.' It includes an introduction and disclaimer, plot synopsis, history, index of former cast members, a photo archive, information on current productions, resources and references. You can also download the lyrics in .gzip format. Although Hair is known as a musical of the late 60's, it questions the standards of morality, sexuality, individualism, racism, violence, drug use, loyalty, and social acceptance which remain problems today.

KEYWORDS   Musical Theater, Popular Music, Rock Music
AUDIENCE   Music Enthusiasts, Musical Theater Enthusiasts, Popular Music Enthusiasts
CONTACT   Toots Harris
           tharris@wellesley.edu
FREE

http://www.mit.edu:8001/people/spwhite/Hair/hair.html

Headquarters Entertainment Corporation Home Page ★★★

This page offers background information on HQE (Headquarters Entertainment Corporation), a Canadian company that buys and sells theatrical real estate, scripts and screenplay licenses, and markets and manages theatrical presentations and corporate events. This site contains schedules of speakers and presentations organized under the auspices of HQE, such as Fiddler on the Roof, a lecture series that highlights speakers such as Lauren Bacall, Candice Bergen and Joan Rivers. A large collection of theater and entertainment-related links are also available.

KEYWORDS   Companies, Entertainment, Events, Theater
AUDIENCE   Actors, Entrepreneurs, Film Professionals, Theater Professionals
CONTACT   HQE Webmaster
           hqexec@fleethouse.com
FREE

http://www.fleethouse.com/fhcanada/hqe_home.htm

The Hungarian Dance Server ★★★

The Hungarian Dance Server offers details about different styles of dance and a list of events in Hungary within the next weeks and months. There is a query form provided as well.

KEYWORDS   Dance, Hungary
AUDIENCE   Dance Enthusiasts, Tourists
FREE

http://www.net-shopper.co.uk/dance/hungary.htm

Connections to Television Soap Operas
"Oh, John . . ."
"Oh, Marsha . . ."

Have you heard the latest about the popular soap opera "Days of Our Lives"? Will Susan Lucci ever win an Emmy award for her portrayal of Erica Kane? She's been nominated bazillions of times but has never won. If you're hooked on soaps, tune into the Internet for answers to these and other burning questions.

By accessing a wide array of sources—many through the Sony Pictures Entertainment site—you can keep abreast of all the dirt on each of the shows, and on all the characters. The primary focus is on bringing you up to date on any episodes you might have missed. There are even collectibles for shows like "General Hospital."

(http://www.spe.Sony.com/Pictures/tv/Soaps)

Index of /Pub/Dance ★★★

This FTP site contains pointers to dance publications and is a dancers' archive. Directories are grouped by geographic regions and by type of dance such as flamenco, tango, ballroom. Other links include video, music and youth programs.

KEYWORDS   Archives, Dancing
AUDIENCE   Dance Enthusiasts, Dance Historians, Dance Students
FREE

ftp://ftp.std.com/pub/dance

Ithaca Swing Dance Network ★★★

This is the site for the Ithaca Swing Dance Network (ISDN), a voluntary organization of swing dance fans who participate in and coordinate dance events in the Ithaca, NY area. The ISDN currently has about 200 members and is growing all the time. The network's activities include listing Ithaca area dance events, arranging workshops, publishing a newsletter, supporting the growth of local dance troupes, providing scholarships, and more. The site also provides links to dance resources world wide.

KEYWORDS   Dance, Dancing, New York, Performing Arts
AUDIENCE   Dancers, New York Residents, Swing Dance Enthusiasts
FREE

http://www.lassp.cornell.edu/newmmc/isdn/

The Kitchen ★★

The Kitchen, and its spinoffs, the Kitchenette and the Electronic Cafe, are arts, music, and dance establishments in New York City. The Kitchen has hosted performances from such artists as Laurie Anderson, Brian Eno, The Talking Heads, Eric Bogosian, and Robert Mapplethorpe. The Kitchen is also hosting new performances from local and international artists, such as Robert Wilson, Van McElwee, and Bonnie Barnett. The Electronic Cafe is a network of experimental art clubs from Paris to New York to California, with such features as interactive networked drum circles. This page contains the performance schedules for each of the three clubs, as well as a catologue of videos from performers.

KEYWORDS Events, Internet Culture, Multimedia, Performance Art
AUDIENCE Artists, Dancers, Multimedia Enthusiasts, Musicians, Performers
CONTACT Panix - Public Access Networks Corporation
webmaster@panix.com
FREE

http://www.panix.com/kitchen

The Lake Arrowhead Classical Ballet Company ★★

This site contains information on current productions by the Lake Arrowhead Classical Ballet Company. It also contains information on the cast, and a brief biography of the director, Sharon McCormick. The producer plans to add a page on the Lake Arrowhead Manor School of Dance.

KEYWORDS Ballet, California, Dance, Performing Arts
AUDIENCE Ballet Enthusiasts, Californians, Dance Enthusiasts
CONTACT webmaster@deltanet.com
FREE

http://www.deltanet.com/ballet/

Laurie Anderson Info ★★★

This page contains information relating to musician Laurie Anderson. Tour dates for current tours are available, as are numerous audio clips from her most recent album. The text of a few excerpted articles on Ms. Anderson are also available, as are numerous links to other sites that contain information relating to her most recent tour or her music in general.

KEYWORDS Music, Performance Art, Postmodernism
AUDIENCE Alternative Music Enthusiasts, Music Enthusiasts
CONTACT Phil Trubey
phil@netpart.com
FREE

http://www.netpart.com/phil/laurie.html

 Les Miserables Home Page ★★★★

This page contains information about the Les Miserables musical (credits, story summary, complete libretto, sounds, graphics and images, tour dates); the novel (the text itself at the Gutenberg project, a Victor Hugo biography, Victor Hugo and French Literature), and Information and Resources (related Web pages, Les Miserables listserv, Les Miserables FAQ) and more. This is the place to go if you need information about Victor Hugo and Les Miserables.

KEYWORDS France, French Literature, Musical Theater
AUDIENCE Fiction Enthusiasts, Francophiles, Musicals Enthusiasts
FREE

http://www.ot.com/lesmis/novpage.html

Lindy Hop in Stockholm ★★★

This site for Lindy Hopping in Stockholm contains information for dancers about where to go to Lindy Hop, how to be a better dancer, as well as a lists of competitions, performances and clubs (particularly Jazz clubs and Swing Societies). There are also many links to other dance resources here, including world wide Lindy Hop clubs.

KEYWORDS Dance, Instructional Materials, Performing Arts, Sweden
AUDIENCE Dance Enthusiasts, Dancers, Lindy Hop Enthusiasts, Sweden Residents, Tourists
CONTACT Oliver Trepte
oliver@fysik4.kth.se
FREE

http://www.fysik4.kth.se/lindy/intl-index.html

The London Stage Gazette ★★★★

The London Stage Gazette site contains information on the London theater including information on individual productions, reviews, general information about theater location and ticket information. One refreshing section called, 'Rumours and Upcoming Shows' gives insider information about what may be forthcoming. The site contains information on London's best-known theaters such as The Royal Shakespeare Company in Stratford, Royal National Theatre, and on other theatrical options including the Barbican Center.

KEYWORDS Drama, London, Performing Arts, Theater
AUDIENCE Actors, Theater Enthusiasts, Theater Professionals, Tourists, United Kingdoms Residents
CONTACT David Fristrom
davidf@tiac.net.
FREE

http://www.tiac.net/users/davidf/london.html

Monserrat Caballe ★★★★

This is one of a series of classical artist pages sponsored by BMG Classics World. This page is dedicated to Monserrat Caballe and includes a portrait, biography, and list of recommended recordings. A discography of over 80 opera, recital and concert recordings supports Caballe's reputation as once of the doyennes of the recording studio. She is equally renowned for her achievements in the area of bel canto singing. Caballe was given the highest title of the Spanish government, the Order of Dona Isabel La Catolica, and France has honored her with the Cross of Commander of Arts and Letters. In 1992, she sang at the Opening Ceremonies of the XXV Olympiad in Barcelona; the performance was viewed by an estimated worldwide television audience of 2 billion.

KEYWORDS Bel Canto Singing, Classical Music, Compact Discs (CDs), Monserrat
AUDIENCE Classical Music Enthusiasts, Compact Disc Users, Music Enthusiasts, Opera Enthusiasts
CONTACT rbourne@panix.com
FREE

http://www.classicalmus.com/artists/caballe.html

New Dramatists Home Page ★★★★

New Dramatists is the nation's oldest nonprofit development and representation organization for new playwrights and directors. This Web page offers information about their programs and personnel, and offers glimpses of recent work completed under the auspices of the program.

KEYWORDS Acting, Drama, Theater, Writing
AUDIENCE Playwrights, Theater Enthusiasts, Theater Professionals, Writers
CONTACT Diana Son
diana@www.itp.tsoa.nyu.edu
FREE

http://www.itp.tsoa.nyu.edu/~diana/ndintro.html

New Heart Company of Artists ★★★★

The New Heart Company of Artists is a performing arts collective in Edmonton, Canada. These Web pages contain schedule information for the various dance, movement and theater pieces they produce, as well as their guiding document, the Mandate, and other background information on the members of New Heart Company.

KEYWORDS Canada, Dance, Performing Arts, Theater Companies
AUDIENCE Canada Residents, Dancers, Performing Artists, Theater Enthusiasts
CONTACT Rohit Sharma
sharma@ee.ualberta.ca
FREE

http://nyquist.ee.ualberta.ca/~sharma/newheart.html

New York City Opera Homepage ★★★

This is the home page for the New York City Opera. It includes an introduction, repertory list, and ticket information for each opera production (ongoing and new). The site includes opera synopses, cast lists, and production schedules. It also contains links to other opera sites on the Web.

KEYWORDS Classical Music, Music, New York, Opera
AUDIENCE Classical Music Enthusiasts, New York Residents, Opera Enthusiasts
CONTACT nycopera@interport.net
FREE

http://www.interport.net:/~nycopera/

New York International Ballet Competition (NYIBC) ★★★

This site provides information about The New York International Ballet Competition that will be held June 3-24, 1996 in the Alice Tully Hall of Lincoln Center New York. Calendar and ticket details are available, as well as the repertoire, rules and procedures, and an application form.

KEYWORDS Ballet, Competitions
AUDIENCE Ballerinas, Ballet Dancers
CONTACT WebLink Inc.
webmaster@weblink.com
FREE

http://www.weblink.com/nyibc/

New York's Capital District Theater ★★★★

This page offers comprehensive theater information for various professional and amateur performing arts groups in and around New York's Capital district (centered in Albany, New York). Notices for auditions in area performances, help wanted ads, schedules, listings of active theater companies (and contact information), and miscellaneous other theater-related resources are available.

- KEYWORDS: Acting, New York, Performing Arts, Schedules
- AUDIENCE: New York Residents, Theater Enthusiasts, Theater Professionals
- CONTACT: Daniel A. Norton danorton@albany.net
- FREE

http://www.albany.net:80/~danorton/theatre/

Northern Ballet Theatre ★★★

The Northern Ballet Theatre (NBT) in the U.K. is presented on the web by Dave McGlade, who adds to the NBT information that came from programs, leaflets and other sources, with his own insights and opinions. The site includes the 1995 tour schedule, productions, artists, and membership information about the Friends of the Northern Ballet Theatre.

- KEYWORDS: Ballet, Theater
- AUDIENCE: Ballet Enthusiasts, Dance Enthusiasts
- CONTACT: Dave McGlade mcglade.win-uk.net
- FREE

http://www.ibmpcug.co.uk/~davem/nbt/home.html

Northwest Flamenco Home Page ★★★

This site contains information about the Portland Flamenco Scene (both listings of events and information about Roberto Lorenz, Flamenco guitarist) as well as a list of Who's Who in the Pacific Northwest (Flamenco dancers and musicians performance groups). It also contains links to other dance and music sites, particularly Flamenco.

- KEYWORDS: Dance, Flamenco, Music, Oregon
- AUDIENCE: Dance Enthusiasts, Dancers, Flamenco Enthusiasts, Oregon Residents
- CONTACT: jdimick@teleport.com
- FREE

http://www.teleport.com/~jdimick/nw.html

Offstage Theater ★★★

Offstage Theater is a nonprofit Virginia-based group of actors who perform 'site-specific' theater—park plays in parks, art gallery plays in art galleries, and their favorites, bar plays in bars. This page contains information about various productions they are or have been involved in, and highlights current script calls.

- KEYWORDS: Acting, Theater, Virginia
- AUDIENCE: Actors, Theater Enthusiasts, Theater Professionals, Virginia Residents
- CONTACT: Offstage Theater Group ldg2h@virginia.edu
- FREE

http://darwin.clas.virginia.edu/~ldg2h/off.html

On Broadway WWW Information Page ★★★

This site contains several links to pages with information about Broadway shows including 'Beauty and the Beast,' 'Cats,' and 'Crazy for You.' These listings are compiled from New York Magazine, the New Yorker and Theatre Week. The site also contains a listing of shows currently playing Off Broadway, e.g., 'All in the Timing,' 'Body Shop,' 'You should be so lucky,' as well as limited runs such as 'Don Juan in Chicago,' or 'Vita and Virginia,' a play about the literary friendship between Virginia Woolf and Vita Sackville-West, starring Vanessa Redgrave and Eileen Atkins. Other links to follow are Theatre WWW sites and Tony Award Listings.

- KEYWORDS: Broadway, Drama, Musicals, New York
- AUDIENCE: Actors, Art Enthusiasts, Performing Artists, Singers, Theater Enthusiasts
- CONTACT: Jogle geigel@psc.edu
- FREE

http://artsnet.heinz.cmu.edu/OnBroadway/

Opera Schedule Server ★★★

The Opera Schedule Server provides information on programs of opera companies around the world. Some of the companies include the New York City Opera, Seattle Opera, the Atlanta Opera and Ente Lirico Arena di Verona (Italian). The information provided varies from company to company but might include seating charts, schedules, financial information, director biographies, and related theatre company information. Other opera-related links are provided such as Current Opera Ezine, The Gilbert & Sullivan Archive, and Basic Opera dictionary by Mario Biondi. There is also a database searchable by city, artist, title, and composer.

- KEYWORDS: Opera, Opera Companies, Performance Schedules, Vocal Music
- AUDIENCE: Music Enthusiasts, Opera Enthusiasts
- CONTACT: Tamas Maray maray@fsz.bme.hu
- FREE

http://www.fsz.bme.hu/opera/main.html

Paris Opera Ballet ★★★

Paris Opera Ballet is maintained by a French Dance enthusiast, Estelle Souche, and contains links to all the ballets in the repertoire, the choreographers, most of the stars, the directors and the 1995-95 season.

- KEYWORDS: Ballet, Paris
- AUDIENCE: Ballet Enthusiasts, Dancers
- CONTACT: Estelle Souche esouche@ens.ens-lyon.fr
- FREE

http://www.ens-lyon.fr/~esouche/danse/POB.html

Placido Domingo ★★★

This is a Sony Corporation featured artist site complete with tour information, music clips, multimedia and miscellaneous artist information. In addition, a biography and discography are provided.

- KEYWORDS: Classical Music, Discographies, Opera
- AUDIENCE: Opera Enthusiasts
- FREE

http://www.music.sony.com/Music/ArtistInfo/PlacidoDomingo.html

Playbill On-Line ★★★

Welcome to Playbill On-Line, the complete on-line theatre information service. Playbill On-Line will ultimately list schedules for more than 800 professional theatres in dozens of cities across America (that will include regional theatres and national tours), plus Canada, London, and even Tokyo. These schedules will be updated weekly and will include all you will want to know about ordering tickets from them. It will also provide news, features, celebrities online, recordings, casting news, theater schools, theater maps, etc.

- KEYWORDS: Acting, Broadway, Drama, Theater
- AUDIENCE: Actors, Drama Enthusiasts, Performers, Theater Enthusiasts, Tourists
- CONTACT: Andrew McGibbon playbill@ix.netcom.com
- FREE

Pope Joan - The World's First Theatrical Workshop Web ★★★★

Pope Joan is a new work of musical theater written by Christopher Moore and produced by Michael Butler and Orlok that will grow as it travels from a Chicago to New York stages. This is the first effort of its kind, a bridge between author, producer, and theater lovers on the World Wide Web. The comments and suggestions that you make will directly affect the way a theater piece is translated to multi-media format, and those same suggestions may effect the direction of the show itself. This Web page includes information about the show and characters, lyrics, selected scenes, historical setting, timeline, critical reviews, and background on The Bailiwick Cast, the author, the producer, and more.

- KEYWORDS: Interactive Theater, Music, Musical Theater, Performing Arts
- AUDIENCE: Music Enthusiasts, Musical Theater Enthusiasts, Performers, Theater Enthusiasts
- CONTACT: orlok@mcs.net
- FREE

http://orlok.vs.mcs.net/

The Princeton Triangle Club ★★★★

The Princeton University's theatrical society, The Triangle Club is the oldest college musical-comedy troupe in the nation and the only college group which creates an original musical comedy each year and then performs it on a national tour. This site contains information on the society, on current, forthcoming and previous productions, sound files, and photographs from past productions. There is also information on

McCarter Theatre, a history of the society, and links to other theater sites on the Net.

KEYWORDS Drama, Musicals, Theater
AUDIENCE Drama Students, New Jersey Residents, Princeton Alumni, Theater Enthusiasts
CONTACT Christian Gilmore
cgilmore@phoenix.princeton.edu
FREE

http://www.princeton.edu/~triangle/sounds/index.html

Round Dance Server ★★

The Round Dance Server is an experimental one still under construction and includes links to cue sheets, round dance clubs in Germany, as well as to square dance and ballroom dancing and four round dance numbers.

KEYWORDS Dance, Square Dancing
AUDIENCE Dance Enthusiasts, Square Dance Enthusiasts
FREE

http://black-beauty.rob.cs.tu-bs.de/

The Royal Ballet ★★★

The British Royal Ballet site contains links to its director, all of the principal dances and to four related ballet sites.

KEYWORDS Ballet, United Kingdom
AUDIENCE Ballet Enthusiasts, Dancers
CONTACT Estelle Souche
esouche@ens.ens-lyon.fr
FREE

http://www.ens-lyon.fr/~esouche/danse/Royal.html

Rutgers Theater Gopher ★★

This gopher archive contains a number of documents useful to those interested in attending theater performances in New York City and London and others with a general interest in Theater. Schedules, theater indexes and addresses, and a few miscellaneous acting and theater-related FAQs are available. A small directory of popular musical theater lyrics is also available.

KEYWORDS Acting, Drama, New York, Performing Arts
AUDIENCE Acting Students, Actors, Theater Enthusiasts, Theater Professionals
CONTACT archive manager
pirmann@cs.rutgers.edu
FREE

gopher://gopher.etext.org/11/Quartz/theater

The San Francisco Ballet ★★★

The San Francisco Ballet is the oldest classical ballet company in the US. The online site is maintained through Stanford University and includes links to the dancers, the San Francisco Ballet School, Corporate Donors, the 1995 Program, and Estelle Souche's dance pages.

KEYWORDS Ballet
AUDIENCE Ballet Enthusiasts, Dance Enthusiasts
CONTACT R. Beal
rbeal@leland.stanford.edu
FREE

http://www-leland.stanford.edu/~rbeal/sfb.html

Tap Dance Homepage ★★★

This site for the International Tap Association links to several tap dance sites and resources, it delineates who's who in tap, provides a glossary, steps, supply reference, as well as some history and general information.

KEYWORDS Dance, Tap Dancing
AUDIENCE Dance Enthusiasts, Tap Dancers
CONTACT Paul Corr
corr@hal.hahnemann.edu
FREE

http://www.hahnemann.edu/tap/

Theater ★★★

This document is a compilation of information resources focused on theater. Resources may include Internet/Bitnet Mailing Lists, Gophers, World Wide Web Sites, Mail Servers, Usenet Newsgroups, FTP Archives, Commercial Online Services, and Bulletin Board Systems. The site also includes general information on how to use the Internet (definitions, search techniques) and an Internet bibliography.

KEYWORDS Meta-Index (Theater), Performing Arts, Stage, Theater
AUDIENCE Media Specialists, Performers, Theater Professionals
CONTACT Deborah Torres
dtorres@umich.edu
FREE

gopher://una.hh.lib.umich.edu:70/00/inetdirsstacks/theater:torresmjvk

ftp://una.hh.lib.umich.edu/inetdirsstacks/theater:torresmjvk

The Theatre Central Web Page ★★★

Theater Central Web Page is a clearinghouse for theater and acting-related resources on the Internet. This page is dedicated to amateur, scholastic, and professional groups, services, and resources. There are links to dozens of sites, including professional acting agencies, amateur, regional, university and professional groups and clubs, magazines, newsgroups, and academic programs in theater around the world. The information covers such areas as theatrical contacts, resources, playwrights, scripts, literature, companies, and calendars.

KEYWORDS Acting, Meta-Index (Theater), Stagecraft, Theater Companies
AUDIENCE Acting Students, Actors, Performing Arts Enthusiasts, Theater Enthusiasts, Theater Professionals
CONTACT Andrew Quixote Kraft
quijote@mit.edu
FREE

http://www.mit.edu:8001/people/quijote/theatre-central.html

TheatreWorks Home Page ★★

This is the home page for TheatreWorks, a theatre company located in the San Francisco Bay Area which is currently celebrating its 25th season. TheatreWorks has grown into a professional company known for its 'electric' performances (San Francisco Chronicle) and 'top-notch work' (San Jose Mercury News). This site offers schedules and information about TheatreWorks' Mainstage productions which range from musicals to dramas, and its Stage2 productions which features contemporary plays. Productions are held at the Mountain View Center for the Performing Arts and the Lucie Stern Theatre in Palo Alto. Announcements about the current and upcoming seasons, directions to the theatres, local restaurant suggestions, and descriptions of the current play are features on this page, as well as a request for contributions of time and funds.

KEYWORDS Acting, Drama, Theater
AUDIENCE Californians, Theater Enthusiasts, Theater Professionals
CONTACT James Sweeney
sweeney@sierra.stanford.edu
FREE

http://none.coolware.com/tworks/

Washington D.C. Swing Dance Server ★★★★

This is a guide to Lindy Hop, Jitterbug, West Coast Swing, Carolina Shag, Hustle, and D.C. Hand Dancing in the Metropolitan Washington Area. The site contains lists of clubs and organizations, instructors, group lessons, weekly dance events and upcoming special events (Dances, Workshops, National Events). One of the highlights of the site is the collection of jpeg images of swing dancers including famous dancers (Fred Astaire and Ginger Rogers, Bill and Hillary Clinton, various champions, and more.). The site also contains links to other US swing dance resources on the net.

KEYWORDS Dance, Instructional Materials, Performing Arts, Washington D.C.
AUDIENCE Dance Enthusiasts, Dancers, Tourists, Washington D.C. Residents
CONTACT Christopher Meyer.
meyer@tiber.nist.gov
FREE

http://its90a.phy.nist.gov/swing/swing.html

Western Square Dancing ★★★

The Western Square Dancing site is quite comprehensive and includes a lot of information about square dance clubs and organizations, dance schedules by area, square dance humor, articles and miscellany, and a glossary of definitions.

KEYWORDS Organizations, Square Dancing
AUDIENCE Dance Enthusiasts, Square Dance Enthusiasts
FREE

http://suif.stanford.edu/~rfrench/wsd/

Winifred Haun & Dancers ★★★

Winifred Haun & Dancers is a Chicago-based dance group that fuses elements of modern, ballet and jazz dance. Visit their site to get who's who details, com-

Performing Arts – Visual Arts

pany reviews, general information, photos, upcoming events and company dance classes.

KEYWORDS	Ballet, Dance
AUDIENCE	Dance Enthusiasts, Illinois Residents
CONTACT	Winifred Haun & Dancers wini@mcs.com
FREE	

http://www.mcs.net/~wini/home.html

The World Wide Web Dance Server (European) ★★★

The World Wide Web European Dance Server is offered by Internet Shopper and includes links to a dance database which allows visitors to add to the list of events in Europe, or, if desired, in the US. Currently there are ten principal categories of links with dozens of subcategories to make a very comprehensive site.

KEYWORDS	Dance, Europe
AUDIENCE	Dance Enthusiasts, Europeans
FREE	

http://www.net-shopper.co.uk/dance/index.htm

Visual Arts

See also
Arts & Music · *Art Galleries*
Arts & Music · *Art Museums*
Arts & Music · *Design*
Arts & Music · *Electronic Arts*
Popular Culture & Entertainment · *Multimedia*

Ansel Adams - Fiat Lux ★★★★

This online exhibition contains photographs of University of California by Ansel Adams. The exhibit contains a brief introductory essay, 'About Ansel Adams—Fiat Lux,' documenting the background of how Ansel Adams agreed to produce a 'current portrait' of the University of California for the Centennial celebration in 1968, an art historical essay on Adams and a chronology, as well as sound files of Adams discussing his photographs. The exhibition is organized into five major areas—Northern UC Campuses, Southern UC Campuses, Agricultural Centers and Field Stations, Natural Reserve System, and Organized Research Units. Brief commentaries accompany the images in each section. The organizers have also compiled an online bookstore where related items may be purchased.

KEYWORDS	Photographers, Photography, Visual Arts
AUDIENCE	Artists, Arts Students, Educators, Photographers, University of California Alumni
CONTACT	James A. Harrod jaharrod@uci.edu
FREE	

http://bookweb.cwis.uci.edu:8042/AdamsHome.html

Australian Centre for the Arts & Technology (ACAT) Homepage ★★★★

The Australian Centre for the Arts and Technology is a center for the teaching, research, recording, publishing, and performance of the music and the dynamic visual arts made with new technology. This site includes information about ACAT's research, facilities and equipment, artistic practice, and course offerings. It will be particularly interesting to Australian residents, but offers information for anyone interested in music, or visual arts and technology.

KEYWORDS	Australia, Classical Music, Electronic Arts, Music Schools
AUDIENCE	Australia Residents, Classical Music Enthusiasts, Music Students
CONTACT	tjk@acat.anu.edu.au
FREE	

http://online.anu.edu.au/ITA/ACAT/ACATHome.html

Connections to Photography Exhibits

A picture is worth a thousands words . . .

It may be a cliché, but nothing speaks volumes like a picture. You can learn virtually everything about photography (as well as visiting exhibits around the world and reading biographies of masters like Ansel Adams) by scouring the Internet.

Whether photography is your hobby or your career, there are places on the World Wide Web that can give you cutting-edge tips and provide information on supplies. One such place is "The Stock Solution," a site offering general products and services as well as access to photographic equipment and supplies.

(http://www.xmission.com/~tssphoto/tssphoto.html)

If you would like to take in an art exhibit near your home (or where you're vacationing), certain Internet sites provide photographic exhibits around the world. Check out The Magic Media Web Pages to see photgraphy works of various artists from around the world.

If you want to view photographic works online in the comfort of your home, you can do that through "Photography—The YellowPages.com."

(http://www.magic.be/) also, **(http://theyellowpages.com/photography.htm)**

Avishai`s Photographs ★★★★

Avishai`s Photographs is a page with a collection of mostly black and white photography. Users will find several images in GIF and JPEG formats, as well as some interesting photography-related finds such as an old 1960 contact sheet and a collection of World War I photos. There are also many links to other photography-related pages.

KEYWORDS	Photographic Arts, Photography
AUDIENCE	Photographers, Photography Enthusiasts
CONTACT	Avishai avishai@amug.org
FREE	

http://www.amug.org/~avishai/morephoto.html

Black Star ★★★★

Black Star is a company that specializes in photography for corporations and others in need of photography professionals. Users can find out about Black Star, as well as browse a large collection of stock photography. There are also links to other sites with photographic information, and an excellent section with photojournalistic essays. Finally, users can browse information on the company and its services.

KEYWORDS Digital Photography, Graphic Design, Photography, Photojournalism
AUDIENCE Graphic Artists, Marketing Professionals, Photographers
CONTACT webmaster@blackstar.com
FREE

http://www.blackstar.com

Cherry Optical Holography ★★

This page contains information on various kinds of holography. Users may obtain descriptions about how the various kinds of holograms work and how to have custom hologram done. There are several images provided as examples.

KEYWORDS Art, Holography, Images, Lasers
AUDIENCE Art Enthusiasts, Art Historians, Artists, Holography Enthusiasts
FREE

http://www.hmt.com/holography/cherry/cherry.html

The 'Classic' Rock Photo Gallery ★★★★

Over fifty photos are presented in this fun and flashy site from former Rolling Stone photographer, Robert Altman. You'll find shots of Mick Jagger, Jim Morrison, Iggy Pop, Tina Turner, Jerry Garcia, and other rock and sixties luminaries, along with shameless self-promotion—'His photographs blew my mind' says Peter Max. Collector's prints of the photos are available, and links to other sites.

KEYWORDS Art Exhibitions, Photography
AUDIENCE Photography Enthusiasts, Rock Fans
FREE

http://www.cea.edu/robert/x.index.html

Covington's Homeless ★★★

John Decker's documentary on drifters in Covington, Kentucky is an original work. There are four groupings—Backpack Bill, Patty and Art, Living in the Streets, and DJ's new apartment. You can experience the photographs one at a time and the narrative provided by the artist links the subjects. Covington's homeless are proof that the Web can be used for creative expression. The site also provides links to other photography sites.

KEYWORDS Documentary Photography, Homelessness, Kentucky
AUDIENCE Arts Community, Homeless Activists, Media Members, Photographers, Social Workers
CONTACT John Decker
jdeck@intac.com
FREE

http://www.iia.org/~deckerj/

The Edgerton Center's Online Photo Gallery ★★★

The Edgerton Center's Online Photo Gallery at the Massachusets Institute of Technology (MIT) offers a number of rather ordinary photographs from MIT students, as well as links to Adobe Photoship tips and The Tech, MIT's student newspaper.

KEYWORDS Photography
AUDIENCE Photography Enthusiasts, Students (Graduate)
FREE

http://the-tech.mit.edu/Gallery/gallery.html

The Electric Gallery ★★★★

The gallery is arranged so the viewer can visit separate wings focused on Haitian Art and Contemporary Southwest Art, as well as The Amazon Project, devoted to the preservation of the art of the indigenous people of the Peruvian Amazon, and the Jazz and Blues Wing which displays paintings and serigraphs capturing the expressions of jazz and the blues. A new wing is also online to present a collection of International Folk Art.

KEYWORDS Contemporary Art, Fine Art, Folk Art, Southwest Art
AUDIENCE Artists, Arts Community, Ethnic Arts Enthusiasts
CONTACT rwpb11@pipeline.com
FREE

http://www.egallery.com/egallery/homepage.html

Fine Art Forum Gallery Page ★★★

This gallery currently presents six room which includes a display of art by Wendy Mills originally presented as Installation Art. These installations were combinations of projected images and electronic sounds activated by a viewer's presence. Also on display are photographs by Celeste Brignac covering digital imaging, fashion, fine arts, and portraits, and works by Paul Brown, Joseph DeLappe and others. Images are accompanied by notes on the works and the artists.

KEYWORDS Art Exhibitions, Performance Art, Photography
AUDIENCE Artists, Arts Community, Graphic Artists, Photographers
CONTACT Paul Brown
pgb2@ra.msstate.edu
FREE

http://www.msstate.edu/Fineart_Online/gallery.html

Fluxus Online ★★★

Fluxus Online was organized by Nam June Paik and Paul Garrin. It contains information about Fluxus projects and an archive of the 1994 festival SeOUL-NyMAX—A Celebration of Art without Borders, which brought together over seventy artists and critics working with dance, music, performance, electronic arts, film, and video. Plans for the future of this site include FluX eMail ArtFest, which will accept ASCII art, uuencoded or binhexed GIFs via the WWW. This site also contains information about Fluxus in Europe, including notes about early Fluxus projects (1962-63).

KEYWORDS Electronic Arts, Video
AUDIENCE Art Historians, Art Students, Artists, Arts Community, Arts Educators, Curators
CONTACT Fluxus@panix.com.
FREE

http://anansi.panix.com:80/fluxus/

The Jazz Photography Of Ray Avery ★★★

This online exhibition presents the jazz photography of Ray Avery. The exhibition is grouped into four major areas—The Lighthouse All Stars, Hermosa Beach & Laguna Beach; Nightclubs, Festivals & Concerts; Recording Sessions—Los Angeles; and Stars of Jazz—TV Series (Billie Holiday, Chet Baker, Jim Hall, Bobby Timmons, Dave Brubeck). Each area contains a few related images and historical commentary. In addition, the curators have assembled a collection of books and CDs that complement this period and feature releases of music recorded at the time and place that many of the photographs were taken. This information and a discography are available in the exhibition bookstore.

KEYWORDS Art Exhibitions, Jazz, Photography
AUDIENCE Art Historians, Arts Community, Jazz Enthusiasts, Music Historians, Photographers
CONTACT James A. Harrod
jaharrod@uci.edu
FREE

http://bookweb.cwis.uci.edu:8042/Jazz/JPRA16.html

Michigan Press Photographers Association ★★

The Michigan Press Photographers Association provides this Web page to offer information on its activities and member benefits. Users will find ethics discussions, contests and commentary on photojournalistic work, and a directory of members. In addition, photographs made available by members can be found on this page.

KEYWORDS Photography, Photojournalism, Press Photography
AUDIENCE Photographers, Photojournalists, Press Photographers
CONTACT ejp@umich.edu
FREE

http://www.cris.com/~mppa/

The National Museum of Photography, Film & Television ★★

The National Museum of Photography Film & Television of the United Kingdom aims to encourage public understanding and appreciation of the science and art of photography, film and television and the relationships between them. This site offers a look at their permanent collection as well as their special attractions. There are links to other United Kingdom sites on the Internet and visual arts web pages.

KEYWORDS Film & Video, Museums, Photography, United Kingdom
AUDIENCE Film Enthusiasts, Film Researchers, Photographers, Video Enthusiasts
CONTACT Bernard Wozny
bpwozny@bradford.ac.uk
FREE

http://www.brad.ac.uk/~bpwozny/NMPFT2/home0.html

Oxford Photographs ★★★★

The Oxford Photographs Web site offers an extensive collection of photographic information on the city of Oxford in England. Users will find photographs of many famous landmarks, including the buildings of venerable Oxford University. This site also hosts local information of use to visitors, as well as a collection of aerial views and other non-traditional types of photographs.

KEYWORDS England, Photography, Photojournalism
AUDIENCE England Residents, Tourists, Travelers
CONTACT Jonathan Bowen
Jonathan.Bowen@comlab.ox.ac.uk
FREE

http://www.comlab.ox.ac.uk/archive/ox/photos.html

A Personal View of Paris ★★★

This site contains photographic images of Paris (c. 1978) and commentary by John Mack. The exhibition, supported by the French government, encourages the viewer to interact by responding to questions posed after viewing each image and text. This site also contains links to other photographic resources.

KEYWORDS Paris, Photography, Travel
AUDIENCE Artists, Arts Community, Francophiles, Humor Enthusiasts, Tourists
CONTACT Jim Mack
jmack@pipeline.com
FREE

http://meteora.ucsd.edu/~norman/paris/Expos/PersonalView/

PHOTON Home Page ★★★★

Billing itself as the first online photography magazine, PHOTON is creating a Web marketplace for those who buy and sell stock photographs. It also covers upcoming photographic competitions, tips on darkroom processing, electronic imaging. This site includes articles on a variety of professional and amateur photographic subjects.

KEYWORDS News Media, Online Magazines, Photography, Stock Photography
AUDIENCE Amateur Photographers, Editors, Photographers, Publishers
CONTACT DavidKilpatrick@photon.scotborders.co.uk
FREE

http://www.scotborders.co.uk/photon/

The Place ★★★★

The place is an art space which is dedicated to using the Web as a medium for exploring the space 'between tool and myth.' Users will find several different exhibitions which incorporate art, photography, and poetry. For example, the Urban Diary contains images from an anonymous urban citizen's diary, and Life With Father is a hypertextual poem with digital photographs. Essays on technology and art are also included, as well as a graphical piece on anatomy and the meaning of the human body.

KEYWORDS Art Galleries, Photography, Poetry
AUDIENCE Art Enthusiasts, Art Students, Artists
CONTACT Joseph Squier
joseph@ux1.cso.uiuc.edu
FREE

http://gertrude.art.uiuc.edu/ludgate/the/place/place2.html

Treebear Studio ★★★★

Treebear Studio is a multi-talented collection of artists who dabble in photography, music, and poetry. This site mostly houses a collection of images created by the Studio, along with a selection of poetry. Users will find a large collection of images organized by the subject matter they capture. Headings available include landscape photography, portraits, and nude photography. Links to other art on the Web are also available here.

KEYWORDS Music, Photographic Arts, Photography, Poetry
AUDIENCE Art Enthusiasts, Photography Enthusiasts
CONTACT Samuel Claiborne
samc@computel.com
FREE

http://www.computel.com/~samc/tb.html

Tunnel Vision Photojournalism Site ★★★★

The Tunnel Vision Photojournalism Site exists to provide a space for the photographer Randall R. Greenwell's work. Users will find a gallery of photojournalistic images in several categories, including a place for newly-updated images. The photographer provides some background information on the images available here, as well as small and large format images for easy downloading. This site also hosts a collection of links to related sites on the Net.

KEYWORDS Photography, Photojournalism
AUDIENCE Photographers, Photography Enthusiasts, Photojournalism Enthusiasts
CONTACT Randall R. Greenwell
randyman@evansville.net
FREE

http://www.evansville.net/~randyman/

Virtual Portfolio ★★★

The Virtual Portfolio site has been created to allow photographers to put up a small portfolio of their work on the Net so that those in need of photographic services can more easily shop for photographers. Users can browse the portfolios by artist, by subject, or for those photography agents that are online, by agent. Information is provided on contacting all of the photographers whose work is displayed here.

KEYWORDS Photographers, Photography, Virtual Portfolios
AUDIENCE Photographers, Photography Consumers
CONTACT Mike Russell
maushaus@dircon.co.uk
FREE

http://www.dircon.co.uk/maushaus/folio.html

The World of Women On-Line ★★★★

This temporary online art gallery of international women's contemporary art is presented in conjunction with the United Nations' Fourth World conference on women to be held in Beijing, China, in 1995. It leads to art work listed by artist's last name and country. What an abundance of art work! Arizona State University provides the memory for these pictures as well as creative research for the project. There are instructions for uploading or snail-mailing women's artwork, so that users or their friends can be part of this international conference.

KEYWORDS Conferences, Contemporary Art, Electronic Arts, Universities
AUDIENCE Art Students, Artists, Feminists, Women
CONTACT Muriel Magenta
atmur@asuvm.inre.asu.edu
FREE

www.asu.edu:80/wwol/

The Zone I Gallery ★★★★

Zone I Gallery is the home page of E.A. Kennedy III, an African American photographer. A newspaper photographer by trade, he concentrates on pictures of people, mainly African Americans. The initial photo, 'Boom Box Homeboy,' is a dramatic profile of a street youth holding a boombox. The home page is an extremely sensitive essay in black and white, of interest to all races and national backgrounds. The first exhibition on the pages is titled, 'Amazing Grace—Portraits from the African American Church.' Kennedy promises to show art of other African American photographers in future cyberspace exhibitions on this page.

KEYWORDS African Americans, Art Exhibitions, Photography, Portraits
AUDIENCE African Americans, Art Educators, Artists, Photographers
CONTACT eak3@gate.net
FREE

www.gate.net/~eak3/

Business & Economics

Accounting	101
Advertising & Marketing	102
Banking	104
Benefits	106
Business Schools	106
Career & Employment	109
Commerce	112
Consumer Issues	116
Economics	117
Finance	118
Home Office	119
Industries	120
International Business	125
Investment	128
Management	133
Non Profits	134
Publishing	136
Real Estate	140
Reference	142
Retail	145
Services	148

Accounting

See also
Business & Economics · *Commerce*
Business & Economics · *Investment*

ANet/The International Accounting Network ★★★★

The International Accounting Network, a group of providers of information on the Internet, exchange ideas and insights about the accounting and auditing professions. The three providers are: the University of Exeter in the UK, Rutgers University in New Jersey, USA, and Southern Cross University in New South Wales, Australia. AN'et online services include Details of Accounting Conferences, ANet Mailing Lists details and hyperlinked archives, a complete list of accounting organizations worldwide, accounting research including a complete list of accounting journals, accounting software and other resources, and much more.

KEYWORDS Accounting, Auditing, Business
AUDIENCE Accountants, Auditors, Business Owners
FREE

http://www.scu.edu.au/ANetHomePage.html

Accounting Services Gopher ★★★

This site offers information about the Accounting Handbook, accounting services training workshops, the University of California, the Berkeley annual financial report, and re-engineering disbursements. There is also a keyword search facility and more.

KEYWORDS Accounting, Education (College/University), Funding
AUDIENCE Accountants, Accounting Educators, Students (University)
CONTACT Carolyn Smith
cmsmith@uclink.berkeley.edu
FREE

gopher://uclink.berkeley.edu:1609/

CTI-AFM (CTI Centre for Accounting Finance and Management) ★★★

The CTI Centre for Accounting Finance and Management (CTI-AFM) contains links to conference proceedings and academic journals. This site is part of a national initiative to promote the effective use of computers in teaching and learning in higher education. The Centre at UEA has built up a considerable resource of software and journals over the last few years. Information about software workshops, conferences and visits to individual departments at the Centre is also available. Other services include a journal Account distributed free to all academics in the relevant disciplines, a catalog of software, information on seminars and demonstrations, general and subject specific electronic discussion lists, an annual conference, and published conference proceedings.

KEYWORDS Accounting, Computer Software, Computing, Journals
AUDIENCE Accountants, Accounting Educators, Accounting Students, Business Owners
FREE

http://www.sys.uea.ac.uk/cti/cti-afm.html

NAARS (National Automated Accounting Research System) ★★★

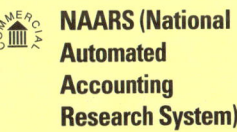

The National Automated Accounting Research System (NAARS) library, provided as a service by agreement with the American Institute of Certified Public Accountants (AICPA), contains a variety of accounting information including annual reports of public corporations, and accounting literature and publications for the accounting professional. Annual reports are annotated with descriptive terms assigned by the AICPA. These terms allow searching of annual report footnotes that illustrate recognized accounting practices.

KEYWORDS Accounting, Annual Reports, Business, Reference
AUDIENCE Accountants, Business Professionals, CPAs, Financial Analysts
CONTACT Mead New Sales Group
COST

http://www.meaddata.com/libcont/naars.html

telnet://nex.meaddata.com

Rutgers Accounting Web (RAW) ★★★★

RAW provides access to an evolving knowledge platform containing a variety of accounting materials. These materials are in hypertext, or in a variety of word processing and presentation graphics formats, and are classified by hierarchy of subjects and by providers. RAW is working with Southern Cross University Centre in New South Wales and with Summa Project at the University of Exeter in England. RAW services provide access to educational materials, a professional accounting program, management faculty, American Accounting Association, certified management accountant programs, accounting resources on the Internet, and web authoring tools. The site also contains information about the National Center For Automated Information Research(NCAIR), which funds RAW.

KEYWORDS Accounting, Auditing, Computing
AUDIENCE Accountants, Accounting Educators, Accounting Students, Auditors, Business Owners

CONTACT   Alex Kogan
           kogan@andromeda.rutgers.edu
FREE

http://www.rutgers.edu/Accounting/raw.html

Advertising & Marketing

See also
Business & Economics · *Industries*
Business & Economics · *Non Profits*
Business & Economics · *Services*
Internet · *Internet Business*

A.C. Nielsen Company

A.C. Nielsen is the global authority on marketing research for consumer packaged goods companies, and media research, including the Nielsen Television Ratings and ANYwhere Online—Nielsen's new venture to measure online commerce. This site provides links to information on Nielson's services, business productivity, market trends, financial information, media research, consumer response, and more.

KEYWORDS   Consumer Goods, Market Research, Television
AUDIENCE   Advertising Professionals, Marketing Professionals, Media Professionals, Researchers
CONTACT   webmaster@nielsen.com.
FREE

http://www.nielsen.com/home/index.html

ADvise Group & Network 2000

The ADvise Group is an information resource for small- to mid-sized advertising agencies with annualized billings up to $50 million. Requring membership, the Group's home page provides information about creating Web sites, a service called Cyberspot Advertising, group consulting, group buying (bulk discount purchases of software, computer systems, and Datatrak time for member agencies), a chat area, a guest log, and an email option.

KEYWORDS   Advertising, Consulting Services, Information Resources, Marketing
AUDIENCE   Advertising Agencies, Advertising Executives, Advertising Professionals, Marketing Specialists
COST

http://www.advize.com/

ARC - American Resource Company

This is a somewhat eclectic gathering of employment advertising listings and links, a connection to Ad Cetera Sports Marketing which sells sports franchise items like t-Shirts, pins, etcetera, and links to HTML programming resources. An electronic feedback form is provided.

KEYWORDS   Advertising, Employment Advertising, Marketing, Sports Marketing
AUDIENCE   Advertisers, Employers, HTML Enthusiasts, Job Seekers, Sports Marketers
FREE

http://www.arcfile.com

Ad Age - It's All About Marketing

The Ad Age Home Page consists of advertising and marketing information culled from the industry's leading magazine, including features such as the Daily Deadline (today's news), interactive media and marketing, smart marketers, interactions, facts and features, transactions, portfolios and awards, and the option to place yourself in the Ad Age database to receive updates and more detailed information. Ad Age has also developed a 'one-stop resource for marketing information', which is a multiple link to the combined information of Hotwired magazine, Ad Age, and Organic Online magazine

KEYWORDS   Advertising, Magazines, Online Magazines
AUDIENCE   Advertisers, Advertising Executives, Business Analysts, Marketing Specialists
FREE

http://www.adage.com/

Alfers Advertising and Publishing, Inc. (The Alfers Zone)

This is the home page for a Nova Scotia advertising agency which is described as an 'all digital, fully electronic advertising agency and publishing company.' Clients include The Halifax Club, Royal Insurance, Nubody's fitness centres, Kids World clothing stores, and NSTN. Links to things automotive and hot links are also provided.

KEYWORDS   Advertising, Internet Marketing, Marketing, Printing
AUDIENCE   Advertisers, Advertising Professionals, Business Professionals, Marketing Specialists
CONTACT   alfers@fox.nstn.ca
FREE

http://fox.nstn.ca/~alfers

Avalanche

Avalanche, an electronic design and production company located in New York City produces interactive media on the WWW, CD-ROMs, and CDi mediums. Their products include online publications, digital press kits, interactive kiosks, corporate media, and complete Internet environments.

KEYWORDS   Design Firms, Multimedia, New York, Online Publications
AUDIENCE   Business Professionals, Marketing Executives
FREE

http://www.avsi.com

CKS Partners Ltd.

CKS Partners Limited is a marketing firm based in the UK. Their web site offers users information about the company's experience in fields such as advertising, marketing, public relations, and Internet presence. Users can see short examples of work done for present and former clients, as well as statistical information on Internet usage.

KEYWORDS   Marketing, Online Marketing, Public Relations
AUDIENCE   Marketers
CONTACT   Brian Fortune
           bfortune@cksp.demon.co.uk
FREE

http://www.cks.com/ukweb/cks/

Carter Waxman's Reststop on the Infogroove

The Carter Waxman Advertising Agency home page is a graphics-rich illustration of the companies marketing capabilities. Due to heavy graphics, the link can be slow at 14.4 baud. The full service agency, located in San Jose, California, provides campaign and spot ads, creative development, collateral, media research and planning, market research, logo development, copywriting, displays and exhibits, public relations, political and community relations, and special events. Links move you through the agency's philosophy, a portfolio of some of their work, a description of their broad client base, and, for your entertainment, an agency-created soap opera spoofing Silicon Valley.

KEYWORDS   Advertising Agencies, Companies, Marketing, Media Research
AUDIENCE   Advertisers, Business Professionals, Marketing Specialists
FREE

http://www.carwax.com

Chiat/Day Idea Factory

Chiat/Day is an large brand promotion, marketing, and media company. Its home site has pages devoted to the inner workings of the company, as well as to its vision of where technology is taking the media and the rest of society. These pages are tied into the theme of the Idea Factory, where ideas are planned and actively created. Users can see areas such as the logistics of how a large media company creates ideas, how persuasion takes place in today's society, and how the technological advances that are taking place today will ultimately affect companies, the media, and the whole society. To that end, users can participate in online surveys (with a special section for advertising professionals and journalists), and future plans include online focus groups.

KEYWORDS   Companies, Internet Culture, Market Research, Sociology
AUDIENCE   Advertising Professionals, General Public, Journalists, Media Critics, Media Industy, Sociologists
CONTACT   webmaster@chiat.com
FREE

http://chiatday.com/factory/

Advertising & Marketing

Communicopia Environmental Research and Communications ★★★★

Communicopia is an environmental communications consulting company that has made the services they offer available online. They provide services to businesses or corporations interested in informing the public about their environment-conscious programs. Communicopia offers a list of previous clients and the papers they have published.

KEYWORDS Consultants, Ecology, Environment, Public Relations
AUDIENCE Business Professionals, Environmentalists, Public Relations Experts
CONTACT communicopia@mindlink.bc.ca
FREE

http://interchange.idc.uvic.ca/communicopia/

Connexx International ★★★★

Connexx International is a business-to-business advertising information provider, marketing itself on the Web, newsgroups, bbs's, Prodigy, and search engines. It provides links on how to subscribe, and information on financial services, venture capital, Mexican investments, domestic and international marketing, distribution, as well as resources and links to other companies.

KEYWORDS Advertising, Information Resources, Internet Marketing, Marketing
AUDIENCE Advertisers, Business Professionals, Internet Marketers, Marketing Specialists
COST

http://www.gc.net

Dun & Bradstreet Information Services ★★★

This is the page of the Dun & Bradstreet Information Services, a resource for global business expertise. Topics include Product Access, Finding A Job, Strategic Business Planning, Tactical Marketing, Predictions, How To Manage Vendors, Research Effectively, and Marketing Business Globally.

KEYWORDS Business Management, Business Planning, Employment
AUDIENCE Employers, Financial Planners, Investors, Job Seekers, Managers, Stockbrokers
CONTACT webmaster@dbisna.com
FREE

http://www.dbisna.com/

The Europa Center ★★★

Europa is a center for commerce, information, and community at the edge of technology. Links are provided to Europa Marketplace, Europa's mall, Europa Kiosks where businesses and organizations place brochures and business cards, Web Search, Home Earth which locates businesses, organizations and users using maps from around the world, and more.

KEYWORDS Business Services, Internet Shopping, Marketing
AUDIENCE Business Professionals, Consumers, Internet Users, Marketing Specialists
CONTACT admin@europa.com
FREE

http://www.europa.com/

Hajjan/Kaufman New Media Lab ★★★★

The Hajjan/Kaufman New Media Lab, a division of Hajjan/Kaufman Advertising located in Marina Del Rey, California, is a leading edge multimedia marketing provider. One of their products is HK Radio, the 'first real-time 'radio station' to broadcast original programming through the Internet.' This portion of the page describes the hardware, software, and downloadable program required to listed to the station through the browser. The lab has a special focus on the publishing, entertainment and financial sectors, and has expertise in websites, ftp sites, gopher sites, mailing lists, Internet broadcast, and teleconferencing.

KEYWORDS Advertising, Internet Marketing, Marketing
AUDIENCE Advertisers, Business Professionals, Internet Users, Marketing Specialists
CONTACT lab@lab.hkweb.com
FREE

http://www.hkweb.com

Insanely Interactive Systems, Inc. ★★★

Insanely Interactive Systems, Inc. is based in Montreal, Quebec, Canada. They provide outsourcing, turn-key and advertising services to corporations of all sizes. You can access their International Traveller's Guide which provides a clickable map of destinations and corresponding information for business travellers. There are also links to a limited number of business resources from their International Business Guide.

KEYWORDS Tourism
AUDIENCE Business Professionals, Canadians, Tourists
CONTACT info@iisys.com
FREE

http://www.iisys.com

Koschs Guide to Network Marketing in Canada ★★★★

This guide is an online book discussing the ins and outs of network marketing specific to the Canadian business environment. Chapters include About Network Marketing, The Right Business for You?, What To Know Before You Start, What to Look for In a Good Network Marketing Company, How To Make Money, How to Use Technology, Using the Net to Market Products, Recommended Companies, Directory of Companies in Canada, references, and further reading.

KEYWORDS Internet Marketing, Marketing, Multi-Level Marketing (MLM)
AUDIENCE Business Professionals, Internet Marketers, Marketing Specialists
FREE

http://www.supernet.ab.ca/Mall/Business/

Marketing & The Internet ★★★★

This is a collection of marketing information resources created to support 'Marketing in a Global Networked Environment', a course in the MBA curriculum at Duke University. Topics include course orchestration, marketing-oriented papers and discussion, marketing applications on the World Wide Web, analyzing Network impact, marketing-oriented lists and search engines, and student projects and submissions.

KEYWORDS Internet Marketing, Marketing, Networking, Universities
AUDIENCE Business Professionals, Business Students, Internet Users
CONTACT johng@mail.duke.edu
FREE

http://www.duke.edu/~mccann/

Marketing By Design, Inc. ★★

Marketing By Design, Inc. specializes in creating, securing and marketing unique designs for sports items. Currently, there is only one link to an Information Super Highway Cap. Most of the products are made in the United States.

KEYWORDS Clothing, Marketing, Sports Marketing
AUDIENCE Athletes, Fashion Enthusiasts, Marketing Professionals, Sports Fans
CONTACT icc@shore.net
FREE

http://northshore.shore.net/icc/mbd.html

Murray Multimedia Page ★★★★

Murray Multimedia's page describes this full service advertising agency specializing in multimedia and print advertising. The agency develops creative concepts for interactive and print media and executes them on time and on budget. Clients include Forbes Magazine, NASA Tech Briefs Magazine, Roche, Schering-Plough, and Chemical/Geosource. Services feature advertising, displays, interactive multimedia presentations, package design, print media, and visual identity systems. The agency asserts itself as a continually leading provider of high technology services by constantly encouraging employees to learn new systems and programs.

KEYWORDS Advertising, Advertising Agencies, Internet Marketing, Multimedia
AUDIENCE Advertisers, Business Professionals, Marketing Specialists
CONTACT john@mm.com
FREE

http://www.murraymedia.com/murray/

National Internet Source Classifieds ★★

The National Internet Source web page offers users a listing of business services and classified advertisements covering a wide variety of areas ranging from electronics companies, to printers, to a fairly comprehensive listing of apartments available across the U.S.

Some of the headings remain empty as the site is still under construction. Users may also post a classified ad at this site for free.

Keywords Apartments, Business Services, Classified Ads
Audience Apartment Hunters, Electronics Buyers, General Public
Free

http://aayt.nis.net/nis/niscom.main.html

Online Classified Advertising ★★★★

The Online Classified Advertising Web site is organized using an easy-to-follow index so that you can locate the ads you're interested in quickly and easily. You can also access the ads on their system through any of the following methods—World Wide Web, Internet auto-response email, BBS download, fax-on-demand and fax phone. Some of the advertisers have provided easy hypertext access directly to the sites.

Keywords BBSs (Bulletin Board Systems), Classified Ads
Audience Business Professionals, Consumers
Contact Support@web-ads.com
Free

http://www.web-ads.com/

Sales and Marketing Exchange (SME) ★★★★

The Sales and Marketing Exchange (SME) home page includes four clickable subcategories: SalesWeb, PRWeb, DesignWeb, and DM (Direct Marketing) Web. Within each of these are linked information resources specifically relating to the subcategories about agencies, associations, forums, information services, industry publications, consultants, seminars and helpful software. Other planned subcategories include the Marketing Web and Ad Web. Each subcategory features a browser electronic form to either sign up as an information user, or as a service provider to be featured on the page.

Keywords Direct Marketing, Marketing, Public Relations, Sales
Audience Marketing Specialists, Public Relations Experts, Sales Professionals
Contact finfo@sme.com
Free

http://www.sme.com/default.html

Smart Choice Technologies Corporation ★

This site is the home of the SmartPoll polling web site. Demonstrations of surveys are given, as are other advertising and marketing tools.

Keywords Internet Business, Marketing
Audience Marketing Executives, Pollsters, Surveyors
Free

http://copeland.smartchoice.com/scdemo

WebTrack ★★★★

WebTrack is an in-depth resource on who is doing what in World Wide Web advertising. The page provides marketers with information to fully leverage the Web as a marketing medium, featuring hyper-directories, newsletters, and tracking software. Information categories include a Web ad database, ad space locator, marketing directory, 'Interad Monthly' newsletter, Web statistics, and an extensive linked listing of popular web sites.

Keywords Advertising, Internet Marketing, Internet Statistics, Marketing
Audience Advertisers, Business Professionals, Internet Marketers, Marketing Specialists
Contact info@webtrack.com
Cost

http://www.webtrack.com

World Wide Yellow Pages ★★★

The World Wide Yellow Pages is a directory of businesses online. For a limited time listings for business on the net will be free—just submit the online form. You can also find information about pricing, request a brochure, or get other information on promoting your business online.

Keywords Internet Marketing, Marketing, Yellow Pages
Audience Business Professionals, Internet Users
Contact info@yellow.com
Free

http://www.yellow.com

Young & Roehr, Inc. Advertising and Public Relations ★★

The Young & Roehr home page provides information about the advertising agency, its mission and services. Young & Roehr is a full service business-to-business marketing and communications company serving the US high-technology, transportation, and paper products industries. The site also contains a page of previous work samples with accompanying GIFs, a short client list, as well as staff bio information.

Keywords Advertising Agencies, Business Services, Marketing, Public Relations
Audience Marketing Communications, Marketing Managers
Contact David White
davidwh@teleport.com
Free

http://www.young-roehr.com/~davidwh

Banking

See also
Business & Economics · *Industries*
Business & Economics · *Services*
Computing & Mathematics · *Software*

Bank America Home Page ★★★

This BankAmerica home page provides information about the bank's various corporate responsibility programs and employment opportunities. Also, ATM locations, special offers, and press releases. There is no specific information on products and services.

Keywords Banking, Companies, Financial Services
Audience Bankers, Banking Industry Analysts, Consumers, Financial Advisors
Free

http://www.bankamerica.com/

Bank of Boston ★

The Bank of Boston's Home page is one text page with no links to other sites or information. The Bank of Boston and its services are briefly described and non-WWW contact information is provided.

Keywords Banking, Financial Services, Massachusetts
Audience Banking Industry Analysts, Financial Advisors, Financial Analysts
Contact bkbinfo@netcom.com
Free

http://www.llnl.gov:80/fstc/bank_of_boston.html

Barclays Group PLC., Home Page ★★★★

This is the Barclays Bank PLC Home page, with links to others describing some of the many services offered by Barclays. Services include Banking Products, Travel Insurance, BarclayCard, and Computer Operations.

Keywords Companies, United Kingdom
Audience Bankers, General Public, Investment Bankers
Contact webmaster@barclays.co.uk
Free

http://www.barclays.co.uk/

Capital One Bank ★★★

This is Capital One Bank's Home Page. They have over five million customers and $7 billion in managed loans. Capital One Bank claims to be one of the top credit card issuers in the country. You can apply for a Visa card online or click to find answers to your financial questions. Capital One Bank is a wholly owned subsidiary of Capital One Financial Corporation (COF), whose common stock is traded on the New York Stock Exchange.

Keywords Banking, Credit Cards, Finance
Audience Consumers, General Public, Internet Users, Investors

CONTACT info@capital1.com
FREE
http://www.capital1.com/CapitalOne/c1-home.html

Chase Global Financial Services

This home page offers Chase Manhattan Bank's annual report, its listing of financial services and products, and a statement about the bank's strategic focus. Links to products and services are also provided.

KEYWORDS Annual Reports, Banking, Finance, Financial Services
AUDIENCE Bankers, Banking Industry Analysts, Financial Advisors, Financial Analysts
FREE
http://www.llnl.gov:80/fstc/chase_manhattan.html

Chemical Bank Home Page

Chemical Bank, one of the leading banks in the world, has established this home page, but as of this compilation, the only working link is to a career services page which lists job openings in New York City, and working conditions and lifestyle issues in the city. Plans for the future of this site include areas for shareholders, employees, customers, and community activities.

KEYWORDS Banking, Finance
AUDIENCE Banking Professionals, Financial Experts, Job Seekers, New York Residents
CONTACT FSTC@cbc.com
FREE
http://fstc.poly.edu/Chemical/Chemhp20.html

Citibank Home Page

The Citibank Home Page provides access to Citibanks' online services. The page has information about banking services, branch locations and other related products. Visitors can also find out some of the bank's services such as the types of accounts, credit cards and loans available through Citibank.

KEYWORDS Companies, Credit Cards, Investment
AUDIENCE Bankers, General Public, Investors
CONTACT citi@www.tti.com
FREE
http://www.tti.com

Cybercash Incorporated

This site provides information about Cybercash Incorporated, which has designed a system of electronic commerce. CyberCash related files within this site include an overview which contains detailed facts and general information about Cybercash, a 'how to' file which should answer any questions about getting started in electronic commerce, and a page which discusses Cybercash Incorparated and its relationships with various banks. In addition, a Cybercash client application form and user's guide can also be obtained through this site.

KEYWORDS Banking, Electronic Commerce
AUDIENCE Business Professionals, Computer Users, Corporartions, General Public
CONTACT info@cybercash.com
FREE
http://www.cybercash.com/

Connections to Cash on the Internet
Will you be paying with cash?

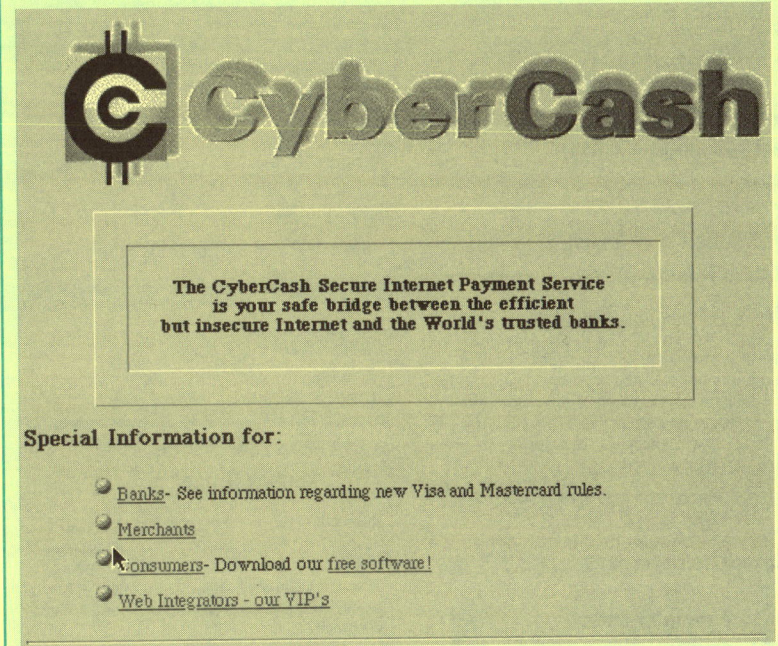

There is an alternative to using your credit card when buying products on the Internet. Internet resources now allow you to pay cash for products and services by connecting you with your bank or an electronic cash service which provides protection for transactions made through your computer.

A variety of digital cash sites are available to set up an account or connect you to a bank so you can make cash transactions on your computer—also know as e-cash or cybercash.

One such Internet site is "CyberCash." This service provides you with an electronic wallet to pay for products you want to purchase over the Internet.

CyberCash provides information on U.S. and Canadian CyberCash banks (such as Wells Fargo, First National Bank of Omaha) and various merchants that sell products for professional, industrial, and home markets. The software is free and there is online assistance for setting up an account and obtaining connections to your bank.
(http://www.cybercash.com/)

also, (http://www.cyberbase.com/software/software.html)

Another service for paying cash via your computer is "DigiCash," a place where you can obtain license payment technology products—chip cards, software- only, and a hybrid of the two—to pay in cash for items you want to buy on the Net. There are also guides on using e-cash, including connections with shops taking e-cash in return for products and services, as well as information on how to set up a transaction and authorize payment.
(http://www.digicash.com/)

also, (http://www.digicash.com/products/projects/projects.html)

FDIC (Federal Deposit Insurance Corporation) Gopher

This server provides information about the Federal Deposit Insurance Corporation (FDIC). The FDIC insures depositors of member banking institutions in the U.S. This server describes the FDIC mission, its history, and

Banking – Business Schools

services. It also provides assorted financial information such as banking statistics, economic statistics, and real estate trend analysis.

KEYWORDS Banking, Federal Deposit Insurance Company (FDIC) (US), Federal Government (US), Finance
AUDIENCE Bankers, Banking Industry Analysts, Economists, General Public
CONTACT POSTMASTER@FDIC.GOV
FREE

gopher://fdic.sura.net:71/

Federal Deposit Insurance Commission Gopher Rating ★★★

The Federal Deposit Insurance Commission Gopher Rating site accesses banking statistics from 1934 to present, with detailed sections on recent banking history. Has directories for Consumer Information, FDIC Assets For Sale, Bibliograghic Information, and recent press releases. This site also has a directory listing other resources for economic statistics.

KEYWORDS Banking, Economics
AUDIENCE Bankers, Banking Industry Analysts
FREE

gopher://fdic.sura.net:71/

First Interstate Bank ★★★

This home page leads to descriptions of First Interstate's consumer and business services and products, a list of bank and ATM locations, and corporate announcements. Business and consumer areas are searchable for specific products or services.

KEYWORDS Banking, Companies, Finance, Loans
AUDIENCE Bankers, Consumers, Creditors
FREE

http://www.hexadecimal.com/fi/

Public Information About the World Bank ★★★

The World Bank Group is the International Bank for Reconstruction and Development (IBRD). It also consists of the International Development Association (IDA), the International Finance Corporation (IFC), and the Multilateral Investment Guarantee Agency (MIGA). The gopher's Public Information Center includes reports on activities and studies by the World Bank, including economic and environmental information as well as contacts for further information.

KEYWORDS Economic Development, International Development, NGOs (Non Governmental Organizations), World Bank
AUDIENCE Economic Development Experts, Economists, Environmental Researchers
CONTACT webmaster@www.worldbank.org
FREE

gopher://ftp.worldbank.org/

U.S. Federal Reserve Board Gopher Site ★★

This gopher site allows for the researching of various data that falls under the purview of the U.S. Federal Reserve, including tracking of banking funds (deposit and non-deposit), mortgage rate information, mortgage financing company data, and the Fed's flow of funds analysis.

KEYWORDS Banking, Commerce, Federal Databases (US)
AUDIENCE Business Analysts, Financial Researchers, Investors
FREE

gopher://town.hall.org/11/other/fed

Benefits

See also
Business & Economics · *Management*

 ## A to Z Insurance Legacy Group ★★★

This site is dedicated to the sale and purchase of insurance in all its varied forms. It is administered by Legacy Group of America, a group of 20 insurance companies, offering a range of insurance packages for the Internet individual, including medical, life, dental and group plans.

KEYWORDS Benefits, Health Insurance, Insurance, Retirement
AUDIENCE Business Professionals, Financial Advisors, General Public
FREE

http://branch.com/legacy/legacy.html

CSCW Research Group - Mikmod Project ★★★★

Mikmod focuses on supplying simulation models for the development and application of microsimulation and typical case models. The goal is to provide strong policy support for the German Federal Administration. Simulation models include—a microsimulation model for the analysis of the 'BAFöG training assistance act' (BAFPLAN), including a model for East Germany, a DSS for analyzing direct and indirect transfers to families with dependent children, (APF), including a microsimulation model for estimating program costs and distributional effects as well as a typical case model for the various pension systems in Germany (ASA).

KEYWORDS Germany, Taxes
AUDIENCE International Financiers, Tax Specialists
CONTACT Dr. Hermann Quinke
Hermann.Quinke@gmd.de
FREE

http://orgwis.gmd.de/MIKMOD/

 ## Employee Benefits ★★★

The Firm concentrates in employee benefits law and includes 16 attorneys who concentrate their practices in employee benefits and eight paralegals. The practice claims to be national in scope, representing employee benefits clients in over 40 states. Their clients include: Sponsors of employee benefit plans. Associations which sponsor health and pension benefit programs for their members. Investment advisors, benefits administration firms, actuaries, insurance companies and health care delivery organizations such as PPOs and HMOs. The National Employee Benefits Institute (a benefits lobbying organization). Multi-employer health and pension plans.

KEYWORDS Employee Benefits, Health Care, Insurance Companies, Pension Plans
AUDIENCE Employees
CONTACT Dave Baker
erisa@magicnet.net
FREE

http://www.rbvdnr.com/eb/eb-main.htm

#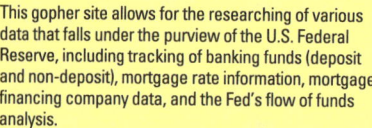

See also
Business & Economics · *Investment*
Business & Economics · *Reference*

Australian Graduate School Of Management ★★

This gopher server provides links to areas on the Internet likely to be of interest to those in the field of management. The site is maintained by the Australian Graduate School of Management (AGSM). There is also information about the AGSM itself including access to library catalogs.

KEYWORDS Business Management, Commerce, Graduate Programs, Universities
AUDIENCE Business Professionals, Business Students, Management Trainers, Managers
CONTACT Pamela Brass
pamb@agsm.unsw.edu.au
FREE

gopher://zap.agsm.unsw.edu.au/

College of Business at Florida State University ★★★

This is a gopher server for the College of Business at Florida State University. Information is provided about admissions, departments, scholarship news, calendars, computing services, Ph.D. and M.B.A. news, a newsletter called The Alumni Connection, seminars, and events.

KEYWORDS Business Management, Education (College/University), Universities
AUDIENCE Business Educators, Business Educators (University), Business Students
CONTACT gopher@cob.fsu.edu
FREE

gopher://cob.fsu.edu:4070/

Dalhousie University, Faculty of Management - Home Page ★★★★

This is the home page of the Dalhousie University Faculty of Management. This page provides both graphical and text-based links to online courses, schools and programs, business and management education centers, and various WWW sites.

KEYWORDS Business Management, Canada

Business Schools   **107**

AUDIENCE   Canada Residents, Students (Secondary/University), Students (University)
CONTACT   Tim Roberts
           www@quasar.sba.dal.ca
FREE

http://quasar.sba.dal.ca:2000/

Fudan Business Student Network ★★★★

The Fudan Business Student Network is focused on providing Fudan alumni and students a place to network. Included to links to Chinese Business Bulletin Board, Business China, Business Asia, Business World, Business Schools, and a Business Students Mailing list.

KEYWORDS   Alumni, Networking
AUDIENCE   Business Professionals, Business Students, Economists, General Public, Managers, Professors
CONTACT   h-zhou@uxa.cso.uiuc.edu
FREE

http://uxa.cso.uiuc.edu/~h-zhou/fudanb.html

Graduate School of Business, Stanford University ★★★

This site is a gopher server of the Graduate School of Business, Stanford University. It offers information about the School, courses, schedules, faculty, library services, research resources, and more. It has links to other gophers.

KEYWORDS   Business, Community Services
AUDIENCE   Business Educators (University), Business Researchers, Business Students
CONTACT   suzanne.sweeney@gsb.stanford.edu
FREE

gopher://gsb.stanford.edu/

Graduate School of Management - Macquarie University, Australia ★★★

This site provides information about the Graduate School of Management at Macquarie University, Australia. The information includes degree program information, research information including online abstracts and business news.

KEYWORDS   Australia, Business Schools, Universities
AUDIENCE   Australians, Business Educators, Business Professionals, Business Students
CONTACT   Mark Silva
           gsm.internet@mq.edu.au
FREE

gopher://gsmgopher.gsm.mq.edu.au/

Connections to the London Business School

The world's economic outlook today is...

To access one of the world's most authoritative resources on economics and business management, turn to the online pages of the London Business School.

The Centre for Economic Forecasting provides quarterly economic forecasts and analysis of both the United Kingdom and various world economies. If you are a corporate executive, a corporate planner, or member of a government and policy-making institution, this site provides invaluable information about tax reform, inflation, exchange rates, and more—all of it independent of national government forecasts and bias.

You can also find out about continuing education courses as well as business management degree programs from the school. Moreover, you'll find extensive information for the school's full-time MBA program for accounting, decision sciences, economics, finance and marketing. You can also obtain information on Ph.D. programs and the Sloan Fellowship Master's Program.

(http://www.lbs.lon.ac.uk/)   also, (http://www.lbs.lon.ac.uk/research/res001.html)

also, (http://www.lbs.lon.ac.uk/mba/index.html)

Groupe Enseignement International des Affaires - Marseille ★★

The International Business School in Marseille has a small site with general information, links to the students, other services and an English page under construction.

KEYWORDS   France, International Business
AUDIENCE   Business Educators, Business Students
FREE

http://serveia.u-3mrs.fr/

Harvard Business School—Marketing Area ★★★★

The Harvard Business School—Marketing Area server provides access to Marketing News, MBA Information, Executive Education, the Doctoral Program, Faculty Biographies, Interactive Marketing sites, and the Harvard Business School home page.

KEYWORDS   Marketing
AUDIENCE   Business Professionals, Business Students, Economists, General Public, Managers, Professors
FREE

http://www.hbs.harvard.edu/marketing/mkt.html

Helsinki School of Economics ★★

The information on this server is about the Helsinki School of Economics and Business in Finland. It provides information on the school's administration, admission criteria for the school, the school's Career

Business & Economics

Business Schools

Services Center, staff email addresses, library services and more.
- KEYWORDS: Computer Networking, Economics, Education, Education (College/University)
- AUDIENCE: Business Educators, Economists, Students (Secondary/University)
- CONTACT: neuvoja@hkkk.fi
- FREE

gopher://gopher.hkkk.fi/

Lancaster University Management School (UK) ★★★

The Management School at Lancaster University comprises six academic departments including Accounting and Finance, Behaviour in Organisations, Economics, Management Learning, Management Science and Marketing, and Management Development. Links are provided for these departments as well as to faculty information and research.
- KEYWORDS: Education (College/University), Faculty, United Kingdom
- AUDIENCE: Business Professionals, Educators (University), Employers, Students (University)
- FREE

http://www.lancs.ac.uk/users/mansch/manageme/index.htm

London Business School ★★★

The London Business School's web site provides access to information on the degree programmes such as the MBA and PH.d. programs in business, the Research Centres, Faculty Information, Publications and more.
- KEYWORDS: MBA Programs, United Kingdom
- AUDIENCE: Business Professionals, Educators (University), Employers, Students (University)
- CONTACT: ANealis@lbs.lon.ac.uk
- FREE

http://www.lbs.lon.ac.uk/

MBA Program ★★★★

The MBA Program for the University of Illinois at Urbana-Champaign site provides links to extensive information about the program. Topics covered include History, FAQs, Financial Aid, Curriculum, Career Services, Job Search E-Zine, Student Resumes, The Alumni Connection, Student Organizations, Housing, Activities, Announcements & Bulletins, the Alumni Newsletter, and more.
- KEYWORDS: Business Education, Business Schools, Graduate Education
- AUDIENCE: Business Professionals, Business Students, Economists, General Public, Managers, Professors
- FREE

http://mba.cba.uiuc.edu/

MIT Sloan School of Management ★★★

The MIT (Massachusetts Institute of Technology) Sloan School of Management home page presents information on its Educational Programs, an online exhibit featuring artists within the MIT community, research centers, current events, community resources, and other Fun Links. Users can access either a text-based only or graphically enhanced menu.
- KEYWORDS: Boston, Education (College/University), Graduate Programs, MBA Programs
- AUDIENCE: Business Professionals, Educators (University), Employers, Students (University)
- FREE

http://www-sloan.mit.edu/

Manchester Business School (UK) ★★★

This home page for the Manchester Business School in England provides access to information about Graduate Degree Programs, Executive Education Programs, Conference Details and Facilities, the Manchester Business School Departments, the Career Management Centre, Employment Opportunities, a Who's Who, internal Telephone Directory, and more.
- KEYWORDS: Education (College/University), MBA Programs, United Kingdom
- AUDIENCE: Business Professionals, Educators (University), Employers, Students (University)
- CONTACT: WEBMASTER@MBS.AC.UK
- FREE

http://www.mbs.ac.uk/

The Masters of Business Administration at United Technologies ★★

The Masters of Business Administration at United Technologies web site offers an overview of this hands-on Technical Business Program where students are educated on site at various participating companies. The site offers a company listing with programs at Pratt & Whitney and Carrier Corporation accompanied by brief descriptions of the educational opportunities offered in the fields of Marketing, Human Resources, Management, and Engineering. Information on rotational programs within these companies and Direct Hire is also available.
- KEYWORDS: Employment, Masters of Business Administration, Professional Recruitment
- AUDIENCE: Business Students, Engineering Job Seekers, Engineers, Technological Businesses
- FREE

http://www.utc.com/BIGIDEA/ideabook.html

Minnesota Carlson School of Management ★★★★

The Minnesota Carlson School of Management web page provides access to its degree programs, calendar of events, research centers, student activities, faculty research and other resources. Users can access a text-based only menu or include graphics.
- KEYWORDS: Education (College/University), Faculty, MBA Programs, Management
- AUDIENCE: Business Professionals, Educators (University), Employers, Students (University)
- CONTACT: www@csom.umn.edu
- FREE

http://www.csom.umn.edu/

Nanyang Technological University—Business School ★★

Welcome to the Nanyang Technological University Business School home page. This server provides information about the school and its teaching and research programmes. There are also links to topics on Economics and Business, Singapore (Infomap), and Other Business School and business-related web servers.
- KEYWORDS: Economics, Education (College/University), Singapore, Southeast Asia
- AUDIENCE: Business Professionals, Educators (University), Employers, Students (University)
- CONTACT: kendall@technet.sg
- FREE

http://www.ntu.ac.sg/~ajdkendall/

Northwestern University J.L. Kellogg Graduate School of Management ★★★

This is a gopher server of the Northwestern University J.L. Kellogg Graduate School of Management. It contains information on the School, academic departments, faculty resumes, seminar schedules, admissions, computer services, the phone book, and more. It has a link to the Northwestern University Gopher.
- KEYWORDS: Education (College/University), Illinois, Management
- AUDIENCE: Business Educators (University), Management Students, Students (Secondary/University)
- CONTACT: gopher@skew.kellogg.nwu.edu
- FREE

gopher://skew.kellogg.nwu.edu/

Swedish School of Economics and Business Administration ★★

This gopher provides information on the Swedish School of Economics and Business Administration which is located not in Sweden, but in Helsinki, Finland. Their server contains information on the School, undergraduate and graduate programs, international exchange programs, departments, and more.
- KEYWORDS: Business, Computer Networking, Economics, Education
- AUDIENCE: Business Educators (University), Economists, Students (Secondary/University)
- FREE

gopher://gopher.shh.fi/

Turku School of Economics and Business Administration ★★

This is a gopher server of the Turku School of Economics and Business Administration in Finland. It contains information on the School, undergraduate and graduate

Business Schools – Career & Employment

programs, international exchange programs, departments, and more.

KEYWORDS Business Schools, Economics, Education (College/University), Finland
AUDIENCE Business Educators (University), Economists, Students (Secondary/University)
FREE

gopher://gopher.tukkk.fi/

UC Berkeley - Walter A. Haas School of Business ★★★★

The UC Berkeley - Walter A. Haas School of Business home page provides access to information on its MBA Programs, Computing at Haas, the Center for Information Technology Management, the Haas Interactive Tour, The New Building, and related links.

KEYWORDS MBA Programs
AUDIENCE Business Educators, Business Professionals, Business Students
CONTACT adam@haas.berkeley.edu
FREE

http://haas.berkeley.edu/

USC (University of Southern California) School of Business Administration ★★★★

The University of Southern California (USC) School of Business Administration Web page provides extensive information on its business programs. Included are links to the Undergraduate Programs, Graduate Programs, Academic Schools, Departments and Programs, Research Centers and Institutes, Academic and Information Resources, Alumni Programs and the USC Business Magazine.

KEYWORDS Research Institutes, Undergraduate Programs
AUDIENCE Business Professionals, Business Students, Economists, Professors
FREE

http://www.usc.edu/dept/sba/

UTK Management Science Program ★★★

This is the site of the Management Science Program at the University of Tennessee which is noted for its academic programs. Topics covered includes some FAQs on Management Science, Programs of Graduate Study, Program Faculty and Facilities, Admission and Financial Aid, The College of Business Administration, and more.

KEYWORDS Education (College/University), Graduate Programs, Management Science, Tennessee
AUDIENCE Business Professionals, Educators (University), Students (University)
CONTACT brogdon@telstar.bus.utk.edu
FREE

http://northstar.bus.utk.edu/mgmtsci/

Vanderbilt University, Owen Graduate School of Management ★★★★

The home page for Vanderbilt University, Owen Graduate School of Management in Nashville, Tennessee provides an easy-to-use image map with various subject areas. Some of these include MBA admissions, MBA student services, faculty, an executive MBA program, executive seminars, alumni services and more.

KEYWORDS Management
AUDIENCE Business Students, Economists, General Public, Managers
CONTACT sulkinds@ctrvax.vanderbilt.edu
FREE

http://www.vanderbilt.edu/Owen/

Washington State University College of Business and Economics ★★★★

The Washington State University College of Business and Economics server provides access to an extensive list of links. The areas include Admission Requirements, Course Outlines, Courses with WWW Interactions, Clubs, Degrees Offered, Employment Connections, Graduate Programs, Scholarships, Grants, and more. There are also links to College and University Programs and other Business Links.

KEYWORDS Scholarships, Universities
AUDIENCE Business Professionals, Business Students, Economists, Managers
FREE

http://www.eecs.wsu.edu/~cbe

West Virginia University College of Business & Economics ★★★★

The West Virginia University College of Business & Economics home page provides access to Academic Departments, Administration, Student Information, Bureau of Business Research, Graduate Programs, Information Technology, Development & Alumni Affairs, Student On-Line Resumés & Career Resources, Publications, and News and Events.

KEYWORDS Business Schools, Universities
AUDIENCE Business Professionals, Business Students, Economists, Professors
CONTACT wolfe@wvubc1.bc.wvu.edu
FREE

http://www.be.wvu.edu

Wharton School of the University of Pennsylvania ★★★★

The Wharton School of the University of Pennsylvania home page provides extensive information on the school and its activities. Included are links to the Wharton Faculty, Academic Departments and Research Centers, the Undergraduate and Graduate Divisions, MBA Program and Wharton Executive MBA Program (WEMBA), Doctoral Programs, Executive Education Division, and Alumni Information. You can also find Wharton publications and computing information online. Many of the documents in the Wharton Information Network are in Adobe Acrobat's Portable Document Format (PDF) which require an Acrobat viewer such as Acrobat Reader or Acrobat Exchange.

KEYWORDS MBA Programs
AUDIENCE Business Educators, Business Professionals, Business Students
CONTACT whitehouse@wharton.upenn.edu
FREE

http://www.wharton.upenn.edu/

Career & Employment

See also
Business & Economics · Industries
Computing & Mathematics · Companies

California Career and Employment Center ★★★

The California Career and Resource Center provides online information about job opportunities in California. Besides allowing potential employers to list job openings, it provides them with resources such as a resume database, where they can establish their own California job opportunity listings for job seekers as well as links to the Online Career Center. The site also provides information for small entrepreneurs and small business owners, such as services and products and links to the Small Business Administration's Web page. And it features information about all types of California colleges for those looking for education resources.

KEYWORDS California, Career, Entrepreneurs, Job Listings
AUDIENCE Employers, Entrepreneurs, Job Seekers, Students
CONTACT Central Coast Employment Services cces@netcom.com
FREE

http://www.webcom.com/~career/

Career Resumes ★★★★

This page is an extension of the Branch Mall and gives information about the company Career Resumes. It advertises its services, and provides information to the user about how to obtain more services.

KEYWORDS Career Services, Companies, Jobs, Resumes
AUDIENCE Job Seekers
FREE

http://branch.com/cr/cr.html

CareerMosaic ★★★★

CareerMosaic(TM) is an online guide to companies and opportunities. Using CareerMosaic, individuals can research companies in a variety of businesses. Users can find out what they do, where they do it, and what their environments are like. All the information has been developed by the employer in cooperation with CareerMosaic. There is also a section for college internships and co-op opportunities, a forms-based search of all UseNet Job categories, and an extensive

Career & Employment

career library containing studies, articles, and tips related to the job market.

KEYWORDS Employment, Internships, Job Listings
AUDIENCE Employment Counselors, Human Resources Departments, Job Recruiters, Job Seekers
CONTACT bmoore@pa.hodes.com
FREE

http://www.careermosaic.com/

The Chicago Tribune Career Finder ★★★★

The Chicago Tribune provides jobs listings from the daily newspaper but with a twist. The site includes articles with related editorial content, such as company profiles, and feature stories on employment, employers, and technology. It also provides recruitment advertising in five computer and electronics-related areas. The ads remain on the Web for two weeks. Supporting editorial material on the Web site includes articles by jobs columnist Carol Kleiman and computer writer James Coates.

KEYWORDS Career, Classified Ads, Jobs, Online Newspapers
AUDIENCE Employers, Illinois Residents, Job Seekers
CONTACT Gene Quinn
genequinn@aol.com
FREE

http://www.chicago.tribune.com

Classified Employment Listings - San Francisco Chronicle and Examiner ★★★★

This page hosts the job listings from the San Francisco Chronicle and Examiner Classified Advertisements. Job opportunities are primarily for companies in Northern California, but they include numerous industries (business, economics, sales, education, etc.). The listings are fairly extensive and up-to-date.

KEYWORDS California, Employment, Job Listings
AUDIENCE Californians, Human Resources Departments, Job Recruiters, Job Seekers
CONTACT George Shirk Gate Content Manager
gshirk@sfgate.com
FREE

http://sfgate.com/classifieds/files/770.html

College Grad Job Hunter—WWW Home Page ★★★★

This is a site useful for college students and college graduates beginning their job search. There is material on the techniques and tactics of job hunting. This site also hosts links to the Online Career Center, as well as other employment networks and bulletin boards with job opportunities.

KEYWORDS Employment, Internet Resources
AUDIENCE Job Seekers, Students (University)

CONTACT knitterb@solaria.sol.net
FREE

http://www.execpc.com/~insider/

Coopers and Lybrand and You ★★★★

Coopers and Lybrand is a member of Coopers and Lybrand International, a limited liability association incorporated in Switzerland. This site is for graduate business placement. In the UK, Coopers is the largest firm of chartered accountants and management consultants, providing services to over half The Times' 100 top companies. In addition, they have a network of offices in over 120 countries worldwide. In particular, they have a presence in every Western European country and are well-established and growing rapidly in Eastern Europe, the Commonwealth of Independent States and in China. The site also contains a European Survey on the information superhighway and multimedia, and a listing of companies.

KEYWORDS Consulting Services, Employment Agencies, International Business, Management
AUDIENCE Business Educators, Business Professionals, Business Students
FREE

http://www.coopers.co.uk/coopers/

Employment Center of Chicano/LatinoNet ★★

The Employment Center posts information on both current and past employment opportunities which are related to Latino, ethnic or linguistic issues. The information ranges from the name/contact of an employer to full job descriptions. The majority of positions offered are within an academic setting, including Deans, Professors, Librarians, and Program Directors.

KEYWORDS Chicano Culture, Job Listings, Universities
AUDIENCE Chicanos, Educators (University), Job Seekers, Latinos
CONTACT CLNET Manager, Chicano Studies Research Center
salinas@latino.sscnet.ucla.edu
FREE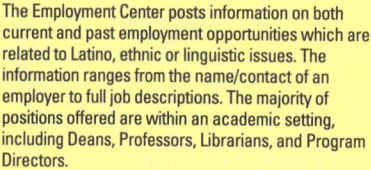

gopher://latino.sscnet.ucla.edu:70/11/Employment%20Center

H.E.A.R.T—Career Connection's OnLine Information System ★★★

H.E.A.R.T. (Human resources Electronic Advertising and Recruiting Tool) is a menu-driven system with presentations of career opportunities. There is no charge to the job seeker, however fees are charged to employers. First-time users must register and select a password. You can search for positions by geographic location or job title, and you can apply for jobs by submitting your resume through this system. Online categories include Accounting, Software Consulting, Engineering, Communications, and Finance.

KEYWORDS Career, Employment, Job Listings
AUDIENCE Job Recruiters, Job Seekers, Students

CONTACT postmaster@career.com
FREE

telnet://career.com/telnet://college.career.com/

IntelliMatch Online Career Services ★★★

IntelliMatch is designed to match job seekers with potential employers such as Samsung, I-Net, and Quality Semiconductor. Their page provides those looking for jobs with 'WATSON' resume forms for their specific fields of expertise. Employers can then order their 'HOLMES' interface in order to browse these potential employee listings and come up with appropriate matches. This site also has current job listings that job seekers can browse without sending in resumes. Also included are FAQs and press releases about the IntelliMatch system, and information about employers who hire through the site.

KEYWORDS Employment, Resumes
AUDIENCE Employers, Job Seekers
CONTACT IntelliMatch Online Services
intelli@netcom.com
FREE

http://www.intellimatch.com/intellimatch/index.html

International Career and Employment Network ★★

This gopher site contains an archive of the International Career and Employment Network Newsletter. Each newsletter has one to three job announcements about jobs located in various points of the world. Recent posts included Engineering jobs with Intel in Malaysia and Banking Internships in Vienna, Austria.

KEYWORDS Employment, Internships
AUDIENCE Job Seekers, Students (University)
FREE

gopher://gopher.indiana.edu:70/11/theuniversity/life/intlcent/icen

Job Finders ★★★

Job Finders contains resume databases and job-related links. It also provides information on colleges and universities in the US and throughout the world. The site has access to comprehensive employment servers such as MSEN's Online Career Center which maintains a Gopher server for employment information, including job offerings and resumes, and pointers to further jobs listings. The comprehensive servers be searched by keyword in job title, company name, job description, resume, state, city, or region. The site also includes recruiters and employment-related information and services.

KEYWORDS Education (College/University), Employment, Job Listings
AUDIENCE Employers, Employment Counselors, Job Seekers
FREE

http://infonext.nrl.navy.mil/job.html

Career & Employment

Job Openings for Economists (JOE) ★★★★

JOE, a project of the American Economic Association, has a large collection of job postings for economists. Most listings are faculty positions in academe, and therefore require a doctoral degree. However, there are also listings from business and non-profit organizations which have less stringent requirements. The listings are both browsable and searchable. The Association publishes a print edition as well, and cooperates with Vanderbilt University to produce this electronic version.

KEYWORDS Economics, Education, Employment, Job Listings
AUDIENCE Economics Students, Economists, Job Seekers
FREE

gopher://vuinfo.vanderbilt.edu:70/11/employment/joe

Job Postings from the Victoria Free-Net ★★

This gopher lists some employment opportunities in Victoria, British Columbia. The jobs are primarily from academic instituitons in Victoria, or computing positions from the BC Systems Corporation.

KEYWORDS Canada, Employment, Job Listings
AUDIENCE Job Seekers
CONTACT Victoria Freenet
vifa@freenet.victoria.bc.ca
FREE

gopher://vifa1.freenet.victoria.bc.ca:70/11/business

Job Search and Employment Opportunities- Best Bets From The Net ★★★

This site offers the Job Search and Employment Opportunities - Best Bets from the Net guide. This guide attempts to list the best sources of job information on the Internet from a variety of professional associations, job listing services, and other semi-professional associations.

KEYWORDS Career, Employment, Information Services, Online Services
AUDIENCE Employees, Job Recruiters, Job Seekers
CONTACT job-guide@umich.edu
FREE

http://asa.ugl.lib.umich.edu/chdocs/employment

Job Search of Southern California ★★

Job Search maintains a database of 40,000 Southern California businesses for those seeking employment in that region. Their Web site gives an introduction to their services, provides a request form for those interested in joining, and allows browsers to receive a brief employer list. After filling out personal data, employment, and industry preference forms, job hunters will receive a an email with a summary of potential employ-ers. After joining Job Search, job seekers can then search the database according to town and industry type.

KEYWORDS California, Companies, Employment, Job Listings
AUDIENCE Business Professionals, Californians, Employment Counselors, Job Seekers
CONTACT Job Search
jobsearch@adnetsol.com
FREE

http://www.adnetsol.com//jsearch/jshome1.html

MBA Students' Guide to the World Wide Web ★★★

The MBA Students' Guide to the World Wide Web focuses on showing MBA students how to survive yet have fun doing it. Topics covered include Career Services & Job Search, The World Of Business, MBA Programs in the US and around the World, MBA Survival Guides, and a section entitled, 'Take a break—surfing to some cool sites!'

KEYWORDS Internet Guides, MBA Programs
AUDIENCE Business Professionals, Economists, General Public, Managers, Professors, Students
CONTACT rwatson@uga.cc.uga.edu
FREE

http://www.cba.uga.edu/tcb/mbaguide/projweb.htm

Monster Board ★★★

Monster Board is a searchable database with over 300 job listings, mostly in the high tech and biotech industries in the Northeastern United States. Surfers may search the database by Industry, Location, company or job title—or by any combination of these categories. The Monster board also contains folios on each company listed, discussing its technology and working environment. The Monster Cave section describes the New England recruiting and advertising firm behind the Monster Board.

KEYWORDS Companies, Employment, Job Listings
AUDIENCE Business Professionals, Employers, Job Seekers, Students (University)
FREE

http://www.monster.com/home.html

National Career Search's Career Magazine ★★★

Career Magazine offers a variety of services for job searchers, recruiters, and networking professionals. Among the areas for users to explore are indexed

---

Connections to JobServe
Find that job in cyberspace

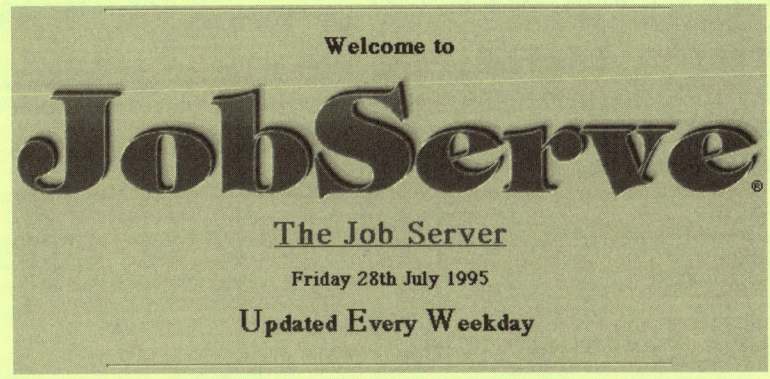

More and more companies are utilizing the World Wide Web to post job openings, especially for those people who want to work in high-technology industries. There are many job opportunities in industry, as well as education and government.

The "JobServe" sites include tips on how to search the JobServe database. When you're ready, just sign onto the Job Server and begin your search. You can respond to ads via the Internet, sending your resume and a cover letter to companies that post on the Web. Often-times, companies will respond within hours of receiving a resume.

There are even areas for consultants, and postings are updated daily. This is one of the best ways to expand your job search without having to go to the local news stand and purchase a dozen or so newspapers, and then begin sending your resume out through snail mail.

(http://www.demon.co.uk/cgi-bin/jobserve/search.pl)

also, (http://www.demon.co.uk/jobserve/)

searches of job-related Usenet groups (searches by location, skills or title), classified ads for career consultants (including a directory of executive recruiters), a collection of articles and news reports about networking, the workplace, and job hunting tips, and a career forum where users can network and share advice online.

KEYWORDS   Employment, Executive Recruiters
AUDIENCE   Human Resources Departments, Job Recruiters, Job Seekers
FREE

http://www.careermag.com/careermag/index.html

Online Career Center ★★★★

The Online Career Center (OCC) is an extensive resource for job seekers. Users can search OCC's list of job openings by job title, keyword, company name, or by geographical region. OCC lists many international jobs as well as North American positions. There is also information about job fairs, resumes and job search skills, as well as recruiting agency listings and other services.

KEYWORDS   Employment, Internships, Job Listings
AUDIENCE   Human Resources Departments, Job Recruiters, Job Seekers
CONTACT   occ@iquest.net
COST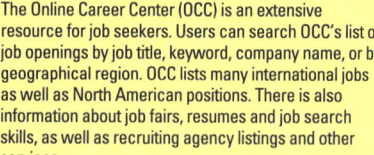

http://www.iquest.net/occ/

gopher://occ.com/

Project Hired ★★★

This is a home page from Project Hired, which gives individuals with disabilities resources and opportunities to compete successfully for employment at all levels in companies throughout Silicon Valley. Here you'll find a list of their accomplishments, contact information, etc.

KEYWORDS   California, Disability Resources, Employment, Silicon Valley
AUDIENCE   Activists, Californians, Disabled People, Job Seekers
CONTACT   prohired@ix.netcom.com
FREE

http://infobase.internex.net:80/impact/190home.html

TIS Recruiting—Top Ten Hot Jobs ★★★

This site developed by TIS Recruiting lists employment opportunities primarily in technical and financial fields. Users may peruse a listing of ten available positions including job title, company and location as well as a brief description. Users may apply for a position by emailing their resume directly to TIS. There is also information on TIS's resume writing services. Job hunters may also conduct a keyword search of other online employment resources from this site.

KEYWORDS   Job Opportunities, Technical Employment
AUDIENCE   Employment Seekers, Engineers, Technical Staff

CONTACT   webmaster@tisny.com
FREE

http://www.tisny.com/tis/hotjobs.html

TKO Personnel, Inc ★★★

TKO specializes in United States and Pacific Rim employment, job opportunities, and recruitment. Their Web site lists information about the company, gives current listings, and provides forms to get further information. The Goldmine Newsletter allows employers to search a list of descriptions of bicultural job candidates in specified fields. Goldmine Opportunities then allows candidates to browse a list of positions in Asia and the U.S. according to job type, describing requirements, duties and salary. They also include a link to the X-Guide, a comprehensive information guide about Japan and U.S.-Japan business relations.

KEYWORDS   Business, Employment, Japan, Job Listings
AUDIENCE   Japan Residents, Job Seekers
CONTACT   TKO Personnel, Inc. kdn@shell.portal.com
FREE

http://www.internet-is.com/tko/index.html

Talent Services ★★★

Talent Services is a Belgian online employment service for graduates or experienced professionals. There are online job opportunities listed.

KEYWORDS   Belgium, Career, Job Listings
AUDIENCE   Belgians, Job Seekers
FREE

http://www.innet.net/talent/fr/

University of Wisconsin, Madison (State Civil Service Listings) ★★

This site contains comprehensive occupational listings including Wisconsin state government job vacancies.

KEYWORDS   Civil Service, Employment, Job Listings, Wisconsin
AUDIENCE   Job Seekers, Wisconsin Residents
FREE

gopher://gopher.adp.wisc.edu

Weekly Job Listings From The Centralized Recruitment and Referral Program ★★★

This gopher site provides a listing of jobs available with the state of Ohio. The list is updated weekly, and contains notices from the Departments of Corrections, Environmental Protections, and Transportation, among others.

KEYWORDS   Employment, Government Agencies, Job Listings, Ohio
AUDIENCE   Job Seekers, Ohio Residents

CONTACT   Ohio Freenet bkalal@freenet.columbus.oh.us
FREE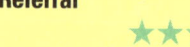

gopher://gizmo.freenet.columbus.oh.us:70/11/governmentcenter/stateofohio/State%20Government%20Job%20Opportunities

World Wide Job Seekers ★★★

This Web site functions as an employment office bulletin board for people all over the world seeking jobs and for those who wish to hire them. Each job-seeker fills out a standardized resume which is then posted at the site, where it is categorized according to type of job sought. Employers can easily browse through the resumes to find a prospective employee that appeals to them. As the site is maintained in Canada there is a bit of Canadian flavor to it. The service is free, and anyone worldwide can post a resume in any field.

KEYWORDS   Job Listings, Resumes
AUDIENCE   Job Seekers, Personnel Managers
CONTACT   webmaster@cban.com
FREE

http://www.cban.com/resume/index.html

Commerce

See also
Business & Economics · *Industries*
Business & Economics · *International Business*
Business & Economics · *Retail*
Law & Criminal Justice · *Business Law*
Popular Culture & Entertainment · *Shopping*

The Access Market Square Home Page ★★★

The Access Market Square Home Page offers a big shopping mall. The unique products and gifts include computer software—mainly multimedia related, electronics (radar jammers and spy supplies, auto audio), clothing, medical products, personal protection products, home-business services (mainly Internet related), jewelry, sports cards, and art (including pseudo 3-dimensional pictures).

KEYWORDS   Clothing, Multimedia, Online Shopping, Shopping Malls
AUDIENCE   Art Enthusiasts, Card Collectors, Computer Users, Shoppers
CONTACT   info@icw.com
FREE

http://www.icw.com/ams.html

Amcham (American Chambers of Commerce Abroad) ★★★

This gopher server offers name, address, phone, and other contact information for American chamber of commerce organizations located abroad. These organizations are affiliates of the American versions,

Commerce

and work to promote mutual economic and business relations between the US and their home countries.

KEYWORDS Business Development, Economic Development, Organizations, Regional Business

AUDIENCE Business Professionals, Business Researchers, Entrepreneurs, International Marketing Professionals

FREE

gopher://sunny.stat-usa.gov:70/11/STAT-USA/NTDB/Amcham

Ann Arbor Chamber of Commerce ★★★

This hosts the Ann Arbor, Michigan Chamber of Commerce. Currently, the available information native to this site consists of a listing of chamber personnel, a local map giving directions, and a cartoon related to the Internet. Users can also find a list of links to reach other local and non-local Internet services.

KEYWORDS Business Development, Michigan, Organizations

AUDIENCE Michigan Residents

CONTACT Branch Information Services and Ann Arbor Area Chamber of Commerce branch-info@branch.com

FREE

http://chamber.ann-arbor.mi.us/

Arizona Home Page ★★★

The Arizona Home Page allows local residents and other users to access information on local area businesses in a wide variety of categories from real estate to electronics dealers. The listings are still somewhat scant, although the page does provide links to CityNet and InfoSeek.

KEYWORDS Arizona, Business, Real Estate

AUDIENCE Arizona Residents, Arizona Tourists, Pheonix Residents

CONTACT KC Vale kc@neta.com

FREE

http://trojan.neta.com/~kc/

Auburn Chamber of Commerce Homepage ★★★

The home page of Auburn, Alabama is sponsored by the Chamber of Commerce and is 'organized for the purpose of advancing the commercial, industrial, civic, and general interest of the City of Auburn and its trade area. The Auburn Chamber is made up of involved members who are committed to improving our community, attracting businesses, having fun, and providing benefits to ourselves and our community.' There are subindexes that cover such topics as local government, an electronic shopping mall, economic development, demographics, education, recreation and retirement.

KEYWORDS Alabama, Economic Development, Organizations, Regional Business

AUDIENCE Alabama Residents, Business Entrepreneurs, Real Estate Entrepreneurs, Tourists

FREE

http://www.viper.net/clients/Au.cc/

 ## BizNet Client Listing ★★★

The BizNet Client Listing of Virginia businesses presents information on local restaurants, consulting firms, real estate brokers, banks, and hospitals. There are several places to shop including Diamonds by WWW, Virginia Tech Bookstore, a clothing shop, a software shop online, a flower shop, and the home page of local grocery store.

KEYWORDS Advertising, Books, Community Networking, Virginia

AUDIENCE Computer Users, Shoppers, Students (University), Virginia Residents

CONTACT biznet@bev.net

FREE

http://www.bnt.com/shopping.html

Cyberspace Malls International ★★★

The Cyberspace Malls International home page from Santa Fe is for people fond of bedding, kitchenware, food, and art. They house several shops offering linens, bed things, furnishing, cookware, and stores like the Santa Fe Chocolate store, Golf Mart, and a couple of local art galleries. This site provides electronic ordering and shows promise of rapid expansion.

KEYWORDS Arts, Chocolate, Internet Shopping, Shopping Malls

AUDIENCE Art Enthusiasts, Home Owners, New Mexico Residents, Shoppers

CONTACT service@cyspacemalls.com

FREE

http://chili.rt66.com/cyspacemalls/

 ## Edge Mall ★★★

This home page from the Edge Internet Services features a small Internet mall oriented mainly toward music professionals. You can find various music supplies here (tapes, professional acoustic pianos, electronic instruments, etc.), a home page of audio and music marketing companies, a couple catalogs of recording companies, and a directory of other commercial sites on the Web.

KEYWORDS Music, Music Industry, Shopping Malls

AUDIENCE Musicians, Shoppers

CONTACT Webmaster@edge.net

FREE

http://www.edge.net/mall/cybermall.html

 ## GENinc's Worldwide Chambers of Commerce ★★

This site for the Community Information and Economic Development Orgs.—World Map (Global Exposure Network, Inc.) claims to feature the pages of local chamber of commerce organizations worldwide. At the time of this writing, however, this site offers only North American organizations in California, Texas, and Colorado. Users are offered either a direct link to pages maintained by the chamber of commerce organizaions, or an index listing the localities with information available. Typically available is information on a local area's population and demographics, transportation, geography, community and government services, business climate, and more.

KEYWORDS Business Development, Economic Development, Organizations, Regional Business

AUDIENCE Business Professionals, Business Researchers, Entrepreneurs, Market Analysts

CONTACT sales@geninc.com

FREE

http://www.geninc.com/geni/maps/chamber_world.html

 ## High Technology Development Corporation Web Server ★★

The High Technology Development Corporation's (HTDC) mission is to facilitate the development of commercial high technology industry in Hawaii. HTDC actively markets and promotes Hawaii as a site for high-technology business and gives advice on policy and planning. HTDC is an agency of the State of Hawaii and is administratively attached to the Department of Business, Economic Development & Tourism (DBEDT). In additon to its own project information, this page contains links to other technology and business organizations such as the Center of Excellence for Research in Ocean Sciences and the Electric Vehicle National Data Center.

KEYWORDS Business, Economic Development, Hawaii, High Technology

AUDIENCE Business Professionals, Economists, Engineers, Marketing Executives

CONTACT webmaster@htdc.mic.hawaii.org

FREE

http://www.mic.hawaii.org/

 ## Home Team (HOME Technology Education And Marketing) ★★★★

The Home Team is a program which involves many industries, all of which are dedicated to spreading the word about the latest technologies for homes. It is primarily directed by trade associations which represent the various industries involved and is managed by Home Systems Network. There are comprehensive links to a wide variety of topics including sections of intelligent homes, proposed standards, lighting controls, security systems, communications systems, entertainment networks, home theaters, energy management, windows, doors and gate controls; plumbing controls, outdoor equipment controls, automation controls and more.

KEYWORDS Home, Home Improvement, Home Technology, Products

AUDIENCE Architects, Home Buyers, Interior Designers

CONTACT creator@hometeam.com

FREE

http://ionet.net/hsn

The IONET Mall

The IONET Mall home page, which is supported by Internet Oklahoma, offers computer resources such as Internet related software/hardware, the services of Johnson Computer & Consulting, and advice on how to automate your home. Also there are fitness and children's books, jewelry, and long distance credit card calling. Orders are usually by phone—no electronic orders.

KEYWORDS   Computer Supplies, Shopping Malls
AUDIENCE   Computer Users, Fitness Enthusiasts, Internet Users, Shoppers
CONTACT   support@ionet.net
FREE

http://www.ionet.net/mall/com_page.html

Internet Business Connection

This home page features The Internet Business Connection—an Online Shopping Center where you can browse through categories and read brief introductions to the products and services offered before reading the full description. Usually, you won't find a real interactive catalog—only promotional home pages of companies offering products or services are available. Some departments in the directory are rather unusual, like Employment, Aquaculture, and Translational Services. All common items for online shopping malls (like computers, finance, travel, and gifts) are present.

KEYWORDS   Computer Products, Gifts, Shopping Malls, Translation
AUDIENCE   Consumers, Job Seekers, Shoppers
CONTACT   ibc@intbc.com
FREE

http://www.charm.net/~ibc/

Internet Shopping Galleria

Another Internet shopping mall—this one looks real. They sell contact lenses, computer software and hardware, books, watches, bikes, automobiles, art, fashion, golf balls, jewelry, food and drinks. The site also includes electronic ordering and nice graphics.

KEYWORDS   Books, Computer Supplies, Shopping Malls, Sportswear
AUDIENCE   Artists, Computer Users, Home Owners, Shoppers, Tourists
CONTACT   rbowen@catcomp.com
FREE

http://intergal.com/

Japan External Trade Organization (JETRO)

This extensive page provides information about doing business in Japan, including import expansion in Japan, industrial cooperation with developed nations, economic exchange with developing nations, international communication, internationalization in Japan, economic data, major publications in English, economic trends in Japan, industry, markets, business practices, and world statistics and data published in Japan.

KEYWORDS   International Trade, Japan, Marketing
AUDIENCE   Business Professionals, International Trade Executives, Marketing Specialists
FREE

http://www.jetro.go.jp/

Journal of Economics and Management Strategy

The Journal of Economics and Management Strategy (JEMS) is a quarterly journal edited by economists and management-strategy scholars. JEMS provides a forum for interaction and research on the competitive strategies of managers and the organizational structure of firms. It features theoretical and empirical industrial organization, applied game theory, and management strategy. There is a link to the rest of the Electronic Newstand.

KEYWORDS   Business, Economics, Human Resources, Management
AUDIENCE   Business Owners, Entrepreneurs, Managers
FREE

gopher://gopher.enews.com:70/11/
business/pubs/business/jems

MEDMarket Healthcare Mfg. Industry Index

This page provides links to all organizations of interest to the healthcare manufacturing industry which have a world wide web Internet presence. Information includes medical product manufacturers and suppliers, vendors to medical product manufacturers and suppliers, auxiliary product and service providers, industry-related organizations, and employment recruiters.

KEYWORDS   Industry, Manufacturing, Medical Manufacturing, Medical Supplies
AUDIENCE   Market Researchers, Marketing Specialists, Medical Professionals, Physicians
CONTACT   csi@frontier.net
FREE

http://www.frontier.net/MEDMarket/
indexes/index.mfr.html

Main Street

This page isn't a usual shopping mall - it's a main street of Downtown Anywhere - a really nice place to visit. Main Street houses a lot of small stores in computers, telecommunications, software, gifts and flowers. Of course, there is no system of payment since every store is a separate entity.

KEYWORDS   Computer Supplies, Gifts, Shopping Malls
AUDIENCE   Collectors, Computer Users, Shoppers, Software Users
CONTACT   downtown@awa.com
FREE

http://awa.com/mainst.html

Online Computer Market Home Page

This home page is something between a directory of computer related sites and a computer store. They keep home pages of several sellers of software/hardware, but their main feature is a number of links to software/hardware producers, computer consultants, calendar of events and trade shows, and computer company profiles.

KEYWORDS   Companies, Computer Consulting, Computer Software, Computer Supplies
AUDIENCE   Computer Professionals, Computer Users, Internet Users
CONTACT   reske@ocm.com
FREE

http://www.ocm.com/

Shecora StarWay USA

A home page from a Shecora StarWay features a lot of different retailers (DIGITAL computers, cat and horse supplies), restaurants, real estate firms, a singles' club, home pages of green companies, and more. Retailers and services providers are ordered by region of the USA, and there is a Worldwide Distribution department.

KEYWORDS   Cats, Computers, Environmental Activism, Shopping Malls
AUDIENCE   Computer Users, Environmentalists, Pet Owners, Shoppers, Single People
CONTACT   info@sai.com
FREE

http://www.sai.com/index.htm

Shopping 2000 Home Page

This home page features a growing list of online catalogs of different consumer goods. Catalogs of flowers, gifts, home electronics, books, pet supplies, kitchen equipment, hosiery, arts and music, etc.

KEYWORDS   Catalogs, Consumer Goods, Internet Commerce, Shopping Malls
AUDIENCE   Collectors, Consumers, General Public, Shoppers
CONTACT   cw@pipeline.com
FREE

http://www.shopping2000.com/

Software.net Home Page

This is an excellent place to shop for a computer software - any platform, any operating system. They have more than 7000 products and guarantee the lowest price. Some products are available for electronic delivery. You can search by product, supplier or operating system, or browse the whole database.

KEYWORDS   Computer Software, Computers, Shopping Malls
AUDIENCE   Computer Users, Internet Users, Macintosh Users, UNIX Users

Commerce

CONTACT webmaster@software.net
FREE

http://software.net/index.htm/
 SK:DDJelhologhjljok

 Surroundings

Surroundings is an online source for western living, a virtual design center. There is a button bar at the bottom of the home page to access a catalog and a room which allows the browser to preview their furniture individually or as completed rooms. There is a catalog of log furniture and two unique services—the one of a kind search and preview service which uses customer profiles to find specific pieces and presents them with pictures prior to purchase, and a virtual design service that uses actual photos or digital images of customers' surroundings to illustrate how their pieces will look with their existing furniture and fixtures. The Surroundings furniture gallery is located in Boulder, Colorado.

KEYWORDS Furniture, Home, Online Catalogs
AUDIENCE Furniture Buyers, Interior Designers
CONTACT wmartens@rmii.com
FREE

http://www.flowerstop.com/~wmartens

 U/Shop Home Page

This home page from the U/Seattle - Seattle's Online Entertainment and Resource Guide - features a small online shop with flowers and videos that you can order electronically. The parent page provides a great amount of information about movies, performances, exhibitions, and nightclubs in Seattle.

KEYWORDS Entertainment, Shopping Malls, Videos
AUDIENCE Shoppers, Tourists, Washington Residents
CONTACT webmaster@uspan.com
FREE

http://useattle.uspan.com/u-shop.html

 **Village Potpourri
Mall's Home Page**

This home page offers merchants and buyers a secure method for carrying out business transactions in an electronic medium. The Village Potpourri Mall serves as a contact point between merchants and buyers on the Internet, providing a site for advertisers's and producers' home pages. Credit card purchases can be made directly—all transactions are secure. Goods and services offered include JCS Computers, pet supplies, pictures of some of the most exotic and beautiful women in Hollywood, and a small coffee company. In the advertising section you can find a lot of travel agencies, investment, consulting, and educational companies.

KEYWORDS Advertising, Computers, Shopping Malls
AUDIENCE Advertisers, Business Professionals, Consumers, Shoppers
CONTACT sales@vpm.com
FREE

http://www.vpm.com/

 Web Street Mall

The Web Street Mall offers several catalogs—fine jewelry, some computer software on CDs, the services

Connections to Worldwide Yellow Pages
If you want bagels from New York . . .

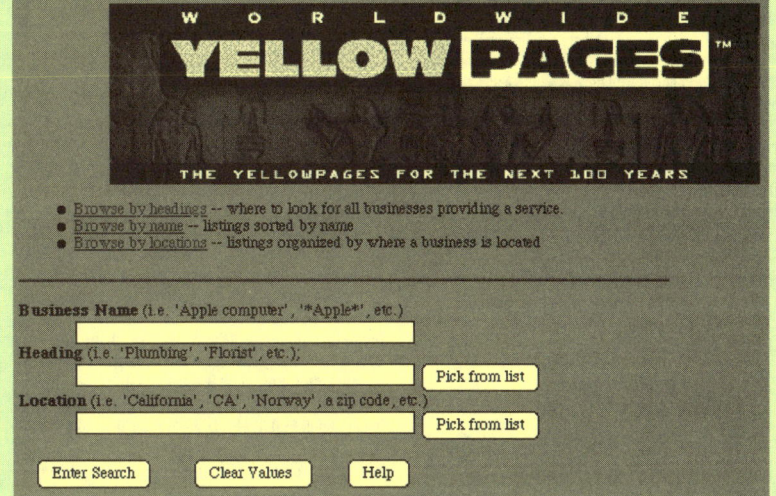

. . . or wish to take belly dancing lessons in Paris, you can let your fingers do the walking through the Yellow Pages directory on the Internet.

At the "Worldwide Yellow Pages" site, you can conduct a quick, online search for a business telephone number and full business address. If you're not quite sure of either, try a search by product category. And if you own a business, submit your business name, address and telephone number, along with product/service information for free inclusion in the directory. Or suppose your favorite neighborhood art supply shop is not yet listed in the Internet Yellow Pages directory; you can submit that store's information for inclusion.

(http://www.yellow.com/)

of Internet specialists, an Internet phone directory on CD, and more. There are also online art works for viewing, but not for sale.

KEYWORDS Advertising, Arts, Computer Software
AUDIENCE Advertisers, Computer Users, Shoppers
CONTACT Marty McCann
  marty@mccann.microserve.com
FREE

http://www.microserve.net:80/~marty/

**Welcome to Computer
Shopper**

This page is the free online edition of Computer Shopper, a Ziff-Davis publication. This page includes the monthly top stories about PC hardware, PC software, PC vendors, new product releases, and PC-related events. It features Pundits & Wizards with product reviews, Benchmarks, which includes a test script for benchmarking systems in Word for Windows format that can be downloaded, and the BBS/User Groups Directory. Computer Shopper will add your BBS or user group to this list for free. 'Shopper Alerts!' includes special deals, links to other sites, and free software demos.

KEYWORDS Computer Products, Online Magazines, Publishing
AUDIENCE Computer Professionals, Computer Users, PC Users, Windows Users

CONTACT webeditor@shopper.ziff.com
FREE

http://www.ziff.com/~cshopper/

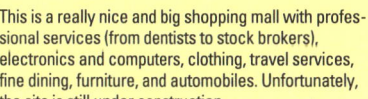 **Welcome to the
Towne Center** ★★★★

This is a really nice and big shopping mall with professional services (from dentists to stock brokers), electronics and computers, clothing, travel services, fine dining, furniture, and automobiles. Unfortunately, the site is still under construction.

KEYWORDS Clothing, Computers, Shopping Malls, Tourism
AUDIENCE Californians, Computer Users, Shoppers, Tourists
CONTACT dberry@packet.net
FREE

http://www.cris.com/~bumm/
 towncntr.html

Commerce – Consumer Issues

Wholesale Coffee/Equipment Resources ★★

According to the producer of this site, this is an informational database which lists wholesale coffee and coffee product vendors. 'This is NOT a coffee product ordering service!' There is a long list of links of vendors including Arbuckle Coffee, Baltimore Coffee & Tea Company, Caffe' d'Arte, Chock Full O' Nuts, Celestial Seasonings Tea , Espresso Resource Guide, Gevalia Kaffe Import Services, Mobile Cart Trendz, Starbucks Coffee, and many more. When you click on the name of the vendor, a brief description of the service or product, and the contact and ordering information (if available) appears.

KEYWORDS Business, Consumer Goods
AUDIENCE Coffee Lovers, Coffee Manufacturers, Coffee Vendors, Restauranteurs
CONTACT Tim Nemec
tim@ins.infonet.net
FREE

http://www.infonet.net/showcase/coffee/wholesl.html

Consumer Issues

See also
Business & Economics · *Non Profits*
Government & Politics · *States*
Law & Criminal Justice · *Business Law*
Law & Criminal Justice · *Ethics*

The Better Business Bureau Home Page ★★★★

This is the home page of the Better Business Bureau (BBB). Links are provided to information on the Council of Better Business Bureaus, Advertising Self-Regulation, Alternative Dispute Resolution, Charity Monitoring and Donor Education, Consumer and Business Education, Reliability Reports on Businesses, Marketplace Complaints and Inquiries, and Scam Alerts and Advisories.

KEYWORDS Agencies, Better Business Bureau (BBB), Business, Consumer Rights
AUDIENCE Business Professionals, Consumers, General Public
CONTACT cbbb@cbbb.org
FREE

http://www.igc.apc.org:80/cbbb/

Commonwealth of Massachusetts Office of Consumer Affairs ★★★

This page is a service of the Commonwealth of Massachusetts Office of Consumer Affairs. Anyone with a complaint against a Massachusetts company can file an online consumer complaint form. There is an Ask for Information service—if you have a question concerning Massachusetts consumer rights, fill out the online form for an answer. In addition, there are various free consumer publications that can be read online, or even ordered using the online forms. Some titles include 'twelve credit card secrets banks don't want you to know' and 'how to get a copy of your credit report.'

KEYWORDS Consumer Affairs, Consumer Protection, Consumer Rights, Massachusetts
AUDIENCE Consumers, Massachusetts Residents, Rip Off Victims
CONTACT The Internet Access Company
support@tiac.net
FREE

http://www.consumer.com/consumer/

Consumer Information Catalog ★★★★

Consumer Information Catalog provides an extensive list of articles and handbooks on consumer credit, financial planning, investment, and banking services. There is information on direct deposit, how to join a federal credit union, making sense of several savings options, choosing and using credit cards, a handbook on consumer protection laws, and much more. There are even hotlinks to such things as the IRS Guide (for tax planning and general information) and an Introduction to Mutual Funds.

KEYWORDS Banking, Consumer Information, Credit
AUDIENCE Consumers, Investors, Taxpayers
CONTACT catalog.pueblo@gsa.gov
FREE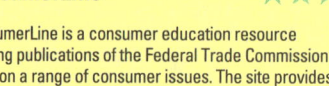

http://www.gsa.gov/cgi-bin/imagemap/cicmap?373,188

ConsumerLine ★★★

ConsumerLine is a consumer education resource offering publications of the Federal Trade Commission (FTC) on a range of consumer issues. The site provides the text of brochures, and often instructions on how to complain or seek more information, in topics such as Automobiles, Consumer Credit, Health and Fitness, Investments, Products, Telemarketing, and Business Publications. There is also a set of answers to a range of common questions about consumer rights.

KEYWORDS Consumer Education, Fair Business Practices, Federal Trade Commission (FTC), Trade Regulation
AUDIENCE Business Professionals, Consumers, Trade Regulators, United States Residents
FREE

gopher://consumer.ftc.gov:2416/11/ConsumerLine

Consumers' Association of Canada ★★

This is the home page of the Consumers' Association of Canada (CAC). Some of the topics cover consumer data, consumer interests, consumer rights, legislation, news, and information on the CAC.

KEYWORDS Canada, Consumer Rights, Legislation, Travel
AUDIENCE Canadians, Consumers, Lawyers
CONTACT John Howard Oxley
aa156@cfn.cs.dal.ca
FREE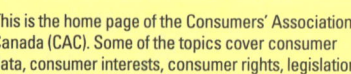

http://www.cfn.cs.dal.ca/Commerce/CAC/cacscript.html

European Guide to the Consumer Market ★★★

This page is a guide to consumer affairs legislation related to the single market and in the European Union. Links include cross-border shopping, canvassing, distance selling, advertising, pharmaceutical products, automobiles, travel and tourism, and legislation of the European Union.

KEYWORDS European Union, Product Information
AUDIENCE Consumers, Europeans, Shoppers, Tourists
FREE

http://www.cec.lu/en/comm/spc/cg/index.htm

Home Improvement Net Tips ★★★

Net Tips gives you up-to-date links to practical information about products and services to help you maintain and upgrade the value of your home. It also offers 'how to' brochures and more detailed information which you can order directly from your computer. Topics include security tips, deadbolts, doorlocks, crime statistics, painting, wallpaper, tiles, wood paneling, and more.

KEYWORDS Home, Home Improvement, Home Ownership, Real Estate
AUDIENCE Carpenters, Home Owners, Home Sellers, Real Estate Brokers
FREE

http://www.webscope.com/nettips/homepage.html

The Home Recording Rights Coalition (HRRC) ★★

The Home Recording Rights Coalition focuses on the public's right to purchase and use home audio and video recording products for noncommercial purposes. Links are provided to significant events in recording rights, digital audio recording rights and legislation, FCC cable compatibility proceedings, HRRC newsletter, archives, and more.

KEYWORDS Video
AUDIENCE Consumers, Retailers
CONTACT hrrc@access.digex.net
FREE

http://www.digex.net/hrrc/hrrc.html

National Consumers Week ★★

This site archives the information released for National Consumers' Week during October 23-29, 1994. Included here is the Consumers' Bill of Rights, contact information for local consumer protection offices nationwide, additional organizations providing consumer information and resources, and a listing of State Agencies on Aging. There are also links to the U.S. Office of Consumer Affairs and Polly Baca, its director.

KEYWORDS Consumer Protection, Consumer Rights, Government Agencies
AUDIENCE Consumers, Merchants, Seniors

Consumer Issues – Economics

CONTACT Issue Dynamics
info@idi.net

FREE

http://apt.org/consumer.html

Shopping Abroad ★★★

The Shopping Abroad site is a chapter of a guide to make you more aware as a consumer and to set out the facts on the European legal perspective on consumer protection. This guide is an introduction to consumer affairs legislation in the European Union. Its purpose is to help consumers understand the complexities of the underlying law. This chapter answers questions and gives information to enable consumers to benefit from the single market.

KEYWORDS Consumer Rights, European Community, European Union, Shopping
AUDIENCE Consumer Affairs Advocates, European Shoppers, Tourists
CONTACT Mrs. Christiane Scrivener
FREE

http://www.cec.lu/en/comm/spc/cg/c1.htm

Taxpayer Assets Project Information Policy Note ★★★

This site is designed by the Taxpayer Assets Project (founded by Ralph Nader) to urge consumers to write to FCC Chairman Reed Hundt and FCC Commissioner James Quello to urge the FCC to lower cable rates. The site provides the user with Hundt's and Quello's telephone number and email address. It also furnishes the user with further information about TAP (Taxpayers Assets Project) and how to access information related to Federal Information Policy.

KEYWORDS Cable Industry, Consumer Watchdog Groups, FCC (Federal Communications Commission), Television
AUDIENCE Communications Specialists, Consumers, Mass Communications Students
CONTACT tap@essential.org
FREE

gopher://gopher.cpsr.org:70/00/taxpayer_assets/Action_Needed_on_Cable

Utility Consumers Action Network (UCAN) ★★

UCAN is a non profit consumer watchdog group formed in 1983 to protect San Diego residential and small business consumers from San Diego Gas & Electric Company's escalating rates. This page provides links to membership information, The Watchdog - UCAN's newsletter for consumers and advocates, San Diego Telecommunications Policy Roundtable (TPR), a UCAN member list, current activities, and history of the group.

KEYWORDS California, Insurance Industry, Utility Companies
AUDIENCE Californians, Consumer Groups, Consumers, Lawyers
CONTACT mshames@powergrid.electriciti.com
FREE

http://www.cts.com/~jgraves/ucan.htm

Connections to Personal Finance
"There's too much month left at the end of my money."

If you've given up hope on winning the lottery as an avenue to financial security—or even if you have won the lottery—the Internet plays host to a vast array of information that can show you how to make your money work for you.

The choices you make about money will have a huge impact on your tomorrow. You can access a service for information and investing advice specifically with regard to mutual funds. It represents probably the largest single resource about such funds. "The Book of Mutual Funds" site allows users to compare facts about individual fund objectives, recent performance, and minimum purchase requirements.

(http://www.iii.net/biz/catalogs/welcome.html)

If you want to check out several options for investment, want to plan for your retirement, or need a loan for your children's education, the Internet's "FinanCenter" is the place to visit. This site provides interactive calculations for evaluating your borrowing and investing options. You can then change your inputs and test various scenarios in order to discover how to minimize your costs or maximize your returns.

(http://plaza.xor.com/resources/index.html)

You can even obtain the latest financial news through various sources on the Internet, including the New York Times, Wall Street Journal, Reuters, and even The Irish Times. If you want to find out what is being done to raise the value of the pound on the world markets, for example, check out the "Finance" section of The Irish Times.

(http://www.ie.unet.ie/cgi-bin/ITindex?/1995/07/07/Finance)

Economics

See also
Business & Economics · *Banking*
Business & Economics · *Finance*
Business & Economics · *Investment*

Berkeley Roundtable on International Economics Web Page ★★★

Administered by the Berkeley Roundtable on the International Economy (BRIE), this web site acts as an index to the academic papers that BRIE publishes. A number of papers are browsable online, while others only have brief abstracts available. The gopher server provides information from the Berkeley Roundtable on the International Economy (BRIE). The server provides resources such as BRIE staff directories, research activities, newsletters, and publications.

KEYWORDS Economic Policy, International Finance
AUDIENCE Business Professionals, Economists, Policymakers, Political Analysts
CONTACT BRIE
brie@garnet.berkeley.edu
FREE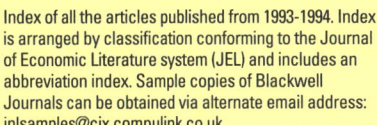

http://server.berkeley.edu/BRIE/wplist.html

gopher://brie.berkeley.edu:2234/

Blackwell Economics Articles Index ★★★★

Index of all the articles published from 1993-1994. Index is arranged by classification conforming to the Journal of Economic Literature system (JEL) and includes an abbreviation index. Sample copies of Blackwell Journals can be obtained via alternate email address: jnlsamples@cix.compulink.co.uk

KEYWORDS Economic Development, Economic Theory, Financial Research
AUDIENCE Economics Researchers, Economics Students
CONTACT Mike Emslie CTI Centre for Economics
cticce@bristol.ac.uk
FREE

http://savage.ecn.bris.ac.uk/cticce/blackeai.htm

The Concord Coalition ★★★

This is a home page from The Concord Coalition—a nonpartisan, grassroots movement to eliminate the deficit and bring entitlements down to a level that's fair to all generations. There There is a guided tour through the page, a list of local offices and contacts in different states.

KEYWORDS Activism, Budget Deficit, Economic Policy, Non Profit Organizations
AUDIENCE Activists, General Public, Nonprofit Organizations, Philanthropists

Economics – Finance

CONTACT concord@sunsite.unc.edu
FREE

http://sunsite.unc.edu/concord/

Department of Economics Gopher Server ★★★★

This site offers access to the University of Texas Economics Department gopher server with information on the departmental news, conferences, data, and faculty and grad students. The site has a keyword search and links to other gophers.

KEYWORDS Economic Development, Economics, Educational Resources
AUDIENCE Academics, Economists, Educators (University), Students (University)
CONTACT John J. Posavatz
posavatz@eco.utexas.edu
FREE

gopher://mundo.eco.utexas.edu/

Economic Information ★★★

This gopher site, maintained by the Red Universitaria Nacional in Chile, offers you general and economic coverage of Chile. Economic information is limited to the general description of the Santiago Stock Exchange and figures on the Chilean economy in 1993-94.

KEYWORDS Chile
AUDIENCE Chileans, Economists, Investors, Latin Americans, Students (University)
CONTACT info@reuna.cl
FREE

gopher://huelen.reuna.cl:70/11/economia/bolsa

Free Trade Treaties ★★★★

An index of treaties related to various aspects of free trade, this page contains links to the text of the recent Maastricht treaty, 1994's WTO/GATT, and the North American Free Trade Agreement (NAFTA).

KEYWORDS Economic Policy, Political Science, Trade, Treaties
AUDIENCE Policy Analysts, Political Scientists, Politicians, Trade Specialists
CONTACT ananse@irv.uit.no
FREE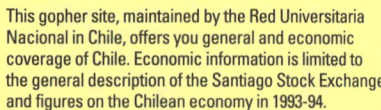

http://ananse.irv.uit.no/trade_law/nav/freetrade.html

Great Lakes Information Network - Economics ★★★

This page provides information and links with regard to business, industry, and commerce in the Great Lakes region. The gopher site includes articles, information, and links such as the Federal Reserve Bank of Chicago, The Great Lakes Circle Tour, pollution prevention and US/Canadian free trade agreeements.

KEYWORDS Business, Great Lakes, Investment, Michigan
AUDIENCE Business Professionals, Illinois Residents, Michigan Residents

FREE

gopher://gopher.great-lakes.net:2200/11/Economics

Industrial Outlook ★★★

Industrial Outlook has been published by the Commerce Department's international trade unit since 1959. The 1994 edition has had more than 130 industry analysts from the Commerce Department and other Federal agencies contribute. It contains the government's forecast for the 1994 US economy. It is very detailed, as there are 40 chapters that focus on particular industries.

KEYWORDS Industry, International Trade, Statistics
AUDIENCE Business Analysts, Investors
CONTACT Jan Zauha
janz@umich.edu
FREE

gopher://una.hh.lib.umich.edu/11/ebb/industry/outlook

International Trade Law Project ★★★★

This page provide links to many sites related to international trade law. Some of the areas covered include WTO/ GATT 1994, United Nations (trade-related organizations), ICC addresses, a comprehensive list of international trade conventions and other relevant trade instruments (including sale of goods and services, procurement of goods, construction and services, carriage of goods, insurance, payment mechanisms, treaties related to greater freedom of trade and/or economic union.

KEYWORDS Economic Policy, International Trade, Law, Treaties
AUDIENCE International Business Professionals, International Lawyers, Trade Specialists
CONTACT ananse@irv.uit.no
FREE

http://ananse.irv.uit.no/trade_law/nav/trade.html

Nber Gopher ★★

The NberGopher provides information on economics from the Publications Department at Harvard University. The information offered includes economics working paper archives and an assoiciated index, as well as files on an FTP site. It has links to economics-oriented gophers.

KEYWORDS Computer Networking, Education (College/University), Publishing
AUDIENCE Academics, Economic Development Experts, Economics Students (University), Economists
CONTACT Daniel Feenberg
feenberg@nber.harvard.edu
FREE

gopher://nber.harvard.edu/

Nebraska Department of Economic Development Gopher ★★★

This gopher describes the Economic Development Department of the University of Nebraska at Lincoln. It contains information on Nebraska's economic development such as contacts, news, press releases, business assistance, technology transfer, and more. It also has links to other gophers.

KEYWORDS Community Networking, Economic Development, Economics, Education (College/University)
AUDIENCE Business Professionals, Economic Development Experts, Economists
CONTACT Steve Williams
stevew@ded1.ded.state.ne.us
FREE

gopher://unlvm.unl.edu:71/

Finance

See also
Business & Economics · *Investment*

Centre for Management of Technology and Entrepreneurship ★★★

The Centre is involved with research into the effective use of computers and communications systems in core businesses involved in the financial services industry. It is multidisciplinary in nature and collaborates with other units at the University of Toronto and with comparable institutions abroad.

KEYWORDS Communications Systems, Computers, Financial Services, Performance Analysis
AUDIENCE Bankers, Financiers, IT Specialists
CONTACT Joseph C. Paradi, Ph.D
paradi@ie.utoronto.ca
FREE

http://www.ie.utoronto.ca/CMTE/cmteintr.html

Debt Counselors of America, Inc. ★★★

Debt Counselors of America, Inc. assists individuals and families with debt and financial difficulties by presenting appropriate resources. This page contains information on debt consolidation, answers to questions about how to deal with collection companies, how to obtain one's credit report, and more. There is no charge for most services, although some specialized services may have minimal fees.

KEYWORDS Consumer Credit, Debt Consolidation, Personal Finance
AUDIENCE Consumers, Debtors, Families, Students (College/Graduate)
CONTACT us003010@interramp.com
FREE

http://www.ip.net:80/shops/GET_OUT_OF_DEBT/

Finance – Home Office

Electronic Credit Repair Kit ★★★★

This document provides background information as well as step by step instructions on how to get incorrect and damaging information off your credit report. The table of contents includes topics such as What is Credit Repair, Inaccurate Credit Reports, Fair Credit Reporting Act, Improving Your Credit Report, Free Credit Reports, Requesting Corrections, and more.

- KEYWORDS Consumer Rights, Credit Bureaus, Credit Reports, Personal Finance
- AUDIENCE Bankers, Credit Enthusiasts, Debtors, General Public
- CONTACT Michael Kielsky
  kielsky@primenet.com
- FREE

http://www.primenet.com/~kielsky/credit.html

FinanceNet WWW Server ★★★

FinanceNet is a network of finance, economic and banking professionals working together with the National Performance Review to design and construct a new National (electronic) Infrastructure—the 'Information Superhighway' that is Vice President Gore's pet project. Located here are comprehensive indices of business-related listservs and other business and economic-related resources. Also provided are schedules of sales and auctions of Federal Government assets and directories of FinanceNet membership.

- KEYWORDS Business, Federal Government (US), Finance
- AUDIENCE Bankers, Business Professionals, Economic Development Experts, Economists
- CONTACT Linda Hoogeveen, Office of Management and Budget
  lhoog@tmn.com
- FREE

http://www.financenet.gov/

Financial Services Technology Consortium ★★★

The Financial Services Technology Consortium (FSTC) is a consortium of financialservices providers, national laboratories, universities, and government agencies which sponsor and participate in collaborative research and development on inter bank technical projects affecting the financial services industry. Their web site provides background information on this non-profit organization as well as a listing of their current projects on issues such as Electronic Commerce and Fraud Prevention and Control. Users can also access a listing of FSTC members.

- KEYWORDS Associations, Electronic Commerce
- AUDIENCE Banks, Electronics Companies, Financial Institutions, Government Agencies, Technical Laboratories, Universities
- FREE

http://www.llnl.gov/fstc/

Financing of Litigation by Sale of Lawsuit Shares ★★

This page describes how to finance lawsuits and virtual law firms through the sale of lawsuit shares. Information is available on Lawsuit Offering Circulars, securities and blue sky laws, bulletin boards for clients and lawyers seeking to discuss possible financing assistance, how to invest in lawsuit stocks, and more.

- KEYWORDS Law Firms, Litigation
- AUDIENCE General Public, Investors, Judges, Lawyers, Legal Professionals, Litigants, Stockbrokers
- CONTACT Carl E. Person
  carlpers@lawmall.com
- FREE

http://www.ocsny.com:80/lawmall/lm_finan.html

ING Bank ★★★★

This is a home page from the Dutch ING Bank International, which is heavily involved in international banking, especially emerging markets. One can find facts and figures about the bank, browse a directory of the bank's locations around the world, read press releases and short information about business partners, perus e research reports on economic and financial subjects, and find out information about international recruitment.

- KEYWORDS Emerging Markets, Financial Research, International Finance, Investment
- AUDIENCE Financial Analysts, Investors, Market Analysts
- FREE

http://www.ing-group.nl/

ITT Hartford Insurance Group ★★★

ITT Hartford Insurance Group is one of the oldest and largest insurance and financial service organizations in the United States. Site topics include the company history, company financial strength, products and services, and news and issues. You can also try the Estate Tax Calculator to learn about the value of a proper estate plan.

- KEYWORDS Companies, Estate Tax, Financial Services, Insurance
- AUDIENCE Business Professionals, Financial Planners, General Public, Investors
- FREE

http://www.itthartford.com/

Individual Investor ★★★

Individual Investor is a monthly personal finance magazine, that offers commentary and opinion on specific investments in stocks and mutual funds. The magazine's primary focus is to provide direct, actionable investment ideas to a lay audience. It is a personal finance magazine that shuns 'soft' features. Instead, it embraces a clear mission: to find and identify profitable investment opportunities. A few of the stories are available to read at the gopher site but to get the full content of stories and features of the magazine one must subscribe. Individual copies are available.

- KEYWORDS Investment, Magazines, Personal Finance
- AUDIENCE Investors
- CONTACT investor@enews.com
- COST

gopher://gopher.enews.com/11/business/pubs/finance/ii

Money: Personal Finance Center ★★★★

Here is Time-Warner's online cousin of Money Magazine, offering feature articles from the print version of the magazine. There are hot links to company reports, loan rates, bulletin boards, and the Fidelity Investments Information Center. 'Marketplace' provides hot links to information on various products, such as cars and computers, and services such as health, finance, and telecommunications. To access the information one must register with Pathfinder, the interactive online service operated by Time Inc. New Media.

- KEYWORDS E-Zines, Investment, Personal Finance
- AUDIENCE Investors
- CONTACT Kevin McKean
  kmckean@pipeline.com
- COST

http://www.pathfinder.com/@@ITwOI5DfZAIAQAEf/money/moneyhome.html

Home Office

See also
Business & Economics · *Non Profits*
Business & Economics · *Retail*
Business & Economics · *Services*
Computing & Mathematics · *Software*
Law & Criminal Justice · *Tax Law*

Application Development Center ★★★

This is a home page from The Application Development Center - a nonprofit organization and resource center providing entrepreneurial networks and support services for software developers located in the Delaware Valley of Pennsylvania. The ADC, a program of the University City Science Center, sponsors monthly executive forums, seminars and workshops and provides services that are focused on the marketing, financing and other business and technical issues of particular interests to the software industry.

- KEYWORDS Business Services, Computer Software, Entrepreneurship, Non Profit Organizations
- AUDIENCE Business Professionals, Computer Programmers, Entrepreneurs, Nonprofit Organizations
- FREE

http://libertynet.org/business/econ-dev/ucsc/adc.html

Big Dreams ★★

The focus of this newsletter is personal development and topics related to starting a small business. The viewer will find information about personal fulfillment and motivation, developing business skills, and ways to combine one's private and corporate lives. Related resources and references such as entrepreneur's

Business & Economics

forums, Usenet newsgroups, and other business home pages can also be found at this site.

Keywords Entrepreneurship, Small Business
Audience Business Professionals, Business Students, Entrepreneurs
Contact Wimsey Information Services
webmaster@wimsey.com
Free

http://www.wimsey.com:80/~duncans/

Entrepreneurs on the Web ★★★

At this site entrepreneurs the world over can find useful business information and offer their goods and services to other entrepreneurs. Entrepreneurs on the Web has two major departments - Goods and Services and Business Information Resources. Goods and Services is where one can list one's service or product. Business Information Resources offers information on doing business on the net, and provides pointers to areas of interest to business users. You can read Brookfield Economics Institute Newsletter for small business owners, or list your firm in a National Directory of Consultants and Consulting Firms and a National Directory of Telecommunications and Related Services - no fee, and go to IDEAbase, which provides online support for new businesses.

Keywords Entrepreneurship, Small Business
Audience Business Professionals, Entrepreneurs, Internet Users
Contact notime@wwa.com
Free

http://sashimi.wwa.com/~notime/eotw/EOTW.html

Entrepreneurs' Exchange Index ★★★

This home page is the Internet version of PRODIGY's Entrepreneurs' Exchange. The Entrepreneurs' Exchange features articles on any subject related to starting or operating a small business — marketing, production, taxes, accounting, and more. The key is that it must be based on the author's experience, and be of interest to other small business people.

Keywords Entrepreneurship, Small Business
Audience Business Entrepreneurs, Business Professionals
Free

http://www.astranet.com/eexchange/jc00indx.htm

Greater Philadelphia Chamber of Commerce ★★★

This is a home page from the nonprofit Greater Philadelphia Chamber of Commerce - a business' most powerful source of information, resources, and assistance whether you're just starting a small business, seeking to grow an existing business, or considering opening a branch of your business in the Philadelphia area. Some services are only for the members.

Keywords Commerce, Entrepreneurship, Non Profit Organizations, Regulations
Audience Business Professionals, Entrepreneurs, Nonprofit Organizations, Pennsylvania Residents
Free

http://libertynet.org/business/econ-dev/chamber/chamber.html

Home Based Wealth ★★

Home Based Wealth provides Home Based Business advice and opportunities from self-made millionaire John Stefanchik. In the past 10 years, John has taught thousands of people how to work from their homes and follow his three entity approach to wealth.

Keywords Business Consulting, Investment, Personal Wealth, Small Business
Audience Consultants, Entrepreneurs, Small Business Owners
Contact Warren Woodford
warren@we.com
Free

http://www.we.com/hbw

Home Business Solution ★★

This site for the Home Business Solutions provides a number of practical tips and information through resources produced by HBC for the home office owner. The various sections promise to help owners with business start-up solutions, advertising and marketing ideas, financial solutions, business to business services, shareware and more. In particular, the HBC site offers information about how their product line of books, manuals, and tapes will help the everyday entrepreneur deal with issues such as 'How to get a business loan' or 'Cheap business cards'.

Keywords Accounting, Consulting Services, Finance, Small Business
Audience Business Professionals, Entrepreneurs
Contact solution@netmar.com
Free

http://netmar.com:80/mall/shops/solution/

Khera Communications' Business Resource Center ★★★

This site is prodcued by Khera Communications, a business consulting firm, and offers a series of guides for small businesses and startup companies. The 'Getting Started' menu offers advice about defining your business and customers, as well as attracting publicity for your company. The 'Marketing Department' provides tips on getting leads and keeping clients. There are more than 20 articles to browse though, along with links to resources in the Washington D.C. area.

Keywords Business Planning, Business Services, Consulting Services, Marketing, Small Business
Audience Business Students, Entrepreneurs, Marketing Professionals, Small Business Owners
Contact Khera Communications, Inc.
www@kciLink.com
Free

http://www.kciLink.com/brc/

Start Up ★★★

This is the home page for the non-profit organization Start Up. Its mission is to promote economic development in and around East Palo Alto by providing business training, capital and other assistance. They offer a Business Feasibility Class, Business Planning Class, Micro-Loan Program, Mentorship, Technical Assistance, Counseling, and Networking Support.

Keywords Business Services, California, Development
Audience Californians, Entrepreneurs
Free

http://infobase.internex.net:80/impact/120home.html

United States Small Business Administration ★★★

Through workshops, individual counseling, publications, and videotapes, the United States Small Business Administration (SBA) helps entrepreneurs understand and meet the challenges of operating businesses— challenges like financing, marketing and management. This site lists the contact information for over 100 SBA offices in the US, listed by region and state. Additional resources such as listings of small business investment companies, calendars of events, and even disaster area offices are listed for each state as well. Other directories include a listing of financial resources for small businesses and a page for programs to expand your business.

Keywords Entrepreneurship, Finance, Government Agencies (US), Small Business Administration
Audience Business Owners, Entrepreneurs, Investors, Managers
Contact Mark Rorabaugh
mark@www.sbaonline.sba.gov
Free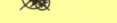

http://www.sbaonline.sba.gov/

gopher://www.sbaonline.sba.gov/

ftp://www.sbaonline.sba.gov/

Industries

See also
Communications · *Communications*
Computing & Mathematics · *Companies*
Engineering & Technology · *Technology*
Health & Medicine · *Medicine*
Popular Culture & Entertainment · *Automobiles*

3M Innovation Network ★★★

3M (Minnesota Mining and Manufacturing Corp.) Innovation Network provides a lot of information for the variety of products the company offers, including Scotch Cellophane Tape, magnetic tapes, recording tapes, and other office equipment. The history of the company and its expansion to worldwide markets is also outlined. There is environmental information

Industries 121

published by the company, and a historical outline of product inventions and introductions by 3M, including Wool Soap Pads, Post-It notepads, and adhesive diaper fastners.

KEYWORDS Copiers, Office Equipment, Office Products
AUDIENCE Consumers, Employees, Investors
CONTACT innovation@mmm.com
FREE

http://www.3m.com/

AT&T ★★★

This AT&T site contains product and service information for its business and consumer users. For users shopping for phone, fax or telecommuting systems, this site offers a variety services and products. Here you can also take a peek at AT&T's vision of the future and find innovative new ideas from Bell Laboratories. In addition, the Global Information Solutions page provides information pertaining to the newest forms of telecommunications, multimedia and network technology. This site also has links to related sites, a story book feature, and a history of AT&T innovations through the past years.

KEYWORDS AT&T, Communications, Companies, Telecommunications
AUDIENCE Business Professionals, General Public, Universities
CONTACT webmaster@att.com
FREE

http://www.att.com

AeroAstro ★★

This site developed by AeroAstro Corporation provides users with company and product information on this developer of space systems. The site outlines various space study products that the company has designed for research institutions and government facilities including NASA and the Massachusetts Institute of Technology. Further information on AeroAstro's personnel and Virginia-based headquarters is also included.

KEYWORDS High Technology, Space Flight, Space Science, Spacecraft Industry
AUDIENCE Engineers, Space Flight Centers, Space Science Centers
CONTACT Peter Goldberg
         peter@aeroastro.com
FREE

http://www.isso.org/Industry/AeroAstro/AeroAstro.html

Allstate Motor Club ★

Visitors to the Allstate Motor Club web site can access information on Emergency Automotive Services including emergency road and tow service, lock out benefits, and theft/hit and run rewards. Information is also available on their custom trip planning services, as well as on car rental and lodging membership discounts.

KEYWORDS Automobile Emergencies, Automobile Insurance, Automobiles, Insurance
AUDIENCE Automobile Owners, Road Trip Planners

Connections to Home Office Resources
From corporate life to self-employment

For many people, setting up a business in the home is the dream of a lifetime. How can you market your talents and find financial success and independence? The best place to get the information you need before you set up a home office is the Internet.

Vast resources—from information on office equipment to legal and financial advice—await the home-based entrepreneur who turns to the World Wide Web to get going.

To find the best deals on office equipment—from fax machines to copiers—turn to the Internet shopping channels that cater to small businesses and home offices. One good place to start is the "Small Business Resource Center" Home Page that give you access to 'Good Stuff Cheap" pages, which specialize in manufacturers' over-supply, close-outs, and must-have items for the small office.

(http:www.webcom.com/~seaquest/)

Advertising your business is the way to get new clients, but if your budget just won't allow it, then you can turn to the Internet to get the word out. The "Home Based Business Yellow Pages" is a way to list your home business for free and jump-start new business ideas in the U.S. and Canada.

(http://www.tab.com/Home.Business/YellowPages/)

Through "Home Business Report," you can read success stories, as well as stories about those who snatched financial victory from the jaws of defeat. You can also turn to 'Business, Economics, and Law Resources" on the Net for help not only in advertising your business, but also for legal advice, set-up forms from the Internal Revenue Service for a home-based business, and assorted financial advice for the small entrepreneur.

(http://www.tab.com/Home.Business/)

also, (http://www.cs.fsu.edu/projects/group5/business.html)

FREE
http://www.shopping2000.com/shopping2000/allstate/

Amsoil - Home Page ★★

The Amsoil home page provides information on the history and use of the first synthetic motor oil to be developed in the US for automobiles. Users may peruse short summaries on the production of the oil as well as its environmental impact. Information is also available for a few other Amsoil products. Users can access ordering information via email.

KEYWORDS Automobiles, Motor Oils
AUDIENCE Automobile Owners, Car Dealers, Mechanics
CONTACT Bob Cameron
         nmau21a@prodigy.com
FREE

http://apollo.co.uk/a/amsoildj/

Auto-By-Tel ★★

The Auto-By-Tel Web page acts mainly as an advertisement for this service which allows customers to purchase cars at wholesale prices by telephone. Prospective car buyers are asked to fill out an online form specifying characteristics they are looking for in a new automobile in addition to contact information. Auto-By-Tel will then contact users by telephone generally within 48 hours. A brief listing of the names of car dealers working in association with this site is included. Very little background information on the service is provided.

KEYWORDS Automobiles, Services, Shopping

Industries

Audience Car Buyers, Car Dealerships
Contact autobytel@aol.com
Free

http://shopping2000.com/shopping2000/auto-by-te/index.html

Autonet ★★

Autonet is designed to provide information about car manufacturers and dealerships across the country, as well as parts and services. You can search for information by car type, cities, or keywords.
Keywords Automobile Care, Automobile Repair, Automobiles, Dealerships
Audience Automobile Owners, Automobile Sellers
Contact rfiege@smartdocs.com
Free

http://www.deltanet.com/autonet/

BM International, Domespace, Homes, Construction ★★★

Domespace sells a unique, pro-environment structure. The dome can be used in many ways, as a home, school, pavillon, or store. Standard-size or custommade, the models can be ready in a short period of time. This site presents detailed information on Domespace and its construction.
Keywords Architecture, Construction, Development, Environmental Design
Audience Architects, Developers, Environmentalists
Free

http://branch.com/dome/dome.html

Black Box OnLine Catalog ★★★★

This site offers an online catalog of products produced by Black Box Corporation. There is access to information on products, technical references, services, and information on data communication problems. There is a search tool for the site, as well as access to order forms.
Keywords Computer Products, Data Communications, Online Catalogs
Audience Communications Specialists, Computer Users, Shoppers, Telecommunications Experts
Contact info@blackbox.com
Free

http://www.blackbox.com/

CBS Incorporated ★★★

This site provides news, listings, season schedules, and program information from CBS Incorporated. Users can employ this site to get the latest information on upcoming CBS sports events, CBS News, remotes, and daily program listings. Users can join the Eye on the Net Club to receive program information. In addition, there is a complete CBS Fall Schedule with show descriptions, cast photos, a scheduling strategy, and news of sales and marketing activities.
Keywords Broadcasting, Communications, Television, Television Networks
Audience Children, General Public, News Buffs, Television Enthusiasts
Free

http://www.cbs.com

Cablevision Systems Corporation ★★★

This site contains facts, statistics and general information about Cablevision, a rapidly growing cable television company. Informative pages include the 'cable report' which provides updates concerning the company's people, programming, operation and future. Cablevision also lists its online services which include a Satellite Weather map, News and Business information, Music, Travel, Sports and Arts. In the future Cablevision hopes to support applications such as 'Interactive Educational Programming,' Home Shopping, Electronic Banking and Video on Demand.
Keywords Cable Television, Media, Telecommunications, Television, Weather
Audience Children, General Public, Television Enthusiasts
Contact webmaster@moon.cablevision.com
Free

http://moon.cablevision.com

Computer Events Directory ★★★★

The Computer Events Directory, maintained by KnowledgeWeb, Inc., is focused on collating a comprehensive list of conferences, exhibitions and trade shows, and then verifying details with individual event organizers. The Directory utilizes computers, communications, and technology events to serve regional, national, and international markets. Their coverage will expand to include more training courses, association, trade, and user group meetings. You can locate events of particular interest by name, date, place, industry, or hot events listing.
Keywords Communications, Conferences, Events, Technology
Audience Computer Users, Internet Users, LAN Administrators, Web Developers
Contact David Fox
info@kweb.com
Free

http://www.kweb.com/kweb

Cooper Lighting ★★★

This is the web site for Cooper Lighting, a manufacturer of area, decorative, and industrial lighting products. 'From deep fly balls in Yankee Stadium, to space exploration at NASA, to landings in the deep of night at Chicago's O'Hare airport, the lights are from Cooper Lighting.' Linked information is available on flood lighting, decorative outdoor lighting, area lighting, and industrial lighting.
Keywords Floodlights, Interior Design, Lighting, Manufacturers
Audience Architects, Landscapers, Manufacturers, Wholesalers
Contact Lance Strahan
strahan@southernnet.com
Free

http://www.southernnet.com/cooper/index.html

Eastern Utilities Associates Home Page ★★

This is a home page for EUA (Eastern Utilities Associates), an electric utility company serving Massachusetts and Rhode Island. Topics include shareholder information, financial community inquiries, financial highlights, core business units, contact information, a list of trustees and EUA Officers, and more.
Keywords Electricity, Utility Companies
Audience Investors, Massachusetts Residents, Rhode Island Residents
Contact Ralph Becker
ralphb@bloss.iii.net
Free

http://www.iii.net/users/ralphb/eua.html

Eastman Kodak Company ★★★

This site offers news and information from the Eastman Kodak Company. Through this site users can access information on topics including document imaging, digital photography, commercial photography, photo journalism, and other detailed technical data. For businesses with Kodak copy machines, information on servicing is available through this site. The site library allows you to download a variety of digital images and also includes a topic oriented search engine.
Keywords Cameras, Film Processing, Photography
Audience Artists, Corparations, General Public, Photographers
Contact webmaster@www.kodak.com
Free

http://www.kodak.com

Enterprise Integration Technologies ★★★

Enterprise Integration Technologies (EIT) is a research, development, and consulting company specializing in information technology for electronic commerce, collaborative engineering, and agile manufacturing. The homepage offers a company overview, employment opportunities and descriptions of current projects for clients. Also included is a personnel directory, company fact sheet and EIT-created WWW software, reports, and mailing lists. EIT are the makers of Secure HTTP.
Keywords Firewalls, Information Technology, Internet, Manufacturing
Audience Computer Programmers, Internet Developers, Web Providers
Contact info@eit.com
Free

http://www.eit.com/

Industries

Federal Information Exchange ★★

This gopher server gives information about a company called Federal Information Exchange, Inc. Federal Information Exchange provides information technology services including database management and software development. This gopher server describes those services and provides telnet access to the company's online services.

Keywords Companies, Databases, Information Technology, Software
Audience Business Professionals, Computer Professionals
Contact comments@fedix.fie.com
Free

gopher://gopher.fie.com/

The Food Resource ★★★★

The Food Resource aims to become a hub of all food-related information on the World Wide Web. Geared to professionals in the food industry as well as home cooks, this site includes information on everything from a long list of organizations, unions, marketers, chemists, the American Butter Institute, et al, to nutritional analyses of various foods, to government resources, to many links to sites which answer culinary queries. But perhaps the most noteworthy feature of The Food Resource is its commitment to bringing you images of all the foods on earth. Here you will find pictures of everything edible, including items as enigmatic as 'foams,' and as homely as 'baked products.' Be sure to check out the fruit and vegetable section, where portraits of cacao, choi, chives, chicory, chayotes and cherries reside with equanimity.

Keywords Food Production, Nutrition
Audience Chefs, Cooks, Food Industry Professionals, Nutritionists
Contact ZoeAnn Holmes, PhD
holmesz@ucs.orst.edu
Free

http://www.orst.edu/food-resource/food.html

GRC Guide to Ribbons and Cartridges ★★★

This is an online buyers guide for printer cartridges and toners. You'll find the replacement toner cartridge for virtually any dot/laser/ink jet printer. They provide a list of GRC stores, but you can't buy your cartridge online.

Keywords Computer Peripherals, Printers
Audience Business Professionals, Computer Users, Shoppers
Free

http://www.printgrc.com/grc/grcguide.html

General Electric Company ★★★

This site provides a wide range of information concerning General Electric, specifically its services and products. Some informative pages listed include a compact view of services and products provided by General Electric, a searchable index for more specific information and the newly introduced product data sheets. 'General Electric World Wide Operations' lists all the countries from which General Electric operates (with G.E. fax and telephone numbers). 'General Electric Company Highlights' describes briefly the company's beginnings and various accomplishments to date. In addition, a list of General Electric individual companies and their profiles are provided.

Keywords Appliances, Electricity, Power, Utilities
Audience General Public, Investment Counselors
Contact geinfo@wwww.ge.com
Free

http://www.ge.com

Global Recycling Network ★★★

'Global Recycling Network (GRN) is a virtual marketplace set up on the Internet to help businesses around the world in finding possible trading partners for the sale of recyclable goods.' GRN offers a markteplace for businesses to post their buy and sell requests for recyclable goods. They can receive personalized search profiles so they automatically receive new leads as they come into the marketplace. Subscription is free for an initial period by filling out the online form. After subscribing, the member can post and access leads from the database.

Keywords Recycling Resources, Trade
Audience Business Professionals, Consumers, Manufacturers
Contact queries@grn.com
Free

http://grn.com:80/grn/

Harriman Associates ★★

This is the home page for Harriman Associates, an Engineering and Architecture Firm in New England. This page covers contact and phone information for the northern New England office.

Keywords Architectural Design, Construction, Engineering
Audience Architects, Builders, Contractors, Engineers, Home Owners
Contact harriman@maine.com
Free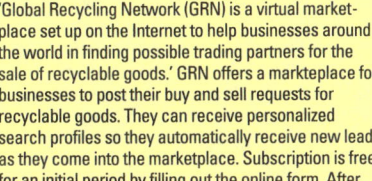

http://w3.maine.com/harriman/

The Hartford Steam Boiler Inspection & Insurance Company ★★★

The Hartford Steam Boiler Inspection & Insurance Company offers boiler and machinery, property, computer, and other types of insurance to commercial clients, as well as a wide range of sophisticated engineering services for risk avoidance and expert plant maintenance.

Keywords Insurance, Machinery, Plant Maintenance, Risk Management
Audience Business Professionals, Business Professionals, Computer Users
Contact dhodges@hsb.com
Free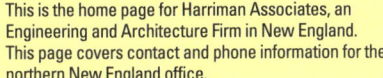

http://www.hsb.com

ISX Corporation ★★

The ISX Corporation's home page provides basic background information on this California-based Advanced Technology Management Company and producer of custom Intelligent Systems. Information on the company's three branches in Southern California, Georgia and Washington D.C. is available at the site. Users may also access more in-depth descriptions of some of ISX's current company projects including various 'Initiative Webs' although many of them require a password for clearance. A company rolodex, calendar of events, and document listing are also available at the site.

Keywords Advanced Technology Management, High Technology, Intelligent Systems
Audience Advanced Technology Management Companies, Computer Programmers, Large Businesses
Contact listserv@isx.com
Free

http://isx.com/

Lunar Resources Company ★★

Visitors to the Lunar Resources Company's home page can access background information on this unique company endeavoring to make space travel a commercial enterprise. Users can access information on some of the company's current projects including the 'Artemis Project' which plans to establish and operate a permanent manned lunar base. Two articles published on the company are included, in addition to an issue of their newsletter. Users may also subscribe to Artemis Magazine a bimonthly magazine combining both nonfiction science articles and some science fiction.

Keywords High Technology, Space Flight, Space Science, Spacecraft Industry
Audience Astrologers, Investors, Space Scientists
Contact Dana Carson
dcarson@access.digex.net
Free

http://www.access.digex.net/~dcarson/Lrc.html

Modeling Agencies ★★

This document provides a list of modeling agencies and phone numbers for a number of states including California, New York, Connecticut, Massachusetts, and more.

Keywords Fashion, Modeling Agencies
Audience Agents, Fashion Designers, Models
Contact ms@genesis.nred.ma.us
Free

http://www.charm.net/~jakec/Agencies.html

NOTIS Systems, Inc. ★★

This gopher site gives information about NOTIS Systems Inc and some of its products. NOTIS Systems specializes in developing graphical user interfaces for client/server systems. Much of this gopher hole centers on information about WinGopher, NOTIS's graphical gopher client.

KEYWORDS Computing, Information Technology, Libraries, OPACs (Online Public Access Catalogs)
AUDIENCE Computer Users, Internet Users
CONTACT wingopher@notis.com
FREE

gopher://wingopher.notis.com/

OFX Direct Online Catalog ★★

OFX Direct Online Catalog is the online arm of Office Furniture Express, Beta Site 0.8. The catalog is not complete, but is fully operational. The goal of OFX Direct is to provide affordable, workable furniture solutions for computer users such as computer desks and ergonomic seating. There are three collections: the Kendall Valley Collection of contemporary-styled casegoods, the Heritage Hill Collection—a collection of traditional-styled casegoods, and the Global Ergonomic Seating Gallery, offering a variety of affordable seating designed to make using a computer more comfortable.

KEYWORDS Furniture, Office Equipment, Online Shopping
AUDIENCE Office Furniture Buyers
CONTACT ofxsales@ofx.com
FREE

http://www.ingress.com/ofx

Olivetti Active Badge System ★★★★

This site features a description of Olivetti's Active Badge System. The Active Badge device transmits a unique infra-red signal every 10 seconds which can be detected by networked sensors within a building. The location of the badge (and hence its wearer) can thus be determined on the basis of information provided by these sensors.

KEYWORDS Companies, Product Information, Technology
AUDIENCE Business Professionals, Security Workers
CONTACT Andy Hopper ah@cam-orl.co.uk
FREE

http://www.cam-orl.co.uk/ab.html

Partners Communication Associates, Inc. ★★

This WWW site describes Partners Communication Associates, Inc., a long distance phone company/provider. By combining purchasing power with mutliple clients, PCA is able to match service quality and pricing offered to large businesses by the big phone companies. Information available on the site is somewhat limited, beyond descriptions of their basic services.

KEYWORDS Business, Telecommunications, Telephones
AUDIENCE Business Professionals, Consumers
CONTACT dan@ccsnet.com
FREE

http://ccsnet.com/kom/kom2.htm

Real/Time Communications Gopher ★★

This gopher server provides access to network services provided by Real/Time Communications. These services currently include information on how to obtain an account on their system, an online book store provided by The Reference Press Inc., and links to important gopher servers. The book store contains resources primarily of interest to business and business investors.

KEYWORDS Books, Business Communications, Companies
AUDIENCE Business Professionals, Computer Users, Investors
CONTACT sales@bga.com
FREE

gopher://gopher.bga.com/

Rhebokskloof Estate ★★★

The Rhebokskloof Estate is in South Africa and dates back to 1692. The virtual online tour starts at the wine shop and features also the winery, restaurants, history, cultivars and viticulture, news items, a price list, payment and delivery information, and the opportunity to place an order. There is also a guest registry when you are finished your tour.

KEYWORDS South Africa, Wineries, Wines
AUDIENCE Wine Enthusiasts
CONTACT mikelane@iafrica.com
FREE

http://www.os2.iaccess.za/rhebok/index.htm

Saturn Corporation ★★★

The Saturn Corporation says this site is a way for them to stay in touch with their customers. Along with information about Saturn's 1995 line of cars, users can retrieve photos of these cars, details about Saturn's features, and product specs. The Magazine section of The Saturn Site is a place for news and 'goings on' around Saturn.

KEYWORDS Automobiles, Companies, Consumer Information
AUDIENCE Automobile Enthusiasts, Consumers, General Public
CONTACT www@organic.com
FREE

http://www.saturncars.com

Schlumberger Information Server ★★

This gopher server provides limited information about an energy company called Schlumberger. It also provides access to the Schlumberger Shareholder Server, containing information primarily of interest to shareholders and investors in the company.

KEYWORDS Companies, Energy, International Business, Investment, Stock Market
AUDIENCE Investors
CONTACT Mary Jo Caliandro caliandro@new-york.sl.slb.com
FREE

gopher://gopher-public.slb.com/

Sony Drive WWW Server Home Page ★★★★

This is the home page for Electronics division of Sony, which sells video/audio equipment, televisions, and electronic devices. You can look at the company profile and structure, see financial results, peruse new Sony products, and read technical recommendations and the company's research reports. There are separate pages for Sony music and multimedia. You'll also find some links to other interesting sites, a schedule of events in Sony showrooms around the world, and you can learn the location of Sony service centers in Japan.

KEYWORDS Electronics, Japan, Manufacturing, Video
AUDIENCE Computer Professionals, Computer Users, Multimedia Enthusiasts
CONTACT webmaster@sony.co.jp
FREE

http://www.sony.co.jp/

Spacecraft Components Corporation Home Page ★★★

Spacecraft Components Corp. has developed this home page to provide consumers with information on their large inventory of electrical connectors and connector accessories to the Aerospace, Airline, Electronic and Electromechanical industries. A free connector consultation and locator service is available at the site as well as an electronic avenue for accessing price and delivery information. Users may also order the eight volume Encyclopedia of Connectors at this web site.

KEYWORDS High Technology, Space Science, Spacecraft Industry
AUDIENCE Spacecraft Distributors, Spacecraft Manufacturers
CONTACT Robert Ray space@spacecraft.com
FREE

http://www.spacecraft.com/spacecraft

Sprint/Centel ANS Home Page ★★★

This site provides information on Sprint/Centel-Florida, and its telephone operations. Information on Sprint/Centel Advanced Network Systems, residential services, business services are described. There are

Industries – International Business

links to Sprint's Corporate Web Server and Sprint/United Telephone-Florida Web Server.

KEYWORDS   Companies, Telecommunications, Telephones, Utilities
AUDIENCE   Consumers, Telecommunications Specialists
FREE

http://cntfl.com/

Sumitomo Chemical Recent Business Trends

This home page developed by Sumitomo Chemical Company, a manufacturer of synthetic resins, allows users to access a collection of short articles providing information on various mergers and other company developments during the latter half of 1994. Some of the articles contain descriptions of Sumitomo's products. The page also includes a link to Sumitomo's home page.

KEYWORDS   Business News, Chemicals, Industry Mergers, Manufacturing
AUDIENCE   Chemical Companies, Investors
FREE

http://www.sumitomo-chem.co.jp/news/newsr_e.html

Toshiba America Incorporated

This site provides information about Toshiba America, a company comprised of five diversified electronics and high technology operating companies that manufacture and market a wide range of business and information systems and products in the United States. Detailed overviews of Toshiba's five independent companies are provided in this site, along with product and services information, a business directory and a Toshiba related news page. Additional information can also be found on the Toshiba Foundation and on Toshiba International Operations.

KEYWORDS   Electronics, Information Systems, Manufacturers
AUDIENCE   General Public, International Business Professionals
FREE

http://www.tais.com

UltraBOND Windshield Repair

UltraBOND repairs automobile windshields. Their site provides information about windshield repair history and their own UltraBOND process, as well as before and after pictures.

KEYWORDS   Automobile Care, Automobile Repair
AUDIENCE   Automobile Enthusiasts, Automobile Mechanics, Automobile Owners
CONTACT   UltraBOND rcampfie@interserv.com
FREE

http://www.ibos.com/pub/ibos/ultrabon/ultra.html

X/Open

X/Open is a not-for-profit international consortium of technical specialists which is dedicated to the advancement of open systems throughout the world. Visitors to their home page can access background information on this organization, including project information, a schedule of committee meetings and events, and publications. Registration information is also available as well as details on their products.

KEYWORDS   Open Systems, Technical Organizations, Technology
AUDIENCE   Technical Associations, Technical Companies
FREE

http://www.xopen.org/

International Business

See also
Computing & Mathematics · *Applications*
Computing & Mathematics · *Companies*
Computing & Mathematics · *Networking*
Government & Politics · *Countries*

Actrade International Ltd Home Page

Actrade International Ltd. is a company which helps small and medium-sized American companies grow through its expertise in Actrade's key areas of export, international trade, investment, and domestic trade finance services. Each branch of the company has a page for its activities, complete with financial reports, graphs, and other statistics. Some specific areas which the company has experience in are Heating, Air Conditioning & Refrigeration Systems, Laundry and Pressing Systems, and Financing and Investments.

KEYWORDS   Business Development, Import-Export, International Trade
AUDIENCE   American Business, International Business Professionals, International Entrepreneurs, Start Up Companies
FREE

http://actrade.interse.com/

Alberta Research Council

The Alberta Research Council (ARC) maintains this server to provide information on its activities and projects. The Council conducts research and business in four major areas - biotechnology, information technology, manufacturing technology, and resource technology. Visitors to this site will find information on research being conducted by the Council, material on the information resources that the Council provides to businesses, and historical information on the Council's mission and purpose. There are also links to ARC's business partners, as well as to other related servers on the Internet.

KEYWORDS   Biotechnology, Engineering, Technology
AUDIENCE   Business Professionals, Information Specialists, Technology Assessment Professionals

CONTACT   techline@arc.ab.ca
FREE

http://www.arc.ab.ca

Asia, Inc. Online

Asia, Inc. Online is the web version of Asia, Inc. magazine, which discusses emerging markets and business issues in the Asia region, including Japan, Thailand, Singapore, India, and Hong Kong. Major departments are Asiafile with regional news, Asia Abroad discussing the business world, The Bottom Line presenting financial analysis, and After Hours providing travel and leisure information. Sample feature articles discuss the Philippine's economic success, Vietnam and ASEAN, and doing business in Asia. The Asia, Inc. Report is a short radio newscast about business trends that is updated three times a week. The conference rooms provide a place where you can read and post information and opinions about related issues, divided up by topic. You can also receive regularly updated financial news from each country covered.

KEYWORDS   Asia, Emerging Markets, International News
AUDIENCE   International Business Professionals, International Stockbrokers
CONTACT   letters@asia-inc.com
FREE

http://www.asia-inc.com/index.html

Australia-Japan Research Center

This site contains annual reports and newsletters regarding Japanese-Australian trade. Other Australian resources are located in various directories on this server.

KEYWORDS   Asia, Australia, Japan, Trade
AUDIENCE   Economists, International Business Professionals, International Development Specialists
CONTACT   sean@coombs.anu.edu.au
FREE

ftp://coombs.anu.edu.au/coombspapers/coombsarchives/asian-pacific-economic-literat/

Bekaert WWW Home Page

Bekaert is a steel wire manufacturer headquartered in Zwevegem, Belgium and founded in 1880. This site provides a history, company profile, company report, and job opportunities at Bekaert and their website producer, Delaware Computing.

KEYWORDS   Belgium, Manufacturing
AUDIENCE   Business Professionals, Purchasing Agents
FREE

http://www.bekaert.com/

Belgian Business Pages

This is a directory of the 2,000 largest companies in Belgium with links to their home pages. Text is in Belgian and English, and all companies are listed alphabetically by business type or industry sector.

KEYWORDS   Belgium, Industry

126 International Business

Business & Economics

AUDIENCE Belgian Business Professionals, Business Analysts, Business Researchers, European Business Professionals, International Marketing Professionals
CONTACT info@larix.com
FREE

http://larix.com/index/

BizHK (Hong Kong)—Doing Business in Hong Kong ★★★

This home page offers you a business directory of Hong Kong. Companies are organized alphabetically and by industry, contact information, and basic company profile. It also provides links to BizAsia, an Asia/Pacific-Rim Business Newsletter, and other information for business professionals.
KEYWORDS Hong Kong, Tourism
AUDIENCE International Business Professionals, International Investors, Managers
CONTACT Raymond Lowe
rlowe@hk.super.net
FREE

http://www.hk.super.net/~rlowe/bizhk/bhhome.html

Board Of Investment ★★★

This gopher site features The Board of Investment of Thailand (BOI) - the principal government agency responsible for providing incentives to stimulate investment in Thailand. The BOI also conducts extensive investment promotion activities both in Thailand and abroad. BOI provides a wide range of investment services, from information on investment opportunities to visa telecommunication access support. A lot of investment information is accessible through this site.
KEYWORDS Asia, Investment, Thailand
AUDIENCE Asians, Business Professionals, International Investors
CONTACT gophadm@chiangmai.ac.th
FREE

gopher://gopher.chiangmai.ac.th/11/.TOURISM/.BOI

China Internet Home Page ★★★

This home page is an introduction to the ChinaNet—an association of Internet users and providers in China. It includes domain name structures, a description of services provided by the ChinaNet, etc. Mainly academic networks are included here, but also some regional and individual sites.
KEYWORDS Asia, China, Internet Networking
AUDIENCE Business Professionals, Chinese, Network Users, Scientists
CONTACT whzhang@ns.cnc.ac.cn
FREE

http://www.cnc.ac.cn:80/

Europages, The European Business Directory ★★

This is the web site of Europages, The European Business Directory. This is a text page which briefly describes and advertises the hard copy edition of this publication. The directory provides free company data on 150,000 suppliers from 25 European countries. This information will help its users find and contact European partners who are positioned for export in any business sector. Business contacts are facilitated by several model letters in five languages.
KEYWORDS Business Directory, Company Profiles, European Businesses, Import-Export
AUDIENCE Business Professionals, Business Students, Entrepreneurs
CONTACT Mme. Stephanie Germain
europage@dialup.francenet.fr
FREE

http://www.europages.com

Free Trade News Online ★★★

This home page offers you Free Trade News—a publication of NAFTA & GATT (now WTO, World Trade Organization) related informational updates, international business news briefs, multi-lateral trade opportunities. It is distributed in the USA, Canada, Mexico, Colombia and Panama.
KEYWORDS Latin America, NAFTA (North American Free Trade Agreement)
AUDIENCE Business Professionals, General Public, Latin Americans, Market Analysts
CONTACT oli@txdirect.net
FREE

http://www.txdirect.net:80/FTN/

INDO Link ★★★

INDO Link is a resource for Indian businesses and communities worldwide. It provides news from India, as well as analysis and legal information pertaining to India. Cultural information includes film and book reviews, poetry, health and fitness information, and recipes. The Global Directory of Services provides advertisements and information for products and businesses with Indian interests. INDO Link also includes regional listings for businesses in US cities with large Indian communities, as well as classified ads.
KEYWORDS Cultural Exchange, India, International News
AUDIENCE Businessman, Indians
CONTACT comments@indolink.com
FREE

http://www.genius.net/indolink/

India Online ★★★

This is the home page of India Online, which is dedicated to providing current information pertaining to India and countries of the Indian subcontinent and serving the advertising needs of its customers. You can find data about Business (export/import offerings, joint ventures, manufacturing, business services, market news, and other business opportunities offered by the newly liberated Indian Economy), Telecommunication (telecommunication services to/from India), Shipping (information on shipping to/from India), Travel (travel related services and places of interest), Food (Indian Restaurants around the world, recipes etc.)
KEYWORDS Commerce, Economic Development, India, Telecommunications
AUDIENCE Business Professionals, Indians, International Investors, Tourists
CONTACT info@IndiaOnline.com
FREE

http://IndiaOnline.com/

India World ★★★★

India World is an electronic magazine designed to provide information about emerging markets in India. The News and Information section provides access to articles from the India Daily, India Weekly, and India Today newspapers and their past archives, as well as airline schedules to Indian cities, festival dates, and diplomatic missions. The Business, Finance and Technology section offers a business directory and company profiles, updates on the Indian markets, analysis of the action in the Indian stock exchange, and Indian business publications. Also included is an Arts section, with relevant books, articles, movie recommendations, and more.
KEYWORDS Business, Emerging Markets, India, International News
AUDIENCE International Business Professionals, International Stockbrokers
CONTACT Rajesh Jain
rajesh@indiaworld.com
COST

http://www.indiaworld.com/

NTT Home Page ★★★

The Nippon Telegraph and Telephone (NTT) Corporation site provides information on Japan's broad range of telecommunications services, including telephone, telegraph, leased circuit, data communication facility, and miscellaneous services. It includes connections to COREnet (COmmunications REsearch Network), a research oriented network at NTT Laboratories. Users will also find information on NTT itself, including links to such information as NTT financial data, its research direction, and links to NTT's subsidiaries.
KEYWORDS International News, Telecommunications
AUDIENCE Computer Users, Internet Users
CONTACT www-admin@seraph.ntt.jp
FREE

http://www.ntt.jp

North Of England Business 'On-Line' ★★★★

North Of England Business is designed to support business professionals who have limited time to surf the Net, but who need to access useful information fast. The site contains international listings of business sites including the Department of Economics, University of Dublin, the Helsinki Economics WWW, Financial Economics (a government site on the University of Helsinki finance page), RiceInfo Gopher, Economics from the Social Sciences Information Gateway, and more.
KEYWORDS British Companies, Consulting Services, Information Services

International Business

AUDIENCE Business Educators, Business Professionals, Business Students (Graduate), Researchers
CONTACT nebol@sourceuk.demon.co.uk
FREE

http://www.demon.co.uk/proact/index.html

Pan Asia Networking (PAN) ★★★

This is a home page from PAN Asia Networking, which promotes collaboration in research and development through information access, use and exchange. PAN supports an electronic communications and networking agenda to connect individuals and institutions for knowledge-sharing across Asia. Environmental organizations, organizations connected with economic development, and scientific institutions are also listed here.

KEYWORDS Asia, Internet Networking, Scientific Research, Technology
AUDIENCE Asians, Environmentalists, International Development Specialists, Scientists
CONTACT PanAsia@idrc.org.sg
FREE

http://www.idrc.org.sg/idrc/pan/intro.html

 ## Partnerships '95 ★

Visitors to the Partnerships '95 home page can access background information on this organization endeavoring to foster international trade between Maine and New Brunswick, Canada. The site provides brief information on the organization's goals as well as a list of membership benefits and a registration form.

KEYWORDS Business Conferences, Canada, Maine
AUDIENCE Maine Companies, New Brunswick Companies
CONTACT amf@unb.ca
FREE

http://www.unb.ca/web/p95/p95.htm

R.I.C.E. (Registered International Correspondents for Exporting) ★★★

This Web site is home to a group called Registered International Correspondents for Exporting, an international business club whose goal is to develop new business opportunities between French and foreign companies. There are links to French and foreign member companies' profiles, information about membership as a correspondent or exporter, and contact information.

KEYWORDS France, Import-Export
AUDIENCE International Business Professionals
FREE

http://www.calvacom.fr/ccio/index.html

Connections to The World Bank
Who is helping the poorest countries?

To get information on financial trends and projects within the world's poorest countries, turn to the "World Bank" Web site.

This site provides a wealth of information on the international financial organization that lends billions of dollars to many of the poorest countries on the planet. You can access information and data on any of the countless projects the bank supports, as well as obtain financial forecasts for virtually every country in the world. This is a great place to learn the history of projects which have brought progress (in the form of industry, and jobs) to countries that have traditionally been overlooked or exploited by the world's wealthier nations.

(http://www.worldbank.org.html/extdr/about.html)

also, (http://www.worldbank.org/html/extpb/Publicaitons.html)

 ## Russian-American Science Home Page ★★

This is the home page for Russian American Science, Inc. They help companies identify, evaluate, and acquire Russian technologies, or aid them in developing their presence in the Russian economy. This includes market and feasibility studies, a technology search (particularly in the aerospace industry), work with the Russian ministries and other government agencies, financing proposals for banks and multilateral financial institutions, translation of specifications, proposals, and other documentation.

KEYWORDS Russia, Technology
AUDIENCE Aerospace Industry Professionals, Business Professionals, Russians
FREE

http://www.catalog.com/ras/Welcome.html

 ## The St. Petersburg Business Journal ★★★

The online version of the monthly St. Petersburg Business Journal features brief updates on local, Russian, European, and national business and financial news in a WWW format.

KEYWORDS Business, Russia
AUDIENCE Anglophones, International Business Professionals, Russians
CONTACT sppress@sovam.com
FREE

http://www.spb.su/spbj/

 ## Sumimoto Corporation Home Page ★★★

This is the home page for the Sumitimo Corporation, an industrial and financial conglomerate in Japan. It provides some information on the company's organization and finances, as well as KEIZAI DOUKOU, a monthly report on the economic trends in Japan and other countries.

KEYWORDS Multimedia, Telecommunications
AUDIENCE Business Professionals, International Investors
CONTACT info@sumitomocorp.co.jp
FREE

http://www.sumitomocorp.co.jp/index-e.html

Technical Research Centre of Finland ★★

This is a gopher server of the Technical Research Centre of Finland (VTT), the largest independent contract research center for industry and the public sector in the Nordic countries. VTT performs research in electronics, information technology, automation, chemical technology, biotechnology, energy and manufacturing. This site contains information on VTT research, services, publications, international activities, staff, and more. It has links to other resources as well.

KEYWORDS Electronics, Finland, Information Science
AUDIENCE Business Professionals, Finns, Scientists
FREE

http://www.vtt.fi/

Thailand ★★★

This home page offers a list of Internet providers in Thailand, with contact persons and addresses included. You can also ascend two layers up and access a list of Internet providers around the world.

KEYWORDS Asia, Internet Networking, Thailand
AUDIENCE Asians, Internet Access Providers, Network Users
CONTACT Benoit LIPS
        lips@pcpm.ucl.ac.be
FREE

http://www.earth.org/~lips/Providers/Thailand.html

Virtual Africa Home Page ★★★

Welcome to The Virtual Africa Home Page. This site connects you to services and information on South African Business. Topics include South African Business Information and Services, Trade with and within South Africa, South African Travel and Tourism, South African Property, and employment resources. The graphics can be very slow in loading.

KEYWORDS International Trade, Real Estate, South Africa, Tourism

International Business – Investment

AUDIENCE African Americans, African Studies Students, South Africans, Tourists
CONTACT Webmaster@africa.com
FREE

http://africa.com

Welcome to Accurate Home Page ★★★

This is a home page from the Malaysian company, Accurate Information System Consultant Sdn. Bhd. Accurate is focused on providing UNIX and network based computer solutions. They do everything from the turnkey installation of large client-server systems, to the installation of individual UNIX workstations, servers, PC-LANs and other devices, to the ongoing provision of maintenance, training and technical support services. Their products and services are presented here.

KEYWORDS Asia, Computer Software, Computer Supplies, Malaysia
AUDIENCE Asians, Business Professionals, Computer Users, UNIX Users
CONTACT roslan@accurate.com.my
FREE

http://accurate.com.my/

Investment

See also
Business & Economics · *Banking*
Government & Politics · *Countries*

About Investing Online ★★★

This home page hosts Investing Online, an electronic monthly newsletter for people who want to use their home computer to gain access to a world of financial information and trading. It contains information about hardware for home investors, new products, phone brokerage services, and a small column with news from the financial world.

KEYWORDS Financial Planning, Investment Advice, Investment Software, Stock Market
AUDIENCE Computer Users, Investors
CONTACT Chuck Epstein
BBMA35A@Prodigy.com
FREE

http://risc.cpbx.net/IOL/about.html

The Ben Franklin Technology Center ★★★

The Ben Franklin Technology Center home page of Southeastern Pennsylvania is a leading non-profit venture capital investment group dedicated to bringing the emerging technologies and ideas of small Pennsylvania companies to market. The center has several funds for newborn companies - Applied Research & Development Fund, Emerging Company Investment Fund, Enterprise Growth Fund, Innovation Investment Fund, and the Business Information Center.

KEYWORDS Finance, Non Profit Organizations, Technology, Technology Transfer
AUDIENCE Business Professionals, Entrepreneurs, Nonprofit Organizations, Pennsylvania Residents
CONTACT bftc@libertynet.org
FREE

http://libertynet.org/business/econ-dev/bftc/bftc.html

Business Way 94 ★★★

Business Way '94 is a handbook concerning Russian companies and the recent process of privatization in St. Petersburg, Russia. It is designed to provide information and advice to potential investors about the investment process, relevant legislation and the changes within these fields. Some of its features include useful statistics about the city, an explanation of the legal processes required to set up a business there, and a comprehensive descriptive list of local companies organized by industry.

KEYWORDS Business, Finance, Investment, Russia
AUDIENCE International Business Professionals, Investors
CONTACT Robert Farrell
farrell@sppress.spb.su
FREE

http://www.spb.su/bw/

Canada Net Mutual Funds ★★★

The Canada Mutual Funds home page provides information about the top 25 percent of Canadian mutual funds—their fees, volatility, simple and compound returns, and ranking. Funds are ordered according to the following criteria: those investing in Canadian Equity, US Equity, International Equity, Special Equity, Resource Equity, Mortgage, Real Estate, Canadian Bond, Foreign Bond, Canadian Money Market, and Foreign Money Market. This information is in the process of transformation to an online database.

KEYWORDS Canada, Mutual Funds, Stock Market
AUDIENCE Financial Analysts, Investors, Stockbrokers
CONTACT Judy Amadatsu
info@visions.com
FREE

http://www.visions.com/netpages/mutuals/mutuals.html

Chemical Company Stock Prices ★★★

Chemical Company Stock Prices presents daily closing prices for 35 major chemical companies. The quotes are organized as follows - This Week's Quotes, Last Week's Quotes, January Quotes, February Quotes, 1994 Quotes.

KEYWORDS Companies, Investment, Stock Market, Stock Quotes
AUDIENCE Investors, Stock Market Players
FREE

http://hackberry.chem.niu.edu:70/1/Stock%20Prices

Chicago Mercantile Exchange Home Page ★★★

This page does not contain quotes and charts. Instead you can find information about the everyday life of the Chicago Mercantile Exchange (CME), history of the CME, biographies of the CME president and chairman, a CME model to consolidate federal financial regulations, and more. Beginning investors can find the Glossary of Futures and Options Terms useful.

KEYWORDS Futures, Illinois
AUDIENCE Financial Analysts, Investors, Market Analysts, Options Traders, Stockbrokers
CONTACT William Burks
wilbirk@cme.com
FREE

http://www.interaccess.com:80/cme/

Colloquium ★★★

This site features an investment newsletter from a New York investment bank, Wertheim Schroder & Co., entitled Colloquium. The newsletter contains information about performance and market perspectives of different companies, ordered by company name. The Colloquium is offered with the hope that Internet users will become comfortable with Wertheim Schroder & Co.'s style of investing and eventually establish an account with the firm. Subscription is free for two months.

KEYWORDS Finance, Market Research, Stock Market
AUDIENCE Business Analysts, Financial Analysts, Investors, Stockbrokers
CONTACT Thomas J. Gillespie
tomg@panix.com
FREE

http://www.hydra.com/ws/colloquium.html

FDIC Insured CDs ★★★

This small promotional home page from CyberBank offers you a service which will find the highest interest rates paid on money market accounts and certificates of deposit in US savings institutions. The CyberBank will help you transfer your money, and the service is free. CyberBank looks only for FDIC-insured saving instruments. Coming soon are similar services in tax-deferred annuities, stocks, bonds, mutual funds, and variable annuities.

KEYWORDS Banking, Financial Services, Interest Rates
AUDIENCE Investors
CONTACT cybrbank@ix.netcom.com
FREE

http://www.webshop.com/cbank/

Fast EDGAR Mutual Funds Reporting ★★★★

EDGAR Mutual Funds is a vast searchable database of mutual fund company filings to the SEC. The database is maintained by the EDGAR Development Project at the NYU Stern School of Business. The mutual fund company filings are arranged by the names of the

Investment

individual company funds. The most useful materials here for the average investor are the 485APOS and 485BPOS filings, which contain prospectuses for the respective funds. Other useful filings include the N-30B and N-30D series which contain quarterly and semi-annual reports of financial and securities holdings data. You will find answers on FAQs (Frequently Asked Questions) about the database at the NYU Edgar development site, a link will be provided after each search.

Keywords Education (College/University), Mutual Funds, Securities, Securities Exchange Commission (SEC)
Audience Business Analysts, Financial Analysts, Investors, Market Analysts
Contact mark@edgar.stern.nyu.edu
Free

http://edgar.stern.nyu.edu/mutual.html

Fidelity Investments Home Page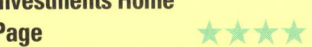

Fidelity Investor Centers offer a variety of informational and educational events. To find out what's happening in your area, visit the Regional Events section of this server. This server offers a convenient way to request literature and applications, as well as to review information about many of the investment products and services provided. Topics of information include what's new, mutual funds, investor tools, contests and games, and brokerage services.

Keywords Brokerage Services, Financial Services, Investment
Audience Financial Planners, Investors
Free

http://www.fid-inv.com/

FinanCenter

This home page features FinanCenter - a personal finance resource center which provides online decision tools and financial services. FinanCenter's interactive calculations allow you to evaluate your borrowing and investing options. You'll find practical reference materials, such as glossaries and professional reports. Section on home loan calculations, information, and services is completed. Auto, education, and credit card information is coming soon as well as evaluation of banks, insurance companies and money management firms, accompanied by the calculations necessary to analyze investments pertaining to each.

Keywords Investment Advice, Loans, Personal Finance, Portfolio Management
Audience Business Professionals, Consumers, Economists, General Public, Investors
Contact finance@primenet.com
Free

http://plaza.xor.com/resources/index.html

Foreign Exchange Rates

This page features a simple currency converter from the Department of Computer Science, Lund University, Sweden. Select two currencies from the list of 23, and exchange rates will appear. The rates are provided by the European Union's Echo service which is solely responsible for accuracy. The given rates are based upon US dollar rates cited by each government's national bank at approximately noon on the given date. The server attempts to update these rates daily at 18.00 Swedish time.

Keywords Currency, Exchange Rates, International Finance
Audience Currency Dealers, Investors
Contact Kurt
kurt@dna.lth.se
Free

http://www.dna.lth.se/cgi-bin/rates

Connections to Trading Cards
There's money in the cards

For a trading card collector, a complete set of the 1955 New York Yankees baseball trading cards is major money in the bank. If you have a collection of trading cards, want to know how to start one, or would like to do some trading, the "Trading Card Grand Central Station" is for you.

If you want to start a collection of non-sport trading cards, there are several sites that will provide you with a list of desirable series to start collecting (such as the Walt Disney Premium Collection or the Batman Forever series). If you keep a close eye out on the Web, you can get in early on collections for upcoming films and events.

(http://nyx10.cs.du.edu:8001/~pbingham/Interests/Games/MagicHomePage.shtml)

There are even some "home pages" of collectors who put their list on the Internet to trade with other collectors. You can also get in touch with collectors and collections around the U.S. and Canada through a vast database that is dedicated to trading cards of all types.

(http://www.wwcd.com/tc/dir.html)

also, (http://lamar.colostate.edu/~mhide/j/mtg.html)

GNN PFC International Investment

This page is an index to the sites of interest for international investors and travellers. It features three resourses covering exchange rates - The Koblas Currency Converter allows you to monitor the performance of the dollar in relation to over 50 foreign currencies on a weekly basis; The Daily Exchange Rate Converter from the Lund University Department of Computer Science in Sweden does nearly the same job with daily currency rates (23 currencies); Spot Exchange Rate Table from the Federal Reserve Bank of New York, published daily, features the midpoints of buying and selling prices, in currency units per dollar, for 12 major international currencies. Other resources available include famous Hong Kong Stocks Reports, exotic RINACO Plus - your jump-point into then Russian stock market, Goethe Investment Heimatseite - German language site focusing on European investments, Money Issues OnLine - Internet version of Canadian personal finance magazine, subscription information on a free electronic mail service Daily China Headline News, and, links to newsgroup Investment FAQs.

KEYWORDS Currency Converter, International Finance, Stock Quotes, Tourism
AUDIENCE Business Analysts, Financial Analysts, Investors, Market Analysts
CONTACT Abbot Chambers
abbot@ora.com
FREE

http://nearnet.gnn.com/gnn/meta/finance/res/invest.country.html

 ### Gruntal & Co. Inc., Weekly Market Summary

This page contains weekly information on the performance of the top 10 and the bottom 10 sectors' stocks for the last week. Some of the index averages presented include Dow Jones, Nasdaq, Standard & Poor's 500, and Russell 1000. It also covers money rates, number of new high/low at NYSE (New York Stock Exchange), NASDAQ, AMEX (American Exchange), earnings announcements expected each week, prices of gold and silver, and inflation and unemployment rates.

KEYWORDS Securities, Stock Market, Stock Quotes
AUDIENCE Business Analysts, Financial Analysts, Investors, Market Analysts
CONTACT Gregg Rosenberg
gregg@acsil.com
FREE

http://www.gruntal.com/investments/wms.html

 ### Heritage West Financial, Inc.

This home page from the Heritage West Financial, Inc. offers you sophisticated strategies of investing in futures markets. The main idea of the strategy concerns good timing in selling and bying options. Heritage West Financial offers advice by experienced traders using state of the art computer software, and security of full diversification among all the futures markets. Subscribers get a free Futures Magazine subscription and discounts on stock price charts.

KEYWORDS Futures, Investment Advice, Portfolio Management
AUDIENCE Financial Analysts, Investors
COST

http://www.infopost.com/heritage/index.html

 ### Hot Stocks Review

This home page features George Chelekis's Hot Stocks Review, Hot Stocks Whispers, and Hot Stocks Alert. George Chelekis has published nine books on investments, bargain-hunting, real estate, and banking. Hot Stock Review deals mainly with small companies that have the potential for extremely rapid growth. Slightly dated issues of the Hot Stocks Report, Hot Stocks Whispers, and Hot Stocks Alert are available free of charge. Subscription information is provided.

KEYWORDS Banking, Financial Forecasting, Investment Advice, Stock Market
AUDIENCE Financial Analysts, Investors, Stockbrokers
CONTACT hotstock@gate.net
FREE

http://www.gate.net/~hotstock/

IOMA Business Page

This home page of The Institute of Management and Administration (IOMA) is an Internet directory of links to sites related to investment, finance, management, and marketing, as well as newsgroups, searchable databases, etc. Main departments are News, Administration, Finance, Management, Sales and Marketing, resources by Industries, and links to directories like E-Net Galaxy Business and Commerce, Whole Internet Catalogue Business and Finance, and Yahoo Guide to the WWW Business. The directory is extensive in the fields of regulations and mutual funds.

KEYWORDS Business, Internet Directories, Mutual Funds, Securities
AUDIENCE Business Professionals, Finance Professionals, Investors
CONTACT sward@ioma.com
FREE

http://ioma.com/ioma/

 ### The Internet Closed-End Fund Investor

The Internet Closed-End Fund Investor provides general information about closed-end funds and charts of Net Asset Value (NAV) and price data on many equity closed-end funds. Data is organized by sector and region. Coverage includes a short introduction and an index to closed-end funds. A list of newsletters and newspapers covering closed-end funds is also included for the sophisticated investor.

KEYWORDS Financial Research, Financial Services, Newsletters
AUDIENCE Financial Analysts, Investors
CONTACT Sam Raja
samraja@icefi.com
COST

http://www.icefi.com/

 ### Investing for the Perplexed

This home page offers you a quarterly investment newsletter plus paid financial advice. This service is for unsophisticated investors—people who have no interest in investments, find business boring, have no idea what the current prime rate is, and don't care. There are registered investment advisors not selling any investment products, offering second opinions on investments an individual is considering, providing financial plans, retirement planning, 3 to 5 year financial plans, and more. Basic questions are free.

KEYWORDS Financial Planning, Investment Advice, Retirement
AUDIENCE Investors, Retirees
COST

http://www.inch.com/~robertny/invest/menu.html

Investment Forecasts For Stocks And Mutual Funds

This home page is from Howard Phillips, Ph.D., a researcher in the field of forecasting theory and artificial intelligence. His stocks and mutual funds advisory has consistently shown a forecasting accuracy in the range of 70% to 90% in 1995 market conditions. Forecasts for 30 stocks from the Dow Jones industrial, 25 stocks in current Alphaline portfolio, and the sector mutual funds are given. Some technical details are discussed, like methodology of estimation forecast accuracy.

KEYWORDS Financial Forecasting, Investment Advice, Mutual Funds, Stocks
AUDIENCE Financial Analysts, Financial Forecasters, Investors, Stockbrokers
CONTACT Howard Phillips
dhp@acpub.duke.edu
FREE

http://www.duke.edu/~dhp/

 ### Investment Solutions Online

Investment Solutions Online is an online stock newsletter that gives daily buy and sell recommendations on stocks. Every evening, subscribers of this newsletter will receive updated recommendations for the following market opening, via internet email. Subscription rates and a sample of the service are available at this site.

KEYWORDS Newsletters, Stock Market
AUDIENCE Stock Market Investors, Stockbrokers
CONTACT info@iso.com
FREE

http://www.iso.com/

 ### Investor's Business Daily

Investor's Business Daily is a national daily newspaper focusing on investment issues, currently in beta-test mode. This Web page offers snapshots of their online service software, which features news summaries, weekly forecasts, and information concerning national issues and business leaders. Elsewhere on this page, users can find several articles excerpted from recent print versions of the newspaper.

KEYWORDS Investment Software, Online Newspapers
AUDIENCE Business Professionals, Business Researchers, Investors, Marketing Professionals
CONTACT Tommy McGloin
ibd_ee@ensemble.com
COST

http://ibd.ensemble.com/tryit.html

Investment

Knight-Ridder Financial Europe ★★★★

This promotional home page from Knight-Ridder Financial (KRF) features services provided by the leading supplier of financial and commodity information, news, historic data, and statistics. Daily information covers Cash, Futures, Agriculture, Stock Indices across 50 exchanges world-wide, and over 500 markets. Knight-Ridder's databases provide investors with charts of historical trends and fundamentals going back decades, combined with the software to update them daily.

- KEYWORDS: Commodities, Financial Research, Stock Quotes
- AUDIENCE: Business Professionals, Economists, Investors, Market Analysts
- CONTACT: bvakil@kridder.cityscape.co.uk
- FREE

http://www.route-one.co.uk/route-one/ridder/

The League of American Investors ★★★★

This home page features an investment game nVESTOR from the League of American Investors. At the beginning, you are given $100,000 in stocks and the weekly Online Weston Manual of Corporate Reports. The League maintains and values your Portfolio. The game is played by email and is absolutely free.

- KEYWORDS: Financial Forecasting, Investment Portfolio, Online Games, Stocks
- AUDIENCE: Business Professionals, Economists, Internet Users, Investors
- FREE

http://www.goldsword.com/pc-signs/nvestor/nvestor.html

MarketWeb ★★★

This home page from InfoVision offers you a free copy of Craig Corcoran's financial newsletter on mutual funds, futures, and intra-day trading. For the sophisticated investor, there is also a list of investment gurus available through InfoVision's MarketInfo phone service, with personal profiles of each advisor included.

- KEYWORDS: Financial Research, Futures, Investment Advice, Mutual Funds
- AUDIENCE: Business Analysts, Investors, Stockbrokers
- CONTACT: Webmaster@infovision.com
- FREE

http://marketweb.com/

Nasdaq Financial Executive Journal ★★★

This page contains the bi-quarterly Nasdaq (National Association of Securities Dealers) Financial Journal. The Journal is a joint project of the Legal Information Institute at Cornell Law School and The Nasdaq (SM) Stock Market. The Journal is an informational service to Nasdaq companies. Nasdaq Financial Journal (NFJ) aims to present a range of expert, professional opinion from prominent, responsible persons on major issues of corporate finance and investor relations.

- KEYWORDS: Finance, NASDAQ, Securities, Stock Market
- AUDIENCE: Financial Analysts, Investors
- FREE

http://nearnet.gnn.com/gnn/meta/finance/res/invest.subjects.html

National Council for Investment Promotion ★★★

This is a home page from the National Council for Investment Promotion of Venezuela (CONAPRI), a joint venture between the Venezuelan business community and the public sector. It was established in 1990 to promote investment in Venezuela and to provide a wide range of services to current and potential investors. CONAPRI provides services free of charge to investors already located in Venezuela — whether international or domestic — and to others who are considering new investments.

- KEYWORDS: International Finance, Venezuela
- AUDIENCE: Business Professionals, Investors, Latin Americans
- CONTACT: conapri@conicit.ve
- FREE

http://lanic.utexas.edu/la/venezuela/conapri/conapri.html

Nestegg ★★★

Nestegg is a home page from IDD (Investment Dealers' Digest) - a diversified financial publishing, database, software and consulting company that specializes in serving the financial services industry. Nestegg mainly advertizes IDD products and financial publications, whose objective is to supply financial information targeted towards the needs of high income and high net worth families. It provides links to IDD products such as Tradeline - a constantly verified database, interactive access to the New York Institute of Finance Bookstore, information about Janus and Invesco groups of mutual funds, Mutual Funds News Index - indexed newspaper, index to the back issues of NestEgg magazine, and to pieces of investment advice for different types of households.

- KEYWORDS: Consulting Services, Financial Services, Investment Advice, Mutual Funds
- AUDIENCE: Economists, Financial Analysts, Investors, Stockbrokers
- CONTACT: jcook@iddis.com
- FREE

http://nestegg.iddis.com/

Networth by GALT Technologies ★★★★

The Networth is a free service which is divided into the following seven separate areas: a mutual fund market manager, an expert panel, equities center, what's new?, welcome and information, market outlook, and an Internet information center. Users can find information on over 5,000 mutual funds, as well as other financial data.

- KEYWORDS: Business, Investment, Mutual Funds, Quotations
- AUDIENCE: Business Professionals, Investors, Stockbrokers
- CONTACT: networth@mfunds.com
- FREE

http://networth.galt.com/

Predicto ★★★★

Predicto is a GA market forecaster. It forecasts day-to-day changes in the S&P 500 market index. Predicto's population of 101 market forecasting algorithms has been continuously evolving since May 20, 1988. The GA (Genetic Algorithm) approach uses processes that have been observed in Darwinian evolution (such as natural selection, mutation, sexual reproduction, and genetic inheritance) to 'evolve' populations of algorithms. When the GA method is applied to economic forecasting, the algorithms evolved comprise market forecasting formulae.

- KEYWORDS: Finance, Investment
- AUDIENCE: Financiers, Investors
- FREE

http://www.quote.com/newsletters/predicto/

RINACO Plus Brokerage House ★★★

This home page from the RINACO Plus, a brokerage house located in Moscow, intends to be your starting point for the Russian stock market. You'll find RINACO Plus's offers and bids, valuable information about current regulations and the institutional environment, recent quotes from futures, stock, and commodities trading, and links to investment resourses provided by the other services. The page is rather eclectic and, regretably, materials are mostly in Russian.

- KEYWORDS: Futures, Investment, Russia, Stock Market
- AUDIENCE: Investors, Russians
- CONTACT: Victor V. Agroskin vvagr@plus.rinaco.msk.su
- FREE

http://www.fe.msk.ru/infomarket/rinacoplus/

Russian Commodity and Raw Materials Home Page ★★★

This home page from the Russian Commodity and Raw Materials Exchange (RCRME) offers you annual reports and results of currency futures trading on the RCRME. If you want a look at a very volatile market, it is here. More data is available in Russian, including Stock, Futures and Commodities Market profiles, current quotes, Presidential personal data, and more.

- KEYWORDS: Futures, Russia, Stocks
- AUDIENCE: Commodities Brokers, Economists, Investors, Stockbrokers
- CONTACT: assa@ivc-rtsb.msk.ru
- FREE

http://www.fe.msk.ru/infomarket/rtsb/ewelcome.html

Security APL Quote Server ★★★★

This site offers 15-minute-delayed securities quotes from North Amercian Quotations, Inc. based in London, Ontario, Canada. Stock and commodity prices are given on an as-needed basis. All quotes are provided free of charge, as this site is used to advertise the commercial-

132 Investment

grade portfolio management software that the company sells.

KEYWORDS Annual Reports, Business, Securities, Stock Market
AUDIENCE Business Analysts, Business Researchers, Financial Researchers, Investors
CONTACT g.www@secapl.com
FREE

http://www.secapl.com/cgi-bin/qs/

The South African Investors' Guide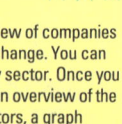

This guide presents a quarterly overview of companies listed on the Johannesburg Stock Exchange. You can select a company alphabetically or by sector. Once you select the company you will receive an overview of the company, history of significant indicators, a graph depicting the company's performance, and other information. You can also take the Technical Analysis Challenge which is a stock trading simulation where you can test your skills and talk and share ideas with experts .

KEYWORDS Company Performance, Investment Guides, South Africa, Stock Exchange
AUDIENCE Business Professionals, Gamblers, Investors, South Africa Residents
FREE

http://africa.com/pages/jse/page1.htm

Stocks PNW

This home page will give you an idea about the performance of stocks of companies in the Pacific Northwest region. Companies are listed by sectors, and for some of them, more detailed information (news releases, corporate overviews, financial information) is provided. The home page tracks performance of the Northwest 50 Index. Also, it houses Walter Raby's Stock Report and provides a link to The Global Gold Investor Digest—The Internet Newsletter for Precious Metal Investors.

KEYWORDS Corporations, Northwest US, Stock Quotes
AUDIENCE Business Analysts, Financial Analysts, Investors, Stockbrokers
CONTACT webmaster@cyberquest.com
FREE

http://www.cyberquest.com/StocksPNW/Welcome.html

Stocks and Commodities

This page is a source of information about stock and commodities. The links are organized in five categories: investment research, securities charting, economics sources, small business assistance, and online brokerage firms.

KEYWORDS Commodities, Stock Market, Wall Street
AUDIENCE Stock Market Investors, Stockbrokers
FREE

http://www.onr.com/stocks.html

Stocks and Stock Reports

From this page you can reach a number of sites with a lot of valuable information: the Market Watch page   which provides a minute-by-minute summary of activity for Dow Jones, S&P (Standard & Poor's), and NYSE (New York Stock Exchange) indexes, the Weekly Market Summary with data on sector trading, index performance, money rates, coming earnings announcements, and gold and silver prices, and QuoteCom, a comprehensive stock market information service (commercial). You'll also find MIT (Massachusets Institute of Technology) Experimental Stock Market Data with same-day price and volume charts for 300 NYSE stocks as well as high, low, and closing price info, Holt's Market Report, and more.

KEYWORDS Financial Services, Information Resources, Securities, Stock Market
AUDIENCE Business Analysts, Financial Analysts, Investors, Market Analysts
CONTACT Abbot Chambers
abbot@ora.com
FREE

http://nearnet.gnn.com/gnn/meta/finance/res/invest.stocks.html

The Syndicate

This page, compiled by Bill Rini, provides a lot of answers on Investment FAQs (frequently asked questions), some nice articles on the mechanics of the stock market, investment advice from investment gurus, ticker symbols for domestic and foreign stocks—currently Asian, Canadian, American, South African, and UK. You'll also find symbols for index options, a list of option exchanges, and jump points to other financial places.

KEYWORDS Bonds, Investment, Securities, Stock Market
AUDIENCE Business Professionals, Financial Analysts, Investors
CONTACT Bill Rini
billman@rain.org
FREE

http://www.rain.org/~billman/syn.html

T-Bill Direct—Your Gateway to Secure Investing

This home page from J.W. Korth & Company advertizes phone access to U.S. Treasury securities—bills, notes, and bonds. You can open an account, or buy and sell securities on the secondary or primary market. Tax tips, answers to FAQs, and a short glossary of terms related to investing in U.S. Treasury securities are included. Link to a New York Federal Reserve Bank site with the latest T-Bills rates is provided.

KEYWORDS Economic Indicators, Government Securities, Investment, Taxes
AUDIENCE Business Professionals, Financial Analysts, Investors
CONTACT webmaster@netfactory.com
COST

http://www.netfactory.com/mondenet/tbdira1.html

Treasury Notes and Bonds Quotes

At this gopher site you can find quotes of US Government securities (bills and notes), commercial paper, federal funds, and certificates of deposit, compiled by the Federal Reserve Bank of New York. For every issue of government securities, bid and ask prices, change of price, and yield are listed.

KEYWORDS Bonds, Certificates Of Deposit, Government Securities (US), Treasury Notes
AUDIENCE Investors
FREE

gopher://una.hh.lib.umich.edu/00/ebb/monetary/quotes.txt

Wall Street Direct

This page, provided by Wall Street DPs is a collection of information for relatively technically sophisticated investors. It contains a large glossary of technical terms used by financial analysts, announcements of future conferences and events in the financial world, book reviews, online bookstore access, methodology showroom, reviews of investor's software, stock market performance forecasts, and more. The site also includes a large number of links to other financial services.

KEYWORDS Securities, Stock Market, Technical Reports, Wall Street
AUDIENCE Business Analysts, Financial Analysts, Investors, Market Analysts
CONTACT wallst@cts.com
FREE

http://www.cts.com/~wallst/index.html

ftp://ftp.cts.com

Welcome to BARRA

This is the home page of BARRA, Inc., an investment technology firm. Company news and information, seminars and workshops, and employment opportunities can be accessed at this site.

KEYWORDS Computer Software, Investment, Stock Market
AUDIENCE Financial Analysts, Traders
CONTACT webmaster@Barra.COM
FREE

http://www.barra.com/

Welcome to WRSL

This is the home page of William R. Storie & Co. Ltd. (WRSL)—an independent financial consulting and management company based in Hamilton, Bermuda. The company offers help in the following areas: offshore insurance and reinsurance, offshore investment management, offshore corporate administration, offshore trusts, and offshore mutual funds. An offshore investment newsletter is available as well as links to other companies providing off-shore consulting.

KEYWORDS Bermuda, Consulting Services, Financial Services
AUDIENCE Business Professionals, Financial Analysts, Financial Planners, Investors
CONTACT Bill Storie, President
wrsl@ibl.bm
FREE

http://www.webcom.com/~wrsl/

Investment – Management **133**

Management

See also
Business & Economics · *Business Schools*
Business & Economics · *Commerce*
Business & Economics · *Investment*

AFL-CIO News OnLine

This page for the AFL-CIO (American Federation of Labor - Congress of Industrial Relations), a labor union organization based in the United States maintains a weekly hyperlinked newsfeed to labor and labor related events and news. Each week contains between 10-15 articles on various labor issues that are meant to be informative about the labor relations movement and process.

KEYWORDS   Industrial Relations, Labor Unions, News
AUDIENCE   AFL-CIO Members, Activists
CONTACT   feedback@aflcio.org
FREE

http://www.aflcio.org/newsonline/

Academy of Management OnLine ★★★★

This Web site is designed to provide the Academy of Management membership with a variety of information related services. Users will find links to AM conference information, publications such as the AM Management Journal, doctoral and junior faculty consortium information, as well as links to other management related resources. In particular, article submission information, style guide and procedures are also offered for potential journal contributors.

KEYWORDS   Business, Research
AUDIENCE   Doctoral Students, Management Professionals, Professors, Students (Graduate)
CONTACT   Mark A. Fuller
            Mark_Fuller@baylor.edu
FREE

http://hsb.baylor.edu/html/fuller/am/am_home.htm

An Analysis of IRS Guidelines for Independent Contractor and Employee Status ★★★

This site presents An Analysis of IRS Guidelines for Independent Contractor and Employee Status. It covers IRS criteria for determining employee versus outside contractor status. Some other areas include training, service rendered personally, hiring, supervising and paying assistants, set hours of work, scheduled payment, and more. For each criteria, the guidelines for both employee and independent contractor are presented and compared.

KEYWORDS   Business, IRS (Internal Revenue Service), Tax Law
AUDIENCE   Accountants, Employees, Employers, Independent Contractors, Tax Preparers
FREE

http://www.primenet.com/~laig/proserve/bulletin/bu0001.htm

Audio Video Campus ★★★

Audio Video Campus produces and markets video training programs which prepare industries, schools, and governments for a global economy. The company also provides links to information about speakers, training resources, ordering, and feedback.

KEYWORDS   Business Management, Motivational Products, Personal Development, Training Programs
AUDIENCE   Business Professionals, Educators, Entrepreneurs, Motivational Speakers, Sales Managers
CONTACT   Christine Didocha
            webs@websrus.com
FREE

http://www.sierra.net:80/avcampus/

Business Ethics Resources on WWW (World Wide Web) ★★★

Business Ethics Resources is a directory with hot links to other Internet sites, such as the Academy of Management On-Line, Better Business Bureau (U.S.), Body Shop, Business Ethics Teaching Society (BETS), Council on Economic Priorities, Harvard Business School - Technology and Operations Management, and more. It also includes hot links to business ethics papers, and some business publications.

KEYWORDS   Business, Ethics
AUDIENCE   Business Students, Ethics Students, Ethics researchers
CONTACT   Chris MacDonald
            chrismac@ethics.ubc.ca
FREE

http://www.ethics.ubc.ca/papers/business.html

Case OnLine Information Systems ★★★

This site offers collections of case histories in personnel management compiled by Harvard Business School, University of Western Ontario, and the European Case Clearing House. It includes technical notes, industry notes, case software, and course materials.

KEYWORDS   Business, Human Resources, Management, Organizational Behavior
AUDIENCE   Business Owners, Employees, Managers
FREE

telnet://vaxmsx.babson.edu

Ethical Business ★★★★

The site for Ethical Business in the UK, founded in March 1995, is an online resource for people interested in ethical and environmental business initiatives and the complex ethical and environmental issues that businesses face. Users will find an updated list of organizations involved in this effort as well as articles, books, bibliographies, and many other resources to encourage ethics in business.

KEYWORDS   Business, Environment, Ethics
AUDIENCE   Business Professionals, Economists, Employees

CONTACT   Craig Mackenzie
            ethical.business@bath.ac.uk
FREE

http://www.bath.ac.uk/Centres/Ethical/

Foundation for Enterprise Development Home Page ★★★★

This site features a home page of The Foundation for Enterprise Development (FED). FED's mission is to foster the development of highly productive, competitive enterprises based on the premise that sharing company ownership and meaningful involvement with employees is a fair and effective means of motivating the workforce and achieving many business objectives. FED's activities focus on providing practical information and assistance to help companies implement equity-based compensation, and strategies for involving employees in improving business operations. You will find a calendar of events and conferences with information about speakers, a FED newsletter, a discussion forum, articles about practical experience in different businesses, and more.

KEYWORDS   Business Strategy, Management
AUDIENCE   Employees, Entrepreneurs, Managers
FREE

http://www.fed.org/fed/

LaborNet @igc ★★★

This site lists unions, organizations, and individuals who are regular participants in LaborNet, part of the Institute for Global Communications network. Although the page is still under development, it does provide a good preliminary list of labor unions and organizations as well as a few hot links to Web pages for organizations already on the WWW. The site also encourages additions to this directory of organizations.

KEYWORDS   Industrial Relations, Labor Unions, Organizations
AUDIENCE   Activists, Employees
CONTACT   labornet.org
FREE

http://www.igc.apc.org/labornet/unions.html

LaborWeb ★★★★

The AFL-CIO (American Federation of Labor - Congress of Industrial Organizations) home page provides policy statements, press releases, boycott lists and other information related to the activities of this American labor institution. The AFL-CIO, a federation of labor unions representing millions of working men and women, committed to the improvement of all lives and communities has further provided information about its campaigns and organizing efforts.

KEYWORDS   Industrial Relations, Labor Unions, Organizations, United States
AUDIENCE   Activists, Employees
CONTACT   feedback@aflcio.org
FREE

http://www.aflcio.org/

Management – Non Profits

Logos Networks Corporation
★★★★

This site offers products and services on how to make decisions and how to negotiate for business professionals. Its goal is to help business professionals successfully navigate through the 90s. It includes audio training tapes, books, and computer programs about leadership and The Five Rings system of negotiation. It also offers the Logasnet which consists of Electronic "training halls" for East-Asian and European negotiators. CALL IN BBS Dial (via modem) the bbs at (510) 527-7439 or email to get windows client software

- **KEYWORDS** Conflict Resolution, Management, Mediation, Training Programs
- **AUDIENCE** Business Professionals, Facilitators, International Business Professionals, Workshop Organizers
- **CONTACT** Tod Brannan
  logas@sys425.chatlink.com
- **FREE**

MCDM WorldScan
★★★

The MCDM WorldScan is the twice yearly newsletter of the International Society on Multiple Criteria Decision Making. The site contains Issues of WorldScan, Objectives of WorldScan, Editorial Advisory Board, Correspondence, and more. You can also access the MCDM directory and the MCDM Calendar of Events.

- **KEYWORDS** Business Strategy, Marketing, Newsletters
- **AUDIENCE** Business Professionals, Economists, General Public, Managers, Professors, Students
- **CONTACT** cpiercy@cbacc.cba.uga.edu
- **FREE**

http://www.cba.uga.edu/mcdm.html

Management Archive ★★★★

The Management Archive gopher provides a free, state of the art electronic forum for management ideas and information of all kinds. The archive includes contributed working papers and preprints in the management and organizational sciences, recent paper calls, course syllabi and teaching materials, conference announcements, archives of Academy of Management and management-related discussion lists.

- **KEYWORDS** Business, Business Ethics, Organizational Behavior
- **AUDIENCE** Management Professionals, Professors, Students (Graduate)
- **CONTACT** Jim Goes
  goes@ursus.jun.alaska.edu
- **FREE**

gopher://ursus.jun.alaska.edu/

Mantis Consultants, Ltd
★★

Mantis Consultants, Ltd. provides business and management consulting. The site offers information such as a corporate summary, a personnel overview, recruitment news, product overviews, detailed product brochures, case studies and technical documents.

- **KEYWORDS** Consulting Services, Services, Software
- **AUDIENCE** Educators (University), Internet Users, Researchers, Students (University)
- **CONTACT** tony@jobstream.co.uk
- **FREE**

http://ftp.mantis.co.uk

The Progressive Business Web Pages ★★★★

The Progressive Business Web Pages is a valuable source of information not only about environmentally conscious businesses on the Net, but also about other environmental organizations, student groups, and publications worldwide. Users may visit their Internet Green Marketplace to order jewelry from Earth Spirit Designs or to subscribe to 'Grassroots Magazine.' The site asserts that all businesses listed here have undergone a screening process using Co-op America Standards.

- **KEYWORDS** Business, Environmental Ethics, Ethics
- **AUDIENCE** Environmental Activists, Health Nuts, Organic Businesses
- **CONTACT** admin@envirolink.org
- **FREE**

http://envirolink.org/products/

Training and Seminar Locators (TASL) ★★★★

This site is the home page of Training and Seminar Locators (TASL) which focuses on helping people in business and industry find training and development resources nationwide. The free access database will provide detailed information on seminars, certificate programs by schools and commercial providers, satellite presentations, industry conferences, computer based training products, training and meeting facilities, and satellite downlink sites. This database that can be searched by type of resource, subject, geographic location, date, and more.

- **KEYWORDS** Directories, Non Profit Organizations, Seminars, Training Programs
- **AUDIENCE** Business Educators, Business Professionals
- **CONTACT** Margie Sweeny
  mms@tasl.com
- **FREE**

http://www.tasl.com/tasl/home.html

Non Profits

See also
Business & Economics · *Career & Employment*
Business & Economics · *Services*
Government & Politics · *Cities*
Science · *Career & Employment*

Bay Area Volunteer Information Center home page ★★★

This site lists almost fifty non-profit and human service organizations that are currently accepting volunteers to work on various projects. Volunteers are needed to do just about anything from repairing computers to picking fruit to making sandwiches. Time commitments can range from a few hours for a single project to as much time as you have available. Some organizations listed here include Big Brothers/Big Sisters, Computer Recycling Center, Habitat For Humanity, and the San Mateo County Food Bank. Contact information, description of volunteer needs, and where applicable, a hot link to the an organization are all provided.

- **KEYWORDS** Philanthropy, Volunteers
- **AUDIENCE** Californians, Foundations, Nonprofit Organizations, Volunteers
- **CONTACT** meernet
  info@meer.net
- **FREE**

http://www.meer.net/~taylor/index.html

Encore Systems ★★★

Encore Systems recycles used furniture to nonprofit organizations. It will collect your surplus furniture if you need a charitable donation. Encore arranges the transfer or disposal of the furniture at no charge to either party.

- **KEYWORDS** Furniture Recycling, Office Furniture
- **AUDIENCE** Business Professionals, Nonprofit Organizations
- **CONTACT** michaell@semaphore.com
- **FREE**

http://www.semaphore.com/encore

INTAC Public Service Venue
★★★

This home page from the Internet provider INTAC Access Corporation is devoted to groups, projects, and news that serve the public good. It houses some sites like Human Rights Web, give links to important services elsewhere and relevant newsgroups.

- **KEYWORDS** Internet Networking
- **AUDIENCE** Activists, Environmentalists, Nonprofit Organizations
- **CONTACT** www@intac.com
- **FREE**

http://www.intac.com/PubService/Service.html

Impact Online ★★★★

This home page features Impact Online, a new organization that can help people get involved with non profits nationwide through the use of technology. They are developing online domains for non profit organizations. Here you can find profiles of some of these charitable organizations, a marketplace, and products and services for non profits. The focus is on economic development and employment, and education.

- **KEYWORDS** Internet Networking
- **AUDIENCE** Activists, Community Activists, Network Users, Nonprofit Organizations
- **CONTACT** ImpactOL@aol.com
- **FREE**

http://www.webcom.com/~iol/

Internet Non-Profit Center ★★★★

The Internet Non-Profit Center, a project of the American Institute of Philanthropy, aims to provide free, fast, and easy access to information on non-profit organizations, wise donating practices, and issues of concern to donors and volunteers. The viewer will find links to and descriptions of non-profit organizations, listed by name, location, and purpose. A library section contains databases of information about various non-profits, generally by sources other than the non-profits themselves. This section includes ratings of non-profits for potential donors, financial data, and articles for donors and non-profits to consider. Other areas include newsletters, announcements, and links to related sites.

KEYWORDS Networking, Philanthropy, Volunteers
AUDIENCE Activists, Foundations, Grantmakers, Non-profit Organizations, Volunteers
FREE

http://human.com/inc/index.html

gopher://gopher.human.com/11/inc

Internet Resources for Non-Profit Organizations ★★★★

This home page presents a guide for non-profit organizations, created in order to help administrators and employees of non profit, public service organizations easily locate relevant information on the Internet. Only resources that are publicly available on the Internet are included. General information can be found about nonprofit activity, relevant business information, government sites and regulations, information on human service programs and activities.

KEYWORDS Grants, Non Profit Organizations
AUDIENCE Activists, Network Users, Nonprofit Organizations, Philantropists
CONTACT public-services@umich.edu
FREE

http://asa.ugl.lib.umich.edu:80/chdocs/nonprofits/nonprofits.h tml

Meta-Index for Non-Profit Organizations ★★★★

This home page offers an extensive index for Non-profits. There are links to other general lists of non-profit organizations, information for nonprofit organizations and activists (including financial and legal aid), news about human rights, civil liberties and politics, health and human services, environmental issues and animal rights.

KEYWORDS Grants, Meta-Indexes, Non Profit Organizations
AUDIENCE Activists, Nonprofit Organizations, Philanthropists
CONTACT ellens@ai.mit.edu
FREE

http://www.ai.mit.edu/people/ellens/non-meta.html#info

Non-profit Energy Savings Investment Program ★★

This is the home page for the Non-profit Energy Savings Investment Program (NESIP), which helps non-profit organizations implement successful energy saving projects by increasing nonprofit managers' and staff's awareness and understanding of energy issues, providing objective and accurate technical expertise and management assistance, providing financial assistance in the form of low-interest loans to implement energy efficiency measures and other energy cost reduction strategies.

KEYWORDS Business Services, Energy, Energy Conservation
AUDIENCE Managers, Nonprofit Organizations, Pennsylvania Residents
FREE

http://libertynet.org/community/nesip/nesip.html

Non-Profit Technology Resources Home Page ★★★

The home page is for the Non-profit Technology Resources (NTR). In the Greater Philadelphia region, NTR provides computer consulting, telephone support and hands-on training to over 200 nonprofit organizations annually. It is the only computer consulting organization in the area devoted exclusively to nonprofits. It can help with accounting systems, fundraising systems, client service records, budget planning tools, mailing lists, merged mailings, print and data communications.

KEYWORDS Accounting, Business Services, Telecommunications
AUDIENCE Computer Users, Nonprofit Organizations, Pennsylvania Residents
CONTACT pokras@libertynet.org
FREE

http://libertynet.org/~pokras/ntr.html

PAW - Non Profit Resources Catalogue ★★★★

This home page from Phillip A. Walker offers you a large and well organized index with a wealth of sites of interest to nonprofits. Information is listed under the following headings: Business and Work, General Nonprofit Resources, General Reference, Health and Human Services, Internet in General, News Sources, Other Nonprofit Issues, Other Personal Interests, United States Government, United Way on the Internet, Weather and Disasters, and more.

KEYWORDS Business Services, Grants, Reference
AUDIENCE Activists, Community Activists, General Public, Nonprofit Organizations
CONTACT pwalker@clark.net
FREE

http://www.clark.net/pub/pwalker/home.html

The PHnet Home Page ★★★

This is a home page from PHNet. The Philippine Network Foundation, Inc. (PFI) is a consortium of institutions, initially from academia and research (also government and private businesses), which aims to establish a national network called PHnet, formerly known as Philnet, with access to the Internet. It includes a directory of members with contact persons, phones, and emails.

KEYWORDS Asia, Internet Networking, Philippines
AUDIENCE Asians, Business Professionals, Network Users, Philippine Residents
FREE

http://www.dost.gov.ph/DOST/DOSTMIS/PHNET/Phnet.html

Connections to Charities

Your help is needed now!

There are hundreds of charities around the world that cater to any number of causes—diseases, human rights, education, and so on— that need your help, both financial and in volunteer services.

If you live in the U.S., there are a number of Internet sites that provide a complete list of charities and descriptions of their focus. If you want a breakdown of Human Service related charities, there are sites that provide that information, including how you can volunteer as well as contribute financially to their causes.

(http://www.charities.org/charity.html)

also, (http://www.charities.org/about.html)

There is even a site with an interactive questionnaire that helps charities discover attitudes about the work being done. Or you can find out about "Tax Efficient Charitable Gifts in the United Kingdom." Did you know that you can tell the tax man to give your tax to charity? You can even participate in an "Online Charity Auction." The money, of course, goes to worthy causes.

(http://mkn.co.uk/help/extra/people/jlfeis)

also, (http://www.futurenet.co.uk/charity/index.html)

also, (http://www.vdospk.com/onlineyp/auction/index.html)

Non Profits – Publishing

The Philanthropy Journal
 ★★★

This page hosts the online sampler of The Philanthropy Journal of North Carolina, a print publication dealing with news, announcements, and connections for nonprofit, volunteer, and fundraising organizations, primarily based in North Carolina. The monthly online journal contains five to ten articles, as well as help wanted ads for philanthropic, nonprofit, and educational institutions. Topics of recent articles include leadership training for nonprofit staff, innovative educational programs, and communication strategies.

- KEYWORDS: Employment, Grants, Philanthropy, Volunteers
- AUDIENCE: Activists, Foundations, Fundraisers, Non-profit Organizations, Volunteers
- CONTACT: webmasters@merlin.nando.net
- FREE

http://www.nando.net/philant/philant.html

Progressive & Non-Profit Organizations on the Net
★★

This page provides a list of links to progressive and non-profit organizations on the net. Topics covered include Youth Organizations and Networks, Socialist and Left Organizations, People of Color Environmental Groups Directory, Women's Rights Organizations, and more.

- KEYWORDS: Environment, Women's Issues
- AUDIENCE: Community Activists, Nonprofit Organizations, Political Activists, Progressives
- CONTACT: edinlinks@garnet.berkeley.edu
- FREE

http://garnet.berkeley.edu:3333/progorgs/progorgs.html

Resources for Grant Writers on the Internet
★★★

This small home page offers useful links to resources for grantwriters available on Internet. These materials are focused either on general information of use to nonprofits, listings of grants available, and sources to contact for grants.

- KEYWORDS: Activism, Business Services, Grants, Non Profit Organizations
- AUDIENCE: Activists, Grantseekers, Nonprofit Organizations
- CONTACT: trinket@umich.edu
- FREE

http://www.umich.edu/~trinket/Resources_for_Grant.html

WWW Guide to Community Networking
★★★

The WWW Guide to Community Networking offers a series of links to communities around the United States that provide a variety of services, such as Disabilities Resources, Weather Updates, Legal, Business or Environment information so that others can learn from their example. CivicNets around the United States, Canada and the world are also linked.

- KEYWORDS: Community, Internet Networking, Non Profit Organizations, Online Guides
- AUDIENCE: Activists, Community Activists, General Public, Nonprofit Organizations
- FREE

http://http2.sils.umich.edu/~ckummer/community.html

Welcome to The Foundation Center's Home Page
★★★

This home page presents The Foundation Center - an independent non profit organization established by several foundations in 1956. Its mission is to increase public understanding of the foundation field. It maintains a comprehensive and up-to-date database on foundations and corporate giving programs, produces directories, and analyzes trends in foundation support of the nonprofit sector. It also publishes The Foundation Directory—the classic reference work for grantseekers—and some 50 other directories, guides and research reports. The information from the database is available electronically through custom searching and online services.

- KEYWORDS: Financial Information, Grants
- AUDIENCE: Activists, Nonprofit Organizations, Philanthropists
- CONTACT: Webmaster@fdncenter.org
- FREE

http://fdncenter.org/

Publishing

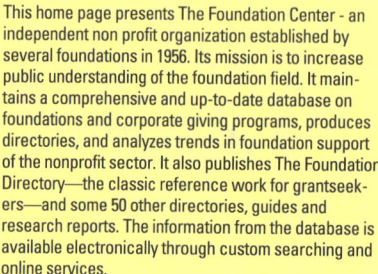

See also
Arts & Music · *Electronic Arts*
Humanities & Social Sciences · *Literature*
Popular Culture & Entertainment · *Books*

A Clean Well Lighted Place For Books
 ★★★

This site is the home of the California bookstore, A Clean Well-Lighted Place for Books. Here you can find events calendars for all of their bookstores, staff favorite booklists, and an order form. They also include a monthly newsletter and a compiled list of translated fiction authors.

- KEYWORDS: Bookstores, California, Literature, Newsletters
- AUDIENCE: Book Readers, Educators, Publishing Students, Writers
- CONTACT: jwscott@well.com
- FREE

http://www.well.com/user/jwscott/index.html

Book Stacks Unlimited, Inc.
 ★★★★

The Book Stacks Web Bookstore offers over 300,000 titles, which you can search by author, title, subject, and ISBN, and you can order right online. Other features include: the ability to save titles in a BookBag, an 800 number for transmitting credit card information, links to favorite authors, the latest book related happenings on the Internet, the Electronic Library where thousands of copyright free ebooks are available, and the Book Cafe for book discussion.

- KEYWORDS: Batman, Books, Bookstores
- AUDIENCE: Book Enthusiasts, Children, Educators, Librarians, Parents, Publishing Students
- CONTACT: Paul Phillips
  paulp@primus.com
- FREE

http://www.books.com/

BookWire Home Page
 ★★★★

BookWire is a collection of all the Internet's resources related to books and the book publishing industries. It contains listings and links to book publishers, sellers, libraries, and electronic publishers with an Internet presence. There is an index of online books, a meta-index of book-related indexes, listings of book and publishing conferences, events, and weekly best-seller listings.

- KEYWORDS: Books, Electronic Publishing, Media, Publishing
- AUDIENCE: Book Enthusiasts, Electronic Publishers, Publishers, Publishing Professionals
- CONTACT: Jamey Bennett
  www@bookwire.com, info@bookwire.com
- FREE

http://www.bookwire.com/

Briarwood WWW System
★★★

This WWW site provides information about Briarwood, an electronic publishing company. It allows subscribers to set up an account to browse through the store. The material produced by the company is primarily educational material aimed at the K-12 grade levels.

- KEYWORDS: Electronic Media, Electronic Publishing, Multimedia, Primary/Secondary Education
- AUDIENCE: Educators (Primary/Secondary), Publishing Educators
- CONTACT: webmaster@briarwood.com
- COST

http://www.briarwood.com/

Cajun CD-ROM Acrobat Journals Using Networks
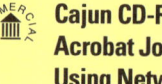  ★★★

Cajun is a project to disseminate the content of various journals over networks and on CD-ROM. Currently, their web site provides access to a selection of seven downloadable articles on electronic publishing collected in the journal, 'Electronic Publishing—Origination Dissemination and Design.' This site is still under construction with plans to include more journals in the future.

- KEYWORDS: Electronic Publishing
- AUDIENCE: Electronic Publishers, Publishers

CONTACT Steve Probets
sgp@cs.nott.ac.uk

FREE

http://www.ep.cs.nott.ac.uk/epoddcaj.html

Combined AAUP Online Catalog/Books ★★★

The Combined AAUP Online Catalog/Books site contains a searchable index of books from publishers in the AAUP (Association of American University Presses). It also has links to online sites of individual academic presses for searching, special academic publishing online projects, and guidelines for preparing an electronic manuscript.

KEYWORDS Books, Internet Guides, Publishing
AUDIENCE Academics, Book Readers, Educators, General Public
CONTACT Chuck Creesy
creesy@pupress.princeton.edu

FREE

http://aaup.pupress.princeton.edu/

Conari ★★★

This is the catalog for Conari Press, publisher of children's books and miscellaneous self-help literature. It contains gifs of cover art, highlights new releases, and allows users to sign onto a mailing list.

KEYWORDS Books, Children's Literature, Publishing
AUDIENCE Book Readers, Children, General Public
CONTACT www@organic.com

FREE

http://www.organic.com/Books/Conari/index.html

Cooperative Internet Catalog ★★★

This site is an on-line catalog of books from several small publishing companies. The catalog is part of the TitleBank Internet Catalog produced by Inforonics, Inc. The catalog has a directory structure and is searchable by author, title or keyword. The topics range from childrens books to computer books and more. There is book ordering information provided.

KEYWORDS Internet Resources, Marketing, Online Services, Publishing
AUDIENCE Booksellers, General Public, Publishers, Reading Enthusiasts
CONTACT info@infor.com

FREE

gopher://infx.infor.com:4300/

Cybernautics Digest ★★★

Cybernautics Digest is a monthly newsletter that summarizes important articles published in the business, technical, and consumer press. The publication focuses on articles that provide insightful analysis of new information technologies, and trends, with a special emphasis on converging information technologies. Each issue includes details on how to retrieve the full text of cited articles via conventional mail or electronic full-text databases. The Web site also features excerpts from back issues. Cybernautics Digest is published monthly and subscription information is available here.

KEYWORDS Information Technology, Multimedia
AUDIENCE Academics, Financial Analysts, Journalists, Researchers
CONTACT twhansen@cuix.pscu.com

FREE

http://www.pscu.com/cyber.html

The Electronic Newsstand ★★★

The Electronic Newsstand provides access to a wide range of magazines. Some of the topics covered include computers, technology, science, business, foreign affairs, and the arts. The contents from all magazines are available, as well as a few articles from the current issue. The magazine collection is searchable by keywords.

KEYWORDS Electronic Media, Electronic Publishing, Magazines, Online Books
AUDIENCE General Public, News Buffs, Reading Enthusiasts
CONTACT comments@enews.com

FREE

gopher://gopher.enews.com/

Connections to Macmillan Publications
Where can I get the latest technology information?

Use the Internet to connect to Macmillan Publishing USA, where the publisher offers an Information SuperLibrary (tm). The site is also home of Macmillan Digital, and the world's largest computer book publisher, Macmillan Computer Publishing.
  Visit Macmillan's imprints - Adobe Press, Brady, Hayden, New Riders, Que, Que College, Sams, and Sams.net to get the latest offerings in software, or information regarding such things as digital artwork. Macmillan's will soon add a General Reference and Macmillan Library Reference will be added to the SuperLibrary.

(http://www.mcp.com/)

Greyden Press Gopher Server ★★★

This gopher is an online bookstore providing publications from Greyden Press. The bookstore may be searched by keyword or by titles, authors, or subjects. The information here includes excerpts and reviews of the publications. It is possible to link to other online bookstores from here.

KEYWORDS Books, Internet Resources, Online Books, Publishing
AUDIENCE Book Readers, Consumers, Publishers
CONTACT info@zip.com

FREE

gopher://gopher.zip.com/

Hermit's Electronic Publishing Page ★★★★

Hermit's Electronic Publishing Page offers a variety of links and information on electronic publishing. Users will find links to many Internet resources with information on publishing electronically, as well as a collection of samples that show effective design techniques.

Additional information on the sites that are linked is provided.

KEYWORDS Electronic Publishing, Internet Publishing, Web Publishing, Zines
AUDIENCE Electronic Publishers, Internet Publishers
CONTACT Hermit
hermit@iglou.com
FREE

http://iglou.com/hermit/epub/epub.html

 Imaja Home Page

The Imaja Home Page offers users information on this California-based graphic software publishing company with downloadable demos and samples of their art, music, and screen saver programs. Users can access a listing of Imaja products, descriptions and prices as well as information on current sales and specials.

KEYWORDS Graphics, Multimedia Publishing, Software Publishing
AUDIENCE Graphic Designers, Macintosh Owners, Software Dealers
CONTACT Greg Jalbert
software@imaja.com
FREE

http://www.imaja.com/imaja/

 Inforonics Gopher Server

This is a gopher menu maintained and organized by Inforonics. The menu offers access to information about publishing companies and their books. A search may be done by title, subject or keyword. There are book reviews and descriptions that give information about individual titles. Books may be purchased by using the fax order forms supplied.

KEYWORDS Books, Catalogs, Companies, Publishing
AUDIENCE Book Dealers, Book Readers, Booksellers, Publishing Professionals
CONTACT Inforonics
info@infor.com
FREE

gopher://gopher.infor.com/

 Interleaf Incorporated

The Interleaf site provides users with information on its integrated document management technology. Specific information is given on Interleaf products, Internet publishing, and a list of organizations now using Interleaf's services. To learn more about Interleaf's style of document management, visit the 'Document Management Library.'

KEYWORDS Document Management, Internet Publishing, Software
AUDIENCE Business Professionals
CONTACT i-direct@ileaf.com
FREE

http://www.ileaf.com

 Jason Aronson Publishers

This is a catalog of books published by Jason Aronson Publishers. Users can browse Judaica books by title or browse Psychotherapy books by subject category. There are also interviews with authors in the two respective categories.

KEYWORDS Books, Judaica, Psychology, Psychotherapy
AUDIENCE Book Readers, Jews, Psychologists
CONTACT jane@aronson.com
FREE

http://www.aronson.com/clients/aronson/

 Manic D Press

The Web site of Manic D Press, a book and comic publisher, provides information about their latest publications. Listings include plot summaries, the genre, and brief reviews, as well as an ordering form for individuals or bookstores/libraries. Also included is a list of upcoming readings and events, and distributors of Manic D Press publications nationwide.

KEYWORDS Comics, Contemporary Literature, Publishing
AUDIENCE Book Enthusiasts, Comics Enthusiasts
CONTACT nadja@sirius.com
FREE

http://www.well.com/user/manicd/index.html

 Nando Times Financial Report

This page is an electronic daily newspaper, containing a short stock report from NYSE (New York Stock Exchange)—indices, volumes (advanced and declined), most active stocks, and the most important business and financial news. Areas covered include investment markets, US and international business, and economic trends. Headlines of key happenings around the world can also be found. The newspaper is produced by the News & Observer Publishing Co. and is a part of commercial NandO.net.

KEYWORDS Economic Indicators, Investment, Online Newspapers, Stock Market
AUDIENCE Business Analysts, Financial Analysts, Investors, Market Analysts
FREE

http://www.nando.net/newsroom/nt/biz.html

 O'Reilly & Associates

This site provides information about the products available from O'Reilly & Associates, a publishing company specializ ing in books about UNIX and the Internet. The information offered includes reviews and excerpts from books, ordering information, sample software from their books, reviews, and bibliographies. The bookstore may be searched by the directories, or by keyword.

KEYWORDS Bookstores, Computing, Online Books, Publishing
AUDIENCE Computer Users, Internet Users, UNIX Users

CONTACT Tim O'Reilly
tim@ora.com
FREE

gopher://gopher.ora.com/

Publishing Resources on the Internet

This document is a compilation of information resources focused on publishing. Topics cover book, magazine, and electronic publishing, rare books, and other publishing issues. Resources may include Internet/Bitnet Mailing Lists, Gophers, World Wide Web Sites, Mail Servers, Usenet Newsgroups, FTP Archives, Commercial Online Services, and Bulletin Board Systems.

KEYWORDS Bibliographies, Books, Electronic Publishing, Publishing
AUDIENCE Book Dealers, Book Readers, Publishers
FREE

ftp://una.hh.lib.umich.edu/inetdirsstacks/publishing:robinson

 Redbear Graphics

Redbear Graphics is a small personal graphic design and WWW publishing company located in Northwest Montana's Glacier Country. The topics include cool links, Montana art & artists, gifts, books, resorts, and real estate and relocation. The page has heavy graphics and may require some patience to download. The current database has over 150,000 licensed and royalty free images for you to view.

KEYWORDS E-Zines, Electronic Publishing, Graphic Design, Montana
AUDIENCE Business Professionals, Internet Users, Montana Residents, Real Estate Professionals
CONTACT Craig R. Kolb
redbear@libby.org
FREE

http://www.libby.org/redbear/rb1.html

 Scholastic Home Page

Scholastic Home Page provides a gateway for the books and other publications produced by Scholastic Inc., whose products are intended for children and their teachers. Services offered are online catalogs of educational materials, online libraries, and newsletters. Products can be ordered through this site.

KEYWORDS Books, Children, Children's Literature, Primary/Secondary Education
AUDIENCE Children, Educators (Primary/Secondary), Parents, Publishing Educators
CONTACT staff@scholastic.com
FREE

http://Scholastic.com:2005/

 Springer-Verlag New York

Springer-Verlag publishes scientific books and journals for the scientist, researcher, student, interested reader, or anyone within the scientific community seeking to further explore the world of science as we now know it.

Publishing

This page contains Springer's newsletters and brochures, an online list of products, and samples and tables of contents from some of Springer-Verlag's publications. Some titles include 'MRI Physics for Radiologists—A Visual Approach,' 'Mathematics and Politics,' and 'The Maize Structure Atlas.' Other files on this site are Text macros, newsletters describing recent publications in Mathematics and Science, electronic journal archives, library news, and a hot list of scientific and mathematics sites.

KEYWORDS Electronic Journals, Publishers, Scientific Publishing
AUDIENCE Science Educators, Science Researchers, Scientists
CONTACT WebMaster@www.springer-ny.com
FREE

http://www.springer-ny.com

 Taugher Books on the World Wide Web

This Web Page contains information on books available at Taugher Books, a bookstore in Belmont, CA. Users can search an index for individual books, as well as find out about ordering and books on sale.

KEYWORDS Books, Bookstores, Fiction, Reference
AUDIENCE Book Readers, General Public
CONTACT Dennis M. Taugher
         taugher@batnet.com
FREE

http://www.batnet.com/taugher/

 Welcome to Booksonline!

This site offers electronic books online in formats for both PC and Macintosh users. There are charges for ordering the books.

KEYWORDS Books, Electronic Books, Publishing
AUDIENCE PC MAC Users
CONTACT Newbridge Communications, Inc.
         service@booksonline.com
COST

http://booksonline.com

 Westlaw Publishing Company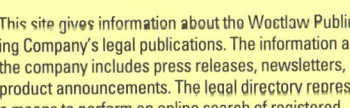

This site gives information about the Westlaw Publishing Company's legal publications. The information about the company includes press releases, newsletters, and product announcements. The legal directory represents a means to perform an online search of registered lawyers and law companies.

KEYWORDS Companies, Law, Legal Research, Publishing
AUDIENCE General Public, Lawyers, Legal Professionals
CONTACT wldhelp@research.westlaw.com
FREE

gopher://wld.westlaw.com/

For Connections To Magazines

Pssst . . . did you hear about Sharon Stone?

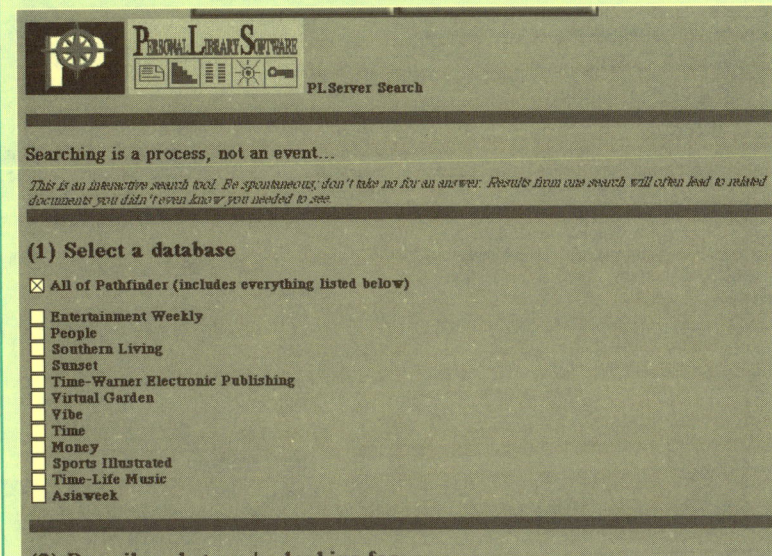

Following American actress Sharon Stone's appearance at the Cannes Film Festival, Hollywood wags began asking the question, "How many people does it take to color Sharon Stone's hair?" The answer, "Ten. One colorist, and nine people in her entourage to watch!"

Such information was in an issue of People magazine. You can get People, US, Time, Newsweek, a bevy of computer publications (such as Home PC), a number of special interest magazines, and magazines from around the world via the Internet.

You can also search a database of magazine articles by category. Select gardening, for instance, and you might pull up a story in Sunset magazine on hanging gardens. You can even look up the latest news on a celebrity by searching the database using that person's name.

(http://www.pathfinder.com/@@FzokcgAAAAAAGjV/cgi-bin/taos_mf.pl?Unix)

Worldwide Publishing Consortium Online

The Worldwide Publishing Consortium is an organization dedicated to shaping the future of publishing. Its mission is to provide an independent international forum for the publishing, graphic arts, communications and multimedia industries to facilitate the exchange of information and the advancement of education. The site is under construction, and contains an outline with many links missing. Some of the areas that are available include mission statements, a who's who of the Board of Directors, information about its corporate sponsors, and a hotlist of publishing and more general Internet Resources.

KEYWORDS Communications, Graphics, Multimedia, Publishing
AUDIENCE Authors, Graphic Designers, Marketing Professionals, Publishers, Writers
CONTACT Bill Wilt
         wilt@rt66.com
FREE

http://rt66.com/twl/WWPC.index.html

 Wyvern Business Library

The Wyvern Business Library is an online bookstore specializing in business titles. At this web site users can access a short listing of business titles including a listing of current new business books for each month. The site also includes a short listing of video and software business products. Users can subscribe to Book-Talk which offers weekly reviews of business materials and can request a free copy of 'Dirty Negotiating Tactics Special Report.'

KEYWORDS Online Bookstores
AUDIENCE Business Publishers, Business Readers
CONTACT wyvern@wyvern.co.uk
FREE

http://www.cityscape.co.uk/users/ab96/

Business & Economics

Real Estate

Business & Economics · Industries
Business & Economics · Investment

ACCNET's Free Real Estate Listing Service ★★

This site provides a free listing service for Real Estate on this Internet. Potential home buyers can search for homes meeting their criteria, including price, location, views, construction materials, tax status, house style, and lot size. There is also information about how to list your house on these pages, as well as how to make money through networking on the Internet.

KEYWORDS	Employment, Home Ownership, Real Estate, Real Estate Listings
AUDIENCE	Home Buyers, Home Owners, Job Seekers, Real Estate Agents, Real Estate Brokers
CONTACT	ACCNET Resource Center root@accnet.com
FREE	

http://accnet.com/homes/index.html

AmericaNet Real Estate Listings ★★★

AmericaNet Real Estate Listings provides links to media concepts, nationwide listings, selling your home on the Internet, and images. Information is provided on Appraisers, Surveyors, Property Inspectors, Movers, Builders, Realtors, as well as Community Profiles.

KEYWORDS	Appraisals, Construction Industry, Loans, United States
AUDIENCE	Investors, Lawyers, Marketing Professionals, Real Estate Professionals
CONTACT	Joe Goldsberry joegold@tiac.net
FREE	

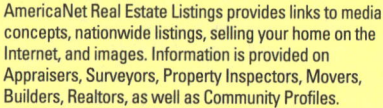

http://www.tiac.net/users/joegold/index.html

Brigadoon.com, Incorporated ★★

Brigadoon.com, Inc. is a parent company with divisions offering Internet services in Real Estate, Electronics, Private Education, and Retail Sales. Their home page provides users with a diverse selection of resources from information on computer networking equipment and private education in the U.S., to accessing a bimonthly Real Estate Magazine and an Internet mall. Corporate information on Brigadoon.com, Inc. is also available.

KEYWORDS	Business Services, Internet Services, Online Marketing
AUDIENCE	Internet Marketers, Internet Shoppers
CONTACT	gsnook@brigadoon.com
FREE	

http://networksnw.com/

Consumer Mortgage Information Network ★★★

This site provides home buyers with a source of information about the financing of a home. A home buyer's qualification program for residential financing can be downloaded for free from here. A library of related articles and government publications as well as a list of links to related sites on the Internet can also be accessed here.

KEYWORDS	Financial Information, Financial Planning, Mortgages
AUDIENCE	Home Buyers, Real Estate Agents, Real Estate Brokers
CONTACT	proactive@human.com
FREE	

http://www.human.com/proactive/index.html

The Corcoran Group ★★★

The Corcoran Group specializes in the sale of luxury co-ops and codominiums in Manhattan. There is an extensive list of links to properties for sale in New York City. The links are organized by area, number of bedrooms, and type of residence. Prices range from a couple of hundred thousand dollars to millions. The Corcoran Report, an in-depth semi-annual pubication of a Survey and Analysis of Conditions and Trends in the New York City Luxury Co-op/Condominium Marketplace, is also available here.

KEYWORDS	Commercial Real Estate, Exclusive Properties, Luxury Condominiums, Manhattan
AUDIENCE	Buyers, New York Residents, Real Estate Brokers
FREE	

http://www.innobits.com/~innobits/sales/corcoran/corcoran.html

Fair Oaks Financial Serivce ★★★★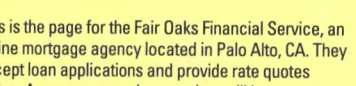

This is the page for the Fair Oaks Financial Service, an online mortgage agency located in Palo Alto, CA. They accept loan applications and provide rate quotes online. As your personal agent, they will locate a competitive home loan, whether it is from a bank, thrift, or other lending institution.

KEYWORDS	California, Home Loans, Mortgages, Real Estate
AUDIENCE	Californians, Home Buyers, Mortgage Brokers, Real Estate Agents
CONTACT	Mark Leaver markl@fofs.com
FREE	

http://fofs.best.com/

GEN Inc.'s Worldwide Real Estate Forum ★★

This site provides links and information to various real estate-related issues and industries. Topics include real estate listings, community information, information on related industries such as appraisers, escrow companies, pest control, home repairs, etc.

KEYWORDS	California, Insurance, Real Estate, Real Estate Listings
AUDIENCE	Appraisers, Home Buyers, Home Sellers, Mortgage Brokers, Real Estate Brokers
CONTACT	webmaster@terminus.com
FREE	

http://www.terminus.com/geni/USA/CA/San_Francisco/RE/index.html

HomeOwners Finance ★★★

This home page from mortgage broker HomeOwners Finance contains everything for home owners and buyers. Here you will find HomeOwners Finance's current loan programs and rates, commentary on the latest trends in interest rates, a wealth of information on getting a loan, actual current loan rates, closing cost estimates, refinancing alternatives, and rates. A glossary of terms and tutorial information on loans is included. You can apply for a loan directly from the page.

KEYWORDS	Interest Rates, Investment Advice, Mortgages, Real Estate
AUDIENCE	Consumers, Home Buyers, Home Owners, Investors
CONTACT	Dick Lepre rlepre@hooked.net
FREE	

http://www.internet-is.com/homeowners/in-new.html

Internet Real Estate Directory ★★★★

The Internet Real Estate Directory strives to be the most complete and useful list of real estate sites on the World Wide Web. This site provides extensive links to real estate-related sites around the world. You can search by state or country, by buying or listing services, or by miscellaneous topics such as financing, open homes, brokers' names, etc.

KEYWORDS	Home, Real Estate, Real Estate Listings
AUDIENCE	Mortgage Brokers, Real Estate Brokers, Real Estate Professionals
CONTACT	Becky Swann becky@onramp.net
FREE	

http://rampages.onramp.net/~becky/relist.html

Mortgage Insurance Frequently Asked Questions ★★

This page provides an FAQ on mortgage insurance. The page is updated ocassionally. Questions include: Are any pre-paid premium amounts refunded if mortgage insurance is cancelled? How do the mortgage insurance escrows get applied to the payment? And does mortgage insurance apply for investor properties? The answers are complete and clear.

KEYWORDS Finance, Home, Loans
AUDIENCE Home Buyers, Home Sellers, Investors, Lenders, Real Estate Professionals
FREE

http://www.homefair.com/homefair/PMI/pmiqa.html

NYSERNet Real Estate Service ★★★

NYSERNet Real Estate Service provides links to listing inventories of real estate companies from California to New York. Some of the companies include Arvida Realty Sales Ltd. - Boca Raton, FL, Residential Real Estate Service, Coldwell Banker, Latter & Blum/Realtors - New Orleans LA, and more.

KEYWORDS Housing, Property Listings, Real Estate Brokers, Residential Real Estate
AUDIENCE Bankers, Buyers, Mortgage Lenders, Real Estate Brokers
CONTACT info@nysernet.org
FREE

http://nysernet.org/cyber/realestate/index.html

Napa Valley Weekly Real Estate Reader Internet Edition ★★★★

The online edition of the Napa Valley Real Estate Reader provides a wealth of real estate information regarding this area of California. Visitors can access numerous descriptions including images of available properties, a large, frequently updated listing of open houses, the area's real estate classified section and even information on local mortgage rates.

KEYWORDS California, Real Estate, Real Estate Employment, Vineyards
AUDIENCE House Hunters, Napa Valley Residents, Real Estate Brokers
CONTACT reader@community.net
FREE

http://odin.community.net/~reader/

National Land Survey of Finland (NLS) ★★★

The National Land Survey of Finland (NLS) works in land-use and mapping services. The NLS maintains the country's real estate registers and archives and manages the national real estate information system. This site presents information on the mapping procedures, geographical information and access to the archives.

KEYWORDS Archives, Finland, Mapping
AUDIENCE Finns, Surveyors
CONTACT webmaster@www.mmh.fi
FREE

http://www.mmh.fi

Connections to World Real Estate
"Be in ever so humble, there's no place like home"

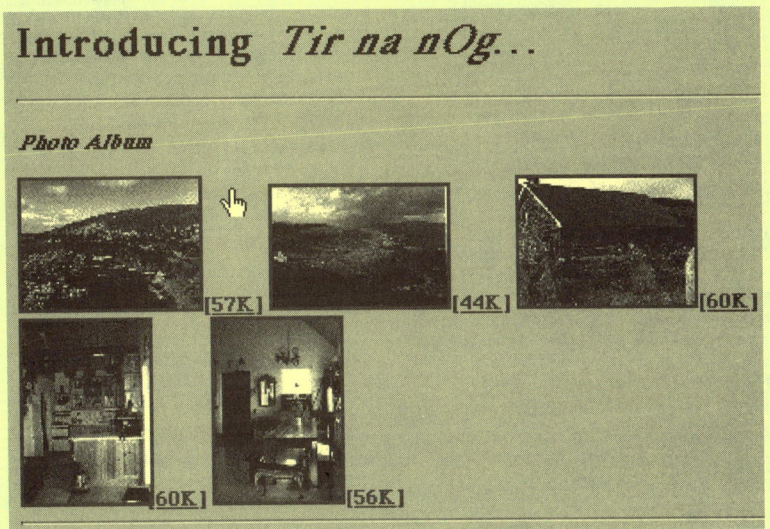

Are you in the market for a new home, a vacation home, or a time share? Or perhaps, you'd rather rent. The Internet furnishes connections to finding a home of your own no matter where you reside. Even if you are in the home-building or mortgage loan businesses, there are sites on the World Wide Web that provide information about development, financing, and construction issues.

(http://www.build.com/)

Whether you want to find a home in Hawaii or Rhode Island, you can get the latest listings and investigate each home and community through the "World of Real Estate" Web site.

(http://pcixous.deltanet.com/archive.html)

If owning a home in England, France, or Thailand is on your agenda, the "Real Estate Related" WWW Pages provide invaluable information and listings on homes and real estate in almost every country around the globe. Whether for sale or rental, the listings are organized by continent, country, state/province, and city or region. You receive complete descriptions of homes, prices, and contacts.

(http://www.xmission.com/~realtor1/relinks.html)

Net Properties Corporation Home Page ★★

The Net Properties Corporation Home Page provides links to HomeNet and CenterNet, which present the company's work in residential and corporate real estate commerce. Net Properties hopes to improve the efficiency of real estate commerce around the world by providing a comprehensive real estate resource online. Currently residential listings are limited to a few states in the United States, but the site also has links to real estate agencies, mortgage calculators, and real estate related news. The CenterNet commercial real estate listings, however, are under construction.

KEYWORDS Corporate Real Estate, Home, Real Estate, Real Estate Listings
AUDIENCE General Public, House Hunters, Movers, Real Estate Brokers
FREE

http://www.intertel.com/

The New York Cooperator—The Co-Op and Condo Monthly ★★★

The New York Cooperator is a magazine that serves the co-op and condo community. Information is provided on all co-op and condo ownership issues, including buying

Real Estate – Reference

and selling, financing, building maintenance, law and legislation, building management, insurance and interior design. The New York Cooperator is offered free to subscribers. You can recieve a free subscription by filling out a form and emailing it to the magazine.

KEYWORDS Co-ops, Condominiums, Housing, Magazines
AUDIENCE Co-op Owners, Condo Owners, Lawyers
CONTACT nycoop@aol.com
FREE

http://www.hia.com/hia/coop

Real Estate in Costa Rica ★★★

This Real Estate page has an online book concerning the legal and administrative details of buying property in Costa Rica, and links to two local legal firms specializing in real estate. You can also find a link to CINDE (Costa Rican Investment and Development), a private, non-profit organization devoted to contacting and advising foreign investors regarding their operations in the country, and a link to tourist information.

KEYWORDS Costa Rica, International Law
AUDIENCE Business Professionals, Latin Americans, Real Estate Brokers, Tourists
CONTACT inter@merica.cool.co.cr
FREE

http://www.cool.co.cr/cgi-bin/prop

Residential Mortgage Guide ★★★

The Residential Mortgage Guide produced by Royal Bank of Canada will show you how to reduce your mortgage costs by Reducing Your Amortization Period, Doubling up and Skipping A Payment, or by locking in a 60-Day Interest Rate Protection program. There are charts representing different terms, rates and payments. There are also links to additional mortgage features offered by this bank.

KEYWORDS Finance, Mortgages
AUDIENCE Canadians, Home Buyers, Home Sellers, Investors, Lenders, Real Estate Professionals
CONTACT Deborah L. Batten
         batten@netbistro.com
FREE

http://vortex.netbistro.com/royal/rmg.html

Sylvan Lawrence Company ★★★

This company, Sylvan Lawrence, advertises office space and real estate property in Manhattan, New York with space and availability information and contact names. Prospective clients can see images of the building, the surrounding views, and a simple floorplan. Other innovative features on this page are MPEG video clips of an aerial view and a 3D walkthough of a proposed office layout. MPEG's are at least 650K in size.

KEYWORDS Advertising, Marketing, New York, Property
AUDIENCE Business Professionals, New York Residents, Real Estate Brokers
CONTACT Jon Zeeff
         branch-info@branch.com
FREE

http://branch.com/sylvan/sylvan.html

Treb Web ★★★

The Treb Web site offers users real estate information for the Northwest Washington State region. The site includes listings of local real estate agencies with contact information as well as images of available properties, accompanied by barely legible descriptions for Island, Skagit, and Whatcom counties. This site is currently under construction and has plans to include information on these three communities in the future.

KEYWORDS Home Buyers, Real Estate Agencies, Washington (USA)
AUDIENCE House Buyers, Real Estate Agencies, Washington Residents
CONTACT treb@pacificrim.net
FREE

http://www.pacificrim.net/~treb/

What's New in Real Estate on the Net ★★★★

What's New in Real Estate on the Net provides links to and information about a wealth of real estate resources on the Internet. Data is presented on moving companies, there's an FAQ on mortgage insurance, information on relocation services, Fannie Mae, Asset-Integrated Mortgages, custom home designs, mortgage rate information, bulletin boards, links for home buyers, finance information, newsgroups, and information on online house tours. This is an informative starting point for all your real estate needs.

KEYWORDS Home, Mortgages
AUDIENCE Home Buyers, Home Sellers, Investors, Lenders, Real Estate Professionals
CONTACT Arnold Kling
         arnoldsk@us.net
FREE

http://www.homefair.com/homefair/otherinf.html

William B. May Company Real Estate Home Page ★★★

William B. May Company is one of the largest full-service real estate brokerages in the New York area, with 5 locations and over 120 agents. On this page you can access information on Communities Served, Property Listings, Company Resources, Customer Support and Services, and Office Locations.

KEYWORDS Brokerage Services, Commercial Real Estate, New York, Property Listings
AUDIENCE New York Residents, Real Estate Brokers, Real Estate Professionals
CONTACT hia2@hia.com
FREE

http://www.hia.com/hia/wbm

Reference

See also
Popular Culture & Entertainment · *General Reference*

Canada (Canadian News and Information Library) ★★★★

The Canadian News and Information Library (Canada) contains Canadian legal news in addition to business and company information. The Canada library contains respected Canadian news publications such as The Toronto Star, The Vancouver Sun, Ottawa Business News and the Montreal Gazette. The Canada library also offers Canadian company profiles, country reports, and Canada's financial database, Cancorp Plus.

KEYWORDS Canada, Commercial Databases, Companies, News Media
AUDIENCE Business Professionals, Canadians, Lawyers
CONTACT Mead New Sales Group
         webmaster@lexis-nexis.com
COST

http://www.meaddata.com

telnet://nex.meaddata.com

Directory of Government Sources of Business and Economic Information on the Internet ★★★★

This is an extensive database of documents and information resources covering a wide range of topics, including agriculture, census data, patent and legal sources. The site also contains official information from many government offices including the USDA, the National Institute of Standards and Technology, the Environmental Protection Agency, and NAFTA documentation.

KEYWORDS Business, Commerce, Economics
AUDIENCE General Public, Government Researchers
CONTACT Terese Austin
         tmurphy@sils.umich.edu
FREE

gopher://una.hh.lib.umich.edu/00/
        inetdirsstacks/
        govdocs%3atsangaustin

Financial Data Finder ★★★★

This home page provides an enormous directory of sources for financial information available on and off the Internet. A number of datasets can be downloaded right from the site. You will find jewels like Annual Historical British Stock Price and Macroeconomic Data since 1700 and Weekly Dow Jones Industrial Average 1900-1989. Other local resources which may interest you include Research Resources in Finance and The Journal of Finance and Educational Resources in Finance.

KEYWORDS Economic Policy, History, Meta-Index (Finance), Stock Market
AUDIENCE Business Analysts, Financial Analysts, Investors, Market Analysts

Reference **143**

CONTACT Tim Opler
topler@magnus.acs.ohio-state.edu

FREE

http://www.cob.ohio-state.edu/dept/fin/osudata.htm

Financial Encyclopedia ★★★★

This home page from Information Innovation is an interactive International Financial Encyclopedia of more than 1000 terms, symbols, financial products, finacial software, technologies used in the financial industry, and more. One can find very rare tidbits of information, such as an acronym for the Kuala Lumpur Stock Exchange and Swift Currency Code for the Kampuchean Riel. You can jump to the extensive management and technology dictionary, or cruise a wide array of links to related information on the Internet.

KEYWORDS   Financial Research, Internet Directories, Terminology
AUDIENCE   Business Professionals, Financial Professionals, Investors, Stockbrokers
CONTACT   Steve Bennett
innovation@euronet.nl

FREE

http://www.euro.net/innovation/Finance_Base/Fin_encyc.html

GNN PFC Company Reports ★★★

This index page provides links to a few company-specific resourses. You can jump to the NETworth List of Public Companies on the Web, which maintains a list of over 100 publicly traded companies with homepages on the WWW (World Wide Web); the SEC's (Securities and Exchange Commission) EDGAR Database - a huge collection of corporate disclosure filings to the Securities and Exchange Commission, and The Texas 500 - the online version of the reference book - The Texas 500 Hoover's Guide to the Top Texas Companies, published by the Reference Press of Austin, Texas.

KEYWORDS   Annual Reports, Companies, Finance, Financial Planning
AUDIENCE   Business Analysts, Investors, Market Analysts
CONTACT   Abbot Chambers
abbot@ora.com

FREE

http://nearnet.gnn.com/gnn/meta/finance/res/invest.reports.html

 Hoover's Online ★★★★

Hoover's Online provides two free Internet databases of company information. It combines the Hoover's MasterList database of information on all publicly-traded U.S. companies and Hoover's Company Profiles database of in-depth information on over 1500 of the world's largest and fastest-growing companies. Hoover's Online includes exclusive news, a database, and search and retrieval features. Don't forget to check out Hoover's Online for The List of Lists and The Top Ten Business News Stories for the current week. An extensive list of business reference products is also available for sale.

KEYWORDS   Stocks
AUDIENCE   Business Professionals, Investors, Librarians, Researchers, Students (University)

CONTACT   Tom Linehan
refpress@bga.com

FREE

http://www.hoovers.com
gopher://gopher.hoovers.com/

Connections to Home Repair
"There's no place like home…"

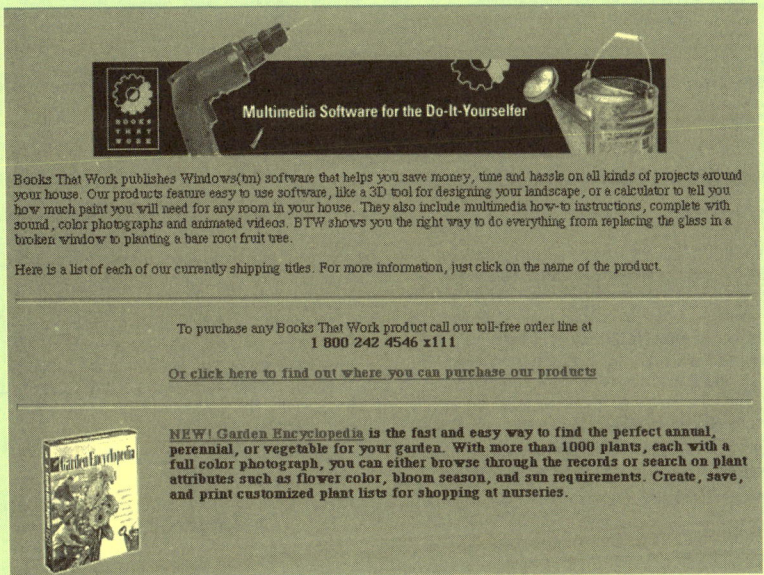

This phrase, which Dorothy repeats three times in the Hollywood classic, "The Wizard of Oz," may not sound so endearing if you have a leaky faucet, dry rot in the attic, or paint peeling from the ceiling. Whatever your home repair or maintenance need, the Internet serves up a wealth of information that can make the job a lot easier.

The best part of Internet home repair services is their visual nature—the user can see the correct way to perform a repair task. For instance, "Books that Work Products" offers interactive Windows software that instructs the user in such jobs as rewiring light fixtures, repairing a leak in the wash room plumbing, or building a bookcase for the den. Prices for the software are in the $20 range. For more ambitious home improvement buffs, there are a number of guides on how to build a deck off the back of your house, then later add a Jacuzzi.

(http://www.btw.com/products/products.htm)

Videos of home improvement tasks are also available— including demonstrations on the use of power tools and installation of doors and windows to the home—all this via the Internet's InfoVidOutlet:Home Improvement.

(hhtp//branch.com:1080/infovid/c320.html)

If you're looking for property to buy and restore, or for construction or restoration equipment, then "Commerce Business Daily" provides the needed resources. This source also furnishes International Government standards for construction in most countries throughout the world.

(http://cos.gdb.org/repos/cdb/cdb-into.html)

INCORPR (Corporation and Partnership Records) ★★★

The Corporation and Partnership Records (INCORPR) library contains current US corporation and partnership filings. The INCORPR library contains current records on corporations and limited partnerships registered with the Office of the Secretary or Department of State. These records include information extracted by the state's staff from articles of incorporation, annual reports, amendments, and other public filings.

KEYWORDS Corporation Guides, Corporations, Filings, Partnerships
AUDIENCE Business Professionals, Lawyers, Regulatory Agencies
COST

http://www.meaddata.com

telnet://nex.meaddata.com

Ideas DIGest Online—Home Page ★★★

Ideas DIGest Online is an electronic magazine about the business of innovation and the development of creative ideas for marketing. Articles cover subjects like ideas, innovation, inventions, patents, and licensing. Links include resource directories on business, intellectual property, product development, market development, and financial services. The home page presents how to incorporate without legal fees, an Investors Corner with thoughts about motivation, and a calendar of events and exhibitions.

KEYWORDS Inventions, Magazines, Small Business
AUDIENCE Entrepreneurs, Inventors
CONTACT idig@wimsey.com
FREE

http://www.wimsey.com/~idig/

Institute of Management & Administration (IOMA) ★★★★

The web site for the Institute Of Management and Administration, Information Services for Professionals offers a meta-index to business resources on the Internet. Topics include finance/accounting, purchasing, institutional investing, manufacturing, human resources, benefits and compensation, property/casualty insurance, design/construction, law firm management, CPA firm management and much more. They also offer trial subscriptions to leading business newsletters.

KEYWORDS (Meta-Index)Business, Law Firms, Management, Newsletters
AUDIENCE Accountants, Business Professionals, Institutional Investors, Lawyers, Managers
CONTACT Kathie Fitzgerald
         kathie@ingress.com
FREE

http://starbase.ingress.com/ioma/

Internet Business Center ★★★★

The Internet Business Center is a World Wide Web-based Internet business information center. The site provides new information about what companies are doing on the Internet and how those companies can conduct business more effectively on the Internet. Areas of focus include - Internet statistics, maps and charts, Internet business sites and services (commercial and non-commercial), vetted Internet information sources, net entertainment establishments. The site also contains information on Internet Marketing and Internet Publishing, available for a small fee, and many links to business related sites.

KEYWORDS Internet Business, Internet Marketing, Internet Publishing, Internet Resources
AUDIENCE Business Owners, Entrepreneurs, Internet Entrepreneurs
FREE

http://tig.com/IBC/Publishing/index.html

Internet Business Journal ★★★★

The Internet Business Journal is a twenty page monthly publication, dedicated to keeping businesses informed of opportunities and developments on the Internet. This Gopher and Web site contains a sampler of articles from the latest edition, as well as supplementary information such as an Advertising on the Internet Guide, The Geography of Cyberspace, and Using the Internet for Marketing. Further information on how to subscribe to the Internet Business Journal, order other publications, or arrange for a speaker, can also be obtained on this page.

KEYWORDS Internet Issues, Internet Marketing, Journals, WWW (World Wide Web)
AUDIENCE Business Professionals, Internet Professionals, Internet Users
FREE

http://www.phoenix.ca/sie/ibj-home.html

gopher://nis.fonorola.net:70/11/Internet%20Business%20Journal

LEXPAT (Patents US) ★★★

The LEXPAT library contains the full text of US patents issued since 1975, the US Patent and Trademark Office Manual of Classification, and the Index to US Patent Classification. The approximately 1,500 patents added to the library each week appear online within four days of their issue. LEXPAT may be searched by individual files for the full text of utility, design or plant patents, or all files can be searched via the 'omni' search. The Manual, Index and Class files can be used to supplement full-text patent searches. LEXPAT allows access to patent information, and also technical details on patented inventions/items. More than 80 percent of the information contained in patents is unavailable in any other form.

KEYWORDS Databases, Inventions, Patent Law, Patents
AUDIENCE Business Researchers, Inventors, Patent Lawyers, Patent Researchers
CONTACT Mead New Sales Group
COST

http://www.meaddata.com/libcont/lexpat.html

telnet://nex.meaddata.com

Money Online ★★★

Money Online provides a digest of the top business news of each day. Each issue contains news about the stock markets, the economy, government decisions, and company announcements. There are links to the previous day's digest, as well as to the Time Daily page, for a summary of non-economic headline stories. Currently there is a link to a promotion from YourFuture, a new personal finance magazine.

KEYWORDS Financial Planning, Money Markets, Online Newspapers
AUDIENCE Business Professionals, Marketing Professionals
CONTACT time-webmaster@www.timeinc.com
FREE

http://pathfinder.com:80/@@d6Y5EsCc@wAAQDqr/time/daily/money/1995/latest.html

National Locator & Data ★★★★

The National Locator & Data web site contains an extensive commercial database of information including Access to Public Records, Background Reports, Commercial Credit, Motor Vehicle Reports, Assets, Missing Persons, Unlisted Phone Numbers, Death Reports, Judgements, Bankruptcies, Address Identifiers, National Kris Cross Plus, and Surname Searches. Combination reports & searches will include a substantial discount depending volume ordered.

KEYWORDS Missing Persons, Public Records, Research
AUDIENCE Business Professionals, Lawyers, Researchers, Writers
CONTACT Richard Hodges
         info-broker@iu.net
FREE

http://iu.net/hodges

Thomas Register Home Page ★★★★

Thomas Register of American Manufacturers provides sourcing information on industrial products and services offered by 150,000 U.S. and Canadian companies in 52,000 categories. On this page you can search on a product or service and retrieve information on the companies who offer that product or service. There are also downloadable files, Information about the CD-ROM edition of the Thomas Register, information on how to list your company in the Thomas Register, and other information about Thomas publications.

KEYWORDS Industrial Products, Manufacturing, Sourcing Information
AUDIENCE Accountants, Business Professionals, Institutional Investors, Lawyers, Managers
CONTACT Vivien Tsu
         online@thomasregister.com
FREE

http://www.thomasregister.com

The Vietnamese Professionals Society ★★★★

The homepage of the Vietnamese Professionals Society is like a virtual guildhall for professionals of Vietnamese-descent all over the world, but mostly in the United States. The site has links to many other Vietnamese listings, including current lists of Vietnamese community meetings around the US, updates on Vietnamese software, newsletters about Vietnam and Vietnamese businesses, Vietnamese translations of professional journal publications, and much more. This is the place to go if you want to get connected to the Vietnamese professional and business community.

KEYWORDS Organizations, Professional Societies, Vietnamese Americans
AUDIENCE Business Analysts, Business Professionals, Vietnamese, Vietnamese Americans
CONTACT hcgvn@netcom.com
FREE

http://www.webcom.com/~hcgvn/

Retail

See also
Business & Economics · *Consumer Issues*
Popular Culture & Entertainment · *Shopping*

A White Dove Flower Shop

A White Dove Flower Shop allows you to order flowers online. Floral arrangements are grouped by arrangement type, such as 24K gold plated roses, tropical flowers and balloons, Disney arrangements, and plants. You can look at pictures of the arrangements and read brief descriptions of each one before using the order form. A reminder service is also available. This allows you to register important dates so that A White Dove can send you a reminder to send flowers several days in advance.

KEYWORDS Flowers, Gifts, Online Shopping
AUDIENCE Florists, Gift Givers, Shoppers
FREE

http://www.branch.com:80/flower-shop/

Animal Mania

Animal Mania is a leading dealer of specialty pets and supplies based in Florida. Their web site features a complete listing of their inventory from the Peruvian Red Tail Boa to a couple types of Scorpions. Headings for Large Cats, Ferrets and Weasels are listed as well, but as yet cannot be opened. The listings that can be opened include one line descriptions of the animals and prices. Animals can be ordered online.

KEYWORDS Exotic Animals, Pet Supplies, Pets
AUDIENCE Pet Buyers, Pet Owners, Pet Stores
CONTACT Michael Pata
         help@animals.com
FREE

http://satelnet.org/animals/

Antiques & Collectibles Guido Shops Locator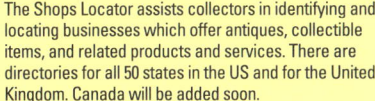

The Shops Locator assists collectors in identifying and locating businesses which offer antiques, collectible items, and related products and services. There are directories for all 50 states in the US and for the United Kingdom. Canada will be added soon.

KEYWORDS Antiques, Collectibles, Directories
AUDIENCE Antique Collectors, Consumers
FREE

http://www.tias.com/antiques/amdir/ShopsLoc.html

Blue Ribbon Orchids

The Blue Ribbon Orchids Web site allows you to order nursery items from a San Diego, California-based orchid grower. You may view pictures of orchid plants and read descriptions of the plants before ordering. Also included are detailed instructions about plant care for each orchid type. Professionals can fill out a form to receive resale order information, and anyone can join their reminder service in order to remember upcoming special and personal holidays.

KEYWORDS Gifts, Online Shopping, Plants
AUDIENCE Florists, Gift Givers, Shoppers
CONTACT Net Sales
         netsales@cts.com
FREE

http://www.cts.com:80/~netsales/bro/index.html

The Body Shop

The Body Shop manufactures and retails skin and hair care cosmetics in well over 1,200 stores in 45 countries. Their business policies and practices are defined by core values— care for the environment, concern for human rights, and opposition to the exploitation of animals. This site provides an opportunity to purchase their products and learn about the history of the company. It also contains information about projects they support including Endangered Species, Human Rights including 'Stop Violence Against Women,' and a missing persons hotline.

KEYWORDS Cosmetics, Hair Care, Human Rights, Social Responsibility
AUDIENCE General Public, Retail Professionals
CONTACT www@bodyshop.co.uk
FREE

http://www.the-body-shop.com/

The Dallas Market Center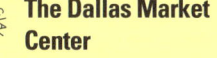

Visitors to The Dallas Market Center can access information on this large trade show facility located in Dallas. The site provides little information to users other than a listing of the different industry shows hosted at the facility, such as a home furnishings and apparel shows.

KEYWORDS Conferences, Retail Business, Texas, Trade Shows
AUDIENCE Dallas Business, Retail Businesses, Trade Show Attendees
CONTACT DMC@the-center.synapse-group.com
FREE

http://the-center.synapse-group.com/

Ember Glo Gifts Flags & Banners

This site advertises Ember Glo Gifts. The company offers flags in 100 possible styles.

KEYWORDS Flags, Product Information
AUDIENCE Consumers, Flag Enthusiasts
FREE

http://branch.com/ember/ember.html

Energy Efficient Environments, Inc.

The Energy Efficient Environments, Inc. home page allows users to browse the pages of this catalogue of energy saving and earth friendly home products. The catalogue includes products such as energy saving light bulbs and plugs, as well as chlorine filtering shower heads, among others. Descriptions and images are included for each product as well as price information. There are also links to other environmentally-related sites.

KEYWORDS Energy Efficient Products, Environmental Products, Home Products
AUDIENCE Home Owners, Environmentally Conscious People
CONTACT energy@mcs.com
FREE

http://www.mcs.net/~energy/home.html

Floreal Floral Arrangements

Floreal is a San Francisco-based floral arrangement company. Their Web site allows you to order from their online catalog, which includes dried leaf arrangements and mobiles inspired by modern artists such as Dali, Kandinski, and Picasso. Included are descriptions of their products and the artists, as well as large pictures. As part of the Electronic Commerce Associates, you can order Floreal arrangements with an online order form and receive them in about 2 weeks.

KEYWORDS Flowers, Gifts, Modern Art
AUDIENCE Florists, Gift Givers, Shoppers
FREE

http://www.eca.com/OLC/floreal/Floreal.html

The Flying Carpet Mall

The Flying Carpet Mall is a collection of Persian Rugs online with photos and descriptions. Currently there are 51 carpets and rugs for viewing, priced in Singapore dollars.

KEYWORDS Antiques, Collectibles, Online Shopping, Persian Rugs
AUDIENCE Antique Collectors, Consumers
CONTACT webmaster@singapore.com
FREE

http://www.singapore.com/products/carpets/carpetmall

Forest Saver

Forest Saver is a manufacturer of recycled stationary and office supplies made from discarded maps. Their home page gives a brief description of these products and allows users to access their web catalogue which includes various map-made products such as envelopes, stationary, note pads, and clip boards. The site also provides links to EcoCentric World and other environment-related sites.

KEYWORDS Office Supplies, Recycled Products, Stationary
AUDIENCE Office Suppliers, Stationary Shoppers, Stationary Supply Stores

146 Retail

Free
http://www.nando.net/prof/eco/forest.html

 Gift Connection Home Page

The Gift Connection sells such items as teddy bears, clocks, picture frames, and other merchandise as individual and corporate gifts. Prices within this short catalog are generally more than $50 (US) per gift. Online ordering, using Netscape's encryption standard is currently available for credit card orders.
Keywords Gifts, Internet Shopping, Merchandise, Online Retailers
Audience Business Professionals, Teddy Bear Enthusiasts
Contact Branch Information Services
Free
http://www.branch.com:80/frames/

 The Gourmet Gardener 1995 Catalogue

The Gourmet Gardener Catalogue offers a dozen categories of items including gourmet herbs, vegetables, spices, edible flowers, etc. Books for gardeners, from budding to seasoned ones, are also available. One can request a printed catalogue or order by phone, fax, or mail.
Keywords Gardening, Mail Order, Online Catalogs, Online Shopping
Audience Gardeners, Gardening Enthusiasts
Free
http://metroux.metrobbs.com/tgg/catalog.htm

 Grant's Florist and Greenhouse

This is the online catalog of Grant's Florist and Greenhouse. It describes the products and services Grant's provides. The picture, price and, a brief description of each product are provided in this catalog, along with an order form.
Keywords Buyers Guides, Companies, Gifts
Audience Consumers, Florists, General Public
Contact Jon Zeeff
branch-info@branch.com
Free
http://branch.com/buning/buning.html

 Harry's Farmers Market, Inc. Home Page

This is the home page of Harry's Farmers Market, Inc. (HFM)—a high quality perishable foods discounter. Harry's Farmers Market states its mission as 'being the leading global resource for fresh food products of exceptional value through the integration of retailing, manufacturing, distribution and information capabilities.' The page is rather weak at present.
Keywords Food, Manufacturing, Retail

Audience Consumers, Cooks, Shoppers
Contact www@hfm.com
Free
http://www.hfm.com:8001/

 Imaginarium OnLine

This is the home page of the specialty toy store Imaginarium. The links include a downloadable form to fill out and turn in at any Imaginarium store to save $5 off any one children's educational software title of your choice. Also provided are links to the 1994 Holiday Highlights and a list of the shopping malls where one of the many Imaginarium stores await you.
Keywords Children, Companies, Software, Toys
Audience Children, Educators, Parents, Santa Claus
Free
http://www.tig.com/Imaginarium/

 J. Sainsbury, PLC

This site is for the J. Sainsbury grocery store chain. It has hundreds of branches in the UK, lists available products and, naturally, allows for purchase by email. Products sold at J. Sainsbury include wine, baked goods, and groceries. The site also contains a brief history of the store chain, and recipes.
Keywords Companies, Food, Supermarkets, Wine
Audience General Public, Shoppers, United Kingdom Residents
Free
http://www.j-sainsbury.co.uk/

 Klehm Nursery

This online nursery has a catalog for tree peonies and peonies, hostas, daylilies and perennials. Email can be sent to obtain a free color catalog. Requests are also taken by phone or fax. In addition, Klehm provides wholesale catalogs for businesses.
Keywords Catalogs, Gardening Supplies, Mail Order, Nurseries
Audience Gardeners, Gardening Enthusiasts
Free
http://www.prairienet.org/business/klehm/list.html

 Lama

This site advertises Lama, an original household construction technique which makes the most of limited space by installing one's bed in the ceiling, so that it lowers at night. This site would interest those looking to free up floor space for things other than a large bed.
Keywords Beds, Construction, Furniture, Home
Audience Designers, Singles, Students
Free
http://branch.com/lama/lama.html

 Mayflower Florist

Mayflower Florists Inc. has a variety of floral arrangements that are available for online ordering through this page. Users can use Netscape's encryption or call a toll free number to order packages such as a Birthday Bouquet, Get Well, Sympathy or Fruit Baskets.
Keywords Flowers, Online Shopping
Audience Flower Enthusiasts, General Public, Gift Givers
Free
http://branch.com:1080/mayflower/mayflow.htm

 Monroe's Pen Shop

If you are interested in buying a vintage pen, The Monroe Pen Shop, a member of Pen Collectors of America Inc., can help. The Web site has links to the magazines Pen World and Pen Finder, catalogs of antique and classic pens for browsing and/or purchase, gifts and accessories, the 'Pen Locator,' and a forum where you can sell your fountain pen.
Keywords Antiques, Collectibles, Online Shopping
Audience Antique Collectors, Consumers
Free
http://www.netaxs.com/people/labenski/monroe.html

 O'Bannon Oriental Carpets

If you enjoy folk art, you can explore the artistry of woven textiles at O'Bannon Oriental Carpets. Follow links to the craftswomen of Turkey using hand-spun wool to create one-of-a-kind carpets and browse several carpet collections. A map is provided to locate the Pittsburgh store.
Keywords Antiques, Collectibles, Oriental Carpets, Pennsylvania
Audience Antique Collectors, Consumers
Contact info@lonewolf.com
Free
http://www.ibp.com/pit/obannon

 Off The Shelf Music & Video Compact Discs and Cassettes

Off The Shelf Music & Video is an online shopping Web site which offers musical compact discs and cassettes. This page leads users to menus for domestic and imports, with the imports divided by CD singles, concert CD's, boxed sets, and new releases. Users can order merchandise online using Netscape's Encryption, telephone, fax, or by mail order.
Keywords Cassettes, Compact Discs (CDs), Music, Online Shopping
Audience General Public, Music Enthusiasts, Popular Culture Enthusiasts
Contact ecmg@empire.na.com
Free
http://empire.na.com/ots/cdcasshp.html

Retail **147**

 Pine Garden Bonsai Company

Pine Garden Bonsai is a family nursery devoted to bonsai. Its online site provides access to bonsai containers, bonsai stock, and finished bonsai. There are classes and tips on the secrets of throwing oval bonsai containers, as well as an order form.

KEYWORDS Gardening, Gardens, Nurseries
AUDIENCE Bonsai Enthusiasts, Gardeners, Gardening Enthusiasts
CONTACT mbraver@aol.com
FREE

http://www.poppyware.com/pgb/

 Sam's Wine Warehouse

Sam's Wine Warehouse has developed an international reputation as one of the leading distributors of wine and spirits in the United States with its commitment to selection, low price, and customer service. Customers can order electronically, fax in orders or call the toll-free line. The Web site includes a chance to design your own wine labels, a calendar of events, selections for the next two months and other selections, a chance to subscribe to Sam's Electronic Newletter, what's new, and other outside related links.

KEYWORDS Chicago, Online Shopping, Wines
AUDIENCE Wine Enthusiasts
FREE

http://www.ravenna.com/sams/

 Sound Wire's Home Page

The Sound Wire site provides access to the store's catalog of the newest music in all genres from country to hip hop. This online catalog offers hundreds of downloadable album covers and sound samples. Album covers are about 100K and the sound samples are in mpeg format and about 130K in size. Sound Wire also offers PGP encrypted transactions for maximum security of electronic transactions using Netcash and First Virtual's method of payment.

KEYWORDS Albums, Compact Discs (CDs), Music, Online Stores
AUDIENCE Consumers, Music Enthusiasts
CONTACT feedback@soundwire.com
FREE

http://soundwire.com

 Tailgate Picnic Products ★★

Tailgate Picnic Products offers users a variety of food related gifts and merchandise. Among the specialty items available for ordering are New York Bagels and Cream Cheese, Gourmet Coffees, Gift Baskets, and assorted items such as Sauces, Candies, and Pates. Users can order merchandise online using Netscape's Encryption, telephone, fax, or by mail order.

KEYWORDS Bagels, Coffee, Food, Online Shopping
AUDIENCE Food Enthusiasts, Gift Givers

Connections to Starting a Business
Financial independence at your fingertips

Business Plans and Business Planning

- Sample business plans
- About business plans
- Business plan outline
- Do you really want to start a business?
- About Business Plan Pro
- Return to Palo Alto Software home page.

Check here to request more information by email.

Some entrepreneurs argue that financial independence can be gained from starting your own business. You can draw on their advice and their experiences, plus get ideas for starting your own business by accessing "Business Start-Up Solutions." This site offers many ideas, including information on how to become a secured credit card distributor or start a mail order business that caters to busy executives.

(http://www.vpm.com/selfhelp/)

Of course, you'll also want to make a business plan if you need to borrow money to start your own boutique or business. Whatever location you choose as your storefront, you'll need some tips for writing a business plan, including advice on how many employees to hire, inventory planning, location, and more. "Business Plans and Business Planning" will give you the outline. You fill in the particulars.

(http://www.pasware.com/bplans.htm)

Once you start your business, you'll need some help ordering office supplies like peel and stick shipping labels, plus advice on the best place to order business stationary and arrange for printing services. You can also obtain mailing lists to help advertise your products and services through the "Services" site on the Internet.

(http://netmar.com/mall/shops/solutions/svcs/)

You can get financial advice about how to keep costs down, plan ahead for paying taxes, and general tips on starting up. The "Small Business Resource Center," which concentrates mostly on starting a small business in the U.S., is also helpful for anyone around the world who wants to succeed the first time out.

(http://www.webcom.com/~seaquest/)

CONTACT ecmg@empire.na.com
FREE

http://empire.na.com/tailgate/tailbask.html

TreEco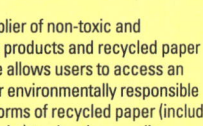

TreEco is a leading supplier of non-toxic and biodegradable cleaning products and recycled paper goods. Their home page allows users to access an online catalogue of their environmentally responsible products from various forms of recycled paper (including some made from denim) to cleaning supplies. Entries include brief descriptions of each product including size and price information. Users may order online.

KEYWORDS Biodegradable Products, Environmental Products, Recycled Products
AUDIENCE Environmentally Conscious Shoppers, Health Food Supermarkets
CONTACT treeco@earthlink.net
FREE

http://www.envirolink.org/treeco/

The Trunk Shop - Nostalgia Signs, Antique Trunks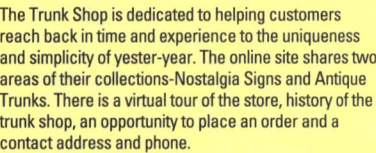

The Trunk Shop is dedicated to helping customers reach back in time and experience to the uniqueness and simplicity of yester-year. The online site shares two areas of their collections-Nostalgia Signs and Antique Trunks. There is a virtual tour of the store, history of the trunk shop, an opportunity to place an order and a contact address and phone.

KEYWORDS Antiques, Collectibles
AUDIENCE Antique Collectors, Consumers
FREE

http://www.ici.net/business/ts/TS.homepage.html

Vintage Direct Wine

Vintage Direct Wine contains access to Australia's great wines at wholesale prices. It is the mail order branch of the Melbourne based Nicks Wine Merchants group. The wines, for delivery within Australia only, are divided by link categories of white, red, champagnes, ports, and special mixed dozen. There is an order form and delivery details.

KEYWORDS Australia, Mail Order, Wines
AUDIENCE Wine Enthusiasts
FREE

http://www.sofcom.com.au/Nicks/index.html

Virgin Pure Spring Water

The Virgin Pure Spring Water web site offers information regarding this beverage supply company. Users can access information on the company's pure drinking water bottled from natural springs in the North Georgia Mountains in addition to information on the purity of the beverage. Further details about ground water is also included at the site.

KEYWORDS Beverages
AUDIENCE Spring Water Dealers, Spring Water Delivery Recipients, Spring Water Drinkers
CONTACT Don Megill
FREE

http://www.mindspring.com/~pure/pure.html

VirtuMall - Shopping in the 21st Century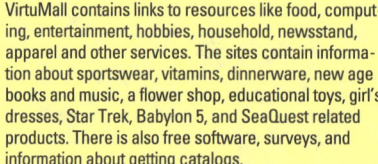

VirtuMall contains links to resources like food, computing, entertainment, hobbies, household, newsstand, apparel and other services. The sites contain information about sportswear, vitamins, dinnerware, new age books and music, a flower shop, educational toys, girl's dresses, Star Trek, Babylon 5, and SeaQuest related products. There is also free software, surveys, and information about getting catalogs.

KEYWORDS Clothing, Health, Online Shopping, Shopping Malls
AUDIENCE Popular Culture Enthusiasts, Shoppers
CONTACT comments@virtumall.com
FREE

http://virtumall.com/fast/virtumall.html

Warehouse Wines and Liquors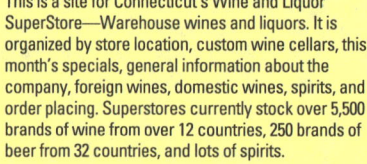

This is a site for Connecticut's Wine and Liquor SuperStore—Warehouse wines and liquors. It is organized by store location, custom wine cellars, this month's specials, general information about the company, foreign wines, domestic wines, spirits, and order placing. Superstores currently stock over 5,500 brands of wine from over 12 countries, 250 brands of beer from 32 countries, and lots of spirits.

KEYWORDS Online Shopping, Spirits, Wines
AUDIENCE Wine Enthusiasts
FREE

http://www.winenliquor.com/wine/wine.htm

Weddings Online

Weddings Online is a unique interactive service designed to simplify planning your wedding. The Master Category Page is the starting point for browsing the actual service pages on the Weddings Online database. The Master Category Page offers a series of 'clickable' images. Categories include bakeries, bands, florists, honeymoons, receptions, hotels, invitations, etc.

KEYWORDS Entertainment, Events, Weddings
AUDIENCE Event Planners, Florists, Parents, Wedding Planners
CONTACT wol@sensemedia.net
FREE

http://www.sensemedia.net/sprawl/9723

Services

See also
Business & Economics · *Advertising & Marketing*
Internet · *Internet Business*

Airtech, Inc.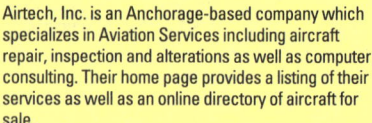

Airtech, Inc. is an Anchorage-based company which specializes in Aviation Services including aircraft repair, inspection and alterations as well as computer consulting. Their home page provides a listing of their services as well as an online directory of aircraft for sale.

KEYWORDS Airlines, Airplane Repair, Aviation, Computers
AUDIENCE Aircraft Owners, Computer Users, Online Marketing Seekers
CONTACT afbwm@alaska.net
FREE

http://www.alaska.net/~afbwm/

Armstrong Design Consultants' Home Page

This home page describes the services and clients of Armstrong Design Consultatants, a computer-based graphic design shop. They specialize in developing visual information systems like identification programs, interactive communications, and publications for corporate, education, and healthcare clients. Their clients include Bellcore, IBM, GTE, Yale and Boston Universities, and MIT. Also included is an extensive online portfolio of examples from these and other clients.

KEYWORDS Computer Graphics, Consulting Services, Graphic Design, Services
AUDIENCE Graphic Designers, Web Designers
CONTACT Frank Armstrong Farmsinger@aol.com
FREE

http://www.nando.net/prof/farmland/farmhouse.html

Bell Productions Services Multimedia, Limited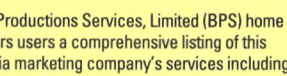

The Bell Productions Services, Limited (BPS) home page offers users a comprehensive listing of this multimedia marketing company's services including video and animation and Internet services among others. Users can also access samples of graphic images produced by BPS.

KEYWORDS Graphics, Marketing, Production Services, Video
AUDIENCE Graphic Designers, Marketing Departments, Presentors
CONTACT bell@inforamp.net
FREE

http://inforamp.net/~bell/

Services **149**

Boston Microcomputer Consulting Home Page ★★

This is the homepage for Boston Microcomputer Consulting, a consulting firm that specializes in creating custom database applications for small to mid-size businesses and non-profit organizations using Microsoft FoxPro for the Windows, DOS and Macintosh platforms. This page provides company information and a FoxPro information and sample application page.

Keywords Consulting Services, Database Management, Windows
Audience Database Managers, Database Users, Foxpro Users, Windows Users
Contact 72147.3617@compuserve.com
Free

http://turnpike.net/emporium/B/bmc/index.html

Connections to Women and Credit Histories
"Are you saying that I don't exist??!!"

Every year, many women are denied credit because they cannot demonstrate a "track record" for previous credit. In many cases, these women have been married and are now divorced, and simply want to open accounts under their own names. Sometimes women who change their names (or revert to their maiden names for professional reasons) find it difficult to establish credit. If you are facing this predicament, there is a way to find out what your rights are, as well as a way to obtain records of previous payments on credit accounts listed under "Mr. and Mrs . . ." The "Facts for Consumers from the Federal Trade Commission" site provides you with advice on how to establish credit, and how to work productively with credit reporting agencies.

This site also provides you with information about federal laws that safeguard your rights to obtain credit; moreover, it advises you on what to do when a creditor fails to report payments you've made to a charge account.

(http://www.webcom.com/~lewrose/brochures/women.html)

Commercial Services on the Net ★★★★

This Web site is a directory of organizations (for profit or not for profit) that have a public presence on the Internet. It is organized by categories, as well as alphabetically. Entries may also be located via searchable keywords. Companies from AAA Advertising to Zilog, as well as organizations such as the US Census Bureau and Australian Consumers' Association are listed.

Keywords Directories, Funding, Internet Commerce, Organizations
Audience Grantmakers, Grantseekers, Internet Users
Contact editors@directory.net
Free

http://www.directory.net/

Commonwealth Inc. Home Page ★★

This site is the home page of Commonwealth Inc., a corporation developing a dual-currency transaction system. It provides an executive summary and registration for its customer newsletter.

Keywords Banking, Currency
Audience Bankers, Business Professionals, Currency Dealers
Contact stevek@commonweal.com
Free

http://commonweal.com/

DataVision— FoxPro Consulting ★

This is the homepage for DataVision, a consulting firm that provides consulting, design, development, and support services for business applications using Microsoft's FoxPro database product. This site provides sample applications and company information.

Keywords Business Services, Consulting Services, Database Management, Software

Audience Database Managers, Database Users, FoxPro Users, Windows Users
Contact dvnet@primenet.com
Free

http://www.primenet.com/~dvnet

Digital Dynamics ★★★★

This page advertises the services of Digital Dynamics, a company that publishes customers' files and data on CDs. Anything from business data to music can be converted.

Keywords Business Services, Computer Administration, Computer Databases, Computing
Audience Computer Users, General Public
Free

http://branch.com/dd/dd.html

Emerging Businesses, Small Businesses and Family-Owned Businesses ★★★★

This page is devoted to providing news, trends, guidance and research from experts, journalists and executives to those in emerging businesses, small businesses and family-owned businesses. Information is updated daily. To access information, one must complete and submit an electronic form for NetMarquee to tailor information to individual needs and for them to email updates directly.

Keywords Business Education, Business Research, Small Business
Audience Business Professionals, Family-Owned Businesses, Small Business Professionals
Contact gumpcom@netmarquee.com
Free

http://nmq.com

Executive Secretarial Services ★★★

The is the home page for Executive Secretarial Services located in New York. Information is included about Executive Secretarial Services, types of services, such as information processing, transcription, database management, as well as the prices and details for the services.

Keywords Business Services, Database Management, Secretarial Services, Transcription
Audience Business Professionals, Business Professionals, Entrepreneurs
Contact ESS@awa.com
Free

http://www.awa.com/ess/ess.html

Federal Express Home Page ★★★★

The Federal Express Home Page provides downloadable Federal Express delivery management software for Windows and DOS users. It provides a nifty online tracking service where you just enter your Airbill Tracking Number and the delivery and/or the scan information for the package will be displayed. Customers can also track via email at track@fedex.com. The site also includes information about FedEx Service Availability, what's new, and the FedEx Money-Back Guarantee.

Keywords Companies, Express Delivery Services, Mailing Services, Shipping
Audience Business Professionals, Business Professionals, General Public
Contact webmaster@fedex.com
Free

http://www.fedex.com/

The Flower Link ★★★

The Flower Link is made up of a consortium of local florists across the US and Canada. There is a search engine, a secure site connection, a flower and plant care information directory, and other links. Flowers can

150 Services

be ordered online. FTD and Direct Ship selections are also available.

KEYWORDS Flowers, Gifts, Online Shopping
AUDIENCE Gardeners, Gardening Enthusiasts, Romantics
FREE

http://www.flowerlink.com/html/menu1.html

Flower Stop Storefront ★★★

The Flower Stop Storefront, run by Chuck Haley, is the Internet's Fresh Flower Market where one can order long-distance roses and flowers. Its nonvirtual storefront, the Flower Stop, is a retail florist located in Colorado Springs, Colorado, the marketing arm of a grower, Pikes Peak Greenhouses, that has been growing and shipping flowers since 1904.

KEYWORDS Flowers, Gifts, Online Shopping
AUDIENCE Flower Enthusiasts, Gardeners, Gardening Enthusiasts
FREE

http://www.flowerstop.com/fstop

Gems—Product & Service Showcase ★★

Gems is a Product & Service Showcase company. Some of the products showcased on this page include The International Picture Personals Magazine which highlights beautiful Russian women. The site also includes products for Desktop Videoconferencing, Patent, Trademark and Copyright protection, and Printed Products, Software and Services For Managing and Promoting Small Businesses.

KEYWORDS Business Services, Online Malls, Personals, Real Estate
AUDIENCE Consumers, Entrepreneurs, Men, Singles, Women
CONTACT info@nysernet.org
FREE

http://www.gems.com/showcase/

Hitachi Business International ★★★

This is a home page for Hitachi Business International, Ltd., a subsidiary of Hitachi, Ltd. in Tokyo, Japan. The company provides various services related to international business in fields like international communications and language services, creative services, office information services, and international trade. An online newsletter and company profile are available here.

KEYWORDS Business Services, Communications, Information Services
AUDIENCE Business Professionals
FREE

http://www.hitachi.co.jp/HBI/hbi.html

Holographics North ★★★

Visitors to the Holographics North web page can access information on this Vermont-based facility which is one of the leading producers of large format holograms. Information on their large format 'stereogram' process is provided, in addition to a partial listing of the company's clients. Some of the images can be accessed in enlarged format at the site. Display kits of the images may be ordered by printing and mailing a form or by calling.

KEYWORDS Holography, Images, Marketing
AUDIENCE Business Professionals, Trade Show Exhibitors
FREE

http://hmt.com/holography/hni/hni.html

Lane and Lenge Florists ★★★

Lane and Lenge Florist has been a leader in the floral wire service industry, now offering their services on the Internet to give customers an easy way to deliver flowers from anywhere in the world. There are links to arrangements, ordering, comments from users, a mailing list and a newspaper article.

KEYWORDS Flowers, Gifts, Plants
AUDIENCE Flower Enthusiasts, Gardeners, Gardening Enthusiasts
FREE

http://plaza.xor.com/lane/start/index.html

Lunds Auction House ★★★

Lunds Auctioneers & Appraisers is a Canadian company based in Victoria, BC. They specialize in collectibles, antiques, and specialty auctions. Follow their links to the auction schedule, catalogues and pictures, benefits of buying or selling at Lunds, or of buying at Lunds and conditions of sale.

KEYWORDS Antiques, Auctioneers, Auctions, Collectibles
AUDIENCE Antique Collectors, Consumers
FREE

http://www.intertrek.com/~lunds/

Net Classifieds ★★★★

Net Classifieds allows you to place an ad or browse existing ads. Simply click on the Flag representing the country in which you want to search, and you will be linked to the directory of that country. For example, if you search classifieds in France, you will find an index for such items as Cars, Bargain Properties, Classified Small Ads, Email Directory, Employment, Personals, and Plants and Machinery. Categories vary by country.

KEYWORDS Classified Ads, Personals
AUDIENCE Consumers, Internet Users
CONTACT Info@Net-Classifieds.co.uk
COST

http://www.net-classifieds.co.uk/

NetTRADER ★★★

The netTRADER is an online classified ad magazine. You can buy, sell, swap, or barter at this site. You will find services, employment, personals, and groups and clubs. The site implements TradeSafe Online, which is an escrow service designed to make online buying, selling, and trading safe and easy. You can search by broadly defined fields such as Buy, Sell or Services, or you can browse through an alphabetical index.

KEYWORDS Bartering, Classified Ads
AUDIENCE Consumers, Internet Users
CONTACT global@sentex.net
COST

http://www.sentex.net/nettrader/

Patscan Patent Searching ★★★

The Patscan web-site provides a newsletter and information on all aspects of intellectual property issues, as well as information on patent and trademark searches and patent copies. Patscan is a patent search service which performs searches which cover Canada, the USA, the United Kingdom and most of Europe. Results are delivered by fax, courier, or to your own computer on the Internet.

KEYWORDS Intellectual Property, Trademarks
AUDIENCE Business Professionals, Entrepreneurs, Inventors, Lawyers
CONTACT jsoroka@unixg.ubc.ca
FREE

http://unixg.ubc.ca:780/~rsimmer/homepage.html

Project Blue Lion ★★

This WWW site provides information about Project Blue Lion, a center of excellence in document management. The following topics are available from the homepage: news and views on document management, conferences and seminars, and a newsletter called Document Management International. Further information about the producer, Project Blue Lion, is also available, as well as links to other sources of information about document management.

KEYWORDS Business, Document Management
AUDIENCE Business Leaders, Documentation Writers, Office Document Architects
CONTACT john@pbl.demon.co.uk
FREE

http://www.ipl.co.uk/pbl

Reyne Hogan Antiques ★★★

Reyne Hogan Antiques buys and sells American and European Art Glass, Depression and Carnival Glass, Estate & Costume Jewelry, and Fine Porcelain and Pottery. There are links to all those items as well as to an Antique Search Index.

KEYWORDS Antiques, Collectibles, Mail Order
AUDIENCE Antique Collectors
FREE

http://www.tias.com/antiques/stores/RHA/index.shtml

Safety Compliance Institute ★★

The Safety Compliance Institute (SCI) Web page briefly summarizes the services provided by this full-service, independent regulatory management consulting firm based in California. The page lists several services rendered by SCI to assist companies in compliance with OSHA requirements. However, none of these services can be selected for further details.

Keywords California, Health, Injury, Regulation
Audience Company Management, Corporate, Small Business
Contact Noah Heldman
noah@websrus.com
Free

http://www.websrus.com/websrus/SCI/

 Simultaneous Wireless Interpretations

Simultaneous Wireless Interpretations provides nationwide reporting and convention coverage. They provide simultaneous wireless interpretation equipment and services, including interpretors, translation of languages by fax or modem, on site cassette recording and duplication in hotel and conference centers nationwide, computer generated transcripts, and more.

Keywords Conventions, Transcription, Translation Services, Wireless Equipment
Audience Interpreters, Media Professionals, Medical Professionals
Free

http://www.branch.com:80/swi/

The Virtual Conference Centre

This site offers access to a series of 'mediated' conferences on technology hosted by The Virtual Conference. The conference is broken up into three groups—social/political, marketing/business, and technology.

Keywords Computer Conferencing, Information Technology, Multimedia, Telecommunications
Audience Conferencing System Users, Consultants, Information Professionals, Researchers
Contact Ian Scales
ians@computing.emap.co.uk
Free

http://www.emap.co.uk/vc/

Business & Economics

Communications

Communications 153
Mass Communications 154
Networking 158
Organizations 161
Telecommunications 163

Communications

See also
Arts & Music · *Electronic Arts*
Business & Economics · *Career & Employment*
Business & Economics · *Publishing*
Popular Culture & Entertainment · *Magazines & Newspapers*

American Communication Association WWW ★★★

This site is produced by the American Communication Association (ACA), which is an organization in the field of communication studies. There is general information about the ACA as well as a long list of links concerning communications law, communication studies, and electronic references.

KEYWORDS Associations, Communications Research
AUDIENCE Communications Specialists, Communications Students, Scholars
CONTACT comminfo@cavern.uark.edu
FREE

http://www.uark.edu/depts/comminfo/www/ACA.html

Artech House Publishers Gopher Site ★★★

This gopher site is an archive for Artech House Publishers, a subsidiary of Horizon House Publications, Inc. Information is provided on its line of professional-level books on telecommunications, optoelectronics, microwave, antennas, and radar. The site includes a complete list of titles as well as information about new and best-selling books, software, video products, and conference information.

KEYWORDS Books, Publishing, Technical Communications, Telecommunications
AUDIENCE Communications Specialists, Communications Students, Engineers, Managers
CONTACT Artech House
artech@world.std.com
FREE

gopher://ftp.std.com:70/11/Book%20Sellers/artech

Bibliography of Organizational Computer-Mediated Communication ★★★

This page offers a bibliography of Computer Mediated Communication sources, with a slant towards organizational communication. It is organized alphabetically, with tags attached to the citations that tell the user the type of document that is being cited (e.g., literature survey, laboratory study, theoretical, discussion, etc.). Users may also link to the Journal of Computer-Mediated Communication from this page.

KEYWORDS Computer Mediated Communication, Electronic Media, Human Communications
AUDIENCE Communications Professionals, Communications Researchers
CONTACT Ian A Rudy
iar1@eng.cam.ac.uk
FREE

http://shum.cc.huji.ac.il/jcmc/rudybib.html

Communication Resources on the Web ★★★★

Communications is the key focus of this extensive list of links to communications resources on the Internet. Users will find links to all manner of communications resources in varying types of media such as radio, TV, print, and online. There are also links to information on media regulation, social issues, communication education, as well as research sources, bibliographies, and library databases.

KEYWORDS Communications, Journalism
AUDIENCE Communications Researchers, Journalists
CONTACT Chandrasekhar Vallath
cvallath@indiana.edu
FREE

http://alnilam.ucs.indiana.edu:1027/

Communication Scholars' Directory ★★★

This page is a listing of communications faculty, students, and professionals from around the world. Users will find full names, titles, phone and email contact information, as well as a brief description of what the person does in the field. Information on adding yourself to the directory is also available.

KEYWORDS Career, Employment
AUDIENCE Academics, Communications Professionals, Communications Researchers
CONTACT Chandrasekhar Vallath
cvallath@indiana.edu
FREE

http://alnilam.ucs.indiana.edu:1027/sources/dirpage.html

Communications Research Group ★★★

The Communications Research Group site at the University of Nottingham contains resources highlighting research into ways to support human communications through computer communications. The group conducts research into the use of computer and communications technologies including virtual reality and distributed systems. Users will find descriptions of

Communications – Mass Communications

the group's current research, projects, publications, and equipment specifications for those interested in details.

- *Keywords* Computer Mediated Communication, Human Communications
- *Audience* Cognitive Scientists, Communications Professionals, Computer Scientists
- *Contact* Dr. Hugh Smith, Dr. Steve Benford
- *Free*

http://www.crg.cs.nott.ac.uk/crg/index.html

David See-Chai Lam Centre for International Communication ★★★

This site is the gopher server for the David See-Chai Lam Centre for International Communication and provides information about its mission, facilities, resources, and more. The David See-Chai Lam Centre for International Communication is part of Simon Fraser University and researches communication methods and problems in the age of modern technology. The resources available on this server include publications, software, and mailing resources.

- *Keywords* Education (College/University), Human Communications, International Communications
- *Audience* Communications Specialists, Communications Students, Educators
- *Contact* Peter Anderson
  anderson@sfu.ca
- *Free*

gopher://hoshi.cic.sfu.ca/

Employment Opportunities and Resume Postings from Gopher Jewels ★★★★

This gopher site contains pointers to job listings throughout the world in almost every field. There are two main directories, Academic Positions and Miscellaneous Resources, and additional subdirectories pointing to specific institutions and services. Resources may be as general as Job Listings From Around the Globe, however there are various headings to look under, including Job Opportunities in the Arts, Law Employers, and more.

- *Keywords* Career, Employment, Jobs, Meta-Index (Jobs)
- *Audience* Educators (University), Job Seekers
- *Contact* USCgopher
  cwis-wizs@usc.edu
- *Free*

gopher://cwis.usc.edu:70/11/
Other_Gophers_and_Information
_Resources/Gophers_by_Subject/
Gopher_Jewels/Istuff/
employment/employment

The Journalism List ★★★★

This page is a comprehensive index of journalism and communications resources available on the Internet. It lists all types of resources, including discussion group mailing lists, finger, ftp, and gopher resources, newsgroups, telnet, wais servers, and World Wide Web pages. In addition, there are sections covering Internet domain names of news organizations, descriptions of journalism schools, and information on journalism software packages.

- *Keywords* Communications, Journalism
- *Audience* CMC Researchers, Communications Researchers, Journalists
- *Contact* John S. Makulowich
  makulow@clark.net
- *Free*

http://www.jou.ufl.edu/commres/jlist.HTM

gopher://una.hh.lib.umich.edu/
inetdirsstacks/journalism

ftp://ftp.clark.net/pub/journalism/
jlist30.txt

MCRLab Home Page ★★★

This site gives information about MCRLab, a Canadian research institute focusing on multimedia. The information covers current research projects and contracts.

- *Keywords* Database Management, Image Processing, Multimedia
- *Audience* Communications Professionals, Communications Specialists, Communications Students
- *Contact* Nicolas D. Georganas
  nngpb@acadvm1.uottawa.ca
- *Free*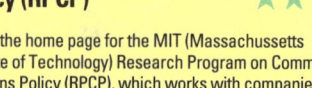

http://mango.genie.uottawa.ca/

MIT Research Program on Communications Policy (RPCP) ★★★

This is the home page for the MIT (Massachussetts Institute of Technology) Research Program on Communications Policy (RPCP), which works with companies, government, and academic leaders to understand and help set the direction for the vast changes related to the rapidly growing communications fields. Linked pages contain information about the RPCP, reports and publications, The Cambridge Roundtable, The Digital Information Infrastructure Guide (DIIG), Networked Multimedia Information Services (NMIS), workshops, seminars, and more.

- *Keywords* Communications, Journals, Massachusetts, Multimedia
- *Audience* Communications Researchers, Researchers
- *Contact* rpcp@farnsworth.mit.edu
- *Free*

http://far.mit.edu

NPR Online ★★★

This home page offers organizational information and some broadcast content for National Public Radio. The site provides program listings and sound clips and pictures of regular newscasters, as well as lists of member stations, NPR jobs, and upcoming events. Content available includes film reviews, recipes, transcripts, and other information on weekly and daily programs. The site also contains sections of documents on important current national and international news.

- *Keywords* Current Events, National Public Radio, Radio
- *Audience* News Buffs, Public Broadcasting Enthusiasts, Radio Enthusiasts, United States Residents
- *Contact* www-info@npr.org
- *Free*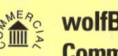

http://www.npr.org/

wolfBayne Communications ★★

The wolfBayne Communications company is a Public Relations firm specializing in multimedia marketing communications. Their home page provides a resume-like listing of PR services rendered and past achievements in the field, including their company charter. Users may contact wolfBayne via email for further information.

- *Keywords* Internet Marketing, Online Marketing, Public Relations, Job Listings
- *Audience* Electronics Companies
- *Contact* Kim M. Bayne
  kimmik@bayne.com
- *Free*

http://www.bayne.com/wolfBayne/

Mass Communications

See also
Education · *Professional Education*
Education · *Universities - United States*
Popular Culture & Entertainment · *Magazines & Newspapers*

AM/FM ★★★

AM/FM is a monthly newsletter covering events throughout the UK radio industry, including BBC network and local radio, Independent National Radio, ILR, satellite radio and the pirates. It is published both in print and as a slightly delayed electronic version which is distributed for free. This WWW database contains back issues of AM/FM, details of how to subscribe to both AM/FM, and its associated UK-Radio mailing list.

- *Keywords* Britain, Radio, Satellite Radio
- *Audience* General Public, Radio Professionals, United Kingdom Residents
- *Contact* amfm@tqmcomms.co.uk
- *Free*

http://www.tecc.co.uk/public/tqm/amfm/index.html

Agile Cable Production Service (ACaPS) ★★★

The Agile Cable Production Service (ACaPS) project focuses on the advanced cable production capabilities needed to offer service over the Internet. ACaPS uses an existing cable harness production and builds on the concepts of the Next-Link project at the Stanford Center for Design Research to apply the software tools now under development at Lockheed AI Center. This site contains an update on the project's status and the experimental software architecture that will enable

Mass Communications

computational agents to facilitate distributed design and engineering.

KEYWORDS Cable Industry, Computer Science, Telecommunications
AUDIENCE Computer Programmers, Computer Specialists, Computer Students
FREE

http://hitchhiker.space.lockheed.com/~acaps/

Amateur Radio ★★★

This site contains a collection of information regarding amateur or ham radio. Users will find a list of callbooks for the UK, Finland, the US and Canada, FAQ's of information from amateur radio newsgroups, and links to numerous radio newsgroups. Also included are pointers to radio-related WWW sites, including individual, commercial and educational pages.

KEYWORDS Ham Radio, Radio Broadcasting
AUDIENCE Amateur Radio Enthusiasts, Radio Enthusiasts
CONTACT John@mcc.ac.uk
FREE

http://www.mcc.ac.uk/OtherPages/AmateurRadio.html

Archive of Cable Regulation Digest's Editions from Multichannel News Magazine ★★★

This site contains the weekly archive activity of Cable Regulation Digest and articles from Multichannel News magazine, both of which cover the television industry.

KEYWORDS Cable Regulation, Cable Television, Communications, Television
AUDIENCE Communications Specialists, Mass Communications Students
CONTACT Professor Neon
         neon@vortex.com
FREE

gopher://gopher.vortex.com:70/11/tv-film-video/cable-reg

The Association of America's Public Television Stations (APTS) ★★★

This site hosts the The Association of America's Public Television Stations (APTS). The APTS is a national advocacy group working on behalf of local public televison stations. The group's objective is to identify, analyze, and share information on the changing media environment and on public television's performance in order to help stations identify and evaluate future options. In addition, the APTS lobbies the U.S. government and others to increase support for public broadcasting. This page hosts Action Alerts, which inform the viewer of upcoming legislation, such as an effort by the federal goverment to cut funding for the Corporation for Public Broadcasting. Other areas maintained on this site include a collection of fact sheets and position papers about Public Broadcasting. Some of the titles available for downloading are: 'Harnessing the Power of Television for Education,' 'Minorities—Important Audiences for Public TV,' and 'How Many Preschool Children Does Public TV Reach?' Viewers can also jump to other Public Broadcasting resources on the Internet.

KEYWORDS Advocacy, Public Television
AUDIENCE Public Broadcasters, Public Broadcasting Activists, Television Professionals
CONTACT Thom Watson
         thom@apts.org
FREE

http://www.universe.digex.net/~apts/

C-SPAN ★★★

This is a server of the C-SPAN (Cable-Satellite Public Affairs Network) television network. The information provided includes C-SPAN programming information. Details of other C-SPAN services, such as C-SPAN audio networks, are also provided.

KEYWORDS Politics, Television
AUDIENCE General Public, Government Watchers, News Buffs
FREE

http://www.c-span.org/

gopher://c-span.org/

The Corporation for Public Broadcasting Home Page ★★

The Corporation for Public Broadcasting (CPB) is a private, nonprofit corporation that oversees the distribution of the annual Federal contribution to 622 public radio stations and to 352 public TV stations throughout the United States and its territories. This page links the viewer to projects sponsored by CPB and its supporters, including parenting and educational programs, job listings, press releases, and other sites like the Annenberg/CPB Project. Users can also read back issues of the newsletter CPB Today, which contains background information about the shows produced by CPB, letters and feedback from viewers, as well as articles about public broadcasting in general.

KEYWORDS Education, Employment, Parenting
AUDIENCE Educators, Parents, Political Activists, Public Broadcasting Activists
CONTACT strait@cpb.org
FREE

http://www.cpb.org/

Connections to 800 Numbers
Never look a gift horse in the mouth

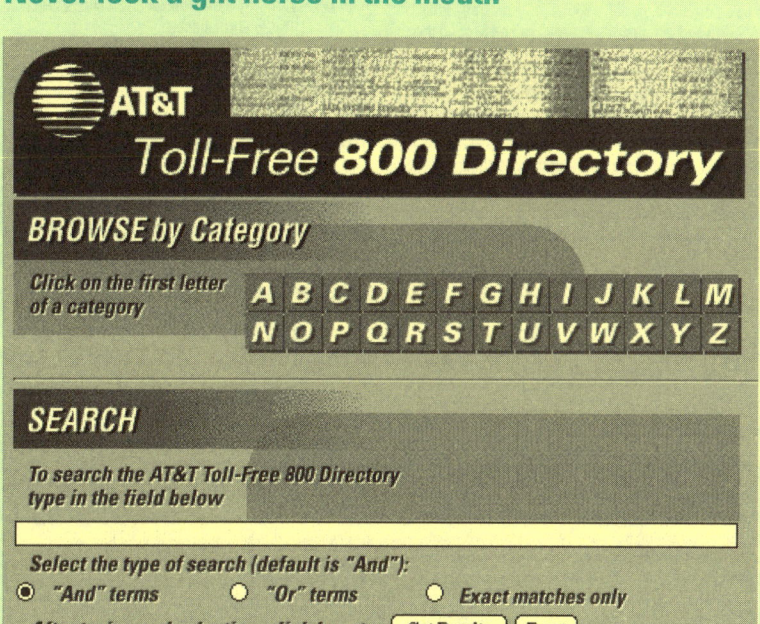

Want to send flowers to your Aunt on her birthday? How 'bout buying some antique brass plates for the door knobs in your home? With the online "AT&T 800 Directory," you can even find the odd things you never thought you'd need.

At this site, the popular directory helps you find any 800 number so that you can call and order the product or items you want. Searches can be initiated by category (i.e. autos, antiques, etc.) or by the name of the company.

(http://att.net/dir800)

Directory of Communication Programs ★★★★

This page details communications programs available at colleges and universities in America and around the world. Users will find decriptions of the various programs, including degrees conferred, departments, and faculty information, as well as contact and local information. Where the college has a server on the Internet, a link is provided to it.

KEYWORDS Communications Programs, Education, Reference, Universities
AUDIENCE Academics, Communications Students, Guidance Counselors, Students (Secondary)
CONTACT Chandrasekhar Vallath
cvallath@indiana.edu
FREE

http://alnilam.ucs.indiana.edu:1027/sources/programs.html

Energy World Wide Web ★

The Energy World Wide Web maintains this site to publicize its radio and television program schedule, contact information, and other details about the Danish student broadcasting service. This site offers links to music charts from Radio Energy, the European Association of University Radio & TV Stations, and a List of University Radio & Television stations in Europe.

KEYWORDS Broadcasting, Denmark, Radio Stations, Television Stations
AUDIENCE Danes, Denmark Residents, Televison Enthusiasts
CONTACT energy@nrg.dtu.dk
FREE

http://www.energy.dtu.dk/english.htm

ftp://ftp.energy.dtu.dk

Fairness & Accuracy In Reporting (FAIR) WWW Pages ★★★★

FAIR (Fairness & Accuracy In Reporting) is an American media watch group offering documented criticism in an effort to correct media bias and imbalance. This site contains excerpts from the current and back issues from Extra, FAIR's bimonthly print magazine. Viewers will also find online editions of FAIR's special reports and related media projects, such as Counterspin and Media Beat. A separate media contact list and an extensive hypertextual index of articles, subjects, and companies is also included on this web page.

KEYWORDS Activism, Journalism
AUDIENCE Journalists, Mass Communications Students, Media Critics, Political Scientists
CONTACT Michael Ernst
mernst@theory.lcs.mit.edu
FREE

http://theory.lcs.mit.edu/~mernst/fair/

Firesign Theatre Home Page ★★★★

This page contains background information on 'Firesign Theatre,' indexes of past programming, links to Firesign Theatre-related FAQs, and information on other sites containing Firesign Theatre materials. Transcripts of selected programming are also available.

KEYWORDS Comedy, Radio, Theater
AUDIENCE Comedy Fans, Humor Enthusiasts, Jokers, Radio Enthusiasts
CONTACT Niles Ritter
ndr@tazboy.jpl.nasa.gov
FREE

http://mtritter.jpl.nasa.gov/firesign.html

Independent Television Service ★★★

This site hosts an archive of the media-forum mailing list which discusses public and independent media. Some recent topics have included 'Gallup Poll' and 'PBS WWW page.' Also on this page are program descriptions and background information for a number of award-winning videos. For example, a number of documentaries related to contemporary issues are described, including 'A Question of Color,' a film about race relations, 'Stolen Moments—Red Hot + Cool,' a documentary about a recent concert to help fund AIDS projects, and 'When Billy Broke His Head...And Other Tales of Wonder', a first person account of disability.

KEYWORDS Filmmaking, Public Television
AUDIENCE Media Analysts, Media Professionals, Political Activists, Public Broadcasting Activists
CONTACT Active Window Productions
info@actwin.com
FREE

http://www.actwin.com:80/ITVS/

Institute of Automation and Communication in Slovakia ★★★★

This site provides information on the administration of the Institute of Automation and Communication, Slovak Academy of Sciences. It also contains information about Internet tools, software, FTP servers in Slovakia, Usenet news, and more. It has links to universities in Slovakia as well as to other gophers.

KEYWORDS Internet Directories, Slovakia
AUDIENCE Academics, Internet Users, Students (University)
FREE

gopher://gopher.uakom.sk/

Media Watch Dog ★★★★

This page contains information on media watch groups which critique the accuracy and expose the biases of the mainstream media. Subjects include media criticism and censorship, and the page presents a listing of censorship-related resources. These include FAIR (Fairness and Accuracy In Reporting), Le Monde Diplomatique, The File Room (an online archive on censorship), Banned Books On-line, Mother Jones Media Watch Resource Guide, and the Society of Professional Journalists.

KEYWORDS Censorship, Media, News
AUDIENCE Civil Rights Activists, Fiction Enthusiasts, Film Enthusiasts, Reading Enthusiasts
CONTACT Michael Ernst
mernst@theory.lcs.mit.edu
FREE

http://theory.lcs.mit.edu/~mernst/media/

National Press Club ★★★★

This site offers a concise collection of Internet resources for journalistic research. It was designed to be a tool for journalists seeking information from the Internet as deadlines approach, and includes access to the Eric Freidheim Library and the Internet Town Hall. Users can also obtain information about the press club, including purpose, history, and geographical information. In addition, lists of past speakers at NPC luncheons are available . (You can download an audio transcript, however the files are 30 megabytes in length.)

KEYWORDS Freedom of Speech, Journalism, National Press Club, News
AUDIENCE Journalism Educators, Journalists, News Readers, Students
CONTACT ClarkNet
global@clark.net
FREE

http://town.hall.org/places/npc/

National Public Radio ★★★

This site hosts listener information for the National Public Radio (NPR) organization. Viewers can choose to link to separate pages for schedules and guides for such NPR programs as All Things Considered, Talk of the Nation, Latino USA, Living on Earth, and The Thistle and Shamrock. Viewers can also jump to pages sponsored by the NPR member stations that have an Internet presence (Web, Gopher, and/or Email addresses). Current events affecting listeners, such as a movement by the federal government to cut funding for public broadcasting, have a separate link. In addition, users can locate past and present program guides listing book, film, and music reviews, recipes, and transcipt retrieval information.

KEYWORDS Employment, Radio
AUDIENCE Job Seekers, Public Broadcasting Activists, Radio Enthusiasts, Reading Enthusiasts
CONTACT www-info@npr.org
FREE

http://www.npr.org/

The Noble Directory of Experts & Spokespersons ★★★

The Noble Directory of Experts & Spokespersons site provides a searchable database of 2,000 experts and spokespersons from a variety of specialized fields and organizations. The directory is designed to be used by media resource locators looking for an expert or spokesperson for interviews, panel discussions, broadcast events or to get access to specialized information. The directory is searchable by expert name, company, or topic. In addition, the site has a monthly news bulletin focusing on advances in medicine, science, technology and other fields.

KEYWORDS Consulting Services, Directories, Mass Media, Public Relations
AUDIENCE Consultants, Media Professionals, Public Relations Professionals, Spokespersons

CONTACT Ms. Lin Doyle
lind@hooked.net
FREE

http://www.experts.com/

Public Broadcasting Service (PBS) Gopher Server ★★★

This server provides information from the Public Broadcasting Service (PBS) television network. The information covers program listings, television-assisted learning courses for adults and children, and descriptions of PBS productions.

KEYWORDS Alternative Education, Broadcasting, Communications, Public Television
AUDIENCE Public Broadcasting Activists, Television Enthusiasts
CONTACT djohnston@pbs.org
FREE

gopher://gopher.pbs.org/

Radio Belche ★★★

This is Belgium's online radio server. It is offered in French and has links to news, music, sports, and more.

KEYWORDS Belgium, Current Events, Radio, Radio Broadcasting
AUDIENCE Internet Users, Radio Enthusiasts
CONTACT Laurent Schumacher
schumacher@tele.ucl.ac.be
FREE

http://www.tele.ucl.ac.be/RadioBelche/index.html

Radio Stations On The Internet ★★★★

This page serves as an index for radio stations across the United States, Canada, Europe and other international communities. Listings include over 200 Radio stations from the U.S. (WMBR Cambridge, KZSU Stanford, WNNX Atlanta, WTBU Boston, etc.), international radio stations (Radio Amsterdam, Stads Radio, 98 FM - Dublin, etc.), and Radio Networks (BBC, Canadian Broadcasting Corparation, Deutsche Welle, National Public Radio, Radio Free Europe, etc).

KEYWORDS Broadcasting, Mass Media, Radio Broadcasting
AUDIENCE Educators, Radio Broadcasters, Radio Enthusiasts, Students (Secondary/College)
CONTACT Jeffrey Schiller
jis@mit.edu
FREE

http://www.mit.edu:8001/activities/wmbr/otherstations.html

RadioSpace ★★★★

RadioSpace is an Internet resource designed for the programming and news staff of radio stations. It provides ready-for-broadcast sound bites, news and programming, and links to radio stations, networks, and other Internet radio resources. The news section provides summaries of current issues as well as links to sources of further information on each topic, including, in some cases, sound clips for broadcast. The inter-views section lists upcoming opportunities for scheduling interviews. A list of other Internet resources includes other sites with audio clips, a sounds archive, and three relevant newsgroups.

KEYWORDS Broadcasting, Radio, Sound Clips
AUDIENCE Media Professionals, News Buffs, Radio Broadcasters
CONTACT dj@radiospace.com
FREE

http://www.radiospace.com/cgi-bin/imagemap/NANBanner?376,18

School of Journalism and Mass Communication ★★★

This is the home page of the School of Journalism and Mass Communication at the University of Wisconsin-Madison. Information on the school, instructional materials, and 'Online Wisconsin' (the school's electronic journal) are included.

KEYWORDS Journalism, Mass Media, Online Journals
AUDIENCE Educators (University), Students (University)
CONTACT online-wisc@macc.wisc.edu
FREE

http://fount.journalism.wisc.edu

Shortwave/Radio Catalog ★★★★

This Shortwave/Radio Catalog page is a set of links to documents, web servers, ftp and gopher sites, telnet services, audio files, pictures, graphs, schedules, software and interactive online programs. The catalog of hypermedia links is split into sets of web pages covering Shortwave and Basic Services, Radio Topics

---

Connections to National Address/Zip Codes

Making The Snail Run Faster . . .

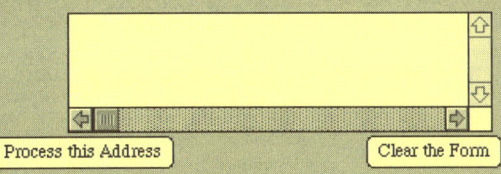

Believe it or not, there are still times when electronic mail won't do. Occasionally you need to send a package across the U.S., or want to send a birthday card to a friend—the old fashioned way (via the U.S. Postal Service).

To make sure the item you send gets there and in a timely manner, you can use the Internet to retrieve the proper mailing addresses of individuals and companies across the U.S. The "Cedar National Address Server" not only provides you with the ZIP Code, but also with the four digits (ZIP Code +4) for specific buildings. You can even retrieve a Postscript file for printing with a barcode, which also speeds up delivery.

(http://www.cedar.buffalo.edu/adserv.html)

(including Medium Wave and FM broadcasting), and Satellite Radio.

KEYWORDS Communications, Radio Broadcasting, Technical Communications
AUDIENCE Radio Enthusiasts, Radio Pirates, Shortwave Radio Users
CONTACT Pete Costello
pec@ios.com
FREE

http://itre.uncecs.edu/radio/

South African Broadcasting Corporation Welcome Page (SABC) ★★

This server contains general information about SABC (South African Broadcasting Corporation) and its programs. There are pages related to SABC's technology, history, Language Center, and employees. Furthermore, the company's internal newsletter, Interkom, which provides news, photographs, and marketing information, is also available.

KEYWORDS Broadcasting, Mass Media
AUDIENCE Mass Communications Students, Media Professionals, South Africans
CONTACT Greg Mallett
mallettg@sabc.co.za
FREE

http://www.sabc.co.za/

TeleRead—Bring the E-Books Home ★★★

TeleRead is a nonpartisan plan to get electronic books into American homes—by way of a national digital library and computers—in an era of declining literacy. TeleRead is also a plan for electronic forms to save billions of dollars in time and money and make the national digital library more affordable. This page gives the viewer more information about the background and potential future of this communications device, as well as a chapter about Teleread that is being published by the American Society for Information Science.

KEYWORDS Education, Electronic Books, Literacy, Multimedia
AUDIENCE Educators, Librarians, Library Users, Reading Enthusiasts
CONTACT ClarkNet
help@clark.net
FREE

http://www.clark.net/pub/rothman/telhome.html

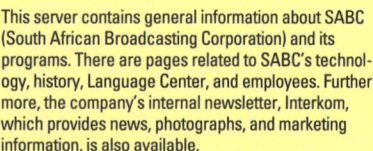

TeleVisions, Inc. ★★★

TeleVisions, Inc. markets multimedia technology from its research of prototypes in academic settings. TeleVisions offers tools, technology, consulting and other services in electronic communications and information dissemination. The page has links to its galleries, technical demonstrations, and electronic books.

KEYWORDS Multimedia, Online Publishing, Television
AUDIENCE Communications Experts, Multimedia Enthusiasts
CONTACT info@tvisions.com
FREE

http://www.tvisions.com/

University of Illinois at Urbana-Champaign College of Communications ★★★

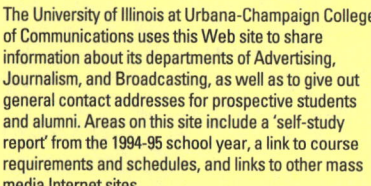

The University of Illinois at Urbana-Champaign College of Communications uses this Web site to share information about its departments of Advertising, Journalism, and Broadcasting, as well as to give out general contact addresses for prospective students and alumni. Areas on this site include a 'self-study report' from the 1994-95 school year, a link to course requirements and schedules, and links to other mass media Internet sites.

KEYWORDS Advertising, Broadcasting, Journalism
AUDIENCE Communications Students, Illinois Residents
CONTACT kazel@uiuc.edu
FREE

http://www.uiuc.edu/providers/comm/

Voice of America Gopher ★★★

One of the U.S. Government's official news agencies, Voice of America (VOA) provides daily broadcasts of international news relating to democracy and America. This gopher contains transcripts of the last seven days of broadcasts in English and other languages, digitized selections of daily broadcasts (updated every 24 hours) in a variety of formats, and background information on the Bureau of Broadcasting and VOA. There are also links to other Government-administered gopher servers at this location.

KEYWORDS Broadcasting, International News, Politics, Radio
AUDIENCE Journalists, News Buffs, Radio Broadcasters, Radio Enthusiasts
FREE

gopher://gopher.VOA.GOV:70/00/newswire/README

WBRS-Waltham 100.1 FM ★★★

WBRS is an all-genre noncommercial radio station located at Brandeis University in Waltham, MA. It is on the air 24 hours daily throughout the year, and is run by students and members of the community. Links are provided to the WBRS board, program guide, live music, contact information, and sponsors.

KEYWORDS Music, Radio
AUDIENCE Music Enthusiasts, Musicians, Radio Enthusiasts, Students (University)
CONTACT wbrs@binah.cc.brandeis.edu
FREE

http://www.wbrs.org/

WXYC ★★★

WXYC, the University of North Carolina's student radio station, is operating the first simulcast over the Internet. If you have a powerful enough Mac, PC, or UNIX machine and a sound card, you can turn your computer into a very expensive radio. This page contains all necessary information for tuning in, including instructions for downloading the software.

KEYWORDS Mass Media, Media, Radio, Simulcast
AUDIENCE MAC Users, PC Users, Radio Enthusiasts, UNIX Users
CONTACT wxyc@unc.edu
FREE

http://sunsite.unc.edu:80/wxyc/

Welcome to BBC ★★★★

This site is the top level for the BBC Broadcasting network. Users will find extensive information on the BBC's radio and television arms, as well as their newer Internet offerings. There is a wide variety of information available here such as program schedules, programming transcripts, news, and much more. Users will also find information on individual programs produced by the BBC, and a collection of links to other media-related servers.

KEYWORDS Broadcasting, Radio, Television, United Kingdom
AUDIENCE BBC Enthusiasts, British, Broadcasting Professionals, Media Professionals
FREE

http://www.bbcnc.org.uk

Wij hebben nieuws voor U (MSR Belgian News) ★★★

This site provides links to all the latest in Belgian news, offered entirely in Dutch (except for a brief information page in English). It is an initiative of the ELIS (Electronic and Information Systems) Department of the University of Gent.

KEYWORDS Belgium, International News, Online Newspapers
AUDIENCE Belgians, Dutch Speakers
FREE

http://www.elis.rug.ac.be/ELISgroups/speech/msr/

Networking

See also
Communications · Telecommunications
Computing & Mathematics · Companies
Computing & Mathematics · Networking
Education · Educational Technology
Engineering & Technology · Technology
Internet · Networking

Academic and Research Network of Greece, Hellenic News ★★★★

This Gopher server at the Network Managment Center of ARIADNE, the Academic and Research Network of Greece, provides access to the Hellenic News database which contains daily news from Greek radio stations in audio and text format. The reports are available in Greek and English.

KEYWORDS Greece, Tourism
AUDIENCE Greek Language Speakers, Greeks
FREE

gopher://alpha.servicenet.ariadne-t.gr

Networking **159**

 Ascend Communications Home Page ★★★

This site offers information about Ascend Communications. There is access to recent news items, new products and press releases, general company information, customer services, as well as a place for feedback. There are also links to other interesting places on subjects such as ISDN, Ascend mailing lists, and more.

KEYWORDS Communications Technology, Companies, Computer Products, Internet Networking
AUDIENCE Business Professionals, Internet Access Providers, Network Users
CONTACT info@ascend.com
FREE

http://www.ascend.com/

Barrnet Gopher/FTP Archives ★★★

This server provides documents and software related to computers and computer networking. This information includes Computer Emergency Response Team (CERT) security advisories, FAQs about the Multicast Backbone (MBONE), information on NFSNet, NREN, an NII, and lists of Internet resources and references. The information is provided by the Bay Area Regional Research Network, based at Stanford University, California.

KEYWORDS Computer Networks, Internet Security, MBONE, Research & Development
AUDIENCE Californians, Computer Users, Internet Users
CONTACT info@barrnet.net
FREE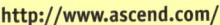

gopher://gopher.barrnet.net/

The Belgian National Support Centre ★★★★

The goal of the MICE (Multimedia Integrated Conferencing for Europe) Project is to pilot networking between European research and sites in the U.S.. This project is funded by the Commission of the European Community (CEC). In addition, it has started an International Seminar Series in multimedia, communications, and networks. This home page is a gateway to the various institutions (mostly in Europe) participating in the project.

KEYWORDS Computer Conferencing, Multimedia, Research
AUDIENCE Communications Specialists, Network Developers
CONTACT mice-nsc@helios.iihe.rtt.be
FREE

http://www.iihe.ac.be:80/mice-nsc/

 **Born Information Services Group** ★★★★

The Born Information Services Group offers this page as a clearinghouse of information for those who are interested in learning about their networking consulting services. There are pages describing the Born Information Services Group in depth, a page of employment opportunities, a page of Born publications available online, and a very extensive hot sheet called 'BORN To Be Wild.'

KEYWORDS Advertisements, Consultants, Employment, Service Providers
AUDIENCE Business Professionals, Purchasing Offices
CONTACT webmaster
  webmaster@born.com
FREE

http://www.born.com/

 CELLWARE's Information Service ★★★

This site offers information about the company Cellware. There is access to information on employees, boards, adapters, systems, and the general company. There is also access to products, software, distributors, and the latest news.

KEYWORDS ATM (Asynchronous Transfer Mode), Computer Hardware, Internet Networking
AUDIENCE ATM (Asynchronous Transfer Mode) Users, Connectivity Hardware Users, Network Users, Software Users
CONTACT info@cellware.de
FREE

http://www.cellware.de/

CSCW Research Group— COMIC Project ★★★★

This site provides information about the COMIC project at Computer Supported Cooperative Work (CSCW) at Lancaster University, which is centered on four major themes. First, an investigation of the organizational context within which CSCW systems are placed and how they can be supported in cooperative systems. Second, an understanding of the means by which CSCW systems are developed and how they are best

---

Connections to World Wide Pen Pals

Perhaps you have a hobby you'd like to share with someone who also likes that hobby. Or maybe you want to communicate with someone halfway around the world who shares your career goals. Chances are you can find that person through the "Start.com—Pen Pal Connection." This is one of many Internet sites that offer ways to build friendships around the world. Friendship aside, the Pen Pal Connection gives you the chance to practice some of your foreign language knowledge, or just communicate with someone in your own language who lives thousands of miles away.

The "E-Mail Pen Pal Connection" is another site that offers a window on far-away lands, a place where you can share your hobbies, philosophies, or cultural backgrounds. Additionally, the "Pen Pal Kids Connection" offers a spot on cyberstreet for youngsters to meet others around the world.

(http://www.start.com/start/penpal2.html)

also, **(http://www.comenius.com/index.html)**

also, **(http://www.scsn.net/~musex/kids.html)**

supported in line with existing development techniques. Third, an examination of the use of notation within CSCW systems and the development of an appropriate role for notation. Fourth, the uncovering of different forms of interaction with and around shared objects and how they can be supported to best facilitate cooperative work. These research themes have been chosen specifically to allow close cooperation across a number of disciplines.

KEYWORDS   Communications, Universities
AUDIENCE   Communications Specialists, Educators, Students (University)
CONTACT   Tom Rodden
        tom@comp.lancs.ac.uk
FREE

http://orgwis.gmd.de/COMIC/

Computing Systems Technology Office of the Advanced Research Projects Agency ★★★

This server provides information about the Computing Systems Technology Office (CSTO) of the Advanced Research Projects Agency (ARPA). It also provides related information about the High Performance Computing and Communications Program. These programs are designed to focus research on scalable computing systems, microsystems, scalable software, national-scale information enterprises, and networking.

KEYWORDS   Information Technology, Software
AUDIENCE   Communications Specialists, Computer Scientists, Software Designers
CONTACT   admin@ftp.arpa.mil
FREE

gopher://ftp.arpa.mil/

Dan Kegel's ISDN Home Page ★★★

This page is an index to information on ISDN (Integrated Services Digital Network). ISDN allows a single connection to transmit voice, video, and data at a much faster rate than traditional analog phone lines. Users will find links to basic information on ISDN, as well as more advanced technical documentation and information on ISDN products and services.

KEYWORDS   Computer Hardware, ISDN, Telecommunications
AUDIENCE   ISDN Providers, ISDN Users, Telecommunications Professionals, Telecommunications Users
CONTACT   Dan Kegel
        dank@alumni.caltech.edu
FREE

http://alumni.caltech.edu/~dank/isdn/

EcuaNet ★★★

This server stores and distributes information about EcuaNet, the major computer network in Ecuador. EcuaNet links Ecuadoran universities, businesses, research institutes, libraries, and government. This server also provides connections to nodes on EcuaNet.

KEYWORDS   Computer Networks, Ecuador, Latin America, Research & Development
AUDIENCE   Educators (University), Government Employees, Researchers
CONTACT   info@ecnet.ec
FREE

gopher://ecua.net.ec/

FortNet Home Page ★★★

FortNet is a public access computer information network whose purpose is to connect Fort Collins area residents and businesses to community resources and to be responsive to the diverse interests of its citizens through the development of electronic partnerships and communities. There is also a direct link to the resources available at the Colorado State University campus located nearby.

KEYWORDS   Government
AUDIENCE   Colorado Residents, Community Groups, Network Developers, Network Users
CONTACT   webmaster@fortnet.org
FREE

http://www.fortnet.org/

France Telecom Network Services ★★★

France Telecom Network Services is based in Stockholm, Sweden and the site is in Swedish. There are links to general information, press releases and clips, other WWW servers, and contact information.

KEYWORDS   France, Sweden
AUDIENCE   Language Enthusiasts, Swedes
CONTACT   ulla@stupi.se
FREE

http://www.transpac.se/

GTE Laboratories Inc. ★★★★

GTE Laboratories is the central research and development arm of GTE, the telephone and electronics corporation. This site provides access to information about the 5 laboratories that make up the core of the services which GTE provides. The labs include Computer and Intelligent Systems, Network Technologies, Systems Technology, Telecommunications Research, and Wireless and Secure Systems. Other areas on this site are Community Services, which gives information about some of the national and local community and educational projects which GTE is involved with. Sponsored Services is a directory of Web Pages which GTE provides support for. These sites include the Knowledge Discovery Mine and Distributed Object Computing pages.

KEYWORDS   Artificial Intelligence, Communications Technology, Mobile Communications
AUDIENCE   Educators, Scientists, Students, Telecommunications Professionals
CONTACT   labsweb@gte.com
FREE

http://info.gte.com/

Global Village ★★★

Global Village makes networking products for networking, fax, and online services. Their Web site provides product information, press releases and announcements, and a product catalog. They also provide a 'tour' of the Internet and access to online software and resources. Their customer support service allows you to find answers to questions about your 'Global Village Product.'

KEYWORDS   Computer Products, Modems, Networking, Customer Support
AUDIENCE   Communications Specialists, Computer Users, Network Users
FREE

http://www.globalcenter.net/index.html

Macom Networking Ltd. ★★★

This is a home page from an Israeli company Macom Networking Ltd. The company is exploring the potential of communication on and through computer networks. Here you'll find information about Israel ranging from political news to tourist sites (including art museums and galleries), from Hebrew ('A Living Language') to real estate. Each topic contains links to related sites on the Web. One of the pages is the site for the Jewish Agency for Israel.

KEYWORDS   Internet Networking, Israel, Museums
AUDIENCE   Israelis, Real Estate Brokers, Tourists
CONTACT   Museums
        info@macom.co.il
FREE

http://www.macom.co.il/

Metricom, Inc. ★★★

Metricom, Inc. develops, manufactures, and markets wireless data communication networks. This site presents information on wireless data services concerning benefits and applications, costs, testimonials from the company's users, coverage, and frequently asked questions. Covering the company itself, there are press releases, product specifications, background information, personal home pages, and information about how the company got started. There is also access to a getting started manual and a programmer's guide.

KEYWORDS   California, Data Communications, Network Servers, Wireless Communications
AUDIENCE   Business Proffessionals, Californians, Network Users
CONTACT   info@metricom.com Technical Support Department: support@metricom.com
FREE

http://www.metricom.com/

NRL Network Research Navigator ★★★

The Naval Research Laboratory (NRL) Network Research Navigator is designed as a research tool to find all available Internet resources that are related to networking. In this site users will find general information about the NRL, the Department of Defense, and their networking projects, as well as on network security and computational science. There is a metaindex of Internet information sites including a general bibliography, links to online books and papers, conference information, and relevant journals. Links are also divided up by subject, such as Multimedia, Signal Processing, and Optical Processing.

KEYWORDS   Computational Sciences, Navy, Network Security

Networking – Organizations

AUDIENCE	Military Personnel, Network Developers, Network Researchers
CONTACT	Dr. Stephen G. Batsell
batsell@itd.nrl.navy.mil
FREE

http://netlab.itd.nrl.navy.mil

Northeast Regional Data Center Home Page ★★★

The Northeast Regional Data Center Home Page provides access to campus resources and data publications. This page has links to the Center's newsletter and online systems. There are additional links to Internet resources in communications and networking.
KEYWORDS	Data Communications, Unix
AUDIENCE	Communications Professionals, Computer Users, Florida Residents, UNIX Users
CONTACT	editor@nervm.nerdc.ufl.edu
FREE

http://www.nerdc.ufl.edu

Plugged In ★★★★

Plugged In provides a multimedia learning environment for the East Palo Alto, California community and other communities. Students otherwise denied access to technology are able to take part in projects that use computer technology in creative ways, thereby gaining exciting learning experiences. Students have completed computer programming classes, cartoon animations, multimedia self-portraits, slide-shows, and interactive newsletters. Many of the student projects are available online for viewing.
KEYWORDS	Multimedia Education, Student Projects
AUDIENCE	Children, Children's Rights Activists, Educators, Parents, Social Workers
CONTACT	webmaster@pluggedin.org
FREE

http://www.pluggedin.org/

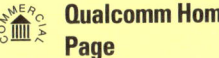 Qualcomm Home Page ★★★

Qualcomm specializes in advanced communications based on digital wireless technologies. This page offers access to information about the company, the company's software technologies and employment opportunities, and CDMA (Code Division Multiple Access) digital cellular technology.
KEYWORDS	Cellular Phones, Mobile Communications, Wireless Communications
AUDIENCE	Cellular Phone Users, Email Users, Mobile Communicators, Software Users
CONTACT	webmaster@qualcomm.com
FREE

http://www.qualcomm.com/QualHome.html

SWITCH ★★★

The information on this site is about SWITCH, the Swiss Academic and Research Network. SWITCH is the main Swiss component of the Internet. In addition to providing information about SWITCH, this server provides links to gophers, databases, libraries, and other services within the SWITCH network.
KEYWORDS	Computer Networks, Research, Switzerland
AUDIENCE	Computer Users, Internet Users, Switzerland Residents
CONTACT	gopher@switch.ch
FREE

gopher://gopher.switch.ch/

Welcome to the Frame Relay Forum ★★★

This site offers a forum on Frame Relay from all over the world. Areas covered include general information, press releases, newsletters, technical papers, marketing, forum information, European forums and user groups, and the Frame Relay newsgroup archives.
KEYWORDS	Broadband Technology, Frame Relay, Newsgroups
AUDIENCE	Communications Professionals, Europeans, Marketing Professionals, Students (University)
CONTACT	Kirsten Machi, Allen Robel
frf@interop.com
robelr@indiana.edu
FREE

http://frame-relay.indiana.edu/

Organizations

See also
Communications · *Telecommunications*
Government & Politics · *States*
Internet · *Internet Access*
Internet · *Internet Resources*

 AMI from MountainNet, Inc. ★★★

MountainNet, Inc., is an Internet service provider in West Virginia. This site provides access to data and databases, covering such topics as agriculture, arts, music, humanities, business resources & services, economics, education, jobs & resume postings, entertainment, environment, history, internet, software libraries, and more.
KEYWORDS	Internet Directories, Internet Tools, Networking
AUDIENCE	Computer Users, Internet Users, Internet Users
CONTACT	info@mountain.net
COST

gopher://gopher.mountain.net/

APT WWW ★★★

This is a home page from The Alliance for Public Technology (APT) - a Washington, DC based non-profit, tax exempt coalition of public interest groups and individuals whose goal is to foster broad access to affordable, usable information and communication services and technology. APT provides an effective grassroots voice for equitable and affordable access to the benefits of telecommunications technology in the Information Age. The site also provides a newsletter, notes on telecommunications policy and networking, calendar of events, and more.
KEYWORDS	Internet Networking, Public Interest, Telecommunications
AUDIENCE	Activists, Network Users, Nonprofit Organizations
CONTACT	apt@apt.org
FREE

http://apt.org/apt.html

The Benton Foundation's Communications Policy Project ★★★

This is a home page for the Benton Foundation, which is working with nonprofit organizations to gain an effective voice for social change and to shape the emerging communications environment, producing media guides, conferences, and demonstration projects. This site offers links to the latest news on communications policy and upcoming events, other nonprofit and telecommunications resources, and information on the Foundation's activities.
KEYWORDS	Activism, Internet Networking, Non Profit Organizations, Telecommunications
AUDIENCE	Activists, Network Users, Nonprofit Organizations
CONTACT	blau@benton.org
FREE

http://www.cdinet.com/Benton/home.html

CMC (Computer-Mediated Communications) Magazine ★★★★

CMC (Computer-Mediated Communications) Magazine is an online publication with current and back issues available in HTML format. This site provides information on computer-mediated communications including forums for discussion, links to other sites, and ways to submit articles to the magazine.
KEYWORDS	Communications Technology, Internet Magazines
AUDIENCE	Communication Researchers, Communications Professionals, Communications Students, Information Scientists
CONTACT	John December
decemj@rpi.edu
FREE

http://www.rpi.edu/~decemj/cmc/mag/index.html

Communications for a Sustainable Future ★★★

This site is maintained by the group Communications for a Sustainable Future, with the goal of using modern information technology to enhance the quality of life in the future. These resources provide discussion groups and information on subjects like the environment and feminism.
KEYWORDS	Communications, Feminism, Information Technology
AUDIENCE	Developers, Environmentalists, Feminists, International Development Specialists

Organizations

CONTACT Don Roper
roper@csf.colorado.edu
FREE

gopher://csf.colorado.edu/

Community Television Producers Association of Hawaii ★★

The Community Television Producers Association (CTPA) home page of Hawaii contains resources for people interested in community television. The CTPA is a non-profit organization established to advocate free speech and provide public access television to the Hawaiian community. Visit the site for information and links to Community Access Television, Video, Film, TV, Virtual Reality, Telecommunications and Entertainment. There are also a number of interesting links to various local sitess, and sightseeing information about Hawaii for potential visitors.

KEYWORDS Free Speech, Hawaii, Non Profit Organizations, Public Access Television
AUDIENCE Civil Liberties Activists, General Public, Hawaii, Video Enthusiasts
CONTACT Brian Lee
ctpa@aloha.net
FREE

http://www.aloha.net/~ctpa

The Cornell American ★★★

This is an archive of the Cornell American, a student publication providing conservative political commentary and opinion. Users will find a complete selection of back issues, as well as articles from the latest issue in ASCII text format. There is an index file with each issue, describing the articles that are available. Articles are available as individual files.

KEYWORDS Journalism, Media, Political Commentary
AUDIENCE Conservatives, Government Watchers, Political Analysts, Political Researchers
CONTACT CA-L@cornell.edu
FREE

ftp://ftp.cit.cornell.edu/pub/special/cornell_american/

Extra! magazine ★★★★

This web site focuses on 'Extra!,' the monthly magazine of FAIR (Fairness and Accuracy in Reporting), a nationwide news media watchdog group. It includes the most recent issues as well as excerpts from back issues. Special items also available here are FAIR's report on Rush Limbaugh's accuracy, an article on FAIR's radio programs and educational services, and more.

KEYWORDS Journalism, Politics
AUDIENCE Journalists, Publishing Professionals, Radio Enthusiasts
CONTACT FAIR
fair@igc.apc.org
FREE

http://theory.lcs.mit.edu/~mernst/fair/

NAB (National Association of Broadcasters) Library and Information Center ★★★

The Library and Information Center of the National Accociation of Broadcasters maintains a collection of URLs for information sources in the broadcasting industries. There are links to information about telecommunications, U.S. and international broadcasting, cable, communications policy, and more.

KEYWORDS Broadcasting, Mass Communications, Technical Communications
AUDIENCE Broadcasters, Communications Professionals, Media Professionals
CONTACT wwurfel@nab.org
FREE

http://www.nab.org/www/userguid/libhome.htm

OSSgopher - Open Source Solutions, Inc. ★★★

This is a gopher server of Open Source Solutions, Inc. (OSS), an organization that finds solutions to Information Age issues of disseminating classified information within government and to the public. It contains information on the OSS, its history, the OSS lunch club, papers & talks by Robert D. Steel, OSS international symposiums, and more.

KEYWORDS Information Retrieval, Information Technology, International Communications
AUDIENCE Computer Users, Government Agencies, Information Brokers, Information Scientists
CONTACT Eric S. Theise
tech@oss.net
FREE

gopher://gopher.oss.net/11/oss

gopher://nic.sura.net/

Society of Professional Journalists ★★★

This ftp archive is maintained by the Society of Professional Journalists, an organization dedicated to serving the needs of professional journalists everywhere. In this directory, users will find information related to journalistic ethics, the Freedom of Information Act, a listing of online newspapers, and more. There is also information available for journalists interested in joining the society.

KEYWORDS Journalism, Mass Communications, Mass Media, Professional Organizations
AUDIENCE Communications Professionals, Communications Students, Journalists
CONTACT Jack D. Lail
jdlail@netcom.com
FREE

ftp://ftp.netcom.com/pub/sp/spj/

Taiwan Network Information Center (TWNIC) Gopher Server ★★★

This is a gopher server of the Taiwan Network Information Center (TWNIC) installed by the Ministry of Education Computer Center. It contains information on TWNIC, registration, information & directory services, Taiwan government documents, and more. It also provides links to other local gophers. Most of the materials are written in Chinese, some in English.

KEYWORDS Internet Directories, Internet Tools, Taiwan
AUDIENCE Educators, Taiwanese Culture Enthusiasts, Taiwanese People
CONTACT hostmaster@twnic.net
FREE

gopher://gopher.twnic.net/

Telemedia, Networks, and Systems Group ★★★

A division of MIT's Laboratory for Computer Science, this group researches topics related to distributed multimedia systems—host interfaces for high speed networks, tool kits for real-time data, visual programming environments, information extraction from video, flexible video models and protocols, networked multimedia peripherals, and ATM network striping. This site offers demos and information on current research projects, links to commercial sites on the Web, and links to multimedia-related sites.

KEYWORDS Computer Applications, Multimedia
AUDIENCE Computer System Designers, Multimedia Enthusiasts
CONTACT webmaster@www.tns.lcs.mit.edu
FREE

http://tns-www.lcs.mit.edu/

The Voice of America ★★★

The Voice of America is the government sponsored short wave radio service. It provides information about the service's mission, its history, and its programming schedule. In addition it provides samples of Voice of America programing in the form of downloadable audio files.

KEYWORDS Current Events, Radio, Shortwave Radio
AUDIENCE General Public, International Travelers, Radio Broadcasters, Radio Enthusiasts
CONTACT info@VOA.GOV
FREE

gopher://ftp.voa.gov/

Telecommunications

See also
Business & Economics · *Industries*
Communications · *Mass Communications*
Computing & Mathematics · *Networking*
Engineering & Technology · *Technology*
Internet · *Networking*

AT&T TalkingPower ★★★★

This site is sponsored by the telecommunications goliath, AT&T. This Web page is a demonstration project that allows users to experience training with networked hypermedia. You can find out about a range of topics, including the distribution of reference documentation for technicians over a network, the delivery of training over a network, the combination of documentation and training in a Performance Support System (PSS), the use and reuse of multimedia resources in documentation and training, how a PSS fits into a large power system, and the use of document standardizing tools (HTML).

KEYWORDS Education, Online Learning, Telephones
AUDIENCE Multimedia Enthusiasts, Telecommunications Professionals
FREE

http://www.att.com/talkingpower/

About Modems ★★★

The information contained here is about modems, protocols, transfer compression, etc. This file contains one chapter from a three-chapter book entitled, The Joy of Telecomputing. This chapter covers topics like 'What you need to know about modems,' to an 'Introduction on buying and using modems.' It covers different modem speeds and future developments. Readers also have the option of ordering The Joy of Telecomputing here.

KEYWORDS Modems, Product Information, Telecommunications, Telecomputing
AUDIENCE Computer Professionals, Computer Users, Modem Users, Telecommunications Experts
CONTACT Kenneth Kirksey
kkirksey@eng.auburn.edu
FREE

ftp://ftp.switch.ch/docs/About_Modems

Advanced Communication Technologies Laboratory ★★★

Students of multimedia will find this site of interest. It includes essays, bibliographies, and past and present multimedia projects. The primary users of the laboratory (and the Internet site) are students enrolled in the class 'The Challenge of Interactive Multimedia,' which is part of the sequence 'Interface, Interaction, and Agency,' taught at the college.

KEYWORDS Education (College/University), Multimedia, Telecommunications
AUDIENCE Multimedia Enthusiasts, Virtual Reality Enthusiasts
CONTACT Professor Allucquere Rosanne (Sandy) Stone
gopher@actlab.rtf.utexas.edu
FREE

http://www.actlab.utexas.edu/

gopher://gopher.actlab.utexas.edu/

AirData Home Page ★★★

This home page has links to all sorts of information on McCaw Cellular's AirData wireless data service, which is based on CDPD technology. It also includes a link to technical assistance for customers, and other wireless data pointers on the Internet.

KEYWORDS Computer Technology, Mobile Communications, Mobile Computing, Wireless Technology
AUDIENCE Business Professionals, Communications Specialists
CONTACT webmaster@airdata.com
FREE

http://www.cellular.com/

Alaska 2001 ★★

This is a text file produced by the Alaska Public Utilities Commission, which describes the present state of Alaska telecommunications capabilties and formulates goals and objectives. Some areas developed within this report are competition and regulation, Universal Service, government use and provision of telecommunications services, and economic development.

KEYWORDS Alaska, Internet Access, Telecommunications
AUDIENCE Alaska Residents, Information Professionals
FREE

http://www.alaska.net/~apuc/2001.html

Ameritech ★★

Ameritech provides Illinois, Indiana, Michigan, Ohio and Wisconsin with local telephone services. It offers cellular, paging, interactive video, and wireless data communications for much of the U.S. and many parts of Europe. This home page provides information on the company's services, statistics on number of customers, type of communications, and areas served. There are also links to what's new, communications solutions, and other Internet information.

KEYWORDS Cellular Communications, Paging, Phone Companies, Video
AUDIENCE Investors, Telecommunications Industry
CONTACT webmaster@www.ameritech.com.
FREE

http://www.ameritech.com

Argus DC Power Systems ★★★

This site offers information on a complete range of products and accessories that provide solutions for all telecommunications power requirements. It provides access to information on power systems, rectifiers, and converters. There is also information on alarms, control panels, fuses, circuit breakers, and front access distribution panels, termination panels, as well as ground and vertical discharge bars.

KEYWORDS Computer Hardware, Telecommunications
AUDIENCE Communications Professionals, Computer Hardware Users, Hardware Engineers, Telecommunications Experts
CONTACT Roger E.Bannister
rbanster@fox.nstn.ns.ca
FREE

http://fox.nstn.ca/~rbanster/index.html

Aurastar Information Systems, Inc. ★★★★

This site offers information on Aurastar Information Systems, a company specializing in frequency management in the area of telecommunications. There is access to information on Aurastar's communication systems of satellites, AM, FM, and television broadcasting, microwave signals, fixed and land mobile radio, cellular radio telephone, and high frequency systems. You'll also gain access to country-specific information in locations where the company is well represented, as well as to their software and consulting services.

KEYWORDS Information Systems, Telecommunications
AUDIENCE Computing Consultants, Managers, Software Users, Telecommunications Experts
CONTACT info@aurastar.com
FREE

http://www.aurastar.com/

Bell Atlantic Corporation ★★

This site gives access to the Bell Atlantic Public Archives. The archives include news releases, speeches, congressional testimony, company history, recent announcements and reports.

KEYWORDS Communications, Companies, Corporations, Telecommunications
AUDIENCE Business Researchers, Telecommunications Professionals
CONTACT Eric Rabe
rabe@ba.com
FREE

gopher://ba.com/

Bellcore Home Page ★★★

This site, offered by Bellcore, allows users to browse through information and resources from this telecommunications research company. Users will find information on ISDN and other upcoming telecommunications technologies, as well as product and research information. There is also information on the company itself, with financial, employment, and historical material provided.

KEYWORDS ISDN, Networking, Telecommunications
AUDIENCE Communications Professionals, Network Designers, Telecommunications Professionals
CONTACT www@ims.bellcore.com
FREE

http://www.bellcore.com

Broadcom Eireann Research Ltd. Home Page

This server is provided by Broadcom Eireann Research Ltd., a telecommunications company located in Dublin, Ireland. Users can browse information on the company and its research projects. There is also material on the current research projects of this prominent telecommunications firm, as well as a collection of technical journals. Finally, tourists to Ireland will enjoy the collection of links to Irish information sites on the net.

KEYWORDS Ireland, Telecommunications Research
AUDIENCE Telecommunications Professionals, Telecommunications Researchers
CONTACT enquiries@broadcom.ie
FREE

http://www.broadcom.ie

Cell Relay Gopher

This is a gopher server of the University Computing Services at Indiana University. This site specializes in cell-relay or broadband technologies (ATM/DQDB/SONET, etc.). It features research papers, standards, product information, mailing list archives, and events such as conferences, workshops, etc.

KEYWORDS Broadband Technology, Information Technology, Mobile Communications, Wireless Technology
AUDIENCE Computer Professionals, Telecommunications Professionals
CONTACT cell-relay-request@indiana.edu
FREE

gopher://cell-relay.indiana.edu/

The Cell Relay Retreat

This site hosts the archives to the cell-relay mailing list, and several other ATM (Asynchronous Transfer Mode)-related mailing lists. There is information on what is new at the retreat, getting started, and upcoming ATM related events. There are search links, several archives, an ATM bibliography, ATM documents, employment opportunity listings, recent trade press articles on ATM, ATM software, and other ATM sites.

KEYWORDS Broadband Technology, Internet Access Providers
AUDIENCE ATM (Asynchronous Transfer Mode) Users, Internet Access Providers, Telecommunications Experts
CONTACT Allen Robel
         robelr@indiana.edu
FREE

http://frame-relay.indiana.edu:80/cell-relay/

Cellular One Home Page

The Cellular One Home Page offers information on cellular phone services. The information covered in this site includes the company's cellular telephones, services and coverage areas, rate plans and billing, and general information. There is also information on their new digital communications services.

KEYWORDS Cellular Phones, Mobile Communications, Services, Wireless Technology
AUDIENCE Cellular Phone Users, Mobile Communicators
CONTACT walowitz@cellone.com
FREE

http://www.elpress.com/cellone/cellone.html

Chicago Journal of Theoretical Computer Science

This is a moderated electronic journal about advanced topics in telecommunications. This page contains information on the journal, as well as information about ordering a subscription.

KEYWORDS Artificial Intelligence, Computer Science, Telecommunications, Ezines
AUDIENCE Computer Programmers, Computer Specialists, Computer Students
CONTACT chicago-journal@cs.uchicago.edu
COST

http://cs-www.uchicago.edu/publications/cjtcs/

Communications Company MARK-ITT

The Communications Company MARK-ITT home page provides access to the Russian Internet. This site has information about the company's history and objectives, software, and services. It also lists what is on the Russian Web and has information about the Republic of Udmurtia, its industry, and trade.

KEYWORDS Information Technology, Software
AUDIENCE Russians, Telecommunications Specialists
FREE

http://www.izhmark.udmurtia.su

Electronic Communications Privacy Act of 1986 (ECPA)

This text file contains the basic text of the Electronic Communications Privacy Act of 1986 (not the final version). In addition to this text, the Act made several changes and/or additions to U.S. Code. See the file in the same directory called 'federal laws' for copies of the new/changed U.S.Code.

KEYWORDS Civil Liberties, Communications
AUDIENCE Communications Students, Email Users, Internet Users, Legal Professionals
CONTACT Peter Townson
         ptownson@eecs.nwu.edu
FREE

http://lcs.mit.edu/telecom-archives/email/ecpa.1986

France Telecom

The CNET (Centre National d'Etudes des Telecommunications), France Telecom's research and development center, has developed many modern telecommunications tools such as digital transmission, electronic switching, satellites, optical fiber, telematics (videotex), and other broadband network services. This site contains information and images pertaining to an exposition in Paris honoring the 50th anniversary of CNET.

KEYWORDS France, Mass Communications, Satellites, Telecommunications
AUDIENCE Communications Professionals, Telecommunications Professionals
FREE

http://www.cnet.fr/

Global Village Customer Support

This is the customer support site for Global Village Communications, a maker of modems, faxes, and network-access products. Global Village develops and markets communication products for personal computer users. Different areas in The Village offer information on communicating from your computer, including faxing, accessing online services and the Internet, and connecting to remote networks.

KEYWORDS Customer Support, Modems, Product Information
AUDIENCE Computer Users, Fax Users, Modem Users, Shoppers
CONTACT webmaster@globalvillag.com
FREE

http://info.globalvillag.com

IITF Web Server

The home page of the Information Infrastructure Task Force (IITF) division of the National Information Infrastructure (NII) provides information about their events and activities. Their Web site includes press releases and contact lists as well as objective information. Committee sections include monthly reports and fact sheets as well as minutes from their meetings. Users may access the online documents, papers and transcripts from the IITF, and access the NII archives.

KEYWORDS Government, Information Superhighway, Information Systems
AUDIENCE Information Scientists, Internet Users, Telecommunications Experts, Telecommunications Professionals
CONTACT nii@ntia.doc.gov
FREE

http://ntiaunix1.ntia.doc.gov

ISDN User's Guide- Appendix A

This page offers information on ISDN equipment and suppliers. There is information on power supplies, terminal adapters, personal computer cards, ISDN telephones, ISDN LAN bridges, communications servers, multiplexers and communications servers, and video conferencing.

KEYWORDS Broadband Technology, ISDN, Internet Access Providers

Telecommunications

AUDIENCE   Business Professionals, Internet Access Providers, Internet Users, Telecommunications Experts, Web Developers
CONTACT   isdn-info@pacbell.com
FREE

http://www.pacbell.com/isdn/book/appen_a.html

 ISDN

This site provides information on ISDN, a high speed connection to the digital highway provided by Pacific Bell. Available information includes an overview, user's guide, service options and rates, how to order, Internet access, video conferencing, telecommuting, and related products and services.

KEYWORDS   Broadband Technology, ISDN, Internet Access Providers
AUDIENCE   Business Professionals, Internet Access Providers, Internet Users, Telecommunications Experts, Web Developers
CONTACT   isdn-info@pacbell.com
FREE

http://www.pacbell.com/isdn/isdn_home.html

Institut National des Telecommunications

This site provides general information concerning the Institut National des Telecommunications in Evry, France.

KEYWORDS   Education (College/University), France, Telecommunications, University Administration
AUDIENCE   Educators, French, Students (University)
CONTACT   Web Group
           web@int-evry.fr
FREE

http://arctique.int-evry.fr/

International Telecommunication Union

This site describes the International Telecommunication Union (ITU) and provides online access to some of its resources. The ITU is an international organization that oversees and coordinates the establishment of telecommunications networks around the world. The resources available through this gopher server include ITU standards, meeting information, press releases, and a list of publications. The accessible databases are the Telecommunication Terminology Database (TERMITE), and ITUDOC, which contains ITU technical papers in the areas of radiocommunication, telecommunication, and development.

KEYWORDS   International Communications, Organizations, Telecommunications
AUDIENCE   Communications Specialists, Network Developers, Telecommunications Experts
CONTACT   Michel Giroux
           giroux@itu.ch
FREE

gopher://gopher.itu.ch/

International Telecommunications Center (ITC)

This extensive web resource is devoted to telecommunications, data communications, and networking. This site has information for anyone using a telephone and a computer. ITC has special telecommunications job listings, a telecom-related advertising area, a telecom magazine area, and more. It also features substantial general telecommunications information.

KEYWORDS   Communications Technology, Computer Software, Jobs, Telecommunications
AUDIENCE   Business Professionals, Consumers, Technology Enthusiasts, Telecommunications Experts
CONTACT   webmaster@telematrix.com
FREE

http://www.telematrix.com/

 **JABRA - Home Page**

This site offers information about the company Jabra, the maker of the Jabra ear phone. There is access to inquiries and ordering information. There is also information on Jabra and the Internet, cellular phones, computers, and the telephone.

KEYWORDS   Communications Technology, Mobile Communications, Wireless Technology
AUDIENCE   Cellular Phone Users, Human Auditory Interface Users, Mobile Communicators, Wireless Communicators
CONTACT   lheller@jabra.com
FREE

http://www.cts.com/browse/jabra/

 Lightning Instrumentation SA

This site offers information on the company Lightning Instrumentation SA. There is access to telecom solutions, a company profile, new information, press releases, medical products, support, and an inquiry card.

KEYWORDS   Internet Networking, Medical Products, Telecommunications
AUDIENCE   Computer Hardware Users, Internet Access Providers, Network Users, Telecommunications Experts
CONTACT   info@lightning.ch
FREE

http://www.lightning.ch/

MIT Research Program on Communications Policy

This gopher server acts as a guide to institutions and organizations doing work and research related to the National Information Infrastructure. The site is maintained by the MIT Research Program on Communications Policy at the Massachusetts Institute of Technology.

KEYWORDS   Communications Research, Information Technology
AUDIENCE   Communications Specialists, Information Scientists
CONTACT   Jonathan Litt
           diig@farnsworth.mit.edu
FREE

gopher://farnsworth.mit.edu/

 McCaw Wireless Data

This site offers information on McCaw Wireless Data, Inc. There is also information on products and services, business solutions, programs, press releases, and hiring opportunities.

KEYWORDS   Cellular Phones, Networking
AUDIENCE   Business Professionals, Channel Partners, Developers, Manufacturers, Network Users
CONTACT   webmaster@airdata.com
FREE

http://www.cellular.com/

 Mobile Office

Mobile Office Magazine specializes in mobile communications. The site provides access to weekly lists of interesting Web sites, weekly news, a directory of links to related material, technology solutions, and the magazine's sponsors.

KEYWORDS   Magazines, Mobile Communications, Wireless Technology
AUDIENCE   Magazine Readers, Mobile Communicators, Sponsors
FREE

http://www.mobileoffice.com/

 Morning Star Technologies Inc.

Morning Star Technologies Inc. makes telecommunication applications and security devices. The page offers extensive information on their products, including pricing IP connectivity. There are user discussion archives and information resources on Internet usage and resources.

KEYWORDS   Internet Access, Internet Security, Product Information, Software
AUDIENCE   Internet Users
CONTACT   Support@MorningStar.Com
FREE

http://www.morningstar.com

Multimedia Communications Laboratory

This site contains information about the Multimedia Lab at Boston University, which investigates issues surrounding the construction of general-purpose distributed multimedia information systems.

KEYWORDS   Electronic Publishing, Multimedia

Telecommunications

AUDIENCE Computer Scientists, Electronic Publishing Enthusiasts, Multimedia Enthusiasts
CONTACT T.D.C. Little
mcl@spiderman.bu.edu
FREE

http://spiderman.bu.edu/

NC-REN (North Carolina Research and Education Network) ★★★

NC-REN (North Carolina Research and Education Network) is a private telecommunications network. The network's purpose is to interconnect universities, research institutions, graduate centers, non-profit organizations, government laboratories, and industries in North Carolina, thus permitting timely participation in research and education projects. Their page provides links to their video and data networks, to the North Carolina Information Highway (NCIH) and other related sites on the Internet.

KEYWORDS Educational Institutions, Networking, North Carolina, Research
AUDIENCE Communications Professionals, Computer Professionals
CONTACT spider@ncren.net
FREE

http://encore.concert.net

 The NORUT Group LTD ★★★

The NORUT Group LTD home page gives information on its applied research group, social science research group, and the NORUT Technology group. The site covers image processing technology, data communications, information systems, data modeling, satellite remote sensing, and image handling. There are links to other sites in Norway and the rest of the Internet.

KEYWORDS Information Technology
AUDIENCE Information Technology Experts, Researchers, Social Scientists, Telecommunications Professionals
CONTACT webmaster@itek.norut.no
FREE

http://www.itek.norut.no

NetCS WWW Home Page ★★★★

NetCS is a company in Berlin, Germany that develops communications products under UNIX. NetCS products are meant to provide telecommunications solutions related to large and complex communications projects. This site gives access to product information and communications technology information. There are links to WWW servers for NetCS' partners.

KEYWORDS Internet Services, Product Information, UNIX
AUDIENCE Telecommunications Experts, UNIX Users
CONTACT Rick Kuhlbars
rick@netcs.com
FREE

http://www.netcs.com/

Office of Telecommunication Services ★★

This gopher server is maintained by the University of Texas at Austin's Office of Telecommunication Services. It provides information on computers, computer networking, and other areas related to telecommunications.

KEYWORDS Computer Networking, Telecommunications, Texas
AUDIENCE Computer Users, Network Users
FREE

gopher://mojo.ots.utexas.edu/

Pacific Bell Internet Gopher Server ★★★

This site gives information about the products and services of Pacific Bell Corporation, a telecommunications company. The information is presented in a directory structure with links to other gopher sites related to Pacific Bell.

KEYWORDS Computer Technology, Telecommunications
AUDIENCE Telecommunications Professionals
CONTACT gopher@PacBell.com
FREE

gopher://gopher.pacbell.com/

PageMart Wireless ★★

PageMart is a nationwide paging company that provides local, regional, and nationwide service with one pager. It also provides text messaging. The site lists the services of Pagemart including email and voice mail. It also includes some GIF (Graphics Imaging Format) images of the pagers.

KEYWORDS Mobile Communications, Wireless Technology
AUDIENCE Business Professionals, General Public, Parents
CONTACT webmaster@pic.net
FREE

http://www.pic.net/business/pagemart/pagemart.html

PolitTeam Project ★★★★

The PoliTeam Project is a telecommunications research program instituted by the German Federal Minister for Research and Technology. The goal of this program is the development of a telecooperation system which supports cooperation between the distributed governmental functions between Bonn and Berlin, as well as the intensification of European cooperation. Specifically, the goal of the POLITeam project consortia is the development of an integrative groupware system that provides comprehensive support for spatially distributed, asynchronous work.

KEYWORDS Europe, Information Technology
AUDIENCE EEC Telecommunications Specialists, Information Technology Experts, Telecommunications Specialists
CONTACT Wolfgang Prinz
Wolfgang.Prinz@gmd.de
FREE

http://orgwis.gmd.de/POLITeam/

RACE ★★★

This is the Web Server of RACE (Research and Technology Development in Advanced Communications Technologies in Europe), whose objective is to introduce Integrated Broadband Communication (IBC) by the end of 1995. There is general information on the RACE project, and specific information on the sub-projects of RACE. Databases are available for RACE information, cost-benefit analysis, and telecom forecasting. There are links to other European commission servers and other information related to telecommunications.

KEYWORDS Audio-Visual Communications, Communications Research
AUDIENCE Internet Access Providers, Telecommunications Experts, Telecommunications Professionals
CONTACT Ade Ajibulu
ade.ajibulu@analysys.co.uk
FREE

http://www.analysys.co.uk/race.htm

Relevantum gopher ★★★

This site offers access to Relevantum, a Finnish training company which deals in data communication courses. Available courses cover subjects including hardware, software, security, networking, and applications. This gopher server also provides links to other networking-related sites on the Internet.

KEYWORDS Communications, Computing, Finland, Networking, Training
AUDIENCE Computer Hardware Users, Computer Students, Computer Users, Computing Consultants
CONTACT Mr. Vesa Parkkari
vesa@relevantum.fi
FREE

gopher://relevantum.fi/

Rockwell Telecommunications Japan ★★

This site is a high-level page that points to several telecommunications technology pages related to Rockwell Japan and the modem products they provide. Press releases and technical specifications for various products are available. Some links may require special permission to access.

KEYWORDS Japan, Modems, Technology, Telecommunications
AUDIENCE Electrical Engineers, Modem Users, Telecommunications Enthusiasts, Telecommunications Professionals
CONTACT palm@tokyo.rockwell.com
FREE

http://www.tokyo.rockwell.com

Telecommunications **167**

Rockwell Telecommunications ★★★

This home page provides information about Rockwell Telecommunications and its services. Rockwell works in automation, avionics, defense electronics, telecommunications, and aerospace technology development. The page offers technical support, product information, and network systems research and development.

Keywords Aerospace Engineering, Computer Networks, Networking, Technical Support
Audience Aerospace Industry Professionals, Computer Scientists, Telecommunications Professionals
Contact webmaster@rns.rockwell.com
Free

http://www.rns.com/

The Satellite TV (and Radio) Page ★★★★

This site offers multiple links to pages related to satellite TV and direct broadcasting information. Information includes scheduling in the U.S. and abroad, and issues related to hardware setup.

Keywords Broadcasting, Mass Communications, Satellite Communications, Television
Audience Telecommunications Experts, Television Enthusiasts
Contact jay@itre.uncecs.edu
Free

http://itre.uncecs.edu/misc/sat.html

Talk N Toss ★★★

This location provides information about Talk n Toss pre-paid phone cards which allow you to call anywhere in the world from anywhere in the U.S. Descriptions, prices, and usage details of the cards are also included.

Keywords Advertising, Marketing, Telecommunications, Telephones
Audience Business Professionals, Consumers, General Public
Contact Jon Zeeff branch-info@branch.com
Free

http://branch.com/talk/talk.html

Telecom Paris WWW Server ★★★

This server offers information on l'Ecole Nationale Supérieure des Télécommunications in France. Users will find material on the facilities and staff of the organization, as well as information on research projects and accomplishments of the group. There are also links to other related telecommunications technology servers on the Internet.

Keywords International Education, Telecommunications
Audience French, Telecommunications Engineers, Telecommunications Professionals
Free

http://web.enst.fr/welcome_uk.html

Connections to Area Code Decoder
Reach out and touch someone . . .

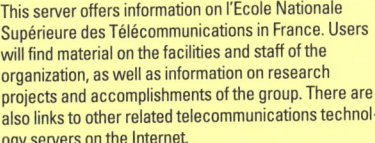

This famous line from AT&T's television commericals might not ring so true if you're not sure of the area code for the number of a friend or relative. At the "AmeriCom Long Distance Area Decoder" site, you can simply specify the city and state you wish to call and in a flash receive the area code.

If you want to make an international call, this service allows you to find out the country and the city code for the number you wish to dial. And if you desire to closely monitor your long-distance costs, you can even find out how much the calling rate is at a particular time of day for any given zone.

(http://www.xmission.com/~americom/aclookup.html)

Telecommunications Council Report—Reforms Toward the Intellectually Creative ★★★

This site offers access to the Japanese report, 'Reforms Toward the Intellectually Creative Society of the 21st Century.' A table of contents offers access to different areas in the report. Topics include transition to an intellectually creative society based on info-communications, the implications of the info-communications infrastructure, characteristics of fiber-optic networks, the goals for building an info-communications infrastructure, developing and introducing applications, establishment of subscriber fiber-optic networks, and recommended measures which should be effected by the government.

Keywords Economic Development, Japan, Telecommunications
Audience Economic Development Experts, Economists, Japan Residents, Telecommunications Experts
Contact feedback@mpt.go.jp
Free

http://www.mpt.go.jp/Report/Report1993No5/contents.html

Telecommunications and Social Interaction ★★★

This is a study of the aspects of social interaction in three areas—networked applications, computer-mediated communication and multimedia applications, and distributed virtual reality.

Keywords Computer Mediated Communication, Multimedia
Audience Scholars, Social Scientists, Sociologists, Students
Free

http://www.nta.no/telektronikk/4.93.dir/Oedegaard_0.html

United Nations International Telecommunications Union Gopher ★★★

The UN International Telecommunications Union (ITU) Gopher offers information on ITU standards, publications, databases, meetings, and press releases. Other directories offered include the ITU Radiocommunication Sector, the ITU Telecommunication Development Sector, Telecommunication Standardization Sector, plus other telecommunications-related topics. The site features search capability for menu titles on the gopher system.

KEYWORDS   Communications Technology, Telecommunications, United Nations
AUDIENCE   Communications Professionals, Communications Specialists, Communications Students
FREE

gopher://info.itu.ch/1

University of Buenos Aires Gopher ★★★

This is the main gopher of the University of Buenos Aires and is maintained by its Center for Scientific Communications. It contains a variety of information about the University, its services, its programs, and local and general events.

KEYWORDS   Argentina, International Education, Scientific Communications
AUDIENCE   International Students, Spanish Speakers, Students, Students (University)
CONTACT   gopher@ccc.uba.ar
FREE

gopher://gopher.uba.ar/

U.C. Santa Cruz Communications & Technology Services ★★★

This is the server for UC Santa Cruz Communications & Technology Services, covering Applications Development & Support, Business Services, Computing Systems Operations, Instructional Computing Laboratories (ICL), Network & Telecommunications Services, Cabling, Network Operations, Network Planning and Development, Telecom Services, etc. Various additional resources, maintained by CATS, can also be accessed directly from this server.

KEYWORDS   California, Computer Systems, Technology, Telecommunications
AUDIENCE   Educators (University), Internet Users, Researchers, Students (University)
FREE

http://ftp.ucsc.edu

Welcome to Ericsson ★★★★

This site offers information about the company Ericsson. There is access to general information about the company including an introduction, presentation, around the world look, and press releases. There is also access to information about their telecommunications products, radio communications, business networks, components, and microwave systems. Additionally, you'll find information about special interests and general services.

KEYWORDS   Internet Networking, Microwave Systems, Radio Communications
AUDIENCE   Microwave System Users, Network Users, Radio Communicators, Telecommunications Experts
CONTACT   webmaster@www.ericsson.nl
FREE

http://www.ericsson.com/

Computing & Mathematics

Analysis	169
Applications	169
Artificial Intelligence	176
Career & Employment	179
Companies	179
Computer Science	185
Hardware	193
Mathematical Formulae	194
Mathematics	195
Networking	201
Operating Systems	203
Organizations	205
Programming	209
Reference	213
Resources	215
Software	220
Standards	228
Statistics	228
Systems	229
Theory	232

Analysis

See also
Computing & Mathematics · *Computer Science*
Engineering & Technology · *Engineering*

Electronic Transactions on Numerical Analysis

This gopher hole gives access to an online journal entitled Electronic Transactions on Numerical Analysis. The journal focuses on recent developments in scientific computing and numerical analysis. This site gives access to recent issues of the journal, provides information on other ways to obtain the journal, and gives information of interest to potential authors. The information is available by keyword search.

KEYWORDS   Computing, Journals, Mathematical Analysis, Numerical Analysis
AUDIENCE   Authors, Computer Scientists, Mathematicians, Numerical Analysts, Scientists
CONTACT   etna@mcs.kent.edu
FREE

http://etna.mcs.kent.edu/

gopher://etna.mcs.kent.edu/

ftp://etna.mcs.kent.edu

State University of New York Group for Stochastic & Computational Mechanics

This site is for the State University of New York's Group for Stochastic & Computational Mechanics. The information provided covers topics including geoscience software and associated documentation, earthquake research, and a programming language called LambdaMOO.

KEYWORDS   Education (College/University), Software, Statistics
AUDIENCE   Academics, Computer Professionals, Computer Users, Students (Secondary/College)
FREE

gopher://venus.eng.buffalo.edu/

Applications

See also
Arts & Music · *Electronic Arts*
Computing & Mathematics · *Companies*
Computing & Mathematics · *Software*
Engineering & Mathematics · *Civil Engineering*

3Com Corporation Gatekeeper

This site is an MIB (Management Information Base) repository. This repository contains a profile on each product line, MIB files, and compiled MIB files for SunNet and Isoview MIB's are a database of managed objects accessed by Network Management Protocols. Most are developed to support SNMP (Simple Network Management Protocol) for remote network applications. MIB compilers and adapter drivers can be found in the binaries' sub-directory. 3Com techical tips, references and bug lists are located in the docs sub-directory. Other sub-directories contain Department of Defense publications such as the Orange-Book.

KEYWORDS   Network Providers, Network Security, Protocols
AUDIENCE   Network Developers, Network Service Providers
CONTACT   Luis Sanchez
ftp@3Com.COM
FREE

ftp://ftp.3com.com/

3DSite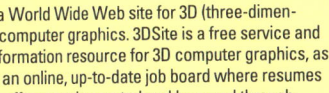

This is a World Wide Web site for 3D (three-dimensional) computer graphics. 3DSite is a free service and is an information resource for 3D computer graphics, as well as an online, up-to-date job board where resumes and job offers can be posted and browsed through.

KEYWORDS   3-D Graphics, Computer Graphics, Graphic Design, Graphics
AUDIENCE   Graphic Artists, Graphic Designers
CONTACT   Daniele Colajacomo
daniele@netcom.com
FREE

http://www.lightside.com/3dsite/

ACM - The First Society in Computing (Association for Computing Machinery)

The Association for Computing Machinery is an organization with a broad interest in the field of computing. Their web server offers access to a wide variety of journals and special interest groups within the field of computing. The Association also offers memberships which include a great many services such as access to local chapters around the world, as well as publications and journals available for a fee.

- KEYWORDS: Computer Applications
- AUDIENCE: Computer Professionals, Computer Scientists, Computer Users
- CONTACT: webmaster@acm.org
- FREE

http://info.acm.org/

ACM Special Interest Group on Multimedia Systems ★★★

The Special Interest Group on Multimedia Systems (SIGMM) provides an international forum for papers, panels, videos, demonstrations, courses, workshops, and exhibits focusing on all aspects of this multi-disciplinary field from underlying technologies to applications and issues, and from theory to practice. Topics include all areas of multimedia and its application. This page mainly provides information on the upcoming events and conferences, but lacks information on membership.

- KEYWORDS: Interactive Media, Multimedia, Virtual Reality
- AUDIENCE: Interactive Program Developers, Multimedia Enthusiasts, Virtual Reality Enthusiasts
- CONTACT: Hui Zhang hzhang@cs.cmu.edu
- FREE

http://info.acm.org/sigmm/

About Cygnus Support ★★★

This is the homepage for the Cygnus Support Information Gallery. Cygnus Support provides commercial support for free GNU software and supports GNU development tools and other sourceware. This site includes press releases, company information, and job openings. It also provides information about the Cygnus Support Developer's Kit with GNU-based software tools and includes the Cygnus Support Online Library which contains past and current issues of Cygnus publications, technical documents about debugging and compiling with GNU tools, and other GNU utilities.

- KEYWORDS: Companies, Gnu, Software, Software Design
- AUDIENCE: GNU Application Developers, GNU Users, Software Developers
- CONTACT: info@cygnus.com
- FREE

http://www.cygnus.com

Applied Systems and Decision Support (ASDS)WWW Server ★★★

This site offers a collection of material related to computer science applications. This site also hosts the UK mirror of the SHASE virtual software library, a large archive of publically accessible software. There are also online manuals for UNIX users, as well as links to other related servers on the Internet.

- KEYWORDS: Computer Science, Software
- AUDIENCE: Computer Scientists, Computer Users
- CONTACT: ofr@doc.ic.ac.uk
- FREE

http://www-asds.doc.ic.ac.uk/

gopher://www-asds.doc.ic.ac.uk/

ftp://www-asds.doc.ic.ac.uk/

Arjuna Project Information ★★★

Arjuna is an object-oriented programming system that provides a set of tools for the construction of fault tolerant distributed applications. This site offers a simple information retrieval system that is accessed via electronic mail. The Info Service has information about a number of topics related to the Arjuna System.

- KEYWORDS: Computer Applications, Object-Oriented Programming
- AUDIENCE: Computer Scientists, Programmers, Researchers, Students
- CONTACT: Stuart Wheater Stuart.Wheater@newcastle.ac.uk
- FREE

http://arjuna.ncl.ac.uk

Basic Support for Cooperative Work (BSCW) ★★★★

Basic Support for Cooperative Work (BSCW) provides facilities for collaboration over the Internet. Its foundation is a 'shared workspace' facility that runs across the most commonly used platforms on PC, Macintosh and Sun. This serves as an integration platform onto which a variety of CSCW applications can be added. The emphasis is on integrating existing tools, rather than constructing new ones. BSCW is based on the World Wide Web.

- KEYWORDS: Internet Resources, Networking
- AUDIENCE: Computer Users, Internet Users
- CONTACT: Richard Bentley bentley@gmd.de
- FREE

http://orgwis.gmd.de/BSCW/

Belmont Research Home Page ★★★

This site is the homepage of Belmont Research, Inc., a company which offers tools, applications, and services to support biomedical research and provides software development and consulting services in several areas, including software for clinical research, object oriented technology and sequencing/genome applications. Information is also available on current job openings and company background.

- KEYWORDS: Biomedical Research, Biomedicine, Biotechnology, Pharmaceutical Companies
- AUDIENCE: Biomedical Researchers, Clinical Researchers, Software Engineers
- FREE

http://www.belmont.com/

Biocomputing and Modeling at The University of Zurich ★★★

This site is an access point into information on biocomputing and molecular modeling. The page also contains links to software at the University of Biocomputing and Molecular Modeling in Zurich.

- KEYWORDS: Artificial Intelligence, Artificial Life, Molecular Modeling
- AUDIENCE: Molecular Biologists, Students (University), Swiss
- CONTACT: Godknecht U. Bernhard rzugo@rzu.unizh.ch
- FREE

http://www-bio.unizh.ch/xmosaic.home

Bugtraq Archives by Thread ★★★★

The Bugtraq archives are a threaded archive of articles from the bugtraq mailing list. The bugtraq mailing list is devoted to exposing and repairing security holes in the UNIX operating system. Users can search the archive by date, subject, or author, and can sort the results by the same criteria.

- KEYWORDS: Computer Security
- AUDIENCE: Network Administrators, UNIX System Administrators, UNIX Users
- CONTACT: Jennifer Myers jmyers@eecs.nwu.edu
- FREE

http://www.eecs.nwu.edu/~jmyers/bugtraq/index.html

Cambridge Crystallographic Data Centre (CCDC) Home Page ★★

The Cambridge Crystallographic Data Centre (CCDC) is responsible for the production of The Cambridge Structural Database, which contains bibliographic, 2D chemical and 3D structural results for organocarbon compounds studied by X-ray or neutron diffraction. Information about the associated software for database searching, visual statistical analysis of data, and molecule display is available here as well.

- KEYWORDS: Biosciences, Databases
- AUDIENCE: Biochemists, Computational Scientists
- CONTACT: pre10@chemcrys.cam.ac.uk
- FREE

http://csdvx2.ccdc.cam.ac.uk

Center for High Assurance Computing Systems Home Page ★★★

The Center for High Assurance Computing Systems (CHACS) conducts research in highly secure computer systems for the US government. Their home page relates aspects of the research in topics such as secure system requirements engineering, cryptographic development, trustworthy network deployment, as well as topics in real-time safety-critical systems. Users will also find CHACS publications, pages about

Applications

specific projects the center is working on, information about personnel, and links to other US government servers.
- KEYWORDS: Computer Security, Cryptography
- AUDIENCE: Computer Security Specialists, Software Engineers
- CONTACT: John D. McLean
  mclean@itd.nrl.navy.mil
- FREE

http://www.itd.nrl.navy.mil/ITD/5540/

Center for Information Systems Management ★★★

The home page of the Center for Information Systems Management contains a wide array of information and resources for information science professionals. Users will find academic research related to the discipline of information science, as well as resources relating to business and professional use of information technology. Of particular interest is the MIS collaborative bulletin board, where users can read about issues in information science, read comments posted by professionals in the field, and add their own comments.
- KEYWORDS: Computer Administration, Computer Applications, Database Applications, Management of Information Systems (MIS)
- AUDIENCE: Business Professionals, Information Scientists, MIS Professionals
- CONTACT: ram@cism.bus.utexas.edu
- FREE

http://cism.bus.utexas.edu/

Center of Excellence for Document Analysis and Recognition ★★★★

The Center of Excellence for Document Analysis and Recognition (CEDAR) interprets handwriting and other texts into digital documents. Their home page provides background information about their staff and facilities, as well as materials about their research. Users may read descriptions about projects, see diagrams such as handwritten address interpretation, and learn about language technology, national address servers, and multimedia image interpretation. This site also includes a list of CEDAR publications, dissertation abstsracts, technical reports and media reports.
- KEYWORDS: Database Applications
- AUDIENCE: Computer Scientists, Database Managers
- CONTACT: Ajay Shekhawat
  ajay@cs.Buffalo.edu
- FREE

http://mirach.cs.buffalo.edu

Chaos Project ★★★★

One key research goal of the Chaos group is to develop methods to produce portable compilers that generate efficient multiprocessor codes for irregular scientific problems, i.e., problems that are unstructured, sparse, adaptive or block-structured. Their Web page contains information about the current projects, papers, and available software as well as information on those involved with the Chaos project.
- KEYWORDS: Chaos Theory, Concurrent Logic, Education (College/University), Software Development

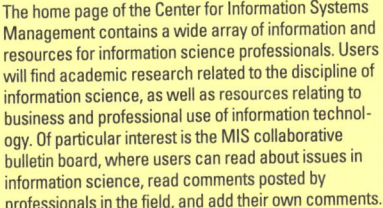

- AUDIENCE: Computer Engineers, Concurrent Logic Programmers, Parallel Computing Programmers
- CONTACT: Wes Stevens
  wes@cs.umd.edu
- FREE

http://www.cs.umd.edu/projects/hpsl.html

Computer Assembler and Simulator for EPROM's (Erasable Programmable Read Only Memory) ★★★★

A cross assembler and simulator for the Acorn RISC machine processor. The assembler, ARM.exe, was created to generate a plain binary file suitable for programming EPROM's (Erasable Programmable Read Only Memory). The simulator was created to be able to test and debug small ARM programmes on virtually any PC.
- KEYWORDS: Computer Programming, Programming Languages
- AUDIENCE: Computer Engineers, Programmers
- CONTACT: Jecel Mattos de Assumpcao Junior
  jecel@lsi.usp
- FREE

ftp://ftp.lsi.usp.br/pub/arm/

Computer Graphics Lab at the Swiss Federal Institute of Technology - LIG - EPFL ★★★

The Computer Graphics Lab (LIG) at the Swiss Federal Institute of Technology (EPFL) focuses on computer animation and virtual reality projects. The Lab is described and data provided on some of the topics and projects they cover such as TRACK motion, walking models, human body deformation, and autonomous virtual actors. Users can also view demo videos of computer generated films that LIG has created, and get information about hardware and software that LIG uses, as well as a list of publications and theses produced by the staff.
- KEYWORDS: Computer Animation, Graphics, Virtual Reality
- AUDIENCE: Animation Enthusiasts, Animators
- CONTACT: Simon Leinen
  simon@lig.di.epfl.ch
- FREE

http://ligsg2.epfl.ch/

Computer Supported Cooperative Work (CSCW) Research Group Homepage ★★★★

The Research Group on Computer Supported Cooperative Work (CSCW) studies the problems of working groups distributed in time and space and works to develop adequate support systems for them. The group has done research on work flow systems, directory systems, organizational knowledge modeling, task management and CSCW development tools. Other topics the group examines are quantitative methods and tools for the analysis of policy planning problems in government agencies.
- KEYWORDS: Networking
- AUDIENCE: Computer Scientists, Systems Administrators
- CONTACT: Dr. Peter Hoschka
  Peter.Hoschka@gmd.de
- FREE

http://orgwis.gmd.de/

Cryptography Export Control Archives ★★★

This page contains information about US export controls on cryptographic technologies. Users may read descriptions of the various regulations and events relating to cryptographic export, or follow links to source documents if desired. There are also links to information about current court cases involving cryptography and its export.
- KEYWORDS: Computer Security, Cryptography
- AUDIENCE: Cryptographers, Privacy Activists
- CONTACT: John Gilmore
  gnu@cygnus.com
- FREE

http://www.cygnus.com/~gnu/export.html

DIMUND (Document Image Understanding) Ftp Site ★★

The DIMUND Document Information Server is provided as a repository for information, data, and public domain code relating to the field of document image understanding. Viewers will find online access to a document understanding bibliography including feature extraction, OCR, online recognition, text/graphics discrimination, signature verification and related document problems. Resources include Programs and Calls for Papers, Frequently Asked Questions, Source Contributions, Technical Reports, and archives from the DIMUND Listserv.
- KEYWORDS: Image Processing, Imaging, Information Retrieval, OCR (Optical Character Recognition)
- AUDIENCE: Computer Scientists, Computer Users
- CONTACT: gopher@dimund.cfar.umd.edu
- FREE

http://dimund.cfar.umd.edu/

gopher://dimund.cfar.umd.edu:70/

ftp://dimund.cfar.umd.edu/

DTP (DeskTop Publishing) Internet Jumplist ★★★

This page contains resources and information related to computer desktop publishing. Users will find links to font and clip art archives, DTP FAQs, help files and other tutorial information, and material on popular applications used by desktop publishers. This site also provides links to other related Internet resources.
- KEYWORDS: Desktop Publishing, Electronic Arts, Graphics, Universities
- AUDIENCE: Desktop Publishers, Graphic Artists, Graphic Designers

Computing & Mathematics

CONTACT Geoffrey William Peters
gwp@cs.purdue.edu
FREE

http://www.cs.purdue.edu/homes/gwp/dtp/dtp.html

Digital Graphics, Inc.

Digital Graphics, Inc. (DGI) is a color imaging center that provides color imaging and finishing services to such markets as industrial design, textile design, corporate graphics, satellite imaging and digital photography. The page gives information about applications for DGI printers and resources for technical problems.

KEYWORDS Companies, Digital Photography, Imaging, Printing
AUDIENCE Designers, Graphic Artists
CONTACT dgi@world.std.com
FREE

http://world.std.com/~dgi/

Digitool, Inc. Home Page

Digitool, Inc. specializes in Macintosh and common Lisp development. The Home Page provides information about their main product, Macintosh Common Lisp (MCL) 3.0, and recent developments. There are also links to user product reviews and special products.

KEYWORDS Computer Applications, Programming Languages, Software
AUDIENCE Mac Users, Programmers
CONTACT info@digitool.com
FREE

http://www.digitool.com

Ewan, A Free Terminal Emulator for Windows

This page describes Ewan, a free telnet and terminal emulator for PCs with Microsoft Windows 3.1 and a Winsock TCP/IP stack installed. This page provides information about DEC VT52, VT100, and ANSI emulation, information about how to create emulation DLLs, and links to sites with the software available and other Winsock-related pages.

KEYWORDS Emulators, Operating Systems, Software
AUDIENCE Computer Professionals, Modem Users, UNIX Users, Windows Users
CONTACT Peter Zander
zander@lysator.liu.se
FREE

http://www.lysator.liu.se:80/~zander/ewan.html

GNU Emacs FAQ

This site contains information on the GNU Emacs, the GNU project's extensible, customizable, self-documenting real-time display editor. An online version of the FAQ is offered with hyperlinks for questions and answers.

KEYWORDS Emacs, Gnu
AUDIENCE Computer Users, Programmers
CONTACT scfaq@indiana.edu
FREE

http://scwww.ucs.indiana.edu/FAQ/Emacs/

Gamsau's (Groupe pour l'Application des Méthodes Scientifiques a l'Architecture et a l'Urbanisme) Home Page

This server maintains information about the cross-section of architecture, urban planning, and computer science. Users will find documentation, software, and research reports from this group, as well as information on future research goals and projects. There are also links to other servers with related information.

KEYWORDS Architecture, Computer Aided Design (CAD), Urban Planning
AUDIENCE Architects, CAD Users, Computer Scientists, Urban Planners
CONTACT Jean-Yves Blaise
jyb@gamsau.cnrs-mrs.fr
FREE

http://www-gams.cnrs-mrs.fr/SOM_ENG.HTM

Graphics, Visualization, and Usability Center Home Page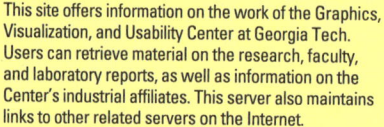

This site offers information on the work of the Graphics, Visualization, and Usability Center at Georgia Tech. Users can retrieve material on the research, faculty, and laboratory reports, as well as information on the Center's industrial affiliates. This server also maintains links to other related servers on the Internet.

KEYWORDS Computer Graphics, Multimedia, Research, Visualization
AUDIENCE Computer Professionals, Computer Scientists, Multimedia Professionals
CONTACT Elizabeth D. Mynatt
beth@cc.gatech.edu
FREE

http://www.cc.gatech.edu/gvu/gvutop.html

Hyperactive Molecules Using Chemical MIME

This site provides a demonstration of an interactive 3-D modeling system for the WWW which requires forms support. It enables you to specify a chemical structure and then have it displayed for your WWW browser.

KEYWORDS Molecular Modeling, Nanotechnology
AUDIENCE Crystallographers, Molecular Biologists
CONTACT Henry Rzepa
rzepa@ic.ac.uk
FREE

http://www.ch.ic.ac.uk/chemical_mime.html

IONA Technologies

The IONA Technologies Home Page is dedicated mostly to Orbix, the central communications mechanism for object oriented applications. It is a developer's kit for integrating software components into full applications where modules can be built on a machine and then spread across a network. This page also provides access to Iona's training and consulting services as well as job opportunities.

KEYWORDS Communications, Computer Programming, Computer Software
AUDIENCE Communications Specialists, Computer Networkers, Developers
CONTACT webmaster@iona.ie
FREE

http://www.iona.ie:8000/www/index.html

Information Science Research Institute

The Information Science Research Institute (ISRI) intends to improve automated technologies for document understanding, utilizing technologies for recognition and retrieval of information from machine-printed documents. This site provides information on ISRI's mission, the organization, the people, and ISRI activities, which includes the annual symposium, text retrieval research, the technology assessment program and development research.

KEYWORDS Computer Science, Information Retrieval
AUDIENCE Computer Scientists, Information Specialists, Technology Researchers
CONTACT isri-info@isri.unlv.edu
FREE

http://www.isri.unlv.edu

Institut für Angewandte Informatik, University of Wuppertal

This site is maintained by the Institute of Applied Computer Science at the University of Wuppertal in Germany. Much of the information here is in German. Users will find information on the University's programs, faculty, staff, and students. In addition, there is some technical information available here, as well as links to other Wuppertal University departments.

KEYWORDS Germany, Informatics
AUDIENCE Computer Educators, Computer Science Students, Computer Scientists, Germans
CONTACT Hans-Jürgen Buhl
webmaster@math.uni-wuppertal.de
FREE

http://wmwap1.math.uni-wuppertal.de

Institut National de Recherche en Informatique et en Automatique

This site contains information on inria-graphlib, a computer graphics services produced by the Institut National de Recherche en Informatique et en Automatique (INRIA), a research institute in France. The server

Applications

Computing & Mathematics

includes information on computer graphics conferences, descriptions of European computer graphics labs, groups on various computer graphics topics, publications, and related FAQs.
- KEYWORDS: Computer Graphics, Conferences, France, Graphics
- AUDIENCE: Graphic Designers, Graphic Designers
- CONTACT: Pierre Jance`ne
  inria-graphlib-post@inria.fr
- FREE

gopher://ftp.inria.fr:71/

Institute of Photogrammetry ★★★

The Institute of Photogrammetry works on research in the fields of digital image understanding, feature extraction, and spatial information systems. This site gives general information about the staff, projects and papers from the institute. There are links to the ftp-server of the institute and a second course on digital photogrammetry.
- KEYWORDS: Computer Science, Germany
- AUDIENCE: Germans, Graphic Artists, Students
- CONTACT: Laszlo Teleki and Stephan Winter
  webmaster@ipb.uni-bonn.de
- FREE

http://www.ipb.uni-bonn.de

Learning Through Collaborative Visualization Project (CoVis) ★★★★

This site offers information on the Learning Through Collaborative Visualization Project at Northwestern University. Users can learn about the project's objective to improve education (particularly K-12) using networking and computer technology. Visitors to this site will find research papers, information on the faculty and staff, video clips and other multimedia materials, and more. There are also detailed descriptions of the technologies that the Project is employing, as well as directories of software and learning materials.
- KEYWORDS: Computer Visualization, Educational Technology, Research, Universities
- AUDIENCE: Computer Scientists, Computer Visualization Specialists, Education Technology Specialists, Educational Porfessionals
- CONTACT: Douglas Gordin
  gordin@covis.nwu.edu
- FREE

http://www.covis.nwu.edu

Lighthouse Design, Ltd. ★★★

Lighthouse Design supplies computer applications such as spreadsheets, databases, presentation graphics, and project management programs. This page provides information on their object oriented development and operating environments. There is access to technical support, downloading of some product software and listings of job opportunities.
- KEYWORDS: Computer Products, Software, Technical Support
- AUDIENCE: Computer Users
- CONTACT: product_name@lighthouse.com
- FREE

http://www.lighthouse.com

Lotus on the Web ★★★

The Lotus on the Web page provides many links to information about the Lotus Corporation and its software for the PC. The software includes 1-2-3, Ami Pro, Approach, Lotus Notes, Freelance, Freelance Graphics, Lotus Organizer, SmarText, SmartSuite Lotus Forms, LotusScript, Lotus Notes, Network Notes, InterNotes Web Publisher, ScreenCam and others. The links provided include Lotus press releases, white papers, technical support, and the Lotus Notes Internet Cookbook, a casual, how-to document about connecting to Internet resources.
- KEYWORDS: Software, Spreadsheet Applications, Utility Software
- AUDIENCE: Computer Professionals, Lotus Users, PC Users, Windows Users
- CONTACT: webmaster@lotus
- FREE

http://www.lotus.com

MIT (Massachuettes Institute of Technology) Laboratory for Computer Science ★★★★

The Laboratory for Computer Science at The Massachussetts Institute of Technology contains information on a wide array of computing topics, from the latest developments in hardware and software to information and systems theory. The Lab is doing advanced research in all aspects of computer science, and has made available much of the results of their work. Those who wish a glimpse of the future of computing should investigate this site.
- KEYWORDS: Computer Applications, Research, Technology, Universities
- AUDIENCE: Computer Engineers, Computer Scientists, Computer Users
- CONTACT: webmaster@www.lcs.mit.edu
- FREE

http://www.lcs.mit.edu/

ftp://ftp.lcs.mit.edu/pub/lcs-pubs

MSU CAST (Mississippi State University Center for Air Sea Technology) ★★★

The Mississippi State University Center for Air Sea Technology's home page offers access to research and software under development. The main focus of the research conducted there is computer-based modeling and simulation of ocean geography and conditions. Users can access information on current and past research conducted by the center, material on the software under development, publications, and descriptions of facilities and staff.
- KEYWORDS: Computer Simulation, Computer Visualization, Oceanography
- AUDIENCE: Computer Visualization Researchers, Oceanographers, Researchers
- CONTACT: James Corbin
  corbin@cast.msstate.edu
- FREE

http://www.cast.msstate.edu/

 MaK Technologies Home Page ★★★

MaK Technologies does research and development work to offer software products that aid in the development, debugging and demonstration of networked distributed simulations and virtual reality systems. The home page provides information about the software products and research projects.
- KEYWORDS: Networking, Operating Systems, Software Development, Virtual Reality
- AUDIENCE: Technology Researchers, Virtual Reality Systems Operators
- CONTACT: info@mak.com
- FREE

http://www.mak.com

Media Lab Welcome ★★★★

Media Lab presents The Massachussetts Institute of Technology's research into information technologies as they relate to various forms of media. There is information about current research projects as well as links to online experiments such as an e-zine, a MOO, and a commodities trading game. There are further links to other sites at MIT.
- KEYWORDS: Computer Applications, Electronic Media, Research, Universities
- AUDIENCE: Arts Community, CMC Researchers, Media Professionals
- CONTACT: webmaster@media.mit.edu
- FREE

http://www.media.mit.edu/

Medical Image Processing Group Home Page ★★★

The Medical Image Processing Group (MIPG) conducts research into medical applications for diagnosis and creating software that will make 3D topographical maps for visualization of medical conditions. Their home page provides information about the group, with staff information. Users can learn about MIPG developed software and projects for which it is currently being used, and see demos and movies about 3DVIEWNIX 1.1.
- KEYWORDS: Algorithms, Medical Software
- AUDIENCE: Medical Professionals, Software Developers
- CONTACT: webmaster@mipg.upenn.edu
- FREE

http://mipgsun.mipg.upenn.edu

Multimedia Home Page ★★★

Multimedia Home Page is presented by the Multimedia Computing Group of the Graphics, Visualization, and Usability Center at Georgia Tech. It offers information on research projects currently underway at the Center, including such topics as computing interfaces for the

Applications

blind, network audio servers, collaborative applications, and VR sound.

- KEYWORDS: Audio-Visual Communications, Multimedia, Research, Research Applications
- AUDIENCE: Computer Professionals, Computer Scientists, Multimedia Enthusiasts, Multimedia Professionals
- CONTACT: Keith Edwards
  keith@cc.gatech.edu
- FREE

http://www.cc.gatech.edu/gvu/multimedia/Multimedia.html

Multimedia World Wide Web PC - How to Distribute Interactive Applications on the Internet ★★★

This home page is for Microsoft Windows users that would like to use, create, and distribute interactive presentations and demonstrations via the World Wide Web. The MM-WWW-PC v. 2.0 consists of a series of configuration settings and a free software application that has been developed using the authoring system Asymetrix Multimedia Toolbook v. 3.0 (R) for Microsoft Windows. Remote users of this system will be able to engage the presentation from within the Web instead of downloading similiar interactive presentations directly. Demo presentations are available for viewing once the user has configured the software.

- KEYWORDS: Companies, Distance Education, Online Learning, Operating Systems
- AUDIENCE: Distance Educators, Educators, Microsoft Windows Users, Students
- CONTACT: nirmng@univ.trieste.it
- FREE

http://www.univ.trieste.it/mmwwwpc/mmwwwpc.html

NAS Home Page (Numerical Aerodynamic Simulation) ★★★

The home page of the Numerical Aerodynamic Simulation Systems Division (NAS) offers access to resources related to the research in computer-simulated aerodynamics. The goal of the NAS is to provide the aerospace research community with a high-performance supercomputing environment capable of simulating all aspects of an aerospace vehicle system. Users can access technical reports, data sets, software, and other resources the NAS has made available to the scientific community.

- KEYWORDS: Aerodynamics, Computer Simulation, Supercomputers
- AUDIENCE: Aerospace Researchers, Researchers
- CONTACT: Marisa K. Chancellor
  marisa@nas.nasa.gov
- FREE

http://www.nas.nasa.gov/home.html

National Center for Supercomputing Applications ★★★★

This site is a gopher server of the National Center for Supercomputing Applications (NCSA) located at the University of Illinois. NCSA is a university-based high-performance computing facility and research center designed to serve the national computational science and engineering community. It provides information about the NCSA, its research, the calendar, NCSA training events, education programs, publications, services, resources, and more. Direct access to the University of Illinois campus Gopher server is provided.

- KEYWORDS: Computer Applications, Education (College/University)
- AUDIENCE: Computer Professionals, Computer Science Students, Computer Specialists, Computer Users
- CONTACT: ncsagopher@ncsa.uiuc.edu
- FREE

gopher://gopher.ncsa.uiuc.edu/

Novell European Support Center ★★★

This site is the server of Novell European Support Center. It includes links to programs, searchable support databases, latest patches and updates for Novell products, sample education material, navigation aids, hints and tips for German speakers, employment opportunities, and more.

- KEYWORDS: Databases, Educational Resources, Europe, Networking Applications
- AUDIENCE: Computer Users, Educators (University), Internet Users, Researchers, Students (University)
- FREE

http://ftp.novell.de

OS/2 Warp vs. Windows95 ★★★

This IBM-produced site provides competitive information that compares OS/2 Warp by IBM Corp and Windows 95 by Microsoft. It compares architecture, multitasking features, user interface, application support, and independent software vendor commitments. A PostScript version of the document is available for downloading.

- KEYWORDS: Computer Systems, Operating Systems
- AUDIENCE: Computer Professionals, PC Users, Software Developers, Windows Users
- CONTACT: pspinfo@austin.ibm.com
- FREE

http://www.austin.ibm.com/pspinfo/os2vschg.html

Official Windows Sockets Web Page ★★★

This page provides access to information about the Windows Sockets API or Winsock, for short. Winsock is a sockets-style communication interface for Microsoft Windows. From this site, you can download files from the Windows Sockets FTP Archive, and access the HTML version of the Winsock specifications, Winsock 2.0 information and overview, Winsock meeting notes, and links to other Winsock sites. This site includes the Lame List, a list of programming no-nos when working with Winsock.

- KEYWORDS: Networking, Operating Systems, Telecommunications
- AUDIENCE: PC Developers, PC Engineers, PC Users, Windows Programmers
- CONTACT: Mark Towfiq
  towfiq@East.Sun.Com
- FREE

http://sunsite.unc.edu/winsock

Open Software Foundation Home Page ★★★★

The Open Software Foundation (OSF) Home Page gives information about OSF technology, their research institute, services and programs. OSF does research and development that provides software solutions that enables multiple computer users to work together in an open system. There are links to job opportunity listings and local tourist information.

- KEYWORDS: Research Applications, Software, Technology
- AUDIENCE: Computer Scientists, Computer Users, Software Developers
- CONTACT: John Bowe
  webmaster@osf.org
- FREE

http://web1.osf.org:8001/

Parallel Computing Archive at HENSA UNIX ★★★★

This archive has special focus on the INMOS Transputer processor, the occam language and the WoTUG user group. It provides organized access to information, binaries, and source codes related to parallel computing.

- KEYWORDS: Computer Programming, Concurrent Systems, Software Archives
- AUDIENCE: Computer Scientists, Concurrent Logic Programmers, Programmers
- CONTACT: Dave Beckett
  D.J.Beckett@ukc.ac.uk
- FREE

http://unix.hensa.ac.uk/parallel/index.html

Phase3 Software Home Page ★★★★

This is Phase3 Software's homepage. This site includes information about Phase3's Windows application development environment, which includes the Windows visual programming tool suite, an Entity-Relationship modeling tool for generating complex data structures, Hyperlink help generator, Phase3 database and report generator, and core documentation. This site also provides company information, product reviews, help, forms to report trouble and make suggestions, online registration, and screen shots and samples. It also includes technical support, FTP access to examples, archives, patches, and templates as well as links to other information sources.

- KEYWORDS: Operating Systems, Software
- AUDIENCE: Database Managers, Software Developers, Windows Application Developers

Applications

FREE

http://www.pacrain.com/~phase3/phase3.html

QMS, Inc. ★★★

QMS, Inc. produces monochrome and color network print systems used for electronic publishing, graphic design, and advanced imaging applications. This page supplies information on their printers, resources, software and technical information.

KEYWORDS Companies, Electronic Publishing, Imaging, Printers, Software
AUDIENCE Computer Users
CONTACT info@qms.com
FREE

http://www.qms.com/

SEED - Software Environments to Support the Early Phases in Building Design ★★★

The SEED page is designed to distribute documents about SEED software for architectural design to internal group users and interested outsiders. Documents are included that describe SEED programming, layout and configuration, with both general overviews and full length instructional documents. There is information about framework applications, reference books, and different groups related to the SEED project.

KEYWORDS Civil Engineering, Engineering, Software
AUDIENCE Civil Engineers, SEED Users, Software Developers
CONTACT seed@edrc.cmu.edu
FREE

http://logan.edrc.cmu.edu

SIGAPP (Special Interest Group for Applied Computing) ★★★

ACM Special Interest Group on Applied Computing gopher server offers practitioners and researchers the opportunity to share mutual interests in innovative applications, technology transfer, experimental computing, strategic research, and the management of computing. This SIG also promotes widespread cooperation among business, government, and academic computing programs

KEYWORDS Computer Applications, Computer News, Technology Transfer
AUDIENCE ACM Members, Computer Professionals, Systems Analysts
CONTACT George E. Hedrick - SIGAPP Chair chair_SIGAPP@acm.org
FREE

gopher://ACM.ORG/
    11%5bthe_files.sig_forums.sigapp.applied_computing_review%5d

SIGGRAPH (Special Interest Group for Computer Graphics) ★★★★

ACM Special Interest Group on Computer Graphics is a forum for the promotion and dissemination of computer graphics research, technologies and applications. Areas include - synthetic images, visualization and modeling, visual communication, interactive techniques, multimedia, visual computer systems and networks. This page provides information on the organization and membership, as well as all sorts of references and information on graphics, graphics techniques, and computer rendering.

KEYWORDS Computer Graphics, Image Processing, Virtual Reality
AUDIENCE Graphic Designers, Programmers, Video Artists
CONTACT Stephen Spencer spencer@siggraph.org
FREE

http://siggraph.org/

SIGLINK (Special Interest Group for Hypertext/Hypermedia) ★★★★

ACM Special Interest Group on Hypertext/Hypermedia is a forum for the promotion, dissemination, and exchange of ideas concerning hypertext research, technologies, and applications among scientists, systems designers, and end-users. This page covers such topics as membership, conferences, and the SIGLINK organization and interests.

KEYWORDS HTML (HyperText Markup Language), Hypermedia, Hypertext
AUDIENCE Computer Scientists, Computer System Designers, Information Scientists
CONTACT Keith Instone instone@acm.org
FREE

http://info.acm.org/siglink/

SIGMOD (Special Interest Group for Management of Data) ★★★★

ACM Special Interest Group on Management of Data investigates the development and application of database technology on a full range of computer organizations. The Web page provides a wide variety of database information ranging from free database software to job openings in database management positions. Both the gopher and web sites provide information on SIGMOD organization, its membership, and its conferences.

KEYWORDS Database Applications, Databases, Information Technology
AUDIENCE Computer Scientists, Database Managers, Information Scientists
CONTACT Won Kim, SIG Chair chair_SIGMOD@acm.org
FREE

http://bunny.cs.uiuc.edu:80/README.html

SIGSIM (Special Interest Group for Simulation) ★★★

ACM Special Interest Group on Simulation and Modeling seeks the advancement of the state-of-the-art in simulation and modeling. By nature extremely cross-disciplinary activities, simulation and modeling cut across a broad range of interests. This gopher site provides information about the SIGSIM organization including membership, conferences, and an annual report.

KEYWORDS Computer Aided Design (CAD), Simulations, Visualization
AUDIENCE ACM Members, Computer Scientists, Engineers, Programmers
CONTACT C. Michael Overstreet SIG Chair chair_SIGSIM@acm.org
FREE

gopher://gopher.acm.org/
    11[the_files.sig_forums.sigsim]

SIGSOUND (Special Interest Group for Sound) ★★★

ACM Special Interest Group on Electronic Forum on SOUND Technology is a forum for the exchange of information on software, algorithms, hardware, and applications for digitally generated and/or manipulated audio signals. The forum provides a mechanism for discussion of research and development, for dissemination of news and announcements, and for establishing an ftp archive for public domain software and FAQ related to sound computation. This gopher site provides information about the SIGSOUND organization including membership, conferences, and an annual report. The Web page is sponsered by the CERL Sound group and features a SIGSOUND forum of messages.

KEYWORDS Audio, Computer Speech Interfaces
AUDIENCE ACM Members, Audio Enthusiasts, Computer Scientists, Programmers
CONTACT Carla Scaletti SIG Chair chair_SIGSound@acm.org
FREE

http://datura.cerl.uiuc.edu/

gopher://gopher.acm.org/
    11[the_files.sig_forums.sigsound]

Santa Fe Institute Home Page ★★★

This is the home page for the Santa Fe institute, one of the foremost institutions in the artificial life/complexity field. This site contains information on a number of their projects, as well as pointers to some of their papers.

KEYWORDS Artificial Intelligence, Artificial Life, Computer Applications
AUDIENCE Computer Engineers, Programmers
CONTACT mike@santafe.edu
FREE

http://www.santafe.edu/

Soar Ifor Project ★★★

This is a project to create an intelligent software agent capable of flying a plane in combat. To date, all of the work has been on flight simulators. This site provides the latest updates on this topic.

- **KEYWORDS** Artificial Intelligence, Computer Science, Flight Simulation
- **AUDIENCE** Computer Science Students, Computer Specialists, Programmers
- **CONTACT** Karl B. Schwamb
- **FREE**

http://www.isi.edu/soar/soar-ifor-project.html

State of the Art Review on Hypermedia Issues And Applications ★★★★

The State of the Art Review on Hypermedia Issues And Applications document is a thorough investigation of the issues and possible applications of hypermedia. Current implementations are centered around hypertext as exemplified throughout the World Wide Web. The document contains sections on hypermedia implementation issues, database issues, user interface issues, information retrieval issues, and applications. Users will also find a postscript version of this document available for downloading.

- **KEYWORDS** Communications, Electronic Media, Hypermedia, Media
- **AUDIENCE** Academics, Media Professionals
- **CONTACT** V. Balasubramanian
  bala@pegasus.rutgers.edu
- **FREE**

http://www.csi.uottawa.ca/~dduchier/misc/hypertext_review/

UNIX Security ★★★★

This page is a collection of various sources of security information for UNIX systems (although there are topics that apply to all computer systems). Users will find general information on security issues, as well as detailed specifics on firewalls, Kerberos, PGP (Pretty Good Privacy), PEM/RIPEM (Privacy Enhanced Mail/Riordan's Internet Privacy Enhanced Mail), anonymous FTP setups, and much more. This archive also includes pointers to security advisories available on the Internet, computer incident reports, as well as pointers to other security-related servers on the net.

- **KEYWORDS** Computer Security, Internet Security, Meta-Index (UNIX Security)
- **AUDIENCE** Cryptographers, Privacy Activists, UNIX Administrators, UNIX Users
- **CONTACT** Jessica Kelley
  jbk@alw.nih.gov
- **FREE**

http://www.alw.nih.gov/Security/security.html

USC Information Sciences Institute ★★★

The Information Sciences Institute at the University Of Southern California is involved in a broad spectrum of information processing research and the development of advanced computer and communication technology systems. There are links to information about research currently being done, as well as information on the technology brokering services the Institute provides to businesses.

- **KEYWORDS** Computer Science, Information Science, Technology
- **AUDIENCE** Academics, Computer Scientists, Information Scientists, Researchers
- **FREE**

http://venera.isi.edu/

ftp://venera.isi.edu/

Wollongong Canada WWW Server ★★★★

The Wollongong Canada WWW Server gives access to software product information, technical support and press releases. The Wollongong Group, Inc. provides software-based networking solutions specializing in protocols, applications, management, and security services using open systems technology. PathWay is a family of TCP/IP-based products that provide operations among computing platforms and mainframe systems.

- **KEYWORDS** Networking, Software
- **AUDIENCE** Computer Users, Networkers
- **CONTACT** Support Staff
  support@lehman.on.ca
- **FREE**

http://www.lehman.on.ca

World Wide Web Robots, Wanderers, and Spiders ★★★★

World Wide Web Robots, Wanderers, and Spiders are all names for programs that traverse the Web automatically. This page is devoted to learning as much about these Spiders, their uses and what pitfalls to avoid.

- **KEYWORDS** Artificial Intelligence, Computer Science
- **AUDIENCE** Computer Science Students, Computer Specialists, Internet Users, Programmers
- **CONTACT** Martijn Koster
  m.koster@nexor.co.uk
- **FREE**

http://web.nexor.co.uk/mak/doc/robots/robots.html

Artificial Intelligence

See also
Computing & Mathematics · *Computer Science*
Engineering & Technology · *Technology*
Humanities & Social Sciences · *Linguistics*
Humanities & Social Science · *Psychology*

AAI/AI-ED (Applied Artificial Intelligence/AI in Education), Computing Department, Lancaster University ★★★

The Applied Artificial Intelligence/AI in Education (AAI/AI-ED) group focuses on the practical applications of artificial intelligence and cognitive modeling, with an emphasis on educational uses. Their home page offers access to information on the research conducted by the group, as well as material on the staff, curricula, and AI in education conferences. Technical reports authored by members of the group are also available.

- **KEYWORDS** Artificial Intelligence, Cognitive Sciences, Computer Applications, Expert Systems
- **AUDIENCE** Academics, Artificial Intelligence Researchers, Educators, Students
- **CONTACT** David Nichols
  dmn@comp.lancs.ac.uk
- **FREE**

http://www.lancs.ac.uk/computing/research/aai-aied/

Artificial Intelligence Applications Institute ★★★

The Artificial Intelligence Applications Institute's work centers around the production/delivery of knowledge-based systems and the direction of future research in practical AI applications. Their home page offers access to descriptions of the projects, products, clients, publications and staff of the Institute. Of particular interest are the full texts of papers written by members of the Institute in postscript and hypertext formats.

- **KEYWORDS** Artificial Intelligence, Cognitive Sciences, Computer Applications, Expert Systems
- **AUDIENCE** Academics, Artificial Intelligence Researchers, Educators, Students
- **CONTACT** AIAI@ed.ac.uk
- **FREE**

http://www.aiai.ed.ac.uk/

Artificial Intelligence Center ★★★

The Artificial Intelligence Center's home page offers access to information on current research projects. Users may obtain material on the staff, public domain software developed by the Center in the field of perception and image analysis, and details on current projects in the field.

- **KEYWORDS** Artificial Intelligence, Cognitive Sciences, Computational Linguistics, Research & Development
- **AUDIENCE** Academics, Artificial Intelligence Researchers, Educators, Students
- **CONTACT** C. Raymond Perrault
  perrault@ai.sri.com
- **FREE**

http://www.ai.sri.com/aic/

Artificial Intelligence FAQs ★★★

The Institute for Information Technology presents this FAQ listing as a service to AI researchers. All questions relating to AI may be answered, from general topics to specific queries. The FAQ links to mailing lists and FTP sites about such areas as genetic algorithms and expert system shells. The Carnegie Mellon University Artificial Intelligence Repository provides a seachable database to most of the AI-related FAQs.

- **KEYWORDS** Artificial Intelligence, Computer Science, FAQs (Frequently Asked Questions), Programming Languages

Artificial Intelligence

AUDIENCE Computer Science Students, Computer Specialists, Programmers
CONTACT Peter Turney
peter@ai.iit.nrc.ca
FREE

http://ai.iit.nrc.ca/ai_faqs.html

Artificial Intelligence Resources ★★★★

The Artificial Intelligence Resources page offers a well-organized index to resources available on the Internet. This list includes pointers to bibliographies, confrences, AI FAQs, journals, news groups, publishers, and more. Users may search this index by keyword.

KEYWORDS Archives, Cognitive Sciences, Computational Linguistics
AUDIENCE Academics, Artificial Intelligence Researchers, Educators, Students
CONTACT Peter Turney
peter@ai.iit.nrc.ca
FREE

http://ai.iit.nrc.ca/ai_point.html

Artificial Life Online ★★★★

This is a journal on artificial life created by MIT (Massachuettes Institute of Technology) and the Santa Fe Institute. It contains pointers to a number of recent documents on artificial life.

KEYWORDS Artificial Intelligence, Artificial Life, Online Journals, Universities
AUDIENCE Computer Science Students, Computer Scientists, Programmers
CONTACT feedback@alife.santafe.edu
FREE

http://alife.santafe.edu/

Association for Uncertainty in Artificial Intelligence ★★

The Association for Uncertainty in Artificial Intelligence (AUAI) is a nonprofit organization with the sole purpose of running the annual Conference on Uncertainty in Artificial Intelligence (UAI). This site contains information on the conferences, as well as a draft edition of The Handbook of Probability in Computing.

KEYWORDS Artificial Intelligence, Computer Science, Conferences, Probability
AUDIENCE Computer Science Students, Computer Specialists, Programmers
FREE

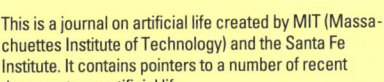
http://ai.eecs.umich.edu/AUAI/

Austrian Research Institute for Artificial Intelligence (OFAI) Home Page ★★★★

This server offers resources and information related to the research ongoing at the Austrian Research Institute for Artificial Intelligence (OFAI) and the Department of Medical Cybernetics and Artificial Intelligence at the University of Vienna (IMKAI). Users will find resources in English and German. There is information on several mailing lists originating here, as well as a collection of AI software. This server also boasts conference information as well as links to other related Internet resources.

KEYWORDS Artificial Intelligence, Computer Science
AUDIENCE Artificial Intelligence Researchers, Computer Scientists
CONTACT Ernst Buchberger
ernst@ai.univie.ac.at
FREE

http://www.ai.univie.ac.at

Chat ★★★

Chat is a natural language information retrieval system, in which users may ask the computer questions in 'natural language' and receive similar replies. Users specify as topics of discussion AIDS, Epilepsy, or Sex Education, as well as having the option to have a simulated conversation with Alice or a dragon.

KEYWORDS Epilepsy, Information Retrieval
AUDIENCE Educators, Sex Educators
CONTACT Thom Whalen
thom@debra.dgbt.doc.ca
FREE

telnet://debra.doc.ca:3000/

Complex Systems Directory ★★★★

This site, located at Charles Stuart University in Australia, contains archived material regarding complex systems. Users can find beginner tutorials on subjects ranging from fuzzy logic and cellular automata to fractals. In addition, this server contains images representing complex systems, and has a large online directory of information on other topics including artificial life, neural networks, cybernetics, and parallel computing. The site also carries Complexity International, a hypermedia journal of original, previously unpublished work in the field of complex systems.

KEYWORDS Artificial Intelligence, Chaos Theory, Complex Systems, Fractals
AUDIENCE Computer Users, Programmers
FREE

http://www.csu.edu.au/./complex_systems/complex.html

gopher://life.anu.edu.au/1/complex_systems

ftp://life.anu.edu.au

Computation and Language E-Print Archive ★★★

This server offers a searchable database and automated retrieval mechanism for academic papers in the field of computational linguistics, which includes natural language and speech processing. Users can search the database by title or author, and obtain abstracts for all available papers.

KEYWORDS Artificial Intelligence, Cognitive Sciences, Computational Linguistics
AUDIENCE Artificial Intelligence Researchers, Educators, Linguistics, Students
CONTACT cl-server@das.harvard.edu
FREE

http://xxx.lanl.gov/cmp-lg/

Experimental Knowledge Systems Laboratory ★★★

The Experimental Knowledge Systems Laboratory focuses on developing autonomous software agents through the use of knowledge-based systems. Users will find detailed descriptions of the Lab's research in such areas as real-time adaptation of autonomous agents, interactive steering of complex systems, artificial intelligence, casual modeling, and more. This server also offers access to demonstrations of the lab's projects, programming resources, and an FTP archive of software and documentation.

KEYWORDS Artificial Intelligence, Expert Systems, Knowledge-Based Systems, Research & Development
AUDIENCE Computer Scientists, Software Engineers
CONTACT eksl-www-admin@cs.umass.edu
FREE

http://eksl-www.cs.umass.edu/eksl.html

Fit.Ki Artificial Intelligence Research Homepage ★★★

The FIT.KI Artificial Intelligence Research Group is an expert sytems and machine learning research team from the German National Research Center for Information Technology. Their Web site provides background information about their research in the areas of Cognitive Robotics, Cooperative Design, and Culture Media Technology. Users can also read short description of past projects and publication lists. Some project software is available for downloading via ftp. A calendar of upcoming events and seminar is provided along with project news

KEYWORDS Cognitive Sciences, Expert Systems, Neural Networks, Robotics
AUDIENCE Artificial Intelligence Researchers, Computer Scientists
CONTACT Josef Bording
josef.boerding@gmd.de
FREE

http://nathan.gmd.de

Human Cognition Research Laboratory (HCRL) Home Page at the Open University ★★★

The Human Cognition Research Laboratory Home Page offers detailed material on current research into human cognition and artificial intelligence. Users will find descriptions of current and future research projects, information on staff and students, and an index of abstracts for technical reports related to cognitive science, some of which are available in postscript format. This server also maintains a collection of links to related resources on the Internet.

KEYWORDS Artificial Intelligence, Cognitive Sciences, Neurosciences
AUDIENCE Artificial Intelligence Researchers, Cognitive Scientists, Neuroscientists

Artificial Intelligence

CONTACT HCRL@open.ac.uk
FREE
http://kmi.open.ac.uk/hcrl-old.html

IIIA (Institut d'Investigacion Intelligencia Artificial) - Artificial Intelligence Research Institute ★★★

The Institut d'Investigacion Intelligencia Artificial (IIIA) is a center dedicated to research in Artificial Intelligence (AI) set up by the Spanish Scientific Research Council (CSIC). Topics of research include expert systems, fuzzy and multivalued logic, machine learning and CASE-based reasoning, AI in medicine, formal specification languages and inequality reasoning, AI languages and shells, reflection and metalevel architectures for AI. Users will find conference and event information, pages from the Catalan Association for Artificial Intelligence, publications, technical reports and more.

KEYWORDS Artificial Intelligence, Expert Systems
AUDIENCE Computer Science Researchers, Computer Scientists, Medical Researchers
CONTACT Enric Plaza
www@iiia.csic.es
FREE
http://www.iiia.csic.es

ftp://ftp.iiia.csic.es

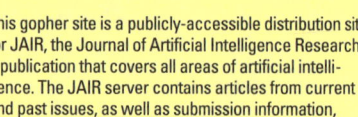

JAIR (Journal of Artificial Intelligence Research) Gopher Server ★★★

This gopher site is a publicly-accessible distribution site for JAIR, the Journal of Artificial Intelligence Research, a publication that covers all areas of artificial intelligence. The JAIR server contains articles from current and past issues, as well as submission information, formatting information, an author index and a table of contents. The articles are presented as PostScript documents.

KEYWORDS Artificial Intelligence, Journals, Publishing
AUDIENCE Computer Scientists, Researchers
CONTACT jair-editor@ptolemy.arc.nasa.gov
FREE
gopher://p.gp.cs.cmu.edu/

LIA Laboratory of Artificial Intelligence ★★★

The LIA Artificial Intelligence Lab at the Ecole Polytechnic Federale du Lausanne (EPFL) focuses on model based reasoning in artificial intelligence. Their web page provides an overview of their activities and research, including definitions of their research areas and project overviews with diagrams. Information about LIA software and hardware is included, as are staff bios and a searchable library catalog. Users may also look at weather images from all over the globe.

KEYWORDS Artificial Intelligence, Cognitive Sciences, Expert Systems, Information Science
AUDIENCE Computer Scientists, Scientists
CONTACT Simon Leinen
simon@lia.di.epfl.ch
FREE
http://liawww.epfl.ch/

Laboratoire Bordelais de Recherche en Informatique ★★★

The Bordeaux Laboratory of Informatics Research works in five categories of study — language theory, algorithms, information release, symbolic programming and image processing. This page gives information about the Laboratory's research, access to publications and information about the Lab. There are links to Mathematic Biliographies, Crystallography sites and other Computer Informatics sites.

KEYWORDS Computer Programming, Image Processing, Mathematics
AUDIENCE French, Informatics Researchers, Mathematicians
CONTACT David Sherman
David.Sherman@LaBRI.U-Bordeaux.FR
FREE
http://www.labri.u-bordeaux.fr

MIT (Massachuettes Institute of Technology) Artificial Intelligence Laboratory Home Page ★★★★

The MIT Artificial Intelligence Lab's Home Page contains a wealth of information about the research projects, publications, and people at one of the most renowned artificial intelligence research groups in the world. This site maintains useful links to other AI resources as well as links to other parts of MIT. Of note are the online AI demonstrations such as the talkbot that answers natural language questions about the Lab in plain English.

KEYWORDS Artificial Intelligence, Computational Neuroscience, Systems Theory, Universities
AUDIENCE Cognitive Scientists, Computational Neuroscientists, Computer Scientists
CONTACT Robert S. Thau
webmaster@ai.mit.edu
FREE
http://www.ai.mit.edu/

ftp://ftp.ai.mit.edu/

Machine Learning Home Page ★★

This site maintains a small amount of material related to artifical intelligence and machine learning. There is an interactive demonstration of an AI 'robot' that users can talk to called 'ELIZA.' ELIZA answers questions and analyzes problems in response to user input. In addition, there is a Slovenian AI magazine called Informatica available here as well as a collection of stereograms for users to view.

KEYWORDS Artificial Intelligence, Interactive Computing
AUDIENCE Artificial Intelligence Researchers, Computer Scientists
FREE
http://www-ai.ijs.si

Serveur WWW de Loria ★★★

The Serveur Loria is made up of two groups, Centre de Recherche en Informatique de Nancy (CRIN) and l'Institut National de Recherche en Informatique et Automatique (INRIA). These groups work on theory and applied research for artificial intelligence and communications. This page provides information about the two groups, their research in speech recognition, pattern recognition, linguistic phenomena, and the implementation of human-computer dialogue systems. There is access to publications and other sites on the web.

KEYWORDS Computer Science, Informatics, Laboratories
AUDIENCE Communications Specialists, Computer Scientists, French, Researchers
CONTACT Danielle Marchand, secrétariat
Danielle.Marchand@loria.fr
FREE
http://www.loria.fr

Sigart Electronic Information Service ★★★

The Sigart Electronic Information Service site provides information about artificial intelligence, including related announcements, calenders, news, conferences, and journals. In addition, the server contains links to other artificial intelligence-related WWW resources. This site is maintained by the Sigart division of the Association for Computing Machinery.

KEYWORDS Artificial Intelligence, Computer Applications, Electronics, Technology
AUDIENCE Computer Professionals, Computer Specialists, Electrical Engineers
CONTACT Chris Welty
weltyc@cs.rpi.edu
FREE
http://sigart.acm.org/

gopher://sigart.acm.org/

Stanford Knowledge Systems Laboratory ★★★

The Stanford Knowledge Systems Laboratory (KSL) conducts research into Artificial Intelligence, engineering knowledge bases and intelligent systems. Included in their home page is the KSL Interactive Networking services, which is a network which allows users to browse 'virtual' documents and receive other knowledge bases services. Also provided are the KSL Technical Reports, listed by author, with brief abstracts. Project reports cover topics such as 'how things work', 'modeling and analysis of Reactive Systems' and 'Knowledge Sharing Techniques'. Descriptions of projects include general overviews and demonstration models. Links are also provided to other AI organizations on the Web.

KEYWORDS Computer Science, Parallel Computing
AUDIENCE Artificial Intelligence Researchers, Computer Scientists, Students

Artificial Intelligence – Companies

CONTACT Stanford Knowledge Systems Laboratory
webmaster@ksl.stanford.edu

FREE

http://ksl.stanford.edu/

UTCS Neural Nets Research Group (University of Texas at Austin) ★★★

This site hosts the Neural Network Research Group of the University of Texas at Austin. The page contains detailed descriptions of current research, including detailed diagrams and charts. In addition, users will find FTP sources for some of the software being developed by the group, as well as an extensive list of pointers to related Internet resources. Publications on topics related to computational neuroscience and artificial intelligence can also be found here.

KEYWORDS Artificial Intelligence, Computational Neuroscience, Neural Networks, Software Development
AUDIENCE Artificial Intelligence Researchers, Neural Network Researchers, Neuroscientists
CONTACT Joseph Sirosh
sirosh@cs.utexas.edu
FREE

http://www.cs.utexas.edu/~nn/

University of Michigan AI Lab Homepage ★★

The University of Michigan Artificial Intelligence Lab Web site discusses issues relating to artificial intelligence and intelligent systems, as well as providing information about the program itself. There is information about educational programs in the AI department, such as decision machines and multiple coordinating vehicles. In addition, this site provides information about the Advanced Technologies Laboratory at the University of Michigan.

KEYWORDS Computer Science, Parallel Computing
AUDIENCE Artificial Intelligence Researchers, Computer Scientists, Students
CONTACT Frank Vincent Koss
koss@umich.edu
FREE

http://ai.eecs.umich.edu/

Vub Ai Lab WWW Home Page ★★★

The Artificial Intelligence Laboratory at the Free University of Brussels provides general information concerning Artifical Intelligence, KADS, KADS-II, KREST, and offers Artificial Intelligence reprints. There is a history of the Laboratory and its research as well as links to other VUB-ULB faculty and department sites.

KEYWORDS Computer Science, Intelligent Agents, Robotics, Scientific Research
AUDIENCE Computer Scientists, Researchers, Students
CONTACT Webmaster
secr@arti.vub.ac.be
FREE

http://arti.vub.ac.be/www/welcome.html

Career & Employment

See also
Engineering & Technology · Career & Employment
Internet · Career & Employment

Career Development Resources for Mathematicians ★★★

This listing is a collection of resources for mathematicians. It includes information and a resume template from the American Mathematical Society, as well as articles related to employment conditions and strategies at academic and commercial institutions.

KEYWORDS Employment, Internships, Societies
AUDIENCE Job Seekers, Mathematicians
CONTACT support@e-math.ams.com
FREE

gopher://e-math.ams.org:70/11/profInfo/Career.Devel

Chancellor and Chancellor, Inc. ★★★

This is the home page of Chancellor and Chancellor, a placement firm for computer professionals in the San Francisco Bay Area. Current openings for contract and permanent positions can be accessed at this site, as well as benefits data, and a company profile.

KEYWORDS Employment, Job Listings
AUDIENCE Computer Professionals, Job Seekers, Managers
CONTACT Andre Vanderbraak
andre@chancellor.com
FREE

http://www.chancellor.com/

Job Board ★★★★

This site run by a professional recruiter offers job listings, mostly computer-related, primarily in Canada, Saudi Arabia, and Connecticut.

KEYWORDS Computing, Employment, Job Listings
AUDIENCE Employers, Job Seekers
FREE

http://www.io.org/~jwsmith/jobs.html

Mathematics Job Market ★★★

This page produced by Geoff Davis, a mathematics graduate student at Dartmouth University, seeks to help both recent and new Ph.D. recipients prepare for the job market. This page has several sections that provide Ph.D.'s with mathematics job market facts, how-to tips, a compiled list of links to other reports, articles, and essays. All in order to offer informational support to ease Ph.D's into the competitive job market.

KEYWORDS Employment, Jobs, Mathematics
AUDIENCE Mathematicians, Students (Graduate)

CONTACT Geoff Davis
gdavis@cs.dartmouth.edu
FREE

http://www.cs.dartmouth.edu/~gdavis/policy/jobmarket.html

Professional Opportunities for Mathematicians ★★★

The American Mathematical Society maintains a list of job openings for those with advanced degrees in mathematics. While the vast majority of positions included are in academe, opportunities in both private business and non-profit organizations are listed as well. Updates to the list occur almost daily. The compilers of the list have standardized entries to a large extent, making the list of over 200 entries relatively simple to scan. There are also separate listings for post-doctoral fellowships.

KEYWORDS Career, Employment, Mathematics
AUDIENCE Job Seekers, Mathematicians
CONTACT support@e-math.ams.com
FREE

gopher://e-math.ams.org.:70/11/profInfo/ProfOp

Companies

See also
Computing & Mathematics · Organizations
Popular Culture & Entertainment · Shopping

3Com Home Page ★★★★

This is 3Com's home page providing access to the computer networking company's background, products and services. Financial reports, employment opportunities, latest 3Com stock report are also available at this site.

KEYWORDS Data Communications, Networking
AUDIENCE Computer Users, Network Administrators, Systems Administrators
CONTACT webmaster@3com.com
FREE

http://www.3com.com

ACC (Advanced Computer Communications) RiverWatch ★★★

This welcome page allows access to the ACC's interactive guide. There is access to the corporate profile, company information, products and technology, information request forms, and announcements.

KEYWORDS ISDN, Internet Access, Manufacturing
AUDIENCE Computer Users, Investors, Network Specialists, Systems Administrators
CONTACT info@acc.com
FREE

http://www.acc.com/

AFSG A/UX FTP Server ★★★★

This server contains unofficial software equivalents of popular UNIX software for Apple's A/UX Operating System. A/UX is UNIX-style software which runs on a Mac. Some of the software is designed to take advantage of Macintosh-specific features, while maintaining a UNIX-type environment on the Mac.

KEYWORDS Computer Products, Software
AUDIENCE Computer Scientists, Programmers
CONTACT Ron Flax
ron@afsg.apple.com
FREE

http://afsg.apple.com/

ftp://afsg.apple.com/pub/

COMMERCIAL AMD (Advanced Micro Devices, Inc.) Home Page ★★★

This is the home page of Advanced Micro Devices, Inc. Information on the company, its products, location, support, events and employment opportunities can be accessed at this site.

KEYWORDS Computer Products, Integrated Circuits
AUDIENCE Computer Manufacturers, Hardware Engineers, Software Engineers
CONTACT webmaster@amd.com
FREE

http://www.amd.com/

COMMERCIAL AT&T Bell Laboratories Research World Wide Web Server ★★★

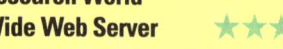

This Web site provides information on research and development at AT&T Bell Laboratories.

KEYWORDS Companies, Technology, Telecommunications, Telephones
AUDIENCE Communications Specialists, Educators, Engineers, Technology Specialists
CONTACT webmaster@research.att.com
FREE

http://www.research.att.com/

ftp://ftp.research.att.com/dist/

COMMERCIAL Access HP (Hewlett-Packard) ★★★★

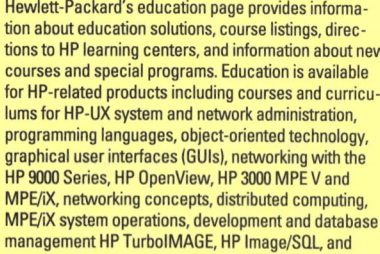

Hewlett-Packard's education page provides information about education solutions, course listings, directions to HP learning centers, and information about new courses and special programs. Education is available for HP-related products including courses and curriculums for HP-UX system and network administration, programming languages, object-oriented technology, graphical user interfaces (GUIs), networking with the HP 9000 Series, HP OpenView, HP 3000 MPE V and MPE/iX, networking concepts, distributed computing, MPE/iX system operations, development and database management HP TurboIMAGE, HP Image/SQL, and more.

KEYWORDS Computer Education, Computer Systems, Operating Systems
AUDIENCE Computer Professionals, Computer System Designers, Programmers
CONTACT webmaster@www.hp.com
FREE

http://www.hp.com/edserver/edserver.html

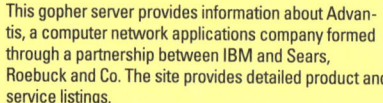

COMMERCIAL Advantis Gopher Server ★★★

This gopher server provides information about Advantis, a computer network applications company formed through a partnership between IBM and Sears, Roebuck and Co. The site provides detailed product and service listings.

KEYWORDS Companies
AUDIENCE Computer Professionals, Network Developers, Network Service Providers
CONTACT jimc@vnet.ibm.com
FREE

gopher://gopher.advantis.com/

COMMERCIAL Amiga Home Page ★★★★

This page is a central location for information and resources for the Amiga family of personal computers. Users will find news and updates about the Amiga and its fate, archives of software written for the Amiga, hardware information, user support groups, and a collection of links to other pages about the Amiga.

KEYWORDS Companies, Computer Graphics, Computer Hardware
AUDIENCE Amiga Users, Computer Users
CONTACT Michael J Witbrock
witbrock@cs.cmu.edu
FREE

http://www.cs.cmu.edu:8001/Web/People/mjw/Computer/Amiga/MainPage.html

COMMERCIAL Apple Computer WWW Server ★★★

This web site contains information about Apple Computer. The resource is designed to provide timely product information, including press releases on Apple's technology and research. It also contains links to Freeware and Shareware sites, support information for users, and information for Macintosh developers and programmers.

KEYWORDS Computer Systems, Technology
AUDIENCE Computer Users, Macintosh Users
CONTACT webmaster@apple.com
FREE

http://www.apple.com/

COMMERCIAL Apple FTP Server ★★

This site is an FTP server containing software for the Apple Macintosh community. Some of the software is MacTCP, Apple Modem Tools, and AppleTalk, among others.

KEYWORDS Software
AUDIENCE Computer Users, Macintosh Users
FREE

gopher://seeding.apple.com/

COMMERCIAL Atria Home Page ★★★

This is the home page of Atria Inc. Its primary product is ClearCase, a source control and configuration management system. Information is available at this site on the company, its products and services, events, technical literature, links to partner and customer home pages, and user group information.

KEYWORDS Software Development, Software Engineering
AUDIENCE Software Developers, Software Engineers
CONTACT webmaster@atria.com
FREE

http://www.atria.com/

COMMERCIAL Bay Networks ★★★★

This is Bay Networks' home page a switched internetworking company. The company's background, news, events, products, and customer support are described, and there's a technical library of documents. However, all of the Bay Networks Technical Library Documents are provided in Portable Document Format (.pdf) and a helper application is required in order to view the documents. Bay Networks recommends the Adobe Acrobat Reader program, which you can download free of charge from Adobe.

KEYWORDS Computer Systems, Networking
AUDIENCE Computer Users, Network Administrators, Systems Administrators
CONTACT webmaster@baynetworks.com
FREE

http://www.baynetworks.com

COMMERCIAL Berkeley Software Design, Inc. Home Page ★★★

Berkeley Software Design provides this site to offer information and support for their BSD UNIX operating system software. Users will find detailed information on the products and services provided by this company. In addition, there are hypertext manual pages for their software, as well as an FTP archive of updates and other software related to the company's products. Information on the BSD/OS users mailing list is also available.

KEYWORDS BSDI, Operating Systems
AUDIENCE BSD/OS Users, Computer Professionals, UNIX Users
CONTACT bsdi-info@bsdi.com
FREE

http://www.bsdi.com

ftp://ftp.bsdi.com/

COMMERCIAL Bristol Products ★★★

This is the Bristol Products homepage providing application cross-development tools for Microsoft Windows and UNIX/Motif. Tools include Wind/U, the Windows to UNIX portability toolkit, HyperHelp, the UNIX online help system, Xprinter, the X Window printing library, and ForeHelp for UNIX. This site provides company information, employment opportunities, product information, and demos of the products. (Most demos have been zipped with gnuzip which can also be downloaded from here.)

KEYWORDS Cross Platform Applications, Operating Systems, Programming, UNIX
AUDIENCE UNIX Users, Windows Users, X Window Users
CONTACT info@bristol.com
FREE

http://bristol.com:80/Products/products.html

CSK Corporation ★★★

This is the company home page from CSK Corporation (including the famous SEGA.) The main divisions of the company are System Integration Services, Professional Services, System Operation Services. You can have a look at their services and software, listen to the Chairman, go to the financial results and company profile page. There's also an online public relations magazine. Generally, you'll find a lot of graphics and sound here.

KEYWORDS Companies, Japanese Business
AUDIENCE Computer Users, Market Analysts, Network Users
CONTACT ndm@cso.csk.co.jp
FREE

http://www.csk.co.jp/

Cadence Design Systems ★★★★

This is the home page of Cadence Design Systems, Inc., a provider of EDA software and services which automates the design of integrated circuits (ICs) and electronic systems. Information on the company, products, financial reports, news, services, locations, and job listings are available at this site.

KEYWORDS Computer Aided Design (CAD), Software
AUDIENCE Electrical Engineers, Software Engineers
FREE

http://www.cadence.com/

Compaq Home Page ★★★

The homepage of Compaq Computers, manufacturer of PC systems, laptops, and desktops, provides product information, service and support, and what's new about their computer systems. FAQs provide information about portables, including the Concerto, Contura, and LTE Elite; desktops, including the Deskpro, Presario, and ProLinea; and systems, including the ProLiant and ProSignia. White papers provide information about Ethernet technology, Compaq desktop management, Compaq insight asynchronous management, and more.

KEYWORDS Computer Hardware, Computer Systems
AUDIENCE Computer Professionals, Computer System Designers, PC Users
CONTACT WebMaster@Compaq.Com
FREE

http://www.compaq.com

Convex Information Server ★★★

This server gives information about Convex computers and Convex Computer Corporation. Most of the information is of interest to users of Convex computers such as technical bulletins, software updates, and release notices.

KEYWORDS Computing, Operating Systems, Software
AUDIENCE Computer Users, Convex Computer Users
CONTACT iserv_admin@convex.com
FREE

gopher://iserv.convex.com/

Cray Research Home Page ★★★★

This is the Cray Research, Inc. World Wide Web information server. The company, which provides large-scale supercomputer systems used in government, industry, and academia offers links to — investor information, their 1994 annual report, historical financial data, facts about the new Cray J932 supercomputer and Cray T90 Series, recent announcements, product information, software, service and support, and a brief company overview.

KEYWORDS Internet Access, Supercomputers
AUDIENCE Computer Professionals, Researchers
FREE

http://ftp.cray.com

CutterNet, Inc. - Network Software Specialists ★★★★

This site describes the products and services of CutterNet Inc. which provides software development utilities related to computer networks. These utilities specialize in interprocess communication, distributed computing, software licensing, and software consulting.

KEYWORDS Computer Products, Internet Networking, Software Development
AUDIENCE Software Designers, Software Developers, Software Engineers
CONTACT info@CutterNet.com
FREE

http://InetBSystems.us.com/CUTTERNET/CutterNet.html

ftp://iccarus.inetbsystems.us.com

Data General Home Page ★★★

Data General produces open systems by providing servers, storage products and services to information systems users. The home page contains information about the company, its profile, products and services. There are links to technical support and other related online servers.

KEYWORDS Data Management, Operating Systems, Systems Engineering
AUDIENCE Server Technicians, Systems Administrators

CONTACT sense@dg.com
FREE

http://www.dg.com/

Dell Computer Home Page ★★★

This is the homepage for Dell Computer Corporation which designs, develops, manufactures, markets, services, and supports a complete line of PCs. Products include bundled PCs such as Latitude Notebooks, Dimension, Omniplex, and Optiplex Desktops. This free site provides FTP access to programs, technical support, and mirror sites for Dell's BBS. Corporate information including financial reports, employment opportunities, and press releases is also available at this site.

KEYWORDS Computer Hardware, Computer Systems
AUDIENCE Computer Professionals, Computer System Designers, PC Users, Windows Users
FREE

http://www.dell.com

Diamond Multimedia Systems, Inc. ★★★

This the homepage for Diamond Multimedia Systems, a supplier of graphics and video accelerator cards, the quad-speed multimedia kits, games accelerator kits, soundcards and fax/modem kits. This site includes product information, software information about GO'95 and InControl Tools, contact information, ftp access to drivers, and links to other sites.

KEYWORDS Computer Hardware, Graphics, Multimedia
AUDIENCE Computer Graphic Designers, Computer Professionals, PC Users
CONTACT webdude@diamondmm.com
FREE

http://www.diamondmm.com

Digital Equipment Corporation ★★★

The Digital Equipment Corporation page provides users with information on its variety of networked computer systems and software. This site allows users to test software on Alpha Servers, learn about Digital's latest research and technology, receive customer service, training, and support. Users can also browse software archives, configure systems, generate quotes, and place orders from Digital Equipment Corporation electronically.

KEYWORDS Digital Electronics, Networking, Software
AUDIENCE Business Professionals, General Public
CONTACT response@mkots3.enet.dec.com
FREE

http://www.digital.com

Edgewood Engineering ★★

This page provides information about Edgewood Engineering, a consulting firm that provides application development for Windows, DOS, and UNIX. There is also information on device drivers for DOS, UNIX, and other operating systems, including Windows VXDs; firmware for microcontrollers, including 8051 and derivatives, and custom computer systems.

KEYWORDS Computer Systems, Operating Systems, Programming
AUDIENCE Computer Professionals, Software Developers, Windows Application Developers
CONTACT Paul Bingman
paul@edgewood.portland.or.us
FREE

http://edgewood.portland.or.us/

FORE Systems, Inc. Home Page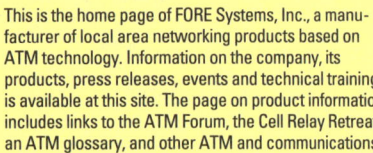

This is the home page of FORE Systems, Inc., a manufacturer of local area networking products based on ATM technology. Information on the company, its products, press releases, events and technical training is available at this site. The page on product information includes links to the ATM Forum, the Cell Relay Retreat, an ATM glossary, and other ATM and communications networking-related material.

KEYWORDS ATM (Asynchronous Transfer Mode), Computer Networking
AUDIENCE Software Professionals, Systems Administrators
CONTACT web@fore.com
FREE

http://www.fore.com/

GraphPad Software Home Page ★★

GraphPad Software designs software exclusively for scientists, who want to simplify data analysis and graphing. Software includes GraphPad Prism, scientific graphics and curve fitting software for Windows, InStat, statistics calculator for DOS or Macintosh, and InTend, a laboratory organizer and calculator for DOS. This site provides information, technical support access and links to other sites.

KEYWORDS Computer Systems, Software
AUDIENCE Macintosh Users, Scientists, Windows Users
FREE

http://www.graphpad.com/

Hewlett-Packard Company ★★★

This site contains a profile and general information on one of the world's largest manufacturers, Hewlett-Packard. Through this site, users will have access to news, products, worldwide contacts, and an information search all pertaining to Hewlett-Packard. Also included are a list of diverse products, an 'Industries and Applications' page, along with information on the directions Hewlett-Packard intends to explore in the future.

KEYWORDS Computer Systems, Computers, Electronic Products, Manufacturers
AUDIENCE Business Professionals, Consumers, General Public
CONTACT webmaster@www.hp.com
FREE

http://www.hp.com

IBM Home Page ★★★★

IBM's homepage presents information about IBM products, services, support, publications, and education for the country of your choice. It provides support for OS/2 and PC DOS platforms and is a source for information about client/server computing, business computing systems, large scale computing, parallel computing, IBM Personal Computers, workstation and server computing, Internet products and services, microelectronics, and networking. Other areas covered include application development, data management, multimedia, networking, operating systems, systems management, transaction processing, and IBM publications.

KEYWORDS Computer Hardware, Networking, Operating Systems, Hardware
AUDIENCE Computer Engineers, Computer Professionals, Computer System Designers, PC Users
CONTACT webmaster@www.ibm.com
FREE

http://www.ibm.com

IKOS Systems, Inc ★★★

This is the home page of IKOS Systems, Inc. an EDA manufacturer and developer of simulation tools. News and press releases, product information, investor and financial information, career opportunities, and employee home pages are all available at this site.

KEYWORDS Computer Aided Design (CAD), Simulation
AUDIENCE Electrical Engineers, Software Engineers
CONTACT WebMaster@ikos.com
FREE

http://www.ikos.com/

Imagicom Home Page ★★★

This is Imagicom's homepage, the site of a free resource and advertisement service designed to aid Windows developers in finding software components. Information is organized by component type (for example, animation and video, audio and sound, editors, spellcheckers, listboxes, grids, image manipulation, spinners and spinboxes, scrollbar and sliders, text display and entry, networking and connectivity) custom control file type (for example, DLLs, OCXs, and VBXs) and alphabetically by vendor and product.

KEYWORDS Operating Systems, Programming, Software
AUDIENCE Computer Professionals, PC Users, Windows Programmers, Windows Users
CONTACT imagicom@xmission.com
FREE

http://www.xmission.com/~imagicom/

Impediment Incorporated Home Page ★★

Impediment Incorporated is a distributor and dealer of workstation products such as Computer Memory. The home page provides information about the company its distribution of products and services.

KEYWORDS Companies, Computer Hardware, Distributors, Workstations
AUDIENCE Business Professionals, Consumers
CONTACT webmaster@impediment.com
COST

http://www.impediment.com/

Inset Home Page ★★★

The Inset company develops and markets the HiJaak Graphics Software Suite, consisting of several Microsoft Windows graphics utilities and editors. This site gives information about this suite of programs, including Hijaak Browser, Smuggler, Touchup, PRO, and Draw. The company also offers help to current and future customers by providing systems requirements, support services and order information.

KEYWORDS Computer Graphics, Graphics, Operating Systems, Software
AUDIENCE Computer Users, Graphic Artists, Microsoft Windows Users, PC Users
CONTACT INFO@insetusa.com
FREE

http://www.insetusa.com/

Intel Home Page ★★★★

This is Intel's home page, with access to information and support for the Intel Pentium processor and other PC processors. Other information and support is included for Proshare data and video conferencing, networking and modem products, support for systems developers, information about components, software development, architectural standards, embedded processors, controllers, flash memory and more. Corporate information includes history, financial reports, and job opportunities. Users can fill out a form to help them select the best PC configuration based on their application needs.

KEYWORDS Computer Hardware, Computer Products
AUDIENCE Computer Engineers, Computer Professionals, Computer System Designers, PC Users
FREE

http://www.intel.com

Interface Electronics, Inc. ★★

This site provides recent news and developments for Microsoft and Novell products. The site is maintained by Interface Electronics, Inc. and also gives information about that company. There are also links to other gophers in Georgia and elsewhere. In addition. users will find a link to Interface's FTP archive with software for PCs, Novell, and general network patches, and more.

KEYWORDS Companies, Computing, Internet Resources, Netware
AUDIENCE MS-DOS Users, Network Administrators, PC Users
CONTACT billy@goofy.interface.com
FREE

gopher://gopher.interface.com/

Companies   **183**

Intergraph International Online   ★★★

Intergraph International Online is the web page for Intergraph Inc., a manufacturer and developer of computer hardware, including workstations, servers, scanners, and plotters. This page has links to product information, contact information within the United States and internationally, order information, a description of various customer services, and a free demo download area where users can obtain demo and evaluation software. In addition, an Intergraph user group link contains descriptions and contact information for Intergraph users.

Keywords Computer Hardware, Servers, Software, Workstations
Audience Business Professionals, Computer Professionals, GIS Professionals, Systems Administrators
Free

http://www.intergraph.com

Iris Development Corporation   ★★★

This is the homepage for Iris Development Corporation, software development and consulting firm, which develops products for the Macintosh, Windows, and General Magic platforms. This site provides information about Email Power Tools (EPT) for Windows and Macintosh. This site is also the access point for the Worldwide Email Information Center.

Keywords Computer Applications, Email, Utility Software
Audience Computer Professionals, Email Users, Macintosh Users, Windows Users
Contact webmaster@irisdev.com
Free

http://irisdev.com/

Lateiner Dataspace Home Page   ★★★★

Lateiner Dataspace is a corporation with research interests in volume visualization, physical simulation techniques, and data structure and representation. The home page makes available papers and technical reports describing this research, as well as providing FTP access to Lateiner's demonstration software and a collection of links to related sites on the Internet.

Keywords Computer Simulation, Computer Visualization, Data Representation, Research
Audience Computer Researchers, Computer Scientists, Researchers
Contact Joshua S. Lateiner
lateiner@dataspace.com
Free

http://www.dataspace.com/

Magical Web   ★★★

This is the Web site of General Magic, Inc. Information on the company's products, Magic Cap operating system and Telescript is available. Job openings, Magic Cap related WWW sites, and PDA information can also be accessed here.

Keywords Computer Applications, Personal Digital Assistants
Audience Computer Users, PDA Users, Software Engineers, Software Professionals
Contact C J Silverio
ceej@genmagic.com
Free

http://www.genmagic.com/

MathSoft Home Page   ★★★★

MathSoft, Inc. develops, markets and supports analytical software tools. The home page provides information on the company, products, and software. The product information describes each of the math programs which includes Mathcad 5.0, S-PLUS 3.2 and Transform and Slicer. There are links to other related mathematics and statistics resources on the Internet.

Keywords Mathematical Software, Product Information, Software
Audience Data Analysts, Educators, Mathematicians, Students, Technical Professionals
Contact webmaster@mathsoft.com
Free

http://www.mathsoft.com

MathWorks, Inc. homepage   ★★★★

MathWorks, Inc. develops and markets interactive engineering and scientific software products specializing in providing high-performance numeric computation and graphics in an easy-to-use environment for university, government, and commercial markets worldwide.

Keywords Companies, Product Information, Software
Audience Engineers, Mathematicians, Scientists
Contact webmaster@mathworks.com
Free

http://www.mathworks.com

Microsoft Corporation World Wide Web Server   ★★★

Microsoft's homepage provides general company information, employment opportunities, and information about new products and upcoming releases. You can access Windows(tm) News, the Microsoft Network, download the Windows Sockets specification (Winsock), and more. This site includes gopher and FTP access to Microsoft's Knowledge Base (including articles, sample code, patches and other support-related products) and a filename searchable version of the Microsoft's Software Library with over 1500 software files.

Keywords Operating Systems, Software
Audience MS-DOS Users, PC Users, Windows Users
Contact www@microsoft.com
Free

http://www.microsoft.com

Midnight Beach   ★★★

Midnight Beach is a software development and consulting company. This archive is used for updates and/or shareware utilities from Midnight Beach. This archive is semi-public in that it is completely unadvertised although anyone can access this site.

Keywords Shareware, Software Development, Software Utilities
Audience Computer Network Users, Computer Systems Users, Computer Users, Internet Access Providers, Programmers
Contact Jon Shemitz
jon@armory.com
Free

ftp://ftp.armory.com/midnight_beach/

NexGen on the Web   ★★★

This is the home page of NexGen, Inc., the maker of Nx586 processor. The Nx586 chip is more affordable than the comparable Pentium processor from Intel. Company information, product information, recent announcements, and NexGen's outlook on the future of computing can be accessed at this site.

Keywords Computer Products, Computer Systems
Audience Computer Manufacturers, Hardware Designers, Software Designers, Software Developers
Contact webmaster@nexgen.com
Free

http://www.nexgen.com/

Novell NetWare Web Page   ★★★★

The official Novell Netware home page is packed with technical information on Netware, especially Netware 4.1, and general business material on the costs and methodology of networking. Also includes information on upcoming Netware conferences and special pricing for certain products.

Keywords Computer Networking, Networking
Audience LAN Administrators, LAN Consultants
Contact webmaster@netpub.com
Free

http://www.netware.com/

Omni Development, Inc.   ★★★

Omni Development, Inc. is a consulting company that works on transaction environments and client-server systems. They develop applications for the WWW, including OmniWeb. The page provides information on the corporation, contact information and software.

Keywords Applications, Client Server Technology, Operating Systems
Audience Business Professionals, Computer Network Users, Computer Users
Contact info@omnigroup.com
Free

http://www.omnigroup.com/

Computing & Mathematics

Companies

PCs Compleat Home Page ★★★

PCs Compleat sells and provides support for IBM and PC compatable computer systems. This site has a Hot Buys page which lists items on sale, such as products by IBM, Packard Bell, and Compaq. A summary of PCs Compleat's services, such as a price guarantee, technical support, and other selling points of the company is provided as well. Users can send email to the company for more information.

KEYWORDS Commercial Vendors, Computer Hardware, Computer Products, Computer Systems
AUDIENCE Consumers, PC Users
CONTACT webmaster@pcscompleat.com
FREE

http://www.ocm.com/pcscompleat/default.htm

Personal Bibliographic Software, Inc. ★★★★

The homepage for Personal Bibliographic Software, Inc. provides data about the company and its software, which consists of ProCite and BiblioLink II. ProCite is a bibliographic management database used for organizing reference information and formatting bibliographies. BiblioLink II is a utility used to transfer records retrieved from other databases into a ProCite database, eliminating the need for manual data entry.

KEYWORDS Bibliographies, Database Management, Publishers, Software
AUDIENCE Librarians, Researchers, Students
CONTACT information@argus-inc.com
FREE

http://argus-inc.com/pbs/pbs.html

gopher://garnet.msen.com/11/vendor/pbsinc

Pure Software, Inc. Home Page ★★★

This is the home page of Pure Software, Inc. a company whose products are intended to facilitate and augment software quality, by removing runtime and performance errors. Information on their products can be accessed at this site, as well as general news about the company.

KEYWORDS Software Development, Software Engineering
AUDIENCE Software Designers, Software Developers, Software Engineers
CONTACT info-home@pure.com
FREE

http://www.rahul.net/ricm/mnl/pure/

Sun User Group Deuschland e.V. (SUGD) ★★★

This is the home page for the Sun User Group Deuschland e.V. (SUGD). The page contains information about the company and its resources including software news. At present, everything is in German, but an English page is under construction.

KEYWORDS Germany, Internet, Software
AUDIENCE Computer Users, Educators (University), Internet Users, Researchers, Students (University)
CONTACT Robert.Zores@dlr.de
FREE

http://ftp.uni-paderborn.de

Supercomputer and Parallel Computer Vendors ★★★

This site provides a list of the vendors of the fastest computers in the world, with accompanying logos and links to vendor home pages. The vendors include Alta Technology, Digital Equipment Corporation, Hewlett-Packard, IBM Power Parallel Systems, NEC, Silicon Graphics, Inc. and others. There are links to over 15 vendors on this page, as well as links to a couple of other pages with similar information.

KEYWORDS Manufacturers, Supercomputers
AUDIENCE Computer Scientists, Educators (University), Researchers, Students (University)
CONTACT Jonathan Hardwick jch@cs.cmu.edu
FREE

http://web.scandal.cs.cmu.edu/www/vendors.html

Sybase Inc. Home Page ★★★

This is the home page of Sybase, Inc., a supplier of client/server-based software products and services for online enterprisewide applications. Information on the company is given, including financial data, news releases, conferences and events, and overviews of their products, Powersoft and Watcom. One may search the Sybase web site by Table of Contents or by keyword.

KEYWORDS Computer Software, Database Applications, Databases
AUDIENCE Database Developers, Database Managers, Database Users
CONTACT webmaster@sybase.com
FREE

http://www.sybase.com/

Symantec Corporation Home Page ★★★★

Symantec Corporation's Home Page provides news, services and support, product and company information about Symantec. This site provides access to the Anti-Virus Reference Center which includes a free Norton AntiVirus Scanner, information about virus detection and repair, virus terminology, and descriptions of specific viruses. This is the home of the Norton Utilities for DOS and Windows, as well as Norton Commander, Norton Backup, Norton Desktop, Norton DiskLock, Norton Speedrive+ and more. It also includes MAC PowerBook utilities and development tools and provides links to other sources of PC and MAC information on the Internet.

KEYWORDS Utility Software, Virus Protection
AUDIENCE Computer Specialists, Macintosh Users, PC Users
CONTACT BWatson@Symantec.COM
FREE

http://www.symantec.com

Taligent Inc. WWW Home Page ★★★

This is the home page of Taligent, Inc., an independent software company owned by Apple, HP and IBM. Information on the company, its products, object technology, developer programs, and career opportunities are available at this site.

KEYWORDS Computer Software, Database Applications
AUDIENCE Software Designers, Software Developers, Software Engineers
CONTACT webmaster@taligent.com
FREE

http://www.taligent.com/

Tandem Computers - WWW Home Page ★★★★

This is the home page of Tandem Computers, Inc., a maker of fault-tolerant online transaction processing (OLTP) systems. Information on the company, including UB Networks, product information, service information, and Tandem applications and solutions information can be accessed at this site.

KEYWORDS Computer Systems, Mainframe Computers
AUDIENCE Information Technology Professionals, MIS Managers, Network Systems Administrators
CONTACT Webmaster@Tandem.com
FREE

http://www.tandem.com/

Telebit Corporation's Gopher ★★★

This site, which is currently under construction, provides information about Telebit Corporation, its products and services. Telebit Corporation speacializes in developing high speed computer communication devices for dial-up and wide area computer networking. The information includes customer support services, product updates, and newsletters. This server is identical to that at apache.telebit.com.

KEYWORDS Companies
AUDIENCE Computer Users, Network Administrators, Network Developers, Network Service Providers
CONTACT support@telebit.com
FREE

gopher://ftp.telebit.com/

Welcome to Oracle ★★★

The Oracle Corporation is a vendor of database software that runs on more than 90 platforms, including

Windows 3.1, Windows for Workgroups, and servers running Netware, OS/2, Windows NT, Unixware, Solaris x86. Oracle provides database and connectivity software for Oracle, as well as development tools for client/server applications and interactive multimedia. Technical support at this site includes access to free support including bulletins, hints, and tips as well as access to fee-based technical support. Corporate information, including financial reports, employment opportunities, and press releases, is available at this site.

KEYWORDS Computer Networking, Database Applications, Database Management, Operating Systems
AUDIENCE Computer Professionals, Database Managers, Database Users, Windows Users
CONTACT webmaster@us.oracle.com
FREE

http://www.oracle.com

Welcome to Sayett Technology ★★★

This is the home page of Sayett Technology, Inc. of New York, which manufactures and distributes high technology presentation equipment utilizing flat panel liquid crystal displays. You can look at the LCD Projection panels manufactured by the Sayett, their technical parameters, and more. There is no electronic ordering.

KEYWORDS Computer Supplies, Shopping Malls
AUDIENCE Business Professionals, Computer Users
CONTACT sayett@eznet.net
FREE

http://www.memo.com/sayett/

Welcome to the MTE Software, Inc. Web Page ★★

This page provides information about MTE Software, a consulting firm that provides print drivers for Windows for Workgroups, Windows NT, and Windows 95.

KEYWORDS Operating Systems, Programming, Software Development
AUDIENCE Computer Professionals, Software Developers, Windows Application Developers
CONTACT Mark Edmead
medmead@electriciti.com
FREE

http://www.electriciti.com/~medmead/

Welcome to Zycad ★★★★

This is the home page of Zycad Corporation which 'offers design verification, rapid prototyping, and test analysis solutions to companies developing high-performance, electronic systems.' Information on the company, its products, customer support, as well as employment opportunities are available at this site.

KEYWORDS Computer Aided Design (CAD), Simulation
AUDIENCE Electrical Engineers, Software Engineers
CONTACT www@zycad.com
FREE

http://www.zycad.com/

Computer Science

See also
Computing & Mathematics · *Mathematics*
Computing & Mathematics · *Programming*
Computing & Mathematics · *Theory*

Advanced Computing Laboratory Gopher ★★

This gopher server gives information on computer visualization research. The resources available include newsletters, publications, images, and software. The server is maintained by the Advanced Computing Laboratory at the Los Alamos National Laboratory, New Mexico. This server also gives access to the Advanced Computing Laboratory's FTP server.

KEYWORDS Computer Technology, Research & Development, Visualization, Workshops
AUDIENCE Computer Engineers, Computer Scientists
CONTACT Chuck Hansen
hansen@acl.lanl.gov
FREE

gopher://www.acl.lanl.gov/

Argonne National Laboratory, Mathematics and Computer Science Division ★★★

This FTP site directory contains mathematics and computer science preprints and technical memoranda, available as either .dvi or .ps files. Sources for these technical reports include the Argonne National Laboratory and Newsletters of the Association for Automated Reasoning.

KEYWORDS Preprints, Programming Environments, Research Institutions, Technical Reports
AUDIENCE Computer Scientists, Mathematicians, Programmers
CONTACT Steve Wright
wright@mcs.anl.gov
FREE

ftp://info.mcs.anl.gov/pub/tech_reports/

Australian National University Supercomputer Facility Web Server ★★★

The Australian National University Supercomputer Facility Web Server provides information on high performance computing (HPC) at the ANU and links to other services relevant to researchers in computational science, engineering and HPC. Documentation about the Center includes annual reports and applications for outside Australian Universities to reserve time or resources with the center. Users can find links to pages on and off this site dedicated to technical reports and other literature, software language aids, a glossary of terms, and specific projects such as an Automated Reasoning Project.

KEYWORDS Supercomputers
AUDIENCE Computer Scientists, Engineers, Researchers, Scientists
CONTACT Drew.Whitehouse@anu.edu.au
FREE

http://anusf.anu.edu.au/

Basser Department of Computer Science Technical Reports, University of Sydney ★★★★

This site contains Computer Science technical reports in compressed postscript format. Some of the more recent titles include 'Customised Hypertext as an Individualised Learning Environment,' and 'Routing on Trees via Matchings.' Some titles appear to be oriented to specific audience such as 'A Program for Constructing High School Timetables' and 'Lies, damned lies and stereotypes - pragmatic approximations of users.'

KEYWORDS Australia, Educational Technology, Programming, Technical Reports
AUDIENCE Computer Scientists, Computer Theorists, Programmers
CONTACT tr-request@cs.usyd.edu.au
FREE

http://www.cs.su.oz.au/Publications/techreports.html

ftp://ftp.cs.su.oz.au/pub/tr

Bilkent University Computer Science Department Technical Reports ★★★

The Bilkent University Computer Science Department has made a number of technical reports and papers available to the publc. All technical reports files are in compressed (gzip) postscript format. Reports are divided by year, and each directory has a text index containing the titles, authors and abstracts from that file. Some files from 1995 are 'A Genetic Algorithm for Multicriteria Inventory Classification' and 'Exploring States of Sparse, Large Markov Chains'

KEYWORDS Algorithms, Research, Technical Reports
AUDIENCE Computer Scientists, Computing Professionals, Computing Students
CONTACT Kemal Oflazer
ko@cs.bilkent.edu.tr
FREE

http://www.cs.bilkent.edu.tr/

gopher://gopher.cs.bilkent.edu.tr/

ftp://ftp.cs.bilkent.edu.tr/pub/tech-reports

CIM (Centre for Intelligent Machines) — McGill University ★★★★

This is the information page for the Centre For Intelligent Machines (CIM) at McGill University. CIM conducts research in fields such as robotics and machine vision. This page offers links to information on CIM and related research, computer related documents such as

The CIM Primer and MATLAB, as well as links to CIM recommended courses and CIM users' home pages.

KEYWORDS Research & Development, Robotics, Universities
AUDIENCE Canadians, Students (University)
CONTACT Steve Robbins
steve@cim.mcgill.ca
FREE

http://www.cim.mcgill.ca/

CLING (Computational Linguistics) Nectar Server ★★

This server is provided by students in the Educational Programme in ComputationalLinguistics at Göteborg University. There is limited English information here. Users will find a brief descripcion of cognitive linguistics, as well as links to the departments that participate in this multi-disciplinary field. There are also links to other Internet resources with similar information.

KEYWORDS Cognitive Sciences, Linguistics, Sweden
AUDIENCE Cognitive Scientists, Computer Scientists, Educators, Linguistic Scientists
CONTACT webmaster@cling.gu.se
FREE

http://www.cling.gu.se

CSCS - Swiss Scientific Computing Center ★★★★

The Swiss Scientific Computing Center (CSCS) is the national center for high performance computing. CSCS provides Switzerland with high-performance computing resources and information. The home page presents information about its services, research, documentation and announcements.

KEYWORDS Europe, Scientific Research, Supercomputers, Switzerland
AUDIENCE Computer Scientists, Computing Specialists, Students
CONTACT Nicole Vecchi
nvecchi@cscs.ch
FREE

http://www.cscs.ch

ftp://ftp.cscs.ch

CSCW Research Group - Konvers Project ★★★★

The goals of this research group are to create an open and object-oriented development environment for CSCW systems, the 'CSCW Shell,' which will simplify the costly development of CSCW systems, and to reimplement and evaluate a functionally extended Task Manager within this environment. This work is carried out in cooperation with European partners from industry and research within the ESPRIT project EuroCODE CSCW Open Development Environment.

KEYWORDS CSCW Systems, Computer Networking, Object-Oriented Programming
AUDIENCE Computer Networkers, Computer Programmers

CONTACT Dr. Thomas Kreifelts
Thomas.Kreifelts@gmd.de
FREE

http://orgwis.gmd.de/Konvers/

Carnegie-Mellon University, Computer Science Department Technical Report Archives ★★★★

This archive has many of the 1991-95 Carnegie Mellon University Computer Science Department Technical Reports in PostScript form Some titles include 'Efficient Parallel Algorithms for Planar DAGs,' 'Stable Function Approximation in Dynamic Programming,' and 'Abstract Models of Memory Management.'

KEYWORDS Programming, Research, Technical Reports
AUDIENCE Computer Researchers, Computer Scientists, Programmers
CONTACT reports@cs.cmu.edu
FREE

http://www.cs.cmu.edu:8001/Web/People/clamen/reports/

ftp://reports.adm.cs.cmu.edu/usr/anon/

Center for Automation Research (CfAR) Home Page ★★★

The Center for Automation Research is an independent research facility in the College of Computer, Mathematical, and Physical Sciences of the University of Maryland. It contains information on the research projects in computer vision, autonomous robotics, and computer/human interaction. It also includes information on the research facilities and staff of the Center, as well as providing links to other Internet sites with related information.

KEYWORDS Automation Research, Computational Vision, Computer Interface Issues, Mathematics, Robotics
AUDIENCE Computational Vision Specialists, Computer Scientists, Robotics Researchers
CONTACT webmaster@cfar.umd.edu
FREE

http://www.cfar.umd.edu

Center for Nonlinear Studies ★★★

The CNLS coordinates a broad range of theoretical, experimental, and computational basic research programs in nonlinear science which incorporates dynamical systems theory (stability and bifurcation theory, chaos, solutions) and statistical mechanics (fractals, scaling) and also includes studies of self-organized structures in computer science (neural nets, artificial life) and in the social sciences including economics. Research papers, contact information, wokshop and conference information, as well as newsletters and links to home pages are available here.

KEYWORDS Fractals, Nonlinear Science, Systems Theory
AUDIENCE Researchers, Scientists

CONTACT Susan Coghlan, Systems Manager
help@cnls.lanl.gov
FREE

http://cnls-www.lanl.gov/

Central Laboratory for Informative and Communicative Technology ★★★

The Central Laboratory for Informative and Communicative Technology at the Technische Universitat Hamburg conducts research on computer systems and software. Their home page includes information about CIP computer pools, and information browsers of software databases. Users may read the laboratory journals in German, discussing topics related to parallel programming and software management. Users may also use the GNU manuals for TUNH databases, read instructions for using the Software Upgrade Protocol, and find out about the Radiance raytracer.

KEYWORDS Algorithms, Computer Systems, Germany, Parallel Computing, Software
AUDIENCE Computer Scientists, Germans, Systems Engineers
CONTACT Hiller@tu-harburg.d400.de
FREE

http://minastirith.cip2b.tu-harburg.de/

Centro Ricerche Informatiche per i Beni Culturali (Center for Cultural Heritage Computing) ★★

The Center for Cultural Heritage Computing is conducting research at the intersection of computer science and the humanities. Users will find information on the research being conducted at the Center, as well as information on the facilities and staff there. This site also provides software, publications, and information on some related conferences and events.

KEYWORDS Computer Interface Issues, Humanities, Italy
AUDIENCE Computer Researchers, Computer Scientists, Humanities Specialists
CONTACT Michele Gianni
gianni@ux1sns.sns.it
FREE

http://www.cribecu.sns.it/ECRIBeCuHome.html

Cilk Project ★★★★

This page is dedicated to information on the Cilk project. Cilk is a package of programs designed for writing multithreaded applications. The page provides access to papers on Cilk, to Multithreaded computational theory, and to the software needed to use Cilk.

KEYWORDS Computer Applications, Programming
AUDIENCE Computer Engineers, Concurrent Logic Programmers, Parallel Programmers

CONTACT   Bradley C. Kuszmaul
           bradley@lcs.mit.edu
FREE

http://theory.lcs.mit.edu/~cilk/

A Collection of Computer Science Bibliographies in BibTeX Format ★★★

This site allows users to access a vast collection of bibliographies of publications in the field of computer science. Users may search via a listserver, or a glimpse-based WWW form. The database is also organized by subject area; users may browse through entries in a particular subject. Information such as author, abstract, keywords, data fields, and keywords is also available.

KEYWORDS   Bibliographies, Databases, Publications
AUDIENCE   Computer Researchers, Computer Scientists, Computer Users
CONTACT   Alf-Christian Achilles
           achilles@ira.uka.de
FREE

http://www.ira.uka.de/ftp/ira/bibliography/index.html

Computation Center Anonymous FTP Server ★★★

This gopher provides access to an FTP server maintained by the Computation Center of the University of Texas at Austin. Some of the resources provided include images, GIF readers and writers, microcomputer software, and UNIX shareware.

KEYWORDS   Computation, Computer Science, Education (College/University), Texas
AUDIENCE   Computer Users, Educators (University), Students (Secondary/University)
CONTACT   remark@ftp.cc.utexas.edu
FREE

gopher://gopher.utexas.edu:3003/

Computational Science Education Project ★★★

The Computational Science Education Project is an electronic publication of the United State Department of Energy. Computational Science is a new field that is rapidly emerging out of collaborative, interdisciplinary research by teams of mathematicians, computer scientists, and scientists and other fields. This site contains a syllabus and support materials for a course in this field as well as background materials on key facets such as computer architecture, programming languages, networks, and scientific visualization. Methods of Computational Science, such as creating algorithms for parallel machines are the next section. Case studies and links to software used within this project are available as well.

KEYWORDS   Computational Sciences, E-Zines, Education, Online Learning, Software
AUDIENCE   Computational Scientists, Computer Scientists, Students (University)
CONTACT   Verena Meiser Umar
           verena@compsci.cas.vanderbilt.edu
FREE

http://csep1.phy.ornl.gov/csep.html

Computer Engineering Group - University of Parma ★★★

The Computer Engineering Group is part of the Department of Information Engineering at the Faculty of Engineering of the University of Parma, Italy. The Group's work falls into the areas of Computer Vision, Distributed Artificial Intelligence, Object-Oriented Programming, Parallel & Distributed Processing, Petri Nets, and Robotics. Users can access directories for research, publications, staff, events, and news. There is currently a call for papers for the Real-Time Imaging Journal on Special-Purpose Architectures for Real-Time Imaging.

KEYWORDS   Artificial Intelligence, Colleges & Universities, Italy, Robotics
AUDIENCE   Computer Scientists, Object Oriented Programmers, Robotics Enthusiasts
CONTACT   Page Manager - Agostino Poggi
           poggi@CE.UniPR.IT
FREE

http://aida.eng.unipr.it

Computer Science Department - Stanford University ★★★

This site offers a wealth of information related to computer science. Produced by Stanford University's Computing Department, this site maintains information on the faculty and staff of the Department, as well as material on current research projects and interests. There are also individual pages for groups such as the artificial intelligence lab within the Department. Users will also find technical documentation and links to other computer science sites on the net.

KEYWORDS   Computer Science, Research, Universities
AUDIENCE   Computer Researchers, Computer Scientists, Computer Users, Students
CONTACT   webmaster@www-cs.stanford.edu
FREE

http://www-cs.stanford.edu

Computer Science Department in the University of Joensuu ★★

This gopher hole serves the Computer Science Department at the University of Joensuu in Finland. The information to be found on this server includes documents about the department, departmental reports, studies and research descriptions, and software related with research projects.

KEYWORDS   Computer Science, Education (College/University)
AUDIENCE   Computer Professionals, Students (Secondary/University)
CONTACT   yllapito@cs.joensuu.fi
FREE

gopher://cs.joensuu.fi:152/

Computer Science House ★★★★

Computer Science House (CSH) is a special interest group housing project at the Rochester Institute of Technology. The home page supplies information about the group, the house and its projects. There are links to member pages, other RIT servers and selected web sites.

KEYWORDS   Education (College/University), Educational Programs, Student Organizations
AUDIENCE   Computer Scientists, Computer Users, RIT Students
CONTACT   webmaster@mail.csh.rit.edu
FREE

http://www.csh.rit.edu

Computer Science, Yale University ★★★

The is the home page for the Computer Science Department at Yale University. Links are provided to information on official public information, graduate admissions information, class syllabi, research groups, the artificial intelligence group, the vision and robotics interdisciplinary research group, the Haskell Project, public FTP file archives, technical reports, department calendars, Internet computer science resources and more.

KEYWORDS   Artificial Intelligence, Computer Science, Robotics
AUDIENCE   Computer Users, Educators (University), Internet Users, Researchers, Students (University)
CONTACT   Root@CS.Yale.edu
FREE

http://ftp.cs.yale.edu

Computer Science ★★★

The gopher server for the University of California at Berkeley provides a general overview of the system and how to use it most easily. The server has links to other relevant servers. Some of the topics to choose from are the computer science division, the Berkeley campus, and more.

KEYWORDS   Computer Science, Computing, Education (College/University)
AUDIENCE   Computer Science Students, Computer Scientists, Educators (University)
CONTACT   Liza Gabato, Michael Short
           gopher-cs@cs.berkeley.edu
FREE

gopher://gopher.cs.berkeley.edu/

Computer Vision Group ★★

The Computer Vision Group works to advance understanding in the areas of computer vision, robotics and the theory of autonomous systems. This is achieved through research and validation in practical applications, many of which assume an industrial nature. Some directories available through this site include Autonomous Robotics and Phase Measurement for Surface Profiling.

KEYWORDS   Research, Robotics
AUDIENCE   Computer Scientists, Robotics Engineers
CONTACT   gjlacey@cs.tcd.ie
FREE

http://cvg.cs.tcd.ie

Computing Research Laboratory (CRL) of New Mexico State University ★★★

CRL, the Computing Research Laboratory at New Mexico State University, is a non-profit research enterprise committed to basic research and software development in advanced computing applications. Research is concentrated in natural language processing, artificial intelligence and graphical user interface design. This site contains information about the laboratory and the CRL Affiliates Program, which allows subcribers to participate directly in CRL research and development projects. Software archives, research projects, FTP archives, and the series CRL's Memoranda in Computer and Cognitive Science are accessible.

KEYWORDS   Artificial Intelligence, New Mexico, Research, Universities
AUDIENCE   Artificial Intelligence Researchers, Computer Scientists, New Mexico Residents
CONTACT   webmaster@nmsu.edu
FREE

http://crl.nmsu.edu/

Concurrent Systems Architecture Group Home Page ★★★★

This page is the home of the Concurrent Systems Architecture Group. Research in the Concurrent Systems Architecture Group focuses on hardware and software architecture issues in parallel computer systems. This page provides information on their projects, and on how to contact their members.

KEYWORDS   Concurrent Logic, Education (College/University), Parallel Computing
AUDIENCE   Computer Engineers, Concurrent Logic Programmers, Parallel Programmers
CONTACT   Andrew A. Chien
          achien@cs.uiuc.edu
FREE

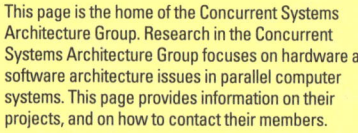

http://www-csag.cs.uiuc.edu/

Cornell Theory Center ★★★★

This site is a gopher server of the Cornell Theory Center in Ithaca, New York. It gives information on the Cornell Theory Center, its services, training, user programs, events, research and technical reports, software lists, tutorials, training exercises, sample programs, and much more. It also has access to the National Science Foundation Meta-Center.

KEYWORDS   Computing, Education (College/University), New York, Universities
AUDIENCE   Computer Professionals, Computer Science Students, Students (University)
CONTACT   Stacy Pendell
          stacyp@tc.cornell.edu
FREE

gopher://gopher.tc.cornell.edu/

Department for Applied Computer Science at the University of Economics and Business Administration - Vienna, Austria ★★

This site at the Department for Applied Computer Science, offers information about the program, including contact information, research and technical reports, details about the department's lecture series, as well as links to related sites and to an arts and architecture project. There is some English, but the majority of the links are written with the German speaking user in mind.

KEYWORDS   Austria, Colleges & Universities, Germany, Student Projects
AUDIENCE   Austrians, Computer Scientists, Students (College)
CONTACT   www@exaic.wu-wien.ac.at
FREE

http://aia.wu-wien.ac.at/welcomee.html

Department of Computer Science (University of Manitoba) ★★★★

The Department of Computer Science Home Page, at the University of Manitoba, presents information about the department, academic programs and research programs. The page has computing resources for setting up home pages and finding publications online. There are links to campus information and other Canadian and computer science resources.

KEYWORDS   Canada, Education (College/University), Research Institutions
AUDIENCE   Canadians, Computer Scientists, Students
CONTACT   www@cs.umanitoba.ca
FREE

http://www.cs.umanitoba.ca

Department of Computer Science, University of Massachusetts at Amherst ★★★★

The Department of Computer Science University of Massachusetts at Amherst presents information about their educational programs. The home page contains links to computer science research groups, the faculty and publications. There are links to campus servers and ACSIOM, the Applied Computing Systems Institute of Massachusetts.

KEYWORDS   Education (College/University), Educational Programs, Massachusetts, Research Institutions
AUDIENCE   Computer Scientists, Educators, Students
CONTACT   www-admin@cs.umass.edu
FREE

http://www.cs.umass.edu

Department of Computer Science and System Analysis at the University of Salzburg, Austria ★★★

This site provides information from the Department of Computer Science and System Analysis at the University of Salzburg. Users will find material on the staff, facilities, and research projects of the Department. There is also information available on PROMS '95, a workshop on protocols for multimedia systems.

KEYWORDS   Computer Education, Computer Science, Systems Analysis
AUDIENCE   Computer Scientists, Computer Users
CONTACT   webmaster@cosy.sbg.ac.at
FREE

http://www.cosy.sbg.ac.at

Department of Computer Science at Victoria University Home Page ★★★

The Department of Computer Science at Victoria University offers information on the academic programs and research undertaken there. Users will find data on professional, graduate, and undergraduate programs, as well as departmental and staff news. There is also material on the consulting, and Internet access services the Department provides, as well as links to regional information on New Zealand.

KEYWORDS   Computer Science, New Zealand, Universities
AUDIENCE   Computer Scientists, Educators, New Zealand Residents, Students
CONTACT   Julian Anderson
          webmaster@comp.vuw.ac.nz
FREE

http://www.comp.vuw.ac.nz

Department of Computer and Systems Sciences at Stockholm University and the Royal Institute of Technology ★★★

This is a gopher server of the Department of Computer and Systems Sciences at Stockholm University and the Royal Institute of Technology (KTH), Sweden. It provides information on the department staff, phone numbers and email addresses, departmental reports, library services, and more. It has links to other gophers as well.

KEYWORDS   Computer Science, Education (College/University), Sweden
AUDIENCE   Academics, Computer Professionals, Educators (University)
CONTACT   dmc@dsv.su.se
FREE

http://gopher.dsv.su.se/

gopher://gopher.dsv.su.se/

Computer Science

Department of Computing, Imperial College, London ★★★

This site is maintained by the Department of Computing at Imperial College, University of London. Users will find information on the curriculum, faculty, and students of the Department. In addition, this server hosts technical materials, software, and research papers in postscript format. There is also material on the campus itself and the surrounding area.

- **KEYWORDS** Computer Science, International Education
- **AUDIENCE** Computer Science Educators, Computer Science Students, Computer Scientists
- **CONTACT** Lee McLoughlin
  L.McLoughlin@doc.ic.ac.uk
- **FREE**

http://web.doc.ic.ac.uk

Distributed Object Computing Group at GTE Laboratories ★★★

The Distributed Object Computing Group at GTE Laboratories works on developing research into object-oriented technology for integrating heterogeneous, autonomous, distributed (HAD) computer systems/resources. This site has pages devoted to the people involved in the research projects, technical reports and papers, assorted notes on distributed systems, and software that incorporates the research that the group performs.

- **KEYWORDS** Distributed Object Management (DOM), Distributed Systems, Programming, Technical Reports
- **AUDIENCE** Computer Programmers, Computer Scientists, Researchers
- **CONTACT** Emon Mortazavi
  emon@gte.com
- **FREE**

http://info.gte.com/gtel/sponsored/doc/doc.html

Facultes Universitaires Notre-Dame de la Paix (FUNDP-University of Namur) ★★★

This short page is home to the Facultés Universitaires Notre-Dame de la Paix (FUNDP) University of Namur in Belgium. It lists its various departments, and offers links to the Computer Science and Science Departments, the history of the school, and the town of Namur. General information is also supplied about the faculty, what's new, and the Belgian network.

- **KEYWORDS** Belgium, Education (College/University), International Education
- **AUDIENCE** Computer Scientists, Researchers, Students
- **CONTACT** webmaster@fundp.ac.be
- **FREE**

http://www.fundp.ac.be/

Gopher Server of the Department of Computer Science of the University of Chile ★★★

The information found on this site is about the Department of Computer Science at the University of Chile in Santiago. The information describes the Department's research and academic programs, allows access to some of their software resources, and provides conference and event information. The bulk of the conference information surrounds VLDB '94, the 20th International Conference on Very Large Databases.

- **KEYWORDS** Chile, Computer Science, Workshops
- **AUDIENCE** Computer Science Students, Computer Scientists, Computing Analysts, Database Managers
- **CONTACT** Claudia Espinosa
  cmespino@dcc.uchile.cl
- **FREE**

gopher://gopher.dcc.uchile.cl/

Gopher-Server der Uni Berne ★★★

The information on this server is mostly about computing. This includes documentation and technical papers about topics like graphical user interfaces, SNMP, security, TCP/IP, and UNIX. This server also provides links to information systems and libraries located within Switzerland. The site is maintained by the University of Berne, Switzerland.

- **KEYWORDS** Computing, Operating Systems, Switzerland, Technical Writing
- **AUDIENCE** Computer Scientists, Systems Administrators
- **CONTACT** Fritz Buetikofer
  btkfr@id.unibe.ch
- **FREE**

gopher://gopher.unibe.ch/

INRIA ★★★★

INRIA, is the French National Institute for Research in Computer Science and Control. This research institute contributes to the evolution of the most advanced techniques in the computer science industry, as well as in the different sectors of application. INRIA's activities consist of basic research, realisation of experimental systems, technology transfers, training through research and knowledge-transfer, Cryptology Etc. Programs of research cover: Parallel architectures, databases, networks and systems: Symbolic computing, programming and software engineering: Artificial intelligence, cognitive sciences and man-machine communication: Robotics, image and vision: Signal processing, control and CIM: Scientific computing, modelling and numerical software. In its areas of expertise, INRIA has become one of the most active and advanced research laboratories in the world.

- **KEYWORDS** Computer Science, Research, Software Engineering, Technology
- **AUDIENCE** Applied Mathematicians, Computer Scientists, Engineers
- **FREE**

http://www.inria.fr/welcome-eng.html

gopher://gopher.inria.fr

ftp://ftp.inria.fr

International Computer Science Institute ★★★

The International Computer Science Institute conducts research in massively parallel computing systems, high speed networks, and distributed multimedia systems. Their home page offers technical reports and overviews describing the Institute's research, information about seminars offered, and other material on the Institute's mission, staff, and facilities. There are also links to detailed descriptions of the projects that the institute is currently working on, as well as public ftp and gopher directories maintained by the institute.

- **KEYWORDS** Artificial Intelligence, Supercomputers
- **AUDIENCE** Computer Researchers, Computer Scientists, Parallel Computing Researchers
- **FREE**

http://http.icsi.berkeley.edu/

gopher://gopher.icsi.berkeley.edu/

Kestrel Institute ★★★

The Kestrel Institute's Web site provides information about their projects and research, which focus on incremental automation of the software process. Their site includes prototypes of the software that they have developed, with graphs and background materials. Research areas are divided up into areas such as language design, algorithm design, and inference, with a general description of the goals of each project. Also provided are publications discussing Kestrel projects and other related topics.

- **KEYWORDS** Algorithms, Computer Systems Architecture, Software Engineering
- **AUDIENCE** Computer Programmers, Software Engineers
- **CONTACT** maria@kestrel.edu
- **FREE**

http://kestrel.edu

LAMI (Laboratoire de Microinformatique) ★★★

This page provides general background about the LAMI projects and activities, which include studying neural networks and building intelligent mobile robots. Information is provided on the divisions and partners in the projects, their computer courses and teaching, and addresses and staff profiles. Users may also find out about their projects, including pictures and profiles of their Robots, and read about and downloading YMosiac, an online help library. Listings and information from the LAMI and other library databases may be linked as well.

- **KEYWORDS** Neural Networks, Robotics, Technology
- **AUDIENCE** Neural Network Researchers
- **CONTACT** Christophe Marguerat
  Christophe.marguerat@di.epfl.ch
- **FREE**

http://lamihp1.epfl.ch/

Computing & Mathematics

Computer Science

LANL (Los Alamos National Laboratory) ACL (Advanced Computing Laboratory) Home Page ★★★

The Advanced Computing Laboratory at Los Alamos National Laboratory maintains this web server to provide information on the Lab's research projects and facilities. There is also a user's guide for those local to the facilities, and information on the staff of the lab. In addition, there are links to information on computer security.

KEYWORDS Computer Science, Research
AUDIENCE Computer Researchers, Computer Scientists
CONTACT webmaster@acl.lanl.gov
FREE

http://www.acl.lanl.gov

Laboratoire de Recherche en Informatique ★★★

Laboratoire de Recherche en Informatique (LRI) is a computer science research laboratory in France doing research in artificial intelligence, computer programming, architecture and parallel processing. This site has information on its research and educational activities, publications and conferences of the lab. There are links to other computer science departments in France and other servers around the world.

KEYWORDS Artificial Intelligence, Programming
AUDIENCE Artificial Intelligence Researchers, Computer Scientists, French
CONTACT mathilde@lri.fr
FREE

http://www.lri.fr

Laboratory of Information Processing Science ★★★

The Laboratory of Information Processing Science at the Helsinki University of Technology, supplies educational programs and research in the area of computer science. The home page offers information on current events, projects, courses and the phone book of the computer science laboratory. There are links to the CS Lab FTP-server, computer science lab guides (in Finnish) and other local resources.

KEYWORDS Education (College/University), Finland, Information Science, Research Labs
AUDIENCE Computer Scientists, Finns, Students
CONTACT www@cs.hut.fi
FREE

http://www.cs.hut.fi

MIT Alewife Project - Home Page ★★★★

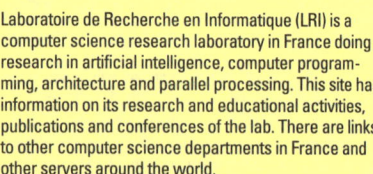

Alewife is a large-scale multiprocessor that integrates both cache-coherent, distributed shared memory and user-level message-passing in a single integrated hardware framework. This page provides information about the Alewife system and various information about the project including people, publications, pictures, and posters.

KEYWORDS Education (College/University), Supercomputers
AUDIENCE Computer Scientists, Hardware Designers
CONTACT Professor Anant Agarwal
  agarwal@cag.lcs.mit.edu
FREE

http://cag-www.lcs.mit.edu/alewife/people/

Mathematics and Computer Science Division ★★★★

The Argonne National Laboratory (ANL) Mathematics and Computer Science Division does research on supercomputing and Information Technologies. The page provides information on their findings in high-performance computing, publications, and some basic information about their division. The Argonne Computing and Communications Infrastructure Futures Laboratory explores and develops computing and communications infrastructure systems. This site gives access to their online book, Designing and Building Parallel Programs, and other resources.

KEYWORDS Information Systems, Scientific Research, Technology
AUDIENCE Communications Experts, Scientists, Software Users, Supercomputing Experts, Technology Researchers
FREE

http://www.mcs.anl.gov

NASA's Software Technology Transfer Center (COSMIC) ★★★★

This server offers information on the activities on NASA's COSMIC, the agency that handles software technology transfer. Their role is to ensure that industry, other government agencies, and academic institutions have access to advanced computer software technology developed for NASA projects. Users can access product demonstrations, technical support information, a product catalog, and ordering information. There is also a search function that allows users to find the product they are looking for.

KEYWORDS Computer Software, Government Agencies, Technology Transfer
AUDIENCE Academic Researchers, Government Researchers, Space Scientists
CONTACT service@cosmic.uga.edu
FREE

http://www.cosmic.uga.edu

gopher://gopher.cosmic.uga.edu/

ftp://ftp.cosmic.uga.edu/

National Chiao Tung University ★★★★

This site describes the National Chiao Tung University, Taiwan. It is maintained by the Department of Computer Science and Information Engineering at the National Chiao Tung University. The information includes the University's administration, academic departments, courses, library resources, centers, FTP sites, Archie searches, software, software related to displaying Chinese characters, and many more. As well, links to other gophers are provided.

KEYWORDS Computer Networking, Education (College/University), Taiwan, University Administration
AUDIENCE Academics, Chinese Speakers, Educators (University), Students
FREE

gopher://gopher.csie.nctu.edu.tw/

National Energy Research Supercomputer Center ★★★★

The National Energy Research Supercomputer Center is a supplier of production high performance computing and networking services to the nationwide energy research community. The programs assist organizations that include the Office of Scientific Computing, Fusion Energy, Basic Energy Sciences, High Energy and Nuclear Physics, and Health and Environmental Research. This page gives extensive links to computing information and resources.

KEYWORDS Energy, Physics, Supercomputers
AUDIENCE Computer Scientists, Energy Researchers
FREE

http://www.nersc.gov

Northeast Parallel Architectures Center Home Page ★★★★

The Northeast Parallel Architectures Center (NPAC) at Syracuse University that focuses on parallel systems, computer communications and technology transfer. This site contains information about the NPAC activities and facilities as well as research materials of numerous projects in subjects such as parallel algorithms and languages. Also included is the online book, 'Parallel Computing Works!' which discusses concurrent computation research from Caltech. The InfoMall virtual corporation and mall, a NDAC project, is also here, as well as the NYNET fiber-optic communications group.

KEYWORDS Algorithms, Parallel Computing, Technology Transfer
AUDIENCE Communications Researchers, Computer Scientists
CONTACT webmaster@npac.syr.edu
FREE

http://minerva.npac.syr.edu/

ORNL (Oak Ridge National Laboratory) Center for Computational Sciences Gopher ★★

Established by the United States Department of Energy (DOE) to provide state-of-the-art resources for Grand Challenge computing, the Center for Computational Sciences, Oak Ridge National Laboratory in Tennessee provides information about the Center and its mission, and provides the results of some recent research such as benchmark tests for computer systems. It aso offers hardware descriptions, calendars, and newsletters.

KEYWORDS Computer Science, Computing, Information Technology, Scientific Research

Computer Science

AUDIENCE Computer Operators, Computer Professionals, Computer Scientists
CONTACT Betsy A. Riley
rileyba@ornl.gov
FREE

http://gopher.ccs.ornl.gov/

gopher://gopher.ccs.ornl.gov/

Online Courses ★★★★

This page offers access to online courses offered by the computer science department at UC Davis. Users may browse courses such as introduction to software, data structures, computer networking, databases, computer architecture, and computer graphics. The individual courses offer homework assignments, lecture notes, syllabi, and more.
KEYWORDS Computer Science
AUDIENCE Computer Users, Educators, Students
CONTACT mosaic@cs.ucdavis.edu
FREE

http://www.cs.ucdavis.edu/online_courses.html

Overview on Lattice Field Theory ★★★★

This page provides background information on the Lattice Field Theory, also known as the Lattice Guage Theory, and on its application. It provides many links to software assisting in Lattice Guage Theory research, and information on the APE Parallel processing machine.
KEYWORDS Concurrent Logic, Mathematics
AUDIENCE Computer Engineers, Concurrent Logic Programmers, Parallel Programmers
CONTACT Marcus Speh
marcus@x4u.desy.de
FREE

http://info.desy.de/www/Lattice.html

Pittsburgh Supercomputing Center ★★★★

Pittsburgh Supercomputing Center (PSC) is a joint project of Carnegie Mellon University and the University of Pittsburgh together with Westinghouse Electric Corporation. The goals of the Center are to provide computational resources to various national programs, advance the techniques and knowledge base of computer science, educate researchers, and assist private sector companies with technological and computing development. This site offers publications such as technical reports and news releases, a hotlist and what's new page, a grants page (with HTML support), a workshop calendar, and links to various research projects under development at the PSC.
KEYWORDS Grants, Institutions, Supercomputers
AUDIENCE Computer Scientists, Educators, Researchers, Scientists, Suprcomputer Users
CONTACT remarks@psc.edu
FREE

http://anon.psc.edu/

Project Pilgrim's Archive ★★★

This gopher site allows users access to the Project Pilgrim archives of the Computer Science Department at the University of Massachusetts at Amherst. The primary goal of Project Pilgrim is the development of an advanced, large-scale, consistent, distributed computing infrastructure. This server provides information on computing environments and Project Pilgrim databases.
KEYWORDS Computer Applications, Information Science, Universities
AUDIENCE Computer Professionals, Computer Scientists, Students (Secondary/University)
CONTACT webmaster@pilgrim.umass.edu
FREE

http://info.pilgrim.umass.edu/

gopher://info.pilgrim.umass.edu/

RISC Info Server ★★★

The Research Institute for Symbolic Computation (RISC) was created to perform research, graduate teaching, and industrial cooperations in the field of symbolic computation. This site contains archives of their work, lists of projects and research areas, and various discussion lists. Current research areas include Computational Category Theory, Combinatorics, Parallel Computation, and Machine Learning.
KEYWORDS Mathematics, Symbolic Algebra
AUDIENCE Computer Programmers, Mathematicians, Numerical Analysts
CONTACT Prof. Dr. Bruno Buchberger
buchberg@groebner.risc.uni-linz.ac.at
FREE

http://info.risc.uni-linz.ac.at/

gopher://info.risc.uni-linz.ac.at/

ftp://info.risc.uni-linz.ac.at/

SICS (Swedish Institute of Computer Science) ★★★★

This is a gopher server of the Swedish Institute of Computer Science (SICS). It offers information on SICS, its phone and email directories, SICS reports, and a EuoPar95, a conference on networking parallel processing computers. SICS is a non-profit research foundation funded by the Swedish National Board for Technical and Industrial Development (NUTEK) and by a group of companies. A short introduction and the Annual Report 1993/94 give a comprehensive description of SICS research and organisation.
KEYWORDS Computer Science, Internet Resources, Sweden
AUDIENCE Academics, Computer Professionals, Internet Users
FREE

http://brahma.sics.se/

gopher://brahma.sics.se/

SRI Computer Science Laboratory ★★★★

This is the SRI Computer Science Laboratory's (CSL) home page. Information is provided on CSL staff members, CSL history (multi-window displays, hypertext, and the mouse were invented at SRI, and the first Internet message was received here.) Links are also provided to programs and activities under the headings Database Interoperability, Dataflow and Intensional Programming, Formal Methods, GEM (Generalized Emulation of Microcircuits), Linear Logic and Proof Theory, Multimedia and Multicast Communications and the Rewriting Program.
KEYWORDS Internet History, Multimedia, Research Institutions, Software
AUDIENCE Educators (University), Internet Users, Researchers, Students (University)
CONTACT Rushby@csl.sri.com
FREE

http://ftp.csl.sri.com

School of Engineering in Computer Science (Ecole pour les Etudes et la Recherche en Informatique et Electronique—EERIE) ★★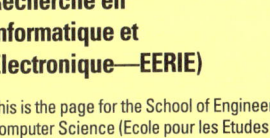

This is the page for the School of Engineering in Computer Science (Ecole pour les Etudes et la Recherche en Informatique et Electronique or EERIE) located in Nîmes, France. Information is provided on the Computer Science Engineering and Production Engineering Laboratory, the Genome server at EERIE, proposed services, local events, and more.
KEYWORDS Computer Science, Engineering, France, Research
AUDIENCE Educators (University), French, Students (University)
CONTACT www@eerie.eerie.fr
FREE

http://eerie.eerie.fr/home_eng.html

Scientific Computing and Visualization Page ★★★

This site offers information from the Scientific Computing and Visualization Group at Boston University. Users will find information on the Group's research initiatives, course offerings, and more. There is also employment information, material on the computing facilities, and links to local information. Users wishing to view information on Boston University in general can use the links provided here to access the top level of the Boston University WWW server.
KEYWORDS Informatics, Scientific Visualization
AUDIENCE Computer Scientists, Computer Visualization Specialists, Scientists
CONTACT Glenn Bresnahan
glenn@lobster.bu.edu
FREE

http://www.bu.edu

Smart Node Program at Cornell University ★★★

This is a gopher server of the Cornell Theory Center Smart Node Program. The Smart Nodes are a consortium of universities, colleges and government research laboratories which distribute supercomputing information, expertise, support, and training to researchers at their sites. It provides information on the program, guidelines, responsibilities, and many more. It also has access to other gopher services on the Internet.

KEYWORDS Computing, Information Technology, Supercomputers, Universities
AUDIENCE Computer Professionals, Internet Users, Researchers, Students (University)
CONTACT sncoord@tc.cornell.edu
FREE

gopher://gopher.tc.cornell.edu:270/

Supercomputing and Parallel Computing Conferences ★★★★

The Supercomputing and Parallel Computing Conferences page contains a database of upcoming conferences and workshops, conference calls for papers in the fields of supercomputing and parallel computing. This site is indexed by name, date, and deadline. These announcements were taken from the comp.parallel, comp.sys.super, and news.announce.conferences newsgroups.

KEYWORDS Databases, Parallel Computing, Supercomputers, Workshops
AUDIENCE Computer Scientists, Educators (University), Researchers, Students (University)
CONTACT Jonathan Hardwick jch@cs.cmu.edu
FREE

http://web.scandal.cs.cmu.edu/www/conferences.html

Supercomputing and Parallel Computing Research Groups ★★★★

This is a meta-index of research groups working in the field of supercomputing and parallel computing, with brief descriptions and links to each group's home pages. Some of the groups listed include the Alewife project at MIT CAG, the CC++ project, the Excalibur group at RIACS, the FM (Fortran M) project at ANL and CRPC, the FLASH project at Stanford, the Omega project at the University of Maryland and many more.

KEYWORDS Meta-Index (Computing), Parallel Computing, Research, Supercomputers
AUDIENCE Computer Scientists, Educators (University), Researchers, Students (University)
CONTACT Jonathan Hardwick jch@cs.cmu.edu
FREE

http://web.scandal.cs.cmu.edu/www/research-groups.html

Trinity College Dublin Computer Science Department ★★★

The Trinity College Dublin Computer Science Department home page presents information about the department, and the history of the college itself. The page has information on the research groups and their activities in such fields as artificial intelligence, computer architecture and image synthesis.

KEYWORDS Artificial Intelligence, Education (College/University), Ireland
AUDIENCE Computer Scientists, Irish, Researchers, Students
CONTACT WebMaster@cs.tcd.ie
FREE

http://www.cs.tcd.ie

UCSTRI—Cover Page (Unified Computer Science Technical Report Index) ★★★

This site maintains a searchable index of technical reports in the field of computer science. Users enter a keyword(s) they wish to search for using a HTML form, and the server comes back with a listing of matched references. Information returned includes author, abstract, contact information, and retrieval source.

KEYWORDS Bibliographies, Databases, Technical Reports
AUDIENCE Computer Researchers, Computer Scientists, Computer Users
CONTACT Marc VanHeyningen mvanheyn@cs.indiana.edu
FREE

http://www.cs.indiana.edu/cstr/search/

University of Bonn Computer Science Department - Parallel Systems and Algorithms ★★★

This page from the University of Bonn Computer Science Department contains information and links related to Parallel Systems and Algorithms. Users can see a listing of events, lectures, staff, projects, publications, and local services. There are also description of the computing services avaialble as well as outside links to computing and Internet resources outside of the university.

KEYWORDS Algorithms, Germany
AUDIENCE Computer Scientists, Germans
CONTACT webmaster@theory.cs.uni-bonn.de
FREE

http://cs.uni-bonn.de

University of Illinois Computer Science Home Page ★★★★

The University of Illinois Computer Science Home Page provides access to the undergraduate and graduate computer science programs. The page contains information about the faculty, research projects and facilities. There are links to other university servers as well as to electrical and computer engineering sites.

KEYWORDS Education (College/University), Educational Programs, Illinois, Research Institutions
AUDIENCE Computer Scientists, Educators, Students
CONTACT srs@cs.uiuc.edu
FREE

http://www.cs.uiuc.edu

University of Minnesota Supercomputer Institute ★★★

The University of Minnesota Supercomputer Institute offers departmental and facilities information through their web site. Users can find out about the goals and research projects at the Institute, or read about their graduate and internship programs. In addition, users can view some of the technical details of the Institute's research, as well as find out about seminars the the Institute hosts.

KEYWORDS Graduate Programs, Parallel Computing, Research, Supercomputers
AUDIENCE Computer Professionals, Computer Researchers, Computer Scientists
CONTACT webmaster@msi.umn.edu
FREE

http://web.msi.umn.edu

gopher://gopher.msi.umn.edu

University of Southampton High Performance Computing Centre (HPCC) homepage ★★★

The University of Southampton High Performance Computing Centre (HPCC) is a collection of resources for Internet and computer users alike. Academic Reports, Software, Programming Tutorials and training programs are available for the user. Some pages on this site describe the local resources (hardware and software) for public use. Research and Development provides interested browsers with papers on several electronic and computer projects.

KEYWORDS Education, United Kingdom
AUDIENCE Computer Science Students, Computer Users, Internet Users, United Kingdom Residents
CONTACT support@par.soton.ac.uk
FREE

http://cs1.soton.ac.uk

Utrecht University Dept. of Computer Science ★★★★

The home page for the Department of Computer Science at Utrecht University in the Netherlands contains information about their educational programs, research facilities and archives. There are links to the other university servers and other Netherland resources.

KEYWORDS Education (College/University), Graduate Programs, Netherlands, Research Institutions
AUDIENCE Computer Scientists, Dutch, Researchers, Students
CONTACT webmaster@cs.ruu.nl
FREE

http://www.cs.ruu.nl

Visualization Laboratory for Scientific Computing ★★★

This is the home page of the Visualization Laboratory for Scientific Computing at the Rensselaer Polytechnic Institute in New York. Users can find out about the staff, faculty, and facilities of the Lab, as well as obtain information on current research projects. In addition, users can obtain technical reports on various topics within Scientific Visualization, as well as access an archive of software to aid in computer visualization.

KEYWORDS Graphics, Scientific Visualization
AUDIENCE Computer Science Researchers, Computer Scientists, Engineers
CONTACT vlsc-support@rpi.edu
FREE

http://wolf3.vlsc.rpi.edu

WWW Computer Architecture Home Page ★★★

This page is an index of resources related to computer architecture. It provides links to computer architecture groups and projects, commercial resources, academic and research efforts, and Usenet news groups devoted to computer architecture issues. Users will also find calls for papers and participation in ongoing research projects, as well as information on contributing a link to this page.

KEYWORDS Computer Hardware, Computer Systems Architecture, Computer Technology
AUDIENCE Computer Hardware Specialists, Computer Scientists, Computer Users
CONTACT Doug Burger
dburger@cs.wisc.edu
FREE

http://www.cs.wisc.edu/~arch/www/

Washington University Computer Science Department ★★★★

The home page for the Washington University Computer Science Department in the School of Engineering contains information on the department's research projects, publications and department. There are links to the research groups such as the applied research laboratory, the artificial intelligence group and the computer visualization laboratory.

KEYWORDS Artificial Intelligence, Education (College/University), Engineering, Research Institutions
AUDIENCE Computer Scientists, Educators, Researchers, Students
CONTACT webmaster@cs.wustl.edu
FREE

http://www.cs.wustl.edu

Wooden Hut Home Page ★★

The Wooden Hut Home Page provides information about the projects and people involved in the supercomputing department of Rechenzentrum Universitaet in Stuttgart, Germany. Their research projects cover such areas as dynamic distributed data, parallel computing, virtual shared reality, and computational chemistry. Their pages include backgrounds of the projects, case studies, and history, as well as research materials. Faculty pages are also provided, and users can access some department documents.

KEYWORDS Distributed Systems, Parallel Computing, Supercomputers, Virtual Reality
AUDIENCE Computer Scientists, Computing Students, Germans

CONTACT Klaus Birken
birken@rus.uni-stuttgart.de
FREE

http://nfhsg3.rus.uni-stuttgart.de

ZGDV Computer Graphics Center ★★★ (COMMERCIAL)

The ZGDV Computer Graphics Center in Germany works on the development and application of computer graphics for research and technological purposes. Their Web site covers their objectives, staff, and provides information about some of their projects, such as Graphical Interface Software, Mobile Information Visualization, and Visual Computing. Papers, FAQ's and other ZGDV documents are provided, with software documentation, GNU software, and specifications.

KEYWORDS Graphics, Scientific Research, Technology Transfer
AUDIENCE Computer Graphic Designers, Germans
CONTACT Herbert Kuhlmann
kuhlmann@igd.fhg.de
FREE

http://medi.igd.fhg.de

Hardware

See also
Computing & Mathematics · *Computer Science*
Internet · *Internet Access*
Popular Culture & Entertainment · *Shopping*

Aligning and Maintaining Floppy Disk Drives ★★★ (COMMERCIAL)

This page is produced by a company that produces floppy disk troubleshooting and repair packages. It offers a brief tutorial on floppy disk alignment. The tutorial covers topics such as head alignment, spindle rotation, diagnosis methods and materials, and functional testing. In addition, users can find out about the various diagnostic/repair software and hardware packages that the company offers for sale.

KEYWORDS Computer Hardware, Floppy Disks, Technology
AUDIENCE Computer Technicians, Computer Users
CONTACT Allan Hughes
ahughes@picosof.com
FREE

http://www.aimnet.com:80/~avasales/

CPU (Central Processing Units) Info Center ★★★

This archive maintains information on computer CPUs (Central Processing Units), the main brain behind today's personal computers. Specifications, announcements, test results, technical papers, and system information can be found on this page. Users can also follow links to other computer hardware information on the Net.

KEYWORDS Central Processing Units (CPUs), Computer Hardware, Technology
AUDIENCE Computer Engineers, Computer Hardware Users, Computer System Designers

CONTACT Tom Burd
burd@eecs.berkeley.edu
FREE

http://infopad.eecs.berkeley.edu/~burd/gpp/cpu.html

Creative Labs Incorporated ★★★ (COMMERCIAL)

The Creative Labs site provides access to a variety of product information. Creative Labs Incorporated is the leader in PC (Personal Computer) sound, video and CD-ROM multimedia solutions with their product, Soundblaster. This company develops, manufactures and markets a large family of multimedia sound and video products, and multimedia kits for entertainment, education and productivity markets. This site can be accessed using ftp, gopher, WWW or wais. Subdirectories cover development information, Soundblaster compatibility, press releases, employment opportunities, technical support, as well as patches and updates for all software supported by this company.

KEYWORDS CD-ROMs, Multimedia, Soundblaster, Technology
AUDIENCE Computer Professionals, Computer Programmers, Multimedia Enthusiasts
CONTACT Tim Bratton
tbratton@creaf.com
FREE

http://www.creaf.com/
ftp://ftp.creaf.com/

DAC Micro Computing ★★★ (COMMERCIAL)

DAC Micro Computing delivers a full line of PC hardware and software solutions. DAC Micro performs services on site hardware maintenence, network installations, software installation and training. There are also links to other computer companies.

KEYWORDS Companies, Computer Hardware, Software
AUDIENCE Business Professionals, Computer Users, Consumers
CONTACT ward@ultranet.com
FREE

http://www.ultranet.com/~ward/

Ganson Engineering, Inc. ★★ (COMMERCIAL)

The Ganson Engineering, Inc. Web site provides information about the company and their line of printing applications. Ganson Engineering Inc. makes network printer interfaces for all platforms focusing on high-quality, high-volume laser, line, and matrix printers and plotters. This site provides product specs, support, and contact information. Most of the site is still under construction.

KEYWORDS Computer Hardware, Interfaces, Networking, Printers
AUDIENCE Business Professionals, Business Professionals, Entrepreneurs
CONTACT Glenn Ganson
jganson@halcyon.com
FREE

http://www.halcyon.com/jganson/GEI/

Microplex Systems, Ltd. ★★★

The Microplex Systems Web page provides information about Microplex Ethernet Printers. Product information includes diagrams, product summaries, technical specifications, and user manuals, as well as press releases and news articles about Microplex products. Users can find technical support for Microplex products through bulletins, upgrades, and downloadable firmware and software. A company overview is also included, with staff profiles and history.

KEYWORDS Computer Hardware, Computer Networks, Computer Peripherals, Networking
AUDIENCE Computer Users, Network Users
CONTACT info@microplex.com
FREE

http://microplex.com

Motorola PowerPC Web Server ★★★

Motorola PowerPC Web Server offers information and resources related to the Motorola/Apple/IBM joint venture, the PowerPC line of RISC (Reduced Instruction Set Computing) microprocessors. Users will find the latest information on the PowerPC architecture, including press releases, future planning, technical references and documentation, and more. There are also sections containing PowerPC FAQs, online support, and links to PowerPC software archives and other PowerPC-related servers.

KEYWORDS Computer Hardware, Computer Peripherals
AUDIENCE Computer Hardware Specialists, Computer Manufacturers, Computer Scientists
CONTACT webmaster@risc.sps.mot.com
FREE

http://www.mot.com/SPS/PowerPC/

Newton Archive ★★★

The Newton Archive is designed as a comprehensive guide to using the Macintosh Newton. Users can access ftp files with archived Newton information divided into categories such as applications, communities, books, utilities, games, software, and demos. Links to Newton news groups, Apple Computer support sites, and software companies on the Web are also provided.

KEYWORDS Computer Hardware, Handheld Computers, Personal Digital Assistants
AUDIENCE Computer Users
CONTACT David A. Rarick
moderator@newton.uiowa.edu
FREE

http://newton.uiowa.edu/

ftp://newton.uiowa.edu.

Stepwise - NeXTSTEP and OpenStep Web Server ★★★★

Stepwise is an information resource for anyone interested in NeXT Computers, or products such as NeXTSTEP, NeXTSTEP Developer, EOF, and NeXTime. The Web pages contain information from NeXTSTEP resellers and developers, over 500 specific NeXT compatible products, archives of Next in Line magazine and the newsgroup comp.sys.next. Users can browse through specific directories for product information, or see files that have been recently added or changed.

KEYWORDS Computer Systems, Computers, Product Information, Workstations
AUDIENCE NeXT Users, NeXt Programmers
FREE

http://digifix.digifix.com/

Welcome to HDS World Headquarters! ★★★

This is the home page for Hitachi Data Systems, which, together with its corporate parent, Hitachi Ltd., designs, manufactures, and markets mainframe computers, storage systems, open systems hardware and software, and services. The site provides news and press releases about the company, its products and services, as well as a regularly updated list of job openings.

KEYWORDS Companies, Mainframe Computers, Manufacturing, Software
AUDIENCE Business Professionals, Computer Users, Internet Users
FREE

http://www.hdshq.com/

Welcome to PC/Computing ★★★★

With the help of some terrific graphics, PC/Computing Online allows users to enjoy this magazine online, free of charge. PC fans can access categories like Bug Bytes to cure their software or system ills, Free Stuff for accessing freeware, shareware, and the like. There is also One-Minute Guide for information seekers who are in a hurry, In Sites to find out about new, interesting Web sites that are cropping up, as well as a graphic, comprehensive Web map, among other features.

KEYWORDS Online Magazines
AUDIENCE Computer Professionals, Computer Users, PC Users, Windows Users
CONTACT webmaster@ziff.com
FREE

http://www.pc-computing.ziff.com/~pccomp/

Mathematical Formulae

Computing & Mathematics · *Applications*
Computing & Mathematics · *Mathematics*
Computing & Mathematics · *Theory*
Science · *Physics*

Axiom ★★★

Axiom is a powerful computer algebra system which provides a complete environment for anyone needing to manipulate and solve mathematical formulae. This site contains a description of Axiom's features, a list of implementations, online support, copies of reports and documentation, and an archive of Axiom code.

KEYWORDS Mathematics, Numerical Analysis, Software, Symbolic Algebra
AUDIENCE Computer Programmers, Mathematicians, Numerical Analysts
CONTACT Michael G. Richardson
miker@nag.co.uk
FREE

http://www.nag.co.uk:70/1h/symbolic/AX.html

gopher://www.nag.co.uk:/11h/symbolic/AX/MKT24

Formulae for Pi ★★★

In this site Roy Williams has written an interesting introduction to the use of arctangent formulas to approximate the numerical value of Pi, the geometrical ratio of the circumference of a circle to its diameter (approximately 3.14).

KEYWORDS Algorithms, Mathematics
AUDIENCE Mathematicians, Numerical Analysts
CONTACT Roy Williams +1 (818) 395-3670
roy@ccsf.caltech.edu
FREE

http://www.ccsf.caltech.edu/~roy/pi.formulas.html

SIGSAM (Special Interest Group on Symbolic & Algebraic Manipulation) Archive ★★★

The Association for Computing Machinery (ACM) Special Interest Group on Symbolic & Algebraic Manipulation (SIGSAM) provides members with a forum in which to exchange ideas about the practical and theoretical aspects of algebraic and symbolic mathematical computation. Its scope of interests includes design, analysis and application of algorithms, data structures, systems and languages. This site provides the ability to subscribe to the group (for a fee) and it contains a partial archive of the SIGSAM Journals.

KEYWORDS Mathematics, Numerical Analysis, Software, Symbolic Algebra
AUDIENCE Computer Programmers, Mathematicians, Numerical Analysts
CONTACT Gene Cooperman
gene@ccs.neu.edu
FREE

http://http.ccs.neu.edu/pub/sigsam/README.html

gopher://gopher.acm.org/11[the_files.sig_forums.sigsam]

ftp://ftp.ccs.neu.edu/pub/sigsam

Spanky Fractal Database ★★★★

The Spanky Fractal Database at Canada's National Meson Research Facility at the University of British Columbia offers a collection of fractal images, papers, software, and other materials. The site provides extensive links to fractal information, graphics, chaos theory, and nonlinear dynamics elsewhere on the Internet.

KEYWORDS   Chaos Theory, Fractals, Mathematics
AUDIENCE   Mathematicians, Numerical Analysts
CONTACT   Noel Giffin
           noel@triumf.ca
FREE

http://spanky.triumf.ca/

ftp://spanky.triumf.ca/

Mathematics

See also
Computing & Mathematics · *Applications*
Computing & Mathematics · *Mathematical Formulae*
Computing & Mathematics · *Theory*
Science · *Physics*

ACM Special Interest Group on Symbolic & Algebraic Manipulation ★★★★

The ACM Special Interest Group on Symbolic & Algebraic Manipulation (SIGSAM) provides members with a forum in which to exchange ideas about the practical and theoretical aspects of algebraic and symbolic mathematical computation. It covers the design, analysis and application of algorithms, data structures, system and languages. This organization provides information on itself, its membership, and its conferences, as well as links to its FTP site and Web journals. The gopher site provides the best entry point with links to the other sources of information.

KEYWORDS   Computation, Design
AUDIENCE   ACM Members, Computer Scientists, Mathematicians, Programmers
CONTACT   Erich Kaltofen SIG Chair
           chair_SIGSAM@acm.org
FREE

http://sigsam.eecs.uic.edu/

gopher://gopher.acm.org/
           11[the_files.sig_forums.sigsam]

ftp://ftp.ccs.neu.edu/pub/sigsam

American Mathematical Society ★★★★

This is the American Mathematical Society's (AMS) resource for delivering electronic products and services to mathematicians. These services include a membership list, abstracts of published articles and preprints, employment information, committee reports, and TeX resources. Various access methods provide different services, and as of this writing, the WWW service was incomplete.

KEYWORDS   Latex, Statistics, TeX
AUDIENCE   Mathematicians, Mathematics Educators, Statisticians, Tex And Latex Users
CONTACT   ams@math.ams.org
FREE

http://e-math.ams.org/

gopher://e-math.ams.org/

ftp://e-math.ams.org/

telnet://e-math.ams.org:2002/

CTI (Computers in Teaching Initiative) Centre for Mathematics and Statistics ★★★

The Centre provides online information about resources for incorporating computer-based materials into the teaching of mathematics and statistics. This site contains descriptions of curriculum programs designed by the Centre for specific Universities and mathematics programs, information on and reviews of software packages for math instruction, and descriptions of past projects of the Computers in Teaching Initiative. There are also pointers to other sites doing research in this area.

KEYWORDS   Computer Aided Instruction, Education (College/University), Educational Software, Mathematical Software
AUDIENCE   Computational Mathematicians, Education Consultants, Mathematics Educators
CONTACT   Pam Bishop
           ctimath@bham.ac.uk
FREE

http://www.bham.ac.uk/ctimath

Centre for Experimental and Constructive Mathematics ★★

This is a gopher service and Web site of the Centre for Experimental and Constructive Mathematics of Simon Fraser University. It provides information on its organization, research, study and work opportunities at CECM, and more. It also provides general information on Simon Fraser University.

KEYWORDS   Education (College/University), Mathematics, Research & Development, Theoretical Mathematics
AUDIENCE   Educators (University), Mathematicians, Students (Graduate)
CONTACT   Brigitte Dorner
           dorner@cecm.sfu.ca
FREE

http://cecm.sfu.ca/

gopher://cecm.sfu.ca/

COMMA (Computing Mathematics) Hotlist Database - Subject Search ★★★

This site allows you to search the Department of Computing Mathematics (COMMA) Hotlist Database, which is compiled from all the readable Mosaic hotlists on the COMMA UNIX systems. Hotlists are submitted by contributors who note interesting web sites and make their hotlists public. You can search by title, subject, or contributor name.

KEYWORDS   Directories, Internet Reference
AUDIENCE   Internet Users

CONTACT   Andrew.Wilson
           Andrew.Wilson@cm.cf.ac.uk
FREE

http://www.cm.cf.ac.uk/htbin/AndrewW/Hotlist/hot_list_search.csh

Computer Algebra Systems ★★★★

This site, located at the University of California at Berkeley, contains a list of currently developed and distributed software for symbolic mathematical applications. Most of the material at this site is obtained from the developers and is kept as up-to-date as possible. Each piece of software has a brief description and the address for users to write or email to for more information.

KEYWORDS   Mathematical Software, Mathematics, Numerical Analysis, Symbolic Algebra
AUDIENCE   Mathematicians, Numerical Analysts
CONTACT   Paulo Ney de Souza
           ca@math.berkeley.edu
FREE

gopher://math.berkeley.edu/11/Symbolic_Soft/

ftp://math.berkeley.edu/pub/Symbolic_Soft/

Departments of Mathematical Sciences at the University of Aarhus ★★★

The Departments of Mathematical Sciences at the University of Aarhus in Denmark provide information on current projects and news. The page has information on biostatistics, hypertext manuals, new servers, courses, and conferences.

KEYWORDS   Education (College/University), Scientific Applications, Statistics
AUDIENCE   Danes, Mathematicians, Scientists, Statisticians, Students
CONTACT   webmaster@mi.aau.dk
FREE

http://www.mi.aau.dk

Department of Mathematics and Computer Science at the Free University of Berlin ★★★

The Department of Mathematics and Computer Science provides information about its research and development, teaching, publications, events and services. The Department has degree programs in such areas as systems software engineering, and includes course listings, publications and reports.

KEYWORDS   Germany, International Education
AUDIENCE   Germans, Mathematicians, Students
FREE

http://www.math.fu-berlin.de

Mathematics

Department of Mathematics, University of Utah ★★★★

The Department of Mathematics page presents research to facilitate communication between mathematicians working on materials-related problems and scientists and engineers in industry and academia. Course information and a departmental roster is provided. There are links to other math- and Utah-related sites.

KEYWORDS Educational Resources, Universities
AUDIENCE Educators, Math Researchers, Mathematicians, Students
CONTACT webmaster@math.utah.edu
FREE

http://www.math.utah.edu

Directory of Scholarly Electronic Conferences in Mathematics and Statistics ★★★

This is an extensive database of electronic conferences pertaining to mathematics and statistics; references include discussion lists, electronic newsletters and Usenet newsgroups. A broad range of mathematical topics are covered—from general interest to highly specific topics in algebra, number theory, and analysis. Conferences for computer software, such as Mathematica and Matlab, are also found in this index.

KEYWORDS Databases, Encryption, Mathematics, Statistics
AUDIENCE Mathematicians, Mathematics Educators, Statisticians
CONTACT Diane Kovacs
dkovacs@kentvm.kent.edu
FREE

gopher://una.hh.lib.umich.edu/00/inetdirsstacks/mathstat%3Aparkmiller

E-Math Digital Resource Center for Mathematics ★★★

The e-Math Digital Resource Center for Mathematics gopher server is provided by the American Mathematical Society and provides access to peer-reviews publications and preprints in TeX form, newsletters, membership directories, and links to other mathematical servers. There is also an archive of resources for the American Mathematical Society's TeX.

KEYWORDS Journals, Mathematics, Scientific Applications, TeX
AUDIENCE LaTeX Users, Mathematicians, Mathematics Educators, TeX Users
CONTACT support@e-math.ams.org
FREE

gopher://e-math.ams.com/

Electronic Journal of Differential Equations ★★★

This is an electronic publication dealing with all aspects of differential equations (o.d.e.'s, p.d.e.'s, integral equations, functional differential equations, etc.) and their applications. It accepts only high quality articles and has a strict referee process. Old articles and abstracts are available.

KEYWORDS Differential Equations, Mathematics
AUDIENCE Mathematicians, Mathematics Educators
CONTACT Alfonso Castro
editor@ejde.math.unt.edu
FREE

http://ejde.math.swt.edu/

gopher://ejde.math.swt.edu/

ftp://ejde.math.swt.edu/

telnet://ejde.math.swt.edu/

Electronic Library for Mathematical Software ★★★

This is an index to available mathematical software. It provides access to databases containing algorithms and code for solving various problems. It includes a searchable index to all the databases. There is also access to newsgroups and various digests.

KEYWORDS Algorithms, Mathematical Software, Mathematics, Numerical Analysis
AUDIENCE Mathematicians, Numerical Analysts, Programmers
CONTACT Henry Thieme
thieme@zib-berlin.de
FREE

http://elib.zib-berlin.de/

gopher://elib.zib-berlin.de/

ftp://elib.zib-berlin.de/

Faculty of Informatics of the Masaryk University, Brno ★★★★

This is the FTP server of the Faculty of Informatics of the Masaryk University, Brno, Czechoslovakia. It provides links to the Math Department, the Institute of Computer Science, and the Supercomputing Centre. It also contains some mirror archives.

KEYWORDS Computer Science, Czechoslovakia, Education (College/University), Information Science
AUDIENCE Computer Scientists, Czechs, Information Scientists
CONTACT Michal Brandejs
brandejs@informatics.muni.cz
FREE

ftp://ftp.muni.cz/pub/

Faculty of Mathematics Gopher Server ★★★

This is a gopher server of the Faculty of Mathematics of the University of Waterloo, Waterloo, Canada. It provides information on the math studies, courses, research, computing resources, events and more. There are also links to other gopher servers of the University of Waterloo.

KEYWORDS Canada, Education (College/University), Mathematics, Universities
AUDIENCE Educators (University), Mathematics Educators, Mathematics Students
CONTACT wcwince@math.uwaterloo.ca
FREE

gopher://jeeves.uwaterloo.ca/

Fractal Microscope ★★★★

The Fractal Microscope offers a collection of information geared towards teachers who wish to enliven their mathematics classes through the use of the complex and beautiful world of fractals. Users will find information on software programs and other teaching aids that can transform a dull subject into a fun and interesting one. This page also has a number of fractal images in many different shapes and colors.

KEYWORDS Electronic Arts
AUDIENCE Educators, Fractal Enthusiasts, Mathematics Educators
CONTACT rpanoff@ncsa.uiuc.edu
FREE

http://www.ncsa.uiuc.edu/Edu/Fractal/Fractal_Home.html

GAMS - Guide to Available Mathematical Software ★★★★

This page houses the Guide to Available Mathematical Software, an index of mathematical software repositories on the Internet. In addition to the comprehensive index of mathematical software, users will find a glossary of terms used on the server, a listing of credits and references, and a set of links to other mathematical resources on the Internet. Users may browse through the index manually, or search by package name, module name, and by what problem(s) the individual software packages solve.

KEYWORDS Computer Software, Mathematics Software
AUDIENCE Computer Scientists, Mathematicians
CONTACT Ronald F. Boisvert
boisvert@nist.gov
FREE

http://gams.nist.gov/

Geometry Center ★★★

The Geometry Center web site provides access to information such as materials available from the Geometry Center, Interactive Web Applications (which require an HTML 2.0 browser), multimedia documents, a downloadable software graphics archive, course materials, workshops, seminars, and courses, and news about math awareness week.

KEYWORDS Education, Geometry, Mathematics, Software
AUDIENCE Math Students, Mathematicians
CONTACT webmaster@geom.umn.edu
FREE

http://freeabel.geom.umn.edu

Geometry Forum ★★★

The Geometry Forum is an electronic community at Swarthmore College focused on geometry and math education. There are links to whats new, forum projects, summer institutes on geometry and the Internet, K-12 sites, research sites, and more.

KEYWORDS Education, Geometry, Mathematics, Universities
AUDIENCE Educators (University), Students (Graduate)
CONTACT forum@forum.swarthmore.edu
FREE

http://forum.swarthmore.edu

gopher://gopher.forum.swarthmore.edu/

History of Mathematics

This site contains a list of over a thousand important mathematicians including all Fields Medal Winners. Over two dozen mathematicians have their own bibliographies. The list can be searched by name, chronology, or geographic region. The page includes pointers to many other sites containing bibliographies and other historical references.

KEYWORDS History, Mathematics
AUDIENCE Historians, History Buffs, Mathematicians, Mathematics Educators
CONTACT David E. Joyce
djoyce@black.clarku.edu
FREE

http://aleph0.clarku.edu/~djoyce/mathhist/mathhist.html

HyperSpace - Australian National University

HyperSpace at the ANU (Australian National University) provides a set of hypertext based services for general relativity (GR) research. This page provides a forms-based program, GR, that searches a list of email and snail mail addresses relevant to the GR community. Also provided is the The General Relativity News Archives containing GR related news, job information, news about postdoctoral fellowships, and conference information. Links are also included for other GR websites, relativity software, electronic journals, research report archives and more.

KEYWORDS Mathematics, Relativity (General)
AUDIENCE General Relativity Scholars, Physicists
CONTACT Ben.Evans@maths.anu.edu.au
FREE

http://einstein.anu.edu.au/hyperspace/

Industrial Mathematics Archive

This gopher server, located at the University of Minnesota, provides information about the Industrial Mathematics Archive (IMA), including newsletters, schedules, and recent announcements. In addition, the site provides users with an archive of LaTeX style files for IMA papers, and information related to the Industrial Mathematics Program at the University of Minnesota.

KEYWORDS Electronic Publishing, Mathematics, Universities
AUDIENCE Mathematicians, Mathematics Educators
FREE

gopher://gopher.ima.umn.edu/

Connections to Mathematics Software

X+Y-Z= . . . A big headache!

Mathematics Software, Tools and Projects

Research projects in Mathematics --- Mathematical Tools

- Research projects and resources:
  - OpenMath Project
  - Multi Modal Mathematics Plexus
  - Fractales à la INRIA
  - The Geometry Forum (including MathMagic)
  - Largest Known Primes Page
  - G&G: a software tool for graphs and their automorphism groups
  - Knot Plot: A Package for Visualizing Mathematical Knots

- Mathematical Tools:
  - Maple V
    - Maple Web Home Page
    - MapleSoft anonymous FTP site
    - Maple at MIT
    - The GRTensor Resource Home Page (Queen's University)
  - Mathematica
    - MathSource: Wolfram's Web server

If you're a professional mathematician, a student of mathematics, or just plain curious about solving some of your own mathematical problems, check out "Mathematics Software, Tools and Projects." At this site, you'll access some of the coolest software products to tackle those knotty problems that twist your brain matter, chew it up, and spit it out!

With these resources you can tap into "Knot Plot," a package for visualizing mathematical knots. We're not just talking "granny" knots here. This places you inside an elaborate program that allows you to visualize and manipulate mathematical knots. You get some 1,000 knots to play with—like the twist-spun knot, knotted sea things, vortex, and sorta Celtic knots, for example.

(http://camel.cecm.sfu.ca/Software/software.html)

If you want to forego the software aspects of mathematics, you can turn to "Interactive Mathematics Text Project," where you'll find some premium interactive math puzzles and problems.

You'll receive a description of the text project, pertinent reports, and samples of project developments. It's designed to improve mathematics education at all levels, from grade school through post-graduate. Here you can also learn about symbolic mathematics and find information on research, tools, and computer systems in the field of computational mathematics.

(gopher://poincare.math.upenn.edu/) also, **(http://symbolicnet.msc.kent.edu/)**

Mathematics

International Congress of Mathematicians - Berlin 1998 ★★★

In 1998 there will be an international mathematics conference in Berlin. This site contains information about the conference, a list of supporters, and a facility for automatically registering. The site also contains a list of other conferences being held in Europe at roughly the same time.

Keywords Conferences, Mathematics
Audience Mathematicians, Mathematics Educators
Contact Prof. Dr. J. Winkler
winkler@math.tu-berlin.de
Free

http://elib.zib-berlin.de:8000/0506AEF6/CICM98

LIFAC - Laboratoire d'Informatique Fondamentale et Appliquée de Cachan ★★

The LIFAC Laboratoire d'Informatique Fondamentale et Appliquée de Cachan is a mathematical laboratory that conducts algorithms, complex communication and neuro-linguistics research. Their home page provides information about their seminars and members, provides publication lists, and lists their international collaborators.

Keywords Algorithms, France, Mathematics
Audience Computer Scientists, Mathematicians
Contact web@weblifac.ens-cachan.fr
Free

http://lifac.ens-cachan.fr/

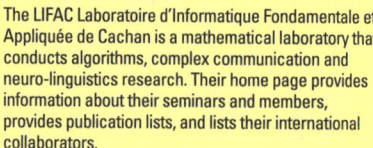 MATLAB Archives ★★★

This site has good collection of files pertaining to MATLAB software for various operating platforms. There are files to fix bugs in the previous versions, as well as add-on tools to simplify MATLAB usage and improve efficiency. There is a public upload site for users to communicate with other MATLAB users about their software development. This site is an archive for MATLAB users to share their ideas and bugs they have encountered in their MATLAB usage.

Keywords MATLAB, Mathematics, Mathematics Software
Audience Internet Users, Mathematicians, Statisticians, Students, Systems Administrators
Contact drea@mathworks.com
Free

ftp://ftp.mathworks.com/Matlab

MacTutor History of Mathematics ★★★★

The MacTutor History of Mathematics is part of the Mathematical MacTutor system developed at the School of Mathematical and Computational Sciences of the University of St. Andrews for learning and experimenting with mathematics. The archive contains the biographies of more than 550 mathematicians. About 200 of these biographies are fairly detailed and most are accompanied by pictures of the mathematicians themselves.

Keywords Biographies, History, Interactive Learning
Audience Biographers, Historians, Mathematicians, Mathematics Educators
Contact John O'Connor
joc@st-andrews.ac.uk
Free

http://www-groups.dcs.st-and.ac.uk:80/~history/

Maple Home Page ★★★

This site was created by the designers of Maple, a computer system for performing symbolic mathematics. The server contains a library of Maple routines and an archive containing the postings and digests of the Maple User's Group (MUG).

Keywords Mathematical Software, Mathematics, Numerical Analysis, Symbolic Algebra
Audience Mathematicians, Numerical Analysts
Contact Lee Qiao
lqiao@daisy.uwaterloo.ca
Free

http://daisy.uwaterloo.ca/home.html

ftp://daisy.uwaterloo.ca/pub/maple/

Math Department of ETH Zurich ★★★

The Math department of ETH Zurich has information on the Institute's programs and studies. There are links to projects and research reports to be downloaded, as well as links to conferences and faculty. The server has links to the Institute and their work. There is access to the other schools within the Institute of Technology and other mathematics departments.

Keywords Operations Research, Statistics, Switzerland
Audience Educators, Mathematicians, Statisticians, Students
Contact Karim Saouli and Sandra Wambold
www@math.ethz.ch
Free

http://www.math.ethz.ch

Math Departments of the Masaryk University ★★★

This site is the FTP server of the Math Department of the Masaryk University in Czechoslovakia. It provides information about lectures, papers and software.

Keywords Computer Science, Czechoslovakia, Education (College/University), Information Science
Audience Computer Scientists, Educators (University), Information Scientists
Contact Michal Brandejs
brandejs@informatics.muni.cz
Free

ftp://ftp.muni.cz/pub/math.muni.cz/

Math Related Graphs and New Software Tools ★★

This site has good collection of files pertaining to MATLAB software for various operating platforms. This section of this site is the upload section where any software that is related to just calculation techniques or plotting software can be found.

Keywords MATLAB, Mathematics, Mathematics Software
Audience Internet Users, Mathematicians, Statisticians, Students, Systems Administrators
Contact drea@mathworks.com
Free

ftp://ftp.mathworks.com/pub

MathSource Gopher ★★★★

This site contains information about the mathematics software package Mathematica. The server is maintained by Wolfram Research, Inc. located in Champaign, Illinois. The information includes general Mathematica material such as documentation and tutorials, as well as more advanced material like enhancements and applications. There are also links to other Mathematica servers around the Internet.

Keywords Mathematics, Software
Audience Computer Users, Educators, Engineers, Mathematicians, Software Users, Students
Contact ms-admin@wri.com
Free

http://mathsource.wri.com/

gopher://mathsource.wri.com/

Mathematics Archives Gopher ★★★

This gopher site provides public domain software and many other materials for teaching mathematics at the university and college level. These materials include a database of both public domain and commercial software relevant to mathematics teaching. It also has pointers to other gophers useful for mathematicians.

Keywords Education (College/University), Educational Software, Mathematics
Audience Education Administrators, Educators, Mathematicians, Mathematics Educators
Contact Earl D. Fife
efife@archives.math.utk.edu
Free

gopher://archives.math.utk.edu/

Mathematics Publications ★★

The information on this gopher server is related to Mathematics. It is located at Duke University, North Carolina. It contains mathematics publications and preprints from the Mathematics Department at Duke University. In addition, it has links to other mathematics gophers.

Keywords Education (College/University), Mathematics, Publishing, Scientific Applications
Audience Educators (University), Mathematicians, Students (University)

Free

gopher://publications.math.duke.edu/

 **Mathworks Archive** ★★★

This site has good collection of files pertaining to MATLAB software for various operating platforms (mostly compressed). This site is an archive for MATLAB users to share their ideas and bugs they have encountered in their MATLAB usage. There are some files with product announcements. This is a public upload site for all the M-files or MEX files.

Keywords MATLAB, Mathematics, Mathematics Software
Audience Internet Users, Mathematicians, Statisticians, Students, Systems Administrators
Contact drea@mathworks.com
Free

ftp://ftp.mathworks.com/in/Matlab/pub/

NA-NET (Numerical Analysis) Home Page ★★★

The NA-NET is a system developed to serve the community of numerical analysts and other researchers. It provides a weekly digest of articles related to numerical analysis, a unique email address for each subscriber, a searchable white pages directory, and a searchable archive of the digest.

Keywords Algorithms, Computer Programming, Mathematics, Numerical Analysis
Audience Mathematicians, Mathematics Educators, Numerical Analysts
Contact nanet@na-net.ornl.gov
Free

http://www.netlib.org/na-net/na_home.html

gopher://www.netlib.org/11/na-digest

ftp://www.netlib.org/na-digest

NetLib Mathematics Archives ★★★

Netlib is a repository of mathematical software, data, documents, address lists, and other useful items. The Mathematics directory includes reports, proofs, and technical manuals generated by about fifty different authors. There are HTML files for users using the Web to access these files.

Keywords Algorithms, Computer Science, Mathematics, Theoretical Mathematics
Audience Computer Scientists, Mathematicians
Contact netlib_maintainers@netlib.org
Free

ftp://netlib.att.com/netlib/att/math/

New York Journal of Mathematics ★★★

The New York Journal of Mathematics is the first electronic general mathematics journal, offered by the University at Albany, New York. The journal covers algebra, modern analysis, and geometry/topology. This site offers information on how to access instructions for

---

Connections to Geometry

It's cool to be square

Various sites on the World Wide Web provide excellent teaching tools (as well as exercises for students) in the arena of geometry. Here you'll learn about measurements, properties, the relationships of points, lines, angles, surfaces, and solids, and how to differentiate an isosceles triangle from a trapezoid.
One such interesting site is the "Department of Descriptive Geometry," where you will find computer graphics and geometry, geometric modeling, and interactive CAD/CAM (Computer Aided Design/Computer Aided Modeling) problems to solve.

(http://abrindy.abrg.uni-miskolc.hu:8080/angol/oktat.html)

At other sites, you can tap into geometry forum newsgroups—an online electronic community designed for challenge and collaboration. You might provide geometry "brain twisters" for others to solve, or you can try solving a geometric puzzle supplied by another user. You can also visit "College Geometry" and the geometry "Forum," a site devoted to dynamic geometry software. Here you can try out the software and learn how to do some problem-solving on your own.

(http://forum.swarthmore.edu/~sarah/HTMLthreads/index.html)

also, (http://forum.swarthmore.edu/research/research.html)

---

submission of papers, journal articles, and other files via gopher and WWW. In addition, the server also contains links to the University at Albany, and to other related mathematics sites on the Internet.

Keywords Mathematics, Research & Development, Technical Writing, Technology
Audience Academics, Educators, Researchers
Contact Mark Steinberger
  mark@sarah.albany.edu
Free

http://nyjm.albany.edu:8000/

gopher://nyjm.albany.edu/

Northwestern University Department of Mathematics ★★★★

The Northwestern University Department of Mathematics contains information about the department's activities and references to items of general interest. It has a listing of faculty, staff, and graduate students. There is information about mathematic research, a seminar calendar, undergraduate and graduate program information, and related information servers. There are some recent department preprints and links to other Northwestern University sites.

Keywords Research, Universities
Audience Educators, Mathematicians, Students
Free

http://www.math.nwu.edu

 Numerical Algorithms Group ★★★

The Numerical Algorithms Group (NAG) produces and distributes numerical, symbolic, statistical and visualization software for the solution of problems in a wide range of applications in such areas as science, engineering, financial analysis and research. This site provides documentation, examples, and packages for NAG products. In addition, there are lists of support and consultancy services in numerical analysis.

Keywords Algorithms, Computer Programming, Mathematical Software, Numerical Analysis, Statistics
Audience Mathematicians, Numerical Analysts, Programmers
Contact webmaster@nag.co.uk
Free

http://www.nag.co.uk:70/

gopher://www.nag.co.uk/

Octave ★★★

This directory at the Department of Mathematics at the University of Zagreb contains the source for Octave, a high-level interactive language for solving numerical problems. See the files README.octave and Announce for more general information, and the file NEWS for a list of recent changes.

Keywords Mathematics
Audience Mathematicians, Numerical Analysts

Mathematics

CONTACT Vladimir Braus
ftp@math.hr

FREE

ftp://cromath.math.hr/mnt/octave/

Penn State Department of Mathematics ★★★★

The Penn State Department of Mathematics provides information about the Department, preprints and mathematics events calendars. Both the Mathematics Department graduate and undergraduate Handbooks are on line with mathematics course descriptions and schedules. There are lists of preprints in the applied mathematics and pure mathematics articles that have appeared in mathematical journals.

KEYWORDS Databases, Statistics, Universities
AUDIENCE Educators, Mathematicians, Students
CONTACT webmaster@math.psu.edu

FREE

http://www.math.psu.edu

gopher://gopher.math.psu.edu/

ftp://ftp.halcyon.com/pub/ii/

SIAM (Society for Industrial and Applied Mathematics) ★★★

This server provides resources related to mathematics. These resources include book reviews, book catalogs, conference dates, and descriptions of journals. The information is provided by the Society for Industrial and Applied Mathematics (SIAM). This gopher hole also contains tunnels to other gopher holes with related information, and the web pages link to other web servers with information on mathematics.

KEYWORDS Industrial Applications, Mathematics, Technology
AUDIENCE Mathematicians, Mathematics Educators, Mathematics Students
CONTACT siam@siam.org

FREE

http://www.siam.org/

gopher://gopher.siam.org/

SIGNUM (Special Interest Group for Numerical Mathematics) ★★

ACM Special Interest Group on Numerical Mathematics draws its membership from computing professionals whose primary concern is computational mathematics. The gopher site provides information about the organization's board of directors and about membership.

KEYWORDS Computation, Mathematics, Numerical Analysis
AUDIENCE ACM Members, Computer Scientists, Mathematicians
CONTACT John R. Gilbert SIG Chair
chair_SIGNUM@acm.org

FREE

gopher://gopher.acm.org/
11[the_files.sig_forums.signum]

School of Mathematics (University of East Anglia) ★★★

The School of Mathematics at the University of East Anglia server contains information about their research, news, seminars and undergraduate programs. The page is arranged with local information links to such areas as recent papers in ergodic theory and a list of publications. There are links to other UEA resources and mathematical information on the Internet.

KEYWORDS Education (College/University)
AUDIENCE Educators, Mathematicians, Researchers, Students
CONTACT www-mth@uea.ac.uk

FREE

http://www.mth.uea.ac.uk

Society of Industrial and Applied Mathematics (SIAM) WWW Undergraduate Page ★★★★

This undergraduate page is sponsored by The Society of Industrial and Applied Mathematics (SIAM). It contains profiles of mathematicians, essays, undergraduate articles, information about SIAM, a student mailing list, job and fellowship information and more. There is also a list of related sites in mathematics.

KEYWORDS Employment, Fellowships, Scientific Applications, Technology
AUDIENCE Job Seekers, Mathematicians, Mathematics Students, Researchers

FREE

http://spicerack.unh.edu:80/~siamug/

Sydney Mathematics & Statistics ★★★

This Sydney Mathematics & Statistics site gives information about members of the school, calendar events, seminars, research, administration and committees. The page offers access to publications, grants, technical reports, and software (Magma computer algebra system). The technical reports can be downloaded or you may view an abstract. There is a searchable database.

KEYWORDS Education (College/University), Research, Software, Statistics
AUDIENCE Australians, Mathematicians, Statisticians
CONTACT Dr Jim Richardson
jimr@maths.usyd.edu.au

FREE

http://www.maths.usyd.edu.au:8000/

Symbolic Mathematical Computation Information Center ★★★

This site maintains an archive of material related to symbolic mathematical computation. Users will find information on research, tools, and computer systems in the field of computational mathematics. There are pointers to FTP libraries of software, tutorial information, and a list of FAQs.

KEYWORDS Algebra, Education, Symbolic Computation
AUDIENCE Computer Scientists, Mathematicians, Mathematics Educators
CONTACT Paul S. Wang
SymbolicNet@mcs.kent.edu

FREE

http://symbolicnet.mcs.kent.edu/

University of Illinois at Champaign-Urbana Mathematics Department ★★★

The University of Illinois at Champaign-Urbana (UIUC) Mathematics Department contains information on the undergraduate and graduate mathematics programs. The page gives access to the course catalog, an education reform project and other research projects. There are links to other departments at the University and other related mathematics servers.

KEYWORDS Archives, Educational Programs
AUDIENCE Educators, Mathematicians, Students
CONTACT Daniel R. Grayson
dan@math.uiuc.edu

FREE

http://www.math.uiuc.edu

University of Minnesota School of Mathematics ★★★

The School of Mathematics page contains information on the professors, students and the current seminar schedule with past schedules being archived for reference. This site has an FTP server link that contains many utilities and applications for mathematicians. There are links to the Minnesota Center for Industrial Mathematics' new research program, and to Math Lab Consultants providing assistance to users.

KEYWORDS Archives, Educational Programs
AUDIENCE Educators, Mathematicians, Students
CONTACT www@math.umn.edu

FREE

http://www.math.umn.edu

University of South Carolina Department of Mathematics ★★★★

The USC Department of Mathematics home page contains information on course materials, faculty, staff, and research projects. The research projects such as the Industrial Mathematics Initiative (IMI) have goals that range from the advancement of theoretical mathematics research to the development of industrial applications to fields like wavelets, computer-aided design and image processing. This site has links to online mathematical research journals, computer science and parallel computing sites.

KEYWORDS Journals, Universities
AUDIENCE Educators, Mathematicians, Students
CONTACT mathwww@math.scarolina.edu
FREE

http://www.math.scarolina.edu

WISDOM (Weizmann Insitute of Science, Department Of Mathematics) ★★★

The WISDOM (Weizmann Institute of Science, Department Of Mathematics) web server provides information on WISDOM's people, computing center facilities, research, publishing of papers and technical reports, a library which is open to the public, and other WWW servers at Weizmann.

KEYWORDS Computer Science, Institutions, Israel, Mathematics
AUDIENCE Mathematics Educators, Mathematics Students
CONTACT Carol Weintraub
carol@wisdom.weizmann.ac.il
FREE

http://www.wisdom.weizmann.ac.il/

ftp://ftp.wisdom.weizmann.ac.il/

Wavelets ★★★

This site contains Wavelets information from the Department of Mathematics at Salzburg University. Wavelets are a way to analyze a signal using base functions which are localized both in time (as diracs, but unlike sine waves), and in frequency (as sine waves, but unlike diracs). They can be used for efficient numerical algorithms and many compression applications. The site consists mainly of pointers to resources elsewhere on the Internet.

KEYWORDS Algorithms, Mathematics, Wavelets
AUDIENCE Educators, Mathematicians
CONTACT Andreas Uhl
uhl@edvz.sbg.ac.at
FREE

http://www.mat.sbg.ac.at/~uhl/wav.html

World Wide Web Virtual Library - Mathematics ★★★★

This is the Mathematics index for the World-Wide Web Virtual Library. It has a thorough listing of different mathematical resources that can be accessed through WWW, Gopher, and news. It includes servers for Mathematics Departments, an index of TeX archives, and a list of electronic math journals.

KEYWORDS Mathematical Software, Meta-Index (Mathematics), TeX
AUDIENCE Mathematicians, Numerical Analysts, Statisticians, Tex And Latex Users
CONTACT webmaster@math.fsu.edu
FREE

http://euclid.math.fsu.edu/Science/math.html

Networking

See also
Communications · *Networking*
Education · *Educational Technology*
Internet · *Networking*

 (r+s)i ★★★

This is a home page from a Brazilian computer firm Redes e Sistemas de Informacio. Its name stands for 'network and information systems,' which specializing in the following areas — Networks (Internet, TCP/IP, Novell), Databases, Software and system development, Methodologies and techniques in computer science, and business informatization processes. The credentials of firm partners and consultants are also presented.

KEYWORDS Brazil, Communications Technology, Information Technology, Software
AUDIENCE Brazilians, Computer Professionals, Computer Users, Internet Users
FREE

http://www.traverse.com/rsi/irsi.htm

ATM (Asynchronous Transfer Mode) Forum ★★★★

This site focuses upon the uses and development of ATM networking technology. Users can find ATM technical information and specifications, development resources, membership information, and an ATM FAQ file. There is also material on the possible uses of the new technology, as well as links to other ATM resources.

KEYWORDS ATM (Asynchronous Transfer Mode), Network Protocols, Networking
AUDIENCE Systems Designers, Telecommunciations Professionals, Telecommunications Engineers
CONTACT Jason Dominguez
webmaster@sbexpos.com
FREE

http://www.atmforum.com

Adaptec Technical Bulletin Board ★★★

Adaptec Technical Bulletin Board is a technical site providing software license agreements as well as several technical documents. Detailed information is provided on new features, Adaptec Host Adaptor support, 32-bit disk access support, CD-ROM drive support, tape drive support, scanner support, set-up command line options, and finally, troubleshooting/limitations. Network installations instructions, configurations for system integration, hardware and software requirements for controllers and SCSI adapters and virtually any other information required to use the Adaptec products are available at this site.

KEYWORDS CD-ROMs, Computer Applications, Computer Hardware
AUDIENCE Computer Hardware Users, Computer Professionals, Computer Scientists, Computer System Designers, Computer Users
FREE

ftp://ftp.adaptec.com/

Advanced Network Architecture People Page ★★

The Advanced Network Architecture People Page offers a brief explanation of the program, which focusses on network architectures, systems and protocols. The main use of this page, however, is to provide contact information and links to the home pages of the professors, graduates students, and administrative staff for this program.

KEYWORDS Computer Systems Architecture, Protocols, Universities
AUDIENCE Computer Designers, Computer Scientists, Computer System Architects
CONTACT Jeff Van Dyke
jvandyke@mit.edu
FREE

http://ana-www.lcs.mit.edu/

BelWu ★★★

Belwu is a German networking system from the University of Stuttgart that links computers and information from all over Germany. Their home page provides information about their projects and net management systems, with project home pages containing research objectives and select papers. There are links to the newsletter Spots, and other networking and communications Web sites. Users may also access the University of Stuttgart directory, through a keyword search or subject list.

KEYWORDS Germany, Telecommunications
AUDIENCE Germans, Network Communication Specialists, Telecommunications Professionals
CONTACT webmaster@belwue.de
FREE

http://nic.belwue.de

Cabletron WWW Home Page ★★★

This site offers information about the company Cabletron Systems. There is access to information on recent news, product catalog, service and technical support, employment, technical papers, LAN care support services, seminars and training, and general company information.

KEYWORDS Internet Networking, Online Catalogs, Technical Support
AUDIENCE Network Administrators, Network Developers, Network Users
CONTACT webmaster@ctron.com
FREE

http://www.ctron.com/

Networking

Cell Relay Retreat ★★★★

The Cell Relay Retreat site hosts the archives to the cell-relay mailing list, and several other ATM (Asynchronous Transfer Mode)-related mailing lists. There is information on what is new at the retreat, getting started, and upcoming ATM related events. There are links to searches for something specific, several archives, an ATM bibliography, ATM documents, employment opportunities, recent trade press articles on ATM, ATM software, and other ATM sites.

KEYWORDS Broadband Technology, Internet Access Providers
AUDIENCE ATM (Asynchronous Transfer Mode) Users, Internet Access Providers, Telecommunications Experts
CONTACT Allen Robel
robelr@indiana.edu
FREE

http://frame-relay.indiana.edu:80/cell-relay/

Chipcom Corporation ★★★★

The Chipcom Corporation produces network platforms and management tools. The Chipcom page supplies information about the company, its products, services and technical support. There are also links to usergroups and product news.

KEYWORDS Companies, Computer Networking, Product Information, Technical Support
AUDIENCE Network Administrators, Systems Administrators
CONTACT webmaster@chipcom.com
FREE

http://www.chipcom.com

Cisco Systems ★★★★

This server provides access to general information on the products and services of Cisco Systems, Inc. Cisco specializes in network routing and internetworking hardware. Guest users of the system can browse product catalogs, brochures, press releases, and some technical documentation. Owners of Cisco products can register with this site to recieve detailed technical support, software, and more.

KEYWORDS Computer Hardware, Internet Networking, Routers
AUDIENCE Cisco Users, Network Administrators, Network Designers, Systems Analysts
FREE

http://www.cisco.com

Computone Corporation Home Page ★★

Computone Corporation provides computer networking hardware and software for users of TCP/IP networks and multiple networked serial devices. Users will find product information, software drivers, technical support information, and contact information. There is also information for potential value-added resellers of Computone products.

KEYWORDS Computer Hardware, Computer Networking, Network Hardware
AUDIENCE Business Professionals, Network Administrators, Network Designers
CONTACT Dave Johnson
dave@computone.com
FREE

http://www.computone.com

Cygnus Network Security ★★★

This site contains information about Cygnus Network Security (CNA), commercial support and security consulting for Kerberos, MIT's Project Athena client-server network security system. It provides access to Kerberos FAQs, documentation and technical papers. There is also information about running Kerberos under Microsoft Windows.

KEYWORDS Networking, Operating Systems, Universities
AUDIENCE GNU Programmers, Network Administrators, Network Developers, Windows Application Developers
CONTACT info@cygnus.com
FREE

http://www.cygnus.com/data/cns/

Develcon Home Page ★★★

This site offers information on Develcon, a company that specializes in developing and marketing local and remote LAN access. There is access to a corporate overview, product information, what's new, service information, contact information, submitting inquiries and comments.

KEYWORDS Electronics, ISDN, Marketing
AUDIENCE Developers, LAN (Local Area Network) Users, Network Users, Telecommunications Experts
CONTACT Info@Develcon.com
FREE

http://www.develcon.com/

Fibronics Mosaic Home Page ★★★

This is a home page for the Israeli-based company, Fibronics International Inc. - an international provider of local area networking, internetworking and network management solutions for the workgroup and the enterprise. Fibronics's customers include USAir, British Airways, KLM, SAS, Swissair, Swiss Bank, Wells Fargo, Bank of America, Bank of Japan, Deutsche Bank, Lloyds of London, Nomura Securities, Societe Generale, and WASA, and a number of large and well known companies worldwide.

KEYWORDS Internet Networking, Israel
AUDIENCE Business Professionals, Internet Users, Israelis
CONTACT Ricky Marek
ricky@fibronics.co.il
FREE

http://www.fibronics.co.il/

HSI-High Speed Interconnect ★★★

This is the CERN High Speed Interconnect Home Page. There are links to technology homepages of ATM (Asynchronous Transfer Mode), FCS (Fibre Channel Standard), HIPPI (High Performance Parallel Interface), SCI (Scalable Coherent Interface), and detector links. There are also links to data acquisition functions of data generators, testing, readout/buffering, event building, processing, and storage.

KEYWORDS Broadband Technology, Internet Access Providers, Technology
AUDIENCE ATM (Asynchronous Transfer Mode) Users (1/1), Communications Professionals, Telecommunications Experts
CONTACT Robert McLaren
Robert.McLaren@cern.ch
FREE

http://www.cern.ch/HSI/Welcome.html

IBM Person to Person Product Family ★★

This page provides information about IBM's person-to-person desktop conferencing product (P2P) for Windows and OS/2. Multiple users on mixed networks can share clipboards, workspaces and meeting minutes. This site includes information about how to conference, and use desktop collaboration tools, and offers user success stories as well.

KEYWORDS Computer Conferencing, Software
AUDIENCE Computer Professionals, PC Users, Windows Users
CONTACT sphipps@vnet.ibm.com
FREE

http://www.hursley.ibm.com/p2p/P2P.html

Industrial Computer Engineering Laboratory ★★★

The Industrial Computer Engineering Laboratory (LIT) at the Swiss Federal Institute of Technology (EPFL) focuses on industrial networking and computer engineering. Their home page describes their projects, which includes the CCE-CNMA communication networks, MMS remote controls and monitoring of industrial devices, and Wireless networking. Each project description includes general backgrounds and overviews, publications, catalogs of products, and reports. Also included on this site is information about the staff and machines, as well as public papers written by LIT staff on topics such as Protocol Testing and Modular Redundancy.

KEYWORDS Communications Technology, Computer Networking
AUDIENCE Computer Specialists, Networking Specialists
CONTACT Jean-Marc Vandel
www@litsun.epfl.ch
FREE

http://lilly.ping.de

Networking – Operating Systems   **203**

 ### Intersolv Home Page

Intersolv is a software company specializing in client/server software development tools. The Company offers a suite of products and related services that are marketed to corporate customers and independent software vendors worldwide. This site offers information about Intersolv's products and services as well as company information such as financial information, job opportunities, global partners, and an online technical support area (including software patches and bug reports).

KEYWORDS Client/Server Technology, Companies, Employment, Software
AUDIENCE MIS Managers, Network Administrators, Programmers
CONTACT webmaster@intersolv.com
FREE

http://www.intersolv.com/

 ### Net Daemons Associates, Inc.

Net Daemons Associates, Inc is a computer network consulting and administration firm. The home page supplies information about the company, their services and tools. The page includes an online manual section for their existing customers.

KEYWORDS Companies, Computer Networking, Consulting Services, Systems Administration
AUDIENCE Business Professionals, Systems Administrators
CONTACT info@nda.com
FREE

http://www.nda.com/

 ### PC-Mac TCP/IP & NFS FAQ list by Rawn Shah

This is PC TCP/IP and NFS Frequently Asked Questions list, which contains lots of information on TCP/IP or NFS product for PC or Macintosh. Moreover a list of TCP/IP and NFS products is also included.

KEYWORDS LANs (Local Area Networks), NFS (Network File System), Protocols
AUDIENCE Computer Networkers, Macintosh Users, PC Users
CONTACT Rawn Shah
 rawn@rtd.com
FREE

http://www.rtd.com/pcnfsfaq/faq.html

 ### Stardust Technologies' WinSock Resource Center

This page is Stardust's Winsock resource center, providing access to information about the Windows Sockets API or Winsock, for short. This site introduces Winsock, WinSock Version 1.1, and WinSock Version 2; provides a Winsock bibliography; and information about Winsock-related events; related Windows-based communications including TAPI Files (Telephony API for Microsoft Windows) and TCP/IP packages; and the Global Winsock Consultants' Network. It also includes a nontechnical Winsock guide, Winsock shareware and freeware, lists of Winsock newsgroups and Winsock mailing lists and more.

KEYWORDS Internet Access Software, Networking, Operating Systems
AUDIENCE Network Developers, PC Programmers, Systems Administrators, Windows Application Developers
CONTACT martinb@stardust.com
FREE

http://www.stardust.com/wsresrce.html

TERENA - Trans-European Research and Education Networking Association

TERENA (Trans-European Research and Education Networking Association) has set a goal 'to promote and participate in the development of a high quality international information and telecommunications infrastructure for the benefit of research and education.' TERENA performs technical activities and provides a platform for discussion and education to encourage the development of a high-quality computer networking infrastructure for the European research community. Links are provided to information on Technical Programme and Working Groups, Procedures (for meetings, etc.) and Liaisons with other organizations.

KEYWORDS Education, European Community, Research & Development, Telecommunications
AUDIENCE Computer Users, Internet Users, Physicists, Researchers
CONTACT secretariat@terena.nl
FREE

http://erasmus.rare.nl

 ### Welcome to Crosswise Corporation!

The homepage for Crosswise Corporation, maker of FacetoFace, is a cross-platform document conferencing software for IBM PCs and compatibles running Microsoft Windows and Macintosh computers. FacetoFace allows multiple users to view and manipulate identical, synchronized images of documents. This site includes demo software, instructions and detailed product information.

KEYWORDS Computer Conferencing, Computer Hardware, Software
AUDIENCE Conferencing System Users, Macintosh Users, PC Users, Windows Users
CONTACT support@crosswise.com
FREE

http://www.crosswise.com/

 ### Welcome to elroNet

This home page introduces you to Elron Electronic Industries' elroNet, an Israeli company that provides LAN interconnection and Internet access. Links are made to tourist information, the interactive TV channel, a shopping mall (mainly comprised of the home pages of hi-tech companies and tourist attractions), and business associations.

KEYWORDS Electronics, Israel, Online Shopping
AUDIENCE Business Professionals, Israelis, Tourists
FREE

http://www.elron.net/

 ### Welcome to Network Computing Devices

Network Computing Devices home page provides products for information access in network computing environments. The information includes color, monochrome and gray-scale X terminals, PC-XWare for both Windows and UNIX access, electronic mail and messaging software (Z-Mail). Corporate information is available at this site for such ares as financial reports, employment opportunities, and press releases.

KEYWORDS Computer Networking, Operating Systems, Utility Software
AUDIENCE Computer Professionals, Network Users, PC Users, Windows Users
CONTACT webmaster@ncd.com
FREE

http://www.ncd.com

 ### Windows Sockets Information

This JSB page provides access to information about the Windows Sockets API or Winsock, for short. This site provides access to information about Virtual Socket Library (VSL) FAQ, software tree, and documentation. Users will also find FTP access to the WinSock version 1.1 specification (in HTML, Word, Postscript, WinHelp, Write, RTF, and text format), Windows Sockets Version 2.0 and new API functions, and slides and notes from Winsock focus group meetings, guidebooks, as well as links to other Winsock sites and information.

KEYWORDS Internet Access Software, Networking, Operating Systems
AUDIENCE Network Developers, PC Users, Systems Administrators, Windows Application Developers
FREE

http://www.jsb.com/prodinfo/winsock/vpws11.html

Operating Systems

See also
Computing & Mathematics · *Applications*
Computing & Mathematics · *Software*

80x86 PC Emulators

This site provides a list and brief review of PC emulators, including emulators to run MS-Windows 3.1 and DOS executables under UNIX, DOS, Windows 95, and Windows NT.

KEYWORDS Emulators, Operating Systems, Utility Software

AUDIENCE Computer Professionals, Software Developers, Windows Application Developers, Windows Programmers
CONTACT erich@uruk.org
FREE

http://www.uruk.org/emu/pc.html

APE Computer at DESY

DESY, the German high energy physics lab, is currently configuring an APE computer. The APE was developed by INFN, Rome, and is now sold under the name Quadrics by Alenia Spazio, S.p.A., Italy. It is a massively parallel SIMD machine, currently used at DESY for Lattice Gauge Theory simulations. DESY provides this page for information on the APE/Quadrics computer including such things as papers on APE, its operating system, compilers, and technical specifications.

KEYWORDS Parallel Computing, Supercomputing
AUDIENCE Computer Engineers, Concurrent Logic Programmers, Parallel Programmers
CONTACT Marcus Speh
  marcus@x4u.desy.de
FREE

http://info.desy.de/www/Lattice/ape.html

Allegro Operating System Home Page

This Allegro homepage provides product information about Allegro, a 32-bit multi-tasking operating system for 386, 486, and Pentium computers that provides network support. The site also has information on Parley, a customizable BBS system that can support thousands of simultaneous users, and Apprehend, a system which provides support for production environments, linking thousands of data collection and process control devices. This site includes product and system configuration information, testimonials, price information, and diagrams.

KEYWORDS Allegro, Computer Hardware, Operating Systems, Software
AUDIENCE Allegro Users, Computer Professionals, PC Users, Software Developers
FREE

http://www.allegrosys.com/index.html

Amoeba Operating System

This site contains technical reports and papers about the Amoeba distributed Operating System. Amoeba is a distributed operating system intended to connect a large number of computers together in a transparent way. Documents within this archive are in Postscript format, and include manuals, an introduction to the operating system, and papers about Amoeba and Orca (a parallel programming language).

KEYWORDS Amoeba, Parallel Computing, Technical Reports
AUDIENCE Amoeba Users, Computer Scientists
CONTACT ftp-adm@cse.ucsc.edu.
FREE

ftp://ftp.cse.ucsc.edu/pub/amoeba/

Chair for Operating Systems University

The Chair for Operating Systems works in the area of distributed, parallel and scalable high performance computing. Students are instructed in operating systems and parallel computing with a special focus on scalable high performance computing. This site gives access to information on the University, the groups projects, papers and publications with links to related sites.

KEYWORDS Germany, Parallel Computing
AUDIENCE Computer Engineers, Germans, Parallel Computing Experts, Students
CONTACT M. Gudjons
  markolf@lfbs.rwth-aachen.de
FREE

http://www.lfbs.rwth-aachen.de

European Microsoft Windows NT Academic Centre

The European Microsoft Windows NT Academic Centre provides computing resources. Topics include the Internet Toolchest for NT, WAIS toolkit, Microsoft Resources, Software Library, Mirrors, NT on the Internet, an FAQ, FTP Sites, Mail, Listservers, Newsgroups, and more.

KEYWORDS Europe, Operating Systems
AUDIENCE Computer Professionals, Computer Users, Internet Users
CONTACT emwac@ed.ac.uk
FREE

http://emwac.ed.ac.uk

European X User Group (EXUG)

This is the home page for the European X User Group (EXUG), a group devoted to the promotion and maintenance of the X Windows operating system. Users will find pointers to collections of X Windows software, information on the latest release of X Windows, EXUG events and membership information, and a collection of FAQs.

KEYWORDS Computer Hardware, X Windows
AUDIENCE UNIX Users, Workstation Users, X Windows Users
CONTACT Rainer Klute
  klute@nads.de
FREE

http://www.nads.de/EXUG/EXUG.html

Linux FTP Directory

This site contains Linux-related files from tsx-11.mit.edu and sunsite.unc.edu collected during November, 1993. In addition, Free Software Foundation sources from prep.ai.mit.edu are included, as these form the basis for most of Linux's utilities. Some sources from ftp.uu.net are included for mail/news programs.

KEYWORDS Mathematics, UNIX
AUDIENCE Computer Specialists, Mathematicians, PC Users, Programmers, UNIX Users

CONTACT Vladimir Braus
  ftp@math.hr
FREE

ftp://cromath.math.hr/mnt/LINUX/

Logdaemon Release 4.5

Logdaemon Release 4.5 subdirectory is an archive of the result of years of transformations on the BSD (Berkeley Software Distribution) source. The code works with SunOS4, SunOS5 (Solaris), Ultrix 4x and other BSD/SYSV4 clones.

KEYWORDS Computer Hardware, Computer Programming, Software Development
AUDIENCE Programmers, Sun Microsystems Users, UNIX Users, Workstation Users
CONTACT Wietse Venema
  wietse@wzv.win.tue.nl
FREE

ftp://ftp.eit.com/jfd/

Minnie's Home Page

Minnie's Home Page is an individual home page dedicated to information about BSD (Berkeley Software Design) PC operating systems. General information provided here includes FAQs, how-to links, and purchasing information for FreeBSD and NetBSD. Links are provided to BSD newsgroups, and a BSD source tree, to find function information about the FreeBSD system. This site also includes links to gateways resources and information.

KEYWORDS Computer Applications, Software Development
AUDIENCE BSD Users, Computer Users, PC Owners
CONTACT Warren Toomey
  wkt@cs.adfa.oz.au
FREE

http://minnie.cs.adfa.oz.au

NCSA (National Center for Supercomputing Applications) Home Page

The National Center for Supercomputing Applications is a high-performance computing and communications facility and research center designed to serve the US computational science and engineering community. NCSA developed the WWW browser Mosaic, as well as other applications for many different types of computers.

KEYWORDS Computer Networking, Computer Science, Supercomputing
AUDIENCE Computer Scientists, General Public, Researchers, Students
CONTACT pubs@ncsa.uiuc.edu
FREE

http://www.ncsa.uiuc.edu/General/NCSAHome.html

Novell Market Messenger Worldwide ★★★★

Novell's homepage provides access to information about operating systems and services. Some of the applications include NetWare, UNIXWare Servers and OLTP Solutions; and home, business and workgroup applications, including Perfect Office, WordPerfect, Presentations 3.0, Quattro Pro, and Internet publishing using Wordperfect. There is technical support that has files, drivers and patches that can be downloaded, a database with search capability, and access to technical documents. Corporate information such as financial reports, employment opportunities, and press releases as well as links to Novell partners, such as 3COM, HP, and Cisco Systems are available at this site.

KEYWORDS   Networking, Networking Software, Software
AUDIENCE   Macintosh Users, Network Administrators, PC Users, Systems Administrators
FREE

http://www.novell.com

Pegasus Stables ★★★

The Pegasus project works to develop operating system support for multimedia systems. The page has information about the researchers, the project and the status of their coffee machines. There are links to the University of Cambridge and the Universiteit Twente.

KEYWORDS   Multimedia, Research & Development, Systems Engineering
AUDIENCE   Europeans, Operating Systems Developers, Researchers
CONTACT   webmaster@pegasus.esprit.ec.org
FREE

http://www.pegasus.esprit.ec.org/

QAID (Question Answer Information Database) ★★★

The QAID (Question Answer Information Database) provides an extensive database of resources, both documented and undocumented, on Windows and Windows 95. It includes links to quick tips and tricks, news and rumors, and an FAQ (Frequently Asked Questions) file. There is also general information and instructions listed by topic.

KEYWORDS   Companies, FAQs (Frequently Asked Questions), Operating Systems, Software
AUDIENCE   PC Users, Programmers, Windows Users
CONTACT   Mike Dixon
          mdixon@whidbey.net
FREE

http://www.whidbey.net/~mdixon/qaid0001.htm

Slackware Linux Version 2.2.0.1 ★★★★

This site provides several detailed documents regarding the latest version of the GNU (GNU's Not UNIX) operating system, Slackware Linux Version 2.2.0.1. An index is provided as to the contents of each subdirectory. This particular version contains libc 4.6.27, Linux kernel 1.2.3 (plus source for many other versions in the source tree including v.0.01) and XFree863.1.1. Linux is a freely distributable implementation of UNIX for 80386 and 80486 machines.

KEYWORDS   Freeware, GNU (GNU's Not Unix), Operating Systems
AUDIENCE   Computer Users, Internet Access Providers, Internet Users, UNIX Users
CONTACT   Patrick Volkerding
          volkerdi@ftp.cdrom.com
FREE

ftp://ftp.execpc.com/pub/linux/slackware/

ftp://ftp.halcyon.com/pub/linux/slackware/

UNIX Reference Desk ★★★★

The UNIX Reference Desk page contains references on computing in the UNIX environment. General information on UNIX, info pages available over the WWW, UNIX on different platforms, X Windows, networking, security and archives on UNIX humor can be accessed at this site.

KEYWORDS   Operating Systems, Unix
AUDIENCE   UNIX System Administrators, UNIX Users
CONTACT   Jennifer Myers
          jmyers@eecs.nwu.edu
FREE

http://www.eecs.nwu.edu/unix.html

USARInfo ★★★

This gopher provides information about a project called UNIX-Server am RZU (USAR) at the University of Zurich. USAR is a project to build a UNIX-based computer network for faculty and students at the university. The provided information includes the logical hardware configuration and the installed software on the system. It also includes instructions on how to access USAR and how to use the installed software. This server is maintained by the Computing Center of the University of Zurich.

KEYWORDS   Education (College/University), Switzerland, Systems Administration, Unix
AUDIENCE   Computer Users, Network Communications Specialists, UNIX System Administrators
CONTACT   gopher@rzu.unizh.ch
FREE

gopher://rzurs1.unizh.ch/

University of Illinois, Urbana-Champaign Choices OS Technical Reports and Papers ★★★

This directory contains a number of technical reports and other documents related to the Encore Multimax, Sun SPARCStation, AT&T 6386, and IBM PS/2 versions of Choices. Most of the documentation, conference papers and technical reports are from the University of Illinois Systems Research Group.

KEYWORDS   Computer Science, Programming
AUDIENCE   Computer Researchers, Computer Scientists, Programmers
CONTACT   David Raila
          raila@cs.uiuc.edu
FREE

ftp://choices.cs.uiuc.edu/Papers/

Organizations

See also
Computing & Mathematics · Companies
Internet · Internet Services

ACM — Association for Computing Machinery ★★★

This is a gopher server of the Association for Computing Machinery (ACM). It provides information on ACM, membership application, ACM network services, ACM forums, ACM pathfinder, the Institute for the Certification of Computing Professionals, and more.

KEYWORDS   Computer Hardware, Computer Technology, Research & Development
AUDIENCE   Computer Professionals, Computer System Designers, Systems Analysts
CONTACT   Michael Allen Clore
          clore@acm.org
FREE

gopher://pascal.acm.org/

AG Group ★★★★

AG Group is a provider of Macintosh-based network management products. Their PEEK software line of network analyzers is their most popular product. This site provides a brief summary on their 4-tape instructional videos, EtherPeek 2.0.4 interface support list, AG Group recommended reading list, U.S. retail pricing from September 1994, as well as product specification data sheets. Also available are slides from their Network Management Seminar (1995), demos for all of their products, ServerScan - an unsupported free utility that provides information on Appleshare file servers, and free upgrades to Netwatchman 2.11, LocalPeek 2.0.4 and EtherPeek 2.0.4.

KEYWORDS   Networking Software, Software, Utility Software
AUDIENCE   Macintosh Users, Network Developers, Network Service Providers, Network Users
CONTACT   info@aggroup.com
FREE

http://www.aggroup.com/

ftp://ftp.aggroup.com/

AMS (American Mathematical Society) ★★★★

This site is the location of the AMS (American Mathematical Society) archive which provides TeX-related software entitled AMS-TeX and AMS-LaTeX. Two 'author packages' can be downloaded from this location each of which include TeX formatting language to typeset manuscripts to shorten time and reduce the price of publications. The packages also contain documentation, instructions, and examples. Current guidelines for publishing papers using the 1991 Mathematical Subjects Classification is available. In addition, a booklet is also available designed to assist

Organizations

students in mathematical sciences who are or will be seeking professional employment.
- KEYWORDS: Mathematics, Software, TeX
- AUDIENCE: Academics, Mathematicians, Numerical Analysts
- CONTACT: tech-support@math.ams.org
- FREE

ftp://e-math.ams.com/

ARPP (Apple Research Partnership Program) WWW Home Page ★★★★

This is the WWW home page of the Apple Research Partnership Program (ARPP) at Carleton University in Ottawa, Ontario. The ARPP is a joint venture between Apple Canada and Carleton University, and is intended to help develop new research applications for Apple equipment. This page offers links to general information on ARPP, MacHTTP resources, and pages dedicated to Ottawa Macintosh developers and users.
- KEYWORDS: Companies, Research & Development
- AUDIENCE: Macintosh Developers, Macintosh Users
- CONTACT: Grant Neufeld @Contact_email:gneufeld@ccs.carleton.ca
- FREE

http://arpp1.carleton.ca/

Association for Computing Machinery ★★★

These sites offer access to the Association for Computing Machinery, an international scientific and educational organization dedicated to advancing the art, science, and application of information technology. The servers provide information about the ACM facilities and staff, and also discuss computing and technology-related issues. In addition, the sites provide links to other similar services on the Internet.
- KEYWORDS: Associations, Computer Applications, Science, Technology
- AUDIENCE: Computer Professionals, Educators, Scientists, Technology Enthusiasts
- CONTACT: Michael Allen Clore clore@acm.org
- FREE

http://info.acm.org/

gopher://info.acm.org/

Australian Computer Society Gopher ★★★

This gopher server provides information on the Australian Computer Society, including its mission statement, related newsgroup, membership information, and contact addresses. The Australian Computer Society is the professional association in Australia for those in the computing and information technology fields.
- KEYWORDS: Australia, Computer Applications, Information Science, Information Technology
- AUDIENCE: Australians, Computer Users
- CONTACT: peterh@acs.org.au
- FREE

gopher://acs-gopher.mit.csu.edu.au:1605/11/acs

Boston Computer Society Home Page ★★★

The Boston Computer Society (BCS) site provides resources to enhance people's computer skills through educational programs, seminars, workshops, and meetings. The page contains access to BCS's calendar of events, user groups and resource center. There are also links to other chapters of the BCS.
- KEYWORDS: Boston, Computer Networking, Educational Programs, Professional Societies
- AUDIENCE: Business Professionals, Computer Networkers, Computer Scientists, Massachusetts Residents
- CONTACT: G. Feldman gaf@bcs.org
- FREE

http://www.bcs.org/bcs/

British Computer Society ★★★

This site contains information on the British Computing Society (BCS). The BCS is the Chartered body for Information Technology professionals. Formed in 1957, it has nearly 34,000 members and in May 1990 became a Chartered Engineering Institution. The society is concerned with the development of computing and its effective application. Under its Royal Charter granted in 1984, it also has responsibilities for education and training, for public awareness, and above all for standards, quality and professionalism. This site provides detailed information on the society, its ethics, organization special projects and code of conduct.
- KEYWORDS: Computer Applications, Informatics, Information Systems, Technology
- AUDIENCE: Computer Professionals, Computer Specialists
- CONTACT: Lynne Coventry lynne@icbl.hw.ac.uk
- FREE

http://www.cityscape.co.uk/bcs/aboutbcs/overview.html

California Education and Research Federation Network ★★★

This gopher describes the California Education and Research Federation Network, a computer network that links educational institutions, research institutions, government, and businesses in California. The documents included describe CERFNet services, its history, usage policies, usage statistics, and services offered to individuals.
- KEYWORDS: California, Computer Networking, Education, Research & Development
- AUDIENCE: Californians, Computer Users, Education Administrators
- CONTACT: help@cerf.net
- FREE

gopher://gopher.cerf.net/

Centre for Intelligent Machines ★★★

This is a gopher server of the Centre for Intelligent Machines (CIM), Montreal, Canada. It provides access to information on CIM, meetings, courses, their phone directory, seminars, its research and technical reports.
- KEYWORDS: Canada, Computer Applications, Education (College/University), Intelligent Agents
- AUDIENCE: Computer Professionals, Computer Students, Students
- CONTACT: Jan Binder jan@cim.mcgill.edu
- FREE

gopher://gopher.cim.mcgill.ca/

Centro Svizzero di Calcolo Scientifico ★★★

This gopher provides information about the Centro Svizzero di Calcolo Scientifico (CSCS), the national scientific computing center for Switzerland. The user will find information about CSCS administration, organization, and industrial collaborations, CSCS supercomputing facilities, CSCS activies and services, and a description of the CSCS infrastructure.
- KEYWORDS: Computer Applications, Computer Science, Supercomputing, Switzerland
- AUDIENCE: Researchers, Science Researchers, Scientists
- CONTACT: info@cscs.ch
- FREE

gopher://pobox.cscs.ch/

Computer & Office Technology Showcase - Index ★★★

This is the Web site for The Computer and Office Technology Showcase which is designed to bring company representatives together with the buyers in their region. The showcase is scheduled to take place in several major cities in the United States on several dates in 1995 and 1996. A list is provided of vendor categories, such as application developers and desktop publishers.
- KEYWORDS: Computer Technology, Conferences
- AUDIENCE: Buyers, Computer Retailers
- CONTACT: webmaster@jkcg.com
- FREE

http://www.jkcg.com/Webmaster/EMS/

Computer Professionals for Social Responsibility ★★★

This is the home page describing the activities of a group called Computer Professionals for Social Responsibility (CPSR). The home page gives access to CPSR policies, publications, lobbies, recent statements, and current and future areas of controversy in high-tech ethical affairs.
- KEYWORDS: Activism, Computer Ethics, Internet Issues, Organizations
- AUDIENCE: Computer Professionals, Policymakers, Political Analysts, Social Scientists

CONTACT   webmaster@cpsr.org
FREE
http://www.cpsr.org/dox/home.html

Computing Systems Technology Office

This gopher site provides selected information about the activities and programs of the Computing Systems Technology Office (CSTO) of the Advanced Research Projects Agency (ARPA). In addition, users can find associated information about the High Performance Computing and Communications Program. CSTO is focused on topics such as scale-able computing systems, scale-able software, national-scale information enterprises, and networking.

KEYWORDS   Computer Applications, Computer Science, Computer Technology, Networking
AUDIENCE   Computer Professionals, Computer Specialists, Network Administrators, Network Users
CONTACT   baa@arpa.mil
FREE
gopher://clyde.isi.edu/

Digital Equipment Computer Users Society

This site is maintained by Digital Equipment Computer Users Society (DECUS). It contains information on DEC, announcements & press releases, DECUS seminars, symposia & tradeshows, the DECUS software library, technical documents, archives, the FTP site, and more. It provides access to other gophers.

KEYWORDS   Computer Peripherals, Computer Systems, Computer Technology
AUDIENCE   Computer Professionals, Computer System Designers
CONTACT   Gopher-Meister@DECUS.Org
FREE
http://www.decus.org/

gopher://decus.org/

Euromath

This is a gopher server of the Euromath Network. The Euromath Network is a project to develop a computer network infrastructure in Eastern Europe and the former Soviet Union to assist research in the mathematically oriented sciences. The Euromath gopher contains resources on mathematics and information science, documents concerned with Euromath, and more.

KEYWORDS   Eastern Europe, Mathematics, Networking
AUDIENCE   Computer Professionals, Internet Users, Mathematicians
CONTACT   Flemming Topsoe
           topsoe@euromath.dk
FREE
gopher://gopher.euromath.dk/

Connections to Online Dictionary of Computing
Don't let the jargon "byte" you

The Free On-line Dictionary of Computing

You may call it "nonsense" if you like, but I've heard nonsense, compared with which that would be as sensible as a dictionary.

About the Dictionary

Contents

Look something up

Case is never significant in searches. An entry is returned if your search string matches its complete heading or, failing that, all entries are returned which have your search string as a substring of their heading.

This is a searchable index. Enter search keywords: [   ]

Help!

If you find any mistakes in the dictionary please mail me. Please do not send any new definitions until further notice, I don't have time to edit them in at the moment and already have quite a backlog.

Confused about the computer jargon you come across in user manuals, or when talking to technical support? Get the answers on the Internet and become computer "literate" (at least with the terms and phrases) without taking a programming course at your local university. The online "Dictionary of Computing" provides a comprehensive set of computing terms and definitions. It also features cross-referencing. Go online and type in the confusing word or phrase and watch for the definition. ASCII and it is given to you!

(http://wombat.doc.ic.ac.uk/)

If you are a bit more conversant with the "language" of computers (particularly an industry insider), there is a site you might want to explore called "The Computists' Communiqué." This weekly newsletter from Computists' International provides information on jobs, grants, and resource leads. Also provided are general news items from within the field of high technology.

(http://www.drci.co.uk/drci/)

Grace Hopper Celebration of Women in Computing Page

This page offers organizational and background information for the Grace Hopper Celebration of Women in Computing, an annual meeting held every year in Washington, D.C. In addition to general information related to the convention, biographies of the various speakers are available.

KEYWORDS   Computer Hardware, Conventions, Women's Issues
AUDIENCE   Computer Professionals, Computer Users, Women
FREE
http://www.digital.com/pub/doc/hopper/info.html

IEEE Computer Society

This is the home page for the IEEE Computer Society, an organization dedicated to sharing knowledge and resources related to the latest advances in computer technology. It offers users abstracts of published papers, descriptions of the committees and boards that make up the IEEE Computer Society, material on current projects and activities, as well as a listing of upcoming computer and engineering conferences. There is also a section containing the Society's publications, a listing of career opportunities, and membership information.

KEYWORDS   Computer Hardware, Computer Technology, Software
AUDIENCE   Computer Engineers, Computer Industry Professionals, Computer Users
CONTACT   admin@computer.org
FREE
http://www.computer.org/

gopher://info.computer.org/

Information and Publishing Department, Mathematical Branch RAS ★★★

This page is from the Mathematics division of the Russian Academy of Sciences (RAS). Users will find information on the different servers operated by the RAS, as well as material specific to the mathematics division. There are links to other related servers on the net, as well as data about the Russian Academy of Sciences itself. Much of the information here is in Russian.

KEYWORDS Mathematics, Russia
AUDIENCE Educators, Mathematicians, Scientists, Students
CONTACT www@www.ras.ru
FREE

http://www.ac.msk.su

Institute for Global Communications (IGC) ★★★

This gopher site disseminates information on the Institute for Global Communications, the US member of the Association for Progressive Communications, a 16-country association of computer networks working for peace, human rights, environmental protection, social justice, and sustainability. It includes online brochures, conference listings and proceedings, anonomyous FTP archives, and job openings information.

KEYWORDS Environmentalism, Labor Issues
AUDIENCE Activists, Environmentalists
CONTACT igc-info@igc.apc.org
FREE

http://www.igc.apc.org/

gopher://gopher.igc.apc.org/

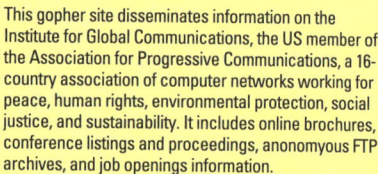

Intel Supercomputer User's Group ★★★

The Intel Supercomputer User's Group (ISUG) provides information and support for Intel computer owners. On their home page users will find materials about their services and becoming an ISUG member, with information about shared resources and training opportunities. Users can read old Intel newsletters, access a calender of upcoming events, and find out about special interest groups. The Intel Supercomputer Web site is also included, with training manuals, a software resource directory, and other Intel computing information. Intel Online, a newsletter for customer help and news, is also archived here.

KEYWORDS Computer User Groups, Supercomputing
AUDIENCE Intel Users, Supercomputer Users
FREE

http://www.ssd.intel.com/ISUG/isug-home.html

International Federation for Information Processing ★★★

This site is the home page for the International Federation for Information Processing and describes its mission, aims, organization, and affiliations. The information is accessed by a table of contents and there are links to other related servers on the Internet as well.

KEYWORDS Associations, Informatics, Information Technology
AUDIENCE Computer Professionals, Information Brokers, Information Scientists
CONTACT Carlos Delgado Kloos
cdk@dit.upm.es
FREE

http://www.dit.upm.es/~cdk/ifip.html

The Internet Project ★★

This is the homepage of the Internet Project created by the PC Users Group (ACT), AUUG, and AUUG, Inc (UNIX User groups) in Canberra, Australia to provide a site for their users. It includes information about the project, contributors, sponsors, and advertisers. Each chapter provides its own page with membership and group information. Free software, tutorials on selected subjects, FAQs, and technical papers are available along with links to related information and and gopher servers.

KEYWORDS Operating Systems
AUDIENCE Computer Users, PC Users, UNIX Users, Windows Users
FREE

http://www.pcug.org.au/cauug/

Luleå Academic Computer Society ★★

This page is the site for the Luleå Academic Computer Society. It provides links to information about the society, services offered to external users, other Nordic computer societies, MUDS, and more.

KEYWORDS Societies, Sweden
AUDIENCE Educators (University), Researchers, Students (University)
CONTACT webmaster@ludd.luth.se
FREE

http://father.ludd.luth.se

Mathemetical Association of America ★★★★

This server is presented by the Mathametical Association of America (MAA). It contains information on MAA, its activites, reports, publications, electronic serivces, and much more. Users will also find a collection of links to other mathematics resources on the Internet.

KEYWORDS Mathematics, Statistics
AUDIENCE Mathematical Biologists, Mathematicians, Mathematics Educators
CONTACT V. Frederick Rickey
rickey@maa.org
FREE

http://www.maa.org/

gopher://math.maa.org/

National Computer Board of Singapore ★★★

This server provides information on the administration and services of the National Computer Board of Singapore. It also provides information about software archives, libraries & catalogs, electronic books, humor & jokes, Usenet news, and more. As well, it has links to other gophers worldwide.

KEYWORDS Computer Science, Singapore
AUDIENCE Computer Professionals, Computer Specialists, Students (Secondary/College)
CONTACT vvijay@ncb.gov.sg
FREE

gopher://gallery.ncb.gov.sg/

SIGDA (Special Interest Group Design Automation) Internet Server at the University of Pittsburgh ★★

This gopher server is for the Special Interest Group, Design Automation (SIGDA), a division of the Association for Computing Machinery. It contains information on SIGDA and its activities, conferences sponsored by SIGDA, and online copies of the SIGDA Newsletter. In addition, this site contains sources for software, newsgroup archives, and links to other related services on the Internet.

KEYWORDS Community Services, Computer Applications, Conferences, University Of Pittsburgh
AUDIENCE Computer Professionals, Computer Specialists, Technical Professionals
CONTACT gopher@ee.pitt.edu
FREE

gopher://kona.ee.pitt.edu/

Share ★★★

This is a gopher server of Share, an association whose member organizations are users of IBM information technology. It provides information on Share, its mission, activities, its history, Share related conferences, news, reports, and more. In addition, it has links to other gophers.

KEYWORDS Computer Professionals, Computer Systems, Computer Technology
AUDIENCE Computer Professionals, Computer System Designers, Computer Users, IBM Users
CONTACT Peter Simon
psimon@share.org
FREE

http://www.share.org/

gopher://share.org/

Stacken Computer Club ★★★

This is a gopher server of the Stacken Computer Club at the Royal Institute of Technology, Sweden. The site offers information on the club, including memberships, contact persons, activities, ongoing projects, courses, and games. This server also contains links to other gopher sites on the Internet.

KEYWORDS Computer Science, Education (College/University), Sweden
AUDIENCE Computer Students, Computer Users, Educators (University)
CONTACT Ake Nordin
moose@stacken.kth.se
FREE

gopher://gopher.stacken.kth.se/

Verlag Heinz Heise ★★★

The Electronic Directory of Vendors offers access to four magazines, the Magazine for Computer Technology, Gateway Data and Telecommunications, ELRAD and Multiuser Multitasking Magazine. There is also access to the WWW and other Internet resources.

KEYWORDS Computer Technology, Online Magazines, Reference, Telecommunications
AUDIENCE Telecommunications Specialists
CONTACT www@ix.de
FREE

http://www.ix.de

Welcome to Softbank Exposition and Conference Company ★★★

This is the home page of Softbank Exposition and Conference Company, which presents trade show events. Its upcoming events are NetWorld+Interop, Seybold Seminars, Digital World and Windows Solutions. Users can also find their corporate background, career opportunities and their publications here.

KEYWORDS Companies, Computer Confrences, Conferences, Events
AUDIENCE Business Professionals, Computer Professionals
CONTACT Jason Dominguez
webmaster@sbexpos.com
FREE

http://www.sbexpos.com/

Programming

See also
Computing & Mathematics · *Applications*
Computing & Mathematics · *Computer Science*
Internet · *Internet Tools*

Aarhus University, Denmark ★★★

This site, based at Aarhus University, Denmark has papers on constraint programming. Some abstracts are available, as well as procedings from conferences such as the Second Principles and Practice of Constraint Programming Workshop, held in Washington State, USA during May of 1994.

KEYWORDS Constraint Programming, Object-Oriented Programming, Technical Reports, User Interfaces
AUDIENCE Computer Programmers
CONTACT Brian H. Mayoh
brian@daimi.aau.dk
FREE

ftp://ftp.daimi.aau.dk/pub/CLP

Ada-Belgium Organization ★★★

Ada is an internationally standardized, general-purpose language used in a wide variety of applications - from missile control to payroll processing to air traffic control. The purpose of the Web site is to be a forum for persons and organizations interested in the Ada programming language, in its applications and in ADA-related technologies such as software engineering methods, environments and tools.

KEYWORDS Belgium, Object-Oriented Programming, Programming Languages
AUDIENCE Programmers, Software Engineers
CONTACT Dirk Craeynest
dirk@cs.kuleuven.ac.be
FREE

http://www.cs.kuleuven.ac.be/~dirk/ada-belgium/

Adding Access Counts To Your Documents ★★★

This document describes how to add an access counter to web pages, so that users can see how many times a particular page has been accessed. Detailed instructions and source code information are provided, along with common problems, questions and answers.

KEYWORDS Internet Publishing, Programming, WWW (World Wide Web)
AUDIENCE Computer Programmers, Internet Professionals, Internet Publishers, Web Developers
CONTACT Chuck Musciano
chuck.musciano@harris.com
FREE

http://melmac.corp.harris.com/access_counts.html

Apple Developer Information for Newton ★★★

This site is designed especially for the Apple software developer. This site provides access to Newton sample code and documentation. Many of the articles at this location pertain to Newton programming and a complete list and synopsis of each article, documentation, samples and developers tools are also available. There is also a question/answer file. The legal issues regarding downloading of software from all Apple subdirectories are clearly outlined. Programs required for downloading software are also described. Each file contains a BinHex license agreement while the remainder of the files are either Compact Pro or Stuffit.

KEYWORDS Handheld Computers, Software Development
AUDIENCE Programmers, Computer Science Students, Software Designers, Software Developers
CONTACT Theresa Lara
engber@applelink.apple.com
FREE

ftp://ftp.apple.com/Newton.and.Starcore.Info/

Apple Support Area and Developer Service ★★★

This site provides information, demos, software and tools necessary for the development of Macintosh software applications. The complete text of the Software License Agreement is also available at this location. The site is organized as follows: 1) All issues of development complete with sample code 2) All issues of Apple Directions 3) Catalogs for ordering development products 4) Developer University demos 5) Technical Documentation 6) Complete sample code and sample applications 7) System software extensions and header files and 8) Tools and examples.

KEYWORDS Computer Applications, Software Development
AUDIENCE Computer Programmers, Computer Science Students, Macintosh Users, Software Developers
CONTACT dpfeedback@applelink.apple.com
FREE

http://www.info.apple.com/

ftp://ftp.info.apple.com/Apple Support Area/Developer_Services/

Arjuna Project FTP Archive ★★

Arjuna is an object oriented programming system that provides a set of tools for the construction of fault tolerant distributed applications. Arjuna provides nested atomic actions (nested atomic transactions) for structuring application programs. Atomic actions operate on objects, which are instances of abstract data types (C++ classes), by making use of remote procedure calls (RPCs). This site contains technical reports and papers of the Arjuna Project Operating System. An index file is provided as well as folders for Papers and Theses.

KEYWORDS Object-Oriented Programming, Technical Reports
AUDIENCE Arjuna Users, Object Oriented Programmers, Programmers
CONTACT Arjuna@newcastle.ac.uk
FREE

ftp://arjuna.ncl.ac.uk/Pub/Docs/

Borland Online ★★★

This is Borland's homepage providing access to information about language and client server products as well as technical support. Language information includes Turbo C++ and Turbo Pascal, database products, including dBASE and Paradox for Windows and DOS, and client server products, including Inter-Base and ReportSmith. Technical support includes files, drivers and patches that can be downloaded, a database with search capability, and access to technical documents. Corporate information including financial reports, employment opportunities, and press releases is available at this site.

KEYWORDS Client Server Technology, Companies, Programming Languages, Utility Software
AUDIENCE Computer Professionals, Computer Programmers, Database Managers, PC Users
FREE

http://www.borland.com

C (Programming Language) FAQ (Frequently Asked Questions) ★★★

This site contains the FAQs for the C programming language. Users can find two versions of the FAQ (one is abridged), as well as a useful guide to C tutorials and books.

KEYWORDS FAQs (Frequently Asked Questions), Programming Languages
AUDIENCE C Programmers, C++ Programmers, Computer Programmers, Computer Scientists
CONTACT scs@eskimo.com
FREE

http://www.cis.ohio-state.edu/hypertext/faq/usenet/C-faq/top.html

CASE Tool Index (Computer Aided Software Engineering) ★★★★

This page presents a sorted list of computer aided software engineering tools. Users can navigate through the list easily if they know the name of the tool or vendor for which they are searching. Tools are listed in alphabetical order, with vendor information available. Alternately, users can browse the list by vendor. Users can then obtain contact information, as well as information about the tools themselves.

KEYWORDS Programming, Programming Environments, Software Engineering
AUDIENCE Computer Programmers, Software Developers, Software Engineers
CONTACT David Lamb
dalamb@qucis.queensu.ca
FREE

http://www.qucis.queensu.ca:1999/Software-Engineering/tools.html

CC++ Programming Language ★★★★

This page contains information on the CC++ language. CC++ is a parallel programming language based on the C++ programming language. The page gives information on where to find a free compiler, and a tutorial for learning CC++. It also has links to other parallel programming pages and information.

KEYWORDS Concurrent Logic, Programming
AUDIENCE Computer Engineers, Concurrent Logic Programmers, Parallel Programmers
FREE

http://www.compbio.caltech.edu/ccpp/

CRIM Parallel Architectures Group ★★★★

CRIM plans to play a leadership role in the growing field of parallel architectures. Activities focus mainly on the development of portable parallel programming environments, performance evaluation and metrics, and the integration of parallel architectures in heterogeneous and distributed environments. Given the fields of application in which CRIM and its partners are involved, the Centre is promoting the application of parallel architectures in signal processing, particularly with regard to speech and images. This page provides information on the CRIM group, its projects and symposium, and on the APAR group.

KEYWORDS Parallel Computing, Spatial Analysis, Speech Recognition
AUDIENCE Concurrent Logic Programmers, Hardware Designers, Microarchitects
CONTACT hancu@crim.ca
FREE

http://www.crim.ca/Domaines_Services/APAR/index-english.html

Cernsting Information Service (Software Technology Interest Group) ★★★

This site was created to provide a forum for the exchange of the latest information and resources in the field of software development. The main focus is on object-oriented design techniques and tools. Users can search the database of articles and papers, a glossary of software engineering terms and jargon, and browse information on C++ and other Object Oriented Programming (OOP) languages.

KEYWORDS Object-Oriented Programming, Programming, Programming Languages, Software Design
AUDIENCE Computer Programmers, Software Developers
CONTACT Mike Sendall
sting@dxcern.cern.ch
FREE

http://dxsting.cern.ch:80/sting/sting.html

Cid System ★★★★

The Cid system is a research parallel programming language (an extension of C) and its implementation, for distributed memory machines such as workstation farms and other scalable platforms. The Cid system implementation has been done at Digital's Cambridge Research Laboratory, and is freely available with sources for research and educational use. This site contains text file related to Cid, the source codes, and contact information for user support.

KEYWORDS Companies, Parallel Computing, Programming Languages
AUDIENCE Computer Programmers, Computer Scientists
CONTACT nikhil@crl.dec.com
FREE

http://www.research.digital.com/CRL/personal/nikhil/cid/home.html

ftp://crl.dec.com:pub/pub/DEC/cid

COMMERCIAL Developer Services and Products ★★★★

This site offers access to a wealth of information and tools for software developers of Apple Computer's machines. Users will find information on Macintosh system software, the latest technical updates and errata, ftp archives of developer's tools, and more. There are also periodicals devoted to Macintosh programming, information on Apple support and training for developers, and sample source code available.

KEYWORDS Programming, Software Development
AUDIENCE Computer Programmers, Macintosh Programmers, Software Developers
CONTACT dpfeedback@applelink.apple.com
FREE

http://www.austin.apple.com:80/dev/

ftp://ftp.info.apple.com/Apple.Support.Area/Developer_Services

Developer's Resource Guide ★★★★

This page by the Vertex Group provides a software development index for MS-DOS, MS-Windows and OS/2 platforms with a special focus on TCP/IP. Topics covered include source code archives, programming languages, magazines, companies, graphics formats, specifications, standards and protocols, Web authors and developers' information, FAQs, mail lists, recruiting companies, other developers' pages and more.

KEYWORDS Operating Systems, Software Development, Software Engineering
AUDIENCE Computer Professionals, Programmers, Software Developers, Windows Application Developers
CONTACT John Fricker
john@mind.net
FREE

http://www.mind.net:80/jfs/devres.html

Distributed Software Engineering Home Page ★★★

This site is maintained by the Distributed Software Engineering Section at the University of London. It offers information on the work the section is doing in software engineering for distributed and parallel computing architectures. Users will find academic papers, departmental and administrative information, and links to other servers with information related to distributed computing and software engineering. There is also a directory with technical documentation available to users.

KEYWORDS Distributed Applications, Parallel Computing, Programming, Software Engineering
AUDIENCE Computer Programmers, Computer Scientists, Software Engineers
CONTACT Nat Pryce
np2@doc.ic.ac.uk
FREE

http://www-dse.doc.ic.ac.uk

EMACs Lisp Introduction ★★★

This page contains information on a variety of the lisp programming language that runs under EMACs in UNIX. Users will find an online hypertext reference manual, and a searchable index of EMACs lisp packages such as Gnus and Ange FTP.

KEYWORDS   EMACs, Programming Languages, Text Processing
AUDIENCE   Computer Programmers, EMACs Users, LISP Programmers, UNIX Users
CONTACT   William M. Perry
wmperry@indiana.edu
FREE

http://www.cs.indiana.edu/elisp/elisp-intro.html

ERL (Earth Resources Laboratory at MIT) nCUBE 2 ★★★

The ERL (Earth Resources Laboratory at MIT) nCUBE 2 web site contains information for programmers of the nCUBE 2. The site provides links to information on the nCUBE parallel web server as well as an online training course, access to sample programs, and a complete set of manual pages. For copyright reasons, access to the sample programs and manual pages is restricted to licensed customers of nCUBE. The site also contains links to nCUBE presentations, technical reports, software and FAQs.

KEYWORDS   Parallel Computing, Software, Universities
AUDIENCE   ComputerUsers, Educators (University) , Programmers, Students (University)
CONTACT   Joe Matarese
charrette@earthcube.mit.edu
FREE

http://earthcube.mit.edu

Eiffel Page ★★★

This page is a central location for information and resources relating to the Eiffel programming language. Users can access Eiffel FAQs, tutorials, product announcements and reviews, organizations devoted to the emerging language, and more. There are also pointers to FTP archives of Eiffel-related materials such as libraries, compilers, and more.

KEYWORDS   Object-Oriented Programming, Programming Languages
AUDIENCE   Computer Programmers, Eiffel Programmers, Object Oriented Programmers
CONTACT   Ted Lawson
Ted.W.Lawson@cm.cf.ac.uk
FREE

http://www.cm.cf.ac.uk:80/CLE/

Home of the Brave Ada Programmers ★★★★

This home page offers a wide variety of resources for those interested in the Ada programming language. Material available includes reference manuals, tools, add-ons, listings of books and other publications, links to free compilers, as well as information about commercial compilers. In addition, there is an online tutorial available.

KEYWORDS   Programming, Programming Languages
AUDIENCE   Ada Programmers, Computer Programmers, Computer Scientists
CONTACT   Magnus Kempe
kempe@di.epfl.ch
FREE

http://lglwww.epfl.ch/Ada/

Connections to Supercomputers
The mother of all computers

To get the low-down on supercomputers, parallel computers, and their manufacturers, access the "Supercomputer and Parallel Computer Vendors" site. It provides access to such vendors as Digital Equipment Corporation, Hewlett-Packard, IBM Power Parallel Systems, NEC, Silicon Graphics, Inc. and more. Here you can learn about the fastest computers in the world. This site is primarily geared for those people most likely to use them—scientists, researchers and educators—though anyone is welcome to visit, of course.

(http://web.scandal.cs.cmu.edu/www.vendors.html)

also, (http://www.cs.cmu.edu/afs/cs.cmu.edu/project/scandal/public/www.vendors.html)

For instance, at the Access HP (Hewlett-Packard) site, you can tap into the company's education page, which provides information about education solutions, course listings, and directions to HP learning centers around the world. There are special learning centers that offer specialized and technical information for the HP-UX system and network administration. There are also courses on programming languages, object-oriented technology, graphical user interfaces, and networking concepts.

(http://www.hp.com/edserver/edserver.html)

Index To Object-Oriented Information Sources ★★★★

This site presents a searchable database of object oriented programming information sources available on the Internet. Users may search by keyword, or browse through the subject headings to obtain the information they want. The index of resources includes a brief description of the individual resources, the name or entity responsible for the resource, and information on where the resource is located. If available, the contact information is presented as a link which users may follow.

Keywords Databases, Programming
Audience Computer Programmers, Computer Scientists, Object Oriented Programmers
Contact scg@iam.unibe.ch
Free

http://cuiwww.unige.ch/OSG/OOinfo/index.html

Internet PostScript Resources ★★★

This page is a central location for resources and information about Adobe's PostScript programming language. It contains pointers to such resources as the PostScript FAQs, tutorials and background information on PS, examples of PostScript code, and PS type 1 fonts available for download.

Keywords FAQs (Frequently Asked Questions), Graphics, Page Description Languages, PostScript
Audience Graphic Designers, Computer Programmers, Desktop Publishers
Contact Aaron Wigley
wigs@yoyo.cc.monash.edu.au
Free

http://yoyo.cc.monash.edu.au:80/~wigs/postscript/

Introduction to the Booch Method ★★★★

This page offers a hypertext overview of the Booch method, a method to help the design, documentation, and implementation of an object oriented program or system. Users can read about the method, learn the various symbols used in the Booch method, and learn how to map the symbols to the C++ programming language.

Keywords Booch Method, Programming
Audience Computer Programmers, Computer Scientists, Object Oriented Programmers
Contact Philipp Schneider
Free

http://www.itr.ch/tt/case/BoochReferenz/

Language List ★★★★

This resource stems from an attempt to catalog every computer language ever published. Users can search the database via an HTML form, and retrieve brief descriptions of the many computer languages that exist. Common languages such as C are described in more detail, and many descriptions include pointers to resources available on the Internet.

Keywords Language Software, Programming, Programming Languages
Audience Computer Programmers, Computer Researchers, Computer Scientists, Computer Users
Contact Bill Kinnersley
billk@cs.ukans.edu
Free

http://cuiwww.unige.ch/langlist

Linux Documentation Project (LDP) ★★★★

This site provides access to the Linux Documentation Project (LDP) in HTML (Hypertext Markup Language) for easy access to the various documents. The documents include the Linux FAQ (Frequently Asked Questions), Linux Info-Sheet (technical overview), Linux Meta-FAQ (list of sources of information, ftp sites, and available documents), Linux GCC FAQ (FAQ about gcc compiler), Linux Software Map (database of software developed and ported to Linux), An Alternative Database Query (to the Linux Software Map based upon the Harvest System), Wais Databases of the Linux Software Map and Linux FAQ, and more.

Keywords Documents, GNU
Audience Internet Access Providers, Linux Users, PC Users, UNIX Users
Contact Matt Welsh
mdw@sunsite.unc.edu
Free

ftp://ftp.halcyon.com/pub/linux/linuxdoc/

Logic Programming Section, Imperial College ★★★

The Logic Programming Section of the Department of Computing at Imperial College conducts research into logic programming and theory on the level of knowledge representation, metalevel, legal and temporal reasoning, and programming language development. Their Web site provides general descriptions of each of these research areas and background about the professors and staff, as well as a few online staff papers. Users will also find online manuals and FAQ's about Artificial Intelligence and programming languages as well as some software available for downloading. Users may also access the public FTP site and directories of the logic programming group for section papers and other archived material.

Keywords Artificial Intelligence, Logic
Audience Computer Science, Programmers
Contact KJ Dryllerakis
K.Dryllerakis@doc.ic.ac.uk
Free

http://laotzu.doc.ic.ac.uk/

PERL (Practical Extraction and Report Language) ★★★★

This site is home to an HTML-formatted and highly indexed PERL programming reference document.

Keywords Programming, Programming Languages
Audience Computer Programmers, Researchers, Students
Contact lwall@netlabs.com
Free

http://www.cs.cmu.edu/Web/People/rgs/perl.html

PERL FAQ (Frequently Asked Questions) ★★★

This site contains the Practical Extraction and Report Language (PERL) FAQs. The topics covered include PERL availability, information sources, programming aids and tips, as well as information on external program interaction.

Keywords FAQs (Frequently Asked Questions), Programming Languages, Scripting Languages
Audience Computer Programmers, PERL Programmers
Contact perlfaq@perl.com
Free

http://www.cis.ohio-state.edu:80/text/faq/usenet/perl-faq/top.html

PERL Programming Language ★★★

This page offers many useful resources for those interested in the PERL programming language. Information is available on the object-oriented version of PERL, Perl5, as well as tutorials, public-domain PERL scripts, and links to other Internet PERL resources. Users can access a search form for easier access to the information available here.

Keywords Programming Languages, Scripting Languages
Audience Computer Programmers, PERL Programmers
Contact Bill Middleton
wjm@metronet.com
Free

http://www.metronet.com/1h/perlinfo

Programming in C ★★★★

This page contains extensive resources for the C programmer. Topics covered include ANSI C, history of the C programming language, literature about C, and C 'culture.' Users will find pointers to free compilers available for download, style guides, source and standards documents, and more.

Keywords Programming, Programming Languages
Audience C Programmers, C++ Programmers, Computer Programmers, Computer Scientists
Contact jutta@cs.tu–berlin.de
Free

http://www.lysator.liu.se/c/index.html

Programming Language Research ★★★★

This site offers resources related to the development of computer programming languages. In addition to an extremely comprehensive listing of developing computer languages, this site offers links to language developers' home pages, information on systems and language design theory, and pointers to journals and papers related to the field of language development.

Keywords Programming, Programming Languages, Programming Theory, Systems Theory
Audience Computer Engineers, Computer Programmers, Computer Scientists
Contact Mark Leone
mleone@cs.cmu.edu
Free

http://www.cs.cmu.edu:8001/afs/cs.cmu.edu/user/mleone/web/language-research.html

Programming – Reference

Python Programming Language ★★★★

This is the home page of the Python programming language. It offers a wealth of resources related to the language, including online tutorials and documentation, quick reference guides, FAQs in text and hypertext, as well as pointers to FTP sites where source and binaries can be downloaded.

Keywords FAQs (Frequently Asked Questions), Object-Oriented Programming, Programming Languages
Audience Computer Programmers, Object Oriented Programmers, Python Programmers
Contact Guido van Rossum Guido.van.Rossum@cwi.nl
Free

http://www.cwi.nl/~guido/Python.html

SIGAda (Special Interest Group for Ada) ★★★★

The Association for Computing Machinery's Special Interest Group on Ada (SIGAda) provides information on the programming language, Ada, and offers pointers to other resources on software. There is also news about the SIGAda organization and its upcoming events, and many links to Ada-related information.

Keywords Programming, Programming Languages, Software
Audience Computer Programmers, Computer Scientists, Computer Students
Contact Brad Balfour bbalfour@acm.org
Free

http://info.acm.org/sigada/

SIGFORTH (Special Interest Group for Forth) ★★★

ACM Special Interest Group on Programming Language FORTH addresses developments and research related to Forth and its professional applications, focusing on the promotion and refinement of concepts, methods, and techniques needed by Forth professionals. The gopher site provides a PC forth compiler, information on the organization, membership, goals, and conferences.

Keywords Engineering, Languages, Programming Languages
Audience Computer Scientists, Engineers, Programmers
Contact Irving Montanez SIG Chair chair_SIGFORTH@acm.org
Free

gopher://gopher.acm.org/
11[the_files.sig_forums.sigFORTH]

SIGPLAN (Special Interest Group for Programming Languages) ★★★

ACM Special Interest Group on Programming Languages explores programming languages concepts and tools, focusing on design, implementation and efficient use. This gopher site provides information on the SIGPLAN organization in the form of membership info, conference information, and an annual report. Also provided are links to several associated Web pages.

Keywords Design, Programming, Programming Languages
Audience Computer Programmers, Computer Scientists, Programming Language Designers
Contact Brent T. Hailpern SIG Chair chair_SIGPLAN@acm.org
Free

gopher://gopher.acm.org/
11[the_files.sig_forums.sigplan]

Software Engineering Lab, EPFL, Switzerland ★★★

The Software Engineering Laboratory at the Ecole Polytechnique Fédérale de Lausanne (EPFL) focuses on software engineering from a developmental methods, tools and design perspective. Visitors will find online documentation, publications, and research information. There is also data on formal methods, as well as departmental and faculty facts. This site also contains links to other software engineering resources on the Internet.

Keywords Computer Science, Object-Oriented Programming, Software Engineering
Audience Computer Scientists, Object-Oriented Programmers, Software Engineers
Contact lgl-www-admin@lglsun.epfl.ch
Free

http://www-lgl.epfl.ch

Windy-FAQ ★★★

This page is an information resource for Windows application developers who need to find programming information on the Internet. It includes USENET groups, gopher sites, FAQs, WWW sites, mailing lists, and print publications. Topics covered include device drivers, text conversion utilities, UNIX/Window NT cross development information, Winsock applications, and more.

Keywords Operating Systems, Programming
Audience Computer Professionals, Programmers, Software Developers
Contact comments@cera.com
Free

http://www.cera.com/windev.htm

Reference

See also
Computing & Mathematics · *Internet*
Computing & Mathematics · *Resources*
Internet · *Internet Protocols*
Internet · *Internet Resources*

Australian Academic & Research Network FTP Site ★★★

This FTP site contains files related to the Australian AARNET network. There are user files such as descriptions of resources available through AARNET, background papers, NIC documents, and X25 Requests for Comments. In addition, there are technical documents, such as usage statistics, monitoring scripts and ways of improving network security.

Keywords Archives, Australia, Software
Audience Australians, Internet Users, Network Administrators
Contact aarnet@aarnet.edu.au
Free

ftp://aarnet.edu.au/

Charles Babbage Institute Home Page ★★★

This site is maintained by the Charles Babbage Institute, which is devoted to the preservation and study of the history of computing. Users will find information about the institute itself, as well as pictures, oral histories, and source documents on the history of information science. There are also extensive bibliographies of material related to computing history, as well as links to other related information sources on the Internet.

Keywords History, Technology
Audience Computer Users, Historians
Contact cbi@vx.cis.umn.edu
Free

http://fs1.itdean.umn.edu/cbi/
cbihome.html

gopher://cutter.lib.umn.edu:70/11/
subject-list/archives-spec/
babbage/

Computer Underground Digest Archive ★★

Computer Underground Digest is an electronic magazine related to hacking and freedom of speech articles. CUD is a forum for the discussion of legal, ethical, social, and other issues regarding computerized information and communications.

Keywords Ethics, Freedom of Speech, Internet Culture, Magazines
Audience Computer Hackers, Computer Users, Internet Issues
Contact Brendan Kehoe, CuD archivist cudarch@eff.org
Free

ftp://ftp.eff.org/pub/Publications/CuD/

Computing Oriented Abbreviation and Acronyms ★★★

The Computing Oriented Abbreviation and Acronyms page is a search engine that allows confused computer users to find out exactly what those abbreviations and acronyms mean. By entering either an acronym or a search string, users will get the term that they're looking for.

Keywords Computer Acronyms, Computer Terminology
Audience Computer Users, Students
Contact mleisher@crl.nmsu.edu
Free

http://crl.nmsu.edu/lists/Babel.html

Ecole Polytechnique Federale de Lausanne ★★★

This server provides access to documents about computing. The documents are organized into general areas such as compilers, editors, shells, and utilities. They cover specific topics such as ksh, tcsh, cfortran, gnat, latex2html, xanim, and more. The server, maintained at the Ecole Polytechnique Federale de Lausanne, is searchable by keyword.

KEYWORDS Computer Applications, Emacs
AUDIENCE Computer Game Developers, Computer Science Students, Programmers, Software Engineers
FREE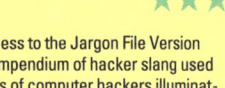

gopher://masg1.epfl.ch/

Hacker Jargon Version 2.9.10 ★★★

This site provides access to the Jargon File Version 2.9.10. This file is a compendium of hacker slang used by various subcultures of computer hackers illuminating hackish tradition, folklore and humour. This is a public domain document, lengthy and detailed. The introduction provides information about this file and about Slang, Jargon and Techspeak. The revision history is also presented. This hacker jargon is collected from technical cultures including MIT AI (Artificial Intelligence) Lab, Stanford AI lab, Bolt Beranek Newman (BBN), Carnegie Mellon University (CMU) and Worcester Polytechnic Institute.

KEYWORDS Hacking, Language, Terminology
AUDIENCE Computer Hackers, Computer Users, Linguists
CONTACT Eric Raymond, Editor
        eric@snark.thyrsus.com
FREE

ftp://ftp.halcyon.com/pub/jargon/

Jargon File ★★★

This site offers a searchable dictionary of terms used in computer science. This is a comprehensive compendium of hacker slang, illuminating many aspects of hackish tradition, folklore, and humor.

KEYWORDS Communications, Computer Science, Dictionaries, Education
AUDIENCE Computer Hackers, Computer Users, Educators
CONTACT Steeve McCauley
        steeve@stoner.eps.mcgill.ca
FREE

http://www.eps.mcgill.ca/jargon/jargon.html/

Ninth Annual Best Buy Awards ★★★★

The Ninth Annual Best Buy Awards page presents the Best for 1994, the best products for PC Computers voted for by readers. Hardware categories include the best 90MHz Pentium System, 486DX2/66 System, Color Notebook Computer, Subnotebook/Palmtop, Multimedia System, and Network Server. Peripheral categories include the best graphic, motion-video and sound boards, monitors, tape backup hard drive, laser printer and more. Software categories include the best operating system, wordprocessor, spreadsheet, database, disk utility, personal information manager, finance/accounting, desktop publishing, presentation-graphics software, and draw/paint/image-edit software.

KEYWORDS Computer Products, Consumer Guides, Online Magazines, Publishers
AUDIENCE Computer Professionals, Computer Users, PC Users, Windows Users
FREE

http://www.ziff.com/~cshopper/features/94best/index.html

Online Dictionary of Computing ★★★★

This site offers a computing dictionary with coverage of terminology, languages, architectures, institutions, history, applications, theories, acronyms and anything else related to computing. There are many cross-references and links to other Internet resources. Queries are monitored, and new entries on popular subjects are added every day.

KEYWORDS Computer Applications, Reference
AUDIENCE Internet Reference, Linguists, Technical Writers
FREE

http://wombat.doc.ic.ac.uk/

PC Novice ★★★
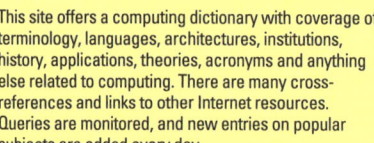

The free online version of PC Novice by Peed Corporation is an information processing company that publishes computer publications on the Web. PC Novice teaches beginners the basics while keeping experienced users up to date on the latest technical innovations and applications. The online version provides a sample of the print magazine, inlcuding the current issue's lead article, next month's table of contents a glossary of commonly-used PC terms and table of contents for PC Novice back issues.

KEYWORDS Computer Applications, Education, Online Magazines
AUDIENCE Computer Professionals, Computer System Designers, Computing Consultants
FREE

http://www.peed.com/pcnovice.html

Pentium Bug FTP Site ★★★

This FTP site contains files from Thomas R. Nicely, the first person to find and report the Pentium FPU bug. Within the Nicely directory, users will find files about Dr. Nicely and the events surrounding the discovery of the bug. A program to test Pentiums for the bug is also included within the directory.

KEYWORDS Debugging, Software
AUDIENCE Computer Users, Mathematicians
FREE

ftp://acavax.lynchburg.edu/nicely/pentbug/

SUNET (Swedish University Network) ★★

This site gives access to archives of online discussions regarding computers and computer networking. The discussion forums covered are Requests For Comments (RFC's) from the Swedish University Network (SUNET). The RFC documents are searchable by keywords.

KEYWORDS Internet Directories, Internet Reference, Sweden
AUDIENCE Internet Users, Network Developers, Network Service Providers
FREE

gopher://sunic.sunet.se:7532/

TidBITS ★★★★

TidBITS home page is Adam Engst's weekly computer newsletter devoted to reporting on computer industry events and new products. Its focus is on the Macintosh computer platform although it covers other platforms as well. Users will find the latest issue of the TidBITS newsletter and a searchable database of past issues. In addition, this page offers useful links to FTP archives of Macintosh software.

KEYWORDS Computer Hardware, Graphical User Interfaces (GUIs)
AUDIENCE Computer Professionals, Computer Users, Macintosh Users
CONTACT Adam C. Engst
        ace@tidbits.com
FREE

http://www.dartmouth.edu/pages/TidBITS/TidBITS.html

Utility Report ★★★

This page is the home of The Utility Page, a weekly report that includes reviews of shareware, freeware, and public domain utilities, add-ons for Windows. Reviews include FTP links for downloading the file(s). A variety of utilities have been reviewed including text editors, screen capture programs, program manager and control manager add-ons, application launchers, resource monitors, pop-up menus, file managers, diagnostic programs, desktop accessories (calendars, calculators, and address book programs), and more.

KEYWORDS Operating Systems, Personal Computers
AUDIENCE Computer Engineers, Programmers, Computer Users, Windows Users
CONTACT David Boyte
        dbandlt@mindspring.com
FREE

http://www.mindspring.com/users/dbandlt/report.html

Welcome to Computer Life ★★★

Ziff-Davis' online publication, Computer Life combines PC and MAC computer information into one source. It provides best-of-the-month selections for reference, personal and entertainment software, computer hardware basics, and multimedia systems. The reviews of PC and Macintosh software and hardware feature main articles and related stories, and how-to projects from upgrades to starting a business. Links to other sites and back issues are available.

KEYWORDS Online Magazines, Publishers
AUDIENCE Computer Users, Macintosh Users, Windows Users
CONTACT webmaster@ziff.com
FREE

http://www.ziff.com/~complife/

Resources

See also
Communications · *Telecommunications*
Computing & Mathematics · *Companies*
Computing & Mathematics · *Reference*
Internet · *Internet Resources*

Apple Computer and Virtual Reality ★★

This site is a repository for Macintosh related virtual reality software and articles, things of general interest and things that may be useful to the community. This site provides interactive demos from Virtus Corporation using Virtus Walkthrough. This software is currently only available to Macintosh users but will eventually be available for Windows at a later date. There are various other software packages available including Gossamer 2.0 and Tierra. This site tries to provide the user with what's new in virtual reality software, what companies are involved, papers, and more.

KEYWORDS	Computer Hardware, Graphics
AUDIENCE	Computer Users, Macintosh Users, Virtual Reality Enthusiasts
CONTACT	Bill Cockayne billc@apple.com
FREE	

ftp://ftp.apple.com/pub/VR/

Bibliographies on Distributed Computing and Networking ★★★★

This Web page is an index of bibliographies and allows you to search the available bibliographies if you are using a forms-capable browser. The bibliographies provide information on topics such as distributed file systems and clusters, process migration, and distributed shells.

KEYWORDS	Bibliographies, Computer Networking, Distributed Computing, Parallel Computing
AUDIENCE	Computer Programmers, Computer Scientists, Concurrent Logic Programmers
CONTACT	Paul Klark paul@cs.arizona.edu
FREE	

http://donkey.CS.Arizona.EDU:1994/bib/Distributed/

Bibliographies on Parallel Processing ★★★★

This Web page is an index of bibliographies and allows you to search the available bibliographies if you are using a forms-capable browser. The bibliographies range from multiprocessing, scheduling and debugging parallel programs to cellular automata, symbolic computation and load balancing.

KEYWORDS	Bibliographies, Computer Programming, Concurrent Systems, Parallel Computing
AUDIENCE	Computer Programmers, Computer Scientists, Concurrent Logic Programmers
CONTACT	Paul Klark paul@cs.arizona.edu
FREE	

http://donkey.CS.Arizona.EDU:1994/bib/Parallel/

COAST Home Page (Computer Operations, Audit, and Security Technology) ★★★

The COAST project involves research into computer security and computer facilities management. The primary focus is on common 'non-trusted' computer systems, with an intent to advance the general state of computer security knowledge. Users can browse copies of the COAST Watch, a newsletter dedicated to describing the events and projects of the COAST project. The project also maintains an extensive (400 MB) ftp archive with alerts, tools, and other material related to computer security.

KEYWORDS	Computer Security, Computer Viruses
AUDIENCE	Computer Security Specialists
FREE	

http://www.cs.purdue.edu/coast/coast.html

ftp://coast.cs.purdue.edu/pub

Computer Paper ★★★

This is the home page of The Computer Paper, a Canadian monthly computer magazine that boasts 350,000 copies of the printed publication distributed each month and over 1,000,000 readers. The current issue as well as back issues of this magazine can be viewed online. In addition, job opportunities with The Computer Paper are listed here, as well as information on computer companies in Canada, and a material on a reader contest with prizes.

KEYWORDS	Computer Magazines, Electronic Magazines
AUDIENCE	Canadians, Computer Professionals, Computer Users
CONTACT	Graeme Bennett graeme@tcp.mindlink.bc.ca
FREE	

http://tcp.ca/

Computer Professionals for Social Responsibility (CPSR) Home Page ★★★★

Computer Professionals for Social Responsibility (CPSR) is a nonprofit, public-interest organization concerned with the effects of computers on society. Of particular interest to CPSR is anything involving computer security, including such topics as encryption, privacy, government information highway policy, and more. Users will find a wealth of information and documents pertaining to these topics.

KEYWORDS	Civil Rights, Computer Security, Encryption
AUDIENCE	Political Activists, Privacy Activists
FREE	

http://cpsr.org/home

gopher://gopher.cpsr.org/

Computer Resources ★★★

This site provides access to data and databases concerned with computer resources. The data covers topics such as AIX, MS-DOS, Mac, MS-Windows, systems, utilities, NeXT, TeX, Linux, and more.

KEYWORDS	Databases, Education (College/University), Portugal, Software
AUDIENCE	Academics, Computer Users, Students
CONTACT	archive@fct.unl.pt
FREE	

gopher://gopher.fct.unl.pt:7072/

Computing Resources and Libraries ★★★

This gopher server is maintained by Stephen D Franklin, Office of Academic Computing, University of California, Irvine. Information provided includes the Anteaters Public Access Catalog (ANTPAC), which includes materials at all UCI Libraries, books, journals, magazines, newspapers, microforms, music scores, films, sound and video recordings, archive and manuscript collections and more. It also makes direct connections to other library gophers and the Internet.

KEYWORDS	Electronic Publishing, Libraries
AUDIENCE	Internet Users, Library Administrators, Library Users
CONTACT	Stephen D Franklin franklin@uci.edu
FREE	

gopher://geneva.acs.uci.edu:1070/

Computing Trailblazer ★★★

The Computing Trailblazer is a Ziff-Davis online publication with many links to PC gopher sites, Web servers, PC publishers, and software companies. Some of the topics covered include Internet resources with links to email, FAQs, howto documents and more; multimedia with links to CD-ROM, video, sound, and developer resources; operating systems with links to DOS, Macintosh system, NeXtSteop, OS/2, Windows, and more; and utilities for DOS/Windows, Macintosh, OS/2, Windows NT, and others. It includes links to hardware manufacturers and software developers, games, and Internet search tools.

KEYWORDS	Online Magazines, Publishers, Software
AUDIENCE	Computer Professionals, Computer Users, Windows Users
CONTACT	webmaster@ziff.com
FREE	

http://www.ziff.com:8032/~zdi/tblazer

Datapro ★★

Datapro is a computer magazine offering a directory of topics covered in past issues, selected current bulletins, and further information on related products and services. The magazine focuses on using computers for effective business marketing strategies. Datapro also offers a wide variety of instructional material and comparison analyses of technology issues.

KEYWORDS	Computer Applications, Electronic Publishing, Magazines, Marketing
AUDIENCE	Business Professionals, Computer Users, Marketing Professionals

FREE
gopher://datapro.mgh.com/

Document Image Understanding and Character Recognition ★★★

This site is a repository for Document Image Understanding and Character Recognition information and resources. The server maintains research announcements, bibliographies, mailing lists, source code, technical reports, database information, and Internet resources for document understanding, character recogntion and some related domains such as information retrieval. Users can get detailed information about these technologies, download software, or link to other sites with related information.

KEYWORDS   Image Processing, OCR (Optical Character Recognition)
AUDIENCE   Computer Scientists, Database Managers, OCR Enthusiasts
CONTACT   webmaster@documents.cfar.umd.edu
FREE

http://documents.cfar.umd.edu/

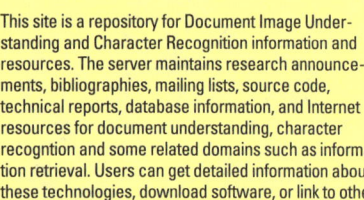 Dr. Dobb's Journal ★★

This is the homepage For Dr. Dobb's Journal with information about languages such as C++, operating systems (Windows/DOS), Linux, and UNIX, and other programming areas, such as online help files and HTML. It also includes Dr. Dobb's Sourcebooks and Dr. Dobb's Developer Update with news analysis, tech focus, conference reports, and news briefs. This site provides selected articles from Dr. Dobb's magazine, the contents of their monthly newsletter, and FTP access to source codes for programs that have appeared in Dr Dobb's magazines.

KEYWORDS   Online Magazines, Programming, Software Development, Software Engineering
AUDIENCE   Computer Engineers, Programmers, Software Designers, Software Developers
CONTACT   msawit@mfi.com
FREE

http://www.ddj.com/

ftp://ftp.mv.com/pub/ddj

Duke University FTP Archive ★★

This is a gopher server of the Duke University. It holds assorted computing and genetics information on areas such as the X11R6 windowing system, GNU, Usenet news, the Chlamydomonas Genetics Center, and more.

KEYWORDS   Biological Sciences, Education (College/University)
AUDIENCE   Computer Professionals, Computer Users, Geneticists
FREE

gopher://ftp.duke.edu/

Eastern European Computer Resources at OSC ★★★

This gopher server provides computer resources for use with Eastern European languages (Latvian, Polish, Russian and Ukrainian). Information includes fonts, translators and software for a variety of systems, including Mac, DOS, UNIX and NeXT computers. The server is provided by the Ohio Supercomputer Center (OSC).

KEYWORDS   Eastern Europe, Russia, Supercomputing
AUDIENCE   Eastern Europeans, Internet Users
CONTACT   Jan Labanowski
          jkl@osc.edu
FREE

gopher://infomeister.osc.edu:74/

Explora Project ★★★★

The Explora Project, based in Germany, offers computer assistance in finding new knowledge in databases. In this project, discovery methods are developed and discovery systems are implemented to support analysis of processes. The prototypes are then introduced and evaluated in practical applications. A prototype has been implemented for the Apple Macintosh and has been used in a lot of practical applications (market research, medicine, election research, natural hazards, political planning, etc.) proving the potentiality of discovery systems.

KEYWORDS   Databases, Information Retrieval, Information Technology, Knowledge-Based Systems
AUDIENCE   Computer Scientists, Database Programmers
FREE

http://orgwis.gmd.de/explora/

Forum of Incident Response and Security Teams (FIRST) ★★★

The Forum of Incident Response and Security Teams is a coalition of computer security incident response teams (such as the Computer Emergency Response Team). The home page is a collection of resources related to computer security issues. Users can read about FIRST's mission, access a CDROM of security tools, and follow links to servers made available by individual members of the coalition.

KEYWORDS   Computer Security, Computer Viruses
AUDIENCE   Computer Security Specialists
CONTACT   first-sec@first.org
FREE

http://csrc.ncsl.nist.gov/first/

FreeBSD Development and Archiving ★★

This site is for miscellaneous extras that the software developers make available as well as FAQ's for FreeBSD UNIX operating systems. This site should be consulted first in times of duress.

KEYWORDS   Freeware, Operating Systems
AUDIENCE   Computer Programmers, Software Developers, Software Engineers, UNIX Users

FREE
ftp://jfreefall.cdrom.com/

Gopher at Vision ★★

Maintained by the Office of Nuclear Safety at the Department of Energy, this gopher server provides information about various aspects of computing and computer culture. The computing data concentrates on OS/2 resources and software, while the computer culture information is provided by a directory dedicated to cyberculture.

KEYWORDS   Internet Culture, Personal Computers
AUDIENCE   Computer Users, Cyberculture Enthusiasts, Internet Users
CONTACT   gopher@budget.cr.doe.gov
FREE

gopher://vision.ns.doe.gov/

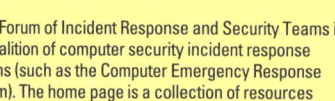 IBM Computer Virus Information Center ★★★

This gopher is IBM's archive of PC-compatible computer viruses. Users can access descriptions of individual computer viruses which include information on the way the virus infects the system as well as its effects on systems. There are also files which detail various methods for eradicating viruses from one's system, virus FAQs, as well as ways users can prevent their systems from ever being infected.

KEYWORDS   Computer Security, Computer Viruses
AUDIENCE   Computer Security Specialists, Computer Users, Network Administrators
CONTACT   David Chess
          chess@watson.ibm.com
FREE

gopher://index.almaden.ibm.com/1virus/virus.70

 IP Stacks Info ★★

Net-Connect's page provides information Windows TCP/IP and Winsock software. This page includes links to Winsock FAQs, Winsock applications, Internet clients for Windows, Winsock shareware libraries, viewer and helper utilities, and NCSA software tools, and more.

KEYWORDS   Operating Systems, Protocols, Utility Software
AUDIENCE   Computer Professionals, Network Administrators, Windows Programmers, Windows Users
CONTACT   sailor@net-connect.net
FREE

http://www.net-connect.net/ipinfo.html

 Index of Utilities ★★★

This is the Born Information Services download page for Windows. It includes Internet tools for Windows, including Eudora, HTML editors, IRC, Trumpet Winsock, Web browsers, and USENET viewers, and Windows utilities, including file compression and archive programs and patches.

KEYWORDS   Internet Tools, Operating Systems, Software, Utility Software

Resources

AUDIENCE Computer Users, Internet Users, PC Users, Windows Users
CONTACT webmaster@born.com
FREE

http://www.born.com/utilities

InfoWorld Home Page ★★★★

The InfoWorld Home Page is an index that lists the issues of InfoWorld magazine. This page is part of the ISN (Internet Shopping Network). Users can browse and search through back issues of InfoWorld, a computer-related magazine with information on the latest developments in the industry. In addition, users can access the Internet Shopping Network via this page.
KEYWORDS Current Events, Internet Shopping, Magazines
AUDIENCE Computer Professionals, Computer Users
CONTACT info@internet.net
FREE

http://www.internet.net/stores/infoworld/index.html

Information Week Home Page ★★★

This is the homepage for the free online version of Information Week published by CMP Publications. Information Week covers the weekly and daily top stories about computer hardware, software, computer vendors, new product releases, and computer-related events. It features Open Labs which conducts in-depth product reviews, first looks, and analyses of the latest computer products and technologies, covering everything from SQL servers and email to ISDN advances and Windows 95.
KEYWORDS Information Week, Online Magazines
AUDIENCE Computer Professionals, Computer Users, PC Users
CONTACT iwkweb@cmp.com
FREE

http://techweb.cmp.com/iwk

InterNET Computer Store ★★

The InterNET Computer Store uses this page to publicize its catalog of computer products which can be ordered over the Internet. Some categories of products include Computers/Peripherals, Accessories/Supplies, and Data Communications. A Hot Deals area is also included. Information about the company, including guarantees, shipping methods, and contact addresses are provided.
KEYWORDS Computer Products, Internet Shopping, Online Shopping
AUDIENCE Computer Users, Online Shoppers
CONTACT products@inetstore.com.
FREE

http://inetstore.com/

Internet Resources for Windows Developers ★★

This page is a collection of resources for the Windows developer. It includes links to many Windows resources, including compiler and development product companies such as Microsoft and Symantec, FAQs, FTP sites, USENET groups, and of developer magazines, and online book stores.
KEYWORDS Operating Systems, Programming, Software Development, Software Engineering
AUDIENCE Computer Professionals, Software Developers, Windows Application Developers
CONTACT Robert Mashlan
rmashlan@r2m.com
FREE

http://www.csn.net/~rmashlan/windev/windev.html

JHuniverse at the Johns Hopkins University ★★★

This site is John Hopkins University's gopher connection to the Internet. It contains computing resources such as introductory manuals, user guides, and newsletters. In addition, this server contains lists of system software, site-licensed software, equipment, and services.
KEYWORDS Computer Applications, Software, User Guides
AUDIENCE Computer Users, Educators (University), Students (Secondary/College)
CONTACT Lee Watkins
lwatkins@jhunix.hcf.jhu.edu
FREE

gopher://jhuniverse.hcf.jhu.edu/

Linux Does The Trick ★★★

This server, run by the University of Linz, offers information on the Linux UNIX operating system for PCs. There is a directory of configuration and other documents, software archives, general UNIX information, and FAQ files. In addition, this server hosts the Austrian Macintosh User Group, which has a number of Macintosh resources in English and German.
KEYWORDS Computer Science, Germany, Operating Systems
AUDIENCE Linux Users, Macintosh Users, PC Users
CONTACT webmaster@wildsau.idv.uni-linz.ac.at
FREE

http://wildsau.idv.uni-linz.ac.at

Macintosh Gopher ★★★

This gopher server at the University of California at Los Angeles offers information that pertains to computers and computer resources. It concentrates on documentation for Macintosh computers and related software.
KEYWORDS Computer Products, Education (College/University)
AUDIENCE Computer Science Students, Computer Users, Students (University)
FREE

gopher://mac-gopher.mic.ucla.edu/

Macintosh Information Web Server ★★

This Web site, maintained by the Computing Service at Newcastle University, is designed as a resource for Power Mac and other Macintosh computer information. A user's guide to Power Macs is included, with links to numerous PowerPC resources on the Web, including newsgroups, FAQs, an online magazine and application information. Also included are information sheets about the different Power Mac series in postscript form. Information about Newcastle University and other local resources are linked.
KEYWORDS Computer Hardware, Personal Computers
AUDIENCE Computer Users, Macintosh Users
CONTACT Tony McDonald
Tony.McDonald@newcastle.ac.uk
FREE

http://launchy.ncl.ac.uk/

NASA Automated Systems Incident Response Capability ★★

The home page of NASA's Automated Systems Incident Response Capability (NASIRC) offers information on the mission and activities of the emergency response team. Users outside of NASA's systems will be unable to access many of the resources available here, but all users can access descriptions of the automated security system NASA has designed to detect security problems, as well as general information about NASIRC. Material is also available on the proper way to respond to security incidents.
KEYWORDS Computer Security, Computer Viruses, NASA (National Aeronautics And Space Administration), Security Issues
AUDIENCE Computer Security Specialists
CONTACT nasirc@nasa.gov
FREE

http://nasirc.nasa.gov/NASIRC_home.html

NIST Computer Security Resource Clearinghouse (National Institute of Standards and Technology) ★★★

This page is a clearinghouse for all computer security related information. The National Institute of Standards and Technology maintains archives of all vulnerability and security alerts issued by the various security incident response teams, as well as indexes of computer viruses, and UNIX security software. Users will also find news and publications relating to computer security, as well as links to other security information servers on the net.
KEYWORDS Computer Security, Computer Viruses
AUDIENCE Computer Security Specialists
CONTACT webmaster@csrc.ncsl.nist.gov
FREE

http://cs-www.ncsl.nist.gov/

National Coordination Office for High Performance Computing and Communications Gopher Server

The information on this gopher server is produced by the National Coordination Office for High Performance Computing and Communications (NCO/HPCC). The mandate of NCO/HPCC is to coordinate the efforts of U.S. federal departments and institutions in their growth of information technology. This gopher server provides information about the NCO/HPCC organization and activities.

KEYWORDS Communications, Government Resources, Information Technology, Supercomputing
AUDIENCE Communications Professionals, Computer Professionals, Government Officials, Information Specialists
CONTACT nco@hpcc.gov
FREE

http://www.hpcc.gov/

gopher://gopher.hpcc.gov/

Ohio Supercomputer Center's Gopher Server

This is a gopher server for the Ohio Supercomputer Center (OSC), a state-funded research project. The OSC's mission is to provide high performance computing services and encourage technologies in a statewide environment for higher education and industry. Information provided includes OSC services, documents, and news releases. In addition, this site provides information on OSC workshops, programs, and has links to other gophers and FTP sites on the Internet.

KEYWORDS Computer Applications, Education (College/University), Research & Development, Supercomputing
AUDIENCE Academics, Computer Professionals, Scientists, Students (Secondary/College)
CONTACT gopher@osc.edu
FREE

gopher://infomeister.osc.edu/

PC Catalog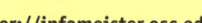

PC Catalog is a product buying resource providing listings of networking, microcomputer, software, peripheral, and new technology products. It includes a Smart Shopper's Checklist and provides comparison information for all major PC categories including systems, modems, monitors, PC boards, PC software, PC storage devices, printers, and more. The information supplied includes vendor's location, business hours, phone/fax numbers, etc. Supplementary resources such as new technology announcements and a shopper's checklist are also available.

KEYWORDS Catalogs, Computer Products, Online Shopping, Software
AUDIENCE Computer Dealers, Consumers, Online Shoppers, PC Users
CONTACT market@pccatalog.peed.com
FREE

gopher://pccatalog.peed.com/1

PC Magazine on the Web

The free online version of PC Magazine, the National Newspaper of Corporate Computing covers the week's top stories about PC hardware, software, vendors, new product releases, and PC-related events. It features PC Labs Online, a hands-on software and hardware evaluation forum; Trends Online; Network Edition with a focus on PC networking issues, Internet Highlights listing sites to visit; and PC Magazine Utilities with download access to the month's featured PC tools and other files.

KEYWORDS Online Magazines, PC Magazine, Publishers
AUDIENCE PC Engineers, PC Programmers, PC Users, Windows Users
CONTACT Tom Giebel
tgiebel@pcmag.ziff.com
FREE

http://zcias3.ziff.com/~pcmag

PC Phone List

This site contains a searchable PC phone list generated by ZEOS tech support as a service to the net community. It is updated approximately once per month. Send email requests for updated list to phone@zeos.com.

KEYWORDS Technical Support, Utility Software
AUDIENCE Computer Professionals, Computer Users, PC Users, Windows Users
CONTACT support@zeos.com
FREE

http://foundation.mit.edu/cgi-bin/search-phone-list

PC-Related Gophers and WWW Servers

This page provides many links to PC gopher sites, Web servers, PC publishers, and software companies. Some of the topics covered include laptops, drivers, LAN networks, and software. The companies with links are Novell (Netware), Ziff Davis, (publisher of magazines including PC Magazine and PC Week), Compaq, Symantec, Dell, Intel, and more. (This page is part of the Internet Computer Index provided by Proper Publishing, a free online reference service.)

KEYWORDS Hardware, Operating Systems, Software
AUDIENCE Computer Engineers, Internet Users, LAN Administrators, PC Users, Windows Users
FREE

http://ici.proper.com/1/pc/gopher-www

SIGCAS (Special Interest Group for Computers and Society)

ACM Special Interest Group on Computers and Society brings together computer professionals, specialists in other fields, and the public at large to address concerns and arouse interest about the impact of computers on society. The gopher link contains some information on the organization and on becoming a member, as well as a few documents on computer ethics.

KEYWORDS Ethics, Social Responsibility
AUDIENCE ACM Members, General Public, Social Scientists, Sociologists
CONTACT C. Dianne Martin SIG Chair
chair_SIGCAS@acm.org
FREE

gopher://gopher.acm.org/
11[the_files.sig_forums.sigcas]

SIGCPR (Special Interest Group for Computer Personnel Research)

The Association for Computing Machinery's Special Interest Group on Computer Personnel Research is a group of approximately 200 information science academics and practitioners who share an interest in the careers, training, attitudes and management of information systems professionals and end users. SIGCPR's journal, Computer Personnel, publishes articles related to these issues, and its annual conference serves as a forum for discussion of current research and practice on IS human resource issues. Its gopher site provides information on the conference, membership, and annual reports.

KEYWORDS Computer Professionals, Personnel, Research & Development
AUDIENCE Computer Professionals, Computer Programers, Computer Specialists, Computer Users
CONTACT Thomas W. Ferratt SIG Chair
chair_SIGCPR@acm.org
FREE

gopher://gopher.acm.org/
11[the_files.sig_forums.sigcpr]

Software Download Page

This Ohio State University page contains the PC User Group's Shareware Library for Windows, Windows NT, and DOS. It provides download links for a few Windows, Windows NT, and DOS shareware programs and some links to other Windows and DOS shareware archives.

KEYWORDS Operating Systems, Shareware, Software Archives, Utility Software
AUDIENCE Computer Professionals, Computer Users, PC Users, Windows Users
FREE

http://krumsee-pc.acs.ohio-state.edu/
software\software.htm

TAP - The Ada Project

The Ada Project (TAP) is a WWW site designed to serve as a clearinghouse for information and resources relating to women in computing. TAP serves primarily as a collection of links to other online resources, rather than as an archive.

KEYWORDS Feminism, Internet Directories, Women's Issues
AUDIENCE Internet Users, Women, Women's Studies Educators, Women's Studies Students
CONTACT Susanne C. Hupfer
hupfer-susanne@cs.yale.edu
FREE

http://www.cs.yale.edu/HTML/YALE/CS/
HyPlans/tap/tap.html

TibKey 1.0 - Tibetan Tools for Windows

TibKey 1.0 is a small utility that makes typing Tibetan text into your Windows applications very easy! This program automatically selects and enters the correct Tibetan ligatures, using a simple Tibetan Keyboard layout. Characters are entered according to the standard Tibetan spelling order. The Tibkey archive was last updated in October 1994.

KEYWORDS Linguistics, Software Development, Tibetans
AUDIENCE Language Students, Microsoft Windows Users, Tibet Enthusiasts, Tibetans
CONTACT coombspapers@coombs.anu.edu.au
FREE

ftp://coombs.anu.edu.au/coombspapers/
otherarchives/asian-studies-
archives/tibetan-archives/tibet-
software/tibkey-windows/

UNIX Information and SICL Help

This gopher site, located at North Carolina State University, provides information on computer resources surrounding the UNIX platform. Users can find material covering various GUI windowing systems, hardware solutions, and information on software including SAS, Splu, and Maple.

KEYWORDS Computer Science, Education (College/University), Internet Resources, Operating Systems
AUDIENCE Computer Science Students, Computer Users
FREE

gopher://eslaba.stat.ncsu.edu/

UNIX Workstation Support Group

This site gives access to data concerned with UNIX workstations. The data cover topics such as AIX (IBM RS-6000), HP-UX, Irix, Mac, Intel, NeXTStep, Solaris, and SunOS. Users will find news and updates on UNIX developments, software, and information on UNIX for various system architectures.

KEYWORDS Computer Hardware, Education (College/University), Operating Systems, Software
AUDIENCE Computer Professionals, Computer Users, UNIX Users, Workstation Users
CONTACT uwsg@indiana.edu
FREE

http://uwsg.ucs.indiana.edu/

gopher://uwsg.ucs.indiana.edu/

WAIS, Inc.

This server offers a demonstration of WAIS, Inc.'s information retrieval systems. Through an HTML form, users can search for any subject by keyword. Users will also find general information on the products and services of WAIS, Inc., including material on the latest developments, job openings at WAIS, and links to WAIS' educational and publishing partners.

KEYWORDS Information Retrieval, Internet Publishing

Connections to Computer Resources
From ThinkPads to Power PCs

For more information contact sales@pcscompleat.com or call 800-294-4727.

Perhaps you have a PC, but want to buy a Macintosh. Or maybe you have a Macintosh and want to buy a PC. If you're facing a computer purchase or you need assistance for custom installation of products or peripherals, the Internet is the best place to "window shop" before you buy. The "PCs Compleat Home Page" is a site that sells and provides support for IBM and PC-compatible computer systems. It includes a "Hot Buys" page that lists items on sale, such as the popular multimedia PCs from Packard Bell, Compaq, and IBM. You also get information on services provided with your purchase, as well as technical support.

(http://www.ocm.com/pcscompleat/default.html)

You can also directly access a computer company to get the information you need—technical help, product information, and technical assistance for rendering your computer more useful to your specific needs. For instance, the "IBM Home Page" provides not only information on IBM products, services, and support, but also allows you to gather information on client/server computing, business computing systems, large scale computing systems, parallel computing systems, workstations and networking solutions. You can also access corporate, financial and stockholder data and reports from this venerable computer giant.

If you are a developer for Macintosh computers—whether a Power Macintosh or a Multimedia Performa—you can tap into Apple Computer, Inc.'s "Developer Services and Products" where you'll learn about the products, get support and training, and access technical documentation and sample codes.

(http://www.ibm.com)

also, (http://www.info.apple.com/dev/developerservices.html)

AUDIENCE Database Managers, Internet Publishers, Internet Users, Professional Researchers
CONTACT frontdesk@wais.com
FREE

http://wais.com

Win/V Page

This is the homepage for WIN/V, a Japanese Language Extension Kit For Microsoft Windows. It allows Windows to run Japanese Windows applications such as Japanese Word for Windows, use Japanese Windows hardware drivers, FEPs Kanji TrueType fonts, browse Japanese Web pages, and input Kanji into English

Windows Applications. This site provides hardware requirements and other FAQs and contact information.

KEYWORDS Operating Systems, Software, Utility Software
AUDIENCE Computer Professionals, PC Users, Windows Users
FREE

http://www.gol.com/winv/winvhome.html

Windows NT FTP Directory

This FTP site provides access to documentation about and utilities for Windows NT. Documentation includes papers about Windows NT issues such as security, and differences between Windows NT and Windows 95, hardware compatability lists for various versions of Windows NT, a catalog of 32-bit applications, and an evaluation kit. Public files include bug reports, FAQs, tools, drivers, fixes, and kits.

KEYWORDS Operating Systems, Software
AUDIENCE Network Administrators, Systems Administrators, Windows NT Developers, Windows Users
FREE

ftp://ftp.microsoft.com/bussys/winnt/

Windows Rag

This is the location of Windows Rags also known as WR Magazine, an online magazine for Windows users. It includes features, comments from readers, articles by staff and readers, reviews and testing, Windows 95 developments, and links to other sites, including past issues of Windows Rag.

KEYWORDS Online Magazines, Operating Systems, Software Reviews
AUDIENCE Computer Science Students, Computer Users, PC Users, Windows Users
CONTACT scrufcat@eskimo.com
FREE

http://www.eskimo.com/~scrufcat/wr.html

Word Processor Filters

This page reviews filters and file format converters used to translate files in Macintosh, Windows, and UNIX formats, such as Rich Text Format (RTF), Word for Windows, WordPerfect, PostScript, LaTeX, QuarkX-Press, Interleaf, troff, and others to HTML. It provides links to the software available for making the translation.

KEYWORDS Computer Hardware, Format Converters, HTML (HyperText Markup Language), Operating Systems
AUDIENCE HTML Users, Technical Writers, Web Developers, Windows Users
FREE

http://www.w3.org/hypertext/WWW/Tools/Word_proc_filters.html

Ziff-Davis Home Page

Come to Ziff-Davis's virtual coffeehouse and you can browse through PC Week, Computer Life, Interactive Week, Computer Shopper and many other computer magazines from this publisher. Relax with your home brewed espresso and your mouse and try some of the magazine tips as you read. You can also keep up-to-date with the latest news scoops such as the Microsoft-Intuit Deal or AOL's plans to preempt Microsoft's plans to provide 'one-button' access.

KEYWORDS Computer Hardware, News, Online Magazines, Publishing
AUDIENCE Computer Users, Internet Users
CONTACT webmaster@ziff.com
FREE

http://www.ziff.com

Software

See also
Computing & Mathematics · *Applications*
Computing & Mathematics · *Programming*
Internet · *Internet Access*
Popular Culture & Entertainment · *Shopping*

1994 Directory of Applications Software for Cray Research Supercomputing

This site within the Cray ftp archive provides information on where to obtain applications software products for the Cray supercomputer. A complete list of applications software developed or simply supported by independent software suppliers as well as by Cray Research Incorporated is provided. The software directory listed software pertaining to computational fluid dynamics, chemistry and chemical engineering, environmental science, simulations and mathematics programming, petroleum seismology and much more.

KEYWORDS Computer Applications, Software, Software Development, Supercomputing
AUDIENCE Chemistry Engineers, Computational Chemists, Computational Mathematicians, Environmental Researchers, Mathematicians
CONTACT webmaster@cray.com
FREE

ftp://ftp.cray.com/applications/

ATI Technologies, Inc.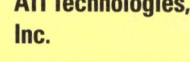

This is the homepage for ATI Technology, providers of graphics, communication, and multimedia video products including MediaMerge, Video-It! and Video Basic (video editing software and low-cost multimedia software for Windows). This site includes information about their products, the company, and support services. Their FTP support site includes updates, drivers and utilities.

KEYWORDS Graphics Software, Multimedia, Operating Systems, Software
AUDIENCE Graphic Artists, Multimedia Developers, Video Artists, Windows Users
CONTACT webmaster@atitech.ca
FREE

http://www.atitech.ca/

Adobe Systems, Incorporated

This Adobe site provides information on technical support and sales for Adobe, Aldus, Prepress and Image Club Graphics Products. A directory for online services and instructions to access their bulletin board is also provided. A list of obsolete products is available but technical information on these products is not available through their bulletin board. System requirements, installation instructions for drivers, technical tips, and software related to Adobe's applications and products is also located at this site.

KEYWORDS Adobe Systems, Computer Graphics, Computer Software, Publishing
AUDIENCE Computer Artists, Computer Graphic Designers, Computer Operators, Computer Users, Desktop Publishers
CONTACT archive-keepers@adobe.com
FREE

http://www.adobe.com/

ftp://ftp.adobe.com/

Apple II Files

This FTP site contains the archive of files relating to Apple II computers. System software, games, utilities, and more are available here.

KEYWORDS Companies, Computer Hardware
AUDIENCE Apple Computer Users, Apple II Users, Computer Users, Programmers
CONTACT Dan DeMaggio, Apple II Archivist
         apple2-archivist@archive.umich.edu
FREE

ftp://mirror.archive.umich.edu/systems/apple2

BE Software Company Home Page

The BE Software Company Home Page offers information about the Behaviour Engine, a new kind of simulation software. It represents behavior of all kinds of motion, including 3D motion and complex sequencing of events, in a general-purpose format that is suitable for use in hypertexts documents.

KEYWORDS Database Applications, Hypertext, Simulation
AUDIENCE Business Professionals, Computer Professionals, Computer Users
CONTACT info@besoft.com
FREE

http://besoft.com/

Best Windows 95 Software

This software archive contains 32-bit shareware programs for Windows 95. Categories include applications, communications, compression utilities, games, graphics, utilities, and Winsock applications, including 32-bit email, FTP, news readers, and Web browsers.

Software   221

(This site will continue to grow with the release of Windows 95.)

KEYWORDS Operating Systems, Shareware, Software Archives, Utility Software
AUDIENCE Computer Professionals, Computer Users, PC Users, Windows Users
CONTACT Phil Jones
jonesp@biology.queensu.ca
FREE

http://biology.queensu.ca/~jonesp/win95/software/software.html

Blueridge Technologies Home Page ★★★

This is the homepage for Blueridge Technologies, provider of OPTIX, a cross-platform document management system for Macintosh and Windows-based computers that incorporates document imaging, archival, text retrieval, workflow, OCR, and FAX capabilities. This site includes product information, technical support, employment opportunities, ordering information, and links to other sites.

KEYWORDS Computer Systems, Document Management, Personal Computers, Software
AUDIENCE Computer Professionals, Document Management Specialists, Macintosh Users, Windows Users
CONTACT webmaster@blueridge.com
FREE

http://www.blueridge.com/

CSUSM (California State University at San Marcos) Windows World ★★★★

The Windows Shareware Archive, part of the CSUSM Campus Wide Information System (CWIS) presents the top-level of a large directory structure. There are shareware programs for Windows accessories including specialty clocks, custom calendars, calculators, address books, dialers, and other related programs. Also, there are File Manager and Program Manager add-ons and alternatives, graphics support, and file conversion programs, screen capture programs, graphic files in different formats and icon tools. System utilities are provided and user applications are covered, including multi-purpose and specialty database programs as well as Internet tools.

KEYWORDS Operating Systems, Shareware, Software Archives
AUDIENCE Computer Engineers, Computer Programmers, PC Users, Windows Users
FREE

http://coyote.csusm.edu/cwis/winworld/winworld.html

CambridgeSoft, We Interrupt This Home Page ★★★

The CambridgeSoft, We Interrupt this Home Page offers information about its new product line including such software as CS ChemOffice Pro for Windows, CS ChemDraw 3.5 for Macintosh, and CS Chem3D Pro 3.2 for Windows.

KEYWORDS Chemistry, Computer Systems, Engineering, Technical Support
AUDIENCE Chemists, Engineers, Researchers
FREE

http://www.camsci.com/

Cantax ★★★

This is the home page of Cantax, an income tax and financial software developer in Canada. Information on all of the Cantax products for both personal and professional markets is available here. There is also detailed information on quality assurance, as well as technical support documents.

KEYWORDS Financial Software, Personal Finance Software, Tax Software
AUDIENCE Accountants, Business Professionals, Canadians
CONTACT cantax@immedia.ca
FREE

http://www.nucleus.com/mall/cantax/

Charles View Software ★★★

The Charles View Software page offers services for preparing software for international markets. The software is for the Far Eastern market focusing on such languages as Japanese, Chinese, and Korean. The page also has information on employment opportunities.

KEYWORDS Computer Software, International Development, Networking, Programming
AUDIENCE International Marketers, Software Developers
CONTACT info@charlesview.com
FREE

http://www.charlesview.com/

Cheyenne Software Home Page ★★★

The Cheyenne Software Home Page offers information about the company, products, support, and downloadable files. Cheyenne Software develops local area networks (LAN) management software products. There is information about technical support and links to other related sites.

KEYWORDS Companies, LANs (Local Area Networks), Networking, Technical Support
AUDIENCE Computer Users, LAN Users, Software Developers
CONTACT webmaster@chey.com
FREE

http://www.chey.com/

Cica Archives ★★★★

This site is Cica's Microsoft Windows Anonymous FTP Service. (Access is also available through mirror sites.) This site serves as the FTP clearinghouse for public domain and shareware Windows-related files covering Windows applications, tips, utilities, drivers, bitmaps, patches, upgrades, program listings from publications, games, icons, sounds, and more. Some specific products covered include Windows desktop utilities, Excel tools, Aldus PageMaker tools, Symantec patches, Winsock applications, Word and WordPerfect utilities, Paradox tools, Borland C++ programs, Turbo Pascal programs, Visual BASIC programs and library files, and Adobe Font manager and Truetype fonts, and more.

KEYWORDS Operating Systems, Shareware, Software Archives, Utility Software
AUDIENCE Computer Professionals, Computer Users, PC Users, Windows Users
FREE

ftp://ftp.cica.indiana.edu

ClipMate for Windows ★★★

This is the site of Thornton Software Solutions, provider of ClipMate, a shareware application for Windows that captures and stores items pasted to the Windows clipboard accessory. At this site, you can download a copy of ClipMate, read press releases, and learn about Thornton Software.

KEYWORDS Operating Systems, Shareware, Utility Software
AUDIENCE Computer Users, Windows Users
CONTACT tsoft@eznet.net
FREE

http://delta.com/tsoft/clipmate.htm

Commercial Timesharing, Inc. ★★★

Commercial Timesharing, Inc. (CTI) is an Engineering and Software Consulting company with vast experience in factory automation and turn key software solutions for manufacturing. CTI is also the creator of the Graphically You (c) Hairstyle Selection System, and HourMaster Spreadsheet (c) programs specifically designed for Cosmetology teachers. The page supplies information about the company and its software tools.

KEYWORDS Consulting Services, Manufacturing, Systems Engineering, Turnkey Systems
AUDIENCE Electrical Engineers, Software Engineers, Systems Administrators
CONTACT Robert D. Brown
sales@comtime.com
FREE

http://dialup.oar.net/~Pcti/

Computer Software at University of Georgia ★★★

This gopher server is located at the University of Georgia, and contains software information and FTP access. A variety of platforms are supported, including Macs, DOS, Windows, NeXT, SGI, Sun, VMS, and Ultrix. This server also provides information and software for BITNET, GNU, Novell, antivirus solutions and various computer utilities.

KEYWORDS Computer Applications, Software, Universities
AUDIENCE Computer Professionals, Internet Users, Students (Secondary/College)
FREE

gopher://server.uga.edu:8001/

Software

CyberMedia's WWW Home Page
 COMMERCIAL ★★

This page is by CyberMedia. It provides product information about First Aid, a program to fix Windows configuration problems, and PC 911, an automatic rescue program and system configuration utility. It also includes demo programs and ordering information.

- **KEYWORDS** Configuration Tools, Operating Systems, Utility Software
- **AUDIENCE** Computer Professionals, PC Users, Windows System Administrators, Windows Users
- **CONTACT** cybermedia@internet-is.com
- **FREE**

http://www.internet-is.com/cybermedia/index.html

DISA Center for Software - Software Management Support
★★★

The DISA Center for Software - Software Management Support Department (SMSD) administers the Department of Defense HBCU/MI Equipment Program. Under the program, SMSD leases new and used computer equipment to designated minority colleges and universities.

- **KEYWORDS** Computer Equipment, Hardware, Software, Software Management Support
- **AUDIENCE** University Administrators
- **FREE**

http://web.fie.com/web/fed/dar/

Dakota Software World Wide Web Page
★★

This is the homepage for Dakota Software, a software development consulting firm. Dakota Software provides custom software applications written in C, C++, and assembly language for UNIX, MS/DOS, or Windows operating systems. This site provides company information and a few links to related information and affiliations.

- **KEYWORDS** Operating Systems, Software Development, Utility Software
- **AUDIENCE** Computer Professionals, PC Users, Software Developers, Windows Users
- **CONTACT** vaughn@indirect.com
- **FREE**

http://www.indirect.com/www/vaughn

Dartmouth Software Development
★★★

This is the home page of Dartmouth College's Software Development group, which provides information on the group's projects and personnel. Some of the projects are freeware, such as BlitzMail, DND, NameD*tective. Fetch is a shareware project. Others projects, InterMapper and SNMPWatcher are available for OEM licensing.

- **KEYWORDS** Freeware, Shareware, Software, Universities
- **AUDIENCE** Macintosh Programmers, Macintosh Users, Network Administrators
- **CONTACT** WebMaster@dartmouth.edu
- **FREE**

http://www.dartmouth.edu/pages/softdev/

Delmarva Power and Light
COMMERCIAL ★★

This Delmarva Power and Light site provides access to a rather miscellaneous grouping of software, documents and source codes. The subdirectories are divided as follows, code, tools and verbiage about Banyan Systems Vines, and a help desk management system developed by Delmarva. There is information about help desks, network management systems, documents about redundant arrays of inexpensive disks (RAID), UNIX and network security, and Raptor Systems' Firewall products. There is code and information for Santa Cruz Operating UNIX (SCO UNIX), documents and files for ENS (ENSign) for SCO UNIX, information for Sparc, Intel Solaris, Sun, and Wellfleet Routers.

- **KEYWORDS** Computer Networking, Freeware
- **AUDIENCE** Computer Networkers, LAN (Local Area Network) Specialists, UNIX System Administrators, UNIX Users
- **CONTACT** John Scoggins
  postmaster@delmarva.com
- **FREE**

ftp://ftp.delmarva.com/

EZ Com-EZ Go
COMMERCIAL ★★

This page provides information about EZ Com-EZ Go, Windows software that facilitates the transmission of files between two modem-equipped PCs. This site includes a demo version and screenshots.

- **KEYWORDS** Communications Software, Modems, Utility Software
- **AUDIENCE** Computer Users, Modem Users, PC Users, Windows Users
- **CONTACT** ezcom@ix.netcom.com
- **FREE**

http://clickshop.com/ezcom/

Exec-PC A-Ware Music Master
COMMERCIAL ★★★★

This site provides access to program updates and utilitiy files for the A-Ware Music Master Music Scheduling System. This information, the latest program update and patch files can also be downloaded from the A-Ware Software BBS (Bulletin Board System). This site provides installation instructions for the patch files as well as the actual patch files.

- **KEYWORDS** Music Software, Technical Support
- **AUDIENCE** Music Educators, Music Enthusiasts, Music Librarians, Music Students
- **CONTACT** Scott Wirt
  a-ware@execpc.com
- **FREE**

ftp://ftp.execpc.com/pub/a-ware/

FTP Software Incorporated, Marketing Information
COMMERCIAL ★★★★

This site provides access to the marketing releases, product descriptions, hardware descriptions and user information regarding the many software products marketed by FTP Software, Incorporated. This marketing information is available for PC/TCP (Personal Computer/Transmission Control Protocol) Development Kit for DOS/Windows, PC/TCP Development Kit for OS/2, Entranx/32 for Windows, Explore OnNet for Windows, LANCatch Trace Utility for DOS, LANWatch Network analyzer for DOS, PC/TCP OnNet version 1.1 for DOS/Windows, and Services OnNet for DOS/Windows.

- **KEYWORDS** Computer Networks, Marketing, Protocols
- **AUDIENCE** Computer Networkers, LAN Consultants, Network Communications Specialists, Network Users
- **CONTACT** info@ftp.com
- **FREE**

http://www.ftp.com/

ftp://ftp.ftp.com/markting/

Fluke Corporation NetDAQ
COMMERCIAL ★★★

This site provides access to three files that include the setup file for reading room temperature at Northwest Nexus Incorporated, a demo version of the Windows application to control NetDAQ instruments via TCP/IP protocol, and finally, a WinSock compliant TCP/IP stack shareware package. The NetDAQ instrument is capable of measuring up to twenty channels of DC (Direct Current) and AC (Alternating Current) voltages, currents, resistance, frequency or temperature (RTDs and thermocouples). Detailed specifications and pricing information are available directly from Fluke Corporation.

- **KEYWORDS** Companies, Computer Networks, Hardware, Networking
- **AUDIENCE** Computer Manufacturers, Internet Developers, Network Researchers, Science Researchers
- **CONTACT** Frank
  frankw@tc.fluke.com
- **FREE**

ftp://ftp.halcyon.com/pub/fluke/

Free Software-Shareware Shack
COMMERCIAL ★★

The Free Software Shack provides links to free software for DOS, Windows, and Macintosh users. Some of the software includes email for DOS, PDQ Mortgage Software for Windows, multimedia novels, a personal information package, shareware games, Internet telephone for Windows, Print Artist for Windows, and Winzip. You may download files from the Web or FTP site.

- **KEYWORDS** Computer Systems, Freeware, Shareware
- **AUDIENCE** Computer Users, Macintosh Users, PC Users

CONTACT jmsmith@pic.net
FREE

http://www.pic.net/uniloc/uniloc.html

ftp://ftp.pic.net/pub/uniloc

Freeware Terminal Emulators

This site provides access to a large number of freeware software utilities that are unsupported by FTP Software Incorporated. Utilities available at this site include freeware terminal emulators such as Tektronix emulation for PC/TPC (Personal Computer/Transmission Control Protocol), public domain freeware version of Silicon Graphics' Flight Simulator which runs over PC/TCP, Etherslip.com packet driver for use with Desqview over SLIP (Serial Line Interface Protocol) which emulates Ethernet, Version 1.1 of FTPNuz NNTP (Network News Transfer Protocol) Newsreader.

KEYWORDS Freeware, Networking, Protocols, Terminal Emulators
AUDIENCE Network Developers, Network Users, PC Users, UNIX Users
CONTACT support@ftp.com
FREE

http://www.ftp.com/

ftp://ftp.ftp.com/pub/dos/

Funk Software's Home Page

Funk Software provides networking utility software for the management and use of Novell LANs. Funk Software add-on products include InWord, Noteworthy, the Worksheet Utilities, P.D.Queue, and Formula Editor. The page gives information about each of the products as well as offering technical support.

KEYWORDS Companies, Networking, Technical Support
AUDIENCE LAN Users, Network Administrators, PC Users
CONTACT webmaster@funk.com
FREE

http://www.funk.com/

InfoImaging Home page

This is InfoImaging's homepage with information about 3D FAX software. This site provides free software to download, product and company information, FAQs, demos, upgrades, tutorials and troubleshooting tips.

KEYWORDS FAX Software, Operating Systems, Software, Utility Software
AUDIENCE Computer Professionals, Fax Users, PC Users, Windows Users
FREE

http://www.infoimaging.com/

International Software Systems, Incorporated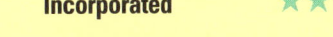

The International Software Systems Home Page offers information on its software product line, employees,

Connections to System Software Resources
From double your RAM to virus protection

Ever put a floppy disk in your computer and get a virus that starts to wreak havoc the minute you finish a long spreadsheet? There are many companies online that provide software to eliminate various problems which occur when you download software, or share disks with your friends and associates.

One way to access the information and products you need to guard against nasty viruses is through software companies that provide virus checkers. The "Symantec Corporation Home Page," for instance, furnishes information on the company's vast array of utilities, including virus checker and RAM doubling applications. You can scan the solutions the company offers for Windows, DOS, Macintosh, and OS/2 computer systems. Also check out company news, including forthcoming upgrades of existing products and new products about to hit the market. You can also receive services and support for the company's products.

(http://www.symantec.com/)

and their home pages. ISSI puts out ProSLCSE, organizational software that has a graphical, adaptable, integrated and intuitive tool set, backed by a complete line of services for process improvement. There are links to financial resources, and other WWW and Internet sites.

KEYWORDS Companies, Computer Applications, Computer Systems
AUDIENCE Business Professionals, Computer Users, Software Shoppers
CONTACT www-admin@issi.com
FREE

http://www.issi.com

James River Group, Inc.

This is the homepage for James River Group, a company that develops and markets software for connecting PCs to UNIX systems. This page provides product information about ICE.TEN.PLUS, ICE.TCP, and RED.FS and includes company information as well.

KEYWORDS Cross Platform Applications, Operating Systems, Personal Computers, UNIX
AUDIENCE Cross-Development Programmers, Software Programmers, UNIX Application Developers, Windows Application Developers
CONTACT teltech@iu.net
FREE

http://www.jriver.com/

Language Engineering Corporation Home Page ★★★

The Language Engineering Corporation (LEC) is a developer of language translation software and natural language processing systems. The home page supplies information about the company and its software products and translation services. LEC software products include LogoVista E to J and Ambassador. There are also links to other language translation related sites.

KEYWORDS Engineering, Linguistics, Natural Language, Software Development
AUDIENCE Linguists, Software Developers, Translators
CONTACT info@hq.lec.com
FREE

http://www.lec.com/

LearnKey ★★★

This WWW site provides information on LearnKey's series of software training video tapes. A number of applications are listed on the home page. Each provides you with the information about the trainer in the video, as well as price and program information for beginner, intermediate and advanced learners.

KEYWORDS Educational Software, Utility Software, Video
AUDIENCE Business Professionals, Computer Users, PC Users, Windows Users
CONTACT learnkey@learnkey.com
FREE

http://www.learnkey.com/

MS-DOS Game Software Repository ★★★

This site is a repository for shareware MS-DOS computer game programs and free demonstration versions of commercial game software.

KEYWORDS Computer Games, Operating Systems, Shareware
AUDIENCE Computer Games Developers, Computer Games Enthusiasts, Games Players
CONTACT Nathan Pieper
  pieper@cs.uwp.edu
FREE

ftp://ftp.uwp.edu/msdos/Games/

MSN (Microsoft Network) Windows 95 ★★★★

This page contains information on Microsoft's Windows 95, including general information and technical advice. The page also has a link to Hot Topics — four additional areas of information about Windows 95 including 'Cost Reductions In Adopting Microsoft Office for Windows 95', 'Microsoft Announces Availability of The Microsoft Network', 'Windows 95 Launch Event Press Release', 'Arrival of Windows 95 in New York.' There is also a link to the Microsoft home page.

KEYWORDS Microsoft Corporation, Operating Systems
AUDIENCE Microsoft Customers, Windows Users
CONTACT www@microsoft.com
FREE

http://wl7.windows.microsoft.com/windows/default.htm

Mac Central ★★★

Mac Central is a place to find Macintosh shareware and freeware available on the Internet. This site has separate directories for Location of Archives, Essential Mac Programs, Fun/Cool Software, and SLIP/PPP software for the Mac. Once you find a program that you want to download, Mac Central will give you a list of FTP sites that store the software. You can then pick the archive site that is nearest you.

KEYWORDS Computer Systems, Meta-Index (Macintosh), Shareware, Software Archives
AUDIENCE Macintosh Users
CONTACT Ahron Balsam
  abtm@ios.com
FREE

http://www2.ios.com/~abtm

Mantis Consultants Ltd ★★★

The Jobstream Group of Mantis Consultants Ltd develops software for client services and offers user training. The page has a corporate summary, product overview and technical documents. The software covers client service organization, in particular, client databases, client accounting and accounts production, portfolio management and valuation, time recording, invoicing and practice accounting.

KEYWORDS Accounting, Companies, Computer Systems, Portfolio Management, Software Development
AUDIENCE Accountants, Business Professionals, Computer Users, Management Consultants
CONTACT Tony Lezard
  admin@mantis.co.uk
FREE

http://www.mantis.co.uk

Marketing Masters - Survey Said for the WEB ★★★

This is the Marketing Masters homepage for Survey Said for the Web and Windows. Survey Said is a survey administration application for taking and tracking Internet surveys, electronic surveys, diskette surveys, kiosk surveys and paper surveys. This site includes company information, product information, and sample surveys, statistics, and screens. A demo version is available for downloading and access to the Survey Said WebNotes Forum is provided.

KEYWORDS Database Applications, Marketing, Operating Systems, Software
AUDIENCE Market Analysts, Market Researchers, Marketing Specialists, Windows Users
CONTACT service@buzzsaw.mv.com
FREE

http://surveysaid.ostech.com:8080/mmasters.htm

Mathematics Software, Tools and Projects ★★★★

The Mathematics Software, Tools and Projects page contains information about mathematics tools, software and online projects provided by the Canadian Mathematical Society. The page has links to various mathematics projects, as well as mathematical software such as Maple, Mathematica, MATLAB, REDUCE, and Magma.

KEYWORDS Mathematics Software
AUDIENCE Mathematicians, Mathematics Educators, Mathematics Students
CONTACT camel@camel.cecm.sfu.ca
FREE

http://camel.cecm.sfu.ca/Software/software.html

Medical Multimedia Systems Home Page ★★★

This page is by Medical Multimedia Systems, provider of Microsoft Windows and Macintosh software for computer-based learning in the biomedical sciences. This page includes product information about Brainiac, SimBioSys, and The Dynamic Spine, and demos. This site also provides ordering information, a mailing list subscription form, and links to other biomedical information and program sources.

KEYWORDS Biomedical Science, Computer Aided Instruction, Computer Systems, Operating Systems
AUDIENCE Macintosh Users, Medical Educators, Medical Students, Windows Users
FREE

http://www.webcom.com/~medmult/welcome.html

Miscellaneous Macintosh Utilities ★★★

This site provides access to many miscellaneous Macintosh freeware utilities. Utilities available at this server include BBEdit-Lite 3.0 (text editor), Compact-Pro, Disinfectant 3.6, Drop Stuff 3.5.1 Installer, Graphic Converter, JPEG Viewer, MACPGP 2.6, Sound Machine 2.1, Sparkle 2.1.5, StripPPC, Stuffit Expander 3.5.1.1, UULite 1.7, U1aw and U1aw Play, macgzip 02.1 and uuUndo 1.0.

KEYWORDS Computer Systems, Freeware
AUDIENCE Computer Users, Macintosh Programmers, Macintosh Users
FREE

ftp://ftp.lightside.com/lightside/MacUtilities/

Software

NEXOR ★★

NEXOR is a British technology company that provides electronic communication software products and services. This page offers marketing, technical and research information. There are links to public WWW servers and staff home pages.

- KEYWORDS: Communications Software, Technology
- AUDIENCE: Computer Professionals, Technology Researchers
- CONTACT: webmaster@nexor.co.uk
- FREE

http://www.nexor.co.uk

Net Ex Unofficial Windows 95 Software Archive ★★★★

The Unofficial Windows 95 site is a software archive (under construction) that contains 32-bit shareware programs for Windows 95. Areas covered include Internet applications (Netscape and others), WinZip 32, and desktop utilities and accessories, such as animated cursors, an MPEG player, and a desktop grabber. (This site will cover more after Windows 95 is released and more shareware is available.)

- KEYWORDS: Operating Systems, Shareware, Software Archives, Utility Software
- AUDIENCE: Computer Professionals, Computer Users, PC Users, Windows Users
- CONTACT: dcosby@infowest.com
- FREE

http://WWW.NetEx.NET/w95/windows95

Network Software and Shareware for NeXT ★★

This site is a Public Site maintained by the Internet Provider MCSNet. This section of this site has Drivers, Compression Software, Patches and Pine software contributed by MCSNet as well as by the other users. It has shareware for UNIX, NeXT, Windows, Linux and Macintosh. This is basically a Public Upload section so the list keeps changing with new sharewares constantly.

- KEYWORDS: Networking, Workstations
- AUDIENCE: Internet Users, Students
- CONTACT: Karl Denningor Karl@mcs.net
- FREE

http://www.mcs.net

gopher://Gopher.mcs.net/

ftp://ftp.mcs.com/pud/dell.software

OS/2 Shareware BBS  ★★★★

The OS/2 Shareware BBS caters to OS/2 users and developers in over 38 countries. The service is available on twenty phone lines plus offers telnet Internet access for subscription members. There are more than 10,700 OS/2 specific downloadable files totalling over 2.2 gigabytes of data in 37 file areas. Special file areas supporting specific software vendors are also available. Full access given on first call with no upload/download ratios enforced. This BBS also carries 64 OS/2-related message conferences.

- KEYWORDS: BBSs (Bulletin Board Systems), Operating Systems, Personal Computers, Shareware
- AUDIENCE: Computer Programmers, Internet Users, Software Developers
- CONTACT: Pete Norloff pnorloff@bbs.os2bbs.com
- FREE

http://www.os2bbs.com

telnet://bbs.os2bbs.com

Pre-Driven Software ★★★

This is the homepage for Pre-Driven Software, offering used game and application software for the IBM-PC for sale. Main areas covered include MS-DOS applications, Windows applications, MS-DOS games, and Windows games. This site also includes Windows and game tips-of-the-week.

- KEYWORDS: Games, Operating Systems, Software, Utility Software
- AUDIENCE: Computer Games Enthusiasts, Computer Users, PC Users, Windows Users
- CONTACT: kevinkj@mcs.com
- FREE

http://www.mcs.net:80/~kevinkj/predrivn.html

Qualcomm Enterprise Software Technologies (QUEST) ★★★

This is the home page for Qualcomm Enterprise Software Technologies (QUEST). Links are provided to documentation, product and ordering information for current and freeware versions of Eudora a leading email software program. There is also a link to a technical help section in addition to general information that Eudora users will find helpful, such as the Quest listserv.

- KEYWORDS: Business Communications, Email, Email Software, Software
- AUDIENCE: Business Professionals, Email Users, Internet Users
- CONTACT: webmaster@qualcomm.com
- FREE

http://www.qualcomm.com/quest/QuestMain.html

RTFTOHTM (Rich Text Format (RTF) to HTML) — Tools  ★

This page provides information about programs that convert Windows word processing files to HTML. It includes reviews, descriptions, and links to archives containing the software. Converters for converting Word for Windows documents to HTML, and for converting Rich Text Format (RTF) to HTML are represented.

- KEYWORDS: Format Converters, Operating Systems, RTF-HTML, Software
- AUDIENCE: HTML Users, Technical Writers, Web Developers, Windows Users
- FREE

http://www.w3.org/hypertext/WWW/Tools/RTFTOHTM.html

Read Chinese in Net Applications ★★★

This page was first created for PC users who have direct Internet connections (including SLIP/PPP/TIA/TwinSock etc. types) running MS-Windows. Currently pointers for other platforms are also included. The page describes the ways that Internet Users can read Chinese symbols on their systems. Setups include installing distinct systems links to gopher and Web Browsers, such as a MS-Windows Chinese System called TwinBridge. Settings changes are given for Mosaic and Netscape users. Other options for users are installing an external Chinese viewer for Web Browsers, obtaining special newsreading software, or using programs like Ghostscript to view specific postscript files. Links to all software options are provided through this page, as well as links to information for non-Windows platforms (Macintosh, X-Windows, etc.)

- KEYWORDS: Chinese Language, International Communications, Internet Software, Internet Tools
- AUDIENCE: Chinese Language Students, Chinese Readers, Language Students, Linguists
- CONTACT: A. Mahendra Rajah, Dept of Computing Services, University of Regina Mahendra@Meena.CC.URegina.CA
- FREE

http://meena.cc.uregina.ca/~liushus/pub/read-chn.html

SST Inc./Windows Programming Tools ★★

This is Systems Software Technology's homepage with information about the TracePlus family of debugging tools for debugging APIs in Windows, Windows 95, and OS/2. This site includes product information, Win32 support, and purchase information. Demo versions are available for TracePlus/Winsock, TracePlus/ODBC, and TracePlus/SQL Server.

- KEYWORDS: Debugging, Operating Systems, Programming
- AUDIENCE: OS/2 Programmers, Programmers, Windows Application Developers
- CONTACT: sstinc@netcom.com
- FREE

http://www.webcom.com/~sstinc/

Seasoft Version 4.212 ★★★★

This ftp server provides access to several files related to Seasoft Version 4.212 from Sea-Bird Electronics Incorporated. Seasoft provides modular, menu-driven routines for acquisition, display, processing and archiving oceanographic data acquired with Sea-Bird electronic equipment. This software is designed to work with IBM XT/AT/386/486/586 or compatible. The files include a description of changes for each version of Seasoft, the Seasoft manual in DOS text format, the Seasoft manual in WordPerfect 5.1 format, Seasoft executable files and Seasoft installation batch file. All of the information can be accessed directly from ftp.seabird.com.

KEYWORDS Oceanography, Software
AUDIENCE Biologists, Database Developers, Marine Biologists, Oceanographers
FREE

ftp://ftp.halcyon.com/pub/seabird/OUT/

Second Nature Software Home Page ★★★

This is Second Nature Software's homepage, publisher of over 60 different screen saver and wallpaper programs for Windows and Macintosh. This site includes Windows and Macintosh samplers, installers, and upgrades that can be downloaded. Sample images from many categories, including space, fantasy, comics, art, and others can be viewed and slide show software can be downloaded. This site also provides product and purchasing information and technical support documentation.

KEYWORDS Computer Systems, Operating Systems, Software, Utility Software
AUDIENCE Computer Users, Graphic Users, PC Users, Windows Users
CONTACT mikebb@secondnature.com
FREE

http://www.secondnature.com/

Serif - Software Products ★★

This is the homepage for Serif, producers of desktop publishing software for Windows, including TypePlus, TablePlus, DrawPlus, PhotoPlus, PagePlus, ArtPack, and FontPack. This site includes information about the company, products, customer service, and technical support. It also includes free software, hints and tricks, and FAQs.

KEYWORDS Desktop Publishing, Graphics Software, Operating Systems
AUDIENCE Desktop Publishers, Documentation Specialists, Technical Writers, Windows Users
CONTACT WebMaster@Serif.Com
FREE

http://www.serif.com/

Software OnLine ★★

Software OnLine allows you to purchase and download software from various developers on the net. Programs include business, personal, educational, management, graphics and games software. Listings include a brief summary and prices.

KEYWORDS Computer Software, Online Shopping, Software Archives
AUDIENCE Computer Users

CONTACT NetRep Explorist
info@netrep.com
FREE

http://saturn.netrep.com:80/home/swol/

Software Research and Development Center ★★★

This site describes the Software Research and Development Center, Turkey. It provides information on the Software Research and Development Center, its research and projects, the anonymous FTP site, documents, and more. As well, it makes connections to other gophers like the METU gopher.

KEYWORDS Computer Applications, Education (College/University), Software, Turkey
AUDIENCE Academics, Computer Professionals, Computer Specialists, Students
FREE

gopher://gopher.srdc.metu.edu.tr/

Software for Theologians ★★★

This gopher contains software archives that are used by theologians and religious studies researchers. The six sections contain Greek and Hebrew font and word processing software, Bible software tools, database and search software, computer assisted language learning software, and theology computing bibliographies. Users may read about each software package before downloading them via ftp.

KEYWORDS Bible, Shareware, Theology
AUDIENCE Religious Studies Educators, Religious Studies Students, Theologians
FREE

gopher://delphi.dur.ac.uk/11/Academic/P-T/Theology/Computing/Software

Software Technology Park of India ★★★

This home page presents Software Technology Park of India (STPI), which was created in order to give a boost to the software exports by the Department of Electronics. Presently, around 210 software units have been given approval by the government to operate under this scheme. Also, a directory of firm exporting software and a list of regional STPI centers is presented.

KEYWORDS Computer Software, India
AUDIENCE Business Professionals, Computer Software Developers, Indians
FREE

http://www.stph.net/

Software.Net ★★★★

Software.Net allows the users to examine and purchase 7800 different discounted computer products and software titles. Listings include prices, order information, demos and reviews for each product, and Software Net also offers customer support for downloaded software and products. They also provide links to online publications PC World and DataQuest Software Quicktakes, and brochures for ACT!, Norton Utilities and Explore OnNet.

KEYWORDS Computer Products, Computer Software, Online Shopping, Software Archives
AUDIENCE Computer Users

CONTACT CyberSource
webmaster@software.net
FREE

http://software.net/index.htm/SK:hbofdlakbegaglpc

Sophos/ACT Anti-Virus Page ★★

This page by Sophos and ACT provides product information about SWEEP, anti-virus specific detection software, for DOS and Windows, Netware, Windows NT, OS/2 and OpenVMS. Other software includes InterCheck client-server, virus checking for workstations; VACCINE cryptographic checksum package for virus-independent detection; D-FENCE memory-resident utility which prevents the use of unauthorized floppy disks and a range of encryption, authentication, and secure erasure products. This page includes ordering information and technical tips.

KEYWORDS Operating Systems, Security Issues, Virus Detection
AUDIENCE Computer Professionals, PC Users, Windows Users
CONTACT tech@infobahn.icubed.com
FREE

http://www.icubed.com/sophos.html

St. Francis Medical Center Software Page ★★★

This page contains information and software related to computer applications in medicine and informatics. It provides DOS and Windows programs for the study of vector and scalar electrocardiography and a list of other software sites and catalogs.

KEYWORDS Medical Applications, Operating Systems
AUDIENCE Macintosh Users, Medical Informatics, Medical Professionals, PC Users
CONTACT leff+@pitt.edu
FREE

http://www.pitt.edu:80/~leff/software/software.html

StatLib Gopher Server ★★

This gopher server provides access to the StatLib archives which contain a collection of statistics software and data. The various directories of information are listed according to subject matter.

KEYWORDS Software, Statistics
AUDIENCE Computer Users, Researchers, Statisticians
CONTACT Mike Meyer
mikem@stat.cmu.edu
FREE

gopher://lib.stat.cmu.edu/

Time Flies Version 2.0 for NeXT ★★★

This site provides access to a demo version of Time Flies Version 2.0, a powerful management tool for NeXT. Time Flies features alarm clocks where the user can create, modify or delete alarms, set alarms to go off at any time, day or month, set alarms to send an email or a screen message and even set an alarm to delete itself when it goes off. The software also features cuckoo clocks and a stopwatch. In addition, a list of Internet archive servers providing access to Time Flies is posted. This software is also available on Paget Press' AppWrapper CD-ROM.

KEYWORDS   Software, Workstations
AUDIENCE   Computer Operators, Computer Users, NeXT Developers, NeXT Users
CONTACT   timebugs@mouthers.wa.com
FREE

ftp://ftp.halcyon.com/pub/nwnexus/next/demos/

Tom's Windows Bargain Bin ★

This page contains a small collection of shareware and freeware Windows utilities that can be downloaded. All programs require VBRUN300.DLL which can be downloaded from this site. Free programs include a Program Manager file access program, a slide (graphic format) viewer, and Notepad replacement.

KEYWORDS   Freeware, Operating Systems, Software, Utility Software
AUDIENCE   Computer Professionals, Computer Users, PC Users, Windows Users
FREE

http://foundation.mit.edu/cgi-bin/search-phone-list

University of Texas at Austin - Computation Center Anonymous FTP Server ★★★

This gopher provides access to an FTP server maintained by the Computation Center of the University of Texas at Austin. Some of the resources provided include images, GIF readers and writers, microcomputer software, and UNIX shareware.

KEYWORDS   Computer Science, Education (College/University), FTP (File Transfer Protocol)
AUDIENCE   Computer Users, Educators (University), Students (Secondary/College)
CONTACT   remark@ftp.cc.utexas.edu
FREE

gopher://bongo.cc.utexas.edu:3003/

 Virtual Roality Home Page ★★★

This page contains comics that are rendered in three dimensions. The author provides information on the applications used to create his comics, and provides MPEG animations of some of the scenes.

KEYWORDS   3-D, Comics, Humor, Images
AUDIENCE   Comics Enthusiasts, Virtual Reality Enthusiasts
CONTACT   Eric Scroger
   scroger@onramp.net
FREE

http://www.onramp.net/~scroger/vreality.html

 Visual Solutions Corporate Home Page ★★

This is the homepage for Visual Solutions, maker of VisSim for Windows, software used by scientists, mathematicians, and engineers. VisSim is a visual block diagram language for nonlinear dynamic simulation. This site provides information about frequency domain analysis, real-time simulation and control, neural nets, and a sample screenshot. A demo version of VisSim is available for downloading.

KEYWORDS   Engineering, Mathematics Software, Operating Systems, Science
AUDIENCE   Engineers, Mathematicians, Scientists, Windows Users
CONTACT   wwinfo@vissol.com
FREE

http://www.ultranet.com/biz/vissim/index.html

 Welcome to MAINSoft ★★★

This is the homepage for MAINSoft, provider of MAINWin, a Windows cross-development technology. MAINWin implements Windows APIs directly on UNIX, allowing Windows application developers to cross-develop their programs for UNIX workstations. This page provides access to a brochure and datasheet, FAQs, price lists, press releases, technical papers, and system requirements.

KEYWORDS   Operating Systems, Programming, Software Development, UNIX
AUDIENCE   Cross-Development Programmers, Software Programmers, UNIX Application Developers, Windows Application Developers
CONTACT   info@mainsoft.com
FREE

http://www.mainsoft.com/

 Welcome to Wavefront ★★★

The home page of Wavefront Technologies offers users information and examples on their professional animation software. There are pages with the latest news and information on Wavefront Technologies, product information, corporate and training information, and a gallery of stills and movies demonstrating the software's capabilities. There is also a collection of links to related servers and newsgroups on the Internet, as well as pages of Wavefront employees.

KEYWORDS   Animation, Computer Graphics, Computer Software
AUDIENCE   Animators, Computer Artists, Graphic Artists, Multimedia Developers
CONTACT   webmaster@wti.com
FREE

http://wavefront.wti.com

 Welcome to Windows Sources on the Web ★★★

This is the online version of Windows Sources, a Ziff-Davis publication. It includes the week's top stories about Windows, Windows NT, and Windows 95, new product releases, and Windows-related events. It provides download access to the month's utilities and shareware for Windows, as well as access to benchmark tests from the Ziff-Davis Benchmark Operation, and an index for Windows Sources back issues.

KEYWORDS   Operating Systems, Publishers
AUDIENCE   Computer Professionals, PC Programmers, PC Users, Windows Users
CONTACT   webeditor@winsources.ziff.com
FREE

http://www.ziff.com/~wsources/

Well Connected Mac ★★★★

This page presents the Macintosh Computer enthusiast with a plethora of useful links. Users will find links to Macintosh software archives, news and FAQs on Macintosh hardware and software, product reviews, as well as links to other Macintosh resources on the Internet.

KEYWORDS   Companies, Computer News, Computer Systems, FAQs (Frequently Asked Questions)
AUDIENCE   GUI Enthusiasts, Macintosh Users
CONTACT   Elliotte Rusty Harold
   elharo@shock.njit.edu
FREE

http://rever.nmsu.edu/~elharo/faq/Macintosh.html

 Wilson WindowWare Home Page ★

This page is the home of Wilson WindowWare which develops, recommends, and sells shareware, including WinBatch, WinEdit, and Address Manager that runs in the Microsoft Windows and Windows NT environments. This site includes Wilson shareware and links to other shareware resources.

KEYWORDS   Operating Systems, Publishing, Shareware
AUDIENCE   Computer Users, PC Users, Shareware Users, Windows Users
CONTACT   morriew@halcyon.com
FREE

http://oneworld.wa.com:80/wilson/pages/index.html

 Windows OnLine/WinOnLine Review ★★

This is the homepage for Windows OnLine, a subscription BBS devoted to Windows, DOS, and OS/2 shareware, and Windows Online Review (WOLR). The free online monthly magazine features Wolly's Shareware Briefs, reviews of Windows shareware, commercial software, hardware, multimedia, and books. There is also access to back issues of WOLR that are available via FTP.

- KEYWORDS: E-Zines, Operating Systems
- AUDIENCE: Computer Professionals, PC Users, Software Developers, Windows Users
- CONTACT: Steven Jay Cohen info@wol.com
- FREE

http://www.cris.com/WOL/

Wuarchive (Washington University Archive) ★★★★

This site is one of the largest publicly-available software archives on the Internet. Software is available for all types of computer systems, including Mac, PC, and UNIX systems. Among the plethora of packages available, users will find Internet software, graphics software, games, and much more.

- KEYWORDS: Freeware, Public Domain Software, Shareware, Washington University
- AUDIENCE: Computer Users, Internet Users
- CONTACT: archives@wugate.wustl.edu
- FREE

http://wuarchive.wustl.edu

ftp://wuarchive.wustl.edu/

Standards

See also
Communications · *Organizations*
Computing & Mathematics · *Organizations*
Internet · *Internet Protocols*

ACM Technical Standards Committee ★★

The mission of the Committee is to coordinate all official ACM participation in standards-related activities. This shall include designation of ACM memberships and liaisons in standards-related organizations and development of policy and procedures for ACM participation in standards-related activities. The committee is also charged with encouraging and coordinating individual SIG standards-related activities, and promoting the dissemination and understanding of standards-related information to ACM members. This page provides information about the committee and its members.

- KEYWORDS: Computing Services, Technical Support
- AUDIENCE: ACM Members, Computer Scientists, Programmers
- CONTACT: Gene Spafford spaf@cs.purdue.edu
- FREE

http://www.cs.purdue.edu/homes/spaf/acm/acm-tsc.html

ATM (Asynchronous Transfer Mode) Forum ★★★★

The ATM (Asynchronous Transfer Mode) Forum is a worldwide organization, aimed at promoting ATM as a technology for the future. ATM provides a multifunctional platform that can support a variety of services and traffic types. In addition, ATM is scalable. Membership information, committee and organization information, press releases, ATM basics, and some frequently asked questions can be accessed at this site.

- KEYWORDS: ATM (Asynchronous Transfer Mode), Associations, Networking, WANs (Wide Area Networks)
- AUDIENCE: Computer Professionals, Computer System Designers, Network Administrators, Systems Administrators
- CONTACT: Jason Dominguez webmaster@sbexpos.com
- FREE

http://www.atmforum.com/

Acropolis Home Page ★★★

The Acropolis is a WWW site dedicated to the advancement of electronic publishing with the Portable Document Format (PDF) and Adobe Acrobat (TM) software. The site includes a list of articles written in PDF format that also generally covers some aspect of publishing using the PDF standard. Some publications available here include issues of Acropolis magazine and SPIN (Service and Product Information Network). Users can also subscribe to Acropolis or read about its origins from a press release page.

- KEYWORDS: E-Zines, Electronic Publishing
- AUDIENCE: Adobe Users, Computer Users, Desktop Publishers, Graphic Artists, PDF Users, Publishers
- CONTACT: webmaster@acropolis.com
- FREE

http://www.interport.net:80/acropolis/

Ethernet Codes ★★★

This file contains information on various codes used on IEEE 802.3 and Ethernet. Ethernet is a set of LAN (Local Area Network) cabling specifications and protocols. Computers using TCP/IP frequently connect to the Internet via an Ethernet. This file also covers Ethernet hardware addresses, hardware, and literally hundreds of codes.

- KEYWORDS: Networking, Telecommunications
- AUDIENCE: Computer Professionals, Engineers, Network Developers, Network Users
- CONTACT: Brent Callaghan Brent.Callaghan@eng.sun.com
- FREE

ftp://ftp.switch.ch/docs/Ethernet-codes/Ethernet-codes

X Consortium ★★★

The primary purpose of the X Consortium at the Massachussetts Institute of Technology is to develop, evolve and maintain the X Window System, a vendor-neutral, system-architecture neutral, network-transparent windowing and user interface standard, and to perform other related research and experimentation in, and implementation of, open systems standards and technology. Links are provided to resources on X Consortium including Release 6 of the X Window System, general information about X, introduction to X Consortium, current projects, job postings and openings, an XJobs mailing list, consortium member organizations, and more.

- KEYWORDS: Employment, User Interface Standard, X Window System
- AUDIENCE: Computer Professionals, Computer Researchers, Mathematicians
- CONTACT: membership@x.org
- FREE

http://export.lcs.mit.edu/

ftp://ftp.x.org/

Statistics

See also
Computing & Mathematics · *Analysis*
Computing & Mathematics · *Applications*
Education · *Resources*

Journal of Statistics Education ★★★

This is a gopher server of the Journal of Statistics Education Information Service at the North Carolina State University. It contains information on the Journals, statistics education discussion archives, software, and more.

- KEYWORDS: Bilingual Education, Electronic Publishing, Statistics
- AUDIENCE: Educators (University), Statisticians, Students (University)
- FREE

gopher://jse.stat.ncsu.edu/

 Resampling Stats Home Page ★★★

The Resampling Stats home page provides information such as articles, books, puzzles and software on the new statistics of resampling. Resampling procedures use the given data to produce simulated 'resamples', the behavior of which is then observed. Readers may download the introductory text by Julian Simon 'Resampling - The New Statistics'. There is also a list of statistical software and links to related sites.

- KEYWORDS: Data Management, Probability, Scientific Research, Software
- AUDIENCE: Engineers, Researchers, Scientists, Statisticians
- CONTACT: Peter Bruce stats@resample.com
- FREE

http://www.statistics.com/

School of Statistics ★★

This server provides statistical software from the University of Minnesota School of Statistics. It also has a collection of announcements in various areas such as computer security and departmental seminar schedules. In addition, there is a collection of World War II memorabilia images.

- KEYWORDS: Software, Statistics
- AUDIENCE: Computer Users, History Buffs, Statisticians
- FREE

gopher://itasca.stat.umn.edu/

Systems

See also
Communications · *Networking*
Computing & Mathematics · *Operating Systems*
Engineering & Technology · *Technology*

Acorn Software Home Page ★★★

The Acorn Software, Inc. company provides storage systems solutions, software, and consulting services for open VMS/VAX and /AXP systems. The Home Page gives information about its products. There is access to the company branches and software development groups as well as links to product demonstrations.

KEYWORDS   Consulting Services, Product Information, Software Development, Technical Support
AUDIENCE   Business Professionals, Computer Users, Systems Administrators
CONTACT   info@acornsw.com
FREE

http://www.acornsw.com/

Center for Applied Parallel Processing ★★★★

The primary goal of the Center for Applied Parallel Processing (CAPP) is to facilitate the solution of Grand Challenge research problems through the deployment of scalable computing, and the development of scalable algorithms for such systems. This page offers information on the CAPP objectives, projects, papers, and parties involved in this research.

KEYWORDS   Concurrent Logic, Distributed Computing, Parallel Computation Research, Supercomputers
AUDIENCE   Computer Engineers, Concurrent Logic Programmers, Parallel Programmers
CONTACT   Oliver A. McBryan, Director
         mcbryan@cs.colorado.edu
FREE

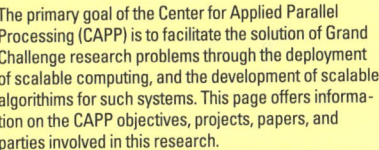

http://www.cs.colorado.edu/home/capp/Home.html

Clam Associates Home Page ★★★

Clam Associates provides development, porting, systems integration, education and support services on UNIX systems. The page presents information about the company's products and services. There are links to other resources on the Internet and job opportunities at CLAM.

KEYWORDS   Companies, Product Information, Systems Administration, Unix
AUDIENCE   Systems Administrators, UNIX Users
CONTACT   webmaster@clam.com
FREE

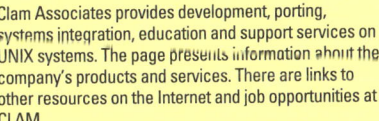

http://www.clam.com/

Computer and Communications Research Center (CCRC) at Washington University ★★★

This is the home page for the Computer and Communications Research Center (CCRC) at Washington University. CCRC provides an interdepartmental research environment in the areas of computer architecture, telecommunications, systems design, and parallel processing. Among the links are student home pages, research findings from the journal, 'IEEE/ACM Transactions on Networking' and news from the Industrial Partnership Program (which contains information about applications of computer networking research). Other items available from this page include educational programs in Computer Engineering and Networking.

KEYWORDS   Telecommunications, Universities
AUDIENCE   Computer Designers, Computer Scientists, Telecommunications Researchers
CONTACT   Chuck Cranor
         chuck@maria.wustl.edu
FREE

http://dworkin.wustl.edu/

ETH Zurich, Electronics Lab, High Performance Computing Home Page ★★

This server offers access to information about the Lab's experimental parallel computers. Users will find pictures, statistics, and schematic information about the computers, as well as some descriptions of their applications. There is also information available about the computers' bus, network architecture and programming environment.

KEYWORDS   Computer Hardware, Supercomputers
AUDIENCE   Computer Researchers, Computer Scientists, Parallel Computing Researchers
CONTACT   Martin Frey
         frey@ife.ee.ethz.ch
FREE

http://www.ife.ee.ethz.ch/music/hpc.html

HaL Computer Systems, Inc. ★★★

This is the home page of HaL Computer Systems, Inc., a UNIX systems company. Users can find company and product information, as well as current job opportunities available here. In addition, various HaL employees' personal home pages can also be browsed through.

KEYWORDS   Computer Systems, Operating Systems
AUDIENCE   Computer Professionals, UNIX Users
CONTACT   webmaster@hal.com
FREE

http://www.hal.com/

Harvard Network Device Test Lab ★★★

This gopher server contains information related to computers and computer networking. The site provides performance test results on bridge, switch and router systems run at the Harvard Network Device Test Lab. It also provides access to the Harvard University telephone directories.

KEYWORDS   Networking, Universities
AUDIENCE   Educators (University), Network Developers
FREE

gopher://ndtl.harvard.edu/

High Rate Mobile Internet Home Page ★★★

This site contains information on the High Data Rate MObile interNET (MONET). MONET will demonstrate the technologies required to develop a Department of Defense network that is interoperable with the future public-carrier networks, and which will provide reliable high data rate connectivity using mobile RF communication links and will support all types of media including data, voice, imagery, fax, and video teleconferencing.

KEYWORDS   Computer Technology, Mobile Computing, Telecommunications
AUDIENCE   Communications Specialists, Computer Researchers
CONTACT   Rico Cheng
         rcheng@nosc.mil
FREE

http://fury.nosc.mil/

IBM Kiosk for Education at the University of Washington ★★★

This gopher is a higher education information service funded by IBM and developed and operated by the Center for Information Systems Optimization at the University of Washington. It offers information such as news, announcements, academic technology services, software, publications and archives. This site also has links to other IBM-related gophers.

KEYWORDS   Community Services, Companies, Universities
AUDIENCE   Computer Professionals, Computer Users, Scientists, Students (Secondary/University)
CONTACT   ike@ike.engr.washington.edu
FREE

http://ike.engr.washington.edu/

gopher://isaac.engr.washington.edu/

Institute for Systems Architecture ★★★

The Institute for Systems Architecture page gives information about micro programming, ISA news, Unix systems and computer programming. The site provides links to the Institute's facilities and other related WWW sites.

KEYWORDS   Computer Programming, Programming Languages, Unix
AUDIENCE   Computer Scientists, Programmers, Systems Architects
CONTACT   webmaster@www.Informatik.th-darmstadt.de
FREE

http://www.isa.informatik.th-darmstadt.de

Institute of Systems Sciences ★★★

The Institute of Systems Sciences does information technology research for the National University of Singapore. The home page offers information on the Institute, current research projects, publications and training programs. This site gives links to information and systems groups as well as the university's facilities.

KEYWORDS Computer Applications, Fuzzy Logic, Information Technology
AUDIENCE Computer Scientists, Information Technologists, Systems Administrators
FREE

http://www.iss.nus.sg

International Computer Science Institute ★★★

The International Computer Science Institute conducts research in massively parallel compuing systems, high speed networks, and distributed multimedia systems. Their home page offers technical reports and overviews describing the Institute's research, information about seminars offered, and other material on the Institute's mission, staff, and facilities. There are also links to detailed descriptions of the institute's current projects, as well as public FTP and gopher directories maintained by the institute.

KEYWORDS Artificial Intelligence, Supercomputers
AUDIENCE Computer Researchers, Computer Scientists, Parallel Computing Researchers, Students
FREE

http://http.icsi.berkeley.edu/

Learnix Educational Services - Catalog ★★

This is the Windows NT support page from Learnix Educational Services. Learnix provides training for system administrators who need to install, configure, optimize, and support the Microsoft Windows NT 3.5 Server. This page provides information about Microsoft Windows NT educational programs.

KEYWORDS Education, Networking, Operating Systems
AUDIENCE Computer Professionals, Network Administrators, Systems Administrators, Windows NT Administrators
FREE

http://www.learnix.ca/cat_mswinnt.html

MIT (Massachusetts Institute of Technology) Parallel and Distributed Operating Systems Group ★★★

The MIT LCS Parallel and Distributed Operating Systems group conducts software research for parallel and distributed computing systems, spanning a wide-range of areas including operating systems, networking, mobile computing, language design, compilers, and architecture. A current project is a new operating system architecture called an exokernel, which works on multiplexing the raw hardware. There are a number of technical reports and publications on this site, covering operating systems, the exokernel, and other research areas.

KEYWORDS Distributed Computing, Parallel Computing, Universities
AUDIENCE Computer Designers, Computer Scientists, Computer System Architects
CONTACT wchsieh@lcs.mit.edu
FREE

http://amsterdam.lcs.mit.edu/

Mediated Information Systems Technology Research Group ★★★

The Mediated Architectures Research Group is dedicated to developing components for mediated information systems. This page provides information about their projects—Persistent Storage Technologies; Intelligent Agent Integration Technology, which is developing a protocol and language for intelligent agents; and the Knowledge Sharing Effort with an agent communication language. Also included are recent papers by staff members on topics such as 'KQML - An Information and Knowledge Exchange Protocol.'

KEYWORDS Communications Research, Information Systems, Programming, Protocols
AUDIENCE Engineers, Information Scientists, Programmers
CONTACT Don McKay
mckay@vfl.paramax.com
FREE

http://louise.vfl.paramax.com/

Microelectromechanical Systems Clearinghouse ★★★

This Clearinghouse is designed to be a resource for information about MicroElectroMechnical Systems (MEMS), created by the ESTO (Electronic Systems Technology Office). Materials included consist of a quarterly newsletter discussing MEMS, and information about materials and projects of the fabrication facilities that do MEMS work, and a moderated discussion group. The Clearinghouse Archives include bibliographies of journals, and dissertation abstracts which offer discussion of topics such as Silicon Micromachined Devices. Also included are links to the ESTO home page, with articles and research materials about the electronics industry.

KEYWORDS Electronics, Information Systems, Nanotechnology
AUDIENCE Computer Scientists, Engineers
CONTACT info-mems@isi.edu
FREE

http://mems.isi.edu

Parallel and Distributed Operatings Systems Group ★★★

The Parallel and Distributed Operating Systems group conducts software research for parallel and distributed computing systems. This site has information on simplifying the parallel and distributed programming process, building efficient distributed systems with off-the-shelf technology that also can be used for parallel supercomputing, and building high performance storage services for these systems.

KEYWORDS Computer Applications, Computer Programming, Telecommunications
AUDIENCE Communications Specialists, Computer Specialists, Computer Students
CONTACT wchsieh@lcs.mit.edu
FREE

http://www.pdos.lcs.mit.edu/

Parallel Computing Archive at Hensa UNIX ★★★

This web archive offers information and resources related to high-performance parallel computing. The site specializes in transputers and the occam language developed to program parallel computers, though it offers a wide variety of parallel computing materials. Users will find indexes of books, bibliographies, FAQs, standards documents, pointers to software libraries, and much more.

KEYWORDS Computer Hardware, Supercomputers
AUDIENCE Computer Researchers, Computer Scientists, Parallel Computing Researchers
CONTACT Dave Beckett
D.J.Beckett@ukc.ac.uk
FREE

http://www.hensa.ac.uk/parallel/

Parallel Tools Consortium ★★★

This page is a resource for research in parallel computing tools, including programming and debugging environments, file browsers, message queuing systems, and operating systems. It offers detailed descriptions and examples of tools in development, material on the staff and facilities, and information on submission of projects to the lab. Users may also access sections on parallel computing conferences, information on the lab by-laws and steering committee, and pointers to other parallel tool projects on the Internet.

KEYWORDS Computer Programming, Supercomputers
AUDIENCE Computer Researchers, Computer Scientists, Parallel Computing Researchers
CONTACT Sam Coleman
scoleman@llnl.gov
FREE

http://www.llnl.gov/ptools/ptools.html

Public Access Computer Systems Review ★★★

This gopher houses the Public Access Computer Systems Review, an electronic newsletter devoted to publically accessible computer systems available in libraries. It covers such topics as electronic publishing, campus-wide information systems, CD-ROM LANs, document delivery systems, and other issues related to public computer systems. Users will find an archive of past issues going back to 1990, as well as the most current issue, a compressed archive of all back issues, author guidelines, and more.

KEYWORDS Computer Systems, Informatics, Magazines
AUDIENCE Computer Users, Educators, Librarians

CONTACT Charles W. Bailey, Jr.
cbailey@uh.edu

FREE

gopher://info.lib.uh.edu/11/articles/e-journals/uhlibrary/pacsreview

SIGARCH (Special Interest Group for Computer Architecture) ★★★★

ACM Special Interest Group on Architecture of Computer Systems serves a unique community of computer professionals working on the forefront of computer design in both industry and academia. It is ACM's primary forum for interchange of ideas about tomorrow's hardware. The gopher server provides information about SIGARCH and becoming a member, as well as links to other hardware design related pages.

KEYWORDS Computer Systems Architecture, Hardware Design, Parallel Computing
AUDIENCE Computer Hardware Users, Computer Professionals, Computer System Designers
CONTACT David A. Patterson - SIG Chair
chair_SIGARCH@acm.org

FREE

gopher://gopher.acm.org/11[the_files.sig_forums.sigarch]

SIGOIS (Special Interest Group for Office Information Systems) ★★★

ACM Special Interest Group on Office Information Systems is interested in topics related to computer-based systems that have a team, group, organizational or societal impact/goal. The scope extends beyond office environments and business to other environments, such as educational, military and hospital. Relevant issues include the design, implementation, evaluation and methodologies that are concerned when researching and developing c-b systems. The gopher site provides information on SIGOIS, its conferences and membership.

KEYWORDS Computer Workgroups, Design, Information Systems
AUDIENCE ACM Members, Computer Professionals, Computer Scientists, Information Scientists
CONTACT Carson Woo SIG Chair
chair_SIGOIS@acm.org

FREE

gopher://gopher.acm.org/11[the_files.sig_forums.sigois]

SIGOPS (Special Interest Group for Operating Systems) ★★★

ACM Special Interest Group on Operating Systems addresses a broad spectrum of issues associated with operating systems research and development. Although many of the members are drawn from industry, academic and government professionals are also represented in the membership. This SIG supports many conferences and workshops, including The SIGOPS European Workshop, held in Europe in alternative years. This gopher site provides information

---

Connections to Shareware
Some of it is free, but all of it's a deal ...

Welcome to RKS Software, Inc.!

RKS Software specializes in high quality shareware programs for the home and office. We are a member of the Association of Shareware Professionals (ASP), and the Shareware Trade Association and Resources (STAR) group.

Perhaps you're looking for software that helps you perform a specific task, but can't find precisely what you need in retail outlets. Are you being overlooked by the mainstream software suppliers? Don't despair. On the Internet there are many software developers and software developer wanna-be's who have created games and productivity applications that you won't find at a retail software outlet or even in a software catalog.

With shareware, you can get programs like "Baseball Stats for Windows," which provides coaching tool software to keep batting, pitching, fielding and stolen base stats. It also helps the user keep track easily by sorting the information as it is updated.

(http://www.peak.org/~beng/whatis.html)

"Gotcha!" is a software shareware program accessed through RKS Software, Inc. that makes it easy for police departments to keep arrest records. It includes a database that gives police the ability to quickly search, access, and maintain records.

(http://www.execpc.com/rks/)

"Aunt Annie's Crafts" provides you with a Windows program for various craft projects. The site includes patterns, illustrated instructions, and informative narratives about handcrafts. Or, you and the kids can try out "Bert's Coloring Programs," which is designed to acquaint children with the computer. You can try the coloring program out before you buy.

(http://www.dnaco.net/~dalafara/annie.html)

---

about the SIGOPS organization including membership, conferences, and an annual report.

KEYWORDS Design, Operating Systems, Research & Development
AUDIENCE ACM Members, Computer Programmers, Computer Scientists, Computer System Designers
CONTACT Henry M. Levy SIG Chair
chair_SIGOPS@acm.org

FREE

gopher://gopher.acm.org/11[the_files.sig_forums.sigops]

Sandia National Labs Massively Parallel Computing Research Laboratory (MPCRL) ★★★★

The Sandia National Labs Massively Parallel Computing Research Laboratory (MPCRL) is conducting research into various aspects of parallel computing. The site offers access to technical reports and research bulletins produced by the lab. Users can also access descriptions of the lab's computers and facilities, as well as a public ftp directory containing source code, papers, and more.

KEYWORDS Computer Hardware, Supercomputers
AUDIENCE Computer Researchers, Computer Scientists, Parallel Computing Researchers
CONTACT www-admin@www.cs.sandia.gov

FREE

http://www.cs.sandia.gov/MPCRL/MPCRL_home_page.html

Scandal Supercomputing Project Home Page ★★★

This site offers information and resources about the Scandal Supercomputing Project, which is developing a portable, interactive programming environment for many different types of supercomputing hardware. They are pursuing two main goals - development of a portable language that supports parallel computing hardware, and an optimization of current algorithmic technology for parallel computing.

KEYWORDS Computer Hardware, Supercomputers
AUDIENCE Computer Researchers, Computer Scientists, Parallel Computing Researchers
CONTACT Jonathan Hardwick
jch@cs.cmu.edu

FREE

http://parallel.scandal.cs.cmu.edu/www/

Systems and Software Technology WWW Server ★★★

This Web site was created by the Systems and Software Technology Division of the Computer Systems Laboratory (CSL) at the National Institute of Standards and Technology (NIST). This site provides background about systems and software technology and gives project and activity reports for the different research groups. Several online publications are included, with federal information about processing standards. Directories to other related research fields are linked, such as multimedia, integrated software engineering, and Xbase.

KEYWORDS Distributed Computing, Software Engineering
AUDIENCE Software Engineers, Systems Engineers
CONTACT Bob Bagwell
robert.bagwill@nist.gov
FREE

http://nemo.ncsl.nist.gov

Wang's Bookshelf (Parallel Computing) ★★★★

This site offers a comprehensive index to many resources related to parallel computing. Users will find links to topics in distributed batch processing, supercomputer labs, fault tolerance issues, compilers and parallelizers, and much more. There is also a section that users can use to search for parallel computing resources available via FTP, gopher, or on the web.

KEYWORDS Computer Hardware, Computer Programming, Supercomputers
AUDIENCE Computer Researchers, Computer Scientists, Parallel Computing Researchers
CONTACT Jonathan Wang
jwang@suned.cs.yale.edu
FREE

http://perch.cs.yale.edu:8001/

World-Wide Web Virtual Library - Concurrent Systems ★★★★

This document contains some pointers to information on concurrent systems available around the world on the World Wide Web. Links for accessing online information in the following categories are available—electronic repositories, research groups and centers, research projects, tools, process algebras, meetings and journals.

KEYWORDS Computer Programming, Concurrent Logic, Concurrent Systems
AUDIENCE Computer Programmers, Computer Scientists, Concurrent Logic Programmers
CONTACT Jonathan Bowen
Jonathan.Bowen@comlab.ox.ac.uk
FREE

http://www.comlab.ox.ac.uk/archive/concurrent.html

Theory

See also
Computing & Mathematics · *Computer Science*
Computing & Mathematics · *Mathematics*
Science · *Physics*

Center for Information Technology at University of Michigan ★★★

This is a gopher server of the Center for Information Technology (CITI) of the University of Michigan. It provides information on CITI projects and CITI technical reports. In addition, access to other gopher servers on campus is provided.

KEYWORDS Computer Applications, Computer Science, Michigan
AUDIENCE Computer Professionals, Computer Students
FREE

gopher://gopher.citi.umich.edu/

Information Mechanics ★★★

This page presents the specialized work of the Information Mechanics Group at the MIT Laboratory of Computer Science. Information mechanics involves the study of the physics of computation and of cellular automata computational machines. Visitors to this site will find detailed information on this research, along with postscript papers and brochures describing the research in more detail. In addition, this server boasts a collection of links to related information on the net.

KEYWORDS Computer Science, Universities
AUDIENCE Computer Scientists, Educators, Electrical Engineers, Students
CONTACT webmaster@im.lcs.mit.edu
FREE

http://www-im.lcs.mit.edu

The Logic Group ★★★

The Logic Group is a research group that primarily focuses on logical systems and information processing systems, and their Web page provides information about their projects. Projects described include CommerceNet, an online electronic 'commerce' system using online catalogs and information services, and RegNet, which is creating a nationwide regulatory system for all types of information. Also included in this site are technical reports for these projects and other Logic Groups Publications, as well as links to educational materials about logic. Users may also access and download software for information manipulation.

KEYWORDS Algorithms, Information Systems, Logic, Programming
AUDIENCE Computer Programmers, Logicians, Mathematicians
CONTACT Michael R. Genesereth
genesereth@cs.stanford.edu
FREE

http://logic.stanford.edu/

Opt-Net Home Page ★★★

Opt-net is an electronic forum designed to meet the needs of the optimization community. It is installed at the Konrad-Zuse-Zentrum fur Informationstechnik in Berlin (ZIB), and it can be accessed through the Internet and most academic and post office networks. The basic services provided by Opt-Net are a weekly digest containing a moderated list of contributions, a unique email address for each subscriber, white page service and an archive of the digest.

KEYWORDS Algorithms, Computer Programming, Numerical Analysis, Optimization
AUDIENCE Mathematicians, Numerical Analysts
CONTACT Mike Dowling
opt-net-adm@zib-berlin.de
FREE

http://moa.math.nat.tu-bs.de/opt-net/opt-net.html

ftp://elib.zib-berlin.de/pub/opt-net

SIGACT (Special Interest Group for Algorithms and Computational Theory) ★★★★

This is the Association for Computing Machinery's page for the special interest group for Theoretical Computer Science (SIGACT). Theoretical Computer Science provides the fundamental concepts, principles, and techniques needed to understand and cope with the rapidly changing field of computer technology. SIGACT's role is to foster and promote the discovery and dissemination of research results, and excellence in instruction at all levels. This page offers information on conferences and synposiums, pointers to other theoretical computer science pages, and SIGACT News.

KEYWORDS Computer Science, Concurrent Logic
AUDIENCE ACM Members, Computer Professionals, Computer Programmers, Computer Scientists
CONTACT Ian Parberry
ian@hercule.csci.unt.edu
FREE

http://hercule.csci.unt.edu:80/sigact/

TOC - Theory of Computation Group ★★★

This is the home page for the Theory of Computation Group at MIT's Computer Science Lab (Massachusetts Institute of Technology). It offers access to information on the Group's projects, facilities, and staff, as well as a listing of other resources related to computational theory. In addition, users will find material on seminars that the Group hosts, as well as an FTP archive of computer algorithms and other related material.

KEYWORDS Algorithms, Massachusetts, Universities
AUDIENCE Computer Scientists, Software Engineers
CONTACT webmaster@theory.lcs.mit.edu
FREE

http://theory.lcs.mit.edu/

Visual Math Institute ★★★

The Visual Math Institute (VMI) at the University of California at Santa Cruz was created in 1975 to administer grants from the State of California and the National Science Foundation. Since 1990, the VMI has been supported by small grants from individuals, to continue the creation of new materials relating to chaos theory, and its applications in the sciences and arts. The VMI server also provides information about the ancient mathematicians Euclid and Hypatia.

KEYWORDS Chaos Theory, Mathematics
AUDIENCE Economists, Historians, Mathematicians
CONTACT Ralph Abraham
rha@cats.ucsc.edu
FREE

http://hypatia.ucsc.edu/

gopher://hypatia.ucsc.edu/

Education

Academic Libraries	233
Alternative Education	237
Career & Employment	237
Continuing Education	239
Curriculum & Instruction	240
Distance Education	241
Educational Issues	242
Educational Policy	243
Educational Projects	244
Educational Technology	246
Funding	249
Government Libraries	250
International Education	250
Language Acquisition	252
Organizations	252
Primary & Secondary Education	255
Professional Education	260
Public Libraries	260
Resources	261
Special Libraries	263
Universities - Africa	264
Universities - Asia	264
Universities - Australia	266
Universities - Canada	267
Universities - Europe	270
Universities - South America	275
Universities - United States	276
Vocational Education	288

Academic Libraries

See also
Education · *Universities - Europe*
Education · *Universities - United States*

Arizona State University Gopher

This is a gopher server of the Arizona State University in Tempe. It contains information on the University Library and its resources and services such as catalogs, electronic books and journals, and more.
KEYWORDS   Education (College/University), Libraries, Library Science, Universities
AUDIENCE   Educators (University), Students (College/University)
FREE

gopher://info.lib.asu.edu/

Atkins Library at UNC Charlotte

This gopher server is a source of information about the Atkins Library at the University of North Carolina at Charlotte. Among the information resources provided here is access to the library catalog, details of opening hours and library services, and a media services directory.
KEYWORDS   Education (College/University), Information Science, Libraries, Library Science
AUDIENCE   Educators, Students (Secondary/University)
FREE

gopher://library.uncc.edu/

Australian National University Electronic Library Information Service

This site provides access to library services at the Australian National University (ANU) and other institutions, access to databases at ANU, and access to library catalogs at most major libraries in the world. The information is maintained by the Australian National University Library. Access to most of Australia's Online Library systems is available from within this gopher site.
KEYWORDS   Information Science, OPACs (Online Public Access Catalogs), Universities (Australia)
AUDIENCE   Educators, Librarians, Library Users, Students
CONTACT   Mark Nearhos
          Mark.Nearhos@anu.edu.au
FREE

gopher://info.anu.edu.au/

Bladen Library WWW Server

The Bladen Library is part of the University of Toronto, and their Web site provides information about their services as well as links to educational and information resources all over the web. Bladen Library materials include library guides, lists of books in their archives and request forms for book ordering. There are also searchable indexes for the University of Toronto archives, with results coming back in citation or full listing form.
KEYWORDS   Internet Resources, Library Access
AUDIENCE   Canada Residents, Educators, Researchers, Students (University)
CONTACT   crichton@macpost.scar.utoronto.ca
FREE

http://library-gopher.scar.utoronto.ca/

Carleton University Libraries

The site is a gopher server of the Carleton University Library in Ottawa, Canada. It provides information on the Carleton University library system, collections, news, library tours and orientation, electronic resources and more. It also includes catalogues of other libraries in Ontario.
KEYWORDS   Canada, Education (College/University), Libraries, Library Science
AUDIENCE   Canadians, Educators (University), Library Users, Students (University)
CONTACT   Rob McDonald
          Rob_McDonald@carleton.ca
FREE

gopher://library3.carleton.ca/

Colorado State University William E Morgan Library

This library's collections are large and wide-ranging. You must telnet to the site and Login as PAC Select 5 for VT100 emulation. To exit, type //exit
KEYWORDS   Germany, Libraries, OPACs (Online Public Access Catalogs), Vietnam War
AUDIENCE   General Public, Researchers, Students
FREE

telnet://pac.carl.org

Duke Library System

This is a gopher server of the Duke University Library system in Durham, North Carolina. It contains information on library resources, phone books, hours, bibliographies, music archives, online catalogs, news, weather, sports, and more. It also has links to other library gophers and gophers on the Internet.
KEYWORDS   Education (College/University), Libraries, Library Science

Academic Libraries

AUDIENCE Educators (University), Library Users, Students (University)

FREE

gopher://iliad.lib.duke.edu/

The Electronic Text Center-University of Virginia ★★★★

The Electronic Text Center at the University of Virginia provides an online archive of thousands of SGML-encoded electronic texts with a library-based Center which contains hardware and software suitable for the creation and analysis of text. The Center provides ongoing training sessions and support of individual teaching and research projects. Topics include The Online Library of Electronic Texts, Training and Users, The Staff, The Online Scholarship Initiative (a new etext service), selected articles concerning electronic texts, projects, and other web servers.

KEYWORDS Electronic Text, Research Projects, Software
AUDIENCE , Computer Professionals, Computer Users, Educators (University), Internet Users, Physicists, Researchers, Students (University)
CONTACT etext@virginia.edu
FREE

http://www.lib.virginia.edu/etext/ETC.html

Indiana University - Purdue University Indianapolis Library ★★★

This page is presented by the Indiana University - Purdue University Indianapolis Library. Users can access a variety of information such as a catalog of the library's resources via telnet, links to other Indiana University campuses, maps, technical documentation, and more.

KEYWORDS OPACs (Online Public Access Catalogs)
AUDIENCE Educators, Students
FREE

http://www-lib.iupui.edu

Iowa State University Library WWW Server ★★★

The Iowa State University Library WWW Server provides information on the Library's hours, calendar of events and collections. This page gives links to other ISU servers and resources.

KEYWORDS Education (College/University), Iowa
AUDIENCE Librarians, Researchers, Students
CONTACT jvc@iastate.edu
FREE

http://www.lib.iastate.edu

James Cook University Library ★★★

This is the gopher server for the main library of James Cook University in Australia. It gives access to the library's catalogs, provides information on the library's facilities and collections, and serves internal newsletters and publications. There are also links to other library sites on the Internet and to the University's gopher server.

KEYWORDS Information Science, Libraries, Library Science, Universities
AUDIENCE Educators, Library Administrators, Library Users, Students
CONTACT jcu.library@jcu.edu.au
FREE

gopher://jculib.jcu.edu.au/

Libraries at Yale University ★★★

This gopher site provides access to resources of the Yale University Libraries—catalogs for libraries both at Yale and elsewhere, and library bulletin boards. There are also connections to manuscript and archive repositories at Johns Hopkins University.

KEYWORDS Education (College/University), Libraries, Library Science
AUDIENCE Academics, Librarians, Students (University)
CONTACT gophadmi@gopher.yale.edu
FREE

gopher://gopher.yale.edu:7000/

Libraries of the University of Toronto ★★★

The site is a gopher server of the University of Toronto Library in Toronto, Canada. It provides a wide variety of policies, calendars, schedules, publications, activities, services, news, and events both in the library and at the University of Toronto in general. In addition, access to other University of Toronto gophers, and worldwide Internet connections are provided.

KEYWORDS Canada, Education (College/University), Libraries, Library Science
AUDIENCE Educators (University), Librarians, Library Users, Students (University)
FREE

gopher://utl.library.utoronto.ca/

Lund University Library ★★★

This is a gopher server of the Lund University Library (UB2), Sweden. It contains information on the Lund University Electronic Library Service, WAIS databases, news, library catalogs, research projects, publications, and more. It has links to other gophers as well.

KEYWORDS Education (College/University), Libraries, Library Science, Sweden
AUDIENCE Educators (University), Students (University), Swedes
CONTACT Anders Ardo anders@munin.ub2.lu.se
FREE

gopher://gopher.ub2.lu.se/

MELVYL System Welcome Page ★★★

The MELVYL system is a computer-based library system created by the University of California that allows users to search a variety of bibliographic databases. Among the items indexed are the entire collections of the University of California campuses, the California State Library in Sacramento, as well as many other collections. Each MELVYL Catalog book record contains all information normally found on catalog cards, as well as the specific location for each holding. Periodical records list title, publisher, holdings notes, subjects, and locations.

KEYWORDS Bibliographies, Information Retrieval, Internet Directories, Library Science
AUDIENCE Academics, Librarians, Library Users, Researchers
CONTACT melvyl@dla.ucop.edu
FREE

http://dla.ucop.edu

ftp://dla.ucop.edu/pub/

telnet://melvyl.ucop.edu

Murdoch University ★★

This is the central gopher server for Murdoch University in Australia. It provides access to the University library's catalogs, gives information about computing facilities at the University, and provides access to other educational sites and resources.

KEYWORDS Australia, OPACs (Online Public Access Catalogs), Universities, University Administration
AUDIENCE Educators, Students
CONTACT Neil Huck huck@csuvax1.csu.murdoch.edu.au
FREE

gopher://infolib.murdoch.edu.au/

North Carolina State University Libraries ★★★

This gopher site provides information about the North Carolina State University Libraries, gives access to government databases, and lets the user browse an online library with catalogs, reference books, dictionaries, and more. The site also provides access to other North Carolina State University resources, as well as providing connections to other gopher holes on the Internet.

KEYWORDS Information Science, Libraries, Library Science, Online Services
AUDIENCE Internet Users, Library Administrators, Library Users, Students
FREE

gopher://dewey.lib.ncsu.edu/

Northwestern University Library Gopher ★★★

This gopher provides access to the Northwestern University Libraries, including descriptions of their holdings and facilities and access to the online catalog. There are also links to other Northwestern University gopher holes and to other library gopher holes across the Internet. Additionally, there are links to some locations on the Internet that provide online news or magazine services.

KEYWORDS Libraries, Library Science, News
AUDIENCE Educators, Library Administrators, Students, Students (University)

Academic Libraries

CONTACT Vincent McCoy
vmccoy@nwu.edu

FREE

gopher://beton.library.nwu.edu/

The Penn Library Gopher ★★★

This site is a gopher server of the University of Pennsylvania Library in Philadelphia. It provides information on Penn Library catalogs, electronic journals, area studies-related resources, biomedical resources, business resources, science resources, humanities resources, social science resources and more. It also contains information on several other library catalogs such as the Temple University Library, the Princeton University Library, the Library of Congress, and other library catalogs.

KEYWORDS Community Services, Education (College/University), Libraries
AUDIENCE Educators (University), Librarians, Library Users, Students (University)
CONTACT librefer@pobox.upenn.edu

FREE

gopher://gopher.library.upenn.edu/

Penn State University Libraries Information Server ★★★

This site is a gopher server of the Pennsylvania State University Libraries in University Park. It contains information on library resources, online catalogs, library computing services, and more. It also has a link to the Penn State University gopher.

KEYWORDS Education (College/University), Libraries, Library Science
AUDIENCE Educators (University), Library Users, Students (University)
CONTACT Gopher@psulias.psu.edu

FREE

gopher://psulias.psu.edu/

Princeton University Libraries' Gopher ★★★

This gopher hole is provided by the Princeton University Libraries. It provides access to the online library catalog. It also gives information about the library's holdings and services.

KEYWORDS Information Science, Libraries, Library Science
AUDIENCE Educators, Librarians, Library Users, Students
CONTACT Marvin Bielawski
marvinb@firestone.Princeton.EDU

FREE

gopher://library.princeton.edu/

Royal Melbourne Institute of Technology Libraries ★★★

The Royal Melbourne Institute of Technology (RMIT) is the largest multi-level university in Australia, training students for careers in applied science, business, design, and engineering. Through RMIT's expansive home page, users can access several libraries' gophers and catalogs, Project Gutenberg's online books through journal databases, and a bounty of departmental information. Links to an eclectic mix of non-academic sites, such as news about Australia and the WWW, are also available. Under the Month's Special and Previous Months' Specials headings, one can find electronic issues of Wired and Time magazines, texts of Northern Territory legislation, and, best of all, Exquisite Corpse, a site consisting of random—often hilarious—phrases like 'sliding gouda is a tragedy waiting to unfold.'

KEYWORDS Information Science, Internet Publishing, Libraries, Universities
AUDIENCE Australians, Librarians, Library Administrators, Library Users, Students
CONTACT Damian Kelly
ryldk@minyos.xx.rmit.edu.au

FREE

http://millbrook.lib.rmit.edu.au/
gopher://millbrook.lib.rmit.edu.au/

The Rutgers University Library ★★

This is a gopher server of Rutgers University Library. It contains information on library resources and services, librarians, the online catalog, and more. In addition, it has links to other library resources available on the Internet.

KEYWORDS Education (College/University), Libraries, Library Science
AUDIENCE Educators (University), Library Users, Students (University)

FREE

gopher://info.rutgers.edu:71/

The SUNY Office of Library Services Gopher ★★

This is a gopher server of the Office of Library Services, State University of New York (SUNY), Central Administration in Albany. It provides access to the SUNY Library Automation and Implementation Program, a network of catalogs for SUNY libraries, as well as to other gophers at all SUNY campuses. It also has links to New York State information resources.

KEYWORDS Education (College/University), Libraries, Library Science
AUDIENCE Educators (University), Library Users, Students (College/University)

FREE

gopher://slscva.ca.sunycentral.edu/

Stanford University Libraries Cecil H Green Library ★★★★

This library's collections are large and wide ranging. To access this site, at the Account prompt, type socrates, At the Type of terminal? prompt, type VT100. To exit type END.

KEYWORDS History, Libraries, OPACs (Online Public Access Catalogs), Transportation
AUDIENCE General Public, Researchers, Students

FREE

telnet://forsythetn.stanford.edu

THOR+ ★★★

THOR+ is the name of the gopher that provides information about the Purdue University libraries in West Lafayette, Indiana. The information on THOR+ is, among other things, about library resources, library administration, and library catalogs. THOR+ provides access to gopher servers at Purdue University and elsewhere.

KEYWORDS Information Science, Libraries, Library Science
AUDIENCE Librarians, Library Users, Students (University)
CONTACT Carl Snow
gophadm@thorplus.lib.purdue.edu

FREE

gopher://thorplus.lib.purdue.edu/

UR Libraries Gopher ★★★

This site gives information about the River Campus Libraries at the University of Rochester in New York. It includes a description of the libraries, their services, and their hours. The gopher also provides a link to their online catalog and links to other library servers across the Internet.

KEYWORDS Information Science, Libraries, New York
AUDIENCE Educators (University), Library Users, Students (University)
CONTACT Margaret Becket
reca@db1.cc.rochester.edu

FREE

gopher://rodent.lib.rochester.edu/

University of Chicago Library ★★★★

This library's collections are large and wide-ranging. At the ENTER CLASS prompt, type lib48. When CONNECTED appears on the screen, press RETURN. To exit, type LOGOUT.

KEYWORDS Drama, Libraries, OPACs (Online Public Access Catalogs), Poetry
AUDIENCE General Public, Researchers, Students

FREE

telnet://olorin.uchicago.edu

The University of Arizona Library Gopher Server ★★★

This gopher site provides resources for The University of Arizona Library users. It includes electronic journals, University of Arizona local resources, national and international resources, and search capabilities using Veronica. It also includes links to other reference resources as well as to other gophers.

KEYWORDS Databases, Information Retrieval, Libraries
AUDIENCE Librarians, Library Administrators, Library Users, Researchers
CONTACT Mohamed Taleb
talebm@ccit.arizona.edu

FREE

gopher://miles.library.arizona.edu/

Academic Libraries

University of California at Berkeley Library ★★★

This is a gopher server of the Library of the University of California at Berkeley. It provides information on libraries, data owner resource tools, electronic journals, information system instructions and support, library electronic mail, the staff, the phone directory, meeting minutes, news and more. In addition, it makes connections to University of California online services and University of California at Berkeley online services.

- **KEYWORDS** Computer Databases, Education (College/University), Libraries
- **AUDIENCE** Librarians, Library Administrators, Library Users, Students (University)
- **CONTACT** Roy Tennant
  rtennant@library.berkeley.edu
- **FREE**

gopher://infolib.berkeley.edu:72/

University of California at San Diego University Libraries ★★★

This library's collections are large and wide ranging. To Login: enter library and Select V for VT100 terminal, then hit ENTER. When The Library is highlighted, Hit ENTER on the Library menu screen (OPAC = INNOPAC.) To exit: Type Q on Library menu Move cursor to QUIT and hit Enter.

- **KEYWORDS** Contemporary Music, Libraries, OPACs (Online Public Access Catalogs), Poetry
- **AUDIENCE** General Public, Researchers, Students
- **FREE**

telnet://library.ucsd.edu

University of Georgia Libraries ★★★

This library's collections are large and wide-ranging including rare books and music. Access Instructions: Username: info Select 3 from menu Enter vt100 for terminal type Select L for library or TN3270 uga.cc.uga.edu Hit TAB twice Type DIAL VTA on the command line On the IBM Systems menu, type L Hit RETURN on the next menu To exit: Type QUIT On the IBM Systems menu, type X

- **KEYWORDS** Libraries, Music, OPACs (Online Public Access Catalogs), Rare Books
- **AUDIENCE** General Public, Researchers, Students
- **FREE**

telnet://gsvms2.cc.gasou.edu

University of Hawaii Thomas Hale Hamilton Library ★★★

This library's collections are large and wide-ranging, including references on Hawaii and Asia. To access: Enter Choice> LIB At the terminal type menu, select 5 for VT100 To exit, type //EXIT

- **KEYWORDS** Asia, Hawaii, Libraries, OPACs (Online Public Access Catalogs)
- **AUDIENCE** General Public, Researchers, Students
- **FREE**

telnet://uhcarl.lib.hawaii.edu

The University of Houston Libraries' Gopher ★★★

This is the University of Houston Libraries' gopher. It provides information on library resources, electronic books and journals, dissertations, reference materials, archival and special collections materials, and more. It has links to other gophers on the Internet.

- **KEYWORDS** Education (College/University), Libraries, Library Science, Texas
- **AUDIENCE** Educators (University), Library Users, Students (University)
- **CONTACT** infogopher@lib.uh.edu
- **FREE**

gopher://info.lib.uh.edu/

University of Iowa Libraries ★★★

This library's collections are large and wide-ranging. To access: Choose option 1 on the menu, OASIS Choose LCAT on the Database selection menu OPAC = NOTIS To exit, type stop

- **KEYWORDS** Libraries, Native American Indians, OPACs (Online Public Access Catalogs), Oral History
- **AUDIENCE** General Public, Researchers, Students
- **FREE**

telnet://oasis.uiowa.edu

University of Maine System Home Page ★★★

The University of Maine System is the educational network for seven Maine campuses. The System has links to off-campus outreach centers and the Ursus Library System. There are links to other services outside of this system.

- **KEYWORDS** Cooperative Networks, Education (College/University), Educational Resources, Maine
- **AUDIENCE** Maine Residents, Students
- **CONTACT** eloise@maine.maine.edu
- **FREE**

http://www.caps.maine.edu

University of Miami Otto G Richter Library ★★★

This library's collections are large and wide-ranging with areas of special interest such as Marine Science and Cuba. To access: Login library Type y OPAC = INNOPAC To exit, type QUIT

- **KEYWORDS** Cuba, Libraries, Marine Sciences, OPACs (Online Public Access Catalogs)
- **AUDIENCE** General Public, Researchers, Students
- **FREE**

telnet://stacks.library.miami.edu

The University of Michigan Library ★★★★

The University of Michigan Library is the central system of general and specialized libraries located on the Ann Arbor campus including the Kresge Business Administration Library, Law Library, Clements Library, the Bentley Historical Library, and the Gerald R. Ford Presidential Library. Libraries are also maintained at the Flint and Dearborn campuses of the University. There are many links to related services on campus and beyond.

- **KEYWORDS** Libraries, Library Science
- **AUDIENCE** Book Reviewers, Librarians, Library Users, Students
- **CONTACT** Library@um.cc.umich.edu
- **FREE**

http://asa.ugl.lib.umich.edu

gopher://gopher.lib.umich.edu/

University of Virginia Library Web ★★★

University of Virginia's (UV) Library Web site offers digital versions of texts, images, music, and many of the other materials that one expects to find in a traditional library, as well as resources that only exist in electronic form. It also has catalog and library resource information, links to other UV library departments, and a listing of library resources worldwide.

- **KEYWORDS** Electronic Arts, Libraries, Library Science
- **AUDIENCE** Academics, Educators, Librarians, Students
- **FREE**

http://www.lib.virginia.edu/

gopher://gopher.lib.virginia.edu/

Wisconsin Interlibrary Services ★★

The Wisconsin Interlibrary Services (WILS) site at the University of Wisconsin provides links and resources regarding Internet libraries and technical services. Included here is the newsletter New Tech News, with articles on topics such as Virtual Libraries, Artificial Life, and Flexible Transistors. This site links to the WILS gopher server, with further information and newsletters from the Wisconsin Interlibrary. Links to various kinds of 'cool' and library-related Web sites are provided, as well as information about the WILS World Conference of Internet Libraries

- **KEYWORDS** Internet Resources
- **AUDIENCE** Internet Users
- **CONTACT** Tom Zillner
  tzillner@macc.wisc.edu
- **FREE**

http://milkyway.wils.wisc.edu

York University Libraries ★★★★

This is a gopher service of libraries of York University in Toronto, Canada. It provides information on the libraries' policies and services, gives access to the library online catalogue, hours of operation, workshops, and more.

- **KEYWORDS** Canada, Databases, Information Retrieval, Libraries
- **AUDIENCE** Educators (University), Library Users, Students (University)
- **CONTACT** Walter Giesbrecht
  walterg@vm2.yorku.ca
- **FREE**

gopher://gamma.library.yorku.ca/

Alternative Education

See also
Education · *Curriculum & Instruction*
Education · *Primary & Secondary Education*
Health & Medicine · *Reference*
Science · *Biology*

Association for Experiential Education Home Page (AEE) ★★

The Association for Experiential Education (AEE) provides resources for the development, practice, and evaluation of experiential learning in all settings. They work in such areas as outdoor adventure programming, mental health, youth services, physical education, management development training, corrections, programming for people with disabilities, and environmental education. Viewers will find membership information, descriptions of the group's listservs, announcements regarding their annual conference, and links to other resources such as first aid for outdoor trips, and information about planning an outdoor learning experience.

KEYWORDS Environmental Education, Outdoor Education
AUDIENCE Educators, Educators (Primary/Secondary), Outdoors Enthusiasts
CONTACT   Rick Curtis, Director, Outdoor Action Program
          Rcurtis@princeton.edu
FREE

http://www.princeton.edu/~rcurtis/aee.html

Australian Defence Force Academy ★★

This gopher server acts as a gateway to resources available on the Internet such as Whois, Usenet news, and Archie. It is maintained by the Australian Defence Force Academy.

KEYWORDS Archie (Internet Tool), Universities, Usenet
AUDIENCE Internet Users
CONTACT   Rowena Childs
          Research@adfa.oz.au
FREE

gopher://ccadfa.cc.adfa.oz.au:4320/

Department of Special Education, University of Kansas ★★★

This is the home page of the Department of Special Education at the University of Kansas, which provides a variety of professional opportunities for students committed to the improvement of lifestyles for children, youth, and adults with disabilities. The page contains information on research and teaching at the University in Special Education, notes on the Dole Human Development Center, disability resources for students with disabilities, a help line, a list of what's new and notes on the Special Education faculty.

KEYWORDS Disability Resources, Special Education
AUDIENCE Disabled People, Special Education Educators
CONTACT   Frank Carey
          fcarey@quest.sped.ukans.edu
FREE

http://www.sped.ukans.edu/spedadmin/welcome.html

Home Education Resources Center (HERC) ★★★

The Home Education Resources Center (HERC) is a site for home schooling and educational resources on the Internet. Viewers will find state home schooling regulations for the entire USA, including information (when available) on parent certification requirements, financial aid advice, and who to contact for more information. A list of national and statewide home school associations and support groups are also available here. Other resources on this site include a sample from the Backyard Scientist, a guide to Keeping your Kids out of the Adult Areas, and a reading list for kids aged 3 and up. Currently under construction is a feedback area where parents can review educational software and other homeschooling resources. HERC offers a full line of educational materials from some of the leaders in education for teachers, home schoolers, and involved parents; an online catalog is available for interested users.

KEYWORDS Educational Resources, Home Schooling, Parenting, Primary/Secondary Education
AUDIENCE Educators, Home Schoolers, Parents
CONTACT   Net Sales, LLC
          netsales@cts.com
FREE

http://www.cts.com/~netsales/herc/

Career & Employment

See also
Arts & Music · *Career & Employment*
Business & Economics · *Career & Employment*
Education · *Resources*
Health & Medicine · *Career & Employment*
Science · *Career & Employment*

Academic Position Network ★★★

The Academic Position Network (APN) is an online service accessible worldwide through Internet. It provides notice of academic position announcements, including faculty, staff and administrative positions. Included are notices of announcements for post-doctoral positions and graduate fellowships/assistantships. The APN files may be browsed as they are organized by country, state and institution. Keyword searches can also be performed at this gopher site.

KEYWORDS Educational Opportunities, Employment, Universities
AUDIENCE Education Administrators, Educators, Educators (University), Job Seekers
CONTACT   apn@epx.cis.umn.edu
FREE

gopher://wcni.cis.umn.edu:11111/

Acadia Counselling Centre ★★★

This is the WWW home page for the Acadia University Counselling Centre. In addition to individual counselling, the Centre offers ongoing Self-Development Groups such as Study Skills, Career Planning, Assertiveness Training, Interpersonal Skills, and Exam Preparation. Other services include Vocational Assessment, a Career Information Room which provides references and career planning aids, and calendars from other Universities. This page provides links to an online counselling service called Uncle Albert, and information on individual counselors.

KEYWORDS Counseling, Education (College/University), Nova Scotia, Universities
AUDIENCE Students (University)
CONTACT   Terry Grignon
          terry.grignon@acadiau.ca
FREE

http://admin.acadiau.ca/counsel/home.html

Arizona State University's Jobs Corner ★★★

This directory carries information about employment opportunities for teachers and professional educators. It contains material that is posted periodically to the Listserv of the American Educational Research Association (AERA@asuvm.inre.asu.edu) as well as pointers to other Internet sources listing jobs for educators. The positions listed here are for persons specializing in the profession of education.

KEYWORDS Educational Opportunities, Employment, Job Listings
AUDIENCE Education Researchers, Educators, Job Seekers
CONTACT   gopher-help@info.asu.edu
FREE

gopher://info.asu.edu:70/11/asu-cwis/education/other/jobs/aera

California State University (CSU) Employment ★★

This site is a gopher server of the California State University (CSU) Employment. The goal of this bulletin board is to provide information about currently available faculty and administrative positions at all 21 campuses of the California State University system.

KEYWORDS Education (College/University), Job Listings, Universities, University Administration
AUDIENCE Administrators, Adults, Educators (University), Job Seekers
FREE

gopher://csueb.sfsu.edu/

Co-Operative Education and Career Services at the University of Waterloo ★★★

This gopher, which is part of the University of Waterloo Information system, was set up for for Administrative Computing information suppliers to use, especially those in the Office of the Registrar, and in Co-Operative Education and Career Services. It also provides information on financial services, courses, exams and access to another gopher servers of the University of Waterloo.

KEYWORDS Canada, Computer Administration, Education (College/University), Universities
AUDIENCE Administrators, Educators (University), Students
CONTACT John Sellens
jmsellens@watdragon.uwaterloo.ca
FREE

gopher://nh1adm.uwaterloo.ca/

Institute of Technology Placement Information ★★

This is a gopher server of the Institute of Technology Placement Information at the University of Minnesota. It contains job listings and job interview schedules.

KEYWORDS Community Services, Education (College/University), Employment, Job Listings
AUDIENCE Academics, Educators (University), Students (Secondary/ University)
CONTACT Herb Harmison
herb@maroon.tc.umn.edu
FREE

gopher://rodent.cis.umn.edu:11114/

Job Openings In and Out of Academe from The Chronicle of Higher Education ★★★★

The Chronicle of Higher Education lists over 700 current positions in higher education and related fields, and includes broad categories of faculty and research openings, administrative and executive positions, and positions outside of academe. These categories are further organized into numerous specific areas for easy browsing. The entire list is searchable by keyword, and the search can be restricted to the Northeast US, the South, West, Midwest, or to jobs outside the US.

KEYWORDS Employment, Job Listings
AUDIENCE Educators (University), Job Recruiters, Job Seekers
CONTACT ads@chronicle.merit.edu
FREE

http://chronicle.merit.edu/.ads/.links.html

National Information Services and Systems (UK) Job Vacancies Directory ★★★

NISS (National Information Services and Systems) provides information services over the UK Joint Academic Network (JANET), and acts as a focus for computer-disseminated information for the academic community. This directory contains entries for a variety of disciplines in England, including Computing, Maths and Sciences, Languages and Literature, Theology, and Library Science. There are also listings for post-graduate opportunities, international vacancies, and short-term projects.

KEYWORDS Employment, England
AUDIENCE Academics, Computer Scientists, Educators (University), Job Seekers
CONTACT NISSBB@NISS.AC.UK
FREE

gopher://gopher.niss.ac.uk:71/11/G

Russian and East European Institute Employment Opportunities ★★★

This URL lists academic and non-academic jobs associated with Russia and Eastern Europe. There are jobs working in Eastern Europe, as well as jobs based in the United States, especially Washington D.C. Positions range from Political Science Lecturer in Hungary to Program Analyst in the Czech Republic. In addition, students can apply for internships based in the United States and Eastern Europe.

KEYWORDS Eastern Europe, Internships, Russia
AUDIENCE Eastern Europe Specialists, Job Seekers, Students (University)
CONTACT ucshelp@indiana.edu,
FREE

gopher://gopher.indiana.edu:70/11/theuniversity/support/reeiaie/reeiemployment

UT Austin Job Listings Gopher ★★★

The job listing section of UT Austin's Gopher Central contains information for academic positions as well as university related employment in the US, Australia, and Canada. This site includes links to university employment resources, general university employment information, as well as job postings for a number of universities. The depth and currency of the information varies from university to university but for the most part users should find some helpful information to start their job search.

KEYWORDS Employment, Higher Education
AUDIENCE Administrators, Job Seekers, Students (Graduate)
CONTACT University of Texas, Austin
FREE

gopher://gopher.utexas.edu:70/11/world/Jobs/Universities

University of Illinois Graduate School of Library and Information Science's Placement Online Search Service ★★★

This database contains all professional job announcements received by the University of Illinois Graduate School of Library and Information Science Placement Office. The database grows by as many as 180 new records each month. Users can search by date, or by experience level.

KEYWORDS Educational Technology, Information Science, Job Listings, Universities
AUDIENCE Academics, Librarians, Media Specialists
FREE

telnet://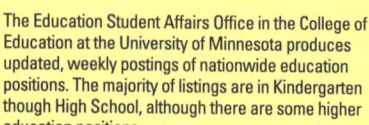
jobs_with_password_Urbaign@alexia.lis.uiuc.edu

University of Minnesota School Of Education Job Search Bulletin Board ★★★

The Education Student Affairs Office in the College of Education at the University of Minnesota produces updated, weekly postings of nationwide education positions. The majority of listings are in Kindergarten though High School, although there are some higher education positions.

KEYWORDS Employment, Job Listings
AUDIENCE Educators (Primary/Secondary), Job Seekers, Students (Secondary/College)
CONTACT University's Microcomputer Helpline at +1 (612) 626-4276
FREE

gopher://rodent.cis.umn.edu:11119/

University of Minnesota ★★★

This University of Minnesota gopher server provides information of interest to current or potential employees including administration details, job descriptions and listings, and more.

KEYWORDS Community Services, Education (College/University), University Administration
AUDIENCE Education Administrators , Educators (University), Students (University)
FREE

gopher://mailbox.mail.umn.edu/

Vanderbilt University Employment Services ★★★

This gopher site contains job listings and information about employment at Vanderbilt University and other locations worldwide. Instructions on how to apply for positions are provided, as well as contact information. Jobs are divided into such areas as Student Employment, Clerical, Executive, Service, Technical, and Temporary positions. Users can also go to employment service links at other universities.

KEYWORDS Academic Jobs, Jobs, Vanderbilt University
AUDIENCE Job Seekers, Tennessee Residents, Vanderbilt Students
CONTACT vuinfo@vanderbilt.edu.
FREE

gopher://vuinfo.vanderbilt.edu/11/employment

Continuing Education

See also
Arts & Music · *Music Organizations*
Business & Economics · *Business Schools*
Education · *Universities - United States*
Health & Medicine · *Medical Schools*
Law & Criminal Justice · *Law Schools*

Acadia's Continuing Education Home Page ★★★★

This is the WWW homepage of Acadia University's Division of Continuing Education. On this page, one can find links to information on the Division's staff, programs, fees, and registration procedures. Links to information on credit and non-credit remote, correspondence, video, and on-site courses offered at Acadia University are also included on this page.

KEYWORDS Continuing Education, Distance Education, Education (College/University), Universities
AUDIENCE Canada Residents, Canadians, Continuing Education Students
CONTACT Terry Grignon
terry.grignon@acadiau.ca
FREE

http://dragon.acadiau.ca/~conted/conted.html

Alabama Extension System Gopher Server ★★★

This gopher server is maintained by the Alabama Cooperative Extension System, a department of Auburn University designed to link the University's resources to the people of the state of Alabama. The resources provided by this gopher server include information on community resource development, family and youth programs, and publications.

KEYWORDS Community Services, Distance Education, Education (College/University), Information Retrieval
AUDIENCE Alabama Residents, Families, Students (University)
CONTACT gopher-admin@acenet.auburn.edu
FREE

gopher://gopher.acenet.auburn.edu/

Antioch New England Graduate School ★★

Antioch New England Graduate School, a graduate school designed for learners over 30 years old, has set up this web site to distribute information about the academic programs, faculty, library facilities, housing and other costs, demographics of the student body, and its philosophy regarding adult and graduate education. The main campus is located in Keene, New Hampshire with alternative campuses in New Hampshire, Connecticut, Maine, Massachusetts, Vermont. The school offers a master's degree in such areas as applied psychology, education, environmental studies/resource management and administration, and organization and management.

KEYWORDS Adult Education, Continuing Education, Graduate Programs
AUDIENCE Adults, Students, Students (Graduate)
CONTACT webmaster@antiochne.edu
FREE

http://sparc.antiochne.edu/

Camosun College ★★★

This server offers information on Camosun College, a public community college serving the people of Southern Vancouver Island, the Saanich Peninsula and the Gulf Islands in Canada. Users will find information on the various schools and departments that make up the college, as well as being able to browse course information. There is also information on the surrounding regional area, culled from a variety of sources.

KEYWORDS Canada, Undergraduate Education
AUDIENCE Canadians, Education Administrators (College), Educators, Students
CONTACT webmaster@camosun.bc.ca
FREE

http://www.camosun.bc.ca

gopher://gopher.camosun.bc.ca/

Campus-Wide Information System for the Alamo Community College District ★★★

This gopher site provides campus-wide information for the Alamo Community Colleges in San Antonio, Texas. The institutions served by this gopher are Palo Alto College, San Antonio College, St. Phillips college, and the Community Education and Service Center. This covers enrollment, registration, the community, academic programs, job opportunities, and other relevant information.

KEYWORDS Computing, Education (College/University), Texas, University Administration
AUDIENCE Educators (University), Students (University), Texas Residents
CONTACT James L.Garrison
SYSWORK1@ACCD.EDU
FREE

gopher://accd.edu/

Continuing & Distance Education Gopher Server at Penn State University ★★

This is the Continuing & Distance Education (C&DE) Gopher Server located at Penn State University. It provides resources and documents relating to Continuing and Distance Education, the Journal of Continuing Higher Education, as well as miscellaneous support documents generated by the Continuing and Distance Education initiatives. It also makes access to other PSU gopher holes.

KEYWORDS Community Networking, Continuing Education, Distance Education
AUDIENCE Distance Educators, Educators (University), Students (University)
CONTACT gopherinfo@omnibus.ce.psu.edu
FREE

gopher://gopher.ce.psu.edu/

Delgado Community College ★★

This is a gopher server of the Delgado Community College in New Orleans. It provides information on the College, software archives, FTP sites, and more. It makes connections to other gophers.

KEYWORDS Education (College/University), Software, University Administration
AUDIENCE Educators (College), Students
CONTACT jdkoch@dcc.edu
FREE

gopher://gopher.dcc.edu/

Estrella Mountain Community College Center ★★★

This is a gopher server of the Estrella Mountain Community College Center, which is the tenth campus of the Maricopa County Community College District. It contains information on academic divisions, administration, campus policies and procedures, computing and communication services, courses, the library, student services, and more.

KEYWORDS Education (College/University), Educational Policy, Schedules, University Administration
AUDIENCE Educators (College), Students (Secondary)
FREE

gopher://gopher.emc.maricopa.edu/

Hartford Graduate Center Gopher ★★★

This site provides information about the graduate degree programs at the Hartford Graduate Center (HGC) in Hartford, Connecticut. There is also news about non-degree programs in leadership and executive development, computer and information systems technology, engineering and management. HGC also offers management and technical programs under contract to business, industrial, and government organizations.

KEYWORDS Business Education, Connecticut, Continuing Education, Engineering
AUDIENCE Business Educators, Business Researchers, Business Students
CONTACT gopher-admin@hgc.edu
FREE

gopher://gopher.hgc.edu/

Honolulu Community College ★★

This gopher site provides information related to Honolulu Community College such as catalogs, staff and student phone books, and orientation data. There are also links to other Hawaiian gophers.

KEYWORDS Continuing Education, Education, Hawaii
AUDIENCE Educators (University), Hawaiians, Students (University)
CONTACT Helen Rapozo
cs_rapozo@hccadb.hcc.hawaii.edu
FREE

gopher://hccadb.hcc.hawaii.edu/

240 Continuing Education – Curriculum & Instruction

The Oregon State University Extension Service ★★★

This is a gopher server of Oregon State University Extension Service. It provides information about the Service, its projects and programs, Oregon State University computing services, the electronic journal of Extension and more. It also makes connections to other gophers.

Keywords Continuing Education, Education (College/University), Oregon
Audience Educators (University), Students (University)
Contact info-mgr@oes.orst.edu
Free

gopher://gopher.oes.orst.edu/

Purdue Cooperative Extension Gopher Site ★★★★

This gopher server gives information about the Cooperative Extension Management System (CEMS) at Purdue University, Indiana. CEMS' goal is to bring the resources of the University to the general public. The information down this gopher hole includes agricultural scholarships, FTP sites, email addresses, publications, computing resources, and more. It has links to other gophers on campus as well as off campus.

Keywords Agriculture, Education (College/University)
Audience Agriculturalists, Educators, Students
Contact cems@ecn.purdue.edu
Free

gopher://hermes.ecn.purdue.edu/

Times Higher Home Page ★★★★

The Times Higher Education Supplement is Britain's best-known higher education magazine. This site offers a quick way to access highlights, headlines and digests from the current issue of The Times Higher Education Supplement, plus providing the opportunity to view all the best employment ads in the higher education sector.

Keywords Employment, Higher Education, The Times
Audience Educators, United Kingdom Residents
Contact theschat@timsup2.demon.co.uk
Free

http://www.timeshigher.newsint.co.uk/

The University and Community College System of Nevada Gopher Server ★★★

This site is a gopher server of the University of Nevada, Reno. It offers information on the University, administrative services, phone books, email addresses, student organizations, graduate programs, job listings, library resources, computing services, and more. It also has access to other gophers.

Keywords Education (College/University), Nevada, University Administration
Audience Educators (University), Students (University)
Contact gophadm@gopher.scs.unr.edu
Free

gopher://gopher.unr.edu/

The University of Wisconsin - Journal of Extension Gopher ★★★

This server provides access to the University of Wisconsin Journal of Extension. The Journal of Extension describes extension programs at the University. Extension programs are aimed to bring the University's resources to the general public. For example, some of the information here is about engineering professional development courses.

Keywords Education (College/University), Engineering, Journals, Wisconsin
Audience Educators (University), Students
Contact Dirk Herr-Hoyman
hoymand@wissago.uwex.edu
Free

gopher://wissago.uwex.edu/

Virginia Cooperative Extension (VCE) Gopher ★★★

This is a gopher server of the Virginia Cooperative Extension (VCE) which provides VCE departmental news releases, information about organizational management, committees and governance, personnel directories, and more.

Keywords Education (College/University), University Administration, Virginia
Audience Educators (University), Students (University)
Contact gopher@gopher.ext.vt.edu
Free

gopher://gopher.ext.vt.edu/

Curriculum & Instruction

See also
Education · *International Education*
Education · *Primary & Secondary Education*
Humanities & Social Sciences · *Literature*
Science · *Biosciences*

Bill Beaty's Homepage ★★★★

This is the Science Hobbyist section of Bill Beaty's World Wide Web Home Page. It contains many links to information of interest to the amateur scientist, including links to the Society of Amateur Science, a physics projects newsletter entitled 'The Belljar, mail order catalogs, and patent information. There are also links to the description of experiments performed by Bill, including an Array Electrometer, a Non-Cryonic Meissner Mglev Cradle, and an Electrostatic Motor made from plastic pop bottles.

Keywords Science, Student Projects
Audience Amateur Scientists, Educators (Primary/Secondary), Hobbyists
Contact Bill Beaty
billb@eskimo.com
Free

http://www.eskimo.com/~billb/amasci.html

The CHANCE Database ★★★

The CHANCE Database provides information about the CHANCE project, an alternative math course designed to give students a better understanding of the significance (or lack thereof) of statistics encountered in the media and elsewhere. It gives access to course materials, course profiles, teaching aids, and student projects associated with the project.

Keywords Databases, Mathematics, Statistics
Audience Mathematics Educators, Mathematics Students
Contact dart.chance@dartmouth.edu
Free

http://www.geom.umn.edu/docs/snell/chance/welcome.html

Classroom & Teacher Resources and Information from the Michigan Department of Education ★★★

This site contains a large collection of materials related to teaching in the state of Michigan. The Classroom & Teacher Resources and Information folder has links to major lesson plan archives, the National Distance Learning Center and Satellite programming schedules, transcripts and other archives like Michigan Gateways program for educators in science and mathematics. Other resources for teachers include daily information updates from CNN and the Daily Report Card, as well as a listing of Freenet Sites which offer free networking resources.

Keywords Lesson Plans, Teacher Resources
Audience Educators, Educators (Primary/Secondary), Michigan Residents
Contact gopher@mdenet.mde.state.mi.us
Free

http://web.mde.state.mi.us:1024/class.html

gopher://mdenet.mde.state.mi.us:70/11/class

Department of English at the University of Georgia ★★

This gopher serves information about the Department of English at the University of Georgia. This information includes announcements, directories, course information, and faculty listings. In addition, it also gives online access to journals and newsletters related to literature, culture, and women's studies.

Keywords English Literature, Poetry, Writing
Audience Literary Scholars, Poetry Enthusiasts, Women's Studies Educators, Women's Studies Students
Free

gopher://parallel.park.uga.edu/

Curriculum & Instruction – Distance Education   **241**

Department of Mathematics at Arizona State University ★★

This gopher provides information about the Department of Mathematics at Arizona State University. This information includes degree programs, research pursuits, departmental directories, and seminar schedules.

KEYWORDS Mathematics, Statistics
AUDIENCE Education Administrators, Mathematicians, Mathematics Educators, Students
FREE

gopher://pi.la.asu.edu/

Infovid Outlet ★★★★

This is a catalog of videos for do-it-yourselfers and educators, a complete guide to the best educational, instructional and informative videos from around the world. The videos are on many subjects, some are academic and others include fitness, child care, computers and hobbies. This page has links to other pages for each of the topics.

KEYWORDS Education, Product Information, Videos
AUDIENCE Consumers, Educators
CONTACT digitali@renoir.cftnet.com
FREE

http://branch.com/infovid/infovid.html

The Minnesota Extension Service Gopher ★★★

This is a gopher server of the EXTEND group of the Educational Development System, Minnesota Extension Service, University of Minnesota. It offers information on courses, special programs, educational materials catalogs, the family consortium clearinghouse, news, weather, market reports, and more. It has links to the national children, youth and family network, as well as other gophers.

KEYWORDS Education, Education (College/University)
AUDIENCE Academics, Educators, Educators (University)
CONTACT Bill Bomash
         wbomash@mes.umn.edu
FREE

gopher://linman.mes.umn.edu/

Mklesson User Guide ★★

This is a brief user guide for mklesson, a tutor-generating program for the World Wide Web (WWW). Mklesson does not require any modification of the local Web server program, and can be maintained and modified by more than one person. This program assumes some prior programming experience. Links to samples of the finished tutorial programs are available.

KEYWORDS Educational Technology, Programming, Tutorials, WWW (World Wide Web)
AUDIENCE Computer Programmers, Computer Science Students, Computer Scientists
CONTACT lgl-www-admin@lglsun.epfl.ch
FREE

http://lglwww.epfl.ch/Ada/Tutorials/Lovelace/userg.html

Super Projects for K-12 Students ★★★★

This directory contains contact information, lesson plans, teacher resources, and archives of student work revolving around interactive and long-distance projects for K-12 students. There are examples of creative writing, home economics, marine biology, art, geography and many other disciplines for teachers and their classes to participate in.

KEYWORDS Interactive Education, Interdisciplinary Studies, Primary/Secondary Education, Student Projects
AUDIENCE Education Administrators, Educators (Primary/Secondary), Students (Primary/Secondary)
CONTACT Donald Perkins
         dperkins@tenet.edu
FREE

gopher://riceinfo.rice.edu:1170/11/Projects

The Text Project ★★★

The Text Project is an attempt by the Globewise Network Academy education consortium to put into hypertext instructional textbooks for several subjects. Thus far, hypertextualized texts include textbooks for courses on Greek mythology, Astronomy, C++, and Internet technical writing. A teacher's resource guide is also provided for learning how to teach courses over the Internet, as well as a guide to putting publications into hypertext.

KEYWORDS Greek Mythology, Hypertext, Online Publishing, Textbooks
AUDIENCE Education Professionals, Professors, Students
CONTACT gna@mcmuse.mc.maricopa.edu
FREE

http://sturgeon.mit.edu:8001/uu-gna/text/index.html

University of Michigan School of Education ★★★

This is a gopher server of the University of Michigan School of Education in Ann Arbor, and it is maintained by the Interactive Communications and Simulations (ICS) project. It contains information on the ICS Project and the School of Education. This gopher also provides access to a public information service called the Metro Detroit Comnet, and to other gophers on and off campus.

KEYWORDS Education (College/University), Michigan
AUDIENCE Academics, Computer Students, Educators, Internet Users
FREE

gopher://ics.soe.umich.edu/

WGBH's Nova Videotapes ★★

Nova, a television show sponsored by public television station WGBH, presents information about the relationship between humanity and science. This site offers users several videotaped series that have been produced by the show. Users can see pictures from, and descriptions of, the shows that are currently available. Some series titles include 'In Search of Human Origins,' 'This Old Pyramid,' and 'The Miracle of Life.' Each series is comprised of several videos which can be ordered individually or as a group. All titles can be ordered online, using Netscape's encryption.

KEYWORDS Biosciences, Online Shopping, Public Television, Science
AUDIENCE Science Educators, Science Enthusiasts
FREE

http://branch.com:1080/nova/nova.html

World Lecture Hall ★★★

The World Lecture Hall page contains links to pages created by faculty worldwide who are using the Web to deliver class materials. Some of the materials provided include course syllabi, assignments, lecture notes, exams, class calendars, multimedia textbooks, and more.

KEYWORDS Curriculum, Distance Education, Education, Multimedia Education
AUDIENCE Distance Educators, Educators (University), General Public, Students (University)
CONTACT www@www.utexas.edu
FREE

http://wwwhost.cc.utexas.edu/world/instruction/index.html

Distance Education

See also
Education · *Educational Technology*
Popular Culture & Entertainment · *Television*

Clive's Virtual Writing Workshop ★★★

This is Clive Brooks' online workshop, specifically devoted to 'Creating Classic Crime Fiction.' Clive Brooks has published a number of original Sherlock Holmes mysteries, and offers online classes for mystery and crime writers. Links include a Visual Resource Bank and an Audio Archive as well as a Sherlock Holmes Story Archive, including such titles as 'Adventure of the Red Leech' and 'Adventure of the Aluminium Crutch' (in etext and html formats). Mr. Brooks' definitive mystery writer is Arthur Conan Doyle. There is also a link to Chris Redmond's Sherlock Holmes home page as a resource. Before enrolling in the full 12-week program, users are required to take a shorter 3-week program in order to ensure that the course is right for themselves.

KEYWORDS English Literature, Writing
AUDIENCE English Literature Enthusiasts, Mystery Novel Enthusiasts, Reading Enthusiasts, Sherlock Holmes Enthusiasts, Writers
FREE

http://theodore-sturgeon.MIT.EDU:8001/~cbrooks/

Distance Education Resources ★★★★

This is a meta-index to major lists of distance education resources. Open universities are one of the specific concentrations, in particular the British Open University, The Dutch Open University and Flanders' EuroStudy Centre for Distance Education.

KEYWORDS International Education, Internet Resources
AUDIENCE Distance Education Teachers, Students

Distance Education – Educational Issues

CONTACT bgls@mailserv.mta.ca
FREE

http://ollc.mta.ca/disted.html

Global Lecture Hall - Conference Records ★★

This directory contains the procedings of a 'Global Lecture Hall Video Conference' held simultaneously in Moscow, Russia, and at the University of Tennessee on July 7, 1994. A major part of the conference dealt with comparing the delivery technologies for setting up a distance learning network. Pros and cons of using TCP/IP, regular telephone service, WWW, CU-SeeME, MBONE, and other methods of delivery are discussed. Some specific strategies related to multimedia systems were discussed. The conference was sponsored by Global University in the USA (GU/USA), a divisional activity of GLOSAS/USA (GLObal Systems Analysis and Simulation Association in the USA)

KEYWORDS Distance Education, International Education, Multimedia Resources, Russia
AUDIENCE Distance Educators, Educators (Primary/Secondary), Educators (University)
CONTACT Donald Perkins
dperkins@tenet.edu
FREE

gopher://riceinfo.rice.edu:1170/11/
Projects/Distance

KQED Center For Education and Lifelong Learning (CELL) ★★★★

This is KQED's Center For Education and Lifelong Learning (CELL) home page. CELL supports a broad range of KQED programming for children, students, childcare providers, parents, adult students, and teachers. This site provides links to School Services, Learning Link, Professional Development, Family Membership, Sesame Street Preschool Education Program, Family Learning Guide, etc. There is also a link to Kidswatch, the KQED Childcare Partnership Newsletter, which provides day-care providers and parents of young children with resources and ideas for making the most of Sesame Street and Mister Rogers' Neighborhood.

KEYWORDS Continuing Education, Parenting, Public Broadcasting
AUDIENCE Childcare Providers, Children, Educators (Primary/Secondary), Parents, Public Television Enthusiasts, Students (Primary/Secondary)
CONTACT sbirnam@kqed.org
FREE

http://www.kqed.org/fromKQED/Cell/
menu.html

Public Broadcasting Service (PBS) Home Page ★★★★

This site is host to the Public Broadcasting Service (PBS). The main feature on this site that is available to users is a searchable monthly program listing with the dates, times and descriptions. There are also educational program guides with activities for K-12 classrooms and a hyperlink directory of Internet sites with K-12 resources and information about college-credit telecourses available through the PBS Adult Learning Service. It includes a clickable map providing information on individual public television stations.

KEYWORDS Education, Public Television, Television Programming
AUDIENCE Educators, Parents, Public Broadcasting Activists
CONTACT www@pbs.org
FREE

http://www.pbs.org/

Solid Waste Recycling Online Correspondence Course ★★

This is the class schedule and syllabus for a Solid Waste Recycling Online Correspondence Course at the University of Wisconsin. Access, registration, and contact information are located here. This correspondance course describes the opportunities available for recycling and the steps necessary to develop a successful recycling program. Correspondence course subscribers will receive complete printed materials, including the extended reference list, answers to the homework questions, and a series of fact sheets with more information and checklists on specific topics, as well as a set of examinations.

KEYWORDS Continuing Education, Environmental Studies, Recycling
AUDIENCE Environmentalists, Students (University)
CONTACT Judy Faber
faber@engr.wisc.edu
FREE

gopher://wissago.uwex.edu:70/11/
.course/recycling/

Technology and Distance Education Branch ★★

This gopher is provided by the office of the Technology and Distance Education Branch of the Ministry of Education, British Columbia. It provides information on the Community Learning Network (CLN) project, a pilot project of the Education Technology Centre, and the Technology and Distance Education Branch of the Ministry of Education.

KEYWORDS Education, Educational Policy, Government, Network Servers
AUDIENCE Adults, Educators, General Public, Students
CONTACT Glen R. Turnbull
gturnbul@cln.etc.bc.ca
FREE

gopher://cln.etc.bc.ca/

TeleEducation New Brunswick ★★★

This is the TeleEducation New Brunswick Gopher Server at Mount Allison University, New Brunswick, Canada. TeleEducation NB is a network of community learning centres in the province of New Brunswick. The site provides information on courses, training programs, and more. It also provides access to some other servers in distance education.

KEYWORDS Alternative Education, Canada, Distance Education, Educational Networks
AUDIENCE Educators, Students

FREE

gopher://tenb.mta.ca/

Educational Issues

See also
Education · Continuing Education
Education · Language Acquisition
Education · Primary & Secondary Education
Humanities & Social Sciences · Linguistics

CRESST Internet Gopher Server ★★★

This site provides information on K-12 education. The information includes results from studies conducted by the National Center for Research on Evaluation, Standards, and Student Testing (CRESST). CRESST researches the abilities of students at the K-12 level and the results of these studies are presented in the form of technical papers and newsletters.

KEYWORDS Education, Educational Resources, Government Resources (US), Primary/Secondary Education
AUDIENCE Education Administrators, Educators, Policymakers
CONTACT comments@cse.ucla.edu
FREE

gopher://spinoza.cse.ucla.edu:71/

FacultyWrites of the University of Minnesota ★★★

FacultyWrites is a gopher server at the University of Minnesota that provides a forum for faculty to interact with one another. It also allows for faculty to communicate with the University's Office of Strategic Planning. Information provided includes strategic planning documents, updates, and comments.

KEYWORDS Community Services, Education (College/University), Faculty, University Administration
AUDIENCE Educators (University), Students (University)
CONTACT FacultyWrites@mailbox.mail.umn.edu
FREE

gopher://mailbox.mail.umn.edu:7000/

LMRINet ★★★

LMRINet is a distribution center for information about linguistic minority research. This information includes newsletters, publications, funding and job opportunities, and discussion arenas for Latino groups, hearing-impaired groups and other groups. LMRINet is funded and operated by University of California's Linguistic Minority Research Institute (LMRI).

KEYWORDS Cultural Studies, Ethnic Studies, Linguistics
AUDIENCE Ethnic Studies Students, Hearing Impaired, Latin Studies Students, Social Scientists
CONTACT InfoDesk@LMRINet.gse.ucsb.edu
FREE

gopher://lmri-net.gse.ucsb.edu/

Educational Issues – Educational Policy

Literacy Research Center and National Center on Adult Literacy's Gopher Server

This site is a source of information about adult literacy. It is maintained by the National Center on Adult Literacy in Philadelphia, Pennsylvania. The information includes newsletters, publications, software, research documents, and discussion groups.

KEYWORDS Continuing Education, Literacy, Writing
AUDIENCE Educators, Linguists
CONTACT Mailbox@literacy.upenn.edu
FREE

gopher://litserver.literacy.upenn.edu/

Times Higher Internet Service

The Times Higher Internet Service is an information base for news in the higher education sector, both in the UK and international. The Service is provided by The Times Higher Education Supplement, the UK's weekly newspaper carrying news and features in all areas of post-compulsory education. This page contains abstracts of articles currently in the print version. There are also links to gopher sites for higher education jobs and conference announcements.

KEYWORDS Employment, Graduate Education, International Education, United Kingdom
AUDIENCE Scholars, Students (University)
CONTACT Tony Durham, Multimedia Editor
         tdurham@timsup2.demon.co.uk
FREE

http://www.timeshigher.newsint.co.uk/

Educational Policy

See also
Government & Politics · *Issues*
Government & Politics · *Policies*
Government & Politics · *States*
Health & Medicine · *Disabilities*

Administrative and Business Services from the University of California-Irving

This gopher provides electronic access to a wide variety of campus administrative and reference information. Information presented includes reference materials (e.g., phone directories, training materials, policy manuals, announcements of events (e.g., workshop schedules, special events), and documents in effect for a short period of time (e.g., fiscal closing instructions, merit cycle information).

KEYWORDS Campus Networks, Education (College/University), University Administration, University Planning
AUDIENCE Administrators, Educators (University), Professors, Students (University)
CONTACT Penny White
         plwhite@uci.edu
FREE

gopher://cbis.cwis.uci.edu:1070/

Board of Regents in Minnesota

This gopher provides information about the Board of Regents at the University of Minnesota in Minneapolis. This includes 1994-95 meeting dates, addresses for Regents, Regents' meeting agendas, and Regents' meeting minutes.

KEYWORDS Education (College/University), Universities, University Administration, University Planning
AUDIENCE Education Administrators, Educators (University)
FREE

gopher://regents.acad.umn.edu/

CSU Gopher

This gopher site is provided by the Office of the Chancellor of the California State University. It provides links to the various California State University campuses as well as giving information from the Chancellor's office itself.

KEYWORDS California, Education (College/University), Universities (History Of), University Administration
AUDIENCE Educators (University), Students (University)
FREE

gopher://gopher.csu.net/

FINS (Finance and Administration Information System)

The acronym FINS stands for Finance and Administration Information System. It is an information service of the Office of Telecommunications at Florida State University. The information on FINS includes documents from the Department of Public Safety, Office of the Controller, and Parking Services. It also provides information about environmental health and safety, and access to the Administrative Information Systems (AIS). AIS is an online service providing information about the administration of Florida State University.

KEYWORDS Finance, Grants, University Administration
AUDIENCE Administrators, Education Administrators, University Administrators
CONTACT gopher@telecom.otc.fsu.edu
FREE

gopher://telecom.otc.fsu.edu/

IEA

This is the gopher site for the IEA Computers in Education study at the University of Minnesota. The International Association for the Evaluation of Educational Achievement (IEA) is an independent international cooperative of research centers from over 40 countries. Its mission is the conducting of comparative studies focusing on educational policies and practices in order to enhance learning within and across national systems of education. It contains summary material for this international study of computers in education.

KEYWORDS Computer Applications, International Development, International Education, Universities
AUDIENCE Education Administrators, Educators (University)

CONTACT rea@vx.cis.umn.edu
FREE

gopher://rodent.cis.umn.edu:11138/

Office of Communications and Publications at Princeton University

This is a gopher server of the Office of Communications and Publications at Princeton University. Information provided includes admissions, graduate studies, the Princeton Weekly Bulletin, campus guides and maps, press releases, and more.

KEYWORDS Education (College/University), University Administration
AUDIENCE Educators (University), Students (Secondary/University)
CONTACT Mahlon Lovett
         mlovett@princeton.edu
FREE

gopher://compub-gopher.princeton.edu/

The Office of the President at the University of California

This is a gopher server of the Office of the President of the University of California in Oakland, California. It provides resources such as a searchable phone book, news, university statistical data, university-wide policies and procedures, and more. It has access to other University of California gophers.

KEYWORDS California, Education (College/University), University Administration
AUDIENCE Administrators, Educators (University), Students (University)
CONTACT infohelp@ucop.edu
FREE

gopher://gopher.ucop.edu/

Richard W. Riley, U.S. Secretary Of Education

The Richard W. Riley site provides a biography of the U.S. Secretary of Education and hot link to the U.S. Department of Education's Home Page. This hot link provides users with information educational projects, budgets, legislation, resources, and more of the education department.

KEYWORDS Educational Policy, Government (US)
AUDIENCE Parents, Students, legislators, teachers
CONTACT wwwadmin@inet.ed.gov
FREE

http://www.ed.gov/offices/OS/riley.html

US Department of Education Home Page

This Web page, administered by the Department of Education's Office of Educational Research and Improvement (OERI), contains a large amount of information on the Department itself as well as links to other education-related sites. Included on these Web pages is s complete Department staff lists and directories, mission statements from the various agencies of the Department, newsletters, news about current projects, and more.

- KEYWORDS Educational Policy, Government Policy (US)
- AUDIENCE Education Administrators, Educators, Journalists, Political Researchers
- CONTACT OERI web administrator
wwwadmin@inet.ed.gov
- FREE

http://www.ed.gov/

Educational Projects

See also
Education · *Distance Education*
Education · *Primary & Secondary Education*
Internet · *Internet Resources*
Science · *Biology*

The Art of Renaissance Science—Galileo and Perspective ★★★

This site hosts a hypermedia presentation entitled, 'The Art of Renaissance Science—Galileo and Perspective.' The work combines about 35 pages of HTML text, 200 GIF images, 10 MPEG video clips and one audio file to educate the viewer about Galileo's early experiments, Renaissance art and mathematics, and Galileo's later theories about the mathematics of motion. The materials used in this presentation were gleaned from a videotape produced by its author, Joseph W. Dauben, and is part of a hypermedia journal sponsored by Science and Engineering Television Network, Inc.

- KEYWORDS Renaissance, Renaissance Art
- AUDIENCE Multimedia Designers, Renaissance Students, Students (Secondary/College)
- CONTACT Gary Welz
gary@setn.org
- FREE

http://www.pd.astro.it/ars/arshtml/arstitle.html

CTDNet (The Center for Talent Development) ★★

This is a gopher server of the CTDNet, a network service at Northwestern University. The mission of the Center for Talent Development is to provide specialized support and services to academically gifted and talented youths. It provides information on the CTDNet, policies, subscription information, and reference materials. CTDNet is an electronic bulletin board, gopher server, and Internet service provider.

- KEYWORDS Alternative Education, Communications, Computer Networking, Gifted Students, Talent Development
- AUDIENCE Computer Users, Educators, Students
- CONTACT operator@ctdnet.acns.nwu.edu
- FREE

gopher://ctdnet.acns.nwu.edu/

The Center for Integrative Studies in the Arts and Humanities ★★

This is a gopher server of Michigan State University's Center for Integrative Studies in the Arts and Humanities (CIS-AH). It provides information on arts and humanities resources, CIS-AH computer documents, course resources and schedules, multimedia collections, news and more. It offers pointers to other Internet resources.

- KEYWORDS Art, Education (College/University), Humanities, Michigan
- AUDIENCE Art Educators, Art Students, Humanists
- CONTACT gopher@ah3.cal.msu.edu
- FREE

gopher://gopher.cal.msu.edu/

The Center for Networked Information Discovery and Retrieval ★★★★

The Center for Networked Information Discovery and Retrieval works on several fronts to gather and distribute information, as well as to help others search on their own. Some projects which CNIDR is involved with (and provides links to) are the Global SchoolHouse, an educational projects for grades 7-12, and freeWAIS-0.3, a search tool. Other Internet based programs are available here, as are papers, contact information, and links to related sites.

- KEYWORDS Primary/Secondary Education, WAIS (Wide Area Information Service)
- AUDIENCE Computer Scientists, Educators, Information Professionals, Librarians
- FREE

http://cnidr.org

Colorado's K-12 Adventures in Supercomputing Project ★★★

The Adventures in Supercomputing is a group project with the Colorado State University and other University research groups across the United States, with the objective being to inspire disadvantaged minority K-12 students to learn about computers and science. Their site includes background information about the project, including activities, events, objectives, and materials about the high schools and primary schools involved. Interested students and administrators can also find out how to get involved with the program and summer workshops, and other K-12 education resources on the Internet are linked.

- KEYWORDS Science, Supercomputing
- AUDIENCE Education Administrators (Primary/Secondary), Education Professionals, Students (Primary/Secondary)
- CONTACT Greg Redder
redder@k12.colostate.edu
- FREE

http://k12.colostate.edu/

Duke University Talent Identification Program ★★

This gopher was created by the Duke University Talent Identification Program (TIP), to identify and cultivate talented youths. The information on this server helps meet those goals by providing access to databases, educational tools and other resources.

- KEYWORDS Alternative Education, Computer Aided Instruction, Databases
- AUDIENCE Education Administrators, Educators, Students
- FREE

gopher://arnold.tip.duke.edu/

EOS - Educational Online Sources ★★★★

EOS offers schools and educational organizations a chance to get information about themselves online. Users can connect to a large list of bulletins and announcements ranging from Rural Curriculum resources to a Math Learning Forum Online Project. The site also contains Frequently Asked Questions on Academic and Internet training issues, as well as pointers to gopher, FTP, and WWW sites in education. There are pages set up for fast connections, slow connections, FTP and gopher.

- KEYWORDS Distance Education, Educational Organizations, Internet Resources
- AUDIENCE Education Administrators, Educators (Primary/Secondary), Librarians
- CONTACT eos@brown.edu
- FREE

http://netspace.students.brown.edu/eos/

gopher://netspace.org

ftp://netspace.org

Eisenhower National Clearinghouse ★★★

This is a gopher server of the Eisenhower National Clearinghouse (ENC). The purpose of the ENC is to encourage the adoption and use of K-12 curriculum materials and programs which support national goals to improve teaching and learning in mathematics and science. It offers information on the ENC, ENC demonstration sites, curriculum resources and materials, and many more. In addition, it has links to other gophers.

- KEYWORDS Networking, Ohio, Primary/Secondary Education, Telecommunications
- AUDIENCE Educators (Primary/Secondary), Students (Primary/Secondary)
- FREE

gopher://enc.org/

From Alligators to Whooping Cranes - A Texas Resource Guide to Endangered Species ★★★

This resource guide contains resources for curriculum and lesson plans dealing with the identification, preservation, and recovery of endangered species. The wide variety of materials available will assist educators in teaching students how to make reasoned decisions regarding conservation of the rich diversity of wildlife and wildlife habitat in Texas. This site lists resources like filmstrips, software, zoos, and people that can be useful in planning a curriculum around endangered species.

KEYWORDS Endangered Species, Primary/Secondary Education, Science
AUDIENCE Animal Lovers, Educators (Primary/Secondary), Environmentalists, Students (Primary/Secondary), Zoologists
CONTACT   Donald Perkins
          dperkins@tenet.edu
FREE

http://riceinfo.rice.edu/armadillo/Endanger/about.html

Global Student Newswire project ★★★

The Global Student Newswire project is a collaboration by a group of student journalists and media scholars dedicated to creating a multimedia source of formal news stories on the Internet. This site consists of a set of standards for writing news stories and a collection of Internet resources devoted to the project.

KEYWORDS Computers, Journalism, Media, Multimedia
AUDIENCE Computer Users, Journalists, Writers
FREE

http://www.jou.ufl.edu/features/

Group Exploring the National Information Infrastructure (GENII) ★★

The Web site of the Group Exploring the National Information Infrastructure (GENII) explains the Australian organization's purpose — to facilitate the training of classroom teachers in skills necessary to use the Internet (the precursor to the National Information Infrastructure). The page provides information about GENII initiatives and its virtual faculty. There are links to educational resources.

KEYWORDS Australia, Education, Internet
AUDIENCE Australians, School Teachers
FREE

http://www.deakin.edu.au/edu/MSEE/GENII/GENII-Home-Page.html

Jason Project ★★★★

This WWW site provides information concerning the Jason exploration projects I-VI—Mediterranean Sea, Lake Ontario & Ships of 1812, Galapagos Islands, Sea of Cortez, Planet Earth and Island Earth, also upcoming expeditions, interactive classroom exercises, discussion forum, and experiments using robotics.

KEYWORDS Earth Sciences, Interactive Excercises, Robotics
AUDIENCE Earth Science Educators, Education Technologists, Students (Primary/Secondary)
CONTACT   Gene Carl Feldman
          gene@seawifs.gsfc.nasa.gov
FREE

http://seawifs.gsfc.nasa.gov/JASON.html

> **Connections to George Lucas Foundation**
> ## "May the Force be with you!"
>
> Not everything about George Lucas is about Star Wars. If you are interested in the educational resources being developed by The George Lucas Educational Foundation, then use the Internet to access this information.
>
> The foundation site on the Internet provides an online newsletter, called "Edutopia," which features a wide variety of information about instruction, learning, and school systems. One issue focused on the crisis in America's school buildings, wherein there are currently some 10,000 fire code violations throughout the nation. Another recent article dealt with school construction and classroom seating arrangements designed to foster a more inviting learning environment.
>
> (http://glef.org/)

K-12 Environmental Health Sciences Education ★★

This is a program description for the development of educational materials related to environmental health sciences in grades K-12 (kindergarten to 12th grade). A rationale is given for spending more resources on K-12 environmental sciences and a brief description of how the National Institute of Environmental Health Science is working to address those concerns. Grant programs and contact information is given as well.

KEYWORDS Environmental Health, Instructional Materials, Public Health, Science
AUDIENCE Educators (Primary/Secondary), Environmental Educators, Students
FREE

http://web.fie.com/web/fed/ehs/prog/ehspgaao.htm

Kids on Campus Home Page - Navigating the Information Superhighway ★★★★

Navigating the Information Superhighway is a program to increase computer awareness and scientific interest among 3rd, 4th, and 5th grade students by using hands-on computer activities, innovative videos, and exciting demonstrations. This page offers demonstrations of links which will provide a sampling of the wide variety of information resources on the Internet.

KEYWORDS Computers, Kids, Science, Videos
AUDIENCE Computer Professionals, Educators (Primary/Secondary), Internet Users, Parents, Students (Primary/Secondary)
FREE

http://www.tc.cornell.edu:80/Kids.on.Campus/

Newton - An Educational Electronic BBS ★★★★

Newton BBS maintains 'Ask a Scientist' programs, where students and the general public can pose questions to mathematicians and scientists and receive an answer geared for their level of understanding. Some typical questions asked have been 'How do refrigerators work?' and 'What is the difference between an aftershock and an earthquake?' There is online lesson support for teachers.

KEYWORDS Computer Aided Instruction, Educational Networks, Science
AUDIENCE Education Administrators, Mathematics Educators, Parents, Science Educators, Students (Primary/Secondary)
CONTACT   cbaker@woody.dep.anl.gov
FREE

http://www.newton.dep.anl.gov/

ftp://newton.dep.anl.gov/

telnet://newton.dep.anl.gov

Office of Educational Research and Improvement ★★★

This Gopher server provides a subset of the information contained in the US Department of Education's Office of Educational Research and Improvement. It provides information on vocational-adult education initiatives, overall goals of the US Department of Education, and legislative initiatives and schoolwide programs involving Elementary and Secondary Education.

KEYWORDS Department Of Education (US), Educational Policy, Vocational Education
AUDIENCE Administrators, Education Administrators, Educators, Sociologists
CONTACT   INet Project Manager
          gopheradm@inet.ed.gov
FREE

gopher://gopher.ed.gov:10001/

Plugged In ★★★★

Plugged In provides a multimedia learning environment for the East Palo Alto, California community and, through electronic communications, to communities elsewhere. Students take part in projects that use computer technology in creative ways in order to provide exciting learning experiences to those who are otherwise denied access to technology. Students have completed computer programming classes, cartoon animations, multimedia self-portraits, slide shows and interactive newsletters. Many of the student projects are available online for viewing.

KEYWORDS Primary/Secondary Education, Student Projects

AUDIENCE   Children, Children's Rights Activists, Educators, Parents, Social Workers
CONTACT   webmaster@pluggedin.org
FREE

http://www.ilt.columbia.edu/LT/curricula.html#top

Press Return- Scholastic Network's Online Magazine ★★★

Press Return gives young writers, poets, and journalists the chance to collaborate with professional editors and to have their work read and viewed by a worldwide audience. Each issue of Press Return is theme-based. Students in grades 6 - 12 can contribute essays, stories, news and/or feature articles, humor, poetry, photos, and cartoons. Submissions to Press Return can only be made by Scholastic Network Members. Viewing this electronic magazine is free, however.

KEYWORDS   Educational Programs, Publishing, Student Projects, Writing
AUDIENCE   Children, Parents, Students (Primary/Secondary)
CONTACT   staff@scholastic.com
FREE

http://scholastic.com:2005/public/PressReturn/Press-Return.html

Scholarly Communications Project of Virginia Polytechnic Institute and State University ★★★★

Virginia Tech's Scholarly Communications Project, a pioneer in electronic communication of scholarly materials, points to nearly a dozen scholarly publications on varied topics. These publications include the Community Services Catalyst, the Journal of Technology Education, the Journal of Veterinary Medical Education, the Journal of Industrial Teacher Education, and others. There are also links to Virginia news, theses and dissertations, and publishing tools.

KEYWORDS   Communications, Conferences, Education, Journals
AUDIENCE   Academics, Educators, Researchers, Scholars
CONTACT   webmaster@scholar.lib.vt.edu
FREE

http://borg.lib.vt.edu/

The Science and Engineering Television Network, Inc., (SETN) ★★

The Science and Engineering Television Network, Inc., (SETN), is a nonprofit consortium of scientific societies, universities, laboratories and corporations organized to foster the development of scientific communication in the medium of television. The Network plans to mirror the best scientific print publications and broadcast news reports, lectures, demonstrations, interviews, conferences and discussions—all concerned with the latest international developments in scientific research and science policy. Currently, the viewer can jump to sites storing work sponsored by the SETN, such as an online hypertext version of 'The Art of Renaissance Science—Galileo and Perspective.' Links to pages of other scientific sites of interest are also provided.

KEYWORDS   Science, Scientific Societies, Television
AUDIENCE   Computer Scientists, Engineers, Mathematicians, Physicists, Researchers, Scientists
CONTACT   Internet Distribution Services marcf@netcom.com
FREE

http://www.service.com/stv/setncall.html

StarkNet Boundary Breakers ★★★

The Boundary Breakers are a group of teachers from several school districts in Stark County, Ohio, USA, who are committed to the idea of 'classrooms without walls.' To achieve this end, they and their classes make use of StarkNet, the county-wide education computer network. Through StarkNet, they are able to participate in cross-district, interdisciplinary, discovery-based learning experiences. The Web page has links to the gopher server, which contains lessons and unit outlines, and other supplementary materials for use in classroom projects.

KEYWORDS   Educational Technology, Educational Theory, Primary/Secondary Education
AUDIENCE   Education Administrators, Educators
CONTACT   Gopher/Web Administrator - Dack Warner dcw2cl@higbird.stark.k12.oh.us
FREE

http://jasper.stark.k12.oh.us/

gopher://199.218.193.6/1

Educational Technology

See also
Communications · Telecommunications
Computing & Mathematics · Networking
Computing & Mathematics · Software
Internet · Internet Access
Internet · Online Games

ACM Special Interest Group on Computer Uses in Education (SIGCUE) ★★★

The ACM Special Interest Group on Computer Uses in Education (SIGCUE) brings together educators at all levels who are interested in using the computer and related technology to aid the educational process. Focus is on the discussion of concepts, methods, and policies that relate to the central issues of instructional computing. The gopher sites provides information on conferences, membership, the board members, and the SIGCUE annual report.

KEYWORDS   Associations, Computer Aided Instruction, Computer Education, Education
AUDIENCE   Computer Educators, Educators
CONTACT   Jim Hightower SIG Chair chair_SIGCUE@acm.org
FREE

gopher://gopher.acm.org/11[the_files.sig_forums.sigcue]

Academic Computing Services ★★★

The Academic Computing Services Web site serves as an anchor sites for several University of Vermont academic projects related to technology. Included here are projects such as the Orient Express Educational Technology and Media Project, the Electronic Classroom, the Hope Hall of Humanities space, which provides a place for online humanities discussion, and the Deep Thought Think Tank, promoting discussion of the influence of the Internet on human existence. Also included are the personal Web pages of numerous University of Vermont students and faculty.

KEYWORDS   Education, Technology
AUDIENCE   Internet Users, Students
CONTACT   sjc@lemming.uvm.edu
FREE

http://lemming.uvm.edu/

Academic Computing Training & User Support ★★

This document is a compilation of information resources focusing on academic computer training and user support. The listservs described here are concerned with setting up operating systems and networks. Here you will find listservs devoted to security, training, mailing lists, billing, and other issues.

KEYWORDS   Campus Networks, Computer Networking, Mailing Lists
AUDIENCE   Computer Users, Management Information Specialists, Network Administrators
CONTACT   mkovacs@mcs.kent.edu
FREE

ftp://una.hh.lib.umich.edu/inetdirsstacks/acadcomp:kovacsm

Academic Consulting & Education (ACE) at UC-Irvine ★★

This gopher site provides access to information on computing support services offered for the University of California at Irvine. It includes suggested solutions for frequently encountered computer problems and a searchable database for computer help.

KEYWORDS   Computer Applications, Educational Technology, Multimedia, Universities
AUDIENCE   Academics, Computer Professionals, Educators, Students
CONTACT   dmbigos@uci.edu
FREE

gopher://ace.cwis.uci.edu:7021/

BVSD Gopher ★★★

The BVSD Gopher is the Boulder Valley School District information server in Boulder, Colorado. The information includes descriptions of the various uses of

Educational Technology

Internet technologies in K-12 curricula, project papers and reports, local information, and links to educational resources on the Internet.

KEYWORDS	Computer Aided Instruction, Primary/Secondary Education
AUDIENCE	Educators (Primary/Secondary), Parents, Students (Primary/Secondary)
CONTACT	Kelly Valdez valdez@bvsd.k12.co.us
FREE	

gopher://bvsd.k12.co.us/

CERT ★★

This is a gopher server of the Communications for North Carolina Education, Research, and Technology (CON-CERT). It provides searchable databases of computer security resources from the Computer Emergency Response Team (CERT). The data contained includes CERT advisories, CERT clippings, documents, and more.

KEYWORDS	Computer Networking, Internet Resources, Internet Security
AUDIENCE	Computer Users, Educators, Internet Users
FREE	

gopher://ncnoc.concert.net/

CICNet Home Page ★★★

CICNet is a project of the Committee on Institutional Cooperation and promotes cooperative academic programs and information resources between educational institutions. This site provides information on CICNet's Internet services, links to Internet directories and resources, a collection of public domain electronic journals, and pointers to sites at CIC universities.

KEYWORDS	Education, Information Retrieval, Information Systems, University Planning
AUDIENCE	Educators, Internet Users, Students (University)
CONTACT	www@www.cic.net
FREE	

http://gopher.cic.net/

gopher://gopher.cic.net/

ftp://ftp.cic.net/pub/

CONICYT ★★★

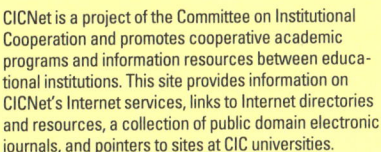

This server provides information about CONICYT, the National Commission for Scientific and Technological Research, Chile. The available information covers areas such as research programs, educational programs, bibliographical and library resources, and Chilean government legislation.

KEYWORDS	Chile, Research & Development, Scientific Research
AUDIENCE	Academics, Science Educators, Science Researchers
CONTACT	info@sophia.conicyt.cl
FREE	

gopher://daniel.conicyt.cl/

Campus Network Services at the University of California at Los Angeles ★★★

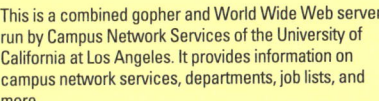

This is a combined gopher and World Wide Web server run by Campus Network Services of the University of California at Los Angeles. It provides information on campus network services, departments, job lists, and more.

KEYWORDS	California, Computer Networking, Education (College/University)
AUDIENCE	Communications Students, Computer Professionals, Computer Students
CONTACT	gopher@cns.ucla.edu
FREE	

gopher://gopher.cns.ucla.edu/

ChemViz ★★★

ChemViz is an National Science Foundation-funded project that uses high-powered computing and communications to help high school students better visualize abstract concepts of chemistry. This program allows the student (or teachers) to make images and animations of calculated atomic and molecular orbitals. Currently the project only supports the Macintosh. A color monitor is necessary to view these files. This directory contains programs, training materials, images, and documentation files for teachers and students to get started.

KEYWORDS	Chemistry, Primary/Secondary Education, Software
AUDIENCE	Chemistry Educators, Chemistry Students (High School/College)
FREE	

ftp://ftp.ncsa.uiuc.edu/Education/ChemViz

Coalition for Networked Information ★★★

The Coalition for Networked Information's gopher site aims to encourage the development of networked educational technology. This server provides a connection to an online search of their databases, gives information about the group, and provides links to their partner groups (Educom and CAUSE).

KEYWORDS	Computer Aided Instruction, Computer Networking, Education
AUDIENCE	Communication Researchers, Education Administrators, Educators
CONTACT	Craig Summerhill craig@cni.org
FREE	

gopher://gopher.cni.org/

The Computation Center ★★★

This site offers information about the University of Texas Computing Center. It provides access to documents and instructions on how to export. It also has graphics, games, mail, editors, and other gophers.

KEYWORDS	Computer Applications, Computer Games
AUDIENCE	Computer Users, Educators (University), Students (University)
CONTACT	remark@ftp.cc.utexas.edu
FREE	

gopher://ftp.cc.utexas.edu:3003/

Curry School of Education ★★★

The Curry School is a foundation dedicated to providing leadership to schools in Virginia, the United States and throughout the world. The Instructional Technology Program and individual faculty members have several Web projects under development such as an Interactive Frog Dissection, a Presentation on School Violence, the Teacher Education Internet Server, and an Education Library.

KEYWORDS	Educational Resources, Interactive Learning, Internet Resources
AUDIENCE	Educators
FREE	

http://curry.edschool.virginia.edu/

Educom ★★★★

Educom is a consortium of higher-education institutions dedicated to increasing the effectiveness of education through the application of the latest developments in information technology. Their World Wide Web and gopher servers offer access to resources designed to support this goal, such as information on educational conferences, publications detailing the latest developments in information technology and educational advancements, material on its lobbying activities and related legislation, and more. Users will also find information on becoming a member of the consortium and the benefits that being a member provides.

KEYWORDS	Information Technology, Interactive Learning, Research & Development
AUDIENCE	Academics, Educators, Information Technology Professionals, Internet Users
CONTACT	info@educom.edu
FREE	

http://educom.edu/

gopher://educom.edu/

Global Schoolhouse (GSH) ★★★

This is a gopher site of the Global Schoolhouse (GSH) Project. The GSH group works to improve education through the use of modern technology. Their gopher contains information on the GSH, its curriculum & policy, Internet tools & training, media coverage & videos, schools, sponsors and more. The Global Schoolhouse (GSH) Project is an internationally recognized activity networking classrooms across the US and overseas to demonstrate the use of the Internet in the K-12 environment. The project utilizes newly emerging last-mile connectivity solutions (CATV), developing collaboration technologies, new interfaces and advanced information discovery and retrieval tools with low-end (MacIntosh or PC) computers.

KEYWORDS	Computer Networking, Curriculum, Internet Resources, Primary/Secondary Education
AUDIENCE	Academics, Educators (Primary/Secondary), Students (Primary/Secondary)
FREE	

gopher://vinca.cnidr.org/

Indiana Higher Education Telecommunication System (IHETS) ★★★

The Indiana Higher Education Telecommunication System (IHETS) is a coalition of 39 public and private Indiana universities that acts as a resource and guiding body for several projects designed to modernize and improve Indiana's networking capabilities. Examples of specific programs that the IHETS works with include 'ACCESS Indiana,' an initiative for community and local schools to increase wide-area networking and Internet access, and Rural Datafication Project, an initiative to wire rural areas for Internet access as well.

KEYWORDS	Computer Networking, Indiana, Internet Networking
AUDIENCE	Indiana Residents
CONTACT	Indiana Higher Education Telecommunication System nic@ind.net
FREE	

http://www.ind.net:80/

Information Systems and Technology (IST) ★★★

The Information Systems and Technology (IST) site has the information on how to obtain a UCLink account. UCLink is a system for use by University of California Berkeley students, staff, and faculty for accessing electronic information resources over the Internet.

KEYWORDS	Computing, University Administration
AUDIENCE	Academics, Computer Users, Students (University)
CONTACT	consult@uclink
FREE	

gopher://uclink.berkeley.edu/

Information Technology Training Initiative ★★★

This site describes the products and resources available from the UK Higher Education Funding Councils' Information Technology Training Initiative (ITTI). ITTI provides computer and paper-based products in the areas of IT Application Skills, Basic IT Skills, Multimedia and Hypertext courseware development tools and training, and Professional IT Skills Training. Prices and addresses for ordering are given.

KEYWORDS	Computer Science, Information Science, Information Technology
AUDIENCE	Educators, Information Scientists, Students
CONTACT	Brian Shields dbs@st-andrews.ac.uk
FREE	

http://www.hull.ac.uk/Hull/ITTI/itti.html

The Institute for Advanced Technology in the Humanities ★★★

This site is a gopher server of the Institute for Advanced Technology in the Humanities (IATH), a research institute at the University of Virginia in Charlottesville. It contains information on the Institute, staff, fellowship opportunities, publications, related readings, software, courses, and more. It has pointers to other resources on the Internet.

KEYWORDS	Education (College/University), Humanities, Technological Advances
AUDIENCE	Educators (University), Humanists, Students (University)
CONTACT	iath@virginia.edu
FREE	

gopher://jefferson.village.virginia.edu/

Lquiz ★★★

LQUIZ is a UNIX program that drills the user in Latin verbs, nouns and pronouns. You must specify one of the options -v, -n or -p to select the verb, noun or pronoun quiz. If invoked without any options, lquiz prompts you to select one mode. It then prompts the user with a question expecting a single answer in Latin - e.g. What is the Imperfect Indicative Active of the verb sum? or What is dative plural of the feminine form of 'is' (that)? The version as of this writing is 1.9, dated March, 1995.

KEYWORDS	Languages, Software, Unix
AUDIENCE	Latin Scholars, Latin Students, UNIX Users
FREE	

ftp://ftp.u.washington.edu/pub/user-supported/libellus/aides/lquiz/

MECCA (Memphis Educational Computer Connectivity Alliance) ★★★

MECCA is the Memphis Educational Computer Connectivity Alliance. MECCA's mission is to facilitate computer networking and information sharing between educational institutions in the Memphis, Tennessee, area. This gopher describes MECCA's activities and has links to member institutions.

KEYWORDS	Computing, Education, Tennessee
AUDIENCE	Education Administrators, Education Administrators (University), Educators, Students (University)
CONTACT	Larry Tague mecca@physio1.utmem.edu
FREE	

gopher://physio1.utmem.edu/

Morris Automated Information Network ★★★★

This is a gopher server of the Morris Automated Information Network (MAIN). MAIN is a computer network for schools and other related institutions in New Jersey. Their gopher provides information on arts, music, entertainment, business, economics, sciences, health, sports, leisure, Morris County, and much more.

KEYWORDS	Computer Networking, Education, Libraries, New Jersey
AUDIENCE	Computer Users, Internet Users
CONTACT	freeholders@main.morris.org
FREE	

gopher://main.morris.org/

New Tools for Teaching ★★★★

This page leads to others that introduce, describe, and exemplify new Internet-based resources for teaching that are already available, and mostly easy to use. There is some information here that is particularly of interest to University of Pennsylvania instructors, but most is for a general audience. Informational resources, arranged in a hypertext fashion, cover topics like Information from/on the Net, The Library, News groups, Gopher, World-Wide Web, and MOO's.

KEYWORDS	Educational Resources, Higher Education, Internet Training, Universities
AUDIENCE	Educators, Educators (University), Information Professionals, Internet Users, Librarians, Students
CONTACT	webmaster@www.sas.upenn.edu
FREE	

http://ccat.sas.upenn.edu/teachdemo

North Dakota Higher Education Computer Network ★★★

This gopher is the main server for the North Dakota Higher Education Computer Network. It provides information about news, campus events, universities in North Dakota, computer resources and Internet resources. In addition, there are also links to other universities' gophers in North Dakota.

KEYWORDS	Computer Networks, Education (College/University), Libraries
AUDIENCE	Educators (University), Students (Secondary/University)
CONTACT	Blayne Puklich puklich@plains.nodak.edu
FREE	

gopher://chiphead.ndsu.nodak.edu/

Open Computing Facility ★★★★

This is a student-run, student-funded organization which is dedicated to the provision of free computing for all University of California at Berkeley students, faculty, and staff. Links are provided to all other information servers located at UC Berkeley including the central campus server and the Cal Berkeley Home page.

KEYWORDS	Education (College/University), Internet Access
AUDIENCE	Educators (University), Students (University)
CONTACT	general-manager@ocf.berkeley.edu
FREE	

http://ocf.berkeley.edu/

gopher://gopher.ocf.berkeley.edu

Project OWLink ★★★

OWLink is an innovative program designed to use the Internet to link Rice University with primary and secondary schools in order to create new collaborative multimedia curricula in Texas studies, environmental science and neuroscience. This linkage will promote shared learning among students, teachers and experts, exploit distance learning, provide access to online resources, and create virtual field trips without leaving the classroom. This WWW Page provides information about this project for the schools involved and the general public. Teachers and administrators can access the lesson plans and curriculum guides as well.

KEYWORDS	Education, Interactive Learning

Educational Technology – Funding

AUDIENCE   Education Administrators, Education Researchers, Educators, Foundations, Students
CONTACT   Donald Perkins
           dperkins@tenet.edu
FREE

http://chico.rice.edu/armadillo/Owlink/

Residential Computing at Stanford University ★★

This is a gopher server of the Residential Computing at the Stanford University. The mission of Residential Computing is to enable students to make effective and efficient use of information technologies in education. It provides information on the Resident Computer Coordinator (RCC) meetings, the RCC/Staff directory, residential computing news, the RCC selection, UNIX help, RCC help files, and more. As well, access to other gophers is provided.

KEYWORDS   Community Services, Education (College/University), Residential Computing
AUDIENCE   Educators (University), Students (Secondary/University)
CONTACT   Kayt Sorhaindo
           kayt@deathstar.stanford.edu
FREE

gopher://deathstar.stanford.edu/

TSW Gopher ★★★

TSW Gopher offers information from The Scholar's Workstation (TSW) Computing Sales Program at the University of California at Berkeley. TSW sells computer products of use to University of California faculty, staff, and students. This information includes product listing and prices, sales policies, and customer eligibility.

KEYWORDS   Education (College/University), Sales
AUDIENCE   Educators, Professors, Students (University)
CONTACT   tswinfo@garnet.berkeley.edu
FREE

gopher://phone.berkeley.edu/

Technology Help & Multimedia Software and Lessons ★★★

This is a directory of resources for teaching with technology. There are files at this site containing hypercard stacks for use with video players and other multimedia files. In addition, users will find information about CD-ROMs and videodiscs for educational use, as well as software and hardware tips for teachers.

KEYWORDS   Computer Aided Instruction, Hypercard, Multimedia, Software
AUDIENCE   Educators (Primary/Secondary)
CONTACT   Donald Perkins
           dperkins@tenet.edu
FREE

gopher://chico.rice.edu:1170/11/Technology

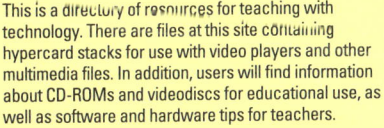

U.S. Department of Education about INET ★★★

This is the WWW server for the U.S. Department of Education's (ED) Institutional Communications Network (INet) project whose goal is to help with communication and information sharing among major education research, development, and dissemination institutions. The server has information about the mission, goals, structure, and newsletters of the U.S. Department of Education.

KEYWORDS   Department Of Education (US), Education, Government (US), Information Technology
AUDIENCE   Education Administrators, Educators, Government Employees
CONTACT   wwwadmin@inet.ed.gov
FREE

http://www.ed.gov/info/about.oeri.html

Virtual School ★★★

This server provides information on computer applications to education. It is part of the Virtual School Project at Maricopa Community College District (MCCD) in Arizona. It contains information on the Virtual School, networked educational environments, and the Globe-wide Network Academy. It has links to other gophers.

KEYWORDS   Distance Education, Education
AUDIENCE   Academics, Educators, Educators (University), Students (University)
CONTACT   nils@mcmuse.mc.maricopa.edu
FREE

gopher://mcmuse.mc.maricopa.edu/

Funding

See also
Arts & Music · *Arts Resources*
Business & Economics · *Career & Employment*

Annual Report, American Indian College Fund ★★★★

This page provides several links to information about the American Indian College Fund. It is a tax-exempt, non-profit organization launched in 1989 by the presidents of the Indian colleges. Its mission is to raise funds from the private sector to provide scholarship aid and developmental assistance to the member institutions and the American Indian Higher Education Consortium that are located in the United States. It also works to increase public awareness of the work of Indian colleges.

KEYWORDS   Education (College/University), Scholarships
AUDIENCE   Business Professionals, Grantmakers, Indian Colleges, Native Americans
CONTACT   Karen M. Strom
           kstrom@hanksville.phast.umass.edu
FREE

http://hanksville.phast.umass.edu/defs/independent/AICF.html

The Doreen B. Townsend Center for the Humanities Gopher ★★★

The Doreen B. Townsend Center for the Humanities at the University of California, Berkeley, offers fellowships to advanced graduate students and untenured faculty on the Berkeley campus and sponsors interdisciplinary graduate research seminars. This site also offers newsletters and other information.

KEYWORDS   Education (College/University), Humanities, Political Science
AUDIENCE   Educators (University), Humanists, Students (University)
CONTACT   Carolyn Smith
           cmsmith@uclink.berkeley.edu
FREE

gopher://uclink.berkeley.edu:1611/

Office of Contract and Grant Administration Gopher ★★

The information down this gopher hole is from the Office of Contract and Grant Administration at the University of California at Irvine (UCI). The information includes research funding opportunities, advice on how to write funding proposals, and funding policy information for both UCI and federal agencies. There is also a variety of employment policy information present on the server.

KEYWORDS   Employment, Finance, University Administration
AUDIENCE   Professors, Researchers, University Administrators
CONTACT   Dennis Wiedeman
           dhwiedem@uci.edu
FREE

gopher://ocga.cwis.uci.edu:7012/

The University of Kansas Research Support and Grant Administration's Gopher ★★★

This site is the University of Kansas Research Support and Grant Administration's gopher server in Lawrence, Kansas. It offers information on news, research services, funding opportunities, the University phone book, research newsletters, and more. It has pointers to other gophers.

KEYWORDS   Education (College/University), Grants, University Administration
AUDIENCE   Academics, Grantseekers, University Administrators
CONTACT   kreed@research.rgsps.ukans.edu
FREE

gopher://gopher.rgsps.ukans.edu/

University of Tennessee Research Services Gopher ★★★

This is the University of Tennessee Research Services gopher server in Knoxville, Tennessee. It offers information on funding opportunities, research policies, publications, professional journals, and more. It makes connections to federal government gophers, as well as other gophers elsewhere on the Internet.

- KEYWORDS Education (College/University), Information Science, Scientific Research
- AUDIENCE Academics, Science Researchers, Scientists, University Administrators
- CONTACT gcole@solar.rtd.utk.edu
- FREE

gopher://gopher.rtd.utk.edu/

Government Libraries

See also
Education · *Academic Libraries*
Education · *Public Libraries*
Education · *Special Libraries*
Government & Politics · *Countries*
Government & Politics · *States*

Data Research Associates, Inc. Information Gateway

This site is a database of the 4.1 million records from the Library of Congress. It contains a catalog from the Books, Maps, Music, Serials, and Visual Materials sections as distributed by the Catalog Distributing Service. This is not the same as the card catalog at the Library of Congress. The last recorded entry at this site was in 1992.

- KEYWORDS Databases, Library of Congress
- AUDIENCE Academics, Cartographers, Library Users, Literary Scholars, Researchers
- CONTACT sales@dra.com
- COST

ftp://dra.com/

telnet://dra.com

LC MARVEL

LC MARVEL, the Library of Congress Machine-Assisted Realization of the Virtual Electronic Library, is the main gopher server for the Library of Congress (LC). It contains information about LC events and facilities, provides online access to LC publications and LC catalogs, and gives links to other important gopher holes.

- KEYWORDS Information Retrieval, Information Science, Libraries, Library of Congress
- AUDIENCE Information Scientists, Librarians, Library Administrators, Researchers
- CONTACT lcmarvel@loc.gov
- FREE

gopher://gopher.loc.gov/

Library Information Server of B.C.

This is the Library Information Server for British Columbia, Canada. It provides information services to employees, project teams, and members of the British Columbian government. Information provided includes printed reference materials, CD-ROM databases, external databases and more. There is a searchable database of abstracts from more than 100 computing and technology periodicals.

- KEYWORDS Government, Information Retrieval, Libraries, Library Science
- AUDIENCE Computer Researchers, Government Officials, Librarians, Literary Scholars
- CONTACT Christine Webb
  cwebb@bcsc02.gov.bc.ca
- FREE

gopher://bcsc02.gov.bc.ca:65522/

The National Library of Australia

The National Library of Australia page provides access to their collections and services. The server has information on events, exhibitions and world wide government information. There are links to the Online Public Access Catalogue (OPAC), the Australian Electronic Journals and other Internet resources.

- KEYWORDS Australia, National Archives
- AUDIENCE Australians, Researchers, Students
- CONTACT Diana Dack
  ddack@nla.gov.au
- FREE

http://www.nla.gov.au/

State Library of North Carolina Gopher Server

The State Library of North Carolina Gopher Server gives access to various gateways of information around the Internet on topics such as business, environment, government, and so on. In addition, it gives access to a limited number of State Library publications.

- KEYWORDS Information Science, Libraries, Library Science, North Carolina
- AUDIENCE Librarians, Library Administrators, Library Users, Researchers
- CONTACT Gary Harden
  gharden@hal.dcr.state.nc.us
- FREE

gopher://hal.ncdcr.gov/

Texas State Electronic Library

The Texas State Electronic Library in Austin, Texas provides access to the collected resources of libraries across the state. These resources include online reference sources, texts of books, electronic journals, and databases. The Texas State Electronic Library is a joint effort of libraries around Texas and is coordinated by the Texas State Library.

- KEYWORDS Information Science, Libraries, Library Science, Texas
- AUDIENCE Librarians, Library Administrators, Library Users, Texas Residents
- CONTACT Christine Masleid
  christin@tsl.texas.gov
- FREE

gopher://link.tsl.texas.gov/

Virginia Library and Information Network (VLIN) Gopher

The VLIN Gopher is part of the services of the Virginia Library and Information Network, sponsored by the Virginia State Library and Archives. The major feature of this gopher is its link to CAVALIR ONLINE, the online union bibiliographic database, which currently contains several million unique bibliographic and holdings records from over 18 Virginia libraries. Other information provided through this gopher service include publications, bulletin boards & freenets, the reference desk, Virginia resources, news, weather, recreation and many more. In addition, users can make connections to other Internet libraries.

- KEYWORDS Computer Databases, Libraries, Library Science, Virginia
- AUDIENCE Librarians, Library Administrators, Library Users, Virginia Residents
- CONTACT Elizabeth Roderick
  eroderic@leo.vsla.edu
- FREE

gopher://gemini.vsla.edu/

Wyoming State Library

This gopher offers limited access to a searchable index of the holdings in Wyoming's State Library, as well as links to other selected libraries on the Internet.

- KEYWORDS United States, Wyoming
- AUDIENCE Librarians, Wyoming Residents
- FREE

gopher://159.238.106.10/

International Education

See also
Computing & Mathematics · *Computer Science*
Education · *Universities - Africa*
Education · *Universities - Asia*
Education · *Universities - Australia*
Education · *Universities - Europe*
Education · *Universities - South America*

Academia Sinica

This site describes the Academia Sinica, Taiwan. It is maintained by the Computing Center of Academia Sinica. The information includes the administration of the Academia Sinica, its institutes, areas of research, publications, library resources/services, Usenet news, courses, and many more.

- KEYWORDS Scientific Research, Taiwan, Universities
- AUDIENCE Academics, Chinese Speakers, Scientists, Students
- CONTACT service@sinica.edu.tw
- FREE

gopher://gopher.sinica.edu.tw/

Commonwealth of Learning - Home Page

This home page describes the mandate, activities, and goals of the Commonwealth of Learning. The Commonwealth of Learning is an international organization established by governments of the British Commonwealth to create and widen access to education and to improve its quality. The server also gives a link to other WWW in the British Commonwealth.

KEYWORDS Commonwealth, International Education
AUDIENCE Educators, International Aid Agencies, International Development Specialists
CONTACT postmaster@col.org
FREE

http://www.col.org/

International Studies at the University of Minnesota ★★★★

This gopher provides information on the University's program in International Studies and some resources relating to the field, including the International Dateline Newsletter, information about the University's China Center, study abroad resources; international courses and opportunities on campus, and information on a project to study Southeast Asian refugees. Also available are resources on campus news and visiting scholars working in related fields.

KEYWORDS Education (College/University), International News, International Studies
AUDIENCE Educators (University), International Studies Students, Minnesota Residents
FREE

gopher://rodent.cis.umn.edu:11137/

OneEurope Magazine ★★★

This is the official and triannual electronic magazine of the AEGEE, a comprehensive European student congress of European nations. Articles and other information related to international education, politics, the environment and numerous other subjects fill these pages. Almost all the materials in OneEurope are written and edited by European university students.

KEYWORDS E-Zines, Europe, International Education
AUDIENCE Educators (University), Europeans, Students (University)
CONTACT Michael Waibel
         wma@freax.fido.de
FREE

http://www.informatik.rwth-aachen.de/AEGEE/oneEurope/

Schulen im WWW, Abteilung Paedagogik und Informatik ★★★

Schulen im WWW gives all the links to German, Austrian and some other European schools with sites on the World Wide Web.

KEYWORDS Austria, Germany, Information Technology
AUDIENCE German Studies Students, Germans
CONTACT webmaster@www.educat.hu-berlin.de
FREE

http://www.educat.hu-berlin.de/schulen/schulen.html

For World History Connections

Just the facts, ma'am

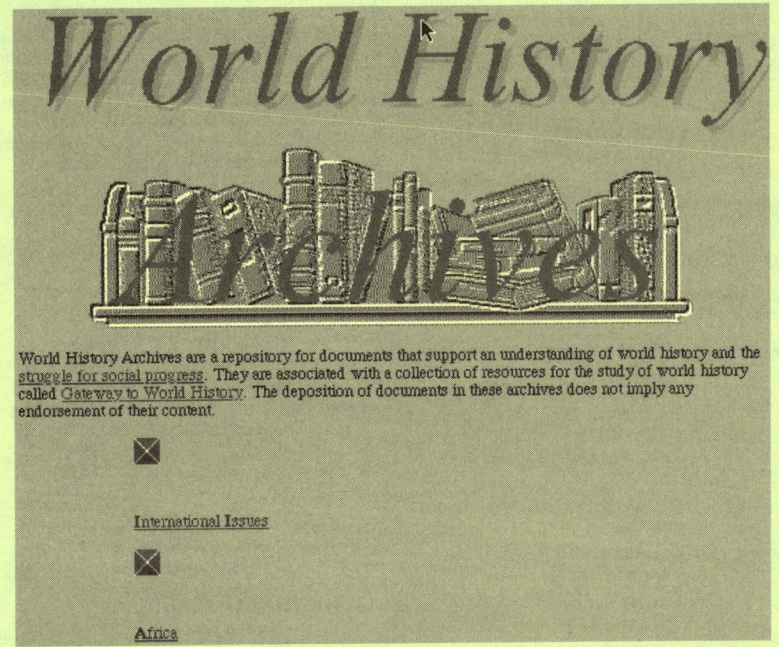

So your homework assignment is to list the dates and locations of the major battles fought in World War II. Where do you go to get the information? The Internet provides a wealth of historical information via a variety of sources that furnish links to other World Wide Web pages which, in turn, provide links to additional historical documents and resources.

If you're involved in a trivia match with a friend and need some historical facts about the non-Western world, where do you turn? If you're smart, it will be the Internet.

While many resources include essays, writings, and analysis, other resources provide just the facts. Only a few places provide history games to make learning fun. One of the easiest and most entertaining places to start your search for historical facts is the World History archives. This site provides the user a link to other Web pages that in turn contain links to documents and other electronic resources related to world history. A majority of the documents, however, comprise examples of "contemporary" world history.

(http://neal.ctstateu.edu/history/world_history/archives/archives.html)

The site also features games that make history relevant and fun. Utilizing the explosion of multimedia, the Gamelink—History CD_ROMs, provides the user with a variety of CD-ROMs that he or she can effortlessly order.

(http://netcenter.com/netcentr/mall/techmart/hightech.html)

If you have ever wondered what the world might be like had American President John F. Kennedy not been assassinated, or if Winston Churchill had never existed, the place to find out is the "Alternative History—What If FAQ" (frequently asked questions). This area is highly entertaining as well as informative, bringing out tidbits of information that might be overlooked through mainstream historical sources.

(http://www.lib.ox.ac.uk/internet/news/faq/archive/history.what-if.html)

International Education – Organizations

The Wladyslaw Poniecki Charitable Foundation

This server provides access to information related to Poland and Eastern Europe. It is provided in part by the The Wladyslaw Poniecki Charitable Foundation, a non-profit group which aims to provide educational materials to Poland. The Foundation is described and there are links to archives with information on Polish culture, and related sites.

Keywords Eastern Europe, Education, Non Profit Organizations, Poland
Audience Europeans, Polish
Contact Darek Milewski
darekm@poniecki.berkeley.edu
Free

gopher://poniecki.berkeley.edu/

Writing Around the World

This World Wide Web Site provides information on the Global Communication through Email project, Cities Writing Project, ESL and other programs sponsored or participated in by the American Language Institute at NYU.

Keywords Communications, ESL (English As A Second Language), Writing
Audience Distance Educators, ESL Teachers, Language Arts Educators
Contact Andrew Hess
hess@acf2.nyu.edu
Free

http://www.nyu.edu/pages/hess/cities.html

Language Acquisition

See also
Communications · *Mass Communications*
Education · *Primary & Secondary Education*
Humanities & Social Sciences · *Languages*
Humanities & Social Sciences · *Linguistics*

The Arabic Tutor

The Arabic Tutor is an Arabic teaching software program for beginners that works with the Microsoft Windows operating system. It features a user-friendly point-and-click feature with sound. This site gives a description of the program, as well as a link to download a demo version. There are several versions of the demo, which includes sound for one of the lessons. Viewers can also look at screen captures to get a sense of what the software can do. Ordering information is given as well.

Keywords Arabic Language, Linguistics
Audience Arabic Students, Iranians, Language Students, Linguists, Middle East Residents
Contact University of Oregon
consult@darkwing.uoregon.edu
Free

http://darkwing.uoregon.edu/~alquds/arabic.html

CELIA (Computer Enhanced Language Instruction Archives)

CELIA (Computer Enhanced Language Instruction Archives) is a collection of computer resources that are useful in teaching languages (CALL, CALI, ...). It consists of public domain, freeware, and shareware files. It also contains Gopher links to other useful resources on the Internet. CELIA is maintained by volunteers. You can help by adding materials, giving feedback, or offering to help. This archive makes use of Gopher links so many items will not appear to the FTP user. Users will find language resources and software for languages such as Chinese, English, Deutsch, Italiano, Japanese, Russian, Espanol, and Thai. There are links to outside systems that contain information and software for learners of French, Polish, and Swedish languages, among others.

Keywords ESL (English As A Second Language), Educational Software, Multilingual Resources, Software
Audience ESL Teachers, English Educators, Language Educators, Language Students
Contact Fred Swartz
fred.swartz@merit.edu
Free

gopher://gopher.archive.merit.edu:7055/11/celia-gopher

ftp://ftp.latrobe.edu.au/pub/celia/

Concordia Programs

This is a list of materials published by Concordia Programs for foreign language instruction. Languages for possible study include Spanish, French, Latin and German as well as English as a Second Language. It contains an annotated list of materials and an order form.

Keywords French, Language Instruction, Spanish
Audience International Students, Language Students
Free

http://www.charm.net/~ibc/ibc2/concord.html

ELSNET's Home Page (European Network in Language and Speech)

ELSNET is the European Network in Language and Speech, one of over a dozen Networks of Excellence established by the European Commission's ESPRIT Division for Basic Research. This Web site addresses the development of language technology in Europe and abroad by helping to coordinate progress on both scientific and technological fronts. Offerings include ELSNET's publications, academic papers, information on current projects, and links to related Internet resources.

Keywords Cognitive Sciences, Communications, Linguistics
Audience Cognitive Scientists, Linguists
Contact elsnet@ed.ac.uk
Free

http://www.cogsci.ed.ac.uk/elsnet/home.html

HyperGlot, The Foreign Language Software Company

This is Hyperglot's home page providing information about foreign language learning software for Spanish, French, German, Italian, Japanese, Chinese, Russian and English for Windows, MS-DOS, and Macintosh. Information at this site includes an online catalog, customer service, technical support, company information, and links to other useful Web pages.

Keywords Language Instruction, Software
Audience Language Educators, Language Students, Macintosh Users, Windows Users
Contact glot@hyperglot.com.
Free

http://www.hyperglot.com/hyperglot.html

The Virtual English Language Center

The Comenius Group is developing this site so that students and teachers of English as a second or foreign language can have online access to relevant materials, products and services. Some areas of this server include 'The Weekly Idiom', a collection of sound files that demonstrate the use of a different idiom per week and 'The Email Pen Pal Connection,' which brings together ESL and other students together in an email exchange. In addition, users can read about John Amos Comenius, a 17th-century pioneer of pansophism and humanistic learning. Links to off-site resources include English MOOs, vocabulary and and dictionary sites.

Keywords ESL (English As A Second Language), ESL (English as a Second Language), Interactive Education, Second Language Acquisition
Audience ESL Teachers, English Educators, Language Educators, Language Students
Contact Interport Communications
webmaster@interport.net
Free

http://www.interport.net/~comenius/

Organizations

See also
Computing & Mathematics · *Organizations*
Government & Politics · *Agencies*
Health & Medicine · *Resources*

The AACE Information Server

This site gives information about the Association for the Advancement of Computing in Education (AACE). AACE is a group whose primary goal is advancing the quality of education through technology. The information provided includes the AACE mission statement, AACE publications, AACE conference dates, and ways to communicate with AACE members.

Keywords Technological Advances
Audience Communication Researchers, Educators
Contact AACE@virginia.edu
Free

gopher://teach.virginia.edu/

ASHA - Berkeley Home Page ★★★

ASHA, a group that helps provide and fund education for underpriviledged children throughout India, offers donation and contact information for their organization on this web page. The most recent ASHA newsletter is also available here, as well as back issues, various press releases, memoranda on current programs, and sponsor lists.

KEYWORDS Activism, India, International Aid, Non Profit Organizations
AUDIENCE Activists, Educators, India Residents, Indians
CONTACT Asha@OCF.Berkeley.Edu
FREE

http://http.icsi.berkeley.edu/~amit/asha/index.html

Academic and Research Network of Slovenia (ARNES) Home Page ★★★

The Academic and Research Network of Slovenia (ARNES) provides network services and expertise to educational and research institutions in Europe. Users can link to the individual institutions, and also to larger organizations of which ARNES is a part. There is information available on ARNES facilities and staff, as well as local news.

KEYWORDS Community Networking, Educational Resources, Networking
AUDIENCE Educators, Network Administrators
CONTACT arnes@arnes.si
FREE

http://www.arnes.si

Alpha Phi Omega Gopher Server ★★★

This gopher holds information about the college student organization Alpha Phi Omega. The Alpha Phi Omega program includes members from the United States and the Republic of the Philippines. Some issues which APO works on are leadership development, community service and friendship. Information on this site includes mailing lists, directories, and newsletters.

KEYWORDS Education (College/University), International Organizations, Student Associations, Universities
AUDIENCE Students (University)
CONTACT Bill Wells
wcwells@uclink.berkeley.edu
FREE

gopher://apo.berkeley.edu:4302/

The American Association of Collegiate Registrars and Admissions Officers ★★★

This gopher site provides access to the American Association of Collegiate Registrars and Admissions Officers, as well as to other higher education professionals. It includes information on services relating to evaluation of foreign educational credentials.

KEYWORDS Educational Organizations, Educational Policy, International Education
AUDIENCE Academics, Administrators, Educators (University), International Students
CONTACT George Spack
spackg@aacrao-dec.nche.edu
FREE

gopher://aacrao-dec.nche.edu/

American Educational Research Association ★★★

The American Educational Research Association is concerned with improving the educational process by encouraging scholarly inquiry related to education and by promoting the dissemination and practical application of research results. The organization has more than 20,000 members representing educators, administrators, researchers, and behavior scientists. There are sections of this Web and Gopher devoted to the interests of its members, some of which have online information available.

KEYWORDS Research & Development
AUDIENCE Behavioral Scientists, Educators
CONTACT Gene V Glass
glass@asu.edu
FREE

http://www.asu.edu/aff/aera/home.html

CAUSE ★★★

This is a gopher server of CAUSE. An international nonprofit association, CAUSE is dedicated to enhancing higher education through the use of information resources. Information provided includes conferences, seminars, awards, the membership directory, libraries, job posting services and more.

KEYWORDS Information Science, Information Technology, International Education
AUDIENCE Educators, International Development Specialists, Students (Secondary/College)
CONTACT info@cause.colorado.edu
FREE

gopher://cause-gopher.colorado.edu/

CREN ★★★

This is a gopher server for the Corporation for Research and Educational Networking (CREN), which gives as its mission the definition and implementation of a number of network servers and services for the realization of a virtual university. The site contains documents, mailing list archives, software, and more.

KEYWORDS Computer Applications, Educational Networks, Research
AUDIENCE Educators (University), Students (University)
FREE

http://www.cren.net

gopher://info.cren.net/

Connections to Learning Another Language

Tres bien, amigo!

University of Trieste
Piazzale Europa, 1
34127 Trieste, ITALY
tel. 040-676 6111

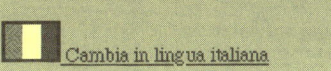 Cambia in lingua italiana

If you know a little about a lot of languages and don't want to embarrass yourself by mixing up what little you know, there are a number of online sites where you can get extensive help. There are even places on the World Wide Web that will teach you Cantonese, rather than Mandarin Chinese.

If you want to learn Italian, what better place than in Italy? Through the Internet you can take your Italian lessons at the University of Trieste, visiting students at the University's Web site. While many of areas on the site are in Italian, these provide a good way to get experience at actually using the language.

(http://www.univ.trieste.it/
e_utshom.html)

Additionally, there are a number of sites where you can learn languages of the Far East. For instance, if you are interested in learning Thai, the "Language FAQ" provides a number of resources for learning about that language; this site includes valuable information on the Thai culture, a pronunciation guide, and a list of universities and libraries around the world that furnish Thai instructional cassette tapes. You can even access studies on the origin of Thai words.

(http://www.nectec.or.th/
soc.culture.thai/language.html)

Centre of University Teaching and Learning Gopher ★★

This site gives information about the Centre for University Teaching and Learning at the University of South Australia. Some resources here include preliminary exercises for writing center programs, a searchable database of educational journal articles, and general resources for information and technology in teaching and learning.

KEYWORDS Continuing Education, Educational Technology, Lesson Plans, Universities
AUDIENCE Education Administrators, Educators
CONTACT Mark de Raad
Mark.deRaad@UniSA.edu.au
FREE

gopher://cutl.city.unisa.edu.au/

Consortium for School Networking ★★★★

The Consortium for School Networking is an American organization for advocating access to the emerging National Information Infrastructure in schools. Users can access the consortium's Technology Resources Page, Technology Planning Resources Guide Funding Opportunities Resources Page, or just pull up notices of the recent activities of the organization. The center also provides key information for national laws affecting technology and education.

KEYWORDS Educational Technology, Politics
AUDIENCE Educators, Lobbyists, Parents, Students, United States Residents
CONTACT webmaster@cosn.org
FREE

http://cosn.org

gopher://cosn.org

Educational Testing Service (ETS) Internet Gopher server ★★★★

Educational Testing Service (ETS), a leader in educational research and testing, is the world's largest private nonprofit educational assessment and measurement institution. This server offers information about some of the tests which ETS administers, including the GRE and the SAT. In addition, the viewer will find information regarding Computer-based Testing, testing students with disabilites, employment listings at ETS, and links to other educational resources.

KEYWORDS Educational Theory, Employment, Research & Development, Standardized Tests
AUDIENCE Educators (University) , Students, Students (Secondary/College)
CONTACT gopher@ets.org
FREE

gopher://gopher.ets.org:70/

FUNET - Finnish University and Research Network ★★★

This site offers information about FUNET (Finnish University and Research Network). FUNET is the primary computer network for research and education in the Scandinavian country of Finland. The information provided includes documents about the various universities connected to FUNET and the research they perform. The server provides links to nodes of FUNET as well as to servers outside of Finland.

KEYWORDS Computer Networking, Education (College/University), Finland, Internet Directories
AUDIENCE Academics, Educators (University), Students (University)
CONTACT gopher-admin@gopher.funet.fi
FREE

gopher://gopher.eunet.fi/

Hong Kong Students Association of The Johns Hopkins University ★★★

The Web page of the Hong Kong Students Association of The Johns Hopkins University details the student group's constitution and membership and provides access to its newsletter. Information about the East Asian country is provided. There are links to similar student groups and the Hong Kong Express, an extensive meta-index.

KEYWORDS Hong Kong
AUDIENCE Hong Kong Natives, Johns Hopkins University Students
FREE

http://metro.turnpike.net/H/hksa/index.html

ICPSR Internet Gopher Server ★★★

The ICPSR Internet Gopher Server provides services and data from the Inter-university Consortium for Political and Social Research (ICPSR). This data includes the 1990 U.S. census, the VARIABLES database, which provides information from many ICPSR surveys, and data archives such as the National Archive of Computerized Data on Aging. Most of the information is searchable by keywords or by WAIS. ICPSR is a non-profit group which acts as a central repository for data of interest to social scientists.

KEYWORDS Political Science, Social Law, Social Sciences
AUDIENCE Academics, Political Scientists, Professors, Social Scientists
CONTACT Peter Joftis
icpsr_netmail@um.cc.umich.edu
FREE

gopher://tdis.icpsr.umich.edu/

Institute for Learning Technologies ★★

The Institute for Learning Technologies, founded in 1986 at Teachers College, Columbia University, works to advance the role of computers and other information technologies in education and society. The Institute works both as an internal funding agency, soliciting proposals and making awards, and as a project development office, organizing and supporting efforts to win grants from external sources. The results are often online. There are several papers and projects that the ILT has produced, as well as links to K-12 and Lifelong Learning Resources.

KEYWORDS New York, Online Guides, Primary/Secondary Education, Research & Development
AUDIENCE Education Researchers, Educators
CONTACT Institute for Learning Technologies
info@ilt.columbia.edu
FREE

http://www.ilt.columbia.edu/ILT/ILTinfo.html#top

Inter-University Consortium for Political and Social Research ★★★

The Inter-University Consortium for Political and Social Research (ICPSR) at the University of Michigan serves social scientists by providing a central repository and dissemination service for machine-readable social science data, training facilities in basic and advanced techniques of quantitative social analysis, and resources that facilitate the use of advanced computer technology by social scientists.

KEYWORDS Computer Aided Instruction, Politics, Social Sciences, Universities
AUDIENCE Academics, Researchers, Social Scientists, Students
CONTACT Peter Joftis
icpsr_netmail@um.cc.umich.edu
FREE

gopher://icpsr.umich.edu/

Latin American and Caribbean Center ★★

The Latin American and Caribbean Center (LACC) provides a table of contents and excerpts from Hemispheres Magazine, as well as resources for Latin American and Caribbean scholars, such as conference announcements, fellowship and grant information, and links to specific institutes, including the Florida Caribbean Institute, the Florida-Mexico Institute, and the Leadership Center of the Americas. There are also links to outside Latin American and Carribean Internet Sites.

KEYWORDS Caribbean, International Education, Latin America, Scholarships
AUDIENCE Latin America Educators, Latin America Residents , Latin America Students
CONTACT University Computer Services
gopher_adm@fiu.edu
FREE

gopher://gopher.fiu.edu:70/11/acadinfo/lacci

MOREnet ★★★

This is a gopher server of the Missouri Research and Education Network (MOREnet). It contains information on MOREnet, its membership workbook, member and staff lists, events, meeting minutes, resources and more. It makes connections to other gophers as well.

KEYWORDS Education, Internet Resources, Networking, Research & Development
AUDIENCE Academics, Computer Users, Educators, Internet Users

Organizations – Primary & Secondary Education

CONTACT nic@more.net
FREE

gopher://services.more.net/

Manitoba Organization of Faculty Associations ★★★

This is a gopher server of the Manitoba Organization of Faculty Associations (MOFA), located in Manitoba, Canada. It provides information on the University of Manitoba Faculty Association, the University of Winnipeg Faculty Association, and related documents, such as collective bargaining agreements. It also gives access to the faculty gophers at institutions throughout Canada and the United States.

KEYWORDS Canada, Educational Resources, Faculty, Labor Issues
AUDIENCE Educators, Educators (University), Labor Organizers, University Faculty
CONTACT Gary Russell
russelg@cc.umanitoba.ca
FREE

gopher://gopher.mofa.mb.ca/

Northwest Regional Educational Laboratory ★★★

This gopher hole provides information about the Northwest Regional Educational Laboratory (NWREL). NWREL is an agency that works to improve educational outcomes for children, youth, and adults. The information on their server includes contacts, publication lists, publication ordering information, and descriptions of NWREL programs.

KEYWORDS Educational Policy, Educational Resources, Research & Development
AUDIENCE Educators
CONTACT Ethel Simon-McWilliams
simone@nwrel.org
FREE

gopher://gopher.nwrel.org/

OERI Gopher Server ★★★

This is a gopher server for the US Department of Education. It provides information about INet, the Department's first Internet node. There is also access to databases and documents containing statistical and research data available through INet. This information centers on the Department's programs to improve teaching and learning skills.

KEYWORDS Computer Networks, Educational Policy, Government Agencies (US), Primary/Secondary Education
AUDIENCE Education Administrators, Educators, Educators (Primary/Secondary)
CONTACT gopheradm@inet.ed.gov
FREE

gopher://gopher.ed.gov/

SOS China Education Fund ★★★

The SOS China Education fund is a nonprofit organization dedicated to bringing educational opportunities to underpriviledged youth in rural China. This server contains information on their current activities as well as articles from the popular press detailing past efforts. A search engine allows users to easily navigate throughout their large archive of Chinese education-related data. This site also features a number of digitized photographs of Chinese schoolchildren, schools, and teachers.

KEYWORDS Children, China, Education, International Aid, Non Profit Organizations
AUDIENCE Activists, China Residents, Chinese, Educators
CONTACT sos@ifcss.org
FREE

http://www.ifcss.org:8001/www/pub/org/sos-edu/.index.html

Scholastic's Internet Center ★★★

Scholastic Press, one of the largest educational publishing organizations, hosts Scholastic's Internet Center. This Web and gopher site contains several databases for classroom activities. Some of the libraries include Middle School Science, Reading and Language Arts, and Integrating Technology Library. Users will also find ordering information for the Education Store, and a listing of titles for teachers and educational administrators. Viewers will also be able to participate in projects like the 1995 International Arctic Project.

KEYWORDS Educational Resources, Primary/Secondary Education, Publishing, Student Projects
AUDIENCE Education Administrators, Educators (Primary/Secondary), Librarians
CONTACT staff@scholastic.com
COST

http://Scholastic.com:2005/

gopher://scholastic.com:2003/

Social Workers Advocating Network Technologies ★★★★

The Social Workers Advocating Network Technologies (SWAN) Home page is a meta-index to activist groups and academic and government resources. Its purpose is to promote professional connectivity as a means of improving the effectiveness of social work. There are links to groups ranging from the American Civil Liberties Union to the World Council of Churches, the Bureau of Census to Washington University, a subject index, and more.

KEYWORDS Public Welfare, Social Work
AUDIENCE Civil Servants, Social Scientists, Social Workers
FREE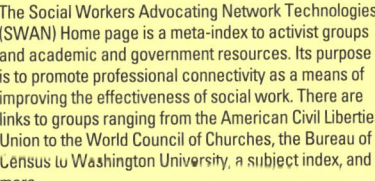

http://falcon.cc.ukans.edu/~pthomas/swan.html

Suisun Marsh Natural History Association (SMNHA) ★★★★

The SMNHA is devoted to encouraging and providing environmental education to school children and other groups across Northern California. Their web pages give information on their educational programs and legal activism - protecting the marsh and surrounding areas from development and pollution, and keeping public access to the marsh guaranteed.

KEYWORDS Activism, Conservation, Environmentalism, Wildlife
AUDIENCE Activists, Conservationists, Environmentalists, Wildlife Biologists, Wildlife Enthusiasts
CONTACT Tim Ligouri
timlig@community.net
FREE

http://community.net/marsh/

Texas Higher Education Coordinating Board Gopher Server ★★★

This gopher server provides information about university and other post-secondary education in the state of Texas. The information is provided by the Texas Higher Education Coordinating Board. The information includes degree programs in Texas, the cost of higher education in Texas, admission requirements for Texas institutions, and links to the institutions themselves.

KEYWORDS Education (College/University), Texas, University Administration
AUDIENCE Educators (University), Students (University), Texas Residents
FREE

gopher://info.thecb.texas.gov/

Primary & Secondary Education

See also
Arts & Music · *Art Resources*
Education · *Educational Projects*
Education · *Resources*
Science · *Biology*

AIDS Now! For Teens ★★★★

This page is an interactive AIDS questionaire for K-12 students. Students answer questions related to AIDS awareness and submit their answers. If they answer correctly, a certificate suitable for printing comes up. There are also links to AIDS Web servers, multimedia resources, and a note to teachers using this resource in the classroom.

KEYWORDS AIDS (Acquired Immune Deficiency Syndrome), Sex Education
AUDIENCE Educators (Primary/Secondary), Health Care Professionals, Health Care Providers, Students (Secondary/College)
CONTACT Jeff Schwartz
webdog@sfsu.edu
FREE

http://edu-52.sfsu.edu/aids/aids.html

Armadillo, The Texas Studies Gopher ★★★★

The Texas Studies Gopher, Armadillo, has been designed with the middle school teacher and student in mind. It presents information about Texas natural and cultural history to support an interdisciplinary course of

Primary & Secondary Education

study around themes of interest to students involved in their surroundings. This server has subdirectories and links to other non-Texas related projects as well.

KEYWORDS History, Primary/Secondary Education, Student Projects, Texas
AUDIENCE Educators (Primary/Secondary), Students (Primary/Secondary), Texan Culture Enthusiasts, Texas Residents
CONTACT Donald Perkins
dperkins@tenet.edu
FREE

gopher://riceinfo.rice.edu:1170/11/

Atlantic View Elementary School ★★★

This is the home page of the Atlantic View Elementary School in Nova Scotia, Canada which has been composed by the students of the third and fourth grades and their teacher. It includes local information focusing on talent, events, student autobiographies, and more. There is also information of interest to Canadian students such as the Earth Day Grocery Bag Project 1994, 1995, and also resources on food allergies in children, and educational information for teachers.

KEYWORDS Canada, Primary/Secondary Education, Student Life
AUDIENCE Canadians, Educators (Primary/Secondary), Students (Primary/Secondary)
CONTACT nbarkhou@fox.nstn.ns.ca
FREE

http://fox.nstn.ca/~nbarkhou/avshome.html

BBC (British Broadcasting Corporation) Education ★★★★

The BBC Education site provides hot links to its interactive service on its programs and resources for all areas of pre-school, children at school, and education resources.

KEYWORDS Educational Resources, Pre-School Education
AUDIENCE Educators, Students, parents
FREE

http://www.bbcnc.org.uk/education/index.html

Best of K-12 on the Internet ★★★

This server is a gateway to information related to K-12 education on the Internet. This information includes gopher and WWW sites at schools, teaching materials, libraries, and mailing lists.

KEYWORDS Curriculum, Internet Resources, Primary/Secondary Education, Schools (Primary/Secondary)
AUDIENCE Educators, Educators (Primary/Secondary), Students (Primary/Secondary)
CONTACT Rhana Jacot
rjacot@cic.net
FREE

gopher://gopher.cic.net:3005/

Colorado K-12 Internet Host Machine's Gopher ★★★

This gopher offers information on K-12 education resources available on the Internet. It includes links to several high schools, access to an Internet K-12 curriculum repository, and various movies and pictures.

KEYWORDS Computers, Primary/Secondary Education
AUDIENCE Educators (Primary/Secondary), Internet Users, Students (Primary/Secondary)
CONTACT Greg Redder
redder@k12.colostate.edu
FREE

gopher://k12.colostate.edu/

Commonwealth Partnership Biology Initiative and Science Education Partnership Awards ★★★

This is a gopher server of the Department of Biological Sciences at Carnegie Mellon University. The purpose of this gopher is to distribute the products of two outreach programs directed at secondary school science teachers. These programs are the Commonwealth Partnership Biology Initiative and the Science Education Partnership Awards. In addition, it contains information on math and science, National Science Foundation educational announcements, networking and K-12 policies, and links to other gophers.

KEYWORDS Biological Sciences, Primary/Secondary Education
AUDIENCE Educators (Primary/Secondary), Educators (University), Students (Primary/Secondary), Students (University)
CONTACT Peter Berget
berget+@cmu.edu
FREE

gopher://sepa1.bio.cmu.edu/

Empire Internet Schoolhouse ★★★

This is a gopher server of the Empire Internet Schoolhouse. The Empire Internet Schoolhouse is a clearinghouse of educational resources provided to the Internet community. It contains information on K-12 resources, projects and discussion groups, library resources, special collections, and more.

KEYWORDS Educational Resources, Networking, Primary/Secondary Education
AUDIENCE Academics, Educators (Primary/Secondary), Internet Users, Students (Primary/Secondary)
FREE

gopher://nysernet.org:3000/

Endangered Species Information on the Internet ★★★

This site contains information and links to outside resources related to endangered species. A lot of the information here was gathered from the U.S. Fish and Wildlife service. Sections of this Web site include Biological and Natural History Information (an endangered species clickable map, databases, images, factsheets and reports), Lesson Plans and Curriculum for K-12 Classes and Schools (Whales for K-5, Vanishing Species for grades 5-8), Projects concerned with Endangered Species (the Jason Project, Monarch Watch, the Journey North), Political Issues, and Regional Information.

KEYWORDS Biological Sciences, Ecology, Education, Endangered Species
AUDIENCE Educators (Primary/Secondary), Parents, Students (Primary/Secondary), Students (Secondary/College)
CONTACT David Cappaert
cappaert@umich.edu
FREE

http://nceet.snre.umich.edu/EndSpp/Endangered.html

Environmental Hazards Management Institute ★★★

The Environmental Hazards Management Institute (EHMI) is a nonpartisan, nonprofit organization dedicated to resolving environmental problems through education and relationship building. The Environmental Education Partnership links sponsoring organizations with their communities, starting with the schools, through sustained, objective environmental education products and programs. The EHMI has developed Automobile Care for the Environment (TM) program to reach out to 10th- and 11th-grade driver's education students with educational kits that can be integrated into existing driver's education programs.

KEYWORDS Automobile Care, Education
AUDIENCE Driver's Education Teachers, Educators (Primary/Secondary), Students (Secondary/College)
FREE

http://www.ehmi.org/

Global Show-n-Tell ★★★

Global Show-n-Tell is a virtual exhibition that lets children show off their favorite projects, possessions, accomplishments and collections to kids (and adults) around the world. The exhibition area consists of links to children's artwork in the form of multimedia pages residing in World Wide Web or FTP servers. Many of the works included here are from children under 10 years old. There are also links to other kids' pages from this site.

KEYWORDS Children, Curriculum, Kids, Online Learning
AUDIENCE Children, Educators (Primary/Secondary), Parents
CONTACT show-n-tell@manymedia.com.
FREE

http://emma.manymedia.com/show-n-tell/

Gopher ESPOL ★★★★

Gopher ESPOL describes the Escuela Superior Politecnica del Litoral (ESPOL) a post-secondary education and research institution in Guayaquil, Ecuador. The information covers ESPOL's history, academics, administration, calendar, computing resources, images. The server's contents are searchable by keywords.

KEYWORDS Education (College/University), Latin America

Primary & Secondary Education

AUDIENCE   Educators (University), Professors, Students (University), University Administrators
FREE

gopher://espol.edu.ec/

Gymboree

The Gymboree Home Page explains the program goals and activities of this parent/child play program. Class information throughout the United States is available. Classes include fun, games, music and activities along with Parachute Time for newborns through five- years- old. Your children can also celebrate their birthdays at Gymboree with bubbles, singing, laughing, climbing, jumping, rolling, and an experienced Gymboree teacher as your host.

KEYWORDS   Children's Programs, Parenting, Pre-School Education
AUDIENCE   Au Pairs, Childcare Providers, Children, Education Administrators, Educators (Primary/Secondary), Families, Parents, Students (Primary/Secondary)
FREE

http://www.service.com/Gymboree/home.html

HPCC and NASA K-12 Internet Project Gopher

This gopher provides information about the various educational programs coordinated by NASA. The major focus is on the K-12 Internet Project. This program attempts to use the computing infrastructure being built through the High Performance Computing and Communications (HPCC) Program to K-12 schools throughout the country. This gopher also gives access to some interactive education software produced by NASA and K-12 Internet sites.

KEYWORDS   Educational Programs, NASA (National Aeronautics And Space Administration), Primary/Secondary Education, Space Science
AUDIENCE   Children, Educators, Educators (Primary/Secondary), Students (Primary/Secondary)
FREE

gopher://quest.arc.nasa.gov/

High School Servers

This is a list of math and science Web sites for high schools in the United States.

KEYWORDS   Mathematics, Primary/Secondary Education
AUDIENCE   Educators (Primary/Secondary), Mathematicians, Statisticians, Students (Primary/Secondary)
CONTACT   webmaster@math.fsu.edu
FREE

http://euclid.math.fsu.edu/Science/highsch.html

Hotlist, Kids Did This!

The Hotlist, Kids Did This! page provides a hotlist of student-produced stuff. Links are provided to science, history, math, language arts, school newspapers, miscellaneous, and more to come. This list is taken from a list of 'Hotlists' of things teachers may find useful. Each hotlist is divided into three main groups - Topics, Science Resources, and Teacher Resources.

KEYWORDS   Children, History, Primary/Secondary Education, School Newspapers
AUDIENCE   Child Care Providers, Educators (Primary/Secondary), Families, Students (Primary/Secondary)
CONTACT   baumann@fi.edu
FREE

http://sln.fi.edu/tfi/hotlists/kids.html

Incomplete Guide to the Internet (K-12)

Incomplete Guide to the Internet is an Internet guide created for teachers and students in grades Kindergarten though 12th grade. This file is available in MS Word for Macintosh and Postscript versions. Many general topics are presented here, including teacher resources, explanations about the Internet, and specific ideas for classroom use.

KEYWORDS   Educational Resources, Educational Technology, Internet Guides, Primary/Secondary Education
AUDIENCE   Education Administrators, Educators (Primary/Secondary), Students (Primary/Secondary)
CONTACT   National Center for Supercomputing Applications ftpadmin@ncsa.uiuc.edu
FREE

ftp://ftp.ncsa.uiuc.edu/Education/Education_Resources/Incomplete_Guide/

Los Alamos Middle School

The Los Alamos Middle School Web site provides information about the school and its students' projects. Users will find events calendars, phone books, and curriculum information for Los Alamos Middle School, as well as student-created home pages. Also included in this site are links to educational resources on the Web, grouped by subject, as well as links to other middle school and college Web sites.

KEYWORDS   Primary/Secondary Education
AUDIENCE   Educators (Secondary), Parents, Students (Secondary)
CONTACT   www@lams.losalamos.nm.us
FREE

http://lams.losalamos.k12.nm.us/

Mathematics in Education

This page, which contains information about various resources for mathematics education, is provided by the Canadian Mathematical Society. The page gives links to information about high school and undergraduate mathematics education, topics and resources, periodicals, and educational communication technology.

KEYWORDS   Computer Aided Instruction, Educational Resources, Mathematics, Primary/Secondary Education
AUDIENCE   Mathematics Educators, Mathematics Students (Primary/Secondary)
CONTACT   camel@camel.cecm.sfu.ca
FREE

http://camel.cecm.sfu.ca/Education/education.html

MidLink Magazine - The Electronic Magazine for Kids in the Middle Grades

MidLink Magazine is an electronic magazine for kids in the middle grades (generally ages 10 to 15). Users can browse through pages of art and writing that link middle school kids all over the world. MidLink will be published bi-monthly, and each issue will have a different theme. There are also outside projects for youths and schools to keep track of or participate in, such as an environmental voyage, native animals, and an informal 'telegrowth' study to see how quickly kids grow.

KEYWORDS   Middle School, Primary/Secondary Education, Zines
AUDIENCE   Children, Mathematics Students (Primary)
CONTACT   Caroline McCullen mccullen@aquarius.cc.ucf.edu
FREE

http://longwood.cs.ucf.edu:80/~MidLink/

Missouri Department of Elementary & Secondary Education

This site contains pointers to educational resources for the state of Missouri. Included here are Missouri K-12 schools on the Web, links to the University of Missouri's Journalism School Online Newspaper (which has teaching and learning sections), the Writery, a writing project, and pointers to outside educational resources on the Internet.

KEYWORDS   Educational Resources, Missouri, Writing Resources
AUDIENCE   Educators, Missouri Residents
CONTACT   admin@services.dese.state.mo.us
FREE

http://oseda.missouri.edu:80/dese/dese.html

gopher://services.dese.state.mo.us/

National Center for Research on Evaluation, Standards, and Student Testing

This is a gopher server of the the National Center for Research on Evaluation, Standards, and Student Testing (CRESST). It provides information about K-12 assessment research, the research on evaluation and testing, products available, CRESST conference 1994, educational resources and more.

KEYWORDS   California, Education, Primary/Secondary Education
AUDIENCE   Educators (Primary/Secondary), Educators (Primary/Secondary)
CONTACT   comments@cse.ucla.edu
FREE

gopher://gopher.cse.ucla.edu/

Primary & Secondary Education

National School Network Testbed ★★

This site gives a description of and access to the National School Network Testbed being developed by Bolt, Beranek, and Newman Inc. The National School Network Testbed is an experimental Internet server designed as a means for 'solving the fundamental problems in building a universally-accessible network of K-12 schools.' The resources currently available include educational materials and access to some schools around the US. Some of the specific items available here include a paper entitled 'Public Access to the Internet,' lesson plans for some traditionally hard to teach areas in genetics and relativity, and information and access to MUSEs in Education (Multi-User Simulation Environments).

Keywords Curriculum, Lesson Plans, Primary/Secondary Education, Research & Development
Audience Education Administrators, Educators, Students (Primary/Secondary)
Contact Martin Huntley
mhuntley@bbn.com
Free

gopher://copernicus.bbn.com/

ORNL Educational Gopher ★★

This server provides information about educational programs sponsored by the Oak Ridge National Laboratory, Tennessee. The information includes newsletters and other publications, software, and funding information. The site also gives links to other education sites around the Internet.

Keywords Internet Reference, Primary/Secondary Education
Audience Administrators, Educators, Educators (Primary/Secondary), Students (Primary/Secondary)
Contact woo@ornl.gov
Free

gopher://woonext.dsrd.ornl.gov/

Ohio Education Computer Network (OECN) gopher site ★★★

This is a prototype/experimental Internet Gopher Server for the use of K-12 public education students and staff in the Ohio Education Computer Network and Internet community. It provides links to numerous other gopher sites containing information that could be useful to teachers and students. This includes publications related to educational research, a searchable German dictionary, economics data, a world area code directory, and social and census information.

Keywords Educational Policy, Interactive Learning, Primary/Secondary Education, Technology
Audience Education Administrators, Educators, Educators (Primary/Secondary), Students
Contact Duane Baker
baker@nwoca1.nwoca.ohio.gov
Free

gopher://nwoca7.nwoca.ohio.gov:72/

Oral History ★★

This directory contains curriculum resources for a K-12 Oral History Project. There is a general outline of questions to ask, as well as a grant proposal listing all materials, time requirements, etc., necessary for incorporating an oral history project into a social studies curriculum. In addition, there is an archive of oral histories done by several elementary school students.

Keywords Curriculum, Oral History, Primary/Secondary Education, Texas
Audience Educators (Primary/Secondary), Historians, Social Studies Educators, Students (Primary/Secondary)
Contact Donald Perkins
dperkins@tenet.edu
Free

gopher://riceinfo.rice.edu:1170/11/Projects/History/Oralhistory

Preschool Page ★★★★

The Preschool Page is a site devoted to information about pre-schoolers for parents and teachers to help improve learning skills as well as provide information about health issues. There are hot links to fun information and games for kids, and hot links to newsgroups for parents and teachers.

Keywords Educational Resources, Pre-School Education
Audience Educators, Parents, Pre-Schoolers, Teachers Aides
Contact kcdillon@dnai.com
Free

http://www.dnai.com/~kcdillon/preschoolers.html

Princeton New Jersey Regional Schools ★★★

This site contains a general information database for the Princeton, New Jersey Regional School District (PRS). Viewers will find information about Princeton High School and the Riverside Elementary School, as well as other educational resources in Princeton and from the outside world. Some items include Princeton High School's online newspaper, course descriptions, and a student profile. In addition, there are some projects online such as 9th-grade creation mythology images and a travel journal by a kindergarten class at Riverside Elementary School.

Keywords Educational Resources, Educational Technology, New Jersey, Student Projects
Audience Education Administrators, Educators, New Jersey Residents
Contact WWW@walnut.prs.k12.nj.us
Free

http://www.prs.k12.nj.us/

Ralph Bunche School ★★★

This is a gopher server of the Ralph Bunche School, an elementary school in New York City. Their gopher contains information on the school, newspaper stories, student science and work projects, and more. It has links to other gophers.

Keywords Computer Science, Education, New York
Audience Educators, Educators (Primary/Secondary), Students
Contact Renso Vasquez
rensov@ralphbunche.rbs.edu
Free

gopher://ralphbunche.rbs.edu/

San Juan Unified School District Gopher ★★★

This site offers access to the Gopher for the San Juan Unified School District in California. Information is provided about the academic courses offered, the Instructional Technology Networking Consortium, software guides, and Internet guides. This site also offers links to other gopher servers.

Keywords California, Networking, Primary/Secondary Education, Schools (Primary/Secondary)
Audience Educators (Primary/Secondary), Parents, Students (Primary/Secondary), Technology Enthusiasts
Contact Dan O'Halloran
dano@sanjuan.edu
Free

gopher://gopher.saintjoe.edu/

SchoolNet of Canada ★★★

This is a gopher server of the Canada School Net. SchoolNet is an educational networking initiative of Industry and Science Canada. It provides information related to elementary and secondary school education. There are also links to the Internet.

Keywords Canada, Educational Networks, Primary/Secondary Education
Audience Computer Users, Educators, Students
Contact schoolnet-admin@carleton.ca
Free

gopher://gopher.schoolnet.carleton.ca:419/

Science at Home ★★★★

This site, Science at Home, provides many links to science activities developed to demystify science for adults and children while fostering scientific inquiry and analysis. Projects are organized according to what room of the house they take place in. Some of these include: the bathroom- caught in the vortex, the kitchen- does a waterdrop have skin? and who makes the best bubbles?, and in the garage-windowsill greenhouse. This is a great place for the family to explore together.

Keywords Children, Parenting
Audience Childcare Providers, Children, Educators (Primary/Secondary), Families, Students (Primary/Secondary)
Contact Robert L. Judd
bj@lanl.gov
Free

http://www.lanl.gov/temp/Education/Contents.html

Texas Education Agency ★★

This is a gopher server of the Texas Education Agency. Its focus is K-12 education in Texas. It contains information such as gopher online help, gopher services, and more.

KEYWORDS Educational Programs, Organizations, Primary/Secondary Education, Texas
AUDIENCE Educators (Primary/Secondary), Students (Primary/Secondary)
CONTACT gopher@tenet.edu
FREE

gopher://gopher.tenet.edu/

University of Massachusetts ★★

The University of Massachusetts gopher server contains information related to K-12 education which includes libraries, online dictionaries, arts, conferences, entertainment, images and fine arts, and more. It also has links to other education-oriented gophers.

KEYWORDS Primary/Secondary Education
AUDIENCE Academics, Educators, Students
FREE

gopher://k12.ucs.umass.edu/

Vanishing Species - Educational Guides ★★★

This directory contains lesson plans, resource materials, and other teacher information for teaching students about endangered species from a multicultural, interdisciplinary perspective. The materials are designed for elementary, middle, and high schools; however, the majority of the online information is most suitable for middle school. There are exercises for writing, biology, music, social studies, and computer skills.

KEYWORDS Endangered Species, Environment, Interdisciplinary Studies
AUDIENCE Animal Rights Activists, Education Administrators, Educators (Primary/Secondary)
CONTACT Donald Perkins
dperkins@tenet.edu
FREE

gopher://riceinfo.rice.edu:1170/11/Texas/Vanishing

Vista Middle School Home Page ★★

Vista Middle School is located in Las Cruces, New Mexico. It hosts approximately 1000 students in 6th, 7th, and 8th grades. This home page joins a Bulletin Board Service within the school's technology program which promotes the use of computers and electronic information in the classroom, as well as innovations in its science and mathematics curriculum. Viewers of this page will find images of Vista Activities, such as its Egyptian day, Metric Olympics, and its sports program. In addition, the school newsletter is online.

KEYWORDS Educational Resources, New Mexico
AUDIENCE Education Administrators, Educators, New Mexico Residents
CONTACT tljones@taipan.nmsu.edu.
FREE

http://128.123.31.49/vista/vista_home.html

Connections to Foreign Language Dictionaries

How do you say "Huh?"

Languages

Welcome to the WWW Virtual Library's Language section. The information located here spans the globe, and is ever-growing. Below, you can find language lessons and tutorials, dictionaries, text and book collections, and even translation services, all available in one form or another on the Internet. It is my goal to keep this list as accurate as possible, so please send corrections and additions to Tyler Jones.

Languages are listed in alphabetical order, with separate sections for book/text collections, multilingual resources, language labs and institutions, and commercial resources on the Net.

Mirrors

- There is a European mirror of the Human-Languages Page available. The Human-Langages Page is what this list is derived from, and contains basically the same information.

Quick Jump

[Multilingual resources] [Books/literature archives] [Linguistics labs and institutions on the Net] [Commercial Resources] [A] [B] [C] [D] [E] [F] [G] [H] [I] [J] [K] [L] [M] [N] [O] [P] [Q] [R] [S] [T] [U] [V] [W] [X] [Y] [Z]

For many of us, traveling to another country and trying to get by on a few simple phrases in another language is a tremendous challenge. If you are traveling between France and Italy and Germany within a short period of time, for instance, you can easily get your vocabulary mixed up.

Through "World Wide Web Library's Language Section" you can access not only valuable travel information, but can also learn simple phrases commonly used by tourists in France. One link provides the user with a French-English/English-French dictionary, in which the user simply inputs words to obtain succinct translations.

And if you're learning French as a second language, this site provides you with excellent practical tutorials.

(http://www.willamette.edu/~tjones/languages/
    WWW_Virtual_Library_Language.html)

A similar site is available for anyone wanting to learn German, or for German-speaking people learning English. Here you'll gain access to German-English and English-German dictionaries. You'll learn familiar phrases and also have access to a pronunciation gazetteer.

(http://www.uni-passau.de/forwiss/mitarbeiter/freie/ramsch/englisch.html)

If you're planning a business trip or vacation to Asia, then learning a bit of the languages spoken in your destination countries is essential. Through the "Japanese/English Dictionary Gateway," for instance, the user is provided a dictionary that gives entries for English words in Japanese characters, and Japanese words in English. The user simply enters the desired word or phrase.

(http://www.wg.omron.co.jp/cgi-bin/j-e)

Welcome to EE-Link ★★★★

The EE-Link is a project of the National Consortium for Environmental Education and Training (NCEET) at the University of Michigan. It is intended to help K-12 environmental educators and it covers current issues and offers its own material as well as material submitted from other organizations. The user can browse EE-Link to find activities that can be implemented in classrooms. It also offers information on how to communicate with others via listservs, newsgroups, and BBSs. These resources include instructional materials, articles, funding sources, and networking opportunities.

KEYWORDS Ecology, Educational Resources, Environment, Primary/Secondary Education
AUDIENCE Educators (Primary/Secondary), Environmentalists, Parents, Students
CONTACT David Cappaert
cappaert@umich.edu
FREE

http://nceet.snre.umich.edu/

gopher://nceet.snre.umich.edu/

Writers in the Schools ★★

WITS (Writers in the Schools) sends professional writers into classrooms to share their love and knowledge of writing with students and their teachers. In this directory, there are a number of experiences that the writers share, along with some of the creative writing produced by the students. There are files containing pointers on how to approach creative writing written by the professional writers, as well as archives of some student writing. The program, as well as the directory, is divided into elementary, middle, and high school projects.

KEYWORDS Creative Writing, Curriculum, English, Language Arts
AUDIENCE Educators (Primary), Educators (Primary/Secondary), English Educators
CONTACT Donald Perkins
dperkins@tenet.edudperkins@tenet.edu
FREE

gopher://riceinfo.rice.edu:1170/11/Projects/LangArt

Professional Education

See also
Communications · *Communications*
Computing & Mathematics · *Resources*

National Institute For Consumer Education (NICE) ★★★

The National Institute For Consumer Education (NICE) is sponsored by the College of Education at Eastern Michigan University. It is a professional development center and resource clearinghouse for consumer, economic, and personal finance education. This page contains links to a calendar of events, resource lists including information on credit problems, mortgages, and legislative information.

KEYWORDS Consumer Education, Personal Finance, Seminars
AUDIENCE Consumers, Educators (University), General Public, Students (University)
CONTACT Rosella Bannister
NICE@emuvax.emich.edu
Rosella.Bannister@emich.edu
FREE

http://www.emich.edu/public/coe/nice/nice.html

The Oregon Graduate Institute of Science & Technology's Gopher ★★

This gopher site provides admissions, program, and enrollment information for the Oregon Graduate Institute of Science & Technology. It includes a searchable faculty index, and a postscript map of how to get to the Institute. An overview of some of Portland, Oregon's Internet Access Providers can also be found on this site.

KEYWORDS Biological Sciences, Engineering, Oregon, Science
AUDIENCE Academics, Engineers, Scientists, Students (Graduate)
CONTACT revel@admin.ogi.edu
FREE

gopher://admin.ogi.edu/

University of Florida College of Journalism and Communications ★★★

The home page of the College of Journalism and Communications at the University of Florida offers a look into the research activities and academic programs available at the College. Users will find information on faculty, students, and staff, as well as material on various courses taught. There are also links to many different communications and journalism resources on the Net.

KEYWORDS Communications, Journalism
AUDIENCE Communications Researchers, Communications Students
CONTACT Gary Ritzenthaler, Sherwood Lawrence
garyz@elm.circa.ufl.edu /
slawrenc@jou.ufl.edu
FREE

http://www.jou.ufl.edu/

Zanesville HKAPA Page ★★★

The Hong Kong Academy for Performing Arts offers professional training in the performing arts. Programs are offered in four disciplines—dance, drama, music and technical arts. Information about these four schools can be found at this site.

KEYWORDS China, Hong Kong, Performing Arts
AUDIENCE Performing Artists
CONTACT Zane Au
zaneau@hk.linkage.net
FREE

http://www.hk.linkage.net/~zaneau/hkapa.htm

Public Libraries

See also
Education · *Academic Libraries*
Education · *Special Libraries*
Humanities & Social Sciences · *Library & Information Studies*
Popular Culture & Entertainment · *Books*

Berkeley Public Library ★★★★

This is the home page of Berkeley Public Library, which is located in Berkeley, California. Some basic information for new users on getting started on the Internet can be found here. Users will also find Berkeley Public Library's Bookmark Index to the Internet, which is a great place to start when looking for information on the Internet. There is also information on the Friends of the Library, as well as book reviews and books on the Internet. Last but not least, Berkeley Public Library's catalog can be accessed via a telnet connection.

KEYWORDS Libraries, California
AUDIENCE Librarians, Library Users
CONTACT Carole Leita
leita@netcom.com
FREE

http://www.ci.berkeley.ca.us/bpl/

Boston Public Library ★★★

This is a gopher server of the Boston Public Library. It contains information on the Library, catalogs, resources, services, special collections, the reference shelf, subject collections, government documents, as well as links to other library gophers.

KEYWORDS Libraries, Library Science, Massachusetts
AUDIENCE Librarians, Library Administrators, Library Users, Students
CONTACT gopher@bpl.org
FREE

gopher://bpl.org/

Cleveland Public Library ★★★

This site is a gopher server of the Cleveland Public Library in Ohio. It contains information on the Library, its resources and services. It also has links to other gophers on the Internet.

KEYWORDS Libraries, Library Science, Networking, Ohio
AUDIENCE Academics, Librarians, Library Administrators, Library Users
FREE

gopher://library.cpl.org/

Colorado Supernet, Inc. ★★★

This site provides access to library-related information in Colorado. It offers access to library resources, databases, systems, the list of participating libraries, and more. It has links to other gophers as well.

KEYWORDS Colorado, Databases, Libraries, Networking
AUDIENCE Colorado Residents, Librarians, Library Administrators, Library Users
FREE

gopher://teal.csn.org:1170/

New York State Library Gopher ★★

This gopher hole is an information service of the New York State Library. This information includes access to Library publications and press releases, a link to the online Library catalog, and assorted state and federal government resources.

KEYWORDS Libraries, Library Science, New York
AUDIENCE Librarians, Library Administrators, Library Users, New York Residents
CONTACT david@unix2.nysed.gov
FREE

gopher://unix2.nysed.gov/

Southern Adirondack and Mohawk Valley Library Systems ★★

This site provides information for and about the Southern Adirondack Library System (SALS) and the Mohawk Valley Library Association (MVLA) in New

York State. This information includes resources for the members of the library systems, such as grant programs and purchasing and cataloging information. It also provides information for the general public such as current programs being run by the library systems, access to library catalogs, and information about this region of New York State.

KEYWORDS Information Science, Libraries, Library Science, New York
AUDIENCE Librarians, Library Administrators, Library Users
CONTACT postmaster@sals.edu
FREE

gopher://sallib.sals.edu/

Resources

See also
Business & Economics · *Publishing*
Humanities & Social Sciences · *Literature*
Internet · *Internet Access*
Law & Criminal Justice · *Legal Resources*

A Professor's Guilt List for English Literature Majors ★★★★

This page provides a 'must' reading list which starts at Alcott, Louisa May, and runs to Yeats, W.B.. There are at least 100 titles listed here, all vital reading for the serious student. This is a terrific resource for any undergraduate wishing to pursue a degree in English Literature. The page was constructed by an English professor at San Jose State University, with his quote 'For many English majors, they don't even have 1/10th of the books listed under their belts before graduation - hence the guilt aspect of it'.

KEYWORDS Books, English Literature, Literature
AUDIENCE Educators (University), English Literature Enthusiasts, Reading Enthusiasts, Students (Secondary/College)
FREE

http://www.next.com/~bong/books/GuiltList.html

AERA Journals ★★★

This page contains information about the five journals published by the American Educational Research Association. The journals are entitled Educational Researcher (ER), American Educational Research Journal (AERJ), Educational Evaluation and Policy Analysis (EEPA), Journal of Educational and Behavioral Statistics (JEBS), and Review of Educational Research (RER).

KEYWORDS Journals, Research
AUDIENCE Behavioral Scientists, Education Administrators, Educators
CONTACT Gene V Glass
glass@asu.edu
FREE

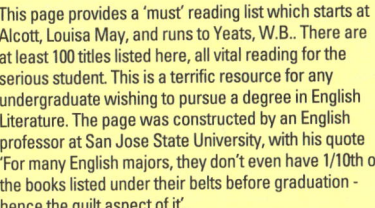

http://www.asu.edu/aff/aera/pubs.html

Action Magazine Pages ★

Action Magazine hosts these pages to publicize itself—a magazine that is currently being distributed throughout schools in the African nations of Zimbabwe, Zambia, Botswana and others. This site summarizes the content and issues covered in the magazine (food, health, environmental issues, wildlife, etc.). Subscription information for educators and parents from other parts of the world are also shown here. Some of its links, including one to a magazine sample edition, were not working during our visit.

KEYWORDS Africa, Children, Magazines, Publishing
AUDIENCE Children, Educators, Parents, Schools
CONTACT Beth Frankl
BFrankl@aol.com
FREE

http://virtumall.com/newsstand/ComedyMag/home.html

AskERIC (Educational Resources Information Center) ★★★★

ERIC (Educational Resources Information Center) provides a meta-index of searchable information on education related resources. AskERIC is comprised of three major components which are the AskERIC Q & A Service, the AskERIC Virtual Library, and the AskERIC R&D. Some of the links include education conferences (calendars and announcements), electronic journals, books, and reference tools, Internet guides and directories, bibliographies, digests, news and announcements, professional and commercial organizations, education listservs archives, lesson plans, FAQs, and more.

KEYWORDS Lesson Plans, Meta-Index (Education)
AUDIENCE Educators (University) , Students (University)
CONTACT Nancy Morgan/Mary Beth McKee
askeric@ericir.syr.edu
FREE

http://eryx.syr.edu

Bibliography Software for Use with FrameMaker ★★

This directory contains Bibliography software for use with FrameMaker 3 and 4. The software creates template files for a thesis that should conform to UC Berkeley thesis guidelines. The template includes title, signature, and copyright pages, as well as an abstract. It also has templates for a single chapter, including numbering for tables, figures, and equations.

KEYWORDS Bibliographies, Graduate Programs, Software, Universities
AUDIENCE Framemaker Users, Thesis Writers, UC Berkeley Grad Students
FREE

ftp://ftp.cs.berkeley.edu/pub/raid/elm/

CNN Classroom Guide ★★★★

This is the CNN gopher menu. Daily entries provide a news briefing, key terms used, and a guide for class discussion. An outline of the day's events is followed by a summary of each news event.

KEYWORDS Current Events, News, Primary/Secondary Education
AUDIENCE Educators (Primary/Secondary), Internet Users , News Buffs, Parents, Researchers, Students (Primary/Secondary)
FREE

gopher://nysernet.org:3000/11/Academic%20Wings/Social%20Studies/CNN%20newsroom

Document Processing Group at the University of Maryland ★★

This is a gopher server of the Document Processing Group at the University of Maryland. Information available includes research announcements, calls for papers and conference programs, the document-list digest archive, online access to a document understanding bibliography, and more. Access to other gophers is provided.

KEYWORDS Computer Applications, Computer Databases, Electronic Publishing
AUDIENCE Computer Users, Database Users
CONTACT Dr. David Doermann
gopher@dimund.cfar.umd.edu
FREE

gopher://dimund.cfar.umd.edu/

E-Text Archives ★★

This gopher server of the University of Michigan provides access to an archive of electronic documents. The documents can be downloaded by anonymous FTP. Some of the subjects include economics, fiction, news, poetry, politics, sports, religion, and more.

KEYWORDS Archives, Electronic Media, Electronic Publishing
AUDIENCE Computer Users, Internet Users
CONTACT Paul Southworth
ftp@etext.archive.umich.edu
FREE

gopher://etext.archive.umich.edu/

Ednet Guide to Usenet Groups ★★★

This document is a guide to help educators find newsgroups. All educational levels and disciplines are represented in this very large list of newsgroups.

KEYWORDS Educational Networks, Educational Resources, Educational Technology, Usenet Newsgroups
AUDIENCE Education Researchers, Educators, Students
CONTACT Prescott Smith
pgsmith@educ.umass.edu
FREE

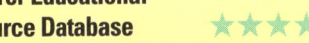

ftp://nic.umass.edu/pub/ednet/edusenet.gde

Explorer Educational Resource Database ★★★★

The Explorer Educational Resource Database allows educators and students to easily navigate through a wide range of educational materials. The majority of materials in this database consists of mathematics and scientific projects. In addition, the files available for downloading are in Macintosh file formats (Clarisworks,

Hypercard). The browsing and searching capabilities use icons that are designed to assist educators in locating resources based on such factors as curricula, process skills, grade levels, and media type. Explorer users can immediately obtain many online resources as well as create new materials for the database.

- **KEYWORDS** Computer Aided Instruction, Lesson Plans
- **AUDIENCE** Educators (Primary/Secondary), Librarians, Parents, Software Designers, Software Developers
- **CONTACT** explorer@unite.tisl.ukans.edu
- **FREE**

http://unite2.tisl.ukans.edu/

Gifted Resources from ERIC (Educational Resources Information Clearinghouse) ★★

This page contains links to the ERIC (Educational Resources Information Center) Special Resources for Gifted and Talented Education program information. Among the links available are a list of digests or short papers about gifted educational issues. The topics include Bibliographies, Resources for Educators, Parents, Middle School, School Reform, Education Restructuring, Mainstreaming the Gifted, Distance Education, and more.

- **KEYWORDS** FAQs (Frequently Asked Questions), Organizations
- **AUDIENCE** Educators, Gifted Students, Parents
- **CONTACT** kmclane@inet.ed.gov
- **FREE**

http://www.eskimo.com/~user/zeric.html

Internet Education Resources ★★★

This gopher is a gateway to educational resources available on the Internet. The gopher holes pointed to by this site include the Academic Positions Network, the Educational Resources Information Center (AskERIC), and the National Center on Adult Literacy.

- **KEYWORDS** Education, Employment, Internet Guides, Literacy
- **AUDIENCE** Academics, Educators, Educators (Primary/Secondary)
- **CONTACT** comments@cse.ucla.edu
- **FREE**

gopher://spinoza.cse.ucla.edu:72/

 ## Kaplan Online ★★★

Kaplan Educational Centers offer students assistance in planning their academic and professional careers through test-taking courses for most standardized tests including the SAT, PSAT, GRE, LSAT, GMAT, TOEFL, MCAT, and NCLEX. This page contains general information and sample questions about these tests, financial aid information, an online ordering page to receive test prep materials, as well as a chat area and BBS. There is also a listing of addresses and phone numbers of Kaplan Centers around the world.

- **KEYWORDS** Graduate Programs, Standardized Tests
- **AUDIENCE** Education Reformers, Educators, Students (Primary/Secondary), Students (Secondary/College), Students (University)
- **CONTACT** webmasters@www.kaplan.com
- **FREE**

http://www.kaplan.com/

Kentucky Department of Education WWW Server - The Kentucky Thoroughbred ★★

This site is designed to be a resource for Kentucky students and teachers to learn to browse the World Wide Web and a starting point for more experienced Web users. There are pointers to school districts within Kentucky that are online, as well as more general educational links. This site also contains the Kentucky Education Technology System (KETS) Files, which contains files related to building the networking infrastructure within the schools of Kentucky. There are several areas that are under development, such as curriculum and teacher certification resources.

- **KEYWORDS** Government Agencies (US), Kentucky, Primary/Secondary Education
- **AUDIENCE** Education Administrators, Educators (Primary/Secondary), Kentucky Residents
- **CONTACT** Robert John Ray, rray@plaza.kde.state.ky.us
- **FREE**

http://www.kde.state.ky.us/

Links to Writing Resources ★★★

This page provides links to tips, guides, and resources for writing such as an Online Writing Lab, The Writer's Block (newsletter), Networked Writing Environment, prose form and outline form resources, Writers' Workshop On-Line Handbook. Most of these resources are sponsored or funded by university and research centers.

- **KEYWORDS** Reference, Writing Resources, Writing Workshops
- **AUDIENCE** Students (University), Writers
- **CONTACT** Eric Crump WLERIC@showme.missouri.edu
- **FREE**

http://www.missouri.edu/~wleric/writehelp.html

NYSERNet, Inc. ★★★

This NYSERNet site gives access to data and databases related to education and sciences. The data cover topics such as education, mathematics, arts, music, languages, sciences, New York State, administrative resources, and more.

- **KEYWORDS** Education, Humanities, New York
- **AUDIENCE** Educators, New York Residents, Students (University)
- **FREE**

gopher://nysernet.org:72/

PORTALS ★★★

PORTALS is an information service of educational institutions in the Portland, Oregon, area. The information provided by PORTALS includes databases, library catalogs, and reference sources.

- **KEYWORDS** Information Science, Libraries, Library Science, Oregon
- **AUDIENCE** Librarians, Library Administrators, Library Users, Oregon Residents
- **CONTACT** zendog@lib.pdx.edu
- **FREE**

gopher://portals.lib.pdx.edu/

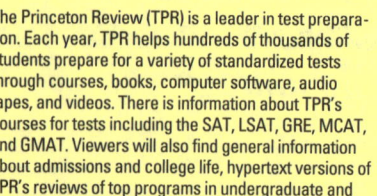 ## The Princeton Review Online ★★★

The Princeton Review (TPR) is a leader in test preparation. Each year, TPR helps hundreds of thousands of students prepare for a variety of standardized tests through courses, books, computer software, audio tapes, and videos. There is information about TPR's courses for tests including the SAT, LSAT, GRE, MCAT, and GMAT. Viewers will also find general information about admissions and college life, hypertext versions of TPR's reviews of top programs in undergraduate and graduate studies, law, business, and medicine. There is also a form for ordering Princeton Review materials.

- **KEYWORDS** Standardized Tests
- **AUDIENCE** Education Reformers, Educators, Students (Primary/Secondary), Students (Secondary/College), Students (University)
- **FREE**

http://www.review.com/

Study Guide to Wheelock ★★

This file is a single (long) document which serves as a guide to Wheelock's Latin, one of the most widely used introductory Latin textbooks used in American colleges and universities. Specifically, this guide is designed to teach basic grammatical concepts to students while learning Latin from Wheelock, and to slow down and recast Wheelock's treatment of the grammar into language which they can understand on their own. The introduction contains notes on how the author, Dale Grote, incorporates this guide into his syllabus and classroom.

- **KEYWORDS** English, Language Instruction
- **AUDIENCE** Educators, Latin Scholars, Latin Students, Linguists
- **CONTACT** Wiretap Online Library gopher@wiretap.spies.com
- **FREE**

gopher://wiretap.spies.com/00/Library/Classic/latin.stu

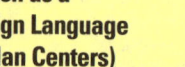 ## TOEFL - Test of English as a Foreign Language (Kaplan Centers) ★★

This page is part of the Kaplan Educational Services Web site, and provides the viewer with information about the TOEFL (Test of English as a Foreign Language) You can find out when the next test is scheduled to be given, contact information if you are taking this test outside of the United States, as well as how the test is scored. In addition, brief information is given about how the TOEFL will change as of July, 1995. Students can order study materials or attend workshops run by Kaplan Services in order to prepare for this exam.

KEYWORDS   ESL (English as a Second Language), International Education, Language Instruction, Standardized Tests
AUDIENCE   International Students
CONTACT   Webmaster
           webmasters@www.kaplan.com.
FREE

http://www.kaplan.com/etc/intl/toefl_top.html

World Wide Web - The Outside Link to Networked Multimedia ★★★

This page is an outline of a Web Workshop which demonstrates Netscape as a teaching tool. The goal of this project is to redirect educational technologies resources from a hypercard/hypertext environment on one computer to one that is networked to the Internet. This site contains extensive information about curriculum planning with the World Wide Web. There are examples of educational resources, cautions to avoid problems, pedagogical justifications for the practices, and lesson plans to get teachers and classes started.

KEYWORDS   Computer Aided Instruction, Interactive Learning, Primary/Secondary Education
AUDIENCE   Education Administrators, Education Researchers, Educators, Educators (Primary/Secondary), Internet Users
CONTACT   Institute for Learning Technologies
           webmaster@ilt.columbia.edu
FREE

http://www.ilt.columbia.edu/LT/webcurr.html

Special Libraries

See also
Education · *Academic Libraries*
Education · *Government Libraries*
Education · *Public Libraries*
Humanities & Social Sciences · *Library & Information Studies*

The 4th Wave Library ★★★

The 4th Wave is an online collection of articles about the Internet and communications. Most of the articles are in Dutch; some are translated into English. Some of the titles include, 'Using the Internet for Marketing-A Publisher's Secrets,' and 'The Internet as a Catalyst for a Paradigm Shift.' There is also the possibility of adding one's own article to the library.

KEYWORDS   Belgium, Virtual Libraries
AUDIENCE   Marketing Managers, Net Surfers, Researchers
FREE

http://www.reference.be/reference/n002100.html

The Association of Research Libraries (ARL) ★★★

This site is a gopher server for the Association of Research Libraries (ARL), an international organization comprised of libraries from post-secondary institutions. It contains information on the ARL, its mission, its programs, its members, its staff, as well as announcements, publications, and research resources.

KEYWORDS   Information Science, Libraries, Library Science, Networking
AUDIENCE   Academics, Librarians, Library Administrators, Library Users
CONTACT   Dru Mogge
           dru@cni.org
FREE

gopher://arl.cni.org/

Connections to People of the Past
What ever happened to . . . ?

Ever wonder what happened to a famous person from the 1970s? Or the '50s? You might ask whether that person faded into obscurity or if... maybe that person died?

If you want to check out those notable names of the past who have since "joined the majority," then cruise the Internet's obituaries sites. Many areas offer obituaries of the famous and infamous. Some obituaries offer a list of the person's accomplishments. Some Internet sites provide information on where the person is buried, along with notes about the funeral or memorials made in honor of the "dearly departed."

Through the "Eternal Surf Archives," you can check out the obituaries of well-known public figures. The items include a picture or drawing, and while the list is currently rather small, more stellar names out of the past are being added daily. This eclectic list includes: William Shakespeare, Howard Hughes, Elvis Presley, Salvador Dali, Franz Kafka, and our ancestor, Cro Magnon Man.

(http://www.obituaries.com/obit/gdead.htm)

Data Research Associates, Inc. ★★★★

Data Research, headquartered in St. Louis, Missouri, is a leading provider of client/server automation systems, networking services and other related services for libraries and other information providers. This page includes free access to a demo library, which includes the Library of Congress Basic Machine Readable Cataloging (MARC) Service (containing over 5 million records.) Users can also access financial data and SEC filings from DRA, as well as press releases and world-wide contact information.

KEYWORDS   Client Server Technology, Library Science, Library of Congress, Networking
AUDIENCE   Librarians, Library Scientists, Researchers

CONTACT webmaster@www.dra.com
FREE

http://dranet.dra.com/

Electronic Data Services at the University of Alberta ★★

This is a gopher service provided and maintained by University of Alberta, located in Canada. This site contains collections of resources for library scientists and other information professionals. Some menu items which can be found here include a Directory of Canadian University Data Libraries & Archives, the Canadian Global Change Program, and Social Science Data Centers and Services.

KEYWORDS Electronic Media, Information Science, Libraries, Social Sciences
AUDIENCE General Public, Library Administrators, Library Users
CONTACT Chuck Humphrey - Data Library Coordinator
chumphre@vm.ucs.ualberta.ca
FREE

gopher://datalib.library.ualberta.ca/

Electronic Library Network of Universities in British Columbia ★★★★

The site is a gopher server of the University of Victoria, British Columbia, Canada. It provides the Electronic Library Network (ELN) service. The ELN was established in 1989 to coordinate and support resource sharing among libraries in 24 British Columbian colleges, institutes, and universities. The ELN's mission is to provide equal, timely, and economical access to information resources beyond institutional library collections and existing services.

KEYWORDS Education (College/University), Information Systems, Libraries, Universities
AUDIENCE Educators, Educators (University), Students
CONTACT Kathryn Paul
kpaul@sol.uvic.ca
FREE

gopher://malahat.library.uvic.ca/

MIDAS (Manchester Information Datasets and Associated Services) ★★★★

The MIDAS (Manchester Information Datasets and Associated Services) Home Page at Manchester Computing Centre provides a National Datasets Service to Universities throughout the UK. Some kinds of dataset available to the UK universities are Census reports, Labor and Child Development Surveys, Macro-Economic Time Series, Digitized maps, and Scientific Databanks.

KEYWORDS Databases, Educational Resources, United Kingdom
AUDIENCE Students (University)
CONTACT info@midas.ac.uk
FREE

http://cs6400.mcc.ac.uk/

The MINITEX Library Information Network ★★

The MINITEX Library Information Network provides information on academic, public, state agency, and other special libraries. MINITEX is produced by the Libraries of the University of Minnesota.

KEYWORDS Education (College/University), Libraries, Library Science
AUDIENCE Educators (University), Library Users, Students (University)
FREE

gopher://rodent.cis.umn.edu:11128/

WORLD (World News and Information) ★★★★

This library contains detailed information about every country in Europe, Asia, the Pacific Rim, Africa, the Middle East, and North and South America. Designed for those who need to monitor world events, organizations, and leaders, this library provides a global view of any subject or topic. WORLD includes information from newspapers and wire services, trade and business journals, as well as company reports, countries and regions, industry and product analysis, business opportunities, selected legal texts and current politics. This site is comprehensive and detailed.

KEYWORDS Business, International News
AUDIENCE Analysts, Business Researchers, Entrepreneurs
COST

http://www.meaddata.com

telnet://nex.meaddata.com

Washington Research Library ★★★

This is a gopher server of the Washington Research Library Consortium, a group of research libraries at George Mason University. The server provides access to member libraries and their catalogs, and to other library catalogs and library-related resources on the Internet.

KEYWORDS Databases, Libraries, Library Science, Maryland
AUDIENCE Librarians, Library Administrators, Library Users
CONTACT Wally Grotophorst
wallyg@fen1.gmu.edu
FREE

gopher://gmutant.wrlc.org/

Universities - Africa

See also
Education · *International Education*

Rhodes University Computing Services ★★★

This site at Rhodes University in South Africa provides information about three departments (Computer Science, Information Systems, and Management), the Astronomy and HAM Radio society, computing services for students and faculty, and the library. Links are also provided for information pertaining to South Africa.

KEYWORDS Education, Ham Radio, South Africa, Universities (Australia)
AUDIENCE Educators (University), South Africans, Students (University)
CONTACT The Registrar, Rhodes University, PO Box 94, GRAHAMSTOWN 6140, South Africa
FREE

http://www.ru.ac.za/

Universities - Asia

See Also
Education · *International Education*

Bilkent University Home Page ★★

This server is the top level of the information system at Bilkent University in Turkey. It offers general information on the Internet and the web for new users, as well as information on the University itself. Users can connect to individual departments at the University, as well as browse a collection of general Internet links geared towards the newbie.

KEYWORDS Universities, Computer Science, Turkey
AUDIENCE Educators, Students, Turkish
CONTACT Mustafa Akgul
akgul@bilkent.edu.tr
FREE

http://www.bilkent.edu.tr

Bogazici University Home Page ★★

This is the home page at Bogazici University, located in Istanbul, Turkey. It contains information on the University and its departments, as well as material on travel and tourism in Turkey. There is also a collection of information for new Internet users, as well as a set of links to major Internet sites. Users can browse the course catalog and search for students and staff at the University as well.

KEYWORDS Universities, Computer Science, Tourism, Turkey
AUDIENCE Educators, Students, Travelers, Turkish
FREE

http://www.boun.edu.tr

gopher://gopher.boun.edu.tr/

Chiang Mai University ★★★

This site provides information on the administration and academic programs of the Chiang Mai University, Thailand. It also contains information about library resources & services, Internet servers in Thailand, tourism, investment & economics, as well as links to other gophers.

KEYWORDS Education (College/University), Thailand, University Administration
AUDIENCE Academics, Educators (University), Students (Secondary/University)
FREE

gopher://gopher.chiangmai.ac.th/

The Chinese University of Hong Kong Home Page ★★★★

This is the home page of the Chinese University of Hong Kong. Users can find departmental information, information about this university, and other WWW servers in Hong Kong. A virtual gallery containing color pictures of Hong Kong is also available at this site.

Keywords China, Universities, Hong Kong
Audience Educators, Students
Contact Philip Leung, Anton Lam
philip-leung@cuhk.hk, anton-lam@cuhk.hk
Free

http://www.cuhk.hk/

City University of Hong Kong Home Page ★★★★

This is the home page of City University of Hong Kong. University information such as the academic structure, research opportunities, teaching and learning facililitesis available here. This site also hosts information on the University's administrative services.

Keywords Universities, Hong Kong
Audience Educators, Students
Contact cc@cityu.edu.hk
Free

http://www.cityu.edu.hk/

Ege University, Turkey ★★★★

This site describes the Ege University, Turkey. It provides documents on the university's administration, electronic books, announcements, the Ege archives, campus news & services, and more. As well, it provides access to other gophers.

Keywords Community Services, Education (College/University), Turkey, University Administration
Audience Academics, Educators (University), Students
Contact sysgroup@vm3090.ege.edu.tr
Free

gopher://gopher.ege.edu.tr/

Hong Kong Baptist University Home Page ★★★★

This is the home page of Hong Kong Baptist University. Information on the university and academic programs can be found at this site. Moreover, campus facilities, student life information and academic calendar of events can be accessed here.

Keywords Baptist University, Hong Kong
Audience Educators, Students
Contact ipro@hkbu.edu.hk
Free

http://www.hkbu.edu.hk/

Keio University Shonan Fujisawa Campus (SFC) ★★★

This site is a campus-wide hypermedia information service for SFC, Keio University, Fujisawa, and Japan. It is equipped with links to the rest of Japan, including cultural, arts, business, and technology links.

Keywords International Business, Internet Services, Japan
Audience International Students, Japanese, Japanese Americans, Students
Contact www-admin@sfc.keio.ac.jp
Free

http://www.sfc.keio.ac.jp/index.en.html

Kyushu University ★★★

The Kyushu University page is an experimental web site giving information about the University, its departments, campus facilities and areas of study. The page contains news about Japan and details about the University's activities. The department links include computer science, economics, aeronautics, electrical engineering and the graduate school of social sciences.

Keywords Curriculum, Japan
Audience Researchers, Scientists, Students
Contact www@www.kyushu-u.ac.jp
Free

http://www.kyushu-u.ac.jp

Nanzan University WWW server ★★★

The Nanzan University (NU) Web server is an entry point to information links about this Japanese university, and WWW servers in Japan and the world. There are links to job information and the NU campus Network.

Keywords Educational Resources, Internet Access, Japan
Audience Educators, Students
Contact www-admin@nanzan-u.ac.jp.
Free

http://www.nanzan-u.ac.jp

National Chung Cheng University ★★

This site contains limited information on National Chung Cheng University, located in Taiwan. Much of the information here is in Chinese. Information includes departmental and academic program information, as well as a brief section with information on Taiwan. There are also links to other Taiwanese servers on the Net.

Keywords Universities, Taiwan
Audience Education Administrators (College), Educators, Students, Taiwan Residents
Contact www@ccunix.ccu.edu.tw
Free

http://www.ccu.edu.tw

gopher://gopher.ccu.edu.tw/

National Sun Yat-sen University ★★★

This site describes the National Sun Yat-sen University, Taiwan. The information includes the University's administration, departments, campus services, library resources & services, anonymous FTP sites, and more. It also contains information on China Times News, books, news, electronic magazines, etc.

Keywords Computer Networking, Education (College/University), Taiwan, University Administration
Audience Academics, Chinese Speakers, Educators (University), Students
Contact mounzon@cc.nsysu.edu.tw
Free

gopher://gopher.nsysu.edu.tw/

National University of Singapore ★★★★

The National University of Singapore Web site provides information about the college, its programs and resources. General information include a cybertour' of the campus, a facility and staff background, and calendars of campus events. Users can find out about campus resources, such as the libraries and networking groups, preview databases, and access the software archives via ftp. Faculty and School listings include study backgrounds and course structure, and the Research Institute listings provide project objectives and background, as well as summaries of University publications.

Keywords Libraries, Singapore
Audience Education Professionals, Singapore Residents, Students
Free

http://nuscc.nus.sg

gopher://nuscc.nus.sg/

Osaka University WWW Server ★★★★

The Osaka University WWW Server provides information about the University, its history and departments. The page has connections to the campus network and Osaka Resources. Some of the departments available include the computation center, the faculty of engineering science and the Genome Information Research Center.

Keywords Asia, Japan, Universities
Audience Educators, Students
Contact www-admin@center.osaka-u.ac.jp
Free

http://www.osaka-u.ac.jp:8080/osaka-u.html

Universiti Sains Malaysia (USM), Penang ★★★

The Universiti Sains Malaysia Home Page presents information about its academic programs, facilities and departments. The page has links to the campus server, calender of events and research programs. There are links to local information and other WWW sites.

Keywords Educational Programs, Malaysia
Audience Educators, Malaysians, Students
Contact sodhy@cs.usm.my
Free

http://www.cs.usm.my

Universities - Asia – Universities - Australia

Welcome to Chulalongkorn University WWW ★★★

This server is provided by Chulalongkorn University, located in Bangkok, Thailand. Visitors can browse through information on the University's history, academic programs, faculty, and facilities. In addition, users can take a 'virtual tour' of the campus, as well as view general information and help files on using the Internet's resources.

KEYWORDS Universities, Thailand, Undergraduate Education
AUDIENCE Education Administrators (College), Educators, Students, Thailand Residents
CONTACT Montree Suntichaikul
montree@netserv.chula.ac.th, www-admin@netserv.chula.ac.th
FREE

http://www.chula.ac.th

gopher://gopher.netserv.chula.ac.th/

ftp://ftp.netserv.chula.ac.th/pub/

Universities - Australia

See also
Computing & Mathematics · *Computer Science*
Computing & Mathematics · *Mathematics*
Education · *International Education*

Australian National University Campus Information Service ★★★

This site is the central gopher server for the Australian National University and provides information about the University and links to the University's other servers. The information available includes administrative manuals, Faculty Handbook, Library Catalogue, Council documents, circulars, internal phone and electronic mail directories.

KEYWORDS Australia, Universities (Australia), University Administration
AUDIENCE Educators, Students
CONTACT Cathy Craig
cais.officer@anu.edu.au
FREE

gopher://polly.anu.edu.au/

Curtin University Campus Information ★★★

This server gives information about news, policies, academic information, staff directories, and more from Curtin University in Australia. There are also links to other Australian gophers.

KEYWORDS Australia, Curriculum, Universities, University Administration
AUDIENCE Australians, Educators, Students
CONTACT R.Taylor@info.curtin.edu.au
FREE

http://www.curtin.edu.au/

gopher://info.curtin.edu.au/

Gopher at University of Western Sydney ★★★

This gopher server provides computing information, class information, administrative information, and more about the University of Western Sydney, Nepean Campus, Australia. Some items available through this site are a Macintosh presentation describing the Centre For Interactive Multimedia In Teaching (CIMIT), class meeting time and room locations for the University, and links to other Internet servers on campus, in Australia, and worldwide.

KEYWORDS Australia, Universities, University Administration
AUDIENCE Australians, Educators, Students
CONTACT M. Houlahan
NepeanGopher@nepean.uws.edu.au
FREE

gopher://gopher.nepean.uws.edu.au/

La Trobe University Gopher Services ★★★

This server gives information about La Trobe University, located in Australia. Directories lead to such information as University administration, campus information, library services, and links to departmental information servers. Users can also link to La Trobe's software archives in order to access files varying from music and educational lesson plans to Internet and general computing utilities.

KEYWORDS Curriculum, Internet Resources, Software Archives, Universities
AUDIENCE Australians, Computer Users, Educators (University), Students
CONTACT Paul Nankervis
P.Nankervis@latrobe.edu.au
FREE

http://www.latrobe.edu.au/

gopher://gopher.latrobe.edu.au/

Monash University - Campus Wide Information Service ★★★

This gopher server provides information about Monash University in Australia, including phone books and directories, student information, library information, administrative information, and more. The server also gives links to other Australian servers and provides further information such as job ads and computer information.

KEYWORDS Australia, Universities, University Administration
AUDIENCE Australians, Educators (University), Students
CONTACT Sue Steele
sue.steele@lib.monash.edu.au
FREE

gopher://cwis.monash.edu.au/

University of Queensland ★★★

This is the main gopher server for the University of Queensland in Brisbane, Australia. It provides information about the University's history and mission, class schedules, degree information, and more. It also provides information about the city of Brisbane.

KEYWORDS Australia, Universities, University Administration
AUDIENCE Australians, Educators, Students
CONTACT Marek Krawus
Marek.Krawus@cc.uq.oz.au
FREE

gopher://gopher.uq.oz.au/

University of Southern Queensland Campus Wide Information Service ★★★

This site, the central gopher server for the University of Southern Queensland, Australia, provides information about the University and the surrounding region. The information includes local events, academic and administrative resources, library catalogs, and links to other servers.

KEYWORDS Australia, Universities, University Administration
AUDIENCE Australians, Educators, Students
CONTACT cwis@helios.usq.edu.au
FREE

gopher://helios.usq.edu.au/

University of Sydney ★★★

This server gives information about the University of Sydney, located in Australia, and includes resources from various University departments and the University archives. The gopher site is due to be replaced by the WWW server in the near future. The archive areas include descriptions of the texts and images from the University and of some of the people and events related to it. Some departments with their own directories include the Law School, the Department of Accounting and the University Library.

KEYWORDS Australia, Universities
AUDIENCE Australia Residents, Australians, Educators, Students
CONTACT Support@isu.usyd.edu.au
FREE

http://www.usyd.edu.au/

gopher://gopher.su.edu.au/

University of Tasmania WWW Service ★★★

This is the server for the University of Tasmania WWW Service. The University of Tasmania comprises several campuses across Australia's island state of Tasmania. It is the only university in the state, with a total enrolment of around 12,000 students. It provides pointers to online services, departmental information, clubs, societies and other organisations, publications, the Tasmania Information File Archive and more.

KEYWORDS Australia, Undergraduate Education, WWW (World Wide Web)
AUDIENCE Educators (University), Internet Users, Researchers, Students (University)
CONTACT web-master@postoffice.utas.edu.au
FREE

http://ftp.utas.edu.au

gopher://info.utas.edu.au/

University of Western Australia ★★★

This site is the main gopher server for the University of Western Australia. It provides directories, research policies, job postings, contact information for University departments, and library catalog access. In addition, users can access a daily calendar of events for the campus, as well as various academic centers such as the Centre for Legumes In Mediterranean Agriculture and the Faculties of Economics & Commerce, Education and Law.

- KEYWORDS Australia, Economics, Educational Programs, Universities
- AUDIENCE Australians, Economists, Educators, Students
- CONTACT bdcoot@ucs.uwa.edu.au
- FREE

gopher://uniwa.uwa.edu.au/

University of Wollongong Gopher ★★★

This is the main gopher server for the University of Wollongong in Australia and gives information about class schedules, University policies, library holdings, and more. There is also a collection of information on how to best navigate the Internet. This server is identical to that at gopher.uow.edu.au.

- KEYWORDS Australia, Universities, University Administration
- AUDIENCE Educators, Students
- CONTACT Steve Cliffe
  gopher@uow.edu.au
- FREE

gopher://wiss.uow.edu.au/

Universities - Canada

See also
Education · *International Education*
Engineering & Technology · *Technology*
Science · *Physics*

Acadia University WWW Home Page ★★★

This site is the top level of Acadia University's WWW information system. Users can find out about the campus, its facilities, faculty, and departments, as well as local information. There is a collection of pictures of the campus available for perusal, and material on student activities. Users can also connect to other servers at Acadia University.

- KEYWORDS Canada, Universities
- AUDIENCE Educators, Students
- CONTACT Paul Steele
  webmaster@acadiau.ca
- FREE

http://www.acadiau.ca

gopher://gopher.acadiau.ca/

Carleton University ★★★

This is a gopher site of Carleton University in Ottawa, Canada. It provides information on and access to admissions, academic records, the calendar, the library, graduate studies, phone directories and more.

- KEYWORDS Canada, Continuing Education, Education (College/University), University Administration
- AUDIENCE Canadians, Educators (University), Students (University)
- CONTACT Jason Goveas
  jgoveas@ccs.carleton.ca
- FREE

gopher://gopher.carleton.ca/

Clarkson University ★★★

This is the Clarkson University home page which provides links to information about the programs, admissions forms, academics, scholarship and research, as well as facts about the Clarkson community, and more.

- KEYWORDS Canada, Clarkson University, Undergraduate Education
- AUDIENCE Computer Professionals, Computer Users, Educators (University), Internet Users, Journalists, Lawyers, LegalProfessionals, Researchers, Students (University)
- CONTACT Pete Deuel. M
  deuelpm@heron.tc.clarkson.edu
- FREE

http://fire.clarkson.edu

Dalhousie University ★★★

This is the home page of Dalhousie University. The page offers links to Dalhousie University general information, WWW and gopher servers, geographic location, searchable student listing, and Internet search tools. In addition, users can view campus publications or take a 'virtual' tour of the university.

- KEYWORDS Canada, Graduated Education, Universities
- AUDIENCE Canada Residents, Students (Secondary/University), Students (University)
- CONTACT Webmaster
  www@ac.dal.ca
- FREE

http://ac.dal.ca/
gopher://ac.dal.ca/

King's Home Page ★★★★

This is the home page of the The University of King's College in Halifax, Nova Scotia, Canada. This page provides links to information on the University's history, library, and admissions staff. Links to information on programs, schools, and institutes are also provided.

- KEYWORDS Canada, Nova Scotia, Universities (History Of)
- AUDIENCE Canada Residents, Students (High School and Up), Students (University)
- CONTACT Stephen Kimber
  skimber@ac.dal.ca
- FREE

http://www.ukings.ns.ca/

Lakehead University Home Page ★★★

This is the WWW home page of Lakehead University in Thunder Bay, Ontario. This page contains links to a searchable University phonebook (forms-based), student home pages, and photos of cross-country skiers. Also included on this page are links to industry information, academic sites, and the University gopher.

- KEYWORDS Canada, Education (College/University)
- AUDIENCE Canada Residents, Students (University)
- CONTACT Paul Inkila
  Paul.Inkila@LakeheadU.Ca
- FREE

http://flash.lakeheadu.ca/
gopher://flash.lakeheadu.ca/

McGill University Home Page ★★★

This is the WWW home page of McGill University in Montreal, Quebec, Canada. This page provides links to information on McGill University's departments, student services, enrollment, and gophers. Also offered on this page are links to all of the Usenet FAQs (frequently asked questions pages), the Virtual Tourist, U.S. and Canadian government pages, and information on the Montreal Canadiens.

- KEYWORDS Montreal, University Administration
- AUDIENCE Canada Residents, Students (Secondary/University), Students (University)
- CONTACT Steve Robbins
  steve@cim.mcgill.ca
- FREE

http://www.mcgill.ca/

McMaster University ★★★

This is the Central McMaster gopher server of McMaster University, Ontario, Canada. It provides information on the University's activities, its policies and procedures, faculty, computing resources, events, publications, libraries, the phone directory, and more. It also provides access to other universities.

- KEYWORDS Canada, Education (College/University), Health Sciences, Universities
- AUDIENCE Educators, Educators (University), Students
- CONTACT go4help@mcmaster.ca
- FREE

gopher://mcmail.cis.mcmaster.ca/

Mount Allison University's WWW Server ★★★

Mount Allison University's WWW Server provides access the University's services and information about the academic programs provided at the University. The page has a virtual campus tour and links to each academic department. There is information about the University bookstore, clubs and societies.

- KEYWORDS Canada, Educational Resources
- AUDIENCE Canadians, Educators, Students
- CONTACT WWW Manager
- FREE

http://www.mta.ca

gopher://gopher.mta.ca/

The Ontario Institute for Studies in Education

This site is a gopher server of the Ontario Institute for Studies in Education in Toronto, Canada. The Ontario Institute for Studies in Education (OISE) is a graduate school of education, affiliated with the University of Toronto. It provides information on OISE degree programs, courses, news, directories, the phone book, and more.

Keywords Canada, Education, Education (College/University), Social Sciences
Audience Canadians, Educators (University), Students (University)
Contact Bob McLean
rmclean@oise.on.ca
Free

gopher://porpoise.oise.on.ca/

Queen's University

This is a gopher server of the Queen's University in Kingston, Ontario, Canada. It provides information on its faculties, courses, libraries, publications, events and more.

Keywords Canada, Education (College/University), International Education, University Administration
Audience Canadians, Educators (University), Students (University)
Contact gopher-admin@post.queensu.ca
Free

gopher://gopher.queensu.ca/

Simon Fraser University

This is a gopher server of the Simon Fraser University, Canada. It provides online access to information about the University and its activities, and also permits browsing and retrieval of information across the Internet.

Keywords Canada, Education (College/University), Social Sciences, Universities
Audience Educators, Educators (University), Students
Contact help@sfu.ca
Free

gopher://gopher.sfu.ca/

Trent University

This is Trent University's Internet Gopher and provides useful information about Trent University to the public. For example, it gives course information, schedules, announcements, and more. Within the Faculty Publications area, users will find texts written or collected by Trent University's faculty which deal with works such as James Joyce, mathematical logic, and religious canticles. Other areas of this gopher server are links to academic, social, and cultural groups on campus, as well as academic departments.

Keywords Canada, Joyce, Universities
Audience Educators (University), Students, Students (Secondary/University)
Contact Ken Brown
kbrown@trentu.ca
Free

gopher://blaze.trentu.ca/

The University of Alberta

This is a gopher server of the Department of Computing Science, University of Alberta in Alberta, Canada. It provides information on the Department, its phone directory, courses, technical reports, instructional supports, software and other University data.

Keywords Canada, Computer Science, Education (College/University), Science
Audience Computer Scientists, Educators (University), Students (University)
Contact Bruce Wm Folliott
bruce@cs.ualberta.ca
Free

gopher://gopher.cs.ualberta.ca/

The University of Calgary

This is a gopher server for the University of Calgary and provides information about the University, its libraries, faculty, student clubs, and more. There are also links to other gopher servers, both at the University of Calgary and elsewhere, and there is more general information about Calgary and southern Alberta available.

Keywords Canada, Education (College/University)
Audience Canadians, Educators, Students
Contact Mike Morrow
morrow@acs.ucalgary.ca
Free

gopher://acs6.acs.ucalgary.ca/

University of Manitoba

This site provides information on the University of Manitoba, its recent events, history, student groups, libraries and more. The University of Manitoba is located in Winnipeg, Manitoba, Canada. The site also provides information about the city of Winnipeg and links to other Canadian WWW servers.

Keywords Canada, Education (College/University), Universities
Audience Canadians, Educators (University), Students (University)
Contact www@umanitoba.ca
Free

http://www.umanitoba.ca/

University of New Brunswick

The site is a gopher server of the University of New Brunswick, New Brunswick, Canada. It provides information on the University's activities, faculty, its phone directory, libraries, campus events, and more.

Keywords Campus Information, Canada, Education (College/University), Social Sciences, Universities
Audience Educators, Educators (Primary/Secondary), Students
Contact Bonnie Mockler
info@unb.ca
Free

gopher://unbmvs1.csd.unb.ca/

University of Saskatchewan

★★★

This is a gopher server of the University of Saskatchewan in Saskatoon, Canada. Information is provided about the University, the University's organizational chart, campus phone book (searchable), faculties, libraries, and more.

KEYWORDS Canada, Education (College/University), Science, Social Sciences
AUDIENCE Canadians, Educators (University), Students (University)
CONTACT Earl Fogel
Earl.Fogel@usask.ca
FREE

gopher://gopher.usask.ca/

University of Toronto

★★★

This gopher site provides access to information on the University of Toronto including the University of Toronto Root Gopher, General Purpose UNIX, Erindale College, Scarborough Campus, Computer Systems Research Institute, Department of Physics, libraries, electronic phone books, campus life, and more.

KEYWORDS Campus Information, Canada, Education (College/University), Universities
AUDIENCE Educators (University), Students
FREE

gopher://vm.utcs.utoronto.ca/

University of Victoria UVicInfo

★★★

The University of Victoria Home Page provides information about the University, its student life, educational programs, and other student services. Weather and travel facts are also offered, along with several different phone directories. Department listings include general research background, personnel information, and publications lists. Users may also access the University of Victoria libraries and gophers resources.

KEYWORDS Canada, Universities
AUDIENCE Education Professionals, Students
CONTACT Joe Sparrow
listman@uvvm.uvic.ca
FREE

http://netinfo.uvic.ca

gopher://info.uvic.ca/

University of Waterloo Campus Wide Information System (UWInfo)

★★★

This is a campuswide information system of the University of Waterloo, Waterloo, Canada. It provides information about the University, its faculty, libraries, courses, exam timetables, student group listings, daily bulletins, and more. It also provides access to other gopher holes on campus.

KEYWORDS Canada, Education (College/University), Social Sciences, Universities
AUDIENCE Educators, Educators (University), Students

CONTACT Faye Abrams
uwinfo-ops@uwinfo.uwaterloo.ca
FREE

gopher://watserv2.uwaterloo.ca/

University of Western Ontario

★★★

This is the gopher server of the University of Western Ontario in London, Canada. It provides information on the University, its faculties, libraries, courses, events and more.

KEYWORDS Canada, Education (College/University), Universities, University Administration
AUDIENCE Canadians, Educators (University), Students (University)
CONTACT gopher@uwo.ca
FREE

gopher://gopher.uwo.ca/

York University

★★★

This is a gopher server of the York University in Toronto, Canada. It provides information about the University's faculties, libraries, its research and publications, the phone book, email directories, computing services, events and more.

KEYWORDS Canada, Education (College/University), Social Sciences, Universities
AUDIENCE Educators, Educators (University), Students

Connections to Self Defense
Watch out, I'm trained in the Martial Arts

SafeSkills, Inc. and TWMA Page

Call (919) 644-1335 or (919) 493-SAFE for class times.

Here's a local Map to SafeSkills, Inc.

Self-Defense For Women Mini-Courses

These very popular mini-courses for women teach both verbal and physical skills that are practical, realistic, and easily remembered. This is not a lecture, nor is it martial arts training. You get safe hands-on practice (we will not throw each other around the room). SafeSkills female instructors have

Ever been mugged? Would you like a greater sense of confidence in your life, help in finding your "center"? Do you need assistance in working through the emotional aftermath of an assault or chronic abuse? The Internet provides a broad spectrum of information on self defense-related matters.

If you want to learn effective self defense techniques, or if you want guildelines for choosing a self defense regimen, then the "Assault Prevention Information Network Index" is a good place to start

(http://galaxy.einet.net/galaxy/Community/Safety/Assault-Prevention/apin/APINindex.html)

You can get a step-by-step video course in self defense. There's also a place that provides information about self defense for women, teaching women both verbal and physicals skills that help protect against an attack. You can even learn about dangerous self defense myths, such as "chemical spray will reliably stop an assailant."

(http://www.cs.duke.edu/~ken/SafeSkills.html)

CONTACT   CWIS Coordinator
          cwis@yorku.ca
FREE

gopher://gopher.yorku.ca/

Universities - Europe

See also
Computing & Mathematics · *Computer Science*
Education · *International Education*
Science · *Physics*

Aalborg University- General Information

This is the top level for Aalborg University's campus-wide information service. There is information on the programs and faculty of the University, as well as library and administrative information. There are also links to Danish resources on the web, as well as to other related scientific and academic institutions. The information in Danish is more comprehensive than that provided in English.

KEYWORDS   Universities, Denmark
AUDIENCE   Education Administrators (College), Educators, Students
CONTACT   www@aud1.auc.dk
FREE

http://www.auc.dk

Abo Akademi University

This site is maintained by Abo Akademi University in Finland. The server provides information on the University, its history, its administration, faculties, academic departments, humanities, psychology, centers, research & studies, computing services, email addresses, phone numbers, news, weather, and more. It has links to other gophers as well.

KEYWORDS   Education (College/University), Finland, Universities, University Administration
AUDIENCE   •Academics, Educators (University), Students (Secondary/University)
CONTACT   uachren@abo.fi
FREE

gopher://gopher.abo.fi/

Adam Mickiewicz University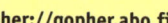

This site offers information on Adam Mickiewicz University in Poznan, Poland. Users will find information on the history, departments, faculty, and facilities of the University. In addition, this server hosts links to other Polish Internet resources, as well as links to related servers around the world.

KEYWORDS   International Education, Poland
AUDIENCE   Educators, Poland Residents, Students
CONTACT   Dorota Nicewicz
           dorota@math.amu.edu.pl
FREE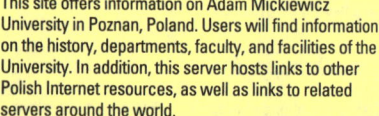

http://www.amu.edu.pl

Centrum voor Wiskunde en Informatica (CWI)

CWI (Centrum voor Wiskunde en Informatica) is the research institute of the SMC (Stichting Mathematisch Centrum). The mission of CWI is to perform frontier research in mathematics and computer science and to transfer new knowledge in these fields to society in general and trade and industry in particular. This page provides pointers to topics under the headings — About CWI, General CWI related items, Departments, Research projects, Library/Other Information Service Announcements, Library and Online Catalogue, and more.

KEYWORDS   Informatics, Netherlands, Research Institutes
AUDIENCE   Educators (University), Internet Users, Researchers, Students (University)
CONTACT   Frank.van.de.Wiel@cwi.nl
FREE

http://ftp.cwi.nl/

Chalmers University of Technology

This site provides information about the Chalmers University of Technology, Gothenburg, Sweden. The server also allows access to policy documents, software, and X.500 catalogues. It has links to other gophers as well.

KEYWORDS   Community Services, Education (College/University), Sweden
AUDIENCE   Academics, Computer Professionals, Educators (University), Students (Secondary/University)
CONTACT   cth-nic@chalmers.se
FREE

gopher://chalmers.se/

City University School of Informatics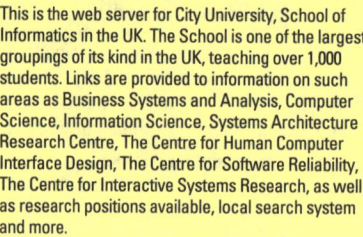

This is the web server for City University, School of Informatics in the UK. The School is one of the largest groupings of its kind in the UK, teaching over 1,000 students. Links are provided to information on such areas as Business Systems and Analysis, Computer Science, Information Science, Systems Architecture Research Centre, The Centre for Human Computer Interface Design, The Centre for Software Reliability, The Centre for Interactive Systems Research, as well as research positions available, local search system and more.

KEYWORDS   Computer Science, Employment, Informatics, United Kingdom
AUDIENCE   Computer Users, Educators (University), Internet Users, Researchers, Students (University)
FREE

http://ftp.cs.city.ac.uk

Cranfield University WWW Information Server

This site offers information provided by Cranfield University in England. Users will find descriptions of the individual departments within the campus, as well as information on the academic and degree programs

available there. This site also hosts computing technical documentation and software directories.

KEYWORDS   Universities, England
AUDIENCE   British, Education Administrators (College), Educators, Students
CONTACT   Alan Pibworth
           a.pibworth@cranfield.ac.uk
FREE

http://www.cranfield.ac.uk

gopher://gopher.cranfield.ac.uk/

Czech Technical University

This site describes the Czech Technical University. The information it provides covers the University's faculties, the computing center, libraries and phonebooks. The site also has a connection to the University's FTP archive.

KEYWORDS   Czech Republic, Engineering Education, Technical Schools, Universities
AUDIENCE   Educators (University), Professors, Students (University)
FREE

gopher://gopher.cvut.cz/

Ecole des Mines de Nancy's Student Server

Ecole des Mines de Nancy's Student Server contains unofficial information about the school, student homepages, and humorous text files about computing, the school, and France.

KEYWORDS   Engineering, France, Student Projects
AUDIENCE   Engineers, France Residents
CONTACT   www@mines.u-nancy.fr
FREE

http://dafne.mines.u-nancy.fr/

Friedrich-Alexander Universitat, Erlangen

The Friedrich-Alexander University of Erlangen-Nuremberg site offers information in German and English about the university itself, the city of Erlangen and the net of the Bavarian Universities. There is access to information from servers all over the world.

KEYWORDS   Germany, Universities, University of Erlangen-Nuernberg
AUDIENCE   Germans, Students, Tourists
CONTACT   Juergen Rothenanger
           Juergen.Rothenanger@RRZE.Uni-Erlangen.de
FREE

http://www.uni-erlangen.de/docs/index.html

Helsinki University of Technology Gopher

This site offers access to the Helsinki University of Technology Information Services. It provides informa-

Universities - Europe

tion in English and Finnish about the faculty and the student union at the University.
- KEYWORDS Computing, Finland, Science, University Administration
- AUDIENCE (College/University), Educators, Finns, Students (University)
- CONTACT Karl Holm
- FREE

gopher://gopher.hut.fi/

IIBS Universities (International Business Studies)

IIBS is a private institute for international business studies based in Munich, Germany. There is detailed information access through the Web site to the MBA and Bachelor of Science Programs. There is a downloadable. printable application form.
- KEYWORDS Business Schools, Germany, MBA Programs, Universities
- AUDIENCE Educators, International Business Students
- CONTACT IIBSinfo@iibs.trans.net
- FREE

http://www.iibs.netplace.com/

Informations-Service an der Universitaet Zuerich

This site offers information about the University of Zurich, Switzerland. This information includes the calendar, library resources, and information for students. The server also acts as a gateway to other gopher sites at the University of Zurich and elsewhere on the Internet.
- KEYWORDS Libraries, Switzerland, University Administration
- AUDIENCE Educators (University) , Professors, Students (University)
- CONTACT gopher@rzu.unizh.ch
- FREE

gopher://gopher.unizh.ch/

Institutt for Informatikk

This is the home page for Institutt for Informatikk in Norway. This server provides information about the school including student activities, lectures and seminars, manuals and dictionaries, and local information. There is an English version of the home page but the links are in Norwegian.
- KEYWORDS Computer Science, Norway
- AUDIENCE Computer Scientists, Educators, Educators (University), Engineers, Physicists, Students (University)
- CONTACT Tor Sørevik
  tor.sorevik@ii.uib.no
- FREE

http://eik.ii.uib.no/index.english.html

University of Joensuu, Finland

The University of Joensuu page offers information on its facilities, faculty and study programs. The University has links to the department of Forestry and the International Studies Programs as well as the University Library.
- KEYWORDS Finland, Humanities, International Relations, Social Sciences
- AUDIENCE Students
- CONTACT intnl@joyl.joensuu.fi
- FREE

http://www.joensuu.fi

Katholieke Universiteit Leuven

The Katholieke Universiteit Leuven in Belgium, which is the oldest catholic university in the world, gives information about the faculty departments at the University, general campus and admissions information. KU Leuven is a center of higher learning and scientific research that has links to the KUL Library, the Belgian Federal Government, the WWW server of BELNET, and other schools on the Internet.
- KEYWORDS Belgium, International Education
- AUDIENCE Belgians, Dutch, Educators, Students
- CONTACT webmaster@kuleuven.ac.be.
- FREE

http://www.kuleuven.ac.be

Kingston University WWW Server

The Kingston University WWW Server gives access to campus facilities, and the School's departments and the faculty. There are links to information about this server, and others in Kingston, a city near London, England. The WWW has been arranged in an informative search outline with links to site categories.
- KEYWORDS Internet Services, Universities
- AUDIENCE Students, United Kingdom Residents
- CONTACT webmaster@kingston.ac.uk
- FREE

http://www.kingston.ac.uk

Leiden University

The Leiden University Web Page offers general information about the University, its faculty, departments, services and student news. The University page has links to related educational resources, other Dutch resources and web sites.
- KEYWORDS Educational Resources, Netherlands
- AUDIENCE Dutch, Educators, Students
- CONTACT Helpdesk@CRI.LeidenUniv.nl
- FREE

http://www.leidenuniv.nl

Linköping University

This is the web server for the Linköping University in Sweden. It provides links to departmental information, other organizations at Linköping University, master's degree programs, student organizations, and some external pointers.
- KEYWORDS Graduate Programs, Universities, Sweden
- AUDIENCE Computer Users, Educators (University) , Internet Users, Researchers, Students (University)
- CONTACT mwe@isy.liu.se
- FREE

http://garbo.isy.liu.se

gopher://gopher.liu.se/

Lund University

This is a gopher server of the Lund University Computing Centre (LDC) in Sweden. It gives information on the University, LDC, its phone books, software, documents, computing resources, and more. It has links to other gophers as well.
- KEYWORDS Computer Science, Education (College/University), Sweden, University Administration
- AUDIENCE Computer Users, Educators (University), Students (University), Swedes
- CONTACT Torgny Hallenmark
  Torgny.Hallenmark@ldc.lu.se
- FREE

gopher://gopher.ldc.lu.se/

Moscow State University Main HTTP Server

The Moscow State University Main HTTP Server gives access to all the departments at the university. There is information on the origins of the university, admissions procedures and requirements. There are links to other universities that have relations with MSU as well as other Russian WWW servers.
- KEYWORDS Educational Resources, Humanities, Russia, Science
- AUDIENCE Russians, Students
- CONTACT Vladimir V Shebordaev
  webmaster@rector.msu.su
- FREE

http://www.rector.msu.su/

Nicolas Copernicus University

This site provides information on the administration and academic programs of the Nicolas Copernicus University in Torun, Poland. It also contains information about the University Library, the UMK Mathmatics Institute, TeX, the city of Torun, and more. As well, links to other gophers are provided.
- KEYWORDS Education (College/University), Poland, University Administration
- AUDIENCE Academics, Educators (University), Mathematicians, Students
- CONTACT Piotr Konstanty
  pk10@pltumk11.bitnet
- FREE

gopher://vm.cc.uni.torun.pl/

Oxford's Centre for Humanities Computing

This site is the Information Service of the Centre for Humanities Computing based at Oxford University Computing Services (OUCS). It describes the various humanities computing projects at OUCS and how to obtain copies of their publications. A complete HTML

version of the Centre's Resources Guide is available here.
- KEYWORDS Computer Aided Instruction, Computing, United Kingdom
- AUDIENCE Academics, Educators (University)
- CONTACT Stuart Lee
Stuart.Lee@oucs.ox.ac.uk
- FREE

http://www.ox.ac.uk/depts/humanities/

Page d'accueil du College de France ★★★

The server for the College of France offers links to the college itself, its faculty, the courses in Paris, Province and abroad and the corresponding address/contact information. Courses are held all over the world in several dozen locations
- KEYWORDS Colleges/Universities, France
- AUDIENCE Education Administrators (College), Educators, Students
- FREE

http://cdfinfo.in2p3.fr/College/college.html

Pohjois-Savo Polytechnic WWW Pages ★★★

The Pohjois-Savo Polytechnic (PSPT) WWW Pages provides information about this Finnish university's degree programs in business administration, technology, crafts and design. The page has links to the different colleges and PSPT member Institutes. There are links to the School's resources and other Finnish servers.
- KEYWORDS Business, Crafts, Finland, Technology
- AUDIENCE Finns, Students, Technology Specialists
- CONTACT webmaster@pspt.fi
- FREE

http://www.pspt.fi

Royal Institute of Technology Gopher ★★★

This site describes the schools and departments, library and computer services at the Royal Institute of Technology in Stockholm, Sweden. In addition, it has links to other gophers, like the European root gopher server.
- KEYWORDS Education (College/University), Sweden, Technology, University Administration
- AUDIENCE Educators (University), Engineers, Students (University)
- CONTACT gopher-info@sunic.sunet.se
- FREE

gopher://gopher.kth.se/

Rug Home Pania ★★★

RUG the Campus Wide Information Server for the University of Groningen in the Netherlands, provides information about the departments, research projects and staff information. There is access to the public libraries as well as tourist information throughout the Netherlands.
- KEYWORDS Educational Resources, Libraries, Netherlands

- AUDIENCE Dutch Persons, Educators, Students
- CONTACT Jan van Beek
J.F.van.Beek@rc.rug.nl
- FREE

http://www.rug.nl/

SIC de la Universitat Jaume I ★★★

This site is the campuswide information system for Universitat Jaume I, a university in Spain. The resources found on this site include the library, the computer center, and student services. In addition, the server provides a special section on political science.
- KEYWORDS Europe, Spain, University Administration
- AUDIENCE Educators (University), Political Scientists, Professors, Students (University)
- CONTACT gopher@si.uji.es
- FREE

gopher://pereiii.uji.es/

Silesian University ★★★

This site describes the Silesian University, Poland. It provides documents on the University's administration, computer center, faculties, academic programs, local news, ads, and more. As well, it provides access to other gophers in Poland as well as in the world.
- KEYWORDS Education (College/University), Poland, University Administration
- AUDIENCE Academics, Educators (University), Students
- CONTACT Maciek Uhlig
muhlig@usctoux1.cto.us.edu.pl
- FREE

gopher://usctoux1.cto.us.edu.pl/

Slovak Academy of Sciences ★★★

This site provides information on the administration and academic programs of Slovak Academy of Sciences. It also provides information about computing resources & services, electronic circuit design & application workshops, and more.
- KEYWORDS Education, Slovakia
- AUDIENCE Academics, Engineers, Scientists, Students (Secondary/University)
- CONTACT hotline@savba.sk
- FREE

gopher://savba.savba.sk/

Stanislaw Staszic University of Mining and Metallurgy in Cracow (UMM) ★★★

This is the home page for Stanislaw Staszic University of Mining and Metallurgy (UMM) in Cracow. It provides information for foreign users, a local gopher, personal home pages at UMM, a UMM phone book, scientific research at UMM, Polish network resources, online books, and more.
- KEYWORDS Metallurgy, Mining, Poland, Stanislaw Staszic University

- AUDIENCE Computer Users, Educators (University), Internet Users, Researchers, Students (University)
- CONTACT Szymon Sokol
szymon@uci.agh.edu.pl
- FREE

http://galaxy.uci.agh.edu.pl

Stockholms Universitet ★★★

Information about Stockholm University, Sweden, is found on this site. This includes a description of the University administration, its departments, library resources, phone books, email addresses, and a musical lyrics archive.
- KEYWORDS Archives, Education (College/University), Sweden, University Administration
- AUDIENCE Educators (University), Students (University), Swedes
- CONTACT Fredrik Reutersw{rd
fr@tele.su.se
- FREE

gopher://circe.su.se/

Technical University - Darmstadt ★★★

This gopher site provides information on the Technical University- Darmstadt, Germany. This includes data on the library, programs, computing services, entrance information, and other academic resource information.
- KEYWORDS Computer Technology, Germany, University Administration
- AUDIENCE Academics, Germans, Professors, Students
- CONTACT Andreas Liebe
liebe@hrz.th-darmstadt.de
- FREE

gopher://gopher.th-darmstadt.de/

The Technical University of Clausthal Gopher Server ★★★

This gopher server provides information on the Technical University of Clausthal such as program requirements, admissions, library and social activities information. It also includes a link to the main campuswide information system and numerous links to worldwide gopher servers.
- KEYWORDS Computer Technology, Germany, University Administration
- AUDIENCE Academics, Professors, Students
- CONTACT Olaf Tegtmeier
tegtmeier@rz.tu-clausthal.de
- FREE

gopher://gopher.tu-clausthal.de/

Technical University of Hamburg-Harburg ★★★

This page contains a brief description of the Technical University of Hamburg-Harburg in Germany including the faculty and staff, equipment and facilities, course descriptions and projects, and thesis-topics offered.
- KEYWORDS Curriculum, Germany, Universities
- AUDIENCE Educators (University), German Students

Universities - Europe

CONTACT muehlthaler@tu-harburg.d400.de
FREE

http://energie1.en.tu-harburg.de/Dept_Energietechnik.html

gopher://hpms.rz.tu-harburg.de/

Tilburg University Home Page ★★★★

The Tilburg University Home page gives access to the departments and institutes located at the University. The page has links to the Institute for Language Technology and Artificial Intelligence, the Department of Economics' Infolab, the Science Shop, and the University Press. There is information and links to other services at Tilburg University and sites on the Internet.

KEYWORDS Computers, Economics, Netherlands
AUDIENCE Dutch, Scientists, Students
CONTACT Maarten van Wijk
Maarten.vanWijk@kub.nl.
FREE

http://www.kub.nl

UCL (University College London) Home Page ★★

This server is the top level of University College London's campus-wide information web. Users will find links to many of the departments at the College, as well as an X.500 directory of faculty, staff, and students. In addition, this server includes many pointers to information on the WWW information system, and links to general information about the school itself.

KEYWORDS Educational Resources, England
AUDIENCE Education Administrators (College), Educators, Students
CONTACT UCL-Info-support@ucl.ac.uk
FREE

http://www-server.bcc.ac.uk

Universidade Nova de Lisboa ★★★

This site describes Universidade Nova de Lisboa, a university in Portugal. It provides documents on the University's administration and departments, software and images, and links to other gophers on the Internet.

KEYWORDS Education (College/University), Portugal, University Administration
AUDIENCE Academics, Educators (University), Portuguese Speakers
CONTACT Joaquim Baptista
archive@fct.unl.pt
FREE

gopher://gopher.fct.unl.pt/

Universitaet Bielefeld, Technische Fakultaet ★★★

This gopher sites provide information on the Faculty of Technology at the University of Bielefeld. This includes programs of study, meal plan, links to other gophers, computing services, and faculty information.

KEYWORDS Computer Technology, Research & Development, University Administration
AUDIENCE Academics, Professors, Students
CONTACT robert@TechFak.Uni-Bielefeld.DE
FREE

gopher://gopher.TechFak.Uni-Bielefeld.de/

Universite Libre de Bruxelles (ULB) ★★

The Free University of Brussels, which is one of the world's leading French-speaking universities, provides an overview of its programs in French and English, and links to various departments, the library, a phone book and other sites on the Internet.

KEYWORDS Belgium, Education (College/University), International Education
AUDIENCE Educators, Researchers, Students
CONTACT Michel Jansens
mjansens@ulb.ac.be
FREE

http://www.ulb.ac.be/

Universiteit Utrecht Informatie Systeem ★★★

The Utrecht University Information System supplies general information on the facilities, the departments, the organizations and the central services at the University. There is a section that gives assistance in finding information on the web. There are also links to other sites in the Netherlands and around the world.

KEYWORDS Educational Resources, Information Systems, Netherlands
AUDIENCE Educators, Netherlands Residents, Students, Tourists
CONTACT Henny.Bekker@cc.ruu.nl
FREE

http://www.ruu.nl/

University College Dublin ★★★

The University College of Dublin (UCD) Web site gives general information about the university, its programs, and the Dublin area. Included here are a college history and general college information, including maps and the text of a recent speech by Mary Robinson. Research areas include high energy astrophysics, magnetics and machines research, and soft condensed matter research, with each research group providing a page of information about their project. Online library catalogs, telephone books and the UCD gopher are available. UCD also compiles Irish archives and electronic directories, and provides links to other relevant Web sites.

KEYWORDS Ireland, Universities
AUDIENCE Irish, Researchers, Students (College)
CONTACT webmaster@nova.ucd.ie
FREE

http://midir.ucd.ie

University College Karlskrona/Ronneby ★★

This is a gopher server of the University College Karlskrona/Ronneby in Sweden. It contains information on the University's departments, addresses, email addresses, student services, and FTP sites. It also provides access to online journals and magazines such as Commerce Business Daily and the Journal of Computer-Medical Communication. It has links to other gopher holes.

KEYWORDS Education (College/University), Journals, Sweden, University Administration
AUDIENCE Educators (University), Students (University), Swedes
CONTACT Mikael Roos
gopher-admin@hk-r.se
FREE

gopher://ronneby.hk-r.se/

University of Antwerp ★★★

The server for the University of Antwerp in Belgium provides access to information on its departments, courses, research, contacts, a search tool to locate students and employees, language courses, specialized seminars, and Internet services. A link is included to Belgium's Web tour.

KEYWORDS Belgium, Education (College/University), International Education
AUDIENCE Educators, Researchers, Students
CONTACT Michel Daulie
ccs.daulie.m@alpha.ufsia.ac.be
FREE

http://www.ufsia.ac.be/

University of Bergen ★★★

This site contains information about the University of Bergen, located in Norway. Information is predominantly in Norwegian, and covers areas such as university departments, courses available, faculty, research and other general areas. In addition, links to other sites, such as local information about Bergen, are available for users.

KEYWORDS Norway, University Administration
AUDIENCE Norwegians, Students (College)
CONTACT Hans Morten Kind
kind@edb.uib.no
FREE

http://www.uib.no/

University of Brighton Home Page ★★★

This server offers information on the University of Brighton in the United Kingdom. Users will find departmental and faculty information, as well as admissions material and course offerings. There are also links to individual departments within the University, and information on the computer facilities there.

KEYWORDS England, University Administration
AUDIENCE Education Administrators (College), Educators, Students
CONTACT Ray Hillman
Ray.Hillman@bton.ac.uk
FREE

http://www.bton.ac.uk

gopher://gopher.bton.ac.uk

Universities - Europe

University of East Anglia (UEA) ★★★

The University of East Anglia is situated on the outskirts of Norwich, in the east of England. There is a link to the main menu that will take the user to areas such as University administration information, academic departments, student resources and links to outside to the university,

- KEYWORDS: Campus Information, England
- AUDIENCE: Students, United Kingdom Residents
- CONTACT: informer@uea.ac.uk
- FREE

http://cpca3.uea.ac.uk

University of Edinburgh's Information Service ★★★

This is the site for the University of Edinburgh's Information Service. It has pointers to News and Events, Telephone, Email and Student email (not available outside Edinburgh), Directories, The University of Edinburgh Library System, Departments and Units, General Information, other web servers at The University of Edinburgh, Online Publications, and informatiion about the City of Edinburgh.

- KEYWORDS: Campus Information, Undergraduate Education
- AUDIENCE: Computer Users, Educators (University), Internet Users, Researchers, Students (University)
- FREE

http://ftp.ed.ac.uk

University of Erlangen-Nurnberg ★★★

The University of Erlangen site provides information about the University and the regions surrounding it. University materials include lists of faculties and institutions of the colleges, a history and overview of the university, and general statistics. Information about the culture, history, and geography of the city of Erlangen is provided, including a city map, contact addresses, and information about local politics. Here the reader may also find the University net of Bavaria, linking to information, maps, and profiles of higher education institutions in the Bavaria region.

- KEYWORDS: Germany, Tourism, Universities
- AUDIENCE: Educators, Germans, Students, Travelers
- CONTACT: Jurgen Rothenanger webmaster@nze.uni-erlange.de
- FREE

http://www.uni-erlangen.de/docs/index_e.html

University of Frankfurt am Main Gopher Server ★★

This gopher server directs users to access University information via their World Wide Web site instead of the gopher site. It offers access to the US Library of Congress, Veronica searches, and many other sites, the majority of which are not written in English.

- KEYWORDS: Germany, Technology, Universities, University Administration
- AUDIENCE: Academics, Educators (University), Students (Secondary/University)
- CONTACT: sysgo@rz.uni-frankfurt.de
- FREE

gopher://gopher.rz.uni-frankfurt.de/

University of Goteborg ★★

This is a gopher server of the University of Goteborg in Sweden. It contains information about the Swedish Social Science Data (SSD) services, SSD holdings of data, the Inter-university Consortium for Political and Social Reseach (ICPSR), the electronic library of the SSD archive, and more. In addition, it has links to other gophers in Sweden as well as in the rest of the world.

- KEYWORDS: Databases, Education (College/University), Social Sciences, Sweden
- AUDIENCE: Educators (University), Social Scientists, Students (University), Swedes
- CONTACT: Birger.Jerlehag@ssd.gu.se
- FREE

gopher://gopher.ssd.gu.se/

University of Helsinki ★★★

This is a gopher server of the University of Helsinki in Finland. It contains information on the University, its administration, admissions, departments and faculties, courses and programs, activities for foreign students, press releases, and library services. It has links to other gophers as well.

- KEYWORDS: Education (College/University), Finland, University Administration
- AUDIENCE: Academics, Educators (University), Students (University)
- CONTACT: Heli@helsinki.fi
- FREE

gopher://gopher.helsinki.fi/

University of Hertfordshire WWW Server ★★★

The University of Hertfordshire WWW Server contains information for the students, faculty, and the outside academic world. Users will find general contact and email addresses, library catalogs, and links to specific divisions such as the School of Information Science, the Division of Electrical Engineering and the Division of Psychology. There are also announcements for upcoming conferences, as well as links to what is new on this server. A collection of links to other Internet servers in the United Kingdom and the rest of the world are provided as well.

- KEYWORDS: United Kingdom, Universities
- AUDIENCE: Students (College), United Kingdom Residents
- CONTACT: webmaster@herts.ac.uk
- FREE

http://altair.herts.ac.uk/

University of Jyvaskyla ★★★

The University of Jyvaskyla gives information on the school departments, faculty, study programs and services. There is information on an upcoming biomechanics conference and links to other sites on the Internet.

- KEYWORDS: Biosciences, Finland
- AUDIENCE: Finnish Persons, Students
- CONTACT: Vesa-Matti Paananen vmpa@math.jyu.fi
- FREE

http://www.jyu.fi
gopher://gopher.jyu.fi/

University of Karlsruhe ★★

This gopher site provides information on the University of Karlsruhe in Germany which includes faculty, registration, the meal plan, admissions, and other aspects of the University. It also includes links to other gophers in Germany and worldwide.

- KEYWORDS: Europe, Germany, University Administration
- AUDIENCE: Academics, Germans, Professors, Students
- CONTACT: Ursula Scheller betzler@rz.uni-karlsruhe.de
- FREE

gopher://gopher.rz.uni-karlsruhe.de/

University of Liege ★★★

The University of Liege in Belgium offers access to its Web site in either French or English. There are over 10 different department servers, links to research information, a WWW FAQ, and miscellaneous other links.

- KEYWORDS: Belgium, Education (College/University), International Education
- AUDIENCE: Researchers, Students
- CONTACT: Webmaster webmaster@ulg.ac.be
- FREE

http://www.ulg.ac.be/

The University of Nottingham ★★★★

The University of Nottingham home page gives access to general information, services, departments and research groups. There are extensive links to each department at the school as well as links to the web.

- KEYWORDS: Educational Programs, Educational Resources, England
- AUDIENCE: Educators, Europeans, Students
- CONTACT: webmaster@nottingham.ac.uk.
- FREE

http://www.nott.ac.uk/

University of Oulu gopher ★★★

This site offers access to the University of Oulu's departments on education, humanities, science, engineering, and more. The computer services center, language center, library, and the Research Institute of Northern Finland are also covered.

- KEYWORDS: Education (College/University), Engineering, Finland, Technology
- AUDIENCE: Academics, Engineers, Finns, Researchers, Scientists
- FREE

gopher://ousrvr.oulu.fi/

Universities - Europe – Universities - South America

University of Tampere ★★

This site provides documents that describe the University of Tampere in Finland. The information includes administration, the calendar, libraries, departments, and news. It has links to other gophers as well.

KEYWORDS Education (College/University), Finland, University Administration
AUDIENCE Academics, Educators (University), Students (Secondary/University)
CONTACT gopher@uta.fi
FREE

gopher://gopher.uta.fi/

University of Trieste ★★★

This site conects to the University's schools, departments, and faculty. There are also links to other interesting Web sites in Italy and Europe. There is an introduction to Italian, Italian literature, and some of Italy's research labs.

KEYWORDS Europe, Foreign Language Repositories, Italy, Mediterranean Culture
AUDIENCE Educators, International Students, Italians, Language Students
CONTACT Flavia Crisma
nirmng@univ.trieste.it
FREE

http://www.univ.trieste.it/e_utshom.html

University of Vaasa ★★★

The University of Vaasa in Finland is described by the documents served on this gopher site. The documents cover topics such as the administration, faculties, departments, the library, publications, news, phone books, calendars, and student services. In addition, the server provides tunnels to other holes in gopher space.

KEYWORDS Education (College/University), Finland, University Administration
AUDIENCE Academics, Educators (University), Students (Secondary/University)
FREE

gopher://gopher.uwasa.fi/

Uppsala Universitet ★★★

This site contains general information about the University of Uppsala in Sweden including reports on research, courses and the campus itself. It also has links to other servers, including many Swedish Universities. Several of the pages are in English, French and German.

KEYWORDS Sweden, Universities
AUDIENCE Researchers, Students (Secondary/University), Swedish Culture Enthusiasts
CONTACT webmaster@sunet.se
FREE

http://www.uu.se/

gopher://gopher.uu.se/

Vision, Speech and Signal Processing (VSSP) Group at the University of Southampton. ★★

This page provides information on the Department of Electronics Vision, Speech and Signal Processing group at the University of Southampton in England. It also includes some miscellaneous linked topics such as Weather Images, The Climbing Archive, trivia, Movie Reviews, an online Multimedia Lab, and NCSA Unix software descriptions.

KEYWORDS Climbing, United Kingdom
AUDIENCE Climbing Enthusiasts, Computer Professionals, Educators (University), Students (University)
CONTACT jkf@soton.ac.uk
FREE

http://elstar.ecs.soton.ac.uk/

Warsaw University ★★★

This site offers information on the administration and academic programs of the Warsaw University, Poland. There's news about academic departments, computing resources and services, library resources and services, campus activities, the Warsaw Academy of Medicine, and much more. It also has links to other resources.

KEYWORDS Education (College/University), Poland, University Administration
AUDIENCE Academics, Educators (University), Medical Professionals, Students
CONTACT chomac@plearn.bitnet
FREE

gopher://plearn.edu.pl/

Universities - South America

See also
Computing & Mathematics · *Mathematics*
Education · *International Education*

Gopher PUC (Pontificia Universidad Catolica de Chile) ★★★

This gopher describes the Pontificia Universidad Catolica de Chile (PUC), a university in Chile. The information includes admission, post-graduate and undergraduate programs, publications, and services. In addition, the server is a gateway to resources on the Internet including news, discussion groups, and other gopher servers.

KEYWORDS Catholicism, Chile, University Administration
AUDIENCE Professors, Students (Secondary/University)
CONTACT g-adm@puc.cl
FREE

gopher://gopher.puc.cl/

Gopher USFQ ★★★

This site holds information about the Universidad San Francisco de Quito, a university in Quito, Ecuador. The information provided covers curricula, administration, libraries, and events. The library resources allow the user to search the library catalog. One can also find maps and images of campus on this gopher.

KEYWORDS Ecuador, Latin America, University Administration
AUDIENCE Academics, Professors, Students (University), University Administrators
CONTACT sistemas@mail.usfq.edu.ec
FREE

gopher://gopher.usfq.edu.ec/

Gopher Universidad Catolica del Norte ★★★

This site offers information about the Universidad Catolica del Norte, a university in Chile. The information includes a history, admission criteria, academic standards, courses, degree programs, and administrative information. In addition, descriptions of current research and access to library resources are provided.

KEYWORDS Chile, University Administration
AUDIENCE Professors, Students (University), University Administrators
CONTACT Nelly Urbina
nurbina@socompa.cecun.ucn.cl
FREE

gopher://socompa.cecun.ucn.cl/

INE Home Page ★★★★

This site offers information about the Federal University of Santa Catarina in Brazil and its Information and Statistics Department, which administers the site. It also provides a general guide to the Brazilian WWW and the Internet.

KEYWORDS Brazil, Computer Applications, Computer Networks, Statistics
AUDIENCE Computer Scientists, Educators (University), Network Developers
CONTACT Jose Eduardo De Lucca
delucca@inf.ufsc.br
FREE

http://www.inf.ufsc.br/

Servicio de Informacion REUNA ★★

This site is a gopher server that provides information about the Red Universitaria Nacional (REUNA), a university in Chile. The information includes a description of the institution, telephone directories, education programs, and library information.

KEYWORDS Chile, University Administration
AUDIENCE Professors, Students (Secondary/University), Students (University), University Administrators
CONTACT info@huelen.reuna.cl
FREE

gopher://huelen.reuna.cl/

Universidad de Concepcion Gopher Server ★★★

This site offers information about the Universidad de Concepcion in Chile. It provides assistance for new users of gophers, a history of the university, seminar dates, faculty and campus information, and an assortment of information about music.

KEYWORDS Chile, University Administration
AUDIENCE Chileans, Music Enthusiasts, Pop Music Enthusiasts, Professors, Students (University)
CONTACT postmast@halcon.dpi.udec.cl
FREE

gopher://halcon.dpi.udec.cl/

Universidad de Santiago de Chile ★★★

This site offers information about the Universidad de Santiago de Chile (The University of Santiago, Chile). The information covers the libraries, faculties, research programs and academic programs. The library information includes a gateway to search the library's online catalogs.

KEYWORDS Chile, Universities, University Administration
AUDIENCE Professors, Students (University), University Administrators
FREE

gopher://ralun.usach.cl/

Universities - United States

See also
Education · *International Education*
Engineering & Technology · *Engineering*
Health & Medicine · *Medical Schools*
Law & Criminal Justice · *Law Schools*

Academic South ★★★

The Academic South site is a gateway to WWW servers operated by universities in the southern United States. The list of servers is provided alphabetically by both institution and state. There is also a facility to submit new additions to the list.

KEYWORDS Computer Networks, Education (College/University), Southern Culture (US)
AUDIENCE Academics, Educators (University), Students (University)
CONTACT Doug Matthews
rdm@unc.edu
FREE

http://sunsite.unc.edu/doug_m/pages/south/academic.html

American Universities ★★★

This site is a list of home pages for American universities. If a certain university does not have its own home page, but a department at the university does, then the department's home page is given. If the university has multiple home pages, then the one that is most interesting and provides the best links to other home pages at that university is given.

KEYWORDS Education (College/University), Internet Guides
AUDIENCE Internet Users, Students (University)

CONTACT mconlon@stat.ufl.edu
FREE

http://www.clas.ufl.edu/CLAS/american-universities.html

ftp://english.hss.cmu.edu/English.Server/Academy/American%20Universities.html

Arizona State University ★★★

This site is the top level of Arizona State University's WWW system. It offers information on the departments and educational programs offered, as well as links to material on the faculty and staff of the University. Users can also browse information on the local area surrounding the University, as well as find out about the computing facilities there. Sports fans will enjoy the links to pages about ASU's popular teams.

KEYWORDS Colleges & Universities, Undergraduate Education, Universities
AUDIENCE Education Administrators (College), Educators, Students
CONTACT Vince Salvato
Vince.Salvato@asu.edu
FREE

http://www.asu.edu

Assumption College Home Page ★★★

The Assumption College Home Page contains information about the university, the local area and alumnae information. There are links to museums and galleries as well as zines and weather reports.

KEYWORDS Colleges & Universities, Computer Networks, Educational Programs, Massachusetts
AUDIENCE Educators, Students
CONTACT Nick Chase
nick15@eve.assumption.edu
FREE

http://www.assumption.edu/

Bates College Campus Wide Information System (CWIS) ★★★

Bates College Campus Wide Information System (CWIS) located in Lewiston, Maine provides information about the course offerings, programs of study, faculty listings and current event and happenings on campus. It also offers links to the university gopher server, electronic databases, libraries, and electronic texts, and other resources on the Internet. Interested users can opt to see the campus via a World Wide Web tour of the college.

KEYWORDS Maine, Campus Information
AUDIENCE Maine Residents, Students (Secondary/University)
CONTACT www@bates.edu
FREE

http://abacus.bates.edu/

gopher://abacus.bates.edu/

Bowdoin College ★★★

The Bowdoin College page provides information about the college, a few departments and local resources in the Maine area. There are links to their gopher server and starting points on the Internet.

KEYWORDS Colleges & Universities, Educational Programs, Educational Resources, Maine
AUDIENCE Educators, Maine Residents, Students
CONTACT webmaster@polar.bowdoin.edu
FREE

http://www.bowdoin.edu

gopher://gopher.bowdoin.edu/

Bowling Green State University Web Site ★★★

Bowling Green State University is located in northwest Ohio, and has more than 18,000 students. Areas on this web site include specific pages for academic departments, such as the Popular Culture, Computer Science and Women's Studies Departments. In addition, users will find information about the city of Bowling Green, admissions information, a photographic tour of the campus, and images from BGSU artists, Thomas Muir, whose work was recently on display at the White House and Smithsonian Institution.

KEYWORDS Ohio, Women's Studies
AUDIENCE Craftspeople, Students (Secondary/College)
CONTACT webmaster@dad.bgsu.edu
FREE

http://dad.bgsu.edu

gopher://dad.bgsu.edu/

Brandeis University ★★★

Brandeis University is a private research university located in Massachusetts. The home page contains information about the degree programs, faculty, research, athletic programs and facilities. There are links to the computer science center, the Center for Complex Systems and the electronic library.

KEYWORDS Computer Science, Educational Programs, Massachusetts, Research
AUDIENCE Educators, Students
CONTACT webmaster@brandeis.edu
FREE

http://www.brandeis.edu/

Brigham Young University ★★

Brigham Young University's WWW server offers information on its academic programs, departments, and more. Users can also take a virtual tour of the campus via an interactive map demonstration. This site also houses administrative information such as the admissions requirements for the University.

KEYWORDS Education (College/University), Utah
AUDIENCE Education Administrators (College), Educators, Students
CONTACT CWIS-team@byu.edu
FREE

http://www.byu.edu

Universities - United States

Brown University ★★★

The Brown University Home Page provides access to information on academic units, the Brown University administration, the Brown University Library, electronic resources, computing and information services, student information and alumni resources.

Keywords   Universities, Libraries, Undergraduate Education
Audience   Computer Users, Educators (University), Internet Users, Researchers, Students (University)
Contact   Webmaster@WWW.Brown.Edu
Free

http://ftp.brown.edu

gopher://gopher.brown.edu:70/

Bucknell University Home Page ★★★

This page provides information on Bucknell University. Users can access material on admissions, maps, and other basic information on the campus. There is also a directory of campus publications availble for viewing, as well as links to individual academic departments within the University.

Keywords   Pennsylvania, University Administration
Audience   Education Administrators (College), Educators, Students
Contact   Bill Erdley
             webmaster@bucknell.edu
Free

http://www.bucknell.edu

gopher://coral.bucknell.edu/

California Polytechnic State University ★★★

This server is provided by California Polytechnic State University to provide information on the campus and its academic programs. Users will find course information, admissions requirements, and links to individual departments within the university. There are also links to student organizations that have a Web presence, as well as information on current research projects at the university.

Keywords   California, Universities, Research Projects, Undergraduate Education
Audience   Education Administrators (College), Educators, Students
Contact   www@oboe.calpoly.edu
Free

http://www.calpoly.edu

gopher://oboe.calpoly.edu/hh/

California State University Long Beach ★★★

This site is the top level of the Cal State University at Long Beach information server. It contains links to information about the campus, its departments, facilities, student groups, courses, and faculty. There are also direct links to many of the more substantial sites hosted by individual departments, as well as to other California State University resources.

Keywords   California, Campus Information
Audience   Californians, Education Administrators (College), Educators, Students
Contact   webmaster@csulb.edu
Free

http://www.acs.csulb.edu

gopher://gopher.csulb.edu/11/

California State University, Hayward ★★★

The California State University, Hayward Home Page is an access point to the University's departments, degree programs, publications and campus information. The Page centers around computing and telecommunications resources, including access to the library.

Keywords   California, Computing Services
Audience   Californians, Mathematicians, Students
Contact   tebo@csuhayward.edu
Free

http://www.mcs.csuhayward.edu

Campus Newspapers on the Internet ★★★★

This page is dedicated to serving readers interested in finding out about issues and events at other universities and colleges around the world from the student-run publications of the various campuses. Listings include resources of interest to the editors and advisers of student-run newspapers.

Keywords   Electronic Media, Online Newspapers
Audience   Academics, Students (Secondary/University), Students (University)
Contact   Jonathan Bell
             jmbell@beacon.asa.utk.edu
Free

http://beacon-www.asa.utk.edu/resources/papers.html

Carleton College WWW ★★

This site offers information on the academic programs at Carleton College. Users will find links to individual departments, admissions information, an other information on the campus and surrounding area. There is also information about Catrleton's study abroad programs and about undergraduate employment at the college.

Keywords   Carleton College, Undergraduate Education
Audience   College Counselors, Educators, Students
Contact   Mark F. Heiman
             mheiman@carleton.edu
Free

http://www.carleton.edu

gopher://gopher.carleton.edu/hh

Clark University ★★★

The Clark University home page contains information about the degree programs, facilities and atheletic programs of the university. The page contains links to the departments and student organizations.

Keywords   Educational Programs, Educational Resources, Massachusetts
Audience   Educators, Massachusetts Residents, Students
Contact   Admissions House
             admissions@vax.clarku.edu
Free

http://www.clarku.edu

Clemson University - Home Page ★★★

This server offers information on Clemson University. Users will find information and links to individual departments within the University. There is also a directory of electronic publications available for browsing here, as well as general information for new users of the Internet.

Keywords   Campus Wide Information Systems, Universities, South Carolina
Audience   Education Administrators (College), Educators, Students
Contact   Barry Johnson
             cyclist@clemson.edu
Free

http://www.clemson.edu

gopher://gopher.clemson.edu

Colby College ★★★★

Colby College is a liberal arts college located in Waterville, Maine. The home page contains information about the college with links to the academic departments and programs. There is information on the admissions and links to student services, organizations and the Colby library collections and services. There are links to selected resources on the Internet.

Keywords   Educational Programs, Educational Resources, Liberal Arts, Maine
Audience   Educators, Maine Residents, Students
Contact   web@colby.edu
Free

http://www.colby.edu

gopher://gopher.colby.edu/

College of the Holy Cross ★★★

The College of the Holy Cross home page provides information about the university and its schools and departments. The page has links to the campus information server, academic departments, and the library and research publications. There are also links to Worcester, Massachusetts information, news, weather, and more.

Audience   Massachussetts Residents, Students
Contact   Colin Murtaugh
             cjmurtaugh@holycross.edu
Free

http://www.holycross.edu

Connecticut College Home Page ★

Connecticut College's Home Page lists information about the school, which is located in New London, Connecticut, USA. Users can choose to link to pages about academic programs, admissions information, academic and student home pages, or the Connecticut College's online magazine, which offers more highlights about the activities of staff, students, and alumni. Some specific departmental programs online include the The Center for Arts & Technology, the Art Department, the Botany Department Herbarium, and the Chemistry Department. Links to Internet sites outside the college are also provided, and there are specific directories of resources for the local and the statewide level.

Keywords Connecticut, Campus Information
Audience Student (High School/College) Connecticut Residents
Contact Susan Faulkner
spfau@conncoll.edu
Free

http://camel.conncoll.edu/

Cornell College ★★★

This site is a gopher server of Cornell College, Iowa. It offers information on admissions, access to databases, library resources, phone books, course materials, and more. In addition, it makes connections to other gophers.

Keywords Education (College/University), Iowa, Science, University Administration
Audience Educators (University), Students (University)
Contact Bruce Cantrall
bruce@cornell-iowa.edu
Free

gopher://gopher.cornell-iowa.edu/

Cornell University ★★★

This is a gopher server of Cornell University. It provides information about the University, admissions, the Graduate School, exams, financial aid, administration, news, housing, human resources, libraries, and departments.

Keywords Education (College/University), New York, University Administration
Audience Educators (University), Students (University)
Contact cuinfo-admin@cornell.edu
Free

gopher://gopher.cit.cornell.edu/

Curio ★★★

Curio is the University of Rochester's campuswide information system. curio contains information about the University, academic departments, administration and support services, calendars, campus phone books and directories, computing and telecommunications, course descriptions and class schedules, and libraries. It also provides access to networked information databases from around the world.

Keywords Campus Information, Education (College/University), New York, University Administration
Audience Educators (University), Students (University)
Contact Barbara Moore
bmoo@db1.cc.rochester.edu
Free

gopher://gopher.cc.rochester.edu/

Dartmouth College ★★★

Dartmouth College has set up this web site to deliver information about the various courses, departments and schools within the educational institution. There are directories set up for academic resources, professional schools, organizations, athletics and recreation. Some items recently added to this site are links to career services, sports teams such as the women's ice hockey team, and a new journal for the humanities and social sciences.

Keywords Ivy League, New Hampshire, Universities
Audience New Hampshire Residents, Students
Contact Andy J. Williams
WebMaster@dartmouth.edu
Free

http://www.dartmouth.edu/

gopher://dartmouth.edu/

Eagleinfo ★★★

This server provides information on American University in Washington, DC. Users will find departmental, faculty, and student information. There is also a set of links to the campus library system, as well as to information and resources about the computing facilities on campus.

Keywords Campus Wide Information Systems, Washington D.C.
Audience Education Administrators (College), Educators, Students
Free

http://www.american.edu

gopher://paladin.american.edu/

Emory University ★★★

This site is provided by Emory University, located in Atlanta, Georgia. Visitors to this site will find admissions information, material on campus life, academic program and departmental information, and more. In addition, this server provides links to campus libraries and computing resources, as well as linking to regional information on the surrounding area.

Keywords Universities, Georgia
Audience Education Administrators (College), Educators, Students
Contact www@www.emory.edu
Free

http://www.cc.emory.edu

gopher://emory.edu/

Fishwrap ★★★

Fishwrap is an experimental personalized newspaper project. It's designed to address the needs of incoming freshmen at MIT. You can create a Fishwrap account if you are a member of the student body, staff or faculty at MIT who is currently connected to an Athena workstation (Dec, Sun, IBM SGI soon). Features in the magazine include Net Surfing with Sam, an advice column, an HTML Primer, and more.

Keywords Online Publications, Undergraduate Education
Audience Educators (University), Students (University)
Contact fishwrap-ombudsman@media.mit.edu
Free

http://fishwrap.mit.edu

Florida State University ★★★★

The Florida State University (FSU) server provides links to a campus map, admission and registration information, facts about the University, news and campus events, job listings, information about FSU Organizations, academic departments and colleges, institutes and centers, student organizations and more.

Keywords Campus Information, Employment, Florida
Audience Computer Users, Educators (University), Internet Users, Researchers, Students (University)
Contact g4adm@mailer.fsu.edu.
Free

http://garnet.acns.fsu.edu

gopher://gopher.fsu.edu/

Florida Tech Education Gopher ★★★

This site is a gopher and Web server of the Florida Institute of Technology in Melbourne, Florida. It provides information for educators such as classroom uses of the Internet, papers, electrical journals, and more. In addition, it provides direct access to other education gopher servers such as EDUCOM, ERIC, CoSN, and more. Other archives available on this server include a collection of Usenet FAQ's (Frequently Asked Questions), local information about Florida Tech (weather, course catalogs, contact information, etc) and a virtual tour of the campus.

Keywords Education (College/University), Educational Technology, Florida
Audience Educators, Educators (University), Information Professionals, Internet Users
Contact www@sci-ed.fit.edu
Free

http://gaia.sci-ed.fit.edu/

gopher://gaia.sci-ed.fit.edu/

GOpherBLUE ★★★★

GOpherBLUE is a campus-wide information system for the University of Michigan in Ann Arbor, Michigan. It provides information about job postings, phone book searches, library resources, software archives, as well as a large amount of data about the academic and research programs at the University of Michigan.

Keywords Education (College/University), Michigan, University Administration
Audience Educators (University), Students (University)
Contact gopherblue@umich.edu
Free

gopher://gopher.uis.itd.umich.edu/

Georgetown University ★★

This site is a gopher server of Georgetown University. It is linked to Georgetown's Academic Computing Center, which contains information about the University, the University calendar, newspaper, academic publications and resources. The server also has information about LISTSERV maintained files, notelogs and meeting minutes from campus groups, and links to other gopher servers on the Internet.

Keywords University Administration, Washington D.C.
Audience Educators (University), Students (Secondary/University)

Universities - United States

FREE
gopher://guvm.ccf.georgetown.edu/

Georgia Tech University ★★★★

Georgia Tech University's Web site is designed to provide information about this university and its products including administration and faculty backgrounds, admissions guidelines, athletic departments, details about campus life and news. The research area provides access to databases of researcher profiles, and information from various engineering, computer, and science related research groups. For example, the Visual Graphics research group provides animations and documents about Virtual Reality, Medical Informatics, Software Visualization and more.

KEYWORDS Computers, Engineering, Science
AUDIENCE Education Professionals, Researchers, Students (College)
CONTACT webmaster@www.gatech.edu
FREE

http://merlin.gatech.edu

Grambling State University Gopher Server ★★★

This site is a gopher server of the Grambling State University in Louisiana. It contains information on computing resources, Internet services, library services, desktop reference services, newspapers, newsletters, magazines, books, directories (names, phone numbers, addresses), and more. In addition, it has links to other gophers.

KEYWORDS Education (College/University), Louisiana
AUDIENCE Academics, Library Users, Students (University)
CONTACT N. Gajendar
system@vax0.gram.edu
FREE

gopher://vax0.gram.edu/

Greenville Technical College Gopher Server ★★★

The Greenville Technical College Gopher Server provides information about computing, resources, library services, and courses. The site also provides access for staff, faculty, and student directories. It also provides links to other servers.

KEYWORDS Computing, Medicine, Physics, South Carolina
AUDIENCE Computer Users, Educators (University), Students (University)
CONTACT GopherAdmin@gvltec.edu
FREE

gopher://gopher.gvltec.edu/

Gustavus Adolphus College Gopher Server ★★★

The Gustavus Adolphus College gopher server provides information about the College, its computer resources, email archives, announcements, calendars, FTP sites, libraries, news, phonebooks, email addresses, and more.

KEYWORDS Education (College/University), Minnesota, University Administration

AUDIENCE Computer Users, Educators (College), Students
CONTACT gopher@gac.edu
FREE

gopher://gopher.gac.edu/

Harvard University WWW home page ★★★★

The Harvard University WWW home page offers a listing of departments, offices, research projects, and student areas with their own individual home pages.

KEYWORDS Massachusetts, Research Projects
AUDIENCE Academics, Librarians, Researchers, Scientists, Students, Students (University)
CONTACT www-admin@harvard.edu
FREE

http://courses.harvard.edu

gopher://gopher.harvard.edu

Harvey Mudd College ★★

This is the home page of Harvey Mudd College. Users can find information on the campus, academic and administrative departments, as well as browse directories of faculty, student and staff and academic computing information.

KEYWORDS California, Universities
AUDIENCE Education Administrators (College), Educators, Students
CONTACT webmaster@hmc.edu
FREE

http://www.hmc.edu/

Hebrew University Information Servers ★★★★

The Hebrew University Campus Information System Home Page provides information in Hebrew and English about - The Jerusalem Mosaic (English), Snunit - Educational Information System (Hebrew), (English) The Journal of Computer-mediated Communication (English), The Institute of Computer Science (English), The Hebrew University - Hadassah Medical School (English), SICSA - Vidal Sassoon International Center for the Study of Anti-Semitism (English), The Melton Centre for Jewish Education in the Diaspora, Business School (English) and the Rothberg School for Overseas Students.

KEYWORDS International Law, Israel, Universities
AUDIENCE Hebrew Scholars, International Students, Israelis
FREE

http://www.huji.ac.il/WWW_DIR/ISLAW00.html

Hofstra's Gopher ★★★

Hofstra's Gopher gives information about Hofstra University in Hempstead, New York. The information includes the academic calendar, athletics, computing services, access to the library's resources, and University publications. The publications available are a collection of online newsletters.

KEYWORDS Cultural Studies, New York, University Administration

AUDIENCE Educators (University), Students (University)
CONTACT Mark Kilarjian
hofstra@hofstra.edu
FREE

gopher://tinker.hofstra.edu/

Home College Tour ★★

This page offers potential students a chance to see information about a number of universities and colleges across the United States and beyond. After registering with the ReZun service (free of charge) the student can browse through a listing of colleges, download software to view an interactive multimedia presentation about a school, submit an application to a school, go to the home page of a school, or send a message to an admissions office requesting more information.

KEYWORDS Admissions, Collectibles, Graduate Education, Universities
AUDIENCE Students (Secondary/University), Students (University), Transfer Students
CONTACT Khera Communications, Inc.
www@kciLink.com.
FREE

http://www.kciLink.com/rezun/

Home Page for Student Governments ★★★

This page contains links to various student government home pages across the world. The links are organized according to protocol and then by country. It is possible to register listings at this site.

KEYWORDS Government, Missouri, Student Associations, Universities
AUDIENCE International Students, Internet Users, Students, Students (University)
CONTACT alecren@umr.edu
FREE

http://www.umr.edu/~stuco/national.html

INFORMU - University of Missouri ★★★

INFORMU is a campus-wide information system for the University of Missouri. The information it provides includes events, activities, faculty and academic information, computing information, and more.

KEYWORDS Missouri, Universities, University Administration
AUDIENCE Educators, Students
FREE

gopher://mizzou1.missouri.edu:801/

Idaho State University Home Page ★★★

The Idaho State University Home Page gives information about academic catalogs, degrees, and course listings. This site provides campus information, events calendars, and workshop schedules. There are links to Internet resources and tools as well as online access to, and information about, the library and Media Center.

KEYWORDS Campus Information, Curriculum, Idaho
AUDIENCE Educators, Students

CONTACT webmaster@isu.edu
FREE
http://www.isu.edu

Indiana University WWW Home Page ★★★

This page is the top level of the Indiana University web. It contains general information on Indiana University as well as links to five of its eight campuses. There is also a searchable 'address book' with information on the people and departments of Indiana University. Users can also access detailed information such as enrollment fees, course programs, departmental information, and more.

KEYWORDS Campus Information, Indiana
AUDIENCE Education Administrators (College), Educators, Students
CONTACT webmaster@indiana.edu
FREE

http://www-iub.indiana.edu

gopher://gopher.indiana.edu/

InfoPath ★★★

InfoPath is an information service maintained by the libraries of the University of California at San Diego. The information is about the library, the campus and the community. All links to other UCSD servers can be found here.

KEYWORDS California, Libraries, Library Science, University Administration
AUDIENCE Educators (University), Professors, Students (University), University Administrators
CONTACT Chris Frymann
         cfrymann@ucsd.edu
FREE

http://www.ucsd.edu/

gopher://infopath.ucsd.edu/

Iowa State University ★★★★

This is a gopher server of the Iowa State University. It contains information on various colleges, departments, offices, library resources, computing services, phone books, news, job lists, and more. Access to other resources on the Internet is provided.

KEYWORDS Campus Information, Education (College/University), Iowa
AUDIENCE Academics, Educators, Educators (University), Students (University)
CONTACT Diana Pounds
         dpounds@iastate.edu
FREE

http://info.iastate.edu/

gopher://info.iastate.edu/

Johns Hopkins University ★★

This Johns Hopkins University's gopher server offers information on the Johns Hopkins University Press, its online catalog of books and journals, and order forms. It also provides some computing resources such as software for Mac and MS/DOS computers, Internet navigators, and more.

KEYWORDS Community Services, Education (College/University), Maryland
AUDIENCE Educators (University), Students (University)
FREE

gopher://jhunix.hcf.jhu.edu:10003/

Kent State University Home Page ★★★

The home page at Kent State University in Ohio provides information about the University and its facilities. KSU has links to other campus gophers and/or HTTP Servers that include the Math and Computer Science home page, the computer services, math and computer science, and the graduate school of education gopher server. There are links to other Campus services and off campus sites.

KEYWORDS Campus Information, Universities, Ohio
AUDIENCE Educators, Students
CONTACT holmberg@scorpio.kent.edu
FREE

http://www.kent.edu

Loyola University Chicago Gopher Server ★★★★

This site is a gopher server of the Loyola University, Chicago. Information available includes admissions, library services/resources, academic calendars, and publications. In addition, it contains information about the Chicago area.

KEYWORDS Education (College/University), Illinois, University Administration
AUDIENCE Educators (University), Students (Secondary/University)
CONTACT gopher-admin@orion.it.luc.edu
FREE

gopher://gopher.luc.edu/

Macalester College ★★★

This site is a gopher server of the Macalester College in St. Paul, Minnesota. It offers information on academic departments, student services, events, library services, and publications.

KEYWORDS Community Services, Education (College/University), Minnesota, University Administration
AUDIENCE Educators (University), Students (Secondary/University)
CONTACT Christopher Doemel
         doemel@macalstr.edu
FREE

gopher://gopher.macalstr.edu/

Michigan State University Home Page ★★★

This is the top level of Michigan State University's campus-wide information system. Users will find links to various University departments, faculty pages, and campus information servers. There are also resources available for current and potential students, as well as information on the local area around the campus.

KEYWORDS Campus Networks, Campus Wide Information Systems, Michigan
AUDIENCE Education Administrators (College), Educators, Students
CONTACT consult@msu.edu
         web@web.msu.edu
FREE

http://web.cl.msu.edu

Middlebury College ★★★

Middlebury College uses this web server to offer information about the academic programs available through this school. The site has information from most of the departments, including major requirements, course offering descriptions, and faculty information. Other areas covered by this site are the university admissions requirements, campus publications, student organizations, and library resources.

KEYWORDS Education (College/University), Vermont
AUDIENCE Students (College), Vermont Residents
CONTACT webmaster@cobalt.middlebury.edu
FREE

http://www.middlebury.edu/

Mississippi State University ★★★

The Mississippi State University (MSU) Web site is designed to provide information about Mississippi State as well as serve as a resource for MSU students and alumni. Included here are maps and photos of the campus, the entire 1994-1995 course catalog, and a directory of deans and faculty. Users can find out about upcoming events and athletic schedules, and read past issues of the campus magazine ALUMNUS. Admissions materials are also included.

KEYWORDS Campus Information, Mississippi, Universities
AUDIENCE Education Professionals, Students (College)
CONTACT Bennet George
         georgeb@ur.msstate.edu
FREE

http://msuinfo.ur.msstate.edu

North Carolina State Home Page ★★

This server maintains information on North Carolina State University. Visitors to this site can retrieve information about the University's courses, departments, faculty and staff, and students. There is a section with admissions information, and material on campus lifestyles. In addition, this server has information on library and computing resources, publications, and links to other educational institutions on the net.

KEYWORDS Campus Information, North Carolina
AUDIENCE Education Administrators (College), Educators, Students
FREE

http://www.acs.ncsu.edu

New York University CWIS ★★★★

This is a gopher server for the New York University campuswide information system. Information available includes academic computing and networking resources, academic departments, programs, admissions, registration, alumni activities, calendars, publications, library facilities, and more. It has access to other gopher holes as well.

KEYWORDS Education (College/University), New York, University Administration
AUDIENCE Educators (University), Students (University), University Administrators
CONTACT cwis@nyu.edu
FREE

gopher://gopher.nyu.edu/

Northwestern University ★★★★

This site is a gopher server of Northwestern University in Illinois. It contains information about the University, its administration, registration procedures, academic departments, courses, library services, computing services, research, and more. Also, connections to other gophers are made.

KEYWORDS Education (College/University), Illinois, University Administration
AUDIENCE Educators (University), Students (University)
CONTACT Tamara Iversen Foster
         nuinfo@nwu.edu
FREE

gopher://gopher.nwu.edu/

Notre Dame's WWW Server ★★★★

Notre Dame's WWW Server supplies information about campus activities, programs and resources. The page gives links to course data, Colleges and departmental information. There is also access to such sites as Notre Dame Football, academic departments and administrative departments.

KEYWORDS Educational Resources, Indiana, Universities
AUDIENCE Educators, Researchers, Students
CONTACT www@www.nd.edu
FREE

http://www.nd.edu

Ohio University ★★★★

This is a gopher server of Ohio University in Athens. It contains information on the University, its admissions, colleges, academic programs, academic departments, job listings, alumni relations, and more. It has links to other gophers on campus.

KEYWORDS Education (College/University), Ohio
AUDIENCE Educators (University), Students (University)
CONTACT John Tysko
         tysko@boss.cs.ohiou.edu
FREE

gopher://ra.cs.ohiou.edu/

Connections to Dictionaries and Reference Guides
Is That All There Is?

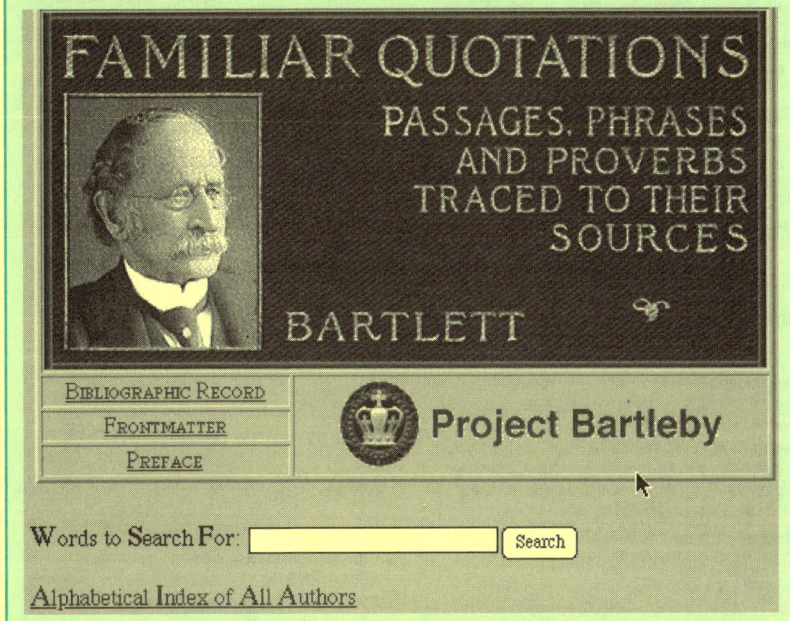

Need to make sure of the correct spelling of "accommodate," or find another word for "changeable"? Or perhaps you need a famous quote to use in a speech you're writing. Need the zip code of a company in Lansing, Michigan, or the telephone country code in Walton-on-Thames, England?

The sites for such information bring this kind of help to your fingertips. You can access references like Websters Dictionary, Barlett's Quotations, and a national 800 telephone book. There is also information on how to get a student loan.

When you're finished and want to relax in front of the television, there's even a weekly listing of all the shows on American network and cable television.

(http://columbia.edu/~sv12/bartlett/)

also, (gopher://odie.niaid.nih.gov/77.thesaurus/index)

also, (http://c.gp.cs.cmu.edu:5103/prog/webster)

also, (http://www.ed.gov/prog_info/SFA/StudentGuide/)   also, (http://tv1.com/)

Oklahoma State University ★★★★

The Oklahoma State University (OSU) page is an access point to the University's resources. The site has admissions information, class schedules and information on the library. There are links to each of the colleges at the University and links to other OSU sites.

KEYWORDS Educational Programs, Oklahoma
AUDIENCE Educators, Oklahoma Residents, Students
CONTACT www-master@www.okstate.edu
FREE

http://www.okstate.edu/

gopher://bubba.ucc.okstate.edu/

Oregon State University ★★★

This site is a gopher and Web server of the Oregon State University. It contains information about the University, libraries, references, directories of people and services, news & events, courses, calendars, graduate programs, computing services, housing, academic departments and colleges, and many more. In addition, it provides links to other Internet sites on and off campus.

KEYWORDS Education (College/University), Oregon, University Administration
AUDIENCE Educators (University), Oregon Residents, Students (University)
CONTACT web@mail.orst.edu
FREE

http://gaia.ucs.orst.edu/

gopher://gaia.ucs.orst.edu/

Universities - United States

Penn State Erie - Behrend College ★★

This is the home page of The Behrend College of Penn State in Erie, Pennsylvnaia. Information provided includes links to general information about the school, information aobut the school of engineering and the Plastics Engineering Technical Center, and other WWW resources at Penn State Erie.

Keywords Engineering, Graduate Programs, Universities

Audience Educators (University), Students (University)

Free

http://euler.bd.psu.edu

Penn State University Information Server ★★★

This is a gopher server of the Penn State University Center for Academic Computing. It provides information about the Penn State University, academic programs, the book store, calendars, news, sports, career interviews & trends, computing resources, courses, departments, and many more. In addition, it contains information about Pennsylvania, such as weather, phone books, services, and more.

Keywords Education (College/University), Pennsylvania, University Administration

Audience Educators (University), Pennsylvania Residents, Students (Secondary/University)

Contact gopherpm@psu.edu

Free

gopher://genesis.ait.psu.edu/

Plymouth State College ★★★

The Plymouth State College page provides information on its academic affairs, departments and programs. The page has campus news and events material and offers access to the library facilities. There are links to local weather, general information and tourist information.

Keywords Educational Programs, Educational Resources, New Hampshire

Audience Educators, New Hampshire Residents, Students

Contact Ted Wisniewski ted@oz.plymouth.edu

Free

http://www.plymouth.edu/

gopher://oz.plymouth.edu/

Purdue University ★★★

This gopher has information about Purdue University. It contains documents concerning the University administration, admissions, research reports, student services, news, and more. It has links to other gopher sites on campus.

Keywords Education (College/University), Indiana, University Administration

Audience Educators (University), Students (University)

Free

gopher://newsgopher.uns.purdue.edu/

Rice University ★★★

This is a gopher server of Rice University in Houston, Texas. It provides information about the University's activities, admissions, courses, calendars, computer resources, libraries, campus events, health and safety, and more. Rice University is home to The Center for Research on Parallel Computation (CRPC) (one of the 25 National Science Foundation Science and Technology Centers), which aims to make massively parallel computer systems truly usable for scientists, engineers and others. It also has a Computer and Information Technology Institute (CITI) established to nurture interdisciplinary research and graduate education in the field of computer and information technology.

Keywords Education (College/University), Texas, University Administration

Audience Educators (University), Students (Secondary/University)

Contact riceinfo@rice.edu

Free

http://www.rice.edu/

gopher://riceinfo.rice.edu:80/hGET%20/

Rutgers University ★★★

This site is a gopher server of Rutgers University. It offers information on academics, registration, departments, schools, courses, support services, computing resources, library resources and services, and more.

Keywords Community Services, Education (College/University), New Jersey, University Administration

Audience Academics, Educators (University), Students (University)

Free

gopher://info.rutgers.edu:72/

School of Education Indiana University ★★

The School of Education at Indiana University Webserver provides links to information about the school's programs, history, faculty, education library, Center for Adolescent Studies, Indiana College Placement and Assessment Center, curriculum and more.

Keywords College Placement, Curriculum, Graduate Programs, Indiana

Audience Educators, Educators (University), Students (University)

Contact T. W. Frick, frick@indiana.edu

Free

http://education.indiana.edu/

St. John's University Academic Computing Services Gopher ★★★

This site offers access to the St. John's University gopher providing information on areas such as education, teaching, mission, and more. The site discusses frequently asked questions about different network systems and other related information. It also has a classifieds and personel ads section.

Keywords Computing, Education (College/University), New York

Audience Computer Students, Computer Users, Educators

Contact $SJU@sjumusic.stjohns.edu

Free

gopher://sjuvm.stjohns.edu/

St. Olaf College ★★★

This is a gopher server of the St. Olaf College in Northfield, Minnesota. It contains information on the College, services, departments, events, announcements, news, and library resources. It provides access to other gophers as well.

Keywords Education (College/University), Minnesota, University Administration

Audience Academics, Educators (University), Students (Secondary/University)

Contact gopher@stolaf.edu

Free

gopher://gopher.stolaf.edu/

Swarthmore College ★★

This site is the top level of Swarthmore College's campus information system. Users can connect to different departments and schools within the college, as well as browse general information on the campus itself. Users can also find out about financial aid at the College, and take a virtual tour of the campus.

Keywords Pennsylvania, Universities

Audience Education Administrators (College), Educators, Students

Contact webmaster@cc.swarthmore.edu

Free

http://www.cc.swarthmore.edu

gopher://gopher.cc.swarthmore.edu/

Syracuse University Campus Wide Information System ★★★

The Syracuse University Campus Wide Information System has information related to four main areas, general information about the University, Academics, Student Concerns, and Administrative, Faculty, and Staff Concerns. There is also information about the city of Syracuse and links to other spots on the World Wide Web.

Keywords New York, Universities

Audience New York Residents, Students (Secondary/University)

Contact SyraCWIS webmaster@www.syr.edu

Free

http://cwis.syr.edu/

gopher://gopher.syr.edu/

Tar Heel Information Service ★★

The Tar Heel Information Service is a gateway to the gopher at the University of North Carolina at Chapel Hill. It provides tunnels to gophers at the University's Office of Information Technology, the CampusWide Information System, and to LaunchPad, a resource center for Sun Microsystems computers.

- KEYWORDS Campus Information, North Carolina
- AUDIENCE Computer Users, Internet Users, Professors, Students (University)
- FREE

gopher://uncvx1.oit.unc.edu/

Texas A & M University

This site gives access to information from various departments and organizations within Texas A & M University. These departments include Admissions and Records, Academic Scholarships, Measurement and Research Services, and others. Each department has its own burrow in the main gopher hole. The information within each varies from one department to the next. Some departments restrict access to users from within Texas A & M University.

- KEYWORDS Information Science, Texas, University Administration
- AUDIENCE Professors, Students (University), University Administrators
- CONTACT Butch.Kemper@tamu.edu
- FREE

gopher://tamuts.tamu.edu/

Tufts University

The Tufts University home page provides information about the university, its schools and departments. The page has links to the campus information server, the library and research publications.

- KEYWORDS Educational Programs, Educational Resources, Massachusetts, Medicine
- AUDIENCE Educators, Massachusetts Residents, Students
- CONTACT webmaster@tufts.edu
- FREE

http://www.tufts.edu/

Tulane University

Tulane University's gopher server gives information about computing services, academic departments, libraries, phone books, the Tulane Cable Access Network (TUCAN), the Tulane student media, and more. It provides access to other gophers on the Internet.

- KEYWORDS Education (College/University), Louisiana, University Administration
- AUDIENCE Academics, Educators (University), Students (University)
- FREE

gopher://gopher.tulane.edu:1070/

UCI's Gopher

This is the main gopher server for the University of California at Irvine. The facilities it contains include program catalogs, admission information, online registration services, online library catalogs, and University history.

- KEYWORDS California, Campus Information, Education (College/University), University Administration
- AUDIENCE Educators, Students
- CONTACT William Parker
  uci-cwis-support@uci.edu
- FREE

gopher://gopher.uci.edu/

UND Computer Center Gopher

This is a gopher server for the University of North Dakota's Computer Center. It provides information about the center, about the University, and about North Dakota Government legislation.

- KEYWORDS Campus Information, Computing, Education (College/University), North Dakota
- AUDIENCE Educators (University), Students (University)
- CONTACT Doris M. Bornhoeft
  bornhoef@vm1.nodak.edu
- FREE

gopher://gopher.cc.und.nodak.edu/

UNHINFO - A Campus-Wide Information System

UNHINFO is a campus wide information system for the University of New Hampshire. The page provides access to the campus server and its facilities. There are links to information on the academic departments, programs, events, directories, schedules, library, computing and information services.

- KEYWORDS Educational Resources, Information Systems, New Hampshire
- AUDIENCE Educators, New Hampshire Residents, Students
- CONTACT jwc
  cwis.admin@unh.edu
- FREE

http://www.unh.edu/

gopher://unhinfo.unh.edu/

The University System of Georgia Interactive Guide

The University System of Georgia Interactive Guide allows users to obtain information about all the education institutions in the state of Georgia. Each college and university has a page, including general background materials, library information and catalogs, and connections to gopher and telnet servers. There's also a General Resource section, in which users can search subject catalogs to find specific information from the entire university system, including employment opportunities, library databases, and university directories. Other information provided includes background about the Board of Regents and educational facts from the State of Georgia.

- KEYWORDS Campus Information, Georgia
- AUDIENCE College Applicants, Georgia Residents, Students (College)
- CONTACT w3admin@oit.peachnet.edu
- FREE

http://k-9.oit.peachnet.edu/USGWEB/USGHome.html

University of Alaska Gopher/WWW Server

This gopher and WWW server offers information on the University of Alaska, its three campuses, and on Alaska in general. Users will find links to the individual campuses of the University of Alaska, as well as departmental and faculty information. There is also information available on Alaska parks, history, politics, and more. Users can also browse technical documentation on Macintosh, PC, and UNIX systems.

- KEYWORDS Alaska, Campus Information, University Of Alaska
- AUDIENCE Alaska Residents, Alaskan Culture Enthusiasts, Educators, Students
- CONTACT sxinfo@orca.alaska.edu
- FREE

http://www.alaska.edu

gopher://www.alaska.edu

University of Arizona

This server, maintained by the University of Arizona, offers users information on the campus, academic departments, student services, and more. There is material on research projects, admissions information, University publications, and local events. Visitors can also view a map of the local area, browse or search through a University phone/address book, or find out about the city of Tuscon.

- KEYWORDS Arizona, Universities
- AUDIENCE Education Administrators (College), Educators, Students
- CONTACT webmaster@www.arizona.edu
- FREE

http://www.arizona.edu

University of Arkansas at Monticello Home Page

This site contains information about the University of Arkansas at Monticello. Users can see the location and history of the University, browse through academic and departmental information, telnet to the library, see a listing of campus events, and scan through a schedule of classes. Links to users home pages, software and listserv archives, and sites off campus are provided as well.

- KEYWORDS Arkansas, Universities
- AUDIENCE Students (Secondary/College)
- CONTACT beeson@uamont.edu
- FREE

http://cotton.uamont.edu

University of Baltimore

This is a gopher server of the University of Baltimore. It contains information on the computing resources and services, the College of Liberal Arts, the Langsdale Library, School of Business, School of Law, phone books, email addresses, and more.

- KEYWORDS Curriculum, Education (College/University), Maryland, University Administration
- AUDIENCE Academics, Educators (University), Students (University)

284 Universities - United States

CONTACT gopher@ube.ub.umd.edu
FREE

gopher://ube.ub.umd.edu/

University of California Information Resources ★★★

This server is a gateway to gopher servers run at all campuses of the University of California. The gateway is maintained at the University of California at Berkeley. The server points to the central gopher server at each campus. The list of gopher servers is provided alphabetically.

KEYWORDS California, Campus Information, Curriculum, University Administration
AUDIENCE Educators, Professors, Students, University Administrators
CONTACT gopher@netinfo.berkeley.edu
FREE

gopher://gopher-registry.berkeley.edu:4322/

The University of Chicago ★★★

The University of Chicago presents campus information for scholars, researchers, and students. The page has data and information links about course schedules, studies available, academic and administration policies. There are links to weather and news in the Chicago area as well as other WWW sites.

KEYWORDS Chicago, Information Resources
AUDIENCE Educators, Illinois Residents, Researchers, Students
CONTACT www@lib.uchicago.edu
FREE

http://www.lib.uchicago.edu

gopher://gopher.uchicago.edu/

University of Colorado at Boulder ★★★

The top level of the University of Colorado at Boulder WWW page offers access to general information about the University. Users will find information on the University administration, academic programs, admissions, student associations, campus, and more. There are also links to individual academic departments, course catalogs, event calendars, and local information.

KEYWORDS Colorado, Universities
AUDIENCE Colorado Residents, Education Administrators (College), Educators, Students
CONTACT Donna Pattee
Donna.Pattee@Colorado.EDU
FREE

http://www.colorado.edu

gopher://gopher.colorado.edu/

University of Connecticut ★★★★

The University of Connecticut Information page contains links to all the University's information servers. The page has information about the schools and departments, faculty, student organizations and University directories. There are also links to Connecticut state resources and web sites.

KEYWORDS Colleges & Universities, Connecticut, Educational Programs, Educational Resources
AUDIENCE Connecticut Residents, Educators, Students
CONTACT ucinfo@uconnvm.uconn.edu
FREE

http://www.uconn.edu

gopher://gopher.uconn.edu/

University of Delaware ★★★

This is the University of Delaware's top-level gopher server. It provides information on the University's activities, phone, email, voice mail and other directories, libraries, faculties, student groups, events and more.

KEYWORDS Delaware, Education (College/University), Social Sciences
AUDIENCE Educators (University), Students (University)
CONTACT Joy Lynam
Joy.Lynam@mvs.udel.edu
FREE

gopher://gopher.udel.edu/

University of Denver ★★★

This server provides information about the University of Denver in Colorado. It contains information on the University's bulletin board, library catalogs, online services, phone books, FTP sites, local weather forecasts, and more. It also has links to other gophers.

KEYWORDS Colorado, Education (College/University), University Administration
AUDIENCE Educators (University), Library Users, Students (University)
CONTACT gopher@gopher.cair.du.edu
FREE

gopher://mercury.cair.du.edu/

University of Florida's Campus-Wide Information System ★★★★

This is a gopher server of the Campus-Wide Information System at the University of Florida in Gainesville, Florida. It contains information about computing and networks, University Press publications, phone and email directories, library resources, and more.

KEYWORDS Education (College/University), Florida, University Administration
AUDIENCE Academics, Educators (University), Students (University)
CONTACT consult@nerdc.ufl.edu
FREE

gopher://gopher.ufl.edu/

University of Hartford ★★★

The University of Hartford uses this Web page to provide the university's faculty, staff, students, and Internet 'guests' with a convenient access point to information and services currently available at the University and on the Internet. Some areas on this site include admissions information, academic departments and schools, general campus information, projects such as the Museum of American Political Life, as well as student home pages.

KEYWORDS Connecticut
AUDIENCE Hartford Residents, Students
CONTACT webmgr@www.hartford.edu
FREE

http://www.hartford.edu/UofHWelcome.html

University of Hawaii - College of Education Gopher Server ★★★

This gopher gives information about the College of Education at the University of Hawaii. This information includes descriptions of the various departments and their academic programs, events, job openings, and network resources.

KEYWORDS Education, Hawaii
AUDIENCE Educational Administrators, Educators, Educators (University), Students (University)
CONTACT edgopher-l@uhunix.uhcc.Hawaii.Edu
FREE

gopher://pegasus.ed.hawaii.edu/

University of Houston's CampusWide Information System ★★★★

This gopher hole provides access to the University of Houston's CampusWide Information Service. It includes administration information, details about various colleges and academic departments, computing and telecommunications resources, library resources & services, and more. Connections to other campus gophers are made.

KEYWORDS Campus Information, Education (College/University), Texas, University Administration
AUDIENCE Academics, Educators (University), Students (University)
CONTACT gopher@uh.edu
FREE

gopher://gopher.uh.edu/

University of Idaho Information & Services ★★★★

This gopher server acts as a resource for the University of Idaho. It contains information about the University, its administration, colleges, departments, computing services, human resources, library resources and services, electronic publications including electronic journals, news, sports, weather, and more.

KEYWORDS Campus Information, Education (College/University), Idaho, University Of Idaho
AUDIENCE Academics, Educators (University), Scientists, Students (University)
CONTACT gopher@uidaho.edu
FREE

gopher://gopher.uidaho.edu/

Universities - United States

University of Illinois Campus Information Gopher ★★★★

This campus-wide information system provides a comprehensive archive of information about the University of Illinois at Urbana-Champaign departments, programs, facilities and services. In addition, users will find an informative collection on disabilities, material on the gopher system itself, links to campus libraries, and information on computer software and hardware. This gopher also includes links to Internet 'phone books' and FTP sites from around the world.

KEYWORDS Illinois, University Administration
AUDIENCE Students (University)
CONTACT   Lynn Bilger
          gopher@uiuc.edu
FREE

gopher://gopher.uiuc.edu/

The University of Illinois at Chicago Gopher Site ★★

This is the wide area information network for the University of Illinois. It is managed by the Academic Data Network and includes a searchable index of the server. Users will find information on enrollment, registration, university policies, campus and community information.

KEYWORDS Computer Administration, Computer Networks, Illinois
AUDIENCE Academics, Students (Secondary/University)
CONTACT   Edward Zawacki
          GOPHER@uicvm.cc.uic.edu
FREE

gopher://uicvm.cc.uic.edu/

The University of Iowa MetaServer ★★★

The University of Iowa MetaServer gives a listing of World Wide Web resources at the University of Iowa. The sites at the Metaserver include the Virtual Hospital, the Iowa Computer Aided Engineering Network, the computer science department, the Iowa Sailing Club and other student computer networks.

KEYWORDS Education (College/University), Educational Resources, Iowa, Online Services
AUDIENCE Internet Users, Iowa Residents, Students
CONTACT   David Lacey
          David-Lacey@uiowa.edu
FREE

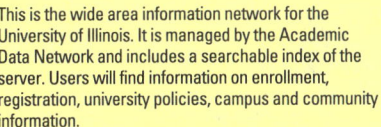

http://www.isca.uiowa.edu

The University of Kansas Gopher Site ★★

This gopher site provides campus-wide information on the University of Kansas in Lawrence. There is information on libraries, course descriptions, computing resources, enrollment, finals, and other campus information.

KEYWORDS Computer Science, Kansas
AUDIENCE Educators (University), Students (University)

CONTACT   Dave Nordland
          Nordlund@ccstaff.cc.ukans.edu
FREE

gopher://ukanaix.cc.ukans.edu/

University of Kentucky Information Services ★★★

This gopher site provides campus-wide information on the University of Kentucky. It offers information on enrollment, registration, the campus, the libraries, University policies and other areas of interest to students, faculty and staff of The University of Kentucky. It also contains links to other gophers, including area weather information and the Internet Navigator search tool.

KEYWORDS Computing, Kentucky, Student Associations
AUDIENCE Educators (University), Students (University)
CONTACT   Robert S. Lee
          sysbob@ukcc.uky.edu
FREE

gopher://ukcc.uky.edu/

The University of Louisville Gopher Site ★★

This gopher site provides information on the University of Louisville in Kentucky. It includes information about the campus, enrollment, courses, programs, and registration as well as other data relevant to the students, faculty and staff of the University of Louisville. It also provides links to other gophers, including a local weather gopher site.

KEYWORDS Computing, Kentucky, University Administration
AUDIENCE Educators (University), Students (University)
CONTACT   Hans Fiedler
          hans@hermes.louisville.edu
FREE

gopher://ulkyvm.louisville.edu/

University of Maine Campus Information ★★★

This is a gopher server of the University of Maine. It provides information about the University, academic departments, degree programs, campus phone directories, events, UM3 course catalog, libraries, campus publications, news, weather and more.

KEYWORDS Education (College/University), Maine
AUDIENCE Educators (University), Library Administrators, Library Users, Students (Secondary/University)
CONTACT   Sam Garwood
          garwood@maine.maine.edu
FREE

gopher://gopher.ume.maine.edu/

University of Maryland Baltimore County ★★★★

This site is a gopher server of the University of Maryland Baltimore County. It contains information on administrative services, academic departments, faculties, computing resources and services, Internet network services, phone and email directories, local and campus newsgroups, student organizations and services, events, announcements and more.

KEYWORDS Education (College/University), Maryland, University Administration
AUDIENCE Educators (University), Students (University)
CONTACT   gopher@gopher.umbc.edu
FREE

gopher://gopher.umbc.edu/

University of Maryland ★★★★

This is a gopher server of the University of Maryland in College Park, Maryland. It offers information on administrative services, computing resources, library resources, student organizations and services, campus events, news, academic resources, colleges, schools, courses, and many more subjects.

KEYWORDS Education (College/University), Maryland, University Administration
AUDIENCE Educators (University), Students (University)
CONTACT   consult@umail.umd.edu
FREE

gopher://gopher.umd.edu/

The University of Memphis WWW Server ★★★

The WWW Server of the University of Memphis in Tennessee offers links to departments, archives and gophers. These department links include biomedical engineering, chemistry, electrical engineering, engineering technology, and the Institute of Egyptian Art and Archaeology. The page offers links to computer services on campus as well as other locations on the Web.

KEYWORDS Computer Networking, Educational Programs, Educational Resources
AUDIENCE Educators, Students
CONTACT   www@cc.memphis.edu
FREE

http://www.memst.edu

gopher://acs1.memst.edu/

The University of Michigan Gopher Server ★★★

This University of Michigan gopher server offers information on FTP archives and users, gopher entries, the World Wide Web, and other Internet resources. It has connections to other gophers with online dictionaries, definitions and computer clubs.

KEYWORDS Internet Reference, Michigan
AUDIENCE Computer Professionals, Computer Specialists, Computer Users, Email Users
CONTACT   gopher@umcc.umich.edu
FREE

gopher://gopher.umcc.umich.edu/

University of Minnesota Information on Courses ★★

This gopher hole contains information on courses at the University of Minnesota in Minneapolis. It provides

Universities - United States

schedules, section status reports, the course guide, and more.
KEYWORDS Education (College/University), Minnesota, University Administration
AUDIENCE Educators (University), Students (University)
FREE

gopher://rodent.cis.umn.edu:11120/

University of Mississippi ★★★

The University of Mississippi site provides connections to academic and administrative departments. The page offers access to the University's resources as well as each school at the University.
KEYWORDS Educational Programs, Educational Resources, Mississippi
AUDIENCE Educators, Mississippi Residents, Students
CONTACT rhovious@sunset.backbone.olemiss.edu
FREE

http://www.olemiss.edu/

University of Montana ★★★

This is a gopher server of the University of Montana. It contains information on the University, its library resources and services, electronic books, reference works, phone books, computing services, schools, departments, sports medicine, and more. It provides access to resources on the Internet.
KEYWORDS Education (College/University), Montana, University Administration
AUDIENCE Educators (University), Students (University)
CONTACT gopher@selway.umt.edu
FREE

gopher://wilcox.umt.edu/

University of Nebraska at Omaha ★★★

This gopher server of the University of Nebraska at Omaha contains a variety of information about the University, including class schedules, student organizations, and department information.
KEYWORDS Campus Information, Nebraska
AUDIENCE Educators (University), Students (University)
FREE

gopher://gopher.unomaha.edu/

University of Nevada, Las Vegas ★★★

The University of Nevada page offers a campus tour and gives access to the alumni association. The site has links to information about the departments at the University as well as the research projects. There are connections to their educational network and other sites on the Web.
KEYWORDS Educational Programs, Nevada, Research
AUDIENCE Educators, Nevada Residents, Researchers, Students
CONTACT www@aurora.nscee.edu.
FREE

http://www.nscee.edu/

gopher://elmore.cs.unlv.edu/

University of North Carolina at Greensboro ★★★

This site is a gopher server of the University of North Carolina at Greensboro. It contains information on computing resources, library resources and services, electronic journals, newsletters, weather and more. It provides access to other gophers on campus as well as off campus.
KEYWORDS Education (College/University), Libraries, North Carolina
AUDIENCE Educators (University), Students (University)
CONTACT Jonathan Thyer
Jonathan_Thyer@uncg.edu
FREE

gopher://gopher.uncg.edu/

University of Oklahoma ★★★★

This is a gopher server of the University of Oklahoma. It contains information on the University, its administrative services, academic departments, library services, job listings, news, events, national archives and records. Data about Oklahoma and surrounding states is included.
KEYWORDS Campus Information, Education (College/University), Oklahoma
AUDIENCE Academics, Educators (University), Students (University)
CONTACT James Deaton
gopher@uoknor.edu
FREE

gopher://gopher.uoknor.edu/

University of Oregon Home Page ★★★★

This is the home page of the University of Oregon. Campus information, administrative and departmental information can be found at this site. An electronic phone book is provided, as well as a current events calendar for campus activities.
KEYWORDS Oregon
AUDIENCE Educators, Students
CONTACT webmaster@www.uoregon.edu
FREE

http://www.uoregon.edu/

gopher://gopher.uoregon.edu/

University of Pennsylvania's Campus-Wide Information System ★★★★

This campus-wide information system provides a comprehensive archive of information about the University of Pennsylvania's departments, programs, facilities and services. There are also links to on-campus libraries, calendars of both school and local events, information on computing, and links to other gophers all over the world.
KEYWORDS Pennsylvania, University Administration
AUDIENCE Educators, Students (University)
CONTACT penninfo-admin@dccs.upenn.edu
FREE

gopher://gopher-penninfo.upenn.edu:71/

University of Rhode Island ★★★

This gopher provides information on the University of Rhode Island's departments, colleges, admissions, registration, administration, undergraduate and graduate programs, conference services, library resources, the phone book, and more. It has pointers to other gophers as well.
KEYWORDS Campus Information, Education (College/University), Rhode Island
AUDIENCE Academics, Educators (University), Students (University)
CONTACT rene@uriacc.uri.edu
FREE

gopher://gopher.uri.edu/

University of South Carolina ★★★

The University of South Carolina maintains this web site to distribute information about the university for current students, alumni, potential applicants and other interested parties. Areas for users to browse through include a what's new page, general campus information, local information for students and faculty, campus libraries, and academic departments.
KEYWORDS South Carolina Universities
AUDIENCE South Carolina Residents, Students
CONTACT wwww@sc.edu
FREE

http://www.csd.scarolina.edu/

gopher://cwis.usc.edu/

The University of South Florida Gopher ★★★

This gopher server offers information about the University of South Florida in Tampa, Florida. It covers the University's different campuses, upcoming events, computing resources, library services, news, newsletters, and more. It provides access to other gophers on campus as well as off campus.
KEYWORDS Education (College/University), Florida, University Administration
AUDIENCE Educators (University), Students (University)
CONTACT Alicia F. Balsera
alicia@usf.edu
FREE

gopher://gopher.usf.edu/

The University of Southern California (UCS) Web site ★★★★

USCweb is the server of the University of Southern California. It provides information on the University's activities, admissions, financial aid, academic departments, courses, calendars, phone books, news, events, libraries and more. It also offers access to other web sites on and off campus. Some new items added to this server are the University of Southern California Brain Project, the Student Senate Communication Sciences Institute, and the Laboratory of Applied Pharmacokinetics.
KEYWORDS California, Campus Information

Universities - United States

AUDIENCE   Californians, Students (Secondary/University)
CONTACT   cwis-wizs@ucs.usc.edu
FREE

http://cwis.usc.edu/

gopher://cwis.usc.edu/

The University of Southern Maine Gopher ★★★★

This is a gopher server of the University of Southern Maine. It contains information on the University, its administrative services, computing resources and services, colleges, departments, library resources and services, academic programs, campus news and events, faculty and staff phone books, and more. It also has links to other gophers on the Internet.

KEYWORDS   Education (College/University), Maine, University Administration
AUDIENCE   Educators (University), Students (University)
CONTACT   houser@usm.maine.edu
FREE

gopher://gopher.usmacs.maine.edu/

The University of Tennessee ★★★

The University of Tennessee Home Page supplies information about the Tennessee university system and its campuses. Campus and Institute pages include general background information and related articles from the Tennessee Alumnus magazine. Administration information as well as news and events and sports calendars are available. Users can also access several University of Tennessee publications online, including course catalogs, a woman's studies newsletter, and the Science Bytes magazine.

KEYWORDS   Tennessee, University Of Campus Information
AUDIENCE   Education Professionals, Professors, Students, Tennessee Residents
CONTACT   Tina Jones
            trjones@utk.edu
FREE

http://loki.ur.utk.edu

gopher://cwis.utk.edu/

University of Texas Gopher Central ★★★

This gopher provides general information on the University of Texas at Austin such as phone directories, education and research programs, newspapers, and libraries. There are also software resources available by FTP and links to important holes in GopherSpace. This gopher serves identical information to that at gopher.utexas.edu.

KEYWORDS   Computer Networks, Computer Science, Education (College/University), Texas
AUDIENCE   Educators (University), Students (Secondary/University)
FREE

gopher://bongo.cc.utexas.edu/

University of Texas at Dallas - CWIS ★★★

This is the Campus Wide Information System (CWIS) for the University of Texas at Dallas (UTD). It contains information on the University, its administration, calendars of events, student services, library services, job opportunities, and more. It has a link to its WWW server and links to other resources on the Internet.

KEYWORDS   Education (College/University), Texas, University Administration, University Of Texas At Dallas
AUDIENCE   Educators (University), Students (University)
FREE

gopher://infoserv.utdallas.edu/

University of Utah ★★★

This site is a gopher server of the University of Utah. It offers information on the University, its academic organizations, news, calendars, telephone directories, libraries, and more. Access to other gophers on campus and around the Internet are also provided.

KEYWORDS   Education (College/University), University Administration, Utah
AUDIENCE   Educators (University), Students (University)
CONTACT   Rhett 'Jonzy' Jones
            jonzy@cc.utah.edu
FREE

gopher://gopher.cc.utah.edu/

University of Vermont ★★★★

This gopher server is located at the University of Vermont. It contains information on the University, student services, computing resources, library services, news and events. It includes links to other Vermont gophers as well as gophers elsewhere on the Internet.

KEYWORDS   Education (College/University), Vermont
AUDIENCE   Academics, Educators (University), Scientists, Students (University)
CONTACT   Allan.Bazinet@uvm.edu
FREE

gopher://gopher.uvm.edu/

The University of Virginia CWIS ★★★★

This is the Campus-Wide Information System for the University of Virginia in Charlottesville, Virginia. It offers information on the University, its administrative services, academic departments, courses, library resources and services, publications, and much more. It has links to other gophers on the Internet.

KEYWORDS   Education (College/University), University Administration, Virginia
AUDIENCE   Educators (University), Students (University)
CONTACT   gwis@virginia.edu
FREE

gopher://gopher.virginia.edu/

University of Western Kentucky Online ★★★★

Western Online contains information about Western Kentucky University (WKU) and the educational programs that it provides. This server gives a virtual walking tour of the campus and the services offered both on and offline. The links provided go to department sites like the Microcomputing Support Center or give access to WKU FTP services, gopher services, and Telnet services.

KEYWORDS   Educational Resources, Kentucky
AUDIENCE   Educators, Kentucky Residents, Students
CONTACT   Baron L. Chandler
            wwwmaint@cristofori.msc.wku.edu
FREE

http://www.msc.wku.edu

gopher://gopher.wku.edu/

University of Wisconsin-Madison Campus Wide Information System ★★★

This gopher server is the University of Wisconsin-Madison Campus Wide Information System (WiscINFO). It provides information on courses, calendars, faculties, libraries, computing resources, news, and employment. In addition, access to the Internet is provided.

KEYWORDS   Campus Information, Education (College/University), University Administration, Wisconsin
AUDIENCE   Educators (University), Students (University)
CONTACT   Barbara Avery
            gopher@doit.wisc.edu
FREE

gopher://gopher.wisc.edu/

Vanderbilt University ★★★

This is a gopher server of Vanderbilt University in Nashville. It offers information on the University, its academic programs, biomedical resource services, campus services, computing resources, email addresses, library services, publications, news, weather, and more. It has pointers to resources on the Internet.

KEYWORDS   Education (College/University), Tennessee, University Administration
AUDIENCE   Educators (University), Students (University)
CONTACT   vuinfo@vanderbilt.edu
FREE

gopher://vuinfo.vanderbilt.edu/

Wake Forest University ★★★

This site is a gopher service of the Wake Forest University. It provides information on the University's administration, schools, academic departments, the library, computer services, student services, news, sports, and more. It also makes connections to off-campus gophers.

KEYWORDS   Campus Information, Education (College/University), North Carolina, University Administration
AUDIENCE   Educators (University), Students (University)
FREE

gopher://gopher.wfu.edu/

Universities - United States – Vocational Education

Washington University in St. Louis ★★★★

The Washington University Home Page provides information about the college and its programs. Users will find alumni, department, and admission information. Athletics schedules and sports information are included, and a constantly updated calendar of school events. A virtual campus tour is included, along with a campus history. Users may also access the library, FTP, and newsgroup information resources, and there are links to local St. Louis Web resources and other Web sites around the world.

KEYWORDS Missouri, Universities
AUDIENCE Educators (University), Students (University)
CONTACT ph-help@ns.wustl.edu
FREE

http://nimue.wustl.edu

gopher://gopher.wustl.edu/

Washington and Lee University ★★★

The Washington and Lee University home page provides information about the college and its resources. Users can find course catalogs, events calendars and student directories, as well as being able to access the Washington and Lee online library catalogs. Washington and Lee department resources are listed by subject, with individual department home pages and relevant text archives and linked web sites. Some general reference information such as a dictionary and glossary of useful terms is also included via gopher, as well as Netlink, a searchable index of useful sites on the Internet.

KEYWORDS Virginia, Universities
AUDIENCE Education Professionals, Students
CONTACT blackmer.h@wlu.edu
FREE

http://liberty.uc.wlu.edu/

gopher://liberty.uc.wlu.edu/

Wayne State University ★★★

This Wayne State University gopher server contains information about the University including its mission, administration, the academic calendar, the no-smoking policy and its phone book. It also offers data on schools, colleges, divisions, departments, student services, library resources, news, and more. It has links to other gophers on campus as well as off campus.

KEYWORDS Education (College/University), Michigan, University Administration
AUDIENCE Educators (University), Students (College/University)
CONTACT Dan Snyder
dsnyder@cms.cc.wayne.edu
FREE

gopher://gopher.wayne.edu/

Welcome to Yale University Home Pages ★★★★

This page is the front door for Yale University's World Wide Web services and departments. From this page, the user can access everything from academic departments and admissions pages to student projects and associations. In addition, special Yale sponsored programs can be found through this site. One example is the 1995 Special Olympics World Summer Games.

KEYWORDS Connecticut, Student Associations, University Administration
AUDIENCE Academics, Researchers, Students (College), Students (Graduate), Yale Students
CONTACT Webmaster@yale.edu
FREE

http://www.cis.yale.edu/FrontDoor/

gopher://gopher.yale.edu/

Willamette University ★★★

This site is a gopher server of the Willamette University in Salem, Oregon. It contains information on the University, its academic departments, library resources, email addresses, news, events and more. Links to other gophers are made.

KEYWORDS Campus Information, Education (College/University), Oregon
AUDIENCE Educators (University), Students (University)
CONTACT gopher@willamette.edu
FREE

gopher://gopher.willamette.edu/

WiscINFO ★★★

WiscINFO is the University of Wisconsin-Madison campuswide information system. It provides information such as courses, calendars, faculties, libraries, computing resources, news, and employment. In addition, access to the Internet is provided.

KEYWORDS Education (College/University), Internet Tools, University Administration, Wisconsin
AUDIENCE Educators (University), Students (Secondary/University)
CONTACT Barbara Avery
gopher@doit.wisc.edu
FREE

gopher://wiscinfo.wisc.edu/

Vocational Education

See also
Computing & Mathematics · *Computer Science*
Computing & Mathematics · *Organizations*
Education · *Educational Projects*
Science · *Biology*
Science · *Physics*

Australian Defence Force Academy ★★

This gopher server is for the Australian Defence Force Academy (ADFA) which provides training to officer cadets in the Australian military. It offers information on the Academy's academic and research programs, staff listings, and facilities.

KEYWORDS Australia, Defense, Military
AUDIENCE Australians, Educators, Military Personnel
CONTACT Rowena Childs
Research@adfa.oz.au
FREE

gopher://gopher.adfa.oz.au/

Hong Kong Polytechnic Institute, Department of Building and Real Estate ★★★

This is the primary site for the Department of Building and Real Estate at the Hong Kong Polytechnic Institutes. It offers various resources about the department itself, its staff, the various programs and degrees, as well as pointers to other resources at the Institute.

KEYWORDS Asia, Hong Kong, International Education, Real Estate
AUDIENCE International Students, Students (University)
CONTACT bre_admin@bs.hkp.hk
FREE

gopher://gopher.bs.hkp.hk/

Metro Tech Career Training Center ★★

At the Metro Tech home page, users can access information on this vocational education institute, where students can receive training in various industries including computer science and practical nursing. The site acts as a brochure for the institute and provides limited information on their finanacial aid options and their training opportunities for high school students. Users access more in-depth information on Metro Tech's Aviation Career Center.

KEYWORDS Computer Science, Nursing, Technical Training, Vocational Education
AUDIENCE Educators, Guidance Counselors, Oklahoma Residents, Students (Secondary/University)
CONTACT metrovt@ionet
FREE

http://ionet.net/nonprofit/metrotech/metro.shtml

The Office of Educational Research and Improvement ★★★

This gopher server provides a subset of the information contained in the US Department of Education's Office of Educational Research and Improvement. It provides information on vocational-adult education initiatives, overall goals of the US Department of Education, and legislative initiatives and schoolwide programs involving Elementary and Secondary Education.

KEYWORDS Education Policy, Educational Resources, Vocational Education
AUDIENCE Educational Administrators, Educators, Parents
CONTACT gopheradm@inet.ed.gov
FREE

gopher://gopher.ed.gov.10001

Society for Handicrafts and Agricultural Work (Obshestwo Propostranienia Truda or ORT)

The information on this server describes the Society for Handicrafts and Agricultural Work (Obshestwo Propostranienia Truda or ORT). ORT is one of the world's largest and oldest international technical training organizations, having been founded in St Petersburg, Russia in 1880 to provide basic trades and agricultural skills. This site contains information on its history, its current activities, ORT skills taught, and ORT statistics.

KEYWORDS Agriculture, Crafts, Russia, Technical Skills
AUDIENCE International Aid Agencies, International Development Specialists, International Students
FREE

gopher://ortnet.ort.org/

USMA Gopher

This is the main gopher server for the United States Military Academy, West Point, New York. The gopher serves up information about the Academy and some of its academic departments, provides access to the library's catalog, and gives links to important Internet sites.

KEYWORDS Military, Military Academies, Military Science, West Point
AUDIENCE Educators (University), Military Personnel, Students (Secondary/University)
CONTACT Jack Robertson
aj4640@trotter.usma.edu
FREE

gopher://euler.math.usma.edu/

Education

Engineering & Technology

Aeronautical Engineering	291
Bioengineering	292
Career & Employment	292
Chemical Engineering	293
Civil Engineering	294
Electrical Engineering	294
Engineering	296
Environmental Engineering	300
Industrial Engineering	301
Material Science	303
Mechanical Engineering	303
Nuclear Engineering	304
Standards	305
Technology	305
Transportation Engineering	311

Aeronautical Engineering

See also
Engineering & Technology · *Transportation Engineering*
Science · *Physics*
Science · *Space Science*
Sports and Recreation · *Aviation*

Aerospace Engineering & Mechanics ★★

This server is maintained by the Aerospace Engineering & Mechanics department of the University of Minnesota. Users will find information on the department's research programs, courses, and faculty. In addition, this site provides links to other University of Minnesota servers on the net.

KEYWORDS Engineering, Mechanical Engineering
AUDIENCE Aerospace Engineers, Educators, Students (University)
CONTACT www@aem.umn.edu
FREE

http://www.aem.umn.edu

Desktop Aeronautics Index Page ★★★

The Desktop Aeronautics' Web Catalog provides easy-to-use aeronautical software for design and education, compatible with Macintosh OS and Microsoft Windows. Programs for aerodynamic analysis and design include LinAir (a multiple nonplanar lifting surface analysis), PANDA (Program for Analysis and Design of Airfoils), SAND (Simulation of Aircraft Nonlinear Dynamics), ADW (Aircraft Design Workshop), and more.

KEYWORDS Aerodynamics, Aeronautics, Software
AUDIENCE Aeronautics Engineers, Macintosh Users, PC Users, Pilots
CONTACT S. Stanaway
 dai@batnet.com
FREE

http://www.batnet.com/dai/

Glenn L. Martin Wind Tunnel ★★

This site describes the facilities and research projects at the Glenn L. Martin Wind Tunnel at the Department of Aerospace Engineering, University of Maryland. Users will find technical details of the tunnel, as well as information on the staff faculty conducting research there. Users can also access descriptions of the aerodynamic research, as well as information on the status of current projects. There are also links to other relevant servers on the Internet.

KEYWORDS Aerodynamics, Physics, Scientific Research
AUDIENCE Aerodynamics Researchers, Aerospace Engineers, Physicists
CONTACT Dr. Jewel Barlow, Director
 barlow@windvane.umd.edu
FREE

http://windvane.umd.edu

NASA Lewis Research Center ★★★

The NASA Lewis Research Center defines and develops advanced technology for new propulsion, power, and communications technologies for application to aeronautics and space. LeRC provides reports for the aircraft engine industry, the energy industry, the automotive industry, the space industry, and other NASA centers. This site gives a searchable index of papers and reports.

KEYWORDS Aeronautics, Communications Technology
AUDIENCE Aeronautic Engineers, Researchers, Space Scientists
CONTACT Omar Syed
 webmaster@lerc.nasa.gov
FREE

http://www.lerc.nasa.gov

NASA's Jet Propulsion Laboratory ★★★★

NASA's Jet Propulsion Laboratory (JPL) at the California Institute of Technology offers news about JPL, online tours, technology transfer, Image/information archives, JPL organizations, FAQs, related home pages, NASA, and the Caltech home page.

KEYWORDS NASA (National Aeronautics And Space Administration), Space Science
AUDIENCE Propulsion Scientists, Space Enthusiasts, Space Scientists
CONTACT newsdesk@jpl.nasa.gov
FREE

http://www.jpl.nasa.gov

NLR Home Page ★★★

The National Aerospace Laboratory NLR is an institute for aerospace research. The Institute provides contributions to activities in aerospace and related fields. NLR is a research organization working in aircraft development, aircraft operations, and space technology. This page offers information on the organization, facilities, research areas and topics. There are links to the NRL FTP and other WWW related sites.

KEYWORDS Netherlands, Scientific Research, Space Science, Technology

292 Aeronautical Engineering – Career & Employment

AUDIENCE Aerospace Engineers, Researchers, Space Scientists, Students
CONTACT info@nlr.nl
FREE

http://www.nlr.nl/

Remote Sensing Thrust Office (CF) ★★★

The Remote Sensing Thrust Office (RSO) develops, advocates, and executes a sensor and data system technology program, in cooperation with industry, to enable advanced NASA and commercial remote sensing missions at reduced costs. Some areas which offer reports and other information include the Solid State Laser Technology, Information Systems, and Passive MicroWave Remote Sensing.

KEYWORDS Lasers, Remote Sensing
AUDIENCE Engineers, NASA Researchers, Space Scientists
CONTACT Milton W. Skolaut, Jr. Milton_S@qmgate.larc.nasa.gov
FREE

http://aesd.larc.nasa.gov/C/CF/CF.html

Bioengineering

See also
Science · Agriculture
Science · Biology
Science · Biosciences
Science · Botany
Science · Zoology

Agricultural Biotechnology Center ★★★

This site contains information on biotechnology issues as they apply to agriculture. The Agricultural Biotechnology Center conducts research into new applications of biotechnology and develops and promotes related agricultural applications. Users can learn about the center through the information at this site, and can find out also more about the research conducted at ABC. In addition, this server maintains links to other agriculture and biotechnology sites on the net.

KEYWORDS Agriculture, Biology, Biotechnology
AUDIENCE Agriculturalists, Biotechnologists, Farmers
CONTACT Peter Fabian www@molmod.abc.hu
FREE

http://www.abc.hu

gopher://hubi.abc.hu:70/

BEC - Bioengineering Center ★★★

This web page is devoted to research and developments in Bioengineering. Its main focus in on simulated surgical procedures and virtual reality, and medical visualization. It lists current projects and researchers involved on this page.

KEYWORDS Bioengineering, Biology, Engineering
AUDIENCE Bioengineers, Doctors, Students, Surgeons

CONTACT Chris Browning gt2038a@prism.gatech.edu
FREE

http://www.oip.gatech.edu/BERC/berctop.html

Genetic Engineering News ★★★

This site, Genetic Engineering News, contains issues of the journal Genetic Engineering News (table of contents and selected articles). Information is also available regarding subscriptions.

KEYWORDS Electronic Journals, Genetics, Molecular Biology
AUDIENCE Bioengineers, Geneticists
FREE

gopher://gopher.enews.com/11/magazines/alphabetic/gl/geng_news

The Rice Institute for Biosciences and Bioengineering ★★

A page which explains the institute, the facilities, the research, and the faculty of the Rice Institute for Biosciences and Bioengineering.

KEYWORDS Engineering, Medicine, Biology
AUDIENCE Doctors, Engineers, Professors, Students
CONTACT David W. Chia dalachia@rice.edu
FREE

http://www-bioc.rice.edu/Institute/IBB.brochure/index.html

U.S. Biotechnology Industry - Facts and Figures 1994/1995 ★★★★

This site contains a range of current information about the biotechnology industry, including sales, markets, companies, research and development, financing and statistics.

KEYWORDS Biotechnology, Companies, Online Publications
AUDIENCE Biologists, Biomedical Researchers, Biotechnologists, Scientists
FREE

http://www.bio.com/bc/bio/2usbio.html

University of Wisconsin Biotechnology Center ★★

This is a gopher site of the University of Wisconsin Biotechnology Center (UWBC). It provides information about biotechnology in the state of Wisconsin, biotechnology-related education resources and opportunities, a biological sciences events listing, a directory of biotechnology researchers, and descriptions of UWBC facilities.

KEYWORDS Biological Research, Biotechnology, Scientific Research, Wisconsin
AUDIENCE Biologists, Biotechnologists

CONTACT Brian Busby brian_busby@gene.biotech.wisc.edu
FREE

gopher://calvin.biotech.wisc.edu/

Career & Employment

See also
Business & Economics · Career & Employment
Computing & Mathematics · Career & Employment
Government & Politics · Agencies

American Society of Engineering Educators Career Development Page ★★★

A large listing of various career development sites including, job listings (engineering and others), Career Magazine, and resume help.

KEYWORDS Careers, Engineering, Jobs, Technology
AUDIENCE Educators, Engineers, Students
CONTACT David Hesprich webmaster@asee.org
FREE

http://www.asee.org/nextgen/career/career.html

Ecole Polytechnique ★★★★

The Ecole Polytechnique, France's most prestigious engineering school, was founded in 1794 during the French Revolution. This site contains a history of the school, in French and English, links to many of the research center's projects, a library catalogue, a list of publications, images of the school and a virtual museum. The site also contains descriptions of the school's doctoral programs and notes on their faculty and alumni.

KEYWORDS Engineering, Mathematics, Multidisciplinary Education, Scientific Research
AUDIENCE Engineering Educators, Engineering Students, French
CONTACT www@www.polytechnique.fr
FREE

http://www.polytechnique.fr/

Human Resources Electronic Advertising and Recruiting Tool (H.E.A.R.T.) - Career Connection Online ★★★

H.E.A.R.T., Human Resources Electronic Advertising and Recruiting Tool, is a menu-driven system that presents career opportunities. There is no charge to the job seeker, however fees are charged to employers. First time users must register and select a password. One can search for positions by geographic location or job title, and one can apply for jobs by submitting a resume through this system. Online categories include:

Accounting, Software Consulting, Engineering, Communications, and Finance.

KEYWORDS Career, Employment, Human Resources, Jobs
AUDIENCE Job Recruiters, Job Seekers, Students
CONTACT postmaster@career.com
FREE

telnet://career.com/telnet://college.career.com/

NASA Ames Research Center Human Resources Information ★★★

This page leads to job announcements at the NASA Ames Research Center. Positions listed are generally for technical or engineering jobs, but there are also secretarial and other office jobs listed. A generic U.S. Federal jobs application is available for downloading, as are general workplace information such as descriptions of benefits, pay structures and internal Ames employee information.

KEYWORDS Employment, Engineering, Human Resources, Jobs
AUDIENCE Federal Employees, Job Seekers
CONTACT Janet Jarmann
janet_jarmann
QMgate.arc.nasa.gov
FREE

http://huminfo.arc.nasa.gov/

TKO Personnel, Inc. ★★★

TKO specializes in United States and Pacific Rim employment, job opportunities and recruitment. This Web site also lists information about the company and provides forms to obtain further information. The Goldmine Newsletter allows employers to search a list of descriptions of bicultural job candidates in specified fields. Goldmine Opportunities then allows candidates to browse a list of positions according to job type, position requirements, duties and salary. They also include a link to the X-Guide, a comprehensive information guide about Japan and U.S.-Japan business relations.

KEYWORDS Employment, International Business, Japan, Jobs
AUDIENCE Japan Residents, Job Seekers
CONTACT kdn@shell.portal.com
FREE

http://www.internet-is.com/tko/index.html

World Wide Job Seekers ★★★

This Web site functions as an electronic employment office bulletin board for job seekers and employers worldwide. Each job-seeker fills out a standardized resume, which is then posted at the site, where it is categorized according to type of job sought. Employers can easily browse through the resumes to find an appealing prospective employee. As the site is maintained in Canada there is a bit of a Canadian flavor to it. The service is free, and anyone in the world can post a resume in any field.

KEYWORDS Employment, Engineering, Jobs
AUDIENCE Job Seekers, Personnel Managers

Connections to Aeronautical Engineering

The sky's the limit

To get off the ground in aeronautics engineering, you need a good launching pad. The Internet can give you the boost to find out about projects (right on the surface of the earth, or way out in space) in which companies and universities are collaborating with the National Aeronautics and Space Administration (NASA). There are even a few sites where you can tap into land-based projects by scientists and researchers which aim to design robots that will one day explore the outer reaches of the galaxy.

Through the "McDonnell Douglas Aerospace" site on the Internet, you can tap into animation and graphics on robotics, or Computer Aided Software Engineering (CASE) projects, or take a look at what the company is doing with Virtual Reality.

At this site you can also peruse demonstration projects like Dante II, an advanced robotic volcano explorer.

(http://pat.mdc.com/)

At the "Glenn L. Martin Wind Tunnel" site, you'll find yourself inside the facilities and research projects at the Department of Aerospace Engineering of the University of Maryland. You'll also find descriptions of aerodynamic research and information on the status of current projects being conducted by the Glenn L. Martin Wind Tunnel facility.

The research projects consist of more than 1,500 tests and projects for conventional airplanes (such as jet fighters), vertical take-off aircraft (helicopters), and even submarines. Some of the projects involve ground vehicles for major car companies, and building construction projects (such as apartment complexes and office facilities).

(http://windvane.umd.edu)

CONTACT webmaster@cban.com
FREE

http://www.cban.com/resume/index.html

Chemical Engineering

See also
Engineering & Technology · *Engineering*
Science · *Chemistry*
Science · *Geosciences*

American Chemical Society ★★★

This is a gopher server of the American Chemical Society (ACS). It contains information on ACS book catalogs, ACS publications, ACS membership, ACS special reports, and more. It has links to other gophers covering chemistry as well as chemistry resources on the Internet.

KEYWORDS Biochemistry, Chemical Engineering, Chemistry, Organizations
AUDIENCE Chemical Engineers, Chemistry Educators, Chemistry Students (Secondary), Chemists
CONTACT gopher@acsinfo.acs.org
FREE

gopher://acsinfo.acs.org/

American Institute of Chemical Engineers ★★★

This site is the official home page of the American Society of Chemical Engineers. It provides information on meetings, employment, and other organizations. It also links to the WWW virtual library of chemical engineering.

KEYWORDS Chemistry, Engineering
AUDIENCE Chemists, Professors, Students, Job Seekers
CONTACT aiche-web@www.che.ufl.edu
FREE

http://www.che.ufl.edu/WWW-CHE/aiche/

Edinburgh Chemical Engineering WWW Home Page ★★

This server is provided by the University of Edinburgh Department of Chemical Engineering. It houses limited information on the department, its faculty, and research interests. Users will find information on both graduate and undergraduate degree programs, as well as information on process and control engineering.

KEYWORDS Chemical Engineering, Chemistry
AUDIENCE Chemical Engineers, Chemists, Education Administrators (College), Educators, Students
CONTACT webmaster@chemeng.ed.ac.uk
FREE

http://www.chemeng.ed.ac.uk

ftp://ftp.chemeng.ed.ac.uk

Hyperactive Molecules Using Chemical MIME ★★★

This site provides a demonstration of an interactive 3-D modeling system for the WWW that requires forms support. It enables the user to specify a chemical structure and then display it for one's WWW browser.

KEYWORDS	Chemistry, Molecular Modeling, Nanotechnology
AUDIENCE	Chemical Engineers, Chemists, Molecular Biologists
CONTACT	Henry Rzepa rzepa@ic.ac.uk
FREE	

http://www.ch.ic.ac.uk/chemical_mime.html

University of Florida Process Improvement Laboratory Home Page

This site is maintained by the Process Improvement Laboratory of the Chemical Engineering Department at the University of Florida. Users will find extensive information about the research that is conducted and material on the facilities and staff at the laboratory. This site also includes links to other chemical engineering and process control sites on the Internet and to the University of Florida itself.

KEYWORDS	Adaptive Control, Chemical Engineering, Engineering, Process Control
AUDIENCE	Chemical Engineers, Educators, Engineers, Students
CONTACT	Dr. Dale W. Kirmse kirmse@che.ufl.edu, webadmin@che.ufl.edu
FREE	

http://www.che.ufl.edu

Civil Engineering

See also
Arts and Music · *Architecture*
Engineering & Technology · *Engineering*
Science · *Physics*

Civil Engineering at Carleton University

The Civil Engineering dpeartment at Carleton University has provided this server to offer information on the academic programs available there. Users will find descriptions of the academic programs, research projects, and student associations of the University. There are some 'exhibits' which demonstrate civil engineering research projects available here, as well as links to related servers on the Internet.

KEYWORDS	Canada, Civil Engineering
AUDIENCE	Civil Engineers, Education Administrators (College), Educators, Students
CONTACT	Neal M. Holtz nholtz@civeng.carleton.ca
FREE	

http://www.civeng.carleton.ca

Department of Civil Engineering at Washington University in St. Louis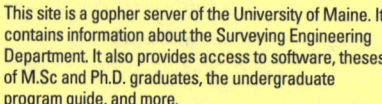

Visitors to the web site of the Department of Civil Engineering at Washington University will find information on the academic programs and research projects found there. There are direct links to pages maintained by the faculty, as well as material on academic degrees conferred and links to other engineering servers on the net.

KEYWORDS	Civil Engineering, Washington State University
AUDIENCE	Civil Engineers, Education Administrators (College), Educators, Students
CONTACT	webmaster@cive.wustl.edu
FREE	

http://www.cive.wustl.edu/cive/

Department of Surveying Engineering at the University of Maine

This site is a gopher server of the University of Maine. It contains information about the Surveying Engineering Department. It also provides access to software, theses of M.Sc and Ph.D. graduates, the undergraduate program guide, and more.

KEYWORDS	Education (College/University), Engineering, Geography, Maine
AUDIENCE	Educators (University), Engineers, Geographers, Students, Surveyors
FREE	

gopher://grouse.umesve.maine.edu/

Service for Earthquake Engineering (NISEE)

The Earthquake Information gopher server has available information services in the fields of earthquake engineering, earthquake hazard mitigation, earthquake disaster response and related disciplines. This site also has links to other related gophers.

KEYWORDS	Diasaster Response, Earth Sciences, Geology, Research & Development
AUDIENCE	Earth Scientists, Engineers, Natural Scientists, Researchers
CONTACT	Jeanette Zerneke seiche@nisee.ce.berkeley.edu
FREE	

gopher://nisee.ce.berkeley.edu/

University of Manitoba Department of Civil and Geological Engineering

This site offers information on the research activities and academic programs of the Department of Civil and Geological Engineering at the University of Manitoba. Users will find graduate and undergraduate program information, as well as links to pages with current research data and descriptions. This server also offers links to many other Internet resources related to civil and geological engineering.

KEYWORDS	Civil Engineering, Colleges & Universities, Geological Engineering
AUDIENCE	Civil Engineers, Educators, Geological Engineers, Geologists, Students
CONTACT	Brian Lucas lucas@ce.umanitoba.ca
FREE	

http://www.ce.umanitoba.ca

Electrical Engineering

See also
Arts and Music · *Electronic Arts*
Computing and Mathematics · *Hardware*
Computing and Mathematics · *Networking*
Science · *Physics*

Center for X-ray Lithography

This gopher provides information about and resources from the Center for X-ray Lithography (CXrL), Wisconsin. The information includes an overview of the CXrL, the center's phone book, and descriptions of current research projects. The resources include software and associated documentation.

KEYWORDS	Electronics, Engineering, Imaging, X-Ray Lythography
AUDIENCE	Computer Engineers, Computer Scientists, Electrical Engineers, Engineers
FREE	

gopher://ishtar.xraylith.wisc.edu/

Department of Electrical Engineering -California Institute of Technology

This is the web server for the Department of Electrical Engineering at the California Institute of Technology. It provides information about the faculty, graduate and undergraduate information, research groups, related web sites, and related departments.

KEYWORDS	California, Electrical Engineering, Graduate Programs
AUDIENCE	Educators, Engineers, Students (University)
CONTACT	www@caltech.edu
FREE	

http://electra.micro.caltech.edu

Department of Electrical Engineering Home Page

The Home Page of the Department of Electrical Engineering at Linköping University gives information about applied electronics, automatic control, computer engineering, image processing, information theory and data transmission. The other departments at Linköping University are linked, and there are external pointers to related sites.

KEYWORDS	Image Processing, Sweden
AUDIENCE	Engineers, Imaging Specialists, Students, Swedes

Electrical Engineering

CONTACT Mikael Wedlin
         mwe@isy.liu.se
FREE
http://www.isy.liu.se

Department of Electrical Engineering at ETH Zurich ★★

This server offers information about the Department of Electrical Engineering at Eidgenoessische Technische Hochschule Zurich (ETH - Zurich), a post-secondary institution in Zurich, Switzerland. The information is limited to a document about the department's fax/modem facilities, and documents about computing resources like AVS, maple, Mathematica, and Quorum.

KEYWORDS Computing, Electrical Engineering, Switzerland
AUDIENCE Computer Scientists, Electrical Engineers, Students (University), Switzerland Residents
CONTACT   karrer@bernina.ethz.ch
FREE
gopher://roseg.ethz.ch/

Department of Electrical Engineering at Tampere University of Technology ★★★

This is the home page of the Department of Electrical Engineering at Tampere University of Technology, located in Tampere, Finland. Information is provided in both English and Finnish. Pointers are given for the laboratories of the departments of physics, measurement technology, Ragnar Granit Institute, and several engineering departments, as well as information on computers and software.

KEYWORDS Engineering, Finland, Physics
AUDIENCE Educators (University), Engineers, Students (University)
CONTACT   webmaster@ee.tut.fi
FREE
http://ee.tut.fi/

EEB Home Page ★★

This site is provided by the Eindhoven University of Technology in the Netherlands. It offers information on the research and academic programs available at the University, and includes links to course descriptions and other resources at the University.

KEYWORDS Circuit Design, Digital Signal Processing, Electrical Engineering, Neural Networks
AUDIENCE Electrical Engineers, Engineers
CONTACT   Heini Withagen
          www@eeb.ele.tue.nl
FREE
http://w3.eeb.ele.tue.nl

Electrical & Computer Engineering Department of University of California at Santa Barbara ★★★

This is a gopher server of the Electrical & Computer Engineering Department (ECE) of the University of California at Santa Barbara. It offers information on ECE, engineering resources, ECE phone books, libraries, news, journals, and more. It provides access to other gophers.

KEYWORDS California, Computer Science, Education (College/University)
AUDIENCE Computer Professionals, Electrical Engineers, Students (Secondary/University)
CONTACT   comsup@ece.ucsb.edu
FREE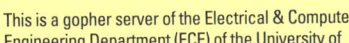
gopher://gopher.ece.ucsb.edu/

Connections to Electrical Engineering
The shocking truth on engineering schools

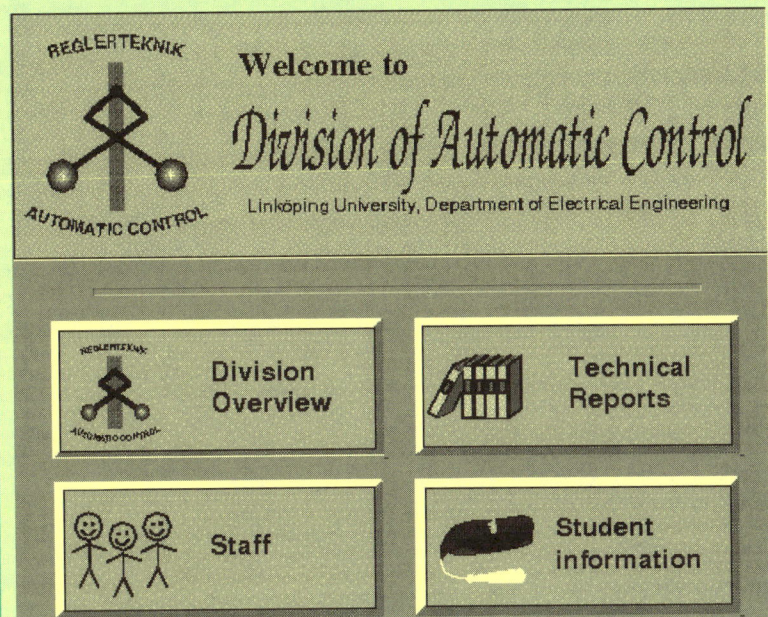

If you're eyeing a career in electrical engineering, you probably already know there are various facets of this field of study. Finding the school with precisely the curriculum you want is a bit harder. If you could search for the best schools anywhere in the world, where would you start?

If you search through the Internet, you get a comprehensive list of major universities that offer courses of study in almost every facet of electrical engineering—from lighting design to aeronautical electrical engineering. You can check out schools ranging from Auburn University in the U.S. to ETH University in Zurich, Switzerland.

You'll not only get course descriptions, but you can also tap into faculty biographies. And definitely check out some of the projects the universities collaborate on with industry, or initiate on their own.

(gopher://roseg.ethz.ch/) also, (http://joakim.isy.liu.se/)

If you lean more toward electronics engineering, there are World Wide Web sites that link you not only to courses of study, but also to products and companies. At the CAEDE (Computer Aided Engineering and Design for Electronics) Page on the Internet you can obtain computer tools from CAEDE at NASA (National Aeronautics and Space Administration) for electrical and optical engineering. You can also find contact lists, and electrical, electronic, and electromechanical parts information management.

(http://longstreet.larc.nasa.gov)

Electrical Engineering Department University of Texas at Arlington ★★★

This server is maintained by the Electrical Engineering Department at the University of Texas. Users will find departmental and course information, as well as a library of downloadable software for electrical engineers. This server also has faculty information, material on current and past research projects, and links to related services on the Internet. Potential students can browse the online brochure to find out more about the department and the local area.

KEYWORDS Electrical Engineering, Engineering

AUDIENCE Educators, Electrical Engineers, Students
CONTACT crowder@eepost.uta.edu,
gradinfo@ee.uta.edu
FREE

http://www-ee.uta.edu

The Faculty of Electronic Engineering of Warsaw University of Technology ★★★

The information in this site describes the Faculty of Electronic Engineering at the Warsaw University of Technology in Poland. This includes local news, faculty lists, Internet addresses of institutes, anonymous FTP, discussion lists, library services, network services, conferences, and more. In addition, it has links to other gophers.

KEYWORDS Education (College/University), Electrical Engineering, Poland
AUDIENCE Academics, Educators (University), Electrical Engineers, Students
CONTACT gopher@elka.pw.edu.pl
FREE

gopher://proton.elka.pw.edu.pl/

The Institute of Electrical and Electronics Engineers ★★★

This gopher site at The Institute of Electrical and Electronics Engineers provides a collection of resources relevant to electrical and electronic engineers. It includes information on the resources offered by the organization such as important publications, standards, new technologies, software, student branch activities, and press releases.

KEYWORDS Biomedical Science, Computer Technology, Electrical Engineering, Engineering
AUDIENCE Electrical Engineers, Engineers, Engineers (Biomedical), Software Engineers
CONTACT gopher-dev@gopher.ieee.org
FREE

gopher://gopher.ieee.org/

Linkoping University, Division of Automatic Control ★★

The Division of Automatic Control at Linkoping University, Sweden, works on control research, and their home page provides information about their nonlinear modelling, hybrid modelling, and system identification projects. Included are all the technical reports from these projects, available by ftp, as well as recent activity reports. This site also links to other educational and professional control engineering Web sites. Information about the staff and students involved in this division is also offered, with general background materials about Linkoping University and Sweden.

KEYWORDS Computer Science, Control Engineering, Systems Engineering
AUDIENCE Electrical Engineers, Engineering Students, Systems Engineers

CONTACT Magnus Sundstedt
masun@isy.liu.se
FREE

http://joakim.isy.liu.se/

Pacific Microelectronics Corporation ★★

The Pacific Microelectronics Corporation (PMC) web site provides information about their whole range of services, capabilities, and process specs for circuit manufacturing and related issues. The PMC provides design, manufacturing and testing services for surface mount printed circuit boards, multichip modules, hybrid circuits and BGA (Ball Grid Arrays) packages. Their product offers a low-fire ceramic technology for packaging hybrids, MCMs (Multichip Modules), and BGAs. Visitors to the site can also download free the MCM cost estimator software, get sales office information as well as a number of links to other related sites.

KEYWORDS Electrical Engineering, Electronics, Manufacturing Industry, Multichips
AUDIENCE Electronic Engineers, IC Designers, Manufacturing Engineers, Packaging Engineers
CONTACT David White
davidwh@teleport.com
FREE

http://www.pmcnet.com/~pmc

Pyrotechnics ★★

The Pyrotechnics page is an introduction to the art of fireworks. Users will find descriptions and pictures of different types of fireworks, a bibliography of pyrotechnic literature, and links to other pyrotechnic resources on the Web. Articles on the basic principlese of pyrotechnic light and electric ignition are included for those interested in creating their own fireworks.

KEYWORDS Fireworks, Pyrotechnics
AUDIENCE Engineers, Fireworks Enthusiasts
FREE

http://cc.oulu.fi/~kempmp/pyro.html

QMU Electronic Engineering Department (Queen Mary and Westfield College) ★★★

This site is the home page of the Electronic Engineering Department at the Queen Mary and Westfield College, University of London. Users will find out about the faculty and students of the Department and about material on courses taught by the professors. Also available is information on the Department's ongoing research projects.

KEYWORDS Electrical Engineering, Engineering
AUDIENCE Electrical Engineering Educators, Electrical Engineering Students, Electrical Engineers
CONTACT Andy Martin
A.P.Martin@qmw.ac.uk
FREE

http://web.elec.qmw.ac.uk

Engineering

See also
Education · *Universities - United States*
Engineering & Technology · *Technology*
Science · *Physics*

ARL's (Applied Research Laboratory) Welcome Page ★★★

This site offers information on the research projects and applications of the Applied Research Laboratory at Washington University. One of the highlights of the Lab is its research into high bandwith ATM networks and their applications in high resolution videoconferencing. Users will find information on this and other research projects, as well as links leading to ARL publications, facilities and staff information, and more.

KEYWORDS ATM (Asynchronous Transfer Mode), Networking
AUDIENCE Engineers, Researchers, Scientists
CONTACT helen@arl.wustl.edu
FREE

http://www.arl.wustl.edu

Adaptive Fuzzy Control ★★

Adaptive Fuzzy Control provides information on the Institute of Systems Science at the National University of Singpore. It gives short description of ongoing projects and contact names.

KEYWORDS Adaptive Control, Research, Singapore
AUDIENCE Engineers, Professors, Researchers, Students
CONTACT Goh Tiong Hwee
thgoh@iss.nus.sg
FREE

http://www.iss.nus.sg/RND/NNFL/Fuzzy_Control.html

CEDAR (Center of Excellence for Document Analysis and Recognition) Home Page ★★★

This site is maintained by the Center of Excellence for Document Analysis and Recognition, an organization that conducts research in document recognition and analysis technology. Users will find information on the people, facilities, publications, and research projects at the Center. This site also provides links to related servers on the Internet.

KEYWORDS Document Analysis, Document Technology, Optical Character Recognition
AUDIENCE Computer Scientists, Document Specialists
CONTACT Ajay Shekhawat
ajay@cedar.Buffalo.EDU
FREE

http://www.cedar.buffalo.edu

Cambridge University Engineering Department Control Group ★★★

The Control Group of the Engineering Department at Cambridge University publishes papers and other academic resources on this site. The Control Group also hosts the Control Engineering branch of the World Wide Web Virtual Library, providing links to many different resources within the field. There is additional information at this site such as research information and publications, as well as links to other servers at Cambridge and beyond.

KEYWORDS   Complex Systems, Control Engineering, United Kingdom
AUDIENCE   Educators, Engineers, Students
CONTACT   Sanjay Lall
   www-control-admin@eng.cam.ac.uk
FREE

http://www-control.eng.cam.ac.uk

Center for Design Research Home Page ★★★

The Center for Design Research (CDR) is engaged in various types of research relating to quality engineering design. Current research includes virtual reality as a designer's tool, computer networks, robotics, and much more. Users can obtain descriptions of research labs and projects, information on the staff, and find out about new happenings at the Center.

KEYWORDS   Design, Engineering Design
AUDIENCE   Designers, Engineers, Researchers
CONTACT   Jack Hong
   hong@sunrise.stanford.edu
FREE

http://gummo.stanford.edu/

Center for the New Engineer ★★★

The Center for the New Engineer is pursuing new practices and technologies for educating engineers who will be effective in the world of the 21st century. The center has worked on projects such as online tutorials on Virtual Memory and Genetic Algorithms, and offline projects such as physically connecting K-12 Schools to the Internet. Ideas on how engineering will develop in the next generation are also advanced on this page. Contact information, research reports, and proceedings from Internet conferences are also available here.

KEYWORDS   Education, Engineering, Internet Access
AUDIENCE   Educators, Engineering Students, Engineers
CONTACT   webmaster@cne.gmu.edu
FREE

http://cne.gmu.edu

Cohen Acoustical Home Page ★★★

This page is presented by Cohen Acoustical, Inc., a company dedicated to acoustics research, sound system design, architectural acoustics, and engineering acoustics. Users will find descriptions of the company's services, samples of their work, and links to related services on the Internet. Most interesting, though, is the collection of research papers on various topics in acoustics research. There is also information about Cohen Acoustical's realtime audio and video broadcasts over the Internet.

KEYWORDS   Acoustics, Audio
AUDIENCE   Acoustic Engineers, Architects, Audiophiles, Professional Audio Engineers
FREE

http://www.cohenacoustical.com/ca/

The College of Engineering of the University of California at Berkeley ★★★

This site is a gopher server of the College of Engineering of the University of California at Berkeley. It provides information on departments, committees, Cooperative Internship Programs, courses, engineering news, undergraduate research, and more.

KEYWORDS   California, Education (College/University), Engineering
AUDIENCE   Educators (University), Engineers, Students (University)
CONTACT   korda@coe.berkeley.edu
FREE

gopher://gopher.coe.berkeley.edu/

Colorado State University College of Engineering ★★★

The Colorado State University Engineering server gives information about the engineering departments and research laboratories. The page has links to each department within the College including atmospheric sciences, civil, mechanical, and electrical engineering. There are links to related engineering homepages for

Connections to Engineering Companies
If you build it... and they will come

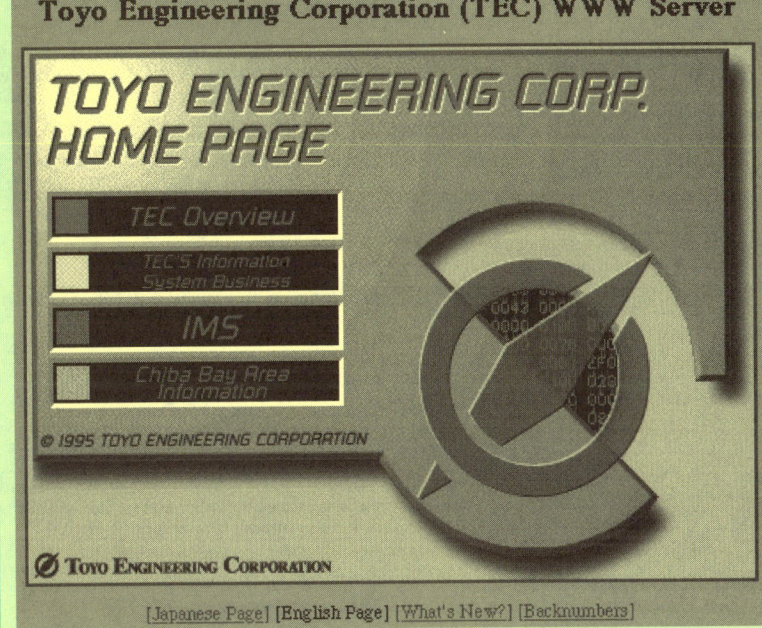

The farmer who needs a silo, the utility company that needs a new plant, and an energy company that requires refining facility equipment share a common goal—they need to get in touch with a company somewhere around the world that can provide them with the product or service they need.

Many engineering companies maintain World Wide Web Sites to not only "advertise" their products and services, but also to provide details of projects for other professionals and students to use in their research.

At the "Toyo Engineering Corporation" site on the Internet, for instance, users not only have access to the company's technology and research projects, but also to the company's offerings on fields of activities such as design, equipment procurement, construction of chemical, nuclear, and electric power, and petrochemical plants.

(http://www.toyo-eng.co.jp/)

computing, structural design and solar energy as well as links to Colorado State University.

KEYWORDS Civil Engineering, Education (College/University), Electrical Engineering, Mechanical Engineering
AUDIENCE Educators, Engineers, Researchers, Students
CONTACT webmaster@lance.colostate.edu
FREE

http://www.lance.colostate.edu

The Cornell Engineering Library Gopher ★★★

The Cornell Engineering Library Gopher provides information on Internet science and engineering resources, the Cornell Engineering Library, the Cornell University Collection Development, the College of Engineering, courses, software and more. There is access to other gophers of engineering coalitions and societies.

KEYWORDS Education (College/University), Engineering, Libraries
AUDIENCE Educators (University), Engineers, Students (Secondary)
CONTACT John Saylor
JMS1@cornell.edu
FREE

gopher://gopher.englib.cornell.edu/

Department of Robotics and Digital Technology ★★★

The Department of Robotics and Digital Technology is one of the nine Departments in the Faculty of Computing & Information Technology at Monash University. The department has interests in Digital Technology, Robotics, Digital Communications, Digital Signal Processing, Image Processing, VLSI, and other related fields. Research activities and technical reports can be found here, as well as contact information, and individual home pages.

KEYWORDS Robotics, Communications Technology
AUDIENCE Engineers, Robot Enthusiasts, Robotics Engineers
CONTACT Jim Breen
webmaster@www.rdt.monash.edu.au
FREE

http://daneel.rdt.monash.edu.au

Design Research Institute ★★★

The Design Research Institute is an organization of collaborating industry and academic scientists and engineers devoted to research bringing computer science and computation technology to bear on problems of engineering design. Services include information capture, computational prototyping, and collaborative technology. Users will find technical documents such as 'A Comparative Analysis of Techniques in Engineering Design' and 'Simulation Methods for Micro-Electro-Mechanical Structures (MEMS) with Application to a Microtweezer.' Instructions are given for any company or individual that wants to participate in this research program or access the library of resources.

KEYWORDS Computer Science, Engineering Design, Industrial Design, Industrial Research
AUDIENCE Engineers, Industry Researchers, Scientists
CONTACT davis@dri.cornell.edu
FREE

http://dri.cornell.edu/

Engineering ★★

This document is a compilation of information resources focused on engineering. The resources vary from listservs about military technology to the Canadian Electro-Acoustics community. Thus, some browsing may be necessary to find an exact resource.

KEYWORDS Electro-Acoustics, Engineering Journals, Military Technology
AUDIENCE Educators, Engineering Students, Engineers, Researchers, Students
FREE

ftp://una.hh.lib.umich.edu/inetdirsstacks/engin:parkmiller

Engineering School of the Catholic University of Chile ★★★

This site is a local information center for the Engineering School of the Catholic University of Chile and its students. It contains an Internet page (in English).

KEYWORDS Chile, Education, Engineering
AUDIENCE Engineers, Students (University)
CONTACT Ingeniera@ing.puc.cl
FREE

http://www.ing.puc.cl/

Engineering Technology Department-Texas A&M University ★★★

This is the home page for the Engineering Technology (ET) Department at Texas A & M University. The ET Department combines laboratories and courses to give students hands-on experience. Links are also provided here to the following items—Listings of Electronics, Mechanical, Manufacturing, and Industrial Distribution Programs and Course Requirements; Electronic Contacts; On-Line Publications; Interactive Pages; Engineering Technology Personal Web Links; and Other Local Sites and Links.

KEYWORDS Electronics, Electronic Engineering
AUDIENCE Engineering Educators, Engineering Students
CONTACT alan@entc.tamu.edu
FREE

http://entcweb.tamu.edu

Engineering Virtual Library ★★★★

The Engineering Virtual Library provides a general overview of a variety of Engineering resources available on the Internet. Fields covered include aerospace, chemical, civil, electrical, mechanical, nuclear and software engineering. Also provided are pointers to general engineering information, government and academic research insitutions and commercial vendors.

KEYWORDS Engineering, Software, Technology
AUDIENCE Engineering Students, Engineers
CONTACT Steve Waterbury
waterbug@epims1.gsfc.nasa.gov
FREE

http://epims1.gsfc.nasa.gov/engineering/engineering.html

The Engineers' Forum ★★★

The Engineers' Forum web pages are comprised mainly of articles and project descriptions from Engineering students at Virginia Technical University. Articles cover the gamut of engineering topics, from vehicle design to electrical engineering and computer science to even more varied topics such as social design and city planning.

KEYWORDS Design, Engineering Journals, Structural Engineering
AUDIENCE Engineering students, Engineers
CONTACT John Cole and Mike Reese
kennedy@vt.edu
FREE

http://www.vt.edu:10021/eng/forum/

Indian Institute of Technology (IIT) - Bombay ★★★

This site at the Computer Science and Engineering Department at the India Institute of Technology (IIT) in Bombay provides imaging software, networking, UNIX, public domain resources of interest to students at IIT and links to other Indian sites. There is also a FAQ.

KEYWORDS Computer Programming, Engineering, India, International Education
AUDIENCE Computer Researchers, Engineering Students, Engineers, Indians
CONTACT Vijay Talati
postmaster@iitb.ernet.in
vijay@iitb.ernet.in
FREE

ftp://ftp.iitb.ernet.in/

Infrastructure Technology Institute ★★★

This server provides information about the development and maintainence of the nation's infrastructure, such as its roads, bridges, and airports. The information is provided by the Infrastructure Technology Institute (ITI) at Northwestern University, Illinois. The information includes descriptions of research prohects at ITI, and access to databases related to the national infrastructure. These databases include government documents, survey results, and studies.

KEYWORDS Construction, Economic Development, Infrastructure, Technological Advances
AUDIENCE Economists, Engineers, Political Analysts, Researchers
FREE

gopher://iti.acns.nwu.edu/

Institut National des Sciences Appliquées de Lyon ★★★★

This page at the Institut National des Sciences Appliquées (INSA) in Lyon offers information on the School's departments and laboratories. INSA has four schools in France for the studies of engineering and technology. This site has information about the School's research for public institutions and there are links to related gophers and FTPs as well as other sites in France and Europe.

KEYWORDS   Electrical Engineering, Mechanics
AUDIENCE   Engineers, French, Researchers, Scientists
CONTACT   Arnaud Girsch
           Arnaud.Girsch@insa-lyon.fr
FREE

http://www.insa-lyon.fr

Institut National des Sciences Appliquées Toulouse ★★★★

The National Institute of Applied Sciences in Toulouse is one of the four INSA Schools in France offering information on engineering studies and research. This server gives information on admission to INSA, the departments, services and the centers. The School's studies include biochemical engineering, mechanical engineering and electrical engineering. There are links to the campus news, a students corner and other WWW and FTP sites.

KEYWORDS   Electrical Engineering, Scientific Research
AUDIENCE   Engineers, French, Researchers, Scientists
CONTACT   Bernard.Salvagnac@dge.insa-tlse.fr
FREE

http://www.insa-tlse.fr

The Institute for Systems Research WWW Home Page ★★★★

This site is the home of the Institute for Systems Research, an engineering research and development labratory operated jointly by the University of Maryland and Harvard University. It maintains a collection of information on the Institute such as material on the faculty and staff, research interests, projects, and more. In addition, users can connect to the Institute's software library, read publications of the Institute, as well as obtain information on research collaborators.

KEYWORDS   Civil Engineering, Industrial Engineering, Systems Engineering
AUDIENCE   Educators, Engineers, Students, Systems Engineers
CONTACT   Amar Vadlamud
           nath@src.umd.edu
FREE

http://wais.isr.umd.edu

ftp://ftp.isr.umd.edu/

Kungl Tekniska Högskolan, KTH ★★★★

The Kungl Tekniska Högskolan (Royal Institute of Technology) is a technical institute for education and research in technology. KTH provides engineering studies and technical research at post-secondary level for Sweden. Their research activities cover a broad spectrum, from natural sciences to all branches of technology, as well as architecture, industrial economics, urban planning, work science and environmental technology. This site gives general information about the school, the students and educational opportunities. There are links to SUNET, the Swedish University Network, and information about Stockholm.

KEYWORDS   Natural Sciences, Sweden
AUDIENCE   Engineers, Students, Swedes, Technical Researchers
CONTACT   webmaster@kth.se
FREE

http://www.kth.se

METU Campus Wide Information System ★★★

The Middle Eastern Technical University (METU) in Turkey focuses on engineering. Users can access information about computer centers in Turkey, and utilize the computer center's online library to access such books as the Turkey Atlas, UNIX manuals, a dictionary, and the Turkish Press Review. Information about the University includes an academic calender, course descriptions, guides to student services, and home pages for the graduate schools.

KEYWORDS   Internet Resources, Turkey, Universities
AUDIENCE   Students, Turks
CONTACT   webmaster@www.metu.edu.tr
FREE

http://knidos.cc.metu.edu.tr/METU/MetuHome.html

Networking for Engineering and Research in Oregon (NERO) ★★★★

The Networking for Engineering and Research in Oregon (NERO) is a project designed to utilize computer networking to enhance engineering education and research. The page gives access to information on the NERO network, research, documentation and applications. The documentation section includes proposals for communication networks and the use of video in NERO projects. This site contains links to the universities and organizations in Oregon that are members of NERO.

KEYWORDS   Computer Aided Design (CAD), Graduate Research, Parallel Computing
AUDIENCE   Educators, Engineers, Researchers, Scientists
CONTACT   Andrew E. Clapp
           clapp@www.nero.net
FREE

http://www.nero.net

Neural Adaptive Control Technology ★★

This page is devoted to research on creating synergy between adaptive control and neural networks.

KEYWORDS   Adaptive Control, Neurology, Research
AUDIENCE   Engineers, Professors, Researchers, Students
CONTACT   Rafal Zbikowski
           rafal@mech.gla.ac.uk
FREE

http://www.mech.gla.ac.uk/~nactftp/nact.html

Photonic Systems Group ★★★★

This is the information page for the McGill University Department of Electrical Engineering's Photonic Systems Group. The objective of the McGill Photonic Systems Group is to design, build and test a representative portion of a free-space optical backplane capable of supporting a terabit/second of aggregate capacity. This page provides links to information on the Photonic Systems Group, its research topics, publications, conferences, and other photonics related Internet resources.

KEYWORDS   Optical Engineering, Research & Development
AUDIENCE   Canada Residents, Engineering Students, Students (Secondary/University), Students (University)
CONTACT   Prof. David Plant
           plant@photonics.ee.mcgill.ca
FREE

http://www.photonics.ee.mcgill.ca/

Region 6 Engineering ★★

The Region 6 Engineering provides information for users of its computing facilities at the Ohio State University. This site provides lab information, including software, hardware, and staff, with a hypertext users guide for the facilities and for Adobe Acrobat. Included in this site are links to the home pages of the departments that utilize the Region 6 facilities, with information about their projects and staff. There are also facts about new software and events taking place at Region 6, as well as information about Ohio State University. Users will also find help topics for creating html documents and Web pages.

KEYWORDS   Chemical Engineering, Computer Systems, Computing, Universities
AUDIENCE   Computer Users, Engineering Students
CONTACT   Geoffrey Hulse
           hulse@kcgl1.eng.ohio-state.edu
FREE

http://kcgl1.eng.ohio-state.edu/

Rockwell Japan RIKK Email Directory ★★

This page is a collection of email addresses for the engineering staff at RIKK, Rockwell Japan, organized alphabetically by last name.

KEYWORDS   Engineering, Japan, Telecommunications
AUDIENCE   Business Professionals, Communications Professionals, Electrical Engineers
CONTACT   Stephen Palm
           palm@tokyo.rockwell.com
FREE

http://www.tokyo.rockwell.com/rikk.mail.eng.html

SWRI Southwest Research Institute ★

This gopher site provides information about the Southwest Research Institute (SWRI), located in San Antonio, Texas. The Southwest Research Institute, founded in 1947, is a nonprofit, applied engineering and physical sciences research and development organization devoted to technology development and transfer.

KEYWORDS   Research, Technology
AUDIENCE   Computer Users, Internet Users
FREE

gopher://espsun.space.swri.edu/

Toyo Engineering Corporation ★★★

This is the company home page from the Toyo Engineering Corporation (TEC). The company specializes in plant design and equipment procurement, as well as construction of chemical, petrochemical, petroleum, oil and gas, fertilizer, nuclear, electric power, and other plants. TEC also figures prominently in the fields of computer-integrated manufacturing, factory automation, and other comprehensive production systems that combine engineering technology with software development. Information about the company's financial results, overseas experience, fields of business, and research department is available.

KEYWORDS   Chemical Engineering, Computer Integrated Manufacturing, Engineering, Japanese Business
AUDIENCE   Business Analysts, Business Professionals, Petroleum Industry Professionals
CONTACT   www@toyo-eng.co.jp
FREE

http://www.toyo-eng.co.jp/

UC Berkeley Electrical Engineering and Computer Science Alumni Registry ★★★

The UC Berkeley Electrical Engineering and Computer Science Alumni Registry provides the names, email and home page addresses, year of graduation, and most recent place of employment for graduates of the Department of Electrical Engineering and Computer Science. The index is browsable by name, year, and place of employment. Alumni can add or change their listings though an online form.

KEYWORDS   Computer Science, Electrical Engineering, Email Addresses
AUDIENCE   Computer Scientists, Electrical Engineers, UC Berkeley Alumni
CONTACT   www@alumni.EECS.Berkeley.EDU
FREE

http://alumni.EECS.Berkeley.EDU/alumreg/index.html

UC San Diego School of Engineering ★★★

This site allows users to access information about the School of Engineering at the University of California at San Diego. There is material on the school itself, as well as departmental and faculty information. There is also a collection of documents about ongoing research projects, links to student resources, and information on the computing facilities at the school. In addition, users can follow links to other servers at UCSD.

KEYWORDS   Engineering, Engineering Education
AUDIENCE   Educators, Engineers, Students
CONTACT   soeweb@soe.ucsd.edu
FREE

http://www-soe.ucsd.edu

UF Process Improvement Laboratory Home Page ★★★★

This site is maintained by the Process Improvement Laboratory of the Chemical Engineering Department at the University of Florida. Users will find extensive information about the research being conducted here, as well as material on the facilities and staff of the Laboratory. This site also includes links to other Chemical Engineering and process control sites on the Interent, as well as to the University of Florida itself.

KEYWORDS   Adaptive Control, Chemical Engineering, Engineering, Process Control
AUDIENCE   Chemical Engineers, Educators, Engineers, Students
CONTACT   Dr. Dale W. Kirmse
          kirmse@che.ufl.edu,
          webadmin@che.ufl.edu
FREE

http://www.che.ufl.edu

The University of Maine College of Engineering ★★★

This is a gopher server of the University of Maine College of Engineering. It contains information on the engineering programs, anonymous FTP sites, news, and weather. It also offers information on the Electrical and Computer Engineering Department. It has links to the Library of Congress Records and other resources.

KEYWORDS   Computer Science, Education (College/University), Engineering, Maine
AUDIENCE   Computer Students, Educators (University), Engineering Students
FREE

gopher://watson.eece.maine.edu/

University of Saskatchewan Engineering Info System ★★★

This is a gopher site of the College of Engineering, University of Saskatchewan, Saskatoon, Canada. It provides information on the College of Engineering, its faculty, research, projects and engineering student societies. There is also data on the University of Saskatchewan and the city of Saskatoon.

KEYWORDS   Canada, Curriculum, Education (College/University), Engineering
AUDIENCE   Civil Engineers, Educators (University), Engineering Students
CONTACT   Ian MacPhedran
          Ian_MacPhedran@engr.usask.ca
FREE

gopher://dvinci.usask.ca/

Wash U. School of Engineering and Applied Science ★★★★

The School of Engineering and Applied Science is home to a group of researchers, teachers, staff, and students doing a variety of research and academic activities. This site gives access to information on each department, its home page, faculty, staff and course schedule. These departments include chemical, civil, electrical and mechanical engineering as well as computer science, systems science and mathematics. There is also information about the organizations, groups and the graduate program at the School.

KEYWORDS   Education (College/University), Washington University
AUDIENCE   Engineers, Researchers, Students, Systems Scientists
CONTACT   webmaster@ecl.wustl.edu
FREE

http://www.ecl.wustl.edu/seas

Environmental Engineering

See also
Government & Politics · *Policies*
Science · *Aquatic Sciences*
Science · *Earth Sciences*
Science · *Environmental Sciences*
Science · *Geosciences*

DWR, Division of Planning ★★★★

This site offers information about the California Department of Water Resources (DWR) Division of Planning, which develops strategies for the wise use and management of California's water resources. Its research is the basis for the California Water Plan, a guide for water management activities throughout the state. The Division's page contains pointers to other DWR servers, current flood information, and several water-related, non-government sites.

KEYWORDS   California, Conservation, Government Agencies (US), Water Resources
AUDIENCE   Californians, Conservationists, Farmers, Geologists
CONTACT   httpd@dop.water.ca.gov
FREE

http://locke.water.ca.gov/

Energy Systems Laboratory Home Page ★★★

This site offers information culled from research into energy systems and conservation. It is maintained by the Energy Systems Laboratory at Texas A&M University. Users will find information on laboratory facilities and staff, energy publications, and energy analysis software. In addition, this site hosts a number of links to Texas A&M and related web servers.

KEYWORDS   Energy, Environmental Engineering
AUDIENCE   Conservationists, Environmental Engineers

CONTACT www@www-esl.tamu.edu
FREE
http://www-esl.tamu.edu

National Key Centre for Design ★★★

This gopher server provides information on the National Key Centre for Design at the Royal Melbourne Institute for Technology (RMIT) in Australia. The information includes staff directories, teaching and research programs, research papers, and environmental design. There are also links to the center's WWW server and other RMIT gopher servers.

KEYWORDS Australia, Design, Education, Environmental Design
AUDIENCE Designers, Educators, Environmental Researchers, Students
CONTACT cfd@rmit.edu.au
FREE
gopher://daedalus.edc.rmit.edu.au/

Solar Radiation Data - Table of Contents ★★★

This page is an access point for solar radiation and climate summary data from selected locations across the US. This data is primarily intended for the siting, specification, and sizing of solar energy equipment. Detailed information on solar energy and methods of collection is also available.

KEYWORDS Climatology, Conservation, Environmental Studies, Solar Energy
AUDIENCE Ecologists, Energy Researchers, Environmentalists, Science Researchers
CONTACT +1 (202) 289-5370
         www-content@solstice.crest.org
FREE
http://solstice.crest.org/renewables/solrad/index.html

Solstice - Sustainable Energy and Development Online! ★★★★

This WWW server provides state-of-the-art information on renewable energy, energy efficiency, the environment, and sustainable community development.

KEYWORDS Conservation, Energy, Environment, Environmental Studies
AUDIENCE Conservationists, Environmentalists, Urban Planners
CONTACT www-content@solstice.crest.org
FREE
http://solstice.crest.org/
gopher://gopher.crest.org/
ftp://solstice.crest.org/pub/

Connections to Environmental Issues
Stop trashing mother earth!

If you're interested in environmental law around the world, or want to download environmental regulations from any of the 50 states in the U.S., you can easily do so on the Internet.

You can even access a handy reference to courses in the environmental sciences at places like The Swedish University, Aberdeen University, or Stanford University.

You can also locate the latest data on acid rain and analysis on how it affects plant and animal life. If you're an environmental activist (or aspire to be), you'll find links to several sites via the Royal Institute of Technology Library in Stockholm, Sweden's "Environmental Sites" on the Internet.

From that point you can learn about the Belgian Antarctic Research Program and visit "Live from Antarctica" to investigate projects ranging from the exploration of Antarctica, to Antarctic plant and animal life, to the hole in the Ozone layer.

(http://www.lib.kth.se/lg.html)

Industrial Engineering

See also
Business & Economics · *Industries*
Computing & Mathematics · *Artificial Intelligence*

 ## Allen-Bradley Home Page ★

The Allen-Bradley Home Page offers a brief summary on this industrial automation supply company based in Wisconsin. Users may access a listing of product areas in which Allen Bradley specializes from Food Processing to Water Treatment, but users must register for free in order to access any more detailed information on the company.

KEYWORDS Engineering, Industrial Automation, Technology
AUDIENCE Engineers, Managers
FREE
http://www.ab.com/

Industrial Engineering

Auburn University Industrial Engineering Department ★★

The WWW server of the Auburn University Industrial Engineering Department is still under construction. The information available now includes profiles of the department's faculty, current research and bibliographical listings of recent publications. In addition, admissions information and general program information is given for undergraduates and graduate students.
- KEYWORDS: Engineering, Industrial Engineering
- AUDIENCE: Engineering Students, Industrial Engineers
- FREE

http://www.eng.auburn.edu/department/ie/iehome.html

Commonwealth Scientific and Industrial Research Organisation ★★★

This gopher server provides a means to search a staff directory database for the Commonwealth Scientific and Industrial Research Organisation (CSIRO), Australia. The database is searchable by keywords. There are also links to other CSIRO gopher servers.
- KEYWORDS: Australia, Industrial Research, Information Retrieval, Scientific Research
- AUDIENCE: Australians, Educators, Science Researchers, Scientists
- FREE

gopher://dingo.tfrc.csiro.au/

Dept. of Industrial Engineering and Operations Research at University of California, Berkeley (IEOR) ★★★★

The WWW server of the UC Berkeley Department of Industrial Engineering and Operations Research provides information about the department's faculty, teaching and research facilities, graduate and undergraduate programs and listings of courses offered in the current and upcoming semesters. The IEOR focuses on two related professions concerned with the efficient operation of complex systems.
- KEYWORDS: Complex Systems, Industrial Engineering, Operations Research
- AUDIENCE: Engineerings Students, Industrial Engineers
- CONTACT: Steve Chick
  chick@delft.berkeley.edu
- FREE

http://maastricht.berkeley.edu/IEOR/

Georgia Institute of Technology School of Industrial and Systems Engineering ★★★

The WWW server of the Georgia Institute of Technology School of Industrial and Systems Engineering provides information about educational programs, research facilities and projects. Course schedules and lists of faculty, staff and students are also available.
- KEYWORDS: Curriculum, Industrial Engineering, Systems Engineering
- AUDIENCE: Engineering Students, Industrial Engineers, Systems Engineers
- CONTACT: T. Govindaraj
  tg@isye.gatech.edu
- FREE

http://isye.gatech.edu/

Industrial Engineering at Clemson University ★★★

The WWW server of the Clemson University Industrial Engineering Department in South Carolina provides detailed information about the undergraduate and graduate programs offered. Also available are a faculty listing and a schedule of upcoming seminars. The site has a searchable index.
- KEYWORDS: Engineering, Industrial Engineering
- AUDIENCE: Engineering Students, Industrial Engineers
- CONTACT: Michael Leonard
  michael.leonard@eng.clemson.edu
- FREE

http://ie.eng.clemson.edu/

gopher://ie.eng.clemson.edu/

Industrial Engineering Virtual Library ★★★

The Industrial Engineering Virtual Library provides pointers to various Internet resources in the field of Industrial Engineering. Currently available are links to the departments of Industrial Engineering of several universities. The site is under continuous contruction - more resources will be added as they become available.
- KEYWORDS: Industrial Engineering, Operations Research
- AUDIENCE: Industrial Engineers
- CONTACT: T. Govindaraj
  tg@isye.gatech.edu
- FREE

http://isye.gatech.edu/www-ie/

Istituto di Tecnologie Industriali e Automazione ★★

The Institute of Industrial Technologies and Automation (ITIA) page gives general information about ITIA, its groups and activities. There is access to people's phone numbers, offices and email addresses
- KEYWORDS: Graduate Education, Scientific Research
- AUDIENCE: Engineers, Science Researchers
- CONTACT: postmaster@itia.mi.cnr.it
- FREE

http://www.itia.mi.cnr.it

Mississippi State University Department of Industrial Engineering ★★★

The WWW server of the Mississippi State University Department of Industrial Engineering is still under construction. What is currently available is a faculty listing and an Industrial Engineering Program Guide for graduate students.
- KEYWORDS: Curriculum, Engineering, Industrial Engineering
- AUDIENCE: Engineering Students, Industrial Engineers
- CONTACT: Wonjang Baek
  baek@engr.msstate.edu
- FREE

http://www.msstate.edu/Dept/IE/

Nanothinc's World of Nanotechnology ★★★

This site contains information about Nanothinc, a company that provides information services concerning nanotechnology.
- KEYWORDS: Companies, Nanotechnology, Product Information
- AUDIENCE: Business Professionals, Nanotechnology Enthusiasts
- CONTACT: webmaster@nanothinc.com
- FREE

http://nanothinc.com/

Peter L. Jackson Homepage ★★★★

Peter L. Jackson is an Associate Professor at the School of Operations Research and Industrial Engineering, Cornell University. His homepage provides detailed hypertext descriptions of a set of educational software tools developed by him and his associates. The software itself is also available at the site. The fields covered by the tools include Manufacturing Systems Design and Engineering Economics.
- KEYWORDS: Educational Software, Engineering Economics, Industrial Engineering
- AUDIENCE: Engineering Students
- CONTACT: Peter L. Jackson
  pj16@cornell.edu
- FREE

ftp://tomcat.synthesis.cornell.edu/pub/Jackson/overview.html

School of Operations Research and Industrial Engineering at Cornell University ★★★★

The WWW server of the School of Operations Research and Industrial Engineering at Cornell University in New York provides a list of courses offered, a list of publications (with some publications available online in PostScript form) and an Annual Report. Also included are links to the homepages of the faculty members.
- KEYWORDS: Curriculum, Engineering, Operations Research
- AUDIENCE: Educators, Engineering Students, Industrial Engineers
- CONTACT: adm@orie.cornell.edu
- FREE

http://ftp.orie.cornell.edu/

Industrial Engineering – Mechanical Engineering

Systems Integration Laboratory at UC Berkeley (SIL) ★★★

The Systems Integration Laboratory (SIL) is a research and educational laboratory in the Department of Industrial Engineering and Operations Research (IEOR) at the University of California at Berkeley. This facility has two main goals - 'hands-on' undergraduate and graduate engineering instruction, and graduate research in manufacturing and engineering systems design. The WWW server also provides information about the laboratory's staff and research. An archive of publications from the SIL and from other research groups is available. The publications are in PostScript form. Abstracts of the lab's work and descriptions of the courses offered are also provided.

KEYWORDS Industrial Engineering, Manufacturing, Operations Research
AUDIENCE Engineering Students, Industrial Engineers
CONTACT Steve Chick
chick@delft.berkeley.edu
FREE

http://maastricht.berkeley.edu/

Material Science

See also
Education · *Universities - Europe*
Education · *Universities - United States*
Science · *Earth Sciences*
Science · *Geosciences*
Science · *Space Science*

J.D. McDonald's Mineral Formula Database-Search ★★★

This is a searchable gopher containing the names and chemical formulae of all 3507 minerals. The database produces ASCII(Text) representations of the chemical formulas of the minerals. A note on the page indicates that the database is still in testing and warns that one should double check any results.

KEYWORDS Geology, Minerals
AUDIENCE Educators (University), Geologists, Mineral Enthusiasts, Students (University)
CONTACT Doug McDonald
mcdonald@aries.scs.uiuc.edu
FREE

gopher://wombat.es.mq.edu.au/1pc%3a/
geology/minerals/mineral.dbf

Los Alamos National Lab Materials Science and Technology Group ★★★

The WWW server of the Los Alamos National Lab Materials Science and Technology Group provides information about the group's research, facilities and members. Links to the homepages of individual researchers are also included, with more detailed information about each member's research.

KEYWORDS Material Science, Materials Engineering, Metallurgy
AUDIENCE Engineers, Materials Scientists

CONTACT Dave Carter
carter@lanl.gov
FREE

http://www.mst6.lanl.gov/

Rockhounds Information Page ★★★★

This page was created by mineral enthusiasts, and contains links to sites of interest to mineral enthusiasts. It also contains the archive for the Rockhounds Mailing List. This is a good starting point for those interested in minerals and rockhounding.

KEYWORDS Earth Sciences, Geology, Minerals
AUDIENCE General Public, Mineral Enthusiasts, Rock Collectors, Students (Primary/Secondary)
CONTACT rockhounds-owner@infodyn.com
FREE

http://www.rahul.net/infodyn/
rockhounds/rockhounds.html

The Royal Institute Of Technology Department of Material Science and Engineering ★★★

The WWW server of The Royal Institute Of Technology Department of Material Science and Engineering in Stockholm, Sweden provides detailed information about the departments' divisions, workers and research areas. Also available is information for students about courses and software tools developed at the department.

KEYWORDS Curriculum, Material Science, Materials Engineering, Sweden
AUDIENCE Engineering Students, Materials Engineers, Materials Scientists
CONTACT mickus@met.kth.se
FREE

http://www.met.kth.se/

Stanislaw Staszic University of Mining and Metallurgy ★★★

This site provides information on the administration of the Stanislaw Staszic University of Mining and Metallurgy, Poland. It also contains information about academic programs, local news, software, library resources & services, public file archives, anonymous FTP, and more. In addition, it makes connections to other gophers.

KEYWORDS Education (College/University), Metallurgy, Mining, Poland
AUDIENCE Eastern Europe Residents, Engineers, Library Users, Mining Professionals
CONTACT Jaroslaw Strzalkowski
js@uci.agh.edu.pl
FREE

gopher://gopher.uci.agh.edu.pl/

Vitoria.html ★★★

The home page of Vitoria, the capital of Alvala and de facto political and institutional capital of the Basque Country, in Spain, presents hypertext information focusing on its indigenous industries, including metallurgy, chemistry, textile, and rubber.

KEYWORDS Chemistry, Metallurgy, Spain, Textiles
AUDIENCE Basque Scholars, Business Entrepreneurs, Spain Residents, Tourists
CONTACT webmaster@we.lc.ehu.es
FREE

http://www.we.lc.ehu.es/BasqueCountry/
Vitoria.html

Mechanical Engineering

See also
Computing & Mathematics · *Applications*
Computing & Mathematics · *Artificial Intelligence*
Computing & Mathematics · *Computer Science*
Science · *Physics*

1995 International BEAM Robot Games ★★★

The BEAM (Biology, Electronics, Aesthetics, and Mechanics) Robot Olympics is an annual competition to design and build working robots that compete against each other to perform specific tasks. This site houses the archives from the 1995 competition, and promises information in the fall for the 1996 competition. Users can find out some background information about the event, see images of robots from the past, download the plans for building certain robots, or visit other sites related to robots and robotcompetitions.

KEYWORDS Artificial Intelligence, Engineering, Robotics, Technology
AUDIENCE Robot Designers, Robot Enthuisasts, Robotics Engineers
CONTACT Mark W. Tilden
mwtilden@lanl.gov
FREE

http://sst.lanl.gov/robot/

Control Technology Corporation ★★★

The Control Technology Corporation produces electronic control systems for automation in the manufacturing process. The company specializes in motion control, analog circuit design, control software engineering, language technology, and user interface design.

KEYWORDS Companies, Control Engineering, Software Engineering, Technology
AUDIENCE Control Engineers, Engineers, Technology Experts
CONTACT info@control.com
FREE

http://www.control.com/

Energy Systems Laboratory ★★★

The Energy Systems Laboratory (ESL) at Texas A&M University conducts research on the subject of alternative energy and energy conservation. Their Web site includes lists of publications by the ESL, organized by subject, as well as information about available ESL software. ESL newsletters are available, with information about ESL projects and articles on topics such as Flow Meters Diagnostics and Air Conditioning and Heat Pump Research.

Keywords Energy Conservation, Software, Solar Energy
Audience Energy Researchers, Mechanical Engineers
Contact www@www-esl.tamu.edu
Free

http://loanstar.tamu.edu/

Lancet.mit.edu ★★

This Web site provides information about the The New Products Program, a collaborative project between the departments of Mechanical Engineering and Electrical Engineering in the School of Engineering at MIT that focuses on product design. Users will find press coverage, background about the project and resource lists, along with a C++ genetic algorithms library. Also included are some current projects created by the group, such as a 'Skeeter' human powered hydrofoil, with background, materials information, and videos.

Keywords Design, Electrical Engineering, Universities
Audience Electrical Engineering Students, Engineering Educators, Mechanical Engineering Students
Contact webmaster@lancet.mit.edu
Free

http://lancet.mit.edu/

The MOSES Project at Leeds and Loughborough ★★★

The MOSES Project at Leeds and Loughborough colleges in England focuses on making reference models for complex systems descriptions. This site provides MOSES project information as well as links to other Loughborough University servers. It includes backgrounds of each of the research areas of the projects, including specification modelling and harmonization. Users will find a bibliography of project publications available in postscript and DVI on subjects such as Assembly Representation with a Product Data Framework and Application Protocols. Users may also access Loughborough University information and the computing services gopher.

Keywords Complex Systems
Audience Engineers, Mechanical Engineers
Contact Pete Dawson
pdawson@leva.leeds.ac.uk
Free

http://levi.lut.ac.uk

Nuclear Engineering

See also
Business & Economics · *Industries*
Computing & Mathematics · *Computer Science*
Government & Politics · *Agencies*
Science · *Environmental Sciences*
Science · *Physics*

Institute for Process Engineering and Power Plant Research ★★★

The Institute for Process Engineering and Power Plant Research (IPEPPR) offers information on its facilities and current research projects. IPEPPR does research in the areas of energy conversion, heat technology, power plant controls, combustion technology, air pollution control, power generation and automatic control. This site gives access to links with information about departments, process engineering, air quality, combustion technology, boiler technology, power generation and automatic control.

Keywords Education, Research
Audience Engineers, Power Plant Operators, Researchers
Contact postmaster@ivd.uni-stuttgart.de
Free

http://www.ivd.uni-stuttgart.de

Joint Institute for Nuclear Research ★★★

The Joint Institute for Nuclear Research (JINR) brings together the efforts, the scientific research and material potential of the eighteen nations involved in studying fundamental properties of matter. JINR's home page provides information about activities, research, conferences and events in the nuclear physics community. This site has links to such laboratories as the Bogoliubov Laboratory of Theoretical Physics and the FrankLaboratory of Neutron Physics.

Keywords Conferences, Nuclear Physics, Particle Physics, Research
Audience Nuclear Physicists, Researchers, Scientists, Theoretical Physicists
Contact main@ssd.jinr.dubna.su
Free

http://www.jinr.dubna.su

Manifest ★★★

This document is an introduction to a hypertext database describing the accident at the Chernobyl Nuclear Power Plant in 1986. The database draws on both an official version of events published in 1992, resources from the Chernobyl Kurchatov Institute Expedition and a number of publications in the scientific press and mass media.

Keywords Energy, Environment, Nuclear Safety
Audience Engineers, Environmental Researchers, Environmental Scientists, Environmentalists
Free

http://polyn.net.kiae.su/polyn/manifest.html

The Nuke server ★★★★

A very large archive of nuclear energy, science, medicine and weapons information, the Nuke server presents hundreds of documents, indices, and links to various aspects of Nuclear Power and related research. Definitive indices of scientists and administrators in every major American nuclear-related endeavor are presented here, as well as a wide array of U.S. Government documents on Nuclear Power, weapons, etc.

Keywords Energy, Nuclear Medicine, Nuclear Safety, Politics
Audience Medical Practitioners, Nuclear Scientists, Physicists, Toxicologists
Contact Benjamin J. Slone, III
sloneb@nuke.handheld.com
Free

http://nuke.handheld.com/

United Nations International Atomic Energy Agency Gopher Service ★★★

This Gopher has directories information about the International Atomic Energy Agency, their programs, and their Public Information News Services. Also included is access to the International Nuclear Information System directory, and the International Information System for the Agricultural Sciences and Technology directory.

Keywords Atomic Energy, Energy, Public Policy, United Nations
Audience Activists, Researchers, Science Researchers
Free

gopher://nesirs01.iaea.or.at:70/1

University of California at Berkeley Department of Nuclear Engineering ★★★

The University of California at Berkeley Department of Nuclear Engineering Web site provides information about the Department and its research projects. Users will find faculty details and student home pages, as well as current course listings. Research areas with technical reports, papers and general news and information include — Fusion, Nuclear Materials, Thermal Hydraulics, Computational Neutronics, and Radioactive Waste Management. The Advanced Designs section provides data about different types of reactors and their purposes. Links to other Nuclear Engineering Web sites and University of California information are also given.

Keywords Computational Neuroscience, Fusion
Audience Engineering Students, Nuclear Engineers, Nuclear Scientists
Contact J. Vujic
tapostma@nuc.berkeley.edu.
Free

http://neutrino.nuc.berkeley.edu

Standards

See also
Computing & Mathematics · *Computer Science*
Engineering & Technology · *Industrial Engineering*
Government & Politics · *Agencies*
Science · *Organizations*

Continuous Quality Improvement ★★

This Clemson University College of Engineering page provides a collection of materials relating to the elimination of defects through comprehensive quality control in industry, government, and universities.
- KEYWORDS: Industrial Engineering, Quality Control
- AUDIENCE: Administrators, Managers
- CONTACT: D.L. Kimbler
  quality@eng.clemson.edu
- FREE

http://deming.eng.clemson.edu

Document Center Home Page ★★★

This is the site for a hard-copy document-delivery service for government and industry specifications and standards. The Document Center has the complete Department of Defense (DoD) Index of Specifications and Standards collection, as well as the complete U.S. collection of the American Society for Testing Materials (ASTM). The Center also has additional industry (ANSI, SAE, IPC, IEEE, EIA, ASME, ISO, IEC, UL) and government (NASA, DLA, FAA) documentation.
- KEYWORDS: Companies, Documents, Information Retrieval, Transportation
- AUDIENCE: Business Researchers, Document Delivery Professionals
- CONTACT: Document Center
  info@doccenter.com
- FREE

http://www.service.com/doccenter/home.html

The Institute of Electrical and Electronics Engineers ★★★

This gopher site at The Institute of Electrical and Electronics Engineers provides a collection of resources relevant to electrical and electronic engineers. It includes information on the resources offered by the organization such as important publications, standards, new technologies, software, student branch activities, and press releases.
- KEYWORDS: Biosciences, Computer Technology, Electrical Engineering, Electronics, Engineering
- AUDIENCE: Biomedical Engineers, Electrical Engineers, Engineers, Software Engineers
- CONTACT: gopher-dev@gopher.ieee.org
- FREE

gopher://gopher.ieee.org/

Manufacturing Systems Integration Division (MSID) ★★★

This Web server provides information on the Manufacturing Systems Integration Division (MSID) of the National Institute of Standards and Technology. MSID contributes to the research and development of standards and technologies leading to the implementation of virtual manufacturing enterprises. MSID uses information technology to implement computer-aided integrated manufacturing systems. This page provides information on the staff, an overview of the department, strategic plan, publications, and more.
- KEYWORDS: Industrial Engineering, Manufacturing, Organizations, Technology
- AUDIENCE: Computer Professionals, Manufacturers
- FREE

http://elib.cme.nist.gov

National Institute of Standards and Technology WWW Homepage ★★★★

The WWW homepage of the U.S. National Institute of Standards and Technology (NIST) contains comprehensive information about NIST. Provided are descriptions of NIST and its research programs, online archives of some NIST publications, news releases, conference announcements and budget information. The site has a searchable index.
- KEYWORDS: Engineering, Research
- AUDIENCE: Engineers, Industrial Professionals
- CONTACT: webmaster@nist.gov
- FREE

http://www.nist.gov/welcome.html

SPA System Gopher ★★

This is a gopher server of the Institute of Electrical and Electronic Engineers, Inc., (IEEE) Standards Department. It contains information on the Standard Process Automation System (SPA), and its FTP archives, which contain software. It also contains information on the Standard Generalized Markup Language (SGML), of which the HyperText Markup Language is a subset.
- KEYWORDS: Computing, Electrical Engineering, Electronics, Hypertext
- AUDIENCE: Computer Engineers, Electrical Engineers, Engineers
- FREE

gopher://stdsbbs.ieee.org/

Technology

See also
Arts & Music · *Architecture*
Arts & Music · *Design*
Computing & Mathematics · *Artificial Intelligence*
Science · *Biosciences*
Science · *Physics*

(ESBA) Electronics and Sensor Based Applications ★★★

The Electronics and Sensor Based Application (ESBA) Unit at the Institute for Systems Engineering and Informatics in Ispra, Italy is a Joint Research Centre for The Commission of the European Communities. It develops software and hardware systems in the fields of Data Acquisition, Data Visualisation, Surveillance, Mobile Robotics and Software Application Development. Their page provides links to their Data Visualisation Group and Mobile Robotics Group.
- KEYWORDS: Italy, Mobile Robotics, Software, Software Development
- AUDIENCE: Engineers, Software Developers
- FREE

http://elec.jrc.it/

Alden Electronics, Inc. ★★★

Alden Electronics, Inc. provides weather data systems, marine electronics and specialized imaging products and papers. The home provides access to company resources and product information.
- KEYWORDS: Companies, Data Systems, Marine Sciences, Weather
- AUDIENCE: GIS Professionals, Marine Biologists, Technologists
- CONTACT: info@alden.com
- FREE

http://www.alden.com/

California Institute of Technology ★★★

The California Institute of Technology WWW site offers information on the academic programs and research projects of this engineering and science technology-oriented school. Users can browse a course catalog, as well as search through a campus phonebook to find the person or department they want. In addition, this server allows users to connect to individual academic departments at Caltech. Users are also able to ftp selected technical reports as well as order reports not publically available.
- KEYWORDS: California, Engineering, Science
- AUDIENCE: Education Administrators (College), Educators, Students
- CONTACT: www@caltech.edu
- FREE

http://www.caltech.edu

ftp://ftp.cs.caltech.edu/tr

Center for the Development of Technological Leadership (CDTL) WWW

This server, offered by the Center for the Development of Technological Leadership, contains material on technological advances and their potential effect on society. Users can browse CenterPoint, the newsletter published by the center, as well as information on degree programs offered by the center. Information and links to other University of Minnesota departments is also available here.

KEYWORDS Management, Technology
AUDIENCE Engineers, System Designers
CONTACT Carl Steadman
carl@cdtl.umn.edu
FREE

http://www.cdtl.umn.edu

Chalmers University of Technology

This site is provided by the Swedish Chalmers University of Technology. It offers information on the academic programs and degrees conferred at the University. Users will also find material on the research interests, staff, and facilities of the University.

KEYWORDS Engineering, Sweden
AUDIENCE Educators, Engineers, Students
CONTACT webmaster@chalmers.se
FREE

http://www.chalmers.se

gopher://gopher.chalmers.se/

Coppe - The Engineering Graduate School and Research Center for the Federal University of Rio de Janeiro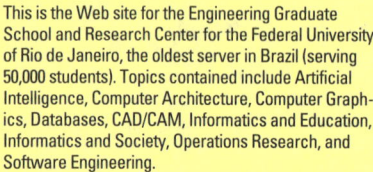

This is the Web site for the Engineering Graduate School and Research Center for the Federal University of Rio de Janeiro, the oldest server in Brazil (serving 50,000 students). Topics contained include Artificial Intelligence, Computer Architecture, Computer Graphics, Databases, CAD/CAM, Informatics and Education, Informatics and Society, Operations Research, and Software Engineering.

KEYWORDS Artificial Intelligence, Brazil, Computer Databases, Computer Technology
AUDIENCE Computer Engineers, Computer Graphic Designers, Computer Users
CONTACT Geraldo Xexeo
xexeo@cos.ufrj.br
FREE

http://guarani.cos.ufrj.br:8000/Home.html

Cornell University - Department of Computer Science Technical Report Library

This site is the online technical report library at the Cornell University Department of Computer Science. This is an entry point to a distributed technical report library developed by the ARPA-sponsored Computer Science Technical Report Project. This library contains technical reports from a number of participating institutions, including Cornell, UC Berkeley, Stanford and Carnegie Mellon Universities.

KEYWORDS Computer Science, Technical Reports
AUDIENCE Computer Scientists, Researchers, Technical Writers
CONTACT tech-reports@cs.cornell.edu.
FREE

http://cs-tr.cs.cornell.edu/

DISA/JIEO Center for Engineering

The Department of Defense Information Systems Agency (DISA) Joint Interoperability and Engineering Organization (JIEO) Center for Engineering (CFE) Web server provides the latest information on technology insertion activities for information systems in the U.S. Department of Defense. Information provided covers several technology insertion projects (ATM Technology Initiative, DISN Router System, etc). An interactive demonstration of the Modular Information Infrastructure Design and Analysis System is also provided.

KEYWORDS Engineering, Information Technology
AUDIENCE Engineers, Information Scientists, Network Developers
CONTACT riehlr@cc.ims.disa.mil
FREE

http://disa11.disa.atd.net/index.html

Department of Advanced Technology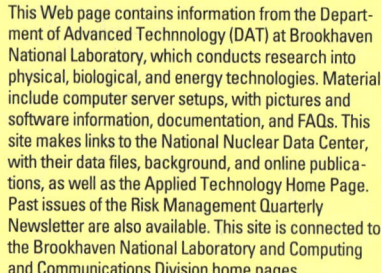

This Web page contains information from the Department of Advanced Technnology (DAT) at Brookhaven National Laboratory, which conducts research into physical, biological, and energy technologies. Materials include computer server setups, with pictures and software information, documentation, and FAQs. This site makes links to the National Nuclear Data Center, with their data files, background, and online publications, as well as the Applied Technology Home Page. Past issues of the Risk Management Quarterly Newsletter are also available. This site is connected to the Brookhaven National Laboratory and Computing and Communications Division home pages.

KEYWORDS Biotechnology, Energy
AUDIENCE Computer Experts, Energy Researchers
CONTACT Yako Sanborn
yako@bnl.gov
FREE

http://necs01.dne.bnl.gov

Department of Robotics and Digital Technology

The Department of Robotics and Digital Technology home page at Monash University supplies information on the research activities, technical reports and staff. There are links to the other departments in computing and information technologies as well as other WWW servers.

KEYWORDS Australia, Education (College/University), Robotics, Technical Reports, Technology
AUDIENCE Australians, Robotic Enthusiasts, Students
CONTACT given.surname@rdt.monash.edu.au
FREE

http://www.rdt.monash.edu.au/

Der Technischen Universitaet Chemnitz-Zwickau

This gopher server provides extensive information on the Technical University of Chemnitz-Zwickau, Germany. This includes data on the different programs, the library, student services, computing services, faculty directory, and other useful information. It also provides links to other gophers.

KEYWORDS Computer Technology, Germany, University Administration
AUDIENCE Academics, Germans, Professors, Students
CONTACT Frank Richter
F.Richter@hrz.tu-chemnitz.de
FREE

gopher://gopher.tu-chemnitz.de/

The ESPRIT Networks of Excellence Information Service

The ESPRIT Specific Research and Technological Development Programme in Information Technology, a division of the European Commission, is designed to be a technological information base for European industrial improvement. Their home page provides Information Technology research project summaries, with objectives, keywords, and contact information, searchable by topic, keyword, or acronym. Links to the various home pages of groups working within ESPRIT are included, with extensive coverage of topics such as computer vision, databases, and distributed systems. Users can also find out about calls for proposals and research funding program opportunities.

KEYWORDS Computing, Distributed Systems, Industry, Information Technology
AUDIENCE Business Professionals, Europeans
CONTACT Nick Cook
nick.cook@newcastle.ac.uk
FREE

http://newcastle.cabernet.esprit.ec.org/index.html

Electrical Engineering at Delft University of Technology Home Page

The Electrical Engineering at Delft University of Technology Home Page is designed to provide information about their faculty and projects. Pages on Telecommunications, Electronics and Control Engineering Laboratory offer research materials, publications listings, news and specific project home pages. The Research Reports from 1989-1993 are also compiled. Users will find materials about the education programs at Delft University in the Netherlands, calendars of upcoming events and conferences, and information about department services.

Keywords Electrical Engineering, Electronics, Telecommunications
Audience Electrical Engineers, Engineering Students, Engineers
Contact webmaster@et.tudelft.nl
Free

http://muresh.et.tudelft.nl

Enterprise Integration Technologies (EIT) ★★★

Enterprise Integration Technologies (EIT) is a research and development and consulting company specializing in information technology for electronic commerce, collaborative engineering and agile manufacturing. There is also a searchable index and links to information about the company.

Keywords Business, Commerce, Information Technology
Audience Commerce Professionals, Engineers
Contact webmaster@eit.com
Free

http://www.eit.com

Faculty of Applied Science at Simon Fraser University ★★★

This is a gopher site of the Faculty of Applied Science at Simon Fraser University (SFU), Burnaby, Canada. It provides information on such areas as communications, computing science, engineering science, the School of Kinesiology and the School of Resource and Environmental Management.

Keywords Canada, Communications, Education (College/University)
Audience Communications Students, Computer Students, Educators (University)
Contact webmaster@cs.sfu.ca
Free

gopher://fas.sfu.ca:80/

Georgia Institute of Technology ★★★

The Georgia Institute of Technology gopher server provides information about registrations, calendars, courses, computing resources, events, the alumni association, campus organizations, as well as continuing education courses. Users can also access information about the Georgia Institute of Technology Electrical and Computer Engineering Industrial Partnership Program. (This is a multi-level support structure designed to create an environment conducive to enhanced and accelerated technology and knowledge transfer between academia and industry.)

Keywords Continuing Education, Education (College/University), University Administration
Audience Educators (University), Students (Secondary/University)
Free

gopher://gopher.gatech.edu/

Gopher du Service Informatique Central ★★★

This site provides information about the Ecole Polytechnique Federale de Lausanne, a university in Lausanne, Switzerland. The information includes descriptions of academic and research programs; user support documents for computing platforms on campus such as DEC, HP, Sun, and Silicon Graphics; and documents about various departments with the university.

Keywords Academics\, Education (College/University), Switzerland, Technical Schools
Audience Educators, Engineers, Europeans, Switzerland Residents
Contact Claude Lecommandeur lecom@sic.epfl.ch
Free

gopher://cognac-f.epfl.ch/

Information Technology Architecture and Standards ★★★

The Information Technology Architecture and Standards page was designed by the University of Pennsyl-

---

Connections to Computer Standards
Is it 000100 or 000110?

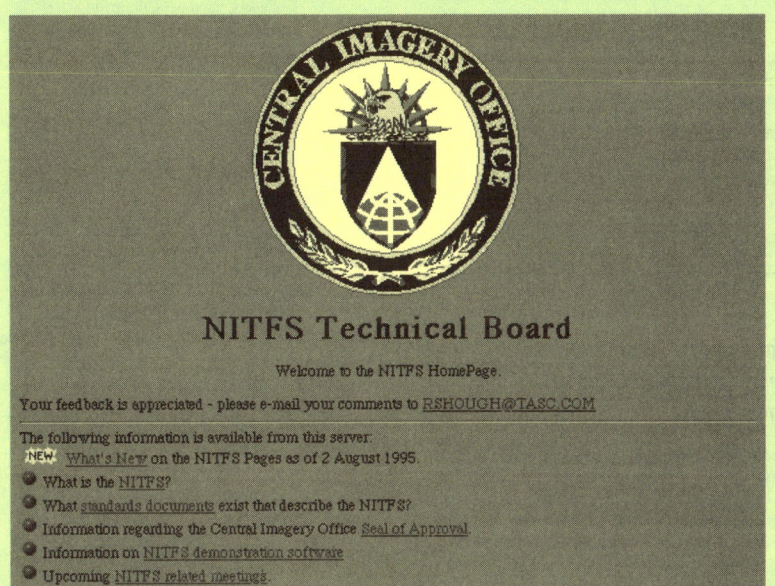

If you need information about the latest in computer (or computing) standards—including the Internet x.500 schema, graphical programming language standards, or the computing standards proposed by IEEE for electrical engineering drawing—the Internet offers a full basket of sites to consult.

You can also find out what the producers of various computing platforms are doing to arrive at a common standard so as to enable disparate computer systems to seamlessly "communicate" with one another— to allow Macintosh users, for instance, to share a PC-formatted disk as easily as if there were no differences in computing standards between Macs and PCs (currently you need special software to do this).

Additionally, you can get the U.S. Defense Department's index of specifications and standards for various products the government buys from private contractors. And you'll find sites devoted to graphical standards for games, as well as computer applications.

(ftp://stdsbbs.ieee.org/pub/)

also (http://info.mcc.ac.uk/CGU/ITTI/Stds/standards_announce.html)

vania to discuss the deployment and acquisition of future technologies. Users will find information about current projects in the fields of Network Architecture, Electronic Mail, and Distributed Computing. Each project description includes access to documents, papers, and research materials. Campus standards materials are also available in Adobe Acrobat form. Articles discussing principles for the use of information technology at the University are also provided, as well as links to other related Web sites.
Keywords Information Technology, Networking
Audience Network Developers
Contact Dr. Noam Arzt
arzt@isc.upenn.edu
Free

http://nextb.dccs.upenn.edu/techarch/itarch.html

The Integrated Science Program at Northwestern University ★★★

This site is a gopher server of the Integrated Science Program (ISP) at Northwestern University, Illinois. It offers information on the ISP, the seminar calendar, the ISP directory, ISP alumni email addresses, and more. It provides access to other gophers on campus as well as off campus.
Keywords Graduate Education, Science, Scientific Research
Audience Educators (University), Mathematicians, Scientists, Students (Secondary)
Free

gopher://gopher.isp.nwu.edu/

Istanbul Technical University ★★★

The Istanbul Technical University (ITU) gives information about the University, its history, the campus, the facilities and educational departments. ITU covers a large area of technology education and research including aeronautics, architecture, physics, civil, mechanical and marine engineering. There are also links to related sites on the Internet, as well as information about Turkey and Istanbul.
Keywords Education (College/University), Engineering, Turkey
Audience Engineers, Students, Technology Enthusiasts, Turks
Contact Hakan Durgut
hakan@itu.edu.tr
Free

http://www.itu.edu.tr

LANL's (Los Alamos National Laboratory) Applied Robotics and Automation ★★★

This document is a guide to the information available from the Applied Robotics and Automation Section of Los Alamos National Laboratory (LANL). Links are provided to Contaminant Analysis Automation Project, Biotechnology Projects such as the Human Genome Project, and other LANL servers.
Keywords Human Genome Project, Research Labs, Robotics
Audience Biologists, Engineers, Researchers
Contact erkkila@lanl.gov
Free

http://eclipse.esa.lanl.gov/

LUT/IT GN - A Gopher/HTTP Server ★★

The Lappeenranta University of Technology does teaching and research for the integration of business and technology. This server supports both Gopher and WWW clients, and in addition to links at the University, it provides links to Sun SparcStation workstations, Matola - CC Snake Workstations, and other networking resources.
Keywords Information Technology, Mechanical Engineering, Scientific Research
Audience Engineers, Information Technologist, Researchers
Free

http://www.it.lut.fi

 ### Lucasfilm's THX Home Page  ★★★

This site offers extensive information on Lucasfilm's THX sound system standard. Users will find information on both home and theatre THX systems, including certification requirements, lists of approved equipment, THX specifications, and more. In addition, users can search for THX equipped theatres around the world, an archive of articles about THX, and much more.
Keywords Audio Technology, Consumer Electronics, Entertainment Technology, Movies
Audience Audio Enthusiasts, Audiophiles, Professional Audio Engineers
Contact admin@lum.com
Free

http://www.thx.com/thx/

Lund Institute of Technology ★★★

The Lund Institute of Technology offers education and research in the fields of chemistry, as well as chemical, civil, mechanical, and electrical engineering, and also engineering physics and architecture. The page gives information about the departments, research activities and facilities. There are links to student societies, information about Sweden and other WWW sites.
Keywords Architecture, Engineering
Audience Computer Scientists, Engineers, Swedes
Contact Christer Holmfors
ch@efd.lth.se
Free

http://www.lth.se

MCNC Site for Information and Electronics ★★★

MCNC (Microelectronics, Computing and Networking Center) is a private, nonprofit corporation whose aim is to support education and industry and to enhance technology-based economic development in North Carolina. Their Site for Information and Electronics provides information about their research in microelectronics, computing and networking.
Keywords Electronics, Supercomputing
Audience Computer Scientists, Engineers, Information Technologists
Contact webcrew@mcnc.org
Free

http://www.mcnc.org

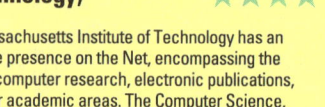 ### MILLIPORE Corporation ★★★

The Millipore Corporation produces purification technology for research and manufacturing needs. The home page offers information about products, services, applications and databases for the company. There are also catalogs for technology in laboratory water purification products, laboratory research products, microelectronics contamination control products and pharmaceutical/biotechnology products.
Keywords Biotechnology, Environment, Microelectronics, Scientific Research
Audience Biotechnologists, Researchers, Scientists
Contact webmaster@www.millipore.com
Free

http://www.millipore.com/

The MIT Home Page (Massachusetts Institute of Technology) ★★★★

The Massachusetts Institute of Technology has an extensive presence on the Net, encompassing the latest in computer research, electronic publications, and other academic areas. The Computer Science, Artificial Intelligence, and Media Labs can be accessed through links found here. There is also a great deal of Internet-related information here, along with a wealth of general-interest information.
Keywords Computer Science, Massachusetts, Technological Advances
Audience Academics, Computer Scientists, Internet Researchers, Students (University)
Contact web-request@mit.edu
Free

http://web.mit.edu/

gopher://gopher.mit.edu

ftp://net-dist.mit.edu

Michigan Technological University ★★★

This site is a gopher server of Michigan Technological University. It provides information on the University, its academic departments, the Center for Computer-Assisted Language Instruction, the Seaman Mineralogi-

Technology

cal Museum, computing resources, the administration, registration, courses, online publications, sports and more. Access to other gophers is also provided.

Keywords Education (College/University), Michigan, University Administration
Audience Educators (University), Students (University)
Contact gmaint@mtu.edu
Free

gopher://opus.mtu.edu/

Mitsubishi Electric Research Laboratories (MERL) ★★★

Mitsubishi Electric Research Laboratories (MERL) conducts basic research on computers and their uses. MERL researchers are developing interactive computer environments to support collaborative learning and working. The home page gives an overview of their objectives and technical staff.

Keywords Computer Technology, Interactive Computing, Research Groups
Audience Computer Users
Contact webmaster@merl.com
Free

http://merl.com

Mizar, Inc. WWW Page ★★★

Mizar produces digital signal processors for Technical Instruments based computers. The boards are available for several BUS architectures includeing VME, PCI and ISA. The Mizar page provides product information, online manuals and technical support.

Keywords Computing, Digital Signal Processing, Hardware, Image Processing
Audience Computer Users, Digital Signal Processors, Technicians
Contact Michael Early
michael_early@mizarvme.com
Free

http://www.mizarvme.com

ftp://ftp.mizarvme.com/public

NASA Commercial Technology Network Home Page ★★★★

The NASA Commercial Technology Network provides information about NASA Technology Transfer programs. The Directory here allows users to look up different NASA technology centers and find out about their programs and projects, as well as accessing online publications and NASA newsletters. Their Agenda for Change document outlines NASA projects and objectives in commercial technologies. Users can also find out how to do research contracting work with NASA's Small Business Innovation Research project, as well as learning about their partnership programs. The TechTracS link provides access to NASA's commercial technology archives and abstracts, searchable by keywords or categories.

Keywords Space, Technology Transfer
Audience Engineers, Small Business Owners

Free

http://nctn.oact.hq.nasa.gov

NASA/JSC Engineering Computational Facility ★★

This is a gopher server maintained by NASA's Johnson Space Center (JSC) Engineering Computational Facility. It provides access to some computing related resources, such as bibliographies, Cray Computer Resources, and Internet service listings. There are also some links to some other NASA gophers.

Keywords Computer Applications, Engineering, NASA (National Aeronautics And Space Administration), Space Science
Audience Aeronautics Engineers, Aerospace Engineers, Computer Specialists
Contact Todd Phillips
todd@ftp.jsc.nasa.gov
Free

gopher://killerbee.jsc.nasa.gov/

New Jersey Institute of Technology ★★★★

New Jersey Institute of Technology (NJIT) is a public research university that has degree programs in engineering, architecture, computer science, management and related science. The NJIT offers access to a departments directory, faculty, support organizations and research centers. There is general information and resources on such topics as academic, administrative and campus events. The page has links to NJIT's campus wide information system as well as other sites on the Internet.

Keywords Computer Science, Educational Resources, Engineering, Technology
Audience Engineers, Researchers, Students, Technical Educators
Contact Alan Leurck
al@njit.edu
Free

http://www.njit.edu/

The Office of Research and Technology Transfer's Gopher Server at the University of Minnesota ★★★

This is the Office of Research and Technology Transfer's (ORTTA) Gopher Server at the University of Minnesota. It contains ORTTA late-breaking news, information about ORTTA contacts, policies and guidelines, rate schedules, funding opportunities, and research publications, as well as other information. It also provides access to other gophers.

Keywords Research, Technology, University Administration
Audience Academics, Business Professionals, Business Professionals, Science Researchers
Contact gopher@ortta.umn.edu
Free

gopher://gopher.ortta.umn.edu/

Oregon Graduate Institute ★★★★

The Oregon Graduate Institute of Science and Technology (OGI) is an academic facility dedicated to research and education in the physical and technological sciences. OGI works on contemporary scientific education, research and services for the region and nation. This site gives access to OGI's catalog, computer science and engineering departments, publications and other online education and research sites.

Keywords Graduated Education, Oregon, Research, Science
Audience Researchers, Scientists, Students, Technologists
Contact Dan Revel
revel@admin.ogi.edu
Free

http://www.ogi.edu/

SAIC - System Development Operation Center and Computer Security Library ★★★

The System Development Ops Center located at the Science Applications International Corporation (SAIC) provides high-technology services and products in areas of energy, environment, health, space science, and systems integration. The Center offers professional Web services with graphical design artist's support. The page gives information about products such as the Computer Misuse Detection System (CMDS) and services. There is also a link to the security library which contains security-related information and programs on the Internet.

Keywords Applications, Companies, Computer Security, Energy, Science, Technology
Audience Computer Security Experts, Government Agencies, Systems Operators
Contact Webmaster@mls.saic.com
Free

http://mls.saic.com

START Technology Partnership ★★★

This is a home page from START Technology Partnership - an independent consortium whose mission is to augment the commercialization activities of universities and research institutions in the Delaware Valley. The consortium brings together the combined expertise and resources of the Ben Franklin Technology Center and the British Technology Group USA (BTG USA) with leading regional venture capital funds, commercial organizations and law firms.

Keywords Intellectual Property, Non Profit Organizations, Technology Transfer
Audience Business Professionals, Entrepreneurs, Nonprofit Organizations, Pennsylvania Residents
Free

http://libertynet.org/business/econ-dev/ucsc/start.html

School of Engineering and Applied Science-University of Pennsylvania

This is the web server for the School of Engineering and Applied Science at the University of Pennsylvania. It provides links to information under these headings—Departments, Student Activities, Class Home Pages, Personal Home Pages, Interdisciplinary Labs and Institutes, Computing and Educational Technology Services, Other Web servers at Penn, and Gopher Information.

Keywords   Applied Sciences, Educational Technology, Engineering
Audience   Engineering Educators, Engineering Students
Contact   webmaster@www.seas.upenn.edu
Free

http://eniac.seas.upenn.edu/

Spatial Audio

This page presents an essay on spatial audio, with emphasis on recent developments. There is a collection of hyperlinked sources presented after the paper, and FTP archives of spatialization software and processed 3D audio files. Users can also link to information on the authors of the papers presented here, as well as to an archive of other reference material.

Keywords   Audio, Multimedia Technologies, Virtual Reality
Audience   Multimedia Enthusiasts, Professional Audio Engineers, Virtual Reality Enthusiasts
Contact   Elizabeth D. Mynatt beth@cc.gatech.edu
Free

http://www.cc.gatech.edu/gvu/multimedia/SpatSound.html

Stevens Institute of Technology EECS page

The Stevens Institute of Technology EECS Home Page provides potential students and other users with general information about the Department of Electrical Engineering and Computer Science. Users will find overviews of the graduate and undergraduate programs, course descriptions and prospectuses, and faculty descriptions and contact addresses. Information about the Stevens Institute Facilities is included, with hardware and software listings and hours of operation. FTP directories of research materials and papers from classes are also provided.

Keywords   Computer Science, Electrical Engineering
Audience   Computer Science Students, Education Professionals, Electrical Engineering Students
Contact   sahirns@menger.eecs.stevens-tech.edu
Free

http://menger.eecs.stevens-tech.edu

Tec de Monterrey

This web site provides information about the Technical Institute in Monterrey, Mexico (El Instituto Tecnológico y de Estudios Superiores de Monterrey). Users can find out about their activities, professors, course information, and other educational materials. Department listings include general information about their areas of specialty and research focuses. A calendar of upcoming events is also provided.

Keywords   Campus Information, Education (College/University), Mexico
Audience   Education Professionals, Mexicans, Students
Contact   webmaster@dch.mty.itesm.mx
Free

http://dch.mty.itesm.mx

The Tech

This server contains back issues of The Tech, MIT's oldest and largest newspaper. The current issue, as well as many issues since 1985, are available and searchable. Links are also provided to other MIT resources including a gallery of digital images, the complete works of William Shakespeare, The Tech Classics Archive, a list of college newspapers of the web, etc.

Keywords   Technological Advances, Technology Journals
Audience   Educators (University), Journalism Students, Shakespeare Enthusiasts, Students (University)
Contact   The Archive Team archive@the-tech.mit.edu
Free

http://the-tech.mit.edu:80/

Technical University in Zvolen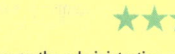

This site provides information on the administration and academic programs of the Technical University in Zvolen, Slovakia. It also contains information about Internet tools & software, FTP servers in Slovakia, Veronica, Archie servers, and more. There are also links to other resources on the Internet.

Keywords   Internet Tools, Slovakia, Technical Schools, University Administration
Audience   Engineers, Internet Users, Slovakia Residents
Contact   info@tuzvo.sk
Free

gopher://vsld.tuzvo.sk/

Technical University of Clausthal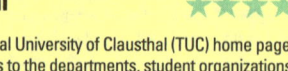

The Technical University of Clausthal (TUC) home page gives access to the departments, student organizations and the TUC special section. The page has information about the central institutions within the university. The special section includes a mineral collection and access to the library. There are links to the region and other information servers on the WWW.

Keywords   Educational Programs, Technology, Universities
Audience   Educators (University), Germans, Students (University)
Contact   webmaster@rz.tu-clausthal.de
Free

http://www.rz.tu-clausthal.de/

Technical University of Gdansk

This site describes the Technical University of Gdansk, Poland. It provides documents on the University's administration, academic programs, faculty, campus news, software, press, multimedia, student associations, and it has links to other gophers.

Keywords   Education (College/University), Poland, University Administration
Audience   Educators (University), Polish, Students (University)
Contact   adcent@pg.gda.pl
Free

gopher://sunrise.pg.gda.pl/

Technology Review Home Page

This site hosts the electronic version of MIT's Technology Review, a magazine about emerging technologies and their implications, which has been published since 1899. Users will find electronic versions of some of the current issue's articles (with related links if available), an online electronic bookstore, information on subscribing to the print version, and information on advertising in the Technology Review.

Keywords   Electronic Media, Newsletters, Technology
Audience   Futurists, General Public, Technology Enthusiasts
Contact   trcomments@mit.edu, technology-review-letters@mit.edu
Free

http://www.mit.edu:8001/afs/athena/org/t/techreview/www/tr.html

Telecom Bretagne Home Page

Telecom Bretagne is a Graduate School for Telecommunications Engineering with several campuses across France. Their home page provides information about the college and its research laboratories with research departments covering fields such as Image Processing, Artificial Intelligence and Cognitions, Parellelism, and Networks and Multimedia. This site allows the user to access library resources in French, and there are listings of departments, services offered, and student life at each campus.

Keywords   Artificial Intelligence, Engineering, France, Telecommunications
Audience   Engineering Students, French, Telecommuncations Researchers
Contact   w3admin@enst-bretagne.fr
Free

http://www.enst-bretagne.fr/Home_page_en.html

U.S.-Japan Center at the University of New Mexico

The US-Japan Center at the University of New Mexico focuses on training scientists in Japanese technology, as well as conducting research and outreach to Japan and its technological systems. Their Web site provides program information, application guidelines, research project backgrounds, and listings of their lecture series. There are also press releases and pictures from Japan, and information about organizations that collaborate with the center.

KEYWORDS Energy, Japan
AUDIENCE Engineers, Researchers, Scientists
CONTACT Jesse S. Casman
jcasman@unm.edu
FREE

http://nobunaga.unm.edu

The UC Berkeley Technical Report Server ★★★★

This server allows you to search for and view technical reports from different divisions within UC Berkeley, as well as from a number of cooperating institutions. This server is a product of the CSTR (Computer Science Technical Report) project, an ARPA sponsored effort to make the technical reports of the nation's top computer science departments available over the Internet.

KEYWORDS Computer Science, Technical Reports
AUDIENCE Computer Scientists, Researchers, Technical Writers
FREE

http://cs-tr.cs.berkeley.edu

University City Science Center ★★★

Welcome to the University City Science Center, a non-profit consortium of leading universities and organizations, one of the world's largest and most successful research parks and business incubators, and home to LibertyNet. Science Center provides three key services to science and technology-based companies - office and laboratory space, business development services, and research management assistance. The page offers you much information on the Center's activities.

KEYWORDS Business Services, Entrepreneurship, Non Profit Organizations, Technology Transfer
AUDIENCE Business Professionals, Entrepreneurs, Nonprofit Organizations, Pennsylvania Residents
CONTACT ucsc@libertynet.org
FREE

http://libertynet.org/business/econ-dev/ucsc/ucsc.html

University of Oregon CIS Software Engineering ★★★

The University of Oregon CIS Software Engineering home page provides information about the department as well as links to student and faculty projects. Included in the Design and Business Course are projects such as the Sierra's interactive movies and role playing games, and the Energy Outlet Electrical Conservation Center. Also included is the NERO distance learning project, with demonstrations and interview transcripts. Users can read a hypertext paper about online shopping and commerce using electronic systems, including diagrams and pictures.

KEYWORDS Computer Science, Internet Shopping, Software Engineering
AUDIENCE Computer Science Educators, Engineering Students, Software Engineers
CONTACT akm@cs.uoregon.edu
FREE

http://maxwell.cs.uoregon.edu/

Connections to Starship Design
"Beam me up, Scotty"

That familiar line from the original Star Trek series was sometimes a plea from a crew member who wanted to leave the surface of some harsh planet and return to the "U.S.S. Starship Enterprise."

The "Starship Design" page allows you to learn more than you ever imagined about the design of starships, while joining (and/or attending) the Lunar Institute of Technology's College of Engineering.

Here you'll learn about Pioneer and Voyager rockets, fission rockets like Orion, and fusion engine rockets like Daedalus and Ramjets. You'll also learn about magnetic sails, solar photon thrusters, and solar and laser sails. To propel the Daedalus-class vehicle, for instance, you would need 27,000 metric tons of helium-3 (which isn't available on earth). To construct this vehicle, you would first need to invent a number of self-reproducing floating "atmosphere mining machines," which would be released in Jupiter's atmosphere. These probes would collect helium-3, and send it to Daedalus—hanging in orbit around the giant red planet.

(http://sunsite.unc.edu/lunar/starship.html)

Transportation Engineering

See also
Government & Politics · *Cities*
Government & Politics · *Issues*
Popular Culture & Entertainment · *Weather & Traffic*
Science · *Environmental Sciences*

Air Force Avionics Directorate ★★

This server provides information about the US Air Force Wright Laboratory and their Avionics Directorate. The Wright Laboratory performs research into aeronautical engineering. This server provides information on the Laboratory's research activities, provides access to technical resources such as library services, and offers news and announcements from the Laboratory.

KEYWORDS Aeronautics, Air Force, Aviation, Engineering
AUDIENCE Aeronautics Engineers, Aerospace Engineers, Military Personnel
CONTACT wl_cc@amspr2.wpafb.af.mil
FREE

gopher://gopher.aa.wpafb.af.mil/

CityTrans/InterTraffic Asia '95 ★★★★

This is the Web site for the City Planning, Transportation and Traffic Engineering Conference scheduled September 21-24 1995 at the World Trade Centre in Singapore. The Conference will focus on Urban Planning, Infrastructure and Transportation: Solutions for the Asia Pacific. The page offers visitor information with a schedule of conferences such as The Future of Public Transportation in the Asia Pacific, and Cities in a Global World. This site also offers details on the conference exhibit, highlighting The Singapore Government Pavilion and more.

KEYWORDS Conferences, Singapore, Transportation, Urban Planning
AUDIENCE Asian Pacific Developers, Business Community, Urban Developers
CONTACT mpconven@singnet.com.sg
FREE

http://silkroute.com/silkroute/convention/mp/citytran/

Cyberspace World Railroad ★★★

The Cyberspace World Railroad was created for railroad lovers and train enthusiasts, as well as professional railroad engineers. Users will find monthly articles about railroads, new trains, and transportation issues. Newsletters and magazines from railroad companies are provided, along with general United Transportation Union news. Pictures of locomotives are provided, and a library of transportation documents, available in Zip format, is also included. The Lounge Car includes personal travel stories involving trains. Users will also find specific timetables for Amtrak, Chicago Metra Commuter Rail System and Canadian Rail & Transit.

KEYWORDS Railroads, Transportation, Travel
AUDIENCE Railroad Enthusiasts, Tourists, Travelers
CONTACT Daniel S. Dawdy
dsdawdy@mcs.com
FREE

http://www.mcs.com/~dsdawdy/cyberoad.html

Partners for Advanced Transit and Highways (PATH) ★★★

The Partners for Advanced Transit and Highways (PATH) page, at the University of California at Berkeley, provides information about its research projects in autonomous vehicle development, freeway services patrol, and traffic simulation and statistics. The PATH page gives announcements, in addition to information about its researchers and newsletter. There are also links to transportation research centers and traffic reports.

KEYWORDS Education (College/University), Technology, Transportation Research
AUDIENCE Educators, Students, Technology Researchers, Transportaion Engineers
CONTACT Karl Petty
pettyk@www-path.eecs.berkeley.edu
FREE

http://www-path.eecs.berkeley.edu/

Railroad-Related Internet Resources ★★★

This WWW server provides pointers to interesting and important railroad-related sources on the Internet. Some model-railroading data is also included. The information is searchable by a table of contents.

KEYWORDS Internet Guides, Railroads, Transportation, Travel
AUDIENCE Railroad Enthusiasts, Tourists, Travelers
CONTACT Robert W. Bowdidge
bowdidge@
FREE

http://www-cse.ucsd.edu/users/bowdidge/railroad/rail-home.html

Government & Politics

Agencies	313
Career & Employment	320
Cities	320
Countries	330
Doctrines	339
History	339
Individuals	340
International	340
Issues	344
Military	346
Policies	349
Political Science	353
Reference	355
Regions	359
States	362

Agencies

See also
Business & Economics · *Finance*
Education · *Organizations*
Government & Politics · *States*
Health & Medicine · *Public Health*

1995 United States Budget Gopher Server ★★★

The 1995 United States Budget Gopher Server is a large archive of budget-related documents, including speeches, the President's Budget Statement, OMB circulars, all the text and various forms of the budget so far, and a search engine to make wading through it all easier. This is administered by the Federal Government.

KEYWORDS   Budget (US), Economics, Federal Government (US), Taxes
AUDIENCE   Business Analysts, Economists, Journalists, Political Scientists
CONTACT   root@sunny.stat-usa.gov
FREE

gopher://sunny.stat-usa.gov/11/BUDGETFY95

Argentina's Ministry of Foreign Affairs ★★★

This home page of Argentina's Ministry of Foreign Affairs provides information on Internet networking, current events, tourist resources, and politics and economics. NAFTA, the United Nations, and the World Bank, are covered and links are made to a number of Chilean and Brazilian servers.

KEYWORDS   Argentina
AUDIENCE   Argentina Residents, Latin Americans, Market Analysts, Tourists
CONTACT   nic-arnet@atina.ar
FREE

http://www.mrec.ar/

gopher://gopher.ar/

CIA Home Page ★★★★

The Central Intelligence Agency's home page contains two searchable databases. The first is the CIA's World Factbook (1994) a compendium of publicly-available information on population, government, terrain, and other information on every nation in the world. The second is the CIA's factbook on intelligence, a volume of information on the CIA and its background, including answers to frequently-asked questions and other data about the Agency and its duties.

KEYWORDS   Federal Government (US), International Relations
AUDIENCE   Government Students, Political Researchers

FREE

http://www.ic.gov/

CLIO — National Archives Gopher/WWW ★★

CLIO is the name of an information system that contains data from the U.S. National Archives and Records Administration (NARA), its holdings, and activities. It offers descriptions of the various government documents and publications held by NARA, and instructions for ordering them. The site also provides access to the Federal Register which acts as the Government's central publication point for laws, Presidential documents, proposed and final Executive Branch regulations, and other legal publications.

KEYWORDS   Federal Documents (US), Federal Government (US), Federal Register (US), Museums
AUDIENCE   Government Employees, Government Officials, Historians, U.S. Citizens
CONTACT   inquire@nara.gov
FREE

http://www.nara.gov/

gopher://gopher.nara.gov/

DOE Headquarters Gopher ★★

The information on this gopher server includes directives, publications, and general information about the Department of Energy of the U.S. Federal Government. This information is mostly of interest to Department employees and contractors. There are also links to other Department of Energy gophers as well as to other government gopher holes.

KEYWORDS   Commerce, Department of Energy (US), Information Retrieval
AUDIENCE   Government Employees, Government Officials
CONTACT   Roger D. Parish u9505rp@vm1.hqadmin.doe.gov
FREE

gopher://vm1.hqadmin.doe.gov/

Defense Technical Information Center (DTIC) ★★★

The Defense Technical Information Center (DTIC) is a major component of the Department of Defense (DoD) Scientific and Technical Information Program. DTIC contributes to the management and conduct of Defense research, development and acquisition efforts. This is done by providing access to and transfer of scientific and technical information for DoD personnel, DoD contractors, and other U.S. Government agency personnel. DTIC holdings include technical reports, management information summaries, independent research, and development summaries. There are special collections such as a referral database and World War II documents.

KEYWORDS Defense, Documents, Military, Technology Transfer
AUDIENCE Defense Industry Followers, Government Officials, Researchers, Students
FREE

http://asc.dtic.dla.mil/

Department of Commerce Home Page ★★★

This is the central home page for all of the U.S. Department of Commerce's individual agencies. It offers pointers to those agencies' own pages and databases, various Federal Government gopher sites, and background information on the Department itself, including statements from the acting Director.

KEYWORDS Banking, Commerce, Department of Commerce (US)
AUDIENCE Business Professionals, Commerce Specialists, Government Researchers, Government Students, Trade Specialists
CONTACT Commerce Dept. Webmaster stat-usa@doc.gov
FREE

http://ecix.doc.gov/

Department of Energy Home Page ★★★

The home page of the U.S. Department of Energy (DOE) contains information on current DOE research projects, schedules of upcoming meetings and community events, training schedules, and much more. Links to other DOE offices and research sites are also located here, as is a front door to OPENNET, a large database of declassified DOE information.

KEYWORDS Energy, Federal Government (US), Physics, Scientific Research
AUDIENCE Energy Researchers, Physicists, Political Researchers, Science Educators, Science Researchers
CONTACT U.S. DOE Office of Scientific and Technical Information webmaster@apollo.osti.gov
FREE

http://www.doe.gov/

Department of Energy Office of Nuclear Safety ★★★

This is a gopher server for the U.S. Department of Energy's (DOE) Office of Nuclear Safety. The Office of Nuclear Safety oversees DOE activities that involve nuclear technology to ensure protection for DOE staff and the general public. This server gives the mission statements of the Office of Nuclear Safety and the DOE, as well as giving access to the Office's newsletter.

KEYWORDS Energy Sources, Government Agencies (US), Health, Nuclear Safety
AUDIENCE Government Employees, Government Officials, Researchers
CONTACT Curtis Fields fields@viper.eh.doe.gov
FREE

gopher://gopher.ns.doe.gov/

Department of Transportation Home Page ★★★

This site provides links to news, information and searches relating to the U.S. Department of Transportation. The site makes available current and past issues of DOT Talk, the department newsletter, which covers the activities and current legislation relevant to the Department. Links in DOT Info lead to general DOT information as well as documents and guidelines for subdepartments such as the Federal Aviation Administration, the FTA, and the Coast Guard. There are also links to broad-based Internet searches.

KEYWORDS Department of Transportation (US), Government Agencies (US), Newsletters, Transportation
AUDIENCE Government Officials, Transportation Professionals, U.S. Citizens
CONTACT gus@dot.gov
FREE

http://www.dot.gov/

Department of the Treasury Internal Revenue Service ★★★

The mission of the U.S. Internal Revenue Service (IRS) is to 'collect the proper amount of tax revenue at the least cost to the public,' and their Web site is designed to aid this process. Users will find copies of the tax forms (available in Adobe Acrobat form) and instructions for filing, as well as information about where to file them. Also included is an FAQ for common tax questions, and information about other tax help services in the US.

KEYWORDS IRS (Internal Revenue Service), Personal Finance, Taxes
AUDIENCE General Public, Taxonomists
CONTACT wwwadmin@www.ustreas.gov
FREE

http://www.ustreas.gov/treasury/bureaus/irs/irs.html

ESnet Gopher Server ★★★

This gopher offers information about the U.S. Department of Energy's computer network called ESNet. This information includes ESNet maps, ESNet statistics, and ESNet policies. It also provides information about areas of science related to the Department of Energy, such as physics.

KEYWORDS Computer Networks, Energy, Environmental Research, Federal Government (US)
AUDIENCE Energy Researchers, Government Employees, Government Officials
CONTACT info@es.net
FREE

gopher://gopher.es.net/

Embassy Page ★★★★

The Embassy Page Web site is a meta-index that provides links to embassies and consulates with a Net presence in the United States, Canada, Japan, and elsewhere. Embassy sites typically provide official information on the home country's economy, international trade, government, culture, travel, and related topics.

KEYWORDS Embassies, Government (US)
AUDIENCE Business Professionals, Journalists, Travelers
CONTACT info@globescope.com
FREE

http://www.globescope.com/web/gsis/embpage.html

Embassy of Spain in Ottawa ★★★★

The Embassy of Spain in Ottawa is an exhaustive resource for students of Spanish culture and Spanish travelers in Canada. It includes an interactive course in Spanish for beginners, and links to major Spanish institutions.

KEYWORDS Geography, Spain, Tourism
AUDIENCE Educators, Students, Travelers
CONTACT Ricardo Mor ar304@freenet.carleton.ca
FREE

http://www.civeng.carleton.ca/SiSpain/

Environmental Protection Agency WWW Server ★★★★

The Environmental Protection Agency WWW Server contains indices and pointers to a large archive of publicly-available EPA environmental information, including the full text of all EPA standards, guidelines and regulations. A search engine, located on the home page, makes searches for particular topics much easier. Due to the large volume of legal, scientific and personnel information here, even browsing the indices can be time consuming.

KEYWORDS Environment, Federal Government (US), Law (US)
AUDIENCE Environmental Scientists, Environmentalists, Naturalists, Nature Lovers
CONTACT EPA Support Staff internet_support@unixmail.rtpnc.epa.gov
FREE

http://www.epa.gov/

Extension Service, U.S. Department of Agriculture Gopher Server ★★★

This is a gopher server of the Extension Service, U.S. Department of Agriculture (USDA). The Extension Service aims to allow the general public access to the information and resources provided by the Department of Agriculture. This gopher gives access to various Extension Service programs related to education, health, family, agriculture and more. In addition, it gives access to USDA resources such as publications and databases.

KEYWORDS Agriculture, Government Documents, Health, Information Retrieval
AUDIENCE Agriculturalists, Economists, General Public, Government Employees, Government Officials

Agencies

CONTACT gopher-admin@esusda.gov
FREE

gopher://esusda.gov/

Federal Bureau of Investigation ★★★

This site provides background information on the FBI and indices of publicly-available publications. A special section on the FBI cases concerns the Unabomber task force, dedicated to apprehending the 'Unabomber,' who has killed numerous people nationwide with home-made mailbombs. A Sketch of the Unabomb suspect is also located here.

KEYWORDS Crime, Federal Government (US), Law (US)
AUDIENCE FBI, Government Employees, Investigators, Journalists, Political Researchers
CONTACT William L. Tafoya, Ph.D.
btafoya@orion.arc.nasa.gov
FREE

http://naic.nasa.gov/fbi/index.html

Federal Communications Commission Web Server ★★★

This server provides information related to the Federal Communications Commission (FCC). Included are links to a WAIS search of all available documents, information on cable TV, private radio and several electronic publications (Common Carrier, Daily Business, Daily Digest, Engineering Technology, Spectrum Management, etc.). Also available are auction information, current events, mass media topics, and FCC forms and fees.

KEYWORDS Government Agencies (US), Television
AUDIENCE Communications Professionals, Communications Specialists, Communications Students
FREE

http://www.fcc.gov/

Federal Emergency Management Agency Home Page ★★★

This page provides links to data about the Federal Emergency Management Agency (FEMA), information about preparing for a disaster, and FEMA's role in helping after a disaster.

KEYWORDS Disaster Relief, Emergency Preparedness, Government Agencies (US), Public Policy
AUDIENCE General Public, Government Employees, Government Officials
FREE

http://www.fema.gov

Federal Networking Council Advisory Committee Information Server ★★★

This gopher serves up information from the Federal Networking Council Advisory Committee, a government body providing assistance to federal agencies in their networking activities. The information found on this server includes reports, papers, and documents.

KEYWORDS Federal Government (US), Government Projects (US), Information Technology, Networking
AUDIENCE Government Agencies, Government Employees, Government Officials
CONTACT Scott Behnke
sbehnke@arpa.mil
FREE

gopher://fncac.fnc.gov/

Fedix/Molis ★★★★

This is a diversified information services company facilitating the partnership of 10 federal agencies under the leadership of the Department of Energy. Federal Information Exchange's system is composed of the Fedix and Molis online information programs. Fedix provides information about opportunities and activities including contracts and products available, as well as minority opportunities and activities within these agencies - Department of Energy (DOE), Air Force Office of Scientific Research (AFOSR), Department of Agriculture (USDA), Federal Aviation Administration (FAA), and the National Aeronautics & Space Administration (NASA).

KEYWORDS Business, Department Of Energy (US), Minority Resources
AUDIENCE Business Owners, Entrepreneurs, Students (Secondary/College)
FREE

http://web.fie.com

Forskningsministeriet ★★★

This site offers reports from the Ministry of Research in Denmark. The Ministry of Research is responsible in the areas of research, telecommunication and the general information technology. There is access to the reports 'From Vision to Action - Info-Society 2000' and 'Info-Society 2000.'

KEYWORDS Denmark, Information Technology, Research
AUDIENCE Danes, Economic Development Experts, Economists, Researchers
CONTACT fsk@fsk.dk
FREE

http://www.sdn.dk/fsk/

General Services Administration Home Page ★★★

This page provides information and links to the offices within the General Services Administration (GSA) and GSA publications. Among the offices listed are the Consumer Information Center, Federal Information Center, Federal Supply Service, Information Technology Service, Regional Offices and Staff Offices, etc. Publications listed include Doing Business with the GSA. There are also links to other U.S. Government Web Servers.

KEYWORDS Consumer Affairs, Government Agencies (US)
AUDIENCE Business Professionals, Business Professionals, Government Officials
CONTACT webmaster@gsa.gov
FREE

http://www.gsa.gov

House of Representatives Home Page ★★★★

The House of Representatives Home Page provides information about the U.S. Government's Legislative Branch and its activities. Users will find legislative schedules, a list of all the state representatives and how to contact them, and general information about the organization and processes of the House of Representatives. The text of bills and resolutions presently in Congress are provided. Users may also access the Internet Law Library and codes for general materials about law in the United states, as well as read educational materials such as the Declaration of Independence and the U.S. Constitution. For visitors, opening hours, and Washington, D.C. transportation guides are included.

KEYWORDS Federal Government (US), House of Representatives (US)
AUDIENCE Government Officials, Government Students, Lawyers, U.S. Citizens
FREE

http://www.house.gov/

Housing and Urban Development on the Internet ★★★

This site provides a link to the Department of Housing and Urban Development (HUD) gopher site, and one to FEDIX, where more information on HUD can be found.

KEYWORDS Department of Housing and Urban Development (HUD), Government (US), Urban Planning
AUDIENCE Home Owners, Real Estate Brokers
CONTACT feedback@www.whitehouse.gov
FREE

http://www.whitehouse.gov/White_House/Cabinet/html/HUD.html

gopher://hud.gov/1

Information Infrastructure Task Force WWW Server ★★★

This site contains information about the Information Infrastructure Task Force offering a list of committees, calendar of events, press releases, and selected legislation. It also provides a contact list of committees and working groups, and access to other Government Web Servers.

KEYWORDS Federal Government (US), Politics, Public Policy, Voting
AUDIENCE General Public, Internet Users, Voters
FREE

http://iitf.doc.gov/

Kokoomus ★★★

The Kokoomus Web page contains details about the attitudes and composition of Finland's Kansallinen Kookoomus (National Coalition) political party. The site chiefly consists of textual information, though there are

email links to the leaders of the centrist group. The text is in Finnish and English.
KEYWORDS Finland, Moderates, Politics
AUDIENCE Finns, International Politics Enthusiasts
CONTACT lassi@koikkis.pp.fi
FREE

http://www.kokoomus.fi/kokoomus/

Manufacturing Systems Integration Division (MSID) ★★★

This Web server provides information on the Manufacturing Systems Integration Division (MSID) of the National Institute of Standards and Technology. MSID contributes to the research and development of standards and technologies leading to the implementation of virtual manufacturing enterprises. MSID uses information technology to implement computer-aided integrated manufacturing systems. This page provides information on the staff, an overview of the department, strategic plan, publications, etc.
KEYWORDS National Institute of Standards and Technology, Technology
AUDIENCE Computer Professionals, Manufacturers
FREE

http://elib.cme.nist.gov

Ministerio de Agricultura de Chile ★★★

This site contains information about the Ministerio de Agricultura de Chile, the Ministry of Agriculture for the Government of Chile. The information consists of statistics on Chilean agriculture.
KEYWORDS Agriculture, Chile, Computer Networks, Government
AUDIENCE Agriculturalists, Chileans, Government Employees
CONTACT root@minagri.gob.cl
FREE

gopher://sanson.minagri.gob.cl/

Ministerio de Relaciones Exteriores del Ecuador ★★★

This site offers information from the Ministry of Foreign Affaires of Ecuador (Ministerio de Relaciones Exteriores del Ecuador). The information consists of access to databases of government documents and economics data. In addition, there is information about the armed conflict between Ecuador and Peru that started in February, 1995.
KEYWORDS Economics, Latin America
AUDIENCE Economists, Government Employees, Policy Analysts, Political Scientists
CONTACT ppadilla@mmrree.gov.ec
FREE

gopher://gopher.mmrree.gov.ec/

Ministry of Economy and Public Works and Services - Argentina ★★★

The World-Wide-Web Server of the Ministry of Economy and Public Works and Services of Argentina gives Internet WWW users access to economic, financial and commercial information of this country. It also includes statistical and census bureau data, investment opportunities, energy, fishing, forestry, mining, tourism, arts and cultural information.
KEYWORDS Argentina, Latin America
AUDIENCE Argentina Residents, Business Professionals, Economists, Investors, Latin Americans, Tourists
CONTACT webmaster@meyosp.mecon.ar
FREE

http://www.mecon.ar/default.htm

Ministry of Science, Technology and Environment ★★

This is a home page from the Ministry of Science, Technology and Environment of Thailand. The Ministry deals with policy, plans, and projects related to science, technology, energy and environment. Nine departments are included in this Ministry including the Department of Pollution Control, the Thailand Institute of Scientific and Technological Research, and the Office of the National Research Council of Thailand. The Ministry deals with policy, plans, and projects related to science, technology, energy and the environment. The structure of the Ministry, its contacts, and the function of every department are presented.
KEYWORDS Asia, Government (US), Thailand
AUDIENCE Asians, Business Professionals, Investors
FREE

http://www.nectec.or.th/bureaux/moste/moste.html

Minority Information Service (USAID) ★★★

This is the site of the Minority Information Service of the US Agency for International Development (USAID). You can search a database for information on grants, procurements, and assistance by deadline date or release date. Other topics include the USAID Organizational Chart, USAID's Overview of its Strategy for Sustainable Development, and information on Protecting the Environment. Minority Programs include Participant Training Project for Europe (Summary), International Development Intern Program, Stay-in-School Program, Summer Aid Program, and the Summer Employment Program.
KEYWORDS Employment, Internships, Minority Information
AUDIENCE Business Professionals, Students (University)
CONTACT webmaster@fedix.fie.com
FREE

http://web.fie.com/web/fed/aid

NASA - JSC Digital Image Collection ★★★

This site provides access to a collection of digital images from NASA missions. Featured are press releases and Earth observation images from the manned space program from Mercury to the present.
KEYWORDS Federal Databases (US), Image Processing, NASA (National Aeronautics And Space Administration), Space
AUDIENCE General Public, Space Science Researchers, Space Scientists, Space Students
CONTACT Kevin C. Marsh K.Marsh@ja6.jsc.nasa.gov
FREE

http://images.jsc.nasa.gov/html/home.htm

NATO Government Server ★★★

This gopher archive, compiled by the University of Maryland Information Server, provides information and documents from the North Atlantic Treaty Organization (NATO). Users will find general contact and location information across the world, texts, declarations, and decisions, and NATO factsheets and newsletters. Speeches, news releases, and the NATO Handbook and NATO Review are also included.
KEYWORDS International Politics, North Atlantic Treaty Organization (NATO), Organizations
AUDIENCE Government Officials, NATO Officials, Politics Enthusiasts
CONTACT consult@umail.umd.edu.
FREE

gopher://gopher.inform.umd.edu/11/Educational_Resources/AcademicResourcesByTopic/UnitedStatesAndWorld/World/International_Agencies/NATO

NIEHS (National Institute of Environmental Health Sciences)/AACR Task Force - Advancement of Minorities in Science ★

This page provides a program description of the NIEHS/AACR Task Force - Advancement of Minorities in Science. It includes the Target Population, FY 1994 accomplishments, written materials related to the project, anticipated future events, and more.
KEYWORDS Biomedical Research, Minority Information, Minority Programs, Science
AUDIENCE Researchers, Students (University)
FREE

http://web.fie.com/web/fed/ehs/prog/ehspgaac.html

National Institute of Standards and Technology (NIST) at Boulder ★★★

This gopher site provides information on the U.S. Department of Commerce National Institute for

Standards and Technology in Boulder, Colorado. This includes information on NIST's research programs, facilities index, Malcolm Baldridge National Quality Award Information, budget and mandate information, as well as specific information on the divisions of the Boulder Campus. It also provides links to NIST's gopher in Gaithersburg, Maryland.

- **KEYWORDS** Commerce, Federal Register (US), National Institute of Standards and Technology, Technology
- **AUDIENCE** Administrators, Computer Specialists, Scientists
- **CONTACT** Scott Paisley paisley@bldrdoc.gov
- **FREE**

gopher://gopher.bldrdoc.gov/

National Institute of Standards and Technology (NIST) ★★★

This gopher site is provided as a service to the organizations and employees of the National Institute of Standards and Technology. It provides remote access login, software available for downloading, conference proceedings, news releases, information on advanced technology programs, and links to other gophers.

- **KEYWORDS** Federal Register (US), National Institute of Standards and Technology, Technology
- **AUDIENCE** Administrators, Computer Specialists, Employees, Scientists
- **CONTACT** Wo Chang wchang@nist.gov
- **FREE**

gopher://gopher-server.nist.gov/

National Oceanic and Atmospheric Administration (NOAA) West Region ★★★

The National Oceanic and Atmospheric Administration (NOAA) West Region has databases on Climatology, Satellite Archives, and special projects such as the Satellite Active Archive Demo and the El Niño Theme Page. Some of the member organizations that make up the NOAA are the Pacific Marine Environmental Laboratory, the Pacific Tides Group, and the Alaska Fisheries Science Center. There are also links to the Education Office, which contains curriculum materials.

- **KEYWORDS** Aquatic Science, Earth Sciences
- **AUDIENCE** Climatologists, Educators, Meteorologists
- **CONTACT** Laura McCarty lmccarty@pmel.noaa.gov
- **FREE**

http://columbia.wrc.noaa.gov

National Parks Service Home Page ★★★★

These Web pages contain park-by-park maps of National Parks Service (NPS) holdings as well as historical and other information on every National Park area. Included are articles and photographs related to a number of NPS projects, from the protection of American Civil War battlefields to a National Archaeological Database and its implementation. There are links here to a number of NPS archives, including the NPS Geospatial Clearinghouse, a National Parks Flora & Fauna database, and other information.

- **KEYWORDS** Environment, Government (US), National Park Service (US), Wildlife
- **AUDIENCE** Environmental Researchers, Environmental Scientists, Environmentalists
- **CONTACT** webmaster@its.nbs.gov
- **FREE**

http://www.nps.gov/nps/

National Science Foundation Home Page ★★★

This page contains information related to the National Science Foundation (NSF), including links to the NSF Grants Proposal Guide, NSF Statistical Reports, the Database of Research Awards, a listing of Directorates, Offices and Programs, and NSF Staff Directories. Also included are recent bulletins and press releases, White House Issuances and Announcements, and a link to other NST information sources (such as the gopher server and publication database).

- **KEYWORDS** Executive Branch (US), Science
- **AUDIENCE** Researchers, Science Educators, Science Researchers
- **CONTACT** webmaster@nsf.gov
- **FREE**

http://stis.nsf.gov/

National Technology Transfer Center Home Page ★★★

This provides information on the National Technology Transfer Center. The goal of the center is transfer technology from science to industry and this home page provides technology transfer resources such as databases, news on shows, conferences, workshops, and job openings. There is also a good deal of information on the center itself.

- **KEYWORDS** Companies, Industry, Science, Technological Advances
- **AUDIENCE** Business Administrators, Entrepreneurs, Job Seekers, Scientists
- **CONTACT** Chuck Monfradi webmaster@nttc.edu
- **FREE**

http://iridium.nttc.edu/nttc.html

National Telecommunications and Information Administration ★★

This is a gopher server for the National Telecommunications and Information Administration, a section of the Department of Commerce. It gives some information about the NTIA, such as access to its phone book, and also provides links to other government sites and documents, such as the Freedom of Information Act and the White House.

- **KEYWORDS** Commerce, Telecommunications, White House
- **AUDIENCE** Government Employees, Government Officials, Telecommunications Experts

---

Connections to Finding Facts: CIA's World Fact Book

This tape will self destruct in five seconds...

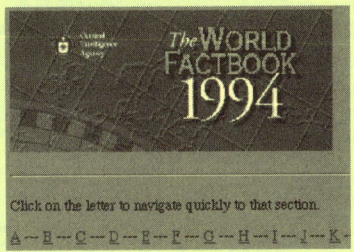

Even the Mission: Impossible crew from the long-running American television adventure series needed help in finding their way around a foreign country. Now, in real life, the Central Intelligence Agency brings its "CIA World Factbook" to the Internet so that travelers, students, and curiosity seekers can investigate the weather conditions, political upheavals, and natural hazards of nearly every country on earth.

Users can also find maps, a weights-and-measures table, and information about population, economic conditions, trade, conflicts, and politics for more than 300 countries and regions of the world. Included are travel advisories for nearly every country as well. Connections to travel guides, such as The Lonely Planet, bring you up-to-the-minute information on things to do and out-of-the way sites to visit.

(http://www.odci.gov/cia/publications/94fact/fb94toc/fb94toc.html)

also, (http://esri.com/)

- **FREE**

gopher://gopher.ntia.doc.gov/

Office of Ocean and Coastal Resource Management ★★★

This Web site describes the work of the Office of Ocean and Coastal Resource Management, a branch of the National Oceanic and Atmospheric Agency (NOAA). Users will find information about departments like the Coastal Programs Division, which supervises conservation and land use of coastal ecosystems. There are links to NOAA, the Environmental Protection Agency, and the Fish and Wildlife Service.

- **KEYWORDS** Conservation, United States
- **AUDIENCE** Civil Servants, Conservationists

Free

http://wave.nos.noaa.gov/ocrm/

Product Development Centre, Canada Communications Group

The Canada Communications Group is affiliated with the Agency of Public Works and Government Services. Its job is to help government clients collect, format, manage, and distribute information. Their services include printing, publishing, and distributing information, both conventionally and through electronic means. The CCG offers Web publishing and bulletin board services to federal agencies and executives, among other services.

Keywords   Canada, Information Services
Audience   Government Agencies, Government Agency Employees
Free

http://www.globalx.net/pdc/

Renewable Energy - A New National Commitment?

This page presents a paper on renewable energy written by the Science Policy Division of the Congressional Research Service at the Library of Congress. The primary focus of this essay is on the Department of Energy's support of renewable energy issues, including budget, energy subsidies, and GATT (General Agreement on Tariffs and Trade) considerations.

Keywords   Energy, Environment, Library of Congress, Public Policy
Audience   Environmentalists, Legislators, Lobbyists, Policymakers
Contact   www-content@solstice.crest.org
Free

http://solstice.crest.org/policy-and-econ/crs/re.html

STAT-USA - A Source of Economic, Business, Social, and Environmental Information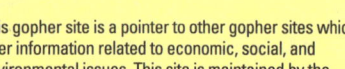

This gopher site is a pointer to other gopher sites which offer information related to economic, social, and environmental issues. This site is maintained by the Department of Commerce of the U.S. Government.

Keywords   Economics, Environmental Research, Social Issues, Statistics
Audience   Business Researchers, Management Information Specialists, Researchers, Social Scientists
Contact   statusa@doc.gov
Free

gopher://gopher.esa.doc.gov/

Social Security Online

The Social Security Online page is designed to provide information about Social Security benefits and services for both individuals and businesses. Users will find the Social Security Handbook, pamphlets with basic benefit information, including retirement, disability, and medicare, as well as numerous Social Security Administration publications in Adobe Acrobat form, covering topics such as 'Your Social Security Taxes' and 'If You are Self-Employed.' Online services which are accessible include Social Security Card applications and benefit estimate software. Other information includes statistical data, policy reports, and social security legislation.

Keywords   Federal Government (US), Social Security, Social Security Administration
Audience   Business Professionals, General Public
Free

http://www.ssa.gov/SSA_Home.html/

gopher://gopher.ssa.gov

Space Systems and Concepts Division

The Space Systems and Concepts Division at NASA Langley Research Center provides links to the goals and objectives of the Division, its personnel, capabilities chart, calendar, activities, and space-related bulletin boards.

Keywords   Research Labs, Space Systems
Audience   Computer Users, Educators (University), Internet Users, Researchers, Students (University)
Contact   r.l.vanvalkenburg@larc.nasa.gov
Free

http://freedom.larc.nasa.gov

Telecommunications and Information Infrastructure Assistance Program (TIIAP) Home Page

The Telecommunications and Information Infrastructure Assistance Program (TIIAP) program is part of the National Telecommunications and Information Administration (NTIA) at the US Department of Commerce. The TIIAP program provides matching grants to state and local governments, health care providers, school districts, libraries, universities, social service organizations, public safety services and other non-profit entities to help them access and use new telecommunications technologies. On this page, the user will find information describing the procedure for applying for grants, an application, all necessary contact information, and other helpful resources.

Keywords   Funding, Grants
Audience   Community Leaders, Education Administrators, Grantseekers, Health Care Professionals
Contact   tiiap@ntia.doc.gov
Free

http://www.ntia.doc.gov/tiiap/tiiap.html

gopher://gopher.ntia.doc.gov/

ftp://ftp.ntia.doc.gov/pub/otia/tiiap/

U.S. Bureau of Mines Gopher

This gopher site provide information about the U.S. Department of the Interior's Bureau of Mines. It includes information on the Bureau's mandates, a searchable file index, links to other U.S. Department of the Interior's gopher sites, and numerous Bureau publications. It also includes budgetary and performance review information.

Keywords   Bureau of Mines (US), Geology, Mining
Audience   Geographers, Geologists, Natural Scientists, Researchers, Scientists
Contact   Matt Klevemann
            klevemmc@gopher.usbm.gov
Free

gopher://miner.usbm.gov/

U.S. Census Bureau Gopher Server

This is a gopher hole for the U.S. Census Bureau. It contains information about the Bureau, its mission, organization, and activities. The main feature on this server is access to the main data bank of the Census Bureau. This database contains results from past surveys, as well as statisical tools and analyses.

Keywords   Census (The), Databases, Statistics
Audience   Business Researchers, Economists, Statisticians
Contact   gatekeeper@census.gov
Free

gopher://gopher.census.gov/

U.S. Consumer Product Safety Commission

This gopher site provides information about the purpose and goals of the U.S. Consumer Product Safety Commission (CPSC). The CPSC works to maintain and ensure the safety of consumer products in the US. Menu Topics include Reporting Product Related Hazards to CPSC, Press Releases, Federal Register Notices, Information for Manufacturers, Retailers and Distributors, How to Receive Information From CPSC, and more. Contact information and resource materials are available here.

Keywords   Consumer Safety, Product Liability, Research
Audience   Consumers, Distributors, General Public, Manufacturers, Retailers, Shoppers
Contact   info@cpsc.gov
Free

gopher://cpsc.gov/

U.S. Department Of Energy Office of Environmental Management (EM)

This is the U.S. Department Of Energy Office of Environmental Management (EM) World Wide Web Server. It provides information services to EM Headquarters, field sites, regulatory agencies, the public, and other stakeholders. Users can access services through menus, a full-text search, or by selecting them directly from the infomap. The menu includes pointers to the

Information Map, EM Public Information Resources, Regulatory Information, Environmental Technology Information, Environmental Information, Other World-Wide Web Servers and Local EM Headquarters Information (Restricted Access).

KEYWORDS Environment, Regulatory Agencies, Technology
AUDIENCE Biologists, Computer Professionals, Educators (University), Environmentalists
CONTACT info@eagle.em.doe.gov
FREE

http://emhpmail.em.doe.gov

U.S. Department of Defense Home Page ★★★

This page provides information on the Office of the Secretary of Defense and links to selected sites of all the branches of the military, including the Air Force, Army and Navy. Also provided are several links to Defense Department agencies (ARPA, Defense Information Systems Agency, Defense Simulation Internet, Defense Technical Information Center, etc.) and information on NATO.

KEYWORDS Federal Government (US), Military
AUDIENCE Defense Analysts, Defense Industry Followers, Military Personnel
FREE

http://www.whitehouse.gov/White_House/Cabinet/html/Department_of_Defense

U.S. Department of State Home Page ★★★

This site provides links to various State Department information sources, including the background and economic/trade practices of a number of countries (from the University of Missouri), Human Rights reports listed by country, NAFTA, speeches by the Secretary of State and Department Travel Advisories.

KEYWORDS Executive Branch (US), Human Rights, US State Department
AUDIENCE Government Officials, Humanists, International Travelers
FREE

http://marvel.loc.gov/11/federal/fedinfo/byagency/executive/state

U.S. Department of Treasury Home Page ★★

This page includes a brief description of the mission of the Treasury Department, links to photos of and biographical information about Treasury Officers, the responsibilities of the Treasury Bureaus, services provided by the Department, and upcoming events and projects.

KEYWORDS Executive Branch (US), Treasury Department (US)
AUDIENCE Business Professionals, Government Officials
FREE

http://www.ustreas.gov

U.S. Department of Veterans Affairs Home Page ★★★★

This page provides background and history of the Department of Veterans Affairs (VA). It has links to information on services and benefits available to veterans, such as pensions, education and training, medical care, home loan assistance and insurance. It also has a section on VA organizations and facilities arranged alphabetically by state.

KEYWORDS Federal Government (US), Military, Veteran Affairs (US)
AUDIENCE Military Personnel, Veterans
FREE

http://www.va.gov/

U.S. Fish and Wildlife Services Home Page ★★★

This home page provides information about the US Government's Fish and Wildlife Services department, and about wildlife and natural resources management in general. Specific topics include endangered species, migratory birds, fisheries, wetlands, and more. The site also features links to related resources.

KEYWORDS Animal Science, Natural History, Wildlife
AUDIENCE Conservationists, Wildlife Biologists, Zoologists
CONTACT Dr. Alan R. Fischer
         fishera@mail.fws.gov
FREE

http://www.fws.gov/

U.S. Government Hypertexts ★★★

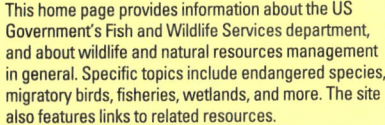

This page covers topics in the news concerning National Policies. Included is White House Information (press releases, the proposed '95 budget, the State of the Union Address), The Bipartisan Commission on Entitlement and Tax Reform, Vice President Gore's program on reinventing America, the National Health Security Plan, and the National Information Infrastructure Proposal with audio and video clips. An audio version of President Clinton's Saturday Radio Addresses is given, as well as access to the National Trade Data Bank.

KEYWORDS Current Events, National Policy, Public Policy, Voting
AUDIENCE Business and Financial Researchers, General Public, Internet Users, Voters
FREE

http://sunsite.unc.edu/govdocs.html

U.S. State Department Travel Warnings and Consular Information Sheets ★★★★

This server provides general travel and consulate information for countries all over the world. Travel information consists of the U.S. State Department public announcements, with comprehensive travel guides and warnings specific to each country, as well as regional maps. Countries are listed alphabetically, with notes marking the last time the country information was updated and whether the site contains a map. Links are also provided to other maps and travel sites on the WWW.

KEYWORDS Consulates, Maps, Tourism
AUDIENCE Travelers, U.S. Citizens
CONTACT cdr@stolaf.edu
FREE

http://www.stolaf.edu/network/travel-advisories.html

Understanding HUD'S (Housing and Urban Development) Mission and Organization ★★

This is the site of HUD's (U.S. Department of Housing & Urban Development) mission statement. HUD is the principal federal agency responsible for programs concerned with housing and community development, fair housing opportunities, and improvement/development of communities in the United States. The different offices of HUD and its roles are outlined.

KEYWORDS Community Development, HUD (Housing & Urban Development), Housing
AUDIENCE Banking Professionals, Mortgage Lenders, Real Estate Brokers
CONTACT fedix@fedix.fie.com
FREE

http://web.fie.com/web/fed/hud/text/hudtbo02.htm

United Nations 50th Anniversary ★★★★

The United Nations is celebrating its 50th anniversary throughout 1995. In particular, two major events mark the anniversary. June 26 marks 50 years since the signing of the UN charter in San Francisco, California., and October 24 marks the date that the UN charter came into effect, which will be celebrated at the UN headquarters in New York. This page provides information about these celebrations as well as numerous links to United Nations related (the Commission on Global Governance, United Nations 50th Anniversary Overview, UN50 Global Projects, UN50 Newsletters, and much more.

KEYWORDS California, Events, NGOs (Non-Governmental Organizations), New York
AUDIENCE Californians, General Public, New York Residents
CONTACT wwww@amdahl.com
FREE

http://www.amdahl.com/internet/events/un50.html

United States Geological Survey (USGS) Homepage ★★★★

This site is the United States Geological Survey (USGS) server, dedicated to all aspects of Geography and geographic data. There are links to directories on public issues and education, USGS environmental research, publications, a GIS tutorial, and descriptions (and examples) of available USGS data products. There is access to online spatial data, and more. There is also an extensive set of links to geography-related resources on the Net.

KEYWORDS Earth Sciences, Environmental Studies, GIS (Geographic Information Systems), Geography
AUDIENCE Earth Scientists, Environmental Researchers, Environmental Scientists, GIS Professionals
CONTACT webmaster@www.usgs.gov
FREE

http://www.usgs.gov/

gopher://info.er.usgs.gov/

United States Postal Service Public WWW Server ★★★

The United States Postal Service Web page provides information for those who have questions about their mail. Users will find a zip code index in order to look up the additional four numbers of a zip code, as well as U.S. postal rates for different package types and weights. Images from the 1995 stamp collection are also included, as are news releases, publications, and general consumer information. Links to other U.S. Postal Service-related Web sites are also provided.

KEYWORDS Postal Service (US)
AUDIENCE General Public, Stamp Collectors, U.S. Citizens
CONTACT jwilli17@email.usps.gov
FREE

http://www.usps.gov/

White House Files ★★★★

The White House Files provides pointers to a variety of information related to the White House that is organized chronologically by year. There is a searchable gopher index, and links to White House information, domestic and international affairs, the economy, budget, and related topics. It contains links to press briefings and conferences, memoranda, executive orders, and proclamations, speeches, and the President's daily schedule.

KEYWORDS Federal Government (US), White House
AUDIENCE Journalists, Political Activists, Political Scientists, Politicians
FREE

http://english-server.hss.cmu.edu/WhiteHouse.html

Career & Employment

See also
Business & Economics · *Career & Employment*
Science · *Career & Employment*

Commonwealth Department of Finance (Australia) - Employment Division ★★★

The Division is responsible for policy advice to Government and guidance to other departments and authorities on public service classification, pay and conditions of service. It is also responsible for policy advice on and superannuation arrangements for Commonwealth public servants and other staff in Commonwealth agencies and authorities. It provides advice on the economic and financial aspects of matters relating to employment, education and training, and more.

KEYWORDS Australia, Commonwealth, Government, Government Policy
AUDIENCE Government Officials, Job Seekers, Public Servants
FREE

http://www.nla.gov.au/finance/emp.html

Department of the Interior Automated Vacancy Announcement System (AVADS) ★★★

The U.S. Department of the Interior Automated Vacancy Announcement System (AVADS) provides electronic access to notices of job opportunities in the Department. The department lists positions for 11 distinct services including the U.S. Geological Survey, Bureau of Mines, and the Fish And Wildlife Service. The positions listed include such titles as chemist, electrician, sign painter, teacher, and fishery biologist. Many positions have specific guidelines for applicants.

KEYWORDS Government Agencies (US)
AUDIENCE Environmentalists, Federal Employees, Job Seekers, Naturalists
FREE

http://info.er.usgs.gov/doi/avads/index.html

Cities

See also
Business & Economics · *Non Profits*
Engineering & Technology · *Transportation Engineering*

Aberystwyth Home Page ★★★

This is the home page for Aberystwyth, a small seaside town on the shores of the Cardigan Bay in Wales. It provides hypertext descriptions and links to the National Library of Wales and one of the constituent colleges of the University of Wales. It also has a hypertext description of the history of the area, as well as related maps, images and descriptions, such as the two Celtic hill forts on Pen Dinas.

KEYWORDS Tourism, Wales
AUDIENCE Librarians, Library Users, Tourists, Wales Residents
CONTACT spk@aber.ac.uk
FREE

http://www.city.net/countries/united_kingdom/wales/aberystwyth/

About Sydney ★★★

The home page of Sydney, the third largest city of Nova Scotia, Canada presents images and hypertext descriptions of interest to tourists. It has subindexes that cover such topics as accommodations, banks, the university, restaurants, shopping areas, police, hospitals, parks, museums, recreational facilities, the airport & bus terminals, and its port, which handles both ferries and cruise ships. Tourist attractions in Sydney include Wentworth park, Cossit House on Charlotte Street, built in 1787, the oldest house in Sydney and now a provincial museum, St. Patrick's Church, and the Jost House on Charlotte Street, a 200-year-old wooded dwelling.

KEYWORDS Canada, Nova Scotia, Tourism
AUDIENCE Canada Residents, History Buffs, Outdoors Enthusiasts, Tourists
CONTACT registrar@sparc.uccb.ns.ca
FREE

http://eagle.uccb.ns.ca/~jhussey/ecma/about_sydney.html

About the City of Aachen ★★★

The Aachen, Germany Home Page is a community network that provides a few hypertext images and descriptions of local history, culture, including the town square and the Cathedral of Aachen. The emphasis is on the images of the area.

KEYWORDS Germany, Images, Tourism
AUDIENCE Europe Scholars, Germany Residents, History Buffs, Tourists
FREE

http://www-i5.informatik.rwth-aachen.de/mjf/stadt-aachen.html

Academ Consulting Services Newsgroups ★★★★

There are several newsgroups at this location, all directly related to the city of Houston, Texas. These Houston newsgroups cover general information, dining, jobs offered, jobs wanted, weather, sports and Internet providers, to name a few. The newsgroups can be accessed using either URL-FTP, URL-gopher or shell access. Detailed access instructions for each newsgroup is provided.

KEYWORDS Texas, Tourism, Usenet Newsgroups
AUDIENCE International Travelers, Texas Residents, Tourists
CONTACT Stan Barber
postmaster@academ.com
FREE

gopher://gopher.academ.com/1/usenet/houston-newsgroups/

ftp://ftp.academ.com/pub/news/houston-newsgroups/

Access Atlanta ★★★

This site is dedicated to the 1996 Olympic Games to be held in Atlanta, Georgia and is not an officially-sponsored Olympic site. The purpose of the site is to provide coverage of the games as they occur. At present, it contains complete events schedules, information on obtaining tickets, a visitor's guide to Atlanta, information about Southern tourist spots, a calendar of events, and more.

KEYWORDS   Georgia, Museums, Olympic Games, Tourism
AUDIENCE   Olympic Games Enthusiasts, Tourists
CONTACT   Mike Gordon
           mg@ajc.com
FREE

http://www.ajc.com/home.htm

The Alexandria Home Page ★★★

This is the home page for Alexandria, the second largest city and the main port of Egypt. Included is a brief history of this city named in honor of Alexander the Great. Links are also provided to a picture gallery, maps of Eastern and Western Alexandria, very specific information on how to reach Alexandria by different modes of transportation, tourist attractions, where to stay including a list of 3, 4 and 5 star hotels, restaurants, related Internet sites and more. The information is taken from the Egyptian Tourist Authority brochure.

KEYWORDS   Egypt, Tourism
AUDIENCE   Fiction Enthusiasts, Historians, History Buffs, Tourists
CONTACT   Alaa K. Ashmawy
           ashmawy@ecn.purdue.edu
FREE

http://ce.ecn.purdue.edu/~ashmawy/ALEX

Alice Springs ★★★

The home page of Alice Springs, located deep in the outback of Central Australia, provides hypermedia images and descriptions of the attractions and facilities of this remote region. This includes buildings of historical interest, lodging, restaurants, museums, a brief history, and contacts for outback safaris.

KEYWORDS   Australia, History, Tourism
AUDIENCE   Australia Residents, Canadians, Hiking Enthusiasts, Tourists
FREE

http://www.world.net/Travel/Australia/NT_info/NTTC/as.html

Amherst Electronic Atrium ★★★★

The home page of Amherst, centrally located in Nova Scotia, Canada, is a community network that provides extensive hypertext descriptions and links to local resources, including the municipal government, the Chamber of Commerce, listings of local businesses, recreation facilities, newspapers, and where to lodge, shop and eat. It is geared to those wishing to relocate or just visit.

KEYWORDS   Community Information, Nova Scotia
AUDIENCE   Canada Residents, Community Activists, Community Groups, Tourists
FREE

http://rs6000.nshpl.library.ns.ca/regionals/cur/atrium.html

Anchorage Community (ATU Telecommunications) ★★★★

The home page of Anchorage, Alaska is a comprehensive, well-structured set of pages that provide useful, interesting information to local residents and tourists alike. It has indices that link to main topics including points of interest, a community calendar, sports and recreation, higher education, the arts, libraries, community services, senior services, and a newcomer's guide. There are links to the Convention & Visitors Bureau and to several pan-Alaskan home pages, as well as one to the University of Alaska, Anchorage and its many features.

KEYWORDS   Alaska, Tourism, Universities
AUDIENCE   Alaska Residents, Art Enthusiasts, Students (University), Tourists
CONTACT   Webmaster@atu.com
FREE

http://www.atu.com/community/community.html

Anglesey Wales Home Page ★★★

The Anglesey, Wales Home Page provides hypermedia images and links to descriptions of local history back to the Roman Empire. A natural history page is under construction. The Isle of Anglesey is situated off the Northwest coast of Wales and contains the town with the longest place name in English— Llanfairpwllgwyngyllgogerychwyrndrobwllllantysiliogogogoch. It includes links to other information about Wales at The University of Wales at Aberystywyth and The University at Cardiff.

KEYWORDS   History, Tourism
AUDIENCE   History Buffs, Tourists, Wales Residents, Wales Scholars
CONTACT   Warren L. Kovach
           WarrenK@kovcomp.demon.co.uk
FREE

http://www.compulink.co.uk/kovcomp/anglesey.html

Ankara - The Capital Out of Steppe ★★★

This is the Home Page of the city of Ankara, which lies in the center of Anatolia on the eastern edge of the great, high Anatolian Plateau in Turkey. It provides hypermedia documentation that describes local history and current attractions, including the climate, transportation and where to lodge, eat and shop. The source of the information is the Ministry of Tourism, Republic of Turkey.

KEYWORDS   Community, Tourism, Turkey
AUDIENCE   History Buffs, Middle East Scholars, Tourists, Turkey Residents
CONTACT   Melih Uzbek
           melih@knidos.cc.metu.edu.tr
FREE

http://www.metu.edu.tr/~melih/turkey/icanadolu/ankara/Ankara.html

Ann Arbor Area Online ★★★

This home page of Ann Arbor, Michigan presents an integrated set of subindexes that balance the information needs of local residents with outsiders interested in the community and with tourists. Ann Arbor Area Online is a community project listing local resources, a photo tour of Ann Arbor, shop at the mall, see what's happening at the universities, or check out a complete list of Ann Arbor organizations online.

KEYWORDS   History, Michigan, Tourism
AUDIENCE   Art Enthusiasts, Michigan Residents, Museum Enthusiasts, Tourists
CONTACT   ellen@merit.edu
FREE

http://online.ann-arbor.mi.us/ann-arbor/online.html

Ann Arbor, Michigan USA ★★★

This home page of Ann Arbor, Michigan, which is sponsored by the Chamber of Commerce, presents free listings for local residents and institutions, and a link to the University of Michigan. There is an Ann Arbor/Detroit events calendar, computer society information, a digital map of SE Michigan, government information, and the local radio station.

KEYWORDS   Michigan, Tourism, Universities
AUDIENCE   Business Entrepreneurs, Michigan Residents, Students (University), Tourists
CONTACT   aaacc@chamber.ann-arbor.mi.us
FREE

http://ann-arbor.com/

Antalya, Turkey ★★★

The home page of Antalya, Turkey provides hypermedia images, descriptions and links to local attractions and facilities of interest to tourists, including historical sites, the natural habitat, museums, art and culture and shopping. It describes sities on the coast to the west, the Coast of Light, and to the east, the Coast of Golden Sand.

KEYWORDS   History, Tourism, Turkey
AUDIENCE   History Buffs, Middle East Scholars, Tourists, Turkey Residents
FREE

http://www.ege.edu.tr/Turkiye/Akdeniz/Antalya.html

Antigonish, Nova Scotia ★★★

This is the home page of Antigonish, Nova Scotia, which is the site of St. Francis Xavier University. It provides hypermedia links to descriptions of local facilities and activities primarily of interest to tourists, including phone numbers, lodging, local activities, restaurants, historical background, maps, transportation and weather.

KEYWORDS   Nova Scotia, Tourism
AUDIENCE   Canada Residents, Canadian Scholars, History Buffs, Tourists

FREE

gopher://gopher.stfx.ca/11/antigonish

Armagh-City of Saints and Scholars ★★★

The Armagh Home Page is a community network for the city in Northern Ireland with hypertext images and descriptions of local institutions, including the Armagh Planetarium, cathedrals, the county museum, the Ardress House, and the Argory. The focus is on the planetarium, with online celestial images available and links to other planetariums.

KEYWORDS Northern Ireland, Planetariums, Tourism
AUDIENCE Astronomers, Astronomy Enthusiasts, Northern Ireland Residents, Tourists
CONTACT Ian Griffin
ipg@star.arm.ac.uk
FREE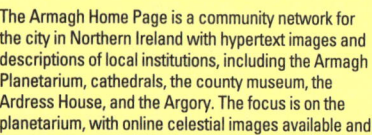

http://star.arm.ac.uk/planet/armagh.html

Atlanta Business Information Exchange ★★★

This home page of Atlanta, Georgia focuses on the interests of businesspeople as they pertain to the city. There are subindexes that cover such topics as an electronic business index, news for business and the information exchange community, associations and organizations, activities and education. There are also government service listings and one for shopping.

KEYWORDS Business, Georgia, Tourism
AUDIENCE Business Entrepreneurs, Real Estate Entrepreneurs
CONTACT webmaster@peachweb.com
FREE

http://www.bie.net/

Austin ★★★

This home page for Austin, Texas provides text and graphics that present 'all sorts of goodies from and about the great city of Austin, Texas.' The subtopics include everything about armadillos (and their importance to Austin), business from 9 to 5, education, fine arts, and food, drink and lodging. There are also subindices that cover city and state government, the media and the movies, non-profit organizations, a gallery of images of Austin and the surrounding area, recreation, general reference (what doesn't fit elsewhere) and services.

KEYWORDS Business, Texas, Tourism
AUDIENCE Art Enthusiasts, Business Entrepreneurs, Museum Enthusiasts, Music Enthusiasts, Texas Residents, Tourists
CONTACT webmaster@quadralay.com
FREE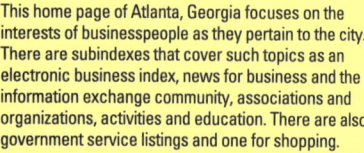

http://www.quadralay.com/www/Austin/Austin.html

Austin Information Center ★★★

This home page is a service of the city government. 'Our mission is to connect you with information, services and the people who make Austin the most livable community in the country. We invite you— citizens, neighbors and visitors—to use the Connection and to help us enhance it, keep it vigorous and make it meaningful.' It has subindices that cover such topics as the document of the city charter, city news releases, Channel 6 schedule, business opportunities with the city and job listings, connections to city services from A to Z, the library and education, health clinics, and things to do, see and hear around and about Austin.

KEYWORDS History, Texas, Tourism
AUDIENCE Community Activists, Texas Residents, Tourists
CONTACT web@ci.austin.tx.us
FREE

http://www.tech.net/austin/

BEV Home Page ★★★

The BEV Home Page is a local community network that describes various groups, activities and functions of the town of Blacksburg, Virginia. It has hypertext links to documents about community activities, local businesses and shops, arts and entertainment, the library and the health care center. It also archives Internet software and provides active links to university and government Web servers.

KEYWORDS Community, Community Networks, Government, Virginia
AUDIENCE Community Activists, Community Groups, Network Developers, Network Users, Virginia Residents
CONTACT webmaker@bev.net
FREE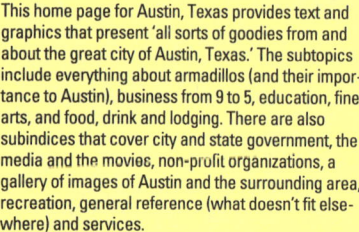

http://crusher.bev.net/index.html

Bakersfield - Kern County ★★★

The home page for Bakersfield, California, which is produced by its major local BBS service, Desert Jewel, presents images and hypertext descriptions of use to local residents, although much of it would be of interest to the tourist. There are subindices covering such topics as the Chamber of Commerce, a current satellite weather map, city and county recreational areas, an online business mall, local entertainment and the arts, and municipal services including schools and medical services.

KEYWORDS Business, California, Tourism
AUDIENCE Art Enthusiasts, Business Entrepreneurs, Californians, Museum Enthusiasts, Tourists
CONTACT jbransom@gem.kern.com
FREE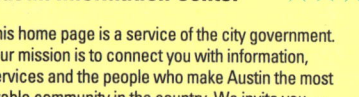

http://www.kern.com/

Bangalore - Welcome to the Garden City ★★★

The Bangador, India Home Page provides hypertext images and descriptions of local attractions and facilities of interest primarily to tourists, especially Gibbon Park, the Lal Bagh botanical gardens and the museums and libraries. It is the only city in India where Kannada, Tamil, Telugu and Hindi are all spoken. It includes a detailed history by Shri Chiranjeev Singh.

KEYWORDS History, India, Languages, Tourism
AUDIENCE History Buffs, India Residents, Linguists, Tourists
CONTACT Dinesh Venkatesh
din_sha@spiderman.bu.edu
FREE

http://spiderman.bu.edu/misc/karnataka/cities/bangalore/

Barossa Valley ★★★

The Barossa Valley Home Page is a community network that provides hypertext descriptions of the local area, with particular emphasis on it being Australia's largest wine producer. It also contains a history and information about the available lodging, and dining.

KEYWORDS Australia, Tourism, Wine
AUDIENCE Australia Residents, History Buffs, Tourists, Wine Enthusiasts
FREE

http://apanix.apana.org.au/~exy/Barossa_Valley.HTML

Belgrade ★★★

The Belgrade, Yugoslavia Home Page is a community network that provides hypermedia images and descriptions that focus on local features of historical interest, including museums, theaters, coffee houses and the Belgrade Fortess - the historical nucleus. It contains multi-media animations.

KEYWORDS Tourism, Yugoslavia
AUDIENCE History Buffs, Multimedia Enthusiasts, Tourists, Yugoslavia Residents
CONTACT lpv@umiacs.umd.edu
FREE

http://www.umiacs.umd.edu/research/lpv/YU/HTML/bg.html

Bellingham-Whatcom County Civic Access ★★★

This home page for Bellingham, Washington presents images and text of primary value to local residents, although travelers could benefit from much of the information. There are subindices that cover such topics as local government information, a history, cultural establishments, educational resources and school board information, state and federal government information, and community events and organizations.

KEYWORDS Business, Tourism, Washington State
AUDIENCE Art Enthusiasts, History Buffs, Tourists, Washington Residents
CONTACT www@nas.com
FREE

http://www.nas.com/civic-access/

Bellingham ★★

This home page for Bellingham, Washington sponsored by the Chamber of Commerce offers images and text of use to local residents, as well as of potential interest to tourists. There are subindices that cover such topics as the Chamber of Commerce, a community calendar of events, current regional business news, and a list of Chamber of Commerce members. There are also links to Washington State Web sites and government services, a weather map and a wine tour.

KEYWORDS Business, Tourism, Washington State

Cities

AUDIENCE Business Entrepreneurs, Tourists, Washington Residents
CONTACT smontgom@pacificrim.net
FREE

http://www.pacificrim.net/~chamber/

Belmont — Access for the Community ★★★

The home page of Belmont, California is produced by the city government and provides information of use primarily to local residents, although it would be of assistance to any travelers pausing there. There are subindices that cover such topics as the Chamber of Commerce, education & the library, local government (with a link to City Hall), links to the Greater Bay Area, organizations, clubs and groups, news and activities, and the town's technology plan.

KEYWORDS Business, California, Tourism
AUDIENCE Business Entrepreneurs, Californians, Tourists
CONTACT info@aimnet.com
FREE

http://www.belmont.gov/

Bend Home Page ★★★

The home page of Bend, Oregon presents GIF graphical images and hypertext descriptions of features and facilities of the area of interest both to local residents and travelers. It has subindices that link to topics such as arts and entertainment, books and libraries, business and services, the community center, education, food and drink, golf, government, history, the marketplace, a newsstand, parks and outdoors, real estate, reference, shopping, special events, tourism and visitors' information.

KEYWORDS History, Oregon, Tourism
AUDIENCE Art Enthusiasts, Business Entrepreneurs, Oregon Residents, Tourists
CONTACT info@bendnet.com
FREE

http://www.bendnet.com/bend.html

Berlin Web ★★

This site provides links to information in English and German about Berlin, its history, and its notable sights, including the Berlin Wall, universities in Berlin, the Brandenburg Gate built 1788-1791, 'Schauspielhaus' concert hall, the former and future house of parliament, built 1884-1894, Olympia stadium (from 1936), and more.

KEYWORDS Germany, History
AUDIENCE Educators, Germans, History Buffs, Tourists
FREE

http://www.chemie.fu-berlin.de/adressen/berlin.html

Bielefeld ★★★

The home page of Bielefeld, Germany provides hypertext images and links to documentation describing features and facilities of the town and the surrounding environs, such as theatres and concerts, shopping, dining, the local industry and commerce, the educational facilities, and sports and recreational opportunities. It has links to Universitat Bielefeld.

KEYWORDS Germany, Tourism

AUDIENCE Germany Residents, Germany Scholars, History Buffs, Tourists
CONTACT Anke Bodzin
anke@SFB360.Uni-Bielefeld.DE
FREE

http://www.techfak.uni-bielefeld.de/blfd/blfdengl.html

Bilbao, Spain ★★★

The home page of Bilbao, Spain, the capital of Bizkaia in the valley of the Nervion River 20 Km from the Cantabrico Sea, provides hypertext images and links to documentation of interest to tourists. It includes history, and where to lodge, dine and shop.

KEYWORDS History, Spain
AUDIENCE History Buffs, Spain Residents, Tourists
CONTACT Jose Maria Alcaide
webmaster@we.lc.ehu.es
FREE

http://www.we.lc.ehu.es/ BasqueCountry/Bilbao.html

Birmingham Web ★★★

The home page of Birmingham, Alabama is a volunteer project to publicize Birmingham on the WWW and to provide free Internet access for area schools and libraries. It has graphical images and hypertext subindexes that cover such topics as events; attractions, museums, and historical sites; schools and libraries (including Jackson State and Samford Universities); government agencies; publications, and arts and dining.

KEYWORDS Alabama, Community Networks, Tourism
AUDIENCE Alabama Residents, Art Enthusiasts, Community Activists, Community Groups
FREE

http://www.the-matrix.com/

Bitola ★★★

The home page of Bitola, the second largest town in the Republic of Macedonia provides hypertext images and documentation primarily focusing on the history of the area, including the ancient ruins of Heraclea Lyncestis on the famous Roman road, Via Egnatia.

KEYWORDS European Culture, Tourism
AUDIENCE History Buffs, Macedonia Residents, Tourists
CONTACT Plamen Bliznakov
Plamen.Bliznakov@ASU.edu
FREE

http://ASUdesign.eas.asu.edu/~bliznako/Macedonia/republic/images/citiesBitola.html

Blacksburg Electronic Village ★★★

The home page of Blacksburg, Virginia presents GIF graphics and html text descriptions that open the town to the outside world and would be of interest to tourists; however, its primary focus is providing Internet services to the local community. It has subindexes that cover such topics as a history of the town, weather, places to stay and eat; the Village mall, an index to local

businesses and shops; community events and news (including senior, arts and entertainment pages); an education center, with local schools on the Web; museums (including the Museum of Natural History); the health care center; and links to other Virginia resources.

KEYWORDS History, Tourism, Virginia
AUDIENCE Tourists, Virginia Rresidents; Community Activists; Community Leaders; Art Enthusiasts; Museum Enthusiasts; History Enthusiasts
CONTACT webmaker@bev.net
FREE

http://www.bev.net/

Bloomington & Indiana University Information ★★★

The home page of Bloomington, Indiana is of interest to residents and visitors. It is composed of graphics and hypertext descriptions containing such topics as the Indiana University Music School Web site, including a listing of local musical and theatrical events; a listing of local parks; restaurant reviews; guides to the local bookstores, music stores and video rental establishments; a guide to recycling, current weather conditions; some images; and links to the Indiana University Computer Science Department and the local computing environment.

KEYWORDS Indiana, Tourism, Universities
AUDIENCE Community Activists, Community Groups, Community Leaders, Indiana Residents
CONTACT webmaster@cs.indiana.edu
FREE

http://www.cs.indiana.edu/inds/localstuff.html

Boca Raton ★★★

The home page of Boca Raton presents images and hypertext that includes information for both visitors and residents - business climate, education, government, recreation facilities, cultural activities, accommodations, and many other aspects of our community. Boca Raton is a dynamic community that melds high-tech industry, culture and sophistication with a warm, hometown appeal. It has indexes that link to such topics as shopping, business, accommodations, real estate, Chamber of Commerce, history, culture, education, recreation, the environment, transportation, government, licenses, health, and worship.

KEYWORDS Community Networks, Florida, Tourism
AUDIENCE Art Enthusiasts, Community Groups, Community Leaders, Florida Residents
CONTACT Chamber@BocaRaton.com
FREE

http://bocaraton.com/

Brussels Eurocapital ★★★

A business-related site, Brussels Eurocapital offers information on the city as a conference or convention place with a schedule of events for the next few years, information on doing business in Brussels, general European information, tourist news, golf resources, and other links.

KEYWORDS Belgium
AUDIENCE International Business Professionals, Tourists

Cities

CONTACT   Olivier Caeymaex
          ocaeymaex@infoboard.be

FREE

http://www.tele.fi/~brussels/

Bryan/College Station WWW Info Service ★★★

This home page for Bryan & College Station, Texas contains commercial, organizational, and city government listings. Each listing holds information ranging from simple lists to online fax ordering. There is also a complete visitor's guide available for virtual tourists which includes a guide to the surrounding communities. There are also links to information on where to lodge, dine and shop.

KEYWORDS History, Texas, Tourism
AUDIENCE Business Entrepreneurs, History Buffs, Texas Residents, Tourists

FREE

http://www.ipt.com/

Buenos Aires ★★★

This is a tourist guide to Buenos Aires in Brazil. It covers the city's history, culture, places to visit, transportation, hotels, restaurants, embassies/consulates, credit card company phone numbers, and other important phone numbers. This information would be of use to any visitor.

KEYWORDS Brazil, Tourism
AUDIENCE Argentina Residents, Business Professionals, Latin Americans, Tourists
CONTACT   www@secyt.gov.ar

FREE

http://www.secyt.gov.ar/bue/buei.html

Burkhard Kirste ★★★

This Berlin, Germany home page provides hypertext images and documents including links that describe available facilities and attractions, including transportation, media, government services, the Berlin Tourist Center, art and music events, and the Berlin Film Festival. There is also a history, and links to other German WWW servers.

KEYWORDS Germany, Tourism
AUDIENCE Film Enthusiasts, Germany Residents, History Buffs, Tourists
CONTACT   kirste@chemie.fu-berlin.de

FREE

http://www.chemie.fu-berlin.de/adressen/berlin.html

Calgary Information Selection Page ★★★

The Calgary, Canada Home Page is a community network that provides hypertext images and links to local attractions and facilities, including accommodations, entertainment, events, dining and adventurous sports.

KEYWORDS Camping, Canada, Community Networking, Tourism
AUDIENCE Art Enthusiasts, Canada Residents, Canadians, Tourists

FREE

http://www.fleethouse.com/fhcanada/western/alta/calgary/cal_pop.html

Calvert Business & Community Organizations ★★★

The home page of Calvert, Texas, presents subindices that cover such topics as the local history, general data about the town, the artisans, businesses and community organizations. In addition, there is information that would benefit tourists, such as lodging, dining and shopping. The primary orientation, however, is toward those interested in either starting a small business there or investing in a current operation.

KEYWORDS Business, Texas, Tourism
AUDIENCE Business Entrepreneurs, History Buffs, Tourists

FREE

http://www.rtis.com/reg/calvert/

Cambridge Civic Network ★★★

The Cambridge Civic Community Network is an Internet project of The Center for Civic Networking, with the participation of individuals and organizations from the Cambridge Community. This site features local and regional information, and links to civic groups and reports on the long-range growth policy plan.

KEYWORDS Community, Community Networking, Government, Massachusetts
AUDIENCE Community Activists, Community Groups, Massachusetts Residents, Network Developers, Network Users
CONTACT   Todd N. Marinoff
          cambmis@ai.mit.edu

FREE

http://www.civic.net:2401/cambridge_civic_network/cambridge_civic_network.html

Carlsbad Community Home Page ★★★★

The Carlsbad Home Page is a local community network that provides information and links to various businesses, services, local government agencies, schools and attractions in the Carlsbad area. This city is located just north of San Diego, CA.

KEYWORDS California, Community, Government, Tourism
AUDIENCE Californians, Community Activists, Community Groups, Network Users
CONTACT   Dan.Anderson
          dan.anderson@bluebird.com

FREE

http://www.bluebird.com/carlsbad/

Charleston Info ★★★

The home page of Charleston, South Carolina presents hypermedia links to information and images of interest both to tourists and to local residents. The subindices include statistical geographical and census data, local events (Spoleto, Worldfest), dining, entertainment, shopping, places to visit, real estate, vacation and apartment rentals, schools, and the weather.

KEYWORDS History, South Carolina, Tourism
AUDIENCE Art Enthusiasts, History Buffs, South Carolina Residents, Tourists
CONTACT   info@sims.com

FREE

http://www.sims.net/places/charleston.html

Chemnitz ★★★

The home page of Chemnitz, Germany provides hypertext images and links to documents describing attractions and facilities primarily of interest to tourists and residents, such as museums, bookstores, hotels, restaurants and contact addresses. It also has a link to the technical university, Chemnitz und Umgebung.

KEYWORDS Germany, Tourism
AUDIENCE German Technicians, Germany Residents, History Buffs, Tourists
CONTACT   Ines Schoenherr
          Ines.Schoenherr@hrz.tu-chemnitz.de

FREE

http://www.tu-chemnitz.de/home/ins/chemnitz.html

Chicago General Information ★★★★

The Chicago! home page is one of several that cover various features and attractions of Chicago, Illinois. It contains hypermedia graphical images and hypertext with subindices that cover such topics as music, philosophy, art, literature, law, politics and Chicago universities. There is also a link to the Chicago Public Library Information Center (CPL) which contains a great deal of information about municipal services, and to VirtualChicago, a MUSE virtual world. Finally, there are links to such subjects as Chicago neighborhoods, the Mercantile Exchange, the Chamber of Commerce, weather and winning lottery numbers.

KEYWORDS Business, Chicago, History, Tourism
AUDIENCE Art Enthusiasts, History Buffs, Illinois Residents, Museum Enthusiasts, Tourists
CONTACT   strange@tezcat.com

FREE

http://www.tezcat.com/web/chicago.html

City of Alexandria VA, Electronic Community ★★★

The home page of Alexandria, Virginia presents images and text in hypermedia format that depict features and facilities of the town of use to local residents and of interest to tourists. There are links to such topics as the local libraries and musuems, city hall, regional information, citizens and neighborhoods, state and federal government agencies, non-profit services, the education and business communities, utilities and transportation.

KEYWORDS Skiing, Tourism, Virginia
AUDIENCE Business Entrepreneurs, Museum Enthusiasts, Students (University), Tourists
CONTACT   ddavis@osf1.gmu.edu

FREE

http://ralph.gmu.edu/alexandria/alexandria.html

Cities

City of Altamonte Springs ★★★

The home page of Altamonte Springs, Florida presents graphics and text that attempt to entice new business into the area. There is a map, a town profile, an overview that includes demographics, labor and location, a description of the quality of life, art and culture, an account of the development of the central business district, city government, taxation, history, city agencies and services, as well as housing.

KEYWORDS Business, Florida, Real Estate
AUDIENCE Business Entrepreneurs, Florida Residents, Real Estate Entrepreneurs, Tourists
CONTACT webmaster@globalnet.net
FREE

http://www.globalnet.net/golda09.html

City of Antwerp ★★★

This is the home page of Antwerp, Belgium, 'the City-on-the-Scheldt.' It provides hypermedia images and descriptions (drawn from a travel brochure) of local attractions, including museums, churches, theaters and sports, such as the town hall, the National Maritime Museum 'Steen,' the city library, the Royal House and the Botanical Gardens.

KEYWORDS Belgium, History, Tourism
AUDIENCE Belgium Residents, Europe Scholars, History Buffs, Tourists
FREE

http://www.ufsia.ac.be/antwerp/antwerp.html

The City of Bari ★★★

The Bari home page provides hypermedia animations, images and descriptions of the city of Bari, located in Apulia in the south of Italy. It also covers the local climate, products and history. The AVI animations were developed by Team on Sistemi Techno-Educativi in Tecnopolis. Their size ranges from 2 to 16 MB. On UNIX machines they can be viewed through Mark Podlipec's XANIM package.

KEYWORDS Italy, Multimedia Resources
AUDIENCE History Buffs, Italy Residents, Multimedia Enthusiasts, Tourists
CONTACT Vincenzo De Florio DeFlorio@Fourier.CSATA.it
FREE

http://fourier.csata.it/bari.html

City of Batavia Homepage ★★★

The home page of Batavia, Illinois (the 'Windmill City' located 35 miles west of Chicago) presents features of the town that would interest and assist local residents, as well as any travelers who might be passing through. Its subindexes cover such topics as the public schools, the Chamber of Commerce, park district, public library, municipal services, civic groups, a community calendar, a history and a link to the Fermi science lab. In addition, there is a postcard walking tour.

KEYWORDS History, Illinois, New York, Tourism
AUDIENCE History Buffs, Illinois Residents, Tourists
CONTACT karl@mcs.net
FREE

http://www.mcs.net/~bhslrc/batavia.html

City of Berkeley Web ★★★★

The home page of Berkeley, California is produced by the city government and contains extensive listings of service departments and other facilities of the city. It contains subindexes that describe such topics as agencies and services, the Rent Stabilization Board, businesses and organizations, email addresses for city officials and departments, general information about the city, government information including city council schedules, the text of the City Charter, libraries (including a link to the University of California library system), museums, the performing arts, and theaters. There are also links out to the wider Bay Area, California State Government and the Federal Government.

KEYWORDS California, Community Networks, Tourism
AUDIENCE Art Enthusiasts, Californians, Museum Enthusiasts, Music Enthusiasts
CONTACT webmaster@ci.berkeley.ca.us
FREE

http://www.ci.berkeley.ca.us/

City of Blue Springs ★★

The home page for Blue Springs, Indiana (in the beginning stages of its development) presents hypertext general information about the town for the public at large. It has links to such topics as the Blue Springs Magazine, a message from the mayor, a new resident's guide, a guide Around City Hall (with a telephone directory), parks and recreation, activities, recycling services, and police deptartment services.

KEYWORDS Community Networks, Indiana, Tourism
AUDIENCE Community Activists, Community Groups, Indiana Residents, Tourists
CONTACT dmckinney@ci.blue-springs.mo.us
FREE

http://www.grapevine.com/bluspr/home.htm

City of Cambridge, Massachusetts ★★★

The home page of Cambridge, Massachusetts concentrates on the city's municipal services, with subindices that provide information concerning the arts, education, employment, the environment, health care, high technology, human services, libraries, museums, tourism, maps, and the local transit services. There are also links to state and federal government services.

KEYWORDS Massachusetts, Tourism
AUDIENCE Art Enthusiasts, Librarians, Massachusetts Residents, Museum Enthusiasts, Tourists
FREE

http://www.ai.mit.edu/projects/iiip/Cambridge/homepage.html

City of Coral Springs, Florida ★★★

The brief home page of Coral Springs, Florida presents hypertext that describes features of the town that would interest potential business developers, entrepreneurs and new residents. The statistics are listed in detail. There are also addresses and contact numbers for lodging and dining establishments.

KEYWORDS Business, Florida, Tourism
AUDIENCE Business Entrepreneurs, Florida Residents, Real Estate Entrepreneurs, Tourists
CONTACT info@compass.net
FREE

http://www.compass.net/~cspring/index.html

City of Evansville Home Page ★★★

The home page of Evansville, Indiana provides text and images that present features and facilities of interest primarily to tourists. There are sublinks to such topics as an area profile, entertainment, education, history, accommodations, churches, area services, and 'YelloWeb Pages.'

KEYWORDS History, Indiana, Tourism
AUDIENCE History Buffs, Indiana Residents, Tourists
CONTACT web@evansville.net
FREE

http://www.evansville.net/eville/

City of Los Angeles Home Page ★★

The City of Los Angeles Home Page is a community network provided and maintained by the Los Angeles Department of Information Services. It provides hypertext and links to various municipal services, including the fire department, the bureau of street lighting, and the Mayor's Committee on Technology Implementation. It also has links to state and federal government agencies.

KEYWORDS California, Community
AUDIENCE Californians, Community Activists, Community Groups, Network Developers, Network Users
CONTACT webmaster@www.ci.la.ca.us
FREE

http://www.ci.la.ca.us/

City of Palo Alto Home Page ★★★

This site is a community network that focuses specifically on the city of Palo Alto, CA. It provides graphical maps, demographics, local commerce, government access, and information of interest to tourists.

KEYWORDS California, Community, Government, Tourism
AUDIENCE Californians, Community Activists, Community Groups, Network Developers
CONTACT wwwadmin@city.palo-alto.ca.us/
FREE

http://www.city.palo-alto.ca.us/home.html

City of San Carlos Home Page ★★★

This WWW site provides community access to the city government of San Carlos, California. There is much information here about many aspects of the local government, such as local elections, city hall announcements, events, and small businesses in San Carlos. The site also provides links to Bay Area newspapers, as well as other city, state and federal government agencies.

KEYWORDS California, Government

Cities

AUDIENCE Community Groups, Government Employees, Government Officials
CONTACT scarlos@crl.com
FREE

http://www.abag.ca.gov/abag/local_gov/city/san_carlos/schome.html

City of San Diego Home Page ★★★★

The City of San Diego Home Page is a community network that offers extensive coverage and links to local tourist attractions and amenities, city and state government agencies, TV and radio stations, and real estate listings. The site provides graphical coverage of the America's Cup race and of the San Diego Chargers, the local professional football team.

KEYWORDS California, Community, Government, Tourism
AUDIENCE Californians, Community Activists, Community Groups, Network Developers
CONTACT info@sannet.gov
FREE

http://white.nosc.mil/sandiego.html

City of Tempe ★★★

The Tempe Home Page is a community network providing comprehensive indices with hypertext documentation and links to a variety of local functions and facilities. Some of the highlights of this site include neighborhood associations, the library and museum, parks, schools, and the upcoming 1996 Superbowl.

KEYWORDS Arizona, Community, Tourism
AUDIENCE Arizona Residents, Community Activists, Community Groups, Network Developers
FREE

http://aztec.asu.edu/government/Tempe/tmpmain.html

City of Vancouver Home Page ★★★

This page is a directory to information about the City of Vancouver, Canada municipal government. Information about municipal services such as police, fire and rescue, libraries, parks and community centres, planning and land use are just a few of the areas covered by this resource. There is also travel and tourism information for people interested in visiting the city.

KEYWORDS Canada, Culture, Municipal Government, Vancouver
AUDIENCE Canadians, Tourists
CONTACT Scott Macrae
mac@wimsey.com
FREE

http://www.city.vancouver.bc.ca

Clear Lake (Houston Suburb) ★★★

The home page of Clear Lake, Texas, a suburb of Houston, presents graphical images and hypertext documentation of interest to both tourists and local residents. It has subindexes which cover such topics as the Chamber of Commerce, churches, transportation, marinas, maps, the weather, and where to lodge, dine and shop. There are also links to major facilities surrounding Houston, such as the Johnson Space Center.

KEYWORDS California, History, Texas, Tourism
AUDIENCE Business Entrepreneurs, Texas Residents, Tourists
CONTACT info@einet.net
FREE

http://www.crl.com/~akmathes/clearlake.html

Cleveland State University's Cleveland Index ★★★

The home page of Cleveland, Ohio presents hypermedia information of interest to tourists, as well as to local residents. It links to such public institutions as Case Western University, the Cleveland Institute of Art and the public library. There is a special focus on the Cleveland professional sports teams (the Browns, the Cavaliers and the Indians) and Web pages for local businesses and institutions, such as the American Cybercasting Corporation, Amerisoft and Aquatic Technology.

KEYWORDS History, Ohio, Tourism, Universities
AUDIENCE Art Enthusiasts, History Buffs, Ohio Residents, Sports Fans, Tourists
CONTACT webmaster@csuohio.edu
FREE

http://www.csuohio.edu/cleveix.html

Colorado Springs Visitor Center ★★★

The home page of Colorado Springs, Colorado, presents graphics and hypertext descriptions of attractions and features of the area of interest both to tourists and to local residents. Colorado Springs sits at the base of Pikes Peak, the 14,110-foot guardian of the Pikes Peak Region. It is a prime site for tourism because of its many natural and man-made features. There are a plethora of various places to enjoy, including the Garden of the Gods, the Flying W Ranch, Seven Falls, the United States Air Force Academy, the United States Olympic Training Center, the Cheyenne Mountain Zoo, the Broadmoor Hotel, the Pikes Peak Center and much more!'

KEYWORDS Colorado, History, Skiing, Tourism
AUDIENCE Canadians, Colorado Residents, Outdoors Enthusiasts, Ski Enthusiasts, Tourists
CONTACT m_frazier@borgil.cxo.dec.com
FREE

http://www.rmii.com/visit/visiter.html

Commission on San Francisco's Environment (CSFE) ★★

The CSFE has prepared a report on the Environmental State of the City providing information on environmental topics such as solid waste management, energy use, air quality, and water management. The goal of CSFE is to bring San Francisco closer to environmental sustainability. The site on the IGC computers contains information about the report, such as the title page and table of contents and the introduction, but it lacks the contents of the actual report.

KEYWORDS Environment, Water Quality
AUDIENCE Californians, Environmentalists
FREE

gopher://gopher.igc.apc.org/11/orgs/sfenvcom

Conroe - Montgomery County, Texas ★★★

The home page of Conroe, Texas provides graphical images and text description that focus on the area's history. The goal of this page is to provide a service to the community which offers information regarding current affairs and perspective about the history of Montgomery County and its citizens. Montgomery County is the home of the historic Crighton Theatre, the Cynthia Woods Mitchell Pavilion, the Woodlands Symphony Orchestra, 22,000-acre Lake Conroe, and one of the largest concentrations of golf courses in the nation.

KEYWORDS History, Texas, Tourism
AUDIENCE Boating Enthusiasts, Fishing Enthusiasts, Golf Enthusiasts, Outdoors Enthusiasts
CONTACT info@mcia.com
FREE

http://mcia.infohwy.com/

Craven County Areas of Interest ★★★

The home page of Craven County, North Carolina presents images and hypertext of interest to local residents as well as tourists. Its mild climate, easy access to water, and friendly people draw visitors from around the world. Activities include sailing, golf, beachcombing, and shopping. The Croatian National Forest is located in the eastern part of Craven County. There are subindexes that link to such topics as arts/leisure, economic development, education, government, health care, history and the weather.

KEYWORDS History, North Carolina, Tourism
AUDIENCE Golf Enthusiasts, North Carolina Residents, Outdoors Enthusiasts, Sailing Enthusiasts
CONTACT helpdesk@coastalnet.com
FREE

http://www.eastnc.coastalnet.com/coastalnet/html/cr_area.htm

Edinburgh - Capital of Scotland ★★★

The Edinburgh home page is a community network with hypertext images and descriptions of local attractions and facilities primarily of interest to tourists and residents including The Official Guide, a city center map, facts and figures, and descriptions of famous Edinburghers.

KEYWORDS Scotland, Tourism
AUDIENCE Community Activists, Community Groups, Network Developers, Network Users
CONTACT Ken Currie
efrkwc@icbl.hw.ac.uk
FREE

http://www.efr.hw.ac.uk/EDC/Edinburgh.html

Cities

Estes Park ★★★

This is the home page of Estes Park, Colorado, gateway to Rocky Mountain National Park. It presents GIF images and text describing features and attractions of the area for tourists and residents. Subindexes link to topics including local lodging, hiking, biking, skiing, and fishing, upcoming events, restaurants (with menus), merchants' access and commercial endeavors, educational opportunities, and doors to the Internet.

KEYWORDS Colorado, History, Tourism
AUDIENCE Colorado Residents, Fishing Enthusiasts, Hiking Enthusiasts, History Buffs
CONTACT arthurvb@Pipeline.com
FREE

http://www.csn.net/~arthurvb/

Eugene Home Page ★★★

The home page of the city of Eugene, Oregon presents graphic images and comprehensive hypertext descriptions of the features, facilities and attractions of the town for the use of residents and tourists. The well-developed indexes contains topics such as business pages, community pages, facts and figures, governmental agencies, a history, media, schools and colleges, the surrounding area, weather, arts and entertainments, events and festivals, maps, parks, recreation, restaurants and cafes, shopping, transportation, hotels and bed & breakfasts, in addition to a major link to all the facilities of the University of Oregon.

KEYWORDS Community Networks, Oregon, Universities
AUDIENCE History Buffs, Oregon Residents, Students (University), Tourists
CONTACT sgazette@efn.org
FREE

http://www.efn.org/~sgazette/eugenehome.html

Fairfax County (Economic Development Authority) ★★★

The home page of Fairfax County, Virginia presents hypertext describing the community, as well as conventions and tourists. Fairfax County, Virginia is home to 23,000 businesses, trade associations, and corporations. Located across the Potomac River from Washington, D.C., Fairfax County offers many advantages for businesses seeking to relocate in the mid-Atlantic region. There are also links here to such topics as selecting a business location or site, arranging a meeting or convention, doing business in Fairfax County, finding partners and suppliers, establishing international operations in Fairfax County, demographic and economic characteristics, and visitor information.

KEYWORDS Business, Tourism, Virginia
AUDIENCE Business Entrepreneurs, Business Professionals, Tourists, Virginia Residents
FREE

http://www.eda.co.fairfax.va.us/fceda

Farragut, Tennessee's World Wide Web ★★

Farragut, Tennessee's World Wide Web page presents information about the Farragut community. Users will find community services, schools, emergency services information, weather, and recreational areas on this site. In addition, there is contact information for the town hall, and link to pages outside Farragut, such as information about Tennessee and Knoxville.

KEYWORDS Cities, Tennessee, Tourism
AUDIENCE Tennessee Residents, Tourists, Travelers
CONTACT Ken Baker
baker@cti-pet.com
FREE

http://denali.cti-pet.com/Farragut_docs/farragut.html

Federal Way ★★★

The home page of Federal Way, Washington is composed of hypertext descriptions of the town's attributes that would be attractive to new businesses. Federal Way is in the Puget Sound region of Washington. This page contains links to such topics as a good place for business, Federal Way government, the quality of life, Vision 2001, historical background, top ten employers, and contact numbers for more information.

KEYWORDS Business, Tourism
AUDIENCE Business Entrepreneurs, Business Professionals, History Buffs, Tourists
CONTACT cher@eskimo.com
FREE

http://www.eskimo.com/~chorus/fedway/index.html

Flagstaff, AZ CityLink ★★★

The Flagstaff CityLink is a community network that is primarily focussed on the interests of tourists, such as food, lodging and shopping facilities. It also has a link, through the Chamber of Commerce, to local government services and businesses.

KEYWORDS Arizona, Community, Tourism
AUDIENCE Arizona Residents, Community Activists, Community Groups
CONTACT citylink@neosoft.com
FREE

http://www.neosoft.com/citylink/flagstaf/default.html

Grenoble ★★★

This provides information about Grenoble, France. The links include the Grenoble University Computing Center (CICG), Pierre Mendès France University, university and research phone book, all the Information Servers of the Grenoble area, theatres and other cultural events. The gopher server is being phased out.

KEYWORDS Computer Networks, France, Scholarly Communication
AUDIENCE Educators (University), Grenoble Residents, Students (Secondary/University)
FREE

http://www.grenet.fr/

gopher://gopher.grenet.fr/

Information on Campbell, California ★★

The new home page of Campbell, California provides cursory listings of local medical services, parks, places to have lunch and the weather. It is being composed by one resident in his spare time.

KEYWORDS Business, California, Tourism
AUDIENCE Business Entrepreneurs, Californians, Tourists
CONTACT Stephen Goldschmidt
goldschm@HaL.com
FREE

http://www.hal.com/~goldschm/campbell.html

Ipswich Web (Queensland, Australia) ★★★★

The home page of Ipswich in Queensland, Australia provides images and hypertext links to areas of interest primarily to tourists and those interested in starting new businesses in the area. Its submenus cover such topics as the city council (including statements from members and official documents), tourism, recreation and leisure, employment, education and training (with a directory of educational and training institutions in the region, and links to a selection of Internet educational resources), business and economic development, instructions and software for exploring the Internet, and WWW pages for local citizens.

KEYWORDS Australia, Business, Tourism
AUDIENCE Australia Residents, Business Entrepreneurs, Community Activists, Tourists
CONTACT ipsweb@gil.ipswichcity.qld.gov.au
FREE

http://gil.ipswichcity.qld.gov.au/home.html

Kobe Earthquake Diary ★★★

The Kobe Earthquake Diary presents a collection of email exchanges from several people involved with the Kobe Earthquake in January 1995. Users will find a personal account of the events and how they affected the region. Correspondence between friends and family, covering everything from concerns for safety to the status of roads, death tolls, and jammed communication lines, can be found here.

KEYWORDS Diaries, Earthquakes, Email, Japan, Natural Disasters
AUDIENCE Disaster Followers, News Buffs
CONTACT Stephen Turnbull
turnbull@shako.sk.tsukuba.ac.jp
FREE

http://turnbull.sk.tsukuba.ac.jp/jishin.html

Kobe Earthquake Information ★★★

This site is a linked index of information relating to the 1995 Kobe, Japan earthquake. The site provides links to news about the disaster and reconstruction of Kobe City with photo images from Kobe City University of Foreign Studies, and much more.

KEYWORDS Earthquakes, Japan
AUDIENCE Japan Residents, Journalists
CONTACT www-admin@rikvax.riken.go.jp
FREE

http://www.riken.go.jp/news/earthquake.html

Government & Politics

Cities

Laguna Beach City Link ★★★

The Laguna Beach Home Page is a community network that provides hypertext descriptions of community facilities and activities, including the arts, points of interests, restaurants, hotels and a calendar of events.

KEYWORDS Community, Tourism
AUDIENCE Californians, Community Activists, Community Groups
CONTACT telesync@ix.netcom.com
FREE

http://www.deltanet.com/telesync/citylink/lagunabeach/index.htm

Little Rock, AR [CityLink] ★★★

The Little Rock, Arkansas Home Page is a community network that provides hypertext descriptions and links to local facilities and activities, including places to lodge, eat and shop. It includes pages concerning General Douglas McArthur's birthplace and the Little Rock Zoo.

KEYWORDS Community, Network Servers
AUDIENCE Arkansas Residents, Community Activists, Community Groups
FREE

http://www.neosoft.com/citylink/lit-rock/default.html

Metcom ★★★

Metcom is a gopher server that provides information about the city of Tuscon, Arizona. This information includes descriptions of the city, its surroundings, and its lifestyle, as well as documents about local arts and entertainment, and information about local business and educational institutions.

KEYWORDS Arizona, Business, Community Networking, Tourism
AUDIENCE Arizona Residents, General Public, Travelers
CONTACT dandrea@econ.tucson.az.us
FREE

gopher://econ.tucson.az.us/

Munster ★★★

The home page of Basel, Germany. It provides hypertext images and descriptions (in German) of local attractions and facilities of interest primarily to tourists, including museums, libraries, the theater and sports. It also has links to local chemistry and pharmaceutical industries.

KEYWORDS Germany, Theater, Tourism
AUDIENCE History Buffs, Italy Residents, Theater Enthusiasts, Tourists
FREE

http://www.urz.unibas.ch/basel/kirch/muenster.htm

National Capital FreeNet ★★★

The Ottawa Freenet is a community network that provides hypertext links to descriptive text and active links concerning social and health services, the Government Center, science, schools, libraries and special interest groups.

KEYWORDS Canada, Community
AUDIENCE Canada Residents, Community Activists, Community Groups
CONTACT office@freenet.carleton.ca
FREE

http://freenet.carleton.ca/

New York's Capital District ★★★

The home page of Albany, New York (Capital District) presents comprehensive GIF graphical images and hypertext descriptions covering features and facilities of the area of use to local residents and of interest to tourists. There are subindexes that cover such topics as academic institutions, dining, entertainment, industry, leisure, maps, media, organizations, politics, retail services, and the weather. There is a link to the myriad services at the State University.

KEYWORDS New York, Tourism, Universities
AUDIENCE History Buffs, New York Residents, Students (University), Tourists
CONTACT rich.louis@albany.net
FREE

http://www.albany.net/~danorton/captdist.html

Paris ★★★

This web site, which is a collaborative effort by individuals in both Paris and the United States, contains an extensive collection of images and text regarding all of the major monuments and museums of Paris, including maps of the Metro and the RER, calendars of events and promotional material relating to local department stores. There is also a visitors' section with up-to-date tourist information on hotels, restaurants, airport schedules and the latest weather images. It includes extensive links to other resources about Paris and France, and a selected bibliography of history and architecture in Paris.

KEYWORDS Art, Cultural Studies, Travel
AUDIENCE Educators, Researchers, Students, Travelers
CONTACT Norman Barth norman@ucsd.edu
FREE

http://meteora.ucsd.edu:80/~norman/paris/

Phoenix, Arizona ★★★

The ArizonaWeb is a community network that provides hypertext information about the Phoenix Metropolitan area and surrounding cities indexed under such subjects as — history, visitors information, transportation, hotels, dining, social services, medical centers, businesses and educational opportunities.

KEYWORDS Community, Tourism
AUDIENCE Arizona Residents, Community Activists, Community Groups, Tourists
FREE

http://Arizonaweb.rtd.com/phoenix

Pueblo OnLine - What's New ★★★

Pueblo Online is a community information service for the city of Pueblo, Colorado. The current version makes critical links between business, government, industry and economic development, with access for residential and private-sector business. The links include real estate listings, local businesses and the Chamber of Commerce.

KEYWORDS Colorado, Community, Government
AUDIENCE Colorado Residents, Community Activists, Community Groups
CONTACT ics@usa.net
FREE

http://usa.net/pueblo/

San Francisco, California ★★

This site is produced by the San Francisco Chamber of Commerce. It includes links to miscellaneous information about San Francisco including geography, history, demographics, education, health and medical facilities, housing, utilities transportation, visitor guides, and restaurants.

KEYWORDS California, Restaurants, Tourism
AUDIENCE Californians, Restaurant Enthusiasts, Shoppers, Tourists
CONTACT Chamber of Commerce, San Francisco webmaster@terminus.com
FREE

http://www.terminus.com/geni/USA/CA/San_Francisco/chamber/index.html

Sault Ste. Marie EDC Homepage ★★★

The home page of Sault Sainte Marie, Ontario, Canada provides images and hypertext descriptions of interest to tourists and residents. It has a tourism subindex covering such topics as history, things to know, attractions, local shopping, accomodations, restaurants, entertainment, and sports facilities. There is also a commercial subindex that covers educational opportunities, electricity, energy, the environment, existing industry, housing, international links location, raw materials, taxation, transportation and wages.

KEYWORDS Canada, Housing, Tourism
AUDIENCE Canada Residents, History Buffs, Tourists
CONTACT ssmedc@soonet.ca
FREE

http://www.soonet.ca/edc/edclgmnu.html

Seattle - The Emerald City ★★★

The Seattle Home Page is a local community network that provides descriptions and links to the Seattle area. The information at this site includes a yellow pages section for business listings and a neighborhood page for personal home pages. The information center page has links to transportation, media, weather, entertainment and general information about Seattle.

KEYWORDS Community, Community Networking, Government, Washington State
AUDIENCE Community Activists, Community Groups, Washington Residents

Cities

CONTACT   seanet@seanet.com
FREE

http://www.seanet.com/Seattle/
SeattleHome.html

Sedona Home Page ★★★

This home page for Sedona, a city in Arizona, offers a community network. Currently under construction, it is working to provide hypertext documents concerning local facilities and activities. It has indexes under the subjects of hiking trails, hotels, Indian ruins, the local newspaper, real estate, resorts, restaurants and nearby sites of interest.

KEYWORDS   Arizona, Community
AUDIENCE   Arizona Residents, Community Activists, Community Groups
CONTACT   arnie@sedona.net
FREE

http://www.sedona.net/sedona.html

Shanghai Home Page ★★★

This is a Web page on Shanghai, the largest industrial and commercial city of China. Users can find a clickable map of Shanghai that shows its major places of interest, as well as pictures of other areas in Shanghai.

KEYWORDS   China
AUDIENCE   Chinese, Shanghai Residents, Tourists
FREE

http://www.engin.swarthmore.edu/~he/shanghai/

Sierra Vista City Home Page ★★★

The Sierra Vista City Page is a community network that provides hypertext descriptions and links to local facilities and services, including government, food, entertainment, travel, shopping and real estate opportunities.

KEYWORDS   Arizona, Community
AUDIENCE   Arizona Residents, Community Activists, Community Groups
CONTACT   Chuck Woodall
           woodallc@cc.ims.disa.mil
FREE

http://www.primenet.com

St. Petersburg Web ★★★

This is a collection of sites in or relevant to the city of St. Petersburg, Russia. Included are a daily news update service; images of local landmarks, visitor information, an online version of 'The Other St. Petersburg,' a guide to the city's 'secret inner life', and links to the home pages of several area periodicals. The text is all in English.

KEYWORDS   Russia, Soviet Union, St. Petersburg
AUDIENCE   Business Professionals, Russians, Travelers
CONTACT   Vadim Denisov
           vd@vd.arcom.spb.su
FREE

http://www.spb.su/

Tallahasee Free-Net Main Menu ★★★
COMMERCIAL

The Tallahassee FreeNet is a community network that provides low-cost access to the Internet to Tallahassee area residents, as well as descriptions and links to social services and organizations, business & professional services, medical & health services and access to the government, science, education, home & garden, and library complexes.

KEYWORDS   Community, Community Networks, Florida, Government
AUDIENCE   Community Activists, Community Groups, Florida Residents
CONTACT   mimi@scri.fsu.edu
FREE

http://freenet3.scri.fsu.edu:81/menus.html

Torino, Italy ★★★

The home page of Torino, Italy is produced by the Politecnico di Torino, which focuses on its research and didactic information, with a phone directory and general information, but it also has a page describing tourist features and attractions of the town of Torino, including such topics as the monetary exchange rates; auto, train, and air transportation schedules and fares, in addition to a map. There are also links to other Italian Web sites.

KEYWORDS   Italy, Tourism
AUDIENCE   Italian Students, Italy Residents, Students (University), Tourists
CONTACT   Alberto Capella
           capella@galileo.polito.it
FREE

http://www.polito.it/travel/travel.html

Town of Amherst ★★★

The home page of Amherst, Massachusetts presents graphics and hypertext that delineate the features and facilities of the area for local residents, although pages of interest to tourists will soon be under construction (June, 1995). There are subindices detailing such topics as town vital statistics, educational opportunities, libraries, fire and police protection, churches, parks, and transportation—and additional pages with addresses and contact numbers for bed & breakfasts, other lodging and dining, and a 'postcard' walking tour.

KEYWORDS   History, Massachusetts, Universities
AUDIENCE   Art Enthusiasts, Community Activists, Massachusetts Residents, Tourists
FREE

http://www-astro.phast.umass.edu/guest/amherst.html

Town of Andover (est. 1646) ★★★

The home page of Andover, Massachusetts presents GIF images and hypertext descriptions that emphasize the town's rich colonial history and its current institutions of education. 'Just twenty-five miles north of Boston, Andover is a town full of history and many picturesque residences - Victorians, Colonials, Cape Cods. Mainly a residential town, Andover also offers Phillips Academy—a distinguished college preparatory school, the Addison Gallery of American Art, and a very highly rated public school system.

KEYWORDS   History, Massachusetts, Tourism
AUDIENCE   Art Enthusiasts, Colonial History Enthusiasts, History Buffs, Massachusetts Residents
CONTACT   webmaster@law.net
FREE

http://metro.turnpike.net/V/victorm/andover.html

Tucson Home Page ★★★

The Tucson Home Page is a community network that serves the Tuscon, Arzona area. It provides hypertext descriptions of local businesses, restaurants and available apartments. It includes school and university offerings and an online dating service.

KEYWORDS   Arizona, Community
AUDIENCE   Arizona Residents, Community Activists, Community Groups
CONTACT   gberns@tucson.com
FREE

http://www.rtd.com/arizona/tucson/index.html

Tulsa Chat ★★
COMMERCIAL

Users must register for access to the Tulsa Chat home page. Currently even a description of what is provided at the site is not available. For non-members, Tulsa Chat provides a link to the Tulsa's home page.

KEYWORDS   Chat Groups, Internet Communications, Oklahoma, Virtual Community
AUDIENCE   Chatters, Oklahoma Residents
COST

http://tonyt.galstar.com/chat.htm

Valencia - A Virtual Trip ★★★

The home page of Valencia, a city on the Mediteranean close to the mouth of the Turia River in Spain, matches text and high-resolution images (with a warning about low bandwidth) focusing on such topics as its festivities, history, business trade fairs, gastronomy, night life, sports, cultural activities, museums, monuments, gardens, as well as what to do and where to shop, go, and sleep. There is a special concentration on its annual Fallas festival, and a detailed history is provided, beginning with Valencia's Roman heritage and founding

KEYWORDS   History, Spain, Tourism
AUDIENCE   History Buffs, Spain Residents, Tourists
CONTACT   vbenet@oo.upv.es
FREE

http://www.upv.es/turista/visit.html

Virtual Chattanooga ★★★

The home page of Chattanooga, Tennessee presents hypermedia information for the benefit of local residents, as well as to attract and serve tourists. It contains subindices that link to such topics as the business environment (provided by the Chamber of Commerce), the Tennessee Aquarium, Lookout Mountain, Rock City, and Ruby Falls. There is also statistical information, including data on schools, the economy, lifestyles and sustainable development. The

Cities – Countries

site is sponsored by a number of local institutions, who are provided with Web space.

Keywords History, Tennessee, Tourism
Audience Art Enthusiasts, Business Entrepreneurs, History Buffs, Tennessee Residents, Tourists
Contact connect@chattanooga.net
Free

http://www.chattanooga.net/

Vukovar ★★★★

The home page of Vukovar, on the Danube River in Croatia, provides graphics and text of interest to those concerned about the area and the effects of present war. It describes the city's location and natural resources, its history, the structure of the municipal government in 1990, a chronology of the war in 1991–'92, photographs, and the rebuilding thereafter. The historical account chronicles over 5,000 years of continuous human settlement.

Keywords Croatia, Tourism
Audience Croatia Residents, History Buffs, Tourists
Free

http://www.rasip.etf.hr/ marios_html/ vukovar/vukovar.html

Webserver in Lahti, Finland ★★★

The Webserver in Lahti, Finland provides information on the Lahti Polytechnic, University of Helsinki, a Lahti research and training centre, and the Technical University of Helsinki in Lahti. There are links to services in Lahti, in Finland, and other countries, as well as links to the congresses in Lahti.

Keywords Education (College/University), Finland
Audience Finns, Students
Contact Webmaster@www.lahti-poly.fi
Free

http://www.lahti-poly.fi

Welcome to Bryan & College Station, Texas ★★★

This home page for Bryan & College Station, Texas presents information for tourists, but is also useful for local residents. There are subpages that cover topics including local businesses, city history, community organizations, news, and entertainment as well as where to dine, shop and lodge.

Keywords History, Texas, Tourism
Audience Business Entrepreneurs, History Buffs, Texas Residents, Tourists
Free

http://www.rtis.com/reg/bcs/

Welcome to Cincinnati ★★★

The home page of Cincinnati, Ohio presents hypermedia information pertinent to local residents, tourists, potential investors and small business entrepreneurs who might like to move there. It has links to such topics as statistical information (1990 Census data and a demographic trend report), geography and a road map. There are links also to schools and universities, libraries, computer organizations, business organizations, entertainment and personal home pages.

Keywords Business, History, Ohio, Tourism
Audience Business Entrepreneurs, History Buffs, Ohio Residents, Tourists
Contact info@iac.net
Free

http://www.iac.net/~bradmc/cinti.html

Welcome to Stockholm! ★★★

The home page of Stockholm, Sweden provides images and hypertext descriptions of interest to tourists, students and local residents. Its subindexes provide links to such topics as general tourist information, museums, information resources (including a map), the Stockholm Water Festival, educational opportunities, the Prime Minister's Office (in Swedish), and the Stockholm Archipelago. There is also coverage of where to lodge, dine and shop.

Keywords Community Services, History, Sweden, Tourism
Audience Art Enthusiasts, History Buffs, Sweden Residents, Tourists
Contact Rickard Schoultz schoultz@sunet.se
Free

http://www.sunet.se/stockholm/

World Wide Web Services in the Tampere Region ★★★

The home page of Tampere, Finland offers links to information about the region (including government and tourist services), education, business, public providers, non-profit organizations, events and contacts. There are maps, links to the Tampere Institute of Technology, the University of Tampere, a description of the elementary school, and tourist information for Finland.

Keywords Finland, History, Tourism
Audience Finland Residents, History Buffs, Students (University), Tourists
Contact webmaster@uta.fi
Free

http://www.uta.fi/region.html

Countries

See also
Business & Economics · *Commerce*
Business & Economics · *International Business*

About Guatemala ★★★

This is a personal home page with information about Guatemalan culture, history, and tourism, with discussions of NAFTA and regional integration. It also contains links to the pages and news services of other Central American countries. In addition, you can learn basic Spanish here.

Keywords Guatemala, Spanish
Audience International Travelers, Latin Americans, Market Analysts, Tourists
Contact Danny Gonzalez DEGONZALEZ@ualr.edu
Free

http://www.ualr.edu/~degonzalez/ guatemala.html

The Age ★★

This online version of Australia's The Age newspaper contains sections (some of which are under construction) such as Computer Age, which has local computer columns, as well as wire services and a shareware repository. Viewers will find a children's section, with stories, jokes, software reviews and links to other kid's pages. There are also areas related to Education, Melbourne, and Sunday Features, as well as a page for special marketing offers.

Keywords Australia, Online Newspapers
Audience Australians, Melbourne Residents, Tourists
Contact support@yarra.vicnet.net.au
Free

http://www.vicnet.net.au/vicnet/ theage.htm

Althingi's Home Page ★★

Althingi (the Icelandic Parliament) was established in 930 A.D., making it one of the oldest surviving governmental institutions in the world. Users can find basic information about this venerable institution, such as material on its members, businesses, and the building which houses the Parliament.

Keywords Iceland, Parliament
Audience Government Researchers, Iceland Residents
Free

http://www.althingi.is/~wwwadm/ upplens.html

An Incomplete Collection of World Flags ★★

This site provides links to information about flag images and how to download them. The four sets of indices available are color in-line images, monochrome in-line images, fewer in-line images (colour display), and fewer in-line images (monochrome display). You will find that each of the lowest level .html files include a reference to the World Factbook, 1993. There are also links to flag associations and other flag-collector resources.

Keywords Collectors, Flags, Images
Audience Artists, Collectors, Graphic Artists, Students (Primary/Secondary), Web Developers
Contact Christopher J.S. Vance jsv@adfa.oz.au
Free

http://www.adfa.oz.au/CS/flg/

Argentina (FAQs) Frequently Asked Questions ★★★★

This FAQ site (in Spanish) contains the directory of FAQs on Argentina. It contains extensive information on Argentina, covering travel information, food, and newspapers. This page contains links to

Countries 331

soc.culture.argentina, soc.answers, and news.answers

KEYWORDS   Argentina, South America, Tourism
AUDIENCE   Argentinians, Business Travelers, Tourists, Travelers
CONTACT   Luis Mandel
           mandel@informatik.uni-muenchen.de
FREE

ftp://rtfm.mit.edu/pub/usenet-by-hierarchy/soc/culture/argentina/

AsiaOne - Daily News and Information on Asia ★★★★

AsiaOne carries daily news and information from Singapore Press Holdings, southeast Asia's premier newspaper and magazine publisher. Links are provided to BusinessTimes Online which contains information on daily news on Singapore and Asia, recent changes and what's coming, choice products and services available on the Net, phone infotainment, and daily highlights.

KEYWORDS   Business, News, Singapore, Southeast Asia
AUDIENCE   Asians, Business Professionals, Researchers, Travelers
CONTACT   Cheah Cheng Poh
           sphepd@singnet.com.sg
FREE

http://www.asia1.com.sg/

Australian System Of Government ★★★

This document provides a detailed description of the Australian system of government, covering its constitution, its political party system and elections, federal, state, and territorial branches of government, and its electoral system.

KEYWORDS   Australia, Government Documents, National Policy, Politics
AUDIENCE   Australian Culture Enthusiasts, Australians, International Lawyers, Political Scientists
FREE

http://www.csu.edu.au/australia/defat/govsys.html

Belgium-Overview ★★★

This Overview site provides general information and links to Belgium including an 'Essay on Belgian Culture.' The general topics include geography and politics, Belgium in Europe, Visiting Belgium, Cities and Regions, Network Services, and miscellaneous Other Belgium overview pages. The site is designed and maintained by Dr. Francisco Heylighen, Senior Research Associate for the Belgian National Fund for Scientific Research at the Free University of Brussels.

KEYWORDS   Belgium, Geography
AUDIENCE   International Business Professionals, Politicians, Tourists
CONTACT   Francis Heylighen
           fheyligh@vnet3.vub.ac.be
FREE

http://pespmc1.vub.ac.be/Belgcul.html

Belgium ★★

This is a general information page about Belgium that lists a great number of figures and statistical facts about the country's geography, people, government, economy, communications, and defense forces. There is only one link to the Central Intelligence Agency home page.

KEYWORDS   Belgium, Geography
AUDIENCE   Belgians, Politicians
FREE

http://www.ic.gov/94fact/country/26.html

Brazil-(FAQs)Frequently Asked Questions ★★★★

This page contains a list of Frequently Asked Questions (and their answers) about the country of Brazil. It is devoted to the discussion of all aspects of Brazil culture, and it references other sites where the reader can obtain specific information on the Internet.

KEYWORDS   Brazil, South America, Tourism
AUDIENCE   Brazilian Culture Enthusiasts, Brazilians, Travelers
CONTACT   Rick Bronson
           rick@rio.moneng.mei.com
FREE

ftp://rtfm.mit.edu/pub/usenet-by-hierarchy/soc/culture/brazil/Soc.Culture.Brazil_Frequent

Bulgaria (FAQs) Frequently Asked Questions ★★★★

This posting contains Frequently Asked Questions (FAQ) about Bulgaria and their answers. The FAQ consists of two parts—general FAQ, and electronic resources FAQ. The page is organized by subject including the following topics—cuisine, art, politics, history, language, and newsgroups.

KEYWORDS   Art, Bulgaria, Culture, Tourism
AUDIENCE   Bulgarian Culture Enthusiasts, Bulgarians, Travelers
CONTACT   Dragomir R. Radev
           radev@news.cs.columbia.edu
FREE

ftp://rtfm.mit.edu/pub/usenet-by-hierarchy/soc/culture/bulgaria/soc.culture.bulgaria_FAQ_%

Canada (FAQs) Frequently Asked Questions ★★

This site contains a list of FAQs (and their answers) about Canadian culture and related matters. It contains a table of contents with subjects such as history, culture, politics, travel, etc.

KEYWORDS   Canada, Culture, History, Tourism
AUDIENCE   Canadian Culture Enthusiasts, Canadians, Tourists, Travelers
CONTACT   Martin Savard
           ag656@freenet.carleton.ca
FREE

ftp://rtfm.mit.edu/pub/usenet-by-hierarchy/soc/culture/canada/

Canadiana—the Canadian Resources Page ★★★★

Canadiana features pointers to Canadian news and information resources, travel updates, government documents, and items of cultural interest.

KEYWORDS   Canada, News, Reference, Tourism
AUDIENCE   Canadians, General Public, Tourists
FREE

http://www.cs.cmu.edu:8001/Web/Unofficial/Canadiana/README.html

Carleton University German Web ★★★

The Carleton University German Web contains links to many German sites such as book online, German civil law, German home pages, German departments in the United States, the German Constitution, news, newsgroups, sports, books, phone numbers, exchange rates, and more.

KEYWORDS   Germany, Internet Resources, Meta-Index (Germany)
AUDIENCE   German Studies Students, Germans
CONTACT   Knut Menard
           kmenard@ccs.carleton.ca
FREE

http://www.carleton.ca/~kmenard/Germanresources.html

China Home Page ★★★

This home page contains a lot of information about China, including scientific, technical, business, and general resources. A list of foreign companies in China is provided, as are links to consulting companies and international travel agencies.

KEYWORDS   Asia, China
AUDIENCE   Asians, Business Professionals, Chinese, Tourists
CONTACT   Rongsheng Xu
           xurs@bepc2.ihep.ac.cn
FREE

http://utkvx1.utk.edu/~xurs/china.html

China In Time And Space (CITAS) Project ★★★

This Gopher is a service of the China In Time And Space (CITAS) project. CITAS is an interdisciplinary effort to develop an electronic database of spatially and temporally referenced data on China that can be used in global change and social science research. It provides information about CITAS goals, activities, and organization, and contains news and announcements, technical and research reports.

KEYWORDS   China, Chinese Studies, Computer Databases
AUDIENCE   Chinese, International Development Specialists, Scientists, Social Scientists
CONTACT   citas@u.washington.edu
FREE

gopher://citas.csde.washington.edu/

Government & Politics

Countries

China News Update ★★★★

China News Digest (CND) is a volunteer-run, non-profit organization aiming at providing news and other information services to readers who are concerned primarily about China-related affairs. The site contains several publications, including CND Global (three issues per week); CND-China (two issues per month), CND-US (two issues per week), CND-Europe/Pacific (one issue per week); CND-Canada (one issue per week). The site also contains links to Chinese literature, including the Zhu Zi Bai Jia (100 scholars) and the I Ching, in both Chinese and English.

KEYWORDS Asia, China, Chinese Literature, International News
AUDIENCE Asian Studies Students, Asians, Educators
FREE

http://www.cnd.org/

City.Net. Germany  ★★★

This page provides links to information on German cities, maps, language resources, travel guides, and more. Information is available on over 35 German cities, including such information as transportation maps and city guides. In addition, this site provides U.S. Government advisory information for U.S. citizens planning travel in Germany.

KEYWORDS German, Germany, History, Tourism
AUDIENCE Educators, Germans, Students (University), Tourists
CONTACT info@city.net
FREE

http://www.city.net/countries/germany/

Colombia WWW Servers ★★★

This site provide links to WWW servers in Colombia, with descriptions of each site. One server is the Universidad del Valle, which provides information about the University, publishes students' work and offers the latest volcano activity in southern Colombia. Another server is Colciencias which describes the CETCOL Network Project, and finally, there's the first WWW server for a commercial organization in Colombia, the Sistemas de Tecnologa Avanzada.

KEYWORDS Colombia, Latin American Studies
AUDIENCE International Business Travelers, Latin American Studies Students, Political Scientists
CONTACT Fernando Jose Gomez F. wwwmngr@univalle.edu.co
FREE

http://www.univalle.edu.co/Colombia.html

Colombia ★★★★

Colombia, a page written by Juan Carlos Dangond provides links to lots of information about the South American nation. The links include an online phone book, History, Government, Economy, Music, Sports, Science, a Clickable Map, and more.

KEYWORDS South America
AUDIENCE International Students, Soccer Fans, Students (University), Tourists
CONTACT Juan Carlos Dangond dangond@eagle.sangamon.edu
FREE

http://www.sangamon.edu/colombia

Comision Nacional de Telecomunicaciones ★★★

This site provides information about Argentina, such as the latest census information, the Argentine constitution, each of its provinces, and has numerous links to other Argentina Internet Resouces. Informacion sobre Argentina, novedades sobre el servicio de gopher, noticias, eventos, informacion en general, etc.

KEYWORDS Argentina, Internet Resources, South America
AUDIENCE Computer Professionals, International Travelers, Spanish Speakers, Tourists
CONTACT Atentos Saludos, Administrador Gopher gopher@secyt.gov.ar
FREE

gopher://gopher.secyt.gov.ar/

Country Information - Brunei ★★

This gopher site provides links to political, economic, and cultural information about the country of Brunei. Sources of information available to the viewer include the US State Department (which documents Human Rights records and travel information for US and other tourists), and the CIA World Factbook, which lists demographics, natural resources, economic, social, and political information.

KEYWORDS Demographics, Human Rights, Indonesia
AUDIENCE Asian Studies Educators, Asian Studies Students, Asians, Political Scientists
CONTACT staff@emailhost.ait.ac.th
FREE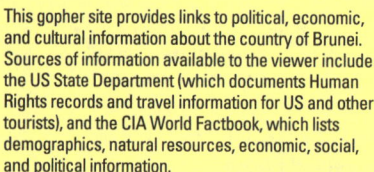

gopher://emailhost.ait.ac.th:70/11/AsiaInfo/CountryInfo/Brunei

Country Information - Cambodia ★★★

This page provides links to information about the country of Cambodia. Sources of information available to the viewer include the Usenet newsgroup, soc.culture.cambodia, the US State Department, the CIA World Factbook (which lists demographics, natural resources, economic, social, and political information), as well as information from the World Bank. In addition, contact information for the United Nations and World Health Organization is linked through this server.

KEYWORDS Demographics, Meta-Index (Cambodia), World Bank
AUDIENCE Asian Studies Educators, Asian Studies Students, Asians, Political Scientists
CONTACT staff@emailhost.ait.ac.th
FREE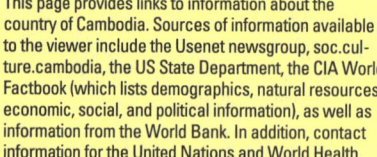

http://emailhost.ait.ac.th/Asia/infocm.html

Country Information - Indonesia ★★★

This page provides links to information about the country of Indonesia. Sources of information available to the viewer include the Usenet newsgroup, soc.culture.indonesia, the United States State Department, the CIA World Factbook (which lists demographics, natural resources, economic, social, and political information), as well as information about the Internet Infrastructure, Criminal Justice, and a lengthy index of projects organized through the World Bank.

KEYWORDS Demographics, Meta-Index (Indonesia), World Bank
AUDIENCE Asian Studies Educators, Asian Studies Students, Asians, Political Scientists
CONTACT staff@emailhost.ait.ac.th
FREE

http://emailhost.ait.ac.th/Asia/infoid.html

Country Information - Malaysia ★★★

This page is a listing of links to information about the country of Malaysia. Users can choose an area of interest like Travel Info, where you may jump to a clickable Touring Map; Country Info, which contains information from the CIA World Fact Book, Malaysia's Stock Exchange, and the Ministry of Finance; and Cultural Information, which includes Usenet archives from soc.culture.malaysia, a list of recipes and restaurants, and football (soccer) information. There is also a listing of World Bank Development projects and a list of current Internet Servers operating within Malaysia.

KEYWORDS Demographics, Malaysia
AUDIENCE Asian Studies Educators, Asian Studies Students, Asians, Political Scientists
CONTACT staff@emailhost.ait.ac.th
FREE

http://emailhost.ait.ac.th/Asia/infomy.html

Country Information - Myanmar (Burma)  ★★

This page provides links to political, economic, and cultural information about the country of Myanmar (Burma). Information sources available to the viewer include the Usenet newsgroup, soc.culture.burma, the US State Department, the CIA World Factbook (which lists demographics, natural resources, economic, social, and political information), as well as information regarding Human Rights. In addition, contact information for the United Nations and World Health Organization is linked through this server.

KEYWORDS Demographics, Human Rights
AUDIENCE Asian Studies Educators, Asian Studies Students, Asians, Political Scientists
CONTACT staff@emailhost.ait.ac.th
FREE

http://emailhost.ait.ac.th/Asia/infobm.html

Country Information - People's Democratic Republic of Laos ★★★

This page provides links to political, economic, and cultural information about the country of Laos. Sources of information available include the Usenet newsgroup, soc.culture.laos, the US State Department, the CIA World Factbook (which lists demographics, natural resources, economic, social, and political information,) as well as information regarding Human Rights. In addition, contact information for the United Nations and World Health Organization is linked through this server.

Keywords Demographics, Human Rights, Meta-Index (Laos)
Audience Asian Studies Educators, Asian Studies Students, Asians, Political Scientists
Contact staff@emailhost.ait.ac.th
Free

http://emailhost.ait.ac.th/Asia/infols.html

Country Information - Singapore ★★★★

This page provides links to information about the country of Singapore. Resources available to the viewer include the Usenet newsgroup, soc.culture.singapore, Trade and Finance sources, and the CIA World Factbook (which lists demographics, natural resources, economic, social, and political information). Tourists will find traveler's information organized by the Singapore Tourism Promotion Board, an online museum of Singapore Art and History, and the current travel advisory from the US State department.

Keywords Demographics, Singapore, Tourism
Audience Asian Studies Educators, Asian Studies Students, Asians, Political Scientists
Contact staff@emailhost.ait.ac.th
Free

http://emailhost.ait.ac.th/Asia/infosg.html

Country Information - Thailand ★★★

This page serves as an index of Internet accessible information about the country of Thailand. From this page, viewers can access other servers containing information about Thailand's political and economic systems from the CIA World Factbook and the Bangkok Post. Also available are a number of Science and Technology servers, reports about AIDS in Thailand, and Thailand's Frequently Asked Questions (FAQ). Tourists will find travelers information organized by region, as well as general information and US State Department Travel Advisories.

Keywords Culture, Meta-Index (Thailand), Tourism
Audience Asian Studies Educators, Asian Studies Students, Asians, Political Scientists
Contact staff@emailhost.ait.ac.th
Free

http://emailhost.ait.ac.th/Asia/infoth.html

Connections To The Library Of Congress
What's "Newt" with you?

The U.S. House of Representatives' Speaker, Newt Gingrich, might be impressed with how quickly and easily he could visit The Library of Congress via the Internet. This site on the World Wide Web provides users with the status of bills being considered in both the House of Representatives and the Senate. It also gives users a state-by-state rundown of congressional members and information about each states

The Library of Congress site also features digitized historical collections, such as clips of presidential inaugurations. If you're planning to visit Washington, D.C. and want to check out exhibits at the Library, start by checking the Net's descriptions—and even photocopies—of special points of interest in exhibits. One exhibit at the Library of Congress in late spring included original drafts of the Declaration of Independence written by Thomas Jefferson, as well as correspondence from one of America's founding fathers—Benjamin Franklin. The Library is also a good resource for historical facts about the United States.

(http://lcweb.loc.gov/homepage/lchp.html)

Country Information - Vietnam ★★★

This page provides links to information about the country of Vietnam. Sources of information available include the Usenet newsgroup, soc.culture.vietnamese, the United States State Department, the CIA World Factbook (which lists demographics, natural resources, economic, social, and political information), as well as information about World Bank development projects. In addition, contact information for the United Nations and World Health Organization is linked through this server. Viewers can also access documents describing Vietnam's telecommunications capacities or search for specific scientists.

Keywords Demographics, World Bank
Audience Asian Studies Educators, Asian Studies Students, Asians, Political Scientists
Contact staff@emailhost.ait.ac.th
Free

http://emailhost.ait.ac.th/Asia/Infovn.html

Crisis in Rwanda ★★★

This site gives information on Rwanda with particular emphasis on the recent civil war and subsequent massacres. A broad variety of information from sources such as the UN, U.S. Government, Amnesty International, and others may be searched. There are also hyperlinks to the sources and other multimedia tools such as an online map of Rwanda.

Keywords African Studies, Current Events, International News, Rwanda
Audience Activists, Africans, General Public, Political Activists

Cuba Gopher Menu ★★

This gopher menu provides links to information on broadcasting to Cuba (Radio and TV Marti) and a Castro speech database, 1959-1994 (in English).

KEYWORDS Cuba, Latin American Studies
AUDIENCE International Students, Latin American Studies Students, Tourists, Travel Agents
CONTACT Info@lanic.utexas.edu
FREE

gopher://lanic.utexas.edu:70/11/la/Cuba

CubaNet ★★★★

CubaNet is a non-profit, non-partisan Internet project in solidarity with the Cuban democracy movement. The two main aspects of this project are, one, to provide world-wide access to information on the underground democracy movement inside Cuba and on related efforts on the part of Cubans abroad, and, two, to forge an electronic link with citizens inside Cuba, skirting censorship by the Cuban government. CubaNet dedicates itself to opening channels of free communication among Cubans inside and outside of the country.

KEYWORDS Censorship, Cuba, Political Freedom
AUDIENCE Cuban Democaracy Activists, Cubans, Political Activists
CONTACT cubanet@bcfreenet.seflin.lib.fl.us
FREE

gopher://gopher.gate.net:70/00/florida/CubaNet/about

Denmark ★★★

This is a page on the country of Denmark. Users can find a description of the country, as well as information on Denmark's geography, geology, climate and various other useful facts. A FAQ in Danish for Danes living abroad is also available.

KEYWORDS Denmark, Europe
AUDIENCE Danes, Tourists
CONTACT info@uni-c.dk
FREE

http://info.denet.dk/denmark.html

Ecuador ★★★

This page provides links to information on Ecuador. Subjects covered include travel information, Internet access, pictures/sites, gopher servers, a journal information data base from the Ministry of Foreign Affairs of Ecuador, Peru/Ecuador conflict, the South American Explorer's Club, study abroad in Cuenca, getting Internet access in Ecuador, and more.

KEYWORDS Ecuador, Latin American Studies
AUDIENCE International Students, Latin American Studies Students, Tourists, Travel Agents
CONTACT eer@seas.upenn.edu
FREE

http://www.seas.upenn.edu:80/~leer/ecuador/

El Salvador ★★★

This page provides links to information on the country of El Salvador including history, travel resources, GDP growth, economic data, trade data, government news, profiles of the Head of State and Cabinet, maps, the Constitution, and more.

KEYWORDS El Salvador, Latin American Studies
AUDIENCE International Students, Latin American Studies Students, Tourists, Travel Agents
CONTACT Info@lanic.utexas.edu
FREE

http://lanic.utexas.edu/la/ca/salvador/

European Home Page ★★★

This site is a gateway to European home pages. The other homepages are accessed by a clickable map. The site also provides access to the EC home page and to the 'World Home Page.'

KEYWORDS Europe, Research, Tourism
AUDIENCE European Internet Surfers, Europeans, Internet Users
CONTACT Jose Miranda
         pinj@di.uminho.pt
FREE

http://s700.uminho.pt/europa.html

FranceWeb ★★★

FranceWeb is a French directory/magazine of Net resources (in French) with direct links and forms to interesting selected sites including news, metro information, currency exchange rates, etc. It also includes a special section of all France or French-speaking resources, a shopping center, and French-speaking forums. The site is updated daily.

KEYWORDS France, Tourism
AUDIENCE France Residents, Francophiles, French Speakers, Tourists
CONTACT FranceWeb@FranceNet.fr.
FREE

http://www.FranceWeb.fr/

Galileo Project ★★★

This site, which is in Spanish, is about Venezuela and the Galileo project. In 1989, a multi-disciplinary team came up with an idea to help Venezuela overcome an internal crisis due to the lack of intellectual leaders. It was called the Galileo program which selected outstanding high school students to be trained in the most prestigious universities of the world. The site provides details of the students' requirements, as well as many other topics .

KEYWORDS Educational Programs, Government, Leadership, Venezuela
AUDIENCE Educators (University), Government Officials, Students (Secondary/College), Venezuelans
CONTACT Hector Briceno
         hbriceno@figment.mit.edu
FREE

gopher://figment.mit.edu:9999/

General Information (Taiwan) ★★★

This is a home page with general information about Taiwan from the CityNet. You'll find basic facts about history, culture, airlines, exchange rate, business hours, national holidays, transportation, and more.

KEYWORDS Asia, Taiwan, Tourism
AUDIENCE Asians, Business Professionals, Chinese, International Travelers
CONTACT Kevin Altis
         altis@city.net
FREE

http://peacock.tnjc.edu.tw/ROC_info.html

Germany ★★★

This site contains links to extensive information on Germany including geography, economy, government, Germany, World Factbook 1994, German News Service, demographics, etc.

KEYWORDS Germany, Government, History, Tourism
AUDIENCE Educators, Germans, Students (University) , Tourists
FREE

http://www.chemie.fu-berlin.de/adressen/brd.html

Guatemala ★★★

This page provides links to information on the country of Guatemala. Subjects covered include maps, history, travel information, geography, economic data, trade data, government information, the Head of State and Cabinet, and the Constitution.

KEYWORDS Guatemala, Latin America
AUDIENCE International Students, Latin American Studies Students, Tourists, Travel Agents
CONTACT info@lanic.utexas.edu
FREE

http://lanic.utexas.edu/la/ca/guatemala/

Guide to Australia ★★★★

This Guide To Australia aims to compile links to all available online information resources about Australia. It includes information on geography, the environment, communications, travel and culture, and government and history of Australia, Australian weather, Australian Usenet groups, health care, etc.

KEYWORDS Australia, Culture, Travel & Tourism , Weather
AUDIENCE Geographers, Native Australians, Travel Agents, Travelers
CONTACT David Green
         David.Green@csu.edu.au
FREE

http://www.csu.edu.au/education/australia.html

Guyana ★★★

This page provides links to information on the country of Guyana, its history, travel information, geography, economic data, trade data, and government information, as well as maps.

KEYWORDS Guyana, Travel & Tourism

Countries 335

AUDIENCE   International Students, Latin American Studies Students, Tourists, Travel Agents
CONTACT   info@lanic.utexas.edu
FREE

http://lanic.utexas.edu/la/sa/guyana/

Honduras ★★★

This page provides links to information on the country of Honduras. Subjects covered include maps, history, travel information, GDP growth, geography, economic data, trade data, government information, Head of State and Cabinet, Constitution, and more.

KEYWORDS   Honduras, Latin America
AUDIENCE   International Students, Latin American Studies Students, Tourists, Travel Agents
CONTACT   info@lanic.utexas.edu
FREE

http://lanic.utexas.edu/la/ca/honduras/

Hungarian Home Page ★★★

This site provides access to a variety of information about Hungary and Internet resources in Hungary. Links are offered to Hungarian WWW sites, the Technical University of Budapest, the Prime Minister's Office, the Institute of Nuclear Research, the Research Laboratory for Mining Chemistry, Juhasz Gyula Teacher Training College, Library databases, a special national email system director, the GNN Currency Converter, Hungarian history, Geography, Hungarian cuisine, and more.

KEYWORDS   Eastern Europe, Hungary
AUDIENCE   Educators (University), Hungarians, Students (University)
CONTACT   www@fsz.bme.hu
FREE

http://www.fsz.bme.hu/hungary/homepage.html

India Homepage ★★★

The India Homepage is designed as an index to link interested users to India resources all over the web. It provides links to diverse subjects relating to the country and culture of India. Topics include tourism, culture and fine arts, religion, cities and states. Included is a large index of images including maps, national leaders, tourist sites, and major cities. Also, you may listen to Indian desert songs, read recipes for Indian cuisine, and learn about national sports.

KEYWORDS   Culture, India, Tourism
AUDIENCE   Ethnic Studies Students, India Culture Enthusiasts, Tourists, Travelers
FREE

http://spiderman.bu.edu/misc/india/index.html

Information Rosenbad ★★★

These pages offer links to a few Swedish federal and local government Internet resources (Census data, election data, and some economic and business information) as well as Swedish and English-language tourism information.

KEYWORDS   Government, Sweden, Tourism
AUDIENCE   International Travelers, Sweden Residents, Swedes, Tourists

CONTACT   Inge Gustafsson
           gus@sb.gov.se
FREE

http://www.sb.gov.se/

Information Servers in Brazil ★★★★

This page provides a hyper-linked list of Brazilian Internet Servers. RNP, Rede Nacional de Pesquisa, is the central WWW server of RNP, the Brazilian Research Network. It provides information about Internet in Brazil and has links to most WWW, gopher and ftp servers in the country. BD, Base de Dados Tropical (Tropical Data Base - BDT) provides information of interest regarding Biotechnology and Biodiversity including Brazilian Directories, Brazilian Patents and the Biodiversity Information Network BIN21) Home Page. UFSC, Department of Informatics provides an index to all Brazilian Network Services, a World Index by Continent (graphic).

KEYWORDS   Biotechnology, Brazil
AUDIENCE   International Business Travelers, Latin American Studies Students, Political Researchers
FREE

http://www.rnp.br/cern.html

Information about Bulgaria ★★★★

This site provides access to a wide variety of online information about Bulgaria. It includes links to information on Bulgarian Jews, an index of articles on Bulgaria, news about Bulgaria, Bulgarian servers, FTP sources, maps, images, sounds and more. It also includes the frequently asked questions with answers for soc.culture.bulgaria.

KEYWORDS   Bulgaria, Cultural Studies, Eastern Europe
AUDIENCE   Bulgarians, Educators (University), Jews, Students (University), Tourists
CONTACT   Penio Penev
           Penev@venezia.Rockefeller.edu
FREE

http://pisa.rockefeller.edu:8080/Bulgaria/

Italian Web Sites ★★★

This site offers a comprehensive set of links to Italian web sites. Included are connections to Italian newspapers, universities, tourist information, a list of resources in Bologna, and more. It even offers a collection of Italian recipes from 'Mama's cookbook.'

KEYWORDS   Europe, Italy, Tourism
AUDIENCE   Italians, Tourists, Travel Agents, Travelers
CONTACT   webmaster@eat.com
FREE

http://www.eat.com/./italian-sites.html

Jamaica ★★★

This page provides links to information on the country of Jamaica. Subjects covered include maps, history, travel information, GDP growth, geography, economic data, trade data, government information, Head of State and Cabinet, Constitution, and more.

KEYWORDS   Jamaica, Travel & Tourism

AUDIENCE   International Students, Tourists, Travel Agents
CONTACT   info@lanic.utexas.edu
FREE

http://lanic.utexas.edu/la/ca/jamaica/

Japanese Information ★★★★

This site provides comprehensive information about Japan available in English or Japanese. Topics include What's New in Japan, National Anthem, Clickable W3 Map for Japan, Japanese Weather Information, National Holidays, Kotowaza (Japanese proverbs), Japan National Tourist Organization, Traveler's Japanese, J-League Forum (Japan Pro Football League), Sumo Information, The Constitution of Japan, Online Publications, and more.

KEYWORDS   Japan, Tourism
AUDIENCE   Educators (University), Researchers, Students (University), Tourists
CONTACT   www-admin@seraph.ntt.jp
FREE

http://www.ntt.jp/japan/index.html

Lebanon (FAQs) Frequently Asked Questions ★★★

This posting contains Frequently Asked Questions (FAQ) about Lebanon. Some of the topics covered include Voice of Lebanon radio service, the Cedars of Lebanon, conservation, ski resort information and economic developments. The second part of the FAQ can be found in the archive, Lebanon-faq/part2.

KEYWORDS   Lebanon, Middle East
AUDIENCE   Lebanese Culture Enthusiasts, Tourists, Travelers
FREE

http://www.lib.ox.ac.uk/internet/news/faq/soc.culture.lebanon.html

ftp://rtfm.mit.edu/pub/usenet/news.answers/lebanon-faq/part1

Manifest ★★★

This document is an introduction to a hypertext database describing the accident at the Chernobyl Nuclear Power Plant in 1986. The database draws on both the official version of events published in 1992, as well as materials of the Chernobyl Kurchatov Institute Expedition and a number of publications in the scientific press and mass media.

KEYWORDS   Chernobyl, Nuclear Power, Nuclear Safety
AUDIENCE   Engineers, Environmental Researchers, Environmental Scientists, Environmentalists
CONTACT   Olga Zimina
           liai@chern1.msk.su
FREE

http://polyn.net.kiae.su/polyn/manifest.html

Mexico ★★★

This page provides links to information on the country of Mexico. Subjects covered include maps, history, articles on Mexico Out of Balance and Mexico's

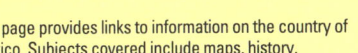
Government & Politics

Electoral Aftermath and Political Future, Conference Memoria, Universities, government information, Head of State and Cabinet, Constitution, North American Free Trade Agreement (NAFTA), and more.
Keywords Mexico, NAFTA (North American Free Trade Agreement)
Audience International Students, Latin American Studies Students, Tourists, Travel Agents
Contact info@lanic.utexas.edu
Free

http://lanic.utexas.edu/la/Mexico/

Natural Resources Canada ★★★

This site describes the responsibilities, activities, and departments of Natural Resources Canada. Natural Resources Canada is a Canadian government department whose goal is to supervise the responsible development of Canada's environment and its natural resources. The information is accessed by a table of contents. There are also links to a great range of other sources of Canadian information on the Net.
Keywords Canada, Environment, Forestry, Government
Audience Canadians, Environmental Researchers, Geologists
Contact Bob Fillmore
fillmore@emr.ca
Free

http://www.emr.ca/

gopher://gopher.emr.ca/

ftp://ftp.emr.ca/pub/

New Zealand / Aotearoa Home Page ★★★

This Best of the Net '93 honoree covers a good deal of what's available on the Net about New Zealand. It includes an illustrated tour, pages on geography, government, tourist information, history, entertainment and sports.
Keywords Geography, New Zealand, South Pacific, Tourism
Audience Educators, New Zealand Residents, Tourists
Contact Michael Witbrock
witbrock@cs.cmu.edu
Free

http://www.cs.cmu.edu:8001/Web/People/mjw/NZ/MainPage.html

New Zealand Government Home Pages ★★★

This is the official home page of the government of New Zealand which is divided into legislative, executive and judiciary sections. This offers good coverage of official information for those ministerial sections that are completed.
Keywords Government, Government Departments, New Zealand
Audience Educators, International Lawyers, New Zealand Residents

Contact Matthew Sheppard
Matthew.Sheppard@vuw.ac.nz
Free

http://www.vuw.ac.nz/govt/

Nicaragua ★★★

This page provides links to information on the country of Nicaragua. Subjects covered include maps, history, travel information, GDP growth, geography, economic data, trade data, government information, Head of State and Cabinet, Constitution, and more.
Keywords Nicaragua, Travel & Tourism
Audience International Students, Latin American Studies Students, Tourists, Travel Agents
Contact info@lanic.utexas.edu
Free

http://lanic.utexas.edu:80/la/ca/nicaragua/

Open Government - Gouvernement Ouvert ★★★

This web site is a pilot project undertaken by Industry Canada to provide greater access to government through information networks. This page contains information on various components of Canada's government such as the Senate, the House of Commons, and the Supreme Court of Canada, as well as providing access to government documents and other wired world governments.
Keywords Canada, Government
Audience Canadians, Educators, Students
Contact Andrew Stephens
stephens@clark.dgim.doc.ca
Free

http://debra.dgbt.doc.ca:80/opengov/

Panama ★★★

This page provides links to information on the country of Panama. Subjects covered include maps, history, travel information, GDP growth, geography, economic data, trade data, government information, Head of State and Cabinet, Constitution, and more.
Keywords Latin America, Panama
Audience International Students, Latin American Studies Students, Tourists, Travel Agents
Contact info@lanic.utexas.edu
Free

http://lanic.utexas.edu/la/ca/panama/

Paraguay ★★★

This page provides links to information on the country of Paraguay. Subjects covered include maps, history, travel information, GDP growth, geography, economic data, trade data, government information, Head of State and Cabinet, Constitution, and more.
Keywords Latin America, Paraguay
Audience International Students, Latin American Studies Students, Tourists, Travel Agents
Contact info@lanic.utexas.edu
Free

http://lanic.utexas.edu/la/sa/paraguay/

Peru

This page provides links to information on the country of Peru. Subjects covered include maps, history, travel information, GDP growth, geography, economic data, trade data, government information, Head of State and Cabinet, Constitution, and more.
Keywords Latin America, Peru
Audience International Students, Latin American Studies Students, Tourists, Travel Agents
Contact info@lanic.utexas.edu
Free

http://lanic.utexas.edu/la/Peru/

Poland Web Server ★★★★

The Poland Web Server offers access to all kinds of information from and about Poland available in English or Polish. Links are provided to the Polish Government Press Office, LOT Airline Schedules, Polish newspapers, the Polish Stock Exchange, the Polish Internet Society, and other cultural and historical resources.
Keywords Cultural Studies, International News, Poland, Tourism
Audience Educators, Polish, Researchers, Students, Travelers
Free

http://info.fuw.edu.pl/pl/PolandHome.html

Political Science in Australia ★★★

This site contains links to information, both historical and current, on various aspects of Australian politics and government. Linked resources include the Australian constitution in searchable hypertext; home pages of various political figures, parties and government offices; political science and government studies departments at Australian universities, and more.
Keywords Australia, Political Science
Audience Australia Residents, Australians, Government Students, Political Researchers, Political Scientists
Contact Rick Kuhn
RAK@www.anu.edu.au
Free

http://www.anu.edu.au/polsci/austpol/austpol

Portugal Web Server ★★★★

This page provides many links to a plethora of information about Portugal in both English and Portuguese. It contains links to such topics as Postal Codes and Telephone Areas, Internet Domains, Public BBSs, Portuguese Virtual Comunities, Portuguese History, Mountain Biking (Summary/Tours in Northern Portugal), Satellite weather images, and more. It also provides links to useful information for Portuguese people including study abroad programs, and Portuguese contacts in the world. Also included is useful information for non-Portuguese (and Portuguese) people including U.S. State department travel information, human rights practices, tourist Information, and more.
Keywords Cultural Studies, Government, Portugal, Tourism
Audience Educators, International Business Professionals, Portugal Residents, Tourists

Countries

CONTACT pinj@di.uminho.pt
FREE

http://s700.uminho.pt/Portugal/portugal.html

Red Cientifica Peruana - WWW Server ★★★

The Red Cientifica Peruana, the Internet network of Peru, is a non-profit organization composed mainly of government (Ministry of Foreign Affairs, and of Industry and Tourism, Congress of Peru) and academic organizations. Information is provided about the network and links are made to other regional WWW servers and gophers.

KEYWORDS Internet Networking, Non Profit Organizations, Peru
AUDIENCE Business Professionals, Latin Americans, Peruvians, Researchers
CONTACT 3Dwww@rcp.net.pe
FREE

http://www.rcp.net.pe/rcp_ingles.html

Reesweb - Russian and East European Studies ★★★★

This page is a meta-index for Russian and East European Studies. Resources are arranged by discipline such as science, business, literature, or type, such as document repositories, interactive databases, software, and more. There are also links to more than 20 national homepages and major sites, Russian Webservers, new items, etc.

KEYWORDS Cultural Studies, Politics, Russia
AUDIENCE Eastern Europeans, Educators, Researchers, Russians, Students (University)
CONTACT Casey Palowitch
 cjp+@pitt.edu
FREE

http://www.pitt.edu/~cjp/rees.html

Republica de Venezuela ★★★★

This site is a sensitive map of Venezuela and provides access to subjects such as economic issues, tourism, and science.

KEYWORDS South America, Venezuela
AUDIENCE International Students, Students (University), Tourists
CONTACT webmaster@venezuela.mit.edu
FREE

http://venezuela.mit.edu/sensitive.html

Rules and Regulations in Russia ★★

This is the home page for the Russian business law publication, 'Rules and Regulations in Russia.' Two issues are currently archived online, covering a wide range of topics related to business and finance, trade and commerce, and law.

KEYWORDS Business, Law, Russia
AUDIENCE Anglophones, Business Professionals, Lawyers

CONTACT sppress@sovam.com
FREE

http://www.spb.su/rulesreg/

Scottish Highlands and Islands Server ★★★

This Web site provides information on Scotland relating to its culture, the Gaelic language, tourism, long-distance education, and work opportunities.

KEYWORDS Cultural Studies, Scotland, Tourism
AUDIENCE Celtic Enthusiasts, Scots, Travelers
CONTACT webmaster@nsa.bt.co.uk
FREE

http://nsa.bt.co.uk/nsa.html

Shima Media Network ★★★★

Keiji Shima, one of Japan's most well-known journalists (and ex-chairman of NHK, the world's largest broadcasting company), presents his own personal news digest. Updated weekly, Shima Media Network presents original articles and reprinted pieces from wire services, as well as special items by noted Japanese journalists and personalities. Subjects are usually specifically related to Japanese trade and Government, but articles on other subjects appear as well.

KEYWORDS International Finance, Japan, Journalism, Politics
AUDIENCE Business Professionals, Japan Residents, Journalists, News Buffs
CONTACT SMN staff
 smn@eccosys.com
FREE

http://www.eccosys.com/SMN/

Slovakia Document Store ★★★★

This page is a meta-index for Slovakian Documents and information. It is organized by page number and then by subject within the page. On page one, country information includes population, nationalities, language, etc. On page two, the information includes the history of Slovakia, human rights reports, economy, religion, currency, exchange rates, cash machines, business, Internet services, time, voltage, video system, telephone, shopping, driving, road maps, emergencies, national holidays, and climate. Page three provides customs duties, insurance companies, travel agencies, tourist information centers, theaters, cinemas, concerts, monuments, and more.

KEYWORDS Eastern Europe, History, Human Rights
AUDIENCE Educators, Linguists, Political Scientists, Tourists, Travel Agents
CONTACT SDS@Slovakia.EU.net
FREE

http://www.eunet.sk/slovakia/slovakia.html

Slovakia Elections 1994/1995 Web Pages ★★★

These pages present complete election information from the 1994 Slovakian General Election, and include both national and regional returns, candidate and ballot initiative information, etc. Preliminary candidate information for the upcoming 1995 regional elections is also available.

KEYWORDS Government, News, Slovakia, Voting
AUDIENCE Political Researchers, Slovakia Residents, Slovaks
CONTACT info@Slovakia.EU.net
FREE

http://www.slovakia.eu.net/slovakia/elections.html

Slovenia ★★★★

This page is a meta-index for Slovenia. Links are provided to an interactive map of Slovenia, towns and places in Slovenia, general information, travel information, science in Slovenia, a historical overview, Slovene language learning materials for English speakers, the Karst route, the Upper Carniolan (Alpine) route, ski resorts, health resorts/spas, and more.

KEYWORDS Slovenia, Tourism
AUDIENCE Fitness Enthusiasts, Skiing Enthusiasts, Slovenia Residents, Tourists
FREE

http://www.ijs.si/slo.html

Southeast Asian Ministers of Education Organization (SEAMEO) ★★

The Southeast Asian Ministers of Education Organization (SEAMEO) page lists the activities, programs and departments. This organization links resources from its 15 member and associate member nations in order to develop excellence in education, science and culture in Southeast Asia. Some areas currently being developed are tropical biology and medicine, archaeology and fine arts, and educational innovation and technology. The files on this server contain contact information, press releases, mission statements, training outlines, and other related materials from their nine regional centers.

KEYWORDS Asian Studies, Educational Policy, Educational Resources, International Education
AUDIENCE Education Administrators, Educators
CONTACT staff@emailhost.ait.ac.th
FREE

http://emailhost.ait.ac.th/Asia/seameo/index.html

Soviet Archives ★★★

This site includes newly opened Soviet archives translated to English, including information about the secret police, the cold war, and more.

KEYWORDS Cold War, Former Soviet Union, Russian Documents
AUDIENCE Educators, Historians, History Buffs, Researchers, Students
FREE

ftp://loc.gov

Suriname ★★★

This page provides links to information on the country of Suriname. Subjects covered include maps, history, travel information, GDP growth, geography, economic

Government & Politics

data, trade data, government information, Head of State and Cabinet, Constitution, and more.

KEYWORDS   Latin America, Suriname
AUDIENCE   International Students, Latin American Studies Students, Tourists, Travel Agents
CONTACT   info@lanic.utexas.edu
FREE

http://lanic.utexas.edu/la/sa/suriname/

Suriname Home Page ★★

This site contains information about the country of Suriname, located in the nothern part of South America. On this page, the viewer will find a travel guide (including general tourist information, the current advisory from the U.S. State Department, and a listing of hotels, travel agencies, and embassies) as well as a walkthough of Paramaribo, the capital of Suriname. There is also information about Suriname's history, languages, and geography. One section covers general knowledge and trivia about Suriname, including CIA World Factbook statistics, information on Anthony Nesty (Suriname's sole Olympic medal winner), and a list of charitable organizations.

KEYWORDS   Guides, South America, Suriname, Tourism
AUDIENCE   Latin American Studies Students, South America Residents, Suriname Residents, Tourists
CONTACT   Erik TKS
           erikt@let.rug.nl
FREE

http://grid.let.rug.nl/~erikt/.Suriname/welcome.html

Technet ★★★★

This site is maintained by Technet, a network supplier in Singapore. There is information about the American Chamber of Commerce, the British Council in Singapore, the Educational Reseach Association, the Industry and Technology Relations Office, the Institute of System Science, the National Science and Technology Board, and a list of major employers in Singapore.

KEYWORDS   Education, Government, Science, Singapore
AUDIENCE   Academics, Students (Secondary/College)
CONTACT   gopher@solomon.technet.sg
FREE

gopher://gopher.technet.sg:2100/

Telephone Numbers In Japan ★★★

This page is a collection of phone numbers for a variety of organizations and informational bureaus in Japan. Many numbers are provided for tourists and travellers to help them find their way around Japan. Included in the list are legal and immigration resources, transportation resources, and emergency numbers.

KEYWORDS   Japan, Telecommunications, Telephone Directories, Tourism
AUDIENCE   Business Professionals, Japan Residents, Tourists
CONTACT   kiwin
           palm@tokyo.rockwell.com
FREE

http://www.tokyo.rockwell.com/jtel2.html

Tennessee Bob's Famous French Links ★★★★

This site sports an incredibly comprehensive list of French links divided into a dozen different categories from 'Finding Things,' to 'French in Business Context.'

KEYWORDS   Art, France, Music
AUDIENCE   French Speakers, Internet Users
FREE

http://192.239.144.18/departments/french/french.html

Thailand - The Big Picture ★★

This Web site maintains a complete list of Internet servers pertaining to and found within Thailand, as well as general information concerning Thailand. There is an extensive set of links to Thai academic institutions.

KEYWORDS   Education, Research, Thailand, Tourism
AUDIENCE   International Students, Researchers, Thailand Residents
CONTACT   Trin Tantsetthi
           webmaster@www.nectec.or.th
FREE

http://www.nectec.or.th/

gopher://gopher.nectec.or.th/

ftp://ftp.nectec.or.th/

Things From Ireland and Other Celtic Lands ★★★★

This site provides access to online resources relating to Ireland and Irish heritage. Some of the topics covered include Politics, Music, News, Radio, Papers, President Robinson's Address, Government Shenanigans, Gaelic Football, Frequently Asked Questions, satellite weather images of Ireland and Britain, and more.

KEYWORDS   Cultural Studies, International Politics, Ireland
AUDIENCE   Irish, Journalists, Political Scientists, Researchers, Tourists
CONTACT   Pat Murphy
           pmurphy@celtic.stanford.edu
FREE

http://celtic.stanford.edu/pmurphy/irish.html

Tibet ★★★★

This site is devoted to Tibet and has links to Tibet Internet Resources - the Central Database, The Tibetan National Flag, The Tibetan Heritage, an informational tour of Tibet, and maps and images of Tibet.

KEYWORDS   Databases, Maps, Tibet, Tourism
AUDIENCE   Political Activists, Tibet Enthusiasts, Tibetans, Tourists
CONTACT   tmciolek@coombs.anu.edu.au
FREE

http://coombs.anu.edu.au/WWWVL-TibetanStudies.html

TimorNet - An Information Service on East Timor ★★★★

TimorNet provides historical information about East Timor, at one time a Portuguese colony. There is information about the land, and ethnology of the Maubere people, as well as an overview of the present conflict. It was annexed by Indonesia, an act that was condemned by the United Nations. There is also a hotlink to people involved in the East-Timor Saga, who left their personal messages for the service site. There is an introductory course for users unfamiliar with the conflict or East Timor.

KEYWORDS   East Timor, Human Rights, Indonesia, Southeast Asia
AUDIENCE   Human Rights Activists, Southeast Asians
CONTACT   TimorNet@mercurio.uc.pt
FREE

http://www.uc.pt/Timor/TimorNet.html

UNISA-South Africa (University of South Africa) ★★★

This is the South Africa page maintained by the University of South Africa, containing information about different regions and major cities, weather conditions, vital statistics, and information about the University of South Africa. There are links to other travel-related resources.

KEYWORDS   Africa, South Africa, Vital Statistics, Weather
AUDIENCE   General Public, International Travelers, South Africans
CONTACT   Aleksandar Radovanovic
           adova@osprey.unisa.ac.za
FREE

http://osprey.unisa.ac.za/0/docs/south-africa.html

Web India ★★★

This home page features Web India, which provides information on Indian businesses and services classified as businesses opportunities in India, and Indian services available worldwide. You can find a wide variety of resources ranging from where to taste spicy Indian food to what business opportunities exist in India. You can contact some Indian businesses through this World Wide Web site. Service is free for non-profit and reasonable for commercial organizations.

KEYWORDS   India
AUDIENCE   Business Analysts, Business Professionals, Indians, Tourists
CONTACT   webmaster@webindia.com
FREE

http://www.webindia.com/

West Bengal Home Page ★★★

This site is full of information about West Bengal, the eastern region of India. Keep up to date on current news in India, read translated Bengali poetry, see Bengali artwork, and look at pictures of writer Tagore. The culture section includes literature, music, art, film, with information about major artists and works. The tourism section covers travel in West Bengal, with pictures, sightseeing tips, transportation details, and

Countries – History   **339**

accomodation and restaurant information for tourist destinations. Also included is general information about the history of the region and the language of Bengal.

KEYWORDS   Culture, India, Indian Art, Tourism
AUDIENCE   Ethnic Studies Students, Indians, Tourists, Travelers
CONTACT   Arghya Chatterjee
           achatt1@umbc8.umbc.edu
FREE

http://www.gl.umbc.edu/~achatt1/wbengal.html

Window-to-Russia ★★★

This site gives the Internet community access to a variety of information available on the Net about Russia. The information is organized into the areas of arts, culture, history, business, science, and other topics. This site provides links to other servers which contain the desired information.

KEYWORDS   History, International Business, Russia, Tourism
AUDIENCE   Business Professionals, Internet Users, Tourists
CONTACT   Eugene Peskin
           eugene@rd.relcom.msk.su
FREE

http://www.kiae.su/www/wtr/

Windows on Italy ★★★★

Windows on Italy provides a hypermap of Italy, a list of towns, historical and regional resources, links to the Constitution, Daily News, cultural tidbits, and a map of Italian WWW servers. There are also a few pictures.

KEYWORDS   European Culture, European History, Italy, Tourism
AUDIENCE   International Students, Italians, Tourists, Travelers
CONTACT   R. Albertini
           woi@siam.mi.cnr.it
FREE

http://www.mi.cnr.it/WOI/

Yugoslavia ★★★

This page provides links to information about the Federal Republic of Yugoslavia consisting of the republics of Montenegro and Serbia. Subjects include facts and figures, the places and people you should see, cuisine, language, tourist information, related resources on the Internet, and more.

KEYWORDS   Tourism, Yugoslavia
AUDIENCE   Educators (University), Serbians, Students (University), Tourists
CONTACT   Nina Milosevic & Vojislav Lalich-Petrich
           lpv@umiacs.umd.edu
FREE

http://www.umiacs.umd.edu/research/lpv/YU/HTML/yu.html

Doctrines

See also
Government & Politics · *Political Science*
Humanities & Social Sciences · *Area & Cultural Studies*
Religion & Philosophy · *Philosophy*
Religion & Philosophy · *Religions*

Foreign Treaties & Covenants Gopher ★★★

This gopher server contains a comprehensive collection of foreign (i.e., non-U.S.) treaties, covenants and constitutions. Also available is a pointer to the World Bank's constitutional archive and a large volume of information on the recent NAFTA and Maastricht treaties, as well as the organizational documents for various international alliances (including the newly-expanded European Community). Search engines are also available to more easily navigate the various documents available here.

KEYWORDS   European Community, Government, International Relations, Treaties
AUDIENCE   Diplomats, Policy Analysts, Political Scientists, Politicians, Trade Specialists
FREE

gopher://gopher.law.cornell.edu:70/11/foreign

United States (U.S.) Constitution and Members of Congress ★★★

This site provides access to specially formatted versions of the United States Constitution. A plain text version (with underlining only) of the U.S. Constitution is also available at this server. The plain text version was formatted from the troff version from the file constitution.troff. A list of all of the Members of the U.S. Congress, with address and other information, is also provided. Files containing information on the Members of Congress are organized according to state.

KEYWORDS   US Constitution
AUDIENCE   Political Activists, U.S. Citizens, U.S. Congress
FREE

ftp://ftp.halcyon.com/pub/activism/

World Constitutions ★★★★

This World Constitutions file contains constitutions and laws from many countries around the world including the Australian Constitution Act of 1900, the Basic Law of Germany, the Japanese Constitution, the Magna Carta, and the United States Constitution.

KEYWORDS   Constitutions, International Documents, International Law, World History
AUDIENCE   Educators, History Buffs, Law Students
FREE

gopher://wiretap.spies.com:70/11/Gov/World

ftp://spies.com/Gov/World/.cap/

History

See also
Humanities & Social Sciences · *History*
Religion & Philosophy · *Philosophy*

Ancient World Web ★★★

The Ancient World Web site is devoted to providing users with a listing of available Internet resources for the study of ancient history, cultures, and art. Indexes are arranged by geography and subject. Largely under construction, this site offers an essay on Trojan gold and a link to the recently-discovered cave paintings in France.

KEYWORDS   Ancient Art, Ancient History, Classics, History
AUDIENCE   Archaeologists, Classicists, Educators, Historians
CONTACT   Julia Hayden
           Julia@Virginia.edu
FREE

http://atlantic.evsc.virginia.edu/julia/AncientWorld.html

Libertarian Party ★★★

The Libertarian Party home page provides official, documentary information about the freedom-loving American political group. Users will find an overview of the party's philosophy, copies of past platforms, pamphlets and documents, a history of party activities, and an event calendar. There are no links to the Net's many unofficial Libertarian sites. Contact information is provided.

KEYWORDS   Libertarianism, Political Parties
AUDIENCE   Journalist, Libertarians, Political Scientists
FREE

http://www.lp.org/lp/

Military Museums of London ★★★

This is the site for information on the Military Museums of London. It contains museum histories and descriptions as well as general information for the museums. The Museums include the Imperial War Museum, the National Maritime Museum and Royal Naval College, the Cabinet War Rooms, the Royal Air Force Museum, National Army Museum, HMS Belfast, and other military-related museums. There are also links to other military history resources on the Net. It includes a travel story on Military Museums of London, and listings for military books stores and antique shops.

KEYWORDS   History (Military), London, Museums, Travel
AUDIENCE   Educators, Military Historians, Researchers, Tourists
CONTACT   abailey@lonestar.utsa.edu
FREE

http://www.cs.ucl.ac.uk/misc/uk/london/london-military-museums.html

Government & Politics

Individuals

See also
Humanities & Social Sciences · *History*
Popular Culture & Entertainment · *Celebrities & Personalities*

Minnesota's 7th Congressional District ★★★★

The activities of Collin Peterson, who represents Minnesota's 7th Congressional District, are made known on this WWW site. Users will find introductory information about Peterson's biography and his participation in the Coalition, a group of centrist Democrats. Press releases and updates of interest to constituents are available regarding Congressional legislation. Contact information is provided, and there are links to the official Web sites of US government offices.

KEYWORDS Congress, Minnesota, Peterson, Politicians
AUDIENCE Journalists, Minnesotans, Political Scientists
CONTACT tocollin@hr.house.gov
FREE

http://www.house.gov/collinpeterson/

Newt Gingrich WWW Fan Club ★★★

The Newt Gingrich WWW Fan Club contains 'all the Newt that's fit to print.' This site provides links to other Newt Gingrich related information including transcripts to Gingrich's college lectures, remarks to the Washington Research Group, the speech at the Republican National Committee, Contract With America, and writings of conservative George Gilder on the so-called Information SuperHighway.

KEYWORDS Politicians
AUDIENCE Conservatives, Libertarians, Republicans
CONTACT RightSide1@aol.com
FREE

http://www.clark.net/pub/jeffd/mr_newt.html

Office of Massachusetts State Representative Anne Paulsen ★★

This site provides a way to contact Massachusetts State Representative Anne Paulsen by email, as well as read official press releases and other information.

KEYWORDS House of Representatives (US), Massachusetts, Politicians
AUDIENCE Massachusetts Residents, New York Residents, Political Scientists, Washington D.C. Residents
CONTACT Tim Miranda
miranda@user1.channel1.com
FREE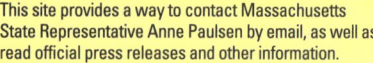

http://www.channel1.com/users/miranda/paulsen.html

Office of Senator Edward Kennedy ★★★

The homepage of the Office of Senator Edward Kennedy provides links to information on Massachusetts, the U.S. Senate and Congress in general, the 1995 U.S. Budget and the Library of Congress. One can browse recent press releases by subject or in alphabetical order. This site has links on the Information Infrastructure Task Force and related topics, and gives Senator Kennedy's email address (senator@kennedy.senate.gov).

KEYWORDS Massachusetts, Politicians
AUDIENCE Massachusetts Residents, Political Activists, Voters
CONTACT Chris Casey
webmaster@kennedy.senate.gov
FREE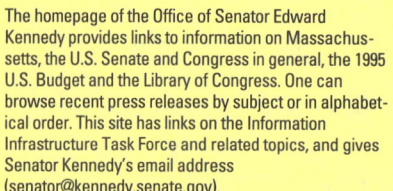

http://www.ai.mit.edu/projects/iiip/Kennedy/homepage.html

gopher://ftp.senate.gov/11/member/ma/kennedy

Ronald Reagan Home Page ★★★

A page dedicated to what the author terms the 'greatest peace-time expansion the United States has ever experienced,' and the President who commanded it, Ronald Reagan. The site includes Reagan background information, facts and figures, numerous photographs, and the former President's address.

KEYWORDS Politicians, Presidents (US)
AUDIENCE Conservatives, Republicans
CONTACT B. Kottman
bkottman@eri.erinet.com
FREE

http://www.erinet.com/bkottman/reagan.html

The Speeches of Newt Gingrich ★★★★

This site maintains a database of transcribed speeches by House Speaker Newt Gingrich. Some of the speeches available here include various pre-election speeches, his acceptance speech, and a recent C-Span television interview.

KEYWORDS Politicians
AUDIENCE Conservatives, Journalists, Political Researchers, Republicans
CONTACT info@dolphin.gulf.net
FREE

http://dolphin.gulf.net/Gingrich.html

International

See also
Business & Economics · *International Business*
Humanities & Social Science · *Area & Cultural Studies*

African National Congress, (ANC) ★★★

The FTP site for the African National Congress has numerous GIFs of prominent political rights activists in South Africa as well as many articles on such topics as lower-class black workers, socialism, the constitution of the ANC, how to join the ANC, and the history of the ANC. It provides important news on a one-or two-day basis, and contains many official press statements.

KEYWORDS Apartheid, Human Rights, International News, South Africa
AUDIENCE Educators, Historians, Political Activists, South Africans
CONTACT ancdip@wn.apc.org
FREE

ftp://wn.apc.org/anc/

Amnesty International ★★★

Amnesty International (AI) attempts to extend human rights and freedoms to people throughout the world by promoting awareness of and adherence to the Universal Declaration of Human Rights. The gopher server contains information about AI and its mission and has reports on many parts of the world such as China, Russia, and the Middle East. Links to other relevant Web sites with more information are also offered.

KEYWORDS Human Rights, Humanitarianism, International Politics, Public Policy
AUDIENCE Humanitarians, International Travelers, Political Activists
FREE

http://www.igc.apc.org/igc/amnesty.html

gopher://gopher.igc.apc.org/11/orgs/ai

ftp://ftp.igc.apc.org/pub/orgs_on_igc/amnesty-info

Belgian Federal Government Online ★★★

Offering a menu of Internet access in Dutch, English, French, and German, this Belgian Government site provides direct links to the elections, feedback, a guest book and more. Click on the language of choice from the Belgian Federal Information Service to see the dozen or so links to government officials, publications, laws, etc. There are even resumes of the king and queen.

KEYWORDS Belgium, Foreign Affairs, Foreign Trade
AUDIENCE Belgians, International Business Professionals
FREE

http://www.belgium.be/belgium/

Brain Gain Network (BGN) ★★

This page contains the text of the the pamphlet of the Brain Gain Network (BGN), a network of professionals and students interested in helping to increase the competitiveness of the Philippine economy in world markets. By promoting entrepreneurial initiative, BGN seeks to reverse the 'brain drain' in all disciplines and industries, especially high technology. The online pamphlet contains topics including the organization of BGN, accomplishments and future directions, how you can become involved in the BGN, and initiators of the brain gain network. This document contains mostly text with very few hyperlinks.

KEYWORDS   Economics, Philippines
AUDIENCE   Educators, Entrepreneurs, Philippinos
CONTACT   pacs@leland.stanford.edu
FREE

http://suncomnet.mozcom.com:80/SCF/BGN/BGNpamph.html

CEDAR - Central European Environmental Data Request Facility ★★★★

The Central European Environmental Data Request Facility (CEDAR) Web site is a resource for professionals to learn more about environmental regulations, projects, meetings, economics and related data in Central Europe. There are a lot of links here, including those to the Austrian Federal Ministry for the Environment, the Central and Eastern European EcoDirectory Project, the World Wildlife Fund (United States), INFOTERRA (the United Nations Environmental Programme) and the UNEP Global Resource Information Database (GRID). Laws, statutes, acts, conventions, and protocols are reproduced verbatim. Newsletters are available, as are searchable databases.

KEYWORDS   Central Europe, Economics, Environment, Environmental Policy
AUDIENCE   Environment Economists, Environment Policymakers, Environmentalists
CONTACT   Bernhard Lorenz
           Bernhard.Lorenz@cedar.univie.ac.at
FREE

http://www.cedar.univie.ac.at/

Center For Civil Society International (CFCSI) Home Page ★★★

The Center for Civil Society International (CFCSI)—which is dedicated to linking up planners in nations that were formerly part of the USSR with resources and organizations in Western countries—produces this Web page. The CFCSI presents a series of indices and links to development-related documents, listservs, archives of documents, and curricula for teaching about development.

KEYWORDS   Former Soviet Union, International Development, Russia
AUDIENCE   International Aid Agencies, International Development Professionals, Russians

CONTACT   Mr. Richard Upjohn
           ccsi@u.washington.edu
FREE

http://solar.rtd.utk.edu/~ccsi/ccsihome.html

Directory of /Gov/World ★★★

Directory of /Gov/World provides a large repository of copies of world government documents such as the Canada Constitution Act, 1867, Constitution of the People's Republic of China 1982, English Bill of Rights 1689, Draft Constitution of Estonian Republic 1992, Hamas Covenant (Islamic Resistance) 1988, the Magna Carta, the Consititution of the United States, the North American Free Trade Agreement, and much more.

KEYWORDS   Bill of Rights, Constitutions, Law, World HIstory
AUDIENCE   Historians, Students K-12, Teachers K-12
CONTACT   archive@wiretap.spies.com
FREE

ftp://wiretap.spies.com/Gov/World/

El Consejo Nacional de Investigaciones Cientificas y Tecnologicas (CONICIT) ★★★

This is the site of the National Council of Scientific and Technological Research of Venezuela, also called the El Consejo Nacional de Investigaciones Cientificas y Tecnologicas (CONICIT). Its main focus is to promote science and technology in Venezuela. It contains information about the following items- Documentacion general de este sistema - Funciones del Conicit y entes asociados al area de C y T - Concursos, becas y programas - Revistas, publicaciones y comunicados - Estadisticas en ciencia y tecnologia en Venezuela - Oportunidades de estudios de Pre y Postgrado en Venezuela - Consulta a Bases de Datos Nacionales e Internacionales - Conexion a otros gophers y servicios internacionales - Otros temas de interes en Ciencia y Tecnologia.

KEYWORDS   International Development, Science & Technology, Spanish, Venezuela
AUDIENCE   Government Officials, Policymakers, Political Scientists, Venezuelans
CONTACT   Jhon Riva
           jrivas@conicit.ve
FREE

gopher://dino.conicit.ve/

Electronic Embassy ★★★

The Electronic Embassy Web site is a meta-index making known the Web presence of members of Washington, D.C.'s embassy community. Users may also access a listing of all of the embassies in the American capital. There are links to U.S. governmental sites, such as the Department of State or the Commerce and Trade Office, American embassies in foreign countries, and nongovernmental organizations.

KEYWORDS   Embassies, Washington D.C.
AUDIENCE   Business Professionals, Diplomats, Expatriates, Journalists
FREE

http://www.embassy.org/

Friends and Partners ★★★★

From Russia and America comes a new information service called 'Friends and Partners,' one of the first information systems jointly developed by citizens of these two nations. To promote better understanding between these nations, it attempts to provide a common base of information about issues affecting relations between the countries, and by providing a common 'meeting place' where Americans and Russians can find and communicate with each other. The menu offers links to resources including History, Geography, Art, Music, Literature, Education and Science. There's also an information base of funding and exchange opportunities, tourism information, and news and weather reports.

KEYWORDS   Cultural Exchange, International Relations, Russia
AUDIENCE   General Public, Russians, Students (Secondary/College)
CONTACT   Natasha Bulashova
           natasha@ibpm.serpukhov.su
           gcole@solar.rtd.utk.edu
FREE

http://solar.rtd.utk.edu/friends/home.html

telnet://april.ibpm.serpukhov.su

Global Democracy Network (GDN) Gopher ★★★★

This site contains a large number of resources (in the form of documents and directories of personnel) for those interested in the GDN's (Global Democracy Network) efforts to improve human rights in various nations and their international development efforts worldwide. The GDN, administered by the nonprofit Congressional Human Rights Foundation, works to 'strengthen democracy worldwide.'

KEYWORDS   Democracy, Human Rights, International Law, Politics
AUDIENCE   Human Rights Activists, International Aid Agencies, International Development Specialists
FREE

gopher://chrf3.gdn.org:70/1

Gorbachev Foundation Home Page ★★★

The Gorbachev Foundation, founded in 1992, was created to 'articulate and address the challenges of the post-Cold War world through the revisioning of global priorities.' These Web pages offer background, structural, contact, and donation information for TGF, as well as articles on specific projects that the organization is involved with.

KEYWORDS   Activism, Education, International Development, Russia
AUDIENCE   Activists, Educators, Russia Residents, Russians
CONTACT   Eric Berg
           info@worldforum.org
FREE

http://www.clark.net/pub/gorbachev/home.html

I'm Europe Home Page ★★★★

Welcome to Information Market - Europe, an initiative of the Directorate-General XIII of the European Community (EC) to provide the World Wide Web with information about Europe and the European electronic information market. Topics on this page include the European Union, European Community Programmes related to the Information Market, Information Market Policy ACTions (IMPACT) Programme, European Commission Host Organisation (ECHO), Community Research and Development Information Service (CORDIS), etc.

Keywords Communications Technology, European Community, Information Services
Audience European Internet Surfers, Europeans, International Business Professionals, Web Developers
Contact webmaster@echo.lu
Free

http://www.echo.lu

IDEX (International Development EXchange) Home Page ★★★

IDEX, an international group that matches small-scale grassroots development efforts in various countries with volunteers, funding and other resources, has archived numerous documents for those interested in international development and related issues at this Web site.

Keywords Education, International Development, Peace, Politics
Audience International Aid Agencies, International Business Educators, International Development Specialists
Contact IDEX
idex@igc.apc.org
Free

http://www.digimark.net/idex/overview.html

IIASA (Institute for Applied Systems Analysis) Home Page ★★★★

The International Institute for Applied Systems Analysis, (IIASA) is an multinational effort to address common environmental problems. Examples of the topics addressed are population, environmentally compatible energy sources, water resources and radiation. The server has extensive information regarding the history and interests of IIASA.

Keywords Environment, Environmental Studies, International Politics, Population Control
Audience Environmental Researchers, Environmentalists, Policymakers
Contact Joerg Messer
joerg@iiasa.ac.at
Free

http://www.iiasa.ac.at/

gopher://gopher.iiasa.ac.at/

Le Ministère de la Culture et de la Francophonie ★★★

This is the site of the French Ministry of Culture. It is presented in French and includes information on Palaeolithic cave paintings in France, a schedule of conferences, debates, and studies, images from an archaeological museum, the age of enlightenment in the paintings of France's national museum, publications, and more.

Keywords France, French Culture, Museums
Audience Archaeologists, Art History Students, Francophiles, Museum Enthusiasts, Tourists
Contact Michel Bottin
bottin@culture.fr
Free

http://web.culture.fr/

Linkages - International Institute for Sustainable Development WWW Server ★★★

Linkages is provided by the International Institute for Sustainable Development (IISD), publishers of the Earth Negotiations Bulletin. The IISD page makes information available on past and future international meetings related to environment and development policy-making, including the Global Forest Policy, the World Summit for Social Development, the Convention to Combat Desertification and Drought, and so forth. IISD's mandate is to promote sustainable development in decision making within government, business, and the daily lives of individuals in Canada and internationally.

Keywords Environmental Organizations, Environmental Policy, Environmental Resources, Policy Research
Audience Environmental Activists, International Aid Agencies, International Development Specialists
Contact reception@iisdpost.iisd.ca
Free

http://www.mbnet.mb.ca:80/linkages/

National Flags ★★★

This site provides a list of links to gif images of national flags of many of the world's countries. The link simply leads to an image without text.

Keywords Flags, Images
Audience Artists, Collectors, Graphic Artists, Students (Primary/Secondary), Web Developers
Free

http://155.187.10.12/flags/nation-flags.html

News Sources for Specific Countries and Regions ★★

This document is a general compilation of information resources focused on news sources for specific countries. Most of the resources here are very specific, such as individual listservs carrying news from Poland, Croatia, or Malasia.

Keywords Croatia, International News, Malaysia, News

Audience General Public, Journalists, Researchers
Free

ftp://una.hh.lib.umich.edu/inetdirstacks/news:robinson

PeaceNet Homepage ★★★

This Web site is a 'front-door' to PeaceNet, a clearinghouse for peace-related political documents, and PeaceNet's gopher server. Information on PeaceNet membership (including a comprehensive membership list) and documents on the Middle East and various topics related to human rights are available here as well as the large archive of documents on the PeaceNet gopher.

Keywords Human Rights, Peace, War
Audience Government Students, Mediators, Policymakers, Political Researchers, Politicians
Contact PeaceNet
peacenet@igc.apc.org
Free

http://www.igc.apc.org/igc/pn.html

People of Color Environmental Groups Directory ★★★

This gopher menu provides a list of links to information international environmental groups. Links are provided to the Institute for Global Communications (IGC) - headline news, EcoNet - Environment, PeaceNet - Peace, Human Rights, and Social Justice, ConflictNet - Conflict Resolution, LaborNet - Labor, and more.

Keywords Environment, Human Rights
Audience Community Activists, Nonprofit Organaizations, Political Activists, Progressives
Contact support@igc.apc.org
Free

gopher://gopher.igc.apc.org:70/11/

Phish Archive ★★

This site provides information about International affairs and environmental affairs from computers connected to PhishNET, a computer network in Massachusetts. Some of the information offered is about foreign aid, the environment, hunger, and the turbulent events in Rwanda.

Keywords Environment, International Development, International News, International Politics
Audience Activists, Environmentalists, International Development Specialists
Free

gopher://archive.phish.net/

ShapeTechnical Centre (STC) WWW Home Page ★★★

The Web server for Shape, NATO's technical research and advice wing, offers background and organizational information as well as data and results of recent unclassified research projects carried out under STC and other NATO/Shape wings.

Keywords Europe, Government, Military, NATO (North Atlantic Treaty Organization)
Audience Military Historians, Military Personnel, Political Researchers, Researchers

CONTACT   Aad van der Zanden
          zanden@stc.nato.int
FREE
http://www.stc.nato.int/

Social Summit ★★★

The Social Summit Web site reports on the events of the World Summit for Social Development in Copenhagen, Denmark, on March 5-12, 1995. Users will find daily reports and final documents from the conference, which was sponsored by the United Nations, as well as materials regarding the several preparatory conferences which preceded the event. There are links to the UN, sovereign governments, and non-governmental organizations.
KEYWORDS   Social Policy, Summits, United Nations
AUDIENCE   International Affairs Students, Journalists
FREE
http://www.iisd.ca/linkages/wssd.html

SummitNet ★★★

The information provided by this gopher server relates primarily to the summit of leaders of the Americas that took place in Miami, Florida, from December 9-11, 1994. The information includes newspaper articles from the Miami Herald, the Christian Science Monitor, and, in Spanish, El Nuevo Herald. Further information includes government documents and publications. The site is maintained by Florida International University.
KEYWORDS   International News, Politics, World Leaders
AUDIENCE   Journalists, Political Analysts, Political Researchers
CONTACT   SUMMIT@SERVAX.FIU.EDU
FREE
gopher://summit.fiu.edu/

UN Population Information Network (POPIN) Gopher ★★★★

The United Nations Population Information Network (POPIN) is funded by the UN Population Fund to improve the flow of population information worldwide and to encourage the exchange of population information and experience among experts. This site provides access to POPIN Information Services, regional POPIN networks, and world demographic trends (UN Population Division), as well as other population gophers.
KEYWORDS   Census (The), Population Control, Research, United Nations
AUDIENCE   Population Experts, United Nations Personnel
CONTACT   Dr. Susan Pasquariella
           popin@undp.org
FREE
gopher://gopher.undp.org:70/11/ungophers/popin

USAID Gopher Server ★★★

This gopher server, administered by the U.S. Agency for International Development (USAID), contains text on USAID itself, as well as articles on USAID's various foreign aid projects, and congressional presentations on behalf of the organization. There are also numerous links to other International Development-related sources on the Internet.
KEYWORDS   Foreign Trade, International Aid, International Development, Politics
AUDIENCE   International Aid Agencies, International Development Specialists
CONTACT   USAID Gopher Administrator
           gopher-admin@info.usaid.gov
FREE
gopher://gopher.info.usaid.gov/1

United Nations ★★★

This is the gopher server for the United Nations. It offers information about the United Nations' background, the United Nations' Charter, UN current information, United Nations documents (General Assembly, ECOSOC, Sec. Council) and United Nations conferences. Also included are links to other UN organizations' gophers—UN Children's Fund (UNICEF), UN Conference on Trade & Development (UNCTAD), North Atlantic Treaty Organization (NATO), UN Educational, Scientific & Cultural Org. (UNESCO) (New York & Paris), UN Environment Programme (UNEP), UN Population Div. (UNDESIPA), UN Research Institute on Social Development (UNRISD) Gopher, UN Volunteers (UNV), World Bank, World Health Organization (WHO), and access to other external databases.
KEYWORDS   International Agencies, International Documents, International Relations, United Nations
AUDIENCE   International Agencies, International Relation Scholars, International Studies Students
FREE
gopher://gopher.un.org/

United Nations Childrens Fund (UNICEF) ★★★

This is a gopher server of the United Nations Children's Fund (UNICEF), an organization devoted to the well-being of the world's children. This site provides information on the work of UNICEF, major UNICEF programs, UNICEF news, UNICEF Library Catalog, the Work Summit for Children, and more.
KEYWORDS   Child Care, Children, International Documents, United Nations

---

Connections to Russia
Russia to the Max!

If you work in business, industry, banking, government or academia, or provide legal, accountancy or other professional services to clients dealing with Russia, you need reliable, authoritative and up-to-date political reference information to operate and transact successfully in this challenging environment. You can get it at "Maximov Companion To Who Governs the Russian Federation" on the World Wide Web.

Maximov is a bi-lingual (English-Russian) publication and has the answers to anyone's questions about dealing with Russia. Systematically organized and easy to use, Maximov's can put you in touch with the right people - 3,400 political decision makers at every level throughout the Russian Federation - officials who have the power to deal with problems and respond to opportunities alike, from privatization, investment and regulatory issues to legislative programs, science policy and local government matters.

(http://www.maximov.com/)

International – Issues

AUDIENCE Child Development Professionals, Childcare Providers, Children's Rights Activists
CONTACT rpadolina@unicef.org
FREE

gopher://hqfaus01.unicef.org/

United Nations Development Programmes (UNDP) Home Page ★★★

The United Nations Development Programme's World Wide Web Server gives access to the UNDP databases, the Sustainable Human Development, public information and recruitment, the United Nations public information, documents, conferences and current information. An extensive list of links to other United Nations organizations and environment-related issues are available.

KEYWORDS International Development, International Documents, Policy Research, United Nations
AUDIENCE International Aid Agencies, International Development Specialists, Volunteers
CONTACT Joao de Souza
jdsouza@undp.org
FREE

http://www.undp.org/

gopher://gopher.undp.org:70/11/undp

United Nations Environment Program CEDAR Gopher ★★★

This gopher offers access to documents on environmental data for Central and Eastern Europe, in addition to The World Wildlife Fund in the U.S. and Russia. There is also access to the UNEP Global Resource Information Database and other environmental gophers.

KEYWORDS Environmental Policy, Environmentalism, United Nations
AUDIENCE Environmental Researchers, Environmental Scientists, Environmentalists, Europeans
FREE

gopher://pan.cedar.univie.ac.at/1

United Nations International Computing Centre WWW ★★★

This home page, maintained by the International Computing Centre, lists the United Nations System Internet Servers. UNICC's purpose is to provide information technology services on networking and computing technology and information management services. Organizations are listed alphabetically to provide easy access to UN-related organizations and such servers as the CERN server, the NSCA server and NASA server.

KEYWORDS Communications Technology, International Relations, United Nations
AUDIENCE Computer Researchers, Information Technology Enthusiasts, International Studies Students

CONTACT helpdesk@unicc.org
FREE

http://www.unicc.org/

United Nations Volunteers (UNV) ★★★★

The United Nations Volunteers programme (UNV) was created to complement the UNDP in development cooperation. Available at this site is information about UNV in general, its activities, UNV vacancies, UNV and the advancement of women, United Nations WWW and Gopher Links, and email directories of UN agencies.

KEYWORDS United Nations, Volunteers
AUDIENCE General Public, International Development Specialists, Job Seekers
CONTACT Alessandro Lanari
ale@unv.ch
FREE

http://suna.unv.ch/

gopher://gopher.unv.ch/

World Bank Gopher ★★★

This Gopher has directories for the Public Information Center, World Bank Publications, Information Bank on African Development Studies, and the World Bank Inspection Panel.

KEYWORDS African Studies, Economics, United Nations, World Bank
AUDIENCE Banking Industry Specialists, Economic Development Specialists, Economists
FREE

gopher://ftp.worldbank.org/1

World Fact Book 1994 ★★★★

The World Fact Book 1994 page provides links to a plethora of information about all the countries of the world. Produced by the CIA, it contains links to information on the United Nations System, weights and measures, international organizations and groups, reference maps of different countries in GIF and JPEG format, subscripton and publication information, and more.

KEYWORDS CIA (Central Intelligence Agency), Maps, Reference
AUDIENCE Educators (Primary/Secondary), Researchers, Students (Primary/Secondary)
FREE

http://www.ic.gov/94fact/fb94toc/fb94toc.html

World Meteorological Organization WWW Server ★★★★

The United Nations World Meteorological Organization server offers press releases, vacancy notices, and a list of the major programs of the World Meteorological Organization (World Weather Watch, World Climate Program, Global Climate Observing System, etc.) Also included are links to the national weather services of Australia, Canada and the U.S., and links to other reports, forecasts, weather maps, and satellite images available on the Web.

KEYWORDS Climatology, Meteorology, United Nations, Weather
AUDIENCE General Public, International Travelers, Meteorologists, Meteorology Students
CONTACT w3server@www.wmo.ch
FREE

http://www.wmo.ch/

Youth Participation in World Summit for Social Development ★★

The Youth Participation in World Summit for Social Development Web site encourages youthful users 'to contribute their ideas on major social issues' to a forum coinciding with the United Nations-sponsored conference, held in March of 1995. Users may participate via email, and can read other postings. There are links to the official Web sites of the conference.

KEYWORDS Social Policy, United Nations, Youth
AUDIENCE International Affairs Students, United Nations Personnel
CONTACT unicefwssd@igc.apc.org
FREE

http://www.intac.com/PubService/rwanda/CONF/un_appeal.html

Issues

See also
Education · *Educational Policy*
Health & Medicine · *Public Health*
Health & Medicine · *Sexually Transmitted Diseases*
Law & Criminal Justice · *Constitutional Law*

Abortion Rights ★★★

The Abortion Rights home page provides information intended for users who are pro-abortion, or pro-choice. The site includes texts of relevant Supreme Court decisions, field reports, and links to Web sites concerning childbirth and other women's issues.

KEYWORDS Abortion, Pro-Choice, United States
AUDIENCE Abortion-Rights Activists, Political Scientists
CONTACT lmann@telerama.lm.com
FREE

http://www.lm.com/~lmann/feminist/abortion.html

Alaska Wilderness League (AWL) ★★★

The Alaska Wilderness League (AWL) is an environmental organization which serves as a watchdog on Alaskan environmental issues. The AWL uses the Econet system to find additional members for the organization. The AWL offers only one page to describe its organization, its focuses, and identifies that one of its key issues is the permanent wilderness designation of the Coastal Plain of the Arctic National Wildlife Refuge.

KEYWORDS Alaska, Conservation, Environmental Policy, Forest Management
AUDIENCE Alaska Residents, Environmentalists, Policy Analysts, Wilderness Enthusiasts

Issues   **345**

CONTACT   awl@igc.apc.org
FREE

gopher://gopher.igc.apc.org/
    0ftp%3Aftp.igc.apc.org@/pub/
    orgs_on_igc/awl

ftp://ftp.igc.apc.org/pub/orgs_on_igc/awl

D.C. Metro Prolife News/Events Line ★★★

The D.C. Metro Prolife News/Events Line Web site presents information supporting the anti-abortion (or prolife) point of view, and provides access to like-minded home pages, such as Lifelinks, as well as Christian sites. There's also a link to the Right Side of the Web home page.

KEYWORDS   Abortion, Women
AUDIENCE   Anti-abortion Activists, Journalists
FREE

http://www.clark.net/pub/jeffd/plnel.html

Electronic Democracy Information Network (EDIN) ★★★★

Electronic Democracy Information Network (EDIN) is sponsored by UC-Berkeley's Center for Community Economic Research (CCER). It provides a directory of issues which focuses on giving a stronger voice to community organizations on the Internet. Some topics provided include race and the California economy, government budget information, Third Parties and electoral reform, labor issues, news services online, political and nonprofit organizations & movements, progressive connections on the Net, the economy, gender and sexuality, trade and the international economy, Right-Wing Politics, Arts, Culture and Humor, and more.

KEYWORDS   Civil Liberties, Internet Issues
AUDIENCE   Educators (College), General Public, Journalists, Political Activists
CONTACT   edinsupporter@garnet.berkeley.edu
FREE

http://garnet.berkeley.edu:3333

gopher://garnet.berkeley.edu:1250/

Enviro Orgs- Environmental Organizations On-Line ★★★

This gopher menu provides links to a lot of information related to environmental organizations. The links include directories and lists on environmental conference schedules, environmental organizations, the process of how to form a nonprofit, and Internet nonprofit centers.

KEYWORDS   Conferences, Environment, Human Rights, Non Profit Organizations
AUDIENCE   Community Activists, Nonprofit Organaizations, Political Activists
CONTACT   Cliff Landesman
            clandesm@panix.com
FREE

gopher://envirolink.org:70/11/.EnviroOrgs

FactBot Database ★★

The FactBot Database Web page presents a barrage of information supporting the anti-abortion (or pro-life) point of view. Material is grouped into categories such as legal, scientific, and factual.

KEYWORDS   Abortion, Women
AUDIENCE   Anti-Abortion Activists, Journalists
FREE

http://www.clark.net/pub/jeffd/factbot.html

First Perspective ★★★

First Perspective is a national newspaper serving the news and information needs of First Nations, the indigenous people of Canada. They publish commentary by indigenous writers, include native law case summaries, pow wow listings, employment listings, education and training opportunities, a digest of events, and more.

KEYWORDS   Canada, Culture
AUDIENCE   Canadians, History Buffs, Indigenous People, Native Canadians
CONTACT   jwastase@mbnet.mb.ca
FREE

http://www.mbnet.mb.ca/firstper/

Flag-Burning Page ★★★

The Flag-Burning Page Web site discusses the hot-button issue of whether it's acceptable to burn this symbol of the United States. Users will find some history of the controversy and track Congressional legislation. Users may also burn a virtual flag. There are links to Interactive Democracy and Congressional sites.

KEYWORDS   Politics, United States
AUDIENCE   Political Activists, Politicians
FREE

http://www.indirect.com/user/warren/flag.html

FoE (Friends of the Earth) Environmental Campaigns ★★★

The FoE states that it is one of the leading environmental pressure groups in the UK. This Web page offers information regarding current environmental campaigns throughout the UK. At the moment, most of the page is under construction, but in the future they say users will be able to access information regarding biodivercity, energy, the atmosphere, industry, pollution, sustainable development and local campaigns.

KEYWORDS   Conservation, Environment
AUDIENCE   British, Environmentalists, Policymakers, Political Activists
CONTACT   Andrew Dilworth
            foe@gn.apc.org
FREE

http://www.foe.co.uk/camps/index.html

Greenpeace WWW ★★★

Greenpeace, a 25-year old International environmental activist group founded in Canada, draws 'attention to an abuse of the environment through their unwavering presence at the scene, whatever the risk'. This Web server presents 'photobooks' of various Greenpeace campaigns and activities; a library of resources for those interested in Greenpeace activities and projects; and an index of environmental multilateral treaties. A link to the Greenpeace gopher is also provided, which contains comprehensive organizational background and contact information, in addition to an archive of transcribed Greenpeace press releases and memoranda.

KEYWORDS   Activism, Conservation, Environmentalism, Wildlife
AUDIENCE   Activists, Conservationists, Environmentalists, Wildlife Biologists, Wildlife Enthusiasts
CONTACT   sysop@greenpeace.org
FREE

http://www.greenpeace.org/

In Pursuit of Justice? ★★★

This Web page, called In Pursuit of Justice?, presents an online book of the same title that is described as a story 'about the abuse of a family by a Child Protective Service agency and the Florida State's Attorney Office.' Users may download the book. There are also links to sites of a similarly anti-government bent.

KEYWORDS   Child Abuse, Federal Government, United States
AUDIENCE   Civil Servants, Parents
FREE

http://www.efn.org/~srl/

Information Infrastructure Task Force (IITF) Web Server ★★★

This site offers information on the Information Infrastructure Task Force (IITF). There is access to new information, a list of committees, working groups, press releases, a calendar of events, speeches, testimonials, documents, and the NII (National Information Infrastructure). There are also links to conferences, communication related web sites, other government web servers, and the Department of Commerce server.

KEYWORDS   Government (US), Information Superhighway
AUDIENCE   Educators, Government Officials, Information Professionals, Internet Activists
CONTACT   nii@ntia.doc.gov
FREE

http://iitf.doc.gov

League for Programming Freedom (LPF) ★★★

This is a brief home page from the League for Programming Freedom - an organization that opposes software patents and user interface copyrights. Discussion, texts of related laws, links to companies opposed and in favor of software patents can be found here along with their newsletter and other resources.

KEYWORDS   Computer Programming, Computer Software, Intellectual Property, Non Profit Organizations
AUDIENCE   Computer Professionals, Computer Programmers, Computer Users

Issues – Military

CONTACT webmasters@lpf.org

FREE

http://www.lpf.org/

The National Association of Regional Councils (NARC) ★★

This site hosts the The National Association of Regional Councils (NARC). The purpose of NARC is to represent the interests of America's regional councils, large and small, urban and rural, at the national level. The NARC also communicates ideas to various regions through the use of conferences, newsletters, and electronic means. Finally the groups maintains databases of information about regional councils and the services that they offer. On this page, the user will find newsletter archives which highlight the activities of the NARC and many of the regional activities of its members. The user can also access the Final Reports of some NARC Task Forces, including the Task Force on Health Care, the Task Force on Water Quality, and the Task Force on Regional Economic Issues

KEYWORDS Conferences, Networking, Regional Councils, Social Studies

AUDIENCE Community Leaders, Political Scientists, Politicians

CONTACT Issue Dynamics
info@idi.net

FREE

http://apt.org/narc.html

Rainforest Action Network Home Page ★★★★

The Rainforest Action Network Home Page is a lively compendium of information related both to the conservation of rain forests and to the Rainforest Action Network's efforts to assist in preserving these ecosystems. At this site you will find data concerning RAN's Action Alerts, current projects in which you can play a role; boycotts and other campaigns; ecotourism; products made using sustainable agriculture or development techniques; a whole truckload of material for kids; educational resources for teachers, and information about people indigenous to the rain forests. There are quite a few links to topics as diverse as music, like-minded organizations, and the media.

KEYWORDS Conservation, Environmentalism

AUDIENCE Children, Conservationists, Environmentalists, Rainforest Action Activists

CONTACT Rainforest Action Network
rainforest@igc.apc.org

FREE

http://www.igc.apc.org/ran/index.html

Sierra Club - Victoria Group Home Page ★★★★

The Sierra Club - Victoria Group Home Page provides many links to other environmental sites - primarily through the EnviroWeb. This Home Page also presents an excellent introduction to the Sierra Club, its activities, policies, and politics. Located here are articles on 'Multinationals and Consumption,' and 'Beyond Timbergate,' as well as other environment oriented documents.

KEYWORDS Activism, Environment, Organizations

AUDIENCE Ecologists, Environmentalists, Sierra Club Members

CONTACT J Wight
jwight@amtsgi.bc.ca

FREE

http://www.islandnet.com/~jwight/enviro

Sierra Club Website (National) ★★★★

The National Sierra Club web site offers complete information about the environmental organization, The Sierra Club. At this site, you will find information about the history of the Club and its environmental policies, summaries of upcoming outings and programs, a list of local Club chapters, material on the various activist groups within the Sierra Club, and a way to join the Club online. There are also links to other environmental sites.

KEYWORDS Activism, Environment, Organizations

AUDIENCE Ecologists, Environmentalists, Sierra Club Members, Wilderness Enthusiasts

CONTACT Dan Anderson
dan.anderson@sierraclub.org

FREE

http://www.sierraclub.org

States of Emergency Database Project ★★★

The States of Emergency Database Project Web page comprises a legal database that contains 'legislative texts and other relevant information on states of emergency in several countries,' such as Malaysia, Northern Ireland, South Africa, and Turkey. Information is organized by country.

KEYWORDS Developing Countries, Government, Human Rights, Law (US)

AUDIENCE Human Rights Activists, Lawyers, Political Scientists

FREE

http://www.law.qub.ac.uk/human.htm

Synergy Solutions ★★★★

Synergy Solutions is a database of WWW resources oriented towards the sharing of solutions. On this page there is a 'Solutions Matrix' where the principal categories are Economics, Education, Health, Politics, Science, and Society and are organized vertically on a grid. Horizontally, the topics include ideas, email, news, organizations, nets, data, publications, and other. You click on the button at the intersection of the two topics such as health and publications and you virtually visit a hyperlinked list of health publications. There is a wealth of accessible information which is provided in a very organized and easy-to-find manner.

KEYWORDS Health, Politics, Sciences

AUDIENCE Educators, Politicians

CONTACT Steven Moyer
space@primenet.com

FREE

http://www.primenet.com/solutions

Military

See also
Education · *Universities - United States*
Education · *Vocational Education*
Government & Politics · *Agencies*
Humanities & Social Sciences · *History*

Air Force Web Page ★★★★

A meta-index of links and pointers to other Air Force web pages and various military Internet resources, this web page also contains a front-door to the Air Force InterNet (AFIN), a transitional network in place while Milnet, the military's 20-year-old internal network, is disassembled and their new network is set up. AFIN houses numerous resources for anyone doing business with the Air Force or working under its command. Also on this web page are individual links to every active Air Force base home page in the world.

KEYWORDS Air Force, Defense, Military

AUDIENCE Defense Analysts, Defense Industry Followers, Military Personnel

CONTACT Capt Matt Jonson
jonson@ddn.af.mil

FREE

http://www.af.mil/

Army Area Handbooks ★★★

The Area Handbooks which are published by and for the Army giving historical, geographical, cultural, and economic information about 10 countries, including China, Israel, Japan, and Somalia.

KEYWORDS Army, International Politics, Military

AUDIENCE Educators, Military Historians, Political Scientists, Students

CONTACT Raleigh Muns, Reference Librarian, Thomas Jefferson Library
srcmuns@umslvma.umsl.edu

FREE

gopher://umslvma.umsl.edu

Army Budget for 1995 ★★★★

This is the complete (at least, the complete section which is unclassified) 1995 President's Budget for the U.S. Army. Programs are indexed by subject and name and the documents themselves are hypertext-annotated to allow for easy navigation between different areas.

KEYWORDS Economics, Federal Government (US), Military

AUDIENCE Activists, Economists, Journalists, Military Personnel

CONTACT RAMSEYE@PENTAGON-ASAFM.ARMY.MIL

FREE

http://134.11.192.15/pubs/greenbk/Budget.htm

Army Corps of Engineers Home Page ★★★

This server carries background information on the Army Corps of Engineers, projects currently under way, newsletters and other topical material. Also included is a large index of geography, mapmaking, and engineer-

ing-related resources from both Government and private-sector sources, and links to those sources that are available over the Internet.
KEYWORDS   Army, Engineering, Geology, Mapmaking
AUDIENCE   Cartographers, Engineers, Government Officials, Military Personnel
CONTACT   U.S. Army Corps of Engineers Internet Publishing Group
           webmaster@www.usace.army.mil
FREE

http://www.usace.army.mil/

Army High Performance Computing Research Center ★★★

This page is created by the Army High Performance Computing Research Center. It describes the research initiatives of the center, as well as providing links to resources such as software and technical documentation. There is also information on the center's educational outreach programs, courses, and links to member institutions which comprise the backbone of this research group.
KEYWORDS   Computer Science, Research
AUDIENCE   Computer Scientists, Military Researchers
CONTACT   Wes Barris
           wesb@msc.edu
FREE

http://www.arc.umn.edu/html/ahpcrc.html

Army Link ★★★★

Army Link is designed as an umbrella site for all of the Army Web pages, as well as providing general information about the U.S. Army. Users will find an alphabetically listed index of 1130 Army organization home pages, both by organization name and subject. Other features include the Army mission statement and information about receiving field manuals or personnel locations. Users may also access the official department of defense publications and fact files via DefenseLink, as well as linking to other U.S. Military Web sites.
KEYWORDS   Army, Military
AUDIENCE   General Public, Military Personnel
CONTACT   webmaster@pentagon-1dms2.army.mil
FREE

http://www.army.mil/

Army Research Laboratory (ARL) Information Server ★★★

This pages describes the activities of the Army Research Laboratory. Users will find basic information on the Lab itself, along with information on technology transfer programs. There are also descriptions of some of the research that the Lab is performing, as well as links to the individual directorates under the ARL umbrella.
KEYWORDS   Military Research, Research Labs
AUDIENCE   Defense contractors, Military Enthusiasts, U.S. Army Officials

CONTACT   webmaster@arl.mil
FREE

http://www.brl.mil

Defence Research Agency ★★★

The Defence Research Agency (DRA) is a Next Steps Agency of the UK Government. Its primary aim is to provide independent, high quality, efficient, and cost-effective scientific and technical services to its customers, primarily to the Ministry of Defence. Users will find images and information about some of the inventions that this agency has created, which include a helmet-mounted pyroelectric camera and small explosives in car safety airbags. Staff home pages, as well as links to other servers supported by the DRA, are provided as well.
KEYWORDS   Military Technology, United Kingdom
AUDIENCE   Computer Scientists, Defense Contractors, Engineers
CONTACT   webmaster@daedalus.dra.hmg.gb
FREE

http://daedalus.dra.hmg.gb

Defense Business Management University Web Page ★★★★

The DBMU, founded in 1992 with a mandate from the Department of Defense to develop and teach certain curricula in order to train the workforce of the DoD more effectively, now gives classes to DoD staff and those working with the DoD on a wide variety of subjects, including a number of technical courses. Their home page offers information on the genesis of the organization, current class and curricula lists (in hypertext or downloadable GUI format), various DBMU newsletters and DBMU organizational charts.
KEYWORDS   Business, Defense, Government, Military
AUDIENCE   Defense Analysts, Government Employees, Government Students, Political Researchers
CONTACT   Steve Hurst DBMU
           sfhurst@nps.navy.mil
FREE

ftp://ftp.nps.navy.mil/pub/dbmu/thesis/tom.html

Defense Technical Information Center (DTIC) Home Page ★★★

The DTIC, which assists in all Department of Defense (DoD) research, engineering and acquisition of new technology efforts, administers this home page. This WWW site offers background information on this, and other wings of the DoD, as well as links to DoD gopher sites and other DoD community information services. Training schedules, job postings, and other DoD data are also indexed at this Web site.
KEYWORDS   Military, Technology
AUDIENCE   Defense Analysts, Government Employees, Government Students, Political Researchers

CONTACT   DTIC Staff
           japistol@dgis.dtic.dla.mil
FREE

http://www.dtic.dla.mil/

gopher://asc.dtic.dla.mil/

Department of Defense Information Systems Technology Insertion ★★★

This Web page, prepared by the Defense Information Systems Agency Technology Insertion program, is a meta-index of projects that upgrade computer-system capabilities throughout the Department of Defense and elsewhere. This process is called 'technology insertion'. Users are provided access to servers such as the Advanced Technology Demonstration Network. There are also links to other military and scientific servers.
KEYWORDS   Computers, Department of Defense (US), United States
AUDIENCE   Computer Scientists, Military Scientists
FREE

http://www.disa.atd.net/

Directorate of Time ★★★

The Directorate of Time Web page is run by the US Naval Observatory and provides information about precision timekeeping. Users will find out about the Observatory and its services, learn about how it creates time scales for the United States and the world, and be able to read about the various clocks that the Observatory uses to keep time. One can sign up to receive the correct time via modem or automated data servers, and by clicking the 'what time is it?' button, one can also get the exact official time for one's time zone.
KEYWORDS   Navy (US)
AUDIENCE   General Public
CONTACT   webmaster@www.usno.navy.mil
FREE

http://tycho.usno.navy.mil/time.html

Economic Conversion Information Exchange Gopher ★★★★

The Economic Conversion Information Exchange (ECIX) gopher provides information related to the economic impact of the downsizing of the United States Defense Department. The information is aimed at those who would be most affected by the changes (communities, industries and workers). The information includes press releases, background information, contacts, finance strategies, and government programs.
KEYWORDS   Community Services, Defense, Economics, Military Policy
AUDIENCE   General Public, Industry Professionals, Military Personnel
CONTACT   epages@doc.gov
FREE

gopher://ecix.doc.gov/

Ftp.Arl.Mil ★★★

This machine is the anonymous file transfer protocol (FTP) repository for The US Army Research Laboratory

Military

(ARL). Some of the repositories located at this site are BRL-CAD Software Repository, BRL-CAD Document Repository, BRL-CAD Bug Tracking System, Historic Computers and Television Images from Operation Desert Storm.

KEYWORDS Research Labs
AUDIENCE Computer Users, Educators (University), Internet Users, Researchers, Students (University)
CONTACT webmaster@arl.mil
FREE

http://ftp.arl.mil

Gulf War Photo Gallery ★★★★

On this server Ronald A. Hoskinson has posted a number of photographs he took during Operation Desert Storm in Kuwait and Baghdad. His personal diary from that period is also available. Over a dozen photographs are available.

KEYWORDS Middle East, Military, War
AUDIENCE Military Historians, Military Personnel, Photographers, Veterans
CONTACT Ronald A. Hoskinson rah2@ra.msstate.edu
FREE

http://www2.msstate.edu/~rah2/gulf-war.html

Jane's Electronic Information System ★★★★

This page is an electronic version of the widely-used Jane's series of indexes and descriptions of military hardware, this allows keyword and boolean searches and will return information on the country of development and the manufacture of any piece of military hardware worldwide. Indexed here are aircraft, ground and aquatic vehicles, munitions, weapons, and other military devices. The demonstration version of the Jane's EIS, shown on this Web site, only contains a subset of Jane's 20+ volumes. Full versions of the database are sold for use on remote systems; the company is considering offering all volumes via their Web site in the near future.

KEYWORDS Indexes, Internet Resources, Vehicles, Weapons
AUDIENCE Military Historians, Military Personnel, Political Researchers
CONTACT Craig Knudsen cknudsen@btg.com
FREE

http://www.btg.com/janes/

NCCOSC West Coast In-Service Engineering Division (NISE) ★★

The NISE West Coast In-Service Engineering Division of the Naval Command, Control and Ocean Surveillance Center (NCCOSC) provides fleet support for the communications and control center for the U.S. Navy. Their home page provides information about the bases that belong to this division and their activities, such as staff and facilties, resources, and objectives. This page also links to the NCCOSC page, with national naval command information, and the Navy Online Web site.

KEYWORDS Engineering, Navy (US)
AUDIENCE Military Personnel, Navy Personnel
CONTACT flo_nisew@nosc.mil
FREE

http://mork.nosc.mil/

NRaD Gopher ★★

This gopher server provides information about the Naval Ocean Systems Center (NOSC) of the United States Navy. The information includes NOSC announcements, policies, meeting and conference schedules, and job openings.

KEYWORDS Defense, Military, Navy (US)
AUDIENCE Military Personnel, Navy Personnel
CONTACT gopher@nosc.mil
FREE

gopher://gopher.nosc.mil/

Naval Command Control and Ocean Surveillance Center ★★★

The Naval Command Control and Ocean Surveillance Center (NCCOSC) Home Page gives access to its research and engineering divisions. NCCOSC is the Navy's warfare center for command, control and communication systems, and ocean surveillance. There are links to other naval pages and related sites on the Internet.

KEYWORDS Government Agencies, National Policy, Navy (US), Research
AUDIENCE Naval Researchers, Navy Personnel
CONTACT webmaster@nosc.mil
FREE

http://www.nosc.mil/

Naval Research Laboratory ★★★★

The Naval Research Laboratory conducts corporate and military research in the Navy environment of sea, sky, and space. This site contains links to information on the directorates within the laboratory, as well as material on some of the research projects and staff of the facility. Users can link to the regional affiliates of the NRL, as well as to other servers on the Net with related information.

KEYWORDS Military Research, Military Science, Naval Research Laboratory, Navy (US)
AUDIENCE Defense Contractors, Military Researchers, Navy Officers
CONTACT webmaster@www.nrl.navy.mil
FREE

http://www.cmf.nrl.navy.mil

Naval Surface Warefare Center, Port Hueneme Division ★★★

The Naval Surface Warfare Center page offers information about the facilities, programs, and engineering at the Port Hueneme Division. There are links and resources for Navy information on the Internet.

KEYWORDS Government Agencies, Navy (US)
AUDIENCE Government Agencies, Navy Personnel
CONTACT Webmaster@phd-nswc
FREE

http://www.nswses.navy.mil/

NavyOnline Home Page ★★★★

The NavyOnline Home Page offers access to Navy information resources to the public and to Navy personnel. Some of the links include the Bureau of Medicine and Surgery (BUMED), Chief of Naval Education and Training (CNET), Engineering Duty Officers and the Fleet Material Support Office (FMSO). Some of the links are restricted to Navy personnel.

KEYWORDS Navy (US)
AUDIENCE General Public, Military Enthusiasts, Naval Personnel, Students
CONTACT webmaster@ncts.navy.mil
FREE

http://www.ncts.navy.mil

Royal Military Academy ★★★

This site for the Belgian Royal Military Academy is fairly comprehensive and includes orientation information, links to seven of the RMA's departments, a chance to listen to the 582k military march of the school and lots of other interesting links.

KEYWORDS Belgium, Military Academies
AUDIENCE Military Students
FREE

http://www.rma.ac.be/

Skunk Works - The Online Military Technology Bulletin Board ★★★

This page presents information about United States Military Technology, and specifically the clandestine Skunk Works aerospace operation coordinated through the Lockheed Corporation. There is an online preview of the book, 'Skunk Works,' by Ben R. Rich, containing dozens of images and first-hand accounts of Lockheed Stealth projects. In addition, there is an online discussion forum related to military technology topics.

KEYWORDS Aeronautics, Military Technology, Space
AUDIENCE Military Historians, Military Personnel, Miltary Enthusiasts, War Historians
CONTACT twep-webmaster@pathfinder.com
FREE

http://bigmouth.pathfinder.com/twep/Features/Skunk_Works/Skunk_Works.html

Survivability/Lethality Analysis Directorate Information Server ★★★

This site offers access to the U.S. Army Research Laboratory's Survivability/Lethality Analysis Directorate (SLAD) Database. Users will find information pertaining to the effectiveness of various weapons systems, simulation software created for the purpose of testing newly-developed weapons, and technical papers related to the Laboratory's research.

KEYWORDS Military Technology, Weapons

Military – Policies

AUDIENCE Ballistics Engineers, Defense Contractors, Military Personnel
CONTACT Lee Butler
butler@arl.mil
FREE

http://web.arl.mil

U.S. Army Corps of Engineers ★★★

This site provides information on the organization, programs, news, facilities, and activities of the US Army Corps of Engineers. With an overview of the ACE's senior staff and various online data services, this site is primarily of interest to persons already affiliated with the ACE; however, many will enjoy the weather information links, and users of all backgrounds will find the History of the Sacramento District a fascinating link, with lavish graphics and interesting historical data.

KEYWORDS Army, Engineering, Government Departments, Military
AUDIENCE Engineers, Military Personnel, Researchers
CONTACT US. Army Corps of Engineers, Internet Publishing Group
webmaster@www.usace.army.mil
FREE

http://www.usace.mil/usace.html

Policies

See also
Business & Economics · *Economics*
Education · *Educational Policy*
Health & Medicine · *Public Health*
Internet · *Internet Issues*

Amnesty International Home Page ★★★

Amnesty International is an independent worldwide human rights movement working impartially for the release of all prisoners of conscience, fair and prompt trials for political prisoners, and an end to torture and executions. Viewers of this site can access Amnesty's Gallery of former prisoners, which features images and stories of people helped by Amnesty. Other items available include the United Nations Universal Declaration of Human Rights, a document outlining the appropriate treatment of humans everywhere, as well as information about joining Amnesty International, or ordering products which help provide financial support for the organization.

KEYWORDS Activism, Human Rights, Organizations
AUDIENCE Activists, Free Speech Activists, Human Rights Activists, Political Activists, Prisoners
CONTACT Organic Online
www@organic.com
FREE

http://www.organic.com:80/Non.profits/Amnesty/

Budget of the United States Government, Fiscal Year 1995 ★★★★

This Web site provides electronic access to U.S. Budget documents. One may use a search engine to

Connections to Military Resources

Get to know all about the Normandy invasion

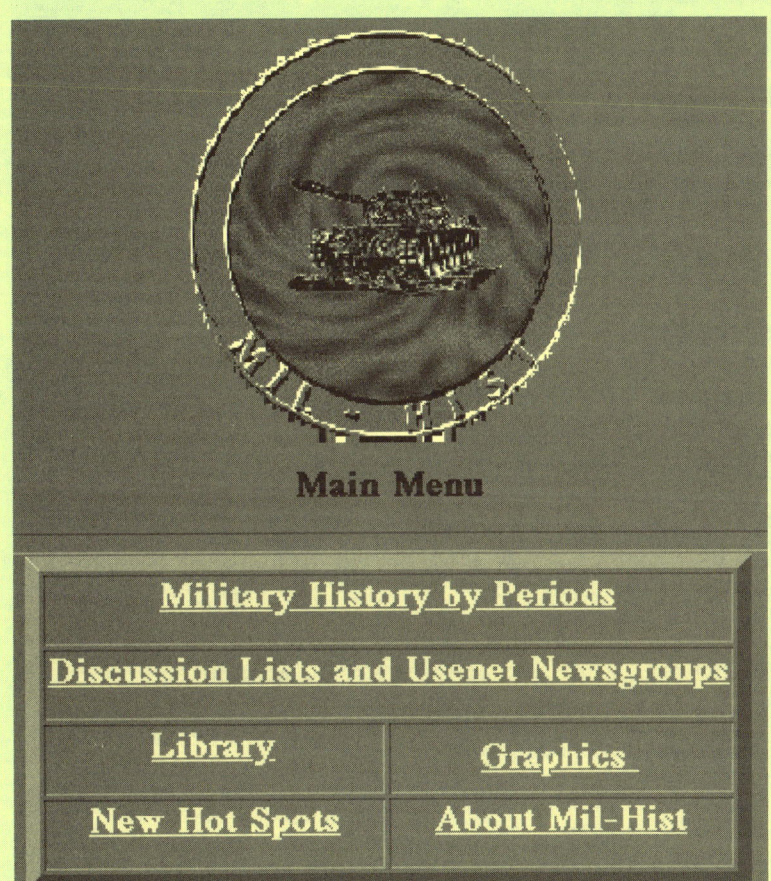

If you're looking for the date, or place a certain battle in World War II was fought, you can scour your local library or an encyclopedia, but the Internet gives you a lot more information.

For instance, The Military History WWW site offers a number of resources arranged according to type of site and historical time period. Users will find photos, maps, texts, bibliographies, and other documents on topics such as World War II, pre-modern war, and the Vietnam War.

In addition, one may access a number of related Internet sites such as libraries and FTP locations. You might not be able to obtain actual combat weapons, but you can get canvas bags, tents, military uniforms, and cooking utensils by exploring the military sites on the Internet.

Also you can check out "The Military Analysis Network," a clearinghouse for the Military Spending Working Group. This site is designed to support the development of a coordinated, long-term campaign to reduce military spending.

The "Electronic Headquarters for the Acquisition of War Knowledge" provides an extensive "Military Science" hot link that features information on logistics, tactics, strategy, technology, and intelligence used in warfare. You'll also find links to military graphics sites for maps.

(http://kuhttp.cc.ukans.edu:80/history/ehawk/)

also (http://www.fas.org/pub/gen/fas/man/)

also, (http://www.wa1a.com/public/tradezone/ammil/ammil.html)

find specific subject areas. The entire budget is available in Portable Document File/Adobe Acrobat form, as well as a Citizen's Guide to the Federal Budget, Analytical Perspectives, and Historical Tables. Users may also access the budget files using the gopher.

KEYWORDS Fiscal Policy, Government (US)
AUDIENCE Government Students, Politics Enthusiasts, U.S. Citizens
CONTACT Amy Williams
amy@sunny.stat-usa.gov
FREE

http://www.doc.gov/inquery/BudgetFY96/BudgetFY96.html

gopher://gopher.stat-usa.gov/11/BudgetFY96

California Abortion and Reproductive Rights Action League ★★★

CARAL (California Abortion and Reproductive Rights Action League), a group which seeks to organize and maintain a constituency of voters interested in guaranteeing women's legal reproductive rights, maintains this Web page. It contains a number of resources including clinic violence updates, information on upcoming CARAL-related events, and various political resources.

KEYWORDS Feminism, Organizations, Politics
AUDIENCE Abortion Rights Advocates, Feminists, Women
CONTACT CARAL
caral@aol.com
FREE

http://www.matisse.net/politics/caral/caral.html

Center for Third World Organizing (CTWO) ★★★

The CTWO is involved in social change organizing through setting up training and leadership development programs. Its model for programs emphasizes multi-racial and multilingual membership. The CTWO page of information briefly discusses the purpose of the organization and some its projects in the USA. The page also offers information on some of its publications and available services.

KEYWORDS Community, Developing Countries, Human Rights, Racial Equality
AUDIENCE Californians, General Public, Political Activists
CONTACT ctwo@igc.apc.org
FREE

gopher://gopher.igc.apc.org/0ftp%3Aftp.igc.apc.org@/pub/orgs_on_igc/ctwo

ftp://ftp.igc.apc.org/pub/orgs_on_igc/ctwo

Coalition to Ban Dihydrogen Monoxide ★★★

This site provides information on the dangerous chemical DHMO (also known as hydric acid), one of the chief ingredients in acid rain and, according to this Coalition, the cause of 'thousands of deaths every year.' Chemical and medical data on this substance, widely used as an industrial solvent and coolant, is available here. There's also information on how you can join the Coalition in its efforts to ban DHMO.

KEYWORDS Activism, Chemistry, Medicine, Politics
AUDIENCE Activists, Chemists, Health Care Policymakers, Policymakers, Politicians
CONTACT Coalition to Ban DHMO
no_dhmo@circus.com
FREE

http://www.circus.com/~no_dhmo/

Conservation Reserve Management Plans ★★★

The Conservation Reserve Management Plans (CRMP) contains plans for two Australian Reserves (Kakadu and Uluru-Kata Tjuta National Parks). The plans were written in 1991, and detail exhaustively the conditions and values of the two parks. They also discuss conservation and development programs for the areas. The gopher server also contains two reef management plans.

KEYWORDS Australia, Conservation, Environment
AUDIENCE Australians, Conservationists, Environmentalists
FREE

http://kaos.erin.gov.au/land/management_plan.html/

gopher://kaos.erin.gov.au/11/areas/manplans/

Contract With America ★★★★

The Contract With America page presents their entire contract text sponsored by Rep. Newt Gingrich, Rep. Dick Armey, and the House Republicans.

KEYWORDS Conservatives, Republican Party
AUDIENCE Conservatives, Libertarians, Republicans
CONTACT RightSide1@aol.com
FREE

http://www.clark.net/pub/jeffd/contract.html

The Death of Affirmative Action ★★

This file is an essay on The Death of Affirmative Action by someone who has benefitted and lost due to affirmative action. He talks about affirmative action being a divisive issue in the 1996 presidential campaign in the US. Other links to affirmative action information are provided.

KEYWORDS Affirmative Action, Legislation
AUDIENCE Asian Americans, Women
CONTACT editor@meanderings.com
FREE

http://www.webcom.com/~sppg/meanderings/me202/me202_1.shtml

Deficit Page ★★★

This page contains a number of documents from the Concord Coalition detailing their Zero Deficit Plan. It also contains a few links to other tax reform organizations' Web pages.

KEYWORDS Budget (US), Federal Government (US), Organizations, Taxes
AUDIENCE Business Analysts, Economists, Government Officials, Political Scientists, Tax Reformers
CONTACT Andrew Norris
andyn@texas.net
FREE

http://www.texas.net/users/andyn/deficit.html

EPIC Alert ★★★★

The biweekly EPIC Alert focuses on privacy in the information age, discussing such subjects as cryptography, national ID cards, medical and consumer records, etc.

KEYWORDS Consumer Protection, Information Technology, Privacy
AUDIENCE Civil Rights Activists, Consumers, Information Technologists
CONTACT Dave Banisar
Banisar@epic.org
FREE

gopher://cpsr.org/11/cpsr/alert/

Emergency Preparedness Information EXchange (EPIX) ★★

This gopher, maintained by the Centre for Policy Research on Science and Technology at Simon Fraser University in Canada, provides information on the Emergency Preparedness Information eXchange (EPIX). It also offers access to various emergency response agencies around the world, summaries of events during recent emergencies, and a list of upcoming conferences.

KEYWORDS Canada, Community Networking, Disaster Relief, Emergency Preparedness
AUDIENCE Administrators, Government Employees, Government Officials, Scientists
CONTACT Peter Anderson
anderson@sfu.ca
FREE

gopher://disaster.cprost.sfu.ca:5555/

Firearms and Liberty Page ★★★

Scott W. Ostrander, who has constructed this page as a 'service to gun owners across America,' has compiled a number of documents (among them the text of the 2nd Amendment of the U.S. Constitution) and links to other firearms-related Web pages. Also included are Mr. Ostrander's own response to the gun control lobby and other personal statements.

KEYWORDS Constitutions, Firearms, Gun Control
AUDIENCE Gun Enthusiasts, Libertarians
CONTACT Scott W. Ostrander
scotto@cica.indiana.edu
FREE

http://www.cica.indiana.edu/hyplan/scotto/firearms/firearms.html

Policies 351

Firearms, Individual Rights, and Politics Page ★★★

This page offers excerpts of texts from various national and state gun-control bills, statements from the NRA and other lobbyists for firearms owners, etc. It is maintained by the Carnegie-Mellon University student gun club.

KEYWORDS Constitutions, Firearms, Gun Control
AUDIENCE Gun Enthusiasts, Libertarians
CONTACT   Karl Kleinpaste
          Karl.Kleinpaste@cs.cmu.edu
FREE

http://www.cs.cmu.edu:8001/afs/cs.cmu.edu/project/nectar/member/karl/html/firearms/firearms.html

Friends of the Earth Home Page ★★★★

In this site the Friends of the Earth, (FoE), a leading environmental pressure group in the UK, provides information regarding environmental campaigns, education, and activities. FoE provides environment-friendly alternatives geared to the citizens of the UK.

KEYWORDS Ecology, Environment, Organizations, United Kingdom
AUDIENCE British, Environmentalists
CONTACT   Andrew Dilworth
          foe@gn.apc.org
FREE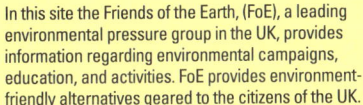

http://www.foe.co.uk/

GATT 1994 ★★★

This site contains the full text and analysis of the General Agreement on Tariffs and Trade. Its sections include text of the agreement establishing the organization (Agreements on Trade in Goods, General Agreement on Trade in Services and Annexes, Agreement on Trade-Related Aspects of Intellectual Property Rights, Including Trade in Counterfeit Goods, Understanding on Rules and Procedures Governing the Settlement of Disputes, Trade Policy Review Mechanism and Plurilateral Trade Agreements), and ministerial decisions and declarations.

KEYWORDS Business, International Trade
AUDIENCE Business Owners, International Business Professionals, Researchers
FREE

http://ananse.irv.uit.no/trade_law/gatt/nav/toc.html

GreenGopher ★★★★

GreenGopher contains information on conservation- and environment-oriented politics pooled from a variety of sources. Subjects include grass roots organizations, various political organizations, and a wide variety of legal, nutrition/food and education-related resources. Links to various other environmentally-themed gophers are also located on this gopher server.

KEYWORDS Environmental Organizations, Law, Legislation, Politics
AUDIENCE Conservationists, Environmentalists, Medical Practitioners, Nutritionists
FREE

gopher://ecosys.drdr.Virginia.EDU:70/00/library/gen/greengopher/intro

Greenpeace International (Amsterdam) ★★★

Greenpeace's server contains information about global environmental concerns such as ozone depletion, climate change and hazardous waste. It does not focus on national topics. Greenpeace also makes available international treaties such as the Montreal Protocol and the Basel Convention. Currently, ozone depletion is the primary topic.

KEYWORDS Environment, Hazardous Materials, Organizations, Ozone
AUDIENCE Environmentalists, Policymakers
CONTACT   sysop@adam.greenpeace.org
FREE

http://www.greenpeace.org/

gopher://gopher.greenpeace.org/

ftp://greenpeace.org/

Institute for Global Communications ★★★★

This page provides links to The Institute for Global Communications Networks (IGC) — PeaceNet, EcoNet, ConflictNet, and LaborNet — which serve individuals and organizations working toward peace, environmental protection, human rights, social and economic justice, sustainable and equitable development, health, and nonviolent conflict resolution. IGC currently links almost 10,000 members and links an additional 10,000 activists and organizations.

KEYWORDS Activism, Economic Justice, Human Rights
AUDIENCE Environmentalists, Human Rights Activists, Political Activists, Women's Rights Activists
CONTACT   support@igc.apc.org
FREE

http://www.igc.apc.org/igc/igcinfo.html

Major Areas of Rand Research ★★★★

This site provides links to Rand research which conducts research in a wide range of subject areas. This research is reported primarily in RAND's publications series, but many studies also appear as books published by commercial publishers and university presses and as articles in professional, scholarly, and technical journals. There are links to a list of RAND's research reports, books, and selected journal articles published from 1992 to 1993 in a specific subject area. Some of the subject areas include arms control, civil justice, drug policy, health, terrorism and subnational conflict, etc.

KEYWORDS Criminal Justice, Economics, Information Systems
AUDIENCE Internet Users, Researchers, Students (University)
FREE

http://www.rand.org/areas/

Connections to Endangered Species

Going... going... gone?

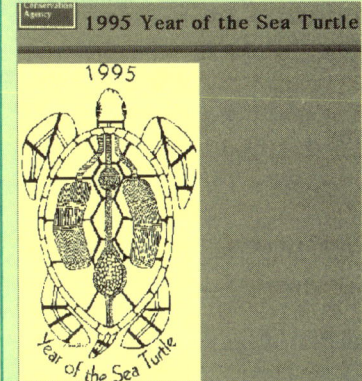

Many Internet sites provide information on the planet's endangered species, with a number of them cataloguing not only by regions of the world, but also listing sanctuaries where many of these species will hopefully survive.

One such site is "Life," a storehouse of general information, legislation, and newsletters, as well as a comprehensive list (including individual descriptions) of endangered animals and plants. You'll find answers to questions about specific species, in addition to action and recovery plans for saving those threatened by extinction.

At the Life site, you'll also learn about the "discovery" of living fossils (creatures once thought to be extinct). Check out the Potoroo, for instance—thought to be extinct for the past 125 years. A few of the Potoroo were found recently in Western Australia.

(http://kaos.erin.gov.au/life/life.html)

You can also tap into the "Convention on International Trade in Endangered Species of Wild Fauna and Flora," which was signed in the U.S., and amended in Germany. This extensive document obligates its signers to protect the given endangered species for generations to come. It also provides clauses against the export or importing of endangered species or animal parts (such as elephant tusks).

(http://kaos.erin.gov.au/human_env/env_leg/cites-con.html)

Government & Politics

Policies

NAFTA ★★★

The full text of the North American Free Trade Agreement is presented, including daily notes dispatched from the White House and a collection of White House press releases dealing with the agreement. The site also contains links to The Tech, a continuous online news service active since 1993 which holds back issues of The Tech, MIT's oldest newspaper as well as links to other information servers in and around MIT.

KEYWORDS Economics, International Trade, NAFTA (North American Free Trade Agreement)
AUDIENCE Business Owners, International Business Professionals, Researchers, Students
FREE

http://the-tech.mit.edu/Bulletins/nafta.html

gopher://niord.shsu.edu/

National Information Infrastructure ★★★

The National Information Infrastructure (NII) page provides information about U.S. Government policy on telecommunications and national networking. Users will find the NII Agenda for Action, with information including the task force, advisory councils, and NII accomplishments. Related documents such as the Government Information Bill and the Technology Initiative Summary are also provided. There'a also a speech by Ronald Brown, the Secretary of Commerce.

KEYWORDS Information Superhighway, Networking, Telecommunications
AUDIENCE Communications Researchers, Internet Users, Telecommunications Specialists, U.S. Citizens
CONTACT Jonathan Magid
jem@sunsite.unc.edu
FREE

http://sunsite.unc.edu/nii/NII-Table-of-Contents.html

National Rifle Association (NRA) Home Page ★★★

The National Rifle Association (NRA) Home Page contains links to numerous firearm and gun control-related documents as well as background information on the NRA (their charter, membership information, etc.) and other organizations with the same aims. Information on the NRA's numerous listservs, local chapters, and promotional items is also available at this site.

KEYWORDS Constitutions, Firearms, Gun Control, Republican Party
AUDIENCE Conservatives, Gun Enthusiasts, Republicans
CONTACT NRA Staff
www@NRA.org
FREE

http://www.nra.org/

North American Institute ★★★★

This site provides information about the North American Institute, a thinktank that was partially responsible for the text of such legislation as the North American Free Trade Agreement (NAFTA). Offered here are numerous documents aimed at helping the citizens and governments of Mexico, America and Canada work together more easily, as well as other information on 'trinational thinking.'

KEYWORDS Law, Organizations, Public Policy, Trade Agreements
AUDIENCE Canadians, General Public, Mexico Residents, Political Scientists, Trade Specialists
CONTACT Justin Longo
naminet@uvvm.uvic.ca
FREE

http://sol.uvic.ca/nami/

ftp://ftp.santafe.edu/pub/NAMINET/

OASIS Gopher ★★★

The OASIS gopher provides emergency readiness information about the state of California. This information includes the latest weather and earthquake bulletins, highway traffic conditions, and emergency plans and contacts. The information is assembled and provided by the California Governor's Office of Emergency Services.

KEYWORDS California, Disaster Relief, Emergency Preparedness
AUDIENCE Californians, General Public, Government Officials
CONTACT oasis@oes.ca.gov
FREE

gopher://oes1.oes.ca.gov:5555/

Penn State Population Research Institute ★★★

This Penn State Population Research Institute site contains information about the Institute, working papers of the Association of Population Centers, staff, and more. It provides access to other sites such as those of the U.S. Census Bureau, UN Population, Population Studies Center at the University of Pennsylvania, and The Australian National University Demography.

KEYWORDS Census (The), Environmental Research, Policy Research, Social Sciences
AUDIENCE Environmental Researchers, Policy Analysts, Social Scientists
CONTACT webmaster@pop.psu.edu
FREE

http://www.pop.psu.edu

gopher://gopher.pop.psu.edu/

Political Participation Project Home Page ★★★

The Political Participation Project, a production of the Massachussetts Institute of Technology, examines how recent advances in the use of interactive technology can help promote voter participation in the political process. In addition to numerous articles on this subject, this site also contains links to a number of other political resources as well as Government databases and other publicly-accessible sources on the Internet.

KEYWORDS Government, Interactive Technology, Politics, Voting
AUDIENCE Government Students, Political Analysts, Political Researchers, Politicians, Voters
CONTACT Mark Bonchek
ppp@ai.mit.edu
FREE

http://www.ai.mit.edu/projects/ppp/home.html

Right to Keep and Bear Arms Page ★★★

A page with information on (and the text of) the second amendment to the U.S. Constitution, and a number of links to other pro-firearms and anti-gun control-themed pages.

KEYWORDS Constitutions, Firearms, Gun Control, Politics
AUDIENCE Civil Liberties Activists, Gun Enthusiasts
CONTACT David M. Putzolu
dputzolu@cs.uiuc.edu
FREE

http://sal.cs.uiuc.edu/rec.guns/rkba.html

Uniform Commercial Code (UCC) ★★★

This site contains the full text of articles one to nine of the Uniform Commercial Code (UCC). The states, not the Federal government, are the primary source of law on commercial transactions in the U.S., but in all 50 states and the District of Columbia at least some of that commercial law is based on the Uniform Commercial Code. The version appearing in this site is the most recent version, and most of its provisions are in effect in most of the US states.

KEYWORDS Business Law, Federal Law
AUDIENCE Business Owners, Corporate Lawyers, Entrepreneurs, Marketing Professionals
CONTACT Peter W. Martin, Legal Information Institute
martin@law.mail.cornell.edu
FREE

http://www.law.cornell.edu/ucc/ucc.table.html

Volunteers in Technical Assistance ★★★

This is a gopher server of the Volunteers in Technical Assistance (VITA). VITA is an organization whose goal is to provided skilled assistance to the victims of natural and human-made disasters. On their gopher one can find information on VITA, international development, and recent disasters such as the Kobe, Japan earthquake and Rwandan civil strife.

KEYWORDS Disaster Relief, International News, Technical Support, Volunteers
AUDIENCE International Aid Agencies, International Development Specialists
FREE

gopher://vita.org/

Political Science

See also
Government & Politics · *Doctrines*
Humanities & Social Sciences · *History*

American Political Science Association Gopher ★★★

This gopher provides information about the American Political Science Association (APSA). The purpose of this gopher is to provide access to online resources useful for political science research and teaching. It is intended to be largely an umbrella gopher, providing links to other gopher servers where the documents are actually maintained. Documents maintained at this site will include those published by the APSA as well as some other documents which are not accessible elsewhere. There is also a directory of political science email addresses.

Keywords Education, Political Science, Research, Social Sciences
Audience Political Analysts, Political Researchers, Political Scientists
Contact Bill Ball
BALL@TRENTON.EDU
Free

gopher://apsa.trenton.edu/

Campaign for Peace and Democracy (CPD) ★★★

The Campaign for Peace and Democracy (CPD), which is based in the US, works for democratic social change around the world. The CPD provides a single page that describes the organization and its activities from its establishment in 1982 up to June 1994. Some of their activities have included demonstrations in support of Aristide in Haiti, protests against the US invasion of Panama, and support for anti-nuclear policies.

Keywords Democracy, Human Rights, International Politics, Peace
Audience General Public, Humanists, Political Activists
Contact camppeacedem@igc.apc.org
Free

http://www.igc.apc.org/igc/people.html
gopher://gopher.igc.apc.org/pub/orgs_on_igc/cpd
ftp://ftp.igc.apc.org/pub/orgs_on_igc/cpd

Chicago Coalition Against Violence Initiative ★★★

The CCAVI was formed to oppose the Violence Initiative, a federal program to research and develop biological controls over inner-city male minority youth. The Coalition has a page on the IGC computers, in order to petition for support of its opposition to claims of biological and genetic bases for intelligence, affluence, criminality, and violence.

Keywords Chicago, Racism, Violence
Audience General Public, Illinois Residents, Political Activists
Contact mlyon@igc.apc.org
Free

gopher://gopher.igc.apc.org:70/0ftp%3Aftp.igc.apc.org@/pub/orgs_on_igc/ccavi
ftp://ftp.igc.apc.org/pub/orgs_on_igc/ccavi

Committees of Correspondence ★★

This gopher server gives information about the Committees of Correspondence (CoC) a politcal movement centered in Berkeley, California. It contains information on the CoC Statement of Principles, registration, CoC member lists, the electronic discussion list of CoC, documents, and more. As well, it holds information about other socialist groups and publications.

Keywords California, Government, Media, Political Activism
Audience Activists, Democratic Socialists, Political Activists, Political Scientists
Free

gopher://garnet.berkeley.edu:2000/

Departement de Science Politique ★★★

This gopher server offers information about the Department of Political Science (Departement de Science Politique) at the University of Geneva, Switzerland. The information includes addresses for the faculty, publications, images of the faculty, and research results.

Keywords Political Science, Politics, Switzerland, University Of Geneva
Audience Political Activists, Political Researchers, Political Scientists, Switzerland Residents
Free

gopher://sposun1.unige.ch/

Economic Democracy Information Network (EDIN) Directory of Issues ★★★★

This is the Economic Democracy Information Network (EDIN) Directory of Issues. It is a key site for a whole range of progressive economic, labor, diversity, gender, socialist, environmental and social welfare information. Some of the issues include The Economy, Defense Conversion and Peace Resources, Labor Issues, Race and Racism, Housing, Health and Poverty, Education and Youth Issues, and much more

Keywords Democracy, Human Rights
Audience Community Activists, Nonprofit Organizations, Political Activists, Progressives
Contact edinlinks@garnet.berkeley.edu
Free

http://garnet.berkeley.edu:3333/EDINlist/EDINlist.html

Electronic Democracy Forum ★★★

The Electronic Democracy Forum (EDF) was started by a group of people concerned with the lack of information available and the lack of debate regarding congressional efforts. This site presents information about the bills and issues before Congress from a non-Republican perspective. The directories of available information include Critiques, Polls and the Text of the Contract with America, Congressional News, and GOP Tax Cut Proposals. Users can also sign up for EDF's mailing list, find the email and postal addresses for the White House and Congress, or go to related links about government and politics.

Keywords Political Activism, Voter Information
Audience Democrats, Political Activists, Political Scientists, Republicans
Free

http://edf.www.media.mit.edu/

Electronic Democracy Information Network (EDIN) Gopher ★★★

A large archive of information on a wide variety of topics, EDIN contains resources created to benefit almost any progressive social project—'from revitalizing inner-city communities to creating sustainable development to converting to a peacetime economy', and more. Documents here range from academic papers written by students and faculty affiliated in some way with EDIN, to directories of services, personnel and other online resources.

Keywords Democracy, Politics, Social Responsibility, Urban Renewal
Audience Activists, Grass-Roots Organizers, Mediators
Contact Nathan 'Nate' Newman
newman@garnet.berkeley.edu
Free

gopher://garnet.berkeley.edu:1252/1

Fourth World Documentation Project - Indigenous Peoples' Information for the Online Community ★★★★

The Fourth World Documentation Project (FWDP) archives contain over 400 documents on Fourth World nations in the Americas, Africa, Asia, Europe, Melanesia and the Pacific. The documents include essays, position papers, resolutions, organizational information, treaties, UN documents, speeches and declarations. The FWDP was organized by the Center For World Indigenous Studies (CWIS) in 1992. The database has distinct directories for different regions of interest. About 5 to 20 documents are added each week, and updates are announced several times a week on the What's New page.

Keywords Human Rights, Indigenous People, International Development
Audience Human Rights Activists, Political Scientists, Researchers, Sociologists

Political Science

CONTACT info@nwnexus.wa.com
FREE

http://www.halcyon.com/FWDP/fwdp.html

gopher://locust.cic.net/11/Politics/Fourth.World

ftp://ftp.halcyon.com/pub/FWDP/

Hunger Web Home Page ★★★★

Brown University's Hunger Web pages tie together various hunger-related resources on the Internet. An email front end allows those who are inclined to email American politicians. A special group of articles on the crisis in Rwanda was recently added, and other resources for hunger activists are available.

KEYWORDS Activism, Disaster Relief, Hunger, International Development
AUDIENCE Activists, Grass-Roots Organizers, Health Care Providers, Health Science Researchers
CONTACT Daniel Zalik
Daniel_Zalik@brown.edu
FREE

http://www.hunger.brown.edu/hungerweb/

James' Liberty Web ★★★

Archivist James has pulled together numerous documents on various aspects of freedom, and the philosophical concept of liberty as well as other constitutionally-themed quotes, documents and abstracts. The material here includes excerpts from Darwin, Aristotle, the Constitution (specifically the Bill of Rights), and the Declaration of Independence.

KEYWORDS Bill Of Rights, Constitutions, Freedom of Speech, Liberty
AUDIENCE General Public, Philosophers, Political Researchers, Political Scientists
CONTACT James
jamesd@netcom.com
FREE

http://nw.com/jamesd/

Jim Warren Gopher ★★

The Jim Warren gopher provides access to data concerned with political action and government. It is a collection of electronic newsletters. Jim Warren is the founder of such computer institutions as Infoworld magazine, Dr. Dobbs Journal magazine, and the West Coast Computer Faire.

KEYWORDS Activism, Computer Ethics, Government, Politics
AUDIENCE Government Officials, Political Activists, Politicians
CONTACT Cliff Figallo
fig@path.net
FREE

gopher://gopher.path.net:8102/

Lead...or Leave ★★★

Lead... or Leave is a Generation X political organization in the United States, and a moving force in the effort to put generational issues on the national political map. This page provides a listing of current situations that are moving on the United States political front, email addresses for politicians and media organizations, and a list of several hundred non-profit, Internet and activist groups ranging from alt.fan.dan-quayle to the Counter Revolutionary Page. There are also links on this page to general information sources, such as the Pilot Online Law Page and Supreme Court Decisions

KEYWORDS Activism, Generation X, Leadership
AUDIENCE Activists, Generation X, Grass-Roots Organizers, Political Science Students
CONTACT Adam Rifkin
adam@cs.caltech.edu
FREE

http://www.cs.caltech.edu/~adam/lead.html

League of Women Voters Home Page ★★★

This site houses a number of documents related to the League of Women Voters as well as a search engine to make studying at the library easier. Also available here is background information on the League and a list of the candidates and projects they've supported—one is California's Motor Voter initiative.

KEYWORDS Organizations, Politics, Voting
AUDIENCE Voters, Women
FREE

http://www.oclc.org/VoteSmart/lwv/lwvhome.htm

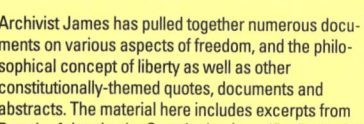 Mother Jones ★★★

This Web site contains online electronic issues of Mother Jones magazine (and Zine), making possible instant electronic feedback to the publishers regarding articles. Mother Jones focuses on social and political analysis, and encourages political activism in its readership.

KEYWORDS Activism, E-Zines, Ethics, Public Policy
AUDIENCE Magazine Readers, Political Activists
CONTACT webserver@mojones.com
FREE

http://www.mojones.com/motherjones.html

National Performance Review Home Page ★★★

This site provides information about President Clinton's and Vice President Gore's plan to reinvent government, and a link to NetResults, the 1994 National Performance Review, as well as an email address for comments and suggestions on the program.

KEYWORDS Presidents (US), Public Policy, Reinventing Government, White House
AUDIENCE General Public, Political Activists, Voters
CONTACT tech-info@www.npr.gsa.gov
FREE

http://www.npr.gov/

Political Participation Project ★★★

The Political Participation Project (PPP) is sponsored by the Intelligent Information Project at the Massachusetts Institute of Technology (MIT). The purpose of the PPP is to discover if interactive media can improve political participation. To that end, the project's activities have included organizing a grassroots organization directory, forming an electronic mailing list of people interested in political behavior and interactive media, and creating a bibliography of articles and books about interactive media and politics, including an online dissertation. There is a summary of the group's findings, as well as organized links to other political resources thoughout this Web server.

KEYWORDS Internet Networking, Political Science
AUDIENCE Political Advisors, Political Scientists, Politicians
FREE

http://www.ai.mit.edu/projects/ppp/home.html

Rand Corporation ★★

This is a gopher server of the RAND Corporation. RAND is a non-profit institution aimed to improve public policy through research. Their gopher includes information on the collaborative work with other institutions, software, RAND's Institute for Civil Justice, and RAND's Institute on Education and Training.

KEYWORDS Civil Rights, Education, Law
AUDIENCE Computer Users, Educators, Law Students, Lawyers
CONTACT gophermaster@rand.org
FREE

gopher://is.rand.org/

Right Side of the Web ★★★★

At last, a place on the Web to give equal time to make up for all of the socialism and moral anarchy (God bless 'em) you find on the Net. What this page provides is a directory of places and resources on the Net for what most people would call the conservative point of view. Some of the links include the Newt Gingrich WWW Fan Club, Rush Limbaugh Information Page, a picture of the gipper, The Right Side's list of people we DO want to see run for the GOP ticket in '96, and more to the right.

KEYWORDS Political Opinions
AUDIENCE Conservatives, Libertarians, Republicans
CONTACT RightSide1@aol.com
FREE

http://www.clark.net/pub/jeffd/index.html

Right-Wing Politics ★★★

Right-Wing Politics provides links to issues concerning ' The Right Side of the Web.' This is a list of conservative, right-wing political links including Lyndon LaRouche, Non Serviam - Johann Schmidt, Radical Religious Right Organizations, Republican Party, Rush Limbaugh, Objectivism/Ayn Rand, and more.

KEYWORDS Conservatives, Internet Resources, Libertarian Party
AUDIENCE Conservatives, Libertarians, Political Activists, Union Members
CONTACT edinlinks@garnet.berkeley.edu
FREE

http://garnet.berkeley.edu:3333/EDINlist/.right/.right.html

Political Science – Reference

Socialist and Left Politics

Socialist and Left Politics page provides links to resources such as the Political Movements Archive, information on socialist theory, DSA- Democratic Socialists of America, NOC- National Organizing Committee (People's Tribune, Rally Comrades), Socialist Party USA, and the Left-Socialist E-lists.

- KEYWORDS: Progressive Politics, Social Theorists, Socialism
- AUDIENCE: Community Activists, Nonprofit Orgaanizations, Political Activists, Progressives
- CONTACT: edinlinks@garnet.berkeley.edu
- FREE

http://garnet.berkeley.edu:3333/EDINlist/.left/.left.html

Socialist Party USA Cybercenter

The Socialist Party USA Cybercenter Home page allows viewers to learn about the socialist movement in America since 1901. The site offers subcriptions to Socialist Party print and electronic newsletters, and a guide for new or potential Socialist party members. Information about the Young People's Socialist League is included, as well as information on how to become a member.

- KEYWORDS: Government, Policy Research, Political Issues, Socialism
- AUDIENCE: Activists, Political Activists, Socialists
- CONTACT: Andrew Hammer hammerand@aol.com
- FREE

http://sunsite.unc.edu/spc/index.html

Texas A&M's White House Archives

Texas A&M's White House Archives contains a wealth of information about the activities of Presidents Bush and Clinton from 1992 through 1995. The textual materials found at the Web site (overlaid on a gopher server) include: statements on domestic and international affairs, texts of press briefings, memoranda and executive orders, public addresses, presidential appointments, and the president's daily schedule. There is a gopher search engine and a link to the White House.

- KEYWORDS: Presidency, United States
- AUDIENCE: Journalists, Political Scientists
- CONTACT: whadmin@tamu.edu
- FREE

http://www.tamu.edu/whitehouse/

Reference

See also
Education · *Government Libraries*
Popular Culture & Entertainment · *General Reference*

Bureau of Labor Statistics' Public Access Server

This server provides access to data from 26 government surveys as well as providing recent news releases. The server is maintained by the Bureau of Labor Statistics. The surveys cover topics such as price data, unemployment statistics, and demographics.

- KEYWORDS: Bureau of Labor Statistics (US), Economics, Labor, Statistics
- AUDIENCE: Business Analysts, Economists
- CONTACT: labstat.helpdesk@bls.gov
- FREE

gopher://stats.bls.gov/

California Online Voter Guide

This site provides a resource center for voters in the California state elections. It gives information on how to register to vote, how to complete the ballots, who is running for what office, links to other election-related sites, and election night results. The site is produced by the California Voter Foundation, a nonprofit, nonprofit, non-partisan organization, and several companies (including Pacific Bell) who provide the Internet access.

- KEYWORDS: California, Elections, Politics (US), Voter Guide
- AUDIENCE: Californians, Government Officials, Politicians, U.S. Citizens, Voters
- CONTACT: Kim Alexander kimalex@netcom.com
- FREE

gopher://gopher.kn.pacbell.com/

Citywatch

This site hosts Citywatch, the San Francisco government cable access channel. The content of the cable channel includes public, educational and government (PEG) programming, including text and other programming about government departments, agencies, boards, commissions and government supported agencies. On this page, users will find schedules of the station's programming; city notices such as grant announcements, neighborhood meetings, and proposals available for comment; city meeting schedules and agendas; locations of all city offices (especially those displaced by earthquake repairs); and contact information for the Board of Supervisors.

- KEYWORDS: Cable Television, Public Television
- AUDIENCE: Activists, Californians, Journalists
- FREE

http://www.well.com:80/www/ctywatch/

Constitution for the United States

This Web page presents the full text of the Constitution of the United States. The signers of the charter are listed, and there is information about ratification by the 13 states that first approved the document. Notes identify clauses that have been altered by amendments. There are links to the text of the amendments and a hot-linked index.

- KEYWORDS: Constitutions, United States
- AUDIENCE: Historians, Political Scientists
- FREE

http://pobox.com/~whig/Constitution.html

Constitutions of the World

This site allows users to access constitutions from countries all over the world. Some of the constitutions are available in English and others are in the language of the country of origin.

- KEYWORDS: Constitutions, Documents, International Politics
- AUDIENCE: Government Students, Politics Enthusiasts, Politics Students
- CONTACT: archive@wiretap.spies.com
- FREE

ftp://wiretap.spies.com/Gov/World/

Counterpoint Publishing Internet Gopher

The gopher server for Counterpoint Publishing, gives the user access to several of its journals produced for the U.S. Federal Government. All users may view parts of the publications and those who pay an annual fee may view the documents in their entirety. Some of the publications available include the U.S. Federal Register, U.S. Commerce Business Daily, Department of Energy Orders, and state environmental regulations.

- KEYWORDS: Government Documents, Publishing, Research
- AUDIENCE: Business Professionals, General Public, Government Employees, Government Officials
- CONTACT: info@counterpoint.com
- COST

gopher://gopher.counterpoint.com/

Declaration of Indcpondence

This University of Indiana Web page presents the text of the Declaration of Independence, written by Thomas Jefferson and proclaimed by the renegade Continental Congress in Philadelphia, Pennsylvania, on July 4, 1776. The site also lists the signers. There are no links.

- KEYWORDS: Declaration of Independence, United States
- AUDIENCE: Historians, Political Scientists
- FREE

http://www.law.indiana.edu/uslawdocs/declaration.html

Democratic Senate Campaign Center (DSCC) Quotebook ★★★

This page contains a number of damaging and embarassing quotations from a variety of Republican politicians who, in many cases, didn't realize their words were being recorded. Racist innendo, sexist and religious jokes and other materials here are supplied by the Democratic Senate Campaign Committee as part of an electronic campaign effort on behalf of various Democratic candidates running for Federal office.

KEYWORDS Humor
AUDIENCE Comedians, Democrats, Humor Enthusiasts, Journalists, Liberals
CONTACT   DSCC Webmaster
          dscc@www.dscc.org
FREE

http://khht.policy.net/d/quotebook.html

Diana- International Human Rights Database ★★★

This Web page, named Diana - International Human Rights Database (after Diana Vincent-Daviss), contains bibliographies, text files, and digitized images for human rights research and advocacy. Material is grouped into primary and secondary sources. There's a link to the Law School Constitutional Repository at the University of the Witwatersrand, Johannesburg, South Africa.

KEYWORDS Human Rights
AUDIENCE Human Rights Activists, Political Scientists
FREE

http://www.law.uc.edu/Diana/

EcoGopher Project at the University of Virginia! ★★★★

EcoGopher is an ongoing project, developed for the purpose of facilitating access to environmental information. This gopher has menu items for over 30 different environmental groups including local University of Virginia clubs, Charlotte organizations and international activist groups. In addition, this site archives the messages from another 30 environmentally related listservs, and contains dozens of other environmental gophers and telnet sites.

KEYWORDS Ecology, Recycling
AUDIENCE Ecologists, Environmental Activists, Environmentalists
CONTACT   gopher@ecosys.drdr.virginia.edu
FREE

gopher://ecosys.drdr.virginia.edu/

Electronic Activist ★★★

This directory contains email addresses for some U.S. Congressmen, statelegislators, newspapers, and television and radio stations, providing citizens with an outlet to reach these various entities. This online directory allows users to click on a name and send an email message to various government officials, legislators, and media outlets through your browser's mailer. This site provides a great way to make your political voice heard through the click of a button!

KEYWORDS Activism, Email Directory, Politics (US)
AUDIENCE Activists, General Public
CONTACT   ifas@crocker.com
FREE

http://www.crocker.com:80/~ifas/activist/

Fast Facts from EDIN ★★★

This site provides links to a list of Fast Facts from Economic Democracy Information Network (EDIN) sponsored by UC-Berkeley's Center for Community Economic Research (CCER). These facts include—Who are the Hungry in the World and the US?, 50 Facts about Poverty, Military Spending & the Budget, Teen Deaths Due to Guns, Union Membership in 1994, and more.

KEYWORDS Human Rights, Hunger
AUDIENCE Community Activists, Nonprofit Organaizations, Political Activists, Progressives
CONTACT   edinlinks@garnet.berkeley.edu
FREE

http://garnet.berkeley.edu:3333/faststats/faststats.html

FedWorld Information Network ★★★★

The FedWorld site is a central location from where users can access the many departments of the U.S. Federal Government and its departments. Resources are indexed by subject and arranged alphabetically for easy access. FedWorld is a clearinghouse of government reports on scientific, technical and business studies. It also provides links to over 200 government servers, arranged by subject matter, such as Administration, Business, Education, Energy, Health Care, Jobs, Legislature, Military, etc.

KEYWORDS Federal Databases (US), Federal Documents (US), Government Documents, Internet Directories
AUDIENCE Business Professionals, General Public, Government Officials, Government Watchers
CONTACT   webmaster@fedworld.gov
FREE

http://www.fedworld.gov/

ftp://fwux.fedworld.gov

telnet://fedworld.gov

Federal Information Exchange, Inc. Home Page ★★★

This page is provided by the Federal Information Exchange, Inc., a company devoted to servicing the data needs of the U.S. Government as well as corporations and educational institutions. Their premiere services, the FEDIX database of federal job openings, and the MOLIS database of minority educational institutions, are available through this Web site, allowing users to browse and search for specific information. In addition, this site also provides information about other Federal Information Exchange services.

KEYWORDS Employment, Information Services
AUDIENCE Education Professionals, Government Officials, Government Watchers, Job Seekers
CONTACT   webmaster@fedix.fie.com
FREE

http://web.fie.com

Federal Web Locator ★★★★

The Federal Web Locator is designed as a meta-index with links to all the federal government pages on the Web, designed by the Villanova Center for Information Law and Policy. Links are listed by agency, and are grouped as federal legislature, judicial branch agencies, independent agencies, executive agencies, government consortium agencies and projects, and related sites that are non-government. Under these categories, links are simply listed alphabetically by institution.

KEYWORDS Federal Government (US), Government Agencies
AUDIENCE Government Students, Law Students, Politics Enthusiasts, U.S. Citizens
CONTACT   Ken Mortensen
          kmortens@mail.law.vill.edu
FREE

http://www.law.vill.edu/Fed-Agency/fedwebloc.html

International Government Resources from MARVEL ★★★★

This gopher contains links to government resources and documents on the Internet, including NATO, United Nations, UNICEF, GATT, treaties and other international government resources, compiled by the Library of Congress. Resources are grouped by organization and subject.

KEYWORDS International Politics, NATO (North Atlantic Treaty Organization), United Nations
AUDIENCE General Public, Government Students, Politics Enthusiasts
CONTACT   lcmarvel@loc.gov
FREE

gopher://marvel.loc.gov/11/federal/intl

Kommunal Rapport ★★★

The Municipal Reporter is a Norwegian newspaper that provides for government officials with news about various municipal operations around the country. This server is part of a project involving the Regional College of Østfold and The Muncipal Reporter. There are links to past and current issues as well as information about those that work on the paper.

KEYWORDS Online Newspapers, Politicians
AUDIENCE Government Employees, Municipal Staff, Norwegian politicians, Norwegians
CONTACT   Micha.Reisel@KR.kommorg.no
FREE

http://www.kr.kommorg.no

Library of Congress Gopher Server ★★★★

The Library of Congress (LC) Machine-Assisted Realization of the Virtual Electronic Library (MARVEL) is a Campus-Wide Information System that combines the vast collection of information available about the Library with easy access to diverse electronic resources over the Internet. Its goal is to serve the staff of LC, as well as the U.S. Congress and constituents throughout the world.

Keywords Government, Library of Congress, Research
Audience General Public, Library Users, Researchers
Free

gopher://marvel.loc.gov/

Library of Congress World Wide Web Home Page ★★★

This site represents the United States Library of Congress's project to distribute its materials and resources over the Internet. Information is available on American Memory Project, the African American Culture and History online exhibit, Country Studies from the Federal Research Division, and access to LC MARVEL (LC's gopher-based campus-wide information system) and LOCIS (the Library of Congress Information System).

Keywords Information Retrieval, Internet Reference, Library of Congress
Audience Educators, General Public, Researchers, U.S. Citizens
Contact lcweb@loc.gov
Free

http://lcweb.loc.gov/homepage/lchp.html

Links to Non-Governmental Organizations ★★★

The Links to Non-Governmental Organizations Web page is a meta-index directing users to non-profit organizations concerned with civil liberties and freedom of communication in the United States and elsewhere. Examples include the Electronic Frontier Foundation Web server and the Fairness & Accuracy in Media home page. Most of the sites are Web pages, though some are gophers.

Keywords Civil Liberties, Non Profit Organizations, United States
Audience Libertarians, Non-governmental Organizations
Free

http://www.eff.org/groups.html

List of U.S. Federal Government WWW Servers ★★★★

This Web site contains listings and links to U.S. Federal Government Web sites. Links are listed by agency, and grouped into servers with multiple agency listings; individual executive, legislative or judicial branch sites; or as consortium servers. Listings then include description of the site/server and its key features that the user may read before linking to the site.

Keywords Federal Government (US), Government Agencies
Audience Government Students, Law Students, Politics Enthusiasts, U.S. Citizens
Contact www-request@fedix.fie.com
Free

http://www.fie.com/www/us_gov.htm

Connections to Maps
"X" marks the spot

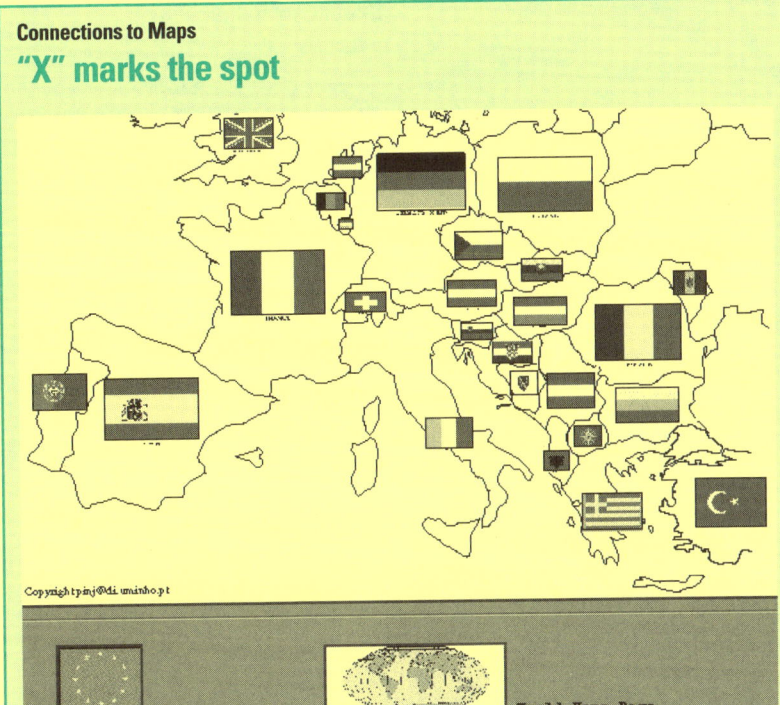

What easier way to view the world or learn geography than with maps? The Internet probably has the biggest collection in the world. You'll find maps that provide vital data about population, the environment, cultural statistics, industry and resources—even the flags of countries—aside from geographical features and political boundaries. Begin your search at the following World Wide Web sites.

(http://www.faf.cuni.cz/world.htm)

Geographic mapping is widely used in business for sales targeting efforts. Certain software allows businesses to combine spreadsheets with mapping to find out how well an advertising campaign has targeted its market. Read up on how businesses employ this technique to refine market research or product penetration.

(http://www.gisworld.com/mag/bg/index.html)

Manchester (UK) Information Datasets and Associated Services (MIDAS) ★★★

The MIDAS service provides online access to, and support for many large and complex data sets, including the 1991 and 1981 UK Census of Population Statistics, continuous UK government surveys, macroeconomic time series databanks, digital map data sets, and scientific data sets. Users will find detailed descriptions of the data sets available, as well as information on becoming a registered user, which allows full access to the data sets.

Keywords Census (The), Demographics, Economics, United Kingdom
Audience British, Educators, Political Analysts
Contact info@midas.ac.uk
Free

http://midas.ac.uk/

gopher://cs6400.mcc.ac.uk/

Maximov's Companion to Who Governs The Russian Federation ★★★★

Maximov's Companion is a powerful, constantly updated reference tool for people who want to know who is in charge of what in Russia and how to contact them. The companion lists over 4,000 officials and 8,000 telephone, fax, and email numbers. The site gives some access to the data and to hot news. An online order form is included. Maximov's goal is to provide accurate and current political reference information so that anyone who wishes to do business or simply operate within Russia may do so.

Keywords Business, Government, Politics, Russia
Audience Business Professionals, Educators, Government Officials., Journalists

CONTACT malina@maximov.com
FREE

http://www.maximov.com/

Political Documents Web Page ★★★★

This site provides an archive of various political documents (including the Magna Carta, the War Powers Act of 1973, and the Gettysburg Address) and indices to such things as multilateral conventions, treaties, rules of war, and charters for many nations and international agencies. This Political Documents collection is maintained and continually under construction by Indiana University's Bill Dueber. Dueber has also recently added a large list of links to other, more modern political and governmental resources, including a wide selection of American federal government Web pages and gopher sites.

KEYWORDS   Constitutions, Documents, Magna Carta, Politics
AUDIENCE   General Public, Philosophers, Political Researchers, Political Scientists
CONTACT   William Dueber wdueber@cs.indiana.edu
FREE

http://www.cs.indiana.edu/inds/politics.html

Primary Human Rights Sources ★★★

The server Diana- International Human Rights Database (after Diana Vincent-Daviss) contains bibliographies, text files, and digitized images for human rights research and advocacy. This Web page contains a listing of Diana's primary sources, materials from the United Nations and the Organization of American States, including the Inter-American Court of Human Rights. The full texts of several documents are available.

KEYWORDS   Human Rights, International Organizations, United Nations
AUDIENCE   Human Rights Activists, Political Scientists
FREE

http://www.law.uc.edu/Diana/pri.html

SICSA The Vidal Sassoon International Center for the Study of Antisemitism ★★★

SICSA, established in 1982 as an interdisciplinary research center dedicatedto an independent, non-political approach to the accumulation and disseminationof knowledge necessary for understanding the phenomenon of antisemitism, provides hotlinks to education cources, conferences and programs, research conducted by the organization, publications on antisemitism, and more. There are hotlinks to other sites for additional information about Jewish culture as well as the United States Holocaust Museum.

KEYWORDS   Antisemitism, Holocaust, Jewish History
AUDIENCE   Historians, Librarians, Researchers, Students
CONTACT   arzt@hum.huji.ac.il
FREE

http://www2.huji.ac.il/www_jcd/top.html

Secondary Human Rights Sources ★★★

The server Diana- International Human Rights Database (after Diana Vincent-Daviss) contains bibliographies, text files, and digitized images for human rights research and advocacy. This Web page contains Diana's secondary sources: bibliographies and an online training course book from the United Nations.

KEYWORDS   Human Rights, United Nations
AUDIENCE   Human Rights Activists, Political Scientists
FREE

http://www.law.uc.edu/Diana/sec.html

U.S. Bureau of the Census Home Page ★★★

This is the home page of the U.S. Census Bureau, which collects data about the people and economy of the United States. Users can access up-to-date population statistics, city and county information, state financial data, and much more.

KEYWORDS   Census Bureau (US), Demographics, Population Control
AUDIENCE   Business Reseachers, Demographers, Government Officials, Statisticians
CONTACT   gatekeeper@census.gov
FREE

http://www.census.gov/

ftp://ftp.census.gov/pub

U.S. Census 1990 ★★★

This gopher site contains all of the Census 1990 information, listed according to state. Users will find sex, age, household type, and race information for each state, as well as general Federal Census information.

KEYWORDS   Census (The), Population Index, Population Studies
AUDIENCE   Government Officials, Population Studies Researchers, U.S. Citizens
CONTACT   consult@umail.umd.edu.
FREE

gopher://gopher.inform.umd.edu/11/
    Educational_Resources/
    AcademicResourcesByTopic/
    UnitedStatesAndWorld/
    United_States/
    National_Agencies/
    ExecutiveBranch/Census-90

U.S. Congress House Directory ★★★

This page contains a listing of the names of all the House members, their email addresses (where applicable), telephone numbers, addresses in Washington, D.C., and their fax numbers. It is arranged alphabetically by each member's state.

KEYWORDS   Email Directory, House of Representatives (US)
AUDIENCE   Email Users, Fax Users, General Public, Journalists

FREE

gopher://gopher.house.gov/1D-1%3a483%3aHouse%20Directory

U.S. Federal Register ★★★

This site gives access to the U.S. Federal Register produced by Counterpoint Publishing Inc. The Register gives the latest regulatory information from U.S. Government agencies. All users may view selected portions of the Register, including the table of contents. Those who have paid an annual fee may view the entire document. The Register is produced daily.

KEYWORDS   Federal Law, Government Documents, Publishing
AUDIENCE   General Public, Government Employees, Government Officials, Lawyers
CONTACT   fedreg@counterpoint.com
COST

gopher://gopher.counterpoint.com:2002/

U.S. House of Representatives' Gopher Service ★★★

This is the gopher server for the U.S. House of Representatives. It contains information about the House and its current members, information about standing House committees, as well as visitor and educational information, such as a description of the procedure for making new laws. The gopher server is searchable by keywords.

KEYWORDS   House of Representatives (US), Politics (US)
AUDIENCE   Educators, General Public, U.S. Citizens, U.S. Congress
CONTACT   househlp@hr.house.gov
FREE

gopher://gopher.house.gov/

United States Senate Gopher Server ★★★

The U.S. Senate's official gopher server maintains an archive of documents voluntarily released by various committees, Senators and other Senate offices detailing their current projects. Press releases, committee membership lists, and miscellaneous information is also available. A search engine allows various directories within the server to be quickly searched by keyword.

KEYWORDS   Federal Government (US), Law (US)
AUDIENCE   Journalists, Lawyers, Media Professionals, Political Researchers
CONTACT   Senate Communications Office guide@scc.senate.gov
FREE

gopher://gopher.senate.gov/

Regions

See also
Government & Politics · *Countries*
Humanities & Social Sciences · *Area & Cultural Studies*

ABAG Online (Access to Bay Area Governments Online)

ABAGOnline is a pilot project, partially funded by a National Telecommunications and Information Administration (NTIA) grant to bring freely accessible government information to Bay Area citizens using personal computers, online databanks, and the Internet. On this site, users will find a local calendar of events for the community featuring items like a workshop on how to obtain funding under the 1995 Crime Bill and a listing for OSHA training classes; a listing of Web Pages for Bay Area Cities and Counties; Informational area like the Transportation Information Page; as well as Who's Who in regional planning and advisory councils.

KEYWORDS   Community Networking, Telecommunications
AUDIENCE   Californians, Community Activists, Community Activists
CONTACT   M. Strata Rose
           strata@virtual.net
FREE

http://www.abag.ca.gov/

gopher://gopher.abag.ca.gov/

About Chebucto Community Net

The Chebucto Community Net is a community network serving the Metropolitan Halifax area. It is run by the Metro Community Access Network Society. The primary index hypertexts documents relating to the Society's activities, including its current activities and archive of its past activities, the names and addresses of its volunteers, and information about its fundraising program.

KEYWORDS   Community, Community Networks, Government, Nova Scotia
AUDIENCE   Canada Residents, Community Activists, Community Groups
CONTACT   userhelp@cfn.cs.dal.ca
FREE

http://www.cfn.cs.dal.ca/

About SEVAnet ★★

SEVAnet is an electronic network that will provide public access to a full range of computerized information and communications services to all of the communities of the Southeastern Virginia Region. When fully operational, SEVAnet will form an electronic link, by modem and by direct wire, between all of the computers in Southeastern Virginia. SEVAnet will also arrange for access by members to the Internet. To help offset some of SEVAnet's operating costs, some features of SEVAnet will require registration and fees.

KEYWORDS   Communications Systems, Community, Southern Culture (US), Virginia

For Connections to Weather Services
When it rains, it pours . . .

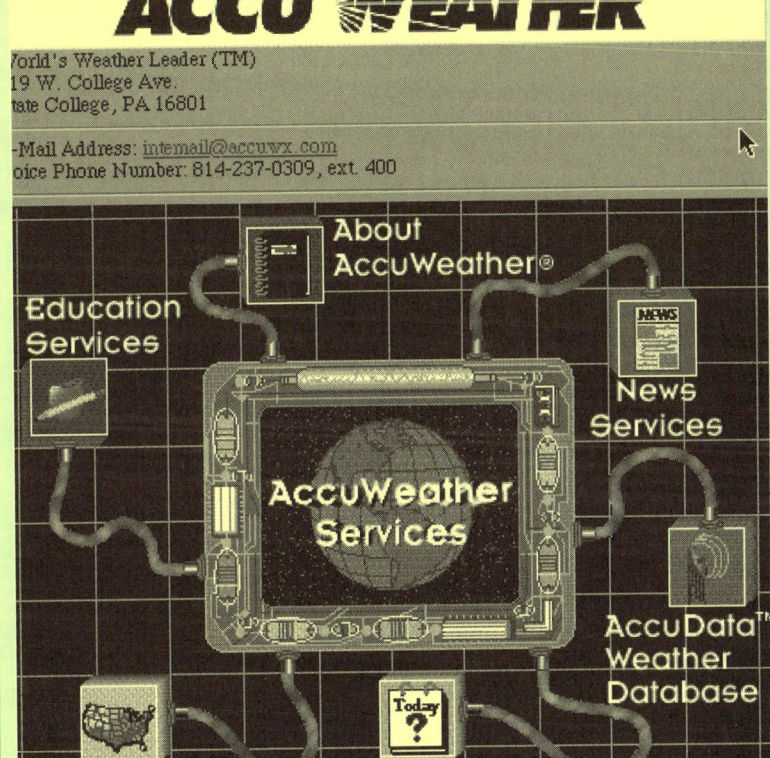

Traveling to Tokyo? Will you need an overcoat? Will you need your "brolly" (umbrella) for an afternoon stroll through London's Covent Gardens? What are the surfing conditions along the beaches of Australia? If you want tomorrow's forecast today, or want to take a peek at the weather forecast for your vacation destination, the Internet is the place to find it.

A wide range of weather resources are available via "WeatherNet," the Internet's source of weather links (some 200 and growing) at:

(http://cirrus.sprl.umich.edu/wxnet/wxnetplus.html), also (http://accuwx.com/)

You can also access The Weather Channel online, which provides updated forecasts and weather conditions each morning on the hour from 5 a.m. to 11 p.m.

(http://www.infi.net/weather/program.html)

If you want earthquake reports from the U.S. Geological Society along with your daily and weekly forecasts, then check out the Internet's "Weather Information Superhighway." This site maintains a vast collection of meteorological data. It also provides satellite photos of atmospheric weather conditions for all major regions of the world—so that you can read what the weather is like, and observe it as well.

(http://thunder.met.fsu.edu/~nws/wxhwy.html)

AUDIENCE Community Activists, Community Groups, Virginia Residents
CONTACT seva@seva.net
COST
http://www.seva.net

Africa - (FAQs) Frequently Asked Questions ★★★

This is the FAQ for the newsgroup, soc.culture.african. The information in the FAQ is organized as an index to information available on the Internet. Topics include working in Africa, history, geography, Internet resources, media, women's issues, music, travel and specific information about different African nations.
KEYWORDS Africa, African Studies, Travel
AUDIENCE Africans, Business Travelers, Students (University), Tourists, Travelers
FREE
http://www.cs.ubc.ca/spider/shaze/africa/tableofcontents3_1.html

Asia-Pacific Information Services ★★★★

This home page is a very good gateway to the information about Asia. It provides general data, Asian Stock Market Closings (Daily), as well as an interactive map with directories of WWW servers and country information.
KEYWORDS Asia, Reference, Travel
AUDIENCE Asians, Business Professionals, Investors, Tourists
CONTACT staff@emailhost.ait.ac.th
FREE
http://emailhost.ait.ac.th/Asia/asia.html

Asian Institute of Technology ★★★★

The top level Web page of the Asian Institute of Technology (AIT) contains extensive information resources. Some of the areas that viewers can find out about include up-to-date links for infoservers and libraries in asian countries; information pages for various Asia-Pacific countries; a clickable map of Thailand with detailed demographic data; links to tourist info by province; searchable abstracts of completed and ongoing research related to the region; and mirrors of subject area indices (to minimize TransPacific traffic).
KEYWORDS Asia, Thailand
AUDIENCE Asian Studies Educators, Asian Studies Students, Asians, Political Scientists
CONTACT staff@emailhost.ait.ac.th
FREE
http://emailhost.ait.ac.th/

Bloemfontein, South Africa ★★★

The home page of Bloemfontein, Capital of the Free State Province in South Africa provides hypertext images and descriptive text of facilities and attractions of primary interest to tourists, including the weather, the natural habitat, local businesses and where to lodge, dine and shop.
KEYWORDS Hiking, South Africa, Tourism
AUDIENCE Camping Enthusiasts, Hiking Enthusiasts, South Africa Residents, Tourists
CONTACT Gawie van Blerk
gawie@pixie.co.za
FREE
http://www.pix.za/0/business/bloemfontein/bloemftn.html
ftp://rtfm.mit.edu/pub/usenet-by-hierarchy/soc/culture/bosna-herzgvna/%5Bmisc.news.

Boulder Community Network ★★★

The goal of the Boulder Community Network is to weave together all the information of a civic, educational, community nature relevant to Boulder County citizens, and ensure access to all. Local information is combined on this site with state, national, and international information sources. Subdirectories under such headings as Education, Art, Business, Employment, and Library list local Boulder resources, followed by national and international links.
KEYWORDS Community Networking
AUDIENCE Colorado Residents, Web Developers
CONTACT BCN Webmaster
webmaster@bcn.boulder.co.edu
FREE
http://bcn.boulder.co.us/

EUnet ★★

This gopher hole provides information about a European computer network called EUNet. EUNet provides networking services to countries in both eastern and western Europe. This gopher describes EUNet services, provides links to sites in member countries, and information about EUNet Traveller, a service to access EUNet sites from abroad.
KEYWORDS Computer Networks, Europe, Internet Resources
AUDIENCE Computer Users, European Internet Users, Europeans, Internet Users
CONTACT info@EU.net
FREE
gopher://eunet.eu.net/

Europa ★★★★

The Europa Web server provides information about the European Union (EU) and its institutions and policies. Users will find the EU history and institution lists, information from the Commission, including commissioner portfolios and speeches, as well as a directory. The Newswire provides daily newsfeeds from the Commission's Spokesperson's Office in French. A guide to the EU policies is also provided, with a consumer guide and information about 'myths' in Europe (for example, that the EC is ruling that all gin bottles must be round rather than square). Key European Union documents are also available, with databases, statistics, and program information.
KEYWORDS European Union, International Politics, Unions
AUDIENCE Europeans, Political Enthusiasts, Politicians
CONTACT europa@di.cec.be
FREE
http://www.cec.lu/Welcome.html

European Community (EC) Home Page ★★★★

This page is part of a service mandated by the Directorate-General XIII of the European Community (EC) as part of a movement to make the EC and component nations' political and trade information available on the Web. This site contains links (in the form of an image map of Europe) to each member country's own national government sites.
KEYWORDS Europe, European Community, Government
AUDIENCE Europeans, Government Students, Political Researchers
CONTACT Jose Miranda
pinj@di.uminho.pt
FREE
http://s700.uminho.pt/ec.html

Hivos ★★★

The Hivos Web site details the Dutch organization's work in promoting development in Africa, Asia, and Latin America. Users will find information about ongoing projects, conferences and other events, and two online magazines and links to like-minded academic, developmental, and environmentalist sites.
KEYWORDS Africa, Development
AUDIENCE Africanists, Economists, Latin Americanists
FREE
http://www.dds.nl/~hivos/

HoosierNet ★★★

HoosierNet is a community-wide digital education, information, and Government & Politics network for Bloomington and Monroe County, Indiana. Its goal is to provide an information infrastructure to enhance the learning capacity and quality of life in the local community through information dissemination and communication.
KEYWORDS Community, Government, Indiana
AUDIENCE Community Activists, Community Groups, Indiana Residents
CONTACT webmaster@access.bloomington.in.us
FREE
http://www.bloomington.in.us

Latin American Gopher Menu ★★★

This page provides links to information on Latin America. Subjects covered include the Association for Public Analysis and Management, Institute for Global Communications (IGC), Peacenet, Rio Grande Free Net, UN-FAO/Food and Agriculture Organization, and more.
KEYWORDS Internet Resources, Latin America
AUDIENCE International Students, Latin American Studies Students, Political Scientists, Tourists
CONTACT info@lanic.utexas.edu
FREE
gopher://lanic.utexas.edu:70/11/la/world

MAGIC-Marin County Government Information Center ★★★

This page provides Marin County Government Information (not all hyper linked), including services offered by county agencies, a directory of county agencies and departments, general information about Marin County government, and phones and email for Marin County Departments.

KEYWORDS California, Government
AUDIENCE Business Professionals, Californians, General Public, Government Officials
CONTACT dhill@marin.org
FREE

http://midas.org/

Marin Information & Data Access System (MIDAS) ★★★★

Welcome to the Marin Information & Data Access System (MIDAS) home page. MIDAS's goals are to increase the public's access to information and expand opportunities for communication among key community resources. The system should benefit local governments, libraries, schools, citizens, private companies, and non-profit agencies. Links are comprehensive and include MAGIC - Marin County Government Information Center, local newspapers, cool links, general information about California, entertainment, restaurants, transportation, weather, Bay Area employment, neighboring communities, and much more.

KEYWORDS California, Community Networking
AUDIENCE Educators, General Public, Marin County Residents, Parents, Public Officials
CONTACT breising@midas.co.marin.ca.us
FREE

http://midas.co.marin.ca.us/

Neighborhood Initiative ★★★★

The Wichita/Sedgwick County Neighborhood Initiative is a county-wide collaborative effort to reduce crime and violence in this region of Kansas. This site provides links to information about this initiative, including topics such as - Key Projects for 1995, The Neighborhood Initiative Coordinating Center, Project Freedom Family and Youth Coalition, Wichita State University Institute for Research on Communities and Crime, and more. Graphics and background cause the loading to be a bit slow, so be patient.

KEYWORDS Crime Prevention, Kansas
AUDIENCE Community Activists, Community Organizations, General Public, Kansas Residents, Urban Planners
CONTACT Pat O'Donnell
         ictcomm@irco.com
FREE

http://www.irco.com/ni/neighbor.html

Oceania — The Atlantis Project ★★★★

This site promotes an organization dedicated to the goal of establishing a new country named Oceania. This country will be devoted to the value of freedom, and will first exist as a sea city in the Caribbean.

KEYWORDS Civil Liberties, Utopia

Connections to World Subway Systems
Where can I catch the Underground?

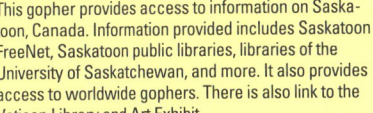

Whether it's called Le Metro, the subway, The Tube, or the Underground, you can find how to use subterranean transit systems around the world by first checking into the Internet.

There are several sites on the World Wide Web for the "Subway Navigator"—some in French, some in German, some in Italian, and some in English—to help you make it from point A to point B on many of the world's underground transit trains.

There are hundreds of navigator systems, including maps, that enable you to specify how to get to your destination from a specific subway station. All you do is enter that information into the specified navigator.

Travel times are evaluated for normal traffic conditions. The list includes the world's largest and most famous cities, such as Tokyo, London, Amsterdam, Singapore, Budapest, Helsinki, Vienna, Paris, Calgary, Marseilles, Madrid, Calcutta, Frankfurt, and New York, to name only a few.

(http://metro.jussieu.fr:10001/english/info.html)

AUDIENCE Activists, Business Professionals, Entrepreneurs, Philosophers
CONTACT oceania@terminus.intermind.net
FREE

http://unicycle.cs.tulane.edu:80/oceania/

Polar Information Sources Gopher ★★★

This directory contains resources related to polar regions. Types of links include libraries in more than a dozen countries, information about polar tourism, and conferences and journals dealing with polar regions.

KEYWORDS Earth Sciences, Libraries, Polar Regions, Tourism
AUDIENCE Earth Scientists, Ecologists, Science Educators, Students (Primary/Secondary)
CONTACT Mary Westell
         westell@acs.ucalgary.ca
FREE

gopher://acs6.acs.ucalgary.ca:70/11/library/polar

Saskatoon FreeNet ★★

This gopher provides access to information on Saskatoon, Canada. Information provided includes Saskatoon FreeNet, Saskatoon public libraries, libraries of the University of Saskatchewan, and more. It also provides access to worldwide gophers. There is also link to the Vatican Library and Art Exhibit.

KEYWORDS Canada, Reference
AUDIENCE Adults, Canadians, Librarians, Library Users, Religious Studies Students
CONTACT D. Fichter
         fichter@willow.usask.ca
FREE

gopher://willow.usask.ca:71/

SunSITE Northern Europe ★★★

The SunSITE Northern Europe Archive provides a wide variety of information about Internet resources, including a list of all WWW servers in the UK; a list of computing-related servers; pointers to the FAQs for all newsgroups; and lots of other information.

KEYWORDS Europe, Information Retrieval, Internet Directories, United Kingdom
AUDIENCE Computer Scientists, Internet Users, United Kingdom Residents, Usenet News Readers

Regions – States

CONTACT wizards@doc.ic.ac.uk
FREE
http://src.doc.ic.ac.uk

States

See also
Government & Politics · Cities
Humanities & Social Sciences · History

1994 California Election Home Page ★★★

This service provides voter information and election returns for the 1994 California general election and is a joint project of the California Secretary of State's Office and Digital Equipment Corporation. The Election Night results were reported here, live on the Internet! The results you see now are the Final Official Canvass. This page contains election returns, voter information, party information and a link to a Spanish version of this information.

KEYWORDS California, Elections, Political Candidates, Voter Information
AUDIENCE Campaign Workers, General Public, Lobbyists, Politicians, Voters
FREE

http://www.election.ca.gov/e/home.html

Alaska Mall ★★★

The Alaska Mall is a statewide network that provides hypertext documentation and links to statewide and local services, such as vacation information, history, calendars of events. It includes active links to businesses grouped by type, such as advertising, books, realty listings and boat charters.

KEYWORDS Business, Community
AUDIENCE Alaska Residents, Community Activists, Community Groups
CONTACT Lynn Moore
  lynnm@alaskan.com
FREE

http://alaskan.com/

CPSR (Computer Professionals for Social Responsibility) Foyer ★★★★

Computer Professionals for Social Responsibility (CPSR) gathers information on publicly available California government resources that are online. Its archives are updated monthly, and may be freely distributed via email and other methods. Submissions of all relevant online resources are accepted. The archive has a number of pointers to sites covering politicians and candidates as well as PACs and other political organizations.

KEYWORDS California, Computer Organizations
AUDIENCE Californians, Political Activists, Political Researchers, Students (University)
CONTACT Chris Mays
  cmays@sfsu.edu
FREE

http://cpsr.org/cpsr/states/california/cal_gov_info_FAQ.html

ftp://cpsr.org/cpsr/states/california/941215.cal_gov_info_FAQ

California Civil Rights Initiative ★★★★

The California Civil Rights Initiative (CCRI) home page provides information about the 1996 plebiscite, which regards affirmative action and gender equity in California. The measure seeks to eliminate race and gender-based standards in government operations, public policy, and public employment. Users will the text of the initiative, press releases, and contact information.

KEYWORDS California, Civil Rights, Plebiscites
AUDIENCE Californians, Journalists, Political Scientists
CONTACT ccri@earthlink.net
FREE

http://www.earthlink.net/~cid/ccri/

California Department of Water Resources Information Systems and Services Office ★★★

This site is a clearinghouse for the California Department of Water Resources Information Systems and Services Office. It offers access to Emergency Information Sources, Weather Images, Maps, and Reports, Law and Government Topics, Economics and Finance Topics, Information Technology Topics, California Irrigation Management Information System, and more.

KEYWORDS California, Water
AUDIENCE Californians, Farmers, Information Scientists, Irrigation Specialists, Meteorologists
CONTACT webmaster@water.ca.gov
FREE

http://www.water.ca.gov/cgi-bin/home.pl

California Economic Recovery & Environmental Restoration (CAREER/PRO) ★★

The California Economic Recovery & Environmental Restoration (CAREER/PRO) was set up to provide information on the redevelopment of closing military facilities in Northern California. CAREER/PRO concerns itself with the closing of the facilities, the following cleanups and future conversion to other uses. The information available dates back to 1993, but it may serve those interested in the base closings.

KEYWORDS California, Defense, Economics, Environment
AUDIENCE Californians, Environmentalists
CONTACT Lenny Siegel
  lsiegel@igc.apc.org
FREE

http://www.igc.apc.org/igc/people.html

gopher://gopher.igc.apc.org/11/environment/toxics/miltox

California State Government Network (CSGnet) ★★★★

Access on this page is given to the WWW servers of California State Departments (Dept. of Fish and Game, Governor's Office of Emergency Services, State Senate, State Lands Commission, Dept. of Transportation, etc.) and gopher servers (Dept. of Education, PUC, State Senate and Secretary of State). Also included are links to federal and local governments, a listing of various topics (such as California Universities, Arts and Entertainment, Sports and Recreation) via the California Virtual Tourist WWW Server, and general Internet resources.

KEYWORDS California, Tourism
AUDIENCE State Officials, Students, Tourists, Voters
CONTACT Webmaster
  WebMaster@teale.ca.gov
FREE

http://www.ca.gov/

ftp://ftp.teale.ca.gov/

California State Senate Gopher Service ★★★

This server provides information from and about the Senate of the State of California. This information includes documents provided by the individual members, descriptions of the activities of Senate committees, and access to bills and legislation from the Senate. There are links to other state and federal government gopher holes.

KEYWORDS California, Politics, Senate
AUDIENCE Californians, Government Officials, Political Analysts, Voters
CONTACT Gopher.Admin@SEN.CA.GOV
FREE

gopher://sen.ca.gov/

California Vehicle Code ★★★

The California Vehicle Code is available by anonymous FTP from the URL and is organized by code number.

KEYWORDS Automobiles, California, Law Enforcement
AUDIENCE Californians, Drivers, Traffic School Instructors
CONTACT Legislative Council Bureau of the State of California
  comments@leginfo.public.ca.gov
FREE

ftp://leginfo.public.ca.gov/pub/code/veh

California Voter Information ★★★★

The California Voter Information Web site provides information and results regarding the state's 1994 general election. Users may access data about statewide and local races and ballot initiatives, including funding information. There's a clickable map that presents returns by county; the material is elsewhere grouped by district. Judicial returns are included. There are links to the home pages of candidates, the major political parties, and other political sites.

KEYWORDS California, Voting
AUDIENCE Californians, Voters

Free

http://www.election.ca.gov/

Colorado National Information Infrastructure Summit ★★

This Web page tells of a National Information Infrastructure (NII) Summit held on December 5, 1994, at the University of Colorado in Boulder. The gathering addressed the telecommunications revolution and its effects on Colorado.

Keywords Colorado, Telecommunications
Audience Coloradans, Telecommunications Experts
Free

http://www.cs.colorado.edu/home/mcbryan/cnii/Home.html

Commonwealth of Kentucky WWW Services ★★★

The goal of the Commonwealth of Kentucky WWW Services site is to create a widely accessible, affordable information resource for Kentucky residents and other interested parties. The top-level menu is broken down into Kentucky State Government information, which lists specific government projects related to its networking infrastructure and Kentucky World Wide Web Services, which contains other entities, such as the Breeders' Cup Home Page, the Kentucky Department of Education, and a number of commercial Web sites.

Keywords Kentucky, Travel, Universities
Audience Kentucky Residents, State Officials, Students, Travelers
Contact Dan L. Whitehouse
dwhiteho@msmail.state.ky.us
Free

http://www.state.ky.us/

Delaware Facts ★★

This page lists facts about the U.S. state of Delaware. Information here includes a description of Delaware's government, physical attributes, chief products, and demographics. Viewers can learn about Delaware's state symbols, such as its official seal, flag, flower, tree, bug, motto, and nickname. There are also links to biographies of Delaware's major elected representatives, a Delaware history page, and an under-construction page devoted to noteworthy Delaware residents.

Keywords Delaware, Demographics, Education (College/University), Tourism
Audience Delaware Residents, Students, Tourists
Contact Scott S. Street or Russell S. Pickett
webmaster@ois.state.de.us
Free

http://www.state.de.us/facts/intro.htm

Hawaii Government Information Servers ★★★

The Nation of Hawaii offers this service to provide information regarding the legal foundation for the restoration of Hawaiian independence, along with cultural perspectives from the people of Hawaii. This site contains legal resources, news articles, historical information, images, and international contact names for more details. In addition, there is a special cultural section entitled, The 24 'Canoe Plants' of Ancient Hawaii, which has a great deal of information about particular plants of the Hawaiian islands, including descriptions, propagation methods, cultural and medicinal uses.

Keywords Hawaii
Audience Hawaiian Activists, Hawaiians, Tourists
Contact webmaster@aloha.net
Free

http://www.hawaii.edu/hawaiihome/gov.html

Hawaii Information Servers ★★★

This page is the top level menu for information about the state of Hawaii, USA. Users can start from this page to see information about Hawaii's goverment structure, tourist information, educational systems, businesses, and civic organizations.

Keywords Hawaii, Local Governments
Audience Business Professionals, Hawaiians, Tourists
Contact webmaster@www.hawaii.net
Free

http://www.hawaii.net/

Hot Topic: January 1995 California Floods ★★★

This page with a regularly changing hot topic is created by Amdahl, a developer of high end hardware and software. Currently the page contains extensive links on the 1995 California floods, which include California Highway Reports (from CalTrans), articles on floods from California newspapers, and much more. Previous Hot Topics, such as United Nations 50th Anniversary, are archived here.

Keywords California, Events, Natural Disasters
Audience Californians, News Buffs
Contact www@amdahl.com
Free

http://www.amdahl.com/internet/events/ca-1-95-floods.html

Indiana State Government - Access Indiana Home Page ★★

The Indiana State Government Home Page contains directories of archives, agencies, and programs. Some of the areas of this site are under constuction, however there are current and up to date pages devoted to the Commission on Public Records, Department of Education, Criminal Justice Institute, and a Job Bank listing employment. In addition, users can jump to outside Indiana servers, such as the Indiana Higher Education Telecommunication System, and the Indiana and Purdue Universities Library system.

Keywords Employment, Government Documents (US), Indiana
Audience Indiana Residents, Lawyers, Researchers
Contact Clark Bohs and Ken Polk
clark_bohs_at_isdlan@ima.isd.state.in.us
ken_polk_at_isdlan@ima.isd.state.in.us
Free

http://www.state.in.us/

Job Files on the FedWorld Information Network ★★★

This directory lists official U.S. Government job announcements from the Office of Personnel Management, available by region or state and updated daily. Positions range from clerical support, to chemists, to auto mechanics and architects.

Keywords Employment, Federal Government (US), Jobs
Audience Job Seekers, Umemployed Workers
Free

ftp://fwux.fedworld.gov/pub/jobs/

Maine State Government Home Page ★★★

This page links the user to offices and agencies of Maine's state government. Among the links for this top level page are the office of Tourism, the Bureau of Elder and Adult Services, the Department of Environmental Protection, the Maine State Library, and the Bureau of Medical Services.

Keywords Maine
Audience Maine Residents, Seniors, Tourists
Contact HELP DESK
webmaster@state.me.us
Free

http://www.state.me.us/

Massachusetts Access to Government Information Service ★★★★

The Massachusetts Access to Government Information Service contains Internet resources for and about Massachusetts. There are several areas on this site that are under construction; however, there are some areas that have current information. Users can see political pages, such as the Massachusetts Governor's Forum which contains a brief biography, inaugural speeches, and budget recommendations. Other areas to view are business-related pages such as a hypertext version of The Vendor Handbook, for vendors interested in doing business with the Commonwealth of Massachusetts. There are also sections like Recreation & Tourism, Kids & Education, and Outside Internet Sites.

Keywords Massachusetts, Politics, Tourism
Audience Business Professionals, Educators, Massachusetts Residents, Tourists
Contact lmacinan@world.std.com
Free

http://www.magnet.state.ma.us/

Missouri Department of Economic Development ★★★

This site hosts online information for anyone with an interest in investing or relocating their business to

Missouri. There is a cross-referenced database, which allows the user to search and display profiles in Community, Products, Economic Development Laws, and available Building and Sites. For example, a search for a specific sized building will bring up a listing of available sites by community, which can be further examined for distance to transportation, educational level of the community, previous use of the site, and more. Under construction is an online request for more information.

KEYWORDS Business Development, Missouri
AUDIENCE Business Analysts, Investors, Missouri Residents, Missouri Residents
CONTACT show-me@cstp.umkc.edu
FREE

http://mmsun5.cstp.umkc.edu/show-me-mo/Welcome.html

Montana Information Delivery System ★★★

This site contains information about the state of Montana, and is designed for networking between residents of Montana, government and private organizations, as well as outside users that are interested in what Montana has to offer. The site contains links to state agencies and departments (some which are under construction), tourist information, employment information, educational institutions, and a page of links to Montana businesses.

KEYWORDS Montana, Tourism
AUDIENCE Montana Residents, Tourists
CONTACT Ed Conrad
cx0032%zip02@mt.gov
FREE

http://www.mt.gov/

NCINFO - NC Local Government on the Internet ★★★★

NCINFO - NC (North Carolina) Local Government on the Internet is an online information resource for anyone interested in North Carolina state and local government. NCINFO is a joint project of the Institute of Government, the North Carolina Association of County Commissioners, and the North Carolina League of Municipalities. In addition to information provided by and about these three organizations, NCINFO links you directly to the most useful resources available on the Internet about local, state, and federal government.

KEYWORDS North Carolina, Research
AUDIENCE Business Professionals, Lawyers, Librarians, Managers, Public Officials
CONTACT Pat Langelier
pal.iog@mhs.unc.edu
FREE

http://ncinfo.iog.unc.edu

gopher://ncinfo.iog.unc.edu

NYSERNet Web ★★★

This site gives information on NYSERNet. NYSERNet (New York State Education and Research Network) is a high-speed data network, connecting New York State to the global community of computing networks. The page provides details of NYSERNet staff, products, special projects and resources.

KEYWORDS Communications, Computer Networks, Information Technology, New York
AUDIENCE Computer Users, Network Service Providers, Network Users, New York Residents
CONTACT Linda Carl
lcarl@nysernet.org
FREE

http://nysernet.org/

New Jersey Gubernatorial Address and Budget Summary ★★

This site contains both the summary of the New Jersey State Budget for the fiscal year 1996 and the text of the governor's budget address on January 23, 1995.

KEYWORDS Economic Indicators, Economics, New Jersey
AUDIENCE Economists, New Jersey Residents, Political Analysts, Politicians
CONTACT Rutgers University Telecommunications Division
ns-www@www-ns.rutgers.edu
FREE

http://www-ns.rutgers.edu/NJ/index.html

New York WWW Sites ★★★

This site, associated with Brandon Plewe's Virtual Tourist project, contains both a clickable New York State area map and an associated text file of most of the information servers in the New York State area. Users can click to reach college and university pages, sites on business and marketing, or lists of pages from New York's neighboring regions in Pennsylvania, Ontario, and New Jersey. There is also a map for finding information about any of the State University of New York (SUNY) campuses.

KEYWORDS Business, New York, Tourism, Universities
AUDIENCE Business Professionals, New York Residents, Students (University), Tourists
CONTACT Brandon Plewe
plewe@acsu.buffalo.edu
FREE

http://wings.buffalo.edu/world/nywww.html

North Carolina Information Highway Home Page ★★★

This site offers information about the NCIH (North Carolina Information Highway). There is access to new information, press releases, frequently asked questions, operational information, information on grant programs, and technical information.

KEYWORDS Broadband Technology, North Carolina, Telecommunications
AUDIENCE Economic Development Experts, Educators, Medical Educators, North Carolina Residents

CONTACT Mark Johnson
Mark.Johnson@ncih.net
FREE

http://ncih.osc.state.nc.us/

Public Transportation ★★

This site is about ITRE's (Institute for Transportation Research and Education) Public Transportation Program. ITRE does research in advanced public transportation (APTS) technologies toward the common goal of increased efficiencies and ridership in North Carolina transit operations. This page outlines the project highlights including Mobility Manager System, which is a test bed for computerized dispatch and related technologies; Apprenticeship and Internship Programs; Public Entrepreneurs Roundtable; Operations Planning Seminar; and more.

KEYWORDS Community Information, North Carolina, Public Transportation
AUDIENCE Engineers, Politicians, Real Estate Professionals, Transportation Professionals
CONTACT Anna M. Nalevanko, Program Director
itre-info@itre.uncecs.edu
FREE

http://itre.uncecs.edu/itre/pubtrans/pubtrans.html

Puerto Rico ★★★★

This is a Web page on Puerto Rico. Users will find facts about Puerto Rico, as well as a list of links to related sites with information on Puerto Rico. There is also a collection of images of Puerto Rico, as well as information on the history and climate of the island.

KEYWORDS Puerto Rico, Tourism
AUDIENCE Puerto Ricans, Tourists, Travelers
CONTACT Jose Pietri
jpietri@hpprdk01.prd.hp.com
FREE

http://hpprdk01.prd.hp.com/

State of Colorado State Officials ★★★

This site is a listing of elected representatives for the State of Colorado. Names, addresses, salary, political affiliations, and expiration of terms are listed. Offices in this site include the Governor, Lt. Governor, Treasurer, Secretary of State, Regents of the University of Colorado, and officers of the Board of Education.

KEYWORDS Colorado, Politics, Voting
AUDIENCE Colorado Residents, Colorado Residents, Political Scientists
CONTACT BCN Webmaster
webmaster@bcn.boulder.co.edu
FREE

http://bcn.boulder.co.us/government/colorado/state-off.html

State of Maine Bureau of Elder and Adult Services Resource Directory ★★★

The State of Maine's Bureau of Elder and Adult Services provides services, education and consultation in order to promote optimal independence for older citizens and for adults in need of protective or supportive services. The Bureau has provided this page as a resource for Maine's eldery and adult population. Many of the resources here are only available to Maine residents. However, there are national organizations and federal agencies listed here as well, plus general information of interest to the elderly of all areas. The Bureau has released a resource guide containing contact information regarding Adult services, Medicare, Employment and Training, Alzheimer's Disease, Veteran Services, and other subjects.

KEYWORDS Alzheimer's Disease, Senior Services
AUDIENCE Maine Residents, Seniors, Social Workers
CONTACT Webmaster_beas@state.me.us
FREE

http://www.state.me.us/beas/dhs_beas.htm

State of Missouri Home Page ★★

This site contains links to Internet resources based in Missouri. Information related to travel, tourism, academic institutions, Missouri state government contacts, or economic development data can be found by by selecting the appropriate hypertext links. A page devoted to the Great Flood of 1993 can also be access from this page.

KEYWORDS Missouri
AUDIENCE Government Employees, Missouri Residents, Tourists
CONTACT Barry Kirk
bkirk1@mail.more.net
FREE

http://www.ecodev.state.mo.us/

State of Wisconsin Information Server ★★★★

This site offers pointers to a number of state government-run sites in Wisconsin, including the Web pages of the Office of the Governor, various Wisconsin state courts, libraries, universities, and more. At this location specifically, historical and other background information about the State of Wisconsin is available.

KEYWORDS Wisconsin
AUDIENCE Political Researchers, Wisconsin Residents
CONTACT wisc-web@badger.state.wi.us
FREE

http://badger.state.wi.us/

TDOC (Texas Department of Commerce) Gopher ★★

This is a gopher hole for the Texas Department of Commerce (TDOC). It provides information on TDOC programs to encourage the development of the Texas economy, such as business development and business finance, as well as providing access to TDOC bibliographies. In addition, it provides access to gopher holes which provide information about the state of Texas.

KEYWORDS Commerce, Economic Development, Texas
AUDIENCE Business Professionals, Government Employees, Texas Residents
FREE

gopher://gopher.tdoc.texas.gov/

Texas Information Highway ★★

The Texas Information Highway is a gopher server providing access to information and resources from and about the government and state of Texas. The information it provides includes legislative information and links to important Internet gopher holes.

KEYWORDS Information Retrieval, Texas
AUDIENCE Business Professionals, Computer Users, Internet Users, Politicians, Texas Residents
CONTACT Wayne McDilda
Wayne@dir.texas.gov
FREE

gopher://info.texas.gov/

 ## Virgin.Mv.Com ★★★

The Virgin.Mv.Com server is operated by Virgin Software, Ltd. as a community service to the residents of New Hampshire. The page contains information about the state of New Hampshire and the town of Epping. The page has links to Internet services in the state, current weather and state politics.

KEYWORDS Internet Services, New Hampshire, Weather
AUDIENCE Community Networks, New Hampshire Residents
CONTACT Bruce Dawson
Bruce_Dawson@16036798740.iddd.tpc.int
FREE

http://virgin.mv.com/

Washington's World-Wide Web Home Page ★★★★

This site acts as a clearinghouse for Washington State political information. Some recently featured items here include the Governor's State of the State address, and daily reports from the State Legislature. Links to various commercial, educational and government institutions in Washington are also available.

KEYWORDS Commerce
AUDIENCE Journalists, Political Researchers, Tourists, Travelers, Washington Residents
CONTACT Jim Culp
culp@dis.wa.gov
FREE

http://olympus.dis.wa.gov/www/wahome.html

Water OnLine ★★★★

Water OnLine helps advance the use of the Internet as a communication and information-sharing tool in order to help solve California's water problems. It does this by enabling federal, state, and municipal water agencies to get quality information online. It facilitates water interest groups' use of the Internet. It also provides a forum for water leaders to discuss policy and technical ramifications of electronic communication/information sharing and provide direction for Water OnLine. The site provides links to Water OnLine's Goals and Objectives, Meeting Minutes, Upcoming Water OnLine workshops, Internet Training & Consulting, and links to Internet tools.

KEYWORDS California, Water
AUDIENCE Consultants, Engineers, Environmentalists, Government Employees
FREE

http://resources.agency.ca.gov/ceres/WOL/home.html

Welcome to California, United States of America ★★

This site, sponsored by GENinc, links to Chambers of Commerce and economic development organizations in California cities, which are listed by county. Chamber of Commerce sites can include community information such as services available locally, local business information, and health and residential information.

KEYWORDS California, Economic Development, Tourism
AUDIENCE Business Professionals, Californians, Investors, Tourists
CONTACT webmaster@terminus.com
FREE

http://www.terminus.com/geni/USA/CA/chamber_ca_menu.html

Health & Medicine

- Addictions 367
- Aging 367
- Alternative Medicine 368
- Biomedicine 370
- Career & Employment 371
- Dental Health 372
- Disabilites 372
- Diseases 374
- Family Health 381
- Health Conditions 383
- Medical Schools 385
- Medical Specialties 389
- Medicine 391
- Mental Health 392
- Organizations 394
- Personal Care 395
- Public Health 396
- Reference 400
- Resources 404
- Services 407
- Sexuality 407
- Sexually Transmitted Diseases 408
- Veterinary Medicine 409
- Women's Health 409

Addictions

See also
Health & Medicine · Women's Health

AL-ANON and ALATEEN ★★★

Al-Anon and Alateen for teenagers are self-help programs for partners and families of alcoholics. Their home page is designed to provide basic information about their programs, and includes the documents The 12 Steps of Alcoholics Anonymous and The 12 Traditions. A questionnaire to see if you need Al-Anon is also provided, as well as lists of phone numbers and addresses of Al-Anon addresses.

KEYWORDS Alcoholism, Organizations, Teenage Issues
AUDIENCE Alcoholics, Families
CONTACT   Don R.
          odat@ccnet.com
FREE

http://solar.rtd.utk.edu/~al-anon/

Drugs in the Workplace ★★★

This site is a monthly publication that provides news and analysis of drug use in the workplace. The issues contain practical news and help for company decision makers, human resource managers, and employee assistance professionals responsible for managing the impact of alcohol and drugs on the workplace. This site focuses on the effects of the federal government's rules and guidelines on the lawful prevention, detection and treatment of substance abuse on the job. Special areas of coverage focus on medical developments and breakthroughs, employee assistance programs, and cutting-edge solutions to common jobsite problems.

KEYWORDS Business, Drugs, Human Resources, Management
AUDIENCE Business Owners, Employees, Managers, Medical Researchers
FREE

gopher://gopher.enews.com:70/11/magazines/alphabetic/a1/diw

HabitSmart ★★★

HabitSmart is designed as a resource for people with destructive habits and addictions of all types, with documents and links to other addiction-related links on the Web. Users will find the document Coping with Addiction, which addresses questions about giving up substance abuse, as well as several documents for parents of children with addictions. A guide to drinking alcohol and blood alcohol levels is also provided, along with tips for reducing smoking and coping with urges. The HabitSmart Archivist newsletter, published bimonthly, prints research information and breakthroughs.

KEYWORDS Alcoholism, Drug Abuse, Smoking
AUDIENCE Alcoholics, Drug Users, Families, Smokers
CONTACT   habtsmrt@cts.com
FREE

http://www.cts.com/~habtsmrt/

Information About Alcoholics Anonymous ★★★

This web site is designed to provide information about the self-help alcohol recovery program Alcoholics Anonymous (AA). Users will find articles written by members of Alcoholics Anonymous about their lives, as well as several AA publications with personal recovery stories. Other online resources include information about upcoming conferences, addresses and phone numbers of centers worldwide, and AA pamphlets and brochures.

KEYWORDS Alcoholism, Organizations
AUDIENCE Alcoholics, Families
CONTACT   Phil W.
          an184160@anon.penet.fi
FREE

http://www.moscow.com/Resources/SelfHelp/AA/

NicNet ★★★

NicNet is The Arizona Nicotine and Tobacco Network web site, with resources and local information regarding tobacco and smoking research. Users will find numerous links to online resources, grouped into categories such as treatment and prevention, policy issues, commercial resources, government resources, journals and databases. Local information includes materials from the University of Arizona Program for Nicotine and Tobacco Research, and users will also find the home pages of several Arizona cancer and health related organizations.

KEYWORDS Smoking
AUDIENCE Smokers, Smoking Researchers
CONTACT   Jacqueline Shober
          jshober@ccit.arizona.edu
FREE

http://www.medlib.arizona.edu/~pubhlth/tobac.html

Aging

See also
Government & Politics · States
Health & Medicine · Biomedicine
Health & Medicine · Mental Health
Science · Agriculture

Aeiveos Corporation ★★★★

Aeiveos Corporation is a biotechnology research and education company dedicated to understanding the causes of aging. Aeiveos develops technologies which minimize the impact of age related diseases and eventually extend the human lifespan. This WWW server contains information about aging, longevity and nutrition related topics, theories on the aging process, pointers to tools for biotechnology research and general information for navigating the Internet. There are links to information about the genes and diseases which are linked to aging, nanotechnology pointers, a who's who in the world of longevity research, and a link to newsgroups which regularly discuss aging issues.

KEYWORDS Aging, Biotechnology, Gerontology, Nutrition
AUDIENCE Biotechnologists, General Public, Gerontologists, Seniors
CONTACT bradbury@aeiveos.wa.com
FREE

http://aeiveos.wa.com/index.html

Aging & Longevity News ★★★

This site contains links to newsgroups focusing on aging, including bionet.molbio.ageing, sci.cryonics, sci.life-extension, and sci.nanotech. There is also an extensive archive of past postings to these newsgroups which is available for browsing. The page also promises that these archives will be searchable in the future.

KEYWORDS Geriatrics, Nutrition, Usenet Newsgroups
AUDIENCE Geriatric Specialists, Health Care Professionals, Seniors
CONTACT Robert Bradbury
         bradbury@aeiveos.wa.com
FREE

http://aeiveos.wa.com/agenews.html

Aging/Longevity Authors ★★★★

This page contains links to names of authors of papers on aging and longevity. Topics include Aging Theory Specialists, Cellular Senescence Specialists, Free Radical Theory Specialists, DNA Mutation Specialists, Dietary Restriction Specialists, Specialists of Aging in Specific Organisms, and Organ Preservation Specialists.

KEYWORDS Aging, Geriatrics, Medical Research, Nanotechnology
AUDIENCE Geriatric Specialists, Health Care Professionals, Medical Researchers, Seniors
CONTACT Robert Bradbury
         bradbury@aeiveos.wa.com
FREE

http://aeiveos.wa.com/au/index.html

Answers Magazine ★★★

'Answers Magazine—The Magazine for Adult Children of Aging Parents' exists for those responsible for or interested in the health and well-being of aging parents. This site contains selected articles on healthcare, insurance, guilt, and more. The magazine covers all aspects of looking after an elderly parent, including how to deal with your feelings and where to get help if you need it.

KEYWORDS Aging, Gerontology, Health Care, Online Magazines
AUDIENCE Geriatric Specialists, Health Care Professionals, Seniors
CONTACT
FREE

http://www.service.com/answers/cover.html

Diet and Nutrition in Aging ★★★

This page focuses on the role of diet and nutrition in the aging process.

KEYWORDS Aging, Diet, Geriatrics, Nutrition
AUDIENCE Geriatric Specialists, Health Care Professionals, Seniors
CONTACT Robert Bradbury
         bradbury@aeiveos.wa.com
FREE

http://aeiveos.wa.com/diet/index.html

Diseases Involved In Aging ★★★

This page provides links to theories about the major causes of death and to WWW sites focusing on the treatment of various diseases.

KEYWORDS Aging, Death, Diseases, Geriatrics
AUDIENCE Geriatric Specialists, Health Care Professionals, Seniors
CONTACT Robert Bradbury
         bradbury@aeiveos.wa.com
FREE

http://aeiveos.wa.com/diseases/index.html

Diseases/Enzymes/Genes Involved with Aging ★★★

This page discusses the diseases, enzymes, and genes involved with aging, including Fanconi's Anemia, Cockaynes's Syndrome, and Xeroderma Pigmentosum.

KEYWORDS Aging, Diseases, Geriatrics, Medical Reference
AUDIENCE Geriatric Specialists, Health Care Professionals, Physicians, Seniors
CONTACT Robert Bradbury
         bradbury@aeiveos.wa.com
FREE

http://aeiveos.wa.com/diseases/agedis.html

Issues Involving Lifespan Extension ★★★★

Issues Involving Lifespan Extension puts forth reasons why maximum lifespans for humans, now believed to be around 120 years, will be eliminated within the next 20 years. With an increasing understanding of the aging process and an application of technologies to significantly extend lifespan, the net result (this site suggests) will be an unlimited maximum lifespan. The result of longer lives could cause overpopulation and economic problems. What do you do with all those extra years? "Don't worry, be happy," answers the author.

KEYWORDS Aging, Geriatrics, Population Studies, Retirement
AUDIENCE Geriatric Specialists, Health Care Professionals, Population Studies Scholars, Seniors
CONTACT Robert Bradbury
         bradbury@aeiveos.wa.com
FREE

http://aeiveos.wa.com/issues.html

List of Theories of Aging ★★★

This list contains links to many theories of the causes of aging including Clinker/Age Pigment Theory, DNA Damage Theory, Hormone/Stress Theory, Immunological Theory, Mitochondrial Theory, and Mutation Theory.

KEYWORDS Aging, Geriatrics, Medical Research, Theory
AUDIENCE Geriatric Specialists, Health Care Professionals, Medical Researchers, Seniors
CONTACT Robert Bradbury
         bradbury@aeiveos.wa.com
FREE

http://aeiveos.wa.com/agethry/

Medline References for Recent Aging Topics ★★★★

This page provides extensive links to abstracts and other information on articles dealing with aging topics current in the medical community. Article source, author name and address, and lists of major and minor indexes in which the article is catalogued are specified with each article, along with the abstract.

KEYWORDS Aging, Geriatrics, Medical Libraries
AUDIENCE Geriatric Specialists, Health Care Professionals, Seniors
CONTACT Robert Bradbury
         bradbury@aeiveos.wa.com
FREE

http://aeiveos.wa.com/agethry/age/

Alternative Medicine

See also
Health & Medicine · *Personal Care*
Popular Culture & Entertainment · *Lifestyles*

Alternative Health and Medicine ★★★★

The purpose of this alternative health and medicine site is to present information about alternative cures and related information to the general public. There is information about herbs, natural health cures, and midwifery. Tips, oxygen therapies and the role of light in health are but a few of the other topics addressed at this site. There is also a major links page to AIDS-related information.

KEYWORDS Alternative Medicine, Health Care, Midwifery
AUDIENCE Alternative Medicine Practitioners, Cancer Patients, Homeopathic Health Care Enthusiasts, Medical Educators
FREE

http://werple.mira.net.au/sumeria/health.html

The Alternative Medicine Home Page ★★★

The Alternative Medicine Home Page is designed as a jumping off point for alternative medicine resources, including homeopathy, massage, and herbal medicine. Users will find lists of newsgroups, mailing lists, and National Institute of Health addresses and contact names. Links to Alternative Medicine web sites are listed with brief descriptions of the contents of each site, as are the database links.

Keywords Herbal Remedies, Homeopathic Medicine, Meta-Indexes
Audience AIDS Patients, Alternative Medicine Practitioners, General Public
Contact Charles B. Wessel, M.L.S
cbw@med.pitt.edu
Free

http://www.pitt.edu/~cbw/altm.html

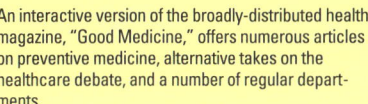 ## Good Medicine Online ★★★★

An interactive version of the broadly-distributed health magazine, "Good Medicine," offers numerous articles on preventive medicine, alternative takes on the healthcare debate, and a number of regular departments.

Keywords Alternative Medicine, Psychology
Audience Doctors, Insurance Professionals, Medical Practitioners, Medical Professionals
Free

http://none.coolware.com/health/good_med/NovIssue.html

Herb Hypercard Stack, Lund Institute of Technology ★★★

This gopher allows access to a downloadable hypercard stack containing information on various herbs. The Lund Institute of Technology forms the Technical Faculty of the University of Lund, Scandinavia's largest establishment for higher education and research.

Keywords Alternative Medicine, Herbal Remedies, Herbs
Audience Alternative Medicine Practitioners, Botanists, Herbalists, Homeopathic Health Care Enthusiasts
Free

gopher://nic.lth.se

Homeopathic Internet Resources List ★★★

This resource list contains information on Internet connections, files, lists, servers, and other online connections to homeopathy—all as an addendum to the 'regular' medical lists. The resources include the Homeopathic Network - Homeonet, libraries which contain homeopathic collections, private databases which can perform homeopathic reference searches, scientific research, homeopathic journals and organizations, and more.

Keywords Holistic Health, Homeopathic Medicine, Medical Resources, Medical Treatment

Connections to Alternative Treatments For Cancer
When traditional treatment fails

 - bar -
Welcome To The Life Extension Foundation

The Life Extension Foundation is **dedicated** to the pursuit of a longer, healthier lifespan. We provide our members with information about the **latest** life extension research, products and therapies. And we offer some of the **most advanced** life extension products in the world at **discount** prices.

- About The Foundation
- Health And Longevity Subjects
- Life Extension Products Catalog
- Life Extension Events

Many people diagnosed with cancer discover that the mainstream western medical treatments—predominantly chemotherapy and radiation—don't work for them. If you want to explore alternative treatments for cancer, you don't have to personally consult with an array of researchers and physicians.

You can access sites that offer advice and detailed information on treatment protocols such as herbal formulae, juice fasting, acupuncture, and others. At the "Life Extension Foundation" site, you'll find loads of information about alternative treatments for cancer, including information on where and from whom to find such treatment. If you live in the U.S., some of these treatments must be approved by the Food and Drug Administration. This site lets you know whether a given alternative treatment is approved for use in the U.S., and if it not, where you can obtain the treatment.

Aside from furnishing names and addresses of providers, the site also supplies cost information for a variety of treatments. Moreover, it maintains a virtual library of articles about different forms of treatment so that you can decide whether or not a particular one is right for you. In general, the Foundation urges users to consult a physician regarding alternative treatments for cancer.

(http://aeiveos.wa.com/lef/)

Audience Holistic Health Enthusiasts, Homeopathic Therapists, Medical Patients, Physicians
Contact Emiel van Galen, M.D.
evgalen@gn.apc.org
Free

http://www.dungeon.com/home/cam/interlst.html

Upcoming Events ★★★★

The upcoming events calendar for Alchemical Medicine Research and Teaching Association (AMRTA) invites contributions and submissions for conferences and events which fall under the domain of alternative medicine and natural healing. Typical events listed include the "3rd World Congress Of Medical Acupuncture and Natural Medicine" and the "Annual Women's Herbal Conference: Honoring the Wisdom of Our Bodies." At any given time, the site features listings for events scheduled up to six months down the road.

Keywords Conferences, Holistic Health

Audience Health Care Providers, Medical Practitioners, Medical Researchers
Contact amrta@amrta.org
Free

http://www.teleport.com/~amrta/events.html

Biomedicine

See also
Health & Medicine · *Medical Specialties*
Science · *Biology*
Science · *Biosciences*

Australian National University's Virus Database ★★

This server contains information on Australian plant viruses and host species. In addition, it provides access to other virus databases, as well as to a wealth of additional virology-related information.

KEYWORDS Genetics, Immunology, Molecular Biology, Virology
AUDIENCE Biomedical Researchers, Botanists, Immunologists, Virologists
FREE

http://life.anu.edu.au/./viruses/virus.html

CGS Biomedical Information Service ★★★
(Commercial)

CGS Biomedical Information Service is an information research company which searches major databases, library collections, the Internet and other resources, specializing in the areas of biomedicine, biotechnology, health care marketing, legal issues, and health related environmental toxicology. On this site users will find links to a description of services and a list of qualifications for the agency.

KEYWORDS Biomedicine, Biotechnology, Marketing, Medical Research
AUDIENCE Attorneys, Biotech Researchers, Health Care Professionals, Legal Professionals, Librarians, Marketing Firms
CONTACT Carole G. Stock
cgs@eskimo.com
FREE

http://www.eskimo.com/~cgs/

Department of Biochemistry of Case Western Reserve University ★★★

This site is a gopher server of the Department of Biochemistry at the School of Medicine of Case Western Reserve University in Cleveland, Ohio. Information is provided about graduate programs, complete with course descriptions, faculty research interests, and more. In addition, there are links to a wide range of BioGophers and biological databases.

KEYWORDS Biochemistry, Education (College/University), Medicine, Ohio
AUDIENCE Biochemists, Educators (University), Students (University)
CONTACT Ashok Aiyar
gopher@biochemistry.cwru.edu
FREE

gopher://biochemistry.bioc.cwru.edu/

EC Enzyme Database ★★★★

The Enzyme database contains information for characterized enzymes, including catalytic activity, cofactors, descriptions, and pointers to diseases associated with a deficiency of the enzyme. The database is searchable by key phrases.

KEYWORDS Bioinformatics, Biomedical Research, Databases, Protein
AUDIENCE Bioinformaticists, Biomedical Researchers, Biotechnologists, Medical Professionals
CONTACT Amos Bairoch
bairoch@cmu.unige.ch
FREE

http://www.gdb.org/Dan/proteins/ec-enzyme.html

Institute Pasteur ★★★★

The homepage of the Institute Pasteur in Paris contains information about the institute and its research activities, staff members, available training courses, a guide of the Paris campus, phone directory, and links to other biology servers.

KEYWORDS Bioinformatics, Genetics, Molecular Biology
AUDIENCE Bioinformaticists, Biologists, Biomedical Researchers, Molecular Biologists
FREE

http://www.pasteur.fr/welcome-uk.html

Jackson Laboratory ★★★★

This is a gopher server of the Jackson Laboratory—a non-profit, independent research institution, founded in 1929 by Dr. Clarence Cook Little. It contains information on the Jackson Laboratory, its research in the fields of basic biomedical sciences and genetics, software, and more. It also provides links to other biomedical gophers.

KEYWORDS Biomedical Research, Cancer, Genetics, Health Sciences
AUDIENCE Biomedical Researchers, Computer Professionals, Students (University)
FREE

gopher://hobbes.jax.org/

McGill Department of BioMedical Engineering ★★★

This is the information page for the BioMedical Engineering department at McGill University. It provides links to information on the Department, its graduate programs, labs, activities, and resources.

KEYWORDS Biomedical Engineering
AUDIENCE Canada Residents, Students (University)
CONTACT Rob Kearney
rob@neuron.biomed.mcgill.ca
FREE

http://www.biomed.mcgill.ca/

Microbiology & Cell Science Department Gopher ★★★

This server provides a collection of resources related to biology. These resources are mainly links to other gophers which have biological articles, databases, and other information useful for biologists.

KEYWORDS Agriculture, Cell Biology, Health Sciences, Microbiology
AUDIENCE Biochemists, Biologists, Health Science Researchers, Scientists
CONTACT Marian Buszko
marian@micro.ifas.ufl.edu
FREE

gopher://micro.ifas.ufl.edu/

The Millipore On-Line Catalog ★★★★
(Commercial)

This site is the online catalog of Millipore. Their products range from environmental testing devices to membranes and filtration systems. The database is searchable by a traditional table of contents as well as by an image-based table of contents. Each product has a detailed description page of qualifications as well as ordering information.

KEYWORDS Genetics, Immunology, Medical Supplies, Molecular Biology
AUDIENCE Biologists, Biomedical Researchers, Biotechnologists, Medical Researchers
CONTACT Dan Jacobson
danj@gdb.org
FREE

http://www.gdb.org/Dan/catal/milli-intro.html

Nanotechnology and Medicine ★★★

This article is a draft for an invited talk at a conference on anti-aging medicine and biomedical technology. Nanotechnology, "the manufacturing technology of the 21st century," is geared toward enabling us to build molecular tools which will repair damage at the molecular and cellular levels and therefore increase lifespan.

KEYWORDS Aging, Geriatrics, Medical Research, Nanotechnology
AUDIENCE Geriatric Specialists, Medical Professionals
CONTACT Ralph C. Merkle
merkle@xerox.com
FREE

ftp://ftp.parc.xerox.com/pub/nano/nanotechAndMedicine.html

National Biomedical Research Foundation ★★★

The University of Houston gopher allows FTP access to the University Gene-Server Software and data archive. The site includes an introduction to molecular graphics, computational molecular biology, and links to other biological gophers.

KEYWORDS Biomedicine, Graphics, Medical Research, Molecular Biology
AUDIENCE Academics, Biologists, Molecular Biologists, Scientists
CONTACT Bill Pearson, Don Gilbert
gene-server@bchs.uh.edu
FREE

gopher://ftp.bchs.uh.edu/

Biomedicine – Career & Employment   **371**

OMIM (Online Mendelian Inheritance in Man) ★★★★

OMIM links clinical medicine with research from the Human Genome Project. It entails a comprehensive catalog of human genes and genetic disorders with full text annotations on current genetic research and clinical disorders. OMIM augments the mapping information available in GDB with clinical references.

KEYWORDS	Bioinformatics, Genetics, Human Genome Project, Molecular Biology
AUDIENCE	Bioinformaticists, Biomedical Researchers, Biotechnologists, Clinicians
CONTACT	mimadm@gdb.org
FREE	

http://gdbwww.gdb.org/omimdoc/omimtop.html

PiHKAL—The Chemical Story ★★★★

This site makes available a body of information concerning the conception, synthesis, definition, and appropriate use of 179 consciousness-changing chemical compounds of the Phenethylamine family. This work is based on the book PiHKAL by Alexander and Ann Shulgin.

KEYWORDS	Drugs
AUDIENCE	Biochemists, Drug Users, Medical Researchers, Neurobiologists, Philosophers
CONTACT	Lamont Granquist lamontg@u.washington.edu
FREE	

http://www.hyperreal.com/drugs/pihkal/

Synapse Root Page ★★★★

This site uses a new software system to provide up-to-date biomedical information to researchers through multimedia (text, movies, and sound). The Synapse library is a demonstration library which contains documents—caremaps, clinical practice guidelines, clinical trial forms, medical education feedback tutorials, CancerNet, a sound library of heart sounds, as well as links to other medical Internet information, and other information resources. A sophisticated WWW search engine is also available.

KEYWORDS	Biomedical Research, Brain Research, Medical Libraries, Multimedia Resources
AUDIENCE	Biomedical Researchers, Health Care Professionals, Neurologists
CONTACT	synapse.info@ualberta.ca
FREE	

http://synapse.uah.ualberta.ca/

University of Southampton Biomedical World Wide Web Server ★★★

The University of Southampton Biomedical World Wide Web server provides medical information and background for the University of Southampton School of Medicine. Included here are the University of Southampton prospectus, U.K. medical site listings, with links to their home pages, and biomedical shareware for users to download. Links are also provided to statistical and biomedical information gophers, libraries and Web sites. Users may also link to the Southampton Biomedical WWW, Gopher, and general WWW servers to do further subject searches.

KEYWORDS	Biomedicine, Medical Reference, Microbiology
AUDIENCE	Biomedical Researchers, Medical Professionals, Medical Students
CONTACT	tnb@soton.ac.uk
FREE	

http://molbiol.soton.ac.uk/

WWW Server for Virology ★★★★

This server contains an extensive database of molecular virology information and tools, including news and journal articles, computer visualizations of viruses, topographical maps of viruses, sequences, alignments, phylogenetic trees, virus classifications, digitized images of viruses by electron microscope, phone books of virologists on the Internet, and many links to other servers. Also included are animations simulating a virus binding to a host cell receptor, and a flight inside a Rhinovirus 16 capsid.

KEYWORDS	Genetics, Immunology, Molecular Biology, Virology
AUDIENCE	Biomedical Researchers, Immunologists, Medical Professionals, Virologists
CONTACT	Stephan Spencer sspencer@rhino.bocklabs.wisc.edu
FREE	

http://www.bocklabs.wisc.edu/

Career & Employment

See also
Science · *Career & Employment*

Academic Physician and Scientist—Job Listings ★★★

Academic Physician and Scientist is the centralized resource for positions in academic medicine. It is mailed free of charge to every faculty physician, scientist, senior resident and fellow at 126 medical schools and their affiliated teaching hospitals. The online version of this publication lists jobs in broad categories such as administrative, basic science, and clinical science, with each category forming its own subclassifications such as Neurology, Emergency Medicine, and Microbiology.

KEYWORDS	Employment, Health Sciences, Job Listings, Medical Schools
AUDIENCE	Doctors, Health Care Professionals, Job Seekers
CONTACT	Laurie Powers, System Admin. +1 (916) 939-7516 lpowers@acad-phy-sci.com
FREE	

gopher://aps.acad-phy-sci.com/

MedSearch America ★★★★

MedSearch America is a major Internet employment advertising and communications network designed specifically for the Healthcare industry. MedSearch America offers detailed employer profiles, job listings, resume postings, industry and career resources, electronic communications, online career discussion groups, online exchange between employers and job seekers, and direct links with related government resources on the Internet. Jobs can be searched by Employer, Title, Location, Primary Industry, and by specific keyword. Some specific headings include Senior Scientist, Clinical Pharmicist, Nurse Practitioner, and Software Engineer.

KEYWORDS	Employment, Health Professions, Internships
AUDIENCE	Doctors, Health Care Professionals, Health Care Providers, Health Science Researchers, Human Resources Departments, Job Recruiters, Job Seekers, Nurses
CONTACT	office@medsearch.com
FREE	

http://www.medsearch.com/

gopher://garnet.msen.com:70/11/vendor/medsearch/

Nurse WWW Information Service ★★

This directory contains a number of resources for finding employment in nursing. Currently, there are very few actual listings on this site, but there are pointers to nursing related job lists in the United States, Canada, and England.

KEYWORDS	Canada, England, Health Professions
AUDIENCE	Health Care Professionals, Health Care Providers, Nurses
CONTACT	cudma@warwick.ac.uk
FREE	

http://www.csv.warwick.ac.uk:8000/

gopher://nurse.csv.warwick.ac.uk/11/jobs

Physicians Employment ★★

This site provides job listings in the U.S. for physicians of all specialties, and information on trends in the medical job market. At this writing, the site offers a form for entering name, specialty, desired area, and email, for later notification of opportunities by email.

KEYWORDS	Health Professions, Job Listings
AUDIENCE	Health Care Professionals, Job Seekers, Medical Students, Physicians
CONTACT	Lynn Waters physemp@fairfield.com
FREE	

http://www.fairfield.com/physemp/index.html

The Virtual Nursing Center ★★★★

The Virtual Nursing Center provides links to many different nursing related references. The topics covered include nursing schools, courses and education resources, graduate and undergraduate health science related courses, the reference desk, time and weather, what's new, browse, and search. There are also links to other virtual centers including medical,

Health & Medicine

pharmacy, veterinary, dental, public health, allied health and nutrition virtual centers.

Keywords Health Professions, Medical Professionals, Midwifery
Audience Health Care Officials, Health Care Professionals, Nurse Practitioners, Nurses, Nutritionists
Contact Jim Martindale
jmartindale@vmsa.oac.uci.edu
Free

http://www-sci.lib.uci.edu:80/~martindale/Nursing.html

Dental Health

See also
Health & Medicine · *Family Health*
Health & Medicine · *Personal Care*
Health & Medicine · *Resources*

Ask an Oral Surgeon ★★★

Ask an Oral Surgeon is a Home Page where lay people, dentists and oral surgeons are invited to ask questions about oral and maxillofacial surgery care. Each week a new question will be selected and answered. The answers are quite comprehensive. Topics discussed have included Tempersomandibular Joint Disease (TMJ), impacted wisdom teeth, and orthognathic and plastic surgery.

Keywords Dentistry, Surgery, Teeth
Audience Dental Patients, Dental Students, Dentists, Oral Surgeons
Contact Kim E. Goldman, DMD
kgoldman@cts.com
Free

http://metro.turnpike.net/O/OMFS/askomfs.html

Dalhousie University Division of Oral and Maxillofacial Radiology ★★★

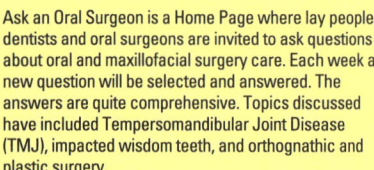

This is the home page of the Dalhousie University Division of Oral and Maxillofacial Radiology. This page offers links to radiology resources, other dental schools, radiation dosimetry and health physics, medical telecommunications and informatics, medical imaging research, listservs for radiology and dentistry, news groups for radiology and dentistry, journals and case studies for radiology, magnetic resonance imaging resources, nuclear medicine resources, and other medical resources. It also provides links to the Dalhousie University information page, various WWW references, and interesting and unusual WWW servers.

Keywords Dentistry, Medical Informatics, Radiology
Audience Canada Residents, Students (Secondary/College), Students (University)
Contact bpass@ac.dal.ca
Free

http://bpass.dentistry.dal.ca/

Dental Related Internet Resources ★★★★

This web site provides a comprehensive index to dental resources on the Internet, produced by the New York University School of Dentistry. Users will find links listed alphabetically under categories such as WWW and gopher sites of US and International dental schools, US Armed Forces sites, commercial and noncommercial sites, and telnet, ftp, listserves and bbs sites.

Keywords Meta-Indexes, New York
Audience Dental Patients, Dentists
Contact dentalweb@nyu.edu
Free

http://www.nyu.edu/Dental/intres.html

The Virtual Dental Center ★★★★

The Virtual Dental Center provides a variety of links to many different dental related references. The topics covered include dental schools, education resources, graduate and undergraduate health science related courses, the reference desk, time and weather, what's new, browse, and search. There are also links to other virtual centers including medical, pharmacy, veterinary, nursing, public health, allied health and nutrition virtual centers.

Keywords Aging, Dentistry, Teeth
Audience Dentists, Nurse Practitioners, Nurses, Pharmacists, Physicians, Veterinarians
Contact Jim Martindale
jmartindale@vmsa.oac.uci.edu
Free

http://www-sci.lib.uci.edu:80/~martindale/Dental.html

Disabilities

See also
Government & Politics · *Issues*
Health & Medicine · *Family Health*
Health & Medicine · *Health Conditions*

ABC Mobility ★★
(Commercial)

ABC Mobility's site describes a new product, an electric scooter - the PaceSaver Plus II, for individuals who cannot walk or have mobility problems. There is ordering information included if you wish to purchase one of their products.

Keywords Mobility Equipment, Product Information, Wheelchairs
Audience Disabled People, Seniors
Free

http://branch.com/abc/abc.html

Apple Computer's Worldwide Disability Solution ★★★★
(Commercial)

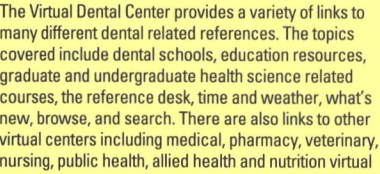

This site is the location of the Macintosh Disability Resources (MDR) database, Version 4.0. It includes 100 commercial products for the Macintosh, enabling computer access by people with disabilities. Each record contains a product description and developer contact information. This software includes tools for people who exhibit motor impairment, blindness, hearing and speech difficulties and/or people with learning disabilities. MDR (Macintosh Disability Resources) can be searched using either keywords, product name, developer's name, disability type or general description.

Keywords Computer Software, Disability Resources
Audience Blind People, Deaf & Disabled People
Contact Theresa Lara
ftp@apple.com
Free

ftp://ftp.apple.com/apple/disability_solutions/

The Arc's Home Page ★★★

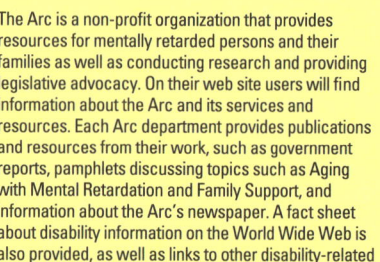

The Arc is a non-profit organization that provides resources for mentally retarded persons and their families as well as conducting research and providing legislative advocacy. On their web site users will find information about the Arc and its services and resources. Each Arc department provides publications and resources from their work, such as government reports, pamphlets discussing topics such as Aging with Mental Retardation and Family Support, and information about the Arc's newspaper. A fact sheet about disability information on the World Wide Web is also provided, as well as links to other disability-related web sites.

Keywords Mental Retardation, Non Profit Organizations
Audience Disabled People, Families, Health Care Providers, Mentally Handicapped People
Contact thearc@metronet.com
Free

http://fohnix.metronet.com/~thearc/welcome.html

CSHSD (Centre for the Study of Health, Sickness and Disablement) Main Index ★★★★

This site mainly provides information about the Centre for the Study of Health, Sickness and Disablement at Brunel University, where the focus of research interests is on motor neuron diseases and neuropathies. Information covers the Centre's faculty, current research, and other biomedical information resources available on the Internet. The site offers archived issues of the research group, as well as access to the University of Alberta's medical library with detailed information on neuromuscular diseases and disorders (including etiology, diagnosis, prognosis and treatment). In addition, the research group provides a list of relevant publications, as well as a recent publication list for other scientists and physicians in the field. The site also makes available computer-assisted qualitative analysis programs (e.g. for modelling survival rates) and specific information about Brunel University.

Keywords Biomedical Research, Disabilities, Medical Research, Neuromuscular Disorders
Audience Biomedical Researchers, Health Care Professionals, Medical Professionals, Neurologists
Contact Stuart Neilson
stuart.neilson@brunel.ac.uk
Free

http://http1.brunel.ac.uk:8080/~hssrsdn/home.html

Cornucopia of Disability Information

CODI is a gopher site, intended to serve as a community resource for consumers and professionals by providing disability-related information in many areas. Some of the information provided includes publications, government services, and employment services.

Keywords   Community Information, Disabilities, Employment
Audience   Disabled People, Health Care Professionals, Physical Therapists, Seniors
Contact   Jay Leavitt
leavitt@ubvmsb.cc.buffalo.edu
Free

gopher://val-dor.cc.buffalo.edu/

Deaf Gopher

The Deaf Gopher provides information about hearing disorders and resources for deaf people. Users will find the information divided into six sections—educational, electronic, Michigan State, Michigan, and General deaf resources and information, and a Deaf Alert with student projects. Before going to the gopher, users may look at brief descriptions of the resources that exist there. A list of other Deaf WWW servers is also included.

Keywords   Deafness, Disability Resources
Audience   Deaf People, Health Care Professionals
Contact   Gary LaPointe
gary@ah3.cal.msu.edu
Free

http://web.cal.msu.edu/deaf/deafintro.html

gopher://burrow.cl.msu.edu/11/msu/dept/deaf

Deaf World Web

The Deaf World Web is designed to be a resource for both deaf and hearing people, including both medical resources and social materials. Cultural information includes deaf-related literature, articles on deaf events, sports news, and databases of sign languages around the world. The References section provides information about organizations and services for deaf people around the world, including media, arts and entertainment, and technology. The Researcher's Forum allows sign linguistics researchers to access materials from research groups all over the world.

Keywords   Deafness, Disability Resources, Linguistics
Audience   Deaf People, General Public, Health Care Professionals
Contact   Jolanta Lapiak
mernix@computel.com
Free

http://www.computel.com/deafworld/

Disabilities Resources

The Disabilities Resources gopher, provided by the University of Maryland, provides resources and information about various disabilities. Users will find adaptive computing and software information, federal and governmental materials and legislature, calendars of disability events, and employment information. A large archive of newsletters, articles and publications relating to disabilities is also included, grouped by subject. Also included is a list of other Internet resources for people with disabilities and disability researchers.

Keywords   Disability Resources, Handicapped People
Audience   Disabled People, Health Care Professionals, Health Care Providers
Contact   consult@umail.umd.edu
Free

gopher://gopher.inform.umd.edu/11/Educational_Resources/AcademicResourcesByTopic/DisabilityResources

Connections to Dental FAQs
The tooth of the matter is . . .

> Martindale's Health Science Guide - '95
> New URL This Page: http://www-sci.lib.uci.edu/HSG/Dental.html
>
> THE "VIRTUAL"- DENTAL CENTER
>
> A "Dental Multimedia Education and Specialized Information Resource Center". Currently the Dental Center contains:
>
> - Metabolic Pathways & Genetic Maps
> - Dental Anatomy & Interactive Anatomy Browsers
> - On-Line Dental Journals & Newsletters
> - Law & Finance - Dental
> - Dental
>   - Dental Schools - Complete Curriculum
>   - Teaching Files & Cases
>   - Courses, Textbooks & Modules
>   - General
>   - Images
>   - Drug Database's & Information
> - Dental Reference Resources
>   - Dental Associations
>   - Dental Profession on the WEB
>   - Dental Schools on the WEB
>   - Dental Reference On the WEB
> - Time & Weather; What's New; Browse; Search
>
> - The Reference Desk; Home Page

So you're thinking about becoming a dentist. Or maybe you just have some questions about dental care. You can get a listing of dental schools around the world as well as dental FAQs (frequently asked questions) at the "Dental Center" site on the World Wide Web. Here you'll access a list of dental schools, curriculums, dental images and a Dental Multimedia Education and Specialized Information Resource area.

(http://www-sci.lib.uci.edu/~martindale/Dental.html)

also, (http://www-sci.lib.uci.edu/HSG/Dental.html)

If you are a dentist just starting out, you can access "The Dental Buying Network" to find out where to order supplies (like the drill bits we all know and love). From this site you'll get a catalog offering supplies and equipment at a 10% to 20% savings.

(http://userwww.service.emory.edu/~bshap02/)

Disability Information Gopher

This is a gopher menu which provides many links to disability-related information. Some of the topics include national information sources on disabilities, Digest of Data on Persons with Disabilities 1992, coming to terms with disabilities, government documents, a directory of independent living centers, employment information, etc. Although some of the sites are primarily applicable to New York and Buffalo students, many are useful for the general public.

Keywords   Disabilities, Disability Resources, Independent Living Centers, Physical Therapy
Audience   Disabled People, Employees, Health Care Professionals, Students (University)
Free

gopher://val-dor.cc.buffalo.edu:70/1

Disabilities – Diseases

Disability Resources on the Web ★★★

The Disabilities Home Page is designed as a metaindex to disability and health resources on the Web. Links are listed by category, such as legal, international, educational, commercial, and other resources, in the order in which they have been added. Users may also access the Disability Mall from this site, wherein they may look at specific products designed by Evan Kemp Associates for disabled persons.

KEYWORDS: Handicapped People, Medical Assistance, Meta-Index (Disabilities)
AUDIENCE: Disabled People, Health Care Professionals, Health Care Providers
CONTACT: webmaster@eka.com
FREE

http://disability.com/cool.html

The Disabled Students of Stanford World Wide Web Page ★★★★

The Disabled Students of Stanford Web page is a resource for people going to Stanford University who have either physical or learning disabilities. Items on this site include local events which involve the differently-abled community. These include ski trips and adaptive aerobics, speakers, general information concerning disabilities, products and services available, information about other universities' disability sites and programs, and a legal section which includes the text of the Americans with Disabilities Act.

KEYWORDS: Alternative Education, Disability Resources, Learning Disabilities
AUDIENCE: Disabled People, Learning Disabled, Students (University)
CONTACT: Michelle Cooke
mcooke@pangea.stanford edu
FREE

http://www-leland.standford.edu/group/dss

Easter Seals OnLine ★★★

This is the site of The Easter Seal Society of Ontario, Canada which helps children with physical disabilities. Topics covered include profiles of the children it serves, programs and services, special events, the research institute, donating information, volunteering opportunities, contact information, and a newsletter.

KEYWORDS: Canada, Children's Programs, Disability Resources, Non Profit Organizations
AUDIENCE: Business Professionals, Children, Deaf & Disabled People, Grantmakers, Grantseekers, Volunteers
FREE

http://www.cyberplex.com/CyberPlex/EasterSeals.html

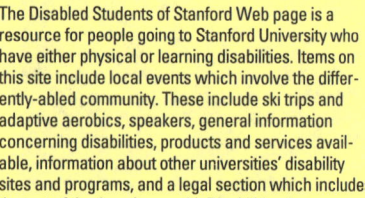

Evan Kemp Associates Disability Resources ★★★

The Disability Home Page offers access to products and services through the Disability Mall, as well as access to political and economic resources through the Disability Marketing Group. There is also consumer protection information, a newsletter serving the needs of the disabled community, and a list of links to related Internet resources.

KEYWORDS: Consumer Protection, Disabilities, Disability Resources
AUDIENCE: Disabled People, Families, Health Care Professionals
CONTACT: webmaster@eka.com
FREE

http://disability.com/

Handicapped Information ★★★★

This site provides access to an extensive archive of information for and about individuals with disabilities and/or handicaps. There are over a hundred files in this server covering such topics as the American Council of the Blind, Americans with Disabilities Act, amputee related files and newsletters, deaf/blind information, Down Syndrome, Special Olympics, handicapped people in the news, strokes/head injuries information, and much more.

KEYWORDS: Computer Technology, Disabilities, Handicaps, Social Issues
AUDIENCE: Disabled People, Medical Patients
CONTACT: Bill
wtm@sheldev.shel.isc-br.com
FREE

ftp://ftp.halcyon.com/pub/handicap/

The Hyperlexia Page ★★★★

The Hyperlexia Web page is an excellent resource for lay people concerned with any of the rare disabilities in the autism spectrum, i.e. PDD, Hyperlexia, and Asperger's Syndrome. The focus is on hyperlexia, a disability which involves very early reading development combined with odd language development and learning and social anomalies. The site has links to articles defining the syndrome, information on schooling, mediation techniques and other online and offline resources.

KEYWORDS: Autism, Hyperlexia, Learning Disabilities, Speech Therapy
AUDIENCE: Health Care Professionals, Parents, Special Education Teachers
CONTACT: Ted and Julie Whaley
whaley@iac.net
FREE

http://www.iac.net/~whaley/gordy.html

Information Technology and Disabilities ★★★

Information Technology and Disabilities is a refereed journal focusing on the development and effective use of new and emerging technologies by computer users with disabilities. Founded by EASI (Equal Access to Software and Information), topics include issues affecting rehabilitation counselors, human resources professionals, and developers of adaptive computer hardware and software products.

KEYWORDS: Disabilities, Disability Resources, Journals
AUDIENCE: Disabled People, Mechanical Engineers, Physical Therapists

FREE

gopher://sjuvm.stjohns.edu/

Trace Center ★★★

This gopher provides information about the Trace Center at the University of Wisconsin, Madison. The Trace Center researches and develops assistive technology for the disabled. Their server offers information on the Center, their outreach programs, papers and publications, software, updates, datasets, the cooperative electronic library, and more. It has links to other disability and rehabilitation resources.

KEYWORDS: Computer Applications, Education (College/University), Software
AUDIENCE: Computer Professionals, Computer Users, Consumers
CONTACT: Bonnie Caparoon
FREE

gopher://trace.waisman.wisc.edu/

The UCLA Disabilities and Computing Program (DCP) ★★★

The UCLA Disabilities and Computing Program (DCP) provides adaptive computing support services to UCLA students, faculty and staff with disabilities, and to campus departments and computing facilities. It provides access to computers, networks and online information. The UCLA DCP Gopher focuses on locally developed resources—publications, planning documents, annual reports, etc.

KEYWORDS: Computing, Disabilities, Education (College/University)
AUDIENCE: Computer Students, Computer Users, Disabled People
CONTACT: Daniel Hilton-Chalfen
hilton-chalfen@mic.ucla.edu
FREE

gopher://gopher.mic.ucla.edu:4334/

Diseases

See also
Health & Medicine · *Health Conditions*
Health & Medicine · *Sexually Transmitted Diseases*

A Book of Basics for Patients ★★★★

This is an online book on Bone Marrow Transplants written for patients. The contents include information about bone marrow, types of transplants, preparing for the transplant, blood cell production, childhood neuroblastoma, Hodgkin's and non-Hodgkin's lymphomas, leukemia, being a donor, being there for the patient, the sibling donor, infections, infertility, insurance issues, and much more.

KEYWORDS: Cancer, Cancer Research, Oncology, Pediatrics
AUDIENCE: Bone Marrow Donors, Cancer Patients, Parents, Physicians, Radiologists, Therapists

FREE
http://cancer.med.upenn.edu:80/0h/
chemo/bmt/contents

AHCPR Quick Reference Guide - Management of Cancer Pain in Adults ★★★

This site contains links to the contents of the AHCPR Quick Reference Guide—Management of Cancer Pain in Adults. The contents of this guide include pain assessment, invasive interventions, treating cancer pain in the elderly, and more. The Clinical Practice Guideline on which this Quick Reference Guide for Clinicians is based was developed by an interdisciplinary, private-sector panel comprised of health care professionals and consumer representatives.

KEYWORDS   Cancer, Medical Research, Oncology
AUDIENCE   Cancer Patients, Clinicians, Health Care Professionals, Oncologists
FREE
http://cancer.med.upenn.edu:80/0h/
med_onc/pain_manage2.html

AIDS Information ★★★

The AIDS section of the gopher of the National Institute of Allergy and Infectious Disease (NIAID) provides background and care information for AIDS patients and doctors. Users will find information about how to nurse HIV/AIDS, CDC daily summaries, and resources from local, national, and international communities. Also included are medical and government AIDS newsletters and reports on AIDS research and disease care.

KEYWORDS   AIDS (Acquired Immune Deficiency Syndrome), Infectious Diseases, Sexually Transmitted Diseases
AUDIENCE   AIDS Activists, AIDS Patients, AIDS Researchers, General Public
FREE
gopher://odie.niaid.nih.gov:70/11/aids

Alzheimer Web Home Page ★★★

This page is a collection of resources concerning Alzheimer's Disease. Users may follow links to research labs, articles written by researchers, news items, and other pages devoted to this affliction.

KEYWORDS   Alzheimer's Disease, Brain Research, Gerontology, Neurobiology
AUDIENCE   Alzheimer's Disease Sufferers, Health Care Professionals, Neurobiologists, Neuroscientists
CONTACT   David Small
          david_small@muwayf.unimelb.edu.au
FREE
http://werple.mira.net.au/~dhs/ad.html

Assessment and Management Tools ★★

This cancer-oriented document contains pain intensity scales organized by simple descriptive and numeric variables (i.e. "no pain" to "worst possible pain") and a

Connections to Disabilities Resources
The world is your oyster

Perhaps the largest collection anywhere of information and resources for people with disabilities can be found on the Internet.

Disabilities resources sites like the "American Disabilities Association," and "Internet Resources for People with Disabilities" provide a full array of services: from World Wide Web sites on where to find disability resources, to information on how to use the Internet, to information on connecting to other people with disabilities around the world.

Through "Internet Resources for People with Disabilities" you can locate general information through sites as varied as the "Down Syndrome Resource," "Blazie Engineering Products for Blind People," and the "Disabilities Directory." You can also find information on education and computer-related disabilities solutions from Apple Computer, Inc. and IBM. This site provides you with access to disabilities resources in such places as Japan, Australia, Germany, and Ireland, as well as the U.S.

The Francophone Resources from France, delivered in both English and French, provides information and education on a number of disabilities topics including blindness, deafness, and other health matters.

(http://lib-www.lib.indiana.edu:8080/resource/easi.html)

Through "Untangling the Web" you'll find information about disability legislation and related laws, advances in treatment of orthopedic, visual, and hearing disabilities, and special education courses. This site also provides a wealth of information on employment opportunities, as well as World Health Handicap News. You can meet friends around the world and learn about new treatments and technologies designed for people with physical, emotional, and learning disabilities. And if you're interested in the transplantation and donation of organs, the Internet provides information for medical professionals and lay persons alike.

(http://www.icdi.wvu.edu/Others.html)

also, (http://www.sped.ukans.edu/speddisabilitiesstuff/speddisabilities-welcome.html)

Diseases

brief inventory form to be filled out by the patient discussing mood, activities, relationships, etc.
KEYWORDS Cancer, Oncology, Patient Resources
AUDIENCE Cancer Patients, Clinicians, Parents, Physicians, Radiologists, Therapists
FREE

http://cancer.med.upenn.edu:80/med_onc/pain_refguide.html

BMT (Bone Marrow Transplant) Newsletters ★★★★

This site contains a collection of 'BMT Newsletters' organized by date, issue number, and subjects in each issue. Subjects include families sharing their stories, BMT's for acute myelogenous leukemia, transplants offering hope to breast cancer patients, stem cell vs. bone marrow transplant, and support groups offering help and hope.
KEYWORDS Cancer, Newsletters, Oncology, Surgery
AUDIENCE Cancer Patients, Families, Health Care Professionals, Oncologists
FREE

http://cancer.med.upenn.edu:80/1s/chemo/bmt/newsletter

Blood Test for Breast and Prostate Cancer ★★★

This document is a brief review of the findings of research into tumor markers that could possibly be used in blood tests for screening and monitoring of breast and prostate cancer. The article is comprised for the most part of extracts from the research findings of Dr. Margaret Hanausek, a faculty member in the Department of Carcinogenesis at the University of Texas.
KEYWORDS Breast Cancer, Medical Research, Prostate Cancer
AUDIENCE Biochemists, Biologists, Health Educators, Medical Practitioners, Medical Researchers, Men, Women
CONTACT Ellen Mayou
ellen_mayou@isqm.mda.uth.tmc.edu
FREE

http://utmdacc.mda.uth.tmc.edu:5003/FALL94/blood.html

Bone Marrow Transplant ★★★

This site provides links to information on Bone Marrow Transplants (BMT) and is patient-oriented. The subjects include what parents should know, risks, benefits, and alternatives to bone marrow transplant. There is a pediatric version for parents, a section on bone marrow donor's experiences, and more.
KEYWORDS Cancer, Oncology, Patient Resources, Surgery
AUDIENCE Cancer Patients, Oncologists, Parents, Radiologists
FREE

http://cancer.med.upenn.edu:80/1s/chemo/bmt

Breast Cancer Information Clearinghouse ★★★

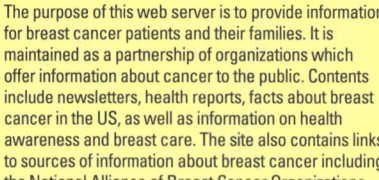

The purpose of this web server is to provide information for breast cancer patients and their families. It is maintained as a partnership of organizations which offer information about cancer to the public. Contents include newsletters, health reports, facts about breast cancer in the US, as well as information on health awareness and breast care. The site also contains links to sources of information about breast cancer including the National Alliance of Breast Cancer Organizations (NABCO).
KEYWORDS Breast Cancer, Health, Women's Issues
AUDIENCE Breast Cancer Patients, Educators, Health Care Professionals, Women
FREE

http://nysernet.org/bcic/

Cancer Information Gopher Server ★★★

This is a gopher server of the University of Pennsylvania School of Medicine in Philadelphia, focusing on cancer information for both the health care professional and the patient. The site offers information about cancer news, meeting announcements, and clinical trials with disease or specialty oriented menus (breast cancer, lung cancer, radiation oncology, pain management, etc.). There are also listings of psychosocial support groups, cancer organizations, and spirituality support groups for patients and caregivers.
KEYWORDS Cancer, Medical Research, Oncology, Patient Resources
AUDIENCE Cancer Patients, Health Care Professionals, Medical Researchers, Oncologists
CONTACT E. Loren Buhle, Jr.
editors@oncolink.upenn.edu
FREE

gopher://cancer.med.upenn.edu:70/11/

CancerGuide ★★★

CancerGuide is designed to be a cancer information resource for cancer patients and a guide providing instructions for accessing research materials. Using either the Tour of CancerGuide or a table of contents, users may access all types of cancer resources. Included here are articles on cancer and statistics, understanding cancer, a list of recommended books, and guides to cancer centers and service organizations. "How To's" include information about researching cancer and accessing medical databases. Other sections provide materials about specific types of cancer, as well as information about alternative therapies and links to information from the MedLine database.
KEYWORDS Cancer, Cancer Research
AUDIENCE Cancer Specialists, Cancer Sufferers, Health Care Professionals
CONTACT Steve Dunn
dunns@bcn.boulder.co.us
FREE

http://bcn.boulder.co.us/health/cancer/canguide.html

CancerNet Web ★★★

The CancerNet Web was designed to allow users to access cancer information from the National Cancer Institute (NCI) of America. Users will find the Physicians Data Query database statements, listed alphabetically by disease, and choose from information listed specifically for either physicians or patients. Materials include treatment, screening, drug, and support information, as well as cancer fact sheets from the NCI.
KEYWORDS Cancer, Cancer Research
AUDIENCE Cancer Specialists, Cancer Sufferers, Health Care Professionals
CONTACT cheryl@icicb.nci.nih.gov
FREE

http://biomed.nus.sg/Cancer/welcome.html

gopher://biomed.nus.sg:70/11/NUS-NCI-CancerNet/

Cansearch—A Guide to Cancer Resources ★★★

Written by a twelve year survivor of cancer, this text document explains, at an introductory level, how to search the Net specifically for cancer information toward becoming "more informed patients and caretakers." The site provides relevant links to outside sites, "what you need to know about your cancer before you search," instructions on effective keyword searches, and other tips (this step-by-step process could be applied to searches in other subject areas).
KEYWORDS Cancer, Diseases, Internet Guides, Medical Education
AUDIENCE Cancer Patients, Health Care Professionals, Internet Users, Physicians
CONTACT Marshall Kragen
mkragen@access.digex.net
FREE

http://www.access.digex.net/~mkragen/cansearch.html

Chemotherapy ★★★

This site provides a list of linked information on chemotherapy, and is intended for patients as well as medical professionals. Some of the subjects include an overview of chemotherapy (patient-oriented), drug precautions for patients, hot pepper candy found to help chemotherapy effects, the new taxoid docetaxel, chemotherapeutic agents used in bladder cancer, and findings on resistance to chemotherapy in cases of ovarian cancer.
KEYWORDS Cancer, Chemotherapy, Oncology, Patient Resources
AUDIENCE Cancer Patients, Health Care Professionals, Oncologists, Pharmacologists
FREE

http://cancer.med.upenn.edu:80/1s/chemo

Dana-Farber Cancer Institute Gopher Server ★★★

This gopher server gives information about the Dana-Farber Cancer Institute at Harvard University. The information includes online phone and email directories, employment opportunities, summaries of research programs, and links to other gophers at Harvard and elsewhere.

KEYWORDS   Cancer, Medical Administration, Medical Research, Organizations
AUDIENCE   Cancer Specialists, Health Care Professionals, Medical Professionals, Medical Researchers
FREE

gopher://farber.dfci.harvard.edu/

Diabetes Knowledgebase ★★★★

The Diabetes Knowledgebase contains a variety of links to areas focusing on diabetes control and complications trials, diabetic eye disease, insulin-dependent diabetes, noninsulin dependent diabetes, and glycemic index.

KEYWORDS   Diabetes, Diseases, Medical Research
AUDIENCE   Diabetics, Health Care Professionals, Physicians
CONTACT   Donald A. Lehn, Ph.D.
           dalehn@facstaff.wisc.edu
FREE

http://www.biostat.wisc.edu/diaknow/index.html

Do Power Lines Cause Cancer? ★★★

This Powerlines—Cancer FAQ is a document that offers scientific and medical discussion of the assertion that electromagnetic fields generated by high-tension power lines cause cancer.

KEYWORDS   Cancer, Medicine
AUDIENCE   Health Care Professionals, Researchers
FREE

ftp://rtfm.mit.edu/pub/usenet/sci.answers/powerlines-cancer-FAQ/

Fred Hutchinson Cancer Research Center Gopher ★★★

This gopher hole is an information resource about cancer. It is maintained by the Fred Hutchinson Cancer Research Center Gopher (FHCRC), a cancer research institute in Seattle, Washington. The resources include FHCRC news, seminar dates, grants and funding information, and research news.

KEYWORDS   Cancer, Diseases, Health Care, Medical Research
AUDIENCE   Health Care Professionals, Health Care Providers, Medical Researchers
CONTACT   Michael Parker
           mparker@fhcrc.org
FREE

gopher://gopher.fhcrc.org/

German Cancer Research Center ★★★★

This site contains medical and biological information concerning cancer and cancer research. Projects like HELIOS-2 - the Advanced Informatics in Medicine project of the European Commission's research program can be accessed here. Additional resources include information on research in Cell Kinetics, collections of scientific images, papers, and technical reports. The site also contains links to other medical servers including Medline and additional national research centers in Germany.

KEYWORDS   Cancer, Germany, Medical Research
AUDIENCE   Cancer Patients, Educators, Health Care Professionals, Medical Students, Oncologists, Researchers
CONTACT   MBI@DKFZ-Heidelberg.de
FREE

http://mbi.dkfz-heidelberg.de/

Connections to AIDS Resources
From testing to treatment options

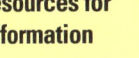

Today, some 350,000 people have died from Acquired Immune Deficiency Syndrome, while millions more are infected with HIV, the virus that causes AIDS. If you have questions about this disease or the virus, the Internet provides a wealth of information gathered from around the world.

Through sci.med.aids of the AIDS FAQ (frequently asked questions), you'll find a question and answer article which addresses commonly asked questions such as "How to prevent infection?", "How is AIDS transmitted?", "How risky is a blood transfusion?", and "Can mosquitoes or other insects transmit HIV?"

The site also provides treatment options and a guide to Social Security Benefits for U.S. citizens. Moreover, you can explore various theories about HIV—from speculation that it's a manmade disease to the possibility that the virus occurs naturally in the human body and is activated by certain behaviors and lifestyles.

(http://www.con.ohio-state.edu/aidsrscs.html)

AIDS is growing fastest among women, as well as for the age group between 25-44. So where can you get information on treatment, hospice care, drugs, and vaccine trials? The Internet's MedWeb: AIDS and HIV pages provide a clearinghouse of information on studies being run around the world, on available treatments, and on hospice care. The site also furnishes access to support groups for those infected, as well as for their caregivers. The Red Ribbon project of MedWeb also provides a place to talk with others about the disease and to get a list of AIDS service organizations in the U.S., Europe, Australia, and Japan.

(http://www.cc.emory.edu/WHSCL/medweb.aids.html)

Global Resources for Cancer Information ★★★★

Global Resources for Cancer Information provides numerous links to extensive cancer-related information. The subjects range from government sites, associations and support groups, to electronic references, hospitals, universities and institutes.

KEYWORDS   Breast Cancer, Cancer, Cancer Research
AUDIENCE   Cancer Patients, Health Care Professionals, Nurses, Physicians

Diseases

FREE

http://cancer.med.upenn.edu/stuff/index.html

H. Lee Moffitt Cancer Center & Research Institute Home Page ★★★

This is the home page for the H. Lee Moffitt Cancer Center & Research Institute at the University of South Florida. It contains links to information on research, education, and links to other cancer related sites. The mission of Moffitt Cancer Center is to contribute to the prevention and cure of cancer. The Moffitt Cancer Center is supported by the teaching and research activities of the USF College of Medicine. The progressive university medical center environment offers patients and the community superior opportunities and advantages in the areas of education, research, detection, diagnosis and treatment.

KEYWORDS   Cancer, Cancer Research, Medical Schools, Oncology
AUDIENCE   Cancer Specialists, Medical Researchers, Medical Students, Oncologists, Physicians
CONTACT   costa@palm.moffitt.usf.edu
FREE

http://daisy.moffitt.usf.edu/

HIV/AIDS Information ★★★

HIV/AIDS Information is a clearinghouse for relevant resources on the Internet. This site provides links to a range of outside resources such as an archive of FAQs from sci.med.aids, an archive of daily AIDS-related news, and semi-annual AIDS statistics from the World Health Organization. There are also links to sites dedicated to political or personal issues, such as ACTUP/Boston and Positive Planet, a Gay and HIV dating magazine, and HIV treatment catalogue.

KEYWORDS   AIDS (Acquired Immune Deficiency Syndrome), FAQs (Frequently Asked Questions), Health Statistics, Internet Directories
AUDIENCE   AIDS Activists, AIDS Researchers, AIDS Sufferers, Gays
CONTACT   QRDstaff@vector.casti.com
FREE

http://www.qrd.org/qrd/www/AIDS.html

Hemochromatosis Disease ★★★

This site gives a brief description of a genetic disorder, hemochromatosis. Hemochromatosis is a disease in which excess iron is absorbed causing accumulation and damage to the joints and vital organs. The information is provided by the Hemochromatosis Foundation which will provide further materials for a minimal charge.

KEYWORDS   Diseases, Genetics, Hemochromatosis
AUDIENCE   Doctors, General Public, Geneticists
FREE

http://branch.com/hemo/hemo.html

Introduction to Breast Cancer ★★★★

This document entails a synopsis of information obtained from the American Cancer Society on breast cancer. It includes general topics such as screening and detection, risk factors, diagnosis, treatment, and psychological considerations. It presents statistical and clinical information on staging and classifying tumors and nodes.

KEYWORDS   Breast Cancer, Cancer Research, Societies, Women's Health
AUDIENCE   Breast Cancer Patients, Health Care Professionals, Women
FREE

http://cancer.med.upenn.edu/Oh/disease/breast/breast-intro.html

Iron and Cancer ★★★

This site provides a short list of some of the pertinent abstracts from a MEDLINE search (1990-1994 references) on iron and cancer. This search stemmed from a question regarding taking iron supplements during/after chemotherapy. No conclusion or opinion is rendered in this listing. Some of the topics covered include body iron stores and risk of colonic neoplasia, suppression of colonic cancer by dietary phytic acid, dietary iron and colorectal cancer risk, and more.

KEYWORDS   Cancer, Chemotherapy, Diet
AUDIENCE   Cancer Patients, Clinicians, Parents, Physicians, Radiologists, Therapists
FREE

http://cancer.med.upenn.edu:80/buhle/chemo/iron_cancer.html

MS Direct Multiple Sclerosis Support ★★★

MS Direct is designed as a guide to Multiple Sclerosis resources on the Internet. Users will find links to Web sites, newsgroups, and BBS's regarding Multiple Sclerosis and other disabilities. Links are listed alphabetically with descriptions of the content of each site. Information about bike rides in support of MS is also provided.

KEYWORDS   Disabilities, Multiple Sclerosis
AUDIENCE   Disability Sufferers, Health Care Professionals, Multiple Sclerosis Sufferers
CONTACT   Dean Sporleder
   dean.sporleder@aquila.com
FREE

http://www.aquila.com/dean.sporleder/ms_home/

Massachusetts General Hospital Functional and Stereotactic Neurosurgery Home Page ★★★

This page presents some of the resources available at the Massachusetts General Hospital Neurosurgical Service. Biographical and contact information about the staff of neurosurgeons is available, including a list of specialists in Parkinson's Disease, chronic pain syndromes, and medically refractory psychiatric diseases. In addition, users can access files about Parkinson's disease, such as the Hoehn and Yahr severity test and articles about pallidotomy. Additional links to outside resources related to Parkinson's Disease and neurosurgery are also available on this page.

KEYWORDS   Hospitals, Neurology, Neurosurgery, Parkinson's Disease
AUDIENCE   Doctors, Health Care Providers, Parkinson's Disease Patients
CONTACT   GateKeeper C. Owen
   owen@helix.mgh.harvard.edu
FREE

http://neurosurgery.mgh.harvard.edu/fnctnlhp.html

Medical Oncology ★★★★

This site contains a list of links to a plethora of cancer-related information. While most of the documents are geared towards the medical community, some are specifically slated as patient-oriented. Some of the topics covered include Bone Marrow Transplant Information (Patient), Assessment and Management Tools for Pain, Chemotherapy, Current Literature, Colorectal Cancer, Therapy of Metastatic Melanoma with Monoclonal Antibodies, and Recommendations on Vitamins, Minerals & Trace Elements.

KEYWORDS   Cancer, Internet Guides, Oncology, Patient Resources
AUDIENCE   Cancer Patients, Oncologists, Radiologists, Therapists
FREE

http://cancer.med.upenn.edu/1s/med_onc

The National Cancer Center Entry Point ★★★

The National Cancer Center Entry Point furnishes links to cancer archives and documents. The page makes connections to the Physician Data Query (PDQ) database that has treatment summaries for health professionals and for patients. There are links to other Japanese and WWW sites.

KEYWORDS   Cancer, Information Resources, Research
AUDIENCE   Cancer Patients, Doctors
CONTACT   www-admin@gan.ncc.go.jp
FREE

http://www.ncc.go.jp

National Institute of Diabetes and Digestive and Kidney Disease (NIDDK) ★★★

The National Institute of Diabetes and Digestive and Kidney Disease (NIDDK) WWW server provides links to a list of patient information documents on subjects including diabetes, digestive diseases and nutrition, endocrine disorders, kidney disorders, and urologic disorders.

KEYWORDS   Diabetes, Digestive Diseases, Kidney Diseases, Patient Resources
AUDIENCE   Diabetics, Health Care Professionals, Patients, Physicians
FREE

http://www.niddk.nih.gov/NIDDK_HomePage.html

The Nature of Cancer ★★★★

This document discusses the nature of cancer and is geared towards medical professionals. Topics include characteristics of malignant cells, carcinogenesis, disease process, staging, and classification of tumors.

KEYWORDS Cancer, Medical Research, Oncology
AUDIENCE Cancer Patients, Health Care Professionals, Oncologists, Radiologists
FREE

http://cancer.med.upenn.edu:80/med_onc/nature_cancer.html

Nutritional Support in Cancer (Patient Oriented) ★★

This document discusses nutritional support for cancer patients written for the patient. Subjects include Nutritional Effects of Cancer such as anorexia, cachexia (a metabolic problem), weight loss, sodium and potassium losses, Nutritional Effects of Therapy including surgery, Resection of the Oral Cavity, as well as stomach, small intestine, radiation treatment and resulting injury, and more.

KEYWORDS Cancer, Nutrition, Oncology, Vitamins
AUDIENCE Cancer Patients, Clinicians, Parents, Physicians, Radiologists, Therapists
FREE

http://cancer.med.upenn.edu:80/med_onc/nutri_support.html

Pain Exercises for Cancer ★★★

This document provides simple exercises for cancer patients to learn pain managment techniques. Descriptions and exercises are given for each category.

KEYWORDS Cancer, Oncology, Patient Resources
AUDIENCE Cancer Patients, Clinicians, Parents, Physicians, Radiologists, Therapists
FREE

http://cancer.med.upenn.edu:80/med_onc/pain_exercise.html

Pallidotomy Restores Mobility to Parkinson's Patient ★★

This page, taken from the Massachusetts General Hospital Functional and Stereotactic Neurosurgery Service (MGH), provides interested viewers with an article about Pallidotomy, a procedure which may be used for treating patients with Parkinson's Disease. This article is taken from the hospital newsletter and highlights a sucessful use of the operation in treating a patient at MGH. This article provides some background information about pallidotomy for the layperson.

KEYWORDS Hospitals, Neurosciences, Neurosurgery, Parkinson's Disease
AUDIENCE Doctors, Health Care Providers, Parkinson's Disease Patients, Supporters of Parkinson's Sufferers
CONTACT GateKeeper C. Owen
owen@helix.mgh.harvard.edu
FREE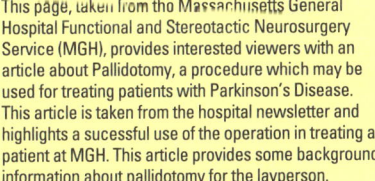

http://neurosurgery.mgh.harvard.edu/pdpallid.html

Connections to Your Heart
Zing went the strings of my heart.

Hearts are broken, some are healed, and some rule the head. If you want to know anything about your heart, the Internet provides a way to check in on your "ticker."
   Through "The Franklin Institute," you can get information on the effects of fried foods, automobiles, elevators, and vacuum cleaners on the heart. As a matter of fact, you will learn that before 1900, very few people died of heart disease. This site also provides opportunities for interactive play with a virtual heart, using visuals and sounds. You can even access information about medicine and treatment for heart disease.

(http://sln.fi.edu/biosci/heart.html)

Parkinson Foundation of Canada—Nova Scotia Division ★★★

The Nova Scotia Division of the Parkinson Foundation of Canada seeks to expand knowledge and understanding about Parkinson's by developing appropriate patient services, by promoting public awareness about Parkinson's, and by providing funding for research into the cause, early detection, effective, accessible treatment, and ultimately the discovery of a cure for Parkinson's. Visitors to this site can find access information for local Parkinson's chapters and support groups in Nova Scotia, read the latest copy of the groups newsletter, and read articles about new research developments for treating Parkinson's Disease (including Pallidotomy). Links to other internet resources are also provided.

KEYWORDS Health Care, Health News, Parkinson's Disease, Support Groups
AUDIENCE Doctors, Health Care Providers, Parkinson's Disease Patients
CONTACT Peter Kidd
pkidd@fox.nstn.ns.ca
FREE

http://www.cfn.cs.dal.ca/~aa163/nsd-pfc.html

Parkinson's Disease Information Center ★★★

The Parkinson's Disease Information Center provides general information about Parkinson's Disease. Included here are definitions of Parkinsonism, a description of the symptoms, and a listing of support groups throughout the world. In addition, the Center has a page devoted to legislation and laws related to the treatment, research, and funding for Parkinson's Disease patients and programs.

KEYWORDS Legislation, Parkinson's Disease, Support Groups
AUDIENCE Doctors, Health Care Providers, Parkinson's Disease Patients
CONTACT Oregon Public Networking/Eugene Freenet
webmaster@efn.org
FREE

http://www.efn.org/~jskaye/pd/index.html

Parkinson's Disease Support Organizations ★★★

This web page provides contact information for a number of support groups, foundations, educational and medical services related to Parkinson's Disease. Each entry contains a brief description of the group and the type of services provided, as well as addresses, phone numbers and contact persons affiliated with the organization. The listing is comprised of predominantly North American services.

KEYWORDS Hospitals, Medical Treatment, Parkinson's Disease, Support Groups

Diseases

AUDIENCE   Doctors, Health Care Providers, Parkinson's Disease Patients

CONTACT   GateKeeper C. Owen
owen@helix.mgh.harvard.edu

FREE

http://neurosurgery.mgh.harvard.edu/pd-suprt.html

Patient Information Documents on Endocrine Disorders ★★★

The Patient Information Documents on Endocrine Disorders page, sponsored by the National Institute of Diabetes and Digestive and Kidney Disease (NIDDK)—a subsidiary of the National Institutes of Health (NIH)—brings users comprehensive information regarding Addison's Disease, Cushing's Syndrome, and Familial Multiple Endocrine Neoplasia Type 1. This site is linked to a broader NIDDK page.

KEYWORDS   Endocrinology, Medical Research, Patient Resources

AUDIENCE   Diabetics, Endocrinologists, Health Care Professionals, Physicians

FREE

http://www.niddk.nih.gov/EndocrineDocs.html

Patient Information Documents on Kidney Diseases ★★

Patient Information Documents on Kidney Diseases End-Stage Renal Disease offers in simple information on Kidney/Urologic Organizations, Professional and Voluntary, and Kidney Stones in Adults. In Kidney Stones in Adults, there is information about: What Is a Kidney Stone?, Who Gets Kidney Stones?, What Causes Kidney Stones?, What Are the Symptoms?, and How Are Kidney Stones Diagnosed?

KEYWORDS   Kidney Diseases, Medical Research, Patient Resources

AUDIENCE   Health Care Professionals, Patients, Physicians

FREE

http://www.niddk.nih.gov/KidneyDocs.html

Patient Information Documents on Urologic Diseases ★★

Patient Information Documents on Urologic Diseases provides a number of articles, such as Interstitial Cystitis, Kidney/Urologic Organizations, Professional and Voluntary, Prostate Enlargement, Urinary Tract Infection, and Interstitial Cystitis, that are written so that anyone can understand the disorders. For instance, under Interstitial Cystitis, the articles covers causes, diagnosis, and treatment of interstitial cystitis as well as information on current research studies that aim to understand and treat the disorder.

KEYWORDS   Medical Research, Patient Resources, Urology

AUDIENCE   Health Care Professionals, Patients, Physicians

FREE

http://www.niddk.nih.gov/UrologicDocs.html

Prostate Cancer ★★★★

This overview of prostate cancer is written for the layperson and covers the following aspects of the disease: signs and symptoms, detection, treatment options and prognosis.

KEYWORDS   Hospital Administration, Medical Treatment, North Carolina, Prostate Cancer

AUDIENCE   Medical Researchers, Men, Prostate Cancer Sufferers

CONTACT   Webmaster
www@sips.state.nc.us

FREE

http://www.sips.state.nc.us/DOI/hosp/hosp04.html

Prostate Cancer Home Page ★★★★

This set of pages contains comprehensive information for the layman about prostate cancer. There is information about the disease process itself, signs and symptoms, diagnostic methods, staging, treatment, and prognosis. In addition there is information about the University of Michigan's own cancer treatment and education programs.

KEYWORDS   Men's Health, Oncology, Prostate Cancer

AUDIENCE   Health Educators, Medical Practitioners, Medical Researchers, Medical Students, Men

CONTACT   Oscar Olivo or Erdwing Coronado
webmaster@cancer.med.umich.edu

FREE

http://www.cancer.med.umich.edu/prostcan/prostcan.html

Prostate Cancer School Report ★★

This is the text of a 6th grade student's school report on Prostate Cancer. It's a very general overview of the disease that contains some useful information on diagnostic methods.

KEYWORDS   Men's Health, Prostate Cancer

AUDIENCE   Health Educators, Men, Science Educators

CONTACT   Barbara Spitz
bspitz@cs.wisc.edu

FREE

http://198.150.8.9/prostatecancer.html

Talaria-Hypermedia Clinical Practice Guidelines for Cancer Pain ★★★★

This site provides Talaria, a hypermedia training and reference tool for healthcare providers managing patients with cancer pain. The clinical practice guideline on cancer pain relief, just released by the Agency for Health Care Policy and Research (AHCPR), formally defines much of the knowledge base for Talaria. The purpose of the program mirrors that of the practice guideline, to improve the management of pain in patients with cancer by informing physicians, nurses and other health care providers about current therapeutic options and principles. Some of the topics covered include assessment of pain in the patient with cancer, pharmacologic management, procedure-related pain in adults and children, barriers to effective pain management, suffering, loss of control, quality of life, pain in special populations, and much more.

KEYWORDS   Cancer

AUDIENCE   Cancer Patients, Health Care Providers, Medical Researchers, Medical Students, Nurses, Oncologists, Physicians, Radiologists

CONTACT   madigan@stat.washington.edu

FREE

http://www.stat.washington.edu/TALARIA/TALARIA.html

Testicular Cancer Page ★★★

This document, a short academic paper compiled by the National Cancer Institute, effectively proves that proper screening methods (self-testing, etc.) can vastly lower the occurence of gravely serious and/or fatal testicular cancer. Self-testing methods are described, and fatality statistics are also presented.

KEYWORDS   Cancer, Men's Health, Oncology, Testicular Cancer

AUDIENCE   Health Educators, Medical Practitioners, Medical Researchers, Medical Students, Men

CONTACT   Webmaster
OncoLink@cancer.med.upenn.edu

FREE

http://cancer.med.upenn.edu:80/0/pdq/304729.txt

Tumor Types and Metastatic Spread (Patient-oriented) ★★

This site provides a list of tumor types and information on metastatic spread rates. This page is merely a listing, there are no hyperlinks to additional information here.

KEYWORDS   Cancer, Medical Research, Oncology

AUDIENCE   Cancer Patients, Health Care Professionals, Oncologists, Surgeons

FREE

http://cancer.med.upenn.edu:80/med_onc/tumor_mets.html

The University of Liverpool CRC Oncology Research Unit ★★

Welcome to the University of Liverpool CRC Oncology Research Unit home pages. The purpose of this site is to centralize the information on cancer which will allow better access to all current information, thus leading to a better understanding of the disease. The site provides links to papers recently released and to remote sites with cancer information.

KEYWORDS   Cancer, Education (College/University), Medical Research, Oncology

Diseases – Family Health

AUDIENCE Cancer Patients, Medical Researchers, Medical Students, Oncologists, Physicians, Radiologists

CONTACT Andrew J Burn
ma92ajb@liverpool.ac.uk

FREE

http://fs2.liv.ac.uk/crconcology.html

University of Texas M. D. Anderson Cancer Center (UTMDACC) ★★★

This is a gopher server of the University of Texas M. D. Anderson Cancer Center (UTMDACC) in Houston. It contains information on the Center, cancer reseach, clinical care & research, computing resources, staff, library resources, and more. It has links to other gophers as well.

KEYWORDS Cancer, Education (College/University), Health Care, Medicine

AUDIENCE Health Care Professionals, Medical Practitioners, Medical Researchers, Texas Residents

CONTACT gopher-admin@utmdacc.uth.tmc.edu

FREE

gopher://utmdacc.uth.tmc.edu/

Family Health

See also
Law & Criminal Justice · *Family Law*
Popular Culture & Entertainment · *Family & Community*
Popular Culture & Entertainment · *Genealogy*

Adolescent Issues Gopher ★★★

This is a gopher menu providing links to information on adolescent issues. Subjects covered include graduating from independence, interviewing adolescents, school health findings, teens with physical disabilities, and more.

KEYWORDS Adolescents, Disabilities, Parenting
AUDIENCE Adolescents, Educators (University), Parents

FREE

gopher://MchNet-server.ichp.ufl.edu:70/1D-1%3A3346%3AAdolescent=%2 0Issues

AdoptioNetwork Home Page ★★★

This page provides links to many adoption-related resources including legal names and phone numbers of state and local government adoption agencies, private adoption agencies, state attorney referrals, national adoption organizations, additional publications and adoption information, quick stats about adoption, conferences and speaking engagements, information for health care professionals and social sciences and other world wide web sites.

KEYWORDS Adoption, Foster Parenting, Infertility, Parenting
AUDIENCE Adoptees, Adoption Agency Professionals, Adoptive Parents

CONTACT Philip W. Schulte
pschulte@adoption.org

FREE

http://www.infi.net:80/adopt/

Chickenpox ★★★★

This article, "Close Encounters of the Poxy Kind," by Valerie Schultz about chickenpox is part of the Family World Publications site. It discusses chickenpox in a humorous, yet informative manner. "Calamine lotion is a nightmare in pink. It is runny and smelly and adheres everywhere except on the pox...Surely God thought up chicken pox as a way for parents to show that they really do love their children unconditionally."

KEYWORDS Humor, Parenting
AUDIENCE Child Care Providers, Parents, Students (Primary/Secondary)
CONTACT family@family.com

FREE

http://family.com/Features/Development/chickenpox.HTML

Childhood Immunizations ★★★

This document discusses the benefits of getting childhood immunizations. A number of infectious diseases are almost completely preventable through routine childhood immunizations. These include diphtheria, pertussis, tetanus, poliomyelitis, Haemophilus influenzae type b infection, measles, mumps, and rubella. Largely as a result of widespread childhood vaccination, these diseases have become considerably less common in the United States.

KEYWORDS Children, Immunology, Infectious Diseases, Pediatrics
AUDIENCE Health Care Providers, Nurses, Parents, Physicians

FREE

gopher://gopher.nlm.nih.gov:70/00/hstat/guide_cps/TEMPgrp12/cps64=..txt

Children's Resources ★★★

This page contains links to many children's resources on the internet. Some of the places include the INFACT Tobacco Industry Campaign against the marketing of tobacco to children, the National Child Rights Alliance, Low-Income Children's Programs, Missing Kids, Parenting, and more.

KEYWORDS Parenting
AUDIENCE Educators (Primary/Secondary), Families, Parents, Students (Primary/Secondary)
CONTACT webmaster@commerce.com

FREE

http://www.commerce.com/global/encyclo/soc/kids/kids_top.html

Connecting Dads With Playgroups ★★

Part of the Family World Inc. site, this article by an at-home dad offers tips on forming a playgroup with other at-home dads. There is also subscription information for the "At-Home Dad," a quarterly newsletter written to help connect the two million fathers who stay home with their children.

KEYWORDS Family, Parenting
AUDIENCE Child Care Providers, Families, Fathers
CONTACT family@family.com

FREE

http://family.com/Features/Dadseye/playgroups.html

CyberPages International—Missing Children ★★

You may contact this site by email, fax, snail mail, or phone if you have lost a child or know someone who has. They will post a picture and/or text here. There are also links to major 'Missing Children' pages on the net including the Heidi Search Centre, the Polly Klaas Foundation and Child Quest.

KEYWORDS Missing Children
AUDIENCE Educators (Primary/Secondary), Parents, Police Personnel, Search and Rescue Professionals
CONTACT lost-persons@cyberpages.com
children@cyberpages.com

FREE

http://www.cyberpages.com/missing.html

EurAupair Intercultural Child Care Programs ★★

EurAupair provides expertise and extensive resources on European au pairs. This site provides information on EurAupair 's Intercultural Child Care Programs. Topics include a description of aupair ('Au pair in French means on par or equal, denoting a reciprocal, caring relationship between the host family and the young person'), appropriate responsibilities for an au pair and U.S. contact information. EurAupair works closely with ASSE International Student Exchange Programs (formerly American Scandinavian Student Exchange), the program sponsor and a United States Information Agency (USIA) designated exchange visitor program founded by Sweden's national Ministry of Education.

KEYWORDS Child Care, Cultural Exchange, Parenting
AUDIENCE Au Pairs, Child Care Providers, Parents, Students (Primary/Secondary)
CONTACT Bruce and Eileen Scherzinger
zinger@fsd.com

FREE

http://turnpike.net/metro/egscherz/aupair.html

Facts for Families ★★★★

Facts for Families hopes to educate parents and families about psychiatric disorders affecting children and adolescents. The American Academy of Child and Adolescent Psychiatry (AACAP) publishes these 46 information sheets which provide concise and up-to-date material on issues such as the depressed child, teen suicide, step-family problems, the adopted child, children who steal, bedwetting, child sexual abuse, and more.

KEYWORDS Child Psychology, Family, Parenting, Sexual Abuse
AUDIENCE Families, Parents, Psychiatrists, Social Workers

Family Health

CONTACT norman.alessi@med.umich.edu
FREE

http://www.med.umich.edu/aacap/facts.index.html

Family World Features Page ★★★

This is the Family World Publications feature page which provides pointers to the following subject areas: health, home tech, activities, recreation and travel, fashion, family files, dad's eye view, education, books and book reviews, baby, parenting, child development, and entertainment.

KEYWORDS Family
AUDIENCE Child Development Professionals, Children, Families, Internet Users, Parents
CONTACT family@family.com
FREE

http://family.com/Features/featuresdocs.html

Family World Text Home Page ★★★

Family World is a collaboration of 30 monthly parenting publications, all members of the national trade association, Parenting Publications of America. They share their activity calendars for parents and children from all sections of the United States and the world. In addition, you will find monthly feature articles, information and articles concerning education, and links to Internet resources for parents, children and schools. Some of the topics of articles include walking without whining, kids and sports, kids and skiing, and more.

KEYWORDS Internet Publishing, Parenting, Sports
AUDIENCE Children, Families, Internet Users, Parents
CONTACT family@family.com
FREE

http://family.com/indexTX.html

The Health Professional's Rainbow Guide to Community Resources in the Midpeninsula Area ★★

The Health Professionals Rainbow Guide to Community Services lists contact information for a variety of health and human services in Palo Alto, San Jose, and the San Francisco Bay Area. The names, addresses, and phone numbers of services devoted to areas like child care, legal assistance, senior services, alcohol and substance abuse, and homemaker and chore services were compiled for patient reference from medical staff. In its electronic form, it is available to all residents of the community.

KEYWORDS Community Services, Human Services, Medical Assistance
AUDIENCE Californians, Medical Professionals, Patients
CONTACT Coolware Inc. webmaster@coolware.com
FREE

http://none.coolware.com/health/pamf/rg/RG.html

Latin American Adoptive Families (LAAF) ★★★

This site provides information on the Latin American Adoptive Families (LAAF). LAAF is an organization of families who have adopted, or are in the process of adopting children from Latin America. It provides adoption information including fact sheets on the adoption situation in Latin America, cultural information on Latin America and a resource list of other adoption related sources. You can become a member of LAAF, share your experiences as an adoptive parent, or assist with the Internet project.

KEYWORDS Latin America, Parenting
AUDIENCE Adoption Agency Professionals, Adoptive Parents, Families
CONTACT Marilyn Rowlands Mrowland@aol.com
FREE

http://www.gems.com/adoption/laaf

Maternal & Child Health Network (MCH-Net) Gopher Server ★★★

This is a gopher server of the Institute for Child Health Policy at the University of Florida. It contains information on systems of care for children, on children with special health care needs, publications, conferences, newsletters, HIV, and much more.

KEYWORDS Child Care, Education (College/University), Health, Health Care
AUDIENCE Child Care Providers, Children's Rights Activists, Health Care Workers
CONTACT gopher@boombox.micro.umn.edu
FREE

gopher://mchnet.ichp.ufl.edu/

Parents Helping Parents ★★★

This page, Parents Helping Parents, is a Family Resource Center for children with any kind of special need (mental, physical, emotional, or learning disabilities). It provides a great number of disabilities-and-child related links including Kid Web, Kids on Campus, US government sites, and much more.

KEYWORDS Children, Disabilities, Parenting
AUDIENCE Child Care Providers, Disabled People, Educators, Parents
CONTACT mcb@wgg.com
FREE

http://www.portal.com/~cbntmkr/php.html

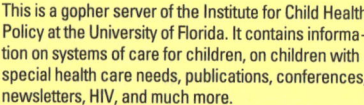
ftp://ftp.netcom.com/cd/pub/LI/LINCS

Poison Safety ★★★★

This is an article on poison safety. Subjects covered include how to prevent unintentional poisoning, teaching safety tips to children, child-resistant containers, Ipecac syrup and poison remedies, statistics on poisoning, and more.

KEYWORDS Children, Emergency Medical Services, Parenting
AUDIENCE Child Care Providers, Children, Emergency Medical Technicians, Parents

CONTACT family@family.com
FREE

http://family.com/Features/Development/PoisonSafe.HTML

The Polly Klaas Foundation ★★★

The Polly Klaas Foundation presents this page of information related to the welfare of children. Since October 1994, the Foundation has assisted in searches for more than one hundred and thirty missing and abducted children. Foundation volunteers have designed, printed, and assisted in the distribution of flyers for thirty five of these search efforts. All but four children have been returned safely. This page contains information on related legislation including "Three Strikes and You're Out," a child safety education program called "Kids and Company," produced by the Adam Walsh Foundation, law enforcement search protocols, and more. There is a list of missing children accompanied by vital information and photos.

KEYWORDS Missing Children
AUDIENCE Educators (Primary/Secondary), Parents, Police Personnel, Search and Rescue Professionals
CONTACT info@northcoast.com
FREE

http://www.northcoast.com/klaas/klaas.html

Solid Foods—A New World For Your Baby ★★★

This article at the Family World site, which discusses when to first feed your infant solid foods, is by Dr. Lillian M. Beard, a practicing pediatrician in Washington, D.C., and an Associate Clinical Professor of Pediatrics at the George Washington University School of Medicine and Health Services. She discusses infant cereal, breast milk, homemade food and store bought food, how to experiment, what to avoid, and more.

KEYWORDS Nutrition, Pediatrics
AUDIENCE Child Care Providers, Child Development Professionals, Fathers, New Mothers
CONTACT family@family.com
FREE

http://family.com/Features/Development/solid_foods.html

A Sport for Your Child ★★★★

This is a discussion of what sport a child should choose. Without considering the range of possibilities, children often want to play the sports their friends play. Parents often encourage children to participate in the sport that the parent played as a child. This document strives to help parents and children make an informed decision about sports. Some of the considerations include team vs. individual, contact level, money, time, and other considerations such as quickness and agility over size.

KEYWORDS Family, Parenting, Sports
AUDIENCE Child Care Providers, Coaches, Parents, Sports Fans

Family Health – Health Conditions   **383**

CONTACT family@family.com
FREE

http://family.com/Features/Recreation/
ChildSports.HTML

USIA Releases Revised Au Pair Regulations ★★

This site contains the text of the USIA's (US Information Agency) final regulations regarding the placement of au pairs with American host families. The new regulations refer to the au pair progam as 'primarily an educational and cultural exchange which incidentally provides some degree of child care.' Requirements set forth items such as stipend amount, ages of au pair and children, allowable work hours per day, and more.

KEYWORDS Child Care, International Education, Parenting
AUDIENCE Au Pairs, Child Care Providers, Parents, Students (Primary/Secondary)
FREE

gopher://198.80.36.82:70/00s/usia/
releases/aupair2.txt

Walking Without Whining ★★★

In this article, which is part of the Family World Publications site, author Sally Mesaroch suggests tricks and games to keep your child from whining on walks. Some of the games include The Stick Trick wherein your children hunt for the very best walking stick they can find, The Trash Detective, which means using trash as clues to the identity of a mysterious person, and Cloud Pictures—"is that a dinosaur up in the sky?"—and more.

KEYWORDS Children, Parenting
AUDIENCE Child Care Providers, Child Development Professionals, Children, Educators (Primary/Secondary), Parents
CONTACT family@family.com
FREE

http://family.com/Features/Development/
WalkWOWhining.HTML

Health Conditions

See also
Health & Medicine · *Diseases*
Health & Medicine · *Personal Care*
Humanities & Social Sciences · *Psychology*
Sports & Recreation · *Personal Fitness*

Allergy Clean Environments ★★★★

This commercial site offers online browsing and ordering of products for people with allergies or asthma, including mattress and pillow products, air cleaners and filters, vacuum cleaners, electronic atmospheric devices, carpet cleaners, mildew inhibitors, masks, and asthma books. Each product in the catalog, which is organized into eight "pages," is pictured and priced.

KEYWORDS Allergies, Asthma, Online Shopping
AUDIENCE Allergists, Allergy Sufferers, Asthma Sufferers, Online Shoppers
FREE

http://www.w2.com/allergy.html

Connections to Naming Your Newborn
What's in a name?

Event Calendars
Feature Stories and Articles
Parents' Forum.
Internet Resources
Shoppertunities
School Articles
People and Information About Family World

Choosing a name for your newborn generally begins many months before the child is born. There are resources on the Internet that can help you pick a name that is striking and unique, or help resolve differences that arise when relatives become involved in naming the child.

One site, "The Family World Home Page," includes a book on "Naming Baby." While offering a wide assortment of names, it also offers advice to expectant parents on how to avoid a family feud after you pick the name you want.

(http://family.com/)

There's even a gopher site for parents who want to give their child a Hindu name. At the "Hindu Names" sites, you are not only given a list of hundreds of boys and girls names, but the English translation of these names as well. How about "Hababala" for a boy? It means "strength."

(gopher://wiretap.spies.com:70/00ULibrary/Article/Language/hindu.nam)

There are additional places to find names on the Internet, such as dictionaries in English, French, Spanish, and several other languages. These typically include world maps and locations as well.

(http://math-www.uni-paderborn.de/HTML/Dictionaries.html)

American Academy of Allergy Asthma and Immunology ★★★

The American Academy of Allergy Asthma and Immunology is a medical society that promotes the knowledge and practice of related health fields. Their home page provides resources for patients and health care providers dealing with allergies and asthma.

Included are AAAAI position statements about issues such as lab procedures, flouride allergies, and controversial techniques. A weekly National Allergy Bureau Report is also provided, which shows how much allergy sufferers will experience symptoms in different regions of the U.S. The site also includes links to other scientific and health related sites.

KEYWORDS Allergies, Asthma, Health Care, Immunology
AUDIENCE Allergy Sufferers, Doctors, Home Care Professionals
CONTACT Paul Rushizky
paulr@csd.uwm.edu
FREE

http://www.uwm.edu/~paulr/aaaai.html

Autism Resources ★★★★

Autism Resources is an intriguing new web site for people interested in developmental disorders related to autism. Here you will find material on what to do if your child is diagnosed autistic, Asperger's or PDD. There are hyperlinks to studies of FC (facilitated communication), the Autism FAQ, data about sensory therapies, and unusual information about sensory problems such as hyperacuity, visual thinking, and communication problems. Most information is written from a high-functioning autistic person's point of view. Online papers, as well as academic and research programs, provide information about helpful treatments and programs for the autistic.

KEYWORDS Autism, Developmental Disabilities, Research, Special Education
AUDIENCE Parents of Autistic Children, Special Education Teachers, Speech Therapists
CONTACT John M. Wobus
jmwobus@mailbox.syr.edu
FREE

http://web.syr.edu/~jmwobus/autism

Children and Adults with Attention Deficit Disorder (CHADD) of Bay County, Chapter 544 Information Page ★★★★

The Children and Adults with Attention Deficit Disorder (CHADD) Information Page is an excellent resource for people coping with Attention Deficit Disorder. Here you will find a myriad of informative electronic documents concerning issues such as parenting a child with Attention Deficit Disorder, living with Adult ADD, treating children with Attention Deficit Disorder, and the legal rights and services available to children who have ADD. The data here is thorough, detailed and fairly exhaustive, and includes material about other disabilities, including Autism, Tourette's Syndrome, Dyslexia, Obsessive-Compulsive Disorder, and Depression. In addition to the various links available, you will also discover ways to contact ADD support groups in your area, as well as to CHADD itself.

KEYWORDS Attention Deficit Disorder, Children's Health, Learning Disabilities
AUDIENCE Attention Deficit Disorder Sufferers, Learning Disabled People, Parents, Special Education Teachers
CONTACT Children and Adults with Attention Deficit Disorder (CHADD) of Bay County
CHADD544@pobox.com
FREE

http://turnpike.net/metro/B/bernstp/chadd544.htm

Chronic Fatigue Syndrome ★★★

The Chronic Fatigue Syndrome (CFS) home page is designed to provide information and news about this health disorder for both sufferers and doctors. Users will find basic introductions to the disease CFS and its symptoms, as well as several electronic newsletters and magazines and their archives. Resource information includes a CFS database, political action files, relevant articles, and numerous FAQs on specific aspects of the disease. A discussion section links users to newsgroups for political and health discussions related to chronic fatigue syndrome. Links to other web sites with CFS information are also listed.

KEYWORDS Chronic Fatigue Syndrome, Medical Resources
AUDIENCE Chronic Fatigue Sufferers, Health Care Professionals
CONTACT Roger Burns
cfs-news-request@list.nih.gov
FREE

http://metro.turnpike.net/C/cfs-news/

Computer Related Repetitive Strain Injury ★★★

Repetitive Strain Injury often occurs as a result of repeated usage of a keyboard or a point-and-click mouse. This site gives basic information about repetitive strain injury, including symptom descriptions, links to health-care resources, and advice for those already suffering symptoms. It also provides illustrations, pictures, and demonstration videos illustrating preventative posture and proper typing techniques.

KEYWORDS Carpal Tunnel Syndrome, Health Care, Repetitive Stress Injuries
AUDIENCE Computer Users, Health Care Professionals, Typists
CONTACT Paul Marxhausen
mpaul@uclinfo.unl.edu
FREE

http://engr-www.unl.edu/ee/eeshop/rsi.html

Diseases and Conditions ★★★

This gopher site provides documents on personal health, covering numerous diseases and conditions such as allergies, the common cold, contagious diseases, headaches, tuberculosis, wounds, and vaccines. Each disease or condition is discussed in an overview, and specific articles may cover topics such as symptoms, self-examinations, medication, and self-care. The site was created by the McKinley Health Center at the University of Illinois.

KEYWORDS Allergies, Diseases, Health Care, Universities
AUDIENCE General Public, Health Care Professionals, Nurses
FREE

gopher://gopher.uiuc.edu/11/UI/CSF/health/heainfo/diseases

The Index to Gluten-Free and Wheat-Free Diets ★★★★

The Index to Gluten-Free and Wheat-Free Diets is an interesting resource for people with inexplicable illnesses. Here you will find material about the Celiac Condition, an immune disorder caused by gluten and wheat intolerance. Suggestions are offered as to how to treat the condition, where and how to get a proper diagnosis, the symptoms and causes of the Celiac Condition, information on how to join the Celiac mailing list, information on the Prodigy Celiac group, and discussion of other sicknesses which are perhaps mistaken for the Celiac Condition, including Irritable Bowel Syndrome (IBS), lactose intolerance, some anemias and dermatitises, and Attention Deficit Disorder (ADD). In addition, some recipes from the book "Gluten Free Cookery" are given.

KEYWORDS Allergies, Diet
AUDIENCE Allergy Sufferers, Gluten-Intolerant People, Irritable Bowel Syndrome Sufferers
CONTACT Peter and Donna Thomson
guides@kendal.demon.co.uk
FREE

http://www.demon.co.uk/webguides/nutrition/diets/glutenfree

NIDD—National Institute of Diabetes and Digestive and Kidney Diseases ★★

The page of the National Institute of Diabetes and Digestive and Kidney Diseases provides information about various digestive, endocrine, diabetic, urologic and kidney disorders. Materials include news releases about health care subjects such as government health studies and weight loss. Also provided is information about health care organizations focusing on specific disorders, organized by disease type, and links to other online health care sites.

KEYWORDS Diabetes, Diseases, Health Care, Kidney Diseases
AUDIENCE Diabetics, Home Care Professionals
CONTACT Walter W. Stewart
stewartw@helix.nih.gov
FREE

http://www.niddk.nih.gov/

The On-Line Allergy Center ★★★

The On-Line Allergy Center offers information to help allergy sufferers. An overview of allergies is provided, as well as descriptions of symptoms and relevant news updates. The Allergy Center also tells the user how to discover if they are allergic to certain foods, and then how to remedy food reactions. There are articles on changing topics, coverage of ear infections and headaches, and a "Parents Page" for parents of children with allergies.

KEYWORDS Allergies, Children's Health, Health Care
AUDIENCE Allergy Sufferers, General Public, Home Care Professionals

CONTACT Russel Roby, M.D.
allergy@sig.net
FREE

http://www.sig.net/~allergy/welcome.html

Skin Web ★★★

Skin Web is the work of the National Skin Centre of Singapore, and is designed to provide information about skin health care in Singapore, as well as educational materials about dermatology. Extensive information about the major dermatology organizations in Singapore is provided, including services and fees. This site includes a comprehensive guide to skin diseases of all types, with descriptions and photographs of symptoms, answers to common questions, and treatment explanations. The publication Dermadigest features articles on topics such as occupational skin diseases in the electronics industry and group therapy for psoriasis. The NSC Bulletin also provides updates on events and breakthroughs in the field of dermatology. It is possible to make an appointment with a dermatologist online.

KEYWORDS Dermatology, Diseases, Health Care, Skin Care
AUDIENCE Dermatologists, Singapore Residents
FREE

http://biomed.nus.sg/nsc/nsc.html

The Sleep Medicine Home Page ★★★

For users suffering from sleep disorders, or just interested in sleep research and medicine, the Sleep Medicine Home Page lists resources covering every aspect of sleep. Links are listed according to sleep topic related newsgroups, sleep disorders, foundations, federal information, medications, book reviews, professional meetings, sleep disorder centers, and business organizations.

KEYWORDS Dreams, Health Care, Insomnia, Medical Research
AUDIENCE Mental Health Sufferers
CONTACT Dr. Michael Thorpy
thorpy@aecom.yu.edu
FREE

http://www.cloud9.net:80/~thorpy/

The Tinnitus FAQ ★★★★

The Tinnitus FAQ is a very thorough document designed to assist tinnitus and related illness sufferers in their search for relief and possible cure. The FAQ covers all facets of the disease, including defining tinnitus, explaining how tinnitus sounds, what causes tinnitus and how to avoided getting the illness, medical and alternative treatments, and masking, ear plugs and other methods of hearing protection. Also mentioned are available and knowledgeable health care providers, addresses for products which help relieve tinnitus, and a list of toxic over-the-counter medications which are linked to tinnitus. Related illnesses such as Meniere's Disease and Hyperacusis are also discussed.

KEYWORDS Deafness, Hearing Science
AUDIENCE Audiologists, Hearing Loss Sufferers, Nose and Throat Specialists, Tinnitus Sufferers

CONTACT Mark Bixby
markb@cccd.edu
FREE

ftp://rtfm.mit.edu/pub/usenet/
news.answers/medicine/tinnitus-faq

Typing Injury FAQ ★★★★

The Typing Injury FAQ provides links to hundreds of relevant typing injury resources all over the Internet, including online publications, mailing lists, WWW sites, and listservs. Information from the ftp.csua.berkeley.edu archives includes files, literature and reviews of products, UNIX software, and pictures. Also included is general information on injuries, a glossary of terms, and some preventive guidelines. A Question and Answer section gives answers to frequently asked questions about typing injuries such as repetitive stress syndromes, as well as information about ergonomics.

KEYWORDS Carpal Tunnel Syndrome, Health, Repetitive Stress Injuries
AUDIENCE Computer Users, Health Care Professionals, Therapists, Typists
CONTACT Dan Wallach
dwallach@CS.princeton.edu
FREE

http://www.cs.princeton.edu/~dwallach/
tifaq/general.html

Medical Schools

See also
Health & Medicine · *Career & Employment*
Health & Medicine · *Medicine*

ALNET ★★★

This site is a gopher server of the Research Information Technology Department at the Albert Einstein College of Medicine (AECOM) in the Bronx, NY. It provides information about AECOM research facilities, AECOM departments and organizations and more. Access to other biology and medicine gopher holes is also provided.

KEYWORDS Biology, Education (College/University), Medical Research, New York
AUDIENCE Medical Educators, Medical Students
CONTACT gopher@aecom.yu.edu
FREE

gopher://gopher.aecom.yu.edu/

Baylor College of Medicine ★★★

The top level of the Baylor College of Medicine's WWW server offers information on the college, including material on admissions, research, educational programs, academic calendars, and more. Users will also find health care information, links to the campus gopher, and general material on the campus and its location.

KEYWORDS Colleges & Universities, Medicine
AUDIENCE Education Administrators (College), Medical Educators, Medical Students, Students (College)

CONTACT www@bcm.tmc.edu
FREE

http://www.bcm.tmc.edu

gopher://gopher.bcm.tmc.edu/

College of Pharmacy Gopher Server at Idaho State University ★★★

This site offers information about the areas of this non-traditional pharmacy program, events, the faculty/staff phone book, and generally about the Idaho State University College of Pharmacy. It also provides links to many other related gopher servers.

KEYWORDS Education (College/University), Pharmaceuticals, Pharmacology, Research & Development
AUDIENCE Academics, Pharmacists, Students
CONTACT gopher@pharmacy.isu.edu
FREE

gopher://pharmacy.isu.edu/

The Cornell University Medical College Gopher ★★★

This is a gopher server for the Cornell University Medical College. It contains information on the College, the faculty listing, the Education Center, facilities, images, phone books, academic computing resources, and much more. It makes connections to other gophers both on and off-campus.

KEYWORDS Biomedicine, Education (College/University), Medical Research, Medicine
AUDIENCE Educators (University), Medical Educators, Students (Secondary/College)
CONTACT Steven_Erde@qmcumc.mail.cornell.edu
FREE

gopher://gopher.med.cornell.edu/

Countway Library of Medicine at Harvard University ★★★

This is a gopher site of the Countway Library of Medicine at Harvard University in Cambridge, Massachusetts. It provides access and linkage to biomedicine-related electronic information, literature, databases, directories, images, library services, and bibliographic tools. There are also links to other Harvard University gophers.

KEYWORDS Education (College/University), Libraries, Medicine, Universities
AUDIENCE Educator (College/Graduate), Medical Educators, Medical Researchers, Medical Students
CONTACT gopher@warren.med.harvard.edu
FREE

gopher://gopher.med.harvard.edu/

Medical Schools

The Gopher Server at the University of Illinois College of Medicine at Urbana-Champaign ★★★

This site is a gopher server of the University of Illinois College of Medicine at Urbana-Champaign. It provides information on the college, clinical guidelines and resources, the library of health sciences, computer resources, news, and fellowships. It makes connections to other gophers.

KEYWORDS Education (College/University), Medical Informatics, Medical Research, Medicine
AUDIENCE Educators (University), Medical Professionals, Students (Secondary/College)
CONTACT a-levy@uiuc.edu
FREE

gopher://gopher.med.uiuc.edu/

The Gopher Server of the North Dakota State University School of Medicine ★★★

This is a gopher server of the School of Medicine at the North Dakota State University (UNDSOM). It contains information on UNDSOM departments, the calendar, the Harley French Library, the phone book, computer resources, terminal services, and road and weather reports. It makes pointers to other gophers on-campus as well as off-campus.

KEYWORDS Cardiopulmonary Medicine, Education (College/University), Medical Treatment, Medicine
AUDIENCE Educators (University), Medical Educators, Students (Secondary/College)
CONTACT Barry.Pederson@medicine.und.nodak.edu
FREE

gopher://gopher.med.und.nodak.edu/

Harvard University Medical Web ★★★★

This page contains links to medical information based at Harvard University. Pointers to Harvard Medical School campuses, programs, departments, and research institutions are given here, as are search tools and links to various library services.

KEYWORDS Medical Schools, Public Health, Universities
AUDIENCE Doctors, Medical Students, Students (University)
CONTACT Timothy Fox
tim_fox@warren.med.harvard.edu
FREE

http://count51.med.harvard.edu

Howard Hughes Medical Institute ★★★

This site is a gopher server of the Howard Hughes Medical Institute of the University of Texas Southwestern Medical Center. It offers information on biology, medicine, computing resources & services, and library resources. It makes connections to other gopher holes on the Internet. The information on this server is identical to that on gopher.swmed.edu.

KEYWORDS Education (College/University), Health, Medicine, Texas
AUDIENCE Educators (University), Medical Educators, Students (Secondary/College)
CONTACT Daniel Joy
joy@howie.swmed.edu
FREE

gopher://iliad.swmed.edu/

John Curtin School of Medical Research ★★

This gopher server gives access to directories, internal newsletters, and annual reports from the John Curtin School of Medical Research. There are also links to gopher sites at the Australian National University.

KEYWORDS Biomedicine, Graduate Education, Medical Education, Medical Research
AUDIENCE Doctors, Medical Educators, Medical Professionals, Medical Students
CONTACT Greg Quinn
Greg.Quinn@anu.edu.au
FREE

gopher://jcsmr.anu.edu.au/

Medical College of Georgia ★★★

This is a gopher server of the Medical College of Georgia. It contains information on allergies, immunology, asthma, health care reform, journal clubs in allergy-immunology, news and more. It has pointers to other medical gophers.

KEYWORDS Education (College/University), Health Sciences, Immunology, Medicine
AUDIENCE Medical Educators, Medical Professionals, Medical Researchers, Medical Students
CONTACT Bill Dolen
deptped.bdolen@mail.mcg.edu
FREE

gopher://lab.allergy.mcg.edu/

Medical College of Wisconsin's Bioethics Online Service ★★★

This site is administered by the Medical College of Wisconsin and gives information about Bioethics. This information includes bulletin board services, news releases, discussion forums, and texts.

KEYWORDS Ethics, Legal Research, Medicine
AUDIENCE Legal Scholars, Medical Professionals
CONTACT Arthur Derse
aderse@its.mcw.edu
FREE

gopher://post.its.mcw.edu:72/

Medical Libraries at Baylor College of Medicine ★★★

This is a gopher of the M.D. Anderson Library at the Baylor College of Medicine in Texas. It contains 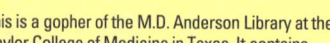 information on medical libraries, resources and services, catalogs, newsletters, and a genetics database called Genbank.

KEYWORDS Education (College/University), Libraries, Medicine, Texas
AUDIENCE Library Users, Medical Educators, Medical Students
FREE

gopher://rmlgopher.uth.tmc.edu/

The Medical University of South Carolina ★★★★

This site is a gopher server of the Medical University of South Carolina. Information is provided about the administration, registration, the departments, colleges, and centers. There are also links to research resources, library resources, computing resources, and other gophers.

KEYWORDS Education (College/University), Medical Schools, Medicine, University Administration
AUDIENCE Academics, Educators (University), Students (Secondary/College)
FREE

gopher://gopher.musc.edu/

The Miner Gopher ★★★

The Miner Gopher provides information about Health Sciences. The information is provided by the Miner Medical Library at the University of Rochester Medical Center. The information provided includes library services, access to Internet resources for the health sciences, and documents about the various faculties and departments at the University of Rochester that are related to Health Sciences.

KEYWORDS Health Sciences, Libraries, Medicine, Nursing
AUDIENCE Health Care Professionals, Health Science Researchers, Medical Students
CONTACT Suzanne Bell
suzanne@medinfo.rochester.edu
FREE

gopher://minergopher.lib.rochester.edu/

NYU Medical Center ★★★★

The NYU Medical Center offers information on their educational opportunities, research, and the Medical Center databases. The page has thumbnail links to seminar listings, a faculty BioSketch, a research database and the NYU-MC Departmental Servers. The extensive department listings include anesthesiology, biochemistry, surgery, cell biology, and microbiology.

KEYWORDS Biomedicine, Databases, Medical Research, New York
AUDIENCE Biomedical Specialists, Medical Researchers, Psychologists, Students
CONTACT Ross Smith
smithp01@mcrcr.med.nyu.edu
FREE

http://www.med.nyu.edu

gopher://gopher.med.nyu.edu/

Osaka Medical College Medical Computation Center

The Home Page of the Osaka Medical College provides access to an assortment of medical information. The page has links to an online version of the Japan Journal of Medical Informatics and the Osaka Medical College gopher server. There are connections to the page in Japanese and other medical sites.

KEYWORDS   Medical Information, Medical Research, Online Journals
AUDIENCE   Educators, Medical Professionals, Students
CONTACT   yamamoto@art.osaka-med.ac.jp
FREE

http://www.osaka-med.ac.jp/SND/main.au

RFHSM Campus Information Service

The Royal Free Hospital School of Medicine (RFHSM) Campus Information Service provides information on the school (located in Hampstead, England) and its resources. The page has links to the medical school, to the department of computing and informatics, and to the library. There are also links to the directory service and the UCL/RFHSM Department of Physiology Personal Home Pages.

KEYWORDS   Educational Resources, England, Medical Informatics, Medical Libraries
AUDIENCE   Medical Researchers, Medical Students, Physicians, United Kingdom Residents
CONTACT   zeus@rfhsm.ac.uk
FREE

http://www.rfhsm.ac.uk/

Rascal Gopher

This is a gopher server of the Harvard Medical School. It contains information on the school, biological resources, email addresses, genetics related software, Internet software, computing resources, and more. It also has links to other medical gophers.

KEYWORDS   Biology, Education (College/University), Genetics, Medicine
AUDIENCE   Medical Educators, Medical Professionals, Medical Researchers, Medical Students
CONTACT   Matthew Temple
         manager@rascal.med.harvard.edu
FREE

gopher://rascal.med.harvard.edu/

Robert Wood Johnson Medical School Gopher

This gopher server provides access to images related to molecular biology, pathology, and radiology. The images are part of an ongoing program at the Robert Wood Johnson Medical School, New Jersey, to develop imaging tools for pathology and clinical biology. The images are available in GIF format.

KEYWORDS   Cell Biology, Imaging, Medicine, Molecular Biology
AUDIENCE   Biomedical Researchers, Molecular Biologists

Connections to Chiropractic
Ohhhh, my aching back!

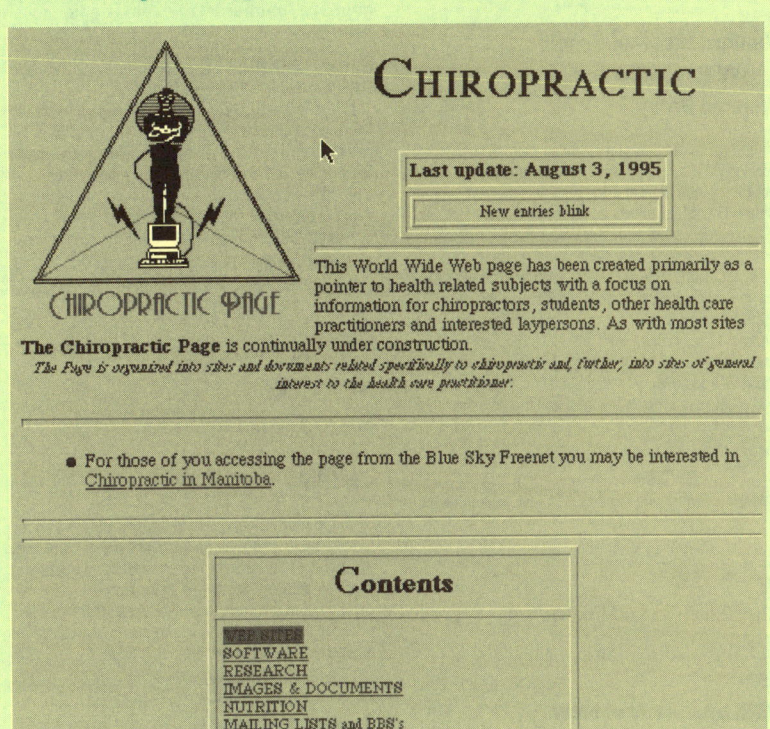

Headaches, back pain, numbness, and tingling sensations are often signs of spinal problems. If you've got any of these symptoms, chiropractic may well provide some solutions. If you have questions about whether that's what you need, then turn to any number of World Wide Web sites for counsel. There you'll be able to search for chiropractors in your area, and find other alternative and holistic healthcare practitioners as well.

(http://www.mbnet.mb.ca/~jwiens/chiro.html)

If you want a national directory of chiropractors in the U.S. (also covering holistic healthcare practitioners), you can find it on "The Gary Null Chiropractic Referral Directory." Here you'll also find a term glossary.

(http://www.mtii.com/chiro/)

CONTACT   djf@mirage.umdnj.edu
FREE

gopher://mirage.umdnj.edu/

SUMC Networking

SUMC Networking is the gopher server of the Stanford University Medical Center (Mednet). SUMC Networking supports networking throughout the Stanford Medical Center. It contains information on its services, the people in the Center, and more.

KEYWORDS   California, Medical Information, Medical Schools, Networking
AUDIENCE   Medical Educators, Medical Professionals, Medical Students, Students (Secondary)
CONTACT   gopher@mednet.stanford.edu
FREE

gopher://mednet.stanford.edu/

The School of Medicine of the Southern Illinois University

This site is a gopher server of the School of Medicine of the Southern Illinois University. It provides access points to other gopher holes such as an Internet software site, medical resources, and Internet tips and tricks.

KEYWORDS   Community Networking, Education (College/University), Illinois, Medicine
AUDIENCE   Educators (University), Medical Professionals, Medical Students

Medical Schools

CONTACT allenw@elmo.c-som.siu.edu
FREE
gopher://gopher.c-som.siu.edu/

Stanford Medical School WWW Page Information Systems Group ★★★

Stanford Medical School Information Systems Group (ISG) WWW Page is designed to provide information about the Medical Center for students at the Medical School. The ISG supports computing programs for the School of Medicine, and their Web site offers data about networking and computing at the Stanford Medical Center, including configuration information and network supports. Also in this site are the archives for the Stanford Medical Center, including medical documents, as well as links to their Home Page where users can find out about all of the Medical Center functions and services. This page also contains links to local resources around Stanford and the Bay Area, as well as to related medical sites and servers.

KEYWORDS Computing, Medical Schools, Medicine, Universities
AUDIENCE Computing Experts, Medical Professionals, Medical Students
CONTACT help@isg.stanford.edu
FREE
http://medisg.stanford.edu/
gopher://medisg.stanford.edu/

State University of New York (SUNY) Health Science Center at Syracuse Gopher ★★★

This gopher server provides information relevant to health sciences at Syracuse University. It includes medical resource information, access to MedSearch America, periodicals, journals, software collections and FTP sites. It also contains links to other gopher sites and searchable indices.

KEYWORDS Biology, Health Sciences, Information Retrieval, Technical Support
AUDIENCE Health Care Professionals, Health Science Researchers, Medical Professionals
CONTACT Larry Polly
  pollyl@vax.cs.hscsyr.edu
FREE
gopher://micro.ec.hscsyr.edu/

Toxic Substances Research and Teaching Program at University of California ★★★

This site is a gopher server of the Toxic Substances Research and Teaching Program at University of California at Davis. It gives information on the 1994 request for proposal summaries.

KEYWORDS Biochemistry, Education (College/University), Medicine, Toxicology
AUDIENCE Biologists, Medical Professionals, Medical Researchers, Toxicologists
CONTACT Melissa Mardesich
  mamardesich@ucdavis.edu
FREE
gopher://gopher.tsrtp.ucdavis.edu/

Tulane Medical Center ★★★★

The Tulane Medical Center (TMC) home page contains information about its two departments—the Tulane-Xavier Center for Bioenvironmental Research and the Department of Pathology and Laboratory Medicine. The page has information about TMC conferences and medical research. There are links to other Tulane University servers and New Orleans area information.

KEYWORDS Medical Research, Pathology
AUDIENCE Biomedical Researchers, Medical Students, Pathologists
CONTACT James H. Harrison, Jr., M.D., Ph.D.
  harrison@tmc.tulane.edu
FREE
http://www.mcl.tulane.edu

UMDinfo ★★★

UMDinfo is the Campus Wide Information System for the University of Medicine and Dentistry of New Jersey (UMDNJ). This site provides information about the UMDNJ, a list of current and upcoming events at UMDNJ, and the phonebook and staff directories. It provides links to the various campuses of UMDNJ and other medical resources on the Internet.

KEYWORDS Dentistry, Education (College/University), Medical Informatics, Medicine
AUDIENCE Dentists, Educators (University), Medical Students
CONTACT gopher@umdnj.edu
FREE
http://rwja.umdnj.edu/
gopher://rwja.umdnj.edu/

University of California Davis Medical Center ★★★★

This site provides information on the The University of California Davis Medical Center (UCDMC), an acute care hospital serving Northern California which offers inpatient and diagnostic services, as well as emergency medical services. The server contains links to the servers for the departments of Radiology, Pathology, and Psychiatry.

KEYWORDS Education (College/University), Hospitals, Radiology, Universities
AUDIENCE Californians, Medical Professionals, Physicians, Students (University)
CONTACT webmaster@ucdmc.ucdavis.edu
FREE
http://edison.ucdmc.ucdavis.edu/ucdmc/index.html

University of Medical Sciences ★★★

This site provides information on the administration and academic programs of the University of Medical Sciences in Poland. It includes data about the Computer Center, libraries, discussion lists, local file archives, images, and more. Also, it has links to other gophers.

KEYWORDS Education (College/University), Medicine, Poland, University Administration
AUDIENCE Medical Educators, Medical Students, Polish
CONTACT ak11@plpuam11.amu.edu.pl
FREE
gopher://hum.amu.edu.pl/

University of Nebraska Medical Center ★★★

This is a gopher server of the University of Nebraska Medical Center. It contains information on biology, medicine, biology email servers, biology FTP servers, biology software, and more. It has links to other medical related gophers such as National Institutes of Health and the National Library of Medicine.

KEYWORDS Biosciences, Community Services, Education (College/University), Medicine
AUDIENCE Biologists, Educators (University), Scientists, Students (Secondary/College)
CONTACT cprice@netserv.unmc.edu
FREE
gopher://netserv.unmc.edu/

University of Texas (UT) Houston Medical School ★★★

The University of Texas (UT) Houston Medical School offers information about specific medical areas such as Analytical Chemistry, Emergency Medicine, Microbiology, Pediatrics, and other specialities. In addition, there is an archive of medical shareware and demo software related to medicine. Links to more sites at the University of Texas and other medical schools are also available. Contact and admissions information is available though the school's gopher server.

KEYWORDS Biomedicine, Medical Software, Universities
AUDIENCE Medical Educators, Medical Students
CONTACT www@dean.med.uth.tmc.edu.
FREE
http://dean.med.uth.tmc.edu
gopher://dean.med.uth.tmc.edu/

University of Washington Radiology Webserver ★★★★

The University of Washington Radiology Webserver presents information and images in radiologic studies. The page provides images of cases which are cross-referenced by specific organ system, anatomic area, or pathologic diagnosis. There is also a listing of radiology career positions offered and sought, some online textbooks, and other teaching materials. There are also links to research projects and software from UW Radiology.

KEYWORDS Imaging, Medical Reference, Radiology
AUDIENCE Medical Students, Radiologists, Researchers
CONTACT Michael L. Richardson, M. D.
  mrich@u.washington.edu
FREE
http://www.rad.washington.edu/

Medical Schools – Medical Specialties

Universität Göttingen Medical Statistics Department ★★★

The Universität Göttingen WWW Server of the Medical Statistics Department features information about the department, the university, and tourist information. There are also links to the university's information systems and medical statistics.

KEYWORDS Archives, Educational Programs, Germany, Statistics
AUDIENCE Germans, Medical Statisticians, Students
CONTACT WWW-Admin@AMS.Medizin.Uni-Goettingen.DE
FREE

http://www.med-stat.gwdg.de

Washington University Division of Comparative Medicine ★★★

This gopher hole was dug at the Washington University Division of Comparative Medicine. It contains information on Veterinary Medicine, on the colleges of Veterinary Medicine, journals & conference proceedings, animal legislation and regulations, mailing lists, Usenet newsgroups, and more. It also has links to other medical related gophers.

KEYWORDS Education (College/University), Health Sciences, Medical Research, Medicine
AUDIENCE Educators (University), Medical Educators, Students (University)
CONTACT Dr. Ken Boschert ken@wudcm.wustl.edu
FREE

gopher://netvet.wustl.edu/

Medical Specialties

See also
Health & Medicine · *Medicine*

5th International Symposium on Presbyopia ★★★

This is the Web page for the 5th International Symposium on Presbyopia which was held on June 5-7, 1995 in Paris France. Conference themes are The Senior Citizen Market, Aging and the Eye, Health and Vision and more. This page provides the schedule of talks, information on the sponsor, Essilor, and links to French Web Sites.

KEYWORDS Conference, Optometry, Presbyopia
AUDIENCE Glasses Makers, Glasses Retailers, Optometrists
CONTACT N. de Brisis essilor@iway.fr
FREE

http://www.iway.fr/essilor/

Connections to Medicine and Health

Is there a doctor on the 'Net?

How would you respond if a child in your home started choking on something? Is there something you can safely take if you're feeling tired all the time? A large number of medical research centers, hospitals, and universities around the world have Web sites for you to consult about your medical needs. Some even focus exclusively on alternative approaches to healthcare.

At "The Health Explorer" site, you'll find answers to common diet/nutrition questions (such as "how many calories should I consume per day?"), women's health issues (including stress management), and men's health issues (such as prostrate cancer). You'll also find the latest information on treatment of childhood diseases such as chicken pox or asthma.

(http://hyrax.med.uth.tmc.edu/ptnt/tocptnt.htm)

At the "Virtual Hospital" site, you can search for health tips, disease prevention advice, and access hotlinks to clinic services and staff. You can also learn some of the latest information available concerning the treatment of cancer and other life-threatening diseases.

(http://indy.radiology.uiowa.edu/VirtualHospital.html)

There are several WWW sites that provide information about alternative forms of medicine (i.e. herbal remedies, homeopathy, etc.). Some sites offer advice on how to treat ailments with common household foods. At the "Sumeria Health" site, for instance, you'll find hotlinks to 50 nutritional tips for treatment of such things as tummy aches (high fiber cookies or peppermint) and asthma (caffeine in coffee). You'll also find guidelines on how to save someone who is choking on food.

(http://lablinks.com/sumeria/health/50tips.html)

AnesUCLA—the UCLA Anesthesiology Gopher Server ★★★

This gopher server, also called AnesUCLA, is for the UCLA Anesthesiology Department. There are connections to other anesthesia gopher servers, UCLA gopher servers, and more.

KEYWORDS Anesthesiology, California, Education (College/University), Medical Schools
AUDIENCE Anesthesiologists, Health Care Professionals, Medical Educators, Medical Students

CONTACT   stan@anes.ucla.edu
FREE

gopher://gopher.anes.ucla.edu/

The Australasian Anesthesia Web Site ★★★

This page contains pointers to medical information including Emergency Protocols, Poisonings, Uncommon Diseases, Anesthesia History, and links to other medicine-related World Wide Web sites. Some of the other sites include Critical Care Medicine, The Visible Human Project, Cardiology, and more.

KEYWORDS   Medical Information, Medical Resources
AUDIENCE   Anethesiologists, Australians, Medical Professionals, Physicians
CONTACT   Chris Thompson
           clt@extro.ucc.su.oz.au
FREE

http://www.usyd.edu.au/su/anaes/anaes.html

The Department of Anesthesiology at the State University of New York ★★

This site is a gopher of the Department of Anesthesiology at the State University of New York. It provides general information about anesthesiology in the form of book reviews, archives, and lecture notes. There are also connections to Internet medical resources.

KEYWORDS   Anesthesiology, Archives, Education (College/University), Medical Research
AUDIENCE   Anesthesiologists, Health Care Professionals, Medical Researchers, Physicians
FREE

gopher://eja.anes.hscsyr.edu/

Department of Pharmacology, University of Texas at Houston ★★

This site is maintained by the Department of Pharmacology at the University of Texas at Houston. Much of the information here is restricted to Department access only. The information available to the general public includes software for Macintosh and PC computers, and various images.

KEYWORDS   Education (College/University), MS-DOS, Pharmacology, Texas
AUDIENCE   Computer Users, Macintosh Users, Medical Professionals, PC Users
CONTACT   dloose@farmr1.med.uth.tmc.edu
FREE

gopher://farmr4.med.uth.tmc.edu/

The Department of Radiology, UC Davis School of Medicine ★★★

This site offers information and resources related to radiology at the University of California at Davis. Users will find detailed information on clinical radiology topics such as Musculoskeletal Radiology and Neuroradiology. This site also hosts research project information as well as departmental and faculty material.

KEYWORDS   Medical Schools, Nuclear Medicine, Radiology
AUDIENCE   Medical Educators, Medical Professionals, Medical Students, Radiologists
CONTACT   Ted Barlow
           webserver@labrad.ucdmc.ucdavis.edu
FREE

http://www-radiology.ucdmc.ucdavis.edu

Global Anesthesiology Server Network ★★★

This site is a gopher server of the Department of Anesthesiology, Medical Center, New York University. It contains information about the Anesthesiology Mailing List digests and the Educational Synopses in Anesthesiology and Critical Care Medicine online journal.

KEYWORDS   Anesthesiology, Education (College/University), Medical Research, Online Journals
AUDIENCE   Anesthesiologists, Health Care Professionals
CONTACT   Keith J Ruskin, MD
           keith@anes.med.nyu.edu
FREE

gopher://gasnet.med.nyu.edu/

Indiana University Radiology ★★★

This is the home page of the Indiana University Radiology Department which contains links to medline, a medical library, the National Institute of Health, and the National Library of Medicine.

KEYWORDS   Indiana, Libraries, Medicine, Radiology
AUDIENCE   Internet Users, Medical Educators, Medical Students
FREE

http://foyt.indyrad.iupui.edu

Massachusetts General Hospital Neurosurgical Service ★★★

The Massachusetts General Hospital Neurosurgical Service page provides access to neuroscience information resources. The page gives links to neurosurgical clinical units, and clinical, research and educational resources.

KEYWORDS   Hospitals, Massachusetts, Medical Resources, Neurology
AUDIENCE   Medical Practitioners, Neuroscientists, Neurosurgeons
CONTACT   Dr. Stephen Tatter
           tatter@helix.mgh.harvard.edu
FREE

http://neurosurgery.mgh.harvard.edu/

Neurology at Massachusetts General Hospital ★★★

This site provides a comprehensive overview of the neurological research going on at the Massachusetts General Hospital. Some interesting details include an online newsletter, a list of current events, research summaries, a physician referral service, home pages of affiliated laboratories, and links to other medical and neurological resources.

KEYWORDS   Medical Research, Neurology
AUDIENCE   Neuroscientists, Physicians
CONTACT   John Lester
           lester@helix.mgh.harvard.edu
FREE

Tropical Medicine ★★

The Tropical Medicine site focuses on the epidemiology of tropical diseases focusing primarily on six diseases (filariasis, leishmaniasis, leprosy, malaria, schistosomiasis, and trypanosomiasis). The National Institute of Allergy and Infectious Diseases (NIAID) defines tropical diseases as those that are associated with poverty, inadequate education, and poor sanitation but are not endemic to the United States or occur at such low frequency that they are not major domestic public health problems. This document outlines research in this area, results, and other related information.

KEYWORDS   Epidemiology, Infectious Diseases, Public Health, Tropical Diseases
AUDIENCE   Biomedical Scientists, Health Care Professionals, Molecular Biologists, Physicians, Researchers
CONTACT   Federal Information Exchange, Inc.
           comments@fedix.fie.com
FREE

http://web.fie.com/web/fed/nih/text/nihtni11.htm

University of Washington Pathology WWW Server ★★★

The University of Washington Department of Pathology provides information on the online resources available for the study of pathology. The page has links to information on the graduate program and related medical sites on the web.

KEYWORDS   Educational Resources, Medical Schools, Pathology, Research
AUDIENCE   Medical Professionals, Pathologists, Researchers
CONTACT   David Adler
           dadler@u.washington.edu
FREE

http://www.pathology.washington.edu/

Medicine

See also
Health & Medicine · *Biomedicine*
Health & Medicine · *Dental Health*
Health & Medicine · *Reference*

The Clinical Decision Making Group (MEDG) ★★★

The Clinical Decision Making Group (MEDG) at MIT works on medical applications utilizing artificial intelligence and computer science. Included in their site is information about their projects, including Guardian Angel patient-centered health information systems, the Heart Failure Program diagnosis system, and the Geninfer genetic risk diagnosis project. Project reports include staff backgrounds, technical reports, documents, and other outside related resources. This site also provides bibliography and ftp sites for accessing MEDG data, as well as links to other related Web sites and documents. Users can also find out about educational programs offered by the group.

Keywords Computer Science, Medical Research, Medical Software
Audience Artificial Intelligence Researchers, Medical Professionals, Medical Researchers
Contact webmaster@medg.lcs.mit.edu
Free

http://medg.lcs.mit.edu/

Dr. Quinn's Online Textbook of Otolaryngology ★★

This site provides access to Dr. Quinn's Online Textbook of Otolaryngology. Otolaryngology is medicine related to the ears, the nose, and the throat, more commonly known as ENT. The site entails a compilation of papers from proceedings of the Department of Otolaryngology of the University of Texas Medical Branch at Galveston. Subjects covered include allergies, ear malformations, and snoring.

Keywords Education (College/University), Medical Treatment, Medicine, Online Books
Audience Doctors, Family Physicians, Medical Practitioners, Physicians
Contact fbquinn@phil.utmb.edu
Free

gopher://phil.utmb.edu/

Karolinska Institute ★★★

This is a gopher server of the Karolinska Institute, Sweden. It contains information on the Karolinska Institue (KI), departments, hospitals, email addresses, media, course literature, phone numbers, and much more. Information also includes public transportation schedules. In addition, it provides links to other medical gophers.

Keywords Education (College/University), Health Sciences, Medicine, Sweden
Audience Educators (University), Health Care Professionals, Medical Professionals
Contact staff@nvg.ki.se
Free

gopher://gopher.mic.ki.se/

Connections to Emergency Services

S.O.S . . .

What do you do after an earthquake or a tornado? If someone starts to choke, would you know how to help them? Get the answers fast on the Internet, even finding organizations available to you following a disaster.

At the "Emergency Services World Wide Web Site" homepage, you can get information on emergency services available online, as well as email addresses and electronic publications for emergency services.

(http://gilligan.uafadm.alaska.edu/www_911.htm)

If you want a quick way to find out what help is available to you after a natural or manmade disaster, then the "Emergency—Guide to Emergency Services World Wide" is the place to visit. It provides a full archive of each organization's services. Additionally, if you want to volunteer or provide financial help, this site will tell you how.

(http://www.catt.citri.edu.au/emergency/)

Medical List-Guide To Internet Clinical Medicine Resources ★★★

The Medical List is a guide to internet clinical medicine resources. It is offered in text form as 'The Medical List' and in a hypertext database as Medical Matrix. Under each topic, URLs are given along with a description of the topic. For example the Cancernet Guide To Cancer Treatment URL is given in text form and then a description of Cancernet in text follows. Other topics include MEDsearch America, an Employment Database, The Virtual Hospital, Disease Categorized Information, and many more.

Keywords Internet Resources, Medicine
Audience General Public, Medical Professionals, Medical Students, Nurses, Physicians
Contact Dr. Gary Malet
gmalet@surfer.win.net
Free

gopher://una.hh.lib.umich.edu:70/00/
inetdirsstacks/medclin:malet

Medical Matrix ★★★

This is an introduction to Medical Matrix. Medical Matrix came about in order to train the medical community to use available Internet resources. It offers physicians and healthworkers point and click access for clinical medicine resources. Commands for complex Internet utilities, in-depth descriptions of medical databases, and specific instructions to access and retrieve information are presented. Steps to promote networking for individuals and institutions are described.

Keywords Internet Resources, Medicine
Audience General Public, Medical Professionals, Medical Students, Nurses, Physicians
Contact Dr. Gary Malet
gmalet@surfer.win.net
Free

http://ukanaix.cc.ukans.edu:80/cwis/
units/medcntr/Lee/INTRO.HTML

The National Library of Medicine Gopher ★★★

This gopher hole is maintained by the National Library of Medicine. It provides a wide variety of information about the library, its services, research activities, visitor information, events, and more. Online services include library catalogs and databases.

KEYWORDS Biomedical Research, Health Journals, Libraries, National Library Of Medicine
AUDIENCE Biomedical Researchers, Medical Practitioners, Medical Researchers, Physicians
CONTACT admin@gopher.nlm.nih.gov
FREE

gopher://gopher.nlm.nih.gov/

The National Physician Assistant Page ★★★

This page serves as an information resource for Physician Assistants and those interested in the profession. The site provides an extensive description of the profession, an overview of educational programs indexed by state, a demographics overview, a summary of current research, job listings (for faculty and primary care positions), an index of organizations and information resources (indexed by state and type), occasional articles, and links to other relevant sites. Users can make entries into the current research and job listings sections with a forms interface.

KEYWORDS Medical Education, Medical Research
AUDIENCE Health Care Professionals, Medical Educators, Medical Students, Physician Assistants
CONTACT John Schira, PA-C pa_editor@halcyon.com
FREE

http://www.halcyon.com/physasst/

TraumaNET Home Page ★★★

TraumaNET provides a broad range of resources on medical trauma and critical care, including information on prevention, treatment, and medical training. This page makes available a monthly case presentation, including summaries, X-rays, and color diagrams of actual trauma cases, a home page for the Shreveport, LA chapter of Mothers Against Drunk Driving, a gopher with relevant files and software (mostly Macintosh), and many links to WWW and FTP sites relevant to trauma and critical care.

KEYWORDS Critical Care, Reference, Surgery
AUDIENCE Health Care Professionals, Medical Trauma Victims, Physicians
CONTACT eblock@lsumc.edu
FREE

http://www.trauma.lsumc.edu/

UMDS Image Processing Group ★★★

The United Medical & Dental Schools (UMDS) Image Processing Group in London conducts research into medical image processing and computer vision, and their home page provides information about their projects as well as links to other medical imaging resources. Their site includes online publications on topics in Data Fusion and Computer Vision, and access to the medical image archives, with head images and radiograms. There's also a calendar of biomedical imaging conferences and newsletters.

KEYWORDS Biomedicine, Medical Imaging, Medical Software, Radiology
AUDIENCE Bioscientists, Medical Image Professionals, Medical Professionals, Radiologists
CONTACT webmaster@ipg.umds.ac.uk
FREE

http://nothung.umds.ac.uk

USC Neurosurgical Information Resource ★★★

Aiming to give the international patient and physician community greater access to neurosurgical care, the USC Neurosurgical Information Resource allows users to submit neurosurgery questions over the Internet, to be answered via email using resources of the USC faculty, staff, and libraries. A separate list shows the department's specialties. An information section provides articles on neurosurgery as well as sketches and current research of the USC Neurosurgical faculty.

KEYWORDS Medical Reference, Medical Schools, Neurosurgery
AUDIENCE Medical Researchers, Medical Students, Neurosurgery Patients, Physicians
CONTACT Peter Gruen, M.D. jpgruen@hsc.usc.edu
FREE

http://www.usc.edu/hsc/neurosurgery/

Vaccine Research and Development ★★★

The National Institute of Allergy and Infectious Diseases (NIAID) is the center of Vaccine Research and Development. The Institute supports wide-reaching research on all types of infectious diseases, their causes, research on the immune system, and cooperation among scientists and researchers in government, industry, and academic institutions. NIAID conducts vaccine research in four major divisions: Division of Microbiology and Infectious Diseases, the Division of Acquired Immunodeficiency Syndrome, the Division of Allergy, Immunology and Transplantation, and the Division of Intramural Research. Research is being done on AIDS vaccines, DNA technology, vaccine-preventable childhood diseases, viral hepatitis, malaria, leprosy, pneumococcal pneumonia, group B streptococcus, tuberculosis, and pertussis (whooping cough). The patient population is varied and includes healthy normal infants to high-risk groups elderly individuals.

KEYWORDS Allergies, Infectious Diseases, Public Health, Vaccine Research
AUDIENCE Biomedical Scientists, Molecular Biologists, Physicians, Researchers
CONTACT Federal Information Exchange, Inc. comments@fedix.fie.com
FREE

http://web.fie.com/web/fed/nih/text/nihtni06.htm

The Virtual Medical Center ★★★★

The Virtual Medical Center provides many links to different medical and hospital related references. The topics covered include medical schools, courses and education resources, graduate and undergraduate health science related courses, the reference desk, and time and weather. There are also links to other virtual centers including dental, pharmacy, veterinary, nursing, public health, allied health and nutrition centers.

KEYWORDS Hospitals, Medical Schools

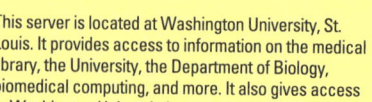

AUDIENCE Dentists, Nurse Practitioners, Nurses, Pharmacists, Physicians, Veterinarians
CONTACT Jim Martindale jmartindale@vmsa.oac.uci.edu
FREE

http://www-sci.lib.uci.edu:80/~martindale/Dental.html

Washington University Medical Gopher ★★★

This server is located at Washington University, St. Louis. It provides access to information on the medical library, the University, the Department of Biology, biomedical computing, and more. It also gives access to Washington University's extensive FTP archives. It has links to other gophers, as well.

KEYWORDS Education (College/University), Libraries, Medical Research, Medicine
AUDIENCE Biologists, Educators (University), Medical Professionals, Students
FREE

gopher://medinfo.wustl.edu:90/

Yale Image Processing and Analysis Group ★★★

The Yale Image Processing and Analysis Group Web site provides information about their projects and research, focusing on 3D diagnostics and Biomedical Images. Users will find research area overviews, with topics such as shape based tracking, magnetic resonance tagging, and biomedical images, with numerous online publications included. Demonstration examples of their research are also provided as MPEG movies and still images. Links to other bioscience sites are also included.

KEYWORDS Biosciences, Medical Imaging, Medical Software, Radiology
AUDIENCE Bioscientists, Medical Image Specialists, Medical Professionals, Radiologists
CONTACT mceachen@noodle.med.yale.edu
FREE

http://noodle.med.yale.edu

Mental Health

See also
Health & Medicine · Public Health
Humanities & Social Sciences · Psychology

The Depression FAQ ★★★

The Depression FAQ is a complete resource of information and materials about depression, taken from the alt.support.depression newsgroup. Users will find basic definitions of different kinds of depression, causes, and medicine and electroconvulsive treatment information. Answers to the frequently asked questions are provided by topic, with cross references to other related questions. Also included are book lists and online links to depression resources, as well as addresses and phone numbers of depression specialists in the U.K.

KEYWORDS Depression, Prozac
AUDIENCE Depression Sufferers, General Public, Health Care Professionals

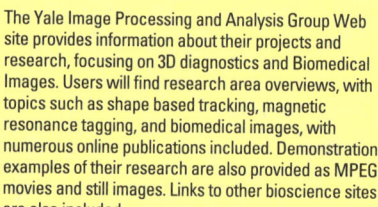

CONTACT Cynthia Frazer
cf12@CORNELL.edu

FREE

http://avocado.pc.helsinki.fi/%7Ejanne/asdfaq/

The Florida Mental Health Institute (FMHI) ★★★

The Florida Mental Health Institute's (FMHI) mission is to strengthen mental health services throughout the state of Florida. FMHI conducts research, education, and demonstration programs. The main topics of research are aging and mental health, child and family studies, community mental health, and mental health law and policy. This gopher server offers information on FMHI, its programs, departments related to health, library facilities and services.

KEYWORDS Aging, Children's Health, Medical Research, Mental Health
AUDIENCE Health Care Professionals, Medical Researchers, Mental Health Professionals
CONTACT Max Dertke
Dertke@hal.fmhi.usf.edu
FREE

gopher://fmhi.usf.edu/

Mood Disorders Server ★★★

The Mood Disorders Server provides information and resources on depression and other mood disorders. The site also contains FAQ's on Prozac and Effexor, an FAQ on depression and other resources related to mood disorders. There are also links to related servers and pages on the web, including HabitSmart which deals with addictions.

KEYWORDS Medicine, Mental Health, Mood Disorders, Prozac
AUDIENCE Health Care Professionals, Mental Health Sufferers, Psychiatrists, Psychologists, Students
CONTACT janne@avocado.pc.helsinki.fi
FREE

http://avocado.pc.helsinki.fi/~janne/mood/mood.html

National Insitute of Mental Health Gopher Server ★★★

This gopher site belongs to the National Institute of Mental Health (NIMH), a division of the National Institutes of Health. The information contains descriptions of the NIMH and its activities, access to some relevant publications, and links to other medical sites on the Internet.

KEYWORDS Medicine, Mental Health, Neurology, Psychiatry
AUDIENCE Medical Researchers, Neuroscientists, Psychiatrists, Psychologists
CONTACT gopher-adm@gopher.nimh.nih.gov
FREE

gopher://gopher.nimh.nih.gov/

gopher://nymph.nimh.nih.gov/

Connections to Parenting

Mama told me there would be days like this

Parenting draws on almost every skill and every experience you've had in life. Naturally, then, most of us need occasional help and advice in raising our children. There are many places on the Internet that provide such support and guidance.

One place to check out is the "Parents Helping Parents" site on the World Wide Web. This site provides support to parents of children with disabilities, and access to a number of disability resources. You'll also learn about health habits for kids, and gain access to the World Health Organization.

(http://www.portal.com/~cbntmkr/php.html)

If you or your child suffer from allergies, you'll find help at the "Online Allergy Center," which provides information and assistance in dealing with a wide variety of allergies—including those related to food.

(http://www.sig.net/~allergy/info.html)

The PSYCGRAD Project of the University of Ottawa ★★★

This is a gopher server of the PSYCGRAD Project maintained by Matthew Simpson of the University of Ottawa in Ottawa, Canada. The PSYCGRAD Project is the electronically based standard of communication among graduate students in the field of psychology. Information provided includes a detailed description of the Project, a copy of The PSYCGRAD Mission Statement, and other miscellaneous items (instructions, how-to, useful tips, etc.), as well as copies of The Psychology Graduate Student Journal and more.

KEYWORDS Canada, Education (College/University), Psychology, Social Sciences
AUDIENCE Psychology Educators, Psychology Students, Students (University)
CONTACT Matthew Simpson
054340@acadvm1.uottawa.ca
FREE

gopher://panda1.uottawa.ca:4010/

Self Help Psychology Magazine ★★★★

Self Help Psychology Magazine online covers many psychological issues including relationships, sexuality, parenting, health, anxiety, and addiction. The articles are written by mental health professionals for the discussion of general psychology as applied to people's everyday lives.

KEYWORDS Magazines, Medicine, Psychiatry, Psychology
AUDIENCE General Public, Psychiatrists, Psychologists
CONTACT Marlene M. Maheu, Ph.D., editor
drm@thegroup.net
FREE

http://www.well.com/www/selfhelp/

Mental Health – Organizations

Vanderbilt University Center for Mental Health Policy

This WWW site provides information on Vanderbilt University's Center for Mental Health Policy (CMHP). Among the documents available from CMHP, users will find publications, reports, unpublished manuscripts concerning the Ft. Bragg Demonstration Project and the Family Empowerment Project, as well as material on new books and other health resources. An ordering form is also available to order some of those manuscripts through the Internet.

KEYWORDS   Education (College/University), Health, Health Sciences, Mental Health
AUDIENCE   Health Care Policymakers, Health Care Professionals, Health Science Researchers, Mental Health Professionals
CONTACT   Mark Kurt
kurt@uansv5.vanderbilt.edu
FREE

http://cmhp.vipps.vanderbilt.edu

Organizations

See also
Health & Medicine · *Addictions*
Health & Medicine · *Disabilities*
Health & Medicine · *Disease*
Health & Medicine · *Public Health*
Health & Medicine · *Women's Health*

American Heart Association

This is a gopher server of the American Heart Association. It provides information on legislative issues, community and educations programs, patient support groups, scientific publications, meetings, news releases, and more. It has links to other gophers as well.

KEYWORDS   Health, Health Care, Health Sciences, Medicine
AUDIENCE   Health Care Professionals, Health Science Researchers, Medical Professionals, Medical Researchers
CONTACT   gopher@amhrt.org
FREE

gopher://gopher.amhrt.org/

The American Physiological Society (APS) Information Server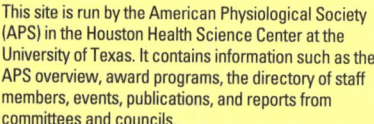

This site is run by the American Physiological Society (APS) in the Houston Health Science Center at the University of Texas. It contains information such as the APS overview, award programs, the directory of staff members, events, publications, and reports from committees and councils.

KEYWORDS   Education (College/University), Health Sciences, Medical Informatics, Medical Research
AUDIENCE   Medical Informatics, Medical Professionals, Medical Researchers, Medical Students

CONTACT   aps_server@oac.hsc.uth.tmc.edu
FREE

gopher://gopher.uth.tmc.edu:3300/

Austin Hospital

This server provides images, telephone directories, medical resources, and software archives from the Austin Hospital at the University of Melbourne, Australia. There are also links to other medicine and biology-oriented servers on the Internet.

KEYWORDS   Hospital Administration, Medical Resources, Medical Treatment, Medicine
AUDIENCE   Doctors, Medical Professionals, Medical Students, Nurses
CONTACT   Daniel O'Callaghan
gopher@austin.unimelb.edu.au
FREE

gopher://gopher.austin.unimelb.edu.au/

CRY (Child Relief and You)

These web pages, administered by CRY (Child Relief and You), contain information on CRY's efforts to supply food, medicine and education to poverty-stricken children across India. Background information on the organization itself and contacts are available.

KEYWORDS   Children, Hunger, India, International Aid, Non Profit Organizations
AUDIENCE   India Residents, Indians
CONTACT   Vijay Vemulapalli
vvemulap@buster.eng.ua.edu
FREE

http://www.acsu.buffalo.edu/~kripa/cry.html

HospitalWeb

The HospitalWeb is a compiled list of hospital web sites, produced by the Department of Neurology at Massachusetts General Hospital, designed to allow users to access information about health care providers around the world. Users will find links listed alphabetically, with location information but no description of the contents of the Web pages themselves. Links to Medical school information are also included.

KEYWORDS   Hospitals, Medical Administration, Meta-Indexes
AUDIENCE   Health Care Professionals, Medical Patients, Medical Researchers
CONTACT   John Lester
lester@helix.mgh.harvard.edu
FREE

http://dem0nmac.mgh.harvard.edu/hospitalweb.html

IMIA

This is a gopher server of the International Medical Informatics Association (IMIA), located at the University of Maryland. It contains information on the International Medical Informatics Association, educational programs in medical informatics, announcements, news, mailing lists, the calendar of upcoming events, and more. It has links to other informatics gophers.

KEYWORDS   Health, Medical Informatics, Medicine

AUDIENCE   Medical Educators, Medical Informatics, Medical Practitioners, Medical Students
FREE

gopher://umabnet.ab.umd.edu:152/

National Institutes of Health (NIH) Home Page

This site gives information into the research activities, resources, events, and facilities at the National Institutes of Health, a Federal biomedical research center. There is a large range of databases about biomedicine online at this site.

KEYWORDS   Biological Research, Biomedicine, Health Care
AUDIENCE   Biologists, Biomedical Researchers, Biotechnologists, Medical Researchers
CONTACT   gopher@gopher.nih.gov
FREE

http://www.nih.gov/index.html

gopher://gopher.nih.gov/

Nightingale Gopher

The menu structure of this University of Tennessee nursing gopher, NIGHTINGALE, is organized from a nursing point-of-view to make it an intuitive tool for all nurses to use. Its purpose is to provide the nursing community with easy access to information which is unique to the profession or especially relevant to its needs, and to facilitate communication within the nursing community. The menu contains items about research, practice, education, professional nursing communications, publications, and other nursing resources.

KEYWORDS   Medical Professionals, Medical Schools, Nursing
AUDIENCE   Health Care Professionals, Nurses
CONTACT   florence@nightingale.con.utk.edu
FREE

gopher://nightingale.con.utk.edu/

Physicians for Human Rights

This gopher serves as a bulletin board and archive for Physicians for Human Rights (PHR), an organization of health professionals and citizens using the medical and forensic sciences to prevent violations of international human rights and humanitarian law. The gopher contains calls to action and notices of current investigations, issue-related archives of information and position statements, e.g. "Doctors and Capital Punishment" and "Chemical Weapons." Also available are a catalog of publications and PHR membership information.

KEYWORDS   Human Rights, Issues, Medicine
AUDIENCE   General Public, Human Rights Activists, Physicians
FREE

gopher://gopher.igc.apc.org:5000/00/int/phr/about/1

Organizations – Personal Care

U.S. Department of Health and Human Services ★★★★

The U.S. Department of Health and Human Services (DHHS) organization provides a selected index of available information by topic, and provides links to other federal government resources. Some of the organizatons included are the Centers for Disease Control (CDC), the Food and Drug Administration (FDA), and the Social Security Administration (SSA). Some of the topics covered include GrantsNet, AIDS Related Information, Cancer Information, and more.

KEYWORDS	Government Agencies, Grants (Medical), Medical Research, Social Security Administration
AUDIENCE	Government Employees, Health Care Professionals, Medical Researchers, Physicians
CONTACT	tthompso@os.dhhs.gov
FREE	

http://www.os.dhhs.gov/

World Health Organization (WHO) ★★★★

The World Health Organization's (WHO) objective is the attainment by all peoples of the highest possible level of health. The server contains information regarding WHO, WHO's major programs, a complete archive of WHO statements on various current international health and medical crises, and guidelines for international health and travel. Also links are provided to related servers. The gopher server of the World Health Organization (WHO) in Switzerland offers information on WHO, email addresses of staff, WHO addresses, WHO descriptions, its programs, news releases, and more.

KEYWORDS	Health, International Aid, Travel, United Nations
AUDIENCE	Environmentalists, General Public, Health Care Professionals
CONTACT	webmaster@who.ch
FREE	

http://www.who.org/

gopher://gopher.who.org/1

Zen Hospice Project Home Page ★★★★

The Zen Hospice Project (ZHP) operates a hospice in San Francisco and various outpatient and education programs. According to this page's author, the ZHP is "dedicated to the care of people approaching death and increasing our understanding of our own impermanence." Their web pages offer numerous articles on this interweaving of Zen Buddhist philosophy and hospice care, including information on the variety of outpatient and educational programs offered by the organization.

KEYWORDS	Terminal Illness, Zen Buddhism
AUDIENCE	Health Care Employees, Health Educators, Hospice Workers, Medical Practitioners, Terminally Ill People
FREE	

http://www.well.com/Community/zenhospice/homepage.html

Connections to Self Help Guides
"Please, I'd rather do it myself!"

America's leading source of self-help legal information. Founded in 1971, Nolo publishes easy-to-use books and software on consumer law subjects such as wills, small claims court, divorce and debt problems. Nolo also provides excellent legal information to small business, including help with incorporation, partnerships, employment law, patents and trademarks.

Nolo Press is dedicated to the simple proposition that the American legal system should be affordable and accessible to all.

Fed Up with the Legal System

If you are an independent, free spirited person, you probably like to do things yourself—whether it's fixing a leaky faucet or defending yourself in small claims court. If you could use some expert advice on how to handle these and other problems, turn to the Internet.

Maybe you want to write your own last will and testament or draw up a tenant lease. Through "Nolo Press Self-Help Law Center," you can see what contracts should look like and get tips about how to prepare legal documents for all occasions. You'll also learn about your rights under the law in a variety of sticky situations.

(http://gnn.com/gnn/bus/nolo/index.html)

Perhaps you want to improve a relationship you have with your boss, a family member or a friend. There are psychological self-help books and magazines available on the Internet to help you do just that. You can find out how to end a bad habit or turn a difficult situation into a positive experience through the "Self-Help Psychology Magazine" site on the World Wide Web. Learn new techniques for self-improvement in forums on "RING!" and in the "Courage to Change Catalog." The latter site provides a list of books, audio tapes, and audio cassettes on subjects including divorce, co-parenting, coping, and positive living.

(http://www.well.com/user/selfhelp/)

also, (http://www.ring.com/miself.html)   also, (http://www.courage.com/ctc.html)

Personal Care

See also
Health & Medicine · *Health Conditions*
Sports & Recreation · *Food & Dining*
Sports & Recreation · *Personal Fitness*

The Food Science & Nutrition Gopher ★★★

This site gives access to data and databases related to food science and nutrition. The Food Science & Nutrition Gopher's intention is to bring current information about the department to students (and prospective students), to the staff and to the faculty. Topics include courses, FoodNet archives, graduate programs, news, and more.

KEYWORDS	Food Sciences, Nutrition, Universities
AUDIENCE	Educators (University), Nutritionists, Students (Secondary/College)
CONTACT	Paul Brady pbrady@che2.che.umn.edu
FREE	

gopher://rodent.cis.umn.edu:11126/

Grant's Health Products - Health Vitamins ★★★
(COMMERCIAL)

This site serves as a catalog for all the health products sold by Grant's, All Golden Pride/Rawleigh brand. Some of the products include vitamins, antioxidant capsules and bee pollen.

KEYWORDS	Health, Nutrition, Product Information, Vitamins
AUDIENCE	Consumers, Nutritionists
FREE	

http://branch.com/health/health.html

International Food Information Council ★★★★

The International Food Information Council Foundation (IFIC) is a nonprofit organization designed to provide scientific information about food and food safety. On their web site users will find background about the IFIC, recent press releases, and IFIC publications on topics such as food biotechnology and pesticides. Information is listed according to the specified audience—consumers, educators, reporters, health care professionals, or parents, with features such as 'Ten Tips for Healthy Eating' and excerpts from IFIC materials. Food Insight, the IFIC newsletter discussing nutrition issues, is provided, along with several FAQs about caffeine, E.coli, and MSG, and general food safety information.

KEYWORDS Consumer Issues, Nutrition
AUDIENCE General Public, Health Care Professionals, Journalists, Nutritionists, Parents
CONTACT carbog@ific.health.org
FREE

http://ificinfo.health.org/

Recommendations— Vitamins, Minerals & Trace Elements ★★★

This document discusses concepts of nutrition and emphasizes the importance of prevention. The author recommends, "think French when eating. Savor your food and eat slowly." He also discusses the merits of a low fat diet, low salt intake, increased fiber, etc. Recommendations for minerals and vitamins with their effects are also provided.

KEYWORDS Cancer, Nutrition, Vitamins
AUDIENCE Cancer Patients, Clinicians, Parents, Physicians, Radiologists, Therapists
FREE

http://cancer.med.upenn.edu:80/med_onc/nutr94.html

The Virtual Nutrition Center ★★★★

The Virtual Nutrition Center provides links to many different nutrition related references. Some of the topics include nutrition, courses and education resources, and graduate and undergraduate nutrition and food science related courses. There are also links to other virtual centers including medical, pharmacy, veterinary, nursing, public health, allied health and dental centers.

KEYWORDS Holistic Health, Nutrition
AUDIENCE Dentists, Nurse Practitioners, Nurses, Pharmacists, Physicians, Veterinarians
CONTACT Jim Martindale
jmartindale@vmsa.oac.uci.edu
FREE

http://www-sci.lib.uci.edu:80/~martindale/Dental.html

Public Health

See also
Health & Medicine · *Medical Specialties*
Health & Medicine · *Mental Health*
Health & Medicine · *Reference*
Popular Culture & Entertainment · *Family & Community*

AIDS FAQ ★★★

This is the FAQ from sci.med.aids, a medical discussion of AIDS causes and treatment.

KEYWORDS AIDS (Acquired Immune Deficiency Syndrome), FAQs (Frequently Asked Questions), Medical Resources
AUDIENCE AIDS Activists, AIDS Patients, Health Care Professionals, Medical Students
FREE

ftp://rtfm.mit.edu/pub/usenet/sci.answers/aids-faq/

AIDS Information via CHAT Database ★★★

The AIDS Information via CHAT Database is a conversational hypertext access technology that will answer plain-English questions about AIDS.

KEYWORDS AIDS (Acquired Immune Deficiency Syndrome), Databases, Immunology, Interactive Education
AUDIENCE AIDS Activists, AIDS Patients, Educators, Health Care Professionals
FREE

telnet://debra.dgbt.doc.ca:3000/

The Cecil G. Sheps Center for Health Services Research ★★★

This is a gopher for the Cecil G. Sheps Center for Health Services Research at the University of North Carolina at Chapel Hill. The Center is mandated to research the structure and effectiveness of the nation's health care system. Their gopher provides information on the Center's programs and research activities. It also provides access to the staff directory.

KEYWORDS Health Sciences, Medical Research, Medicine, Public Health
AUDIENCE Health Care Policy Makers, Health Care Professionals
CONTACT Kathleen Crook
Kathleen_Crook@unc.edu
FREE

gopher://sheps.schsr.unc.edu/

Center for Food Safety and Applied Nutrition— CFSAN ★★★

The Center for Food Safety and Applied Nutrition (CFSAN) is a division of the Food and Drug Administration which ensures that food and cosmetics in the U.S. are safe and the food nutritious. Users will find press releases about current food issues, such as biotechnology and genetically altered tomatoes, as well as information about food additives and pesticides, foodborne illnesses, and food labeling. Cosmetics materials include labeling guidelines and regulation information. Several advice columns are included on food issues such as vegetarian diets and properly preparing ground meat. Access to the FDA gopher and databases with further nutrition materials is also provided.

KEYWORDS Consumer Issues, Food And Drug Administration (FDA), Nutrition
AUDIENCE General Public, Nutritionists
CONTACT Larry Dusold
lrd@vm.cfsan.fda.gov
FREE

http://vm.cfsan.fda.gov/list.html

The Centers for Disease Control and Prevention Website ★★★★

The Centers for Disease Control Website contains a great deal of relevant information for people interested in patterns of illness among Americans. Here you will find data about the CDC and links to all of its branches, including the National Center for Environmental Health, the National Center for Occupational Safety and Health, the Epidemiology Program Office, and the National Immunization Program. CDC journals are archived here, including the Morbidity and Mortality Weekly Report. There is a link to the Hazardous Substance Release/Health Effects Database (HAZDAT), as well as links to the National Institute of Health, the Department of Health & Human Services Gopher, the World Health Organization (WHO) Gopher and the Library of Congress Gopher, and others.

KEYWORDS Centers For Disease Control, Diseases, Epidemiology, Occupational Health & Safety
AUDIENCE Doctors, Epidemiologists, Health Care Professionals
CONTACT netinfo@cdc1.cdc.gov
FREE

http://www.cdc.gov/

College of Human Ecology and Division of Nutritional Sciences Gopher Server ★★★

On this server you will find information about the College of Human Ecology and the Division of Nutritional Sciences at Cornell, in Ithica, New York. Included are descriptions of the departments and administrative units, faculty, staff and student directories, seminar listings, and much more. In addition, links to other sources of information on the Internet are available.

KEYWORDS Ecology, Nutrition, University Administration
AUDIENCE Ecologists, Educators (University), Nutritionists, Students (University)
CONTACT Lynne Worsfold
ljw6@cornell.edu
FREE

gopher://gopher.human.cornell.edu/

Comprehensive Epidemiologic Data Resource ★★★

This site offers access to the Comprehensive Epidemiologic Data Resource (CEDR) data catalog. There are instructions and customer service information available for users of the resource. The main focus of these services has been the Health and Mortality Study of the DOE work force. The epidemiologic data currently available through the CEDR Program consist of analytic data sets, working data sets, and their associated documentation files. Detailed definitions of these data sets and files are provided in the CEDR Catalog.

KEYWORDS Databases, Epidemiology, Health Statistics, Public Health
AUDIENCE Epidemiologists, Health Care Professionals, Health Science Researchers

Public Health 397

CONTACT Dr. Mark Durst
MJDurst@lbl.gov
FREE
gopher://cedr.lbl.gov/

Department of Food Science & Nutrition- University of Minnesota ★★★★

The Department of Food Science and Nutrition at the University of Minnesota offers undergraduate and graduate programs in Nutrition and in Food Science that prepare students for careers related to food and health. This server provides links to a photographic tour, a searchable index, Twin Cities information, announcements, Internet Supported Courses, and more.

KEYWORDS Distance Education, Food Sciences, Nutrition
AUDIENCE Computer Users, Educators (University), Internet Users, Researchers, Students (University)
FREE
http://fscn1.fsci.umn.edu

FDA Center for Food Safety & Applied Nutrition ★★★

The FDA Center for Food Safety & Applied Nutrition server is maintained by the Center for Food Safety and Nutrition, a department of the Food and Drug Administration. The site provides access to several FDA/CFSAN documents and links to other U.S. government servers.

KEYWORDS Food And Drug Administration (FDA), Government Agencies, Health News, Nutrition
AUDIENCE General Public, Government Employees, Nutritionists
CONTACT lrd@vm.cfsan.fda.gov
FREE
http://vm.cfsan.fda.gov/index.html

Finnish Institute of Occupational Health (FIOH) ★★★★

The Finnish Institute of Occupational Health (FIOH) generates information on the interaction of work and health to promote healthier and safer working conditions. The Institute does research projects on occupational health services, work-related health problems, and occupational hygiene studies. There are links to other occupational health foundations world wide.

KEYWORDS Finland, Medical Information, Medical Research, Occupational Health & Safety
AUDIENCE Doctors, Employees, Health Care Professionals
CONTACT Ville Pilviö
vpil@occuphealth.fi
FREE
http://www.occuphealth.fi/

Connections to Nutrition
Eat your vegetables

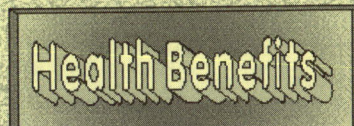

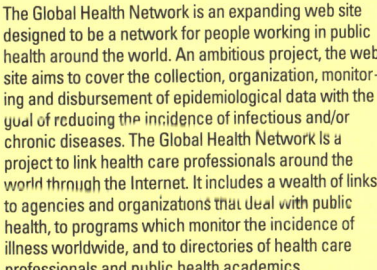

If you're counting calories, or want to find out the best diet for sports training, you'll find on the World Wide Web a veritable health spa of information on nutrition—most of which comes from registered dietitians. These sites explain, among other things, why dieting often doesn't work. You don't have to live on bean sprouts to lose weight! You can eat a balanced diet that satisfies you, too. You can even order dietary supplements, and get a nutrition expert's advice on what kind of foods you should be eating for a longer, healthier life.

(http://www.kaiwan.com/~health/info.html)

also, (http://www-sci.lib.uci.edu/HSG/Nutrition.html)

If you want nutritional counseling or wish to obtain an online personal nutrition profile, you have several sites to choose from. Look for "Ten Tips to Healthy Eating" and "Coping with Food Cravings."

(http://health.mirical.com/)

The Global Health Network ★★★★

The Global Health Network is an expanding web site designed to be a network for people working in public health around the world. An ambitious project, the web site aims to cover the collection, organization, monitoring and disbursement of epidemiological data with the goal of reducing the incidence of infectious and/or chronic diseases. The Global Health Network is a project to link health care professionals around the world through the Internet. It includes a wealth of links to agencies and organizations that deal with public health, to programs which monitor the incidence of illness worldwide, and to directories of health care professionals and public health academics.

KEYWORDS Epidemiology, Immunology, Infectious Diseases, Public Health
AUDIENCE Doctors, Epidemiologists, Health Care Policy Makers, Health Care Professionals
CONTACT rlaporte@vms.cis.pitt.edu
FREE
http://info.pitt.edu/HOME/GHNet/GHNet.html

The HIVNET Gopher ★★★

This gopher site provides information on HIVNET, the European arm of the Global Electronic Network for AIDS (GENA). Associated organizations in GENA are AEGIS, based in the U.S., APC via Greennet and Gaylink. GENA provides its connected sites with daily feeds of discussion and data areas, as well as many of the available newsletters, such as AIDS Treatment News and the CDC Daily AIDS Summary. In addition, certain library items are provided, such as the Amsterdam and Berlin conference abstracts.

KEYWORDS AIDS (Acquired Immune Deficiency Syndrome), Diseases, Medical Information
AUDIENCE AIDS Activists, AIDS Researchers, Gays, Medical Researchers
CONTACT info@hivnet.org
FREE
gopher://gopher.hivnet.org/

Harvard University School of Public Health ★★★

This site provides information about Harvard University's School of Public Health (HSPH). The server contains descriptions of departments, admissions policies, courses, course schedules, and available computer services. In addition, this site contains links to other gopher servers at Harvard University.

- KEYWORDS Computer Science, Public Health
- AUDIENCE Computer Students, Educators (University), Students (Secondary/University)
- FREE

gopher://hsph.harvard.edu/

INFACT's Tobacco Industry Campaign Page ★★★★

This series of web pages and linked documents is one part of INFACT's organized boycott of Philip Morris Tobacco, Inc. and their related companies (Kraft, Jell-o, and more). Within these pages are a number of articles of interest to anti-smoking activists, including statements from R.J. Reynolds and Philip Morris officials, and the texts of several pieces of anti-smoking legislation.

- KEYWORDS Activism, Boycott, Smoke-Free Environments, Tobacco
- AUDIENCE Medical Practitioners, Medical Researchers, Smokers
- CONTACT Thomas Boutell boutell@netcom.com
- FREE

http://sunsite.unc.edu/boutell/infact/infact.html

Immunization Action Coalition ★★★

This home page provides excerpts from newsletters and current projects of the Immunization Action Coalition, an organization promoting immunization of people of all ages against vaccine-preventable diseases. The page contains excerpts from 'Needle Tips,' the Coalition's newsletter, as well as information and news on the Hepatitis B Coalition program.

- KEYWORDS Hepatitis, Newsletters, Public Health
- AUDIENCE Doctors, Health Care Professionals, Health Care Students, Immunologists
- CONTACT immunize@winternet.com
- FREE

http://www.winternet.com/~immunize/

MUSOM RuralNet Gopher ★★

This site provides information about rural health care. The Department of Academic Computing maintains this site at the Marshall University School of Medicine in Huntington, West Virginia. The resources on this gopher include descriptions of and information about the School, rural health care resources such as the results of studies and descriptions of government programs, and links to other health care Internet sites.

- KEYWORDS Health Care, Health Sciences, Rural Development
- AUDIENCE Health Care Professionals, Health Care Providers, Medical Educators
- CONTACT Andy Jarrell gopher@musom01.mu.wvnet.edu
- FREE

gopher://ruralnet.mu.wvnet.edu/

The Malaria Database ★★★★

The Malaria Database is a complex Web site providing important references to researchers. It is more pertinent to the microbiologist, parasitologist, geneticist or medical professional than to the entomologist—this because nucleotide and protein sequence data, and malaria genome or strain information are available here. It also contains a bibliography of malaria antigens, links telling the accessor about upcoming conferences and other related Internet resources, grant information, and several links to other malaria, tropical disease or parasitology Web sites.

- KEYWORDS Malaria, Microbiology, Parasitology, Tropical Diseases
- AUDIENCE Geneticists, Medical Researchers, Microbiologists, Tropical Disease Specialists
- CONTACT Ross Coppel/The Department of Microbiology, Monash University ross.coppel@med.monash.edu.au
- FREE

http://www.wehi.edu.au/biology/malaria/who.html

Minnesota Department of Health (MDH) ★★

This gopher contains the staff directory for the Minnesota Department of Health (MDH), as well as the technical support staff information, plus an array of public domain software that MDH has found useful. There are also links to U.S. health-related resources, and other Minnesota and worldwide gopher sites.

- KEYWORDS Health Care, Internet Software, Medical Resources, Medical Schools
- AUDIENCE Health Care Professionals, Minnesota Residents
- CONTACT Elbert LaGrew Elbert.Lagrew@health.state.mn.us
- FREE

gopher://sunny.health.state.mn.us/1

NCTR Gopher Server ★★

This gopher is maintained by the National Center for Toxicology Research (NCTR), a Food and Drug Administration (FDA) research center. The mandate of the NCTR is to perform research assessing the FDA's regulatory needs. This gopher provides information about the NCTR's activities.

- KEYWORDS Biomedical Research, Government Agencies, Medical Research, Toxicology
- AUDIENCE Government Employees, Government Officials, Health Science Researchers, Toxicologists
- CONTACT gopher@fdant.nctr.fda.gov
- FREE

gopher://gopher.nctr.fda.gov/

National Institute of Allergy and Infectious Disease Gopher Server ★★★

This gopher server is maintained by the National Institute of Allergy and Infectious Disease (NIAID). It provides a variety of medicine and health sciences information, including a large number of documents on AIDS and sexually transmitted diseases. In addition, it provides access to the NIAID databases for those hosts within the National Institute of Health domain.

- KEYWORDS AIDS (Acquired Immune Deficiency Syndrome), Allergies, Infectious Diseases, Medicine
- AUDIENCE General Public, Infectious Disease Sufferers, Medical Researchers
- CONTACT Brent Sessions sessions@nih.gov
- FREE

gopher://gopher.niaid.nih.gov/

PIE (Policy Information Exchange) Online ★★★

PIE Online is a Web site put together by the Policy Information Exchange, a nonprofit institution which disseminates unbiased United States health care policy information to physical and mental health care professionals. Users will find data about current national health policy, including verbatim testimonies before the House of Representatives, budget outlines and grant information, articles about health care reform (these appeared initially in PIE's newsletter Policy in Perspective), and reviews of related articles. They'll also find bibliographies pertaining to case management issues and information on how to join PIE.

- KEYWORDS Health Care, Health Care Policy, Mental Health
- AUDIENCE Health Care Policymakers, Health Care Professionals, Health Care Reformers, Mental Health Professionals
- CONTACT pie@pie.org
- FREE

http://pie.org

SEVA Foundation home page ★★

The SEVA Foundation is a charitable organization which states its mission is 'to prevent and relieve suffering and generate hope through compassionate action.' They offer a page detailing their activities providing health and education services around the world, and their history over the last 15 years.

- KEYWORDS Health Promotion, International Aid, Non Profit Organizations
- AUDIENCE Health Care Employees, Health Educators, Medical Practitioners, Nonprofit Professionals
- FREE

http://www.well.com/Community/Seva/

SIRI FTP/Gopher File Library ★★

The SIRI FTP/Gopher File Library has various files which will be of use in developing a health and safety program. These files include the archives of newsletters on chemical safety. The archives are searchable by keyword and there are pointers to other relevant gopher sites.

- KEYWORDS Chemistry, Education (College/University), Health Care Policy, Public Access Archives
- AUDIENCE Chemists, Educators (University), Students (University)

CONTACT Ralph Stuart
rstuart@moose.uvm.edu

FREE

gopher://siri.uvm.edu/

Technical Information Services - ES&H Orders and Notices ★★★

This gopher hole is part of the Technical Information Service (TIS), sponsored by the U.S. Department of Energy's Office of Environment, Safety, and Health (ES&H). TIS provides information related to safety issues. This URL accesses a database of ES&H orders and notices about safety issues, covering issues including hazardous waste handling, maintenance management, and motor vehicle safety. The database is searchable by keywords.

KEYWORDS Government Documents, Occupational Health & Safety, Work Environment
AUDIENCE Business Professionals, Government Officials, Industrial Professionals, Professionals
CONTACT support@tis.inel.gov
FREE

gopher://dewey.tis.inel.gov:2011/

gopher://dewey.tis.inel.gov:2010/

Technical Information Services—Occupational Safety and Health Act ★★★

This gopher hole is part of the Techinical Information Service (TIS), a service sponsored by the US Department of Energy's (DOE) Office of Environment, Safety, and Health (ES&H). TIS provides information related to safety issues. This gopher provides a series of documents interpreting the 1970 Occupational Safety and Health Act. The documents are searchable by keywords.

KEYWORDS Government Agencies, Legislation, Occupational Health & Safety, Work Environment
AUDIENCE Business Professionals, Government Officials, Industrial Professionals, Professionals
CONTACT support@tis.inel.gov
FREE

gopher://dewey.tis.inel.gov:2019/

Technical Information Services—Publications of the Office of Environment, Safety and Health ★★★

This gopher hole is part of the Technical Information Service (TIS), sponsored by the U.S. Department of Energy's (DOE) Office of Environment, Safety, and Health (ES&H). TIS provides information related to safety issues. This gopher provides online access to publications from ES&H, ranging in topic from safety

Connections to Ergonomics
How to avoid a painful desk job . . .

Ever felt a pain in your lower back after working for hours in front of a computer? Perhaps your work is repetitive and you are feeling a bit like you have "tennis elbow" or "keyboard shoulder."

If your work requires repetitive motion, or if you sit for long hours at a desk . . . get up! Take a break! Then get online to find out how to reduce stress and avoid the discomfort of back and neck pain.

The World Wide Web brings together information about ergonomics from all over the world. There are many studies available on the subject, and you can get tips on how to avoid some of the common aches and pains that result from extended periods of keyboarding or other repetitive motion activities.

At the "Video Display Terminal Ergonomics," you can learn how to evaluate the ergonomic risks of your job. This site also provides educational hypermedia and information links on reducing stress that derives from sitting at a desk too long. You'll also find an array of ideas on how to take an optimal stretch break. You can even take a VDT Familiarity Exercise to find out how much you know. For instance, for the best viewing distance from a VDT screen, should your face be 18 inches, 10 inches, or 24 inches away? Or, can you get a headache from reflected glare on a VDT screen?

(http://www.virginia.edu/~enhealth/toc.html)

If you want to learn more about ergonomic studies and how industries like office seating manufacturers are responding for the well-being of employees around the world, you might tap into "Ergonomics Activities in Lulea University, Sweden."

(http://www.ludd.lutyh.se/~anthony/ergo/ergo.html)

400 Public Health – Reference

and health bulletins to a journal about occupational safety. The library is searchable by keywords.

- **KEYWORDS** Government Documents, Occupational Health & Safety, Online Journals, Work Environment
- **AUDIENCE** Business Professionals, Government Officials, Industrial Professionals, Professionals
- **CONTACT** support@tis.inel.gov
- **FREE**

gopher://dewey.tis.inel.gov:2013/

The University of Texas School of Public Health ★★★

This site is a gopher server of the University of Texas School of Public Health. It contains information on the school, admissions, Centers, Institutes, programs, facilities, the Library, research projects, and more. It also makes connections to other gophers both on and off campus.

- **KEYWORDS** Education (College/University), Health, Health Care, Medicine
- **AUDIENCE** Health Care Professionals, Medical Researchers, Students (Secondary/University)
- **FREE**

gopher://utsph.sph.uth.tmc.edu/

The Virtual Public Health Center ★★★★

The Virtual Public Health Center provides an assortment of links to many different public health related references. The topics covered include public health schools, courses and education resources, graduate and undergraduate health science related courses, the reference desk, time and weather, what's new, browse, and search. There are also links to other virtual centers including medical, pharmacy, veterinary, nursing, dental, allied health and nutrition virtual centers.

- **KEYWORDS** Medicine, Public Health
- **AUDIENCE** Health Care Officials, Health Care Professionals, Students (University)
- **CONTACT** Jim Martindale jmartindale@vmsa.oac.uci.edu
- **FREE**

http://www-sci.lib.uci.edu:80/~martindale/PHealth.html

Reference

See also
Health & Medicine · *Medicine*
Health & Medicine · *Resources*

Anatomy Teaching Modules ★★★

This site provides online anatomy teaching modules including text and images. Modules include normal knee anatomy, normal distal thigh anatomy, and TMJ Tutorial.

- **KEYWORDS** Medical Education, Medicine, Radiology
- **AUDIENCE** Artists, Educators, Health Care Professionals, Medical Residents, Medical Students
- **CONTACT** Michael L. Richardson, M.D. mrich@u.washington.edu
- **FREE**

http://www.rad.washington.edu/AnatomyModuleList.html

Austin Hospital ★★

This site provides a list of resources about HTML and academic discussion forums available on the Internet. The site is maintained at Austin Hospital in Melbourne, Australia. The HTML resources are supposed to appear in a hypertext document, but the list appears as plain text. The database of discussion forums is searchable by keywords.

- **KEYWORDS** Internet Guides, Medical Informatics, Usenet Newsgroups
- **AUDIENCE** Academics, Internet Users, Usenet News Readers
- **CONTACT** Daniel O'Callaghan gopher@austin.unimelb.edu.au
- **FREE**

http://www.austin.unimelb.edu.au:800/

The Charles A. Dana Medical Library ★★

This server provides medicine and healthcare-related information. The server is maintained by the medical library at the University of Vermont. It provides information about medical research and clinical medicine, medical consumer information, and library policy and facility information.

- **KEYWORDS** Education, Libraries, Medical Informatics, Medicine
- **AUDIENCE** Clinicians, Health Care Consumers, Health Care Providers, Medical Researchers
- **CONTACT** Elizabeth Dow edow@salus.med.uvm.edu
- **FREE**

gopher://salus.med.uvm.edu/

Explore The Virtual Heart ★★★★

This site is presented in an outline format with a plethora of links to information on the heart. The links are divided into categories such as the structure of the heart, the fluid of the heart and the vessels of the heart. There are text, images and movies on such areas as exercise, healthy eating, drug-free lifestyles, diabetes, bypass surgery, the pulmonary system, how to take your pulse, EKGs, and more.

- **KEYWORDS** Exercise, Heart, Primary/Secondary Education, Pulmonary System
- **AUDIENCE** Educators (Primary/Secondary), Internet Users, Students (Primary/Secondary)
- **FREE**

http://sln.fi.edu/TOC.biosci.html

Factsheets ★★★

This is a gopher menu of factsheet links put out by the NY Department of Health. Some of the the diseases indexed include chickenpox, botulism, gonorrhea, hepatitis A, B and C, Herpes II, Influenza, Kawasaki syndrome, leprosy, Lyme disease, rabies, ringworm, and many more.

- **KEYWORDS** Diseases, Health, Medicine, Rabies
- **AUDIENCE** General Public, Nurses, Parents, Patients, Physicians
- **FREE**

gopher://gopher.health.state.ny.us:70/11/.consumer/.factsheets

Health Explorer - Men's Health ★★★★

This page, a subsection of the MEDIC (Medical Education Information Center) system at the University of Texas' Medical School, focuses on male health issues but also contains useful health information of a more general nature such as articles on exercise and nutrition.

- **KEYWORDS** Men's Health, Men's Issues, Prostate Cancer, Weight Loss
- **AUDIENCE** Health Educators, Medical Practitioners, Men, Women
- **CONTACT** Dr. Anne LeMaistre lemaist@casper.med.uth.tmc.edu
- **FREE**

http://hyrax.med.uth.tmc.edu/ptnt/00000391.htm

Health Information ★★★

This gopher, produced by the McKinley Center at the University of Illinois, contains information about general health care and health related issues. Users will find topics such as diseases/conditions, drugs and alcohol, fitness, nutrition, sexuality, women's health, and stress, as well as materials about medications and tests.

- **KEYWORDS** Health Care, Nutrition, Women's Health
- **AUDIENCE** General Public, Health Care Professionals, Women
- **CONTACT** Lynn Bilger gopher@uiuc.edu
- **FREE**

gopher://gopher.uiuc.edu/11/UI/CSF/health/heainfo

Hippocratic Oath ★★

This site presents the full text of the Hippocratic Oath. There is an introductory note about the law of Hippocrates and the oath of Hippocrates.

- **KEYWORDS** Hippocratic Oath, Medical Ethics, Medicine
- **AUDIENCE** Doctors, Health Care Professionals, Medical Students
- **FREE**

ftp://ftp.std.com/obi/Hippocrates/Hippocratic.Oath

HyperDoc ★★★★

HyperDOC is a Multimedia/Hypertext Resource of the U.S. National Library of Medicine (NLM). This site provides access to the National Library of Medicine and their databases, exhibits, and images. The library's Medical Literature Analysis and Retrieval System (MEDLARS), a pioneering effort in rapid online bibliographic retrieval, provides an avenue for preparing bibliographic publications such as Index Medicus, as well as access to online bibliographic retrieval. The site includes information on Intramural Programs, including the National Center for Biotechnology, the Visible Human Project and the Lister Hill National Center for

Biomedical Communication. The site contains links to information on extramural programs, and grants and contracts. It also provides visitor information and current events listings.

KEYWORDS   Biotechnology, Medicine, Multimedia
AUDIENCE   Educators, Health Care Professionals, Researchers, Students
FREE

http://www.nlm.nih.gov

Internet Health Resources ★★★

This Web site is designed to provide access to health information for both San Francisco, CA residents and a global audience of consumers and health care providers. Users will find the Family Fertility Center home page, which provides materials about egg donation and surrogacy, address lists for state and national health organizations, and the Medical Reporter, with articles and general information about basic health conditions. Other features include links to other health focused Web sites, listed according to the subject focus of each site, a compiled list of online and hard copy health magazines, and health care legislation information. San Francisco residents will find health information specific to the Bay Area region.

KEYWORDS   Health Care, Medicine
AUDIENCE   General Public, Health Care Professionals
CONTACT   Cliff Bernstein
          cliffb@hooked.net
FREE

http://www.ihr.com/

Jonathon Tward's Multimedia Medical Reference Library ★★★★

Jonathon Tward's Multimedia Medical Reference Library is designed as a guide to medical information on the Internet. Users will find the Multimedia Medical Library Index, with links to Internet resources listed by disease, with a brief description of the source. The Medical School Curriculum index lists medical school curriculums by the focus of their departments (such as embryology or anatomy). Other features include an index of medical imaging and video web sites, online sounds and downloadable software, and an alphabetical list of medical schools in the U.S. Also included is a list of other medical indexes.

KEYWORDS   Medical Education, Medical Information, Medical Research
AUDIENCE   Medical Professionals, Medical Researchers, Medical Students
CONTACT   JTWARD@tiac.net
FREE

http://www.tiac.net/users/jtward/index.html

Life-Threatening Medical Emergencies ★★★

The Life-Threatening Medical Emergencies site contains information concerning what to do in case of medical emergencies. The emergencies covered include when an adult or child is choking, or has stopped breathing and when either an adult or a child's heart stops beating. The site also has a link to the author's home page.

KEYWORDS   Emergency Medical Services, First Aid, Health, Medicine
AUDIENCE   General Public, Health Care Professionals
CONTACT   lzeltser@seas.upenn.edu
FREE

http://www.seas.upenn.edu/~lzeltser/first.aid.html

Lifetime Health Letter ★★★

The Lifetime Health Letter is a periodical published by the University of Texas at Houston's Campus Health Center, containing articles concerned with health, fitness, nutrition and general wellbeing.

KEYWORDS   Health Journals, Men's Health, Men's Issues
AUDIENCE   Health Educators, Medical Practitioners, Medical Researchers, Men, Nutritionists, Women
CONTACT   Beth Ardoin
          bardoin@oac.hsc.uth.tmc.edu
FREE

http://www.uth.tmc.edu/lifetime/life.html

The Magnesium Catastrophe ★★★★

This site provides access to twelve articles regarding the world-wide magnesium catastrophe. Magnesium deficiency appears to have caused 8 million sudden coronary deaths in America alone from 1940-1994, based on census data and studies of similar deaths conducted in other countries. These articles deal with the current status of the magnesium catastrophe, the calculation of American deaths caused by magnesium deficiency, justification of these calculations, citizens' petition to FDA (Food and Drug Administration) to support voluntary fortification of beverages with magnesium, and the economics of magnesium fortification. Also included is a history of the United States magnesium catastrophe, a letter to the Freedom of Information Act office, a summary of a recent magnesium seminar, magnesium deficiency and suicide in Finland, a personal experience with magnesium, magnesium deficiency and asthma, and finally, magnesium levels in various water sources.

KEYWORDS   Dietary Deficiency, Magnesium, Nutrition, World Health
AUDIENCE   Dietitians, Government Agency Employees, Nutritionists, Physicians
CONTACT   Paul Mason
          magnesium@ix.netcom.com
FREE

ftp://ftp.execpc.com/pub/magnesium/

Medical Education Information Center ★★★★

The Medical Education Information Center is part of the Department of Pathology and Laboratory Medicine at the University of Texas Medical School, Houston. This site provides access to education programs, a library of publications, and other medical-related infomation. The specific contents include self-instructional programs, allied health, and medical graduate education, a forum on available services and consultations at UT/Hermann Hospital, continuing medical education programs, a range of issues in medical informatics and its impact on the practice of medicine, and a clinical forum specific to pathology. The site also contains a health explorer, a forum for patients and the community.

KEYWORDS   Information Services, Medical Education, Medicine
AUDIENCE   Educators, Health Care Professionals, Students
CONTACT   Anne LeMaistre, M.D.
          lemaist@casper.med.uth.tmc.edu
FREE

http://hyrax.med.uth.tmc.edu/

Medical Education Page ★★★

The Medical Education Page is a meta-index providing links to medical information on the WWW, produced by students at Loma Linda University. Users will find links listed alphabetically according to type of Internet resources, with WWW sites subcategories of reference, indices, learning tools, medical schools, medical centers, and medicine and computing. No descriptions of the site are provided. The Medical School Interview Page allows users to read and contribute to a list of questionnaires about the interview processes at various medical schools in the United States.

KEYWORDS   Medical Information, Medical Resources, Medical Schools
AUDIENCE   Medical Professionals, Medical Researchers, Medical Students
CONTACT   Gregory Allen
          gwa@primenet.com
FREE

http://www1.primenet.com/%7Egwa/med.ed/

Medical Research Library of Brooklyn ★★★

This is a gopher server of the Medical Research Library of Brooklyn, located at the State University of New York, Health Science Center. It contains information related to medicine, academic programs, courses, and more. In addition, it provides links to other medical school gophers.

KEYWORDS   Community Services, Education (College/University), Medicine, University Administration
AUDIENCE   Educators (University), Medical Educators, Students (University)
CONTACT   Y. Kathy Kwanb
          kwan@medlib.hscbklyn.edu
FREE

gopher://gopher1.medlib.hscbklyn.edu/

Medical and Mental Health Problems ★★★

This Web site is a collection of links to other resources on the WWW relating to medical conditions and mental health problems. Users will find links listed alphabetically by problem, such as anxiety or depression, as well as groupings of sources for general health information.

KEYWORDS Medical Resources, Mental Health
AUDIENCE General Public
CONTACT Jeanine Wade
mmjw@bga.com
FREE

http://www.realtime.net/~mmjw/

Medline ★★★

The Medline telnet interface allows for the browsing of a library index of the reports and journals (past and current) from the database of the Food and Drug Administration.

KEYWORDS Drugs, Food And Drug Administration (FDA), Journals, Medical Reference
AUDIENCE Consumers, Health Care Professionals, Medical Researchers, Nutritionists
FREE

telnet://library.umdnj.edu

Men's Health ★★★

The Healthy Devil system, named after Duke University's Blue Devil mascot, offers articles and self-testing procedures for various gender specific ailments. This page offers information on a variety of men's health problems, including erectile dysfunctions and various forms of cancer.

KEYWORDS Cancer, Men's Issues, Sexuality
AUDIENCE Health Care Professionals, Medical Practitioners, Men, Urologists
CONTACT Linda Carl
carl0001@mc.duke.edu
FREE

http://152.3.65.120/h-devil/men/men.htm

Men's Health Issues Gopher ★★★

This gopher server offers a few articles on men's health issues, including articles on impotence screening and cancer screening.

KEYWORDS Men's Health, Men's Issues, Sexuality
AUDIENCE Health Educators, Men, Sex Educators
FREE

gopher://gizmo.freenet.columbus.oh.us/11/healthservices/OSU%20Medical%20Center/Health%20Promotion%20and%20Disease%20Prevention%20Information/Men's%20Health%20Issues

Men's Issues Page ★★★

The Men's Issues Page offers pointers to a wide variety of resources related in some way to men's issues. Subjects such as health, legal issues, marriage and divorce, children, drugs and many others are represented here. This site provides answers to frequently asked questions concerning fathers' rights in family law, single parenting, child support, annotated bibliographies, men's organizations and statistics.

KEYWORDS Cancer, Gender Studies, Men's Issues, Sexuality
AUDIENCE Health Care Professionals, Lawyers, Men
CONTACT David R. Throop
throop@cs.utexas.edu
FREE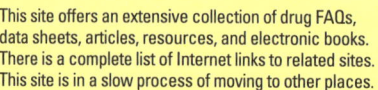

http://www.vix.com/pub/men/index.html

Neuropharmacological Anarchy ★★★

This site offers an extensive collection of drug FAQs, data sheets, articles, resources, and electronic books. There is a complete list of Internet links to related sites. This site is in a slow process of moving to other places.

KEYWORDS Drug Use, Drugs, Pharmacology, Psychedelics
AUDIENCE Drug Educators, Drug Users, Pharmacologists
CONTACT Lamont Granquist
lamontg@u.washington.edu
FREE

http://www.hyperreal.com/drugs

North American Venomous Snakebite-Emergency First Aid ★★

This document provides emergency first aid information for the North American Venomous Snakebite. It covers what to do and what not to do, contacts in a snakebite emergency, and links to the worldwide Poisons Information Database.

KEYWORDS Snakes
AUDIENCE Camping Enthusiasts, Educators, Families, Parents
CONTACT grenard@herpmed.com
FREE

http://www.xmission.com/~gastown/herpmed/snbite.html

The Obituary Page ★★★

The Obituary Page offers virtual commemoration of deaths, both in a Virtual Memorial Garden (anyone on the Internet can contribute to this listing) and a listing of public figures compiled by the maintainer of the site. Listings include dates of birth and death, occupation, and words of remembrance. These can be submitted with an entry form, which allows for inserting links as well.

KEYWORDS Death, Family, Obituaries
AUDIENCE Families, Internet Users, Mourners
CONTACT Lindsay Marshall
Lindsay.Marshall@newcastle.ac.uk
FREE

http://catless.ncl.ac.uk/Obituary/README.html

OncoLink ★★★★

OncoLink is an incredibly thorough resource for patients, family, friends, and professionals working with cancer patients. This award winning web site (Best of the Web - Best Professional Service Award, 1994) features an incredible amount of up-to-the-minute information on such topics as chemo- and radiotherapy, new cancer treatments, and current and upcoming clinical trials. There are comprehensive menus oriented by disease and specialty (including medical physics, pain management, veterinary oncology, gynelogical oncology and pediatric oncology, for example). Information about upcoming conferences and meetings are posted. Links to support groups and on and offline resources abound here, and cover such disparate subjects as caregiver education courses, sexuality and cancer, grief and spirituality resources, and hospice information. Related illnesses are discussed as well, including AIDS and syndromes related to Agent Orange.

KEYWORDS AIDS (Acquired Immune Deficiency Syndrome), Cancer, Experimental Medicine, Oncology
AUDIENCE Cancer Patients, Hospice Workers, Medical Professionals, Oncologists
CONTACT Oncolink@oncolink.upenn.edu
FREE

http://cancer.med.upenn.edu/

Pharmacy World Wide Web Sites ★★★★

The Pharmacy World Wide Web Sites contains links to numerous pharmacy related Internet resources. The links are seperated by countries covered which include Australia, Austria (Institute of Pharmaceutical Chemistry), Canada (Pharmacology at Dalhousie University), Denmark, Germany (Institute for Pharmaceutical Technology), Japan (Mizuno Pharmacie), Singapore, the United Kingdom and the USA.

KEYWORDS Biosciences, Medicine, Meta-Index (Pharmacy), Pharmacy
AUDIENCE Health Care Professionals, Medical Researchers, Pharmacists
CONTACT David Bourne
david-bourne@uokhsc.edu
FREE

http://157.142.72.77/pharmacy/pharmint.html

Physicians GenRx ★★★★

Physicians GenRx allows WWW browsing of a database of the most current information available on prescription pharmaceuticals. The results of keyword searches (for drug name or category of ailment) can be viewed in their entirety, or only specific elements of a record can be pulled, e.g. drug interactions, warnings, adverse reactions, or precautions. Each of these elements contains lengthy explanations and tables.

KEYWORDS Databases, Pharmacology, Reference
AUDIENCE Medical Patients, Medical Researchers, Pharmacists, Physicians
CONTACT staff@icsi.net
COST

http://www.icsi.net/GenRx.html

Poisons Information Database ★★★★

The Poisons Information Database provides information on Natural Toxins and Poisons, such as those from plants, snakes and animals, links to directories of antivenoms, toxicologists, and Poison Control Centers around the world.

Keywords First Aid, Poisons
Audience Camping Enthusiasts, Educators, Medical Professionals
Contact P. Gopalakrishnakone
antgopal@leonis.nus.sg
Free

http://biomed.nus.sg:80/PID/PID.html

The Ruth Lilly Medical Library Gopher Server at the Indiana University School of Medicine ★★★

This is a gopher server of the Indiana University (IU) School of Medicine Ruth Lilly Medical Library. It contains information on the Medical School, Ruth Lilly Medical Library (RLML) services and data, electronic books and journals, medical sciences resources, bio-databases, and more. Direct access to other gophers, both on and off-campus, is provided.

Keywords Graduate Education, Health Sciences, Medical Informatics, Medicine
Audience Educators (University), Medical Educators, Students (Secondary/College)
Contact James Jay Morgan
morganj@indyvax.iupui.edu
Free

gopher://gopher.medlib.iupui.edu/

Topics in Primary Care ★★★★

The Master List of Primary Care Teaching Topics for health care professionals was taken from the teaching files of General Medicine faculty, UHS practitioners, and residents, to be processed into web-format as a resource for comprehensive patient care. The topics covered include health promotion and prevention, urology, gynecology, neurology, dermatology, ophthalmology, hematology and oncology, endocrine, infectious disease, musculoskeletal and rheumatologic, neurology, endocrine, ENT and allergy, psychiatry, nutrition, cardiovascular, pulmonary, surgical, geriatric, medication and pharmacy. The site also contains links to other Primary Care Resources and Mental Health Resources on the Web.

Keywords Geriatrics, Infectious Diseases, Medicine, Primary Care
Audience Educators, Health Care Professionals, Patients, Students
Contact Matthew Ryan
matt@uhs.bsd.uchicago.edu
Free

http://uhs.bsd.uchicago.edu/uhs/topics/uhs-teaching.html

Connections to Nutrients and Drugs
Get Smart

Having trouble remembering where you left your sunglasses? Are you feeling dumb and dumber with each passing day? Fear not; help is only an Internet site away.

At the "Smart Nutrients and Drugs" site on the World Wide Web, you'll find a host of information showing that certain nutrients and drugs improve learning and memory through their beneficial effect on brain chemistry.

Take for instance Acetyl-l-Carnitine: this is a brain stimulating nutrient that improves mental performance. You might also take Piracetam—a brain stimulant that synchronizes the spheres of the brain, thereby increasing concentration and cognition, and improving learning and memory capabilities.

This site provides invaluable information for anyone feeling inclined to experiment with mental enhancement of this kind. Take note, however, that while some of the therapies are available in the U.S., others can only be obtained through mail-order companies in other countries.

(http://www.c2.org/~smart/SmartDrugsAndNutrients/)

U.S. National Library of Medicine (NLM) ★★★★

The US National Library of Medicine (NLM) offers extensive online information services dealing with clinical care, toxicology and environmental health, and basic biomedical research. NLM is the world's largest library dealing with a single scientific/professional topic. It cares for over 4.5 million holdings including books, journal, reports, manuscripts and audio-visual items, and has several active research and development components, houses an extensive History of Medicine collection, and provides several programs designed to improve the nation's medical library system. It offers a wide array of information about the library, its services, research activities, visitor information, events, and more. Online services include library catalogs and databases.

Keywords Biomedical Research, Libraries, Medical Research, National Institutes of Health
Audience Biomedical Researchers, Medical Researchers, Medical Students, Physicians
Contact hyperdoc@nlm.nih.gov
Free

http://www.nlm.nih.gov/

The University of Tennessee Health Sciences Library ★★★

This is a gopher server of the Health Sciences Library, University of Tennessee, Memphis. It contains information on library online catalogs, article citation databases, academic departments, and more. It provides access to other gophers as well.

Keywords Education (College/University), Information Science, Libraries, Medical Informatics
Audience Educators (University), Librarians, Students (University)

Health & Medicine

CONTACT   Lois Bellamy
          lbellamy@gopher.lib.utmem.edu
FREE

gopher://gopher.lib.utmem.edu/

University of Utah Spencer S. Eccles Health Sciences Library ★★★

Welcome to the University of Utah Spencer S. Eccles Health Sciences Library. This Web server provides access to information about library services, faculty, workshops, seminars, and special events, as well as links to multimedia resources in the health sciences.

KEYWORDS   Health Sciences, Libraries
AUDIENCE   Medical Educators, Physicians, Students (University)
CONTACT   sdennis@ecclab.med.utah.edu
FREE

http://el-gopher.med.utah.edu

Virtual Hospital ★★★

The Virtual Hospital (VH) is a continuously updated medical multimedia database accessible 24 hours a day. The site provides distance learning to practicing physicians and may be used for Continuing Medical Education (CME). It also contains a database of medical information designed for use by healthcare professionals and patients.

KEYWORDS   Distance Education, Health Sciences, Medical Informatics, Medicine
AUDIENCE   Biologists, General Public, Health Care Professionals, Medical Professionals, Medical Students
CONTACT   librarian@vh.radiology.uiowa.edu
FREE

http://indy.radiology.uiowa.edu/VirtualHospital.html

The William H. Welch Medical Library Gopher ★★

This site is a gopher server of the William H. Welch Medical Library at the Johns Hopkins Medical Institutions. It provides access to the library resources, and other gophers on campus.

KEYWORDS   Education (College/University), Libraries, Library Science, Medicine
AUDIENCE   Medical Educators, Medical Practitioners, Medical Students
CONTACT   go4comm@welchlink.welch.jhu.edu
FREE

gopher://welchlink.welch.jhu.edu/

Women's Health Resources on the Internet ★★★★

This site offers a guide to Internet resources that relate to women's health concerns. It includes many subjects such as drinking and dieting, eating disorders, stress, birth control, cancer and support groups. There is also an index which organizes the resources by the tool used to obtain them. Sources of a general nature are also included.

KEYWORDS   Gynecology, Sexuality, Women's Health
AUDIENCE   Health Care Professionals, Students (Secondary/College), Women, Women's Studies Students
CONTACT   Tricia Segal, Julie Lea
           women-health@umich.edu
FREE

http://asa.ugl.lib.umich.edu./chdocs/womenhealth/womens_health.html

gopher://una.hh.lib.umich.edu/00/inetdirsstacks/womenhealth%asegalea

Resources

See also
Health & Medicine · *Medicine*
Health & Medicine · *Reference*

Adoption Information ★★★

Adoption Information on the Internet is posted at the beginning of each month to alt.adoption, alt.adoption agency, alt.infertility, alt.support.foster-parents, misc.kids, misc.kids.info, misc.kids.pregnancy, alt.answers, misc.answers, and news.answers. This page offers information and access to the adoption related newsgroups, mailing lists, email help, and other web sites. This is a fruitful resource for those interested in any aspect of adoption.

KEYWORDS   Adoption, Foster Families, Infertility, Parenting
AUDIENCE   Adoptees, Adoptive Parents, Families, Foster Parents
CONTACT   Annette Thompson
           annette69@delphi.com
FREE

http://www.gems.com/adoption/others.html

Austin Hospital PET Centre Image Database ★★★

This database provides access to representative PET-scan images for various human medical conditions. The images are stored in a JPEG format so you will need a JPEG viewing program to see them. There are two parts to each scan—a description of the patient aetiology and the accompanying scan, and the JPEG file of the images themselves. The two have the same name, but differ in the extension (.txt /.jpg).

KEYWORDS   Medical Imaging, Medical Reference, Radiology, X-Rays
AUDIENCE   Health Care Professionals, Medical Researchers, Radiologists
FREE

gopher://gopher.austin.unimelb.edu.au:70/11/images

Facial Animation ★★★★

The Perceptual Science Laboratory at the University of California—Santa Cruz conducts research into perception and cognition. A major research area concerning speech perception involves efforts in facial animation. The focus of this Web site is on an NSF sponsored Facial Animation Workshop. Papers and studies presented at the workshop are presented as synopses providing details into the techniques and approaches taken in the realistic rendering of facial animations.

KEYWORDS   Animation, Perception, Speech
AUDIENCE   Artists, Computer Artists, Computer Graphic Designers, Graphic Designers
CONTACT   Michael M. Cohen
           mmcohen@mambo.ucsc.edu
FREE

http://mambo.ucsc.edu/psl/fan.html

Healthwise ★★★★

The Healthwise Web site produced by the Columbia University Health Education and Wellness program provides medical and health advice. Their Go Ask Alice! feature allows users to send questions in to professional or peer health educators and receive advice. Users may also search previous questions and answers using a keyword search or a subject index. Other features include the Healthwise Highlight archives, with articles discussing different health topics.

KEYWORDS   Advice, Medical Assistance, Mental Health
AUDIENCE   General Public, Health Care Consumers, Students (College)
FREE

http://www.columbia.edu/cu/healthwise/

Helios Server ★★

The Helios site is intended to provide development information about the Helios project, which involves research into simplifying medical application software for the Commission of the European Community. Included in this site are papers discussing the project, a style guide for the Helios software including online graphics, and a reference manual. Also included is a demo model of the project with graphs explaining the function of each process.

KEYWORDS   European Community, Medical Software, Medicine
AUDIENCE   Medical Informatics Specialists, Software Developers
CONTACT   Eva Olsson, Bengt Göransson, Erik Borälv, Bengt Sandblad
           Helios@cmd.uu.se
FREE

http://korint.cmd.uu.se

History of Medicine Division ★★★★

This is the site for the National Institutes of Health's History of Medicine Division. The Library's resources for historical scholarship in the medical and related sciences are among the richest of any institution in the world. They include rarities (e.g. collections of Arabic and oriental medical literature) and exhaustive materials for the support of studies in the history of human health and disease. This site provides access to online images (a database of nearly 60,000 images from the prints and photographs collection), and online exhibitions (e.g. A History of Cesarean Section, Perez on Medicine—The Whimsical Art of Jose Perez, and A History of the US Public Health Service).

KEYWORDS   History, National Institutes Of Health
AUDIENCE   Educators, Health Care Professionals, Historians, Medical Students, Physicians, Researchers

Resources

FREE

http://www.nlm.nih.gov/hmd.dir/hmd.html

Index of Disease Resources

This is a list of disease links from the Medical Matrix Project of disease resources. The information includes listservs, medicine documents, catalogue information, educational services, medical students forums, images, journals, software, and more. Some of the diseases include diabetes, epilepsy, lyme disease, multiple sclerosis, cancer, and autism.

KEYWORDS Internet Resources, Medicine
AUDIENCE General Public, Medical Professionals, Medical Students, Nurses, Physicians
CONTACT Dr. Gary Malet
gmalet@surfer.win.net
FREE

http://ukanaix.cc.ukans.edu:80/cwis/units/medcntr/Lee/

Internal Medicine Network Services

This gopher server provides information about the Department of Internal Medicine at Washington University, St. Louis. The information available on the server includes departmental contact information, awards and fellowships, conference facilities and centers, and research facilities/centers. The site also provides links to medicine-related gophers on the Internet such as the National Institutes of Health.

KEYWORDS Medical Research, Medical Schools, Medicine
AUDIENCE Doctors, Medical Practitioners, Medical Students, Physicians
CONTACT css@visar.wustl.edu
FREE

gopher://telesphere.wustl.edu/

Internet Health Resources Home Page

The Internet Health Resources Home Page provides access to a wide range of practical health information. From this page you can link to local/regional health resources including events, local health care providers, local support groups, fitness centers, and Internet-wide sources which include universal practical health information for all locales.

KEYWORDS Community Information, Health, Medical Reference, Meta-Index (Medical)
AUDIENCE Community Leaders, General Public, Health Care Professionals, Physicians
CONTACT cliffb@hooked.net
FREE

http://www.hooked.net/site/health/nethome1.html

The Lawson Research Institute

New medical imaging systems such as computed tomography (CT), ultrasound, digital radiography and magnetic resonance imaging (MRI) are offering views of the human body previously unavailable. This Web site provides us with a collection of some of the imagery created as part of research conducted by The Lawson Research Institute of St. Joseph's Hospital in London, Ontario, Canada.

KEYWORDS Canada, Digital Radiography, Medical Images, Ultrasound
AUDIENCE Computer Artists, Computer Graphic Designers, Graphic Designers
CONTACT webmaster@irus.rri.uwo.ca
FREE

http://www.stjosephs.london.on.ca/lri.html

MEDCOR WWW Site (Medical Computing Resource)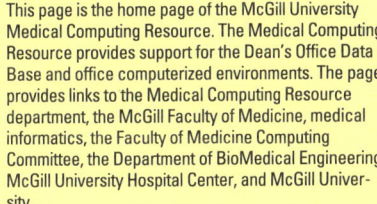

This page is the home page of the McGill University Medical Computing Resource. The Medical Computing Resource provides support for the Dean's Office Data Base and office computerized environments. The page provides links to the Medical Computing Resource department, the McGill Faculty of Medicine, medical informatics, the Faculty of Medicine Computing Committee, the Department of BioMedical Engineering, McGill University Hospital Center, and McGill University.

KEYWORDS Medical Informatics, Medical Research, Universities
AUDIENCE Canada Residents, Students (Secondary/College), Students (University)
CONTACT Luis Siles
siles@palace.medcor.mcgill.ca
FREE

http://www.medcor.mcgill.ca/

MNI Home Page (Montreal Neurological Institute)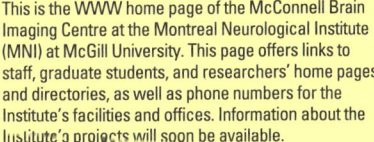

This is the WWW home page of the McConnell Brain Imaging Centre at the Montreal Neurological Institute (MNI) at McGill University. This page offers links to staff, graduate students, and researchers' home pages and directories, as well as phone numbers for the Institute's facilities and offices. Information about the Institute's projects will soon be available.

KEYWORDS Brain Research, Medical Imaging, Neurology, Universities
AUDIENCE Canada Residents, Medical Students, Students (University)
CONTACT web@pet.mni.mcgill.ca
FREE

http://www.mni.mcgill.ca/

MedLink

MedLink distributes medical information over the Web, to all the doctors and nurses in Sweden. This site gives links to information about laboratory studies, medicine, other professionals and publications.

KEYWORDS Medical Resources, Sweden
AUDIENCE Doctors, Nurses
CONTACT Mats E Brante
edward@ls.se webmaster@ls.se
FREE

http://www.ls.se/medlink/homepage.html

Medical Instructional Resources

This site, maintained by the University of Calgary, provides information about medical instructional resources. There is a comprehensive list of links to medical educational Web sites, descriptions of various upcoming medical conferences in America and Canada, and online medical courses. Internet sites that include information about family medicine and general medical health are also listed. Users can also access University of Calgary information and home pages via ftp, gopher, or the World Wide Web.

KEYWORDS Medical Education, Universities
AUDIENCE Health Care Professionals, Medical Professionals, Medical Students
FREE

http://mir.med.ucalgary.ca

Medical Photography Forum

The Medical Photography Forum provides a place where people can share their ideas on medical photography and other audio visual media pertaining to the medical field. There are links to news and events and information about The Institute of Medical Illustrators, as well as other links to related sites.

KEYWORDS Audio Technology, Medical Photography
AUDIENCE Medical Illustrators, Medical Professionals, Physicians
CONTACT Andrew.Johnson@ncl.ac.uk
FREE

http://www.ncl.ac.uk/~napj/index.html

Medical Resources

This ftp server presents a large guide to medical resources available on the Internet. Coverage includes major ailments, and other major repositories of medical information.

KEYWORDS Internet Guides, Medical Resources, Meta-Index (Medical)
AUDIENCE Health Care Professionals, Medical Researchers, Medical Students, Physicians
FREE

ftp://ftp.tunet.fi/pub/sci/medical/medical.resources.10-9

Medical Software

The Medical Software site provides Macintosh software for medical science professionals to download. The menu allows access to a demo, hypercards, and utilities. The site contains an index with the physical pathways to software, dated 1988-1993.

KEYWORDS Medicine, Neurology, Software
AUDIENCE Health Care Professionals, Medical Students

Resources

CONTACT comments@mac.archive.umich.edu
FREE

gopher://gopher.vifp.monash.edu.au:70/11/Medical/medcal/software

ftp://mac.archive.umich.edu/

Medical and Health Information (Albert Einstein College of Medicine) ★★★

The Medical and Health Information site gives access to medical resources that include bioethic, medical school, and biomedical gophers. There are links to such medical institutions as the National Institutes of Health (NIH), the Food and Drug Administration FDA, the National Institute of Allergy and Infectious Diseases (NIAID), the National Institute of Environmental Health Sciences, the National Toxicology Program (NTP), and the World Health Organization (WHO).

KEYWORDS Bioinformatics, Cancer Research, Medical Resources, Medical Schools
AUDIENCE Cancer Specialists, Health Care Professionals, Medical Researchers, Medical Students
FREE

gopher://gopher.aecom.yu.edu:70/11/inet/medical

Medscape—The Online Resource For Better Patient Care ★★★★

Medscape, The Online Resource For Better Patient Care is a free web site for health professionals and interested consumers. Practice-oriented information is peer-reviewed and edited by leaders in the fields of AIDS, infectious diseases, urology, and surgery. Highly-structured articles and full-color graphics are supplemented with stored literature searches and annotated links to relevant Internet resources. This site is produced by SCP Communications, Inc., a publisher of medical journals and medical education programs.

KEYWORDS Infectious Diseases, Surgery
AUDIENCE Consumers, Health Care Professionals, Medical Professionals, Physicians, Researchers
CONTACT Bill Seitz
         seitz@scp.com
FREE

http://www.medscape.com

Nursing Services Home Page ★★

The Nursing Services Home Page, launched in August 1994 and administered by the Duke University Medical Center, gives online access to current issues of Nursing Connections, a department publication. This site also provides links to other nursing and health-related web sites.

KEYWORDS Medical Professionals, Nursing
AUDIENCE Health Care Professionals, Nurses, Students (Secondary/College)

CONTACT Wendy Robinson
         robin001@mc.duke.edu
FREE

http://nursing-www.mc.duke.edu/nursing/nshomepg.htm

Pharmaceutical Information Network ★★★★

PharmInfoNet is dedicated to the dissemination of pharmaceutical product information to health care professionals, students, and patients. This site provides access to a database of drug information arranged alphabetically by trade name. The PharmMall is an area where pharmaceutical manufacturers, publishers, pharmacy software developers, and other companies can place their home pages, catalogs, and product information. Also on this page is a list of frequently-asked questions about prescription drugs (featuring authoritative answers), a rotating exhibit of pharmaceutical and pharmacy-related art, photographs and interactive multimedia museum tours, and links to other pharmaceutical areas on the Internet.

KEYWORDS Drugs, Health, Medicine
AUDIENCE General Public, Health Care Professionals, Medical Students, Pharmaceutical Companies
CONTACT John Mack
         jmack@pipeline.com
FREE

http://pharminfo.com/

The Polio Survivors' Page ★★★★

The Polio Survivors' Page is a website for people who have had polio and the people who care for them. Here you will find a large variety of resources for polio and post-polio syndrome survivors and patients. These include articles about polio and post-polio syndrome by survivors and health care professionals, lists of medical articles and literature, information about rehabilitation and coping with the illnesses, a "Do's and Don'ts" guide for post-polio patients, newsletters from the Atlanta Post-Polio Association, a section on famous people who have had polio, (including Frida Kahlo), very detailed information about the virus, a search area for other polio information on the internet, and information about on and offline support groups and resources for polio survivors. A lot of the information comes from the Easter Seal Society of Washington. All of the information is interesting and informative.

KEYWORDS Neurology, Physical Therapy, Polio
AUDIENCE Neurologists, Physical Therapists, Polio Survivors
CONTACT Tom Dempsey
         dempt@eskimo.com
FREE

http://www.eskimo.com

The University of Washington Health Sciences Center for Educational Resources ★★

This is a gopher server of the University of Washington Health Sciences Center for Educational Resources. It provides images of the University of Washington, educational multimedia references, the Globewide Network Academy (GNA) catalog, information about the library, and more.

KEYWORDS Education, Education (College/University), Health Sciences
AUDIENCE Educators (University), Internet Users, Students (University)
CONTACT Bob McGough
         bobmcg@u.washington.edu
FREE

gopher://newman.hs.washington.edu/

The Virtual Allied Health Center ★★★★

The Virtual Allied Health Center provides links to different allied health related resources. The topics include dental schools, education resources, graduate and undergraduate health science related courses, the reference desk, and more. There are also links to other virtual centers.

KEYWORDS Dentistry, Medicine
AUDIENCE Dentists, Nurses, Pharmacists, Physicians, Veterinarians
CONTACT Jim Martindale
         jmartindale@vmsa.oac.uci.edu
FREE

http://www-sci.lib.uci.edu:80/~martindale/Dental.html

The Virtual Pharmacy Center ★★★★

The Virtual Pharmacy Center provides an array of links to many different health related references. The topics covered include pharmacy schools, education resources, graduate and undergraduate health science related courses, the reference desk, time and weather, what's new, browse, and search. There are also links to other virtual centers including medical, dental, veterinary, nursing, public health, allied health and nutrition virtual centers.

KEYWORDS Drugs, Health, Medicine
AUDIENCE Dentists, Nurse Practitioners, Nurses, Pharmacists, Physicians, Veterinarians
CONTACT Jim Martindale
         jmartindale@vmsa.oac.uci.edu
FREE

http://www-sci.lib.uci.edu:80/~martindale/Pharmacy.html

World Wide Drugs ★★★★

This site provides many links to other health-related servers and sites on the Internet. Some of the resources include Martindale's Virtual Pharmacy Center, the University of California, the San Francisco WebServers, the Pharmaceutical Information Network, Harvard medicine, medical resources on the Internet and more. This is a good place to start searching for health-related sites.

KEYWORDS Drugs, Health, Medicine, Pharmacology
AUDIENCE Dentists, Nurse Practitioners, Nurses, Pharmacists, Physicians, Veterinarians
CONTACT Neil Sandow, Pharm.D.
         neils@community.net
FREE

http://community.net/~neils/new.html

Resources – Sexuality

The World Wide Web
Virtual Library-Pharmacy ★★★★

This page includes a plethora of links to pharmacy related Internet resources. The links include pharmacy web sites from Australia to Austria, and Japan to the United States. Many Schools of Pharmacy are listed, along with associations such as the American Association of Pharmaceutical Scientists (AAPS), International Pharmaceutical Federation (FIP). There are links to hospitals such as Center for Imaging and Pharmaceutical Research at Massachusetts General Hospital, pharmaceutical and biotechnology companies such as Eli Lilly and Company, Monsanto Company, and Searle Pharmaceutical Products. It also includes access to an online career center, grant information, Federal Register, and more.

Keywords Drugs, Health, Meta-Index (Pharmacy), Pharmacology
Audience Health Care Professionals, Medical Students, Patients, Pharmaceutical Companies
Contact David Bourne, david-bourne@uokhsc.edu
Free

http://www.cpb.uokhsc.edu/pharmacy/pharmint.html

Services

See also
Health & Medicine · *Alternative Medicine*
Health & Medicine · *Medical Specialties*

University of Arizona
Health Sciences Center ★★★

This page provides general information about the University of Arizona Health Sciences Center. Sections on teaching, health care, research, and support services explain the Center's overall goals and current activities. The page also links to descriptions of the Center's different schools, including the Colleges of Medicine, Nursing, Pharmacy, and Health Related Professions. An 'Outreach Services' section explains programs and services made available across Arizona by the Center. The page also offers a search tool for finding people affiliated with the Center and health information.

Keywords Arizona, Health Sciences, Health Services, Medical Education
Audience Arizona Residents, Doctors, Medical Educators, Medical Students
Contact webteam@hinet.arizona.edu
Free

http://128.196.106.42/ahsc.html

Connections to Poison Control
Don't panic, help is on the way!

Ever wondered what antitoxins you should take for snake bites or exactly what poison oak looks like before you walk through a patch on a hiking trail? There are several online sites that provide information on venomous animals, poisoning, toxicity, and chemical hazards—and what to do for treatment. Sites that give you this type of information include the "Arizona Poison Page" and "Trailside Poison Ivy Barrier." The latter is a treatment you can order for minimizing irritation after exposure to poison ivy.

(http://amber.medlib.arizona.edu/poison.html)

also, **(http://www.mc2usa.com/hydromer/trailsid.html)**

If you want to know how to identify venomous snakes in their native habitats or obtain medical information about snake bites, plant toxins and animal toxins, one site that provides extensive information is the "Poisons Information Database (Singapore)." The database includes a directory of Poison Control Centers around the world—invaluable when you need help fast.

(http://biomed.nus.sg/PID/PID.html)

Sexuality

See also
Health & Medicine · *Reference*
Health & Medicine · *Sexually Transmitted Diseases*
Health & Medicine · *Women's Health*
Humanities & Social Sciences · *Sociology*
Popular Culture & Entertainment · *Lifestyles*

The Blowfish Sexuality
Information Center ★★★★

This page provides many links to sexuality resources on the Internet. Topics available include general resources, sex and health, sexuality, gender, censorship, erotic arts and entertainment, and more. Some of the specific subjects include a piercing and tattoo FAQ, AIDS information, the Bad Sex Prize, a British award for the worst description of sex in a novel, and the prostitution FAQ—an encyclopedic collection of information about prostitution from all over the world.

Keywords Gender Issues, Sexuality
Audience Gays, Lesbians, Men, Sex Enthusiasts, Sex Industry Workers, Women
Contact blowfish@blowfish.com
Free

http://www.best.com/~blowfish/blowsic.html

Circumcision Issues Page ★★

This page offers articles that deal with various aspects of male circumcision, particularly the negative aspects of this procedure. A few bibliographic references toward books on related subjects are also available, as is an article on foreskin restoration.

Keywords Circumcision, Men's Health, Men's Issues, Sexuality
Audience Health Care Professionals, Medical Practitioners, Men

407

Health & Medicine

CONTACT Gary Burlingame
gburlin@eskimo.com

FREE

http://www.eskimo.com/%7Egburlin/circ.html

GLAAD/Dallas Home Page ★★★

This is the home page for the Dallas Chapter of the National Gay and Lesbian Alliance Against Defamation. The information presented here is about the organization, its mission, and its membership. The site also houses recent GLAAD/Dallas newsletters, provides links to newsletters of other chapters, and archives information on contacting local and national news media.

KEYWORDS Lesbianism, Newsletters, Texas
AUDIENCE Bisexuals, Gay Rights Activists, Gays, Texas Residents
CONTACT Wynn Wagner
webmaster@global.org

FREE

http://oaklawn.global.org/glaad

The Gaze Support BBS Home Page ★★★★

This page provides a description of The Gaze Support BBS, a gay-positive, gay-run bulletin board. It details the board's purpose, hours of availability, software and hardware, access requirements, and network affiliations. The topics range from gay life all over the world, descriptions and contact information for organizations, to events and services, and film and book reviews.

KEYWORDS Homosexuality, Lesbianism
AUDIENCE BBS Users, Bisexuals, Gays, Lesbians
CONTACT Ken Tyrrell
kentyrr@teleport.com

FREE

http://www.teleport.com/~kentyrr/

Gender and Sexuality ★★★

This page is a collection of papers, academic and otherwise, on gender and sexuality issues. Users will find a wide selection of papers appealing to many interests - gay and lesbian sexual issues, women's issues, transsexual and transgender issues, and much more. The papers are indexed alphabetically, allowing users to follow a link to retrieve a plaintext version of the paper.

KEYWORDS Gender Issues, Sexual Orientation, Sexuality, Sociology
AUDIENCE Educators, Gender Studies Students, Humanists, Women's Studies Students
CONTACT postmaster@english.hss.cmu.edu

FREE

http://english-server.hss.cmu.edu/Gender.html

Men's Health ★★

This file offers abstracts and other short descriptive information for various common afflictions and dysfunctions of the male reproductive system. A thorough description of the most common medical test used to diagnose prostate cancer is also presented.

KEYWORDS Cancer, Men's Health, Sexuality
AUDIENCE Health Educators, Medical Practitioners, Men, Urologists
CONTACT Boynton Health Services, MIS Department
mis@vax.bhs.umn.edu

FREE

gopher://rodent.cis.umn.edu:11141/00/services_offered/general_medical/menshealth/menshlth.txt

The Safer Sex Page ★★★★

The Safer Sex Web site is an archive created by a grad student at the University of California San Francisco, with all kinds of information about sex and how to have it safely. Users will find brochures on topics such as Sex Myths, Risks of Oral Sex, and How to Put on a Condom, with diagrams and general information. Sex and Health Education Counselors will also find specific brochures and information for their work, including news releases about current health issues. An AIDS section deals directly with different aspects of the disease and preventing it. The Safer Sex Forum allows users to have virtual discussions about changing safe sex topics. Multimedia safe sex videos and demonstrations are also linked under one subcategory, as are links to other Safe Sex WWW sites.

KEYWORDS Safe Sex, Sex Education, Sexuality
AUDIENCE General Public, Sex Enthusiasts, Teenagers
CONTACT troyer@cgl.ucsf.edu

FREE

http://www.cmpharm.ucsf.edu/~troyer/safesex.html

Sex Information ★★★

This gopher directory contains a number of informative documents which offer treatment and screening information on a variety of sexually transmitted diseases, various ailments of the reproductive system, and miscellaneous sexual dysfunctions.

KEYWORDS Medical Treatment, Sexuality, Sexually Transmitted Diseases
AUDIENCE Health Educators, Men, Sex Enthusiasts, Students (University), Women
CONTACT gopher administrator
health@selway.umt.edu

FREE

gopher://umt.umt.edu:700/11/sex

Usenet Newsgroup Soc.bi Home Page ★★★★

Detailed information about the newsgroup Soc.bi is housed at this site, including a thorough FAQ (with details about bisexuality in general as well as guidelines for posting to the newsgroup), a link to the gopher site, newsgroup statistics, biographies of participants, and a collection of recipes from the group. The page also provides information about the 1995 UK Bisexual Conference, and a partial list of other Internet resources concerning the topic of bisexuality.

KEYWORDS Bisexuality, Newsgroups, Sexual Orientation, Sexuality
AUDIENCE Bisexual Activists, Bisexuals

CONTACT Jon Harley
J.W.Harley@bham.ac.uk

FREE

http://sun1.bham.ac.uk/~harleyjw/soc-bi.html

Sexually Transmitted Diseases

See also
Health & Medicine · *Diseases*
Health & Medicine · *Sexuality*
Health & Medicine · *Women's Health*
Humanities & Social Sciences · *Sociology*

ACTUP/Boston Home Page ★★

The ACTUP/Boston Home Page links the user to other sites with information about AIDS and safe sex. It provides a standard of care chart and a recent issue of ATTITUDE! newsletter. Baseline Treatments for common infections can be found as well as a main link to the HIV Infoweb Home Page.

KEYWORDS AIDS (Acquired Immune Deficiency Syndrome), Sexuality
AUDIENCE AIDS Activists, Bisexuals, Gays, Lesbians
CONTACT Robert DeBenedictis
contact@actup.org

FREE

AIDS Action Committee of Massachusetts ★★

The AIDS Action Committee of Massachusetts is New England's oldest AIDS service. The mission of the AIDS Action committee is comprised of three interdependent goals: to provide services to people living with HIV and to the people who live and care for them, to combat the AIDS epidemic through education, and to advocate for fair and effective AIDS policy and funding. This page summarizes the work that the AAC is doing, but provides little else for people outside of the New England Area.

KEYWORDS AIDS (Acquired Immune Deficiency Syndrome), Education, Health Care, New England
AUDIENCE AIDS Patients, AIDS Support Groups, Educators, Massachussetts Residents, New England Residents

FREE

http://bighorn.terra.net/aac/

Preventing HIV and AIDS ★★★★

This page about AIDS/HIV prevention, provides links to advice, information, and suggestions on how to get involved in the issue. It includes a link to a form for mailing to the CDC National AIDS clearinghouse.

KEYWORDS AIDS (Acquired Immune Deficiency Syndrome), Gay Rights, Health Care
AUDIENCE Activists, HIV Positive People, Health Care Consumers, Health Care Providers

CONTACT biancaTroll Productions
bianca@bianca.com

FREE

http://bianca.com/lolla/politics/aids/aids.html

Veterinary Medicine

See also
Science · *Biosciences*
Sports & Recreation · *Pets & Animals*

American Veterinary Computer Society Home Page ★★

This site houses a searchable archive of the American Veterinary Computer Society (ACVS) Newsletter.

KEYWORDS Computers, Veterinary Medicine, Veterinary Science
AUDIENCE Computer Users, Veterinarians
FREE

http://netvet.wustl.edu/avcs.htm

gopher://netvet.wustl.edu:70/10n:/vet/avcs/

The Internet Vet Column ★★★★

The Internet Vet Column is a mailing list for people who have questions about pet illnesses. It functions more like a 'Pet Advice Column' than a mailing list. Questions are sent to the mailing list at internet-vet@netcom.com and are then answered by the "Internet Vet," Jeff Parke, DVM in the mailing list. The list is distributed weekly. Animals most often covered are dogs and cats, but more exotic pets are also often mentioned.

KEYWORDS Pets, Veterinary Care
AUDIENCE Animal Lovers, Pet Owners, Veterinarians Owners
CONTACT The Internet Vet
internet-vet@netcom.com
FREE

http://www.zmall.com/pet/tittle/pets/1vc/homepage.html

NetVet Veterinary Resources ★★★

This collection of veterinary and animal-related computer resources includes archives of animal legislation and regulation, listings for colleges of Veterinary Medicine, conference information, and animal-related databases, including the Electronic Zoo. It also features links to other animal and veterinary-related systems.

KEYWORDS Animal Science, Animals, Veterinary Medicine
AUDIENCE Animal Lovers, Veterinarians
CONTACT ken@wudcm.wustl.edu
FREE

http://netvet.wustl.edu/

gopher://netvet.wustl.edu:70/11n:/vet

Connections to Sexuality
Male, female . . . whatever

The Society for Human Sexuality

Please be aware that the files in our online library, the links on this home page, and the messages on our mailing list will explicitly discuss sexual matters. If you may not legally possess or view these materials in your area, or if your interaction with these materials could put Society for Human Sexuality (or its members) at any risk of legal action, then please do not use any of these resources. If you are under the age of 21, quit now. Be aware that there is no erotic fiction and that there are no erotic images of any kind at this site.

Where can you find information on human sexuality? At the "Gender and Human Sexuality" site on the World Wide Web, you'll find a host of information about men's issues, planned parenthood, romance, and feminist/activist resources.

There are even information servers that put you in touch with counseling services for STDs (sexually transmitted diseases) such as herpes and AIDS. Here you'll also find links to alternative lifestyles, such as gay, lesbian, S & M, abstinence, and others.

(http://www.cs.colorado.edu/homes/mebryan/public_html/bb/77/summary.html)

At the SHS Library site on the Internet, you'll find links to information and controversies about birth control pills and other contraceptives, as well as to political activities seeking to repeal what many believe to be outdated laws on sexual activity. There are also links to information on nutrition, how to handle coming out of the "closet," and fact sheets on a variety of sexually transmitted diseases.

(http://weber.u.washington.edu/~sfpse/ftpsite.html)

Vet Web Information Network ★★★

A page maintained by the Purdue University School of Veterinary Medicine. There are medical illustrations, a history of veterinary medicine, and educational resources. The site also includes information on the Purdue School of Veterinary Medicine.

KEYWORDS Animals, Pets, Veterinary Medicine
AUDIENCE Pet Owners, Students, veterinarians
CONTACT webmaster@vet.purdue.edu
FREE

http://vet.purdue.edu/

Women's Health

See also
Health & Medicine · *Diseases*
Humanities & Social Sciences · *Women's Studies*

Abortion & Reproductive Rights Internet Resources ★★★★

The Abortion & Reproductive Rights Internet Resources page provides links to pro-choice and anti-choice information. Some of the articles concern birth, father rights and responsibilities, feminists for life, anti-choice reading list, guide for active feminists, a miscellaneous pro-choice page, the full text of Roe v. Wade, the freedom of choice act, methods of contraception, and more.

KEYWORDS Abortion, Feminism, Reproductive Rights
AUDIENCE Fathers, Feminists, Mothers, Pro-Choice Activists

CONTACT Kathy Watkins
caral@aol.com
FREE

http://www.matisse.net/politics/caral/abortion.html

Atlanta Reproductive Health Center Home Page ★★★★

This site provides pointers to information in areas of women's health including infertility, endometriosis, contraception, menopause, sexually transmitted diseases, adoption and premenstrual syndrome.

KEYWORDS Infertility, Menopause
AUDIENCE Health Care Professionals, Obstetricians, Pregnant Women, Women
CONTACT Dr. Mark Perloe.
mperloe@mindspring.com
FREE

http://www.mindspring.com/~mperloe/index.html

Barnard/Columbia Women's Handbook Gopher Menu ★★★★

This site is the gopher menu for the Barnard/Columbia Women's Handbook which provides comprehensive information on health issues affecting women. Some of the subjects covered include gynecological disorders, HIV and AIDS, pregnancy and abortion, therapy and mental health, medication and 12 step programs, compulsive eating, alcoholism, lesbian issues, disabilities, rape, battering, and more.

KEYWORDS Eating Disorders, Gynecology, Pregnancy, Women's Health

AUDIENCE Alcoholics, Anorexia Nervosa Sufferers, Bulimia Nervosa Sufferers, Drug Users, Health Care Providers, Women

FREE

gopher://dag.cc.columbia.edu:71/11/publications/women

Birth, Pregnancy and Midwifery Resources ★★★★

This site provides an index of birth-related and midwifery information. Some are files, some just give basic contact information, others are web nodes themselves. Some of the topics include Childbirth and Parent Education Association, American College of Nurse-Midwives, The Rural Medical Computer Network, Waterbirth information, and some usenet groups, misc.kids.pregnancy, misc.health.alternatives, and more.

KEYWORDS Midwifery, Pregnancy
AUDIENCE Childcare Providers, Midwives, Mothers, Obstetricians, Parents, Pregnant Women
CONTACT Donna Dolezal Zelzer
djz@efn.org
FREE

http://www.efn.org/~djz/birth/resources.html

Birth-Tech—Tests and Technology in Pregnancy and Birth ★★★

This page summarizes the book "Birth-Tech—Tests and Technology in Pregnancy and Birth," by Anne Charlish and Linda Hughey Holt, M.D. This book addresses the array of prenatal technologies and the many questions and concerns expectant mothers may have. Birth-Tech comprehensively and concisely deals with the prenatal care, hospital procedures, and medical techniques used to assist the safe delivery of a healthy baby.

KEYWORDS Infertility, Pregnancy
AUDIENCE Health Care Professionals, Men, Midwives, Pregnant Women
FREE

gopher://gopher.infor.com:4600/0exec%3A-v%20a%20R994671-997932-=/.text/Main%

Breast Cancer Awareness Month ★★★★

This document, which is part of the Family World Publications site, discusses what women need to know about mammography. Subjects covered include What is a mammogram? What is it like to have a mammogram? Are mammograms safe? When should I have a mammogram? Where should I go for a mammogram? How will I pay for a mammogram? It also gives an American Cancer Society information line.

KEYWORDS Breast Cancer, Societies
AUDIENCE Health Care Professionals, Women
CONTACT family@family.com
FREE

http://family.com/Features/Development/BreastCancer.HTML

Breastfeeding Information ★★★

This page is an index of birth-related information. Links are provided to information on breastfeeding, nutrition tips for pregnancy, breastfeeding and feminism, non-standard lactation, and more.

KEYWORDS Pregnancy, Women's Health
AUDIENCE Lactating Women, Mothers, Obstetricians, Pregnant Women
CONTACT Donna Dolezal Zelzer
djz@efn.org
FREE

http://www.efn.org/~djz/birth/breastfeeding.html

CARAL—California Abortion and Reproductive Rights Action League—North ★★★★

The California Abortion and Reproductive Rights Action League (CARAL) page provides links to information on abortion and California politics. CARAL North, California Abortion and Reproductive Rights Action, is a non-profit, independent, political and educational organization located in San Francisco, California. The mission of CARAL is to develop and sustain a constituency that uses the political process to guarantee the full range of reproductive health services to all women. CARAL is funded by individual donations.

KEYWORDS Abortion, California, Health Care, Women's Issues
AUDIENCE Health Care Professionals, Men, Obstetricians, Political Activists, Pro-Choice Activists, Women
CONTACT Kathy Watkins
caral@aol.com
FREE

http://www.matisse.net/politics/caral/caral.html

Guide To Women's Health Issues ★★★★

This site contains a table of contents with links for The Women's Health Guide produced by the University of Michigan, School of Information and Library Studies. The topics are varied and include body image/eating disorders, drug/alcohol problems, gynecological exams, birth control, menopause, menstruation, pregnancy, and more.

KEYWORDS Eating Disorders, Menopause, Pregnancy
AUDIENCE Health Care Professionals, Health Care Providers, Mothers, Pregnant Women, Women
CONTACT women-health@umich.edu
FREE

http://asa.ugl.lib.umich.edu/chdocs/womenhealth/toc.html

gopher://una.hh.lib.umich.edu/00/inetdirsstacks/womenhealth%3asegalea

High Risk Situations and Complications in Pregnancy, Labor and Birth ★★★

This page on High Risk Situations And Complications In Pregnancy, Labor And Birth provides links to information on possible problems and what to do about them. Subjects include fetal screening, testing, risk scoring, physical violence and sexual abuse, and dealing with HIV and AIDs in pregnancy.

KEYWORDS Obstetrics, Pregnancy
AUDIENCE Husbands, Pregnant Women
CONTACT Donna Dolezal Zelzer
djz@efn.org
FREE

http://www.efn.org/~djz/birth/complications.html

Midwifery, Pregnancy and Birth Related Information ★★★

This site contains links to other pregnancy-related sites including articles and files such as The Homebirth Choice, Types of Midwives, Gracious Births, etc. Pointers to other directories include lactation, breastfeeding, infant nutrition, nutrition and pregnancy, high risk situations and complications in pregnancy, labor and birth, and more.

KEYWORDS Midwifery, Pregnancy
AUDIENCE Health Care Professionals, Midwives, Obstetricians, Pregnant Women
CONTACT Donna Dolezal Zelzer
djz@efn.org
FREE

http://www.efn.org/~djz/birth/birthindex.html

OBGYN ★★★★

This OBGYN gopher menu includes links to information on estrogen prophylaxis, genital herpes simplex, postmenopausal osteoporosis, chlamydial infection, and pregnancy.

KEYWORDS Pregnancy, Sexually Transmitted Diseases
AUDIENCE Obstetricians, Pregnant Women, Women
FREE

gopher://info.med.yale.edu:70/11/Disciplines/Discipline/OBGYN

Screening for Congenital Birth Defects ★★★★

This is a document on screening for congenital birth defects. It recommends that amniocentesis for karyotyping should be offered to pregnant women aged 35 and older. Subjects covered include the efficacy of screening tests, early detection, clinical intervention, and references.

KEYWORDS Obstetrics, Pregnancy
AUDIENCE Health Care Professionals, Obstetricians, Pregnant Women, Women

Free

gopher://gopher.nlm.nih.gov:70/00/hstat/
guide_cps/TEMPgrp8/cps4= 6.txt

Screening for Fetal Distress ★★★★

This document at the National Institutes Of Health focuses on screening for fetal distress. It recommends that fetal heart rate should be measured by auscultation on all women in labor to detect signs of fetal distress. However, electronic fetal monitoring should be reserved for pregnancies at increased risk for fetal distress. Subjects covered include the efficacy of screening tests, early detection, clinical intervention, and references.

Keywords Obstetrics, Pregnancy
Audience Midwives, Obstetricians, Pregnant Women, Women
Free

gopher://gopher.nlm.nih.gov:70/00/hstat/
guide_cps/TEMPgrp8/cps4= 7.txt

Screening for Intrauterine Growth Retardation ★★★★

This document provided by the National Institutes of Health promotes screening for intrauterine growth retardation. It suggests that women at increased risk for delivering a growth-retarded infant should receive ultrasound examinations early in the second trimester to determine gestational age and in the third trimester to measure the size of critical fetal structures. Subjects covered include the efficacy of screening tests, early detection, clinical intervention, and references.

Keywords Obstetrics, Pregnancy
Audience Health Care Professionals, Obstetricians, Pregnant Women, Women
Free

gopher://gopher.nlm.nih.gov:70/00/hstat/
guide_cps/TEMPgrp8/cps4= 2.txt

Screening for Rh Incompatibility ★★★★

This is a document provided by the National Institutes of Health on screening for Rh incompatibility, which recommends that all pregnant women should receive ABO/Rh blood typing and testing for anti-Rh(D) antibody at their first prenatal visit. Subjects covered include the efficacy of screening tests, early detection, clinical intervention, and references.

Keywords Obstetrics, Pregnancy
Audience Health Care Professionals, Obstetricians, Pregnant Women, Women
Free

gopher://gopher.nlm.nih.gov:70/00/hstat/
guide_cps/TEMPgrp8/cps4= 5.txt

Water Birth—Safe, Gentle, Joyous Childbirth ★★★★

This site offers an article by Karil Daniels of Point of View Productions on the advantages of water births and water deliveries. Links are provided to further information including water-baby experiences, water birth videotape, how to make a video documentary about water birth, and water baby materials you can order. There is also a link to a graphic portrayal of a mother giving birth in water.

Keywords Pregnancy, Women's Health
Audience Men, Midwives, Obstetricians, Pregnant Women
Free

http://www.path.net:80/karil/

Health & Medicine

Humanities & Social Sciences

Anthropology 413
Archaeology 414
Area & Cultural Studies 414
Classics 422
Geography 423
History 424
Languages 427
Library & Information Studies 429
Linguistics 431
Literature 433
Psychology 445
Sociology 446
Women's Studies 450

Anthropology

See also
Arts & Music · *Visual Arts*
Humanities & Social Sciences · *Classics*
Popular Culture & Entertainment · *Museums & Theme Parks*
Science · *Environmental Sciences*

Aboriginal Super Information Highway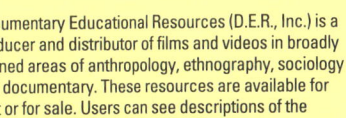

The Aboriginal Super Information Highway Web page provides a selection of information on Canada's Indian peoples, primarily those in Manitoba. Topics include government and events of interest to the Indian community. Users may also access images of contemporary Indian artwork and subscribe via online form to a magazine about Indian culture.

KEYWORDS Canada, Indians
AUDIENCE Indians, Manitobans
FREE

http://www.abinfohwy.ca/abinfohwy/

Anthropology, Cross Cultural Studies, & Archaeology ★★

This document is a compilation of information resources focused on anthropology, cross cultural studies, and archaeology. Resources may include Internet/Bitnet Mailing Lists, Gophers, World Wide Web Sites, Mail Servers, Usenet Newsgroups, FTP Archives, Commercial Online Services, and Bulletin Board Systems.

KEYWORDS Cross Cultural Studies, Universities
AUDIENCE Anthropologists, Archaeologists, Educators, Students
CONTACT gbell@kentvm.kent.edu
FREE

ftp://una.hh.lib.umich.edu/inetdirsstacks/anthro:bell

The Curia Project, Thesaurus Lunguarum Hibernae ★★★★

This page presents one Irish Literary work, The Dream of Oengus, in Gaelic, accompanied by bibliographic and technical details. The Curia Project is described as an archive of literary and historical materials pertaining to early, medieval and modern Ireland. One of the page's useful features is that key characters and event/place names in the story are highlighted as links - when you click on them, a database search occurs, resulting in a Gaelic language definition or explanation of the term.

KEYWORDS Ireland, Irish Literature
AUDIENCE Fiction Enthusiasts, Gaelic Language Scholars, Irish Literature Enthusiasts, Literary Scholars
FREE

http://curia.ucc.ie/curia/texts/oengus.html

Documentary Educational Resources ★★★

Documentary Educational Resources (D.E.R., Inc.) is a producer and distributor of films and videos in broadly defined areas of anthropology, ethnography, sociology and documentary. These resources are available for rent or for sale. Users can see descriptions of the hundreds of videos and film that are in the archives. These resources can be browsed by title, filmmaker, geographical area, or by subject area.

KEYWORDS Documentaries, Educational Resources, Ethnography
AUDIENCE Anthropologists, Documentary Makers, Educators, Filmmakers, Sociologists
CONTACT Pete Bastien
         ptbast@cs.wpi.edu
FREE

http://cs.wpi.edu/~ptbast/der/homepage.html

NativeWeb ★★★★

The NativeWeb home page provides access to (mostly textual) resources about 'native' or indigenous peoples, particularly in the United States and other Western countries. Information is primarily organized by subject, geography, and ethnicity. There is also a meta-index that includes pointers to Usenet groups and listservs.

KEYWORDS Anthropology, Indigenous People
AUDIENCE Anthropologists, Native Peoples
FREE

http://kuhttp.cc.ukans.edu/~marc/native_main.html

Social Science Centre of University of Western Ontario ★★★

This is a gopher server of the Social Science Centre (SSC) at the University of Western Ontario in Canada. It covers social science topics, provides information on SSC, anthropology, the Center for Administrative & Information Studies, the Social Science Computing Laboratory, and more.

KEYWORDS Canada, Computing, Education (College/University), Social Sciences
AUDIENCE Educators (University), Social Scientists, Students (University)

414   Anthropology – Area & Cultural Studies

CONTACT   gopher@sscl.uwo.ca

FREE

gopher://gopher.sscl.uwo.ca/

Archaeology

See also
Arts & Music · *Art History*
Humanities & Social Sciences · *Classics*
Popular Culture & Entertainment · *Museums & Theme Parks*
Science · *Geosciences*

Ancient Palestine Gallery with Biblical References ★★★★

A multimedia Biblical Archaeology museum, this site covers the Middle and Late Bronze Age and the Iron Age. It includes overviews, images of pottery and other artifacts, archaeological illustrations, photographs of sites, and multimedia reference materials. Also available are a syllabus, lecture notes, and student papers from an Introduction to Biblical Terminology course.

KEYWORDS   Biblical History, Bronze Age
AUDIENCE   Archaeologists, Archaeology Educators, Archaeology Students, Biblical History Students
CONTACT   John R. Abercrombie
jacka@ccat.sas.upenn.edu
FREE

http://philae.sas.upenn.edu/ANEP/ANEP.html

Archaeological Field Work Server ★★★★

This service is designed to allow those seeking archaeological fieldwork opportunities to browse postings submitted by those who have them to offer. Included here are positions for volunteers, paid workers, field schools, contract jobs — whatever is submitted or found on various lists and news groups. This server does not contain position announcements for professional academic or staff archaeologists. The positions are listed by the region of the world where the jobs are located.

KEYWORDS   Jobs, Volunteers
AUDIENCE   Archaeologists, Archaeology Students
CONTACT   kps1@cornell.edu
FREE

http://durendal.cit.cornell.edu/TestPit.html

Artifacts-R-Us ★★★★

Artifacts-R-Us is a commercial website which advertises itself as 'Your One Stop Shop for Rare Artifacts.' It is that, and quite a bit more. Here you can purchase your very own entire dinosaur skeleton, or, if perhaps space is a problem for you, a few triceratops toe bones, a saber tooth tiger skull, a fossil of a dragonfly, or a dinosaur egg with an embryo still inside. Dinosaur nests with eggs are also available, as are several different items from the oligocene, eocene, and devonian periods. If you are not that fond of dinosaurs, you may still find the perfect gift here. A meteorite may spark your interest instead. There is a catch, though.....you need to have a lot of money to buy any of these things. Prices range from $200 for a very few items to $2 million for four Hypacrosaurus Stebbengeri dinosaur skeletons. Serious inquiries only!

KEYWORDS   Astronomy, Dinosaurs, Paleontology
AUDIENCE   Children, Dinosaur Enthusiasts, Fossil Collectors, Natural History Museum Curators
CONTACT   questions@maple.nis.net (NIS)
FREE

http://www.nis.net/artifacts

Discovery of a Palaeolithic Painted Cave at Vallon - Pont-d'Arc (Ardèche) ★★★

An exceptionally important archaeological discovery has recently been made in the Ardèche gorges (southern France), on the edge of a national reserve, in the form of a vast underground network of caves decorated with paintings and engravings dating from the Palaeolithic age (17,000 - 20,000 years ago). The discovery was made on December 25, near the village of Vallon-Pont-d'Arc during an archaeological survey. The site provides images of several paintings and a comprehensive report on the condition and contents of the find. The site also provides links to research into prehistoric wall paintings elsewhere.

KEYWORDS   Archaeology, Art, Cave Paintings, Palaeolithic Age
AUDIENCE   Archaeologists, Art Historians, Educators, Palaeolithic Age Scholars, Students
FREE

http://www.culture.fr/gvpda-en.htm

Egyptian Artifacts Exhibit ★★★★

The Egyptian Artifacts Exhibit offers a collection of information and images about Egyptian artifacts at the University of Memphis. Users can view the images, and browse through background information on each one. In addition, this site provides information on how the artifacts were obtained, as well as links to other Egyptian resources on the Net.

KEYWORDS   Archaeology, Egyptian Archaeology, Egyptian Artifacts
AUDIENCE   Archaeologists, Archaeology Enthusiasts, Egyptian Culture Enthusiasts, Egyptologists
FREE

http://www.memphis.edu/egypt/artifact.html

Internet Resources for Heritage Conservation, Historic Preservation, and Archaeology ★★★

This document is a compilation of information resources focused on archaeology, historic preservation, and heritage conservation. Resources may include Internet/Bitnet Mailing Lists, Gophers, World Wide Web Sites, Mail Servers, Usenet Newsgroups, FTP Archives, Commercial Online Services, and Bulletin Board Systems.

KEYWORDS   Anthropology, Historic Preservation, History, Meta-Index (Archaeology)
AUDIENCE   Archaeologists, Architects, Art Historians, Historians, Researchers, Students
FREE

ftp://una.hh.lib.umich.edu/inetdirsstacks/archpres:stott

Maya Adventure ★★★

The Maya Adventure is presented by the Science Museum of Minnesota. The exhibit includes information related to ancient and modern Maya culture. Topics include Mayan Sites, Activities, Mayan Photo Archive, and more. You can perform an experiment to learn how limestone dissolves forming cenotes (caves) in Chichen Itza. Then you can view images of these cenotes or other ruins. Sites on your adventure include Altar de Sacrificios, Chiapas Highlands, Uxmal, and others.

KEYWORDS   Anthropology, History, Museums
AUDIENCE   Anthropologists, Historians, Mayans, Students (University), Tourists
FREE

http://ties.k12.mn.us/~smm/

The University of Memphis Institute of Egyptian Art and Archaeology ★★★

The University of Memphis Institute of Egyptian Art and Archaeology site includes information on the institute which is dedicated to the study of the art and culture of ancient Egypt through teaching, research, exhibition, and community education, an online exhibition of Egyptian Artifacts from the institute's collection, and a color tour of Egypt.

KEYWORDS   Ancient Egypt, Artifacts, Egypt, Museums
AUDIENCE   Archaeologists, Artists, Egyptian Culture Enthusiasts, Egyptologists
FREE

http://www.memphis.edu/egypt/main.html

Area & Cultural Studies

See also
Arts & Music · *Art History*
Government & Politics · *Cities*
Government & Politics · *Countries*
Government & Politics · *States*
Humanities & Social Sciences · *Languages*

ANU Asian Studies Virtual Library ★★★★

This document keeps track of leading information facilities in the field of Asian Studies, and contains links to 195 related WWW servers worldwide, indexed by country and region.

KEYWORDS   Asian Studies, Australia, Information Retrieval, Virtual Libraries
AUDIENCE   Asian Studies Educators, Asian Studies Students, Internet Users, Researchers

CONTACT Dr. T. Matthew Ciolek
tmciolek@coombs.anu.edu.au

FREE

http://coombs.anu.edu.au/WWWVL-AsianStudies.html

ANU Social Sciences and Asian-Pacific Studies Information Service ★★★

This gopher server acts as a resource center for the social sciences of the Australian and Asia-Pacific Region. The services offered include archives, directories, databases, electronic mailing lists, resource catalogues, etc. The service is maintained by the Australian National University.

KEYWORDS Asia, Cultural Studies, Social Sciences, Universities
AUDIENCE Asian Studies Educators, Australians, Educators, Social Scientists
CONTACT T. Matthew Ciolek
coombspapers@coombs.anu.edu.au
FREE

gopher://coombs.anu.edu.au/

Aboriginal Studies Electronic Data Archive (ASEDA) ★★★

The Australian Institute of Aboriginal and Torres Strait Islander Studies holds computerized material in the Aboriginal Studies Electronic Data Archive (ASEDA). Items in this data archive are available to researchers by request, and include texts, dictionaries, theses in Australian languages, as well as non-linguistic materials such as font packages, software, and graphics. In addition, the researcher can request documents pertaining to Land Claims and the Royal Commission into Aboriginal Deaths in Custody. The Archive is available to researchers, subject to deposit and access conditions. By accessing information in electronic form researchers can locate references that are not available by keyword searching of catalogues. In addition, the linguistic collection of over 280 languages allows users to engage in comparative linguistic work. The archive also stores the work of researchers for free.

KEYWORDS Aboriginal Studies, Australia, Languages
AUDIENCE Aboriginal Researchers, Australians, Linguists
CONTACT Dr T.Matthew Ciolek, Australian National University
tmciolek@coombs.anu.edu.au
FREE

http://coombs.anu.edu.au/SpecialProj/ASEDA/ASEDA.html

African American Directory ★★★

This Web site provides information on African American art and culture. A list of cultural sites of interest is provided on the home page, as well as an online art gallery of works by African Americans. There is information available on African American music and writing, as well as links to African American businesses, writers, and personal home pages. There is also a section with online personal ads for African Americans.

KEYWORDS Africa, American Culture, Art, Cultural Studies
AUDIENCE African Americans, American Studies Students, Art Enthusiasts
CONTACT Joe Jones
joejones@lainet.com
FREE

http://www.lainet.com/~joejones

American Misconceptions about Japan ★★★

This FAQ file focuses on common American misconceptions about Japan, which is a controversial topic not covered in the other FAQ files for <soc.culture.japan>. These misconceptions also affect Asian Americans.

KEYWORDS Ethnocentrism, Japan
AUDIENCE Asian Americans, General Public, Japanese Americans, United States Residents
CONTACT TANAKA Tomoyuki (Tanaka is my family name) Eigenmann Hall 393, Bloomington, IN
tanaka@indiana.edu
FREE

ftp://rtfm.mit.edu/pub/usenet-by-hierarchy/soc/culture/asian/american/American_misconceptions_about_Japan_FAQ

American Studies Web ★★★★

This site is a meta-index of American Studies Resources on the Internet. There are hundreds of links organized by topic and by subtopic under those. Topics and subtopics include history, politics and economics, race and ethnicity, gender and sexuality, environment, visual arts, architecture, performing arts, philosophy and religion, social sciences, and more.

KEYWORDS Gender Issues, Libraries, Performing Arts
AUDIENCE American Studies Students, Internet Users, Researchers, Students (University)
CONTACT David Phillips
davidp@minerva.cis.yale.edu
FREE

http://www.cis.yale.edu/~davidp/amstud.html#amsty

Art of China Home Page ★★★

This page serves to promote Chinese culture world wide. It provides access to Chinese art, Chinese music, Chinese scenery, Chinese cuisine, the zodiac and other Chinese related sites. In the Chinese art section, paintings, crafts such as carved ivory, and chinese calligraphy are included. The music section covers violin solos, songs, and contemporary music. The scenery section includes pictures of such places as the Forbidden City, Great Wall, Imperial Gardens, Yellow Mountain as well as some online trips. Photographs and recipes of some authentic Chinese dishes are also provided. A chart is included to help determine your sign in the Chinese Zodiac, which is based on a twelve year cycle with each year represented by an animal. Last but not least, there is an audio tutorial of Chinese, for greeting, shopping, dining and traveling. It is audible

---

Connections to Birthdays

Do you share the same birthday with a famous person?

Curious about famous people who share your birth date? What momentous historical events have happened on your birth date? Through the Internet, you can discover fascinating facts from history and around the globe that tie-in to your birthday.

Perhaps you feel a kindred spirit toward a famous person. You might want to check to see if that person shares your birthday. Through "Grey Kitten's List o' Birthdays, Famous Birthday" sites, you'll not only get a list of the rich and famous who share your birthday, but biographies of those persons. For instance, if your "soul mate" is a movie star, you'll get a filmography. You can even find out if someone famous (or notorious) died on your birthday.

(http://oeonline.com/~edog/bday.html)

also, (http://www.con.wesleyan.edu/~kitten/birthday.html)

also, (http://www.eb.com/cgi-bin/bio.pl)

Maybe you want to shop for a unique birthday gift—perhaps something "virtual"? Post your birthday on the Web and "meet" other Internet surfers who have the same birthday. Get together online and celebrate.

(http://sunsit.unc.edu/btbin/birthday)

also, (http://castor.u-aizu.ac.jp/VirtualReality/WWW.Animation/Birthday/)

via Sound Machine for Macintosh and GoldWave for Windows.
KEYWORDS China, Food, Tourism
AUDIENCE Art Enthusiasts, Art Organizations, Artists, Chinese
CONTACT Remy Rong Guo
rguo@ecn.purdue.edu
FREE

http://pasture.ecn.purdue.edu/~agenhtml/agenmc/china/china.html

Asian American Resources ★★★

This site contains extensive links to Asian American Resources on the net. Subjects include WWW Servers, Events, Magazine Info, Online Journals, Files and Individual Home Pages. Some of these links are the Filipino Club of Honolulu Community College, Southeast Asian Archive, Transpacific Magazine, Harvard Chinese American Magazine, Asian American Census Statistics, Asian American Small Businesses, and much more.
KEYWORDS Asian Americans, Ethnic Studies
AUDIENCE Asian Americans, Chinese, Filipinos, Small Business Owners
CONTACT Brian Yamauchi
yamauchi@alpha.ces.cwru.edu
FREE

http://yuggoth.ces.cwru.edu/yamauchi/aar.html

Australian Gophers ★★★

This is an Australian gopher menu with links to a large variety of topics including bushwalking, film, personals, computers, education, electronics, games, jobs, legal, music, religion, theatre, jokes and beyond.
KEYWORDS Australia, Bushwalking, Games, Jobs
AUDIENCE Australians, Game Enthusiasts, Internet Users
CONTACT David Green
D.Green@csu.edu.au
FREE

gopher://services.canberra.edu.au:4320/1nntp%20ls%20aus%20

Australian Indigenous Population ★★★

The Australian Indigenous Population Web page provides textual information about the life and history of Australia's Aborigines. Topics include population, history, art, and religion. There is also material about the Aborigines' modern life and political status. Users may access links to Web sites dealing with aboriginal and indigenous populations worldwide.
KEYWORDS Aboriginals, Australia
AUDIENCE Aboriginals, Anthropologists
FREE

http://webnet.com.au/koori/homekori.html

Australian National University Coombsweb Social Sciences Server ★★★

This server from the Australian National University is for Social Sciences with links to Asian Studies. It is divided into links to virtual libraries, multimedia publishing services, and miscellaneous indexes.
KEYWORDS Asian Studies, Social Sciences, Sociology, Universities
AUDIENCE Scholars, Social Scientists, Sociologists, Students
FREE

http://coombs.anu.edu.au/CoombsHome.html

Australian National University Demography Program Archive ★★★

This is a site of the Research Schools of Social Sciences & Pacific and Asian Studies at the Australian National University devoted to Demography and Population Studies, and it has a multitude of links to all kinds of related research papers/abstracts, Virtual Libraries, newsletters and databases.
KEYWORDS Demography, Social Sciences, Sociology, Universities
AUDIENCE Scholars, Social Scientists, Sociologists, Students
CONTACT Diana Crow
Diana.Crow@anu.edu.au
FREE

http://coombs.anu.edu.au/ResFacilities/ANUDemogPage.html

CARNet Gopher ★★

The CARNet Gopher is dedicated to disseminating news about Croatia. Although resources listed include the United States Embassy in Zagreb, and Information Services in Croatia, many of the links don't work, or are only available in Croatian.
KEYWORDS Croatia, Cultural Studies, Eastern Europe, International News
AUDIENCE Croatians, Educators, Journalists, Students
FREE

gopher://rujan.srce.hr

CLNET ★★★

The Chicano/Latino Electronic Network (CLENet) brings online the Chicano/Latino research as well as linguistic minority and educational research efforts being carried out at UCLA and elsewhere, and serves as a gateway between faculty, staff and students who have research and curricular efforts in these areas. It offers an opportunity to Chicanos and Latinos to produce their own personal Web pages to be added to the CLNET directory, as well as links to a library, bookstores, museums and cultural events. It also has an employment center, conference center, student center and research center.
KEYWORDS Chicano Culture, Social Sciences, Sociology
AUDIENCE Chicanos, Latinos, Scholars, Social Scientists, Sociologists, Students
CONTACT Richard Chabran
chabran@latino.sscnet.ucla.edu
FREE

http://latino.sscnet.ucla.edu/

Carnegie Mellon University English Server ★★★★

The English Server contains a collection of documents, images and pointers to resources on a wide variety of topics in English, Classics and Social studies. There are also works relating to film and television, the Internet, computers, music, and much more. Practically any discipline that can be considered 'liberal arts' can be found here.
KEYWORDS Cultural Studies, Humanities, Literature, Social Sciences
AUDIENCE Book Readers, English Educators, Fiction Enthusiasts, General Public, Students
CONTACT Geoff Sauer
postmaster@english-server.hss.cmu.edu
FREE

gopher://english-server.hss.cmu.edu/

Center For the Study of Southern Culture Home Page ★★★

This is the home page for The Center for the Study of Southern Culture at the University of Mississippi. This center has become a focal point for innovative education and research on the American South. In addition to its degree programs the center encourages public understanding of the South through publications, media productions, lectures, perfomances, and exhibitions. Included online are The Southern Register (which is the Newsletter of the Center for the Study of Southern Culture), Living Blues -A Journal of the African American Blues Tradition, Living Blues-Blues Directory, a comprehensive guide to the blues music industry, and Reckon-The Magazine of Southern Culture.
KEYWORDS American Studies, Research, Southern Culture (US), Universities
AUDIENCE Educators (University), Students (University)
CONTACT tracy@imp.cssc.olemiss.edu
FREE

http://imp.cssc.olemiss.edu/

Chicano/LatinoNet ★★★★

Chicano/LatinoNet is a computer resource to distribute information about Latin American studies. It includes information about courses in Chicano/Latino related topics, Chicano/Latino community resources, a collection of online library catalogs and reference sources, and more. Chicano/LatinoNet is maintained by the Chicano Studies Research Center at the University of California at Los Angeles.
KEYWORDS Chicano Culture, Latin American Studies, Universities
AUDIENCE Chicanos, Latin American Studies Students, Latinos
CONTACT Romelia Salinas
salinas@latino.sscnet.ucla.edu
FREE

gopher://latino.sscnet.ucla.edu/

Chinese-Language-Related Information Page ★★★★

The Chinese-Language-Related Information Page is a comprehensive navigational tool pointing you to Chinese language resources on the Internet. There are links to online language courses and teaching materials, sources of Chinese text files, linguistic resources, and information for librarians who maintain Asian resources. There are also pointers to other resources with Chinese-related information.

KEYWORDS China, Foreign Language Instruction, Meta-Index (Chinese), Tourism
AUDIENCE Chinese, Chinese Speakers, Linguists, Translators
CONTACT Carlos McEvilly
mcevilly@netcom.com
FREE

http://www.c3.lanl.gov/~cim/chinese.html

Cultronix ★★★

Cultronix is a quarterly cultural studies journal which, in a hypertext format, incorporates video, sound, interactive use of forms, and more. The publication covers, among other issues, the relationship between a machine-centered culture and human development.

KEYWORDS Cultural Studies, Internet Magazines, Journals
AUDIENCE Academics, Communication Researchers, Cultural Studies Students, Literary Theorists
CONTACT Editor
cultronix@english-server.hss.cmu.edu
FREE

http://english.hss.cmu.edu/cultronix.html

DRUM Home Page ★★★

It is Drum's mission to provide connectivity to the Internet, National Information Highway, and various State Information Highways for the African and African American community. Some areas of information available here include pages on African American Universities, Arts, Civil Rights, Speeches, and Organizations.

KEYWORDS African American Studies
AUDIENCE African Americans, Africans
CONTACT Charles Isbell
isbell@ai.mit.edu
FREE

http://drum.ncsc.org/

Directory of Usenet Soc.Culture (Country Information) ★★★★

This is the Usenet directory for soc.culture which contains links to information on many countries worldwide.

KEYWORDS Countries, Cultural Studies, Tourism
AUDIENCE Business Travelers, Students (University), Tourists, Travelers
FREE

ftp://rtfm.mit.edu/pub/usenet-by-hierarchy/soc/culture/

Connections to Islam
From Ramadan to Prayers in Islam

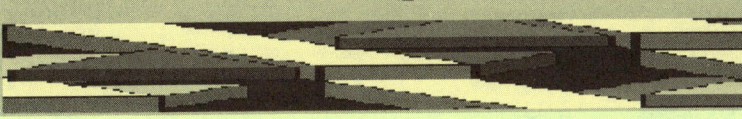
Meet Allah, His Book, His Prophets: Muhammad, Jesus, Moses etc.
Welcome to the Mosque of the Internet

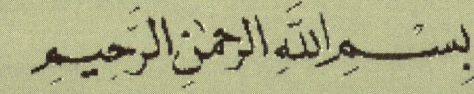
In the Name of Allah, the most Gracious, the most Merciful

Islamic Resources
Open to muslims and non-muslims worldwide.

Islamic Resources Home Page

For information about Islam—including articles, prayers, and Ramadan (the month of fasting in Islam)—the Internet is a superior resource. If your questions are very basic (What is Islam?), or if you want to get at the fundamental principals of the religion, there are a number of available sources, including FAQs (frequently asked questions) and the "Meta Page."

At these sites, you can access cultural, news, and issues forums pertaining to Islam; addressed here are (among other topics) marriage laws, women in Islam, life after death, Islamic ethics and morality, human rights, and the Islamic calendar.

At the Meta Page you'll find links to "Islamic Resources on the Internet," which provide a list of Halal Foods, and books and videos on Islamic literature. You'll also find information on the Islamic concept of worship, God, and prophesy.

(http://wings.buffalo.edu/student-life/sa/muslim/isi.html)

If you are interested in the Renaissance of Islam or would like to make a virtual visit to the Azhar Mosque, you can easily connect to the materials and information available on the Net. If you want to access FAQs, the Usenet FAQs are the place to start. Here you can learn about Farrakhism and gain access to other Islamic resources on the World Wide Web.

(http://www.cis.ohio-state.edu/hypertext/faq/hngusenet/soc/religion/islam/top.html)

also, (http://thales.nmia.com/~mosque/)

FELIPE'S Things Latino Page-Connecting toCyberRaza ★★★★

FELIPE'S Things Latino Page-Connecting toCyberRaza page provides an extensive list of links to Latino resources on the net. The topics include Latin American Centers, Links to places Latino, and places about Latinos, such as MayaQuest Learning Adventure, and Chicano History, The Tejano Music Home Page, Arte, Comida, Y Cultura Mexicana, Tourism Canada's Latin American and Carribean Page, Links to some Latino or Latino related publications, the Automatic Spanish verb conjugator, a long list of UseNet Newsgroups, and general information.

KEYWORDS History, Latin American Studies
AUDIENCE Hispanics, Latin Americans, Mexican Americans, Spanish Speakers, Students (University)
CONTACT felipe@bongo.cc.utexas.edu
FREE

http://edb518ea.edb.utexas.edu/html/latinos.html

Area & Cultural Studies

Film/Video Materials for Programs on Hispanics ★★★

Film/Video Materials for Programs on Hispanics is a non-hyperlinked list of films by and/or for Hispanics. Each film is listed by title, followed by the length of the film, the language, a brief description of the film, the producer, who may use the film and what year it was produced. Subjects range from the story of twenty-two undocumented workers who stood up for their rights and took their employer to court, to performance artist Guillermo Gomez-Pena.

Keywords Film, Hispanic Americans, Video
Audience Film Enthusiasts, Film Makers, Hispanics
Free

gopher://english.hss.cmu.edu/0F-2%3A5662%3AHispanic%20Experience

The Handbook of Latin American Studies ★★★

The Handbook of Latin American Studies (HLAS) is a bibliographical publication in the field of Latin American studies. The database contains abstracts and complete bibliographic information for published works from and about Latin America on a range of topics in the humanities and social sciences. This handbook has been published for the last 58 years.

Keywords Indigenous Studies, Latin American Studies
Audience Human Rights Activists, Latin American Researchers, Political Scientists, Sociologists
Free

telnet://locis.loc.gov:23/

Hispanic Pages In The USA ★★★★

This site provides links to Hispanic Pages in the USA. Some of the topics covered include COLOQUIO, Revista Cultural Hispana, a Spanish language magazine, famous Hispanics in the world and history, los paises Hispanos (Hispanic Countries), la tauromaquia (the art of bullfighting), American Revolution, REFORMA to promote library services to the Hispanic population, spanish art, and more.

Keywords Bullfighting, History
Audience Chicanos, Hispanics, Latin Americans, Mexican Americans
Contact Javier Bustamante gbustam@clark.net
Free

http://www.clark.net/pub/jgbustam/heritage/heritage.html

Human Rights and Universal Responsibility ★★★

This site contains a speech by his Holiness the Dalai Lama of Tibet. The speech was first given at the United Nations World Conference on Human Rights on June 15, 1993 in Vienna, Austria. There is also a link to the Journal of Buddhist Ethics.

Keywords Ethics, Human Rights, Tibet
Audience Human Rights Activists, Humanists, Tibetans
Free

http://www.cac.psu.edu/jbe/dalai1.html

Index of Native American Resources on the Internet ★★

This is a brief hyperlinked Index of Native American Resources on the Internet. It includes educational resources, cultural resources, art resources, government resources, and more.

Keywords Cultural Studies, History, Native Americans
Audience History Buffs, Indigenous People, Native Americans
Contact kstrom@hanksville.phast.umass.edu
Free

http://hanksville.phast.umass.edu/misc/NAresources.html

Indian Pueblo Cultural Center ★★★

This site contains images and information on over 15 different Pueblo Indian sites and tribes. It also contains a list of facilities offered by the Pueblo Cultural Center and a page with Pueblo etiquette and rules.

Keywords Native Americans, New Mexico
Audience Educators, Historians, Native Americans, Pueblo Indians, Students
Contact Karen M. Strom kstrom@hanksville.phast.umass.edu
Free

http://hanksville.phast.umass.edu/defs/independent/PCC/PCC.html

Indigenous/Native/Aboriginal Related Online Information ★★★

This is a list of Internet/BITnet mailing lists and news services that focus on or relate to Indigenous, Native, or Aboriginal people, culture, and issues. The latest copy can be found at the Netcom FTP site

Keywords Aboriginal Studies, Cultural Studies, Indigenous Studies, Native Americans
Audience Anthropologists, Indigeneous People, Native Americans, Researchers
Contact amcgee@netcom.com
Free

gopher://acs6.acs.ucalgary.ca:70/00/library/polar/infofiles/native

ftp://ftp.netcom.com/pub/amcgee/indigenous/

Indonesian Students at Calvin College & Seminary ★★

The Indonesian Students at Calvin College & Seminary presents the home pages of students at the Grand Rapids, Michigan, school. Users may also access information about Indonesia, including travel, culture, and other topics. There is a clickable map and a thumbnail sketch of the East Asian country, and a few links.

Keywords Colleges/Universities, Indonesia, Students
Audience Calvin College Students, Indonesians
Free

http://www.calvin.edu/~rsetia67/indonesian/indonesian.html

The Institute of Latin American Studies in the University of Texas at Austin ★★★

This is a gopher server of the Institute of Latin American Studies (ILAS) in the University of Texas at Austin. It contains information on Latin America, publications, libraries, and more. It also has links to other gophers.

Keywords Latin American Studies, South America, Universities
Audience Humanists, Latin American Studies Students, Social Scientists
Contact Ning Lin info@lanic.utexas.edu
Free

gopher://lanic-gopher.utexas.edu/

Iranian Cultural & Information Center ★★★

This site has a collection of resources for students or enthusiasts of Iranian culture. There are links to areas such as Iranian art, literature, cuisine, and movies. In addition, users can look up information about Iranian related conferences, schools and universities, and other Iranian Internet sites. Several Persian text editors and utilities are available for downloading here. In addition, a clickable map allows the viewer to find out more information about the different geographic regions in Iran.

Keywords Iran, Persia, Persian Language
Audience Iran Residents, Iranian Culture Enthusiasts, Persian Writers
Contact webmaster@Tehran.stanford.edu
Free

http://tehran.stanford.edu/

ftp://tehran.stanford.edu/

Iranshahr ★★★

The Iranshahr Web site contains textual and graphic resources for users interested in Iran. Topics include history, literature, and music. There's also information on conferences and newsgroups, plus a thumbnail sketch of the country and its people. Users may access links to Web sites dealing with Iran and the Middle East.

Keywords Cultural Studies, History, Iran
Audience Academics, Iranians
Free

http://weber.u.washington.edu/~iranshar/

Irish Resources on the Internet ★★★★

Collected by Dennis Doyle, this page is a list of sites with links to Irish universities, geneology, language, literature and theater. Mr. Doyle also posts usenet newsgroups of Celtic interest and quite a number of mail lists with listserv subscription instructions. Lists include such titles as 'Solitary Pagan Practitioner Digest' and 'Modern British and Irish Literature 1895-19+'. Also listed are files from University College, Dublin, Anonymous FTP files, files about Irish or Celtic culture on America Online, Telnet sites, and other useful addresses such as the Irish electronic yellow pages.

KEYWORDS Celtic Culture, Ireland
AUDIENCE English Literature Enthusiasts, Irish, Reading Enthusiasts, Students (University)
CONTACT ddoyle@cello.gina.calstate.edu
FREE

http://futon.sfsu.edu/%7Ejtm/Gaelic/irish_srcs.html

Kurdish Information Network (KIN) ★★★

This site contains a wealth of information about the Kurdish and the geographical region of Kurdistan. This archive has facts and figures about the land, ecology, people, language, religion, and demographic trends. There are also several articles about Kurdish history, and cultural issues. In addition, there are written lessons on the Kurdish language, a small archive of images, and links and contacts to other Kurdish organizations on and off the Internet.

KEYWORDS Cultural Studies, Kurdish Culture
AUDIENCE Kurdistan Scholars, Kurds, Students
FREE

http://nucst11.neep.wisc.edu/

La Union Chicana por Aztlan (LUChA) at MIT ★★★

La Union Chicana por Aztlan (LUChA) at MIT, is dedicated to providing both cultural and academic support to students who identify in any way with Mexican American culture. This page has many links to areas such as the East Coast Chicano Student Forum (ECCSF), recent issues of Que Pasa? the official LUChA newsletter, Pocho Magazine On-Line - Aztlan's rudest humor magazine, the charter and some related files for the soc.culture.mexican.american Usenet newsgroup, California Proposition 187 information, and links to other Chicano/Latino pages on the Internet.

KEYWORDS Chicano Culture, Latin American Studies, Latino/Chicano Culture, Mexico
AUDIENCE Chicanos, Hispanics, Latin Americans, Latinas, Mexican Americans, Spanish Speakers, Students (University)
FREE

http://www.mit.edu:8001/activities/lucha/homepage.html

Latin America ★★★

This site provides access to links relating to the study of Latin America such as the Latin American and Caribbean Center (LACC) at Florida International University, and the Latin America on Heidelberg History Gopher, Online Colegios, a newsletter devoted to the study of Colonial Latin American philosophy, Latino and Chicano Studies, a home page for the Latin American Solidarity group at the University of Kansas, and more.

KEYWORDS Caribbean, Latin American Studies, Politics

Connections to Sobre CLNet
Que pasa?

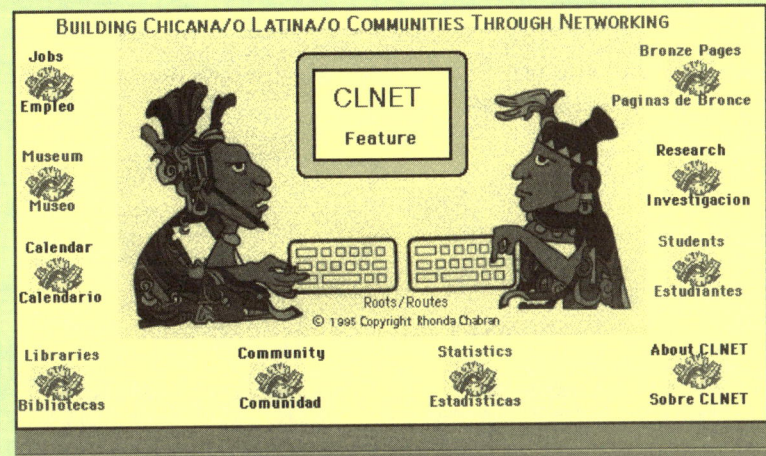

The "Chicano/Latino Electronic Network" puts you in touch with a healthy cross-section of Internet resources for the Chicano/Latino community. In English and in Spanish, this site includes job listings, a resume service, and career advice for the Latino community.

The site has now grown to cover a broad swath of Chicano and Latino culture. The CLNet calendar consists of events pertaining to Latino and linguistic minority research issues. CLNET also provides the community with a place to get information on social services, legal services, housing, and transportation issues and resources for a wide selection of cities around the U.S. CLNet lets users create their own Web page to communicate with other minorities and foster communication within the Chicano/Latino community.

Additionally, there are features on topics like Cinco de Mayo festivals, historical perspectives on Latino culture, and literature of Latin America and the third world. CLNET also hosts a site for information about cultural customs and traditions.

(http://latino.sscnet.ucla.edu/) also,

(http://latino.sscnet.ucla.edu/community.html)

AUDIENCE Educators (University), Latin Americans, Students (University)
FREE

http://history.cc.ukans.edu/history/reading_rooms/latin_america.html

LatinoWeb ★★★★

The LatinoWeb home page is a meta-index containing numerous links in these fields — art and music; business and employment; education; history; current events; government agencies, nonprofit organizations, and advocacy groups; and newspapers and magazines. The site is fairly exhaustive in its coverage.

KEYWORDS Business, Cultural Studies, Government, Latin Americans
AUDIENCE Latin Americans, United States Residents
FREE

http://www.catalog.com/favision/latnoweb

List of Hindu Names ★★★

This site contains a list of Hindu names and their meanings.
KEYWORDS Hindu Culture
AUDIENCE General Public, Hindus, Researchers, Students
FREE

gopher://wiretap.spies.com:70/00/Library/Article/Language/hindu.nam

ftp://spies.com/Library/Article/Language/hindu.nam

Little Russia ★★★★

This site provides links to resources related to the history and culture of Russia. Any document on this server can be viewed either through the WAIS gateway or directly from the menu. Topics covered include major Russian attractions such as Moscow Architecture of

420 Area & Cultural Studies

XIII-XIX centuries. The Music page contains the largest online catalog of Russian CDs and more than 200 audio clips, the collection of Russian romantic songs, and Pop Music. Other links include Russian network maps and a list of the Internet servers, computer games and fonts, Russification of the Macintosh computer, A Brief Visit to Russia, How to buy Russian articles in the USA, Getting US visas, work permits, green cards, and more.

KEYWORDS Cultural Studies, Music, Politics, Russia
AUDIENCE Macintosh Users, Music Enthusiasts, Russians, Tourists
CONTACT Vladimir Pekkel
pekkel@uthscsa.edu
FREE

http://mars.uthscsa.edu/Russia/

Middle East Resource Center ★★★

The Middle East Resource Center is a public service effort of the Global Publishing Group. What distinguishes the work presented here is the promotion of Persian/Arabic hypertext (HTML). Some of the information on this site requires an ISIRI-3342 browser (like PMosaic), or an external viewer. This site offers viewers access to organizations with a Middle Eastern focus, such as the Association for Persian Logic, Language and Computing and the Iranian Human Rights Working Group. In addition, a number of publications are available online, such as Computer Report, Az Iroon, news reports related to the Middle East, as well as articles and poetry in Arabic and Persian.

KEYWORDS Arabic, Middle Eastern Studies
AUDIENCE Iranians, Middle East Residents, Middle East Scholars, Persia Residents
CONTACT Global Publication Group
webmaster@gpg.com
FREE

http://gpg.com/MERC/

The Milarepa Fund ★★

The Milarepa Fund was established to inform the public about the Tibetan civilization, and to inform people about what they can do to stop the destruction of Tibetan culture.

KEYWORDS Cultural Studies, Tibet
AUDIENCE Activists, Buddhists, Tibetans
FREE

http://bianca.com/lolla/politics/milarepa/milarepa.html

Native American Resources on the Internet ★★★★

This page contains a list of links to other major Native American resources on the Internet. The list includes NativeNet WWW Home Page, The National Museum of the American Indian, Native Americans at Princeton, The American Indian College Fund, Center For World Indigenous Studies, A Guide to the Great Sioux Nation, Bureau of Indian Affairs, Native Education Initiative, The American Indian Culture Home Page, and more.

KEYWORDS Indigenous Studies, Native Americans
AUDIENCE Ethnic Studies Students, Native Americans
FREE

http://hanksville.phast.umass.edu/misc/NAresources.html

Native Education Centre ★★

This is a gopher server of the the Native Education Centre (NEC), located in British Columbia, Canada. Users will find information on the NEC and the Family Violence Resource Centre. Some resources available here include the NEC electronic library, and electronic library resources. Examples of files produced or compiled by the NEC are reviews of books and films with Native themes, speeches focussing on Native issues, and links to further sites related to Native peoples around the world. The Family Violence Resource Center is a collection of links related to women, children, families, and domestic violence.

KEYWORDS Aboriginal Studies, Educational Resources, Native Americans
AUDIENCE Aboriginal Studies Students, Educators, Families, Indigenous People, Native Americans
CONTACT gopher@native-ed.bc.ca
FREE

gopher://gopher.native-ed.bc.ca/

Oneida Indian Nation of New York ★★★

This Web site presents historical and cultural information about the Onyota', aka, the Oneida Indian Nation, or the People of the Standing Stone. The Oneida Indian Nation, one of the original members of the Iroquois Confederacy, enjoys a unique role in America's history, having supported the Colonies in the struggle for independence from England. The Nation exists as a sovereign political unit which predates the Constitution of the United States. This page contains links to Treaties Project, The Shako - Wi Project, Economic Sovereignty Mind, Body, and Spirit, and links to other Native American information sites.

KEYWORDS Native Americans, New York
AUDIENCE Educators (University), Native Americans, Students (University)
CONTACT oneida1@transit.nyser.net
FREE

http://nysernet.org:80/oneida/

Other Fourth World Resources on the Internet ★★★★

The Other Fourth World Resources on the Internet page provides a long linked list of resources on the Internet related to indigenous and aboriginal people around the world. The goal of the Fourth World Documentation Project is to document and make available to tribal governments, researchers and organizations important documents relating to the social, political, strategic, economic and human rights situations being faced by indigenous and aboriginal people. Four hundred documents are organized according to region - African Documents, European and Asian Documents, Melanesian, Polynesian and Micronesian Documents, North, Central and South American Documents, Internationally focused documents, and United Nations Documents.

KEYWORDS Native Americans, Tribal Governments (US)
AUDIENCE Historians, Human Rights Activists, N. Indigenous Cultures, Native Americans, Researchers
CONTACT John Burrows
jburrows@halcyon.com
FREE

http://www.halcyon.com/FWDP/othernet.html

Pigulki ★★

This server gives acess to Pigulki, an electronic collection of news analysis, press reviews, and humor from/about Poland and the Polish community abroad. The newsletters are given in both Polish and English.

KEYWORDS News, Poland
AUDIENCE Polish Culture Enthusiasts, Polish Speakers
CONTACT Marek SamocNews
mjs111@phyvs0.anu.edu.au
FREE

gopher://laserspark.anu.edu.au/

Pueblo Cultural Center ★★★

The Indian Pueblo Cultural Center offers information and resources related to the Pueblo Indians of New Mexico. Users will find information on the various clans within the Pueblo Indian family such as the Tesuque and Zuni clans. There is also detailed information on the facilities of the cultural center, including museum and theater programs, event schedules, directions for those who wish to visit the center, as well as center rules and 'Pueblo etiquette' guides.

KEYWORDS Cultural Studies, Museums, Native Americans
AUDIENCE American Indian Culture Enthusiasts, Archaeologists, Museum Enthusiasts, Native Americans
CONTACT Karen M. Strom
kstrom@hanksville.phast.umass.edu
FREE

http://hanksville.phast.umass.edu:80/defs/independent/PCC/PCC.html

Scottish Borders ★★★

The Scottish Borders pages has information on Scottish subjects including arts like children's tales, Rob Hain, Jesse Rae (virtual Rock); writers like James Hogg, Howard Purdie, Sir Walter Scott; history, culture and leisure, and publications including Photon Magazine. The site also contains links to Tweednet, the Scottish server. The Scottish Border virutal gallery will contain works of art in various media (paintings, photography, calligraphy).

KEYWORDS Museums, Scotland, Visual Arts
AUDIENCE Educators, Scots, Scottish Culture Enthusiasts, Tourists
FREE

http://www.scotborders.co.uk/

Singapore Online (TM) ★★★★

This page offers travelers and business professionals information about Singapore. Users can search for registered companies in Singapore, and receive information on various businesses and tourist activities.

The site also offers many general information links regarding Singapore.

KEYWORDS International Travel, South Pacific, Southeast Asia, Tourism
AUDIENCE Business Researchers, International Business Professionals, International Development Specialists, Internet Developers
CONTACT webmaster@singapore.com
FREE

http://www.singapore.com/

Southeast Asian Archive ★★

The Southeast Asian Archive describes the archive and how to access it. The Archive collects materials relating to the resettlement of Southeast Asian refugees and immigrants in the United States (and to a lesser extent, worldwide), the 'boat people' and land refugees, and the culture and history of Cambodia, Laos, and Vietnam. There is a special focus on materials pertaining to Southeast Asians in Orange County, CA. The holdings include books, refugee orientation materials, government documents, reports and surveys, periodicals, journal articles, newspaper clippings, video and audio recordings, ephemera, personal and institutional papers. There is particular attention given to collecting theses and dissertations.

KEYWORDS History, Refugees, Southeast Asia, Vietnamese Americans
AUDIENCE Educators, Researchers, Southeast Asians, Students (University), Vietnamese
CONTACT Anne Frank
         afrank@uci.edu
FREE

http://www.lib.uci.edu/sea/seahome.html

Sun Tzu - The Art of War ★★★★

This is an electronic text version of Sun Tzu's The Art of War, written in the Big 5 Chinese dialect. Knowledge of this dialect will be required to understand content.

KEYWORDS China, Literature
AUDIENCE Chinese Literature Enthusiasts, Fiction Enthusiasts, Literary Scholars, Students (University)
FREE

http://biomed.nus.sg/CM/cweb/sunzi/b5/sunzi.b5.html

University of Texas — Latin American Network Information Center ★★★★

The objective of the University of Texas — Latin American Network Information Center (UT-LANIC) is to provide Latin American users with access to academic databases and information services throughout the Internet world, and to provide Latin Americanists around the world with access to information on and from Latin America. Users will find links to Web home pages and other resources for general Latin American information, as well as specific directories for more than 25 Latin American countries, library systems, and publications.

KEYWORDS Latin American Studies, Universities
AUDIENCE Human Rights Activists, Latin American Researchers, Political Scientists, Sociologists

Connections to Judaism
From Kosher foods to Literature

The World Wide Web comprises an incredible resource of information on practically every aspect of, and perspective on, Judaism. One superior site is the Judaism page for the "A to Z guide on Judaism." This site furnishes general information on the culture of Israel, as well as on Jewish customs. Here you can study, among other items, the Dead Sea Scrolls. If you're interested in Jewish literature or want to peruse the English and Hebrew calendar, then try "Judaism (Religion)" on the Internet. At this site you can access the A to Z Guide through "Judaica Collection," and the Dead Sea Scrolls from "Religion, Judaism" (which is part of the World Wide Web Virtual Library).

(http://www.cs.cmu.edu/afs/cs.cmu/edu/user/clamen/misc/Judaica/README.html)

also, (http:www.biologie.uni-freiburg.del/~amueller/religion/Judaism.html)

If you are looking for Kosher foods for Passover or guidelines on the kinds of foods to serve at Passover, then you'd be advised to contact "Kosher Express." You can also obtain general culture information via "Weizmann Physics, Judaism and Israel."

(http://www.weizmann.ac.il/physics/jew_il.html)

also, (http://www.marketnet.com/mknet/kosher/)

FREE

http://lanic.utexas.edu/
gopher://lanic.utexas.edu/

The Virtual Baguette ★★★

The Virtual Baguette is an online French culture magazine with a focus on humor and satire. Sections include the Entendre music section, with sound files of French music, the electronic gastronomy section with regional recipes, and Mots, which allows users to create poetry in either French or English. There are satirical guides to French culture, such as the Virtual Lourdes, which provides a 'tour' of this historically important religious site, and a gallery of images of Le Bidet. The Virtual Forum is a discussion area for Virtual Baguette readers and also includes a guide to current French events and culture web sites.

KEYWORDS France, French, Humor
AUDIENCE French Citizens, French Enthusiasts
FREE

http://www.mmania.com/

Welcome to Malaysia ★★★

This guide aims to compile available information resources about Malaysia for distribution via World Wide Web. Topics such as travel information, immigration, religion, culture, and more, are covered. In addition, users can access environmental and governmental information, as well as sound clips and graphics related to Malaysia.

KEYWORDS International Travel, Malaysia, South Pacific, Southeast Asia
AUDIENCE Malaysians, Students, Tourists, Travelers
CONTACT webmaster@jaring.my
FREE

http://www.jaring.my/

The World-Wide Web Virtual Library Latin American Studies ★★★★

This virtual library provides a great deal of information on Latin America. You can go to a particular country and see a menu of general information. There are links to the home pages of international organizations, business and trade organizations, information about Internet networking, and more to be found in this comprehensive source of information.

KEYWORDS Internet Guides, Latin American Studies
AUDIENCE Business Professionals, International Travelers, Latin Americans, Researchers, Tourists

Area & Cultural Studies – Classics

CONTACT Ning Lin
info@lanic.utexas.edu

FREE

http://lanic.utexas.edu/las.html

Yeshe De Project ★★★

Established in 1983, the Yeshe De Project is dedicated to preserving the texts of the Tibetan Buddhist tradition, encouraging scholarly research, and promoting translation of traditional Buddhist texts. Under its auspices, the entire Kanjur and Tanjur, the Tibetan Buddhist Canon in 120 Western-style volumes, was reprinted, and 600 additional volumes containing 75,000 precious texts were gathered from monasteries and libraries around the world. This page has a detailed history of the project and some of its texts as well as links to other sites related to Tibet.

KEYWORDS Books, Tibet
AUDIENCE Humanists, Scholars, Tibetans
CONTACT Will Spiegelman
wgs@leland.stanford.edu

FREE

http://www-leland.stanford.edu:80/~wgs/yd.html

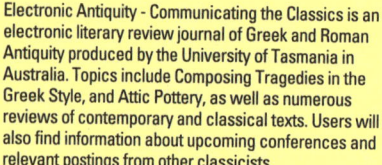

Classics

See also
Arts & Music · *Art History*
Humanities & Social Sciences · *Literature*
Religion & Philosophy · *Mythology*

Books Online ★★★

This site contains hundreds of full-text online books, including many classics such as Anna Karenina and The Complete Works of William Shakespeare. It has a searchable index and also provides links to other book resources.

KEYWORDS Books, Classics, Dramatists, Online Books
AUDIENCE Book Readers, Literature Students, Reading Enthusiasts, Students (Secondary/College)

FREE

http://www.cs.cmu.edu/Web/books.html

Books Online, Listed by Title ★★★★

This site lists mostly books that are available as electronic text. It can be browsed by title or by author, and contains links to other online book resources. The book titles are classics such The Brothers Karamazov by Dostoevsky, Candide by Voltaire, The Complete Works by Shakespeare, Daisy Miller by Henry James and many more.

KEYWORDS Authors, Books, Classics, Fiction
AUDIENCE Book Readers, Fiction Enthusiasts, General Public, Students (University)
CONTACT spok@cs.cmu.edu

FREE

http://www.cs.cmu.edu:8001/Web/booktitles.html

Classic Chinese Text ★★★★

This is an archive of classic Chinese literature texts in electronic format, posted in the Big 5 Chinese dialect and text. A helpful pronunciation glossary is included (Big 5 character words are listed with english character words). There are hundreds of texts located at this site. Knowledge of this dialect is required to understand content.

KEYWORDS China, Chinese Literature, Literature
AUDIENCE Chinese Literature Enthusiasts, Fiction Enthusiasts, Literary Scholars, Students (University)

FREE

gopher://dongpo.math.ncu.edu.tw/11/chinese

Department of Classical Studies Gopher ★★★

This Department of Classical Studies at University of Michigan gopher site offers information about anthropology and archeology. Some of the areas covered include Britain, the Orient, and general world heritage. This site has links to other gopher servers, projects, and databases.

KEYWORDS Anthropology, Archaeology, Classics
AUDIENCE Academics, Anthropologists, Archaeologists, Art Historians
CONTACT Sebastian Heath
sfsh@umich.edu

FREE

gopher://rome.classics.lsa.umich.edu/

Electronic Antiquity - Communicating the Classics ★★

Electronic Antiquity - Communicating the Classics is an electronic literary review journal of Greek and Roman Antiquity produced by the University of Tasmania in Australia. Topics include Composing Tragedies in the Greek Style, and Attic Pottery, as well as numerous reviews of contemporary and classical texts. Users will also find information about upcoming conferences and relevant postings from other classicists.

KEYWORDS Ancient Greece, Literary Criticism
AUDIENCE Classicists, Classics Students, Greek Studies Specialists
CONTACT antiquity-editor@classics.utas.edu.au.

FREE

gopher://info.utas.edu.au/11/Publications/Electronic%20Antiquity%20:%20Communicating%20The%20Classics/

The Facts On File Encyclopedia of World Mythology and Legend ★★★★

A Natural Book Club Main Selection, this book is 'exhaustive in its coverage...encompassing myths and legends from around the world...' according to the author at this gopher site. The Encyclopedia of World Mythology and Legend by Anthony S. Mercatante contains more than 2,500 entries ranging from Aesop's fables to the myths of Micronesia to Voodoo. Purchase and ISBN information are available here.

KEYWORDS Literature, Mythology
AUDIENCE Educators (University), Fiction Enthusiasts, Literary Scholars, Mythology Enthusiasts, Students (University)

FREE

gopher://ns1.infor.com:4600/1exec%3AR24753842477570-/.te:

Greek and Roman Mythology A to Z - A Young Reader's Companion ★★★★

This is a valuable resource for K-12 students and educators interested in the essence of the mythology in Greek and Roman literature. Booklist is quoted, 'It is recommended for purchase by school and public libraries serving students in the middle grades and up.' Purchase and ISBN information are available here.

KEYWORDS Children's Literature, Literature, Mythology
AUDIENCE Educators (Primary/Secondary), Librarians, Literary Scholars, Mythology Enthusiasts, Students (Primary/Secondary)

FREE

gopher://ns1.infor.com:4600/1exec%AR2941543-2943426/.te:

The HELLAS List Home Page ★★★

The Hellenic discussion List is a forum for exchange of information about various subjects concerning Greece and Greeks at home or abroad. Users will find online subscription information for this mailing list, as well as collected resources related to Greece and Greek culture. There are links to the home pages of subscribers to Hellas, as well as to sites such as the Cypress Home Page, the Hellenic Society, Greek current events, and others.

KEYWORDS Ancient Greece, Hellenic Culture
AUDIENCE Greece Residents, Greek Culture Enthusiasts, Greeks
CONTACT webmaster@velox.stanford.edu

FREE

http://velox.stanford.edu/hellas/

Internationales Shakespeare Globe ★★★

This site is the international Shakespeare headquarters of the Internet and is based at the University of Cologne in Germany. The links are not only to Shakespearean sites on the Web, but to articles, the Globe in London, workshops and conferences in Germany and contact information.

KEYWORDS Classics, Dramatists, Germany, Literature
AUDIENCE Drama Enthusiasts, Shakespeare Enthusiasts

CONTACT Andreas Schlenger
ame14@rrz.uni-koeln.de

FREE

http://www.rrz.uni-koeln.de/phil-fak/
englisch/shakespeare/index.html

Shakespeare Gopher

This site organizes the Shakespeare Corpus into the following categories - Comedies, Romances, Histories, Tragedies, Roman, and Poetry. The texts are available for keyword search or full-text browsing. Keyword search can search the genre categories or individual works, returning the paragraph in which the keyword was found. The gopher site also provides a glossary of Shakespearean words.

KEYWORDS Classics, Dramatists, Elizabethan Drama, Poetry
AUDIENCE Educators, General Public, Shakespeare Enthusiasts, Shakespeare Scholars
FREE

gopher://ccat.sas.upenn.edu:70/11/
Archive/SHAKESPEARE

The Shakespeare Web

These pages are dedicated to playwright, William Shakespeare. Acknowledged father of what we know today as dramatic theater, this site contains numerous Shakespeare works, as well as biographies, a complete bibliography, FAQs, lists of film versions of his work, and links to a number of other Shakespeare-related resources on the Internet.

KEYWORDS Classics, Literature, Theater
AUDIENCE Actors, Playwrights, Shakespeare Enthusiasts
CONTACT Webmaster
dna@svpal.org
FREE

http://sashimi.wwa.com/~culturew/
Shakesweb/shakesweb.html

Tables of Contents of Interest to Classicists

The Tables of Contents of Interest to Classicists gopher is designed as a compilation of brief abstracts of classical journals. After browsing a list of the journals included in this gopher, users can either search the journals with a subject or title search, or pick the archaeology, classics, or religious studies files.

KEYWORDS Journals, Reference
AUDIENCE Classicists, Classics Researchers, Classics Students
CONTACT Philippa MW Matheson
amphoras@epas.utoronto.ca
FREE

gopher://gopher.lib.virginia.edu:70/11/
alpha/tocs

The Tech Classics Archive

The Tech Classics Archive is an online collection of 184 classical works by 17 authors, including Aristotle, Aristophanes, Euripedes, Hippocrates, Plato and Plutarch. Users may browse a list of titles and authors or conduct a subject search, after which they have a choice to read a complete work or the unformatted text. Certain key texts, such as the Hippocratic Oath and Homer's Iliad, are featured. Links to other online literature, classics, and electronic book Web sites are also provided.

KEYWORDS Literature, Online Books, Philosophy
AUDIENCE Classics Researchers, Classics Students, English Students, Fiction Enthusiasts
CONTACT Daniel C. Stevenson
classics@the-tech.mit.edu
FREE

http://the-tech.mit.edu/Classics/

War and Peace

This is an electronic text version of Leo Tolstoy's War and Peace. The file is over two megabytes in size, and will take a long time to receive over slow links.

KEYWORDS Literature, Russian Literature

Connections to Rare Books
Book worms beware!

A rare book is not necessarily old or monetarily valuable. Rather, it is a book with research or intellectual value that would be difficult or impossible to replace. Rare Books preserves approximately 50,000 titles dating from a leaf of the Gutenberg Bible (ca. 1456) to recent first editions. It also houses a wide range of formats, from miniatures no larger than one inch high, to magnificent volumes forty inches tall; from five-hundred year-old books in as fine a condition as the day they were printed to twentieth-century first editions crumbling from the acidity of their paper.

Besides individual books, Rare Books houses book collections that bring together groupings of volumes on a particular topic. Subject areas represented are broad, but areas of special strength are

- natural history
- the American Revolution
- American travel accounts
- British shire histories
- nineteenth and twentieth century English language fiction
- Romanov Russian history and travel
- science fiction
- Swiss history
- works published by the Kelmscott Press

If the book you want is out of print, or the print-run was limited, you don't have to search through rare book stores all over town. Use the Internet for connections to finding those rare and collectible books.

Do you want a copy of a First Grade Reader from the 1920s or an historical book on the British Museum? Find it through various sites on the Internet.

Maybe your interest leans toward science fiction from the 1950s, or books of maps from the 19th century. One of many likely places you will find what you want is through "Rare Books"; or check the "KBC Online Book Store List." At the latter site, you can locate rare manuscripts as well.

(http://www.tulane.edu/~lmiller/RareBooks.html)

also, (http://kbc.com/html/bookstor.htm)

AUDIENCE Literary Critics, Literary Scholars, Reading Enthusiasts, Russian Literature Enthusiasts
FREE

gopher://gopher.vt.edu:10010/11/151

Geography

See also
Computing & Mathematics · *Computer Science*
Government & Politics · *Agencies*
Science · *Earth Sciences*
Science · *Geosciences*

Xerox PARC Map Viewer

The Xerox PARC Map Viewer allows users to look at an interactive map of the world, by clicking on a region. The zoom in and zoom out buttons bring the map into closer detail in increments of 2, 5, 10, and 25. The map can be viewed in color, elliptically, rectangularly, or as a square, or one can see a map of the United States only. Other features included are river and border markings and latitude/longitude coordinates.

- **KEYWORDS** Interactive Learning, Maps
- **AUDIENCE** Cartographers, General Public, Geography Enthusiasts
- **CONTACT** webmaster@xerox.com
- **FREE**

http://pubweb.parc.xerox.com/map

History

See also
Arts & Music · *Art History*
Government & Politics · *Countries*
Government & Politics · *Doctrines*
Sports & Recreation · *Travel & Tourism*

American Memory

American Memory consists of collections of primary source and archival material relating to American culture and history. Most of these offerings are from the Library of Congress. The elements in each American Memory collection include cataloging, digital reproductions of the items, and various accompaniments. Photographic, recorded sound, manuscript and early motion picture collections have been prepared for Internet access.

- **KEYWORDS** American Studies, Education, Social Studies
- **AUDIENCE** Educators (Primary/Secondary), Historians, Students, Students (Secondary/University)
- **FREE**

http://lcweb2.loc.gov/amhome.html

American Studies ★★★

This is a gopher server for the the American Studies Program and the History Department at the University of Texas (UT) at Austin. It contains information on American Studies, history, libraries, staff, faculty, and more. It has links to the UT main gopher as well as other gophers on the Internet.

- **KEYWORDS** American Studies, Education, History, Universities
- **AUDIENCE** Educators (University), Historians, History Students
- **CONTACT** Greg Hiner
  hiner@mail.utexas.edu
- **FREE**

gopher://whitman.gar.utexas.edu/

Anne Frank Site ★★★★

This site contains information relating to Anne Frank, a young woman who for a time succesfully hid in Amsterdam from the Nazi Government, but was discovered and killed. The diary Anne kept while in hiding has been an important reminder of the Holocaust for Jews and all others who fear replication of this type of event. Selections from Frank's own writing are available here, as are articles about the book and her life. Photographs and other miscellany relating to the holocaust and authenticity (proven by the Netherlands State Institute for War Documentation) are also available.

- **KEYWORDS** Holocaust, Judaism, World War II
- **AUDIENCE** Historians, Holocaust Survivors, Jews, Students
- **CONTACT** Thang D. Nguyen
  tdnguyen@cs.washington.edu
- **FREE**

http://www.cs.washington.edu/homes/tdnguyen/Anne_Frank.html

Bodleian Library Manuscript Collections ★★★

This site, maintained at the famous Bodleian Library in Oxford, England, provides images and accompanying annotation (with hypertext links to other documents) of manuscript illustrations from the Bodleian's world-respected collection. Online images include the following manuscripts—Marguerite de Navarre's 'La Coche ou le Debat de l'Amour,' a Book of Hours (Flanders, c.1360), the Bible Moralisee (Paris, c.1235-45), and a medical miscellany (England, late 13th century).

- **KEYWORDS** Art Collections, Manuscript Collections, Rare Books, Renaissance Studies
- **AUDIENCE** Art Historians, Medievalists, Researchers, Students (University)
- **CONTACT** djp@rsl.ox.ac.uk
- **FREE**

http://rsl.ox.ac.uk/imacat.html

Bryn Mawr Gopher ★★

This gopher is the home of two online history journals, the Bryn Mawr Classical Review and the Bryn Mawr Medieval Review. Each discusses various aspects of culture and literature in their respective time periods. The information is provided by the libraries of the University of Virginia.

- **KEYWORDS** Classics, Education, History, Medieval Studies
- **AUDIENCE** Historians, Literary Scholars, Medieval Scholars
- **FREE**

gopher://gopher.lib.virginia.edu:70/11/journals/

The California Missions ★★

U.S. Highway 101 closely parallels the historic Mission Trail, the chain of 21 missions established in the 18th century by the Spanish padres. This page provides cursory information on these missions in California. It includes a few links and some brief descriptions of some of the missions. There are also links to the Chambers of Commerce/EDO's, Travel/Tourism & Convention & Visitor Bureaus and the Real Estate Forum .

- **KEYWORDS** California, History, Native Americans, Religion
- **AUDIENCE** Californians, Educators (Primary/Secondary), History Buffs, Students (Primary/Secondary)
- **CONTACT** webmaster@terminus.com
- **FREE**

http://www.foundation.tricon.com/triicon_home/CA/missions.html

Canadian Heritage Information Network ★★★★

This is the information page for The Canadian Heritage Information Network (CHIN). The Canadian Heritage Information Network is a computer-based network that serves museums, libraries and other heritage institutions internationally. They supply access to over 20 databases, provide advice on information standards, explore and evaluate multimedia technologies, and offer specialized training in museum practices and Internet use. This page provides links to the network's brochure and newsletters, reference databases, the Conservation Information Network, multimedia projects, museum documentation training, publications, and CHIN's Guide to Canadian Museums. The page may also be viewed in French.

- **KEYWORDS** Canada, History, Meta-Index (Multimedia), Museums
- **AUDIENCE** Canada Residents , Canadian Culture Enthusiasts
- **CONTACT** kfilipps@www.chin.doc.ca
- **FREE**

http://www.chin.doc.ca

Common Knowledge

This site provides access to information regarding the serial publication 'Common Knowledge' a journal of intellectual history and cultural studies. Common Knowledge publishes work in the arts, social sciences, cultural studies and intellectual history that redefines divisive terms and figures of the past and present. The journal features rotating columns, book reviews, reviews of articles from other journals, works in progress, poetry, fiction and verse plays, and innovations in scholarly style. Common Knowledge is published by the University of Oxford Press. A complete table of contents for each back issue is also available at this location as well as access statistics for this server.

- **KEYWORDS** Cultural Studies, Intellectual History, Journals
- **AUDIENCE** Intellectuals, Scholars, Sociologists
- **CONTACT** Robert Nelson
  nelson@utdallas.edu
- **FREE**

ftp://ftp.halcyon.com/local/Common_Knowledge/

D-Day

This page provides links and information on D-Day. The information includes World War II material collected from Government and Military archives and from Stars and Stripes newspaper, a collection from the Army and Navy News reels Archive, a collection of famous speeches from the National Archives, Army and Navy sources, a collection of maps and battle plans from the Center for Military History, and more. (This page was created by the students and faculty of Patch High School in Stuttgart, Germany.)

- **KEYWORDS** History (US), Military Archives (US), World War II
- **AUDIENCE** History Buffs, Students (Secondary/College)

History　　425

CONTACT　WWW@patch-ahs.dsi.net
　　　　bdyer@patch-ahs.dsi.net
FREE

http://192.253.114.31/D-Day/
Table_of_contents.html

Dr. Richard Sutherland's German Archives

Dr. Richard Sutherland's German Archives site is accessible via ftp and has 22 file categories with multiple subcategories available for downloading through the United States Air Force Academy Anonymous ftp server. All downloads and uploads are logged.

KEYWORDS　Archives, Germany, Internet Resources
AUDIENCE　German Studies Students, Historians
FREE

ftp://ftp.usafa.af.mil/

Empires Beyond the Great Wall — The Heritage of Genghis Khan

Gold saddle ornaments, delicate porcelain wares, intricate bronze statues and priceless funeral paintings have recently been discovered on China's last archaeological frontier. Now, for the first time in the West, Empires Beyond the Great Wall - The Heritage of Genghis Khan brings these treasures and ancient artifacts from the steps of Inner Mongolia to the Royal British Columbia Museum, March 31 to September 10, 1995. This site contains images of many artifacts from the exhibition along with historical notes explaining both the artifacts and Genghis Kahn's role in history by exhibition curator Dr. Adam Kessler. The site also contains information on how to obtain tickets for the exhibition.

KEYWORDS　History, Mongolia
AUDIENCE　Arts Community, Educators, Historians, Students
FREE

http://vvv.com/khan/

Events and People In Black History

This page provides information and links to events and people in Black history. You can search through the Black History site for historical events that happened on a particular day in a particular month. There are also references to such items as 'I Have A Dream' by Martin Luther King, Jr. and a list of black inventors.

KEYWORDS　African Amercians, American History, Cultural Studies, Ethnic Studies
AUDIENCE　African Americans, African Descendants, Historians, Students
CONTACT　Charles Isbell
　　　　isbell@ai.mit.edu
FREE

http://www.ai.mit.edu/~isbell/HFh/black/
bhcal-toc.html

Connections to Black/African Resources

Black/African people around the globe

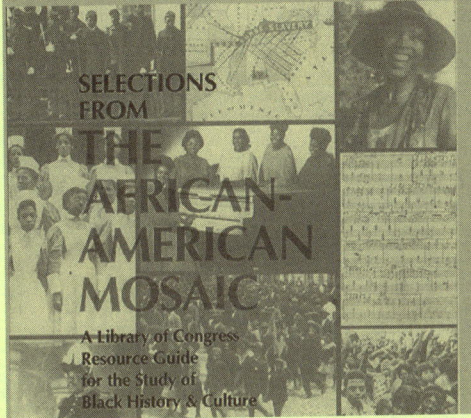

There are a growing number of Internet sites which provide a virtual storehouse of information on Black/African people around the world. One of these is the "K-12 Africa Guide," which provides an exhaustive electronic reference for the wide range of Black/African resources available on the Internet.

The "K-12 Africa Guide" will bring you up to speed on the civil rights movement in the U.S. and the history of the anti-Apartheid movement in South Africa, while furnishing country-specific information about Black/African people in government, business, education, the arts, entertainment, and more.

(http://www.sas.upenn.edu/African_Studies/Home_Page/AFR_GIDE.html)

"K-12 African Studies" provides information on a variety of leaders, past and present (from Marcus Garvey to George Washington Carver to Desmond Tutu), as well as on noted poets, writers, and actors of African descent. It also furnishes health information and information on governments worldwide. Additionally, you can learn about the complexity of the racism issue throughout the world, study the history of African dance, and endless other topics.

(http://www.sas.upenn.edu/African_Studies/K-12/menu_K-12.html)

Other resources provide folklore, traditional stories, and inspirational quotes by Black/African people. Through the "IGC's African American Resources," you'll access an array of information pertaining to legislation, technology, and education issues of specific concern to African Americans. This site includes a special focus on African American women and women's issues.

(http://www.igc.apc.org/igc/www.africanam.html)

The Flour Wars, A Humorous Aztec Story

The Flour Wars, A Humorous Aztec Story provides a historical account from the ancient Aztec Empire 'about a long simmering feud and near apocalyptic war in ancient Mexico.' Throughout this humorous story there are links to the glossary. The story chapters include The Great Feast, Plans of War, Quetzadilla — The Mystical Advisor, Shower of Tortillas Ends Feud, and The Moral of the Story.

KEYWORDS　Aztec History
AUDIENCE　History Buffs, Humor Enthusiasts, Internet Users, Latin Americans
CONTACT　pocho24@aol.com
FREE

http://saint.media.mit.edu:8001/~cast/
fwars1.html

Fortress of Louisbourg

Visit the 18th century French fortress of Louisbourg in Nova Scotia, Canada. From the home page here, or the main menu of the CD which you can order from this page, you can click on buttons to learn more about the key battles, life styles of the people at that time and the reconstruction of the fortress. The CD-ROM itself is about two hours long, and contains 500 photographs, about 40 minutes of video, animation of the two great battles, a 3D mode of the Fortress Town as it was in 1745, narration, music and 400 pages of printable text. The Fortress of Louisbourg Web Page and the CD are being presented in conjunction with the 250th Anniversary of the First Seige of the Fortress by the English in 1745.

KEYWORDS CD-ROMs, Fortresses, Historic Battles, Nova Scotia
AUDIENCE Canadians, Educators (Primary/Secondary), History Buffs, Students (Primary/Secondary)
CONTACT   owenfitz@fox.nstn.ns.ca
FREE

http://eagle.uccb.ns.ca/~jhussey/owenfitz/home.html

German History Gopher Menu ★★★

This German History gopher site provides access to a wide variety of files including such articles as 'Some remarks on the history of the DDR,' 'Hitler's Insanity,' 'Recreation in the Third Reich,' and more.

KEYWORDS Germany, Gophers, Internet Resources
AUDIENCE Germans, Historians
FREE

gopher://gopher.urz.uni-heidelberg.de/11/subject/hd/fak7/h ist/o1/logs/gc/de/e5

HNSource The Central Information Server For Historians ★★★

This is the page for the University of Kansas Historians' Information Server. Here you will find a wealth of history related resources including — Heritage, The Center for Kansas Genealogy and Family and Local History; libraries, including Carrie — the full text electronic library; research sources and resources; books and articles; bibliographies; guides and discussion list archives; links to other Humanities sites on the web; and more.

KEYWORDS Genealogy, History (US), Kansas, Research
AUDIENCE Educators, Historians, Humanists, Students (University)
FREE

http://kuhttp.cc.ukans.edu/history/hnsource_main.html

Historical Documents Gopher Menu ★★★★

This page is a gopher menu of a dozen of the greatest documents and speeches in the English language. This includes the Declaration of Independence, the Emancipation Proclamation, the Magna Carta, Martin Luther King's 'I Have a Dream' speech, Nelson Mandela's Inauguration Speech, The United States Constitution, and more.

KEYWORDS Historical Documents, History (US)
AUDIENCE Historians, Politicians, Speechwriters, Students (Secondary/College)
FREE

gopher://vax.queens.lib.ny.us/11[gopher._ss._histdocs]

I*EARN Holocaust/Genocide Project (HGP). ★★★

This page is devoted to information about I*EARN Holocaust/Genocide Project (HGP). The HGP is currently offering much data and up-to-date information about the Holocaust, genocide, and several related topics. HGP encourages teachers and students to research in order to better understand the historical events, political processes and human action in regard to the Holocaust. Genocidal occurrences in history, and current events of bias and hate are also highlighted in this resource. You will be able to read exclusive interviews with Holocaust survivors and the rescuers who struggled in World War II. You will also find out how to join the annual Poland/Israel Study Mission, how to contribute to a student magazine, An End To Intolerance, and you will receive updates on current events. The project allows teachers of various subjects to introduce their students to the Holocaust and to genocide from their preferred approach.

KEYWORDS Genocide, Holocaust, Israel
AUDIENCE Germans, History Buffs, Holocaust Survivors, Jews, War Veterans
CONTACT   coldspring@igc.apc.org
FREE

http://www.peg.apc.org/~iearn/hgpproject.html

gopher://gopher.igc.apc.org:7009/1

Johns Hopkins University Archives Gopher Server ★★★

This is a source of information on the collections of the Johns Hopkins University Library's Department of Special Collections and Archives. It contains information about Special Collections, Archival Inventories, Manuscript Registers, and pointers to other gopher sites about archives and manuscript repositories.

KEYWORDS Archives, Libraries, Universities
AUDIENCE Educators (University), Historians, Librarians, Students (University)
CONTACT   Brian Harrington, Library Network Guy brian@musicbox.mse.jhu.edu
FREE

gopher://musicbox.mse.jhu.edu:70/

Kingdom of the Sun God - A History of the Andes and Their People ★★★★

This is the complete story of the Chilean Andes from an eminent writer of geographic history, including a '...detailed account of the...cultural heritage from prehistoric times to the modern era,' according to the reviewer at this gopher site. Purchase and ISBN information are available here.

KEYWORDS Literature, Mythology, South America
AUDIENCE Chileans, Fiction Enthusiasts, Literary Scholars, Mythology Enthusiasts
FREE

gopher://ns1.infor.com:4600/1exec%3AR3657099-3658305-/.te:

Letters from an Iowa Soldier in the Civil War ★★★

These letters are part of a collection written by a 21-year-old soldier, Newton Robert Scott, Private, Company A, of the 36th Infantry, Iowa Volunteers. Scott's letters, written between 1862 and 1865, are filled with rich details of the war and the living conditions in the Union camps in Mississippi, Missouri, Iowa and Arkansas. He tells of the terrible diseases that took a heavier toll than Confederate bullets, and the soldiers' frustration and impatience with the politicians in Washington.

KEYWORDS American Studies, Civil War, Education, History (US)
AUDIENCE Historians, History Buffs, Students (Secondary/College)
FREE

http://www.ucsc.edu/civil-war-letters/home.html

Mark Twain on the Philippines ★★★

This URL is a hypertext resource about American author Mark Twain and his opposition to the Philippine-American War of 1899-1902. As the vice president of the Anti-Imperialist League for the last ten years of his life, Twain wrote numerous critiques of the war, addressed to both political leaders and American citizens. This page contains the text of these articles and essays, as well as political cartoons regarding Twain and the Imperialists. Users can view these texts online (pages are formatted for Netscape) or download the passages amd pictures in generic formats. Other links are available for browsing on general topics of Mark Twain, other writings, the Anti-Imperialist League, and on the Philippines.

KEYWORDS Authors, Literature, Philippines
AUDIENCE Activists, Literary Scholars, Mark Twain Enthusiasts, Political Scientists
FREE

http://web.syr.edu/~fjzwick/twain_ph.html

Pulitzer Prize-History ★★★

This is a non-hyperlinked list of book winners of the Pulitzer Prize for History awarded by the Graduate School of Journalism at Columbia University. The awards are arranged chronologically by year from 1917 to the present year. Some of the winners include A Midwife's Tale - The Life of Martha Ballard, Based on Her Diary, 1785-1812, by Laurel Thatcher Ulrich , Battle Cry Freedom - The Civil War Era, by James M McPherson, and The Transformation of Virginia, 1740-1790, by Rhys L. Isaac .

KEYWORDS Books, History, Literary Awards, Literature
AUDIENCE Fiction Enthusiasts, History Buffs, Librarians, Reading Enthusiasts
CONTACT   Derrik Walker dwalker@books.com
FREE

http://www.books.com/awards/pulhist.htm

The Spectacular State - Fascism and the Modern Imagination ★★★

This site contains extensive program information and historical context for 'The Spectacular State,' a 1994 conference on Fascism and modernity held at Simon Fraser University. In addition to essays on the theoretical and political aims of the conference, there are descriptions and notes on lectures, films and videos, art exhibitions, and people participating in the conference. The site offers an annotated list of links to many topics touched on by the conference.

KEYWORDS Conferences, Europe, Holocaust
AUDIENCE Activists, Cultural Critics, Historians, Political Theorists
CONTACT Weston Triemstra
triemstr@sfu.ca
FREE

http://hoshi.cic.sfu.ca/~spec-state/

The United States Holocaust Memorial Museum ★★★

The United States Holocaust Memorial Museum Web site provides background history of the establishment and activities of the museum, as well as descriptions of their programs and visitor information. Also available are educational materials about the Holocaust, including a brief history of World War II, an article about children in the Holocaust, and a videography of resources. This site also gives an overview of the programs, publications, and archives of the United States Holocaust Research Institute.

KEYWORDS History, Holocaust, Judaism, Museums
AUDIENCE Holocaust Researchers, Israelis, Jews, Students
CONTACT Arnold Kramer
akramer@ushmm.org
FREE

http://www.ushmm.org/

University of Pennsylvania History Department Gopher ★★★★

This is a gopher server of the University of Pennsylvania History Department. It gives information on the Department, its staff, office hours, undergraduate and graduate programs, course descriptions, fellowships and more. It has links to other history gophers.

KEYWORDS Education, Historical Documents, History, Universities
AUDIENCE History Educators, History Students, Students (University)
FREE

gopher://hiker.sas.upenn.edu:72/

Worlds of Late Antiquity ★★★

Worlds of Late Antiquity is a home page for educational materials relating to the culture of the Mediterranean world in late antiquity (roughly 200-700 C.E.), including syllabi, bibliographies, original-language texts, paintings, and student discussions. Material is organized under headings such as Augustine, Boethius, the Christian Bible, Cassiodorus, Erasmus, Gregory the Great, and Palaeography.

KEYWORDS Christianity, Classical Studies, Distance Education, Mediterranean Culture
AUDIENCE General Public, Humanists, Religious Studies Scholars, Researchers, Students
CONTACT James J. O'Donnell
jod@ccat.sas.upenn.edu
FREE

http://ccat.sas.upenn.edu/jod/wola.html

Languages

See also
Humanities & Social Sciences · Linguistics
Humanities & Social Sciences · Literature

ARTFL Project, University of Chicago ★★★

The main goal of the American and French Research on the Treasury of the French Language (ARTFL) is to create a database of French language texts for researchers. Their Web site provides information about the project, several online publications and articles relating to their work, and ARTFL newsletters. Users may also search the bibliography section of the ARTFL database, or if from a subscribing university, the entire text database and the Provencal poetry database. Other available databases are a French bible, a french dictionary, and a morphological analysis. Information about ARTFL imaging projects is also included.

KEYWORDS French, French Literature
AUDIENCE French, French Studies Students, Language Researchers
CONTACT Mark Olsen
mark@gide.uchicago.edu
FREE

http://web.cnam.fr/fr/

Catalan Language Introductory Page ★★

Catalan is a Romance Language which has aspects in common with the Iberian romance languages and the Gaule romance languages. Catalan is used mainly in Spain, but also in Andorra, France and Italy (on Sardinia). This page offers the reader background information about the language, as well as maps of the areas within its linguistic domain. All information is given in English, with an option to view the pages in Catalan.

KEYWORDS Catalan, Languages, Linguistics, Spanish
AUDIENCE Catalan Speakers, Language Students, Linguists, Spanish
CONTACT Tyler Jones
TJones@willamette.edu
FREE

http://www.willamette.edu/~tjones/languages/Catalan/webcat1.html

Concilium Romarici Montis (The Council of Remiremont) ★★

This site provides the Latin reader with the text of the 12th century Latin poem called Concilium Romarici Montis (The Council of Remiremont). This is a story about nuns who are just a little bit naughty and settle down with each other to talk about what sort of men they like - the knight or the clerk as lovers. The poem is written as a hypertext document, so the reader can click on a particular unfamiliar word to see a comment or explanation. Explanations were written by a team of scholars at Bryn Mawr College, and assumes the reader's knowledge of the basics of morphology, vocabulary, and grammar, and offer additional assistance and annotations that will help the beginning reader.

KEYWORDS Latin, Linguistics, Poetry
AUDIENCE Classics Students, Language Students, Latin Scholars, Latin Students, Linguists
CONTACT J.J. O'Donnell
jod@ccat.sas.upenn.edu
FREE

http://ccat.sas.upenn.edu/jod/remiremont.html

Finno-Ugric Languages and Cultures Home Page ★★

This site presents information related to Finno-Ugric Languages (Hungarian, Finnish, Estonian, the threatened minority languages of Russia, and related topics such as Palaeosiberian, Uralic affinities, and more). Viewers will find specific resources for Hungarian, Finnish, Estonian, and other smaller languages from the region. Other links on this site include lists of Uralic Languages with demographics, information and archives for a Finno-Ugric mailing list, as well as upcoming conference announcements.

KEYWORDS Languages, Linguistics, Slavic Languages
AUDIENCE Language Specialists, Linguists, Slavic Linguists
FREE

http://amacrine.berkeley.edu/finnugr/home.html

The French Page ★★★★

This site offers 'Les Capetiens - Les Croisades,' a sound, image, and text presentation based on Hugues Capet, covering French civilization and religious history from 987, as well as a link to downloadable files including a French Reader and games in French.

KEYWORDS France, History
AUDIENCE Distance Educators, Francophiles, French Language Educators, French Language Students
FREE

http://philae.sas.upenn.edu/French/french.html

German Studies Trails on the Internet ★★★

This site lists useful German Studies resources. It contains links to German language literature, film, and music resources. It also provides access to popular German magazines, libraries, university archives, and other points of interest.

KEYWORDS German, Language Instruction, Languages
AUDIENCE Germans, Language Educators, Language Students, Researchers

CONTACT Andreas Lixl-Purcell
         lixlpurc@fagan.uncg.edu
FREE

http://www.uncg.edu:80/~lixlpurc/german.html

Hellenistic Greek Linguistics ★★★

This site contains information related to Hellenistic Greek linguistics. Some of the areas for viewers to explore are the reference grammar project, the Greek-grammar mailing list (including archives), archives of papers, software and Greek fonts, bibliographies, and the Center for the Computer Analysis of Texts' tagged Greek New Testament.

KEYWORDS Grammar, Greek Culture, Languages, Linguistics
AUDIENCE Greek Scholars, Greeks, Language Students, Linguists
CONTACT   Toivo Pedaste
          toivo@ucs.uwa.edu.au
FREE

http://styx.uwa.edu.au/HGrk/

Hindi Program at University of Pennsylvania ★★★

The Hindi Program at University of Pennsylvania contains a collection of audio files for learning Hindi, several Quicktime Movies (nearly 8 MB in length), and a number of images from Northern India. There is a description of the Hindi Program as well as of the University of Pennsylvania.

KEYWORDS Hindi, Language Instruction, Languages, Universities
AUDIENCE Hindi Scholars, Hindis, Language Specialists, Linguists
CONTACT   Michael Nenashev, System Administrator
          michael@ccat.sas.upenn.edu
FREE

http://philae.sas.upenn.edu/Hindi/

Italian Language and Literature ★★★★

This page is a large initial source for research material on Italian language and literature. There are brief descriptive paragraphs arranged by linguistic/literary categories and by significant authors. The time period covered runs from the origins of Italian literature to contemporary authors. The links to Italian language and literature resources include Dartmouth Department of Italian Language and Literature, Dante Project, Il Circolo Italiano Information, and Language Resource Center Holdings (Cassettes, Videos, Books) resources, plus outside resources including general Italian language, online dictionaries, Italian usenet newsgroups, news services, magazines, Moo's, electronic texts and language software.

KEYWORDS Italian Language, Italian Literature, Linguistics
AUDIENCE Educators (University), Reading Enthusiasts, Students (University)

CONTACT Riccardo.Scateni@crs4.it
FREE

http://www.crs4.it/~riccardo/Letteratura/Misc/Storia /html

Lojban - A Realization Of Loglan ★★★

Lojban is an artificial language, the major accomplishment of Dr. James Cooke Brown's 35-year research project into the nature of human language. As others became involved in the research, a variety of other goals arose in linguistics research, computers and artificial intelligence, intercultural communication, and education. This site contains a number of background and introductory materials for learners of this language, (grammar, phonetics, roots, metaphors, etc.), contact information for Lojban clubs and the officials listserv, as well as links to other resources.

KEYWORDS Human Languages, Linguistics
AUDIENCE Language Students, Linguists, Loglan Speakers, Lojban Speakers
FREE

http://xiron.pc.helsinki.fi/lojban/

Rasta/Patois Dictionary ★

This page is a Rasta/Patois Dictionary. Although short, (about five pages) a number of sayings, idioms, and terms are translated into ordinary English. Sources for this page come from Reggae International, KSBR 88.5 FM in Laguna Beach, CA, the rec.music.reggae newsgroup, and from the reggae archives maintainer.

KEYWORDS Dictionaries, Jamaica
AUDIENCE Jamaicans, Language Students, Linguists, Rastafarians, Reggae Enthusiasts
FREE

http://www.willamette.edu/~tjones/languages/rasta-lang.html

Soc.culture.thai.language Frequently Asked Questions ★★★

This part of the soc.culture.thai FAQ describes information on language and linguistics. Some specific areas that are covered by the FAQ include the de facto Thai transcription scheme for soc.culture.thai; Learning Thai abroad; Learning Thai in Thailand; Poetry; and the word 'farang.'

KEYWORDS Languages, Linguistics, Thai Language
AUDIENCE Language Scholars, Linguists, Thai Culture Enthusiasts, Thailand Residents, Thais
FREE

http://www.nectec.or.th/soc.culture.thai/language.html

gopher://gopher.nectec.or.th:70/11/sct-faq/language

ftp://ftp.nectec.or.th/soc.culture.thai/language

Språkbanken - Language Bank of Swedish ★★

The purpose of the Language Bank is to collect and make available machine-readable linguistic data in systematic form. The online information on this site includes descriptions of what kinds of data are available from the Language Bank. There are Modern and Historical Swedish texts, as well as several kinds of Lexical Data.

KEYWORDS Languages, Linguistics
AUDIENCE Language Specialists, Linguists, Swedes
CONTACT   Martin Gellerstam
          gellerstam@svenska.gu.se
FREE

http://logos.svenska.gu.se/lbeng.html

gopher://logos.svenska.gu.se/11/The Language Bank

Texts in the Latin Language ★

This site has two archives of Latin texts and commentaries. The first is from Malin and contains collections such as The Statutes of the Commune of Bugelle (Biella), Ausonius' Mosella, and the text from the Verdun Altar in Klosterneuburg. Another directory is from the Project Libellus and is devoted to archiving texts and translations from the late 19th and early 20th century compilers, featuring works such as Apuleius-Cupid et Psyche, Caesar- De Bello Gallico, Book I, Livy-Ab Urbe Condita, and a number of other texts. Some of these texts are in a raw and unformatted format.

KEYWORDS Latin, Linguistics
AUDIENCE Classics Students, Language Students, Latin Scholars, Latin Students, Linguists
CONTACT   Wiretap Online Library
          gopher@wiretap.spies.com
FREE

gopher://wiretap.spies.com/11/Library/Classic/Latin

University of Michigan Linguistics Archive ★★★

This site contains a collection of public domain, freeware, shareware, and other files that may be useful to linguists. The directories available to the user includes fonts, software programs, texts, and listservs. Programs are available for the Macintosh, DOS, and Windows platforms. Texts includes papers, bibliographical information, and linguistics course syllabi. The listservs directory contains short descriptions and subscription information for a variety of listservs related to general linguistics, specific theories and particular languages.

KEYWORDS Educational Software, Languages, Linguistics, Universities
AUDIENCE Language Scholars, Linguists
CONTACT   linguistics-archivist@archive.umich.edu
FREE

gopher://gopher.archive.merit.edu:7055/11/linguistics/

Y'a du français sur ce %$#&* de Web! ★★★

This site is a comprehensive launching point for any French-language Web sites. Currently there are a total of 110 links in this Canadian-based site. This is an extremely worthwhile site, particularly to linguists, and students of French. The page is in French.

KEYWORDS Canada, France, French, Languages
AUDIENCE French Speakers, Language Educators, Students
CONTACT Jean-Hugues Roy
hugo@eureka.qc.ca
FREE

http://www.lanternette.com/hugo/francais.html

Yamada Language Guides ★★★★

The Yamada Language Guides is a resource to language information on the Internet. Users may browse an alphabetical, geographical, or language family list of languages. Each listing contains links to resources on the Internet directly related to that language as well as downloadable font software. Or, users may browse the entire font archive of language fonts for non-English Web browsing, with descriptions and examples. Links to multi-language and interactive Internet language learning web sites are also grouped together.

KEYWORDS Educational Software, Fonts, Languages
AUDIENCE Language Researchers, Language Specialists, Language Students
CONTACT ylc@oregon.uoregon.edu
FREE

http://babel.uoregon.edu/yamada/guides.html

Library & Information Studies

See also
Education · *Academic Libraries*
Education · *Government Libraries*
Education · *Libraries*
Education · *Public Libraries*
Education · *Special Libraries*
Science · *Organizations*

Bibsys ★★★★

Bibsys is a shared library system of Norwegian libraries. Users can search the database by keyword to access a database of over 1.6 million bibliographies. This database can be interfaced via the web, gopher, email, or telnet.

KEYWORDS Bibliographies, Libraries, Norway
AUDIENCE Educators, Library Users, Norwegians, Students
CONTACT info@bibsys.no
FREE

http://www.bibsys.no/english.html

gopher://gopher.bibsys.no:70/1

Britannica Online ★★★★

Britannica Online is the online hypertext version of the Encyclopaedia Britannica. The database allows searches by keyword, presenting the user with a set of active links. Users may demo the service, though there is a subscription fee for full use.

KEYWORDS Encyclopedias, Information Retrieval, Reference
AUDIENCE Educators, Librarians, Researchers, Students
CONTACT support@eb.com
COST

http://www.eb.com/

Center for Information Technology Experimental Gopher Service ★★★

This gopher server provides information on current technological trends including recent journal articles and technical reports. It also includes links to other gophers including the main University of Michigan gopher.

KEYWORDS Information Technology, Technical Reports
AUDIENCE Computer Scientists, Information Scientists, Students (University), Systems Operators
CONTACT info@citi.umich.edu
FREE

gopher://metro.citi.umich.edu/

Cultural Studies and Critical Theory ★★★★

This page provides links to some of the works which may help to introduce the issues and concerns raised by cultural studies and critical theory. This list draws from the fields of literary criticism, sociology, gender studies, cultural anthropology, feminism, history and psychoanalysis in order to discuss contemporary texts and cultural practices. Some of the works included on this page are Adams-Poor Relief, Dolan - Crisis in the Gulf, Foucault, Jameson, Sartre, Girls, Girls, Girls, Nymphomania, Significance of Visual Form, Violence and Sacred Notes, and more.

KEYWORDS Critical Theory, Cultural Studies, Feminism, Libraries, Literary Criticism
AUDIENCE Academics, Critics, Educators (University), Students (Secondary/University)
FREE

http://english.hss.cmu.edu/Theory.html

Cyberville Library ★★★

This web page is a compendium of links to online libraries throughout the world, with an emphasis on Asia. There are reference works such as Roget's Thesaurus available, gopher and web links to book and music libraries, and a good list of library-related projects on the net.

KEYWORDS Books, Cultural Studies, Libraries, Library Science
AUDIENCE Academics, Asian Studies Educators, Librarians, Students
CONTACT kianjin@ncb.gov.sg
FREE

http://www.ncb.gov.sg/cyber/library.html

Connections to Madagascar

What's happening on the Rainbow Island?

Madagascar is undeniably one of the world's most beautiful and exotic locations. Now you can travel to the "Rainbow Island" via the Internet and learn about the culture, ethnology, music, and history of this diverse, tropical land.

Through the "Ethnology of Madagascar" sites you will find that Madagascar's people comprise a mixture of Indonesian and African ethnicities, and that 19 tribes make up the 11 million inhabitants of this east African island. You say you like sisal carpets? That's one of Madagascar's major exports, in addition to vanilla, clove, pepper, coffee and tobacco.

From the main Madagascar site on the Internet, you can link to maps, as well as a practical guide to the sites and towns on the island, including yearly festivals and weekly markets.

(http://lalo.inria.fr/~andry/Ethnies.html)

also, (http://lalo.inria.fr/~andry/Tana.html)

ESRC Data Archive ★★★★

The ESRC Data Archive at the University of Essex in the United Kingdom houses the largest collection of accessible computer-readable data in the social sciences and humanities in the UK. It is a national resource center that has approximately 4,500 datasets of interest to researchers in all sectors and from many different disciplines. Specific to researchers of English literature, within the page you can telnet to BIRON, the Archive's Online Catalogue and Subject Index. Also available are the ESRC Data Archive Bulletin, WAIS search of the archive's catalogue, ordering data from the archive and more. This is a very large resource for

English literature and the humanities and social science in general.

KEYWORDS Libraries, Literary Studies, Literature, Research
AUDIENCE Educators (University), English Literature Enthusiasts, Literary Scholars, Reading Enthusiasts, Students (University)
CONTACT hann2@essex.ac.uk
FREE

http://dawww.essex.ac.uk

Graduate School of Library and Information Studies at McGill University ★★★★

This is the information page for the Graduate School of Library and Information Studies at McGill University in Montreal, Quebec, Canada. This page contains links to information on the goals and objectives, history, admission requirements, facilities, and research facilities of the school. It also offers links to information on the school's faculty, instructional programs, and courses.

KEYWORDS Information Science, Library Science, Universities
AUDIENCE Canada Residents, Librarians, Students (University)
CONTACT su@gslis.lan.mcgill.ca
FREE

http://www.gslis.mcgill.ca/homepage.html

Informatique pour les Sciences Sociales ★★★

This server provides information about the Faculty of Social Sciences (Section des Sciences Sociales) at the University of Geneva, Switzerland. The information includes research activities within the faculty, announcements, descriptions of computer resources available through the faculty such as the Exploratory Data Analysis (EDA) software package and the ECPR Standing Group of Computer Users, and links to data archives, databases, and other social science resources on the Internet.

KEYWORDS Database Management, Social Sciences, Switzerland, Universities
AUDIENCE Researchers, Social Scientists, Sociologists
CONTACT Eugene Horber
        Horber@uni2a.unige.ch
FREE

gopher://sposun2.unige.ch/

Inter-University Consortium for Political and Social Research (ICPSR) ★★★

The Inter-University Consortium for Political and Social Research (ICPSR) serves social scientists by providing a central repository and dissemination service for machine-readable social science data, training facilities in basic and advanced techniques of quantitative social analysis, and resources that facilitate the use of advanced computer technology by social scientists.

KEYWORDS International Research, Politics, Scientific Research, Social Sciences
AUDIENCE Academics, Researchers, Social Scientists, Students
CONTACT Peter Joftis
        icpsr_netmail@um.cc.umich.edu
FREE

gopher://gopher.icpsr.umich.edu/

Internet Connections - A Librarian's Guide to Dial-up Access and Use ★★★

This directory contains the chapters to the book, Internet Connections—A Librarian's Guide to Dial-up Access and Use. The book is designed for librarians and library patrons that are not currently online or who have just become online. The book details the major Internet tools, including email, Gopher, FTP and WWW. There are portions of the book that are appropriate for all users, however, the focus of the work is on how the Internet can benefit libraries and librarians.

KEYWORDS Internet Guides, Libraries
AUDIENCE Librarians, Library Administrators, Library Users
FREE

ftp://dla.ucop.edu/pub/internet/connections/

Le Serveur Gopher de l'Universite de Geneve ★★★

Le Serveur Gopher de l'Universite de Geneve server provides access to library resources at the University of Geneva, Switzerland, as well as other gopher and information servers in Switzerland.

KEYWORDS Education, Libraries, Switzerland, Universities
AUDIENCE Library Users, Professors, Students (University), Switzerland Residents
CONTACT naef@divsun.unige.ch
FREE

gopher://gopher.unige.ch/

RLG's (Research Libraries Group, Inc.) Home Page ★★★

The Research Libraries Group, Inc. is a non-profit collective organization comprised of universities, museums, libraries, and others devoted to improving access to information. They offer document indexing and retrieval systems, as well as research information. There is also a searchable bibliographic database and a Z39.50 document retrieval system.

KEYWORDS Library Science, Research
AUDIENCE Information Specialists, Librarians, Researchers
CONTACT bl.btw@rlg.stanford.edu
FREE

http://www-rlg.stanford.edu

The Royal Library ★★★

This is a gopher server for the Royal Library of Denmark. It contains an overview of the Library and its resources and services. It also offers email addresses, news, announcements, and more.

KEYWORDS Denmark, Libraries, Library Science
AUDIENCE Internet Users, Librarians, Library Administrators, Library Users
CONTACT Mikael Hansen
        meh@admin.kb.bib.dk
FREE

gopher://gopher.kb.bib.dk/

School of Information and Library Science at the University of North Carolina Chapel Hill ★★★★

This is a gopher server of the School of Information and Library Science at the University of North Carolina Chapel Hill. It provides information about the School and its academic programs, courses and schedules, calendars, faculty, Internet electronic journals and books, and more. In addition, it makes connections to other gophers on campus.

KEYWORDS Education (College/University), Information Science, Library Science
AUDIENCE Educators (University), Librarians, Students (University)
CONTACT Scott Barker
        barker@ils.unc.edu
FREE

gopher://ils.unc.edu/

Social Science Information Gateway (SOSIG) ★★★

The Social Science Information Gateway (SOSIG) is an index to a wealth of resources on the World Wide Web in the Social Sciences. It is extremely clear, and is consisely organized for easy access to any of the social sciences from Education and Feminism to Sociology and Statistics. It has a search feature and the latest news including job vacancies.

KEYWORDS Social Sciences, Sociology
AUDIENCE Anthropologists, Feminists, Geographers, Psychologists, Social Scientists, Sociologists
CONTACT sosig-info@bris.ac.uk
FREE

http://sosig.esrc.bris.ac.uk/

UK Office for Library and Information Networking ★★★

The UK Office for Library and Information Networking (UKOLN) conducts research in the area of libraries and information networking. Their Web server offers information on the research conducted at the Office, as well as providing links to some of the resources they have found useful in this research. They also offer material such as lecture transcripts and other publications related to their mission.

KEYWORDS Information Science, Networking

AUDIENCE	Information Scientists, Library Scientists, Network Administrators
CONTACT	Chris Brown c.p.brown@bath.ac.uk
FREE	

http://ukoln.bath.ac.uk/ukoln/home.html

The University of Virginia Library Science ★★★

This University of Virginia gopher server gives information about the Library Science Department. It offers a calendar of library staff events, library short courses, policies, guidelines, reports, organizations, library departments, training documents, and more. In addition, it provides access to other library gophers on the Internet.

KEYWORDS	Community Services, Education (College/University), Libraries, Library Science
AUDIENCE	Educators (University), Librarians, Students (University)
CONTACT	gwis@virginia.edu
FREE	

gopher://orion.lib.virginia.edu:2001/

World Systems Archive ★★★

The World-Systems Archive is located at the Communications for the Sustainable Future (CSF) at the University of Colorado at Boulder and is maintained in association with the World-Systems electronic network also running at the University of Colorado. The purpose of this electronic archive is to promote the free exchange of information relevant to the study and understanding of the modern world system and earlier intersocietal networks. The archive contains documents, books, data, biographical information, newsletters, bibliographies, and announcements.

KEYWORDS	Archives, Social Sciences, Sociology
AUDIENCE	Librarians, Scholars, Social Scientists, Sociologists, Students
CONTACT	Chris Chase-Dunn chriscd@jhu.edu
FREE	

http://csf.colorado.edu/wsystems/wsarch.html

Linguistics

See also
Computing & Mathematics · *Artificial Intelligence*
Education · *Educational Issues*
Humanities & Social Sciences · *Languages*
Popular Culture & Entertainment · *General Reference*

The Anagram Server ★★★

This Web site provides an anagram generator. Simply enter any word into the form, press return, and you will receive a list of all possible variations of words with those letters. For those new to anagrams, the Anagram Server also provides general information about anagrams, and an anagram hall of fame.

KEYWORDS	Anagrams, Games, Language
AUDIENCE	Anagram Enthusiasts, General Public

Connections to the Holocaust
The Holocaust of World War II

Welcome to the homepage of
SICSA
THE VIDAL SASSOON INTERNATIONAL CENTER FOR THE STUDY OF ANTISEMITISM
THE HEBREW UNIVERSITY OF JERUSALEM
This site will always be under construction. Please send comments and suggestions to ruzit@hum.huji.ac.il

About SICSA
Research Projects
SICSA Publications
SICSA Newsletter #10: Summer-Fall 1994

The most shocking awareness to emerge from World War II concerned the Holocaust. Today, the Holocaust continues to spark controversy, with revisionists claiming it never happened. There are many sites on the World Wide Web that provide indisputable evidence that the Holocaust occurred, including SICSA - Vidal Sassoon International Center for the Study of Antisemitism.

(http://www2.huji.ac.il/www_jcd/top.html)

If you are interested in Holocaust narratives (including that of Anne Frank, on which the movie The Diary of Anne Frank was based), or want to view an archive of materials about the Nazi death camps which exhaustively documents the atrocities suffered by millions of Jews during the war, there are several excellent sites to search.

(http://www.peg.apc.org/~iearn/hgpproject.html)

Additionally, there are places to access aerial photographs of the infamous Treblinka death camp, as well as links to a network of organizations and individuals who work to provide programming, awareness, and education on the Holocaust. You can even explore the United States Holocaust Memorial Museum, which offers a wealth of information on the Holocaust.

(http://www.kaiwan.com/~greg.ihr/jhr/v15n1p25_Raven.html)

also, (http://www.ushmm.org/organizations/list.html)

CONTACT	wsmith@wordsmith.org
FREE	

http://www.wordsmith.org/awad-cgibin/anagram

The Archive of the Linguist Mailing List ★★★

This site is an archive of postings to the Linguist mailing list, which provides a forum where academic linguists can discuss issues and information in the field. The chronological archiving of the daily postings makes browsing awkward.

KEYWORDS	Linguistics, Mailing Lists, Universities
AUDIENCE	Language Educators, Language Students, Linguists
CONTACT	Graham Katz
FREE	

http://www.ling.rochester.edu/linguist/contents.html

CSLI (Center for the Study of Language and Information) at Stanford University ★★★★

CSLI was founded early in 1983 to further research and development of integrated theories of language, information, and computation. Areas on this site include upcoming events at the Center, such as seminars on the Movement of Technology from University to Industry. Also available are Research Projects, including project abstracts, reports, and bibliographic data for areas like Intelligent Machines, Human/Computer Interaction and Logic as a Theory of Information Processing. In addition, the Publications area contains a catalog of work generated by the center (dissertations, lecture notes, books, etc) as well as an online reports area (for example, Objectivism, Biological Naturalism and Searle.) Other items of interest include a listing of Industrial Affiliations, and a listing of related groups at Stanford and elsewhere on the Internet.

KEYWORDS	Computing, Language, Logic, Universities
AUDIENCE	Computer Scientists, Language Students, Linguists, Logicians

CONTACT csli@csli.stanford.edu
FREE

http://csli-www.stanford.edu/

gopher://Csli-gopher.Stanford.EDU.:70/11/CSLI

ftp://csli.stanford.edu/

Colibri Home Page ★★★

Colibri - An electronic newsletter and WWW service for people interested in the fields of language, speech, logic and/or information. The Colibri newsletter is sent out every week from the OTS. This website has access to the latest issue of the magazine, as well as an index for searching past issues. In addition, it contains pointers to other language and logic related sites around the internet.

KEYWORDS Linguistics, Natural Language, Newsletters
AUDIENCE Language Specialists, Language Students, Linguists
CONTACT colibri@let.ruu.nl
FREE

http://colibri.let.ruu.nl/

Department of Linguistics & Modern English Language, Lancaster University ★★★

This is the World Wide Web Service of the Department of Linguistics and Modern English Language at Lancaster University in the United Kingdom. In addition to department and research information, this site also provides users with current news, recreation and travel tips, and links to many WWW sites.

KEYWORDS English, Language, Linguistics, United Kingdom
AUDIENCE Educators, Educators (University), Linguistics Scholars, Students (University)
CONTACT Zack Evans
Z.Evans@lancs.ac.uk
FREE

http://www.lancs.ac.uk/

Foreign Language Chat Groups (More about MOOs) ★★★

According to this site, MOOs are Internet accessible, text-mediated virtual environments well suited for distance learning. MUDs are Multi-User Domains and MUSHs are defined here as Multi-user Shared Hallucinations. This is a very good site to access Foreign language MOOs and MUDs. There is clarification here about how to 'speak' in a MOO, MOO commands and how to logon to a MOO.

KEYWORDS Chat Groups, IRS (Internal Revenue Service), Internet Communications, Languages
AUDIENCE Foreign Language Enthusiasts, International Students
CONTACT Steve Thorne
thorne@garnet.berkeley.edu
FREE

http://www.itp.berkeley.edu/~thorne/MOO.html

Foreign Language and Culture ★★★★

The Foreign Language and Culture Web site is a guide to all kinds of foreign lands from Asia, Bulgaria and Brazil to Vietnam, the Welsh and Yugoslavia. There is general foreign stuff such as the CIA World Factbooks, and the European Home Page, as well as all the specific country links. A keyword search tool and main list make navigation easier.

KEYWORDS Dictionaries, European Culture, Foreign Languages, Language Instruction
AUDIENCE Educators, Internet Users
CONTACT Douglas Brick
dbrick@speakeasy.org
FREE

http://www.speakeasy.org/~dbrick/Hot/foreign.html

The Human Language Page ★★★★

The Human Language Page is an enormous site containing links to a spectrum of linguistic and literature selections which are broadly categorized according to language. The site can be explored for tutorials and other multilingual resources, such as language histories and dictionaries of contemporary, archaic, and dead languages. A link is provided for commercial resources, such as translation services and linguistics software, although the site is non-commercial. The home page can be read in seven languages and it provides links to information and instruction in over fifty languages.

KEYWORDS Ethnic Studies, Linguistics, Multilingual Resources, Philology
AUDIENCE Interpreters, Language Specialists, Language Students, Linguists
CONTACT Tyler Jones
tjones@willamette.edu
FREE

http://www.willamette.edu/~tjones/language-page.html

Indigenous People's Literature ★★★

The Indigenous People's Literature site is a guide to indigenous writing, language, and culture, as well as Internet resources about indigenous literature. Users will find extensive information about language and literature in different regions of the world, and materials about and by artists, leaders, and writers. Included in this site is music, poetry, art, stories, and other documents from indigenous tribal leaders. This site is also part of the NativeWeb.

KEYWORDS Cultural Studies, Indigenous People
AUDIENCE Indigenous People, Literature, Literature Students

CONTACT Glenn Welker
gwelker@mail.lmi.org
FREE

http://kuhttp.cc.ukans.edu/~marc/natlit/natlit.html

Language Bank of Sweden - Sprakbanken ★★

The Language Bank of Sweden at Goteborg University was created to systematize machine-readable linguistic data. Besides providing information about their projects and their staff, their home page allows users to access their archives and look at word searches for historical and modern Swedish texts, as well as finding out about frequency-based word lexical data and word lists for spelling.

KEYWORDS Computational Linguistics, Language Software, Sweden
AUDIENCE Language Researchers, Linguists, Swedes
CONTACT Martin Gellerstam
gellerstam@svenska.gu.se
FREE

http://logos.svenska.gu.se

Linguistics, Language, Literature - BUBL Information Service, United Kingdom ★★★★

The Linguistics, Language, Literature gopher directory at Bath University is an extremely deep, varied and complex list of electronic text sources, including English, Scottish, German, French, Italian, Spanish and Classical literature, plus sources to libraries, various universities and some searchable databases. This is a rich readers' and academicians' research tool.

KEYWORDS General Literature, Literary Criticism
AUDIENCE Classical Literature Enthusiasts, English Literature Enthusiasts, French, Germans, Italians, Literary Critics, Literary Scholars, Scots, Spanish
FREE

gopher://ukoln.bath.ac.uk:7070/11/Link/Tree/Literature/

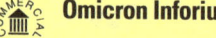 Omicron Inforium ★★★

The Omicron Inforium is a place for persons with scholarly interests to find useful information on the WWW about places, events, products and services. Special attention is given to books and links related to the Cognitive Sciences including language behavior and linguistics.

KEYWORDS Cognitive Sciences, Linguistics
AUDIENCE Educators, Scholars
CONTACT gwilcox@www.omicron.com
FREE

http://www.maine.com/inforium

Linguistics – Literature **433**

University of North Carolina, Department of German and Russian ★★★

The German Studies Page of Professor Andreas Lixl-Purcell at the University of North Carolina at Greensboro lists some of the most useful German literature and culture resources and research trails on the World Wide Web. The interdisciplinary links to Europe and the German-speaking countries are organized around academic fields such as German Language and Culture, Arts and Humanities, Economics and Business, Education and Research, International Affairs, Science and Technology, and the experimental Web site - the German Internet Project.

KEYWORDS	German Studies, Germany, Internet Directories
AUDIENCE	Educators, German Studies Students
CONTACT	Professor Andreas Lixl-Purcell lixlpurc@fagan.uncg.edu
FREE	

http://www.uncg.edu/~lixlpurc/german.html

The Word Detective ★★

The Word Detective is a bimonthly newsletter on words and language, exploring where words came from and where the English language is headed. Visitors to this home page can read a sample article and send in their questions. Free sample issues are also available. Subscription information is also available here.

KEYWORDS	Humor, Language
AUDIENCE	Educators, Linguistics Enthusiasts, Reading Enthusiasts, Writers
CONTACT	Evan Morris words1@escape.com words1@pipeline.com
FREE	

http://www.escape.com/~words1/index.html

The Yuen Ren Society for the Promotion of Chinese Dialect Fieldwork ★★

The Yuen Ren Society is devoted to the practice of descriptive dialect fieldwork and the collection and distribution of fresh Chinese dialect data in quantity. As part of this work, the Society holds periodic conferences and publishes an occasional journal and a monograph under the title, the Treasury of Chinese Dialect Data. The viewer of this page will find the table of contents and ordering information for this journal, as well as upcoming conference details. Links to other Web Pages concerned with Dialectology & Fieldwork, General Linguistics, and China & Chinese in general available here as well.

KEYWORDS	Chinese Language, Languages, Linguistics, Yuen Ren Chao
AUDIENCE	Asian Literature Enthusiasts, Chinese Linguists
CONTACT	help@cac.washington.edu
FREE	

http://weber.u.washington.edu/~yuenren/Circular.html

Literature

See also
Business & Economics · *Publishing*
Humanities & Social Sciences · *Area & Cultural Studies*
Humanities & Social Sciences · *Classics*
Popular Culture & Entertainment · *Books*

A Web of One's Own ★★

A Web of One's Own, based on Virginia Woolf's book, 'A Room of One's Own' is a Cyberwomen locale, with essays, reviews and interviews written by women, mostly in Dutch.

KEYWORDS	Belgium, Women's Studies
AUDIENCE	Activists, Feminists, Students, Women
FREE	

http://www.reference.be/womweb/

Abbey's Web ★★★★

This page is dedicated to the life and collected works of author, outdoorsman and activist Edward Abbey. Although known and criticized most for works that his detractors say promote 'ecoterrorism,' (The Monkeywrench Gang, etc.), Abbey also wrote numerous non-political tales of nature and the American southwest. Both a complete biography and a bibliography are available.

KEYWORDS	Conservation, Environmental Activism, Environmental Studies, Literature
AUDIENCE	Conservationists, Environmentalists, Fiction Enthusiasts, Political Researchers, Reading Enthusiasts
CONTACT	Christer Lindh clindh@abalon.se
FREE	

http://www.abalon.se/beach/aw/abbey.html

Alex - A Catalogue of Electronic Texts on the Internet ★★★

Alex is a catalogue of books and other works on the Internet, and includes almost 1800 entries. The Catalogue is divided into the following sections - search the catalog, browse the catalog by author, date, host, language, subject, or title, and information about cataloging Internet resources. Alex allows users to find and retrieve the full-text of documents on the Internet

KEYWORDS	Electronic Texts, Fiction, Online Books
AUDIENCE	Book Enthusiasts, Internet Users, Librarians, Students (University)
CONTACT	Eric Lease Morgan eric_morgan@ncsu.edu
FREE	

http://www.lib.ncsu.edu:80/stacks/alex-index.html

gopher://rsl.ox.ac.uk:70/11/lib-corn/hunter

Annual Bibliography of English Language and Literature OnLine ★★★★

ABELL OnLine, published by the Modern Humanities Research Association, annually lists all scholarly articles, doctoral dissertations, books and reviews concerning the English language, literature and related topics published anywhere in the world. The first volume, covering 1920, appeared in 1921; the most recent volume to be published is Volume 67 for 1992. The ABELL database currently holds more than 20,000 entries for the 1991 and 1992 volumes. This is a very large database with worldwide resources.

KEYWORDS	Bibliographies, Electronic Texts, English, English Literature
AUDIENCE	Educators (University), English Literature Enthusiasts, Literary Critics, Literary Scholars, Literary Theorists, Students (University)
CONTACT	abell@ula.cam.ac.uk
FREE	

http://www.hull.ac.uk/Hull/FR_Web/abell.html

Avalon ★★★★

The Avalon Arthurian Legend web site is a compilation of all types of King Arthur related texts and resources. Besides a basic introduction to the King Arthur legend, with a list of names, pictures of shields, the ten rules of chivalry and an FAQ, users will find numerous online book reviews and articles relating to King Arthur literature. True Arthur lovers will also find the entire Monty Python Holy Grail script and a list of other Arthur films. Numerous other Arthurian online texts and resources are also linked.

KEYWORDS	Monty Python, Mythology
AUDIENCE	Arthururian Enthusiasts, Fiction Enthusiasts, Mythology Enthusiasts
CONTACT	Chris Thornborrow ct@epcc.ed.ac.uk
FREE	

http://www.epcc.ed.ac.uk/~ct/arthur.html

Baltimore 1998 Worldcon Bid ★★

This site presents information on the upcoming 1998 56th World Science Fiction Convention. The maintainers of this site are bidding to hold the conference in Baltimore, Maryland. Users can find information on this bid, as well as information on the sponsoring group (known as the Pirates of Fenzance). This site also includes information and links to other Science Fiction conventions, as well as information on how to vote on the bid.

KEYWORDS	Fantasy Literature, Literature, Science Fiction
AUDIENCE	Fiction Enthusiasts, Science Fiction Enthusiasts
CONTACT	Dana Carson dcarson@access.digex.net, baltimore98@access.digex.net
FREE	

http://www.access.digex.net/~balt98

Banned Books Online ★★★★

This site is devoted to notable literary texts that have been subject to censorship or censorship attempts. Books include Joyce's Ulysses, Voltaire's Candide, Cleland's Fanny Hill, Aristophanes' Lysistrata, Chaucer's Canterbury Tales, Boccaccio's Decameron and many more. The whys and wherefores of censorship are discussed, and more information is available at the exhibit based at Carnegie Mellon University.

KEYWORDS Censorship, English Literature, Literary Criticism, Literature
AUDIENCE English Literature Enthusiasts, Fiction Enthusiasts, Literary Scholars
FREE

http://www.cs.cmu.edu:8001/Web/People/spok/banned-books.html

The Bartleby Project ★★★★

Project Bartleby, named for the famous short story by Herman Melville, Bartleby, The Scrivener (1853) transcribes full-text versions of selected books into online text versions. This is currently one of the largest public collections of online literature, and is maintained with strict editorial and quality control procedures. Titles include The Odysseys of Homer, Emily Dickinson's Poems, John Keats' Poetical Works, Bartlett's Familiar Quotations, Shelley's Complete Poetical Works (under development), Walt Whitman's Leaves of Grass, Oscar Wilde's Poems, and William Wordsworth's Complete Poetical Works. These are large electronic files requiring significant downloading time.

KEYWORDS Classics, English Literature, Literary Criticism, Literature
AUDIENCE Educators (University), English Literature Enthusiasts, Literary Critics, Literary Scholars, Reading Enthusiasts, Students (University)
FREE

http://www.columbia.edu

The Blue Penny Quarterly ★★★

Available only in a self-running Macintosh format, The Blue Penny Quarterly (BPQ) acts as a 'bridge between the literary and online communities,' disseminating original and previously-published award winning literature and poetry by critically acclaimed authors. Authors included in recent issues of BPQ have included Deborah Eisenberg and Guggenheim winner Robert Sward.

KEYWORDS Contemporary Literature, Fiction, Magazines, Poetry
AUDIENCE Fiction Enthusiasts, Poetry Enthusiasts, Poets, Reading Enthusiasts, Writers
CONTACT Doug Lawson
         dll5e@fermi.clas.virginia.edu
FREE

ftp://ftp.luth.se/pub/mac/misc/BPQ/

Book Stacks-Hall of Fame ★★★★

This page contains a hyperlinked list of well-known book awards, including the name and the purpose of the award. The list includes the Book Critic's Circle Awards, the Book Critic's choice for the best books of the year, the Booker Prize, The United Kingdom's Book Trusts' Prize, the Caldecott Medal, the American Library Association's award for the best in illustrated children's literature, the Nobel Prize awarded by the Nobel Foundation for literature, and the Pulitzer Prize given by the Graduate School of Journalism at Columbia University in biography, drama, history, non-fiction, and poetry.

KEYWORDS Literary Awards, Literary Criticism, Poetry
AUDIENCE Fiction Enthusiasts, Librarians, Reading Enthusiasts
CONTACT Derrik Walke
         dwalker@books.com
FREE

http://www.books.com/awards.htm

Books On-Line, New Listings ★★★★

This site contains recent additions to a larger list called Books On-Line, Listed By Title. This list has links to other book lists such as the Gutenberg Project.

KEYWORDS Books, Classics, Fiction
AUDIENCE Book Readers, General Public
CONTACT spok@cs.cmu.edu
FREE

http://www.cs.cmu.edu:8001/Web/booknew.html

Books of South Asian Literature Written in English ★★★★

This is an extensive resource of books written by South Asian authors, offered in both English translation (61 texts) and original languages. Categories include English, Translated, Other Books About South Asia (including many historical and political texts by authors like Gandhi, Nehru and others), and South Asian Feminist Literature. Most of the authors quoted here are of Indian or Singaporean origin.

KEYWORDS Literature
AUDIENCE Feminists, Fiction Enthusiasts, Indian Literature Enthusiasts, Literary Scholars
FREE

http://www.ntu.ac.sg/~mmurali/sabooks.html

Bosnian Literature ★★

This is an ftp directory containing files regarding many aspects of current events in Bosnia. Of particular interest is the file 'pjesme/', which houses a number of Bosnian poetry and story documents. All files are in Bosnian/Hertzegovinian/Yugoslavian languages. Files are compressed; MacGZip, a Windows-oriented unZip program or a UNIX unzip command will be required to open the files for viewing.

KEYWORDS Bosnia, Literary Criticism, Literature
AUDIENCE Bosnians, Fiction Enthusiasts, Historians, Literary Scholars, Literature Enthusiasts
FREE

ftp://triples.math.mcgill.ca/pub/bosnia

Bricolage ★★★★

Bricolage is an online magazine designed to provide both original documents about writing and links to Internet resources for writers. Users will find monthly feature articles on subjects such as PGP digital signatures and writers newsgroups. Resources are grouped into four categories, with both remote and local information - Bureau, with general writing links; Lounge, with market and contact information; Seminary, with information for beginning writers; and a list of Web sites that are relevant for writers. Information includes everything from George Polti's 36 Dramatic Situations to a list of definitions of figures of speech. Registered writers may also enter the Bourse forum for writing discussions.

KEYWORDS E-Zines, Journalism, Writing
AUDIENCE Authors, Journalists, Writers
CONTACT Trevor Lawrence
         t.lawrence@bbcnc.org.uk
FREE

http://bel.avonibp.co.uk/bricolage/welcome.html

British Poetry 1780-1910 ★★★

The British Poetry 1780-1910 web site contains archived Romantic and Victorian era texts by numerous British poets. Texts include works by Lewis Carroll, Samuel Coleridge, Alfred Lord Tennyson, and Mary Robinson. Some texts include illustrations from the original texts, and/or annotations.

KEYWORDS British Literature, Electronic Texts, Poetry, Romantic Poets
AUDIENCE Literature Enthuisiasts, Poetry Enthusiasts
CONTACT Jerome McGann
         jjm2f@lizzie.engl.virginia.edu
FREE

http://www.lib.virginia.edu/etext/britpo/britpo.html

C.S. Lewis Home Page ★★★★

Devoted to the scholar and spiritual writer C.S. Lewis, this page presents a biography, desriptions of 20 of his best works, a birthday tribute, quotes, and some downloadable stories. This is a resource for those interested in the influence of Anglican, Baptist, Lutheran, Methodist, Pentecostal, Presbyterian, and Roman Catholic religious beliefs in literature and society.

KEYWORDS Christianity, English Literature, Religious Literature
AUDIENCE English Literature Enthusiasts, Literary Scholars, Religious Studies Educators, Religious Studies Students
FREE

http://paul.spu.edu/~loren/lewis/

Censorship of Literature ★★★★

This page contains an extensive list of links to works of literature that have been censured or banned at some point, as well as some related information. Some of the links include Lady Chatterly's Lover, D.H. Lawrence, The Bible, The Koran, Machiavelli's 'Discorsi' and 'Il Principe', Holt, Rinehart and Winston Health Textbook, the works of Jean-Jacques Rousseau, Hawthorne's 'The Scarlet Letter, a Romance', the French Banned Books List of 1961, Hemingway's Novels, and more.

KEYWORDS Books, Censorship, Literature
AUDIENCE Civil Rights Activists, Fiction Enthusiasts, Historians, Reading Enthusiasts, Writers

Literature   **435**

FREE
http://fileroom.aaup.uic.edu/FileRoom/
documents/Mliterature.html

Children's Literature Web Guide ★★★★

This site contains extensive information on children's literature and provides links to various topics. Within each topic there are many more links. Some of the topics include Lists of Recommended Books, Information about Authors, Current Movie Tie-ins, Electronic Journals and Discussion Groups, Research Guides to Children's Literature, Resources for Parents and Teachers, and more.

KEYWORDS   Books, Children's Literature
AUDIENCE   Book Dealers, Children, Educators (Primary/Secondary), Parents, Students (Primary/Secondary)
FREE

http://www.ucalgary.ca/~dkbrown/
index.html

Chinese Literature Directory at the National Central University of Taiwan ★★★★

This is a gopher menu of files containing miscellaneous Chinese literature, books of Buddhism, poetry, a books catalog and more. All tests are in Big 5 code Chinese dialect.

KEYWORDS   Buddhism, China, Chinese Literature
AUDIENCE   Chinese, Chinese Literature Enthusiasts, Chinese Poetry Enthusiasts, Literary Scholars
FREE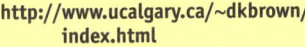

gopher://gopher.mgt.ncu.edu.tw/11/
Chinese

Chinese Poetry ★★★★

A collection of Chinese poems is offered here. They date from the Tang Shi, Shi Jing and other periods, listed in the Big 5 Chinese dialect/text. Several hundred texts are here in electronic format. Ability to read this dialect will be required to understand content.

KEYWORDS   Chinese Literature, Literature, Poetry
AUDIENCE   Chinese Literature Enthusiasts, Chinese Poetry Enthusiasts, Fiction Enthusiasts, Poetry Enthusiasts
CONTACT   shann@math.ncu.edu.tw
FREE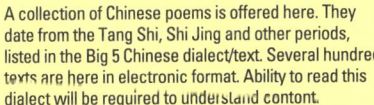

gopher://dongpo.math.ncu.edu.tw/11/
poem

The City Heiress ★★★★

The City Heiress is part the Electronic Text Center, Alderman Library, University of Virginia and contains a lengthy play about society in 17th Century London written in 1677 by Aphra Benn. The characters' speeches and the plot are similar to Shakespeare but the play lacks the depth of classical reference and double entendre of Shakespeare's work. However, the site will interest students of English literature and women's studies.

KEYWORDS   Drama, English Literature, Women's Studies
AUDIENCE   Educators (University), English Literature Enthusiasts, Literary Critics, Literary Scholars, Reading Enthusiasts, Students (University)
FREE

http://etext.lib.virginia.edu/
modeng.browse.html

Classical Chinese Poetry Page ★★★★

This page is an in-depth source of Chinese poetry, including Big 5 code Chinese dialect and English ascii versions of poems from seven major poets, 300 selected poems from the Tang Dynasty, and more.

KEYWORDS   China, Chinese Literature
AUDIENCE   Chinese Poetry Enthusiasts, Fiction Enthusiasts, Poetry Enthusiasts, Poetry Scholars
FREE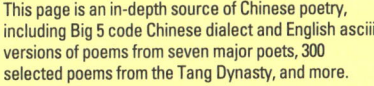

http://www.mordor.com/pei/poetry1.html

The Collected Works of Shakespeare ★★★★

This page contains the collected works of William Shakespeare in either etext or html format (20 are currently in html). You can browse through a chronological list of works in order of composition by category (Histories, Comedies, Tragedies, Poetry, Glossary), you can search for specific phrases, or if you have forms support, you can fill in a form for a specific search. This is a growing and valuable resource, especially given the choice of etext or html documents.

KEYWORDS   English Literature, Playwrights, Poetry, Theater
AUDIENCE   English Literature Enthusiasts, Poetry Enthusiasts, Reading Enthusiasts, Students (University)
CONTACT   matty@www.gh.cs.usyd.edu
FREE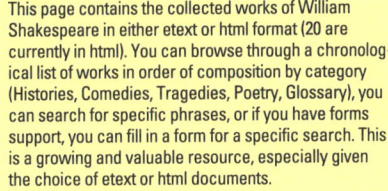

http://www.gh.cs.usyd.edu.an/~matty/
Shakespeare/index.html

The Complete Shorter Fiction ★★★★

This is a page holding a complete catalog of Oscar Wilde's short works in electronic text, including 14 short stories and six poems in prose.

KEYWORDS   English Literature, Poetry, Short Stories
AUDIENCE   English Literature Enthusiasts, Literary Scholars, Poetry Enthusiasts, Reading Enthusiasts
FREE

http://www.datatext.co.uk/library/wilde/
stories/chapters.htm

Comte de Lautreamont ★★★★

This is a comprehensive page about the Comte de Lautreamont, also known as Isidore Duacasse, (1846-70) and his works. According to the author of the page, 'His writing is drenched with an unrestrained savagery and menace, and it possesses a remarkable hallucinatory quality.' Biographical information about the author, his novel Les Chants de Maldoror, Poems, Letters, and the Lautreamont Collection are linked at this site.

KEYWORDS   French Literature, Literary Criticism, Literature
AUDIENCE   French Students, Literary Scholars, Reading Enthusiasts, Students (University)
FREE

http://www.lsi.usp.br/usp/rod/text/
lautreamont/lautreamont.html

Contes Per a Extraterrestres ★★★★

Contes per a extraterrestres, an electronic journal of short fiction, reviews and dossiers, publishes a number of short stories by authors around the world in each trilingual issue. The majority of the contents are in Spanish only, but a number of pieces are in Catalan and English.

KEYWORDS   Contemporary Literature, Fiction, Online Magazines, Spanish Language
AUDIENCE   Reading Enthusiasts, Spanish Culture Enthusiasts, Spanish Speakers, Writers
CONTACT   Carles Bellver and Josep M. Chorda extraterrestres@guest.uji.es
FREE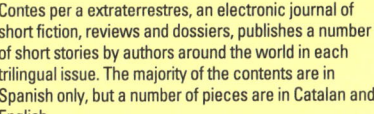

http://www.uji.es/CPE/

David Eddings Web Page ★★★★

These pages contain an FAQ, bibliography and biographical information related to fantasy fiction author David Eddings and his books (the most popular being his Belgariad series). Information on the fictional characters and places that fill his stories is also available at this site.

KEYWORDS   Fantasy, Science Fiction
AUDIENCE   Fantasy Enthusiasts, Reading Enthusiasts, Students (University)
CONTACT   James Carter
jfc5@york.ac.uk
FREE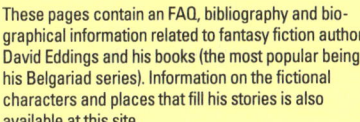

http://www.york.ac.uk/~jfc5/eddings/
eddings.html

Descriptions of an Imaginary University (DIU) ★★★

An irregular journal of poetry and poetics, Descriptions of an Imaginary University (DIU) offers poets the chance to publish their work anonymously (or pseudonymously—writing may be attached to names, but rarely are these names the actual names of people). Submissions come from poets and authors across the globe, and are not constrained to particular topics.

KEYWORDS   Contemporary Literature, Journals, Poetry
AUDIENCE   Poetry Enthusiasts, Poets
CONTACT   Chris Funkhouser
cf2785@albnyvms.bitnet
FREE

gopher://wings.buffalo.edu/internet/
library/e-journals/ub/rift/
journals/list/diu

Dogwood Blossoms - The Online Journal of Haiku ★★★★

An online electronic journal about Haiku poetry, Dogwood Blossoms is a '...place where Haiku can be shared and discussed with other lovers of art.' Information includes the current edition, capability to FTP to back issues, submissions by readers, discussions of the art, and published works of Haiku.

KEYWORDS Art, Haiku, Japanese Literature, Poetry
AUDIENCE English Literature Enthusiasts, Haiku Poetry Enthusiasts, Japanese Literature Enthusiasts, Poetry Enthusiasts
CONTACT glwarner@samford.edu
FREE

http://glwarner.samford.edu/haiku.html

Eden Etext Archive ★★★

The Eden Etext Archives is one individual's collection of 'the best' electronic texts available over the Internet, including everything from popular culture articles to classic novels. Electronic texts are listed alphabetically by genre, such as articles, classic text (subcategorized by authors such as Shakespeare and Edgar Allen Poe), historical and political documents, FAQs, Humor, Religious Texts, Sports and Television.

KEYWORDS Electronic Texts, Online Books, Playwrights
AUDIENCE Fiction Enthusiasts, Popular Culture Enthusiasts
CONTACT Adam Frey
adam@eden.apana.org.au
FREE

http://www.cs.rmit.edu.au/etext/

gopher://turtle.apana.org.au.

ftp://ftp.cs.rmit.edu.au in /pub/etext

Electronic Archives for Teaching the American Literatures ★★★★

The Electronic Archives for Teaching the American Literatures page provides links to essays, syllabi, bibliographies, and other resources for teaching the multiple literatures of the United States. The Archives are designed as a complementary resource to the electronic discussion list, t-amlit.

KEYWORDS Curriculum, Education, Languages, Teacher Resources
AUDIENCE American Literature Enthusiasts, Educators, Literary Scholars, Students (University)
CONTACT Randy Bass, Director
tamlit@gusun.georgetown.edu
FREE

http://www.georgetown.edu:80/tamlit/tamlit-home.html

Electronic Children's Books Gopher ★

This searchable gopher resource contains electronic children's books that are in the public domain. These include both classic and contemporary titles. Sample titles include Sherlock Holmes, Little Women, Peter Pan, and the Wizard of Oz. Sample authors include Charles Dickens, Rudyard Kippling, Daniel Defoe and Joseph Konrad.

KEYWORDS Children's Literature, Fantasy
AUDIENCE Children, Educators (Primary/Secondary), Librarians, Parents
CONTACT Donnie Curtis
dcurtis@lib.nmsu.edu
FREE

gopher://lib.nmsu.edu/11/.subjects/Education/.childlit/.childbooks

Electronic Poetry Center ★★★

The Electronic Poetry Center is an online library of electronic and hypertextual poetry. Local information includes the Center ezine, RIFT, with poetry and reviews, and the Poetics discussion area for poetry, with access to the archives of past discussions. Users will find the poetry texts available from the Poetry Center listed by author, small press, sound file, and poetics documents libraries. Listings include author/press backgrounds and actual literary texts. A meta-index of other poetry sites is also provided.

KEYWORDS E-Zines, Electronic Texts, Poetry
AUDIENCE Fiction Enthusiasts, Poetry Enthusiasts
CONTACT Loss Glazier
lolpoet@acsu.buffalo.edu
FREE

http://wings.buffalo.edu/internet/library/e-journals/ub/rift/

The Electronic Text (E-Text) Archives ★★★

The Gutenberg Project's goal is to provide a collection of 10,000 of the most used books by the year 2001. This gopher site hosts the project as well as a collection of other literary works such as poetry, drama and magazines.

KEYWORDS Drama, English Literature, Online Books, Poetry
AUDIENCE Book Lovers, General Public
FREE

gopher://fir.cic.net/

Elements of Style ★★★

Elements of Style by William Strunk has been used for over 70 years as a guide for writing and editing. This online edition was created by Project Bartleby at Columbia University, and contains the hypertextual version of the original publication. The main sections of the book discuss Elementary Rules of Usage and Elementary Principles of Composition, as well as form, common words and expressions, and common spelling errors.

KEYWORDS Online Books, Textbooks, Writing
AUDIENCE Educators, Journalists, Students, Writers
CONTACT Steven van Leeuwen
publications@columbia.edu
FREE

http://www.columbia.edu/~svl2/strunk/

English Server ★★★

This large and eclectic collection of humanities resources contains archives of conventional humanities materials, such as historical documents and classic books in electronic form, but it also offers more unusual and hard to find resources, particularly in the field of popular culture and media. It features access to many humanities and culture-related online journals such as Bad Subjects, FineArt Forum, and Postmodern Culture, and has links to a wide variety of related Internet sites and resources.

KEYWORDS English Literature, Humanities, Popular Culture
AUDIENCE Educators (University), General Public, Researchers, Students (University)
FREE

http://english-server.hss.cmu.edu

Ever The Twain Shall Meet ★★★★

In addition to biographical information on Mark Twain (a pseudonym for Samuel Clemens), this site contains several pieces of his work - both fiction and essay - in hypertext, and links to other sites on the Web where the vast majority of his work is stored.

KEYWORDS American Literature, Literature
AUDIENCE Fiction Enthusiasts, Historians
CONTACT joseph@telerama.lm.com
FREE

http://www.lm.com/~joseph/mtwain.html

The File Room - Works Censored on the Grounds of Sexual and Gender Orientation ★★★★

This page is part of an ongoing project called The File Room, which provides documention of censorship in the United States. It contains a list of works of art (books, photos, advertisements, films, and more) which were censored due to their sexual orientation. For each work the date and circumstances surrounding the censorship or censorship attempt are given. Viewers may also move to different topics or submit their own entries.

KEYWORDS Art, Books, Censorship, Sexual Orientation
AUDIENCE Art Historians, Arts Community, Educators, Literary Critics, Students
CONTACT Maria Roussos
mroussos@eecs.uic.edu
FREE

http://fileroom.aaup.uic.edu/FileRoom/documents/Gsex_gender.html

Frequently Asked Questions about Isaac Asimov ★★★★

This document contains links to answers of frequently asked questions about science fiction author, Isaac Asimov, and his works. It is posted periodically to the Usenet newsgroups alt.books.isaac-asimov, alt.answers, and news.answers. The contents of the file include a list of all of Asimov's books, biographical material (non-literary and literary) Foundation/Robot Series questions, and information on Asimov records, audio tapes, videotapes, and software.

KEYWORDS Science Fiction, Science Fiction/Fantasy

Literature 437

AUDIENCE   Asimov Enthusiasts, Robot Enthusiasts, Science Fiction Enthusiasts
CONTACT   Fred Condo
           fred@lightside.com
FREE

http://www.lightside.com/SpecialInterest/asimov/asimov-faq.html

ftp://rtfm.mit.edu/pub/usenet/alt.books.isaac-asimov/Isaac_Asimov_FAQ

The Goldsmiths Playlist ★★★★

The Goldsmiths Playlist is a work in progress. When complete, it will be a searchable index of thousands of English language plays and musicals, with citations for individual performances, biographical information on authors and those involved with notable performances, and other information.

KEYWORDS   Authors, Drama, Musicals
AUDIENCE   Actors, Playwrights, Theater Enthusiasts, Theater Professionals
CONTACT   Chris Hayes
           tgpmail@gold.ac.uk
FREE

http://www.gold.ac.uk/tgp/Welcome.html

Gopher Menu Collection of Classic Chinese Literature ★★★★

This resource is a gopher menu of Classic Chinese Literature, all in Big 5 code Chinese dialect. Authors include Confucius, Laogi, ancient and modern texts, and more.

KEYWORDS   China, Chinese Literature
AUDIENCE   Chinese, Chinese Literature Enthusiasts, Chinese Poetry Enthusiasts, Literary Scholars
FREE

gopher://sunsite.unc.edu/11/../.pub/docs/books/Chinese

Great Expectations ★★★★

This is an electronic text version of Charles Dickens' Great Expectations. There is a large amount of data here, requiring extensive downloading time.

KEYWORDS   English Literature, Literary Criticism
AUDIENCE   English Literature Enthusiasts, Literary Critics, Literary Scholars, Reading Enthusiasts
FREE

http://www.datatext.co.uk/library/dickens/greatexp/chapters.htm

Grimm's Fairy Tales ★★★★

This gopher directory provides the text of almost 100 of Grimm's fairy tales. Tales include 'Cinderella,' 'The Little Mermaid,' 'Three Little Pigs,' and 'The Story of Thumbelina.' Each story is an individual text file.

KEYWORDS   Children's Literature, Fairy Tales, Stories
AUDIENCE   Children, Fantasy Enthusiasts, Fiction Enthusiasts, Storytellers
FREE

gopher://ftp.std.com:70/11/obi/book/Fairy.Tales/Grimm

Gutenberg Etext World Wide Web Home Page ★★★

This is the home page for Project Gutenberg, whose goal is to provide electronic versions of 10,000 of the most used books by the year 2001. Many popular works of English literature are indexed here.

KEYWORDS   Books, Electronic Books, Electronic Publishing, English Literature
AUDIENCE   Book Readers, Educators, General Public, Students
CONTACT   Evan Mair
           emair@bu.edu
FREE

http://med-amsa.bu.edu/Gutenberg/Welcome.html

ftp://ftp.cdrom.com/pub/gutenberg/

Connections to Books on Tape
Reading alone is no fun.

Welcome to Our Library of Audio Rental Books

"Time is our most precious asset."

"Reading is our window to the world."

Tired of listening to traffic reports as you drive? There are alternatives—aside from those tired old music tapes on the cassette player! Through "Books on Tape," you'll gain hours of "reading" fun while you commute or travel on a long cross-country trip.

The Internet provides a virtual library of audio tapes of numerous classic and contemporary works, such as Trilogy by Stephen King.

Many people have found that a book worth reading is also worth listening to. Sometimes famous authors and actors provide the voice on the tape. Remember when your parents used to read you bedtime stories? If so, you know how stories can come alive through an aural medium.

(http://www.iquest.net/te/audiobks.html)

Want to know the right places to look for love? "Cupid's Book Store" offers a catalog of books on tape geared toward lovers, romance, and finding a lover. Do you know the top five avenues for finding a mate? They're on the Net.

(http://www.apk.net/cupid/bookstor/audtapes.html)

Children can find "Annie Sunshine and the White Owl of the Cedars" on the Internet. At this site, you can access a coloring/activity book and accompanying audio tape.

(http://apollo.co.uk/a/asunshine/)

Haiku for People! ★★★★

This is a very detailed page concerning Japanese Haiku poetry. The features of this site include 'What is Haiku?,' Haiku's political influence, how to write Haiku-poems, published poems, Haiku submissions by readers by subject category, and links other Haiku pages.

KEYWORDS   Art, Haiku, Poetry, Writing Resources
AUDIENCE   English Literature Enthusiasts, Haiku Poetry Enthusiasts, Japanese Literature Enthusiasts, Poetry Enthusiasts
CONTACT   Kei Toyomasu
           keitoy@oslonett.no
FREE

http://www.oslonett.no/home/keitoy/haiku.html

Humanities Text Initiative ★★★★

The Humanities Text Initiative (HTI) is a project of the University of Michigan Libraries, the UM Press, and the School of Library and Information Studies. The HTI is responsible for creating and maintaining new textual collections, primarily in SGML, with an initial focus on Middle English materials and American verse. Links to sources include dictionaries and lexicographic resources, English language and literature collections, religious texts, Latin texts, journals and more. This is a scholarly English literature research resource.

- KEYWORDS: Dictionaries, English Literature, Literary Criticism
- AUDIENCE: Bibliographers, Educators (University), English Educators, Literary Scholars, Reading Enthusiasts
- CONTACT: hti@umich.edu
- FREE

http://www.hti.umich.edu/

Humanum Gopher ★★★★

Humanum Gopher is a gopher menu of electronic texts including Boccaccio, Byron, Cervantes, Chaucer, Dickens, Dumas, Fielding, Lawrence, Milton, Montaigne, Swift, Verne and dozens of others. While the author list is extensive, the number of texts per author are limited to a few of their most famous works. Many files are quite large and will require significant downloading time.

- KEYWORDS: Electronic Texts, English Literature, Literary Criticism, Literature
- AUDIENCE: Educators (University), English Literature Enthusiasts, Fiction Enthusiasts, Literary Scholars, Students (University)
- FREE

gopher://humanum.arts.cuhk/11/humftp/E-text/Literature

Hyperizons Hypertext Fiction ★★★

Hyperizons is a guide to hypertext books and literary theory on the Web. Users will find links to two types of online books, original hypertext compositions (meaning literature that has never been published in print form), and converted print literature. Criteria for inclusion on the list is true hypertexuality, meaning more than simple 'turn the page' buttons. Literature and essays that discuss theory and technique aspects of hypertext fiction publishing are also provided, as well as individual and class projects in hypertext publishing.

- KEYWORDS: Hypertext, Online Books
- AUDIENCE: Book Enthusiasts, Fiction Enthusiasts
- CONTACT: Michael Shumate mshumate@acpub.duke.edu
- FREE

http://www.duke.edu/~mshumate/hyperfic.html

IFS - Johannes Kepler University Linz ★★★★

This page at the Kepler University in Linz, Austria provides resources for researching Austrian literature, including libraries, dictionaries, general starting points for searching, an object-oriented bibliography, world wide web sources, hypermedia, information filtering and retrieval, and an overview of publishers.

- KEYWORDS: Austria, Libraries, Literature, Universities
- AUDIENCE: Austrians, Educators (University), Germans, Literary Scholars, Reading Enthusiasts, Students (University)
- CONTACT: webmaster@ifs.uni-linz.ac.at
- FREE

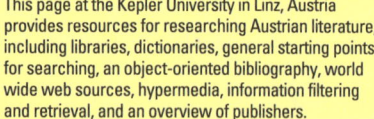

http://www.ifs.uni-linz.ac.at/ifs/literature

INKSPOT - Resource for Children's Writers ★★★

INKSPOT is a resource for those who write for children. This site contains many links and on-site documents of use to writers in general as well as those who write for children. Topics include reference materials, online books, writing workshops, authors, publishers, booksellers, publications and associations, libraries, grammar and style guides, and resources for young writers.

- KEYWORDS: Authors, Children's Literature, Reference, Writing Resources
- AUDIENCE: Children, Educators, Fiction Enthusiasts, Parents, Writers
- CONTACT: morgaine@utcc.utoronto.ca
- FREE

http://www.interlog.com/~ohi/dmo-pages/writers.html

Index - Jeff Frost's English Literature Links ★★★

Jeff Frost provides links to poetry, writing resources, electronic texts including the English server, a large storehouse of E-texts, and the English and literature server at the University of Pennsylvania, research assistance resources, the Shakespeare Web (an interactive hypermedia environment dedicated to the understanding of Shakespeare's plays and works), and a list of 31 of Frost's favorite works, including Tennyson, Poe, Dickens, Wilde, Chaucer and more. This is a fairly eclectic collection based on his interests, but provides excellent links to comprehensive English literature sources.

- KEYWORDS: Electronic Texts, English Literature, Playwrights, Poetry
- AUDIENCE: Academics, English Literature Enthusiasts, Literary Critics, Poetry Enthusiasts, Reading Enthusiasts, Students (University), Writers
- CONTACT: batalion@wsnet.com
- FREE

http://www.wsnet.com

Index of Chinese Classics at China News Digest ★★★★

This is a resource of Chinese literature text, mostly in Big 5 code Chinese dialect with some English ascii translations. Texts includes a developing list of 100 Chinese scholars (Lao Tse, Chuang Tsu, Confucius and more), plus the I Ching, novels, poetry, and primers.

- KEYWORDS: China, Chinese Literature
- AUDIENCE: Chinese Literature Enthusiasts, Chinese Poetry Enthusiasts, Fiction Enthusiasts, Literary Scholars
- FREE

http://www.cnd.org/Classics/index.html

Indigenous Peoples' Literature ★★★

The Indigenous Peoples' Literature Web site provides access to selected literary works and reference materials regarding indigenous peoples, primarily American Indians. The archive includes music and poetry, political documents, and stories.

- KEYWORDS: Literature
- AUDIENCE: Anthropologists, Native Americans
- FREE

http://kuhttp.cc.ukans.edu/~marc/natlit/native_lit_main.html

The Infinite Goof ★★★

This web page contains miscellaneous background and bibliographic information on contemporary American author Tom Robbins. Information on a few of his novels (which include Skinny Legs And All, Even Cowgirls Get The Blues, Still Life With Woodpecker, and more) and digitized images of some of their covers are also available.

- KEYWORDS: American Literature, Fiction
- AUDIENCE: American Literature Students, Fiction Enthusiasts, Reading Enthusiasts
- CONTACT: Matthew Cooperberg mrc@dartmouth.edu
- FREE

http://coos.dartmouth.edu/~cygnus/robbins.html

Internet Poetry Archive ★★★★

The Internet Poetry Archive, is in its first phase of an ongoing project by the University of North Carolina Press and the UNC Office of Information Technology. It will include the work of living poets from around the world; the two now included are Czeslaw Milosz and Seamus Heaney. Six more are scheduled to be presented here. Poets' pages will include electronic texts, audio clips of poets reading poems, poets' comments about their work, photographs and associated graphics. The page is intended to be as fully interactive as possible to present multi-dimensional aspects of a poet's work utilizing all aspects of network and multimedia technology.

- KEYWORDS: English Literature, Poetry, Poets
- AUDIENCE: English Literature Enthusiasts, Literary Critics, Literary Scholars, Poetry Enthusiasts
- CONTACT: Paul_Jones@unc.edu
- FREE

http://sunsite.unc.edu/dykki/poetry/home.html

Italian Literature Selections in HTML ★★★★

This is an in-depth resource of Italian literature texts, all written in Italian and in html format, by Dante, Boccaccio, Pirandello, Pagliaro, Ferrarri, San Francisco d'Assissi and many other authors. Areas covered include poetry, novels, narratives, contemporary authors, religious texts, philosophy, satire, theater, and miscellaneous.

- KEYWORDS: Italian Literature, Poetry
- AUDIENCE: Fiction Enthusiasts, Italian Literature Enthusiasts, Italians, Literary Critics, Literary Scholars
- FREE

http://www.crs4.it/HTML/Literature.html

The J.R.R. Tolkein Information Page ★★★★

This page contains links to net resources concerning the works and life of J.R.R. Tolkien. Some of the topics include frequently asked questions (FAQs), a book list, games list, Tolkien mailing lists, movie information on The Hobbit, Lord of the Rings, Return of the King, and more. Links to newsgroups, online texts, Tengwar fonts, graphics, and Tolkien societies, are also provided.

KEYWORDS	Children's Literature
AUDIENCE	Children, Fantasy Enthusiasts, Fiction Enthusiasts
CONTACT	Eric Lippert
FREE	

http://csclub.uwaterloo.ca/u/relipper/tolkien/rootpage.html

Jack Vance Archive ★★★★

This site contains all manner of information relating to science fiction author Jack Vance and his books, including bibliographies and background information in several languages, and scanned book covers from some of his more popular volumes, and 'The Vance Phile' - a small, independently published magazine devoted to Vance and his work.

KEYWORDS	Science Fiction
AUDIENCE	Fantasy Enthusiasts, Reading Enthusiasts, Science Fiction Enthusiasts
CONTACT	Remy Wetzels vance-archive@stack.urc.tue.nl
FREE	

http://www.stack.urc.tue.nl/~remy/

Jane Austen Info Page ★★★★

This page offers a comprehensive look at the life and work of Jane Austen, a prominent English author and social activist. A number of her novels (as well as numerous shorter works, both fiction and non) are available in annotated hypertext. The exhaustive biographical information presented here has been taken from a number of different books and biographies of Austen.

KEYWORDS	British Literature, Literature
AUDIENCE	Fiction Enthusiasts, Reading Enthusiasts, Writers
CONTACT	Henry Churchyard churchh@uts.cc.utexas.edu
FREE	

http://uts.cc.utexas.edu/~churchh/janeinfo.html

The Karoline von Gunderrode Pages ★★★

These pages are dedicated to 18th and 19th-century author Karoline von Gunderrode and the ongoing discussion of her work, usually within the framework of gender studies and philosophy. A biography of von Gunderrode and a continually growing collection of her work in hypertext (in both English and the original German) are also available.

KEYWORDS	Gender Issues, German Literature, Philosophy
AUDIENCE	Fiction Enthusiasts, Germans, Philosophers, Reading Enthusiasts, Women's Studies Educators
CONTACT	Christine Campbell ccampbel@reed.edu
FREE	

http://www.reed.edu/~ccampbel/Guenderrode.html

Kim ★★★★

This is an electronic text version of the novel Kim, by Rudyard Kipling. Antony, the poster of this text at Datatext, would like anyone who wishes to send him an introduction to the novel.

KEYWORDS	Books, English Literature, India
AUDIENCE	English Literature Enthusiasts, Literary Scholars, Reading Enthusiasts
CONTACT	antony@datatext.co.uk
FREE	

http://www.datatext.co.uk/library/kipling/kim/chapters.htm

Labyrinth ★★★

This site is the online version of Labyrinth magazine. It offers a selection of visual and literary work from students at Indiana University in Bloomington. Poetry from a number of local poets is also included.

KEYWORDS	Art, Literature, Poetry
AUDIENCE	Artists, Poets, Students (University), Writers
CONTACT	The Labyrinth Electronic Publishing Project labstaff@yod.honors.indiana.edu
FREE	

http://www.honors.indiana.edu/docs/lab/

Labyrinth Library of Medieval Studies ★★★★

This page is a tremendous resource of medieval literary information. It covers Latin, French, Italian and Middle English literature. The Latin area, for example, includes Latin bible texts, liturgical texts, classical Greek texts that influenced Latin traditions, classical and late classical latin texts (Virgil, Ovid, Pliny the Younger, Tacitus, Lucretius, Ausonius), early Patristic writings, medieval Latin texts and translations, grammatical curriculum texts and more. This is a highly recommended source for medieval studies students, educators and enthusiasts.

KEYWORDS	Classical Studies, English Literature, Literature, Medieval Studies
AUDIENCE	English Literature Enthusiasts, Literary Scholars, Medieval Literature Enthusiasts, Students (University)
FREE	

http://www.georgetown.edu/labyrinth/library/

Le Serveur Litterature de l'universite de Montreal ★★★★

Le Serveur Litterature de l'universite de Montreal is a gopher menu of literary information, sources and texts at the University of Montreal. All documents are written in French. Included are a presentation of French gopher literature, the Department of French Studies at the University of Montreal, literary reviews, library resources, electronic texts and more.

KEYWORDS	French Literature, Libraries, Literature, Universities
AUDIENCE	Fiction Enthusiasts, French Literature Enthusiasts, Literary Scholars, Students (University)
FREE	

gopher://gopher.litteratures.umontreal.ca:7070/1

Lewis Carroll Home Page ★★★★

This page contains writing from, and information about, Lewis Carroll, the author of such children's stories as Alice's Adventures in Wonderland and Through the Looking-Glass. Contact information for several literary organizations concerned with his life and work are available, as are annotated hypertext versions of selected Carroll writings. Complete biographical information is also presented.

KEYWORDS	Children's Literature, Literature
AUDIENCE	Children, Educators (Primary/Secondary), Fiction Enthusiasts, Reading Enthusiasts
CONTACT	Joel M. Birenbaum joel.birenbaum@att.com
FREE	

http://ux4.cso.uiuc.edu/~jbirenba/carroll.html

Literary Zines ★★

This directory contains about 15 different Literary Zines. Titles include Asian Voices, Athene, Blloball, Morpo Review, Taproot, and InterText.

KEYWORDS	Asian Literature, E-Zines, Human Communications, Literature
AUDIENCE	Cyberculture Enthusiasts, Cybernauts, Fiction Enthusiasts
CONTACT	rita@etext.archive.umich.edu
FREE	

ftp://etext.archive.umich.edu/pub/Zines-by-subject/Literary/

Literatur Online ★★★

Literatur Online provides German-language links to dictionaries, encyclopedias, glossaries, news from Germany, German libraries, books and reports. There is a section of the social aspects of computerized communication.

KEYWORDS	Current Events, Databases, German Literature, Libraries
AUDIENCE	German Enthusiasts, German Language Students, Germans
CONTACT	Achim Jung junga@informatik.tu-muenchen.de
FREE	

http://www.leo.org/infosys/lit/

Literature ★★★★

The Literature page is devoted to digitized Russian literature. The works include four books of poems by Russian poet Sasha Cherniy (228 poems), a collection of poems by Anna Ahmatova, an extensive collection of Russian proverbs, and classics by Leo Tolstory (Anna Karenina, War and Peace) and Fyodor Dostoevsky (The

Brothers Karamozov). Also provided is an index of 100 classic books in electronic form and quite a few links to English, Irish, Scandinavian, Greek, Latin, and Medieval literature.

KEYWORDS Classics, Poetry, Proverbs, Russian Literature
AUDIENCE Educators (University), English Literature Enthusiasts, Literary Critics, Russian Literature Enthusiasts, Students (University)
FREE

http://solar.rtd.utk.edu/friends/literature/literature.html

Literature - Collections of Great Works ★★★★

This collection of electronic texts includes Austen, Browning, Hardy, Henry, Melville, Milton, Shelley, Wells, Yeats and many more. The Collection of Great Works is a good source for electronic texts of classic English literature. Many files are very large and will require significant downloading time.

KEYWORDS Electronic Texts, English Literature, Literary Criticism, Literature
AUDIENCE Educators (University), English Literature Enthusiasts, Literary Critics, Literary Scholars, Students (University)
FREE

gopher://clevxd.cpl.org:70/11staff_gopher%3A%5B_literature%5D

Literature Peruana ★★★★

Literatura Peruana is a site featuring books in Spanish about Peru or from Peruvian authors, specifically related to the province of Pacasmayo. Titles in electronic text format include Estampas Pacasmayinas, Pacasmayo Historico, Libro de coros, and Recetas peruanas.

KEYWORDS Literature, Spanish Language
AUDIENCE Fiction Enthusiasts, Linguists, Literary Scholars, Peruvian Literature Enthusiasts
CONTACT felipe@vnet.ibm.com
FREE

http://tfnet.ils.unc.edu/~felipe/

Literature Related Mailing Lists ★★★

The Literature Related Mailing Lists site offers brief descriptions and access information for a number of Internet mailing lists. Users will find material about lists devoted to Spanish Baroque poetry, Balzac, French literature, the Latin Language, and more. These mailing lists are primarily related to the study of non-English literature.

KEYWORDS Discussion Lists, Literary Forums, Literature, Mailing Lists
AUDIENCE Fiction Enthusiasts, Literary Educators, Literary Students, Literary Theorists
FREE

gopher://gopher.english.upenn.edu/11/Lists/Other/

Literaturliste Internet ★★★

This Internet Literature list offered by Dr. Oliver Obst of the University of Muenster in Germany provides links to all German-language books on the Net, mail order books, Internet books in English, and miscellaneous book lists.

KEYWORDS Books, German Literature, Internet Resources
AUDIENCE German Studies Students, Germans
CONTACT Dr. Oliver Obst
obsto@uni-muenster.de
FREE

http://medsun06.uni-muenster.de/zbm/liti.html

Litterature Francophone et Textes en Francais ★★★★

This site contains links to French literature pages on the net. Some of the pages include literary Gophers, Erofile (French and Italian language texts), Les Fables de La Fontaine, ARTFL (a project for American and French Research of Treasury of the French Language), an anthology of Verlaine, Online French texts, French dictionaries, and more.

KEYWORDS Bible, Dictionaries, French Literature
AUDIENCE Critics, Educators, Francophiles, French Speakers, Students
FREE

http://www.cnam.fr/fr/litterature.html

Mal og Menning - Catalog of Icelandic Books ★★★★

This is an extensive alphabetical catalog of Icelandic books, provided by Malog Menning in Iceland, including author, site, a brief description of each book, and a reference number. A web browser form page is available to order books. Payment is by Cash on Delivery, Credit Card, or you can pick up your book at Mal og Menning in Iceland.

KEYWORDS Literary Criticism, Literature
AUDIENCE Fiction Enthusiasts, Icelanders, Icelandic Literature Enthusiasts, Literary Scholars
FREE

http://www.centrum.is

Mark Twain Resources on the WWW ★★★

This Web site is designed as a meta-index to Mark Twain reference materials on the Internet. Users will find links to exhibits, writings, popular culture such as television and film, tourism, and educational materials relating to Mark Twain and his literature. Links are listed according to type of resource, with a brief description of the contents of each site.

KEYWORDS Authors
AUDIENCE Fiction Enthusiasts, Literature Researchers, Literature Students
CONTACT Jim Zwick
fjzwick@mailbox.syr.edu
FREE

http://web.syr.edu/~fjzwick/twainwww.html

Mindflow Magazine ★★★

Available in both ascii and an MS-DOS executable (replete with VGA graphics and scrollable menus), Mindflow is a monthly e-zine that features poems, short stories, brainstorms, random thoughts, essays and commentary authored, for the most part, by American university students.

KEYWORDS Contemporary Literature, E-Zines, Poetry
AUDIENCE Poetry Enthusiasts, Poets, Reading Enthusiasts, Students, Writers
CONTACT Keith Shapiro
kdshap0@mik.uky.edu
FREE

gopher://gopher.etext.org/11/Zines/Mindflow/

Nepali Literature Home Page ★★★

The Nepali Literature Home Page is a site for different kinds of Nepali literature and cultural information. Users will find menu items for Nepali poems, short stories, plays, music, and children's literature. In addition, areas under construction (and are in need of contributions) include essays, letters, comedies, travel literature, folk tales, literary news, and book reviews. Other areas on this site include the International Nepali Literary Society's and the Nepal Human Rights Committee. Outside links to the Nepali home page, and to Nepal related newsgroup are also provided.

KEYWORDS Cultural Studies, Nepal, Poetry, Travel Literature
AUDIENCE Nepal Residents, Nepali Culture Enthusiasts
CONTACT George Mason University
system@site.gmu.edu
FREE

http://www.site.gmu.edu:80/~psubedi/

Nineteenth-Century German Stories ★★★

This WWW site provides hypertext versions of stories by the Grimm Brothers, Wilhelm Busch and Heinrich Hoffman in original German with English translations (including some by Mark Twain) and some original manuscript illustrations.

KEYWORDS German Literature, Illustrations, Stories
AUDIENCE German Language Educators, German Language Students, Librarians, Storytellers
CONTACT Robert Godwin-Jones
rgjones@cabell.vcu.edu
FREE

http://www.fln.vcu.edu/menu.html

Nobel Prize for Literature ★★★★

This is a hyperlinked list of book winners of the Nobel Prize for Literature awarded by the Nobel Foundation For Literature. The awards are arranged chronologically by year. Each category provides the year and a hyperlinked author's name. When you click on the author's name a page with a hyperlinked list of the author's works appears which in turn supplies you with the title, author, publisher, date, and price. From this page you can buy this book online if you choose after opening an account.

KEYWORDS Authors, Books, Literary Awards, Literature
AUDIENCE Fiction Enthusiasts, Librarians, Reading Enthusiasts
CONTACT Derrik Walker
dwalker@books.com
FREE

http://www.books.com/awards/nobel.htm

The North American Science Fiction Convention ★★★

This site presents information on the North American Science Fiction Convention. Users will find material on attending the latest conference as well as hotel booking and sponsor information. There are also pages on the local area where the conference is being held, as well as material on future conferences and events related to the Science Fiction world.

KEYWORDS Literature, Science Fiction
AUDIENCE Book Readers, Fiction Enthusiasts, Science Fiction Enthusiasts
CONTACT nasfic@dragoncon.org
FREE

http://www.dragoncon.org/dragoncon/

The On-Line Books Page ★★★★

This is the front page for an index of hundreds of on-line books. It also points to some common repositories of online books and other documents. The local index includes more than 450 English works in various formats, including text and HTML. All should be free for personal, noncommercial use. This page also provides pointers to specialty or foreign-language repositories, book catalogues and retailers, special exhibits such as Banned Books On-Line, etc.

KEYWORDS Electronic Texts, Fiction, Online Books
AUDIENCE Book Readers, Internet Users, Librarians, Students (University)
CONTACT spok@cs.cmu.edu
FREE

http://www.cs.cmu.edu:8001/Web/books.html

On-Line French Texts ★★★

The University of Virginia's online French text site is very comprehensive and may be browsed or searched.

KEYWORDS French Literature, Online Books, Universities
AUDIENCE French Literature Enthusiasts, French Students
FREE

http://etext.lib.virginia.edu/french.html

On-Line Writing Lab ★★★

Purdue University's On-Line Writing Lab is designed to provide basic writing information for students and other writers. Users will find instructional materials divided into categories such as parts of speech, punctuation, spelling, English as a second language, and writing resumes, research papers, and citations. All documents are in the form of handouts and include definitions and writing examples.

KEYWORDS Grammar, Universities, Writing
AUDIENCE General Public, Journalists, Students, Writers
CONTACT Muriel Harris and Dave Taylor
owl@sage.cc.purdue.edu.
FREE

http://owl.trc.purdue.edu/by-topic.html

The Online Book Initiative ★★

The Online Book Initiative is designed to be a library of freely redistributable texts such as book collections, information from conferences, catalogues, and other online publications. The publications are listed alphabetically by name, title or subject, such as Emily Dickenson, Sun Microsystems, or Conspiracy, with no other particular organizational form. Texts are in gopher form. An FAQ is provided for general questions, as well as mailing list information.

KEYWORDS Books, Online Books, Poets
AUDIENCE Book Enthusiasts, Fiction Enthusiasts, General Public
CONTACT Barry Shein
bzs@world.std.com
FREE

gopher://gopher.std.com/11/obi/

Online Chaucer Bibliography ★★★

The Online Chaucer Bibliography site offers a searchable online bibliography of research papers and books related to the study of Geoffrey Chaucer's works. The gopher site offers access instructions, as well as a link to the telnet site itself. Once in the database, users can search for information by author, subject, and title.

KEYWORDS Authors, Medieval Period, OPACs (Online Public Access Catalogs), Old English
AUDIENCE English Students, Literary Critics, Literary Scholars
FREE

gopher://gopher.epas.utoronto.ca/11/cch/disciplines/medieval_studies/chaucer

telnet://utsaibm.utsa.edu/

Oroonoko; or, The Royal Slave ★★★★

This is the story of a West Indies slave as told from the perspective of an English gentleman, written by Aphra Benn in 1688. The prose, as is typical of popular 17th century British writing, can be somewhat dense and wandering; the story goes into great detail about the life and struggles of a Caribbean slave during the period.

KEYWORDS English Literature, Online Books
AUDIENCE Educators (University), English Literature Enthusiasts, Reading Enthusiasts, Students (University)
FREE

gopher://english.hss.cmv.edu/0F2%3A49%3ABehn-Oroonoko

Persian Literature ★★★★

This page presents two biographies, and reviews of books about Iran, Persia, and classic Persian literary texts. A poetry section is under development.

KEYWORDS Iran, Literature, Middle Eastern Literature
AUDIENCE Iranians, Literary Scholars, Middle East Scholars, Reading Enthusiasts
FREE

http://tehran.stanford.edu/Literature/literature.html

Philippine Literature Home Page ★★★

This page celebrates Philippine culture through literature. The viewer will find short stories, poems, novel excerpts, cover art, and other areas on this server. There are sections that are devoted to Filipina authors and to issues for women of Philippine descent. Some authors highlighted on this page are Linda Ty-Casper, Jessica Hagedorn, Carlos Bulosan, and Jose 'Pete' Lacaba. The page includes English and Tagalog writers, modern and classical authors, scholarly dissertations and Filipino folklore.

KEYWORDS Authors, Philippine Literature
AUDIENCE Asian Studies Educators, Asian Studies Students, Filipinos, Literature Students
CONTACT wwww@teleport.com. T
FREE

http://www.teleport.com/~ria/index.html

Postmodern Culture ★★★★
(COMMERCIAL)

Postmodern Culture is an Electronic Journal of Interdisciplinary Criticism. There are links to postmodern theory and postmodern literature.

KEYWORDS Journals, Postmodernism
AUDIENCE Academics, Critics, Scholars
CONTACT eaeg@unity.ncsu.edu
FREE

http://jefferson.village.virginia.edu/pmc/contents.all.html

gopher://jefferson.village.virginia.edu/11/pubs/pmc

Praxis - A Journal of Graduate Criticism and Theory ★★

This page has information and links to articles from PRAXIS, a journal of Graduate Criticism and Theory. PRAXIS welcomes submissions on cultural and textual interpretation from graduate students in various disciplines, and in particular inquiries into pedagogic, aesthetic and ideological practices. Information on subscriptons and submission of manuscripts is given.

KEYWORDS Literary Criticism, Pedagogy
AUDIENCE Critics, Educators (University), Philosophers, Students (University)
CONTACT cobrien@cancer.rutgers.edu
FREE

http://www.rutgers.edu/praxis/PRAXIS.html

Project Gutenberg ★★★

The goal of Project Gutenberg is to 'make information, books and other materials available to the general public in forms a vast majority of the computers, programs and people can easily read, use, quote, and search' in the form of electronic texts. Their Web site contains access to their etext archives, via several ftp sites across the United States. All texts are Public Domain, which means that the author has been deceased for fifty years, and include US Governmental documents, the Bible, and many Shakespeare texts. Users may browse alphabetical title, author, or subject listings. The Project Gutenberg newsletters and an archive of articles about the project are also included.

KEYWORDS Electronic Texts, Online Books, Playwrights
AUDIENCE Book Lovers, Fiction Enthusiasts
CONTACT   Karin L. Trgovac
          dircompg@jg.cso.uiuc.edu
FREE

http://jg.cso.uiuc.edu/pg_home.html

Project Muse Home Page ★★★★

Project Muse is a collaborative experiment attempting to put all of Johns Hopkins University's scholarly journals into an online searchable database. Users may browse through articles from three sample journals discussing literature and French. Or, users can access the entire Project Muse article database, using subject searches, or a table of contents divided into alphabetical, subject, or graphic listings, with descriptions of each journal and subscription information. Access to actual articles from the database will eventually be restricted to Johns Hopkins students and faculty.

KEYWORDS Electronic Publishing, Journals, Universities
AUDIENCE Literature, Students
CONTACT   Todd Kelley
          Todd.Kelley@jhu.edu
FREE

http://muse.mse.jhu.edu

Project Runeberg ★★★

This page provides links to an alphabetical index of over 50 titles. It also has mirror pages in several different Nordic languages. Project Runeberg, founded in December 1992, is an open and voluntary initiative to create and collect free electronic editions of classic Nordic literature and art. Project Runeberg fans meet and discuss various topics on an electronic mailing list.

KEYWORDS Electronic Texts, Geography, Nordic Literature
AUDIENCE   Librarians, Nordic Literature Enthusiasts, Students (University)
CONTACT   Lars Aronsson
           aronsson@lysator.liu.se
FREE

http://www.lysator.liu.se/runeberg/Main.html

gopher://gopher.lysator.liu.se/runeberg/

ftp://ftp.lysator.liu.se/runeberg/

Pulitzer Prize-Biography or Autobiography ★★★

This is a non-hyperlinked list of book winners of the Pulitzer Prize for Biography or Autobiography awarded by the Graduate School of Journalism at Columbia University. The awards are arranged chronologically by year from 1917 to the present year. Some of the winners include W.E.B. DuBois, by D. Lewis, Machiavelli in Hell, by Sebastian Grazia, and The Power Broker, by Robert Moses and the Fall of New York, by Robert Caro.

KEYWORDS Books, Literary Awards, Literature
AUDIENCE Fiction Enthusiasts, Librarians, Reading Enthusiasts
CONTACT   Derrik Walker
          dwalker@books.com
FREE

http://www.books.com/awards/pulbio.htm

Pulitzer Prize-Drama ★★★

This is a non-hyperlinked list of book winners of the Pulitzer Prize for Drama awarded by the Graduate School of Journalism at Columbia University. The awards are arranged chronologically by year from 1917 to the present year. Some of the winners include Lost in Yonkers, by Neil Simon, Driving Miss Daisy, by Alfred Uhry, and A Chorus Line, by James Kirkwood and Nicholas Dante.

KEYWORDS Books, Drama, Literary Awards, Literature
AUDIENCE Drama Enthusiasts, Fiction Enthusiasts, Librarians, Reading Enthusiasts
CONTACT   Derrik Walker
          dwalker@books.com
FREE

http://www.books.com/awards/puldram.htm

Pulitzer Prize-General Non-Fiction ★★★

This is a non-hyperlinked list of book winners of the Pulitzer Prize for General Non-Fiction awarded by the Graduate School of Journalism at Columbia University. The awards are arranged chronologically by year from 1917 to the present year. Some of the winners include The Ants, by Bert Holldobler and Edward O. Wilson, Is There No Place on Earth for Me, by Susan Sheehan, and Beautiful Swimmers, by William W. Warner.

KEYWORDS Books, Literary Awards, Literature
AUDIENCE Fiction Enthusiasts, Librarians, Non-Fiction Enthusiasts, Reading Enthusiasts, Writers
CONTACT   Derrik Walker
          dwalker@books.com
FREE

http://www.books.com/awards/pulnfic.htm

Quote of the Moment ★★★

The Quote of the Moment is a website which provides a quotation from a literary source. One quote at a time is provided but you may 'Reload this document for a new quote.' The word 'reload' is hyperlinked and when you click on it a new quote replaces the former quote. A fun page to visit.

KEYWORDS Authors, Books, Literature, Quotations
AUDIENCE Children, Educators (Primary/Secondary), Librarians, Parents, Reading Enthusiasts, Students (Primary/Secondary)
CONTACT   Derrik Walker
          dwalker@books.com
FREE

http://melville.books.com/scripts/quotes.exe?sid~Oh6LevtLJ93EQHo

Reading is Fundamental - Chris Lehmann Home Page ★★★

This is a casual but enthuastic list by Chris Lehmann, a British and American Literature major, of his 'Read It and Quite Possibly Weep List' of books he has enjoyed. His list includes The Great Gatsby, F. Scott Fitzgerald; Written on the Body, Jeanette Winterson; The Tempest, William Shakespeare; Humboldt's Gift, Saul Bellow; and Generation X, Douglas Copeland. This self-described amateur book critic also accepts submissions of favorite authors/titles, and lists 'anything by H.L. Mencken'; Yellow Raft on Blue Water, Michael Dorris; and Gravity's Rainbow, Thomas Pynchon. This is a page to reference if you're not sure what you'd like to read next.

KEYWORDS English Literature, Literature, Popular Culture
AUDIENCE Fiction Enthusiasts, Reading Enthusiasts
CONTACT   cdl@access.digex.net
FREE

http://www.access.digex.net/~cdl/books.html

Reginald in Russia ★★★★

This is a collection of classic short stories by H.H. Munro (Saki), prepared by Anders Thulin. Titles include Reginald in Russia, the Reticence of Lady Anne, The Lost Sanjak, and 12 others.

KEYWORDS English Literature, Short Stories
AUDIENCE English Literature Enthusiasts, Literary Critics, Literary Scholars, Reading Enthusiasts
CONTACT   ath@linkoping.trab.se
FREE

gopher://wiretap.spies.com/00/Library/Classic/russia.hh

Rice University Collection of Literature, Electronic Books and Journals ★★★★

This is a source of gopher directories, literary electronic texts and resources collected from all over the Internet. You can research by subject area, or download texts which range from Aesop's Fables to Essays in Radical Empiricism by William James. The site is a very large pan-global literary resource.

KEYWORDS English Literature, Libraries, Literature, Universities
AUDIENCE Educators (University), English Literature Enthusiasts, Literary Scholars, Reading Enthusiasts, Students (University)
CONTACT   cwis@rice.edu
FREE

gopher://chico.rice.edu/11/Subject/LitBooks

Rimbaud ★★★

This short page dedicated to the French poet Arthur Rimbaud contains some text in French and a half a dozen links to various poems written by him.

KEYWORDS Authors, French Literature, Poetry
AUDIENCE French Speakers, Poetry Enthusiasts
FREE

http://acacia.ens.fr:8080/home/cbonnet/ailleurs/rimbaud.html

Sappho and Phaon ★★★★

The Anecdotes of a Grecian Poetess, written by Mary Robinson in 1796, is an analysis of classical Greek poetry as explored by many British authors of the period. Ms. Robinson specifically explores Greek sapphic myths in certain texts. The scope of poetry covered here includes The Legitimate Sonnet, Petrarch, Shakespeare, Johnson, and more.

KEYWORDS English Literature, Poetry
AUDIENCE English Literature Enthusiasts, Literary Scholars, Reading Enthusiasts
FREE

http://www.lib.virginia.edu/etext/britpo/sappho

Science Fiction Resource Guide ★★★★

This page contains an extensive database of science fiction information which can be accessed by hyperlinks. Subject areas include archives, authors, bibliographies and lists, movies, bookstores, role-playing games, zines, etc. Some of the topics include Anne Rice, Bram Stoker, Jules Verne, H G Wells, Star Wars, Star Trek, nanotechnology, vampire fiction, and more.

KEYWORDS Bookstores
AUDIENCE Book Readers, Science Fiction Enthusiasts, Star Trek Enthusiasts, Students (Primary/Secondary)
CONTACT Gareth Rees
FREE

ftp://gandalf.rutgers.edu/pub/sfl/sf-resource.guide.html

Scottish Folktales Gopher ★★

This gopher provides access to a collection of well-told Scottish Folktales, and includes Celtic songs and poetry.

KEYWORDS Gaelic Poetry, Scottish Folklore
AUDIENCE Educators (Primary/Secondary), Librarians, Storytellers, Students
FREE

gopher://leapfrog.almac.co.uk/11/scotland/dalriada/myths/scottish

Selected American Library Association Children's Newbery Award Winners ★★★

The Selected American Library Association Children's Newbery Award Winners page contains links to a list of winners for children's literature including the title, publisher, retail price, year of award, a brief description of each story and the capability to click and browse at the first few chapters of each book. Information is also available for the background on the Newbery Awards program, terms and criteria on which the awards are based, and the functioning of the awards committee.

KEYWORDS Books, Bookstores, Literary Awards, Publishing
AUDIENCE Children, Educators (Primary/Secondary), Fiction Enthusiasts, Librarians, Parents, Reading Enthusiasts, Students (Primary/Secondary), Writers
CONTACT webmaster@psi.com
FREE

http://dab.psi.net/ChapterOne/children/index.html

Connections to Men's Issues
Bridging the gender gap

Planning for your child's future
Birth Father Rights and Responsibilities

For almost fifty years, birth parents have trusted Bethany as their partner in making some of the most difficult decisions in their lives. We understand what you're going through.

Birth parents who work with Bethany can expect

- confidentiality and respect
- freedom from pressure
- information about community resources, if they decide to parent
- well-researched profiles of adoptive families from which they select a family, if they choose adoption
- follow-up counseling after the baby's birth

You can trust Bethany because the counselors are more than qualified professionals -- they truly care.

Bethany wants to help you with the unanswered questions you may have. We are concerned with your feelings. You can expect straight talk about life-affirming choices from Bethany.

My girlfriend is pregnant and won't talk to me about what she's going to do with my baby. How do I get her to listen and include me in the decision?

Interested in drumming? How 'bout the Men's Movement? Maybe you have issues about employment for men. How do you deal with fatherhood or being fatherless? The Internet can put you onto a broad base of resources for men.

You can learn more about the responsibilities connected with being a birth-father, or how to be a better father, husband, or lover. You can access a number of sites and forums that discuss various issues, including "Friends of Choice for Men"—a group advocating reproductive rights for men, or the "Reproductive Rights for Men" site.

(http://www.bethany.org/bethany/bfather.html)

If you're interested in getting in touch with your "inner child," or being a part of a men's movement organization, then "Men's Issues: Legal Issues and Resources" provides a Men's Issue page that provides you with links to those resources. There is also a wide assortment of information about domestic violence, employment, false rape charges, abuse and molestation, health issues (such as prostrate cancer), child custody, divorce, and romance. There is also a site on sexuality (which features discussions on homosexuality, homophobia, jealousy, sexual satisfaction in marriage, and outdated sexual and gender conditioning).

(http://www.vix.com/pub/men/law/law.html)

The Shakespeare Web ★★★★

This site contains Shakespeare-related topics of a whimsical nature. The page provides a link, Today in Shakespeare History, which brings you to what happened in the 1600's on the same day. Also included is a quotation contest, a Shakespeare queries page, The Shakespeare FAQ List, information on Shakespeare Festivals and Repertory Theater Companies, and more. The Shakespeare Web aims to provide a one-stop shopping center for all your bard-related needs and desires.

KEYWORDS Festivals, Playwrights
AUDIENCE Actors, Drama Enthusiasts, Literary Scholars, Shakespeare Enthusiasts
CONTACT dna@svpal.org
FREE

http://www.culturewave.com/culturewave/shakespeare/

Humanities & Social Sciences

Sheba Feminist Press ★★

This page gives information on Sheba, a publisher of writings by women of color, lesbians, working-class women and women who continue to be discriminated against. Sheba has found a strong and growing demand from many UK lesbians for well-written, explicit, woman-centered erotic material. A number of prominent Black U.S. writers have been published in the UK by Sheba, including bell hooks, Audre Lorde, and Jewelle Gomez. Extracts from some Sheba publications are included.

Keywords African American Authors, Feminist Literature, United Kingdom
Audience Authors, Women, Women Writers
Contact emizzell@echonyc.com
Free

gopher://echonyc.com:70/00/Women/sheba

Somerville Stories ★★

This site provides links to a collection of very short stories the author has written over the last two years for the newsgroup talk.bizarre. All of them more or less concern his life while living in his apartment in Somerville. The stories, besides all being amusing, are interwoven through the magic of hypertext. You can access them by character, by chronological order, by subject/keyword, or by title.

Keywords Comedy, Fiction, Short Stories
Audience Fiction Enthusiasts, Internet Users
Contact Thomas Colthurst
thomasc@athena.mit.edu
Free

http://www.mit.edu:8001/afs/athena.mit.edu/user/t/h/thomasc/Public/stories/stories.html

Terry Pratchett Home Page ★★★

This group of pages contains pictures, interviews, and miscellaneous excerpted text relating to or from the novels of Terry Pratchett, the popular science fiction author. A full bibliography of Mr. Pratchett's work, as well as biographical information about him, is available. An FAQ relating to the reality that most of his novels share is also featured.

Keywords Science Fiction, Science Fiction/Fantasy
Audience Fantasy Enthusiasts, Reading Enthusiasts, Science Fiction Enthusiasts
Contact Robert R. Collier
mautx@csv.warwick.ac.uk
Free

http://www.csv.warwick.ac.uk/~mautx/PTerry/PTerry.html

Thomas Keneally ★★★★

This page is dedicated to Thomas Kenneally, one of Australia's most prominent contemporary authors. Abstracts of much of his work, both fiction and non-fiction, are available here, as are the digitized cover images from those books.

Keywords Australia, Literature
Audience Australians, Fiction Enthusiasts, Holocaust Survivors, Jews, Reading Enthusiasts

Contact J.K. Cohen
jkcohen@uci.edu
Free

http://bookweb.cwis.uci.edu:8042/Keneally.html

Turkish Poetry Homepage ★★★★

This is a large collection of Turkish poetry written in Turkish and in English translation. Turkey has a long tradition of poetic expression which goes back as far as the 11th century, and poetry has always remained an important part of Turkish culture and feeling.

Keywords Literature, Poetry, Turkey
Audience Fiction Enthusiasts, Literary Scholars, Poetry Enthusiasts, Turkish Literature Enthusiasts
Contact sibel@cs.umd.edu
Free

http://www.cs.umd.edu/~sibel/poetry/poetry.html

University of Glasgow - Faculty of Arts ★★★

The WWW page for the University of Glasgow's (Scotland) Faculty of Arts offers a small number of links to humanities and literature servers on the Internet such as the Language Center and COMET, the English literature texts server. The site includes access to various locations such as 'The Whole Internet Catalogue,' the BBC, and the University of Glasgow's home page.

Keywords University Departments, University of Glasgow
Audience Humanities Scholars, University of Glasgow Students
Contact rda@arts.gla.ac.uk
Free

http://www.arts.gla.ac.uk/homepage.html

Voice of the Shuttle - Literatures Page ★★★★

This is an extremely rich site which provides resources on classical literature, literature and language (largely Greek), philosophy, and literature from France, Ireland (Gaelic/Celtic), Germany, Islam, Italy, Japan, Poland, Russia, Spain, and Turkey. This is a highly recommended literature resource page.

Keywords Classics, Languages, Literary Criticism, Literature
Audience Educators (University), Fiction Enthusiasts, Literary Critics, Literary Scholars, Reading Enthusiasts, Students (University)
Contact ayliu@humanitas.ucsb.edu
Free

http://humanitas.ucsb.edu/shuttle/

Wei-Chang Shann's Big-5 Chinese Literature Archive ★★★★

This gopher site is a menu list of many Chinese literature and poetry texts, all in Big 5 code Chinese dialect.

Keywords China, Chinese Literature

Audience Chinese, Chinese Literature Enthusiasts, Chinese Poetry Enthusiasts, Literary Scholars
Free

gopher://dongpo.math.ncu.edu.tw/

Whales In Literature ★★

This site discusses whales in literature and has links to the text of Melville's 'Moby-Dick,' Bierce's 'The Devil's Dictionary,' and one satirist's defintion of a whale, 'Leviathan.' An enormous aquatic animal mentioned by Job, some suppose it to have been the whale. But that distinguished ichthyologer, Dr Jordan, of Stanford University, maintains with considerable heat that it was a species of gigantic tadpole. The text offers a brief discussion about whales.

Keywords American Literature, Books, Literary Motifs
Audience Reading Enthusiasts, Whale Enthusiasts
Contact Andrew Graham
asd13@cc.keele.ac.uk
Free

http://www.physics.helsinki.fi/whale/literature/graham.html

The William S. Burroughs Files ★★★★

This page offers a collection of resources related to the prolific beat-era author William S. Burroughs. Users will find a series of audio clips from Burroughs readings, information on the author's recent projects and activities, and biographical and historical information. There is also a bibliography of the author's writings, links to online texts by the author, and a compendium of links to other William S. Burroughs information on the net.

Keywords American Literature, Beat Generation, Literary Studies, Literature
Audience Fiction Enthusiasts, Literary Critics, Literary Theorists, Students
Contact Malcolm Humes
mal@emf.net
Free

http://www.hyperreal.com/wsb/index.html

WorldCon '96 ★★★

The WorldCon '96 site offers information on the 1996 World Science Fiction Society to be held in Los Angeles, California. Alternatively known as LACon III, WorldCon '96 offers vendor information, writer showcases and workshops, lectures, and other events of interest to science fiction and fantasy literature fans. Users will find event participation information including proposed schedules, a celebrities and guests attendee list, and the Hugo Award programs. Travel and accomodations information is also provided.

Keywords Conventions, Fantasy, Literature, Science Fiction
Audience Book Readers, Fantasy Literature Enthusiasts, Science Fiction Enthusiasts
Contact lacon3-info@netcom.com
Free

http://sundry.hsc.usc.edu/lacon3/

ftp://ftp.netcom.com/pub/la/lacon3-info/index.html

Literature – Psychology

The World Wide Web Virtual Library, Literature ★★★

The Internet Book Information Center is maintained by the University of N. Carolina for The World Wide Web Virtual Library and is a smorgasbord of links to various Internet book projects. It has pointers to review resources, online booksellers, and newsgroups related to books, to name a few. It is evolving, having no overall apparent structure.

KEYWORDS Books, Fiction, Journalism, Meta-Index (Electronic Texts)
AUDIENCE Book Readers, Literary Critics, Publishing Professionals, Students (University)
CONTACT ibic@sunsite.unc.edu
FREE

http://sunsite.unc.edu/ibic/IBIC-homepage.html

Psychology

See also
Health & Medicine · *Mental Health*
Humanities & Social Sciences · *Sociology*

American Psychological Society (APS) ★★★

The American Psychological Society (APS) site has information for psychology researchers and teachers. It details how to become a member of the Society and provides information on the current officers of the APS. It also offers teaching aids for professors, links to sites with research information, services for graduate students, a software archive for DOS/Mac Software, and job listings.

KEYWORDS Job Listings, Organizations, Psychology, Software
AUDIENCE Job Seekers, Psychologists, Psychology Educators, Students (University)
FREE

http://psych.hanover.edu/APS/

The Art of Imaging ★

'The Art of Imaging' offers a human performance mental imagery training program. The program is intended for motivated individuals and small groups (2 to 4 people) seeking creative transformation. The training utilizes a multi-disciplinary approach and is centered in the use of sound to help amplify the imaging process. Using Eidetic images in your mind to focus on and create new perceptual skills, this seminar may allow the client to grow in significant ways. Schedules, costs, and locations are given on this page as well.

KEYWORDS Memory, Mental Imagery, Sports Visualization
AUDIENCE Californians, Management Trainers
CONTACT Coolware Inc.
webmaster@coolware.com
FREE

http://none.coolware.com/health/imaging/TheArtofImaging.html

Cognitive and Psychological Sciences ★★★

This Cognitive and Psychological Sciences resource at the Stanford University Psychology Department contains links to academic programs, organizations and conference lists, journals and magazines, Usenet newsgroups, discussion lists, and other general information regarding cognitive science.

KEYWORDS Cognitive Sciences, Psychology
AUDIENCE Cognitive Scientists, Neuroscientists, Psychiatrists, Psychologists
CONTACT Scott Mainwaring
sdm@psych.stanford.edu
FREE

http://matia.stanford.edu/cogsci.html

Dictionary of Symbolism - Cultural Icons and the Meanings Behind them ★★★★

This is a review and source reference for the Dictionary of Symbolism-Cultural Icons and the Meanings Behind Them, by Hans Biedermann, translated by James Hulbert. Purchase and ISBN information are available here.

KEYWORDS Literature, Mythology
AUDIENCE Literary Scholars, Mythology Enthusiasts, Reading Enthusiasts
FREE

gopher://gopher.infor.com:4600/0exec%3A-v%20a20R1686920

Northwestern University Psychology Department ★★★★

The Northwestern University Psychology Department's home page supplies information about its faculty, courses and programs. The page contains listings of the people, graduate and undergraduate academic programs, class schedules and course descriptions. There is class information for (C28) Cognitive Psychology including handouts and exam questions. There are links to information resources such as the Northwestern Psychology Department MacLab Library and other Internet sites.

KEYWORDS Cognitive Sciences, Education (College/University), Educational Programs
AUDIENCE Psychologists, Students
CONTACT aminoff@nwu.edu
FREE

http://www.psych.nwu.edu/

PORE (Public Orgonomic Research Exchange) ★★★

PORE (Public Orgonomic Research Exchange) is an organization devoted to the discussion of, and exchange of information about, the psychologist Wilhelm Reich, and his study of an elemental energy which he entitled 'Orgonomy.' At this Home Page you will find an electronic newsletter about Orgone Energy, a list of organizations and groups pertaining to Dr. Reich, information on orgonomics and classified ads for things like Orgone Boxes. There are also a number of links to Web search engines and other resources available here.

KEYWORDS Psychologists, Psychology
AUDIENCE Alternative Health Care Enthusiasts, Orgone Energy Enthusiasts
CONTACT PORE (Public Orgonomic Research Exchange)
pore@aol.com
FREE

http://www.mainelink.net/~jogg

The Princeton University's Gopher Server ★★★

This Princeton University gopher server gives access to resources in the areas of psychology and psychiatry. These resources include online journals and access to the Princeton University library catalog.

KEYWORDS Psychiatry, Psychology, Scientific Journals
AUDIENCE Educators, Medical Researchers, Psychologists, Sociologists, Students
CONTACT gopher@princeton.edu
FREE

gopher://gopher.princeton.edu:9000/

Psychiatry On Line ★★★★

Psychiatry On Line is a monthly 'Online International Journal of Psychiatry' designed for mental health professionals. Articles at the website generally address current concerns in psychiatry, among which could be depression, dementia, organic brain disorders, resources for mental health, SSRI's and other psychotropic medications, religion and psychiatry and sexual dysfunction. Case studies are presented, as is information on academic programs in psychiatry, psychology and related disciplines. Psychiatry On Line accepts manuscript submissions - guidelines are posted here. Letters are also accepted, and you will find a lively debate about the topics therein. Also available here are links to other pertinent Internet sites.

KEYWORDS Mental Health, Psychiatry, Psychology, Psychopharmacology
AUDIENCE Mental Health Professionals, Psychiatrists, Psychologists, Psychopharmacologists
CONTACT Dr. Ben Green
ad88@cityscape.co.uk
FREE

http://www.cityscape.co.uk/users/ad88/psych.htm

Psychology Department at the University of Pennsylvania ★★★

This is a gopher server of the Psychology Department of the University of Pennsylvania. It provides information on the Department, the graduate program, the undergraduate program, courses, journals, publications, psychology-related software, data archives, and more.

KEYWORDS Psychology, Social Sciences
AUDIENCE Psychologists, Psychology Educators, Psychology Students

Psychology – Sociology

CONTACT gopher@psych.upenn.edu
FREE

gopher://psych.upenn.edu/

The Psychology Gopher Service ★★

This service provides access to information and resources related to the Department of Psychology at the University of Illinois Urbana-Champaign. This information includes departmental news and events, computing resources at the department, library resources, and course material.

KEYWORDS Psychology, Psychotherapy, Universities
AUDIENCE Professors, Psychologists, Psychology Students (Graduate), Students (University)
CONTACT John Boyd
jboyd@s.psych.uiuc.edu
FREE

gopher://s.psych.uiuc.edu/

Psycoloquy ★★★★

Psycoloquy is an international, interdisciplinary electronic journal of open peer commentary in the biobehavioral and cognitive sciences, supported on an experimental basis by the American Psychological Association. Psycoloquy is attempting to provide a model for electronic scholarly periodicals. All contributions are refereed; the journal has an editorial board and draws upon experts in the pertinent subspecialties (psychology, neuroscience, behavioral biology, cognitive science, philosophy, linguistics, and computer science). In addition to refereed 'target articles,' Psycoloquy publishes refereed peer commentary on those articles, as well as authors'responses to those commentaries.

KEYWORDS Cognitive Sciences, Electronic Journals, Neurosciences, Psychology
AUDIENCE Mental Health Professionals, Psychiatrists, Psychologists, Psychology Students
CONTACT Stevan Harnad
harnad@ecs.soton.ac.uk
FREE

gopher://gopher.Princeton.EDU:70/1ftp%3Aprinceton.edu@/pub/harnad/Psycoloquy/Background/

RDZ ★★★

RDZ is a gopher site maintained by the Department of Psychology at St. Johns University in Jamaica, New York. It is part of the UNIBASE network which focuses on providing Internet connectivity for schools and small libraries. It contains information about FTP sites, databases, professional development activities, special interest centers, and more. It has pointers to other resources on the Internet.

KEYWORDS Education, Libraries, Networking, New York
AUDIENCE Educators, Librarians, Library Users
CONTACT Dr. Zenhausern
drz@sjuvm.stjohns.edu
FREE

gopher://rdz.stjohns.edu/

Sociology

See also
Humanities & Social Sciences · Area & Cultural Studies
Humanities & Social Sciences · Library & Information Studies

American Communication Association WWW-Social Science Communication Research ★★★

This Social Science Research Resource WWW site is full of links to resources valuable to communication research. It is run by the American Communication Association from a server at the University of Arkansas and contains such links as U.S. Statistical Data, Steinmetz Data Archive, the Virtual MeetMarket, Behavior Analysis, and the CHANCE Database.

KEYWORDS Psychology, Research, Sociology
AUDIENCE Social Scientists, Sociologists
CONTACT comminfo@cavern.uark.edu
FREE

http://cavern.uark.edu/comminfo/www/social.science.html

Cyberspace Report ★★★

This site offers recent episodes, of a public affairs show on Los Angeles radio, called 'The Cyberspace Report'. The show explores the social issues of computing through interviews and topic shows. Users can listen to recent episodes by clicking on the desired choice.

KEYWORDS Cyberspace, Internet Culture
AUDIENCE Computer Users, General Public, Internet Users
CONTACT Lisa M. Covi
covi@ICS.UCI.EDU
FREE

http://www.ics.uci.edu/~ejw/csr/cyber.html

Daily Work by an Ordinary News Photographer ★★

This page contains photographs by photojournalist Allen Rose. Rose is a newspaper photographer for the Fort Worth Star-Telegram, working in Arlington, Texas and his project shows what he photographs each day. Photographs include sports, children, local personalities and feature stories and events. Each photograph includes a caption and the collection creates a visual collage of contemporary Arlington.

KEYWORDS Journalism, News, Photography, Texas
AUDIENCE Journalists, News Buffs, Photographers
CONTACT Allen Rose
arose@metronet.com
FREE

http://www.metronet.com/~arose/today/workhome.html

Department of Sociology, Princeton University ★★★

This is the Web site for Princeton University's Department of Sociology, that is continuously updated or 'under construction' as they express it. It has excellent scholarly links as well as some information on their graduate and undergraduate programs, faculty and recently taught courses. The style is very academic and research oriented as might be expected from the Ivy League.

KEYWORDS Social Sciences, Sociology, Universities
AUDIENCE Scholars, Social Scientists, Sociologists, Students
CONTACT Princeton University, Department of Sociology
sociolog@princeton.edu
FREE

http://www.princeton.edu/~sociolog

Electronic Journal of Sociology ★★★

The Electronic Journal of Sociology is available free of charge online and is published as plain ascii text. It is a refereed electronic journal which specializes in publishing articles and commentaries for those who wish rapid feedback about current or proposed projects, while retaining standards of scholarly content. The files are available for anonymous ftp at the University of Alberta, Canada and from the Coombs Computer Center at the Australian National University. Disks are available for a fee of $15 Canadian.

KEYWORDS Electronic Journals, Social Sciences, Sociology
AUDIENCE Scholars, Social Scientists, Sociologists, Students
CONTACT Mike Sosteric, Guy Germain
msosteri@gpu.srv.ualberta.ca;
ggermain@gpu.srv.ualberta.ca
FREE

http://gpu.srv.ualberta.ca:8010/

ftp://ftp.srv.ualberta.ca

Institute for Policy Research ★★

The Institute for Policy Research (IPR) is a multidisciplinary research organization at the University of Cincinnati composed of a number of research centers and programs. In addition, the Institute conducts 'The Ohio Poll,' a quarterly cost-shared survey of Ohio residents, a semi-annual omnibus survey in Greater Cincinnati and the 'University of Cincinnati National Health Survey.' The site is designed with extra large type for net surfers and researchers who have perhaps been hunched over their machines for hours, and links are provided to the latest press releases from 'The Ohio Poll,' 'The University of Cincinnati National Health Survey,' IPR Research and Methodology Seminars, Papers by IPR and IPR Staff and an IPR Directory of Internet Resources.

KEYWORDS Research, Research Institutes, Sociology
AUDIENCE Social Scientists, Sociologists
CONTACT Dr. Alfred J. Tuchfarber, Director
Alfred.Tuchfarber@uc.edu
FREE

http://www.uc.edu/~sordc/iprhomepage.html

Sociology **447**

Institute for Social Studies, University of Warsaw ★★★

The Institute for Social Studies, located at the University of Warsaw, has resources including papers in English and Polish, conference announcements, contact information for various committees and sub-councils, as well as links to outside research institutions that offer related information. A survey on Polish society is also available here, which reports demographics and social trends.

Keywords Poland, Social Sciences, Warsaw
Audience Eastern Europeans, Polish, Social Scientists
Contact M. Jacek Szamrej
jasza@samba.iss.uw.edu.pl
Free

http://andante.iss.uw.edu.pl/

The International Society for Human Ethology Website ★★★

The International Society for Human Ethology website is a site for professionals in the fields of human ethology, human biology, urban ethology and related disciplines. Here you will find information about the society, its goals, history and membership materials, announcements of upcoming conferences and abstracts of papers recently given, explications of programs, videotapes, freeware useful to behaviorists, information about grants, articles from relevant electronic publications, and multimedia links to other pertinent websites.

Keywords Behavioral Science, Primatology, Urban Studies
Audience Behaviorists, Ethologists, Primatologists
Contact Dr. Karl Grammer
karl.grammer@univie.ac.at
Free

http://evolution.humb.univie.ac.at

Journal of World-Systems Research ★★★

The Journal of World-Systems Research (JWSR) is an electronic journal dedicated to scholarly research on the modern world-system and earlier, smaller intersocietal networks. JWSR is published under the sponsorship of the Program in Comparative International Development in the Sociology Department of Johns Hopkins University. The site offers links to articles, staff, editorial policy, subscriptions and operations, information for submitting articles, and more.

Keywords Journals, Social Sciences, Subscriptions, Universities
Audience Social Scientists, Sociologists
Contact chriscd@jhu.edu
Free

http://csf.colorado.edu/wsystems/jwsr.html

National Center for the Workplace ★★★

This is a gopher server for the National Center for the Workplace at the University of California at Berkeley. It offers information on the Center, its mission, staff and researchers, events, activities, projects, publications, and more.

Keywords California, Education (College/University), Humanities
Audience Academics, Social Scientists, Students (University)
Contact ncw@uclink.berkeley.edu
Free

gopher://uclink.berkeley.edu:3030/

Connections to Television Talk Shows
"I married my sister's girlfriend's aunt's cousin, who's a cross-dressing stripper at a road-side cafe. Boy, have I got troubles."

You could watch other people "spill the beans" about their problems on a variety of talk shows, or you could do something like watch C/Net. You can even go online with C/Net and hear actual Internet phone calls or search the virtual software library for the best tools to get the most from the Web.

C/Net on television and on the Internet give you the latest information about technology and how it will change your life.

But even if you're into Ricki Lake, Phil Donohue, or Oprah, rest assured that there's a web site that caters to your interests. You can download photos of the hosts, video clips, and audio clips, and generally keep abreast of the most compelling and lurid stories western culture has to offer. To find out more, tune into the next . . . on the Internet.

(http://www.cnet.com/)

448 Sociolgy

Norwegian Social Science Data Service (NSD) ★★★

The Norwegian Social Science Data Services (NSD) is an organization based in Norway, servicing the research community. Its main task is to develop databases and relevant software to secure easy access to empirical data. The Web site offers access to general information including staff email addresses, statistical databases and software, the EU Referendum for Finland, Sweden and Norway, a data catalog (in Norwegian), miscellaneous articles and publications and other social science data archives.

KEYWORDS   Databases, Norway, Research, Social Sciences
AUDIENCE   Social Scientists, Sociologists
CONTACT   dbh@nsd.uib.no
FREE

http://www.uib.no/nsd/nsd-eng.html

Population Index ★★★★

This site provides the full contents of all 1993 and 1994 issues (Volumes 59 and 60) of the Population Index, a widely respected quarterly demographic bibliography. Each issue is indexed geographically and by author. A comprehensive author index to all 1993-1994 issues is also provided. Eventually all issues dating back as far as 1986 will be available in the same format.

KEYWORDS   Demographics, Migration, Reference
AUDIENCE   Population Researchers, Researchers, Sociologists
CONTACT   popindex@princeton.edu
FREE

http://opr.princeton.edu/pi/pindex.htm

Population Studies Center - University of Michigan ★★★★

The Population Studies Center (PSC) at the University of Michigan is a demographic research and training center. The page offers information on the staff, publications and a PSC description. There are links to other departments at the University of Michigan and population resources on the WWW.

KEYWORDS   Community Information, Demographics, Education (College/University)
AUDIENCE   Population Studies Students, Sociologists, Students
CONTACT   webmaster@psc.lsa.umich.edu
FREE

http://www.psc.lsa.umich.edu/

Population Studies Center, University of Pennsylvania ★★★

This gopher server provides information obtained from population studies and surveys. The information was collected by the Population Studies Center at the University of Pennsylvania. The data includes results from surveys and censuses from Africa, Latin America, and the USA. In addition, this server provides papers and publications from the Population Studies Center.

KEYWORDS   Census (The), Environment, Geography, International Research
AUDIENCE   Geographers, Health Care Policy Makers
FREE

gopher://lexis.pop.upenn.edu/

Progressive Sociology Network ★★

The Progressive Sociology Network site is an index to sociology archives, authors, gopher sites and various other Progressive Sociology and Progressive Population Network links. The Progressive Sociologists Network (PSN) began as a listserv in April 1992 with the goal of bringing together sociologists from all over the world concerned with progressive issues and values such as working class struggles, civil rights struggles, women's rights, racial and ethnic minorities' rights, community development, justice, ecological and environmental issues, and more.

KEYWORDS   Gophers, Population, Sociology
AUDIENCE   Social Scientists, Sociologists
FREE

http://csf.colorado.edu/psn/

Race ★★★★

This is an extensive meta-index for Black and American Studies. It is a page of 100+ links including the African-American Bibliography, Asian Envy, The Death of Affirmative Action, Douglass - My Escape from Slavery, Eaten up by Stereotypes, King - Free At Last, Networking the Nations, NAACP, Race and the Religious Right, Truth - Ain't I a Woman?, Who are the World's Indigenous?, and many more.

KEYWORDS   Affirmative Action, Race Relations
AUDIENCE   African Americans, Hispanics
FREE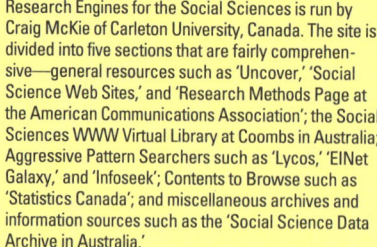

http://english-www.hss.cmu.edu/Race.html

Research Engines For The Social Sciences ★★★

Research Engines for the Social Sciences is run by Craig McKie of Carleton University, Canada. The site is divided into five sections that are fairly comprehensive—general resources such as 'Uncover,' 'Social Science Web Sites,' and 'Research Methods Page at the American Communications Association'; the Social Sciences WWW Virtual Library at Coombs in Australia; Aggressive Pattern Searchers such as 'Lycos,' 'ElNet Galaxy,' and 'Infoseek'; Contents to Browse such as 'Statistics Canada'; and miscellaneous archives and information sources such as the 'Social Science Data Archive in Australia.'

KEYWORDS   Internet Resources, Research, Social Sciences, Sociology
AUDIENCE   Social Scientists, Sociologists
CONTACT   oab024@freenet.carleton.ca
FREE

http://www.carleton.ca/~cmckie/research.html

The Social Science Computing Gopher at the University of Pennsylvania ★★

This is a gopher server of the Social Science Computing Center at the University of Pennsylvania. It provides information such as Social Science Computing policy statements, computing resources and services, announcements, data holdings, and Internet services. It also provides access to other gophers.

KEYWORDS   Computing, Education (College/University), Social Sciences, Social Work
AUDIENCE   Computing Analysts, Educators (University), Social Scientists, Social Workers
CONTACT   Andrew White
   awhite@mcneil.sas.upenn.edu
FREE

gopher://gopher.ssc.upenn.edu/

Social Science Methodology School Home Page ★★★

The Social Science Methodology School Home Page is based at the University of Essex in the United Kingdom and offers an overview of the 'Twenty-Eighth Essex Summer School in Social Science Data Analysis and Collection.' The site contains links to all the courses, the computing facilities and to general information.

KEYWORDS   Research Methodology, Social Sciences, United Kingdom
AUDIENCE   Social Scientists, Sociologists, Students
CONTACT   sum_sch@essex.ac.uk
FREE

http://www.essex.ac.uk/social-science-methodology-school

Sociology Department, Lancaster University, UK ★★★

This is the site of the Department of Sociology at Lancaster University in the United Kingdom. It is very scholarly oriented and is a good launching point for academics and researchers. It has the usual links to staff, postgraduate students and courses and sociology sites of interest. The most valuable link is perhaps to the ESRC Social Sciences Information Gateway, for a wealth of Social Sciences resources, a site maintained by Bristol University.

KEYWORDS   Social Sciences, Sociology
AUDIENCE   Scholars, Social Scientists, Sociologists, Students
CONTACT   Catherine Fletcher, Jon O'Brien
   soa012@cent1.lancs.ac.uk;
   soajeo@cent1.lancs.ac.uk
FREE

http://www.comp.lancs.ac.uk/sociology/

Sociology at the University of Surrey (United Kingdom) ★★★

This is the Web site of the Department of Sociology at the University of Surrey in the United Kingdom. It is very well organized and research focused, and for those who like images and being able to visualize a physical location, they provide a visual guided tour of their department.

KEYWORDS Social Sciences, Sociology
AUDIENCE Scholars, Social Scientists, Sociologists, Students
CONTACT Department of Sociology, University of Surrey
www@soc.surrey.ac.uk
FREE

http://www.soc.surrey.ac.uk/

The Sociology of Cyberspace ★★★

The Sociology of Cyberspace is a collaborative project taught by professors from a variety of disciplines including sociology, physics, philosophy, business, art, English, women's studies, and computer science. It is being offered as a course at Bradley University in Peoria, Illinois, and this site accesses links to the class syllabus, required texts, and articles.

KEYWORDS Cyberspace, Sociology, Universities, University Courses
AUDIENCE Social Scientists, Sociologists, Students
CONTACT Steve Stone
stone@bradley.bradley.edu
FREE

http://lydia.bradley.edu/las/soc/syl/391/index.html

University of Pennsylvania - Department of Sociology ★★★

The University of Pennsylvania Department of Sociology focuses its attention upon five broad areas—Demography, Family-Gender Studies, Medical Sociology, Race and Ethnic Relations, Organizations and Work, and the Sociology of Culture. There are links to the faculty and their areas of expertise, to the graduate and undergraduate programs including requirements and admissions, and course descriptions. Other pointers lead to related sites, and the Population Studies Center.

KEYWORDS Pennsylvania, Sociology, Universities
AUDIENCE Social Scientists, Sociologists
CONTACT Diane Waters, Computer Resource Coordinator
waters@soc.sas.upenn.edu
FREE

http://www.ssc.upenn.edu/soc/Overview.html

University of Washington - Other Social Science Sites ★★★

This is an excellent source of social science links to use as a launching point for any sociology search. There are well over a hundred links to such things as the UK Social Science Resources, the US Office of Population Research, the University of Michigan, and the National Archives Center for Electronic Records.

KEYWORDS Internet Resources, Meta-Index (Social Science), Social Sciences, Sociology
AUDIENCE Social Scientists, Sociologists

Connections to Women's Issues
Women: careers, health, and public policy

Where can you find information about breast cancer, or self defense, or on juggling both home and a career? The Internet puts women in touch with an array of sources for help and collaboration on just about any issue women face today.

One unmoderated forum site, called "CyberSisters," is a place where women artists, performers, and writers explore their art, discuss creative issues, and network with other women. If you're interested in a gallery and publication vehicle for women artists, Cyber-Sisters provides access. You can also tap into "Women's Wire" for news and information about a wide range of women's issues.

(http://www.pmedia.com/Sisters) also, (http://gopher.wwire.net:8101/)

The Internet features forums and sites for women in German, Chinese, and English where users are invited to discuss feminist research, teachings, and other issues. The sites also provide information on upcoming conferences for, about, and by women that will be held throughout the world. Some sites are currently furnishing information on the UN Conference in Beijing. The agenda is expected to address the status of women in various countries, domestic violence, racism, marriage practices, international feminist movements, health, prostitution, and lesbian rights.

You can tap into an unmoderated forum on breast-cancer to learn how women face this and other life-threatening diseases. You can learn about various medical treatments via "The Gender-Related Electronic Forums." At this site you'll also tap into discussions for activists, educators and researchers run by CCOAR—the Coalition of Campus Organizations Addressing Rape. You'll also find information on careers for women in science and technology.

(http://cec.wustl.edu/~cs142/gender.html)

Also on the Net is the CMU Women's Center, which provides "chat lines" where women can discuss important issues. It serves as an outlet for the full range of viewpoints.

CONTACT Fred Nick,
fred@u.washington.edu
FREE

http://augustus.csscr.washington.edu/other_ss.html

WWW Virtual Library - Sociology ★★★

This is the launching point for a thorough surfing of Sociology and related fields such as Anthropology. It is run by Fordham University and includes visits to several other institutions' departments of Sociology, such as Princeton and the University of Colorado, as well as Specialized Resources such as archives, sociology topics and newsletters. General Resources are included as well.

KEYWORDS Libraries, Social Sciences, Sociology, Virtual Libraries
AUDIENCE Scholars, Social Scientists, Sociologists, Students
CONTACT Dr. Samuel R. Brown
brown@murray.fordham.edu
FREE

http://www.w3.org/hypertext/DataSources/bySubject/Sociology/Overview.html

Sociology – Women's Studies

West Chester University WWW Virtual Library for Sociology ★★★

This is the virtual library for Sociology maintained by West Chester University. It currently contains links to 26 sociology studies, as well as to the West Chester University Home Page.

KEYWORDS Social Sciences, Sociology
AUDIENCE Scholars, Social Scientists, Sociologists, Students
FREE

http://albie.wcupa.edu/ttreadwell/index.html

York University - Department of Sociology ★★

This Web site is in its infancy and detailed information for the Sociology department at York University in the United Kingdom is not yet available. However the site does have links to the current research interests which include media and popular culture, cultural change, language and conversation analysis, and modern European social thought. There are pointers to postgraduate sociology degrees and undergraduate courses, and more general information about studying at York as a postgraduate or undergraduate.

KEYWORDS Europe, Sociology, Universities
AUDIENCE Social Scientists, Sociologists, Students
FREE

http://www.york.ac.uk/aux/init/depts/soci-w.htm

Women's Studies

See also
Arts & Music · *Film & Video*
Computing & Mathematics · *Organizations*
Health & Medicine · *Reference*
Health & Medicine · *Sexuality*
Humanities & Social Sciences · *History*

Catt's Claws, a Frequently-Appearing Feminist Newsletter ★★★

This is a feminist newsletter which is emailed approximately three times a week. Not an interactive discussion net but an exchange of information, it is not sponsored by any organization. Some of the issues covered include a television movie dealing with lesbians and how to send your support to the station for airing a controversial movie, the nomination of the new Surgeon General by President Clinton, White House and congressional email addresses for mailing your comments, women's health issues, and anything else which is political and affects women.

KEYWORDS Feminism, Women's Issues
AUDIENCE Feminists, Men, Women, Women's Studies Students
CONTACT irenestuber@delphi.com
FREE

http://www.lm.com/~lmann/feminist/cattsclaws.html

Cybergrrl! ★★★★

This page provides links to a miscellany of Internet sites on the Internet. Some of the locations include Women's Issues on the 'Net, Non-Profit Info and Related Resources, Paris (via San Diego), The Louvre Museum, The CIA, Edgar Allen Poe - The Compleat Collection, HotWired, Anne Frank Page, PC Week Best Home Pages, HTML for Beginners, and more.

KEYWORDS France, Non Profit Organizations, Women's Issues
AUDIENCE Internet Users, Students (Secondary/University), Tourists, Women
CONTACT asherman@interport.net
FREE

http://www.interport.net/~asherman/surf.html

Directory of Professional Women's Organizations ★★★★

This is a gopher directory of organizations including the American Association Of University Women (AAUW), Association of Junior Leagues, The Black Women Physicians Project, Catalyst, The National Association for Female Executives, Inc. (NAFE), Soroptimist International of the Americas, and Women in Communications, Inc.

KEYWORDS Professional Organizations, Women's Groups, Women's Issues
AUDIENCE Men, Professional Women, Women, Women Business Owners
FREE

gopher://path.net:8101/00/Work/women%27s_professional_orgs

Feminist Activist Resources on the Net ★★★★

This guide is particularly oriented toward connecting Feminists to useful resources on the Internet. Some of the linked resources include current feminist issues, reproductive rights, domestic violence, women and work, women's organizations, general resources for political activists, suggestions for current feminist action, feminist fun and games, soc.feminism, gender-related electronic forums etc.

KEYWORDS Feminism, Political Activism, Reproductive Rights, Women's Issues
AUDIENCE Feminists, Political Activists, Women, Women's Studies Students
CONTACT Sarah Stapleton-Gray
sarahg@netcom.com
FREE

http://www.clark.net/pub/s-gray/feminist.html

Feminist WWW Sites ★★★★

This FTP site provides a collection of WWW sites related to women's studies, feminism, lesbian issues, gender issues, and more. Some of the references inlcude employment opportunities, college courses, womens health issues, current feminist issues, news and information, a Women's Guide to the Internet, Usenet groups, women in computing, domestic partner benefits, gay youth, women in comics, women in TV and film, Nancy Drew, music, Internet tools, and much more.

KEYWORDS Employment, Feminism, WWW (World Wide Web), Women's Health
AUDIENCE Actors, Artists, Feminists, Gays, Internet Users, Lesbians
CONTACT Amy Goodloe
agoodloe@best.com
FREE

ftp://ftp.best.com/pub/agoodloe/internet-women/feminist-websites.txt

Gender Issues Directory ★★★★

The Gender Issues Directory publishes texts on gender studies, women, and feminism, with a particular focus on women in computing. There are pointers to articles such as 'Gender Differences in Computer-Mediated Communication' and 'Why Are There So Few Female Computer Scientists?' There are also links to a gender issues bibliography and other gender-related sites including information on soc.feminism and the Women's Studies gopher at the University of Maryland.

KEYWORDS Gender Issues, Women's Issues, Women's Studies
AUDIENCE Communications Researchers, Computer Professionals, Women, Women's Rights Activists
FREE

http://cpsr.org/cpsr/gender/gender.html

Gender Issues and Computing ★★

This directory contains files related to gender and computing. There are several papers concerned with women participating in discussion groups, harassment of women within Usenet, email and chats, as well as women entering the field of computing.

KEYWORDS Computing, Feminism, Gender Issues, Internet Issues
AUDIENCE Feminists, Men, Sociologists, Women
CONTACT amcgee@netcom.com
FREE

ftp://ftp.netcom.com/pub/amcgee/gender/

Internet-Women FTP Directory ★★★

This ftp directory is for files and archives of interest to the subscribers to internet-women-help and internet-women-info. Many of the files include copies of interesting posts from one or both of the lists. Other documents have been collected from other sources. Some of the topics include feminist websites, finding good lists, lesbian-gay lists, newsgroup -FAQ lists, and more.

KEYWORDS Feminism, History, Lesbianism, Women's Issues
AUDIENCE Feminists, Internet Users, Lesbians, Women
CONTACT Amy Goodloe
agoodloe@best.com
FREE

ftp://ftp.best.com/pub/agoodloe/internet-women/

Karoline von Guenderrode Pages ★★★★

Devoted to the life and works of German intellectual Karoline von Guenderrode (1780-1806), this page includes a small number of her works, two bibliographies, several textual excursi, and two maps of Germany from the turn of the 19th century. The page may expand into a larger series focusing on German women intellectuals in the late 18th and early 19th centuries. This is an intriguing source for materials in a largely unexplored area of German literature and women's intellectual expression.

KEYWORDS Germany, Literature, Women's Issues, Women's Studies
AUDIENCE Educators (University), Germans, Literary Scholars, Students (University)
CONTACT ccampbe@reed.edu
FREE

http://www.reed.edu/~ccampbel/Guenderrode.html

The Minnesota Women's Center (MWC) ★★

The Minnesota Women's Center (MWC) gives information on resources, services, programs and activities of interest to women and related to women's issues.

KEYWORDS Databases, Feminism, Women's Issues, Women's Studies
AUDIENCE Educators (University), Women, Women's Studies Students
CONTACT mnwomen@maroon.tc.umn.edu
FREE

gopher://rodent.cis.umn.edu:11112/

Women ★★★

This page is a list of resources related to women's issues. Links include information on abortion and reproductive rights, breast cancer, midwifery and home birth, and women in politics.

KEYWORDS Asia, Feminism
AUDIENCE Feminists, General Public, Women
CONTACT igc-info@igc.apc.org
FREE

http://www.igc.apc.org/igc/www.women.html

Womon Gopher ★★★

A large gopher site containing numerous resources for those interested in feminism and women's health topics. Examples of resources include African-American Women in the Sciences, Women's Public Policy, Women's Environment and Development Organization, Women's and Gender Studies, Center for Women's studies in Education, Koordinationsstelle fuer Frauenforschung, Linz Austria and Chicana-Latina Studies at UCLA. Pointers to many other gophers and mailing lists are also included.

KEYWORDS Feminism, Politics, Women's Health, Women's Studies
AUDIENCE Activists, Feminists, Sociologists, Women
CONTACT Calvin Boyer
cjboyer@uci.edu
FREE

gopher://peg.cwis.uci.edu:7000/11/gopher.welcome/peg/women

Women of Achievement and Herstory, a Frequently-Appearing Newsletter ★★

This is a newsletter about notable women in history. Anniversaries of famous women are given such as Susan B. Anthony and Sarah Fuller. There are also book reviews and daily quotations.

KEYWORDS Feminism, History, Women's Issues
AUDIENCE Feminists, Historians, Men, Women, Women's Studies Students
CONTACT irenestuber@delphi.com
FREE

http://www.lm.com/~lmann/feminist/achievement.html

Women's Homepage ★★★★

This site offers a collection of online writings and resources by, about, and for women. It gives further references to a large and varied collection of gopher and WWW sites which relate to women. The topics include Women in Computer Science and Engineering, Women's Studies Programs, Women in Academia and Industry, Gender and Sexuality, Women's Health, etc.

KEYWORDS Feminism, Women's Issues, Women's Studies
AUDIENCE Researchers, Students (Secondary/University), Women, Women's Studies Educators
CONTACT Jesssie Stickgold-Sarah
sorokin@mit.edu
FREE

http://www.mit.edu:8001/people/sorokin/women/index.html

Internet

Career & Employment	453
Internet Access	453
Internet Business	455
Internet Communications	458
Internet Issues	461
Internet Protocols	462
Internet Resources	462
Internet Security	470
Internet Services	472
Internet Tools	476
Networking	480
Organizations	482
Virtual Communities	482

Career & Employment

See also
Education · *Universities - Europe*
Popular Culture & Entertainment · *Multimedia*

Bay Area Multimedia Technology Alliance Home Page

The Bay Area Multimedia Technology Alliance (BAMTA) Home Page, part of the Web Form Technology Development Project, provides Web space for job postings of multimedia, Internet and Web technology related jobs. Companies and organizations are encouraged to submit job openings using an online form, while individuals can browse through the opening lists or search interested openings found in the BAMTA searchable databank.

KEYWORDS	Employment, Internet, Jobs, Multimedia
AUDIENCE	Job Seekers, Multimedia Artists, Web Developers
CONTACT	Dr. Susie W. Chu chu@mlds-www.arc.nasa.gov
FREE	

http://equinox.arc.nasa.gov:80/form/BAMTA/

This Is Cyberzone

Cyberzone is an online job and career resource. It bills itself as a continuously evolving frontier, featuring cutting-edge ways to keep up on the ever-changing landscape of life, careers, and culture. Employer profiles and information on the high technology job scene are positioned particularly prominently.

KEYWORDS	Computers, Employment, Technology
AUDIENCE	Internet Users, Students, Technology professionals
FREE	

http://monster.monster.com:81/b/imagemap/homestrip2?191,45

Internet Access

See also
Communications · *Telecommunications*
Computing & Mathematics · *Companies*
Internet · *Internet Services*

America Online

The America Online ftp site provides access to America Online TCP/IP (Transmission Control Protocol/Internet Protocol) client software. The beta version of this software is currently available but they do not provide technical support until it is released as production software. This client enables access to the America Online private information network where you can play online games, download software etc. Beta testing bug lists and corrections are available. A program to Unzip files and an index of files available at this site can also be accessed. Installation instructions for Macintosh users and the upgrade process for America Online for Windows are also documented at this site.

KEYWORDS	Commercial Online Services, Computer Networks, Software, TCP/IP
AUDIENCE	Computer Game Enthusiasts, Computer Users, Macintosh Users, Windows Users
CONTACT	Bob postmaster@aol.com
FREE	

ftp://ftp.aol.com/

Funet Information Services

Funet is a non-profit organization providing communication services to its members. It also provides access to different information services (Gopher, WAIS, World Wide Web) and mail gateways (X.400, Elisa, Mailnet, IBM X.400). An extensive public domain file archive nic.funet.fi is one of the biggest in the Internet. There are more than 20 gigabytes of free software, documents, manuals, etc. available.

KEYWORDS	Finland, Internet Service Providers
AUDIENCE	Computer Users, Educators (University), Internet Users, Researchers, Students (University)
CONTACT	info@funet.fi
FREE	

http://ftp.funet.fi/funet/FUNET-english.html

Hamilton-Wentworth FreeNet

The Hamilton-Wentworth FreeNet provides Usenet news, email, and much more to local subscribers and interested individuals. Information about Hamilton, Ontario, and its surrounding area is available here. Additional links include information about the FreeNet Community Networking projects, as well as telnet, gopher, and WWW links to other FreeNets across Canada and the rest of the world.

KEYWORDS	Canada, Virtual Communities
AUDIENCE	Canadians, Internet Users
CONTACT	Pat Toal pat@freenet.hamilton.on.ca
FREE	

http://www.freenet.hamilton.on.ca

telnet://freenet.hamilton.on.ca

How To Select an Internet Service Provider ★★★

This page is a guide on how to select an Internet Service Provider and is written by the president and CEO of UUNET Technologies, Inc. The selection criteria presented includes network topology, network link speeds, high speed backbone, technology, and staff. This text gives new users a good idea of what kinds of questions to ask themselves and the providers as they shop around for service.

KEYWORDS   Consumer Guides, Internet Access Providers, Internet Service Providers
AUDIENCE   Business Professionals, Computer Users, Education Administrators, Internet Users
CONTACT   alternet-info@uunet.uu.net
FREE

http://web.cnam.fr:80/Network/Internet-access/how_to_select.html

Human Factor ★★★

The Human Factor is dedicated to helping unconnected humans navigate the information pathways of the Internet. This page contains links to a variety of areas including shareware, downloadable images, videos and animation, utilities and tools, a 'hot links' page, etc. To keep with the spirit of the Internet, the producers are offering free pages to anyone doing worthwhile non-profit types of things.

KEYWORDS   Internet Guides, Shareware
AUDIENCE   Business Professionals, Computer Users, Internet Users, Nonprofit Organizations
CONTACT   scott@human.com
FREE

http://www.human.com:80/index.html

Kaapelisolmu - Kabelknuten - Knot at the Cable ★★

Located at the Helsinki City Library, The Knot at the Cable gives the public free access to the Internet. It functions as an electronic publishing house for non-governmental organizations, cultural movements, and individuals. This site gives links to information about Finland as well as links to other sites on the Internet.

KEYWORDS   Finland, Internet Issues
AUDIENCE   Finns, Helsinki Residents
CONTACT   solmu@kaapeli.fi
FREE

http://www.kaapeli.fi

List of W3 Servers in France ★★★

This is a meta-index to all of the Web servers in France with maps, keyword search, and the opportunity to register a new server that is listed.

KEYWORDS   France, Networks
AUDIENCE   Business Professionals, French, Travelers
FREE

http://web.urec.fr/docs/www_list_fr.html

Networking Computing Devices, Inc. ★★★★

Network Computing Devices, Inc. is a manufacturer of information access products that enable Internet users to conduct financial transactions over the Internet. Their products Z-Mail, a cross-platform (Windows, UNIX, Mac, and character terminals) email system, and Mariner, an Internet access and navigation tool, offer access to Internet resources. This page gives access to the company backround, career opportunities and product information.

KEYWORDS   Computer Networks, Information Technology, Internet Services, Z-Mail
AUDIENCE   Computer Networkers, Email Users, Internet Users
CONTACT   webmaster@ncd.com
COST

http://www.ncd.com

Omaha Free-Net ★★

Omaha Free-Net is a communication and Internet service that provides citizens with free electronic access to valuable community information. Some of the items available to users are links to local Omaha resources on the Internet, such as schools, medical centers, housing, jobs, and libraries. Other links are to general information about Omaha and to the home pages of Omaha Free-Net's sponsors.

KEYWORDS   Community Networks, Freenets, Nebraska
AUDIENCE   Community Activists, Nebraska Residents
CONTACT   nherzog@unomaha.edu
FREE

http://omahafreenet.org/

P/F/M News & Mail Uebersicht ★★★

P/F/M...News & Mail is a German-language Web site produced by an Internet Provider. Besides general Internet hookup information, tools and statistics, there are several examples of servers run by their clients and an opportunity to directly send an email for further questions.

KEYWORDS   Germany, Internet Access Providers, Internet Tools
AUDIENCE   German-Speaking World
CONTACT   info@PFM-Mainz.de
FREE

http://www.PFM-Mainz.DE/

Providers of Commercial Internet Access (POCIA) ★★★

POCIA is a directory of commercial Internet access providers in the US and Canada as well as other countries. A complete list of regional and nationwide service providers (for US and Canada) is available.

KEYWORDS   Internet Access Providers, Internet Service Providers
AUDIENCE   Business Professionals, Internet Users, Marketing Specialists
CONTACT   celestin@olympus.net
FREE

http://www.teleport.com/~cci/directories/pocia/pocia.html

Sunshine Coast ★★★★

The Sunshine Coast Community Network provides Internet services to the many small communities of the Sunshine Coast, 20 miles from Vancouver. It includes links to government resources, other Canadian WWW sites, resources for exploring the Net, and technical support - including software and books.

KEYWORDS   Canada, Internet Access Providers
AUDIENCE   Canada Residents, Community Activists, Community Groups, Network Developers, Network Users
CONTACT   webmaster@sunshine.net
COST

http://www.sunshine.net/sunshine.html

Surfnet InfoServices Home Page ★★★

The Surfnet InfoServices Home Page contains information on the networks that it supplies for education and research groups. The page contains links to Surfnet, a network for the academic and research community, and VSNU, an association of Universities in the Netherlands. There are links to gophers, FTP archives, and pointers to other Web servers.

KEYWORDS   Information Services, Network Servers
AUDIENCE   Dutch, Educators, Researchers, Students
CONTACT   infoservices@surfnet.nl
FREE

http://www.nic.surfnet.nl

Three Rivers Free-Net ★★★★

The Three Rivers Free-Net serves the Pittsburgh, Pennsylvania area as a central place for community networking and resource sharing. Users can find local programs and projects for education, health care, sports, social events, and business connections. Although this FreeNet does not currently offer email accounts, it does provide lists of Internet providers as a public service.

KEYWORDS   Community Networks, Freenets, Pennsylvania
AUDIENCE   Community Activists, Pennsylvania Residents
CONTACT   webmaster@trfn.pgh.pa.us
FREE

http://trfn.pgh.pa.us/

The Well ★★★

The Well is an online service which offers Internet resources such as Telnet, FTP, Gopher, Usenet News, and online conferencing. No SLIP/PPP services are offered at this time. Dial-up lines are available and access is available through the CPN Compuserve Network. The Well's gopher site offers information on issues concerning cyberSpace, the environment, and many social issues. Information on rates can be attained by connecting to their gopher server. Those dialup users who are members of MCI's Friends and

Family can receive 20% off the costs of their calls to the Well's dialup lines.

KEYWORDS Chat Groups, Commercial Online Services, Telnet
AUDIENCE Activists, BBS Users, Californians, Computer Users
CONTACT   info@well.com
COST

gopher://gopher.well.sf.ca.us

telnet://well.sf.ca.us

Youngstown Free-Net ★★★

This is a gopher server of the Youngstown Free-Net, located at Youngstown State University, Ohio. It contains information about the community of Youngstown, Ohio, such as the animal hospital, businesses, the industrial park, the government center, library systems, the post office, television and radio stations, and Youngstown State University. This network allows users to access the Internet's resources for free.

KEYWORDS Internet Access Providers, Ohio
AUDIENCE Computer Users, Educators, Internet Users, Students
CONTACT   Lou Anschuetz
          lou@ysu.edu
FREE

http://yfn.ysu.edu/

gopher://yfn.ysu.edu/

Internet Business

See also
Business & Economics · *Advertising & Marketing*
Internet · *Internet Services*
Popular Culture & Entertainment · *Shopping*

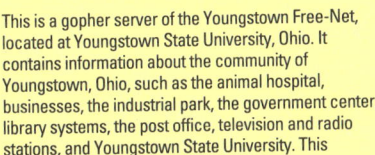 Ads International ★★★

This is the WWW site of Ads International, an online advertisement agency based in Victoria, British Columbia. Some of the services and products advertised include real estate, artists, art work, alternative medicine, hotel chains, investment opportunities, and stamps.

KEYWORDS Advertising, Canada, Internet Directories
AUDIENCE Commercial Advertisers, Internet Users
CONTACT   Steve Switzer
          sswitzer@dataflux.bc.ca
FREE

http://vvv.com/adsint

 BizWeb ★★★

BizWeb is an Internet based information server designed to bring product information together in one place, making shopping quick and easy. Users click on categories which will bring up links to commercial sites. The site lists over 600 different business pages with a few big graphics that take a long time to download. Categories of goods and services links from this site include areas such traditional areas as computing, consulting, and networking, as well as other areas like publishing, music, clothes, and florists.

KEYWORDS Commerce, Internet Marketing, Online Shopping
AUDIENCE Business Professionals, Clients, Computer Professionals, Consumers
CONTACT   Bob Baggerman
          bob@bizweb.com
FREE

http://www.bizweb.com/

Connections to Careers
Get a life!

Briskin's Internet Career Finder!

Many of today's hottest jobs aren't listed in the newspaper--they're here, on the Web--and Jeff Briskin can help you find them. Simply connect with one or more of the following dedicated free searchable on-line employment databases. They all provide keyword access to thousands of positions, most of which you can apply for electronically. Company profiles and career advice are also offered, and several services allow you to store your resume in a resume library that employers can search to find you! So, let Briskin's Internet Career Finder put the power of the Internet to work for your career.

Thinking of changing careers? There are many questions to consider. What will it take to start over? What kind of salary can I expect? Where can I find help for getting a job? The Internet provides a plethora of information, resources and job listings to help get you started in a new career.

Maybe you're happy with your career but feel your skills are unappreciated at your current workplace. You can find specific career sites on the Internet to help narrow your search down. Many career sites provide invaluable information about your chances of obtaining a new job in a given field (including advice on moving to another part of the world to get the job and salary you want). If you are over 40 years old, you can even find sites that cater to those making a transition after losing a job.

Get an insider look at jobs available, but not advertised in the newspaper, by checking out "Briskin's Internet Career Finder." This site provides assistance in searching dedicated online employment databases at many corporations in the U.S. and around the world. There's even a connection to large U.S. recruitment agencies, as well as an online resume bank.

(http://web.ixl.net:8000/briskin/)

If your career choice is in the arts and entertainment industries, then "ArtsNet Career Services Center" provides links to databases for jobs in film, theater, television, etc.

(http://artsnet.heinz.cmu.edu/career/career.html)

There is also the "Careers Service" site to help you if you're looking to enroll in postgraduate courses to enhance your chances of getting a job. It also delineates specific steps in making a career change.

(http://www.staffs.ac.uk/sands/care/careers/html)

Business Sources on the Net (BSN) ★★

This gopher contains more than 200 business related Internet resources including gopher holes, World Wide Web pages, ftp sites, listservs, and newsgroups. Subdirectories such as Accounting, Investments, Personnel, Management, and America help to divide the list of resources into more manageable segments.

KEYWORDS Accounting, Investment, Management, Meta-Index (Business/Economics)

456 Internet Business

AUDIENCE Acountants, Economists, Human Resources Departments, Investors, Managers
CONTACT Diane Kovacs
dkovacs@kentvm
FREE

gopher://refmac.kent.edu:70/1D-1%3A2577%3ABusiness

 ### Come In From Out Of The Spam

Come in from Out of the Spam is the website of Strangelove Internet Enterprises (SIE), an Internet business publishing, consulting, and training organization. SIE published 'The Internet Business Journal' in 1993, and 'How to Advertise on the Internet' in 1994. This page has links to these two publications as well as to The Internet Training Company, Internet Advertising Review, Strangelove's Essays, and more.

KEYWORDS Advertising, Internet Publishing, Training
AUDIENCE Advertising Professionals, Internet Professionals, Marketing Professionals, Publishers, Web Developers
CONTACT Michael Strangelove
sie@strangelove.com
FREE

http://www.phoenix.ca/sie

 ### Cybersight

Cybersight is part of an Internet marketing firm, focusing on interactivity in their Web sites. On their Web page, users may find examples of their products and fun interactive games to play. Features include an interactive Graffiti Wall upon which users may design their own graffiti contributions, a Realtime Chatter Web IRC, and a Choose Your Own Adventure story that is designed by users. You may also play a game of scrabble or try to decipher a picture puzzle.

KEYWORDS Interactivity, Internet Relay Chat, Puzzles
AUDIENCE Internet Users, Web Developers
CONTACT imi@cybersight.com
FREE

http://cybersight.com/cgi-bin/cs/s?main.gmml

DigiCash Home Page

This is the home page for DigiCash, an electronic payment system that allows for secure electronic transfer of funds along with the anonymity of spending paper cash. Users can obtain detailed information about the DigiCash system, including information on how security and anonymity is implemented, as well as obtaining the client software necessary to use DigiCash. There is also information available on becoming a DigiCash merchant, as well as links to merchants that accept DigiCash.

KEYWORDS Electronic Money Transfers, Financial Services, Internet Commerce
AUDIENCE Banking Industry Analysts, Business Professionals, Electronic Money Users, Internet Users
CONTACT info@digicash.com
FREE

http://www.digicash.com/

Economics and the Internet

This directory, updated on 11/14/93, contains a series of four articles about the Internet and Economics. One article entitled 'Some Economics of the Internet' details the history, technology, and cost structure of the Internet. The authors describe a possible smart-market mechanism for pricing traffic on the Internet, arguing that usage-based pricing is likely to come sooner or later and that some serious thought should be devoted to devising a sensible, rather than haphazard, system of usage-based pricing.

KEYWORDS Economics, Internet Marketing
AUDIENCE Business Analysts, Business Researchers, Business Students, Internet Users
CONTACT Hal R. Varian
Hal.Varian@umich.edu
FREE

ftp://gopher.econ.lsa.umich.edu/pub/Papers/

 ### First Virtual Home Page

This is the home page of First Virtual, an entity that has established an electronic payment system whereby users can securely transfer funds over a network like the Internet. First Virtual differs from other electronic payment schemes in that it does not rely on some form of encryption to keep transactions from being compromised. Instead, it uses a telephone call verification system combined with regular email to securely transfer payments electronically. Users can obtain information on the First Virtual payment system, sign up for an account, or get info on becoming a merchant with the First Virtual system.

KEYWORDS Digital Transactions, Electronic Money Transfers, Internet Commerce, Secure Transactions
AUDIENCE Banking Industry Analysts, Business Professionals, Electronic Money Users, Internet Users
CONTACT webmaster@fv.com, info@fv.com
FREE

http://www.fv.com/

 ### I/PRO (Internet Profiles Corporation)

I/PRO (Internet Profiles Corporation) provides systems that allow the independent measurement and analysis of Web site usage. These systems enable organizations that own or manage Web sites to understand how and by whom their sites are being used. I/PRO is a member of the CommerceNet consortium. This system allows you to analyze the usage of your World Wide Web server, combining information from your server's log files with I/PRO's large database of site and user profiles. You can receive summary statistics on usage, demographics of the people and companies accessing your site, and even analyses of the efficiency with which your Web server is constructed. You can obtain a guest account to test the system which allows you to see how these reports actually work.

KEYWORDS Internet Marketing, Internet Statistics, Web Statistics
AUDIENCE Advertising Professionals, Internet Marketing Professionals, Web Managers
CONTACT info@ipro.com
FREE

http://www.ipro.com./

 ### Interactive Publishing Alert

Interactive Publishing Alert is a twice-monthly newsletter tracking trends and developments in the electronic newspaper and magazine field. Topics include publishing on the Web, content provider deals, online advertising models, attracting women to online publications, and using electronic publishing in global markets. There are interviews of leading industry personalities such as Netscape's Marc Andreessen and Omni's Keith Ferrell, as well as reviews of online publications such as HotWired. According to the site producers, 'subscribers include Microsoft, America Online, Ziff-Davis, The Los Angeles Times, US News & World Report, The Financial Times of London, La Nacion of Argentina, and many other major media and technology companies worldwide.'

KEYWORDS Advertising, Electronic Publishing, Online Magazines
AUDIENCE Advertising Professionals, Internet Professionals, Marketing Professionals, Publishers, Web Developers
CONTACT Rosalind Resnick
rosalind@harrison.win.net
FREE

http://www.netcreations.com/ipa/

 ### Internet Business Journal

A monthly magazine published both on paper and electronically, the Internet Business Journal contains articles for those who seek to advance their business through utilizing the Internet either as a medium for advertising or a total business environment. Numerous indices of services and people using the Internet in their business campaigns are also available.

KEYWORDS Consulting, Internet Commerce, Internet Marketing
AUDIENCE Business Analysts, Business Professionals, Business Researchers, Entrepreneurs
CONTACT Aneurin Bosley
abosley@ott.hookup.net
FREE

gopher://gopher.fonorola.net/11/Internet%20Business%20Journal/

ftp://ftp.fonorola.net/Internet%20Business%20Journal/

 ### Internet Distribution Services

Internet Distribution Services, Inc. provides electronic marketing, publishing, and distribution services on the Internet. This site allows users to link to some of the sites that IDS has built for its customers, and provides information on the products and services of the company.

KEYWORDS Consulting, Internet Commerce, Internet Marketing, Internet Publishing
AUDIENCE Internet Users, Marketing Professionals

CONTACT   marcf@netcom.com
FREE

http://www.center.org

Internet Group ★★★

The Internet Group is a Web center of information about conducting business on the Internet. It is regularly updated with Internet industry statistics, featured articles on Internet business issues and references to sources of information about conducting business on the Internet. The site also has a listing of selected new commercial sites.

KEYWORDS   Consulting, Internet Commerce, Internet Services
AUDIENCE   Business Professionals, Entrepreneurs
CONTACT   Michael Bauer
           bauer@tig.com
FREE

http://tig.com/IBC/

The Internet Marketing Group (IMG) Incorporated ★★★★

This site provides access to a small organization known as the Internet Marketing Group (IMG), Gateway to the Borderless Marketplace. The purpose of the IMG is to bring the vast resources of the Internet to the small and medium-sized business owner worldwide. The IMG offers its services in advertising, online retail sales, Web page development, computer hardware/software, and technical support. Some of the resources here include - Marketplace (classified advertisements for local Seattle vendors), a list of non-profit organizations on the WWW, a guide to Pacific Northwest Cyberspace, and information about IMG Incorporated.

KEYWORDS   Internet Marketing, Small Business
AUDIENCE   Business Owners, Business Professionals, Marketing Professionals, Small Businesses Owners
CONTACT   Ken Brown
           brownie@halcyon.com
FREE

ftp://ftp.halcyon.com/local/IMG/

Internet Registration Templates ★★★

This site contains templates for users who wish to register with InterNIC (Network Information Center). There are templates in this directory for specific regional areas including the United States, Canada, Europe, and Asia, as well as general instructions, and forms for higher registrations such as for connected networks.

KEYWORDS   DNS (Domain Name Server), Internet Protocols, Internet Standards, Networking
AUDIENCE   Internet Access Providers, Internet Users
CONTACT   Hung Vu
           hungv@fonorola.com
FREE

gopher://nis.fonorola.net:70/11/templates

Connections to Wish Lists

. . . and another thing I'd like is . . .

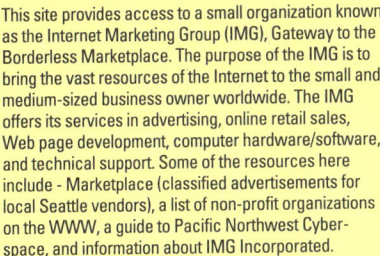

If you spend a lot of time surfing the 'Net, you might have a few suggestions that would make the Internet more complete than it is at present.

Now you can sound off and voice your opinions about what you would like to see on the World Wide Web that isn't currently there, or present ideas to better organize the Internet.

The "Things I'd Like to See in CyberSpace" site gives you an opportunity to email your wishes and have them posted on the site's home page.

Thus far, for instance, participants have suggested consolidating the search engines (www, ftp, gopher) and creating a home page for political leaders in which constituents could post their complaints about the performance of that leader, as well as air their views on critical issues.

Got an idea?

(http://www.clark.net/pub/journalism/wishes.html)

Liberty Hill Cyberwerks ★★★

This gopher server gives information about Liberty Hill Cyberwerks, an Internet consulting firm. The company provides training and education services about the Internet, and develops and maintains Internet resources, such as gopher and WWW servers, for clients. The server also gives a list of upcoming seminars being arranged by the company.

KEYWORDS   Consulting, Internet Training
AUDIENCE   Business Professionals, Computer Users, Computing Consultants
CONTACT   Eric S. Theise
           verve@cyberwerks.com
FREE

gopher://cyberwerks.com/

Multimedia Ink Design Internet Ad Emporium ★★★

The Internet Ad Emporium is an online 'mall' which allows businesses to advertise their products. The main focus is on travel-related companies; users will find in-depth information about several cruise lines and travel service providers, and links to smaller retailers of more diverse products. Interested businesses can find information about advertising their products.

KEYWORDS   Online Shopping, Retailers
AUDIENCE   Internet Shoppers, Travelers
CONTACT   Rick Degelsmith
           rdegel@mmink.com
FREE

http://mmink.cts.com

NetBill Project Home Page ★★★

The home page of the NetBill Project offers access to information about the project under development at the Information Networking Institute of Carnegie Mellon University. NetBill is an Internet commerce system optimized for network-delivered services. Its creators envision users being able to automatically pay for documents, CPU cycles, or other network resources.

KEYWORDS   Digital Transactions
AUDIENCE   Banking Industry Analysts, Business Professionals, Electronic Money Users, Internet Users
CONTACT   Marvin A. Sirbu
           sirbu+@cmu.edu
FREE

http://www.ini.cmu.edu/netbill/

NetCheque Electronic Payment System ★★★

This page provides a brief description of the NetCheque electronic payment system, which allows users to send electronic payments via email. Users can access information about the NetCheque payment system, read academic papers written by NetCheque's creators, or sign up for an account so that they can use the NetCheque system.

KEYWORDS Digital Transactions, Electronic Money Transfers
AUDIENCE Banking Industry Analysts, Business Professionals, Electronic Money Users, Internet Users
CONTACT netcheque@isi.edu
FREE

http://nii-server.isi.edu/info/NetCheque/

Network Payment Mechanisms and Digital Cash ★★★★

This page contains resources related to secure electronic money transfers over networks such as the Internet. There are many different schemes being implemented by different companies, and this page indexes them all. Users will find detailed background information on the various schemes, as well as pointers to the individual digital cash systems.

KEYWORDS Digital Transactions, Electronic Money Transfers
AUDIENCE Banking Industry Analysts, Business Professionals, Electronic Money Users, Internet Users
CONTACT Michael Peirce
mepeirce@alf2.tcd.ie
FREE

http://ganges.cs.tcd.ie/mepeirce/project.html

Print Publications Related to Business Use of the Internet ★★★★

This page contains basic information on publications related to the Internet, giving the title, author, publisher, price, links to the publication's home page, (if it has one), along with links from Net Happenings and the Internet Marketing Archives that announce or review the publication.

KEYWORDS Books, Internet Business
AUDIENCE Business Professionals, Internet Users
CONTACT Cliff Kurtzman
Cliff.Kurtzman@Tenagra.com
FREE

http://arganet.tenagra.com/Tenagra/books.html

Strangelove Internet Enterprises ★★★★

Strangelove Internet Enterprises (SIE) is an Internet business publishing, consulting, and training organization. This site contains links to the Internet Business Journal, one of the first outlets for discussion and commentary of commercial resources on the Internet. Other areas include the Internet Advertising Review, which contains excerpts of articles evaluating the content and design of commercial sites, as well as Erotica and Internet Marketing, which examines the use of erotica on the Internet. In addition, Strangelove Enterprises sponsors a contest which encourages Internet users to vote for their favorite Internet entrepreneur or storefront.

KEYWORDS Internet Issues, Internet Marketing
AUDIENCE Business Professionals, Internet Professionals, Internet Users, Marketing Professionals
FREE

http://www.phoenix.ca/sie/index.html

Virtual Office Home Page ★★★★

The Virtual Office Home Page presents a directory of Internet resources under some of the most popular headings. Each area has its own contact information and consulting services for interested businesses and individuals. Users can browse through categories such as Daily (news, weather, TV listings), Kids (educational and kids sites), Shop (online malls), Business (securities, investing, economics) HospitalNet (medical and health resources), Fun (sports, games, horoscopes) and much more.

KEYWORDS Internet Business
AUDIENCE General Public, Internet Users
CONTACT feedback@virtual.office.com
FREE

http://virtual.office.com/

Welcome to Pizza Hut! ★★★★

Users can order a pizza to be delivered by providing their name, address and phone number. At the time of this writing, this delivery service is available only in Santa Cruz, California USA.

KEYWORDS Pizzas
AUDIENCE General Public, Food Enthusiasts
CONTACT webmaster@PizzaHut.com
FREE

http://www.pizzahut.com/

Welcome to Web Communications ★★★

Web Communications is a company in the business of providing server space for WWW pages and FTP directories. Information is available on setting up an account with Web Commnications, pricing and services provided, as well as a selection of pointers to HTML and WWW tutorials. Users can also browse through the current sites available through Web Communications.

KEYWORDS Internet Publishing, Internet Service Providers
AUDIENCE Internet Publishers, Internet Users
CONTACT Thomas Leavitt
info@webcom.com
FREE

http://www.webcom.com/

ftp://ftp.webcom.com/

World Wide Web Development by Webhead Inc. ★★★

Webhead is a high-end Web Development company based in San Francisco, California. Webhead specializes in creating Web sites using advanced programming techniques including Java, and real or virtual spaces with VRML modeling. The site has useful resources including a wide variety of Web development information in conjunction with a published book.

KEYWORDS Consulting Services, VRML, Web Development, Web Services
AUDIENCE HTML Users, Internet Users, Programmers
CONTACT Behram Antia
behram@webhead.com
FREE

http://www.webhead.com/

Internet Communications

See also
Communications · *Telecommunications*
Internet · *Internet Services*
Internet · *Networking*

Best of the Web ★★★

The best of the Web Awards for 1994 are listed on this site, as well as information regarding the Best of the Web 1995 nominations. The Best of the Web awards serve to recognize the strides that have been made using the World Wide Web as a communications medium. There were 13 categories in 1994, some of which included the best in Commercial Services, Educational Services, Entertainment Sites, Professional Services, Navigational Aids, and Best Overall Site. There were also awards for technical categories such as interactivity, design, and use of multimedia.

KEYWORDS Web Design, Web Browsing, Internet Communications
AUDIENCE Internet Professionals, Internet Users, Librarians
CONTACT CWIS at SUNY Buffalo
wings@wings.buffalo.edu
FREE

http://wings.buffalo.edu/contest/

Bulletin Board Home Page ★★★

This group of 'bulletin boards' works not unlike Usenet - each area has a distinct topic, usually related to stories and themes published in articles within Time-Warner's Pathfinder, and users can read each other's comments and post their own for public viewing. Currently, dozens of different topics are available, indexed both by subject and related publication. Many Time-Warner magazines (Vibe, People, Entertainment Weekly, Time) are represented.

Keywords Hollywood, Magazines, Personalities
Audience Film Enthusiasts, Gossips, Internet Users, Music Enthusiasts
Contact webmaster@pathfinder.com
Free

http://bigmouth.pathfinder.com:80/pathfinder/bbs-home.html

CUD (Computer Underground Digest)

The CUD (Computer Underground Digest) directory lists dozens of archived 'Zines,' or electronic magazines that cater to specific audiences. This directory is organized by subject matter, including headings like Cyberculture, Music, Non Fiction, and Religious categories

Keywords Electronic Magazines, Magazines, Zines
Audience Cyberculture Enthusiasts, Cybernauts, Internet Users, Music Enthusiasts
Contact rita@etext.archive.umich.edu
Free

ftp://etext.archive.umich.edu/pub/Zines-by-subject/

Finding Email Addresses

This document offers tips on finding email addresses. How to find an email address for someone who may be in college, in the military, a Usenet contributor, a 'Net Personality,' or who has some other useful characterization that can be used.

Keywords Email, Internet Communications, Internet Search Tools
Audience Email Users, Internet Newcomers, Internet Users
Contact ftpkeeper@sunsite.unc.edu
Free

ftp://sunsite.unc.edu/pub/docs/about-the-net/libsoft/email_address.txt

Frame Relay Forum ★★★

This page provides access to information about the Frame Relay Forum, an association of corporate members comprised of vendors, carriers, users and consultants committed to the implementation of Frame Relay in accordance with national and international standards. The group was formed in 1991 and maintains chapters in North America, Europe, Australia/New Zealand and recently in Japan. Besides offering the information on the membership and meeting schedules of the Frame Relay Forum, there are technical resources such as the Frame Relay Application Guide, Frame Relay Glossary, Carrier and User Profile Update, and a registry of technical documents on Frame Relay.

Keywords Associations, Frame Relay, Networking, WANs (Wide Area Networks)
Audience Computer Professionals, Computer System Designers, Network Administrators, Systems Administrators

Connections to Etiquette
CAN I DO THIS?

If you want quick and easy tips on netiquette, look at some of the pointers in "Net Etiquette." Among other things, these warn against spreading a hoax over the Internet, and remind you not to casually capitalize words in messages, since it will indicate that you are ANGRY. Also, be careful what you write about another person on the Internet. Such messages are easily forwarded.

(http://ixc.net/toc.html) also, (http://rs6000.adm.fau.edu/rinaldi/net/elec.html)

At the "Ethics and Etiquette of Internet Information Resources" site, you can find principles and pointers relevant to ethics and etiquette concerning the use and development of networked information resources. This site provides a number of documents that address questions about being a good citizen on the Internet, advertising on the World Wide Web, and appropriate Internet conduct.

(http://coombs.anu.edu.au/SpecialProj/QLTY/QltyEtiq.html)

Do you want to learn about table manners or need advice on proper etiquette? How much should you tip at a restaurant for exceptional service? Are you aware that it is proper to buy the chef a glass of champagne for a well-cooked meal? How much should you tip the bell-boy at a hotel? What should you do after you sneeze at a formal dinner? Should you return an engagement ring if you break off the engagement? The "Tipping" site provides answers to interesting questions about etiquette around the globe.

(http://www.cpmc.columbia.edu/homepages/gonzalu/tipping.html)

CONTACT Kirsten Machi
frf@interop.com

FREE

http://frame-relay.indiana.edu

Hotwired

The Hotwired site provides users with a variety of doorways into the Digital Revolution. These include providing coverage of where to go and what to see on the Net, spreading industry gossip, reviewing advances—and regressions—in communications technology, and providing highly personal hypertext essays and bulletins from around the globe as pointers to the 'Way New journalism' that is possible on the Web, among many others. The site also encourages the user to browse personal ads, shop for WiredWare, subscribe to the magazine, and explore Wired's library.

KEYWORDS Communications Technology, Digital Revolution, Internet Publishing, Multimedia
AUDIENCE Artists, News Buffs, Philosophers, Writers
CONTACT support@hotwired.com

FREE

http://www.hotwired.com

IRC (Internet Relay Chat) ★★★

This site contains the software for accessing IRC (Internet Relay Chat) a multi-user, multi-channel chatting network. It allows people all over the Internet to 'talk' to one another interactively and in real time. There are versions in the appropriate directories for UNIX-, Macintosh-, and PC-compatible architectures. The topics encountered through IRC range from sexually oriented discussions to educational conferences and the latest news from disaster areas like Kobe, Japan during its earthquake.

KEYWORDS Internet Tools, Shareware, Virtual Community
AUDIENCE General Public, IRC Users, Internet Users
FREE

ftp://cs-ftp.bu.edu/irc

Inter-Network Mail Guide ★★

This file documents methods of sending mail from one network to another. It represents the aggregate knowledge of the readers of comp.mail.misc and many contributors elsewhere. The purpose of this document is to help users on different networks (e.g. Compuserve, Fidonet, Bitnet, etc.) to address email messages to each other by listing the different address formats.

KEYWORDS Email, Networking, Reference
AUDIENCE Email Users, Internet Users
CONTACT University of Wisconsin-Milwaukee
help@uwm.edu

FREE

http://alpha.acast.nova.edu/cgi-bin/inmgq.pl

ftp://ftp.csd.uwm.edu/pub/internetwork-mail-guide

InternetMCI

This is MCI's Internet Home Page. You can download free Internet and utility software from MCI. For virtual shopping you can visit the MCI marketplace which contains electronic goods, sporting goods, software, flowers, computer products, and more. You can also find FAQs about InternetMCI.

KEYWORDS Internet Tools, Online Shopping, Software, Virtual Shopping
AUDIENCE Software Users, Virtual Shoppers

FREE

http://www.internetmci.com/

Internet Talk Radio Archives ★★

This gopher server provides access to archives about Internet Talk Radio, an online radio show about the Internet. The archives include selections from Talk Radio's programming, a history of the show, and FAQs. The archive is maintained at the Los Alamos National Laboratory.

KEYWORDS Communications Technology, Internet Communications, Public Access Archives
AUDIENCE Internet Users, Radio Enthusiasts, Radio Pirates

FREE

gopher://juggler.lanl.gov/

Muenster-The Friendly German Channel ★★★

Muenster,' the friendly German channel' is an Internet Relay Chat channel based in the small town in the northwestern part of Germany. Next to the IRC, Germany, which is also accessible through this site, Muenster is the most frequented German-language IRC. Most of the conversation is in German, although all other languages are accepted. There is a link to IRC channels within their own WWW pages.

KEYWORDS Germany, IRS (Internal Revenue Service), Internet Protocols
AUDIENCE Germans, Internet Users
CONTACT janssen@rz.uni-karlsruhe.de

FREE

http://www.uni-karlsruhe.de/~Urs.Janssen/irc/muenster.html

Netiquette Home Page ★★★

The Netiquette Home Page contains contents from the guide The Net - User Guidelines and Netiquette by Arlene Rinaldi, which explains user responsibility for their actions when networking. Users can learn about the appropriate behavior and protocols for email, telnet, FTP, discussion groups and electronic communities. FAQs for questions about email privacy, receipts and rudeness, and losing Internet access are also provided.

KEYWORDS Internet Protocols, Netiquette
AUDIENCE Home Page Creators, Internet Users, Web Developers
CONTACT Arlene Rinaldi
rinaldi@acc.fau.edu

FREE

http://rs6000.adm.fau.edu/rinaldi/netiquette.html

Smileys and Other Standard Symbols ★★★

This site provides access to The Smiley Dictionary. This dictionary provides information regarding Smileys and other standard symbols. Smileys, which are also known as 'emoticons,' are used to indicate an emotional state in email or news. Although originally intended as jokes, emoticons are practically required under certain circumstances. They provide visual cues to statements that were intended to be humorous, sarcastic or ironic, thus preventing them from being misinterpreted.

KEYWORDS Dictionaries, Internet Standards
AUDIENCE Email Users, Network Communications Specialists, Usenet News Readers
CONTACT Per Goetterup
ballerup@freja.diku.dk

FREE

ftp://ftp.halcyon.com/pub/ii/internet/smileys.txt/

TIN Newsreader FAQ (Frequently Asked Questions) ★★★★

This site provides access to an FAQ regarding the TIN Newsreader. TIN is a netnews (Usenet) newsreader that provides a full screen, easy to use text-based interface, with online help at all levels. This FAQ provides general information regarding the newsreader, information regarding compilation, configuration, a list of known bugs, and acknowledgments.

KEYWORDS Usenet
AUDIENCE Internet Users, TIN Newsreader Users
CONTACT Iain Lea
iain.lea@erlm.siemens.de

FREE

ftp://ftp.halcyon.com/pub/ii/internet/tin_faq.txt/

WWW Daily ★★★★

This page is a listing of links to commercial news services on the WWW. Links include services outside the US.

KEYWORDS Communications Technology, Electronic Media, Mass Communications, Newspapers
AUDIENCE News Buffs
CONTACT Kathy Valladares
electnws@jou.ufl.edu

FREE

http://www.jou.ufl.edu/commres/newsmap.map?247,162

The Web Voyeur ★★★★

The Web Voyeur is a collection of links to images from live video and CUSeeMe feeds all over the world. Wondering what the skyline of San Francisco looks like? The Web Voyeur will link you to a Webcam site that will show you. Links are grouped by subject, such as outdoor scenes, offices and labs, the virtual zoo, and 'simply strange' sites, with brief descriptions of each feed. Users may link to the sites to either access information about the site and Webcam, or simply link directly to the images.

KEYWORDS CUSeeMe, Conferencing, Telecommunications

AUDIENCE Internet Users, Voyeurs
CONTACT irving@eskimo.com
FREE

http://www.eskimo.com/%7Eirving/web-voyeur/

Internet Issues

See also
Communications · *Telecommunications*
Government & Politics · *Policies*
Internet · *Organizations*

Boardwatch Interactive ★★★

Boardwatch Magazine - Guide to Electronic Bulletin Boards and the Internet, the widely-distributed paper magazine, has brought an archive of its past issues to the World Wide Web. The full text of every article in Boardwatch is available on their website, including illustrations and special resources of use to technophiles and BBS users. Links to other BBS-related sites, comprehensive national and international listings, as well as other items can be found in these pages. It is not only for those who want to use online services usefully and economically, but also for those who operate online services and develop products for the online industry.

KEYWORDS Internet Networking, Magazines, Technology, Telecommunications
AUDIENCE BBS Users, Internet Business Professionals, Internet Users
CONTACT Administrator
subscriptions@boardwatch.com
FREE

http://www.boardwatch.com/

Computer Policy and Critiques Archive ★★★

This collection of educational and network computer policies is a compilation of policies found in CAF (Computers and Academic Freedom) and EFF (Electronic Frontier Foundation) archives. The collection also includes critiques of some of the policies (i.e., Acceptable Use Policy) written from an academic freedom point of view. The index is arranged in alphabetical order and by type of network the policy is written for (Colleges, Organizations, Governmental, Free-nets, etc.).

KEYWORDS Computer Policy, Education Policy
AUDIENCE Administrators, Educational Administrators, Network Administrators
CONTACT gopher@eff.org
FREE

gopher://gopher.eff.org:70/11/CAF/policies

ftp://ftp.eff.org/pub/CAF/policies

Cyberspace Law Review Bibliography ★★★

This site provides a bibliograhy (not hyperlinked) of Cyberspace Law related works. Some of the wrtings include The Liability of Computer Bulletin Boards for Defamation Posted by Others, The Constitution in Cyberspace-The Fundamental Rights of Computer Users, Operator Liability Associated with Maintaining a Computer Bulletin Board, E-Law- Legal Issues Affecting Computer Information Systems and System Operator Liability, and much more.

KEYWORDS Freedom of Speech, Intellectual Property, Legal Issues
AUDIENCE General Public, Law Students, Lawyers, Legal Professionals, Litigants
CONTACT Eric Schlachter
eschlach@netcom.com
FREE

http://starbase.ingress.com/tsw/rcl/eric.html

IT Online/Out There Magazine ★★★

Out There and IT online are two intertwining experimental publications produced by the Swedish Institute of Computer Science. Both are dedicated to exploring new uses for the Internet, especially integrating disciplines and people who have, up until now, not used the Internet or seen its applicability in their field. The current issue contains a number of articles on the intersection of technology and art, and the implications of such a paradigm shift to artists around the world.

KEYWORDS Art, Communications
AUDIENCE Art Educators, Art Students, Computer Artists
CONTACT it-found@sics.se
FREE

http://www.ot.sics.se/

Information About the Electronic Frontier Foundation ★★★★

This page contains links to information on the Electronic Frontier Foundation (EFF) including its legal services, civil liberties work, how to join, resources for online activists, and more. Since its inception, EFF has worked to shape the nation's communications infrastructure and the policies that govern it in order to maintain and enhance First Amendment, privacy, and other democratic values. EFF sponsors legal cases where users' online civil liberties have been violated. EFF has been working to make sure that network providers uphold civil liberties, freedom of speech, and more.

KEYWORDS Civil Liberties, Freedom of Speech, Internet Issues, Internet Policy
AUDIENCE ACLU Members, Activists, Civil Liberties Activists, Lawyers
CONTACT ask@eff.org
FREE

http://www.eff.org/EFFdocs/about_eff.html

Internet Monthly Reports ★★

This newsletter is a monthly communication to the Internet Research Group. This is a technical report on activities by the leaders of Internet research and development.

KEYWORDS Internet Issues, Internet Standards, Newsletters, Organizations
AUDIENCE Internet Specialists, Internet Users
CONTACT nic-info@nic.merit.edu
FREE

ftp://nic.merit.edu/internet/newsletters/internet.monthly.report/

Internet US Domain ★★

This site provides access to a document regarding the Internet US (United States) Domain. It contains an introduction defining the US Domain as an official top-level domain in the Domain Name System (DNS). The US Domain hierarchy is based on political geography - states, then cities and so on. The article continues with information regarding membership, administration, delegation, groups, other networks, unique names, wild cards, servers, and more. The last article at this location is the US Domain Questionnaire for Host Entry. The information in this questionnaire must be provided to the US Domain registrar, Ann Westine Cooper, for entry into the US Domain.

KEYWORDS Domain Name System (DNS), Internet Access, Organizations
AUDIENCE Commercial Advertisers, Government Agency Employees, Internet Access Providers
CONTACT Ann Westine Cooper
cooper@isi.edu
FREE

ftp://ftp.execpc.com/pub/info/us-domain.txt/

Law on the Internet ★★★

This article, Law on the Internet, has links to information about the Internet, The Legal List, Information to Read or Download, Notable Internet Email Addresses, Books About the Internet, and more. This article originally appeared in the Spring, 1994 issue of the Nolo News.

KEYWORDS Internet Issues, Legal Advice, Legal Issues, Publishers
AUDIENCE Internet Professionals, Internet Users, Legal Professionals
CONTACT cs@NoloPress.com
FREE

http://nearnet.gnn.com/gnn/bus/nolo/lawnet.html

Public Access to the Internet Symposium Archives ★★

This archive contains records from the Public Access to the Internet Symposium held at the Harvard University, John F. Kennedy School of Government in May, 1993. This conference dealt with how to combine human and computer information services to meet public needs.

KEYWORDS Internet Issues, Internet Networking, Organizations
AUDIENCE Internet Users, Management Information Specialists, Media Specialists
CONTACT nic-info@nic.merit.edu
FREE

ftp://nic.merit.edu/conference.proceedings/

Internet Protocols

See also
Computing & Mathematics · *Standards*
Internet · *Internet Resources*

FTP (File Transfer Protocol) Primer ★★★

This site provides access to a document entitled 'FTP Primer'. Part I of this document provides step-by-step instructions on how to FTP (File Transfer Protocol) a file. It includes a complete listing of prompts and replies and describes how to use the UNIX FTP interface. Part II of this document describes in detail the process of first downloading files to your microcomputer and then decoding it, using special utility programs. This document appears to have been written for the Internet newcomer.

KEYWORDS	FTP (File Transfer Protocol)
AUDIENCE	Internet Access Providers, Internet Newcomers, Internet Users
CONTACT	Ray Beausoleil beausol@u.washington.edu
FREE	

ftp://ftp.lightside.com/lightside/FTP_Primer/

IHAC Documents du CCAI ★★★

This site hosts information for the Canadian Information Highway Advisory Council. There is access to information on how to use this site and an essay competition called Call For Papers. There is also access to announcements of membership, policy papers, minutes of meetings, submissions to the council, a study on Canada's information highway, the subject of privacy, and a subcommittee report on copyright laws.

KEYWORDS	Canada, Information Superhighway, Internet Policy, Issues
AUDIENCE	Copyright Activists, Policy Analysts, Policymakers, Privacy Activists
CONTACT	council@istc.ca
FREE	

http://debra.dgbt.doc.ca/info-highway/ih.html

MBONE Information Web (Virtual Internet Backbone for Multicast IP) ★★★

This page is a collection of resources related to the Internet MBONE, a tunneling protocol that allows real-time video and audio to be sent over the Internet. Users can get full details of how MBONE works from this site, as well as background information and the technical specification. There are also pointers to FTP sites where MBONE software can be downloaded, as well as instructions on how to set up MBONE on your system.

KEYWORDS	Real-Time Networking, Software
AUDIENCE	Internet Users, MBONE Users, Multimedia Enthusiasts
CONTACT	Vinay Kumar vinay@eit.com
FREE	

http://www.eit.com/techinfo/mbone/mbone.html

Overview of HTTP ★★★★

This page provides information about HTTP, the Internet protocol used by WWW servers and browser clients. HTTP is an application-level protocol with the lightness and speed necessary for distributed, collaborative hyper media information systems such as the Web. There are links to detailed information about HTTP, including technical specifications, version upgrade plans, and security concerns.

KEYWORDS	HTTP (HyperText Transport Protocol), Hypermedia, Internet Networking, Internet Protocols
AUDIENCE	Computer Scientists, Internet Developers, WWW Developers, Web Users
CONTACT	webmaster@info.cern.ch
FREE	

http://info.cern.ch/hypertext/WWW/Protocols/Overview.html

Reseaux IP Europeens - Network Coordination Centre ★★★

This is a gopher server of the RIPE (Reseaux IP Europeens) in the Netherlands. RIPE is a collaborative organization open to all European Internet service providers. The objective of RIPE is to ensure the necessary administrative and technical coordination to allow the operation of a pan-European IP network. It contains information on RIPE, its documents, its forms and templates, the list of local Internet registries in Europe, RIPE meetings, and more.

KEYWORDS	Netherlands
AUDIENCE	Internet Users, Network Administrators, Network Service Providers
CONTACT	Anne Lord ncc@ripe.net
FREE	

gopher://gopher.ripe.net/

Internet Resources

See also
Business & Economics · *Publishing*
Computing & Mathematics · *Resources*

Ask The Webmaster ★★★★

Using a form-based interface, visitors to this page can 'ask the webmaster' virtually any question and receive a unique (albeit often unhelpful and usually funny) answer. A large archive of past questions and answers is also available for browsing.

KEYWORDS	Internet Culture
AUDIENCE	Astrologers, Astrology Enthusiasts, Humor Enthusiasts
CONTACT	The Webmaster duke@mvb.saic.com
FREE	

http://se.saic.com/home/duke/askweb.html

AstraNet ★★★

AstraNet, the WWW information site sponsored by Prodigy Services Company, provides lists of outside WWW links in the following categories - news, business, travel, government, sports, entertainment, shopping, and general reference. Additionally, AstraNet makes specialized information in these categories available to its subscribers.

KEYWORDS	News, Online Services
AUDIENCE	Internet Newcomers, Internet Users, News Buffs, Online Service Users
CONTACT	webmaster@www.astranet.com
FREE	

http://www.astranet.com/

Australian WWW Servers ★★★

This site is a meta-index of World Wide Web servers located in Australia. Sites are indexed alphabetically by name, topic, state and by the type of service they offer. This is an Australian starting point for users to follow links to search the web.

KEYWORDS	Australia, Databases, Internet Access, WWW (World Wide Web)
AUDIENCE	Australian Culture Enthusiasts, Australians, Internet Specialists, Internet Users
CONTACT	David Green DGreen@csu.edu.au
FREE	

http://www.csu.edu.au/links/ozweb.html

Bobaworld ★★★★

Bobaworld is one individual's gigantic page of cool links, a venerable directory for worthwhile World Wide Web pages. His links are organized into sections for 'cool' sites, events listings, Web and Net information sites, 'useful' sites, 'fun' sites, and 'eclectic' sites. He includes a navigator for easy access to his pages, and FAQ's, WWW survey information, and a Top Ten list.

KEYWORDS	Internet Guides, Web Authoring
AUDIENCE	Internet Users, Students
CONTACT	Bob Allison boba@wwa.com
FREE	

http://gagme.wwa.com/~boba/bobaworld.html

California World Wide Web Servers ★★★★

The California WWW Servers Page includes pointers to all known servers within the state. Being a Lawrence Livermore National Laboratory page, it is funded by the U.S. Department of Energy. There are pointers to federal, state, and local governments and agencies. There are also links to several NASA-administered sites and US Navy servers. There are no descriptions of the sites.

KEYWORDS California, Meta-Index (California)

Internet Resources

AUDIENCE Californians, Political Researchers, Students (University)
CONTACT Jerry L. Owens
jlowens@llnl.gov
FREE

http://www.llnl.gov/ptools/california.servers.html

CompuServe Web Home Page ★★★★

The CompuServe WWW site provides information on the company (an overview, news releases about the company, and updates on special events), lists of notable WWW links, a current events section, and a utility for finding CompuServe services, mail addresses, and resources. Also available are a detailed explanation of services offered, and a 'Join' section to sign up for service.

KEYWORDS Commercial Online Services, Internet Companies, Online Services
AUDIENCE Dial-Up Internet Users, Internet Newcomers, Internet Users, Online Service Users
CONTACT webmaster@compuserve.com
FREE

http://www.compuserve.com/

Cool Site of the Day ★★★★

This Cool Site of the Day site is produced by Glenn Davis of InfiNet, with links to his favorite Web sites. Besides a mystery link to the daily 'Cool Site,' he includes links to previous 'Cool Sites,' listed monthly. Also included is an FAQ and guide to the Cool Site index, and a comment form for submissions and requests.

KEYWORDS Internet Guides
AUDIENCE General Public, Internet Users
CONTACT Glenn Davis
cool@infi.net
FREE

http://www.infi.net/cool.html

CyberQuest ★★★★

CyberQuest is a page of links to Internet lists, with a focus on keeping the weary Internet surfer safe from the recent avalanche of commercial sites. Links are provided to some of the best Internet directories, including Yahoo, Global Network Navigator, The NetGuide, EINet Galaxy, and The Whole Internet Catalog. You'll also find many other handy Internet tools, such as a Finger gateway, a Whois gateway, Gopher Sites, and so on. Also here, but not quite as useful as the rest of the page, are links to entertainment and educational sites the producer personally finds cool. People producing Web pages should check this one out to get some ideas on how to make a page truly useful!

KEYWORDS Internet Culture, Internet Directories
AUDIENCE Cyberculture Enthusiasts, Internet Users, Web Developers
CONTACT Di-Spy
di-spy@pb.net
FREE

http://www.pb.net/~dispy

Connections to the Internet Business Center

If you're looking to expand your business beyond your local community, the Internet can put you in touch with advertising services on various World Wide Web sites. Targeting your audience is easier with Internet demographic data, all of which is available via the "Internet Business Center."

You'll be able to expand your customer base from a few thousand to many millions, and you can even make contact with venture capital firms on the World Wide Web to help expand the products and services you offer. If you want to know more, the IBC can provide you with studies on Internet shopping behavior and attitudes so that you can adjust your marketing efforts to attain the best results.

The "Internet Business & Marketing Center Home Page" can help you find business opportunities, and even set up an advertising account online to get your "open for business" message out to millions of subscribers worldwide.

(http://www.intnet.net/ibmc/) also, (http://www.gnn.com/gnn/wic/bus.23.html)

Daniel's Icon Archive ★★★★

This is a large (4000+) collection of icons, intended primarily for use in creating WWW pages. Users may browse through the archive or download the entire archive at once.

KEYWORDS Clip Art, Computer Art, WWW (World Wide Web)
AUDIENCE Graphic Designers, Internet Publishers, Internet Specialists, Web Developers
CONTACT Daniel McCoy
mccoy@gothamcity.jsc.nasa.gov
FREE

http://www.jsc.nasa.gov/~mccoy/Icons/index.html

Deepthought Anonymous Utilities ★★★

This site provides access to a very large number of software utilities. The utilities are broken down into these main categories - Administrative utilities (mostly scripts), html (hypertext markup language) and http (hypertext transfer protocol) utilities, utilities for the Midnight Beach software, compiled binaries for SCO UNIX and SCO XENIX systems, general purpose utilities, source for various utilities, textual material such as documentation on TCP/IP (Transmission Control Protocol/Internet Protocol) network setup and administration. The site also includes archives that do not fall into any of these categories such as a serial infrared remote controller write-up and driver, and finally archives maintained by deepthought.armory.com users.

KEYWORDS Software, Software Utilities, TCP/IP, UNIX
AUDIENCE Computer Programmers, Computer Systems Users, Computer Users, Internet Access Providers

Free

http://www.armory.com/

ftp://ftp.armory.com/

Delphi Internet ★★★

This home page of Delphi Internet provides links to the fX Television Network and various other resources based on HarperCollins affiliations and products. The site emphasizes popular entertainment and books in its featured content, offering sample sound clips, book excerpts, and product ordering information. Also available are press releases on recent Delphi corporate news, product giveaways, and a 'Best of the Web.'

Keywords Internet Access Providers, Online Services
Audience Internet Users, Online Service Users, Television Enthusiasts
Contact talkback@delphi.com
Free

http://www.delphi.com/

ElNet Galaxy ★★★★

The Galaxy is a guide to worldwide information and services and is provided as a public service by ElNet and Galaxy guest editors. The information is organized by topic and each of the ten main areas have appropriate subcategories of topics to choose from. The directory can also be searched. In the current version, different information spaces, such as Gopher or WAIS, are searched individually (one at a time, according to the user's choices from the Galaxy menu). Depending on your criteria, a search request can go through over 100,000 web pages in ElNet's database. In addition, you can add your own information to Galaxy. ElNet also sells a number of information products and services for interested parties.

Keywords Databases, Internet Directories, Meta-Index (Internet)
Audience Information Professionals, Internet Professionals, Internet Users, Librarians
Contact ElNet Galaxy
Free

http://www.einet.net/galaxy.html

Educator's Guide to Email Lists ★★★

This document is a guide to help educators find email listservs. All educational levels and disciplines are represented in this very large list of email addresses.

Keywords Directories, Educational Technology, Email
Audience Educators, Educators (Primary/Secondary), Researchers, Students (Secondary/College)
Contact Prescott Smith
pgsmith@educ.umass.edu
Free

ftp://nic.umass.edu/pub/ednet/educatrs.lst

Electronic Frontier Foundation's (Extended) Guide to the Internet (EFF) ★★★★

This free document is a comprensive book about the Internet, currently organized by the Electronic Frontier Foundation (EFF). There are explanations of how various parts of the Internet are put together. Topics covered include Email, Ftp, Telnet, Usenet News, Gopher and World Wide Web. The book also lists Internet access providers in the United States, Canada, and selected other countries and cities. Users can look for resources within subject area or network tool, such as Agricultural Telnet sites or Science Fiction related Ftp sites. There is also a large number of related articles about Internet culture, EFF, Netiquette, and other useful online thoughts. EFF is a nonprofit organization based in Washington, DC, dedicated to ensuring that everyone has access to the newly emerging communications technologies vital to active participation in the events of our world.

Keywords Freedom of Information, Information Superhighway
Audience Information Professionals, Internet Trainers, Internet Users, Librarians
Contact Electronic Frontier Foundation
webmaster@eff.org
Free

http://www.eff.org/papers/eegtti/eegttitop.html

gopher://gopher.eff.org:70/hh/Net_info/EFF_Net_Guide

ftp://ftp.eff.org/pub/Net_info/EFF_Net_Guide/

Elm Software ★★★★

This site provides a copy of Elm Software, V. 2.4 PL24, as well as worldwide Internet addresses of sites willing to distribute and support this software. This site only has a Beta version of the software available and is unsupported. Elm is a 'user agent' email system designed to run with 'sendmail' or 'bin/mail' of any other UNIX mail transport system. Elm mail system also contains programs to list a table of contents of your mail, paginates mail files, has an auto-reply system, is screen-oriented, user-friendly, and intelligent.

Keywords Email, UNIX
Audience Academics, Business Professionals, Email Users, Internet Users, Software Users, UNIX Users
Contact Dave Taylor
taylor@intuitive.com
Free

ftp://dsinc.dsi.com/pub/elm/

Eureka! Internet Guide ★★★

Eureka! is an individual home page that provides an index to Internet resources on various topics, focusing on World Wide Web and Internet issues. Links are grouped into categories such as FAQs, Gopher, HTML, Maps, Servers, and PERL, with materials about publishing and creating HTML documents on the Web. Other documents include BBC television schedules, information about Sex, Censorship and the Internet, and an online 'cafe' with information about coffees and Web sites.

Keywords HTML (HyperText Markup Language), Internet Guides
Audience Internet Users, World Wide Web Publishers
Contact Martin Hamilton
martin@mrrl.lut.ac.uk
Free

http://mrrl.lut.ac.uk

Four11 Directory Services (SLED) ★★★★

The Four11 Online User Directory is a directory of online users and their email addresses, with almost half a million listings. It allows you to search by any combination of first name, last name, location, old email address, and current or past organizations. An optional paid membership provides additional services, including an expanded list, search agents, links to a Web page, and PGP key services.

Keywords Directories, Email, Internet Reference
Audience Computer Users, Internet Users
Contact comments@Four11.com
Free

http://www.four11.com/Sled.html

Free Access Foundation (FAF) ★★

The goal of this foundation is to provide every computer user with a modem access to the Internet. The word 'free' does not necessarily imply no-cost access but the information provided at this server regarding Internet access is 'free'. The Free Access Foundation (FAF) hopes to soon provide a telnet accessible site-server, a mail-to newsgroup forwarding system, an automated mailserver and a gopher for interactive viewing/searching of FAF archives. FAF currently has archives providing information on public access Internet sites they can locate and contact. Finally, this archive contains a large list of Internet account providers (pub/faf/Remote-Sites) sorted via geographic area.

Keywords Internet Access, Internet Providers, Organizations
Audience Computer Games Enthusiasts, Internet Users, Modem Users
Contact faf@faf.org
Free

ftp://ftp.halcyon.com/pub/faf/

GEnie Web Site ★★★

This site provides information and resources for the GEnie online service. The page contains notices of updates to the GEnie service, a link to the GEnie gopher, and the latest software and help files available to download or via FTP.

Keywords Internet Companies, Online Services
Audience Internet Newcomers, Online Service Users
Contact Andy Finkenstadt
andy@genie.com
Free

http://www.genie.com/

Gopher FAQ ★★★

This file contains answers to Frequently Asked Questions (FAQs) about gophers from the USENET newsgroup comp.infosystems.gopher. Gopher is a navigational program for finding files and resources on the Internet.

Keywords FAQs (Frequently Asked Questions), Gopher, Internet Reference
Audience Internet Newcomers, Internet Users

CONTACT ftp-bugs@rtfm.mit.edu
FREE

gopher://mudhoney.micro.umn.edu:70/00/Gopher.FAQ

ftp://pit-manager.mit.edu/pub/usenet/news.answers/gopher-faq

Graduate and Undergraduate Admissions Email Addresses ★★★

This document is a list of email addresses with which to contact people/offices who can give information about graduate and undergraduate programs in that department at that university.

KEYWORDS Email
AUDIENCE Students (Primary/Secondary), Students (Secondary/University), Students (University)
FREE

ftp://pit-manager.mit.edu/pub/usenet-by-group/soc.college

Green Eggs Report ★★★★

The Green Eggs report is a collection of URLs that have been spotted by the Rumor Database System. Rumor collects about 1,500 new and unique URLs every day from selected newsgroups. URLs are arranged solely by their first appearance in a newsgroup. (If a message was cross-posted, it will appear only once.)

KEYWORDS Internet Tools, URLs (Universal Resource Locaters), Usenet Newsgroups
AUDIENCE Internet Professionals, Internet Users
FREE

http://ibd.ar.com/ger/

Growth of the World Wide Web ★★★

This site provides the most recent results from `The World Wide Web Wanderer' (W4), a PERL script designed to surf the Web and estimate its size. The site gives an interpretation of recent net traffic statistics and also provides a list of all WWW sites detected by W4. The addresses are listed according to domain name (eg. .edu, .gov, .ca). The usefulness of this site is limited by the Web's rapid growth.

KEYWORDS Computer Networks, Internet Statistics, Internet Tools, Internet Traffic
AUDIENCE Internet Users, Network Administrators
CONTACT Matthew K. Gray
         Mkgray@mit.edu
FREE

http://www.mit.edu:8001/people/mkgray/web-growth.html

Guide to Cyberspace 6.1 ★★★★

The Guide to Cyberspace 6.1 server provides a guide to the WWW, the Internet, hypertext, Mosaic, and related subjects. The information is accessed by a table of contents and includes many images and other media to help explain the subject. There are also links to other 'helpdesk' sites and to interesting places on the net.

KEYWORDS Hypermedia
AUDIENCE Computer Users, Internet Users
CONTACT Kevin Hughes
         kevinh@eit.com
FREE

http://www.eit.com/web/www.guide/

Hitchhiker's Guide to the Internet ★★

This document, dated September, 1989, gives a history of the Internet from its inception as ARPANET, a wide-area experimental network connecting hosts and terminal servers together. The history is somewhat technical, however, there is a glossary and other basic information.

KEYWORDS Internet Culture, Internet Guides
AUDIENCE Internet Specialists, Internet Users, Network Developers
CONTACT Merit Network Information Center
         nic-info@nic.merit.edu
FREE

ftp://nic.merit.edu/documents/rfc/rfc1118.txt

How To Put Your Data on the Web ★★★

This web site offers comprehensive information on setting up your own WWW server on the Internet. There are help and documentation files, style guides, links to sites where the necessary server and HTML editing software may be downloaded, and much more.

KEYWORDS Internet Training, WWW (World Wide Web), Web Development
AUDIENCE Internet Developers, Web Developers, Web Users
CONTACT www-bug@info.cern.ch
FREE

http://info.cern.ch/hypertext/WWW/Provider/Overview.html

How to Publish on the Internet ★★★

How to Publish on the Internet is a how-to book about publishing on the World Wide Web. This Web site describes the book and contains further notes and updates to the published book. A lot of the information in this site is presented with hypertext headings, so users can easily get more commentary about subjects like online communities or legal aspects of the Internet. Other links on this site lead to software mentioned in the book, a hotlist of HTML publishing links, or to a bulletin board discussion area at the Pathfinder site.

KEYWORDS Internet Guides, Internet Publishing, Web Authoring, Web Development
AUDIENCE HTML Authors, Internet Access Providers, Internet Professionals
CONTACT twep-webmaster@pathfinder.com
FREE

http://pathfinder.com/twep/Features/How_Pub_Web/How_Pub_Web.html

Index - Gateway to Free-Nets and Community Computer Networks via World-Wide Web ★★★

The Gateway to Free-Nets and Community Computer Networks via World Wide Web is an international index of Web sites related to community organizing. There is a large listing of known FreeNets here which lists Web addresses of FreeNets from Australia to the Ukraine to the United States and Canada. Links to other community resource indexes are also provided.

KEYWORDS Community Organizing, Freenets, Meta-Index (Communities)
AUDIENCE Community Activists, FreeNet Users, International Organizers
FREE

http://freenet.victoria.bc.ca/freenets.html

Infobot Hotlist Database ★★★

This page is a collection of popular links on the World Wide Web. Users can mail their hotlists to an infobot, which ranks individual links according to their popularity. The infobot updates this page hourly.

KEYWORDS Internet Resources, WWW (World Wide Web)
AUDIENCE Internet Specialists, Internet Users, Web Users
CONTACT ksedgwic@bonsai.com
FREE

ftp://ftp.netcom.com/pub/ks/ksedgwic/hotlist/hotlist.html

Information Bank ★★

This collection of Internet links contains over 700 items organized into about 75 categories. The user can see an alphabetical list, a subject oriented list, or a subject oriented tree (which shows all branches). The top level allows you to access collections of What's New pages, Internet Search Pages, Current Events, and interactive applications (MUDs and MOOs).

KEYWORDS Internet Resources, Meta-Index (Internet)
AUDIENCE Internet Professionals, Internet Users, Librarians
CONTACT ClarkNet
         office@clark.net
FREE

http://www.clark.net/pub/global/front.html

Information by Sites ★★★

This home page from Red Cientifica y Tecnologica Nacional contains a list of information on Internet resources in Argentina. This consists mainly of government and academic sites; there are also some international organizations.

KEYWORDS Argentina, Internet Resources
AUDIENCE Argentina Residents, Investors, Latin Americans, Tourists
CONTACT www@secyt.gov.ar
FREE

http://www.secyt.gov.ar/xsite.html

Information by Subject Areas ★★★★

This directory maintained by Rice University contains links to resources organized by subject matter. The resources themselves cover a wide range of topics available on the Internet. The resource collection is similar to that available on other major gopher servers such as InterNIC because they merge similar collections maintained elsewhere. These resources may be unavailable at any time due to many factors, however, the lists are extensive and are updated about once a week.

KEYWORDS	Internet Directories, Internet Resources
AUDIENCE	General Public, Internet Newcomers, Internet Users, Researchers
CONTACT	Prentiss Riddle cwis@rice.edu
FREE	

gopher://riceinfo.rice.edu:70/11/Subject/

Internet Computer Index ★★★★

The Internet Computer Index (ICI) is an easy-to-use, free service that leads Internet users to all of the information available on the Internet relating to PCs, Macintoshes, and UNIX computers. ICI users can find out answers to their hardware and software questions, solve networking problems, research buying decisions, and stay up-to-date about their systems.

KEYWORDS	Computer Hardware, Personal Computers
AUDIENCE	Computer Hardware Users, Computer Users
CONTACT	info@proper.com
FREE	

http://ici.proper.com/

gopher://proper.com/

Internet Cruise ★★

This site contains a computer-based tutorial for new and experienced Internet navigators. It provides an introduction to Internet resources as diverse as supercomputing, minorities, multimedia, cooking, and so on. It also offers information about the tools needed to access those resources.

KEYWORDS	Electronic Literacy, Internet Software, Internet Training, Online Guides
AUDIENCE	Internet Newcomers, Internet Users, Macintosh Users, PC Users
CONTACT	Merit Network Information Center nic-info@nic.merit.edu
FREE	

ftp://nic.merit.edu/internet/resources/

 Internet Initiative Japan ★★★★

This site offers extensive information on the Internet, with an emphasis on providing tools for Japanese users of the Net. Internet Initiative Japan is a company that provides Internet access in Japan. Users will find information on Internet Initiative Japan, as well as archives of PC, Mac, and UNIX software. There is also information on IIJ's Internet services, and pointers to all types of Internet resources.

KEYWORDS	Computer Networks, Internet Access Providers, Internet Resources, Japan
AUDIENCE	Computer Users, Internet Researchers, Internet Users
CONTACT	ftp@ftp.iij.ad.jp
FREE	

http://www.iij.ad.jp/

ftp://ftp.iij.ad.jp/

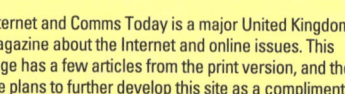 Internet and Comms Today ★★★

Internet and Comms Today is a major United Kingdom magazine about the Internet and online issues. This page has a few articles from the print version, and there are plans to further develop this site as a compliment to the hard copy. The articles currently online have been related to topics such as MUDs, the Joint Academic NETwork (JANET), and an introduction to videoconferencing.

KEYWORDS	Media, Online Magazines, United Kingdom
AUDIENCE	Internet Users, United Kingdom Residents
CONTACT	Dave Westley, Editor davew@paragon.co.uk
FREE	

http://www.atlas.co.uk/paragon/ict1.html

Intrrr Nrrrd Magazine ★★★

Intrrr Nrrrd Magazine is a constantly changing collection of software and 'hacks' for those involved in the 'diy' (do-it-yourself) punk subculture. It offers articles, stories, a software archive with video and audio conferencing programs for Macs and PCs as well as links to other sites. The editor, Brian Cors, welcomes practically any submission he can get.

KEYWORDS	Cyberculture, Internet Publishing, Magazines, Zines
AUDIENCE	Cyberculture Enthusiasts, Internet Publishers, Internet Users
CONTACT	Brian Cors corsbria@student.msu.edu
FREE	

http://www.etext.org/Zines/Intrrr.Nrrrd/intrrr.html

Jasper's Home Page ★★★★

Jasper's Home Page is a collection of resources about fonts, the electronic information exchange standard SGML, and other Internet information, produced by a member of O'Reilly and Associates. At this site, users can obtain information about the TeX WWW interface and find online help, as well as read information about fonts and the newsgroup comp fonts, with FAQs and the Internet Font Archive. SGML information includes tutorials, documentation, and reference pages, as well as links to other SGML information on the Web.

KEYWORDS	HTML (HyperText Markup Language, Internet Tools
AUDIENCE	Internet Producers, Internet Users
CONTACT	Norman Walsh norm@ora.com
FREE	

http://jasper.ora.com/homepage.cgi

Justin's Links from the Underground ★★★★

Justin's Links from the Underground is one individual's effort to compile an index to all the 'weird, wild and wonderful' sites on the World Wide Web. Links are grouped into subject categories, such as interactive pages, 'sexy stuff,' spirituality and worship, and 'eye candy,' with descriptions of each link and markings of new sites. Justin has also provided a guide to creating your own home page and using the WWW, an advice section, recipes, and an online maze.

KEYWORDS	Internet Guides
AUDIENCE	General Public, Internet Users
CONTACT	justin@cyborgasmic.com
FREE	

http://www.links.net/

LEO - Link Everything Online ★★★

Link Everything Online is a central entrance point for the Net Surfer based in Munich, Germany and leading to any subject of interest. Since the server is located in Germany, some of its information is only available in German. The home page is divided into links pointing to Munich, LEO Software Archives, LEO Mailing list Archives, Entering the World Wide Web, Various Search-Indices in LEO, and LEO, the project.

KEYWORDS	Archives, Germany, Meta-Index (Germany)
AUDIENCE	Germans, Internet Users
CONTACT	Beate Fuhrmann webmaster@informatik.tu-muenchen.de
FREE	

http://www.leo.org/index.html

Listserv Guide for General Users ★★

The Listserv Guide for General users site is an online user manual for use of the Listserv server. The Listserv server is used primarily for creating and maintaining mailing lists for users on the BITNET/EARN networks or for those people who can connect to the BITNET/EARN networks. Listserv also acts as a file server and a database.

KEYWORDS	Bitnet, Databases, Listservs, Mailing Lists
AUDIENCE	Computer Users, Email Users, Internet Users
CONTACT	Nadine Grange EARNDOC@earncc.earn.net
FREE	

http://www.earn.net/lug/notice.html

Mailbase ★★★

The Mailbase is a mailing list service from the United Kingdom. Their Website provides information about their services and provides Gopher access to their mailing list archives. Mailing list menus include descriptions of the issues covered, members and moderators, mail archives, and joining information. Lists covering topics such as Library, Medical and Social Sciences are organized by subject. Also included is an FAQ for users interested in starting their own mailing lists.

KEYWORDS	Internet Service Providers, Mailing Lists
AUDIENCE	Internet Users, Mailing List Users

CONTACT mailbase-helpline@mailbase.ac.uk
FREE
http://mailbase.ac.uk/

Mark Maimone's World Wide Web Tutorial Slides ★★★

This is a hypertext tutorial on the World Wide Web from Mark Maimone, a graduate student in the Computer Science Department at Carnegie Mellon University. It covers the basic questions such as 'What Is the Web?' through advanced topics such as setting up a web server, imagemaps, and more. It is graphics-intensive, as it was originally designed to be a slide presentation.

KEYWORDS Computer Science
AUDIENCE Internet Specialists, Internet Users, Web Developers, Web Users
CONTACT Mark Maimone
mwm@cmu.edu
FREE
http://www.cs.cmu.edu:8001/afs/cs/usr/mwm/www/tutorial/

Merit Network Information Center Services ★★★★

This site provides a large collection of Internet guides and information, serving as a clearinghouse for many Internet guides, documents, and utilities. It includes Internet FAQs, bibliographies, glossaries, and user guides such as Zen and the Art of the Internet, and The Internet Companion. It also has archives of various Internet documents listing service providers, acceptable use policies, and resources. Many software programs for navigating the Internet are also available here for a wide variety of platforms.

KEYWORDS Internet Guides, Internet Issues, Internet Resources, Meta-Index (Internet)
AUDIENCE Internet Users, Network Administrators, Network Developers
CONTACT nic-info@nic.merit.edu
FREE
ftp://nic.merit.edu/

Mirsky's Worst of the Web ★★★

Mirsky's Worst of the Web is a humorous site dedicated to pointing out the very worst Web sites. Users may browse the daily entries or go through back archives of terrible pages, with descriptions of each link and just why it is so bad. Users may also enter the Worst of the Web contest.

KEYWORDS Internet Guides, Web Authoring
AUDIENCE Internet Users, Web Users
CONTACT Mr. Mirsky
mirsky@volant.com
FREE
http://turnpike.net/metro/mirsky/Worst.html

Connections to The McKinley
Make it simple, make it fast

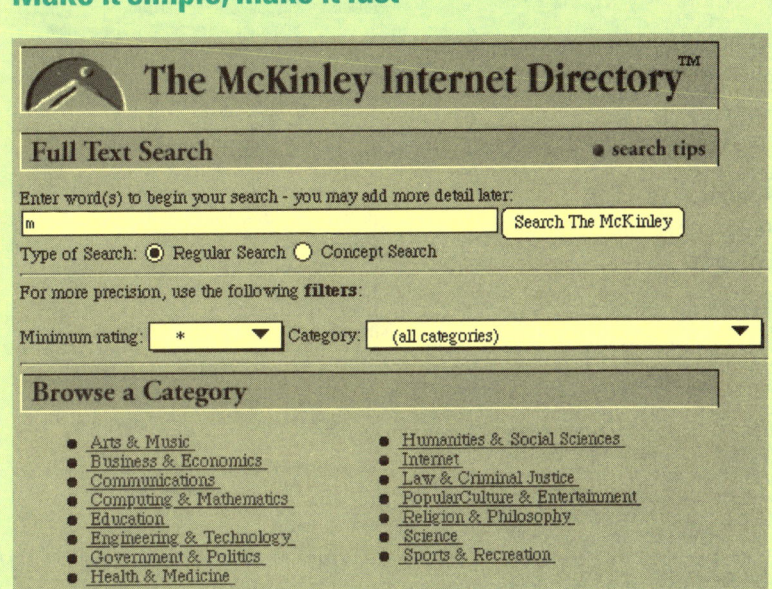

You are assigned the task to find the latest information on Spiral Galaxy M100 or to purchase a software utility that automates a specialized function in the company's spreadsheet software program. Where to you begin your search?

If you're smart, you'll use the Internet and get the fastest "assistant" to help you — The McKinley.

Searching the Internet for a specific item or article is very much like looking for the proverbial "needle in a haystack." The mountain of information that comprise the World Wide Web is daunting. You can spend hours and money trying to "find" something that is hidden somewhere in a database server half way around the world.

With The McKinley, your search is quick and its simple. You can get to the file, article, or information you need quickerthanyoucanreadthis.

Best of all, The McKinley evaluates sites for their ease-of-use, content up-to-dateness, and organization, so you don't waste time looking through a site that may not have what you want.

If time and money are too valuable to waste, check out The McKinley.

(http://www.mckinley.com/)

Miscellaneous Internet Documents ★★★

This site provides access to several short documents regarding Internet-related problems. For example, the 'subscribe_all_newsgroups' subdirectory provides information on how to subscribe to all newsgroups via TRN, NN and other newsreaders. The 'archie_ftp_uncompression' subdirectory provides a quick reference for using an Archie client to find files, using FTP (File Transfer Protocol) to get files, uncompressing files, using the less and more commands and deciding whether a file is ASCII or binary. The 'kermit_transfers' subdirectory provides information on how to transfer files with DOS Kermit. The 'killing' subdirectory describes how to globally 'kill' an author (ie. have your newsreader mark his/her articles as 'read' in all newsgroups. This is for NN, TRN and RN newsreaders).

KEYWORDS FTP (File Transfer Protocol), Newsgroups
AUDIENCE Internet Newsgroup Subscribers, Internet Users, Internet Users
CONTACT Nancy McGough
nancym@ii.com
FREE
ftp://ftp.halcyon.com/pub/ii/internet/

NETCOM OnLine Communication Services, Inc. ★★★

This WWW site provides information about Netcom, a commerical provider of Internet access in the United States. Information available includes - a list of local access numbers for dial-up Internet connection, listings for jobs available at the company, a company overview, news and press releases on current company events, a list of products and services, and information on

Netcom software. There are also links to favorite Internet destinations and an Internet Assistance and Information page.

KEYWORDS Internet Access Providers, Internet Companies
AUDIENCE Dial-Up Internet Users, Internet Newcomers
CONTACT glee@netcom.com
FREE

http://www.netcom.com/

NN Newsreader FAQ (Frequently Asked Questions) ★★★★

This site provides access to a wealth of information regarding the NN Newsreader. The 'getting-started.txt' subdirectory contains an FAQ that provides a comprehensive introduction to news and the NN newsreader. It also includes a lot of general news concepts and strategies that might be useful with other newsreaders. This FAQ provides information on how to get the latest version of the FAQ, a brief introduction to NN, customizing NN, efficiently reading lots of news, virtual newsgroups, creating a custom menu of articles, saving articles, posting, glossary, contributors and copyright information. This FAQ is also located in the 'NN/GettingStarted/getting-started' subdirectory.

KEYWORDS FAQs (Frequently Asked Questions), Newsgroups, Usenet Newsgroups
AUDIENCE Internet Users, NN Newsreader Users, Usenet News Readers
CONTACT Nancy McGough nancym@ii.com
FREE

http://www.cis.ohio-state.edu/hypertext/ faq/usenet/usenet/software/ nn/ getting-started/faq.html

ftp://ftp.halcyon.com/pub/ii/internet/NN/

NetUSE Kommunikationstechnologie GmbH ★★★

The NetUSE Kommunikationstechnologie GmbH Web is a German Internet guide, and their Web site contains a meta-index of information and guides to using the Internet. Users can browse their database using a full text search or graphical subject listings. Subject areas include NetUSE services, Northern German information services, business listings, education, and news, with links to hundreds of German and English Web sites.

KEYWORDS Germany, Internet Guides, Meta-Index (Germany)
AUDIENCE Germans, Internet Users
CONTACT Info@NetUSE.de
FREE

http://nuki.netuse.de

Network Information Retrieval (NIR) ★★★★

These compiled resources provide information describing the Internet and Network Information Retrieval systems. The author, John December, organizes these resources into Utilities (e.g. Finger, Netfind), Tools (Archie, FTP), Systems (Gopher, WAIS, WWW), and Interfaces (Mosiac, Hytelnet). Direct links to the programs December describes are included in the HTML version

KEYWORDS Internet Training, Online Guides
AUDIENCE Educators, Internet Users, Management Information Specialists, Researchers
FREE

http://www.rpi.edu/Internet/Guides/ decemj/itools/nir.html

ftp://ftp.rpi.edu/pub/communications/

Networks & Community Resources ★★★

This document is a compilation of information resources focused on networks and communities. Resources may include Internet/Bitnet Mailing Lists, Gophers, World Wide Web Sites, Mail Servers, Usenet Newsgroups, FTP Archives, Commercial Online Services, and Bulletin Board Systems.

KEYWORDS Activism, Community Networking, Privacy, Virtual Community
AUDIENCE Community Activists, Free-Net Organizers, Fundraisers, Network Developers
FREE

ftp://una.hh.lib.umich.edu/inetdirsstacks/ nets:sternberg

Patrick Crispen's Internet Roadmap ★★★

This site contains a six week tutorial for learning about the Internet, broken into about 30 files. Its producer, Patrick Crispen, wrote this tutorial for a subscribed audience of 55,000 email users. The complete set of lessons, including quizzes and homework answers, are archived on this site. Topics of lessons include email, telnet, ftp, gopher, WWW, MOOs and MUDs, as well as Internet culture issues such as spamming, advertising, and the future of the Net. Topics tend to start out with the basics, and grow to include some more advanced topics. Homework typically will include going out on the Internet and using the specific lesson information to retrieve information or files.

KEYWORDS Internet Guides, Internet Tools, Internet Training, Online Guides
AUDIENCE Information Professionals, Internet Trainers, Internet Users, Librarians
CONTACT Neil Enns ennsnr@brandonu.ca
FREE

http://www.brandonu.ca/~ennsnr/ Resources/Roadmap/Welcome.html

Planet Earth Home Page ★★★★

Run by the Department of Navy, the Planet Earth Home Page is an important resource guide for using and surfing the Internet. It offers information on using the Internet, provides links so you can search the Internet via Yahoo, Lycos, WWW Worm, the Meta-Index, Galaxy, etc. It also contains links arranged by university and subject matter.

KEYWORDS Internet Directories, Internet Reference
AUDIENCE General Public, Internet Users
CONTACT Richard P. Bocker bocker@nosc.mil
FREE

http://white.nosc.mil/info.html

Portuguese Root Gopher ★★★★

This is the Portuguese Root Gopher. It is maintained by the Departamento de Informatica at the Universidade Nova de Lisboa, Portugal. This server intends to be the root of all Portuguese gopher servers. It serves as a collecting point for Internet resources in and about Portugal for Portuguese users or users from elsewhere.

KEYWORDS Internet Directories, Internet Guides, Portugal
AUDIENCE Academics, Internet Users, Portuguese Speakers, Students
CONTACT Joaquim Baptista archive@fct.unl.pt
FREE

gopher://gopher.fct.unl.pt:4320/

Primer on Internet & TCP/IP Tools ★★★★

This document is an introductory guide to some of the TCP/IP and Internet tools that allow users to access the wide variety of information. It also describes discussion lists accessible from the Internet, ways to obtain Internet documents, and resources that help users weave their way through the Internet. This memo may be used as a tutorial for individual learning, a step-by-step laboratory manual for a course, or as the basis for a site user's manual.

KEYWORDS Internet Issues, Internet Protocols, Organizations, TCP/IP
AUDIENCE Internet Newcomers, Internet Users, Network Service Providers, Network Users
CONTACT nic-info@nic.merit.edu
FREE

ftp://nic.merit.edu/documents/rfc/ rfc1739.txt

Publicly Accessible Mailing Lists ★★★

This is a list of several thousand mailing lists available primarily through the Internet and the UUCP network. A mailing list is different from a newsgroup because you do not receive anything unless you specifically request it. The information included with each list varies, but most will have at least a sentence of description (sometimes a paragraph), and contact information to reach the moderator or listowner. Subject areas with the widest range of groups include Computers, Cultural, Education, Music, Regional, and Sports.

KEYWORDS Email, Listservs, Mailing Lists
AUDIENCE Email Users, General Public, Information Professionals, Librarians
CONTACT Peter da Silva peter@taronga.com
FREE

http://www.neosoft.com/internet/paml/

ftp://rtfm.mit.edu/pub/usenet/ news.answers/mail/mailing-lists/

Internet Resources

Stanford Netnews Filtering Service ★★★★

The Stanford Netnews Filtering Service homepage is a free service provided by Stanford to the Internet Community. The Netnews Filtering Server allows users to submit profiles of Usenet articles they would be interested in, and the server will return articles of interest to the user via email. The filter can handle complex profiles, and allows users to send feedback which will improve the server's filtering capabilities. The web page contains instructions on how to use the filter, information on how the filter works, and a HTML form which users can use to submit profiles and updates to the server.

KEYWORDS Internet Search Tools, News Media, Usenet Newsgroups
AUDIENCE Internet Users, Usenet News Readers
CONTACT tyan@cs.stanford.edu
FREE

http://woodstock.stanford.edu:2000/

Submit It! ★★★★

The Submit It! page was designed for Web publishers who want to submit their Web creations to the various online guides and search engines. At this site, users can fill out a form to briefly describe their site, mark off the destinations that they wish to submit it to, and send it off. Search engines included in the list are Lycos, WebCrawler, Yahoo, What's New and more.

KEYWORDS Web Authoring, Web Development
AUDIENCE Internet Users, Web Developers
CONTACT Scott Banister
         banister@uiuc.edu
FREE

http://www.cen.uiuc.edu/~banister/submit-it/

Understanding the Internet ★★★

Understanding the Internet is a guide for beginning Internet users, deriving from the special television series on the Discovery Channel. The site is divided into two parts - 'The Program' with a information from the television documentary, and 'Exploring The Internet' with links to outside resources on the Net. In 'The Program,' users will find information about the people interviewed on the TV show, with links to their home pages. The Beginners Guide to exploring the Internet includes pointers to sites with overviews of the Web, resource lists, explanations of Netiquette, and explanations of different types of applications such as WWW and email.

KEYWORDS Internet Guides, Netiquette
AUDIENCE Internet Users, Web Users
CONTACT understanding@screen.com
FREE

http://www.screen.com/start

Useless WWW Pages ★★★★

The Useless WWW Pages contains links to thousands of completely useless Web sites, from Biff the Bear's Potty Cam to T.V. Test Patterns. As the author writes, the only thing these sites have in common is the humorous quality that arises from their complete irrelevance to Web users. Besides browsing the alphabetical list of constantly changing useless pages, users may utilize features such as the Useless Site of the Week and the Pick of the Day.

KEYWORDS Internet Guides, Web Authoring
AUDIENCE Humor Enthusiasts, Internet Users
CONTACT useless@primus.com
FREE

http://www.primus.com/staff/paulp/useless.html

Usenet FAQ's ★★★

This Web site contains a hypertext list of the hundreds of FAQs found in news.answers, so that users may be able to find the FAQ for the topics they have questions about. FAQs are listed alphabetically by subject, with an introduction to the FAQ, a listing of the contents, information about using it, and directions for obtaining it. A subject search engine is also provided.

KEYWORDS FAQs (Frequently Asked Questions), Internet Reference, Usenet Newsgroups
AUDIENCE Internet Users, Usenet News Readers
CONTACT Thomas A. Fine
         fine@cis.ohio-state.edu
FREE

http://www.cis.ohio-state.edu/hypertext/faq/usenet/FAQ-List.html

What Is Usenet? ★★★

These documents describe the nature of Usenet, the worldwide distributed discussion system. The document explains what Usenet is, what it is not, and some tips for maximizing your productivity while using Usenet.

KEYWORDS Internet Guides, Netiquette, Newsgroups, Usenet Newsgroups
AUDIENCE Internet Newcomers, Internet Users, Researchers, Usenet News Readers
CONTACT ftp-bugs@rtfm.mit.edu
FREE

ftp://rtfm.mit.edu/pub/usenet/news.answers/usenet/what-is/part1

Connections to Child Safety on the Information Highway

Don't touch that dial!

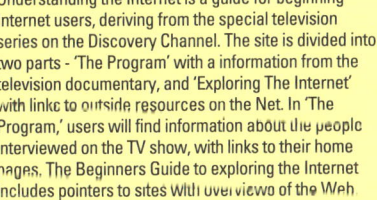

With more and more computers appearing in the home and people signing on daily to the Internet, there is the danger that as your children learn to access the Internet, they could be exposed to unsuitable material.

Many online service providers give parents a way to "block" out undesirable "chat" rooms and forums. But even innocent forums can turn ugly, or someone can sign on and "raid" a site before the service provider can disconnect that user.

Parents are encouraged to read tips and guidelines about using the Internet and protecting their children. You can instruct your children not to give out the home phone number and your address to anyone he or she meets on the Internet. Other tips include encouraging children to report to you any email or bulletin board messages that they consider demeaning or belligerent.

There are many more guidelines available to follow for insuring that your child's trip down the information superhighway is safe.

(http://www.riverdale.k12.or.us/safety.html)

Internet Resources – Internet Security

Who's Online ★★★

Who's Online is a collective experiment towards a non-commercial, decentralized Hyperbiographical database of people on the Internet. The database can be searched by profession, alphabetically, or by a keyword search. People on the Internet can submit the addresses of their home pages to the database for inclusion.

KEYWORDS Bibliographies, Databases, Hypermedia
AUDIENCE Computer Users, Internet Users
CONTACT   Enrique Canessa
          canessae@ictp.trieste.it
FREE

http://www.ictp.trieste.it/Canessa/whoiswho.html

Whole Internet Catalog ★★★

The Online Whole Internet Catalog is a collection of links to about a thousand of the best resources on the Internet, divided into easy-to-surf subject areas. Entries have been taken from the the Global Network Navigator's book, The Whole Internet User's Guide & Catalog. Each link is summarized on its own page within the Catalog, and links to indexes are labeled for the user. A listing of appropriate Usenet newsgroups are given in each category (without links). A search mechanism is available, as well as a top 25 page, an editor's choice page, and a 'guest celebrity' page, featuring an internet celebrity and their favorite links.

KEYWORDS Internet Directories, Meta-Index (Internet), Networking
AUDIENCE General Public, Internet Professionals, Internet Users, Librarians
CONTACT   Global Network Navigator
          orum@gnn.com
FREE

http://www.gnn.com/wic/newrescat.toc.html/

World Wide Web FAQ ★★★★

This web site contains frequently asked questions and answers about WWW, a distributed hypermedia system first developed by CERN. The document is fully HTML-based, allowing easy navigation using a WWW browser.

KEYWORDS Information Retrieval, Internet Reference
AUDIENCE Computer Scientists, Internet Users, Web Developers, Web Users
CONTACT   boutell@netcom.com
FREE

http://sunsite.unc.edu/boutell/faq/www_faq.html

ftp://ftp.netcom.com/pub/bo/boutell/faq/www_faq.html

World Wide Web Initiative - The Project ★★★★

The Project, produced by the W3 consortium, contains links to all kinds of information regarding the WWW. Among the more notable links are the extensive list of WWW servers worldwide, retrieval sites for WWW client and server software, WWW standards and technical details, and of course, the WWW FAQ.

KEYWORDS FAQs (Frequently Asked Questions), Internet Resources, Internet Services, WWW (World Wide Web)
AUDIENCE Internet Users, Web Developers, Web Users
CONTACT   Tim Berners-Lee
          timbl@w3.org
FREE

http://info.cern.ch/hypertext/WWW/TheProject.html

World Wide Web Mailing Lists ★★★

This document contains information on mailing lists and Usenet groups on topics related to the World Wide Web. Brief descriptions of the various newsgroups and mailing lists are given, often with links to sites where additional information can be found.

KEYWORDS Email, Usenet Newsgroups
AUDIENCE Internet Users, Network Administrators
CONTACT   Brian Kelly
          B.Kelly@leeds.ac.uk
FREE

http://www.leeds.ac.uk/ucs/WWW/WWW_mailing_lists

World Wide Web Worm ★★★

The World Wide Web Worm is an Internet searching robot program which indexes titles, URLs, and reference links. Viewers use the WWW Worm to search for information on the Internet. By inputing certain criteria, the user can search for a specific kind of file by type (html, txt, mpg, jpeg, etc) or in a particular country, or for information from different sources that are related to the same thing (worldwide references to NASA, for example).

KEYWORDS Internet Reference, Internet Tools, WWW (World Wide Web)
AUDIENCE Internet Users, Librarians, Researchers, Students
CONTACT   webmaster@cs.colorado.edu
FREE

http://www.cs.colorado.edu/home/mcbryan/WWWW.html

Internet Security

See also
Computing & Mathematics · *Applications*
Government & Politic · *Policies*
Internet · *Organizations*
Law & Criminal Justice · *Reference*

ActivCard on the Net ★★★

ActivCard on the Net is a program introducing security to the world of remote services. The Web site offers general information on Internet security, training and education, press releases, demo software, and more.

KEYWORDS France, Software, Training, Wireless Technology
AUDIENCE Internet Business Professionals, Internet Security Specialists
FREE

http://www.francenet.fr/activcard/

BorderWare - Janus Internet Firewall Server ★★★

BorderWare is a plug and play firewall and Internet server for companies with a dedicated Internet connection. This page offers information about the several product packages and services which are available. There are also a few pages which explain the reasons why firewall security is needed for different users and how the security systems work. An FAQ and a white paper are also on this site. Finally, users can read about different support services and configurations that are available.

KEYWORDS Firewalls, Hacking, Network Security
AUDIENCE Computer Professionals, Internet Providers, Network Security Professionals
FREE

http://lykos.netpart.com/janus/

CERT Coordination Center (Computer Emergency Response Team) ★★★

The Computer Emergency Response Team is a group dedicated to exposing and correcting security problems on the Internet, as well as directly involving itself with security incidents worldwide. Users can access the text of advisories that the team has published recently, and find out details of security vulnerabilities in various programs and applications. There is also a FAQ file and a public FTP directory, as well as a searchable database of computer security material.

KEYWORDS Computer Viruses, Internet Security, Organizations
AUDIENCE Computer Security Specialists, Systems Analysts
CONTACT   cert@cert.org
FREE

http://www.sei.cmu.edu/SEI/programs/cert.html

gopher://gopher.first.org/

Computer Ethics ★★★

This page is a collection of resources and links to information on the subject of computer ethics. Users will find material on computer security, privacy issues, FAQs and mailing lists, and other computer ethics information. In addition, users will find links to such organizations as the Electronic Frontier Foundation and the Cypherpunks, as well as links to computer ethics newsgroups.

KEYWORDS Computer Ethics, Computer Security, Internet Issues
AUDIENCE Computer Professionals, Computer Researchers, Computer Users
CONTACT   Meng Weng Wong
          mengwong@seas.upenn.edu
FREE

http://www.seas.upenn.edu/~mengwong/comp.ethics.html

Internet Security

Computer and Network Security Reference Index

The Telstra Corporation's Computer and Network Security Reference Index provides a gateway to computer security resources available on the Internet. It includes links to FAQs, online document archives, advisories, news, mailing lists, and more. The information is accessible through a table of contents.

Keywords Computer Security, Internet Security
Audience Computer Scientists, Internet Users, Network Administrators
Contact Rodney Campbell
rodney@tansu.com.au
Free

http://www.telstra.com.au/info/security.html

Cypherpunks Home Page

This site maintains an archive of material related to cryptography and privacy. Users can download cryptography programs for various systems, find out about anonymous remailer servers, read essays on the need for strong cryptography, and more. It is maintained by the Cypherpunks, a loose group of individuals dedicated to maintaining personal privacy in an increasingly public time.

Keywords Cryptography, Encryption, Internet Security, Privacy
Audience Cryptographers, Cypherpunks, Internet Users, Privacy Activists
Contact Sameer Parekh
sameer@c2.org
Free

http://www.csua.berkeley.edu/cypherpunks/Home.html

ftp://ftp.csua.berkeley.edu/pub/cypherpunks/

Internet Security Products Information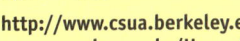

This site provides access to a list of vendors who provide network security products and services. The presentation of specific vendors in this archive does not imply recommendation, warranty or anything else on the part of Great Circle Associates. Vendors represented at this location include Ans, Bnti, Border, Checkpoint, Great Circle, Lsli, Raptor and Tis. All files are in compressed zip format. In the firewalls/info subdirectory there is an ftp 'PASV' passive mode patch and a second file containing authentication devices. Both of these patches can be downloaded from this location and are in compressed format.

Keywords Firewalls, Internet Security, Networking, Software
Audience Internet Access Providers, Internet Access Providers, Internet Developers, Internet Security Specialists
Contact Brent Chapman
Brent@GreatCircle.com
Free

ftp://ftp.greatcircle.com/pub/firewalls/info/

Connections to The Personals
One is the loneliest number . . .

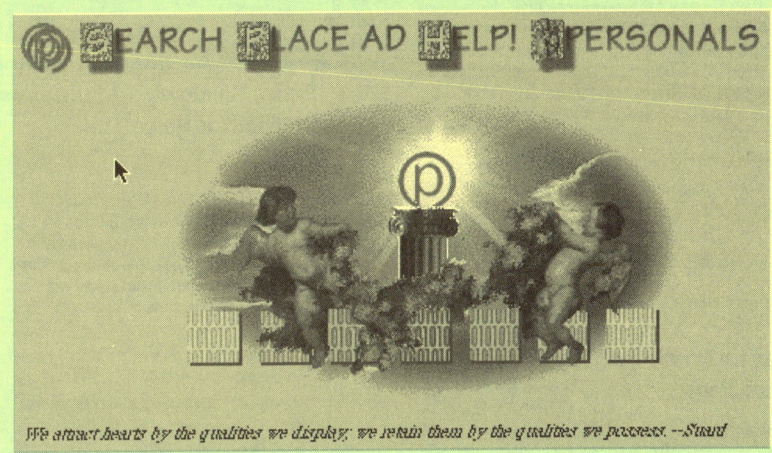

Want to make new friends? Take a trip with someone new? Find a mate? Through the Internet, you'll find 1-900 telephone numbers galore for dating services, connections to travel mates, or access to thousands upon thousands of personal ads. As in the "real world," personals on the Internet tend to be broken down by interests, or by sexual orientation, religion, and political affiliation. Many sites are in English, but there are also sites for Spanish, Italian, French, and Swedish speaking users.

Many sites will help you access personal ads placed by singles and couples looking to meet someone just like you. If you want to find a friend to share in an interactive online game, participate in a mutual hobby, or discuss earth sciences with, then you can send that person an email and designate a time to meet over the Internet.

You can access many types of people who are searching through the Internet for a special friend, a mate, or someone who shares common interests. "Welcome to the public.com Personals" is a gathering place where specific forums allow people from around the world to connect and talk about interests, careers, life goals, and desires. There are also "Personals" sites in several other languages beside English.

(http://www.public.com/personals/) also, (http://evalu0.ific.uv.es/miembros.html) also, (http://www.eunet.fi/˜EUnet/Personal.html)

Papers Available Regarding Firewalls

This site provides access to Brent Chapman's relevant papers on firewalls. Brent Chapman is an employee of Great Circle Associates and the Firewalls mailing list manager. The readme file in this directory provides the original sources for the papers provided, for two reasons - the first is that the user will get the latest and greatest information directly from the original source and secondly, GreatCircle.com only has a slow 9.6 kb/s link to the internet. This author list includes their last name, email address and anonymous ftp URL.

Keywords Firewalls, Internet Publishing
Audience Internet Access Providers, Internet Access Providers, Internet Developers, Internet Security Specialists
Contact Brent Chapman
Brent@GreatCircle.com
Free

ftp://ftp.greatcircle.com/pub/firewalls/papers/

Quadralay Cryptography Archive

The Quadralay Cryptography Archive contains information about the Quadralay Corporation and about cryptography in general. This site has an extensive list of FAQs about various encryption schemes used today. Substantial information about the Clipper Chip and the National Security Agency is also provided. You may also find out about the program PGP (Pretty Good Privacy), RIPEM (Riordan's Internet Privacy Enhanced Mail), and RSA's public-key crypto systems.

Keywords Cryptography, Encryption, Internet Security, Privacy
Audience Internet Specialists, Security Workers
Contact Brian Combs
combs@quadralay.com
Free

http://www.quadralay.com/www/Crypt/Crypt.html

RSA Data Security, Inc. ★★★★

RSA Data Security, Inc. works in cryptography developing software encryption. The home page gives information about their products, services, technical support, and laboratories. Their products include a developer's cryptographic toolkit, a certificate issuing system and RSA Secure a disk and file encryption product. There is also price information available.

KEYWORDS Cryptography, Data Communications
AUDIENCE Computer Professionals, Cryptographers, Data Communicators
CONTACT Internet: info@rsa.com
FREE

http://www.rsa.com/

Rutgers WWW-Security Index Page ★★★★

This Web page indexes information on security for the World Wide Web, HTTP, HTML, and related software/protocols. Issues for WWW security, information on related mailing lists, the IETF Web Transaction Security Working Group and a list of related documents are available here.

KEYWORDS Internet Security, Privacy, WWW (World Wide Web)
AUDIENCE Web Developers, Web Providers, Web Users
CONTACT www-security-team@www-ns.rutgers.edu
FREE

http://www-ns.rutgers.edu/www-security/index.html

Site Security Handbook ★★★★

This document describes procedures that network administrators can implement to help make their Internet-linked network more secure. The document includes information on why adminstrators need to implement security policy, risk assessment, common security procedures, and more. Users will also find an extensive bibliography with hypertext links to sources available online.

KEYWORDS Firewalls, Internet Security
AUDIENCE Internet Providers, Internet Users, Network Administrators
CONTACT J. Paul Holbrook, Joyce K. Reynolds
holbrook@cic.net
FREE

http://www.cis.ohio-state.edu/htbin/rfc/rfc1244.html

Internet Services

See also
Business & Economics · *Publishing*
Internet · *Internet Access*

Active Window Productions Home Page ★★★

The Active Window Productions (AWP) provides solutions ranging from WWW homepage creation to electronic storefronts and information services with a broad range of interactivity. The home page provides a listing of companies and organizations linked with AWP. There are links to local servers for Boston, fish resources and to MediaNation.

KEYWORDS Companies, Electronic Storefronts, Internet Marketing, Web Authoring
AUDIENCE Internet Users, Massachusetts Residents, Publishers
CONTACT Mark Rosenstein
mar@actwin.com
COST

http://www.actwin.com

Atom Co., Ltd. ★★★

This home page offers a virtual gallery, video disk sales and previews, Virtual Maclife (an electronic magazine), Japanese independent music awards, voice options, musical bytes, sales and information from the Voyager Co. There is also general information about Japan.

KEYWORDS Japan, Multimedia
AUDIENCE Computer System Designers, Computer Users, Internet Professionals, Internet Users
CONTACT info@atom.co.jp
FREE

http://www.atom.co.jp/index.html

BBN Planet ★★★

BBN Planet offers Internet service packages to business and organization. The Company handles all aspects of the network, including project management, technology, infrastructure, security, system management, and ongoing service and support. This page has information on their service offerings, customer profiles and job opportunities.

KEYWORDS Internet Networking, Internet Security, Telecommunications
AUDIENCE Business Professionals, Internet Security Managers, Internet Users
CONTACT net-info@bbnplanet.com
COST

http://www.near.net

CESnet ★★★

This server provides information on the Czech Educational and Scientific NETwork (CESnet), the main Internet network in the Czech republic. The information covers networking in the Czech Republic, links to various network services, contact addresses, the Gopher protocol and software, and software and documents written in Czech Republic.

KEYWORDS Computer Networks, Czech Republic, Research & Development
AUDIENCE Academics, Educators, Researchers
CONTACT Petr Kolar
gopheradm@vslib.cz
FREE

gopher://gopher.cesnet.cz/

CVaNet - Central Virginia's Free-Net ★★★

The Central Virginia Free-Net (CVaNet), uses this Web site to describe its services as a community networking tool. CVaNet users can read and send email as well as subscribe to Usenet newsgroups. There is also an online conferencing area, a commercial-free community zone, and a commerce area, as well as an extensive help area for new or confused users.

KEYWORDS Community Networking, Freenets, Virginia
AUDIENCE Community Activists, Virginia Residents
CONTACT help@freenet.vcu.edu
FREE

http://freenet.vcu.edu/

CommerceNet Home ★★

CommerceNet is a company that is attempting to create a wide ranging infrastructure to support electronic commerce over the Internet. Users will find information on the various services that the company offers, including descriptions of future implementations and possibilities. In addition, users can browse offerings from companies that are members of CommerceNet. This server also offers background information on CommerceNet itself, as well as material on joining their network of businesses.

KEYWORDS Consulting, Internet Business, Internet Commerce, Online Shopping
AUDIENCE Business Professionals, Internet Professionals, Marketing Professionals
CONTACT info@commerce.net
FREE

http://www.commerce.net

Greater Detroit Free-Net ★★★

The Greater Detroit Free-Net (GDFN) is a Michigan non-profit corporation. This site publicizes its services of providing the residents of Metropolitan Detroit (including Windsor, Ontario) with free, electronic access to community-related information. Users can use the FreeNet for email, interactive conferences, and to access news about living in the Detroit area. This site also provides Web and Gopher links to community resources such as schools, libraries, and other general reference sites.

KEYWORDS Freenets, Michigan
AUDIENCE FreeNet Users, Michigan Residents, Ontario Residents
CONTACT webmaster@detroit.freenet.org
FREE

http://detroit.freenet.org/

Home Pages, Inc.

This is the home page of Home Pages, Inc., a World Wide Web (WWW) authoring firm. They offer HTML authoring services, as well as offering more complex scripting, search engines, and other high-profile Web services. Users will find information on the services available, as well as links to demonstrations, pricing information, and more.

KEYWORDS   Consulting, Internet Publishing, WWW (World Wide Web)
AUDIENCE   Business Professionals, Small Business Owners
CONTACT   feedback@HomePages.com
FREE

http://www.homepages.com/

I.S.A.R. Netwerke

The Internet Service, Administration and Routing (ISAR) Netwerke provides information about addresses and emails of German Networks. This site provides links to weather maps, the European Community Database ECHO, German universities and other WWW servers.

KEYWORDS   Computer Networking, Europe, Germany, Information Services
AUDIENCE   Computer Networkers, Europeans, Germans
CONTACT   info@ISAR.de
FREE

http://www.isar.de

Internet Multicasting Service

The Internet Multicasting Service is a public cyberstation dedicated to public data, software, standards, and other infrastructure technologies. There are links to information on such events as Earth Day and the Internet 1996 World Exposition and Radio on the Internet.

KEYWORDS   Internet Communications, Telecommunications
AUDIENCE   Internet Users, Online Businesses, Telecommunications Professionals
CONTACT   questions@radio.com
FREE

http://www.media.org

Kapor Enterprises, Inc.

The Kapor Enterprises page is intended to highlight some projects in Boston designed to increase community access to technology. Some of the participants of this project include Freedom House, the United South End Settlements, the MIT Community Fellows Program and the Civil Rights Project, Inc. There are links to the staff's home pages as well as to the participating groups.

KEYWORDS   Community Networking, Internet Issues
AUDIENCE   Civil Rights Activists, Internet Users, Massachusetts Residents

---

Find The Meaning Of Acronyms
R. U. N. Sync? (Meaning: Are you in synchronization?)

Do acronyms have you stumped? On the Internet, acronyms comprise a key portion of the online language itself. If you're not sure what to do with the FTPs (File Transfer Protocol), https (Hypertext Transfer Protocol), and MUDs (Multi-User Dungeon) you encounter on the Internet, you can get help on the Net itself. The "WorldWideWeb Acronym and Abbreviation Server" provides a list of more than 6,000 acronyms and abbreviations which is constantly updated. And if you know of an acronym that's not currently in the glossary, you can submit it for inclusion.

(http://curia.ucc.ie/info/net/acronyms/acro.html)

CONTACT   Christopher Davis
           ckd@kei.com
FREE

http://www.kei.com

Mercury, News-Gopher Gateway Server

Mercury offers USENET news to Gopher clients. Users can read news in the order it was received at the news server, or in subject-threaded order. Subjects are sorted in alphabetical order, and articles within a subject are sorted in the order they were received by the news server. Mercury also returns a 'bookmark' containing the identifier of the last article currently available in the current group. Keep in mind that Mercury is a read-only gateway—posting is not possible on this server. Experimental service as of December, 1994. It's an extemely busy site (130 000 calls per day as of December, 1994.)

KEYWORDS   News, Usenet Newsgroups
AUDIENCE   Internet Users, News Buffs, Usenet News Readers
CONTACT   Dennis Boone
           drb@gopher.msu.edu
FREE

gopher://gopher.msu.edu:3441/

NLnet/NLUUG Hallway

The NLnet and NLUUG Hallway page is an access point to the Internet in the Netherlands. From this point you may access NLnet and NLUUG home pages in both English and Dutch. The links provide information about the Netherlands and Europe.

KEYWORDS   Community Networks, Computer Networking, Internet Access Providers, Netherlands
AUDIENCE   Computer Networkers, Dutch, Internet Users
FREE

http://www.nl.net/

NYSERNet (New York State Education and Research Network)

This site gives information on NYSERNet. NYSERNet (New York State Education and Research Network) is a high-speed data network, connecting New York State to the global community of computing networks. The NYSERNet mission is to advance effective network access to information and computational resources, collaborative tools and leading edge technologies to all individuals and sectors within the State of New York. The page provides details of NYSERNet staff, products, special projects and resources. The Special Collections include resources such as breast cancer information, business and economic development, community networks, the Empire Internet Schoolhouse (K-12), higher education and Internet help.

KEYWORDS Communications, Computer Networks, Information Technology, New York
AUDIENCE Computer Users, Network Service Providers, New York Residents, Usenet News Readers
CONTACT Linda Carl
lcarl@nysernet.org
FREE

gopher://nysernet.org/

National Hosts Home Page ★★★★

The National Hosts Home Page provides information on servers in different countries, the Advanced Communications Technologies and Services (ACTS) program and proposal requirements. It gives details on each of the National Hosts and links to the National Host servers currently running. It also has details of the workplan for ACTS and links to other sites containing ACTS information.

KEYWORDS Broadband Technology
AUDIENCE Communications Professionals, Internet Access Providers
CONTACT Jim Warwick
jim.warwick@analysys.co.uk
FREE

http://www.analysys.co.uk/acts/default.htm

Net Impact ★★★

Net Impact creates web sites for companies in the recreation and travel industries. The Home Page presents examples of their work in such areas as ski resorts, tourism and recreation.

KEYWORDS Internet Services, Marketing, Recreation, Web Authoring
AUDIENCE Business Professionals, Recreational Companies
CONTACT info@netimpact.com
FREE

http://www.ultranet.com/biz/netimpact/

Netherlands BBS ★★★

The Netherlands BBS is a Bulletin Board Service based in Michigan (not the Netherlands.) Users will find a description of the BBS, as well as links to helpful pages within the Web site. For example, users can click to a guide to for newbies or to resources for learning HTML. Other areas on this site is the Virtual City of NetherCity, a linked Web environment with places such as the NetherCity Tower Complex, City Hall, Users' Condos, and the FunLand Amusement Park.

KEYWORDS BBSs (Bulletin Board Systems), Michigan
AUDIENCE Internet Users, Michigan Residents
CONTACT BBS Staff
help@nether.net
FREE

http://netherlands.ypsi.mi.us/

North Sea Consulting's Web Server ★★★

North Sea Consulting maintains this web server to offer information on their Internet consulting services. The company develops and maintains Internet gateways, webservers, infobots, large-scale hypertext repositories, customized search engines and secure email systems. The site also provides information on various Web robots and search engines, as well as providing links to useful Internet tools and documentation.

KEYWORDS Consulting, Internet Access, Software
AUDIENCE Internet Publishers, Internet Users
CONTACT Stan Norton
norton@northsea.com
FREE

http://www.northsea.com/

ftp://ftp.northsea.com

Oregon Web Servers ★★★★

This page contains links to Oregon-area Web servers. The list of the Web servers is sorted by the city they are in, and includes businesses, service providers, colleges, and more.

KEYWORDS Oregon, WWW (World Wide Web), Web Servers
AUDIENCE Internet Users, Oregon Residents, Web Providers
CONTACT Tyler Jones
Tjones@willamette.edu
FREE

http://www.willamette.edu/~tjones/Oregonmap.html

Oslonett AS ★★★★

The Oslonett AS page provides information about their UNIX Internet connections. The page gives information about Oslonett's consulting services and marketplace. There are links to Scandanavian resources and other Internet sites.

KEYWORDS Computer Networking, Internet Access Providers, UNIX
AUDIENCE Computer Networkers, Internet Users, Norwegians
CONTACT oslonett@oslonett.no
FREE

http://www.oslonett.no/

Red Cientifica Peruana, the Internet Network of Peru ★★★★

The Red Cientifica Peruana (Red Internet del Peru) is an access point to the Internet Network of Peru. The pages may be viewed in a graphics version or in text. The site has information about Peru, links to the Peruvian Scientific Network and to the Ministry of Foreign Affairs, the University of Lima and more.

KEYWORDS Computer Networks, Internet Access, Peru
AUDIENCE Educators, Peruvians, Scientists, Students
FREE

http://www.rcp.net.pe/

RedEye Interactive ★★★

RedEye Interactive is a Bulletin Board Service based in New York which focuses on networking between multimedia professionals and enthusiasts. This Web site has contact information and downloadable software for anyone wishing to find out more about this resource. RedEye's resources include public bulletin boards where people can post and sell their work online, as well as read news and reviews of the latest developments in multimedia. The content of this describes the BBS, which has a subscription fee for its users.

KEYWORDS BBSs (Bulletin Board Systems), Multimedia, Networking, New York
AUDIENCE Interactive Artists, Multimedia Developers, Programmers
CONTACT redeye@wwa.com
FREE

http://sashimi.wwa.com/redeye/

Rhein Information Services ★★★

This is the site of the Rhein Information Services Individual Network in the Bonn area, Germany with pointers to Individual Network e.V. (German), Rhein.DE (Regionalnetz Bonn e.V.) (German), this host and Golden-Net, Individuals, Mailing-Lists.

KEYWORDS Germany, Information Services
AUDIENCE Computer Users, Educators (University), Internet Users, Researchers, Students (University)
CONTACT webmaster@www.rhein.de
FREE

http://gak.rhein.de

Sistemas de Tecnologia Avanzada S.A./STA/S.T.A. ★★

This is a home page from the Columbian company Sistemas de Tecnologia Avanzada S.A., which provides system integrator and consulting services, resells commodities, etc. It focuses primarily on RISC, PC and Networks hardware and software. Here you can find out about their products and services, and even subscribe to their online magazine, Status.

KEYWORDS Colombia, Software
AUDIENCE Colombians, Computer Users, Latin Americans, Usenet News Readers
CONTACT daniel@sta.sistecol.com
FREE

http://www.sistecol.com/ingles.htm

Tallahasee Free-Net Home Page ★★★★

The Tallahasee Free-Net is a publicly supported community networking resource for the Tallahassee Florida Community. Users will find a wealth of community and informational resources in areas ranging in diversity from Agriculture, to Homes and Gardens, to Religion and Philosophy. Other areas available for browsing are city and government pages, libraries, local and state activist groups, and medical and health information. There is even a local Pollen Count Page. Links to other FreeNet and Internet information is provided as well.

KEYWORDS Community Organizing, Florida, Freenets
AUDIENCE Community Activists, Florida Residents, FreeNet Users
CONTACT ppp-admin@freenet.scri.fsu.edu
FREE

http://freenet3.scri.fsu.edu:81/

UUCP (UNIX-to-UNX Copy Program) Gopher Database ★★

This Gopher Gateway performs searches of the UUCP (UNIX-to-UNIX Copy Program) database to find out path and host information. The Path function tries to return the most optimium path for an Internet host. The Host function returns the data registered for the UUCP host in the UUCP maps.

KEYWORDS Email, Internet Protocols, Software, UNIX
AUDIENCE Computer Users, Students, Systems Operators, UNIX Users
FREE

gopher://agate.berkeley.edu:4324/

Vancouver FreeNet ★★★

The Vancouver FreeNet, funded by member and corporate support, is a community information system available to everyone in Vancouver's Lower Mainland. This Web page has a variety of resources for users, such as the FreeNet News, the online newsletter of the VRFA, local Web pages of FreeNet users like the Vancouver International Film Festival, and listings of home pages for useful sites in Canada, British Columbia, and other FreeNet locations.

KEYWORDS Freenets, Vancouver
AUDIENCE Community Activists, Vancouver Residents
CONTACT web-admin@freenet.vancouver.bc.ca
FREE

http://freenet.vancouver.bc.ca/

Victoria Free-Net Home Page ★★★★

The Victoria Free-Net is a community computing information system provided to the city of Victoria, at no cost to users. This page lists information about how the Free-Net works, how people can contribute to it, and instructions on how to access the Free-Net via telnet. Users can research community and educational resources through listings of libraries, music sites, literary sites, local organizations, and other areas maintained or linked through this server.

KEYWORDS Community Networking, Freenets
AUDIENCE Community Activists, Victoria Residents
FREE

http://freenet.victoria.bc.ca/vifa.html

WWW Servers in Hong Kong ★★★

This page contains links to Web servers in Hong Kong. The list of the Web servers is sorted by alphabetic order and includes colleges and universities, government agencies, music industry, network service providers, etc.

KEYWORDS Hong Kong, WWW (World Wide Web), Web Servers
AUDIENCE Chinese Culture Enthusiasts, Internet Users, Web Providers
CONTACT HK Network Information Centre hknic@cuhk.hk
FREE

http://www.cuhk.hk/hkwww.html

Connections to Shopping
Shopping: The art, the craft, the life

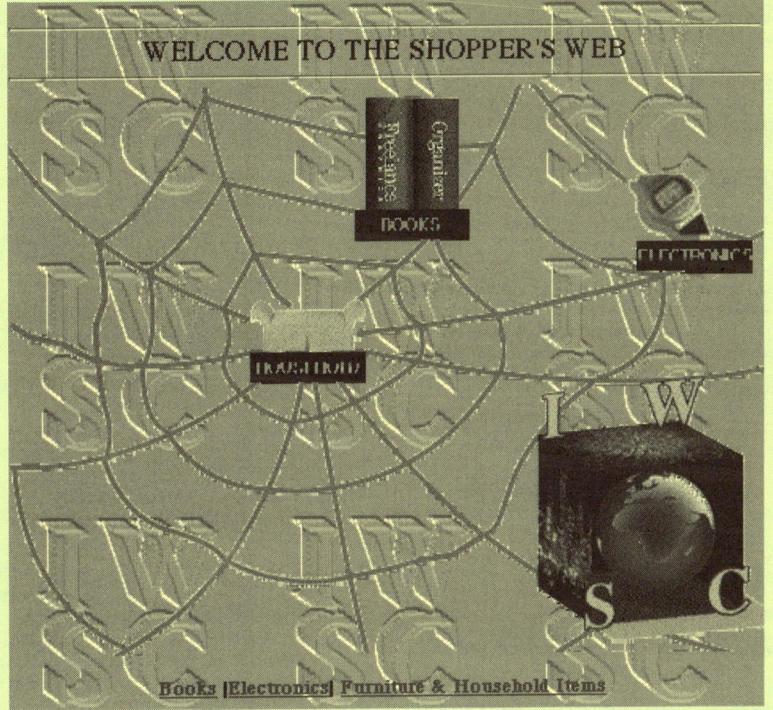

If shopping is your thing, you don't have to tire yourself out walking around a mega-mall looking for items like jade earrings or pink socks. You can do your shopping in your home, through the hundreds of catalogs, shops, and boutiques on the Internet.

Save gas, your time, and your energy. Browse through bookstores, jewelry stores, gift stores, wine warehouses, cheese shops, coffee emporiums, and lingerie shops. If you doubt you'll ever find what you want, think again! From Apples to Zithers, you can find it in any one of the virtual shopping malls. There's the Shoppers Mall, The Global Shoppers Web, World Square, The Internet Mall, Mall of the Universe, Net Catalogs, and a lot, lot more, waiting for you to visit.

You can even learn how to save money on groceries and other household items via the Internet. You'll find birdhouses, chocolates, and plants. Get out those credit cards . . . CHARGE!

(http://www.kona-coffee.com/) also, (http://infolique.lm.com/power.html)

also, (http://www.drag.net/shoppers/shoppers.html)

also, (http://www.webcom.com/~thinque/isis/)

also, (http://community.net/~csamir/aisshop.html)

WebPost ★★★

WebPost is a service for posting to the Internet directories and search engines on the World Wide Web. WebPost is accessible to any company designing, developing or marketing Web sites. All the user has to do is fill in standard information about the Web site they wish to publicize, including name, URL, description, and keywords. WebPost supports over 25 major

Internet directories, search engines, 'What's New' sites and mailing lists.

KEYWORDS   Internet Directories, Internet Marketing, Internet Search Tools
AUDIENCE   Internet Access Providers, Public Relations Agencies, Web Developers
CONTACT   Mr. Bill Younker
           byounker@sme.com
FREE

http://www.sme.com/webpost/

Women Online ★★★

This site is an online brochure for Women Online, a Macintosh and Internet consulting referral service for women in the San Francisco Bay Area. 'The primary focus of this service is on meeting the individual needs of women as personal users of Macintosh computers and/or the Internet. Plans for Windows support are on the way. The online brochure includes a description of the Macintosh and Internet support offered, a database of Women consultants in this area, the business philosophy, and information on subscribing to the Internet.

KEYWORDS   Consulting, Women's Issues
AUDIENCE   Californians, Internet Professionals, Macintosh Users, Women, Women Entrepreneurs
CONTACT   Amy T. Goodloe
           Women-Online@agoodloe.vip.best.com
FREE

http://www.best.com:80/~agoodloe/wo-brochure.html

Internet Tools

See also
Computing & Mathematics · *Resources*
Education · *International Education*
Internet · *Internet Communications*

 ### Air Mosaic Download Area ★★

Users can download the Air Mosaic Web browsing software from this site on the Netcenter online mall. Air Mosaic is also incorporated into an online service that users can use for their Internet access. Users will find announcements about the product and service as well as other promotional messages, including some ALL CAPS advertisements for their eyes, as well as an offer about 'how to earn a living selling Internet Accounts from the comforts of home.'

KEYWORDS   Air Mosaic, Internet Services, MS Windows, Web Browsers
AUDIENCE   Internet Users, Microsoft Windows Users
CONTACT   lite@ix.netcom.com
FREE

http://netcenter.com/air/air.html

Archie ★★★

This is an Archie server designed to allow people to do a keyword search for resources available on the Internet. It is located in Australia but otherwise identical to similar servers located elsewhere.

KEYWORDS   Archie, Information Retrieval, Internet Resources
AUDIENCE   Australians, Computer Users, Internet Users
FREE

gopher://archie.au:4320/

A Beginner's Guide to HTML ★★★★

The Beginner's Guide to HTML describes the basics of writing in HTML (HyperText Markup Language). This site provides a primer for producing documents in HTML, the markup language used by web browsers such as Mosaic to display information. It assumes that you have access to and a general understanding of how a browser works. The information is very detailed and has links to each basic markup tag, other documents, in-line images, troubleshooting, sounds, animations, examples and more.

KEYWORDS   Computer Applications, HTML (HyperText Markup Language), Internet Tools, WWW (World Wide Web)
AUDIENCE   Graphic Artists, HTML Users, Internet Users, Web Developers
CONTACT   pubs@ncsa.uiuc.edu
FREE

http://www.ncsa.uiuc.edu/General/Internet/WWW/HTMLPrimer.html

Browser Watch ★★★

Browser watch was designed as a resource for Web developers and users to provide information about new browsers, servers, CGIs, HTML editors and software related to WWW use. Users will find features such as news updates about Internet developments and a page with tables of different types of browsers, their features, and links to their home pages. Access statistics of browsers and IP addresses available as well.

KEYWORDS   Internet Browsers, WWW (World Wide Web)
AUDIENCE   Internet Users, Web Developers
CONTACT   Dave J. Garaffa
           d-garaffa@ski.mskcc.org
FREE

http://www.ski.mskcc.org:80/browserwatch/index.html

CIRIL (Centre Interuniversitaire de Ressources Informatiques de Lorraine) Internet Tools ★★★

This gopher is a gateway to Internet tools. The tools include Whois at ciril.fr, umn.edu, and ripe.net, Usenet news at ciril.fr, Archie searches at ciril.fr, and a finger database also at ciril.fr. The service is maintained by the Centre Interuniversitaire de Ressources Informatiques de Lorraine (CIRIL), a network information center in France.

KEYWORDS   Archie, Internet Access, Internet Tools, Whois
AUDIENCE   European Internet Users, Free-Net Organizers, French Students, Internet Users
FREE

gopher://gopher.ciril.fr:8100/

Carlos' Forms Tutorial ★★★★

This page allows users to begin an interactive tutorial on HTML (HyperText Markup Language) forms. Forms allow WWW users to input information directly on to WWW pages, and are a feature of HTML level 2. This is a fun tutorial that guides you through each step in understanding HTML and the WWW.

KEYWORDS   HTML (HyperText Markup Language), Tutorials, WWW (World Wide Web)
AUDIENCE   Computer Programmers, Internet Publishers, Internet Specialists, Web Developers
CONTACT   Carlos A. Pero
           c-pero@uiuc.edu
FREE

http://robot0.ge.uiuc.edu/~carlosp/cs317/cft.html

Cello - An Internet Browser from the Legal Information Institute ★★★★

Cello is a multipurpose Internet browser produced by the Legal Information Institute at Cornell Law School which allows access to the myriad information resources of the Internet. It supports WorldWideWeb, Gopher, FTP, CSO/ph/qi, and Usenet News retrievals natively, and other protocols (WAIS, Hytelnet, Telnet, and TN3270) through external clients and public gateways. Users will find a veritable cornucopia of links here, ranging from the serious (a listing of all the gophers in the world, a comprehensive list of FTP sites, the EIT list of network information services) to the stimulating (online tours of the Vatican Exhibit and Dead Sea Scrolls Exhibit) to the downright silly (links to several Internet-accessible Coke machines).

KEYWORDS   Information Retrieval, Internet Browsers, Internet Tools
AUDIENCE   Internet Users
CONTACT   cellobug@fatty.law.cornell.edu
FREE

ftp://ftp.law.cornell.edu/pub/LII/Cello/default.htm

Cello FAQ ★★★★

This is a site containing common questions and answers about Cello, a multipurpose Internet browser. The browser supports World Wide Web, Gopher, FTP, CSO/pf/qi, and Usenet News retrievals natively, and other protocols (WAIS, Hytelnet, Telnet, and TN3270) through external clients and public gateways.

KEYWORDS   FAQs (Frequently Asked Questions), Internet Tools, Reference
AUDIENCE   Internet Newcomers, Internet Professionals, PC Users
CONTACT   bruce@flair.law.ubc.ca,
           will@polecat.law.indiana.edu
FREE

http://www.law.cornell.edu/cello/cellofaq.html

Comparison of Mailing List Software ★★★

This site provides access to a document presenting a comparison of three mailing list software applications,

Majordomo, ProcMail and Listserver and those parts of the software related to mailing, list management, archival digests, list maintenance, and more. In the list-manager's directory there are also tools of potential use to any mailing list-manager. There are no documents available describing these tools and they are only available in compressed format.

- KEYWORDS Mailing List Management, Mailing Lists, Software Reviews
- AUDIENCE Internet Mailing List Managers, Mass Communications Educators, Software Developers, Software Users
- CONTACT Ralph Manfredi
ram@eiffel.com
- FREE

ftp://ftp.greatcircle.com/pub/list-managers/software.review/

Converters To and From HTML ★★★

This page, provided by HyperNews, contains a collection of links to shareware and tools to convert text to and from HTML. Links contain a description of the contents of each program and tool, and are grouped into HTML, SGML, Text, Mail, News, Postscript, and other Web and word processing tools. Users may also post questions and responses about HTML conversion issues.

- KEYWORDS HTML (HyperText Markup Language, Shareware
- AUDIENCE HTML Authors, Web Developers
- CONTACT Daniel LaLiberte
liberte@ncsa.uiuc.edu
- FREE

http://union.ncsa.uiuc.edu/HyperNews/get/www/html/converters.html

Crash Course on Writing Documents for the Web ★★★★

This site provides a crash course for producing documents in HTML, the markup language used by the World Wide Web. It's designed for someone who wants to put a page on the web but could care less about most of the technical details. Links are provided to topics such as the absolute essentials, HTML philosophy, the body of the document, links, images, and more. This information provides the beginner with enough HTML information to produce a web page rather easily. Links to other web tools are provided for more advanced HTML documents.

- KEYWORDS HTML (HyperText Markup Language), How to Guides, Internet Resources
- AUDIENCE Graphic Artists, HTML Users, Internet Users, Web Developers, Windows Users
- FREE

http://www.pcweek.ziff.com/~eamonn/crash_course.html

Entering the World-Wide-Web - A Guide to Cyberspace ★★

This site houses a hypertexted article entitled 'Entering the World-Wide Web - A Guide to Cyberspace.' It offers a good description of what the WWW is and how it works. The site maintains helpful links to other sites related to the WWW and the Internet in general which are useful for Internet beginners.

- KEYWORDS How to Guides, Internet Guides, Internet Tools, WWW (World Wide Web)
- AUDIENCE Internet Users, Web Users
- FREE

http://www.hcc.hawaii.edu/guide/www.guide.html

Epilogue Technology Corporation Archie.el Version 2.0 ★★★

This subdirectory of the Epilogue Technology Corporation provides access to a copy of Archie.el version 2.0. This utility is a mock interface to Archie for EMAC's (Editing MACro's). This file is not part of the many GNU EMAC's ('GNU's Not UNIX' Editing MACro's) but the same permissions and terms of usage apply. This site includes documentation complete with installation instructions, usage and customization variables. In the 'Archie.el.diff' subdirectory is the source code for the diffs developed for Archie.el version 2.0. The last modification date noted was October, 1992.

- KEYWORDS Archie, Emacs, Internet Search Tools
- AUDIENCE Internet Developers, Internet Professionals, Internet Researchers, Internet Users
- CONTACT Jack Repenning
jackr@sgi.com
- FREE

ftp://ftp.epilogue.com/pub/sra/src/archie.el/

Gopher ★★★★

Gopher is an Internet access tool that locates and retrieves resources using a graph of menus. In this directory are subdirectories containing the current versions of internet Gopher clients and servers. Technical information, user's guides, versions for different hardware platforms, and other resources can be located from this URL. You will also find a copy of the conference proceedings from the 1994 Gopher Conference.

- KEYWORDS Gopher, Internet Directories, Internet Tools
- AUDIENCE Information Brokers, Internet Users, Network Administrators, Network Developers
- CONTACT gopher@boombox.micro.umn.edu
- FREE

gopher://boombox.micro.umn.edu/

ftp://boombox.micro.umn.edu/pub/gopher/

Guide to Network Resource Tools ★★★

This page offers a complete description of the tools available to users of the Internet. It covers the major resources such as gophers and the World Wide Web, as well as less-popular tools such as Netfind and Trickle. Users will find detailed descriptions of the individual tools, instructions on how to access them, examples of their use, and pointers for users interested in learning more about the tools.

- KEYWORDS Internet Culture, Internet Guides, Internet Issues
- AUDIENCE Internet Users
- CONTACT Nadine Grange
grange@earncc.earn.net
- FREE

http://www.earn.net/gnrt/notice.html

HTML 3.0 DTD ★★★

This page is the current DTD (document type definition) of HyperText Markup Language(HTML) 3.0, formerly known as HTML+. As of this writing, HTML 3.0 is still under development.

- KEYWORDS Internet Standards, WWW (World Wide Web)
- AUDIENCE Computer Programmers, Internet Specialists, Network Developers, Web Developers
- FREE

http://info.cern.ch/hypertext/WWW/MarkUp/html3-dtd.txt

HTML Assistant FAQ (Frequently Asked Question) ★★★★

This site gives information on HTML Assistant and how to obtain it. HTML Assistant is a hypertext editor for creating and editing documents used on the World Wide Web. In addition to its editing facilities, HTML Assistant incorporates features which can help you to organize and keep track of the Internet resources that you use. It runs under MS Windows so you need to have Windows on your system in order to use it. HTML Assistant is available via anonymous FTP as freeware.

- KEYWORDS FAQs (Frequently Asked Questions), HTML (HyperText Markup Language), Internet Tools, Web Authoring
- AUDIENCE Internet Providers, Internet Users, Web Users
- CONTACT Howard Harawitz
harawitz@brooknorth.bedford.ns.ca
- FREE

ftp://ftp.cs.dal.ca/htmlasst/htmlafaq.htm

HTML Documentation Table of Contents (HyperText Markup Language) ★★★★

This page is a starting point for those interested in learning HTML. Issues covered include HTML basics, server and software information, style and structure guidelines, advanced HTML and HTML +, and more.

- KEYWORDS HTML (HyperText Markup Language), Programming Languages
- AUDIENCE Internet Developers, Internet Users, Web Developers, Web Users
- CONTACT Dr. Ian Graham
igraham@utirc.utoronto.ca
- FREE

http://www.utirc.utoronto.ca/HTMLdocs/NewHTML/htmlindex.html

Internet Tools

HTML FAQ ★★★

Frequently asked questions and answers about HTML (Hypertext Markup Language), the language used by WWW developers. The FAQ covers the practices of creating new documents specifically for the WWW format, as well as transforming existing materials into WWW documents.

- **KEYWORDS** Computer Science, Reference, WWW (World Wide Web)
- **AUDIENCE** Computer Scientists, Web Developers, Web Users
- **CONTACT** Iain O'Cain
  ec@umcc.umich.edu
- **FREE**

http://www.umcc.umich.edu/~ec/www/html_faq.html

HTML_Editors ★★★★

This page provides links to information on HTML (HyperText Markup Language) editors. HTML editors allow you to create hypertext documents used on the World Wide Web. Both Windows and Macintosh editors are included.

- **KEYWORDS** HTML (HyperText Markup Language, Internet Tools, WWW (World Wide Web), Web Authoring
- **AUDIENCE** HTML Users, Macintosh Users, Web Developers, Windows Users
- **CONTACT** Alan Richmond
  Cyberweb@Stars.com
- **FREE**

http://WWW.Stars.com/Vlib/Providers/HTML_Editors.html

HotJava Home Page ★★★
(COMMERCIAL)

This is the home page of Sun Microsystem's HotJava, a World Wide Web browser that can execute applets, which are interactive programs written in the Java language that can run from within a Web page. A tutorial on writing applets in Java is offered, as well as documentation on Java and HotJava, downloading instructions for the software, examples of what can be done with the Java language and the World Wide Web, known bugs, frequently requested features and frequently asked questions.

- **KEYWORDS** Internet Browsers
- **AUDIENCE** Computer Professionals, Computer Programmers, Network Administrators, Software Engineers
- **CONTACT** java@java.sun.com
- **FREE**

http://java.sun.com

Icon Browser ★★

This site provides an archive of icons suitable for inclusion in HTML documents. There is a index for searching the icons by name. There is a listed in a series of 114 pages displaying collages of the icons that the user can the click on to obtain the desired icon.

- **KEYWORDS** Computer Graphics, Internet Resources
- **AUDIENCE** Computer Users, Internet Users
- **CONTACT** gio@virgilio.di.unipi.it
- **FREE**

http://www.di.unipi.it/iconbrowser/icons.html

InterNIC Directory Services ★★★★
(COMMERCIAL)

This web site provides free access to Internet directory services such as X.500, WHOIS, and Netfind white pages. Through these services, one may attempt to find anyone who is connected to the Internet, using information such as name, geographic location, and workplace or domain.

- **KEYWORDS** Directories, Internet Tools
- **AUDIENCE** General Public, Internet Users
- **CONTACT** admin@ds.internic.net
- **FREE**

http://ds.internic.net/ds/dspgwp.html

Internet Tools for MACTCP (Macintosh Transmission Contol Protocol) and TidBITS ★★★★

This site provides access to the serial known as TidBITS, a Macintosh-based publication. The 'issues' subdirectory contains every issue of TidBITS, in text format, and sorted by year. The 'misc' subdirectory contains files such as caring for your wrists, easyview, Mac updates and message-splitting. The 'select' subdirectory contains important Internet tools for the MACTCP-based connection such as interviews, interslip, jpegview, macppp, MacTCP, anarchie, blueskies, bookmarks, disinfectant, dropstuff, Eudora, fetch, finger and ISKM Internet Software Updates. The subdirectory 'thewordbook' contains files in conjunction with 'The Word Book' for Macintosh users dealing almost exclusively with MS Word. Finally, the 'tisk' subdirectory is a selective mirror of Info-MacArchive's/comm (info-mac/comm).

- **KEYWORDS** Archives, Internet Search Tools
- **AUDIENCE** Computer Users, Internet Users, Macintosh Users
- **CONTACT** Adam C. Engst
  ace@tidbits.com
- **FREE**

ftp://ftp.halcyon.com/pub/tidbits/

LibWWW-PERL - Distribution Information ★★★

This page provides access to a freely available PERL (programming language) library specifically devoted to the World Wide Web. Programmers can find many tools here such as wwwbot.pl, a package for implementing the robot exclusion protocol.

- **KEYWORDS** Internet Tools
- **AUDIENCE** Computer Programmers, Internet Publishers, Internet Specialists, Web Developers
- **CONTACT** Roy Fielding
  fielding@ics.uci.edu
- **FREE**

http://www.ics.uci.edu/WebSoft/libwww-perl/

List of WWW Archie Services ★★★

This is a list of Archie servers available via WWW around the world, some of which offer HTML forms support. Archie is a tool which can locate files anywhere on the Internet that are available for FTP, using a filename keyword search.

- **KEYWORDS** Internet Resources, Internet Tools
- **AUDIENCE** Internet Users
- **CONTACT** Martijn Koster
  m.koster@nexor.co.uk
- **FREE**

http://web.nexor.co.uk/archie.html

Mosaic Home Page ★★★★

This is the welcome page to the National Center for Supercomputing Applications (NCSA) World Wide Web server, which features the Mosaic WWW application. There are links here to help you find a copy of Mosaic and other Internet software, as well as starting points from which to explore the vast resources of the WWW.

- **KEYWORDS** Internet Tools, WWW (World Wide Web)
- **AUDIENCE** Internet Users
- **CONTACT** mosaic@ncsa.uiuc.edu
- **FREE**

http://www.ncsa.uiuc.edu/SDG/Software/Mosaic/NCSAMosaicHome.html

ftp://ftp.ncsa.uiuc.edu

Netscape Navigator Extensions to HTML ★★★
(COMMERCIAL)

This page is a reference guide for Netscape's extensions to the HTML standard. Users will find descriptions and syntax of the extensions, as well as some examples of their use.

- **KEYWORDS** WWW (World Wide Web)
- **AUDIENCE** Netscape Users, Web Developers, Web Users
- **CONTACT** info@mcom.com
- **FREE**

http://www.netscape.com/home/services_docs/html-extensions.html

Nicname/Whois ★★

Whois is an Internet access tool that provides information on registered network names. The server is accessible across the Internet from user programs running on local hosts, and it delivers the full name, U.S. mailing address, telephone number, and network mailbox for DDN users who are registered in the NIC database. This document describes its uses and procedures.

- **KEYWORDS** Internet Guides, Internet Networking, Internet Tools, Whois
- **AUDIENCE** Internet Users
- **CONTACT** nic-info@nic.merit.edu
- **FREE**

ftp://nic.merit.edu/documents/rfc/rfc0954.txt

PMosaic - Localized Persian/Arabic Mosaic ★★★

PMosaic is an enhanced NCSA Mosaic 2.4 UNIX/X11 WWW browser supporting Trilingual Persian, Arabic and English text. Currently, versions of this browser will run on UNIX platforms including SGI 5.2/5.3, Sun 4.1.3, Solaris 2.3, HP 7xx, IBM RS6000, DEC Ultrix, alpha, and Linux. Visitors will find instructions on how to create bilingual HTML documents for PMosaic, as well as sample documents.

KEYWORDS   WWW (World Wide Web)
AUDIENCE   Arabic Writers, Iranians, Middle East Residents, Persians
CONTACT   Global Publication Group
           pmosaic@simorgh.gpg.com
FREE

http://gpg.com/pmosaic/

ftp://Tehran.stanford.edu/Iran_Lib/PMosaic/

Site-Index.Pl—Indexing Your Web Site ★★★

This page offers information on and access to a PERL script that automates Aliweb site-indexing for those running NCSA's Web Server.

KEYWORDS   WWW Servers
AUDIENCE   Computer Programmers, Internet Publishers, Internet Specialists, Web Developers
CONTACT   Robert Thau
           rst@ai.mit.edu
FREE

http://www.ai.mit.edu/tools/site-index.html

Sources for Internet Browsers and Client Software ★★

This site provides an incomplete list of sources for Internet browsers and client software.

KEYWORDS   Internet Tools, WWW Servers
AUDIENCE   Internet Users
CONTACT   David Green
           David.Green@anu.edu.au
FREE

http://life.anu.edu.au/links/syslib.html

Texture Land! ★★★

Texture Land! is a terrific graphic resource for Web developers and home page creators who wish to take advantage of the background capabilities of Netscape 1.1., providing numerous graphic textures for users to download. Users may choose from lists of Normal Textures or AbNorMal Textures, and download them simply by clicking on the image that they want and 'saving the image as.' This site then provides instructions for how to integrate the graphic into your HTML documents. Users may also download all of the textures at once in a zip file.

KEYWORDS   Graphics, HTML (HyperText Markup Language)
AUDIENCE   HTML Authors, Home Page Creators, Web Developers
CONTACT   Chris Pearce
           yyz@europa.com
FREE

http://www.europa.com/~yyz/textures/textures.html

Tools for WWW Providers ★★★★

This page contains pointers to HTML and WWW tools for many computer platforms.

KEYWORDS   Internet Resources, WWW (World Wide Web)
AUDIENCE   Internet Publishers, Internet Specialists, Web Developers, Web Users
CONTACT   Tim Berners-Lee
           timbl@w3.org
FREE

http://info.cern.ch/hypertext/WWW/Tools/

Connections to HotJava
Spice it up!

When you want to spice up your spreadsheet for a presentation, or create a game that has lots of "bells and whistles," turn to the "HotJava" site.

This site enables you to access the HotJava browser so as to better appreciate a page on the Internet that contains sophisticated graphics, for instance. Or to access "applets" which serve to spice up a presentation, a resume, a business report, a spreadsheet, or a word-game you've created.

There are educational applets, such as 3D chemical models, fractal figures, or blinking text. You can also access a variety of games and other diversions at this site—perfect when you're in the mood to directly experience the benefits of applets, rather than incorporate them into your work.

(http://java.sun.com/applets/)

UR* and The Names and Addresses of WWW Objects ★★★

This page describes in detail the addressing scheme of the WWW, which uses Uniform Resource Identifiers (URIs), Uniform Resource Locators (URLs), Uniform Resource Names (URNs), and Uniform Resource Citations (URCs). Links can be followed to RFC specification documents, background material, and mailing list archives related to the Uniform Resource addressing scheme.

KEYWORDS   Internet Standards, WWW (World Wide Web)
AUDIENCE   Internet Developers, Web Developers, Web Users
CONTACT   Tim Berners-Lee
           timbl@w3.org
FREE

http://www11.w3.org/hypertext/WWW/Addressing/Addressing.html

W3 and HTML Tools ★★★

The W3 Consortium for Web development has created this site as a resource for Web publishers and HTML authors. It contains HTML tools and shareware for Web development, available from both local and outside Web sources. Users will find a CGI Archive, sites for generating HTML, HTML authors and editing, and other useful scripts. Each tool is listed with a description of its function.

KEYWORDS HTML (HyperText Markup Language), Shareware)
AUDIENCE HTML Authors, Home Page Creators, Web Developers
CONTACT webmaster@w3.org
FREE

http://www.w3.org/hypertext/WWW/Tools/

WAIS (Wide Area Information Servers) FAQ ★★

Common questions and answers about WAIS (Wide Area Information Servers), a networked full-text retrieval system. WAIS can be used to search documents on a particular site for keywords and transfer the document to the user. This FAQ gives information about how to obtain and use the software.

KEYWORDS FAQs (Frequently Asked Questions), Internet Tools, WAIS (Wide Area Information Service)
AUDIENCE Computer Scientists, Internet Users, Researchers, Students
CONTACT ftp-bugs@rtfm.mit.edu
FREE

ftp://rtfm.mit.edu/pub/usenet-by-group/news.answers/wais-faq/getting-started

Web Communications Comprehensive Guide to Publishing on the Web ★★★

The Web Communications Comprehensive Guide to Publishing on the Web is designed as a resource for creating home pages and HTML documents. Users can read their instructions for basic HTML (HyperText Markup Language) programming, including creating fill-out forms and tag templates, as well as finding general guidelines for creating a site and publicizing it. An icon index and a collection of free WWW browsers and tools are also provided.

KEYWORDS HTML (HyperText Markup Language), Web Development
AUDIENCE HTML Authors, Web Developers
CONTACT support@webcom.com
FREE

http://www.webcom.com/~webcom/html/

 Weblint ★★★★

This page allows users to enter a URL (Uniform Resource Locator) or HTML code and have it checked for mistakes, proper structure, and integrity.

KEYWORDS Internet, WWW (World Wide Web)
AUDIENCE Internet Publishers, Internet Specialists, Web Developers, Web Users
CONTACT webster@unipress.com
FREE

http://www.unipress.com/weblint/

 **Welcome to Aliweb** ★★★★

Aliweb is a searchable database of descriptions of available resources on the World Wide Web. It is based upon the principal that the people responsible for a site are in the best position to describe its contents accurately. Site maintainers fill out a standardized form describing their site, and Aliweb retrieves these documents hourly to refine its database. Users may then search by keyword, and have access to up-to-date information. Site maintainers may also add their servers to the Aliweb database.

KEYWORDS Databases, Internet Search Tools
AUDIENCE Internet Users, Web Developers, Web Users
CONTACT Martijn Koster
m.koster@nexor.co.uk
FREE

http://web.nexor.co.uk/public/aliweb/aliweb.html

Welcome to ArchiePlex ★★★

This is a direct gateway to various archie servers around the world, allowing customization of searches via HTML forms support. Archie is a tool which can locate files anywhere on the Internet that are available for FTP, using a filename keyword search.

KEYWORDS Internet Resources, Internet Tools
AUDIENCE Internet Users
CONTACT Martijn Koster
m.koster@nexor.co.uk
FREE

http://web.nexor.co.uk/public/archie/archieplex/archieplex.html

Wide World Web Wonder Widget — Mozilla Printing ★★★

The Wide World Web Wonder Widget is an experimental tool for acquiring a PostScript document from a URL chosen by the browser.

KEYWORDS Internet Browsers, Internet Tools
AUDIENCE Internet Browsers, Internet Users
CONTACT mtoy@mcom.com
FREE

http://home.mcom.com/people/mtoy/cgi/www-print.cgi

Windows Internet Software ★★★

This site provides access to a small number files of Internet Software for Windows. Files located in this subdirectory include a self-extracting archive containing PC Eudora email client, Windows 32-bit extensions, WinWeb WWW Browser (substitute for Mosaic), WinIRC Internet Relay Chat for Windows, DOS Internet Toolkit, Finger 3.1, and more. The 'lightside/WinUtilities' subdirectory contains four Windows utilities; pkzip, uuencode, uudecode and winzip.

KEYWORDS Freeware, Internet Search Tools
AUDIENCE Internet Users, PC Users, Windows Users

FREE

ftp://ftp.lightside.com/lightside/WinInternetSoftware/

 Yahoo ★★★★

Yahoo - Yet Another Hierarchical Officious Oracle - is a hierarchical index of the World Wide Web. This index primarily targets their list towards HTML documents, however they do include other URLs when they are useful. Current capabilities of the Yahoo index include a menubar which can take you to the next higher level of a specific category, a forms based search of the URL's, titles, and comments within Yahoo's directory, and an 'add your own entry' form. Other specific pages on Yahoo can link the user to sites that are either New, Popular, Cool, or Random. In addition, a legend system indicates a new site (within the first 3 days). Under construction is a simple rating system which can indicate a recommended site.

KEYWORDS Internet Directories, Meta-Index (Internet), WWW (World Wide Web)
AUDIENCE Information Professionals, Internet Professionals, Internet Users, Librarians
CONTACT yahoo@akebono.stanford.edu
FREE

http://www.yahoo.com/

Networking

See also
Computing & Mathematics · *Software*
Education · *Educational Technology*
Internet · *Internet Access*

Bellcore Metamail V.2.7 ★★★

This site provides a generic implementation of MIME (Multipurpose Internet Mail Extentions) to extend existing email software. This software implements MIME standards and extends email into multimedia mail. It incorporates into existing mail programs and converts the program to a multimedia one. In addition to the standard ASCII text format it sends mail using an image format, audio, arbitrary binary and/or richtext format. Publications are also available at this site regarding the current state of 'Ethernet' as well as papers complete with slides and audio-files in genuine MIME multimedia format.

KEYWORDS Email, Multimedia
AUDIENCE Academics, Business Professionals, Email Users, Internet Users
CONTACT Nathaniel S. Borenstein
nsb@bellcore.com
FREE

ftp://thumper.bellcore.com/

Ebone ★★★

This gopher describes Ebone which stands for European Backbone. Ebone is a European international network backbone connecting research network service providers. The server also provides access to nodes on the Ebone network, provides searches of Ebone WAIS, Archie, and Veronica, servers, and acts as a gateway to information services in European cities.

KEYWORDS Computer Hardware, Computer Networks, Europe

AUDIENCE European Internet Users, German Internet Users, Internet Users
FREE
gopher://gopher.ebone.net/

IP (Internet Protocol) - Next Generation ★★★

This page provides access to information about the next generation of Internet Protocols being developed by the Internet Engineering Task Force (IETF). Users may access a series of postscript documents describing various technical specifications of the emerging protocol.
KEYWORDS Internet Networking, Internet Protocols, Internet Standards
AUDIENCE Internet Engineering Task Force Members, Internet Providers, Internet Users
CONTACT ietf-web@cnri.reston.va.us
FREE

http://www.ietf.cnri.reston.va.us/ipng/ipng.html

InterNIC Home Page ★★★★

The InterNIC networking organization, a collaborative project which provides information in three key areas - accessing and using the Internet, assistance in locating resources on the network, and registering network components for Internet connectivity. The overall goal of the InterNIC is to make networking and networked information more easily accessible to researchers, educators, and the general public.
KEYWORDS Computer Science, Information Retrieval, Networked Information Retrieval
AUDIENCE General Public, Internet Users, Researchers, Students
CONTACT guide@internic.net
FREE

http://www.internic.net/

Internetworking Company of Southern Africa ★★★

The gopher server for the Internetworking Company of Southern Africa describes its history, products, and services. There are also links to important gopher sites around the Internet.
KEYWORDS Companies, Networking, South Africa
AUDIENCE Africans, Computer Users, Network Developers, South Africans
CONTACT info@ticsa.com
FREE

gopher://gopher.ticsa.com/

Merit Network, Inc. ★★★

Merit Network, Inc. is an Internet service run by 11 Michigan universities to connect to information resources from various state organizations and education providers. Their home page covers their projects in areas such as routing technology and NSFNET, with overviews, tools and documents, papers, and users' guides. Users may also access the MichNet Gopher, a Merit regional research and educational network, with Internet documents and software archives. Other resources provided include an introductory guide to using the Internet and directories to online resources.
KEYWORDS Information Systems, Internet Services, Networking, Routing Algorithms
AUDIENCE Internet Users, Michigan Residents
CONTACT info@merit.edu
FREE

http://nic.merit.edu

NC-REN Network ★★

This gopher site describes the North Carolina Research and Education (NC-REN) Network. NC-REN Network is a privately owned computer and telecommunications network in North Carolina. The server provides information about the network's facilities for data and video transmission. It also provides information about Internet services provided to individuals and corporations by NC-REN Network.
KEYWORDS Internet Access, Internet Service Providers, Telecommunications
AUDIENCE Computer Users, Internet Users
FREE

gopher://jazz.concert.net:71/

NORDUnet ★★

This is a gopher server of the NORDUnet in Sweden. NORDUnet is a regional UNIX-based computer network covering the countries of Scandinavia. Their server offers information on NORDUnet, its organization, its services, Internet engineering work, and more. It has links to gophers in Denmark, Finland, Iceland, and Norway.
KEYWORDS Internet Tools, Networking, Sweden
AUDIENCE Computer Users, Internet Users
CONTACT gopher-info@nic.nordu.net
FREE

gopher://nic.nordu.net/

PSGNet ★★★

This gopher gives information about computer networks and computer networking in the developing world. The site is maintained by PSGnet and RAINet. Some of the information covered includes information on networking in Africa and Latin America, and a mechanism to submit documents to the database.
KEYWORDS Africa, Computer Networking, International Development, Latin America
AUDIENCE International Business Educators, International Development Specialists
CONTACT lowcost-net@psg.com
FREE

gopher://gopher.psg.com/

A Revised Catalog of Available X.500 Implementations ★★

A catalog of available X.500 Implementations, a globally distributed Internet directory service. This document is the result of a survey that gathered new or updated descriptions of currently available implementations of X.500, including commercial products and openly available offerings. This document is a revision of RFC 1292. This document contains detailed descriptions of 26 different X.500 implementations—DSAs, DUAs, and DUA interfaces.
KEYWORDS Internet Issues, Internet Networking, Internet Standards, X.500
AUDIENCE Internet Specialists, Network Administrators, Network Developers
CONTACT nic-info@nic.merit.edu
FREE

ftp://nic.merit.edu/documents/fyi/fyi_11.txt

Sprintlink Gopher Server ★★★

This gopher server will provide information about Internetworking as well as Sprint information of interest and relevence to the Internet community. Users will find information on Sprint and its activities, technical material on Internetworking, and world news. In addition, this gopher provides links to other gophers around the world, as well as links to Internet phone books.
KEYWORDS Networking, Phone Books, Telecommunications
AUDIENCE Internet Users, Network Users
CONTACT Richard Martin
       rmartin@sprintlink.net
FREE

gopher://ftp.sprintlink.net

Switch Swiss Academic and Research Network ★★★★

The Switch Swiss Academic and Research Network connects the resources of numerous Swiss universities, companies, and other institutions. Their Web site provides information about their services and how to access them, as well as providing the Netnews BBS discussing the Internet Community. Links to the Web sites of all of the educational organizations and research laboratories associated with the Network are included. Users may also browse through a list of educational libraries, with information about their resources and connections via WWW or Telnet.
KEYWORDS Information Systems, Internet Access Providers, Switzerland
AUDIENCE Educators, Internet Users, Researchers, Swiss
CONTACT webmaster@www.switch.ch
       English, German
FREE

http://nic.switch.ch/

WINLAB Home Page ★★★

WINLAB (Wireless Information Network Laboratory) mission is to 'collaborate with industry and government to advance the future of wireless communications through research and education.' This site gives access to brochures, a prospectus, sponsors, people, study groups, publications, and events about WINLAB. There is access to information on the Fifth WINLAB Workshop and sponsor related material. There are links to other sites of both wireless and general interest information.
KEYWORDS Information Services, Research, Wireless Communications

AUDIENCE Government Employees, Industry Employees, Students (University), Wireless Communicators
CONTACT webmaster@winwww.rutgers.edu
FREE

http://winwww.rutgers.edu/

Organizations

See also
Computing & Mathematics · *Organizations*
Internet · *Internet Issues*
Internet · *Internet Resources*

Coalition for Networked Information ★★★

This is the home page for the Coalition for Networked Information, a joint project of the Association of Research Libraries, CAUSE, and EDUCOM. The Coalition's mission is to promote the creation of and access to information resources in networked environments in order to enrich scholarship and to promote intellectual productivity.
KEYWORDS Computer Networking, Information Retrieval
AUDIENCE Internet Users, Researchers
CONTACT info@cni.org
FREE

http://www.cni.org/CNI.homepage.html

gopher://gopher.cni.org/

ftp://ftp.cni.org/

telnet://a.cni.org

First WWW Conference ★★★

This site gives information about the First WWW Conference held in May 1994 in Geneva, Switzerland. It provides lists of the people, companies, and institutions that participated, summaries of workshops and panel discussions, preliminary proceedings, and more.
KEYWORDS Conferences, Information Technology, Organizations, WWW (World Wide Web)
AUDIENCE Computer Professionals, Computer Scientists, Information Scientists
CONTACT Robert Cailliau CAILLIAU@www1.cern.ch
FREE

http://www1.cern.ch/WWW94/Welcome.html

HyperNews ★★★

This site is a part of the HyperNews Project, which is an attempt to combine Usenet News with WWW hypertext capabilities. Newsgroup posters can use HTML to specify links in their articles, which allows readers to directly connect with source documents if desired. The service is in its infancy, and there are not many articles available currently. Note that the site is not directly connected with Usenet news.
KEYWORDS HTML (HyperText Markup Language), Usenet Newsgroups
AUDIENCE Internet Users, Usenet News Readers
CONTACT Daniel LaLiberte iberte@ncsa.uiuc.edu
FREE

http://union.ncsa.uiuc.edu:80/HyperNews/get/hypernews.html

IETF Home Page (Internet Engineering Task Force) ★★★

This is the home page of the Internet Engineering Task Force, a loosely organized collection of professional volunteers who oversee the engineering protocols development of the Internet. Users can access hypertext and gopher versions of the proceedings of IETF meetings, which are held three times a year. In addition, users will find information on IETF working groups and their projects. IETF working groups are the entities that actually perform the hardcore engineering work needed to further Internet protocol standardization as well as development of the Internet.
KEYWORDS Internet Issues, Internet Networking, Internet Protocols, Organizations
AUDIENCE Internet Engineering Task Force Members, Internet Providers, Internet Users
CONTACT ietf-info@cnri.reston.va.us
FREE

http://www.ietf.cnri.reston.va.us/home.html

Institute for Global Communications (IGC) Gopher ★★★

This gopher site provides information about computer networks, such as PeaceNet, EcoNet, ConflictNet, and LaborNet, maintained by the Institute for Global Communications in San Francisco (IGC). IGC is part of an international consortium working for political causes. In addition to providing information about IGC, this gopher provides links to resources on the various networks which in turn provide information on areas such as peace, human rights, environmental protection, social justice, and sustainability.
KEYWORDS Computer Networks, International Politics, Peace
AUDIENCE Activists, Environmentalists, Political Activists
CONTACT igc-info@igc.apc.org
FREE

gopher://gopher.econet.apc.org/

International Internet Association Gopher Site ★★★

This gopher site provides information on the International Internet Organization (IIA), a non-profit provider of free Internet access and services in the world. The organization, based in Washington D.C. (with the technical office in New Jersey), is primarily composed of engineers and computer network professionals dedicated to promoting the availability of online resources and connection to all aspects of society. The site includes account information, associations of the organization, access to a telephone line to connect, and other relevant resource information.
KEYWORDS Cyberspace, Internet Issues, Organizations, Virtual Community
AUDIENCE Computer Users, Information Scientists, Internet Users
FREE

gopher://gopher.iia.org/

Internet Society Gopher Server ★★★

This gopher server provides information on the Internet Society. This includes information on membership, publications, conference proceedings, financial and conduct information.
KEYWORDS Computer Technology, Internet Security, Internet Tools
AUDIENCE Business Professionals, Computer Professionals, Internet Users
CONTACT amr@isoc.org
FREE

gopher://gopher.isoc.org/

Virtual Communities

See also
Internet · *Online Games*
Sports & Recreation · *Games*

(Evil!) Mud ★★

This adult site offers a virtual world that stresses the dark and evil nature of mankind. There are several text adventure-style puzzles available for you to solve.
KEYWORDS Computer Games, MUDs (Multi-User Dimensions), Puzzles, Role-Playing
AUDIENCE Adults, MUD Users, Role-Playing Enthusiasts
FREE

telnet://intac.com:4201

5th Dimension ★★★

This site is a virtual world for the City of Terminus. The theme is a standard adventure game but violence is not stressed.
KEYWORDS MUDs (Multi-User Dimensions), Online Games, Role-Playing, Virtual Communities
AUDIENCE MUD Users, Role-Playing Enthusiasts
FREE

telnet://gauss.ifm.liu.se:3000

Abyss IV ★★★★

This is a standard adventure game with a virtual world partly patterned after Tolkien's 'The Lord of the Rings'.
KEYWORDS MUDs (Multi-User Dimensions), Online Games, Role-Playing
AUDIENCE MUD Users, Role-Playing Enthusiasts
FREE

telnet://129.89.68.89:4000

Adamant ★★★

This MUD (Multi-User Dimension), Adamant, is based on the standard adventure game of Dungeons and Dragons. Starting from Luzi's Memorial Church, you can travel to nearby locations including the Palace of

Galltus, the Library, the Jail, and the Market Place, with more exotic places found further on. This MUD is located in Germany, and although the language used is English, you can often find players chatting in German.

KEYWORDS   MUDs (Multi-User Dimensions), Online Games, Role-Playing
AUDIENCE   MUD Users, Role-Playing Enthusiasts
FREE

telnet://rm600.rbg.informatik.th-darmstadt.de:4711

Addventure

Addventure is an addicting variation on the 'Choose your own adventure' story. Users can click to go to a possible outcome and add their own twists to the storyline. This interactive creative writing project can consume more time than you expected, as each one of several running adventures has thousands of potential outcomes. There are specific adventures being developed for children and for 'mature audiences.'

KEYWORDS   Adventure Games, Interactive Entertainment
AUDIENCE   Experimental People, Internet Users, Role Playing Enthusiasts
CONTACT   prisoner@addventure.com
FREE

http://www.addventure.com/

Albion Mud

This is a standard Dungeons and Dragons fantasy adventure. The object is to gain experience by completing quests and fighting enemies.

KEYWORDS   MUDs (Multi-User Dimensions), Online Games, Role-Playing, Virtual Communities
AUDIENCE   MUD Users, Role-Playing Enthusiasts
CONTACT   mud@veda.is
FREE

telnet://veda.is:4000

BEV - Blacksburg Electronic Village

The Blacksburg Electronic Village is a cooperative project of Virginia Tech, Bell Atlantic of Virginia, and the Town of Blacksburg, that links its citizens, via computers, to each other and to the worldwide Internet. Some of the areas to check out are the chamber of commerce, village mall, calendar of events, local organizations, local schools, and official town information. In fact there is even a database of medical information compiled by a local physician.

KEYWORDS   Internet Access, Internet Culture, Virginia
AUDIENCE   Blacksburg Residents, Internet Access Providers, Internet Users, Virginia Residents
CONTACT   webmaker@bev.net
FREE

http://crusher.bev.net/

gopher://gopher.bev.net/

Bolo

This site provides access to all of the files necessary to play Bolo, an interactive multi-user network tank/war game. The only text file available at this location is one entitled 'Puppy Love's Unofficial Bolo Tactics and Strategy Guide'. This guide is not suitable for new Bolo players but is aimed at individuals who have played enough Bolo to warrant paying the shareware fee. Shareware fees are not posted in this document but may be present in one of several compressed Bolo files available for FTP from this server.

KEYWORDS   Games, Shareware
AUDIENCE   Computer Game Enthusiasts, Computer Users, Game Enthusiasts, Interactive Game Players
CONTACT   miller@minerva.cis.yale.edu
FREE

ftp://ftp.lightside.com/lightside/Bolo/

Cajun Nights MUSH (Multi-User Shared Hallucination)

The Cajun Nights MUSH [Multi-User Shared Hallucination] is based on White Wolf's Storyteller system. It is set in the World of Darkness, and more specifically takes place in New Orleans and Baton Rouge, Louisiana.

KEYWORDS   Cajun Culture, Role-Playing, Science Fiction, Virtual Communities
AUDIENCE   MUD Users, Role-Playing Enthusiasts, Science Fiction Enthusiasts
CONTACT   blackthorn@delphi.glendon.yorku.ca
FREE

telnet://krynn.solace.mh.se:7373/

Camelot MUSH (Multi-User Shared Hallucination)

Camelot MUSH is a MUSH [Multi-User Shared Hallucination] set in the legendary time of King Arthur and the Knights of the Round Table. Character concepts are open, and registration is optional (but has benefits).

KEYWORDS   MUDs (Multi-User Dimensions), Role-Playing, Virtual Communities
AUDIENCE   Anglophiles, Cyberculture Enthusiasts, MUD Users, Role-Playing Enthusiasts
CONTACT   Morgana
           leia@csulb.edu
FREE

telnet://cadman.rit.buffalo.edu:5440/

Cardiff's Video Game Database Browser

This system is dedicated to stand-alone video games such as the Atari Jaguar, Genesis, 0, Sega, and Nintendo. You can search for a particular game and see how the game was rated.

KEYWORDS   Online Games, Recreation
AUDIENCE   Computer Game Enthusiasts
CONTACT   Simon Smith
           Simon.N.Smith@cm.cf.ac.uk
FREE

http://www.cm.cf.ac.uk/Games/

CrystalMUSH (Multi-User Shared Hallucination)

CrystalMUSH [Multi-User Shared Hallucination] is based on Anne McCaffrey's 'CrystalSinger' novels, and is set on the planet Ballybran. The text descriptions are less stylized and contain more vivid imagery than most MUSHes, reading almost like a story.

KEYWORDS   MUDs (Multi-User Dimensions), Role-Playing, Science Fiction, Virtual Communities
AUDIENCE   MUD Users, Role-Playing Enthusiasts, Science Fiction Enthusiasts
FREE

telnet://moink.nmsu.edu:6886/

Dawn Sisters MUSH (Multi-User Shared Hallucination)

Dawn Sisters is a MUSH [Multi-User Shared Hallucination] based on Anne McCaffrey's Dragonrider novels. It is set in post-Ninth-Pass Pern, after 'All the Weyrs of Pern.'

KEYWORDS   MUDs (Multi-User Dimensions), Role-Playing, Science Fiction, Virtual Communities
AUDIENCE   MUD Users, Role-Playing Enthusiasts, Science Fiction Enthusiasts
CONTACT   khyri@netcom.com
FREE

telnet://arms.gps.caltech.edu:9944/

Death's Domain

This MUD is patterned after the standard Dungeons and Dragons fantasy adventure game.

KEYWORDS   Computer Games, MUDs (Multi-User Dimensions), Online Games, Role-Playing
AUDIENCE   MUD Users, Role-Playing Enthusiasts
FREE

telnet://cybernet.cse.fau.edu:9000

Deep Seas

Deep Seas is a social MUSH [Multi-User Shared Hallucination] in an underwater setting. Character registration is required. Mail requests for a character to the contact email address.

KEYWORDS   Games, MUDs (Multi-User Dimensions), Role-Playing, Virtual Communities
AUDIENCE   Cyberculture Enthusiasts, MUD Users, Role-Playing Enthusiasts
CONTACT   deepseas-request@muds.okstate.edu
FREE

telnet://muds.okstate.edu:6250/

Discordia MUSH (Multi-User Shared Hallucination)

Discordia MUSH is a small, relaxed social MUSH [Multi-User Shared Hallucination]. Guest characters

Virtual Communities

can explore for up to 30 minutes. Send requests for registered characters to the contact email.

KEYWORDS Games, MUDs (Multi-User Dimensions), Role-Playing, Virtual Communities
AUDIENCE Cyberculture Enthusiasts, MUD Users, Role-Playing Enthusiasts
CONTACT poyner@pc2.pc.maricopa.edu
FREE

telnet://discordia.phya.utoledo.edu:4201/

DoggieMUSH (Multi-User Shared Hallucination)

DoggieMUSH is a small, relaxed, sometimes silly social MUSH [Multi-User Shared Hallucination] with a canine flavor. Neophyte MUSHers can find a good 'help trail' to follow as an introduction.

KEYWORDS MUDs (Multi-User Dimensions), Role-Playing, Virtual Communities
AUDIENCE Cyberculture Enthusiasts, MUD Users, Role-Playing Enthusiasts
FREE

telnet://aladdin.dataflux.bc.ca:8888/

DragonDawn

This MUSH [Multi-User Shared Hallucination] is based on Anne McCaffrey's Dragonrider series. It is set on Pern during the Second Pass of the Red Star.

KEYWORDS MUDs (Multi-User Dimensions), Role-Playing, Science Fiction, Virtual Communities
AUDIENCE MUD Users, Role-Playing Enthusiasts, Science Fiction Enthusiasts
FREE

telnet://cashew.enmu.edu:2222/

DragonMUD [Multi-User Dimension]

The DragonMUD is set in 18th-century London. Emphasis is on puzzles and adventure, and the text is less stylized and contains more vivid imagery than most MUDS.

KEYWORDS London, MUDs (Multi-User Dimensions), Role-Playing, Virtual Communities
AUDIENCE Anglophiles, Cyberculture Enthusiasts, MUD Users, Role-Playing Enthusiasts
FREE

telnet://satan.ucsd.edu:4201/

E-Ville Dialogues

The E-Ville Dialogues is an electronic fictional place that the author describes as a multi-meta layered, fully illustrated book. The subject and object are to be the study of mediated thought processes by way of the spatial and visual manifestations of the ideas discussed. For ordinary citizens, E-Ville is a very difficult place to live, unless one is invited into the dining room. If one is never invited into The Restaurant this means one thing - eternal damnation.

KEYWORDS Cyberspace, MUDs (Multi-User Dimensions)
AUDIENCE Cybernauts, Fiction Enthusiasts, Interactive Game Players, Internet Users

CONTACT Shana M. Fisher
shana@www.itp.tsoa.nyu.edu
FREE

http://www.itp.tsoa.nyu.edu/~shana/Dialogues/cover.html

ElendorMush Home Page

This site offers information on the ElendorMush, an online role-playing game based on J.R.R. Tolkien's works. It contains references to places and people from Tolkien's books.

KEYWORDS Cyberculture, Cyberpunk Games
AUDIENCE Fantasy Enthusiasts, Internet Users, MUSH Enthusiasts
FREE

http://where.com/Elendor/Welcome.html

Globe

The Globe is an entertainment site full of games, software, and online chats. Features include several different chat rooms for real time discussions, a Message Center where users may write or review commentaries about numerous topics, and a gallery with art and animation. Other fun links include comics, games, and links to software. The Global Consortium is a collection of pages from entertainment sites, Internet access providers, and other commercial and non-commercial Web sites.

KEYWORDS Internet Games, Internet Relay Chat
AUDIENCE IRC Enthusiasts, Internet Users, WWW Browsers
CONTACT tvk1@cornell.edu
FREE

http://globe1.csuglab.cornell.edu/global/homepage.html

Grimne MUD

This MUD (Multi-User Dimension) is heavily combat oriented, and prides itself on being known as one of the worst hack-and-slash MUDs around. It is based in a sword-and-sorcery setting.

KEYWORDS Cyberculture, MUDs (Multi-User Dimensions), Role-Playing, Virtual Communities
AUDIENCE Cyberculture Enthusiasts, MUD Users, Role-Playing Enthusiasts
CONTACT haralde@pvv.unit.no
FREE

http://www.pvv.unit.no/~haralde/grimne/

telnet://iq.pvv.unit.no:4000/

Guide to Select BBS's on the Internet

The Guide to Select BBS's on the Internet is a comprehensive collection of pointers to over 300 Bulletin Board Systems around the world. Users will find the guide in two forms - the full guided tour, with descriptions of each BBS, its location, and a telnet or Web link; and the quick tour, with listings of only names and addresses, with links. A What's New list with the most recent

additions to the BBS list, as well as general information about it, are also provided.

KEYWORDS BBSs (Bulletin Board Systems), Networking, Telecommunications
AUDIENCE BBS Users, Internet Users
CONTACT cerebus@dkmail.dkeep.com
FREE

http://dkeep.com/sbi.htm

HtMUD

This is a distributed graphical MUD (Multi-User Dimension), accessible through a Web browser. Unlike most MUDs, which are completely textual, htMUD allows the use of graphics to display of your system.

KEYWORDS Cyberculture, MUDs (Multi-User Dimensions), Role-Playing, Virtual Communities
AUDIENCE Cyberculture Enthusiasts, MUD Users, Role-Playing Enthusiasts
CONTACT phi@www.arisia.org
FREE

http://www.elf.com/~phi/htmud/

Hypertext MUD Lists

Hypertext MUDs page is one individual's collection of links to different MUDs all over the Internet, created to provide easy access to hundreds of existing virtual communities. Users may connect to each MUD via name or number, and links are grouped into categories such as Aber MUDs, Diku MUDs, LP Muds, MUSHes, and MOOs. Links are grouped by MUD type, but the contents are not described.

KEYWORDS MUDs (Multi-User Dimensions), Role-Playing
AUDIENCE MUD Enthusiasts, MUD Users
CONTACT arp3@eskimo.com
FREE

http://www.eskimo.com/~tarp3/muds.html

IRC Related Documents

This Web site contains information about IRC (Internet Relay Chat) and virtual conversations. Users will find links to documents with reference materials, policy and administration information, and essays on the sociological aspects of IRC. Links to IRC channels with Web sites are provided, as well as telnet links to a few selected IRC channels. Logs from IRC discussion during important events (such as the Gulf War or the 1994 California Earthquake) are also provided, as well as links to other IRC Web pages and newsgroups. Each listing contains a description of the quality and contents of the page.

KEYWORDS IRC (Internet Relay Chat)
AUDIENCE IRC Users, Internet Users
CONTACT Paul Graham
pjg@acsu.buffalo.edu
FREE

http://urth.acsu.buffalo.edu/irc/WWW/ircdocs.html

Internationale Stadt Overview ★★★

This site describes a virtual 'city' on the net called Internationale Stadt. Based in Berlin, Germany, this site offers information on joining this community, as well as allowing users to explore the spaces that this community offers. There is material on music, art, culture, and market services. There is also information on community Internet access for the city's users.

KEYWORDS Community Networks, Internet Communities, Internet Culture, Virtual Communities
AUDIENCE Cyberculture Enthusiasts, Internet Users
CONTACT is@contrib.de
FREE

http://www.is.in-berlin.de/IS/IS_MAP.engl.html

Jay's House MOO ★★

This is a social interaction MOOs (Object-Oriented MUD). It has an experimental Web interface as well as the standard telnet access. Most of the interaction occurs in Jay's House, but there is plenty to explore outside as well.

KEYWORDS Cyberculture, MOOs (Object Oriented MUDs), Role-Playing, Virtual Communities
AUDIENCE Cyberculture Enthusiasts, MUD Users, Role-Playing Enthusiasts
FREE

http://jh.ccs.neu.edu:7043/

telnet://jhm.ccs.neu.edu:1709/

Kingdoms ★★

Kingdoms is a MUD (Multi-User Dimension) that follows a fantasy type theme leaning towards the medieval time period. Players must solve quests and gain experience points by killing monsters and each other in a heavily combat-oriented setting.

KEYWORDS Cyberculture, MUDs (Multi-User Dimensions), Role-Playing, Virtual Communities
AUDIENCE Cyberculture Enthusiasts, MUD Users, Role-Playing Enthusiasts
CONTACT Scott A. Jackson
saj1@ra.msstate.edu
FREE

http://eru.dd.chalmers.se/~kingdoms/

telnet://gwaihir.dd.chalmers.se:1812/

Land of Drogon ★★★★

This MUD (Multiple-User Dimension) is based in a fantasy adventure setting. Players control a small amount of magic.

KEYWORDS Role-Playing, Virtual Communities
AUDIENCE Cyberculture Enthusiasts, MUD Users, Role-Playing Enthusiasts
FREE

http://www.meiko.com/drogon/whatis.html

telnet://drogon.meiko.com:6381/

For Connections to Internet Games
Just playing around

Looking to have some fun? The Internet features several connections for you. There are many games that children can play—a number of them educational. If you're a fan of Star Trek, there are some games that have Star Trek themes and can be played by several people online.

(http://:factoryx.factoryx.com)

If action games and playing against an opponent is more your speed, then you should try "The Internet Nexus" [Gaming], where there is a wide variety of multi-player games available. You can even call up a friend and challenge him or her to a game over the Internet. This site is also where the most popular multi-player games are available, such as DOOM, Heretic and Descent. Another way to find people to play the popular games online is through Modem Player-DOOM.

(http://:www.hooked.net/user/tprice)

MUD Resource Collection ★★★

This Website is a collection of links to information about MUDs, MUSHes, and other virtual communities in which users can role play in different rooms. Links are grouped into FAQs and documents available online, MUDlists and MudWHO collections of MUD information, and links to other Web servers and games interfaces, FTP archives, and newsgroups. Each link is listed with a description of the document or site and its contents.

KEYWORDS MUDs (Multi-User Dimensions), Role-Playing
AUDIENCE MUD Enthusiasts, MUD Users
CONTACT Lydia Leong
lwl@graphics.cis.upenn.edu
FREE

http://www.cis.upenn.edu/~lwl/mudinfo.html

NannyMUD ★★

This MUD (Multi-User Dimension) claims to be one of the oldest LPMuds still left, and also the one with the most quests. It has a medieval fantasy setting.

KEYWORDS Cyberculture, MUDs (Multi-User Dimensions), Role-Playing, Virtual Communities
AUDIENCE Cyberculture Enthusiasts, MUD Users, Role-Playing Enthusiasts
FREE

http://www.lysator.liu.se:7500/mud/nannymud/nannymud.html

telnet://mud.lysator.liu.se:2000/

Oriental MUD ★★★

This site offers an adventure game, Oriental MUD (Multi-User Dimension) with a theme based on ancient Chinese culture.

KEYWORDS Games, MUDs (Multi-User Dimensions), Role-Playing
AUDIENCE Chinese, MUD Users, Role-Playing Enthusiasts
CONTACT mud@ntu.ac.sg
FREE

telnet://ntuix.ntu.ac.sg:5000

The Postcard Store ★★★

This electric postcard server is easy to use. You can choose an image from the virtual card rack, compose and address a message to a friend, and send the card. Your friend will receive an email message with a claim number that can be redeemed for the card at the site's pick-up window.

KEYWORDS Postcards
AUDIENCE General Public
CONTACT Judith S. Donath
judith@media.mit.edu
FREE

http://persona.www.media.mit.edu/postcards/

Realms MUD ★★★

This is a standard adventure game in the style of Dungeons and Dragons. Donations are accepted for those who want better access to the MUD during busy times of the day.

KEYWORDS   Games, MUDs (Multi-User Dimensions), Online Games, Role-Playing
AUDIENCE   MUD Users, Role-Playing Enthusiasts
FREE

telnet://amanda.dorsai.org:1501

SPACESIM (Space Simulation)- An Electronic Newsletter for Space Simulation Enthusiasts ★★★

This site provides links to current and past issues of the monthly newsletter SPACESIM, an electronic newsletter for Space Simulation Enthusiasts. Articles cover cutting-edge presentations and projects in this field, as well as opportunities to simulate current actual space missions in Internet-wired classrooms. Articles offer classroom exercises, lab activities, and curriculum examples. The newsletter also explores real-time telecommunicated simulations between classrooms at a distance.

KEYWORDS   Science Education, Simulation, Space Science
AUDIENCE   Science Educators, Science Students, Space Scientists, Space Simulation Enthusiasts
CONTACT   Chris Rowan
           chris@tenet.edu
FREE

http://chico.rice.edu/armadillo/Simulations/ssimv1n2.html

Talker ★★★

Talker is a real time chat community, part of the InfiNet Web site. Users can hold conversations with other Talker users in several different 'rooms.' They may also identify themselves by choosing a graphic image to go by their contributions to the conversation.

KEYWORDS   Internet Networking, Internet Relay Chat, Telecommunications
AUDIENCE   General Public, Internet Users
CONTACT   talker@infi.net
FREE

http://www.infi.net/talker/

Texas Twilight MUSH (Multi-User Shared Hallucination) ★★★★

Texas Twilight MUSH is based on White Wolf's World of Darkness, and uses the Storyteller system. The setting is gothic-punk Dallas in 1996. Mages, Vampires, and Werewolves are supported.

KEYWORDS   Role-Playing, Virtual Community
AUDIENCE   Cyberculture Enthusiasts, MUD Users, Role-Playing Enthusiasts
CONTACT   jharvey@netcom.com
FREE

telnet://seds.lpl.arizona.edu:6250/

Toon MUSH 3 (Multi-User Shared Hallucination) ★★★★

Toon MUSH 3 bases itself in a cartoon world, where characters are cartoons.

KEYWORDS   Role-Playing, Virtual Community
AUDIENCE   Cyberculture Enthusiasts, MUD Users, Role-Playing Enthusiasts
FREE

telnet://brahe.phys.unm.edu:9999/

Transformers MUSH (Multi-User Shared Hallucination) ★★★★

Transformers MUSH (Multi-User Shared Hallucination) bases itself on the Hasbro Transformer toys and animated series.

KEYWORDS   Role-Playing, Virtual Community
AUDIENCE   Cyberculture Enthusiasts, MUD Users, Role-Playing Enthusiasts
FREE

telnet://megavolt.cc.vt.edu:4201/

TrippyMUSH (Multi-User Shared Hallucination) ★★★★

TrippyMUSH is an unthemed social MUSH, geared somewhat towards silliness.

KEYWORDS   Role-Playing, Virtual Community
AUDIENCE   Cyberculture Enthusiasts, MUD Users, Role-Playing Enthusiasts
FREE

telnet://pebkac.satelnet.org:7567/

Two Moons ★★★★

Two Moons is a MUSH (Multi-User Shared Hallucination) based on the ElfQuest comics and uses some of the ElfQuest roleplaying game rules.

KEYWORDS   Role-Playing, Virtual Community
AUDIENCE   Cyberculture Enthusiasts, MUD Users, Role-Playing Enthusiasts
FREE

telnet://lupine.org:4201/

Wacko MUSH (Multi-User Shared Hallucination) ★★★★

Wacko MUSH is unthemed.

KEYWORDS   Role-Playing, Virtual Community
AUDIENCE   Cyberculture Enthusiasts, MUD Users, Role-Playing Enthusiasts
FREE

telnet://red-branch.mit.edu:6003/

Webchat ★★★★

Webchat is an Internet Relay Chat-like system that allows Web users to have real-time conversations with each other via the Web. After downloading the free software and getting a 'handle,' users may exchange conversations, images, and multimedia information in a series of different 'rooms,' each with a different topic focus (such as politics or music). Webchat also includes regular interviews at the Internet Roundtable with educators, government officials, and writers, with transcripts available after the event. Users may also look at mailing lists, FAQs and code documentation.

KEYWORDS   Chat Groups, Internet Communications
AUDIENCE   General Public, Internet Users
CONTACT   webchat@irsociety.com
FREE

http://www.irsociety.com/webchat/webchat.html

Welcome to the Worlds, Inc ★★★★

(COMMERCIAL)

World's Chat is a 3-D online chat environment. You can download the freeware to participate in this 3-D interactive area. Users are represented by Digital Actors that move through 3-D spaces and interact with other users. Worlds, Inc. has a commercial division that will consult with companies to design and help build their own multi-user virtual world. You will need at least a 486 PC and a modem. As of May, 1995, a Macintosh-based version was in the works but not yet available. Keep checking the site for further information and updates.

KEYWORDS   3D Webs, Internet Communications, Online Chat, Virtual Reality
AUDIENCE   3D Designers, Chat Enthusiasts, Internet Users
CONTACT   techsupport@kaworlds.com
FREE

http://www.kaworlds.com/

World Wide Web Dating Game ★★★★

This is an online dating game. Each game will consist of one entrant choosing between three contestants. The entrant submits five questions for the contestants to answer, then the Internet community can vote on whose answers they like best. Of course, the entrant can choose whomever he or she likes best. After the date, the entrant will report back on how it went. Instructions on how to become a contestant can be found at this site, as well as the contestants of the latest game.

KEYWORDS   Dating
AUDIENCE   General Public, Single People
CONTACT   Eve Astrid Andersson
           eveander@cco.caltech.edu
FREE

http://www.cid.com/cid/date/

Write MUSH ★★★★

This MUSH (Multi-User Shared Hallucination) is a combination social and classroom environment for the teaching, discussion, workshopping, and appreciation of creative writing. An educator's guide to using Write

MUSH for interactive creative writing classes is available at the FTP site.

Keywords Cyberculture, MUDs (Multi-User Dimensions), Role-Playing, Virtual Communities

Audience Cyberculture Enthusiasts, MUD Users, Role-Playing Enthusiasts

Free

ftp://netcom.com/pub/marcia

telnet://palmer.sacc.colostate.edu:6250/

Law & Criminal Justice

Business Law	489
Career & Employment	490
Conferences & Events	490
Constitutional Law	490
Criminal Justice	492
Environmental Law	492
Ethics	493
Family Law	494
Intellectual Property	495
International & Comparative Law	496
Judicial Branch	497
Law Schools	498
Legal History & Theory	500
Legal Issues	500
Legal Resources	500
Litigation & Procedures	502
Reference	503
Statutes	505
Tax Law	506
Torts	506

Business Law

See also
Business & Economics · *Management*
Government & Politics · *Countries*
Law & Criminal Justice · *Intellectual Property*
Law & Criminal Justice · *Legal Resources*

Advertising Law Internet Site ★★★★

This Advertising Law Internet Site maintained by the law firm Arent Fox, Kintner Plotkin & Kahn provides general information concerning advertising, consumer rights, and intellectual property. There are over 225 internal links at this site as well as a searchable database. Some of the resources include news on the Federal Trade Commission's statements and acts, articles about advertising law, FTC advertising guidelines and enforcement policy statements, trade regulation rules, consumer brochures, European consumer and advertising law, and more.

KEYWORDS Advertising, Consumer Rights, Federal Trade Commission (FTC), Law Firms
AUDIENCE Advertising Professionals, Lawyers, Legal Professionals
CONTACT Lewis Rose
lewrose@netcom.com
FREE

http://www.webcom.com/~lewrose/home.html

California Penal Code Section 502—Computer Crimes ★★★

This page contains a copy of section 502 of the California Penal Code, relating to computer crimes. It legally defines the boundaries of computer crime, gives legal definitions of computer terms, and describes penalties for those convicted of the crimes described in the document.

KEYWORDS Computer Security, Crime, Legal Issues, Statutes
AUDIENCE Computer Hackers, Computer Users, Lawyers
FREE

http://rocky.humboldt.edu/CPC502.html

Care Of Your Small Corporation ★★★

This article focuses on incorporating a small business, which is an important and sometimes exhausting task. This article originally appeared in the Summer, 1994 issue of the Nolo News. The author, Anthony Mancuso, is the author of Nolo Press's new book, Taking Care of Your Corporation.

KEYWORDS Legal Advice, Legal Issues, Legal Resources, Small Business
AUDIENCE Business Professionals, Entrepreneurs, Legal Professionals
CONTACT cs@NoloPress.com
FREE

http://nearnet.gnn.com/gnn/bus/nolo/careco.html

Center for Corporate Law ★★★

The World Wide Web server of The Center for Corporate Law at the University of Cincinnati College of Law contains electronic data that will assist lawyers in the practice of corporate and securities law. The data offered consists of the text of the federal securities laws and their accompanying rules and forms. The laws include full texts of the most important corporate acts of the post-Depression era.

KEYWORDS Corporate Law, Corporations, Securities, Securities Exchange Commission (SEC)
AUDIENCE Business Owners, Corporate Lawyers, Entrepreneurs, Law Educators
FREE

http://www.law.uc.edu/CCL/

The Consumer Law Page ★★★

Collected here are some links to articles on topics of interest to consumers, and to the Plaintiff's Bar. Topics covered in articles include: Products Liability (such as Update on Breast Implant—The New Evidence Against Dow Chemical), All-Terrain Vehicles—Deaths and Injuries to Children, Toxic Torts (such as The Cancer War Needs an Informed Public—Known Carcinogens to be Avoided), Proving Toxic Torts—A Primer on Pharmacokinetics, Traumatic Brain Injuries, Wrongful Adoption—Fraud by Adoption Agencies, Representing Survivors of Crime, and more.

KEYWORDS Adoption, Consumer Law, Product Liability
AUDIENCE General Public, Law Students, Lawyers, Legal Professionals, Litigants
CONTACT Richard Alexander
talf@netcom.com
FREE

http://starbase.ingress.com/tsw/talf/txt/intro.html

Indiana Code—Title 23 ★★★★

This hypertext version of the Indiana Code allows users to search the state's code through hyperlinked sections of the code. The source for the Indiana Code was provided by the Indiana State Library. Users can either browse through the linear links of each part of the code or can conduct a full text search using the search function supplied.

KEYWORDS Codes, Corporate Law, Indiana, States

AUDIENCE Activists, Attorneys, Indiana Residents, Political Science Students
CONTACT   Will Sadler
          webmaster@polecat.law.indiana.edu
FREE

http://www.law.indiana.edu/codes/in/23/title-23.html

Pepper & Corazzini, L.L.P.

This site offers the services of the communications law firm, Pepper & Corazzini, L.L.P. They specialize in radio, television, satellite, microwave, mobile radio, and cellular communications. The firm deals with the FCC (Federal Communications Commission) and other federal agencies on a regular basis. Users can access a company profile, information on the company's activities, as well as a collection of links to other legal resources on the net.

KEYWORDS Communications, Law Firms, Telecommunications
AUDIENCE Lawyers
CONTACT   Neal Friedman
          njf@commlaw.com
FREE

http://www.iis.com:80/p-and-c/

Trade Law Library Internet Sites for Law, Commerce, Finance and Economics ★★★★

This is the page for Trade Law Library which provides links to Internet sites for law, commerce, finance and economics. Some of the topics covered include general lists of various law services such as Yahoo and EINet, Galaxy Law and Regulation List, Indiana University Law School, CTI Law Technology Centre at Warwick University, and more. Commerce-related material includes Virtual Library finance, economics, investment and tax information, The World Bank, European Union Information, and more. Law databases, law publishers, libraries, bookstores, and additional references are also linked.

KEYWORDS Commerce, Economics, Meta-Index (Law), World Bank
AUDIENCE Business Professionals, Economists, Law Students, Lawyers, Legal Professionals, Politicians
CONTACT   ananse@irv.uit.no
FREE

http://ananse.irv.uit.no/trade_law/nav/law_ref.html

When You Have to Let Someone Go

This article originally appeared in the Winter, 1994 issue of Nolo News and is adapted from Attorney Fred Steingold's new book The Employer's Legal Handbook from Nolo Press. Coverage includes advice on firing an employee, contractual commitments, lawful reasons for firing, Nolo Press products on employee relations, and more.

KEYWORDS Law, Legal Issues, Legal Publishers

AUDIENCE Employers, Entrepreneurs, General Public, Lawyers, Legal Professionals
CONTACT   cs@NoloPress.com
FREE

http://nearnet.gnn.com/gnn/bus/nolo/letgo.html

Career & Employment

See also
Education · *Career & Employment*

The Law Practice Management Page

Collected on this page are articles that relate to Law Practice Management. These articles relate to the 'nuts and bolts' of the day-to-day operation and long range planning and management of a law practice. The topics covered include: essential factors to consider when selecting client accounting software for use on a personal computer, practical issues and professional liability, organizing your law practice for success, how to define the capital account in your law partnership agreement, factors in setting law firm goals and objectives, management training for attorneys—an unfulfilled need, and other subjects.

KEYWORDS Law Firms, Legal Advice, Legal Software, Management
AUDIENCE General Public, Law Students, Lawyers, Legal Professionals, Litigants
CONTACT   jjacques@ccnet.com
FREE

http://starbase.ingress.com/tsw/jpw/manage.html

Legal Professionals Lounge ★★★★

This site is a link from the Lectric Law Library home page. It contains material directed to those in the legal professions, and features numerous articles and resources which pertain to the Judicial branch (both state and federal). There is even a section entitled "Of Interest to Judges." Miscellaneous materials concern, among other things, news on criminal and civil procedures, and reports on federal judicial caseloads.

KEYWORDS Judges, Judicial Branch, Legal Professions
AUDIENCE Judges, Law Students, Lawyers, Legal Researchers
CONTACT   staff@inter-law.com
FREE

http://www.inter-law.com/pro.html

Conferences & Events

European Association of Law and Economics ★★★★

The European Association of Law and Economics (EALE) comprises an institutional response to the increasing importance of economic analysis of law in Europe. The association provides assistance for scholars embarking on this new field of research. Its annual conference has become an important forum for the exchange of information and ideas. The EALE also arranges seminars jointly with other organizations, and locally in different countries. Several conference volumes have been published and the association has a periodical newsletter.

KEYWORDS Economics, Law (International)
AUDIENCE Business Professionals, Economists, Lawyers, Researchers
CONTACT   Sam Rea , Werner Antweiler Jr.
          reas@epas.utoronto.ca
          werner@epas.utoronto.ca
FREE

http://www.epas.utoronto.ca:5680/eale/eale.html

Constitutional Law

See also
Government & Politics · *Doctrines*
Government & Politics · *Policies*
Government & Politics · *Political Science*
Law & Criminal Justice · *International & Comparative Law*

ACLU of Illinois Home Page ★★★★

This site is the American Civil Liberties Union Ilinois Chapter's home page. It is devoted to promoting the state and national organization, as well as the U.S. Constitution, the Bill of Rights, and protecting unpopular political opinions of all persuasions. Numerous links include connections to the First Amendment Fund, the Reproductive Rights Project, groups concerned with AIDS, poverty, and more. There are also links to Current Cases, Press Releases, and the Illinois Legislative Report.

KEYWORDS Civil Liberties, Illinois U.S. Constitution, Organizations
AUDIENCE Civil Libertarians, Law Students, Lawyers, U.S. Citizens
CONTACT   acluil@aol.com
FREE

http://www.aclu-il.org/

American Civil Liberties Union Free Reading Room ★★★★

This site contains a collection of materials and resources provided by the American Civil Liberties Union. Some of the material offered includes publications, press releases, FAQs, and information about

Constitutional Law

upcoming events. The site is maintained by the Pipeline Network, Inc.

KEYWORDS Civil Liberties, Civil Rights, Legal Issues, Organizations
AUDIENCE Activists, Civil Libertarians, Legal Scholars
CONTACT   infoaclu@aclu.org
FREE

gopher://gopher.pipeline.com:6601/

Civil Liberties Index

CLI is an index to newsworthy Netnews articles about civil liberties issues related to computers. It is available via a mailing list (titles only) or via the World Wide Web. The articles include titles such as 'Crime Bill Debate Heating Up' and 'Florida Group Will Not Press for Anti-Gay Amendment.'

KEYWORDS Civil Liberties, Computer Ethics, Ethics, U.S. Constitution
AUDIENCE Computer Users, Legal Professionals, Media Professionals
CONTACT   Carl Kadie
          kadie@eff.org
FREE

http://www.eff.org/CAF/cl-index.html

Computers and Academic Freedom ★★★

This page entails a collection of resources related to computers and academic freedom. Users will find material on topics such as censorship on university campuses, civil liberty, sex and the Internet, banned and challenged academic information, and more. Users can also access several FAQ files on computers and academic freedom, material on creating a sensible information policy, as well legal and case study information. This site also provides a collection of links to related Internet resources.

KEYWORDS Censorship, Civil Liberties, Computer Ethics, Internet Issues
AUDIENCE Computer Users, Internet Users, Network Administrators, Systems Administrators
CONTACT   kadie@eff.org
FREE

http://www.eff.org:80/CAF/

The Information Law Web ★★★★

The Information Law Web provides a collection of people, places, and things that can help you understand your rights in the emerging Information Age. Some of the linked topics include: Sandra Day O'Connor (the U.S. Supreme Court Justice who wrote the majority opinion for the landmark Information Law ruling), Feist Publications v. Rural Telephone Service, academics who specialize in information law, intellectual property, trademark and copyright sites, statutes that govern information law, Cyberspace Law Review Bibliography, Copyright FAQ, U.S. Supreme Court intellectual property decisions, and more.

KEYWORDS Intellectual Property, Internet Issues, Patent Law
AUDIENCE General Public, Law Students, Lawyers, Legal Professionals

CONTACT   Ralph C. Losey,
          wisdom@digital.net
FREE

http://starbase.ingress.com/tsw/rcl/infolaw.html

Legal Beat

This site offers a digest of controversial crime and freedom of speech issues related to Cyberspace. Most of the incidents here relate to sexual materials and their distribution, copyright infringement, or unauthorized entry into computer systems. The maintainer has cross-referenced the digests with subsequent court cases, legislative bills, and newspaper reports regarding each case.

KEYWORDS Censorship, Cyberculture, Freedom of Speech, Legal Issues, Mass Communications
AUDIENCE First Amendment Activists, Legal Scholars, Legislators
CONTACT   support@hotwired.com
FREE

http://www.hotwired.com/Staff/justin/dox/law.html

Phil Zimmerman Defense Fund

The Phil Zimmerman Defense Fund page appeals to those interested in America's first, fourth, and fifth amendment rights. This page provides access to the Federal case against Phil Zimmerman, the developer of the PGP ('Pretty Good Privacy') encryption mechanism in widespread use on the Internet. According to the government, Zimmerman violated Federal restrictions on the export of encryption technology. This site provides details on how to contribute your time and/or your money.

KEYWORDS Civil Liberties, Encryption, U.S. Constitution
AUDIENCE Law Professors, Law Students, Lawyers, Legal Professionals, Researchers
CONTACT   zldf@clark.net
FREE

http://www.netresponse.com/zldf/appeal.html

Preserve, Protect, and Defend the Internet

This page is devoted to distributing information regarding proposed U.S. legislation S. 314 and H.R. 1004, the Communications Decency Act. A critique of the legislation by the Center for Democracy and Technology is provided, along with the full text of the bill. In addition, an electronic petition is available for signing. The author of this page posts updated information about this legislation about once a week.

KEYWORDS Censorship, Communications, Internet Issues
AUDIENCE ACLU Supporters, Activists, Internet Users, Politicians
FREE

http://www.phantom.com/~slowdog/

ftp://wookie.net/pub/users/slowdog/

Connections to Business Law

How "safe" are the products you buy?

Laws covering advertising, product safety, and patents vary widely from country to country. In many cases, tourists can be "burned" by false advertising claims for products and services in countries where "let the buyer beware" is taken literally. On the other hand, companies whose market extends beyond their home-country's borders may find that product and service claims in another country are far stricter (and sometimes far costlier).

To find out about legal issues in trade and advertising throughout the world, you don't have to hire a lawyer to do the labor-intensive research. Save yourself a lot of money by doing your initial research on the Internet.

One of many useful sites is called "Advertising Law," where you can connect to more than 225 internal links on advertising, consumer rights and intellectual property around the world. You can also find trade regulation rules, consumer brochures, and details on European consumer and advertising laws.

At the "General Product Safety" site in the "European Consumer and Advertising Laws" area of the Internet, you can learn what measures have been taken to ensure the safety of products that are bought and sold throughout the European Common Market. You can also find out what legal obligations manufacturers have to consumers.

(http://www.webcom.com/~lewrose/home.html)

Constitutional Law – Environmental Law

U.S. Constitution ★★★★

The U.S. Constitution page produced by Cornell University contains links to the full text of the U.S. Constitution. It includes links to articles I through VII, the preamble, the signers and the amendments.

KEYWORDS Civil Rights, U.S. Constitution
AUDIENCE Business Professionals, Law Professors, Law Students, Lawyers, Legal Professionals
CONTACT martin@law.mail.cornell.edu
FREE

http://www.law.cornell.edu/constitution/constitution.overview.html

Criminal Justice

See also
Law & Criminal Justice · *Business Law*
Law & Criminal Justice · *International & Comparative Law*

The California Criminal Law Observer's Page ★★★

This page provides links to information on criminal law. Topics and information covered include the New Immigrant's Guide to the Consequences of a Felony Conviction in California, a basic glossary of criminal law terms and jargon, quirky crimes and punishments, weapons, computers, and the criminal law. You'll also learn about criminal records—how to clear, improve upon, correct, expunge, destroy, seal and otherwise deal with the serious matter of police, court, California Department of Justice, and Federal Bureau of Investigation records. (If you enjoy filling out your own tax returns or reading telephone directories, you will love this section.)

KEYWORDS California, Crime, FBI (Federal Bureau Of Investigation), Legal Terminology
AUDIENCE General Public, Law Students, Lawyers, Legal Professionals, Litigants
CONTACT Jerome P. Mullins
alawyer@eworld.com
FREE

http://starbase.ingress.com/tsw/alawyer/criminal.html

Criminal Justice Resources ★★★★

Cecil Greek's page on Criminal Justice Resources opens with a large photo of OJ Simpson and his defense team. This page provides an extensive list of links to Criminal Justice Resources on the Web. Some of the links include: Searchable Law Databases, International Criminal Justice Sources, Juvenile Delinquency & Drug and Alcohol Information, Prisons and the Death Penalty, Due Process and Civil Rights, Online Criminal Justice Discussion Groups, E-Journals, and more.

KEYWORDS Civil Rights, Death Penalty, Juvenile Delinquency, Law
AUDIENCE Law Students, Lawyers, Legal Professionals, Researchers
FREE

http://www.stpt.usf.edu/~greek/cj.html

Defense Fund for the Victims of a Modern Massachusetts Witch Hunt ★★

The Defense Fund for the Victims of a Modern Massachusetts Witch Hunt is a brief document that outlines how one can support the Amirault family. During the height of the ritual abuse craze, the Amiraults were convicted for heinous crimes against children.

KEYWORDS Law, Massachusetts , Organizations
AUDIENCE Law Students, Lawyers, Legal Professionals, Researchers
CONTACT Jonathan G. Harris
harris@mit.edu
FREE

http://web.mit.edu/harris/www/defensefund.html

The K9 Academy For Law Enforcement ★★

The K9 Academy For Law Enforcement is a business made up of police officers dedicated to the training of police K9 handlers. The K9 Academy can send dog trainers anywhere in the world to work on specific training or consulting projects. This site contains contact information for this consulting company, including the areas of expertise for each staff person. In addition, users will find a listing of books written by Robert S. Eden, the company president, a number of court decisions dealing with K9 Case Law, conference announcements for law enforcement officers, as well as K9 database software, training tips and links to other law enforcement resources on the Internet.

KEYWORDS Dogs, Educational Programs, Law Enforcement, Police
AUDIENCE N. Law Enforcement Professionals, Service Dog Trainers
CONTACT Best Internet Communications, Inc.
www@best.com
FREE

http://www.best.com/~policek9/k9home.htm

Prison Legal News ★★★

The Prison Legal News is a monthly newsletter published and edited by Washington State prisoners Ed Mead and Paul Wright. The PLN has been regularly published since May of 1990. While the paper's focus is on Washington State, the PLN also features coverage of prison-related news and analyses from across the country and around the world. The PLN reports on court decisions affecting prisoners and contains information designed to help prisoners vindicate their rights in the judicial system.

KEYWORDS Legal Advice, Newsletters
AUDIENCE Criminal Lawyers, Law Students, Lawyers, Prisoners, Probation Counselors
CONTACT Prison Legal News
ellens@ai.mit.edu
FREE

http://www.ai.mit.edu/people/ellens/PLN/pln.html

Three Strikes and You're Out Law ★★★★

This site explores the implications of the 1994 ballot initiative approved by California voters known as 'Three Strikes and You're Out.' Analysis covers the ballot initiative (i.e.Proposition 184) itself, the actual statute that was passed, and three other code sections that identify the types of violations that count as 'strikes' against you. There are a variety of links which go into greater detail about given sub-categories, as well as a link back to the home page of Jerome Mullins' law office.

KEYWORDS California, Codes, Crime
AUDIENCE Californians, Civil Libertarians, Defendents
CONTACT Jerome P. Mullins
lawyer@eworld.com
FREE

http://starbase.ingress.com/tsw/alawyer/3strikes.html

United Nations Justice Network (UNCJIN) ★★★★

This a gopher menu for the United Nations Justice Network (UNCJIN), including pointers to United Nations Rules, U.N. Criminal Justice Country Profiles, the CIA World Factbook 1992, an FBI gopher site, and more. The goal of UNCJIN is to establish a worldwide network to enhance the exchange of information concerning criminal justice and crime prevention issues among policy makers, planners, practitioners, scholars and other experts, as well as United Nations national correspondents and research institutions.

KEYWORDS Criminal Justice, Law, United Nations
AUDIENCE Lawyers, Legal Professionals, Legal Scholars, Policymakers
CONTACT Adam Bouloukos
ab5202@uacsc1.albany.edu
FREE

gopher://UACSC2.ALBANY.EDU/11/newman/

Environmental Law

See also
Government & Policies · *Policies*
Science · *Environmental Sciences*

ENERGY ★★★★

The Energy News and Information (ENERGY) library consists of news, legal, and regulatory information.The ENERGY library contains more than 50 full-text sources concentrating on energy-related news and issues. Also available are decisions and orders of the United States Federal Power Commission, Federal Energy Regulatory Commission, and Nuclear Regulatory Commission. At the state level, the site covers administrative decisions and orders for 17 states. Energy industry research reports from InvestextR are also available.

KEYWORDS Energy, Legislation, Regulations
AUDIENCE Energy Researchers, Environmentalists
COST

http://www.meaddata.com

telnet://nex.meaddata.com

Environmental Law – Ethics **493**

 ENVIRN (Environment Library)

The Environment (ENVIRN) Library contains a variety of environment-related news and legal information. Specifically it features a combination of environmental information that can provide critical insight into environmental hazards, EPA ratings, specific company investigations, evaluations of potentially hazardous chemicals, and parties responsible for cleanup of specific hazardous sites. Additionally, ENVIRN provides a wealth of environment-related information: legislation, regulations, and court and agency decisions at both the federal and state levels, news, the Environmental Law Reporter, and American Law Reports.

KEYWORDS   Environmental Law, Legislation
AUDIENCE   Business Professionals, Environmental Researchers
COST

http://www.meaddata.com

telnet://nex.meaddata.com

Environmental Law ★★★

This page provides links for searching environmental law resources in Israel and the world. Some of the text can be searched in both Hebrew or English and includes information such as Treaties and Agreements, Environmental Law Archives, United States Law Libraries, and Library of Congress (LOCIS).

KEYWORDS   Environmental Law, International Law, Israel
AUDIENCE   Environmentalists, International Lawyers, Israelis, Jews, Lawyers, Researchers
FREE

http://www.huji.ac.il/www_teva/law.html

Environmental Legislation and Agreements ★★★★

The Environmental Legislation and Agreements (ELA) Web page offers a score of Australian Legislation and Agreements and International Agreements on the environment. The legislations and agreements range from the year 1900 to the present. They also cover diverse topics such as bird migrations and climate change, as well as forest policy, endangered species, and preparedness for nuclear disasters.

KEYWORDS   Environmental Health, Environmental Law, Legislation, Public Policy
AUDIENCE   Australians, Environmentalists, General Public, Policymakers
CONTACT   +61 (6) 274 1199
FREE

http://kaos.erin.gov.au/human_env/env_leg/env_leg.html/

gopher://kaos.erin.gov.au/11/legislation/

National Biological Service Home Page ★★★

The National Biological Service (NBS), a new U.S. Department of the Interior bureau, offers a collection of biological information. 'The mission of the NBS is to work with others to provide the scientific understanding and technologies necessary to manage the nation's biological resources. This information can be useful to landowners interested in protecting resources and those who have questions about environmental law and legislation.

KEYWORDS   Biology, Environmental Law, Government, Legislation
AUDIENCE   Activists, Biologists, Environmentalists, Farmers, Legal Professionals
CONTACT   webmaster@its.nbs.gov
FREE

http://www.its.nbs.gov/nbs/

Connections to Family Law
Stop or I'll sue!

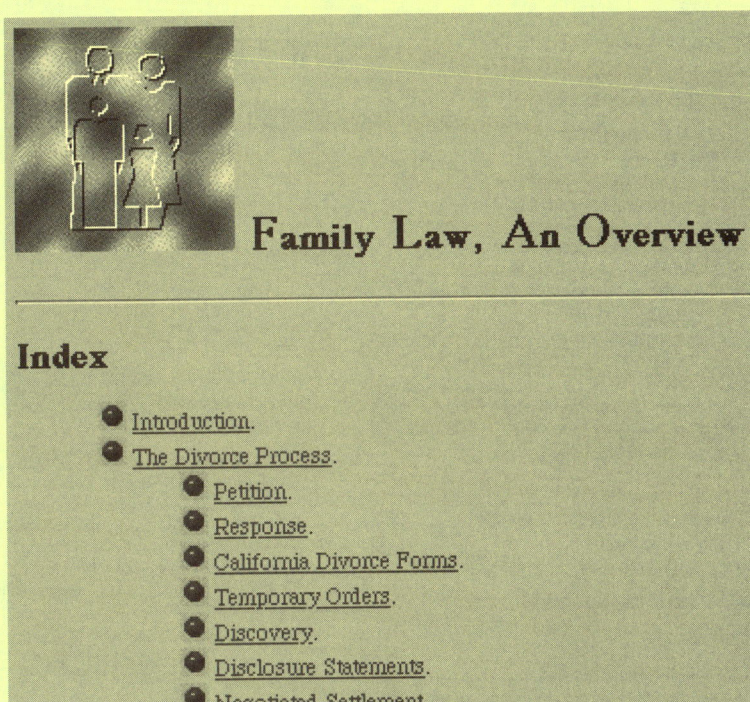

Need to get a restraining order to keep an estranged spouse out of your hair? Involved in a battle for child custody? There is much you can learn and do before you actually take the step of hiring an attorney.

Through the "Family Law" site on the Internet, you can access information on divorce laws, child custody rights, and negotiating settlements. For California residents, this Internet site provides users with state divorce forms, as well as pointers if you have to go to trial.

(http:www.legal.net/family.html)

Ethics

See also
Business & Economics · *Management*
Government & Policies · *Political Science*
Religion & Philosophy · *Philosophy*

The Critical Criminology American Sheriffs Association (ASA) Section ★★★

The Critical Criminology WWW site for the American Sheriffs Association (ASA) provides Internet resources in fields such as prisons, the death penalty, prisoner litigation, and legal codes. Users will find links to major American databases that include the U.S. Department of Justice and the San Francisco Chronicle.

KEYWORDS   California, Criminology, Death Penalty, Organizations

Law & Criminal Justice

AUDIENCE   Criminologists, Law Enforcement Professionals, Lawyers
CONTACT   Jim Thomas
            critcrim@sun.soci.niu.edu
FREE

http://sun.soci.niu.edu/~critcrim/

Expert Witnesses on a Contingent-Fee Basis ★★

The Code of Professional Responsibility, which has been adopted in one form or another in virtually every state, states that it is unethical for a lawyer to employ an expert witness on a contingent-fee basis. This article discusses the possibility of using or becoming an expert witness on a contingent-fee basis.

KEYWORDS   Law, Legal Ethics, Professional Responsibility
AUDIENCE   Expert Witnesses, General Public, Investors, Judges, Lawyers, Legal Professionals
CONTACT   Carl E. Person
            carlpers@lawmall.com
FREE

http://www.ocsny.com:80/lawmall/lm_exper.html

Legal and Ethical Internet Resources ★★★★

The Legal and Ethical Internet Resources site represents a compilation of resources available online to assist universities and university administrators when dealing with legal and ethical Internet issues. Resources include articles, discussion lists, legal pointers, and examples of Internet legal battles. There are also hotlinks to legal/ethical counsel from groups like the ACLU, Computer Professionals for Social Responsibility, the U.S. Supreme Court's Project Hermes, and more.

KEYWORDS   Internet Issues, Legal Ethics
AUDIENCE   Educators, Internet Users, Lawyers, Students
CONTACT   John Campbell
            jdc@nuxi.ucc.nau.edu
FREE

http://www.nau.edu/legal.html

Militia Watch & Other Progressive Causes ★★★★

Miltia Watch is part of the a larger web site called The Left Side of The Web. In this section, users will find current news stories about militia, right wing, and hate groups throughout the United States and the rest of the world. A number of older articles detailing these groups' activities are provided here as well. Other links at this site are for progressive and liberal home pages across the Internet.

KEYWORDS   Militias, Organizations, Paramilitary Groups
AUDIENCE   Gun Control Advocates, Progressives
FREE

http://paul.spu.edu/~sinnfein/progressive.html

Rules of Professional Conduct Governing Lawyers ★★★★

This site exhaustively describes and documents the official rules of professional and ethical conduct by lawyers. It begins by focusing on domains like responsibility, competence, and confidentiality. Areas of particularly lengthy and intense concentration include Conflict of Interest, Public Service, and Advocacy. There are also plenty of links to related areas throughout the site.

KEYWORDS   Ethics, Legal Professions, Professional Responsibility
AUDIENCE   Defendents, Law Students, Lawyers, Legal Researchers
CONTACT   Cornell Law School
            martin@law.mail.cornell.edu
FREE

http://www.law.cornell.edu:80/lawyers/rules.credits.html

Vincent Chin Case ★★★

The Vincent Chin Case Web site is devoted to providing the public with essays and documentation concerning the death of Vincent Chin in 1982. The site contains two essays, a partial transcript from the film 'Who Killed Vincent Chin?' and letters written by Mr. Chin to various Asian American student associations.

KEYWORDS   Asian American Issues, Crime, Ethics
AUDIENCE   Activists, Asian-Americans, Chinese, Humanists
CONTACT   TANAKA Tomoyuki
            tanaka@indiana.edu
FREE

http://bronze.ucs.indiana.edu/~tanaka/vincent/vincent.html

Family Law

See also
Popular Culture & Entertainment · *Family & Community*

Child Custody ★★★

When parents split up, one of the most wrenching decisions to be made concerns the children. This article deals with the law in child custody disputes. It originally appeared in the Spring, 1994 issue of the Nolo News. The authors, Robin Leonard and Stephen Elias, wrote the new third edition of Nolo's Pocket Guide to Family Law.

KEYWORDS   Child Custody, Legal Advice, Legal Publishers, Legal Resources
AUDIENCE   Divorced People, Families
CONTACT   cs@NoloPress.com
FREE

http://nearnet.gnn.com/gnn/bus/nolo/custod.html

Family And Medical Leave ★★★

The Family and Medical Leave Act (FMLA) is the subject of this article. These articles are adapted from the second edition of Your Rights in the Workplace, available from Nolo Press.

KEYWORDS   Employment, Family Law, Legal Advice, Medical
AUDIENCE   Employees, Families, Women
CONTACT   cs@NoloPress.com
FREE

http://nearnet.gnn.com/gnn/bus/nolo/work.html

Family Law, An Overview ★★★

This page describes family law or the divorce process. Links are included to petition, response, California divorce forms, temporary orders, discovery, disclosure statements, negotiated settlement, trial, and more.

KEYWORDS   California, Child Custody, Divorce Law, Legal Advice
AUDIENCE   Divorced People, Husbands, Lawyers, Legal Professionals, Wives
CONTACT   Editor@Legal.Net (tm)
FREE

http://www.legal.net/family.htm

Forms for a California Divorce ★★

On this page you fill out forms to initiate (or respond to) a California divorce or legal separation procedure. By answering the questions on this Web page, a completed Summons, Petition, and Confidential Counseling Statement will be prepared and mailed to you. Upon receipt of the documents, you must file them with the court and serve a copy of the documents on your spouse.

KEYWORDS   California, Child Support, Divorce Law, Legal Resources
AUDIENCE   Husbands, Lawyers, Legal Professionals, Wives
CONTACT   Editor@Legal.Net (tm)
FREE

http://www.Legal.Net/divorce.htm

National Child Rights Alliance ★★★★

This site provides pointers to documents which adhere to the philosophy of the NCRA, The National Child Rights Alliance. The NCRA seeks to change economic, social, legal, medical, cultural and parental practices that harm youth. Some of the documents provided include the Youth Bill of Rights, Foster Kids and the Law, When a Child Wants a Divorce, Hillary Clinton—In Her Own Words, Barriers to School-Based HIV Prevention, and more.

KEYWORDS   Children's Rights, Health Care, Law
AUDIENCE   Child Care Providers, Educators (Primary/Secondary), Judges, Lawyers
CONTACT   Jim Senter
            JIMSENTER@delphi.com
FREE

http://www.ai.mit.edu/people/ellens/NCRA/ncra.html

Simple California Support Calculation

This page provides a form for determining approximately what you should pay or receive in child support. You enter the six most important factors in determining California support, namely gross income of the parties, tax filing status, number of children, number of children from other relationships, the percentage of time the non-physical custodial parent spends with his or her children, and child care expenses. SupportPro (tm), a computer program used to help courts calculate the proper amount of support, is available for sale online at this Web site.

KEYWORDS California, Child Support, Divorce Law, Legal Information
AUDIENCE Divorced People, Husbands, Lawyers, Wives
CONTACT Editor@Legal.Net (tm)
FREE

http://www.Legal.Net/support.htm

Who Needs A Living Trust?

If you're considering setting up a living trust to avoid probate, this article will address your concerns. It originally appeared in the Fall, 1994 issue of the Nolo News. The author, attorney Mary Randolph, is on the Nolo Press staff.

KEYWORDS Legal Advice, Legal Issues, Legal Resources
AUDIENCE Families, General Public, Seniors
CONTACT cs@NoloPress.com
FREE

http://nearnet.gnn.com/gnn/bus/nolo/trust.html

Intellectual Property

See also
Business & Economics · *Services*
Internet · *Internet Issues*
Law & Criminal Justice · *Constitutional Law*

Bernstein Shur Sawyer & Nelson Counselors at Law

The Bernstein Shur Sawyer & Nelson Counselors home page includes information in the following areas of law: Litigation, Intellectual Property, Municipal, Administrative, Public Finance, and Legislative Practice, Commercial Bankruptcy and Creditors' Rights Litigation, Corporations and Tax, Media Law, Trusts and Estates, Employment and Labor Law, Utility Matters, and more.

KEYWORDS Law Firms, Litigation, Trusts and Estates
AUDIENCE General Public, Lawyers, Legal Professionals, Litigants
CONTACT pfrinsko@mainelaw.com
FREE

http://www.biddeford.com/bssn/

Connections to Intellectual Property Rights
Don your product with a trade dress

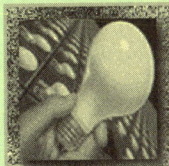
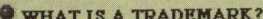

So you've started a business. You've also decided on a name you want to use for your company. You then invent a product and settle on a name for it. Then you design some distinctive packaging for the product. What do you do next?

If you aren't careful, you could run into problems with another company that has already established a trademark name, as well as a trade dress (packaging) for its product that matches the one you want to use. You can't afford to run the risk of a lawsuit. The place to start checking to make sure you don't "infringe" on another company's name or product (and vice versa) is the "Intellectual Property" site on the World Wide Web. There you'll get the legal low-down on the information you need, including a legal definition of a trademark, a trade name, a fictitious business name, a corporate name, a trade dress, and more.

At this site, you can also learn how the GATT trade agreement between the U.S. and the European community alters U.S. patent law.

(http://www.legal.net/intellrt.html)

Copyright Act of 1976

This hypertext document taken from the U.S. Code of Federal Regulations allows users to search and access the U.S. Code on intellectual property including the Semiconductor Chip Act of 1994 and the Audio Home Recording Act of 1992. Both full text search and a browse feature are offered to assist the user.

KEYWORDS Business Law, Codes, Copyright Law
AUDIENCE Attorneys, Business Professionals, General Public
CONTACT Peter W. Martin
martin@law.mail.cornell.edu
FREE

http://www.law.cornell.edu:80/usc/17/overview.html

The Institute for Learning Technologies Guide to Copyright and Related Resources

This page provides information (including links to Internet resources) of interest to educators and others relating to copyrights. Resources include U.S. Supreme Court decisions, Guides to Copyrights for Educators, Librarians, and Multimedia, and other organizations on the Internet related to copyrights.

KEYWORDS Copyright Law, Education
AUDIENCE Academics, Copyright Lawyers, Educators, Law Students, Legal Professionals

CONTACT   webmaster@ilt.columbia.edu
FREE

http://www.ilt.columbia.edu/gen/ref/ILTcopy.html

Intellectual Property ★★

This page describes intellectual property law. Topics include trademark, trade name, fictitious business name, corporate name, registering your trademark/service mark, trade dress, and more.
KEYWORDS   California, Corporations, Patent Law, Trademarks
AUDIENCE   Business Professionals, Lawyers, Legal Professionals, Mediators, Patent Lawyers
FREE

http://www.legal.net/intellct.htm

Source Translation & Optimization's (STO) Internet Patent Search System ★★

This site allows the viewer to search for patent information. Searches are based on the categories of inventions of United States Patent and Trademark Office (PTO), which number over 400 areas and are divided into Electronic, Chemical, Engineering, and Mechanical. Using this search system, you can obtain a list of titles to patents in any class or subclass. This site also links the user to documents such as PTO contact information, standards for submitting drawings within patent applications, a copy of the U.S. Patent Laws, as well as information about international patents.
KEYWORDS   Inventions, Patent Law, Trademarks
AUDIENCE   Engineers, Inventors, Patent Lawyers, Patent Researchers, Trademark Attorneys
CONTACT   Sunsite at University of North Carolina WebMaster@SunSITE.unc.edu
FREE

http://sunsite.unc.edu/patents/intropat.html

Trademark Act of 1946 ('Lanham Act'), As Amended ★★★★

This site provides a hypertext version of the U.S. Trademark Act of 1946 (the 'Lanham Act'), As Amended 1994, Title 15, United States Code, Sections 1051–1127. Fully HTML-ized.
KEYWORDS   Commerce, Trademarks
AUDIENCE   Business Researchers, Lawyers, Politicians
CONTACT   Peter W. Martin
          martin@law.mail.cornell.edu
FREE

http://www.law.cornell.edu/lanham/lanham.table.html

U.S. Patent and Trademark Office Home Page ★★★

The U.S. Patent and Trademark Office site contains the text of several pamphlets and newsletters related to intellectual property law, trademarks, patents, and copyrights. Transcripts are available of numerous PTO hearings on topics such as biotechnology, software patents, and the Internet. Job vacancies and other internal PTO information are also here.
KEYWORDS   Copyright Law, Law, Patent Law, Trademarks
AUDIENCE   Entrepreneurs, Inventors, Patent Lawyers, Patent Researchers, Researchers
CONTACT   www@uspto.gov
FREE

http://www.uspto.gov/

U.S. Patent Act, As Amended ★★★★

This resource contains full-text documentation regarding the U.S. Patent Act (Title 35, United States Code, Sections 1-376). It is fully hypertexted for ease of navigation.
KEYWORDS   Law, Patent Law
AUDIENCE   Business Professionals, Law Students, Legal Professionals, Legislators
CONTACT   Peter W. Martin
          martin@law.mail.cornell.edu
FREE

http://www.law.cornell.edu/usc/35/i_iv/overview.html

International & Comparative Law

See also
Business & Economics · *Economics*
Government & Politics · *International*
Law & Criminal Justice · *Reference*

Estonian Law Translations ★★★

This page contains links to unofficial translations of some Estonian law texts into English. Some of the information includes the Estonian Constitution, laws on aliens, citizenship, education, private schools, etc.
KEYWORDS   Constitutions, Estonia, Law (International), Legal Resources
AUDIENCE   Estonians, International Lawyers, Lawyers, Legal Professionals
FREE

http://www.eenet.ee/english/law/index.html

Fabritius Tengnagel & Heine ★★★

Fabritius Tengnagel & Heine is a Copenhagen-based law firm providing assistance in all matters pertaining to Danish law. Fabritius Tengnagel & Heine's Homepage is the first of its kind in continental Europe. The homepage has a full English version with links provided to the law firm's areas of practice, staff biographies, history, hours, and a Danish newsletter.
KEYWORDS   Danish Law, Denmark, Europe, Law
AUDIENCE   Denmark Residents, Lawyers, Litigants
CONTACT   Martin von Haller Groenbaek
          dklaw@inet.uni-c.dk
FREE

http://www.mondo.dk/mm/advoweb/fth/

Internet Law Library - Laws of Other Nations ★★★★

This Internet Directory produced by the Internet Law Library, contains a hyperlinked list of various countries as a source of comparison for the laws of other nations. Each country link contains a wide variety of information, with provisions of the constitution when possible, plus a varying collection (depending on country) of law publications, articles, and links to listservs for legal issues and professionals around the world.
KEYWORDS   Comparative Law, International Law, Law of Nations
AUDIENCE   Attorneys, Paralegals, Professors
CONTACT   usc@hr.house.gov
FREE

http://www.pls.com:8001/his/52.htm

Internet Law Library - Treaties and International Law ★★★

This page from the Internet Law Library provides a list of links to various international treaties, laws, and agreements honored between the countries of the world. A wide-ranging collection of topics is covered including nuclear weapons, human rights, and trade agreements, to name just a few. There are also hyperlinks to gopher sites that contain the text of important treaties such as The Law of the Sea or the Geneva Conventions.
KEYWORDS   International Law, International Relations, Law of Nations, Treaties
AUDIENCE   Activists, Attorneys, Professors
CONTACT   usc@hr.house.gov
FREE

http://www.pls.com:8001/his/89.htm

Irish Law Page ★★★

This site provides links to The Irish Law list which is an email discussion list of members worldwide. Some of the accessible information includes news on the Irish Government, the Irish Constitution, Queen's University Belfast Law, and links to other law-related Internet sites.
KEYWORDS   Constitutions, Government, Ireland, Law (Ireland)
AUDIENCE   International Lawyers, Irish, Legal Professionals
CONTACT   Darius Whelan
          dwh@staffmail.rtc-tallaght.ie
FREE

http://www.maths.tcd.ie/pub/IrishLaw/irlaw.html

International & Comparative Law – Judicial Branch

United Nations Criminal Justice Information Network (UNCJIN) Gopher ★★

United Nations Criminal Justice Information Network (UNCJIN) was established as a global crime prevention and criminal justice information network. This gopher aims to assist in the exchange of information concerning criminal justice and crime prevention issues. Some of the information provided includes UNCJIN objectives, and UN criminal justice country profiles and statistics. There are links that range from PAVNET Online, the World Criminal Justice Library Network, to the CIA World Factbook, the FBI Gopher, and the National Criminal Justice Reference Service (NCJRS).

- KEYWORDS: Criminal Justice, International Law, United Nations
- AUDIENCE: Criminal Lawyers, International Law Students
- CONTACT: Adam Bouloukos AB5202@UACSC1.ALBANY.EDU
- FREE

gopher://uacsc2.albany.edu:70/11/newman

The University of Chicago Law School's Center for the Study of Constitutionalism in Eastern Europe ★★★

This gopher site, administered by the University of Chicago Law School's Center for the Study of Constitutionalism in Eastern Europe, contains the Center's journal, 'Eastern European Constitutional Review,' other papers and documents related to the field, a catalog of the Center's archives, and other resources for those interested in the subject.

- KEYWORDS: Constitutions, Eastern Europe, Law (International), Legal Research
- AUDIENCE: Eastern Europeans, International Lawyers, Law Students
- CONTACT: June Farris jpf3@midway.uchicago.edu
- FREE

gopher://lawnext.uchicago.edu/11/.center

The University of Saarland ★★★

The University of Saarland provides access to the Department of Justice information and resources on the Internet. This site gives access to news bulletins from the German Federal Constitutional Court and the Federal Supreme Courts of Germany. There are links to related law information as well as to other sites on the Internet.

- KEYWORDS: Germany, Law Schools, Lawyers
- AUDIENCE: Germans, Law Students, Lawyers
- CONTACT: jura@phil.uni-sb.de
- FREE

http://www.jura.uni-sb.de

Connections to Law Schools
Of bad eyes, bad backs, and pale skin

Law students read a lot—probably hundreds of pounds of books during the course of their studies.

If you want to make law your field of study, render your task of finding a law school virtually paper free by surveying the myriad of law school sites on the Internet.

You can generate lists of curricula at law schools from Aberdeen to Zurich. Typically you can access admissions information, and even online legal documents. One such place includes the University of Sydney which provides users with links to archives of electronic discussion groups, staff directories, and library catalogs.

(gopher://sulaw.law.su.oz.au/)

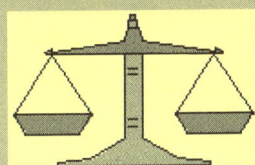

Another place to search before, or even after, you decide on the law school you want to attend, is the "Law School Admission Services" site. For U.S. residents, this site provides a host of information on the LSAT (Law School Admission Test), including test dates and locations. There is also a way to link to law schools and law firms on the Web. The "Law Services Directory" site furnishes LSAT registration information, as well as scoring and reporting.

(http://www.lsac.org/index.html)

Judicial Branch

See also
Government & Politics · *Agencies*
Law & Criminal Justice · *Legal History & Theory*
Law & Criminal Justice · *Legal Resources*
Law & Criminal Justice · *Litigation & Procedures*

Decisions of the U.S. Supreme Court ★★★

This site contains recent United States Supreme Court decisions (1990-1994) indexed by topic or searchable by keyword. The cases are also arranged on a year-to-year basis by name. There are selected Pre-1990 decisions on such topics as administrative and patent law, decisions bearing on school prayer, and Roe v. Wade.

- KEYWORDS: Federal Law, Government Documents (US), Legal Resources, US Supreme Court
- AUDIENCE: Judges, Law Students, Legal Scholars
- CONTACT: Brian T. Shelden bts1@cornell.edu
- FREE

http://www.law.cornell.edu/supct/

Eleventh Circuit Published Opinions ★★★

This site features the published decisions of the U.S. Court of Appeals for the Eleventh Circuit. This material is provided in compressed .ZIP archive files as a public service. Due to the enormous amount of material in any given ruling, only the last three months of opinions are available. There are also links to the Federal Judicial

Center, the Administrative Office of U.S. Courts, and the Emory University Law Library, among other sites.

KEYWORDS Appeals, Federal Courts (US)
AUDIENCE Judges, Law Students, Lawyers, Legal Researchers
CONTACT wmundy@mindspring.com
FREE

http://www.mindspring.com/~wmundy/opinions.html

Law Schools

See also
Education · *Professional Education*
Health & Medicine · *Medical Schools*

29 Reasons Not to Go to Law School

This article provides a tongue-in-cheek look at law and lawyers. Nolo Press concluded long ago that there are only four things wrong with jumping on the lawyer track—law students, law school, becoming a lawyer, and practicing law. This article originally appeared in the Winter, 1994 issue of the Nolo News. It is an excerpt from the new 4th edition of 29 Reasons Not to Go to Law School, written by Ralph Warner, Toni Ihara, Mari Stein and Barbara Kate Repa, and illustrated by Mari Stein (Nolo Press).

KEYWORDS Humor, Law Schools, Legal Publishers
AUDIENCE Consumers, General Public, Lawyers, Legal Professionals, Students (University)
CONTACT cs@NoloPress.com
FREE

http://nearnet.gnn.com/gnn/bus/nolo/29rart.html

Case Western Reserve University Law School

This site is a gopher server of the Case Western Reserve University Law School, Ohio. It contains information on the School and its degree prgrams, admissions, the library, and more. It has links to other law gophers on the Internet.

KEYWORDS Education (College/University), Law, Ohio
AUDIENCE Educators (University), Law Students, Lawyers
FREE

gopher://holmes.law.cwru.edu/

Chicago-Kent College of Law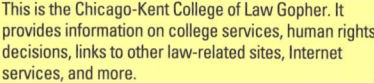

This is the Chicago-Kent College of Law Gopher. It provides information on college services, human rights decisions, links to other law-related sites, Internet services, and more.

KEYWORDS Graduate Education, Illinois, Law, Law Schools
AUDIENCE Law Students, Lawyers, Legal Professionals
CONTACT ldonahue@chicagokent.kentlaw.edu
FREE

gopher://chicagokent.kentlaw.edu/

Cleveland-Marshall College of Law

The Cleveland-Marshall College of Law server provides access to information regarding the law school, library, technical help, related law software, and services. The page has links to Ohio servers and other law-related sites that deal with legal education, law, and law librarianship.

KEYWORDS Law Libraries, Ohio
AUDIENCE Law Students, Lawyers, Ohio Residents
CONTACT webmaster@www.law.csuohio.edu
FREE

http://www.law.csuohio.edu

The Cleveland State University Law Library

The Cleveland State University Law Library's gopher server gives information on electronic publications, news, FTP sevices, local WAIS sources, Usenet services, library resources, and much more. Access to OhioLINK, other library resources, and other gophers are provided.

KEYWORDS Education (College/University), Law Schools, Ohio
AUDIENCE Law Students, Lawyers, Legal Professionals
FREE

gopher://gopher.law.csuohio.edu/

Cornell Law School Gopher Server

This site is a gopher server of the Cornell Law School at Cornell University in Ithaca, New York. It contains the weekly calendar of events, a directory of legal academia, library resources, periodicals, and journals. In addition, it makes connections to other legal gopher holes on the Internet.

KEYWORDS Law, Law Schools, Legal Research, New York
AUDIENCE Educators (University), Law Students, Lawyers
CONTACT Thomas R. Bruce
feedback@fatty.law.cornell.edu
FREE

gopher://www.law.cornell.edu/

D'Angelo Law Library, University of Chicago

This gopher hole provides information about the D'Angelo Law Library and the Law School at the University of Chicago. The information includes the Law School calendar, publications, access to the Library catalog, and the Library handbook.

KEYWORDS Law, Legal Research, Libraries, Universities
AUDIENCE Law Students, Lawyers, Legal Professionals, Legal Scholars
CONTACT Bill Schwesig
w-schwesig@uchicago.edu
FREE

gopher://lawnext.uchicago.edu/

Electronic Easement—A Property Law Web Site

The Electronic Easement—A Property Law Web Site includes teaching materials, notices of recent developments, full text submissions, and a directory of law instructors, and more. The purpose of The Electronic Easement is to provide a convenient means through which law instructors interested in the areas of property and trusts can communicate with each other and share information. It has been designed as a form of newsletter to which anyone can make a contribution. In its initial form, this Web site is designed to serve a Canadian audience. However, in due course, it will be useful to the international community.

KEYWORDS Canada, Law, Property Law
AUDIENCE Canadians, Law Educators, Law Students, Legal Scholars, Real Estate Lawyers
CONTACT Brent Poohkay
bpoohkay@law.ualberta.ca
FREE

http://gpu.srv.ualberta.ca/~bpoohkay/ee/ee.html

Florida State University School of Law

The Florida State University School of Law Web site provides materials about the law programs and other Florida State University resources. Users will find deparment materials such as faculty biographies, placement services, and course catalogs, and can also access the online library catalogs and electronic books via gopher. Also included are a compiled list of on-line law resources and networking/Internet guides.

KEYWORDS Law, Law Schools, Universities
AUDIENCE Education Professionals, Law Professors, Law Students
FREE

http://law.fsu.edu/

Law Schools and Law Firms on the WWW

This page contains a list with links to law schools and law firms on the Internet. Some of the sites include the University of Alberta Faculty of Law, the Northern California Association of Law Libraries, the Deutsch-Amerikanische Juristenvereinigung (German-American Lawyers Association), Hastings College of Law, the firm of Heller, Ehrman, White, & McAuliffe, the University of Salzburg in Austria, the University of Warwick CTI Law Technology Centre (UK). The list is international and extensive.

KEYWORDS Law (International), Law Firms, Law Libraries, Law Schools
AUDIENCE International Lawyers, Law Students, Lawyers, Legal Professionals
FREE

http://www.law.indiana.edu/law/lawother.html

Ohio Northern University Law School

This site provides information relevant to the Law School at Ohio Northern University. This information includes past examinations, documentation about their gopher software, and links to the main Ohio Northern University gopher. The site also provides online access to the US Declaration of Independence and the US Constitution.

Keywords Law Reviews, Law Schools, Legal Research, Ohio
Audience Educators (University), Law Students
Free

http://taggart.onu.edu/

gopher://taggart.onu.edu/

Sydney University Law School ★★★

This site is a gopher server for the Sydney University Law School in Australia. It provides access to staff directories, archives of electronic discussion groups, online legal documents, and library catalogs. There is also a link to the main Sydney University gopher and to other law school gophers.

Keywords Australia, International Education, Law (International), Law Schools
Audience Educators (University), Law Students, Lawyers, Legal Scholars
Contact Nelson Velasquez
nelsonv@sulaw.law.su.OZ.AU
Free

gopher://sulaw.law.su.oz.au/

University of Arkansas School of Law ★★

The University of Arkansas School of Law web site provides information about the college and its resources. Users will find the school catalog and faculty profiles along with materials from courses such as AIDS and the Law or Legal Writing. Library resources include book lists, old exams, Arkansas law cases, and general library information. Links to other law or Arkansas related Web materials are also provided.

Keywords Law, Law Schools
Audience Law Professors, Law Students
Contact ken@law.uark.edu
Free

http://law-gopher.uark.edu/

University of Utah College of Law Gopher Server ★★★

This is a gopher server of the University of Utah College of Law. It provides information on the College bulletin, the library, events, Utah State legal materials, and more. It connects to the University main campus gopher as well as other gophers on the Internet.

Keywords Education (College/University), Law, Law Schools, Utah
Audience Educators (University), Law Students, Lawyers, Students
Contact perkins@admn1.law.utah.edu
Free

gopher://gopher.law.utah.edu/

Connections to Legal Resources
The long arm of the law reaches around the world

You don't have to hire a lawyer (or solicitor) to find out what your legal rights are: there's a wealth of information on the World Wide Web that covers a broad spectrum of law—and organized country by country.

If you have questions about international law, you can access the "World Criminal Justice Library Network" to find out rulings and laws enacted at various locations around the world. There is also a "Foreign and International Law" site that enables you to look at primary documents and receive pertinent commentary.

You'll find recent U.S. Supreme Court Decisions posted so that you can keep tabs on precedent-setting rulings handed down by America's highest court. If number-crunching is your cup of tea, there's a site called the "Bureau of Justice Statistics" where you can find such things as the latest crime statistics. You can even access The World Health Organization and general information on laws in various countries. All of this and more can be reached via:

(gopher://UACSC2.ALBANY.EDU:70//11/newman)

At the "P-Law Legal Resource Locator," every American law is immediately at your fingertips—right down to state-by-state laws and constitutions. Through the "Library of Congress" site, you'll find information on copyright protocol and a comprehensive listing. If you've invented a widget, you can search copyright registrations and recorded copyright assignments to see if anyone else has beaten you to the punch. There are even sites that cover multimedia law and software licensing. If you want to check the latest unemployment figures in the U.S., you can access the Bureau of Labor Statistics. Finally, at tax time, you can download all of the Internal Revenue Service (IRS) forms you'll need to give Uncle Sam his due.

(http://www.dorsai.org/p-law/p-lawhp.html)

Legal History & Theory

See also
Humanities & Social Sciences · *History*
Law & Criminal Justice · *Reference*
Religion & Philosophy · *Philosophy*

Arbitration and Mediation, Brief History ★★★

A Brief History of Arbitration and Mediation is a short text document that discusses mediation and arbitration as traditional methods of dispute resolution.

KEYWORDS Arbitration, Conflict Resolution, Legal History, Mediation
AUDIENCE Law Students, Lawyers, Legal Professionals, Researchers
FREE

http://www.gama.com/his2.htm

Roman Law ★★★

This homepage is a collection of information concerning Roman Law. This is a hypertext representation of small parts of the Corpus Iuris Iustiniani and corresponding medieval comments. Texts available by link in Latin include The Life of Papinianus, The Life of Ulpianus, The Life of Accursius, The Life of Vivianus and some pages on the history of furtum by Heiko Recktenwald.

KEYWORDS Jurisprudence, Legal History, Roman Law
AUDIENCE Law Students, Lawyers, Legal Professionals, Researchers
CONTACT   Thomas Ruefner
          homas.ruefner@student.uni-tuebingen.de
FREE

http://www.jura.uni-sb.de/Rechtsgeschichte/Ius.Romanum/english.html

Why Lawyers Make Bad Judges ★★★

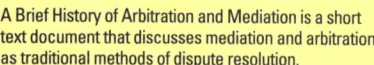

This article originally appeared in the Summer, 1993 issue of the Nolo News. Ralph Warner is co-founder of Nolo Press and a prolific writer and editor of Nolo self-help law books. The articles on this page include Law School—No Place to Grow Judges, No Schools for Judges, Breaking the Stranglehold, Montana Judges Hog-Tie Non-Lawyers, and more.

KEYWORDS Judicial Branch, Law, Legal Issues
AUDIENCE Consumers, General Public, Lawyers, Legal Professionals
CONTACT   cs@NoloPress.com
FREE

http://nearnet.gnn.com/gnn/bus/nolo/badlaw.html

Legal Issues

See also
Law & Criminal Justice · *Business Law*
Law & Criminal Justice · *Family Law*
Law & Criminal Justice · *Legal Resources*

Beating the Insurance Racket ★★

This article originally appeared in the Fall, 1993 issue of Nolo News and is adapted from Beat the Nursing Home Trap—A Consumer's Guide to Choosing and Financing Long-Term Care (Nolo Press). It describes the pitfalls of many long-term care policies and details some other possible ways to finance nursing home care.

KEYWORDS Health Care, Insurance, Legal Issues, Medicare
AUDIENCE Consumers, Lawyers
CONTACT   cs@NoloPress.com
FREE

http://nearnet.gnn.com/gnn/bus/nolo/nurart.html

Legal Resources

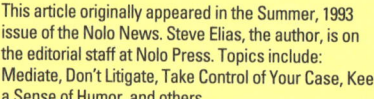

See also
Law & Criminal Justice · *Business Law*
Law & Criminal Justice · *International & Comparative Law*
Law & Criminal Justice · *Judicial Branch*

10 Tips for Staying Sane in Court ★★★

This article originally appeared in the Summer, 1993 issue of the Nolo News. Steve Elias, the author, is on the editorial staff at Nolo Press. Topics include: Mediate, Don't Litigate, Take Control of Your Case, Keep a Sense of Humor, and others.

KEYWORDS Legal Issues, Mediation
AUDIENCE Consumers, General Public, Lawyers, Legal Professionals
CONTACT   cs@NoloPress.com
FREE

http://nearnet.gnn.com/gnn/bus/nolo/saneco.html

Directory of Legal Services ★★★

The Directory of Legal Services provides a list of attorneys from around the country. It describes their qualifications and areas of practice. The Directory also provides a list of businesses that offer support services to the legal community.

KEYWORDS California, Law (US), Lawyers
AUDIENCE Business Professionals, Lawyers, Legal Professionals, Mediators, Patent Lawyers
CONTACT   Editor@Legal.Net (tm)
FREE

http://www.legal.net/directry.htm

The Global Arbitration Mediation Association Inc. (GAMA) ★★★

This page is sponsored by The Global Arbitration Mediation Association, Inc. (GAMA). It provides links to GAMA legal forms and other legal forms, information on arbitration and mediation, online Agreements to Mediate or to Arbitrate through GAMA, Inc., and links to other law-related Internet sites.

KEYWORDS Legal Resources, Mediation
AUDIENCE General Public, Judges, Lawyers, Legal Professionals, Litigants
CONTACT   T. K. Read
          theresa@wwa.com
FREE

http://www.gama.com/

The Law Office Technology Homepage ★★★

This is the site of Dana Shultz & Associates, which specializes in office technology. This page provides various links to information related to law office technology such as: using technology to avoid malpractice and conflicts of interest, how technology can increase revenue, advice on earnings and client satisfaction, technology management—three keys to success, client-server relationships, negotiating computer contracts, and more.

KEYWORDS Information Technology, Law Firms, Legal Resources
AUDIENCE General Public, Law Students, Lawyers, Legal Professionals, Litigants
CONTACT   Dana Shultz
          dhshultz@ds-a.com
FREE

http://starbase.ingress.com/tsw/ds/ds.html

LawMall ★★★★

LawMall is a law information site which serves lawyers and legal professionals, as well as clients and laypersons. LawMall's goal is 'to provide the most complete collection of legal information and sources on the Internet.' It also provides a 'law course' for Internet surfers, a clearing house for expert witnesses willing to work on a contingent-fee basis, development of virtual law practices (emphasizing litigation), downloadable pamphlets which deal with legal, economic, business and political issues, a place where clients, lawyers, and related professions can find each other, and more.

KEYWORDS Legal Resources, Mediation
AUDIENCE General Public, Judges, Lawyers, Legal Professionals, Litigants
CONTACT   Carl E. Person
          carlpers@lawmall.com
FREE

http://www.ocsny.com:80/lawmall/

Legal Resources

The Legal Network for Everyone ★★★★

Welcome! Legal.Net (tm) is for those who provide, regulate, support, or are merely interested in knowing about, legal services. Lawyers and legal support businesses can advertise here, and individuals and businesses can find the names and qualifications of attorneys and law firms. Lawyers can find other lawyers to refer cases to or associate with. There are articles written by lawyers, judges, and laypersons about issues that are of interest to the legal profession and general public. Laypersons can post questions that are responded to by lawyers.

KEYWORDS   Law, Law Firms, Legal Advice, Legal Resources
AUDIENCE   General Public, Lawyers, Legal Professionals, Litigants
CONTACT   Editor@Legal.Net (tm)
FREE

http://www.Legal.Net/

Legal Publishers ★★★

This list is part of AMG's Directory of Legal Resources. It provides links to legal publishers on the Internet and contact information for those not on the Internet. Some of the publishers include Dialog, West Publishing, Butterworth Legal Publishers, and more.

KEYWORDS   Internet Publishing, Law, Legal Publishers
AUDIENCE   Law Students, Lawyers, Legal Professionals, Legal Publishers, Legal Scholars
CONTACT   Alan Gahtan
         agahtan@io.org
FREE

http://www.io.org/~agahtan/lawpubl.htm

Noisy Neighbors ★★★

This site presents information on how to deal with noisy neighbors, nuisances, boundaries, trees, etc. This article originally appeared in the Fall, 1994 issue of the Nolo News. It was adapted from Neighbor Law—Trees, Fences, Boundaries), published by Nolo Press.

KEYWORDS   Legal Advice, Property Law, Real Estate
AUDIENCE   General Public, Home Owners
CONTACT   cs@NoloPress.com
FREE

http://nearnet.gnn.com/gnn/bus/nolo/noise.html

Personal Injury Claims ★★★

The article entitled Taking The Mystery Out Of Personal Injury Claims—Five Commonly Asked Questions discusses how settling an injury claim with an insurance company can be quite simple. In most cases you do not need a lawyer, and you don't need to know technical language or complex legal rules. This article originally appeared in the Summer, 1993 issue of the Nolo News. It was adapted from How to Win Your Personal Injury Claim, by Joseph L. Matthews (Nolo Press).

KEYWORDS   Insurance, Legal Advice, Personal Injury
AUDIENCE   General Public, Lawyers

Connections to Adoptions

And baby makes three . . .

Internet Adoption Photolisting *by* Precious in HIS Sight

Welcome to the Internet Adoption Photolisting by Precious in HIS Sight! This is a photolisting of children available for **international adoption** as well as collection of adoption information and links other sites for adoptive parents. Adoptive families (Christians and non-Christians) are currently being sought for these particular children by various US adoption agencies. We hope that you will be encouraged to consider adoption and tell others about the life changing difference they can make in the world of a child through adoption. If you see a child you are interested in, just call or write the agency that appears at the bottom of the listing. The listing is updated no less than once a month. The photolisting is best viewed using Netscape 1.1 or greater.

● ** Browse the Photolistings in Chronological Order, Country, Age, or Sex.

● My Visit to an Ethiopian Orphanage

● General Information About Adoption

● FAQ for Adoptive Parents - Adoption Information on the Internet

---

Looking to expand your family? Many children are left as orphans in war-torn parts of the world, while others are given up for adoption because the birth-parents are unable to care for the child. If you have ever considered adoption as a way to expand your family unit, there are sites that cater to specific regions such as Latin America or Asia. A number of international adoption agencies now post child listings online—some government-affiliated and some private.

The "Precious in HIS Sight" Web site provides photo listings of children available for international adoption by any licensed U.S. or Canadian adoption agency that would like to participate.

(http://www.gems.com/adoption/)

You can also access "Latin American Adoptive Families," which provides information to people considering adopting a child from Latin America; this group also furnishes prospective parents with cultural information on countries in Latin America.

(http://www.gems.com/adoption/laaf/)

The "Adoption Network" home page provides names and phone numbers of local government and private adoption agencies, attorneys, support groups, national adoption organizations, and various publications that deal with adoption.

(http://www.infi.net:80/adopt/)

If you are an adoptive parent and want to share your experiences as well as find information about support groups or special-needs children, the "Minnesota Children Youth & Family Consortium" can provide you with an outlet, as well as a wealth of helpful information.

(http://www.fsci.umn.edu/cyfc/AdoptINFO.html)

Law & Criminal Justice

Legal Resources – Litigation & Procedures

CONTACT cs@NoloPress.com
FREE

http://nearnet.gnn.com/gnn/bus/nolo/injur.html

Peter W. Huber Home Page ★★★

This site offers information about Peter W. Huber, a lawyer and writer. It also offers access to information about books that he has either authored or edited, including The Geodesic Network, The Geodesic Network II, Federal Telecommunications Law, and many others. Also provided is access to his regular column in Forbes magazine.

KEYWORDS Books, Telecommunications
AUDIENCE Book Readers, Market Analysts, Market Researchers, Telecommunications Experts
CONTACT Peter W. Huber
huber@khht.com
FREE

http://khht.com/huber/home.html

The Seamless Website—Law and Legal Resources ★★★

The Seamless Website is a commercial Web site that is devoted entirely to law, lawyers, law students, and the practice of law. It features original articles on topics relating to law, and cyberspace, the home pages of lawyers, law firms and legal service providers, and links to other law related sites.

KEYWORDS Business, Law, Law Firms, Lawyers
AUDIENCE General Public, Law Students, Lawyers, Legal Professionals, Litigants
CONTACT Kevin Lee Thomason, J.D
kevinlee@crl.com
FREE

http://seamless.com/

U.S. Department of Justice Home Page ★★★★

A number of documents are available here, from the text of the Violent Crime and Law Enforcement Act of 1994, to information on the detaining of Cuban refugees, as well as data on other Justice Department actions. Also provided are statements by the Attorney General and links to various Department of Justice gophers (the Press Release gopher, a job vacancies index, and a general information Department of Justice gopher).

KEYWORDS Crime, Federal Agencies (US), Job Listings
AUDIENCE Investigators, Law Enforcement Personnel, Lawyers, Political Researchers
CONTACT Dept. of Justice Web Administrator
web@usdoj.gov
FREE

http://www.usdoj.gov/

Villanova Center for Information Law and Policy ★★★★

The Villanova Center for Information Law and Policy provides comprehensive online legal information and law resources from government institutions, specifically focusing on technology development. The site contains publications such as the Villanova Information Law Chronicle, the Tax Law Compendium, and the Networking Technotes (which includes papers, articles and news about these topics). Users can look up rules and decisions from federal courts on the Web, indexed by name, years, or keywords. Patent information, tax laws, and legal writing resources are also provided. Villanova provides links to related discussion groups.

KEYWORDS Public Policy, Tax Law
AUDIENCE Law Educators, Law Students, Legal Professionals
CONTACT Kenneth P. Mortensen
kmortens@mail.law.vill.edu
FREE

http://ming.law.vill.edu

The Virtual Law Firm Described ★★

This page, produced by Carl E. Person, describes and outlines the virtues of the Virtual Law Firm. It proposes that this evolution of the law firm would have practical benefits such as reducing labor costs, allowing several individual legal professionals to work together by each performing a separate function, and helping small law firms to find the resources necessary to work efficiently.

KEYWORDS Law, Law Firms
AUDIENCE Expert Witnesses, Investors, Judges, Lawyers, Legal Professionals
CONTACT Carl E. Person
carlpers@lawmall.com
FREE

http://www.ocsny.com:80/lawmall/lm_virtu.html

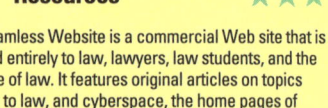

Litigation & Procedures

See also
Business & Economics · *Finance*
Law & Criminal Justice · *Intellectual Property*

Dataline Gopher Menu ★★★★

This page is a gopher menu for Dataline, an organization which works on glass-ceiling cases. Dataline writes about job and gender discrimination lawsuits and looks for ways to support the plaintiffs. Dataline's goal is to engage people online in discussing these issues, and solicit interest and support for some of the plaintiffs whose cases it has followed. Some of the subjects included are mentoring, sexual harassment, women in academic medicine—Stanford University Medical School, and more.

KEYWORDS Gender Discrimination, Women's Issues
AUDIENCE Men, Professional Women, Women, Women Employees

CONTACT ronce@well.sf.ca.us
FREE

gopher://gopher.cyberwerks.com:70/11/dataline

Drafting of Civil Complaint ★★

This document, 'Drafting of Civil Complaint—the Highest Leverage Obtainable in a Lawsuit' discusses inventive pleadings where the 'outcome of the case will be quite dependent on the quality and inventiveness of the complaint.' This site offers suggestions and cautions about the filing process.

KEYWORDS Divorce Law, Law Reviews
AUDIENCE Expert Witnesses, Investors, Judges, Lawyers, Legal Professionals
CONTACT Carl E. Person
carlpers@lawmall.com
FREE

http://www.ocsny.com:80/lawmall/lm_draft.html

Federal Rules of Evidence ★★★★

This hypertext publication pertains to federal rules and procedures regarding the admission of evidence within courts in the U.S. There are an abundance of hot links to specific areas like Witnesses, Expert Testimony, Hearsay, Authentication and Identification, and many more. The site also features a full text search capability to help users find specific information quickly.

KEYWORDS Evidence, Judicial Branch, Statutes
AUDIENCE Judges, Law Students, Lawyers, Legal Researchers
CONTACT Peter W. Martin, Legal Information Institute
martin@law.mail.cornell.edu
FREE

http://www.law.cornell.edu/rules/fre/overview.html

Litigation Arts ★★★

This is a commercial Web site for Litigation Arts. Litigation Arts offers a full range of multimedia services for the legal industry. For over nine years Litigation Arts has been providing courtroom exhibits, animations, videography, and laserdisc and CD-ROM authoring for legal professionals. Links are provided to exhibits, charts, graphs, and diagrams, animations and simulations, laserdisc archiving with bar code accessiblity, video-depositions, day in the life simulations, and site walk-throughs.

KEYWORDS Law, Legal Resources, Multimedia Applications, Video
AUDIENCE Law Students, Lawyers, Legal Professionals, Litigants
CONTACT artguys@crl.com
FREE

http://seamless.com/litarts/lahome.html

Public Citizen Litigation Group 1994 Case Reviews ★★★

This page is the 1994 Annual Report of The Public Citizen Litigation Group which works in five major areas: government and corporate accountability, fighting

Litigation & Procedures – Reference 503

secrecy, regulation of the professions, separation of powers, and worker rights. This report is not a financial report, but a summary of the group's cases in these areas as well as information about the emerging areas of class action and preemption law. The document is organized under these areas of law and summarizes 1994's work by the PCLG.

KEYWORDS Class Action Suits, Preemption Law, Public Interest Law
AUDIENCE Consumer Groups, Consumers, Employees, Labor Unions, Union Members
FREE

gopher://essential.essential.org:70/00/ftp/pub/public_citizen/pclg/1994_annrpt

Using Computer Generated Evidence ★★★

This paper explores the use of computer animation in the courtroom. It is a basic primer on these types of animations, and includes advice to litigators who wish to use this type of evidence. It covers everything from What Does Computer Evidence Mean? to Does Computer Evidence Mislead the Jury? to What are the State Standards for Admissibility of Substantive Computer Evidence?

KEYWORDS Computers, Law, Legal Information
AUDIENCE General Public, Law Students, Lawyers, Legal Professionals, Litigants
CONTACT kevinlee@crl.com
FREE

http://seamless.com/evidence/evidence.html

Connections to Legal References

The perils of being a "motor-mouth"

Cyberspace Law Review Bibliography
by Eric Schlachter, Esq.

eschlach@netcom.com

(Editor's note: this bibliography was written by Eric Schlachter, Esq., and is reprinted with his permission. Readers may also wish to read Electronic Networks and Computer Bulletin Boards, which was also written by Mr. Schlachter).

Electronic Networks and Computer Bulletin Boards: Developing a Legal Regime to Fit the Technology
by Eric Schlachter [*] [updated Spring, 1994]

Nota bene readers may also wish to see Mr. Schlacter's in-depth bibliography of cyberpace law, which appears courtesy of the Information Law Web.

So you want to know what you can and can't say on the Internet? To learn precisely that fine line between slander and "just kidding around"? There is a site on the Internet devoted specifically to answering questions users commonly have about the legal issues regarding computer bulletin boards, email and cyberspace in general.

The "Cyberspace Law Review Bibliography" is a good source to find cyberspace law-related information. Some writings include "The Liability of Computer Bulletin Boards for Defamation Posted by Others," and "Legal Issues Affecting Computer Information Systems and System Operator Liability." The site also contains information about "The Fundamental Rights of Computer Users."

(http://starbase.ingress.com/tsw/rcl/eric.html)

Reference

See also
Government & Politics · *Doctrines*
Law & Criminal Justice · *Judicial Branch*

'Lectric Law Library ★★★★

Upon entering the 'Lectric Law Library,' the user is facetiously urged to 'take a walk around and view the art-work and artifacts on loan from the world's finest museums and galleries.' This relatively new site in fact functions as an online law library, albeit an irreverent one. Interesting sections include: the The Laypeople's Law Lounge—featuring a self-help section with material of special interest to prose litigators, an area devoted to the interests of various professional groups including judges, attorneys, and paralegals, and The Periodical Reading Room.

KEYWORDS Directories, Law
AUDIENCE Attorneys, General Public, Law Students, Legal Researchers
FREE

http://www.inter-law.com/

Chicago-Kent's Guide to Legal Resources ★★★★

This Home Page features a scrolling box with a full array of legal topics for the user to access; these range from Business Issues, Computer Law, and Constitutional Issues, to Foreign Law, Human Rights, Political Action, and Tax and Tort issues, to name just a few. Another prominent feature is 'The Law Link of the Week,' a hot link to an ever-changing legal site of particular interest and usefulness. There is also an 'Other Legal Resources' link, furnishing access to a highly diverse group of resource providers.

KEYWORDS Business Law, Constitutional Law, Legal Issues
AUDIENCE General Public, Law Students, Lawyers, Legal Researchers
CONTACT Chicago-Kent College of Law webmaster@chicagokent.kentlaw.edu
FREE

http://www.kentlaw.edu/lawnet/lawlinks.html

Federal Legal Research Template ★★★

The Federal Legal Research Template constitutes a legal index, education resource, and reference for legal tools to be found on the Internet. There is information about Legislative History, the U.S. Constiution and U.S. Code, Case Law, Federal Regulations, and more. There are also a wide array of hotlinks providing direct access to everything from U.S. Supreme Court decisions to the American Bar Association homepage to the entire Federal Register.

KEYWORDS Legal History
AUDIENCE Law Students, Lawyers, Legal Professionals

CONTACT Jerry Lawson netlegal@cais.com.
FREE

http://www.netrail.net/~sunburst/

Internet Law Library - Attorney and Legal Profession Directories ★★★★

This Internet directory of attorneys and legal professions, part of the Internet Law Library, provides a hyperlinked list of various academic and professional individuals, firms, and company directories. Users will find resources such as West Publishing's Legal Directory or the New Zealand Lawyers Email directory.

KEYWORDS Directories, Legal Professions
AUDIENCE Attorneys, Law Professors, Paralegals
CONTACT usc@hr.house.gov
FREE

http://www.pls.com:8001/his/115.htm

Law and Legal Documents ★★

This gopher serves up various legal resources such as the citizen's guide on using the Freedom of Information Act and the Privacy Act, court opinions, policy documents, the White House, and more. The site is maintained at Syracuse University. It also makes connections to other gophers.

KEYWORDS Government, Law (US), Legal Information, Privacy
AUDIENCE General Public, Law Students, Lawyers
CONTACT   elgouri@dataserver.syr.edu
FREE

gopher://eryx.syr.edu/

Legal Briefs ★★★

This page of legal briefs provides articles about laws that affect people daily. Some of the articles discuss why lawyers make bad judges, keeping legal fees down during a divorce, beating the insurance racket, making gifts to children, and more.

KEYWORDS Law, Legal Advice, Legal Issues, Legal Publishers
AUDIENCE Consumers, Lawyers, Legal Professionals
CONTACT   cs@NoloPress.com
FREE

http://nearnet.gnn.com/gnn/bus/nolo/briefs.html

The Legal Domain Network ★★★

The Legal Domain Network provides read-only access to an archive of law-related Usenet discussions as well as a list of law-related mailing lists. The Usenet discussions can be searched by keywords.

KEYWORDS Law, Legal Research, Usenet
AUDIENCE Law Students, Lawyers, Legal Professionals, Legal Scholars
CONTACT   Laurence S. Donahue, Jr.
          webmaster@chicagokent.kentlaw.edu
FREE

http://www.kentlaw.edu/lawnet/lawnet.html

The Legal Information Institute ★★★★

The Legal Information Institute explores new ways of distributing legal documents and information. Its activities include the distribution of course supplements on disk in a hypertextual format, and the dissemination of legal information via the Internet. This server offers links to Supreme Court decisions, recent decisions of the New York Court of Appeals, the full U.S. Code, email address directory of faculty and staff at U.S. law schools, the Cornell Law Review, hypertext law materials on disk, and information about Cornell Law School and the Cornell Law Library.

KEYWORDS Document Distribution, Law Libraries, Law Schools, Universities
AUDIENCE Computer Professionals, Computer Users, Educators (University), Internet Users
CONTACT   lii@fatty.law.cornell.edu
FREE

http://fatty.law.cornell.edu

Legislate, Inc. Gopher ★★★

This commercial service offers a browsable database of the complete text of all federal bills and laws back to 1976 and various search engines to navigate through the data. Legislate, Inc. provides this gopher server as a 'sampler' of their services. They provide the complete (thus far) archives of bills for the 103rd and 104th Congresses (1993/94 and 1995/96) as well as ordering information, information on Legislate's 'custom' database packages, information on 'hot bills' currently on the floor, and various federal register documents.

KEYWORDS Federal Databases (US), Legislation
AUDIENCE Activists, Government Students, Journalists, Legislators, Political Scientists
CONTACT   legislate@gopher.legislate.com
FREE

gopher://gopher.legislate.com/

Nolo Press Home Page ★★★

The Nolo Press Home Page provides links to their catalogue, current features, sample chapters from some of their books and software, etc. Nolo publishes easy-to-use books and software on consumer law subjects such as wills, small claims court, divorce, and debt problems. Nolo also prepares excellent legal information for small businesses, including help with incorporation, partnerships, employment law, patents, and trademarks. Nolo Press is dedicated to the simple proposition that the American legal system should be affordable and accessible to all.

KEYWORDS Law, Legal Issues, Legal Publishers
AUDIENCE Consumers, General Public, Lawyers, Legal Professionals, Small Business Owners
CONTACT   cs@NoloPress.com
FREE

http://nearnet.gnn.com/gnn/bus/nolo/index.html

Periodical Reading Room ★★★★

This site represents a link from the 'Lectric Law Library home page, and features a wide-ranging collection of legal research materials. For example, the user will find 'The ACLU Collection: A selection of material on topics of broad interest by the world's leading pinko bleeding heart liberals,' The Drug Collection—with reports and articles pertaining to the legal effects of America's drug prohibition, and The Eclectic Law Review, a grab-bag of various legal resources, both standard and bizarre.

KEYWORDS Law, Libraries, Research
AUDIENCE General Public, Law Students, Lawyers, Legal Researchers
CONTACT   staff@inter-law.com
FREE

http://www.inter-law.com/per.html

Self-Help Pamphlets - Problems ★★★

This page provides self-help pamphlets on legal, economic, business, and political problems. Information is provided for topics including job termination or demotion, whistleblowing, developing and marketing your creativity, starting a new business in NYC, controlling litigation costs—for lawyers and clients, virtual law practice—how it works, how to protect your ideas, and more.

KEYWORDS Legal Resources, Self-Help Programs
AUDIENCE General Public, Judges, Lawyers, Legal Professionals, Litigants
CONTACT   Carl E. Person
          carlpers@lawmall.com
FREE

http://www.ocsny.com:80/lawmall/lm_pamph.html

Thomas—Legislative Information on the Internet. ★★★

This page provides links to legislative information on the Internet. Links include the full text of all versions of House and Senate bills searchable by keyword(s) or by bill number, full text of the daily account of proceedings on the House and Senate Floors searchable by keyword(s), an explanation of the lawmaking process, the House of Representatives and Senate Gopher, Library of Congress, and more.

KEYWORDS Law, Legislation, Library of Congress
AUDIENCE Democrats, Internet users, Political Scientists, Republicans, Students
CONTACT   thomas@loc.gov
FREE

http://thomas.loc.gov/

University of Southern California Law Center and Law Library ★★★★

The University of Southern California Law Center and Law Library provides information about the Library's resources and hours, and offers a great number of law-related links on the Internet—government resources, law journals, directories of law schools, law firms, and more. There is also related computer and WWW information.

KEYWORDS California, Law Libraries, Law Schools, Legal Research
AUDIENCE Law Students, Lawyers, Legal Professionals, Legal Scholars
CONTACT   Darin Fox
          dfox@law.usc.edu
FREE

http://www.usc.edu/dept/law-lib/usclaw.html

The WWW Virtual Library —Law ★★★★

The WWW Virtual Library provides an extensive database of law resources available on the Internet. Resources include virtually anything related to law, e.g. law schools, legal publications, other law servers, international sources, Library of Congress, Courts of Appeal, technology reviews, United Nations, U.S. Government, and more.

KEYWORDS International Law, Law, Law Schools, Legal Resources

Reference – Statutes

AUDIENCE   Judges, Law Students, Lawyers, Legal Scholars
CONTACT   wwwlaw@polecat.law.indiana.edu
FREE

http://www.law.indiana.edu:80/law/lawindex.html

Statutes

See also
Law & Criminal Justice · *Business Law*

Attorney-General's Chambers ★★★

The Attorney-General's Chambers represents an education and resource site pertaining to the domain of Singapore's Attorney General, and by extension, this country's overall legal code. Departments include a Legislative division, a Civil division, a Crime division, and a Computer Information Services section. If you're planning to travel or do business in Singapore, this site offers comprehensive information to ensure that you don't run afoul of the country's notoriously strict laws. There are also hotlinks to 'What's hot,' 'What's cool,' and more.

KEYWORDS   International Law, Law, Singapore
AUDIENCE   Business Professionals, Singapore Residents, Travelers
CONTACT   webster@www.sg
FREE

http://www.sg/infomap/gov/agc.html

California Codes ★★★★

This site makes available California's legislative information through the Internet via its public access computer. Legislative information is organized by a list of hyperlinked California codes, arranged by area such as Business and Professional Code or the Vehicle Code to name just a few. This electronic version of the code provides users a way to view by chapter and section each code listed.

KEYWORDS   California, Codes, States
AUDIENCE   Activists, Attorneys, Californians
CONTACT   Ken Shirriff
            shirriff@eng.sun.com
FREE

http://www.law.indiana.edu/codes/ca/codes.html

FEAR—Forfeiture Endangers American Rights ★★★★

The FEAR (Forfeiture Endangers American Rights) home page provides resources on property rights and forfeiture laws. Topics include victims, legislation, lobbying, court news, police, prosecutors, libraries, news archives and more.

KEYWORDS   California, Civil Rights, Constitutional Law, Property Rights
AUDIENCE   Law Students, Lawyers, Legal Professionals, Researchers
CONTACT   F.E.A.R.
            fearno1@nbn.com
FREE

http://www.calyx.com/~fear/

Florida Legislature On-Line Sunshine ★★★★

This page, produced by the Florida Legislature as a public service, provides comprehensive electronic access to Florida Statutes (Full Volume 1993). Included are those statutes published in odd-numbered years, those sections of the statutes affected in a particular year, and those published in even-numbered years. Users will also be able to conduct a keyword search of the Florida statutes either by full text or by chapter names.

KEYWORDS   Codes, Florida, Legislature, States
AUDIENCE   Activists, Attorneys, Florida Residents
CONTACT   wane@scri.fsu.edu
FREE

http://www.scri.fsu.edu/fla-leg/statutes/

Indiana Legal Information ★★★

This page hosts information about the Indiana Legal System. Included here is a hypertext version of the Indiana Code 1994-'95, which is organized into 33 titles, such as Taxation, Education, and Corrections, each of which contains subheadings of Articles, Chapters, and Sections. There are also links to hypertext versions of the Indiana Constitution and a special hypertext section devoted to the Indiana Uniform Fraudulent Transfer Act. Under construction is a Courts directory which will list information regarding the Indiana Supreme Court and other contacts.

KEYWORDS   Constitutions, Indiana, Law (US), Legal Information
AUDIENCE   Indiana Residents, Law Students, Lawyers, Legal Professionals, Legal Scholars

---

Connections To Finding Your Family
Who am I?

For many adoptees, finding birth parents is part of an emotional and spiritual search for one's roots. In other cases, adoptees face life-threatening diseases that may be hereditary and need to know who their birth parents are so as to obtain a medical history. In either case, this quest can be controversial for both sides involved. The Internet now provides a more efficient and confidential way to find your birth-family; this service is currently designed primarily for U.S. residents.

Additionally, there are special support groups for adoptees, whether focusing on emotional issues around being an adoptee, to help in approaching the birth-parents once they are located. The "Information for Adoptees" site provides a full search service, support groups by states, and several genealogical links.

(http://www.infi.net/adopt/adoptee.html)

CONTACT webmaster@polecat.law.indiana.edu
FREE

http://www.law.indiana.edu/law/in.html

Information About the Federal Crime Control Bill

This page contains the full text and some supplementary information about the Federal Crime Control Bill introduced in the U.S. Congress in 1994. Users will find a table of contents, the entire text arranged by chapter, notes such as the official legislative history, and explanatory statements about the bill.

KEYWORDS Crime, Legislation
AUDIENCE Legislators, Political Scientists, Prosecutors, United States Residents
CONTACT Richard Zorza, Counsel for Technology zorzar@vera.org
FREE

http://broadway.vera.org/pub/crimebill/cb.html

Internet Law Library - U.S. Code

This site is a product of the US House of Representatives, and entails an experiment in electronic democracy. It aims to demonstrate the potential and benefit of making the entire US Code available to the public at no charge. This massive body of information is made manageable though the sophisticated Personal Library Software, accessible on-site.

KEYWORDS Codes, Democracy, United States
AUDIENCE General Public, Lawyers, Legal Researchers, Students
CONTACT U.S. House of Representatives Comments@hr.house.gov
FREE

http://www.pls.com:8001/his/usc.html

New York State Statutes

This gopher contains a series of files with all consolidated laws and selected unconsolidated laws of New York State. This information comprises a tree structure of menus which leads the user to various sections of law, e.g., State Education Law, Alcohol and Beverage Control Law. Each separate law is divided into files containing the various sections of that law. This database will not reflect statutory changes each time a new chapter of law is signed. It will be updated on a less frequent basis.

KEYWORDS Codes, New York, States
AUDIENCE Activists, Attorneys, New York Residents
CONTACT comment@senate.state.ny.us
FREE

gopher://lbdc.senate.state.ny.us:70/11/.laws/

Tax Law

See also
Business & Economic · *Finance*
Government & Politics · *Agencies*

Hot Tax Topics

The Hot Tax Topics site provides information on topics like the effectiveness of current U.S. government tax strategies, the latest taxpayer victories and defeats in the courts and with the IRS, the proposed 'flat tax,' and the Congressional Report on Expatriation Tax Avoidance. The 'hot topics' format is easy to access and engrossing, like a print-based newsweekly. Information is useful and thorough, though hotlinks to other areas are limited.

KEYWORDS Government Agencies, IRS, Taxes
AUDIENCE Lawyers, Tax Accountants, Tax Payers
CONTACT Robert L. Sommers, taxman@taxprophet.com
FREE

http://www.taxprophet.com/hottopics.html

Internal Revenue Code, Section 501

This home page offers a hypertext version of the U.S. Internal Revenue Code, specifically Section 501. Information is included on tax exemptions for corporations, certain trusts which are very important to nonprofit organizations. The information is hyperlinked.

KEYWORDS Internal Revenue Code, Non Profit Organizations, Regulations, Taxation
AUDIENCE Activists, Nonprofit Organizations, Philanthropists
CONTACT kelvin@fourmilab.ch
FREE

http://www.fourmilab.ch/ustax/www/t26-A-1-F-I- 501.html

Tax Issues and Internet Links

This Kent-Law School site features an assortment of links to other Web sites and resources pertaining to Tax Law. Resources range from the Villanova Law School Tax Law Compendium, to Tax Net-UK Residents, to The False Claims Act Legal Center. Also featured is an electronic compendium of information related to the filing of Income Tax forms, as well as links providing direct access to federal and state tax forms and agencies.

KEYWORDS Codes, Tax Forms, Taxes
AUDIENCE Accountants, Law Students, Lawyers, Taxpayers
CONTACT Chicago-Kent Law webmaster@chicagokent.kentlaw.edu
FREE

http://www.kentlaw.edu/cgi-bin/lawlinks.subject.cgi

Tax Topics Contents

This site pertains to the British tax code and practices. It addresses questions such as - what to do with a tax return? Does everyone get a tax return? Who are your contacts at the Inland Revenue? It also focuses on the best ways to calculate one's taxes, and how to generate tax-free income. There are seemingly endless links to other locations for specialized information, from interest payments to self-employment.

KEYWORDS Britain, Codes, Taxes
AUDIENCE Accountants, British, International Business Professionals, Lawyers
CONTACT Purple Training Limited tax@purple.co.uk
FREE

http://www.purple.co.uk/purplet/tax/contents.html

U.S. Income Tax Law

This site comprises a chapter on U.S. Income Tax Law from a publication of the Government Printing Office (GPO). Aside from furnishing comprehensive information about the U.S. Income Tax code, the site also provides useful hotlinks to the U.S. House of Representatives, the U.S. Senate, the entire Federal Register, the Legal Information Institute at Cornell Law School, and more. This site represents an experiment by the House Information Systems to place U.S. government functions and resources online.

KEYWORDS Codes, Legislation, Taxes
AUDIENCE General Public, Law Students, Lawyers, Tax Accountants
CONTACT Government Printing Office help@eids05.eids.gpo.gov
FREE

http://www.best.com/~ftmexpat/html/taxsites/law-legi.html

Torts

See also
Law & Criminal Justice · *Litigation & Procedures*

Franklin, Cardwell & Jones, P.C.

This site is the homepage of a Houston-based firm of trial attorneys which claims to have established itself as one of the first law firms with a presence on the World Wide Web. This server is intended to provide potential clients with information about the firm's practice and with links to a variety of free legal resources on the Internet. Curiously, there's even a hot link to the "1995 Cutting Horse World Champion, Suzan Cardwell."

KEYWORDS Criminals, Lawyers, Legal Services
AUDIENCE Lawyers, Legal Clients, Legal Researchers
FREE

http://www.fcj.com/

Internet Law Library - Tort Law

This page, part of the U.S. House of Representatives Internet Law Library, presents a list of links to several tort-related articles discussing such issues as product liability, punitive damages, and liability in general. In addition, it offers a number of links to other closely related tort topics.

KEYWORDS   Civil Law, Consumer Rights, Liability
AUDIENCE   Activists, Attorneys, General Public
CONTACT   usc@hr.house.gov
FREE

http://www.pls.com:8001/his/110.htm

Law Link—Tort Resources ★★★★

This site provides fairly extensive coverage of legal Torts. Sub-categories include slander and defamation, privacy issues, and consumer-related torts. Some specific titles include 'Legal Pitfalls in Cyberspace: Defamation on Computer Networks,' 'Principles for Providing and Using Personal Information,' and a collection of articles on topics of interest to consumers and the Plaintiff's Bar. Much of the coverage focuses on cyberspace-related issues.

KEYWORDS   Consumer Rights, Internet, Legal Issues
AUDIENCE   General Public, Law Students, Lawyers, Legal Researchers
CONTACT   Chicago-Kent Law
           webmaster@chicagokent.kentlaw.edu
FREE

http://www.kentlaw.edu/cgi-bin/lawlinks.subject.cgi

Professor Newt's Contract with Corporations ★★★★

Professor Newt's Contract with Corporations is an article published by Nolo Press. It is a searing analysis and critique of House Speaker Newt Gingrich's proposals to limit the amounts that can be recovered in personal-injury cases, and to discourage lawsuits by making losing litigants pay the other side's attorney fees. The site also features hotlinks to several other areas, including a critique of America's broken legal system, and catalog information about Nolo products and publications.

KEYWORDS   Federal Law, Politicians
AUDIENCE   Lawyers, Legal Researchers, Political Reformers, Students
FREE

http://nearnet.gnn.com/gnn/bus/nolo/newt.html

Torts Law Materials ★★★★

This page produced by Cornell Law School's Legal Information Institute offers a short list of tort related law materials on the Internet. The resources are divided into two sections, one being a list of links to primary sources while the other list of links leads to reference type sources concerning tort information.

KEYWORDS   Civil Law, Consumer Rights
AUDIENCE   Activists, Attorneys, General Public
CONTACT   Peter W. Martin
           martin@law.mail.cornell.edu
FREE

http://www.law.cornell.edu/topics/torts.html

Popular Culture & Entertainment

Automobiles	509
Books	511
Celebrities & Personalities	516
Family & Community	517
Fashion	522
Genealogy	522
General Reference	523
Humor	525
Lifestyles	530
Magazines & Newspapers	533
Movies	541
Multimedia	543
Museums & Theme Parks	544
Shopping	545
Television	550
Unexplained Phenomena	552
Weather & Traffic	554

Automobiles

See also
Business & Economics · *Industries*
Sports & Recreation · *Motor Sports*

Alldata WWW Server

★★★★

This site offers access to the ALLDATA-LINK information retrieval system for PCs. This service helps car owners maintain, service and troubleshoot their vehicles. The ALLDATA-LINK diagnostic and repair database provides access to over 10,000 repair facilities nationwide.

KEYWORDS Automobile Repair, Automobiles, Information Retrieval, Software
AUDIENCE Automobile Enthusiasts, Automobile Owners, General Public
CONTACT Theresa@alldata.com
FREE

http://irsociety.com/0c:/alldata.html

Auto Financing Page

★★★

This page allows you to fill in the blanks and submit a form which will return to you all the details of your automobile financing. The process works by filling in the blanks that you know, leave the others empty and they will be computed when you submit the form. The system can compute any single field from the other three. The fields include interest rate (annual percentage), principal amount (amount of loan), number of months, and monthly payment.

KEYWORDS Automobile Financing, Automobiles, Used Cars
AUDIENCE Automobile Buyers, Automobile Dealers
CONTACT Michael Littman
mlittman@cs.brown.edu
FREE

http://www.cs.brown.edu/cgi-bin/financing.pl

AutoNetwork

★★★

This is a virtual car lot with over 3,000 vehicles that are available. Select the make of the car in the list provided, and then select the model which interests you most. Information on where the car is available, options that come with the car, and contact information is given for each selection you make.

KEYWORDS Auto Showrooms, Automobiles, Consumer Affairs, Transportation
AUDIENCE Automobile Buyers, Automobile Enthusiasts, Automobile Mechanics

FREE

http://www.cbo.com/auto/makevsmodels.html

Automobile-Related Home Pages

★★★

This Web site contains links to a large number of automobile-related home pages, produced by a proud Acura NSX enthusiast. Pointers to Web sites are listed alphabetically by car brand, with brief descriptions of the contents of the sites. Links to Formula One and racing Web sites are also included, as well as a page of automotive resources for specific automobile issues.

KEYWORDS Home Pages, Motor Sports
AUDIENCE Automobile Enthusiasts, Automobile Owners
CONTACT David Hwang
david@ganglion.anes.med.umich.edu
FREE

http://ganglion.anes.med.umich.edu/NSX/misc/other-pages.html

Beverly Hills Motoring Accessories

★★★

Beverly Hills Motoring Accessories sells car covers, floor mats, utilities and 'protective' accessories for automobiles. Their Web site provides material on each product, including pictures, and gives ordering information.

KEYWORDS Automobile Care, Automobiles, Shopping
AUDIENCE Automobile Enthusiasts, Automobile Owners, Californians

FREE

http://www.shopping2000.com/shopping2000/bev-hills/

Car Audio Page

★★★

This page contains links and information on car audio. Links are provided to schematics as well as crossover basics and tables for crossover construction. Planned additions to this page include basic electronic formulas pertaining to car audio installation, tips, techniques, and tricks on all sorts of topics, and product reviews on a variety of products.

KEYWORDS Auto Audio, Auto Audio Installation, Automobiles, Used Cars
AUDIENCE Audio Enthusiasts, Automobile Buyers, Automobile Dealers, Automobile Owners
CONTACT John Thompson,
spdtrap@ksu.ksu.edu
FREE

http://www.ksu.ksu.edu/~spdtrap/caraudio/CarAudio.html

Automobiles

 Car Price Network

This site offers pricing information on new and used prices for cars, trucks, and vans. For new vehicles, you can access prices, specifications and options, etc. and tips on how to deal with the dealer, how to make your best deal, and how much to pay. For used cars, you can also get mileage charts, prices for options, tips on what to expect when you buy, sell, or trade a used car. You can also access rebate information, factory incentives, lease tips, delivery options, etc. You can order the report online.

KEYWORDS   Auto Showrooms, Automobile Financing, Automobiles, Used Cars
AUDIENCE   Automobile Buyers, Automobile Sellers, Consumers, Drivers
CONTACT   info@infomed.com
FREE

http://www.w2.com/car1.html

Car Show and Event Listing Page

This page is a Web vision dedicated to all car lovers the world over, from the simplicity of the antique automobiles of the past to the auto industries' wonders of today and beyond. Featured on this page are notices of car shows, events, or organized 'cruising' areas where car owners and enthusiasts can show off their machines or check out what's new on the block. Viewers will find event names, locations, fees, contact information, directions and a brief description of the event. Information is organized by month. The actual locations range from a restaurant parking lot in Alberta, Canada, to a plaza in Baja, Mexico.

KEYWORDS   Antiques, Automobile Care, Automobiles, Events
AUDIENCE   Automobile Enthusiasts, Automobile Mechanics, Automobile Owners
CONTACT   cody@kbt.com
FREE

http://kbt.com/carshow/

 Classic Car Connection

Classic Car Connection is the first international electronic database monitoring classic car prices internationally. The latest prices for a wide range of popular and exotic classics are listed. This is a unique database of contacts for great deals, clubs, events, spare parts, insurance, shipping services, accessories, restoration services and a wealth of other information about classic and collectible vehicles around the world.

KEYWORDS   Auto Showrooms, Automobiles, Classic Cars, Collectors
AUDIENCE   Audio Enthusiasts, Automobile Buyers, Automobile Dealers, Classic Car Enthusiasts
FREE

http://www.primenet.com/~dadalus/classic.html

 DealerNet - The Virtual Showroom

The Virtual Showroom offers a wide range of information about domestic and international automobiles. From here you can access various automobile manufacturers and participating dealers, view actual video footage of current models, browse a variety of related financing and insurance products, or hunt for the ideal previously owned car. Use DealerNet to search for elusive automobile parts, choice accessories and quality service, check in with Autoworld for the history, news and future of the industry, and, for recreational information, explore the Boats, RVs and Trailers page.

KEYWORDS   Auto Manufacturers, Auto Showrooms, Automobiles, Transportation
AUDIENCE   Audio Enthusiasts, Automobile Buyers, Automobile Mechanics, Automobile Repair
CONTACT   info@dealernet.com
FREE

http://www.dealernet.com/

 Goodyear Tire and Rubber Company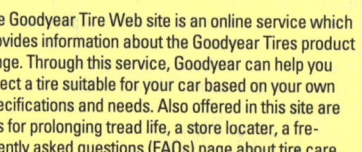

The Goodyear Tire Web site is an online service which provides information about the Goodyear Tires product range. Through this service, Goodyear can help you select a tire suitable for your car based on your own specifications and needs. Also offered in this site are tips for prolonging tread life, a store locater, a frequently asked questions (FAQs) page about tire care, and a calendar of events for racing and blimp activities. In addition, links to other driving-related features can be found.

KEYWORDS   Automobile Equipment, Companies, Motor Sports, Tires
AUDIENCE   Drivers, General Public, Mechanics, Race Car Drivers
CONTACT   webmaster@goodyear.com
FREE

http://www.goodyear.com

 Imall Automotive Want Ads

This page lists links to automotive want ads located on the Imall. The links range from individual cars to auto conventions.

KEYWORDS   Auto Showrooms, Automobiles, Online Advertising
AUDIENCE   Automobile Buyers, Automobile Dealers, Automobile Enthusiasts, Classic Car Enthusiasts
CONTACT   management@imall.com
FREE

http://www.imall.com/cgi-bin/alisearch?IMALL.*Automotive,want-ads

 Rent-A-Wreck of America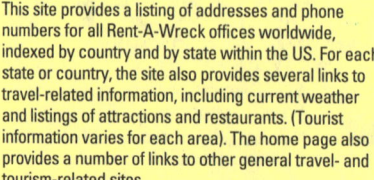

This site provides a listing of addresses and phone numbers for all Rent-A-Wreck offices worldwide, indexed by country and by state within the US. For each state or country, the site also provides several links to travel-related information, including current weather and listings of attractions and restaurants. (Tourist information varies for each area). The home page also provides a number of links to other general travel- and tourism-related sites.

KEYWORDS   Auto Rental, Travel, Used Cars
AUDIENCE   Automobile Enthusiasts, Automobile Renters, Drivers, Tourists
CONTACT   Ken Blum   Ken@charm.net
FREE

http://www.charm.net:80/~ken/

 Sotheby's Car Auctions

This page provides information on Sotheby's Car Auctions. They cover major sales of collectible vehicles and automobilia from around the world. You can preview important auctions in more detail than has ever been possible before, and then get the results faster and in greater depth than any printed publication can deliver them to you. In one Sotheby's sale held at the Royal Air Force Museum in England, over 500 lots were on offer, ranging through a remarkable diversity of collectors' cars, and commercial, horse-drawn, military, and steam vehicles, as well as automobilia.

KEYWORDS   Auctions, Automobiles, Used Cars
AUDIENCE   Automobile Dealers, Automobile Enthusiasts, Classic Cars Enthusiasts
FREE

http://www.primenet.com/~dadalus/auction.html

Team.Net Automotive Information Archives

This home page provides access to information on automobiles assembled on the Internet by various individuals on the Net and also gives links to other WWW sites with a similar focus. The resources includes images, movies, and sounds.

KEYWORDS   Automobiles, Motorcycles, Transportation
AUDIENCE   Automobile Enthusiasts, Automobile Owners, Automobile Racers, Motorcycle Enthusiasts
CONTACT   Mark J. Bradakis   mjb@triumph.cs.utah.edu
FREE

http://triumph.cs.utah.edu/team.net.html

 Trivial Information

This is list of trivial facts with links related to automobiles. Topics covered include gasoline FAQ, coolant, calculations of gear ratios, oxygen sensors, tires, oil, break-ins, etc.

KEYWORDS   Automobiles, Classic Cars, Information Resources, Mechanical Engineering
AUDIENCE   Automobile Buyers, Automobile Dealers, Automobile Enthusiasts, Classic Car Enthusiasts
CONTACT   Kyle Hamar   khamar@mailhost.tcs.tulane.edu
FREE

http://ram.chem.tulane.edu:8080/f-body/trivia/trivia.html

Webfoot's Used Car Lot

This page has links to many used car lots on the WWW as well as information about automobiles. This is a free service for both buyers and sellers. You simply click on

Popular Culture & Entertainment

the location of the lot (city) and off you go. You can also access all kinds of other auto information such as specific makes or models, automotive operations/maintenance information, newsgroups, finding a car, car finances, accessories, parts, services, bicycles, boats, aircraft, and more.

KEYWORDS Auto Showrooms, Automobile Care, Automobiles, Used Cars
AUDIENCE Automobile Buyers, Automobile Dealers, Automobile Enthusiasts, Classic Car Enthusiasts
CONTACT Kaitlin Duck Sherwood
ducky@netcom.com
FREE

http://www.webfoot.com/lots/international.car.lot.html

Books

See also
Arts & Music · *Electronic Arts*
Business & Economics · *Publishing*
Education · *Public Libraries*
Humanities & Social Sciences · *Literature*

ABAA Booknet

ABAA Booknet is a resource for people interested in old, rare books. It includes an infopage for the ABAA (Antiquarian Booksellers' Association of America) and links to newsletters, a list of booksellers, a search form for specific books and authors, information about book fairs, research and discussion groups, and a Book Security bulletin.

KEYWORDS Antiquarian Books, Books, Publishing, Rare Books
AUDIENCE Antique Collectors, Book Dealers, Publishing Professionals, Reading Enthusiasts
CONTACT the booknet team
booknet@rmharris.com
FREE

http://www.clark.net/pub/rmharris/booknet1.html

Alan Rankin Rare Books

Alan Rankin Rare Books is a Scotland-based dealer of vintage books and manuscripts. Users will find an online catalog in HTML and Adobe Acrobat (PDF) formats. The catalog contains over a hundred entries, with categories of books such as Poetry, Science, Scotland, and Theology. Catalogs include prices, conditions of the works, a brief description, and details about any unique characteristics. Links to related book and collecting pages are also included.

KEYWORDS Online Bookstores, Poetry, Rare Books, Scotland
AUDIENCE Book Collectors, Bookworms, Poetry Enthusiasts, Rare Book Dealers, Scottish Book Collectors
CONTACT Ad82@CityScape.co.uk
FREE

http://www.cityscape.co.uk/users/ad82/index.html

Connections to Buying Classic Automobiles
Take a ride in my Oldsmobile

If you're hunting for classic cars, garage equipment, advertising items, or repair tools, check out the Highway One site on the World Wide Web. Collector cars including Jaguars, Austins, and the Ford Model TT one-ton vans are on sale.

The site includes not only a list of available cars, but also those recently sold, and a currency chart for exchange rates the day of the sale. The Classified Ads section includes photos of classic cars on sale, as well as tips on buying, selling, and renovating classic automobiles. Automobile buffs from around the world can access this site through the following address:

(http://www.highway-one.com/)

Alternative Textbooks [IMS]

The Alternative Textbooks home page provides a place for higher education students to purchase used and new textbooks at discount prices. Currently, the site is under construction. It only offers a listing of some courses at Stanford University and their required texts with stock and price information. A map to the store located in Palo Alto and store hours are also provided.

KEYWORDS Education, Textbooks, Used Textbooks
AUDIENCE Professors, Stanford University Professors, Students, Students (University), Textbook Buyers
CONTACT jpc@internex.net
FREE

http://netmedia.com/ims/alttext/home.html

Atomic Books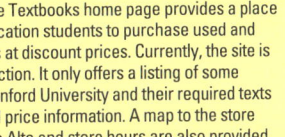

The Atomic Books web site offers a comprehensive listing of alternative and rare comics from the likes of Robert Crumb and Lynda Barry. Entries include issues available and price information. Some entries may be accessed for cover images. The site also includes a listing of comic book compilations and listings for special interest groups.

KEYWORDS Comics, Rare Comic Books
AUDIENCE Comic Book Collectors, Comics Enthusiasts
FREE

http://www.clark.net/pub/atomicbk/catalog/altcomic.html

Audio Bestsellers

Audio Bestsellers provides links to the audio books (books-on-tape) and publishers on the Bestseller list. Audio books are chosen for their groundbreaking subject matter, production, or packaging. A broad range of categories were selected in an attempt to include as many audio genres as possible. Topics include best of the best audio books on politics, unabridged fiction, nonfiction, erotica, multi-cast, memoir/autobiography, sports, live performance, and many more. You simply click on a topic or type of book which brings up a list of bestsellers under that category.

KEYWORDS Audio Books, Books, Literature
AUDIENCE Fiction Enthusiasts, Librarians, Reading Enthusiasts, Writers
CONTACT Derrik Walker
dwalker@books.com
FREE

http://www.books.com/audio1.htm

Authornet

Through Authornet, you are introduced to new writers and their works. The site usually features excerpts from

Books

a new or soon-to-be-published novel, and also includes a hypertext link to a mail-order bookstore where you can order the book if you like the extract presented here. Authornet also allows you to leave comments for the author to read, and tells where you can meet the author at bookstore appearances. Be forewarned that the books and authors featured here are not chosen necessarily for their quality; it's a commercial service for which publishers pay to get exposure for their products.

KEYWORDS Books, Publishing, Writers
AUDIENCE Book Readers, Book Reviewers, Literary Critics, Writers
CONTACT Richard Carrington
FREE

http://www.imgnet.com/auth/index.html

Bay Area Bookstore Events ★★★

Bay Area Bookstore Events provides links to a collection of monthly calendars of events and occasional additional items from ten San Francisco Bay Area bookstores. The events described in these calendars are free and open to the public unless otherwise noted. The ten calendars are for A Clean Well-Lighted Place for Books-Cupertino, Larkspur and San Francisco; Book Passages-Corte Madera; The Booksmith-San Francisco; Black Oak Books, Cody's Books, and Gaia Bookstore & Community Center-Berkeley, CA; Kepler's Books - Menlo Park; and Printers Inc. Bookstores-Palo Alto and Mountain View.

KEYWORDS Authors, Bookstores, California, Events
AUDIENCE Book Dealers, Book Readers, Californians
CONTACT Eric De Mund
         ead@netcom.com
FREE

http://www.culturewave.com/culturewave/ba-bookstore-events/

gopher://gopher kksf.tbo.com/ KKSF, Smooth Jazz 103.7/ Entertainment/Books/Bay Area Bookstore Events

ftp://wwa.com/pub/culturewave/ba-bookstore-events/

Bestsellers ★★★

Bestsellers is a website which provides links to the books on the Bestseller list. (There is also a 'If you only had one book to read' link for those who want a general list). Topics include hardcover fiction and nonfiction, paperback mass market, paperback trade, and audio bestsellers. You simply click on a topic or type of book which brings up a list of bestsellers under that category. The books are organized by title (hyperklinked). Then under each title is the author, publisher, price and ISBN number. When you click on the title, a page with bestseller information appears which supplies you with the title, author, publisher, date, and price. You can buy a book online after opening an account.

KEYWORDS Audio Books, Books, Literature
AUDIENCE Fiction Enthusiasts, Librarians, Reading Enthusiasts, Writers
CONTACT Derrik Walker
         dwalker@books.com
FREE

http://www.books.com/best1.htm

BiblioBytes - Books on Computer ★★★

The Bibliobytes home page provides users with a listing of fiction and non-fiction books currently available online. Users can perform a search by genre or a complete listing of titles is available alphabetically by author's last name. Users may purchase titles online. Each day one book is available free for the downloading.

KEYWORDS Books, Bookstores, Literature, Online Books
AUDIENCE Reading Enthusiasts, Writers
CONTACT comment@bb.com
FREE

http://www.bb.com/

Book Catalogues and Book Clubs List ★★★

The Book Catalogues and Book Clubs List offers the names, addresses and a brief description of book publishers, stores and clubs. There are some catalogues and ordering information online.

KEYWORDS Book Clubs, Books, Publishing
AUDIENCE Academics, Book Dealers, Book Readers
CONTACT Cindy Tittle Moore
         tittle@netcom.com
FREE

http://io.com/user/tittle/books/catalogues.html

Bookport ★★★

Bookport is a Web site that provides access to and information about online and printed books. Through this site you can receive sample chapters, press releases, and book and author info from featured books. Bookport indexes and links online reading lists, publishers and booksellers, according to genre and interest, as well as online books.

KEYWORDS Books, Internet Guides, Online Books, Publishing
AUDIENCE Book Readers, Booksellers, Publishers
CONTACT info@bookport.com
FREE

http://www.bookport.com/htbin/welcome/9535.html

BookWeb ★★★

The BookWeb home page sponsored by the American Booksellers Association provides an excellent resource for publishing industry people and book worms worldwide. Users can access the current issue of 'Bookselling This Week' or check out an updated calendar of author readings and appearances on television, radio and in-person across the U.S. A listing of U.S. bookstores is also provided along with links to their home pages. In the future BookWeb has plans to incorporate industry research and news on the freedom of expression at the site.

KEYWORDS Book News, Bookstores, Literary Events
AUDIENCE Booksellers, Publishers, Reading Enthusiasts

FREE

http://www.ambook.org/

Dial-A-Book ★★★

Dial-A-Book is an online bookstore that allows you to download complete texts fo some books and browse first chapters and tables of contents. The hyperlinked linked choices include books from major university presses, Newbery Award Children's books, chess books, excerpts from eleven Bibles translations, Ziff-Davis and Albion Books computer Books, and more.

KEYWORDS Children's Literature, Online Publications
AUDIENCE Children, Educators (Primary/Secondary), Fiction Enthusiasts, Librarians, Parents, Reading Enthusiasts, Students (Primary/Secondary), Writers
CONTACT webmaster@psi.com
FREE

http://dab.psi.net/DialABook/index.html

Douglas Adams Worship Page ★★★

This page contains FAQs relating to Douglas Adams' popular series of novels (beginning with The Hitchhiker's Guide to the Galaxy) as well as other outgrowths of his work (including Infocom's text-based computer game version of the first book). Background information on the author as well as abstracts of the novels themselves are available.

KEYWORDS Adams, Douglas, Internet Guides, Science Fiction
AUDIENCE Humor Enthusiasts, Science Fiction Enthusiasts
CONTACT Nathan Hughes
         nhughes@umich.edu
FREE

http://www.umd.umich.edu/~nhughes/dna/

Dr. Seuss Books In Print (BIP) ★★★

Dr. Seuss Books In Print (BIP) page contains a long list of Dr. Seuss titles taken from the 1994-95 Books in Print (BIP). The categories provided include books, special collections, and books and cassettes in Spanish. Each title is accompanied by the number of pages, publication date listed in BIP, ISBN # for regular edition and grade level listed.

KEYWORDS Cassettes, Children's Literature, Dr. Seuss
AUDIENCE Children, Librarians, Parents, Students (Primary/Secondary)
CONTACT David Bedno
         drseuss@gorn.iuma.com
FREE

http://klinzhai.iuma.com/~drseuss/seuss/seuss.books.html

Dr. Seuss Parody Page ★★

The Dr. Seuss Parody Page contains items that are either parodies of Dr. Seuss books, Dr. Seuss' style, or are just related to Dr. Seuss. The topics covered include Freudian Analysis of Cat in the Hat, Dr. Seuss's Inferno, Reproductive Habits of the North-Going Zax, The

Pentium Problem Explained and On the Problem of North-Going Zaxen.

KEYWORDS Children's Literature, Dr. Seuss, Humor
AUDIENCE Children, Humorists, Librarians, Parents, Students (Primary/Secondary)
CONTACT David Bedno
drseuss@gorn.iuma.com
FREE

http://klinzhai.iuma.com/~drseuss/seuss/seuss.parody.html

FAQ - Shakespeare ★★★

This is a limited FAQ within the Shakespeare Web page answering three questions about William Shakespeare, namely 'Is there a place on the Web where I can find and download the Droeshout engraving to a JPEG view format?'; 'What are the controversies people discuss today in regard to Shakespeare and his plays?'; and 'Was Shakespeare gay?' This is a limited source, and submissions of queries for analysis are welcome.

KEYWORDS History, Literature (English), Poetry, Shakespeare, William
AUDIENCE Academics, English Literature Enthusiasts, History Buffs, Literary Scholars
CONTACT dna@sypal.org
FREE

http://sashimi.wwa.com/~culturew/Shakesweb/shakesfaq.html

Goldney Books ★★★
(COMMERCIAL)

The Goldney Books home page provides users with a listing of this UK-based book dealer's inventory of rare books. The site includes listings for Goldney's large collection of first editions of fiction and literature dating back to the late 19th Century and indexed alphabetically by the author's last name. They also carry rare works of children's literature as well as wine books. Entries include basic information as well as some specific details regarding special characteristics and conditions of the work.

KEYWORDS Book Collecting, Books, Online Bookstores, Rare Books, United Kingdom
AUDIENCE Book Collectors, Book Dealers, Bookworms
CONTACT GoldneyBooks@cityscape.co.uk
FREE

http://www.gold.net/users/ea48/

Hardcover Bestsellers-Fiction ★★★★
(COMMERCIAL)

Hardcover Bestsellers-Fiction is a Website which provides links to fiction hardcover books on the Bestseller list. This list is provided with permission from Publisher's Weekly. The bestseller book list is organized by title (hyperlinked). Then under each title is the author, publisher, price and ISBN number. When you click on the title, a page with bestseller inofrmation appears which in turn also supplies you with the title, author, publisher, date, and price. From this page you can buy this book online if you choose after opening an account. The bestseller list is updated frequesntly as required.

KEYWORDS Books, Fiction, Literature
AUDIENCE Fiction Enthusiasts, Librarians, Reading Enthusiasts, Writers

Connections to Nostradamus
Find out the future today

The legendary soothsayer Nostradamus accurately prophesied about earthquakes in China and California which actually occurred hundreds of years later, or so say those who have studied his works. To peruse Nostradamus' extensive prophecies and predictions, turn to the Internet.

A site called "Nostradamus" provides a wealth of information, including much of the text of the soothsayer's predictions. Now you don't have to wait until next week, next year, or the next decade to find out what the news headlines will be. You can even chart the information so as to place yourself "in the right place at the right time" by heeding what the seer sees for the world tomorrow.

(http://www.deltanet.com/nostradamus/what_is.htm)

CONTACT Derrik Walker
dwalker@books.com
FREE

http://www.books.com/best2.htm

Hitchhiker's Guide to the Galaxy Home Page ★★★★

This page is dedicated to Douglas Adams books and fan clubs. It offers links to other sites that allow searches of his novels, as well as several fan club sites. Soundmachine files of characters from TV or movie spinoffs are also provided.

KEYWORDS Books, Fiction, Science Fiction
AUDIENCE Science Fiction Enthusiasts
CONTACT Jean-Paul Davis
JDavis@galcit.caltech.edu
FREE

http://www.galcit.caltech.edu/~jdavis/hhgttg.html

Hugo Awards ★★★★
(COMMERCIAL)

This is a hyperlinked list of book winners of the Hugo Awards given by the World Science Fiction Convention. The book winners are arranged chronologically by year. Each category provides the title and a hyperlinked author's name. When you click on the author's name, a hyperlinked list of the author's works appears which in turn supplies you with the title, author, publisher, date, price etc. From this page you can buy this book online if you choose after opening an account. Some of the books include Green Mars by Kim Stanley Robinson, The Snow Queen by Joan D. Vinge, and Fountain's Edge by Isaac Asimov.

KEYWORDS Awards, Books, Literary Criticism, Science Fiction
AUDIENCE Librarians, Reading Enthusiasts, Science Fiction Enthusiasts
CONTACT Derrik Walker
dwalker@books.com
FREE

http://www.books.com/awards/hugo.htm

Lambda Literary Award Winners ★★★★
(COMMERCIAL)

This is a hyperlinked list of book winners of the Lambda Literary Award for the best in gay and lesbian literature. The awards are arranged chronologically by year and then within each year by one lesbian and one gay man recipient in each of the following categories - fiction, non-fiction, poetry, mystery, science fiction/fantasy, anthologies, small press, humor, and children's/young adult literature. Each category is divided between lesbian and gay men's. Each category provides the title and a hyperlinked author's name. When you click on the author's name a page with a hyperlinked list of the author's works appears which in turn supplies you with

Popular Culture & Entertainment

Books

the title, author, publisher, date, price, and more. From this page you can buy this book online if you choose after opening an account.

KEYWORDS Awards, Books, Lesbian/Gay Literature, Literary Criticism
AUDIENCE Children, Educators (Primary/Secondary), Librarians, Parents
CONTACT Derrik Walker
dwalker@books.com
FREE

http://www.books.com/awards/lambwin.htm

Moon Travel Handbooks

Moon Travel publishes travel guides for North America, Asia and the Pacific Islands. Their Web site provides travel information about these regions including health advice, useful excerpts from their books, and an Asia travel booklist for recommended reading. Also included is Road Trip USA, in which North American travelers can contribute to rough drafts a comprehensive 'blue highway' guide.

KEYWORDS Books, North America, Publishing, Tourism
AUDIENCE Book Enthusiasts, Travelers
CONTACT travel@moon.com
FREE

http://www.moon.com:7000/

gopher://gopher.moon.com

Music Book Society

Music Book Society is a specialty book club offering books, compact disks, videos and other materials in the area of classical music and opera. Their home page lists current monthly offerings with descriptions of the published material as well as author, publisher, and discount price information. Users may apply for club membership via email.

KEYWORDS Classical Music, Music Books, Music Societies, Opera
AUDIENCE Classical Music Enthusiasts, Musicians, Opera Fans
CONTACT musicbk@tiac.net
FREE

http://www.tiac.net/users/musicbk/

Online Bookstore Home Page

The Online Bookstore is a large Web site where users can look for book titles, read excerpts from chapters, find out about conferences and events, and read some perspectives into digital culture. Although many of the books available here are related to the Internet or have a technological bent, a number of selections are of general interest - biographies, history, fiction are just a few examples. The layout of the site can be daunting, given the wealth of the material.

KEYWORDS Bookstores, Internet Guides, Publishing, Reference
AUDIENCE Book Readers, Fiction Enthusiasts, Writers

CONTACT obs@obs-us.com
FREE

http://marketplace.com/obs/obshome.html

Online Islamic Bookstore

The Online Islamic Bookstore home page allows users to browse through their extensive inventory of books and mixed media materials on Islamic culture. The listing includes works by Al-Ghazali, Martin Lings, and others. Users can access a number of book reviews at the site and may order online. Students receive a five percent discount on all books. Links are provided to other sites related to Islamic culture.

KEYWORDS Islamic Books, Islamic Culture, Online Bookstores
AUDIENCE Islamic Book Collectors, Islamic Culture Enthusiasts
CONTACT khan@sharaaz.com
FREE

http://www.shana.com/

Page of Apocalypse

This is a page dedicated to the X-Men comic book. This site contains links to ftp image sites, X-Men news groups, collectors lists, and related comics pages.

KEYWORDS Comics
AUDIENCE Collectors, Comics Enthusiasts
CONTACT m-blase@ux4.cso.uiuc.edu
FREE

http://ux4.cso.uiuc.edu/~m-blase/x-page.html

Paperback Bestsellers - Mass Market

Paperback Bestsellers-Mass Market is a website which provides links to 'popular' books on the Bestseller list which might appeal to the mass market or a broad audience. Some of the 1995 titles have included The Chamber by John Grisham, Tom Clancy's Op-Center, and The Robber Bride by Margaret Atwood. This list is provided with permission from Publisher's Weekly. The bestseller paperback book list is organized by title (hyperlinked). Then under each title is the author, publisher, price and ISBN number. When you click on the title, a page with bestseller information appears which in turn also supplies you with the title, author, publisher, date, and price. From this page you can buy this book online if you choose after opening an account. The bestseller list is updated as frequently as required.

KEYWORDS Books, Literature, Mass Market
AUDIENCE Fiction Enthusiasts, Librarians, Reading Enthusiasts, Writers
CONTACT Derrik Walker
dwalker@books.com
FREE

http://www.books.com/best4.htm

Philip Kindred Dick FAQ

This hypertext FAQ provides a comprehensive source of information relating to author Philip K. Dick and his work. A complete biography is presented, as well as the text of much of his work that include photographs, interviews, quotes and miscellaneous articles excerpted from various journalistic sources. There is information about movie spin-offs, references in popular music, newsletters, and a bibliography which credits those who contribute information.

KEYWORDS Fiction, Science Fiction
AUDIENCE Fantasy Enthusiasts, Fiction Enthusiasts, Science Fiction Enthusiasts
CONTACT Regulus
regulus@interport.net
FREE

http://www.interport.net/~regulus/pkd/pkd-int.html

Read USA Mail Order

This is site is an online mail order service offering general interest and computer books, audio books, and multimedia titles. Orders can be placed by filling out an online order form. All payment, shipping, and return policies are documented in detail.

KEYWORDS Advertising, Books, Internet Marketing, Multimedia
AUDIENCE Computer Users, General Public
CONTACT +1 (516) 878-6675
FREE

http://branch.com/readusa/readusa.html

Reiter's Books

Reiter's Books is an online bookstore with a wide selection of non-fiction titles. Visitors to their home page can go through their inventory either by using a full text search or by choosing from a listing of subject headings ranging from Cyberlife to Astrophysics. Users may order titles online using a personal payment password.

KEYWORDS Books, Computer Books, Online Bookstores, Text Books
AUDIENCE Book Buyers, Reading Enthusiasts
CONTACT Downtown@awa.com
FREE

http://www.awa.com/reiters/index.html

Roswell Computer Books

Visitor's to the Roswell Computer Books web site can access the entire inventory of this online bookstore specializing in computer titles. Visitors may perform a direct search by author, title, or ISBN or may browse the collection using subject headings. Entries include basic information with little or no content description. The site includes a selection of book reviews, and a listing of specials for the month. Users may order online and may open accounts with Roswell electronically.

KEYWORDS Computer Books, Online Bookstores
AUDIENCE Computer Book Readers, Nonfiction Readers

CONTACT roswell@fox.nstn.ca
FREE

http://www.nstn.ca/cybermall/roswell/roswell.html

Science Fiction Resource Guide - Awards, Biblio's and Lists, Bookstores ★★★★

This site provides a meta-index of science fiction resources. Awards include the best science fiction novel published in the UK; horror fiction; winners 1990-present; best gay and lesbian science fiction and fantasy novels; and more. There is a large collection of author bibliographies, as well as subject bibliographies including Cyberpunk, Feminist Science Fiction Page, Internet Top 100 SF/Fantasy List, SF references in music, Vampires, Nanotechnology, and more. There are also lists of bookstores worldwide as well as online.

KEYWORDS Bibliographies, Bookstores, Science Fiction
AUDIENCE Reading Enthusiasts, Science Fiction Enthusiasts
CONTACT hazel@netcom.com
FREE

http://www.lamp.ac.uk/~spc/sf/sf-resource.html

Shadowlands - A Writers Collective ★★★

Shadowlands - A Writers Collective is an experimental Internet site that allows the visitor to either observe a work of fiction being written or participate through email in the actual writing of the book.

KEYWORDS Books, Fiction, Interactive, Writing
AUDIENCE Fiction Enthusiasts, Reading Enthusiasts, Writers
CONTACT Robert Martin
romartin@heartland.bradley.edu
FREE

http://rhf.bradley.edu/~romartin/

Sheri S. Tepper Home Page ★★★

This page contains a complete bibliography of the works of feminist science fiction author Sheri S. Tepper, as well as links to other feminist science fiction-related resources on the Internet.

KEYWORDS Feminism, Science Fiction
AUDIENCE Feminists, Mystery Fiction Enthusiasts, Reading Enthusiasts, Science Fiction Enthusiasts
CONTACT Laura Doyle
U28884@uicvm.uic.edu
FREE

http://tigger.cc.uic.edu/~lauramd/tepper.html

Speculative Fiction Authors ★★★★

This page serves as a meta-index of speculative fiction authors. Along with listings of their publications, you will also find bibliographies and FAQs (Frequently Asked Questions). Writers include Douglas Adams, author of 'Hitchhiker's Guide to the Galaxy,' and Isaac Asimov. The site also contains a link to the newsgroup alt.books.isaac-asimov, a forum for discussing his novels and other works.

KEYWORDS Books, Literature (Fantasy), Meta-Index (Authors), Science Fiction
AUDIENCE Book Readers, Fiction Enthusiasts, Fiction Writers, Science Fiction Enthusiasts
CONTACT John Leavitt
jrrl@cmu.edu
FREE

http://thule.mt.cs.cmu.edu:8001/sf-clearing-house/authors/

Connections to Golf Resources
FORE!

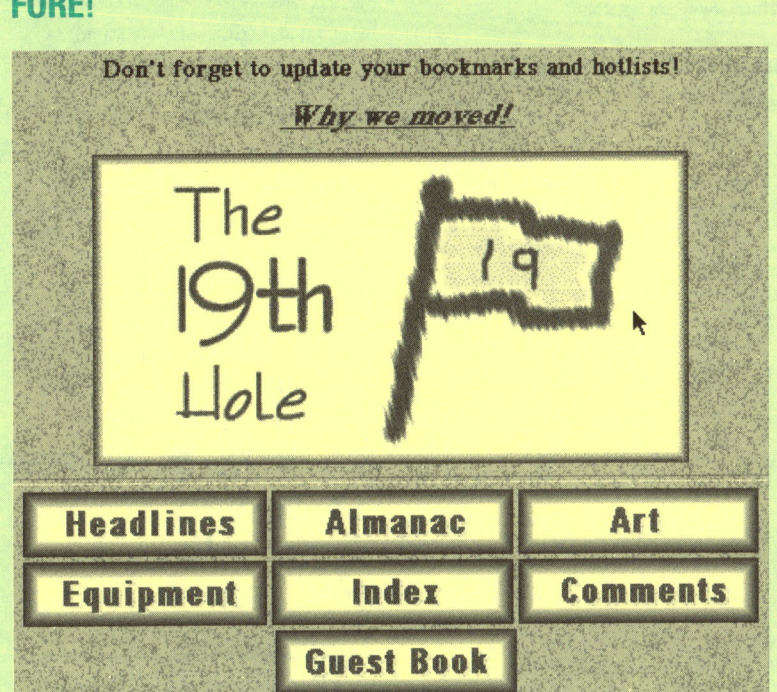

Before you take off for the golf course, check into the Internet's resources for the latest information on courses and paraphernalia, specifically designed for the golf "pro-at-heart."

If you need a golf necktie, golf socks, or want to learn about some of the more exotic fairways around the world, then "LPI: Golf Guides," "Cool Golf Places," or even "Golfer's Delight" are but a few of many sites that offer information about golfing from Alberta, Canada to Bermuda to Utah. You can also get the latest tournament info from the Ladies Professional Golfers Association, the major PGA men's tour, and others. Moreover, you'll find a wide variety of golfing publications, such as Divot, your online link for golf fiction, opinion, and commentary.

If you want to improve your swing, there are places on the Web that point you to appropriate schools. You can also order video tapes of instruction from the real golf pros or explore the latest developments in golf equipment.

(http://www.sport.net/golf/) also, (http://www.webcom.com/~dms/golf.html)

also, (http://www.sonic.net/~lanier/golfguide.html)

Stacey's Professional Bookstore ★★★

Stacey's Professional Bookstore home page acts as an online catalogue for this San Francisco-based professional bookstore. Users can access a comprehensive listing of computer, business, non-fiction, and fiction titles each with short content descriptions and prices. The site also includes a listing of Stacey's branch stores with area maps. The site includes featured publishers of the month, sample chapters, and information on author appearances and other store events.

KEYWORDS Bookstores, Fiction, Technical Books
AUDIENCE Business Readers, Technical Readers

Books – Celebrities & Personalities

CONTACT staceysbk@aol.com
FREE
http://www.staceys.com

UCI Bookstore, University of California, Irvine ★★★

This site represents the online version of the Univeristy of California at Irvine Bookstore. The bookstore offers all kinds of books, including academic, general, technical, and medical. There are music exhibits, samples from the collection of over 30,000 classical and jazz CDs, sweatshirts, t-shirts, and other emblematic items from UCI.

KEYWORDS Books, Music, University Bookstores
AUDIENCE Book Readers, General Public, Music Enthusiasts, Students (University)
CONTACT K. Cohen
jkcohen@uci.edu
FREE
http://bookweb.cwis.uci.edu:8042/HomeTest.html

UNCAT Database ★★★

UNCAT is an online catalogue of uncatalogued titles including research reports, pamphlets, brochures, catalogs, newsletters, booklets, books, videocassettes, audio cassettes, diskettes and CD-ROMs not available in a bookstore or library. The site provides listings of publications in a selection of categories including Arts, Products, Human Relationships, and Social Action among others. Each entry includes price, specification, author, and issue information as well as a brief descriptions of the publications and order information.

KEYWORDS Online Book Catalogue, Online Bookstores
AUDIENCE Book Buyers, Book Dealers, Non-Profit Organizations, Researchers
CONTACT Michael R. Prolman
UNCAT@Sapphire.com
FREE
http://www.digimark.net/UNCAT/

Unofficial Xanth Page ★★★★

The Unofficial Xanth Page page contains links to science fiction- and Piers Anthony-fan newsgroups, text files from Anthony's work, trivia about Anthony's fictional world of Xanth, images and information related to Anthony's fiction in general, and a list of other science fiction-related pages on the Web.

KEYWORDS Fiction, Science Fiction
AUDIENCE Science Fiction Enthusiasts
CONTACT Andrew Lee Wooldridge
awooldri@indiana.edu
FREE
http://www.cs.indiana.edu/hyplan/awooldri/Xanth.html

Ursula K. LeGuin ★★★

This provides a bibliographical listing of LeGuin's works and criticism about her. It contains a link to short reviews from magazines.

KEYWORDS Books, Children's Fiction, Fiction, Science Fiction
AUDIENCE Reading Enthusiasts, Science Fiction Enthusiasts
FREE
http://tigger.cc.uic.edu/~lauramd/leguin.html

Zaphod Beeblebrox Home Page! ★★★

The Zaphod Beeblebrox Home Page! contains trivia relating to Douglas Adams' work, such as artwork, fictional character references, sound files from the radio series, as well as links to related sites.

KEYWORDS Books, Fiction, Science Fiction
AUDIENCE Science Fiction Enthusiasts
CONTACT Paul Mulka
beblbrox@rhf.bradley.edu
FREE
http://rhf.bradley.edu/~beblbrox/

Celebrities & Personalities

See also
Popular Culture & Entertainment · *Magazines & Newspapers*

Alex Bennett's World ★★★★

This site was created by Bay Area radio personality Alex Bennett. It includes pictures of Bennett and his staff, as well as lists of upcoming events on his show, and local comedic and musical events. The site also reflects Bennett's radio sensibility, featuring multimedia representations of recent topics discussed on his show. And, it has Kurt Cobain's Death Certificate and autopsy photo.

KEYWORDS Alex, Bennett, Comedy, Music, Radio Disk Jockeys
AUDIENCE Alternative Music Enthusiasts, Californians, Radio Enthusiasts
CONTACT Alex Bennett
alex@hooked.net
FREE
http://www.hooked.net/alex/

Britannica's Lives ★★★

Ever wondered which famous celebrities you share your birthday with? This Web site allows users to enter their birth date and the age range of the celebrities and world leaders that they want to read about, and then receive brief biographies of each. All birthday records are also listed by year of birth and by generation. Records come from the Britannica Online database.

KEYWORDS Birthdays, World Leaders
AUDIENCE Celebrity Enthusiasts, General Public
CONTACT support@eb.com
FREE
http://www.eb.com/calendar/calendar.html

Chatter ★★★

Chatter is a regular department of the online version of People Magazine, which includes selected quotes (some funny, some interesting, some purportedly embarrassing) from celebrities. Recent profiles and 'mini-interviews' have included such stars as Helen Mirren, Sean Connery, and Barbra Streisand.

KEYWORDS Celebrities, Hollywood, People Magazine, Personalities
AUDIENCE Celebrity Enthusiasts, Film Enthusiasts, Gossips
CONTACT People Webmaster
people-webmaster@pathfinder.com
FREE
http://bigmouth.pathfinder.com:80/people/950227/chatter.html

Jim Carrey Web Page ★★★

This page contains background and appearance information relating to the popular comedian and film star Jim Carrey. Images from movies and television shows he has appeared in are also available, as are a few transcribed interviews.

KEYWORDS Comedy, Humor
AUDIENCE Comedy Enthusiasts, Comedy Fans
CONTACT Randy B. Brown
browner@halcyon.com
FREE
http://www.halcyon.com/browner/

The Master of Suspense ★★★★

'There is no terror in the bang, only in the anticipation of it' - and Alfred Hitchcock was the master of this. Ah! but shall we keep you in suspense - and not disclose the thrilling pieces of information behind these blue links. Come to these pages, if you dare. They appear to be perfectly harmless. However, once you have clicked on the 'indiscreet' blue text what you find behind may be 'a little more sinister-looking than the link itself.' Have fun and beware. Everything Hitchcock is here from his wit to a gallery of the Psycho shower scene.

KEYWORDS Movies
AUDIENCE Movie Enthusiasts, Suspense Enthusiasts
CONTACT Patricio López Guzmán
plopezg@nextdch.mty.itesm.mx
FREE
http://nextdch.mty.itesm.mx/~plopezg/Kaplan/Hitchcock.html

Family & Community

See also
Business & Economics · *Consumer Issues*
Health & Medicine · *Family Health*
Law & Criminal Justice · *Family Law*
Popular Culture & Entertainment · *Genealogy*

Academy of Family Mediators (AFM) ★★★

The Academy of Family Mediators (AFM) is a non-profit educational organization that supports professional and public mediation education. The site offers information about AFM and how to join, the resources available as a member, as well as educational and marketing products that include video and audio tapes about mediation.

KEYWORDS Conflict Resolution, Family, Mediation, Psychology
AUDIENCE Families, General Public, Mediators, Social Workers
CONTACT afmoffice@igc.apc.org
FREE

http://wideopen.igc.org/~dkern/AFM/AFMHome.html

gopher://gopher.igc.apc.org/00/orgs/afm

Adoptees Mailing List Home Page ★★

This page contains links to adoption-related resources. Some of the links include the Adoption Information Exchange, the Genealogy Home Page, the Lost in America missing person's page, and information on the alt.adoption newsgroup.

KEYWORDS Adoption, Children, Genealogy, Parenting
AUDIENCE Adoptees, Adoption Agencies Professionals, Adoptive Parents, Genealogy Enthusiasts
CONTACT Jeff Hartung
hartung@crl.ucsd.edu
FREE

http://psy.ucsd.edu/jhartung/adoptees.html

Adoption Information Exchange 1995 ★★★★

The Adoption Information Exchange includes information regarding adoption education and resources available in Washington. The list has been available since 1977, and is distributed through Adoption Information Service, a tax-exempt, non-profit volunteer organization committed to making information about adoption available to the community.

KEYWORDS Adoption, Legal Resources, Parenting, Washington State
AUDIENCE Adoptees, Adoptive Parents, Lawyers, Social Workers
FREE

http://www.halcyon.com/adoption/exchange.html

African American Women ★★

This is a gopher menu for information related to African American Women. There is a searchable gopher index. Other topics include - a Minority Education Partnership, Office of Minority and Special Student Affairs, The Places of Women—Perspectives on the Roles of Women in Religious Traditions and Structures, Young Women's and Self-Empowerment Groups, Organizations, Women of Color Discussion Group, and more.

KEYWORDS African American Studies, Educational Opportunities
AUDIENCE African Americans, Women

FREE

gopher://rodent.cis.umn.edu:11112/11/Organizations%20and%20Publications/By%20Community/African%20American%20Women

Aloha United Way Home Pages ★★★

Aloha United Way Home Pages (AUW) host information about this organization's activities throughout the state of Hawaii. AUW is a full-service organization involved in fund-raising, allocations, community problem-solving, public/private partnerships, and public information. This page lists the addresses, descriptions, and the amount of money that AUW provides for 64 different social service organizations, including the Hawaii chapters of the American Red Cross, Boys and Girls Clubs, Catholic Charities, Mental Health Association, and others.

KEYWORDS Community Networking, Directories, Hawaii, Social Work
AUDIENCE Charities, Hawaiians, Health Care Providers, Social Workers
CONTACT Hawaiian Electric Industries
webmaster@hei.com
FREE

http://www.hei.com/community/auw.html

American Childcare Solutions ★★★

The American Childcare Solutions site, provides information on childcare alternatives. It does not provide links to local childcare references but what it does provide are links and information on related law and legislation, and tips on how to find a good childcare provider. There is also information on national agencies, nannies, aupairs resources, educational and training resources, toy and product suppliers, and access to children's pages on the Net. You can find software advice, health links, child gifted and talented resources, parent and child magazines, related government agencies, publications and more.

KEYWORDS Child Care, Legal Resources, Parenting, Primary/Secondary Education
AUDIENCE Childcare Providers, Education Administrators, Educators (Primary/Secondary), Parents
CONTACT Bruce and Eileen Scherzinger
zinger@fsd.com
FREE

http://turnpike.net/metro/egscherz/index.html

Area Wide Association for Responsible Education (AWARE) ★

The Area Wide Association for Responsible Education Organization (AWARE), strives to aid young minds to develop sound basic education needs. The organization endeavors to provide social and emotional support by reinforcing the idea of self-esteem and positive self-imaging. AWARE provides free services for students in the East Bay area of California. This Web page contains the group's mission statement, outlines of its program,

and contact information for schools, students, parents, and volunteers.

KEYWORDS Educational Programs, Self-Esteem, Volunteers
AUDIENCE Californians, Educators, Parents
CONTACT Leonard Aldridge
sysop@irie.com
FREE

http://www.dnai.com/~kenseq/aware.html

CYFERNet ES/NAL/ACE USDA Gopher ★★★

This gopher gives access to several information services of the United States Government. These services include the Children Youth Family Education Research Network (CYFERNet) and the Extension Service Gopher Server. The information relates to health and family issues. This server is maintained by the United States Department of Agriculture.

KEYWORDS Family, Health
AUDIENCE Adults, Children, Educators, Families
CONTACT admin@cyfer.esusda.gov
FREE

gopher://cyfer.esusda.gov/

CYFERNet ★★★★

This is a CYFERNet, the Children Youth and Family Network in the state of Minnesota. It contains information on child care, family resiliency, science and technology literacy, youth at risk community-based projects, journals, newsletters, and many more. It has links to other CYF servers.

KEYWORDS Child Care, Community Services, Computer Networking, Family
AUDIENCE Child Care Providers, Children's Rights Activists, Educators, Family Planners
CONTACT Trudy Dunham
tdunham@mes.umn.edu
FREE

gopher://tinman.mes.umn.edu:4242/

Child Quest International, Inc. ★★★★

This site provides pages of photographs of missing children and related information. Child Quest International is a nonprofit corporation devoted to the recovery and protection of missing, abused and exploited children. Child Quest differs from other nonprofit organizations in that it utilizes many new and exciting technologies, including computer photo digitizing pictures of missing children, computerized age enhancement to current age, as well as on-site scanning, poster-making, and distribution of the child and abductor(s). It offers its services free of charge, made possible through donations and fundraising.

KEYWORDS Abused Children, Missing Children
AUDIENCE Child Care Providers, Children's Rights Activists, Law Enforcement Professionals
CONTACT Dean Nelson
musicman@bitchen.Eng.Sun.COM
FREE

http://www.omega.com/adima/bands/child_quest/cqmain.html

518   Family & Community

Childcare National Network Gopher   ★★★

This is the Childcare National Network Gopher which contains the menu for the National Network for Child Care. This Childcare Network works with University Extension systems nationally through human and technological dissemination to increase and strengthen quality child care environments by providing research and resources. Some of the linked topics include Business Management, Child Development, Community Development, Curriculum and Daily Planning, Health and Safety, Parent Involvement and Education, and more.

- **KEYWORDS**   Child Care, Community Development, Education
- **AUDIENCE**   Child Care Providers, Educators (University), Parents, Students (University)
- **CONTACT**   Ina Lynn McClain/Karen B. DeBord NNCCINFO@mes.umn.edu
- **FREE**

gopher://tinman.mes.umn.edu:4242/11/ChildCare/

Children's Page Stories, Poems, Pictures and Sounds   ★★★★

This page contains many links to information for children such as games, LEGO, Winnie the Pooh, children's programs and Interactive Gallery from the California Museum of Photography, pictures from Disney, chocolate page, Santa Claus, Theodore Tugboat activity center, and more.

- **KEYWORDS**   Children, Children's Programs, Dinosaurs, Interactive Games
- **AUDIENCE**   Child Care Providers, Children, Educators (Primary/Secondary), Parents, Students (Primary/Secondary)
- **FREE**

http://www.comlab.ox.ac.uk/oucl/users/jonathan.bowen/children.html

Children's Pages at WombatNet   ★★★★

The Children's Pages at WombatNet contains links to sites for children. Subjects include animals, dinosaurs, high schools, hobbies, libraries, magazines, museums, news, space, toys, travel, and more.

- **KEYWORDS**   Dinosaurs, Kids, Space, Toys
- **AUDIENCE**   Children, Educators (Primary/Secondary), Parents, Students (Primary/Secondary), Teenagers
- **FREE**

http://www.batnet.com/wombat/children.html

Community Board Program (CBP)   ★★★

The CBP is a national nonprofit conflict resolution organization established in 1976 in San Francisco. CBP provides free dispute resolution to all residents. The goals of CBP are to build safe neighborhoods and schools and to create stronger relationships in families and the community. The gopher site on the IGC computers lists information regarding school peer mediation programs, available training, and dispute resolution resources. However, much of the site is currently (2/5/95) under construction.

- **KEYWORDS**   Community, Conflict Resolution, Mediation
- **AUDIENCE**   Californians, General Public, Mediators
- **CONTACT**   cmbrds@igc.apc.org
- **FREE**

gopher://gopher.igc.apc.org/11/orgs/cb

Concerned Singles   ★★★

Concerned Singles is an introduction service that uses the IGC computers to make available information about their service. The goal of Concerned Singles is to bring together people from around the world who share humanistic concerns. The gopher page contains information about membership ($55) and privileges of membership.

- **KEYWORDS**   Human Rights, Peace, Racial Equality, Singles
- **AUDIENCE**   Humanists, Single People
- **CONTACT**   concernsingl@igc.apc.org
- **FREE**

gopher://gopher.igc.apc.org/0ftp%3Aftp.igc.apc.org@/pub/orgs_on_igc/concernsingl

ftp://ftp.igc.apc.org/pub/orgs_on_igc/concernsingl

CyberKids   ★★★★

CyberKids is a free online magazine for kids by kids (with a little help from their friends at Mountain Lake Software and Woodwind Consulting). It contains stories, artwork, puzzles, and more. They expect to publish four issues in 1995.

- **KEYWORDS**   Parenting, Primary/Secondary Education, Stories
- **AUDIENCE**   Childcare Providers, Educators (Primary/Secondary), Parents, Students (Primary/Secondary)
- **CONTACT**   cyberkids@mtlake.com
- **FREE**

http://www.woodwind.com/mtlake/CyberKids/CyberKids.html

Domestic Violence Resources   ★★★★

This site contains links to other Internet sites dealing with domestic violence issues. The resources include statistics, the Domestic Violence Handbook, bibliographies, shelter numbers for battered women and their children, and links to other women's issues resources on the web.

- **KEYWORDS**   Crime, Domestic Violence
- **AUDIENCE**   Battered Women, Domestic Mediators, Husbands, Psychologists, Therapists, Wives
- **CONTACT**   asherman@interport.net
- **FREE**

http://www.interport.net/~asherman/dv.html

Environmental Recycling Hotline   ★★★

The Environmental Recycling Hotline provides a searchable database organized by zip code for five states - Arizona, Nevada, Hawaii, Texas, and Colorado. You enter the zip code on the online form and then click on the button 'Please tell me about recycling in my areas.' More states will be added. The search is available in English or Spanish.

- **KEYWORDS**   Community Services, Recycling, Recycling Locations
- **AUDIENCE**   Business Professionals, General Public, Recycling Enthusiasts, United States Residents
- **CONTACT**   Jim Lippard lippard@primenet.com
- **FREE**

http://www.primenet.com/erh.html

FatherNet   ★★★★

FatherNet is an electronic forum for the discussion of the role of men as parents. It is based on a national conference on the matter, called 'Family Re-Union III, The Role of Men in Children's Lives, held July 11, 1994 in Nashville, Tennessee. This server contains information on conference proceedings, research on men and children, an electronic bulletin board and online chat service, information about the Fathers' Resource Center, and newsletters.

- **KEYWORDS**   Children, Education (College/University), Fathers, Men
- **AUDIENCE**   Child Care Providers, Child Development Professionals, Educators, Men
- **CONTACT**   Jan cyfstaff@maroon.tc.umn.edu
- **FREE**

gopher://tinman.mes.umn.edu:80/

The Human Factor   ★★★★

The Human Factor is a gopher menu for many sites relating to nonprofit organizations, including links to enviromental organizations, foundation centers, FAQs (Frequently Asked Questions) About nonprofits, and the Guide To Internet Resources for Non-Profit.

- **KEYWORDS**   Corporate Giving, Grants
- **AUDIENCE**   Business Professionals, Grantmakers, Grantseekers, Nonprofit Organizations, Volunteers
- **FREE**

gopher://human.com/11/inc/sites

ISN (International Student Wire) KidNews   ★★★

ISN KidNews is a news service for students and teachers around the world. Anyone may use stories from the service, and anyone may submit stories. It covers topics such as report card jitters, dances, drinking and smoking problems, people profiles such as favorite teachers or friends, how-to stories from hockey to making bracelets, reviews of books, movies, restaurants, sports stories of local 'heroes,' poetry and fiction written by students, and discussion sections for students and teachers.

- **KEYWORDS**   News, Primary/Secondary Education, Student Life

Family & Community   519

AUDIENCE Educators (Primary/Secondary), Parents, Students (Primary/Secondary)
CONTACT Dr. Peter Owens
IN%"kidnews@umassd.edu
FREE

http://www.umassd.edu/SpecialPrograms/ISN/KidNews.html

Inter-Tribal Network, CNS, Inc.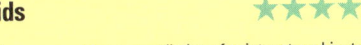

This gopher contains online resources for Native Americans. Users will find information on government policy, individual tribes and reservation lands, Native American medicine, and more. There are also links to other related gophers on the Internet.

KEYWORDS Internet Resources, Native American Culture, Native Americans
AUDIENCE Educators, Native Americans, Students, United States Residents
FREE

gopher://earth.usa.net:70/11/News%20and%20Information/itn

Interesting Places for Kids ★★★★

This page provides a compilation of pointers to subjects that might be interesting to kids who have access to the Internet. Some of the topics covered are—art and literature, museums and other exhibits, toys and games, movies and TV shows, and Web pages set up by (or for) kids.

KEYWORDS Children's Literature, Children's Activities, Movies, Museums
AUDIENCE Children, Educators (Primary/Secondary), Internet Users, Parents, Students (Primary/Secondary)
CONTACT Stephen Savitzky
steve@crc.ricoh.com
FREE

http://www.crc.ricoh.com/people/steve/kids.html

KidPub ★★★★

KidPub is a place for children to publish stories on the World Wide Web and to read stories published by others. The site also provides instructions on how to publish your story and statistics about KidPub access (updated hourly).

KEYWORDS Internet Publishing, Parenting, Primary/Secondary Education
AUDIENCE Children, Educators (Primary/Secondary), Parents, Students (Primary/Secondary)
FREE

http://www.en-garde.com/kidpub/

Kids Internet Delight (KID)

Gathered here are pointers to sites that children might enjoy. Some of the links include Catch a Cold Virus on the Web!, The Children Page, Educational Mail Archives, Exploratorium, Games Domain, KidLink, Plugged In, RoboColt, Youth Consumers Database, and more.

KEYWORDS Children, Education, Games, Parenting
AUDIENCE Childcare Providers, Children, Parents, Schools, Students (Primary/Secondary)
CONTACT John S. Makulowich
makulow@trainer.com
FREE

http://www.clark.net/pub/journalism/kid.html

Lion King Coloring Book ★★★★

Welcome to the Lion King coloring book. You can download the JPEG pictures of line art from The Lion King or you can print them. The images include the Hyenas, Scar, Mufasa and Simba, Rafiki, Simba and Nala, Simba, Timon, and Pumbaa, Zazu, and a movie poster. This page is a true delight for the children in your life.

KEYWORDS Children, Disney, Movies
AUDIENCE Child Care Providers, Children, Parents
FREE

http://www.wdp.com/cgi-bin/htimage/BVPM/LionKing/images/LionKing.ma p?327,225

Connections to Au Pairs and Child Care Providers
Calling Mary Poppins

What Is EurAupair?

EurAupair is an organization with its roots in Europe. EurAupair works closely with ASSE International Student Exchange Programs (formerly American Scandinavian Student Exchange), the program sponsor and a United States Information Agency (USIA) designated exchange visitor program founded by Sweden's national Ministry of Education. The American based ASSE is the largest, oldest and most prominent international student exchange organization in Europe. Consequently, EurAupair's expertise and extensive resources primarily concentrate on European au pairs. EurAupair is a U.S. **not-for-profit**, public benefit organization founded to improve understanding among people of different countries through cultural exchange. Together, EurAupair and ASSE's worldwide organization sponsors more than 60,000 young exchange participants annually and well over half a million in the past 57 years.

For many people, the quintessential au pair was the lovable Mary Poppins from the Hollywood movie by Walt Disney. If you're looking for an au pair, you can begin your search by exploring the possibilities on the "EurAupair" site—a place where you can find responsible young adults from Europe who provide child care in exchange for inclusion in a family's life and exposure to a new culture. Au pairs do more than babysit. They are trained in infant care and in entertaining and instructing preschoolers through reading, singing, and game playing. Some may even shop for groceries and prepare meals when things get hectic. This intercultural child-care program works closely with the International Student Exchange Programs to enable students to spend a year with a family abroad. You'll also find au pair address exchanges and other information at this site.

(http://turnpike.net/metro/egscherz/aupair.html)

There is also assistance awaiting at the "American Childcare Solutions" site which provides suggestions on what to look for in a childcare provider, as well as links to games and books for kids at the "Children's Page" site. The site includes pictures, sounds, and fun games for children.

(http://www.comlab.ox.ac.uk/oucl/users/jonathan.bowen/children.html)

National Civic League ★★★

The National Civic League (NCL) is an advocacy organization promoting the principles of collaborative problem-solving in local community building. NCL accomplishes this mission through technical assistance, training, publishing, research, and an awards program. This page lists a summary of the organization's programs and projects, as well as examples of successful community actions such as setting up shopping areas, reducing drug dealing, and improving health care.

KEYWORDS Activism, Community Networking, Community Services, Research
AUDIENCE Activists, Community Groups, Community Leaders, Grass-Roots Organizers, Politicians
FREE

http://www.csn.net:80/ncl/

National Parent Information Network ★★★★

The National Parent Information Network (NPIN) site is sponsored by two ERIC (Educational Resources Information Center) clearinghouses - the ERIC Clearinghouse on Urban Education and the ERIC Clearinghouse on Elementary and Early Childhood Education. Its purpose is to provide information to parents and resources to people and organizations who work with parents. This site provides links to the following topics of information- Parent News (Updated Weekly), Short Items Especially for Parents, Parents AskERIC (an email question and answer service), Ideas for Community Programs and Activities, The Market Place, Resources for Parent Educators, ERIC Digests, and ERIC Bibliographies.

KEYWORDS Child Care, Educational Resources, Parenting, Primary/Secondary Education
AUDIENCE Childcare Providers, Educators, Educators (Primary/Secondary), Parents, Researchers
CONTACT Dianne Rothenberg rothenbe@uiuc.edu
FREE

http://www.prairienet.org/htmls/eric/npin/npinhome.html

Nationwide Nannies! ★★★

Nationwide Nannies Inc. is an innovative service that provides you with resumes of candidates seeking live-in positions as nannies, housekeepers and elderly care givers. The concept is that you can search for help from a national labor pool. Candidates should be willing to relocate. Select the candidates best suited to your family's needs and contact them directly. The cost is only $149.00 for a full month of service. There is no charge to search the database. Links are provided to topics inlcluding Searching the Nationwide Nannies Database, After You Have Found Candidates, Before Hiring Your Nanny, After Hiring Your Nanny, and more.

KEYWORDS Child Care, Parenting
AUDIENCE Au Pairs, Childcare Providers, Parents
CONTACT nannies-info@paradise.net
FREE

http://www.nannies.com/

Philadelphia Unemployment Project ★★

This is the home page from The Philadelphia Unemployment Project (PUP), an organization dedicated to educating and organizing area unemployed and low-wage people around services,and dealing with issues and policies affecting their lives. PUP provides legal and consultative services.

KEYWORDS Community, Non Profit Organizations, Unemployment
AUDIENCE Job Seekers, Pennsylvania Residents
CONTACT brownt@libertynet.org
FREE

http://libertynet.org/community/hs/pup.html

Phoenix Police Department Community Relations Page ★★★

This page presents information about and by the Phoenix Police Department in Arizona, U.S.A. Users will find items like Phoenix's Silent Witness program, which features pictures and descriptions of suspects; information on several community programs that deal with gangs, drugs, graffiti, and other social ills; and a page devoted to 'Blue By You,' the fastest police car in Arizona. General information about the history of the police department and its museum is also given.

KEYWORDS Arizona, Community Services, Museums, Police
AUDIENCE Arizona Residents, Community Leaders, Law Enforcement Professionals
CONTACT Getnet International gia@getnet.com
FREE

http://www.getnet.com/silent/phx_police.html

Plumbing Controls ★★★

This site contains an overview of intelligent plumbing controls and related devices as well as an international list of plumbing controls resources and standards proposals. The site also contains information about other home control resources including the Home Systems Network, a concept based on the communication between devices that control home utilities through a centralized intelligence system of controls. Although the page describes various devices, only the educational materials are available for purchase through the site.

KEYWORDS Distributed Intelligence Systems, Home Automation, Home Repair, Plumbing
AUDIENCE Home Owners, Plumbers
CONTACT creator@hometeam.com
FREE

http://www.ionet.net/hsn/plumbing.shtml

Rainbow Family of Living Light Home Page ★★★★

Although this is not an official Rainbow Family-endorsed page, the Rainbow Family of Living Light home page has a wide range of information about the history, current activities and future plans of the Rainbow Family, a loosely knit tribe of 'hippies' and their annual Rainbow Gatherings. Included here are Rainbow-related events, such as information on this year's gathering, and a calendar of global and local events. Historical information on this site include excerpts from media sources as well as explanations of the movement. Images from previous gatherings and forest fires in Wyoming are here, as are archives from other Rainbow sources (newsgroups, FTP archives, and other individuals).

KEYWORDS Environmental Awareness, Peace
AUDIENCE Deadheads, Environmentalists, Peace Activists, Rainbow Family Members, Sociologists
FREE

http://darkstar.cygnus.com/rainbow.html

Recycling Factoids ★★★

Recycling Factoids provides links to information on recycling. The topics include definitions, material factoids, recycling at home, landfills, energy reduction, rain forests, junk mail, publications, organizations, and quotes from kids.

KEYWORDS Community Services, Energy Conservation, Recycling
AUDIENCE Families, Recycling Proponents, Virginia Residents
CONTACT Shay Mitchell jsm8f@ecosys.drdr.virginia.edu
FREE

http://ecosys.drdr.virginia.edu/factoids.html

Soc.Couples.Wedding WWW page ★★★

This Web site contains archives from the wedding newsgroup Soc.couples.wedding, which discusses how to throw weddings. Users will find collected information from the newgroup and FAQs grouped by topic, such as wedding rings, etiquette, wedding photography, music, ceremonies, invitations, attire, and registries. Information includes everything from listings of bridal apparel stores to a guide for choosing diamonds. Links to commercial Web sites that are related to weddings, marriage, or honeymoons are also included, as well as personal reviews of wedding services, including restaurants and DJs, grouped by region. Users may also put up home pages for their own wedding here.

KEYWORDS Holidays, Marriage, Weddings
AUDIENCE Brides, Couples
CONTACT Sonja Kueppers sek@wam.umd.edu
FREE

http://www.wam.umd.edu/~sek/wedding.html

Storytelling Resources on the Web ★★★★

Sherri Johnson has turned her love for storytelling into a useful resource. Here she has gathered together everything she could find on the Net relating to storytelling, both in terms of folklore and as a performance art aimed at children. Easy hypertext links enable the viewer to find everything from the original Aesop's Fables online at the Gutenberg Projec, to stories written and told by children themselves, to profiles of professional storytellers. This site in itself contains very little information, but has many well-organized links to the world of storytelling throughout the Web.

KEYWORDS Children's Activities, Folklore, Performance Art, Storytelling
AUDIENCE Children, Folklorists, Storytellers
CONTACT Sherri Johnson sjohnson@cc.swarthmore.edu
FREE

http://www.swarthmore.edu:80/~sjohnson/stories/

Sweeps Vacuum & Repair Center Inc. ★★★

This location provides information such as price, quality, description, and an order form for the MIELE vacuum cleaner, claimed to be best for asthma and allergy sufferers.

KEYWORDS Allergies, Asthma, Home, Household Products, Product Information
AUDIENCE Consumers, General Public, Health Care Consumers

CONTACT Jon Zeeff
         branch-info@branch.com
FREE

http://branch.com/sweeps/sweeps.html

Teel Family Home Page ★★★

This site provides something for the entire family. The Alaska page has pictures, a book list, and links to other Alaskan sites. The Homeschool page has software reviews, wintertime curriculum, and the newest addition—a place to learn about polar bears and walruses. Don't miss printing out your own 'Binky' (Alaska's most famous polar bear) puppet. Matthew's page has the downloadable wallpaper of the week, pictures and more to come. The kid's page is about snow and includes how to make your own 'best ever' snowflake and edible glacier.

KEYWORDS Alaska, Children, Family, Tourism
AUDIENCE Alaska Residents, Children, Educators (Primary/Secondary), Parents, Students (Primary/Secondary)
FREE

http://www.alaska.net:80/~mteel/

Uncle Bob's Kid's Page ★★★★

This page is a treasure chest of links (over 1200) for children which have been cleaned, checked, and annotated, with spotlights on special subjects. Topics include Spider's Pick of the Day, editing a picture online, space telescopes, Sega news, VolcanoWorld and Sea World, the Apollo 11, the moon mission, Barbie, dinosaurs in Hawaii, stereograms, Star Trek, Theodore Tugboat Children's Activity Center, and much more. This is a site for the whole family.

KEYWORDS Children's Activities, Educational Resources, Kids, Pre-Teens
AUDIENCE Children, Educators (Primary/Secondary), Internet Users, Parents, Students (Primary/Secondary)
FREE

http://gagme.wwa.com/~boba/kids.html

Webster's Page, Internet—A Parents Guide ★★★

This site is an online directory geared towards children and parents. It contains information which can also be found in Webster's forthcoming book 'Internet—A Parents Guide.' Some of the topics include art, language arts, social studies, sports and hobbies, etc.

KEYWORDS Children's Online Directory, Family Life, Online Directories, Sports
AUDIENCE Children, Educators (Primary/Secondary), Parents, Students (Primary/Secondary)
CONTACT   rbpress@halcyon.com
FREE

http://www.halcyon.com/ResPress/kids.html

Youth Networks-Movements ★★

This site provides a list of links to information on youth issues. Links are provided to Progressive Student 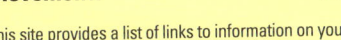 Network, Queer Youth Organizations, Student Environmental Action Coalition (SEACNET), National Association of Graduate/Professional Students, Alliance for Student Aid, and more.

KEYWORDS Environment, Youth
AUDIENCE Community Activists, Nonprofit Organizations, Political Activists, Progressives
CONTACT   edinlinks@garnet.berkeley.edu
FREE

http://garnet.berkeley.edu:3333/EDINlist/.educ/.youth/.youth.html

---

Connections to Wedding Planning

Get me to the church on time . . .

EVENT PLANNING INFO

- Balloon Aviation
- Catering
- Wedding and Event Planners
- Floral Design
- Formal Wear
- Hair & Makeup Design
- Limousines & Transportation
- Locations
- Ministers
- Musicians/Entertainers
- Party Rentals
- Photography
- Theatrical Lighting
- Valet Services
- Video
- Wedding Cakes and Bakeries

Are you planning a wedding? Conquer this logistical challenge using the World Wide Web.

There are software programs that help you with organizing invitations, gifts, RSVPs, thank you notes, and the expenses related to tying the knot on special dates.

If you need a catering service, floral design, formal wear, hair and make-up design, limousines, ministers, musicians, party rentals, or photography sources, you can tap into any of several online resources, including "Bridesmaid for Windows" and "Event Planning & Special Occasions." Do you dream of getting married in a hot air balloon? There are places on the Web that will help you find the ballooning companies to make that dream come true.

(http://www.freerun.com/napavalley/spocs/spocs.html)

also, (http://www.upside.com/infolane/simple/bride.html)

also, (http://sensemedia.net/sprawl/13313)

If you need to cut costs or prefer a small wedding, check out resources like "Make a Wedding" that can help you "decorate" your wedding on $100. This site includes tips on making floral designs out of butcher paper.

(http://www.sisna.com/DILL/HOME.htm)

Fashion

See also
Business & Economics · *Industries*
Business & Economics · *Retail*
Popular Culture & Entertainment · *Shopping*

Fashion Bibliography ★★

This is a bibliography of fashion books, articles, and fashion-related items.

KEYWORDS Fashion, Publishing
AUDIENCE Agents, Fashion Designers, Models, Women, Youth

Family & Community – Genealogy

CONTACT ms@genesis.nred.ma.us
FREE

http://www.charm.net/~jakec/Biblio.html

Fashion Magazines

This document provides a list of fashion magazines including the title, publisher, subscription information, contact information, and more.

KEYWORDS Fashion, Publishing
AUDIENCE Agents, Fashion Designers, Models, Women, Youth
CONTACT ms@genesis.nred.ma.us
FREE

http://www.charm.net/~jakec/Magazines.html

Home of Codpiece International

The Home of Codpiece International is a Web site totally devoted to the 'resurrection of the codpiece.' Here you will find answered all the questions you have ever posed regarding this 'brassiere for men' and 'carrying case for coins and the family jewels.' You can join the 'Bring Back the Codpiece Campaign' at this site, learn the noble history of the no-longer-forgotten codpiece and even purchase a t-shirt stating your adherence to one of the party lines, 'Indulge Your Bulge,' 'A New Dimension in Men's Clothing,' and others. Soon to come—a modern codpiece!

KEYWORDS Clothing, Design, Fashion
AUDIENCE Codpiece Enthusiasts, Fashion Designers, Historians, Men
CONTACT Jennifer Strait and Richard Appleyard codpiece@teleport.com
FREE

http://www.teleport.com/~codpiece

La Collection - Designer Accessories

La Collection is a women's fashion accessories showroom in New York City, which represents designers (24 at this writing), of jewelry, hats, belts, bags, scarves, gloves, and home accessories. Currently, the only other information here is the company's email address, other contact information, and a link to the TAG Online Mall. The content of this page will be geared towards retail stores that are on the Internet.

KEYWORDS Fashion, Fashion Designers, New York
AUDIENCE Fashion Enthusiasts, Fashion Industry Professionals, New York Residents
CONTACT TAG Online Mall webmaster@tagsys.com
FREE

http://www.tagsys.com:80/Ads/LaCollection/

Nicole Miller Online

Nicole Miller is a fashion designer known for her 'designer clothes at fun prices.' In addition to the growing number of boutiques, Nicole Miller's designs are sold at major department stores throughout North America. Her designs include ties, vests, scarves, shoes, handbags, socks, stationery, and men's and women's swimwear. This Web site contains background information about Nicole Miller and her career.

KEYWORDS Designer Apparel, Fashion, Fashion Designers, Online Shopping
AUDIENCE Fashion Industry Professionals, New York Residents, Popular Culture Enthusiasts
FREE

http://www.interactive.line.com/nicole/.cover_nicole.html

Sposabella Bridal- La Sposa Veil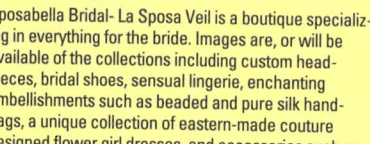

Sposabella Bridal- La Sposa Veil is a boutique specializing in everything for the bride. Images are, or will be available of the collections including custom headpieces, bridal shoes, sensual lingerie, enchanting embellishments such as beaded and pure silk handbags, a unique collection of eastern-made couture designed flower girl dresses, and accessories such as bridal books, quills, garters and undergarments.

KEYWORDS Boutiques, Bridal Apparel, Clothing, Weddings
AUDIENCE Brides-to-Be, Fashion Designers, Wedding Planners
FREE

http://www.hydra.com/sposa/sposa.html

Write With Light Shirts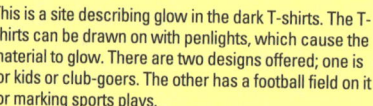

This is a site describing glow in the dark T-shirts. The T-shirts can be drawn on with penlights, which cause the material to glow. There are two designs offered; one is for kids or club-goers. The other has a football field on it for marking sports plays.

KEYWORDS Children, Fashion, Product Information, Sports
AUDIENCE Children, Cyberculture Enthusiasts, Football Fans
FREE

http://adware.com/mall/neovideo/welcome.html

X-Large Clothing

This site provides catalogs, store information and order forms for X-Large and X-Girl casual clothing. Besides information about their clothing, they have a several short films and sound files and an ongoing guide to 'video game lifestyles.'

KEYWORDS Clothing, Online Shopping, People Of Size, Retail
AUDIENCE Fashion Enthusiasts, Large People, Online Shoppers, Women
FREE

http://www.cinenet.net:80/XLarge

Genealogy

See also
Popular Culture & Entertainment · *Family & Community*
Science · *Biosciences*

Everton Publishers Genealogy Page

The Genealogy page, produced by the Everton genealogy publishers, serves as a collection of information about genealogy for those interested in discovering their family histories. Users will find a guide to getting started with your genealogy, and online archives of the electronic version of the magazine Everton's Genealogical Helper, which includes an interview with the staff of the Family History Library's Automated Resource Center and an article on Virtual Libraries. Information about genealogical archives and libraries is included, with pointers to ones on the Internet. Other highlights include genealogical software information and reviews, lists of US, international, and group resources.

KEYWORDS Birth Records, Family, Heritage
AUDIENCE Families, Genealogists, General Public, Historians, Researchers
CONTACT jayhall@xmission.com
FREE

http://www.xmission.com/~jayhall/

Genealogy Home Page

This page contains links to a great wealth of genealogy information with guides to genealogy research and information about research in such key areas as— Starting Genealogy, Communicating with Other Genealogists, Maps, Libraries with Genealogy Collections, Genealogy Software, Online Genealogy Information, etc. Information can also be found about commercial genealogical services.

KEYWORDS Birth Records, Family History, Genealogy, Heritage
AUDIENCE Adoptees, Genealogists, General Public, Historians, Researchers
CONTACT saw@ftp.cac.psu.edu
FREE

http://ftp.cac.psu.edu/~saw/genealogy.html

Genealogy Toolbox

The Genealogy Toolbox contains comprensive lists of genealogy resources on the World Wide Web. Users will find over 600 links to Web sites containing information in the form of genealogy guides, family data and histories, different types of resources, groups and associations, and genealogy software. A surname index is also included, in which users can hunt through Internet databases, family histories, and pedigree charts to find a name. Users will also find information about heraldry, historical Web sites, and links to commercial resources.

KEYWORDS Birth Records, Family, Heritage
AUDIENCE Families, Genealogists, General Public, Historians, Researchers
CONTACT helm@alexia.lis.uiuc.edu
FREE

http://ux1.cso.uiuc.edu/~al-helm/genealogy.html

Genealogy – General Reference

Global Heritage Center

 ★★★

This is a site for the Global Heritage Center, a company which produces software and storage systems for genealogical research and other data intensive uses. This site describes its genealogical software and CD-ROM systems.

Keywords Data Storage, Family History, Genealogy
Audience Families, Genealogists
Contact sjledet@netcom.com
Free

http://www.mindspring.com/~sledet/genealogy/ghc.html

General Reference

See also
Business & Economics · *Reference*
Government & Politics · *Reference*
Internet · *Internet Resources*

Apollo 11 Mission to the Moon

★★★

This NASA site allows you to travel back 25 years through time to view images and hear sounds from the first United States mission to the moon. You can read the astronauts' memories and important White House papers, enjoy the collection of mission patches or travel to the many installations around the world that make up the National Aeronautics and Space Administration (NASA).

Keywords Aeronautics, NASA (National Aeronautics And Space Administration), Space Science
Audience Educators (Primary/Secondary), History Buffs, Space Enthusiasts, Students (Primary/Secondary)
Contact comments@www.nasa.gov
Free

http://www.gsfc.nasa.gov/hqpao/apollo_11.html

Award Winners- Book, Movie, and Music Award Lists

★★★★

This site is an extensive gopher menu of award winners for books, movies, and music. The many hyperlinked topics include Nominees for the 1995 Pen Literary Awards Best Picture (movies), Caldecott (children's), Coretta Scott King (children's), Hugo (science fiction), Los Angeles Times, National Book Awards, Nebula (science fiction), Newbery (children's), Gay/Lesbian Book Awards, Pulitzer Prizes, and more.

Keywords Books, Movies, Music
Audience Fiction Enthusiasts, Librarians, Parents, Reading Enthusiasts
Free

http://gopher.metronet.com:70/1/borders/awards

Connections to Fashion
Eeeeeuuuoooo . . . call the fashion police!

Fabulous, Yet Friendly, Fashion Tips

Once upon a time, the only discussions of fashion on the Internet would have led you to believe all users dressed like this. And it probably was true. Now that commercial sites are springing up like dandelions in an empty lot, anyone with a PPP connection can be a fashion victim.

Sorry, No Copyright Violations Here!

If you came looking for the supermodel .gifs attributed to this site on page 43 of the latest magazine to hop on the Internet bandwagon, *the net*, you're out of luck. I wouldn't have supermodel .gifs because
- Scantily clad women aren't my thing,
- I do copyright permissions work and know what the deal is, and
- I come to bury supermodels, not to praise them.

Another victory for journalistic excellence!

Not sure what to wear today? Perhaps you want a new look. Through Fabulous, Yet Friendly Tips you can get fashion tips, or investigate fashion throughout the world. You can order some new duds for an upcoming party.

Also access "What do you expect for free, Vogue?", or learn how to make Clear Plastic Fashions (like a plastic raincoat) via

(http://www.sils.umich.edu/~sooty/fashion.html)

If you want to look at some ancient fashion plates, or get historical information about fashion around the world, there are a number of Internet sites that provide it. At MODA, the spotlight is on Filipino fashion. You can see how people of that island nation mix fuschia and apple green, blue jeans and finely embroidered barong. There is information on Filipino personalities who made it in the world of fashion, such as designers Rey Valera, Pitoy Moreno, and Auggie Cordero.

(http://pubweb.acns.nwu.edu/~flip/fashion.html)

If you want to order clothes, there are even places on the Internet where you can get in touch with company catalogs for both men and women, such as "Above and Beyond," and "The Tall & All Mall".

(http://www.abmall.com/ca.above.html)

You'll also find the "International Male" catalog for ordering clothes and accessories.

(http://www.intmale.com/intmale/intmale.htm)

Other sites include NetBoutique, Sheplers, Spiegel, and even Wal-Mart.

DeLorme Mapping

 ★★★

DeLorme Mapping specializes in mapping software and databases and publishes printed atlases for individual states. DeLorme's Atlas & Gazetteer series offers recreational mapping that covers each state's topography and major highways, jeep trails, boat ramps, lakes, streams, campgrounds, mountains, forests and waterfalls. The page has information on their maps, ordering information and online maps.

Keywords Maps, States, Tourism, Travel
Audience Business Professionals, Educators, Tourists, Travelers
Free

http://www.delorme.com/

Eastgates Favorites

★★★

This is a page of Eastgate Systems' favorite Web sites. These sites include QuarkWeb, The E-Ville Dialogues, Artists For a Better Image, stock price charts, robots, disc golf, and links to other sites.

Keywords Art, Online Directories, Stocks
Audience Artists, Golfers, Internet Users, Investors
Free

http://www.shore.net/~eastgate/Others.html

Flick's Home Page

★★

Flick's home page provides access to miscellaneous links, such as Ham Radio, The Event Horizon, Employment Opportunities Browser, etc.

Keywords Employment, Radio, Scientific Research

524 General Reference

AUDIENCE Computer Professionals, Computer Users, Educators (University), Internet Users, Researchers, Students (University)
CONTACT mckim@lerc.nasa.gov
FREE

http://flick.lerc.nasa.gov/

Guide To Lockpicking ★★★★

This site offers a fully hypertexted guide on picking locks. It covers several different types of locks, from the standard pin and tumbler kind to more complex and difficult to pick locks. Users will find detailed diagrams and exercises to follow in order to master the art of lockpicking. There are also sections which cover more advanced lockpicking topics such as vibration picking, as well as a section which goes over legal issues. Finally, this guide has information on how to build your own lockpicking tools.

KEYWORDS Crime, Locksmiths, Police
AUDIENCE Computer Hackers, Criminals, Locksmiths, Police
CONTACT Mattias Wingstedt
         wing@lysator.liu.se
FREE

http://www.lysator.liu.se/mit-guide/mit-guide.html

Japanese/English Dictionary Gateway ★★★

The Japanese/English Dictionary Gateway is a dictionary that gives entries for English words in Japanese characters. It can also give Japanese characters for words in English or Japanese which are entered by the user in the Western alphabet.

KEYWORDS Japanese Language Software
AUDIENCE Academics, Japanese Culture Enthusiasts, Linguists
CONTACT Jeffrey Fried
         jfried@omron.co.jp
FREE

http://www.cs.cmu.edu:8001/cgi-bin/j-e/tty/gateway?SASE-tty/dict#does

John James - Weekly Horoscopes ★★★

John James examines the collective unconscious in his weekly CyberStar Horoscopes. You simply click on your zodiac sign and your future awaits you! There is also a link to The Funky Times which delivers extensive links to the best news, weather, comic strips, features, and links in one Online Daily Index.

KEYWORDS Astrology, Horoscopes, News
AUDIENCE Horoscope Readers, Internet Users, News Buffs
CONTACT Stephen Lord
         stephen@realitycom.com
FREE

http://www.realitycom.com/cybstars/stars.html

LEGO Information ★★★

The LEGO page is full of information for Lego lovers, including pictures and descriptions from the catalogs of the 1994 and 1995 product lines and set lists for Lego accessories. There are pictures of Lego constructions made by individuals and Lego Robots, as well as building ideas. Lego users can also find out how to play different games with their Legos and information is provided about Lego clubs, the Lego factory, and other Lego Internet sites.

KEYWORDS Children's Toys, Games
AUDIENCE Children, Parents
CONTACT David Koblas
         koblas@homepages.com
FREE

http://legowww.homepages.com/

MTU Volcanoes Page ★★★★

This Volcanoes Page is sponsored by the Keweenaw Volcano Observatory, and contains comprehensive information on volcanoes. Some of the descriptions, such as 'Ice volcanoes of Lake Superior's South Shore—Observations of a Chilling Phenomenon,' are geared towards a general audience, whereas other, more technical, pages are geared towards volcanologists. The pages contain JPEG images of eruptions, geologic interest pictures, and satellite photos.

KEYWORDS Earth Sciences, Geology, Volcanos
AUDIENCE Educators (Primary/Secondary), General Public, Geologists, Students (Primary/Secondary), Volcanologists
CONTACT Robert "Sparge" Landsparger
         rel@mtu.edu
FREE

http://www.geo.mtu.edu/volcanoes/

Matt's UK Nature Information ★★★

Matt's UK Nature Information is an alphabetical linked index of topics relating to nature such as animals, BBC Wildlife Magazine, Common Spotted Orchid, dragonflies and much more. The menu can also be searched thematically through broad categories such as 'Plants.' This page also provides a link to the uk.nature newsgroup and an FAQ regarding the newsgroup.

KEYWORDS Nature, Personal Page
AUDIENCE Ecologists, Nature Fans
FREE

http://www.rfhsm.ac.uk:81/golly/naturpag.html

Menu of Journals ★★

This is a menu of electronic journals, databases, etc., for researchers, journalists, etc. This page is a list of non-descriptive links to other hypertext pages.

KEYWORDS Databases, Electronic Journals, Research
AUDIENCE Computer Professionals, Computer Users, Educators (University), Internet Users, Journalists, Lawyers, Legal Professionals, Researchers, Students (University)
FREE

http://fiasco.snre.umich.edu

O'Reilly Home Page ★★★

This is the O'Reilly Publishers Home Page, which contains information in separate newsletters focusing on The Internet, Using UNIX & X, System Administration, Programming, Business and Travel, O'Reilly News, and more. There is also online book ordering information on many of these various subjects.

KEYWORDS International News, Internet Resources, Programming, Travel
AUDIENCE Computer Users, Educators (University), Internet Users, Researchers, Students (University)
FREE

http://ftp.ora.com

Pathfinder O.J. Central ★★★★

This page, sponsored by Time Inc.'s Pathfinder Web Site, contains resources related to the O.J. Simpson Murder Trial in Los Angeles of 1994/5. You can find information related to the crime scene and evidence, a daily calendar listing the media reports from June 1994 to the present, a Who's Who of all the players in the legal process, an archive of trial transcripts updated daily, legal papers associated with the case, and a bulletin board discussion area for people to discuss their opinions of this crime and trial. Most of the material available here is presented in hypertext format, so readers can easily find related news stories and sidebar materials.

KEYWORDS Abuse, Law, Law Reviews, O.J. Simpson
AUDIENCE Lawyers, Legal Professionals, News Buffs, Trial Lawyers
CONTACT pathfinder-webmaster@pathfinder.com
FREE

http://bigmouth.pathfinder.com/pathfinder/features/oj/central1.html

Pure Information ★★★

This is a page of miscellaneous hotlists and links to a potpourri of subjects. Some of the resources include tourist information on many different countries, maps, astronomy, the Exploratorium Musuem, the Virtual Hospital, and cooking. There is also the Encyclopedia Britannica, census data, the U.S. Constitution, web how-to information such as Zen and the Art of the Internet, Laserdisc information, Net BBS list, and more.

KEYWORDS Cyberculture, HTML (HyperText Markup Language
AUDIENCE Cyberpunks, Internet Users, Researchers
CONTACT Andrew Tong
         werdna@ugcs.caltech.edu
FREE

http://www.ugcs.caltech.edu/~werdna/hotlist/pinfo.html

Views Of The Solar System ★★★★

Views of the Solar System has been created as an educational tour of the solar system. It contains images and information about the Sun, planets, moons, asteroids, comets, and meteoroids. This tour uses

General Reference – Humor

hypertext to allow space travel by simply clicking on a desired planet. There is a glossary of unusual terms, a statistics page, and information about the history of space exploration.

Keywords Astronomy, NASA (National Aeronautics And Space Administration), Space Exploration
Audience Astronomy Enthusiasts, Educators (Primary/Secondary), Students (Primary/Secondary)
Free

http://www.c3.lanl.gov/~cjhamil/SolarSystem/homepage.html

What's Hot This Week In Entertainment? ★★★

This site offers reviews of recent items in the popular culture, courtesy of Time and VIBE magazine. There are feature items each week, as well as a searchable archive of past reviews. Reviews fall under the categories of Music, Television, Books, Movies, and Multimedia. There is also a Bulletin Board area for fans to write their own reviews and offer feedback for particular shows and books.

Keywords Multimedia, Pop Music, Reviews
Audience Book Readers, Movie Enthusiasts, Music Enthusiasts, Reading Enthusiasts, Television Enthusiasts
Contact webmaster@pathfinder.com
Free

http://bigmouth.pathfinder.com/pathfinder/reviews/reviews.html

World Wide Web Acronym Server ★★★★

This is the site to go to when you want to know what an abbreviation or acronym means. The Acronym Translator can be used via email or through the WWW to locate the full English wording of the submitted acronym, and users may also suggest definitions to unknown acronyms. The site also contains info on how to use the related email dictionary and thesaurus service.

Keywords Acronyms, Dictionaries, Linguistics, Online Guides
Audience Linguists, Researchers
Free

http://curia.ucc.ie/info/net/acronyms/acro.html

World Port Classified Advertising ★★★

This classified advertisement service will post your ads for employment, real estate (by state), computing, transportation, pets, and more. There is an extensive business-to-business directory as well.

Keywords Advertising, Classified Ads
Audience Buyers, Human Resources Departments, Job Recruiters, Job Seekers, Real Estate Brokers

---

Connections to Horoscopes
Your future is revealed

Even a stubborn, bull-headed Aries does some planning. If you want an astrological update on what to expect tomorrow or even six months from now, you might want to check out any of the dozen or so astrological forecasts on the Internet. One of several popular World Wide Web sites include "Jonathan Cainer's Daily Horoscope" (from the Daily Mail of London). This site provides a daily zodiac forecast, and includes weekly predictions, as well year-ahead horoscopes. If you're not sure what your sign is, you can confirm it on-line with Cainer. If you have questions about the zodiac, there's even an FAQ site that provides answers. There are also links to other Internet horoscopes services, such as "Spirit WWW—Astrology" and the "Underground Astrologer."

(http://www.realitycom.com/webstars/index.html)

Contact webmaster@worldport.com
Free

http://www.worldport.com/classified/

Humor

See also
Humanities & Social Sciences · *Literature*
Law & Criminal Justice · *Law Schools*
Sports & Recreation · *Recreation*

A Little UNIX Humor ★★★★

This page contains a few funny articles relating in some way to the UNIX operating system or various help-line situations. The famous 'Bastard Operator from Hell' series is also available in its entirety.

Keywords Computers, Jokes, Programming Languages, UNIX
Audience Computer Users, Humor Enthusiasts, UNIX Systems Administrators, UNIX Users
Contact Chris D. Halverson cdh@ties.k12.mn.us
Free

http://www.ties.k12.mn.us:80/~cdh/unix_humor.html

Amazing Adventures of Bromwyn Bunny ★★★

These pages contain accounts of the world-traveling exploits Bromwyn Bunny, a stuffed animal who has (according to the narrative and photographs available) traveled across the world, and visited many exotic and interesting regions along the way.

Keywords Humor
Audience Children, Humor Enthusiasts
Contact Lee E. J. Arnould lee_eja@postoffice.utas.edu.au
Free

http://leja.cs.utas.edu.au/bromwyn/bromwyn.html

Humor

Amusing Stories

This page contains links to dozens of amusing stories and articles, some factual and some not. Also available here are several of the more well-known 'April fools' faux-newspaper articles and press releases that have been posted to USENET newsgroups recently.

- **KEYWORDS** Comedy, Jokes, Satire
- **AUDIENCE** Comedy Fans, Jokers, Journalists, News Buffs, Practical Jokers
- **CONTACT** Jay Zylstra
  zylstra@spu.edu
- **FREE**

http://paul.spu.edu/~zylstra/comedy/stories/index.html

April Fools on the Internet

This site contains a large archive, indexed by year, of 'April fools' posts to various USENET newsgroups. The index currently contains articles posted to USENET between the late '80s and the present.

- **KEYWORDS** April Fools Day, Humor, Jokes
- **AUDIENCE** Humor Enthusiasts, Internet Users, Jokers, Practical Jokers
- **CONTACT** David Barbieri
  barberi@sunsite.unc.edu
- **FREE**

http://sunsite.unc.edu/dbarberi/april-fools.html

Australian Humour Gopher

This gopher server contains dozens of collections of jokes (grouped by subject), as well as a search engine to make navigating their 'canonical list of lightbulb jokes' easier. Collections of humorous acronyms, song lyrics, research papers and epigrams are also available.

- **KEYWORDS** Comedy, Jokes, Meta-Index (Jokes), Satire
- **AUDIENCE** Comedians, Humor Enthusiasts, Jokers
- **FREE**

gopher://155.187.10.12:70/11/fun/humour

C/3F What Snooze?

What Snooze? is an uncensored parody of the 'What's New' page found on most Web-surfing programs like Netscape and Mosaic. The creators of What Snooze? declare that it 'contains a list of links to the hundreds of thousands of new Web pages that have been created and announced in the last 10 minutes.' Of course none of the hypertext links work, but that doesn't matter, as you'll be falling off your chair laughing at the incisive satirical descriptions of nonexistent Web sites such as 'NetWebVirtuMall USA' and the 'Union of Concerned Kamikazes.'

- **KEYWORDS** Humor, Internet Culture, Satire
- **AUDIENCE** Cyberculture Enthusiasts, Internet Users, Web Developers
- **FREE**

http://www.digimark.net/mfu/whatsnoo.html

Calvin and Hobbes Archive

This is the home page of Calvin and Hobbes. Users can find pictures of Calvin and Hobbes, as well as related newsgroups and FTP sites. This site also lists other Calvin & Hobbes Web pages.

- **KEYWORDS** Calvin And Hobbes, Comics, Humor
- **AUDIENCE** Comics Enthusiasts, General Public
- **CONTACT** Justin Higuchi
  jhiguch@wiliki.eng.hawaii.edu
- **FREE**

http://www.eng.hawaii.edu/Contribs/justin/Archive/Index.html

Canonical Collection of Light-Bulb Jokes

This is a large and comprehensive list of light bulb jokes, in the vein of 'How many X does it take to screw in a light bulb?', where X is a particular recognizable group or type of individual(s).

- **KEYWORDS** Comedy, Jokes
- **AUDIENCE** Comedians, Electricians, Humor Enthusiasts, Jokers
- **CONTACT** Bob Antia
  antia@ksr.com
- **FREE**

http://www.ksr.com/~antia/Light_Bulb_jokes.txt

Cartoons by Tom Tomorrow

This site is devoted to the comic strip This Modern World. It is updated weekly, and is maintained by the author. The site was created online for people that have papers that do not carry the comic strip.

- **KEYWORDS** Cartoons, Comedy, Comics, Humor
- **AUDIENCE** Comics Enthusiasts, Humor Enthusiasts
- **CONTACT** Tom Tomorrow
  tomorrow@well.com
- **FREE**

http://www.well.com/Community/comic/

Church of Euthanasia

The Church of Euthanasia is an avant garde satirical humor cabal, and their Web page is a cavalcade of disembowelled sacred cows and violated taboos. Working under the banner 'Suicide, Abortion, Cannibalism, Sodomy,' the Church actively promotes the end of human life on earth, mainly through the promotion of the above-mentioned activities. Hyperlinks lead to the Church's official magazine 'Snuff It,' bursting with serious and not-so-serious ruminations on the best way to end human life, to church sermons on topics you'd rather not ponder, and of course to an online catalog of Church paraphenalia.

- **KEYWORDS** Humor, Religion, Satire
- **AUDIENCE** Curiosity Seekers, Humor Enthusiasts, Jokers
- **CONTACT** R. Scott LaMorte
  static@netcom.com
- **FREE**

http://www.paranoia.com/coe/

Citizen Poke Magazine

Citizen Poke is a monthly electronic magazine of humor and comics made available by a group of students at the University of Massachussetts in Amherst. Every issue contains satirical articles and columns, collections of jokes, riddles, and puns, as well as a number of comics and cartoons. The issues of Citizen Poke may be downloaded from the web site in a Adobe Acrobat format. The Acrobat reader is also available for a variety of platforms (Mac, PC and Sun).

- **KEYWORDS** E-Zines, Humor, Jokes, Magazines
- **AUDIENCE** Comedy Fans, Humor Enthusiasts, Jokers
- **CONTACT** Citizen Poke Staff
  poke@amherst.edu
- **FREE**

http://www.amherst.edu:80/~poke/

Comics 'n Stuff

The Comics 'n Stuff Web site is a meta-index to cartoons and comics on the World Wide Web, with links to hundreds of Web sites. Comics are listed alphabetically, with some brief descriptions and loading information. Users will also find the 'Comic of the Week' feature and a list of comic related pages on the Web.

- **KEYWORDS** Cartoons, Comics
- **AUDIENCE** Comics Enthusiasts, General Public, Humor Enthusiasts
- **CONTACT** Christian Cosas
  c617145@showme.missouri.edu
- **FREE**

http://www.missouri.edu/~c617145/comix.html

Computer Humor

This short document provides links to a few computer-related humorous documents. Available from this location are a digital form for composing 'flames' (inflammatory and usually angry individual responses), an article examining the effects of excessive cross-posting on one's karma, and more.

- **KEYWORDS** Flames, Humor, Jokes, Netiquette
- **AUDIENCE** Computer Users, Humor Enthusiasts, Programmers, UNIX Systems Administrators
- **CONTACT** Michael Sattler
  msattler@jungle.com
- **FREE**

http://www.indstate.edu/msattler/culture/comp/humor/index.html

Confession Booth

This page is an online confessional. Users can submit their sins and be absolved of their wrongdoing by performing the penance which the online priest gives out. The confessor can choose from a list of sins to confess to, including Murder, Sloth, Deception, Misplaced Priorities, and Fish in Microwave. The service is whimsical, although users can take this service as seriously as they like.

- **KEYWORDS** Confession, Entertainment, Humor
- **AUDIENCE** Humor Enthusiasts, Jokers

CONTACT anwar@cs.cmu.edu
caruana@cs.cmu.edu

FREE

http://anther.learning.cs.cmu.edu/priest.html

Coolest Hostnames On The Net ★★★★

Meng Weng Wong maintains this list of sometimes outrageously silly host names for machines at various locations on the Internet. Names that are puns, jokes, or just plain silly are listed. Wong updates this list regularly.

KEYWORDS Humor, Internet Host Names
AUDIENCE Humor Enthusiasts, Internet Users, Systems Operators, UNIX Systems Administrators
CONTACT Meng Weng Wong
mengwong@seas.upenn.edu
FREE

http://www.seas.upenn.edu:80/~mengwong/coolhosts.html

Countdown ★★★

The Countdown! page provides a clock that gives the exact number of seconds until the new millenium, either January 1, 2000, or January 1, 2001, depending how you perceive it. Users may also look up how many seconds have passed or will pass between two times in the past or future by entering dates and times into the watch form.

KEYWORDS Futurism
AUDIENCE General Public, Internet Users
CONTACT spiders@spiders.com
FREE

http://www.spiders.com/cgi-bin/countdown

Dennis' Private Joke Collection ★★★

Mr. Rears' collection of jokes includes a number of Waco/Branch Davidian jokes, a listing of possible marriage counseling courses for both men and women, and other (some risque) material.

KEYWORDS Jokes, Satire, Sexual Innuendo
AUDIENCE Humor Enthusiasts, Husbands, Jokers, Wives
CONTACT Dennis G. Rears
drears@pica.army.mil
FREE

http://polar.pica.army.mil/people/drears/humor/humor.html

Dilbert Zone ★★★

This is a home page on Dilbert, a popular character in comics. Users can find a two-week Dilbert cartoon archive, some prehistory of Delbert and a photo tour of how Dilbert is created. In addition, the Dilbert licensed vendor list and the Dilbert Zone FAQ is also available.

KEYWORDS Comics, Computer Humor
AUDIENCE Comics Enthusiasts

Connections to Generation X
Old boring people have all the money...

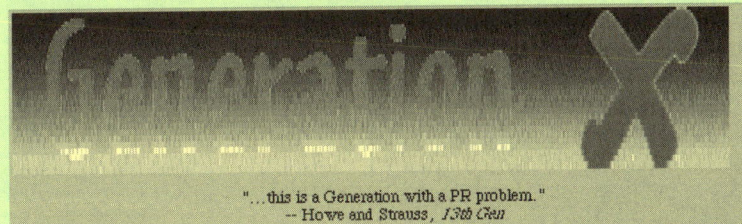

If you're part of the greatly misunderstood Generation X and are dying to share your alienation with others of your kind around the world, the optimal way is clearly via the Internet.

You can subscribe to an online newsletter that focuses exclusively on the culture of Gen X. You can speak out about your frustrations, brag about your successes, and discuss your wide-ranging political and social views. Through one of many popular sites on the Internet, "alt.society.generation-x at play," you can even access a gallery of pictures of Generation X-ers.

(http://www.io.org/~spamily/Tingle_Pictures.html)

also, (http://www.cybernetics.net/users/rdavis/GenX.html)

You can visit the "YaZone," a site for Generation Xers interested in music, other places, finding key-pals, and posting responses to common life issues. You can get news about fads, clothing trends, and popular culture. If a little brother or sister is bugging you about getting on the Web, then YaZone offers a playground for kids ages 8-12, to get them out of your hair.

(http://www.spectracom.com/yazone/)

CONTACT webmaster@unitedmedia.com
FREE

http://www.unitedmedia.com/comics/dilbert/

Economist Jokes ★★★

This file contains a few dozen economics and economist-related jokes, riddles, and humorous anecdotes. The maintainer of this page claims that even Adam Smith would have laughed at these jokes.

KEYWORDS Humor, Jokes
AUDIENCE Business Professionals, Economics Students, Economists, Joke Enthusiasts
CONTACT Pasi Kuoppam
pkm@etla.fi
FREE

http://www.etla.fi/pkm/joke.html

Funky Site of the Day ★★★

Funky Site of the Day provides a brand new, hand-picked, dew drenched, lip-smacking Web site each and every day. It also includes a list of previous Funky Sites.

KEYWORDS Computers, WWW (World Wide Web)
AUDIENCE Internet Users
CONTACT Stephen Lord
stephen@realitycom.com
FREE

http://www.realitycom.com/cybstars/index.html

Harold Reynolds' Humour Collection ★★★★

Harold Reynolds' Humour Collection is my personal choice for Funniest Spot on the World Wide Web. If you have even the slightest acquaintance with dogs or cats, especially through ownership or companionship (take your pick), saunter on over to this site and take a gander at some of the lists and diagrams available. Then mail them to yourself and send them to your

Humor

friends, acquaintances, co-workers, relatives, neighbors, pet shop and the funny-looking guy down the hall.

KEYWORDS Cats, Dogs, Humor, Pets
AUDIENCE Animal Lovers, Cat Lovers, Dog Owners, Pet Owners
CONTACT Harold Reynolds
reynolds@geog.utoronto.ca
FREE

http://geog.utoronto.ca/reynolds/humour.html

The House of Slime ★★★★

The House of Slime is the Internet site that answers that ever present question, 'What is Slime?' Not confined to a simple definition, the House of Slime brings a multiplicity of references to the average slime aficionado, including, but not limited to - slime as it relates to entertainment, computing, slime molds, slugs and their botanical cousin, the kombucha mushroom. The House of Slime then takes a slight departure to concentrate on a purely textural kinsman, mucus. Also available here are links to sex, drugs and rock 'n' roll topics, terminating in a link to the ultimate slime extravaganza, death.

KEYWORDS Computing, Death, Entertainment, Jokes
AUDIENCE Allergy Sufferers, Humor Enthusiasts, Mushroom Enthusiasts, Slug Enthusiasts
CONTACT John L. Stone
jleon@teleport.com
FREE

http://www.teleport.com/~jleon/index.html

Humorous Quotations ★★★★

This site contains a very large archive of humorous quotes, one-liners and short nonsequiturs from a variety of comedians, entertainers, authors and fictional characters. Numerous links to other humor resources are also available.

KEYWORDS Comedy, Jokes, Meta-Index (Humor)
AUDIENCE Comedians, Humor Enthusiasts, Jokers
CONTACT Don Geddis
Geddis@CS.Stanford.EDU
FREE

http://meta.stanford.edu/quotes.html

The IMRF (Internet Multimedia Research Foundation) Choose Your Own Adventure Story ★★

This page is home to the Internet Multimedia Research Foundation (IMRF) Choose your Own Adventure Story. This story works on the principle of the reader choosing what the main character will do next. It is also possible to add to the story in progress. Note that the story which appears here has been written predominantly by college physics students, and contains bizarre choices and consequences including vomiting, bleeding, exposure to gamma radiation, and other actions which may not be suitable for very young children. The IMRF is an organization committed to stretching the boundaries of multimedia technology by using existing multimedia technology in new, surprising, and often stupid ways.

KEYWORDS Fiction, Humor, Internet Games

AUDIENCE Adventurers, Fiction Enthusiasts, Humor Enthusiasts
CONTACT Sho Kuwamoto
sho@physics.purdue.edu
FREE

http://physics.purdue.edu/~sho/imrf.html

Insomniac's Humor Collection ★★★

This site contains dozens of humorous items, including a comprehensive list of David Letterman's monologues, a few hundred political jokes (mostly written for a conservative audience), and more.

KEYWORDS Comedy, Jokes
AUDIENCE Conservatives, Humor Enthusiasts, Jokers, Republicans, Television Enthusiasts
CONTACT Insomniac
elewis@rohan.sdsu.edu
FREE

http://rohan.sdsu.edu:80/home/elewis/Humor.html

The Jean-Paul Sartre Cookbook ★★★

The Jean-Paul Sartre Cookbook is the original creation of Alastair Sutherland of the 'Free Agent' alternative newspaper in Portland, Oregon, who claims to have been lucky enough to discover several previously lost diaries of French philosopher Jean-Paul Sartre stuck in between the cushions of his office sofa. The diaries reveal a young Sartre obsessed not with the void, but with food. Join Sartre as he keeps 'creating omelets one after another, like soldiers marching into the sea, but each one seems empty, hollow, like stone,' and as he feeds Malraux his original recipe that included cigarettes, coffee and four tiny stones, Malraux comments by puking.

KEYWORDS Cookbooks, Cooking, Humor, Online Publications
AUDIENCE Humor Enthusiasts, Humorists
CONTACT Dan Bornstein
danfuzz@kaleida.com
FREE

http://web.kaleida.com/u/danfuzz/info/words/stories/sartre_cookbook.html

Joe Kung's Jokespace ★★★

Page administrator Joe Kung has collected at this site a few joke collections, a large list of embarassing quotes from ex-Vice President J. Danforth Quayle, and a cgi-script that generates random disco songs every time a user access it.

KEYWORDS Dan, Humor, Jokes, Quale
AUDIENCE Democrats, Humor Enthusiasts, Jokers, Journalists, Liberals, Political Researchers
CONTACT Joe Kung
jtkung@netcom.com
FREE

http://cecelia.media.mit.edu:8080/htdocs/jokes.html

Joke Of The Day ★★★

This page presents a new joke in French every day. The page administrator, Bruno Rossi, takes most of the jokes from the Usenet newsgroup fr.rec.humour.

KEYWORDS France, French, Jokes
AUDIENCE France Residents, Francophiles, French Speakers, French Students, Jokers
CONTACT Bruno Rossi
rossi@ascom.cica.fr
FREE

http://ascom.cica.fr:80/~rossi/perso/motd.html

Jokes For The Rainy Days ★★

This document contains a large number of jokes, riddles, humorous 'English' written by foreign-language speakers, funny error messages generated in UNIX and DOS operating systems, and much more. There is no index or search engine available; to find specific entries the entire document must be browsed.

KEYWORDS Comedy, Computers, Jokes
AUDIENCE Comedians, Humor Enthusiasts, Jokers
FREE

http://www.mips.com/HTMLs/Joke_B.html

Lawyer Jokes ★★★

This location contains a very comprehensive list of lawyer jokes, mostly in question-and-answer format. Students and faculty at the Cornell School of Law, where this document is located, have apparently added to the list, which originally came from usenet newsgroup rec.humor.

KEYWORDS Humor, Jokes
AUDIENCE Comedians, Humor Enthusiasts, Jokers, Law Students, Lawyers, Legal Professionals
FREE

http://gopher.law.cornell.edu:70/0/misc/Humor/lawyer_jokes

Macintosh Humor ★★★★

This page contains jokes related to Apple Macintosh products and a number of 'April fool's posts,' mostly fake press releases that Apple never released including such items as 'Power Macintosh Discontinued Due to Shocking Speed,' 'Microsoft Icons Contain Evil Hidden Messages,' and 'Apple Releases Caffeine Manager.'

KEYWORDS Computers, Jokes
AUDIENCE Computer Users, Humor Enthusiasts, Macintosh Users, Practical Jokers
CONTACT Robert Lentz
lentz@rossi.astro.nwu.edu
FREE

http://www.astro.nwu.edu/lentz/mac/humor/home-mac-humor.html

Miscellaneous Diversions ★★★★

This site contains links to the Dr. Fun cartoon (updated daily), various Internet jokes and humor archives, and other non-humor entertainment such as sports schedules.

KEYWORDS Cartoons, Jokes

Humor   529

AUDIENCE   Comedians, Humor Enthusiasts, Jokers, Sports Fans
CONTACT   Ashutosh Sanzgiri
         sanzgiri@hepr1.tamu.edu
FREE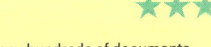

http://hepr1.tamu.edu/fun.html

Mother Of All Humor Archives ★★★

This archive contains many hundreds of documents, and many of those contain hundreds of individual jokes, riddles, accounts of practical jokes, anecdotes, excerpts from popular press, amusing stories, and more.

KEYWORDS   Humor, Jokes
AUDIENCE   Humor Enthusiasts, Internet Users, Jokers, Practical Jokers, Reading Enthusiasts
CONTACT   Christopher Kline
         ckline@acm.org
FREE

http://www.tc.cornell.edu/~ckline/humor/maillist.html

Page-O Bizarro ★★★

These pages contain excerpts from the popular USENET newsgroup talk.bizarre, as well as links to the home pages of several celebrated talk.bizarre denizens. A small archive of humorous posts is available.

KEYWORDS   Fiction, Humor, Jokes
AUDIENCE   Cartoon Enthusiasts, Fiction Enthusiasts, Humor Enthusiasts, Reading Enthusiasts
CONTACT   John Perry
         jperry@cs.ucla.edu
FREE

http://www.best.com/~johnp/bizarro.html

Palindrome Page ★★★★

This document contains (listed in no particular order) dozens of palindromes - words or phrases that read identically both backwards and forwards.

KEYWORDS   Linguistics
AUDIENCE   Humor Enthusiasts, Linguists, Palindrome Enthusiasts
CONTACT   Beej
         beej@ecst.csuchico.edu
FREE

http://www2.ecst.csuchico.edu/~beej/palindromes.html

Practical Jokes Archive ★★★

This document is a very large (over 180k) collection of practical jokes collected from the Alt.shenanigans USENET newsgroup over the past few years. There is no index or search engine available at this time.

KEYWORDS   Humor, Jokes
AUDIENCE   Humor Enthusiasts, Jokers, Practical Jokers
CONTACT   Richard Ormered
         Richard.Ormered@newcastle.ac.uk
FREE

http://www.umd.umich.edu/~nhughes/htmldocs/pracjokes.html

Connections To Jokes
To err is human

Down in the dumps? Feel like you made a complete fool of yourself at the office party? Made any gaffes you wish you could take back?

You might want to visit the "Jokes For The Rainy Days" site. This site, interestingly enough, focuses particularly on the difficulty non-English speaking cultures have in trying to accommodate English-speaking tourists with advice and directions.

For instance, a sign spotted at a Bangkok dry cleaners: "Drop your trousers here for best results." Or a sign spotted at a Copenhagen airline ticket counter: "We take your bags and send them in all directions."

Included at this site are courtroom bloopers, taken (apparently) from recorded proceedings at trials. One such example:
Attorney: "Where you acquainted with the deceased?"
Witness: "Yes, sir."
Attorney: "Before or after he died?"

(http://www.mips.com/HTMLs/Joke_B.html)

Shakespearian Insult Kit ★★★★

This document contains instructions and a form for use in generating convincingly silly Shakespearian insults. Users may take a word from each of three columns and string them together, forming such epithets as 'thou churlish beef-witted pignut,' and 'thou yeasty toad-spotted canker-blossom.'

KEYWORDS   Insults, Jokes
AUDIENCE   Humor Enthusiasts, Jokers, Shakespeare Enthusiasts
CONTACT   Adrian Forte
         gforte@uxa.ecn.bgu.edu
FREE

http://www.ecn.bgu.edu/users/gforte/shakespear.insult.html

Smiles Ha Ha Ha ★★★

This page contains a number of links to jokes collections and other humorous ephemera. Among the items available here are a canonical list of funny answering machine messages, the do's and don't's of dating, and miscellaneous university-related humor.

KEYWORDS   Dating, Education (College/University), Humor, Jokes
AUDIENCE   Answering Machine Owners, Jokers, Students (University)
CONTACT   Lenny Zeltser
         lzeltser@seas.upenn.edu
FREE

http://www.seas.upenn.edu:80/~lzeltser/Funny/index.html

Today's Horoscope ★★★★

This page contains humorous horoscopes, custom written each day by page creator Ron E. Lunde with the aid of 'precise planetary positions, a custom-made analog computer, and ancient Norwegian meditation techniques.' Mr. Lunde admits that mostly he just 'spins a carrot' to arrive at his conclusions.

Keywords Humor, Jokes
Audience Astrology Enthusiasts, Horoscope Readers, Humor Enthusiasts, Jokers
Contact Ron E. Lunde
ronl@teleport.com
Free

http://www.teleport.com/~ronl/horo.html

Twenty-Eight-Hour Day

This page presents a worldwide movement to change the clocks and the way we live and work. The author proposes a new time system, based on twenty-eight hour days, which would increase productivity, reduce the workweek to four days, and save on commuting and mental energies. Side effects of the system are the elimination of Mondays and the lack of sun on Thursdays.

Keywords Humor, Sleeping
Audience Clock Manufacturers, Humor Enthusiasts, Jokers
Contact Kaplan OnLine
webmasters@www.kaplan.com
Free

http://www.kaplan.com/etc/bosh/28-hr.html

Underholding Humor Page ★★★

These pages contain documents which are all in Norwegian. Some of the files available here are canonical lists of jokes about blondes, O.J. Simpson, sororities/fraternities and other genres. The links are in a variety of languages, including English, to humor-related sites worldwide.

Keywords Comedy, Jokes, Norway
Audience Comedians, Comedy Fans, Humor Enthusiasts, Jokers, Norwegians
Contact jon@gfi.uib.no
Free

http://yr.gfi.uib.no/fun/humor.html

University of Michigan Humor Archive ★★★

This site contains a large collection of jokes, song lyrics, riddles, puns, and uncategorizeable humorous texts on a wide variety of topics. Some of the joke-filled subdirectories here include 'Sex,' 'Monty Python,' 'Politics,' 'Religion,' and 'Computers.'

Keywords Jokes, Meta-Index (Humor), Monty Python
Audience Comedians, Humor Enthusiasts, Jokers, Reading Enthusiasts
Contact Paul Southworth, Archivist
ftp@etext.archive.umich.edu
Free

gopher://etext.archive.umich.edu:70/11/Quartz/humor

Vitsove... Vitsove... Vitsove... ★★★

This page contains a large archive of jokes in Bulgarian. Most are from Bulgarian culture, although a few are merely translations of non-nation-specific jokes originally in English and other languages.

Keywords Bulgaria, Humor
Audience Bulgaria Residents, Bulgarian Speakers, Bulgarians, Humor Enthusiasts, Linguists
Contact Ivo Sargoytchev
ivor@interlog.com
Free

http://www.interlog.com/~ivor/vitsove.html

Wayne State Humor Archive ★★★

This gopher site contains a number of documents, most being transcriptions of humorous songs or stories, joke collections, and other articles focusing on the subject of comedy.

Keywords Comedy, Jokes, Songs
Audience Humor Enthusiasts, Jokers
Contact Michael Edelman
mje@pookie.pass.wayne.edu
Free

gopher://pookie.pass.wayne.edu:70/11/humor

Lifestyles

See also
Health & Medicine · Sexuality
Humanities & Social Sciences · Women's Studies
Popular Culture & Entertainment · Family & Community

Active Window's LesBiGay Pages ★★★

The Active Window's LesBiGay Pages collection of gay/lesbian/bisexual-related information features prose and photographic documentation of the recent Stonewall 25th anniversary, and the march on the United Nations. Information on news, editorials, and activist information, although somewhat outdated is included with a short list of links to other sites of interest.

Keywords Activism, Homosexuality, Lesbianism
Audience Bisexuals, Gay Rights Activists, Gays, Lesbians
Contact Jay Laird
jaide@actwin.com
Free

http://www.actwin.com/lesbigay/index.html

African American Haven ★★★

The African American Haven home page is a meta-index linking users to Web sites about black music, art, and history. There are also links to African American business sites, and to other meta-indexes.

Keywords African Americans, Business, Culture
Audience African Americans, Business Professionals

Free

http://www.auc.edu/~tpearson/haven.html

Alt.Romance.Chat Archive ★★★

This is the home page for the USENET newsgroup Alt.romance.chat. Users can find the FAQ list, a picture gallery of scanned photographs of ARC.folk, home pages of some ARCitizens. Links to other romance-related sites are also included.

Keywords Romance, Romantics
Audience Adults, Romantics, Single People
Contact Cheshire Cat
smccoy@harris.com
Free

http://minerva.doe.mtu.edu/arc/

Alternative Sexuality Resource List ★★★

The Alternative Sexuality Resource List is designed to be a reference guide for non-pornographic sexual resources on the Internet. Links are grouped into topics such as body art, bondage, polyandry, politics, and queer issues, and divided up by type of Internet resource. Several transgender links are also included.

Keywords Homosexuality, Sexual Fetishes, Sexual Orientation
Audience Gays, Sex Enthusiasts
Contact reive@phantom.com
Free

http://www.phantom.com:80/~reive/altsex.html

Blars' Renaissance Faire Page ★★★

Blar's Renaissance Faire Page gives a complete and updated listing of Renaissance fantasy fairs happening in central California. Blar includes brief, insightful reviews of some past fairs as well as contact phone numbers for most of the events. This page also has links to other sites for followers of Renaissance culture and entertainment.

Keywords California, Renaissance Fairs, Renaissance History, Science Fiction
Audience Renaissance Fantasy Buffs, Renaissance Historians, Science Fiction Enthusiasts
Contact blarson@blars.la.ca.us
Free

http://sundry.hsc.usc.edu/faire.html

Chi-Town Squares ★★★

The home page for the Chi-Town Squares, a Chicago-area gay and lesbian square dance organization, includes a club schedule and information about past and upcoming square dance conventions. Much of the page is still under construction.

Keywords Dancing, Lesbianism, Square Dancing
Audience Bisexuals, Dance Enthusiasts, Folk Dancers, Gays

Lifestyles **531**

CONTACT Steven R. Messamer
messamer@msc.com

FREE

http://www.mcs.net/~messamer/http/chitown.html

Columbia Almanac of Information Pertaining to Sexual Orientation ★★★

This gopher site contains a comprehensive list of resources for the gay and lesbian community of Columbia University and New York City. Among the topics are Columbia's official policies regarding sexual orientation, student and community groups in the area, and local advocacy and counseling resources.

KEYWORDS Bisexuality, Homosexuality, New York, Sexual Orientation
AUDIENCE Bisexuals, Gays, New York Residents, Students (University)
FREE

gopher://gopher.cc.columbia.edu:71/00/community/calipso/calipso10

Cosmic Home Page ★★★★

The Cosmic Home Page is a vast compendium of resources of interest to people who wish to better the planet and those who reside on it physically, emotionally and spiritually. Available are links to all of the major vegetarian sites on the Web, including but not limited to the Vegetarian Resource Group Home Page, the Vegetarian Pages, Ben's Mega-Veggie Index and the Vegan Action Home Page; as well as links to all sorts of alternative thought sites, encompassing topics such as reincarnation, lightwork, Out-of-Body Experiences, natural medicines, and UFOs. There is a link to get a computerized tarot reading, a link to a home page concerned with Ferraris, several links to museums and even quite a few to art sites on the Net.

KEYWORDS New Age Philosophy, Spirituality, Veganism, Vegetarianism
AUDIENCE Holistic Health Care Practitioners, New Age Enthusiasts, Vegans, Vegetarians
CONTACT Brad Urani
Cosmicfr@inlink.com
FREE

http://www.inlink.com/~cosmicfr/homepage.html

Divoroo Home Page ★★★

This is a support center for the divorced, never married but hurting from a failed love, and the separated. Some phone numbers and links for divorce support can be found. Fathers Rights and Equality Exchange (FREE) is a place to begin for men. Both a domestic and an international list of FREE Area Coordinators can also be found here.

KEYWORDS Divorce, Relationships
AUDIENCE Adults, Single People
CONTACT Dean Hughson
dean@primenet.com
FREE

http://www3.primenet.com/~dean/

Connections to Anarchy Online
Anarchists of the World Unite!

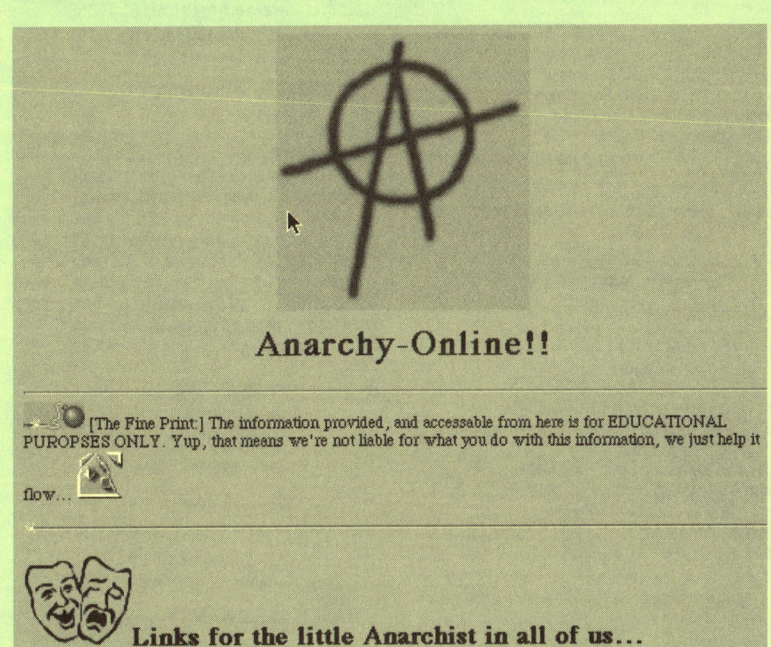

Think the free-market system stinks? Should all laws should be abolished? Does government exist solely for the benefit of the rich and powerful? Or maybe you just want to find sound files of new CD releases. "Anarchy Online" features a wide array of controversial subjects and viewpoints. It's also a place to get into the "Music Kitchen" and check out the sound files of such artists as the Beastie Boys, Bonnie Raitt, and World Domination Records.

Additionally, you'll find Phrack Magazine here, one of the longest-running electronic magazines on the Internet. This 'zine has long been a source of controversy since it's seen by law enforcement officials as a direct link to the "secret society" of computer hackers—a claim its editors scoff at.

Anarchy Online also puts you in touch with a variety of people most aptly described as dissidents—those actively opposing government brutality and the repression of human rights.

(http://anarchy-online.com/)

Dublin Pub Review ★★

This site offers reviews of Dublin's social and nightlife venues, and is divided into two sections, pubs and nightclubs. Along with descriptions of ambiance and clientele, reviews rate beer prices and offer a subjective overall rating for each venue. Many reviews also specify street addresses. The list, compiled and written by an individual, is not comprehensive.

KEYWORDS Beer, Pubs
AUDIENCE Beer Enthusiasts, Ireland Residents, Nightlife Enthusiasts, Tourists
CONTACT czimmerm@dsg.cs.tcd.ie
FREE

http://www.dsg.cs.tcd.ie/dsg_people/czimmerm/pubs.html

Gays ★★★

This site is a meta index for Gays on the World Wide Web. It includes Shopping, Videos, Pictures, Information, personal ads and Gay related resources. There are special offers for consumers, distributors, resellers and tv channels. This site is suitable for adults only.

KEYWORDS Adult Videos, Homosexuality, Personal Ads, Shopping
AUDIENCE Adults, Gays, Men, Sex Enthusiasts, Women
CONTACT Noel Boller
nboller@gays.com
FREE

http://www.gays.com

ftp://ftp.gays.com

Popular Culture & Entertainment

Lifestyles

International Association of Gay Square Dance Clubs ★★★

This is the home page for the International Association of Gay Square Dance Clubs. Its main purpose is to provide information about upcoming conventions and related events, both in the San Francisco Bay Area and nationwide. It also houses a list of member clubs and email contacts, as well as links to other square dancing resources and gay-lesbian information sites.

KEYWORDS Lesbianism, Recreation, Square Dancing
AUDIENCE Bisexuals, Dance Enthusiasts, Folk Dancers, Gays, Lesbians
CONTACT Sheldon Green
agxsg@nasagiss.giss.nasa.gov
FREE

http://hawg.stanford.edu/~sgreen/IAGSDC/.html

OutNOW! Alive ★★★

OutNOW is a biweekly newspaper for Northern California's gay, lesbian, and bisexual community and friends. The circulation of 12,000 print copies are distributed throughout the San Francisco Bay Area, as well as a limited national distribution. The online edition contains most of the features from the print version. Each issue features articles under such categories as Northern California, the Nation and World, Opinions and Commentary, Out On The Town and Classifieds.

KEYWORDS Bisexuals, Lesbianism, Online Newspapers
AUDIENCE AIDS Activists, Bisexuals, Californians, Gays, Lesbians
CONTACT Zoom.Com
webmaster@zoom.com
FREE

http://www.zoom.com/outnow/

Queer Information ★★★★

This site houses an extensive and informative collection of articles regarding various aspects of gay history, culture, politics, and religion. It also includes a brief list of links to other gay-related sites.

KEYWORDS Bisexuals, Homosexuality, Lesbianism
AUDIENCE Bisexuals, Gay Rights Activists, Gays, Lesbians
CONTACT Scott Safier
corwin+@cmu.edu
FREE

http://www.cs.cmu.edu:8001/afs/cs.cmu.edu/user/scotts/bulgarians/mainpage.html

Queer Lounge ★★★

This page is a very eclectic mixture of information, most of which is related to gay and lesbian issues. Some of the topics found here include current events and politics; product advertisements and endorsements; upcoming real-life and electronic events; online resources and publications; Internet help; and general interest links.

KEYWORDS Homosexuality, Internet Resources, Lesbianism
AUDIENCE Bisexuals, Gays, Internet Users, Lesbians
CONTACT Tom Hicks
tomh@cyberzine.org
FREE

http://cyberzine.org/html/GLAIDS/glaidshomepage.html

Sex in America ★★★

This Web page is devoted to sexually-oriented topics, with some emphasis on American culture. The basis of this site is the bestselling book, Sex in America—A Definitive Survey, published by Little, Brown, and Company (1994). Users will find excerpts from the book, statistical data, and related articles like '101 Best Places for a Quickie.' These are adult areas, and viewer discretion is highly advised. In addition to the online reference area, there is a bulletin board discussion center, where people discuss topics such as 'Playing Games,' and 'Masturbation' and 'Mature Men at College.'

KEYWORDS Counseling, Sex, Sexual Orientation
AUDIENCE Psychologists, Sex Counselors, Sex Enthusiasts, United States Residents
CONTACT twep-webmaster@pathfinder.com
FREE

http://bigmouth.pathfinder.com/twep/Features/Sex/Sex.html

Tall Club of New York City ★★

The Tall Club of New York City (TCNYC) is a not-for-profit social club for tall people. The purpose of the club is to promote friendships among tall people and to sponsor activities of interest for its members and cooperation with other Tall Clubs. This page contains links for upcoming events, a photo gallery of its members, and the club's online newsletter, the Tall Metropolis. There is also a page devoted to Marfan's Syndrome Foundation, the charity supported by Tall Clubs International.

KEYWORDS Community Networks, Social Events
AUDIENCE New York Residents, Tall People
CONTACT Richard Stoller
rstoller@panix.com
FREE

http://www.panix.com/~rstoller/

UC Berkeley Gay/Lesbian/Queer Home Page ★★★

This site contains extensive information of interest to gays, lesbians, and bisexuals. It includes listings of local (San Francisco Bay Area) current events, job listings, and exhibits; information about UC Berkeley's campus resources, such as courses and student groups; documents relating to local and national groups and resources; and many links to other infoservers and newsgroups. Most of this information is also available via gopher.

KEYWORDS Bisexuality, Homosexuality, Lesbianism
AUDIENCE Bisexuals, Gays, Lesbians, Students (University)
CONTACT queer@server.berkeley.edu
FREE

http://server.berkeley.edu:80/mblga/

Vegetarian Resource Group (VRG) ★★★★

This site offers back issues of the Vegetarian Journal (organized by subject and by issue), as well as other resources on veganism and vegetarianism. Some of the resources include articles, brochures, and tips on topics such as nutrition, cooking, animal rights, new products, travel, scientific studies, and relevant books and software. One section covers vegetarian foods for institutions. There is also a link to an outside animal rights resource.

KEYWORDS Food, Nutrition, Vegetarianism
AUDIENCE Food Enthusiasts, Nutritionists, Researchers, Vegetarians
CONTACT brad@clark.net
FREE

http://envirolink.org/arrs/VRG/home.html

WEB Personals ★★★

WEB Personals is a semi-moderated free service that is intended for people who want to meet others for romance, companionship, or other activities. Choose to explore romance connections, pen pals, or friend and group activities. Ads have been placed from most states and countries. You can now include your photo in your ad, as well as respond anonymously. Currently, this page receives 3500 visitors a day. A site in Japanese is also available.

KEYWORDS Love, Online Services, Personals, Romance
AUDIENCE Friends, Lonely People, Men, Personal Ad Readers, Romantics, Women
CONTACT Internet Media Services
ims@netmedia.com
FREE

http://www.netmedia.com:80/date/

Welcome to the Public.Com Personals ★★★★

Welcome to the Public.com Personals allows surfers to browse personals from around the world and place ads at the service of their choice. It contains links to about 20 independent personals services. It also accommodates diverse preferences.

KEYWORDS Communications, Dating, Personals
AUDIENCE Internet Users, Single People
FREE

http://www.public.com/personals/

Magazines & Newspapers

See also
Arts & Music · *Electronic Arts*
Business & Economics · *Publishing*
Humanities & Social Sciences · *Literature*

21C - The Magazine of the 21st Century ★★★

21 C The Magazine of the 21st Century is an online magazine with eclectic futuristic type articles. Some of the feature articles deal with subjects such as the paradox of time travel, travelling at warp speed, time

Lifestyles – Magazines & Newspapers

warps, black holes and multiple universes. The articles also deal with individuals or companies such as Murdoch, Disney, Sony and Nintendo the winners and losers of a digital dog-eat-dog world, Rodney Brooks' artificial intelligence robots, and Vaclav Havel, the president of the Czech Republic who describes his vision of the future.

KEYWORDS Artificial Intelligence, Internet Magazines, Space Science
AUDIENCE Cyberpunks, Internet Users, Students (High School/Graduate), Writers
CONTACT Ed@21C.com.au
FREE

http://www.acci.com.au/21c/21c_homepage.html

ABCDEFG E-Zine ★★★

ABCDEFG E-Zine is a libertarian activist 'Zine, put out by Phillip Winn, a born-again Christian with a lot on his mind. A typical article from this irregularly published zine, sarcastically entitled 'Our Savior, Newt Gingrich,' exposes what Mr. Winn hates about The Speaker of the House - that he's too much of a normal liberal politician, and not enough of an anti-government revolutionary. Elsewhere the author defends his condemnation of the FCC, and wrestles with the countless ethical conflicts that arise in someone who wants unlimited freedom AND a nationally enforced Christian moral code.

KEYWORDS E-Zines, Libertarianism, Political Commentary
AUDIENCE Christians, Libertarians, Political Activists
CONTACT Phillip Winn
         pwinn@dakota.net
FREE

http://www.dakota.net/~pwinn/abcdefg/

Alternative X-Home Page ★★★

This is an online magazine about Generation X (people aged from late teens to 20s') and counterculture themes, with emphasis on literary and artistic expression. It contains columns, excerpts and profiles, plus info on Black Ice Fiction, an avant-pop publisher.

KEYWORDS Contemporary Literature, Generation X, Internet Magazines, Zines
AUDIENCE General Public, Generation X, Internet Users, Popular Culture Enthusiasts
CONTACT X@marketplace.com
FREE

http://marketplace.com/0/alt.x/althome.html

Asahi Shimbun ★★★

Asahi Shimbun is an online version of the Asahi Shimbun News of Tokyo. This site is the English online version of Japan's second largest newspaper. This is an orderly site with links for current news, news releases, and information from the newsroom, along with abundant photographs and colorful graphics. Also included is the ASAMUL Test, an entertaining and educational test of the reader's multimedia and technological literacy.

KEYWORDS International News, Japan, News
AUDIENCE International Business Professionals, Japanese Culture Enthusiasts
CONTACT Asahi Shimbun
         newsroom@mx.asahi-np.co.jp
FREE

http://www.asahi.com/english/english.html

Bad Subjects ★★★

This gopher provides access to an online political magazine called Bad Subjects. Bad Subjects discusses leftist-socialist politics and the study of popular culture. The server is located at the University of California at Berkeley. It contains issues from 1992-1995, policy discussions, and links to further distribution sites.

KEYWORDS Humanities, Magazines, Politics
AUDIENCE Educators (University), Political Activists, Students (Secondary/University)
CONTACT badsubjects-request@uclink.berkeley.edu
FREE

gopher://uclink.berkeley.edu:52673/

Beat Magazine ★★★

Beat Magazine is an online magazine sponsored by Australia Online which provides entertainment and cultural news. It contains features, reviews and listings of music film, and art events throughout Australia, and specifically in Sydney and Melbourne. It is updated weekly on Wednesdays.

KEYWORDS Australia, Online Magazines
AUDIENCE Australian Music Enthusiasts, Music Enthusiasts
CONTACT Beat Magazine
         beat@ozonline.com.au
FREE

http://www.ozonline.com.au/beat/

Best Of Free Spirit Magazine ★★★

Free Spirit is a journal of personal transformation. It is designed to present stimulating ideas and resources for people who are on a pathway of personal growth. Free Spirit has print editions in New York and Los Angeles, and has an extensive marketplace section for those looking for professional services, products, events and gatherings in the community. Online viewers will be able to access selected articles, such as Food And Your Health and the WoodStock Journal. An up to date New York City Community Calendar advertises services and events such as Meditation, Kung Fu, Stretching, Dance, Yoga, Women's Support, and more.

KEYWORDS Mental Health, Personal Transformation, Self Help Programs, Vegetarianism
AUDIENCE Counselors, New York City Vegetarians, New York Residents, Vegetarians
CONTACT TAG Online Mall
         webmaster@tagsys.com
FREE

http://www.tagsys.com:80/Ads/FreeSpirit/

Capital Homepage ★★★

This site is the online version of The Capital newspaper, serving the Annapolis, Maryland area. Local Entertainment, Home Improvement, Sports, and the nearby U.S. Naval Academy are some of the paper's regular topics. There is also a Business section, a Home Computing page, and plans are in the works for Personals and Classified sections. Some areas available here, but not in the print version of the Capital, are a 1995 calendar of local events, searchable archives, and links to interesting items around the Internet.

KEYWORDS Maryland, Navy, News, Online Newspapers
AUDIENCE Maryland Residents, News Readers
CONTACT InfiNet, L.C.
         www@infi.net
FREE

http://www.infi.net/capital/

China News Digest ★★★★

This is a gopher for an organization aimed at providing news and information about China and China-related affairs. Recent issues of their magazine are available (in Chinese) as are images of China and links to other China-related servers.

KEYWORDS China, Chinese Language, Chinese Studies, Electronic Publishing
AUDIENCE Chinese, International Development Specialists, International Students, Students
CONTACT admin@cnd.org
FREE

gopher://cnd.org/

ClariNet e.News ★★★

ClariNet Communications Corp. publishes the ClariNet e.News, a commercial electronic news service on the Internet. The e.News offers general, international, sports, technology, entertainment and financial news, as well as special features, comics, and columns. Sources for e.News include AP/Reuters News, Techwire, Newsbytes, Matrix News, and Bay City News (San Francisco Bay Area) as well as the ClariNet Stock report, covering computer and technology stocks.

KEYWORDS Electronic Media, Internet Publications, News
AUDIENCE Californians, Internet Access Providers, Journalists, News Readers
CONTACT webmaster@clarinet.com
COST

http://www.clarinet.com/

Daily News - Free Internet Sources ★★

This page is an index of places on the Internet that publish publicly accessible and significant news on a daily basis. Users will find links to news services covering all areas of the globe, as well as specialty news outlets providing weather updates, Internet news, and more. This server also provides information on radio and television news sources, as well as material for aspiring journalists and a list of alternative news sources.

KEYWORDS Current Events, Internet Directories, Journalism, Media, News Media
AUDIENCE General Public, Journalists, Media Professionals, News Buffs
CONTACT Sam Sternberg
         samsam@vm1.yorku.ca
FREE

http://www.helsinki.fi/~lsaarine/news.html

534 Magazines & Newspapers

gopher://gopher.nstn.ca:70/11/Cybrary/News/news

 Der Spiegel ★★★

Der Spiegel is the online home of the German news magazine. It includes articles from the current and past issues of the print edition of Der Spiegel, covering topics such as German political coalitions, and the international criminal, Jurgen Schneider. Also provided is information about the Internet, as well as links to numerous other online magazines and newspapers. An order form is given for people interested in subscribing to the print version.

Keywords Der Spiegel, Germany, International News, Magazines
Audience Germans
Contact 74431.736@compuserve.com
Free

http://www.hamburg.pop.de/bda/int/spiegel/

 Detroit Free Press ★

The Detroit Free Press maintains this page as a service to journalists, researchers and other members of the public looking for information regarding Detroit, Michigan, and the newspaper itself. Users can find contact information for reporters and departments of the newspaper, but not current articles. There are a number of links to outside resources such as gopher sites and weather information.

Keywords Journalism, Michigan, Online Newspapers
Audience Information Professionals, Journalists, Michigan Residents
Free

http://gopher.det-freepress.com:9002/

 Die Tageszeitung ★★★

Die Tageszeitung is a young and liberal daily German newspaper from Berlin. The web site contains articles from the newspaper, updated on a daily basis. Articles are organized according to topic - front page news, domestic news, economy, world news, literature, Berlin news, and more. Readers can also scroll through lists of headlines and article summaries. Also included is the comic strip Tom and special photo highlights.

Keywords Germany, International News
Audience Germans, Researchers, Tourists
Contact taz@prz.tu-berlin.de
Free

http://www.prz.tu-berlin.de:80/~taz/

 Die Welt ★★★

Die Welt is a large conservative daily newspaper from Berlin, Germany. After 8pm German time, the reader can find news articles from the next day's morning edition. News is organized by topic - world news, front page news, German news, culture, economy, and sports. The user can also browse a list of headlines with brief article summaries.

Keywords Germany, International News, Tourism
Audience Germans, Researchers, Tourists

Contact Michael Fuchs
fuchs@www.welt.de
Free

http://www.welt.de/welcome.html

ETEXT Archives ★★★

The ETEXT Archives contains pointers to electronic periodicals of all kinds including Electronic Books, a mirror of the Computer Professionals for Social Responsibility archives, political material ranging from zines to essays, a mirror of the computer underground digest archives, mailing lists archived by month, mainstream and not-so-mainstream religious periodicals and texts, sports information including Dorian Kim's baseball archives, and legal documents and essays.

Keywords Archives, E-Zines, Journals, Social Responsibility
Audience Computer Users, Educators (University), Internet Users, Researchers, Students (University)
Contact www@etext.org
Free

http://ftp.etext.org

 Electronic Telegraph ★★★★

This page is the online version of the Daily Telegraph, published in London, England. The user can access the Telegraph's front page stories, city, national and international news pages, sports, and special features. Many stories contain links to related articles and opinion pieces. In addition, there is an archive of previous issues dating back to November, 1994. A Marketplace section of this online newspaper contains advertisements for commercial companies and enterprises.

Keywords International News, Journalism, London, Online Newspapers
Audience Anglophiles, British, Europeans, Journalists, News Readers, United Kingdoms Residents
Contact webmaster@telegraph.co.uk
Free

http://www.telegraph.co.uk/

Eye Magazine ★★★

Eye Magazine contains information about the arts and entertainment in Toronto and southern Ontario. Eye focuses on alternative politics and entertainment news, film, theatre, music, comedy, dance, and photography. Most issues contain diverse art reviews and feature articles as well as archives that contain past columns and issues, such as a collection of eye's Enviro columns from Bob Hunter, co-founder of Greenpeace and ecology specialist with CITY-TV.

Keywords Art Criticism, Movie Reviews, Music, Theater Reviews
Audience Arts Community, Canada Residents, General Public, Tourists
Contact eye@interlog.com
Free

http://www.interlog.com/eye/

 Feed ★★★★

The editors of Feed, an online magazine, seek to create a journal that 'probes the mentality of contemporary technoculture and politics.' The inaugural issue contains analyses by several commentators on Newt Gengrich's Reinhardt lectures, electronic roundtable discussions, and a feature article on the New Zealand rock music scene. Commentators in the initial issue include Dr. George Keyworth, Dr Alvin Toffler and Ester Dyson.

Keywords Internet, Political Commentary, Satire
Audience Activists, General Public, Internet Users
Contact Steve Johnson
feed@emedia.net
Free

http://www.emedia.net/feed/

 Free Spirit Magazine ★★★

Free Spirit magazine's web pages present a few selected articles from the printed version as well as subscription and rate information. The magazine itself deals with a wide array of personal development, growth and spirituality issues.

Keywords New Age Philosophy, Spirituality
Audience New Age Enthusiasts, New Age Music Enthusiasts, Popular Culture Enthusiasts
Contact office@tagsys.com
Free

http://www.tagsys.com/Ads/FreeSpirit/

 GSB Online ★★★

GSB Online is the Web site of Graeme Bennett, managing editor of Canada's largest monthly computer magazine, 'The Computer Paper.' Here you'll find a wealth of computer information, nifty Web Tricks, crossword puzzles, riddles, QuickTime movies, children's stories, MIDI files, RealAudio broadcasts, plays, and artwork. This site offers three different graphical interfaces designed for Macintosh, Windows, and OS/2 users.

Keywords Computer Magazines, Online Magazines, Windows
Audience Children, Computer Users, Musicians, Publishers
Contact Graeme Bennett
graeme@tcp.mindlink.bc.ca
Free

http://tcp.ca/gsb

 The Gate ★★★

The online editions of the San Francisco Chronicle and the San Francisco Examiner are combined on this site. Readers will find the daily versions of these newspapers, including News, Business, Sports, Editorial, and Datebook sections. The articles of both newspapers are arranged into areas like columnists, cybersports, the Internet, and Here and Now. Related links are included in each section, such as specific sports related links in the Cybersports section. In addition, viewers can peruse the combined classified advertisements.

Keywords California, News, Online Newspapers
Audience Californians, Journalists, News readers

FREE
http://sfgate.com/

Halifax Herald Limited ★★

This server provides readers with timely, relevant coverage of events, issues and people that are important to Nova Scotians. At its NewsCentre page, you can view samples of stories from current editions of The Chronicle-Herald or The Mail-Star, send news tips, letters to the editor, and/or comments. In addition, you can get contact numbers for the reporters and staff, as well as subscription information about related information services. Links to services outside of this site include tourism pages for Nova Scotia, New Brunswick, and Prince Edward Island.

KEYWORDS Canada, News, Nova Scotia, Online Newspapers
AUDIENCE Canada Residents, Canadians, News Readers, Tourists
FREE
http://www.herald.ns.ca/

The Herald Sun ★★★★

The Herald Sun is Australia's largest selling newspaper (Melbourne), and currently has its computer and technology section, Get Wired, online. This site contains links to other sites on the net, an extensive Games Guide, reviews of the latest software and hardware, and much more. It also features a Gadgets, Chip Chat, Computer Features, Cool Sites sections, and a Seminar Room. Quite intelligent and graphic intensive.

KEYWORDS Australia, Computers, Online Newspapers, Technology
AUDIENCE Australians, International Business Professionals, Technology Enthusiasts
CONTACT   Jason Hill
          jhill@ozonline.com.au
FREE
http://www.ozonline.com.au/getwired

Hip Webzine ★★★★

Hip magazine's graphic-intense web pages contain a large collection of humor writing, poetry from a number of different sources, and some short fiction. Regular features also include columns, letters, and reviews of various media.

KEYWORDS Fiction, Poetry
AUDIENCE Poets, Reading Enthusiasts, Writers
CONTACT   systems@hip.com
FREE
http://www.hip.com/cover.htm

The Hitlist ★★★★

Billing itself as 'the next step and last stop for hiphop,' The Hitlist is a monthly magazine that contains articles, links to artist homepages, downloadable samples and video images from a wide variety of hiphop artists, and much more.

KEYWORDS Hip-Hop, Music, Rap Music
AUDIENCE Hiphop Enthusiasts, Musicians, Rap Music Enthusiasts

---

Connections to Confession Booths
To err is human

Having an affair with your best-friend's wife? Stole a pen from the company's supply cabinet, or an ashtray from a hotel? There's a way to tell someone about your "sins" and get them off your chest. You can do it on the Internet—and anonymously! It's the next best thing to going on a television talk show and really embarrassing yourself.

These areas on the Internet are heavily copyrighted, and are designed for those people grappling with a guilty conscience. You can admit your incessant slothing at work or your lies to impress people, confess to having back-stabbed a coworker in the office or "murdered" someone for not paying back a personal loan. You won't get off easily, however. Those who come to the confession booths must "pay" for their sins. The "digital" priest hands out atonement, and it ranges (depending on the severity of your sin) from learning the chemical elements table to reciting a Shakespearean sonnet. You might even have to write a thousand times, "I will not lie again." You can enter an Internet Confession Booth via The Scroll Of Sins' multiple sites.

(http://bashir.til.tu-harburg.de/priest.html)

also, (http://anther.learning.cs.cmu.edu/sinscroll2.html)

also, (http://anther.learning.cs.cmu.edu/sinscroll.html)

CONTACT Hitlist Editor
         aja@cldc.howard.edu
FREE
http://www.cldc.howard.edu/%7Eaja/hitlist/

Inquisitor Magazine ★★★

A quarterly magazine on numerous subjects, Inquisitor's tongue-in-cheek articles deal with such topics as Godzilla, New York City, marketing, women and language, and 'recursive television.'

KEYWORDS Culture, Technology
AUDIENCE Esoterica Enthusiasts, New York Residents, Reading Enthusiasts

CONTACT   Laurel Sutton
          inquisitor@echonyc.com
FREE
http://mosaic.echonyc.com/~xixax/Inquisitor/

Inside Cable Magazine ★★★★

This site offers a selection of articles from the Inside Cable Magazine. This information is dedicated exclusively to reporting the UK cable industry and its services, including local programming and the development of local services.

KEYWORDS Cable Industry, Television, United Kingdom
AUDIENCE Communications Specialists, Mass Communications Students, Mass Communications Technicians

536 Magazines & Newspapers

FREE
http://scitsc.wlv.ac.uk/university/sles/sm/incable.html

Insider - North Carolina State Government News Service ★★

This page hosts The Inside, a commercial service of The News & Observer Co, based in North Carolina. Issues are published five days a week, although there is a one-week lag time before it is freely available on this network. Each issue contains a news summary, a review of activities in North Carolina's House and Senate, schedules for various utility and advisory committees, and calendars for the North Carolina Supreme Court. In addition, civic information such as contact information for local legislators, poll results, and a hospitalization charges guide for North Carolina are listed.

KEYWORDS   Government Documents, North Carolina
AUDIENCE   Activists, Community Leaders, North Carolina Residents, Political Scientists
CONTACT   webmasters@merlin.nando.net
FREE

http://www.nando.net/insider/insiders.html

The Insider ★★★

The Insider is a department of the online version of People Magazine, offering 'inside information' about the lives and relationships of Hollywood stars. Updated weekly, the service has recently featured short pieces on Jim Carrey's divorce, Florence Henderson, and the owners of the Planet Hollywood restaurants.

KEYWORDS   Celebrities, Hollywood, People Magazine
AUDIENCE   Celebrity Enthusiasts, Film Enthusiasts, Gossips
CONTACT   People Webmaster
           people-webmaster@pathfinder.com
FREE

http://bigmouth.pathfinder.com:80/people/950227/insider.html

InterFace Magazine ★★★

Dedicated to exploring creative uses for new technology, this Vancouver, Canada-based magazine (also available in printed form) showcases digital art, and articles by and for those who work or play with computers that are not what the editors call 'technobabble'. New features on this Web site include 'virtual resumes' and a gallery of artwork by artists on the Internet, a classified ads section, and more.

KEYWORDS   Computer Art, Journalism, Magazines, Technology
AUDIENCE   Computer Artists, General Public, Technology Enthusiasts
CONTACT   Robert McCourty
           interface@dataflux.bc.ca
FREE

http://www.dataflux.bc.ca/v3/interface/

International Teletimes ★★

Teletimes is a bi-monthly general interest and culture magazine which showcases different ideas and viewpoints from around the world. Readers can also contribute submissions such as articles, photographs, and graphics that address the specific topic for the month. Previous themes have been Problems in Education, Tourism, and Political Systems. Another section exists for semi-regular topics such as Films, Cuisine, and Music Notes. The 'World' section offers content with international scope which is independent of the issue's theme.

KEYWORDS   Cultural Exchange, International Communications, Photography
AUDIENCE   Artists, International Travelers, Photographers, Reading Enthusiasts, Writers
CONTACT   Joe Germuska, HTML Consultant
           j-germuska@nwu.edu
FREE

http://www.wimsey.com/teletimes.root/teletimes_home_page.html

Irish Times On The Web ★★★

This is the index to The Irish Times On The Web newspaper in electronic form. Topics include news, sports, finance, and editorials. Archives go back two months and are searchable by date.

KEYWORDS   Ireland, News, Online Newspapers
AUDIENCE   Irish
CONTACT   Stephen Barrett
           postmaster@irish-times.ie
FREE

http://www.ieunet.ie/ois/irishtimes/index.shtml

The Jerusalem Post ★★★★

The Jerusalem Post is Israel's only English-language daily newspaper. Its site includes news, opinion, business, people and places, marketplace, what's happening, and columns.

KEYWORDS   International News, Israel, Middle East, Online Newspapers
AUDIENCE   International Business Professionals, Israelis, Jews, Tourists
CONTACT   Nina Keren-David or Derek Fattal
           jpost@zeus.datasrv.co.il
FREE

http://www.jpost.co.il/

John Labovitz's E-zine-List ★★★

This is a directory of electronic magazines that are generally non-mainstream and mostly published by a small group of people for fun or personal reasons. Titles range from Netsurfer Digest, St. Louis Sports Online, The Weekly Something or Other, to SMILE, Quanta, and the Smashing Pumpkins e-zine. There are short descriptions, contact information and links for each of the sites.

KEYWORDS   Directories, E-Zines, Internet Magazines, Internet Publishing
AUDIENCE   Cyberpunks, Popular Culture Enthusiasts
CONTACT   John Labovitz
           johnl@ora.com
FREE

http://www.meer.net/~johnl/e-zine-list/index.html

Kyodo Cyber Express ★★

Kyodo News is a well known international news agency based in Japan. In this experimental Kyodo Cyber Express, the viewer is offered a choice of news and features from Kyodo's operations. There are contact sheets of photographs from the Kobe Earthquake of 1995, which can be clicked on to bring up full-size images with captions. Under constuction is a World Heritage page, linking the viewer to pictures and stories about areas such as the Grand Canyon, the Great Barrier Reef, and Istanbul.

KEYWORDS   Geography, International News, Online Newspapers, Tourism
AUDIENCE   Asian Studies Students, Asians, Journalists, Photographers, Tourists
CONTACT   Cyber Publishing Japan server
           feedback@tmc.toppan.co.jp
FREE

http://www.toppan.co.jp/kyodo/

La Nacion ★★★★

This online version of La Nacion, a newspaper from the Costa Rican capital of San Jose, provides local, regional, and international news coverage. Naturally the main edition is in Spanish, but the site has a link to English-language news briefs. The site is fairly slick in appearance, with photos and interesting graphics, and a variety of coverage areas. Financial news of the Latin American world receives considerable attention.

KEYWORDS   Costa Rica, International News, Latin America, Online Newspapers
AUDIENCE   Central Americans, Costa Ricans, International Business Professionals, Tourists
CONTACT   webmaster@nacion.co.cr
FREE

http://www.nacion.co.cr/

 The Lynx Magazine ★★

The Lynx states that its mission is 'to publish a real magazine on the World Wide Web on a regular basis.' The magazine covers the more alternative sides of the Web and the Internet, and aims to be amusing, informative, and slightly anarchic. Issue #1 covered the WWW '94 conference.

KEYWORDS   Magazines, WWW (World Wide Web)
AUDIENCE   Internet Users
CONTACT   Tony Jewell
           tony@cityscape.co.uk
FREE

http://www.gold.net/lynx/

M.E.N. Magazine ★★★

M.E.N. Magazine is published by Seattle M.E.N., Men's Evolvement Network, whose mission is to provide 'information, support and advocacy for men.' It has a national as well as regional focus. Pages for viewers to peruse include Men's stories, Articles, Poetry, Humor, and Editorials. Articles have focused on men and grief, domestic violence, gender reconciliation, love and betrayal, recovering from the wounds of child sexual abuse, drumming and the use of Native American traditions, and reports on national men's conferences. Commentary such as Where are We Going, Letters to the Editor, and Editorials present a variety of opinions about men's issues. In addition, there is a page of conference and event listings, as well as a large collection of reviews of books, audio materials, and videotapes.

KEYWORDS Gender Issues, Health Services, Men, Men's Issues
AUDIENCE Men, Sociologists, Women
CONTACT menmag@wln.com
FREE

http://info-sys.home.vix.com/menmag/

Connections to the Witchcraft and the Occult
"Double, Double toil and trouble…"

Whether your knowledge of witches, witchcraft and the occult comes from the American television program "Bewitched" or from Shakespeare's "MacBeth," you can find the more serious side of witches and witchcraft on the Internet.

Witches have come out of the "broom closet" to educate the public on the religion of Wicca and the historical roots of modern practices. You can get in touch with Wiccan religious organizations around the world—from Europe to Australia. Many sites, like "About Witchcraft, Witchcraft—General Practices," provide a wide range of information.

(http://www.cog.org/cog/general/iabout.html)

also, (http://www.cog.org.cog.general/iprac.html)

There are also a variety of Wicca FAQs (frequently asked questions) and pagan news-groups. You can retrieve a list of witches in Belgium from the 13th to 16th centuries. You can obtain descriptions of people accused of witchcraft, as well as a time line of important events in the history of witchcraft. If you're interested, check out the list of pagan festivals at "Joan's Witch Directory."

(http://www.ucmb.ulb.ac.be/~joan/witches/witch_dir.html)

Masthead ★★★

Cyberkind is an online literary magagine that focus on poetry, prose and art. Its current issue includes 15 sundry nonfiction articles, six pieces of short fiction, seven poems and three GIF art images.

KEYWORDS Contemporary Literature, Internet Publishing
AUDIENCE Book Readers, Literary Critics, Online Publishers, Publishing Professionals
CONTACT Shannon Turlington
shannon@sunsite.unc.edu
FREE

http://sunsite.unc.edu/ckind/

Media List ★★★

The Media List is a text-based listing of newspapers, magazines, newsletters, TV and radio stations, and other media outlets that accept submissions via email. It indexes the outlets by media type, listing each alphabetically, and provides email contact addresses. The List contains addresses for media organizations around the world, but focuses primarily on U.S. media outlets. Organizations that have more than one department with email are fully indexed.

KEYWORDS Mass Media, Media
AUDIENCE Communications Researchers, General Public, Media Professionals
CONTACT Adam Gaffin
adamg@world.std.com
FREE

ftp://ftp.std.com/customers/periodicals/Middlesex-News/medialist

Melvin Electronic Magazine ★★★

This biweekly magazine turns pop culture on its head with a collection of stories, blurbs, and news articles for Internet surfers. Sections of Melvin include homegrown news stories, interviews with music artists, and hypertextual articles that are humorous, self-promotional, and a change of pace from the standard Net fare. There are marketplace areas of this online magazine, as well as surveys and sweepstakes to enter.

KEYWORDS Internet Magazines, News, Popular Culture, Zines
AUDIENCE Adults, Artists, Multimedia Enthusiasts, Web Designers, Web Users
CONTACT info@melvin.com
FREE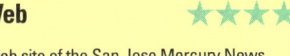

http://www.melvin.com/

Mercury Center Web ★★★★

This is the web site of the San Jose Mercury News which contains the text contents of the newspaper and some photos. The site is updated daily and includes late-breaking wire service reports. Also included are links to Internet-specific information and advertisers.

KEYWORDS Online Newspapers, Silicon Valley
AUDIENCE Californians
CONTACT Bill Mitchell
bmitch@sjmercury.com
FREE

http://www.sjmercury.com/

Milford Cabinet and Wilton Journal ★★★

The Milford Cabinet and Wilton Journal is a weekly online newspaper serving the southern New Hampshire area. The home page provides links to back issues of weekly front pages, a town index of local news stories, and town hall information for areas covered by the newspaper. There are links to the rest of the newspaper including classifieds, editorials and the Southern New Hampshire Business Directory.

KEYWORDS Community Information, Community Networking, Electronic Publishing, Newspapers
AUDIENCE Community Networkers, Journalists, New Hampshire Residents
CONTACT John Leslie Consulting
support@jlc.net
FREE

http://www.cabinet.com/Cabinet/Home.html

Mofile Place ★★★★

Mofile Place is an online magazine that discusses all aspects of Finnish news and culture. Regular sections include music reviews, religious information, interviews with important Finnish businessmen and politicians, and art by Finnish artists and photographers. Business and commerce in Finland is also covered, with directories of companies, economic forecasts, and information brokers. There's current news from Finland, and sports updates, as well as general background materials.

KEYWORDS Cultural Studies, Finland, News, Travel
AUDIENCE Cultural Studies Enthusiasts, Finns, Travelers
CONTACT Jarno Tarkoma
webmaster@mofile.fi
FREE

http://mofile.fi/

Money and Investing Update ★★★★

Money and Investing Update is the online source of financial news and analysis from The Wall Street Journal. The site provides continuous update of financial and market news, market columns and features, and access to past copies of the newspaper covering personal finance, investing, taxes, and more. The service is initially free but will be by subscription basis only at some point in the future.

KEYWORDS Investments, Newspapers, Personal Finance
AUDIENCE Business Professionals, Businesswomen, Educators, Investors, Market Analysts

CONTACT Neil Budde
         budde@nrs.dowjones.com
COST

http://update.wsj.com/

Mother Jones Magazine and Mother Jones Interactive ★★★

Mother Jones Interactive, the 'digital sister' of Mother Jones magazine, provides a wide array of articles with advice for grass-roots activists hoping to tackle social problems in America. These web pages also carry the entire text of the most recent issue of the magazine, and an archive of a few back issues.

KEYWORDS Activism, Magazines
AUDIENCE Activists, Liberals
CONTACT   Editor
          backtalk@mojones.com
FREE

http://www.mojones.com/

NandO.Net ★★★★

This server hosts the online editions of the News and Observer (NandO), based in North Carolina, USA. Users can see a digest of international, national, business, technology, and sports stories. Articles within these categories are archived on the daily digest page. In addition to news reporting, there are varied features sponsored through Nando.Net. For example, the Cyrano server creates email love letters; The Jesse Helms Sampler provides an archive of North Carolina's outspoken senator; and North Carolina Discoveries highlights a summer of traveling through the Tar Heel State. A number of professional marketing and media organizations can be found here as well.

KEYWORDS Business, International News, North Carolina, Sports
AUDIENCE Business Professionals, Conservatives, Lovers, News Readers, North Carolina Residents
CONTACT   webmasters@merlin.nando.net
FREE

http://www.nando.net/

NetMedia by Karl Rademacher ★★

The NetMedia list is a plaintext listing of newspapers and other mass media outlets that have some form of Internet contact. It primarily contains media organizations' email addresses. The list is organized geographically, with entries from all over the world, focusing primarily on United States media outlets. There is also a section of organizations that either cannot be classified geographically or were not classified at the time of the list's publishing.

KEYWORDS Communications, Mass Media, News Media, Publishing
AUDIENCE Communications Professionals, Media Professionals

CONTACT Karl Rademacher
         gsu0010@bgu.edu
FREE

http://www.jou.ufl.edu/commres/netmedia.htm

Newspaper and Journalism Links ★★★

This page is a collection of links to newpapers and journalism resources on the Internet. The primary focus is on college and high school publications, but there are links for commercial publications as well as TV and radio resources. Users will also find information and links on other journalism resources on the Internet.

KEYWORDS Electronic Media, Journalism, News Media, Online Newspapers
AUDIENCE Journalists, Media Professionals, Newspaper Publishers, Students
CONTACT   Kelly Campbell
          camk@ksu.ksu.edu
FREE

http://www.spub.ksu.edu/other/journ.html

Omphalos Magazine ★★★

A journal of speculative fiction, Omphalos presents a large number of reviews of new science fiction and fantasy books and magazines, as well as commentary on the SF genre by Editor John Leavitt.

KEYWORDS Books, Fiction, Magazines, Science Fiction
AUDIENCE Science Fiction Enthusiasts, Writers
CONTACT   John Leavitt, Editor
          jrrl@cs.cmu.edu
FREE

http://thule.mt.cs.cmu.edu:8001/sf-clearing-house/zines/omphalos/

Online Newspapers ★★★★

This page is devoted to newspaper publishers with online services. There are many types of online services including—Newspaper local dial-up services (BBSs), Newspaper services on commercial online services (America Online, Compuserve, etc.), US dailies/US weeklies and others/Links only to all papers, and miscellaneous electronic newspaper services. The site also provides links to free news services available online including college newspapers and consultants.

KEYWORDS Journalism, Media, News, Online Newspapers
AUDIENCE News Buffs
CONTACT   Steve Outing
          outings@netcom.com
FREE

http://marketplace.com/e-papers.list.www/e-papers.home.page.html

PC Week ★★★

This page is the free online version of PC Week, the National Newspaper of Corporate Computing, published by Ziff Davis. PC Week Online covers the week's top stories about PC hardware, PC software, PC vendors, new product releases, and PC related events. It includes weekly columns such as Rumor Central and Coop's Corner, and features PC Week Labs, a hands-on software and hardware evaluation forum. PC Week's FAQ answers questions about both online and print versions of the publication.

KEYWORDS Online Magazines, Ziff-Davis Publishing
AUDIENCE PC Engineers, PC Programmers, PC Users, Windows Users
CONTACT   Jeffrey Frentzen
          jfrentzen@pcweek.ziff.com
FREE

http://www.pcweek.ziff.com/~pcweek/

Pathfinder ★★★★

Pathfinder is an index to Time Warner publications online. It includes, Time, Vibe, Sports Illustrated, Money, Fortune, and the Virtual Garden. Also provided are email addresses for the editors, bulletin boards on Finance, MultiMedia, and more.

KEYWORDS Journalism, Popular Culture
AUDIENCE Educators, Graphic Artists, Publishers, Students, Writers
CONTACT   webmaster@pathfinder.com
FREE

http://www.timeinc.com/pathfinder/Home_low.html

People Magazine ★★★

This page hosts the online version of People Magazine. The top stories and cover pages are available online. Other sections for readers to browse are the Insiders, a gossip column; Passages, which reports milestones in the entertainment world; Chatter, which list quotations attributed to celebrities, and Pics and Pans, a review of recent televison shows, movies, music releases and books. There is a searchable index as well as a link to Bulletin Boards where people can exchange opinions about topics in the news and popular culture.

KEYWORDS Celebrities, Internet Magazines, People Magazine, Television
AUDIENCE Magazine Readers, Movie Enthusiasts, Television Enthusiasts
CONTACT   people-webmaster@pathfinder.com
FREE

http://pathfinder.com/people/Welcome.html

Progressive Magazines and OnLine News Services ★★★

This page provides a list of links to progressive magazines and online news services. Some of the links include CrossRoads, Bad Subjects, FAIR—Fairness & Accuracy in Reporting, Mother Jones Magazine, News for a People's World—SF Bay Area Progressive Newspaper, AlterNet—News on the Culture War, and more.

KEYWORDS Internet Magazines, Journalism, News, Progressive Magazines
AUDIENCE Community Activists, Nonprofit Organaizations, Political Activists, Progressives

CONTACT edinlinks@garnet.berkeley.edu
FREE

http://garnet.berkeley.edu:3333/.mags/.mags.html

Putrid Afterthought ★★★★

Putrid Afterthought is a Web-based art zine that reflects the darker side of American culture. Users will find art and stories under such headings as 'Internet Crime Archives,' 'Generation Hex,' and 'Digichrist.' Those who are easily offended should avoid visiting this site. The thicker-skinned will enjoy the dark humor and irreverence that this site displays.

KEYWORDS Humor
AUDIENCE Counterculture Enthusiasts, Popular Culture Enthusiasts
CONTACT Antonio Mendoza
elvision@earthlink.net
FREE

http://underground.net/Art/mendoza.html

Quill Magazine ★★★

This site offers an online sample of the Quill Magazine, a publication of the Society of Professional Journalists. It contains news and information of interest to the journalistic community, such as ethical perspectives on current news stories, Freedom of Information issues, and more. There is also information on trade conferences, journalism workshops, and other timely resources of interest to journalism professionals.

KEYWORDS Internet Magazines, Journalism, Mass Media, Media
AUDIENCE Communications Professionals, Journalists, News Buffs, Students
CONTACT Brian Steffens
76330.1376@CompuServe.Com
FREE

ftp://ftp.netcom.com/pub/sp/spj/html/quill.html

Shift Online Magazine ★★★

Shift Online presents numerous resources for those interested or involved in the creation and dissemination of new interactive media and the use of new technologies to enhance existing mediums of communication. The magazine also offers a 'toolbox' where readers can download the latest freely-distributable versions of the Mosaic and Netscape browsers.

KEYWORDS Interactive Media, Interactivity, New Media
AUDIENCE Interactive Program Developers, Multimedia Enthusiasts, Musicians, New Media Artists
CONTACT info@shift.com
FREE

http://www.e-commerce.com/Shift.home

Shogakukan Bookshop ★★

Shogakukan is a Japanese publisher of magazines for children, comic magazines, weeklies, dictionaries, encyclopedias and art books. Their home page provides access to a selection of articles from publications such as Japan's 'Weekly Post' and 'Sapio' on Asian life and culture. Users can also access information on new products available in Japan as well as on upcoming Japanese events. A version of the site is available in Japanese as well as in English.

KEYWORDS International News, Japanese Culture, Japanese News
AUDIENCE Asian Culture Enthusiasts, Japanese, Japanese Speakers
FREE

http://www.toppan.co.jp/bookshop/

Southern Living ★★★

Southern Living is America's largest regional magazine. Each month, this online version provides the text and many of the graphics related to gardening and horticulture gleaned from the print version. Some of the articles that have recently appeared include 'Great Garden Shops' (across the South) and 'The Season's First Flowers,' a guide to flower arranging. There are links to other gardening magazines like Sunset Magazine and Homeground.

KEYWORDS Gardening, Horticulture, Internet Magazines, Southern Culture (US)
AUDIENCE Gardeners, Home Owners, Horticulturalists, News Readers

---

Connections To Channeling and Astrology
Elvis has channeled through me . . .

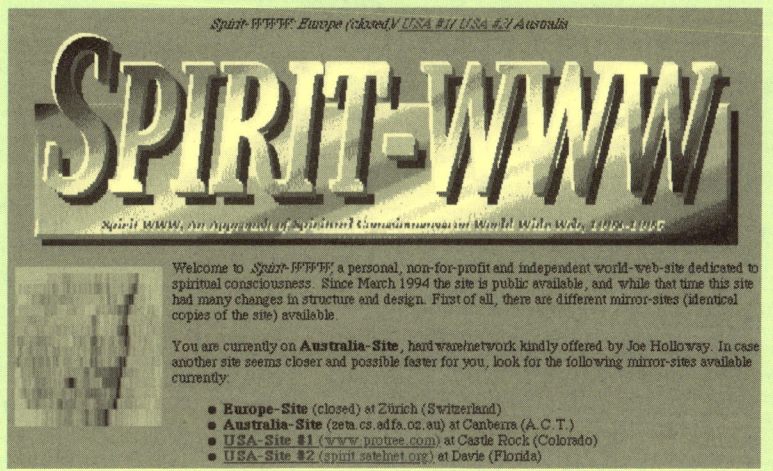

Ever felt like you had an out-of-body experience? Perhaps your interest lies in UFOs, or maybe you practice yoga. Now there's a way to connect with similar-minded folks online.

The "Spirit-WWW" site connects you to an area which focuses on, among other things, channeling (in which the spirit of a disembodied being enters the channeler's body to convey information to another person). Moreover, information on the study and philosophy of many Eastern and esoteric religions, as well as a section on reincarnation, are available at this site. Movie clips, new age music, astrological charts, and even calendars for religious observances around the world can also be found via Spirit-WWW.

(http://zeta.cs.adfa.oz.au/Spirit.html)

CONTACT vg-webmaster@www.timeinc.com
FREE

http://pathfinder.com:80/@@Uo8kU4BigwAAQD2r/vg/Magazine-Rack/SoLiving/

Spontaneous Combustion Webzine ★★★

These pages house the Web-based counterpart of Spontaneous Combustion, a magazine devoted to profiles of and interviews with punk and hardcore/alternative rock bands. Fans of bands such as Superconductor, The Offspring, and 7 Seconds will find this material of interest. Back issues of the 8-year-old magazine are also available in electronic form.

KEYWORDS Alternative Music, Punk Rock, Rock Music
AUDIENCE Alternative Music Enthusiasts, Musicians, Punks, Rock Fans
CONTACT Mike Fischer
mxv@spontaneous.com
FREE

http://www.interaccess.com/users/mxv/

Sports World ★★★★

Sports World provides up-to-date information on a variety of sports, including baseball, football, hockey,

Magazines & Newspapers

golf, racing, tennis, and more. There are special events hotlinks, such as the U.S. Open, Indianapolis 500, and discussion groups, schedules, statistics on all major sporting events. There is real-time up-to-the minute scores provided for games in progress, such as baseball, basketball, or football.

Keywords Baseball, Basketball, Football, Golf, Racing, Tennis
Audience Men, Sports Fans, Women
Contact webmaster@sportsworld.line.com
Free

http://199.97.97.3/cgi-bin/sports/

St. Petersburg Press Home Page

The St. Petersburg Press is a weekly newspaper with a print run of 15,000 copies. The front page of each online issue hosts a main story, photos and links to articles under Top Stories, News, Business, Commentary, Classified Ads, and Culture. The current issue and back issues, dating back to September 1994, are available online.

Keywords International News, Online Newspapers, Russia, St. Petersburg
Audience Florida Residents, News Readers, Russians, Tourists
Contact Nicholai Gluzdov ng@sppress.spb.su
Free

http://www.spb.su/sppress/index.html

StarPhoenix

The StarPhoenix is a mid-size daily newspaper in Saskatoon, Saskatchewan, Canada. It is currently building local news links you can enter such as The Newsroom—where you will find links to news sources in Canada, the U.S., and around the world. Other features include The Locker Room (sports), The Weather Office, the Cultural Center, the Board Room (business), the Market Place (advertising), the Theme Park (specialty publications and themed home pages), and the First Nations Home Page—a collection of links connecting First Nations resources on the Net. Finally, the Funky Site of the Day is a special treat.

Keywords Canada, Newspapers, Online Newspapers
Audience Canadians, International Business Professionals, Pop-Culture Enthusiasts
Contact Doug Lacombe dlacombe@eagle.wbm.ca
Free

http://www.wbm.ca/users/sphoenix/index.html

State51's Hub

An electronic counterpart to the monthly British magazine State51, this webzine covers humor, football (soccer in America), experiments in hypermedia and other uncategorizable material. State51 also contains within its rapidly changing pages jumping off points to a number of other British webzines and publications.

Keywords England, New Media
Audience English, Humor Enthusiasts, Soccer Fans
Contact Editor intouch@state51.demon.co.uk
Free

http://www.state51.co.uk/state51/hub.html

Sunset Magazine

Sunset is one of the America's largest regional magazines, and the publisher of Sunset's Western Garden Book, the preeminent horticultural reference work for Western gardeners. This page hosts the online edition, covering only the horticultural aspects of the magazine. (More coverage is planned in the future). Users can peruse articles like 'Sacramento's Most Colorful Public Garden' and 'Tomatoes that Stay in Bounds.' Currently, only the text from the magazine articles are available online.

Keywords Gardening, Horticulture, Internet Magazines, Magazines
Audience Californians, Gardeners, Home Owners, Horticulturalists, Magazine Readers, News Readers
Contact vg-webmaster@www.timeinc.com
Free

http://pathfinder.com:80/@@Uo8kU4BigwAAQD2r/vg/Magazine-Rack/Sunset/

Tico Times

The Tico Times is Central America's leading English-language weekly. Based in San Jose, Costa Rica, The Tico Times covers news, business, entertainment and travel in Costa Rica and neighboring countries. The online version provides a varied sampling of the weekly print edition. Departments include Top Stories, News Briefs, Business, Exploring Costa Rica, and Central America, among others. There are numerous links which are said to be updated every Friday.

Keywords Central America, Costa Rica, Online Newspapers
Audience Costa Ricans, International Business Professionals, Tourists
Contact Steve Outing outings@netcom.com
Free

http://infoweb.magi.com/calypso/ttimes.html

Time Magazine

This page provides the full text of each week's Time Magazine, a leading American newsmagazine. Photos and advertisements have been omitted. Viewers can use the Times On Capital Hill, a guide which displays how national representatives voted in Congress. Back issues dating to January 1994, are also available for browsing.

Keywords Media, Online Newspapers
Audience Magazine Readers, News Buffs
Contact time-webmaster@www.timeinc.com
Free

http://pathfinder.com:80/@@Jb@zCRDqGQMAQC@r/time/magazine/magazine.html

TimesFax Internet Edition (from The New York Times)

TimesFax Internet Edition is an electronically delivered version of TimesFax, the digest of The New York Times sent daily to over 150,000 readers around the world. This eight-page digest includes stories from the front page and business section, the top foreign and national stories of the day, as well as sports, a recent NYT crossword puzzle, and selections from the Times's editorial and Op-Ed pages. This free service requires an Adobe Acrobat Reader, which can be downloaded through this Web page.

Keywords Media, News, Online Newspapers
Audience Business Professionals, Crossword Enthusiasts, New York Times Enthusiasts
Free

http://nytimesfax.com/

To Be Continued

To Be Continued is an all-text magazine of science-fiction and fantasy stories, articles and book reviews with a hypertext index page that gives access to a number of back issues as well as the current issue.

Keywords Fantasy, Fiction, Science Fiction
Audience Reading Enthusiasts, Science Fiction Enthusiasts
Contact R. Allen Jervis, co-director voyager@irishmvs.cc.nd.edu
Free

http://thule.mt.cs.cmu.edu:8001/sf-clearing-house/zines/to-be-continued/

USA Today

USA Today provides an up-to-date version of the national newspaper, major stories in news, sports, money, life, and weather. The online version is graphically a copy of the day's version but is available through subscription only.

Keywords International News, Newspapers, United States
Audience Educators, Reading Enthusiasts, Sports Fans, Students
Cost

http://www.usatoday.com/

Undaground Rap Blastin' Asiatic Newsletter (URBAN)

Every issue of URBAN contains humorous reviews of albums and new films. There are many articles about hacking and various technologies (e.g., voice mail boxes) and other minor mischief.

Keywords Film, Hacking, Hip-Hop, Rap Music
Audience Computer Hackers, Hip-Hop Enthusiasts, Rap Music Enthusiasts
Contact mtc@gagme.wwa.com
Free

gopher://gopher.etext.org/11/Zines/Urban/

Urban Desires Magazine ★★★

Urban Desires is an extensive collection of reviews, articles, book excerpts, reprints from other magazines and media, and original fiction and reporting. Subjects range from the sex industry and drugs, to literature and journalism.

- KEYWORDS: Contemporary Literature, Culture, Journalism, Magazines
- AUDIENCE: Fiction Enthusiasts, Magazine Readers
- CONTACT: Kyle Shannon
  kyle@indienet.com
- FREE

http://desires.com/

Verbiage Magazine ★★★★

Verbiage Magazine showcases very short stories. It has published three issues with about ten stories in each. The writing is terse. Judge the quality for yourself.

- KEYWORDS: Contemporary Literature, Fiction, Internet Publishing, Short Stories
- AUDIENCE: Book Readers, Literary Critics, Publishing Professionals
- CONTACT: Tom Boutell
  boutell@netcom.com
- FREE

http://sunsite.unc.edu/boutell/verbiage/

The Virtual Mirror ★★★★

Virtual Mirror is an extremely broad-subjected journal and arts review with articles on everything from IBM email client software to gardening and flower bulbs.

- KEYWORDS: Film, Gardening
- AUDIENCE: Art Enthusiasts, Gardeners, General Public, IBM users
- CONTACT: Bob Stewart
  mirror@wwa.com
- FREE

http://mirror.wwa.com/mirror/

Washingtonian Magazine Online ★★★
COMMERCIAL

This site is the online version of Washingtonian magazine. It offers a variety of articles of interest to residents and visitors. Information about restaurants, transportation, and lodging is provided, as well as news about upcoming events in the Washington metropolitan area.

- KEYWORDS: Tourism, Washington D.C.
- AUDIENCE: Tourists, Washington D.C. Residents
- FREE

http://www.infi.net/washmag/

Weekly Mail & Guardian ★★★
COMMERCIAL

This site contains information about The Weekly Mail & Guardian, the South African independent newspaper. Users will find subscription information for the electronic version, which includes all material supplied by The Weekly Mail but NOT from outside news sources. There is also a notice for subscribers who wish to participate in an email news forum to discuss the issues brought out through the newspaper. Also on this site is a monthly column on computing and the Internet. Although the current editions of the Weekly Mail & Guardian are not available on the Web, there is a link to searchable back issues which has a one-month lag time.

- KEYWORDS: Online Newspapers, South Africa
- AUDIENCE: South Africa Researchers, South Africans
- CONTACT: Internet Solution
  webmaster@is.co.za
- COST

http://www.is.co.za/services/wmail/wmail.html

Women of Greater Atlanta Online Magazine! ★★★

This site provides pointers to feature articles in the online magazine, Women of Greater Atlanta. Some of the subjects covered include It's the Nineties, The Wandering Palate, A Menopause Moment, Financial Focus, Get Outta Town, Beauty Tip, A Man's Point of View, Legal Briefs, etc.

- KEYWORDS: Beauty, Georgia, Magazines, Women's Issues
- AUDIENCE: Magazine Readers, Tourists, Women
- CONTACT: Sue Wright - Publisher
  swright@america.net
- FREE

http://www.america.net/com/prestige/wgahome.html

Zero Hora ★★★
COMMERCIAL

This is the major newspaper of the south of Brazil, which publishes its Portuguese computer supplement of the newspaper on the Internet.

- KEYWORDS: Brazil, Newspapers, Online Newspapers, South America
- AUDIENCE: Brazilians, Computer Professionals, International Business Professionals
- CONTACT: zhinfo@ax.apc.org
- FREE

http://www.embratel.net.br/infoserv/zerohora/index.html

ZipZap ★★★

Zipzap is one of a number of new online underground magazines. The editors put together an eclectic mix of offbeat fiction, interviews with avant garde scenesters, and obtuse discussions of the subculture of art movements. The first isssue contains articles such as 'What Is Avant-Pop?' and downloadable sound files of poets reading their work.

- KEYWORDS: Art Criticism, E-Zines, Fiction
- AUDIENCE: Alternative Music Enthusiasts, Curiosity Seekers, Writers
- FREE

http://zipzap.com/cover.html

Movies

See also
Arts & Music · *Film & Video*
Popular Culture & Entertainment · *Celebrities & Personalities*
Popular Culture & Entertainment · *Television*

Best Video ★★★
COMMERCIAL

Best Video offers over 24,000 titles, accumulating at a rate of 125 per week. They carry an extensive selection of foreign and classic films and a comprehensive range of film genres, as well as CDs. Chances are that you'll find what you're looking for among the more than 230 video categories this catalogue covers. Videos are available for rental for those in the Fairfield, Hartford, Waterbury, and Shoreline areas of Connecticut. Videos are also offered for purchase from the online catalogue.

- KEYWORDS: Connecticut, Film, Rental Services, Video
- AUDIENCE: Connecticut Residents, Movie Enthusiasts, Television Enthusiasts, Video Enthusiasts
- CONTACT: BestVid@aol.com
- FREE

http://www.tagsys.com:80/ads/bestvideo/

Flanders International Film Festival ★★★

This Web site is the result of a collaborative project between the International Flanders Film Festival in Ghent and the University of Ghent. Each October, some 100 films from all over the world are presented to an audience of some 60,000 spectators. The links at the site include general information, the program, useful addresses, dates, and a festival newsletter.

- KEYWORDS: Belgium, Film Festivals
- AUDIENCE: Actors, Directors, Film Enthusiasts, Screenwriters
- FREE

http://www.rug.ac.be/filmfestival/Welcome.html

Hollyweb Online Film Guide ★★★★

The Hollyweb Online Film Guide is a collection of information and resources devoted to film and cinema. Users will find movie reviews, film news, information on independent and major studio movies currently in production, current box-office statistics, and more. There is a comprehensive list of film related Internet links as well as information for those who wish to contribute to the production of the site.

- KEYWORDS: Cinema, Film, Hollywood, Mass Communications
- AUDIENCE: Film Enthusiasts, Movie Buffs, Popular Culture Enthusiasts
- CONTACT: Scott M. Pease
  Spease@netcom.com
- FREE

http://www.ingress.com/users/spease/hw/hollyweb.html

Movies

Hong Kong Cinema

This page provides access to a Hong Kong Movie Database, information about Hong Kong movies playing in the San Francisco Bay Area, Hong Kong Cinema box office reports, recent articles on the Hong Kong film industry, various awards to Hong Kong movies and also various related links such as The Hong Kong Popstars Archive.

- KEYWORDS: Hong Kong, Hong Kong Movies
- AUDIENCE: Chinese Culture Enthusiasts, Movie Enthusiasts
- CONTACT: jmf@egret0.stanford.edu
- FREE

http://egret0.stanford.edu:80/hk

Internet Movie Database

This site offers a database of movie titles and television series complete with ratings, cross-referenced by actor, director, and supporting cast. The database is searchable by title and keyword. Ratings from 1-10 are provided by the database users themselves, and visitors to the site are encouraged to vote.

- KEYWORDS: Cinema, Film, Television, Videos
- AUDIENCE: General Public, Movie Enthusiasts, Television Enthusiasts, Video Enthusiasts
- CONTACT: Rob Hartill
  Robert.Hartill@cm.cf.ac.uk
- FREE

http://www.msstate.edu/Movies/

Lion King

This site provides moviegoers and the press with up-to-date previews of the recently released Walt Disney production, Lion King. There are QuickTime movie clips as well as interviews and pictures.

- KEYWORDS: Film, Movies, Previews
- AUDIENCE: Children, Critics, Film Enthusiasts, Movie Buffs
- FREE

http://bvp.wdp.com/BVPM/PressRoom/LionKing/LionKing.html

MCA/Universal's V/IP (Visual/ Interactive Previews)

This is MCA/Universal's V/IP (Visual/ Interactive Previews) of future films. Links are provided to the different movies via a mixture of text and graphics. Some of Universal's movies include Casper, Village of the Damned, and Tales from the Crypt.

- KEYWORDS: Film, Movies
- AUDIENCE: Film Enthusiasts, Filmmakers, Movie Directors, Movie Enthusiasts
- FREE

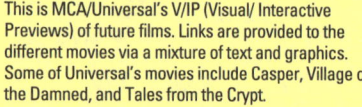

http://www.mca.com/universal_pictures/index.html

Main Page - The Internet Movie Database at Cardiff UK

This WWW front end to the Rec.arts.movies movie database aims to make useful and up to date movie information freely available online, across as many systems and platforms as possible. Users may search the database for actors, directors, characters, and movies. Users can also rate movies in the database or add movies that don't exist in the database.

- KEYWORDS: Interactive Media, Movies, Popular Culture, Television
- AUDIENCE: Film Enthusiasts, Film Researchers, Movie Buffs
- CONTACT: Rob Hartill
  Movie.Database@cm.cf.ac.uk
- FREE

http://www.msstate.edu/Movies

New Line Cinema ★★

This is New Line Cinema's preview page for movies such as 'Dumb and Dumber' with Jim Carrey. The home page is almost all graphics so it takes awhile to load. Then you can click on the graphic for the movie you want to preview and more graphics appear... slowly. You can click further to learn more about the movie, cast and soundtrack album. There is no mechanism to use text-only at this time.

- KEYWORDS: Movies, Video
- AUDIENCE: Film Enthusiasts, Filmmakers, Movie Enthusiasts, Television Enthusiasts
- FREE

http://cybertimes.com/NewLine/Welcome.html

Paramount Pictures ★★

This is where you can preview movies and see what's coming from Paramount Pictures. This home page has a number of graphics, so be patient when loading it. Each movie title includes a very brief description and graphics, and is hyperlinked to a text document that further describes the movie, provides snapshots, and has interviews and insight from the actors and directors regarding the movie. You can also choose further information in either text or graphics mode. In the graphics mode you can download previews and photos, see credits, read biographies of the cast and filmmakers, and more.

- KEYWORDS: Movies, Television
- AUDIENCE: Film Enthusiasts, Filmmakers, Movie Enthusiasts, Television Enthusiasts
- FREE

http://paramount.com

Sony Pictures Entertainment Home Page ★★

Sony Pictures Entertainment Home Page provides information on theater, movies and television. The pages contain many graphics so the loading can be very slow depending on your Internet connection speed. You can preview movies, find out the location of Sony theaters near you, and find pictures, movies, sound files, what's new, and more information on your favorite television shows.

- KEYWORDS: Film Technology, Television
- AUDIENCE: Film Enthusiasts, Film Researchers, Movie Enthusiasts, Television Enthusiasts
- FREE

http://www.spe.sony.com/Pictures/index.html

Teen Movie Critic ★★

Teen Movie Critic contains reviews written by a 16-year-old who lives in Minneapolis, of current movies. Some of the films reviewed include Blue Velvet, Elephant Man and Wild at Heart. The site also contains an archive of previous reviews, listed alphabetically, and links to other critics pages.

- KEYWORDS: Movie Reviews, Movies
- AUDIENCE: Minnesota Residents, Movie Enthusiasts, Teenagers
- CONTACT: Roger Davidson
  magic@skypoint.com
- FREE

http://www.skypoint.com/members/magic/roger/teencritic.html

Terry Gilliam's Brazil FAQs (Frequently Asked Questions) Version 1.2.4 ★★★

This ftp site provides access to extensive documentation of FAQs (Frequently Asked Questions) based on the Terry Gilliam movie 'Brazil'. This FAQ was created to answer such frequently posted questions as what the film is about, how many versions have been released, what the title is supposed to mean and much more.

- KEYWORDS: Brazil, Filmmaking, Movies
- AUDIENCE: Film Enthusiasts, Film Researchers, Filmmakers, Fim Directors, Movie Directors
- CONTACT: David S. Cowen (David Eschatfische)
  esch@fische.com
- FREE

ftp://ftp.execpc.com/pub/esch/brazil-faq/

Multimedia

See also
Arts & Music · *Electronic Arts*
Popular Culture & Entertainment · *Television*

CD-I Home Page ★★★

This page contains a wealth of information on the compact-disc interactive (CD-I) format. Users will find a listing of all of the latest CD-I releases, information for developers, and an FAQ (Frequently Asked Questions) file for owners and potential owners of a CD-I machine. In addition, this site maintains a listing of other resources about CD-I, as well as information on the Usenet newsgroup devoted to CD-I users.

- KEYWORDS: Consumer Electronics, Education, Interactive Technology, Multimedia
- AUDIENCE: CD-I Developers, CD-I Users, Interactive Entertainment Enthusiasts

CONTACT erik@acs.brockport.edu

FREE

http://www.acs.brockport.edu/cd-i/

ftp://ftp.acs.brockport.edu/incoming/cd-i/

Electronic Catalog at Walnut Creek CDROM! ★★★★

This is the site of the Electronic Catalog at Walnut Creek CDROM. It provides access to an Alphabetical Index of CD-ROMs, Shareware CD-ROMs, awesome graphics, fractals, and programs, operating systems, jobs listings, discs and paraphernalia, and more. Contact or ordering information from Walnut Creek CDROM is also provided here.

KEYWORDS CD ROM, Electronic Catalog, Employment, Shareware

AUDIENCE Computer Users, Educators (University), Internet Users, Researchers, Students (University)

CONTACT www@wcarchive.cdrom.com

FREE

http://ftp.cdrom.com

ftp://ftp.cdrom.com

Index to Multimedia Resources ★★★★

Multimedia Information Resources is a meta-index of multimedia resources sponsored by the University of Geneva. It has extensive links under the following categories - Ratings & Guides, FAQ's, Newsgroup Archives, Media Archives, Research Archives, Bibliographies, Digital Museums and Galleries, Commercial Networks, Magazines, Publishers, Hypertext and Virtual Reality.

KEYWORDS Communications Technology, Media, Virtual Reality

AUDIENCE Artists, Computer Users, Internet Users, Multimedia Enthusiasts, Video Artists

CONTACT Simon Gibbs
simon@cui.unige.ch

FREE

http://fourier.dur.ac.uk:8000/mm.html

Internet Town Hall ★★★

The Internet Town Hall provides a variety of multimedia resources including virtual tourism, music, radio, US Government databases, digital shopping, and more. There are links to the various organizations providing these services and to the organizations supporting the Internet Town Hall.

KEYWORDS Internet Directories, Internet Guides

AUDIENCE Internet Users

CONTACT info@radio.com

FREE

http://www.town.hall.org/

gopher://town.hall.org/

Lysator ★★

Lysator is a gopher server of the Lysator, a students' computer society at Linkoping University, Sweden. It contains information on Lysator, electronic texts, the science fiction archive, games, and more. It has links to other gophers like the Swedish root server.

KEYWORDS Computer Networking, Computer Science, Education (College/University), Sweden

AUDIENCE Educators (University), Science Fiction Enthusiasts

CONTACT Tommy Persson
gopher@lysator.liu.se

FREE

gopher://gopher.lysator.liu.se/

Mani's Front Door ★★★

This is a true multimedia site. Come to this page to experience sounds, an art gallery, cool links, and graphics. There is also a link to Mani's Backcountry World which features hiking, a BRYCE page, biking, backpacking, climbing, and the preservation of the outdoors.

KEYWORDS Cyberbusiness, Cyberculture, Hiking, Multimedia, Tourism

AUDIENCE Computer Users, Hiking Enthusiasts, Outdoors Enthusiasts, Tourists

CONTACT Michael Gerstein
maniman@well.com

FREE

http://www.well.com/user/maniman/

Thalia's Funpage ★★

This is a page of miscellaneous fun links which can be accessed in English or Dutch. Subjects include the Muppets, Samuri Pizza Cats, The Dutch Top 40, The cabaret page with Monty Python, some MPEG movies, and the daily Babe-test for the truly unenlightened. Some of this material is not appropriate for children.

KEYWORDS Games, Humor, Netherlands

AUDIENCE Internet Users, Parents

CONTACT Thalia
rhebben@sci.kun.nl

FREE

http://www.sci.kun.nl/thalia/funpage/fun_en.html

UWI (UnderWorld Industries) Cultural Playground ★★★★

The UWI (UnderWorld Industries) Cultural Playground provides informtion and links to a variety of websites. Subjects include an art/poetry web-zine, periodicals, roadtrip journals, UWI Shopping Maul (stuff to get - music, books, misc.), glossary of mayhem, fashion design, animation pages, experimental music, art, video, news, and miscellaneous. Summary tags are also provided for each link letting the surfer know what kind of site it is. Categories include normal, worthy, urgent, experiment, contribute, links offsite, and document.

KEYWORDS Art, Music, Shareware, Zines

AUDIENCE Art Enthusiasts, Artists, Computer Artists, Multimedia Enthusiasts, Music Enthusiasts

CONTACT jon@kzsu.stanford.edu

FREE

http://kzsu.stanford.edu/uwi.html

Welcome to Image Club Graphics ★★★★

Image Club Graphics is a provider of clipart, photo-graphic images, and font collections for PC and Macintosh computers. Online product information for the collections include samples that can be viewed and downloaded. This site also includes new Image Club releases, a monthly countdown of best selling products, and company information.

KEYWORDS Graphics, Macintosh Tools, PC Tools, Software

AUDIENCE Desktop Publishers, Graphic Designers, Macintosh Users, PC Users

CONTACT ghutchin@adobe.com

FREE

http://www.adobe.com/imageclub/

Museums & Theme Parks

See also
Arts & Music · *Anthropology*
Arts & Music · *Archaeology*
Popular Culture & Entertainment · *Family & Community*

Animal Information Data Base ★★★★

This is the introduction page of the Animal Information Data Base, provided by Sea World Incorporated. It contains information aimed at educators and students about animals and their environments. Links on this page lead to information 'booklets' on several animals including manatees, bottlenose dolphins and gorillas.

KEYWORDS Education, Sea Mammals, Sea World, Wildlife

AUDIENCE Educators (Primary/Secondary), Nature Lovers, Students (Primary/Secondary)

CONTACT Sea.World@bev.net

FREE

http://www.bev.net/education/SeaWorld/infobook.html

Bishop Museum ★★★

This is a gopher server for the Bishop Museum in Hawaii. It contains information on the Museum such as hours, admissions, services, the email user list, and news. It has links to University of Hawaii's gopher as well as other museum gophers.

KEYWORDS Cultural Studies, Education (College/University), Hawaii, Museums

AUDIENCE Academics, Students, Tourists

CONTACT Edward Yagi
gopher@bishop.bishop.hawaii.org

FREE

gopher://bishop.bishop.hawaii.org/

544   Museums & Theme Parks

California Academy of Science ★★

The information on this server is related to the California Academy of Science (CAS). CAS is a a natural history museum, aquarium, and planetarium in San Francisco. This server provides information on the CAS, its mission, hours, admission, public exhibits, events, newsletters, and CAS programs.

Keywords   California, Natural History Museum, Networking, Scientists
Audience   Academics, Scholars, Science Researchers, Scientists
Free

gopher://cas.calacademy.org/

Canadian Museum of Civilization Corporation (CMCC) ★★★★

The CMCC comprises the Canadian Museum of Civilization (CMC) and its affiliate, the Canadian War Museum (CWM). The combined holdings of the CMC and the CWM exceeds 4 million artifacts. The main body of the collection presented online covers archaeology (Canadian pre-history) and ethnology (Canadian Indian, Inuit, Metis), history, and folk culture. Temporary exhibitions, and the Children's Museum are also covered, and there is information on the National Postal Museum. The site also contains general information about the museums, historical introductions, a calendar of events, and a summary listing of exhibit openings, film presentations, live performances.

Keywords   Archaeology, Artifacts, Canadian Heritage, Ethnology
Audience   Archaeologists, Canadians, Ethnologists, Inuits, Native Americans, Tourists
Contact   Stephen Alsford
           stephen.alsford@cmcc.muse.digital.ca
Free

http://www.cmcc.muse.digital.ca/cmc/cmcfra/welcmfra.html

The Exploratorium ★★★

This is home page of the Exploratorium, a museum of science, technology, and human perception in San Francisco. It contains Information on events, programs, publications, press releases, and more. In addition, it makes connections to associated organizations, physics resources, and astronomical resources.

Keywords   Education, Museums, Recreation
Audience   Children, Educators, Science Hobbyists, Students
Contact   Ron Hipschman
           ronh@exploratorium.edu
Free

http://www.exploratorium.edu/

gopher://gopher.exploratorium.edu

Field Museum of Natural History Experimental WWW Server ★★★★

The Field Museum of Natural History Experimental WWW Server is a site full of sounds, animations, hypertext and other multimedia elements put together to reveal secrets about evolution and the history of life. Here you will be able to access images of specimens from the Chicago museum's collection of over 20 million objects, or 'Take the Tour' of the current exhibition. Topics can include dinosaurs, early humanoids and early mammals, the first stirrings of life on this planet, and perhaps even prehistoric plants. There are also links to other exhibits at the museum, (for example, to the Javanese Mask Collection) and related sites and information.

Keywords   Anthropology, Evolution, Natural History
Audience   Children, Dinosaur Enthusiasts, Natural History Enthusiasts, Students (Primary/Secondary)
Contact   Mary Rasmussen
           Mary@evl.eecs.uic.edu
Free

http://www.bvis.uic.edu

Franklin Institute Science Museum ★★★

This museum site contains several virtual exhibits and an educational hot list which points to educational hotspots on the Internet. The exhibitions include 'Benjamin Franklin - Glimpses of The Man' and 'The Heart - A Virtual Exploration.' The site also contains a publications library and sample science programs and demonstrations as well as information for those planning a visit to the Institute which includes the Fels Planetarium. There are also links to other science resources.

Keywords   Educational Resources, Virtual Art, Virtual Gallery
Audience   Educators, General Public, Graduate Students, Students
Free

http://sln.fi.edu/

Marine World Africa USA ★★

This is the home page for Marine World Africa USA, a theme park located in Vallejo, California. On this page, the viewer will find public relations materials, consisting of mostly images of the animals and marine life at the park. In addition, directions and hours are given for patrons.

Keywords   Animals, Marine World Africa, USA, Wildlife
Audience   Animal Lovers, Californians, Parents
Contact   FreeRun Technologies
           comments@freerun.com
Free

http://www.freerun.com/napavalley/outdoor/marinewo/marinewo.html

Maya Adventure ★★★

The Maya Adventure is presented by the Science Museum of Minnesota. The exhibit includes information related to ancient and modern Maya culture. Topics include Maya Sites, Activities, Maya Photo Archive, and more. You can perform an experiment to learn how limestone dissolves forming cenotes (caves) in Chichen Itza. Then you can view images of these cenotes or other ruins. Sites on your adventure include Altar de Sacrificios, Chiapas Highlands, Uxmal, and others.

Keywords   Anthropology, History, Mayan Culture, Science Museum Of Minnesota
Audience   Anthropologists, Historians, Mayans, Students (University), Tourists
Free

http://ties.k12.mn.us/~smm/

Museum Of New Zealand - Te PapaTongarewa ★★★

The National Museum of New Zealand represents the mix of the National Museum and National Art Gallery. The site contains images from, and information about, the Maori collections (art and history), Natural History in New Zealand, and decorative art collections. There are sound files for many of the images.

Keywords   Anthropology, Art Collections, Museums, Natural History Museum
Audience   Anthropologists, Art Historians, Maoris, New Zealand Culture Enthusiasts
Free

http://hyperg.tu-graz.ac.at:80/E411AAF1/CNew_Zealand

Museums and Galleries (Washington, D.C.) ★★★

This site contains addresses and general information about museums and collections in the Washington, D.C. area. The sites include the Ansel Adams Collection, the National Archives, The Phillips Collection, Arlington Arts Center, Dumbarton Oaks, The Folger Shakespeare Library, Fondo del Sol Visual Arts Center, the Corcoran Gallery of Art, the Daughters of the American Revolution Museum, etc.

Keywords   Art Collections, Art Museums, Tourism, Washington D.C.
Audience   Arts Community, Families, Tourists, Washington D.C. Residents
Free

http://www.co.arlington.va.us/museums.htm

Natural History Museum, Berne (NMBE) ★★★★

This site contains a history of the Natural History Museum with images, current events and exhibitions (e.g., Wild in der Küche—an exhibit about man, game, hunting, meat, and prehistory), a short tour of the museum and special notes. Founded in the early 19th century, the museum is internationally renowned for its diorama displays showing Swiss and foreign birds and mammals in their natural surroundings; the museum's strengths include earth sciences, invertebrate animals, and vertebrate animals. The site also contains general museum information, including contact information.

Keywords   Animal Science, Earth Sciences, Natural Sciences, Zoology
Audience   Animal Lovers, Earth Scientists, Educators, Natural Scientists
Contact   Marc Nussbaumer
           nussbaumer@nmbe.unibe.ch
Free

http://www-nmbe.unibe.ch/

Museums & Theme Parks – Shopping

Ocean Planet Online ★★★★

Ocean Planet Online is the Web page for the 1995 Smithsonian exhibit of the same name. The exhibit explores current environmental issues affecting the health of the world's oceans. Visitors can take several guided tours of the exhibit, which include themes such as Biodiversity, Women and the Sea, Pollution, and Sea Surprises. Each tour offers short commentaries, definitions and impressive (though sometimes bandwidth intensive) photos. Users can also look up facts or images by searching a specific theme, or get ordering information from the museum shop. A link to the Smithsonian is provided.

KEYWORDS Ecology, Environment, Ocean
AUDIENCE Environmentalists, Marine Biologists
CONTACT Gene Carl Feldman
gene@seawifs.gsfc.nasa.gov
FREE

http://seawifs.gsfc.nasa.gov/ocean_planet.html

Renaissance Faire ★★★★

Renaissance Faire Web page provides resources and references for people who organize Renaissance Faires. This page offers an Introduction to Renaissance Faires, costuming and costumes, language and pronunciation accessories, acting, working with the public, and more. The site also provides links to Faire Resources and to specifics on the California Renaissance Faire.

KEYWORDS Events, Renaissance Faires
AUDIENCE Period Actors, Promoters, Renaissance Faire Organizers
CONTACT banshee@resort.com
FREE

http://www.resort.com/~banshee/Faire/index.html

St. Louis Science Center ★★★★

The St. Louis Science Center home page contains information on exhibits, current films, and science education. Visitors can tour the center, find information on fossils, ecology, the environment, and other science information. This site is especially good for children who want to learn more about science.

KEYWORDS Biosciences, Ecology, Natural Sciences, Primary/Secondary Education
AUDIENCE Children, Science Educators, Science Researchers, Scientists, Students (Primary/Secondary)
FREE

http://slsc.wustl.edu/~slsc/

Smithsonian Institution's Natural History Gopher ★★★★

This site offers information about the Smithsonian Institute of Natural History museum. Some of the areas discussed are botany, entomology, paleobiology, and much more. This server also has links to other related sites.

KEYWORDS Entomology, Museums, Natural History, Smithsonian Institution
AUDIENCE Academics, Entomologists, Historians, History Buffs
CONTACT Don Gourley
don@smithson.si.edu
FREE

gopher://nmnhgoph.si.edu/

Subway ★★★★

This web site features an interactive Subway, a tool linking users to museums and WWW servers around the world. It also hosts a multimedia museum from UC Berkeley's Museum of Paleontology.

KEYWORDS Museums, Paleontology
AUDIENCE Dinosaur Enthusiasts, Internet Users, Paleontologists
CONTACT David Polly
davip@ucmp1.berkeley.edu
FREE

http://ucmp1.berkeley.edu/subway.html

UC Museum of Paleontology ★★★★

This is the home page for the UC Berkeley Museum of Paleontology. The Museum's enormous collections are ranked 4th in America in size, and the paleontological materials include protists, plants, invertebrates and vertebrates. The collections are available to researchers at the Museum or through an extensive loan program. The page contains images and information from the museum collections, the history of paleontology, catalogs, information about seminars, etc. There is also a link to a home page for imageless users, and links to other palentology- and natural science-related sites on the Web.

KEYWORDS Fossils, Invertebrates, Natural History, Plants
AUDIENCE Educators, General Public, Paleontologists, Students
CONTACT Robert Guralnick
robg@fossil.berkeley.edu
FREE

http://ucmp1.berkeley.edu/museum.html

Shopping

See also
Business & Economics · *Commerce*
Business & Economics · *Retail*
Popular Culture & Entertainment · *Fashion*

$tarving $hirley's $avings Page ★★

$tarving $hirley's $avings Page is an online bargain shopping guide. It provides tips for shopping thrift stores and yard sales, and for reselling at consignment stores. She also discusses coupon-cutting, double or triple coupon savings, and you can subscribe to $tarving $hirley's $avings $heet or order a sample copy.

KEYWORDS Bargains, Consignment
AUDIENCE Bargain Hunters, Consumers, Shoppers
CONTACT mkinga@aol.com
FREE

http://www.mindspring.com/~kmims/ss.html

800 numbers ★★★

This site offers a listing of AT&T's 800 numbers, accessible by name or category. It's designed to help you shop for the things you need and want without ever leaving the comfort of your home or office. You can use this Directory to buy almost anything from anywhere in the United States, from gifts and flowers to things for the home and unique and hard-to-find items.

KEYWORDS AT&T (American Telephone & Telegraph), Communications, Information Retrieval, Online Services
AUDIENCE Business Professionals, General Public
CONTACT dir800@mail.att.net
FREE

http://att.net/dir800

Amboan & Badinia Furniture of Spain ★★★

Amboan and Badinia are two of the worlds highest quality manufacturers of classic, hand-finished furniture. The furniture is available worldwide through offices in Europe, the Orient, the US and Canada. Online, the browser can view a select few pieces from their portfolios. The photos are rotated to be able to show off a greater portion of their 200 models. There is a catalog of inlays by Marqueteria Ricardo Llorca as well as a World Directory of Sales Representatives.

KEYWORDS Furniture, Home, Spain
AUDIENCE Furniture Buyers, Interior Designers
CONTACT mjd@amboan.roc.servtech.com
FREE

http://www.servtech.com/public/amboan

Barclay Square ★★★

Barclay Square is a cybermall with a number of stores. The interface is designed to resemble a top view of a mall floor plan. Users can click on the image map location of the store they want to visit. Stores include Toys'R'Us, Blackwell's Books, Campus Travel and more. Stores list a sampling of their products, which can be ordered directly online. This site is part of a growing electronic city called Supernet.

KEYWORDS Cybermalls, Retail
AUDIENCE Advertisers, Retailers, Shoppers
FREE

http://www.itl.net/barclaysquare/

The Bonsai Boy of New York ★★★

This is the online catalog of the Bonsai Boy of New York. It lists the types of bonsai trees being offered in this shop. The picture, price and a brief description of each type of miniaturized tree are provided in this catalog. An order form is also included.

KEYWORDS Bonsai Trees, Buyers Guides, Product Information, Recreation
AUDIENCE Bonsai Enthusiasts, Consumers
CONTACT Jon Zeeff
branch-info@branch.com
FREE

http://branch.com/bonsai/bonsai.html

Branch Mall ★★★

Branch Information Services, one of the oldest 'Internet Malls,' offers shopping to customers and leases storefronts and electronic catalogs to vendors. A wide variety of products and services are available, such as food, clothing, electronics, business and legal services, travel services, and more. There are also links to other online shopping malls on the Internet.

KEYWORDS Advertising, Consumer Goods, Internet Shopping, Shopping
AUDIENCE Consumers, Merchants, Shoppers
CONTACT Jon Zeeff
jon@branch.com
FREE

http://branch.com/

gopher://branch.com/

Catalogue.com, Incorporated ★★

Catalogue.com, Incorporated offers to build and distribute full fledged online catalogues for traditional mail order catalogue companies. At the time of review no mail order companies were featured, but a couple of sports related pages/magazine offers were featured as well as 'catalog.comix,' and a few sites related to the producers/designers of the page.

KEYWORDS Mail Order, Sports Magazines
AUDIENCE Mail Order Companies, Shoppers
CONTACT info@catalogue.com
FREE

http://www.catalogue.com/

Cigar Specialist ★★★

The Cigar Specialist Web page markets handmade cigars, featuring brands like Ashton and Partegas. Detailed product information is provided, and users may order by online form.

KEYWORDS Cigars, Smoking
AUDIENCE Shoppers, Smokers
FREE

http://www.infohwy.com/cyberia/cigar

Dargate Auction Galleries ★★★

The Dargate Auction Galleries home page provides information on this Pittsburgh-based auctioneer. Users can access a current schedule of upcoming auctions and previews including some listings of merchandise available including fine art, furniture, historical items, and oriental rugs. A map to Dargate's is also included at the site as well as information on their Conditions of Sale.

KEYWORDS Antique Auctions, Antiques, Antiques Galleries, Auctions
AUDIENCE Antique Collectors, Antique Dealers, Art Buyers, Art Collectors, Auction Attenders
FREE

http://www.ibp.com/pit/dargate

Deep Space Mall ★★★

Deep Space Mall is a cybermall offering products from a number of stores. Stores include Counterfeit Perfumes, The Flag Store, Self Defense Store, South Western Shop and more. Each store offers a nice size sampling of its products which can be ordered by phone or mail, and the producers promise soon by email. This site provides a link to other stores and a link on how to get and use PGP (Pretty Good Privacy). The site also has images relating to the US Space program.

KEYWORDS Cybermalls, Shopping
AUDIENCE Advertizers, Shoppers
CONTACT webmaster@deepspace.com
FREE

http://www.deepspace.com/deepspace.html

Defense Reutilization and Marketing Service (DRMS) ★★★

The Defense Reutilization and Marketing Service (DRMS) sells surplus Department of Defense (DoD) property to the general public. This includes everything from computers to vehicles, aircraft parts to clothing, furniture to scrap metal, and more. The general public can buy this merchandise at two types of sales— local and international. Links to information on the sales including dates, locations, support telephone numbers, catalogs, sale items are provided.

KEYWORDS Automobiles, Consumer Goods, Sales
AUDIENCE Automobile Buyers, Consumers, General Public
CONTACT webmasters@drms.dla.mil
FREE

http://131.87.1.51/index.html

Elsewear, T-shirts, Computer Gifts, Clothing ★★★★

This site is an online mail order service selling t-shirts with computer-generated graphics printed on them. Several designs are displayed, and other designs are described, including color combinations.

KEYWORDS Advertising, Clothing, Online Shopping, Product Information
AUDIENCE Consumers, General Public, Internet Users
CONTACT +1 (802) 424-6303, +1 (800) 425-6303
FREE

http://branch.com/shirts/shirts.html

Forman Interactive Corp. Vendor List ★★★

This home page offers you a lot of quite different things - swimwear and tuxedos, metalworking machinery, CD ROMs, sporting goods, ballet shoes, health services, and plastic surgery. In general, there seems to be an emphasis on hardware and services. One can order by phone. The page is presently under construction, but some stores are already open.

KEYWORDS Clothing, Health, Music, Shopping Malls
AUDIENCE Dance Enthusiasts, Fitness Enthusiasts, Health Care Consumers, Shoppers
CONTACT info@forman.com
FREE

http://www.forman.com/

Fossilized Shark Tooth Jewelry - Peter Boesley ★★★

Peter Boesley has developed this Web site in order to market his jewelry made from 15 - 30 million-year-old fossilized shark teeth at reduced prices. Images can be accessed for both men's and women's jewelry sets which include earrings and necklace pendants available in various sizes and colors. In the future, users will also be able to access information on the history of these fossils. Online ordering is available at the site.

KEYWORDS Crafts, Fashion, Jewelry
AUDIENCE Craft Shoppers, Jewelry Shoppers, Nature Lovers
CONTACT Peter Boesley
shark@haven.uniserve.com
FREE

http://haven.uniserve.com/~shark/welcome.html

Hand in Hand ★★★

The Hand in Hand catalogue offers for sale over 400 carefully chosen products for infants, toddlers, and pre-schoolers. It carries high quality toys, games and puzzles, books and videos, art supplies, musical instruments, CDs and cassettes, multicultural books and toys, strollers, safety products, furniture and storage items.

KEYWORDS Baby Products, Child Care, Parenting, Toys
AUDIENCE Childcare Providers, Children, Parents, Schools
CONTACT fsd@world.std.com
FREE

http://www.digital.com/gnn/bus/handhand/index.html

I-Mart ★★

This Web site developed by the Internet Marketing Group, Ltd. allows users to access various goods and services available online. Currently, there are subject headings for such goods as arts, crafts, flowers and gifts in addition to consulting and marketing services. Coming attractions include the addition of an online art gallery, an Internet association, and multicultural center.

KEYWORDS Online Malls, Online Marketing, Online Shopping
AUDIENCE Internet Advertisers, Internet Shoppers
CONTACT img-info@wcci.com
FREE

http://www.wcci.com

Internet Catalog Mart ★★★

The Catalog Mart boasts more than 10,000 catalogs in over 800 topics. Each of these catalogs are available for

Shopping 547

free. Simply select any topic you are interested in and fill out the electronic order form. Your catalog request will automatically be forwarded to all appropriate catalog houses. Topics cover virtually all areas from hockey to homebuilding to hunting to horseshoes. There is also a form for vendors interested in adding their free catalogs to the list.

KEYWORDS Catalogs, Internet Shopping, Marketing
AUDIENCE General Public, Internet Shoppers
FREE

http://catalog.savvy.com/

Internet Company Gateway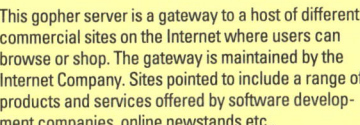

This gopher server is a gateway to a host of different commercial sites on the Internet where users can browse or shop. The gateway is maintained by the Internet Company. Sites pointed to include a range of products and services offered by software development companies, online newstands etc..

KEYWORDS Companies, Internet Guides, Shopping
AUDIENCE Business Professionals, Consumers, General Public, Internet Users
CONTACT info@internet.com
FREE

gopher://gopher.internet.com/

Internet Information Mall

This is an online shopping mall called The Internet Information Mall managed by Cyberspace Development, Inc. Some of the stores currently open include bookstores and software companies. The mall allows for online, real time credit card payments and electronic delivery of some goods.

KEYWORDS Business, Internet Marketing, Marketing, Shopping
AUDIENCE Consumers, General Public, Internet Users
CONTACT office@marketplace.com
FREE

gopher://marketplace.com/

Internet Plaza

This site provides an online shopping mall called Internet Plaza. The products are provided by different companies. Some of the products sold include books, software, computer networking, and flowers. Internet Plaza is a registered trademark of XOR Network Engineering, Inc.

KEYWORDS Computer Products, Internet Marketing, Marketing, Shopping
AUDIENCE Business Professionals, Consumers, General Public, Marketing Professionals
CONTACT Shopping
plaza@plaza.xor.com
FREE

gopher://chimchim.xor.com/

Internet Shopping Network

The Internet Shopping Network is owned by the Home Shopping Network. By connecting to their WWW site you gain access to over 600 companies' products. ISN offers a text-only and a graphical-based format for their pages. Ordering from ISN requires a free membership which may be attained with a credit card. ISN offers mainly computer-related products at this time.

KEYWORDS Computer Products, Sales, Shopping
AUDIENCE Computer System Designers, Computer Users
CONTACT feedback@internet.net
FREE

http://www.internet.net/index.html

Connections to Flea Markets

One person's garbage is another's treasure

A hand-crank ice cream maker from the 1950s, brass candle holders, beach towels from the 1960s, and wind-up toys are just a few of the items you'll find for sale at flea markets, garage sales, and church bazaars on the Internet. That's right—on the Internet.

If you are looking for something to add to a knick-knack collection, or to dress up the hearth, you'll likely find it at one of several sites on the Internet.

There's even a magazine on the Internet that is dedicated solely to vintage collectibles from the 1940s through the 1970s, including profiles of notable collectors. The items generally go for extremely reasonable prices, too.

(http://www.tias.com/antiques/pubs/gcr/flea_market/)

Maybe you have something to sell—an old typewriter (remember them?), a vintage wedding dress, brass door knobs, or any number of outdated but collectible kitchen gadgets. You can post your item at Flea Market @ FUW. If you're looking for an item—an old rotary telephone, a collection of albums from the 1960s, or even an old computer, you might find it at this site. The site provides long and short forms of descriptions of items. If you post an item and sell it, you can immediately delete the advertisement. If you're looking for something specific, you can search by category to make it quick and efficient.

(http://info.fuw.edu.pl/market/market.html)

Kauai Exotix

Kauai Exotix grows and ships tropical flowers to anywhere in the United States within 48 hours. The site provides information on various types of exotic flower arrangements available, farm-direct from Hawaii. Tips on flower care and a book on how to arrange these exotic blooms are also available at the site. Surprisingly, the Kauai flower farms are home to three bed and breakfasts, which are also described. There is also a link to Planet Hawaii.

KEYWORDS Flowers, Gifts, Tropical Flowers
AUDIENCE Event Planners, Florists, Gift Shoppers

548 Shopping

CONTACT Suzanne Eastman
kexotix@aloha.net
FREE

http://planet-hawaii.com/~exotix/

Luxury Linens Home Page ★★

This is the home page of Luxury Linens, a division of Burlington Coat Factory. They offer one of the largest selections of name brands and designer labels Sheets, Pillow cases, Towels, Comforters, Blankets, Table Linens, Bath Accessories advertised at 25% to 50% off regular retail prices elsewhere. Links are provided to a Store Locator image map to find the store locations as well as corporate data.

KEYWORDS Bath Accessories, Discount Shopping, Household Items, Linens
AUDIENCE Consumers, Interior Decorators
CONTACT luxury.linens@coat.com
FREE

http://www.coat.com/linens.html

MCS Instructional Videos ★★

The Marketing Concepts & Strategies Company distributes several video cassette series on subjects ranging from pets to the Internet to gambling. This page gives a brief description of the videotapes, and allows the user to order them by phone or mail. Users can also request more information about the products or the company via an online form.

KEYWORDS Instructional Videos, Internet Training, Online Shopping, Pets
AUDIENCE Gamblers, Internet Users, Management Trainers, Pet Lovers
CONTACT w3@unipress.com
FREE

http://main.street.net/mcs/

MarketBase Online Catalog ★★★

This is an online shopping forum where buyers and sellers can exchange their needs and goods. Access can be obtained by gopher, telnet, FTP, or dial-up modems. Access is free to purchasers.

KEYWORDS Business, Companies, Internet Resources, Shopping
AUDIENCE Business Professionals, Consumers, Merchants
CONTACT info@mb.com
FREE

gopher://mb.com/

Multi Media Japan ★★★

This is a home page from MMJP (Multi Media Japan), a new corporate information medium produced by Atson, Inc., the company that created ASAHI Net. There are various business enterprises' electronic catalogs (Sun Corporation with computer hardware and software), online shops (TransCosmos with Internet software and services), and news services.

KEYWORDS Internet Commerce, Japanese Business, Online Shopping

AUDIENCE Computer Users, Network Users
FREE

http://www.mmjp.or.jp/

Net Sweats and Tees ★★★

The Net Sweats and Tees web site is an online store for Internet-related sweatshirts and T-shirts. Visitors to the site can view this collection of hacker fashions, join the T-shirt of the month club, or purchase the shirts online. The site provides links to other online retailers of casual gear.

KEYWORDS Online Shopping, Sweatshirts
AUDIENCE Clothes Shoppers, T-Shirt Collectors
CONTACT duenorth@icw.com
FREE

http://www.icw.com/netsweat/netsweat.html

NovaSource ★★

The NovaSource web page is a general forum for online advertisements. Visitors are linked somewhat randomly to a short list of home pages ranging from travel lodges to sugar-free products. Information on NovaSource's marketing services is also provided. At the site users are also encouraged to register for a free 'NovaSource Membership' although membership is left undefined.

KEYWORDS Online Marketing, Online Shopping
AUDIENCE Business Professionals, Consumers, Marketers
CONTACT novasrc@oasis.efn.org
FREE

http://oasis.efn.org/novasrc/ns.html

OfficeMax Online ★★

This page offers you some office supplies from Office-Max, mainly computers and phones/faxes. The page is a part of a big cyberstore, maintained by MCI, and also features electronic ordering and an electronic shopping basket.

KEYWORDS Communications, Computers, Office Equipment, Online Shopping
AUDIENCE Business Professionals, Computer Users, Shoppers
CONTACT OfficeMax@internetMCI.com
FREE

http://www2.pcy.mci.net/marketplace/omax/

Officially Licensed Super Bowl Commemorative Coins ★★

This site developed by Jacobson & Jardine, Inc. provides information on this company's complete collection of Super Bowl commemorative coins. This collection dates back to the very first Super Bowl ever played in 1967. Images of the coins as well as ordering information is provided.

KEYWORDS Coin Collecting, Commemorative Coins, Sports Events

AUDIENCE Coin Collectors, Football Fans
FREE

http://www.imall.com/imall/Collectibles/superbowl/superbowl.html

The Shops at Carolina Furniture ★★★

The Shops at Carolina Furniture in Williamsburg, VA specializes in furniture in rustic and provincial styles. They also carry Karastan Oriental carpets and hand-knotted rugs from India, Pakistan and Tibet, the complete line of Virginia Metalcrafters & Baldwin Brass, lighting and textiles as well as Pennsylvania House solid cherry, oak, maple and pine furniture in traditional and country styles. There is an online order opportunity as well as a request form for further information and catalogs.

KEYWORDS Furniture, Home, Online Shopping
AUDIENCE Consumers, Furniture Buyers
CONTACT The Virtual Company
furnish@tvc.com, its@tvc.com
FREE

http://www.wmbg.com/vlm/carolina_furniture/toc.html

Sophisticated Chocolates ★★★

This site is an advertisement for a gourmet chocolate company, Sophisticated Chocolates. Descriptions and prices of a few products given. Orders are taken by phone and products are shipped via Federal Express. Sophisticated Chocolates will sell you chocolate-filled Gift Baskets, Chocolate Corporate Logos, Chocolate Covered Strawberries, Chocolate Covered Grapes, and more.

KEYWORDS Food, Gifts, Gourmet Food, Online Shopping
AUDIENCE Chocolate Lovers, General Public
CONTACT +1 (800) 437-6507
FREE

http://branch.com/sophisticated

Speak To Me Catalog of Talking Products ★★★★

This is a catalog of products that actually talk. A selection of personal electronics and novelties can be browsed, and an order for items can also be placed.

KEYWORDS Advertising, Electronics, Shopping, Storefronts
AUDIENCE Consumers, Internet Users
CONTACT Seth Russell
seth@halcyon.com
FREE

http://clickshop.com/speak/

The Store ★★

This site allows you to browse or purchase NFL (National Football League)-licensed merchandise. It is operated by the All Sports.com Company Store. A special toll-free number is provided for ordering.

KEYWORDS Football, Product Information, Shopping, Sports

AUDIENCE Football Fans, Internet Users
CONTACT mgolden@justlaw.com
FREE

http://allsports.questtech.com/nfl/store.html

Towne Center ★★★

The Towne Center is a cybermall whose slogan is 'Shop Saratosa's Finest'. The Mall offers a selection of professional services, bookstores, clothing stores, travel services, dining information/advertisements, furniture stores, and auto retailers. The catalogues for the various companies -many that are national or local chains such as Hold Everything - offer a small sampling of their products with illustrations. Information on how to order by phone or mail is provided. This site is very bandwidth intensive.

KEYWORDS Cybermalls, Shopping
AUDIENCE Advertizers, Shoppers
CONTACT dberry@packet.net
FREE

http://www.coolsite.com/towncntr.html

Virtual Vineyards ★★★

This Virtual Vineyard contains Master Sommelier Peter Granoff's personal wine selections. He includes his tasting notes to to aid you in your search for wines. Virtual Vineyards will deliver directly to you, with a guarantee, the wines you choose from the online catalogue. Because Virtual Vineyards is one of the first companies on the Internet that operates a secure-transaction Netscape Commerce Server, you can use your credit card. Here you can also find specials and samplers including Chardonnays, Merlots, and Cabernets. Bon Appetit!

KEYWORDS Food, Vineyards, Wine, Wine Tasting
AUDIENCE Entertainers, Restauranteurs, Wine Enthusiasts
CONTACT corkdork@virtualvin.com
FREE

http://www.virtualvin.com/

WorldWide Marketplace ★★★

This home page offers promises that a huge mall with lots of departments will be here in the future, but currently it's practically empty. It does house travel services, Internet services, consulting, telecommunications providers, a couple of bookstores, a real estate agency, sport cards and comics dealers. You can place your own business here. There's no electronic ordering. User must telephone the companies to order products.

KEYWORDS Computer Consulting, Shopping Malls, Telecommunications, Travel
AUDIENCE Computer Users, Internet Users, Tourists
CONTACT Info-Request@cygnus.nb.ca
FREE

http://www.cygnus.nb.ca/mall/mall.html

Connections to Television Game Shows
What is Euphrates?

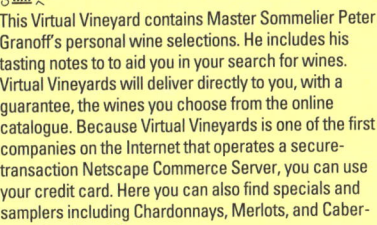

So you can't get enough of Alex Trebek, the host of the popular U.S. television show Jeopardy! Or maybe you want to find out more about Vanna White, co-host and "chief letter turner" on 'Wheel of Fortune.' Then turn to the Internet, where millions of people around the world are already asking "Who is . . .?" and "What is . . .?"

Through the Internet, you have access to a wealth of information about virtually every game show, including news about the stars, the rules of the various games, who won the biggest prizes, and even the challenge of playing some of the games online.

Through the shows' World Wide Web sites, you can get video clips, audio clips, and photographs of the hosts, as well as all the pertinent data (such as game prizes).

(http://www.spe.sony.com/Pictures/tv/games.html)

Television

See also
Arts & Music · *Film & Video*
Popular Culture & Entertainment · *Celebrities & Personalities*
Popular Culture & Entertainment · *Movies*

Association of America's Public Television Stations ★★★

This site is a collection of resources related to public television in the United States. The information ranges from general public television issues, such as governmental regulations, and funding and press releases, to access issues, and public television's role in education. There is an extensive set of links to other public television stations and related resources.

KEYWORDS Mass Communications, Media, Public Television, Television
AUDIENCE Activists, Media Professionals, Public Television Enthusiasts, Television Enthusiasts
CONTACT Thom Watson
         thom@apts.org
FREE

http://www.universe.digex.net:80/~apts/

C/Net Online ★★★★

C/Net Online is the Internet version of the U.S. cable television show that covers the vast field of technology and computers. At this site, you get reviews of computer software and hardware (including games and networks), information about technological innovations such as digital cameras, hotlinks to Internet sites of companies covered by C/Net's television program, and much more.

KEYWORDS   Computer Technology, E-Zines, Internet, Online Magazines
AUDIENCE   Computer Users, Consumers, Games Enthusiasts, Internet Users
CONTACT   support@cnet.com
FREE

http://cnet.com/

CableLabs Home Page ★★★

This is the home page for CableLabs, which is a consortium of Cable Television providers that focus on the cable industry's research and development. They offer press releases, publications, and information on conferences related to the cable industry. The cable technology newsletter provides a collection of resources related to the cable and telecommunications industries.

KEYWORDS   Cable Television, Mass Communications, Media, Television
AUDIENCE   Broadcasters, Cable Television Providers, Media Professionals, Television Professionals
CONTACT   webmaster@cablelabs.com
FREE

http://www.cablelabs.com/

Deutsche Welle WWW ★★★

The Deutsche Welle radio and TV site provides access to news reports and analyses, lists of German and international television and radio programs, international television and radio frequencies, and information on transcription services.

KEYWORDS   Germany, Radio, Television
AUDIENCE   Radio Enthusiasts, Television Enthusiasts
CONTACT   GMD
           web-editors@gmd.de, dw@dw.gmd.de
FREE

http://www-dw.gmd.de/deutsch/index.html

Doug Krause's WWW Television Server ★★★

This server offers access to information and resources about popular television programs such as M*A*S*H*, Saturday Night Live, and Gilligan's Island. Users will find FAQ files related to each show, including pictures and other related information. A comprehensive list provides TV network contacts, addresses, and phone numbers.

KEYWORDS   Mass Communications, Media, Popular Culture, Television
AUDIENCE   Popular Culture Enthusiasts, Television Enthusiasts
CONTACT   Doug Krause
           dijon@best.com
FREE

http://www.best.com/~dijon/tv/

Film and Television ★★

This page is a collection of links to film and television resources on the Internet. Users will find resources such as the C-Span gopher, the Beavis and Butthead home page, David Letterman's top ten lists, Monty Python's home page, and more. This server provides a wide variety of film and TV resources that are alphabetically organized.

KEYWORDS   Film, Mass Communications, Media, Television
AUDIENCE   Film Enthusiasts, Popular Culture Enthusiasts, Television Enthusiasts
CONTACT   Geoffrey Sauer
           postmaster@english.hss.cmu.edu
FREE

http://english-server.hss.cmu.edu/Film&TV.html

The Gillian Anderson Home Page ★★★

Either you love 'The X-Files' or you don't, and if you don't, I'd recommend that you stay far away from this site. The Gillian Anderson Home Page is a worshipful paean to the actress who plays Special Agent Dana Scully on televison's weekly exploration of the unknown. You'll find here far, far more than you ever wanted to know about this up-and-coming TV star, from interviews and soundbites to downloadable movie clips and details on every aspect of her persona, both on-screen and off-screen.

KEYWORDS   Science Fiction, Television
AUDIENCE   Television Enthusiasts
CONTACT   Victor Chan
           vichan@gpu.srv.ualberta.ca
FREE

http://gpu3.srv.ualberta.ca/~mlwalter/GAHP.html

I Saw It On TV - A Guide To Broadcast Programming Sources ★★

This site contains information about ordering specific television programs that have aired on any of the major United States television networks. It tells the user the price of the program and provides an address or phone number to have a videotape sent to your home/office. Additionally, the user will find addresses and phone numbers of the television program distributors and production companies, in addition to U.S. and Canadian television networks.

KEYWORDS   Cable Television, Television, Videos
AUDIENCE   Communications Specialists, Mass Communications Students, Television Enthusiasts
CONTACT   Corrine H. Smith
           chs@psulias.psu.edu
FREE

ftp://ftp.std.com/pub/tv-networks/broadcast-sources.txt

KCAL-TV Ch 9 Independent ★★

This site developed by KCAL, Channel 9 television in Los Angeles, California provides a comprehensive listing of the station's staff including detailed background information and photos. No information on programming or local news is offered at the site, although there is a link to TV Net.

KEYWORDS   California, California News, Television Stations
AUDIENCE   Californians, Los Angeles Tourists
CONTACT   kcaltv@aol.com
FREE

http://tvnet.com/TV/CAtv/KCAL.html

KMSP-TV UPN 9 ★★★★

The KMSP-TV UPN 9 Web page is a well-organized and up-to-date page, chock full of valuable information for residents of the Twin Cities and other KMSP viewers. The site offers not only access to local and global news but also includes a program listing for the new viewing season with image-accompanied descriptions for programs such as 'Star Trek' and 'Baywatch.' The site provides information on local entertainment as well as a link to the Twin Cities Computer Network site.

KEYWORDS   Minnesota, Television News, Television Programming, Television Stations
AUDIENCE   Minnesota Residents, Minnesota Tourists
CONTACT   upn9@kmsp.com
FREE

http://tccn.com/kmsp/upn9.html

Klingon Language Institute ★★★

The Klingon Language Institute has two main missions - first, to promote, foster, and develop the Klingon language, and second, to bring together Klingon language enthusiasts from around the world and provide them with a common forum for the discussion and the exchange of ideas. The membership of the Klingon Language Institute spans 20 nations of the globe. This site contains information about the Klingon Language system, archives of the Klingon Language Mailing List, ordering information for learning Klingon on your own (price of postage only!) and information about several creative projects including Klingon translation of the Bible and William Shakespeare's Works.

KEYWORDS   Language, Linguistics
AUDIENCE   Language Scholars, Linguists, Star Trek Enthusiasts, Trekkies
CONTACT   Mark E. Shoulson
           shoulson@cs.columbia.edu
FREE

http://www.kli.org/KLIhome.html

MTV Music Television ★★★

The MTV Music Television Web site is created to be an entertaining site that provides MTV-related material. Users will find MTV Oddities animation, with changing quicktime clips from MTV's newest animation show, information about the MTV Beach House, and Beach TV schedules.

KEYWORDS Animation, Music
AUDIENCE Music Enthusiasts, Teenagers, Television Enthusiasts
CONTACT feedback@mtv.com
FREE

http://mtv.com

Network 23 - XXIII ★★★

This site is the home site for a service provider in New York City Named Network 23, after the television network from the series Max Headroom. It has links to other sites specifically dedicated to the program containing an episode list, images, sounds, and scripts from the series.

KEYWORDS Comedy, Cyberculture, Television
AUDIENCE Comedy Fans, Science Fiction Enthusiasts
CONTACT Nick Jarecki
max@net23.com
FREE

http://www.net23.com

Rockford Files Homepage ★★★

This site is dedicated to the television series, The Rockford Files. It offers stills from the series, episodes, scripts, and links to other parts of the Net where the user might find related information.

KEYWORDS Detectives, Mystery Fiction, Television
AUDIENCE Rockford Files Fans, Television Enthusiasts
CONTACT Aaron Sumner
asumner@falcon.cc.ukans.edu
FREE

http://falcon.cc.ukans.edu/~asumner/rockford/

Star Trek - Voyager Web Site ★★★★

Paramount and Viacom have created an interactive fantasy Web site to support the new Star Trek - Voyager series. Upon entering the site, you are treated as a newly awakened member of the Voyager's crew. You are able to use the site as a 'PADD - personal access display device' containing information about the U.S.S. Voyager's mission, crew, and technology. Once you have learned all of the details, you can take an online evaluation. If you pass, you are praised by a video of the captain.

KEYWORDS Movies, Space, Television
AUDIENCE Broadcasters, Space Enthusiasts, Star Trek Enthusiasts
CONTACT voyager@paramount.com
FREE

http://voyager.paramount.com/

Sci-Fi Channel ★★★

This site provides an informative overview of The Science Fiction Channel and offers a wide variety of topics to investigate. The site includes daily program listings, documents with downloadable graphics and sound files, pages about science fiction programs, and a script writing exercise. Also offered are daily program plot summaries, science fiction Internet news, and other science fiction related resources.

KEYWORDS Movies, Science Fiction, Television
AUDIENCE General Public, Movie Enthusiasts, Science Fiction Enthusiasts, Television Enthusiasts
FREE

http://www.scifi.com

Sea Quest FTP site ★★★

This FTP site features sounds, newletters, character profiles, and guides relating to the television series Sea Quest.

KEYWORDS Drama, Science Fiction, Television, Television Programming
AUDIENCE General Public, Science Fiction Enthusiasts, Television Enthusiasts
FREE

http://www.hyperion.com:80/ftp/pub/TV/seaQuest/

Star Trek Humor ★★★

This page contains a few Star Trek-inspired bits of comedy, including fictitious sketches in which characters from the Star Trek television programs and films interact in ways that they certainly never did on-screen.

KEYWORDS Satire, Science Fiction, Television
AUDIENCE Jokers, Science Fiction Enthusiasts, Star Trek Enthusiasts, Trekkies

---

Connections to Sports
Fishing for compliments?

Whether you like to watch or participate in sports, the Internet is unmatched for its coverage of sports activities. If you're into bodybuilding, lacrosse, paddling, or spelunking, the Internet is the comprehensive international source for all sports.

One of the premier suppliers of international sports on the Internet is ESPN, the cable television purveyor, which beams Australian Football, Brazilian Soccer, and Wimbledon Tennis into millions of homes worldwide. ESPN is now doing the same thing on the Internet, and is doing so in English, Portuguese, Spanish, Mandarin, and Cantonese.

Besides ESPN's monthly television listings for all the major regions of the world, its Web site provides coverage of all varieties of sporting activities. Users can even download sound bites and photos of specific games while they are "in-progress." Users can also send questions via email to ESPN about its sports coverage. And now ESPN is featuring coverage of non-professional outdoor sports as well.

(http://web1.starwave.com/editors/studios/)

If your interest lies in archery, caving, chess, fishing, or skate-boarding, then check out the World-Wide Web Virtual Library - Sport Usenet Groups. There are currently more than 50 sports listed.

(http://www.atm.ch.cam.ac.uk/sports/usenet.html)

With the number growing all the time. At another site, "Sports (Leisure and Recreation)," you can find topics for discussion on air hockey, bodybuilding, cycling, and more at.

(http:www.einet.net/galaxy/Leisure-and Recreation/Sports.html)

Television – Unexplained Phenomena

CONTACT Christopher Dent
cdent@indiana.edu

FREE

http://www.honors.indiana.edu/%7echrome/trek/index.html

Steve Rapport's Young Ones' Page ★★

This site is dedicated to the British comedy series, The Young Ones. It offers scripts and sample sounds from the series.

KEYWORDS British Comedy, Comedy, Communications, Television
AUDIENCE Television Enthusiasts
CONTACT hammers@netcom.com

FREE

http://sashimi.wwa.com/hammers/comedy/youngone/youngone.htm

Street Cents Online ★★★★

This page presents the online extension of Street Cents, a Canadian television show devoted to showing young audiences how to get money honestly and how to avoid scams and ripoffs when spending it. Each edition of Street Cents Online includes product reviews, such as frozen pizzas or Crest toothpaste, viewer/reader surveys like 'What would you change in advertising?', and reports on money issues like part time job income and stocks and bonds. Other areas of this Web site focus on recent movies, music artists, and television shows.

KEYWORDS Adolescence, Consumer Protection, Teenage Issues
AUDIENCE Canadians, Children, Consumers, Parents, Teenagers
CONTACT Cochran Interactive Incorporated
ajh@cochran.com

FREE

http://www.screen.com/streetcents.html

TV Net The Ultimate TV List ★★★★

The Ultimate TV List is an index of Internet resources related to television programs in the United States and elsewhere. The resource list, including current listings, ranges from newsgroups and listservers to World Wide Web pages. Users can browse the alphabetical list by program names, program genres, or by resource type. There is a section where users can add their own favorite shows or resources to the list.

KEYWORDS Broadcasting, Mass Communications, Popular Culture, Television
AUDIENCE Broadcasters, Popular Culture Enthusiasts, Television Enthusiasts
CONTACT David Cronshaw
david@tvnet.com

FREE

http://www.tvnet.com/UTVL/utvl.html

Transformers ★★★★

This is a page of links specific to the Transformers TV series. Included are links to ftp sites, fan fiction, and episode transcripts.

KEYWORDS Science Fiction, Television, Transformers
AUDIENCE Comics Enthusiasts, Television Enthusiasts
CONTACT tf@vt.edu

FREE

http://www.vt.edu:10021/other/transformers/

Unofficial Picket Fences Home Page ★★★

This site is dedicated to the television series, Picket Fences. It features cast descriptions, an episodes list, as well as links to other sites related to the show.

KEYWORDS Picket Fences, TV Drama, Television
AUDIENCE Television Enthusiasts
CONTACT Jeff Mealiffe
jeff.mealiffe@smtpgw.sdcs.k12.ca.us

FREE

http://199.245.131.7/fences/fences.html

Vanderbilt Television News Archive ★★★★

The Vanderbilt Television News Archive is a collection of over 23,000 television news broadcasts dating back to 1968, and over 8,000 hours of news-related programming. Users can browse text indexes with abstracts of the Archive's collection, as well as obtain information about borrowing tapes of individual broadcasts and compiled broadcast tapes. This server also offers links to related information resources on the Internet.

KEYWORDS Archives, News, News Media, Television
AUDIENCE News Buffs, Researchers, Television Enthusiasts, Television News Enthusiasts
CONTACT tvnews@tvnews.Vanderbilt.Edu

FREE

http://tvnews.vanderbilt.edu/

gopher://tvnews.Vanderbilt.Edu:70/

WDIV-TV Channel 4 (Detroit) ★★★

The WDIV-TV home page allows users to access detailed information about this Detroit-based television station's staff. The site also provides information on their current programming schedule with links to the home pages of many popular NBC sitcoms. Users can access information on a selection of news and sports features. For weather information users are provided with links to other online weather resources.

KEYWORDS Michigan, NBC Television, Television Stations
AUDIENCE Michigan Residents
CONTACT Mike Wendland
mikew@wdiv.com

FREE

http://www.wdiv.com/

Unexplained Phenomena

See also
Popular Culture & Entertainment · Television

Dark Side of the Web ★★★

The Dark Side of the Web is a guide to strange, macabre, and occult-related Internet sites. Users will find links listed alphabetically by subject, with no description of the site. Subject categories include art and images, cemeteries and death, gothic pages, halloween, horror, movies and music-related pages, paranormal, paganism, and vampire pages.

KEYWORDS Death, Paganism, Vampires
AUDIENCE Internet Users, Occult Enthusiasts
CONTACT Carrie Carolin
carrie@cascade.net

FREE

http://www.cascade.net/darkweb.html

Department of Conspiracy Investigation and Propagation ★★★

The Department of Conspiracy Investigation & Propagation is a spoof of Conspiracy and Government information on the Web. The page offers some conspiracy theories, implicating organizations like Rock the Vote, Microsoft Corporation and The Bavarian Illuminati. Links are provided to the real home pages of the organizations 'implicated'. Users can add their own conspiracy theory to the site.

KEYWORDS Conspiracy, Humor, Satire, Spoof
AUDIENCE Conspiracy Theory Enthusiasts, Satire Enthusiasts
CONTACT aiken@conspiracy.org

FREE

http://www.conspiracy.org/conspiracy/conspiracy.html

Electric Dreams Magazine ★★★

This site contains articles for those interested in dreams and their interpretation. Electric Dreams includes dream transcriptions, journals and other material on the interpretation and theory of the meanings of dream imagery.

KEYWORDS Dream Interpretation, Dreams, Health, Psychology
AUDIENCE Dreamers, Psychiatrists, Psychologists, Reading Enthusiasts
CONTACT Catherine Decker
cathy@cassandra.ucr.edu

FREE

ftp://sppc1952.uwsp.edu/

Encyclopedia of Ghosts and Spirits ★★★★

This is a review and resource for The Encyclopedia of Ghosts and Spirits by Rosemary Ellen Guiley with more

than 400 A to Z entries and 70 illustrations about paranormal activitiy worldwide. Purchase and ISBN information are available here.

Keywords General Literature, Mythology
Audience Reading Enthusiasts, Students (Secondary/College), Students (Secondary/University)
Free

gopher://ns1.infor.com:4600/
    1exec%3AR1969010-1971796-/
    .te:

FAQ - Alt.Vampyres ★★★

This Web site, an FAQ for the Usenet group alt.vampyres, covers introductory ground. There is also a list of the forms vampires take in different cultures, an extensive bibliography, and information for contacting societies interested in vampires.

Keywords Mythology, Vampires
Audience Mythologians, Sociologists, Vampire Enthusiasts
Free

http://csclub.uwaterloo.ca/~fyao/vamp/vampfaq

Hastings UFO Society ★★★

This page contains satirical UFO-related 'news' bulletins and other articles for those who do not believe in the existence of Unidentified Flying Objects. Weekly spoken bulletins are also available in various audio formats.

Keywords Aliens, Humor, Satire, UFO (Unidentified Flying Objects)
Audience Humor Enthusiasts, Practical Jokers
Contact Hastings UFO Society
    scott@santarosa.edu
Free

http://www.santarosa.edu/hufos/

High Weirdness by E-Mail ★★

This is a guide to some interesting sources of information online. This zine focuses mainly on bizarre philosophies, such as Discordia and SubGenius. Contents include offbeat religions, spirituality, paganism, magic, occultism, UFOs, and paranormal phenomena.

Keywords Hacking, Paganism, Paranormal, Zines
Audience Computer Hackers, Cyberculture Enthusiasts, Cybernauts, Popular Culture Enthusiasts
Contact rita@etext.archive.umich.edu
Free

ftp://etext.archive.umich.edu/pub/Zines/Weirdness

Jonathan Cainer's Daily Horoscopes ★★★

This site provides Jonathan Cainer's daily horoscopes taken from the Daily Mail, Britain's Daily Newspaper. You simply click on your zodiac sign and your future awaits you! There is also a link to 'The Funky Times,' which delivers extensive links to the best Daily News weather, comic strips, and features. You can also check out your personal horoscopes and 'Year Ahead Horoscopes' via the Internet. Also available are his weekly forecasts in Real Audio format. Listen while you surf!

Keywords Astrology, Horoscopes
Audience Horoscope Readers, Internet Users, News Buffs
Contact Stephen Lord
    stephen@realitycom.com
Free

http://www.realitycom.com/webstars/index.html

Magical Blend Magazine Online ★★★

Magical Blend magazine covers many different subjects, from the occult, homeopathic medicine, ambient and house music, to science fiction, philosophy and psychology. While it may be hard to pin a single restrictive description on Magical Blend, the subjects are varied enough to interest almost anyone.

Keywords Alternative Music, Homeopathic Medicine, Occult, Science Fiction
Audience Music Enthusiasts, Occult Enthusiasts, Science Fiction Enthusiasts
Contact Editor
    magical@eden.com
Free

http://www.eden.com/magical/main.html

Real Astrology ★★★★

Real Astrology is an online Horoscope page written by Rob Brezsny, whose humorous Astrology pages are found in the San Francisco Weekly and Details Maga-

---

Connections to Ghosts
BOO!

Archive X
Paranormal Phenomena

x \'eks\ vt x-ed also x'd or xed \'ekst\; 1: to mark with an x 2: to cancel or obliterate with a series of x's -- usu. used with out

para.nor.mal \,par-*-'nor-m*l\ adj (ca 1920) : not scientifically explainable : SUPERNATURAL

Archive X is a series of Web pages devoted towards Paranormal Phenomena. It is a portion of The Virtual Library. Information is gathered from various news groups as well as submissions from interested parties and case histories from officially documented hauntings and paranormal activities.

Archive X was created by Brandon Gillespie brandon@paradise.declab.usu.edu, and maintained by him through 1994 and part of 1995"

Disclaimer: Because information may exist in this listing does not mean I personally endorse it nor believe it. I am simply creating an archive of other's experiences as they recounted or were recorded.

Recent Changes to **Archive X**

Everything you always wanted to know about ghosts but were afraid to ask, can be found on the Internet. There's a virtual library of ghost stories from around the world, a ghost stories mailing list and games about ghosts.

"Archive X" on the World Wide Web provides you with hotlinks for hunting ghosts. You can also touch base with the "Space Ghost" and choose from a wide selection of ghost stories to read before you go to bed.

(http://www.crown.net/X/)

If you are more interested in finding out about ghost towns to visit, try the "Arizona Treasure Hunters Ghost Town Guide" site. The site features maps of ghost towns, an index of guides and historical material on several ghost towns in Arizona, plus links to other ghost towns in the American West.

(http://www.halcyon.com/treasure/books/states/stateaz.html)

If you have been visited by ghosts or other things that go bump in the night, you can haunt the "Folklore/Ghost-Stories" site and share your personal ghost stories.

(http://www.crown.net/X/)

zine. Users can find their weekly horoscopes, updated every Thursday.

KEYWORDS   Astrology, Horoscopes
AUDIENCE   Astrology Enthusiasts, Horoscope Readers
CONTACT   Rob Breszny
           zenpride@well.sf.ca.us
FREE

http://www.butterfly.net/astro/

Shawn's Occult Resources ★★★

Shawn's Occult Resources is a meta-index to magic and mysticism pages on the Web. Links are listed alphabetically by topic, such as alchemy, gnosis, mythology, neopaganism, and tarot, with a one-sentence description of each site. Also included is the terminology dictionary, the Magic Code, a take-off on the Geek Code, and a guide to other individual occult indexes.

KEYWORDS   Magic, Mysticism, Occult
AUDIENCE   Magic Enthusiasts, Occult Enthusiasts
CONTACT   Shawn Knight
           knightster+@cmu.edu
FREE

http://www.contrib.andrew.cmu.edu/~eclectic/occult.html

World Wide Web Ouija ★★

The World Wide Web Ouija is an online version of the popular prophecy game, in which a pointer that participants have lightly set their hands on spells out messages on a gameboard. A 'Ouija board' is provided, upon which users are supposed to place their mouse after having asked a question and then spun around 20 times. This page is a self-proclaimed game, rather than a serious attempt at prophecy, and designed for entertainment purposes.

KEYWORDS   Games, Prophecy
AUDIENCE   Games Enthusiasts, Occult Enthusiasts
CONTACT   black@vidalia.unh.edu
FREE

http://www.math.unh.edu/~black/cgi-bin/ouija.cgi

Weather & Traffic

See also
Engineering & Technology · *Technology*
Science · *Earth Sciences*
Science · *Geosciences*

Current Weather Maps/Movies ★★★

This Web site, which is updated hourly, offers meteorological data, images, and maps from locations around the world. Visual and infrared maps are supplied from current satellite data. This site also provides links to archives containing software needed to access interactive weather browsers on the net.

KEYWORDS   Climatology, Meteorology, Weather
AUDIENCE   Climatologists, General Public, Meteorologists, Meteorology Students
CONTACT   Charles Henrich
           henrich@crh.cl.msu.edu
FREE

http://clunix.cl.msu.edu:80/weather/

German Railway Timetables and Information ★★★

This server provides information on fares and schedules of German passenger railroads. Inquiries are made by filling out a form. Responses are emailed to the user. There is also limited information about railroads in the rest of Europe.

KEYWORDS   Germany, Online Services, Railroads, Tourism
AUDIENCE   Germans, Students, Tourists, Travelers
CONTACT   ule3@rz.uni-karlsruhe.de
FREE

http://rzstud1.rz.uni-karlsruhe.de/~ule3/info-trn.html

IntelliCast ★★★

The Intellicast WWW site offers users a simple index for finding weather forecasts for major American cities and ski resorts. Indexes are organized according to city, type of forecast, and region. In addition, one may also view images of individual cities and examine weather histories.

KEYWORDS   Meteorology, Ski Conditions, Weather
AUDIENCE   Skiing Enthusiasts, Tourists
CONTACT   info@intellicast.com
FREE

http://www.intellicast.com/

KKTV-TV (Colorado Springs, CO) Netline Weather ★★★

This is the Weather Forecast Web page for KKTV-TV serving Colorado Springs, Colorado. The site provides daily updated weather maps for Colorado and the United States, as well as an audio copy of the local weatherman's forecast. The site also provides a link to a satellite loop and to a camera scanning Colorado's Pikes Peak.

KEYWORDS   Colorado, Meteorology, Television, Weather Forecasts
AUDIENCE   Colorado Springs Residents, Meteorologists
CONTACT   kktv@softronics.com
FREE

http://www.kktv.com/_weather/wthr_loc.htm

Meteorological Operations Division Gopher ★★★★

This site offers access to national weather reports. The reports consist of climatic summaries, current conditions, extended forcasts, and forecasts. The server also has special weather statements, radar summaries, storm warnings, radar summaries, and state police road conditions.

KEYWORDS   Geography, Meteorology, Weather, Weather Reports
AUDIENCE   Adults, General Public, Meteorologists
FREE

gopher://ux2.cso.uiuc.edu:16000/

New York City Subway System ★★★

This site is a guide to the New York City Subway System, used by over 3.3 million people every day. Site visitors can zoom in on a subway map to find the closest station to their destination. Contact information for the Metropolitan Transportation Authority and other local commuter rail services are also available.

KEYWORDS   Maps, New York, Public Transportation, Subways
AUDIENCE   Public Transportation Users, Tourists, New York Residents
CONTACT   webmaster@mediabridge.com
FREE

http://www.mediabridge.com/nyc/transportation/subways/

Oregon Climate Service (OCS) Home Page ★★★★

The Oregon Climate Service (OCS) home page provides access to weather information for the local area and the United States. The OCS page contains weather forecasts, precipitation reports, warnings, publications and data archives. The page has an outline listing of links for marine forecasts, road conditions, snow reports and forecasts for Oregon, the Pacific Northwest, the US and the Globe. There are links to the Corvallis (Hyslop) Reports, the State Summaries of Weather and Climate and the USGS Water Availability Report.

KEYWORDS   Climatology, Meteorology, Snow Reports, Weather
AUDIENCE   Climatologists, Meteorologists, Oregon Residents, Students
CONTACT   oregon@ats.orst.edu
FREE

http://ocs.ats.orst.edu/

San Francisco Bay Area Traffic Information ★★★★

The Transit Information Project is a public service to provide instant online access to transit information for the San Francisco Bay Area. The site is divided into a number of sections such as Announcements, Transit Carriers, Regional Information, and Administrative information about the project itself. Users will find not only a fairly comprehensive list with links to the different modes of transporation available (Buses, Trains, Ferries, Air Transporation, etc.) but links to schedules and general information useful to visitors and residents alike.

KEYWORDS   California, Public Transportation, Traffic Reports, Transportation
AUDIENCE   Californians, Policymakers, Tourists

CONTACT   Traffic Information Administrator
          transit@server.berkeley.edu
FREE

http://server.berkeley.edu/Transit/
index.html

Southern California Real-Time Traffic Report ★★★★

This site is an experimental server designed to give real time traffic reports for the Los Angeles area. The traffic reports are given by a series of maps or by a quick summary of trouble spots. Users may choose a map updated in real time or, if their connection is slow, updated every five minutes. Users may then click on any spot on the map for more detailed information about that area. The site also provides weather forecasts for the Los Angeles area.

KEYWORDS California, Civil Engineering, Computer Applications, Travel
AUDIENCE Californians, Civil Engineers, General Public
CONTACT   William J. Proffer
          proffer@scubed.com
FREE

http://www.scubed.com:8001/caltrans/
transnet.html

Southwest Agricultural Weather Service Center ★★★★

The National Weather Services' Southwest Agricultural Weather Service Center page provides local agricultural forecasts, warnings, and reports. The page has reports for weekly and monthly drought, sunshine, and crop reports. There are educational materials on reporting as well as links to related weather, atmosphere, and oceanography sites.

KEYWORDS Agriculture, Atmospheric Sciences, Weather
AUDIENCE Agricultural Researchers, Farmers, Southwest Residents
CONTACT   James A. Nelson Jr.
          jnelson@swami.tamu.edu
FREE

http://swami.tamu.edu/

Storm '95 RAINwatch ★★

The Storm '95 RAINwatch Web site is provided by the Regional Alliance for Information Networking. It offers information on the 1995 rain season in California, which has sustained much damage due to the extensive flooding. Users will find state damage reports, as well as reports from the Federal Emergency Management Agency. Information on the status of California roads is also provided.

KEYWORDS California
AUDIENCE Californians
CONTACT   storm95@rain.org
FREE

http://www.rain.org/storm95/

USA Today Weather ★★★

At the USA Today Weather web site users can access daily weather reports nationwide. There are general

Connections to UFOs
Take me to your leader

UFO Sightings by Astronauts
UFO Joe February 17, 1993
Contents:
- Major Gordon Cooper
- Ed White & James McDivitt
- James Lovell and Frank Borman
- Neil Armstrong & Edwin "Buzz" Aldrin
- Donald Slayton
- Major Robert White
- NASA Pilot Joseph A. Walker
- Commander Eugene Cernan
- NASA's Maurice Chatelain
- NASA's Scott Carpenter

Do you believe in UFOs? Do you feel you've been taken aboard an extraterrestrial craft? The Internet allows you access to vast resources about UFOs, from the point of view of both believers and skeptics.

You may question some of the stories you read on the Internet; some you may believe. There are Internet sites about UFO Sightings by U.S. astronauts. One is from one of the original U.S. Mercury missions in which Major Gordon Cooper reported seeing a "glowing, greenish object" ahead of the capsule.

(http://www.cs.bgsu.edu/~jzawodn/ufo/astro-sightings.html)

You can also read about UFOs, the New Physics, and a situation report on the acquisition of advanced technology and human interaction with alien cultures. There's even information about animal mutilation and UFOs at this site.

(http://spirit/satelnet.org/Spirit/krill.html)

also, (http://www.hia.com/hia/pcr/ufo.html)

You can also access a UFO bibliography, as well as books and CD-ROMs on UFO abductions; these are available on various Net sites.

(http://www.cis.ksu.edu/~psiber/substand/UFO.html)

reports for the West, Midwest, South and East. One may also read the day's headlines as reported by USA Today.

KEYWORDS News, Newspapers, Weather
AUDIENCE General Public, US Newspaper Readers, United States Residents
FREE

http://www.usatoday.com/web5.htm

WDIV-TV (Detroit, MI) WeatherWatch ★★★

This is the Weather page for WDIV-TV in Detroit, Michigan. The page provides an introduction to the staff, local weather forecasts and ten day temperature forecast. The site is linked to national weather forecasts pages, satellite images and current weather maps and movies.

KEYWORDS Meteorology, Michigan, Television, Weather Forecasts
AUDIENCE Michigan Residents, Weather Forecasters
CONTACT   wdiv@aol.com
FREE

http://www.ruct.net/WDTV/
weatherwatch.html

WISC-TV Weather ★★★★

The WISC-TV Weather home page provides comprehensive information on weather conditions and forecasts for the city of Madison, Wisconsin and other areas. The forecast is updated twice daily, and there are predications for upcoming days. A national satellite picture may also be viewed.

KEYWORDS Weather, Wisconsin
AUDIENCE Wisconsin Residents, Weather Enthusiasts
FREE

http://wwwdev.binc.net:497/weather.htm

Washington State Department of Transportation

This site for the Washington State Department of Transportation contains information for all traffic and transportation related information for the state. The site includes a link to a traffic flow page with a continually updated image map of Puget Sound area. Users can click on an area of the map to get corresponding information to various transporation construction projects and projections for the area. In addition, bulletins of projects, issues, incidents, as well as the Sunshine Report (detailed construction project listings with cost, completion date, and mileage information) are included.

KEYWORDS Traffic Reports, Transportation, Washington State
AUDIENCE Policymakers, Transporation Engineers, Washington State Residents
CONTACT Michael Forbis
trafficmaster@wsdot.wa.gov
FREE

http://198.238.212.10/regions/northwest/

Weather Watch Magazine

Weather Watch Magazine offers this Web site to describe its magazine and offer a preview of the latest edition of the magazine. Users will find material on the staff, subscription information, and more. There are links to many weather information sites on the net available from this site.

KEYWORDS Magazines, Publications, Weather
AUDIENCE Climatologists, Weather Enthusiasts
CONTACT William Hipkins
wxcentral@aol.com
FREE

http://northshore.shore.net/~wxcentrl/

WebWeather

WebWeather is designed to provide users with quick and easy access to weather conditions and forecasts throughout the world. One may conduct searches by region and city. In addition, users may look up the latest marine forecasts for any ocean in the world.

KEYWORDS Meteorology, Weather
AUDIENCE General Public, Tourists, Travelers
CONTACT Ben Davenport
bpd@princeton.edu
FREE

http://www.princeton.edu/Webweather/ww.html

Religion & Philosophy

Doctrines 557
Mythology 557
Philosophy 558
Religions 559
Religious Artifacts 562
Religious History 562
Resources 562

Doctrines

See also
Humanities & Social Sciences · *Classics*
Humanities & Social Sciences · *History*

Atheism ★★

The Alt.Atheism Web contains information from the alt.atheism Usenet newsgroups. Users will find overviews of the contents of the newsgroups, FAQs and a general introduction to atheism. Also provided are address lists for atheist organizations and links to resources on the Web.

Keywords Atheism, Philosophy, Religious Studies
Audience Atheists, Religious Studies Students
Contact mathew@mantis.co.uk
Free

http://www.mantis.co.uk/atheism/

Marx and Engels' Writings ★★★★

This page, provided by the Progressive Sociologists' Network, contains links to an extensive collection of texts about Marx and Engels. Some of the works include Young Marx (before editing Rheinische Zeitung), On the Jewish Question, The Communist Manifesto, Poland and the Russian Menace, The Civil War in France, Engels' Speech at Karl Marx's Grave, and more.

Keywords Communism, Political Science
Audience Classical Philosophers, Marxists, Political Scientists, Socialists
Free

http://english-www.hss.cmu.edu/

UNARIUS Academy of Science ★★★

This site describes the New Age-oriented UNARIUS Academy of Science, a tax-exempt, non-profit, educational foundation that publishes books and videos of New World Teaching. UNARIUS stands for UNiversal ARticulate Interdimensional Understanding of Science.

Keywords New Age Philosophy
Audience Educators, New Age Enthusiasts, Scientists, Students (Secondary/College)
Contact unarius@cts.com
Free

http://crash.cts.com/~unarius/

Zen Buddhist Texts ★★★

This site entails a comprehensive listing of Zen Buddhist texts, electronic information, and links. There is information available on Zen groups and meditation meetings. The site is updated by the students at the Southwest Chogye Zen Center.

Keywords Journals, Philosophy, Taoism, Zen Buddhism
Audience Buddhists, Educators (University), Philosophers, Students
Contact Steven Newton
snewton@oac.hsc.uth.tms.edu
Free

http://oac11.hsc.uth.tmc.edu/zen/index.html

Mythology

See also
Humanities & Social Sciences · *Classics*
Religion · *Religions*

Myths, Legends, and Folklore ★★★

Myths, Legends, and Folklore provides links to mythology and legend resources on the Internet. It is organized by geography (Greek and Roman) and genre (Gothic Horror).

Keywords History, Myths, Pagans, Religion
Audience Educators, Literary Scholars, Mythology Enthusiasts, Students
Contact graymouser@mit.edu
Free

http://www.mit.edu:8001/people/mouser/myth.html

Oxford Arthurian Society ★★★

This is the home page of the Oxford Arthurian Society. It provides information on the society and its current schedule. It also provides links to other Arthurian sites on the web.

Keywords Celtic Culture, History, Legends, Myths
Audience History Buffs, Mythology Enthusiasts, Scholars, Students
Contact arthursoc@sable.o%.ac.uk
Free

http://info.ox.ac.uk/~arthsoc/

World of the Vikings, The ★★★

World of the Vikings is a page devoted to Vikings and the research and mythology that surrounds them. It provides links to research, education, and museums.

Keywords Myths, Scholars, Students
Audience Educators, History Researchers, Mythology Enthusiasts, Mythology Students

CONTACT jeremy@jjohnson.demon.co.uk
FREE

http://www.demon.co.uk/history/index.html

Philosophy

See also
Humanities & Social Sciences · *Anthropology*
Humanities & Social Sciences · *Literature*

American Philosophical Association (APA) ★★★

This site, acting as a crossroads to philosophy-related sites on the Internet, organizes its links into sites with philosophical content, societies, institutes, centers and departments, software for philosophers, other meta-indexes, publishers, and libraries and collections. There is also a link to the APA Electronic Bulletin Board, a gopher with email address books, events calendars, grant information, calls for papers, and other resources.

KEYWORDS Meta-Index (Philosophy), Organizations
AUDIENCE Internet Users, Librarians, Philosophers, Philosophy Students
CONTACT Saul Traiger
         traiger@oxy.edu
FREE

http://www.oxy.edu/apa/apa.html

gopher://gate.oxy.eud/

Department of Philosophy at Indiana University ★★★

The resources on this philosophy gopher server include access to a philosophy journal called the Electronic Journal of Analytic Philosophy, and a bibliography on belief revision and non-monotonicity which is searchable by keywords. The site also provides links to other gopher holes in the Indiana University academic system.

KEYWORDS Education (College/University), Journals, Philosophy
AUDIENCE Philosophers, Philosophy Educators, Professors, Students (University)
CONTACT gopher@phil.indiana.edu
FREE

gopher://tarski.phil.indiana.edu/

Edward N. Zalta Home Page ★★★

The home page of Edward N. Zalta, a Senior Researcher at the Center for the Study of Language and Information, an independent research institution on the Stanford University campus. Zalta has a Ph.D. in Philosophy; his research specialties include—Metaphysics and Ontology, Philosophy of Language and Intensional Logic, and Philosophy of the Mind and Intentionality. Links are provided to courses and syllabi, publications, and places lectured.

KEYWORDS Logic, Metaphysics, Philosophy
AUDIENCE Linguists, Metaphysics Enthusiasts, Philosophers, Students (University)
CONTACT
FREE

http://mally.stanford.edu/zalta.html

Indiana University Philosophy Department ★★★★

The Indiana University Philosophy Department offers information about its graduate studies program. The page has course descriptions, seminar schedules and an electronic journal. There are links to philosophy resources on the Internet and other departments at Indiana University.

KEYWORDS Analytical Philosophy, Cognitive Sciences, Education (College/University), Educational Programs
AUDIENCE Educators, Philosophers, Students
CONTACT information@phil.indiana.edu
FREE

http://www.phil.indiana.edu/

McGill Philosophy Home Page ★★★

This is the information page for the McGill University Department of Philosophy. Its purposes are to make information about the Department available over the Internet, and to make the Internet easily accessible to the members of the Department. It has links to pages about the Web, McGill University, and the Philosophy Department. There are additional links to various Internet philosophy resources and to the University's mainframe computers (available to McGill faculty, students and staff only).

KEYWORDS Philosophy
AUDIENCE Canada Residents, Students (Secondary/University), Students (University)
CONTACT Andrew Burday
         andy@philo.mcgill.ca
FREE

http://godel.philo.mcgill.ca/

Philosophy in Cyberspace ★★★

Philosophy in Cyberspace is a lengthy guide to gophers, FTPs, listservs, USENET newsgroups, telnet addresses, and WWW sites related to philosophy. Drawn up with a particular interest in resources on feminism and political philosophy, this guide contains information on online bibliographies, libraries, and books. There is information on how to connect with people, on-line journals, articles, and other resources in specific branches of philosophy. Mailing lists and newsgroups are divided into content areas such as 'Aesthetics' and 'Political Philosophy'. The guide also contains information on postgraduate and undergraduate programs in philosophy.

KEYWORDS Aesthetics, Meta-Index (Philosophy), Philosophy
AUDIENCE Internet Users, Librarians, Philosophers, Philosophy Students
CONTACT 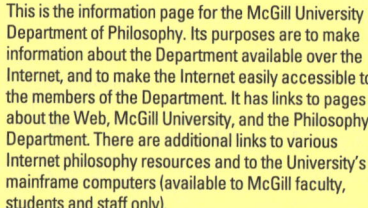 Dey Alexander
         dey@silas.cc.monash.edu.au
FREE

http://www.bris.ac.uk/Depts/Philosophy/Cyber/philcyb.html

gopher://info.monash.edu.au

ftp://ftp.cc.monash.edu.au/pub/

School of Wisdom ★★★

The School of Wisdom is a philosophy group dedicated to finding an understanding of chance, chaos and the order behind them using The Wheel developed by Professor Keyserling as a model. On their home page they provide information about this philosophy, with a description of the Wheel and its meaning, the Wisdom Laws of order, and an explanation of the importance of numbers in fractal geometry and chaos theory. Users will also find essays regarding the origin of the Universe and the meta-politics of the Internet, as well as descriptions of the essays given by guest speakers at the School of Wisdom conferences with the theme of Understanding.

KEYWORDS Chaos Theory, Mathematical Philosophy
AUDIENCE Philosophy Enthusiasts, Philosophy Students, Philosophy Teachers
CONTACT Ralph Losey
         wisdom@digital.net
FREE

http://www.webcom.com/~metanoic/wisdom/

UCI Philosophy Gopher ★★★

This gopher server, sponsored by the Department of Philosophy at University of California, Irvine, provides bibliographies, course details, FAQs, and links to online journals related to philosophy.

KEYWORDS Bibliographies, Journals, Philosophy
AUDIENCE Philosophers, Philosophy Educators, Professors, Students (University)
CONTACT Peter Woodruff
         philoso@gopher-server.cwis.uci.edu
FREE

gopher://philosophy.cwis.uci.edu:7016/

Ultimate Philosophy Page ★★★★

This site acts as a crossroads to Internet resources on philosophy, divided into the following categories - gopher sites, philosophy projects, university departments, individual philosophers' works and discussions, home pages of selected philosophers, and journals. Journals listed cover a range of subjects, including continental and analytic philosophy, religious ethics, complexity, artificial intelligence, and Australian philosophy.

KEYWORDS Ethics, Meta-Index (Philosophy)
AUDIENCE Internet Users, Librarians, Philosophers, Philosophy Students
CONTACT Sean Cearley
         cearls@rpi.edu
FREE

http://www.rpi.edu/~cearls/phil.html

Welcome to the Principia Cybernetica Web ★★★★

Welcome to the Principia Cybernetica Web promotes the computer-supported collaborative development of an evolutionary-systemic philosophy. This project tackles philosophical questions with the help of cybernetic theories and technologies.

KEYWORDS Evolution, Philosophy

AUDIENCE   Evolutionists, Philosophers, Systems Administrators
CONTACT   Francis Heylighen
           fheyligh@vnet3.vub.ac.be
FREE

http://pespmc1.vub.ac.be/

Religions

See also
Humanities & Social Sciences · *Archaeology*
Religion · *Doctrines*

143 Biblical Contradictions ★★

This Web site contains replies to 143 purported Bible contradictions including an interactive dialogue on the subject. It has an index of the contradictions and allows the user to add comments.

KEYWORDS   Bible, Christianity, History, Theology
AUDIENCE   Bible Scholars, Christians, Religious Studies Students, Theologians
CONTACT   Andrew Tong
           werdna@ugcs.caltech.edu
FREE

http://www.ugcs.caltech.edu/cgi-bin/webnews/read/contradictions/0

Book of Mormon ★★

This gopher from the Presbyterian College provides the entire Book of Mormon in electronic text form, listed by book.

KEYWORDS   Mormonism, Religious Studies, Religious Texts
AUDIENCE   Mormons, Religious Studies Educators, Religious Studies Students
CONTACT   Jon Bell
           jtbell@presby.edu
FREE

gopher://cs1.presby.edu/11/religion/Mormon

Campus Crosswalk ★★★

This is a periodical for Christian college-level students who are having trouble with conflicts between their faith and their university surroundings. Campus CrossWalk features question-and-answer forums, articles, reviews of popular films and music, and a number of special features in every issue.

KEYWORDS   Christianity, Religious Magazines, Religious Studies
AUDIENCE   Christians, Clergy, Counselors, Students (University)
CONTACT   Milton Jones
           editor@ccw.acu.edu
FREE

http://ccw.acu.edu/

Connections to Religions

Now, let us give thanks . . .

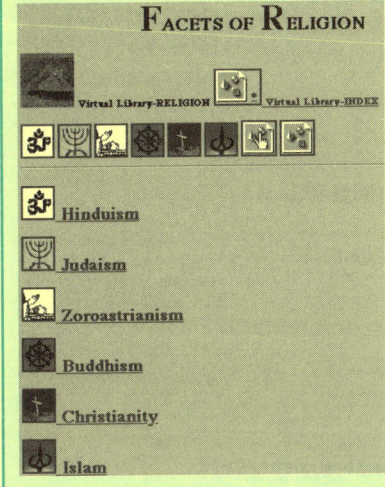

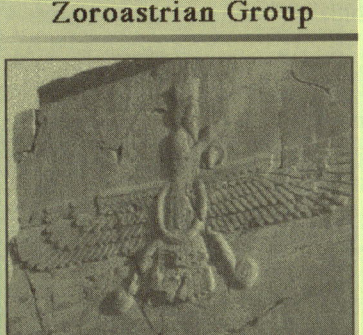
Faravahar or Farohar

Some of the busiest sites on the Internet are those that pertain to religion—whether Islam, Christianity, Judaism, or Buddhism.

If you want to understand more about the fundamental religious beliefs and teachings of the world's religions, or to make contact with others who share your religious beliefs, the Internet has several sites.

The "Religion" site on the World Wide Web offers users a connection to a virtual library on nearly all of the world's religions—from the Baha'i Faith to Zoroastrianism. The site provides basic religious doctrine and suggested readings for each of the religions as well.

(http://www.biologie.uni-freiburg.de/~amueller/religion/)

Other sites offer CD-ROMS of major religious texts, including The Bible and The Koran, as well as more marginalized works—all in a multimedia format.

(http://www.interlog.com/~pjm/cdshop/ibm/cat38.html) for IBM compatible PCs, also, (http://www.interlog.com/~pjm/cdshop/mac/cat38.html) for Macs.

Catholic Resources on the Net ★★★★

The Catholic Resources on the Net site provides links to Internet resources having to do with Catholicism. Links are grouped into subject categories such as liturgy and worship, scripture, writings from the early Church, Catholic organizations, and Catholic books. Brief descriptions of source of the resources is provided. The site is maintained by students at Carnegie Mellon University in Pennsylvania, so regional Catholic resources including worship service information are also provided.

KEYWORDS   Catholicism, Religious Studies
AUDIENCE   Catholics, Religious Studies Educators, Religious Studies Students
CONTACT   John Ockerbloom
           spok+catholic@cs.cmu.edu
FREE

http://www.cs.cmu.edu/Web/People/spok/catholic.html

Central Organization for Jewish Education ★★★

This gopher provides information related to Judaism. The Central Organization for Jewish Education maintains the offerings which include the Lubavitch Library, the Chabad LISTSERV mailing list, weekly and daily Torah studies, Jewish life, women in Judaism, and more.

KEYWORDS   Education, Judaism, Libraries, Organizations
AUDIENCE   Jews, Librarians, Students (University), Women
CONTACT   Yosef Y. Kazen, Jewish Organizations
           yyk@chabad.org
FREE

gopher://lubavitch.chabad.org/

Christian Internet Resources ★★★★

A gopher site which provides access to other Christianity related gophers, a catalog of contemporary Christian music, an online copy of Christian Resources Internet Guide, and a comprehensive guide to resources related to classical Christianity.

KEYWORDS   Christian Music, Christianity, Theology

AUDIENCE   Christians, General Public, Musicians, Theology Students
FREE

gopher://gopher.mc.edu:70/11/lnr/christian

Christian Resource List ★★★★

This site acts as a crossroads to Christian Internet resources, and is divided into categories including: What is Christianity?, Bibles, History and Culture, writings on music and literature, commercial sites, conferences, and newsgroups and mailing lists. The extensive category 'Christian Organizations and Churches' features sub-categories which include individual churches, larger church bodies, missions and ministries, schools and universities, and arts organizations.

KEYWORDS   Bible, Christian Music, Christianity
AUDIENCE   Christians, Historians, Internet Users, Religious Studies Scholars
CONTACT   Simon Damberger
            damberge@beagle.colorado.edu
FREE

http://saturn.colorado.edu:8080/Christian/list.html

College of Biblical and Family Studies ★★★

This gopher gives information about the degree programs offered at the College of Biblical and Family Studies at Abilene Christian University (ACU), Abilene, Texas. There is also information about ACU missions, biblical and theological resources, and other religious information available on the Internet.

KEYWORDS   Bible, Christianity, Education, Evangelism
AUDIENCE   Christians, Families, Religious Studies Educators, Religious Studies Students
CONTACT   info@bible.acu.edu
FREE

gopher://bible.acu.edu/

Cousins ★★★

An occasional e-zine/newsletter for those interested in or currently practicing the spiritual arts. Topics discussed here are witchcraft, WICCA, various forms of magic, tarot and other similar subjects. A strong emphasis on the legends of Sherwood Forest in England is also part of the theme of this publication.

KEYWORDS   Magazines, Spirituality, WICCA, Witchcraft
AUDIENCE   Popular Culture Enthusiasts
CONTACT   Susan Gavula
            sjgavula@terminator.rs.itd.umich.edu
FREE

gopher://locust.cic.net:70/00/Zines/Cousins/

Information about The Baha'i Faith ★★★

This site contains a magazine of the Baha'i Faith. Articles include 'Baha'u'llah—A Statement,' 'Sacred Texts, Baha'i Writings,' 'Baha'i Statement to the UN Conference on the Environment,' and 'U.S. Congress condemns repression of Baha'is.' The site also provides a link to a Baha'i discussion group.

KEYWORDS   Religious Texts
AUDIENCE   Religious Studies Educators, Religious Studies Students
CONTACT   Terry Maton
            Terry.Maton@usask.ca
FREE

http://duke.usask.ca/~maton/bahai.html

Islamic Resources Gopher Server ★★

This gopher gives information about Islam including FAQs, bibliographies, and summaries of beliefs and practices. There are links to other resources related to Islam including an online version of the Koran.

KEYWORDS   Associations, Islam, Religion, Religious Texts
AUDIENCE   Muslims, Religious Studies Educators
CONTACT   yaakob@latif.com
FREE

gopher://latif.com/

Judaism and Jewish Resources ★★★★

Judaism and Jewish Resources provides a gateway to a range of Jewish resources on the Internet. The extensive table of contents includes gophers, FTP archives, updates on 'The State of Israel', news and media, FAQ and reading lists from the newsgroup Soc.culture.jewish, products and services, and sections on Jewish communities, museums and exhibitions, archeology, libraries, books, and other Jewish Web sites.

KEYWORDS   Israel, Judaism, Libraries, Museums
AUDIENCE   Educators (University), Jews, Judaica Scholars, News Buffs
CONTACT   Andrew Tannenbaum
            trb@spdcc.com
FREE

http://shamash.nysernet.org/trb/judaism.html

Liturgical Texts on the Internet ★★★

This gopher site is a meta-index to texts and commentaries on all aspects of Christian liturgies. Some books include—The Book of Common Prayer (1979 American) and DILS (The Work of Professor Sarah L. Keefer), with papers that include CANTUS—Database for Gregorian Chants for the Divine Office; Pius XII On Sacred Music (1955); and Vat II—Lumen Gentium (Constitution on the Church).

KEYWORDS   Liturgy, Theology
AUDIENCE   Historians, Priests, Theologians, Theology Students
FREE

gopher://delphi.dur.ac.uk:70/11/Academic/P-T/Theology/Computing/Liturgy

The NYSERNet-Shamash Consortium Gopher ★★★

This site offers access to information about Judaism and discusses areas such as Jewish campus life, Culture Net, Project Genesis, forum lists, Holocaust information, and more. The purpose is to unify Jewish organizations with common resources which are in close geographical proximity.

KEYWORDS   Holocaust, Jewish Politics, Judaism, Religion
AUDIENCE   Holocaust Survivors, Jews, Religious Studies Educators, Religious Studies Students
CONTACT   info@judaism.com
FREE

gopher://israel.nysernet.org/

Qur'an ★★

Qur'an contains the Islamic religious text the Qur'an (or Koran) in English translation, produced by the Presbyterian College. Chapters are listed individually.

KEYWORDS   Islam, Qur'an, Religious Texts
AUDIENCE   Muslims, Religious Studies Educators, Religious Studies Students
FREE

gopher://cs1.presby.edu/11/religion/Quran/

SDANet (Seventh Day Adventist Gopher) ★★★

This is a gopher site which provides access to multiple items of interest about and by Seventh-Day Adventists, including essays, digests, electronic books, and a newsletter-style series of information.

KEYWORDS   Evangelism, Religion, Seventh Day Adventists, Theology
AUDIENCE   Christians, Seventh Day Adventists, Theology Students
CONTACT   gophermaster@sdanet.org
FREE

gopher://gopher.sdanet.org

Sikhism Home Page ★★★

The Sikhism home page provides information about the Sikh religion. It includes the background of the religious philosophy, translations of key scriptures, and historical details. Biographies of key Sikh Gurus and other religious figures are included, as well as pictures and information about important temples and religious texts. A glossary of terms, a list of religious symbols, and a calendar of dates from Sikh history are also provided.

KEYWORDS   India, Religion, Sikhism
AUDIENCE   Religious Studies Students, Sikhs
CONTACT   Sandeep Singh Brar
            sandeep@io.org
FREE

http://www.io.org/~sandeep/sikhism.htm

Surprises on the Character of God

This site provides access to the complete text of an electronic book entitled, 'Surprises on the Character of God—Studies and Conclusions Toward a God of Pure Love,' by Jim Redman. Using both the Hebrew and Greek Scriptures of the Christian Holy Bible, the author discusses several aspects of God, the Church, and Christianity. The author has concluded that Jesus Christ is the ultimate Bible authority and must therefore not be contradicted by the writings of the Apostle Paul or others. A newsletter is planned regarding the issues in this book. A donation/payment of $15.00 US is requested for each copy of this book.

KEYWORDS Christianity, God
AUDIENCE Bible Readers, Christians, Jews, Religious Studies Educators, Religious Studies Students
CONTACT Jim Redman
hyssop@earth.execpc.com
FREE

ftp://ftp.execpc.com/pub/hyssop-out/

University Lutheran Church (ELCA)- Cambridge, Massachussetts

The University Lutheran Church page provides information about the church in Cambridge, Massachussetts, and its activities. The page has a letter from the Pastor with a connection to the Ten Commandments and an online version of the Bible.

KEYWORDS Churches, Education (College/University), Lutheranism, Massachusetts
AUDIENCE Massachusetts Residents, Religious Studies Students, Theologians
CONTACT lutheran@hcs.harvard.edu
FREE

http://web.mit.edu/lem/www/unilu-home.html

Virtual Christianity - Bibles

The Virtual Christianity Bible page is a meta index that provides links to different versions of the Bible in hypertext. Users will find Bible links grouped into English Bibles with multiple translations, King James Version, search utilities, and Bibles in foreign languages. Each Bible link describes the Bible that is available and its organizational form.

KEYWORDS Bible, Christianity, Religious Texts
AUDIENCE Bible Scholars, Christians, Religious Studies Educators, Religious Studies Students
CONTACT Aaron Bryce Cárdenas
aaronc@mit.edu
FREE

http://www.mit.edu:8001/people/aaronc/bibles.html

Zen@SunSITE

This site offers a variety of information regarding Zen, including a supply of 'koans' (a short story, often a dialogue between a student and a teacher that points

Connections to Mythology
"Thorry" I "mythed" that!

Did you know that in Roman mythology, the gods were not really worshipped, but were more objects of entertainment? The Greeks took their gods and a given god's legend a bit more seriously, however. If you cruise the Internet, you can find a wealth of information about mythology—including Greek and Roman, Finnish, Norse/Teutonic, and Near Eastern.

At the "Myths and Legends" site, you'll find articles on mythology, as well as a rundown on the gods and their legends. Even British and Celtic mythology is covered here; you can learn about Gaelic languages, culture, and lifestyles, while perusing the lesser known history of King Arthur.

If you want to learn something about Assyro-Babylonian Mythology, you can focus on either the "older gods" or the "younger gods"—two groups that seemed to be at loggerheads over who would rule Mesopotamia (the area of the Tigris and Euphrates rivers). Apsu, the underworld ocean god, is the begetter of the skies and the earth, but had trouble quelling the noise of his children and grandchildren. To find out how he dealt with them, check out "The Assyro-Babylonian Mythology FAQ."

(http://www.mit.edu:8001/people/mouser/assyrbaby/1-faq.html)

towards some essence of the spirit of Zen) which can be updated constantly using your browser's reload mechanism. Some of the subjects covered include The Gateless Gate, FAQs (Frequently Asked Questions) from Alt.zen, Zen Buddhist Texts, Zen Hospice Project, and more. There are also links to other Zen sites and The Dharma Web.

KEYWORDS	Philosophy, Religion, Zen Buddhism
AUDIENCE	Buddhists, Educators (University), Philosophers, Students
CONTACT	Ben Walter bjw@gnu.ai.mit.
FREE	

http://sunsite.unc.edu/zen/

Religious Artifacts

See also
Religion · *Doctrines*
Religion · *Religious History*

Dead Sea Scrolls ★★★

The Dead Sea Scrolls exhibit at the Library of Congress created this Web site to provide information about the exhibit and the Qumran culture from which these scrolls came. The historical and cultural background of the time of the Dead Sea Scrolls, images from the scrolls and English translations of the information are provided. Information and images of other artifacts from the Qumran community are also given, such as textiles, pottery, and coins. For those interested in visiting the exhibit at the Library of Congress, further readings and location information is included.

KEYWORDS	Archeology, Biblical Texts, Dead Sea Scrolls, Historical Documents
AUDIENCE	Archaeologists, Historians
CONTACT	K.D. Ellis kell@seq1.loc.gov
FREE	

http://sunsite.unc.edu/expo/deadsea.scrolls.exhibit/intro.html

Shroud of Turin Home Page ★★★

This home page provides links to literature, history, and scientific research about The Shroud of Turin, as well as having a good image of the shroud itself. It has been rated as one of the top 5% websites on the Internet and includes links to other religion sites on the Internet.

KEYWORDS	Christianity, History, Religion, Religious Leaders
AUDIENCE	Christians, Historians, Religion Scholars, Researchers
CONTACT	npacheco@cais.com
FREE	

http://www.cais.com/npacheco/shroud/turin.html

Religious History

See also
Humanities & Social Sciences · *History*

Calvin Institute ★★★

Calvin Institute focuses on the history and theology of Christian religion. It has links to the reformation, Westminster studies, Church government and many others. It is part of what is known as The Center for the Advancement of Paleo Orthodoxy.

KEYWORDS	History, Religion, Religious Studies
AUDIENCE	History Buffs, Religion Scholars, Scholars, Students
CONTACT	Mark A. Buckner covpca@usit.net
FREE	

http://www.usit.net/public/CAPO/ccalvin.html

Religion in England ★★★

This page provides an overview of Religion in England. It has links to Biblical typology, the Church of England, Roman Catholicism and alternative traditions and religions.

KEYWORDS	Great Britain, History, Religion
AUDIENCE	Educators, History Buffs, Literary Scholars, Religion Scholars, Scholars, Students
CONTACT	ds@pion.het.brown.edu
FREE	

http://www.iris.brown.edu/iris/RIE/Religion_OV.html

Resources

See also
Government & Politics · *Doctrines*

1-800-Judaism Online ★★★
(COMMERCIAL)

This is the gopher server for 1-800-JUDAISM, a mail order company specializing in selling books, tapes, and videos related to Judaism. This server offers information about their books and provides ordering information.

KEYWORDS	Judaism, Videos
AUDIENCE	Jews, Judaica Scholars, Religious Studies Educators
CONTACT	info@judaism.com
FREE	

gopher://judaism.com/

Andrews University Gopher Server ★★★

This gopher site describes Andrews University, a Seventh-Day Adventist institution located in southwestern Michigan. It provides information on the campus, as well as descriptions of the various academic departments and their programs.

KEYWORDS	Christianity, Michigan, Seventh Day Adventists, University Administration
AUDIENCE	Christians, Educators, Students
CONTACT	gophermaster@andrews.edu
FREE	

gopher://gopher.andrews.edu/

Art House Internet Site ★★★★

This site contains information on Art House, a nonprofit organization in Nashville, Tennessee, whose goal is to provide education for artists and non-artists in 'development of the Christian mind.' This group aims to supplement the teachings of the church, and it offers articles about Christian/art issues from Art House Newsletters.

KEYWORDS	Art, Christianity, Community Services
AUDIENCE	Artists, Christians, Theologians
CONTACT	Nick Barre http://www.netcentral.net/netcentral/nick.html
FREE	

http://www.netcentral.net/arthouse/cp_and_ah.html

Bethany Christian Services WWW Server ★★★

This is the home page of a Christian organization in Grand Rapids, Michigan that is committed to the protection of children and families. It contains information about the organization's services and resource lists of other Christian sites.

KEYWORDS	Charities, Children, Community Services, Family
AUDIENCE	Christians, Families
CONTACT	Andrew J. Bass andyb@bethany.org
FREE	

http://www.bethany.org/bethany/about_bcs.html

gopher://gopher.bethany.org/

Bible Gateway ★★★

This home page contains a hypertext version of the Bible in English, German, Swedish, Latin, French, and Tagalog. One can also search for specific words, passages and verses. Instructions are included for using the Bible Gateway to turn scripture references into hyperlink in your own documents.

KEYWORDS	Bible, Christianity, History
AUDIENCE	Bible Scholars, Christians, Historians, Theologians, Web Developers
CONTACT	Nick Hengeveld nick@calvin.edu
FREE	

http://www.calvin.edu/cgi-bin/bible/

Calvin's GoWeb Server ★★★

This is a gopher for the Calvin College and the Calvin Theological Seminary. It summarizes both the academic and theological programs, as well as providing information about the campus, campus publications, and student groups. There are also links to Christian resources on the Internet.

KEYWORDS Campus Information, Christianity, Education (College/University), University Administration
AUDIENCE Christians, Educators, Students, Theologians
CONTACT gopher-admin@calvin.edu
FREE

gopher://gopher.calvin.edu/

http://calvin.edu/

Center for Computer Analysis of Texts ★★★

This gopher is supported by the staff in Educational Technology Services and is located on a workstation server supporting the departments of Classical Studies and Religious Studies at the University of Pennsylvania. The resources include partial access to the Center's archives and access to software via an FTP server. The archives contain text and images from classical and religious works.

KEYWORDS Archives, Religion
AUDIENCE Educators, Religious Studies Educators, Religious Studies Students, Students
CONTACT Jay Treat
jtreat@ccat.sas.upenn.edu
FREE

gopher://ccat.sas.upenn.edu/

Encyclopedia of Gods - Over 2,500 Deities of the World ★★★★

This gopher site contains a review of, and ordering information for 'The Encyclopedia of Gods - Over 2,500 Deities of the World,' by Michael Jordan. Information ranges from the most ancient gods of polytheistic societies—Hittite, Sumerian, Mesopotamian—to the most contemporary gods of the major monotheistic religions. Purchase and ISBN information are available here.

KEYWORDS General Literature, Mythology, Religion
AUDIENCE Literary Scholars, Mythology Enthusiasts, Religious Studies Educators, Religious Studies Students
FREE

gopher://ns1.infor.com:4600/
1exec%3AR1979124-1982098-/
.text/Main%3A/.bin/views

Global Jewish Networking ★★★★

This server is a central gathering place and clearinghouse for issues of Jewish concern. The site porovides hot links to Jewish libraries and catalogs, many Jewish servers and archives around the globe, some Jewish virtual museums (including The Society for Preservation of Nature in Israel, Hebrew—A Living Language, and The United States Holocaust Memorial Museum), Jewish conferences and discussions, Jewish education resources, software resources for Hebrew support, and more.

KEYWORDS Educational Resources, Judaism, Museums

Connections to Philosophy
It's the logical place to be

Is there reality in virtual reality? Can an aesthetic experience be experienced through sociological practices? If you have questions about the vast field of "the logical" or if you think it's illogical to be reasonable, then there are a number of Net sites you'll want to check out.

Some of these explore topics like "the aesthetics of human virtue" by way of other sciences such as psychology, ethnology, or history. You can even access a collection of work on musical-aesthetics, or learn about "electric language."

If you want to know about metaphysics in virtual reality, there is a place to get that information. If you want to indulge in the lighter side of logic, then try "Philosophy and Monty Python"—focusing on the classic and brilliant British television comedy series. Conversely, you can get real serious and study the philosophy of Ayn Rand or investigate philosophy and religion. There's even a link to the "Anthology of the Work of Carl Jung."

(http://college.antioch.edu/~smauldin/)

also, (http://www.arts.cuhk.hk/Philo.html)

AUDIENCE Jews, Judaica Scholars, Librarians, Politics Enthusiasts
CONTACT jewishnt@bguvm.bgu.ac.il
FREE

http://www.mofet.macam98.ac.il/~dovw/
t01.html

Islamic Literature and Study Plan ★★★★

This site, via FTP, is a compilation of numerous articles and directories which offer many sources (and a good study plan, as the header indicates) for those who wish to be acquainted with Islamic literature and other subjects. Included are a broad overview of Islam (religion and culture), the Quran, a list of Islamic booksellers and translations of various Islamic works.

KEYWORDS Islam, Islamic Literature, Religious Texts

AUDIENCE N. Islam Religion/Culture Enthusiasts, Religious Studies Educators, Religious Studies Students
FREE

http://www.sas.upenn.edu/
African_Studies/Software/
Islamic_Literature_12227.html

ftp://ftp.mcs.kent.edu

Journal of Buddhist Ethics ★★★

The Journal of Buddhist Ethics interprets in a broad sense in various subject matters from a Buddhist perspective. It exists as a 'Journal' only in the electronic sense of the word, and has not yet reached the traditional presses. The site offers global links to other

Buddhist resources as well as information on an online conference for students. The Journal also offers subscriptions and accepts submissions.

KEYWORDS   Buddhism, Philosophy, Taoism, Theology
AUDIENCE   Buddhists, Philosophers, Philosophy Students, Students
CONTACT   Dr. Wayne R. Husted
            wrh@psu.edu.
FREE

http://www.cac.psu.edu/jbe/jbe.html

Lambert Dolphin's Resource Files

This page is a collection of essays on contemporary Christianity written by Lambert Dolphin, a former geophysicist who now devotes his time to Christian theology and geophysical consulting services. There is a large collection of essays available on such topics as science and the Bible, sexuality, and biblical interpretation. There is also a compendium of links to other Christianity resources on the Net, as well as some material on geophysical research and Dolphin's consulting services.

KEYWORDS   Bible, Christianity, Spirituality
AUDIENCE   Christians, Religious Studies Educators, Religious Studies Students, Spirituality Seekers
CONTACT   Lambert Dolphin
            dolphin@best.com
FREE

http://www.best.com/~dolphin/

ftp://ftp.best.com/~dolphin/

The Monk Page

Welcome to Russell's Monastic Den where you will find information on monks, monasteries and the Scriptorium, which is a center for writings on monks. You will find lots of monk and monastic-related links such as Monastic Art and Architecture, Monasticism, Saint Benedict, Coptic Sites in Egypt and St. John's Abbey. You will also end up in a very surprising place if you push the 'Don't Push This Button' button.

KEYWORDS   Monasteries, Religion, Sociology
AUDIENCE   Monks, Saints, Social Scientists, Sociologists
CONTACT   russelln@efn.org
FREE

http://www.efn.org/~russelln

Spirit WWW

The Spirit WWW is a collection of documents and links to Web resources dealing with spirituality and religion. Users will find sections with compiled information on channelling, lightwork, healing, reincarnation, UFOs, Yoga, Out-of-Body Experiences, Astrology, and other spiritual consciousness topics. Each section contains essays discussing the topic, sorted by author and subject, and links to directly related Internet sources for each section. Numerous print and online zines are compiled, along with newsgroups, listservs, and other networking resources. A search engine is provided, and users may also browse through paintings, movies, sound files, and reviews relating to spirituality.

KEYWORDS   Religious Studies, Spirituality

Connections to Christian Resources

"Now, I lay me down to sleep, I pray the Lord my soul to keep"

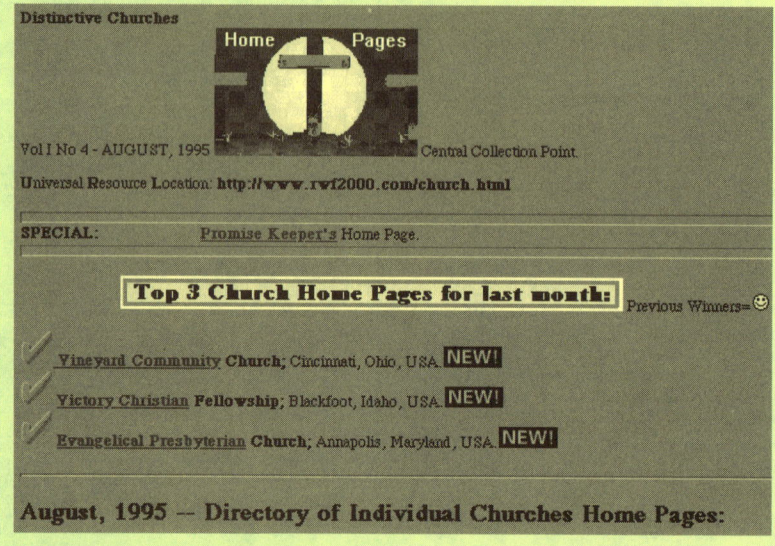

Like many religious forums and sites on the Internet, the Christian-oriented network of resources is quite busy. Moreover, within this arena, one may obtain translations of the Bible in 11 languages, as well as a vast database of books and other material relevant to Christian life.

Sites provide connections to various churches (most of them in the U.S.), "chat" forums about issues (ranging from marriage to morality to old age), and stories of missions around the world. You can even find sites where you can study sacred Christian texts, view Christian art, and more.

(http://osiris.colorado.edu/~brumbaug/CHURCH/resources.html),

also, **(http://www.iclnet.org/pub/resources/res3.html)**

AUDIENCE   Religious Studies Enthusiasts, Spirituality Enthusiasts
CONTACT   René K. Müller
            kiwi@iis.ee.ethz.ch
FREE

http://www.protree.com/Spirit.html

What the Bible Says About Mohammed

This site contains a lecture by Ahmed Deedat on Mohammed, the major prophet of Islamic belief. The lecture comments on Jewish and Christian scriptures specifically explaining how the Muslims might interpret these scriptures. The site also offers free Muslim literature.

KEYWORDS   Islam, Muslims, Religious Studies, Theology
AUDIENCE   Christians, Jews, Muslims, Religious Studies Students, Theologians
FREE

http://www.wam.umd.edu/~ibrahim/
    Muhammad.in.Bible.html

Science

Agriculture	565
Aquatic Sciences	568
Astronomy	571
Biology	574
Biosciences	579
Botany	582
Career & Employment	584
Chemistry	585
Earth Sciences	587
Environmental Sciences	591
Geosciences	597
Individuals	600
Neurosciences	600
Organizations	601
Paleontology	603
Physics	603
Space Science	609
Zoology	613

Agriculture

See also
Health & Medicine · *Veterinary Medicine*
Sports & Recreation · *Pets & Animals*

AESNet - The New York State Agricultural Experiment Station Network ★★

This is the New York State Agricultural Experiment Station Network, which offers information concerning entomology, food science, horticulture, and plant pathology resources at Cornell University.

KEYWORDS Agriculture, Entomology, Horticulture, Plants
AUDIENCE Botanists, Entomologists, Horticulturalists, Students
CONTACT M.R.McLellan
M-R-McLellan@Cornell.edu
FREE

gopher://aruba.nysaes.cornell.edu/

Agricultural Biotechnology Center ★★★

This site contains information on biotechnology issues as they apply to agriculture. The Agricultural Biotechnology Center conducts research into new applications of biotechnology and develops and promotes their agricultural applications. Users can find out about the center through the information at this site, as well as information about the research conducted there. In addition, this server maintains links to other agriculture and biotechnology sites on the net.

KEYWORDS Agriculture, Biological Research, Biotechnology
AUDIENCE Agriculturalists, Biotechnologists, Farmers
CONTACT Peter Fabian
www@molmod.abc.hu
FREE

http://www.abc.hu

gopher://hubi.abc.hu:70/

Agricultural Genome World Wide Web Server ★★★★

This is the information page for the Agricultural Genome World Wide Web (AGWWW) Server. The AGWWW is a service provided by the USDA (United States Department of Agriculture), National Agricultural Library in Beltsville, Maryland, USA. The information contained on the server consists of a database of genome information for agriculturally important organisms including links to plant genome information, animal genome information, and the Agricultural Genome Gopher. This page also contains links to a search for projects and researchers, the National Agricultural Library Gopher Server, and the National Agricultural Library Phone List.

KEYWORDS Agriculture, Biodiversity, Genomes, Research
AUDIENCE Agriculturalists, Biologists, Ecologists, Researchers
FREE

http://probe.nalusda.gov/

gopher://gopher.nalusda.gov/

ftp://probe.nalusda.gov/pub

Alternative Farming Systems Center ★★

This server provides access to various alternative farming resources. The Alternative Farming Systems Information Center (AFSIC) is one of eleven Information Centers at the National Agricultural Library (NAL), located in Beltsville, Maryland.

KEYWORDS Education (College/University)
AUDIENCE Agriculturalists, Environmentalists, Farmers
CONTACT consult@umail.umd.edu
FREE

gopher://info.umd.edu:1800/00/
Alternative_Farming_Systems_In
formation_Center/intro.asc

The Apiculture Ink and Issues (APIS) Home Page ★★★★

The Apiculture Ink and Issues (APIS) Home Page is an informative place for the beekeeper to stop whilst caught in the Web. This site has complete texts of the last three years of the APIS Newsletter, set in a useful index. The articles are thoughtful and lucid, whether the subject is general beekeeping, breeding programs, 'apitherapy' (the medicinal use of honey bee products), apicultural conferences, the National Honey Board, pollination, or the Dreaded Africanized Honey Bee. Produced in Florida, some of the material is local to the state, but most is pertinent to the bee.

KEYWORDS Beekeeping, Bees, Entomology
AUDIENCE Apiarists, Beekeepers, Entomologists, Florida Residents
CONTACT Dr. Malcolm (Tom) Sanford, Extension Beekeeping Specialist
mts@gnv.ifas.ufl.edu
FREE

http://gnv.ifas.ufl.edu/~entweb/apis/
apis.html

The Beekeeping Home Page ★★★★

Whether you are an apiculturist or an unassuming beekeeper, The Beekeeping Home Page has information that will keep you enthralled for hours. An incredibly thorough resource, this Web site comprises everything Internet related to bees. Looking for a little film about the bee? Some photos? Perhaps some recipes for making mead? How about links to all of the beekeeping archives, from the APIS Newsletters to logs for the mailing list Bee-L? Perhaps a link to the Usenet newsgroup sci.agriculture.beekeeping? Links to all other beekeeping Web sites? It's all here.

KEYWORDS Beekeeping, Bees
AUDIENCE Apiarists, Beekeepers, Entomologists
CONTACT   Jordan Luther King Schwartz
          jlks@u.washington.edu
FREE

http://weber.u.washington.edu/~jlks/bee.html

BioLink Newsletter ★★★

BioLink is the quarterly newsletter of the USAID-funded Agricultural Biotechnology for Sustainable Productivity (ABSP) Project. The newsletter covers topics such as Global Biotechnology Programs for the improvement and implementation of agricultural growth in industrialized countries. ICI Seeds, Inc. a seed company that is actively involved in the development of stable maize hybrids, is also involved in the USAID project. The Newsletter also covers workshops aimed at examining the current status of biosafety guides and regulations. Countries involved in this project include Latin America, Egypt, Kenya and Indonesia.

KEYWORDS Agriculture, Biology, Biotechnology
AUDIENCE Agriculturalists, Biologists, Biotechnologists, Scientists
FREE

ftp://bdt.ftpt.br/download/BioLink_1-4_TXT

Centre de Coopération Internationale en Recherche Agronomique pour le Développement ★★★

This server is produced by the Centre de Coopération Internationale en Recherche Agronomique pour le Développement (CIRAD). It contains information on agriculture, with agricultural databases and other information available. Most of the material on this server is in French.

KEYWORDS Agriculture, Farming, France
AUDIENCE Agricultural Researchers, Agriculturalists, Farmers
CONTACT   Gilles Fournié
          fournie@cirad.fr
FREE

http://www.cirad.fr/EN/welcome.shtml

City Farmer's Urban Agriculture Notes ★★★★

This page has information and links to articles on urban agriculture. The page is provided by City Farmer, in Vancouver, British Columbia, Canada. Urban Agriculture Notes is written for those who want to start up their own 'Office of Urban Agriculture' and for gardeners who are curious about what City Farmer refers to as political horticulture. Links on this page lead to information on a variety of urban farming topics including urban home composting, dealing with a rat in a compost bin, community gardens, and international urban agriculture.

KEYWORDS Activism, Ecology, Recycling, Urban Agriculture
AUDIENCE Ecologists, Recyclers, Urban Farming Activists
CONTACT   cityfarm@unixg.ubc.ca
FREE

http://unixg.ubc.ca:780/~cityfarm/urbagnotes1.html

Extension Service USDA Gopher ★★★★

The Extension Service USDA gopher covers agricultural issues ranging from policies to surrounding agencies within the USDA and the federal government. There is specific information like flood and disaster-related information and coverage of major legislation and policy issues such as healthcare, NAFTA, National Information Infrastructure, and the National Performance Review.

KEYWORDS Agriculture, Economics, Government, Policy Research
AUDIENCE Agriculture Students, Government Researchers
CONTACT   gopher-admin@esusda.gov
FREE

gopher://esusda.gov/1/

Florida Agricultural Information Retrieval System (FAIRS) ★★★★

This page links documents on the Florida Agricultural Information Retrieval System (FAIRS). FAIRS is a comprehensive research library produced by the University of Florida's Institute of Food and Agricultural Sciences (IFAS), covering topics such as agriculture, energy, food safety and nutrition, natural resources, pesticides and pesticide safety, turfgrass, water quality and wildlife. FAIRS has thousands of documents, illustrations, photographs and tables from major programs within IFAS, including information on beneficial insects, alternative crops, plant disease, and dairy science.

KEYWORDS Ecology, Information Retrieval, Natural Resources
AUDIENCE Agriculturalists, Conservationists, Ecologists, Florida Residents
CONTACT   fairsweb@gnv.ifas.ufl.edu
FREE

http://hammock.ifas.ufl.edu/

Food and Agriculture Organization of the United Nations ★★

This gopher server provides access to the archives of the Food and Agriculture Organization of the United Nations. The archives include agricultural statistics, forestry resources, and international development resources.

KEYWORDS Agriculture, Food Production, Forestry, United Nations
AUDIENCE International Aid Agencies, International Development Specialists, Scientists
CONTACT   Laurie Federgreen
          Laurie.Federgreen@fao.org
FREE

gopher://gopher.fao.org/

Global Entomology Agriculture Research Server- (GEARS) ★★★★

GEARS, the Global Entomology Agriculture Research Server is an exciting new resource concerning the role that insects—often bees—play in agriculture. There is a wide variety of information here geared to all types of people; including children, interested adults, and entomological and agricultural professionals. Among the many links here are those to the Carl Hayden Bee Research Center in Tucson, Arizona, This Week's Inside Look at Research and News in Entomology, information about Africanized honeybees, other related Web sites, and articles on a range of subjects. There are links to the 'Insect Theater Online.'

KEYWORDS Agriculture, Beekeeping, Entomology, Insects
AUDIENCE Beekeepers, Entomologists, Insect Enthusiasts
CONTACT   Dr. Stephen Buchmann
          buchmann@ccit.arizona.edu
FREE

http://gears.tucson.ars.ag.gov/

Grain Genes Gopher ★★★

The GrainGenes gopher server is part of the National Agricultural Library and the US Department of Agriculture Plant Genome Program. It contains molecular and phenotypic information about wheat, barley, oats, and other small grains. Information available includes databases, images, the wheat gene catalog, newsletters, and publications. It also has links to other gophers.

KEYWORDS Agriculture, Biology, Databases, Genetics
AUDIENCE Agriculturalists, Biologists, Botanists, Geneticists, Molecular Biologists
CONTACT   Olin Anderson
          oandersn@pw.usda.gov
FREE

gopher://greengenes.cit.cornell.edu/

The Maize Genome Database Gopher ★★★

This server is part of the Agricultural Genome Gopher Server of the National Agricultural Library of the US Department of Agriculture. The information on this server focuses on genetic data for maize, otherwise known as corn. The database is searchable by keywords. This server also provides documentation about the database and links to the rest of the database. This portion of the Agricultural Genome Gopher Server is located at the University of Missouri.

KEYWORDS Agriculture, Databases, Genetics, Research
AUDIENCE Agriculturalists, Biologists, Geneticists
CONTACT   Denis Hancock
          dhancock@teosinte.agron.missouri.edu
FREE

gopher://teosinte.agron.missouri.edu/

National Genetic Resources Program of the U.S. Department of Agriculture's Agricultural Research Service (ARS) ★★★

The National Genetic Resources Program, of the U.S. Department of Agriculture's Agricultural Research Service (ARS), provides germplasm information about plants, animals, microbes and insects. It also provides links to other gophers related to agriculture and genetics.

KEYWORDS	Agriculture, Biotechnology, Botany, Entomology
AUDIENCE	Agriculturalists, Biologists, Entomologists, Zoologists
CONTACT	Jimmie Mowder dbmujm@sol.ars-grin.gov
FREE	

gopher://gopher.ars-grin.gov/

National Soil Erosion Research Laboratory (NSERL) Home Page ★★★

This is the World Wide Web home page of the United States Department of Agriculture - Agricultural Research Service (USDA-ARS), National Soil Erosion Research Lab (NSERL). NSERL is the focal point for the U.S. Government's national research program in soil erosion. Major program thrusts of the NSERL include fundamental erosion process research, erosion control research, and delivery of improved erosion prediction technology. This page provides links to a database on soil erosion topics which can be accessed by hyperlinks. It also contains links to information on NSERL software and work completed on the Lab's CD-ROM project.

KEYWORDS	Agriculture, Environmental Research, Federal Government (US), Soil Science
AUDIENCE	Agriculturalists, Conservationists, Ecologists, Farmers
CONTACT	David Whittemore del@ecn.purdue.edu
FREE	

http://purgatory.ecn.purdue.edu:20002/

Pesticide Information Service (PESTIS) ★★★

The Pesticide Information Service (PESTIS) is an online database for the pesticide use reform and sustainable agriculture communities, made available on the EcoNet computer network. This database has over 400 news items, action alerts, newsletter articles and fact sheets. The site may be searched by the index.

KEYWORDS	Agriculture, Ecology, Environment
AUDIENCE	Environmental Educators, Environmentalists, Students (Secondary/University)
CONTACT	The Institute for Global Communications (IGC) support@igc.apc.org
FREE	

gopher://gopher.igc.apc.org/11/orgs/panna/pestis

Connections to Flora and Fauna
Look, but don't touch

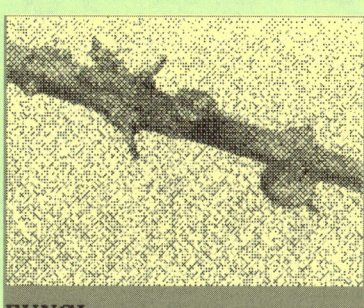

On Australia's "Flora and Fauna" page, you'll find an extensive "library" of photographs of the unique flora and fauna of this island continent—a land which has served as a sanctuary for some 55 million years to such "critters" as kangaroos, koala bears, and the duckbill platypus.

(http://rs306.ccs.bbk.ac.uk/flora/welcome.html)

You can also access a wide selection of photographs and information on the flora and fauna of Hungary. From this site, simply click on the "snapshots" to gain a more expansive view of the plants and animals in question. Through the 'First Light Mud Homepage" you can read in Hungarian or in English about the flora of the country, and link to a beginner's handbook on the country's back roads and rural areas where the hillsides and fields are abundant with a wide variety of flora.

(http://www.sch.bme.hu/cool.html)

also, (http://www.uni-giessen.de/~gdg3/mud/firstl.html)

Through the "Fauna of Madagascar" site, you can take a look at the plant and animal life of the island that some claim is similar in diversity and scope to the Biblical Noah's Ark: peruse some 300 species of butterflies, 256 species of birds, 28 kinds of bats, 144 types of frogs and 257 types of reptiles. The island is also a sanctuary for lemurs, a monkey-like primate, found only on Madagascar.

(http://lalo.inria.fr/~andry/Mada.html)

The RiceGenes Gopher ★★★

This server is part of the Agricultural Genome Gopher Server at the National Agricultural Library of the US Department of Agriculture. The information on this server focuses on genetic information about varieties of rice. The database is searchable by keywords. This server also provides documentation about the database and links to the rest of the database.

KEYWORDS	Genetics, Libraries, Molecular Biology
AUDIENCE	Biochemists, Botanists, Geneticists, Molecular Biologists
CONTACT	Doug Bigwood
FREE	

gopher://locus.nalusda.gov:7007/

SolGenes Gopher ★★★

This site offers information about SolGenes, a solanaceae genome database. It is a compilation of molecular and phenotypic information, primarily for tomato, potato and pepper. Some of the areas discussed are genetic maps, DNA probes, autoradiogram images of survey blots, and germplasm records.

KEYWORDS	Agriculture, Genetics, Molecular Biology, Plant Science
AUDIENCE	Geneticists, Molecular Biologists, Molecular Biotechnologists
CONTACT	Steve Tanksley steve_tanksley@qmrelay.mail.cornell.edu
FREE	

gopher://nightshade.cit.cornell.edu:71/

The Soybase Gopher ★★★

This server is part of the Agricultural Genome Gopher Server at the National Agricultural Library of US Department of Agriculture. The information on this server focuses on genetic information about members of the soy family. The database is searchable by keywords. This server also provides documentation about the database and links to the rest of the database.

KEYWORDS	Genetics, Libraries, Molecular Biology
AUDIENCE	Biochemists, Botanists, Geneticists, Molecular Biologists
CONTACT	Doug Bigwood
FREE	

gopher://locus.nalusda.gov:7005/

Agriculture – Aquatic Sciences

The TAMU/TAEX GN/Gopher/WWW Server ★★★

This site offers access to research-based agricultural and environmental information. Available resources include newsletters, publications, 4-H community development information, and a master gardener page.

KEYWORDS Agriculture, Environmental Resources, Gardens, Texas
AUDIENCE Academics, Agriculturalists, Agriculture Students, Environmental Researchers
CONTACT Dr. Zerle L. Carpenter
z-carpenter@tamu.edu
FREE

http://leviathan.tamu.edu/

gopher://leviathan.tamu.edu/

ftp://leviathan.tamu.edu/

Texas A&M University Home Page ★★★

The Texas A&M Home page contains pointers to — Texas A&M University College of Agriculture and Life Sciences, the departments of Agricultural Economics, Agricultural Engineering, Nutrition Program (Interdisciplinary), Plant Pathology and Microbiology, Poultry Science, Rangeland Ecology and Management, and their College of Education. Full information about campus life can also be found there.

KEYWORDS Agriculture, Engineering, Universities
AUDIENCE Agriculturalists, Agronomists, Engineers, Students (University), Texas Residents
CONTACT Hal Mueller
FREE

http://www.tamu.edu/

gopher://opal.tamu.edu

U.S. Department of Agriculture's Economics and Statistics System ★★★

This site gives access to data and databases concerned with agriculture and agricultural biology. The data covers topics such as textile fiber production, farm production expenses, milk and dairy product sales, and fertilizer use. The databases has a keyword search and is presented in a Lotus 1-2-3 format.

KEYWORDS Agriculture, Databases, Economics, Government Documents
AUDIENCE Agriculturalists, Economists
CONTACT Oya Rieger
oyr1@cornell.edu
FREE

gopher://usda.mannlib.cornell.edu/

University of Agriculture in Nitra ★★★

This site gives information on the administration and academic programs of the University of Agriculture in Nitra, Slovak Republic. It also provides information on the university's departments, faculty, courses, FTP servers, and the Slovakia document store. Access to other gophers is provided.

KEYWORDS Agriculture, Central Europe, Education (College/University), Farm Economics
AUDIENCE Academics, Educators (University), Scientists, Students (Secondary/College)
CONTACT gph@uniag.sk
FREE

gopher://uvt.uniag.sk/

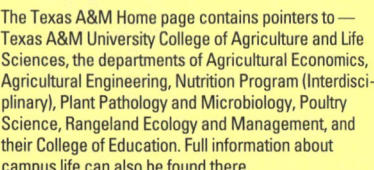

Aquatic Sciences

See also
Government & Politics · *Agencies*
Science · *Biosciences*

Aquaculture Network Information Center (AquaNIC) ★★★

AquaNIC (The Aquaculture Network Information Center) is a launching pad for those interested in aquaculture information available on the Internet. It is maintained by Purdue University with the support of many organizations. It has a considerable amount of information regarding the farming of aquatic animals and plants, and what it sees as a booming industry in the century to come.

KEYWORDS Aquaculture, Ecology, Environment
AUDIENCE Agriculturalists, Aquatic Farmers, Environmentalists
CONTACT Mark Einstein
meintei@hub.ansc.purdue.edu
FREE

gopher://thorplus.lib.purdue.edu/11/databases/AquaNIC/

telnet://thorplus.lib.purdue.edu/

Australian Oceanographic Data Centre (AODC) ★★★★

The Australian Oceanographic Data Centre (AODC) was established to improve communication of oceanographic information and data within the defense and civil communities. The AODC is responsible for providing maritime environmental support. This site contains general information about AODC, its products and services, the systems AODC uses, as well as projects AODC is involved in.

KEYWORDS Aquatic Science, Australia, Environment, Oceanography
AUDIENCE Australians, Environmentalists, Oceanographers
CONTACT ben@AODC.gov.au
FREE

http://www.aodc.gov.au/AODC.html

Catalog of Freshwater Fish ★★★

The Catalog of Freshwater Fish site contains a collection of pictures of freshwater fish categorized by type, scientific name or common name. Fish include angels, barbs, cats, goldfish, some sharks, tetras, and more.

KEYWORDS Aquariums, Freshwater Fish, Marine Biology
AUDIENCE Aquarium Owners, Fish Enthusiasts, Internet Users
CONTACT Mark Rosenstein
mar@actwin.com
FREE

http://www.actwin.com/fish/fresh-species.html

Center for Coastal Studies, Scripps Institution of Oceanography, University of California, San Diego ★★

The Center for Coastal Studies (CCS) sponsors research into the coastal environment. The CCS Home Page details the people and projects at the Center, and provides a front end to the Data Zoo, an archive of oceanographic data concerning, among other topics, waves, currents, tides, sedimentation, and marine archaeology.

KEYWORDS Coastal Marine Biology, Marine Biology, Ocean Ecology, Oceanography
AUDIENCE Enviromental Activists, Oceanographers, Researchers
CONTACT WebMaster@www-ccs.ucsd.edu
FREE

http://coast.ucsd.edu/

gopher://gopher-ccs.ucsd.edu:70/11

ftp://coast.ucsd.edu

Common Heritage ★★★

The Common Heritage Page is dedicated to the deep ocean as it relates to technology, sustainable development, and more. This site contains a collection of articles such as Ocean Policy and Law, Humans as Marine Mammals, Haiti, the New Atlantis. This site also tells users how to contact the Common Heritage Corporation to increase their coastal industry profit.

KEYWORDS Deep Ocean Technology, Marine Life, Substainable Development
AUDIENCE Environmnentalists, Marine Biologists, Oceanographers
FREE

http://www.aloha.com/~craven/

Distributed Ocean Data System ★★

The Distributed Ocean Data System (DODS) is a project of the Oceanography Society, currently under development. It will be a client-server based distributed system for access to oceanographic data over the Internet, and its structure is being defined in series of national workshops, the results of which are archived at this Web site.

KEYWORDS Information Retrieval, Oceanography
AUDIENCE Oceanographers, Researchers

CONTACT   Glenn Flierl
           glenn@lake.mit.edu
FREE

http://lake.mit.edu/dods.html

Institute of Oceanographic Sciences Deacon Laboratory (IOSDL) ★★★

The Institute of Oceanographic Sciences Deacon Laboratory (IOSDL) serves to advance the understanding of the oceanic environment and processes of environmental change in the oceans, and to predict future change. The Web server is intended to provide information for IOSDL's locality (e.g. phone numbers, map) as well as detail the activities of IOSDL. Among some of the current activities are ocean processes, seafloor processes, and ocean technology. IOSDL's Web site is geared less toward the environmentalist than the oceanographer.

KEYWORDS   Environment, Oceanography, Oceans, United Kingdom
AUDIENCE   British, Environmentalists, Oceanographers
CONTACT   44-428-684141 (Vox), 44-428-683066 (Fax)
           Andrew C. Coward, acc@ub.nso.ac.uk
FREE

http://www.nwo.ac.uk/

Inter-Institutional Database of Fish Biodiversity in the Neotropics (NEODAT) Fish Biodiversity Gopher ★★

The Inter-Institutional Database of Fish Biodiversity in the Neotropics (NEODAT) is an international cooperative effort to make available systematic and geographic data on neotropical freshwater fish specimen deposited in various collections. This gopher contains information on specimens from fish collections, fish species, ichthyologists and ichthyological collections, and collection management software. There are links to bibliographic databases and related gophers and information services.

KEYWORDS   Biodiversity, Fish, Marine Sciences, Zoology
AUDIENCE   Biodiversity Activists, Marine Biologists, Scientists
CONTACT   neodat@say.acnatsci.org
FREE

gopher://fowler.acnatsci.org/

International Council for the Exploration of the Sea (ICES) Home Page ★★★★

The International Council for the Exploration of the Sea (ICES) Home Page is devoted to physical oceanography and marine biology, with a concentration centered around the North Atlantic Ocean and the Baltic Sea. Here you will find information concerning the various projects and programs ICES organizes, ICES meetings, conferences and workshops concerning fisheries science, mariculture, estuaries, and commercial fishing. Also available are several databases, related to oceanography, fish assessment and environmental pollution.

KEYWORDS   Marine Biology, Oceanography
AUDIENCE   Climatologists, Fishery Scientists, Marine Biologists, Oceanographers
CONTACT   Harry Dooley
           Postmaster@server.ices.inst.dk
FREE

http://www.ices.inst.dk

Joint Research Center Marine Environment Unit ★★★

The Marine Environment Unit of the Joint Research Center (JRC) studies ocean color and sea surface temperatures, and develops hydrodynamic models. Open domain documents include sea surface temperature readings, and documents and animation of pigment concentration. Results are shown for the research projects on Baltic Sea and North Atlantic Florescence. An interactive DMS model demonstrates the ventilation of these sulphuric gases to the atmosphere. Links are included to the JRC home page and the Centre for Earth Observation, as well as marine environment related Web documents.

KEYWORDS   Climatology, Marine Biology, Ocean Ecology, Oceanography
AUDIENCE   Marine Biologists, Oceanographers
CONTACT   www-admin.me-unit@jrc.it
FREE

http://me-www.jrc.it:80/home.html

Connections to the Arctic Region
From the top of the world

What kind of wildlife will you find in the Arctic? Does this frozen region have a history? If you long to learn about Arctic explorers, pick up information on marine life in the Arctic Ocean, or find out just how thick the polar icecap is, turn to the "Polar Regions" home page—your ticket to exploring and discovering the Arctic.

In the "Polar Regions" Web-site, you'll learn about the Arctic's "inhabitants" (polar bears and seals among them), or tap into the history of the region without having to don a heavy coat or mittens. You'll also discover how veteran explorer, author, and educator, Will Steger, and his team of international explorers and scientists fared on their trek across the top of the world.

(http://www.stud.unit.no/~sveinw/arctic/)

also, (http://scholastic.com:2005/public/IAP/IAP-Home.html)

There are a number of Internet sites that provide biographies of noted explorers out of the past; one of these is the "Byrd Polar Research Center" for collections on Arctic life. This site features Admiral Byrd's letters, radiograms, charts, and artifacts, as well as information on special research support programs.

(http://www.bprc.mps.ohio-state.edu/BPRCAP.html)

also, (http://www.einet.net/galaxy/Social-Sciences/History/Polar-Regions.html)

Aquatic Sciences

Land and Water - Terrestrial and Inland Aquatic Landscape Systems - Australia

The Land and Water Web page offers information about components of the landscape, such as landscape disturbances (natural and human-induced), geology and soil, vegetation, and inland aquatic systems. Some of the files are online and there are links to other servers. The information contained could be used as a general introduction to the components of landscapes.

KEYWORDS Australia, Ecology, Environment, Geology
AUDIENCE Australians, Ecologists, Environmentalists
FREE

http://kaos.erin.gov.au/land/land.html

The MBL/WHOI (Marine Biological Laboratory and the Woods Hole Oceanographic Institution) Library Gopher Server

This is a gopher hole that leads to the joint libraries of the Marine Biological Laboratory and the Woods Hole Oceanographic Institution (MBL/WHOI). It provides online access to the MBL/WHOI Library catalogs as well as other library resources and services. It also has links to other gopher servers with marine biology information.

KEYWORDS Biological Research, Libraries, Marine Biology, Oceanography
AUDIENCE Biologists, Marine Biologists, Scientists
CONTACT Maggie Rioux
mrioux@mbl.edu
FREE

gopher://hoh.mbl.edu:71/

MariNet Home Page

MariNet is a commercial online information service for the Marine Technology community. MariNet is a free service that provides industry news, a list of companies, organizations, and professional societies online. There are links to information on marine recreation, publications, job opportunities and other sites related to marine technology.

KEYWORDS Databases, Marine Sciences, Online Services
AUDIENCE Marine Biologists, Marine Enthusiasts, Marine Technologists
CONTACT office@marinet.com
FREE

http://www.marinet.com

The Marine Biological Laboratory

This is a gopher server of the Marine Biological Laboratory (MBL). MBL is an independent, non-profit research institute located in Massachusetts and is America's oldest marine lab. Their gopher site contains information on MBL, and gives access to MBL databases, the library, the resource center, jobs listings, and more.

KEYWORDS Biological Research, Biosciences, Marine Biology, Oceanography
AUDIENCE Biologists, Marine Biologists, Scientists
CONTACT dremsen@mbl.edu
FREE

gopher://hoh.mbl.edu/

NATO/SACLANTCEN Home Page

The NATO/SACLANTCEN Home Page offers a searchable database of its web pages. The Centre conducts undersea research to assist SACLANT. The page gives information on the principal research activities of the SACLANT Undersea Research Centre. There are links to publications, databases and their recruitment program.

KEYWORDS Government Agencies, Marine Sciences, Oceanography
AUDIENCE NATO employees, Oceanographers, Researchers
CONTACT www@saclantc.nato.int
FREE

http://www.saclantc.nato.int/

NEMA Oceanographic Data Server

The NEMO Oceanographic data server allows the user to access some of the Scripps collection of oceanography data sets. Although most data sets are available through ftp, users can look through some online gopher directories. WWW directory topics include public domain hydrography, shores, and winds.

KEYWORDS Marine Sciences, Oceanography
AUDIENCE Marine Biologists, Oceanographers
CONTACT David Newton
dnewton@ucsd.edu
FREE

http://nemo.ucsd.edu/

telnet://telnet nemo.ucsd.edu

National Oceanographic Data Center (NODC) Home Page

The National Oceanographic Data Center (NODC) is a national environmental data center. The NODC provides ocean data management and ocean data services to researchers and others. This site provides NODC products, services and publications as well as links to the NODC Oceanographic Databases.

KEYWORDS Government Agencies, Oceanography
AUDIENCE Ecologists, Oceanographers, Researchers, Scientists
CONTACT Natalie Wong
nwong@nodc.noaa.gov
FREE

http://www.nodc.noaa.gov/

gopher://ariel.nodc.noaa.gov/

The Ocean Research Insitute WWW Server

Ocean Research Institute promotes research in order to better understand the complex problems found in marine science. The page gives information about the research facilities, vessels, research and other ORI services, and offers links to other oceanographic institutions and data centers.

KEYWORDS Marine Sciences, Ocean Ecology, Oceanography, Research
AUDIENCE Aquatic Scientists, Ecologists, Oceanographers
CONTACT webmasters@ori.u-tokyo.ac.jp
FREE

http://www.ori.u-tokyo.ac.jp/

Scripps Institution of Oceanography, Physical Oceanography Research Division (PORD)

The Scripps Institute of Oceanography, Physical Oceanography Research Division (PORD) at the University of California San Diego (UCSD), focuses on the study of the ocean and the atmosphere. Their home page provides information about the program, including addresses and materials about UCSD and pages PORD projects. The Joint Environmental Data Analysis Center researches the temperature of the ocean floor, and their page provides animation, images and graphs of global ocean temperatures. The NEMO Hydrographic Data Center provides data sets on climatology and hydrography through a telnet connection.

KEYWORDS Climatology, Marine Biology, Ocean Ecology, Oceanography
AUDIENCE Ocean Researchers, Oceanography Students
CONTACT www@jedac.ucsd.edu
FREE

http://jedac2.ucsd.edu/

gopher://sio.ucsd.edu/

Turtle Trax

This page is devoted to Marine Turtles and was created to provide awareness of the threatened or endangered state of turtle species. The site highlights a particularly gruesome threat to the green sea turtle, the fibropapilloma tumor, and tells the story of one particular group of Hawaiian green sea turtles, the Honokowai group of Maui. The site contains numerous images (drawings and photos) as well as information on the turtles depicted, and their habitats. It also has links to many aquatic related resources varying from the US National Marine Fisheries Service to The Lahaina News.

KEYWORDS Endangered Species, Hawaii, Marine Ecology, Turtles
AUDIENCE Animal Rights Activists, Ecologists, Turtle Enthusiasts
CONTACT Peter Bennett and Ursula Keuper-Bennett
bunrab@io.org
FREE

http://www.io.org/~bunrab/trax.jpg

Universities Water Information Network ★★

This site is a gopher server of the Universities Water Information Network, located at Southern Illinois University. It contains information such as research abstracts, the water resources expert directory, the state institutes directory, calendars of water events as well as agriculture-related resources.

KEYWORDS Geology, Information Resources, Water Quality
AUDIENCE Environmental Scientists, Environmentalists, Geologists
CONTACT Faye Anderson
faye@uwin.siu.edu
FREE

gopher://uwin.c-wr.siu.edu/

Welcome to Oceanic ★★★

This site allows access to information provided by the Ocean Information Center at the University of Delaware. Detailed information is available on research projects such as the World Ocean Circulation Experiment, as well as material on the Center's research ships and cruise schedules. There are also links to other oceanographic servers in the net.

KEYWORDS Marine Biology, Marine Geology, Oceanography, Research
AUDIENCE Marine Biologists, Oceanographers
CONTACT oceanic@diu.cms.udel.edu
FREE

http://www.cms.udel.edu

The Woods Hole Oceanographic Institution Gopher Server ★★★★

This is a gopher server of the Woods Hole Oceanographic Institution (WHOI). It contains information about the WHOI, its research, its library, its education programs, software, WHOI oceanographic databases, news, phone books, and much more. It also has links to other gophers.

KEYWORDS Environment, Geography, Oceanography, Oceans
AUDIENCE Marine Biologists, Oceanographers
CONTACT Julie Allen
jallen@whoi.edu
FREE

gopher://pearl.whoi.edu/

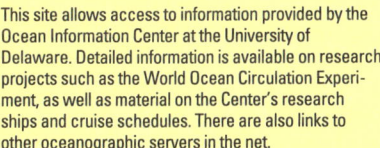

Astronomy

See also
Science · *Physics*
Science · *Space Science*

APO (Apache Point Observatory) Home Page ★★★

This server offers information on the Apache Point Observatory in New Mexico. Users can browse information on the telescopes and other equipment at the observatory, read the viewing schedules, and find out about local weather conditions. There are also links to other astronomy resources on the net, as well as information on positions available at the observatory.

KEYWORDS Astronomy, Telescopes
AUDIENCE Astronomers, Astronomy Enthusiasts, Space Scientists
CONTACT Russell Owen
owen@astro.washington.edu
FREE

http://www.apo.nmsu.edu

Astronomy ★★★

This document is a compilation of information resources focusing on astronomy. Resources may include Internet/Bitnet Mailing Lists, Gophers, World Wide Web sites, Mail Servers, Usenet Newsgroups, FTP Archives, Commercial Online Services, and Bulletin Board Systems.

KEYWORDS Astronomy, Journals, Meta-Index (Astronomy), Space Science
AUDIENCE Astronomers, Astrophysicists, Space Enthusiasts
FREE

ftp://una.hh.lib.umich.edu/inetdirsstacks/acadlist.astronom

Center for Extreme Ultraviolet Astrophysics ★★★★

The Center for Extreme Ultraviolet Astrophysics maintains this site at the University of California at Berkeley. It is the clearinghouse for data from the Extreme Ultraviolet Explorer (EUVE), a NASA satellite launched in 1992. This site provides access to details about the EUVE Guest Observer Center and the EUVE Public Archive of Mission Data and Information. There are also excellent science education projects for K-12 students. Some educational resources are in bilingual (Spanish-English), see the Science Online link.

KEYWORDS Education, NASA (National Aeronautics And Space Administration), Satellites, Space Science
AUDIENCE Astronomers, Astrophysicists, Scholars
CONTACT egoinfo@cea.berkeley.edu
bboyd@cea.berkeley.edu
FREE

http://cea-ftp.cea.berkeley.edu/

Cerro Tololo Interamerican Observatory (CTIO) ★★

Cerro Tololo Interamerican Observatory (CTIO) is a complex of astronomical telescopes and instruments located approximately 80 km to the East of La Serena, Chile at an altitude of 2200 Meters. CTIO's facilities are available for use for approved projects by all qualified astronomers in the western hemisphere. Some of the areas available here are newsletters, press releases, details about the Cerro Tololo observatory, and environmental reports compiled with data from CTIO. Descriptions of the different telescopes used at the observatory are given using both illustrations and technical specifications.

KEYWORDS Chile, Space, Telescopes
AUDIENCE Astronomers, Astronomy Students, Astrophysicists
CONTACT jhughes@noao.edu
FREE

http://ctios2.ctio.noao.edu/ctio.html

Dominion Radio Astrophysical Observatory (DRAO) ★★★

DRAO is a national facility operated by the National Research Council of Canada through its Herzberg Institute of Astrophysics. This page provides links to information on DRAO including Facilities such as Synthesis Telescope (& Proposal Forms), 26 meter telescope, Solar Flux Monitoring, Visitors and Seminars, DRAO Newsletter, DRAO Annual Report, Activities, Meetings, Astronomical email, and more.

KEYWORDS Canada, Observatories, Telescopes
AUDIENCE Computer Users, Educators (University), Internet Users, Researchers, Students (University)
CONTACT hoffmann@drao.nrc.ca)
FREE

http://ftp.drao.nrc.ca

Guide to Backyard Astronomy ★★★
COMMERCIAL

This site describes the Guide to Backyard Astronomy, a 40-minute instructional videotape offering an introduction to astronomy. Information about what it covers and how to purchase it is provided. There are also a few links to other astronomy sites on the Web.

KEYWORDS Astronomy, Product Information, Video
AUDIENCE Astronomers
CONTACT connie@crescent.com
FREE

http://crescent.com/crescent.html

The Herzberg Institute of Astrophysics ★★★

The Herzberg Institute of Astrophysics is the scientific institute within the National Research Council of Canada which has the mandate from Parliament to 'operate and administer any astronomical observatories established or maintained by the Government of Canada.' There is information and distinct pages set up for areas such as the Canadian France Hawaii Telescope, Dominion Radio Astrophysical Observatory, and Solar Terrestrial Physics. There are also submissions, and contact information links from this page.

KEYWORDS Canada, Physics
AUDIENCE Astronomers, Astrophysicists
CONTACT www@dao.nrc.ca
FREE

http://dao.nrc.ca/

Hubble Space Telescope Astrometry Science Team ★★★★

The Hubble Space Telescope Astrometry Science Team uses the Fine Guidance Sensors aboard the Hubble Space Telescope (HST) to measure star positions, study binary stars, and study stellar motions. Papers about the work done by the Astrometry Team are available at this site and include topics such as The

Astronomy

Fine Guidance Sensors and The Wide-Field / Planetary Camera. Users can also download software created by the staff such as a model fitting system and a graphical observation planning program. There are also images of the work done by the team, coupled with descriptions.

KEYWORDS	Telescopes
AUDIENCE	Astronomers, Astronomy Students, Space Enthusiasts
CONTACT	G. F. Benedict fritz@dorrit.as.utexas.edu
FREE	

http://dorrit.as.utexas.edu/

IUCAA (Inter-University Centre for Astronomy and Astrophysics) ★★★

The Inter-University Centre for Astronomy and Astrophysics, (IUCAA) was set up to promote the growth of active groups in astronomy and astrophysics in India. Information on the center's research and staff is available, as well as links to other astronomical resources on the Net.

KEYWORDS	Astronomy, Education, Research
AUDIENCE	Astronomers, Astrophysicists, Researchers, Students
CONTACT	amk@iucaa.ernet.in
FREE	

http://iucaa.iucaa.ernet.in/welcome.html

Isaac Newton Group ★★★★

This site offers astronomy resources. The site is maintained by the Isaac Newton Group, a division of the Instituto de Astrofisica de Canarias (IAC). IAC operate several important astronomical facilities on the Canary Islands. The resources available through this gopher include software, telescope information, user bulletins, and preprints.

KEYWORDS	Astronomy, Telescopes
AUDIENCE	Astronomers, Astrophysicists, Space Enthusiasts
CONTACT	Reynier Peletier naw@ing.iac.es
FREE	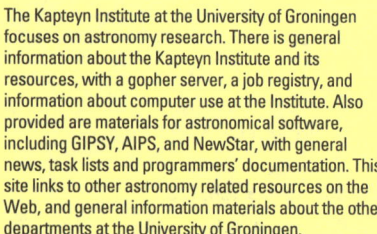

gopher://vega.ing.iac.es/

The Kapteyn Institute Information Server ★★

The Kapteyn Institute at the University of Groningen focuses on astronomy research. There is general information about the Kapteyn Institute and its resources, with a gopher server, a job registry, and information about computer use at the Institute. Also provided are materials for astronomical software, including GIPSY, AIPS, and NewStar, with general news, task lists and programmers' documentation. This site links to other astronomy related resources on the Web, and general information materials about the other departments at the University of Groningen.

KEYWORDS	Computers, Universities
AUDIENCE	Astronomers, Astronomy Students
FREE	

http://kapteyn.astro.rug.nl

Lund Observatory ★★★★

The Lund Observatory's home page provides information about their research projects and services as well as resources about astronomy. Research projects such as those on Astronomical Image Processing and Solar Terrestrial Research, each have home pages which provide descriptions, course information, and reprints/preprints. Users will also find material and images from their Nordic Optical Telescope and other local satellite weather images.

KEYWORDS	Meteorology, Weather
AUDIENCE	Astronomers, Astrophysicists
CONTACT	peter@astro.lu.se
FREE	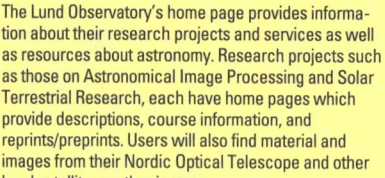

http://nastol.astro.lu.se/Html/home.html

Max-Planck-Institut für Radioastronomie ★★

The Max-Planck-Institut für Radioastronomie offers information on the Institute's research and its 100-m radio telescope. The page has links to the research groups and their projects. Information about the construction of the telescope is provided with information about making proposal requests for using the 100-m telescope. There are links to other astronomy sites and research projects on the Internet.

KEYWORDS	Radio Astronomy, Space Science, Telescopes
AUDIENCE	Astronomers, Researchers, Space Scientists
CONTACT	Peter Müller peter@mpifr-bonn.mpg.de
FREE	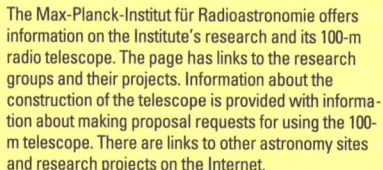

http://www.mpifr-bonn.mpg.de

NASA Astrophysics Data System Home page ★★★★

NASA's Astrophysics Data System is a distributed processing software that provides users with access to over 190 astronomical catalogs and approximately 125,000 astronomical abstracts. Astronomical data can be imported to or exported from analysis systems. ADS also provides direct access to the HEASARC Browse tool, NSSDC's Online Data and Information Service (NODIS), the NASA/IPAC Extragalactic Database (NED), SIMBAD (Set of Identifications, Measurements, and Bibliography for Astronomical Data). The user is able to access all of this information via a simple-to-use Graphical User Interface (GUI).

KEYWORDS	Databases, NASA (National Aeronautics And Space Administration)
AUDIENCE	Astronomers, Astrophysicists, Educators, Scientists, Students (University)
CONTACT	ads@cuads.colorado.edu
FREE	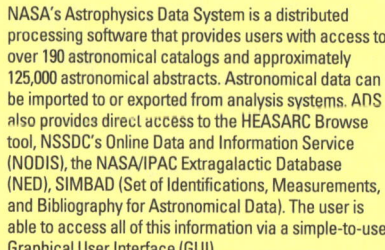

http://adswww.colorado.edu/adswww/adshomepg.html

NASA/IPAC Extragalactic Database (NED) ★★★

The NASA/IPAC Extragalactic Database (NED) is an object-oriented database, built around a master list of 250,000 extragalactic objects for which cross-identifications of names have been established, accurate positions and redshifts entered to the extent possible along with some basic data collected. There are 450,000 bibliographic references relevant to the individual objects, including abstracts of extragalactic interest which are kept online. Detailed and referenced photometry data has been taken from large compilations and will eventually be collected from the literature.

KEYWORDS	Astronomy, Databases, Extragalactic Phenomena
AUDIENCE	Astronomers, Astrophysicists, Scientists, Space Enthusiasts, Space Students
CONTACT	G. Helou, B. Madore, M. Schmitz ned@ipac.caltech.edu
FREE	

ftp://ned.ipac.caltech.edu/pub/ned

telnet://ned@ned.ipac.caltech.edu

National Astronomy and Ionosphere Center Arecibo Observatory ★★★

The National Astronomy and Ionosphere Center Arecibo Observatory is home of the largest radar-radio telescope in the world. The high sensitivity of the Arecibo main antenna enables scientists to peer more deeply into the Universe, and to study the detailed behavior of pulsars which are often not detectable by other telescopes. This site has information culled from its data and compiled in areas such as Radio Astronomy and Atmospheric Science. There is also current information available, such as the Telescope Schedule, Visitor Information, and a publication listing that is dated from July, 1991 to June, 1995.

KEYWORDS	Astronomy, Ionosphere, Observatories, Space Science
AUDIENCE	Astronomers, Puerto Rico Residents, Space Enthusiasts
CONTACT	Murray Lewis blewis@naic.edu
FREE	

http://aosun.naic.edu/

National Optical Astronomy Observatories ★★★★

The National Optical Astronomy Observatories (NOAO) page provides information on their general services, special events and research projects. The page has links to the NOAO observatories, FTP archives and science events such as images of planetary nebulae, Kitt Peak Observatory and the Gemini Project.

KEYWORDS	Images, Research
AUDIENCE	Astronomers, Astrophysicists, Researchers, Scientists
CONTACT	jbarnes@noao.edu
FREE	

http://www.noao.edu/

The Nine Planets ★★★

The Nine Planets is a 'multimedia tour' of the solar system, written for beginning astronomy enthusiasts, with incredible archives of basic information about the planets. The 'tour' includes pictures, scientific facts, history, and a general description of each of the nine planets of the solar system, as well as their moons, with sound files and movie clips. Users will find a hypertextual outline of the contents as well as appendices and glossaries of technical terms. Information about spacecraft and space exploration is also included.

KEYWORDS Planets, Solar System, Space
AUDIENCE Astronomy Enthusiasts, Space Enthusiasts, Students
CONTACT William A. Arnett
billa@znet.com
FREE

http://seds.lpl.arizona.edu/nineplanets/nineplanets/nineplanets.html

Optical and Infrared Astronomy Division ★★★★

The Optical and Infrared Astronomy Division's main focus is extragalactic and galactic astronomy. Studies emphasized include the large-scale structure of the universe, clusters of stars and of galaxies, and the formation and evolution of stars by using data from satellites, balloons, spacecraft, and ground-based observations and development of spectroscopy and imaging techniques. There is a link to commentary about the structure of the universe explained in layman's terms. Links are also provided to major observatory sites like the Whipple Observatory in Tucson Arizona, The Telescope Data center in Cambridge Mass., and the Oakridge Observatory in Harvard, Mass.

KEYWORDS Astronomy, Spectroscopy
AUDIENCE Astronomers, Astronomy Enthusiasts
FREE

http://oir-www.harvard.edu/

Osservatorio Astronomico Di Palermo Home Page ★★★

This site offers users a glimpse into the activities of the Osservatorio Astronomico Di Palermo. Users will find descriptions of the research in stellar, solar, and x-ray astronomy. There is a comprehensive collection of links to other astronomy resources on the net, as well as a bibliographic index and historical archive.

KEYWORDS Astronomy, Italy, Space Science, X-Ray Astronomy
AUDIENCE Astronomers, Italians, Science Historians, Scientists
CONTACT webmaster@oapa.astropa.unipa.it
FREE

http://www.astropa.unipa.it

Space Environment Laboratory ★★★★

The home page for the Space Environment Laboratory gives access to a large variety of resources produced by the lab including recent solar images, space weather forecasts. One can also obtain publications and products from the lab and the resources are accessed by a multimedia presentation.

KEYWORDS Environment, Physics, Research
AUDIENCE Astrophysicists, Space Science Researchers, Space Scientists
CONTACT Vern Raben
vraben@sel.noaa.gov
FREE

http://www.sel.bldrdoc.gov/

Space Telescope Electronic Information Service ★★★

This site has information and links pertaining to NASA's Hubble Space Telescope. The Space Telescope Electronic Information Service caters to both scientists and the general public. One can find astronomical and scientific software here as well as GIFs and JPEGs from the space telescope. There are also many links to astronomy-related subjects for researchers, journalists, and those interested in astronomy.

KEYWORDS Astronomy, Telescopes
AUDIENCE Astronomers, Astronomy Enthusiasts, Astrophysicists, Students (Graduate), Students (University)

Connections to the Hubble Space Telescope
Far out!!

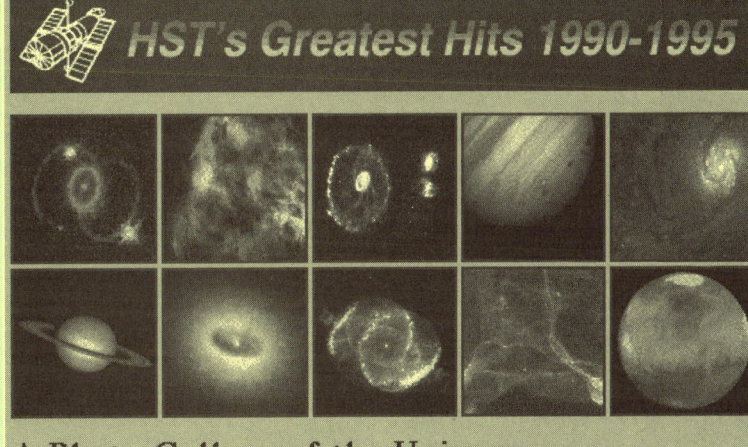

Want to travel to the Orion Nebula? How about visiting Saturn? You can do it through "Connections to the Hubble Space Telescope." This site provides you with pictures of the universe taken from the lens of the most famous telescope in outer space.

You can visit "Hubble's Greatest Hits" (1990 -1995), and learn about second-generation instruments installed on the telescope which provide infrared imaging and spectroscopic observations of astronomical targets.

Next to taking a Viking mission trip to Jupiter, these are the clearest pictures you will likely ever see of deep space, since the telescope is positioned well beyond any interference from the earth's ozone layer. You can explore what science has learned so far from Hubble's data—ranging from knowledge about planets in our solar system to novas and black holes hundreds of thousands of light-years away. Through "Space Telescope— European Coordinating Facility," you'll have online access to Hubble's entire data archive.

(http://www.stsci.edu/pubinfo/BestOfHST95.html)

CONTACT Chris O'Dea
webmaster@stsci.edu
FREE

http://marvel.stsci.edu/

Space Telescope Science Institute (STScI) ★★★★

This page is the top level menu for the Space Telescope Science Institute (STScI) WWW Server, which provides documentation, images, software, and other information related to the Hubble Space Telescope. There is a link to Internet resources for astronomers, as well as a large public area containing items such as images, movies, and press releases. A large archive of information from past Hubble projects is also available online. This site uploads new images and information on a regular basis, including full color pictures of planets within the solar system and charts images of outside galaxies.

KEYWORDS Astronomy, Images, NASA (National Aeronautics And Space Administration), Telescopes

Astronomy – Biology

AUDIENCE Astronomers, Astronomy Students, Space Enthusiasts
CONTACT Chris O'Dea
webmaster@stsci.edu
FREE

http://stsci.edu/

The University of California Search for Extraterrestrial Civilizations ★★★

A Web site containing information on the UC Berkeley SETI Program, SERENDIP (Search for Extraterrestrial Radio Emissions from Nearby Developed Intelligent Populations), an ongoing scientific research effort aimed at detecting radio signals from extraterrestrial civilizations. Details about the program and updates on current research activities are also accessible.

KEYWORDS Astronomy
AUDIENCE Academics, Astronomers, Astronomy Enthusiasts, Astrophysicists
CONTACT sereninfo@ssl.berkeley.edu
FREE

http://albert.ssl.berkeley.edu:80/serendip/

Warsaw University Astronomical Observatory ★★★★

The Warsaw University Astronomical Observatory maintains this WWW server to offer information on the Observatory's activities and research projects. Users will find facilities and staff information, as well as descriptions and detailed scientific data about their current research projects. There is also information available on scientific software in use at the observatory, and a collection of links to outside servers with astronomical information.

KEYWORDS Astronomy, Poland, Space Science
AUDIENCE Astronomers, Scientists, Space Scientists
CONTACT Andrzej Udalski
udalski@sirius.astrouw.edu.pl
FREE

http://www.astrouw.edu.pl

Biology

See also
Engineering & Technology · *Bioengineering*
Health & Medicine · *Biomedicine*
Science · *Biosciences*

16 S RNA Database ★★★★

This 16 S RNA Database contains a list of representative complete or nearly complete 16S and 16S-like RNA sequences, their GenBank/EMBL accession numbers and entries, and secondary structure diagrams for select organisms. Also available is a list of mitochondrial and chloroplast structures, and representative Archaea, (eu)Bacterial, and Eucarya structures.

KEYWORDS Biological Research, Biology, Genetics, Molecular Biology
AUDIENCE Bioinformaticists, Biologists, Biomedical Researchers, Biotechnologists
CONTACT robin.gutell@colorado.edu
FREE

http://pundit.colorado.edu:8080/RNA/16S/16s.html

AGEN Biomedical ★★★★

This site is the homepage of AGEN Biomedical, a biotechnology company which produces medical and veterinary diagnostic products based on monoclonal antibody technology. Special fields include human haemostasis and infectious diseases, while veterinary diagnostics include companion animal diseases, canine heartworm, FIV and FeLV. Also included is information about research and development, manufacturing capability, regulatory affairs, corporate objectives, products and distributors.

KEYWORDS Biotechnology, Companies, Molecular Biology
AUDIENCE Biologists, Biomedical Researchers, Biotechnologists, Veterinarians
CONTACT richards@agen.com.au
FREE

http://www.agen.com.au/

Actinomycete-Streptomyces Internet Resource Center (ASIRC) ★★★★

The ASIRC (Actinomycete-Streptomyces Internet Resource Center) provides announcements and information regarding Actinomycete-Streptomyces research, including future meeting dates and programs, methods and techniques, secondary metabolite structures, photographs, micrographs, and job postings.

KEYWORDS Biological Research, Genetics, Molecular Biology
AUDIENCE Bioinformaticists, Biologists, Biomedical Researchers, Biotechnologists
CONTACT asirc@molbio.cbs.umn.edu
FREE

http://molbio.cbs.umn.edu/asirc/

Alces Candida Albicans Database ★★★★

This is an extensive database on the genetics of the yeast Candida Albicans. The information included here is mostly unpublished and there are many links to molecular genetic information. In addition, this site contains a large virtual genome center with access to many genetics programs and information.

KEYWORDS Bioinformatics, Databases, Genetics, Molecular Biology
AUDIENCE Bioinformaticists, Biologists, Biomedical Researchers, Biotechnologists
CONTACT Stew Scherer
stew@lenti.med.umn.edu
FREE

http://alces.med.umn.edu/start.html

Archive of Biology Software and Data at Indiana University (IUBio) ★★★★

IUBio Archive is an archive of biology, chemistry, and molecular biology data and software. The archive includes items to browse, search and fetch molecular data; software; biology news and documents; as well as links to remote information sources in biology and elsewhere. The main area of concentration of this archive is molecular biology. It is recommended to first read the file Archive.doc, which has considerable information about and instructions for using the archive.

KEYWORDS Archives, Chemistry, Education (College/University), Molecular Biology
AUDIENCE Biologists, Molecular Biologists, Molecular Biotechnologists, Students
CONTACT archive@bio.indiana.edu
FREE

ftp://ftp.bio.indiana.edu

Arris Pharmaceutical Corp. ★★★★

This site is the homepage of Arris Pharmaceutical Corp., a biotechnology company engaged in the discovery and development of synthetic small molecule therapeutics that modulate the activity of medically important proteins. The company is focusing its initial product development programs on protease-based therapies for human inflammatory diseases and on oral cytokine and growth factor mimetics. The company's structure-based drug design approach combines the disciplines of chemistry and biology with crystallography and applied mathematics in the form of artificial intelligence (AI) paradigms designed to shorten the drug discovery and development cycle. Information is also available on recent company news and job opportunities.

KEYWORDS Biotechnology, Companies, Molecular Biology
AUDIENCE Biologists, Biomedical Researchers, Biotechnologists, Scientists
FREE

http://www.arris.com/

BIO Online ★★★★

This site is the homepage of BIO Online, a comprehensive site for biotechnology-related information and services on the Internet, combining the resources of biotechnology companies, biotechnology centers, universities and other research and academic institutions, industry suppliers and vendors, government agencies, and non-profit special interest groups. Also provided are events calendars, career management materials, news, job postings, product catalogs/technical support and investor relations information.

KEYWORDS Bioinformatics, Biotechnology, Companies
AUDIENCE Biologists, Biomedical Researchers, Biotechnologists, Scientists
FREE

http://www.bio.com/

BIOSIS ★★★★

BIOSIS, established in 1926, is a not-for-profit organization whose mission is to foster the growth, communica-

tion and use of biological knowledge for the common good. This site contains the world's largest collection of abstracts and bibliographic references to worldwide biological and medical literature.
KEYWORDS   Biotechnology, Companies, Publications
AUDIENCE   Biologists, Biomedical Researchers, Biotechnologists, Scientists
CONTACT   info@mail.biosis.org
FREE

http://www.biosis.org/htmls/common/biosis.html

BIOSYM Technologies

BIOSYM Technologies is the world's largest supplier of molecular modeling software and strategies for biological, chemical, and materials research. Also available are newsletters and company information.
KEYWORDS   Biophysics, Biotechnology, Companies
AUDIENCE   Biologists, Biomedical Researchers, Biotechnologists, Scientists
CONTACT   webmaster@biosym.com
FREE

http://www.biosym.com/

BioData, Inc.

This site is the homepage of BioData, Inc., a provider of computer system integration services to biotechnology and pharmaceutical companies. The company provides services to biotechnology start-ups and large biotechnology and pharmaceutical corporations. Information is also available on current job openings, personnel and vendor listings.
KEYWORDS   Bioinformatics, Biotechnology, Companies
AUDIENCE   Biologists, Biomedical Researchers, Biotechnologists, Scientists
CONTACT   webmaster@BioData.COM
FREE

http://www.biodata.com/

BioLogical Research Network, Int'l. (BRNI)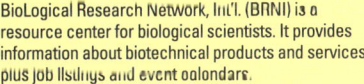

BioLogical Research Network, Int'l. (BRNI) is a resource center for biological scientists. It provides information about biotechnical products and services, plus job listings and event calendars.
KEYWORDS   Biological Research, Biology, Biosciences, Job Listings
AUDIENCE   Biologists, Biomedical Researchers
CONTACT   brni@bio.com
FREE

http://cns.bio.com/brni.html

Biological Sciences Newsgroup Forums

BIOSCI and Bionet are a series of electronic communication forums (i.e. electronic bulletin boards or newsgroups) for use by biological scientists and related professionals worldwide. This site offers extensive information for biologists as well as links to other gopher and WWW sites.
KEYWORDS   Biological Research, Biology, Biosciences, Biotechnology
AUDIENCE   Biochemists, Biologists, Biomedical Researchers, Biotechnologists
CONTACT   Mack, David
          biosci-help@net.bio.net
FREE

gopher://gopher.bio.net/

Biology Database Searches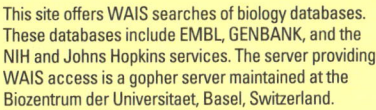

This site offers WAIS searches of biology databases. These databases include EMBL, GENBANK, and the NIH and Johns Hopkins services. The server providing WAIS access is a gopher server maintained at the Biozentrum der Universitaet, Basel, Switzerland.
KEYWORDS   Bioinformatics, Biology, Databases, Genetics
AUDIENCE   Biologists, Computer Users, Geneticists
CONTACT   Reinhard Doelz
          doelz@urz.unibas.ch
FREE

gopher://biox.embnet.unibas.ch:13020/

Biology Internet Tools

This site offers Internet services related to biology. This includes a finger service of computers at the Biozentrum der Universitaet, Basel, Switzerland, access to biology-related Usenet news, and a WAIS query service of the Getz biology database. The server providing these services is a gopher server maintained at the Biozentrum der Universitaet, Basel, Switzerland.
KEYWORDS   Biology, Biosciences, Databases, Usenet Newsgroups
AUDIENCE   Biologists, Computer Users
CONTACT   Reinhard Doelz
          doelz@urz.unibas.ch
FREE

gopher://gopher.embnet.unibas.ch:12999/

Biomechanics, Inc.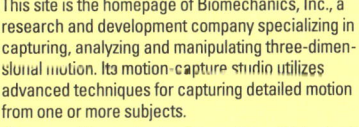

This site is the homepage of Biomechanics, Inc., a research and development company specializing in capturing, analyzing and manipulating three-dimensional motion. Its motion-capture studio utilizes advanced techniques for capturing detailed motion from one or more subjects.
KEYWORDS   Biomechanics, Biomedicine, Biotechnology, Companies
AUDIENCE   Biologists, Biomedical Researchers, Biotechnologists, Scientists
FREE

http://www.crl.com/~biomech/

Biotechnology Law Web Server

Biotechnology Law Web Server was designed by the Biotechnology Practice Group with the objective of offering legal and scientific information of interest to biotechnology researchers. Available resources include a patent primer, intellectual property resource center and agricultural biotech information.
KEYWORDS   Biotechnology, Biotechnology Law, Companies, Patents
AUDIENCE   Biologists, Biomedical Researchers, Biotechnologists, Scientists
CONTACT   PBCJ@ari.net
FREE

http://biotechlaw.ari.net/

CAOS/CAMM Center, The Netherlands

The CAOS/CAMM Center is a national facility containing a large selection of software and databases in the areas of molecular modeling, genomics, bioinformatics and computational chemistry.
KEYWORDS   Bioinformatics, Genetics, Molecular Biology, Molecular Modeling
AUDIENCE   Bioinformaticists, Biologists, Chemists, Molecular Biologists, Physicists
CONTACT   Jack A.M. Leunissen
          jackl@caos.kun.nl
FREE

http://cammsg3.caos.kun.nl:8000/

Cambridge Healthtech Institute

Cambridge Healthtech Institute was established to facilitate the discussion and exchange of technical and commercial information through the organization and sponsorship of biomedical conferences and biotechnology researchers. Conference listings are posted on a variety of biomedical topics.
KEYWORDS   Biomedical Conferences, Biomedicine, Biotechnology, Companies
AUDIENCE   Biologists, Biomedical Researchers, Biotechnologists, Scientists
CONTACT   chi@world.std.com
FREE

http://www.xensei.com/users/chi/homepg.html

Chromosome X Database

This is a searchable database of human chromosome X containing physical and genetic mapping data. In addition, information is available on sequences, YACs, probes, loci and genes
KEYWORDS   Biomedical Research, Chromosomes, Genetics, Molecular Biology
AUDIENCE   Bioinformaticists, Biologists, Biomedical Researchers, Biotechnologists
FREE

http://probe.nalusda.gov:8300/cgi-bin/nph-3.sh/hchx/hchx?c

Ciba

This site is the homepage of Ciba-Geigy, the Swiss Biotechnology Company and includes financial information, research and development, contacts, media information, and healthcare news.
KEYWORDS   Biotechnology, Companies, Pharmaceuticals

AUDIENCE Biologists, Biomedical Researchers, Biotechnologists, Scientists
FREE

http://www.ciba.com/

Computational Biology ★★★

This is a gopher server of the Johns Hopkins University Computational Biology Center. It contains information about computational biology and genetics. There are biology FTP sites, software and data archives for browsing from here. In addition, it has links to other gophers on the Internet.

KEYWORDS Biology, Biosciences, Computer Applications, Computing
AUDIENCE Academics, Biologists, Computer Professionals, Scientists
CONTACT Dan Jacobson
danj@mail.gdb.org
FREE

gopher://merlot.welch.jhu.edu/

Course in Cell Biology (French) ★★★

This Gopher site contains a tutorial in French on cell biology appropriate for more advanced students. It covers such topics as cell cycle, cell membrane, internal organelles, cytoskeleton, genetic material, and related topics. It contains no pictures but does have a searchable index of key words.

KEYWORDS Cell Biology, Distance Learning, Genetics, Molecular Biology
AUDIENCE Biomedical Researchers, Biotechnologists, Medical Educators, Students
FREE

gopher://brise.ere.umontreal.ca/11/bb/textes/notes

Course/Tutorial on Cell Biology ★★★★

This Web site contains a very informative tutorial on cell biology appropriate for the novice or more advanced students. It covers such topics as a definition of a cell, and provides information on plants, bacteria, procaryotes, eucaryotes, cell membranes, phospholipids, internal organelles, cytoskeleton, genetic material, and related topics. Includes color pictures and diagrams to aid in understanding.

KEYWORDS Bioinformatics, Cell Biology, Distance Learning, Genetics
AUDIENCE Biomedical Researchers, Biotechnologists, Students (University)
FREE

http://lenti.med.umn.edu/~mwd/cell_www/cell.html

DSHB (Developmental Studies Hybridoma Bank) ★★★★

The Developmental Studies Hybridoma Bank supplies investigators with monoclonal antibodies useful for studies in developmental and cell biology. They may be ordered as tissue culture supernatants, ascites, or partially purified immunoglobulin and selected hybridomas are also available.

KEYWORDS Biomedical Research, Cell Biology, Immunology, Molecular Biology
AUDIENCE Biologists, Biomedical Researchers, Biotechnologists, Medical Researchers
CONTACT dshb@welchlink.welch.jhu.edu
FREE

http://www.gdb.org/Dan/DSHB/dshb.intro.html

European Molecular Biology Network Homepage ★★★

The European Molecular Biology Network (EMBnet) was created to link European laboratories using biocomputing and bioinformatics in molecular biology research. This site describes some of the projects being conducted in this field and maintains links to close to 20 servers in each member country.

KEYWORDS Bioinformatics, Biomedical Computing, Microbiology, Molecular Biology
AUDIENCE Molecular Biologists, Nanotechnology Enthusiasts
CONTACT R. Doelz
doelz@urz.unibas.ch
FREE

http://beta.embnet.unibas.ch/embnet/info.html

Genlink - A Human Genetics Resource ★★★★

GenLink is a multimedia database resource for human genetics. GenLink provides links for mapping information and software tools to produce unified maps of the human genome. Researchers interested in identifying genes based on map positions should find the resource helpful. The resource includes information about human chromosome workshops, viewing of human meiotic maps, 1993 Genome screen maps, and comprehensive microsatellite maps. There are also links to other genetic resources.

KEYWORDS Bioinformatics, Biological Research, Genetics, Molecular Biology
AUDIENCE Bioinformaticists, Biologists, Biomedical Researchers, Biotechnologists
CONTACT genlink@hdklab.wustl.edu
FREE

http://www.genlink.wustl.edu/

Genome Net WWW Server ★★★★

GenomeNet is a Japanese site for genome research and related research in molecular biology. Extensive information is available on the Human Genome Project in Japan and on genetics in general. Also available are sequence interpretation tools, searchable genetics information and links to many Molecular Biology servers.

KEYWORDS Bioinformatics, Biological Research, Genetics, Molecular Biology
AUDIENCE Bioinformaticists, Biologists, Biomedical Researchers, Biotechnologists
CONTACT www@genome.ad.jp
FREE

http://www.genome.ad.jp/

Haartman Institute ★★★

The Haartman Institute conducts biology research at the University of Helsinki in Finland. Included at their site is the electronic newsletter Meilehti, with an index of past newsletters, organized both chronologically and by subject. Articles in both Finnish and English concern such topics as BioComputing and Networked Sequence Services, and BioComputing and Global Communication. Users will also find links to other biology sites on the Web, as well as information about the University of Helsinki.

KEYWORDS Biosciences, Biotechnology
AUDIENCE Biologists, Biology Researchers, Biology Students
CONTACT Pekka Salonen
Pekka.Salonen@Helsinki.FI
FREE

http://kirke.helsinki.fi/

The Jackson Laboratory Bioinformatics Server ★★★★

The Jackson Laboratory Bioinformatics Server contains the Mouse Genome Database (MGD) which has data on experiments on the genetics of mice. There are tools to help users submit their own data, information on how to access the Encyclopedia of the Mouse Genome, and links to other bioinformatics servers.

KEYWORDS Bioinformatics, Genetics, Genomes, Mice
AUDIENCE Bioinformaticists, Geneticists
CONTACT Mouse Genome Informatics User Support, The Jackson Laboratory, 600 Main Street, mgi-help@informatics.jax.org
FREE

http://www.informatics.jax.org/

Johns Hopkins University BioInformatics Web Server ★★★★

This site contains Prot-Web (a collection of protein databases), extensive links to other biology servers around the world, electronic publications in biology, as well as links to other biology databases at Johns Hopkins.

KEYWORDS Bioinformatics, Databases, Molecular Biology, Proteins
AUDIENCE Bioinformaticists, Biologists, Biomedical Researchers, Biotechnologists
CONTACT Dan Jacobson
danj@gdb.org
FREE

http://www.gdb.org/

Lawrence Berkeley Laboratory Human Genome Center Web Server ★★★

This is the home page for the Lawrence Berkeley Laboratory (LBL) Human Genome Center, which studies human genetics. The Center's research activities, facilities, and personnel are described, and a gateway is provided to other biology resources on the Web.

KEYWORDS	Biological Research, Genetics, Research Institutes
AUDIENCE	Biologists, Educators (University), Geneticists, Researchers
CONTACT	HGC Web Master
FREE	

http://www-hgc.lbl.gov/GenomeHome.html

Meat Animal Research Center ★★★★

The Meat Animal Research Center provides information about research on swine and cattle genomes. Included are genome maps for both animals, as well as links to related resources.

KEYWORDS	Biological Research, Genetics, Molecular Biology
AUDIENCE	Bioinformaticists, Biologists, Biomedical Researchers, Biotechnologists
CONTACT	bradley@aux.marc.usda.gov
FREE	

http://sol.marc.usda.gov/

Microbial Germplasm Database ★★★

This gopher server provides access to a database of strains of bacteria, viruses, fungi, and other microbes. The database is maintained by Oregon State University. Most of the microbes are those that affect the areas of botany and agricultural botany. The database is partially searchable by a keyword search. There are also links to other biological and scientific gophers.

KEYWORDS	Botany, Microbiology, Plant Pathology, Viruses
AUDIENCE	Biologists, Botanists
CONTACT	Larry Moore mgd-feedback@bcc.orst.edu
FREE	

gopher://ava.bcc.orst.edu/

Microbial Pathogenesis ★★

This site contains issues of the journal Microbial Pathogenesis, presented as a table of contents only. The journal publishes papers on basic mechanisms in the infectious process, including current methodological advances in molecular biology. Information is also available on subscriptions and instructions to authors.

KEYWORDS	Biology Journals, Biotechnology, Microbiology, Molecular Biology
AUDIENCE	Biologists, Biomedical Researchers, Biotechnologists, Microbiologists

FREE

gopher://ukoln.bath.ac.uk:7070/11/Link/Tree/Publishing/AcademicPress/APJournals/APJ71

Molecular Biology Computation Resource ★★★

The Molecular Biology Computational Resource (MCBR) Guide provides online support for users of the MCBR at Baylor University, and serves as a resource for molecular biology questions. Included in this site are links to databases covering subjects such as sequence similarity searches, organismal information, and biological data, as well as links to other web sites focusing on issues of biology and genetics. This site also includes information about the MCBR and Baylor University, with staff profiles, programs, and scientific software that MCBR produces.

KEYWORDS	Genetics, Molecular Biology
AUDIENCE	Biology Students, Geneticists, Molecular Biologists
CONTACT	mbcrhelp@mbcr.bcm.tmc.edu
FREE	

http://mbcr.bcm.tmc.edu/home.html

Connections to Women and Science
From Astronomy to Zoology

Many women in general, and minority women in particular, have made major contributions to the fields of science and engineering.

If you are thinking about pursuing a career in science and engineering, you owe it to yourself to check out the educational grants and fellowships available through the Internet. This is also a great way for young women interested in science to find out about minority women who have made it in their fields—women such as Dr. Shirley Jackson, a theoretical physicist, and Dorothy McClendon, a microbiologist.

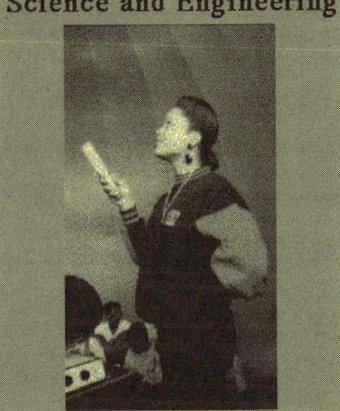

The "Women and Minorities in Science and Engineering" site provides links with key organizations, such the Society of Women Engineers, and Women in Geoscience. These organizations typically maintain gopher addresses so that you can link to comprehensive information concerning chapter history, personalities, and research work being conducted by women affiliated with the organization.

You can also access profiles of accomplished female scientists through the "Women in Science and Engineering" site, as well as an exhaustive bibliography from Dorothy Hill, noted geologist and paleontologist.

(http://www.ai.mit.edu/people/ellens/Gender/wom_and_min.html)

also, (http://www.lib.lsu.edu/lib/chem/display/faces.html)

also, (gopher://flint.mines.colorado.4501/1)

Molecular Biology Techniques Manual ★★

This manual contains information and instructional material for two molecular techniques—Sodium Dodecyl Sulphate Polyacrylamide Gel Electrophoresis, and Immunoelectroblotting ('Western' Blotting) of Proteins. Detailed information, protocols, and safety concerns are available for each technique.

KEYWORDS	Bioinformatics, Genetics, Molecular Biology
AUDIENCE	Biologists, Biology Educators, Biology Students, Biomedical Researchers, Molecular Biologists
CONTACT	www@uct.ac.za
FREE	

http://www.uct.ac.za/microbiology/manualln.html

Molecules R US ★★★★

The Molecules R US site provides an online engine for searching the Brookhaven Protein Data Bank (PDB) of both proteins and nucleic acids' crystallographic structures. The PDB is a repository of published crystal structures. The user can perform text-based searches of the database contents and display molecular structures if the local client is correctly configured. For the latter case, configuration instructions are provided online. Structure files in PDB format may be downloaded to the local host.

KEYWORDS	Biomedical Research, Crystallography, Proteins, Research

AUDIENCE: Biochemists, Bioinformaticists, Biomedical Researchers, Molecular Biologists
CONTACT: Peter C. FitzGerald pf4q@nih.gov
FREE

http://www.nih.gov/www94/molrus

NIH Molecular Modeling Home Page ★★★★

This document provides a source of information concerning the major facets of molecular modeling methods and its biological applications. The site is maintained by the National Institutes of Health (NIH). It provides access to software, NIH research activities, databases and educational resources.

KEYWORDS: Biochemistry, Biomedical Research, Molecular Biology, Research Institutes
AUDIENCE: Biomedical Researchers, Educators, Molecular Biologists, Molecular Biotechnologists
CONTACT: cmb@hawk.dcrt.nih.gov
FREE

http://www.nih.gov/molecular_modeling/mmhome.html

NRSub - A Non-Redundant Database for Bacillus Subtilis ★★★★

The NRSub (A Non-Redundant Database for Bacillus subtilis) database provides access to a non-redundant set of DNA sequences from Bacillus subtilis. All of the duplications from the general sequence collections have been removed and all detected overlapping sequences have been merged into contigs. Additional data is available on gene mapping and codon usage, as well as cross-references with EMBL, Swiss-Prot, and Enzyme collections.

KEYWORDS: Biological Research, Genetics, Molecular Biology
AUDIENCE: Bioinformaticists, Biologists, Biomedical Researchers, Biotechnologists
CONTACT: moszer@pasteur.fr
FREE

http://ddbjs4h.genes.nig.ac.jp/

OGMP (Organelle Genome Megasequencing Program) ★★★★

This OGMP (Organelle Genome Megasequencing Program) provides information about the OGMP, a collaborative team of seven research groups from Eastern Canada, each of which is interested in molecular evolution. This site is mainly focused on mitochondria, plastids and bacteria.

KEYWORDS: Biological Research, Genetics, Molecular Biology
AUDIENCE: Bioinformaticists, Biologists, Biomedical Researchers, Biotechnologists
CONTACT: tim@BCH.UMontreal.CA
FREE

http://megasun.bch.umontreal.ca/welcome.html

PID (Protist Image Data) ★★★★

Protist Image Data (PID) provides pictures and short descriptions of selected protist genera, especially those genera whose species are frequently used as experimental organisms or are important in studies of organismal evolution. Information is available on morphology, taxonomy and phylogenetic relationships of these organisms.

KEYWORDS: Bioinformatics, Biological Research, Genetics, Molecular Biology
AUDIENCE: Bioinformaticists, Biologists, Biomedical Researchers, Biotechnologists
CONTACT: okellyc@bch.umontreal.ca
FREE

http://megasun.bch.umontreal.ca/protists/protists.html

RDP (Ribosomal Database Project) ★★★

This RDP (Ribosomal Database Project) contains information on the large and small ribosomal subunits of both prokaryotic and eukaryotic organisms. Users can also find information on phylogenetic trees and secondary structure diagrams, as well as download sequence analysis software.

KEYWORDS: Biological Research, Cell Biology, Genetics, Molecular Biology
AUDIENCE: Bioinformaticists, Biologists, Biomedical Researchers, Biotechnologists
CONTACT: mrmike@uiuc.edu
FREE

http://geta.life.uiuc.edu/index.html

The Tree of Life - A Phylogenetic Navigation System for the Internet ★★★

The Tree of Life Phylogenetic Navigator is a system designed to link biological information available on the Internet. It provides taxonomic and systematic information (diversity, phylogeny) of various groups of organisms. The display of these links is in the form of a phylogenetic tree linking the organisms.

KEYWORDS: Bioinformatics, Biological Research, Biology, Biosciences
AUDIENCE: Bioinformaticists, Biologists, Biomedical Researchers, Biotechnologists
CONTACT: tree@phylogeny.arizona.edu
FREE

http://phylogeny.arizona.edu/tree/phylogeny.html

U.S. Biotechnology Industry - Facts and Figures 1994/1995 ★★★★

This site contains a wealth of current information about the biotechnology industry, including sales and markets, companies, research and development, financing and statistics.

KEYWORDS: Biotechnology, Companies, Online Publications, Publications
AUDIENCE: Biologists, Biomedical Researchers, Biotechnologists, Scientists
FREE

http://www.bio.com/bc/bio/2usbio.html

UCSC Perceptual Science Laboratory ★★★

The UCSC Perceptual Science Laboratory (PSL) conducts research into human perception, including speech perception and facial animation. This site contains information about the PSL, including papers by PSL staff, project descriptions, and links to related sites on the Web. Subjects covered include facial analysis, lipreading, and speech, with links to other Web sites that deal with each of these subjects. Users can also look at animations of facial movements.

KEYWORDS: Human Physiology, Perception, Speech Recognition
AUDIENCE: Cognitive Scientists, Speech Therapists
CONTACT: mmcohen@mambo.ucsc.edu
FREE

http://mambo.ucsc.edu/

U.S. Geological Server Biology Server ★★★

In this site the US Geological Survey provides a compendium of bioscience-related Internet links to hundreds of Web sites and gopher servers around the world. Some of the links include Baylor College of Medicine Genome Center, Johns Hopkins University—BioInformatics Web Server, and Johns Hopkins University—BioInformatics Web Server.

KEYWORDS: Bioinformatics, Biological Research, Biology, Biosciences
AUDIENCE: Biologists, Biotechnologists, Researchers
CONTACT: webmaster@info.er.usgs.gov
FREE

http://info.er.usgs.gov/network/science/biology/index.html

University of Houston Gene-Server Protein Information Resource (PIR) Archive ★★★

University of Houston's Protein Information Resource (PIR) makes the International Protein Sequence Database available via this gopher server. It is sponsored by the National Biomedical Research Foundation and it has pointers to other biological resources on the Internet.

KEYWORDS: Biosciences, Databases, Molecular Biology, Proteins
AUDIENCE: Biochemists, Biomedical Researchers, Geneticists, Molecular Biologists
CONTACT: Dan Davison davison@uh.edu
FREE

gopher://evolution.bchs.uh.edu/

University of Michigan Human Genome Center ★★★

The University of Michigan Human Genome Center Home Page is an online resource for genomic studies. This site provides a search for a genetic map of a mouse as well as regularly updated physical map data for clones and STS. Also included are instructions for telnet access to the DNA Sequencing database and archived chromatograms, as well as guides and instructions for users of the Genome Center's computing facilties. A comprehensive list of links to other Biology and Genome Informatics Web sites is also provided.

KEYWORDS   Biosciences, Genetics, Genomes, Human Physiology
AUDIENCE   Geneticists, Genome Researchers
CONTACT   Spencer W. Thomas
Spencer.Thomas@med.umich.edu
FREE

http://mendel.hgp.med.umich.edu

Visible Human Project ★★★

The Visible Human Project is an outgrowth of the National Library of Medicine's 1986 Long-Range Plan to create a complete, anatomically detailed, three-dimensional representation of the male and female human body. The long-term goal of the Visible Human Project is to produce a system of knowledge structures that will transparently link visual knowledge forms to symbolic knowledge formats such as the names of body parts.

KEYWORDS   Anatomy, Biomedical Research, Imaging, Magnetic Resonance
AUDIENCE   Biomedical Researchers, Medical Practitioners, Medical Researchers
CONTACT   hyperdoc@nlm.nih.gov
FREE

http://www.nlm.nih.gov/extramural_research.dir/visible_human.html

Worcester Foundation for Experimental Biology (WFEB) Gopher ★★★

The WFEB Gopher offers biology and experimental biology information. WFEB stands for the Worcester Foundation for Experimental Biology, a research group in Massachusetts. The site provides computer and computer networking information and biology information which includes granting agencies, databases, and more.

KEYWORDS   Bioinformatics, Biological Research, Biology, Research
AUDIENCE   Biologists, Medical Researchers
CONTACT   Foteos Macrides
MACRIDES@SCI.WFEB.EDU
FREE

gopher://sci.wfeb.edu/

Worm Literature Index ★★★★

This site houses the Worm Breeder's Gazette, a journal for biologists studying various species of worms. Users can search the archive, as well as an index of academic papers related to the study of worms. In addition, there is a large bibliography of worm-related material here for perusal.

KEYWORDS   Biological Research, Electronic Journals, Genetics
AUDIENCE   Biologists, Biomedical Researchers, Biotechnologists
CONTACT   Leon Avery
leon@eatworms.swmed.edu
FREE

http://eatworms.swmed.edu/htbin/wbgart/

Biosciences

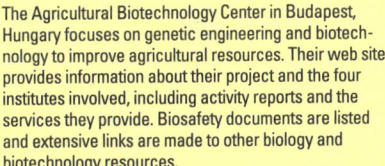

See also
Engineering & Technology · *Bioengineering*
Health & Medicine · *Biomedicine*

Agricultural Biotechnology Center ★★★

The Agricultural Biotechnology Center in Budapest, Hungary focuses on genetic engineering and biotechnology to improve agricultural resources. Their web site provides information about their project and the four institutes involved, including activity reports and the services they provide. Biosafety documents are listed and extensive links are made to other biology and biotechnology resources.

KEYWORDS   Agriculture, Biotechnology
AUDIENCE   Agriculturalists, Biotechnologists, Genetic Engineers
CONTACT   éter Fábián
www@molmod.abc.hu
FREE

http://molmod.abc.hu

BDT Base de Dados Tropical Web ★★★★

The Base de Dados Tropical (BDT) Tropical Database is a department within the Fundacao Tropical de Pesquisas e Tecnologia (FTPT) 'Andre Tosello', a Brazilian not-for-profit foundation. The information available is extensive in subjects such as biodiversity, environmental education, botany, molecular biology, zoology, meteorology, and environmental legislation. FTPT also maintains the BIN21 (Biodiversity Information Network). The BDT offers access to publications, as well as links to other biodiversity sources on the Internet.

KEYWORDS   Biodiversity, Brazil, Environment, Tropical Databases
AUDIENCE   Biologists, Botanists, Ecologists, Environmental Researchers, Zoologists
CONTACT   Dr. Vanderlei Perez Canhos
vcanhos@ftpt.br
FREE

http://ftpt.br/

gopher://ftpt.br/

Biologist's Control Panel ★★★★

This site is a master search engine for most molecular biology utilities. It allows the visitor to search many different biology databases at a single site and contains extensive references and pointers.

KEYWORDS   Bioinformatics, Genetics, Genomes, Molecular Biology
AUDIENCE   Bioinformaticists, Biologists, Biomedical Researchers, Biotechnologists
CONTACT   gc-help@bcm.tmc.edu
FREE

http://gc.bcm.tmc.edu:8088/bio/

Birkbeck College, Department of Crystallography Home Page ★★★

This site offers extensive information on the science of crystallography. Produced by the Crystallography Department at Birkbeck College, it offers material such as an Internet course titled 'The Principles of Protein Structure,' and information on the courses and degree programs available. There are also links to some professional societies and WWW servers with related information. Users will also find general information for new users of the Internet.

KEYWORDS   Crystallography, Molecular Biology
AUDIENCE   Bioscience Professionals, Crystallographers, Molecular Biologists
FREE

http://www.cryst.bbk.ac.uk

The Blue Goose Server ★★★★

The Blue Goose Server provides information about the U.S. National Wildlife System, and topics related to wildlife management and natural resources management. It details the different programs that National Wildlife is involved with regarding wildlife, habitat, and natural resources.

KEYWORDS   Environment, National Wildlife System, Natural Resources, Wildlife
AUDIENCE   Environmentalists, General Public, Policymakers
CONTACT   Sean Furniss
FurnissS@mail.fws.gov
FREE

http://bluegoose.arw.r9.fws.gov/

DDBJ (DNA Databank of Japan) ★★★★

DDBJ is the sole DNA sequence data bank in Japan which is officially certified to collect DNA sequences from researchers and which can issue accession numbers to the data submitters. This database collects data mainly from Japanese researchers and exchanges the data daily with EMBL, GenBank, and GSDB.

KEYWORDS   Databases, Genetics, Genomes, Japan
AUDIENCE   Bioinformaticists, Biologists, Biomedical Researchers, Biotechnologists
CONTACT   ftp@nig.ac.jp
FREE

gopher://gopher.nig.ac.jp/1

Biosciences

E. coli Genetic Stock Center ★★★★

This site is a database of genetic information on the bacterium E. coli. There is information including genotypes and reference information for several thousand strains, map and gene information, and specific mutations.

KEYWORDS	Biomedical Research, Gene Mapping, Genetics, Molecular Biology
AUDIENCE	Bioinformaticists, Biologists, Biomedical Researchers, Biotechnologists
CONTACT	Stan Letovsky letovsky@cs.yale.edu
FREE	

http://cgsc.biology.yale.edu/top.html

gopher://cgsc.biology.yale.edu/

EIHG (Eccles Institute of Human Genetics) ★★★★

Eccles Institute of Human Genetics (EIHG) provides announcements and information about upcoming talks and seminars at EIHG, links to other WWW servers, links to those WWW servers related to genetics, the home pages of several people at the EIHG, various labs' protocols, and a gateway interface to EIHG Genetics database.

KEYWORDS	Biological Research, Genetics, Molecular Biology
AUDIENCE	Bioinformaticists, Biomedical Researchers, Biotechnologists, Geneticists
CONTACT	www-admin@www-genetics.med.utah.edu
FREE	

http://www-genetics.med.utah.edu/

Fish Net ★★★★

This site is a database of information on efforts to map genes in zebrafish. The information here includes zebrafish genetic maps, strains, molecular probes, DNA libraries, cloned genes, mutations, news, and references.

KEYWORDS	Fish, Gene Mapping, Genetics, Molecular Biology
AUDIENCE	Bioinformaticists, Biologists, Biomedical Researchers, Biotechnologists
CONTACT	Pat Edwards edwards@uoneuro.uoregon.edu
FREE	

http://zfish.uoregon.edu/

GenBank ★★★★

GenBank is the NIH (National Institutes of Health) genetic sequence database, a collection of all known DNA sequences. The extensive database, with over 269,500 sequences, has a search index via several methods. NCBI is continuously developing new tools and enhancing existing ones to improve both submission and access to GenBank.

KEYWORDS	Bioinformatics, Databases, Gene Mapping, Genetics
AUDIENCE	Bioinformaticists, Biologists, Biomedical Researchers, Biotechnologists
CONTACT	www@ncbi.nlm.nih.gov
FREE	

http://www.ncbi.nlm.nih.gov/Genbank/index.html

GenQuest - The Q Server ★★★★

This site is an integrated interface to the sequence comparison server at the Oak Ridge National Lab. It was designed for rapid and sensitive comparison of DNA and protein sequence to existing DNA and protein sequence databases and the rapid retrieval of the full database entries of any sequence.

KEYWORDS	Bioinformatics, Databases, Molecular Biology, Protein Chemistry
AUDIENCE	Bioinformaticists, Biologists, Biomedical Researchers, Biotechnologists
CONTACT	Dan Jacobson danj@gdb.org
FREE	

http://www.gdb.org/Dan/gq/gq.form.html

Genetic Engineering News ★★★

This site, Genetic Engineering News, contains issues of the journal Genetic Engineering News (table of contents and selected articles). Information is also available on subscriptions.

KEYWORDS	Electronic Journals, Genetics, Molecular Biology
AUDIENCE	Bioengineers, Geneticists
FREE	

gopher://gopher.enews.com/11/magazines/alphabetic/gl/geng_news

Group 1 Intron Database ★★★★

The Group 1 Intron Database contains information on group I introns. Information is available on secondary structure diagrams (Postscript format), references, accession numbers, and papers.

KEYWORDS	Biological Research, Genetics, Molecular Biology
AUDIENCE	Bioinformaticists, Biologists, Biomedical Researchers, Biotechnologists
CONTACT	damberge@beagle.colorado.edu
FREE	

http://pundit.colorado.edu:8080/RNA/GRPI/introns.html

HGMIS (Human Genome Management Information System) ★★★★

This site is a clearinghouse of information on the U.S. human genome project and includes a newsletter and many pointers to genome-related sites.

KEYWORDS	Bioinformatics, Genetics, Human Genome Project, Molecular Biology
AUDIENCE	Bioinformaticists, Biologists, Biomedical Researchers, Biotechnologists
CONTACT	martinsa@ornl.gov
FREE	

http://www.ornl.gov/TechResources/Human_Genome/home.html

The Illinois Natural History Survey Home Page ★★★★

The Illinois Natural History Survey Home Page maintains an overview of the ecosystems of Illinois. This site has material about the flora and fauna of the state, and the projects the Illinois Natural History Survey is conducting to preserve them. You can also link to the various collections held there, including the entomology collection (over 6,000,000 strong), the herbarium, 645,000 fish specimen, a crustacean collection, and a collection of mollusks. The various centers which comprise the survey are linked as well. Among them are the Center for Equatic Ecology, the Center for Biodiversity, and the Center for Economic Entomology.

KEYWORDS	Biodiversity, Entomology, Illinois, Natural History
AUDIENCE	Entomologists, Illinois Residents, Natural Historians, Natural History Enthusiasts
CONTACT	The Illinois Natural History Survey inhs-www@denr1.igis.uiuc.edu
FREE	

http://www.inhs.uiuc.edu:70

Institut Jacques Monod ★★★★

This site at Institut Jacques Monod in France contains information on its research activities, phone books, library and seminars. It also provides links to other biotechnology-related sites.

KEYWORDS	Cell Biology, Genetics, Molecular Biology
AUDIENCE	Bioinformaticists, Biologists, Biomedical Researchers, Biotechnologists
FREE	

http://bioldev1.ijm.jussieu.fr/DefaultE.html

The Jackson Laboratory WWW Server ★★★★

The Jackson Laboratory conducts research in basic genetics and the role of genes in health and disease. The laboratory provides access to the mouse genome project and other genetic resources to the world. This site gives information and links on current projects, research and training programs.

KEYWORDS	Biomedical Research, Gene Mapping, Genomes
AUDIENCE	Biomedical Researchers, Geneticists, Scientists
CONTACT	csb@jax.org
FREE	

http://www.jax.org

Journal Conferences, and Current Awareness Services (Biosciences) ★★★★

Journal Conferences, and Current Awareness Services is a meta-index containing selected online journals,

Biosciences

academic conferences, and home pages concerning biology and medicine. Comprehensive listings by service provider and subject matter provide hundreds of links to resources, including the US National Institute of Health, European Molecular Biology Network, and the World Lecture Hall.

KEYWORDS Biological Resources, Biomedical Science, Conferences, Journals
AUDIENCE Biologists, Molecular Biologists, Researchers
CONTACT Keith Robinson, Steve Brenner krobinson@nucleus.harvard.edu, s.e.brenner@bioc.cam.ac.uk
FREE

http://golgi.harvard.edu/journals.html

MOTIF Bioinformatics Web Site ★★★

The MOTIF Bioinformatics Web Site is a comprehensive meta index of Bioinformatics and Genome Web sites on the Web. Users will find links grouped into Bioinformatics Databases and Searching, Bioinformatics Centers, Bioinformatics Archives and Lists, and Genome Databases, Genome Centers, and other Biomedical Servers. Users will also find links to the Department of Biochemistry at Stanford University.

KEYWORDS Biochemistry, Bioinformatics, Biomedicine, Genomes
AUDIENCE Bioinformaticists, Biomedical Specialists, Geneticists
CONTACT Tod M. Klingler klingler@cmgm.stanford.edu
FREE

http://motif.stanford.edu/

Molecular Ecology Home Page ★★

This Web Site provides a forum for cooperation among those interested in or actively engaged in molecular ecological research. Some of the items available to viewers are a searchable list of biologists worldwide, pointers to molecular biology servers, and a collection of databases for ribosomal RNA, enzymes, genomes, and proteins. There is also a bulletin board system where readers can read and respond to each other's messages and queries.

KEYWORDS Biology Research, Ecology, Oceanography, Research
AUDIENCE Biologists, Ecologists, Molecular Ecologists, Oceanographers, Scientists
CONTACT kemp@bnl.gov
FREE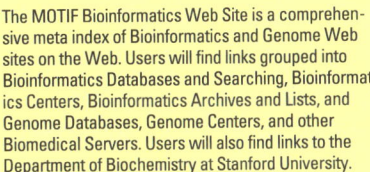

http://bnloc7.das.bnl.gov/molecol/index.html

MycDB (Mycobacterium Database) ★★★★

This site is an extensive database of information on Mycobacteria research. This site includes genetic data, information on stocks, physical mapping, and tuberculosis research.

KEYWORDS Biological Resources, Biomedical Research, Genetics, Molecular Biology
AUDIENCE Bioinformaticists, Biologists, Biomedical Researchers, Biotechnologists

CONTACT Stewart Cole stcole@pasteur.fr
FREE

http://kiev.physchem.kth.se/MycDB.html

Nature Genetics ★★★

This site contains the table of contents and selected articles from the journal Nature Genetics. Information is also available regarding subscriptions.

KEYWORDS Electronic Journals, Genetics, Molecular Biology
AUDIENCE Biologists, Biomedical Researchers, Geneticists
FREE

gopher://gopher.enews.com/11/magazines/alphabetic/mr/ng

The Nucleic Acid Database ★★★

The Nucleic Acid Database (NDB) Web server allows users to access the summaries of key information from the project database, such as the names of structures, structure feature summaries, cell dimensions, protein/DNA complexes, and other Nucleic Acid information. Materials about the NDB project are also provided, including newsletters, an online manual, and a NDB structure atlas and dictionaries.

KEYWORDS Cell Biology, Genetics
AUDIENCE Biologists, Geneticists
FREE

http://ndb.rutgers.edu

Oxford Molecular Group ★★★

The Oxford Molecular Group page presents information about its divisions, design software, and visualization tools and services. The Group is made up of four divisions—Oxford Molecular Ltd, IntelliGenetics Inc., CAChe Scientific Inc., and the Drug Design Divison. The page contains links to product information that includes integrated drug design services, tools for analyzing protein structures, computer-aided molecular design and chemistry software, and bioinformatics tools and related services.

KEYWORDS Bioinformatics, Computer Aided Design (CAD), Genetics, Research Laboratories
AUDIENCE Bioscientists, Geneticists, Molecular Chemists
CONTACT webmaster@oxmol.co.uk
FREE

http://www.ig.com/

Primer on Molecular Genetics ★★★★

This site contains a tutorial on genetics that the layperson will find useful. Topics covered include DNA, genes, chromosomes, mapping the human genome, and model organisms.

KEYWORDS Education, Genetics, Human Genome Project, Molecular Biology
AUDIENCE Biologists, Biomedical Researchers, Biotechnologists, Science Educators

CONTACT Dan Jacobson danj@gdb.org
FREE

http://www.gdb.org/Dan/DOE/intro.html

TBASE - The Transgenic/Targeted Mutation Database ★★★★

TBASE is a searchable database of information on transgenic mice. Since the development of technology to manipulate the germline of animals over a decade ago, a large number of transgenic animals have been produced worldwide for use in both basic and applied research. The information available includes targeted mutations, phenotypes, and transgenic technology.

KEYWORDS Bioinformatics, Biotechnology, Genealogy, Genetics
AUDIENCE Bioinformaticists, Biologists, Biomedical Researchers, Biotechnologists
CONTACT Dan Jacobson danj@gdb.org
FREE

http://www.gdb.org/Dan/tbase/tbase.html

Theoretical Biophysics Group Home Page ★★★★

The Theoretical Biophysics Group develops tools to employ high performance parallel computers for research in structural biology. The group does molecular dynamics simulations to develop software for molecular dynamics and 3D viewing of molecular systems. This page offers access to information on their research, resources, publications and grant information. The research they perform includes such areas as structural biology, medicinal chemistry, immobilized artificial membranes and muscle proteins.

KEYWORDS Biophysics, Computer Applications
AUDIENCE Biologists, Biophysicists, Students, Theoretical Scientists
CONTACT k-hamer@uiuc.edu
FREE

http://www.ks.uiuc.edu

W.M. Keck Center for Genome Informatics ★★★★

This W.M. Keck Center for Genome Informatics contains information on the Center and provides a genus-species database for genome informatics and information on upcoming seminars.

KEYWORDS Bioinformatics, Genetics, Molecular Biology
AUDIENCE Bioinformaticists, Biologists, Biomedical Researchers, Biotechnologists
CONTACT leland@straylight.tamu.edu
FREE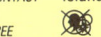

http://keck.tamu.edu/cgi/cgi.html

gopher://keck.tamu.edu/00/.keck_ibt_tamu/Keck_IBT_TAMU

Biosciences – Botany

Weizmann Institute of Science, Israel ★★★★

This site is the homepage of Weizmann Institute, Israel, and contains information about the Institute, indexed versions of the major molecular biology databases (GenBank, SWISSPROT, PIR, PDB, TFD, Prosite, LiMB), links to similar databases at other sites, a large collection of public domain software, newsletters, information on grants and directory services.

KEYWORDS   Bioinformatics, Genetics, Molecular Biology
AUDIENCE   Bioinformaticists, Biologists, Biomedical Researchers, Biotechnologists
CONTACT   Jaime Prilusky
          lsprilus@weizmann.weizmann.ac.il
FREE

http://bioinformatics.weizmann.ac.il:70/

Whitehead Institute Center for Genome Research ★★★★

Whitehead Institute Center for Genome Research maintains extensive information on genetics research. Users will find genetics databases, papers and technical documents, and information on mailing lists and discussion groups devoted to genetics. In addition, this server has a collection of links to other genetic resources on the net.

KEYWORDS   Biology, Genetics, Molecular Biology
AUDIENCE   Biologists, Geneticists, Molecular Biologists
CONTACT   Lincoln Stein
          lstein@genome.wi.mit.edu
FREE

http://www-genome.wi.mit.edu

dbEST ★★★★

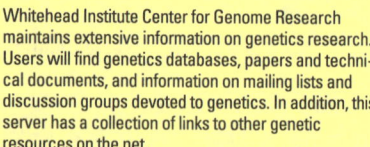

dbEST is a National Center for Biotechnology Information (NCBI) resource, that contains sequence and mapping data on partial, 'single-pass' cDNA sequences or Expressed Sequence Tags. It is a division of NCBI's Genbank expressly for cDNA data. Users will find information on various methods for accessing dBest, and material on submitting data to the collection.

KEYWORDS   Bioinformatics, Genetics, Genomes, Molecular Biology
AUDIENCE   Bioinformaticists, Biomedical Researchers, Biotechnologists, Geneticists, Molecular Biologists
CONTACT   Carolyn Tolstoshev, Mark Boguski
          carolyn@ncbi.nlm.nih.gov
          boguski@ncbi.nlm.nih.gov
FREE

http://www.ncbi.nlm.nih.gov/dbEST/index.html

Botany

See also
Engineering & Technology · *Bioengineering*
Science · *Environmental Sciences*
Sports & Recreation · *Gardening*

AAtDB - An Arabidopsis Thaliana Database ★★★★

This site is a comprehensive database of genetic information on the weed Arabidopsis thaliana. Plant researchers use this small flowering plant as a model organism to study plant developmental processes. Included are genetic and physical maps of the Arabidopsis thaliana chromosomes, some sequence information, and additional general information such as literature and pictures.

KEYWORDS   Genetics, Horticulture, Molecular Biology, Plants
AUDIENCE   Agriculturalists, Biomedical Researchers, Biotechnologists, Horticulturalists
CONTACT   John Morris
          john.morris@frodo.mgh.harvard.edu
FREE

http://weeds.mgh.harvard.edu/
gopher://weeds.mgh.harvard.edu/

American Association of Botanical Gardens and Arboreta (AABGA) ★★★

The American Association of Botanical Gardens and Arboreta (AABGA) is the professional association for public gardens in North America, supporting the public horticulture community in its mission to study, display and conserve plants. The page contains information on the AABG's history and future plans, a list of institutional members (botanical gardens and aboreta), society updates, information on membership, and links to related flora and fauna sites.

KEYWORDS   Conservation, Gardens, Horticulture, Plants
AUDIENCE   Botanical Garden Enthusists, Botanists
CONTACT   Kristin L. Hansen
          hansen@gene.med.umn.edu
FREE

http://192.104.39.4/AABGA/aabga1.html

Arabidopsis Information Management System (AIMS) (Arabidopsis thaliana Database) ★★★★

This site is a database of genetic information on the weed Arabidopsis thaliana. Plant researchers use this small flowering plant as a model organism to study plant developmental processes. Stocks, genetic mapping data, and links to newsletters and suppliers are included here.

KEYWORDS   Genetics, Molecular Biology, Plants
AUDIENCE   Agriculturalists, Biomedical Researchers, Biotechnologists, Horticulturalists
CONTACT   aims-manager@genesys.cps.msu.edu
FREE

http://genesys.cps.msu.edu:3333/

Australian National Botanic Gardens Biodiversity Server ★★★★

The Australian National Botanic Gardens Biodiversity (ANBG) Server offers access to information and resources related to Australia's flora. News is available on current research projects, the collection of the Botanical Gardens, an aviary maintained by the ANBG, tours and educational services offered, and Australia's geographic features. Users may also search the database by keyword to more efficiently locate information.

KEYWORDS   Biodiversity, Flora, Gardens, Plant Science
AUDIENCE   Australian Culture Enthusiasts, Australians, Botanists, Gardeners
CONTACT   Jim Croft
          rc@anbg.gov.au
FREE

http://155.187.10.12:80/anbg/anbg.html
gopher://osprey.erin.gov.au/

Bibliographies for Biodiversity and Plant Conservation ★★★

Bibliographies for Biodiversity and Plant Conservation (BBPC) is a gopher server that offers a searchable option to six different bibliography lists (Kangaroo, Threatened Species, Nature Conservation, Cocos [Keeling] Islands, Remnants of Vegetation). The BBPC may prove useful to the conservation or environmental researcher, but is probabaly not useful for the general reader.

KEYWORDS   Bibliographies, Biodiversity, Ecology, Environmental Resources
AUDIENCE   Conservationists, Environmental Researchers, Environmentalists
FREE

gopher://155.187.10.12/11/library/bibliography/

Botany Image Archive ★★

This directory contains a collection of almost 400 images of flowers, plants, and fungi from around the world which were created by scanning transparencies taken by museum and herbarium collectors during expeditions. These images are cataloged and can be searched under such criteria as scientific name, family, order, species, common name, location of original image, and sponsoring agency responsible for obtaining the image.

KEYWORDS   Horticulture, Images, Plants
AUDIENCE   Biologists, Botanists, Flower Enthusiasts, Horticulturalists
CONTACT   Julian Humphries
          jmh3@cornell.edu
FREE

http://muse.bio.cornell.edu/images/

gopher://muse.bio.cornell.edu:70/11/images

California Exotic Pest Plant Council (CEPPC) ★★

The California Exotic Pest Plant Council (CEPPC) was created to facilitate the compilation and distribution of information on exotic pest plant control topics. The gopher server offers information regarding different plants along with agricultural news from different parts of North America.

KEYWORDS   Agriculture, Botany, California, Plant Science
AUDIENCE   Botanists, Californians, Ecologists
CONTACT   Steve Harris
sharris@igc.apc.org
FREE

gopher://gopher.igc.apc.org/11/orgs/ceppc

Canoe Plants of Ancient Hawaii ★★★★

Canoe Plants of Hawaii is an informative and unusual site concerning the plants Hawaii's original residents brought to the islands by canoe. The material here is quite thorough and clear enough to be appreciated by professionals and by interested lay people. Here you will find complete slices of both anthropological and botanical information, including descriptions of the plants, methods of propagation, drawings or photographs of most plants, cultural and medicinal uses for the plants, an alphabetical list of the plants organized by their Hawaiian names, and links to several other Polynesia or Hawain sites.

KEYWORDS   Botany, Hawaii
AUDIENCE   Botanists, Ethnobotanists, Gardeners, Polynesians
CONTACT   Lynton Dove White
exec@hawaii-nation.org
FREE

http://hawaii-nation.org/nation/canoe/canoe.html

Carnivorous Plants Database ★★★★

The Carnivorous Plants Database/Web page, sponsored by the International Carnivorous Plant Society, is for people interested in the cultivation, propagation, or appreciation of carniverous plants. Contents include a searchable database of over 3,000 carnivorous plants, with photographs of the plants and other vital information. There are links to the Carnivorous Plants Mailing List, the Carnivorous Plants Archive, and several regional and international Carnivorous Plant Societies (e.g., the International Carnivorous Plant Society).

KEYWORDS   Botanical Taxonomy, Carnivorous Plants, Horticulture, Plants
AUDIENCE   Botanists, Carniverous Plant Enthusiasts, Gardeners, Horticulturalists
CONTACT   Rick Walker
walker@opus.hpl.hp.com
FREE

http://www.hpl.hp.com/bot/cp_home

Connections to the Antarctic
News from down under . . . way down under

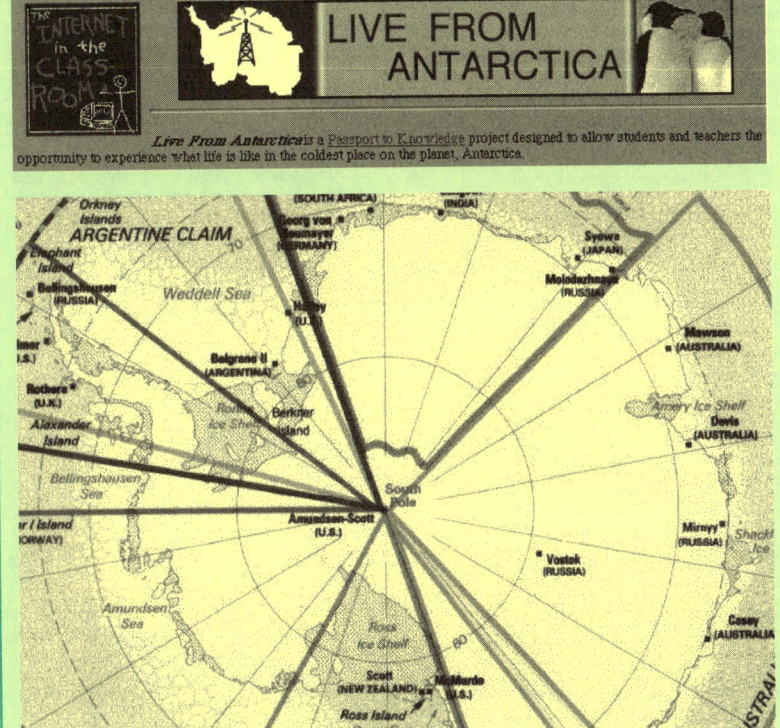

The Antarctic is not only the coldest region on earth, but is also the windiest place to be any time of the year, as well as featuring the highest average elevation of any continent. While it has no permanent human residents, it does hold "grave yards" where a number of unfortunate explorers from long ago lie in eternal rest. This remote, inhospitable environment provides the impetus for some extremely stimulating educational sites on the World Wide Web.

"Live From Antarctica" is part of the U.S. Public Broadcasting System's series focusing on research taking place in the Antarctic. This site gives students the chance to interact with scientists at work and get a feel for what life is like in the coldest place on the planet. Another site, called "Antarctica," provides vital statistical information, including the fact that the continent is capped by an ice sheet over four kilometers thick in many places.

(http://www.nbs.ac.uk/public/info/antarctica.html)

also, (http://quest.arc.nasa.gov/livefrom/livefrom.html)

If you're interested in joining an expedition to this great white region, then check out the "Gateway to Antarctica Tourism" page. Features include cruising information to Antarctica and sub-Antarctic Islands (bring a sweater and an extra pair of warm socks!). You can also browse through and order gifts (posters, etc.) from the latest Antarctic Shop Catalog.

(http://icair.iac.org.nz/tourism.index.html)

Georgeson Botanical Garden ★★

The Georgeson Botanical Garden is a research program dedicated to the propagation, cultivation and conservation of native and introduced plant species in the subarctic North. Links are available to current happenings, history, publications, tours and demonstrations, gardening trivia, class information and membership information.

KEYWORDS   Alaska, Botanical Gardens, Gardens, Research
AUDIENCE   Gardeners, Gardening Enthusiasts
FREE

http://www.lter.alaska.edu/html/gbg.html

Botany – Career & Employment

Lehle Seeds

This site is the home page for Lehle Seeds, a commercial producer of Arabidopsis seeds. Plant researchers use this small flowering plant as a model organism to study plant developmental processes. Included are extensive links to research-related topics, such as resources, online science journals, vendors of scientific supplies, and genetic data.

Keywords Genetics, Plant Science, Plants
Audience Agriculturalists, Biomedical Researchers, Biotechnologists, Horticulturalists
Contact webmaster@arabidopsis.com
Free

http://www.arabidopsis.com/

Missouri Botanical Garden Home Page ★★★★

The Missouri Botanical Gardens, (MBG) offers extensive online information about exhibits and research at MBG. The server has information on MBG's horticulture, ongoing flora projects, and educational programs. MBG makes available its research data and also offers links to other botanical resources around the globe.

Keywords Botany, Conservation, Education, Environment
Audience Botanists, Environmentalists, Students (Primary/Secondary)
Contact Alan V. Tucker
tucker@mobot.org
Free

http://straylight.tamu.edu/MoBot/welcom.html/

gopher://mobot.org/11/

Nottingham Arabidopsis Stock Centre Home Page ★★★

The Nottingham Arabidopsis Stock Centre Home Page is designed to be a comprehensive guide to the Arabidopsis plant, a small flowering plant commonly used by plant science researchers for studying plant developmental processes. Users can browse the stock catalog according to stock type, as well as look at a picture book of over 400 varieties and mutants, before using an order form to order seeds. This site also provides general growing information, pest control guides, and genetic maps. Links to other Arabidopsis Web research sites are included.

Keywords Biotechnology, Plant Science
Audience Biotechnologists, Plant Scientists
Contact Mary Anderson
arabidopsis@nottingham.ac.uk
Free

http://nasc.life.nott.ac.uk

Otj.cat ★★★

This site offers a catalog listing of the favorite beneficial plants and botanical products from the botanical collection of a family/team of plant lovers and researchers dedicated to preservation and propagation.

Keywords Drugs, Entheogens, Hallucinogenics, Horticulture
Audience Botanists, Drug Users, Educators, Ethnobotanists, Gardeners, Horticulturalists
Free

ftp://www.clark.net/pub/murple/local/otj.cat

The Royal Botanic Gardens ★★★

The Royal Botanic Gardens server in Kew, United Kingdom gives access to a visit to the gardens, other collections, scientific research, conservation, general information for visitors and other botanical and horticultural servers.

Keywords Botanical Gardens, Gardens, Horticulture, United Kingdom
Audience Gardeners, Gardening Enthusiasts
Contact webmaster@rbgkew.org.uk
Free

http://www.rbgkew.org.uk/

WWW Server of the University of Costa Rica ★★★

This WWW server is a focal point to all other university servers in Costa Rica. It contains a virtual botanical garden with pictures and descriptions of a wide variety of Central American flowers.

Keywords Biology, Botany, Costa Rica, Travel
Audience Biologists, Botanists, International Travelers
Contact Gladys Hidalgo Chaves
gladish@cariari.ucr.ac.cr
Free

http://www.ucr.ac.cr/

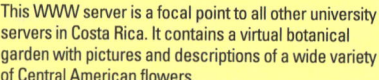

Career & Employment

See also
Engineering & Technology · *Career & Employment*
Health & Medicine · *Career & Employment*

American Astronomical Society Job Register ★★★

This page lists the monthly employment listings from the American Astronomical Society. Many of the positions are for postdoctoral research positions. Jobs include scientific publishing, astronomical centers, academic positions, research positions, etc. Job listings for the previous months (with results) are also filed here.

Keywords Astronomy, Employment, Job Listings
Audience Astronomers, Astrophysicists, Job Seekers, Science Researchers
Contact webmaster@aas.org
Free

http://blackhole.aas.org/JobRegister/aasjobs.html

ftp://blackhole.aas.org/jobs/

Careers for Physicists Homepage ★★★

The Careers for Physicists Homepage presents information about the career seminar series held in the physics department at the University of Washington in Seattle, WA. The purpose of the project is to bring young physicists in contact with physicists who are following diverse careers paths. Although much of the information is of particular interest to UW graduate students, other useful infromation for non-UW physics students includes general information, seminar schedules, as well as pointers to newsgroups and mailing lists.

Keywords Career, Employment, Jobs, Physics
Audience Physicists, Scientists, Students (Graduate)
Contact Steve Sutlief
sutlief@phys.washington.edu
Free

http://squark.phys.washington.edu://people/Sutlief/careers/

Lawrence Berkeley Laboratory ★★

This gopher server is maintained at the Lawrence Berkeley Laboratory, Berkeley, California. This server has been superceded by a WWW server. The information provided here includes job openings and images.

Keywords Employment, Laboratories, Research, Research & Development
Audience Job Seekers, Researchers, Science Researchers
Free

gopher://gopher.lbl.gov/

Minority Access to Research Careers

This program is an effort to attract highly qualified underrepresented minorities to professional careers in the Biomedical Sciences.

Keywords Biomedical Research, Biomedical Science, Minority Programs
Audience Researchers, Students (Post Graduate)
Free

http://web.fie.com/web/fed/ehs/prog/ehspgaah.htm

Online Academic Chemistry Employment Clearinghouse ★★

The Online Academic Chemistry Employment Clearinghouse lists employment opportunities in the chemical academic community, including jobs at the professor, instructor, post-doctoral, and graduate research assistant levels. Employment opportunities are broken down into five categories or disciplines - analytical, inorganic, organic and physical chemistry and biochemistry. The number of listings varies according the discipline.

Keywords Academia, Chemistry, Employment
Audience Chemical Engineers, Chemists, Job Seekers

CONTACT   Steven Bachrach
          smb@smb.chem.niu.edu
FREE

http://hackberry.chem.niu.edu:70/0/
      webpage.html

gopher://hackberry.chem.niu.edu:70/11/
      ChemJob

The Young Scientists' Network ★★★

The Young Scientists' Network site contains various job listings, funding, and career resources archived from the YSN mailing list. The digest includes an organized chronicle of mailing list back issues searchable by author, subject, and issue number relating to all aspects of job prospects and preparation for scientists and Ph.D.'s entering the job market. Users can also find links to mentoring and employment networking advice to assist in the professional development process.

KEYWORDS   Employment, Jobs, Professional Development
AUDIENCE   Scientists, Students (Graduate)
CONTACT   Arthur Smith
           asmith@mammoth.chem.washington.edu
FREE

http://snorri.chem.washington.edu:80/
      ysnarchive/

Chemistry

See also
Engineering & Technology · *Chemical Engineering*

American Chemical Society Gopher ★★★

Contains information about books and journals available from the American Chemical Society. The list contains descriptions of each book and is searchable by author, title key word, or key word in document. Order forms for journals and books are also available.

KEYWORDS   Books, Chemistry, Online Books, Organizations
AUDIENCE   Chemistry Educators, Chemistry Engineers, Chemistry Students, Chemists, Students (University)
FREE

gopher://acs.infor.com:4500/

Amino Acids ★★★★

This site contains a catalog of amino acids showing color space-filling models, characteristics, linear formulas, and various attributes. Links are given for each amino acid to related information in the database.

KEYWORDS   Biochemistry, Bioinformatics, Crystallography
AUDIENCE   Biochemists, Bioinformaticists, Biomedical Researchers, Chemists
CONTACT   Vera Heinau
           heinau@chemie.fu-berlin.de
FREE

http://www.chemie.fu-berlin.de/
      chemistry/bio/amino-acids.html

Connections to Chemistry on the Internet
Atom-smashing news goes online

Whether you want to know more about atom smashing or molecular modeling, you'll find what you need through the "Chemistry Information" site. Here you'll gain access to the Fullerene Database, maintained by the University of Arizona, which provides a wide selection of information on, for, and about chemistry.

You'll not only gain access to the Periodic Table of the Elements, but also to a database on proteins maintained at Brookhaven National Laboratory. Moreover, you can tap into hundreds of chemistry resources at universities around the world. You can go to such Web sites as the Birkbeck College (in England) for its crystallography's tutorial and HTML Workshop, or connect to news and programming from the British Biophysical Society.

This site will also provide you with information on SCARECROW, a project for the graphical display and analysis of molecular dynamics trajectories.

(http://hackberry.chem.niu.edu:70/0/cheminf.html)

Atlas of Side-Chain and Main-Chain Hydrogen Bonding ★★★★

This site contains a graphical summary of hydrogen bonding in a dataset of high-resolution protein structures. It shows the distributions of the frequencies and geometries of hydrogen bonds formed by main-chain and side-chain donors and acceptors.

KEYWORDS   Biochemistry, Bioinformatics, Chemistry, Crystallography
AUDIENCE   Biochemists, Bioinformaticists, Biomedical Researchers, Chemists
CONTACT   Ian Mcdonald
           mcdonald@bsm.bioc.ucl.ac.uk
FREE

http://www.biochem.ucl.ac.uk/~mcdonald/
      atlas/

Australian Chemistry Network ★★★★

The Australian Chemistry Network has a variety of resources for anyone interested in chemistry. Some of the areas of this site available to the user include the administrative pages, which list chemistry institutes and university departments, along with journals and abstracts from various sources; a Research Resource page provides links to research projects; the Teaching page lists chemistry-related educational resources across the world, and the Software section points to several archives of chemistry and scientific software. Links to other sites in Australia and the rest of the world are provided.

KEYWORDS   Australia, Chemistry, Journals, Research
AUDIENCE   Chemical Engineers, Chemistry Students, Chemists
CONTACT   Alan Arnold
           apa@adfa.oz.au
FREE

http://apamac.ch.adfa.oz.au/

Cambridge University Chemical Laboratory Home Page ★★★

The Cambridge University Chemical Laboratory Home Page provides information about the Chemical Engineering Department and its projects. This site includes background about the Laboratory, its staff and research projects, and lists upcoming colloquia for each of the research topic areas - organic, inorganic, and theoretical chemistry. Users may also read materials about specific chemistry courses. Links are included to other chemical information sites and servers on the Web, as well as to the Cambridge University Home Pages.

KEYWORDS	Chemical Analysis, Organic Chemistry, Universities
AUDIENCE	Chemical Engineers, Chemistry Researchers, Chemistry Students
CONTACT	Dr J M Goodman jmg11@cus.cam.ac.uk
FREE	

http://mria.ch.cam.ac.uk

Dukechem Directory Page ★★★★

This site is maintained by the Department of Chemistry at Duke University. It provides links to the chemistry library, a phone directory of Duke students and faculty, as well as information on the academic and research programs at the Department. In addition, this site offers course material, and links to other chemistry sites on the Net.

KEYWORDS	Biochemistry, Chemical Engineering, Chemistry, Universities
AUDIENCE	Chemical Engineers, Chemists, Education Administrators (College), Educators, Students
CONTACT	Yuji Shinozaki yuji@chem.duke.edu
FREE	

http://www.chem.duke.edu

Freie Universitat, Berlin CHEMnet WWW ★★★★

This site is a database of software and documents on chemistry, amino acids, analytical chemistry, alchemy, crystallography, and other chemical information. In addition, there are many pointers to other chemical and bilingual databases in Europe and the U.S.

KEYWORDS	Biochemistry, Biological Research, Proteins, Software
AUDIENCE	Biochemists, Bioinformaticists, Biomedical Researchers, Chemists
CONTACT	webmaster@chemie.fu-berlin.de
FREE	

http://www.chemie.fu-berlin.de/index_e.html

Institute of Chemical Technology ★★★

This site offers access to resources provided by the Institute of Chemical Technology, Prague, Czech Republic. These resources include Czech journals such as Zpravodaj CSMUG, Zpravodaj VSCHT, Chemicky prumysl 93, and Chemicky prumysl 94, as well as archives of Statistical Mechanics of Liquids. The server also provides some information about the Institute of Chemical Technology such as its history, enrollment, and funding.

KEYWORDS	Chemistry, Theoretical Chemistry
AUDIENCE	Chemical Engineers, Chemists, Science Researchers, Students (University)
FREE	

gopher://gopher.vscht.cz/

Institute of Chemistry ★★★

The Institute of Chemistry page provides links to the facilities at the University of Campinas in Brazil. There is information about the facility, graduate studies program, software and computing facilities.

KEYWORDS	Computer Networking, Organic Chemistry, Research, Software
AUDIENCE	Brazilians, Chemists, Students
CONTACT	www@iqm.unicamp.br
FREE	

http://www.iqm.unicamp.br

J. D. McDonald's Mineral Formula Database-Search ★★★

This is a searchable gopher containing the names and chemical formulae of all 3507 minerals. The database produces ascii (Text) representations of the chemical formulas of the minerals. A note on the page indicates that the database is still being tested and warns that the user should double check results.

KEYWORDS	Databases, Education, Geology, Minerals
AUDIENCE	Educators (College), Geologists, Mineral Enthusiasts, Students (University)
CONTACT	Doug McDonald mcdonald@aries.scs.uiuc.edu
FREE	

gopher://wombat.es.mq.edu.au/1pc%3a/geology/minerals/mineral.dbf

The Miller Group of Theoretical Chemistry ★★

The Miller Group of Theoretical Chemistry at the Universtiy of California Berkeley focuses on the study of chemical reactions at the molecular level. Their home page provides background about their research interests, information about the group's personnel, and a list of publications that the group has authored.

KEYWORDS	Chemical Engineering, Theoretical Chemistry
AUDIENCE	Chemistry Educators, Chemistry Engineers, Chemistry Students
CONTACT	Professor William H. Miller miller@neon.cchem.berkeley.edu
FREE	

http://neon.cchem.berkeley.edu

Molecular Animations ★★★★

This site contains molecular movies and very high-resolution images including flight through a membrane model, dynamics of the bilayer, molecular dynamics run of an argon cluster, vibrations, quantum dynamics movies, proton transfer, and more. These images are extremely large because of their high resolution, and as a result take more time to download.

KEYWORDS	Chemistry, Molecular Biology, Molecular Modeling, Physics
AUDIENCE	Chemists, Molecular Biologists, Physicists, Researchers
CONTACT	Hoorst Vollhardt horstv@pc.chemie.th-darmstadt.de
FREE	

http://www.pc.chemie.th-darmstadt.de/molcad/movie.html

Molecular Simulations Incorporated (MSI) ★★★★

(COMMERCIAL)

Molecular Simulations Incorporated (MSI) home page presents information on its scientific software and chemical-computing products. The page gives access to product details about the Cerius2 software environment, as well as information on the Catalyst and Quanta Life Science product lines. The software tools may be used for protein design, combinatorial chemistry and macromolecular structure determination. The page contains demonstrations of X-ray Crystallography and Nuclear Magnetic Resonance Workbenches as well as links to related genetic, molecular, and chemistry sites.

KEYWORDS	Life Sciences, Material Science, Molecular Imaging, Scientific Software
AUDIENCE	Chemists, Molecture Structure Analyzers, Molecular Biologists, Pharmaceutical Designers
FREE	

http://www.msi.com/

National University of Singapore BioGopher ★★★

This gopher offers information about biochemistry. It is maintained by the Department of Biochemistry at the National University of Singapore. The information includes details about the IUBMB 3rd International Conference 1995, descriptions of the University, access to the Singapore biotechnology database, and more. In addition, it has links to other resources.

KEYWORDS	Biochemistry, Biology, Education (College/University), Singapore
AUDIENCE	Academics, Biochemists, Educators (University), Students (University)
CONTACT	Dr Tan Tin Wee bchtantw@leonis.nus.sg
FREE	

gopher://biomed.nus.sg/

OSC's Computational Chemistry List ★★★

This is a gopher server of the Ohio Supercomputer Center (OSC). It contains information on OSC's Computational Chemistry List (CCL). Information available includes data, documents, hardware, software, instructions, jobs, periodicals, and more.

KEYWORDS	Chemical Engineering, Computational Chemistry, Education (College/University), Supercomputing

Chemistry – Earth Sciences

AUDIENCE	Chemical Engineers, Chemistry Educators, Chemistry Students (Secondary), Chemists
CONTACT	Jan Labanowski jkl@osc.edu
FREE	

gopher://infomeister.osc.edu:73/

Some Chemistry Resources on the Internet ★★★

This document is a compilation of information resources focused on chemistry. Resources may include Internet/bitnet mailing lists, gophers, World Wide Web sites, mail servers, Usenet newsgroups, FTP archives, commercial online services, and bulletin board systems.

KEYWORDS	Education, Meta-Index (Chemistry), Quantum Chemistry, Theoretical Chemistry
AUDIENCE	Chemical Engineers, Chemistry Educators, Chemists, Scientists, Students
FREE	

ftp://una.hh.lib.umich.edu/inetdirsstacks/chemistry:wiggins

Earth Sciences

See also
Humanities & Social Sciences · *Geography*
Popular Culture & Entertainment · *Weather & Traffic*
Science · *Geosciences*

Alfred Wegener Institute ★★★

This site at Germany's Alfred Wegener Institute archives information retrieved by the Institute's various projects in polar and marine research. Specific topics include glaciology, ocean floor mapping, marine biology, ozone measurement, and long-term global change.

KEYWORDS	Germany, Marine Biology, Oceanography, Polar Regions
AUDIENCE	Biologists, Geologists, Researchers
CONTACT	Chris Dodge cdodge@awi-bremerhaven.de
FREE	

http://www.awi-bremerhaven.de/

Atmospheric Science at the State University of New York at Albany ★★★

This is gopher server of the Department of Atmospheric Science at the State University of New York at Albany (SUNY Albany). It contains information about Albany forecast products, national forecast products, surface maps, hourly weather roundups, and more. It also has connections to other gophers on campus and on the Internet.

KEYWORDS	Atmospheric Sciences, Climatology, New York, Scientific Research
AUDIENCE	Science Researchers, Scientists
CONTACT	gopher@atmos.albany.edu
FREE	

gopher://gopher.atmos.albany.edu/

Blue-Skies Gopher ★★★

Blue-Skies is a gopher server providing weather information for the United States. It includes forecasts, current conditions, images, and climate data. There are images of other parts of the world available, as well as educational material for the K-12 level.

KEYWORDS	Atmospheric Sciences, Meteorology, Primary/Secondary Education, Weather
AUDIENCE	Educators (Primary/Secondary), General Public, Meteorologists
CONTACT	blueskies@umich.edu
FREE	

gopher://downwind.sprl.umich.edu/

Bureau of Meteorology ★★★★

This gopher server provides information on Australian weather including up-to-date forecasts, current conditions, warnings, and images. The site also provides information on Australian climate data. The information is provided by the Australian Bureau of Meteorology.

KEYWORDS	Australia, Climatology, Meteorology, Weather
AUDIENCE	Australian Culture Enthusiasts, Climatologists, General Public, Meteorologists
CONTACT	Justin Baker gopher@bom.gov.au
FREE	

gopher://babel.ho.bom.gov.au/

CIESIN (Consortium for International Earth Science Information Network) ★★★

This is a server of the Consortium for International Earth Science Information Network (CIESIN). It provides information about Earth sciences and the environment, such as environmental change, world resources, and population growth. It gives information on CIESIN, its mission, members, facilities, services, programs, press releases, the human dimensions programme, CIESIN electronic bookshelf, and more. It has links to other earth science resources on the Internet.

KEYWORDS	Environment, Environmental Resources, Environmental Sciences
AUDIENCE	Environmental Researchers, Environmental Scientists, Scientists
FREE	

http://www.ciesin.org/
gopher://gopher.ciesin.org/
ftp://ftp.ciesin.org/

Center for Wave Phenomena CWP/SU Seismic Software ★★★

CWP/SU Seismic Software is a free software package created at the Center for Wave Phenomena, Colorado School of Mines. The package is an 'instant exploration seismic research and processing environment' for UNIX-based machines. The package contains tools for reading/writing tapes in the SEG-Y format, manipulating seismic data in the SEG-Y format, Fourier transforms, filtering, synthetic data generation, and seismic migration.

KEYWORDS	Geology, Geophysics, Seismology, Software
AUDIENCE	Geologists, Geophysicists, Seismologists
CONTACT	John Stockwell, Jack K. Cohen john@dix.mines.colorado.edu jkc@dix.mines.colorado.edu
FREE	

http://gn.mines.colorado.edu/1/csm/software/

gopher://hilbert.mines.colorado.edu:3852/11s/cwpcodes

Centre for Atmospheric Science ★★★

The Centre for Atmospheric Sciences (CAS) is a joint venture between the Chemistry Department and the Department of Applied Mathematics and Theoretical Physics at Cambridge University to develop models for Earth's atmosphere. This site offers seminars on atmospheric-related topics as well as publication lists of researchers at CAS. There are tentative plans to make the publications available online at some future date.

KEYWORDS	Atmospheric Sciences, Environmental Sciences, Meteorology, Universities
AUDIENCE	Atmospheric Researchers, Environmental Scientists, Meteorologists
FREE	

http://www.atm.ch.cam.ac.uk/

Climate, Meteorology and Environmental Monitoring ★★★

This site is part of the FTPT (Fundacao Tropical de Pesquisas e Tecnologia), a Brazilian not-for-profit foundation. The site contains global resources for atmospheric data, as well as satellite images. Much of the information is about the Brazilian environment, either from data taken via remote sensing or satellite images.

KEYWORDS	Atmospheric Sciences, Brazil, Environmental Sciences, Meteorology
AUDIENCE	Brazilians, Climatologists, Environmentalists, Meteorologists
CONTACT	Dr. Vanderlei Perez Canhos vcanhos@ftpt.br
FREE	

http://ftpt.br/structure/climate.html

Climatic Research Unit Home Page ★★★

This site offers meteorologcal and climatological data and research information. Provided by the Climatic Research Unit at the University of East Anglia in England, this site offers current weather information, research papers, online publications, and information on the degrees that the Unit offers. There are also links to related sites on the WWW.

KEYWORDS	Atmospheric Sciences, Climatology, Meteorology
AUDIENCE	Climatologists, Earth Scientists, Educators, Meteorologists, Students

CONTACT Mike Salmon
         m.salmon@uea.ac.uk
FREE

http://www.cru.uea.ac.uk

College of Natural Resources at the University of California at Berkeley ★★★

This gopher is for the College of Natural Resources at the University of California at Berkeley. It provides information on agricultural and resource economics, environmental science, policy, management, nutritional sciences, plant biology, and forest products. It also offers information on email addresses at the College and at the University. In addition, it has links to other gophers on campus and on the Internet.

KEYWORDS Biology, Education (College/University), Environmental Sciences, Natural Sciences
AUDIENCE Biologists, Ecologists, Economists, Natural Scientists
FREE

gopher://nature.berkeley.edu/

Department of Forest Genetics Gopher at the Swedish University of Agricultural Sciences ★★★

This is the Department of Forest Genetics Gopher at the Swedish University of Agricultural Sciences (SLU). It contains information on the Department, addresses, fax and phone numbers, details about research at Forest Genetics, a photo gallery of the staff, and more. It also gives information on SLU and has links to other gophers and WWW servers.

KEYWORDS Education (College/University), Forestry, Genetics, Sweden
AUDIENCE Academics, Educators (University), Foresters, Geneticists
CONTACT   Roland.Gronroos@sgen.slu.se
FREE

gopher://gopher.sgen.slu.se/

The ECS Data Handling System (EDHS) ★★★

The ECS Data Handling System (EDHS) is the online distribution, storage, and retrieval system for documents and information about the EOSDIS (Earth Observing System Data and Information System) Core System (ECS). You can perform a quicksearch to search for document numbers, titles, or keywords or a full text search. Topics covered include EOSDIS Product Use Survey, ECS COTS Procurement Information, ECS Reviews, Facility Maps, EDHS How To's, and more.

KEYWORDS NASA (National Aeronautics And Space Administration)
AUDIENCE Computer Users, Earth Scientists, Researchers, Scientists, Students (University)
CONTACT   Kris Wheeler
          kwheeler@eos.hitc.com
FREE

http://edhs1.gsfc.nasa.gov/

Earth Observing System Information Server ★★★

The Earth Observing System Information Server attempts to provide convenient access to program information for those involved or interested in the EOS (Earth Observing System) program. Links are included to EOS Project Related Servers or one may select a DAAC (Distributed Active Archive Center) site from a clickable map. DAACs are institutions that generate EOS standard products and carry out NASA's responsibilities for data archive, distribution, and management.

KEYWORDS Earth Observing System, NASA (National Aeronautics And Space Administration)
AUDIENCE Computer Professionals, Computer Users, Earth Scientists, Educators (University), Engineers, Internet Users
CONTACT   www@eos.nasa.gov.
FREE

http://eos.nasa.gov

Environment Canada ★★★★

This server provides weather forecasts for Canada which are updated many times a day, as well as charts, maps and satellite images. There is also information about modernizing the weather service, plus links to the home page of the Minister of the Environment, to the Canadian Meterological Centre, and to other regional Environment Canada sites.

KEYWORDS Canada, Climatology, Environment, Weather
AUDIENCE Canadians, Environmentalists, Weather Forecasters
FREE

http://cmits02.dow.on.doe.ca/

FSU Meteorology Department Gopher Server ★★★★

This gopher site at the Meteorology Department of Florida State University in Tallahassee offers meteorological information on radar, aviation model plots, and links to other weather servers on the Internet.

KEYWORDS Atmospheric Sciences, Meteorology, Satellites, Universities
AUDIENCE Earth Scientists, Meteorologists, Meteorology Students, Scientists
CONTACT   hudson@met.fsu.edu
FREE

gopher://metlab1.met.fsu.edu/

GPS (Global Positioning System) Information Sources ★★★★

This is a digital text file which lists and describes worldwide GPS information sources. Included are the U.S. Government GPS Information Center (operated by the U.S. Coast Guard), various electronic information sources such as BBSs, Internet sites, mailing lists, Usenet groups, and a listing of hardcopy sources such as journals, magazines, newsletters, books, papers, and monographs.

KEYWORDS Geography, Information Systems, Mapping, Satellites

AUDIENCE Earth Scientists, Geographers, Oceanographers, Sailors
CONTACT   Richard Langley
          lang@unb.ca
FREE

ftp://unbmvs1.csd.unb.ca/
   PUB.CANSPACE.GPS.INFO.SOURCES

Incorporated Research Institutions for Seismology (IRIS) ★★★★

The Incorporated Research Institutions for Seismology (IRIS) is a consortium of eighty universities in the United States which have research programs in seismology. IRIS is funded by the U.S. National Science Foundation and by the Air Force Office of Scientific Research. Users will find links to specific arms of the organization such as the Global Seismic Network or the Data Management Systems pages. General seismological software, reports, and products are available for downloading as well.

KEYWORDS Earthquakes, Seismology
AUDIENCE Earth Scientists, Earthquake Enthusiasts, Earthquake Researchers, Seismologists
CONTACT   braman@iris.washington.edu
FREE

http://dmc.iris.washington.edu/

Kilburn Earth Sciences Page ★★★

The Kilburn Earth Sciences Page at Keene State College is designed to provide information and links to resources about Earth Sciences. Hundreds of links are included to Web sites in the areas of Earth Science, Environmental Science, Higher Education, Computer and the Internet, organized in no apparent manner. The Internet pages include a guide to writing HTML documents and links to courses being conducted over the Web. Also included are links to Keene State College information, including specific materials about the Environmental Science program.

KEYWORDS Environmental Sciences, Geology, Internet Guides
AUDIENCE Earth Scientists, Environmental Researchers, Science Students
CONTACT   Tim Allen
          tallen@keene.edu
FREE

http://kilburn.keene.edu/

gopher://kilburn.keene.edu/

Lamont-Doherty Earth Observatory of Columbia University's World Wide Web (WWW) Server ★★★

The Lamont-Doherty Earth Observatory researches how planet Earth operates, with scientific inquiries ranging from the origin and history to the processes taking place in and on the planet. This research includes seismology, marine geology and geophysics, terrestrial geology, geochemistry, atmospheric science, oceanography and paleontology. This page offers links to current research projects and related web sites.

KEYWORDS	Education (College/University), GIS (Geographic Information Systems), Geosciences, Scientific Research
AUDIENCE	Earth Scientists, Geologists, Researchers, Scientists, Students
CONTACT	Dale Chayes and Deborah Barnes. webmaster@ldeo.columbia.edu
FREE	

http://www.ldeo.columbia.edu

Langley Distributed Active Archive Center (DAAC) ★★★★

The Langley DAAC (Distributed Active Archive Center) archives and distributes NASA science data in the areas of radiation budget, clouds, aerosols, and tropospheric chemistry. The Langley DAAC will archive some of the datasets which result from the Earth Observing System (EOS) program and other elements of Mission to Planet Earth. This page provides information on Projects Supported, Future Data Products, Accessing Data, Documentation, User and Data Services, DAAC Frequently Asked Questions, and other DAACs.

KEYWORDS	Chemistry, Earth Observing System
AUDIENCE	Computer Professionals, Computer Users, Earth Scientists, Educators (University), Engineers, Internet Users
CONTACT	Jeff Cleveland III jeffc@magician.larc.nasa.gov
FREE	

http://eosdis.larc.nasa.gov

Los Alamos National Laboratory Weather Machine ★★

This gopher server provides weather information in the form of observations and forecasts for New Mexico. The server is maintained at the Los Alamos National Laboratory. Users will find satellite maps, GIF and Postscript files of current conditions, and a collection of links to other meteorological sites on the Internet.

KEYWORDS	Atmospheric Sciences, Internet Tools, Meteorology, Weather
AUDIENCE	Climatologists, General Public, Internet Users, Meteorologists
CONTACT	Lee Ankeny laa@lanl.gov
FREE	

gopher://sibyl.lanl.gov/

Massachusetts Institute of Technology (MIT) Earth Resources Laboratory's Gopher ★★★

The MIT Earth Resources Laboratory Home Page provides information of interest to any field in the earth sciences. Of particular interest to the MIT lab are applied geophysics, seismology (especially seismic exploration), environmental engineering, and parallel computing. Users will find documents pertaining to GIS and GPS systems, computational analysis in the geosciences, and information on borehole acoustic analysis. There are also links to other servers on the Internet with related information.

KEYWORDS	Earth Sciences, Education (College/University), Geology, Geosciences
AUDIENCE	Earth Scientists, Scientists, Students (University)
CONTACT	Joe Matarese matarese@erl.mit.edu
FREE	

gopher://www-erl.mit.edu/

The NCAR/UCAR Gopher ★★★

This is the gopher server for the National Center for Atmospheric Research and the University Committee for Atmospheric Research, a consortium of research interests in Boulder, Colorado, who are studying the Earth's Atmosphere. The information provided here is relevant to atmospheric science and includes access to weather forecasts, remote sensing images, online library access, and more.

KEYWORDS	Atmospheric Sciences, Climatology, Meteorology
AUDIENCE	Earth Scientists, Educators, Students
CONTACT	gopher@ucar.edu
FREE	

gopher://atd.ucar.edu/

National Center for Atmospheric Research Atmospheric Technology Division WWW Home Page ★★★

This site offers information from the National Center for Atmospheric Research, Atmospheric Technology Division. Users will find material on research projects, atmospheric graphs, charts, and other data, and scientific reports and papers written at the Center. There are also links to other divisions at the center, as well as to other meteorological and scientific sites.

KEYWORDS	Atmospheric Sciences, Meteorology, National Center For Atmospheric Research (NCAR)
AUDIENCE	Atmospheric Scientists, Meteorologists, Researchers, Scientists
CONTACT	webmaster@stout.atd.ucar.edu
FREE	

http://www.atd.ucar.edu

gopher://www.ucar.edu/

The National Climatic Data Center (NCDC) ★★★★

The National Climatic Data Center (NCDC) page offers information on its products and archived data on climatology. The page gives access to papers, technical reports and bulletins concerning the analysis of climate data. NCDC performs functions related to data management, data synthesis, modeling, and information publication. This site has a link to the National Oceanic and Atmospheric Administration.

KEYWORDS	Atmospheric Sciences, Climatology, Information Resources, Meteorology
AUDIENCE	Atmospheric Scientists, Climatologists, Environmental Researchers, Researchers
CONTACT	www@ncdc.noaa.gov
FREE	

http://www.ncdc.noaa.gov

National Data Buoy Center (NDBC) Home Page ★★★★

The National Data Buoy Center (NDBC), through various mediums, 'serves as the focal point for data buoy and associated automated meteorological monitoring system technology of the United States.' Their web pages contain the same data they provide to forecasters and meteorological/environmental researchers. Data on the server is updated continuously, and the volume of information available here is extremely large. Dozens of links to other government-run environment, oceanography and meteorology-related sites are also available.

KEYWORDS	Environmental Sciences, Federal Government (US), Meteorology
AUDIENCE	Environmental Researchers, Environmental Scientists, Marine Biologists, Meteorologists
CONTACT	Ian M. Palao ipalao@tsc.ndbc.noaa.gov
FREE	

http://seaboard.ndbc.noaa.gov/

National Earthquake Information Center (NEIC) ★★★★

The National Earthquake Information Center (NEIC), a part of the U.S. Department of the Interior, U.S. Geological Survey, is located in Golden, Colorado, 10 miles west of Denver. The NEIC rapidly collects and disseminates information on earthquakes within the United States and worldwide. It is the national data center and archive for earthquake information. The NEIC routinely publishes earthquake data volumes and bulletins, and reports on earthquake occurrences and earthquake effects.

KEYWORDS	Earthquakes, Maps
AUDIENCE	Earth Scientists, Educators, Geologists, Students
FREE	

http://oemg.er.usgs.gov/fact-sheets/earth-science-information/earthquake.html

National Geophysical Data Center ★★★★

The National Geophysical Data Center (NDGC) conducts data management for research in environmentally related areas, including geophysics, marine geology, and paleoclimatology. At this site NGDC provides data and information for each of these research areas, including photographs, graphs, data tables, and other information resources. For example, the Solid Earth Geophysics page includes data and activities for Global Science, Coastal Activities, Regional Geophysics and Educational Products. Users can also find materials about NDGC services and other related data services.

| KEYWORDS | Climatology, Environmental Research, Geophysics, Marine Geology |

Earth Sciences

AUDIENCE Environmental Researchers, Geophysicists, Marine Geologists
CONTACT Marc Ertle
mertle@ngdc.noaa.gov
FREE

http://meridian.ngdc.noaa.gov/

gopher://gopher.ngdc.noaa.gov/

National Oceanic and Atmospheric Administration ★★★★

The National Oceanic and Atmospheric Administration offers extensive information on their services, research and ecological fields of interest. The page has information on seminars for NOAA employees and links to their programs and data information services.

KEYWORDS Atmospheric Sciences, Government Agencies, Oceanography
AUDIENCE Ecologists, Environmental Scientist, Oceanographers
CONTACT webmaster@www.noaa.gov
FREE

http://www.noaa.gov/

National Water Data Exchange Home Page (NAWDEX) ★★★★

The National Water Data Exchange (NAWDEX) is a group of water-oriented organizations working together to improve the access to water data and water information. Its publications include—Definitions of Database Files and Fields of the Personal Computer-Based Water Data Sources Directory, a Directory of Assistance Centers of the National Water Data Exchange, and a Directory of Member Organizations of the National Water Data Exchange. Membership in NAWDEX is voluntary and is open to any water-oriented organization that wishes to take an active role.

KEYWORDS Hydrology, Water Quality, Water Resources
AUDIENCE Environmentalists, Hydrologists, Water Conservationists
CONTACT J.W. Green
wgreen@nxdxqvarsa.er.usgs.gov
FREE

http://h2o.usgs.gov/public/nawdex/nawdex.html

OS WWW Server ★★★

The National Energy Authority (NEA) of Iceland advises the Icelandic government on energy policy by performing research and planning to find the most economical utilization of available energy resources, such as developing the geothermal and hydropower potential of Iceland. This page provides information about Iceland, and offers links to sites such as Hewlett Packard in Iceland, pictures and maps of Iceland, and other WWW servers in Iceland.

KEYWORDS Energy, Geosciences, Iceland
AUDIENCE Energy Researchers, Icelandic People, Scientists
CONTACT Jón Haukur Gulaugsson
jhg@os.is
FREE

http://www.os.is/

Planet Earth Home Page Images ★★★

This Web site contains archived images from all over the Web that home page developers will find useful. Users will find links to images in subject categories such as space images, NASA images, travel images, and medical images, as well as icon and flag archives. Links to other image servers on the Web are also included.

KEYWORDS Archives, Pictures
AUDIENCE General Public, Home Page Developers, Internet Users
CONTACT Richard P. Bocker
bocker@nosc.mil
FREE

http://www.nosc.mil/planet_earth/images.html

The Purdue University Weather Processor Gopher Server ★★★

This gopher site at Purdue University in West Lafayette, Indiana provides meterological information including technical information on software called The Weather Processor. It includes radar reports, satellite images, forecasts, and links to other gophers.

KEYWORDS Atmospheric Sciences, Software Defects, Universities, Weather
AUDIENCE Meteorologists, Meteorology Students
CONTACT Frank Koontz
devo@cell.atms.purdue.edu
FREE

gopher://meteor.atms.purdue.edu/

The Southern Regional Climate Center Gopher Server ★★★

This is the Southern Regional Climate Center (SRCC) Gopher Server at Louisiana State University, Baton Rouge, Louisiana. It contains information on SRCC administration and policies, electronic climate atlas, surface weather observations, forecasts, climate summaries, images, and more. It has pointers to other gophers.

KEYWORDS Climatology, Education (College/University), Meteorology, Weather
AUDIENCE Climatologists, General Public, Meteorologists
CONTACT gophermaint@maestro.srcc.lsu.edu
FREE

gopher://nevado.srcc.lsu.edu/

Space Shuttle Earth Observation Project Photography Database ★★★

The Space Shuttle Earth Observation Project photography database of the Flight Science Support Office (FSSO) contains references to over 120,000 photographs of Earth from space during the last 3 decades. There are also some digitized images. The images are stored in binary DAT files. There are two types of photos available - 1024 x 1024, and 512 x 512. These images may be viewed in Adobe Photoshop (Macintosh).

KEYWORDS Environmental Sciences, Geography, Remote Sensing
AUDIENCE Environmental Researchers, Environmental Scientists, Geographers
CONTACT David E. Pitts
pitts@sn.jsc.nasa.gov
FREE

ftp://sseop.jsc.nasa.gov/

U.S. Long Term Ecological Research (LTER) ★★★

The U.S. Long Term Ecological Research Group (LTER) was created to promote collaborative efforts between nationwide research groups dedicated to ecology issues, focusing on population studies, organic and inorganic patterns, and site disturbances. Their home page provides information about their programs, participating researchers and students, general ecology data, and a map of ecosystems across the U.S. that the LTER is investigating, with information about specific regions and satellite photos. Data catalogs and research materials, organized by project focus, are also included.

KEYWORDS Ecology, Environmental Sciences, Population Studies, Research
AUDIENCE Earth Scientists, Ecologists, Environmental Activists, Research Scientists
CONTACT Office@LTERnet.edu
FREE

http://lternet.washington.edu/

USGS Atlantic Marine Geology ★★

This site, maintained by the U.S. Geological Survey (USGS), is used to make available marine geological data for public access and internal use. This server offers access to databases of information related to marine geology, including ship tracks, gridded-data sets, and sediment texture.

KEYWORDS Geology, Mapping, Oceans, U.S. Geological Survey (USGS)
AUDIENCE Earth Scientists, Geographers, Geologists, Science Researchers
CONTACT James Robb
jrobb@nobska.er.usgs.gov
FREE

gopher://bramble.er.usgs.gov/

Unidata Gopher Service ★★★

This is a gopher server at the Unidata Program Center in Boulder, Colorado. Unidata is a meteorology and atmospheric science database center. It offers information such as software packages, projects, publications, weather maps and images, and more.

KEYWORDS Atmospheric Sciences, Education (College/University), Meteorology, Weather
AUDIENCE Science Researchers, Scientists
CONTACT support@unidata.ucar.edu
FREE

gopher://unidata.ucar.edu/

University of Hawaii at Manoa Ocean, Earth Science and Technology Home Page ★★★

This site contains images from the Japanese Geostationary Meteorological Satellite (GMS) and NOAA Advanced Very High Resolution Radar Satellite (AVHRR), as well as meteorological data—local, regional, national, and worldwide weather data sets, and Pacific oceanographic data.

KEYWORDS Meteorology, Oceanography, Satellites, Weather
AUDIENCE Environmental Researchers, Environmental Scientists, Geographers, Oceanographers
CONTACT sat_lab@soest.hawaii.edu
FREE

http://www.soest.hawaii.edu

ftp://satftp.soest.hawaii.edu/

Weather and Satellite Images from Nottingham University and University of Edinburgh ★★★

This site contains satellite images held by the University of Nottingham and retrieved from Meteosat, usually within a few minutes of the pictures original broadcast. All are in JPEG format. There are infra-red and visible light images of Europe, Scandinavia, the U.K., and the world, and links to various weather information sites.

KEYWORDS Meteorology, Remote Sensing, Satellite Data, Weather
AUDIENCE Geographers, Meteorologists
CONTACT Steve Marchant
satpcrec@met.ed.ac.uk
FREE

http://web.nexor.co.uk/places/satellite.html

Connections to the Ecology

S.O.S: Calling all earthlings

How have plants evolved over eons of time as they adjust to the effects of humanity? What kinds of ecological studies are currently underway? You can find the answers to these questions and more by utilizing the Internet.

A wide selection of links are provided for ecological studies in Costa Rica, Antarctica, and elsewhere on the planet. There are numerous sites from universities and ecological institutes around the globe that amassed a plethora of information on ecological matters.

If you're wondering which animals and plants are on the endangered-species list, the Internet provides sources to find that information. At the International Center for Tropical Ecology, you have access to Australian Environmental Resources Information, the Tropical Forest Research Center, Habitat Ecology at Bedford Institute of Oceanography, and more; you can even visit some botanical gardens.

You can also access information on the recent Man and Biosphere study, and obtain the latest data on tropical rainforests in Surinam and Brazil.

(http://ecology.umsl.edu/)

Environmental Sciences

See also
Engineering & Technology · *Environmental Engineering*
Law & Criminal Justice · *Environmental Law*
Popular Culture & Entertainment · *Weather & Traffic*

1994 National Environmental Scorecard ★★★

This is an image-map of the United States that allows users to click on any state or region and examine the voting record of various politicians on environmental legislation. There are indices of legislators with high scores (voted to protect natural resources), low scores (put development before environmental protection), or those who voted specifically against protecting particular environmental resources.

KEYWORDS Environmental Policy, Government, Legislation
AUDIENCE Environmental Researchers, Environmentalists, General Public, Journalists, Voters
CONTACT lcv@econet.apc.org
FREE

http://www.econet.apc.org/lcv/scorecard.html

gopher://gopher.econet.apc.org/11/orgs/lcv/1994

American Rivers Gopher ★★★

American Rivers (AR) is an environmental advocacy group that seeks to protect American waterways and the wildlife that lives in those ecosystems. This gopher contains information on various symposia and conferences organized by or with AR, as well as a list of open intern positions with the organization, current canvassing and letter-writing campaigns, and information on various pending environmental legislation.

KEYWORDS   Activism, Environment, Rivers, Wildlife
AUDIENCE   Activists, Environmentalists, Fish Enthusiasts, Wilderness Enthusiasts, Wildlife Biologists
CONTACT   Kirsten Bevinetto Artman
FREE

gopher://gopher.igc.apc.org/11/orgs/amrivers

American Wind Energy Association (AWEA) Home Page ★★★

The American Wind Energy Association (AWEA) proposes wind energy as an alternative source for the energy demands throughout the world. The AWEA offers information on energy technologies as a public service at no cost. Some of the information offered is concerned with climate change, sustainable development, and an archive on wind energy.

KEYWORDS   Alternative Energy, Archives, Research, Wind Energy
AUDIENCE   Energy Researchers, Environmentalists, General Public
CONTACT   Nat Holder
           www-content@solstice.crest.org
FREE

http://solstice.crest.org/renewables/awea/Homepage.html

The Arid Lands Newsletter Home Page ★★★★

The Arid Lands Newsletter Home Page is an exciting, diverse, informative and appealing Website dedicated to dispersing information about desert ecosystems. Here you will find an array of information concerning these arid lands, from the scientific to the poetic. Topics covered to date have included cooking with unusual vegetables and fruits, desert architecture and the environment, information about ecological programs, both botanical and zoological, the desert in literature, and various viewpoints on biodiversity and conservation. This site also has some stimulating and unique links.

KEYWORDS   Biodiversity, Ecology
AUDIENCE   Biologists, Botanists, Conservationists, Desert Enthusiasts
CONTACT   John Bancroft
           jbanc@ag.arizona.edu
FREE

http://ag.arizona.edu/OALS/ALN/ALNHome.html

Atmospheric Physics Group ★★★

The Atmospheric Physics Group (APG) at The University of Adelaide in Australia investigates the dynamical nature of the Earth's atmosphere from the ground up to a height of about 100 km. The group employs various tools to conduct research, including 5 atmospheric radars. This site details its field sites, research facilities, personnel, and publications.

KEYWORDS   Atmospheric Sciences, Australia, Environment, Physics
AUDIENCE   Atmospheric Researchers, Australians, Climatologists, Environmentalists
CONTACT   Brenton Vandepeer
           bvandepe@physics.adelaide.edu.au
FREE

http://bragg.physics.adelaide.edu.au/atmospheric/home.html

Australian Environmental Resources Information Network (ERIN) ★★★★

This gopher contains a wide range of Australian environmental information. Coverage includes biodiversity, protected areas, terrestrial and marine environments, environmental protection and legislation, international agreements, and general information about ERIN. The site also houses a newsletter archive and provides many links to other related Internet resources.

KEYWORDS   Australia, Biodiversity, Ecology, Environment
AUDIENCE   Ecologists, Environmentalists, Researchers
FREE

http://kaos.erin.gov.au/erin.html

gopher://kaos.erin.gov.au:70/

Biofuel Database ★★

The Alternative Motor Fuels Act of 1988 (AMFA) is a federal statute (Public Law 100-494) that encourages the development and widespread use of methanol, ethanol, and natural gas as transportation fuels. This site has a biofuels database search, refueling site information, and maps. The site uses a password screen.

KEYWORDS   Mapping, Natural Resources, Transportation, Transportation Law
AUDIENCE   Automobile Users, Business And Financial Researchers, Business Professionals
CONTACT   strawnw@tcplink.nrel.gov
FREE

gopher://afdc.nrel.gov/

CERES - California Environmental Resources Evaluation System ★★★

The California Environmental Resources Evaluation System (CERES) system allows users to access a wide variety of California environmental information such as environmental impact reports, satellite images, animal population and habitats, meteorological data, and more. Users may also access individual departments such as the Department of Fish and Game or the California Coastal Commission for more specific resources.

KEYWORDS   California, Environment, Environmental Resources, Meteorology
AUDIENCE   Educators, Environmental Activists, Environmental Researchers, Meteorologists
CONTACT   httpd@agency.resources.ca.gov
FREE

http://resources.agency.ca.gov/

Carbon Dioxide Information Analysis Center ★★★

Sponsored by the US Department of Energy's Global Change Research Program, the Carbon Dioxide Information Analysis Center (CDIAC) provides information regarding the complex environmental issues associated with elevated levels of atmospheric carbon dioxide and other radiatively active trace gases. This site features a descriptive list of numerical data packages (NDPs), information products containing data sets and text from scientific studies that the user may download.

KEYWORDS   Atmospheric Sciences, Climatology, Department Of Energy (US), Environmental Sciences
AUDIENCE   Climatologists, Environmental Researchers, Environmentalists
CONTACT   webmaster@www.esd.ornl.gov
FREE

http://cdiac.esd.ornl.gov:80/cdiac/

ftp://cdiac.esd.ornl.gov/pub/

Consortium for International Earth Science Information Network (CIESIN) Human Dimensions Kiosk ★★★

An interactive forum for the discussion of 'human dimensions of global environmental change,' this series of Web pages offers a large index and the full text of a number of unpublished academic papers, as well as an 'electronic bookshelf' that contains a membership directory, various global change declarations, and other information. Links to a number of other related sites are also available.

KEYWORDS   Conservation, Earth Sciences, Environment
AUDIENCE   International Development Professionals, Social Scientists, Sociologists
CONTACT   CIESIN User Services
           ciesn.info@ciesn.org
FREE

http://www.ciesin.org/kiosk/home.html

The Dendrome Gopher ★★★

The Dendrome Gopher Server provides information about the Dendrome Project, a collection of databases containing genetic information about trees. The gopher server gives information about the project in general and provides access to the database. Users will also find a directory of related publications, additional information on plant genetics, and a collection of links to related resources on the Internet.

KEYWORDS   Biology, Botany, Databases, Genetics
AUDIENCE   Biochemists, Environmental Scientists, Geneticists, Molecular Biologists
CONTACT   David B. Neale
           dendrome@s27w007.pswfs.gov
FREE

gopher://s27w007.pswfs.gov/

Environmental Sciences

Earthwatch ★★★★

Earthwatch is an organization that sponsors expeditions and research teams investigating environmental phenomena, the state of the Earth, and the interaction between the planet and its inhabitants. This site lists dozens of activities that are available for people to join. Their missions (which require a financial as well as a time committment) range from cave and volcano explorations to studying whales in the Indian Ocean, are descibed in detail, with features such as Field Conditions, Costs, Subject Specialties recommended, and contact information.

- KEYWORDS: Environmental Research, Expeditions, Tourism
- AUDIENCE: Automobile Users, Environmental Researchers, Environmentalists, Scientists, Students (College)
- CONTACT: mmi@earthwatch.org
- FREE

http://gaia.earthwatch.org/

EcoLogic ★★★★

EcoLogic is the environmental project of Rensselaer Student Pugwash, a student organization. The documents in this site are the electronic outreach efforts of the group as a whole. This WWW site focuses mainly on environmental improvements, recycling, and vegetarianism. Schedules of EcoLogic meetings and available group positions are also available.

- KEYWORDS: Environment, Environmental Sciences, Recycling
- AUDIENCE: Analysts, Educators, Students, Vegetarians
- CONTACT: Bobbi Chase chaser@rpi.edu
- FREE

http://www.rpi.edu/~daughb/ecologic/ecologic_home.html

EcoNet ★★★★

EcoNet serves organizations and individuals working for environmental preservation and sustainability. A partial list of EcoNet's resources includes General Environment, Agriculture and Trade, Climate, Energy, Forests, Water. The WWW page contains many hotlinks to other environmental sites.

- KEYWORDS: Climatology, Conservation, Energy, Environment
- AUDIENCE: Ecologists, Environmentalists, General Public, Meteorologists
- CONTACT: econet@econet.apc.org
- FREE

http://www.igc.apc.org/igc/en.html

gopher://gopher.igc.apc.org/11/environment

EnviroFreeNet ★★★★

The EnviroFreenet is a project of the EnviroLink Network. The items in the FreeNet offer services such as email, environmental conferences, Usenet news groups and more features (for users with accounts). The resources included are accesses to the EnviroGopher, the EnviroWeb, and the EnviroProducts (Hypertext of Green Products and Services).

- KEYWORDS: Ecology, Education (College/University), Environment, Environment-Safe Products
- AUDIENCE: Environmentalists, Free-Net Users, General Public, Students (University)
- CONTACT: Paul Hansen phansen@together.net
- FREE

telnet://envirolink.org/23

The EnviroLink Network ★★★★

The EnviroLink Web site deals with a number of environmental issues and provides links to various sources of ecology-related information across the Internet. Many images, facts, and educational information on the environment are included.

- KEYWORDS: Ecology, Environmental Resources, Research
- AUDIENCE: Ecologists, Environmentalists, General Public, Students
- CONTACT: admin@envirolink.org
- FREE

http://envirolink.org/

gopher://envirolink.org/

ftp://envirolink.org/

telnet://envirolink.org

Environment and Conservation Research ★★★

The Way Kambas Project was undertaken to survey the Asian elephant and Sumatran rhino to provide data on their size, age structure, habitat usage and distribution around the National Way Kambas Park. The site offers summaries of the project for the years 1993 and 1994, and is still under construction.

- KEYWORDS: Animal Rights, Elephants, National Parks, Rhinoceros
- AUDIENCE: Animal Rights Activists, Conservationists, Environmentalists
- CONTACT: Ben Anderson B.Anderson@lut.ac.uk
- FREE

http://pipkin.lut.ac.uk/~ben/enres/envres.html/

Environment Canada ★★★★

As one of the many Environment Canada sites, this one covers Weather, Climatological Information, Initiatives, and Programs of the four Atlantic provinces of Canada (Nova Scotia, New Brunswick, Prince Edward Island, Newfoundland and Labrador). Specific topics included within the weather section are graphical interfaces, forecasts (land and marine), ozone reports for Canada, and warnings (updated only when necessary). Other major attractions of this site include an interesting FAQ list, and a list of public consultations and events. Information on contacting the Minister of the Environment (Canada) is also found here.

- KEYWORDS: Ecology, Environment, Environmental Sciences
- AUDIENCE: Climatologists, Ecologists, Environmentalists, General Public
- CONTACT: fred@holmes.bed.ns.doe.ca
- FREE

http://www.ns.doe.ca/how.html

Environment Institute (EI) at Joint Research Centre (JRC) ★★★

Environment Institute (EI) at Joint Research Centre (JRC) is involved in many different areas of environmental science. Some of the different areas are atmospheric physics, atmosphere-biospheric interactions, and environmental chemicals. Currently, none of the areas have any information available online. Also, this web site seems to be aimed at the hard scientist rather than the ordinary environmentalist.

- KEYWORDS: Atmospheric Sciences, Environment, Italy
- AUDIENCE: Chemists, Environmentalists, Physicists
- CONTACT: wwwmaster@ei.jrc.it
- FREE

http://me-www.jrc.it/jrc.html

Environmental Education Conferences ★★★

This directory lists conferences, calls for papers and proposals, and service learning seminars related to environmental education. This list is updated at least twice a month and contains announcements approximately six months in advance.

- KEYWORDS: Conferences, Ecology, Environmental Education
- AUDIENCE: Educators (Primary/Secondary), Environmental Educators, Parents, Students (Secondary/College)
- CONTACT: David Cappaert cappaert@umich.edu
- FREE

gopher://nceet.snre.umich.edu:70/11/networking/.conferences

Environmental Information ★★★

The Environmental Information page, sponsored by the Department of Energy, provides resources on current programs and legislation related to environmental management in the US. Resources, which cover such issues as waste management, pollution prevention, decommissioning, and recycling, include minutes and announcements of DOE meetings, site reports, status of current projects and programs, and some technical information.

- KEYWORDS: Environmental Sciences, Government Projects, Pollution Prevention
- AUDIENCE: Activists, Business Professionals, Environmentalists, United States Residents
- CONTACT: info@eagle.em.doe.gov
- FREE

http://www.em.doe.gov/emnet6.html

Environmental Portfolio Newsletters (EPN) ★★★★

The EPN is a compilation of ten different Australian newsletters containing topics such as wildlife protection, biodiversity, sustainable living, and Australian birds. The Web page is useful as it has brought together on one page the archives of many different newsletters.

- KEYWORDS: Australia, Biodiversity, Endangered Species, Environment

AUDIENCE   Australians, Environmentalists
FREE

http://kaos.erin.gov.au/general/
    newsletters.html

gopher://kaos.erin.gov.au

Environmental Research Laboratories ★★★★

The Environmental Research Laboratories (ERL) web site contains information describing the labs' structure and research. Items include the ERL weekly report, a map of the ERL laboratories and a searchable directory of the National Oceanic and Atmospheric Administration. Links to the homepages of ERL facilities are also provided.

KEYWORDS   Earth Sciences, Environment, Environmental Sciences
AUDIENCE   Environmental Researchers, Environmental Scientists
CONTACT   Perry S. Hillegas
           Perry@erl.noaa.gov
FREE

http://www.erl.gov/erlhome.html

Environmental and Environment-Related Acronyms ★★★★

The Acronym Web page offers a form-based search form to find what an acronym stands for or acronyms that contain a certain word(s). The database contains common computer terms, chemical compounds, acronyms for overseas environmental and aid agencies, as well as environment and environment-related agencies within Australia. Searching is easy to do, but there is no guarantee that their list of acronyms is either exhaustive or up-to-date.

KEYWORDS   Australia, Environment
AUDIENCE   Australians, Environmentalists
FREE

http://kaos.erin.gov.au/general/
    acronyms.html

FireNet ★★★★

FireNet is an online information service for everyone interested in rural and landscape fires. The information concerns all aspects of fire science and management. The first FireNet node was established at the Australian National University in 1993 by Malcolm Gill. Information includes FireNet news, weather, indexes, searches, etc.

KEYWORDS   Earth Sciences, Environment, Fire Science
AUDIENCE   Educators, Fire Fighters, General Public, Researchers, Students
CONTACT   Malcolm Gill
           malcolm@pican.pi.csiro.au
FREE

http://life.anu.edu.au/firenet/firenet.html

gopher://life.anu.edu.au:70/11/
    landscape_ecology/firenet

ftp://life.anu.edu.au/Pub/firenet/

Gateway to Antarctica Home Page ★★★

The International Centre for Antarctic Information and Research (ICAIR) seeks to disseminate scientific and environmental information on Antarctica and the Southern Ocean by increasing the accessibility of environmental data to scientists, and transforming scientific data and knowledge on Antarctica into forms more easily understood and applied by decision makers, politicians, educators and the general public. The ICAIR Web site provides access to documents and databases dealing with Antarctic politics, environment, tourism, education, and science issues.

KEYWORDS   Antarctica, Environmental Sciences
AUDIENCE   Antarctica Enthusiasts, Environmental Scientists, Researchers
CONTACT   Dean Ashby
           ashby@icair.iac.org.nz
FREE

http://icair.iac.org.nz/

Greenness Index For Australia ★★★★

This page provides a video sequence of the Greenness Index. ERIN (Environmental Resources Information Network) routinely monitors the density of green plant cover over all Australia. This is carried out by using a 'Greenness Index' derived from satellite data. This index, properly termed the Normalized Difference Vegetation Index (NDVI), is derived from data obtained daily from the Advanced Very High Resolution Radiometer (AVHRR) carried aboard the U.S. National Oceanographic & Atmospheric Administration's satellites.

KEYWORDS   Environment, Environmental Monitoring, Plant Science, Satellite Data
AUDIENCE   Agronomists, Botanists, Environmentalists, Students (University)
FREE

http://kaos.erin.gov.au/sat_pics/ndvi.html

International Ground Water Modeling Center at the University of Colorado ★★★

This is a gopher server of the Univeristy of Colorado International Ground Water Modeling Center. It offers information on the Center, its history, its mission, modeling methodologies, software, education and training of users, managers, publications, and much more.

KEYWORDS   Education (College/University), Environment, Geography, Water Quality
AUDIENCE   Academics, Agriculturalists, Scientists, Students (University)
FREE

gopher://igwmc.mines.colorado.edu:3851/

Long Term Ecological Research Program ★★★

This gopher is set up to retrieve and browse part of the Konza-LTER (Long Term Ecological Research) database. The site is primarily of interest to Konza-LTER investigators in the U.S.A. or other countries.

KEYWORDS   Biology Research, Ecology, Research
AUDIENCE   Biologists, Ecologists
CONTACT   Konza-LTER
           jmb@andro.konza.ksu.edu
FREE

gopher://bison.konza.ksu.edu/

Measurement of Air Pollution from Satellites (MAPS) ★★★★

This site provides information and data from the MAPS experiment, a NASA program to measure the global distribution of carbon monoxide in the free troposphere. This site offers detailed accounts of mission objectives, operations, current status, and results, including color maps indicating global distribution of carbon monoxide. A project overview details the mechanism of the MAPS instrument hardware and some of the scientific principles behind its detection. The current flight of the MAPS experiment is taking measurements to evaluate seasonal changes in carbon monoxide sources and chemistry.

KEYWORDS   Environmental Sciences, NASA (National Aeronautics And Space Administration), Pollution Prevention, Satellite Data
AUDIENCE   Activists, Business Professionals, Environmentalists, Government Officials
CONTACT   Scott Nolf
           s.r.nolf@larc.nasa.gov
FREE

http://stormy.larc.nasa.gov/overview.html

National Center for Atmospheric Research (NCAR) Data Support Section (DSS) ★★★

At this site, Data Support Section (DSS) provides access to catalogs, documentation, programs, and data files from the extensive collection of the National Center for Atmospheric Research (NCAR). The news directory contains recent developments such as new data and updates. Most data files are not contained within this system, but many smaller sets are made available in the subdirectory upon request.

KEYWORDS   Atmospheric Sciences, Environmental Sciences, Meteorology, Research Institutes
AUDIENCE   Atmospheric Scientists, Environmental Scientists, Meteorologists
CONTACT   datahelp@ncar.ucar.edu
FREE

ftp://ncardata.ucar.edu/

National Institute of Environmental Health Sciences (NIEHS) ★★★

The National Institute of Environmental Health Sciences (NIEHS) studies how the environment, genes, and time interact to affect our health. The contents of this page contain links to grant information, research programs, education and training programs, minority program information, and employment opportunities.

KEYWORDS   Environmental Organizations, Grants, Minority Programs, Research
AUDIENCE   Health Sciences Researchers, Health Sciences Students

Environmental Sciences

CONTACT Dr. Michael Galvin
         webmaster@fedix.fie.com
FREE
http://web.fie.com/web/fed/ehs/

National Wetlands Inventory Web Page ★★★★

The U.S. Fish & Wildlife Service's National Wetlands Inventory Web pages contain a large database of wetlands-related information. Information available on this site ranges from a complete list of wetlands plant species, to resource maps and other GIS information, to conservation-related legislation and law.

KEYWORDS Environment, GIS (Geographic Information Systems), Law, Wetlands
AUDIENCE Environmental Researchers, Environmentalists, Legal Professionals
CONTACT   Don Cheesman
          op@enterprise.nwi.fws.gov
FREE
http://www.nwi.fws.gov/

Pacific Marine Environmental Laboratory ★★★

Pacific Marine Environmental Laboratory conducts scientific research in oceanography, marine meteorology, geochemistry, and related subjects. The page provides access to information on current research projects, seminars and publications. There are links to other NOAA organiazations, the Library, and ship information.

KEYWORDS Environmental Research, Geosciences, Marine Sciences, Oceanography
AUDIENCE Environmental Specialists, Marine Biologists, Oceanographers
CONTACT   lmccarty@pmel.noaa.gov
FREE
http://www.pmel.noaa.gov/

Puget Sound Demonstration Database ★★★

This gopher server is provided by People For Puget Sound, Seattle Public Library, and Future InfoSystems, Inc., and gives information about environmental conditions in Puget Sound, Washington. The information is obtained from government and research group sources and includes databases and newsletters. It is intended to show the feasibility of free public access databases.

KEYWORDS Databases, Environment, Environmental Sciences, Public Access Archives
AUDIENCE Environmental Researchers, Environmental Scientists, General Public
CONTACT   Willem Scholten
          willem@futureinfo.com
FREE
gopher://pegun.futureinfo.com/

Rachel's Environment and Health Weekly ★★★

This weekly journal contains information about the environment, with emphasis on toxic chemicals and their effects on human health. Other related topics that are reported include news of legislative proposals and bills, risk assessment, media studies, activism, and solid waste issues. Each weekly newsletter focuses on one topic, and is roughly 5-7 pages long. The four hundred back issues available are listed in reverse chronological order by title. Journals titles include 'The End of Regulation? [risk assessment],' 'The Pesticide Opportunity,' and 'More Studies Show Human Sperm Loss.'

KEYWORDS Environmental Awareness, Environmental Resources, Health News, Toxicology
AUDIENCE Environmentalists, Health Care Professionals, Medical Researchers
CONTACT   The World
          staff@world.std.com
FREE
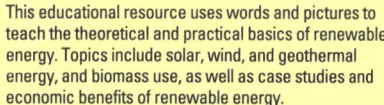
gopher://ftp.std.com:70/11/FTP/world/periodicals/rachel

ftp://ftp.std.com/periodicals/rachel/

Renewable Energy Education Module ★★★★

This educational resource uses words and pictures to teach the theoretical and practical basics of renewable energy. Topics include solar, wind, and geothermal energy, and biomass use, as well as case studies and economic benefits of renewable energy.

KEYWORDS Conservation, Environmental Sciences
AUDIENCE Educators, Environmentalists, Students
CONTACT   Christopher Gronbeck
          www-content@solstice.crest.org
FREE
http://solstice.crest.org/renewables/re-kiosk/index.shtml

Resource Renewal Institute Home Page ★★★

This site contains information about the Resource Renewal Institute and its Green Plans (strategies for efficient management of natural resources), as well as other issues related to environmental health and sustainability.

KEYWORDS Conservation, Environmental Health, Environmental Sciences
AUDIENCE Environmental Researchers, Environmentalists
CONTACT   Tyler Johnson
          rsrnin@well.com
FREE
http://www.well.com/Community/Tyler/rri.html

Tasmanian Parks and Wildlife Service ★★★★

The Tasmanian Parks and Wildlife Service (TPWS) has set up a Web site to provide information regarding the Tasmanian environment, wildlife, environmental protection methods, and more. The site is geared toward interests of local concerns, though the general environmentalist may still find items of interest.

KEYWORDS Biodiversity, Environment, Environmental Protection, Tasmania
AUDIENCE Conservationists, Environmental Researchers, Environmentalists, Tasmanians
CONTACT   webmaster@parks.parks.tas.gov.au
FREE
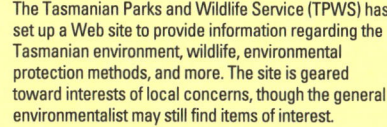
http://www.parks.tas.gov.au/tpws.html

Connections to Recycling
What is old, can be new

Don't even think about trashing your old computer. Your printer, used printer cartridges, and printer ribbons can be recycled. If you have questions about what to recycle, how to recycle, and recycling companies in your community, find out over the Internet.

Through a number of online resources you can discover recycling programs, typically organized by zip codes. All you have to do is click a button on the desired zip code and you get specific information and locations (anywhere in the U.S.).

(http://www.primenet.com/erh.html)

You can find out what types of recycling services are available in Scotland, and in England as well. The following site enables you to access a recycling hotline which will answer your questions about recycling almost anything, including old computers and printers.

(http://www.envirolink.org/orgs/greeaction/recycle.html)

also, **(http://www.earthcycle.com/g/p/_7233ca69/nmen/about.html)**

Technical Information Services - Environmental Guidance Memos ★★★

This gopher is part of the US Department of Energy's (DOE) Office of Environment, Safety, and Health's Technical Information Service (TIS). TIS provides information related to safety issues. This gopher hole is a collection of Environmental Guidance Memos issued by the DOE. These documents are related to government acts such as the Clean Air Act, the Clean Water Act, and other environmental issues such as radioactive and toxic waste. The database is searchable by keywords.

KEYWORDS Environmental Reports, Federal Government (US), Health, Information Technology
AUDIENCE Government Employees, Government Officials, Professionals
CONTACT support@tis.inel.gov
FREE

gopher://dewey.tis.inel.gov:2012/

UCLA Center for Clean Technology ★★★

The UCLA Center for Clean Technology page provides resources on issues in the design of clean, economically competitive technologies. The site offers detailed overviews and substantive information (including charts) about issues arising in the Center's six research programs, focusing on pollution prevention, combustion, water treatment, chemical transport, remediation, and risk analysis. Also available is information on graduate student fellowships and undergraduate internships in pollution prevention as part of the Center.

KEYWORDS Environmental Sciences, Pollution Prevention, Technology, Universities
AUDIENCE Business Professionals, Environmental Science Students, Environmental Scientists
CONTACT cct@seas.ucla.edu
FREE

http://cct.seas.ucla.edu/cct.home.html

United Nations Environment Programme Home Page ★★★★

The Home Page of United Nations Environment Programme offers information on climate change, toxic chemicals, endangered species and global resources. Also included are links the U.N.'s Desertification Convention, the Earthwatch program, a section on trade and the environment, and a link to other environmental services on the World Wide Web.

KEYWORDS Environmental Awareness, Environmental Policy, Environmental Sciences, United Nations
AUDIENCE Environmental Researchers, Environmental Scientists, Environmentalists
CONTACT Webmaster@unep.ch
FREE

http://www.unep.ch/

United Nations Environmental Programme CEDAR Home Page ★★★

CEDAR (The Central European Environmental Data Request Facility) Home Page provides links to information on various environmental organizations. Included are several European environmental sites, such as the Regional Environmental Center for Central and Eastern Europe, the World Wildlife Fund in the U.S., the Global Resource Information Database, and other environmental WWW and Gopher Servers. CEDAR is a regional service center for the United Nations Environment Programme's INFOTERRA Network, a global information network to coordinate information resources and activities.

KEYWORDS Environmental Policy, Europe, Information Resources, United Nations
AUDIENCE Environmental Researchers, Environmental Scientists, Environmentalists, Europeans
CONTACT Douglas J. Kahn, Manager
FREE

http://pan.cedar.univie.ac.at/

United Nations List of Protected Areas 1993 ★★★★

The World Conservation Monitoring Centre has provided a form-searchable database of the 1993 UN List of National Parks and Protected Areas. To search the database, the user need only find the country or area of interest in a supplied list, and the National Parks and Protected Areas of the selection will then be supplied.

KEYWORDS Biodiversity, Conservation, Environment, Protected Lands
AUDIENCE Conservationists, Environmentalists, Policymakers
CONTACT Ian Barnes
Ian.Barnes@wcmc.org.uk
FREE

http://www.wcmc.org.uk/data/database/un_combo.html/

U.S. Environmental Protection Agency's Public Access Server ★★★

This gopher site provides public information on initiatives of the U.S. Environmental Protection Agency. It includes a keyword search for information, links to other government and EPA gophers that are accessible by the public, and links to other EPA gophers where access is restricted to EPA personnel. It also provides a mechanism for file transfers and gives instructions on how to join mailing lists covering environmental issues.

KEYWORDS Environment, Environmental Policy, Environmental Protection, Federal Government (US)
AUDIENCE Business Professionals, Energy Researchers, Environmentalists
CONTACT John Shirey
internet_support@unixmail.rtpnc.epa.gov
FREE

gopher://gopher.epa.gov/

U.S. Long-Term Ecological Research Network ★★★

This gopher hole is a source of information on ecology and environmental science, particularly as applied to the United States. The information has been assembled by the Long-Term Ecological Research (LTER) Program of the National Science Foundation. LTER's mandate is to support research on long-term ecological phenomena in the United States. The information provided includes descriptions of research, databases, publications, and images.

KEYWORDS Ecology, Environment, Research & Development
AUDIENCE Ecologists, Environmental Researchers, Environmental Scientists
FREE

gopher://lternet.edu/

Waste Management Technology Analysis and Decision Support (WTMADS) ★★★★

The Waste Management Technology Analysis and Decision Support Center at Los Alamos National Laboratory (WTMADS) is a database system that compiles information about hazardous and radioactive waste. Their Web site is designed to instruct concerned citizens about how to get rid of their toxic waste, with searches for possible treatments. National waste facilities are also listed by state, with inventory charts, as well as information about support tools. A searchable database is included for information about projects and technologies at different U.S. laboratories. Users will also find a convenient acronym directory.

KEYWORDS Environmental Protection, Nuclear Safety, Toxicology, Waste Management
AUDIENCE Business Professionals, Environmental Scientists
CONTACT palmer@lanl.gov
FREE

http://muse.mse.jhu.edu/

World Conservation Monitoring Centre Home Page ★★★★

The World Conservation Monitoring Centre Home Page is an exceptional place for environmental researchers, scholars and scientists, or those simply interested in the preservation of our world. There are a variety of searchable indices, which comprise information including, but not limited to, endangered and threatened species, an incredibly comprehensive catalogue of all national parks and protected areas worldwide, an FAQ concerning the 'Top 20 Endangered Species,' links to many other search engines, links to sites related to biodiversity, conservation, botany, meteorology, indigenous peoples, biology and microbiology, and a link to the invincible coffee machine at Cambridge University.

KEYWORDS Biodiversity, Conservation, Endangered Species
AUDIENCE Biologists, Conservationists, Ecologists, Environmental Scientists

Environmental Sciences – Geosciences

CONTACT info@wcmc.org.uk
FREE
http://www.wcmc.org.uk

Geosciences

See also
Humanities & Social Sciences · *Geography*
Popular Culture & Entertainment · *Weather & Traffic*
Science · *Earth Sciences*

Arizona Geographic Information Council ★★★

The mission of the Arizona Geographic Information Council (AGIC) is to coordinate the development and management of geographic information systems (GIS) and geographic data in Arizona. Users will find information about AGIC's meetings, conferences, newsletters, listservers. The minutes and other reports are available from AGIC's subcommittees - Education, Data Resources, Technology, and Information Exchange. There are also links to other GIS resources nationwide.

KEYWORDS Education, Geography, Information Resources
AUDIENCE GIS Professionals
CONTACT Michael Collins
mcollins@lnd.state.az.us
FREE

http://www.state.az.us/gis3/agic/agichome.html

Australian Geological Survey Organisation (AGSO) WWW Server ★★

This server provides information about the Australian Geological Survey Organisation (AGSO) and includes topics such as the Environment, Geology and Geophysics, Groundwater, Hazards, Minerals and Petroleum. The AGSO Operating Plan 94-95 and the AGSO Yearbook 92-93 are also available, as is a set of visual indexes into the standard Australian map series.

KEYWORDS Environment, Geography, Geology
AUDIENCE Environmental Researchers, Environmental Scientists, Geographers, Geologists
CONTACT Peter Miller
pmiller@agso.gov.au
FREE

http://garnet.bmr.gov.au/

British Geological Survey (BGS) Homepage ★★★

This site contains British Geological Survey (BGS) publications, library collections, unpublished archives (including maps, reports, registers, photographs and collections of material) and datasets and databases. The directory links to information on the products and services of different divisions or groups within the BGS. Another option supports topic search by hypertext links, geographical location, keywords, author names and specialist indexes.

KEYWORDS Earth Sciences, Geography, Geology, Mapping
AUDIENCE Earth Scientists, Geographers, Geologists

CONTACT www-bgs@ua.nkw.ac.uk
FREE
http://www.nkw.ac.uk/bgs/

CSIRO Division of Minerals - Perth ★★★★

The CSIRO Division of Minerals in Perth does research in flocculation processes and heavy minerals. The page has information about associated research groups within CSIRO and links to their servers. There are links to libraries, chemistry related sites and reference materials.

KEYWORDS Australia, Minerals, Research
AUDIENCE Australians, Geoscientists
CONTACT Curator
Webmaster@per.dmp.csiro.au
FREE

http://www.per.dmp.csiro.au/

Canada Centre for Mapping of Natural Resources Canada ★★★

This is an experimental gopher server for the Canada Centre for Mapping of Natural Resources Canada, in Ottawa, Canada. Information provided includes national systems of geodetic and cadastral surveying, topographic and national atlas mapping, remote sensing and geographical information systems.

KEYWORDS Geology, Mapping, Remote Sensing, Research
AUDIENCE Geologists, Science Researchers, Students (University)
CONTACT Ben Lowsci
benlow@emr.ca
FREE

gopher://ccm-10.ccm.emr.ca/

Center for Wave Phenomena (CWP) ★★

This is a gopher server of the Center for Wave Phenomena (CWP) at University of Colorado. CWP supports an interdisciplinary (geophysics and mathematics) research and educational program in seismic exploration. It provides information on the CWP, its FTP site, the free software, sample seismic data, the neural net code, and more.

KEYWORDS Colorado, Education (College/University), Geophysics, Mathematics
AUDIENCE Geologists, Geoscientists, Mathematicians
FREE

gopher://cwp.mines.colorado.edu:3852/

Conferences in Meteorology ★★

This site lists international meetings, conferences, and calls for papers in the field of meteorology. The entries are sorted by date in English and in German. There is also information about other geophysical disciplines.

KEYWORDS Climatology, Geophysics, Geosciences, Meteorology
AUDIENCE Geoscientists, Meteorologists, Scientists

CONTACT Dennis Schulze
www@www.met.fu-berlin.de
FREE

http://www.met.fu-berlin.de/konferenzen/index.html

Crustal Dynamics Data Information System ★★★

The Crustal Dynamics Data Information System (CDDIS) supports data archiving and distribution activities for the space geodesy and geodynamics community. The main objectives of the system are to store space geodesy- and geodynamics-related data products in a central data bank, and to disseminate this information to NASA investigators and cooperating institutions. The site includes links to information on the NASA Space Geodesy Program (SGP), the NASA Dynamics of the Solid Earth (DOSE) Investigation, and a Catalog of Site Information.

KEYWORDS Geodesy, Geology, NASA (National Aeronautics And Space Administration)
AUDIENCE Geologists
CONTACT Carey Noll
noll@cddis.gsfc.nasa.gov
FREE

http://cddis.gsfc.nasa.gov/

Department of Earth and Planetary Sciences ★★★★

This is the information page for The Department of Earth and Planetary Sciences (EPS) at McGill University in Montreal, Quebec, Canada. It provides links to more information about EPS, including the EPS Gopher and EPS FTP site, Earth Science-related pages, and Canadian Superconducting Gravimeter information. This page also lists several contacts in the EPS Department regarding graduate and undergraduate studies.

KEYWORDS Earth Sciences, Geology
AUDIENCE Canada Residents, Students (University), Students(Secondary/College)
CONTACT Anne Kosowski
anne@geosci.lan.mcgill.ca
FREE

http://stoner.eps.mcgill.ca/

Department of Petroleum and Geosystems Engineering at The University of Texas ★★★

This is a gopher server of the Department of Petroleum and Geosystems Engineering at The University of Texas at Austin. The information provided includes archive tools, library catalogs, the public FTP directory, weather, and more. This site makes connections to other gophers on campus as well as on the Internet.

KEYWORDS Education (College/University), Engineering, Petroleum
AUDIENCE Educators (University), Engineers, Scientists, Students(Secondary/College)
CONTACT gopher@pe.utexas.edu
FREE

gopher://gopher.pe.utexas.edu/

Geosciences

EROS/Ames Home Page ★★★

This page provides specific information on geographic information systems, and remote sensing projects at EROS/Ames. Project mission taken from the web page - 'Our mission is to take advantage of our presence at Ames for promoting the use of remote sensing and related geographic information by providing a bridge between basic research and practical applications for earth science and resource management.' The information is of use to all GIS users conducting research on changes in the environment.

KEYWORDS Geography, Mapping, NASA (National Aeronautics And Space Administration), Remote Sensing
AUDIENCE Educators (College), Environmental Researchers, GIS Professionals, GIS Users
CONTACT lgaydos@gaia.arc.nasa.gov
FREE

http://geo.arc.nasa.gov/usgs/erosames.html

ESRI Federal GIS (Geographic Information Systems) Page ★★★★

This Environmental Systems Research Institute, Inc. (ESRI) page focuses on the use of GIS by the federal government and offers a way to find information on how federal ARC/INFO users around the nation share information, ideas, and ways to effectively use or implement a GIS. In addition, users will also find current federal projects using GIS, links to its quarterly newsletter 'ARC News' and ESRI-L discussion list, both offered to help facilitate communication between ARC/INFO users.

KEYWORDS Earth Sciences, GIS (Geographic Information Servers), Geography, Software
AUDIENCE Environmentalists, Geologists
CONTACT info@esri.com
FREE

http://www.esri.com/company/federal/federal.html

GIS by ESRI ★★★★

This major geographic information site includes earth sciences information and materials including GIS applications, as well as news and other educational materials (such as online data sets and maps). Sections titled 'Books and Publications,' 'News,' 'Jobs,' 'Products,' and 'User Services,' guide visitors to lists of information and sources. The page also contains additional free information and products, as well as ordering information for commercial products.

KEYWORDS Earth Sciences, GIS (Geographic Information Servers, Geography, Jobs
AUDIENCE Earth Science Educators, Environmentalists, Geologists, Students
CONTACT webmaster@esri.com
FREE

http://www.esri.com/

GIS Jobs Clearinghouse ★★★

The GJC was started to help consolidate GIS/IP/GPS position announcements in one easy-to-use place. The last four months of listings are accessible here, with older listings available via the FTP site. This is a small but specialized resource, and as such, most postings are in the university or government arenas with a few listings from private industries.

KEYWORDS Employment, Forestry, GIS (Geographic Information Systems), Geography
AUDIENCE GIS Users, GIS and IP Professionals, Job Recruiters, Job Seekers
CONTACT gopher@walleye.forestry.umn.edu
sdlime@torpedo.forestry.umn.edu
FREE

http://wwwrsl.forestry.umn.edu:10000/rsgisinfo/jobs.html

gopher://walleye.forestry.umn.edu:70/11/gopher/rsgisinfo/gisjobs

ftp://torpedo.forestry.umn.edu/pub/gisjobs/

GIS Solutions for Everyone ★★★★

This page for ESRI, Environmental Systems Research Institute, Inc. offers information about its geographic information system (GIS) software. Users will find this page an easy way to review the core ESRI software product line, related published information, as well as downloadable versions of certain ArcView software. The page also contains a link to an ESRI software overview for those unfamiliar to its line of products.

KEYWORDS Earth Sciences, GIS (Geographic Information Servers), Geography, Software
AUDIENCE Environmentalists, Geologists, Urban Planners
CONTACT info@esri.com
FREE

http://www.esri.com/products/products.html

GIS/Remote Sensing/GPS/Geoscience ★★★★

This page is a central location for a wide variety of geographical information, including weather resources, GIS and Global Positioning System (GPS) information, and links to geoscience laboratories and resources worldwide.

KEYWORDS Geography, Geosciences, Remote Sensing, Weather GIF Images
AUDIENCE GIS and IP Professionals, Researchers, Students
CONTACT Hal Mueller
hal@zilker.net
FREE

http://www.zilker.net/~hal/geoscience/

Geologic Thin-Plate Finite Element Software Programs for Tectonophysics Modeling ★★★

This site contains two programs for modeling plate deformation. They can be used to model deformation of the lithosphere, formulate tectonic hypotheses, fit geodetic data, estimate long-term seismic hazard, study the rheology of the plates, or teach students. Also found at the site is an interactive graphics post-processor.

KEYWORDS Computer Modeling, Earth Sciences, Geology, Geophysics
AUDIENCE Earth Scientists, Geologists, Science Researchers
CONTACT Peter Bird
pbird@ess.ucla.edu
FREE

ftp://pong.igpp.ucla.edu/pub/pbird

Harvard Design & Mapping ★★★

The Harvard Design & Mapping Co., Inc. produces Geographic Information Systems (GIS) applications development technology. The company provides system solutions for environmental, transportation and utilities applications. The page presents a list of clients and profiles of past work.

KEYWORDS Environment, GIS (Geographic Information Systems), Technology, Transportation
AUDIENCE Environmentalists, Geoscientists, Systems Designers
FREE

http://www.harvardnet.com/hdm/welcome.html

Internet GIS and R/S (Remote Sensing) Information Sites ★★

This site yields a comprehensive list of online GIS (Geographic Information Systems) Remote Sensing (generally satellite) information sources. Entries are arranged in alphabetical order. The title of an entry may be derived from the name of producer, name of site, or name of data set. This list includes academic, government and commercial Internet sites.

KEYWORDS GIS (Geographic Information Systems), Geography, Mapping, Satellites
AUDIENCE Earth Scientists, GIS Professionals, GIS Users, Geographers
CONTACT Michael McDermott
mcdermom@gisdog.gis.queensu.ca
FREE

ftp://ftp.census.gov/pub/geo/gissites.txt

Manual of Federal Geographic Data Products ★★★★

The manual describes Federal geographic data products that are national in scope and commonly distributed to the public. Geographic data products include maps, digital data, aerial photographs and multispectral images, and other referenced data sets. These products are described in a standard format and grouped by each resource's producing agency.

KEYWORDS Federal Databases (US), GIS (Geographic Information Systems), Geography, Mapping
AUDIENCE Earth Scientists, GIS Professionals, GIS Users, Geographers, Geologists
FREE

http://info.er.usgs.gov/fgdc-catalog/title.html

Geosciences 599

Montana Natural Resource Information System ★★★

The Montana Natural Resource Information System, located in the Montana State Library, provides comprehensive access to information about Montana's natural resources, storage, retrieval, and dissemination of that information in meaningful form.

KEYWORDS Ecology, Endangered Species, GIS (Geographic Information Systems), Natural Resources
AUDIENCE Animal Rights Activists, Ecologists, Environmentalists, GIS Users, Montana Residents
CONTACT gerry@nris.msl.mt.gov
FREE

http://nris.msl.mt.gov/

National Geodetic Survey ★★★

The National Geodetic Survey develops and maintains information on geographical movement through the National Spatial Reference System (NSRS) Network. The page gives access to the organization's mission, products, services and project documentation. There are links to related organizations and Web sites.

KEYWORDS Archives, Geography, Information Resources, Mapping
AUDIENCE Geographers, Geoscientists, Researchers
FREE

http://www.ngs.noaa.gov

National Geophysical Data Center ★★★

The National Geophysical Data Center conducts research in solid earth geophysics, solar-terrestrial physics, marine geology and geophysics. Users will find extensive datasets in their searchable GOLD (Geophysical OnLine Data) database, as well as detailed information on the Center's research projects.

KEYWORDS Earth Sciences, Geology, Geophysics
AUDIENCE Geologists, Geophysicists
CONTACT info@ngdc.noaa.gov
FREE

http://www.ngdc.noaa.gov/

gopher://gopher.ngdc.noaa.gov

ftp://ftp.ngdc.noaa.gov/

Remote Sensing Public Access Center (RSPAC) ★★★

The Remote Sensing Public Access Center (RSPAC) supports and stimulates broad public use, via the Internet, of the remote sensing databases maintained by NASA and other agencies. This site contains links to information about the RSPAC Program and the 18 RSPAC projects nationwide, whose locations are shown by a locator map, a 16 kB clickable image. The site also links to the Digital Library Technology (DLT) Project which supports the development of new technologies to facilitate public access to NASA data via computer networks, as well as links to sources of remote sensing data and information on the Internet.

KEYWORDS Environmental Sciences, Geography, Remote Sensing

Connections to Elements Tables
When was iron discovered?

Where can you find complete information on the periodic table of elements? You'll find a number of sites online, practically all of which provide excellent hypertext links. These sources comprise a great research reference, given their almost unparalleled currency and thoroughness.

Two sources to check out include the "Periodic Table of Elements" and "WebElements." WebElements is a bit more graphical, but like the Periodic Table of Elements, it allows the user to click on a given symbol and go directly to information about that element.

With iron, for instance, you'll learn that its date of "discovery" was around 2500 B.C., that its covalent is 116, and you'll also find data on its effective nuclear charge and bond enthalpies. You don't have to be a scientist to use and appreciate this site. The information provided is what you might typically find on your next chemistry test.

(http://www.gnn.com/gnn/wic/chem.04.html)

also, **(http://www.cchem.berkeley.edu/Table/index.html)**

AUDIENCE Earth Scientists, Environmental Researchers, Environmental Scientists, Geographers
CONTACT Jeff de La BeaujardiEre webmaster@camille.gsfc.nasa.go
FREE

http://rsd.gsfc.nasa.gov/rsd/

The USGS Northern California Seismic Network ★★★

This site developed by The USGS Northern California Seismic Network lists earthquakes of a magnitude 2 or greater recorded during the past 3 days. The list provides the date and exact time of the earthquakes, including their longitudinal and latitudinal coordinates and seismic ratings. The site also provides the addresses of other earthquake-related sites on the Web.

KEYWORDS California, Earthquakes, Seismic Data
AUDIENCE Californian Residents, Seismologists
CONTACT quake@andreas.wr.usgs.gov
FREE

http://www.cs.indiana.edu/finger/andreas.wr.usgs.gov/quake/w

University of California, Santa Barbara Geological Sciences Gopher ★★★

This gopher contains information on the Geological Sciences Department with links to gopher resources of interest to earth scientists. The Geology Department information includes information on geology course descriptions (Paleontology, Oceanography, Seismology, and more), and on the happenings of the local department. The Geology Research description contains links to many earth science gophers (United States Geological Survey, Quick Epicenter Determination telnet connection, University of California Berkeley), and a link to the department ftp site which includes information on Niles and Associates Endnote bibliography program.

KEYWORDS Earth Sciences, Education (College/University), Geology, Seismology
AUDIENCE Earth Scientists, Geologists, Students (University)
CONTACT Dave Robbins
dave@magic.geol.ucsb.edu
FREE

gopher://gopher.geol.ucsb.edu/

VolcanoWorld ★★★★

The VolcanoWorld WWW page offers remote sensing images, other related data, and interactive experiments for those interested in teaching or learning about volcanoes and related sciences. The site has links from its data with principles of geology, and provides algorithms with which users can analyze images available. The sections include topics such as recent volcanic activity, how volcanoes work, historic eruptions, and 'Ask a Volcanologist'-an interactive Q&A.

KEYWORDS Earth Sciences, Educational Resources, Geology, Research
AUDIENCE Geologists, Science Educators, Students, Volcano Enthusiasts
CONTACT Prabhu Ram
ram@cs.und.nodak.edu
FREE

http://volcano.und.nodak.edu/vwdocs/vwteam/vwteam.html

Water Resources of Colorado ★★★

This site contains resources and data related to water supply in the state of Colorado. Users will find current data such as recent weather, snowpacks, and more. This site also provides links to other geological resources as well as other U.S. Geological Survey sites on the net.

KEYWORDS Colorado, Geography, Geosciences, US Geological Survey
AUDIENCE Environmental Scientists, Geologists, Geoscientists
CONTACT webmaster@webserver.cr.usgs.gov
FREE

http://webserver.cr.usgs.gov

Weather & Global Monitoring ★★★★

This page contains links to information and maps on current weather satellite images worldwide. The subjects range from weather reports and forecasts to environmental issues and environmental monitoring from space.

KEYWORDS Climatology, Geography, Meteorology, Weather Satellites
AUDIENCE Geographers, Students (University)
CONTACT Dr. David Green
d.green@csu.edu.au
FREE

http://www.csu.edu.au/weather.html

Individuals

See also
Humanities & Social Sciences · *History*

The Faces of Science - African Americans in the Sciences ★★★

This site presents a hyperlinked list of African Americans in the Sciences. The list is categorized into past, present and future happenings. Some of the 'past' names include chemurgist Dr. George Washington Carver, theoretical physicist Dr. Shirley Jackson, and microbiologist Dorothy McClendon. The 'present' includes information on the AFRITECH '95 Electronic Conference whose theme is 'Impact of Technology on the African American Experience.' Graphs and charts are included showing the rise in Ph.Ds in science for African Americans from 1876 through 1993, and a breakdown of African Americans earning Science Ph.Ds issued from 1860 through 1969. Also included is a guide to resources available for the history, participation, and encouragement of minorities in the sciences. The 'future' section gives information on the LSU chemistry department and its enrollment of a record-setting 20 African American students in the doctoral program for the 1994 fall semester.

KEYWORDS Role Models, Scientists
AUDIENCE African Americans, Chemists, Educators (University), Scientists, Students (University)
CONTACT Mitchell C. Brown
notmcb@lsuvm.sncc.lsu.edu
FREE

http://www.lib.lsu.edu/lib/chem/display/faces.html

Famous Electricians Hall ★★★

This site contains brief biographies (with portraits) of the following electrical discoverers/Inventors—A.M. Ampere, Ch. de Coulomb, M. Faraday, L. Foucault, B. Franklin, C.F. Gauss, von Helmholtz, H. Hertz, Kirchhoff, J.C. Maxwell, J. Watt, and others. The texts are in French although the introduction is in English.

KEYWORDS Biographies, Electrical Engineering, History, Inventors
AUDIENCE Electrical Engineers, Science Enthusiasts, Scientists
FREE

http://www.rma.ac.be/elec/famous.html

Minorities in Science - Guide to Selected Resources ★★★

This page provides a non-hyperlinked list of resources for minorities in science. It contains directories of people such as members of various science departments, federal R&D agencies, dissertations, employees, government statistics and reports, general biographies (African Americans in Sciences and in general), applications for proposals, curriculum materials, indexes, and the LSU (Louisiana State University) library catalogue.

KEYWORDS Directories, Minority Resources
AUDIENCE African Americans, Chemists, Educators (University), Scientists, Students (University)
CONTACT Mitchell C. Brown
notmcb@lsuvm.sncc.lsu.edu
FREE

http://www.lib.lsu.edu/lib/chem/display/srs119.html

Neurosciences

See also
Health & Medicine · *Diseases*
Health & Medicine · *Resources*
Science · *Biosciences*

Computational Neurobiology Lab ★★

This site provides information about the people working at the Computational Neurobiology Laboratory at Baylor College of Medicine, and about the projects and simulations currently being developed there. It also has links to other biology sites on the web.

KEYWORDS Computer Simulation, Education (College/University), Medicine, Neurology
AUDIENCE Biological Researchers, Biologists, Neuroscientists, Students
CONTACT Christophe Person
chrisp@dirac.bcm.tmc.edu
FREE

http://dirac.bcm.tmc.edu/

Department of Cognitive and Linguistic Sciences at Brown University ★★★

This page offers information on the research initiatives and academic programs of the Department of Cognitive and Linguistic Sciences at Brown University. Users will find course descriptions, information on the degree programs available, and material on the faculty and staff of the Department. There are also links to general information on Brown University, as well as to information on life in Providence, Rhode Island.

KEYWORDS Cognitive Sciences, Linguistics, Rhode Island, Universities
AUDIENCE Cognitive Scientists, Educators, Linguistic Scientists, Students
CONTACT Margaret Doll
margaret_doll@brown.edu
FREE

http://www.cog.brown.edu

Institute for Behavioral Research ★★★

The Institute for Behavioral Research (IBR) is a multidisciplinary research organization at the University of Georgia, the purpose of which is to encourage a pooling of the expertise of faculty Fellows and graduate students from various departments to attack significant

Neurosciences – Organizations **601**

social and behavioral problems at both basic and applied levels.
KEYWORDS   Alternative Education, Behavioral Science, Social Work
AUDIENCE   Educators (University), Researchers, Students (University)
FREE
gopher://gopher.ibr.uga.edu/

Society for Neuroscience Gopher Server ★★★

This gopher serves publications from the Society for Neuroscience, and gives information about this international organization of scientists and physicians who study the brain and nervous system. The publications include the society's newsletter and lists of other publications that can be ordered.
KEYWORDS   Brain Research, Neurobiology, Neurology
AUDIENCE   Doctors, Neurobiologists, Neuroscientists
CONTACT   gopher-admin@sfn.org
FREE
gopher://gopher.sfn.org/

Organizations
See also
Computing & Mathematics · *Computer Science*
Science · *Environmental Science*

American Association of Zookeepers (AAZK) ★★★★

This is the World Wide Web Home Page of the American Association on Zookeepers (AAZK). AAZK is a non-profit volunteer organization made up of professional zookeepers dedicated to professional animal care and conservation. This page contains links to information on AAZK's services, including the AAZK FTP server, AAZK GOPHER server, a collection of large animal pictures, fund-raising events, and the Elephant Managers Association home page. A link is also provided to the Zoological Email Directory, a searchable list of worldwide zoological professionals.
KEYWORDS   Animal Science, Animals, Zoos
AUDIENCE   Nature Lovers, Zoo Enthusiasts, Zookeepers
CONTACT   hpear3@aazk.ind.net
FREE
http://aazk.ind.net/
gopher://adams.ind.net/1
ftp://adams.ind.net/pub/

American Geological Society ★★★

The gopher site for the American Geological Society includes information about the Society and information on how to access GeoRef, a bibliographic database of geoscience literature of the world. It also lists current government proposals that affect the geosciences.
KEYWORDS   Environmental Policy, Geosciences, Literature, Scientific Research
AUDIENCE   Geologists, Students (University)
FREE
gopher://agi.umd.edu:71/11/

Australian Commonwealth Scientific and Industrial Research Organisation (CSIRO) ★★★

The Australian Commonwealth Scientific and Industrial Research Organisation (CSIRO) is an independent statutory authority constituted and operating under the provisions of the Science and Industry Research Act 1949. CSIRO provides research on a variety of topics of interest to scientists and staticians.
KEYWORDS   Australia, Demographics, Research, Scientific Research
AUDIENCE   Australians, Researchers, Scientists
CONTACT   web@its.csiro.au
FREE
http://commsun.its.csiro.au/

BUBL Information Service ★★★

The BUBL Information Service serves U.K. Library and Information Science Professionals and the wider academic and research communities they support. It provides sources on library information, Internet resources, computer networking, and more.
KEYWORDS   Information Science, Libraries, Library Science, United Kingdom
AUDIENCE   British, Librarians, Library Administrators, Library Users
CONTACT   cijs27@uk.ac.strathclyde.vaxb
FREE
gopher://ukoln.bath.ac.uk:7070/

Beckman Institute for Advanced Science and Technology ★★★★

The Beckman Institute, a research institute at the University of Illinois at Urbana-Champaign, takes an interdisciplinary approach to scientific research in three primary areas- biological intelligence, human-computer intelligent interaction, and molecular and electronic nanostructures. Users will find information on the research underway at the Institute, as well as on the facilities and staff there. Material on the history, publications, and events of the Institute is also available.
KEYWORDS   Artificial Intelligence, Molecular Physics, Nanotechnology
AUDIENCE   Artificial Intelligence Researchers, Researchers, Scientists
CONTACT   Jiri Jonas
j-jonas@uiuc.edu
webmaster@www.beckman.uiuc.edu
FREE
http://www.beckman.uiuc.edu

BioMOO, The Biologists' Virtual Meeting Place ★★★★

BioMOO is a virtual meeting place for biologists, connected to the Globewide Network Academy. The main physical part of the BioMOO is located at the BioInformatics Unit of the Weizmann Institute of Science, Israel. BioMOO is a professional community of Biology researchers. It is a place to come meet and brainstorm with colleagues in biological studies and related fields, to hold colloquia and conferences, and to explore the serious side of this new medium.
KEYWORDS   Bioinformatics, Genetics, Molecular Biology, Organizations
AUDIENCE   Bioinformaticists, Biologists, Biomedical Researchers, Biotechnologists
CONTACT   Gustavo Glusman
Gustavo@bioinformatics.weizmann.ac.il
FREE
http://bioinformatics.weizmann.ac.il:70/1s/biomoo

Consiglio Nazionale delle Ricerche, Area Della Ricerca di Firenze (National Research Council, Florence Research Area) ★★★

The National Research Council of Italy conducts scientific research in a wide variety of areas, including agriculture, biotechnology, physics, space sciences, electrical engineering and more. Users will find information on each of these areas, as well as links to servers with related information. There is also a directory of newspapers and publications, and a link to European Union information.
KEYWORDS   Research, Science
AUDIENCE   Italians, Scientists
CONTACT   ced@server.area.fi.cnr.it
FREE
http://www.area.fi.cnr.it/default.html

Consiglio Nazionale delle Ricerche ★★★

The National Council of Research provides access to all the institutes, groups and organizations performing research in Italy. The fields of research range from physics, chemistry and biology to information technology, molecular biology, telecommunications and sociology. Organizations may be searched by geographical location or by field of study with some links to their home page.
KEYWORDS   Italy, Research, Technology
AUDIENCE   Italians, Researchers, Scientists, Technologists
CONTACT   webmaster@www.cnr.it
FREE
http://www.mi.cnr.it

Organizations

DOE (Department of Energy) Human Subjects Database ★★★★

This U.S. Department of Energy database contains descriptions of the methods used in all research projects involving human subjects that are currently funded by the Department of Energy or are performed at DOE facilities with support from others. Summary information on all of the studies has been provided, as well as the capability to do interactive searches.

KEYWORDS Biomedicine, Genetics, Medical Research, Scientific Research
AUDIENCE Biomedical Researchers, Biotechnologists, Medical Researchers, Science Researchers
CONTACT Dan Jacobson
danj@gdb.org
FREE

http://www.gdb.org/HTB/htb.html

Federation of American Scientists ★★

This is a gopher server for the Federation of American Scientists. It provides information on issues of interest to the Federation, such as U.S. government policies, government secrecy, and the arms race. This information is provided in the form of documents and newsletters.

KEYWORDS Activism, Federal Government (US), International Politics, Scientists
AUDIENCE Activists, Scientists
CONTACT jstone@igc.apc.org
FREE

gopher://fas.psych.nwu.edu/

Indigo Instruments Homepage ★★★★

The Indigo Instruments Home Page is a commercial site for ordering scientific supplies. Items sold are useful for professionals, educators and serious hobbyists. Among the products offered are a variety of magnifiers, scientific glassware (including beakers, Erlenmeyer flasks, pipettes, volumetric flasks, et al.), several types of forceps, drawing instruments, in addition to biology (zoology/botany), physiology, or molecular model kits. Each item is pictured and there is also an index of images.

KEYWORDS Biology, Science, Scientific Instruments, Scientific Research
AUDIENCE Biologists, Botanists, Science Educators, Science Hobbyists
CONTACT Slogan@indigo.com
FREE

http://ds.internic.net/indigo/index.html

The Institute of Physical and Chemical Research (RIKEN) ★★★★

The Institute of Physical and Chemical Research (RIKEN) does exstensive research within the fields of science and technology. The home page gives information about the Institute, its research laboratories and research groups. This site has specific information on the accelerator facilities, the optical engineering laboratories and the computing center. There are links to microorganism databases, nuclear and high energy physics sites on the WWW.

KEYWORDS Biophysics, Chemistry, Physics, Scientific Research
AUDIENCE Biologists, Chemists, Engineers, Physicists
CONTACT www-admin@rikvax.riken.go.jp
FREE

http://www.riken.go.jp/

International Union of Crystallography ★★★

The International Union of Crystallography (IUC) presents its efforts to unify research in the field of crystallography. There are extensive resources ranging from the Crystallographic Information File to IUC journals, reports, upcoming meetings and related information resources. There are links to the International Union of Crystallography, and the World Database of Crystallographers.

KEYWORDS Computer Applications, Crystallography
AUDIENCE Communications Specialists, Crystallographers, Researchers
CONTACT Brian McMahon
bm@iucr.ac.uk
FREE

http://www.iucr.ac.uk

Lawrence Livermore National Laboratory ★★★

This is the top-level page for Lawrence Livermore National Laboratory. Users can follow the many subdirectories to obtain detailed information on the lab such as its history, past and present research, publications, facilities and staff, and more. There are also links to other related sites on the Internet.

KEYWORDS Scientific Research, Universities, Research Laboratories
AUDIENCE Educators, Researchers, Scientists
CONTACT Bob Lormand
lormand1@llnl.gov
FREE

http://www-atp.llnl.gov

Los Alamos National Laboratory ★★★

This gopher server is maintained by the Las Alamos National Laboratory (LANL), New Mexico. The LANL's intention is to develop world-class science and technology and to apply them to the nation's security and well-being. The information presented includes current news and events from LANL, access to the LANL phone book, job information, library access, and software archives. In addition, information about the various research activities of LANL is provided.

KEYWORDS Federal Government (US), Research & Development, Technology
AUDIENCE Researchers, Science Researchers, Scientists
CONTACT gopher@lanl.gov
FREE

gopher://gopher.lanl.gov/

Mark Sheehan's Nature Conservancy Page ★★★

The Nature Conservancy is an established, effective international organization whose aim is to preserve the diversity of living things through habitat protection. This page provides links to the Natural Heritage Programs and Conservation Data Centers, Biodiversity Support Program, Great Lakes Biodiversity Project, East Maui (Hawai'i) Watershed Partnership, Waikamoi Preserve, and other related projects.

KEYWORDS Biodiversity, Environmental Protection, Habitats, Nature
AUDIENCE Biologists, Environmentalists, Politicians, Students
CONTACT sheehan@indiana.edu
FREE

http://copper.ucs.indiana.edu/~sheehan/conservancy.html

Natural History Web ★★★★

The Natural History Web, maintained by the Smithsonian National Museum of Natural History, provides information about the museum's research projects and national collections. The site provides a museum guide, with floor plans and information about current exhibits, as well as a calendar of public programs and events. Overviews are given of studies being done by seven different programs and laboratories, and scientific departments are divided into subjects such as anthropology, invertebrate zoology, and paleobiology, with listings of the resources of those departments and access to some of their archives. A list with links to other Natural Science Web sites is also provided.

KEYWORDS Museums, Natural History, Zoology
AUDIENCE Anthropologists, Natural History Scientists, Natural Scientists, Students, Zoologists
CONTACT Don Gourley
don@smithson.si.edu
FREE

http://nmnhgoph.si.edu

Publications of the National Science Foundation ★★★

This gopher server was built to provide access to the publications from the National Science Foundation (NSF). The publications can be browsed according to subject matter (biology, computing, etc.), or there is an index searchable by keywords or call number. This server is one component of NSF's Science and Technology Information System (STIS). There are also some documents about STIS itself online at this gopher site.

KEYWORDS Government Documents, Publishing, Science, Scientific Journals
AUDIENCE Government Employees, Scientists
CONTACT stis@nsf.gov
FREE

gopher://gopher.nsf.gov/

Russian Academy of Sciences ★★★★

This site contains the Russian Academy of Science's home page and links to other WWW servers, highlighting science servers. The Academy of Science page includes links to the departments of Mathematics, General Physics and Astronomy, General Biology, Nuclear Physics, Physical Chemistry, Mechanics, Informatics, etc. The page is under construction and soon will have pages for History, Philosophy, Ocean Research, Economy, World Literature, and more.

KEYWORDS   Chemistry, Informatics, Mathematics, Physics
AUDIENCE   Chemists, Educators, Physicists, Researchers, Scientists
CONTACT   www@www.ras.ru.
FREE

http://www.ras.ru/

Rutherford Appleton Laboratory ★★★

The Rutherford Appleton Laboratory is a research laboratory in London, England. RAL has research programs that include astronomy, biology, chemistry, computing, engineering, particle physics, radio communications and space science. This page gives links to the programs and supplies information about their research.

KEYWORDS   Computer Science, Engineering, Physics, Scientific Research
AUDIENCE   Communications Specialists, Computer Scientists, Researchers, Scientists
CONTACT   Tony Buckley
           A.G.Buckley@daresbury.ac.uk
FREE

http://www.rl.ac.uk/

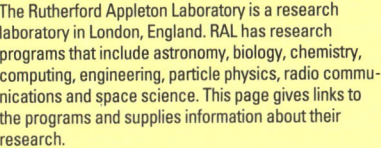
Paleontology

See also
Humanities & Social Sciences · *Archaeology*
Popular Culture & Entertainment · *Museums & Theme Parks*
Science · *Geosciences*

DNA to Dinosaurs ★★★★

This site provides access to QuickTime movies, 'scary' pictures, and sounds of dinosaurs. Included is a movie 'See Triceratops Run' and sounds of the 100-million-year Triassic forecast. In order to see the movie and hear the sound one needs an mpeg viewer and an audio player that will play AU files.

KEYWORDS   Animation, Dinosaurs, Prehistoric Animals, Primary/Secondary Education
AUDIENCE   Children, Educators (Primary/Secondary), Parents, Students (Primary/Secondary)
FREE

http://www.bvis.uic.edu/museum/Media_page.html

UC Museum of Paleontology Website ★★★★

The UC Museum of Paleontology Website is an excellent resource for professionals in the field and other individuals interested in paleontology. The user will find, along with information about the museum itself and its outreach programs, a searchable index of scholarly publications written by people associated with the museum (researchers, graduate students, et al.), other equally searchable indices of museum collections-including those devoted to vertebrates, invertebrates, mollusks, and Pacific Rim biodiversity, links to similar online resources, and information about the weather in Berkeley, California. There is also information available about current exhibitions, presented in an 'interactive museum' format and a resource called 'Paleo Pals' which is a place to have all your pressing paleo-questions discussed and answered.

KEYWORDS   Dinosaurs, Museums, Paleontology
AUDIENCE   Californians, Dinosaur Enthusiasts, Paleontologists
CONTACT   Jere H. Lipps (Director) Allen Collins (sysadmin), Robert Guralnick (Internet co
FREE

http://ucmp1.berkeley.edu
gopher://ucmp1.berkeley.edu/

Dino Russ' Lair ★★★★

Dino Russ' Lair is an exciting Web site for all sorts of dinosaur, paleontology, and earth and geosciences professionals and aficionados. There are quite a few links here, including ones to vertebrate paleontology, over 200 earth sciences sites, and many other sites concerning dinosaurs. All sorts of related pictures abound, linked through many internationally known museums and archives. Available earth and geoscience information covers a lot of ground, including meteorology, paleontology, crystallography and volcanology. Field programs and digs looking for participants recruit here too.

KEYWORDS   Dinosaurs, Natural History, Paleontology
AUDIENCE   Children, Dinosaur Enthusiasts, Earth Scientists, Paleontologists
CONTACT   Dino Russ aka Russel J. Jacobson
           jacobson@geoserv.isgs.uiuc.edu
FREE

http://jacobson.isgs.uiuc.edu/

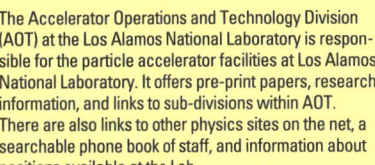
Physics

See also
Computing & Mathematics · *Mathematics*
Science · *Astronomy*
Science · *Space Science*

Accelerator Laboratory LMU and TU Munich ★★

This site offers limited information on the particle accelerator facilities located in Munich, Germany. Most of the information available here is in German, although there is some basic information in English. Users will find descriptions of the Laboratory and its research projects, as well as material on the computing facilities.

KEYWORDS   Germany, Particle Accelerators, Physics Research
AUDIENCE   Educators, Germans, Physicists, Students
CONTACT   Rechnergruppe@Physik.Uni-Muenchen.DE
FREE

http://www.bl.physik.tu-muenchen.de/index_english/index_english.html

Accelerator Operations & Technology Welcome ★★★

The Accelerator Operations and Technology Division (AOT) at the Los Alamos National Laboratory is responsible for the particle accelerator facilities at Los Alamos National Laboratory. It offers pre-print papers, research information, and links to sub-divisions within AOT. There are also links to other physics sites on the net, a searchable phone book of staff, and information about positions available at the Lab.

KEYWORDS   Laboratories, Particle Accelerators, Physics Research, Quantum Mechanics
AUDIENCE   Physicists, Physics Researchers, Scientists
CONTACT   gvaughn@lanl.gov , fkrawczyk@lanl.gov
FREE

http://www.atdiv.lanl.gov

Advanced Photon Source ★★★

The Advanced Photon Source at Argonne National Laboratory is a national user facility designed to produce insertion-device- and bending-magnet-based synchrotron radiation to be used in forefront research in science and technology. Topics on this page are Accelerator Status, APS Information Services, Accelerator Systems Division, Experimental Facilities Division, APS User Organization, Collaborative Access Team (CAT) Home Pages, EPICS Information, Selected Offsite Information and Selected Meetings and Conferences.

KEYWORDS   Laboratories, Photons, Technology
AUDIENCE   Physicists, Researchers
CONTACT   Bill McDowell
           wpm@aps.anl.gov
FREE

http://epics.aps.anl.gov

American Institute of Physics ★★★

This is a gopher server of the American Institute of Physics (AIP). It contains information on AIP, its FTP archives, FYI archives, physics eduction news archives, AIP's online physics information network, and more. In addition, it has links to other science-related gophers.

KEYWORDS   Archives, Education (College/University), Physics, Theoretical Physics
AUDIENCE   Academics, Educators, Physicists, Scientists
CONTACT   admin@aip.org
FREE

gopher://pinet.aip.org/

Background Material ★★★

This site offers material describing the nature of and current physics research into quarks and other elementary particles. It focuses primarily on the search for the sixth quark, the top quark.

KEYWORDS   Particle Physics, Physics, Quantum Physics, Quark
AUDIENCE   Physicists, Researchers, Students
CONTACT   webmaster@fnal.gov
FREE

http://fnnews.fnal.gov/top_background.html

Brock University Department of Physics ★★★★

The home page for the Brock University Department of Physics in Ontario gives extensive information about the department, University and experimental physics. The site has sections about physics news, department faculty and staff, and academic courses There are many links to physics sites on the Internet as well as guides to using the Internet.

KEYWORDS Education (College/University), Educational Programs, Scientific Research, Theoretical Physics
AUDIENCE Educators, Physicists, Researchers, Students
CONTACT Ed Sternin
edik@Brocko.ca
FREE

http://www.physics.brocku.ca/

Brookhaven National Laboratory Home Page ★★★

Brookhaven National Laboratory (BNL) is a multi-disciplinary laboratory that carries out basic and applied research in the physical, biomedical and environmental sciences and in selected energy technologies. The BNL Home page provides links to its departments and divisions which include the Departments of Advanced Technology, of Applied Science, of Biology, of Chemistry and the Center for Accelerator Physics.

KEYWORDS Biosciences, High Energy Physics, Scientific Research
AUDIENCE Physicists, Scientists, Students (University)
CONTACT Peter Sutherland
suther@suntid.bnl.gov
FREE

http://www.bnl.gov/

Brown University Department of Physics ★★★★

The Brown University Department of Physics home page supplies information about seminars, graduate programs, lectures and research groups. The page has a listing of physics events in particle theory, condensed matter theory and astrophysics. There are links to information about high energy physics, preprints, computing resources used in physics and Brown University information servers.

KEYWORDS Education (College/University), Educational Programs, High Energy Physics, Particle Physics
AUDIENCE Educators, Physicists, Researchers, Students
CONTACT webmaster@barus.physics.brown.edu
FREE

http://www.physics.brown.edu/

CERN - European Laboratory for Particle Physics (Conseil Europeen pour la Recherche Nucleaire) ★★★★

CERN is one of the world's largest scientific laboratories and an outstanding example of international collaboration of its many member states. Besides being the birthplace for the World Wide Web, CERN does work within the fields of Accelerators, Computing, Research and Development, and Systems and Services. There are links to other physics areas within CERN and the rest of the Internet.

KEYWORDS Computer Science, Research & Development, Switzerland
AUDIENCE Physicists, Scientists
CONTACT www-support@www.cern.ch
FREE

http://delinfo.cern.ch/

CERN Preprint Server ★★★★

CERN Preprint Server links thousands of preprints related to science and engineering to anyone searching for articles in these fields. Some of the topics include—High Energy Physics Phenomenology and Theory, Astrophysics, Quantum Cosmology, Nuclear Theory, and Experimental Physics. Scientists can send in preprints in paper or electronic formats to be converted to PDF and Postscript file types. Titles, authors or collaboration, number of pages and publication information are extracted and displayed next to the preprint numbers, as well as abstracts when available.

KEYWORDS Science Research, Scientific Publishing, Astrophysics
AUDIENCE Astrophysicists, Nuclear Researchers, Physicists
CONTACT support@preprints.cern.ch
FREE

http://darssrv1.cern.ch/

Centre de Physique des Particules de Marseille (CPPM) ★★★

This is the home page for the Center of Particle Physics in Marseille, France. The Center's focus corresponds to the activity of rediscovering the fundamentals in particle physics, the physics of the infinitely small, the elementary particles and the study of the forces that define matter. There is information on what CPPM does and how to get there.

KEYWORDS France, Particle Physics, Physics, Scientific Research
AUDIENCE Physicists, Scientists, Students (University)
CONTACT Michel RICARD
ricard@cppm.in2p3.fr
FREE

http://marwww.in2p3.fr/

The Compact Muon Solenoid ★★★

The Compact Muon Solenoid is a general purpose detector used in conjunction with a particle collider. It has been optimized to detect a SM Higgs boson over a mass range from 90 GeV to 1 TeV, but it also allows detection of a wide range of possible signatures from alternative electro-weak symmetry breaking mechanisms. This site provides papers and technical reports from the projects, as well as images, future plans and links to related sites.

KEYWORDS Particle Accelerators, Technical Reports
AUDIENCE Particle Physicists
CONTACT docmaster@cmsinfo.cern.ch
FREE

http://cmsinfo.cern.ch

Condensed Matter Theory Group ★★★

The Condensed Matter Theory Group at the Institute of Physics of Johannes-Gutenberg University offers this server to provide information on their current research projects and staff. Visitors to this site will find material on individual staff members, collections of academic papers relating to the research into the physics of condensed matter, and a collection of outside resources of interest to physicists. There is also a collection of technical documentation, and an event calendar with information on physics confrences and seminars.

KEYWORDS Physics Research, Theories
AUDIENCE Educators, Physicists, Physics Researchers, Students
CONTACT Volker Tries
tries@chaplin.physik.uni-mainz.de
FREE

http://www.cond-mat.physik.uni-mainz.de

Contemporary Physics Education Project (CPEP) ★★★

The Contemporary Physics Education Project (CPEP) is a non-profit organization of teachers, educators, and physicists. CPEP materials present the current understanding of the fundamental nature of matter and energy, incorporating the major research findings of the past three decades. This site presents the 1995 Chart of Fundamental Particles and Interactions, links to a bibliography, education programs and other physics education sites.

KEYWORDS Education, High Energy Physics, Particle Physics
AUDIENCE Educators, Physicists, Scientists, Students
CONTACT Michael Barnett
pdg@lbl.gov
FREE

http://www-pdg.lbl.gov/cpep.html

Continuous Electron Beam Accelerator Facility ★★★

This site provides information on the Continuous Electron Beam Accelerator Facility operated by the Southeastern Universities Research Association (SURA) for the Department of Energy. Users will find detailed information regarding the facility's research and physical plant. In addition, this site allows access to data collected by the staff of the facility, as well as information on the procedures involved with experi-

mentation. This site also provides links to other sites with related information.
- KEYWORDS Organizations, Particle Accelerators, Physics Research
- AUDIENCE Physicists, Physics Researchers, Scientists
- CONTACT Karen Hokansson kchok@cebaf.gov, webmaster@cebaf.gov
- FREE

http://www.cebaf.gov

DELPHI, DEtector for Lepton, Photon and Hadron Identification ★★★★

DELPHI, or the DEtector for Lepton, Photon and Hadron Identification is an accelerator of electrons, antiparticles, and positrons. Measuring 27 kilometers in circumference, it took over seven years to build. Information from DELPHI is distributed to about 500 physicists in 47 universities and institutes in 20 countries worldwide.
- KEYWORDS Particle Accelerators, Particle Physics
- AUDIENCE Particle Physicists, Physicists
- CONTACT Mark Dönszelmann duns@delonline.cern.ch
- FREE

http://deloffline.cern.ch/

Deutsches Elektronen-Synchrotron (DESY) ★★★★

This is the Web server for the Deutsches Elektronen-Synchrotron (DESY) in Hamburg. The laboratory performs basic research in high-energy and particle physics as well as in the production and application of synchrotron radiation. The laboratory has locations in Hamburg and Zeuthen, Germany. Information is provided on User Support Groups, Application Software Group, DESY Library, DESY reports, a conference list, electronic journals, a list of journals available in the DESY library, instructions for submitting papers to electronic archives, Collaborations, DESY Software Support and Newsgroups.
- KEYWORDS Germany, Journals, Synchrotron Radiation
- AUDIENCE Educators (University), Internet Users, Researchers, Students (University)
- CONTACT webmaster@desy.de
- FREE

http://ftp.desy.de

ENSLAPP (Ecole Normale Superieure of Lyon) Laboratory for Theoretical Physics ★★★

The ENSLAPP (Ecole Normale Superieure of Lyon) Laboratory for Theoretical Physics site provides information on the following topics—scientific activities including activity reports, the prepublication server, scientific manifestations such as seminars, staff description, information servers including title/abstract preprint WAIS servers, common bibliography database, technical Information about the local computer network, and other information servers.
- KEYWORDS Databases, France, Physics, Theoretical Physics
- AUDIENCE Educators (University), Physicists, Students (University)
- FREE

http://enslapp.ens-lyon.fr/Lyon/Lyon.html

The Fermilab Library ★★★

The Fermilab Library contains the files of, and books used by the Fermi National Accelerator Laboratory. From this Web site users may access their library files via telnet, or read about recent library acquisitions. Also included are periodicals and CDROM reference listings, as well as information about using the desks and technical services. Users will also find links to Quark news, High Energy Physics Web sites, and preprint servers from Los Alamos, CERN and KEK.
- KEYWORDS High Energy Physics, Libraries, Particle Physics, Quark
- AUDIENCE High-Energy Physics Researchers, Physicists
- CONTACT library@fnal.gov
- FREE

http://libmc1.fnal.gov/

Fermilab Theoretical Physics Department ★★★

This page is part of the Fermi National Accelerator Laboratory, a Department of Energy National Laboratory, which provides information on the Fermilab Theoretical Physics Department with links to seminars, physics information, positions available in the theoretical physics department, a superstring model building home page, a directory of group members, and more.
- KEYWORDS Laboratories, Job Listings, Theoretical Physics
- AUDIENCE Physicists, Scientists
- CONTACT mackenzie@fnal.gov
- FREE

http://fnth02.fnal.gov/

HEPIC - High Energy Physics Information Center ★★★★

The High Energy Physics Information Center is an Internet starting point for high energy physics. This site offers information and links to CERNLIB writeups and the U.S. mirror sites, HEPnet Newsgroups, documentation, HEP preprints and publication information, information about HEP experiments, and software used for HEP research.
- KEYWORDS High Energy Physics, Internet Networking, Physics, Software
- AUDIENCE Physicists, Scientists, Students (University)
- CONTACT Jeff Dingbaum dingbaum@hep.net
- FREE

http://www.hep.net/

HERMES Home Page ★★★

This site is the entry point for information about the HERMES project. The HERMES experiment is an internal target experiment in the HERA electron beam. It will measure the spin dependent structure functions of protons and neutrons and will determine the fundamental Bjorken Sum Rule. Data taking has just started in spring 1995. Selected files available from this site include technical papers related to the project, images and movies, and links to specific HERMES sites. Users can link to other sites related to physics, such as Hamburg, Germany, and other locations on the Internet.
- KEYWORDS Particle Physics, Scientific Publishing
- AUDIENCE Atomic Physicists, Physicists
- CONTACT Michael Dueren dueren@hermes.desy.de
- FREE

http://dxhra1.desy.de

Connections to Physics

I had a dream about condensed matter physics

If you spend much of your time worrying about epitaxial growth of compound semiconductors, there is an online site for you!

Actually, this location focuses on semiconductors which are components of the solar cells needed for the generation of power in satellites, deep-space probes, and NASA's space station. These cells must be able to survive the harsh environment of space. It is because of them that we are able to get really neat close-up photos of planets and galaxies. Aside from allowing us to view other worlds, this technology also gives us infrared shots of our planet from weather satellites.

(http://www.physics.auburn.edu/condmat.html)

Harvard Condensed Matter Theory Group ★★

The Harvard Condensed Matter Theory Group makes available manuals and technical documents related to Unix, Mosaic, Physics, and other items of local interest to Harvard users. Tutorials, Man Pages, and user home pages are some of the areas available to visitors. A feature of this site is the TeX and UNIX help hypertext learning systems for new users, and some of the areas have been rewritten with specific references to the Harvard Physics Department.

KEYWORDS Physics, TeX, UNIX
AUDIENCE Mosaic Users, Students (University), UNIX Users
CONTACT webmaster@cmt
FREE

http://cmtw.harvard.edu/

The High Energy Physics Department's (NIKHEF-H) WWW server ★★★

NIKHEF is the National Institute for Nuclear Physics and High-Energy Physics in the Netherlands. The page provides access to information on people at the Institute, seminars and experiments. There are links to preprints, Web sites in the Netherlands and other sites related to physics.

KEYWORDS High Energy Physics, Nuclear Physics, Particle Accelerators
AUDIENCE Nuclear Physicists, Physicists, Researchers
CONTACT webmaster@nikhef.nl
FREE

http://www.nikhef.nl

High Energy Physics Division at Argonne National Laboratory ★★★★

The High Energy Physics Division at Argonne National Laboratory (in Idaho and Illinois) conducts research in theoretical and experimental particle physics as well as accelerator development. This site provides access to experimental and theoretical research, accelerator research and development, and support services.

KEYWORDS High Energy Physics, Particle Physics
AUDIENCE Physicists, Scientists, Students (University)
CONTACT ls@hep.anl.gov
FREE

http://www.hep.anl.gov/

ICTP (International Centre for Theoretical Physics) ★★★

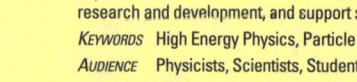

This International Centre for Theoretical Physics (ICTP) gopher disseminates information regarding the scientific activities carried out at the Centre in Trieste, Italy. Information is also provided on the scientific publications, courses, and other services offered by the Third World Academy of Sciences in Trieste and on other Internet physics resources worldwide.

KEYWORDS Europe, Italy, Physics, Theoretical Physics
AUDIENCE Physicists, Theoretical Physicists
CONTACT admin@ictp.trieste.it
FREE

http://gopher.ictp.trieste.it/
gopher://gopher.ictp.trieste.it:70/

Imperial College Theoretical Physics Group ★★★

This is the web server for the Imperial College Theoretical Physics Group in London. It provides links to seminars, research, preprints, theoretical physics and cosmology on-line journals, other physics information including pointers to the American Physical Society and the High Energy Physics Servers Index.

KEYWORDS Cosmology, Imperial College (UK), Physics, Theoretical Physics
AUDIENCE Physicists, Researchers
CONTACT Christopher Parker
c.s.parker@ic.ac.uk
FREE

http://euclid.tp.ph.ic.ac.uk/

Institute of Nuclear Physics Moscow State University ★★★

The Institute of Nuclear Physics Moscow State University home page offers access to information regarding their departments of research. The institute conducts fundamental and applied scientific research in high energy physics, space, solid state, atomic, low and medium energy nuclear physics, microelectronics and quantum electronics. There are links to general information, WWW resources and other MSU servers.

KEYWORDS High Energy Physics, Nuclear Physics, Quantum Electronics, Russia
AUDIENCE Physicists, Researchers
CONTACT Prof. Mikhail I. Panasyuk
panasyuk@srdlan.npi.msu.su
FREE

http://www.npi.msu.su/

International Institute of Theoretical and Applied Physics ★★★

The International Institute Of Theoretical And Applied Physics works to build relations between US scientists and scientists in developing countries with the goal being the pursuit of scientific research and education. This page provides information on lectures and seminars related to the fields of mathematics and physical sciences. There are also links to information servers in physics and mathematics.

KEYWORDS Applied Mathematics, Educational Resources, Particle Physics, Theoretical Physics
AUDIENCE International Scientists, Lecturers, Physicists, Students
CONTACT iitap@iastate.edu
FREE

http://www.physics.iastate.edu/

Joint Institute for Nuclear Research ★★★

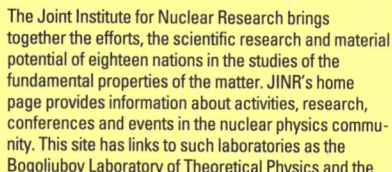

The Joint Institute for Nuclear Research brings together the efforts, the scientific research and material potential of eighteen nations in the studies of the fundamental properties of the matter. JINR's home page provides information about activities, research, conferences and events in the nuclear physics community. This site has links to such laboratories as the Bogoliubov Laboratory of Theoretical Physics and the Frank Laboratory of Neutron Physics.

KEYWORDS Conferences, Networking, Nuclear Physics, Particle Physics
AUDIENCE Nuclear Physicists, Researchers, Scientists, Theoretical Physicists
CONTACT main@ssd.jinr.dubna.su
FREE

http://www.jinr.dubna.su

LANL Nonlinear Science Information Service ★★★

This gopher hole provides access to papers and preprints in the area of non-linear science. The papers are organized according to their subject. There is also an index of all papers. This gopher hole is located at the Los Alamos National Laboratory, New Mexico.

KEYWORDS Chaos Theory, Online Books, Physics
AUDIENCE Physicists, Scientists
CONTACT gopher-admin@xyz.lanl.gov
FREE

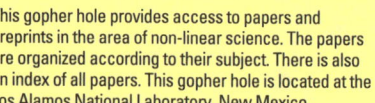

gopher://xyz.lanl.gov/

LEPICS Gopher ★★★

This gopher provides information about the LEPICS computer system, a private computing facility for the L3 experiment at the CERN particle accelerator in Switzerland. This server has information on the current status of LEPICS, such as its CPU load, current jobs, and current users. It also offers help files and project documents for LEPICS. In addition, information about the L3 experiment itself, such as publications from L3 collaborators, L3 news, and L3 experiment tools, is also given.

KEYWORDS Computer Systems, Particle Accelerators, Particle Physics, Quantum Physics
AUDIENCE Particle Physicists, Physicists, Science Researchers
FREE

gopher://lepics.cern.ch/

Laboratoire d'Energie Solaire et de Physique du Bâtiment- (LESO B) ★★★

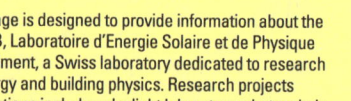

This page is designed to provide information about the LESO B, Laboratoire d'Energie Solaire et de Physique du Bâtiment, a Swiss laboratory dedicated to research of energy and building physics. Research projects descriptions include a daylight laboratory, photovoltaic building elements, and building ventilation, with pictures, objectives, and tool information. Also included are materials on several types of LESO B Software, including a program that measures the acoustics of

Physics

indoor spaces, with demo examples. Educational resources for energy research are also listed.

KEYWORDS Architecture, Energy, Software, Solar Energy
AUDIENCE Energy Researchers, Physics Students
CONTACT R. Compagnon
compagnon@eldp.epfl.ch
FREE

http://lesosun1.epfl.ch/

Laboratory of Seismics and Acoustics ★★★★

This page provides links to information on research performed by the Laboratory of Seismics and Acoustics at the Department of Applied Physics and the Department of Technology at Delft University in the Netherlands. The Laboratory performs research on acoustic and elastodynamic wave theory, with applications in acoustic imaging and acoustic control.

KEYWORDS Geosciences, Research, Seismology
AUDIENCE Applied Physicists, Structural Engineers
CONTACT webmaster@wwwak.tn.tudelft.nl
FREE

http://wwwak.tn.tudelft.nl/index.html

Lawrence Berkeley Laboratory (LBL) ★★★★

Lawrence Berkeley Laboratory (LBL) conducts research in biosciences, particle physics, environmental sciences, chemistry and engineering. LBL brings together scientists, engineers, technicians, and students of a wide spectrum of talents to do research. This page gives extensive information and links to research and educational projects as well as technology transfer and computing information.

KEYWORDS Biosciences, Chemistry, Engineering, Scientific Research
AUDIENCE Researchers, Scientists
CONTACT Jeff Kahn
JBKahn@lbl.gov
FREE

http://www.lbl.gov

Los Alamos Physics Information Server ★★★★

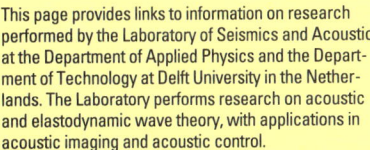

The Los Alamos Physics Information Server is an archive of searchable data from their research papers. A search engine allows users to search Los Alamos preprints and abstracts, or publications and authors, which are listed by subject for the last 3, 6 or 12 months. Subject listings include Accelerator Physics, Nuclear Theory, Chemical Physics, General Relativity and Quantum Mechanics, and High Energy.

KEYWORDS Relativity, Scientific Research
AUDIENCE Nuclear Physicists, Physicists
CONTACT www-admin@mentor.lanl.gov
FREE

http://mentor.lanl.gov

McMaster University, Department of Physics and Astronomy ★★★★

The McMaster University Department of Physics and Astronomy provides information on its research areas, graduate programs, databases, and preprints. The page offers links to faculty and department pages. There are links to other WWW servers in astronomy and physics.

KEYWORDS Astronomy, Canada, Education (College/University)
AUDIENCE Astronomers, Physicists, Students
CONTACT physics@mcmaster.ca
FREE

http://www.physics.mcmaster.ca/

National Synchrotron Light Source ★★★

The National Synchrotron Light Source operates an X-Ray Ring and a VUV (Vacuum Ultra Violet) Ring with the radiation from the storage rings being guided into over 83 beamlines, or experimental stations, where it is used in many fields of research. This site has information on the beamline, research & development, support systems and accelerator physics.

KEYWORDS Biosciences, Crystallography, High Energy Physics, Scientific Research
AUDIENCE Biologists, Chemists, Engineers, Metallurgists, Solid State Physicists
FREE

http://www.nsls.bnl.gov/

Nuclear Physics Electronic ★★★

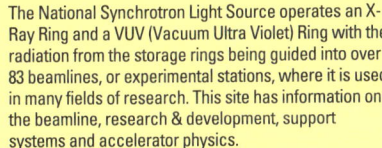

Nuclear Physics Electronic aims to supplement the information in the journals Nuclear Physics A and B. The page has an online index that may be searched, or browsed to access full-text information. There is information about Nuclear Physics Electronics and how to subscribe.

KEYWORDS Journals, Nuclear Physics, Online Magazines, Scientific Research
AUDIENCE Nuclear Physicists, Researchers, Scientists
CONTACT Jan Visser
J.Visser@Elsevier.nl
COST

http://www.nucphys.nl

Office of Fusion Energy ★★★

This server gives information on the Office of Fusion of the U.S. Department of Energy, its member labs, its programs, and research. The mission of the Office of Fusion Energy is to develop fusion as an environmentally attractive, commercially viable, and sustainable energy source for the nation and the world. There are also links to other Department of Energy servers.

KEYWORDS Environmental Research, Fusion, Nuclear Safety, Physics
AUDIENCE Environmental Researchers, Physicists
CONTACT willis@er.doe.gov
FREE

http://wwwofe.er.doe.gov/

P-24 Plasma Physics Group ★★★

The Plasma Physics Group of Los Alamos National Laboratory applies extensive knowledge of plasma, atomic, and laser-matter interaction physics, and laboratory experiments to study high-energy density matter in the plasma state. This group addresses problems of national significance in inertial and magnetic fusion, nuclear weapons stewardship, conventional defense, environmental management, and plasma-based advanced manufacturing. The Plasma Physics Group page provides access to information about its facilities with links to other LANL and physics pages.

KEYWORDS Fusion, Government, Plasma Physics, Technology
AUDIENCE Plasma Physicist, Researchers, Scientists, Students
CONTACT Cris W. Barnes
cbarnes@lanl.gov
FREE

http://fjwsys.lanl.gov/

Particle Data Group ★★★

The PDG reviews the field of Particle Physics, and compiles and analyzes data on particle properties. This site presents information as Postscript files on the review of particle properties, a particle properties interactive database, books, booklets, diaries, and atlases. There are links to a directory of high-energy physics laboratories and agencies as well as educational materials and other major high-energy physics databases.

KEYWORDS High Energy Physics, Particle Physics, Scientific Research
AUDIENCE Educators, Physicists, Scientists, Students
CONTACT Betty Armstrong
B_Armstrong@lbl.gov
FREE

http://www-pdg.lbl.gov/

Paul Scherrer Institut (PSI) WWW Information Services ★★★★

The Paul Scherrer Institut (PSI) does research for Switzerland. The home page gives information about the Institute, its research and central services. PSI maintains research in the areas of nuclear and particle physics, life sciences, and solid-state physics. The Institute supplies information on sustainable development for Switzerland and universities. There are links to other WWW servers in Switzerland.

KEYWORDS Nuclear Physics, Solid State Physics
AUDIENCE Physicists, Scientists
CONTACT Ernst Gujer
gujer@cvax.psi.ch
FREE

http://www.psi.ch/

Physics Department, Hamburg University ★★★

This site is conducted (mostly in German) from the Physics department of Hamburg University. Users will find general information on Hamburg University such as courses offered, libraries available, and more. In addition, this server hosts a number of electronic documents related to physics, as well as detailed material on the department itself.

KEYWORDS Germany, International Education
AUDIENCE Germans, Physics Educators, Physics Students
CONTACT fib@physnet.uni-hamburg.de
FREE

http://wserver.physnet.uni-hamburg.de

Physics HyperTexts ★★

This site maintains several hypertext physics documents. Users will find such topics as muon and neutrino detectors, nucleon decay, and high-energy physics. In addition, this server offers the lighter side of physics, with a document on 'meta-physical' issues, as well as pages on the physics of music.

KEYWORDS Instructional Materials, Physics
AUDIENCE Physicists, Physics Educators, Physics Researchers, Physics Students
CONTACT Vladimir Chaloupka
        vladi@u.washington.edu
FREE

http://web.phys.washington.edu

Physik Institut der Universitaet Zuerich ★★

This site offers information related to physics. This includes answers to frequently asked questions, archives of what's new on the Net in physics, and archives of the journal Physics News. The server is located at the Physics Institute at the University of Zurich. It also provides information about quantum chemistry, computing, and phone numbers at the Institute.

KEYWORDS Education (College/University), Physics, Quantum Chemistry, Theoretical Physics
AUDIENCE Physicists, Science Researchers
CONTACT gopher-adm@physik.unizh.ch
FREE

gopher://gopher.physik.unizh.ch/

Prague Welcome ★★

This page, maintained by the Division of Elementary Particle Physics at the Academy of Sciences of the Czech Republic, contains materials related to physics research. Users will find links to major European laboratories, physics conference information, and a collection of documents related to the research conducted by the Division. In addition, this server houses research project information and links to other physics resources on the Web.

KEYWORDS Particle Physics, Physics
AUDIENCE Educators, Physicists, Students
CONTACT Julius Hrivnac
        Julius.Hrivnac@cern.ch, hrivnac@fzu.cz
FREE

http://www-hep.fzu.cz

RHIC - Relativistic Heavy Ion Collider Home Page ★★★★

The Relativistic Heavy Ion Collider (RHIC), the newest of BNL's big machines, is currently under construction with commissioning scheduled for 1999. RHIC will collide subatomic particles called heavy ions at high energies to recreate the hot, dense plasma of quarks and gluons believed to have existed in the early universe immediately after the Big Bang. This site presents information about accelerator physics, the Collider Ring Division, the Detector Group, the installation status and instrumentation.

KEYWORDS High Energy Physics, Particle Accelerators, Particle Physics, Relativity
AUDIENCE Physicists, Scientists, Students (University)
CONTACT http_admin@acnsun10.rhic.bnl.gov
FREE

http://acnsun10.rhic.bnl.gov:80/RHIC/index.html

The Radiophysics Laboratory Home Page ★★★

This site offers information on the activities of the Radiophysics Laboratory at the Commonwealth Scientific Industrial Research Organisation in Australia. Users will find research information, material on the computing facilities, and links to related professional organizations. There is also staff and general facilities information, and databases of scientific data derived from the Lab's research.

KEYWORDS Astronomy, Radio Physics, Radio Telescopes, Space Science
AUDIENCE Astronomers, Physicists, Radio Astronomers
CONTACT Jim Argyros
        jargyros@atnf.csiro.au
FREE

http://www.atnf.csiro.au

SLAC (Stanford Linear Accelerator Center) Home Page ★★★

This page contains information about the SLAC (Stanford Linear Accelerator Center). SLAC is a particle accelerator laboratory at Stanford University. Users will find information on the facilities and faculty at the laboratory, and information on many research projects that are underway there. This server also maintains links to a great number of physics resources on the Web, as well as links to other Stanford University departments.

KEYWORDS Particle Accelerators, Particle Physics, Physics
AUDIENCE Educators, Physicists, Students
CONTACT Joan M. Winters
        winters@slac.stanford.edu
FREE

http://www-slac.slac.stanford.edu

TRIUMF Home Page ★★★

TRIUMF - Canada's National Meson Research Facility gives detailed information about the facility, staff and research. The Home Page is broken into categories - general, computing, people, groups, activities, experiments and collaborations. There is an extensive listing of HEP sites and information services, selected world links, and reference material.

KEYWORDS High Energy Physics, Particle Physics, Scientific Research
AUDIENCE Educators, Physicists, Scientists, Students
CONTACT Computing Services Group
        wj@triumf.ca
FREE

http://www.triumf.ca/

Universitat Oldenburg Physics ★★

The Universitat Oldenburg Physics page gives information about the department, the University and publications. The site also has information on clusters in atomic physics, physics facts, databases and other Internet services.

KEYWORDS Education (College/University), Educational Resources, Particle Physics
AUDIENCE Educators, Germans, Physicists, Students
CONTACT stamer@merlin.physik.uni-oldenburg.de
FREE

http://www.physik.uni-oldenburg.de/

University of Pennsylvania Department of Physics and Astronomy ★★★★

This site contains a variety of information related to physics, astronomy, and astrophysics. Distinct menus allow the user to choose from educational materials, such as course materials, and items, such as the Shoemaker-Levy 9 Impacts Archives, Computer Information, such as Unix documentation, the National Scalable Cluster Project, and FTP archives, Seminars and Colloquia, including High Energy Physics Theory Seminars, and Departmental Information including contact information.

KEYWORDS Astronomy, Universities
AUDIENCE Astronomers, Physicists, Scientists, Students
CONTACT Donald Benton
        benton@dept.physics.upenn.edu
FREE

http://dept.physics.upenn.edu/

University of Pittsburgh Relativity Group ★★★

The Relativity Group at the University of Pittsburgh provides general information concerning relativity, the Numerical Relativity Project, the Binary Black Hole Grand Challenge Collaboration, and the global relativity scene. This server also provides reprints, relativity tools, and other general science information.

KEYWORDS Physics, Relativity, Research, Theoretical Physics
AUDIENCE Physicists, Researchers, Space Students, Students
FREE

http://artemis.phyast.pitt.edu

Warsaw University - Physics Department Home Page

This page is the home of the Physics Department at Warsaw University. Users will find information on the department, its research, staff, and students, and a collection of links to other physics-related servers on the Internet. In addition, this server offers local material such as maps, network information, and a 'flea market' where users can browse and post ads for a wide variety of goods and services.

KEYWORDS   Physics, Poland
AUDIENCE   Physicists, Physics Educators, Physics Students
FREE

http://www.fuw.edu.pl/

Welcome to INFN-LNGS (Istituto Nazionale di Fisica Nucleare- Laboratori Nazionali del Gran Sasso)

This page is maintained by the Laboratori Nazionali del Gran Sasso (Gran Sasso National Laboratory). It provides information on their underground laboratory for particle physics and astrophysics. Users will find technical and physical details of the lab, as well as material on research conducted there. Links to other related servers and general Internet information is available as well.

KEYWORDS   Italy, Nuclear Physics, Particle Accelerators, Scientific Research
AUDIENCE   Physicists, Physics Educators, Physics Students
CONTACT   Alberto D'Ambrosio
           dambrosio@lngs.infn.it
FREE

http://wsgs00.lngs.infn.it

Wilson Synchrotron Laboratory

This site is maintained by the Wilson Synchrotron Laboratory at Cornell University. The Wilson Laboratory is a high-energy physics research center which houses the 10 GeV Cornell Electron-positron Storage Ring 'CESR,' the high energy particle detector 'CLEO,' and the Cornell High Energy Synchrotron Source 'CHESS.' Users will find academic papers, information on research projects and facilities, and links to other related servers on the Internet.

KEYWORDS   Research, Universities
AUDIENCE   High-Energy Physics Researchers, Physicists, Physics Educators, Physics Students
CONTACT   webmaster@lns598.lns.cornell.edu
FREE

http://w4.lns.cornell.edu

Connections to Physics Education
What's a Quark?

Contemporary Physics Education Project (CPEP)

If you ever wondered what holds the world together, or if you want to know more about particles such as quarks, gluons, and neutrinos, check out the "Contemporary Physics Education Project" (CPEP). Here you'll get hands-on instruction in a variety of topics related to physics. This site comprises a non-profit organization of teachers, educators, and physicists, dedicated to presenting the latest understanding of the fundamental nature of matter and energy. The group incorporates within its curriculum major research findings of the past three decades.

The site also furnishes software that employs graphics to illustrate key concepts. Additionally, you'll find a packet of classroom activities with worksheets which expand on the concepts of matter and energy. There are also workshops for teachers at various sites around the U.S., designed to make the learning process more fun and relevant.

(http://www-pdg.lbl.gov/cpep.html)

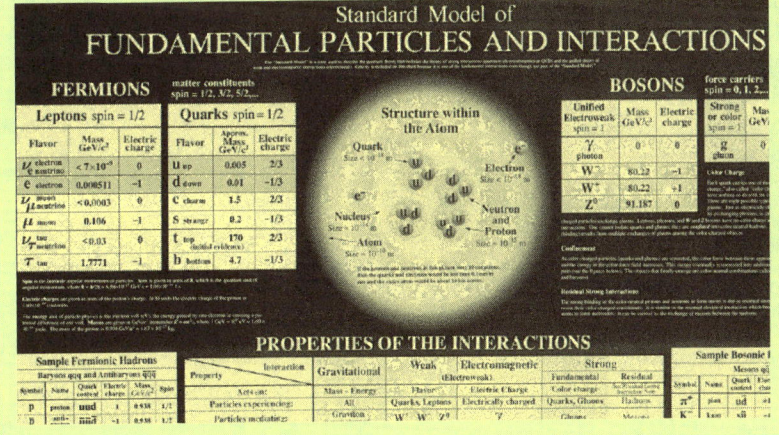

Space Science

See also
Government & Politics · Agencies
Science · Astronomy
Science · Earth Sciences

Aeronautics Consolidated Supercomputing Facility (ACSF)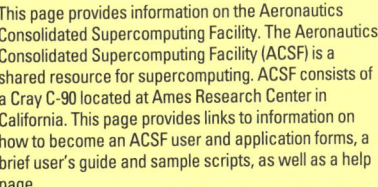

This page provides information on the Aeronautics Consolidated Supercomputing Facility. The Aeronautics Consolidated Supercomputing Facility (ACSF) is a shared resource for supercomputing. ACSF consists of a Cray C-90 located at Ames Research Center in California. This page provides links to information on how to become an ACSF user and application forms, a brief user's guide and sample scripts, as well as a help page.

KEYWORDS   Aeronautics, Engineering, Research & Development, Supercomputing
AUDIENCE   Aerospace Engineers, Aerospace Industry Professionals, Aerospace Researchers
CONTACT   Lona Howser
           l.m.howser@larc.nasa.gov
FREE

http://cabsparc.larc.nasa.gov/ACSF/acsf.html

Aerospace Electronics Systems Division (GL)

Aerospace Electronics Systems Division handles electronic, electro-optical, and control systems for NASA Langley Research Center's atmospheric, aeronautic, spaceflight, and laboratory programs. The division designs, fabricates, tests, and operates ground and flight instrumentation equipment for Center flight projects. Users can see summaries of what each department does, and some areas have technical reports, images, contact information and other useful information.

KEYWORDS   Aerospace Engineering, NASA (National Aeronautics And Space Administration)
AUDIENCE   Aerospace Researchers, Engineers, NASA Researchers
CONTACT   aesd@larc.nasa.gov
FREE

http://aesd.larc.nasa.gov

Space Science

Aviation Week Information Services

This server gives information about Aviation Week and Space Technology magazine and other related products. The other products include newsletters, aviation directories, and online magazines. None of the products are accessible through this gopher, but there is purchasing information provided.

- KEYWORDS: Aeronautics, Aviation, Technology, Transportation Law
- AUDIENCE: Aeronautics Engineers, Aerospace Engineers, Aviators, Space Scientists
- CONTACT: Cindy Lister avweek@mgh.com
- FREE

gopher://datapro.mgh.com:71/

CERT (Centre d'Études et de Recherches de Toulouse) ONERA (Office National d'Études et de Recherches Aérospatiales) Home Page

This site provides access to information on the activities and research of the Centre d'Études et de Recherches de Toulouse (CERT), a division of the Office National d'Études et de Recherches Aérospatiales (ONERA). Users will find descriptions of the research facilities, goals, and projects of the Center. This site also provides links to related sites on the Internet.

- KEYWORDS: Aerospace Engineering, Astronomy, Space Science
- AUDIENCE: Aerospace Engineers, Astronomers
- FREE

http://www.cert.fr/index.a.html

Canada-France-Hawaii Telescope Home Page ★★★

The Canada-France-Hawaii Telescope observatory is located atop the summit of Mauna Kea in Hawaii. This site offers information on the research going on at the observatory, and archives of astronomical data, computer software, and an astronomical library. Users will also find links to other astronomical Internet resources, as well as observing schedules, newsletters, and astronomical calendars.

- KEYWORDS: Astronomy, Observatories, Space Science, Telescopes
- AUDIENCE: Astronomers, Astrophysicists, Space Scientists
- CONTACT: webmaster@cfht.hawaii.edu
- FREE

http://www.cfht.hawaii.edu

Center for Atmospheric and Space Sciences

This site provides information provided by the Center for Atmospheric and Space Sciences at Utah State University. Users will find material on the research projects and facilities at the Center, as well as links to other related servers on the Internet.

- KEYWORDS: Astronomy, Atmospheric Sciences, Space Science
- AUDIENCE: Atmospheric Scientists, Educators, Space Scientists, Students
- CONTACT: thompson@usu.edu
- FREE

http://www.cass.usu.edu

Compton Observatory Science Support Center (COSSC)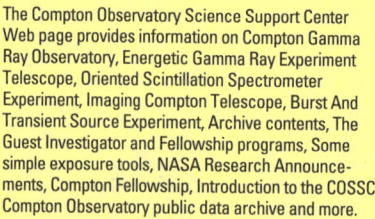

The Compton Observatory Science Support Center Web page provides information on Compton Gamma Ray Observatory, Energetic Gamma Ray Experiment Telescope, Oriented Scintillation Spectrometer Experiment, Imaging Compton Telescope, Burst And Transient Source Experiment, Archive contents, The Guest Investigator and Fellowship programs, Some simple exposure tools, NASA Research Announcements, Compton Fellowship, Introduction to the COSSC, Compton Observatory public data archive and more.

- KEYWORDS: Astronomy, Fellowships, Observatories, Telescopes
- AUDIENCE: Computer Users, Educators (University), Internet Users, Researchers, Students (University)
- CONTACT: feedback@ascasrv.gsfc.nasa.gov
- FREE

http://enemy.gsfc.nasa.gov

Dryden Flight Research Center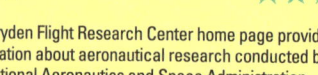

The Dryden Flight Research Center home page provides information about aeronautical research conducted by the National Aeronautics and Space Administration (NASA) at the Edwards, California, base. Users will find reports of past and ongoing research projects, an extensive photo server, a search engine, and links to other NASA sites.

- KEYWORDS: Aeronautical Research, NASA (National Aeronautics And Space Administration)
- AUDIENCE: Space Enthusiasts, Space Scientists
- FREE

http://www.dfrf.nasa.gov/dryden.html

Endeavor Astro-2 Space Mission ★★★★

These WWW pages will allow the user to learn more about the Astro-2 high-tech observatory that flew for 16 days with the Space Shuttle Endeavour during the STS-67 mission between March 2 and March 18, 1995. You can learn more about the Astro-2 experiments and the discoveries made. Just click on a button to meet the astronauts, and NASA team, to examine the flight log, see the telescopes, come aboard the Astro-2 flight deck, and take a virtual reality trip around the Astro-2 payload. (Download the Mac or Window file and you will be able to fly around the Astro-2 Payload) or take a virtual spacewalk where you will see some great GIF images of the shuttle spaceship.

- KEYWORDS: Astronomy, NASA (National Aeronautics And Space Administration), Space Shuttle
- AUDIENCE: General Public, Internet Users, Scientists, Space Enthusiasts, Students (Primary/Secondary)
- CONTACT: Stephen.Maher@gsfc.nasa.gov
- FREE

http://astro-2.msfc.nasa.gov/

Experimental Hypersonics Branch Home Page ★★★

This page is the home of the Experimental Hypersonics Branch at NASA's Langley research facilities. Research is conducted in high-velocity/high-temperature environments to test space vehicle delivery systems. Users will find a description and pictures of the test facilities, information on the current research focus, and more. In addition, this server hosts a collection of other space science resources, as well as a collection of links to other related servers on the Internet.

- KEYWORDS: Aerodynamics, Space Science
- AUDIENCE: Aerodynamics Engineers, Aerospace Engineers, Space Scientists
- CONTACT: Dr. Scott D. Holland s.d.holland@larc.nasa.gov
- FREE

http://wolfpack.larc.nasa.gov/EHB.html

Goddard Space Flight Center (GSFC) Gopher

This site provides access to the gopher for the National Aeronautics and Space Administration's Goddard Space Flight Center (GSFC) in Greenbelt, Maryland. The information provided by that server includes a section about the GSFC containing contact information, maps, and images, as well as a section of computing information pertaining to SunOS, Solaris, and VMS.

- KEYWORDS: Computing, NASA (National Aeronautics And Space Administration), Satellites, Scientific Research
- AUDIENCE: Aeronautics Engineers, Space Scientists, Space Students
- CONTACT: gopher@gopher.gsfc.nasa.gov
- FREE

gopher://gopher.gsfc.nasa.gov/

Hubble Space Telescope (HST) and the Space Telescope Science Institute Public Information Files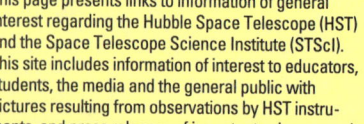

This page presents links to information of general interest regarding the Hubble Space Telescope (HST) and the Space Telescope Science Institute (STScI). This site includes information of interest to educators, students, the media and the general public with pictures resulting from observations by HST instruments, and press releases of important science results made possible by HST observations.

- KEYWORDS: Astronomy, Education, NASA (National Aeronautics And Space Administration), Telescopes
- AUDIENCE: Astronomers, Astronomy Students, General Public, Space Enthusiasts

CONTACT Zolt Levay
         levay@stsci.edu
FREE
http://stsci.edu/public.html

Infrared Processing & Analysis Center ★★★

The Infrared Processing and Analysis Center (IPAC) produces data-intensive processing tasks for NASA's infrared astronomy program, and provides scientific expertise to the astronomy community. This site gives information about the projects, news and information at IPAC. Services available at IPAC include IRSKY, an observation planning tool that allows IRAS image displaying and overlaying of catalogs on the images, IBIS (IRSKY Batch Inquiry System), and XCATSCAN, a catalog scanning tool that provides interactive queries of the IRAS databases, as well as many other major catalogs.

KEYWORDS Astronomy, Infrared Processing
AUDIENCE Astronomers, Researchers, Space Scientists, Students
CONTACT   www@ipac.caltech.edu
FREE
http://www.ipac.caltech.edu

The Institute for Space and Terrestrial Science ★★★

The Institute for Space and Terrestrial Science (ISTS) provides resources in multidisciplinary space and terrestrial sciences, engineering, and education to stimulate collaborative research and industrial development. ISTS research covers such areas as human performance in space, small satellite payloads, space instrumentation, and environmental change. This site gives links to ISTS administration, earth observation laboratories and space related sites.

KEYWORDS Education, Engineering, Scientific Research
AUDIENCE Engineers, Scientists, Space Scientists
CONTACT   webadmin@ists.ca
FREE
http://www.ists.ca

Ithaco, Inc. ★★

The Ithaco Incorporated home page provides information on this New York-based developer of spacecraft attitude determination and control systems. Information on their equipment such as earth sensors, momentum/reaction wheels and momentum managing electromagnets is included and accompanied by images of products. Information on Ithaco's analysis service is also provided.

KEYWORDS Companies, Space Equipment, Space Systems, Space Technology
AUDIENCE NASA Managers, Space Scientists
FREE
http://www.isso.org/Industry/Ithaco/ithaco.html

Kennedy Space Center ★★★

This server provides information about NASA's Kennedy Space Center. This information includes history, maps, access to image archives, directories, and space shuttle operation details. The server provides links to the Center's FTP site as well as to its WWW server.

KEYWORDS Engineering, Images, NASA (National Aeronautics And Space Administration), Satellites
AUDIENCE Engineers, Space Enthusiasts, Space Professionals
FREE
gopher://www.ksc.nasa.gov/
http://www.ksc.nasa.gov

MDA - Houston (McDonnell Douglas Aerospace) ★★★

The home page of McDonnell Douglas Aerospace in Houston provides access to information on current research in aerospace and computer technology. MDA provides a range of engineering support to NASA and the aerospace community. This document also includes links to related Internet resources.

KEYWORDS Aeronautics, Aerospace Engineering, Computer Technology, Space Science
AUDIENCE Aerospace Engineers, Aerospace Industry Professionals, Computer Scientists, Engineers
CONTACT   Craig Zook
          zook@pat.mdc.com
FREE
http://pat.mdc.com/

Mars Mission Research Center (M2RC) ★★★★

The Mars Mission Research Center home page aims to broaden the nation's engineering capability to meet the critical needs of the civilian space program. M2RC develops educational and research programs that focus on the technology necessary for efficient space transportation. This site gives information on the project, research, documents and links to related sites.

KEYWORDS Engineering, Planets, Research, Technology
AUDIENCE Engineers, NASA Researchers, Space Scientists, Students
CONTACT   www_admin@mmrc.ncsu.edu
FREE
http://www.mmrc.ncsu.edu

Max Planck Institute for Astrophysics ★★★

The Max Planck Institute for Astrophysics page gives information on the people, seminars and research of the Institute. The research groups study such areas as binaries, cosmology, galaxy formation and gravitational lenses. This site provides links to the research groups and their current projects. There are files that may be downloaded.

KEYWORDS Astrophysics, Cosmology, Germany, Research
AUDIENCE Astrophysicists, Cosmologists, Researchers, Space Scientists, Students
CONTACT   webmaster@mpa-garching.mpg.de
FREE
http://www.mpa-garching.mpg.de

The Mission Operations and Data Systems Directorate (MO&DSD) - Code 500 ★★★★

The Mission Operations and Data Systems Directorate (MO&DSD) is comprised of institutional mission operations facilities which provide for mission planning and scheduling, command management, health and safety monitoring, real-time command and control, network configuration and performance monitoring, communications interface, orbit and attitude computations, data capture, processing, and distribution. This server also lists specific related directories.

KEYWORDS Government Agencies (US), NASA (National Aeronautics And Space Administration)
AUDIENCE Engineers, NASA Researchers, Space Scientists
CONTACT   Donald Wilson
          wilson@joy.gsfc.nasa.gov
FREE
http://ddwilson.gsfc.nasa.gov

NASA Ames Imaging Library System (AILS) ★★★

NASA's Ames Imaging Library System (AILS) contains databases of images taken from the Ames Imaging Technology Branch. Directories here include photos, illustration, and artistic images for Aircraft, the Space Shuttle, Outer Space, High Altitude Aerial Shots, and more. The database has a simple search engine for faster location of files.

KEYWORDS Aeronautics, Graphics, Images, NASA (National Aeronautics And Space Administration)
AUDIENCE General Public, Graphics Enthusiasts, Space Enthusiasts
CONTACT   Shahriar Kianersi
          kianersi@atlas.arc.nasa.gov
FREE
http://ails.arc.nasa.gov

The NASA Astrophysics Data System Home Page ★★★

The Astrophysics Data System (ADS) is an environment for astronomers which provides a wealth of astronomical data to the scientific user community in electronic form. Users will find directories for astronomy/astrophysics, containing approximately 210,000 abstracts and space instrumentation.

KEYWORDS Astronomy, Technical Reports
AUDIENCE Astronomers, Astrophysicists, Space Scientists
CONTACT   ads@cfa.harvard.edu
FREE
http://adswww.harvard.edu/

Space Science

NASA Center Home Pages ★★★★

This site contains a list of links to all the National Aeronautics and Space Administration's (NASA) Center Home Pages. Organized under each Center's name - such as NASA Headquarters, Goddard Space Flight Center, Jet Propulsion Lab, and more. Information is provided about past and present NASA research. There is access given to mission photographs and live shuttle transmissions.

- **KEYWORDS** Astronomy, NASA (National Aeronautics And Space Administration), Photography, Scientific Research
- **AUDIENCE** General Public, Internet Users, Science Researchers, Space Professionals
- **CONTACT** James Gass
gass@ndadsa.gsfc.nasa.gov
- **FREE**

http://www.hq.nasa.gov/office/mtpe/

NASA Center for AeroSpace Information ★★★

This gopher server is maintained by the NASA Scientific and Technical Information (STI) program. It provides information of interest to professionals in the aerospace industry. The information is in the form of an online journal titled 'Selected Current Aerospace Notices (SCAN)'. In addition to SCAN, this gopher also provides access to an online catalog for an aerospace library titled the Aerospace Research Information Network.

- **KEYWORDS** Aerodynamics, NASA (National Aeronautics And Space Administration), Research, Scientific Journals
- **AUDIENCE** Aerospace Engineers, Aerospace Industry Professionals, Science Researchers, Space Scientists
- **CONTACT** casigopher@sti.nasa.gov
- **FREE**

gopher://gopher.sti.nasa.gov/

NASA Jet Propulsion Laboratory ★★★

The Jet Propulsion Laboratory (JPL) home page describes the Pasadena, California, research laboratory's ongoing work in space exploration. The site provides press releases (such as news of the Jupiter-bound Galileo spacecraft), general descriptions of JPL's work, image and information archives, and other resources. There are links to the National Aeronautics and Space Administration (NASA), JPL's parent body, and Caltech, which administers the laboratory.

- **KEYWORDS** California, NASA (National Aeronautics And Space Administration), Research Labs
- **AUDIENCE** Journalists, Space Scientists
- **CONTACT** newsdesk@jpl.nasa.gov
- **FREE**

http://www.jpl.nasa.gov/

NASA Langley Research Center Home Page ★★★★

This is the WWW home page for the NASA Langley Research Center (LaRC). The mission of LaRC includes performing innovative aerospace research, transferring technology to users, and supporting U.S. government agencies, U.S. industry, NASA centers, and the educational community. Detailed and comprehensive links to all LaRC resources are provided. There are also links to Langley Technology Access Services, including the Technology Experts Locator Service (TELS), the Technology Opportunities Showcase (TOPS), the Langley Software Server (LSS), and the Langley Technical Report Server (LTRS). Links are also provided to Langley projects, teams and initiatives, other NASA information, and Langley Organizations Online.

- **KEYWORDS** Aeronautics, NASA (National Aeronautics And Space Administration), Research, Technology
- **AUDIENCE** Aeronautics Engineers, Aerospace Engineers, Aerospace Industry Professionals, Space Enthusiasts, Space Scientists, Students
- **CONTACT** Michael Nelson
m.l.nelson@larc.nasa.gov
- **FREE**

http://mosaic.larc.nasa.gov/larc.html

NASA Scientific and Technical Information Office ★★★

This is the server for the NASA Scientific and Technical Information Office. This server is run by the NASA Center for AeroSpace Information (CASI). It provides pointers to products and other NASA resources.

- **KEYWORDS** NASA (National Aeronautics And Space Administration), Research Institutes, Technology
- **AUDIENCE** Educators (University), Internet Users, Researchers, Students (University)
- **CONTACT** hanson@sti.nasa.gov
- **FREE**

http://ftp.sti.nasa.gov

Planetary Data System Microwave Subnode ★★★

The Microwave Subnode is a subsidiary of the Geosciences Node of NASA's Planetary Data System. The Subnode archives and distributes digital data related to the study of the surfaces and interiors of planetary bodies using active and passive microwave sensing techniques. This page has pointers to a variety of other NASA sites, each of which contains related information. On this server, the user can find data sets and images from spaceborne measurements of the planet Venus. Preprints about Venus are also available here.

- **KEYWORDS** Archives, Geosciences, NASA (National Aeronautics And Space Administration)
- **AUDIENCE** Astronomers, Astrophysicists, NASA Researchers
- **CONTACT** Peter G. Ford
pds-requests@space.mit.edu
- **FREE**

http://delcano.mit.edu/

Shuttle Launch Countdown ★★★

This WWW page, called Shuttle Launch Countdown, provides up-to-date information about US space shuttle missions, specifically the liftoff phase. There is an online version of the countdown clock. Users will also find descriptions and imagery of recent shuttle missions, details of all the shuttle flights, and background information about the space shuttle program. There are links to other National Aeronautics and Space Administration sites.

- **KEYWORDS** Florida, NASA (National Aeronautics And Space Administration), Space Shuttle Program
- **AUDIENCE** Journalists, Space Enthusiasts
- **CONTACT** dumoulin@titan.ksc.nasa.gov
- **FREE**

http://www.ksc.nasa.gov/shuttle/countdown/

Space Activism Home Page ★★★★

The Space Activism home page promotes the furthering of space exploration through lobbying. Presented at this site are the names, email and US postal addresses of various administrators and elected officials responsible for funding American space programs. Links to other space-related Web pages and numerous NASA sites are also located here.

- **KEYWORDS** Activism, Astronomy, Politics, Space
- **AUDIENCE** Researchers, Space Enthusiasts, Space Flight Enthusiasts
- **CONTACT** John Lewis
jlewis@qrc.com
- **FREE**

http://muon.qrc.com/space/start.html

Space Calendar ★★★★

The Jet Propulsion Laboratory site features a Space Calendar, which lists space-related events and anniversaries for the coming year. Links throughout the calendar provide the user with the opportunity to learn more about the scientists, missions, and celestial objects mentioned.

- **KEYWORDS** Astronomy, Calendars, NASA (National Aeronautics And Space Administration), Space
- **AUDIENCE** Astronomers, Space Enthusiasts
- **CONTACT** Ron Baalke
baalke@kelvin.jpl.nasa.gov
- **FREE**

http://newproducts.jpl.nasa.gov/calendar/calendar.html

The Space Telescope - European Coordinating Facility ★★★

This site, The Space Telescope - European Coordinating Facility, assists astronomy researchers in Europe in taking advantage of the information provided by the Hubble Space Telescope. Links include STAN, Space Telescope Analysis Newsletters, bulletin boards, archives, meetings, public images, visitor information, staff homepages, conferences, updates, new items listed, etc.

- **KEYWORDS** Astronomy, Europe, Telescopes
- **AUDIENCE** Astronomers, Europeans, Physicists, Researchers

CONTACT   murtagh@eso.org
FREE
http://ecf.hq.eso.org/

Spacecraft Systems Division Home Page ★★★★

The Spacecraft Systems Division (SSD) Home Page provides users with information about the spacecraft programs of the Office of Space Access and Technology at NASA, which engineers exploratory spacecraft. This site includes information about their technology divisions, including news releases, objectives, and technical program plans. Users can read about SSD's projects and accomplishments such as Dante II, a tethered exploratory robot, and view current images being sent back by the robot. Some of the other accomplishments described include advanced microsensors, the ASTRO Star Tracker, and a Plasma Contactor.

KEYWORDS   Aeronautics, Engineering, NASA (National Aeronautics And Space Administration)
AUDIENCE   Aeronautics Engineers, Aerospace Industry Professionals
CONTACT   Dave Lavery
dave.lavery@hq.nasa.gov
FREE
http://ranier.oact.hq.nasa.gov/SCRS_Page/SCHP.html

Starship Design ★★★

Lunar Institute of Technology's College of Engineering sponsors the School of Starship Design Web Page. This page gives detailed information on past, present and future starship design projects, including specifications and propulsion, classes, and how to join the school. There are links to the School library, the LIT Home Page and other Web sites.

KEYWORDS   Engineering Design, Future Technology, Space
AUDIENCE   Engineers, Propulsion Experts, Space Enthusiasts
CONTACT   David Levine
lunar@sunsite.unc.edu
FREE
http://sunsite.unc.edu/lunar/sdhp.html

United Nations Office for Outer Space Affairs FTP ★★★

The United Nations Office for Outer Space Affairs FTP focuses on the promotion of international cooperation in the use of space technology and to ensure that space activities do not damage space or Earth's environment. This site gives information about their charter, background and responsibilities. There are also links to other sources of space-related information and space agencies.

KEYWORDS   Aeronautics, Space, United Nations
AUDIENCE   Aerospace Industry Professionals, Space Enthusiasts
CONTACT   R. Albrecht
ralbrech@eso.org
FREE
ftp://ns3.hq.eso.org/pub/un/un-homepage.html

Connections to Outer Space
E.T. . . . you're home

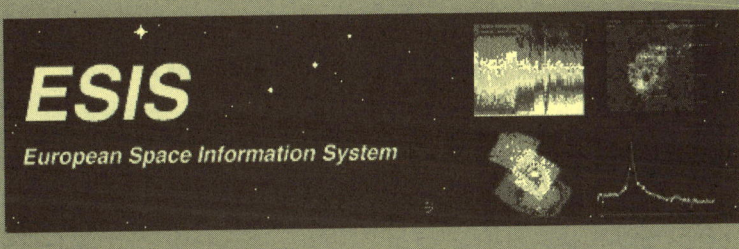

You don't need to sign up for astronaut training with the National Aeronautics Space Administration (NASA) to explore outer space. You don't even have to wait for a visit from an extra-terrestrial to get a glimpse of the greater universe.

On the Internet, there are connections to several space programs throughout the world, including sites originating in Finland and France. There is even a Space-Time Travel Machine which enables you to explore the birth of the universe and the formation of galaxies and planets. You'll find extensive information on quantum mechanics, fog, snow, and fractal synthesis of cloud dynamics. There is also a wide selection of artistic representations of prime numbers, the hydrogen atom, and a black hole.

(http://mesis.esrin.esa.it/html/esis.html)

The largest online connection to outer space comes through the Nasa Kennedy Space Center where you can visit a launch photo directory, as well as take an extensive historical look at space travel—including the Spacelab Mission, the Russian MIR rendezvous with SpaceLab 3, and the McDonnell Douglas Space and Defense Systems. Through this site, you have NASA Online Information (for the latest launch data), connections to the European Space Agency, the Canadian Astronomy Data Center, and the Space Remote Sensing Center.

(http://www.ksc.nasa.gov/ksc.html)

University of Wisconsin-Madison Space Science and Engineering Center Gopher Server ★★★

This site is the University of Wisconsin-Madison Space Science and Engineering Center Gopher Server. The information it contains includes images, software, newsletters, satellite data, and real-time southern hemisphere composite images. This site provides access to other gophers related to space sciences.

KEYWORDS   Astronomy, Education (College/University), Engineering, Satellite Data
AUDIENCE   Engineers, Space Science Researchers, Space Scientists, Space Students
FREE
gopher://gopher.ssec.wisc.edu/

Zoology

See also
Popular Culture & Entertainment · *Museums & Theme Parks*
Science · *Aquatic Sciences*
Science · *Organizations*

AVES ★★★

AVES is an archive of bird GIFS and bird-related information. The server provides an index of all the GIFS. The other information includes descriptions and audio tracks of bird calls.

KEYWORDS   Biology, Birds, Computer Graphics, Ornithology
AUDIENCE   Biologists, Bird Watchers, Ornithologists
CONTACT   Russ Glaeser
rglaeser@macaw.cecer.army.mil
FREE
gopher://vitruvius.cecer.army.mil/

Zoology

The American Association of Zookeepers' (AAZK) Home Page ★★★★

An exciting and unusual Web site, the American Association of Zookeepers' (AAZK) Home Page is sure to fascinate the curious, inform the professional, and perhaps even guide those seeking a new career. Not only will you find many photographs of all different types of animals at this spot, including birds, dinosaurs, otters, reptiles, dung beetles, fringetails, orandas, buffleheads, bees and a small directory of toucans, but also information on how to become a zookeeper yourself. The colleges that offer animal management courses are noted, especially those which include large or exotic animal training and husbandry. There are links to other related sites here as well, including those to the Bowling for Rhinos and Elephant Managers Associations, as well as links to similarly oriented gopher servers.

KEYWORDS Animal Husbandry, Animals, Zookeeping, Zoos
AUDIENCE Animal Behaviorists, Animal Lovers, Animal Trainers, Zookeepers
CONTACT hpear@aazk.ind.net
FREE

http://aazk.ind.net

Animal Behavior Society Website ★★★★

The Animal Behavior Society Website is a site designed for members and contributors to the Animal Behavior Society and its various journals. The site contains links to the Animal Behavior Society (ABS) Gopher, the ABS Newsletter, the electronic mailing list ABSNet, archives for the study of animal behavior and information about the journals 'Evolution' and 'Ethology.' Here you will also find information on how to submit manuscripts for publication in professional journals, how to write grant proposals, which grants are available for animal behavior researchers and reviews and data on acquiring computer programs specific to the field.

KEYWORDS Animal Science, Biology, Evolution, Zoology
AUDIENCE Animal Psychologists, Behaviorists, Biologists, Ethologists
CONTACT Hugh Dingle, President
cisab@loris.cisab.indiana.edu
FREE

http://www.cisab.indiana.edu/
animal_behaviour.html

Animal Rights Resource Site (ARRS) ★★★★

This site offers a wide range of resources for those exploring issues in animal rights, and includes much information on veganism and vegetarianism. Resources include news, pictures, essays, guides, journals, leaflets, reference (including FAQ's), and a list of action alerts and projects. Written material and pictures are divided into subject categories, and include the journals AnimaLife and Vegan News. News covers current US politics and activism. Users can browse using search engines as well as 'subject wrappers' which organize all the site's resources into sub-categories such as 'The Dairy Industry.'

KEYWORDS Animal Rights, Animals, Endangered Species
AUDIENCE Animal Rights Activists, Nutritionists, Vegans, Vegetarians
CONTACT Donald Graft
dgraft@gate.net
FREE

http://envirolink.org/arrs/index.html

Bat Conservation International Home Page ★★★★

The Bat Conservation International Home Page provides a lot of information about bats. There is a list and pictures of the 43 different types of North American bats including Peter's Ghost Faced Bat, the Lappet-Browed Bat, the Hoary Bat, the Pallid Bat, and both the Northern and Southern Yellows. The site also includes information on how to join or assist Bat Conservation International in their quest to preserve all bat species, references to books on bats, information on how to attract bats, a few hints and one handy, inexpensive title on how to construct your own bat houses.

KEYWORDS Bats, Mammals, Wildlife Conservation
AUDIENCE Animal Lovers, Bat Conservation International Members, Conservationists
FREE

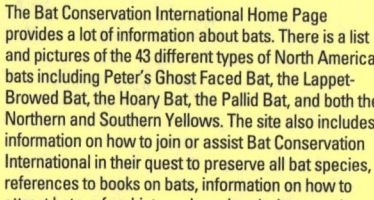

http://www.hipark.austin.isd.tenet.edu/
bat/main.html

The Birds of Fermilab ★★★★

The Birds of Fermilab is an unusual spot on the World Wide Web. Fermilab, perhaps better known as the Fermi National Accelerator Laboratory, is not only one of the better known high energy physics laboratories, but it is also situated on some of the best bird watching territory in the Chicago, Illinois area. Here you will find a comprehensive, well-organized chart covering the many birds who have been seen in the area of Fermilab. In addition, a thorough account of how to find and observe birds at Fermilab is available, as well as a companion map indicating the exact locations noted in the text.

KEYWORDS Birds, Ornithology
AUDIENCE Bird Watchers, Illinois Residents, Nature Enthusiasts, Wildlife Enthusiasts
CONTACT Peter Kasper
kasper@fnal.gov
FREE

http://www.fnal.gov/ecology/wildlife/
list.html

Butterfly Pictures ★★★★

This site contains quality images of butterflies which can be downloaded and viewed in JPEG format.

KEYWORDS Biology, Entomology, Insects, Primary/Secondary Education
AUDIENCE Biologists, Biomedical Researchers, Entomologists, Science Educators
CONTACT Philip Greenspun
philg@mit.edu
FREE

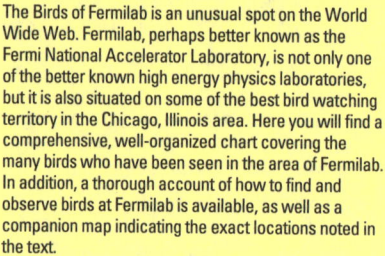

http://www-swiss.ai.mit.edu/~philg/
photo/butterflies/

CICA Project Biology ★★★

This site presents animations of Siamese Fighting Fish (Betta) to test the behavior of real fish when an animation was shown on a monitor next to the fish tank. Variables in the animation such as color, size, speed, and movement of the fish could be easily changed and recorded to videotape their effects on the fish noted. There are RGB images and MPEG's that may be downloaded.

KEYWORDS Fish, Freshwater Fish, Psychology, Science Research
AUDIENCE Biologists, Psychologists, Zoologists
CONTACT Allison Halpern, Bill Rowland
webmaster@cica.indiana.edu
FREE

http://www.cica.indiana.edu/projects/
Biology/index.html

The Department of Entomology- Michigan State University ★★★

This is the Web server of The Department of Entomology at Michigan State University. It provides a description of the Department of Entomology, faculty information, seminar series information, and other entomology-related Internet information.

KEYWORDS Entomology, Insects
AUDIENCE Educators (University), Entomologists
CONTACT webmaster@esalsun10.ent.msu.edu
FREE

http://esalsun10.ent.msu.edu

Electronic Zoo ★★

This document is a list of animal-related computer resources (Internet/Bitnet Mailing Lists, Gophers, World Wide Web Sites, Mail Servers, Usenet Newsgroups, FTP Archives, Commercial Online Services, and Bulletin Board Systems) This extensive list of resources ranges from the Canadian Society for Theoretical Biology to the East Bay Vegan Newsletter.

KEYWORDS Animal Rights, Animal Science, Veterinary Science, Zoos
AUDIENCE Animal Lovers, Biologists, Educators, Veterinarians, Zoologists
CONTACT ken@wudcm.wustl.edu
FREE

ftp://una.hh.lib.umich.edu/inetdirsstacks/
animals:boschert

The Elephant Managers Association (EMA) Home Page ★★★★

Interested in becoming a manager of elephants..... or just look like one? This is the place for you! For those of us lucky enough to have learned the arts of elephant training and husbandry and those whose job is to keep elephants in comfort and proper status in zoos around the globe, as well as people who simply prefer pachyderms, the Elephant Managers Association Web site will enthrall, entertain and enlighten. Here you will find texts of the Journal of the Elephant Managers Association, which often include interviews with professionals in the field, regional reports, information about sanctuaries and wildlife preserves, and notable events in the elephant world; material on joining the Elephant Managers Association; a rather difficult for the novice elephant trivia quiz; a link to the Indianapolis Zoo's Elephant Program, and also to a few other related sites.

- KEYWORDS Animal Husbandry, Animals, Elephants, Zookeeping
- AUDIENCE Elephant Enthusiasts, Elephant Managers, Zoo Enthusiasts, Zookeepers
- CONTACT tpolk@dialin.ind.net
- FREE

http://aazk.ind.net/ema/emahome.html

Entomology Image Gallery of Iowa State ★★★★

This site is a large image gallery of insects. Included are pictures of mosquitos of the Midwestern U.S., a beetle movie, tick movies, still images of ticks with such notables as the Lone Star Tick, images of lice and a tick dissection sequence. All images are of very high quality and are viewable by JPEG after downloading.

- KEYWORDS Entomology, Insect Biology, Insects, Molecular Biology
- AUDIENCE Biologists, Biomedical Researchers, Entomologists, Science Educators
- FREE

http://www.public.iastate.edu/~entomology/ImageGallery.html

Entomology at Colorado State University ★★★★

An up-to-date Web site containing online photos of insects, entomology-related educational programs, and extensive Internet entomology links. Available information includes material related to the entomology program at Colorado State University, entomology events and job openings around the world, and links to insect-related publications available on the Web.

- KEYWORDS Biology, Educational Programs, Entomology, Insect Biology
- AUDIENCE Entomologists, Insect Enthusiasts, Researchers, Students
- CONTACT Lou Bjostad
  lbjostad@lamar.colostate.edu
- FREE

http://www.colostate.edu/Depts/Entomology/ent.html

gopher://gopher.colostate.edu/11/ON/ACADEMIC/AGSCI/ENTOMOLO

A Fine Kettle of Fish ★★★

This is the Icthyology Database for Cornell University's MUSEServer. This site offers queries of their database by taxonomy and geography, catalog number or field number. There are also links to other Ichthyological Resources such as the NEODAT Gopher and the Neodat Project collection, the Desert Fishes Council, The MNHN (Paris) Fish Collection, Cornell Fish Collection, and the Cornell Ichthyology Collections.

- KEYWORDS Biodiversity, Ichthyology, Universities
- AUDIENCE Biodiversity Researchers, Fishery Scientists, Oceanographers
- CONTACT Julian Humphries
  jmh3@cornell.edu
- FREE

http://muse.bio.cornell.edu/taxonomy/fish.html

Fish Information Service (FINS) Index ★★★

This is an archive of information about aquariums. It covers both freshwater and marine, tropical and temperate, and reef tanks. The site provides FAQs, catalogs, pictures, movies, and links to other web sites.

- KEYWORDS Aquariums, Biology, Fish
- AUDIENCE Aquarium Keepers, Biologists, Fish Enthusiasts

- CONTACT Mark Rosenstein
  mar@actwin.com
- FREE

http://www.actwin.com/fish/index.html

FlyBase ★★★★

This site is an extensive database of genetic and molecular data for Drosophila (fruit fly) which can be accessed by hyperlinks. Information is available on Drosophila genes, chromosomal aberrations, stocks, sequences, genomic clones, and researchers. In addition, genetic and physical mapping data are available.

- KEYWORDS Bioinformatics, Drosophila, Genetics, Molecular Biology
- AUDIENCE Bioinformaticists, Biologists, Biomedical Researchers, Biotechnologists

---

Connections to Zoology
Froggies, birdies, and fishies

The online "Zoo" is always open. At many of the zoological sites on the Internet you can get in touch with virtually all the creatures that hop on the ground, swim in the ocean, or fly in the air.

Not only are there universities that provide sites for zoological information and research, but if you want to make it your career, you can access a list of the graduate and undergraduate courses at places like the University of Toronto or the University of Maine.

(http://www.zoo.latrobe.edu.au/) also, (http://www.zoo.utoronto.ca/)

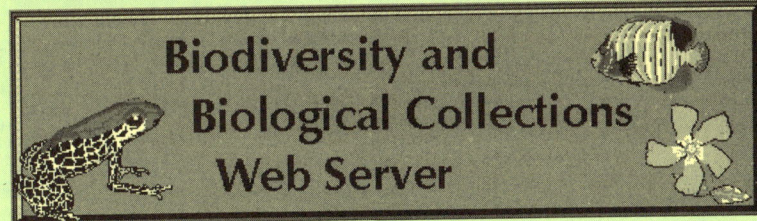

If amoebas and protozoa are your thing, there's a site devoted to these microscopic critters, as well as to the study of all animals—even humans. This site, "Zoology Information for Secondary School Students," provides easy access to the diverse field of zoology by subdividing it into highly manageable areas.

(http://www.zoo.utoronto.ca/secondary.html)

If you want to obtain a comprehensive list of zoological names and categories, check out the "International Code of Zoological Nomenclature." Here you'll find up-to-date information on the "governing" body that regulates the naming of taxa in zoology.

(http://www.york.biosis.org/zrdocs/iczn/code.html)

CONTACT flybase-help@morgan.harvard.edu
FREE

http://morgan.harvard.edu/

Furman University Insect Collection ★★★★

This site contains images of butterflies and moths. Although it is strongest in Order Lepidoptera, the collection adequately describes most other orders found in the American Southeast.

KEYWORDS Biology, Entomology, Insect Biology, Insects
AUDIENCE Biologists, Biomedical Researchers, Entomologists, Science Educators
FREE

http://www.furman.edu/~snyder/butterfly/index.html

Herp Pictures ★★★★

This site provides an extensive database of photos of reptiles. You can view the thumbnail icons first or go directly to the list of photos. Some of the photos include Cat Eating Snake, Horned Lizard with egg clutch, many frogs, Galopagos Tortoise, Rainbow Boa, American Alligator, Water Dragon, Figi Island Iguana, and many more.

KEYWORDS Animals, Herpetology, Reptiles
AUDIENCE Educators (Primary/Secondary), Reptile Enthusiasts, Students (Primary/Secondary), Zoologists
CONTACT Mike Pingleton
pingleto@ncsa.uiuc.edu
FREE

http://gto.ncsa.uiuc.edu/pingleto/lobby.html

Herpetology - Texas Natural History Collection ★★★

The Herpetology Collection is one of the research divisions of the Texas Natural History Collection in the Texas Memorial Museum at the University of Texas at Austin. The holdings consist of about 53,000 catalogued specimen. Links are provided to Preserved Specimen, Skeletons, Tape Recordings, Frozen Tissues, OnLine Database, Geographic Coverage, Taxonomic coverage, and Loans and Visits.

KEYWORDS Herpetology, Museums, Natural History, Universities
AUDIENCE Herpetologists, Researchers, Scientists
CONTACT David Cannatella
catfish@mail.utexas.edu.
FREE

http://www.utexas.edu:80/ftp/pub/tnhc/.www/herps/herps.html

Images of the Drosophila Brain ★★★★

This site at the Nagoshi Drosophila Lab at Iowa State University is an image gallery of the drosophila (fruit fly) brain. Included are serial sections of wild-type adult fly brains in GIF format. It includes names of major brain structures.

KEYWORDS Drosophila, Entomology, Insect Biology, Molecular Biology
AUDIENCE Biologists, Biomedical Researchers, Entomologists, Science Educators
FREE

ftp://ftp.bio.indiana.edu/11/Flybase/allied-data/images/brain-k-ito

Interactive Frog Dissection Kit Info Page ★★★

This site shows an interactive simulation of the dissection of a computer-generated frog. Other images and papers relevant to the program are provided.

KEYWORDS Biology, Interactive Learning, Simulation
AUDIENCE Biologists, Educators, Students
CONTACT Bill Johnston
wejohnston@lbl.gov
FREE

http://george.lbl.gov/ITG.hm.pg.docs/dissect/info.html

The Johns Hopkins Center for Alternatives to Animal Testing ★★★

The home page of the Johns Hopkins Center for Alternatives to Animal Testing (CAAT) provides an overview of the Center's history, mission, and ongoing programs, as well as an online newsletter.

KEYWORDS Animal Rights, Animal Science, Animals
AUDIENCE Activists, Animal Lovers, Researchers
CONTACT caat@jhuhyg.sph.jhu.edu
FREE

http://www.jhu.edu/~caat/

The Online Book of Parrots ★★★★

The Online Book of Parrots is destined to become one of the Websites most visited by people interested in ornithology or keeping parrots. The information here is extensive. It includes an excellent, comprehensive and simple to use taxonomic tree delineating the genealogy of every type of parrot, from the kakapo to the king. There are also a variety of indices here, including an index of pictures of psittacines and several searchable gopher indices. Some links to related sites are also available here.

KEYWORDS Birds, Ornithology, Parrots
AUDIENCE Bird Lovers, Ornithologists, Pet Owners, Taxonomists
CONTACT H -J Pfeffer
pfeffer@club.tu-clausthal.de
FREE

http://www.ub.tu-clausthal.de/p_welcome.html

Penises of the Animal Kingdom ★★★

Penises of the Animal Kingdom is the name of a scientifically accurate chart illustrated with many photographs available through the Scientific Novelty Company by mail or phone order, and advertised over the Internet. The poster, which costs $8.95, compares and contrasts the male members of various animals, including humans, giraffes, porpoises and whales. According to the online copy, Penises of the Animal Kingdom is 'More than a Reference - [it's] a Work of Art.'

KEYWORDS Animals, Humor
AUDIENCE Anatomists, Biologists, Marine Biologists, Sex Enthusiasts
CONTACT The Scientific Novelty Company
FREE

http://www.tagsys.com/Ads/SciNovelty/index.html

Program in Animal Behavior at Indiana University ★★★

This page introduces Indiana University's Center for the Integrative Study of Animal Behavior Program in Bloomington, Indiana. The center studies a variety of organisms including rabbits, bats, rodents, birds, amphibians, fish, molluscs, flies, and wasps, in a variety of settings. This page provides links to the Research Training Group (RTG) at the center, information about the faculty, and computer software archives for the study of animal behavior.

KEYWORDS Animal Science, Software, Zookeepers, Zoology
AUDIENCE Animal Behaviorists, Biologists, Nature Lovers, Zoologists
CONTACT Shan Duncan
sdduncan@indiana.edu
FREE

http://www.cisab.indiana.edu/index.html

Strange Mutants ★★★★

This site at the Nagoshi Drosophila Lab at Iowa State University is an image gallery of drosophila (fruit fly) mutants. The site is subtitled 'Some Ugly Flies We've Come Across,' and includes a headless fly and a fly with one eye transformed into an antenna.

KEYWORDS Drosophila, Entomology, Insect Biology, Molecular Biology
AUDIENCE Biologists, Biomedical Researchers, Entomologists, Science Educators
CONTACT Eric Johnson
eric-johnson@uiowa.edu
FREE

http://fly2.biology.uiowa.edu/Fly/Mutants.html

Terry Polk's Zoological Email Directory ★★★★

Terry Polk's Zoological Email Directory aims to create a hypertext, searchable index of all people currently working at zoos, aquariums, animal-related organizations and societies, schools and universities, wildlife rehabilitators, and people who research animal-related issues. The database is searchable through a myriad of keywords or search strings, and includes information on each professional's name, institution, division, geographical area, title, animals worked with, and finally, his or her Internet address. It is updated frequently.

KEYWORDS Wildlife Rehabilitation, Zoology
AUDIENCE Ethologists, Marine Biologists, Wildlife Rehabilitationists, Zoologists

CONTACT   Terry Polk
          t.polk@dialin.ind.net
FREE

http://www.wcmc.org.uk/infoserv/
    zoodir.html

Wisconsin Regional Primate Research Center ★★★★

The HTTP and Gopher servers of the Wisconsin Regional Primate Research Center (WRPRC) host the Primate Info Net, a comprehensive collection of links and information regarding primates and primatology. There are links to the Primate Center software archives and the University of Wisconsin at Madison.

KEYWORDS Animal Science, Animals, Zoology
AUDIENCE Animal Lovers, Primatologists
CONTACT   Larry Jacobsen
          jacobsen@primate.wisc.edu
FREE

http://www.primate.wisc.edu/

gopher://saimiri.primate.wisc.edu:70/1

Zoological Record Home Page ★★★★

This is the World Wide Web Home Page for the Zoological Record. The Zoological Record is an index to worldwide zoological literature, produced by BIOSIS UK, a company based in York, England. It is the oldest continuing scientific indexing service in the world, and was founded in 1864 by a group of zoologists associated with the Zoological Society of London and the Natural History Museum. This page contains links to information on BIOSIS and The Zoological Record, a link to BIOSIS' WWW server, information provided by the International Commission on Zoological Nomenclature, and a glossary of nomenclatural terms used in zoology.

KEYWORDS Animals, Education (College/University), Literature, Zoological Record
AUDIENCE Educators (University), Students (Secondary/College), Zoologists
CONTACT   Judith M. Howcroft
          jhowcroft@york.biosis.org
FREE

http://www.york.biosis.org/

Sports & Recreation

Aquatic Sports	619
Aviation	620
Career & Employment	621
Crafts & Hobbies	621
Food & Dining	624
Games	634
Gardening	636
Motor Sports	638
Organizations	639
Outdoor Recreation	640
Personal Fitness	642
Pets & Animals	643
Recreation	648
Sports	648
Travel & Tourism	653

Aquatic Sports

See also
Sports & Recreation · *Outdoor Recreation*

Aquanaut ★★★

Aquanaut is the Internet's first online magazine dedicated to the recreational and technical scuba diving community. The page contains the latest scuba news, commercial services (housing, equipment), reviews of popular dive destinations, lists of diving schools and clubs, scuba images, information including weather reports, and links to other online scuba archives.

KEYWORDS Journals, Scuba Diving, Sports Equipment, Tourism
AUDIENCE Aquatic Sports Enthusiasts, Athletes, Scuba Divers
CONTACT aquanaut@opal.com.
FREE

http://www.terra.net/aquanaut.

The Barefoot Water Skiing Page ★★★

The Barefoot Water Skiing Page is dedicated to promotion of the sport of barefoot water skiing. The page contains the men's and women's ABC national standings lists, 1995 tournament schedule, and Junior World's information as well as information about the American Barefoot Club (ABC). Other topics include Learn to Barefoot, Advanced Tricks and Starts, Equipment Information, The AWSA and ABC, Rules of Competition, Tournament Results, National Standings, Figure 8 Challenge, Footin' Images and Links, and more.

KEYWORDS Skiing, Sports Equipment, Water Skiing
AUDIENCE Athletes, Barefoot Skiing Enthusiasts, Skiing Enthusiasts
CONTACT Charlie Hill
hillcs@picard.ml.wpafb.af.mil
FREE

http://www.primenet.com/~jodell/foot/BarefootPage.html

Bruce's Paddling Page ★★★★

Bruce's Paddling Page is an exciting spot devoted to watersports which involve paddles... such as kayaking and canoeing. Although some of the material here relates specifically to the Delaware area, including local paddling organizations, weather forecasts, reports of nearby tidal levels and river flow, there is information for paddlers from all over. At this site you will find several FAQ's related to paddling, links to intriguing home pages and other Internet resources, recipes for outdoor cooking, and data concerning travel to the more far-flung paddling regions on the globe.

KEYWORDS Canoeing, Delaware, Kayaking
AUDIENCE Camping Enthusiasts, Canoers, Kayakers
CONTACT Bruce Fisher
bef@ssnet.com
FREE

http://ssnet.com/~bef/BrucesPaddlingPage.html

The Complete Surfing Guide for Coaches ★★★

This page contains excerpts from the book 'The Complete Surfing Guide for Coaches, Including Historical Notes' by renowned surfer Bruce Gabrielson. The sections include Surf Team Coaching, Judging Contests, Learning to Surf, Shaping Surfboards, and more. There is also a biography of the author and a history of the Huntington Beach Surf Clubs.

KEYWORDS Surfing
AUDIENCE Surfing Coaches, Surfing Enthusiasts
CONTACT Bruce C. Gabrielson, Ph.D.
ses@BlackMagic.Com
FREE

http://www.blackmagic.com/ses/book/toc.html

Diving Bermuda ★★★

Diving Bermuda considers itself a one-stop WWW page for all the information you need about recreational scuba diving in Bermuda. The contents include What's New? (a variety of water related links including boating information, and snorkeling and diving at carribean islands, St Kitts and Nevis), General Bermuda Scuba Information, Dive Shops and Equipment Vendors, Dive Sites, information on the Bermuda Sub-Aqua Club, information about the Bermuda Aquarium and other items of interest.

KEYWORDS Aquariums, Bermuda, Sailing, Scuba Diving
AUDIENCE Bermuda Residents, Diving Enthusiasts, Fish Enthusiasts, Scuba Divers, Tourists
FREE

http://turnpike.net.80/emporium/D/diving/

H.O. Sports Inc. ★★★

This page contains information on equipment for water skiing and knee boards. At this site, you will find information on and images of the 1995 HO Extreme Skis, the 1995 Hyperlite Wakeboards, the Hyperlite Snowboards and the1995 Heat Wave Wetsuits. This page also provides links to other ski resource pages on the Net and includes the 4th annual 'Learn to Ski' clinic schedule.

KEYWORDS Canada, Knee Boards, Skiing, Sports Equipment
AUDIENCE Sports Fans, Water Skiers
CONTACT ho_sports@halcyon.com
FREE

http://www.hosports.com/hosports

Mark Rosenstein's Sailing Page ★★★★

Mr. Rosenstein's Sailing Page is a list of Internet sailing resources. Information on races, such as the America's Cup, can be found, as well as links to sites devoted to particular classes of ships, plus maritime-related government and educational sites.

KEYWORDS	Boating, Sailing
AUDIENCE	Boating Enthusiasts, Sailors
CONTACT	Mark Rosenstein mbr@bellcore.com
FREE	

http://community.bellcore.com/mbr/sailing-page.html

The Windsurfer's Mailing List & Web Page ★

The Windsurfer's Web page is the Internet's first global mailing list designed to discuss the sport of windsurfing. In addition to details about joining the mailing list, this site also has links to other windsurfing-related Web sites, including several pages from members of the mailing list.

KEYWORDS	Outdoor Recreation, Water Sports, Windsurfing
AUDIENCE	Surfing Enthusiasts, Water Sports Enthusiasts, Windsurfing Enthusiasts
CONTACT	webmaster@fly.com
FREE	

http://www.fly.com/Fly/Wml/wml_welcome.html

WoodenBoat ★★★

This site for WoodenBoat, a magazine for Wooden boat owners, builders, and designers has information from WoodenBoat and Professional BoatBuilder publications. Users can subscribe online as well as order products from the company. This web site also includes information about a boating school and an online catalog.

KEYWORDS	Boat Construction, Boating
AUDIENCE	Boat Builders, Boat Owners, Boaters, Boating Enthusiasts
CONTACT	woodenboat@hypernet.com
FREE	

http://media1.hypernet.com/WoodenBoat.html

Aviation

See also
Engineering & Technology · *Aeronautical Engineering*
Government & Politics · *Agencies*

Aeronet Aviation Airlines ★★★

This home page features Aeronet - a network for aviation industry. Here you'll find links to home pages of airlines, airports, aircraft producers, Aviation News newsletter, aviation conferences, universities, regulations, etc.

KEYWORDS	Air Transportation, Airlines, United Kingdom
AUDIENCE	Aerospace Industry Professionals, Aviators, Business Professionals, International Travelers, Tourists
CONTACT	Peter@aeronet.demon.co.uk
FREE	

http://www.demon.co.uk/aeronet/

Aircraft Index By Type ★★★

This page provides a long list of links to information about all kinds of aircraft. You will find specifications, descriptions, and performance information. There are no graphics.

KEYWORDS	Airplanes, Aviation
AUDIENCE	Aerospace Industry Professionals, Aviation Enthusiasts, Aviators, Pilots
FREE	

http://www.brooklyn.cuny.edu/rec/air/aircraft/types/types.html

Fly With Us ★★★

If you are ready for the thrill and the challenge of a lifetime, you can take the controls of a high-performance fighter jet in Moscow and break the speed of sound with one of the best pilots in the world as your co-pilot! Fly With Us, the original Russian purveyor of military flights for civilians, is your host on this vacation of a lifetime. You'll fly to exotic, enchanting Moscow and stay in a first-class hotel. At your choice, you can visit some of the world's best theaters, restaurants, museums and exotic nightclubs and casinos. All information about this vacation is linked to this page.

KEYWORDS	Aviation, Russia, Tourism
AUDIENCE	Aviation Enthusiasts, Pilots, Travelers
CONTACT	Ro Nagey RoNagey@design-design.com
FREE	

http://www.IntNet.net/mig29/

Minnesota Department of Transportation's Aeronautical Information Server ★★★

This site offers a variety of general and educational resources related to Airplanes, Aviation, and Aeronautics. The Sky's the Limit is a series of books featuring people who have made contributions to the field of aviation. Minnesota's Aviation Information Directory lists career and scholarship information for future pilots, as well as a listing of educational institutions that offer aviation degrees. In addition, there are several collections of aviation and aeronautics lesson plans for elementary and kindergarten school science programs.

KEYWORDS	Aeronautics, Airplanes, Aviation, Minnesota
AUDIENCE	Aeronautics Enthusiasts, Airplane Enthusiasts, Aviation Enthusiasts, Aviators
CONTACT	mdot@augsburg.edu
FREE	

http://bbs.augsburg.edu/mdot/mdot.html

Paramotor Home Page ★★

The Paramotor is a motorized paraglider. One of the safest and smallest aircraft in the world, the paramotor is launched from the ground and requires no license. This page is sponsored by the manufacturer, and describes more about what a Paramotor is, and contains several pictures and video clips to illustrate how the Paramotor works. In addition ordering and contact information is given online.

KEYWORDS	Adventure Travel, Aviation, Parasailing, Product Information
AUDIENCE	Aviators, Paragliders, Parasailors, Thrill Seekers
CONTACT	Cyberactive
FREE	

http://cyberactive-1.com/paramotor/html/para2.html

Rec.Aviation Gopher Hole ★★★

This gopher server contains information and resources related to aviation and acts as an archive site for discussions on the Usenet group rec.aviation. Some of the material provided includes articles, ride reports, flight planning sheets, and weather.

KEYWORDS	Airplanes, Aviation, Flight Simulation, Usenet Newsgroups
AUDIENCE	Aerospace Engineers, Aviators, Pilots
CONTACT	William LeFebvre lefebvre@dis.anl.gov
FREE	

gopher://av.eecs.nwu.edu/

The World-Wide Web Virtual Library - Aviation ★★★★

This is an excellent meta-index with a great number of links to universities specializing in aviation education, home pages of airlines and airports, and technical reports. Also provided are pictures, history, military aircrafts, publications, and links to other aviation sites.

KEYWORDS	Aviation
AUDIENCE	Aerospace Industry Professionals, Aviators, Business Professionals, Tourists
CONTACT	Brian Gamage gamageb@cts.db.erau.edu
FREE	

http://www.db.erau.edu/www_virtual_lib/aviation.html

Career & Employment

Arts & Music · *Career & Employment*

EOA (Employment Opportunities in Australia), Opportunities In - Sports ★★★

Employment Opportunities in Australia provides job listings for sports and sport-related positions.

Keywords Australia, Career, Sports
Audience Professional sports players, coaches, managers
Contact eoainfo@eoa.com.au
Free

http://www.employment.com.au/sport.html

Crafts & Hobbies

See also
Arts & Music · *Decorative Arts*
Arts & Music · *Design*
Humanities & Social Sciences · *Area & Cultural Studies*

Antiquarian Booksellers' Association of America ★★★

The Antiquarian Booksellers' Association of America was founded in 1949 to encourage interest in rare books and manuscripts and to maintain the highest standards in the antiquarian book trade. The WWW site provides information about ABAA members and their specialties. It is intended for the use of all those who may desire professional service in the purchase, sale or appraisal of antiquarian books and manuscripts.

Keywords Antiquarian Books, Antiques, Books, Collectibles
Audience Antique Collectors
Contact abaa@panix.com
Free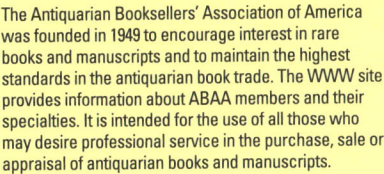

http://www.clark.net/pub/rmharris/abaa.html

Antique Tractor Forum ★★★

The Antique Tractor Forum's second page has no link to a first page. However the resources available through this site include a gopher server, a 'Tractor Image Depot,' subscription services, the Ageless Iron Expo, the Antique Mechanics Home Page, several FAQs, and a search tool.

Keywords Antiques, Associations, Collectibles
Audience Antique Collectors
Free

http://ledger.co.forsyth.nc.us/www/tractor/at_forum_page_2.html

Connections to Scuba Diving
Glub, glub, glub . . .

Some of nature's best handiwork is found below sea level, and if you are interested in seeing marine life or learning how to get to the best diving sites, the World Wide Web can take you there.

Whether it is scuba diving off the coast of Belize (some say it's the best in the world) or the Great Barrier Reef in Australia, you can find out how to get there, what it will cost, if there are group diving tours, and the best time to go. One of several Internet connections you can check is Rick's Master Scuba Links, which includes dive destinations and an adventure tours directory.

(http://www.evansville.net/~mmd/rscuba.html)

also, (http://www.travelsource.com/scuba/)

also, (http://www.travelsource.com/exotic/blackbird.html)

If you are interested in joining a scuba diving club or want to take lessons, there are many sites on the Web with the information you need. Want to find out what's happening at the University of Queensland Underwater Club or hear sounds from a diving expedition? Just check out Scuba Diving or Matti Leinio (SCUBA index) on the Internet.

(http://www.hut.fi/~mleinio/scubai.html)

Antiques Index ★★★

This is the Mankato, Minnesota Web Index for Antiques and Collectibles. The site also includes guidelines to help choose and negotiate with an antique dealer. The purpose of this server is to provide information about and images of antiques to people who are now to collecting.

Keywords Antiques, Collectibles, Meta-Index (Antiques)
Audience Antique Collectors
Free

http://www.ic.mankato.mn.us/antiques/Antiques.html

Antiques and The Arts Weekly ★★★

Antiques and The Arts Weekly advertises itself as the 'nation's leading weekly publication covering the antiques trade.' Each week, Antiques and The Arts Weekly averages 200 pages, including hundreds of detailed listings of auctions with photos, a calendar of antiques shows, and extensive coverage of museum and gallery exhibitions, historical society programs, book reviews, and antiques show and auction coverage from around the country. Visit the site for sample articles and subscription information.

Keywords Antiques, Collectibles, Magazines
Audience Antique Collectors
Free

http://www.connix.com/thebee/aweb/aa.htm

Callsigns for Ham Radio ★★★

Users interested in accessing the call numbers and names of amateur ham radio callsigns will find the database they need at this site. By entering the callsign, users can find out the license name, class, and address.

Keywords Ham Radio, Radio
Audience Ham Radio Enthusiasts, Internet Users
Contact Mark Eichin
eichin@mit.edu.
Free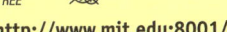

http://www.mit.edu:8001/callsign/

telnet://callsign.cs.buffalo.edu

Crafts & Hobbies

Canadian Vintage Radio Society ★★★

The Canadian Vintage Radio Society is a registered non-profit organization dedicated to the Preservation, Restoration & Collecting of Antique Radios & Related Items. Online links are to the Radio Waves publication, classified ads, fact sheets, and more.

KEYWORDS Antiques, Collectibles, Societies
AUDIENCE Antique Collectors
FREE

http://www.supernet.ab.ca/Mall/Recreation/cvrs.html

The Ceramics Gopher ★★

The SDSU Ceramics Gopher is a database of glazes, with general information about ceramics and glazes. Users will find articles about ceramics, databases with analyses of ceramics materials and glazes, and archived information from the ClayArt newsgroup. This gopher also includes environmental and safety information in addition to listings of ceramic suppliers.

KEYWORDS Art, Ceramics
AUDIENCE Ceramic Artists, Crafts Enthusiasts
CONTACT Richard Burkett
    rburkett@ucssun1.sdsu.edu
FREE

gopher://gopher.sdsu.edu:70/11/SDSU%20Campus%20Topics/Departmental%20Information/Art%20Department/The%20Ceramics%20Gopher

Classified Flea Market ★★★
COMMERCIAL

The Classified Flea Market (CFM) is a weekly 100,000-reader-circulation shopping publication distributed free in the San Francisco East Bay area. Each issue contains over 3,000 ads. Users will find categories of ads such as business, music, real estate, and services. In addition, a listing of and links to retail establishments that carry CFM weekly is available.

KEYWORDS Antiques, Classified Ads, Collectibles, Flea Markets
AUDIENCE Antique Collectors, Californians
FREE

http://www.cfm.com/cfm/

Collectible Web Services - Free Advertising! ★★★

Collectible Web Services offers free ad service on the Internet for collectors. There are links to for sale ads, wanted ads and electronic storefront services, as well as links to the WWW Virtual Library of Collecting.

KEYWORDS Antiques, Classified Ads, Collectibles
AUDIENCE Advertisers, Antique Collectors
FREE

http://iquest.com/~cws/free_ads

Collectors' Network ★★★

An electronic magazine for collectors of any kind, the pages of Collectors' Network contain comprehensive indices of collectors' resources on the Internet as well as pointers to the various Usenet newsgroups of interest to collectors. Also within these pages are schedules of regional collectors' and antique shows, as well as other information.

KEYWORDS Antiques, Collectibles
AUDIENCE Collectors
CONTACT Mark Paterson
    collector@netcom.com
FREE

ftp://ftp.netcom.com/pub/co/collector/collect.html

Diana's Textile Server ★★★

Diana's Textile Server contains links to Web sites that will be useful for those interested in crafts or sewing. Users will find a bulletin board for crafters, where individuals can post questions or hold discussions on different topics; and a store search form, which allows users to look up over 1200 crafts materials stores around the world. Links to other resources are listed by topics, such as crocheting, embroidery, knitting, spinning, and weaving, with sources of goods, organizations, listservs, and individual projects related to each category.

KEYWORDS Knitting, Sewing, Textiles
AUDIENCE Crafts Enthusiasts, Crafts Materials Suppliers, Sewing Enthusiasts
FREE

http://palver.terminus.com/crafts/index.html

Gemological Survey ★★

GemNET Precious stone index and survey presents an online catalogue of popular precious and semi-precious gems which are currently purchased, worn, or collected by individuals who utilize the Web.

KEYWORDS Antiques, Collectibles, Gem Dealers, Meta-Index (Gems)
AUDIENCE Antique Collectors
FREE

http://www.intac.com/~edwards/ngems.html

General Woodworking Information ★★★

This site provides links to various pages which relate to the topic of woodworking. These pages include various FAQs and information about other woodworking aficionados.

KEYWORDS Crafts, Hobbies, Woodworking
AUDIENCE Crafts Enthusiasts, Woodworkers
CONTACT Michael D. Sullivan
    mds@access.digex.net
FREE

http://access.digex.com/~mds/woodwork.html

Glass Insulators ★★★

Glass Insular collecting is a relatively new hobby, with approximately 2500 collectors involved in organizations and/or subscribing to publications. Information on this hobby is available online under the categories of books, magazines, the National Insulator Association, Insulator Clubs, a mailing list and color photographs.

KEYWORDS Antiques, Collectibles, Glass Insulators, Hobbies
AUDIENCE Antique Collectors
FREE

http://www.resilience.com/insulators

Herb and Tobacco Flip Pipe ★★
COMMERCIAL

The Herb and Tobacco Flip Pipe Web page advertises foldable pipes made of wood. The product is 'designed and intended for tobacco and legal herb use only.' Users may order via postal mail.

KEYWORDS Pipe Smoking, Wood
AUDIENCE Shoppers, Smokers
FREE

http://www.infotank.com/FlipPipe/

The Internet Antique Shop ★★★

The TIAS Internet Antique Shop is an excellent launching point for a search of antiques and collectibles sites on the Net. It has an antiques mall, services, publications, and loads of other resources on the Web.

KEYWORDS Antiques, Collectibles, Online Shopping
AUDIENCE Antique Collectors
FREE

http://www.rivendell.com/antiques

The Internet Auction List ★★★

The Internet Auction List is a central listing of auction Web pages, created by USA Web. The goal is to present the most complete and useful listing of Auction Web sites available. There are about 40 different auctions currently listed and new ones added all the time.

KEYWORDS Antiques, Auctions, Collectibles
AUDIENCE Antique Collectors
FREE

http://www.usaweb.com/usaweb/auction.html

Joseph Wu's Origami Page ★★★

Anyone who is interested in the Japanese art of paper folding, Origami, will find a cornucopia of useful information at Joseph Wu's Origami Page. Besides an overview of the art and history of origami, information about origami organizations around the world, and instructions on how to create your own origami, this site contains a gallery of photos of original origami. This site also includes diagrams and files for learning origami, available in postscript, PDF, gopher and FTP form. A collection of pointers to other origami Web sites is also compiled, along with related origami Web documents.

KEYWORDS Images, Japanese Art, Origami
AUDIENCE Crafts Enthusiasts, Japanese Culture Enthusiasts

Crafts & Hobbies   623

CONTACT jwu@cs.ubc.ca
FREE
http://www.cs.ubc.ca/spider/jwu/origami.html

Katsu Custom Works

The Katsu Custom Works web site offers product information on this company's hand painted, ornamental wall lights. The site provides images of a few of the lights including price and delivery information.

KEYWORDS Crafts, Decorative Lights
AUDIENCE Craft Shoppers, Gallery Shoppers, Light Dealers
FREE
http://www.usis.com/~dneal/katsu/

Maine Antique Digest Magazine

The Maine Antique Digest is a monthly newspaper that covers the marketplace for antiques and art in the U.S., Canada, and England. The online site provides links to the Digest's Table of Contents and some articles, book reviews, advertisements, auctions, resources, subscription and email information.

KEYWORDS Antiques, Auctions, Collectibles, Magazines
AUDIENCE Antique Collectors
FREE
http://www.maine.com/mad/Welcome.html

Mike's Clock Clinic

Mike is the expert on the Atmos clock, including the 150th anniversary special edition Atmos by Jaeger-LeCoultre. The Web site offers advice on the Atmos clock, its care and operation, and a system for dating the Atmos. There are links to a clock repair page and to two FTP sites, as well as a newsgroup.

KEYWORDS Antiques, Clocks, Collectibles, Horology
AUDIENCE Antique Collectors
FREE
http://www.webcom.com/~z4murray/

Non-Sports Cards Pages

This page brings you information sports cards—NOT! It is dedicated to non-sports card collecting including promo cards for the new Star Wars Card Sets and the Topps X-Files (Season 1) Cards, the newsgroups such as rec.collecting.cards.non-sports (deals with ONLY Non-Sport Cards), rec.arts.comics.marketplace (deals with comic-related materials), rec.arts.sf.marketplace (deals with science fiction materials); cartoons, comics, and artwork, as well as television, and more.

KEYWORDS Card Collecting, Cartoons, Newsgroups, Star Wars
AUDIENCE Collectors, Educators (University), Science Fiction Enthusiasts, Students (University)
CONTACT rkohlbus@dining.umd.edu
FREE
http://empire.umd.edu

Connections To Finding A Hobby
Idle hands are the devil's workshop

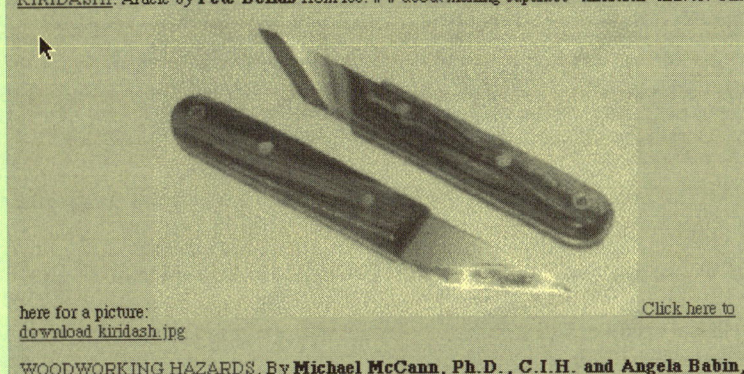

If you're into collecting stamps, wooden toys, vintage clothing— or woodworking, knitting, creating handbags, or doing beadwork—you will find thousands of people on the Internet who share your interests.

You can find out how to obtain a quilting supplier's address, catalogues on sewing machines and rubber stamps, even movie collectibles such as Star Trek memorabilia, and more.

Did you know that to bend wood you should spend one hour per inch-thickness steaming the block of wood? This age-old technique was used by ship builders and carpenters for wooden ornaments made of oak and mahogany. Such information can be found at the "General Woodworking Information" site on the World Wide Web.

(http://access.digex.com/~mds/woodwork.html)

Orientique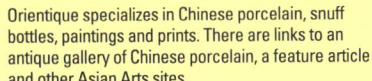

Orientique specializes in Chinese porcelain, snuff bottles, paintings and prints. There are links to an antique gallery of Chinese porcelain, a feature article and other Asian Arts sites.

KEYWORDS Antiques, China, Collectibles
AUDIENCE Antique Collectors
CONTACT joef@hk.super.net
FREE
http://www.hk.super.net/~joeyf/orientiq/orientiq.htm

Random House - House of Collectibles

This is the homepage for the House of Collectibles publishers. Here you'll find information for collectors and dealers of all types of antiques and collectibles. Links are to New Titles for 1995, Tours and Promotional Information, HOC Newsletters, Collectorware, and a Suggestion Box. There are also pointers to other collectibles resources online.

KEYWORDS Antiques, Books, Collectibles, Random House
AUDIENCE Antique Collectors
FREE
http://www.randomhouse.com/HC/

Rockhounds Information Page

The page was created by mineral enthusiasts, and contains links to sites of interest to mineral enthusiasts. It also contains the archive for the Rockhounds Mailing List. This is a good starting point for those interested in minerals and rockhounding.

KEYWORDS Earth Sciences, Geology, Minerals
AUDIENCE General Public, Mineral Enthusiasts, Rock Collectors, Students (Primary/Secondary)
CONTACT rockhounds-owner@infodyn.com
FREE
http://www.rahul.net/infodyn/rockhounds/rockhounds.html

W6YX- Stanford Amateur Radio Club ★★★

The Stanford Amateur Radio Club's home pages offer information on the Club's activities and current projects. Users can obtain information on Amateur Radio License courses given by the club, as well as license exam dates and locations. There are links to amateur radio resources such as the up-to-date FCC callsign database, and to other amateur radio clubs around the world.

- KEYWORDS: Ham Radio, Radio
- AUDIENCE: Amateur Radio Enthusiasts, Communications Engineers, Ham Radio Enthusiasts, Radio Enthusiasts
- CONTACT: Stanford Amateur Radio Club - W6YX
  w6yx-info@w6yx.stanford.edu
- FREE

http://w6yx.stanford.edu

W^5 Wood Working on the World Wide Web ★★★

The Wood Working on the World Wide Web (W^5) page was created to provide a forum for woodworkers all over the world to exchange information. Users will find general woodworking tips, information about different types of tools/machines such as saws, and excerpts from the book Woodsmith. Woodworkers may also post questions or responses in the HELP-LINE section. A compilation of pointers to other wood crafts sites are also provided, as well as downloadable shareware CAD programs.

- KEYWORDS: Carpentry, Woodworking
- AUDIENCE: Crafts Enthusiasts, Woodworkers
- CONTACT: Gary Straub
  gstraub@mail.coin.missouri.edu
- FREE

http://cyclops.iucf.indiana.edu/~brown/hyplan/wood.html

Wits' End Antiques ★★★

Wits' End Antiques buys and sells American and European Art Glass, Fine & Costume Jewelry, and Fine China. Its online site offers an antique search feature, an antique shop, a survey, a show schedule, and a suggestion box.

- KEYWORDS: Antiques, Collectibles, Online Shopping
- AUDIENCE: Antique Collectors
- CONTACT: rwexler@tias.com
- FREE

http://www.rivendell.com/witsend/

The Wooden Toy ★★★

This site contains images of wooden toys and brief histories. The contents of the site include selections of outdoor toys and games (wagons and soldiers), school and learning (desks with abaci, blocks), handcrafted and industrial toys (wooden Mickey Mouses, Pinocchios), games (football, horse races), etc. Most of the toys date from the early 20th century and are European (Italian and French) in origin.

- KEYWORDS: Art Exhibitions, Collectibles, Toys, Woodworking
- AUDIENCE: Children, Educators, Toy Collectors

FREE

http://www.pd.astro.it/forms/mostra/mostra_i.html

World Wide Quilting ★★★

The World Wide Quilting page provides an archive of all types of information for quilting enthusiasts and craftspeople. Users will find basic quilting information and techniques, diagrams, and foundations for making quilts. Calendars of quilts shows and exhibitions, book reviews, and information about different quilting organizations are also included. Quilters may also get in touch with each other through the quilting newsgroups, or through the trading posts.

- KEYWORDS: Book Reviews, Quilting, Sewing, Textiles
- AUDIENCE: Crafts Enthusiasts, Quilting Enthusiasts, Sewing Enthusiasts
- CONTACT: QHomePage@ttsw.com
- FREE

http://ttsw.com/MainQuiltingPage.html

Food & Dining

See also
Health & Medicine · Reference
Popular Culture & Entertainment · Lifestyles

A List of Food and Cooking Sites ★★★

This site is fully devoted to listing food and cooking sites on the Web. It is produced by Amy Gale out of New Zealand and contains links to recipes from the rec.food.recipes newsgroup archives, general recipe sites such as 'Callahan's Cookbook,' 'Fat Free Recipe Archive,' and the 'Internet Kitchen;' ethnic recipe sites such as 'La Comida Mexicana,' and an Indian recipes FTP site; vegetarian recipes and information; drinks; restaurants; commercial sites; and miscellaneous sites such as 'The Jean-Paul Sartre Cookbook,' for some good ol' down-home existential fare.

- KEYWORDS: Archives, Cooking, Meta-Index (Recipes), Recipes
- AUDIENCE: Cooking Enthusiasts, Cooks
- CONTACT: Larry W. Virden
  lwv26@cas.org
- FREE

http://www.vuw.ac.nz/who/Amy.Gale/recipes/other-sites.html

A Napa Valley Virtual Visit ★★★

The Napa Valley Virtual Visit takes us on an indepth online tour of California's Napa Valley. Wine, wineries, restaurants, dining, events, sightseeing, shopping, lodging, personal and corporate travel information are all represented. There are lots of images and some QuickTime video clips available.

- KEYWORDS: California, Wineries, Winery Tours, Wines
- AUDIENCE: Wine Enthusiasts
- FREE

http://www.freerun.com/

A World of Tea ★★★ (COMMERCIAL)

This page is sponsored by the Stash Tea Company. It provides a source for tea information, tea news, tea recipes, tea history, tea quotes, teapots and tea trivia. Many links to other tea-related sites are also available.

- KEYWORDS: Herbs, Tea
- AUDIENCE: Cooks, History Buffs, Tea Enthusiasts, Tourists
- CONTACT: Dave Schooler
  dave@stashtea.com
- FREE

http://www.stashtea.com/~tea

Acats Internet Bar Pages ★★★

The Acats Aristocats Bar and Party Crew Internet Bar Page was created by a group of bartenders to provide information about making and serving wine, cocktails, and long drinks. Users will find a drink database, where they may look up the recipes for their favorite drinks or drink contents, bartending job listings, and fictional stories about tending bars. The Online Drink List contains the top drinks that the Acat bartenders are producing, and the Ultimate Drink contains recipes contributed by readers. Other features include the Drink of the Week recipe, a bulletin board for questions, and the IKEA guide to building your own bar.

- KEYWORDS: Alcohol, Bartending, Wine
- AUDIENCE: Cocktail Drinker, Entertainers, Wine Drinkers
- CONTACT: mikwe@isy.liu.se
- FREE

http://www.isy.liu.se/~mikwe/acats.html

American Wine on the Web ★★★★

American Wine on the Web offers reports on the wines, wineries, people and events of the wine regions in the US and the Americas. In addition to interviews and articles on wine culture and wine in culture (e.g. the role of wine in Passover and Easter), there are wine country reports from regional editors in six winemaking regions of the US (which include information on local wineries and wine clubs and events).

- KEYWORDS: Magazines, Wine, Wine Tasting, Wines
- AUDIENCE: Festival Enthusiasts, Restaurant Enthusiasts, Wine Enthusiasts
- CONTACT: Gerry Troy
  wine@2way.com
- FREE

http://www.deltanet.com:80/food/wine/

The Atlanta Restaurant Guide ★★★

Researched and entered by students at the Georgia Institute of Technology, the Atlanta Restaurant Review links to restaurants by price and food type and provides further information about Atlanta.

- KEYWORDS: Georgia, Restaurant Guides, Restaurants
- AUDIENCE: Dining Enthusiasts, Gourmets, Tourists

Food & Dining

CONTACT gt5548b@prism.gatech.edu
FREE

http://www.gatech.edu/3020/restaurants/atlanta.restaurants.html

Austrian Restaurant Guide ★★

This brief guide to Austrian Restaurants compiled by Keith Waclena of the University of Chicago during a family trip in 1994, makes no attempt at completeness. It is written by an American for Americans traveling to Austria and corrections or comments are welcome, especially from native Austrians. There is also a companion guide to Austrian beer available as a link. The site is interesting to visit, but very weak on links.

KEYWORDS Austria, Dining Out, Food, Restaurants
AUDIENCE Tourists
CONTACT k-waclena@uchicago.edu
FREE

http://www.lib.uchicago.edu/keith/austria/restaurants.html

Beer Hunting In Belgium ★★★

This site is home to a seven-part series on beer and brewing in Belgium. It is interesting and informative and evidently updated frequently. It does, however, have no visual enhancements that would greatly add to the tour. There are no links to other Web sites.

KEYWORDS Beer, Belgium, Collectibles, Travel
AUDIENCE Beer Enthusiasts, Belgians, Tourists
FREE

http://karikukko.pc.helsinki.fi/BeerHunting/Intro.html

Beer and Wine Reference Information ★★★★

The Beer and Wine Reference Information pages list hundreds of links to beer, wine, ale, and pub related pages on the Net. Some of the links include the Belgian Beer List, personal beer pages, pub guides (in Cambridge, Dublin, NYC), individual breweries, wine FAQs, information about Hungarian wine, wine societies and vineyards, and more.

KEYWORDS Alcohol, Beer, Wine
AUDIENCE Beer Enthusiasts, Tourists
FREE

http://www.panix.com/~clay/beer.html

Ben's Mega Veggie Index ★★★★

Ben's Mega Veggie Index is a Web site devoted to vegetarian issues and animal rights. There are links to many articles here, devoted to a number of issues, as well as to various vegetarian societies both in England and the United States. There is also a link to the Meta-Index of Animal Rights Information. The alphabetical index of vegetarian issues includes everything from getting enough vitamin B12 to vegetarian beers to factory farming to gardening to osteoporosis to keeping dogs and cats on vegetarian diets. This is not a site for finding recipes or restaurants, but to explore the ethical and medical issues to become, and remain non-carnivorous.

KEYWORDS Animal Rights, Health, Veganism, Vegetarianism
AUDIENCE Animal Rights Activists, Fitness Enthusiasts, Researchers, Vegans, Vegetarians
CONTACT Ben Leamy
leamy@uel.ac.uk
FREE

http://www.uel.ac.uk/pers/1420/vegindex.html

The Best Of Free Spirit Health Restaurant Guide ★★★

Free Spirit provides New York City vegetarians with some contact information for vegetarian and near-vegetarian restaurants and clubs throughout Manhattan and New York City. This text file listing is organized by location (such as East Village, 14th-58th Midtown, Brooklyn), and by strictness of vegetarianism. Some examples are Totally Vegetarian, Vegetarian with Fish &/or Dairy, and Not Totally Vegetarian. Street locations and hours are listed.

KEYWORDS New York, Restaurants, Vegetarianism
AUDIENCE New York City Vegetarians, New York Residents, Vegetarians
CONTACT TAG Online Mall
webmaster@tagsys.com
FREE

http://www.tagsys.com/Ads/FreeSpirit/restaurant.html

The Blue Directory of Food & Beverage Businesses ★★★

The Blue Directory of Food and Beverage Businesses provides access to companies whose services can aid do benefit the Food and Beverage Industry, including Associations and Organizations, Delivery Services-Specialty Gifts, Educational Centers such as Culinary Arts and Trade Schools, Food Sciences sites, Manufacturers, Publications and References, Restaurants, Retailers and Wholesalers. It is produced by Winzig-Sayles Corporation as a service. Winzig-Sayles provides WEB consulting and production of Corporate Pages for the Food, Beverage and Foodservice Industries.

KEYWORDS Beverages, Cooking, Food
AUDIENCE Business Professionals, Cooking Enthusiasts, Cooks
CONTACT Webmaster
BPAF74B@prodigy.com
FREE

http://www.2way.com/food/pvo/bluedir.html

Bologna - Restaurants ★★

This site describing a dozen restaurants in the Bologna, Italy area is rather light, but does include good descriptions. The restaurants are predominantly Italian, with one Mexican and one Greek selection.

KEYWORDS International Cuisine, Italy, Restaurants
AUDIENCE Dining Enthusiasts
CONTACT dore.cxr@ds.net.it
FREE

http://www.dsnet.it/Bologna/engl_ristoranti.html

Boston Restaurants by Cuisine ★★★

Boston Restaurants by Cuisine is organized A to Z by cuisine type from Afghan to Brazilian to Continental, Indonesian, Mexican, or Vietnamese. They are also organized by area and there is an opportunity to send in your own restaurant review to keep the site up-to-date.

KEYWORDS Boston, Cuisine, Restaurant Guides, Restaurants
AUDIENCE Dining Enthusiasts, Gourmets, Tourists
FREE

http://genoa.osf.org:8001/boston-food/boston-by-cuisine.html

The Boyer Coffee Company Home Page ★★★★

The Boyer Coffee Company Home Page is a coffee, tea or spice lover's dreamscape mirage glistening in the confines of the World Wide Web. For the hot drink connoisseur, the mecca of The Boyer Coffee Company awaits, complete with a collection of reasonably-priced coffees along with some more expensive and exotic types, including Celebes Kalossi Select, Jamaican Blue Mountain, Genuine Yemen Mocha, Ethiopian Yrgacheffe, and Tanzanian Peaberry. There is an equally impressive selection of teas and spices, including whole cumin, whole hibiscus flowers, ground jalapeno peppers, many different types of peppercorns, and powdered vanilla. Also available are coffee and tea accessories, gift boxes, flavored syrups and currently, a nifty little recipe for macaroons.

KEYWORDS Coffee, Food, Spices, Tea
AUDIENCE Chefs, Coffee Lovers, Cooks, Students, Tea Enthusiasts
CONTACT William Boyer
boyers@usa.net
FREE

http://www.bid.com/bid/boyers

CheeseNet ★★★★

The marvellous CheeseNet has become the supreme cheeserie of the World Wide Web. Dazzling curdled milk afficionados with the most remarkable cheese poetry, this site gracefully links to the purveyors of Internet cheeses and the archives of cheese recipes, and disseminates the incredible History of Cheese. This is the place to find out what mozzarella is really made of, partake in an interactive cheesemaking demonstration, learn the lusty language of cheese (find out if your cheese is 'dry matter,' 'earthy,' 'barnyardy, or 'open' and 'supple'), behold a picture-perfect panorama of provolone , or simply ask a question of Dr. Cheese. Find out for good whether your cheese is innocuous and virtually unnoticeable or bland, rank and buttery.

KEYWORDS Cooking, Poetry, Recipes
AUDIENCE Cheese Lovers, Cooks

Food & Dining

CONTACT Kyle P. Whelliston
kpw@efn.org

FREE

http://www.efn.org/~kpw/cheesenet.html

Chile Today Hot Tamale ★★★
COMMERCIAL

According to this site, 'After salt, the chile pepper has become the most frequently-used seasoning and condiment in the world.' Here, one can join the Chile of the Month Club, or the Hot Sauce of the Month Club, buy some gift boxes, or learn some facts about the spicy peppers. One can order online or by fax or phone.

KEYWORDS Condiments, Gifts
AUDIENCE Chili Pepper Enthusiasts, Cooks, Shoppers, Spicy Food Enthusiasts
CONTACT Chile Today Hot Tamale
chile@emall.com
FREE

http://eMall.Com/Chile/Chile1.html

The Chile-Heads Home Page ★★★★

The Chile-Heads Home Page is an outstanding resource for all of your hot and spicy food and gardening needs. Here you will find out everything conceivable about chile peppers, from Asia to South America. There is a vast searchable database of recipes waiting for you here, which includes chutneys, alcoholic beverages, soups, salads, salsas, jams, stews, muffins...and more. There is even a recipe for Mexican Jalapeno Chocolate Cream Cake. In addition to recipes, available at this site is a list of United States restaurants, organized by region—primarily chile hot spots—appealing to chile devotees; a link to the Creole and Cajun Recipe Page; a great deal of information about growing, harvesting, and preserving peppers; links to additional online resources for books, magazines, cookbooks and catalogs; phone numbers and addresses of similar businesses that are not yet online; a list of over 500 hot sauces; directions for making chile ristras, and finally, the answer to the age- old question 'What is the hottest pepper?'

KEYWORDS Chili Peppers, Food, Recipes
AUDIENCE Chile Pepper Enthusiasts, Cooks, Gardeners, Spicy Food Enthusiasts
CONTACT Mike Bowers
Mikeb@radonc.ucdmc.ucdavis.edu
FREE

http://chile.ucdmc.ucdavis.edu:8000/www/chile.html

The Chocolate Page ★★★★

The Chocolate Page is a Web site devoted to all the possible uses of chocolate. Along with quite a few recipes for dishes ranging from chocolate cheesecake to 'Chocolate Chirpie Chip Cookies' (chocolate recipes which include insects), you will find chocolate trivia, online sources for chocolate and the FAQ for the Usenet newsgroup Alt.Food.Chocolate. Washington D.C. dwellers will find special merits here, as one link concerns the best places to eat chocolate in the nation's capitol.

KEYWORDS Chocolate, Food, Recipes
AUDIENCE Chocolate Lovers, Cooks, Washington D.C. Residents

FREE

http://www.qrc.com/~sholubek/choco/start.htm

Clos La Chance Wines ★★★
COMMERCIAL

Clos LaChance Wines is a small, private company dedicated to the production of top-quality Chardonnay, Pinot Noir and Cabernet Sauvignon wines. The Web site is divided into a company overview, news, products and services and contact and support. There is an online order form for wines and gifts.

KEYWORDS Online Shopping, Wineries, Wines
AUDIENCE Wine Enthusiasts
CONTACT webmaster@commerce.com
FREE

http://www.commerce.com/clos/clos-top.html

Club Oenologie Francois Rabelais ★★★

Club Oenologie is a wine tasting organization based in Paris, France. Their wine site offers comprehensive worldwide links to wine sites as well as information about the club, its members, sponsors, etc. There is a huge graphic of France in the middle of their home page that you might want to turn off as it takes a very long time to download.

KEYWORDS Associations, France, Wine Tasting Organizations, Wines
AUDIENCE Wine Enthusiasts
FREE

http://ici-paris.ensta.fr/~oinos/

Coffee Reference Desk ★★★

Coffee lovers, this is the page is for you! It provides linked references to many coffee-related subject including Coffee Varieties, Blends & Roasts, Coffee & Tea Books, The Coffee Recipe Collection, Tons of Biscotti Recipes, Getting Started With A French Press, Opinions On Various Espresso Machines, On The Kona Quality Dispute, Nicknames For Coffee, The Caffeine - a poem by BADBOB, and much more.

KEYWORDS Coffee, Espresso Machines, Mail Order Business
AUDIENCE Coffee Lovers, Coffee Manufacturers, Coffee Vendors
CONTACT Tim Nemec
tim@ins.infonet.net
FREE

http://www.netins.net/showcase/coffee/refdesk.html

The Condiments Web Page ★★★

The Condiments Web Page is a somewhat tongue-in-cheek site reviewing various condiments found in supermarkets and fast-food restaurants. Included are comments on mayonnaise, catsup and other common food toppers, from common sites like Safeway, Taco Bell, Burger King, and Jack in the Box. There is also a condiment glossary at this site.

KEYWORDS Condiments, Fast Food, Spices

AUDIENCE Fast Food Enthusiasts, Students (Secondary), Students (University)
CONTACT Adam Machanic
amachani@gwhs.denver.k12.co.us
FREE

http://164.92.126.21/Etcetera/Condiments

The Creole and Cajun Recipe Page ★★★

Chuck Taggart's Creole and Cajun Recipe Page is prepared with care by a native New Orleanian who is a Culinary Arts student at UCLA, going to what he calls 'gradual school.' It highlights the 'marvelous' Creole cuisine of New Orleans, and the 'hearty cooking' of Acadiana or 'Cajun country.' This site is a subsite of 'The Gumbo Pages,' a large musical, cultural and culinary World Wide Web site concentrating on New Orleans, southern Louisiana and the wide world of non-commercial radio. Besides oodles of recipes and a comment by Mark Twain (who visited the site in 1884—the real world site, that is) that 'New Orleans food is as delicious as the less criminal forms of sin,' one can read an introduction to the joys of Cajun and Creole cuisine and get more acquainted with basic Creole and Acadian ingredients.

KEYWORDS Cajun Cuisine, Cooking, Creole Cooking, Recipes
AUDIENCE Cooking Enthusiasts, Cooks
CONTACT eamon@netcom.com
FREE

http://www.webcom.com/~gumbo/recipe-page.html

Croatia and Wine ★★

This site by Robert Kostelac of Croatia is a little difficult to reach at its direct URL, so if you don't succeed in connecting to the direct address, you might want to try the address without the crowine.html, then click on the wine site. This is probably the only place on the Internet to find out about Croatian wine and more about Croatia itself.

KEYWORDS Croatia, Wine History, Wines
AUDIENCE Wine Enthusiasts
FREE

http://tjev.tel.etf.hr/~kostelac/crowine.html

The Culinary Professional's Resource Center ★★★

The Van Nostrand Reinhold division of Thomson Publishing Catalogs (VNR) offers this online resource for culinary professionals to help professionals and students in culinary arts use electronic services to locate information and develop professional contacts. There are such links as 'Food and Wine Online,' 'New Publications,' 'Chefs on the Internet Mailing List,' 'ChefNet BBS,' 'HotelNet BBS,' 'FoodNet,' and 'The New England Culinary Institute.'

KEYWORDS Chefs, Cooking, Food
AUDIENCE Culinary Students, Professional Cooks

Food & Dining

CONTACT webmaster@list.thomson.com
FREE
http://www.vnr.com/cul.html

Cyber Café Guide ★★★

The Cyber Cafe Guide is a guide to physical restaurants across the world that have a combination of coffee and computers, such as coffeehouses with Internet access. Users will find listings of working cyber cafes, listed by location, as well as listings of cyber cafes that are on the way or rumored to exist soon. Each listing links to a description of the cafe, with addresses and opening hours, and contact information. Cyber Cafe enthusiasts will find other links of relevance to coffee on the Web.

KEYWORDS Cafes, Caffeine, Coffee
AUDIENCE Cafe Enthusiasts, Coffee Lovers, Internet Users
CONTACT Mark Dziecielewski
markdz@easynet.co.uk
FREE
http://www.easynet.co.uk/pages/cafe/ccafe.htm

Cyberia Food and Drink ★★★

Cyberia Food and Drink, a site based in Houston, Texas, links to all sorts of recipe master lists such as 'The Recipe Folder,' and Food and Drink sites such as 'eGG e-zine,' 'Coffee,' 'Chili Recipe Collection,' 'Bread Baking.'

KEYWORDS Cooking, Recipes, Texas
AUDIENCE Cooking Enthusiasts, Cooks
CONTACT info@infohwy.com
FREE
http://houston.infohwy.com/cyberia/food.htm

DC Dining Guide ★★★

The DC Dining Guide is divided by cuisine with links to a newsgroup, a district area dining guide and Washingtonian's Dining & Entertainment. There is a sophisticated search tool and over 1400 restaurants are listed. Reviews are available for the 100 best restaurants, best bargain restaurants, a reader restaurant survey, and more.

KEYWORDS Restaurant Guides, Restaurant Reviews, Restaurants
AUDIENCE Dining Enthusiasts, Gourmets, Tourists
FREE
http://dcpages.ari.net/dcdining/dcdining.html

The Definitive Review of Dublin's Watering Holes ★★★

This is the home page for the Dublin Pub Review, an online review of the public houses, inns and pubs of Dublin, Ireland. Due to the huge number of pubs in Dublin, the page is limited to those judged to be the best. Each pub is described, located and rated according to cost and environment. It also contains links to other pub related sites.

KEYWORDS Alcohol, Ales, Beer, Ireland
AUDIENCE Dublin Residents, Tourists

CONTACT czimmermm@dsg.cs.tcd.ie
FREE
http://www.dsg.cs.tcd.ie:80/dsg_people/czimmerm/pubs.html

The Digital Restaurant Guide to San Francisco ★★★

The Digital Restaurant Guide to San Francisco has a food glossary and a search feature by Best, Alphabetical, by Cuisine and by World Origin. Soon it will also be searchable by neighborhood. Links upcoming include San Francisco sites, entertainment, and hotels.

KEYWORDS Restaurant Guides, Restaurants
AUDIENCE Dining Enthusiasts, Gourmets, Tourists
CONTACT okon@sf.net
FREE
http://www.sf.net/lantern/start.html

Dining Out on the Web ★★★

Dining out on the Web is a exclusive list of restaurant guides on the Web, with no recipes, cookbooks, or alcohol sites. Users will find links to restaurant sites listed under comprehensive sites, or by physical location in the U.S., or around the world. This site contains links to both commercial sites, such as home pages of restaurants, and noncommercial guides to dining out. Listings include a few words of description regarding the contents of each site.

KEYWORDS Food, Meta-Index (Beverages), Restaurants
AUDIENCE Food Enthusiasts, Gourmets, Tourists
CONTACT Dan Whaley
dan@sunnyside.com
FREE
http://www.ird.net/diningout.html

FatFree Recipe Archive ★★★★

The FatFree Recipe Archive contains recipes of interest to people following the McDougall, Ornish or similar plans; for vegetarians and for health-conscious people in general. There is great variety to the recipes archived here, everything from salsa to cornbreads to 'meat analogues' to many different kinds of dessert. International recipes are also offered. Everything is either completely fat-free or extremely low in fat; all recipes are also either vegan or vegetarian. This site also gives information on how to join the FatFree Mailing List.

KEYWORDS Cooking, Recipes, Vegetarianism
AUDIENCE Cooks, Fitness Enthusiasts, Vegans, Vegetarians
CONTACT Michelle Dick
artemis@rahul.net
FREE
ftp://geod.emr.ca/pub/Recipes/FatFree/

From the King's Kitchen ★★

This site advertises and offers order information for a cookbook, described as a 'superb book of recipes, some Jewish, some not (155 pages).' Many of the recipes were handed down from Jewish mothers and grandmothers and include such all-time favorites as Challah (plaited bread) and Matzo Balls (to float in your chicken soup). There is a sample recipe for Rabbi Michelson's Grandmas' Chicken Soup. For orders outside Australia or New Zealand, the minimum order quantity is 10 books. Unfortunately, only those with forms capability can order the book as no publisher name, address, phone or email is given.

KEYWORDS Celebrities, Cookbooks, Recipes
AUDIENCE Cooking Enthusiasts, Cooks, Jewish Mothers
CONTACT sofcom@sofcom.com.au
FREE
http://www.sofcom.com.au/Cookbook/Cookbook.html

Godiva On-Line ★★★★

Godiva On-Line is a commercial Website put together by Chocolatier Magazine and Godiva Chocolatier. At the site, you can order a subscription to Chocolatier Magazine or pounds of Godiva Chocolates online, but there's also an array of interesting recipes, (most, of course, incorporating chocolate) and a glossary of baking terms. For the more studious chocolate fancier, there is also a brief history of chocolate, and even a history of the Godiva Company. You can also send comments to the owners of Godiva and Chocolatier.

KEYWORDS Chocolate, Cooking, Food, Recipes
AUDIENCE Chefs, Chocolate Lovers, Cooks, Food Enthusiasts, Online Shoppers
CONTACT Godiva Chocolatier
webmaster@godiva.com
FREE
http://www.godiva.com

HOTHOTHOT ★★★★

HOTHOTHOT is a commercial Web site catering to people who like their food to steam, scorch, burn, or totally inflame. The site sells hot sauces and other spicy items, organized by ingredients, place of origin, name and level of heat. Information on Scoville units is also provided, as is a list of the Ten Hottest Sauces. There is a link to the Chile-Heads Mailing List (a list for discussing the cultivation, heat ratio and taste of various chiles). Items in the catalog bear names like Nuclear Hell, Inner Beauty Real Hot Sauce, Texas Tears, Hot, Sweet and Sticky, and Spitfire Sauce. Candies and other condiments are available. One can order online.

KEYWORDS Food, Food Delivery
AUDIENCE Chefs, Chile Pepper Enthusiasts, Cooks, Spicy Food Enthusiasts
CONTACT hothothot@earthlink.net
FREE
http://www.hot.presence.com/g/p/H3/__16990d93/h3-home.html

Houston Restaurant Database ★★★

Houston's Interactive Restaurant Database is an anonymous service that allows new restaurants to be added and currently online restaurants to have reviews added.

KEYWORDS Databases, Restaurants, Texas
AUDIENCE Dining Enthusiasts, Gourmets, Tourists
FREE
http://pgsa.rice.edu/restdb.html

Food & Dining

Indian Recipes ★★

This site acts as a crossroads to resources providing recipes and other information on cooking and eating Indian food. The site links to vegetarian collections containing Indian recipes, exclusively Indian recipe collections, and FAQ's on food, cooking, and vegetarianism. Some collections focus on regional Indian food (e.g. 'Cuisine of Tamilnadu, South India'), other collections provide quick or fat-free dishes.

KEYWORDS	Food, India, Recipes, Restaurants
AUDIENCE	Cooks, Ethnic Food Enthusiasts, Restaurant Enthusiasts, Vegetarians
CONTACT	sridhar@asuvax.eas.asu.edu
FREE	

http://spiderman.bu.edu/misc/india/recipes.html

Insect Recipes ★★★

Iowa State University's Tasty Insect Recipes is certainly a unique site with all kinds of wonderfully inviting delicacies offered such as 'Banana Worm Bread, ' (YUM!), 'Rootworm Beetle Dip,' and 'Chocolate Chirpie Cookies.' Don't forget to keep a good supply of dry-roasted crickets, dry-roasted rootworm beetles, and dry-roasted army worms. The site might want to add a link to some dry-roasted insect outlets to make these buggy batches of crispy critters readily available.

KEYWORDS	Cooking, Food, Insects, Recipes
AUDIENCE	Cooking Enthusiasts, Cooks, Innovators
FREE	

http://www.public.iastate.edu/%7Eentomology/InsectsAsFood.html

The Internet Epicurean ★★★★

Simply the Food Lovers Internet Extravaganza. As we embark upon our trip through this miraculous virtual land of food, we enter a small themed area, say 'Picnic in the Park' or 'Valentine's Day,' which is linked to several similarly-oriented recipe or commercial sites by way of a menu. Also available at this mini-stop are a few rather goofy stories related to the topic of the month. As we continue along our way, we are jostled from one seemingly innocuous spot to the next. Surprise, however awaits you with minty breath. Start with the simply titled, Recipes (which contains nearly all recipes known to humankind), then proceed along to billions and billions of Home Pages, Commercial sites, Restaurant Guides (both General and Regional), Art Spots, and Usenet Newsgroups, all pertinent to the food or wine aficionado. This Fine Food World awaits. It is free, and it is yours.

KEYWORDS	Food, Gifts, Recipes, Restaurants
AUDIENCE	Chefs, Cooks, Food Enthusiasts, Restaurant Enthusiasts
CONTACT	ricsmith@onramp.net
FREE	

http://rampages.onramp.net/~ricsmith/epicure.html

Jell-O Recipes/Why I Love Jell-O ★★★★

Jell-O Recipes/Why I Love Jello is the Oxford English Dictionary of alcoholic and non-alcoholic recipes, all using the gentle gelatin, Jell-O. Here you will find virtually everything you could possibly need to know to create your next wild Jell-O Cocktail Party. In addition to the recipes (for everything from Margaritas to Sex on the Beaches) you will find a confession written by the proud compiler, entitled, 'How I Got Started With Jell-O and Alcohol.' A blast.

KEYWORDS	Alcohol, Food, Recipes
AUDIENCE	Bartenders, Cooks, Jell-O Enthusiasts, Partygoers
CONTACT	CMJ Baden (Chas) hazel-chas@netcom.com
FREE	

ftp://ftp.netcom.com/pub/ha/hazel/jello

Korean Cooking ★★★

Korean Cooking is part of a Web site devoted to the business and culture of Korea. There are several traditional recipes here, for meat dishes, kimchee, rice and seaweed. The entire site is readable in either Hangul or English.

KEYWORDS	Cooking, Food, Korea, Recipes
AUDIENCE	Chefs, Cooks, Food Enthusiasts, Koreans
CONTACT	june@korea.com
FREE	

http://www.Korea.com/SIGHTSEE/recipe1.htm

Kosher Restaurant Database ★★★

The Kosher Restaurant Database works by query and searches the New York Metropolitan area and many other areas around the world for kosher restaurants by city and category.

KEYWORDS	Databases, Kosher Foods, Restaurants
AUDIENCE	Dining Enthusiasts, Gourmets, Tourists
FREE	

http://shamash.nysernet.org/kosher/krestquery.html

La Bouillabaisse Home Page ★★★

La Bouillabaisse is a fairly well-known French restaurant in Brooklyn Heights, New York that features mostly Provencale fare, which trades traditional heavy cream and butter sauces for lighter and healthier olive oil, wine, spices and reduced stocks. The site introduces us to the owners and staff, complete with pictures of Amanda Green, one of the founding partners, and her new baby, Nick, as well as the cuisine, menu, and hours, with reservation policy. There are reviews of the restaurant, home pages for the owners, and links to other restaurant pages.

KEYWORDS	Bouillabaisse, Cooking, Louisiana, Restaurants
AUDIENCE	Cooking Enthusiasts, Cooks, Restauraunt Enthsuiasts
CONTACT	Steve Manes manes@magpie.com
FREE	

http://genesis.wnet.org/~manes/bouil.html

La Comida Mexicana ★★★

La Comida Mexicana is an online cookbook, created by the University of Guadalajara, filled with traditional Mexican recipes. The 'cookbook' contains recipes for soup, eggs, meat dishes, vegetables, and salsas. Each entry includes pictures of the food, and a recipe written in Spanish. A history of Mexican cuisine is also included, along with classic recipes for pozole and birra (beer).

KEYWORDS	Mexico, Recipes
AUDIENCE	Cooks, Food Enthusiasts
CONTACT	maguey@rulfo.dca.udg.mx
FREE	

http://www.udg.mx/Cocina/menu.html

Le Cordon Bleu ★★★

This site is part of the Paris Exhibit 'L'Art Culinaire.' The menus presented here are from the world-famous cooking school in Paris- 'Le Cordon Bleu.' Many of the recipes are taught at Le Cordon Bleu school by a team of master chefs from France's various Michelin-star restaurants. Start your tour on Saturday and continue to the following Friday sampling each of seven full menus available. Check into the history link for Le Cordon Bleu and go back almost one hundred years to January 14, 1896 to Paris's Palais Royal.

KEYWORDS	Cooking, Paris, Recipes
AUDIENCE	Cooking Enthusiasts, Cooking Students, Cooks
CONTACT	Frans van Hoesel hoesel@chem.rug.nl
FREE	

http://sunsite.unc.edu/expo/restaurant/restaurant.html

Le Cyber-Routard ★★★

Ly Cyber-Routard offers a search of restaurants and cafes in Paris, all over Europe, in Africa, Asia and the United States. The Paris list is the most comprehensive with over 105 possibilities to choose from, while there's only one restaurant suggestion for Senegal. One can search in English or French by name, price, type of food, and location, or one can add an address or comment. This site has potential, but there aren't that many listings included here yet.

KEYWORDS	France, International Cuisine, Restaurants
AUDIENCE	French, Restaurant Goers, Tourists
FREE	

http://olympe.polytechnique.fr/~niania/CyberRout/

Mama's Cookbook ★★★★

This site offers 'a million different recipes,' a cooking glossary, and a pasta glossary. The user has the ability to scroll through the site and look for various dishes or do an item search. Mama provides her favorite new dish every week.

KEYWORDS	Cooking, Mediterranean Culture, Recipes
AUDIENCE	Chefs, Cooks, Food Enthusiasts , Italians
CONTACT	Mama Cucina info@frymulti.com
FREE	

http://www.eat.com/cookbook/index.html

Food & Dining   **629**

Master Cook Home Page

The Master Cook Website operates graphically through six book icons under the topics of Recipes, Master-Cook, Cooking Info, News, Other Sites and Product Support. It is produced by Arion Software, which makes a computer CD-ROM program called MasterCook. The program allows users to put all their favorite recipes on disk, generate automatic shopping lists, access a rich database of recipes, and perform a nutritional analysis on the meals you prepare. The Web site accesses a demonstration of the program, product information and ordering forms, as well as product support.

- **KEYWORDS** Archives, Chefs, Cooking, Recipes
- **AUDIENCE** Cooking Enthusiasts, Cooks
- **CONTACT** Technical Support
  tech@arion.com
- **FREE**

http://www.arion.com/mstrcook.html

The Mead Maker's Page

The Mead Maker's Page is offered by Forrest Cook who works at the Research Data Program of the National Center for Atmospheric Research located in Boulder, Colorado. The site offers all kinds of information including mead styles and ingredients, recipes, synonyms, papers & articles, mead groups and miscellaneous links to brewing sites and a beekeeping home page.

- **KEYWORDS** Cooking, Winemaking, Wines
- **AUDIENCE** Wine Enthusiasts
- **FREE**

http://www.atd.ucar.edu/rdp/gfc/mead/mead.html

Mentos FAQs (Frequently Asked Questions) Version 2.0

This site provides access to FAQs (Frequently Asked Questions) regarding the popular candy called Mentos. Synopses of the Mentos commercials are given, as well as information about the candies themselves including packaging, ingredients, manufacturer, imitations and history. Currently there are five varieties of candy - mint, mixed fruit, strawberry cinnamon and spearmint.

- **KEYWORDS** Candy, Food
- **AUDIENCE** Candy Lovers, Culinary Professionals, Dessert Enthusiasts
- **CONTACT** Health Doerr
  doerrhb@expert.cc.purdue.edu
- **FREE**

ftp://ftp.execpc.com/pub/esch/mentos-faq/

Midland Harvest Burgers

Midland Harvest Burgers is a commercial Website for the Midland Harvest Burger Company. The company offers burgers and other 'meat' loaves for sale. Items are vegetarian, using no animal products, and low-fat. One may order directly through the URL.

- **KEYWORDS** Animal Rights, Cooking, Food
- **AUDIENCE** Animal Rights Activists, Cooks, Vegans, Vegetarians
- **CONTACT** Springs of Life
  Springs@emall
- **FREE**

http://emall.com/Harvest/Harvest1.html

The Mofile Place Coffee Page ★★★

As it says on this particular Home Page (the Mofile Place Coffee Page), 'Most or part of the rise of the Computer Age and certainly of Internet can be attributed to the powers of Coffee.' Here you will find a heap of material devoted to proving just that, as well as introducing the novice to, and titillating the expert about, the fabulous bean. Available here are bits of coffee history, coffee plant taxonomy, links to all of the Usenet Newsgroups related to coffee and caffeine, and a few coffee recipes. The Page's concluding quote - 'Coffee. What's that?' By the time you get there, you'll know.

- **KEYWORDS** Caffeine, Coffee, Finland, Recipes
- **AUDIENCE** Coffee Lovers, Cooks, Finland Residents
- **CONTACT** Jarno Tarkoma
  coffee@mofile.fi or jta@mofile.fi
- **FREE**

http://www.mofile.fi/coffee/default.htm

Napa Valley Dining ★★★

Napa Valley Dining is divided into 6 links of featured restaurants, a listing of all Napa Valley restaurants, Calistoga restaurants, St. Helena restaurants, postings, and read postings.

- **KEYWORDS** California, Restaurant Guides, Restaurants
- **AUDIENCE** Dining Enthusiasts, Gourmets, Tourists

Connections to Recipes

Food for thought

Herbs & Spices
By Jeffrey Dawkins and Ron Lunde

How much marjoram should you add to spice up those green beans? Maybe some Tamil-nadu cuisine would go nice with your yogurt drink. On the Internet there are literally thousands of recipes to satisfy virtually every taste bud on the planet.

For instance, at the "Herbs & Spices" site (one of several devoted to these delicacies), you'll not only find hundreds of recipes for incorporating some 60 herbs and spices, but also tips on how to grow your own herbs. There are even esoteric recipes for using herbs to ward off werewolves or create an aphrodisiac.

(http://www.teleport.com/~ronl/herbs.html)

It would literally be hard to avoid finding a new way to cook any edible meat or vegetable at the "Recipes Archives" site, a list of thousands of recipes from Usenet. There are concoctions for meat and vegetarian entrees, sweet-and-sour side dishes, alcoholic and non-alcoholic desserts, and more.

(http://www.NeoSoft.com:80/recipes/index.html)

If your sweet tooth can't ever seem to get enough chocolate, you'll be happy to know that there are several Web sites guaranteed to saturate your cocoa cravings. At the "I Need My Chocolate!" site, you'll find recipes which incorporate various types of chocolate from around the world (such as German, Viennese, and Dutch). You can even commiserate with other chocoholics online.

(http://www.qrc.com/~sholubek/choco/start.html)

CONTACT forbes@freerun.com
FREE

http://www.freerun.com/napavalley/restrnts.html

New York City Dining Information ★★★

From Armenian to Zimbabwean fare, chances are you'll find it in New York. This online guide offers dining tips and search tools by area, by cuisine, by famous restaurants and by FoodPhone. There is a chance to critique a New York City restaurant as well.

KEYWORDS New York, Restaurant Guides, Restaurant Reviews, Restaurants
AUDIENCE Dining Enthusiasts, Gourmets, Tourists
FREE

http://www.cs.columbia.edu/nyc/dining/l

Old Harbor Brewing Company ★★

This is the home page of the Old Harbor Brewing Company, a Massachusetts company that brews Pilgrim Ale in addition to other ales. Visitors can find images of the Pilgrim Label, product information, a list of some of the many locations that carry Old Harbor products, links to Great Bottle Opener products as well as other beer-related web pages.

KEYWORDS Alcoholic Beverages, Ales, Beer Brewing
AUDIENCE Beer Drinkers, Entertainers, Restauranteurs
CONTACT cc@shore.net
FREE

http://northshore.shore.net/icc/pilgrim.html

Over the Coffee ★★★

Over the Coffee is a Web site containing information about coffee online and in the physical world. Besides the coffee reference desk, with information about different types of coffee and the art of brewing, art, and opinions relating to coffee, this site provides a comprehensive list of links to coffee-related and commercial coffee Web sites. The Business section contains information about commercial coffee companies, with alphabetical listings of hundreds of coffee roasters, cafes, and coffee vendors around the world. Addresses, contact information, and background information about their products is also provided. The Wall of Java allows coffee lovers to contribute to a discussion about their caffeine addiction!

KEYWORDS Cafes, Caffeine, Coffee
AUDIENCE Caffeine Lovers, Coffee Lovers, Coffeehouse Owners
CONTACT tim@gryffin.com
FREE

http://www.infonet.net/showcase/coffee/

Paris Restaurant Guide ★★★★

The Paris Restaurant Guide describes the best hotels and restaurants in Paris with searching capabilities based on maps and various criteria. The criteria used includes price, features such as music and valet parking, and types of cuisine including French, regional and foreign. There is also an extensive pull down list of restaurants and/or hotels listed by name.

KEYWORDS Maps, Paris, Restaurants, Tourism
AUDIENCE Cooks, French Food Enthusiasts, Internet users, Tourists, general public, individuals
CONTACT P Marissal
         marissal@world-net.sct.fr
FREE

http://oda.sct.fr

Paulig Recipe Page ★★★★

The Paulig Recipe Page is a Web site devoted entirely to recipes where a prominent ingredient is coffee. As Gustav Paulig, Ltd is a coffee company, this is perhaps to be expected. The recipes at this site, however, are both intriguing and simple. Although some seem familiar (coffee milkshakes, for example), most have an exotic turn to them. Among the recipes currently available are those which mix coffee and cola, and a Hawaiian coffee recipe which includes grapefruit juice, pineapple juice, vanilla ice cream, whipped cream and brown sugar. There are also a variety of espresso bar-type drink recipes here. New recipes are added weekly.

KEYWORDS Coffee, Cooking, Finland, Recipes
AUDIENCE Chefs, Coffee Lovers, Cooks
CONTACT Gustav Paulig, Ltd.
FREE

http://www.mofile.fi/biz/paulig/recep.htm

Pub Hiker's Guide - Introduction ★★★

The Pub Hiker's Guide aims to provide information for those who would like to stay in interesting public houses on their walking holidays in the United Kingdom. Currently the guide focuses on the South Pennines and Dark Peak, but it will expand to cover pubs in the Yorkshire Dales and the Lake Region by the end of summer, 1995. The guide also includes weather and accommodation reports.

KEYWORDS Alcohol, Beer, Pubs, United Kingdom
AUDIENCE Tourists
CONTACT hiker@dobx.demon.co.uk
FREE

http://www.demon.co.uk/dobx/hike.html

Ragu Presents - Mama's Cucina ★★★★

This site is presented by Ragu, and has an extensive collection of links to browse. Users can browse through dozens of recipes or choose to learn about Italy's culture (architecture, language, geography). Other links on this site show consumers the ingredients, nutritional information and some recipes for Ragu's products (tomato sauces, pizza sauces, and chicken flavorings.) In addition, viewers can read and write in their favorite dinner anecdotes, order coupons, T-shirts, and other promotions, or enter a trip to Italy sweepstakes.

KEYWORDS Italian Food, Italy, Recipes
AUDIENCE Chefs, Cooks, Dining Enthusiasts, Internet Users, Italians

CONTACT Fry Multimedia
         info@frymulti.com.
FREE

http://www.eat.com/

Rec.Food.Veg's Most Frequently Asked Question's List ★★★★

The Rec.Food.Veg FAQ is an extensive and highly detailed manuscript for vegetarians and those interested in vegetarian eating habits. It includes information relevant to both the novice and experienced vegetarian. Topics covered are the vegetarian vocabulary, the availability and flavor of various vegetarian products, feeding pets a non-meat diet (and several animal rights issues), literature and restaurants.

KEYWORDS Animal Rights, Cooking, Diets, Vegetarianism
AUDIENCE Animal Rights Activists, Chefs, Cooks, Ecologists, Vegetarians
CONTACT Michael Traub
         traub@btcs.bt.co.uk
FREE

ftp://rtfm.mit.edu/pub/usenet/news.answers/vegetarian/faq

Recipe Server at Technical University, Berlin ★★★

The Cooking Database with over 12,000 recipes is offered through the Interdepartmental Research Center for Process Control Applications of the Technical University of Berlin. One can query the database, find a list of drinks and access many German-language recipe links. There are hyperlinks to other servers such as 'The Recipes Folder' and 'A Malt Whisky Tour.' Avoid the overlarge graphic at the top of the homepage by turning to text-only browsing.

KEYWORDS Cooking, Databases, Germany, Recipes
AUDIENCE Cooking Enthusiasts, Cooks
CONTACT Carl Berger
         carl.berger@synapse.org
FREE

http://www.prz.tu-berlin.de/~nicolai/topics/meal/meal.html

Recipes Archives ★★★

This archive contains the collected recipes from the Usenet group rec.food.recipes. There are thousands of recipes here, ranging from appetizers to soups, lamb to sauces, and breads to desserts. The directory is organized by recipe type, and alphabetical order within each type. Given the worldwide nature of the Internet, recipes will range from vegetable soup to jellied moose nose.

KEYWORDS Archives, Diets, Food, Recipes
AUDIENCE Chefs, Cooks, Food Enthusiasts, Restaurateurs
CONTACT Peter da Silva
         peter@taronga.com
FREE

http://www.NeoSoft.com:80/recipes/index.html

Food & Dining

The Recipes! ★★★

The Recipes! is a unique Web site containing a variety of recipes geared to use during camping, kayaking, canoeing, and climbing trips. Most recipes are vegetarian, or have directions for adapting them. Instructions are provided for making main courses, desserts and snacks, and new recipes are added frequently. Some of the dishes here are to be made before you leave on your adventure; others are designed to be prepared over an open flame with the scent of nature combining with that of woodsmoke.

KEYWORDS Camping, Canoeing, Recipes
AUDIENCE Camping Enthusiasts, Canoers, Climbing Enthusiasts, Cooks, Kayakers
CONTACT Bruce Fisher
bef@ssnet.com
FREE

http://ssnet.com/~bef/Recipies.html

Recipes ★★★★

Whether you are intrigued by learning how to fetch your dinner from a sizzling pit in your backyard, dine on Malaysian or Turkish cuisine that you've cooked yourself, sample a cricket or grasshopper immersed in a sticky sauce, or simply fix up a new and different batch of hamburgers, veggie burgers or an Italian Rum Cake, this is the site to consult. An astounding array of links to practically all recipe sites on the World Wide Web (and including some Gopher and FTP sites as well), the succinctly titled Recipes, is exactly that. Perfect in its way, and complete, Recipes contains only recipes, and more than enough to vex or fascinate even the most competent home chef for at least a year.

KEYWORDS Cooking, Food, Recipe Archives, Recipes
AUDIENCE Chefs, Cooks, Food Enthusiasts, Vegetarians
CONTACT ricsmith@onramp.net
FREE

http://rampages.onramp.net/~ricsmith/recipe.html

Restaurants in Stockholm, Sweden ★★

The Stockholm Restaurant guide reviews a small number of the over 2500 restaurants in Stockholm, Sweden, and accumulates new listings all the time. The guide is good for tourists as it is entirely in English.

KEYWORDS Restaurants, Sweden
AUDIENCE Dining Enthusiasts, Tourists
CONTACT Ulla
ulla@stupi.se
FREE

http://www.us.stupi.se/Food

Robin Garr's Wine Bargain Page ★★★

Robin Garr's Wine Bargain Page is a cyberwine consumer report and resource for wine lovers. There is a query forum where one can ask a question about wine and receive an answer within 24 hours. There are tasting notes, a wine value archive organized chronologically within region and type to make it easy to find specific wines of interest and an off-line club for Net-wired wine lovers in the Ann Arbor/Detroit, Michigan area. This is a very unique and often-updated site

where one can learn a lot about wine and have some fun doing it.

KEYWORDS Wine Bargains, Wine Tasting, Wines
AUDIENCE Wine Enthusiasts
FREE

http://iglou.com/why/wine.html

Connections to Restaurants Around the World
Waiter, there's a critic in my soup!

Hungry? If you want to find a great restaurant in your area, browse the menu, check out how much it will cost for a couple or a family of six, the Internet is the place to start.

Many restaurant Net-sites are designed for specific cities, and yes, there is a worldwide dining guide. You pick the country and city, and you'll invariably find the best places to eat.

If you want only Kosher restaurants, or you're a fan of the U.S. chain of Chili's restaurants, you'll find the appropriate listing on the Web. You can also get in touch with other people who have eaten at particular restaurants and find out their opinions of the eatery. Whether you're dining your way through New Orleans, San Francisco, or Kiev, you'll find reviews and menus to suit your palate.

(http://www.sunnyside.com/diningout.html)

also, (http://www.webcom.com/~gumbo/food/norstfaq.txt)

also, (http://genoa.osf.org:8001/boston/info-serv.html)

If you plan to visit London, Paris, or Rio, you can plan your dining experience ahead of time. The Internet allows you to effortlessly search out the hot spots, vegetarian restaurants, kosher restaurants, or even the best place to get gnocchi. Through "Dining Out on the Web," an extensive database provides information on where to eat in nearly every city in the world. You get reviews and menus on many of these sites. Beware. The URL is expected to change but if you have a search engine for the Internet, you can access it by typing in the words "Dining Out on the Web."

(http:www.cmpharm.ucsf.edu/~troyer/diningout.html)

Slovenian Recipes ★★★★

Slovenian Recipes is one part of a Web site devoted to the culture of the Slovenians. If you are interested in learning how to make traditional Slovenian food, this is the site for you. Available are all types of recipes, from meat and fish entrees to side dishes, vegetables and desserts. In addition to the recipes, you will find here a table of cooking measurement conversions from Slovenian to English/American, and a short guide to the

632 Food & Dining

pronunciation of Slovenian. You can also click to hear the names of the recipes spoken aloud.

KEYWORDS Food, Recipes, Slovenia
AUDIENCE Chefs, Cooks, Home Economics Teachers, Slovaks
CONTACT Dr. Danilo Zavrtanik (president) or Mark Martinec (cyberguy) mark.martinec@ijs.si
FREE

http://www.ijs.si/recipes/

The Solar Cooking Archive ★★

The Solar Cooking Archive was created by Solar Box Cookers Northwest to help spread solar cooking throughout the world. The Archive provides access to an image gallery, slide show with text narration, news, and a document search for such things as 'Introducing Solar Ovens to Rural Kenya.'

KEYWORDS Archives, Cooking, Meta-Index (Cooking), Solar Cooking
AUDIENCE Cooking Enthusiasts, Cooks, Environmentalists
CONTACT tsponheim@accessone.com
FREE

http://www.xmission.com/~seer/sbcn/index.htm

Spencer's Beer Page ★★★

Spencer's Beer Page is designed as a resource for homebrewers, with information about making and bottling beer. Users will find documents of beer brewing intructions as well as beer recipes. An archive of beer label images is also provided, which users may browse with or without captions. Other documents include fermentation experiments, the results of the Great American Beer Festivals, and searchable archives from several Homebrew Digests and brewing mailing lists. A large list of pointers to other beer resources on the Internet is also included.

KEYWORDS Alcoholic Beverages, Beer
AUDIENCE Beer Brewers, Beer Enthusiasts
CONTACT Spencer W. Thomas spencer@umich.edu
FREE

http://guraldi.itn.med.umich.edu/Beer/

The Strawberry Facts Page ★★★

This is a Web page on strawberries. Users can find links to strawberry recipes, information about the growing of strawberries, and strawberry trivia. Moreover, this site lists strawberry-related music and musicians, and has an index of various graphic files of strawberries.

KEYWORDS Fruits
AUDIENCE Cooks, General Public
CONTACT Jenni A. Mott jmott@wimsey.com
FREE

http://www.wimsey.com/~jmott/sbfacts/sbfacts.html

Taste Unlimited ★★★

Taste Unlimited is an online catalog of specialty food and wines available for online or off line ordering. Delivery is available anywhere in the continental United States. The site is divided into the Gifts of Taste Holiday Catalog, the Simple Pleasures giftpack shop, the Savory Sauces rack, and the Fall 1994 newsletter What's New link.

KEYWORDS Catalogs, Catering, Specialty Foods, Wine
AUDIENCE Gourmets
FREE

http://www.ip.net/tu/

Technet - Austin Dining Guide ★★★

The Tech.net Austin Dining Guide is a part of the Austin Information Center, a public service provided by TechNet. The Guide contains information and reviews of restaurants in the Austin, Texas area that may be browsed by restaurants of the week/month, recent changes, best of Austin, alphabetic listing, listing by cuisine, or area listing.

KEYWORDS Restaurant Guides, Restaurants, Texas
AUDIENCE Dining Enthusiasts, Gourmets, Tourists
CONTACT info@tech.net
FREE

http://www.tech.net/austin/dining/index.html

Themes - Cuisine ★★★

Themes Cuisine is a French site for recipes written in French and English. Most of the recipes have been culled from the Usenet groups' fr.rec.cuisine' and 'francom.alimentation.' The recipes are search-accessible by entree, side dish, main dish, dessert, drinks and sauce. There are measurement conversion tables available, links to other cooking pages, and an introduction and warnings from the author. Readers are invited to take a photo of their prepared recipe and put it in .gif format to be able to display it next to the recipe in the index in the future.

KEYWORDS Cooking, Cuisine, France, Recipes
AUDIENCE Cooking Enthusiasts, Cooks
CONTACT ivicente@cenaath.cena.dgac.fr
FREE

http://www.cenaath.cena.dgac.fr/themes/cuisine

This is Real Good Taste! ★★★

This is real good taste! provides a variety of information on Thai food, on restaurants in both the U.S. and Thailand, popular Thai recipes, and much more.

KEYWORDS Restaurants, Thai Culture, Thai Food, Travel
AUDIENCE Chefs, Cooks, Food Enthusiasts, Thailand Residents
CONTACT Wut Apirakkhit songwut@seas.upenn.edu
FREE

http://www.seas.upenn.edu/~songwut/food.html

Vancouver's Virtual Dining Guide ★★

Vancouver's Virtual Dining Guide is where you will find all sorts of interesting information on the fine foods and spirits of British Columbia. Its goal is to offer the best Vancouver has to offer to the rest of the world. As this is a new site, links are not yet complete, but it will eventually include restaurant listings, cafe listings, a recipe archive, restaurant reviews, and a feature restaurant of the week. Some of the restaurant listings can be browsed currently and they are divided by type of food from African and All You Can Eat to Vegetarian and Vietnamese, carrying address and phone information.

KEYWORDS Canada, Restaurants, Vancouver
AUDIENCE Canadians, Dining Enthusiasts
FREE

http://imagineer.com/VDG/

The Vegetarian Pages ★★★★

The Vegetarian Pages is an encyclopedia of vegetarian resources on the Internet. A tremendous amount of information of use to vegetarians, animal rights activists, people interested in healthful living and people in search of new ideas for cooking and dining, are covered. Among the resources available are 'The World Guide to Vegetarianism,' a comprehensive international list of vegetarian restaurants, organizations and natural food stores; a hypertext guide to other vegetarian-oriented Internet sites; a vegetarian glossary, and a myriad of recipes with vegetarian appeal.

KEYWORDS Animal Rights, Cooking, Food, Vegetarianism
AUDIENCE Animal Rights Activists, Cooks, Travelers, Vegetarians
FREE

http://catless.ncl.ac.uk/vegetarian/

Veggies Unite! ★★★

Veggies Unite! is a searchable online cookbook with over 2000 vegetarian and vegan recipes. Users will find recipes for bean dishes, casseroles, drinks, ethnic foods, meat substitutes, sweets and snacks, and tofu. A master index is also provided, with all recipes listed alphabetically. Links to other vegetarian, health, and nutrition resources on the Internet are also compiled.

KEYWORDS Cookbooks, Health, Recipes, Vegetarianism
AUDIENCE Cooks, Food Enthusiasts, Gourmets, Vegetarians
CONTACT Yvette Norem veggie@jalapeno.ucs.indiana.edu
FREE

http://www-sc.ucssc.indiana.edu/cgi-bin/recipes/

The VineNet ★★★

VineNet is offered as a public service to wine enthusiasts by Knowledge-Based Technologies, Inc. and is the place to find the latest information on New England wine events, wine tastings and other wine news as well as a good starting point to explore the world of wine on the Internet.

KEYWORDS New England, Wine Tasting, Wineries, Wines
AUDIENCE Wine Enthusiasts

Food & Dining

FREE

http://linux.kbt.com/vinenet/welcome.html

The Virtual Pub and Beer Emporium ★★★

The Virtual Pub and Beer Emporium is a forum for beer aficionados to learn about drinking and brewing beer. Users will find links to beer-related Web sites across the world, with a brief description of each site, and FAQs and archived documents from different beer groups online. Local information includes an archive of beer tasting reviews, a patron's list with pictures of famous brewers, and a guide to drinking beer in Germany, Belgium, and the Netherlands.

KEYWORDS   Alcohol, Bartending, Beer, Netherlands
AUDIENCE   Beer Enthusiasts
CONTACT   Joel Plutchak
          plutchak@lager.geo.brown.edu
FREE

http://lager.geo.brown.edu:8080/virtual-pub/

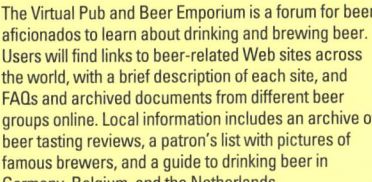 **Waiters On Wheels' World Wide Web Server** ★★

This service is an online food delivery network, linking residents of networked cities to dozens of restaurants in their area. Restaurants on the system range from American cafes to Japanese and Italian food. Currently, this service is available in the San Francisco Bay Area, the Seattle and Spokane areas, and future plans include Las Vegas. The city page lists a description, address and hours of operation, as well as menus of each restaurant. The menus are form-based, so the user need only list the quantity of each desired item on the menu. Users are required to join the service and may receive discounts on delivery charges.

KEYWORDS   Food, Restaurants
AUDIENCE   Californians, Washington Residents
CONTACT   Sunnyside Computing, Inc.
          doorbell@sunnyside.com
FREE

http://www.sunnyside.com/cgi/get?wow/index:QEMEFiIh

Web Compendium of Alcohol Beverages ★★★★

This site acts as a crossroads to commercial and non-commercial resources devoted to wine, beer and spirits. Sites are organized by Internet resource type, then by beverage. This meta-index lists newsgroups, mailing lists, gophers, FTP sites, WWW sites, bulletin boards, commercial online forums (e.g., America Online's Wine & Dine Online), and virtual malls. Resources include archives, glossaries, newsletters, organizational rules and statistics, FAQs, brewing instructions, and producers' sites.

KEYWORDS   Beer, Meta-Index (Beverages), Wine
AUDIENCE   Dining Enthusiasts, Internet Users, Wine Enthusiasts
CONTACT   Dean Tudor
          dtudor@acs.ryerson.ca
FREE

http://www.interlog.com/eye/Food-drink/Drinks/tudor.htm

Welcome to Sally's Place ★★★

Welcome to Sally's Place, A Worldwide Perspective on the Finer Things in Life. As Sally's guest, you can make yourself comfortable and stay to browse numerous food sites (cooking, recipes, news, products, announcements), drink sites (Wine, Beer, Coffee, Tea), Dining sites (Restaurant Reviews, Listings, Announcements) as well as links to Travel, Fun, Business, Libraries, and What's New. Sally Bernstein is a charter member of the International Association of Culinary Professionals and makes her home in the San Francisco Bay Area after having studied at La Varenne, Le Pot a Feu, and Cordon Bleu cooking schools in Paris, France.

KEYWORDS   Cooking, Dining Out, Drinks, Restaurants
AUDIENCE   Dining Enthusiasts, Food Enthusiasts, World
FREE

http://www.bpe.com/

 Whisling Wings Farm ★★★

Whisling Wings Farm sells organic berry products that are grown without pesticides, using insects to control insects, while concentrating on quality and taste. The Home Page supplies information about purchasing these berries and gift baskets. There is also information on berry news, nurseries and recipes, farming sites in Maine and on the Internet.

KEYWORDS   Farming, Food Production, Fruits, Organic Foods
AUDIENCE   Berry Enthusiasts, Consumers, Farmers
CONTACT   Don and Julie Harper
          dharper@wwfarm.com
FREE

http://www.biddeford.com/~dtaylor/ww/ww1.html

Wine Net News ★★★★

This site provides the text of Wine Net News, an online newsletter of reviews by wine lovers on the Internet. The concise reviews, covering wines from Australia, California, France, Chile, Italy, Spain, Portugal, Oregon, and Washington State, specify wine price and use the 100-point system. The bimonthly newsletter also provides special reports on vineyard growth and crop forecasts. Back issues of the newsletter are also available. There is also a list of other wine resources on the Internet.

KEYWORDS   Restaurant Reviews, Vineyards, Wine
AUDIENCE   Dining Enthusiasts, Gourmets, Restaurant Enthusiasts, Wine Enthusiasts
CONTACT   sethg@cs.berkeley.edu
FREE

http://http.cs.berkeley.edu/~sethg/Wine/

 The WineWeb ★★★

The WineWeb allows for online searching, browsing, and purchasing of wines from around the world. Wines can be searched by winery, country, county, grape type, vintage, and price. Wineries can be searched by location, appellation, and by annual production. There's also legal information on receiving wine shipments and press releases from WineWeb companies.

KEYWORDS   Online Shopping, Wine
AUDIENCE   Online Shoppers, Restaurant Enthusiasts, Restaurateurs, Wine Enthusiasts
CONTACT   rkreutz@wineweb.com
FREE

http://beep.roadrunner.com:80/wine/

Wines of Slovenia ★★

The Wines of Slovenia is a unique site giving the history of the wine-growing regions of Slovenia, a global history of winemaking, some wine archives, specialized wine shops, and a link to the Vino '95 wine fair.

KEYWORDS   Slovenia, Vineyards, Wine History, Wines
AUDIENCE   Wine Enthusiasts
FREE

http://www.ijs.si/wine_uvod.html

 **Wit Beer - Spring Street Brewing Company** ★★★

The Wit Beer information page, from the Spring Street Brewing Company uses this page to document the history of the brewery and specific beers, give information about the master brewers, and to provide contact information for local Wit beer retailers and distributors thoughout the area. This page also includes a public stock offering, order form for promotional merchandise (clothes, glassware, etc.) and other miscellaneous items related to brewing.

KEYWORDS   Alcoholic Beverages, Beer, Brewing, New York
AUDIENCE   Beer Enthusiasts, Distributors, New York Residents
CONTACT   witbeer@interport.net
FREE

http://www.interport.net:80/witbeer

The EGG (The Electronic Gourmet Guide) ★★★★

This site hosts the eGG (The Electronic Gourmet Guide), the e-zine dedicated to food and gourmet cooking. Users can find features on master chefs, recipes, wine and coffee, and links to other Internet food resources.

KEYWORDS   Cooking, Gourmet Food, Wine, Zines
AUDIENCE   Chefs, Cooks, Culinary Professionals, Gourmets, Wine Enthusiasts
CONTACT   Kate Heyhoe
          egg@deltanet.com
FREE

http://www.deltanet.com:80/2way/egg/

Games

See also
Internet · Online Games
Sports & Recreation · Recreation

The Asylum ★★★

The Asylum is an 'interactive playground' designed by Creative Internet to showcase the interactive entertainment potential of the WWW (World Wide Web). Users will find the WWW Lite Brite, with 'art' that users may manipulate, archives of past creations, the Revolving Door Hotlist, on which users may add or delete links, and a Fiction Therapy area for multi-author writing projects. There is also a scratch pad for doodles, a Poll Booth for user discussions, and a 'Dump' with a page about the children's show character Barney.

KEYWORDS Interactive Media, Internet Games
AUDIENCE Games Enthusiasts, Interactive Game Players, Internet Users
CONTACT Aure Prochazka and Joe Cates
aure@galcit.caltech.edu and joe@galcit.caltech.edu
FREE

http://www.galcit.caltech.edu/~ta/cgi-bin/asylhome-ta

BlackJack Server ★★★★

This page contains an interactive Blackjack game created by Universal Access. Users can play the dealer, and may even make bets with virtual money.

KEYWORDS Card Games, Interactive Media, Internet Games
AUDIENCE Games Enthusiasts, Interactive Game Players, Internet Users
CONTACT Henry Minsky
hqm@ua.com
FREE

http://www.ua.com/blackjack/bj.html

Bridge on the Web ★★★

Bridge on the Web is a comprehensive guide to bridge links all over the Internet. Included are links to current and recent tournaments, newsgroups and daily bulletins, and Web pages of various bridge clubs. Also included is a copy of the book Laws of Bridge, a comprehensive guide to playing bridge.

KEYWORDS Bridge, Card Games, Games
AUDIENCE Bridge Enthusiasts, Games Enthusiasts
CONTACT Hans van Staveren
sater@cs.vu.nl
FREE

http://www.cs.vu.nl/~sater/bridge/bridge-on-the-web.html

Chess Nuts ★★★

Chess Nuts is a meta-index designed to link interested chess enthusiasts to chess sites all over the Web. Local files include a games archive, plays from classic games, world chess rankings, and articles from the newsgroup rec.games.chess. Links are grouped according by Web sites, FTP sites, newsgroups, email correspondence chess, and IRC real time chess.

KEYWORDS Chess, Games
AUDIENCE Chess Players, Games Enthusiasts
CONTACT David Bell
bd374@gre.ac.uk
FREE

http://www.gre.ac.uk/~bd374/

Computer Gaming World ★★★

Computer Gaming World is the online version of the games magazine from Ziff-Davis. Features include previews of games such as Magic - the Gathering, and reviews and articles about current role playing, adventure, actions, sports and simulation games. The shareware showcase and Patches allows user to download free software from over the Web.

KEYWORDS Computer Games, Online Magazines
AUDIENCE Computer Games Enthusiasts, Games Enthusiasts
CONTACT webmaster@ziff.com
FREE

http://www.ziff.com/~gaming/

Doom Gate ★★★

The Doom Gate page provides information and resources for the computer game Doom. Users may look at spoilers, screen shots, read up on game tools, and download shareware for Doom, Heretic, Strife and Descent. A list of links to Doom Nodes on the Web, with descriptions of their contents, is also included. Other game information includes addons, documents and FAQs for general game instruction, and utilities that will aid in playing Doom. The Forum section provides links, newsgroups, IRC's and mailing lists for Doom discussion and help.

KEYWORDS Computer Games
AUDIENCE Doom Enthusiasts, Games Enthusiasts
CONTACT Piotr Kapiszewski and Steve Young
webmaster@doomgate.cs.buffalo.edu
FREE

http://doomgate.cs.buffalo.edu/

First Internet Backgammon Server ★★★★

This site lets users play Backgammon in real time against other players.

KEYWORDS Computer Games, Online Games
AUDIENCE Backgammon Players, Game Enthusiasts
CONTACT Andreas Schneider
marvin@fraggel65.mdstud.chalmers.se
FREE

telnet://fraggel65.mdstud.chalmers.se:4321/

GNU WebChess ★★★

GNU WebChess is an online chess game that matches players with the computers. Users may manipulate variables such as which player goes first and the time limit for each play. Although the original screen image of the chessboard takes a long time to download, subsequent plays are quick. FAQs, general rules for chess, and links to other chess resources are also available here.

KEYWORDS Chess, Interactive Media, Internet Games
AUDIENCE Chess Enthusiasts, Games Enthusiasts
CONTACT dj@delorie.com
FREE

http://www.delorie.com/game-room/chess/

Game Bytes ★★★★

A large volume of information on computer gaming fills the pages of this electronic publication. Game Bytes provides reviews, screen shots, previews of soon-to-be-released titles and much more for the computer game player. Attention is given to a wide variety of games, including simulations, arcade games, and strategy. Also on the Web pages are links to other game-related sites.

KEYWORDS Computer Games, Computer Graphics, Games
AUDIENCE Computer Game Developers, Computer Game Enthusiasts, Game Enthusiasts
CONTACT Ross Erickson
rwe@bangate.compaq.com
FREE

http://wcl-rs.bham.ac.uk/GameBytes

gopher://gopher.cic.net/e-serials/alphabetic/g/game-bytes

ftp://ftp.uml.edu/msdos/Games/Game_Bytes/

The Games Domain ★★★★

The Games Domain contains links to hundreds of game sites all over the Web. Users can access lists with links to hundreds of games, ftp sites, and game information, organized into groups such as patches, commercial sites, FAQs, games related ftp and Web sites, walk-throughs, and magazines. Also included is the Games Domain Review with articles and reviews of the gaming industry, freeware and shareware games, and hardware. Other features include the direct download directory, for directly accessing demos and games, and the Games Nexus information archive for games programmers.

KEYWORDS Computer Games, Internet Games, Shareware
AUDIENCE Computer Games Enthusiasts, Games Enthusiasts, General Public, Internet Users
CONTACT djh@gamesdom.demon.co.uk
FREE

http://wcl-rs.bham.ac.uk/GamesDomain

Go FTP Archives ★★★

This is a repository for GO-related material. This site contains graphic interfaces for the Internet GO Server, text files for GO rules and strategy, and GO-playing computer programs.

KEYWORDS Computer Games, Games, Go
AUDIENCE Chinese, Computer Game Enthusiasts, Game Enthusiasts
FREE

ftp://bsdserver.ucsf.edu/Go/

Games

HGJ's Chess Pages ★★★

HGJ's Chess pages are a series of World Wide Web pages that have pointers to more than 200 chess sites across the Internet. The sites are arranged in categories such as Main Chess Links & Local Articles, New Links, Clubs, Chess Clubs & Organizations, Computer Chess & Chess Programs, and Tournaments and Events. There is also an area for humorous stories, FTP sites, and chess-like games.

Keywords Board Games, Chess, Strategy Games
Audience Board Games Players, Chess Enthusiasts
Contact Herbert Groot Jebbink
hgj@xs4all.nl
Free

http://www.xs4all.nl/~hgj/chess.html

Internet Chess Server (USA) ★★★★

This site allows chess enthusiasts to play chess or watch games being played in real time. It features automatic chess ratings and a user base ranging from novice chessplayers to Grand Masters. This system is operated by a group of volunteers.

Keywords Chess, Games, Online Games
Audience Chess Enthusiasts, Chess Players, Game Enthusiasts
Contact Daniel Sleator
sleator@cs.cmu.edu
Free

ftp://ics.onenet.net/pub/chess/

telnet://chess.lm.com:5000

The Internet Chinese Chess Server (ICCS) ★★★★

This site lets users play Chinese chess against other players in real-time.

Keywords Chess, Computer Games, Online Games
Audience Chinese, Game Enthusiasts
Contact xichen@coolidge.harvard.edu
Free

telnet://coolidge.harvard.edu:5555

Internet Go Server ★★★★

Users play the Asian board game 'GO' in real time at this site. Graphic interfaces are available for many computers. GO tournaments are held periodically.

Keywords Games, Go, Online Games, Virtual Community
Audience Chinese, Game Enthusiasts
Contact igs-adm@igs.nuri.net
Free

telnet://igs.nuri.net:6969

Mr. Potato Head ★★★★

This is an interactive game of Mr. Potato Head that you play on the Internet. Just select a feature with the radio buttons, and then select finished to redraw the image. Or select reset to get a blank head.

Keywords Children, Interactive Games
Audience Children, Internet Users, Parents, Students (Primary/Secondary)
Free

http://www.acsu.buffalo.edu/cgi-bin/potato

OKbridge Bridge on the Internet ★★★

OKbridge is an online bridge club, established so that users can play bridge on the Internet, and this Web site provides information about OKbridge and guidelines to becoming a member. Although participating in bridge games is restricted to paid members, the OKbridge Web site provides a manual, ethical guidelines, and a mailing list. It is possible to try a sample game and look at a photo album of OKbridge members. Also included are links to other bridge clubs, newsgroups, and bridge archives on the Web.

Keywords Bridge, Card Games, Games
Audience Bridge Enthusiasts, Card Players
Contact Matthew Clegg
info@OKbridge.com
Cost

http://www.cts.com/~okbridge/

Play by Mail Home Page ★★★

This page contains information and pointers to games that can be played via email or snail mail. Users will find an FAQ about play by mail games, taken from rec.games.pbm, as well as a huge list of games, with information about the sponsoring company, game types, duration, costs, and general description. The Galactic View tables are also provided, as well as a Play-by-Email fanzine available online. Links to Play by Mail Web sites are also included.

Keywords Email, Internet Games
Audience Games Enthusiasts, Internet Users
Contact Greg Lindahl
gl8f@virginia.edu
Free

http://fermi.clas.virginia.edu/~gl8f/pbm.html

Sliding Tile Puzzle ★★★

This site offers a 4x4 tile puzzle which the user can complete by clicking on individual tiles with the goal of fixing a scrambled image. The page, including all of its images, reloads every time one clicks on a tile, so this site requires above-average bandwidth. The site also links to some information about the puzzle and how it works, and to a collection of more sliding tile puzzles.

Keywords Games, Tile Puzzles
Audience Children, Game Enthusiasts, Web Developers, Web Users
Contact Andrew Wilson
Andrew.Wilson@cm.cf.ac.uk
Free

http://www.cm.cf.ac.uk/htbin/AndrewW/Puzzle/puzzle4x4image

Soccer Games ★★

This page includes a a non-hyperlinked directory of sites where computer soccer games can be located. The games include Italian Football Manager for PCs, Football Manager Game for Windows, Football Manager for the PC (DOS), One - Nil for the PC (DOS), and Italian Football Manager PC game (3.05).

Keywords Computer Games, Soccer
Audience Computer Games Enthusiasts, Soccer Fans, Sports Fans, Students (Primary/Secondary)
Free

http://www.atm.ch.cam.ac.uk:80/sports/games.html

Super Nintendo Entertainment System ★★★★

This is a page with some bits and pieces about the Super Nintendo Entertainment System. Included are links to other WWW Nintendo sources, hundreds of video game FAQs including Saga, Aladdin, Galen Komatsu's Art of Fighting, Alien vs. Predator, Knuckleheads, Mortal Kombat, Samurai Shodown, Super Mario, etc.; Nick's Super Nintendo Game Ratings, and links to the newsgroup rec.games.video.nintendo.

Keywords Games, Video Games
Audience Internet Users, Nintendo Enthusiasts, Video Games Players
Contact s.b.hill@bris.ac.uk
Free

http://sbh.cse.bris.ac.uk/Nintendo.html

ftp://ftp.netcom.com/pub/vi/videogames/faqs

Time Hunter's Page for Gamers ★★

TimeHunter's Page for Gamers contains information and links for some of the most popular action games for DOS computers. Most of the links here are related to Doom, Descent, or Heretic, although there are also links to general gaming sites as well. In addition, almost all of the links from this page go to other sites where the actual content and/or software is located.

Keywords Computer Games, Heretic
Audience Computer Game Enthusiasts, Descent Players, Doom Players
Free

http://aspin.asu.edu/provider/dcgovier/gamer.html

The Week in Chess ★★★★

This site allows you to view live chess games as well as those played in recent tournaments around the world. It also includes chess-related news and analyses.

Keywords Board Games, Chess, News
Audience Chess Enthusiasts, Chess Players
Free

http://www.brad.ac.uk/~mdcrowth/chess.html/

World Snooker Archive ★★★

The World Snooker Archive is designed to be a comprehensive guide for snooker players all over the world, providing material on snooker and links to other resources on the Web. Besides general information about tournaments and championships, this site includes an archive of pictures and a video of top-ranking snooker players, useful addresses and phone numbers, and a bibliography of books. Miscellaneous items, such as a timeline of the history of snooker, various world records, and information about becoming professional are included.

KEYWORDS Games, Online Games, Snooker, Table Games
AUDIENCE Games Enthusiasts, Snooker Players
CONTACT M.S. Braithwaite
M.S.Braithwaite@bradford.ac.uk
FREE

http://www.brad.ac.uk/~msbraith/S/s.html

Zarf's List of Interactive Games on the Web ★★★

This site is a directory of games and entertaining diversions which are played in real time on the World Wide Web. The list has Interactive games such as multi-player games, user-versus-computer games, adventure games, and anything else that sounds like a game. In addition, users can access a list of Interactive Toys.

KEYWORDS Computer Games, Online Games
AUDIENCE Computer Game Enthusiasts, Game Enthusiasts, Web Users
CONTACT Andrew Plotkin
erkyrath@cmu.edu
FREE

http://www.cs.cmu.edu/afs/andrew/org/kgb/www/zarf/games.html

Gardening

See also
Health & Medicine · *Alternative Medicine*
Science · *Botany*
Science · *Environment Science*

Art in the Garden ★★★★

Art in the Garden is the Home page for the event by the same name sponsored by the Evanston Chamber of Commerce, Illinois. The event, which takes place every summer, is a fair for urban garden designers to show off their work. The page contains a description of the event with dates, a map on how to get there, an application for artists, past award winners and a link to the Evanston chamber of commerce.

KEYWORDS Gardens, Illinois
AUDIENCE Evanston Residents, Gardeners, Landscape Designers
CONTACT EvChamber@aol.com
FREE

http://www.cola.chi.il.us/cola/artinthegarden

Atlanta Garden Connection ★★

Atlanta Garden Connection gives gardeners in Atlanta an Internet destination where they can learn where to find gardening resources and information. Upcoming features include online conversations with other Atlanta gardeners, information about gardening attractions in Georgia and nearby states and calendars of upcoming gardening events.

KEYWORDS Gardening, Gardens, Georgia, Internet Resources
AUDIENCE Gardeners, Gardening Enthusiasts
FREE

http://www.atlgarden.com/

Bonsai Home Page ★★

This page is devoted to the art of growing bonsai trees. There are images of trees grown by various contributors to this archive. In addition, viewers can access links to bonsai clubs, bonsai FAQs, a bonsai dictionary, and bonsai book lists and reviews.

KEYWORDS Bonsai Trees, Gardening, Horticulture, Plants
AUDIENCE Bonsai Enthusiasts, Botanists, Florists, Flower Enthusiasts, Gardeners, Horticulturalists
CONTACT Michael Dinsmore
dinsmore@world.std.com
FREE

http://www.pass.wayne.edu/~dan/

gopher://bonsai.pass.wayne.edu/

ftp://bonsai.pass.wayne.edu/

Brooklyn Botanic Garden ★★★

Brooklyn Botanic Garden blooms in the middle of one of the largest cities in the world. More than 12,000 kinds of plants from around the globe are displayed on 52 acres and in the Steinhardt Conservatory. Its Website provides access to membership information, sample articles from its publication 'Plants & Gardens News,' and a membership form.

KEYWORDS Botanical Gardens, Club Memberships, Gardening
AUDIENCE Gardeners, Gardening Enthusiasts
FREE

http://mirror.wwa.com/mirror/orgs/bbg/bbg.htm

The Carniverous Plant Archive Page ★★★★

The Carniverous Plant Archive Page is a premium cache of information about Droseras, Pings, Nepenthes, VFTs, and quite a few more of these fascinating plants. Here you will encounter a bibliography of many related books and articles, a variety of suppliers' lists from around the world, including commercial nurseries and grow and trade lists of other aficionados; an international listing of carnivorous plant societies; information on how to legally import the plants; information on the care and housing of meat-eating plants, and a link to the taxonomic database at the Carniverous Plant Home Page.

KEYWORDS Botany, Gardening, Horticulture
AUDIENCE Botanists, Carniverous Plant Enthusiasts, Gardeners, Horticulturalists
CONTACT Chris Frazier
cfrazie@unm.edu
FREE

http://randomaccess.unm.edu/www/cp/cparchive.html

The Cyber-Plantsman ★★★

The Cyber-Plantsman is an online publication of Barry Glick, advertised as the source of 'all sorts of valuable and interesting information for the serious gardener.' Links to various flower shows, symposiums, book 'raviews' (books to rave about), horticultural heroes, and much, much more.

KEYWORDS Flower Shows, Gardening, Horticulture, Online Publications
AUDIENCE Gardeners, Gardening Enthusiasts
FREE

http://mirror.wwa.com/mirror/garden/cyberplt.htm

Don't Panic Eat Organic ★★★

This organic gardening home page is by Noah's Ark, one of the world's suppliers of organic cherimoya, and includes dozens of links for organic farmers, gardeners and other natural foods enthusiasts.

KEYWORDS Gardening Supplies, Natural Foods, Organic Gardening
AUDIENCE Agriculturalists, Gardeners, Natural Foods Enthusiasts
FREE

http://www.rain.org/~sals/my.html

The Garden Patch ★★★
COMMERCIAL

This is the Virtual Mirror's Garden Patch, a central index of garden pages. It is a commercial publication with advertising within its pages provided by a business directory, and links to page sponsors and relevant advertisers in product reviews.

KEYWORDS Directories, Garden Tips, Perennials, Planting
AUDIENCE Gardeners, Gardening Enthusiasts
FREE

http://mirror.wwa.com/mirror/garden/patch.htm

GardenNet ★★★

GardenNet is a resource center for garden enthusiasts and links to GardenNet Magazine, Gardens OnLine, a catalog center, book center, visitor's center, events calendar, garden associations and other Internet garden resources.

KEYWORDS Gardening Supplies, Gardens, Internet Resources, Online Catalogs
AUDIENCE Gardeners, Gardening Enthusiasts
CONTACT webmaster@olympus.net
FREE

http://www.olympus.net/gardens/welcome.html

Gardens & Gardening ★★★

The Gardens and Gardening site, run by Peter Henry and Laura Jantek, gives access to their monthly column, 'Fine Gardens,' , provides a forum for gardening questions or the opportunity to write to Laura and Peter, explores environmental issues, and provides pointers to selected Internet resources.

KEYWORDS Environmental Issues, Gardening, Gardens, Plant Clubs

Gardening **637**

AUDIENCE Environmentalists, Gardeners, Gardening Enthusiasts
CONTACT aa036@cfn.cs.dal.ca
FREE

http://www.cfn.cs.dal.ca/Recreation/Gardening/G_G_Home.html

Herbs & Spices

Ron Lunde's Herb site includes an index of herbs and spices, recipes, sources, how to grow your own, history, geography, and references.

KEYWORDS Herbs, Internet Resources, Online Publications, Spices
AUDIENCE Gardeners, Gardening Enthusiasts
FREE

http://www.teleport.com/~ronl/herbs/herbs.html

Horticulture Solutions

The Horticulture Solutions Web site provides information and tips for gardening. Users will find information grouped by topic, such as flowers, houseplants, pests, soils and fertilizers, and vegetables. Information in each section is listed alphabetically, with general background about plants, growing tips, and problem recognition. A glossary of terms is also included.

KEYWORDS Horticulture, Plants
AUDIENCE Gardeners, Gardening Enthusiasts, Horticulturalists, Nature Lovers
CONTACT solutions@ilces.ag.uiuc.edu
FREE

http://www.ag.uiuc.edu/~robsond/solutions/hort.html

Hortus-A Gardening Journal

Hortus, A Gardening Journal, produced in the UK, advertises itself as the 'most intelligent magazine in the world.' It is a privately published quarterly journal which addresses itself to intelligent and lively-minded gardeners throughout the English-speaking world.

KEYWORDS Gardening, Gardens, Magazines
AUDIENCE Gardeners, Gardening Enthusiasts
CONTACT services@kc3ltd.demon.co.uk
FREE

http://www.kc3ltd.co.uk/business/hortus.html

InfoVid Outlet- Gardening & Flowers

InfoVid Outlet is an educational and how-to video warehouse. Its online catalog lists 25 gardening and flower videos available to order with links to an order form.

KEYWORDS Flowers, Gardening, Online Catalogs, Videos
AUDIENCE Gardeners, Gardening Enthusiasts
FREE

http://branch.com:1080/infovid/c318.html

Connections to Gardening
A rose by any other name . . .

Once you've weeded the crab grass in your back yard and planted a few cucumbers along the hedge row, why not explore the world's online gardens?

You can stroll through the Australian National Botanic Gardens, see the "Flowers of the Week," or discover sub-Antarctic island plants. Even critters like frogs and birds are allocated Web space at the gardening site. Additionally, you'll find interesting hotlinks, as well as suggested reading materials for the novice and professional gardener alike.

(http://155.187.10.12:80/anbg/anbg.html)

If you want to access all the latest gardening tips from Time-Life, Inc.'s vast gardening publications division (including magazines such as Sunset and Southern Living), then "The Virtual Garden" is the place to browse. In addition to this site, there are dozens of others that provide a wealth of hotlinks and information on botanical gardens. You'll gain access to plant authorities who can advise you how to treat the insect infestation of daffodils or root-rot in an elm tree.

(http://www.pathfinder.com/@@CwXHcwAAAAAAAED8/vg/)

Pilatus- Luwasa Hydroculture Plant Protection System

This site developed by Pilatus Direct markets their line of Luwasa planters to online users. The page outlines the Luwasa plant feeding system and allows users to order the planters online.

KEYWORDS Botany, Gardening, Plants
AUDIENCE Environmentalists, Gardeners, Home Decorators, Home Makers
FREE

http://usa.net/pilatus/

Pukeiti Rhododendron Trust

The Pukeiti Rhododendron Trust Home page covers one of New Zealand's premier public gardens, with over 2,000 species of Rhododendrons. Many images of Rhododendrons can also be viewed here.

KEYWORDS Gardening, New Zealand
AUDIENCE Gardeners, Horticulturalists, New Zealand Residents
CONTACT H.Bolitho h.bolitho@taranaki.ac.nz & m.plant@taranaki.ac.nz
FREE

http://pluto.taranaki.ac.nz/pukeiti/pukinfo.html

Sunshine Farm & Gardens ★★★

Sunshine Farm & Gardens is the home, farm, garden, arboretum and nursery of Barry Glick, aka the Cyber-Plantsman. Barry exchanges seeds and plants with hundreds of botanical gardens and individual plant collectors and gardeners the world over. Visitors are welcome with advance notice and plants from the collection are available for sale to the public.

KEYWORDS Arboretums, Gardens, Organizations, Plant Collections
AUDIENCE Gardeners, Gardening Enthusiasts
FREE

http://mirror.wwa.com/mirror/busdir/sunshine/sunshine.htm

University of Florida Herbarium ★★★

The University of Florida Herbarium is an integral unit in the Department of Natural Sciences of the Florida Museum of Natural History. Pointers are provided to the Vascular Plant collection, news and announcements, and a catalog.

KEYWORDS Botanical Gardens, Gardening, Herbarium
AUDIENCE Botanists, Gardeners, Gardening Enthusiasts
FREE

http://nabalu.flas.ufl.edu/flashome.html

Virtual Garden ★★★★

COMMERCIAL

The Virtual Garden Homepage is devoted to all aspects of home gardening. It is created by Time-Life and often quotes articles printed in their publications, such as Sunset Magazine. However, this is a worthwhile resource in its own right, consisting of a searchable database of approximately 2000 North American houseplants (searchable by a wide array of choices, including type, height or color of plant); a directory of flowering houseplants organized by Latin botanical name, with a link to each plant; a directory of foliage houseplants, similarly organized; sections on picking out and the care and maintenance of houseplants; and a zone finder, so you can be sure of the planting zone you are in. The Magazine Rack section has links to articles from Sunset, Southern Living and Homeground, and links to advertisements for Time-Life books on gardening.

KEYWORDS Gardening, Horticulture
AUDIENCE Botanists, Gardeners, Horticulturalists, House Plant Enthusiasts
CONTACT vg-webmaster@www.timeinc.com
FREE

http://www.timeinc.com/vg/

Motor Sports

See also
Popular Culture & Entertainment · Automobiles
Sports & Recreation · Weather & Traffic

1955 Dodge La Femme ★★

COMMERCIAL

This page highlights the 1955 and 1956 Dodge La Femme, the only mass produced cars designed specifically for women. The 1955 La Femme was pink and white, with pink rosebud upholstery, a factory-equipped pink leather purse, pink umbrella, rain hat and rain coat. The viewer can read a very large document describing the car and the public's reaction, as well as see images of this car.

KEYWORDS Collectibles
AUDIENCE Antique Dealers, Automobile Collectors, Feminists, Historians
CONTACT xxltony@cts.com
FREE

http://www.cts.com/~xxltony/1955-la-femme.html

Alfa Romeo Home Page (Unofficial) ★★★

This page is an noncommercial web site devoted to Alfa Romeo automobiles. Users will find different kinds of information about Alfa Romeos including details about particular models (Spiders, 145's, Milanos, etc.) and general information such as technical specifications, contact information for local Alfa Romeo car clubs, where to find spare parts, history of the Alfa Romeo car line, pictures, and even a listing of movies in which Alfa Romeos have appeared. Several articles related to Alfa Romeo's pullout of the American car market can be found here. The server is located in Australia, and has information collected from a variety of international sources.

KEYWORDS Automobiles, Italy, Sports Cars
AUDIENCE Automobile Enthusiasts, Automobile Racing Enthusiasts, Drivers, Mechanics
CONTACT baragry@amdahl1.cs.latrobe.odu.au
FREE

http://amdahl1.lat.oz.au:8080/~baragry/AlfaRomeo/

BMW K-Bike Motorcycles ★★★★

This page provides everything you ever wanted to know about BMW motorcyIces. There is also detailed information about the BMW motorcycle organization (which apparently has around 20,000 members). There is a major list of hot links addressing every how-to question ever posed regarding these motorcycles.

KEYWORDS Mechanics, Motor Sports, Motorcycles
AUDIENCE BMW Motorcycle Riders, Motorcycle Enthusiasts
FREE

http://www.cms.udel.edu/~walt/BMW.html

Brit-Iron ★★★

Welcome to the home page for the British motorcycle mailing list, Brit-Iron. The purpose of Brit-Iron is to provide a forum for riders, restorers and admirers of these classic machines to share information and experiences. There is also a long list of hot links to motorcycling around the world.

KEYWORDS Britain, Mechanics, Motor Sports, Motorcycles
AUDIENCE Brit-Iron Enthusiasts, Motorcycle Enthusiasts
FREE

http://bronze.ucs.indiana.edu/~cstringe/brit.html

Cameron Simpson's Moto Page ★★★★

This page contains links to information about events, people and other motorcycle-related pages. Trip reports are also included. There are links to commercial sites, club information, magazine information, and more.

KEYWORDS Clubs, Mechanics, Motor Sports, Motorcycles
AUDIENCE Motorcycle Riders, Motorcyle Enthusiasts
FREE

http://www.dap.csiro.au/~cameron/moto/

Chrysler Neon Homepage (Unofficial) ★★★

This is an unofficial homepage for the Chysler Neon. It presents a variety of information put together from various sources by Neon enthusiasts. What viewers will find here are images of the Neon, a listing of options available for the car, and a hypertext listing of Neon's TSB's (Technical Service Bulletins), which are useful for diagnosing specific car problems.

KEYWORDS Automobile Maintenance, Automobiles
AUDIENCE Automobile Buyers, Drivers
FREE

http://www.public.iastate.edu/~sheldon/neon.html

Coming General Motor Events ★★★

This page provides a calendar of motorcycling events around Australia. This includes rallies, runs, test days, etc. Races are not included. There are links to calendars of events elsewhere in Australia.

KEYWORDS Australia, Motor Racing, Motor Sports, Motorcycles
AUDIENCE Australians, Motorcycle Enthusiasts
FREE

http://ledoux.arbld.unimelb.edu.au/~mtc/motorbike/comingup.html

ESPNET SportsZone Auto Racing ★★★

ESPNET SportsZone Auto Racing provides news and information on top stories of the day such as 'McLaren driving team drops Mansell,' and feature stories including Indy advertisements and 'Ask Dr. Jerry

Motor Sports – Organizations

Punch.' One section is devoted to the Indianapolis 500 (or the current big race) including a daily update, starting lineup, or the current big race.

KEYWORDS Auto Racing, Indianapolis 500
AUDIENCE Automobile Enthusiasts, Automobile Racing Enthusiasts, Sports Fans
CONTACT ESPNET SportsZone
espnet.sportszone@starwave.com
FREE

http://espnet.sportszone.com/car

Harley-Davidson Web Site ★★★

Everything you ever wanted to know about Harley-Davidsons can be found here at the Harley Web Site. All the different models are described in detail. Tool kit information and lists of recall notes can also be found.

KEYWORDS Mechanics, Motor Sports, Motorcycles
AUDIENCE Harley-Davidson Enthusiasts, Motorbike Enthusiasts
FREE

http://www.halcyon.com/zipgun/wwg/wwg.html

Motorcycle Online is Here ★★★★

For motorcycle enthusiasts with time on their hands to browse, Motorcycle Online is a good site to start with! There's a major section on antique bikes, a 'Nuts and Bolts' section, links to the Motorcycle Online Bulletin Board, and the Complete Motorcycle Database.

KEYWORDS Motor Racing, Motor Sports, Motorcycles
AUDIENCE Motorcycle Enthusiasts
FREE

http://motorcycle.com/motorcycle.html

R.A.S. Racer Archive ★★★

Welcome to the r.a.s. Racer Archive. Here you will find information on Formula 1, IndyCar, and NASCAR racing. There are links to the Formula 1 World Championship, CART PPG IndyCar Championship, NASCAR Winston Cup Championship, GIF and JPEG racing pictures, and links to the newsgroups.

AUDIENCE Automobile Racers, Automobile Racing Enthusiasts, Motor Sports Enthusiasts
CONTACT Jay Carina
carina@wiliki.eng.hawaii.edu
FREE

http://www.eng.hawaii.edu/Contribs/carina/ra.home.page.html

Rec.Motorcycles.Reviews Archives Home Page ★★★★

The Rec.Motorcycles.Reviews Archives contains a plethora of bike and accessories reviews, written by rec.motorcycle NewsNet readers based on their own experiences. A wide variety of bike images gathered off the Net can also be found here along with hot links to home pages for specific motorcycle makes, including ones for Honda, Buell, BMW, and others.

KEYWORDS Mechanics, Motor Sports, Motorcycles
AUDIENCE Motorcycle Enthusiasts, Motorcycle Riders

Connections to Car Clubs
On your mark . . . get set . . . Go!

All around the world, car owners are linking up via the Internet and forming clubs that celebrate a certain make and model of car.

For example, the Scottish Kit Car Club provides information on club events, such as car shows, club visits to car museums and a race for owners of kit and special cars. Included in its annual membership is a monthly newsletter, a quarterly magazine, free passes or discounts to any car shows the group particpates in, as well as discounts from suppliers. You can even share your expertise in the care and "feeding" of many special cars, including the Westfield, Lancia or BMW.

(http://www.tay.ac.uk/mcsweb/staff/amm/skcc.html)

Cybercars is one of the largest car collection sites on the Internet. This area offers Kit Car Manufacturer's catalogs and full-size replicas of Cobras, Ferraris, Lamborghinis.

(http://www.cybercars.com/)

FREE

http://www.cecm.sfu.ca/RMR_home.html

Red Line Highway ★★

Red Line Highway is the motorcycle enthusiast's center for information, gear etc. If you're passionate about motorcycling, whether you're into touring, racing, rallies, cruising, canyon carving, dirt, the latest, the oldest, or the fastest, it's all here.

KEYWORDS Motor Racing, Motor Sports, Motorcycles
AUDIENCE Motorcycle Enthusiasts, Motorcycle Racing Enthusiasts
FREE

http://www.dnai.com/~infored/

Organizations

See also
Sports & Recreation · *Recreation*
Sports & Recreation · *Sports*

Monthly Optics for Birding FAQ ★★★★

The Monthly Optics for Birding FAQ is an adjunct to both the Usenet Newsgroup rec.birds and the Wildbirds FAQ. It is a very detailed account of current optical devices used for bird watching. Covering primarily binoculars of all types and price ranges, as well as telescopes. This FAQ is also thorough in its discussion of peripherals (ie. tripods, window mounts, etc.). Bird watching magazines are also noted.

KEYWORDS Birds, Ornithology, Wildlife
AUDIENCE Astronomers, Bird Watchers, Ornithologists, Wilderness Enthusiasts
CONTACT Ed Matthews
edm@aib.com
FREE

ftp://rtfm.mit.edu/pub/usenet-by-group/rec.birds/rec.birds_Monthly_Optics_for_Birding_FAQ

NBA Information Pages ★★★

The site contains the NBA Information Pages. Topics include video highlights for yesterday's NBA games, the NBA Schedule, NBA team home pages, Eric Richard's Professional Basketball Server, Gate Cybersports NBA Page, NBAStats Project, basketball FAQ, Satchel Sports NBA, Nerdo.Net Covering the NBA, etc.

KEYWORDS Basketball, Newspapers
AUDIENCE Basketball Fans, Coaches, Sports Fans
FREE

http://www.tns.lcs.mit.edu/cgi-bin/sports/nba

Organizations – Outdoor Recreation

Surfrider Online ★★★

This is the page for the Surfrider Foundation. Surfrider is a non-profit environmental organization dedicated to the protection and enhancement of the world's waves and beaches through conservation, activism, research and education. The site contains information on surfing conditions world wide and on problems that effect surfing conditions including pollution, and legislation aimed at protecting the surfing environment. The site also contains GIF format images of surfing, news clippings related to the subject and an online version of the Surfrider newsletter.

KEYWORDS California, Environmental Protection, Surfing
AUDIENCE Californians, Environmentalists, Surfing Enthusiasts
CONTACT Mike Roberts
mike@swirl.com/miker@progress.com
FREE

http://www.sdsc.edu/surfrider.html

University of Utah Ski Reports ★★

This University of Utah gopher server provides skiers and local residents with information on backcountry avalanche bulletins, advisories, and warnings. The site also provides access to headlines and excerpts from the Salt Lake Tribune newspaper.

KEYWORDS News, Skiing, Utah, Weather
AUDIENCE Skiing Enthusiasts, Sports Fans, Utah Residents
CONTACT jonzy@cc.utah.edu
FREE

gopher://u.cc.utah.edu/

Outdoor Recreation

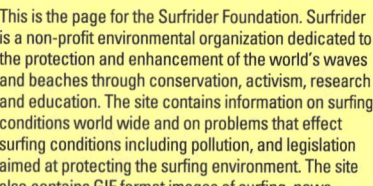

See also
Science · *Environmental Sciences*
Sports & Recreation · *Aquatic Sports*

Adventuring/IGLOO ★★★★

Adventuring is a nonprofit organization providing opportunites for group outdoor activities to the Washington DC gay and lesbian community. Their home page provides information about the group and its parent organization, IGLOO (the International Gay and Lesbian Outdoor Organization), upcoming activities, and related topics.

KEYWORDS Organizations, Outdoor Education
AUDIENCE Bisexuals, Gays, Lesbians, Washington D.C. Residents, Wilderness Enthusiasts
CONTACT erewhon@digex.com
FREE

http://access.digex.net/~erewhon/

Australian Alpine Information Service ★★★

This page provides up-to-the minute information for those interested in skiing in Australia and New Zealand. It features detailed area maps, which the user may use to look up information about resort and lift ticket prices in any desired region. Also featured are—a list of upcoming downhill and cross-country events; recent weather reports and satellite pictures; information on skiing-related associations and newsgroups; and collections of ski stories, pictures, and Web resources.

KEYWORDS Australia, New Zealand, Ski Resorts, Skiing
AUDIENCE Australians, Skiing Enthusiasts
CONTACT Joe Holloway
Joe.Holloway@adfa.oz.au
FREE

http://www.adfa.oz.au/aais/

The Backcountry Home Page ★★★

This page is an attempt to organize and archive the backcountry-related information that is available on the Internet. Backcountry in this context refers to all kinds of wilderness recreation. There is an emphasis of information on locations inside the United States, though there are International pointers to be found as well.

KEYWORDS Hiking, Outdoor Recreation, Travel, Wilderness
AUDIENCE Hiking Enthusiasts, International Travelers, Outdoors Enthusiasts
CONTACT Stephen Johns
johns@swri.edu
FREE

http://io.datasys.swri.edu/Overview.html

The Bay Area Mountain Rescue Unit (BAMRU) ★

This page describes the activities of the The Bay Area Mountain Rescue Unit (BAMRU), which is a Search and Rescue team working in the San Francisco Bay Area. Users will see a a description of the volunteer organization's services and skills. There are links from this page to other Emergency and Search and Rescue organizations like the Red Cross and the Victoria State Emergency Services. Other items include a text file describing an optimal Wilderness EMS Medical Kit.

KEYWORDS Emergency Medical Services, Search And Rescue (SAR)
AUDIENCE Californians, Emergency Medical Technicians, Mountaineers
FREE

http://baby.indstate.edu/msattler/culture/travel/bamru.html

Bay Area Orienteering Club (BAOC) ★★

In orienteering, you use a map and compass to find your way across unfamiliar terrain. Using your imagination and navigational skills, you try to select the best route to each marker point. There are many versions of orienteering (on foot, bicycle, or skis; at night; in relays, and so forth), but the idea is essentially the same. Furthermore, most orienteering events are in some way, shape or form, a competition (for those inclined). Rogaining is a form of Orienteering where the competition lasts from 12 to 24 or more hours. This page is devoted to the activities of the San Francisco Bay Area chapter (BAOC). Information about Bay Area Orienteering is provided, including information about the BAOC mailing list. Viewers will find schedules of upcoming events, results of previous competitions, rankings, trim (permanent) courses, directions to BAOC-mapped areas, and links to other California and International Orienteering Internet sites and resources.

KEYWORDS Orienteering
AUDIENCE Californians, Orienteering Enthusiasts
CONTACT wriley@leland.stanford.edu
FREE

http://www-leland.stanford.edu/~wriley/baoc.html

Bicycle Racing Results Gopher ★★★★

The purpose of the Millsaps Results gopher is to track results of all forms of bicycle racing, including amateur, collegiate, and professional. Most of the information is compiled from the Usenet newsgroup rec.bicycles.racing, but individuals can contribute local race results to the gopher as well. Besides results, the gopher has pointers to race calendars, television broadcast schedules, and wire reports.

KEYWORDS Bicycle Racing, Bicycling, Mountain Biking
AUDIENCE Bicycle Racers, Bicycling Enthusiasts, Mountain Biking Enthusiasts
CONTACT kingst@okra03.millsaps.edu
FREE

gopher://gopher.millsaps.edu/11GOPHER_ROOT_FOODSERV:[racing]

The Climbing Archive! ★★★

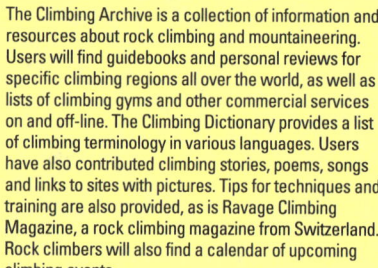

The Climbing Archive is a collection of information and resources about rock climbing and mountaineering. Users will find guidebooks and personal reviews for specific climbing regions all over the world, as well as lists of climbing gyms and other commercial services on and off-line. The Climbing Dictionary provides a list of climbing terminology in various languages. Users have also contributed climbing stories, poems, songs and links to sites with pictures. Tips for techniques and training are also provided, as is Ravage Climbing Magazine, a rock climbing magazine from Switzerland. Rock climbers will also find a calendar of upcoming climbing events.

KEYWORDS Hiking, Mountaineering, Rock Climbing
AUDIENCE Mountaineers, Nature Lovers, Rock Climbers
CONTACT d0asta@dtek.chalmers.se
FREE

http://www.dtek.chalmers.se/Climbing/index.html

Cyberboarder Electronic Magazine - (Snowboarding) ★★★

Cyberboarder Electronic Magazine contains a wealth of information for snowboarders including up-to-the minute snow conditions on the slopes across America (especially in the mountains of Northern California). A number of snowboard-related articles also fill these pages.

KEYWORDS Skiing, Snowboarding, Weather
AUDIENCE Outdoors Enthusiasts, Skiing Enthusiasts, Snowboarders

Outdoor Recreation

Free

http://www-leland.stanford.edu/~etchiu/Cyberboarder/

gopher://dunkin.princeton.edu/

Ebikes ★★

This site contains resources for bicyclists in New York City. The site is based on the Ebikes mailing list, and there are archives available for this list. There is also contact information and descriptions of bicycle organizations such as Transportation Alternatives, Critical Mass, and the Tri-State Transportation Campaign. In addition, viewers can see Frequently Asked Questions from the Ebikes Mailing list, which describes places to bicycle, bicycle shops and clubs, and bridges that allow bicycle accessibilty.

Keywords   Bicycling, Cycling, New York, Transportation
Audience   Bicycling Enthusiasts, Bicycling Enthusiasts, New York Residents
Contact   Danny Lieberman
             dfl@panix.com
Free

http://www.panix.com/ebikes/ebikes.html

gopher://gopher.panix.com:70/11/ebikes

GORP - The Great Outdoor Recreation Pages ★★★

GORP - The Great Outdoor Recreation Pages promises to be the most complete resource for wilderness activities online. Here you will find links on all types of outdoor sport and recreation, from kayaking to bird-watching, from wildlife trips to orienteering. All links are organized by activity type and location, and often include information from all over the world. In addition to learning about the parks, wilderness areas, national wildlife refuges and other sites of interest, there is also a lot of material at this site about outdoor volunteer opportunities, relevant books, and online vendors of appropriate accoutrements as well as organizers of trekking and fishing trips.

Keywords   Adventure Travel, Camping, Wildlife
Audience   Adventure Travelers, Camping Enthusiasts, Fishing Enthusiasts, Wilderness Enthusiasts
Contact   GORP, Greer Consulting Services, Inc.
             postmaster@www.gorp.com
Free

http://www.gorp.com

The Global Cycling Network (VeloNet) ★★★★

This site provides links to many cycling sites on the Web. Some of the information includes Bicycle Organizations (contacts, newsletters, ride calendars, etc), Other Organizations Relevant to Cycling, Upcoming Public Meetings Relevant to Bicycling, Mailing Lists at cycling.org, Regional Information by Geographic Location, The Reading Room, and more.

Keywords   Cycling, Fitness, Sports
Audience   Bicycling Enthusiasts, Fitness Enthusiasts, Sports Fans
Free

http://cycling.org/

Connections to Rock Climbing Resources
Going up?

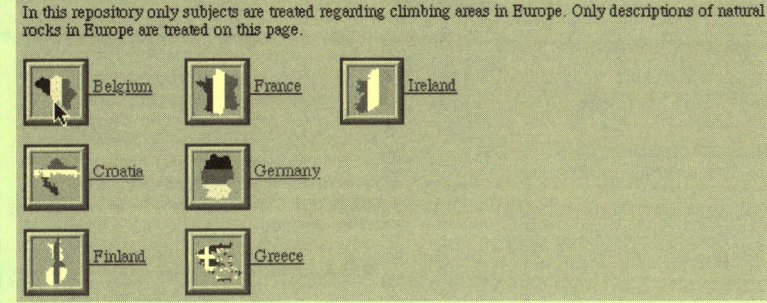

If your idea of adventure or sport is climbing up a rock, then get in touch with resources catering to rock climbing enthusiasts on the Internet.

World Wide Web resources can put you in touch not only with other rock climbers, but provide tales on some of the best places around the world for this sport. You can also get access to up-to-date training, rock climbing gyms (to hone your skills or find out if you like the sport), and the equipment you'll need before you head up.

One place to get essential equipment is a listing of rock climbing companies. But you can also get information on equipment through the "Rock Climbing in Europe" pages. Rock Climbing in Europe provides connections to rock climbing gyms and lists the best places for rock climbing throughout Europe. How about the Alps?

(http://www.eeb.ele.tue.nl/climbing/)

also, (http://www.outdoornet.com/rock/roclist.html)

If you want to know even more about climbing in the Swiss Alps, then read the online version of Ravage—The Swiss Climbing Journal. Here you not only get information about the Swiss climbing scene, but maps, technical articles, stories, pictures and competitions.

(http://www.dtek.chalmers.se/Climbing/Ravage/index.html)

If you are interested in rock climbing in the U.S., there are pages that cater to different regions of the country. The Deep South Climber's Companion, provides hundreds of places in Alabama, Georgia and Tennessee where you can climb. There are photos, maps and a directory of climbing clubs that offer assistance and advice to enthusiasts.

(http://east.isx.com/~lrumanes/climbing/deepsouth.html)

Golf Archives ★★★★

This site contains archives of golf-related information. Specifically, users will find the latest Golf FAQs (Frequently Asked Questions) posted to rec.sport.golf and the GOLF-L Listserv. In addition, there is a listing of people and companies that manufacture custom-designed golf clubs, as well as tips for clubmakers. Golf images, information about specific courses, and general information about the sport. Other Internet links are available within other directories on this server.

Keywords   Archives, Golf
Audience   Golf Club Manufacturers, Golfers
Free

http://dunkin.princeton.edu/.golf/

gopher://dunkin.Princeton.EDU:70/1ftp%3Adunkin.Princeton.EDU@pub/golf/

ftp://dunkin.Princeton.EDU/pub/golf/

The Great Outdoors ★★★

Camping, bicycling, hiking fishing and hunting, skiing, scuba diving, and walking are all available to those looking for recreation in the greater Seattle area. This site, The Great Outdoors, has links to pages that focus on these recreational activities.

Keywords   Hiking, Outdoor Recreation, Pacific Northwest, Washington State
Audience   Outdoors Enthusiasts, Tourists, Washington Residents
Free

http://www.seanet.com/Seattle/Parks/outdoors.html

Hang Gliding WWW Server ★★★

The Hang Gliding WWW Server is an archive of pictures of hang gliders, as well as documents related

Outdoor Recreation – Personal Fitness

to hang gliding. Users will find numerous ways to browse through the photographs, indexed by date and alphabetically by title. Each picture contains information about the pilot, the photographers, and general information about the flight itself. Also provided are hang gliding digests, with information and documents from the 1192-1995 hang gliding mailing lists. Numerous links to other related sites are compiled, such as weather servers, downloadable software for hang gliding, glider designs, and FAQs, as local resources and as pointers to other Web sites.

KEYWORDS Aviation, Hang Gliding
AUDIENCE Aviation Enthusiasts, Hang Gliding Enthusiasts
CONTACT Alec Proudfoot
alec@cougar.stanford.edu
FREE

http://cougar.stanford.edu:7878/HGMPSHomePage.html

J.P.'s Fishing Page ★★

J.P.'s Fishing Page provides a meta-index of information about fishing, with pointers to numerous fishing resources on the Web. Users will find pages with images of flies and fish, links to fishing newsgroups, and a non-ordered list of fishing Web pages. An anonymous ftp server provides users with access to information files from other fishers and fishing enthusiasts.

KEYWORDS Fish, Fishing
AUDIENCE Fishing Enthusiasts, Sports Fans
CONTACT J.P. Suchoski
jsuchosk@mtu.edu
FREE

http://www.geo.mtu.edu/~jsuchosk/fish/fishpage

Mountain Biking ★★

The Mountain Biking page offers news and information to mountain bikers in the San Francisco Bay Area, as well as links to pages about bicycling worldwide. Users will find news flashes of interest to bikers, such as speed limit enforcement in local parks, and notices of municipal and social meetings related to mountain biking. Viewers can see general descriptions of biking trails from Santa Cruz to Lake Tahoe. Descriptions may also include a rating factor for technical, and effort, and overall impressions.

KEYWORDS California, Cycling, Mountain Biking, National Parks
AUDIENCE Bicycling Enthusiasts, Mountain Biking Enthusiasts, Outdoors Enthusiasts
CONTACT webmaster@CS.Stanford.EDU
FREE

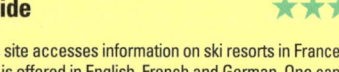

http://xenon.stanford.edu/~rsf/mtn-bike.html

Ski IN - The Global Ski Guide ★★★

This site accesses information on ski resorts in France and is offered in English, French and German. One can look for resorts by region or by alphabetical resort listing, or check out a listing of the author's favorite resorts for skiing, skiing off the beaten track, and children. There will be links to snowboarding and cross-country skiing available soon.

KEYWORDS France, Guides, Ski Resorts
AUDIENCE French, Skiing Enthusiasts
FREE

http://www.idnet.fr/ski/

Skydive! Archive ★★★

Skydive! is an archive of information and links to resources on the Web that have to do with skydiving. Users will find documents grouped into categories such as organizations, relative work, equipment, safety and training, and places to go. Information includes Federal Aviation Regulations, Skydiving Malfunction Survey Results, and a list of Drop Zones, Clubs, and Schools online. Instructions about how to do certain kinds of drops such as sitflying, freeflying, skysurfing, or freestyle, are also included.

KEYWORDS Aviation, Skydiving
AUDIENCE Aviation Enthusiasts, Skydiving Enthusiasts
CONTACT Bradley C. Spatz and Eric S. Johnson
bcs@cis.ufl.edu
FREE

http://www.cis.ufl.edu/skydive/

Speleology Server Home Page ★★★

The Speleology Home Page provides information about speleology, the sport of caving. Users will find information about the National Speleology Society, as well as other speleology organizations. Other materials include an archive of caving pictures, clip art and cartoons, as well as more serious files with software for cave mapping and surveying. Caving documents include archives of the Cavers Digest newsgroup and Caving Online newsletter regarding spelunking resources on the Internet. Users will also find a public calendar of speleological events, and information about commercial equipment retailers.

KEYWORDS Caving, Spelunking
AUDIENCE Adventure Sport Enthusiasts, Caving Enthusiasts
CONTACT Robert M. Hubley
Hubley-Robert@CS.YALE.EDU
FREE

http://speleology.cs.yale.edu/

The WWW Bicycle Lane ★★★★

The WWW Bicycle Lane has pointers to many bicycle-related sites - over a dozen WWW sites, several FTP sites, gophers, and mailing lists. The page also contains six large JPEG images of famous moments in professional cycling history. One very interesting subdirectory has pointers to online USCF (United States Cycling Federation) teams. The page also has a few nice online images.

KEYWORDS Bicycle Racing, Bicycling, Cycling
AUDIENCE Bicycle Racers, Bicycling Enthusiasts
CONTACT Bryn Dole
dole@cs.purdue.edu
FREE

http://www.cs.purdue.edu/homes/dole/bike.html

Womens' Mountain Bike and Tea Society (WOMBATS) ★★

WOMBATS (Womens' Mountain Bike and Tea Society) is a network of mountain biking clubs whose mission is 'to sustain a women's off-road cycling network so that members may—find a riding partner, encourage girls and women to try cycling for the fun of it, learn the trails in their area, improve riding skills, keep up with the latest news of interest on 'women who love mud too much', enhance awareness of bicycles as a mode of transportation, and in short, change the world.'

KEYWORDS Cycling, Mountain Biking, Women's Sports
AUDIENCE Bicycling Enthusiasts, Mountain Biking Enthusiasts, Women
CONTACT Echo
jhhl@echonyc.com, hadley@echonyc.com
FREE

http://www.echonyc.com/~hadley/wombats/wombats.html

Personal Fitness

See also
Health & Medicine · *Personal Care*
Popular Culture & Entertainment · *Lifestyles*

Cray Research Incorporated Fitness Files ★★★

This site provides access to an abbreviated database on health and nutrition. A complete nutrition database is available at this site from the same original US Government location. A FAQ (Frequently Asked Questions) file can be accessed here regarding miscellaneous fitness information.

KEYWORDS Diet, Fitness, Health News, Nutrition
AUDIENCE Dietitians, Employees, Fitness Enthusiasts, Health Care Providers, Nutritionists
CONTACT Jeff Gleixner
glex@cray.com
FREE

ftp://ftp.cray.com/pub/misc.fitness/

The Female Bodybuilder Home Page ★★★

'This page is about female bodybuilding and so you can expect that there will be some pictures of female bodybuilders posing, working out, etc.' There are also links to home pages of several female bodybuilders, and many links to photographs. If you are offended by pictures of female bodybuilders, consider yourself warned. There are also links to newsgroups, magazines, products, etc.

KEYWORDS Fitness, Sports
AUDIENCE Athletes, Bodybuilders, Fitness Enthusiasts, Weight Trainers
FREE

http://www.ama.caltech.edu/~mrm/body.html

ftp://ftp.cray.com in the /pub/misc.fitness directory.

Personal Fitness – Pets & Animals   **643**

Stretching and Flexibility

This site contains links to a wealth of information on stretching and flexibility. Linked topics include the physiology of stretching, flexibility, types of stretching, how to stretch, references on stretching, working toward the splits, and normal ranges of joint motion.

- KEYWORDS: Athletics, Fitness, Sports Physiology, Stretching
- AUDIENCE: Athletes, Bodybuilders, Fitness Enthusiasts, Weight Trainers
- FREE

http://archie.ac.il/papers/rma/stretching_1.html

The Weightlifting Page! ★★★

This page contains links to information on weightlifting. The topics include newsgroups, mailing lists, the abdominal training FAQ, nutrition, Olympic-style lifting and powerlifting, bodybuilding, Reebok's site, etc.

- KEYWORDS: Fitness, Sports
- AUDIENCE: Athletes, Bodybuilders, Fitness Enthusiasts, Weight Trainers
- CONTACT: Kyle Wilson   ksw@cs.odu.edu
- FREE

http://www.cs.odu.edu/~ksw/weights.html

Connections to English Soccer

Use your head

So how has the Wimbledon Football Club done this season? Are the Nottingham Forest and the Queen's Park Rangers in the running for first place? If you're interested in English Soccer, the Internet is the place to find all of the statistics and game scores. You can also get information on team facts, such as the club using the most players in a match (Ipswich), or the one that uses the most substitutes (Norwich).

If you don't understand the game or its rules, you can tap into a number of Internet sites that will provide that information, such as the FAQ (frequently asked questions) site, or "Soccermania" home page.

If you are in the U.S. but want to watch some of the European matches, you can get to a site called "Soccer on U.S. TV" that will give you the desired information.

(http://www.rosat.mpe-garching.mpg.de/~mjf/.FCB/RSS.FAQ)

also, (http://cswww2.sx.ac.uk/users/jrtobi/soccer/)

also, (http://www.best.com/~olivert/soccer/tv-info.html)

Soccer is a game played worldwide, so many of these sites target specific team play in such places as Kuwait, Australia, and Argentina. You can also get a brief history of the game, bookmaker's odds on a given team's championship chances, and more team scores from around the globe.

(http://cypress.mcsr.olemiss.edu/~ccadeff/arg/soccer/campeon/)

also, (http://www.liii.com/~hajeri/sports.html)

Pets & Animals

See also
Health & Medicine · *Veterinary Medicine*
Popular Culture & Entertainment · *Family & Community*
Science · *Zoology*

Adam's Fox Box ★★★★

Adam's Fox Box is the pre-eminent spot for foxes on the World Wide Web. Whether you are a fox yourself, or are interested in getting to know a few, this could easily be your first stop. Available here are lots of fox stories, poems, songs, legends, myths and other literary miscellany; many pictures of foxes; links and information to just about anything you can think of that includes the word fox (for example, the foxtrot); a little movie of a fox preparing a vole for dinner; quite a list of books about foxes, and links to many imaginable and a few unimaginable related sites, from alt.skunks to alt.fan.furries.

- KEYWORDS: Animal Rights, Foxes
- AUDIENCE: Animal Lovers, Dog Owners, Fox Enthusiasts
- CONTACT: Adam D. Moss   mossap@essex.ac.uk
- FREE

http://tavi.acomp.usf.edu/foxbox/

Adopt-A-Lemur ★★★★

Adopt-A-Lemur is a program sponsored by the Duke University Primate Center, a research facility prominent in the study of prosimian primate behavior, diet and reproduction. The Adopt-A-Lemur program allows you to 'adopt' the prosimian of your choice by paying a reasonable fee equivalent to the animal's feeding and upkeep for one year. Animals available include lemurs, lorises, bushbabies and pottos.

- KEYWORDS: Animals, Conservation, Endangered Species, Lemurs, Primatology
- AUDIENCE: Animal Lovers, Conservationists, Lemur Lovers, Primatologists
- CONTACT: Duke University Primate Center   primate@acpub.duke.edu
- FREE

http://www.dupc.org/adopt.html

The African Bird Club Home Page ★★★★

The African Bird Club Home Page is a stimulating spot on the Web for people interested in the birds, wildlife and environmental protection of Africa. Available at this site are detailed descriptions of certain African birds, their habits, taxonomy, and distribution; as well as tips on identifying and locating these animals in the wild. In addition, there is material about the conservation of ecosystems in Africa, bird and wildlife ecology, biodiversity, deforestation, and other environmental issues pertinent to this continent. You will also find a hypertext list of numerous ornithological Internet sites.

- KEYWORDS: Africa, Birds, Ornithology
- AUDIENCE: Africans, Bird Watchers, Ornithologists, Wilderness Enthusiasts
- CONTACT: Iain Robertson   100415.1146@compuserve.com
- FREE

http://www.gold.net/users/dj10/abchome.html

 Aquatic Technology ★★

The Aquatic Technology home page offers a comprehensive listing of aquarium supplies from aquarium chemicals, pets, decor, and literature. The site offers information on current specials and sales.

- KEYWORDS: Aquariums, Fish
- AUDIENCE: Aquarium Buyers, Aquarium Dealers, Aquarium Owners
- CONTACT: aquatic-technology@actwin.com
- FREE

http://www.actwin.com/AquaticTech/index.html

Bird Studies in the Australian National Botanic Gardens ★★★★

For the devotee of the extraordinary avifauna of Australia, this is a native site which will capture you, at least for a while. You can take a leisurely stroll among the cyber-flora while looking at pictures of some of the local birds, including the maned duck, pied currawong, ubiquitous kookaburra, and superb fairy wren; you can peruse a checklist of birds seen in the gardens, or listen to some of their calls. Although the sounds of kookaburra and wren may be mellifluous, they are accompanied here by the screams of two types of cockatoo. Useful for terrifying family, friends, and co-workers, perhaps these would also work as warning signals when your computer is about to crash? Links to many related Australian sites are also accessible from here.

- KEYWORDS: Australia, Birds, Birdwatching
- AUDIENCE: Australians, Bird Lovers, Bird Watchers, Nature Lovers

Pets & Animals

CONTACT Jim Croft
jrc@anbg.gov.au

FREE

http://osprey.erin.gov.au/projects/birds/bird-studies.html

Birding on the Web ★★★★

Birding on the Web is a fairly comprehensive site dedicated to the love of bird watching. Here you will find daily updates on 'hot birds' that you can see (organized by date and region), recent postings from a variety of birding and/or migration mailing lists including, but not limited to, 'Bird Chat,' 'SeaBird,' 'Avifauna,' 'MarVaDel-L,' 'EuroBirdNet' and 'Leps-L', a link to the Usenet newsgroup rec.birds, many photographs of birds, some newsletters, a variety of birding FAQs, descriptions of different birdwatching tools, including books, videotapes, and CD-ROMs, bird societies' announcements, and a myriad of checklists from all around the world.

KEYWORDS Birds, Birdwatching, Ornithology
AUDIENCE Bird Lovers, Bird Watchers, Naturalists, Ornithologists
CONTACT siler@wharton.upenn.edu
FREE

http://compstat.wharton.upenn.edu:8001/~siler/birding.html

Bowling for Rhinos' Home Page ★★★★

For those interested in both wildlife conservation and the noble art of bowling, Bowling for Rhinos is a singular stop along the information superhighway. Whether you wish to take off your shoes and relax whilst reading about the Ngare Sergoi Wildlife Preserve or the Ujunkulon National Park in Java, Indonesia or instead would prefer to become a more active participant in the fight for seriously endangered species of rhinoceri by staging your own event, you will be fascinated by this site.

KEYWORDS Bowling, Endangered Species, Wildlife Conservation
AUDIENCE Animal Lovers, Bowlers, Conservationists, Rhinoceros Enthusiasts
CONTACT hpear@aazk.ind.net
FREE

http://aazk.ind.net/bfr/BFR-home.html

The Colorado Herpetological Society - Internet Resources Page ★★★★

The Colorado Herpetological Society - Internet Resources Page is a thorough and thoroughly rewarding list of links to all sorts of herpetological WWW resources. Here you will be able to jump to all sorts of herp-oriented sites, from those which concern Australian herps to those aimed at fulfilling your curiosity about Subarctic species. In addition, information about other herpetological societies is available through this site, as are links to the Home Pages of fellow reptile and amphibian aficionados.

KEYWORDS Amphibians, Herpetology, Reptiles
AUDIENCE Herpetologists, Pet Owners, Reptile Enthusiasts

CONTACT Rebecca Sobol
sobol@stout.atd.ucar.edu

FREE

http://www.atd.ucar.edu/rdp/ris/chs_pointers.html

The Companion Rabbit FAQ ★★★★

The Companion Rabbit FAQ covers the essentials of home rabbit care and provides pointers to other, more detailed, sources of information. Discussed in this FAQ are the hows, whys and whens of spaying or neutering your pet rabbit; tips for training rabbits not to have behavioral problems; litter box training techniques, and an extensive guide to feeding your pet. Also presented are ways to contact the House Rabbit Society and how to get the House Rabbit Journal.

KEYWORDS Animals, Pets, Rabbits, Rodents
AUDIENCE Animal Lovers, Pet Lovers, Pet Owners, Veterinarians
CONTACT Laura Tessmer
69763@strauss.udel.edu
FREE

ftp://leibniz.math.fu-berlin.de/pub/doc/petbunny/faq/

Dogs-FAQ/Email Lists ★★★★

The Dogs-FAQ/Email Lists is an inventory of all dog-related mailing lists on the Internet. Each entry contains a short description of the list, and information on how to contact or subscribe to it. Many are marked as to how much traffic the list receives. Mailing list topics range from the general to the activity- specific (i.e., an Obedience list, a list on Herding, one on Conformation, another on Holistic Veterinary Care). There are also quite a few breed-specific lists. Pointers on how to use and set up your own mailing list are also included in this FAQ.

KEYWORDS Dogs, Pets
AUDIENCE Dog Breeders, Dog Owners, Law Enforcement Professionals, Show Dog Owners
CONTACT Cindy Tittle Moore
tittle@netcom.com
FREE

http://www.io.com/user/tittle/dogs-faq/lists/email-list.html

Equestrian Information, Pictures and Texts ★★★★

This equestrian page provides a comprehensive list of equine and related subjects presented as links to, Web, gopher, FTP and telnet resources. There are links to netvet and online vet. The many horse links include The Thoroughbred Page, 1996 Olympic equestrian events, Housing, Husbandry, and Welfare of Horses, United States Dressage Foundation, Zebra Information, Arabian Breeders' Marketing Network, Navicular Disease, Buying a Horse, Books about Horses, etc. The cow pages include Dairy Software, American Jersey Cattle Club, Beef Cattle Information, USDA—AMS Livestock Reports, Bovine Somatotropin, Calf Feeding, Cows Caught in the Web, etc.

KEYWORDS Animals, Cows, Events, Horses
AUDIENCE Animal Lovers, Equestrians, Farmers, Horse Lovers, Veterinarians

CONTACT Peter.D.Asprey
u02pda@abdn.ac.uk

FREE

http://www.abdn.ac.uk/~u02pda/infoboot.html

Fact and Fiction About Armadillos ★★

This gopher site contains legends, folklore, and facts about armadillos, a Texas mascot. You will find trivia about armadillos, advertisements for places one can go to see armadillos, and more!

KEYWORDS Animals, Armadillos, Folklore, Texas
AUDIENCE Animal Lovers, Armadillo Enthusiasts, Texas Residents
CONTACT Donald Perkins
dperkins@tenet.edu
FREE

gopher://chico.rice.edu:1170/11/Armadillos

Ferret Central ★★★

This site contains information about ferrets. On this page, users will find a Ferret FAQ list (Frequently Asked Questions) in text and HTML format, as well as the Ferret Photo Gallery. Some features of this site are a state-by-state and international listing of veterinarians and ferret clubs, a listing of health and medical resources related to ferrets, and a listing of places where owning a ferret is illegal.

KEYWORDS Animals, Ferrets, Pets, Veterinary Medicine
AUDIENCE Ferret Enthusiasts
FREE

http://www.optics.rochester.edu:8080/users/pgreene/central.html

Himisuluv Cat Breeder's Page ★★★★

The Himisuluv Cat Breeder's Page is a jolly little site devoted to cats, specifically the Persian-furred, Siamese-colored breed called the Himalayan. Beginning with a photograph of their Grand Champion, Kiss, a Seal Point Himalayan (he became Grand Champion in two shows!) and continuing on to some serious information about the breed, this Page is a well-organized, delightful introduction to this cuddly and loveable, yet regal animal. Here you will also find links to some of the better cat-oriented Home Pages on the World Wide Web, including the Fanciers' Home Page; information on subscribing to 'The Cat Fancier's Journal,' a serious off-line magazine for breeders and cat lovers, and a link to the live fishcam which may be of particular interest to your cat more than to you. There are also a few non-cat related links here, but it's okay, you can ignore them.

KEYWORDS Animal Breeding, Animals, Cats, Pets
AUDIENCE Cat Breeders, Cat Lovers, Pet Owners
FREE

http://www.wimsey.com/~sfullard/index.html

Pets & Animals

JC's Birdwatching and Natural History Links

JC's Birdwatching and Natural History Links is a Home Page made up entirely of links to other interesting sites. Unlike many such hubs of WWW materials, this particular site's concentration is not limited to information concerning North America. It also includes comprehensive data from Switzerland, Scotland, England, Wales and other countries. All of the birdwatching FAQs are available here too, as well as a link to the Usenet newsgroup rec.birds.

KEYWORDS Animals, Birds, Natural History
AUDIENCE Bird Watchers, Naturalists, Nature Lovers, Wildlife Enthusiasts
CONTACT James Cracknell
jgc3@aber.ac.uk
FREE

http://www.aber.ac.uk/~jgc3/birding.html

Kakapo Place

Kakapo Place (also named 'The Fabulous Kakapo') is a Web site devoted solely to one of the rarest creatures in the world, the ground-dwelling, flightless, nocturnal kakapo parrot. Here you will learn all about this bird, from its size (approximately eight pounds!) to the number remaining on Earth (56) to its lifespan (60+ years), as well as more particular information. There is also a history of the conservation of the kakapo over the last 20 years, a listing of organizations dedicated to preserving the species, summaries of books, papers and a videotape about this strange psittacine and several photographs for you to scrutinize.

KEYWORDS Birds, Conservation, Endangered Species, Parrots
AUDIENCE Animal Lovers, Bird Lovers, Conservationists, Ecologists
CONTACT ruhue@atrium.resort.com
FREE

http://www.resort.com/~ruhue/kakapo.html

Koala's Page

Koala's page is one of a small handful of sites on the Internet devoted to that small handful of mammal, the koala. Here you will find a lot of facts about koalas, including their history and prehistory, life cycle, physiology, eating habits and sociability; some koala ASCII art, a few well-written synopses of koala books, some koala stories, and information on where to find koalas in the wild and in captivity. There are a few links here too, notably one to the Qantas Koala Page, an interesting and funny page which occasionally even works!

KEYWORDS Animals, Australia
AUDIENCE Animal Lovers, Children, Koala Enthusiasts, Marsupial Enthusiasts
CONTACT Judy Peng
jpeng@ocf.berkeley.edu
FREE

http://www.ocf.berkeley.edu/~jpeng/koala.html

Connections to Pets
Heeere Rover. Good boy!

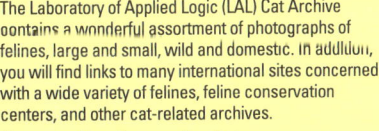

Whether your "faithful" companion is an iguana, pig, parakeet, dog, or cat, you can find out about their typical behavior, tips on training them, where to get "holistic" veterinary care, and how to breed them, through a variety of Internet sites.

Many of the sites are discussion forums for pet owners, with the largest collection of such forums focusing on dogs; you'll find hundreds of forums for owners of a wide variety of breeds, including the Australian Sheep Dog, Vizslas, Portuguese Water Dogs, and Bouvier Des Flandres.

(http://www.io.com/~tittle/dogs-faq/activities/obedience.html)

Ever thought about raising an armadillo—commonly known as the "national" mascot of Texas? There is even a site for the critter that discusses its habits, what it likes to eat, and its history in Texas folk lore.

(gopher://chico.rice.edu:1170/11/Armadillos)

Cat owners might want to check out the "Cat Home Page" for discussion groups (by breed), and learn some helpful "holistic" approaches for the care and feeding of your feline, as well as how to train your cat (instead of the other way around!)

(http://www.io.com/~tittle/cats-faq/homepage.html)

Laboratory of Applied Logic (LAL) Cat Archive

The Laboratory of Applied Logic (LAL) Cat Archive contains a wonderful assortment of photographs of felines, large and small, wild and domestic. In addition, you will find links to many international sites concerned with a wide variety of felines, feline conservation centers, and other cat-related archives.

KEYWORDS Cats, Conservation, Pets
AUDIENCE Animal Lovers, Cat Lovers, Pet Owners
CONTACT Kelly Hall
hall@cs.byu.edu
FREE

http://lal.cs.byu.edu/cats/cats.html

LlamaWeb

LlamaWeb is a wondrous site specializing in llamas, alpacas and other camelids which includes information as diverse as camelid veterinary medicine and a 'Name That Llama' contest. Available here are materials about llama care and training, llama intelligence and behavior, llama trekking, llama books, llama fibers, llama farming equipment, eccentric llama stories, recommended llama veterinarians, and links to other online llama farms and related resources. You can play a llama trivia game here, find out 'Things To Do with Llamas,' and learn where the nearest hot spot is for an upcoming llama show. Don't forget while you're there to check out everything you always wanted to know about llama spit but were afraid to ask.

KEYWORDS Farming, Veterinary Care
AUDIENCE Animal Lovers, Llama Enthusiasts, Veterinarians
CONTACT Dale Graham
degraham@webcom.com
FREE

http://www.webcom.com/~degraham

Mike's Herpetocultural Home Page

Mike's Herpetological Home Page is an excellent resource for your reptile and amphibian needs. Including information on all type of herps, from turtles to chamaeleons, in captivity and in the wild, Mike's Page makes good use of both photographs and written information to captivate and educate those interested in a wide range of cold-blooded animals. Here you will find many exciting documents, including a variety of related FAQs. Many links to other pertinent Websites are also available here.

KEYWORDS Amphibians, Herpetology, Pets, Reptiles
AUDIENCE Amphibian Enthusiasts, Herpetologists, Pet Owners, Reptile Enthusiasts
CONTACT pingleto@ncsa.uiuc.edu
FREE

http://gto.ncsa.uiuc.edu/pingleto/herp.html

The National Anti-Hunt Campaign Website ★★★★

The National Anti-Hunt Campaign Website is a place for animal rights activists to learn news about anti-hunting activities, primarily taking place in Great Britain. The Campaign promotes non-violent protest against hunting and other blood sports. Information about legal matters, including laws and acts concerning animal rights are listed here. Also provided is information on how to join the NAHC, or how to help the cause.

KEYWORDS Animal Protection, Hunting
AUDIENCE Animal Lovers, Animal Rights Activists, Anti-Hunting Activists
FREE

http://envirolink.org/adn/NAHC/info.html

The National Zoo, Washington, DC Home Page ★★★

This Home Page tells you all you need to know before you visit The National Zoo in Washington, D.C. Here you will find directions to the Zoo, as well as its hours; late-breaking news about upcoming exhibits, events, and new members of the Zoo's animal family; developments in the Zoo's zoological and botanical projects, and information specifically designed for teachers.

KEYWORDS Animals, Zoos
AUDIENCE Animal Lovers, Tourists, Washington D.C. Residents, Zoo Enthusiasts
CONTACT The National Zoo
nzpem053@sivm.si.edu
FREE

gopher://gopher.american.edu/11/de/zoo

The North American Breeding Bird Survey Home Page ★★★★

The North American Breeding Bird Survey Home Page is a repository for information about the counts of breeding birds taken in North America during June and May. Here you will find detailed information about the counts, as well as fine maps, graphs, and indices of North American bird populations; you will also find pictures of North American birds, and audio clips of North American bird songs. A lively addition to this page is its Bird Identification Quizzes, which change every hour and are both difficult and fascinating.

KEYWORDS Birds, Birdwatching, Wildlife

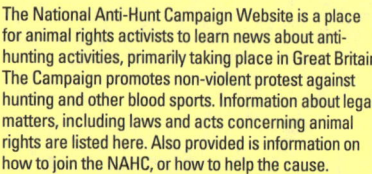

AUDIENCE Bird Lovers, Bird Watchers, Bird Watchers, Environmentalists
CONTACT Jim Hines
jim_hines@nbs.gov
FREE

http://www.im.nbs.gov/bbs

The Penguin Page ★★★★

This is the penguin lover's page. There are links to information about the emperor penguin, the yellow-eyed penguin, the macaroni penguin. A penguin FAQ is included as well as information about penguin behaviour, a review of the literature, links to other animal-related pages, and humorous and nonsensical penguins.

KEYWORDS Animals, Penguins
AUDIENCE Animal Lovers, Animal Trainers, Penguin Lovers, Veterinarians
CONTACT welch@mail.sas.upenn.edu.
FREE

http://www.sas.upenn.edu/~kwelch/penguin.html

Quadralay's Armadillo Home Page ★★★★

Quadralay's Armadillo Home Page is a sprightly little site full of lore about two celebrated denizens of Texas—the omnipresent Hog of the Road, the wild armadillo, and the equally wild, yet somewhat less abundant, human resident of Austin. Here you will find a bit of factual information about the armadillo; some armadillo jokes and historical references; a few touches here and there of information about Armadillo-Con, Austin's Sci Fi Convention; Austin, Texas and its 'most famous nightclub,' Armadillo World Headquarters.

KEYWORDS Armadillos, Humor, Texas
AUDIENCE Animal Lovers, Armadillo Enthusiasts, Texas Residents
CONTACT Quadralay Corporation
info@quadralay.com
FREE

http://www.quadralay.com/www/Austin/Dillo/index.html

The Rabbit Page ★★★★

The Rabbit Page is a Web site devoted to the humble yet proud house rabbit. You will find quite a few photographs here, as well as information vital to the care, feeding and well-being of your bunny. The Petbunny FAQ is available at this site, as are other related FAQs (for example, the hay FAQ and at least one veterinary medicine FAQ). Links to other Net sites concerning rabbits are plentiful, as are data about off-line resources including various House Rabbit Societies located around the United States. There are links to sites concerning other pets here, too.

KEYWORDS Pets, Rabbits, Rodents, Veterinary Medicine
AUDIENCE Pet Lovers, Rabbit Lovers, Rodent Lovers, Veterinarians
CONTACT Thor and Velvet D. Bunny
2bunnys@cpcug.org
FREE

http://cpcug.org/user/2bunnys/

gopher://cpcug.org:79/02bunnys

Rebecca Sobol's Herp Page ★★★★

Rebecca Sobol's Herp Page largely concerns her snakes - several pythons, several boas. She also has a rather lovely turtle, who is featured as well. It is an interesting page with several photographs, some information on how you can best care for your snake, and a link to the Colorado Herpetological Society, where Ms. Sobol is Secretary/Treasurer. Be sure to learn about the mysterious 'snow snake' at this site, especially if you are a skiier as well as a herp fan, as there is limited data available from other quarters about the species.

KEYWORDS Herpetology, Pets, Reptiles, Snakes
AUDIENCE Herpetologists, Pet Owners, Reptile Enthusiasts
CONTACT Rebecca Sobol
sobol@stout.atd.ucar.edu
FREE

http://www.atd.ucar.edu/rdp/ris/ris_herp.html

The Rec.Pets.* Grief and Pet-Loss FAQ ★★★★

The Rec.Pets.* Grief and Pet Loss FAQ is designed for people who have just lost a beloved companion animal. The tone is serious and the material fairly extensive. Topics covered include—which pets cause the strongest attachments, the manifestations of grief, how to help children when their pet dies, the pros and cons of euthanasia (i.e., will the animal be able to enjoy life if not euthanized?) and a short section on the responsibility of the veterinarian to assist the grieving family. A reference list for adults and children can be found at the end of this FAQ.

KEYWORDS Pets, Veterinary Care
AUDIENCE Pet Owners, Veterinarians
CONTACT Cindy Tittle Moore
tittle@netcom.com
FREE

http://www.lib.ox.ac.uk/internet/news/faq/archive/pets.pet-loss.html

Rec.Pets.Birds FAQ ★★★★

The Rec.Pets.Birds FAQ contains information for people who read the Usenet newsgroup rec.pets.birds and pet bird enthusiasts in general. It is a very complete, four-part reference tool which covers many areas of interest to bird owners.

KEYWORDS Animals, Birds, Ornithology, Pets
AUDIENCE Animal Lovers, Bird Watchers, Ornithologists, Pet Owners
CONTACT giannini@nova.umd.edu
FREE

ftp://rtfm.mit.edu/pub/usenet/rec.pets.birds/

Pets & Animals

Rec.Pets.Dogs Canine Activities - Obedience Trials FAQ

The Canine Activities - Obedience Trials FAQ is a thorough resource for people interested in entering their dogs in dog shows which feature obedience as an event. Included are a history of the American Kennel Club's Obedience Trials; a list of organizations which offer Obedience Trials; overviews of the AKC and other groups' exercises and requirements for titles; opportunities for mixed breed dogs; help with show stress, hints for handlers and hints on dogs' attire. An acronym list, glossary, and resources are also provided. Currently the FAQ's main focus is North America; they are interested in obtaining more material on international trials.

- KEYWORDS Dogs, Pets
- AUDIENCE American Kennel Club Members, Dog Owners, Dog Show Personnel, Show Dog Owners
- CONTACT Cindy Tittle Moore
tittle@netcom.com
- FREE

http://www.io.com/~tittle/dogs-faq/activities/obedience.html

The Save The Manatee Club Manatee Information Home Page

The Save The Manatee Club Manatee Information Home Page is an excellent place to learn about the splendid marine mammal, the manatee. A relative to the dugong and sea cow, there are only 1800 manatees left in the United States. The Save The Manatee Club offers not only information about the species, but an opportunity to assist in its survival by becoming the proud adoptive parent of one of the Club's tagged manatee friends. Also available here are news clips about this mock mermaid and links to easy-to-read summaries of the Marine Mammal Protection Act and the Endangered Species Act, as well as a link to the United States Fish and Wildlife Service.

- KEYWORDS Aquatic Science, Endangered Species, Zoology
- AUDIENCE Children, Conservationists, Ecologists, Manatee Enthusiasts
- CONTACT Save The Manatee Club
fucshia@hue.org
- FREE

http://www.satelnet.org/manatee

The Singapore Zoological Gardens Home Page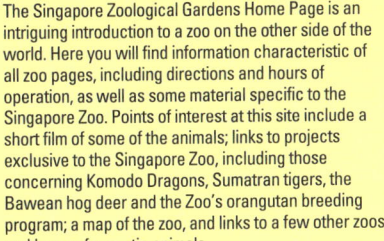

The Singapore Zoological Gardens Home Page is an intriguing introduction to a zoo on the other side of the world. Here you will find information characteristic of all zoo pages, including directions and hours of operation, as well as some material specific to the Singapore Zoo. Points of interest at this site include a short film of some of the animals; links to projects exclusive to the Singapore Zoo, including those concerning Komodo Dragons, Sumatran tigers, the Bawean hog deer and the Zoo's orangutan breeding program; a map of the zoo, and links to a few other zoos and homes for exotic animals.

- KEYWORDS Animals, Singapore, Zoos
- AUDIENCE Animal Lovers, Singapore Residents, Travelers, Zoo Enthusiasts
- FREE

http://www.ncb.gov.sg/sog/att/abal/zoo.html

The Squashed Bug Zoo

The Squashed Bug Zoo is a Home Page devoted to the smallest of roadkill, the insect. Here, however you will not only find pictures of the oozy remnants of life ended in a brief moment of collision, but several roach-type-things and blood engorged ticks. One can only imagine where these were found (until viewing them, that is). Newly available is a small vertebrate section. This site also takes submissions.

- KEYWORDS Entomology, Humor, Insects
- AUDIENCE Biologists, Entomologists, Insect Enthusiasts, Virginia Residents
- CONTACT David Meeker
dcmc3c@virgina.edu
- FREE

http://albert.ccae.Virginia.edu/~dcm3c/zoo.html

Those Wonderful Cats of Panther's Cave

Often updated and rarely overrated, the Wonderful Cats of Panther's Cave contains more information, photographs and links concerning our feline friends than even the most fervent feline fancier could focus upon in a day. From Home Pages to a candid shot of the President's cat, Socks, and even a sample of his voice (Socks' not Bill's), this site will entertain all but the most recalcitrant. Included and highlighted are feline Public Service Announcements, and you will find in addition to the merriment, some serious animal welfare and rescue links, a link to the all-FAQ rec.pets.cats site, and a couple kitty commercial companies.

- KEYWORDS Animal Welfare, Cats, Felids, Pets
- AUDIENCE Animal Lovers, Cat Breeders, Cat Lovers
- CONTACT panther@eskimo.com, panther@aloha.com, panther@pixi.com
- FREE

http://www.eskimo.com/~panther/cats.html

Trendy's House of Herpetology

Trendy's House of Herpetology is a Web site devoted to reptiles and amphibians, unique in that it is not only dedicated to herps, but also sponsored by one. Trendy, an iguana, is open to answering all of your herpetology queries (but only visually, unless you speak iguana) through a video camera linked to this site. Additional information here concerns the care and feeding of herps, how to obtain that special herp, and a small trove of quite funny herp-related humor. There are links to other reptile and amphibian sites available as well.

- KEYWORDS Amphibians, Herpetology, Reptiles
- AUDIENCE Amphibian Enthusiasts, Herpetologists, Pet Owners, Reptile Enthusiasts
- CONTACT Liza Daly
ldaly@bu.edu
- FREE

http://www.concorde.com/~chaos/herps

University of Kentucky Horse Racing Archives

This site, the University of Kentucky Horse Racing Archives, provides other links to horse racing-related World Wide Web sites. Some of the topics include Derby Mailing List, Don MacBeth Fund, AXCIS (Trackmaster), Churchill Downs, Agricomm, Espnet, 1995 North American Racing Dates, and more.

- KEYWORDS Horse Racing
- AUDIENCE Gamblers, Horse Breeders, Horse Racing Enthusiasts
- CONTACT stevem@inslab.uky.edu
- FREE

http://www.inslab.uky.edu/~stevem/horses/racing.html

Welcome to the Cathouse! The Exotic Feline Breeding Compound and Feline Conservation Center Home Page

If the idea of being less than three feet away from a wild cat that you have never seen or perhaps even imagined before piques your interest, get to know the Cathouse! The Exotic Feline Breeding Compound and Feline Conservation Center is a home page deserving of scrutiny by people interested in the preservation of all large cats. Pictures of the Cathouse's cats are available, including those of their fishing cats, jaguars, jaguarundis, Chinese leopards, snow leopards, a margay and perhaps even a bobcat or two or three; as are information about joining or becoming a volunteer at the Center; descriptions of the special events planned for the upcoming year, which include a Twilight Tour where you can get your picture taken with an ocelot or leopard, and the Fabulous Feline Follies (ocassionally attended by a tiger); and links to other animal sites. A worthy cause and an interesting site.

- KEYWORDS Endangered Species, Felids, Wildlife Rehabilitation
- AUDIENCE Animal Lovers, Cat Lovers, Conservationists, Wildlife Rehabilitators
- CONTACT info@cathouse-fcc.org
- FREE

http://www.cathouse-fcc.org

The Wild Bird Society of Japan's Bird and Green Information Center Home Page

The Wild Bird Society of Japan's Bird and Green Information Center Home Page is a lively site providing information about the society, its publications and some data of interest to those who go birdwatching in Japan and other parts of Asia. You will find here detailed tables of contents of the publications 'Yacho' (Wild Birds) and 'Strix' (a Journal of Field Ornithology); information on wildlife sanctuaries and protection in Japan; summaries of books on Japanese and Asian birdwatching, written in English, and available through the Society; photographs of 'small visitors' seen at the Center, and a thorough, engaging description of the

Society's goals, operations, activities and accomplishments.

KEYWORDS Birds, Birdwatching, Japan, Ornithology
AUDIENCE Bird Lovers, Bird Watchers, Japan Residents, Ornithologists
CONTACT Satoshi Marutani
marutani@st.rim.or.jp
FREE

http://www.st.rim.or.jp/~marutani

Wildbirds FAQ ★★★★

The Wildbirds FAQ is the FAQ for the Usenet newsgroup, rec.birds, the gathering place of bird watchers on the Internet. The FAQ is divided into two parts, the first of which includes information pertinent to bird watchers and people interested in wild bird rehabilitation. Topics covered include, but are not limited to, the Annual Bird Counts, wild bird checklists, rare bird sightings, banded birds and supplies for bird watchers. The second part covers wild bird magazines and organizations, software and available Internet sites for checklists, information on and recommendations of all types of field guides (including, for example, on eggs) and recordings of bird sounds. Internet sites of interest to birders, including digitized images are also listed.

KEYWORDS Birds, Ornithology, Wildlife
AUDIENCE Animal Lovers, Bird Watchers, Wilderness Enthusiasts
FREE

ftp://rtfm.mit.edu/pub/usenet-by-group/
rec.birds/
rec.birds_Frequently_Asked_Questions_
(FAQ)_(Part_1_2)

The World Wide Raccoon Web ★★★

The World Wide Raccoon Web is your one-stop shop for Internet links to raccoon information. At the site itself you will find material encompassing both scientific and fancier information about raccoons, a lengthy and expanding raccoon bibliography, notes on how to feed wild raccoons, a story or two about these furry beasts, a link to the Raccoon Lovers' Mailing List, and another to the Usenet newsgroup alt.animals.raccoons. There are also some links to other animal pages available here.

KEYWORDS Veterinary Care, Veterinary Medicine
AUDIENCE Animal Lovers, Children, Raccoon Enthusiasts, Veterinarians
CONTACT Seth J Morabito
sjm1@cornell.edu
FREE

http://deja-vu.oldiron.cornell.edu/~sjm1/
raccoons

Recreation

See also
Arts & Music · Decorative Arts
Internet · Online Games
Sports & Recreation · Outdoor Recreation

Paintball Headquarters ★★★

The Paintball Headquarters markets guns, clothing, and accessories for the weekend warrior who takes paintball contests seriously, and wants the be properly accoutered. The site features a catalog which users may request by online form.

KEYWORDS Paintball, War Games
AUDIENCE Military Enthusiasts, Paintballers
FREE

http://www.infop.com/paint/index.html

SnowPage ★★★★

The SnowPage includes everything you ever wanted to know about snow and then some. Subjects include Skiing (Alpine/Nordic), Snowboarding, EZines - Electronic Online Magazines, Winter Resort Reports, Trail Maps, Picture Gallery, Snow People on the Web (personal home pages), and an extensive list of other snow-related Web sites. Come here and be snowed by an avalanche of information.

KEYWORDS Skiing, Snowboarding
AUDIENCE Children, Ice Skaters, Parents, Skiing Enthusiasts, Snowboarders
CONTACT Dan Homolka.
d.homolka@ic.ac.uk
FREE

http://rmd-www.mr.ic.ac.uk/snow/
snowpage.html

Top Hand Trails ★★

The Top Hand Trails Web site advertises horseback riding trips in the Santa Catalina Mountains of Arizona. Users may access JPEG images of the local fauna. Price information is provided.

KEYWORDS Fauna, Horseback Riding
AUDIENCE Horseback Riders, Tourists
FREE

http://www.infop.com/tophand/index.html

Sports

See also
Sports & Recreation · Aquatic Sports
Sports & Recreation · Motor Sports

1996 Centennial Olympic Games ★★★★

This is the official page of the 1996 Summer Olympic Games. The contents include a brief welcome, a history of the sports and their venues for the Games, the official programme, travel information, ticket information, official products, and sponsors' news on the cultural Olympiad. There is also a virtual Olympic Stadium flythrough (3.9mb AVI). For Games zealots, the site also contains a countdown of days to the 1996 Olympics.

KEYWORDS Georgia, Homosexuality, Olympic Games, Tourism
AUDIENCE Athletes, Educators, Olympics Enthusiasts, Sports Fans, Tourists
FREE

http://www.atlanta.olympic.org/
index.html

The 19th Hole ★★★

This page provides links to all kinds of information for golfers. Access is provided to golf equipment, a 1-800 Directory of Golf Companies, the Daily Golf News, a Scorecard Archive, Golf Art and Pictures, and more.

KEYWORDS Golf, Tourism
AUDIENCE Golf Enthusiasts, Golfers
CONTACT James E. ('Jimbo')
jimbo@bandw.panam.edu
FREE

http://www.tr-riscs.panam.edu/golf/
19thhole.html

All Sports Web Server ★★★

All Sports.com is a presentation of Quest Technologies. It was set up by sports fans, for sports fans. The viewers of this page can link to specific directories for baseball, football, soccer, basketball, and hockey Internet sites, as well as a miscellaneous sports directory. The links in this site are updated weekly, according to the author. There is also a link to the author's officially licensed sports catalog.

KEYWORDS Baseball, Football, Soccer, Sports News
AUDIENCE Baseball Fans, Basketball Fans, Hockey Enthusiasts, Sports Fans
FREE

http://allsports.questtech.com/nfl/
nfl.html

The Basketball Server ★★★★

This server hosts scores, articles, features, and other news about the sport of basketball. Coverage extends from the NBA (National Basketball Association) to college level, with a special section devoted to the Atlantic Coast Conference (ACC). Concerning the NBA, box scores, game highlights, daily news summaries, and regular feature pieces about players, teams, and business transactions are provided. There is also extensive coverage of individual teams in the NBA.

KEYWORDS Basketball, Online Newspapers
AUDIENCE Basketball Fans, NBA Enthusiasts, Sports Fans
CONTACT zonker@nando.net
FREE

http://www.nando.net/sports/bkb/1994/
bkbserv.html

The Belgian Soccer Archive ★★★

The Belgian Soccer Archive is produced by a fan of Belgian soccer who has been collecting results of games played by Belgian teams for about two years.

The site contains links to these results, to the Usenet newsgroup, rec.sport.soccer as well as numerous other related links.

KEYWORDS Archives, Belgium, Soccer
AUDIENCE Soccer Fans
FREE

http://www.wi.leidenuniv.nl/home/andries/belgian_soccer.html

The Brown Curling Club

The Brown University Curling Club page is designed to promote the unique sport of curling. Those who are unfamiliar with curling will find an animated demonstration and written explanation, along with a brief history of the sport and pictures from historical archives. Information about the Brown Curling Club is also provided for University Students, as well as addresses for those interested in starting their own curling clubs.

KEYWORDS Curling, Outdoor Recreation, Universities
AUDIENCE Curling Enthusiasts, Game Enthusiasts, Students (University)
CONTACT   The Brown Curling Club
          curling@brown.edu
FREE

http://www.brown.edu:80/Students/Brown_Curling_Club/

The Canonical Hockey Links Page

The Canonical Hockey Links Page is an impressive compilation of pointers to Web sites and Internet resources having to do with the game of Hockey, created by one hockey enthusiast. Users will find hundreds of links listed in categories such as meta-indexes, general links, league links leagues, and individual team home pages, with numerous subcategories.

KEYWORDS Hockey
AUDIENCE Hockey Enthusiasts, Sports Fans
CONTACT   Doug Norris
          n9143349@henson.cc.wwu.edu
FREE

http://rowlf.cc.wwu.edu:8080/~n9143349/links.html

College Football Spring Notes

College Football Spring Notes provides a hyperlinked list on each of the college football conferences. When you click on a specific conference another hyperlinked list appears with a link to each team in that conference. For each team there is an analysis of the team, and interesting scoops on specific players.

KEYWORDS College Sports, Football
AUDIENCE Football Fans, Sports Fans, Students (University)
CONTACT   ESPNET SportsZone
          espnet.sportszone@starwave.com
FREE

http://espnet.sportszone.com/ncf/editors/features/conflist.html

---

Connections to Adventure Vacations

How about kayaking in the Himalayas?

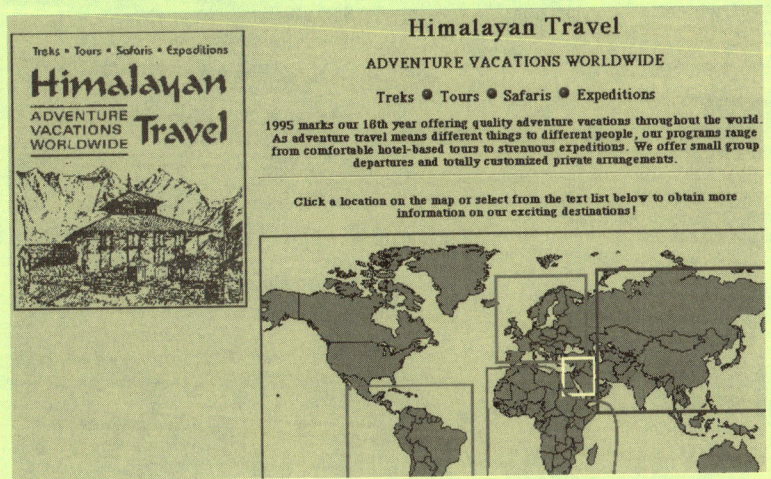

If you want to have a more exciting vacation than lying on a beach, there are hundreds of vacation alternatives on the Internet.

Some sites are specific to certain regions, but if you are interested in a Safari Expedition to exotic places around the world, then the Himalayan Travel site is one of many that offers the adventure-minded a connection to the vacation of a lifetime.

(http://www.gorp.com/himtravel.htm)

If you are interested in prospecting for gold in Alaska, or taking a journey through geologic time on a raft down the Grand Canyon in the U.S., try the Adrift Adventures site.

(http://www.netpub.com/adrift/adwelc.htm)

Now, about kayaking in the Himalayas.... If kayaking appeals to you, there is a site on the World Wide Web that gives you kayaking instructions, a list of schools dedicated solely to the sport and a schedule of upcoming kayak trips.

(http://jstart.com/kayak/kayak.html)

College Lacrosse USA

This site on College Lacrosse USA provides links to the different college lacrosse divisions, conferences, men's and women's NCAA tournaments, scores of recent games, college lacrosse news, conference standings, NCAA Lacrosse Radio Network, and archives. When you click on a specific conference another hyperlinked list appears with a link to each team in that conference.

KEYWORDS College Sports, Lacrosse
AUDIENCE Athletes, Lacrosse Enthusiasts, Sports Fans, Students (University)
CONTACT   Steve Ulrich/Marcy Dubroff
          CNC_SFU@admin.FandM.edu
FREE

http://www.fandm.edu/centennialconference/lacrosse/mainmenu

CricInfo

This gopher site, CricInfo, provides information on the CricInfo's database. It contains cricket statistics, scorecards, articles, humour, and more. It also provides information such as news and links to other gophers.

KEYWORDS Cricket, Sports
AUDIENCE Cricket Enthusiasts, Sports Fans
CONTACT   cricinfo@ogi.edu
FREE

gopher://cricinfo.cse.ogi.edu:7070/

Dave's 1996 Olympic Web Site List

This site provides links to a variety of World Wide Web sites with information on the 1996 Centennial Olympic Games to be held in Atlanta, Georgia. This page contains useful information for anyone attending the Olympics or simply planning to visit Atlanta. Contents include a link to the official Olympic Games program page, information on sponsors (IBM and Nationsbank), articles from the Atlanta Journal-Constitutional, plus information on housing, art, entertainment, and restaurants.

KEYWORDS Georgia, Olympic Games, Tourism
AUDIENCE Athletes, Olympics Enthusiasts, Sports Fans, Tourists

CONTACT Dave Rosselle, Supervisor Network Planning, AT&T
rosselle@mindspring.com

FREE

http://www.atlanta.olympic.org/

European Football Qualifying Championships 1996 ★★

This site, Qualifying of the European Championship 1996 in England, presents a summary of scores, teams, and history of the event. The information is presented in German and English.

KEYWORDS International Soccer
AUDIENCE Soccer Fans, Sports Fans
CONTACT Reinhard Kahle
Kahle@iam.unibe.ch

FREE

http://iamwww.unibe.ch/~ftiwww/Sonstiges/Tabellen/EM/em1996.html

Footbag Worldwide ★★★

This page is devoted to the sport of footbag, also known as 'Hacky-Sack.' Information on the proper equipment and sportswear is available here, as well as material on different game variations. Users can also find footbag rules and regulations, tips and techniques, links to related servers, and more.

KEYWORDS Sports
AUDIENCE Footbag Enthusiasts, Hacky-Sack Enthusiasts, Sports Fans
CONTACT Jim Curtis
jim_curtis@cup.hp.com

FREE

http://www.footbag.org/

The Football Server ★★★★

This server hosts scores and highlights, team statistics, full-color images, and general news about the sport of Football (USA). Both the National Football League and NCAA Division 1 teams are represented on these pages. Viewers will find highlights of the 1994 season, including Super Bowl news, as well as current news about trades, injuries, and business. Each team has its own page on this server, complete with statistics, rosters, and features. (Some areas are under construction and/or may not be available during the off-season.) On the college side, viewers will find AP and CNN Top 25 coverage, as well as regional conference statistics, images, and highlights.

KEYWORDS Football, Online Newspapers
AUDIENCE Football Fans
CONTACT zonker@nando.net

FREE

http://www.nando.net/football/1994/fbserv.html

GNN Women's Basketball ★★★

Welcome to the Women's Basketball Page in the GNN Sports Center. The Sports Center will be combining the best of the Net with a satellite feed from SportsTicker to give you team reports, schedules, and new servers, along with up-to-the-minute box scores, game reports, and special features. Some of the linked topics on this page include GNN Women's Basketball Archives, The Scoop in Women's Hoops, Associated Press Top 25 Women's College Basketball Poll, NCAA Division II Women's Basketball Poll, and player spotlights.

KEYWORDS Basketball, Women's Sports
AUDIENCE Athletes, Basketball Fans, Students, Women, Women's Sports Enthusiasts
CONTACT Ellie Cutler, Editor
ellie@ora.com

FREE

http://gnn.com/gnn/meta/sports/basketball/women/index.html

German Bundesliga Results ★★★

German Bundesliga Results provides information about German soccer leagues. It gives rankings for all games for Bundesliga 1 and 2, including details on each round, lists of best scorers, and surveys on results. Also included are German Cup Results and links to information on regional German soccer leagues, as well as dates for future German national team games.

KEYWORDS Germany, Soccer, Sports Schedules
AUDIENCE Germans, Soccer Fans
CONTACT Thomas Hofmeister
hofmeist@Ls2.infomatik.uni-dortmund.de

FREE

http://ls2-www.informatik.uni-dortmund.de/Buli/Buli.html

GolfWeb Home Page ★★★

GolfWeb's Home Page contains all manner of information related to golf. Users will find PGA tour news, golf rules, golf resorts and courses around the world, information on golf schools, and more. Users can also visit an online pro shop with clothes, golfing equipment, books, videos, and other related accessories.

KEYWORDS Golf, Golf Courses, Online Shopping
AUDIENCE Golf Enthusiasts, Sports Fans
CONTACT comments@golfweb.com

FREE

http://www.golfweb.com/

Indiana Women's Basketball OnLine ★★★★

This is Indiana University's Women's Basketball OnLine page. It contains links to information including recent Big Ten action, schedules and results for all other Big Ten teams, NCAA statistics, Big Ten champions year-by-year, and other women's basketball home pages.

KEYWORDS Basketball, Women's Sports
AUDIENCE Athletes, Basketball Fans, Students (University), Women, Women's Sports Enthusiasts
CONTACT Chris Lambert
wlambert@indiana.edu

FREE

http://copper.ucs.indiana.edu/~wlambert/hoosiers.html

InfoVid Outlet- Sports ★★

This site presents a collection of how-to videos for various sports and recreation activities. Some of the available topics include archery, bowling, camping, skiing, and more. Users can access descriptions of the content of the videotapes, and place an order online.

KEYWORDS Sports, Videos
AUDIENCE Consumers, Sports Fans
CONTACT digitali@renoir.cftnet.com

FREE

http://w3.branch.com/branch/infovid/c330.html

Jesper Lauridsen's Football Page ★★★★

Jesper Lauridsen's Football Page offers extensive links to soccer (called football in the United Kingdom) sites on the Web. Some of the sites include profiles of great Liverpool players, Bundesliga tipping competition, Premiership FAQ, updated results and tables from all competitions, International Football I and International Football II.

KEYWORDS Football, Soccer, Sports
AUDIENCE Football Fans, Soccer Fans, Sports Fans, Students (Primary/Secondary)
CONTACT Jesper Lauridsen
rorschak@daimi.aau.dk

FREE

http://www.daimi.aau.dk/~rorschak/fodbold.html

Juggling Information Service ★★★★

This is the web page of the Juggling Information Service, a site serving the Internet juggling community by providing links to all of the juggling related sources that can be found. Home pages of jugglers, related USENET newsgroups, juggling pictures and juggling videos can also be found. Moreover, users can also obtain juggling help and get information on joining a juggling group. Even information on juggling related software can be obtained here.

KEYWORDS Hobbies, Juggling
AUDIENCE Jugglers, Juggling Enthusiasts
CONTACT juggle@hal.com

FREE

http://www.hal.com/services/juggle/

The Little Dream of Flying - Trampoline Page ★★★

The Little Dream of Flying Web site is dedicated to the sport of trampolining. This site gives the general information about the sport, such as rules and history, contains competition schedules, and gives statistics for various leagues. Also included is a mailing list for trampoline enthusiasts, and reviews and reports from past competitions. This page also provides links to other sports and German pages.

KEYWORDS Germany, Sports, Sports Schedules, Trampoline

Sports **651**

AUDIENCE Germans, Gymnasts, Sports Fans, Trampoline Enthusiasts
CONTACT Ralph Busse
busse@darmstadt.gmd.de
FREE

http://este.darmstadt.gmd.de:5000/misc/tramp/trhome_en.html

NBA Playoff Schedule and Results ★★★★

This site publishes the NBA Playoff Schedule and Results. The name of the teams and scores are hyperlinked so you can read the past highlights of any game. You can read about the playoff matchups, an analysis of the matchups, and what the coaches and players are discussing. It's almost as good as being in the dressing room.

KEYWORDS Basketball, NBA (National Basketball Association), Scores
AUDIENCE Basketball Fans, Sports Fans
CONTACT ESPNET SportsZone
espnet.sportszone@starwave.com
FREE

http://espnet.sportszone.com/nba/playoffs/schedule.html

NHL Schedule and Results ★★★★

This site publishes the NHL Playoff Schedule and Results. The name of the teams and scores are hyperlinked so you can read the past highlights of any game. You can read about the playoff matchups, an analysis of the matchups, and what the coaches and players are discussing. It's almost as good as being there without being cold.

KEYWORDS Hockey, Scores
AUDIENCE Hockey Enthusiasts, Sports Fans
CONTACT ESPNET SportsZone
espnet.sportszone@starwave.com
FREE

http://espnet.sportszone.com/nhl/playoffs/schedule.html

New York City Inline Skating Guide ★★★

This page contains information and resources for in-line skating in New York City. Listed here is legal information, locations of good and bad places to skate throughout Manhattan and the metropolitan New York area, in-line skating clubs and organizations, and information on related activities like roller hockey and roller basketball. In addition, the Web author has listed various businesses that are particularly friendly or unfriendly to in-line skaters.

KEYWORDS In-Line Skating, New York, Organizations, Outdoor Recreation
AUDIENCE In-Line Skaters, New York In-Line Skaters
CONTACT Robert B. Schmunk
rbs@panix.com
FREE

http://www.giss.nasa.gov/Staff/SchmunkRB.html

OU Croquet Club Home Page ★★★

Welcome to the Oxford University Croquet Club's home page. Croquet is extremely popular in the University and is played in almost every college. There is a huge Cuppers tournament in the summer and plenty of other activities. This page has links to those activities and other information regarding the 1995 Oxford Tournament, Croquet By-laws, Coaching Notes, and the Croquet Association.

KEYWORDS Croquet, England, Sports
AUDIENCE Anglophiles, Croquet Enthusiasts, Sports Fans, Students (University)
CONTACT prosser@vax.ox.ac.uk
FREE

http://info.ox.ac.uk:80/~croquet/

Outside Online ★★★★

The Outside Online site is a collection of resources for the outdoor sports enthusiast. Users will find articles on various sporting topics, location reports from recreational areas throughout the nation, and an area where members of Outside Online can discuss sporting topics. In addition, this site maintains comprehensive links to other sports resources on the Internet.

KEYWORDS Sports, Sports Equipment, Sports Schedules
AUDIENCE Consumers, Outdoor Sports Enthusiasts, Sports Fans
CONTACT info@starwave.com
FREE

http://web2.starwave.com/outside/

Rec.Sports.Soccer - The WEB Page ★★★

The Rec.Sport.Soccer web page contains everything found in the FAQ as well as links to other soccer related sites. Topics include the FIFA (Federation Internationale de Football Association) rules, terminology, World Cup USA '94, Soccer Games for the Computer, and more.

KEYWORDS Soccer, Sports
AUDIENCE Soccer Fans, Sports Fans, Students (Primary/Secondary)
CONTACT John Stringer
johns@avs.uniras.dk
FREE

http://www.atm.ch.cam.ac.uk:80/sports/

Rob's Magic Directory ★★★

This site contains descriptions of products which can be ordered online from Rob's Magic, Juggling & Kite Shop. As the name implies, users will find merchandise such as kites, juggling equipment, and magic trick material. There is a wide variety of merchandise available here, and there is a description for each item, as well as pricing information.

KEYWORDS Juggling, Sports
AUDIENCE Clowns, Jugglers, Kite Flying Enthusiasts, Magicians, Sports Fans
FREE

http://www.rt66.com/olworld/mall/mall_us/c_toys/m_robs/index.html

Scott Perlstein Enterprises Essential Tennis ★★★

A review and foreword for the book ESSENTIAL TENNIS is provided with price and ordering information.

KEYWORDS Advertising, Marketing, Sports, Tennis
AUDIENCE Book Readers, Sports Fans, Tennis Enthusiasts
CONTACT Jon Zeeff
branch-info@branch.com
FREE

http://branch.com/tennis/tennis.html

Ski Web ★★★

The Ski Web is a self proclaimed guide to skiing 'for Skiers by Skiers (and Snowboarders,too!).' Users will find information provided by region, with lists of all the ski resorts in the area and descriptions of their mountains. Each region also includes listings about highways and roads, weather, recreational activities in the area, lodging, and regularly updated ski condition reports, as both local sources and links to outside Web resources. An archive of trail maps is included, along with information about Alpine World Magazine and other commercial skiing postings.

KEYWORDS Ski Resorts, Skiing, Snowboarding
AUDIENCE Skiing Enthusiasts, Snowboarding Enthusiasts
CONTACT skiweb@sierra.net
FREE

http://diamond.sierra.net/SkiWeb/

Skilton's Baseball Links ★★★

Skilton's Baseball Links is one individual's collection of pointers to baseball resources on the World Wide Web. Links are listed in categories such as major and minor league scores and statistics, league information, individual team pages for major, minor, amateur, and college teams, merchandise, baseball cards, and baseball newsgroups. All listings are alphabetical, and very few contain any description of the sites.

KEYWORDS Baseball
AUDIENCE Baseball Fans, Sports Fans
CONTACT John Skilton
skilton@ssnet.com
FREE

http://ssnet.com/~skilton/baseball.html

SnowLink, the Ski Industries America Web Site! ★★★★

The SIA is a trade association representing many of the manufacturers in the Ski Industry. Many of the SIA members have joined together to create this multimedia forum in order to broaden the channels of communication between skiers, dealers, and manufacturers. This page contains information on snow skis and snowboards, Apparel (Cold Earth Wear), Hiking (Merrell Footwear, Raichle boots), and Ski Accessories (Pro Case, Hertel). There are also links to other snow-related sites.

KEYWORDS Hiking, Skiing, Winter Sports
AUDIENCE Athletes, Skiing Enthusiasts

652 Sports

FREE

http://www.hosports.com/cgi-bin/
htimage/opt/httpd/image-map/
mainbar.conf?132,12

Sports Information Server ★★★

Welcome to the Sports Information Server. Here you can access every little piece of data about your favorite professional sports teams. The Professional Hockey Server provides box scores, team schedules, and current standings. The Professional Basketball Server gives recent scores, team schedules, and player statistics. The Professional Football Server supplies the results of the NFL Draft, box scores, and a few other tidbits of information.

KEYWORDS Basketball, Football, Hockey
AUDIENCE Basketball Fans, Football Fans, Hockey Enthusiasts, Sports Fans
CONTACT sis-comments@netgen.com
FREE

http://www.netgen.com/sis/sports.html

SportsLine USA ★★★★

SportsLine USA provides sports information, entertainment and merchandise. SportsLine USA services intends to eventually provide subscribers with final scores, standings, team and player statistics, limited edition memorabilia, commentary, bulletin boards, electronic mail, fantasy leagues, real-time chat and proprietary games and contests. In the future, SportsLine USA also aims to be interactive so that subscribers can communicate with other sports fans as well as former and current sports personalities. You must submit an online registration form to use the free services.

KEYWORDS Entertainment, Scores
AUDIENCE Athletes, Consumers, Event Planners, Sports Fans
CONTACT feedback@sportsline.com
FREE

http://www.sportsline.com

The Sports Server ★★★

The Sports Server provides readers with coverage of most of the world's major sporting events. Users can choose a summary of the top 15 sports news articles worldwide. There are also separate pages devoted to Baseball, Basketball, and Football (U.S.), as well as a general page covering stories in Racing, Soccer, Tennis, Golf, Olympics, Boxing, and Ice Hockey. Each section lists news stories in reverse chronological order, so users can see archives of old stories in the same directories as the new ones. In addition, there are individual categories within certain sports, so that topical articles, such as the 1994/5 baseball strike can be grouped together.

KEYWORDS Baseball, Basketball, Football, Sports News
AUDIENCE Baseball Fans, Basketball Fans, Football Fans, Sports Fans
CONTACT webmasters@merlin.nando.net
FREE

http://www.nando.net/sptsserv.html

Thoroughbred Horse Racing and Breeding ★★★★

This site, Thoroughbred Horse Racing and Breeding, provides other links to horse racing-related World Wide Web sites. Some of the topics include Thoroughbred Horse Racing Information Link from Las Vegas, Sports Central, daily results, and entries from the US. Other links include the Santa Anita Web page, The Churchill Downs Web page and the Kentucky Derby, the University of Kentucky's Horse Racing Archives, Breeders' Cup, pages for handicappers including T.H.R.I.L. (Thoroughbred Horse Racing Information Link), and the 'TRC Thoroughbred Notebook.' Alt.sport.horse-racing newsgroup, Derby mailing list, EQUINET, and racehorse ownership partnerships are also on the Web.

KEYWORDS Horse Racing, Thoroughbred Horses
AUDIENCE Gamblers, Horse Breeders, Horse Racing Enthusiasts, Jockeys
CONTACT Jeff Klenner
hyperion@swcp.com
FREE

http://www.swcp.com/~hyperion/
horse.html

 Tum Yetto Ghetto ★★★

Tum Yetto Ghetto offers information, pictures, and attitudes about the increasingly popular sports skateboarding, surfing, and snowboarding. In addition, this offbeat site hosts a Web-based magazine called 'Foxy,' as well as a collection of random tidbits, computer art, and music-related information. Through this site, users can also access product information for a number of sports equipment manufacturers, record labels, and other related commercial entities.

KEYWORDS Skateboarding, Snowboarding, Surfing
AUDIENCE Cyberculture Enthusiasts, Skateboarders, Snowboarding Enthusiasts, Surfing Enthusiasts
CONTACT Tony Sanfilippo
tony@tumyeto.com
FREE

http://www.tumyeto.com/

UI Rugby WWW Server ★★★

This World Wide Web rugby information service provides access to all significant data on the game of rugby to be found on the Internet. The linked sites include basics of rugby, rules of rugby, trivia and frequently asked questions, schedules of international games including World Cup, and rugby culture such as songs and jokes.

KEYWORDS Rugby, Sports
AUDIENCE Rugby Fans, Sports Fans
CONTACT pbickers@phys.uidaho.edu
FREE

http://rugby.phys.uidaho.edu/rugby.html

Ultimate Frisbee ★★★

This page is designed as a 'course' on Ultimate Frisbee in Germany, designed to teach the basics to a new Ultimate player. It provides information about how the game is played, rules and regulations, it defines specific terms used during the game, and gives a brief history of the sport. Also included are instructions about specific techniques and tactics for frisbee throwing and receiving. Links are included to other Ultimate Frisbee Web sites, such as the Internet Frisbee Shops, as well as addresses for Ultimate organizations.

KEYWORDS Frisbee, Germany, Sports Training
AUDIENCE Frisbee Enthusiasts, Sports Fans
CONTACT Judith Grabandt
judy@bonsai.educat.hu-berlin.de
FREE

http://www.educat.hu-berlin.de/ultimate/

Volleyball WorldWide ★★★★

Welcome to Volleyball WorldWide! This server attempts to centralize information on the sport of Volleyball. Some of the topics covered include USAV-USA Volleyball (formerly USVBA), Federation Internationale de Volley-Ball (FIVB), professional volleyball (AVP, WPVA, NVA), introduction/history of volleyball, rec.sport.volleyball frequently asked questions (faq), magazines, wallyball.

KEYWORDS Sports, Volleyball
AUDIENCE Sports Fans, Students (University), Volleyball Enthusiasts
CONTACT Tom Jack
taj@cup.hp.com
FREE

http://www.cup.hp.com/~vball/

White Water Rafting Guide ★★★

This site contains information and resources for the sport of white water river rafting. Users will find beginners' guides, as well as information on classifying rivers in terms of skill level. There is also listings of some popular equipment providers available here, as well as rivers especially suited for the sport.

KEYWORDS Rivers, Water Sports
AUDIENCE Sports Fans, Water Sports Enthusiasts, White Water Rafting Enthusiasts
CONTACT Ricky Houghton
ricky.houghton@cs.cmu.edu
FREE

http://whirl.speech.cs.cmu.edu/
WhiteWaterRafting.html

World Wide Web of Sports ★★★★

This page is a meta-index of sports information. It is organized by sport, and your search can be customized to selections with or without pictures. Some of the pointers include basketball (NBA and NCAA), Sailing and America's Cup, National Hockey League, miscellaneous athletic games such as the Olympics and Good Will Games, frisbee, rugby, golf, rowing, cricket, and much more. This is a good place to start a sports search.

KEYWORDS Basketball, Sailing, bicycling
AUDIENCE Children, Coaches, Parents, Sports Fans
FREE

http://www.tns.lcs.mit.edu/cgi-bin/
sports/

The XVIII Olympic Winter Games ★★★

This is the site for the 1998 Winter Olympics in Nagano, Japan, available in both English and Japanese. There are links to the descriptions of all the events, descriptions of venues and what event will take place there, access directions to Nagano inlcuding transportation types, and a page devoted to the official mascot of the Nagano Olympics, the Snowlet, which is an owl found in the forests of Nagano.

KEYWORDS Japan, Olympic Games, Sports, Sports News
AUDIENCE Ice Hockey Fans, Olympic Enthusiasts, Owl Enthusiasts, Skaters, Skiing Enthusiasts, Winter Sports Enthusiasts
CONTACT naoc@hq.linc.or.jp
FREE

http://www.linc.or.jp/Nagano/index.html

Travel & Tourism

See also
Arts & Music · *Art Galleries*
Government & Politics · *Countries*
Humanities & Social Sciences · *Area & Cultural Studies*
Popular Culture & Entertainment · *Museums & Theme Parks*
Popular Culture & Entertainment · *Weather & Traffic*

1996 Summer Olympic Games Information ★★

This page provides material on the 1996 Summer Olympics in Atlanta, Georgia. Much of the information is geared towards people who will be attending the games. Information includes maps and other local details about Atlanta, where to find private housing during the games, merchandising, transportation, and more.

KEYWORDS Atlanta (Georgia), Olympic Games, Travel Information
AUDIENCE Olympics Enthusiasts, Sports Fans
CONTACT royal@mindspring.com
FREE

http://www.mindspring.com/~royal/olympic.html

A Guide to Old Covered Bridges of the Philadelphia Region ★★★★

This page provides links to documents which are a guide to the old covered bridges of the greater Philadelphia region. Covered bridges symbolize small-town America, something from the nineteenth century, picturesque and sentimental, 'kissing bridges' recall a time when life was simpler and closer to the land. Photogenic and often remote from the Interstate Highways and cities of the twentieth century, covered bridges lure the explorer to find the little streams and dirt roads. The guide presents the bridges by county, structural type, driving tour, seasons, and FAQs.

KEYWORDS Bridges, History (US)
AUDIENCE Artists, History Buffs, Internet Users, Philadelphia Residents, Photographers

Connections to Caving (Spelunking)

Going down . . .

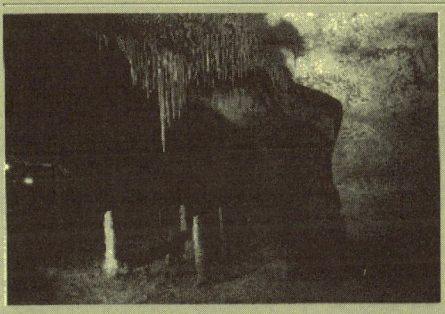

Hull University Speleological Society Expedition to Romania

INTRODUCTION

Romania is one of the least visited of the 'eastern bloc' countries, especially by cavers from the west. This is a shame since Romania contains some of eastern Europe's most spectacular karst scenery along with some spectacular caves. Topographically, Romania resembles a huge amphitheatre. The lofty peaks of the Carpathian Mountains rise to more than 8,240 feet, composed of broken massifs often covered with thick forests, surrounding the Transylvania plateau, which averages 2,640 feet above sea level. The valleys contain several small villages, each a cluster of a dozen or do wooden frame buildings along an unpaved road. Romania is only about half the size of France, however over 11,000 caves have been documented.

Andrew Knight

Get down with speleology! Through the Internet, you can access the most vital caving (or spelunking) information sites around the world. Whether you practice your sport in Australia, Europe, or the U.S., resources on the World Wide Web give you the answers and best places to visit.

With the fall of communism in Eastern Europe, some of the lesser-known, first-rate caving locations are now opening up to the western spelunkers. The Hull University Speleological Society Expedition to Romania provides a vast amount of information on caving in the former Eastern Bloc country. Resources include locations, pictures, and travel advice.

(http://rschp2.anu.edu.au:8080/cave/romania.html)

There are a number of Internet sites that provide extensive information about places to go caving throughout the world. Many of the Internet sites provide easy-to-access information about geography, as well as expeditions for groups and individuals in Australia, the U.S., Sweden, and elsewhere. Through Caving WWW Sites, you'll also find information on caving via scuba dives. You'll access caving clubs to find out what they are up to as well as read about their experiences on caving in various locations around the world. There are even pages dedicated to Slovenia's exotic Karst region, not far from Trieste and the Adriatic.

(http://www.ijs.si/slo-karst-route.html)

also, (http://150.203.35.27:8080/cave/cavelink.html)

also, (http://www.mit.edu:8001/activities/spelunk/home.html)

also, (http://zenon.inria.fr:8003/agos/sis/CavingWeb.html)

FREE

http://www.honors.drexel.edu/top/bridge1/CB1.HTML

A Photographic Tour of Lesvos ★★★

The home page of Lesvos, Greece, the birthplace of Sappho, provides images and hypertext descriptions of attractions and facilities primarily of interest to tourists, especially those with an interest in photography. It is an Aegean island located on the gulf of Adramyti. It includes high-resolution photographs of petrified trees, an ancient theater (Mytilini) and a number of items in the Theofilos Museum.

KEYWORDS Greece, Photography, Tourism
AUDIENCE Greece Residents, History Buffs, Photography Enthusiasts, Tourists
CONTACT Yannis G. Kavaklis
kavaklis@stepc.gr
FREE

http://www.stepc.gr/yannis/lesvos-m.html

About Graz and Styria ★★★★

The home page of Graz, capital of the province of Styria, Austria, provides images and hypertext descriptions primarily of interest to tourists. It has links to such features as the annual Styriarte Festival, the Armory museum, with 30,000 pieces of armor preserved in their original state since the seventeenth century, the Stubing Open-air Museum, Piber, where the Lipizzaner horses are bred for the Spanish Court Riding School in Vienna. There is also coverage of local theater and opera, numerous sporting events from tennis to gliding, the Provincial Arsenal and Parliament, Herz-Jesu Church and Eggenberg Palace—and, of course, where to lodge, dine and shop.

KEYWORDS Austria, History, Horses, Tourism
AUDIENCE Art Enthusiasts, Austria Residents, Outdoors Enthusiasts, Sailing Enthusiasts, Tourists
FREE

http://hgiicm.tu-graz.ac.at/E6A04D9F/Cmmisdata

Advice and Adventures on Budget Travel in Europe ★★★

Nick Cockcroft, a globetrotting student, shares his penny-wise travel tips with like-minded adventurers. A great deal of the information focuses on Nick's personal tales, and he's free with unadulterated praise and condemnation for the European destinations he loved and hated. Concrete travel advice is scattered here and there, but don't rely on Nick as your sole source of travel intelligence. In the future he plans to cover Asia as well.

KEYWORDS Adventure Travel, Budget Travel, Europe, Travel Planning
AUDIENCE Budget Travelers, Students (University), Tourists, Travel Agents
CONTACT Nick Cockcroft
cockcr01@wharton.upenn.edu
FREE

http://futures.wharton.upenn.edu/~cockcr01

Aerial Views of Switzerland ★★★

The M.A.C. AG in Switzerland is an electronic publishing company that offers their spectacular new multimedia CD, Aerial Views of Switzerland over the Web. In cooperation with Swissair and the Swiss Tourist Office, M.A.C. offers a tour of Switzerland by air for 89 Swiss francs. The 1000 images include sightseeing (ancient castles, medieval towns, favorite tourist regions), Mittelholzer (pioneering flight photographs), Alpine World (views of the highest Swiss Alps), and a historical selection of images taken from the archives.

KEYWORDS CD-ROMs, Multimedia, Photography, Switzerland
AUDIENCE Swiss, Swiss Culture Enthusiasts, Tourists, Travel Agents
CONTACT multimedia@dial.eunet.ch
COST

http://www.eunet.ch/Customers/multimedia/index.html

Africa Camping Safari Itinerary ★★

This site presents an itinerary for a Camping Safari in Kenya. Travel takes place in a 4-wheel drive safari truck, train, and on foot. The safari includes a trip to the Masai Mara Game Park and a trek up Mt. Kenya. Optional side excursions include a week on the coast of Kenya or a one-week trip to climb Mt. Kilimanjaro. The land cost, airfare to Nairobi, and hiking difficulty are included on the page. However, there is no information about who to contact or who to pay or who is organizing the trip, so be sure to make note of the contact information provided here.

KEYWORDS Camping, Kenya, Safari
AUDIENCE Safari Enthusiasts, Tourists, Travel Agents
CONTACT Canadian Himalayan Expeditions Ltd.
webmaster@netpart.com
FREE

http://www.netpart.com/che/acs.html

Akiko International Home Page ★★★

The Akiko site offers a wide variety of information related to New Zealand. Users will find material on traveling in New Zealand, a New Zealand FAQ, information on businesses and the Internet in New Zealand, and more.

KEYWORDS International Travel, New Zealand, Southeast Asia, Tourism
AUDIENCE New Zealand Culture Enthusiasts, Tourists, Travelers
CONTACT akiko@nz.com
FREE

http://www.akiko.lm.com/

The Alaska Travel Guide ★★★

The Alaska Travel Guide is a statewide indexed network of hypertext documents and links to organizations and locales of interest to travelers. It includes links to cities, fishing and hunting sites, transportation, parks and travel agencies.

KEYWORDS Alaska, Fishing, Tourism
AUDIENCE Community Groups, Fishing Enthusiasts, Network Users, Tourists, Travel Agents
CONTACT howard@travel.alaska.net
FREE

http://www.alaska.net:80/~travel/

Amsterdam Airport Schiphol ★★★★

This is an extremely good home page about Amsterdam International Airport Schiphol. You'll find virtually everything you need—flight schedules, a detailed guide to the airport, maps, how to get to and from the airport, a description of the Visitor Center, and more.

KEYWORDS Aviation, Netherlands, Transportation
AUDIENCE Business Professionals, Dutch, International Travelers, Tourists
CONTACT schiphol@xxlink.nl
FREE

http://www.xxlink.nl/schiphol/

Anaheim/Orange County CA CityLink ★★★

The Anaheim, California Home Page is a community network that provides hypertext descriptions of facilities and sights of interest to tourists. This site provides an index of links to local places to stay, eat and shop.

KEYWORDS California, Community Information
AUDIENCE Californians, Community Activists, Community Groups, Network Developers, Network Users
FREE

http://www.neosoft.com/citylink/anaheim/default.html

Anchorage CityLink ★★★

Anchorage CityLink is a community network oriented toward the features of the city which are of interest to tourists. This site provides hypertext descriptions and links to various features and services, such as where to eat, stay and shop.

KEYWORDS Alaska, Community Information
AUDIENCE Alaska Residents, Community Activists, Community Groups, Network Developers, Network Users, Tourists
CONTACT citylink@neosoft.com
FREE

http://www.neosoft.com/citylink/anchor/default.html

Asia Online ★★★★

This Web site offers a complete economic and business-related outlook on one of the world's largest regions, Asia. Information on travel, business and finance, and Asian culture is presented in a clear, well-organized format. Highlights of this cybermall include InTechTra's Hong Kong securities reports, TravelASIA's tourism information for countries in Asia and the Pacific Rim, and Asian business listings.

KEYWORDS Asia, Pacific Rim, Travel Information
AUDIENCE Asian Culture Enthusiasts, International Business Professionals, International Development Specialists, International Travelers
FREE

http://www.branch.com:80/silkroute/

Travel & Tourism **655**

Aspen Snowmass Online ★★★

This community network focuses on information about Snowmass, a nearby ski resort to Aspen, Colorado, including ski conditions, lodging availability, and travel plans. This current data is in addition to civic and commercial groups operating both in Snowmass and in Aspen.

KEYWORDS   Community Information, Government, Outdoor Recreation, Skiing
AUDIENCE   Aspen Residents, Community Activists, Community Groups, Network Developers, Skiing Enthusiasts, Tourists
CONTACT   aspenonline@infosphere.com
FREE

http://www.aspenonline.com/aspenonline

Atlanta! T.R.A.V.E.L.I.N.K Inc. ★★★

This home page for Atlanta, Georgia was produced and is being maintained by students in technical writing courses at Georgia Tech University and presents images and text combined in an effort to attract tourists.

KEYWORDS   Georgia, Tourism
AUDIENCE   Art Enthusiasts, Georgia Residents, Students (University), Tourists
CONTACT   andy@mordred.gatech.edu
FREE

http://www.gatech.edu/3020/travelink/homepage.html

Austin Travel Guide ★★★

This home page presents graphics and hypertext that attempt to entice the tourist, including a stand of 'postcards,' a list of hotels by area, a list of restaurants by type, car rental agencies & limo services, places to see, Austin night clubs, radio stations, maps, golf courses, and additional information.

KEYWORDS   Music, Texas, Tourism
AUDIENCE   Art Enthusiasts, Music Enthusiasts, Texas Residents, Tourists
CONTACT   tomb@tab.com
FREE

http://www.tab.com/Travel/Austin/Austin.html

 ## The Bay Area Online Home Page ★★★

The Bay Area Online service is a compilation of guides that focus on the San Francisco Bay area, including the Oakland and San Jose areas. The headings included in this guide include Restaurants, Places to See, and Shopping Centers. Each of these three guides contains basic contact information for thousands of retail establishments and attractions throughout the Bay Area. The Restaurants page includes a form for user reviews of each establishment.

KEYWORDS   Restaurants, Shopping Malls
AUDIENCE   Californians, Travelers
CONTACT   Internet Media Services
           ims@netmedia.com
FREE

http://www.netmedia.com/bayonline/

Belize ★★★

This page provides general links to information on Belize. Included are links to maps, history, travel information, growth, economic data, trade data, government information, and more.

KEYWORDS   Belize, Caribbean, Central America, Travel Information
AUDIENCE   International Students, Latin American Studies Students, Tourists, Travel Agents
CONTACT   info@lanic.utexas.edu
FREE

http://lanic.utexas.edu/la/ca/belize/

Berkshire County ★★★

The home page of Berkshire County, Massachusetts presents GIF images and hypertext descriptions of attractions and facilities of the area that are mainly of interest to tourists. There are subindices that cover such topics as visitor information, lodging, restaurants, recreation, night life, a calendar of events, shopping, attractions, theaters and concerts, and a local area map, as well as local weather, demographics and news. There is special focus on the world-renowned Tanglewood Music Festival (the summer home of the Boston Symphony Orchestra).

KEYWORDS   Massachusetts, Tanglewood Music Festival, Tourism
AUDIENCE   Art Enthusiasts, Camping Enthusiasts, Golf Enthusiasts, Hiking Enthusiasts
CONTACT   info@ultranet.com
FREE

http://www.ultranet.com/~isite/berkshire.html

Bolivia ★★★★

This page provides links to information on the country of Bolivia. Subjects covered include maps, history, travel information, growth, economic data, trade data, government information, and Amazonian Peoples' Organizations in Bolivia.

KEYWORDS   Bolivia, Latin America, Tourism, Travel Information
AUDIENCE   International Students, Latin American Studies Students, Tourists, Travel Agents
CONTACT   info@lanic.utexas.edu
FREE

http://lanic.utexas.edu/la/sa/bolivia/

Boynton Beach ★★★

The home page of Boynton Beach, Florida presents images and hypertext that describe features and facilities of interest primarily to tourists. Boynton Beach is located 15 minutes from West Palm Beach International Airport, and halfway between the exclusive Palm Beaches and Boca Raton. Boynton Beach has some of the finest water sports in the state of Florida, including drift fishing, excellent scuba diving, wide sandy beaches, World class golf courses, dozens of restaurants and pubs, relaxed shopping in the Boynton Beach Mall, other speciality shops in the area and the day's scuba diving conditions.

KEYWORDS   Fishing, Florida, Tourism
AUDIENCE   Fishing Enthusiasts, Florida Residents, Golf Enthusiasts, Outdoors Enthusiasts, Tourists
CONTACT   admin@emi.net
FREE

http://www.emi.net/~bdenton/bbeach1.html

Brest 96 ★★★

The home page of Brest, France provides hypertext images and links to documentation pertaining to attractions and facilities of the town and its environment of particular interest to tourists. It focuses on its harbor and sailing features, particularly the annual regatta between Brest and Douanamez. It also details where to lodge, dine and shop.

KEYWORDS   France, Sailing, Tourism
AUDIENCE   France Residents, Hiking Enthusiasts, Sailing Enthusiasts, Tourists
CONTACT   brest96@enst-bretagne.fr
FREE

http://www.enst-bretagne.fr:3000/anglais/ Home_page_gb.html

Brighton, England, United Kingdom ★★★★

The home page of Brighton, on the South Coast of England provides hypertext images and descriptions of local attractions and facilities, including The Lanes, originally the village of Brighthelmstone, which is full of shops, clubs and 'twisty little passages,' and such hotels as The Grand and The Metropole. There is a brief history and information of interest to tourists concerning places to lodge, dine and shop.

KEYWORDS   England, Tourism
AUDIENCE   England Residents, History Buffs, Sunbathers, Tourists
CONTACT   Andy Holyer
           andyh@pavilion.co.uk
FREE

http://www.pavilion.co.uk/SouthCoastScene/area.htm

Brisbane, Australia ★★★

The home page of Brisbane, capital of the state of Queensland, Australia, provides hypertext images and links to attractions and facilities of particular interest to tourists, including weather, sights and attractions, the Parklands complex, which contains the Queensland Museum, State Library, and the Queensland Performing Arts Complex. It is the gateway to Rainforest national parks and the Great Barrier reef.

KEYWORDS   Australia, Hiking, Scuba Diving, Tourism
AUDIENCE   Australia Residents, Camping Enthusiasts, Hiking Enthusiasts, Tourists
CONTACT   Contact_emailashley@dstc.edu.au
FREE

http://www.dstc.edu.au/events/icodp95/brisbane.html

Burnie, Tasmania ★★★

The home page of the city of Burnie, in the state of Tasmania, Australia, provides hypertext images and links to documents describing the region's features and facilities of primary interest to tourists, such as its pulp and paper mill, and the city port serving the region's

Sports & Recreation

mining industry. The attractions described include Fern Glade, Bernie Park and trout fishing at Lake Kara. The Pioneer Village Museum offers a taste of what life was like at the turn of the century.

KEYWORDS   Australia, Tasmania, Tourism
AUDIENCE   Australia Residents, Fishing Enthusiasts, Hiking Enthusiasts, Tourists
CONTACT   Justin.Ridge@its.utas.edu.au
FREE

http://info.utas.edu.au/docs/tastour/nw/burnie.html

Calistoga ★★★

The is the home page for a town famous for its hot springs - Calistoga, in the Napa Valley of Northern California. The site presents graphical images and hypertext descriptions of interest to tourists and those seeking mineral, mud, and steam baths. It has subindices that provide information about the area's spas, lodging, restaurants, outdoor activities, and annual events and includes a map of the region.

KEYWORDS   California, Tourism
AUDIENCE   Californians, Outdoors Enthusiasts, Spa Enthusiasts, Tourists
CONTACT   Frank Forbes
           forbes@freerun.com
FREE

http://www.freerun.com/napavalley/calistog/calistog.html

Cambridge, United Kingdom ★★★★

The Cambridge, England home page provides hypertext images and links both to attractions and facilities of interest primarily to tourists, and to those interested in Cambridge University (with links directly to the University's computer network). The tourist links include cinemas, museums, dentists, taxis, banks, police and to the Tourist Information Centre.

KEYWORDS   England, Tourism, Universities
AUDIENCE   England Residents, England Scholars, History Buffs, Tourists
CONTACT   webmaster@cl.cam.ac.uk
FREE

http://www.cs.ucl.ac.uk/misc/uk/cambridge.html

gopher://gopher.cam.ac.uk/11/CambArea

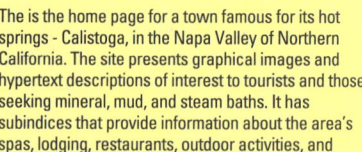

Canadian Airlines International ★★★

The Canadian Airlines International (CAI) Page gives access to the airline's services, destinations and weather information. The server has facts about the airline and its current flight destinations. Viewers may find out schedule information and about the types of aircraft CAI flies. There are links to the WWW and the top ten comercial web sites.

KEYWORDS   Airlines, Canada, Weather
AUDIENCE   Canada Residents, Tourists, Travelers
CONTACT   webmaster@www.CdnAir.CA
FREE

http://www.ntf.ca/

Cape Ann WebSite ★★★

The home page for Cape Ann, Massachusetts presents sublinks to hypertext descriptions of the area with attractions for tourists, including beaches, parks, hiking and camping attractions, whale watching, fishing, and boating and sailing opportunities. Among the annual events listed are the Rocky Neck Art Colony seasonal opening in May, the New Fish Festival in June and the holiday parade in July. Cape Ann is home to a number of artist colonies and galleries.

KEYWORDS   Massachusetts, Tourism
AUDIENCE   Camping Enthusiasts, Fishing Enthusiasts, Hiking Enthusiasts, Massachusetts Residents, Outdoors Enthusiasts, Sailing Enthusiasts, Tourists
CONTACT   info@intermktg.com
FREE

http://wizard.pn.com/capeann/

Cape Cod Home Page ★★★

The home page for Cape Cod, Massachusetts focuses on information, both through GIF images and hypertext descriptions and sublinks, of interest to tourists and those who might wish to move there. There are links to such topics as the Cape Cod real estate database, local town information, artists of New England, Cape Cod bed and breakfasts, hotels and inns, the online MarketSpace, and how to order overnight delivery of living Cape Cod lobsters.

KEYWORDS   Massachusetts, Real Estate, Tourism
AUDIENCE   Camping Enthusiasts, Hiking Enthusiasts, Outdoors Enthusiasts, Sailing Enthusiasts, Tourists
CONTACT   dmedia@oa.net
FREE

http://www.dmc.oa.net:8001/

Capetown & Vicinity ★★★

The home page of Cape Town, South Africa provides hypertext images and links to documents pertaining to features and facilities of the local area of primary interest to tourists, including Table Mountain, the waterfront, gardens (Kirstenbosch) and museums, Cape Point Nature Preserve, Hoet Bay, and where to lodge, dine and shop. St. George's open market is completely 'pedestrianised' with street performers and other entertaining diversions.

KEYWORDS   Hiking, South Africa, Tourism
AUDIENCE   Community Activists, Community Groups, Network Developers, Network Users
CONTACT   Philip Hazel
           ph10@cus.cam.ac.uk
FREE

http://www.city.net/countries/south_africa/cape_town/

Cardiff, Wales, United Kingdom ★★★

The home page of Cardiff, the capital of Wales, provides hyptertext images and links to documents presenting information primarily of interest to tourists, such as a historical guide, the nearby Brecon Beacons mountains, the waterfalls of the Afon Mellte valley, and the Taff Trail. There is a map of the town center and a link to the WWW server at the University of Cardiff.

KEYWORDS   Tourism, Wales
AUDIENCE   Hiking Enthusiasts, Tourists, Wales Residents, Wales Scholars
CONTACT   Robert.Hartill
           Robert.Hartill@cm.cf.ac.uk
FREE

http://www.cs.ucl.ac.uk/misc/uk/cardiff.html

Cassoviapolis Home Page ★★★

The home page of Kosice, Slovakia provides images and hypertext descriptions of local features and attractions primarily of interest to tourists, with an emphasis on the history of the region beginning with the 12th century when it was called Pentapolitana. There are also images and an account of a nearby children's railway built prior to World War II that still operates a steam locomotive from the railway workshops of 20 Spisska Nova Ves. There are also links to pages about the local technical university and, in town, where to lodge, dine and shop.

KEYWORDS   History, Slovakia, Tourism
AUDIENCE   History Buffs, Railroad Enthusiasts, Slovakia Residents, Tourists
CONTACT   kupcik@ccsun.tuke.sk
FREE

http://www.tuke.sk/kosice/kosice1-a.html

Cathay Pacific (USA) Home Page ★★★

This is the home page from Cathay Pacific Airways — the only daily non-smoking, non-stop B747-400 service between Los Angeles and Hong Kong. Currently, flight schedules are not available. However, one can enter a contest to win a free ticket for two, learn about their tourist packages, and get some useful link to Asian infoservers.

KEYWORDS   Airlines, Hong Kong, Tourism, Transportation
AUDIENCE   Asians, Business Professionals, Tourists
FREE

http://www.cathay-usa.com/

Chambre de Commerce de Sfax ★

The home page of Sfax, Tunisia provides images and hypertext descriptions (in French) primarily of interest to tourists. Under construction, it has basic links to information about where to lodge, dine and shop. It also has a brief history and description of cultural activities (both under construction).

KEYWORDS   Culture, History, Tunisia
AUDIENCE   Art Enthusiasts, History Buffs, Tourists, Tunisia Residents
FREE

gopher://alyssa.rsinet.tn/1

Travel & Tourism

Champaign-Urbana Convention and Visitors Bureau ★★★

The home page of Champaign-Urbana, Illinois is a start-up site presented by the Champaign-Urbana Hotel and Motel Association that presents addresses and contact numbers for local lodging, dining and shopping. It also provides information about local attractions, including Allerton Park, Anita Purves Nature Center, the Octave Chanute Aerospace Museum, the Champaign County Historical Archives, and the County Historical Museum.

KEYWORDS	Illinois, Tourism
AUDIENCE	Art Enthusiasts, Illinois Residents, Museum Enthusiasts, Tourists
CONTACT	info@prairienet.org
FREE	

http://www.prairienet.org/community/convention/home.html

Charleston Info ★★★

The home page of Charlotte, North Carolina presents hypermedia information primarily of interest to tourists, although it would also be of use to local and regional residents. It contains subindices that link to a map, a calendar of events, sports and recreation, arts, culture and history, shopping, local business and industry, lodging and restaurants.

KEYWORDS	History, North Carolina, Tourism
AUDIENCE	Art Enthusiasts, Museum Enthusiasts, North Carolina Residents, Tourists
CONTACT	John Ellis web-ncnet@www.hickory.nc.us
FREE	

http://www.hickory.nc.us/ncnetworks/clt-intr.html

The Charlottesville Guide ★★★

The home page of Charlottesville, Virginia, which is sponsored by CVille Weekly, provides graphics and hypertext images of features and attractions of interest to tourists and local residents. It has subindices concerning such topics as antiques and galleries, bed and breakfasts, day-tripping, events, phone numbers, hotels, newcomer services, points of interest, real estate, restaurants and shops.

KEYWORDS	History, Tourism, Virginia
AUDIENCE	Art Enthusiasts, History Buffs, North Carolina Residents, Tourists
CONTACT	liz_brooks@krj.ccmail.compuserve.com
FREE	

http://www.whitlock.com/kcj/guide/

Chicago's Home Page ★★★

Chicago's home page is one of several that cover various features and attractions of the city. It contains graphics and hypertext descriptions that present attractions and features primarily of interest to tourists. It contains links to such topics as sightseeing, museums, galleries, sports and scheduled events as well as restaurants, hotels and entertainment.

KEYWORDS	Chicago, History, Tourism, Visual Arts
AUDIENCE	Art Enthusiasts, History Buffs, Illinois Residents, Museum Enthusiasts, Tourists

Connections to Cruise Lines
It's no longer just for the shuffle-board crowd

If you think that taking a cruise is just for the "older" generation, then think again. The popularity of cruise vacations is growing the fastest among singles and young families. Through the Internet you can find the ship tailored to the type of vacation you seek. There are cruises to suit every taste, including small ships, megaships, party ships, quiet ships, tall ships, sports cruises, river cruises, and watersports cruises.

Nearly every cruise line in the world—including the Windjammer cruises for sailing enthusiasts—is accessible through the Internet. Service includes information on cruise times, ports of call, and costs. You can even find out whether you'll have to dress up for an evening meal (some cruise lines are designed for casual wear only). Some Internet sites to browse for your sailing experience include Costa Travel On-Line, and Rec.Travel.Cruises.

(http://mmink.cts.com/costa.html)

also, **(http://www.digimark.net/rec-travel/cruises/rtc.html)**

If sailing on a Windjammer cruise is more like what you're looking for, several sites provide access, including "Welcome to Let's Fly & Cruise." Here you can also arrange to take a cruise for business, educational, and sports purposes, arrange a pilgrimage to the Holy Land, or even learn how to get a job on a cruise ship.

(http://market.net/travel/tc/cruises/index.html)

For information about specific cruise lines, you can access dedicated Internet sites, including Carnival Cruise Line and Royal Carribean Cruise Line. Their pages (like many of the cruise line pages) provide you with a vast array of information about the vacation spots their ships visit, as well as connections to travel agents to help you arrange your next trip.

(http:mmink.com/mmink/carnival/carnival.html)

also, **(http:mmink.com/mmink/kiosks/costa/rccl.html)**

Did you know that 54% of the people who go on a cruise are female? That 34% of the people who take cruises have household incomes of between $20,000 and $40,000 per year? If you have questions about cruise vacations (who take them, etc.), the Internet provides information and references about cruising and many of the popular cruise lines.

(http://www.explore.com/E_cruise.html)

CONTACT webcore@webcore.com
FREE
http://www.webcore.com/chicago/

Chile ★★

This page is in Spanish and primarily provides links to Chilean servers, universities and government information. The links to universities include the Universidad de Chile, Universidad de Concepcion, Universidad de Santiago de Chile, and more. There is a link to the National Commission for Science and Technology and COPESA, the electronic newspaper.

KEYWORDS Chile, Latin America, Universities
AUDIENCE International Students, Latin American Studies Students, Tourists, Travel Agents
CONTACT info@lanic.utexas.edu
FREE
http://lanic.utexas.edu/la/Chile.html

City of Joensuu, Finland ★★★

The home page of the city of Joensuu, Finland provides images and hypertext links to descriptions primarily of interest to tourists. It has subindexes that link to city information, travelling the surrounding region of Karela, cultural life, maps, transportation, and where to lodge, dine and shop. There is a special focus on the annual Housing Fair. There are also links to the University of Joensuu, North Karelia Polytechnic College, the Finnish Forest Research Institute and the European Forest Institute.

KEYWORDS Finland, History, Tourism
AUDIENCE Art Enthusiasts, Finland Residents, History Buffs, Tourists
CONTACT Perttu.Kulmala@Jns.Fi
FREE
http://www.jns.fi/eng/def_eng.htm

The City of Melbourne and Monash University ★★★

The home page of Melbourne, Australia provides images and hypertext descriptions primarily of interest to tourists and those concerned with Monash University in nearby Clayton. The links to the university are extensive but those related to the city of Melbourne consist of 'snapshots' of the city and accompanying descriptions. There are also links to Melbourne theatre reviews, sports and a geneology page.

KEYWORDS Australia, Tourism
AUDIENCE Australia Residents, Australia Scholars, Theater Enthusiasts, Tourists
CONTACT Gary Hardy
garyh@vicnet.net.au
FREE
http://www.cs.monash.edu.au/melbourne/index.html

City of St. John's ★★★

The home page of St. John's, Newfoundland, Canada provides JPEG images and HTML text descriptions of interest to tourists, business developers and local residents. Its subindexes provide links to such topics as local golf courses, tours of St. John's Harbour, the Freshwater Resource Center, and the Provincial Museum. There are extensive listings of local government and tourist services. It also covers where to lodge (with hotel rates and contact numbers), dine (organized under ethnic headings), and shop.

KEYWORDS Business Development, Canada, Tourism
AUDIENCE Art Enthusiasts, Canada Residents, Sailing Enthusiasts, Tourists
CONTACT info@compusult.nf.ca
FREE
http://www.compusult.nf.ca/nfld/tourism/stjohns/stjohns.html

The City of Thessaloniki ★★★

The home page of Thessaloniki, the second-largest city in Greece and one of the oldest cities in Europe, provides hypertext documentation concerning the city's long history, and many images of ancient preserved monuments.

KEYWORDS Greece, Tourism
AUDIENCE Byzantine Scholars, Greece Residents, Greek Scholars, History Buffs, Tourists
CONTACT Lambros Makris
lmak@eng.auth.gr
FREE
http://uranus.eng.auth.gr/new/eng/thessaloniki.html

City.Net ★★★★

City.Net allows users to obtain information about cities and regions from all over the world. Users can search the database by city name, or browse a hierarchical list of world regions and cities.

KEYWORDS Cities, International Travel, Meta-Index (International Cities), Tourism
AUDIENCE General Public, Tourists, Travel Agents
CONTACT support@city.net
FREE
http://www.city.net/

Color Tour of Egypt ★★★

The Color Tour of Egypt page provides thumbnail graphical linked images. Some of the pictures include a view of the Nile, Pool of Lotus, and Papyrus in front of the Cairo Museum; The god Hapy with the symbol of the unification of Egypt; The Step Pyramid of King Djoser of the Old Kingdom; The Temple of Isis on the island of Philae; and more.

KEYWORDS Africa, Culture, Egypt, Pyramids
AUDIENCE Art History Students, Educators, Egyptians, Photographers, Tourists, Travelers
FREE
http://www.memphis.edu/egypt/egypt.html

Commonwealth of Kentucky Tourism Cabinet ★★

The Commonwealth of Kentucky Tourism Cabinet site allows the viewer to take a virtual tour of the state of Kentucky. Viewers may choose from the regions of bluegrass highlands, western waterlands, scenic wonderlands, or eastern highlands. From each region, you can jump to contact information and descriptions of attractions, accommodations, golf courses, campgrounds, and other features.

KEYWORDS Events, Horse Racing, Kentucky, National Parks
AUDIENCE Horse Racing Enthusiasts, Kentucky Residents, Spelunkers, Tourists
CONTACT Dan L. Whitehouse
dwhiteho@msmail.state.ky.us
FREE
http://www.state.ky.us/tour/tour.htm

Cork City ★★★

The Cork, Ireland home page provides hypertext images and descriptions of local attractions and facilities primarily of interest to tourists, including a map of city centre, transportation to and from, hotels, sightseeing, restaurants and pubs. It includes a link to Ringaskiddy Ferry Port and the Royal Crosshaven Yacht Club, the oldest in the world.

KEYWORDS Ireland, Sailing, Tourism
AUDIENCE Ireland Residents, Sailing Enthusiasts, Tourists, Yachting Enthusiasts
CONTACT niall@symphony.ucc.ie
FREE
http://symphony.ucc.ie/ ~niall/cork.html

Costa Rica ★★★

This page provides links to information on the country of Costa Rica. There are resources for learning about Costa Rica with subjects that cover history, travel, economic data, trade, and government. There are maps of Costa Rica as well as information on the head of state, cabinet and constitution.

KEYWORDS Central America, Costa Rica, Government, Tourism
AUDIENCE International Students, Latin American Studies Students, Tourists, Travel Agents
CONTACT Info@lanic.utexas.edu
FREE
http://lanic.utexas.edu/la/ca/cr

Crash ★★★★

A journal of adventurous travel, the editorial mission of Crash is not only to help travelers plan and experience their trips, but to help us all—as a quote from G.K. Chesterton in the Crash masthead illustrates— 'set foot (in our) own country as a foreign land.' Crash sets out to fulfill their aim with highly-researched and detailed alternative travel stories, journals, letters, reviews and other material for the 'underground traveler.'

KEYWORDS Travel, Vacations
AUDIENCE Explorers, Tourists, Travelers
CONTACT John Labovitz
johnl@ora.com
FREE
gopher://gopher.etext.org/Zines/Crash
ftp://ftp.etext.org/pub/Zines/Crash/

Danes Abroad FAQ ★★

This site contains an FAQ (Frequently Asked Question) or a Dansk OSS in Danish for Danes living abroad. A variety of topics are covered including information about telephones, videos, computers, televison, Japan, and more.

KEYWORDS Denmark, Expatriates, FAQs (Frequently Asked Questions), Travel Information
AUDIENCE Danes, Journalists, Students (College/Graduate) Tourists
CONTACT Steen Koefoed Larsen
steenkl@dircon.co.uk
FREE

http://info.denet.dk/danskoss/oss.html

Darmstadt City Home Page ★★★

The home page of Darmstadt, located in the Rhein region of Germany, provides images and hypertext links to documentation primarily of interest to tourists and those interested in history. It has a general introduction, a short history, data about the region, and transportation facts.

KEYWORDS Germany, History, Tourism
AUDIENCE Art Enthusiasts, Germany Residents, History Buffs, Tourists
FREE

http://www.th-darmstadt.de/hrz/netz/hannes/darmstadt/daengl.html

Den Haag ★★★

The home page of Den Haag, the Netherlands, provides hypertext images and links to documents pertaining to facilities and attractions primarily of interest to tourists, including casinos, museums, coming events, hiking and camping, and banking services. It also offers vital information about where to lodge, dine and shop. There is information about local services (Haagse Hogeschool, Digitale Hofstad) in Dutch.

KEYWORDS Camping, Netherlands, Tourism
AUDIENCE Camping Enthusiasts, Hiking Enthusiasts, Netherlands Residents, Tourists
CONTACT comments@xxlink.nl
FREE

http://www.xxlink.nl/cities/den_haag

Der Virtuelle Tourist ★★★

Der virtuelle Tourist or 'The Virtual Tourist' provides links to all kinds of country overviews, pointers to travel newsgroups libraries, travel reports and train connections in Germany. Most of the site is in German.

KEYWORDS Germany, Maps, Transportation, Travel Information
AUDIENCE Germans, Tourists
CONTACT Markus Stumpf
stumpf@Informatik.TU-Muenchen.de
FREE

http://www.leo.org/infosys/tourist/

Digitale Regio Friesland ★★★

The home page of Friesland, The Netherlands, provides images and links to documentation (in Dutch) that provide information primarily of interest to tourists. It includes an index with links to cultural activities, theatre and music, hotels and restaurants, local politics, Het Bedrijvencentrum and Het Winkelcentrum.

KEYWORDS History, Netherlands, Tourism

AUDIENCE History Buffs, Music Enthusiasts, Netherlands Residents, Theater Enthusiasts, Tourists
CONTACT regiobestuur@knoware.nl
FREE

http://dru.knoware.nl/friesland/index.htm

Duesseldorf ★★★

The home page of Dusseldorf, on the Rhine River in Germany, provides hypertext images and links to documentation describing facilities and attractions primarily of interest to tourists, including a hotel directory, the Trade Fair Company, sightseeing opportunities, geography, and upcoming events.

KEYWORDS Germany, Rhine, Tourism
AUDIENCE Camping Enthusiasts, Germany Residents, History Buffs, Tourists
FREE

http://www.rz.uni-duesseldorf.de/WWW/D/home_e.html

El Paso ★★★

The home page of El Paso, Texas presents images and html text descriptions that attempt to draw tourists to the region. There are indices that link to such topics as the location, climate, surrounding cities, events, a calendar, hotels & motels, as well as museums & historic sites.

KEYWORDS History, Texas, Tourism
AUDIENCE Art Enthusiasts, History Buffs, Texas Residents, Tourists
CONTACT chitta@cs.utep.edu
FREE

http://cs.utep.edu/elpaso/main.html

Ferrara, Italy ★★★

The home page of Ferrara, Italy, provides hypertext images and links to documents describing the town's facilities and attractions, primarily of interest to tourists. Its main index has links to maps, addresses, artistic and cultural happenings, a history, hotels, restaurants, famous citizens, and sights and monuments.

KEYWORDS History, Italy, Tourism
AUDIENCE Art Enthusiasts, History Buffs, Italy Residents, Tourists
FREE

http://csufrisc.unife.it:8080/ferrara/ferrar_.html

Flag International ★★★★

This World Wide Web server contains detailed information about the 96 Flag motels and hotels around Victoria, Australia, searchable by name, location, or other keyword. Users may make reservations by filling out the online form.

KEYWORDS Accomodations, Australia, Hotels, Tourism
AUDIENCE Australian Culture Enthusiasts, Tourists, Travelers
CONTACT flag@aus.net
FREE

http://www.aus.net/00/flag/flaghome.html

Frankfurt/Main City Information ★★★

The home page of Frankfurt, located in the Rhein-Main region of Germany, provides images and hypertext links to facilities and attractions primarily of interest to tourists, including historical and cultural information, tourist features (such as the Taunus Mountains with a medley of pretty villages and famous spas or the romantic wine-growing regions lining the hills along the Rhine), and commercial information.

KEYWORDS Business, Germany, Tourism
AUDIENCE Art Enthusiasts, Business Entrepreneurs, Germany Residents, History Buffs, Tourists
CONTACT webmaster@nacamar.de
FREE

http://www.nacamar.de/city/frankfurt/e_frankfurt.html

Gawler ★★★

The home page of Gawler, South Australia, located 40 kilometers from Adelaide as a gateway to the Barossa Valley wine region, provides images and hypertext descriptions of attractions and facilities primarily of interest to tourists. It has an index with links to Gawler facilities, the Barossa Valley, Para Wira National Park, the Roseworthy Campus, and the April 23rd Anzac Parade.

KEYWORDS Australia, Tourism, Wines
AUDIENCE Australia Residents, Hiking Enthusiasts, History Buffs, Tourists, Wine Enthusiasts
CONTACT Eric Youle
exy@apanix.apana.org.au
FREE

http://apanix.apana.org.au/~exy/gawler.html

Genoa ★★★

The home page of Genoa, Italy provides images and hypertext links to descriptions of facilities and attractions primarily of interest to tourists, including transportation (air and rail schedules and fares), consulates, theatres, museums, calendar of cultural events and the activities program of the cultural association, Valore Liguria (including a typical Ligurian restaurant menu).

KEYWORDS History, Italy, Tourism
AUDIENCE Art Enthusiasts, History Buffs, Italy Residents, Theater Enthusiasts, Tourists
CONTACT Paolo Franchi
www@afrodite.lira.dist.unige.it
FREE

http://www.doit.it/Tourism/genova/genoa.html

Ghent, Belgium ★★★

The home page of Ghent, the main city of East Flanders in The Netherlands provides images and hypertext documents describing attractions primarily of interest to tourists. It was composed by a resident who has set up a set of images of historical sites in the city and a description of their history, including The Saint Catholic Church, the Saint Baaf Cathedral, the truly medieval Castle of the Counts (with its torture chamber). It also has images of the yearly 10-day festival during July celebrating the ascension of King Leonard to the throne in 1831.

KEYWORDS Belgium, History, Tourism
AUDIENCE Catholic Scholars, History Buffs, Medievalists, Netherlands Residents, Tourists
FREE

http://www.cs.unm.edu/~patrik/ghent.html

GolfData Web ★★★

This page contains links to Golf Travel Packages, Golf Publications, Tournaments and Associations, Golf Equipment Vendors, The Golf Channel, Course Information, and more.

KEYWORDS Golf, Sports, Tourism
AUDIENCE Golf Enthusiasts, Traveleers
CONTACT   david@gdol.com
FREE

http://www.gdol.com/

Grand Canyon National Park Home Page ★★★

The Grand Canyon National Park Home Page provides information for potential visitors about this national famous natural landmark. Users will find information about how to get there and seasonal weather tables, as well as maps of regions and backcountry trails, with descriptions and a photo gallery. Users may also take a 'virtual tour' of the Grand Canyon, with photos and descriptions. A bibliography of useful materials is listed, as well as information about different types of park services and other attractions in the Grand Canyon area.

KEYWORDS Backpacking, Geological Landmarks, National Parks
AUDIENCE Backpacking Enthusiasts, Hiking Enthusiasts, Nature Lovers, Tourists, Travelers
CONTACT   Bob Ribokas
          bob@kbt.com
FREE

http://www.kbt.com/gc/gc_home.html

Greater Baton Rouge Internet Rest Area ★★★

The home page of Baton Rouge, the capital of Louisiana, provides images and hypertext that expose the city's features and attractions that would primarily be of interest to tourists. The descriptive pages are organized around a sequence of photographs of major features of the area, including the U.S.S. Kidd Nautical Historical Center, Baton Rouge Magnet High School (with the only high school FM radio station on the air 24 hours a day, 365 days a year), a Gothic Revival castle, and the Greater Baton Rouge Bridge, gateway to the city from the west.

KEYWORDS History (US), Louisiana, Tourism
AUDIENCE History Buffs, Louisiana Residents, Museum Enthusiasts, Tourists
FREE

http://www.tyrell.net/~aevinc/aev2gbr.html

Grenoble, Ishre France ★★★

The home page of Grenoble, in the Rhine-Alpes in France provides images and hypertext links to descriptions of attractions and facilities primarily of interest to tourists and business entrepreneurs. Its main index provides links to educational opportunities, including research, the environment and quality of life and the business climate. It also covers such festivals as the Berloiz and the Chamrousse Festival of Humorous Films.

KEYWORDS Business, France, Tourism
AUDIENCE Business Entrepreneurs, France Residents, History Buffs, Tourists
FREE

http://www.grenet.fr/gid/anglais/

The Gumbo Pages ★★★★

The Gumbo Pages are a musical, culinary and cultural information source about New Orleans and French Louisiana, with essential information for the visitor to New Orleans and Acadiana (or 'Cajun country'). The contents of the site include music, culture and food in New Orleans, a Creole Cajun Recipe page, and 'Acadiana - Les Paroisses Acadiennes,' a guide to Cajun country. The site also contains information about the page's author's gumbo radio home show, and other music related information including recommended (Cajun/Zydeco) albums.

KEYWORDS Cajun Food, Dance, Louisiana, Tourism
AUDIENCE Cajun Food Enthusiasts, Louisiana Residents, Tourists, Zydeco Music Enthusiasts
CONTACT   Chuck Taggart
          eamon@netcom.com
FREE

http://www.webcom.com/~gumbo/

Hafnarfjvrpur, Iceland ★★★

The home page of Hafnarfjvrpur, ten minutes from Reykjavik, Iceland provides images and descriptions of local attractions and facilities of interest to tourists, with an emphasis on its historical sites. It includes a link to information concerning the annual Viking Festival.

KEYWORDS History, Iceland, Tourism
AUDIENCE Art Enthusiasts, History Buffs, Iceland Residents, Tourists
CONTACT   Thorgrimur P. Thorgrimsson
          thorthor@ismennt.is
FREE

http://rvik.ismennt.is/~thorthor/hafnarfj.html

Haifa, Israel Home Page ★★★

The home page of Haifa, Israel provides images and hypertext descriptions of attractions primarily of interest to tourists — with a strong focus on several museums, such as the Israel National Museum of Science and the Reuben and Edith Hecht Museum.

KEYWORDS Israel, Museums, Tourism
AUDIENCE Art Enthusiasts, Israel Residents, Museum Enthusiasts, Tourists
CONTACT   info@elron.net
FREE

http://www.city.net/countries/israel/haifa

Halifax, Nova Scotia, Canada ★★★

The home page of Halifax, Nova Scotia provides images and hypertext descriptions of attractions, events and facilities primarily of interest to tourists. It includes maps, transportation information, where to lodge, dine and shop, history, art and culture, and scenic walks. There is a sub-index with links to tours, nightlife and local news.

KEYWORDS History, Nova Scotia, Tourism
AUDIENCE Tourists
CONTACT   Tim Roberts
          tjr@sbacoop.sba.dal.ca
FREE

http://ttg.sba.dal.ca/nstour/halifax/index.htm

Hamburg, Germany ★★★

The home page of Hamburg, Germany provides images and hypertext descriptions of primary interest to tourists. Its primary index is a listing of links to maps, geography, thorough history, commercial activities, and cultural opportunities. The text is in German.

KEYWORDS Germany, History, Tourism
AUDIENCE Art Enthusiasts, Germany Residents, History Buffs, Tourists
CONTACT   Klaus Rosenfeld
          rosenfeld@rrz.uni-hamburg.de
FREE

http://www.uni-hamburg.de/Hamburg/HH_homepage.html

Hartsfield International Airport Home Page ★★★

This is a home page describing Hartsfield International Airport. It includes a list of airlines serving the airport with phones, a map, and a list of services. The page is a part of Atlanta (host of the '96 Olympics) home page.

KEYWORDS Air Transportation, Airports, Georgia, Travel
AUDIENCE Business Professionals, International Travelers, Sports Fans, Tourists
CONTACT   Andy
          andy@mordred.gatech.edu
FREE

http://www.gatech.edu/3020/travelink/airport.homepage.html

Hawaii Home Page ★★★★

The Hawaii Home Page is designed to provide users with a comprehensive listing of materials about Hawaii and its information resources. Information Services are divided up into the categories of business, education, government, organizations, and visitor centers. Each topic area includes graphics and links to individual resources listed alphabetically.

KEYWORDS Hawaii
AUDIENCE Hawaii Residents, Internet Users, Tourists, Travelers
CONTACT   webmaster@www.hawaii.net
FREE

http://nic.hawaii.net/

Travel & Tourism

Hawaii Visitors Bureau ★★★★

This page links the viewer to information about the Hawaiian Islands. There are pages devoted to the islands of Hawaii, Maui, Oahu, and others. Each Island page gives the viewer some history, background, a listing and several images of the attractions of the area. There are also pages devoted to activities for residents and tourists, accomodation links where each hotel or bed & breakfast has its own home page (with online reservations under construction). The calendar of events describes daily activities months in advance.

KEYWORDS	Hawaii, Hawaiian Culture, Hotels, Travel Information
AUDIENCE	Hawaiians, Tourists
CONTACT	Hawaii Visitors Bureau webmaster@www.visit.hawaii.org
FREE	

http://www.visit.hawaii.org/

HyperGuide to Manchester ★★★

The home page of Manchester, England provides images and hypertext descriptions primarily of interest to tourists. It begins with extensive auto, bus and rail travel instructions, including a complete guide to the sprawl of the University of Manchester campus. Being a university town, the sub-menus detail information about bookstores, art galleries, pubs, and student life.

KEYWORDS	England, Tourism, Universities
AUDIENCE	Art Enthusiasts, England Residents, History Buffs, Tourists
CONTACT	Matt Hall Matt.Hall@man.ac.uk
FREE	

http://info.mcc.ac.uk/Geology/HyperGuide/HyperGuide.html

Hong Kong Online Site ★★★

This is an online guide of Hong Kong. Users can find information on airlines, hotels, restaurants, as well as a shopping guide, tourist spots, Hong Kong culture, and more.

KEYWORDS	Hong Kong, Online Guides
AUDIENCE	Chinese Culture Enthusiasts, Hong Kong Residents
CONTACT	webzone@hk.super.net
FREE	

http://www.hk.super.net/~webzone/hk.html

In, From and Around Munich ★★★★

This is the Link Everything Online (LEO) guide to Munich, Germany. There is a City Guide, Public Transport, Cinema Program information, Pubs and Hangouts, Opening times, a Guide to the City Council and Administration, an Overview about Munich's History, Museums, Events and Oktoberfest. There is a very detailed page of links to Munich information systems; a software archive is also accessible from the site.

KEYWORDS	Germany, Travel Information
AUDIENCE	Business Travellers, Students, Tourists

Connections to Travel
On a slow boat to China

If you want to satisfy your wanderlust, or if you are curious about travel in Uzbeskistan or Morocco, look no further than the Internet. Many World Wide Web sites cater to the vagabond in all of us—opening up the world in ways that the travel pages in your newspaper could never do.

If you want to go trekking in Tibet, you can get weather information for various times of the year, advice on ethical issues concerning travel to this Chinese-occupied country, and information on how to get a Visa, surveillance of foreigners, and the costs of organized tours. The site provides maps, points of view on whether it is best to travel alone or with a group, as well as the best time of year to visit.

(http://www.manymedia.com/tibet/TibetTravel.html)

Once you've decided on a destination, your next online task might be to check airline schedules. You can even get answers to commonly asked questions about airline travel (and other modes of transportation) via the "Easy Sabre."

(http://www.lib.ox.ac.uk/internet/news/faq/archive/travel.air.online-info.html)

If you are interested in a career in travel, you can access information on the Internet that tells you how to set up a business and how to start selling airline tickets, car rentals, hotels, cruise and tour bookings, train tickets and more via "Above All Travel."

(http://www.aboveall.com/)

If you simply want to find some great travel bargains (flying for free or at drastically reduced rates), the "InteleTravel Agent Information" site can help, as well as "Travel— Clever Ways to Travel for Free or at Little Cost."

(http://inteletravel.com/inteletravel/agent.html)

also, (http://adam.cs.uwec.edu/~andersts/travel.html)

Travel & Tourism

CONTACT Markus Stumpf
stumpf@Informatik.TU-Muenchen.DE
FREE

http://www.leo.org/muenchen/

Information about Utrecht ★★★

The home page of the city of Utrecht in the The Netherlands, has text combined with graphical links to such topics as its attractions, bicycle and boat rental, bungalow parks, camping sites, coach rental, events, banking and tourists services, hotels, restaurants, several museums, riding schools, and local tourist boards. It also contains a set of links to other Web servers and projects.

KEYWORDS History, Tourism
AUDIENCE Art Enthusiasts, History Buffs, Museum Enthusiasts, Netherland Residents, Tourists
CONTACT comments@xxlink.nl
FREE

http://www.xxlink.nl/cities/utrecht

Information on Turkiye (Turkey) ★★★★

This is a home page providing information on Turkey. The user will find a multimedia tour, as well as resources about Turkey's culture, history, religion, science, arts, literature, electronic newspapers, magazines and sports.

KEYWORDS Culture, Turkey
AUDIENCE General Public, Turkish
CONTACT Benan Basoglu
benan@utkvx.utk.edu
FREE

http://www.cs.utk.edu/~basoglu/turkiye.html

InterAshland ★★★

The home page of Ashland, Oregon, focuses on the world-renowned Shakespeare Festival, but also presents graphics and hypertext descriptions of local features and attractions of potential interest to tourists and residents. Theaters include the Actors Theatre, the Ashland Community Theatre and the Camelot Theatre Company. There are subindices with topics including local schools and academies, hotels and motels, transportation, and a city history produced by the Chamber of Commerce.

KEYWORDS Oregon, Shakespeare Festival, Tourism
AUDIENCE Art Enthusiasts, Oregon Residents, Shakespeare Enthusiasts, Tourists
FREE

http://www.mind.net/ashland/

InterMind's Las Vegas On-Line ★★

This site presents information about Las Vegas, Nevada. Viewers can find links to local hotels, attractions, restaurants, and news. Where appropriate, information includes telephone numbers, descriptions, and reservation instructions. Plans for the future include online reservations.

KEYWORDS Gambling, Nevada, Travel Information
AUDIENCE Gamblers, Nevada Residents, Tourists
CONTACT Intermind Corporation
webmaster@terminus.intermind.net
FREE

http://www.intermind.net/las.vegas.on-line/homepage.html

Introduction to Wanaka ★★★

The home page of the town of Wanaka in New Zealand presents text descriptions combined with graphics of local features, attractions and facilities of interest to tourists, including how to get there, and information about skiing, a wide range of hotels, and a photo gallery of local sightseeing settings. There are extensive camping, trekking and horseback riding notations, not to mention a special emphasis on the area's paragliding school and activities.

KEYWORDS History, New Zealand, Tourism
AUDIENCE New Zealand Residents, Outdoors Enthusiasts, Paragliders, Tourists
CONTACT Martin Lennon
FREE

http://www3.waikato.ac.nz/wanaka/

The Irish Tourist and Holiday Facilities Page ★★

This WWW site provides accommodation recommendations for those travel enthusiasts who wish to enjoy their holiday in Ireland. A detailed discription of several accommodations is available, including material on Abbeyview Holiday Homes in Kinsale, and Trident Holiday Homes. A link to The Irish Jobs page is also provided for travelers who intend to stay for long periods of time.

KEYWORDS Ireland, Tourism, Travel, Travel Information
AUDIENCE Families, Irish Culture Enthusiasts, Travel Agents, Traveleers
CONTACT John Feeley
swexp@internet-eireann.ie
FREE

http://www.internet-eireann.ie/Ireland/tourist.html

Isfahan - Home Page ★★★

The home page of Isfahan, Iran provides images and hypertext links describing numerous architectural cites in the city, grouped by type — such as mosques, minarets, palaces and various other sites.

KEYWORDS Architecture, Iran, Tourism
AUDIENCE Architecture Enthusiasts, Architecture Scholars, History Buffs, Iran Residents, Persian Culture Enthusiasts, Tourists
CONTACT trochford@bridge.anglia.ac.uk
FREE

http://www.anglia.ac.uk/~trochford/isfahan.html

The Island of Crete - A Guide ★★

The home page of the Island of Crete, in the Mediterranean off of Greece, provides hypertext images and links to preliminary documentation primarily of interest to tourists. It has a very brief description of the charms and history of the isle, and is, at present, under construction.

KEYWORDS Crete, Greece, History, Tourism
AUDIENCE Crete Residents, Greek Scholars, History Buffs, Tourists
CONTACT Stelios Sartzetakis
stelios@ics.forth.gr
FREE

http://www.forthnet.gr/crete/index.html

Israel Information Service ★★★

The Israel Information Service gopher provides information that covers such topics as Israeli-Arab relations, Israeli Economic News, Education and Student Programs, Archaeology, Culture Media and Communications, and Tourism.

KEYWORDS Israel, Travel
AUDIENCE Educators, Israelis, Jews, Students, Travelers
FREE

gopher://israel-info.gov.il

The Jerusalem Mosaic ★★★★

The home page of Jerusalem, Israel provides images and hypertext descriptions of attractions and facilities primarily of interest to tourists and those interested in the history of the city that is the central core of three of the world's major religions. The images, which are keyed to maps, are mainly of religious sites and remains.

KEYWORDS History, Israel, Tourism
AUDIENCE History Buffs, Israel Residents, Religion Scholars, Tourists
CONTACT Dudu Rashty
Rashty@WWW.HUJI.AC.IL
FREE

http://www.city.net/countries/israel/jerusalem

Jerusalem Tour ★★★

This site offers a virtual tour of the ancient city of Jerusalem. It provides a view of the city from the sky, views of Jerusalem Gate, as well as varied historical, religious, and cultural information. There are links to other Jerusalem and Israeli sites.

KEYWORDS Culture, Israel, Travel
AUDIENCE Educators, Historians, Students, Travelers
FREE

http://shum.cc.huji.ac.il/jeru/jerusalem.html

Juneau, AK CityLink ★★★

The Juneau CityLink is a community network that provides hypertext documentation and active links to tourist attractions and services. It includes indexes that link to scuba diving, glacier excursions, bed and breakfasts, and dining and lodging facilities.

KEYWORDS Alaska, Community Information, Tourism
AUDIENCE Alaska Residents, Community Activists, Community Groups, Network Developers, Network Users

Travel & Tourism

CONTACT citylink@neosoft.com
FREE

http://www.neosoft.com/citylink/juneau/default.html

Kyushu Home Page ★★★

The home page of Kyushu, Japan provides images and hypertext descriptions primarily of interest to tourists, detailing where to lodge, dine and shop. There are also subindices that give tourist information regarding the nearby cities of Fukuoka, Saga, Nagasaki, Kumamoto Oita, Miyazaki, and Kagoshima.

KEYWORDS History, Japan, Tourism
AUDIENCE History Buffs, Japan Residents, Tourists
CONTACT www-admin@nic.karrn.ad.jp
FREE

http://www.karrn.ad.jp/index-e.html

 ## LOT Polish Airlines - Schedule ★★

This home page is just a text file with a schedule of all the LOT flights, internal and international. Very badly organized and presented, but the information is hard to find elsewhere. This is a part of the Warsaw University Physics Department home page, some information about Poland can also be found here.

KEYWORDS Air Transportation, Airlines, Poland
AUDIENCE Business Professionals, International Travelers, Polish, Tourists
CONTACT Kacper Nowicki
    Kacper.Nowicki@fuw.edu.pl
FREE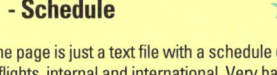

http://info.fuw.edu.pl/pl/LOT-schedule.txt

Let Frederickton Entertain You ★★★

The home page of Frederickton, the capital of New Brunswick, Canada, provides images and hypertext links to documents primarily of interest to tourists. The town features a living history program, which includes a tour of the town, including the changing of the Guard at Officers' Square, complete with white helmets and black boots, and outdoor performances by the Calithumpians.

KEYWORDS Canada, Tourism
AUDIENCE Canada Residents, Theater Enthusiasts, Tourists
FREE

http://www.cygnus.nb.ca/fredericton/fredfin.html

Let's Meet in Brussels ★★★

The home page of Brussels, Belgium provides hypertext descriptions of attractions and facilities primarily of interest to tourists. It includes a regional description, its economy, and useful tips such as transportation schedules and fares, weather, and where to lodge, dine and shop. It is presented by the Belgium Congress, which is a nonprofit organization that encourages conferences and conventions in the area.

KEYWORDS Belgium, History, Tourism
AUDIENCE Belgium Residents, History Buffs, Tourists

CONTACT tech.G7@interpac.be
FREE

http://www.ib.be/meet/

Lethbridge, Alberta, Canada ★★★

The home page of Lethbridge, Alberta, Canada provides images and hypertext descriptions primarily of interest to tourists, including where to lodge, dine, and shop. The site on which Lethbridge now sits was the home of Fort Whoop-Up, a notorious site where traders illegally sold liquor to Indians. The city of Lethbridge is also home to a large Japanese-Canadian population due to the compulsory relocation of Japanese-Canadians from the West coast of British Columbia during World War II when they were suspected of being potential subversives. As such, the city is home to the Nikka Yuko Japanese Garden, one of the most authentic Japanese Gardens in North America.

KEYWORDS Canada, Tourism
AUDIENCE Canada Residents, History Buffs, Japan Scholars, Tourists
CONTACT Brad Wallacee
    brad@ras.ucalgary.ca
FREE

http://www.cuug.ab.ca:8001/VT/lethbridge.html

Lima - Capital del Peru ★★★

The home page of Lima, Peru provides images and hypertext descriptions primarily of interest to tourists. Aside from details as to where to lodge and shop, it provides links to a number of beaches, city plazas, museums and churches.

KEYWORDS History, Peru, Tourism
AUDIENCE History Buffs, Peru Residents, Tourists
CONTACT webmaster@rcp.net.pee
FREE

http://www.rcp.net.pe/peru/lima/lima.html

Ljubljana ★★★

The home page of Ljubljana, the capital of Slovenia, provides images and hypertext descriptions primarily of interest to tourists. The images focus on its thousand-year old castle which has views of the Kmnik, Julian and Karawanken Alps.

KEYWORDS History, Slovenia, Tourism
AUDIENCE Art Enthusiasts, History Buffs, Slovenia Residents, Tourists
CONTACT mark.martinec@ijs.si
FREE

http://www.ijs.si/slo-ljubljana.html

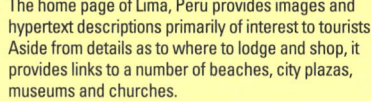 ## The Long Island Web ★★

The Long Island Web contains information about things to do in Long Island, New York. Listed here are directory items such as hotels and motels, restaurants arranged by type of cuisine, museums, wineries and beaches. There is also travel information, nature sites, shopping locations, and nightlife spots. Each item contains contact information, a short description, and occasionally an image. Other items of interest on this page are historical facts, trivia about Long Island, and annual weather information, with a link to current weather conditions.

KEYWORDS Museums, New York, Restaurants, Shopping
AUDIENCE New York Residents, Tourists
FREE

http://cyberactive-1.com/html/li-web.html

Louisville, Kentucky Visitor Center ★★

This site hosts travel and tourism information for the city of Louisville, Kentucky, the home of the Kentucky Derby, the Louisille Falls Fountain, and Jefferson Memorial Forest. On this page you will find hotel and restaurant listings, and contact information for a number of Louisville's attractions. The attractions available are under such categories as Sports, Television and Radio Stations, Nature and Recreation, Shopping, Museums, Parks, Antiques, Performing Arts, and Historic Places.

KEYWORDS Events, Horse Racing, Kentucky, Restaurants
AUDIENCE Kentucky Residents, Tourists
CONTACT IgLou -The Internet Gateway of Louisville
    info@iglou.com
FREE

http://iglou.com/louisville.html

 ## Lufthansa-Timetable ★★★

This is a searchable database of the flight schedule of Lufthansa, the airline of Germany. You enter your destination and departure points, and the date you wish to travel, and you get a list of Lufthansa flights. Return flight information is also immediately available.

KEYWORDS Air Transportation, Airlines, Germany
AUDIENCE Germans, International Travelers, Tourists
CONTACT rutter@tkz.fh-rpl.de
FREE

http://www.tkz.fh-rpl.de/tii/lh/lhflug-e.html

Madawaska-Victoria ★★★

The home page of Madawaska-Victoria provides images and hypertext descriptions primarily of interest to tourists. Its subindexes detailed information on transportation, maps, a calendar of events, history, and where to lodge, dine and shop. There is a special focus on the New Brunswick Botanical Garden and the Falls and Gorge of Grand Falls, and La Foire Brayonne and the Grand Falls Regional Potato Festival, as well as coverage of outdoor activities, such as golf, hunting and fishing, sailing, hiking, tennis and swimming.

KEYWORDS Canada, Tourism
AUDIENCE Camping Enthusiasts, Canada Residents, Hiking Enthusiasts, History Buffs, Outdoors Enthusiasts, Tourists
FREE

http://www.cuslm.ca/madvic/emada-vi.htm

Magnificent Madras

The home page of Madras, the capital of Tamil Madu on the shores of the Bay of Bengal in India, provides images and hypertext descriptions primarily of interest to tourists. Its subindices reveal detailed information about its history, places of interest, Fort St. George, the Marina, the Ice House, Snake Park, several museums, The Anna Zoological Park, the Planetarium and Kapaleeswarar Temple.

- **KEYWORDS** History, India, Tourism
- **AUDIENCE** Art Enthusiasts, History Buffs, India Residents, Tourists
- **CONTACT** Anthony Rajakumar arajakum@mtu.edu
- **FREE**

http://www.list.ufl.edu/~sriraj/madras.html

Maine Tourism Web Site

This site provides a wealth of information about tourism in the US state of Maine. Topics covered here include Regional Information; Helpful Information, such as State Symbols, event calendars and transportation; Special Attractions, like Lighthouses and Covered Bridges; Activities, including sports, shopping, and historical sites; and features such as Photographs of Maine and A Child's Fantasyland. Viewers can also jump to pages sponsored by specific tourist attractions, such as local skiing resorts.

- **KEYWORDS** Maine, Shopping, Skiing, Travel Information
- **AUDIENCE** Maine Residents, Tourists
- **CONTACT** webmaster_tour@state.me.us
- **FREE**

http://www.state.me.us/decd/tour/welcome.html

Malmoe (Sweden)

The home page of Malmoe, Sweden provides hypertext descriptions of the town primarily of interest to tourists. They are part of a project in a university course at MacNemkarna University in Malmoe and are not presently being updated. The pages have menus that offer detailed information about theatre performances, movies, art exhihitions, lectures, and concerts.

- **KEYWORDS** History, Sweden, Tourism
- **AUDIENCE** Art Enthusiasts, History Buffs, Sweden Residents, Tourists
- **CONTACT** Ulrika Andersson ulrika.andersson@student.mm.se
- **FREE**

http://www.project.mm.se/malmoe/engelska

Manchester Home Page

The home page for Manchester-By-The-Sea, Massachusetts presents images and hypertext that offer an introduction to the town for tourists. It has sublinks to such topics as beaches, hiking, parks, museums, an artist colony, musical festivals and whale watching, as well as boating and sailing, golf courses and special events. There are also addresses and telephone numbers for lodging, dining and shopping. See Link for history of Manchester-by-the-Sea.

- **KEYWORDS** England, Massachusetts, Sailing, Tourism
- **AUDIENCE** Camping Enthusiasts, Hiking Enthusiasts, Massachusetts Residents, Outdoors Enthusiasts, Sailing Enthusiasts, Tourists
- **CONTACT** info@intermktg.com
- **FREE**

http://wizard.pn.com/capeann/manchester.html

Maribor Main Page

The home page of Maribor, the second largest city in Slovenia, situated at the cross-section of traffic routes leading from central to southeastern Europe, presents descriptions and images of interest to tourists, potential business developers, and local residents. From a peaceful provincial town, inhabited by merchants, craftsmen associated with several guild-organizations, a sprinkling of clerks and soldiers, and a few members of the nobility, Maribor has been transformed into an economically and culturally dynamic city. There are indexes related to lodging, shopping and dining (especially wine), the arts, literature, and music.

- **KEYWORDS** Culture, Slovenia, Tourism, Wines
- **AUDIENCE** Art Enthusiasts, History Buffs, Slovenia Residents, Tourists, Wine Enthusiasts
- **CONTACT** rcum@uni-mb.si
- **FREE**

http://www.uni-mb.si/maribor.html

Milan

The home page of Milan, Italy provides images and hypertext descriptions primarily of interest to tourists. It has four views of the city from the roof of the Duomo, a history, entertainment, theatres, museums, first-class and less expensive hotels, pubs, phrases, events, and transportation information.

- **KEYWORDS** History, Italy, Tourism
- **AUDIENCE** Art Enthusiasts, History Buffs, Italy Residents, Tourists
- **CONTACT** senonm@ghost.sm.dsi.unimi.it
- **FREE**

http://www.dsi.unimi.it/Users/Students/markus/milan/milan.html

Minnesota Department of Transportation - World Wide Web

This site contains information for travelers in the state of Minnesota, USA, as well as links to general transportation resources. Viewers can find local driving conditions for Minnesota, and links to information from the University of Illinois at Urbana-Champaign's Department of Atmospheric Science.

- **KEYWORDS** Aeronautics, Minnesota, Transportation, Weather Reports
- **AUDIENCE** Minnesota Residents, Tourists, Transportation Professionals
- **CONTACT** webmaster@dot.state.mn.us
- **FREE**

http://www.dot.state.mn.us/

gopher://gopher.dot.state.mn.us

Multimediashow Linz

The home page of Linz, the capital of Upper Austria situated on the Danube River between Vienna and Salzburg, provides images and hypertext descriptions mainly of interest to tourists. The text, primarily in German, details where to lodge, dine and shop, and provides links to cultural activities, museums, art galleries, and sports activities. There is a link to many activities at the University at Linz.

- **KEYWORDS** Germany, History, Tourism
- **AUDIENCE** Art Enthusiasts, Germany Residents, History Buffs, Tourists
- **CONTACT** Manfred Pils Pils@idv.uni-linz.ac.at
- **FREE**

http://www.idv.uni-linz.ac.at/linzinfo/Linzhome.htm

The Nando Entertainment Server

Communities from a specific part of the United States can find useful information here. This site serves the cities of Raleigh, Chapel Hill, Durham and other localities within the Triangle Area in North Carolina, USA, providing information about entertainment options. Listings include Movies, Community Announcements, Concerts, Local Music, Recreation, Books, Lectures, Comedy, Nightlife, Theater, and Dance.

- **KEYWORDS** Entertainment, North Carolina
- **AUDIENCE** North Carolina Residents, Tourists
- **CONTACT** webmasters@merlin.nando.net
- **FREE**

http://merlin.nando.net/

The New York Web

The New York Web offers pages of interest to New York City residents and tourists looking for interesting things to see and do in Manhattan. Among the pages within this site are searchable guides to New York City's Night Life, which lists clubs, bars, and restaurants, City Life contains links to NYC events like the Thanksgiving day parade and the New York City Marathon, as well as to local tour operators.

- **KEYWORDS** Events, Multimedia, New York, Restaurants
- **AUDIENCE** New York Residents, Tourists
- **CONTACT** The New York Web nysurf@nyweb.com
- **FREE**

http://nyweb.com/

Norfolk International Airport

This well-organized site offers an online guide to the Norfolk International Airport in Virginia. You'll find a flight schedule, directions to the airport, and maps and layouts of the terminal. There are also other WWW links, and an In-Flight Survey—fill it out and you could win a prize.

- **KEYWORDS** Aviation, Transportation, Virginia

Travel & Tourism   **665**

AUDIENCE Business Professionals, Tourists, Virginia Residents
CONTACT airport@infi.net
FREE

http://www.infi.net/orf/

Nova Scotia Tourism ★★★

This is the Nova Scotia Tourism information page. The page provides links to information on Nova Scotia's weather, crafts, and the Greater Halifax Visitor Guide.

KEYWORDS Nova Scotia, Tourism, Travel
AUDIENCE Canada Residents, Canadians, Traveleers
CONTACT Tim Roberts
tjr@sbacoop.sba.dal.ca
FREE

http://ttg.sba.dal.ca:80/nstour/

Novo Mesto ★★★

The home page of the town, Novo Mesto, on the river Krka in Slovenia, has indexes that link to text and GIF-formatted images with a strong focus on the region's history, from its founding in 1365 through its commercial and manufacturing development in the middle of the last century, focusing on its central market. There are images of the two main churches, one of which has a famous altar image of St. Nicolaus by J.B. Tintoretto.

KEYWORDS History, Slovenia, Tourism
AUDIENCE Art Enthusiasts, History Buffs, Slovenia Residents, Tourists
CONTACT Iztok Umek
iztok@fer.uni-lj.si
FREE

http://www.fer.uni-lj.si/~iztok/Novo_mesto.html

The Paperless Guide to New York City ★★★

The Paperless Guide presents an extensive listing of things to do and see while visiting New York City. The viewer can choose from menu items such as Sights, Museums, Food/Dining, Entertainment, Hotels and Lodging, and Shopping to get a sense of what experiences await them when they arrive in NYC. Each menu item provides a listing of venues, complete with a description, address, hours of operation, and admission prices. Useful features for tourists include a street locating index, and a link to local weather conditions. In addition, some extra features on this server include a page devoted to New York City's history and trivia, a current events page, and special announcements like a contest on how to celebrate New Year's Eve 2000 in Times Square.

KEYWORDS New York, Restaurants, Shopping
AUDIENCE New York Culture Enthusiasts, New York Residents, Tourists, Travelers
CONTACT Mediabridge Infosystems Inc
nyc@mediabridge.com
FREE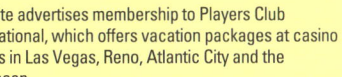

http://www.mediabridge.com/nyc/

Connections to Shopping Abroad
Searching Bonn for German chocolates

CHAPTER 1 SHOPPING ABROAD
SHOPPING ABROAD – NO PROBLEM?

Buying a camera, filling the boot with wine or foodstuffs, buying a flat or investing money abroad - this will soon be an everyday occurrence.

To make the most of the Single Market, consumers must be sure that their interests are protected. So they need objective information, a clear legislative framework and possibly even legal assistance.

However, the Single Market, being of recent vintage, is synonymous both with common rules on quality, safety and health and, in the legal domain, with greater risks.

This chapter surveys what has been done to enable consumers to benefit from the Single Market. Specific sectors are dealt with in greater detail in other chapters of this Guide.

? I never thought of shopping abroad on a big scale - what's in it for me?

? But what do our neighbours have that is so interesting?

With the European Common Market ever-expanding, your ability to purchase various products abroad is too—and without restrictive tariffs from one country to the next, either.
But what about your rights as a consumer? If you're planning a serious shopping trip to Belgium, France, or Italy, you'd probably like to know what you can buy, what the consumer's rights are, some information about product quality, and even the general hours the shops are open. You can get these answers and more before you make your trip by exploring the "Single Market" site on the World Wide Web. Here you'll find products or brands that are available only in a particular region of a given country. You'll also find yourself able to search out investment possibilities in areas like real estate and artwork.

(http://www.cec.lu/en/comm/spc/cg/c1.htm)

Players Club International ★★★★

This site advertises membership to Players Club International, which offers vacation packages at casino resorts in Las Vegas, Reno, Atlantic City and the Caribbean.

KEYWORDS Advertising, Gambling, Tourism
AUDIENCE Gamblers, Tourists
CONTACT +1 (800) 275-6000
FREE

http://branch.com/players/players.html

Portland International Airport ★★★

A home page from the Portland International Airport offers standard information - such as maps and how to get there, but in addition, it provides a list of Air Traffic Control services. This will be useful not only to passengers, but also to pilots. The page is a part of the Portland City Net home page.

KEYWORDS Air Transportation, Airports, Oregon, Travel
AUDIENCE Aviators, Business Professionals, International Travelers, Oregon Residents, Tourists
CONTACT roger@westlinn.com
FREE

http://www.teleport.com/~rogerb/kpdx/

Qantas Airways Ltd Home Page ★★★

This home page provides information about the Australian airline, Qantas Airways. Besides company information, there are flight schedules, career opportunities, fares and tariffs, links to some other airlines' and airports' home pages, AMTRAK information, and airline phone numbers.

KEYWORDS Air Transportation, Airlines, Australia
AUDIENCE Australians, International Travelers, Tourists
CONTACT David@Anzac.com
FREE

http://www.anzac.com/qantas/qantas.htm

Quoi de Neuf sur Lausanne ★★★

The home page of Lausanne, Switzerland provides images and hypertext descriptions of facilities and attractions primarily of interest to tourists, with the links organized based on the image of a walking tour starting from the Rue de Bourg. The tour includes the local art galleries and museums and includes details as to where to lodge, dine and shop.

KEYWORDS France, History, Switzerland, Tourism
AUDIENCE Art Enthusiasts, History Buffs, Switzerland Residents, Tourists

Sports & Recreation

CONTACT info@fastnet.ch
FREE

http://www.fastnet.ch/LSNE/lsne.html

Road Warrior Outpost ★★★

Road Warrior Outpost is a resource for portable computer users, providing information, news, products, travel information, a trading post, service for laptop and notebook computer users, and links to other interesting Internet sources. FAQs cover connecting to digital phone systems, how cellular communication works, battery life, and the nickel metal hydride (Ni-MH) battery tip. Viewers may register for free and receive Road Warrior News through email.

KEYWORDS Electronic Magazines
AUDIENCE Computer Professionals, Laptop Users, Macintosh Users, PC Users
CONTACT command@warrior.com
FREE

http://warrior.com

Rockport Home Page ★★★

This is the home page for Rockport, a town at the tip of Cape Ann in Massachusetts. It presents graphics and hypertext that serve to introduce the town to tourists. It offers sublinks to such subjects as beaches, hiking, parks, museums, an artist colony, musical festivals and whale watching, as well as boating and sailing, guided land and sea tours, golf courses and special events. There are also addresses and contact numbers for accommodations, shopping and dining establishments.

KEYWORDS Massachusetts, Sailing, Tourism
AUDIENCE Camping Enthusiasts, Hiking Enthusiasts, Massachusetts Residents, Museum Enthusiasts, Tourists
CONTACT info@intermktg.com
FREE

http://wizard.pn.com/capeann/rockport.html

Round-The-World Travel Guide ★★★★

This site offers a round-the-world travel guide. Structured similarly to many FAQ files, this site presents a table of contents with direct hypertext links to useful information. This guide covers all aspects of world travel, including advice on making pre-travel decisions, money matters, route planning, and more. It also includes pointers to other sites with more information than is provided in this document.

KEYWORDS Travel, Travel Information, Travel Planning
AUDIENCE Travel Agents, Travelers
CONTACT Marc Brosius
        brosius@fit.edu
FREE

http://www.digimark.net/rec-travel/rtw/html/faq.html

Sailing the Greek Isles ★★★

The home page of Kalymnos, a Mediterranean seaport in Greece, provides images and hypertext descriptions of the seaport's attractions primarily of interest to sailors and tourists. It describes the local weather and navigation conditions, and the local nautical rules and regulations, as well as providing detailed information about local charters.

KEYWORDS Greece, Sailing, Tourism
AUDIENCE Greece Residents, Sailing Enthusiasts, Tourists
CONTACT dianee@eskimo.com
FREE

http://www.eskimo.com/~dianee

Shamash ★★★

This Shamash gopher site is part of this group's efforts to 'help bring the Jewish community into the center lanes of the Information Superhighway.' The menu contains gopher how-to instructions, information about Jewish resources, the current Hebrew date, and more.

KEYWORDS Israel, Travel
AUDIENCE Educators, Jews, Students, Travelers
FREE

gopher://israel.nysernet.org

Singapore Online Guide ★★★★

This page is a comprehensive collection of information on the city of Singapore for foreign travelers. Available links include information on Singapore's climate and appropriate attire, attractions and entertainment, local customs and laws, and hotels and restaurants.

KEYWORDS Singapore, Thailand
AUDIENCE Chinese Culture Enthusiasts, Travelers
FREE

http://www.ncb.gov.sg/sog/sog.html

Slavonski Brod ★★★

The home page of Slavonski Brod, the third largest city in southern Slavonia, presents text, paintings and photos of interest to tourists. It has indexes that focus on its history, museums (esecially the Brosdsko Posavlje), and galleries. There are also details concerning where to lodge, dine and shop.

KEYWORDS Croatia, History, Tourism
AUDIENCE Art Enthusiasts, Croatia Residents, History Buffs, Tourists
CONTACT www@tel.etf.hr
FREE

http://tjev.tel.etf.hr/hrvatska/HRgradovi/Brod/Brod.html

Sofia ★★★

The home page of Sofia, capital and largest city of Bulgaria, presents accounts of regional facilities and attractions of interest to students and tourists, focusing on such educational institutions as Kliment Ohridski University, the University of National and World Economics, The Higher Institute of Architecture and Civil Engineering, The Medical Academy, The Academy of Fine Arts, and The Higher School of Drama.

KEYWORDS Bulgaria, Education, Tourism
AUDIENCE Art Enthusiasts, Bulgaria Residents, History Buffs, Students (University), Tourists
FREE

http://www.cs.columbia.edu/~radev/bulgaria/Sofia.html

Solothurn ★★★

The home page of the Canton of Solothurn, Switzerland offers text taken from brochures provided by the Solothurn Regional Tourist Office. The presentation simulates a tour around the city with photographs augmented by written narration. The sights include the Old Arsenal Museum, a hermit's cave, the neighborhoods of Soleure and Soletta, and sports and leisure facilities. The pages have focused on what can be seen in one day, with more extended features under construction.

KEYWORDS History, Switzerland, Tourism
AUDIENCE Art Enthusiasts, History Buffs, Switzerland Residents, Tourists
CONTACT marcel.marchon@iwi.unisg.ch
FREE

http://www-iwi.unisg.ch/~mmarchon/solothu/index.html

Southwest Airlines Home Gate ★★★★

This absolutely wonderful page serves up a description of the 46 airports Southwest serves, flight schedules, fares, tourist information, reservations phones, fun pack vacations, group travel, financial reports - nearly everything one wants to know about an airline.

KEYWORDS Air Transportation, Airlines, United States
AUDIENCE Business Professionals, General Public, Tourists
FREE

http://www.iflyswa.com/

Split Soon... ★★★

The home page of Split, the largest city of Dalmatia, Croatia offers images and text presenting the region's rich historical and cultural artifacts. There is a focus on Diocletian's Palace, and various museums and galleries, including the Cathedral Treasury, the Gallery of fine Arts, the Museum of the Croatian Navy and the archaeological, ethnographic, and municipal museums.

KEYWORDS Croatia, Culture, History, Tourism
AUDIENCE Art Enthusiasts, Croatia Residents, History Buffs, Tourists
CONTACT www@tel.etf.hr
FREE

http://tjev.tel.etf.hr/hrvatska/HRgradovi/Split/Split.ht ml

St. Galler Stadt Information ★★★

The home page of Gallen, Switzerland (in German) presents indexes that provide links to such topics as hotels, restaurants, sports, theaters, concerts, museums, and libraries. The detailed data (dates, contact numbers, addresses) are of potential value to both tourists and local residents.

KEYWORDS History, Switzerland, Tourism
AUDIENCE Art Enthusiasts, Germany Residents, History Buffs, Tourists
CONTACT postmaster@swissinfo.ch
FREE

http://www.swissinfo.ch/swissinfo/local/sg/sg.html

Sports & Recreation

Travel & Tourism

Stadt Leipzig ★★★

The home page of Leipzig, Germany provides images and hypertext descriptions primarily of interest to tourists, including a brief history, sightseeing images, local parks, and where to lodge, dine and shop. The text is primarily in German, with a short summary in English. The sights include the Old Bourse, the Old Weighing House and the Old City Hall.

Keywords Art, Germany, Tourism
Audience Art Enthusiasts, Germany Residents, History Buffs, Tourists
Contact Dr. Klaus Kunze
kunze@rz.uni-leipzig.de
Free

http://www.uni-leipzig.de/leipzig/

Star Clippers ★★

This is the site for Star Clippers, a company that offers cruises in the Caribbean on boats modelled after nineteenth century clipper ships. They emphasize their casually elegant approach, and provide descriptions of the ships and itineraries.

Keywords Cruises, Tourism
Audience Business Professionals, Cruise Enthusiasts, Tourists, Travel Agents
Contact cruise@explore.com
Free

http://www.explore.com/sc/SC.html

Stubbs Island Whale Watching ★★

The Stubbs Island Whale Watching site offers information on daily whale watching tours given by Stubbs Island Charters, Ltd., in British Columbia, Canada. Information on cruises, hydroplanes, and senior and/or group rates are given.

Keywords Canada, Charter Services, Stubbs Island, Whale Watching
Audience Marine Biologists, Tourists, Whale Enthusiasts
Free

http://www.physics.helsinki.fi/whale/canada/stubbs.html

Subway Navigator (Indicateur des Metros) ★★★

This site is an interactive, navigational tool for both English and French speakers. The user can plot his way throughout several cities in Europe and North America. The user must input departure and arrival locations, and the program will plot a graphical route utilizing a rough map of the particular city, as well as an estimate of travel time.

Keywords International Travel, Transportation, Travel Planning
Audience Europeans, Tourists, Travel Agents, Urban Planners
Contact Pierre David
Pierre.David@prism.uvsq.fr
Free

http://metro.jussieu.fr:10001/

Sunday River ★★★

The home page of Bethel, Maine provides images & hypertext that attempt to entice the skier & tourist to its slopes. 'Come on in and have a seat in the comfy chair, grab a cup of coffee, take off your boots (aaaaahhhh!), clear off your goggles, put your gloves and jacket over by the fireplace, and get ready to have a great time at one of the best places on earth.' The skiing information includes cross-country, trails (and their difficulty), general information on Sunday River, and (apres-ski) restaurant and nightlife information, as well as a year's list of upcoming events.

Keywords Maine, Skiing, Tourism
Audience Camping Enthusiasts, Hiking Enthusiasts, Maine Residents, Outdoors Enthusiasts, Ski Enthusiasts, Tourists
Contact oneill@cs.uml.edu
Free

http://www.uml.edu/~koverber/Sunday.html

Sydney, Australia ★★★

The home page of Sydney, Australia provides images and hypertext descriptions of value to tourists, theatregoers, and residents. The pages are arranged in the form of a pictoral tour of the city with accompanying written narrative. There is also a major link to the primary symbol of Sydney, the Opera House, with its vast network of stages that present theatre, musicals, opera, contemporary dance, ballet, and every form of music from symphony concerts to jazz.

Keywords Australia, Theater, Tourism
Audience Australia Residents, Music Enthusiasts, Theater Enthusiasts, Tourists
Contact andrew@bio.uts.edu.au
Free

http://www.bio.uts.edu.au/sydney/sydney.html

Szabolcs-Szatmar-Bereg ★★★

The aim of the home page of Szabolcs-Szatmar-Bereg, three hours' drive from Budapest, in easternmost Hungary, is to acquaint the visitor with this region. It presents text and images related to its natural, architectural and cultural assets. It also provides general data about the economy of the country.

Keywords Art Exhibitions, Hungary, Tourism
Audience Art Enthusiasts, Hungarian Internet Users, Hungary Residents, Tourists
Contact Istvan Komsdi
komodii@ny1.bgytf.hu
Free

http://www.bgytf.hu/~komodi/megye/english/folap.shtml

Szeged (Hungary) ★★★

The home page of Szeged, Hungary, provided by Jszsef Attila University, presents text concerning the local institutions of higher learning, including the Liszt Ferenc Academy of Music, the Biological Research Centre of the Hungarian Academy of Sciences, and the Albert Szent-Gyvgyi Medical University. There are many photos of the region provided by the University Association from the air or upper regions of various historical buildings.

Keywords History, Tourism
Audience History Buffs, Hungary Residents, Students (University), Tourists
Contact solarium@cc.u-szeged.hu
Free

http://www.jate.u-szeged.hu/szeged/

Tasmania - Launceston ★★★

The home page of Launceston, located on the Tamar River in Tasmania, Australia, provides images and hypertext descriptions of interest primarily to tourists, especially hikers and campers. There are pages with details concerning such natural habitats as the Cataract Gorge Reserve. The chairlift crossing the Gorge is the longest single span in the world. Activities include rock climbing and white-water rafting. There are also descriptions of the Penny Royal Watermill and the Waverley Woollen Mills.

Keywords History, Tasmania, Tourism
Audience Australia Residents, Camping Enthusiasts, Hiking Enthusiasts, Mountain Climbing Enthusiasts, Tourists, White-Water Rafters
Contact Justin.Ridge@its.utas.edu.au
Free

http://info.utas.edu.au/docs/tastour/ne/launceston.html

Taxi ★★

This page provides information about Taxi for the Macintosh or Windows, a software application that helps travelers plan trips and make reservations. It combines Zagat Survey's hotel and restaurant database with city maps and route mapping by Middlegate. This site provides a demo version of Taxi that can be downloaded.

Keywords Maps, PC Tools, Software, Travel Planning
Audience Computer Users, Macintosh Users, Travel Agents, Windows Users
Contact cw@pipeline.com
Free

http://shopping2000.com/shopping2000/taxi/taxi.html

Things To Do In & Around Tralee ★★★

The home page of Tralee, the capital of County Kerry, Ireland, presents images and hypertext descriptions of interest to tourists, including such topics as the Kerry County Museum, the Tralee-Blennerville Steam Railway, the Blennerville Windmill, the Fenit Seaworld Aquarium, the Aquadome and other activities. There is also a link to the provider, the Regional Technical College (RTC), which covers the schools of Science, Engineering & Construction Studies, Business & Social Studies, and which has its own link to information on what to do in town.

Keywords Ireland, Tourism
Audience Art Enthusiasts, Ireland Residents, Museum Enthusiasts, Students (University), Tourists

668 Travel & Tourism

CONTACT Paul Collins
paulc@staffmail.rtc-tralee.ie
FREE

http://ns.rtc-tralee.ie/TraleeTown/traleehp.html

Timisoara Home Page ★★★

The home page of Timisoara, the most Westernized Romanian city, provides images and hypertext descriptions of interest to tourists, including such topics as its elegant baroque squares, churches and cathedrals, new German and French libraries and it pedestrian-only downtown square. There is data about its selection of beer patios, cafes, restaurants, gelato stands and gift shops, as well as its large university. There are cultural accounts of the ethnic diversity converging there—including Germans, Hungarians, Serbs, Slovaks and a Jewish community. There are maps, a list of currency exchange rates, and relevant phone numbers and addresses.

KEYWORDS History, Tourism
AUDIENCE Art Enthusiasts, History Buffs, Romania Residents, Tourists
CONTACT DAIR-info@vpm.com
FREE

http://www.gate.net/~atoth1/timisoara.html

Tokyo Q ★★★

The home page of Tokyo, Japan focuses on timely items of interest to tourists, including such subjects as what is happening in Tokyo, what happened last week and what is on the agenda for next week, a suggested list of good restaurants, the best baths, and adventurous little city tours.

KEYWORDS History, Japan, Tourism
AUDIENCE Art Enthusiasts, History Buffs, Japan Scholars, Tourists
CONTACT rok@shrine.cyber.ad.jp
FREE

http://shrine.cyber.ad.jp/~rok/lastweek.html

Torcaza Trails-Trekking in the Venezuelan Andes ★★★

This page provides links to information on an adventurous trek into the Venezuelan Andes via the Torcaza Trails. Torcaza Trails offers the adventurous traveler the chance to explore the Sierra Nevada National Park in the Venezuelan Andes. The trek is designed to be of minimum impact to both the environment and the traditions of the local people. The income that these remote communities receive from tourism is intended to help preserve rural life that is being threatened by the encroachment of modern society.

KEYWORDS Hiking, Venezuela
AUDIENCE International Students, South Americans, Students (University), Tourists
CONTACT Rowena Hill/Andres Fajardo
rdrake@ing.ula.ve
FREE

http://Venezuela.mit.edu/tourism/torcaza/torcaza1.html

Tour of Liverpool ★★★

The home page of Liverpool, England provides images and hypertext links to descriptions primarily of interest to tourists. The focus of the pages centers on the exhibits devoted to the Beatles. There are subindices with pages devoted to a history of Liverpool, entertainment and the arts, a pub & club guide, football and other sports, and the Albert Dock (a restored commercial center).

KEYWORDS England, Tourism
AUDIENCE Beatles Fans, England Residents, Music Enthusiasts, Tourists
CONTACT www@csc.liv.ac.uk
FREE

http://www.csc.liv.ac.uk/users/webtour/city/tour.html

Tourist Guide to Hong Kong ★★

This is a short introductory guide to Hong Kong - its history, culture, where to dine and entertain, what to see. The page is a part of City Net.

KEYWORDS Asia, Hong Kong, Tourism
AUDIENCE Hong Kong Residents, Tourists
CONTACT info@infolink.net
FREE

http://www.infolink.net/hongkong/hongkong.html

Tourist Guide to Kyoto ★★★

The home page of Kyoto, the cultural and artistic center of Japan, provides images and hypertext links to features and facilities primarily of interest to tourists. More than 600 Buddhist shrines as well as the site of the Imperial Palace fill the subindices of images and accounts of the city's rich religious and political tradition. There are also subpages specifically designed for tourists, with links to travel arrangements, accommodations, dining, shopping, sightseeing & walking tours, and maps.

KEYWORDS History, Japan, Tourism
AUDIENCE Buddhism Scholars, History Buffs, Japan Residents, Tourists
CONTACT jw@fuji.stanford.edu
FREE

http://www.ntt.jp/japan/JNTO/Kyoto/

Travel Information About Belgium ★★★

This site currently provides facts about Belgium's history, culture, weather, transportation, money, hotels, and regional information. Soon to come is a restaurant list which covers regional specialties, but there is already a list of cafes, and links to two beer pages. There are at least a half dozen other excellent links.

KEYWORDS Belgium
AUDIENCE Business Professionals, Tourists
CONTACT Erik Evrard
evrard@dice2.desy.de
FREE

http://www.iihe.ac.be/hep/pp/evrard/travel.html

Trento & Trentino ★★★

The home page of Trento, Italy focuses on facilities and attractions of interest to tourists, including its castles, lakes, parks, museums, and general information about the town. The Web pages are provided by the University of Trento, which also has links to its own internal operations, including the departments of physics, mathematics, economics, law, computer and management services, and the information engineering lab.

KEYWORDS Italy, Tourism
AUDIENCE Italy Residents, Museum Enthusiasts, Students (University), Tourists
FREE

http://www.unitn.it/trentino/trentino.html

UbU's PaGe LiSbOn ★★★

The home page of Lisbon, Portugal provides images and hypertext descriptions primarily of interest to tourists. It contains subindices to pages concerning a description of the city, museums, interesting sites, and a special focus on the upcoming Expo'98, a world exhibit on oceans. It includes detailed bus schedules to and from all the sites mentioned.

KEYWORDS Portugal, Spain, Tourism
AUDIENCE Art Enthusiasts, History Buffs, Portugal Residents, Tourists
CONTACT ubu@individual.puug.pt
FREE

http://www.puug.pt/Lisboa/ubu_e.htm

Ubeda and Baeza Home Page ★★★

The home page of Ubeda, Spain, less than two hours by car from Granada, combines photographs with a history and descriptions of many of the buildings that have served to preserve its character as a model Renaissance town.

KEYWORDS History, Spain, Tourism
AUDIENCE Art Enthusiasts, History Buffs, Renaissance Scholars, Spain Residents, Tourists
CONTACT J.J. Merelo
jmerelo@kal-el.ugr.es
FREE

http://kal-el.ugr.es/ubeda.html

United Kingdom Guide ★★★★

This unofficial guide to the UK provides an interactive map of the UK with data on different towns and cities, and virtual tours. It also offers weather maps updated daily, excerpts from several newspapers and a variety of tourist-related, statistical and government information.

KEYWORDS Ireland, Travel Information, United Kingdom, Weather
AUDIENCE British, Irish, Scots, Students, Travelers
FREE

http://www.cs.ucl.ac.uk/misc/uk/intro.html

Universita' degli Studi dell'Aquila

The home page of L'Aquila, the capital of Abruzzo, Italy provides images and hypertext descriptions primarily of interest to tourists and students of Italian and Roman history. Images are available of many local historical sites organized around the central Maria di Roio Square, including the Palazzo Rivera and the Basilica of Maria di Collemaggio.

Keywords History, Italy, Tourism
Audience History Buffs, Italy Residents, Tourists
Contact mosaic@www.univaq.it
Free

http://www.univaq.it/

Vancouver Home Page

The home page of Vancouver, British Columbia, Canada, provides graphics and text links to such subjects as local accommodations, attractions, entertainment, activities, dining, events, and transportation.

Keywords Canada, History, Tourism
Audience Art Enthusiasts, Canada Residents, History Buffs, Tourists
Contact mgarnett@pie.vancouver.bc.ca
Free

http://www.aurora.net/pie/htm/first.html

Vegas.Com

Vegas.Com provides the viewer with information about Las Vegas, Nevada. This site has descriptions and contact information for casinos, hotels, restaurants, attractions, and more. For new bettors, a hypertext book offers the basics of most gambling games. In addition, reservations and online ordering forms for some car rental agencies, hotels, restaurants, videos and even weddings have been created for use with your credit cards. This site also contains calendar listings of shows playing at Las Vegas Resorts.

Keywords Entertainment, Gambling, Nevada
Audience Gamblers, Nevada Residents, Tourists
Contact Kimberly Coon - media
kimberly@vegas.com
Free

http://www.vegas.com/

Village of St. Claude

The home page of St. Claude, Manitoba, 100 km from Winnipeg, Canada, population 615, provides images and hypertext descriptions of interest to tourists and potential business developers, as well as data pertaining to services of value to local residents. Its subindexes provide links to such topics as the location, demographic information, local government, community services, shopping, business and industry, recreation and tourism, in addition to community contacts.

Keywords Canada, Community Services, Tourism
Audience Art Enthusiasts, Canada Residents, History Buffs, Tourists
Contact Bill Reid
Bill_Reid@MBnet.MB.CA
Free

http://www.mbnet.mb.ca/cp/st.claude.html

Connections to Wines and Wineries

Now, here's an amusing little wine . . .

Discover Cuvee Hedwighof (Cabernet/Swigelt) Barrique, 1991, or a Gelber Muskateller from Austria on the Internet. Matter of fact, you don't have to visit your local liquor and wine shop to buy your favorite wines.

Through the World Wide Web, you can order wines from all over the world. Whether you prefer a California Chardonnay or a French Burgundy, you can can purchase it online.

"The Virtual Wine Country" site provides hotlinks to various wineries in the U.S., and to one of the first European wineries on the Internet.

(http://www.wines.com/virtual.html)

You can tap into Wine-related newsgroups and individual winery sites online. At many sites you get a list of wines available, price lists and a history (with photos) of the winery. If you enjoy Burgundy, for instance, "The Burgundy Cellar Home Page" is the place to find the best wines. You can even get maps of wine-making regions and vintners. If you are a novice and want to become a connoisseur, the "Wine Web" is a good source for understanding, selecting ,and acquiring wines from around the world.

(http://www.covesoft.com/wine/)

also, (http://www.iii.net/biz/burgcellar/burghome.html)

If you prefer California wines from the various growing regions, including the Sonoma and Napa Valleys, you can go online with many of the wineries and get their wine list plus historical information about the wineries. If you are planning to visit the regions, maps and other data (like dining choices and nearby spas and mud baths) will make your wine tasting tour more fun. The Internet's "World Wide Wine Connection" gives you global exposure to famous wine regions.

(http://www.geninc.com/geni/wine/index.html)

Village of Treherne

The home page of Treherne, located in southern Manitoba, Canada provides images and hypertext descriptions of interest to tourists, covering such subjects as its location, a history, demographics (including a population breakdown by age and employment statistics), local government, community services, shopping, business and industry, recreation and community contacts.

Keywords Canada, History, Tourism
Audience Canada Residents, History Buffs, Tourists

Free

http://www.mbnet.mb.ca/cp/treherne.html

Ville de Magog / City of Magog

The home page of Magog, Quebec (in Canada) provides images and hypertext descriptions primarily of interest to tourists. It is under construction, but provides maps, travel information, a brief history of Magog, and where to lodge and dine.

Keywords Canada, Tourism

AUDIENCE   Art Enthusiasts, Canada Residents, History Buffs, Tourists
CONTACT   Roland Clairvoyant
FREE

http://www.fmmo.ca/roland/city.html

Virgin Atlantic Homepage

This is a home page from the British Airline Virgin Atlantic. It offers very well-structured information about fares and schedules—you can view all their options, conditions, etc. There are also phone numbers for making reservations in different cities. This a great place to visit for do-it-yourself travel arrangements.

KEYWORDS   Air Transportation, Airlines, Britain
AUDIENCE   British, Business Professionals, International Travelers, Tourists
CONTACT   Info@aeronet.demon.co.uk
FREE

http://www.demon.co.uk/atlantic/

WETVenice Home Page

The home page of Venice, Italy, presents photos, paintings and hypertext descriptions of relevance to tourists, covering such topics as its cultural and religious heritage, shows, sports and entertainment, maps, transportation to and from the Venice Carnival, accommodations and dining. Concerning the center of the city, there are subindices related to some restaurants, public transit, language courses, and where to stay. There is coverage of religious events, the International Art Exhibition, the Festival of Contemporary Music, the International Film Festival, the Marathon and regattas. There is also, of course, plenty of information about rowing.

KEYWORDS   History, Italy, Tourism
AUDIENCE   Art Enthusiasts, History Buffs, Italy Residents, Tourists
CONTACT   Corrado Petrucco
           conrad@cidoc.iuav.unive.it c/o
FREE

http://www.iuav.unive.it/wetvenice/wetvenice.html

The Webfoot's Guide to Italy

This site provides information on all aspects of Italy. The page breaks Italy down into regions and cities and contains facts on lodging, transportation, travelogues, language, literature, culture, sports, government, and commerce. There is also a tip guide for tourists.

KEYWORDS   Europe, Italy, Tourism, Travel
AUDIENCE   International Students, Italians, Tourists, Travelers
CONTACT   Kate Sherwood
           ducky@netcom.com
FREE

http://www.webfoot.com/travel/guides/italy/italy.html

Welcome To The Unofficial Haitian Home Page

The home page of the Island of Haiti provides images and hypertext descriptions of facilities, attractions, history and current events primarily of interest to tourists and political activists. It has extensive links to cultural pages ranging from Haitian proverbs through literature and painting to contemporary Voodoo Rock. It also has pages devoted to the tumultuous history of the island and the contemporary events that have been in the world's spotlight.

KEYWORDS   Haiti, History, Politics, Tourism
AUDIENCE   Haiti Residents, History Buffs, Tourists
CONTACT   RafReid@primenet.com
FREE

http://www.primenet.com/~rafreid/

Welcome to Canadian Airlines International

This site offers schedules and other related information from Canadian Airlines International. Users will find destination charts, airplane maintenance information, and instructions on reserving a seat on a flight. This server also provides travel and weather information, as well as links to tourism sites on the Net.

KEYWORDS   Air Transportation, Airlines, Canada, Travel
AUDIENCE   Business Professionals, Canadians, Tourists, Travelers
CONTACT   webmaster@www.CdnAir.CA
FREE

http://www.cdnair.ca

Welcome to Caswell Beach, NC

The home page of Caswell Beach, North Carolina presents graphical images and hypertext descriptions of the town's features for tourists. Named after Fort Caswell at the top of the island, Caswell Beach is home to the brightest lighthouse in the U.S. and hosts a Coast Guard Station reminiscent of the old coastal life-saving stations. There is no commercial development and thus it is a quiet place to vacation.

KEYWORDS   History, North Carolina, Tourism
AUDIENCE   History Buffs, North Carolina Residents, Tourists
CONTACT   info@webcom.com
FREE

http://www.webcom.com/~towns/caswell/caswell.html

Welcome to Cocoa Beach

The home page of Cocoa Beach, Florida presents GIF images and text links containing information of interest to tourists and anyone who might like to relocate there. There are sublinks to topics including commerce, education, real estate, recreation, restaurants, shopping, and transportation.

KEYWORDS   Florida, History, Tourism

AUDIENCE   Business Entrepreneurs, Florida Residents, History Buffs, Tourists
CONTACT   info@iu.net
FREE

http://www.iu.net/cocoa.beach/

Welcome to Gladstone, Manitoba, Canada

The home page of Gladstone, located on the Yellowhead Highway, 120 kilometers northwest of Winnipeg in Manitoba, Canada, provides images and hypertext descriptions primarily of interest to tourists. Its index page offers links to its location, demographic information, local government, community services, shopping and business, in addition to recreation and tourism.

KEYWORDS   Canada, Tourism
AUDIENCE   Canada Residents, Tourists
FREE

http://www.mbnet.mb.ca/cp/gladstone.html

Welcome to ITG Tours

This WWW site provides information on the services offered by ITG Tours, an American-based travel agency. Their products include tour packages to over 100 cities throughtout the United States, with no membership fee. Additional information includes customized price lists, instructions on tour booking and information about ITG itself.

KEYWORDS   Tourism, Travel Agencies, Travel Planning
AUDIENCE   Families, Travel Agents, Travelers
CONTACT   Kevin B. O'Connell, President
           info@itgtours.com
FREE

http://www.itgtours.com/itg

Whidbey Island Homepage

This site provides a comprehensive guide to beautiful Whidbey Island, a 50-mile-long island located in the Puget Sound just north of Seattle. The Home Page includes a schedule of festivals, lodging, ferry schedules, and other relevant information for travelers. This page also provides links to great sites for children, national weather information, state and federal government links, financial news, and more.

KEYWORDS   Camping, Northwest US, Washington State
AUDIENCE   Bicycling Enthusiasts, Boaters, Camping Enthusiasts, Tourists
CONTACT   admin@whidbey.net
FREE

http://www.whidbey.net

World Guide to Vegetarianism - California

The World Guide to Vegetarianism - California is a list of businesses and organizations useful to vegetarians living in or visiting California. Included is material about restaurants, health food stores, vegetarian organizations and festivals, et al. Contact information, telephone numbers and addresses are provided.

Keywords California, Food, Nutrition, Vegetarianism
Audience Animal Rights Activists, Buddhists, Cooks, Vegetarians
Contact Mark Wisdom
mwisdom@bnr.ca
Free

http://catless.ncl.ac.uk/Vegetarian/

**ftp://rtfm.mit.edu/pub/usenet/
news.answers/vegetarian/guide/
california**

Email and Mailing Lists

Arts & Music	675
Business & Economics	678
Communications	679
Computing & Mathematics	679
Education	684
Engineering & Technology	686
Government & Politics	687
Health & Medicine	688
Humanities & Social Sciences	690
Internet	693
Law & Criminal Justice	695
Popular Culture & Entertainment	696
Religion & Philosophy	698
Science	699
Sports & Recreation	701

Electronic Mail

Sending and receiving electronic mail (Email) is the Internet's most widely used function. At one time it was thought that letter-writing would go the way of the horse and buggy, but email has revived and transformed the art of writing letters into something new, fresh, immediate and compelling. People the world over are 'meeting' and making friends with like-minded people via the Internet. Email breaks down the boundaries of time and distance the same way the advent of the telephone revolutionized everyday communication.

Instead of being delivered by the post office, electronic mail messages are sent directly to your computer by way of a modem or by a high speed telecommunications connection. This not only vastly accelerates the speed with which messages can be transmitted, but provides numerous advantages to individuals as well as businesses in regards to efficiency, organization, and convenience.

Businesses, for instance can compose a single message and distribute it simultaneously to a worldwide sales staff that is Internet connected . Other significant advances in the workplace is the use of email for collaborative projects between people all the world. It is now quite easy to attach documents, files, programs, graphics, and even sound files to electronic mail you send to people who are thousands of miles away. Physical distance is no longer a barrier to this type of work situation.

Mailing Lists

What is a Mailing List?

By providing an efficient and inexpensive way to exchange information and messages simultaneously between many people all over the world, email has spawned the development of mailing lists. Mailing lists, similar to Usenet newsgroups, cover thousands of topics and interests. The continued growth is limited only by the initiative and imagination of the people who create them. Mailing lists were created by people who wanted an easy, reliable way for a group of people with a common interest to communicate by email.

The difference between newsgroups and mailing lists lies mostly in how the messages are delivered and the control in readership and content that mailing lists offer.

Email messages for a particular mailing list are sent to the administrator (either human or automated), and then in turn delivered by email to those who have subscribed to the mailing list. These messages are delivered to your email box like any other email message.

In a way, mailing lists are similar to subscribing to a hardcopy magazine like *Time* and relying on receiving a new copy each week except mailing list delivery schedules vary from list to list.

For example, individuals interested in discussing blues music can choose to subscribe to a mailing list called BLUES-L. Once subscribed, you will start receiving copies of all email messages posted to that particular mailing list. You can just be a 'lurker' (reader) of those messages, or you can choose to participate by responding publically to the entire mailing list or privately to just one of the list subscribers.

Other Things to Know about Mailing Lists

Moderated vs. Unmoderated

Moderated mailing lists tend to have fewer messages because an editor or moderator is screening and posting only those messages that are pertinent to the subject of the mailing list. This cuts down on 'noise', a problem common to newsgroups in which messages unsuited or unrelated to the subject are posted. But the majority of lists are unmoderated and therefore messages are most often automatically distributed.

Mailing List Digests

A digest is a single email message that contains a collection of individual messages in the body of one email message. This is a convenient and possibly even a money saving feature (i.e., your service charges you a per message fee), especially for those mailing lists that have a high level of message traffic.

Helpful Hints about Mailing Lists

Don't overload your mailbox! If you subscribe to many different mailing lists at the same time, you will receive vast amounts of email. It is not impossible to receive several hundred email messages in a single day if you are not careful!

Another Way to Find Out about Mailing Lists to Join Visit the Mailing List FAQ Page and scroll through the entries there. When you find one of interest, you can click your mouse and receive the FAQ for that particular mailing list. In addition to The McKinley, FAQs (Frequently Asked Questions) are very helpful documents in terms of helping you find a particular mailing list of interest to you. Check out the FAQ site provided below.

FAQ-Maintainer and FAQ-Maintainer-Announce Mailing Lists ★★★★

This site provides access to two mailing lists; The FAQ-Maintainer and the FAQ-Maintainer-Announce. These two mailing lists are intended for discussion among or announcements for people who maintain FAQs (Frequently Asked Questions) postings. This information is sent to all new subscribers and is posted to the mailing lists approximately every 90 days. Archives of these two mailing lists are available, as well as a list of the adminstrators of these lists. To make a submission, address mail to faq-maintainer@mit.edu or faq-maintainer-announce@mit.edu. The 'announce' mailing list includes the other mailing list, therefore do not send the same posting to both mailing lists. The 'announce' mailing list is moderated.

KEYWORDS   FAQs (Frequently Asked Questions), Mailing Lists, Internet Tools
AUDIENCE   Internet Enthusiasts, Internet Mailing List Managers, Mailing List Users
CONTACT   Nancy McGough
            nancym@ii.com
FREE

ftp://ftp.halcyon.com/pub/ii/internet/
    FAQMaintainer/mail-list-policy/

Mailing List Basics

You can subscribe to any listing that has a URL address beginning with **mailto**; simply email the administrator address for the mailing list to process your subscription request. You then get an email in return verifying that you have been added to the mailing list. The response time will often vary depending on whether the mailing list is managed by a person or mailing list software.

It is also very important to remember that there is an essential difference between sending messages for administrative reasons (i.e., subscribing and unsubscribing) and sending messages to the mailing list for subscribers to read. Subscribing, unsubscribing, and anything that affects your subscription to the mailing list should go to the administrative address.

For example, the mailing list AUSTEN-L@cm1.mcgil.ca is managed by the mailing list software listserv.

To subscribe, you should write to:

listserv@cm1.mcgil.ca

Any messages for all mailing list subscribers to read should be sent to the listname address at:

austen-l@vm1.mcgil.ca

But in both cases, notice that the tail end of the address does not change.

How to Subscribe and Unsubscribe

To subscribe to a mailing list, you first need to find out whether you are sending your request to a software program or a human being. Knowing the difference between a list that has a human moderator and one that is controlled by software is important because it determines how you request a subscription.

You can usually tell by the mailto: address. If the address contains the information **listserv@** for example, the resource is handled by a software program; sometimes if the address contains the information **-request@** then it is a toss up as to whether there is a human or software at the other end. If you see what appears to be a regular email address, then there most likely is a human intermediary that handles the subscription and information requests as well as maintains the distribution list.

We have listed six major mailing list software programs that are used. They differ slightly in how to join and leave a mailing list, so do note the distinctions, however slight.

There are also other types of mailing list software and how to subscribe or unsubscribe is difficult to figure out. If this is so, you may have to send an email message with the standard format of *list-name-request@host.domain* to receive a message regarding how to subscribe.

For example, to find out information about the ORCHIDS mailing list with the mailto: address ORCHIDS@scuacc.scu.edu, you should write:

ORCHIDS-request@scuacc.scu.edu

In return, you should receive instructions on how to subscribe to the ORCHIDS mailing list. Most of the mailing lists however, fall under one of the six major programs that are available. Included below is information on how to subscribe and unsubcibe to each one.

(Note: the words SUB and UNSUB stand for subscribe and unsubscribe.)

Mailing List Software

listserv

SUB <listname> <first name> <last name>
UNSUB <listname>

Example:

AUSTEN-L@cm1.mcgil.ca (A mailing list about Jane Austen)

Mail subscription request to:

listserv@vm1.mcgil.ca

In the body of the message type either:

SUB AUSTEN-L Christine Smith

or

UNSUB AUSTEN-L

majordomo

subscribe <listname>
unsubscribe <listname>

Example:

BERMUDA-LOVERS@world.std.com (A mailing list for people who love Bermuda)

Mail subscription request to:

majordomo@world.std.com

In the body of the message type either:

Subscribe BERMUDA-LOVERS

or

Unsubscribe BERMUDA-LOVERS

almanac -

subscribe <listname> <first name>
                              <last name>
unsubscribe <listname>

Example:

CITE-JOBS-MG@esusda.edu (Technology, Information, and Communication Job announcements)

Mail subscription request to:

almanac@esusda.edu

In the body of the message type either:

subscribe CITE-JOBS-MG Christine Smith

or

unsubscribe CITE-JOBS-MG

listproc-

subscribe <listname> <first name> <last name>

unsubscribe listname

Example:

AUDIO-L@bgu.edu (Discussion of hearing defects)

Mail subscription request to:

listproc@bgu.edu

In the body of the message type either:

subscribe AUDIO-L Christine Smith

or

unsubscribe AUDIO-L

mailbase

join <listname> <firstname> <lastname>
leave <listname>

Example:

WEB-SUPPORT@mailbase.ac.uk (Discussion of WWW issues, browsers, and servers)

Mail subscription request to:

mailbase@mailbase.ac.uk

In the body of the message type either:

join WEB-SUPPORT Christine Smith

or

leave WEB-SUPPORT

mailserv

The web mailserv differs from the other mailing list programs in that it is designed to work over the World Wide Web. It provides what is called a forms-based interface in which the user simply fills in a form to complete a subscription request. Currently, it requires PERL and HTTPD 1.2 in order to work, and operates in conjunction with either Netscape or Mosaic for Windows or XWindows.

It supports forms for listproc, listserv, majordomo, smartlist, and manually administered mailing lists. To subscribe or unsubscribe is done via the click of a button.

Final Reminders

1. Send the subscription request in most cases to the **administrative address**.
2. Place the subscribe request in the **body of the message**.
3. In most cases, leave the **subject line blank**.
4. When you subscribe to a list, you will usually receive a 'Welcome' message with basic information and instructions that you will most definitely need at a later time. **Save this message!**
5. Mailing lists can be a wonderful way for the everyday person to keep informed about a variety of topics simply and economically. There are thousands of mailing lists and The McKinley has made it easier to find the one that is right for you.

Arts & Music

Architecture

GEODESIC
Discussion of Buckminster Fuller and His Amazing Geodesic Domes
mailto:LISTSERV@UBVM.CC.BUFFALO.EDU

Art History

AMART-L
Discussion of American Art and Architecture
mailto:LISTSERV@CUNYVM.CUNY.EDU

Art Resources

ART-SUPPORT
Art related issues and technology in the UK
mailto:MAILBASE@MAILBASE.AC.UK

ARTNET
Discussion of technology use in art
mailto:MAILBASE@MAILBASE.AC.UK

Design

DESIGN-L
Basic Design and Applied Design in Art and Architecture
mailto:LISTSERV@PSUVM.PSU.EDU

FACXCH-L
Discussion Among Faculty Members in Art and Architecture, Visual and Basic Design
mailto:LISTSERV@PSUVM.PSU.EDU

IDFORUM
Discussion Among Industrial Designers, Industrial Design Educational Institutions, and Design Research Centers
mailto:LISTSERV@VM1.YORKU.CA

YUNUS
A discussion of the TeX typesetting system with special emphasis on Turkish TeX
mailto:LISTSERV@VM.CC.METU.EDU.TR

Electronic Arts

ART-MG
Computer Based Art and Resources
mailto:ALMANAC@ESUSDA.GOV

FINEART
Professional discussion of collaboration between artists and computer scientists
mailto:FINEART-REQUEST@ECS.UMASS.EDU

GRAPHUK
Computer graphics issues
mailto:GRAPHUK-REQUEST@CS.MAN.AC.UK

Film & Video

FILM-L
Different Points of View About Cinema
mailto:LISTSERV@ITESMVF1.RZS.ITESM.MX

FILMUS-L
Discussion of Dramatic Music for Film and TV
mailto:LISTSERV@IUBVM.UCS.INDIANA.EDU

LABORFILMS
Discussion of Labor Film History and Issues
mailto:LABORFILMS-REQUEST@COUGAR.COM

SCREEN-L
A wide-ranging discussion for those who study, research, or teach film and television
mailto:LISTSERV@UA1VM.UA.EDU

Music

ACCORDION
User discussion of accordion and free-reed instruments
mailto:ACCORDION-REQUEST@CS.CMU.EDU

ALLMUSIC
All Music in All Its Aspects
mailto:LISTSERV@AMERICAN.EDU

BAGPIPE
Any topic on bagpipe technique and equipment
mailto:BAGPIPE-REQUEST@CS.DARTMOUTH.EDU

DOUBLEREED-L
Announcements, techniques and construction of reed instruments
mailto:LISTPROC@ACC.WUACC.EDU

FINLANDIA
Discussion of Finnish classical and modern composers
mailto:MAJORDOMO@PHOENIX.OULU.FI

FLUTE-M
Flute playing techniques and music issues
mailto:FLUTE-M-REQUEST@UNIXG.UBC.CA

HARP-L
Harmonica techniques, equipment and issues
mailto:MXSERVER@WKUVX1.WKU.EDU

HORN
French horn techniques and theory
mailto:MUGREENE@MERLIN.NLU.EDU

KLARINET
A general discussion of the clarinet including news, research and teaching
mailto:LISTSERV%VCCSCENT.BITNET@VTBIT.CC.VT.EDU

KS32
Discussion of ENSONIQ synthesizer keyboards
mailto:KS32-REQUEST@CYGNUS.COM

Arts & Music

LA-RADIO
Discussion of Metropolitan Los Angeles Radio
mailto:LA-RADIO-REQUEST@HELEN.SURFCTY.COM

LATAMMUS
A discussion of Latin American music
mailto:LISTSERV@ASUVM.INRE.ASU.EDU

LUTE
Discussion of Lute Music
mailto:LUTE-REQUEST@CS.DARTMOUTH.EDU

MICAT-L
Academic Discussion of Musical Instrument Technology
mailto:MAILSERV@NRM.SE

MTO-LIST
Professional Discussion of Music Theory and Related Disciplines
mailto:LISTPROC@HUSC.HARVARD.EDU

MUSIC-AND-MOVING-PICTURES
Professional discussion of making music for film
mailto:MAILBASE@MAILBASE.AC.UK

MUSICAL-AESTHETICS
Analyses and problems with musical aesthetics
mailto:MAILBASE@MAILBASE.AC.UK

NM
Discussion of experimental or cutting edge music
mailto:MAJORDOMO@XMISSION.COM

PIANO-L
Discussion of piano performance, theory, and techniques
mailto:PIANO-L-REQUEST@UAMONT.EDU

PIPORG-L
A discussion of musical, technical, and historical issues of all kinds of organs
mailto:LISTSERV@ALBANY.EDU

RMMGA
Gateway to newsgroup on acoustic guitars
mailto:RMMGA-REQUEST@JHUNIX.HCF.JHU.EDU

VOCALIST
Discussion of vocal techniques, practice and recording
mailto:MAJORDOMO@PHOENIX.OULU.FI

Music Genres

BBSHOP
Barbershop organization singing and activities
mailto:BBSHOP-REQUEST@CRAY.COM

BGRASS L
Bluegrass Music
mailto:LISTSERV@UKCC.UKY.EDU

BLUES-L
Blues Music and Performers
mailto:LISTSERV@BROWNVM.BROWN.EDU

BRASS
Brass musical performance topics and discussion
mailto:brass-request@geomag.gly.fsu.edu

CLASSM-L
Discussion of All Classical Music
mailto:LISTSERV@BROWNVM.BROWN.EDU

DREAMPOP-L
Discussion of Dream Pop Music and Related Bands
mailto:LISTSERV@NETCOM.COM

EARLYM-L
Discussion of Medieval, Renaissance, and Baroque Music
mailto:LISTSERV@AEARN.EDVZ.UNIVIE.AC.AT

EXOTICA
Discussion of 1950's and 1960s ususual LP releases
mailto:MAJORDOMO@XMISSION.COM

FOLKTALK
Traditional and Contemporary Folk Music
mailto:LISTSERV@WMVM1.CC.WM.EDU

FOLK_MUSIC
Discussion of Recent American Folk-style Singer/Songwriters
mailto:LISTSERV@NYSERNET.ORG

FUNKY-MUSIC
Discussion of Funk music and its History
mailto:FUNKY-MUSIC-REQUEST@MIT.EDU

GRUNGE-L
Discussion of Grunge Rock
mailto:LISTSERV@UBVM.CC.BUFFALO.EDU

HPSCHD-L
Discussion of All Early Stringed Keyboard Instruments Except Modern Piano
mailto:LISTSERV@ALBANY.EDU

JPOP
Japanese popular music issues
mailto:JPOP-REQUEST@FERKEL.UCSB.EDU

KIWIMUSIC
Discussion of New Zealand Pop Bands
mailto:KIWIMUSIC-REQUEST@ATHENA.MIT.EDU

SOCO-L
A discussion of Southern Rock Music and related topics
mailto:LISTSERV@UBVM.CC.BUFFALO.EDU

TRUMPET
Discussion of the Trumpet
mailto:LISTSERV@ACAD1.DANA.EDU

Music Organizations

CUNYMUS
Discussion Among Graduate Students of Music Programs at City University of New York
mailto:LISTSERV@CUNYVMS1.CC.CUNY.EDU

IAML-L
The International Association of Music Libraries discussion group
mailto:IAML-REQUEST@NRM.SE

Music Resources

ANALOGUE
Discussion of Vintage Analogue Electronic Music Equipment
mailto:ANALOGUE-REQUEST@MAGNUS.ACS.OHIO-STATE.EDU

CHANTER-LISTE
Major list of multilingual French Musique mailing lists
mailto:MAJORDOMO@WIMSEY.COM

CHANTEUSE-LISTE
Multilingual mailing list for female French singer fans
mailto:MAJORDOMO@WIMSEY.COM

INFOCD
Discussion of Compact Audio Discs and Related Hardware
mailto:MIKEY@PERCH.NOSC.MIL

KS32
Discussion for Users of Ensoniq Synthesizer Instruments
mailto:KS32-REQUEST@CYGNUS.COM

MUSICA
Commentary and review of international musical happenings
mailto:MAJORDOMO@PANTHEON.IT

MUSPRF-L
Music Information and Pedagogy
mailto:LISTSERV@CMSUVMB.CMSU.EDU

Musical Groups

ADOLPH-A-CARROT
Discussion of Australian rock group Severed Heads
mailto:ADOLPH-A-CARROT-REQUEST@ANDREW.CMU.EDU

ELO-LIST
Discussion of Rock Group Electric Light Orchestra
mailto:ELO-LIST-REQUEST@ANDREW.CMU.EDU

LOST-CHORDS
Discussion of Musical Group the Moody Blues
mailto:LOST-CHORDS-REQUEST@MIT.EDU

ROXETTE
Discussion of Swedish band Roxette
mailto:OWNER-ROXETTE@EIUNIX.TUWIEN.AC.AT

STRANGE FRUIT
Discussion of the English band Catherine Wheel
mailto:FRUIT-REQUEST@GDB.ORG

U2
Discussion of Irish rock band U2
mailto:GRACE@DELPHI.COM

Musicians

ALICEFAN
Discussion of Alice Cooper
mailto:LISTSERV@WKUVX1.BITNET

ATAVACHRON
Discussion of works of guitarist Allan Holdsworth
mailto:ATAVACHRON@MOREKYPR.MOREHEAD-ST.EDU

BOLTON
Discussion of performing artist Michael Bolton
mailto:bwoolf@pro-woolf.clark.net

BTL
Discussion of Musician Debbie Gibson
mailto:mkwong@scf.nmsu.edu

COSTELLO
Discussion of Musician Elvis Costello
mailto:COSTELLO-REQUEST@GNU.AI.MIT.EDU

ENO-L
Discussion of pop music composer Brian Eno
mailto:ENO-L-REQUEST@UDLAPVMS.PUE.UDLAP.MX

HEY-JOE
Discussion of Rock Musician Jimi Hendrix
mailto:HEY-JOE-REQUEST@MS.UKY.EDU

HWY61-L
Access to and Delivery of a Bob Dylan Newsgroup
mailto:LISTSERV@UBVM.CC.BUFFALO.EDU

JAMIE-L
A discussion of the musician Jamie Notarthomas
mailto:LISTSERV@CORNELL.EDU

JOHN DENVER INTERNET FAN CLUB
Discussion of Country Musician John Denver
mailto:EMILYPARRIS@DELPHI.COM

Arts & Music

Mailing Lists

MIKE OLDFIELD-MUSIC
Discussion of Mike Oldfield and his Music
mailto:HART@VTCC1.CC.VT.EDU

ONO-NET
Art, Music, and Writings of Yoko Ono
mailto:LISTSERV@VM1.SPCS.UMN.EDU

SINATRA
Frank Sinatra and Related Facts
mailto:LISTSERV@VM.TEMPLE.EDU

STORMCOCK
Discussion of folk-rock musician Roy Harper
mailto:STORMCOCK-REQUEST@CS.QMW.AC.UK

AON
Discussion of the rock group The Art of Noise
mailto:aon-request@POLYSLO.CALPOLY.EDU

BEASTIELIST
Discussion of rap group the Beastie Boys
mailto:MAJORDOMO@WORLD.STD.COM

BPM
Discussion of Novice and Professional DJ Issues and Resources
mailto:BPM-REQUEST@ANDREW.CMU.EDU

BUZZ-FACTORY
The Screaming Trees and All Pertinent Subjects
mailto:LISTSERV@NOSFERATU.CAS.USF.EDU

CHALKHILLS
Discussion of the rock band XTC
mailto:CHALKHILLS-REQUEST@PRESTO.IG.COM

CHANTEUR-LISTE
Mailing list for male French music fans
mailto:MAJORDOMO@WIMSEY.COM

CLOUD-ZERO
Discussion of punk rock musician Edward Ka-Spel
mailto:CLOUD-ZERO-REQUEST@CS.MCGILL.CA

CONGA
Discussion of pop band Gloria Estefan and Miami Sound Machine
mailto:CONGA-REQUEST@HUSTLE.RAHUL.NET

DEAD-FLAMES
Discussion of rock group the Grateful Dead
mailto:DEAD-FLAMES-REQUEST@VIRGINIA.EDU

DEAD-HEADS
Announcements and ticket information for the Grateful Dead
mailto:DEAD-HEADS-REQUEST@VIRGINIA.EDU

DEWY-FIELDS
Discussion of Norwegian pop band Bel Canto
mailto:DEWY-FIELDS-REQUEST@IFI.UIO.NO

DISCIPLINE
Discussion of pop band King Crimson
mailto:DISCIPLINE-REQUEST@CS.MAN.AC.UK

GRAHAM-PARKER
Discussion of pop musician Graham Parker
mailto:MAJORDOMO@PRIMENET.COM

INDIGO-GIRLS
Discussion of folk music group Indigo Girls
mailto:INDIGO-GIRLS-REQUEST@CGRG.OHIO-STATE.EDU

JOURNEY-L
Discussion of pop band Journey
mailto:JOURNEY-L-REQUEST@WKUVX1.WKU.EDU

JULIEMASSE-LISTE
Mailing list for French musician Julie Masse
mailto:MAJORDOMO@WIMSEY.COM

JUMP-IN-THE-RIVER
Discussion of musician Sinead O' Connor
mailto:JITR-REQUEST@PRESTO.IG.COM

K-D-LANG
Discussion of country musician k.d. lang
mailto:MAJORDOMO@WORLD.STD.COM

KISSARMY
Discussion of rock group KISS
mailto:MXSERVER@WKUVX1.WKU.EDU

KOSMOS
Discussion of pop musician Paul Weller
mailto:KOSMOS-REQUEST@MIT.EDU

LIFE-TALKING
Discussion of pop group Life Talking
mailto:LIFE-TALKING-REQUEST@FERKEL.UCSB.EDU

LOVE-HOUNDS
Discussion of pop musician Kate Bush
mailto:LOVE-HOUNDS-REQUEST@EDDIE.MIT.EDU

LUCKYTOWN
Discussion of rock musician Bruce Springsteen
mailto:LUCKYTOWN-REQUEST@NETCOM.COM

MONKEES
Discussion of TV show and musical group The Monkees
mailto:MAJORDOMO@PRIMENET.COM

POI-POUNDERS
Discussion of rock band Poi Dog Pondering
mailto:POI-POUNDERS-REQUEST@PRESTO.IG.COM

POLICE
Discussion of rock group The Police
mailto:MAJORDOMO@XMISSON.COM

POWDERWORKS
Discussion of Australian rock group Midnight Oil
mailto:MAJORDOMO@CS.COLORADO.EDU

TADREAM
Discussion of pop band Tangerine Dream
mailto:TADREAM-REQUEST@CS.UWP.EDU

UNDERCOVER
Discussion of the rock group the Rolling Stones
mailto:undercover-request@tempest.cis.uoguelph.ca

ZEPPELIN-L
Led Zeppelin
mailto:LISTSERV@CORNELL.EDU

Performing Arts

BALLET-MODERN-DANCE
Ballet
mailto:LISTSERV@NETCOM.COM

BALLROOM
Announcments, information, and techniques on ballroom and swing dancing
mailto:ballroom-request@athena.mit.edu

COLLAB-L
Professional discussion of new performance scriptwriting
mailto:SAS14@PSU.EDU

DANCE-L
A discussion for those who are interested in folk dance and traditional dance
mailto:LISTSERV@NIC.SURFNET.NL

FUZZY-RAMBLINGS
Discussion of the rock group Fuzzbox
mailto:FUZZY-RAMBLINGS-REQUEST@FERKEL.UCSB.EDU

NERDNOSH
An open discussion forum for storytellers
mailto:listserv@clovis.nerdnosh.org

SAVOYNET
A discussion of Gilbert and/or Sullivan related issues
mailto:LISTSERV@BRIDGEWATER.EDU

STAGECRAFT
Stage work techniques, production and discussion
mailto:STAGECRAFT-REQUEST@JAGUAR.UTAH.EDU

TANGO-L
A discussion of the Argentine Tango and related topics
mailto:listserv@mitvma.mit.edu

TAP-JAZZ
Discussion of Tap and Jazz-style dances, history, and technique
mailto:MAJORODMO@WORLD.STD.COM

THEATRE
A discussion forum in which to share experiences and ideas about theater
mailto:LISTSERV@PUCC.PRINCETON.EDU

UK-SF
Discussion of UK science fiction and fantasy shows
mailto:LISTPROC@UEL.AC.UK

Visual Arts

3D
3-D photography announcements and general information
mailto:3D-REQUEST@LBL.GOV

ALT-PHOTO-PROCESS
Discussion of Alternative Photo Processes
mailto:LISTPROC@VAST.UNSW.EDU.AU

ARTCRIT
Visual Art Critical Discourse
mailto:LISTSERV@VM1.YORKU.CA

INGRAFX
Cartography, Information Graphics, and Scientific Visualization
mailto:LISTSERV@UBVM.CC.BUFFALO.EDU

LEICA CAMERAS
Discussion of Leica Photographic Equipment and Practice
mailto:reid@mejac.palo-alto.ca.us

PHOTO-L
Discussion of photographic equipment and technique
mailto:LISTPROC@CSUOHIO.EDU

PHOTOFORUM
An open discussion forum and databank for photo educators and the photo community at large
mailto:LISTSERV@LISTSERVER.ISC.RIT.EDU

PHOTOHST
A discussion of the history of photography and related areas of interest
mailto:LISTSERV@ASUVM.INRE.ASU.EDU

STOCKPHOTO
Professional discussion of stock photography trends and practices
mailto:LISTPROC@INFO.CURTIN.EDU.AU

Business & Economics

Advertising & Marketing

BIZ-MARKETING-CONSULTING
Professional Discussion of Marketing in a Consulting Role
mailto:MAJORDOMO@WORLD.STD.COM

HTMARCOM
Discussion of Marketing Communications in Relation to Computer/Electronics
mailto:LISTSERV@CSCNS.COM

MARKET-L
A general discussion forum for marketing professionals, students, and educators
mailto:LISTSERV@NERVM.NERDC.UFL.EDU

MARTECH
A discussion of marketing with technology
mailto:LISTSERV@CSCNS.COM

Banking

CU-TALK
Discussion of Credit Union Issues
mailto:LISTSERV@USA.NET

Business Schools

MBA-L
A discussion and forum for MBA programs and their administrations
mailto:LISTSERV@VM.MARIST.EDU

Career & Employment

AV-JOBS
Aviation Industry Employment Openings
mailto:LISTSERV@ROTOR.COM

CITE-JOBS-MG
Technology, Information and Communication Job Announcements
mailto:ALMANAC@ESUSDA.GOV

EAP
Discussion of Employee Assistance Counseling Issues
mailto:LISTPROC@PGE.COM

SCWK-L
Social Work Professionals and Related Topics
mailto:LISTSERV@ISTO1.FERRIS.EDU

Commerce

APPLE-CROP-MG
Discussion of Apple Production and Marketing Issues
mailto:ALMANAC@ESUSDA.GOV

BEEF-L
Discussion of Beef Research and Commercial Activities
mailto:LISTPROC@LISTPROC.WSU.EDU

BIZ-WIRE
Business and Creation of New Businesses
mailto:LISTSERV@AIS.NET

BMW
Discussion of BMW Automobiles
mailto:BMW-REQUEST@BALLTOWN.CMA.COM

BMW
Discussion of BMW Motorcycles
mailto:BMW-REQUEST@RIDER.CACTUS.ORG

GOVSALES
Government Assets Sale News, Notices and Announcements
mailto:LISTPROC@FINANCENET.GOV

SMALLFRUIT-MG
Professional Discussion of Small Fruit Production
mailto:ALMANAC@ESUSDA.GOV

WHATSNEW
Announcements of Chinese-Music Compact Discs
mailto:NEWWAVE@RAHUL.NET

Consumer Issues

CONSSCI
Discussion Among Consumer Advocates
mailto:LISTSERV@UKCC.UKY.EDU

COROLLA
Discussion of Toyota Corollas, Chevy Novas and Geo Prizms
mailto:COROLLA-REQUEST@MCS.COM

FOODLINK
Food Safety
mailto:LISTSERV@WSUVM1.CSC.WSU.EDU

OXYFRESH
Discussion of The OxyFresh Line of Health Care Products
mailto:LISTSERV@ISTO1.FERRIS.EDU

Economics

BUDGET-NET
Discussion of United States Governmental Economic Policy Issues
mailto:LISTPROC@FINANCENET.GOV

CET-MG
Discussion of Community Economics Issues
mailto:ALMANAC@ESUSDA.GOV

CET-NEWS
Discussion of Community Economic Assistance Issues
mailto:ALMANAC@ESUSDA.GOV

ECON-DEV
Professional Discussion of Economic Development Issues
mailto:MAJORDOMO@CSN.ORG

E-EUROPE
Links Business Students and Professionals to Eastern European Countries Making the Transition to Market Economies
mailto:LISTSERV@PUCC.PRINCETON.EDU

ECOL-ECON
Discussion of Ecological Economics Issues
mailto:TOOR@CSF.COLORADO.EDU

POL-ECON
Serious Discussion of Political Economic Theory
mailto:MXSERVER@SHSU.EDU

Industries

AMFM
United Kingdom Radio Industry
mailto:LISTSERV@TQMCOMMS.CO.UK

AMFM
United Kingdom Radio Industry (duplicate)
mailto:listserv@orbital.demon.co.uk

JANITOR
A discussion janitorial services
mailto:LISTSERV@UKANVM.CC.UKANS.EDU

NEWPROD
Professional Discussion of New Product Development Process
mailto:MAJORDOMO@WORLD.STD.COM

NPPA-L
Discussion Among Professional Visual Communicators
mailto:LISTSERV@CMUVM.CSV.CMICH.EDU

NRCH
Discussion Among Health Care Information Systems Executives and Clinicians
mailto:LISTSERV@USA.NET

RADIO-RIDER
Computers and Radio Show Preparation
mailto:LISTSERV@RADIO-ONLINE.COM

RADIO-RIDER
Computers and Radio Show Preparation (duplicate?)
mailto:LISTSERV@RADIO-ONLINE.COM

VIDEO-WIRE
Video Software Industry
mailto:LISTSERV@AIS.NET

International Business

AJBS-L
Association of Japanese Business Studies
mailto:LISTSERV@PUCC.PRINCETON.EDU

CARIBBEAN-ECONOMY
Discussion of Caribbean Basin Economies
mailto:CARIBBEAN-ECONOMY-REQUEST@VELA.ACS.OAKLAND.EDU

ECA-L
Post-Communist Transformation in Eastern Europe
mailto:LISTSERV@GSUVM1.GSU.EDU

ECONOMY
Economy of Less Developed Countries
mailto:LISTSERV@TECMTYVM.MTY.ITESM.MX

IPE-ISA-L
International Political Economy
mailto:LISTSERV@MACH1.WLU.CA

Investment

WALLSTREET-DIRECT-LIST
Discussion of Trading and Investment Services and Products
mailto:WALLSTREET-DIRECT-LIST-REQUEST@CTS.COM

Labor

FLEXWORK
Flexible Work Situations
mailto:LISTSERV@PSUHMC.HMC.PSU.EDU

GUILDNET-L
Discussion of Working Conditions in the Journalism Industry
mailto:MAJORDOMO@ACS.RYERSON.CA

Management

APOGEES
A discussion of critical and strategic information management
mailto:LISTSERV@FRMOP11.CNUSC.FR

CHANGE
Professional Discussion of Initiating Change in Organizations
mailto:MAJORDOMO@MINDSPRING.COM

QUALITY
A discussion of Total Quality Management in manufacturing and service industries
mailto:LISTSERV@PUCC.PRINCETON.EDU

Publishing

CARR-L
The Use of Computers in Journalism
mailto:LISTSERV@ULKYVM.LOUISVILLE.EDU

Real Estate

COMMERCIAL.REALESTATE
Information and Classifieds for Commercial Real Estate Professionals
mailto:COMMERCIAL.REALESTATE@DATABASE.COM

Services

ESBDC-L
Discussion of Small Business Development Centers and Economic Climate for Small Businesses
mailto:LISTSERV@ISTO1.FERRIS.EDU

Communications

Mass Communications

NIIBYCTV
A discussion concerning access to the National Information Infrastructure via Cable Television
mailto:LISTSERV@MIAMIU.MUOHIO.EDU

XPRESS-LIST
A discussion of the X*Press X*Change data service available on some cable television systems
mailto:LISTSERV@GROT.STARCONN.COM

Organizations

CKI-L
Issues of Running a Circle-K International Chapter
mailto:LISTSERV@TAMVM1.TAMU.EDU

Society

BALT-L
Communications to and about Baltic Republics
mailto:LISTSERV@UBVM.CC.BUFFALO.EDU

CERES-L
Building Knowledge Networks to Disseminate Environmental Information
mailto:LISTSERV@WVNVM.WVNET.EDU

Telecommunications

AFRICANA
Information Technology Progress in Africa
mailto:LISTSERV@wmvm1.cc.wm.edu

BIN-L
Community Telecommunication in Central Kentucky
mailto:LISTSERV@UKCC.UKY.EDU

HUMAN-NETS
Global computer and telecommunications issues
mailto:HUMAN-NETS-REQUEST@ARAMIS.RUTGERS.EDU

TELECOM
Technical aspects of telecommunications systems and archives
mailto:TELECOM-REQUEST@EECS.NWU.EDU

Computing & Mathematics

Analysis

CONTENT
Discussion of quantitative analysis of texts and images
mailto:CONTENT-REQUEST@LIST.GATECH.EDU

EVALTEN
Discussion of data analysis in mental health systems
mailto:MAJORDOMO@WORLD.STD.COM

Applications

AI-CHI
AI applications to Human-Computer Interface design issues
mailto:wiley!ai-chi-request@LLL-LCC.LLNL.GOV

ANMI-L
Distribution of VT/ANSI animation files
mailto:ANMI-L@RMCS.CRANFIELD.AC.UK

APE-INFO
Discussion of visualization software package apE
mailto:apE-info-request@ferkel.ucsb.edu

ASCIIART
Line Printer Artwork
mailto:LISTSERV@UKCC.UKY.EDU

BILLINGHEARN
Billing and Chargeback of Computer Resources
mailto:LISTSERV@LISTSERV.NET

BLISSTERS
BLISS programming language discussion
mailto:BLISSTERS-REQUEST@WKUVX1.WKU.EDU

CASE-L
Computer Aided Software Engineering
mailto:LISTSERV@UCCVMA.UCOP.EDU

CCNET-L
A discussion of the use of Chinese on computers and related hardware, software, and technology
mailto:LISTSERV@UGA.UGA.EDU

CLAY=XLDEV
Microsoft Excel strategies and discussion
mailto:CLAY=XLDEV-ADD@CS.CMU.EDU

COMPUMED
High-performance Computing in the Medical Profession
mailto:LISTSERV@SJUVM.STJOHNS.EDU

CPRI-L
Discussion of Totally Computerized Patient Records
mailto:LISTSERV@UKANAIX.CC.UKANS.EDU

CUSSNET
Discussion of Use of Computers in Human Services
mailto:LISTSERV@STAT.COM

DIGVID-L
Discussion of Digitally Stored Video
mailto:LISTSERV@UCDAVIS.EDU

E-HUG
Hebrew and Computers
mailto:LISTSERV@DARTCMS1.DARTMOUTH.EDU

EDI-L
Electronic Data Interchange Issues
mailto:LISTSERV@UCCVMA.UCOP.EDU

EPUBS-MG
Discussion of ES/CES Electronic Publishing Issues
mailto:ALMANAC@ESUSDA.GOV

FLIGHT-SIM
Flight simulation issues
mailto:FLIGHT-SIM@-REQUESTGROVE.IUP.EDU

FRAC-L
Computer Graphical Generation of Fractal Images
mailto:LISTSERV@GITVM1.GATECH.EDU

GUG-SYSADMIN
CAD-Tool genesil bugfixes and rumors
mailto:GUG-SYSADMINS-REQUEST@VLSIVIE.TUWIEN.AC.AT

HL7
Professional discussion of the HL7 interface protocol
mailto:MAJORDOMO@VIRGINIA.EDU

HQ-L
Discussion of HealthQuest Products
mailto:LISTSERV@PSUHMC.HMC.PSU.EDU

HUMANIST
Discussion of the Application of Computers to Humanities Scholarship
mailto:LISTSERV@BROWNVM.BROWN.EDU

HYPERAMI
Discussion of Hypermedia Projects on the Amiga
mailto:LISTSERV@ARCHIVE.OIT.UNC.EDU

ILUG
Professional discussion of the ImageVision Library
mailto:ILUG-REQUEST@SGI.COM

IMAGE-L
Image Processing and Related Issues
mailto:LISTSERV@VM3090.EGE.EDU.TR

LITHO-L
Discussion of Desktop Publishing, Printing, Photocopying, and Binding
mailto:LISTSERV@UNB.CA

MACCHAT
Information for Production-Oriented Graphics Professionals Using Macintosh
mailto:LISTSERV@VM.TEMPLE.EDU

Computing & Mathematics

MACMULTI
Discussion of Multimedia on Macintosh
mailto:LISTSERV%FCCJ.BITNET@LISTSERV.NET

MAE-ANNOUNCE
Announcements and Information on the Macintosh Application Environment
mailto:LISTPROC@MEDRAUT.APPLE.COM

MAE-BUGS
Macintosh Application Environment Bug Submission and Information
mailto:LISTPROC@MEDRAUT.APPLE.COM

MAE-USERS
Informal Discussion of the Macintosh Application Environment
mailto:LISTPROC@MEDRAUT.APPLE.COM

PHOTOSHOP
Adobe Photoshop problems and suggestions
mailto:PHOTOSHOP@HIPP.ETSU.EDU

THEORIST
A discussion and information exchange for users of Theorist, a symbolic mathematics and graphics program
mailto:LISTSERV@UTKVM1.UTK.EDU

WINNEWS
Microsoft Windows information and issues
mailto:ENEWS@MICROSOFT.NWNET.COM

WINSOCK-L
Professional and general discussion of Windows Sockets
mailto:LIST-ADMIN@PAPA.INDSTATE.EDU

WINSOCK-L
Windows Sockets information
mailto:LISTPROC@LISTPROC.NET

WORD-PC
User discussion of Microsoft Word for DOS and Windows
mailto:MAILSERV@UFOBI1.UNI-FORST.GWDG.DE

XWIN-L
A discussion of X-Windows protocol including programming
mailto:LISTSERV@VM3090.EGE.EDU.TR

Artificial Intelligence

AI-ED
Use of artificial intelligence in education issues
mailto:AI-Ed-Request@SUN.COM

AI-MEDICINE
Using artifical intelligence in medical education
mailto:ai-medicine-request@med.stanford.edu

AIL-L
Artificial Intelligence and Law
mailto:listserv@austin.onu.edu

DISTRIBUTED-AI
Distributed Artificial Intelligence issues and research
mailto:MAILBASE@MAILBASE.AC.UK

NL-KR
Language understanding in artificial intelligence
mailto:NL-KR-REQUEST@CS.RPI.EDU

PARAMIND
Computer-generated writing issues
mailto:PARAMIND@ESKIMO.COM

Career & Employment

ADVISE-L
A discussion for students who work in university computer centers as advisors or consultants
mailto:LISTSERV@NAC.NETNORTH.CA

CIS-L
Discussion of Careers in Information Systems
mailto:LISTSERV@UBE.UBALT.EDU

CJI
Monthly Updated Document Regarding Computer Jobs in Israel
mailto:LISTSERV@JERUSALEM1.DATASRV.CO.IL

Computer Science

CSEMLIST
A discussion of Computer Science in Economics and Management
mailto:LISTSERV%HASARA11.BITNET@VM1.NODAK.EDU

CYBSYS-L
Systems Science, Cybernetics, and Related Fields
mailto:LISTSERV@BINGVMB.CC.BINGHAMTON.EDU

IR-LIST
A discussion of varied topics related to Information Retrieval
mailto:LISTSERV@LISTSERV.NET

MICRO-L
A general discussion of microcomputers
mailto:LISTSERV@VM.ITS.RPI.EDU

Hardware

9370-L
A discussion of the IBM 9370 family and the VM/IS packaging system
mailto:LISTSERV@NIC.SURFNET.NL

AMIGA
AMIGA Computers
mailto:listserver@varano.ing.como.polimi.it

APOLLO
User discussion of Apollo computers
mailto:APOLLO-REQUEST@IIMIX.CC.UMICH.EDU

APOLLO-L
Discussion Among Apollo Computer Users
mailto:LISTSERV@UMRVMB.UMR.EDU

ASMICRO-L
All aspects of use of Application Specific Microprocessors
mailto:ASMICRO-REQUEST@VME131.LSI.USP.ANSP.BR

BIGM-L
Bigmouth and PowerLine Voice Mail PC Cards
mailto:LISTSERV@VM.SAS.COM

CD-ROM
Information for Buyers and Sellers of New and Used CD-ROM Disks and Drives
mailto:LISTSERV@DAYTONSHAREWARE.COM

CDROM-L
Design, Production, and Use of CD-ROM
mailto:LISTSERV@UCCVMA.UCOP.EDU

CDROMLAN
Information on CD-ROM Products, LAN Environments, Hardware
mailto:LISTSERV@IDBSU.IDBSU.EDU

CELLULAR-AUTOMATA
Cellular automata and application information
mailto:CELLULAR-AUTOMATA-REQUEST@THINK.COM

CHINESE-CDROM
Chinese CD-ROM Product Announcements
mailto:NEWWAVE@RAHUL.NET

FASTBS-L
A discussion of news and information relating to FASTBUS
mailto:LISTSERV@VM.UCS.UALBERTA.CA

GRID
GRID Compass computer collector issues
mailto:JANS@TEKCRL.TEK.COM

GSDSP
Discussion of the GS/DSP co-processor board for Apple II computers
mailto:GSDSP-REQUEST@OCF.BERKELEY.EDU

HEATH-PEOPLE
Heath or Zenith terminal and computer discussion
mailto:HEATH-PEOPLE-REQUEST@MC.LCS.MIT.EDU

HP-28
A discussion of HP-28C/HP-28S calculators
mailto:LISTSERV@VM1.NODAK.EDU

IMAGEN-L
Discussion of Imagen Laser Printers
mailto:LISTSERV@BOLIS.SF-BAY.ORG

INFO-APPLE
Discussion of Apple II series computers
mailto:INFO-APPLE-REQUEST@BRL.MIL

INFO-ATARI16
Discussion of 16-bit Atari computers
mailto:INFO-ATARI16-REQUEST@NAUCSE.CSE.NAU.EDU

INFO-ATARI16
Discussion of Atari Computers
mailto:LISTSERV@VM.MARIST.EDU

INFO-MAC
Apple Macintosh computer issues
mailto:INFO-MAC-REQUEST@SUMEX.STANFORD.EDU

INFO-PDP11
Digital's PDP-11 series minicomputer issues
mailto:INFO-PDP11-REQUEST@TRANSARC.COM

INFO-PYRAMID-REQUEST
Discussion of Pyramid computers
mailto:INFO-PYRAMID-REQUEST@MIMSY.UMD.EDU

INFO-TAHOE
Discussions of Tahoe CPU computers
mailto:INFO-TAHOE-REQUEST@UWM.EDU

INFO-VAX
Digital Equipment Corporation VAX computer questions and answers
mailto:INFO-VAX-REQUEST@MVB.SAIC.COM

IPSC-MANAGERS
Discussion of the Intel iPSC line of parallel computers
mailto:LISTPROC@NAS.NASA.GOV

IPSC-USERS
Serious discussion of the Intel iPSC line of parallel computers
mailto:LISTPROC@NAS.NASA.GOV

Computing & Mathematics

MACPB-L
Discussion of the Macintosh Powerbook
mailto:LISTSERV@YALEVM.CIS.YALE.EDU

MACPB-L
A discussion of Macintosh Powerbook issues
mailto:LISTSERV@YALEVM.YCC.YALE.EDU

MACPPC-L
Discussion of Macintosh Power PC
mailto:LISTSERV@YALEVM.CIS.YALE.EDU

MODEMS-L
A discussion forum for modem users
mailto:LISTSERV@VM.ITS.RPI.EDU

NEWTON-L
A discussion of the Newton Personal Digital Assistant from Apple
mailto:LISTSERV@DARTCMS1.DARTMOUTH.EDU

PAS-LOVERS
Discussion of Pro Audio Spectrum PC sound cards
mailto:MAJORDOMO@QICLAB.SCN.RAIN.COM

PCBUILD
A discussion concerning building IBM PC clone computers
mailto:LISTSERV@TSCVM.TRENTON.EDU

PDP8-LOVERS
Discussion of the 'antique' DEC computers
mailto:PDP8-LOVERS-REQUEST@AI.MIT.EDU

PORTMASTER-USERS
Discussion of Livingston Portmaster line of terminal servers and routers
mailto:MAJORDOMO@MAIL.MSEN.COM

POVGUI-L
Graphical Interface to DKB/POV Ray Tracer
mailto:LISTSERV@VM3090.EGE.EDU.TR

POWER-PC
A discussion of the IBM POWER-PC computers
mailto:LISTSERV@UGA.CC.UGA.EDU

SLUG
Information on the Symbolics Lisp machines
mailto:SLUG-REQUEST@AI.SRI.COM

ULTRALITE-LIST
A general discussion of the NEC Ultralite notebook, models PC-17-01/02
mailto:LISTSERV@GROT.STARCONN.COM

WORKS
Discussion of personal work station computers
mailto:WORKS-REQUEST@RUTGERS.EDU

Mathematics

CRYPTO-L
Discussion of Cryptology and Related Mathematics
mailto:LISTSERV%JPNIUVM0.BITNET@PUCC.PRINCETON.EDU

CUBE-LOVERS
Discussion of mathematical solutions to the Rubik's Cube
mailto:CUBE-LOVERS-REQUEST@AI.AI.MIT.EDU

ILAS-NET
Activities in Linear Algebra
mailto:LISTSERV@TECHNION.TECHNION.AC.IL

QMLIST
Information Exchange Regarding Quantitative Morphology
mailto:LISTSERVER@TBONE.BIOL.SCAROLINA.EDU

Networking

BANYAN-L
Discussion of Banyan Networks
mailto:LISTSERV@LISTSERV.NET

HEADER-PEOPLE
Message header format discussion and issues
mailto:HEADER-PEOPLE-REQUEST@MC.LCS.MIT.EDU

INFO-APPLETALK
Discussion of Applebus networking scheme
mailto:INFO-APPLETALK-REQUEST@ANDREW.CMU.EDU

INFO-CLUSTERS
Clustered Computing issues and discussion
mailto:INFO-CLUSTERS-REQUEST@LARC.NASA.GOV

LANMAN-L
A discussion of Microsoft LAN Manager and variants
mailto:LISTSERV@LIST.NIH.GOV

LANSRV-L
IBM LAN Server Network Operating System problems and maintenance
mailto:LISTPROC@BGU.EDU

NOVELL
A discussion forum for users of the Novell Netware Network Operating System in Higher Education
mailto:LISTSERV@SUVM.ACS.SYR.EDU

QM-L
A discussion of CE Software's QuickMail initiated by Yale University to share common experiences and problems
mailto:LISTSERV@YALEVM.YCC.YALE.EDU

SUN-NETS
Sun networking configuration, problems and services issues
mailto:SUN-NETS-REQUEST@UMIACS.UMD.EDU

TECHWR-L
A discussion of technical communication and related issues
mailto:LISTSERV@VM1.UCC.OKSTATE.EDU

Operating Systems

AIX-L
A discussion of the AIX operating system which disseminates information and technical details
mailto:LISTSERV@BUACCA.BU.EDU

AIXNEWS
UNIX, RS6000 Platform
mailto:LISTSERV@PUCC.PRINCETON.EDU

DATA-PROTECTION
Professional discussion of data security
mailto:MAILBASE@MAILBASE.AC.UK

GOULDBUGS
Bug reports for GOULD UTX/32 (UNIX) operating system and software
mailto:GOULDBUGS-REQUEST@BRL.MIL

HPMINI-L
Hewlett Packard 9000 Series
mailto:LISTSERV@UAFSYSB.UARK.EDU

HPUX-ADMIN
HP-UX system administration issues
mailto:MAJORDOMO@CV.RUU.NL

IBM-NETS
Discussion of IBM Mainframes and Networking
mailto:LISTSERV@BITNIC.EDUCOM.EDU

INFO-1100
Discussion of the Xerox/Envos Lisp environment and its protocols
mailto:INFO-1100-REQUEST@ANZUS.COM

INFO-ANDREW-BUGS
Andrew distribution bug reports
mailto:INFO-ANDREW-BUGS-REQUEST@ANDREW.CMU.EDU

INFO-IRIS
Discussion of Silicon Graphics workstations and software
mailto:INFO-IRIS-REQUEST@ARL.MIL

MAC-SECURITY
Discussion of Macintosh System 7.0 security
mailto:MAJORDOMO@NDA.COM

MACTURK
A discussion of academic computing on the Macintosh in Turkey
mailto:LISTSERV@VM3090.EGE.EDU.TR

MINIX-L
A discussion of the Minix Operating System
mailto:LISTSERV@VM1.NODAK.EDU

NEXTSTEP
Discussion of NeXTstep Operating Environment
mailto:LISTSERV@VMA.CC.ND.EDU

PCTECH-L
An unmoderated discussion of MS-DOS personal computers
mailto:LISTSERV@VM3090.EGE.EDU.TR

POWER-L
A discussion of the IBM RISC System/6000 family
mailto:LISTSERV@VM1.NODAK.EDU

TOPS20
TOPS20 product information and discussion
mailto:TOPS20-REQUEST@PANDA.COM

UNIX-WIZARDS
Information for UNIX operating system users
mailto:UNIX-WIZARDS-REQUEST@BRL.MIL

UTS-L
A discussion of Amdahl's UTS/580 implementation of Unix and of software running in the UTS environment
mailto:LISTSERV@VM.GMD.DE

VIRUS-L
A discussion of virus related topics and experiences
mailto:LISTSERV@CC.ITU.EDU.TR

VM-UTIL
A list for the redistribution of and discussion of the utilities used by the VM/SP and CMS operating systems
mailto:LISTSERV@VM.GMD.DE

VMVIRUS
A discussion of VM viruses and worms
mailto:LISTSERV%PCCVM.BITNET@CMSA.BERKELEY.EDU

Organizations

CISA-L
Information about and Access to Ferris State University Computer Information Systems Association
mailto:LISTSERV@IST01.FERRIS.EDU

CPSR
Announcements and Information from Computer Professionals for Social Responsibility
mailto:LISTSERV@GWUVM.GWU.EDU

Programming

AMIGA-M2
Programming language Modula-2 information
mailto:amiga-m2-request@VIRGINIA.EDU

APL-L
Implementation and Application of APL Language
mailto:LISTSERV@UNB.CA

APPC-L
IBM's Advanced Program-to-Program Communication
mailto:LISTSERV@AMERICAN.EDU

AREXX-L
REXX Programming Language
mailto:LISTSERV@UCF1VM.CC.UCF.EDU

ASM370
Programming in IBM System/370 Assembly Language
mailto:LISTSERV@UCF1VM.CC.UCF.EDU

ASSMPC-L
An interactive discussion of the PC Assembly languages
mailto:LISTSERV%USACHVM1.BITNET@
    VM1.NODAK.EDU

C370-L
The C Programming Language on 370-Architecture Machines
mailto:LISTSERV@CMUVM.CSV.CMICH.EDU

CENVI-CMM
Professional discussion of the Cmm programming language
mailto:MAJORDOMO@WORLD.STD.COM

CLP.X
Announcements, techniques, and discussion of programming languages
mailto:CLP-REQUEST.X@XEROX.COM

FRANZ-FRIENDS
Franz LISP Language discussion and topics
mailto:FRANZ-FRIENDS-REQUEST@BERKELEY.EDU

ICON-GROUP
Icon programming language techniques and issues
mailto:ICON-GROUP-REQUEST@ARIZONA.EDU

INFO-ADA
Announcments and discussion of the Ada programming language
mailto:INFO-ADA-REQUEST@AJPO.SEI.CMU.EDU

INFO-C
Discussions of the C programming language
mailto:INFO-C-REQUEST@RESEARCH.ATT.COM

INFO-M2
Modula-2 Programming Language
mailto:LISTSERV@BITNIC.EDUCOM.EDU

INFO-PROGRAPH
Information on icon-based object-oriented programming language Prograph
mailto:INFO-PROGRAPH-REQUEST@
    GROVE.IUP.EDU

MACRO32
Discussion of the MACRO-32 programming language
mailto:MXSERVER@WKUVX1.WKU.EDU

MACRO32-DIGEST
Digest version of MACRO32 discussion
mailto:MXSERVER@WKUVX1.WKU.EDU

PERL-USERS
Digest discussion of programming language PERL
mailto:PERL-USERS-REQUEST@VIRGINIA.EDU

RC
Discussion of the Tom Duff-designed RC shell
mailto:RC-REQUEST@
    HAWKWIND.UTCS.TORONTO.EDU

VMSNET-INTERNALS
Discussion of VAX/VMS systems programming
mailto:MXSERVER@WKUVX1.WKU.EDU

VMSNET-INTERNALS-DIGEST
Digest version discussion of VAX/VMS systems programming
mailto:MXSERVER@WKUVX1.WKU.EDU

Software

ACCESS-L
ACCESS Database
mailto:LISTSERV@INDYCMS.IUPUI.EDU

AMSSIS-L
The American Management System Student Information System
mailto:LISTSERV@uafsysb.uark.edu

ANDREW-DEMOS
Demonstrations of Andrew system software
mailto:ANDREW-DEMOS-REQUEST@
    ANDREW.CMU.EDU

ANU-NEWS
ANU-NEWS Software VAX/VMS Systems
mailto:LISTSERV@VM1.NoDak.EDU

AUTOCAD
Autocad
mailto:LISTSERV@JHUVM.HCF.JHU.EDU

AWARE
Authorware Professional Users
mailto:LISTSERV@CC1.KULEUVEN.AC.BE

BCS_CAD-SIG
Discussion of CAD software operation and issues
mailto:MAJORDOMO@WORLD.STD.COM

BMDP-L
A user-oriented discussion of BMDP software
mailto:LISTSERV@VM1.MCGILL.CA

BRS-L
A discussion of the full-text retrieval software program BRS/Search
mailto:LISTSERV@VM.USC.EDU

CD-ROM ONLINE
CD-ROM Online Magazine
mailto:CDRMAG@NSIMULTIMEDIA.COM

CD-ROM ONLINE
CD-ROM Online Magazine Information and Resources
mailto:CDRMAG@NSIMULTIMEDIA.COM

CUPLE-L
Comprehensive Unified Physics Learning Environment Software and Related Topics
mailto:LISTSERV@UBVM.CC.BUFFALO.EDU

DATAPERF
Users of DataPerfect Database Software
mailto:LISTSERV@WSUVM1.CSC.WSU.EDU

DDTS-USERS
Discussion of DDT defect tracking software
mailto:MAJORDOMO@BIGBIRD.BU.EDU

DECRDB-L
Discussion of Digital Corp.'s Relational Database Products
mailto:LISTSERV@CCVM.SUNYSB.EDU

DFHSM-L
IBM's Hierarchical Storage Manager Software
mailto:LISTSERV@EMUVM1.CC.EMORY.EDU

DIRECT-L
MacroMind Director Software for the Macintosh
mailto:LISTSERV@UAFSYSB.UARK.EDU

DKB-L
Discussion of DKB/POV Raytracer Graphics Software
mailto:LISTSERV@VM3090.EGE.EDU.TR

ECTL
Computer speech interface discussion and research
mailto:ECTL-REQUEST@
    SNOWHITE.CIS.UOGUELPH.CA

EGRET-L
Discussion of EGRET Software Package
mailto:LISTSERV@DARTCMS1.DARTMOUTH.EDU

EXPLORE
CREN's ListProcessor List-Management Issues
mailto:LISTPROC@LISTPROC.NET

FDDI
Fiber Distributed Data Interface technology issues
mailto:FDDI-SUBSCRIBE@LIST.KEAN.EDU

FOLIO-L
Folio Views Hypertext Management Products
mailto:LISTSERV@SIVM.SI.EDU

FRAMERS
Discussion of FrameMaker desktop publishing package
mailto:MAJORDOMO@MATH.MCGILL.CA

GLELIST
Discussion Among GLE Graphics Package Users
mailto:LISTSERVER@TBONE.BIOL.SCAROLINA.EDU

HYPERCRD
Hypercard for Apple Macintosh
mailto:LISTSERV@MSU.EDU

HYTEL-L
Announcements Regarding HYTELNET
mailto:LISTSERV@KENTVM.KENT.EDU

I-BBOARD
BBoard package discussion and issues
mailto:I-BBREQ@SPCVXA.SPC.EDU

I-FINGER
Finger program and related utilities discussion and issues
mailto:I-FINREQ@SPCVXA.SPC.EDU

IBMPC-KIDS
IBM PC and compatible computer children's software discussion
mailto:IBMPC-KIDS-REQUEST@
    MINERVA.SWS.UIUC.EDU

IBMTCP-L
IBM TCP/IP For VM Program
mailto:LISTSERV@PUCC.PRINCETON.EDU

IDMS-L
Cullinet Software
mailto:LISTSERV@UGA.CC.UGA.EDU

INFINI-D
Information Exchange Regarding Infini-D Software
mailto:LISTSERV@UAFSYSB.UARK.EDU

INFO-GNU-MSDOS
GNU Software
mailto:LISTSERV@SUN.SOE.CLARKSON.EDU

INFO-ZIP
Announcements for the Portable Zip and UnZip software packages
mailto:MXSERVER@WKUVX1.WKU.EDU

INFORMIX-LIST
Informix software questions and anwers
mailto:INFORMIX-LIST-REQUEST@
    RMY.EMORY.EDU

INTERFACES-P-M
User-interface research, design and implementation issues
mailto:INTERFACES-P-M-REQUEST@CRIM.CA

ITALIC-L
Irish Tex and Latex, GML and SGML
mailto:LISTSERV@IRLEARN.UCD.IE

JPSOFT
A discussion of the 4DOS command interpreter and other software by JP software
mailto:LISTSERV@VMA.CC.ND.EDU

LIMDEP-L
Discussion of Limdep Software
mailto:LISTSERV@GSB.USYD.EDU.AU

LITHOBID
User Support List for Printers and Suppliers Using LithoBid
mailto:LISTSERV@UNB.CA

LSOFT-ANNOUNCE
Announcements from L-Soft
mailto:LISTSERV@LISTSERV.NET

METACARD-LIST
An unmoderated discussion of the MetaCard software
mailto:LISTSERV@GROT.STARCONN.COM

MX-LIST
Bug reports and announcements for electronic mail package Message Exchange
mailto:MX-LIST-REQUEST@WKUVX1.WKU.EDU

OCR
General Optical Character Recognition issues
mailto:OCR-REQUEST@PHIL.RUU.NL

PAGEMAKER
Aldus Pagemaker and Desktop Publishing
mailto:LISTSERV@INDYCMS.IUPUI.EDU

POWERH-L
Discussion of PowerHouse 4GL Package
mailto:LISTSERV@UNB.CA

PROCMAIL
Discussion of UNIX mail processing package 'procmail'
mailto:PROCMAIL-REQUEST@INFORMATIK.RWTH-AACHEN.DE

PSTAT-L
Information Exchange about P-STAT Data Management and Statistics Package
mailto:LISTSERV@IRLEARN.UCD.IE

SMAIL3-USERS
Discussion of smail3.X mailers problems and fixes
mailto:SMAIL3-USERS-REQUEST@CS.ATHABASCAU.CA

SMAIL3-WIZARDS
Discussion for smail3.X mailer users
mailto:SMAIL3-WIZARDS-REQUEST@CS.ATHABASCAU.CA

SMARTCAM
Discussion of SmartCam software
mailto:MAJORDOMO@WORLD.STD.COM

SMARTLIST
SmartList mailing list management package questions and information
mailto:SMARTLIST-REQUEST@INFORMATIK.RWTH-AACHEN.DE

TOOLB-L
A discussion of Asymetrix ToolBook software and its integration into multimedia environments
mailto:LISTSERV@AFSYSB.UARK.EDU

UNIX-LISTPROC
Discussion of ListProcessor (an email list management package)
mailto:LISTPROC@AVS.COM

UUPC-ANNOUNCE
Announcements about UUPC/Extended Software
mailto:LISTSERV@KEW.COM

UUPC-INFO
High-volume Discussion of UUPC/Extended Software
mailto:LISTSERV@KEW.COM

VTCAD-L
A broad discussion of CAD programs and the CAD industry
mailto:LISTSERV@VTVM2.CC.VT.EDU

WILDCAT-L
User discussion of Wildcat BBS software and other MSI products
mailto:WILDCAT-L@TERMINAL-ONE.COM

WIN3-L
A general discussion about Microsoft Windows
mailto:LISTSERV@UICVM.UIC.EDU

WINHLP-L
An archived discussion of the Windows Help Compiler (WINHELP)
mailto:LISTSERV@ADMIN.HUMBERC.ON.CA

WORD-MAC
A discussion of Microsoft Word for the Macintosh
mailto:LISTSERV@ALSVID.UNE.EDU.AU

Standards

COMP-FORTRAN-90
Fortran 90 and HPF standards for Fortran information
mailto:MAILBASE@MAILBASE.AC.UK

PROTOCOL
An open discussion of computer protocols including communication protocols and internal formats
mailto:LISTSERV@VMD.CSO.UIUC.EDU

SGML
News, reviews and discussion of SGML and related standards
mailto:MAILBASE@MAILBASE.AC.UK

STD-UNIX
Discussion of UNIX standards and archives
mailto:STD-UNIX-REQUEST@UUNET.UU.NET

Statistics

DAILY
Statistical data and publications from Statistics Canada
mailto:LISTPROC@STATCAN.CA

Systems

AAI
Automated AUTODIN Interface system information
mailto:AAI-REQUEST@ST-LOUIS-EMH2.ARMY.MIL

ACCENTSERVER
Publication for UNIX operating system and application information
mailto:ACCENTSERVER@NIS.COM

AI-KAPPA-PC
Kappa PC and OOP/Expert System development issues
mailto:mailbase@mailbase.ac.uk

ALPHA-OSF-MANAGERS
Trouble shooting aid for Alpha AXP systems administrators
mailto:MAJORDOMO@ORNL.GOV

CARISUSE
User discussion of the CARIS geographic information system (GIS)
mailto:ROGER@SUN1.COGS.NS.CA

CCMAIL-L
CC-Mail LAN-Based Email System
mailto:LISTSERV@VM1.UCC.OKSTATE.EDU

CICSTALK
Discussion of CICS Transaction Processing System and UNIX
mailto:LISTSERV@IMC.COM

CPM-L
Discussion of CPM Operating System
mailto:LISTSERV@VM.ITS.RPI.EDU

CYBER-L
Information for Installers/Supporters of Control Data Systems
mailto:LISTSERV@BITNIC.EDUCOM.EDU

DB2-L
Discussion of IBM's DB/2 Database Products
mailto:LISTSERV@AMERICAN.EDU

DECSTATION-MANAGERS
Discussion of DECstation management
mailto:MAJORDOMO@ORNL.GOV

EMBED
Embedded computer system engineering issues
mailto:EMBED-REQUEST@SYNCHRO.COM

ENCTALK
Discussion of Encina Transaction Processing System Topics
mailto:LISTSERV@IMC.COM

IBM-SRD
IBM Screen Reader Product
mailto:LISTSERV@VM1.NODAK.EDU

INFO-68K
OS user discussion of small 68000 systems
mailto:INFO-68K-REQUEST@BERKELEY.EDU

INFO-ANDREW
General discussion of Andrew distribution
mailto:INFO-ANDREW-REQUEST@ANDREW.CMU.EDU

INFO-DATABASIX
Discussion of Databasix Information Systems in Libraries and Museums
mailto:INFO-DATABASIX-REQUEST@DIS.NL

INFO-GNU
Discussion of the Unix-compatible Software System GNU
mailto:INFO-GNU-REQUEST@PREP.AI.MIT.EDU

INFO-INGRES
Discussion of INGRES RDBMS in different computing environments
mailto:INFO-INGRES-REQUEST@MATH.AMS.ORG

INFO-SOLBOURNE
Information on Solbourne computers, workstations and servers
mailto:INFO-SOLBOURNE-REQUEST@ACSU.BUFFALO.EDU

INFO-UNIX
UNIX system questions and answers
mailto:INFO-UNIX-REQUEST@BRL.MIL

IRIS-ON-LINE
Monthly News Magazine for Silicon Graphics Systems Information
mailto:LIST-MANAGER@SGI.COM

LINUX-ACTIVISTS
Discussion of Linux Operating System Hacking
mailto:LINUX-ACTIVISTS-REQUEST@NIKSULA.HUT.FI

Computing & Mathematics – Education

Mailing Lists

MAC-MGRS
Professional discussion of Macintosh systems and networks
mailto:MAJORDOMO@WORLD.STD.COM

MUSIC-RESEARCH-DIGEST
Discussion of Computer Technology in Music Research
mailto:MUSIC-RESEARCH-REQUEST@
CATTELL.PSYCH.UPENN.EDU

RISKS
Computer system and public safety issues
mailto:RISKS-REQUEST@CSL.SRI.COM

SUN-386I
Sun 386i system issues and discussion
mailto:SUN-386I-REQUEST@RICE.EDU

SUN-MANAGERS
Professional discussion of Sun systems
mailto:SUN-MANAGERS-REQUEST@EECS.NWU.EDU

SYBASE-L
Discussion of Sybase Product Complex Across All Platforms
mailto:LISTSERV@VM.USC.EDU

Sun Security Bulletins
Customer Warning System bulletins from Sun Security
mailto:SECURITY-ALERT@SUN.COM

TE-TALK
Top End Transaction Processing System
mailto:LISTSERV@IMC.COM

UNICTR-L
Discussion of CA-Unicenter
mailto:LISTSERVE@BYU.EDU

VMXA-L
Installation, Operation, and Maintenance of VM/XA Systems
mailto:LISTSERV@UGA.CC.UGA.EDU

X-ADA
Discussion of the X Window system with ADA
mailto:X-ADA-REQUEST@EXPO.LCS.MIT.EDU

X11-3D
Discussion of 3D extensions to the X Window System
mailto:X11-3D-REQUEST@ATHENA.MIT.EDU

XIMAGE
Discussion of image processing with the X Window System
mailto:XIMAGE-REQUEST@EXPO.LCS.MIT.EDU

XPERT
General discussion on the X window system
mailto:XPERT-REQUEST@ATHENA.MIT.EDU

XVIDEO
Discussion live and still video in the X Window System
mailto:XVIDEO-REQUEST@EXPO.LCS.MIT.EDU

Theory

Q-METHOD
Discussion of Q-Methodology
mailto:LISTSERV@KENTVM.KENT.EDU

VSAM-L
A discussion of the Virtual Storage Access Method
mailto:LISTSERV@VM3090.EGE.EDU.TR

Education

Alternative Education

EDSTYLE
The Learning Styles Movement
mailto:LISTSERV@SJUVM.STJOHNS.EDU

HOME-ED
Home education issues and methods
mailto:HOME-ED-REQUEST@THINK.COM

Curriculum & Instruction

ASTA-L
String Teaching
mailto:LISTSERV@CMSUVMB.CMSU.EDU

CHEMISTRYTM
Intenational chemistry telementoring academic discussion group
mailto:CHEMISTRYTM-REQUEST@
DHVX20.CSUDH.EDU

ENGLISH-TEACHERS
Discussion of English curriculum in K-12
mailto:MAJORDOMO@UX1.CSO.UIUC.EDU

ISSS
A discussion of the International Student Space Simulation curriculum
mailto:LISTSERV@JHUVM.HCF.JHU.EDU

PAR-L
A moderated discussion forum which allows users of test-making, test-scoring, and electronic gradebook software to communicate and share ideas
mailto:LISTSERV@CCAT.SAS.UPENN.EDU

PHYS-L
A discussion forum for college and university physics teachers
mailto:LISTSERV@UWF.CC.UWF.EDU

PRECALC
A discussion of the problems in teaching precalculus/developmental mathematics
mailto:LISTSERV%IPFWVM.BITNET@
UICVM.UIC.EDU

SAIS-L
A forum to exchange ideas on making the sciences more appealing to students
mailto:LISTSERV@UNB.CA

T-AMLIT
A pedagogical and critical discussion of American literature
mailto:LISTSERV@BITNIC.EDUCOM.EDU

TAG-L
A discussion of Talented and Gifted Education
mailto:LISTSERV@VM1.NODAK.EDU

TOURISM
Discussion of developing education programs with tourism industry
mailto:ALMANAC@ESUSDA.GOV

WORLD-L
discussion of the pedogogy of teaching a scientific and non-Eurocentric world history
mailto:LISTSERV@UBVM.CC.BUFFALO.EDU

Distance Education

DEOS-L
Discussion of Distance Education
mailto:LISTSERV@PSUVM.PSU.EDU

EDISTA
A discussion of distance education and UNIDIS (The University Distance Program) at the University of Santiago in Chile
mailto:LISTSERV%USACHVM1.BITNET@
VM1.NODAK.EDU

Educational Issues

EFLIST
Discussion of Environment and Education Issues and Advocacy
mailto:EFLIST-REQUEST@HTBBS.COM

LEARNING
Child-centered learning techniques and discussion
mailto:LEARNING-REQUEST@SEA.EAST.SUN.COM

MULT-ED
Academic Discussion of Multicultural Education Issues
mailto:LISTPROC@GMU.EDU

NEWEDU-L
A discussion of new paradigms in education and how they may be implemented
mailto:LISTSERV@VM.USC.EDU

Educational Policy

EDPOLYAN
Education Policy Analysis
mailto:LISTSERV@ASUVM.INRE.ASU.EDU

EDPOLYAR
Articles on Education Policy Analysis
mailto:LISTSERV@ASUVM.INRE.ASU.EDU

Educational Projects

AVP-L
Professional discussion of Alternative to Violence Project, Inc
mailto:PRH4@CORNELL.EDU

FORSUM-L
Interactive Environmental Education Project
mailto:LISTSERV@BROWNVM.BROWN.EDU

Educational Technology

ACSOFT-L
Academic Software Development and Types
mailto:LISTSERV@WUVMD.WUSTL.EDU

AECM-L
Using hardware and software in college/university accounting education
mailto:MAILSERV@LOYOLA.EDU

COMPUTERSUPPORT-LAW-SCHOOLS
Discussion for computer support officers in law schools
mailto:MAILBASE@MAILBASE.AC.UK

CTI-COMPLIT
Computer literacy in higher education issues
mailto:MAILBASE@MAILBASE.AC.UK

CTI-L
Computers in Teaching
mailto:LISTSERV@IRLEARN.UCD.IE

DECNEWS
Information about Digital Corp. to Users in Educational/Research Institutions
mailto:LISTSERV@UBVM.CC.BUFFALO.EDU

EDNET
Educational Potential of the Internet
mailto:LISTSERV@NIC.UMASS.EDU

EDTECH
A discussion of educational technology research, advances and schools
mailto:LISTSERV%0HSTVMA.BITNET@VM1.NODAK.EDU

EDUCOM-W
Issues in Technology and Education of Interest to Women
mailto:LISTSERV@BITNIC.EDUCOM.EDU

INCLASS
Academic Discussion of Internet Use in the Classroom
mailto:LISTPROC@SCHOOLNET.CARLETON.CA

KIDSNET
Global education network for K-12 students and teachers
mailto:KIDSNET-REQUEST@VMS.CIS.PITT.EDU

LABMGR
A discussion about the management of microcomputer labs in academia
mailto:LISTSERV@UKCC.UKY.EDU

LASPAU-L
A discussion of the development and use of academic networks in Latin America
mailto:LISTSERV@HARVARDA.HARVARD.EDU

MEDIA-L
A forum for media service professionals about educational communication and technology
mailto:LISTSERV@BINGVMB.CC.BINGHAMTON.EDU

PEN-PALS
Forum for children to communicate with each other online
mailto:PEN-PALS-REQUEST@MAINSTREAM.COM

SATEDU-L
A discussion of Satellite Education and its integration into the classroom
mailto:LISTSERV@MAINVM.WCUPA.EDU

VIDNET-L
A discussion forum for problems and concerns in operating a campus-wide video network
mailto:LISTSERV@UGA.CC.UGA.EDU

WRICOM
Discussion of computer use in writing
mailto:MAILBASE@MAILBASE.AC.UK

Funding

GRANTS-L
Discussion of Contract and Grant Preparation and Administration
mailto:LISTSERV@GSUVM1.GSU.EDU

International Education

CIE-NEWS
Information from UC Irvine's Center for International Education Regarding International Study, Work, and Research Opportunities
mailto:LISTSERV@UCI.EDU

GLBL-HS
Discussion Among Students and Teachers of Global Studies or World Cultures
mailto:LISTSERV@OCMVM.ONONDAGA.BOCES.K12.NY.US

HILAT-L
Information Interchange about Research on Higher Education in Latin America
mailto:LISTSERV@LISTSERV.NET

INTDEV-L
Study and Instruction of International Development
mailto:LISTSERV@URIACC.URI.EDU

Language Acquisition

BILINGUE-L
Bilingual Education Assistance
mailto:LISTSERV@REYNOLDS.K12.OR.US

ESPAN-L
Discussion of Spanish Language Pedagogy Issues
mailto:LISTSERV@VM.TAU.AC.IL

JTIT-L
A discussion of the teaching of Japanese and Japanese language programs
mailto:LISTSERV@PSUVM.PSU.EDU

TESLK-12
A professional discussion of K-12 TESL issues
mailto:LISTSERV@CUNYVM.CUNY.EDU

Libraries

ADVANC-L
GEAC Advance Library System and Advance Hardware and Software
mailto:LISTSERV@LISTSERV.NET

CALIBK12
Discussion Among California Library Media Teachers
mailto:LISTSERV@SJSUVM1.SJSU.EDU

COLLBARG
Current Trends in Professional Status of Academic Librarians in Relation to Collective Bargaining
mailto:LISTSERV@CMS.CC.WAYNE.EDU

GAY-LIBN
DiscussionHEALTHRE Among Gay, Lesbian, and Bisexual Librarians
mailto:LISTSERV@VM.USC.EDU

LOANSTAR
Professional Discussion of Library Needs, Information, and Technologies
mailto:LOANSTAR-REQUEST@TWU.EDU

Organizations

AAESA-L
Education Service Agencies in North America
mailto:MAILSERV@ADMIN.ACES.K12.CT.US

NREN-DISCUSS
Discussion of National Research and Education Network
mailto:NREN-DISCUSS-REQUEST@PSI.COM

Primary & Secondary Education

CHILDRENS-VOICE
Information on and publishing of pre-school to 8th children's writing
mailto:LISTPROC@SCHOOLNET.CARLETON.CA

K12ADMIN
A discussion forum for K-12 school administrators
mailto:LISTSERV@SUVM.SYR.EDU

WORDLY-L
Delivery system for K-12 educational games KeyWord and Rhyme-n-Reason
mailto:MAISER@EVBHORT.UOGUELPH.CA

WORDPLAY-L
Educational game of English idioms WordPlay-L
mailto:MAILSERV@LEVELS.UNISA.EDU.AU

Universities

ACADV
Professional Academic Advising
mailto:LISTSERV@VM1.NODAK.EDU

ACTNOW-L
College Activism/Information
mailto:LISTSERV@BROWNVM.BROWN.EDU

APO-L
Alpha Phi Omega Fraternity Members Discussion
mailto:LISTSERV@VM.CC.PURDUE.EDU

APOSOC-L
Alpha Phi Omega Fraternity Members Discussion
mailto:LISTSERV@PSUVM.PSU.EDU

ASHE-L
Issues within the Association for the Study of Higher Education
mailto:LISTSERV@LISTSERV.NET

ASSESS
Assessment Issues and Policies in Higher Education
mailto:LISTSERV@UKCC.UKY.EDU

BRUNONIA
Brown University and Related Topics
mailto:LISTSERV@BROWNVM.BROWN.EDU

BUSFAC-L
Business Faculties' Problems, Solutions, and Research Ideas
mailto:LISTSERV@CMUVM.CSV.CMICH.EDU

CAMPCLIM
College Campuses' Personal, Educational, and Physical Environments
mailto:LISTSERV@UAFSYSB.UARK.EDU

CATALYST
Journal Providing Articles on Continuing/Community Education Practices
mailto:LISTSERV@VTVM1.CC.VT.EDU

CBEHIGH
Computers as Higher Education Tools
mailto:LISTSERV@CC1.KULEUVEN.AC.BE

CHAIRS-L
Professional discussion of academic chairperson issues and problems
mailto:CHAIRS-REQUEST@ACC.FAU.EDU

Education – Engineering & Technology

CIRCUITS-L
Strategies and issues in circuit course for electrical engineering students
mailto:CIRCUITS-REQUEST@UWPLATT.EDU

CPARK-L
Campus Parking Services Information Exchange
mailto:LISTSERV@PSUVM.PSU.EDU

CREWRT-L
Discussion of Creative Writing's Role in College/University Curricula
mailto:LISTSERV@UMCVMB.MISSOURI.EDU

CUMREC-L
A discussion concerning computer use in administration at the college and university level
mailto:LISTSERV%NDSUVM1.BITNET@CUNYVM.CUNY.EDU

CWIS-L
A discussion pertaining to the creation of campus-wide information systems
mailto:LISTSERV%WUVMD.BITNET@VM1.NODAK.EDU

DJ-L
Discussion of College Radio Today
mailto:LISTSERV@VM1.NODAK.EDU

DSSHE-L
Disabled Student Services
mailto:LISTSERV@UBVM.CC.BUFFALO.EDU

FACSER-L
College/University Facilities and Services
mailto:LISTSERV@WVNVM.WVNET.EDU

FAU-L
Florida Atlantic University issues and news
mailto:FAU-REQUEST@ACC.FAU.EDU

FINAID-L
Discussion Among University Student Financial Aid Administrators
mailto:LISTSERV@PSUVM.PSU.EDU

GAYNET
Lesbian and gay issues on college campuses
mailto:GAYNET-REQUEST@ATHENA.MIT.EDU

GC-L
Internationalization of Curricula by Email
mailto:LISTSERV@URIACC.URI.EDU

H-AMSTDY
Discussion of Issues within American Studies Field
mailto:LISTSERV@UICVM.UIC.EDU

HEPROC-L
Discussion of Major Issues in Higher Education
mailto:LISTSERV@AMERICAN.EDU

HONORS
Discussion and News of the National Collegiate Honors Council
mailto:LISTSERV@LISTSERV.NET

IPCT-L
Pedagogical Issues in Higher Education Involving Teaching with Technology
mailto:LISTSERV@GUVM.GEORGETOWN.EDU

IUPRESSL
Information about Indiana University Press Publications and Activities
mailto:LISTSERV@IUBVM.UCS.INDIANA.EDU

LATINO-L
Latino college and university students issues and concerns
mailto:LATINO-L-REQUEST@AMHERST.EDU

MET-STUD
Academic Discussion of Meteorological Studies
mailto:LISTPROC@BIBO.MET.FU-BERLIN.DE

PSYGRD-J
Psychology Graduate Student Journal
mailto:LISTSERV@ACADVM1.UOTTAWA.CA

STUDIUM
Scholarly and interdisciplinary discussion of higher education history
mailto:FFAAI01@CC1.KULEUVEN.AC.BE

T-ASSIST
A discussion of the teaching assistant position and related topics
mailto:LISTSERV@UNMVMA.UNM.EDU

TCC-L
Discussion Among Community College Teachers
mailto:LISTSERV@UHCCVM.UHCC.HAWAII.EDU

TQM-L
A discussion of Total Quality Management concepts and their implementation in colleges and universities
mailto:LISTSERV@UKANVM.CC.UKANS.EDU

UNINFSEC
A closed (one must apply) discussion of job related issues for university information security practitioners
mailto:LISTSERV@CUVMC.AIS.COLUMBIA.EDU

WISA
Women in Student Affairs
mailto:LISTSERV@ULKYVM.LOUISVILLE.EDU

Vocational Education

VOCNET
A discussion of vocational education
mailto:LISTSERV@CMSA.BERKELEY.EDU

Engineering & Technology

Chemical Engineering

IFPHEN-L
Discussion of Interfacial Phenomena
mailto:LISTSERV@WSUVM1.CSC.WSU.EDU

Civil Engineering

SEWER-LIST
Practical discussion of sewer system issues
mailto:LISTPROC@MCFEELEY.CC.UTEXAS.EDU

Engineering

BUILT-ENVIRONMENT
Discussion of Engineering and Construction
mailto:MAILBASE@MAILBASE.AC.UK

CCES-L
Discussion Among Canadian Engineering Students
mailto:LISTSERV@UNB.CA

Environmental Engineering

AE
Alternative Energy Sources
mailto:LISTSERV@SJSUVM1.SJSU.EDU

ENVENG-L
Discussion of Environmental Engineering Education and Research Issues
mailto:LISTPROC@LISTPROC.NET

Industrial Engineering

VISION-LIST
Discussion of vision issues in technology
mailto:VISION-LIST-REQUEST@TELEOS.COM

Material Science

GEOSYN
Professional discussion of geosynthetics industry
mailto:MAJORDOMO@CSN.ORG

METALLURGY-L
Academic and professional discussion of metallurgy
mailto:MAJORDOMO@MTU.EDU

SOFC
Solid oxide fuel cell stack design and manufacturing issues
mailto:MAILBASE@MAILBASE.AC.UK

TEXTILES
An acedemic discussion of textile and clothing related sciences
mailto:LISTSERV@VM3090.EGE.EDU.TR

Mechanical Engineering

MECH-L
A discussion of Mechanical Engineering and related topics
mailto:LISTSERV@UTARLVM1.UTA.EDU

Nuclear Engineering

CDN-NUCL-L
Discussion of Nuclear Energy, Research and Education Issues
mailto:LISTPROC@MCMASTER.CA

Technology

78-L
Recordings of the Pre-LP Era
mailto:LISTSERV@CORNELL.EDU

AUDIO-L
Audio Theories, Equipment, and Applications
mailto:LISTSERV@ITESMVF1.RZS.ITESM.MX

DASP-L
Digital Acoustic Signal Processing and Related Subjects
mailto:LISTSERV@EARN.CVUT.CZ

EV
Current State and Future Direction of Electric Vehicles
mailto:LISTSERV@SJSUVM1.SJSU.EDU

FIRE-LIST
Professional discussion of fire suppression systems
mailto:MAJORDOMO@HALCYON.COM

HIT
A discussion concerning imagined and real technological developments in the near/far future
mailto:LISTSERV%UFRJ.BITNET@CUNYVM.CUNY.EDU

HPV
Discussion of human-powered vehicle construction and operation
mailto:MAJORDOMO@ZIPPY.SONOMA.EDU

I-TV
Discussion of Two-Way Interactive Television Related to Education and Community Development
mailto:LISTSERV@KNOWLEDGEWORK.COM

INFO-FUTURES
Discussion of technology's effects in industry
mailto:INFO-FUTURES-REQUEST@WORLD.STD.COM

INFO-HIGH-AUDIO
High end audio equipment techniques and opinions
mailto:INFO-HIGH-AUDIO-REQUEST@INTROL.COM

PHOTO-CD
Kodak CD Products and Technology
mailto:LISTSERV@INFO.KODAK.COM

SATNEWS
Satellite television industry newsletter
mailto:SATNEWS-REQUEST@MRRL.LUT.AC.UK

SD3D
Discussion of 3D imaging platforms and disciplines
mailto:SD3D-REQUEST@SDSC.EDU

TECHNOLOGY-TRANSFER-LIST
Professional discussion of technology transfer issues
mailto:TECHNOLOGY-TRANSFER-LIST-REQUEST@SEI.CMU.EDU

VHF
Very High Frequency radio issues
mailto:VHF-REQUEST@W6YX.STANFORD.EDU

Transportation Engineering

RACEFAB
Serious discussion of race car and bike engineering
mailto:RACEFAB-REQUEST@PMS076.PMS.FORD.COM

Government & Politics

Career & Employment

FEDJOBS
Postings of Federal Job Openings
mailto:LISTSERV@DARTCMS1.DARTMOUTH.EDU

Cities

MUNINET
Discussion of Municipality Economics and Development
mailto:LISTPROC@FINANCENET.GOV

Countries

BRAS-NET
Discussion for Brazilians
mailto:BRAS-NET-REQUEST@CS.COLUMBIA.EDU

IRL-POL
Current Irish Politics
mailto:LISTSERV@IRLEARN.UCD.IE

SUDAN-L
A discussion of issues concerning Sudan
mailto:LISTSERV@EMUVM1.CC.EMORY.EDU

Doctrines

C-NEWS
General information on conservative political issues
mailto:MAJORDOMO@WORLD.STD.COM

LIBERNET
Libertarian and classical liberal discussions
mailto:LIBERNET-REQUEST@DARTMOUTH.EDU

MARXISM
Discussion of Marxist tradtions
mailto:MAJORDOMO@WORLD.STD.COM

Individuals

PEROT
Information on H. Ross Perot and his Candidacy and Campaign
mailto:LISTSERV@VM.MARIST.EDU

International

ENVCEE
Discussion of Environmental Issues in Central and Eastern Europe
mailto:LISTSERV@REC.HU

MIDEAST-PEACE
An open discussion of issues surrounding the peace process in the mideast
mailto:LISTSERV@AIS.NET

MODERATENET
Discussion of the Middle East Peace Talks
mailto:RAYHANANIA@DELPHI.COM

WORLDGOV
World government discussion
mailto:WORLDGOV-REQUEST@TOMAHAWK.WELCH.JHU.EDU

YOUTH-GLOBAL-ED-CIT
Youth global citizenship education resources
mailto:ALMANAC@ESUSDA.GOV

Issues

ACT-UP
ACT-UP Events and Ideas Worldwide
mailto:ACT-UP-REQUEST@WORLD.STD.COM

AMNESTY
Amnesty International Urgent Action Appeals
mailto:LISTSERV@JHUVM.HCF.JHU.EDU

ANIMAL-RIGHTS
Serious discussion of animal rights issues
mailto:Animal-Rights-Request@XANTH.CS.ODU.EDU

AR-Alerts
Discussion of animal rights issues
mailto:majordomo@ny.neavs.com

ARMS-L
War, Weapons, and The Arms Race
mailto:LISTSERV@BUACCA.BU.EDU

CONG-REFORM
Insider Information on Congressional Reform Issues
mailto:LISTSERVER@ESSENTIAL.ORG

DISARM-L
Discussion of Accelerating World Disarmament of Weapons
mailto:LISTSERV@UACSC2.ALBANY.EDU

ECOCT-A
Discussion of Sustainable Urban Development Issues
mailto:LISTSERV@SEARN.SUNET.SE

EFF-ACTIVISTS
Discussion Regarding Activist and Campaign Information
mailto:LISTSERV@EFF.ORG

ELAN
Discussion of the Environment in Latin America
mailto:LISTSERV@CSF.COLORADO.EDU

ENVIRONMENT-L
Discussion of Environment and New York State in Particular
mailto:LISTSERV@CORNELL.EDU

FIREARMS-POLITICS
Firearms legislation and issues in the United States
mailto:FIREARMS-POLITICS-REQUEST@CS.CMU.EDU

FORCED-MIGRATION
Forced migration issues and discussion
mailto:MAILBASE@MAILBASE.AC.UK

HEALTHRE
Discussion of Health Care Reform
mailto:LISTSERV@UKCC.UKY.EDU

HR-L
Human rights issues and discussion
mailto:HR-L-REQUEST@VMS.CIS.PITT.EDU

IFREEDOM
Canadian discussion on censorship and freedom of speech
mailto:IFREEDOM-REQUEST@SNOOPY.UCIS.DAL.CA

INFOTERRA
Environmental information, announcements and publications
mailto:LISTPROC@PAN.CEDAR.UNIVIE.AC.AT

POLITICS
An open, but serious forum for the discussion of politics
mailto:LISTSERV@UCF1VM.CC.UCF.EDU

PRESS-RELEASE
National Rifle Association of America press releases and announcements
mailto:PRESS-RELEASE-REQUEST@NRA.ORG

QN
Queer Nation discussion, announcements and information
mailto:QN-REQUEST@QUEERNET.ORG

RKBA-ALERT
Announcements from the National Rifle Association of America
mailto:RKBA-ALERT-REQUEST@NRA.ORG

UWSA
United States We Stand America issues and interests
mailto:TELCON@SHELL.PORTAL.COM

Military

MILITARY-HISTORY
Discussion of military history
mailto:MAILBASE@MAILBASE.AC.UK

Policies

ASYLUM-L
Discussion of legal asylum and refugee status standards
mailto:MAJORDOMO@UFSIA.AC.BE

GOP-L
Friendly, Insulated Discussion of Republican and Conservative Policies
mailto:LISTSERV%PCCVM.BITNET@CMSA.BERKELEY.EDU

NEWS
Distribution of Local, State, and Federal Government Financial News
mailto:LISTPROC@FINANCENET.GOV

NHCTEN
Discussion of national health care reform effects on mental health systems
mailto:MAJORDOMO@WORLD.STD.COM

PUBPOL-L
A discussion of public policy, public administration, and public planning
mailto:LISTSERV@VM1.SPCS.UMN.EDU

TAP-RESOURCES
A candid assessment and discussion of the management of publicly owned natural resources
mailto:LISTSERVER@ESSENTIAL.ORG

Political Science

POLI-SCI
Discussion of Unites States election process and technologies
mailto:POLI-SCI-REQUEST@RUTGERS.EDU

PSRT-L
A moderated discussion of political science issues for researchers and teachers
mailto:LISTSERV@MIZZOU1.MISSOURI.EDU

Reference

WH-SUMMARY
Summaries from White House archives
mailto:ALMANAC@ESUSDA.GOV

Regions

PRA
Participatory Community Development
mailto:LISTSERV@UOGUELPH.CA

States

KENTUCKY
A discussion of civic and political issues in Kentucky
mailto:LISTSERV@UKCC.UKY.EDU

MN-POLITICS
Discussion of Minnesota politics and public policy
mailto:MAJORDOMO@MR.NET

STATE-COUNTY
State and county government finance issues
mailto:LISTPROC@FINANCENET.GOV

WVA-L
West Virginia news, culture, and history
mailto:MAJORDOMO@WORLD.STD.COM

Health & Medicine

Addictions

ADDICT-L
Addictions Awareness, Research, Education, and Recovery
mailto:LISTSERV@KENTVM.KENT.EDU

ALCOHOL
Alcohol and Drug Abuse
mailto:LISTSERV@LMUACAD.BITNET

Aging

LONGEVITY
Discussion of Ways to Extend Human Life
mailto:LISTSERV@VM3090.EGE.EDU.TR

Alternative Medicine

CHIRO-LIST
Chiropractor mailing list
mailto:MAJORDOMO@SILCOM.COM

HOLISTIC
Discussion of Holistic Concepts and Methods of Living
mailto:LISTSERV@SIUCVMB.SIU.EDU

Biomedicine

BIOMED-L
A discussion of Biomedical Ethics on a variety of topics
mailto:LISTSERV@LISTSERV.NET

Conferences & Events

CROMED-L
Current Medical Events in Croatia
mailto:LISTSERV@AEARN.EDVZ.UNIVIE.AC.AT

Dental Health

AMALGAM
Dental 'Silver' Tooth Fillings and Chronic Mercury Poisoning
mailto:LISTSERV@GMD.DE

D-ORAL-L
Scientists'/Clinicians' Problems with Human/Mammalian Oral Microbiota
mailto:LISTSERV@LIST.NIH.GOV

DENTALWEB
Discussion of the Dental Education Community and the Internet
mailto:LISTPROC@BITE.DB.UTH.TMC.EDU

Disabilities

ADD-PARENTS
Attention Deficit/Hyperactivity Disorder Information and Support
mailto:ADD-PARENTS-REQUEST@MV.MV.COM

AUDIOL-L
Discussion of Hearing defects and Related Issues
mailto:LISTPROC@BGU.EDU

AUTISM
Autism and Developmental Disability
mailto:LISTSERV@SJUVM.STJOHNS.EDU

BLINDFAM
Blindness and its Effects on Family Life
mailto:LISTSERV@SJUVM.STJOHNS.EDU

DADVOCAT
Discussion Among Fathers of Disabled Children and Interested Persons/Professionals
mailto:LISTSERV@UKCC.UKY.EDU

DEAFBLND
Discussion of Dual Sensory Impairment Professionals, Individuals, Families, and Friends
mailto:LISTSERV@UKCC.UKY.EDU

L-HCAP
A discusssion of technology for the handicapped
mailto:LISTSERV@VM1.NODAK.EDU

MOBILITY
Access and Mobility for Disabled Persons
mailto:LISTSERV@SJUVM.STJOHNS.EDU

STUT-HLP
Discussion and support for stutterers and their families
mailto:LISTPROC@BGU.EDU

STUTT-L
A research and clinical discussion of stuttering
mailto:LISTSERV@VM.TEMPLE.EDU

Diseases

OCD-L
Obsessive Compulsive Disorder
mailto:LISTSERV@VM.MARIST.EDU

Health & Medical Professionals

EMED-L
Professional discussion of emergency health practices
mailto:MAJORDOMO@ITSA.UCSF.EDU

GRADNRSE
Discussion for Practicing Nurses
mailto:LISTSERV@KENTVM.KENT.EDU

MEDPHYS
Professional Discussion of Medical Physics
mailto:MEDPHYS-REQUEST@RADONC.DUKE.EDU

NRSING-L
A discussion of Nursing and health care informatics
mailto:LISTSERV@NIC.UMASS.EDU

Health & Medicine

NURSENET
A wide-ranging discussion of nursing issues for health professionals
mailto:LISTSERV@VM.UTCC.UTORONTO.CA

PICU
Professional discussion of pediatric intensive care
mailto:LISTPROC@ITS.MCW.EDU

RESIDENTS
Discussion of Residency Issues
mailto:LISTSERV@UTMB.EDU

SNURSE-L
A discussion for student nurses and nursing issues
mailto:LISTSERV@UBVM.CC.BUFFALO.EDU

Health Conditions

AIDS
Medical, social and political AIDS issues
mailto:AIDS-REQUEST@CS.UCLA.EDU

ALS Interest Group List
Discussion of Amyotrophic Lateral Sclerosis
mailto:bro@huey.met.fsu.edu

BIFIDA-L
Spina Bifida
mailto:LISTSERV@MERCURY.DSU.EDU

BOSTON-RSI
Repetitive stress injury information for the Boston area
mailto:Boston-RSI-request@world.std.com

BREAST-CANCER
Breast Cancer and All Related Issues
mailto:LISTSERVER@MORGAN.UCS.MUN.CA

CANCERNET
Information statements from the National Cancer Institute
mailto:CANCERNET@ICICB.NCI.NIH.GOV

CATHAR-M
People Who Have or Are Involved with Chronic Fatigue Syndrome
mailto:LISTSERV@SJUVM.STJOHNS.EDU

CELIAC
Discussion of Celiac Disease, Dermatitis Herpetiformis, and Various Intolerances
mailto:LISTSERV@SJUVM.STJOHNS.EDU

CFIDS-L
Political Action Issues Concerning Chronic Fatigue Syndrome
mailto:LISTSERV@AMERICAN.EDU

CFS-D
A discussion of information relating to Chronic Fatigue Syndrome
mailto:LISTSERV%ALBNYDH2@ALBANY.EDU

CFS-FILE
Resource and Information Files on Chronic Fatigue Syndrome
mailto:LISTSERV@SJUVM.STJOHNS.EDU

CFS-L
Discussion of Chronic Fatigue Syndrome
mailto:LISTSERV@LIST.NIH.GOV

CFS-MED
Physicians' Discussion of Chronic Fatigue Syndrome
mailto:LISTSERV@LIST.NIH.GOV

CFS-NEWS
Information on Chronic Fatigue Syndrome
mailto:LISTSERV@LIST.NIH.GOV

CFS-WIRE
News Items Regarding Chronic Fatigue Syndrome
mailto:LISTSERV@LIST.NIH.GOV

CYSTIC-L
Holistic Impact of Cystic Fibrosis
mailto:LISTSERV@YALEVM.CIS.YALE.EDU

DIABETIC
Discussion Among Diabetics
mailto:LISTSERV@LEHIGH.EDU

HEPV-L
Discussion Among Sufferers of Chronic Hepatitis and Indirectly Involved Persons
mailto:LISTSERV@SJUVM.STJOHNS.EDU

IBDLIST
Discussion of Inflammatory Bowel Diseases issues
mailto:IBDLIST-REQUEST%MVAC23@UDEL.EDU

IMMUNE
Information and support for immune-system breakdown victims
mailto:IMMUNE-REQUEST@WEBER.UCSD.EDU

LYMENET-L
A discussion of current developments in treating Lyme disease
mailto:LISTSERV@Lehigh.EDU

MUSC-DYS-LIST
General Discussion of Muscular Dystrophy
mailto:MD-LIST-REQUEST@DATA.BASIX.COM

OVARIAN-CANCER
Ovarian Cancer
mailto:LISTSERV@IST01.FERRIS.EDU

PARKINSN
An international exchange forum for people interested in Parkinson's Disease
mailto:LISTSERV@VM.UTCC.UTORONTO.CA

POLIO
Sufferers of or Those Affected by Polio
mailto:LISTSERV@SJUVM.STJOHNS.EDU

RPLIST
Retinitis Pigmentosa and Related Issues
mailto:LISTSERV@SJUVM.STJOHNS.EDU

SOREHAND
Typing Related Injuries
mailto:LISTSERV@UCSFVM.UCSF.EDU

STROKE-L
Discussion Regarding Cerebrovascular Accidents (Strokes)
mailto:LISTSERV@UKCC.UKY.EDU

WITSENDO
A discussion of all aspects of the disease Endometriosis
mailto:LISTSERV@DARTCMS1.DARTMOUTH.EDU

YEAST-L
A discussion of yeast-related health problems and their treatment, and yeast-free recipes
mailto:LISTSERV@PSUHMC.HMC.PSU.EDU

Medical Schools

MEDSTU-L
A discussion and information exchange for medical students worldwide
mailto:LISTSERV@UNMVMA.UNM.EDU

Medicine

EYE-MOVEMENT
Scientific discussion of eye movement studies
mailto:MAILBASE@MAILBASE.AC.UK

HYPBAR-L
Discussion of Medicine in Relation to Diving
mailto:LISTSERV@TECHNION.TECHNION.AC.IL

IVTHERAPY-L
A forum about I.V. therapy treatment and professionals
mailto:LISTSERV@NETCOM.COM

RC_WORLD
A discussion of Respiratory Therapy or Care issues
mailto:LISTSERV@INDYCMS.IUPUI.EDU

Mental Health

AR
Discussion of Achievement Barriers
mailto:MoreMind@aol.COM

CHILD-PSYCHIATRY
Child and adolescent psychiatry issues and discussion
mailto:MAILBASE@MAILBASE.AC.UK

CLINICAL-PSYCHOPHYSIOLOGY
Discussion of Clinical Psychophysiology issues
mailto:MAILBASE@MAILBASE.AC.UK

DEPRESSION
Academic discussion of mood disorders in clinical and research settings
mailto:MAILBASE@MAILBASE.AC.UK

EMERGENCY-PSYCHIATRY
Professional Discussion of Emergency Psychiatry
mailto:MAILBASE@MAILBASE.AC.UK

FORENSIC-PSYCHIATRY
Scholarly Discussion of Forensic Psychiatry
mailto:MAILBASE@MAILBASE.AC.UK

OUTCOMETEN
Professional discussion of mental health improvement projects
mailto:MAJORDOMO@WORLD.STD.COM

PSYCHIATRY
Professional discussion of psychiatric findings and issues
mailto:MAILBASE@MAILBASE.AC.UK

PSYCHO-PHARM
Professional discussion of clinical psychopharmacology
mailto:MAJORDOMO@NETCOM.COM

PSYCHOANALYSIS
Professional discussion of psychoanalysic issues
mailto:MAILBASE@MAILBASE.AC.UK

TRANSCULTURAL-PSYCHOLOGY
Professional discussion of mental health services in diverse culture
mailto:MAILBASE@MAILBASE.AC.UK

TRAUMATIC-STRESS
Discussion of traumatic stress events
mailto:MAILBASE@MAILBASE.AC.UK

WALKERS
Discussion and support for depression sufferers and their families
mailto:MAJORDOMO@WORLD.STD.COM

Personal Care

DIET
Support and Discussion of Weight Loss
mailto:LISTSERV@UBVM.CC.BUFFALO.EDU

FIT-L
Discussion of Wellness, Exercise, and Diet
mailto:LISTSERV@ETSUADMN.ETSU.EDU

Public Health

FOODLINK
Food Safety Specialists Discussion of Foodborne Illness Outbreaks
mailto:LISTPROC@LISTPROC.WSU.EDU

MANAGED-BEHAVIOURAL-HEALTHCARE
Discussion of Health Care Reform in the United States and Worldwide
mailto:MAILBASE@MAILBASE.AC.UK

PUBLIC-HEALH
Professional discussion and information on public health
mailto:MAILBASE@MAILBASE.AC.UK

Reference

ACCRI-L
Anaesthesia and Critical Care Internet Resources
mailto:LISTSERV@UABDPO.DPO.UAB.EDU

ANEST-L
Anaesthesiology
mailto:LISTSERV@UBVM.CC.BUFFALO.EDU

DERM-L
Discussion Among Dermatologists
mailto:LISTSERV@YALEVM.CIS.YALE.EDU

LASMED-L
A discussion of lasers in medicine
mailto:LISTSERV@VM.TAU.AC.IL

OPHTHAL
Ophthalmology and Clinical Ophthalmology
mailto:LISTSERV@UBVM.CC.BUFFALO.EDU

Resources

HSPNET-L
A discussion concerning the connecting of rural hospitals with major medical centers
mailto:LISTSERV%ALBNYDH2.BITNET@UACSC2.ALBANY.EDU

MED-TECH
A discussion of medical technology
mailto:LISTSERV@IST01.FERRIS.EDU

MEDINF-L
A discussion of the medical data processing and informatics fields
mailto:LISTSERV@VM.GMD.DE

MEDNETS
A discussion of medical telecommunication networks relating to clinical practice, medical research, and administration
mailto:LISTSERV@VM1.NODAK.EDU

MEDNEWS
A discussion and distribution list for the Health Info-Com Network medical newsletter
mailto:LISTSERV@ASUVM.INRE.ASU.EDU

NURSERES
Discussion Among Nurse Researchers
mailto:LISTSERV@KENTVM.KENT.EDU

OPTIMAL
Professional Discussion of Ophthalmic Photography Research
mailto:MAISER@VISION.EEI.UPMC.EDU

REHAB-RU
Physical Medicine and Rehabilitation in Rural/Community Settings
mailto:LISTSERV@UKCC.UKY.EDU

TRNSPLNT
A discussion of the trauma and day-to-day coping involved in organ transplant
mailto:LISTSERV@WUVMD.WUSTL.EDU

Veterinary Medicine

VETINFO
Veterinary Informatics
mailto:LISTSERV@LISTSERV.NET

WLREHAB
Wildlife Rehabilitation
mailto:LISTSERV@VM1.NODAK.EDU

Humanities & Social Sciences

Anthropology

ANTHRO-L
A discussion of techniques and areas of research in Anthropology
mailto:LISTSERV@UBVM.CC.BUFFALO.EDU

BIBLIONUMIS-L
Literature Dealing with Numismatics
mailto:LISTSERV@NETCOM.COM

Archaeology

ARCH-L
Problems Related to Archaeological Projects
mailto:LISTSERV@IBM.GWDG.DE

ARCH-THEORY
Archeaological theory in Europe research
mailto:MAILBASE@MAILBASE.AC.UK

DARWIN-L
Discussion of History and Theory of Historical Sciences
mailto:LISTSERV@UKANAIX.CC.UKANS.EDU

Area & Cultural Studies

AFRICA-L
African Continent, Countries, and Peoples
mailto:LISTSERV@VM1.LCC.UFMG.BR

ARAB-AMERICAN
Discussion of Arab-American issues
mailto:MAILSERV@CARLETON.EDU

ARGENTINA
Discussion of Argentina and Argentinian Issues
mailto:ARGENTINA-REQUEST@OIS.DB.TORONTO.EDU

BASQUE-L
Basque Culture Information
mailto:LISTSERV@CUNYVM.CUNY.EDU

BERITA-L
Malaysia, Singapore, and Pertinent Asian Countries
mailto:LISTSERV@VMD.CSO.UIUC.EDU

BUBBA-L
Southern United States culture, language, and lifestyle issues
mailto:LISTPROC@KNUTH.MTSU.EDU

CANADA-L
Political, Social, Cultural, and Economic Issues in Canada
mailto:LISTSERV@VM1.MCGILL.CA

CERRO-L
Regional Development and Related Research in Central Europe
mailto:LISTSERV@aearn.edvz.uni-linz.ac.at

DEVEL-L
Technology Transfer in International Development
mailto:LISTSERV@AUVM.AMERICAN.EDU

EC
The European Community
mailto:LISTSERV@VM.CC.METU.EDU.TR

GAELIC-L
News and Information in Gaelic
mailto:LISTSERV@IRLEARN.UCD.IE

GENERAL
Italian University Student General Discussion Group
mailto:LISTPROC@CSR.UNIBO.IT

HUNGARY
Discussion of Hungarian Issues
mailto:LISTSERV@GWUVM.GWU.EDU

INDIA-L
News to People of the Indian Subcontinent
mailto:LISTSERV@VM.TEMPLE.EDU

INDOLOGY
Discussion Among Scholars of Classical India
mailto:LISTSERV@LIVERPOOL.AC.UK

LLAJTA
Discussion of All Topics Relating to Bolivia
mailto:LISTSERV@IO.DSD.LITTON.COM

LSA-L
Discussion of Topics Related to Liberia
mailto:LISTSERV@UGA.CC.UGA.EDU

MALAWI
Discussion of Malawian Culture
mailto:NYASANET-REQUEST@UNH.EDU

NAT-WORK
Native American Work and Employment
mailto:LISTSERV@VM1.CC.UAKRON.EDU

PAGLIA-L
Dr. Camille Paglia's ideas and writings discussed
mailto:MAILSERV@AC.DAL.CA

PERU
Discussion of Peru and other issues
mailto:OWNER-PERU@CS.SFSU.EDU

POLAND-L
A discussion of Polish culture and events
mailto:LISTSERV@UBVM.CC.BUFFALO.EDU

SAUDADESDOBRASIL
Discussion of Brazilian cultural issues
mailto:LISTPROC@LISTS.PRINCETON.EDU

UKRAINA
The Ukraine
mailto:LISTSERV@UKANAIX.CC.UKANS.EDU

URBAN-L
A discussion and information exchange on Urban Planning
mailto:LISTSERV%TREARN.BITNET@VM1.NODAK.EDU

VA-HIST
Research and Writing about Virginia History
mailto:LISTSERVER@LEO.VSLA.EDU

Humanities & Social Sciences

Career & Employment

JOBPLACE
A discussion of job search techniques for individuals
mailto:LISTSERV@UKCC.UKY.EDU

LIBJOB
Announcements of Library Employment Opportunities
mailto:LISTPROC@FIREFLY.PRAIRIENET.ORG

TRDEV-L
An academic discussion of the training and development of human resources
mailto:LISTSERV@PSUVM.PSU.EDU

Classics

CLASSICS
Discussion of Ancient Greek and Latin Subjects
mailto:LISTSERV@UWAVM.U.WASHINGTON.EDU

Geography

GEOGRAPH
Discussion of Geography
mailto:LISTSERV@SEARN.SUNET.SE

History

AEROSP-L
Effects of Aerospace on Twentieth Century
mailto:LISTSERV@SIVM.SI.EDU

ANCIEN-L
History of the Ancient Mediterranean
mailto:LISTSERV@ULKYVM.LOUISVILLE.EDU

ANSAXNET
Discussion of Pre-1100 English History
mailto:U47C2@WVNVM.WVNET.EDU

C18-L
A discussion concerning varied aspects of the 18th century
mailto:LISTSERV%PSUVM.BITNET@VM1.NODAK.EDU

C18-STUDIES
Discussion of 18th Century Studies
mailto:JANET%"MAILBASE@MAILBASE.AC.UK"

H-URBAN
Discussion Among Scholars of Urban History
mailto:LISTSERV@UICVM.UIC.EDU

HISLAW-L
Discussion Among Students and Scholars of the History of the Law
mailto:LISTSERV@ULKYVM.LOUISVILLE.EDU

HISTEC-L
Academic, Non-Sectarian Discussion Among Students and Scholars of the History of Evangelical Christianity
mailto:LISTSERV@UKANVM.CC.UKANS.EDU

HOLOCAUS
The Holocaust, Anti-Semitism, and Jewish History of the 1930's and 1940's
mailto:LISTSERV@UICVM.UIC.EDU

HOPOS-L
Discussion Among Scholars of the History of Philosophy of Science
mailto:LISTSERV@UKCC.UKY.EDU

LT-ANTIQ
Discussion of Topics Related to Late Antiquity
mailto:LISTSERV@UNIVSCVM.CSD.SCAROLINA.EDU

MEDIEV-L
An academic discussion forum about the Middle Ages (A.D. 283-1500)
mailto:LISTSERV@UKANVM.CC.UKANS.EDU

MEDSCI-L
A discussion of Medieval and Rennaissance science
mailto:LISTSERV@BROWNVM.BROWN.EDU

PREZHIST
An open discussion of Presidential History from 1789-1992
mailto:LISTSERV@KASEY.UMKC.EDU

RENAIS-L
A discussion and debate forum for students and scholars of the history of the Rennaissance
mailto:LISTSERV@ULKYVM.LOUISVILLE.EDU

RUSHIST
A discussion of any aspect of Russian history
mailto:LISTSERV@VM.USC.EDU

SCAHRLDS
Discussion of Heraldry within the Society for Creative Anachronism
mailto:LISTSERV@PUCC.PRINCETON.EDU

SHOTHC-L
An academic forum for scholars to discuss the history of technology and the subtopic of information, computing and society
mailto:LISTSERV@SIVM.SI.EDU

VICTORIA
19th-Century British Culture and Society
mailto:LISTSERV@IUBVM.UCS.INDIANA.EDU

VWAR-L
A discussion of the Vietnam War
mailto:LISTSERV@UBVM.CC.BUFFALO.EDU

WWII-L
A discussion of the history, society, and strategy of World War II
mailto:LISTSERV@UBVM.CC.BUFFALO.EDU

Languages

COPYEDITING-L
Discussion Among Copy Editors
mailto:LISTSERV@CORNELL.EDU

HONYAKU
Professional discussion for Japanese/English translators
mailto:HONYAKU-REQUEST@NETCOM.COM

INDIA-IN-LANGUAGES
Discussion of major languages of Indian subcontinent
mailto:INDIA-IN-LANGUAGES-REQUEST@EE.ROCHESTER.EDU

ITISALAT
A moderated discussion of Arabic language and Technology
mailto:LISTSERV@GUVM.GEORGETOWN.CCF.EDU

LANTRA-L
A discussion of translation and interpreting issues
mailto:LISTSERV@SEARN.SUNET.SE

LATIN-L
A discussion of Latin and related issues
mailto:LISTSERV@PSUVM.PSU.EDU

NIHONGO
A discussion of the verbal and written Japanese language
mailto:LISTSERV@MITVMA.MIT.EDU

RUSTEX-L
A discussion of the Russian language version of the TeX typesetting system
mailto:LISTSERV@UBVM.CC.BUFFALO.EDU

WELSH-L
A discussion of the Welsh language and culture
mailto:LISTSERV@IRLEARN.UCD.IE

Library & Information Studies

AACRL
Discussion Among Alabama Academic/Research Library Professionals
mailto:LISTSERV@UABDPO.DPO.UAB.EDU

AFAS-L
African American Studies and Librarianship
mailto:LISTSERV@KENTVM.KENT.EDU

ALA-PLAN
Conferences of the American Library Association
mailto:LISTSERV@SUN.CC.WESTGA.EDU

AMIA-L
Society of Art Libraries Discussion List
mailto:LISTSERV@UKCC.UKY.EDU

ARCHIVES
Archival Theory and Practice
mailto:LISTSERV@INDYCMS.IUPUI.EDU

BI-L
Assisting Patrons in Effectively Using Library Resources
mailto:LISTSERV@BINGVMB.CC.BINGHAMTON.EDU

BIBSOCAN
Bibliography Techniques and Problems
mailto:LISTSERV@VM.UTCC.UTORONTO.CA

BIBSOFT
Bibliographic Database Management Software
mailto:LISTSERV@INDYCMS.IUPUI.EDU

CIDOC-L
Discussion of Museum Documentation Issues
mailto:MAILSERV@NRM.SE

COLLDV-L
Discussion Among Those Involved with Library Collection Development
mailto:LISTSERV@VM.USC.EDU

CONSDIST
Professional discussion of archive material conservation
mailto:CONSDIST-REQUEST@LINDY.STANFORD.EDU

COOPCAT
Information Aiding in the Formation of Cooperative Cataloging Arrangements Between Libraries
mailto:LISTSERV@NERVM.NERDC.UFL.EDU

EMEDIA
Bibliographic strategies and issues for electronic media
mailto:MXSERVER@VAX1.ELON.EDU

GOVDOC-L
Information Dissemination Through Federal Depository Libraries
mailto:LISTSERV@PSUVM.PSU.EDU

Mailing Lists

Humanities & Social Sciences

INDEX-L
Discussion of Index Preparation
mailto:LISTSERV@BINGVMB.CC.BINGHAMTON.EDU

INT-LAW
Exchange of Foreign, Comparative, and International Legal Materials/Issues
mailto:LISTSERV@VM1.SPCS.UMN.EDU

LIBADMIN
A discussion of library administration and management
mailto:LISTSERV@UMAB.UMD.EDU

LIBIDAHO
Discussion of Idaho Libraries and Librarians
mailto:LISTSERV@IDBSU.IDBSU.EDU

LIBMASTR
An informal discussion for users of the Library Master bibliographic and textual database manegement system
mailto:LISTSERV@ACADVM1.UOTTAWA.CA

LIBRARY
A general discussion of library issues
mailto:LISTSERV@MIAMIU.MUOHIO.EDU

LIBREF-L
A discussion of reference libraries and related issues
mailto:LISTSERV@KENTVM.KENT.EDU

LIBRES
A discussion of the impact of new technologies on gender roles in the library
mailto:LISTSERV@KENTVM.KENT.EDU

LIBWAT-L
A discussion of the impact of new technologies on gender roles in the library
mailto:LISTSERV@UBVM.CC.BUFFALO.EDU

LIS-L
A discussion forum for students of library and information science
mailto:LISTSERV@VMD.CSO.UIUC.EDU

LM_NET
A discussion forum about school library media services
mailto:LISTSERV@SUVM.SYR.EDU

MARYLIB
Discussion Among Maryland-Area Librarians and Information Professionals
mailto:LISTSERV@UMAB.UMD.EDU

MEDLIB-L
A discussion forum for health science librarians
mailto:LISTSERV@UBVM.CC.BUFFALO.EDU

MELIBS-L
Discussion of Library Service in Maine and Related Topics
mailto:LISTSERV@MAINE.MAINE.EDU

MEMO-NET
Discussion for Library/Media and Technology Professionals
mailto:LISTSERV@VAX1.MANKATO.MSUS.EDU

NATRESLIB-L
Discussion of natural resource librarianship
mailto:ANNHED@CC.USU.EDU

NETADMIN
A discussion forum for managers of regional or statewide library networks
mailto:LISTSERVER@LEO.VSLA.EDU

PUBLIB
A discussion of all aspects of public libraries
mailto:LISTSERV@NYSERNET.ORG

PUBLIB-NET
A focused discussion about the use of the Internet in public libraries
mailto:LISTSERV@NYSERNET.ORG

PUBYAC
A practical discussion of all aspects of library services to children and young adults
mailto:LISTSERV@LIS.PITT.EDU

SLA-BOSTON
A discussion for the membership of the Boston Special Libraries Association
mailto:LISTSERV@BABSON.EDU

SLAITE-L
A discussion of topics relevent to the membership of the Special Libraries Association Information Technology Division
mailto:LISTSERV@BABSON.EDU

STS-L
Discussion Among Science and Technology Librarians
mailto:LISTSERV@UTKVM1.UTK.EDU

Linguistics

LINGUIST
Discussion of Linguistics and Related Fields
mailto:LISTSERV@TAMVM1.TAMU.EDU

LOJBAN-LIST
Academic discussion of artificial language Lobjan
mailto:LOJBAN-LIST-REQUEST@SNARK.THYRSUS.COM

PSY-LANGUAGE
Research, theories and discussion of psychopathology
mailto:MAILBASE@MAILBASE.AC.UK

SLLING-L
Sign Language Linguistics
mailto:LISTSERV@YALEVM.YCC.YALE.EDU

WORDS-L
A multi-topic discussion of anything that relates to the English language
mailto:LISTSERV@UGA.CC.UGA.EDU

Literature

AMLIT-L
American Literature
mailto:LISTSERV@UMCVMB.MISSOURI.EDU

APPLIT
Appalachian Literature and History
mailto:LISTSERV@MSUACAD.MOREHEAD-ST.EDU

AUSTEN-L
Works of Jane Austen and her Contemporaries
mailto:LISTSERV@vm1.mcgill.ca

BENSON
Discussion of author EF Benson's works
mailto:MAJORDOMO@WORLD.STD.COM

BIBLIO
Discussion of Fine Book Collecting
mailto:BIBLIO-REQUEST@IRIS.CLAREMONT.EDU

BLAKE ONLINE
Discussion of Poet and Artist William Blake
mailto:blake-request@albion.com

BLISTER
General mailing list for books
mailto:MAJORDOMO@WORLD.STD.COM

BRONTE
Discussion of the Bronte sisters and their works
mailto:MAJORDOMO@WORLD.STD.COM

CANLIT-L
Discussion of Canadian Literature
mailto:MAILSERV@NLC-BNC.CA

CHAUCER
Discussion of Medieval English Literature
mailto:LISTSERV@SIUCVMB.SIU.EDU

CHAUCER
Discussion of Chaucer and Medieval English Literature
mailto:LISTSERV@UNLINFO.UNL.EDU

CHILDLIT
Discussion of Children's Literature
mailto:LISTSERV@RUTVM1.RUTGERS.EDU

CHPOEM-L
Sharing and Discussion of Chinese Poems
mailto:LISTSERV@UBVM.CC.BUFFALO.EDU

CHRISTLIT
Discussion of Interrelations Between Christianity and Literature
mailto:LISTSERV@BETHEL.EDU

COMPARATIVE-LITERATURE
Comparative literature study and disciplines
mailto:MAILBASE@MAILBASE.AC.UK

E-POETRY
Distribution of an Interactive Literary Journal
mailto:LISTSERV@UBVM.CC.BUFFALO.EDU

FICTION
Discussion of Fiction Writing
mailto:LISTSERV@PSUVM.PSU.EDU

FWAKE-L
Discussion of Joyce's Finnegan's Wake
mailto:LISTSERV@IRLEARN.UCD.IE

GOTHIC LITERATURE
Discussion of Gothic Literature
mailto:JANET%"MAILBASE@MAILBASE.AC.UK"

HEMING-L
Discussion of Ernest Hemingway's life and works
mailto:MAJORDOMO@MTU.EDU

KIND_SPIRIT
Discussion of 'Anne of Green Gables' author Lucy Maud Montgomery
mailto:KIND_SPIRIT-REQUEST@IRUS.RRI.UWO.CA

LITERARY
A general discussion of literature
mailto:LISTSERV@UCF1VM.CC.UCF.EDU

MAGIC-L
A discussion of the books and philosophy of Tom Robbins
mailto:LISTSERV@AMERICAN.EDU

MEMOIR-L
A discussion of published first-person accounts such as memoirs, diaries, and journals
mailto:LISTSERV@VM.CC.LATECH.EDU

MILIEU
Discussion of Writer Julian May and her Works
mailto:MILIEU-REQUEST@YOYO.CC.MONASH.EDU.AU

MODERN-BRITISH-FICTION
Post-war British fiction discussion
mailto:MAILBASE@MAILBASE.AC.UK

NABOKV-L
Scholarly Discussion of Nabokov's Writings
mailto:LISTSERV@UCSBVM.UCSB.EDU

NAT-EDU
An open discussion of Native American Literature
mailto:LISTSERV@INDYCMS.IUPUI.EDU

NATIVELIT-L
An open discussion of Native American Literature
mailto:LISTSERV@CORNELL.EDU

NIGHT-L
Folklore, fact and fiction on supernatural creatures
mailto:LISTPROC@UNICORN.ACS.TTU.EDU

Humanities & Social Sciences – Internet

ORFEO
Renaissance and Baroque Hispanic poetry discussion
mailto:LISTPROC@UNICORN.ACS.TTU.EDU

POET
International poet workshop
mailto:MAJORDOMO@SCRUZ.UCSC.EDU

POLANYI
Discussion of 'post-critical' academic Michael Polanyi
mailto:OWNER-POLANYI@SBU.EDU

PURTOPOI
A discussion of issues in rhetoric and composition, professional writing, and language research
mailto:LISTSERV@VM.CC.PURDUE.EDU

RRA-L
A moderated discussion for readers of romance fiction
mailto:LISTSERV@KENTVM.KENT.EDU

SHAKSPER
A scholarly discussion of current Shakespearean research
mailto:LISTSERV@VM.EPAS.UTORONTO.CA

SUPERGUY
A forum for the posting of sci-fi/fantasy stories as per the list's guidelines
mailto:LISTSERV@UCF1VM.CC.UCF.EDU

TOLKIEN
A discussion of topics related to the writing J.R.R. Tolkien
mailto:LISTSERV@JHUVM.HCF.JHU.EDU

TROLLOPE
Discussion of 19th century English author Anthony Trollope
mailto:MAJORDOMO@WORLD.STD.COM

TWAIN-L
An academic discussion of the life and writings of Mark Twain
mailto:LISTSERV@VM1.YORKU.CA

WEIRD-L
A discussion devoted to weird writing
mailto:LISTSERV@BROWNVM.BROWN.EDU

WRITERS
Discussion of the art, craft, and business of writing
mailto:LISTSERV@VM1.NODAK.EDU

Psychology

ALCOHOL-PSYCHOL
Professional discussion of alchohol comsumption
mailto:MAILBASE@MAILBASE.AC.UK

ATTACHMENT
Discussion of Bowlby-Ainsworth's Theory of Attachment
mailto:MAILBASE@MAILBASE.AC.UK

CLINICAL-PSYCHOLOGY
Clinical psychology issues and practices
mailto:MAILBASE@MAILBASE.AC.UK

COMPUTERS-AND-PSYCHOLOGY
Psychological aspects of computers discussion and issues
mailto:MAILBASE@MAILBASE.AC.UK

CREATIVITY
Philosophy, Sociology, and Psychology of Creativity
mailto:LISTSERV@THINK.NET

HELPLESSNESS
Serious discussion of learned helplessness
mailto:MAILBASE@MAILBASE.AC.UK

IAPSY-L
Communication and Collaboration Among Psychologists Throughout the Americas
mailto:LISTSERV@UACSC2.ALBANY.EDU

IMAGINATION
Electronic Journal for Discussions of the Imagination
mailto:LISTPROC@BOUN.EDU.TR

IOOB-L
Discussion of Industrial/Organizational Psychology
mailto:LISTSERV@UGA.CC.UGA.EDU

OBLOMOV
Discussion of Procrastination Research
mailto:LISTPROC@RUG.NL

PCP
Personal Construct Psychology methodology and theory
mailto:MAILBASE@MAILBASE.AC.UK

PSYC
A moderated E-journal sponsored by the American Psychological Association with articles and general information
mailto:LISTSERV@PUCC.PRINCETON.EDU

PSYCGRAD
An open discussion forum for graduate students in psychology
mailto:LISTSERV@ACADVM1.UOTTAWA.CA

PSYCH-COUNS
Academic and scientific discussion of counselling psychology
mailto:MAILBASE@MAILBASE.AC.UK

PSYCH-EXPTS
Professional psychology discussion of experiment generator packages
mailto:MAILBASE@MAILBASE.AC.UK

PSYCHE-D
A discussion on the subject of consciousness
mailto:LISTSERV@IRIS.RFMH.ORG

PSYCHIATRY-ASSESSMENT
Psychological testing research and clinical issues
mailto:MAILBASE@MAILBASE.AC.UK

PSYCHIATRY-RESOURCES
Discussion of psychiatric and abnormal psychology resource guide
mailto:MAILBASE@MAILBASE.AC.UK

PSYGAME
Psychological, sociological and ethical effects of computer game design
mailto:LISTPROC@U.WASHINGTON.EDU

SCHIZ-L
A forum for communication among researchers interested in schizophrenia
mailto:LISTSERV@UMAB.UMD.EDU

THERAPIST-L
Professional and academic discussion of clinical psychology
mailto:JTM@NETCOM.COM

Sociology

ADOPTEES
Adoption Discussion for Adult Adoptees
mailto:ADOPTEES-REQUEST@UCSD.EDU

CJMOVIES
Reviews and Original Essays on the Intersection of Popular Culture with Criminal Justice
mailto:LISTSERV@ALBANY.EDU

DISASTER RESEARCH
Discussion of Human Behavior in Disasters
mailto:myers_mf@CUBLDR.COLORADO.EDU

FAMLYSCI
Family Science, Therapy, and Sociology
mailto:LISTSERV@UKCC.UKY.EDU

HRS-L
Discussion Among Scholars Interested in the Scientific Study of Human Rights
mailto:LISTSERV@BINGVMB.CC.BINGHAMTON.EDU

NEIGHBORHOOD-DANCE
Discussion of social topics in dance groups
mailto:MAJORDOMO@WORLD.STD.COM

SHARP-L
An interdisciplinary discussion of the history of the printed word
mailto:LISTSERV@IUBVM.UCS.INDIANA.EDU

SOCETH-L
A discussion devoted to interdisciplinary approaches to Social Ethics
mailto:LISTSERV@VM.USC.EDU

SOCIAL-THEORY
Serious discussion of individual and social processes
mailto:MAILBASE@MAILBASE.AC.UK

SOCINFO
Social science discussion of technology and society
mailto:MAILBASE@MAILBASE.AC.UK

Women's Studies

FEMISA
Discussion of Feminism, Gender, Women and International Relations
mailto:LISTSERV@CSF.COLORADO.EDU

FIST
Discussion of women in science and technology
mailto:FIST-REQUEST@HAMP.HAMPSHIRE.EDU

WMST-L
An academic discussion of the teaching, research and administration involved in Women's Studies programs
mailto:LISTSERV@UMDD.UMD.EDU

Internet

Internet Access

COMP-ORG-EFF-NEWS
News to Mail Gateway for Newsgroup comp.org.eff.news
mailto:LISTSERV@EFF.ORG

COMP-ORG-EFF-TALK
Mail to News Gateway for Newsgroup comp.org.eff.talk
mailto:LISTSERV@EFF.ORG

NAMEDROPPERS
Discussion of domain style names
mailto:MAJORDOMO@INTERNIC.NET

UNIX-SOURCES
Gateway for distribution of the newsgroup comp.sources.unix
mailto:UNIX-SOURCES-REQUEST@BRL.MIL

Internet Business

IBJ-L
Electronic Text of the Internet Business Journal
mailto:LISTSERV@PONIECKI.BERKELEY.EDU

IMALL-CHAT
Discussion about Internet Mall Vendors
mailto:LISTSERV@NETCOM.COM

IMALL-L
Emailed Listings of Internet Mall Shops
mailto:LISTSERV@NETCOM.COM

INET-MARKETING
Marketing goods and services on the Internet
mailto:LISTPROC@EINET.NET

Internet Communications

CB-NET
Internet Communication Between China and Western Countries
mailto:LISTPROC@BGU.EDU

ONLINE-NEWS
Discussion of online newspapers and magazine development
mailto:MAJORDOMO@MARKETPLACE.COM

OPERLIST
Discussion of Internet Relay Chat and New Versions
mailto:OPERLIST-REQUEST@EFF.ORG

RXIRC-L
A discussion of technical and usage issues relating to the rxIRC client software which allows one to communicate with Internet Relay Chat servers
mailto:LISTSERV@VMTECQRO.QRO.ITESM.MX

Internet Issues

COM-PRIV
Internet commercialization issues and discussion
mailto:COM-PRIV-REQUEST@PSI.COM

CWD-L
Brock Meek's news service on Internet issues
mailto:MAJORDOMO@CYBERWERKS.COM

CYBERMIND
Discussion of cyberspace effects on subjectivity
mailto:MAJORDOMO@WORLD.STD.COM

HACK-L
Discussion of pirated files posted on worldwide BBS systems
mailto:MAJORDOMO@ALIVE.ERSYS.EDMONTON.AB.CA

HELPNET
A discussion of the uses of global computer networks in times of disaster
mailto:LISTSERV@VM1.NODAK.EDU

IST-MANAGERS
Discussion of Internet mailing list issues
mailto:MAJORDOMO@GREATCIRCLE.COM

MAJORDOMO-USERS
Discussion of Majordomo mailing list problems
mailto:MAJORDOMO-USERS-REQUEST@GREATCIRCLE.COM

NETIQUETTE
Discussion of Internet Etiquette
mailto:NETIQUETTE-REQUEST@ALBION.COM

PRLIST
List for connecting online Puerto Ricans
mailto:PRLIST-REQUEST@HTBBS.COM

QUAKE-L
A discussion of how the Internet may be helpful in the event of an earthquake
mailto:LISTSERV@VM1.NODAK.EDU

WEB4LIB
A discussion about creating and managing library-based World-Wide Web servers and clients
mailto:LISTSERV@LIBRARY.BERKELEY.EDU

Internet Protocols

FSP-DISCUSSION
Discussion of the connection-less FSP protocol
mailto:LISTMASTER@GERMANY.EU.NET

INFO-KERMIT
Kermit user discussion on maintanance, bugs, and general topics
mailto:INFO-KERMIT-REQUEST@WATSON.CC.COLUMBIA.EDU

MHSNEWS
CCITT X.400 (MHS) message handling protocols questions and answers
mailto:MHSNEWS-REQUEST@UNINETT.NO

MSP-L
Message Send Protocol 2
mailto:LISTSERV@ALBANY.EDU

PCIP
A discussion of any TCP/IP implementations for Intel-based computers including Windows Sockets
mailto:LISTSERV@LIST.NIH.GOV

POP
Post Office Protocol and Implementations
mailto:LISTSERV@JHUNIX.HCF.JHU.EDU

RFC Announcements
Announcements of publications from Internet protocal community
mailto:RFC-REQUEST@NIC.DDN.MIL

TCP-IP
TCP/IP protocol professional discussion
mailto:TCP-IP-REQUEST@NIC.DDN.MIL

WINTCP-L
A multi-topic discussion of the Wollongong company's TCP/IP program WINTCP
mailto:LISTSERV@UBVM.CC.BUFFALO.EDU

Internet Resources

ALM-NEWS
Almanac Email Information Server Issues
mailto:ALMANAC@ESUSDA.GOV

ANN-LOTS
Pointers to Sources of Online Information, Indexes, and Lists
mailto:LISTSERV@VM1.NODAK.EDU

BBS-L
Bulletin Board Systems
mailto:LISTSERV@SAUPM00.BITNET

COMP-GOPHER-DIFFS
Distribution and Discussion of Bookmarks to New Gopher Material
mailto:LISTSERV@EFF.ORG

HELP-NET
Discussion about Solving User Problems with Internet/Bitnet Utilities and Software
mailto:LISTSERV@VM.TEMPLE.EDU

MSDOS-ANN
New Additions to Internet Archives
mailto:LISTSERV@SIMTEL.COAST.NET

NET-GUIDE
Updates to EFF's Guide to the Internet
mailto:LISTSERV@EFF.ORG

NET-HAPPENINGS
Distribution of professional networker information service
mailto:MAJORDOMO@IS.INTERNIC.NET

NETTRAIN
Discussion Among Those Involved in Teaching Use of Bitnet and Internet
mailto:LISTSERV@UBVM.CC.BUFFALO.EDU

ORA-NEWS
Announcements from Internet Publisher O'Reilly & Associates
mailto:LISTPROC@ONLINE.ORA.COM

PRACTICE
Practice of LISTSERV Commands
mailto:LISTSERV@ASUVM.INRE.ASU.EDU

ROADMAP
A Free Internet Training Workshop
mailto:LISTSERV@UA1VM.UA.EDU

SCIFAQ-L
A moderated list of articles from Usenet newsgroup sci.answers allowing easy access via email to Usenet FAQ documents
mailto:LISTSERV@YALEVM.CIS.YALE.EDU

VIRTU-L
A discussion of all aspects of virtual reality based on the Use-net newsgroup sci.virtual-worlds
mailto:LISTSERV@VMD.CSO.UIUC.EDU

VPIEJ-L
A discussion of electronic publishing issues with special emphasis on scholarly electronic journals
mailto:LISTSERV@VTVM1.CC.VT.EDU

WWW-ANNOUNCE
The WWW
mailto:LISTSERV@INFO.CERN.CH

Internet Security

DIGIANARCH
Internet censorship issues and discussion
mailto:DIGIANARCH@IDS.NET

FIREWALLS
Discussion of maintaining Internet firewalls
mailto:MAJORDOMO@GREATCIRCLE.COM

INFO-PGP
Discussion of Public Key Encryption Programs
mailto:INFO-PGP-REQUEST@LUCPUL.IT.LUC.EDU

JUDGES-L
Security System to Protect Network News System Against Overload from Multiple Posts
mailto:LISTSERV@UBVM.CC.BUFFALO.EDU

PGP-PUBLIC-KEYS
Pretty Good Privacy public key distribution mailing list
mailto:MAJORDOMO@C2.ORG

WWW-SECURITY
WWW security standards and implementation
mailto:WWW-SECURITY-REQUEST@NSMX.RUTGERS.EDU

Internet Services

LYCOS-USERS
Discussion of the WWW lycos server developments and applications
mailto:MAJORDOMO@MAIL.MSEN.COM

NET-HAPPENINGS
A forum for the announcements of events, tools, lists, and conferences on the internet
mailto:LISTSERV@IS.INTERNIC.NET

NEW-LIST
A forum for the posting of new public mailing lists
mailto:LISTSERV@VM1.NODAK.EDU

NOTGNU
Discussion of the NotGNU Internet Service
mailto:NOTGNU-REQUEST@NETCOM.COM

USENET-ORACLE
Newsgroup offering answers to any and all questions
mailto:ORACLE-ADMIN@CS.INDIANA.EDU

WEB-SUPPORT
Discussion of WWW issues, browsers and servers
mailto:MAILBASE@MAILBASE.AC.UK

WWW-BUYINFO
WWW purchased information issues and resources
mailto:WWW-BUYINFO-REQUEST@ALLEGRA.ATT.COM

WWW-MANAGERS
Questions and answers for WWW server maintenance
mailto:MAJORDOMO@LISTS.STANFORD.EDU

WWW-SPEED
Discussion of WWW performance issues
mailto:WWW-SPEED-REQUEST@TIPPER.OIT.UNC.EDU

WWWORDER
Discussion of WWW catalog creation and related issues
mailto:LISTPROC@EINET.NET

Internet Tools

ARIE-L
Usage of the Ariel Document Transmission System for the Internet
mailto:LISTSERV@LISTSERV.NET

BIND
Berkeley Internet Name Domain (BIND) domain software information
mailto:bind-request@uunet.uu.net

DOSLYNX-DEV
Distribution of DosLynx-related Information, Updates, and Development Discussion
mailto:LISTSERV@UKANAIX.CC.UKANS.EDU

IFIP-GTWY
IFIP 6.5 Task Group on Gateways issues and discussion
mailto:IFIP-GTWY-REQUEST@ICS.UCI.EDU

IRCHAT
Discussion of GNU's Interface to the Internet Relay Chat
mailto:IRCHAT-REQUEST@CC.TUT.FI

KIOSKS-L
Discussion of Kiosk Hardware and Software
mailto:KIOSKS-L-REQUEST@LANL.GOV

LDBASE-L
A forum discussing the Listserve Database Search facility
mailto:LISTSERV@UKANVM.CC.UKANS.EDU

MOSAIC-L
Mosaic Users and Developers
mailto:LISTSERV@UICVM.UIC.EDU

NETBLAZER-USERS
Discussion of Telebit NetBlazer products
mailto:NETBLAZER-USERS-REQUEST@TELEBIT.COM

NETJAM
Internet Collaboration on Musical Compositions Through
mailto:NETJAM-REQUEST@XCF.BERKELEY.EDU

NNMVS-L
An open discussion of the MVS/TSO NNTP News Reader
mailto:LISTSERV@VM.USC.EDU

NUNTIUS-L
A discussion of the Nuntius Newsreader for Macintoshes
mailto:LISTSERV@CORNELL.EDU

WAIS-DISCUSSION
A moderated discussion about WAIS related topics
mailto:LISTSERV@THINK.COM

WAIS-TALK
An interactive discussion of WAIS for implementors
mailto:LISTSERV@THINK.COM

WWW-HTML
HTML Language
mailto:LISTSERV@INFO.CERN.CH

WWW-PROXY
WWW Proxies, Caching, and Servers
mailto:LISTSERV@INFO.CERN.CH

WWW-RDB
Gatewaying Relational Databases into WWW
mailto:LISTSERV@INFO.CERN.CH

WWW-TALK
Technical Design Discussion of WWW Software
mailto:LISTSERV@INFO.CERN.CH

Networking

BIG-LAN
Issues in Designing and Operating Campus-size LANs
mailto:BIG-LAN-REQUEST@SUVM.SYR.EDU or LISTSERV@SUVM.ACS.SYR.EDU

CISCO
Cisco Systems, Inc. network product information and problems
mailto:CISCO-REQUEST@SPOT.COLORADO.EDU

COMMUNET
Issues, Technologies, Implications of Computer-based Networking
mailto:LISTSERV@UVMVM.UVM.EDU

CW-EMAIL
Discussion of Campus-wide Email Systems
mailto:LISTSERV@EARNCC.EARN.NET

GNET
Documents on bring the Internet to poorer nations
mailto:GNET_REQUEST@DHVX20.CSUDH.EDU

INFO-NETS-REQUEST
Networking questions, discussions, and information
mailto:INFO-NETS-REQUEST@THINK.COM

NAMNET
Discussion of Electronic Networking in Namibia
mailto:NAMNET-REQUEST@LISSE.NA

NETW4-L
Discussion of Internet System Software Novell Netware
mailto:LISTPROC@BGU.EDU

SCOUT-REPORT
Weekly publication on Internet network activities
mailto:MAJORDOMO@IS.INTERNIC.NET

SCOUT-REPORT-HTML
Mailing list for newsletter on Internet networking activities
mailto:MAJORDOMO@IS.INTERNIC.NET

Organizations

BITNEWS
A discussion centering on BitNet news and administrative developments
mailto:LISTSERV@BITNIC.EDUCOM.EDU

IETF
Discussion for the Internet Engineering Task Force
mailto:IETF-REQUEST@NRI.RESTON.VA.US

IETF-ANNOUNCE
Announcements for the Internet Engineering Task Force
mailto:IETF-ANNOUNCE-REQUEST@NRI.RESTON.VA.US

IMR
Monthly Newsletter on Internet Research Group Accomplishments
mailto:IMR-REQUEST@ISI.EDU

Virtual Communities

IND-NET
Electronic community dialogue on American Indian issues
mailto:LISTPROC@LISTPROC.WSU.EDU

WWW-VRML
Discussion of WWW virtual reality design
mailto:MAJORDOMO@WIRED.COM

Law & Criminal Justice

Constitutional Law

AWD
Discussion of the Americans with Disabilities Act litigation and regulations
mailto:MAJORDOMO@COUNTERPOINT.COM

Criminal Justice

LEGALTEN
Discussion of law in mental health system
mailto:MAJORDOMO@WORLD.STD.COM

PRISON-L
Discussions Among Prison Teachers
mailto:LISTSERV@DARTCMS1.DARTMOUTH.EDU

Family Law

FREE-L
Exchange of Information about Fathers' Rights
mailto:LISTSERV@INDYCMS.IUPUI.EDU

Y-RIGHTS
A discussion on the legal and societal rights of youths
mailto:LISTSERV@SJUVM.STJOHNS.EDU

International & Comparative Law

IRISHLAW
Discussion of Irish Law
mailto:LISTSERV@IRLEARN.UCD.IE

Law Schools

LAWSCH-L
A discussion of issues affecting all law students
mailto:LISTSERV%AUVM.BITNET@VM1.NODAK.EDU

STUDENTLAWTECH
Discussion Among Law Students about Law and Technology
mailto:LISTSERV@LISTSERV.LAW.CORNELL.EDU

Legal History & Theory

LAWSOC-L
Inter-disciplinary discussion of Canadian law theory
mailto:LAWSOC-L-REQUEST@CC.UMANITOBA.CA

RELIGIONLAW
Discussion of Religion and the Law
mailto:LISTSERV@GRIZZLY.UCLA.EDU

Legal Resources

INFO-LAW
Discussion of computer use in law
mailto:INFO-LAW-REQUEST@BRL.MIL

NOCALL-LIST
Northern California Association of Law Libraries issues
mailto:MAJORDOMO@NETCOM.COM

Litigation & Procedures

EDLAW
Discussion Among Education Law Instructors and Practitioners
mailto:LISTSERV@UKCC.UKY.EDU

FORENS-L
Discussion of forensic use in court
mailto:FORENS-REQUEST@ACC.FAU.EDU

Organizations

ALL-OF-ELSA
European Law Students Assocation discussion
mailto:akj@jus.uio.no

JUST-L
Professional and Academic Discussion of Justice Administration Issues
mailto:LISTPROC@BGU.EDU

Reference

LAWLIBREF-L
Discussion List for Reference Librarians in Law Libraries
mailto:LISTSERV@ACC.WUACC.EDU

Popular Culture & Entertainment

Automobiles

BRITISH-CARS
British automobile appreciation, information and resources
mailto:BRITISH-CARS-REQUEST@AUTOX.TEAM.NET

DATSUN-ROADSTERS
Discussion of Datsun Roadsters
mailto:DATSUN-ROADSTERS-REQUEST@AUTOX.TEAM.NET

EXOTIC-CARS
Discussion of Limited Production Automobiles
mailto:EXOTIC-CARS-REQUEST@SOL.ASL.HITACHI.COM

F-BODY
Discussion of Camaros and Firebirds
mailto:F-BODY-REQUEST@SPDCC.COM

FORDNATICS
Discussion of High performance Fords
mailto:FORDNATICS-REQUEST@FREUD.ARC.NASA.GOV

HARLEYS
Discussion of Harley-Davidson Motorcycles
mailto:HARLEY-REQUEST@THINKAGE.ON.CA

HONDA
Discussion of Honda and Acura automobiles
mailto:HONDA-REQUEST@MSRC.SUNYSB.EDU

HOTROD
Discussion of High performance Vehicles
mailto:HOTROD-REQUEST@DIXIE.COM

ITALIAN-CARS
Discussion of Italian made automobiles
mailto:ITALIAN-CARS-REQUEST@BALLTOWN.CMA.COM

JAG-LOVERS
Maintenance, restoration and information of Jaguar automobiles
mailto:scott@psy.uwa.edu.au

LOTUS-CARS
Discussion of Colin Chapman-designed Road and Race Cars
mailto:LOTUS-CARS-REQUEST@NETCOM.COM

MAZDA-LIST
Discussion of Mazda Vehicles
mailto:MAZDA-LIST-REQUEST@MS.UKY.EDU

MIATA
Discussion of the Mazda Miata Automobile
mailto:MIATA-REQUEST@JHUNIX.HCF.JHU.EDU

MOPAR
Discussion and Appreciation of Chrysler Corporation Motor Vehicles
mailto:MOPAR-REQUEST@THOR.ISP.NWU.EDU

MR2-INTEREST
Discussion of Toyota MR2s
mailto:MR2-INTEREST-REQUEST@VALIDGH.COM

MUSTANGS
Discussion of Late Model Ford Mustangs
mailto:mustangs-request@cup.hp.com

OFFROAD
Discussion of Offfroad Adventuring
mailto:OFFROAD-REQUEST@AI.GTRI.GATECH.EDU

PORSCHEPHILES
Porsche automobiles discussion of maintenance and sales
mailto:PORSCHEPHILES-REQUEST@TTA.COM

QUATTRO
Discussion of Audi cars, primarily AWD quattro models
mailto:QUATTRO-REQUEST@ARIES.EAST.SUN.COM

SAAB_NETWORK
Discussion of SAAB automobiles
mailto:SAAB@NETWORK.MHS.COMPUSERVE.COM

SWEDISHBRICKS
International discussion of Volvo automobiles
mailto:SWEDISHBRICKS-REQUEST@ME.ROCHESTER.EDU

VINTAGVW
A discussion on maintenance and care of early model Volkswagens
mailto:LISTSERV@SJSUVM1.SJSU.EDU

Z-CARS
Datsun/Nissan Z cars discussion
mailto:Z-CAR-REQUEST@DIXIE.COM

Books

A.RICE
Discussion of the works of Anne Rice
mailto:NGUSTAS%HAMPVMS.BITNET@VM1.NODAK.EDU

BOOK-TALK
Upcoming Book, CD, and Video Titles
mailto:LISTSERV@COLUMBIA.ILC.COM

BOOKNEWS
Reviews of Upcoming Books, CDs, and Videos
mailto:listserv@columbia.ilc.com

BOSTON-BOOK
Discussion for Boston area book lovers
mailto:MAJORDOMO@WORLD.STD.COM

COMIX
Discussion of mainstream and alternative comic books
mailto:MAJORDOMO@WORLD.STD.COM

DERYNI-L
Discussion of science fiction writer Katherine Kurtz
mailto:MAIL-SERVER@MINTIR.NEW-ORLEANS.LA.US

DOROTHYL
Discussion Among Mystery Lovers
mailto:LISTSERV@KENTVM.KENT.EDU

FANTASY
Fantasy fiction discussion
mailto:LISTPROC@UNICORN.ACS.TTU.EDU

MERCEDES-LACKEY
Discussion of fantasy writer Mercedes Lackey
mailto:LISTPROC@UEL.AC.UK

Popular Culture & Entertainment

QUANTA-ASCII
Electronic journal of Science Fiction and Fantasy
mailto:MAJORDOMO@NETCOM.COM

QUANTA-NOTICE
Notification message for new versions of Quanta science fiction journal
mailto:MAJORDOMO@NETCOM.COM

QUANTA-POSTSCRIPT
Electronic science fiction magazine Quanta
mailto:MAJORDOMO@NETCOM.COM

SF-LIST
Science fiction genre discussion
mailto:LISTPROC@UNICORN.ACS.TTU.EDU

SF-LIT
Science fiction and fantasy in media issues and discussion
mailto:LISTPROC@LOC.GOV

SF-LOVERS
Science fiction in pop culture discussion
mailto:SF-LOVERS-REQUEST@RUTGERS.EDU

SPECTRUM-BOL
Spectrum-Bol online publishing announcements and discussion
mailto:73774.2733@COMPUSERVE.COM

THRILLPOWER
Discussion of British comic 2000AD and related materials
mailto:THRILLPOWER-REQUEST@THEPOINT.COM

UK-SF-BOOKS
Discussion of UK science fiction authors and their books
mailto:LISTPROC@UEL.AC.UK

VAMPYRES
Vampire Stories
mailto:LISTSERV@GUVM.CCF.GEORGETOWN.EDU

Celebrities & Personalities

KEANU-L
A discussion of Keanu Reeves
mailto:LISTSERV@CORNELL.EDU

Family & Community

BRTHPRNT
Discussion Among Birthparents of Adopted Children
mailto:LISTSERV@INDYCMS.IUPUI.EDU

CHILDFREE
Digest version of child-free information and support mailing list
mailto:CHILDFREE-REQUEST-DIGEST@LUNCH.ASD.SGI.COM

CHILDFREE
Information and support for child-free people
mailto:CHILDFREE-REQUEST@LUNCH.ASD.SGI.COM

TEXWOHIST-L
Discussion by and of Texan women
mailto:TEXWOHIST-L-REQUEST@VENUS.TWU.EDU

TWINS
Discussion of twins-related issues
mailto:OWNER-TWINS@ATHENA.MIT.EDU

URBANITES
Discussion of self-sufficiency in urban life
mailto:URBANITES-REQUEST@PSYCHE.MIT.EDU

Fashion

F-COSTUME
Fantasy costume and clothing resources and techniques
mailto:F-COSTUME-REQUEST@LUNCH.ASD.SGI.COM

H-COSTUME
Discussion of Accurate Historical Clothing Reproduction
mailto:H-COSTUME-REQUEST@ANDREW.CMU.EDU

VINTAGE
Restoration discussion and sale announcements of vintage clothing and jewelry
mailto:VINTAGE-REQUEST@LUNCH.ASD.SGI.COM

WEARABLE
Discussion of wearable art and original clothing creation
mailto:WEARABLE-REQUEST@LUNCH.ASD.SGI.COM

Genealogy

LINES-L
A discussion of the Lifelines Genialogical Database and Report Generator
mailto:LISTSERV@VM1.NODAK.EDU

ROOTS-L
A discussion of tools, techniques, and requests for genealogical research
mailto:LISTSERV@VM1.NODAK.EDU

Humor

BONG-L
Weekly Humor Newsletter
mailto:LISTSERV@NETCOM.COM

HUMOR
Humor of All Types, Topics, and Tastes
mailto:LISTSERV@UGA.CC.UGA.EDU

REHU-L
Religious Humor
mailto:LISTSERV@BGU.EDU

STHL-L
Star Trek Humor
mailto:LISTSERV@NIC.SURFNET.NL

TOP5
A David Letterman-Style Comedy List
mailto:LISTSERV@GITVM1.GATECH.EDU

Lifestyles

BISEXU-L
Bisexuality and Related Issues
mailto:LISTSERV@BROWNVM.BROWN.EDU

COUPLES-L
Discussion of Heterosexual Relationships
mailto:LISTSERV@CORNELL.EDU

GENERATION X
Discussion of Generation X Issues and Lifestyles
mailto:MMILOTAY@GALAXY.GOV.BC.CA

GLB-NEWS
Read-only Information for Gay, Lesbian, Bisexual, Transsexual, Transgender, and Sympathetic Persons
mailto:LISTSERV@BROWNVM.BROWN.EDU

MAXLIFE
A discussion of issues relating to a positive and healthy life style
mailto:LISTSERV@LISTSERV.UNC.EDU

SINGLES
Discussion of the Single Life and Related Topics
mailto:LISTSERV@UTMB.EDU

UK-DANCE
A discussion of rave culture in the United Kingdom
mailto:LISTSERV@ORBITAL.DEMON.CO.UK

Media

FRANCE-MEDIA
French broadcasting media research and information
mailto:MAILBASE@MAILBASE.AC.UK

PROG-PUBS
Progressive and alternative publication and media
mailto:PROG-PUBS-REQUEST@FUGGLES.ACC.VIRGINIA.EDU

RADIOPREP
Radio show issues
mailto:MAJORDOMO@HALCYON.COM

Movies

HIGHLA-L
Discussion of the Highlander Movies and TV Series
mailto:LISTSERV@PSUVM.PSU.EDU

HORROR
Discussion of Horror Films and Fiction
mailto:LISTSERV@PACEVM.DAC.PACE.EDU

MOVIES-SEIVOM
Discussion of Self-referential Movies that Break the Fourth Wall
mailto:MOVIES-SEIVOM@KINEXIS.COM

Multimedia

CDPUB
CDROM publishing systems, standards, and hardware issues
mailto:MAIL-SERVER@KNEX.VIA.MIND.ORG

PERSPECTIVE
Newsletter on interactive program industry and applications
mailto:PERSPECTIVE-REQUEST@DIGMEDIA.COM

Museums & Theme Parks

MUSEUM-L
A general discussion of museums for all museum professionals and other interested people
mailto:LISTSERV@UNMVMA.UNM.EDU

Television

90210
Fox TV show Beverly Hills 90210 discussion
mailto:90210-request@ferkel.ucsb.edu

B5-REVIEW-L
The Babylon 5 Television Series and Related Information
mailto:LISTSERV@CORNELL.EDU

CLARISSA
Discussion of Clarissa Explains It All
mailto:CLARISSA-REQUEST@FERKEL.UCSB.EDU

DRWHO-L
Discussion of science fiction show Dr. Who
mailto:LISTPROC@UEL.AC.UK

FAB-L
Discussion of Producer Gerry Anderson
mailto:LISTPROC@UEL.AC.UK

FAB-UFO
Discussion of Gerry Anderson-Produced Science Fiction Show UFO
mailto:LISTPROC@UEL.AC.UK

FLAMINGO
Discussion of TV series 'Parker Lewis'
mailto:FLAMINGO-REQUEST@LENNY.CORP.SGI.COM

GARGOYLES
Discussion of Disney animated series Gargoyles
mailto:MAJORDOMO@SARD.MV.NET

GLDISCLIST
Discussion of the soap opera Guiding Light
mailto:GLDISCLIST-OWNER@UCLINK.BERKELEY.EDU

GUIDINGLIST
Discussion of the soap opera Guiding Light
mailto:GUIDINGLIST-OWNER@UCLINK.BERKELEY.EDU

KFTLC-L
Discussion of TV Show, Kung Fu—The Legend Continues
mailto:LISTSERV@PSUVM.PSU.EDU

LATE-SHOW-NEWS
Weekly Electronic Newsletter on Late-Night Talk Shows
mailto:LISTPROC@ECHONYC.COM

LOVINGLIST
Discussion of soap opera Loving
mailto:LOVINGLIST-OWNER@UCLINK.BERKELEY.EDU

MAYBERRY
A discussion of telivision shows starring Andy Griffith
mailto:LISTSERV@BOLIS.SF-BAY.ORG

Party-of-Five
Discussion of Fox series 'Party of Five'
mailto:PARTY-OF-FIVE-REQUEST@WWA.COM

REDDWARF
Discussion of UK comedy 'Red Dwarf'
mailto:LISTPROC@UEL.AC.UK

STARTREK
A discussion based in Europe of all aspects of Star Trek
mailto:LISTSERVER@LE.AC.UK

STREK-L
A wide-ranging discussion of the television program Star Trek
mailto:LISTSERV%PCCVM.BITNET@CMSA.BERKELEY.EDU

TREK-REVIEW-L
An edited fanzine of reviews and commentary for the entire Star Trek series
mailto:LISTSERV@CORNELL.EDU

TREKWRTR
Discussions Among Star Trek Script Writers
mailto:LISTSERV@PCCVM.SYCRCI.PCC.EDU

TV-L
A general discussion of television programs
mailto:LISTSERV%TREARN.BITNET@VM1.NODAK.EDU

TV2NITE-L
A Daily Guide to Prime Time Network and Cable Television
mailto:LISTSERV@NETCOM.COM

VULCAN-L
Star Trek Planet and Culture of Vulcan
mailto:LISTSERV@NETCOM.COM

WILDWEST
Discussion of western TV show The Wild Wild West
mailto:LISTPROC@MOOSE.UVM.EDU

Unexplained Phenomena

PSI-L
A discussion of experiences with and research in PSI (e.g. ESP, out-of-body experiences)
mailto:LISTSERV@VM.ITS.RPI.EDU

Weather & Traffic

WX-TALK
A discussion of weather-related phenomena
mailto:LISTSERV@VMD.CSO.UIUC.EDU

Religion & Philosophy

Doctrines

APOLOGIA-L
Discussion for Biblical Christian apologetics
mailto:MAJORDOMO@NETCOM.COM

B-GREEK
Serious discussion of the Greek Bible
mailto:MAJORDOMO@VIRGINIA.EDU

CATHOLIC
Discussion of Orthodox Catholic Theology Issues
mailto:CATHOLIC-REQUEST@SARTO.GAITHERSBURG.MD.US

HINDU-D
Discussion of Various Hindu Doctrines as Applied to Daily Living
mailto:LISTSERV@ARIZVM1.CCIT.ARIZONA.EDU

JEWISH
Non-abusive Discussion of Jewish Topics and Jewish Law
mailto:LISTSERV@ISRAEL.NYSERNET.ORG

Individuals

BATAILLE
Philosophy of Bataille
mailto:LISTSERV@THINK.NET

BAUDRILLARD
Philosophy of Jean Baudrillard
mailto:LISTSERV@THINK.NET

BELIEF-L
Personal Ideologies, Morals, and Ethics
mailto:LISTSERV@BROWNVM.BROWN.EDU

BENJAMIN
Philosophy of Walter Benjamin
mailto:LISTSERV@THINK.NET

DERRIDA
Discussion of Jacques Derrida
mailto:LISTSERV%CFRVM.BITNET@uga.cc.uga.edu

FOUCAULT
Discussion of Michel Foucault
mailto:LISTSERV@THINK.NET

KIERKEGAARD
Library, discussion and questions on philosopher Soren Kierkegaard
mailto:KIERKEGAARD-REQUEST@STOLAF.EDU

NIETZSCH
Scholarly and Interdisciplinary Discussions of Friedrich Nietzsche
mailto:LISTSERV@DARTMOUTH.EDU

PEIRCE-L
Discussion of philosopher and scientists Charles Sanders Peirce
mailto:LISTPROC@UNICORN.ACS.TTU.EDU

Philosophy

ECOTHEOL
Discussion of ecology from a theological perspective
mailto:MAILBASE@MAILBASE.AC.UK

ENVIROETHICS
Academic Discussion of Environmental Ethics
mailto:MAILBASE@MAILBASE.AC.UK

FICTION-OF-PHILOSOPHY
Discussion of philosophy in fiction
mailto:MAJORDOMO@WORLD.STD.COM

LOGIC-L
A pedagogical and theoretical discussion of elementary logic
mailto:LISTSERV@BUCKNELL.EDU

MDVLPHIL
A discussion of the philosophy and socio-political thought of the middle ages
mailto:LISTSERV@LSUVM.SNCC.LSU.EDU

MOCHIN
Intelligence's Role in World Transformation
mailto:LISTSERV@ISRAEL.NYSERNET.ORG

PHIL-LIT
A discussion and exchange forum which links the fields of philosophy and literature
mailto:LISTSERV@TAMVM1.TAMU.EDU

PHILOSOP
A discussion forum for topics relating to adademic philosophy
mailto:LISTSERV@VM1.YORKU.CA

SEMIOS-L
A discussion of various topics relating to semiotics
mailto:LISTSERV@ULKYVM.LOUISVILLE.EDU

SOPHIA
A discussion of Ancient Philosophy
mailto:LISTSERV@LIVERPOOL.AC.UK

UUS-L
A discussion of the Unitarian Universalist philosophy and a forum for the distribution of UU-related information
mailto:LISTSERV@UBVM.CC.BUFFALO.EDU

Religions

AMERCATH
History of American Catholicism
mailto:LISTSERV@UKCC.UKY.EDU

Religion & Philosophy – Science

BALTUVA
Issues of Concern to Observant Jews
mailto:LISTSERV@VM1.MCGILL.CA

BAPTIST
Baptist Experience
mailto:LISTSERV@UKCC.UKY.EDU

BUDDHA-L
Buddhism for Serious Academic Discussion
mailto:LISTSERV@ULKYVM.LOUISVILLE.EDU

BUDDHIST-PHILOSOPHY
Buddhist Philosophy
mailto:LISTSERV@THINK.NET

CATHOLIC
Discussion of Roman Catholic, Anglo-Catholic, and Orthodox Catholic Approaches to Christianity
mailto:LISTSERV@AMERICAN.EDU

CATHOLIC-ACTION
Discussion of Catholic Religion Values and Issues
mailto:RFREEMAN@VPNET.CHI.IL.US

CELL-CHURCH
Discussion of the nontraditional religion 'Cell Church'
mailto:CELL-CHURCH-REQUEST@BIBLE.ACU.EDU

IHP-NET
Inter-faith discussion of spirituality and health issues
mailto:MAJORDOMO@INTERACCESS.COM

JAIN-L
Discussion of the non-Vedic Indian Religion Jainism
mailto:JAIN-REQUEST@INDIRECT.COM

LITURGY
Inter-disciplinary discussion of Christian liturgy history and tradition
mailto:MAILBASE@MAILBASE.AC.UK

LTHRN-L
Discussion of Lutheran Church Social and Theological Issues
mailto:LISTPROC2@BGU.EDU

MENNO
A moderated discussion of the Anabaptist/Mennonite religions
mailto:LISTSERV@UCI.COM

OLDCATH-L
The Independent Catholic Movement and The Old Catholic Communion
mailto:LISTSERV@STOUR.IINET.COM.AU

PJAL
A discussion forum for Jewish organizations and activists who operate according to organized principles
mailto:LISTSERV@ISRAEL.NYSERNET.ORG

PJML
An open forum for progressive Jews and progressive Jewish activists and organizations
mailto:LISTSERV@ISRAEL.NYSERNET.ORG

QUAKER-L
Discussion of Quakerism
mailto:LISTSERV@VMD.CSO.UIUC.EDU

RELIGION-ALL
Religion-related list distribution information
mailto:MAILBASE@MAILBASE.AC.UK

SHABBATSHALOM
A Jewish Spiritual Connection for Non-Practicing Jews
mailto:LISTSERV@ISRAEL.NYSERNET.ORG

SHAKER
A wide-ranging discussion of the history, culture, and beliefs of the Shakers
mailto:LISTSERV@UKCC.UKY.EDU

SPIRIT-L
Spirituality in Secular Roman Catholic Life
mailto:LISTSERV@AMERICAN.EDU

TECHSPIRIT-L
Implications of Technospirituality
mailto:LISTSERVER@WILLIAMS.EDU

WITTENBERG
Lutheran Church history announcments and research
mailto:MAILSERV@CRF.CUIS.EDU

Religious History

ECCHST-L
MIDEAST-PEACE is a discussion list for Middle East scholars, businesspeople, and/or residents. Discussions of all issues related to the peace processes between the PLO and Israel, and between Jordan and Israel, are welcome here
mailto:LISTSERV@AIS.NET

H-AMREL
Discussion of Religion's Influence on American Society from Pre-Colonial Era to Present
mailto:LISTSERV@MSU.EDU

IOUDAIOS
An academic discussion of first-century Judaism with special attention to the writings of Philo of Alexandria and Flavius Josephus
mailto:LISTSERV@VM1.YORKU.CA

ISLAM-L
A discussion of the history of Islam
mailto:LISTSERV@ULKYVM.LOUISVILLE.EDU

Resources

AIBI-L
Computerized Analysis of the Bible and Related Texts
mailto:LISTSERV@ACADVM1.UOTTAWA.CA

BIBLE-L
The Bible
mailto:LISTSERV@GITVM1.GATECH.EDU

FEMREL-L
Discussion and Resources Concerning Women, Religion, and Feminist Theology
mailto:LISTSERV@MIZZOU1.MISSOURI.EDU

PARANORMAL
Parapsychology theoretical and philosophical issues and projects
mailto:MAILBASE@MAILBASE.AC.UK

Science

Agriculture

AG-EXP-L
Expert Systems in Agricultural Production and Management
mailto:LISTSERV@VM1.NODAK.EDU

ERS-REPORTS
US Department of Agriculture Situation and Outlook Reports
mailto:ALMANAC@ESUSDA.GOV

GOATS
Goat management questions and answers
mailto:LISTPROC@LISTPROC.WSU.EDU

LEAFMULCH-MG
Environmental/Agricultural Discussion of Leaf Mulching
mailto:ALMANAC@ESUSDA.GOV

PIGFARM
Pig breeding and production issues
mailto:MAISER@IST01.FERRIS.EDU

TRICKLE-L
An unmoderated discussion of trickle or drip irrigation
mailto:LISTSERV@UNL.EDU

USDA.DVM
Newsletter for veterinary medicine, science, and agriculture
mailto:ALMANAC@ESUSDA.GOV

VEG-PROD-MG
Discussion of vegetable production, marketing and research
mailto:ALMANAC@ESUSDA.GOV

Aquatic Sciences

AQUA-L
Science, Technology, and Business of Breeding Aquatic Species
mailto:LISTSERV@VM.UOGUELPH.CA

CICHLID-L
Discussion of Cichlidae Freshwater Fish
mailto:MAILSERV@NRM.SE

DEEPSEA
Deep-sea and Hydrothermal Vent Biologists
mailto:LISTSERV@UVVM.UVIC.CA

Astronomy

ASTRO
Discussion of Astronomy
mailto:LISTSERV@GITVM1.GATECH.EDU

Biology

BEE-L
Biology about Bees
mailto:LISTSERV@UACSC2.ALBANY.EDU

BIO-SOFTWARE
Discussion of software for the biological sciences
mailto:BIOSCI%NET.BIO.NET@VM1.NODAK.EDU

BNFNET-L
Biological Nitrogen Fixation
mailto:LISTSERV@FINHUTC.HUT.FI

CAMEL-L
Camel Research and Studies
mailto:LISTSERV@LISTSERV.NET

CDN-L
Human head growth and development information
mailto:MAJORDOMO@PO.CWRU.EDU

CBT-GENERAL
Professional discussion of biological timing research news and comments
mailto:CBT-GENERAL-REQUEST@VIRGINIA.EDU

CELLWALL
Discussion of Plant Cell Wall Biology
mailto:LISTSERV@VM1.NoDak.EDU

CRUST-L
Discussion of Crustacean Biology
mailto:LISTSERV@SIVM.SI.EDU

CVNET
Communication for vision and color research
mailto:CVNET@VM1.YORKU.CA

Mailing Lists

HUMAN-GENOME-PROGRAM
Genome-related issues and discussion
mailto:BIOSCI-SERVER@NET.BIO.NET

HUMBIO-L
Variety of biological science topics
mailto:HUMBIO-REQUEST@ACC.FAU.EDU

HUMEVO
Human Biological Evolution
mailto:LISTSERV@GWUVM.GWU.EDU

LACTACID
A discussion of the biology and uses of lactic acid bacteria
mailto:LISTSERV@SEARN.SUNET.SE

OPTICS
Optic field announcements, ideas and discussion
mailto:MAILSERV@TOE.TOWSON.EDU

PLANT-HORMONES
Plant hormone research discussion
mailto:MAILBASE@MAILBASE.AC.UK

PLANT-TAXONOMY
Plant taxonomy discussion and announcements
mailto:MAILBASE@MAILBASE.AC.UK

POPULATION-BIOLOGY
Serious academic discussion of population biology
mailto:BIOSCI-SERVER@NET.BIO.NET

PORIFERA
All aspects of sponge biology and chemistry
mailto:MAILBASE@MAILBASE.AC.UK

PRIMATOLOGY
Human and non-human primate studies and research
mailto:MAILBASE@MAILBASE.AC.UK

RADIOBIOLOGY
Informal professional discussion of radiobiology issues
mailto:MAILBASE@MAILBASE.AC.UK

SOCINSCT
A university level research discussion of social insect biology focussing on but not limited to Eusocial insects
mailto:LISTSERV@ALBANY.EDU

Biosciences

BIODICEN-L
Biodiversity Data and Information
mailto:LISTSERV@UCJEPS.BERKELEY.EDU

BIOMCH-L
Biomechanics and Human or Animal Movement Science
mailto:LISTSERV@NIC.SURFNET.NL

BIOPHYS
Academic discussion of all aspects of biophysics
mailto:BIOSCI-SERVER@NET.BIO.NET

BIOTECH
Discussion of Biotechnology
mailto:LISTSERV@LISTSERV.NET

CYTONET
Scientific discussion of biosciences
mailto:BIOSCI-SERVER@NET.BIO.NET

GENTALK
Discussion of Genetics and Genetic Engineering Issues
mailto:LISTSERV@USA.NET

HUM-MOLGEN
Discussion and Announcements Related to Human Molecular Genetics
mailto:LISTSERV@NIC.SURFNET.NL

MOLBIO_NYSAES-L
A discussion of issues in plant molecular Biology and related topics
mailto:LISTSERV@CORNELL.EDU

Botany

BEN
Newsletter on botany and plant ecology in Canada and Pacific Northwest
mailto:aceska@cue.bc.ca

BROM-L
The Bromeliaceae Plant Family and Related Subjects
mailto:LISTSERV@FTPT.BR

Career & Employment

FROGJOBS
Scientific Employment Opportunities in France
mailto:LISTPROC@LISTPROC.NET

WISENET
A discussion of women's careers in science, mathematics, or engineering
mailto:LISTSERV@UICVM.UIC.EDU

Chemistry

CHEMCOM
Discussion of Chemistry in the Community
mailto:LISTSERV@UBVM.CC.BUFFALO.EDU

CHEMISTRY
Computational Chemistry List on chemistry software and methodology
mailto:CHEMISTRY-REQUEST@OSC.EDU

CHMINF-L
Discussion of All Topics Related to Chemistry
mailto:LISTSERV@IUBVM.UCS.INDIANA.EDU

Earth Sciences

C14-L
Technical, Informed Discussion of Radioisotope Dating
mailto:LISTSERV@LISTSERV.ARIZONA.EDU

CLIMLIST
Professional discussion and announcments about climatology
mailto:JOHNA@MAGNUS.ACS.OHIO-STATE.EDU

EARTHANDSKY
Weekly earth science and astronomy publication
mailto:MAJORDOMO@LISTS.UTEXAS.EDU

Environmental Sciences

APPL-BIODIV
Ecological diversity in resource and land management
mailto:APPL-BIODIV-REQUEST@UNIXG.UBC.CA

ASEH-L
Discussion of Environmental History and Issues
mailto:LISTPROC@UNICORN.ACS.TTU.EDU

BIOSPH-L
A discussion of issues and events relating to the BioSphere
mailto:LISTSERV%UBVM.BITNET@VM1.NODAK.EDU

COASTNET
Coastal Management and Resources
mailto:LISTSERV@URIACC.URI.EDU

COMPOST
Discussion of Home Composting
mailto:LISTPROC@LISTPROC.WSU.EDU

HUDSON-R
Discussion of Hudson River ecology and pollution
mailto:MAJORDOMO@MATRIX.NEWPALTZ.EDU

HYDROGEN
Exchange of Information Regarding Hydrogen as an Alternative Fuel
mailto:LISTSERV@URIACC.URI.EDU

NATLIT-L
Environmental science educational resources
mailto:LISTPROC@ENVIROLINK.ORG

REACTIVE
A forum for discussion and exchange of information on air sampling
mailto:LISTSERV@VM1.MCGILL.CA

RES-ECON
Communication and discussion of land and resource economics
mailto:RES-ECON-REQUEST@UNIXG.UBC.CA

TWSGIS-L
A discussion of information on the use and abuse of GIS and Remote Sensing Technology
mailto:LISTSERV@VM1.NODAK.EDU

Geosciences

EXP-PET
Discussion of experimental geosciences
mailto:MAJORDOMO@S100.ES.LLNL.GOV

HIMNET
Professional discussion for geologists and geographers in Himalayan countries
mailto:HIMNET@ERDW.ETHZ.CH

Neurosciences

CREA-CPS
Creative Thinking and Problem Solving
mailto:LISTSERV@NIC.SURFNET.NL

INTUDM-L
Discussion of Intuition in Decision Making
mailto:LISTSERV@UTEPVM.EP.UTEXAS.EDU

NEURON
Academic information on all aspects of neural networks
mailto:NEURON-REQUEST@CATTELL.PSYCH.UPENN.EDU

Organizations

MEMSNET
A forum for the Mineral Economics and Management Society
mailto:LISTSERV@UABDPO.DPO.UAB.EDU

NATOSCI
Information on Various NATO Topics
mailto:NATOSCI@STC.NATO.INT

Paleontology

DINOSAUR
Serious discussion of evidence related to dinosaurs
mailto:LISTPROC@LEPOMIS.PSYCH.UPENN.EDU

Physics

AMP-L
Atomic and Molecular Physics
mailto:LISTSERV@VM.GMD.DE

BURG-CEN
Fluid Mechanics
mailto:LISTSERV@NIC.SURFNET.NL

CFD
Discussion of Computational Fluid Dynamics
mailto:LISTSERV@UKCC.UKY.EDU

FUSION
Nuclear Fusion
mailto:LISTSERV@VM1.NODAK.EDU

PHYSICS
Professional discussion of theoretical and experimental physics
mailto:PHYSICS-REQUEST@QEDQCD.RYE.NY.US

POLYMERP
A discussion of Polymer Physics
mailto:LISTSERV@LISTSERV.NET

Space Science

EXTRATERRESTRIALS
Academic and scientific discussion of extraterrestrial life
mailto:MAILBASE@MAILBASE.AC.UK

Veterinary Science

AAVLD-L
Veterinary Diagnostics and Animal Health
mailto:LISTSERV@LISTSERV.NET

Sports & Recreation

Aquatic Sports

ICYRA
Discussion of collegiate yacht racing
mailto:ICYRA-REQUEST@MAILHOST.TCS.TULANE.EDU

SCUBA
A discussion for scuba and skin diving enthusiasts
mailto:LISTSERV@CC.ITU.EDU.TR

SCUBA-D
A discussion based on the newsgroup rec.scuba
mailto:LISTSERV@BROWNVM.BROWN.EDU

SCUBA-L
A discussion of all aspects of scuba diving
mailto:LISTSERV@BROWNVM.BROWN.EDU

SWIM-L
A fun discussion of all aspects of swimming
mailto:LISTSERV@UAFSYSB.UARK.EDU

SYNCHRO-S
Syncronized swimming discussion
mailto:SYNCHRO-S-REQUEST@UNIXG.UBC.CA

WAVE_LENGTH
Discussion of aquatic paddle sports
mailto:WAVE_LENGTH-REQUEST@BBS.SD68.NANAIMO.BC.CA

WHITEWATER
Discussion of kayak and canoeing techniques and equipment
mailto:WHITEWATER-REQUEST@GYNKO.CIRC.UPENN.EDU

WINDSURFING
Discussion of windsurfing equipment and technique
mailto:WINDSURFING-REQUEST@FLY.COM

YACHT-L
A discussion of yachting and related topics
mailto:LISTSERV@HEARN.NIC.SURFNET.NL

Aviation

AERONAUTICS
Moderated version of aviation newsgroup sci.aeronautics
mailto:aeronautics-request@rascal.ics.utexas.edu

AIRLINE
Civil Aircraft and Commercial Airlines
mailto:LISTSERV@CUNYVM.CUNY.EDU

AIRPLANE-CLUBS
Aviation Management and Operation Issues
mailto:AIRPLANE-CLUBS-REQUEST@DG-RTP.DG.COM

AV-ROTOR
Helicopter Advice and Experience
mailto:LISTSERV@ROTOR.COM

ULTRALIGHT-FLIGHT
Discussion and information on ultralight aircraft
mailto:ULTRALIGHT-FLIGHT-REQUEST@MS.UKY.EDU

Crafts & Hobbies

BALLOON
Balloon sculpting techniques and reviews
mailto:BALLOON-REQUEST@ENT.ROCHESTER.EDU

BONSAI
Bonsai and Related Crafts
mailto:LISTSERV@CMS.CC.WAYNE.EDU

BUGNET
General Discussion of Insects
mailto:LISTSERV@WSUVM1.CSC.WSU.EDU

CARDS
Sport trading cards discussion and sales
mailto:CARDS-REQUEST@TANSTAAFL.UCHICAGO.EDU

CLAYART
Discussion of Ceramic Arts and Pottery Field Issues
mailto:LISTSERV@UKCC.UKY.EDU

CLOCKS
Discussion of All Aspects of Clock and Watch Work
mailto:LISTSERV@SUVM.SYR.EDU

COLLECTORS-NET-REQUEST
Announcments, ads and information on all types of collecting
mailto:COLLECTORS-REQUEST-NET@NETCOM.COM

CP
Discussion of Cultivation, Propagation, and Trading of Carnivorous Plants
mailto:LISTSERV@HPL-OPUS.HPL.HP.COM

DOLLH-L
Discussion of Doll House and Miniature Enthusiasts
mailto:LISTSERV@IST01.FERRIS.EDU

HONDA-L
Discussion of Honda Automobiles
mailto:LISTSERV@BROWNVM.BROWN.EDU

INTERQUILT
Discussion of Quilts and Quilting
mailto:MBISHOP@CCMAIL.SUNYSB.EDU

JEWELRY
Discussion of Jewelry-Making and Related Disciplines
mailto:LISTPROC@MISHIMA.MN.ORG

KNIT
A discussion of knitting and spinning
mailto:LISTSERV@GEOM.UMN.EDU

MBISHOP+PFAFF
Discussion of Pfaff Sewing Machines
mailto:MBISHOP@CCMAIL.SUNYSB.EDU

MINOLTA-L
Discussion about Minolta Cameras
mailto:LISTSERV@RIT.EDU

MISTNET
Sightings of Migratory Birds
mailto:LISTSERV@VM.STLAWU.EDU

NUMISM-L
Numismatics of Antiquity and the Middle Ages
mailto:LISTSERV@UNIVSCVM.CSD.SCAROLINA.EDU

ORIGAMI-L
Techniques, organizations, and materials for origami
mailto:ORIGAMI-L-REQUEST@NSTN.NS.CA

PHOTO-3D
Stereo and 3D Photos
mailto:LISTSERV@CSG.LBL.GOV

POSTCARD
A discussion for the exchange or collecting of picture postcards
mailto:LISTSERV@IDBSU.IDBSU.EDU

Q-XCHG
A list for the exchange of quilt related materials and patterns
mailto:LISTSERV@EMUVM1.CC.EMORY.EDU

QUILTNET
A discussion of general quilting information
mailto:LISTSERV@EMUVM1.CC.EMORY.EDU

RAILROAD
A discussion of anything about real or model railroads
mailto:LISTSERV@CUNYVM.CUNY.EDU

ROCKHOUNDS
Discussion of gem and mineral collecting
mailto:ROCKHOUNDS-REQUEST@INFODYN.COM

ROCKS-AND-FOSSILS
Discussion and information on rock collecting
mailto:MAJORODMO@WORLD.STD.COM

SCA
Society for Creative Anachronism information
mailto:SCA-REQUEST@MC.LCS.MIT.EDU

STAMPS
A discussion of stamps for collectors and enthusiasts
mailto:LISTSERV@CUNYVM.CUNY.EDU

TEDDY-BEARS
Teddy bear collecting and announcements
mailto:TEDDY-BEAR-REQUEST@RHEIN.DE

Sports & Recreation

WOODWORK
A discussion concerning the tools, methods, and techniques of woodworking
mailto:LISTSERV%IPFWVM.BITNET@VM1.NODAK.EDU

Food & Dining

BREAD
All aspects of bread making
mailto:BREAD-DIGEST-REQUEST@CYKICK.INFORES.COM

CHILE-HEADS
Discussion of Chile Peppers
mailto:CHILE-HEADS-REQUEST@CHILE.UCDMC.UCDAVIS.EDU

FATFREE
Discussion of Extremely Lowfat Vegetarianism
mailto:FATFREE-REQUEST@HUSTLE.RAHUL.NET

FOODWINE
Serious Discussion of Food and Its Accompaniments
mailto:LISTSERV@CMUVM.CSV.CMICH.EDU

HOMEBREW
Discussion of beer making and tasting
mailto:HOMEBREW-REQUEST%HPFCMR@HPLABS.HP.COM

J-FOOD-L
A discussion Japanese food and culture
mailto:LISTSERV%JPNKNU10.BITNET@CUNYVM.CUNY.EDU

OZWINE
Discussion of Australian and New Zealand wines
mailto:MAISER@KOALA.CS.COWAN.EDU.AU

POI-DIGEST
I think this is a discussion of the Hawaiian food 'poi'
mailto:POI-POUNDERS-REQUEST@PRESTO.IG.COM

Games

ADND-L
A discussion of all aspects of Dungeons and Dragons and Advanced Dungeons and Dragons
mailto:LISTSERV@UTARLVM1.UTA.EDU

BROOMS-L
Broomball
mailto:LISTSERV@GITVM1.GATECH.EDU

CARWAR-L
Discussion of the Game of Car Wars
mailto:LISTSERV@UBVM.BUFFALO.EDU

CHESS-L
A discussion of the game of chess including information on chess tournaments
mailto:LISTSERV@NIC.SURFNET.NL

CHILL
Contemporary horror role playing issues and techniques
mailto:CHILL-REQUEST@CALLAMER.COM

DERBY
Discussion of Horse racing Strategies
mailto:DERBY-REQUEST@EKRL.COM

DIPL-L
The Game of Diplomacy
mailto:LISTSERV@MITVMA.MIT.EDU

FNN
Fantasy Role-playing Games
mailto:LISTSERVER@LE.AC.UK

GAMES-L
Computer Games
mailto:LISTSERV@BROWNVM.BROWN.EDU

JAE+SW-RPG
Discussion of rules and strategies for the Star Wars Role Playing Game
mailto:MAILSERV@DRYCAS.CLUB.CC.CMU.EDU

MONOPOLY
The Monopoly Board Game
mailto:LISTSERV@IST01.FERRIS.EDU

REALMS
Discussion of Forgotten Realms FRP game setting
mailto:MAJORDOMO@OSSI.COM

REALMS-DIGEST
Digest version of forgotten Realms FRP game setting discussion
mailto:MAJORDOMO@OSSI.COM

SCA-WEST
Discussion of the medieval play group 'Society of Creative Anachronism'
mailto:SCA-WEST-OWNER@ECST.CSUCHICO.EDU

SHADOWRN
A discussion of the fantasy game ShadowRun
mailto:LISTSERV@HEARN.NIC.SURFNET.NL

SHOGI-L
A discussion about the strategic board game Shogi
mailto:LISTSERV@TECHNION.TECHNION.AC.IL

SPELLJAMMER
A specific discussion limited to the Spelljammer campaign in Advanced Dungeons and Dragons
mailto:LISTSERVER@LE.AC.UK

STRAT-O-MATIC
Discussion of Strat-O-Matic board and computer games
mailto:SCOTRICH@CWIS.ISU.EDU

TRAVELLER
Discussion and strategies of TRAVELLER role playing game
mailto:TRAVELLER-REQUEST@ENGRG.UWO.CA

WAR40K
Discussion of Warhammer products and games
mailto:MAJORDOMO@BISMARCK.GATECH.EDU

Gardening

GARDENS
Home Gardening
mailto:LISTSERV@UKCC.UKY.EDU

Motor Sports

AUTOX
Autocrossing techniques and issues
mailto:AUTOX-REQUEST@AUTOX.TEAM.NET

WHEELTOWHEEL
Discussion of auto racing
mailto:WHEELTOWHEEL-REQUEST@ABINGDON.ENG.SUN.COM

Organizations

CBA
Discussion of Continental Basketball Association Issues and Resources
mailto:CBA-REQUEST@GS1.COM

SCOUTS-L
A varied discussion of scouting throughout the world
mailto:LISTSERV%TCUBVM.BITNET@CUNYVM.CUNY.EDU

Outdoor Recreation

BALLOON
General ballooning issues for commercial and sport users
mailto:BALLOON-REQUEST@LUT.AC.UK

BICYCLE
Bicycling techniques, advocacy, and racing issues
mailto:LISTPROC@LISTPROC.NET

BIKECOMMUTE
Bicycle commuting issues and advocacy
mailto:BIKECOMMUTE-REQUEST@BIKE2WORK.SUN.COM

BIKECURRENT
Bicycle lighting and electronics issues
mailto:BIKECURRENT-REQUEST@SCUBA.ENG.SUN.COM

BIKEPEOPLE
Bicycle activism in Santa Cruz County, California
mailto:BIKEPEOPLE-REQUEST@DAIZU.UCSC.EDU

BLACK-POWDER
Discussion of black powder arms
mailto:Majordomo@catnip.Berkeley.CA.US

CAVERS-DIGEST
Discussion of Caves and Spelunking
mailto:LISTPROC@SPELEOLOGY.CS.YALE.EDU

FIREARMS
Hunting and firearms safety issues and discussion
mailto:FIREARMS-REQUEST@CS.CMU.EDU

GUTSFRISBEE-L
Discussion of sport of Guts Frisbee
mailto:MAJORDOMO@MTU.EDU

HANG-GLIDING
Discussion of Hang-gliding and Ballooning
mailto:HANG-GLIDING-REQUEST@VIRGINIA.EDU

HUNTING
Discussion of Hunting
mailto:LISTSERV@TAMVM1.TAMU.EDU

KITES
Discussion of Kite Making, Flying, and Products
mailto:KITES-REQUEST@HARVARD.HARVARD.EDU

MGARDEN
Master Gardener environmental and cultural awareness topics
mailto:LISTPROC@LISTPROC.WSU.EDU

NORDIC-SKI
Discussion of Nordic Skiing
mailto:NORDIC-SKI-REQUEST@GRAPHICS.CORNELL.EDU

ORIENTEERING
Discussion of Orienteering and Rogaining
mailto:ORIENTEERING-REQUEST@GRAPHICS.CORNELL.EDU

SLEDDOG
Discussion of Northern Breed and Working dog sports and labor
mailto:MAJORDOMO@CSN.ORG

TAG-NET
Discussion of caving in the Southeastern United States
mailto:MAJORDOMO@NETCOM.COM

Sports & Recreation

TANDEM
A discussion and information forum for tandem bicycle enthusiasts
mailto:LISTSERV@HOBBES.UCSD.EDU

UNICYCLING
Discussion of unicycling techniques and sales
mailto:UNICYCLING-REQUEST@MCS.KENT.EDU

Personal Fitness

AIKIDO-L
Aikido
mailto:LISTSERV@PSUVM.PSU.EDU

SPORTSCI
Academic and professional discussion of scientific methods in sport
mailto:MAJORDOMO@STONEBOW.OTAGO.AC.NZ

WEIGHTS
Discussion of weightlifting routines, nutrition, and experiences
mailto:WEIGHTS-REQUEST@MICKEY.DISNEY.COM

WELLNESSLIST
Personal fitness publications, announcements and discussion
mailto:MAJORDOMO@WELLNESSMART.COM

WISHPERD
A discussion of women and fitness
mailto:LISTSERV@SJSUVM1.SJSU.EDU

Pets & Animals

AQUARIUM
Keeping Aquatic Life in an Aquarium
mailto:LISTSERV@EMUVM1.CC.EMORY.EDU

BETTAS
Keeping/Breeding of Betta Splendens (Siamese Fighting Fish)
mailto:LISTSERV@ARIZVM1.CCIT.ARIZONA.EDU

BIRDEAST, BIRDCHAT, BIRDCNTR, BIRDWEST
Bird Watching Hotlines
mailto:LISTSERV@ARIZVM1.CCIT.ARIZONA.EDU

CANINE-L
Discussion Among Dog Owners
mailto:LISTSERV@PSUVM.PSU.EDU

EQUINE-L
Discussion of Horses
mailto:LISTSERV@PSUVM.PSU.EDU

EXOTIC-L
Exotic Pet Birds
mailto:LISTSERV@PLEARN.EDU.PL

FELINE-L
Discussion of Cats
mailto:LISTSERV@PSUVM.PSU.EDU

FERRET
Discussion of Ferrets
mailto:LISTSERV@CUNYVM.CUNY.EDU

GOLDEN
Discussions Among Golden Retriever Enthusiasts
mailto:LISTSERV@HOBBES.UCSD.EDU

HORSE
Discussion of Equestrian Issues
mailto:EQUESTRIANS-REQUEST@WORLD.STD.COM

OBED
Dog training technique and discussion
mailto:OBEDREQ@REEPICHEEP.GCN.UOKNOR.EDU

PETBUNNY
Care and Behavior of Pet Rabbits
mailto:LISTSERV@UKCC.UKY.EDU

Recreation

CAUSERIE
Chatting in French
mailto:LISTSERV@UQUEBEC.CA

MOCAVES
Caving in Missouri
mailto:LISTSERV@UMSLVMA.UMSL.EDU

OVR-CAVE
Caving and Caves in Kentucky, Indiana, and Ohio
mailto:LISTSERV@UKCC.UKY.EDU

Sports

BA-FOOTBAG
Discussion of Footbag Resources and Events
mailto:BA-FOOTBAG-REQUEST@HPMPES2.CUP.HP.COM

BASEBALL-CHAT
Discussion of General Baseball Issues
mailto:LISTPROC@MEDRAUT.APPLE.COM

BOSOX
Discussion of Boston Red Sox
mailto:MAJORDOMO@WORLD.STD.COM

BOSOX-DIGEST
Digest of Boston Red Sox mailing list
mailto:MAJORDOMO@WORLD.STD.COM

CAT-CHAT
Discussion of University of Kentucky Wildcats Basketball
mailto:LISTSERV@UKCC.UKY.EDU

CELTICS
Discussion of the Boston Celtics
mailto:MAJORDOMO@CISCO.COM

CELTICS
Discussion of Boston Celtics basketball team
mailto:MAJORDOMO@HILLEL.COM

CELTICS-DIGEST
Digest of Boston Celtics discussion
mailto:MAJORDOMO@CISCO.COM

DRS
Discussion Among Runners of All Levels
mailto:LISTSERV@DARTCMS1.DARTMOUTH.EDU

GIANTS
San Francisco Giants Discussion and Information
mailto:LISTPROC@MEDRAUT.APPLE.COM

GIANTS-SCORES
San Francisco Giants' Box scores, League Standings, and Transactions
mailto:LISTPROC@MEDRAUT.APPLE.COM

GIANTS-TICKETS
San Francisco Giants Ticket Buying and Selling
mailto:LISTPROC@MEDRAUT.APPLE.COM

Golf-L
Discussion of Golf and Related Topics
mailto:LISTSERV@UBVM.CC.BUFFALO.EDU

GYMN
Gymnastics discussion and related topics
mailto:OWNER-GYMN@MIT.EDU

HOCKEY-D
Provides Information, but not Discussion on HOCKEY-L
mailto:LISTSERV@MAINE.MAINE.EDU

HOCKEY-L
Discussion of Collegiate Ice Hockey
mailto:LISTSERV@MAINE.MAINE.EDU

JAYS
Toronto Blue Jays scores, highlights, and player information
mailto:JAYS-REQUEST@HIVNET.UBC.CA

KARATE
An unmoderated discussion of Karate and related styles
mailto:LISTSERV@UKANAIX.CC.UKANS.EDU

LACROSSE
A discussion of the sport lacrosse
mailto:LISTSERV@SUVM.SYR.EDU

MARTIAL-ARTS
Discussion of Martial arts Training and Philosophy
mailto:MARTIAL-ARTS-REQUEST@DRAGON.CSO.UIUC.EDU

OLYMPUCK
Olympic Ice Hockey
mailto:LISTSERV@MAINE.MAINE.EDU

SOMWPS
Women's basketball discussion forum and information
mailto:MAIL-SERVER@KNEX.VIA.MIND.ORG

UK-HOCKEY
Discussion of UK ice hockey
mailto:MAJORDOMO@CEE.HW.AC.UK

VBALL
Announcements and discussion of Boston area volleyball
mailto:VBALL-ADMIN@INTELLIGENCE.COM

WHL
Western Hockey League and Memorial Cup discussion
mailto:KLOOTZAK@U.WASHINGTON.EDU

Travel & Tourism

BERMUDA-LOVERS
Discussion of travel and tourism in Bermuda
mailto:MAJORDOMO@WORLD.STD.COM

GREEN.TRAVEL
Discussion of Environmentally Sustainable Tourism
mailto:MENDICOTT@IGC.APC.ORG

HOSPEX
Database List for Netwide Hospitality Exchange
mailto:LISTSERV@PLEARN.EDU.PL

HOSPEX-L
Discussion of Netwide Hospitality Exchanges
mailto:LISTSERV@PLEARN.EDU.PL

NEW-ORLEANS
New Orleans history, entertainment, and culture
mailto:MAIL-SERVER@MINTIR.NEW-ORLEANS.LA.US

NYCKAYAKER
Discussion of New York City attractions
mailto:MAJORDOMO@WORLD.STD.COM

TRAVEL-L
A discussion of tourism
mailto:LISTSERV%TREARN.BITNET@VM1.NODAK.EDU

Newsgroups

- Arts & Music 708
- Business & Economics 709
- Communications 711
- Computing & Mathematics 711
- Education 718
- Engineering & Technology 719
- Government & Politics 719
- Health & Medicine 720
- Humanities & Social Sciences 722
- Internet 724
- Law & Criminal Justice 726
- Popular Culture & Entertainment 726
- Religion & Philosophy 733
- Science 734
- Sports & Recreation 735

Usenet Newsgroups

What is Usenet?

The Internet plays host to a number of unique ways to communicate with others around the world. One very popular and often baffling way to communicate is Usenet. This is the name given to describe a large collection of newsgroups (discussion groups) that number literally in the tens of thousands and is used by people all over the world.

Newsgroups tend to focus on very specific topics. Examples include skiing, political rhetoric, women's health issues, religious theology, sex, divorce, romance, or workplace issues. Some are unusual, but a vast majority represent typical discussion topics you might have within your own circle of friends. The context of the discussions may vary from relevant current or historical events to personal anecdotes or just plain information sharing. Through these newsgroups you will find experts and enthusiasts who share similar (and many times dissimilar) views on a particular subject.

It is often said that Usenet represents the heart of Internet because it is a medium that draws people from all over the world to communicate on various topics with a wide variety of opinions and perspectives. In this way, Usenet is a true example of the 'virtual community' in this age of communications technology, unhindered by the geography, ideology, or government policy that normally control our surroundings.

How is Usenet Organized?

There are several broad but basic categories of Usenet groups that are distributed world-wide throughout the entire Usenet (see table below). But not all of the newsgroups share in such wide distribution. There are some sites, for example, that comprise a subset of another group and may be distributed primarily within a given geographic region or country.

In addition to the standard newsgroup hierarchy, there is an alternative newsgroup hierarchy that comes from a variety of sources and does not operate under the more formal procedures of the 7 standard hierarchies. Access to these alternative hierarchies depends largely on which newsgroups your service provider decides to carry through their service. Descriptions of some of these alternative hierarchies have been provided for you later in the introduction.

The Seven Standard Hierarchies of Usenet

Name	Description
comp.	Newsgroups for computer professionals and enthusiasts
news.	Newsgroups on the administration and use of the Usenet
rec.	Newsgroups covering hobbies, arts, sports and related topics
sci.	Newsgroups on the wide world of science
soc.	Newsgroups about social sciences, social issues, and socializing
talk.	Newsgroups for controversy and no-holds-barred debate
misc.	Newsgroups for topics not covered in the above categories

How does Usenet work?

Usenet messages or 'postings' are distributed by a system that relies on certain computer communications standards or 'protocols' to distribute a message to the different networks (including Internet) and online services with a Usenet connection. Once a message is posted using a newsreader (see 'How to Access Usenet'), it is sent out and copied from machine to machine throughout Usenet until it is fully distributed.

Anatomy of a Message

The format of the message contains two parts - the header (the part that contains information about the subject of the posting) and the body (the part that contains the actual text of the message).

History of Usenet

Usenet, though part of the Internet, should not be confused with the Internet. Usenet began in 1979 when two Duke University graduate students wanted to hook computers together in order to exchange information with the UNIX community (UNIX is an operating system). They wrote the first

Usenet Newsreaders

NAME	PLATFORM	FTP SITE*	DIRECTORY
FNEWS	VAX/VMS/UNIX	ftp.tui.marc.cri.nz	/pub/fnews
rn	UNIX	ftp.academ.com	
trn	UNIX	ftp.uu.net	/networking/news/readers/trn
nn	UNIX	ftp.uniwa.uwa.edu.au	/pub/nn
tin	UNIX	ftp.germany.eu.net	/pub/news/tin
Pine	UNIX	ftp.cac.washington.edu	/pine/pine.tar/Z
trumpet	DOS	ftp.utas.edu.au	/pc/trumpet/
wintrumpet	Windows	ftp.utas.edu.au	/pc/trumpet/wintrump/*.*
Hypernews	Macintosh	ftp.apple.com	
Newswatcher	Macintosh	ftp.acns.nwu.edu	/pub/newswatcher
Nuntius	Macintosh	ftp.frederik.ruc.dk	

*Some ftp addresses include the specific directories in which you will find the program. For example, to download FNEWS, you connect to the ftp address and then go to the /pub/ (public) directory and then into the /fnews/ directory.

version of news software and started out with two sites, "unc" and "duke." Over time, the number of sites grew, the information flow increased, and the software went through several modifications. In 1986 the Network News Transfer Protocol (NNTP) was released allowing sites to exchange information via TCP/IP (Transmission Control Protocol/Internet Protocol) connections rather than uucp (UNIX-to-UNIX copy program) connections. Since then, NNTP and its variations has become the standard for the Usenet.

How to access Usenet

To access Usenet, you must be connected to the Internet and have access to some type of newsreader program. Newsreader programs vary in difficulty of use, quality, or by the type of service used. National commercial providers such as Netcom, America OnLine, Delphi, Genie, Compuserve, and a large number of local and regional Internet providers provide access to a newsreader. If your Internet connection does not provide a newsreader program, all is not lost. There are many newsreader programs available both commercially and for free on the Internet.

A short list of the more popular programs and their ftp location is provided for your convenience so that you may download the program of your choice. See the table at the top of this page.

Usenet Rules of Thumb

A newsgroup is a place to discuss, express opinions, and share information. Keep in mind that the more controversial the subject, the greater the chance that users are engaged in a discussion that you may find inane or even unrelated to the topic at hand. This is the nature of the newsgroup community.

Another rule of thumb is not to jump into a newsgroup and start making inappropriate or judgmental statements that demonstrate your personal indignation over a particular belief, behavior, or desire. As with any community, get a sense of the tone and temperment of the people before you 'jump' into the conversation. This is a simple act of netiquette that will carry you a long way.

One final rule of thumb, be sure to read the FAQs (Frequently Asked Questions) of the newsgroup, if one exists, before posting an article to the newsgroup. FAQs are documents of practical use that provide useful and informative answers to frequently asked questions about the newsgroup. To find out if a particular newsgroup has a FAQ, simply logon by anonymous ftp to:

ftp://rtfm.mit.edu

Description of the Standard Newsgroup Hierarchies

comp

This hierarchy covers those newsgroups for computer professionals and computer enthusiasts. Hundreds of sites provide readers with a vast storehouse of knowledge for every aspect of computers, both hardware and software. For instance, **comp.multimedia** is a newsgroup in which every aspect of multimedia presentations on computers is discussed— sound, full-motion video, graphics, programming languages, and even aesthetic issues. Hardware products such as motherboards, chips, chip technology, and computer peripherals like printers, also have newsgroup sites.

news

This hierarchy covers Usenet itself, focusing on discussions about Usenet network administration and Usenet newsgroups as a topic. By accessing news lists, you can obtain information about the top newsgroups on Usenet, whether they discuss a specific movie, a particular sport, or a health issue.

rec

This hierarchy is where discussions and information are exchanged on hobbies, crafts, the arts, and sports, not to mention such topics as cooking, dining, sewing, photography, and hiking, to name just a few. The newsgroups under this hierarchy number in the thousands and grow daily. There are probably close to 80,000 such groups in which enthusiasts and professionals alike discuss, query, and exchange experiences on a recreational topic. For instance, **rec.video,** is a news group that covers home and hobby video cameras, recorders and image processing, emphasizing the technology rather than the aesthetics.

sci

This hierarchy covers the wide world of science. These newsgroups are typically concerned with practical knowledge related to such things as research or established applications of science. The field is wide open and consists of all of the sciences (i.e., zoology, botany, astronomy) with specific groups discussing particular topics under each of the category areas. There are literally thousands of such groups. For instance, under **sci.aquaria,** scientific aspects of aquatic life are discussed and more broadly, this group covers many aspects of marine biology.

soc

This hierarchy is concerned with social sciences, social issues, and socializing. Its focus can be as broad as the culture and people of Ecuador, as in **soc.culture.ecuador,** or as specific as **soc.religion.christian.youthwork,** a newsgroup that discusses Christian youth workers. There is also the ever-popular **soc.singles** which covers single-related issues such as depression, dating, and scheduled singles events throughout the world. Overall, there are thousands of sites, much like that of the **rec** category.

talk
This hierarchy covers controversial issues and is a kind of no-holds-barred forum for debate among those interested in specific topics. For instance, **talk.politics.animals** concerns animal rights, or fishing rights in international waters. Another newsgroup, **talk.philosophy,** discusses philosophies about politics and culture around the world. There are also talk newsgroups which cover lifestyles, such as gay issues (i.e., homophobia), and current issues (such as the pros and cons of the United Nations stance on Bosnia). Many countries and cultures are represented in this newsgroup and discussions cover every aspect of politics and ethics.

misc
This hierarchy covers anything that isn't easily covered in the above groups, or combines two related topics under one news group. This area also serves as the Usenet Marketplace, where users can also find items—particularly computer equipment—for sale. For example, **misc.mac.multimedia.games** is a group that discusses issues (rules) for certain games for anyone with a Macintosh multimedia computer

Descriptions of Alternative Newsgroup Hierarchies

alt
The alternative newsgroup contains countless discussion groups on a wide variety of subjects. Some alternative newsgroups pertain to specific languages and may or may not be available in both English and that language. For example, the **de** designation signifies those newsgroups that contain German hierarchies and **relcom** signifies those newsgroups containing Russian hierarchies. There are even local and national newsgroups in which people exchange information on specific topics or discuss local issues in general. Some include: **ba** for the San Francisco Bay Area; **uk** for the United Kingdom; **mtl** for Montreal, Canada, **it** for Italy, and **nz** for New Zealand.

This alternative hierarchy contains probably the largest group of discussion forums, numbering in the thousands and growing daily. For instance, **alt.sport.***** includes discussions of sports not covered in **rec.sports,** plus some devoted to professional sports, like hockey, soccer, football, and basketball. Those marked by **alt.bbs.***,** are bulletin board systems that break down discussion areas into very specific subjects such as a local (city or regional) bulletin board to discuss a concert playing at a park (i.e., **alt.bbs.austin.concert**). You can also find newsgroups for religion, sex, music, and even personals. If you see **alt.binaries.*,** you'll know that a wide variety of binary files—including multimedia, pictures and sounds—are available.

bionet
This hierarchy features sites dedicated to biology, biochemistry, biophysics, and other sciences not found in **sci**. These newsgroups' coverage runs the gamut of science news from research theories to professional organizations. You can, for instance, find out how to join an organization dedicated to a specific science, or locate research statistics on matter and energy.

bit
This hierarchy consists of echoes (automatic copies) of a wide selection of mailing lists carried on BITNET, an academic-oriented network composed of mainframes at North American (U.S. and Canada) and European colleges and universities. A mailing list is a way of distributing discussion by electronic mail, with all subscribers receiving a copy of each message.

biz
This hierarchy is devoted to business and information about businesses. It includes a breakdown of certain industries such as computer, medical service, or food service. These sites will include information about a specific company (i.e., **biz.ibm**), including press releases, the latest financial information (whether the company is publicly traded on world stock markets), and even the profiles of executives. Products and services are also covered, including new features and purchase locations.

clari
This hierarchy is where, for a price, you can get news 'hot off the press' so to speak. These newsgroups feature real news (like in a newspaper) and input from wire services around the world, like Reuters or the Associated Press. These sites generally edit and repackage the articles into Usenet format and then send them out over the Internet. Typically, the newsgroups provide the full printed text of news stories, as well as sidebars to the main stories.

ddn
This hierarchy is the Defense Data Network. The unclassified portion of the ddn is the Military Network (MILNET). The ddn is being phased out and transformed so that the four Defense Data Networks will be under the Department Of Defense (DOD) Inter-networking Data Service (Defense Information Systems Network, DISN).

gnu
This hierarchy is where you will find discussions of Free Software Foundation products including software requirements, overviews of a program's parameters, and descriptions/reviews of products. Some newsgroups provide help in installing a program, or tips on modifying a program to suit specific purposes.

humanities
This hierarchy is a new addition (instituted in 1995) in the newsgroup family and will focus on a variety of topics in the arts and humanities (fine arts and literature). Dave Lawrence, moderator of **news.announce.newgroups** issued a new group control message for humanities.misc on April 17th. Future group proposals in the new **humanities.*** hierarchy will proceed via the normal mechanisms of news.announce.newgroups and will be listed in newsgroup lists by the moderator of news.announce.newgroups. This means that humanities will be joined to the **'Big 7'** (i.e. comp, sci, news, soc, rec, talk, misc) in Usenet administration.

ieee
This hierarchy of newsgroups, created by the Institute of Electrical and Electronics Engineers (IEEE), typically hosts discussions related to the engineering and electronics fields. Here you can find information on professional organizations and on companies that offer specific services and products; you'll also find research pertaining to such down-to-earth things as electrical timing devices for home appliances or office equipment.

info
This hierarchy covers issues (technical and non-technical) about large computer systems, networked computer systems, computer programming, software, hardware, and computer operating systems. It also covers discussions of administrative issues about the Internet by information newsgroups on the Internet.

K12
This hierarchy provides information about primary and secondary education, with sites focusing on topics relevant to schools, curriculum, educational training

Newsgroups

projects, textbooks, and professional organizations. Here instructors can find resources and thousands of lesson plans for many areas of curriculum. **K12** also provides links for continuing education programs, and even forums for discussing current events.

sci.bio
This hierarchy offers discussion groups on topics concerning biology theories and research— such as **sci.bio.evolution**, which focuses on the evolution of plants and animals.

relcom
The relcom hierarchy is a news interface created in Russia. The Relcom Network was created in 1990 as a small professional network providing an internal communications network to the developers and users of computer systems at the Kurchatov Institute of Atomic Energy (now the Russian scientific center "Kurchatovsky Institute") and several other Moscow scientific organizations.

vmsnet
This hierarchy provides newsgroups for discussion of products and services for the mainframe computer systems of Digital Equipment Corporation (DEC). These newsgroups are technical discussions centering on the fine points of these complex computer systems. Some pertain to networking, others to software development and programming issues.

Final Reminders
The Usenet-distributed conferencing system is a great way to make friends and engage in thousands of interesting conversation topics. Some you might enjoy, and others you might find offensive. If you come across a topic name (i.e., White Supremacy) that offends you, then don't go into that newsgroup.

Also remember that newsgroups do not belong to and are not run by any one "body" or administrator. They really do represent the heartbeat and pulse of the Internet community at large.

Arts & Music

Architecture
alt.architecture
 Building design/construction and related topics
alt.architecture.alternative
 Non-traditional building designs
alt.architecture.int-design
 Interior design of man-made spaces
alt.landscape.architecture
 Landscape design and planning

Decorative Arts
rec.antiques
 Discussing antiques and vintage items
rec.antiques.marketplace
 Buying/selling/trading antiques
rec.arts.bodyart
 Tattoos and body decoration discussions
rec.crafts.textiles.misc
 Fiber and textile crafts not covered elsewhere
rec.crafts.textiles.needlework
 Any form of decorative stitching done by hand
rec.crafts.textiles.quilting
 All about quilts and other quilted items
rec.crafts.textiles.sewing
 Sewing: clothes, furnishings, costumes, etc
rec.crafts.textiles.yarn
 Yarn making & use: spin, dye, knit, weave, etc

Electronic Arts
alt.animation.warner-bros
 Discussions about Warner Brothers cartoons
alt.ascii-art
 Pictures composed of ASCII characters
alt.ascii-art.animation
 Movies composed of ASCII characters
alt.graphics.pixutils
 Discussion of pixmap utilities
bit.listserv.ingrafx
 Information Graphics
rec.arts.ascii
 ASCII art, info on archives, art, & artists
relcom.comp.animation
 Discussions on computer animation programs

Film & Video
alt.fan.ceiling
 Overused in movie fight scenes around the world
alt.movies.silent
 Shhhhhhhhhhh!
bit.listserv.cinema-l
 Discussions on all forms of cinema
bit.listserv.film-l
 Film making and reviews list
rec.arts.movies.production
 Filmmaking, amateur and professional
rec.video
 Video and video components
rec.video.cable-tv
 Technical and regulatory issues of cable television
rec.video.desktop
 Amateur, computer-based video editing and production
rec.video.production
 Making professional quality video productions
rec.video.releases
 Pre-recorded video releases on laserdisc and videotape
rec.video.satellite.dbs
 DBS systems and technologies
rec.video.satellite.europe
 European satellite broadcasting
rec.video.satellite.misc
 Non-TVRO and non-DBS satellite information
rec.video.satellite.tvro
 "Large Dish" ("BUD") systems and technologies

Music Genres
alt.exotic-music
 Exotic music discussions
alt.music.alternative
 For groups having 2 or less Platinum-selling albums
alt.music.alternative.female
 Discussing alternative music by female artists
alt.music.big-band
 Sounds from the Big Band era
alt.music.black-metal
 Iron instruments
alt.music.canada
 Oh, Canada, eh?
alt.music.chapel-hill
 You might think hymnals and chants, but you'd be wrong
alt.music.dance
 Music to dance to
alt.music.ebm
 Electronic (or not?) Body Music
alt.music.filk
 SF/fantasy related folk music
alt.music.hawaiian
 The music of the Hawaiian islands
alt.music.jewish
 Music from the Jewish heritage
alt.music.polkas
 Weird Al or not, polka is popular
alt.music.progressive
 Yes, Marillion, Asia, King Crimson, etc
alt.music.psychedelic
 All types of psychedelic music
alt.music.rockabilly
 Rockabilly
alt.music.ska
 Discussions of ska (skank) music, bands, and suchlike
alt.music.soul
 Discussion of sweet soul music
alt.music.swedish-pop
 ABBA and beyond
alt.music.synth.roland.u20
 The Roland U20 synthesizer
alt.music.synthpop
 Depeche Mode, Erasure, Pet Shop Boys, and much more!
alt.music.techno
 Bring on the bass!
alt.music.video-games
 Music that appears in video games
alt.music.world
 Discussion of music from around the world
alt.random.noise
 Bitstream Underground's Random Noise
alt.rap.sucks
 The anti-rap crowd sounds off
alt.rave
 Techno-culture: music, dancing, drugs, dancing, etc
alt.rock-n-roll
 Counterpart to alt.sex and alt.drugs
alt.rock-n-roll.classic
 Classic rock, both the music and its marketing
alt.rock-n-roll.hard
 Music where stance is everything
alt.rock-n-roll.metal
 For the headbangers on the net
alt.rock-n-roll.metal.death
 "Death metal" and newgroup overkill
alt.rock-n-roll.metal.heavy
 Non-sissyboy metal bands
alt.rock-n-roll.metal.progressive
 Slayer teams up with Tom Cora
alt.rock-n-roll.oldies
 Discussion of rock and roll music from 1950-1970

alt.thrash
  Thrashlife
bit.listserv.bgrass-l
  Bluegrass Music List
bit.listserv.blues-l
  Blues Music List
rec.music.bluenote
  Discussion of jazz, blues, and related types of music
rec.music.bluenote.blues
  The Blues in all forms and all aspects
rec.music.celtic
  Traditional and modern music with a Celtic flavor
rec.music.christian
  Christian music, both contemporary and traditional
rec.music.classical
  Discussion about classical music
rec.music.classical.guitar
  Classical music performed on guitar
rec.music.classical.performing
  Performing classical (including early) music
rec.music.classical.recordings
  Classical music on CD, vinyl, cassette, etc
rec.music.compose
  Creating musical and lyrical works
rec.music.country.old-time
  Southern fiddle/banjo music and beyond
rec.music.country.western
  C&W music, performers, performances, etc
rec.music.dementia
  Discussion of comedy and novelty music
rec.music.dylan
  Discussion of Bob's works & music
rec.music.early
  Discussion of pre-classical European music
rec.music.folk
  Folks discussing folk music of various sorts
rec.music.funky
  Funk, soul, rhythm & blues and related
rec.music.indian.classical
  Hindustani and Carnatic Indian classical music
rec.music.indian.misc
  Discussing Indian music in general
rec.music.industrial
  Discussion of all industrial-related music styles
rec.music.info
  News and announcements on musical topics
rec.music.makers
  For performers and their discussions
rec.music.makers.bagpipe
  Music and playing of all types of bagpipes
rec.music.makers.bands
  For musicians who play in groups with others
rec.music.makers.bass
  Upright bass and bass guitar techniques and equipment
rec.music.makers.bowed-strings
  Violin family (current & old) performance
rec.music.makers.builders
  Design, building, repair of musical instruments
rec.music.movies
  Music for movies and television
rec.music.newage
  "New Age" music discussions
rec.music.opera
  All aspects of opera
rec.music.progressive
  Symphonic rock, art rock, fusion, Canterbury, RIO, etc
rec.music.promotional
  Information and promo materials from record companies
rec.music.ragtime
  Ragtime and related music styles
rec.music.reggae
  Roots, Rockers, Dancehall Reggae

Performing Arts

alt.arts.ballet
  All aspects of ballet & modern dance as performing art
alt.arts.storytelling
  Discussion of storytelling in all its forms
alt.comedy.firesgn-thtre
  Firesign Theatre in all its flaming glory
alt.magic
  For discussion about stage magic
alt.stagecraft
  Technical theatre issues
rec.arts.dance
  Any aspects of dance not covered in another newsgroup
rec.arts.theatre.misc
  Miscellaneous topics and issues in theatre
rec.arts.theatre.musicals
  Musical theatre around the world
rec.arts.theatre.plays
  Dramaturgy and discussion of plays
rec.arts.theatre.stagecraft
  Issues in stagecraft and production
rec.music.a-cappella
  Vocal music without instrumental accompaniment

Visual Arts

alt.animation.spumco
  The Danes call it Quality
alt.journalism.photo
  The work of photo journalists
bit.listserv.nppa-l
  National Press Photographers Association
rec.arts.animation
  Discussion of various kinds of animation
rec.arts.anime
  Japanese animation discussion
rec.arts.anime.info
  Announcements about Japanese animation
rec.arts.anime.marketplace
  Things for sale in the Japanese animation world
rec.arts.anime.stories
  All about Japanese comic fanzines
rec.arts.fine
  Fine arts & artists
rec.arts.misc
  Discussions about the arts not in other groups
rec.photo.advanced
  Advanced topics (equipment and technique)
rec.photo.darkroom
  Developing, printing and other darkroom issues
rec.photo.help
  Beginners questions about photography (and answers)
rec.photo.marketplace
  Trading of personal photographic equipment
rec.photo.misc
  General issues related to photography
rec.photo.moderated
  The art and science of photography

Business & Economics

Accounting

biz.comp.accounting
  Dialogue specific to the accounting software industry

Advertising & Marketing

biz.marketplace.computers.discussion
  Discussion of computer merchandising

Banking

relcom.banktech
  Discussions on banking technologies

Career & Employment

biz.jobs.offered
  Position announcements
misc.jobs.contract
  Discussions about contract labor
misc.jobs.misc
  Discussion about employment, workplaces, careers
misc.jobs.offered
  Announcements of positions available
misc.jobs.offered.entry
  Job listings only for entry-level positions
misc.jobs.resumes
  Postings of resumes and "situation wanted" articles
relcom.commerce.jobs
  Jobs offered/wanted

Commerce

alt.business.misc
  All aspects of commerce
alt.business.multi-level
  Multi-level (network) marketing businesses
alt.org.jaycees
  Junior Chamber of Commerce
misc.industry.pulp-and-paper
  Technical topics in the pulp and paper industry
misc.industry.quality
  Quality standards and other issues
misc.transport.rail.misc
  Miscellaneous rail issues & discussions
misc.transport.trucking
  Commercial trucking related issues
relcom.commerce.money
  Credits, deposits, currency
relcom.commerce.other
  Miscelannia

Consumer Issues

misc.consumers
  Consumer interests, product reviews, etc
misc.consumers.house
  Discussion about owning and maintaining a house
misc.kids.consumers
  Products related to kids

Business & Economics

Newsgroups

Economics

sci.econ
 The science of economics
sci.econ.research
 Research in all fields of economics

Finance

clari.apbl.reports.finance
 Reports on the money supply

Industries

alt.business.insurance
 All about the insurance industry
alt.industrial
 The Industrial Computing Society claimed this name
alt.manufacturing.misc
 All about manufacturing
misc.industry.utilities.electric
 The electric utility industry

International Business

alt.business.import-export
 Business aspects of international trade
bit.listserv.e-europe
 Eastern Europe Business Network
bit.listserv.japan
 Japanese Business and Economics Network
biz.marketplace.international
 International commerce opportunities
biz.marketplace.international.discussion
 Talk of international commerce
misc.invest.canada
 Investing in Canadian financial markets
relcom.wtc
 Commercial proposals of World Trade Centers

Investment

misc.invest
 Investments and the handling of money
misc.invest.funds
 Sharing info about bond, stock, real estate funds
misc.invest.futures
 Physical commodity and financial futures markets
misc.invest.stocks
 Forum for sharing info about stocks and options
misc.invest.technical
 Analyzing market trends with technical methods
relcom.commerce.stocks
 Stocks and bonds
relcom.infomarket.talk
 Discussion on security market development

Labor

alt.society.labor-unions
 Theory and practice of labor unions

Management

bit.listserv.quality
 TQM in Manufacturing and Service Industries
misc.business.consulting
 The business of consulting

misc.business.records-mgmt
 All aspects of professional records management

Non Profits

soc.org.nonprofit
 Nonprofit organizations

Organizations

alt.aapg.general
 The American Association of Petroleum Geologists

Real Estate

misc.invest.real-estate
 Property investments
relcom.commerce.estate
 Real estate

Reference

biz.books.technical
 Technical bookstore & publisher advertising & info
biz.clarinet.sample
 Samples of ClariNet newsgroups for the outside world
biz.general
 Dialogue related to business operations and offerings
biz.misc
 Miscellaneous postings of a commercial nature
biz.stolen
 Postings about stolen merchandise
clari.apbl.biz.briefs
 Hourly business newsbrief from the AP
clari.apbl.biz.headlines
 Headlines of top business stories
clari.apbl.reports.commodity
 Chicago Board of Trade report
clari.apbl.reports.dollar_gold
 Daily gold and dollar prices
clari.apbl.stocks
 General stock market reports
clari.apbl.stocks.analysis
 Market analysis from the insiders
clari.apbl.stocks.dow
 Dow Jones averages
clari.apbl.stocks.tech
 *clariNews TechWire stock reports
clari.biz.briefs
 Business newsbriefs
clari.biz.earnings
 Businesses' earnings, profits, losses
clari.biz.economy
 Economic news and indicators
clari.biz.economy.world
 Economy stories for non-US countries
clari.biz.features
 Business feature stories
clari.biz.finance
 Finance, currency, Corporate finance
clari.biz.industry.agriculture
 Agriculture, fishing, forestry
clari.biz.industry.automotive
 The car and truck industry
clari.biz.industry.aviation
 Airlines and airports
clari.biz.industry.banking
 Banks and S&Ls
clari.biz.industry.broadcasting
 The television and radio industry

clari.biz.industry.construction
 The construction industry
clari.biz.industry.dry_goods
 Consumer goods, clothing, furniture
clari.biz.industry.energy
 Oil, gas, coal, alternatives
clari.biz.industry.food
 Food processing, markets, restaurants
clari.biz.industry.health
 The health care business
clari.biz.industry.insurance
 The insurance industry
clari.biz.industry.manufacturing
 Heavy industry
clari.biz.industry.mining
 Mining for metals, minerals
clari.biz.industry.print_media
 Newspapers, publishers, magazines
clari.biz.industry.real_estate
 Housing and real estate
clari.biz.industry.retail
 Retail stores and shops
clari.biz.industry.services
 Consulting, brokerages, services
clari.biz.industry.tourism
 The tourism and hotel industry
clari.biz.industry.transportation
 Trains, buses, transit, shipping
clari.biz.market.commodities
 Commodity reports
clari.biz.market.misc
 Bonds, money market funds, other instruments
clari.biz.market.news
 News affecting the financial markets
clari.biz.market.report
 General market reports, S&P, etc
clari.biz.market.report.asia
 Asian market reports
clari.biz.market.report.europe
 European market reports
clari.biz.market.report.top
 Overview of the markets
clari.biz.market.report.usa
 U.S. market reports
clari.biz.market.report.usa.nyse
 New York Stock Exchange reports
clari.biz.mergers
 Mergers and acquisitions
clari.biz.misc
 Other business news
clari.biz.review
 Daily review of business news
clari.biz.top
 Top business news
clari.biz.urgent
 Breaking business news
clari.biz.world_trade
 GATT, free trade, trade disputes
relcom.commerce.infoserv
 Information services
relcom.currency
 Exchange rates in CIS countries

Services

biz.americast
 AmeriCast announcements
biz.americast.samples
 Samples of AmeriCast (Moderated)
biz.comp.services
 Generic commercial service postings
biz.marketplace.computers.mac
 Mac hardware/software offered/wanted
biz.marketplace.computers.other
 Other computer hardware/software
biz.marketplace.computers.pc-clone
 PC-compatible hardware/software

biz.marketplace.computers.workstation
  Workstation hardware /software
biz.marketplace.discussion
  Discussion of biz.marketplace issues
biz.marketplace.non-computer
  Non-computer merchandise offered/wanted
biz.marketplace.services.computers
  Computer services offered/sought
biz.marketplace.services.discussion
  Discussion of business services
biz.marketplace.services.non-computer
  Non-computer services offered/wanted
misc.business.facilitators
  Discussions for all types of facilitators
relcom.commerce.orgtech
  Office equipment
relcom.commerce.transport
  Vehicles and spare parts
ref.biz.sco.general
  Q&A, discussions and comments on SCO products

Communications

Mass Communications

alt.journalism
  Shop talk by journalists and journalism students
alt.journalism.criticism
  I write, therefore I'm biased
alt.journalism.gonzo
  Hunter S. Thompson's approach to reporting
alt.journalism.print
  For newspaper, magazine and online reporters
alt.journalism.students
  People studying to be journalists
alt.radio.digital
  Digital radio signals
alt.radio.uk
  Radio in the United Kingdom

Telecommunications

alt.cellular-phone-tech
  Brilliant telephony mind blows netnews naming
alt.cellular.oki.900
  A whole group for a telephone model
alt.dcom.telecom
  Discussion of telecommunications technology
alt.ntia.avail
  NTIA Virtual Conference: Affordability and Availability

Computing & Mathematics

Analysis

comp.cad.synthesis
  Research and production in the field of logic synthesis

Artificial Intelligence

comp.ai
  Artificial Intelligence discussions
comp.ai.alife
  Research about artificial life
comp.ai.edu
  Applications of Artificial Intelligence to Education
comp.ai.fuzzy
  Fuzzy set theory, aka fuzzy logic
comp.ai.games
  Artificial Intelligence in games and game-playing
comp.ai.genetic
  Genetic algorithms in computing
comp.ai.jair.announce
  Announcements & abstracts of the Journal of AI Research
comp.ai.jair.papers
  Papers published by the Journal of AI Research
comp.ai.nat-lang
  Natural language processing by computers
comp.ai.neural-nets
  All aspects of neural networks
comp.ai.nlang-know-rep
  Natural Language and Knowledge Representation
comp.ai.philosophy
  Philosophical aspects of Artificial Intelligence
comp.ai.shells
  Expert systems and other artificial intelligence shells
comp.ai.vision
  Artificial Intelligence Vision Research
comp.human-factors
  Issues related to human-computer interaction (HCI)

Career & Employment

alt.computer.consultants
  The business of consulting about computers
alt.computer.consultants.ads
  Soliciting for computer consultants
comp.os.os2.marketplace
  For sale/wanted; shopping; commercial ads; job postings
info.labmgr
  Computer lab managers list
vmsnet.employment
  Jobs sought/offered, & employment related issues

Computer Science

comp.compression
  Data compression algorithms and theory
comp.constraints
  Constraint processing and related topics
comp.edu
  computerscience education
comp.graphics.visualization
  Info on scientific visualization
sci.crypt
  Different methods of data en/decryption

Hardware

alt.bbs.pcbuucp
  The commerical PCBoard gateway, PCB-UUCP
alt.bbs.powerboard
  For discussion about the Powerboard BBS package
alt.cd-rom
  Discussions of optical storage media
alt.cd-rom.reviews
  Reviews of various published things available on CD-ROM
alt.comp.hardware.homebuilt
  Designing devious devices in the den
alt.comp.msx
  Some sort of computer system
alt.comp.periphs.mainboard.asus
  ASUS motherboards
alt.periphs.pcmcia
  Credit card sized plug in peripherals (PCMCIA, JEDIA)
alt.sys.icl
  International Computers Limited hardware and software
alt.sys.intergraph
  Support for Intergraph machines
alt.sys.pc-clone.zeos
  Zeos computer systems
bit.listserv.9370-l
  IBM 9370 and VM/IS specific topics list
bit.listserv.calc-ti
  Texas Instruments Graphics Calulators
bit.listserv.graph-ti
  Discussion of the TI-8x Series Calculator
bit.listserv.ibm-main
  IBM Mainframe discussion list
bit.listserv.l-vmctr
  VMCENTER Components discussion list
bit.listserv.opers-l
  Mainframe Operations discussion list
bit.listserv.page-l
  IBM 3812/3820 Tips and problems discussion list
bit.listserv.power-l
  POWER-L IBM RS/6000 POWER Family
bit.listserv.vse-l
  IBM VSE/ESA discussion list
biz.comp.hardware
  Generic commercial hardware postings
biz.dec
  DEC equipment & software
biz.dec.decathena
  DECathena discussions
comp.arch.storage
  Storage system issues, both hardware and software
comp.benchmarks
  Discussion of benchmarking techniques and results
comp.dcom.sys.cisco
  Info on Cisco routers and bridges
comp.emulators.apple2
  Emulators of Apple // systems
comp.emulators.cbm
  Emulators of C-64, C-128, PET, and VIC-20 systems
comp.emulators.misc
  Emulators of miscellaneous computersystems
comp.ivideodisc
  Interactive videodiscs — uses, potential, etc
comp.laser-printers
  Laser printers, hardware & software
comp.lsi
  Large scale integrated circuits
comp.os.ms-windows.programmer.drivers
  Drivers & VxDs — no driver requests!
comp.os.ms-windows.video
  Video adapters and drivers for Windows
comp.os.msdos.4dos
  The 4DOS command processor for MS-DOS
comp.os.msdos.pcgeos
  GeoWorks PC/GEOS and PC/GEOS-based packages
comp.os.vms
  DEC's VAX* line of computers& VMS
comp.periphs
  Peripheral devices
comp.periphs.printers
  Information on printers
comp.periphs.scsi
  Discussion of SCSI-based peripheral devices
comp.protocols.appletalk
  Applebus hardware & software
comp.publish.cdrom.hardware
  Hardware used in publishing with CD-ROM
comp.robotics
  All aspects of robots and their applications
comp.robotics.misc
  All aspects of robots and their applications

Computing & Mathematics

comp.robotics.research
 Academic, government & industry research in robotics
comp.sys.acorn.hardware
 Acorn hardware
comp.sys.amiga.reviews
 Reviews of Amiga software, hardware
comp.sys.amiga.uucp
 Amiga UUCP packages
comp.sys.amstrad.8bit
 Amstrad CPC/PcW/GX4000 software/hardware
comp.sys.apollo
 Apollo computer systems
comp.sys.apple2.marketplace
 Buying, selling and trading Apple II equipment
comp.sys.arm
 The ARM processor architecture and support chips
comp.sys.atari.advocacy
 Attacking and defending Atari computers
comp.sys.encore
 Encore's MultiMax computers
comp.sys.handhelds
 Handheld computers and programmable calculators
comp.sys.hp48
 Hewlett-Packard's HP48 and HP28 calculators
comp.sys.hp.hpux
 Issues pertaining to HP-UX & 9000 series computers
comp.sys.hp.mpe
 Issues pertaining to MPE & 3000 series computers
comp.sys.ibm.pc.games.strategic
 Strategy/planning games on PCs
comp.sys.ibm.pc.hardware.cd-rom
 CD-ROM drives and interfaces for the PC
comp.sys.ibm.pc.hardware.chips
 Processor, cache, memory chips, etc
comp.sys.ibm.pc.hardware.comm
 Modems & communication cards for the PC
comp.sys.ibm.pc.hardware.misc
 Miscellaneous PC hardware topics
comp.sys.ibm.pc.hardware.networking
 Network hardware & equipment for the PC
comp.sys.ibm.pc.hardware.storage
 Hard drives & other PC storage devices
comp.sys.ibm.pc.hardware.systems
 Whole IBM PC computer & clone systems
comp.sys.ibm.pc.hardware.video
 Video cards & monitors for the PC
comp.sys.ibm.pc.misc
 Discussion about IBM personal computers
comp.sys.ibm.pc.rt
 Topics related to IBM's RT computer
comp.sys.ibm.pc.soundcard.advocacy
 Advocacy for a particular soundcard
comp.sys.ibm.pc.soundcard.games
 Questions about using soundcards with games
comp.sys.ibm.pc.soundcard.misc
 Soundcards in general
comp.sys.ibm.pc.soundcard.music
 Music and sound questions using soundcards
comp.sys.ibm.pc.soundcard.tech
 Technical questions about pc soundcards
comp.sys.ibm.ps2.hardware
 Microchannel hardware, any vendor
comp.sys.intel.ipsc310
 Anything related to the Intel 310
comp.sys.isis
 The ISIS distributed system from Cornell
comp.sys.laptops
 Laptop (portable) computers
comp.sys.m6809
 Discussion about 6809's
comp.sys.m68k
 Discussion about 68k's
comp.sys.m68k.pc
 Discussion about 68k-based PCs
comp.sys.m88k
 Discussion about 88k-based computers

comp.sys.mac.hardware
 Macintosh hardware issues & discussions
comp.sys.mac.hardware.misc
 General Mac hardware topics not already covered
comp.sys.mac.hardware.storage
 All forms of Mac storage hardware and media
comp.sys.mac.hardware.video
 Video input and output hardware on the Mac
comp.sys.mac.hypercard
 The Macintosh Hypercard: info & uses
comp.sys.mac.misc
 General discussions about the Apple Macintosh
comp.sys.mac.portables
 Discussion particular to laptop Macintoshes
comp.sys.mac.printing
 All about printing hardware and software on the Mac
comp.sys.mentor
 Mentor Graphics products & the Silicon *compiler System
comp.sys.msx
 The MSX home computersystem
comp.sys.ncr
 Discussion about NCR computers
comp.sys.newton.announce
 Newton information posts
comp.sys.newton.misc
 Miscellaneous discussion about Newton systems
comp.sys.sun.hardware
 Sun Microsystems hardware
comp.sys.super
 Super*computers
comp.sys.xerox
 Xerox 1100 workstations and protocols
comp.sys.zenith
 Heath terminals and related Zenith products
comp.sys.zenith.z100
 The Zenith Z-100 (Heath H-100) family of computers
comp.terminals
 All sorts of terminals
info.slug
 Care and feeding of Symbolics Lisp machines
info.solbourne
 Disc. & info on Solbourne computers
relcom.commerce.computers
 Computer hardware
relcom.comp.crosstools
 Cross-tools for embedded systems. Single-chip computers
relcom.fido.su.hardw
 FIDOnet, computer hardware

Mathematical Formulae

comp.apps.spreadsheets
 Spreadsheets on various platforms
comp.arch.bus.vmebus
 Hardware and software for VMEbus Systems
sci.materials.ceramics
 Ceramic science
sci.math
 Mathematical discussions and pursuits
sci.math.research
 Discussion of current mathematical research
sci.math.symbolic
 Symbolic algebra discussion

Mathematics

alt.math.iams
 Internet Amateur Mathematics Society
bit.listserv.frac-l
 FRACTAL Discussion List
comp.arch
 computer architecture

comp.arch.arithmetic
 Implementing arithmetic on computers/digital systems
sci.math.num-analysis
 Numerical Analysis

Networking

alt.filesystems.afs
 The Andrew Filesystem
alt.winsock
 Windows Sockets
alt.winsock.voice
 Winsock voice communication
bit.listserv.appc-l
 APPC Discussion List
bit.listserv.banyan-l
 Banyan Vines Network Software Discussions
bit.listserv.big-lan
 Campus-Size LAN Discussion Group
bit.listserv.cdromlan
 CD-ROM on Local Area Networks
bit.listserv.csg-l
 Control System Group Network
bit.listserv.cwis-l
 Campus-Wide Information Systems
bit.listserv.edi-l
 Electronic Data Interchange Issues
bit.listserv.linkfail
 Link failure announcements
bit.listserv.nettrain
 Network Trainers list
bit.listserv.nodmgt-l
 Node Management
bit.listserv.novell
 Novell LAN interest group
bit.listserv.sfs-l
 VM Shared File System discussion list
bit.sci.purposive-behavior
 Control System Group Network
comp.arch.fpga
 Field Programmable Gate Array based computing systems
comp.databases.olap
 Analytical Processing, Multidimensional DBMS, EIS, DSS
comp.databases.pick
 Pick-like, post-relational, database systems
comp.dcom.net-management
 Network management methods and applications
comp.graphics.apps.data-explorer
 IBM's Visualization Data Explorer (DX)
comp.graphics.avs
 The Application Visualization System
comp.infosystems
 Any discussion about information systems
comp.lsi.testing
 Testing of electronic circuits
comp.mail.sendmail
 Configuring and using the BSD sendmail agent
comp.mail.smail
 Administering & using the smail email transport system
comp.mail.uucp
 Mail in the uucp network environment
comp.mail.zmail
 The various Z-Mail products and their configurability
comp.music
 Applications of computers in music research
comp.networks.noctools.announce
 Info and announcements about NOC tools
comp.networks.noctools.bugs
 Bug reports and fixes for NOC tools
comp.networks.noctools.d
 Discussion about NOC tools
comp.networks.noctools.submissions
 New NOC tools submissions

Computing & Mathematics

comp.networks.noctools.tools
Descriptions of available NOC tools
comp.networks.noctools.wanted
Requests for NOC software
comp.os.ms-windows.nt.misc
General discussion about Windows NT
comp.os.ms-windows.nt.setup
Configuring Windows NT systems
comp.os.ms-windows.programmer.memory
Memory management issues
comp.parallel.mpi
Message Passing Interface (MPI)
comp.parallel.pvm
The PVM system of multi-computer parallelization
comp.protocols.ibm
Networking with IBM mainframes
comp.protocols.iso.x400
X400 mail protocol discussions
comp.protocols.iso.x400.gateway
X400 mail gateway discussions
comp.protocols.kerberos
The Kerberos authentication server
comp.protocols.nfs
Discussion about the Network File System protocol
comp.protocols.pcnet
Topics related to PCNET (a personal computer network)
comp.protocols.snmp
The Simple Network Management Protocol
comp.protocols.tcp-ip
TCP and IP network protocols
comp.protocols.time.ntp
The network time protocol
comp.security.misc
Security issues of computers and networks
comp.sys.acorn.networking
Networking of Acorn computers
comp.sys.amiga.networking
Amiga networking software/hardware
comp.sys.apple2.comm
Apple II data communications
comp.sys.novell
Discussion of Novell Netware products
info.bytecounters
NSstat network analysis program.
info.ietf.njm
Joint Monitoring Access btwn Adjacent Networks/IETF group
info.nets
Inter-network connectivity
info.snmp
Simple Gateway/Network Monitoring Protocol
info.sun-managers
Sun-managers digest
info.sun-nets
Sun-nets (nee Sun Spots) digest
misc.test
For testing of network software. Very boring
relcom.comp.security
Computer data security discussions
vmsnet.networks.management.misc
Other network management solutions

Operating Systems

alt.windows.cde
The Common Desktop Environment
bit.listserv.aix-l
IBM AIX Discussion List
bit.listserv.cmspip-l
VM/SP CMS Pipelines Discussion List
bit.listserv.notis-l
NOTIS/DOBIS Discussion group List
bit.listserv.os2-l
OS/2 Discussion
bit.listserv.rscs-l
VM/RSCS mailing list
bit.listserv.rscsmods
The RSCS modifications list
bit.listserv.vmesa-l
VM/ESA mailing list
bit.listserv.vmxa-l
VM/XA discussion list
bit.listserv.win3-l
Microsoft Windows Version 3 forum
comp.arch.embedded
Embedded computer systems topics
comp.bugs.2bsd
Reports of UNIX* version 2BSD related bugs
comp.bugs.4bsd
Reports of UNIX version 4BSD related bugs
comp.bugs.4bsd.ucb-fixes
Bug reports/fixes for BSD Unix
comp.bugs.misc
General UNIX bug reports and fixes (incl V7, uucp)
comp.os.linux.announce
Announcements important to the Linux community
comp.os.linux.answers
FAQs, How-To's, READMEs, etc. about Linux
comp.os.linux.development.apps
Writing Linux applications, porting to Linux
comp.os.linux.development.system
Linux kernels, device drivers, modules
comp.os.linux.hardware
Hardware compatibility with the Linux operating system
comp.os.linux.misc
Linux-specific topics not covered by other groups
comp.os.linux.networking
Networking and communications under Linux
comp.os.linux.setup
Linux installation and system administration
comp.os.linux.x
Linux X Window System servers, clients, libs and fonts
comp.os.lynx
Discussion of LynxOS and Lynx Real-Time Systems
comp.os.mach
The MACH OS from CMU & other places
comp.os.minix
Discussion of Tanenbaum's MINIX system
comp.os.misc
General OS-oriented discussion not carried elsewhere
comp.os.os2.advocacy
Supporting and flaming OS/2
comp.os.os2.announce
Notable news and announcements related to OS/2
comp.os.os2.apps
Discussions of applications under OS/2
comp.os.os2.beta
All aspects of beta releases of OS/2 systems software
comp.os.os2.bugs
OS/2 system bug reports, fixes and work-arounds
comp.os.os2.com
Modem/Fax hardware/drivers/apps/utils under OS/2
comp.os.os2.games
Running games under OS/2
comp.os.os2.mail-news
Mail and news apps/utils (on- & offline) under OS/2
comp.os.os2.misc
Miscellaneous topics about the OS/2 system
comp.os.os2.multimedia
Multi-media on OS/2 systems
comp.os.os2.networking.misc
Miscellaneous networking issues of OS/2
comp.os.os2.networking.tcp-ip
TCP/IP under OS/2
comp.os.os2.networking.www
World Wide Web (WWW) apps/utils under OS/2
comp.os.os2.programmer.misc
Programming OS/2 machines
comp.os.os2.programmer.oop
Programming system objects (SOM, WPS, etc)
comp.os.os2.programmer.porting
Porting software to OS/2 machines
comp.os.os2.programmer.tools
compilers, assemblers, interpreters under OS/2
comp.os.os2.setup
Installing and configuring OS/2 systems
comp.os.os2.setup.misc
Installing/configuring OS/2; misc. hardware/drivers
comp.os.os2.setup.storage
Disk/Tape/CD-ROM hardware/drivers under OS/2
comp.os.os2.setup.video
Base video hardware/drivers under OS/2
comp.os.os2.utilities
General purpose utilities (shells/backup/compression/etc)
comp.os.os9
Discussions about the os9 operating system
comp.os.parix
Forum for users of the parallel operating system PARIX
comp.os.qnx
Using and developing under the QNX operating system
comp.os.research
Operating systems and related areas
comp.os.rsts
Topics related to the PDP-11 RSTS/E operating system
comp.os.v
The V distributed operating system from Stanford
comp.os.vxworks
The VxWorks real-time operating system
comp.os.xinu
The XINU operating system from Purdue (D. Comer)
comp.security.unix
Discussion of Unix security
comp.soft-sys.andrew
The Andrew system from CMU
comp.sources.unix
Postings of complete, UNIX-oriented sources
comp.std.lisp
User group (ALU) supported standards
comp.std.mumps
Discussions about Mumps standards
comp.std.unix
Discussion for the P1003 committee on UNIX
comp.sys.3b1
Discussion and support of AT&T 7300/3B1/UnixPC
comp.sys.acorn
Discussion on Acorn and ARM-based computers
comp.sys.acorn.announce
Announcements for Acorn and ARM users
comp.sys.acorn.misc
Acorn computing in general
comp.sys.acorn.tech
Software and hardware aspects of Acorn and ARM products
comp.sys.apple2.gno
The Apple IIgs GNO multitasking environment
comp.sys.convex
Convex computer systems hardware and software
comp.sys.dec
Discussions about DEC computer systems
comp.sys.harris
Harris computer systems, especially real-time systems
comp.sys.hp.hardware
Discussion of Hewlett Packard system hardware
comp.sys.hp.misc
Issues not covered in any other comp.sys.hp. group
comp.sys.ibm.pc.digest
The IBM PC, PC-XT, and PC-AT
comp.sys.intel
Discussions about Intel systems and parts
comp.sys.mac.oop.macapp3
Version 3 of the MacApp object oriented system
comp.sys.mac.system
Discussions of Macintosh system software

Computing & Mathematics

comp.sys.mips
Systems based on MIPS chips
comp.sys.next.advocacy
The NeXT religion
comp.sys.next.announce
Announcements related to the NeXT computer system
comp.sys.next.bugs
Discussion and solutions for known NeXT bugs
comp.sys.next.hardware
Discussing the physical aspects of NeXT computers
comp.sys.next.marketplace
NeXT hardware, software and jobs
comp.sys.next.misc
General discussion about the NeXT computersystem
comp.sys.next.sysadmin
Discussions related to NeXT system administration
comp.sys.nsc.32k
National Semiconductor 32000 series chips
comp.sys.palmtops
Super-powered calculators in the palm of your hand
comp.sys.pen
Interacting with computers through pen gestures
comp.sys.powerpc
General PowerPC discussion
comp.sys.prime
Prime computer products
comp.sys.proteon
Proteon gateway products
comp.sys.psion
Discussion about PSION Personal computers & Organizers
comp.sys.pyramid
Pyramid 90x computers
comp.sys.ridge
Ridge 32 computersand ROS
comp.sys.sequent
Sequent systems, (Balance and Symmetry)
comp.sys.sgi.admin
System administration on Silicon Graphics's Irises
comp.sys.sgi.announce
Announcements for the SGI community
comp.sys.sgi.apps
Applications which run on the Iris
comp.sys.sgi.audio
Audio on SGI systems
comp.sys.sgi.bugs
Bugs found in the IRIX operating system
comp.sys.ti.explorer
The Texas Instruments Explorer
comp.sys.unisys
Sperry, Burroughs, Convergent and Unisys systems
comp.unix.admin
Administering a UNIX-based system
comp.unix.advocacy
Arguments for and against UNIX and UNIX versions
comp.unix.aix
IBM's version of UNIX
comp.unix.amiga
Minix, SYSV4 and other nix on an Amiga
comp.unix.aux
The version of UNIX for Apple Macintosh II computers
comp.unix.bsd.386bsd.announce
Announcements pertaining to 386BSD
comp.unix.bsd.386bsd.misc
386BSD operating system
comp.unix.bsd.bsdi.announce
Announcements pertaining to BSD/OS
comp.unix.bsd.bsdi.misc
BSD/OS operating system
comp.unix.bsd.freebsd.announce
Announcements pertaining to FreeBSD
comp.unix.bsd.freebsd.misc
FreeBSD operating system
comp.unix.bsd.misc
BSD operating systems
comp.unix.bsd.netbsd.announce
Announcements pertaining to NetBSD
comp.unix.bsd.netbsd.misc
NetBSD operating system
comp.unix.cray
Cray computers and their operating systems
comp.unix.dos-under-unix
MS-DOS running under UNIX by whatever means
comp.unix.internals
Discussions on hacking UNIX internals
comp.unix.large
UNIX on mainframes and in large networks
comp.unix.machten
The MachTen operating system and related issues
comp.unix.misc
Various topics that don't fit other groups
comp.unix.pc-clone.16bit
UNIX on 286 architectures
comp.unix.pc-clone.32bit
UNIX on 386 and 486 architectures
comp.unix.programmer
Q&A for people programming under UNIX
comp.unix.questions
UNIX neophytes group
comp.unix.sco.announce
SCO and related product announcements
comp.unix.sco.misc
SCO Unix, Systems, and Environments
comp.unix.sco.programmer
Programming in and for SCO Environments
comp.unix.shell
Using and programming the UNIX shell
comp.unix.solaris
Discussions about the Solaris operating system
comp.unix.sys3
System III UNIX discussions
comp.unix.sys5.misc
Versions of System V which predate Release 3
comp.unix.sys5.r3
Discussing System V Release 3
comp.unix.sys5.r4
Discussing System V Release 4
comp.unix.unixware
Discussion about Novell's UNIXWare products
comp.unix.unixware.announce
Announcements related to UNIXWare
comp.unix.unixware.misc
Products of Novell's UNIX Systems Group
comp.unix.user-friendly
Discussion of UNIX user-friendliness
comp.unix.wizards
For only true UNIX wizards
comp.unix.xenix.misc
General discussions regarding XENIX (except SCO)
comp.unix.xenix.sco
XENIX versions from the Santa Cruz Operation
comp.virus
Computer viruses & security
comp.windows.garnet
The Garnet user interface development environment
comp.windows.interviews
The InterViews object-oriented windowing system
comp.windows.misc
Various issues about windowing systems
comp.windows.news
Sun Microsystems' NeWS window system
comp.windows.open-look
Discussion about the Open Look GUI
comp.windows.suit
The SUIT user-interface toolkit
comp.windows.ui-builders.uimx
Using and augmenting the UIM/X UI Builder
comp.windows.x
Discussion about the X Window System
comp.windows.x.announce
X Window System announcements
comp.windows.x.apps
Getting and using, not programming, applications for X
comp.windows.x.i386unix
The XFree86 window system and others
comp.windows.x.intrinsics
Discussion of the X toolkit
comp.windows.x.motif
The Motif GUI for the X Window System
comp.windows.x.pex
The PEX extension of the X Window System
info.mach
The Mach operating system
relcom.comp.os.os2
OS/2 operational system
relcom.comp.os.vms
VMS operational system
relcom.comp.os.windows
FIDOnet area, MS-Windows operational system
relcom.comp.os.windows.prog
FIDOnet area, programming under MS-Windows
relcom.fido.ru.unix
Inter-network challenge to OS UNIX
relcom.x
X Windows discussion
vmsnet.alpha
Discussion about Alpha AXP architecture, systems, porting, etc
vmsnet.announce
General announcements of interest to all
vmsnet.decus.journal
The DECUServe Journal
vmsnet.decus.lugs
Discussion of DECUS Local User Groups and related issues
vmsnet.epsilon-cd
DEC's free, unsupported OpenVMS AXP CD
vmsnet.internals
VMS internals, MACRO-32, Bliss, gatewayed to MACRO32 list
vmsnet.misc
General VMS topics not covered elsewhere
vmsnet.networks.desktop.misc
Other desktop integration software

Organizations

alt.current-events.cebit95
CeBIT'95 at Hannover
comp.org.cpsr.announce
Computer Professionals for Social Responsibility
comp.org.cpsr.talk
Issues of *computing and social responsibility
comp.org.eff.news
News from the Electronic Frontier Foundation
comp.org.eff.talk
Discussion of EFF goals, strategies, etc
comp.org.fidonet
FidoNews digest, official news of FidoNet Assoc
comp.org.ieee
Issues and announcements about the IEEE & its members
comp.org.isoc.interest
Discussion about the Internet Society
comp.org.issnnet
The International Student Society for Neural Networks
comp.org.lisp-users
Association of Lisp Users related discussions
comp.org.sug
Talk about/for the The Sun User's Group
comp.org.usenix
USENIX Association events and announcements
comp.org.usenix.roomshare
Finding lodging during Usenix conferences
comp.research.japan
The nature of research in Japan

Computing & Mathematics

comp.society.cu-digest
  The Computer Underground Digest
comp.society.futures
  Events in technology affecting future computing
comp.unix.osf.misc
  Various aspects of Open Software Foundation products
comp.unix.osf.osf1
  The Open Software Foundation's OSF/1
gnu.gnusenet.config
  GNU's Not Usenet administration and configuration
rec.org.mensa
  Talking with members of the high IQ society Mensa

Programming

alt.cobol
  Relationship between programming and stone axes
alt.fan.netcom.hack.hack.hack
  Barbarians at the gate
alt.hackers
  Descriptions of projects currently under development
alt.hackers.malicious
  The really bad guys — don't take candy from them
alt.hackintosh
  Clever programming on Apple's Macintosh
alt.hypertext
  Discussion of hypertext — uses, transport, etc
alt.lang.asm
  Assembly languages of various flavors
alt.lang.basic
  The Language That Would Not Die
alt.lang.ca-realizer
  The CA Realizer GUI programming environment
alt.lang.design
  Discussion for the design of computer languges
alt.msdos.programmer
  For the serious MS/DOS programmer (no for sale ads)
alt.sb.programmer
  Programming the Sound Blaster PC sound card
alt.sys.amiga.blitz
  The Blitz Basic programming language
alt.winsock.programming
  Programming Windows Sockets
bit.listserv.asm370
  IBM 370 Assembly Programming Discussions
bit.listserv.script-l
  IBM vs Waterloo SCRIPT Discussion Group
bit.listserv.simula
  The SIMULA language list
bit.listserv.sqlinfo
  Forum for SQL/DS and related topics
bit.listserv.vfort-l
  V3-Fortran discussion list
comp.cog-eng
  Cognitive engineering
comp.graphics.api.misc
  Application Programmer Interface issues, methods
comp.graphics.api.opengl
  The OpenGL 3D application programming interface
comp.graphics.api.pexlib
  The PEXlib application programming interface
comp.lang.ada
  Discussion about Ada
comp.lang.apl
  Discussion about APL
comp.lang.asm.x86
  General 80x86 assembly language programming
comp.lang.asm370
  Programming in IBM System/370 Assembly Language
comp.lang.basic.misc
  Other dialects and aspects of BASIC
comp.lang.basic.visual.3rdparty
  Add-ins for Visual Basic
comp.lang.basic.visual.announce
  Official information on Visual Basic
comp.lang.basic.visual.database
  Database aspects of Visual Basic
comp.lang.basic.visual.misc
  Visual Basic in general
comp.lang.beta
  The object-oriented programming language BETA
comp.lang.c
  Discussion about C
comp.lang.c++
  The object-oriented C++ language
comp.lang.c++.leda
  All aspects of the LEDA library
comp.lang.c.moderated
  The C programming language
comp.lang.clipper
  Clipper and Visual Objects programming languages
comp.lang.clos
  Common Lisp Object System discussions
comp.lang.clu
  The CLU language & related topics
comp.lang.cobol
  The COBOL language and software
comp.lang.dylan
  For discussion of the Dylan language
comp.lang.eiffel
  The object-oriented Eiffel language
comp.lang.forth
  Discussion about Forth
comp.lang.forth.mac
  The CSI MacForth programming environment
comp.lang.fortran
  Discussion about FORTRAN
comp.lang.functional
  Discussion about functional languages
comp.lang.hermes
  The Hermes language for distributed applications
comp.lang.icon
  Topics related to the ICON programming language
comp.lang.idl
  IDL (Interface Description Language) related topics
comp.lang.idl-pvwave
  IDL and PV-Wave language discussions
comp.lang.lisp
  Discussion about LISP
comp.lang.lisp.franz
  The Franz Lisp programming language
comp.lang.lisp.mcl
  Discussing Apple's Macintosh Common Lisp
comp.lang.lisp.x
  The XLISP language system
comp.lang.logo
  The Logo teaching and learning language
comp.lang.misc
  Different computer languages not specifically listed
comp.lang.ml
  ML languages including Standard ML, CAML, Lazy ML, etc
comp.lang.modula2
  Discussion about Modula-2
comp.lang.modula3
  Discussion about the Modula-3 language
comp.lang.mumps
  The M (MUMPS) language & technology, in general
comp.lang.oberon
  The Oberon language and system
comp.lang.objective-c
  The Objective-C language and environment
comp.lang.pascal
  Discussion about Pascal
comp.lang.perl
  Discussion of Larry Wall's Perl system
comp.lang.perl.announce
  Announcements about Perl
comp.lang.perl.misc
  The Perl language in general
comp.lang.pop
  Pop11 and the Plug user group
comp.lang.postscript
  The PostScript Page Description Language
comp.lang.prograph
  Prograph, a visual object-oriented dataflow language
comp.lang.prolog
  Discussion about PROLOG
comp.lang.python
  The Python computer language
comp.lang.rexx
  The REXX command language
comp.lang.sather
  The object-oriented computer language Sather
comp.lang.scheme
  The Scheme Programming language
comp.lang.scheme.c
  The Scheme language environment
comp.lang.sigplan
  Info & announcements from ACM SIGPLAN
comp.lang.smalltalk
  Discussion about Smalltalk 80
comp.lang.tcl
  The Tcl programming language and related tools
comp.lang.verilog
  Discussing Verilog and PLI
comp.lang.vhdl
  VHSIC Hardware Description Language, IEEE 1076/87
comp.lang.visual
  General discussion of visual programming languages
comp.lsi.cad
  Electrical computerAided Design
comp.object
  Object-oriented programming and languages
comp.object.logic
  Integrating object-oriented and logic programming
comp.org.acm
  Topics about the Association for *computing Machinery
comp.os.ms-windows.programmer.controls
  Controls, dialogs and VBXs
comp.os.ms-windows.programmer.misc
  Programming Microsoft Windows
comp.os.ms-windows.programmer.multimedia
  Multimedia programming
comp.os.ms-windows.programmer.networks
  Network programming
comp.os.ms-windows.programmer.ole
  OLE2, COM and DDE programming
comp.os.ms-windows.programmer.win32
  32-bit Windows programming interfaces
comp.os.msdos.programmer
  Programming MS-DOS machines
comp.programming
  Programming issues that transcend languages and OSs
comp.programming.literate
  Knuth's "literate programming" method and tools
comp.protocols.dicom
  Digital Imaging and Communications in Medicine
comp.protocols.iso
  The ISO protocol stack
comp.protocols.iso.dev-environ
  The ISO Development Environment
comp.sources.hp48
  Programs for the HP48 and HP28 calculators
comp.sources.postscript
  Source code for programs written in PostScript
comp.sources.reviewed
  Source code evaluated by peer review
comp.specification
  Languages and methodologies for formal specification
comp.specification.larch
  Larch family of formal specification languages

Newsgroups

comp.specification.z
Discussion about the formal specification notation Z
comp.std.c
Discussion about C language standards
comp.std.c++
Discussion about C++ language, library, standards
comp.sys.acorn.programmer
Programming of Acorn computers
comp.sys.amiga.programmer
Developers & hobbyists discuss code
comp.sys.apple2.programmer
Programming on the Apple II
comp.sys.atari.programmer
Programming on the Atari computer
comp.sys.mac.oop.misc
Object oriented programming issues on the Mac
comp.sys.mac.programmer.codewarrior
Mac programming using CodeWarrior
comp.sys.mac.programmer.help
Help with Macintosh programming
comp.sys.mac.programmer.info
Frequently requested information
comp.sys.mac.programmer.misc
Other issues of Macintosh programming
comp.sys.mac.programmer.tools
Macintosh programming tools
comp.sys.next.programmer
NeXT related programming issues
comp.sys.transputer
The Transputer computer and OCCAM language
comp.text.sgml
ISO 8879 SGML, structured documents, markup languages
gnu.emacs.sources
ONLY (please!) C and Lisp source code for GNU Emacs
relcom.comp.binaries
Binary codes of computer programs
relcom.comp.binaries.d
Discussions of binary codes
relcom.comp.lang.forth
Forth programming language
relcom.comp.lang.pascal
Using of Pascal programming language
relcom.comp.virus
Computer viruses
relcom.fido.ru.hacker
FIDOnet, hackers and crackers (legal!)
relcom.fido.su.c-c++
FIDOnet, C & C++ language

Software

alt.1d
One-dimensional imaging, & the thinking behind it
alt.3d
Three-dimensional imaging
alt.3d.misc
Same as alt.3d, only better
alt.3d.sirds
Especially for Single Image Random Dot Stereograms
alt.3d.studio
For 3D Studio users
alt.aldus.freehand
The other hand is busy-computer graphics
alt.aldus.pagemaker
Don't use expensive user support, come here instead
alt.authorware
About Authorware, produced by Authorware. So subtle
alt.binaries.clip-art
Distribution of DOS, Mac and UNIX clipart
alt.cad
Computer Aided Design
alt.cad.autocad
CAD as practiced by customers of Autodesk
alt.cad.cadkey
Cadkey, Datacad, and other Cadkey, Inc. products
alt.comp.shareware
"Try Before You Buy" software marketing
alt.comp.shareware.for-kids
"Try Before You Buy" for children
alt.comp.virus
An unmoderated forum for discussing viruses
alt.corel.graphics
The PClone package Corel Draw & related products
alt.fractal-design.painter
Fractal Design's "Natural Media" painting
alt.fringeware
Riding the radical edge of the software wave
alt.soft-sys.corel.draw
The Corel Draw graphics package
alt.sources
Alternative source code, unmoderated. Caveat Emptor
alt.sources.amiga
Source code for the Amiga
alt.sources.d
Discussion of posted sources
alt.sources.index
Pointers to source code in alt.sources.*
alt.sources.mac
Source code for Apple Macintosh computers
alt.sources.wanted
Requests for source code
alt.toolkits.xview
The X windows XView toolkit
bit.listserv.c370-l
C/370 discussion list
bit.listserv.cics-l
CICS discussion list
bit.listserv.dasig
Database Administration
bit.listserv.db2-l
DB2 Data Base discussion list
bit.listserv.license
Software licensing list
bit.listserv.pagemakr
PageMaker for Desktop Publishers
bit.listserv.uigis-l
User Interface for Geographical Info Systems
bit.listserv.wpcorp-l
WordPerfect Corporation products discussions
bit.listserv.wpwin-l
WordPerfect for Windows
bit.mailserv.word-mac
Word Processing on the Macintosh
bit.mailserv.word-pc
Word Processing on the IBM PC
bit.software.international
International Software list
biz.comp.software
Generic commercial software postings
comp.archives.msdos.announce
Announcements about MSDOS archives
comp.archives.msdos.d
Discussion of materials available in MSDOS archives
comp.binaries.ibm.pc.wanted
Requests for IBM PC and compatible programs
comp.binaries.mac
Encoded Macintosh programs in binary
comp.binaries.ms-windows
Binary programs for Microsoft Windows
comp.binaries.newton
Apple Newton binaries, sources, books, etc
comp.binaries.os2
Binaries for use under the OS/2 ABI
comp.binaries.psion
Binaries for the range of Psion computers
comp.cad.compass
compass Design Automation EDA tools
comp.cad.autocad
AutoDesk's AutoCAD software
comp.cad.i-deas
SDRC I-DEAS Masters Series software
comp.cad.microstation
MicroStation CAD software and related products
comp.cad.pro-engineer
Parametric Technology's Pro/Engineer design package
comp.databases.informix
Informix database management software discussions
comp.databases.ms-access
MS Windows' relational database system, Access
comp.databases.object
Object-oriented paradigms in database systems
comp.databases.oracle
The SQL database products of the Oracle Corporation
comp.databases.paradox
Borland's database for DOS & MS Windows
comp.databases.progress
The Progress 4GL & RDBMS
comp.databases.rdb
The relational database engine RDB from DEC
comp.databases.theory
Discussing advances in database technology
comp.databases.xbase.fox
Fox Software's xBase system and compatibles
comp.databases.xbase.misc
Discussion of xBase (dBASE-like) products
comp.dcom.fax
Fax hardware, software, and protocols
comp.editors
Topics related to computerized text editing
comp.emulators.ms-windows.wine
A free MS-Windows emulator under X
comp.graphics.apps.alias
3-D graphics software from Alias Research
comp.graphics.apps.avs
The Application Visualization System
comp.graphics.misc
computer graphics miscellany
comp.graphics.opengl
The OpenGL 3D application programming interface
comp.graphics.packages.3dstudio
Autodesk's 3D Studio software
comp.graphics.packages.alias
3-D graphics software from Alias Research
comp.graphics.packages.lightwave
NewTek's Lightwave3D and related topics
comp.graphics.raytracing
Ray tracing software, tools and methods
comp.graphics.rendering.misc
Rendering comparisons, approaches, methods
comp.graphics.rendering.raytracing
Ray tracing software, tools and methods
comp.graphics.rendering.renderman
RenderMan interface & shading language
comp.graphics.research
Highly technical computer graphics discussion
comp.groupware
Software and hardware for shared interactive environments
comp.groupware.lotus-notes.misc
Lotus Notes related discussions
comp.mail.list-admin.policy
Policy issues in running mailing lists
comp.mail.list-admin.software
Software used in the running of mailing lists
comp.multimedia
Interactive multimedia technologies of all kinds
comp.os.cpm.amethyst
Discussion of Amethyst, CP/M-80 software package
comp.os.ms-windows.advocacy
Speculation and debate about Microsoft Windows
comp.os.ms-windows.announce
Announcements relating to Windows

Computing & Mathematics

comp.os.ms-windows.apps.comm
MS-Windows communication applications
comp.os.ms-windows.apps.financial
MS-Windows financial & tax software
comp.os.ms-windows.apps.misc
MS-Windows applications
comp.os.ms-windows.apps.utilities
MS-Windows utilities
comp.os.ms-windows.apps.word-proc
MS-Windows word-processing applications
comp.os.ms-windows.misc
General discussions about Windows issues
comp.os.ms-windows.networking.misc
Windows and other networks
comp.os.ms-windows.networking.tcp-ip
Windows and TCP/IP networking
comp.os.ms-windows.networking.windows
Windows' built-in networking
comp.os.ms-windows.programmer.tools
Development tools in Windows
comp.os.ms-windows.programmer.winhelp
WinHelp/Multimedia Viewer development
comp.os.ms-windows.setup
Installing and configuring Microsoft Windows
comp.os.msdos.apps
Discussion of applications that run under MS-DOS
comp.os.msdos.desqview
QuarterDeck's Desqview and related products
comp.os.msdos.djgpp
DOS GNU C/C++ applications and programming environment
comp.os.msdos.mail-news
Administering mail & network news systems under MS-DOS
comp.os.msdos.misc
Miscellaneous topics about MS-DOS machines
comp.publish.cdrom.multimedia
Software for multimedia authoring & publishing
comp.publish.cdrom.software
Software used in publishing with CD-ROM
comp.publish.prepress
Electronic prepress
comp.soft-sys.dce
The Distributed computing Environment (DCE)
comp.soft-sys.khoros
The Khoros X11 visualization system
comp.soft-sys.math.mathematica
Mathematica discussion group
comp.soft-sys.matlab
The MathWorks calculation and visualization package
comp.soft-sys.nextstep
The NeXTstep computing environment
comp.soft-sys.powerbuilder
Application development tools from PowerSoft
comp.soft-sys.ptolemy
The Ptolemy simulation/code generation environment
comp.soft-sys.sas
The SAS statistics package
comp.soft-sys.shazam
The SHAZAM econometrics computer program
comp.soft-sys.spss
The SPSS statistics package
comp.soft-sys.wavefront
Wavefront software products, problems, etc
comp.software-eng
Software Engineering and related topics
comp.software.config-mgmt
Configuration management, tools and procedures
comp.software.international
Finding, using, & writing non-English software
comp.software.licensing
Software licensing technology
comp.sources.games
Postings of recreational software
comp.sources.games.bugs
Bug reports and fixes for posted game software

comp.sources.mac
Software for the Apple Macintosh
comp.sources.misc
Posting of software
comp.sources.sun
Software for Sun workstations
comp.sources.testers
Finding people to test software
comp.sources.wanted
Requests for software and fixes
comp.sources.x
Software for the X Window System
comp.sw.components
Software components and related technology
comp.sys.acorn.apps
Acorn software applications
comp.sys.amiga.emulations
Various hardware & software emulators
comp.sys.amiga.games
Discussion of games for the Commodore Amiga
comp.sys.apple2
Discussion about Apple II micros
comp.sys.hp.apps
Discussion of software and apps on all HP platforms
comp.sys.ibm.pc.demos
Demonstration programs which showcase programmer skill
comp.sys.ibm.pc.games.action
Arcade-style games on PCs
comp.sys.ibm.pc.games.adventure
Adventure (non-rpg) games on PCs
comp.sys.ibm.pc.games.announce
Announcements for all PC gamers
comp.sys.ibm.pc.games.flight-sim
Flight simulators on PCs
comp.sys.ibm.pc.games.marketplace
PC clone games wanted and for sale
comp.sys.ibm.pc.games.misc
Games not covered by other PC groups
comp.sys.ibm.pc.games.rpg
Role-playing games on the PC
comp.sys.mac.announce
Important notices for Macintosh users
comp.sys.mac.comm
Discussion of Macintosh communications
comp.sys.mac.databases
Database systems for the Apple Macintosh
comp.sys.mac.digest
Apple Macintosh: info&uses, but no programs
comp.sys.mac.games
Discussions of games on the Macintosh
comp.sys.mac.games.action
Action games for the Macintosh
comp.sys.mac.games.adventure
Adventure games for the Macintosh
comp.sys.mac.games.announce
Announcements for Mac gamers
comp.sys.mac.games.flight-sim
Flight simulator gameplay on the Mac
comp.sys.mac.games.marketplace
Macintosh games for sale and trade
comp.sys.mac.games.misc
Macintosh games not covered in other groups
comp.sys.mac.games.strategic
Strategy/planning games on the Macintosh
comp.sys.mac.graphics
Macintosh graphics: paint, draw, 3D, CAD, animation
comp.sys.newton.programmer
Discussion of Newton software development
comp.sys.next.software
Function, use and availability of NeXT programs
comp.sys.sun.apps
Software applications for Sun computersystems
comp.text
Text processing issues and methods
comp.text.frame
Desktop publishing with FrameMaker

comp.text.interleaf
Applications and use of Interleaf software
comp.text.pdf
Adobe Acrobat and Portable Document Format technology
comp.text.tex
Discussion about the TeX and LaTeX systems & macros
gnu.announce
Status and announcements from the Project
gnu.bash.bug
Bourne Again SHell bug reports and suggested fixes
gnu.chess
Announcements about the GNU Chess program
gnu.emacs.announce
Announcements about GNU Emacs
gnu.emacs.bug
GNU Emacs bug reports and suggested fixes
gnu.emacs.help
User queries and answers
gnu.emacs.vm.bug
Bug reports on the Emacs VM mail package
gnu.emacs.vm.info
Information about the Emacs VM mail package
gnu.emacs.vms
VMS port of GNU Emacs
gnu.epoch.misc
The Epoch X11 extensions to Emacs
gnu.g++.announce
Announcements about the GNU C++ Compiler
gnu.g++.bug
Bug reports and suggested fixes for g++
gnu.g++.help
GNU C++ compiler (G++) user queries and answers
gnu.g++.lib.bug
g++ library bug reports/suggested fixes
gnu.gcc.announce
Announcements about the GNU C Compiler
gnu.gcc.bug
GNU C Compiler bug reports/suggested fixes
gnu.gcc.help
GNU C Compiler (gcc) user queries and answers
gnu.gdb.bug
gcc/g++ DeBugger bugs and suggested fixes
gnu.ghostscript.bug
GNU Ghostscript interpreter bugs
gnu.gnusenet.test
GNU's Not Usenet alternative hierarchy testing
gnu.groff.bug
Bugs in the GNU roff programs
gnu.misc.discuss
Serious discussion about GNU and freed software
gnu.smalltalk.bug
Bugs in GNU Smalltalk
gnu.utils.bug
GNU utilities bugs (e.g., make, gawk, ls)
info.brl-cad
BRL's Solid Modeling CAD system
info.nysersnmp
The SNMP software distributed by PSI
info.unix-sw
Software available FTP
relcom.commerce.software
Software
relcom.commerce.software.demo
Demo versions of commercial software
relcom.comp.clarion
CLARION database management system
relcom.comp.dbms.clipper
Clipper database development system
relcom.comp.dbms.foxpro
FoxPro database development system
relcom.comp.dbms.vista
db_Vista discussions
relcom.comp.demo
Demo versions of various software
relcom.comp.demo.d
Discussions on demo software

Computing & Mathematics – Education

relcom.comp.sources.d
  Discussions on sources
relcom.comp.sources.misc
  Software sources
relcom.fido.ru.strack
  FIDOnet, digitized sound
relcom.msdos
  MS-DOS software
vmsnet.infosystems.gopher
  Gopher software for VMS, gateway to VMSGopher-L
vmsnet.infosystems.misc
  Misc. infosystem software for VMS (WAIS, WWW)
vmsnet.networks.management.decmcc
  DECmcc and related software
vmsnet.sources.games
  Recreational software postings
vmsnet.uucp
  DECUS uucp software, gatewayed to vmsnet mailing list

Standards

comp.std.announce
  Announcements about standards activities
comp.std.internat
  Discussion about international standards
comp.std.misc
  Discussion about various standards
comp.std.wireless
  Examining standards for wireless network technology

Statistics

sci.stat.math
  Statistics from a strictly mathematical viewpoint

Theory

comp.databases
  Database and data management issues and theory
comp.realtime
  Issues related to real-time computing
comp.society
  The impact of technology on society
comp.theory
  Theoretical computer science
comp.theory.dynamic-sys
  Ergodic Theory and Dynamical Systems
comp.theory.self-org-sys
  Topics related to self-organization
info.theorynt
  Theory list

Education

Alternative Education

alt.cesium
  College Educated Students in Universal Mainland
alt.education.alternative
  School doesn't have to suck!
alt.education.disabled
  Education for people with physical/mental disabilities
alt.education.home-school.christian
  Christian home-schoolers
k12.ed.special
  Educating students with handicaps and/or special needs
misc.education.home-school.christian
  Christian home-schooling
misc.education.home-school.misc
  Almost anything about home-schooling

Continuing Education

misc.education.adult
  Adult education and adult literacy practice/research

Curriculum & Instruction

alt.education.email-project
  The email project for teaching English
alt.teachers.lesson-planning
  Helping teachers plan their instruction
k12.ed.art
  Arts & crafts curricula in K-12 education
k12.ed.business
  Business education curricula in grades K-12
k12.ed.comp.literacy
  Teaching computer literacy in grades K-12
k12.ed.health-pe
  Health and Physical Ed. curricula in grades K-12
k12.ed.life-skills
  Home Economics, career education, and school counseling
k12.ed.math
  Mathematics curriculum in K-12 education
k12.ed.music
  Music and Performing Arts curriculum in K-12 education
k12.ed.science
  Science curriculum in K-12 education
k12.ed.soc-studies
  Social Studies/History curriculum K-12 education
k12.ed.tag
  K-12 education for gifted and talented students
k12.lang.deutsch-eng
  Bilingual German/English practice with native speakers
k12.lang.esp-eng
  Bilingual Spanish/English practice with native speakers
k12.lang.francais
  French practice with native speakers
k12.lang.japanese
  Bilingual Japanese/English ith native speakers
k12.lang.russian
  Bilingual Russian/English practice with native speakers
soc.college.teaching-asst
  Issues affecting collegiate teaching assistants

Distance Education

alt.education.distance
  Learning from teachers who are far away

Educational Issues

alt.comp.acad-freedom.news
  Academic freedom issues related to computers
alt.comp.acad-freedom.talk
  Academic freedom issues related to computers
alt.education.ib.tok
  International Baccalaureates in Theory of Knowledge
misc.education.science
  Issues related to science education
sci.edu
  The science of education

Educational Policy

bit.listserv.ashe-l
  Higher Ed policy and research
bit.listserv.edpolyan
  Education Policy Analysis forum

Educational Technology

bit.listserv.aect-l
  Educational Communication and Technology
bit.listserv.dectei-l
  DECUS Education Software Library Discussions
bit.listserv.edtech
  EDTECH - Educational Technology

Libraries

relcom.sci.libraries
  Discussion of libraries and related info
soc.libraries.talk
  Discussing all aspects of libraries

Primary & Secondary Education

alt.society.high-school
  The vaguely alternative world of high school
bit.listserv.physhare
  K-12 Physics list
bit.listserv.tecmat-l
  Technology in secondary math
bit.listserv.wac-l
  Writing Across the Curriculum
k12.chat.teacher
  Casual conversation for teachers of grades K-12
k12.lang.art
  The art of teaching language skills in grades K-12
k12.sys.channel0
  Current projects
k12.sys.channel1
  Current projects
k12.sys.channel10
  Current projects
k12.sys.channel11
  Current projects
k12.sys.channel12
  Current projects
k12.sys.channel2
  Current projects
k12.sys.channel3
  Current projects
k12.sys.channel4
  Current projects
k12.sys.channel5
  Current projects
k12.sys.channel6
  Current projects
k12.sys.channel7
  Current projects
k12.sys.channel8
  Current projects
k12.sys.channel9
  Current projects
k12.sys.projects
  Discussion of potential projects

Resources

alt.education.higher.stu-affairs
  Student Affairs principles & practices

alt.education.research
Studying about studying
alt.education.university.vision2020
Models for a university in 2020
alt.literacy.adult
Adults, Literacy, Reading, Writing
alt.military.cadet
Preparing for the coming apocalypse
alt.school.homework-help
Looking for assistance with schoolwork
bit.listserv.aera
American Educational Research Association
bit.listserv.edusig-l
EDUSIG Discussions
bit.listserv.ibm-hesc
IBM Higher Education Consortium
bit.listserv.sganet
Student Government Global Mail Network
misc.education
Discussion of the educational system
relcom.education
Education discussions, from pre-school to higher

Vocational Education

bit.listserv.vocnet
Vocational Education Discussion Group
k12.ed.tech
Industrial arts & vocational education in grades K-12
misc.education.multimedia
Multimedia for education

Engineering & Technology

Aeronautical Engineering

clari.tw.aerospace
Aerospace industry and companies

Bioengineering

sci.engr.biomed
Discussing the field of biomedical engineering
sci.life-extension
Slowing, stopping or reversing the ageing process

Chemical Engineering

sci.engr.chem
All aspects of chemical engineering

Civil Engineering

relcom.commerce.construction
Construction materials and equipment
sci.engr.civil
Topics related to civil engineering

Electrical Engineering

alt.electronics.analog.vlsi
VLSI system design
ieee.announce
General Announcements for IEEE community
ieee.config
Postings about managing the ieee.* groups

ieee.general
IEEE - General discussion
ieee.pcnfs
Discussion & tips on PC-NFS
ieee.rab.announce
Regional Activities Board - Announcements
ieee.rab.general
Regional Activities Board - General discussion
ieee.region1
Region 1 Announcements
ieee.tab.announce
Technical Activities Board - Announcements
ieee.tab.general
Technical Activities Board - General discussion
ieee.tcos
The Technical Committee on Operating Systems
ieee.usab.announce
USAB - Announcements
ieee.usab.general
USAB - General discussion
sci.electronics
Circuits, theory, electrons and discussions
sci.electronics.cad
Schematic drafting, printed circuit layout, simulation
sci.electronics.repair
Fixing electronic equipment
sci.engr.semiconductors
Semiconductor devices, processes, materials, physics
sci.engr.television.advanced
HDTV/DATV standards, equipment, practices, etc
sci.engr.television.broadcast
Broadcast facility equipment and practices

Environmental Engineering

alt.hvac
Heating, venting and air conditioning
sci.engr.geomechanics
Geomechanics issues and related topics
sci.engr.heat-vent-ac
Heating, ventilating, air conditioning & refrigeration
sci.engr.lighting
Light, vision & color in architecture, media, etc

Material Science

alt.lycra
The WunderFabrik
relcom.commerce.metals
Metals and metal products
sci.engr.metallurgy
Metallurgical Engineering
sci.materials
All aspects of materials engineering

Mechanical Engineering

sci.engr.mech
The field of mechanical engineering
sci.mech.fluids
All aspects of fluid mechanics

Government & Politics

Agencies

alt.law-enforcement.R_C_M_P
The Royal Canadian Mounted Police
alt.politics.org.batf
Politics of the U.S. firearms (etc.) regulation agency
alt.politics.org.cia
The United States Central Intelligence Agency
alt.politics.org.fbi
The United States Federal Bureau of Investigation
alt.politics.org.misc
Political organizations
alt.politics.org.nsa
The ultrasecret security arm of the US government
alt.visa.us
Discussion/information on visas pertaining to US

Career & Employment

alt.peace-corps
The works of the Peace Corps

Countries

alt.culture.okusi-ambeno
Discussion about the Sultanate of Okusi-Ambeno
alt.culture.tuva
Topics related to the Republic of Tuva, South Siberia
alt.current-events.bosnia
The strife of Bosnia-Herzegovina
alt.current-events.haiti
News about Haiti
alt.current-events.korean-crisis
North Korea's nuclear armament
alt.current-events.russia
Current happenings in Russia
alt.current-events.ukraine
Current and fast paced Ukrainian events
alt.current-events.usa
What's new in the United States
alt.dear.whitehouse
When Hints from Heloise aren't enough
alt.india.progressive
Progressive politics in the Indian sub-continent
alt.politics.usa.congress
Discussions relating to U.S. House and Senate
alt.politics.usa.misc
Miscellaneous USA politics
misc.immigration.canada
Canada immigration issues

Doctrines

alt.flame.right-wing-conservatives
Sticking it to the ultra-conservatives
alt.magick.order
Discussion of magickopolitical hierarchy
alt.politics.democrats.d
U.S. Democratic party
alt.politics.libertarian
The libertarian ideology
alt.politics.nationalism.white
People who believe in White Supremacy
alt.politics.radical-left
Who remains after the radicals left?

alt.politics.socialism.trotsky
   Trotskyite socialism discussions
alt.politics.usa.constitution
   U.S. Constitutional politics
alt.politics.usa.republican
   Discussions of the USA Republican Party

Issues

alt.activism
   Activities for activists
alt.activism.d
   A place to discuss issues in alt.activism
alt.activism.death-penalty
   For people opposed to capital punishment
alt.freedom.of.information.act
   All about the FOIA
alt.government.abuse
   Our Government Abuses its Power
alt.impeach.clinton
   Some think he performs as though he is impaired
alt.law-enforcement
   No, ossifer, there's nothing illegal going on in alt
alt.politics.datahighway
   Electronic interstate infrastructure
alt.politics.economics
   War == Poverty, & other discussions
alt.politics.elections
   All about the process of electing leaders
alt.politics.homosexuality
   As the name implies
alt.politics.media
   How the mass media is involved in shaping politics
alt.politics.reform
   Political reform
alt.politics.scorched-earth
   An environmentally oriented group
alt.revisionism
   "It CAN'T be that way 'cause here's the FACTS"
alt.revolution.counter
   Discussions of counter-revolutionary issues
alt.society.civil-liberty
   Same as alt.society.civil-liberties
alt.society.conservatism
   Social, cultural, and political conservatism
alt.society.revolution
   Espousing Jeffersonian ideals
bit.listserv.devmedia
   Media for Development and Domocracy
bit.listserv.disarm-l
   Disarmament Discussion List
bit.listserv.govdoc-l
   Discussion of Government Document Issues
bit.listserv.politics
   Forum for Discussion of Politics
info.firearms.politics
   Pol. firearms discussions
misc.activism.militia
   Citizens bearing arms for the common defense
misc.immigration.misc
   Miscellaneous countries immigration issues
misc.immigration.usa
   USA immigration issues
relcom.politics
   Political discussions
soc.rights.human
   Human rights & activism (e.g., Amnesty International)
talk.politics.crypto
   The relation between cryptography and government
talk.politics.drugs
   The politics of drug issues
talk.politics.guns
   The politics of firearm ownership and (mis)use
talk.politics.libertarian
   Libertarian politics & political philosophy

talk.politics.misc
   Political discussions and ravings of all kinds
talk.politics.theory
   Theory of politics and political systems

Political Science

alt.society.anarchy
   Societies without rulers

Regions

alt.culture.virtual.oceania
   Oceania project discussion and news
alt.great-lakes
   Discussions of the Great Lakes and adjacent places
bit.listserv.berita.d
   Discussions about b.l.berita
bit.listserv.catala
   Catalan Discussion List
talk.politics.china
   Discussion of political issues related to China
talk.politics.european-union
   The EU and political integration in Europe
talk.politics.mideast
   Discussion & debate over Middle Eastern events
talk.politics.soviet
   Discussion of Soviet politics, domestic and foreign
talk.politics.tibet
   The politics of Tibet and the Tibetan people

Health & Medicine

Addictions

alt.recovery
   For people in recovery programs (e.g., AA, ACA, GA)
alt.recovery.aa
   Recovery and Alcoholics Anonymous
alt.recovery.na
   Recovery and Narcotics Anonymous
alt.support.eating-disord
   People over the edge about weight loss
alt.support.ex-cult
   Recovering from religious cult experiences
alt.support.stop-smoking
   Getting over the nicotine addiction

Aging

alt.support.menopause
   Helping women through menopause

Alternative Medicine

alt.folklore.aromatherapy
   Discussion of aromatherapy
alt.folklore.herbs
   Discussion of all aspects of herbs and their uses
alt.health.ayurveda
   Really old medicine from India
alt.hypnosis
   When you awaken, you will forget about this newsgroup
misc.health.alternative
   Alternative, complementary and holistic health care

Biomedicine

alt.human-brain
   A delicacy in some corners of the planet
bionet.biology.cardiovascular
   Scientists engaged in cardiovascular research

Career & Employment

misc.emerg-services
   Forum for paramedics & other first responders

Dental Health

sci.med.dentistry
   Dentally related topics; all about teeth

Disabilities

alt.support.learning-disab
   For individuals with learning disabilities
alt.support.stuttering
   Support for people who stutter
alt.support.tourette
   Support for folks with Tourette's Syndrome
bit.listserv.autism
   Autism list
bit.listserv.axslib-l
   Library Access for People with Disabilities
bit.listserv.blindnws
   Blindness issues and discussions
bit.listserv.deaf-l
   Deaf List
bit.listserv.down-syn
   Downs Syndrome discussion group
bit.listserv.easi
   Computer Access for People with Disabilities
bit.listserv.l-hcap
   Handicap list

Diseases

alt.med.fibromyalgia
   Fibromyalgia Fibrositis list

Family Health

alt.support.foster-parents
   People who are foster parents
alt.support.househusbands
   Men who stay home to tend the house
alt.support.single-parents
   Single parenting solutions and support
alt.support.step-parents
   Dealing with step parents

Health & Medical Professionals

alt.med.phys-assts
   The profession of physician's assistant
bit.listserv.snurse-l
   International Nursing Student Group
sci.med.nursing
   Nursing questions and discussion
sci.med.telemedicine
   Hospital/physician networks. No diagnosis questions
sci.med.transcription
   Information for and about medical transcriptionists

Health & Medicine

Health Conditions

alt.abuse.recovery
Helping victims of abuse to recover
alt.alcohol
Don't drink and drive on the Info...no, I can't say it
alt.health.cfids-action
Chronic Fatigue Snydrome Action Group
alt.med.allergy
Helping people with allergies
alt.med.cfs
Chronic Fatigue Syndrome discussions
alt.support-heart
Support for people with heart trouble
alt.support.arthritis
Helping people with stiff joints
alt.support.asthma
Dealing with labored breathing
alt.support.cancer
Emotional aid for people with cancer
alt.support.cancer.prostate
Helping men with prostate cancer
alt.support.cerebral-palsy
Cerebral Palsy support
alt.support.crohns-colitis
Support for sufferers of ulcerative colitis
alt.support.diabetes.kids
Support for kids w/diabetes and their families
alt.support.dwarfism
Support for unusually short people
alt.support.dystonia
The cyberspace support group for dystonia
alt.support.epilepsy
Epilepsy support
alt.support.headaches.migraine
Discussion of migraine and headache ailments
alt.support.musc-dystrophy
A support group for muscular dystrophy
alt.support.post-polio
Post Polio Syndrome discussion area
alt.support.prostate.prostatitis
For individuals with prostatitis
alt.support.sleep-disorder
For all types of sleep disorders
alt.support.tinnitus
Coping with ringing ears and other head noises
bit.listserv.c+health
Computer and Health discussion list
bit.listserv.cfs.newsletter
Chronic Fatigue Syndrome newsletter
bit.med.resp-care.world
Respiratory Care World
misc.handicap
Items of interest for/about the handicapped
misc.health.aids
AIDS issues and support
misc.health.arthritis
Arthritis and related disorders
misc.health.diabetes
Discussion of diabetes management in day to day life
sci.med.diseases.cancer
Diagnosis, treatment, and prevention of cancer
sci.med.immunology
Medical/scientific aspects of immune illness
sci.med.nutrition
Physiological impacts of diet
sci.med.occupational
Repetitive Strain Injuries (RSI) & job injury issues
sci.med.orthopedics
Orthopedic Surgery, related issues and management
sci.med.vision
Human vision, visual correction, and visual science
talk.euthanasia
All aspects of euthanasia

Medical Schools

bit.listserv.medforum
Medical Students discussions
misc.education.medical
Issues related to medical education
sci.med.pharmacy
The teaching and practice of pharmacy

Medicine

alt.med.equipment
Discussion of medical equipment
alt.med.outpat.clinic
Outpatient clinic issues, discussions
bit.listserv.mxdiag-l
Molecular Pathology and Diagnostics
bit.listserv.transplant
Transplant Recipients List
sci.med
Medicine and its related products and regulations
sci.med.aids
AIDS: treatment, pathology/biology of HIV, prevention
sci.med.pathology
Pathology and laboratory medicine
sci.med.radiology
All aspects of radiology
sci.techniques.mag-resonance
Magnetic resonance imaging and spectroscopy
sci.techniques.mass-spec
All areas of mass spectrometry
sci.techniques.microscopy
The field of microscopy
sci.techniques.spectroscopy
Spectrum analysis

Mental Health

alt.abuse.transcendence
Non-standard ways to deal with all forms of abuse
alt.angst
Anxiety in the modern world
alt.society.mental-health
Keeping your marbles in the modern world
alt.support
Dealing with emotional situations & experiences
alt.support.anxiety-panic
Support for people who have panic attacks
alt.support.attn-deficit
Attention Deficit Disorder
alt.support.depression
Depression and mood disorders
alt.support.depression.manic
Extremely serious depression problems
alt.support.dissociation
For persons with dissociative disorders
alt.support.grief
Support group for the grieving
alt.support.loneliness
It's not easy being green
alt.support.ocd
For overcoming Obsessive-Compulsive Disorder
alt.support.personality
Group for those with personality disorders
alt.support.schizophrenia
Mutual support for schizophrenics
alt.support.shyness
Um, er, <blush>, well, maybe I will post, after all
alt.support.social-phobia
Helping Xenophobes
sci.med.psychobiology
Dialog and news in psychiatry and psychobiology
soc.support.fat-acceptance
Self-acceptance for fat people. No diet talk
soc.support.transgendered
Transgendered and intersexed persons

Personal Care

alt.hygiene.male
There is still a reason for circumcision
alt.meditation
General discussion of meditation
alt.meditation.quanyin
The Quan Yin method of meditation
alt.meditation.transcendental
Contemplation of states beyond the teeth
alt.support.diet
Seeking enlightenment through weight loss
alt.support.obesity
Support/resources to treat obesity
alt.support.short
Short people commiserate
alt.support.tall
Issues of interest to tall people

Public Health

alt.abortion.inequity
Paternal obligations of failing to abort unwanted child
alt.adoption
For those involved with or contemplating adoption
alt.adoption.agency
Licensed non-profit adoption agency information
alt.suicide.holiday
Talk of why suicides increase at holidays
alt.support.non-smokers
Discussing issues relating to second-hand smoke
alt.support.non-smokers.moderated
The dangers of secondhand smoke
talk.abortion
All sorts of discussions and arguments on abortion

Reference

sci.med.informatics
Computer applications in medical care
sci.med.physics
Issues of physics in medical testing/care

Resources

alt.image.medical
Medical image exchange discussions
bit.listserv.medlib-l
Medical Libraries discussion list
bit.listserv.mednews
Health Info-Com Network Newsletter
bit.listserv.tbi-support
Traumatic Brain Injury Support list
misc.kids.health
Children's health
misc.kids.info
Informational posts related to misc.kids hierarchy
relcom.commerce.medicine
Medical services, equipment, drugs
soc.veterans
Social issues relating to military veterans
talk.politics.medicine
The politics and ethics involved with health care

Health & Medicine – Humanities & Social Sciences

Sexuality

alt.foreplay
Not just for golf enthusiasts
alt.infertility
Discussion of infertility causes and treatments
alt.magick.sex
Pursuing spirituality through sexuality and vice versa
alt.recovery.addiction.sexual
Recovering sex addicts
soc.motss
Issues pertaining to homosexuality

Women's Health

misc.kids.pregnancy
Pre-pregnancy planning, pregnancy, childbirth

Humanities & Social Sciences

Anthropology

alt.scottish.clans
Discussions about Scottish Clans

Archaeology

alt.archaeology
Use sci.archaeology instead

Area & Cultural Studies

alt.california
The state and the state of mind
alt.chinese.text
Postings in Chinese; Chinese language software
alt.chinese.text.big5
Posting in Chinese[BIG 5]
alt.culture.alaska
Is this where the ice weasels come from?
alt.culture.argentina
Use soc.culture.argentina instead
alt.culture.beaches
Surf's up!
alt.culture.bullfight
To understand and appreciate the bullfight
alt.culture.cajun
Cajun culture, history, genealogy, events
alt.culture.egyptian
Use soc.culture.egyptian instead
alt.culture.hawaii
Ua Mau Ke Ea O Ka 'Aina I Ka Pono
alt.culture.indonesia
Use soc.culture.indonesia instead
alt.culture.internet
The culture(s) of the Internet
alt.culture.karnataka
Culture and language of the Indian state of Karnataka
alt.culture.net-viking
Norsemen on the net
alt.culture.ny-upstate
New York State, above Westchester
alt.culture.oregon
Discussion about the state of Oregon
alt.culture.saudi
The life and times of the people of Saudi Arabia
alt.culture.us.1970s
At least pick a _good_ decade to be stuck in the past
alt.culture.us.1980s
The Me Decade
alt.culture.us.asian-indian
Asian Indians in the US and Canada
alt.culture.us.southwest
Basking in the sun of the US's lower left
alt.mexico
The people of Central America's largest nation
alt.native
People indigenous to an area before modern colonisation
alt.news.macedonia
News concerning Macedonia in the Balkan Region
alt.planning.urban
Urban development
alt.silly-group.persian
Casual, non-political or religious chat about Persia
alt.skinheads
The skinhead culture/anti-culture
alt.skinheads.moderated
The skinhead culture/anti-culture
alt.society.futures
Musing on where we're all headed
alt.society.paradigms
Social and cultural patterns
alt.surrealism
Surrealist ideologies and their influences
alt.sustainable.agriculture
Such as the Mekong delta before Agent Orange
alt.talk.korean
A lighthearted place for discussions concerning Koreans
bit.lang.neder-l
Dutch Language and Literature list
bit.listserv.basque-l
Basque Culture List
bit.listserv.berita
News about Malaysia and Singapore
bit.listserv.bosnet
Bosnia News
bit.listserv.euearn-l
Eastern Europe list
bit.listserv.hellas
The Hellenic discussion list
bit.listserv.hungary
Hungarian discussion list
bit.listserv.mideur-l
Middle Europe discussion list
bit.listserv.muslims
Islamic Information and News Network
bit.listserv.seasia-l
Southeast Asia discussion list
bit.listserv.slovak-l
Slovak discussion list
bit.listserv.sthcult
Southern Cultures discussions
humanities.misc
General topics in the arts & humanities
soc.culture.afghanistan
Discussion of the Afghan society
soc.culture.african
Discussions about Africa & things African
soc.culture.african.american
Discussions about Afro-American issues
soc.culture.albanian
Albania and Albanians around the world
soc.culture.arabic
Technological & cultural issues, *not* politics
soc.culture.argentina
All about life in Argentina
soc.culture.asean
Countries of the Assoc. of SE Asian Nations
soc.culture.asian.american
Issues & discussion about Asian-Americans
soc.culture.assyrian
Assyrian culture, history, language, current diaspora
soc.culture.australian
Australian culture and society
soc.culture.austria
Austria and its people
soc.culture.baltics
People of the Baltic states
soc.culture.bangladesh
Issues & discussion about Bangladesh
soc.culture.belgium
Belgian society, culture(s) and people
soc.culture.bengali
Sociocultural identity of worldwide Bengali population
soc.culture.berber
The berber language, history, and culture
soc.culture.bolivia
Bolivian people and culture
soc.culture.bosna-herzgvna
The independent state of Bosnia and Herzegovina
soc.culture.brazil
Talking about the people and country of Brazil
soc.culture.british
Issues about Britain & those of British descent
soc.culture.bulgaria
Discussing Bulgarian society
soc.culture.burma
Politics, culture, news, discussion about Burma
soc.culture.cambodia
Cambodia and its people
soc.culture.canada
Discussions of Canada and its people
soc.culture.caribbean
Life in the Caribbean
soc.culture.celtic
Irish, Scottish, Breton, Cornish, Manx & Welsh
soc.culture.chile
All about Chile and its people
soc.culture.china
About China and Chinese culture
soc.culture.colombia
Colombian talk, social, politics, science
soc.culture.croatia
The lives of people of Croatia
soc.culture.cuba
Cuban culture, society and politics
soc.culture.czecho-slovak
Bohemian, Slovak, Moravian and Silesian life
soc.culture.dominican-rep
The life and people of the Dominican Republic
soc.culture.ecuador
The culture and people of Ecuador
soc.culture.egyptian
Egypt, and its society, culture, heritage, etc
soc.culture.esperanto
The neutral international language Esperanto
soc.culture.estonia
Estonian culture, language, news, politics
soc.culture.europe
Discussing all aspects of all-European society
soc.culture.filipino
Group about the Filipino culture
soc.culture.french
French culture, history, and related discussions
soc.culture.german
Discussions about German culture and history
soc.culture.greek
Group about Greeks
soc.culture.hongkong
Discussions pertaining to Hong Kong
soc.culture.hongkong.entertainment
Entertainment in Hong Kong
soc.culture.indian
Group for discussion about India & things Indian
soc.culture.indian.info
Info group for soc.culture.indian, etc
soc.culture.indian.kerala
Culture of the people of Keralite origin

Humanities & Social Sciences

soc.culture.indian.marathi
  Discussion related to Marathi Culture
soc.culture.indian.telugu
  The culture of the Telugu people of India
soc.culture.indonesia
  All about the Indonesian nation
soc.culture.iranian
  Discussions about Iran and things Iranian/Persian
soc.culture.iraq
  Iraq, its society, culture and heritage
soc.culture.irish
  Ireland and Irish culture
soc.culture.israel
  Israel and Israelis
soc.culture.italian
  The Italian people and their culture
soc.culture.japan
  Everything Japanese, except the Japanese language
soc.culture.jewish
  Jewish culture & religion. (cf. talk.politics.mideast)
soc.culture.jewish.holocaust
  The Shoah
soc.culture.jordan
  All topics concerning The Hashemite Kingdom of Jordan
soc.culture.korean
  Discussions about Korea & things Korean
soc.culture.kurdish
  People from Kurdistan and Kurds around the world
soc.culture.kuwait
  Kuwaiti culture, society, and history
soc.culture.laos
  Cultural and Social Aspects of Laos
soc.culture.latin-america
  Topics about Latin-America
soc.culture.lebanon
  Discussion about things Lebanese
soc.culture.maghreb
  North African society and culture
soc.culture.magyar
  The Hungarian people & their culture
soc.culture.malagasy
  Madagascar and the Malagasy culture
soc.culture.malaysia
  All about Malaysian society
soc.culture.mexican
  Discussion of Mexico's society
soc.culture.mexican.american
  Mexican-American/Chicano culture and issues
soc.culture.misc
  Group for discussion about other cultures
soc.culture.mongolian
  Everything related to Mongols and Mongolia
soc.culture.native
  Aboriginal people around the world
soc.culture.nepal
  Discussion of people and things in & from Nepal
soc.culture.netherlands
  People from the Netherlands and Belgium
soc.culture.new-zealand
  Discussion of topics related to New Zealand
soc.culture.nigeria
  Nigerian affairs, society, cultures, and peoples
soc.culture.nordic
  Discussion about culture up north
soc.culture.pakistan
  Topics of discussion about Pakistan
soc.culture.palestine
  Palestinian people, culture and politics
soc.culture.peru
  All about the people of Peru
soc.culture.polish
  Polish culture, Polish past, and Polish politics
soc.culture.portuguese
  Discussion of the people of Portugal
soc.culture.puerto-rico
  Puerto Rican culture, society and politics

soc.culture.punjab
  Punjab and Punjabi culture
soc.culture.quebec
  Quebec society and culture
soc.culture.romanian
  Discussion of Romanian and Moldavian people
soc.culture.russian
  All things Russian in the broadest sense
soc.culture.scientists
  Cultural issues about scientists & scientific projects
soc.culture.scottish
  Anything regarding Scotland or things Scots
soc.culture.sierra-leone
  The culture of Sierra Leone
soc.culture.singapore
  The past, present and future of Singapore
soc.culture.slovenia
  Slovenia and Slovenian people
soc.culture.somalia
  Somalian affairs, society, and culture
soc.culture.south-africa
  South African society, culture, & politics
soc.culture.soviet
  Topics relating to Russian or Soviet culture
soc.culture.spain
  Spain and the Spanish
soc.culture.sri-lanka
  Things & people from Sri Lanka
soc.culture.swiss
  Swiss culture
soc.culture.syria
  Syrian cultural matters and affairs
soc.culture.taiwan
  Discussion about things Taiwanese
soc.culture.tamil
  Tamil language, history and culture
soc.culture.thai
  Thai people and their culture
soc.culture.turkish
  Discussion about things Turkish
soc.culture.ukrainian
  The lives and times of the Ukrainian people
soc.culture.uruguay
  Discussions of Uruguay for those at home and abroad
soc.culture.usa
  The culture of the United States of America
soc.culture.venezuela
  Discussion of topics related to Venezuela
soc.culture.vietnamese
  Issues and discussions of Vietnamese culture
soc.culture.welsh
  The people, language and history of Wales
soc.culture.yugoslavia
  Discussions of Yugoslavia and its people
soc.genealogy.benelux
  Genealogy in Belgium, the Netherlands and Luxembourg

Classics

sci.classics
  Studying classical history, languages, art and more

Geography

alt.appalachian
  Appalachian region awareness, events, and culture
bit.listserv.endnote
  Bibsoft Endnote discussions
bit.listserv.geograph
  Geography list
relcom.comp.gis
  Geographical information systems

History

alt.history.future
  Discussion of possible history of the future
alt.history.living
  A forum for discussing the hobby of living history
alt.history.what-if
  What would the net have been like without this group?
alt.revolution.american.second
  Jeffersonian dreams
alt.war
  Not just collateral damage
alt.war.civil.usa
  Discussion of the U.S. Civil War (1861-1865)
alt.war.vietnam
  Discussion of all aspects of the Vietnam War
bit.listserv.c18-l
  18th Century Interdisciplinary Discussion
bit.listserv.history
  History List
soc.history
  Discussions of things historical
soc.history.living
  Living history and reenactment, issues and info
soc.history.moderated
  All aspects of history
soc.history.science
  History of science and related areas
soc.history.war.misc
  History & events of wars in general
soc.history.war.vietnam
  The Vietnam War
soc.history.war.world-war-ii
  History & events of World War Two
soc.history.what-if
  Alternate history

Languages

alt.japanese.text
  Postings in Japanese; Japanese language software
alt.language.urdu.poetry
  Poetry in the Indic Urdu language
alt.usage.english
  English grammar, word usages, and related topics
alt.usage.german
  Questions and answers about the German language
alt.uu.lang.esperanto.misc
  Learning Esperanto at the Usenet University
alt.uu.lang.russian.misc
  Learning Russian at the Usenet University
ooi.lang
  Natural languages, communication, etc
sci.lang.japan
  The Japanese language, both spoken and written
sci.lang.translation
  Problems and concerns of translators/interpreters

Library & Information Studies

bit.listserv.advanc-l
  Geac Advanced Integrated Library System Users
bit.listserv.arie-l
  RLG Ariel Document Transmission Group
bit.listserv.asis-l
  American Society of Information Science
bit.listserv.autocat
  Library Cataloging and Authorities List
bit.listserv.circplus
  Circulation Reserve and Related Library Issues

bit.listserv.imagelib
  Image Databases in Libraries
bit.listserv.libref-l
  Library Reference Issues
bit.listserv.libres
  Library and Information Science Research
bit.listserv.lis-l
  Library and Information Science Students
k12.library
  Implementing info technologies in school libraries

Linguistics

bit.listserv.words-l
  English Language Discussion Group

Literature

alt.horror
  The horror genre
alt.horror.creative
  Original horror fiction, poems, pictures
alt.lesbian.feminist.poetry
  Everyone has their niche
alt.prose
  Postings of original writings, fictional & otherwise
bit.listserv.authorware
  Authorware Professional Authoring Program
bit.listserv.geodesic
  List for the discussion of Buckminster Fuller
bit.listserv.gutnberg
  GUTNBERG discussion list
bit.listserv.literary
  Discussions about Literature
bit.listserv.superguy
  Superguy Story list
bit.listserv.techwr-l
  Technical Writing list
relcom.arts.epic
  Literary arts of epical kind (more then 10 Kbytes)
relcom.arts.qwerty
  Literary arts of small forms (less then 10 Kbytes)
relcom.fido.su.tolkien
  FIDOnet, creations of J.R.R Tolkien

Psychology

alt.consciousness.4th-way
  The Fourth Way, Gurdjieff, Ouspensky
alt.clearing.technology
  Traumatic Incident Reduction and Clearing
alt.consciousness
  Discussions on the study of the human consciousness
alt.consciousness.mysticism
  The quest for ultimate reality
alt.dreams
  What do they mean?
alt.dreams.lucid
  What do they really mean?
alt.psychoactives
  Better living through chemistry
alt.psychology.help
  An alt.support group away from home
alt.psychology.mistake-theory
  Research and discussion about mistakes
alt.psychology.nlp
  Neuro-linguistic programming
alt.psychology.personality
  Personality taxonomy, such as Myers-Briggs
alt.recovery.adult-children
  For adults from dysfunctional families
alt.recovery.codependency
  Mutually destructive relationships
alt.revenge
  Two wrongs trying to make a right
bit.listserv.ioob-l
  Industrial Psychology
bit.listserv.psycgrad
  Psychology Grad Student Discussions
sci.psychology
  Topics related to psychology
sci.psychology.digest
  PSYCOLOQUY: Refereed Psychology Journal and Newsletter
sci.psychology.research
  Research issues in psychology

Sociology

alt.discrimination
  Quotas, affirmative action, bigotry, persecution
alt.folklore.science
  The folklore of science, not the science of folklore
alt.mens-rights
  We hold these truths to be self-evident
alt.misanthropy
  People who hate people
alt.sci.sociology
  People are really interesting when you watch them
bit.listserv.qualrs-l
  Qualitative Research of the Human Sciences
bit.listserv.sos-data
  Social Science Data List
misc.activism.progressive
  Information for Progressive activists
misc.kids
  Children, their behavior and activities
soc.answers
  Repository for periodic USENET articles
soc.bi
  Discussions of bisexuality
soc.couples
  Discussions for couples (cf. soc.singles)
soc.couples.intercultural
  Inter-cultural and inter-racial relationships
soc.couples.wedding
  Wedding planning
soc.men
  Issues related to men, their problems & relationships
soc.misc
  Socially-oriented topics not in other groups
soc.org.service-clubs.misc
  General info on all service topics
soc.singles
  Newsgroup for single people, their activities, etc
soc.support.youth.gay-lesbian-bi
  Gay youths helping each other

Women's Studies

alt.feminazis
  For people who hate radical feminists
alt.feminism.individualism
  Discussions about feminism and individualism
alt.women.attitudes
  The different attitudes that women have
soc.feminism
  Discussion of feminism & feminist issues
soc.women
  Issues related to women, their problems & relationships
talk.rape
  Discussions on stopping rape; not to be crossposted

Internet

Internet Access

alt.aol-sucks
  Why some people hate AOL and its users
alt.aol.rejects
  Another forum for gripes about America Online
alt.bbs
  Computer BBS systems & software
alt.bbs.ads
  Ads for various computer BBS's
alt.bbs.citadel
  The Citadel BBS
alt.bbs.doors
  Bulletin board system add-on executables, or "doors"
alt.fan.mozilla
  Discussions of Netscape's WWW browser Mozilla
alt.fan.zbig-tyrlik
  A Cleveland Internet provider
alt.freenet
  Free access to computer networks
alt.netcom.sucks
  Work out your troubles with support@netcom.com
alt.online-service
  Large commercial online services, and the Internet
alt.online-service.america-online
  Or should that be "America Offline?"
alt.online-service.compuserve
  Discussions and questions about Compuserve
alt.online-service.delphi
  Run! It's the Delphoids!
alt.online-service.freenet
  Public FreeNet systems
alt.online-service.genie
  Discussions and questions about GEnie
alt.online-service.imagination
  Discussion of The Imagination Network
alt.online-service.interramp
  For discussions about the ISP InterRamp
alt.sys.mac.newuser-help
  A forum for Macintosh users new to the Internet
alt.winsock.ivc
  Windows Sockets, Internet Voice Chat
alt.winsock.trumpet
  The Trumpet newsreader
bit.listserv.cw-email
  Campus-Wide E-mail discussion list
bit.listserv.domain-l
  Domains discussion group
bit.listserv.gguide
  BITNIC GGUIDE list
bit.listserv.innopac
  Innovative Interfaces Online Public Access
bit.listserv.jnet-l
  BITNIC JNET-L list
bit.listserv.liaison
  BITNIC LIAISON
bit.listserv.mail-l
  BITNIC MAIL-L list
bit.listserv.pacs-l
  Public-Access Computer System Forum
bit.listserv.tech-l
  BITNIC TECH-L list
bit.listserv.trans-l
  BITNIC TRANS-L list
bit.listserv.www-vm
  World-wide Web on VM Platform list
biz.comp.mcs
  MCSNet
biz.comp.telebit.netblazer
  The Telebit Netblazer

comp.infosystems.www.advocacy
    Comments and arguments over the best and worst
comp.infosystems.www.announce
    World-Wide Web announcements
info.nsfnet.status
    NSFnet status reports
vmsnet.networks.misc
    General networking topics not covered elsewhere
vmsnet.networks.tcp-ip.cmu-tek
    CMU-TEK TCP/Ipackage,
vmsnet.networks.tcp-ip.misc
    Other TCP/IP solutions for VMS
vmsnet.networks.tcp-ip.multinet
    TGV's Multinet TCP/IP, g-wayed to infomultinet
vmsnet.networks.tcp-ip.tcpware
    Process Software's TCPWARE TCP/IP software
vmsnet.networks.tcp-ip.ucxDEC's
    VMS/Ultrix Connection (TCP/IP services for VMS)

Internet Communications

alt.fan.longest-thread
    Fans of the Longest Thread Ever
alt.flame.spelling
    USENET's favourite fallacious argoomint
alt.irc.announce
    Announcements about Internet Relay Chat (IRC)
alt.irc.hottub
    Discussion of the IRC channel #hottub
alt.irc.ircii
    IRC, the sequel
alt.irc.jeopardy
    For discussion of the IRC channel #jeopardy
alt.irc.questions
    How-to questions for IRC (International Relay Chat)
alt.irc.undernet
    The alternative IRC
alt.irc.undernet.30plus
    30 + the alternative IRC
alt.irc.undernet.chatzone
    Discussion group for #chatzone on Undernet IRC
bit.listserv.pmail
    Pegasus mail discussions
bit.listserv.pmdf-l
    PMDF distribution list
bit.listserv.ucp-l
    University Computing Project mailing list
bit.listserv.xmailer
    Crosswell Mailer
comp.infosystems.www.authoring.cgi
    Writing CGI scripts for the Web
comp.internet.net-happenings
    Announcements of network happenings
info.ietf.smtp
    IETF SMTP extension discussions
info.nupop
    Northwestern University's POP for PCs
info.pem-dev
    IETF privacy enhanced mail discussions
relcom.comp.newmedia
    Global networks as a new mass media
relcom.postmasters
    For RELCOM postmasters, official
relcom.postmasters.d
    Discussion of postmaster's troubles and bright ideas
vmsnet.mail.misc
    Other electronic mail software
vmsnet.mail.mx
    MX email system, gatewayed to MX mailing list
vmsnet.mail.pmdf
    PMDF email system, gatewayed to ipmdf mailing list

Internet Issues

alt.conspiracy.usenet-cabal
    Discussion of fears about a non-existent group
alt.current-events.net-abuse
    Usenet spamming, Green Card and the like
alt.current-events.net-abuse.spam
    Tracking inundations
alt.destroy.the.internet
    Demons in the wire
alt.internet.media-coverage
    The coverage of the Internet by the media
alt.irc.bots
    Daemons on the Internet Relay Chat
alt.privacy
    Privacy issues in cyberspace
alt.privacy.anon-server
    Issues surrounding programs that aid anonymity
alt.pub-ban.homolka
    About the publication ban on the Karla Homolka trial
alt.stop.spamming
    Trying to prevent net abuse
alt.stupidity
    Discussion about stupid newsgroups
alt.uu.future
    Does Usenet University have a viable future?
bit.listserv.lstsrv-l
    Forum on LISTSERV
comp.infosystems.www.authoring.misc
    Miscellaneous Web authoring issues
comp.infosystems.www.users
    WWW user issues (Mosaic, Lynx, etc)
info.big-internet
    Issues facing a huge Internet
info.ietf.hosts
    *IETF host requirements discussions
news.admin.policy
    Policy issues of USENET
news.lists.ps-maps
    Maps relating to USENET traffic flows
news.misc
    Discussions of USENET itself
relcom.fido.ru.networks
    Inter-network discussion of global nets

Internet Protocols

bit.listserv.ibm7171
    Protocol Converter list
bit.listserv.ibmtcp-l
    IBM TCP/IP list
bit.listserv.tn3270-l
    tn3270 protocol discussion list
bit.listserv.x400-l
    x.400 Protocol list
biz.dec.ip
    IP networking on DEC machines
comp.protocols.misc
    Various forms and types of protocol
comp.protocols.ppp
    Discussion of the Internet Point to Point Protocol
news.software.nntp
    The Network News Transfer Protocol
relcom.tcpip
    TCP/IP protocols and their implementation
vmsnet.networks.tcp-ip.wintcp
    The Wollongong Group's WIN-TCP TCP/IP software

Internet Resources

alt.culture.usenet
    A self-referential oxymoron
alt.culture.www
    World Wide Web culture
alt.etext
    Texts made available for electronic redistribution
alt.internet.talk-radio
    Carl Malamud's Internet Talk Radio program
alt.net.scandal
    Outrageous happenings on the net
alt.newbie
    The altnet housewarming committee
alt.newbies
    Housewarming for a group
alt.online-service.prodigy
    The Sears Prodigy system
alt.online-service.well
    Talk about The Whole Earth 'Lectronic Link @well.com
alt.test
    Alternative subnetwork testing
alt.usenet.offline-reader
    Getting your fix offline
alt.uu.announce
    Announcements of Usenet University
bit.admin
    bit. newgroups discussions
bit.general
    Discussions relating to BitNet/Usenet
bit.listserv.advise-l
    User Services list
bit.listserv.applicat
    Applications under BITNET
bit.listserv.bitnews
    News about BitNet
bit.listserv.hdesk-l
    Help Desk Operations
bit.listserv.help-net
    Help on BitNet and the Internet
bit.listserv.lsoft-announce
    ListServ Announcements
bit.listserv.netnws-l
    NETNWS-L Netnews list
bit.listserv.new-list
    NEW-LIST - New List Announcements
bit.listserv.test
    Test Newsgroup
bit.listserv.tex-l
    The TeXnical topics list
bit.listserv.ug-l
    Usage Guidelines
biz.config
    Biz Usenet configuration and administration
biz.test
    Biz newsgroup test messages
clari.matrix_news
    Monthly journal on the internet
comp.infosystems.announce
    Announcements of internet information services
comp.infosystems.www.misc
    Miscellaneous World Wide Web discussion
comp.internet.library
    Discussing electronic libraries
info.admin
    Admin. messages regarding info.groups
info.nsfnet.cert
    Comp. Emerg.Response Team announcements
info.rfc
    Announcements of newly released RFCs
news.announce.conferences
    Calls for papers and conference announcements
news.announce.important
    General announcements of interest to all
news.announce.newgroups
    Calls for newgroups & announcements of same
news.announce.newusers
    Explanatory postings for new users
news.answers
    Repository for periodic USENET articles
news.groups
    Discussions and lists of newsgroups

news.groups.questions
  Where can I find talk about topic X?
news.groups.reviews
  What is going on in group or mailing list named X
news.lists
  News-related statistics and lists
news.newusers.questions
  Q & A for users new to the Usenet
rec.answers
  Repository for periodic USENET articles
relcom.archives
  Messages about new items on archive sites
relcom.fido.su.general
  FIDOnet, about everything and nothing
relcom.fido.su.softw
  FIDOnet, software in general
relcom.netnews
  Announcements and articles important for all netters
relcom.netnews.big
  General BIG articles
relcom.newusers
  Q&A of new Relcom users
relcom.terms
  Discussion of various terms and terminology
vmsnet.announce.newusers
  Orientation info for new users
vmsnet.groups
  Administration of the VMSnet newsgroups

Internet Security

alt.privacy.clipper
  The USA administration's Clipper encryption plan
alt.security.index
  Pointers to good stuff in alt.security
alt.security.pgp
  The Pretty Good Privacy package
alt.sigs.and.quotes
  Showing off signature files
lt.security
  Security issues on computer systems
relcom.fido.su.virus
  FIDOnet, viruses and vaccines

Internet Services

alt.bbs.allsysop
  SysOp concerns of ALL networks and technologies
alt.internet.services
  Not available in the uucp world, even via email
comp.infosystems.kiosks
  Informational and transactional kiosks
news.admin.hierarchies
  Network news hierarchies
news.admin.misc
  General topics of network news administration

Virtual Communities

soc.net-people
  Announcements, requests, etc. about people on the net

Law & Criminal Justice

Constitutional Law

alt.censorship
  Discussion about restricting speech/press

Ethics

misc.legal
  Legalities and the ethics of law

Individuals

bit.listserv.ada-law
  ADA Law discussions

Intellectual Property

misc.int-property
  Discussion of intellectual property rights

Law Schools

bit.listserv.lawsch-l
  Law School discussion list
bit.listserv.lawsch.internships
  Law School Internships

Legal Issues

alt.prisons
  Can I get an alt. feed in the slammer?
misc.legal.moderated
  All aspects of law

Reference

alt.crime
  Crime in general, not just the crimes in alt.

Tax Law

alt.business.internal-audit
  Discussion of internal auditing
misc.taxes
  Tax laws and advice

Popular Culture & Entertainment

Automobiles

alt.autos.antique
  Discussion of all facets of older automobiles
alt.autos.camaro.firebird
  A couple of American sports cars
alt.autos.macho-trucks
  For macho truck enthusiasts. Big block or bust
alt.autos.rod-n-custom
  Vehicles with modified engines and/or appearance
alt.cars.Ford-Probe
  "PROBE ME" —— actual Viriginia woman's license plate
alt.fan.dragons
  People love automobiles at Pennsic
rec.autos.4x4
  The on and off-road four wheel drive vehicle
rec.autos.antique
  Discussing all aspects of automobiles over 25 years old
rec.autos.driving
  Driving automobiles
rec.autos.makers.chrysler
  Dodge, Plymouth, Jeep, Eagle, etc info/talk
rec.autos.makers.saturn
  All about Saturn cars, fans and company
rec.autos.marketplace
  Buy/Sell/Trade automobiles, parts, tools, accessories
rec.autos.misc
  Miscellaneous discussion about automobiles
rec.autos.rod-n-custom
  High performance automobiles
rec.autos.simulators
  Discussion of automotive simulators
rec.autos.sport.f1
  Formula 1 motor racing
rec.autos.sport.indy
  Indy Car motor racing
rec.autos.sport.info
  Auto racing news, results, announcements
rec.autos.sport.misc
  Organized, legal auto competitions
rec.autos.sport.nascar
  NASCAR and other professional stock car racing
rec.autos.sport.tech
  Technical aspects & technology of auto racing
rec.autos.tech
  Technical aspects of automobiles, et. al
rec.autos.vw
  Issues pertaining to Volkswagen products

Books

alt.books.anne-rice
  The Vampire Thermostat
alt.books.beatgeneration
  Beat authors, Burroughs, Kerouac, etc
alt.books.brian-lumley
  Books by Brian Lumley
alt.books.deryni
  Katherine Kurtz's books, especially the Deryni series
alt.books.isaac-asimov
  Fans of the late SF/science author Isaac Asimov
alt.books.kurt-vonnegut
  Discussion of Kurt Vonnegut's works
alt.books.m-lackey
  Author Mercedes Lackey and her books
alt.books.phil-k-dick
  Discussion about the works of Phillip K. Dick
alt.books.reviews
  "If you want to know how it turns out, read it!"
alt.books.sf.melanie-rawn
  discussion of Melanie Rawn's writings
alt.books.stephen-king
  The works of horror writer Stephen King
alt.books.technical
  Discussion of technical books
alt.books.tom-clancy
  The group for discussion of Mr. Techno-Thriller
alt.comics.alternative
  You could try a book without pictures, for example
alt.comics.batman
  Marketing mania

Popular Culture & Entertainment

alt.comics.classic
For the discussion of golden and silver age comic books
alt.comics.elfquest
W & R Pini's ElfQuest series
alt.comics.fan-fiction
Original works using existing comic characters
alt.comics.lnh
Interactive net.madness in the superhero genre
alt.comics.peanuts
For the discussion of the Peanuts comic strip
alt.comics.superman
No one knows it is also alt.clark.kent
alt.fan.authors.stephen-king
Modern master of the spooky story
alt.fan.david-sternlight
David Sternlight, sci.crypt crusader
alt.fan.douglas-adams
Author of "The Meaning of Liff", & other fine works
alt.fan.dune
Herbert's drinking buddies
alt.fan.eddings
The works of writer David Eddings
alt.fan.furry
Fans of funny animals, ala Steve Gallacci's book
alt.fan.heinlein
Fans of SF author Robert Heinlein grok this group
alt.fan.hofstadter
Douglas Hofstadter and Godel, Escher, Bach
alt.fan.holmes
Elementary, my dear Watson. Like he ever said that
alt.fan.pern
Anne McCaffery's SF oeuvre
alt.fan.philip-dick
Philip K. Dick, writer
alt.fan.piers-anthony
For fans of the s-f author Piers Anthony
alt.fan.pooh
Winnie-the-Pooh and Piglet too
alt.fan.pratchett
For fans of Terry Pratchett, s-f humor writer
alt.fan.rumpole
Rumpole of the Bailey
alt.fan.tolkien
Mortal Men doomed to die
alt.fan.tom-robbins
31 flavours for readers
alt.fan.wodehouse
Discussion of the works of author P.G. Wodehouse
alt.galactic-guide
Hitch Hiker's Guide to the Known Galaxy Project
alt.misc.forteana
Charles Fort, his books, and general weird happenings
alt.pulp
Paperback fiction, newsprint production, orange juice
alt.shared-reality.sf-and-fantasy
"Worlds Beyond" shared universe
bit.listserv.rra-l
Romance Readers Anonymous
clari.living.books
News about books and authors
misc.books.technical
Discussion of books about technical topics
rec.arts.books
Books of all genres, and the publishing industry
rec.arts.books.childrens
All aspects of children's literature
rec.arts.books.hist-fiction
Historical fictions (novels) in general
rec.arts.books.marketplace
Buying and selling of books
rec.arts.books.reviews
Book reviews
rec.arts.books.tolkien
The works of J.R.R. Tolkien
rec.arts.erotica
Erotic fiction and verse
rec.arts.int-fiction
Discussions about interactive fiction
rec.arts.manga
All aspects of the Japanese storytelling art form
rec.arts.mystery
Mystery and crime books, plays and films
rec.arts.poems
For the posting of poems
rec.arts.prose
Short works of prose fiction and followup discussion
rec.arts.sf.announce
Major announcements of the SF world
rec.arts.sf.fandom
Discussions of SF fan activities
rec.arts.sf.marketplace
Personal forsale notices of SF materials
rec.arts.sf.misc
Science fiction lovers' newsgroup
rec.arts.sf.reviews
Reviews of science fiction/fantasy/horror works
rec.arts.sf.science
Real and speculative aspects of SF science
rec.arts.sf.written
Discussion of written science fiction and fantasy
rec.arts.sf.written.robert-jordan
Books by author Robert Jordan
relcom.commerce.publishing
Books, publishing services
relcom.fido.su.books
FIDOnet, for book readers and lovers

Celebrities & Personalities

alt.celebrities
Famous people and their sycophants
alt.fan.asprin
I'm fond of buffered analgesics. Robert Lynn Asprin too
alt.fan.bill-gates
Fans of the original micro-softie
alt.fan.bob-dole
A US Congressman
alt.fan.brad-pitt
A young actor the women seem to be crazy about
alt.fan.chris-elliott
Get a Life, you Letterman flunky
alt.fan.conan-obrien
Late Night with a big red pompadour
alt.fan.dan-quayle
For discussion of a past US Vice President
alt.fan.dennis-miller
Comedian Dennis Miller
alt.fan.don-imus
Fans of radio host Imus
alt.fan.don-n-mike
Two radio guys
alt.fan.drmellow
A place to worship Dr. Mellow
alt.fan.fabio
A hunk of pecs
alt.fan.g-gordon-liddy
Crime does pay, or we wouldn't have so much of it
alt.fan.greaseman
Fans of Doug Tracht, the DJ
alt.fan.harrison-ford
From Blade Runner to Indian Jones to Clancy stories
alt.fan.heather-locklear
TJ Hooker's hottest cop
alt.fan.howard-stern
Fans of the abrasive radio & TV personality
alt.fan.jay-leno
Fans of The Tonight Show with Jay Leno
alt.fan.jim-carrey
Wild and wacky comedian Jame Carrey
alt.fan.john-palmer
With an army of lawyers from a Michigan warren
alt.fan.judge-ito
The Ringmaster
alt.fan.kevin-mitnick
Hooked hacker
alt.fan.letterman
One of the top 10 reasons to get the alt groups
alt.fan.lucia-chen
Lucia "Chen Lu" Chen of Mexicali, Mexico
alt.fan.marcia-clark
No one would know her, but she prosecutes O.J. Simpson
alt.fan.mel-brooks
Actor/directory/funnyman Mel Brooks
alt.fan.nathan.brazil
The Well of Souls and all things Markovian
alt.fan.newt-gingrich
Conservatives return with a vengence
alt.fan.noam-chomsky
Noam Chomsky's writings and opinions
alt.fan.oj-simpson
Juice! Juice! Juice!
alt.fan.paul-bernardo
Until death do us part
alt.fan.phoebe-cates
Princess Caraboo
alt.fan.ronald-reagan
Jellybeans and all
alt.fan.rush-limbaugh
Derogation of others for fun and profit
alt.fan.samantha-fox
For fans of the famous Page 3 Girl/pop singer
alt.fan.schwarzenegger
Imitated but never duplicated
alt.fan.tarantino
Filmmaker Quentin Tarantino
alt.fan.teen.idols
Boys and men that teenagers worship
alt.fan.teen.starlets
Girls and women that teenagers worship
alt.fan.vic-reeves
Britain's top light entertainer and formation mollusc
alt.fan.villains
Antagonists as protagonists
alt.fan.warlord
The War Lord of the West Preservation Fan Club
alt.fan.weird-al
He's rather a lot like Kibo, actually
alt.fan.winona-ryder
Generation X's gorgeous, elfin, brainy, goddess actress
alt.fan.woody-allen
The diminutive neurotic
alt.fandom.cons
Announcements of conventions (SciFi and others)
alt.non.sequitur
Richard Nixon
alt.obituaries
Notices of dead folks
alt.oj.coverage.gone.overboard
The overdone O.J. Simpson coverage
alt.rush-limbaugh
Fans of the conservative activist radio announcer
alt.showbiz.gossip
A misguided attempt to centralize gossip
alt.talk.royalty
Discussion of royalty and nobility
clari.living.celebrities
Famous people in the news

Family & Community

alt.child-support
Raising children in a split family

alt.co-ops
  Discussion about cooperatives
alt.community.intentional
  Some spinoff from alt.co-ops
alt.dads-rights
  Rights of fathers
alt.kids-talk
  A place for the pre-college set on the net
alt.masonic.members
  Freemasons
alt.masonic.youth
  Children of Freemasons
alt.missing-kids
  Locating missing children
alt.parents-teens
  Parent-teenager relationships
alt.psychotic.roommates
  Single white female seeks roommate
alt.support.depression.flame
  People with no tolerance for depressed people
alt.support.divorce
  Discussion of marital breakups
alt.teens
  Teenagers
alt.toys.hi-tech
  Optimus Prime is my hero
alt.toys.transformers
  From robots to vehicles and back again
alt.true-crime
  Criminal acts around the world
alt.wedding
  Til death or our lawyers do us part
bit.listserv.free-l
  Fathers Rights and Equality Discussion List
relcom.commerce.household
  All for house - furniture, freezers, ovens, etc
relcom.kids
  About kids

Fashion

alt.fan.elite
  Maker of Supermodels
alt.fashion
  All facets of the fashion industry discussed
alt.gothic.fashion
  Discussion on pointy boots, hair dye, and makeup tips!
alt.punk.straight-edge
  Shaving eyebrows for fun and profit
alt.society.underwear
  What's the big deal, anyway?
alt.supermodels
  Discussing famous & beautiful models
alt.supermodels.cindy-crawford
  House of Style's overexposed host
clari.living
  Fashion, leisure, lifestyle

Genealogy

soc.genealogy.computing
  Genealogical computing & net resources
soc.genealogy.french
  Francophone genealogy
soc.genealogy.german
  Family history including a German background
soc.genealogy.jewish
  Jewish genealogy group
soc.genealogy.medieval
  Genealogy in the period from roughly AD500 to AD1600
soc.genealogy.methods
  Genealogical methods and resources

soc.genealogy.misc
  General genealogical discussions
soc.genealogy.surnames
  Surname queries & tafels

Humor

alt.anagrams
  Playing with words
alt.callahans
  Callahan's bar for puns and fellowship
alt.canadian.beaver
  More from "Things that make you go, 'eh?'"
alt.captain.sarcastic
  For the captain's minions
alt.comedy.british
  Discussion of British comedy in a variety of media
alt.comedy.british.blackadder
  The Black Adder programme
alt.comedy.improvisation
  Group improvisational comedies
alt.comedy.slapstick
  Slapstick: comedy stressing farce and horseplay
alt.comedy.slapstick.3-stooges
  Hey, Mo!
alt.comedy.standup
  Discussion of stand-up comedy and comedians
alt.fan.letterman.top-ten
  Top Ten lists from the Letterman show
alt.fan.penn-n-teller
  The magicians Penn Jillette & Teller
alt.fun.with.matt
  No arms and no legs on a doorstep; how fun could it be?
alt.graffiti
  The writing is on the wall
alt.humor.best-of-usenet
  What the moderator thinks is funniest
alt.humor.best-of-usenet.d
  Discussion of alt.humor.best-of-usenet posts
alt.humor.bluesman
  Humor from the 105th St. BluesMan's world
alt.humor.puns
  Not here
alt.jokes.pentium
  Playing with the problems plaguing Pentium
alt.shenanigans
  Practical jokes, pranks, randomness, etc
alt.silly.little.newsgroup
  With a silly.big.name
alt.slack
  Posting relating to the Church of the Subgenius
alt.spam
  What is that stuff that doth jiggle in the breeze?
alt.spam.barf.barf.barf
  The SPAM-haters group
alt.tasteless
  Truly disgusting
alt.tasteless.jokes
  Sometimes insulting rather than disgusting or humorous
alt.timewasters
  A pretty good summary of making the list of alt groups
rec.humor
  Jokes and the like. May be somewhat offensive
rec.humor.d
  Discussions on the content of rec.humor articles
rec.humor.funny
  Jokes that are funny (in the moderator's opinion)
rec.humor.oracle
  Sagacious advice from the USENET Oracle
rec.humor.oracle.d
  Comments about the USENET Oracle's comments
relcom.humor
  Ha-ha-ha. Jokes, you know them, funny

relcom.humor.lus
  Moderated humor and jokes

Lifestyles

alt.amazon-women.admirers
  Worshiping women you have to look up to
alt.chinese.fengshui
  Creating harmonious work and living environments
alt.cult.nudism
  Crackpots in the nudist movement
alt.cyberpunk
  High-tech low-life
alt.cyberpunk.chatsubo
  Literary virtual reality in a cyberpunk hangout
alt.cyberpunk.movement
  A little laxative might help
alt.cyberspace
  Cyberspace and how it should work
alt.cyberspace.rebels
  Tough individualists on the net
alt.discordia
  All hail Eris, etc
alt.discordia.scc
  Discussion of topics relevant to the Sno(w) Chao Cabal
alt.fan.skinny
  Fat fetishes have no place here
alt.flame.roommate
  Putting the pig on a spit
alt.fraternity.sorority
  Discussions of fraternity/sorority life and issues
alt.gathering.rainbow
  For discussing the annual Rainbow Gathering
alt.geek
  To fulfill an observed need
alt.good.news
  A place for some news that's good news
alt.gothic
  The gothic movement: things mournful and dark
alt.hangover
  Pass the aspirin and a barrel of coffee
alt.homosexual
  Same as alt.sex.homosexual
alt.journalism.gay-press
  News from a homosexual viewpoint
alt.lifestyle.barefoot
  Discussions related to going barefoot
alt.niteclub.alternative
  Alternative music nightclubs
alt.niteclub.commercial
  Commercially owned nightclubs
alt.niteclub.independent
  Promoters of independent nightclubs
alt.party
  Parties, celebration and general debauchery
alt.peeves
  Discussion of peeves
alt.politics.white-power
  People who believe in White Supremacy
alt.polyamory
  For those with multiple loves
alt.romance
  Discussion about the romantic side of love
alt.romance.chat
  Talk about no sex
alt.romance.unhappy
  alt.angst on the run
alt.self-improve
  Self-improvement in less than 14 characters
alt.shoe.lesbians
  A discussion for shoe lesbians and their friends
alt.smokers
  Puffing on tobacco
alt.smokers.cigars
  From stogies to cubans

Popular Culture & Entertainment

alt.smokers.pipes
  Briars, meerschaums, and calabashes
alt.society.generation-x
  Lifestyles of those born 1960-early-1970s
alt.society.neutopia
  A place to further the cause of peace and love
alt.suburbs
  Living on the skirt of the city
alt.transgendered
  Boys will be girls, and vice-versa
alt.usenet.kooks
  I have a theory about why we have such crazy theories
bit.listserv.gaynet
  GayNet Discussion List
misc.rural
  Devoted to issues concerning rural living

Magazines & Newspapers

alt.mag.playboy
  Four decades of appreciation or degradation
alt.motherjones
  Mother Jones magazine
alt.readers.ym
  Fans of "ym" magazine
alt.wired
  Wired Magazine
alt.zines
  Small magazines, mostly noncommercial
bit.listserv.pakistan
  Pakistan News Service
bit.listserv.pns-l
  Pakistan News Service Discussions
clari.apbl.briefs
  Hourly newsbrief from the Associated Press
clari.apbl.entertainment
  Entertainment news
clari.apbl.movies
  News on movies and filmmaking
clari.apbl.music
  News on music and the music industry
clari.apbl.reports.economy
  General economic reports
clari.apbl.review
  Daily review of the news
clari.apbl.today_history
  Today in History feature
clari.apbl.tv
  News on television and broadcasting
clari.apbl.weather
  World weather reports
clari.apbl.weather.misc
  Miscellaneous weather-related articles
clari.apbl.weather.storms
  Major storms
clari.apbl.weather.usa
  U.S. weather reports
clari.feature.bizarro
  Daily Bizarro comic panel by Dan Piraro
clari.feature.dave_barry
  Columns of humourist Dave Barry
clari.feature.dilbert
  The daily comic strip "Dilbert" (MIME/uuencoded GIF)
clari.feature.imprb_research
  Excerpts from the Annals of Improbable Research
clari.feature.joebob
  Joe Bob Briggs goes to the Drive-in
clari.feature.mike_royko
  Chicago Opinion Columnist Mike Royko
clari.feature.miss_manners
  Judith Martin's humourous etiquette advice
clari.feature.worldviews
  Views of the World: International editorial cartoons

clari.living.animals
  Human interest stories about animals
clari.living.arts
  News of the arts
clari.living.bizarre
  Unusual or funny news stories
clari.living.entertainment
  Entertainment news
clari.living.goodnews
  Stories of success and survival
clari.living.history
  News and human interest about history
clari.living.history.today
  Today in History feature
clari.living.human_interest
  General Human interest stories
clari.living.music
  News of the music scene
clari.living.tv
  News of television programs and events
clari.local.alabama
  News of Alabama
clari.local.alaska
  News of Alaska
clari.local.arizona
  News of Arizona
clari.local.arkansas
  News of Arkansas
clari.local.california
  News of California
clari.local.chicago
  News of Chicago
clari.local.colorado
  News of Colorado
clari.local.connecticut
  News of Connecticut
clari.local.delaware
  News of Delaware
clari.local.florida
  News of Florida
clari.local.georgia
  News of Georgia
clari.local.hawaii
  News of Hawaii
clari.local.idaho
  News of Idaho
clari.local.illinois
  News of Illinois
clari.local.indiana
  News of Indiana
clari.local.iowa
  News of Iowa
clari.local.kansas
  News of Kansas
clari.local.kentucky
  News of Kentucky
clari.local.los_angeles
  News of Los Angeles, California
clari.local.louisiana
  News of Louisiana
clari.local.maine
  News of Maine
clari.local.maryland
  News of Maryland
clari.local.massachusetts
  News of Massachusetts
clari.local.michigan
  News of Michigan
clari.local.minnesota
  News of Minnesota
clari.local.mississippi
  News of Mississippi
clari.local.missouri
  News of Missouri
clari.local.montana
  News of Montana
clari.local.nebraska
  News of Nebraska

clari.local.nevada
  News of Nevada
clari.local.new_hampshire
  News of New Hampshire
clari.local.new_jersey
  News of New Jersey
clari.local.new_mexico
  News of New Mexico
clari.local.new_york
  News of New York
clari.local.north_carolina
  News of North Carolina
clari.local.north_dakota
  News of North Dakota
clari.local.nyc
  News of New York City, New York
clari.local.ohio
  News of Ohio
clari.local.oklahoma
  News of Oklahoma
clari.local.oregon
  News of Oregon
clari.local.pennsylvania
  News of Pennsylvania
clari.local.rhode_island
  News of Rhode Island
clari.local.sfbay
  News of San Francisco Bay Area
clari.local.south_carolina
  News of South Carolina
clari.local.south_dakota
  News of South Dakota
clari.local.tennessee
  News of Tennessee
clari.local.texas
  News of Texas
clari.local.utah
  News of Utah
clari.local.vermont
  News of Vermont
clari.local.virginia+dc
  News of Virginia and Washington DC
clari.local.washington
  News of Washington State
clari.local.west_virginia
  News of West Virginia
clari.local.wisconsin
  News of Wisconsin
clari.local.wyoming
  News of Wyoming
clari.net.talk.news
  Discussion of events in the news — NOT moderated
clari.news.aging
  News of senior citizens and aging
clari.news.alcohol
  Drunk driving, alcoholism
clari.news.blacks
  Black news
clari.news.briefs
  Regular news summaries
clari.news.censorship
  Censorship, government control of media
clari.news.civil_rights
  Freedom, civil rights, human rights
clari.news.conflict
  War, conflict, peace talks
clari.news.corruption
  Corruption in government
clari.news.crime.abductions
  Kidnappings, hostage-taking
clari.news.crime.abuse
  Spouse and child abuse
clari.news.crime.issue
  The social issue of crime
clari.news.crime.juvenile
  Crimes by children and teenagers
clari.news.crime.misc
  Other crimes

Popular Culture & Entertainment

clari.news.crime.murders
Murders and shootings
clari.news.crime.organized
Organized crime
clari.news.crime.sex
Sex crimes, child pornography
clari.news.crime.top
Well-known crimes
clari.news.crime.white_collar
Insider trading, fraud, embezzlement
clari.news.disaster
Major problems, accidents & natural disasters
clari.news.drugs
Drug abuse and social policy
clari.news.education
Primary and secondary education
clari.news.education.higher
Colleges and universities
clari.news.ethnicity
Ethnicity issues
clari.news.family
Families, adoption, marriage
clari.news.features
Unclassified feature stories
clari.news.flash
Ultra-important once-a-year news flashes
clari.news.gays
Homosexuality and gay rights
clari.news.guns
Gun control and other gun news
clari.news.hot.japan_quake
News on the Kobe quake and related issues
clari.news.immigration
Refugees, immigration, migration
clari.news.jews
Jewish news
clari.news.labor
Unions, strikes
clari.news.labor.layoff
Layoffs in the news
clari.news.labor.strike
Strikes
clari.news.poverty
Poverty, homelessness, hunger
clari.news.punishment
Prison conditions, torture, death penalty
clari.news.religion
Religion, religious leaders, televangelists
clari.news.reproduction
Abortion, contraception, fertility
clari.news.review
Daily news review
clari.news.sex
Sexual issues, sex-related political stories
clari.news.smoking
Smoking and tobacco issues
clari.news.terrorism
Terrorist actions & related news around the world
clari.news.top
Top US news stories
clari.news.trouble
Less major accidents, problems & mishaps
clari.news.urgent
Major breaking stories of the day
clari.news.usa.gov.financial
Fiscal and financial US policy
clari.news.usa.gov.foreign_policy
U.S. foreign policy
clari.news.usa.gov.misc
Miscellaneous U.S. domestic policy
clari.news.usa.gov.personalities
Personalities and private lives
clari.news.usa.gov.politics
Party politics and electioneering
clari.news.usa.gov.state+local
State and local governments
clari.news.usa.gov.white_house
Presidential news

clari.news.usa.law
Legal news and U.S. lawsuits
clari.news.usa.law.supreme
The U.S. Supreme Court
clari.news.usa.military
News of the U.S. military
clari.news.weather
Weather and temperature reports
clari.news.women
Womens' issues: sexism, harassment
clari.sfbay.briefs
Twice daily news roundups for SF Bay Area
clari.sfbay.entertain
Reviews and entertainment news for SF Bay Area
clari.sfbay.fire
Stories from Fire Depts. of the SF Bay
clari.sfbay.general
Main stories for SF Bay Area
clari.sfbay.misc
Shorter general items for SF Bay Area
clari.sfbay.police
Stories from the Police Depts. of the SF Bay
clari.sfbay.roads
Reports from Caltrans and the CHP
clari.sfbay.short
Very short items for SF Bay Area
clari.sfbay.weather
SF Bay and California Weather reports
clari.sports.baseball
Baseball scores, stories, stats
clari.sports.baseball.games
Baseball games & box scores
clari.sports.basketball
Basketball coverage
clari.sports.basketball.college
College basketball coverage
clari.sports.briefs
General sports scoreboard
clari.sports.features
Sports feature stories
clari.sports.football
Pro football coverage
clari.sports.football.college
College football coverage
clari.sports.football.games
Coverage of individual pro games
clari.sports.golf
Golf coverage
clari.sports.hockey
NHL coverage
clari.sports.misc
Other sports, plus general sports news
clari.sports.motor
Racing, Motor Sports
clari.sports.olympic
The Olympic Games
clari.sports.review
Daily review of sports
clari.sports.tennis
Tennis news & scores
clari.sports.top
Top sports news
clari.tw.biotechnology
Biotechnology news
clari.tw.computers
Computer industry, applications and developments
clari.tw.defense
Defense industry issues
clari.tw.electronics
Electronics makers and sellers
clari.tw.environment
Environmental news, hazardous waste, forests
clari.tw.health
Disease, medicine, health care, sick celebs
clari.tw.health.aids
AIDS stories, research, political issues
clari.tw.misc
General technical industry stories

clari.tw.new_media
Online services, multimedia, the Internet
clari.tw.nuclear
Nuclear power & waste
clari.tw.science
General science stories
clari.tw.space
NASA, Astronomy & spaceflight
clari.tw.stocks
Regular reports on computer & technology stock prices
clari.tw.telecom
Phones, Satellites, Media & general Telecom
clari.tw.top
Top technical stories
clari.world.africa
Translated reports from Africa
clari.world.africa.south_africa
News from South Africa
clari.world.americas.canada
General Canadian news
clari.world.americas.canada.business
Canadian business news
clari.world.americas.canada.review
Daily review of Canadian news
clari.world.americas.caribbean
News of the Caribbean island nations
clari.world.americas.central
News of Central America
clari.world.americas.mexico
News of Mexico
clari.world.americas.south
News of South America
clari.world.asia.central
Ex-Soviet republics in Central Asia
clari.world.asia.china
News of China
clari.world.asia.hong_kong
News of Hong Kong
clari.world.asia.india
News of India
clari.world.asia.japan
News of Japan
clari.world.asia.koreas
News of North and South Korea
clari.world.asia.south
News of South Asia (Pakistan, Bangladesh, etc.)
clari.world.asia.southeast
News of Southeast Asia
clari.world.asia.taiwan
News of the Republic of China (Taiwan)
clari.world.briefs
Brief of world events
clari.world.europe.alpine
Austria, Switzerland, Liechtenstein
clari.world.europe.balkans
Former Yugoslavia, Romania, Bulgaria
clari.world.europe.benelux
Belgium, the Netherlands, Luxembourg
clari.world.europe.central
Poland, Czech Rep., Slovakia, Hungary
clari.world.europe.eastern
Translated reports from Eastern Europe
clari.world.europe.france
News of France and Monaco
clari.world.europe.germany
News of Germany
clari.world.europe.greece
News of Greece
clari.world.europe.iberia
Spain, Portugal, and Andorra
clari.world.europe.ireland
News of the Republic of Ireland
clari.world.europe.italy
News of Italy and San Marino
clari.world.europe.northern
Scandinavia, Finland, Iceland

Popular Culture & Entertainment

clari.world.europe.russia
    News of Russia
clari.world.europe.uk
    News of the United Kingdom
clari.world.europe.union
    News about the European Union
clari.world.mideast
    News from the Middle East
clari.world.mideast.arabia
    News of the Arabian Peninsula
clari.world.mideast.iran
    News of Iran
clari.world.mideast.iraq
    News of Iraq
clari.world.mideast.israel
    News of Israel and occupied lands
clari.world.mideast.turkey
    News of Turkey
clari.world.oceania
    News of Oceania
clari.world.oceania.australia
    News of Australia
clari.world.oceania.new_zealand
    News of New Zealand
clari.world.organizations
    The UN and other organizations
clari.world.top
    Top news from around the world
rec.arts.comics.alternative
    Alternative (non-mainstream) comic books
rec.arts.comics.creative
    Encouraging good superhero-style writing
rec.arts.comics.dc.universe
    DC Comics' shared universe and characters
rec.arts.comics.elfquest
    The Elfquest universe and characters
rec.arts.comics.info
    Reviews, convention information and other comics news
rec.arts.comics.marketplace
    The exchange of comics and comic related items
rec.arts.comics.marvel.universe
    Marvel Comics' shared universe and characters
rec.arts.comics.misc
    Comic books, graphic novels, sequential art
rec.arts.comics.other-media
    Comic book spinoffs in other media
rec.arts.comics.strips
    Discussion of short-form comics
rec.arts.comics.xbooks
    The Mutant Universe of Marvel Comics
rec.mag
    Magazine summaries, tables of contents, etc
rec.mag.dargon
    DargonZine fantasy fiction emag issues and discussion

Media

alt.fan.kroq
    LA radio station KROQ, FM 106.7. Great monster name
alt.news-media
    Don't believe the hype
alt.radio.online-tonight
    OnLine Tonight radio show discussion
alt.radio.talk
    Radio talk and call-in shows
misc.news.bosnia
    News, articles, reports & information on Bosnia
misc.news.east-europe.rferl
    Radio Free Europe/Radio Liberty Daily Report
misc.news.southasia
    News from Bangladesh, India, Nepal, etc
misc.writing
    Discussion of writing in all of its forms

rec.arts.disney
    Discussion of any Disney-related subjects
rec.arts.wobegon
    "A Prairie Home Companion" radio show discussion

Movies

Virgin! Virgin! Virgin!
    Virgin!
alt.asian-movies
    Movies from Hong Kong, Taiwan and the Chinese mainland
alt.cult-movies
    Movies with a cult following
alt.cult-movies.evil-deads
    The Evil Dead movie series
alt.fan.actors
    Discussion of actors, make and female
alt.fan.blade-runner
    The movie Blade Runner
alt.fan.bruce-campbell
    From the Evil Dead to Brisco County, Jr
alt.fan.ed-wood
    Ed Wood
alt.fan.james-bond
    On his Majesty's Secret Service (& secret linen too)
alt.fan.lion-king
    Discussion of Disney's "The Lion King"
alt.fan.mike-jittlov
    Electronic fan club for animator Mike Jittlov
alt.fan.scarecrow
    The Wiz is a WOW!
alt.fan.spinal-tap
    Down on the sex farm
alt.fan.tank-girl
    No, she doesn't make noises like a squirrel. Really
alt.movies.branagh-thmpsn
    Films of Kenneth Branagh and Emma Thompson
alt.movies.joe-vs-volcano
    Fans discuss the movie Joe versus the Volcano
alt.movies.kubrick
    For the discussion of Stanley Kubrick's movies
alt.movies.monster
    Godzilla! The Wolfman! The Thing! Aiiieee!!
alt.movies.scorsese
    Are you talking to me? You think I'm funny?
alt.movies.spielberg
    Films of blockbuster director Steven Spielberg
alt.movies.tim-burton
    The brooding works of Tim Burton
alt.movies.visual-effects
    Discussion of visual f/x for movies and tv
clari.living.movies
    News of film and movies
rec.arts.movies
    Discussions of movies and movie making
rec.arts.movies.announce
    Newsworthy events in the movie business
rec.arts.movies.current-films
    The latest movie releases
rec.arts.movies.lists+surveys
    Top-N lists and general surveys
rec.arts.movies.misc
    General aspects of movies not covered by other groups
rec.arts.movies.movie-going
    Going-to-movies experiences
rec.arts.movies.past-films
    Past movies
rec.arts.movies.people
    People in the movie business
rec.arts.movies.reviews
    Reviews of movies
rec.arts.movies.tech
    Technical aspects of movies
rec.arts.sf.movies
    Discussing SF motion pictures

rec.arts.sf.starwars
    Discussion of the Star Wars universe
rec.arts.sf.starwars.collecting
    Topics relating to Star Wars collecting
rec.arts.sf.starwars.info
    General information pertaining to Star Wars
rec.arts.sf.starwars.misc
    Miscellaneous topics pertaining to Star Wars

Museums & Theme Parks

alt.fairs.renaissance
    Discussions of Renaissance fairs and festivals
bit.listserv.museum-l
    Museum Discussion List
rec.parks.theme
    Entertainment theme parks
rec.roller-coaster
    Roller coasters and other amusement park rides

Shopping

alt.clothing.lingerie
    The special secrets under wraps
alt.clothing.sneakers
    Sports, casual, collection, or just one pair
alt.consumers.free-stuff
    Free offers and how to take advantage of them
alt.coupons
    /koo pahns/, not /kew pahns/. Try it
clari.living.consumer
    Consumer issues and products
misc.wanted
    Requests for things that are needed (NOT software)
relcom.ads
    Non-commercial ads
relcom.commerce.consume
    Cosmetics, parfumes, dresses, shoes
relcom.consumers
    Consumer info on products and services. No ads

Television

alt.aeffle.und.pferdle
    German TV cartoon characters das Aeffle und das Pferdle
alt.babylon5.uk
    Use uk.media.tv.sf.babylon5 instead
alt.drwho.creative
    Writing about long scarves and time machines
alt.dss
    Discussion of the new Digital Satellite Systems
alt.ensign.wesley.die.die.die
    We just can't get enough of him
alt.fan.disney.afternoon
    Disney Afternoon characters & shows
alt.fan.gene-scott
    Some TV preacher and horsebreeder
alt.fan.greg-kinnear
    The host of "TalkSoup" on the E! Entertainment Channel
alt.fan.hawaii-five-o
    Book 'em, Dano
alt.fan.michaela.strachan
    British children's TV presenter
alt.fan.monty-python
    Electronic fan club for those wacky Brits
alt.fan.pam-anderson
    Playmate and Baywatch lifeguard
alt.fan.power-rangers
    Discussion of important Power Rangers facts
alt.fan.q
    Omnipotent being from either Star Trek or James Bond

Popular Culture & Entertainment

alt.fan.ren-and-stimpy
  For folks who couldn't find alt.tv.ren-n-stimpy
alt.fan.surak
  That wild and crazy Vulcan
alt.fan.wings
  Fans of the telly show Wings
alt.mtv-sucks
  Video killed the radio star
alt.org.starfleet
  The "Starfleet" Star Trek fan organization
alt.ql.creative
  Quantum Leap fiction for the typographically challenged
alt.satellite.tv.europe
  All about European satellite tv
alt.shared-reality.startrek.klingon
  Klingons: Blood, Honor and Tribbles
alt.starfleet.rpg
  Starfleet role playing stories
alt.startrek.creative
  Stories and parodies related to Star Trek
alt.startrek.klingon
  AcK! What is that thing on your head?!
alt.tv.90210
  Use alt.tv.bh90210 instead
alt.tv.absolutely-fabulous
  People who love television
alt.tv.absolutely_fabulous
  People who love television
alt.tv.air-farce
  Royal Canadian Air Farce
alt.tv.animaniacs
  Steven Spielberg's Animaniacs!
alt.tv.babylon-5
  Use rec.arts.sf.tv.babylon5 instead
alt.tv.barney
  He's everywhere. Now appearing in several alt groups
alt.tv.beakmans-world
  Some sort of science and comedy show
alt.tv.beavis-n-butthead
  Uh huh huh huh uh uh huh uh huh -MTV program
alt.tv.bh90210
  Fans of "Beverly Hills 90210" TV show
alt.tv.brisco-county
  A western comedy adventure
alt.tv.chicago-hope
  Discussion of the TV Show Chicago Hope
alt.tv.china-beach
  China Beach
alt.tv.comedy-central
  Just what the hell is going on here?
alt.tv.commercials
  Keep them on the boob tube and off the net
alt.tv.dinosaurs
  A live action animated sitcom
alt.tv.dinosaurs.barney.die.die.die
  Squish the saccharine newt
alt.tv.discovery
  Programmes on The Discovery Channel
alt.tv.discovery.ca
  The Discovery Channel Canada discussion group
alt.tv.discovery.canada
  The Discovery Channel Canada discussion group
alt.tv.duckman
  The Duckman animated sitcom
alt.tv.earth2
  Discussion of _Earth 2_ television series
alt.tv.eek-the-cat
  Fans of the television show Eek the Cat
alt.tv.er
  Discussion of the television show E.R
alt.tv.forever-knight
  The Forever Knight television programme
alt.tv.frasier
  Kelsey Grammer as Frasier
alt.tv.friends
  Discussion of NBC's comedy Friends

alt.tv.game-shows
  Just look at these wonderful prizes
alt.tv.hermans-head
  Fans of those inside (and outside) of Herman's Head
alt.tv.highlander
  There was only one, then a bad sequel, now a TV show
alt.tv.home-improvement
  Discussions on the ABC sitcom Home Improvement
alt.tv.homicide
  A shotgun does an impressive job of destroying a TV
alt.tv.infomercials
  30 minutes to sell you a vacuum hair cutting system
alt.tv.kids-in-hall
  The Kids in the Hall comedy skits
alt.tv.knight-rider
  Discussions about Knight Rider
alt.tv.kungfu
  "Kung-fu" and "Kung-fu, The Legend Continues"
alt.tv.liquid-tv
  Animated variety
alt.tv.lois-n-clark
  The new adventures of the man from Krypton, Superman
alt.tv.lost-in-space.danger.will-robinson.danger.danger.danger
  Lost in Space
alt.tv.mad-about-you
  Some people really love their televisions
alt.tv.magnum-pi
  Tom Selleck stars as a hunky private investigator
alt.tv.mash
  Nothing like a good comedy about war and dying
alt.tv.max-headroom
  Blipverts will kill ya
alt.tv.melrose-place
  Cat fights and sleaziness, Wednesdays on FOX
alt.tv.models-inc
  A spinoff of Melrose Place
alt.tv.mtv
  I want my MTV
alt.tv.muppets
  Miss Piggy on the tube
alt.tv.mwc
  "Married... With Children"
alt.tv.my-s-c-life
  My So-Called Life and Operation Life Support
alt.tv.networks.cbc
  Shows on the Canadian Broadcasting Corporation (CBC)
alt.tv.news-shows
  Tabloid journalism on the televison
alt.tv.nickelodeon
  The first network for kids
alt.tv.northern-exp
  For the TV show with moss growing on it
alt.tv.nypd-blue
  For fans of the NYPD Blue TV show
alt.tv.party-of-five
  Fans of Fox's Party of Five
alt.tv.party-of-five.puke.puke.puke
  Detractors of Fox's Party of Five
alt.tv.picket-fences
  The Picket Fences show
alt.tv.prisoner
  The Prisoner television series from years ago
alt.tv.public-access
  Public access and community television
alt.tv.quantum-leap.creative
  Fanfiction relating to the show Quantum Leap
alt.tv.real-world
  Discussion of the MTV programme "The Real World"
alt.tv.red-dwarf
  The British sci-fi/comedy show
alt.tv.ren-n-stimpy
  Some change from Lassie, eh?

alt.tv.robotech
  The Robotech animated SF TV series
alt.tv.rockford-files
  But he won't do windows
alt.tv.roseanne
  In all her glory
alt.tv.sctv
  SCTV (Second City TV) & alumni discussions
alt.tv.saved-bell
  Saved by the Bell, a sitcom for teens
alt.tv.seaquest
  Deep sea adventures in the future
alt.tv.seinfeld
  A funny guy
alt.tv.sentai
  Live action Asian SF/Fantasy discussion, etc
alt.tv.sesame-street
  Sunny day
alt.tv.simpsons
  Don't have a cow, man!
alt.tv.simpsons.itchy-scratchy
  The cartoon-within-a-cartoon
alt.tv.snl
  Saturday Night Live, older but not better
alt.tv.star-trek.voyager
  Another Star Trek universe show: Voyager
alt.tv.talkshows.late
  Late night wars on the major networks
alt.tv.tekwar
  A discussion of the television TekWar series
alt.tv.time-traxx
  Back from the future in Time Traxx
alt.tv.tiny-toon
  Discussion about the "Tiny Toon Adventures" show
alt.tv.tiny-toon.fandom
  Apparently one fan group could not bind them all
alt.tv.tv-nation
  Some show called "TV Nation"
alt.tv.twilight.zone
  Rod Serling fantasies
alt.tv.twin-peaks
  Discussion about the popular (and unusual) TV show
alt.tv.wiseguy
  A wise guy
alt.tv.x-files
  Extra-terrestrial coverup conspiracies
alt.tv.x-files.creative
  Creative writings for the The X-Files
alt.tv.xuxa
  That Connie Dobbs clone, her tv show, and her double Xs
alt.video.laserdisc
  LD players and selections available for them
alt.video.tape-trading
  Trading of legally copied videos
alt.videos.bootlegs
  People pirating shows
bit.listserv.screen-l
  Film and Television Discussion List
rec.arts.drwho
  Discussion about Dr. Who
rec.arts.sf.tv
  Discussing general television SF
rec.arts.sf.tv.babylon5
  Babylon 5 creators meet Babylon 5 fans
rec.arts.sf.tv.quantum-leap
  Quantum Leap TV, comics, cons, etc
rec.arts.startrek.current
  New Star Trek shows, movies and books
rec.arts.startrek.fandom
  Star Trek conventions and memorabilia
rec.arts.startrek.info
  Information about the universe of Star Trek
rec.arts.startrek.misc
  General discussions of Star Trek
rec.arts.startrek.reviews
  Reviews of Star Trek books, episodes, films, &c

rec.arts.startrek.tech
   Star Trek's depiction of future technologies
rec.arts.tv
   The boob tube, its history, and past and current shows
rec.arts.tv.interactive
   Developments in interactive television
rec.arts.tv.mst3k
   For fans of Mystery Science Theater 3000
rec.arts.tv.mst3k.announce
   Mystery Science Theater 3000 announcements
rec.arts.tv.mst3k.misc
   For fans of Mystery Science Theater 3000
rec.arts.tv.soaps.abc
   Soap operas produced by or for the ABC network
rec.arts.tv.soaps.cbs
   Soap operas produced by or for the CBS network
rec.arts.tv.soaps.misc
   Postings of interest to all soap opera viewers
rec.arts.tv.uk
   Discussions of telly shows from the UK
rec.arts.tv.uk.comedy
   Regarding UK-based comedy shows
rec.arts.tv.uk.coronation-st
   Regarding the UK based show Coronation Street
rec.arts.tv.uk.eastenders
   Regarding the UK based show Eastenders
rec.arts.tv.uk.misc
   Miscellaneous topics about UK-based television

Unexplained Phenomena

alt.alien.research
   Extraterrestial body snatching for fun and profit
alt.alien.visitors
   Space Aliens on Earth! Abduction! Gov't Coverup!
alt.bigfoot
   Dr. Scholl's gone native
alt.bigfoot.research
   Serious discussion by Bigfoot researchers
alt.consciousness.near-death-exp
   Discussion of near-death experiences
alt.conspiracy
   Be paranoid — they're out to get you
alt.conspiracy.area51
   The US Government has a secret they're not telling you
alt.conspiracy.retards
   For those not impressed with the conspiracy-minded
alt.divination
   Divination techniques (e.g., I Ching, Tarot, runes)
alt.horror.werewolves
   They were wolves, now they're something to be wary of
alt.magick
   For discussion about supernatural arts
alt.magick.chaos
   Do not meddle in the affairs of wizards
alt.magick.moderated
   Serious discussion of magickal practices
alt.mindcontrol
   Are you sure those thoughts are really your own?
alt.out-of-body
   Out of Body Experiences
alt.paranet.metaphysics
   Philosphical ontology, cosmology and cosmetology
alt.paranet.paranormal
   "If it exists, how can supernatural be beyond natural?"
alt.paranet.psi
   "How much pressure can you generate with your brain?"
alt.paranet.science
   "Maybe if we dissect the psychic ..."
alt.paranet.skeptic
   "I don't believe they turned you into a newt."
alt.paranet.ufo
   "Heck, I guess naming it ``UFO'' identifies it."
alt.paranormal
   Phenomena which are not scientifically explicable
alt.paranormal.channeling
   Spiritual mediumship, channeling and channelers
bit.listserv.skeptic
   Discussion of Extraordinary Things
rec.org.sca
   Society for Creative Anachronism
relcom.fido.su.magic
   FIDOnet, magic and occult sciences

Weather & Traffic

alt.law-enforcement.traffic
   Highway laws and their enforcement
bit.listserv.wx-talk
   Weather Issues Discussions

Religion & Philosophy

Mythology

alt.mythology
   Zeus rules
alt.mythology.mythic-animals
   Creatures of myth, fantasy, and imagination

Philosophy

alt.christnet.philosophy
   Philosophical implications of Christianity
alt.individualism
   Philosophies where individual rights are paramount
alt.magick.ethics
   Discussion of the ethics/morals of magickal work
alt.memetics
   The evolution of ideas in societies
alt.necromicon
   Big time death wish
alt.philosophy.debate
   Back to basics
alt.philosophy.jarf
   The Jarf philosphy/metaphysics/religion/culture
alt.philosophy.objectivism
   A product of the Ayn Rand corporation
alt.philosophy.zen
   Meditating on how the alt.* namespace works
alt.postmodern
   Postmodernism, semiotics, deconstruction, and the like
alt.prophecies.nostradamus
   Mystic verse
alt.religion.computers
   Tiresome technical tirades
relcom.sci.philosophy
   Philosophic discussions and related projects
sci.philosophy.meta
   Discussions within the scope of "MetaPhilosophy"
talk.origins
   Evolution versus creationism (sometimes hot!)
talk.philosophy.humanism
   Humanism in the modern world
talk.philosophy.misc
   Philosophical musings on all topics

Religions

alt.atheism
   Godless heathens
alt.atheism.moderated
   Focused Godless heathens
alt.atheism.satire
   Atheism-related humour and satire
alt.bible.prophecy
   Discussion of the Bible and its prophecies
alt.christnet
   Gathering place for Christian ministers and users
alt.christnet.bible
   Bible discussion and research
alt.christnet.christianlife
   How to live what Christians believe
alt.christnet.evangelical
   Some aspect of evangelism
alt.christnet.hypocrisy
   "Vengeance is mine!" sayeth jfurr
alt.christnet.prayer
   Prayer in the lives of Christians
alt.christnet.second-coming.real-soon-now
   It could happen
alt.christnet.theology
   The distinctives of God of Christian theology
alt.fan.jalaludin_rumi
   Works of the mystic Sufi Jalaludin Rumi (1207-1273 AD)
alt.fan.jesus-christ
   Israel in 4 BC had no mass communication
alt.hindu
   The Hindu religion
alt.islam.sufism
   Discussions of the mystical dimensions of Islam
alt.magick.tyagi
   Magick as revealed by Mordred Nagasiva
alt.pagan
   Discussions about paganism & religion
alt.recovery.catholicism
   Getting over a Roman Catholic upbringing
alt.recovery.religion
   The twelve steps from the Ten Commandments
alt.religion.all-worlds
   Grokking the Church of All Worlds from Heinlein's book
alt.religion.broadcast
   Say Amen, somebody!
alt.religion.buddhism.nichiren
   Nichiren believers unite
alt.religion.buddhism.tibetan
   The teachings of Buddha as studied in Tibet
alt.religion.christian
   Unmoderated forum for discussing Christianity
alt.religion.christian.boston-church
   The international Church of Christ
alt.religion.eckankar
   Eckankar, the religion of the Light and Sound of God
alt.religion.gnostic
   History and philosophies of the Gnostic sects
alt.religion.islam
   Discussion of Islamic Faith & Soc.Religion.Islam
alt.religion.jonism
   Discussion of the Jonist spiritual tradition
alt.religion.mormon
   Mormon religion
alt.religion.rabbet
   The Rabbet sect
alt.religion.scientology
   L. Ron Hubbard's Church of Scientology
alt.religion.secular.atavism
   Ontogeny recapitulates phylogeny!
alt.religion.sexuality
   The politics of sexuality and religion
alt.religion.universal-life
   Universal Life Church

Newsgroups

alt.religion.vaisnava
  Discussion of the Vaisnava spiritual tradition
alt.religion.wicca
  Discussion of witchery
alt.religion.zoroastrianism
  Zoraster's/Zarathustra's religion, mazdaism
alt.satanism
  Not such a bad dude once you get to know him
alt.sufi
  "Come, come, whoever you are, this caravan is not of despair..."
alt.the-jihad
  Religious crusading anyone?
alt.zen
  It is
bit.listserv.catholic
  Free Catholic List
bit.listserv.christia
  Practical Christian Life
bit.listserv.uus-l
  Unitarian-Universalist List
soc.religion.bahai
  Discussion of the Baha'i Faith
soc.religion.christian
  Christianity and related topics
soc.religion.christian.bible-study
  Examining the Holy Bible
soc.religion.christian.youth-work
  Christians working with young people
soc.religion.eastern
  Discussions of Eastern religions
soc.religion.gnosis
  Gnosis, marifat, jnana & direct sacred experience
soc.religion.islam
  Discussions of the Islamic faith
soc.religion.quaker
  The Religious Society of Friends
soc.religion.shamanism
  Discussion of the full range of shamanic experience
soc.religion.sikhism
  Sikh Religion and Sikhs all over the world
soc.religion.unitarian-univ
  Unitarian-Universalism & non-creedal religions
talk.religion.buddhism
  All aspects of Buddhism as religion and philosophy
talk.religion.misc
  Religious, ethical, & moral implications
talk.religion.newage
  Esoteric and minority religions & philosophies

Religious History

alt.messianic
  Messianic traditions

Resources

alt.org.promisekeepers
  The Christian Organization PromiseKeepers

Science

Agriculture

alt.agriculture.fruit
  Fruit production
alt.agriculture.misc
  Use sci.agriculture instead
sci.agriculture
  Farming, agriculture and related topics
sci.agriculture.beekeeping
  Beekeeping, bee-culture and hive products

Aquatic Sciences

rec.ponds
  Pond issues: plants, fish, design, maintenance
sci.aquaria
  Only scientifically-oriented postings about aquaria
sci.bio.fisheries
  All aspects of fisheries science and fish biology
sci.bio.microbiology
  Protists, fungi, algae, other microscopic organisms
sci.geo.oceanography
  Oceanography, oceanology and marine science

Astronomy

alt.sci.planetary
  Studies in planetary science
sci.astro
  Astronomy discussions and information
sci.astro.amateur
  Amateur astronomy equipment, techniques, info, etc
sci.astro.fits
  Issues related to the Flexible Image Transport System
sci.astro.hubble
  Processing Hubble Space Telescope data
sci.astro.planetarium
  Discussion of planetariums
sci.astro.research
  Forum in astronomy/astrophysics research
sci.geo.meteorology
  Discussion of meteorology and related topics
sci.space.shuttle
  The space shuttle and the STS program

Biology

bionet.agroforestry
  Discussion of Agroforestry
bionet.announce
  Announcements of widespread interest to biologists
bionet.biology.computational
  Computer and mathematical applications
bionet.biology.grasses
  The biology of grasses: cereal, forage, turf, etc
bionet.biology.n2-fixation
  Research issues on biological nitrogen fixation
bionet.biology.tropical
  Discussions about tropical biology
bionet.celegans
  The model organism Caenorhabditis elegans
bionet.cellbiol
  Discussions about cell biology
bionet.cellbiol.cytonet
  The cytoskeleton, plasma membrane and cell wall
bionet.chlamydomonas
  Discussions about the green alga Chlamydomonas
bionet.drosophila
  Discussions about the biology of fruit flies
bionet.info-theory
  Discussions about biological information theory
bionet.journals.contents
  Contents of biology journal publications
bionet.journals.note
  Advice on dealing with journals in biology
bionet.microbiology
  The science and profession of microbiology
bionet.mycology
  Discussions about filamentous fungi
bionet.photosynthesis
  Discussions about research on photosynthesis
bionet.plants
  Discussion about all aspects of plant biology
bionet.population-bio
  Technical discussions about population biology
bionet.prof-society.faseb
  Fed. of American Societies for Experimental Biology
bionet.software
  Information about software for biology
bionet.software.www
  Information about WWW sources of interest to biologists
bionet.users.addresses
  Who's who in Biology
sci.bio
  Biology and related sciences
sci.bio.conservation
  Conservation biology research
sci.bio.ecology
  Ecological research
sci.bio.entomology.lepidoptera
  Lepidoptera: butterflies & moths
sci.bio.entomology.misc
  General insect study and related issues
sci.bio.ethology
  Animal behavior and behavioral ecology
sci.bio.evolution
  Discussions of evolutionary biology
sci.bio.food-science
  Topics related to food science and technology
sci.bio.herp
  Biology of amphibians and reptiles

Botany

alt.bonsai
  Little trees and battle screams
rec.arts.bonsai
  Dwarfish trees and shrubbery

Career & Employment

bionet.jobs
  Scientific Job opportunities
bionet.jobs.wanted
  Requests for employment in the biological sciences
bionet.women-in-bio
  Discussions about women in biology
sci.research.careers
  Issues relevant to careers in scientific research
sci.research.postdoc
  Anything about post-doctoral studies, including offers
sci.stat.consult
  Statistical consulting
sci.stat.edu
  Statistics education

Chemistry

alt.advanced.placed.or.honors.chemistry.2
  High.schoolers.with.newgroup
alt.drugs.chemistry
  Discussion of drug chemistry and synthesis
relcom.commerce.chemical
  Chemical production
sci.chem
  Chemistry and related sciences
sci.chem.electrochem
  The field of electrochemistry
sci.chem.labware
  Chemical laboratory equipment
sci.chem.organomet
  Organometallic chemistry

Environmental Sciences

alt.energy.renewable
Fueling ourselves without depleting everything
alt.save.the.earth
Environmentalist causes
alt.solar.thermal
Sun. Heat. An obvious connexion to most
bit.listserv.biosph-l
Biosphere, ecology, Discussion List
bit.listserv.envbeh-l
Forum on Environment and Human Behavior
info.isode
The ISO Development Environment package
sci.environment
Discussions about the environment and ecology
talk.environment
Discussion the state of the environment & what to do

Geosciences

alt.disasters.earthquake
Did the 'big one' shut down the 'net?
sci.geo.earthquakes
For discussion of earthquakes and related matters
sci.geo.eos
NASA's Earth Observation System (EOS)
sci.geo.fluids
Discussion of geophysical fluid dynamics
sci.geo.geology
Discussion of solid earth sciences
sci.geo.petroleum
All aspects of petroleum and the petroleum industry

Human Physiology

sci.anthropology
All aspects of studying humankind

Neurosciences

sci.cognitive
Perception, memory, judgement and reasoning

Organizations

alt.alumni.bronx-science
Those crazy kids from Bronx-Sci
alt.sci.tech.indonesian
Science and technology in Indonesia
bionet.prof-society.ascb
The American Society for Cell Biology
bionet.prof-society.biophysics
Biophysical Society official announcements
bionet.prof-society.cfbs
Canadian Federation of Biological Societies
bionet.prof-society.csm
Canadian Society of Microbiologists
bit.listserv.earntech
EARN Technical Group
info.nsf.grants
NSF grant notes
sci.skeptic
Skeptics discussing pseudo-science

Paleontology

sci.anthropology.paleo
Evolution of man and other primates
sci.archaeology
Studying antiquities of the world
sci.archaeology.mesoamerican
The field of mesoamerican archaeology
sci.bio.paleontology
Life of the past (but no creation vs evolution!)

Physics

alt.fan.serge-rudaz
Discussion of the famous physicist
alt.sci.physics.acoustics
The soundness of the science of sound
alt.sci.physics.new-theories
Scientific theories you won't find in journals
alt.sci.time-travel
Theory of time travel
bit.listserv.spires-l
SPIRES Conference list
sci.optics
Discussion relating to the science of optics
sci.physics
Physical laws, properties, etc
sci.physics.accelerators
Particle accelerators and the physics of beams
sci.physics.computational.fluid-dynamics
Computational fluid dynamics
sci.physics.cond-matter
Condensed matter physics, theory and experiment
sci.physics.electromag
Electromagnetic theory and applications
sci.physics.fusion
Info on fusion, esp. "cold" fusion
sci.physics.particle
Particle physics discussions
sci.physics.plasma
Plasma Science & Technology community exchange
sci.physics.research
Current physics research
sci.polymers
All aspects of polymer science
sci.techniques.xtallography
The field of crystallography

Space Science

sci.aeronautics
The science of aeronautics & related technology
sci.aeronautics.airliners
Airliner technology
sci.aeronautics.simulation
Aerospace simulation technology
sci.geo.satellite-nav
Satellite navigation systems, especially GPS
sci.nonlinear
Chaotic systems and other nonlinear scientific study
sci.space.news
Announcements of space-related news items
sci.space.policy
Discussions about space policy
sci.space.science
Space and planetary science and related technical work
sci.space.tech
Technical and general issues related to space flight

Sports & Recreation

Aquatic Sports

alt.sailing.asa
The American Sailing Association
bit.listserv.scuba-l
Scuba diving Discussion List
rec.boats.building
Boat building, design, restoration, and repair

Aviation

alt.disasters.aviation
Plane Lands Safely at Airfield, Film at 11
rec.aviation.announce
Events of interest to the aviation community
rec.aviation.answers
Frequently asked questions about aviation
rec.aviation.hang-gliding
Hang-gliding, para-gliding, foot-launched flight
rec.aviation.homebuilt
Selecting, designing, building, and restoring aircraft
rec.aviation.ifr
Flying under Instrument Flight Rules
rec.aviation.marketplace
Aviation classifieds
rec.aviation.military
Military aircraft of the past, present and future
rec.aviation.misc
Miscellaneous topics in aviation
rec.aviation.owning
Information on owning airplanes
rec.aviation.piloting
General discussion for aviators
rec.aviation.products
Reviews and discussion of products useful to pilots
rec.aviation.questions
Aviation questions and answers
rec.aviation.rotorcraft
Helicopters and other rotary wing aircraft
rec.aviation.simulators
Flight simulation on all levels
rec.aviation.soaring
All aspects of sailplanes and hang-gliders
rec.aviation.stories
Anecdotes of flight experiences
rec.aviation.student
Learning to fly
rec.aviation.ultralight
Light aircraft in general, all topics

Career & Employment

alt.sport.officiating
Being a referee

Crafts & Hobbies

alt.aquaria
The aquarium & related as a hobby
alt.aquaria.killies
Killifish, members of family cyprinodontidae
alt.beadworld
We must appease the Bead Gods
alt.boomerang
The angular throwing club, not the Eddie Murphy flick
alt.collecting.autographs
WOW! You got Pete Rose's? What about Kibo's?
alt.crafts.plastic-canvas
Using plastic and canvas in artful creations
alt.home.repair
Bob Vila would love this group
alt.horology
A group for the science of clocks and watches
alt.inventors
People with new ideas
alt.masonic.demolay
Demonstrating how to build a basement

alt.sewing
  A group that is not as it seams
bit.listserv.candle-l
  Candle Products discussion list
bit.listserv.postcard
  Postcard Collectors discussion group
info.firearms
  Non-political firearms discussions
rec.collecting
  Discussion among collectors of many things
rec.collecting.cards.discuss
  Discussion of sports and non-sports cards
rec.collecting.cards.non-sports
  Non-sports cards
rec.collecting.coins
  Coin, currency, medal, etc. collecting forum
rec.collecting.dolls
  Doll and bear collecting and crafting
rec.collecting.sport.baseball
  Baseball memorabilia (cards, photos, etc)
rec.collecting.sport.basketball
  Basketball memorabilia (cards, photos, etc)
rec.collecting.sport.football
  Football memorabilia (cards, photos, etc)
rec.collecting.sport.hockey
  Hockey memorabilia (cards, photos, etc)
rec.collecting.sport.misc
  Sports memorabilia not in any other group
rec.collecting.stamps
  Discussion of all things related to philately
rec.crafts.beads
  Making, collecting, and using beads
rec.crafts.brewing
  The art of making beers and meads
rec.crafts.jewelry
  All aspects of jewelry making and lapidary work
rec.crafts.marketplace
  Small-scale ads for craft products of all kinds
rec.crafts.metalworking
  All aspects of working with metal
rec.crafts.misc
  Handiwork arts not covered elsewhere
rec.crafts.polymer-clay
  Techniques & resources relating to polymer clay
rec.crafts.winemaking
  The tasteful art of making wine
rec.folk-dancing
  Folk dances, dancers, and dancing
rec.games.trading-cards.announce
  Important news about trading card games
rec.games.trading-cards.jyhad
  Jyhad trading card game discussions
rec.games.trading-cards.magic.misc
  General "Magic: the Gathering" postings
rec.games.trading-cards.magic.rules
  "Magic: the Gathering" rules Q&A
rec.games.trading-cards.magic.strategy
  "Magic: the Gathering" strategy
rec.games.trading-cards.marketplace
  Sales, auctions, trades of game cards
rec.games.trading-cards.misc
  Other trading card game discussions
rec.games.trivia
  Discussion about trivia
rec.games.vectrex
  The Vectrex game system
rec.guns
  Discussions about firearms
rec.heraldry
  Discussion of coats of arms
rec.juggling
  Juggling techniques, equipment and events
rec.kites
  Talk about kites and kiting
rec.models.railroad
  Model railroads of all scales
rec.models.rc
  Radio-controlled models for hobbyists
rec.models.rockets
  Model rockets for hobbyists
rec.models.scale
  Construction of models
rec.pyrotechnics
  Fireworks, rocketry, safety, & other topics
rec.radio.amateur.antenna
  Antennas: theory, techniques and construction
rec.radio.amateur.digital.misc
  Packet radio and other digital radio modes
rec.radio.amateur.equipment
  All about production amateur radio hardware
rec.radio.amateur.homebrew
  Amateur radio construction and experimentation
rec.radio.amateur.misc
  Amateur radio practices, contests, events, rules, etc
rec.radio.amateur.policy
  Radio use & regulation policy
rec.radio.amateur.space
  Amateur radio transmissions through space
rec.radio.broadcasting
  Discussion of global domestic broadcast radio
rec.radio.cb
  Citizen-band radio
rec.radio.info
  Informational postings related to radio
rec.radio.noncomm
  Topics relating to noncommercial radio
rec.radio.scanner
  "Utility" broadcasting traffic above 30 MHz
rec.radio.shortwave
  Shortwave radio enthusiasts
rec.radio.swap
  Offers to trade and swap radio equipment
rec.railroad
  For fans of real trains, ferroequinologists
rec.sport.waterski
  Waterskiing and other boat-towed activities
rec.toys.cars
  Toy car collecting
rec.toys.lego
  Discussion of Lego, Duplo (and compatible) toys
rec.toys.misc
  Discussion of toys that lack a specific newsgroup
rec.woodworking
  Hobbyists interested in woodworking

Food & Dining

alt.bacchus
  Disciples of the god of wine
alt.beer
  Good for what ales ya
alt.cereal
  Breakfast cereals and their (m)ilk
alt.coffee
  Another group worshipping caffeine
alt.crackers
  Snack food in little bits or big bytes
alt.culture.sardines
  Sardine culture and religion
alt.cybercafes
  Cyber/Computer/Internet Cafes or Coffeeshops
alt.drinks.kool-aid
  Beverage break on the Information Superhighway
alt.drinks.snapple
  Made from the Best Stuff on Earth
alt.drugs.caffeine
  All about the world's most-used stimulant drug
alt.fan.super-big-gulp
  Brain freeze!
alt.fan.wavey.davey
  Ocean Spray's latest flavour
alt.food
  Use rec.food.cooking instead
alt.food.chocolate
  Aphrodisiac confections
alt.food.cocacola
  An American Classic. Buy our nostalgic art
alt.food.coffee
  Black gold of another sort. Colombian tea
alt.food.fast-food
  Fast food restaurants
alt.food.fat-free
  Very low fat foods; not necessarily about weight loss
alt.food.ice-cream
  I scream, you scream, we all scream for ice cream
alt.food.low-fat
  Low fat diets, food, and cooking
alt.food.mcdonalds
  Carl Sagan's favourite burger place
alt.food.professionals
  Fruit of the Loom
alt.food.red-lobster
  Seafood'n'stuff
alt.food.sushi
  The ancient art of preparing raw fish
alt.food.taco-bell
  Make a run for the border
alt.food.waffle-house
  Not just for breakfast anymore
alt.food.wine
  All about wine, for oeneophiles
alt.gourmand
  Recipes & cooking info
alt.ketchup
  Whak* Whak* ...shake... Whak* Damn, all over my tie
alt.mcdonalds
  Can I get fries with that?
alt.pub.coffeehouse.amethyst
  Realistic place to meet and chat with friends
alt.pub.dragons-inn
  Fantasy virtual reality pub similar to alt.callahans
alt.pub.havens-rest
  Fantasy virtual reality pub similar to alt.callahans
alt.tequila
  It becomes hard to spell when you drink too much
alt.zima
  A clear malt beverage, better with lime
rec.food.chocolate
  Chocolate
rec.food.cooking
  Food, cooking, cookbooks, and recipes
rec.food.drink
  Wines and spirits
rec.food.drink.beer
  All things beer
rec.food.drink.coffee
  The making and drinking of coffee
rec.food.drink.tea
  Tea as beverage and culture
rec.food.historic
  The history of food making arts
rec.food.preserving
  Preserving foodstuffs, herbs, and medicinals
rec.food.recipes
  Recipes for interesting food and drink
rec.food.restaurants
  Discussion of dining out
rec.food.sourdough
  Making and baking with sourdough
rec.food.veg
  Vegetarians
rec.food.veg.cooking
  Vegetarian recipes, cooking, nutrition
relcom.commerce.food
  Food
relcom.commerce.food.drinks
  Spirits and soft drinks
relcom.commerce.food.sweet
  Sweeties, sugar

Games

alt.cardgame.magic
Use rec.games.trading-cards.magic.misc instead
alt.cardgame.spellfire
TSR's SpellFire game
alt.chess.ics
The Internet Chess Server
alt.fan.sonic-hedgehog
Sega's spinning blue hero
alt.games.air-warrior
The Air Warrior combat computer game
alt.games.apogee
A real high point in any gamer's day
alt.games.cosmic-wimpout
A dice game popular in the computer crowd
alt.games.dark-forces
Discussion of Star Wars related game
alt.games.dice
Games that use dice
alt.games.doom
A really popular PC game
alt.games.doom.announce
Announcements about the PC game Doom
alt.games.doom.newplayers
Helping people new to a really popular PC game
alt.games.dune-ii.virgin-games
Virgin Games computer game Dune II
alt.games.final-fantasy
The Final Fantasy game
alt.games.frp.dnd-util
Computer utilities for Dungeons and Dragons
alt.games.frp.tekumel
Empire of the Petal Throne FRPG by M. A. R. Barker
alt.games.jyhad
Another trading card game, like Magic, the Gathering
alt.games.lynx
The Atari Lynx
alt.games.marathon
Discussion of the Macintosh Sci-Fi game Marathon
alt.games.milkcaps
An old game rejuvenated
alt.games.milkcaps.pogs
Like alt.games.milkcaps
alt.games.mk
Struggling in Mortal Kombat!
alt.games.mtrek
Multi-Trek, a multi-user Star Trek-like game
alt.games.netrek.paradise
Discussion of the paradise version of netrek
alt.games.nomic
Ask scott@glia.biostr.washington.edu
alt.games.nomic.unomic
A USENET Experiment, a game of NOMIC via USENET
alt.games.playmaker-football
Playmaker Football Discussion Area
alt.games.sf2
The video game Street Fighter 2
alt.games.tiddlywinks
Flip the discs —- fun for hours on end!
alt.games.torg
Gateway for TORG mailing list
alt.games.ultima.dragons
Hints for Ultima games
alt.games.vga-planets
Discussion of Tim Wisseman's VGA Planets
alt.games.video.classic
Video games from before the mid-1980s
alt.games.video.sony-playstation
Sony's Playstation
alt.games.warcraft
The craft of war
alt.games.wc3
A sequel to the infamous Water Closet games
alt.games.whitewolf
Discussion of WhiteWolf's line of gothic/horror RPGs
alt.games.xpilot
Discussion on all aspects of the X11 game Xpilot
alt.games.xtrek
The networked game Xtrek
alt.mac.games.binaries
Game binaries for the Macintosh
alt.sega.genesis
Another addiction
alt.sport.croquet
A venerable lawn game
alt.sport.darts
Look what you've done to the wall!
alt.sport.foosball
Table soccer and dizzy little men
alt.sport.lacrosse
The game of lacrosse
alt.sport.lasertag
Indoor splatball with infrared lasers
alt.sport.pool
Knock your balls into your pockets for fun
bit.listserv.games-l
Computer Games List
rec.arts.sf.starwars.games
Star Wars games: RPG, computer, card, etc
rec.gambling
Articles on games of chance & betting
rec.gambling.blackjack
Analysis of and strategy for blackjack, aka 21
rec.gambling.craps
Analysis of and strategy for the dice game craps
rec.gambling.lottery
Strategy and news of lotteries and sweepstakes
rec.gambling.misc
All other gambling topics including travel
rec.gambling.other-games
Gambling games not covered elsewhere
rec.gambling.poker
Analysis and strategy of live poker games
rec.gambling.racing
Wagering on animal races
rec.gambling.sports
Wagering on human sporting events
rec.games.abstract
Perfect information, pure strategy games
rec.games.backgammon
Discussion of the game of backgammon
rec.games.board
Discussion and hints on board games
rec.games.board.ce
The Cosmic Encounter board game
rec.games.board.marketplace
Trading and selling of board games
rec.games.bolo
The networked strategy war game Bolo
rec.games.bridge
Hobbyists interested in bridge
rec.games.chess
Chess & computer chess
rec.games.chinese-chess
Discussion of the game of Chinese chess, Xiangqi
rec.games.diplomacy
The conquest game Diplomacy
rec.games.empire
Discussion and hints about Empire
rec.games.frp.advocacy
Flames and rebuttals about various role-playing systems
rec.games.frp.announce
Announcements of happenings in the role-playing world
rec.games.frp.archives
Archivable fantasy stories and other projects
rec.games.frp.cyber
Discussions of cyberpunk related roleplaying games
rec.games.frp.dnd
Fantasy role-playing with TSR's Dungeons and Dragons
rec.games.frp.gurps
The GURPS role playing game
rec.games.frp.live-action
Live-action roleplaying games
rec.games.frp.marketplace
Role-playing game materials wanted and for sale
rec.games.frp.misc
General discussions of role-playing games
rec.games.go
Discussion about Go
rec.games.int-fiction
All aspects of interactive fiction games
rec.games.mecha
Giant robot games
rec.games.miniatures
Tabletop wargaming
rec.games.miniatures.historical
Historical and modern tabletop wargaming
rec.games.miniatures.misc
Miniatures and various tabletop wargames
rec.games.miniatures.warhammer
Wargaming in the Warhammer Universe
rec.games.pbm
Discussion about Play by Mail games
rec.games.pinball
Discussing pinball-related issues
rec.games.playing-cards
Recreational (non-gambling) card playing
rec.games.programmer
Discussion of adventure game programming
rec.games.video.3do
Discussion of 3DO video game systems
rec.games.video.advocacy
Debate on merits of various video game systems
rec.games.video.arcade
Discussions about coin-operated video games
rec.games.video.arcade.collecting
Collecting, converting, repairing etc
rec.games.video.atari
Discussion of Atari's video game systems
rec.games.video.cd-i
CD-i topics with emphasis on games
rec.games.video.classic
Older home video entertainment systems
rec.games.video.marketplace
Home video game stuff for sale or trade
rec.games.video.misc
General discussion about home video games
rec.games.video.nintendo
All Nintendo video game systems and software
rec.games.video.sega
All Sega video game systems and software
rec.games.video.sony
Sony game hardware and software
rec.games.xtank.play
Strategy and tactics for the distributed game Xtank
rec.games.xtank.programmer
Coding the Xtank game and its robots
rec.puzzles
Puzzles, problems, and quizzes
rec.puzzles.crosswords
Making and playing gridded word puzzles
relcom.games
Discussion of computer, play-by-mail and other games

Gardening

rec.gardens
Gardening, methods and results
rec.gardens.orchids
Growing, hybridizing, and general care of orchids
rec.gardens.roses
Gardening information related to roses

Motor Sports

alt.hotrod
  High speed automobiles
alt.scooter
  Motor scooters, like Vespas, Lambrettas, etc
rec.motorcycles
  Motorcycles and related products and laws
rec.motorcycles.dirt
  Riding motorcycles and ATVs off-road
rec.motorcycles.harley
  All aspects of Harley-Davidson motorcycles
rec.motorcycles.racing
  Discussion of all aspects of racing motorcycles

Organizations

alt.drumcorps
  Use rec.arts.marching.drumcorps instead
rec.scouting
  Scouting youth organizations worldwide

Outdoor Recreation

alt.mining.recreational
  Digging rock as a hobby
alt.mountain-bike
  Use rec.bicycles.off-road instead
alt.org.audubon
  Regarding the Audubon Society
alt.org.earth-first
  Discussion of the Earth First! society
alt.org.sierra-club
  Regarding the Sierra Club
alt.pinecone
  The heart of camp arts & crafts
alt.skate-board
  Discussion of all apsects of skate-boarding
alt.snowmobiles
  For bikers who don't like two wheels in snow and ice
alt.sport.bungee
  Like alt.suicide with rubber bands
alt.sport.jet-ski
  Discussion of personal watercraft
alt.sport.paintball
  Splat, you're it
alt.surfing
  Riding the ocean waves
rec.backcountry
  Activities in the Great Outdoors
rec.hunting
  Discussions about hunting
relcom.rec.tourism
  Sport outgoing: hiking, water, etc

Personal Fitness

alt.backrubs
  Lower...to the right...aaaah!
alt.yoga
  All forms and aspects of yoga
misc.fitness
  Physical fitness, exercise, bodybuilding, etc
misc.fitness.aerobic
  All forms of aerobic activity
misc.fitness.misc
  All other general fitness topics
misc.fitness.weights
  Bodybuilding, weightlifting, resistance

Pets & Animals

alt.animals.badgers
  Wombat love
alt.animals.bears
  Bear love and "Da Bears"!
alt.animals.dolphins
  Flipper, Darwin, and all their friends
alt.animals.felines
  Cats of all types
alt.animals.felines.lions
  Royalty of the Beasts
alt.animals.foxes
  For those wild and crazy guys
alt.animals.raccoons
  discussion of raccoons and raccoon-related topics
alt.chinchilla
  The nature of chinchilla farming in America today
alt.fan.lemurs
  Little critters with BIG eyes
alt.lemmings
  Rodents with a death wish
alt.pets.hamsters
  Make that wheel go 'round
alt.pets.rabbits
  Coneys abound. See also alt.fan.john-palmer
alt.skunks
  Le pew
alt.sport.falconry
  Hunting with birds of prey
alt.sports.falconry
  Falconry
alt.sport.horse-racing
  Run for the roses: breeding, betting on, & racing horses
alt.wolves
  Discussing wolves & wolf-mix dogs
rec.animals.wildlife
  Wildlife related discussions/information
rec.aquaria
  Keeping fish and aquaria as a hobby
rec.birds
  Hobbyists interested in bird watching
rec.pets
  Pets, pet care, and household animals in general
rec.pets.birds
  The culture and care of indoor birds
rec.pets.cats
  Discussion about domestic cats
rec.pets.dogs.activities
  Dog events: showing, obedience, agility, etc
rec.pets.dogs.behavior
  Behaviors and problems: housetraining, chewing, etc
rec.pets.dogs.breeds
  Breed specific — breed traits, finding breeders, etc
rec.pets.dogs.health
  Info about health problems & how to care for dogs
rec.pets.dogs.info
  General information and FAQs posted here
rec.pets.dogs.misc
  All other topics, chat, humor, etc
rec.pets.dogs.rescue
  Information about breed rescue, placing and adopting
rec.pets.herp
  Reptiles, amphibians and other exotic vivarium pets
talk.politics.animals
  The use and/or abuse of animals

Recreation

alt.archery
  Robin Hood had the right idea
alt.caving
  Spelunk
alt.spleen
  Venting as a biological function
misc.survivalism
  Disaster and long-term survival techniques and theory
rec.misc
  General topics about recreational/participant sports
rec.nude
  Hobbyists interested in naturist/nudist activities
rec.outdoors.fishing
  All aspects of sport and commercial fishing
rec.outdoors.fishing.fly
  Fly fishing in general
rec.outdoors.fishing.saltwater
  Saltwater fishing, methods, gear, Q&A
rec.running
  Running for enjoyment, sport, exercise, etc
rec.scuba
  Hobbyists interested in SCUBA diving
rec.skate
  Ice skating and roller skating
rec.skiing.alpine
  Downhill skiing technique, equipment, etc
rec.skiing.announce
  FAQ, competition results, automated snow reports

Sports

alt.college.college-bowl
  Discussions of the College Bowl competition
alt.fan.nancy-kerrigan.ouch.ouch.ouch
  Another Nancy & Tonya saga group
alt.fan.robert-jordan
  Baseball's most popular minor leaguer
alt.flame.football.notre-dame
  Flames directed towards Notre Dame football
alt.lacrosse
  Use alt.sport.lacrosse instead
alt.org.h-h-harriers
  Running + drinking w/the Hash House Harriers
alt.sport.basketball.pro.fantasy
  Rotisserie league basketball
alt.sport.bowling
  In the gutter again
alt.sport.korfball
  Discussion of the sport of Korfball
alt.sport.maulball
  The brutal sport of maulball
alt.sport.racquetball
  All aspects of indoor racquetball and related sports
alt.sport.squash
  With the proper technique, vegetables can go very fast
alt.sports.badminton
  Discussion about badminton
alt.sports.baseball.atlanta-braves
  Atlanta Braves major league baseball
alt.sports.baseball.balt-orioles
  Baltimore Orioles major league baseball
alt.sports.baseball.bos-redsox
  Boston Red Sox major league baseball
alt.sports.baseball.calif-angels
  California Angles major league baseball
alt.sports.baseball.chi-whitesox
  Chicago White Sox major league baseball
alt.sports.baseball.chicago-cubs
  Chicago Cubs major league baseball
alt.sports.baseball.cinci-reds
  Cincinnati Reds major league baseball
alt.sports.baseball.cleve-indians
  Cleveland Indians major league baseball
alt.sports.baseball.col-rockies
  Colorado Rockies major league baseball
alt.sports.baseball.detroit-tigers
  Detroit Tigers major league baseball

Sports & Recreation

alt.sports.baseball.fla-marlins
  Florida Marlins major league baseball
alt.sports.baseball.houston-astros
  Houston Astros major league baseball
alt.sports.baseball.kc-royals
  Kansas City Royals major league baseball
alt.sports.baseball.la-dodgers
  Los Angeles Dodgers major league baseball
alt.sports.baseball.minor-leagues
  Minor league baseball talk
alt.sports.baseball.mke-brewers
  Milwaukee Brewers major league baseball
alt.sports.baseball.mn-twins
  Minnesota Twins major league baseball
alt.sports.baseball.montreal-expos
  Montreal Expos major league baseball
alt.sports.baseball.ny-mets
  New York Mets baseball talk
alt.sports.baseball.ny-yankees
  New York Yankees baseball talk
alt.sports.baseball.oakland-as
  Oakland As major league baseball
alt.sports.baseball.phila-phillies
  Philadelphia Phillies baseball talk
alt.sports.baseball.pitt-pirates
  Pittsburg Pirates major league baseball
alt.sports.baseball.sd-padres
  San Diego Padres major league baseball talk
alt.sports.baseball.sea-mariners
  Seattle Mariners major league baseball
alt.sports.baseball.sf-giants
  San Francisco Giants baseball talk
alt.sports.baseball.stl-cardinals
  St Louis Cardinals baseball talk
alt.sports.baseball.texas-rangers
  Texas Rangers major league baseball
alt.sports.baseball.tor-bluejays
  Toronto Blue Jays baseball talk
alt.sports.basketball.college.big-5
  Big 5 college basketball
alt.sports.basketball.ivy.penn
  U of Pennsylvania (NOT Penn State!) basketball
alt.sports.basketball.nba.atlanta-hawks
  Atlanta Hawks NBA basketball
alt.sports.basketball.nba.boston-celtics
  Boston Celtics NBA basketball
alt.sports.basketball.nba.char-hornets
  Charlotte Hornets NBA basketball
alt.sports.basketball.nba.chicago-bulls
  Chicago Bulls NBA basketball
alt.sports.basketball.nba.denver-nuggets
  Denver Nuggets NBA basketball
alt.sports.basketball.nba.det-pistons
  Detroit Pistons NBA basketball talk
alt.sports.basketball.nba.gs-warriors
  Golden State Warriors NBA basketball
alt.sports.basketball.nba.hou-rockets
  Houston Rockets NBA basketball
alt.sports.basketball.nba.la-lakers
  Los Angeles Lakers NBA basketball
alt.sports.basketball.nba.miami-heat
  Miami Heat NBA basketball
alt.sports.basketball.nba.mil-bucks
  Milwaukee Bucks NBA basketball
alt.sports.basketball.nba.mn-wolves
  Minnesota Timberwolves NBA basketball
alt.sports.basketball.nba.orlando-magic
  Orlando Magic NBA basketball talk
alt.sports.basketball.nba.phila-76ers
  Philadelphia 76ers NBA basketball talk
alt.sports.basketball.nba.phx-suns
  Phoenix Suns NBA basketball talk
alt.sports.basketball.nba.sa-spurs
  San Antonio Spurs basketball talk
alt.sports.basketball.nba.sac-kings
  Sacramento Kings NBA TEAM
alt.sports.basketball.nba.seattle-sonics
  Seattle Sonics NBA basketball

alt.sports.basketball.nba.utah-jazz
  Utah Jazz NBA basketball talk
alt.sports.basketball.nba.wash-bullets
  Washington Bullets NBA basketball
alt.sports.basketball.pro.ny-knicks
  New York Knicks NBA basketball talk
alt.sports.college.acc
  Discussions about the Atlantic Coast Conference
alt.sports.college.big-east
  Discussions of college sports in the big-east
alt.sports.college.ivy-league
  Ivy League athletics
alt.sports.college.nc-state
  NC State sports teams
alt.sports.college.ohio-state
  OSU Sports plus a whole lot more
alt.sports.college.pac-10
  Discussions of college sports in the Pac 10
alt.sports.football.arena
  Arena football (US-style, not soccer)
alt.sports.football.college.fsu-seminoles
  Florida U Seminoles football
alt.sports.football.mn-vikings
  Minnesota Vikings football talk
alt.sports.football.pro.atl-falcons
  Atlanta Falcons NFL Football talk
alt.sports.football.pro.buffalo-bills
  Buffalo Bills NFL football talk
alt.sports.football.pro.car-panthers
  Carolina Panthers NFL football talk
alt.sports.football.pro.chicago-bears
  Chicago Bears NFL football talk
alt.sports.football.pro.cinci-bengals
  Cincinnati Bengals NFL football talk
alt.sports.football.pro.cleve-browns
  Cleveland Browns NFL football talk
alt.sports.football.pro.dallas-cowboys
  Dallas Cowboys NFL football talk
alt.sports.football.pro.denver-broncos
  Denver Broncos NFL football talk
alt.sports.football.pro.detroit-lions
  Detroit Lions NFL football
alt.sports.football.pro.gb-packers
  Green Bay Packers NFL football talk
alt.sports.football.pro.houston-oilers
  Houston Oilers NFL football talk
alt.sports.football.pro.kc-chiefs
  Kansas City Chiefs NFL football talk
alt.sports.football.pro.la-raiders
  Los Angeles Raiders NFL football talk
alt.sports.football.pro.la-rams
  Los Angeles Rams NFL football talk
alt.sports.football.pro.miami-dolphins
  Miami Dolphins NFL football talk
alt.sports.football.pro.ne-patriots
  New England Patriots NFL football talk
alt.sports.football.pro.no-saints
  New Orleans Saints NFL football talk
alt.sports.football.pro.ny-giants
  New York Giants NFL football talk
alt.sports.football.pro.ny-jets
  New York Jets NFL football talk
alt.sports.football.pro.phila-eagles
  Philadelphia Eagles NFL football talk
alt.sports.football.pro.phoe-cardinals
  Phoenix Cardinals NFL football talk
alt.sports.football.pro.pitt-steelers
  Pittsburgh Steelers NFL football talk
alt.sports.football.pro.sd-chargers
  San Diego Chargers NFL football talk
alt.sports.football.pro.sea-seahawks
  Seattle Seahawks NFL football talk
alt.sports.football.pro.sf-49ers
  San Francisco 49ers NFL football talk
alt.sports.football.pro.tampabay-bucs
  Tampa Bay Bucaneers NFL football talk
alt.sports.football.pro.wash-redskins
  Washington Redskins NFL football talk

alt.sports.hocket.nhl.det-redwings
  Detroit Red Wings NHL hocket talk
alt.sports.hockey.echl
  EC Hockey League
alt.sports.hockey.fantasy
  Rotisserie league ice hockey
alt.sports.hockey.ihl
  I Hockey Leage
alt.sports.hockey.nhl.boston-bruins
  Boston Bruins NHL hockey talk
alt.sports.hockey.nhl.buffalo-sabres
  The NHL Buffalo Sabres
alt.sports.hockey.nhl.chi-blackhawks
  Chicago Blackhawks NHL hockey talk
alt.sports.hockey.nhl.clgry-flames
  Calgary Flames NHL hockey talk
alt.sports.hockey.nhl.det-redwings
  Detroit Redwings NHL hockey talk
alt.sports.hockey.nhl.edm-oilers
  Edmonton Oilers NHL hockey talk
alt.sports.hockey.nhl.hford-whalers
  Hartford Whalers NHL hockey talk
alt.sports.hockey.nhl.la-kings
  Los Angeles Kings NHL hockey talk
alt.sports.hockey.nhl.mtl-canadiens
  Montreal Canadiens NHL hockey talk
alt.sports.hockey.nhl.nj-devils
  New Jersey Devils NHL hockey talk
alt.sports.hockey.nhl.ny-islanders
  New York Islanders NHL hockey talk
alt.sports.hockey.nhl.ny-rangers
  New York Rangers NHL hockey talk
alt.sports.hockey.nhl.phila-flyers
  Philadelphia Flyers NHL hockey talk
alt.sports.hockey.nhl.pit-penguins
  Pittsburgh Penguins NHL hockey talk
alt.sports.hockey.nhl.que-nordiques
  The NHL Quebec Nordiques
alt.sports.hockey.nhl.sj-sharks
  San Jose Sharks NHL hockey talk
alt.sports.hockey.nhl.tor-mapleleafs
  Toronto Maple Leafs NHL hockey talk
alt.sports.hockey.nhl.vanc-canucks
  Vancouver Canucks NHL hockey talk
alt.sports.hockey.nhl.wash-capitals
  Washington Captials NHL hockey talk
alt.sports.hockey.nhl.winnipeg-jets
  Winnipeg Jets NHL hockey talk
alt.sports.oj-simpson
  His time is passed, but some want to still discuss it
alt.sports.soccer.european
  Football, European-style
bit.listserv.sportpsy
  Exercise and Sports Psychology
rec.bicycles.marketplace
  Buying, selling & reviewing items for cycling
rec.bicycles.misc
  General discussion of bicycling
rec.bicycles.off-road
  All aspects of off-road bicycling
rec.bicycles.racing
  Bicycle racing techniques, rules and results
rec.bicycles.rides
  Discussions of tours and training or commuting routes
rec.bicycles.soc
  Societal issues of bicycling
rec.bicycles.tech
  Cycling product design, construction, maintenance, etc
rec.boats
  Hobbyists interested in boating
rec.boats.cruising
  Cruising in boats
rec.boats.marketplace
  Boating products for sale and wanted
rec.boats.paddle
  Talk about any boats with oars, paddles, etc

rec.boats.racing
  Boat racing
rec.climbing
  Climbing techniques, competition announcements, etc
rec.equestrian
  Discussion of things equestrian
rec.martial-arts
  Discussion of the various martial art forms
rec.skiing.backcountry
  Backcountry skiing
rec.skiing.marketplace
  Items for sale/wanted
rec.skiing.nordic
  Cross-country skiing technique, equipment, etc
rec.skiing.resorts.europe
  Skiing in Europe
rec.skiing.resorts.misc
  Skiing in other than Europe and North America
rec.skiing.resorts.north-america
  Skiing in North America
rec.skiing.snowboard
  Snowboarding technique, equipment, etc
rec.skydiving
  Hobbyists interested in skydiving
rec.sport.baseball
  Discussion about baseball
rec.sport.baseball.analysis
  Analysis & discussion of baseball
rec.sport.baseball.college
  Baseball on the collegiate level
rec.sport.baseball.data
  Raw baseball data (Stats, birthdays, scheds)
rec.sport.baseball.fantasy
  Rotisserie (fantasy) baseball play
rec.sport.basketball.college
  Hoops on the collegiate level
rec.sport.basketball.misc
  Discussion about basketball
rec.sport.basketball.pro
  Talk of professional basketball
rec.sport.basketball.women
  Women's basketball at all levels
rec.sport.billiard
  Billiard sports, including pool, snooker, carom games
rec.sport.boxing
  Boxing in all its pugilistic facets and forms
rec.sport.cricket
  Discussion about the sport of cricket
rec.sport.cricket.info
  News, scores and info related to cricket
rec.sport.disc
  Discussion of flying disc based sports
rec.sport.fencing
  All aspects of swordplay
rec.sport.football.australian
  Discussion of Australian (Rules) Football
rec.sport.football.canadian
  All about Canadian rules football
rec.sport.football.college
  US-style college football
rec.sport.football.fantasy
  Rotisserie (fantasy) football play
rec.sport.football.misc
  Discussion about American-style football
rec.sport.football.pro
  US-style professional football
rec.sport.golf
  Discussion about all aspects of golfing
rec.sport.hockey
  Discussion about ice hockey
rec.sport.hockey.field
  Discussion of the sport of field hockey
rec.sport.misc
  Spectator sports
rec.sport.olympics
  All aspects of the Olympic Games

rec.sport.orienteering
  All matters related to the sport of orienteering
rec.sport.paintball
  Discussing all aspects of the survival game paintball
rec.sport.pro-wrestling
  Discussion about professional wrestling
rec.sport.pro-wrestling.fantasy
  Rotisserie league professional wrestling
rec.sport.rowing
  Crew for competition or fitness
rec.sport.rugby
  Discussion about the game of rugby
rec.sport.skating.ice.figure
  Figure/artistic skating
rec.sport.skating.ice.recreational
  Recreational ice skating
rec.sport.skating.inline
  Inline skating, aka Rollerblading
rec.sport.skating.misc
  Miscellaneous skating topics
rec.sport.skating.racing
  Racing and speed skating
rec.sport.skating.roller
  Conventional (quad) roller skating
rec.sport.soccer
  Discussion about soccer (Association Football)
rec.sport.swimming
  Training for and competing in swimming events
rec.sport.table-soccer
  Table-soccer of all types: foosball and subbuteo
rec.sport.table-tennis
  Things related to table tennis (aka Ping Pong)
rec.sport.tennis
  Things related to the sport of tennis
rec.sport.triathlon
  Discussing all aspects of multi-event sports
rec.sport.unicycling
  All sorts of fun on one wheel
rec.sport.volleyball
  Discussion about volleyball
rec.sport.water-polo
  Discussion of water polo
rec.windsurfing
  Riding the waves as a hobby

Travel & Tourism

alt.flame.airlines
  Problems and complaints with the airlines
alt.las-vegas.gambling
  Throwing money away in Nevada
alt.rv
  Rotten varmints or recreational vehicles, you decide
alt.travel.canada
  All about travelling to Canada
alt.travel.canada.ontario
  All about travelling to Ontario
alt.travel.canada.ontario.toronto
  All about travelling to Toronto
alt.travel.road-trip
  Ever go to Montreal for pizza —— from Albany?
alt.vacation.las-vegas
  Everything you always wanted to know about Vegas
bit.listserv.travel-l
  Tourism Discussions
misc.kids.vacation
  Discussion on all forms of family-oriented vacationing
misc.transport.air-industry
  Airlines, airports, commercial aircraft
misc.transport.rail.americas
  Railroads & railways in North & South America
misc.transport.rail.australia-nz
  Railways in Australia & New Zealand
misc.transport.rail.europe
  Railroads & railways in all of Europe

rec.travel.air
  Airline travel around the world
rec.travel.asia
  Travel in Asia
rec.travel.cruises
  Travel by cruise ship
rec.travel.europe
  Travel in Europe
rec.travel.marketplace
  Tickets and accomodations wanted and for sale
rec.travel.misc
  Everything and anything about travel
rec.travel.usa-canada
  Travel in the United States and Canada
relcom.commerce.tour
  Tourism, leisure and entertainment opportunities

Commercial Online Services

America Online 741
AT&T WorldNet Services 741
BIX 742
CompuServe 742
Delphi 747
eWorld 747
GEnie 748
IBM's infoMarket 751
InternetMCI 751
MSN (Microsoft Network) 752
NETCOM 752
Prodigy 752
The WELL 753
Women's Wire 756

Commercial Online Services and the Internet

For many years, researchers and scientists in the government and the military had access to what we now call the Internet through their institutional affiliations.

But the emergence of home computers, telecommunications products such as modems, and overall technological growth spawned a new industry.

Many individuals, small businesses, and organizations saw the enormous potential in using this new communications medium to enhance their work through expanded access to online resources and communication.

Commercial online services such as America OnLine, Compuserve, and Prodigy began catering to the needs of the new customers by providing electronic mail (email), online chat groups or forums, and a varied collection of online research resources.

These online services are now beginning to offer limited if not complete access to the Internet. We have tried to offer you a small overview of online services that are currently available. Each service is described, including mention of special features, sign up information, cost of services, points of presence, and contact information to help you choose the right service for you.

America Online

America Online is a provider of communication, information, and entertainment services to consumers and businesses. AOL services include an array of on-line education and research resources, a fax services, an e-mail service to other AOL users as well as Internet users, and numerous news services, including the American ABC Television network, The New York Times, and major news wire services like UPI and Reuters.

Additionally, AOL offers weather services, financial news and stock quotes. AOL recently added Global Network navigator (GNN) for navigating the tens of thousands of Internet services. AOL also offers WebCrawler a fast and easy-to-use full-text Internet search tool. The company also offers Home Shopping Network Interactive an online shopping mall for books works of art and music, jewelry and fine gifts. Other retail outlet available through AOL is 1-800 Flowers, Shopper's Express, AutoVantage, Lands End, and Starbucks Coffee catalogs.

Entertainment options include Nickelodeon OnLine (scheduled to begin in late summer '95) where kids can play games, watch video clips, and get programming information for the American cable television network. AOL also plans to bring its online services to users in Western and Eastern Europe, with Germany, France and the United Kingdom to come online in late '95.

Who it's for: Individuals and businesses.

Points of Presence: All 50 states. Eastern and Western Europe to be added starting late '95.

Cost: Basic rate is $9.95 per month, which includes five hours of on-line time, with few additional charges ($2.95 for each hour beyond five hours and some per-page charges for faxes and paper mail messages).

Contact: American Online at http://www.aol.com/;
Email to **postmaster@aol.com**;
or Voice 1 (800) 827-6364

AT&T WorldNet Services

AT&T WorldNet Services is in the planning stages, and trials for Internet access is planned by the end of 1995. The company is working with NetScape, and other content providers to have AT&T hosted or AT&T provided content services. The service will include email, an extensive directory to find places, resources and people on the

Internet (which is in addition to its 1-(800) directory. The provider has also licensed to use The McKinley database, a standalone directory of pre-defined subject categories. An Internet exploration station will help provide a series of theme areas for family entertainment and education.

Who it's for: Individuals and businesses (Macintosh and Windows users).

Points of Presence: Worldwide.

Cost: n/a

Contact: AT&T WorldNet Services, Email: webmaster@att.com, Call +1 (800) 831-5259, URL: http://www.att.com/

BIX

Among the specialized Internet Provider Services, BIX is one that is dedicated solely to the building industry worldwide. It provides links for commerce and infrastructure, businesses and governement, public and private sectors. BIX provides resources from the U.S. government, universities, and major businesses. The service provider also features educational, communication, and informational resources. It even provides a health and safety center, an environmental protection center, and a weather and travel service.

There are some 47 Industry Classifications within the building industry — from architecture to real estate. Related businesses, such as attorneys and manufactuers and distributors of construction products is included. It is operated by the Building Industry Exchange Foundation. Among its other services, it provides an interactive ligbrary and bookstore for graphical and interactive presentations related to the building industry.

It also provides a global business directory, and a virtual industrial park, which showcases the industry's businesses, products and people from around the world. There is even a career and employment center that includes a resume writing service and career counselors. Much of the online services are free.

Who's it for Anyone in the building industry or related industries.

Points of Presence International.

Costs - Free.

Contact Building Industry Exchange; Email to BIX@building.com; URL http://www.building.com/bix/;

Telephone + 1 (302) 996-2511; Fax + 1 (302) 996-5818.

CompuServe

One of the oldest online service providers, CompuServe offers a wide range of resources and services for business and home users. CompuServe services include news and financial information, research databases, and some 1,500 discussion forums. Moreover, it offers an extensive email service that allows users to choose among 13 mail systems, including MCI Mail and the Internet.

News services available through CompuServe include Associated Press Online and Newspaper Archives, which jointly provide access to more than 50 major U.S. newspapers. There are travel services, with support for Eaasy Sabre and Worldspan Travelshopper. CompuServe also features a wide selection of games, with a Multiplayer Games Forum, shareware games to download, and a wide range of game publishers forums. Additionally, CompuServe furnishes access to the World Wide Web via its NetLauncher web browser, which is available on a variety of operating systems (Windows, Macintosh, Unix, OS/2, etc.).

As for business services, users can download as many as 20 up-to-the-minute quotes for stocks, options, indexes, exchange rates, and mutual funds. Finally, research databases cover a variety of domains including health, high technology, and general-interest magazines. Full text and abstracts are available for hundreds of periodicals. CompuServe also provides Usenet and FTP access, with full Internet access planned before the end of 1995.

Who it's for: Business and individual users. Strongest for business users.

Points of Presence: Throughout the U.S.

Cost: Subscription is $9.95 per month for use of any of 100 basic services, including news, weather, Eaasy Sabre, and the equivalent of 60 three-page CompuServe email messages. Extended services (at up to $4.80 per hour) include CNN Online, European railway schedules, and AP Sports Wire.

Contact: CompuServe Inc., Email: 70006,101@compuserve.com, or call (800) 848-8199

Key
- • means Basic Service, free of additional charge
- + Extended Services, $4.80 per hour
- $ Premium Service (prices vary from service to service)

Arts & Music

Art Resources

ARCHIVE	+	Archive Photos Forum
COMANIM	+	Computer Animation Forum
COMART	+	Computer Art Forum
BLASTER	+	Creative Labs Forum
DAVINCI	+	Da Vinci Forum
FINEARTS	+	Fine Arts Forum
GRAPHBVEN	+	Graphics B Vendor Forum
CORNER	+	Graphics Corner Forum
GRAPHDEV	+	Graphics Developers Forum
GRAPHFF	+	Graphics File Finder
GRAPHICS	+	Graphics Forums
GALLERY	+	Graphics Gallery Forum
GRAPHPLUS	+	Graphics Plus Forum
GRFSHOW	+	Graphics Showcase Forum
GRAPHSUPPORT	+	Graphics Support Forum
GRAPHVEN	+	Graphics Vendor Forum
GRVENC	+	Graphics Vendors C Forum
GRFINDEX	+	Graphics Visual Index For
GRFWELCOME	+	Graphics Welcome Center F
LENS	•	Lens Express

Film & Video

FCINEMA	+	526 France Cinema Forum
ARCFILM	+	67 Archive Films Forum

Music Genres

AMGCLASSICAL	•	All Music Guide Classical
ALLMUSIC	•	All-Music Guide
AMGPOP	+	All-Music Guide Forum
BARRY	+	Arista Records Download A
ARTIST	+	Artist Forum
DEUFUNK	+	Deutsches Funk Forum
SOUL	+	Electric Soul Forum
JAZZ	+	Jazz Beat Forum

Music Organizations

CD	•	BMG Compact Disc Club
FREECD	•	Columbia House Music Club
JR	•	Justice Records

Music Resources

BBCM	•	BBC Music Magazine

Musicians

CLINT	+	Download Clint Black Single
GARTH	+	Garth Brooks Spotlight

Business & Economics

Accounting

ACCOUNTING	+	Accounting Vendor Forum
BILLING	•	Billing Information

Advertising & Marketing

IQINT	+	418 Download Pricing Data

Banking

COGERMAN	$	Deutsche Firmendatenbank

Career & Employment

CAPARTNERS	+	CA Business Partners Forum
CAREERS	+	Career Management Forum

Compuserve

CBAFORUM • CBA Administrators Forum
ESPAN • E-Span Online Job Listing

Companies
BASCOMPANY • Basic Company Snapshot

Consumer Issues
CONFORUM + Consumer Forum
CONSUMER • Consumer Reports
CRAUTO • Consumer Reports Auto.
DRUGS • Consumer Reports Drug Ref.

Finance
MONEY + Finance
FINFORUM + Financial Forums
INTERFACES + Financial Interfaces
FINVEN + Financial Software Forum
FINHELP • Financial Surcharge List
MQINT $ Issue Pricing Interface

Industries
IWFOR + IndustryWeek Forum
INDWEEK • IndustryWeek Interactive
IW • IndustryWeek Management Centre

International Business
GLOREP $ 559 Global Report
GRP + ADP's Global Report
TRADE + International Trade Forum

Investment
GQUOTES • 122 Basic Global Quotes
BAS-74 • 123 Basic Quotes
COMMODITIES + 262 Commodities
CPRICE $ 263 Commodity Pricing
DISCLOSURE • 412 Disclosure SEC($E)
BONDS $ Bonds Listing
QQUOTE $ Current Day Quotes
SNAPSHOT + Current Market Snapshot
DIVIDENDS $ Dividends and Splits
DR • Dreyfus Corporation
DBDEUTSCH $ Dun&Bradstreet Deutschl.
DBFRANCE $ Dun&Bradstreet France
DBINTL $ Dun&Bradstreet Internat.
DUNBUK $ Dun&Bradstreet UK
DBCAN $ Dun's Canadian Mkt. Ident
DYP $ Dun's Elect Business Dir
DMI $ Dun's Market Identifiers
ETRADE + E*TRADE Securities
ETGAME + E*TRADE Stock Market Game
MQUOTE + Financial File/MQUOTE II
EARNINGS + Financial Forecasts
FPERINV + Fortune Personal Investing
FUNDWATCH • FundWatch by Money Mag.
IBES $ IBES Earnings Est Rpto(E)
DBINT $ Int'l Dun's Mkt Identifier
INVTEXT $ InvesText
INV + Investext
IB • Investor's Business Daily
JPMORGAN + JP Morgan

Legal Aspects
UKTRADEMARK $ British Trade Marks
CORP + Company Corporation, The
MMM-73 + CompuServe Tax Connection
CORPACTION + Corporate Actions Notification
FINHLP + Financial Documentation
TAXFORMS + IRS Tax Forms/Documents

Management
ADMINI • Administrator's Workstation

Organizations
FEDERATION + Fed. Of Int'l Distributors
FFS-1 • Florida Fruit Shippers

GOODYEAR • Goodyear Online

Personal Finance
FINTOL + Calculate Net Worth
CF • CheckFree

Publishing
COMBUS $ Commerce Business Daily
ENT • Entrepreneur Magazine
FORTUNE • FORTUNE

Real Estate
HOMEFORUM + Calif. Assoc. Realtors PUBLIC
CTB • Centerbank Mortgage Company
CMS • CMS Home Mortgage Corp
EAM • Express America Mortgage
HF • HOMEFINDER BY AMS

Reference
CSYMBOL + 264 Commodity Symbol Lookup
BIZFILE $ Biz*File
BUSDB $ Business Database Plus
BUSDEM $ Business Demographics
INC • Business Incorp. Guide
CENDATA + CENDATA
BIZNEWS + CNN Business Forum
ANALYZER $ Company Analyzer
MMM-70 + Company Information
AFFILIATIONS $ Corporate Affiliations
DECNIDEV + Digital Business Partner
EUROLIB $ European Co. Research Centre
COEURO $ European Company Library
EXECUTIVE • Executive Service Option
INFOCTR • Financial Services Info. Ctr.
FORT500 + Fortune 500 Lists
FFORUM + FORTUNE Forum
FRCOMPANIES $ French Company Info
GERLIB $ German Company Research Center
HOOVER • Hoover Company Database
ICCDIR $ ICC Directory of UK Comp.
INNOVATION + Ideas & Inventions Forum
BIZALMANAC • Info-Please Business Almanac
INVFORUM + Investors Forum
IQBUSINESS + IQUEST Business InfoCenter
KEYBRIT $ Key British Enterprises

Services
COSCREEN $ Company Screening(EW)
CARD • CompuServe Visa Card
CIC-12 • Continental Insurance Center
CRE • Credentials Services
CONVENTION + Electronic Convention Ctr
TAXRETURN | Electronic Filing
ENTMAGAZINE + Entrep. Small Business Square
ENS $ Executive News Service
FILTRN + Financial File Transfer
HRB • H&R Block
INFOCHECK $ Infocheck

Communications

Career & Employment
BPFORUM + Broadcast Pro Forum
MBAWARE + MBAware Forum

Communications
DATAQUEST + Dataquest Online
NEWS3X400 + Duke Communications Forum

HAMNET + Hamnet Forum

Mass Communications
MEDIADAILY + Cowles/SIMBA Media Daily
JFORUM + Journalism Forum

Networking
INTELFORUM + Comm. & Networking Forum

Organizations
ENS $ Associated Press
GTE • GTE Phone Mart

Telecommunications
MAIL • CompuServe Mail
MAILHELP • CompuServe Mail Center
PTALK + CompuServe Mail for PowerTalk
MAILHUB + CompuServe Mail Hub

Computing & Mathematics

Applications
AMIGAFF + Amiga File Finder
ATARIFF + Atari File Finder
NEWBASIC • Basic Conversion Area
MSNETWORKS + Client Server Computing Forum
CBMAPP + Commodore Applications Forum

Career & Employment
CONSULT + Computer Consult. Forum
DCIEXPO + Digital Consulting - DCI

Companies
ADOBE + Adobe Systems, Inc.
AMIGAVENDOR + Amiga Vendor Forum
APPLENEWS $ Apple News Clips
THREECOM + Ask3Com
ASKFORUM + Ask3Com Forum
BB • Broderbund Software
CTRON + Cabletron System, Inc.
CTRONFORUM + Cabletron Systems Forum
VIVAMODEM + Computer Peripheral, Inc.
DA • Dalco Computer Electronics
DACCESS + Data Access Corp. Forum
DEC + Digital Equipment Corp.
DVORAK + Dvorak Development Forum
HAYES + Hayes
HAYFORUM + Hayes Online
INTEL + Intel Corporation
INTUIT + Intuit Forum
LOGITECH + Logitech Forum
LOTUSNEWS + Lotus Press Release Forum

Computer Science
DBADVISOR + Data Based Advisor Forum

Hardware
ADOBESYS + Adobe Systems Forum
APLFBK • Apple Feedback
APPUSER + Apple II Users Forum
APIIVEN + Apple II Vendor Forum
APLSUP + Apple Support Forum
ATARINET + Atari Users Network
ATARIVEN + Atari Vendor Forum
MACCLARIS + Claris Macintosh Forum
COCO + Color Computer Forum
CBMNEWS + Commodore Newsletter
CBMSERVICE + Commodore Service Forum
CBMNET + Commodore Users Network
CPQFORUM + Compaq Connection
COMPBG $ Computer Buyers' Guide
CLUB + Computer Club Forum

Compuserve

DECPC + DEC PC Forum
DECUNET + DEC Users Network
DECPCI + DECPCI Forum
DELL + Dell Forum
PCDIREKT + Deutsches PC Direkt Forum
PCPRO + Deutsches PCpro-Forum
DD • Digital's PC Store
EPSON + Epson Forum
HARDWARE + Hardware Forums
HPHAND + HP Handheld Forum
HPOMNIBOOK + HP OmniBook Forum
HPPER + HP Peripherals Forum
HPSPEC + HP Specials
IBMCOS + IBM COS Network Solution Forum
IBMDATA + IBM Data Products Forum
IBMDB2 + IBM DB2 Database Forum
IBMDESK + IBM Desktop Forum
IBMIMAGE + IBM ImagePlus Forum
LMUFORUM + IBM LMU2 Forum
IBMOBJ + IBM Object Technology Forum
BUYIBM • IBM PC Direct
IBMSVR + IBM PC Server Forum
POWERPC + IBM PowerPC Forum
IBMPS2 + IBM PS2 Forum
OS2UGER + IBM PSM Deutschland Forum
PSPAPROD + IBM PSP A Products Forum
IBMSPEC + IBM Special Needs Forum
THINKPAD + IBM ThinkPad Forum
VALUEPOINT + IBM ValuePoint Forum
VOICETYPE + IBM VoiceType Forum
VISUAL + IBM WRAD Support Forum
INTELARCH + Intel Architecture Labs Forum
INTELCORP + Intel Components/Embedded
JDR • JDR Microdevices

Networking
LANBVEN + LAN B Vendor Forum
LANVEN + Lan Vendor Forum

Operating Systems
DCIMSOFT • 364 DOSCIM Information Area
CITRIX + Citrix Systems Forum
CPMFORUM + CP/M Users Group Forum
CTOS + CTOS/Pathway Forum
DMCIMSU • Deutsches MacCIM Forum
GERWIN + Deutsches Windows Mag Forum
DCIMSUPPORT • DOSCIM Support Forum
GATEWAY + Gateway 2000 Forum
HPSYS + HP Systems Forum
HYBRID • Hybrid Technical Systems
IBMPS1 + IBM Aptiva & PS/1 Forum
IBMENG + IBM CAD/CAM Forum
OS2BVEN + IBM OS/2 B Vendors Forum
OS2DF1 + IBM OS/2 Developer 1 Forum
OS2DF2 + IBM OS/2 Developer 2 Forum
OS2HELP + IBM OS/2 Help Database
OS2SERV + IBM OS/2 Service Pak
OS2SUPPORT + IBM OS/2 Support Forum
OS2USER + IBM OS/2 Users Forum
OS2AVEN + IBM OS/2 Vendor Forum

Programming
APPROG + Apple II Prog. Forum
BANFORUM + Banyan Forum
BORLAND + BORLAND
BORAPP + Borland Application Forum
BCPPDOS + Borland C++/DOS Forum
BCPPWIN + Borland C++ for Win/OS2 Forum
BORCONN + Borland Connections Forum
BORDB + Borland DB Products Forum
DBASEWIN + Borland dBASE For Windows
DBASEDOS + Borland dBASE Forum
BDEVTOOLS + Borland Dev. Tools Forum
BORGER + Borland Germany
BORGMBH + Borland GmbH Forum
PDOXDOS + Borland Paradox/Dos Forum
PDOXWIN + Borland Paradox/Windows Forum
IBMLANG + IBM Languages Forum

Reference
PHONES • Access Numbers
PHONE • Access Phone Numbers
ACIUS + ACI US Forum
AIEXPERT + AI EXPERT Forum
AMIGATECH + Amiga Tech Forum
AMIGAUSER + Amiga User's Forum
APLTIL + Apple Tech Info Library
APLNEW + Apple What's New Library
ASCIIDEV + ASCII Developers Forum
ASPCD + ASP CD-ROM Forum
ASTFORUM + AST Forum
BASIS + BASIS International Forum
CADENCE + Cadence Forum
CANOPUS + Canopus Forum
CLATECH + Claris TechInfo Database
CAI + Computer Associates Forums
COMPDB $ Computer Database Plus
CE • Computer Express
COMPLIB + Computer Library
LIFE + Computer Life
CLIFEUK + Computer Life UK Forum
CRN + Computer Reseller News Forum
UKSHOPPER + Computer Shopper (UK) Forum
DPTRAIN + Computer Training Forum
PCTV + Computers on Television Forum
COMPUTERS • Computing Support
TRACE $ COMPUTRACE
FORTH + Creative Solutions/Forth Forum
DPNEWS $ Data-Process. Newsletter
DBMSFORUM + DBMS Magazine Forum
GERNET + Deutsches Computer Forum
MSDR + Developer Relations Forum
DBDIGITALK + Digitalk Database
DDJFORUM + Dr. Dobb's Journal Forum
NEUHAUS + Dr. Neuhaus Forum
GENCOM + General Computing Forum
NETVIEW + IBM Netview Family Forum
INFOMANAGE + Information Management Forum
IAWEEK + Inter@ctive Week Forum
LANMAG + Lan Magazine Forum

Software
CADDVEN + 180 CADD/CAM/CAE Vendor Forum
CASEFORUM + 181 CASE DCI Forum
CAPRIVIEW + 224 Capricorn Download Area
ACTION + Action Games Forum
ADOBEA + Adobe Applications Forum
AMIGAARTS + Amiga Arts Forum
ARTISOFT + Artisoft Forum
ASPFORUM + ASP/Shareware Forum
ACAD + Autodesk AutoCAD Forum
ASOFT + Autodesk Multimedia Forum
ARETAIL + Autodesk Retail Products Forum
ASHOWCASE + Autodesk Showcase Forum
CADDBVEN + CADD/CAM/CAE B Vendor Forum
CDVEN + CD-ROM A Vendor Forum
CDVENB + CD-ROM B Vendor Forum
CDROM + CDROM Forum
CHEYENNE + Cheyenne Software Forum
CLARFR + Claris France Forum
CLARIS + Claris Information Center
WINCLARIS + Claris Windows Forum
CBMART + Commodore Arts/Games Forum
CS4GEOS • CompuServe for GEOS Software
NOTES + CS Lotus Notes Information Ser
WCSNAVSUP + CSNav-Win Support Forum
DASHBOARD + Dashboard 3.0 for Windows
DELRINA379 + Delrina Technology Forum
DIAGSOFT + DiagSoft Forum
DIGITALK + Digitalk Forum
FONTBANK + FontBank Online
FOXFORUM + Fox Software Forum
FTCFILES • FTC FREE Downloads
GAMDEV + Game Developers Forum
GCPSUPPORT + Golden CommPass Support
IBMPSP + IBM Personal Software Products
SOFSOL + IBM Software Solutions Forum
IBMSTORAGE + IBM Storage Systems Forum
IMAGAVEN + Imaging Vendor A Forum
CHIPSOFT + Intuit Support Forum
IRIFORUM + IRI Software Forum
ANTIVIRUS + KAOS AntiVirus
KODAK + Kodak CD Forum
LOTUSA + LDC Spreadsheets Forum
LOTUSWP + LDC Word Processing Forum
LOTUSB + LDC Words & Pixels Forum
LOTUS123W + Lotus 123 For Windows Upgrade
LOTUSCOMM + Lotus Communications Forum
LOTGER + Lotus GmbH Forum
LOTUSTECH + Lotus Technical Library
MACUP + MACup Verlag Forum

Standards
BENCHMARK + Benchmark & Standards Forum

Telecomputing
CISSOFT • CompuServe Software

Education

Colleges & Universities
STUFOB + College & Adult Student Forum

International Education
DATAEASE + DataEase International Forum

Resources
ASPELL • A WinCIM Spell-Check
DISSERTATION $ Dissertation Abstracts
EDFORUM + Education Forum
EDRESEARCH + Educational Res. Forum
ERIC $ ERIC - Education Research
IQEDUCATION + IQUEST Education InfoCenter

Engineering & Technology

Engineering
- AESNET + Audio Engineering Society
- COMPENDEX $ Ei Compendex Plus
- LEAP + Engineering Automation Forum
- IQENGINEER + IQUEST Engineering InfoCenter

Technology
- EICON + Eicon Technology Forum
- IQTECHNOLOGY + IQUEST Technology InfoCenter

Government & Politics

Agencies
- STATE • Department of State

Countries
- BOSNIA $ 1Bosnia Clipping Folder
- BELFORUM + Belgium Forum

International
- CRISIS + 558 Global Crises Forum

Policies
- BUDGET • Congressional Tracking

Reference
- APFRANCE • AP France en Ligne
- FRELECT $ Elections Francaises
- INFOUSA + Government Giveaways Forum
- GPO + Government Publications
- LESKO + Information USA
- IUM • Information USA Mall
- ISSUESFORUM + Issues Forum

Health & Medicine

Alternative Medicine
- HOLISTIC + Holistic Health Forum

Disabilities
- DISABILITIES + Disabilities Forum
- HANDICAPPED • Handicapped User's Data

Diseases
- CANCER + Cancer Forum

Health Conditions
- ADD + Attn. Deficit Disorder Forum
- DIABETES + Diabetes Forum

Organizations
- AARP + AARP Forum
- NURSE + American Nurses Association

Personal Care
- GOODHEALTH + Health & Fitness Forum
- HVE • Health & Vitamin Express
- FITNESS + Health/Fitness
- HNT • HealthNet

Reference
- AIDSNEWS + Aids News Clips
- CCMLAIDS $ CCML AIDS Articles
- HLTDB $ Health Database Plus
- IBMHEALTH + IBM Clinton Health Plan
- IQMEDICAL + IQUEST Medical InfoCenter

Resources
- CL • Contact Lens Supply

Sexuality
- HSX200 + HSX Adult Forum
- HSX100 + HSX Open Forum
- HUMAN + Human Sexuality Databank

Humanities & Social Sciences

Area & Cultural Studies
- AFRO + African American Culture
- LEGENDS + British Legends

Classics
- TMC-45 + Classic Quotes

Geography
- CALFORUM + California Forum
- CDNFORUM + Canada Forum
- CANADA • Canada Services Menu
- ATL • Canada's Atlantic Coast
- CHICAGO + Chicago Spotlight
- CNL • Connecticut National Life
- CUBA $ Cuba News Clips
- DETROIT + Detroit Free Press Forum
- DFM + Detroit Free Press Store
- INFOGER + Deutschland Info
- GERLINE + Deutschland Online Forum
- EURFORUM + European Forum
- FLORIDA + Florida Forum
- FLATODAY + Florida Today Forum
- HAITI $ Haiti News Clips
- HKFORUM + Hong Kong Forum
- INFOFR + Informatique France Forum
- ISLAND + Island of Kesmai
- ISRAEL + Israel Forum
- ITALFOR + Italian Forum
- JAPAN + Japan Forum
- MAGELLAN + MAGELLAN Geographix Maps

History
- LIVING + Living History Forum

Languages
- FLEFO + Foreign Language Forum

Library & Information Studies
- DICTIONARY • American Heritage Dictionary
- ENCYCLOPEDIA • Grolier Encyclopedia
- IQUEST $ IQuest
- KI $ Knowledge Index

Literature
- TWAUTHORS + Authors Forum

Internet

Internet Access
- TSHIRT + 299 CompuServe T-Shirt Contest
- CCD • 305 CompuServeCD
- CCDSUP • 306 CompuServeCD Forum
- PASSWORD • Change Your Password Program
- EUROPE + CompuServe Europe
- TOP + CompuServe Main Menu
- MACNAV • CompuServe Navigator, Mac
- CSNAV • CompuServe Navigator, Windows
- CHOICES • CompuServe Pricing Plans
- RATES • CompuServe Rates
- INDEX • CompuServe Subject Index
- TOUR • CompuServe Tour
- CSHELP • Customer Servive Help Database
- DTC • Directory of Catalogs
- FEEDBACK • Feedback to Customer Service
- FORUMS • Forums
- ISDN + ISDN Forum

Internet Resources
- COMPUADD + CompuAdd Forum
- CSAPPS + CompuServe Applications Forum
- HELPFORUM + CompuServe Help Forum
- FREE3D + CompuServe Magazine 3-D Image
- MAPI + CompuServe MS Mail Driver
- CSNEWS + CompuServe News Forum
- RULES + CompuServe Operating Rules

Internet Services
- PACFORUM + CompuServe Pacific Forum
- TELNET + CompuServe Telnet Access
- CYBERFORUM + Cyber Forum
- CYBERWAREHOUSE • CyberWarehouse
- INETCLUB • Internet Club
- INETFORUM + Internet New Users Forum
- INETPUBLISH + Internet Publishing Forum
- INETRESOURCE + Internet Resources Forum
- INTERNET • Internet Services
- IWORLD + Internet World Forum

Internet Tools
- VOICEMAIL • A WinCIM Add-on: VOICE EMAIL
- QUESTIONS • Commonly Asked Questions
- FTP + File Transfer Protocol

Networking
- BAYNETWORKS + Bay Networks Forum

Organizations
- CRUISE • Compu-Cruise by Rosenbluth
- OLI • CompuServe Magazine
- EFFSIG + Electronic Frontier Foundation

Programming
- DELPHI + Borland Delphi Forum

Law & Criminal Justice

Legal Resources
- LEGALRC $ Legal Research Center

Reference
- CRFORUM + Court Reporters Forum
- LAWSIG + Legal Forum

Popular Culture & Entertainment

Automobiles
- AI • 100 Automobile Info Center
- AUTOLIVE • 101 Automobile Live
- AUTOFORUM + 102 Automobile Magazine Forum
- AUTOSTORE • 103 Automobile Magazine Store

Commercial Online Services

AUTO +	104	Automotive Information
NEWCAR $	93	AutoNet New Car Showroom
ATV •	94	AutoVantage OnLine
CARS +	99	Automobile Forum

Books

BOMC •	139	Book Of The Month Club
PREVIEW +	140	Book Preview Forum
BOOKREVIEW $	141	Book Review Digest
BOT-1 +	142	Books On Tape
BOOKS $	143	Books in Print
BBIP +	160	British Books in Print
EBOOKS +	453	Electronic Books
LOS +	746	Library Of Science Book Club
AB •	88	Audio Book Club

Celebrities & Personalities

HOLLYWOOD •	606	Hollywood Hotline
HOLFILE +	607	Hollywood Online DL Area

Family & Community

MYFAMILY +	490	Family Services Forum
DAD •	492	Father's Day Online
STUFOA +	725	Kids & Teens Student Forum

Genealogy

ROOTS +	548	Genealogy Forum
GENSUP +	549	Genealogy Support Forum

General Reference

GRAMS +	352	CupidGrams
ENCOUNTERS +	458	Encounters Forum
ECENTER +	461	Entertainment Center
EDRIVE +	462	Entertainment Drive
EFORUM +	463	Entertainment Drive Forum
EWK •	465	Entertainment Works
TMC-101 +	686	Intelligence Test
ATTACHMATE +	84	Attachmate Corporation
XTALK +	85	Attachmate Crosstalk Forum
ATTM +	86	Attachmate Forum

Humor

FUNFOR +	531	Funnies Forum

Magazines & Newspapers

CNNFORUM +	202	CNN Forum
CNNONLINE +	203	CNN Online
COMICPUB +	257	Comics Publishers Forum
COMIC +	258	Comics/Animation Forum
DTPONLINE +	367	DTPONLINE
SPIEGEL +	381	Der Spiegel Forum
DTPFORUM +	382	Desktop Publishing Forum
DTP +	386	Desktop/Electronic Publ.
EUROPROMO +	475	European Newspaper Promotion
GENX +	552	Generation X Comics Download
GLAMOUR +	557	Glamour Graphics Forum
GUARDIAN +	579	Guardian newspaper
LEMONDE +	741	Le Monde
APONLINE +	76	Associated Press Online
AAPONLINE +	91	Australian Associated Press

Miscellaneous

ASTROLOGY +	77	Astrological Charting

Movies

CCV •	349	Critic's Choice Video
DTVFORUM +	385	Desktop Video Forum
VIEWER +	438	EDRIVE Movie Viewer
EMOVIES +	439	EDRIVE'S Movie Forum
ALLMOVIE +	44	All-Movie Guide
EDRIVE +	446	Edrive Enhanced Menu
ANVENA +	57	Animation Vendor A Forum
FLICKS +	608	Hollywood Online Forum
SCENE •	721	Jurassic Park
LionKing +	748	Lion King Download Area

Multimedia

EMEDIA +	464	Entertainment Multimedia Area
FAST +	481	FAST Multimedia

Shopping

FGS (800-Flowers) •		1-800-Flowers and Gifthouse
BASSETT +	125	Bassett Furniture
BH +	158	Breton Harbor Gift Services
BR •	165	Brooks Brothers
CADILLAC +	212	Cadillac
CLASSIFIEDS +	245	Classifieds
CVA •	252	Colonel Audio Video
CVA •	253	Colonel Video & Audio
CBK +	278	CompuBooks
DB +	373	Data Based Advisor Mall Store
DTPAVEN +	383	Desktop Publishing Vendor A
DTPBVEN +	384	Desktop Publishing Vendor B
BEDS •	402	Dial-A-Mattress
ALASKA •	42	Alaska Peddler
ESTORE +	437	EDRIVE Limited
FTD •	487	FTD Online
AC •	51	Americana Clothing
FS •	514	Flower Stop
FC •	518	Ford Credit
FORD +	519	Ford Motor Company
FOO •	527	Free Offer Outlet
HAL •	591	Hallmark Connections
MMSS +	6	A2Z Multimedia SuperShop
JCPENNEY •	709	JCPenney
WILEY +	718	John Wiley Book Store
LEGGS +	730	L'eggs Hanes Bali Playtex
LA •	739	Lands End
LINCOLN +	747	Lincoln/Mercury Showroom

Telecommunications

BEL •	129	BellSouth Cellular

Weather & Traffic

AAROADWATCH •	7	AA Roadwatch

Religion & Philosophy

Religions

CATHOLIC +		Catholic Online Forum

Resources

CCF •		Christian Children's Fund

Science

Astronomy

ASTROFORUM +		Astronomy Forum

COMET +		Comet/Jupiter Collision Files
URANUS +		Hubble Uranus Images

Biosciences

BIORHYTHM •		Biorhythms

Earth Sciences

EARTH +		Earth Forum

Environmental Sciences

AIRDATA +	39	AirData Forum

Paleontology

DINO +		Dinosaur Forum

Sports & Recreation

Aquatic Sports

AMERICASCUP +		America's Cup Forum
FISHNET +		Aquaria / Fish Forum

Aviation

ATCONTROL +		Air Traffic Controller
AVSIG +		Aviation Forum (AVSIG)
AVIATION +		Aviation Menu
ASI +		Aviation Safety Institute
AVSUP +		Aviation Support Forum
AWG-1 +		Aviation Week Group
AWO-4 +		Aviation Week Group Forum
EMI $		EMI Aviation Services
FSFORUM +		Flight Simulation Forum

Countries

MAGIC +		General Magic Forum

Crafts & Hobbies

CEFORUMS +	330	Consumer Electronics Forums
CANON +		Canon Support
CBCLUB +		CB Club
CBFORUM +		CB Forum
HANDLE +		CB Handle
CBPROFILES +		CB Profiles
CB +		CB Simulator
CUPCAKE +		CB Society
CB +		Citizens Band Simulator
COLLECT +		Collectibles Forum
DOLLS +		Dolls Forum
HANDYMAN +		Family Handyman Forum
FIBERCRAFTS +		Fibercrafts Forum
FIREARMS +		Firearms Forum
FUJI +		Fuji Photo Film USA Forum
GARDENING +		Gardening Forum
GW •		Garrett Wade Woodworking
HANDCRAFTS +		Handcrafts Forum
UKINTERFLORA +		Interflora

Food & Dining

AIF •		Adventures In Food
WINEFORUM +		Bacchus Wine Forum
CHEFS •		Chef's Catalog
COF •		Coffee Anyone???
COOKS +		Cook's Online Forum
ETHELM •		Ethel M Chocolates
GIM •		Gimmee Jimmy's Cookies
GMR •		Green Mountain Coffee Roasters
HAM •		HoneyBaked Ham
LBW •		Liquor By Wire

Games

BLACKDRAGON •	136	BlackDragon
KAQUIZ •	726	Knowledge Adventure Quiz
ATARIGAMING +		Atari GAMING Forum
ATARIPRO +		Atari ST Prod. Forum
BRIDGE +		Bridge Forum

CQUEST •	CastleQuest
CHESSFORUM +	Chess Forum
GAMEWORLD +	Computer Gaming World
EGAMER •	Electronic Gamer(tm)
EPIC +	Epic MegaGames Forum
ADVENT •	Fantasy/Role-Playing Adv.
GAMECON +	Game Forums and News
GAMBETA +	Game Publisher Beta Forum
GAMAPUB +	Game Publishers A Forum
GAMBPUB +	Game Publishers B Forum
GAMCPUB +	Game Publishers C Forum
GAMDPUB +	Game Publishers D Forum
GAMPUB •	Game Publishers Forums
GAMERS •	Gamers Forum
HANGMAN •	Hangman
HOTGAMES +	Hot Games Download Area

Organizations
CLADVENT • Classic Adventure

Recreation
ENADVENT • Enhanced Adventure

Sports
SPORTS $ AP Sports
GOLF • Austad's
JORDANS $ JordanWatch
GOLF • Lanier Golf Database

Travel & Tourism
UKTRAVEL •	AA Travel Services
ABC +	ABC Worldwide Hotel Guide
AIT +	Adventures in Travel
AIRCANADA •	Air Canada Forum
AF •	Air France
ASU •	Airline Services Unlimited
AL •	Alamo Rent-A-Car
AMZ •	Amazing Vacations
INNS •	Bed & Breakfast Database
SABRE •	EAASY SABRE
SABRECIM •	EAASY SABRE (CIM)
RAILWAY +	European Rail
GTC-1 •	Getting Through Customs
HYA •	Hyatt Hotels & Resorts
INNFORUM +	Inn and Lodging Forum

Delphi

The Delphi Internet Services Corporation develops and markets interactive entertainment, information, and communications services for personal computer users worldwide, and provides full access to the Internet.

Delphi furnishes users with email service, special forums and a wide selection of news, references, computer information, and downloadable files. News services include UPI, The Business Wire, PR Newswire, and Reuters. Dialog, one of the largest information databases in the world, is accessible through Delphi. Stock market and other financial market information is also available. Reference resources include Grolier's Encyclopedia and the Dictionary of Cultural Literacy, to name a few. A variety of games are available through Delphi—such as Wumpu—and modem to modem interactive play is available for games like chess and Go. Delphi does not offer a "basic services" area (as do many other providers) wherein you browse without accumulating hourly charges.

Who it's for: Individuals, businesses, children.

Points of Presence: U.S. and Canada.

Cost: Basic plan is four hours free at $10 a month, with additional connect-time billed at $4 an hour. Another plan offers 20 hours of use per month for $20, with additional connect-time billed at $1.80 per hour.

Contact: Call (800) 695-4005, Dial up modem (800) 365-4636, **telnet://delphi.com**

Arts & Music

ALTERNATIVE MUSIC DEBATE (OPEN)	FORUM 376
MOSH MADNESS (OPEN)	FORUM 392

Business & Economics

HOME IMPROVEMENTS & REPAIRS (OPEN)	FORUM 274
THE WORK PLACE (OPEN)	FORUM 427

Communications

THE MEDIA SF FORUM (OPEN)	FORUM 86

Education

CALC ONLINE CAMPUS (OPEN)	FORUM 378

Engineering & Technology

MODERN TECH (OPEN)	FORUM 110

Government & Politics

DIXIE STATES FORUM (OPEN)	FORUM 381
POLITINET (OPEN)	FORUM 031
RURAL ROUTE (OPEN)	FORUM 207
THE CALL OF THE HIGHLANDS (OPEN)	FORUM 170

Humanities & Social Sciences

ASIAN AMERICAN DISCUSSION FORUM (OPEN)	FORUM 377
HISTORY	FORUM 243
LATINO SOCIAL WORK (APPLICATION ONLY)	FORUM 164
THE ROMANCE WRITERS WORKSHOP (OPEN)	FORUM 329

Internet

THE EFF FORUM (OPEN)	FORUM 118

Law & Criminal Justice

LAMBDA LINKS (OPEN)	FORUM 383

Popular Culture & Entertainment

DRAGON'S LAIR (OPEN)	FORUM 415
FLAME-FREE VIEWS FORUM (OPEN)	FORUM 423
FUTURE ADOPTIVE FAMILIES (OPEN)	FORUM 304
OLDIES FORUM (OPEN)	FORUM 315
PHANTASMIC VOYAGE (APPLICATION ONLY)	FORUM 451
RAINBOWS AND UNICORNS (OPEN)	FORUM 369
RELATIONSHIPS ONLINE (OPEN)	FORUM 433
TEEN/YOUTH FORUM (OPEN)	FORUM 038
THE BOOK AND CANDLE PUB (OPEN)	FORUM 080
THE COMICS FORUM (OPEN)	FORUM 052
THE COSMIC SOFA (PSYCHIC FORUM) (OPEN)	FORUM 134
THE DRAGONET (OPEN)	FORUM 025
THE MOMMY TRACK (OPEN)	FORUM 148
THE ROMANCE WRITERS WORKSHOP (OPEN)	FORUM 329
WALDEN THREE (OPEN)	FORUM 417

Religion & Philosophy

PAGAN CENTRAL (OPEN)	FORUM 259

Sports & Recreation

NATIONAL ONLINE QUILTERS (OPEN)	FORUM 220
PET LOVERS' FORUM (OPEN)	FORUM 047
SCOUT SUPPORT FORUM (OPEN)	FORUM 231

eWorld

eWorld is Apple Computer Inc.'s online provider service. eWorld's strong point is that it represents the only place to get direct, online computing support from Apple. It provides users with an on-ramp to the Internet and uses a Town Square metaphor (a group of buildings) to help guide users around the information services it provides.

eWorld provides information and group forums that focus on entertainment, education, design and small business needs. When traveling, users can access their eWorld account from almost anywhere in the world by checking into the Info Booth for access numbers. eWorld also provides email service for its members.

Who it's for: Individuals, home businesses, small businesses, education, publishing and design groups, and the entertainment field.

Points of Presence: Available in English to the U.S., Canada, United Kingdom, Ireland, Australia, and New Zealand (additional countries are currently being added). A Windows version is expected soon.

Cost: Basic service rates are $8.95 per month for four free hours (rates differ from country to country). There is no charge for Internet access and direct, online Apple support.

Contact: Email to subscribe@eworld.com

Arts & Music

MuchMusic Online
A "chat" room where musicians and music lovers meet to talk about music.
Intimate & Interactive

Playbill Online
A "chat" room where users talk about theater.
Playbill Chat

Urban Music Connections
A "chat" room where users talk about urban music.
Urban Music Live

Computing & Mathematics

Apple Customer Center
Where special guest of Apple Computer talk to users.
Apple Cafe

Straight to the Source
Places where users can chat with mroe than 100 computer companies about products and issues.
Company Conferences

Ziffnet/Mac
Where users can talk about computer products.
ZMac Cafe

Education

Blackberry Creek
A place where youngsters talk and play "learning" games.
The Hungry Ear

eWorld Educator Connection
A "chat" room where users can talk with educators, business people and parents about educational topics.
The Faculty Lounge

Health & Medicine

Disability Connections
A "chat" room for scheduled and impromptu conversations.
The Water Cooler

Natural Connection
A "chat" room where users talk about health, healing and holistic approaches to wellness.
The Main Conference Room

Present Moment
A "chat" room where users talk about homeopathy, herbs, and philosophy of alternative health.
The Tea Room

Transformations
Around the clock conversations
Twelve Steps Online

Transformations
"Chat" rooms where user meet for scheduled support group meetings.
Support Group Meetings

10 Percent
A "chat" room where gays and lesbians meet to talk about a variety of issues, events, as well as to meet.
The Gay & Lesbian Cafe

Popular Culture & Entertainment

Entertainment A-Z
Where users talk about games and a variety of popular culture events and issues.
Entertainment Talk

Film & Video Emporium
A "chat" room where users talk about creatvie videos and films.
The Producer's Lounge

Imagine Engine
A place where kids can talk about books and creativity.
The Station House

Inside Games
A "chat" room where users can talk to gaming peers, game publishers, and game developers.
Game talk

Music Universe
A "chat" room where user talk about a variety of musical topics.
Open Mic

The Online Bookstore
Meet with authors in the "Author, Author" chat room, and join electronic booksignings.
Author, Author

Tube Time
Where users talk about television events, shows, and issues.
Studio A

Women Online Worldwide
A "chat" room where users talk about women's issues and ideas.
Women's Space

WorldPaper Online
A "chat" room where users can discuss the latest news or issues of the day.
Face to Face

Writer's Digest
A "chat" room where writers, authors and publishers talk about issues and works.
Author to Author

Youth Central
A place where kids and teens can talk about a variety of topics.
Youth Yak

Yoyodyne
A "chat" room where users talk about life and games.
Yoyodyne Coffeehouse

Science

Earthwatch
A "chat" room where users talk to EarthCorps members and scientists.
EW Base Camp

Sports & Recreation

Stat Factory
A "chat" room where users talk about sports drafts and special sporting events.
Stat Factory Live

GEnie

GEnie Online Service provides its users with connections to investment companies such as Charles Schwab Brokerage Services and Dow Jones News/Retrieval. The service provider focuses on RoundTables, which are special interest subjects that range from computers to comics to collectible items like toys, stamps and cars. There are Interactive Conferences and Special Events each night featuring a person well-known in his or her field. GEnie also creates newsletters and magazines for many of its RoundTables.

GEnie publishes a monthly multimedia magazine, LiveWire, for all major computing platforms, including DOS, Windows, Mac and Amiga. The magazine features information about particular aspects of the online service—such as shareware, games, and personalities in film, sports, and business who make "special appearances" at RoundTables and Interactive Conferences. GEnie also provides users with email service and is moving toward full Internet access.

Who it's for: Individuals and businesses. It is geared more for individual users.

Points of Presence: Throughout the U.S. and Canada.

Cost: Monthly fee of $8.95 provides up to four hours of standard connect time, with a charge of $3.00 an hour for each hour beyond the initial allotment. Premium service (costs vary) includes Charles Schwab Brokerage Services (not available in Canada), Travel Service, and a clipping service.

Contact: Call (800) 638-9636 for a free disk of GEnie for Windows or Macintosh. At the time of sign-up, GEnie offers $50 worth of free services during the first month.

Arts & Music

Design
DTP.RT	Desktop Publishing RoundTable

Electronic Arts
FLANAGAN	BITSTREAM RoundTable
DEB	Gallery 44
IMAGE1	Graphic Images RoundTable

Music
SM	The Music RoundTable

Music Resources
SM	MIDI & Computer Musicians RoundTable

Visual Arts
PHOTOBASE	Archive Photos
PHOTOBASE	Photo & Video RoundTable
PSI$	PhotoSource International
JODY	Visual ARTS & Crafts RoundTable

Business & Economics

Career & Employment
SUPPORT	Career & Professional Services
SUPPORT	Corporate Affiliates Research Center
DR.JOB	Dr. Job
WORKPLACE$	WorkPlace RoundTable

Commerce
SUPPORT	Business Week

Companies
SUPPORT	D&B Asia/Pacific Company Profiles
SUPPORT	D&B Canadian Company Profiles
SUPPORT	D&B European Company Profiles
SUPPORT	D&B International Company Profiles
SUPPORT	D&B U.S. Company Profiles

Home Office
J.ATTARD	Home Office/Small Business RoundTable

International
WELCOM	World Economic Forum Private RoundTable

International Business
SUPPORT	Canadian Business Center
SUPPORT	Dun & Bradstreet Databases

Investment
SCHWAB	Charles Schwab Brokerage Services
SUPPORT	Closing Stock Quotes
SUPPORT	Investment Reports
INVEST$	Investors' RoundTable
SOS	SOS Registered Investment Advisors
SUPPORT	The Investment ANALY$T

Legal Aspects
INCORPORATE	Business Incorporating Guide
SUPPORT	Trade Names Database
SUPPORT	Trademark Center
SUPPORT	Worldwide Patent Center

Personal Finance
CHECKFREE	CheckFree Corporation
SUPPORT	GEnie Loan Calculator
SUPPORT	Personal Finance & Investing Services
J.ATTARD	Tax RoundTable

Reference
SUPPORT	Commerce Business Daily
SUPPORT	D&B U.S. Business Locator
SUPPORT	Dialog Database Center
DJCS	Dow Jones News/Retrieval
DIRECTORY$	The Business Resource Directory
SUPPORT	Thomas Register
SUPPORT	TRW Business Credit Profiles

Services
SUPPORT	Business Services
CORPORATION	The Company Corporation

Computing & Mathematics

Career & Employment
E-SPAN	E-Span JobSearch

Companies
FEEDBACK	Apple/Macintosh Products & Services
DARLAH	Atari 8-Bit RoundTable
FEEDBACK	Atari & Jaguar Products and Services
DARLAH	Atari ST & Jaguar RoundTable
COMMODORE$	Commodore 64/128 RoundTable
HAYES.TECH	Hayes RoundTable
STARSHIP$	Other Commodore & Amiga Services

Hardware
DAVESMALL	Gadgets By Small RoundTable
ICDINC	ICD RoundTable
MARK.YOUNG	Newton RoundTable
PORT$	Portfolio RoundTable
PPC.DONNIE	PPC RoundTable
HOGAN	Tandy RoundTable by Mike Hogan
BW.MILLER	TI RoundTable

Networking
DATACOMM$	DataComm & Interconnectivity RoundTable

Operating Systems
STROM	IBM PC RoundTable by Charles Strom
STROM	IBM PC/Tandy-TRS-80 & Compatibles
MAC.HELP	Macintosh RoundTable
STROM	OS/2 RoundTable
UNIX$	Unix RoundTable

Programming
DEB	Amiga Pro/Am RoundTable
ATARIDEV	Atari Developers RoundTable
BORLAND$	Borland RoundTable
MS.LAWRENCE	Computer Game Developers RoundTable
ELLIOTT.C	Forth Interest Group RoundTable
IBM$	IBM PC Programmers & Developers RoundTable
MACPRO.HELP	Macintosh Programmers/Developers RoundTable
KATE.DANIEL	PostScript RoundTable
PPCPRO.HELP	PowerPC Programmers' RoundTable
PLRT$	Programming & Programming Languages
MOTO$	SPECTRO

Reference
SUPPORT	Computer & Electronics NewsCenter
NEWSBYTES	Newsbytes News Network
SUPPORT	Product Support Services
SUPPORT	Special Interest Groups

Software
TURBO$	Amiga Aladdin RoundTable
A2PRO.HELP	Apple II Programmers RoundTable
A2.HELP	Apple II RoundTable
SCOTTV	Autodesk Retail Products RoundTable
DBMS	Database RoundTable
BRIAN.D	ENABLE RoundTable
SWATSON	FreeSoft RoundTable
TONY.C	Geoworks RoundTable by Tony Cuozzo
STROM	IBM Product Support RoundTable
CHIPSOFT-1	Intuit RoundTable
MAC.HELP	Macintosh Vendors RoundTable
MSPRT$	Microsoft Press RoundTable
MSRT.MAIL$	Microsoft RoundTable
WIN95$	Microsoft Windows 95 RoundTable
MUSTANG.INC	MUSTANG Software RoundTable
ALADDIN$	PC Aladdin Support RoundTable
SL-TECH	Soft-Logik Publishing RoundTable
SOFTDISK	Softdisk Publishing
STARSHIP$	*StarShip* Amiga RoundTable
TIMEWORKS	TimeWorks RoundTable
VIR-SEC$	Virus/Computer Security RoundTable
WIN95$	Windows 95 News Highlight Center
STROM	Windows RoundTable
WP.DAVE	WordPerfect RoundTable

Systems
BW.MILLER	CP/M RoundTable
MFRT$	Mini/Mainframe RoundTable

Telecommunications
BBS.MGMT$	BBS & Telecommunications RoundTable

Telecomputing
SOFTRONICS-2	Softronics RoundTable

Education

Colleges & Universities
RENSSELAER	Rensselaer Polytechnic RoundTable

Distance Education
CALC	CALC Online Campus

Funding
NCSL	College Aid Sources for Higher Ed.

Libraries
SUPPORT	Bibliographic Citations Center

Resources
SUPPORT	Dissertation Abstracts
RJP	Education RoundTable
SUPPORT	Education Services
SUPPORT	Educator's Center
GROLIERS	Grolier's Electronic Encyclopedia
SUPPORT	Peterson's College Guide
SUPPORT	Peterson's Graduate School Guide

Government & Politics

Career & Employment
D.FLORY	A Law Enforcement RoundTable

Countries
CANADA	Canada RoundTable
USA.EUROPE	Deutschland RoundTable
USA.EUROPE	Europe RoundTable
JAPAN-RT	Japan RoundTable
SUPPORT	U.S. Federal Center
WHRT$	White House RoundTable

International
SUPPORT	Symposiums on Global Issues

Military
SAFSB2	Air Force Small Business RoundTable
MIL-SPEC	Military RoundTable

Regions
WEST$	American West RoundTable
GARY-B	USA East RoundTable
GARY-B	USA MidWest RoundTable

States
FEEDBACK	California Apartment Association

Health & Medicine

Conferences & Events
KUMBAYA	Kumbaya RoundTable
RHONDA.M	Medical RoundTable

Disabilities
ABLE-DAVE	DisAbilities RoundTable

Health & Medical Professionals
SUPPORT	Medical Professional's Center

Resources
SUPPORT	AIDS Research Center
SUPPORT	Consumer Medicine

Services
CONTACT	Contact Lens Supply, Inc.

Sexuality
GAY.RT	Gay and Lesbian Issues RoundTable

Humanities & Social Sciences

History
HISTORYRT$	History RoundTable

Literature
CAROLE.NWA	National Writers' Association RoundTable
POWER.PAM	Writers' Ink RoundTable

Internet

Communications
FEEDBACK	GEnie Communications Products

Internet Access
FEEDBACK	Billing & Account Information
FEEDBACK	Front Ends for GEnie Games
FEEDBACK	GEnie Front Ends
SUPPORT	GEnie Reference Center
SUPPORT	GEnie Research & Reference Services
FEEDBACK	Gift Of Time
INDEX.WRITER	Index of Products & Services
ANDY	Internet Gateway
FEEDBACK	New Members' Information
FEEDBACK	Phone Access Directory
FEEDBACK	Policies & Guidelines

Internet Communications
FEEDBACK	GE Mail

Internet Resources
FEEDBACK	Account Information
None Availab	CD-ROM World Magazine
GENIELAMP	Computing on GEnie Newsletter
FEEDBACK	GE Information Services
GENIEMAC$	GEnie for MAC Support RoundTable
GENIEWIN$	GEnie for Windows Support RoundTable
FEEDBACK	GEnie Help
FEEDBACK	GEnie Information
FEEDBACK	GEnie Online User's Manual
FEEDBACK	GEnie Rate Information
FEEDBACK	GEnie Reminder Service
FEEDBACK	GEnie User Profiles
GENIEUS$	GENIEus RoundTable
FEEDBACK	Hot & Happening Events on GEnie
ANDY	Internet Education Center
INTERNET$	Internet RoundTable
SUPPORT	NetGuide Magazine
FEEDBACK	New Member Practice RoundTable
SUPPORT	PC-VAN Gateway
TURBO$	ST Aladdin RoundTable

Internet Services
FEEDBACK	GEnie$Premium Pricing Information

Internet Tools
FEEDBACK	GE Mail to FAX

Online Games
BOB.MAPLES	Castle Quest by Bob Maples
CYBERSTRIKE	CyberStrike(tm) by Simutronics
SATCHI	Mud II: The Quest for Immortality

Resources
FEEDBACK	Computing on GEnie
FEEDBACK	National Real-Time Conference

Services
FEEDBACK	GEnie Business Booster

Virtual Communities
PFNNI	GEnie Chat Lines
PENNI	GEnie Chat Lines Help and Hints

Law & Criminal Justice

Conferences & Events
ROBERT.LEWIS	Law RoundTable

Legal Resources
SUPPORT	Law Center

Popular Culture & Entertainment

Automobiles
GREG.AMY	Automotive RoundTable
AUTOVANTAGE	AutoVantage Online (R)

Books
SF-NIC	First Science Fiction & Fantasy RoundTable
SUPPORT	GEnie's BookShelf
RAINBO	Rainbo Electronic Reviews
POWER.PAM	Readers RoundTable
PATO	Romance & Women's Fiction RoundTable
BOOKMARK	Signed Editions
SF-2000	Third Science Fiction & Fantasy RoundTable

Celebrities & Personalities
JERRYP	Jerry Pournelle RoundTable

Family & Community
EMERGENCY$	Emergency RoundTable
FAMILYRT$	Family and Personal Growth RoundTable
LASS	Home & Real Estate RoundTable
SUPPORT	Public Opinion Online Database

Food & Dining
COOKIE-LADY	Food & Wine RoundTable

Genealogy
GRTSYSOP$	Genealogy RoundTable

General Reference
FEEDBACK	Entertainment Services
SM	ODMR Capsule Reviews
GARY-B	The Disney RoundTable

Lifestyles
NEWAGE.MAIL$	New Age RoundTable

Magazines & Newspapers
SUPPORT	Boston Globe
SUPPORT	Chicago Tribune
SUPPORT	Columnists and News Features
POWER.PAM	Comics RoundTable
SUPPORT	Entertainment Weekly
SUPPORT	Fortune Magazine
SUPPORT	GEnie QuikNews
SUPPORT	GEnie's NewsStand
SUPPORT	Life Magazine
FEEDBACK	LiveWire Online Magazine
SUPPORT	Los Angeles Times
SUPPORT	MONEY Magazine
SUPPORT	News, Sports & Features
SUPPORT	People Magazine
SUPPORT	Reuters Newswires
SUPPORT	San Francisco Chronicle
SUPPORT	Sports Illustrated
SUPPORT	Time Magazine
SUPPORT	USA Today
SUPPORT	Washington Post

Media
STARR	Second Science Fiction & Fantasy RoundTable
HOTLINE	ShowBizQuiz(tm)

Miscellaneous
ASTRO.MAIL$	Astrological Forecasts Online
ASTRO-COMM	Astrology by Astro
ASTRO.MAIL$	Astrology RoundTable
PF$	Public Forum*NonProfit Connection RoundTable
SUPPORT	Quotations Online
RADIO.RT	Radio & Electronics RoundTable

Movies
CINEMAN	CINEMAN Entertainment Information
MOVIES	Show Biz RoundTable

Multimedia
GENIELAMP	Digitial Publishing RoundTable
SUPPORT	GEnie Banner Maker
MULTIMEDIA$	Multimedia Product Center
MULTIMEDIA$	Multimedia RoundTable

Shopping

AUTOQUOT-R	AutoQuot-r Information Center
CHIPS	Chips & Bits
PHARMACY	Court Pharmacy
DIRECTMICRO	Direct Micro
MUSIC.VIDEOS	Entertainment Works
FEEDBACK	GEnie Classified Ads
MALL	GEnie Mall Merchants
GENIEPRODS1	GEnie Products
GENIESTORE	GEnie Products Store
SUPPORT	GEnie Shopping Services
GERMAN	Great German Gifts
GIFTS	Just Terrific Gifts
LANDSEND	Lands End
LDROSES	Long Distance Roses
MARYMAC	MaryMac Industries
MC-SOFTWARE	Mission Control
NOTEWORTHY	Noteworthy Music
OMNITECH	Omni Technics
PARSONS	Parsons Technology
PC.CATALOG	PC Catalog - PC Comparison Shopping
PENNYWISE	Penny Wise Office Products
SAFEWARE	Safeware Computer Insurance
COMPUSTORE	Shoppers Advantage Online
SHADES-MORE	Sunglasses, Shavers & More
FEDII.2	The Software Club by SoftClub
TITAN-GAMES	Titan Games
KNOLL	Walter Knoll Florist

Television

CTV-DREW	Inside CTV RoundTable
NBC5	NBC Online RoundTable
BANKS1414	Soap Opera Summaries

Unexplained Phenomena

REVENANT	PSI-Net RoundTable

Weather & Traffic

FRANK.REDDY	Space & Science Weather Center

Religion & Philosophy

Resources

A.WERRY	Religion & Philosophy RoundTable

Science

Astronomy

MICHAELH	Planetary Society RoundTable
FRANK.REDDY	Space & Science Information Center
FRANK.REDDY	Space & Science RoundTable

Chemistry

BW.MILLER	Chemistry RoundTable

Environmental Sciences

SUPPORT	Environmental Center

Sports & Recreation

Aquatic Sports

DIVEMASTER	Scuba RoundTable

Aviation

AVIATION$	Aviation RoundTable
NATCA-RT$	National Air Traffic Controllers RoundTable

Crafts & Hobbies

JODY	Collectibles RoundTable
LASS	Home Improvement RoundTable
SUPPORT	Leisure Pursuits & Hobbies
HOBBYSTORE	Master Hobbies
PAUL	Modeling RoundTable
JODY	NeedleARTS RoundTable
NARIPAT	Remodeling Marketplace RoundTable
STAMPS.RT	Stamp Collecting RoundTable
COOKIE-LADY	Zymurgy RoundTable

Food & Dining

COFFEE2GO	Coffee Anyone ??? (R)
COOKIES	Gimmee Jimmy's Cookies

Games

BOB.MAPLES	Adventure 550
KESMAI	Air Warrior(tm) by Kesmai
BOB.MAPLES	Black Dragon by Bob Maples
SUPPORT	Classic Games
SUPPORT	Dor Sageth by Runge and Thonssen
AUSI-SUPPORT	Dragon's Gate by AUSI
SPORTS	Fantasy Sports Leagues RoundTable
FEDII.2	Federation II
MBJ	Galaxy I by Mark Jacobs
SCORPIA	Games RoundTable by Scorpia
GS3FEEDBACK$	GemStone III: Shadow World
GENCON	Gencon(R)/Origins(TM)
SUPPORT	GEnie Game Room
SUPPORT	GEnie Multi-player Games
HY$	Hundred Years War RoundTable
HY$	Hundred Years War(tm) by DENO
KESMAI	Island of Kesmai by Kesmai Corp.
MPBT.SUPPORT	MultiPlayer BattleTech (R)
SCORPIA	Multiplayer Games RoundTable
KESMAI	MultiPlayer Harpoon(tm) by Kesmai
NTN3	NTN Trivia
OWHELP$	Orb Wars
SUPPORT	Original Adventure
QB1	QB1 from NTN Communications, Inc.
JWEAVERJR	RSCARDS Backgammon
JWEAVERJR	RSCARDS Blackjack
JWEAVERJR	RSCARDS Bridge
JWEAVERJR	RSCARDS Checkers
JWEAVERJR	RSCARDS Chess
JWEAVERJR	RSCARDS Multi-player Games
JWEAVERJR	RSCARDS Poker
JWEAVERJR	RSCARDS Reversi
STEVE.COLE	SFB Update Area by ADB
SIMU-RT$	Simutronics RoundTable
DARK.EMPIRE	Stellar Emperor
DARK.EMPIRE	Stellar Warrior
VANDER-JACK	TSR Online RoundTable
SCORPIA	Video Games RoundTable

Gardening

PALM.MOM	International Palm Society RoundTable
PAUL	Gardening RoundTable

Motor Sports

MOTO$	Motorcycling RoundTable

Outdoor Recreation

PAUL	Outdoors RoundTable

Pets & Animals

MAGGIEMAE	Maggie Mae's PET-NET RoundTable

Shopping

LEASE	American Lease Exchange

Sports

SPORTS	GEnie NFL Football Pool
SPORTS	Sports RoundTable

Travel & Tourism

CALKOBRIN	Adventure Atlas
EAASY.SABRE	American Airlines EAASY SABRE
USA.EUROPE	British Isles RoundTable
OAG-HELP	Official Airline Guides
GARY-B	Travel RoundTable
FEEDBACK	Travel Services

IBM's infoMarket

IBM's infoMarket Search is an online Internet access service, available for free during its beta test period. This service provides users with a way to search for documents, news, and references on the Internet through such data sources as The McKinley Group, Inc., Open Text Corporation, Yahoo, and Usenet News.

These facilities provide individual users and businesses with access to directory resources for the Internet, major world news organizations (including newspapers and magazines), weather services, virtual online shopping malls, catalogs, entertainment and educational resources, and newsgroups.

Additionally, IBM's Web Explorer allows users to search the Internet for a wide variety of information, whether for business, educational, or entertainment purposes.

Who it's for: Individuals and businesses.

Points of Presence: International.

Cost: During the beta test of the product (expected to last to the end of 1995), the service is free. A user fee schedule had not been established at press time.

Contact: IBM infoMarket Search, email: info@www.infomkt.ibm.com, URL: http://www.infomkt.ibm.com/info

InternetMCI

InternetMCI offers consumers and businesses a full range of Internet offerings with a nationwide dial-up access to the Internet, as well as its own MarketplaceMCI, an electronic shopping area, where members have access to such places as Dun & Bradstreet Information Services, Hammacher Schlemmer & Co., OfficeMax, Inc., Intercontinental Florist, Aetna Life and Casualty, Amtrack, Dell Computers, Healthrider, Sara Lee (L'eggs and Superior Coffee), Reveal Computer Products, and National Wildlife Galleries, Inc. (Art Access). Another service is NetworkMCI

Commercial Online Services

which includes email, faxing, videoconferencing, and whiteboard conferencing. For sending and receiving email on the Internet, internetMCI customers can purchase emailMCI separately.

Who it's for: Individuals and businesses (Windows users).

Points of Presence: U.S. (initially 64 U.S. cities)

Cost: Basic rate is $9.95 per month, including the first five hours of local access ($2.50 for each additional hour). Users who wish to dial in via MCI's 800 service will pay $6.50 for each hour of access.

Contact: MCI,
Email: **mcinews@mcimail.com**,
Call + 1 (800) 955-5210,
URL: **http://www.internetMCI.com/**

MSN (Microsoft Network)

Microsoft Network is one of the newest interactive online services. It aims primarily to provide individuals and businesses with email, bulletin boards, and "chat rooms" on a range of topics. The service was introduced concurrently with the release of Windows '95 (late August, 1995), and covers arts and entertainment, news and weather, business and finance, sports, health, fitness, science, computers and software.

Each of the forums are facilitated by a select group of Forum Managers, who bring to their positions specialized knowledge, credibility, and respect in their areas of expertise. Other services include product and support information for Microsoft products, as well as for providers of peripheral Windows products. There is a special section providing specific Microsoft support for customers.

Who it's for: Individuals and businesses.

Points of Presence: Initially available in 35 countries. Localized in 20 languages.

Cost: Unavailable but expected to be in line with other service provider costs

Contact: n/a

NETCOM

This online company's core service involves providing a subscription to the Internet. It also offers Windows users worldwide email, and allows users to interact online with millions of people worldwide. A subscription includes NetCruiser Internet software, which provides a graphical user interface for the Internet. With NetCruiser, users also gain access to USENET News—a world-wide bulletin board with more than 10,000 categories for users to read, post, and download articles on any topic of interest.

Coverage spans a variety of subjects including the entertainment business, education, and special interest topics. Users can also access a map of publicly accessible computers (at research institutions, educational institutions, and government centers) in all 50 states in the U.S. NetCruiser supports two major Internet browsing tools—World Wide Web and Gopher.

Who it's for: Individuals and businesses (Windows users only).

Points of Presence: In 41 states and growing, and four Canadian provinces.

Cost: NetCruiser software is free. An individual account is priced at $19.95 per month, which includes 40 hours of peak hour access (Monday through Friday 9 a.m. to Midnight). Access during off-peak hours is unlimited and not charged. A business account is $239.40 yearly (prepaid a year in advance), plus a $50 set-up fee to establish an account.

Contact: NETCOM On-Line Communication Services, Inc., call (800) 353-6000,
URL: **http://www.netcom.com/**

Prodigy

Prodigy offers a wide range of services for personal computer users, especially children. (Prodigy claims to constantly monitor content so that children are not exposed to offensive material.) Besides entertainment and shopping services, Prodigy features up-to-the-minute sports coverage (including information on events in progress on the ESPN cable television network).

Prodigy offers users email service plus Internet email. Prodigy also offers access to Usenet Newsgroups and a World Wide Web browser. The company has plans to use the wide bandwidth of cable technology to enable users to view, on-demand, video clips of live sporting events on their PCs. Additionally, there are places for users to meet celebrities in various fields of interest—from well-known financial advisers to famous actors.

There are also more than 1,000 bulletin boards, including a separate section for younger children to play interactive games. Access to Homework Helper, a database of some 35 periodicals and 700 reference books, is available to youngsters in grades K-12.

Who it's for: Individuals, particularly children, using Windows.

Points of Presence: Throughout the U.S.

Cost: A subscription is $9.95 per month, which includes five hours of connect time. After five hours, it costs $2.95 per hour.

Contact: Call (800) 776-3449

Arts & Music

Art Resources
Antiques [& Collecting]
Arts

Music
Music 1
Music 2

Music Genres
Country Music

Performing Arts
Playbill

Business & Economics

Career & Employment
Careers

Economics
Money Talk

Management
Your Business

Reference
Marketplace

Communications

Human Communications
Chat
My Turn Online
New Member
Service Clubs
The Club

Telecommunications
Information Highway

Computing & Mathematics

Computer Science
Computer

Hardware
Hardware Support

Software
Software Support

Education

Colleges & Universities
College

Distance Education
Homework Helper

Educational Issues
Education

International Education
Foreign Languages

Resources
Learning Adventure

Government & Politics

Issues
News

Issues
Veterans

Health & Medicine

Aging
Seniors

Family Health
Parenting

Health Conditions
Health

Resources
Medical Support

Humanities & Social Sciences

Area & Cultural Studies
Black Experience
Canada
Cultures
Native American

Literature
Books & Writing

Internet

Networking
Internet Forum

Law & Criminal Justice

Criminal Justice
Cops & Crime

Legal Issues
Legal Exchange

Popular Culture & Entertainment

Family & Community
Adoption
Singles
Teens

Genealogy
Genealogy

General Reference
Gateway 2000
Myth & Fantasy
Radio
Science Fiction

Humor
Comedy
Comics

Lifestyles
Gay & Lesbian
Lifestyles

Magazines & Newspapers
Newsweek
Tekno Comix

Miscellaneous
Astrology
Disney Fans
Trivia

Movies
Movies

Multimedia
Video Gamoo

Television
Star Trek
TV
TV Networks

Unexplained Phenomena
Supernatural

Religion & Philosophy

Doctrines
Religion Concourse 1

General Reference
Religion Concourse 2

Science

Earth Sciences
Science [& Environment]

Sports & Recreation

Automobiles
Automotive

Crafts & Hobbies
Collecting 1
Collecting 2
Crafts
Crafts 2
Trading Cards

Food & Dining
Food
Wine [Beer & Spirits]

Games
Games
Role Playing Games

Gardening
Home & Garden

Motor Sports
Auto Racing
Motorcycles

Pets & Animals
Pets

Sports
Baseball
Basketball
Football
Hockey
NFL
SI for Kids
Sports
Sports Play
Wrestling

Travel & Tourism
Travel

The WELL

The WELL bills itself as the birthplace of citizen-based virtual community. The service has more than 260 conferences on subjects including media, art, literature, Generation X, jazz, The Grateful Dead, parenting, music and spirituality. It also provides connection to full Internet services, including Usenet newsgroups, the World Wide Web, Gopher and its own MUSE (Multi-User Simulation Environment).

The WELL also provides users with electronic mail, conferencing for business and personal groups. The provider draws on a confluence of diverse social and professional elements, including writers,

The WELL

artists, educators, programmers, lawyers, entrepreneurs, hobbyist, parents, and musicians. Conferences and conversations tend to range from the technical and specific to the abstract and intellectual.

There is connection to the Internet, and users are provided Usenet newsgroups, gopher, and various net searching capabilities. The WELL even hosts classes on Internet Training, which provides users with hands-on experience with The WELL and how to explore the Internet through The Whole Works Internet Toolkit. In addition there is an online The Whole Internet Catalog for seaching the WWW, as well as a hotlink to Yahoo. There is also a Web self-publishing Service, called Web Express, which offers members the option to create their own web self-publishing directory.

Who it's for: Individuals using Windows and Macintosh systems - primarily for adults.

Points of Presence: New York City and San Francisco Bay Area.

Cost: Individual subscription is $15 a month, which includes five hours of connect time per month, with additional hours billed at $2.50. There is a one-time set-up fee of $15. There are other membership plans for more frequent users and users that already have an Internet account.

Contact: The WELL;
Email to **web-info@well.com;**
URL **http://www.well.com/;**
or Voice 1 (415) 332-4335.

Arts & Music

Art Organizations
NAPLPS	g naplps

Artists
Arts	g arts
Creativity	g creativity
New York Scene	g nylive

Books
Science Fiction	g sf

Design
Design	g design
Graphic Arts	g graph

Electronic Arts
Art Com Electronic Net	g acen
Muchomedia	g mucho
Radio	g rad

Film & Video
Filmmaking	g film
Movies	g movies
Video	g vid

Miscellaneous
Feedback	g feedback

Music
Audio	g aud
Feedback	g feedback
MIDI	g midi
Mirrorshades	g mirror
Music	g music
NY Live Music	g nylive
Tapes	g tapes
Tickets	g tix
Tours	g tours

Music Genres
Classical Music	g classic
Country and Western	g country
HORDE bands	g horde
Jazz	g jazz

Music Groups
Beatles	g beat
Bob Dylan	g dylan
GD Hour	g gdh
Grateful Dead	g gd
HORDE bands	g horde
House Music	g house
Jazz	g jazz

Musical
Digital Recording	g digital

Performing Arts
Bay Area Tonight	g bat
Life Stories	g life
Theater	g theat

Visual Arts
Photography	g pho

Business & Economics

Career & Employment
Classifieds	g cla
Entrepreneurs	g entre

Commerce
Agriculture	g agri
One Person Business	g oneperbiz
The Future	g fut
Transportation	g transport

Consumer Issues
Consumers	g cons

International Business
Translators	g trans

Investment
Investments	g invest
Thrift	g thrift
Towards Sustainability	g sust

Legal Aspects
Legal	g legal

Management
Consultants	g consult

Personal Finance
Homeowners	g home

Reference
Business	g biz
Business and Technology	g biztech
Work and Workplace	g work

Communications

Career & Employment
Computer Journalism	g cpj
Freelance Writing	g byline

Communications
Current Events	g current
Digital Recording	g digital
Indexing	g indexing
Information	g info
Languages	g language
Muchomedia: Multimedia	g mucho

Human Communications
Kids (penpals)	g kidlink

Mass Communications
Advertising	g ad
Media	g media
Radio	g rad
Technical Writers	g tec
Television	g tv

Mobile Communications
Wireless Personal Communication	g wireless

Telecommunications
Telecommunications	g tele
The Internet	g inet

Computing & Mathematics

Companies
Amiga	g amiga
Apple II	g apple
Business and Technology	g biztech
Forth Interest Group	g fig
IBM PC	g ibm
Macintosh	g mac
Mactech	g mactech
Mirrorshades	g mirror
NAPLPS	g naplps

Hardware
Computers (Mainframes, etc.)	g compu
Hypercard	g hype
Laptop	g lap
MIDI	g midi
Personal Digital Assistant	g pda
Printers	g print

Networking
Mac Network Admin	g macadm

Operating Systems
Mac System7	g mac7
NeXT	g next
OS/2	g os2
Unix	g unix
Windows	g windows
Windows Tech	g wintech

Reference
Berkeley MAC Users Group	g bmug
Hacking	g hack

Software
Art and Graphics	g gra
Desktop Publishing	g desk
Software Support	g ssc
Software/Programming	g software
Word Processing	g word

Systems
Scientific Computing	g scicomp

Telecomputing
Internet	g inet
LANs	g lan
Wireless Personal Communication	g wireless
World Wide Web	g web

Theory
AI/Forth/Realtime	g realtime
Virtual Reality	g vr

Education

Educational Issues
Education	g ed

Government & Politics

Cities
Peninsula, South Bay Area	g pen

Countries
Britain	g britain
Canada	g canada
Tibet	g tibet

Doctrines
Socialism	g workers
Unity	g unity

International
Travel	g tra

Issues
Amnesty International	g amnesty
Berkeley	g berk
Computer Professionals for Social Responsibility	g cpsr
Computers, Freedom & Privacy	g cfp
Electronic Frontier Foundation	g eff
Environment	g env
Firearms	g firearms
First Amendment	g first
Geography	g geo
Liberty	g liberty
Non-Profits	g non
Peace	g peace

Military
Veterans	g vets
War	g war

Political Science
Politics	g pol

Regions
Desert	g dry
Earth	g earth
East Coast USA	g east
Hawaii	g aloha
Midwest USA	g midwest
New York	g ny
North Bay	g north
Northwest USA	g nw
Oakland	g oak
Outdoors	g out
Pacific Rim	g pacrim
Rocky Mountains	g rocky
San Francisco	g sanfran
Southern California	g socal
Southern USA	g south

States
Texas/Southwest USA	g rodeo

Health & Medicine

Aging
Aging	g gray

Health Conditions
AIDS	g aids
Disability	g disability

Resources
Dreams	g dream
Drugs	g drugs
Eros	g eros
Health	g heal
Holistic	g holi
Hospice	g heal
Jewish	g jew
Mind	g mind
Myers/Briggs Type Indicator	g mbti
Optical	g eyes
Self-Help	g selfhelp
Therapy	g therapy

Services
Brainstorm	g brain

Sexuality
Sexuality	g sex

Humanities & Social Sciences

Area & Cultural Studies
French	g france
German	g german
Irish	g irish
Jewish	g jew
Language	g language
Pacific Rim	g pacrim
Spanish	g spanish
Tibet	g tibet

History
History	g hist

Libraries
Library Users Conference	g luc

Psychology
Psychology	g psy

Internet

Internet Communications
Hosts	g host
News (WELL community news)	g news
WELLTales	g tales

Internet Issues
Deeper technical view	g deeper
Party	g party
Policy	g policy
The Internet	g internet
Usenet	g usenet

Internet References
Digest (of the news conf)	g digest

Internet Resources
Best of the WELL	g best
Blair Newman Memorial Conf	g blair
Highway (native plant) Project	g highway
the WELL Archives	g archives

Internet Tools
Front-End Development	g front
General technical	g gentech
Index of new WELL topics	g newtops
MetaWELL	g meta
Muds, Muses, MOOs	g mu
MUSEs, MUDs, and WELLmuse	g mu
Offline WELL reader for ibm	g sweeper
Public Software & Programmers	g public
System Newsbriefs	g sysnews
Test	g test
The World-Wide-Web	g web
Tips (pointers to topics)	g tips
Usenet ("net news")	g usenet
WELLcome and help	g well
World Wide Web	g web

Virtual Communities
Virtual Communities	g vc

Law & Criminal Justice

Ethics
Ethics	g ethics

Popular Culture & Entertainment

Books
Books	g books
Comics	g comics
Dead Literature	g deadlit
Deadlit	g deadlit
Mysteries	g noir
Poetry	g poetry
Words	g words
Writers	g wri

Family & Community
Parenting	g par
Singles	g singles
WELL Kids	g wellkids

Genealogy
Genealogy	g roots

Humor
Jokes	g jokes

Lifestyles
Couples	g love
Gay	g gay
Generation X	g genx

Magazines & Newspapers
bOING bOING	g bb
Details Magazine	g details
Gnosis Magazine	g gnosis
Interview	g interview
L.A. Reader	g lareader
Microtimes	g microx
Mondo 2000	g mondo
Periodicals/Newsletters	g per
Whole Earth Review	g we
Wired	g wired
Zine on the WELL	g zine
Zines/Fanzine Scene	g f5

The WELL – Women's Wire

Miscellaneous	
Bent	g bent
CDs	g cd
Cyberfoo-First Night Party	g foo
Fringeware	g fw
Interpersonal Communication	g in
Lies	g lies
Life Stories	g life
Miscellaneous	g misc
Nightowls: 12 - 6am PCT	g owl
Pop Culture	g popcult
Popular Culture	g popcult
Redheads on the WELL	g row
Statements	g stmt
True Confessions	g tru
Unclear	g unclear
Weird	g weird

Movies	
Movies	g movies

Shopping	
Fashion	g plumage

Television	
Star Trek	g trek
Television	g tv

Unexplained Phenomena	
Scams	g scam

Religion & Philosophy

Doctrines	
Christian	g cross

Philosophy	
Fringes of Reason	g fringes
Philosophy	g phi

Religions	
Buddhist	g wonderland
Religion	g relig
Spirituality	g spirit

Science

Biology	
Biology and Info	g bioinfo
Biosphere II	g bio2

Environmental Sciences	
Environment	g environ

Geosciences	
Earthquake	g quake

Physics	
Energy	g power

Scientists	
Brainstorm	g brainstorm
Cohousing	g coho
Science	g science

Space Science	
Atmosphere	g atmosphere

Sports & Recreation

Crafts & Hobbies	
Chess	g chess
Collecting and Antiques	g collect
Crafts	g crafts
Games	g games

Food & Dining	
Cooking	g cook
Drinks	g drinks
NY Food	g nyfood
Restaurants	g rest

Gardening	
Gardening	g gard

Motor Sports	
Motorcycling	g ride
Motoring	g car

Outdoor Recreation	
Outdoor Recreation	g out

Pets & Animals	
Pets	g pets
Wildlife	g wild

Recreation	
Party	g party

Sports	
Bicycles	g bike
Boating	g boat
Golf	g golf
NY Sports	g nysports
Sports	g sports

Travel & Tourism	
Flying	g flying
Travel	g tra

Women's Wire

This online service provider is the first interactive service designed to specifically address the personal and professional interests of women. Subscribers will find women-oriented news, resources, and discussion groups, as well as access to an array of Usenet newsgroups and the Internet. These newsgroups provide information from periodicals, government sources, newswires, women's organizations, and resource books.

Another service is Interactive Exchanges, enabling subscribers to obtain information on computers and technology, political and social issues, and health, fitness, and alternative medical resources. Under the career and finance areas of Women's Wire, users can join in on talks about career planning and management, investing, and starting a business. There is even a job forecast for women.

Finally, users can find out about local and regional cultural events, support groups, and resources for parenting and education.

Who it's for: Primarily Women.

Points of Presence: Worldwide.

Cost: Fee is $9.95 a month for first three hours, and $3.95 per hour for every hour after that.

Contact: Women's Wire, call (800) 210-8998 within the U.S. and (415) 378-6500 outside the U.S. URL: http://www.women.com/

Arts & Music

Cinema Forum
Films

Business & Economics

Women Investing
Investing issues

Communications

News Cafe
For journalists/writers

Humanities & Social Sciences

Business Roundtable
Managing Career/Women in Business/Professional Coach management

Career Coach
Career Counselor

Gender, Race, Class
Social Issues

Library Forum
Books

Shrink/Wrap
Online psychiatrist and discussions

Internet

On the Internet
All things online

Law & Criminal Justice

Legal Line
Legal advice and discussion

Popular Culture & Entertainment

Club Grill
Discussion for the the 20-something generation. GenX

New Media Women
Multimedia/Technology discussions

Parents in Clubhouse
Moms and family

A Whimsical Internet Tour

Welcome to The McKinley Whimsical Web Tour!

This is an adventure-filled Internet cruise–accompanied by your personal escort, the McKinley Directory. (Before settling into your seat and beginning the voyage, however, you'll need a World Wide Web browser. Web browsers help users navigate among various sites located on the Internet, and enable them to view graphics, which is particularly exciting.)

Let McKinley open the door and guide you through cyberspace. Your itinerary includes some of the most entertaining, informative, and useful sites on the World Wide Web–and the tour lasts as long as your whim!

Bon voyage!

The Tour

Kick off your tour with **Arts & Music**. Treasures like those found in the famous **Louvre** Museum in Paris can be transported right into your living room.

http://meteora.ucsd.edu:80/~norman/paris/Musees/Louvre/

After visiting the Louvre, you might want to visit the **Leonardo da Vinci Museum**,

http://movieweb.com/museum/main.html

or the **Smithsonian Institution's** homepage which points to many of its museums.

http://www.si.edu/start.html

Art has also moved off the gallery wall and online. Visit some **online galleries** and find out all about **arts conferences**, **competitions** and what's up in **performance art**.

http://www.tmn.com/Oh/Artswire/www/about.html

http://www.msstate.edu/Fineart_Online/

Maybe it's time to get down to business or do your taxes. You can get in touch with the **IRS** before they get in touch with you;

http://www.ustreas.gov/treasury/bureaus/irs/irs.html

or see what's up or down on the **stock market**.

http://www.quote.com//

Looking for insider information on **international investments**? Check out the following:

Hong Kong

http://160.96.7.121:1080/news/intra/index.html/

Canada

http://networth.galt.com/www/home/capital/ticktalk/ticktalk.ht/

Europe

http://www.spb.su/spbj//

Perhaps you've joined the ranks of those who are working from a home office or you're starting up a small business. Chances are it would be helpful to find useful information about:

Accessories for your Apple computer

http://www.apple.com//

Insurance

http://branch.com/legacy/legacy.html/

Business publications

http://www-mitpress.mit.edu/

Business training seminars

http://www.tasl.com/tasl/home.html/

Women and Computer Science

http://www.ai.mit.edu/people/ellens/gender.html

Internet Women Help List

http://www.best.com:80/~agoodloe/iw-help.html

Women Online

http://www.best.com:80/~agoodloe/wo-brochure.html

Now, after all that work, how about exploring some **international vacation packages**!

http://www.branch.com:80/silkroute//

Speaking of vacation packages, Sports and Recreation is our next stop. Time for some R & R! Are you a movie buff? An adventure seeker? A stalwart backpacker? How about the following:

A **trip around the world**?

http://wings.buffalo.edu/world//

Maui - The Valley Island

http://204.182.52.1//

An **armchair journey**?

http://nearnet.gnn.com/gnn/meta/travel/index.html/

Hiking and camping in the great outdoors?

http://www.gorp.com//"

EcoTourism is a great way to enjoy the world and let others enjoy it, too. If you want to travel "green" and you'd like to learn more about **earth-friendly vacations**, cruise on down the cyber-river to this listserv.

mailto:Majordomo@igc.apc.org

http://www.gate.net/good-green-fun/

If travel's not what your looking for, but you still want to get out and be active, check out these sites.

How about a quick set of **tennis**?

http://arganet.tenagra.com/Racquet_Workshop/Tennis.html/

Or a day on the links playing a round of **golf**?

http://www.tr-riscs.panam.edu/golf/19thhole.html

Or a rousing **soccer** game?

http://www.tns.lcs.mit.edu/cgi-bin/sports//

You could also visit the **Olympics** and see your country's bid for glory,

http://www.mindspring.com/~royal/olympic.html/

or the **1995 America's Cup** where you can meet the first ever all-women crew of America[3].

http://www.ac95.org/30/30.html/

Have you had enough relaxation? You could take a more serious look at our global village by checking out Government & Politics sites like the following:

International affairs and **governments**

http://http://www.meaddata.com/

Country and National facts

http://wings.buffalo.edu/world//

Want to get facts quickly about the world's governing bodies? Check the Net's extensive databases of **government references**,

http://www.fedworld.gov/

or peruse the Net archives of **historical events, places, and politics**. You can read up on The Magna Carta,

http://www.cs.indiana.edu/inds/politics.html/

or what happened at the **Berlin Wall**.

http://www.chemie.fu-berlin.de/adressen/berlin.html/

Culture mavens will want to cruise Humanities & Social Science sites. Satisfy your curiosity about how other people live by clicking on World, Culture, and Community sites.

Discover the ancient traditions of **Asian culture**,

http://coombs.anu.edu.au/CoombsHome.html/

or the **poetry, music, and social customs of Chile, Ecuador, and Peru**.

http://history.cc.ukans.edu/history/reading_rooms/latin_america.html

Take a look at **village life and city life in emerging African nations**,

http://www.cs.ubc.ca/spider/shaze/africa/tableofcontents3_1.html/

find out about **nations that are "plugged in"** to the Internet,

http://wings.buffalo.edu/world/vt2//

or sample a few "bytes" of **international cuisine**.

http://www.deltanet.com/2way/egg/

Does **your community** have resources in cyberspace? Find out about **online resources** at this site.

http://www.city.net//

Scholars can sift through an extensive list of resources for **international research**.

http://www.ic.gov/94fact/fb94toc/fb94toc.html/

Try searching for the truth about human existence. Religion and Philosophy sites can help you find out:

Facts about **Islam**

http://gopher://latif.com/information about Islam/

Who **Buddha** was, and what **Nirvana** is

http://www.cac.psu.edu/jbe/jbe.html/

About the sage of China, **Confucius**

http://excalibur.rz.unipotsdam.de/texte/books/confuciu/analects.tx

The differences among myriad of **Christian groups**

http://saturn.colorado.edu:8080/Christian/list.html/

What the Promised Land represents in **Judaism**

gopher://israel.nysernet.org//

About **New Age Philosophy**, with its angels, auras, and ascending masters

http://bigmouth.pathfinder.com/%7Etwep/Celestine/bbs//

Or perhaps it's time to visit the **virtual confession booth**. What will your penance be?

http://anther.learning.cs.cmu.edu/priest.html/

What's more important than your health? Concerned about that pain in your neck? Need to check a First Aid fact? What's the best medicine for common ailments? Are you headed for job burn-out? Health & Medicine sites can offer help.

Do you suffer symptoms of **stress** like headaches and insomia?

http://asa.ugl.lib.umich.edu/chdocs/womenhealth/emotional.html#Stress/

Do you want to quit **smoking**?

http://cancer.med.upenn.edu:80/1s/topics/

If you want to find out about the latest in research for major diseases, try looking up the following:

Cancer

http://www.ncc.go.jp/cnet.html/

Heart disease

http://avnode.wustl.edu//

AIDS

http://gpawww.who.ch/gpahome.htm

If you're a parent, you not only have health questions about yourself, but also about your children. These sites might provide some answers.

Are **childhood immunizations** safe?

gopher://gopher.nlm.nih.gov:70/00/hstat/guide_cps/TEMPgrp12/cps64.txt/

Is there good advice for raising **kids with special needs**?

http://wonder.mit.edu/our-kids.html/

What is **good parenting**?

http://www.portal.com/~cbntmkr/php.html/

If you're disabled or the parent of a disabled child, you might like to glance at the following:

Disabilities and resources for the disabled

http://www.eskimo.com/~jlubin/disabled.html/

Locating well-trained **assistance dogs**

http://grunt.berkeley.edu/cci.html/

Do you need to find specific information on women and health care, women and employment, or women and general resources? Try these sites:

Women's resources

http://sunsite.unc.edu/cheryb/women/

Women's health

http://asa.ugl.lib.umich.edu/chdocs/womenhealth/toc.html/

Stress

http://asa.ugl.lib.umich.edu/chdocs/womenhealth/emotional.html#Stress/

Nutrition

http://asa.ugl.lib.umich.edu/chdocs/womenhealth/physical.html#Nutrition/

Work and the glass ceiling

gopher://gopher.cyberwerks.com:70/11/dataline

The Net is not just a vast information resource. It can also bring parents and children quality time together. The fun begins with:

Playing together on the Internet

http://gagme.wwa.com/~boba/kids.html/

Creating your own **stories**

http://www.cochran.com/tt.html/

Games families play

http://wcl-rs.bham.ac.uk/GamesDomain/

Learning about science in the kitchen. Why does a souffle rise?

http://www.lanl.gov/temp/Education/Contents.html/

Perhaps you are searching for **the perfect family pet**. How about **pygmy pigs, rats, or rabbits**?

http://netvet.wustl.edu//

Maybe you're choosing **your child's college**,

http://www.review.com//

or looking for **a better job** to finance that college tuition.

http://www.iquest.net/Career_Taxi/taxi.html/

While you're traveling the Net, keep an eye out for local wildlife.

You can look at–but don't feed–the different species located at **The Electronic Zoo**

http://netvet.wustl.edu/On:\e-zoo.htm|/

and then giggle at pictures of **froggies**

http://www.cs.yale.edu/HTML/YALE/CS/HyPlans/loosemore-sandra/froggy.html/

or gasp at real **dinosaurs**.

http://www.hcc.hawaii.edu/dinos/dinos.1.html/

What you don't know about Law & Criminal Justice can hurt you. So, you need a lawyer... or do you? Do you need help with adoption? Is your driving record online? Are you interested in the **laws** of:

Israel?

http://www.eenet.ee/english/law/index.html/

Estonia?

http://www.eenet.ee/english/law/index.html/

Do you need help **filing for divorce**?

http://www.Legal.Net (tm)/divorce.htm/

Do you know your **consumer rights**?

http://tsw.ingress.com/tsw/talf/txt/intro.html/

Are you interested in:

Immigration procedures?

http://www.ingress.com/users/tonyb/immigrat/index.htm/

Proposition 187 in California?

http://www.election.ca.gov/e/prop/187/home.html/

A career in law? Visit a **law school** on the Net.

http://www.law.indiana.edu/law/lawother.html/

There is so much information on the Net regarding developments in communications and software that it is difficult to keep up to date. To help you out, try these sites on for size:

Artificial Intelligence

http://http.ici.berkeley.edu/

Telecommunications in Europe

http://www.analysys.co.uk/race.htm

Software for researchers and Internet developers

ftp://ftp.halcyon.com/pub/fluke

The latest from **Apple Computers**

http://www.apple.com/documents/productsupport.html

If you're on a budget, or you like the idea of **Shareware**, you might like this site.

http://www.jumbo.com/

Further Touring

Whew. Quite a trip. Now what? Where do you go from here?

That decision is up to you. But rest assured the McKinley Directory will help you continue on your journey. The McKinley Internet Directory is now available online. Be sure to check out the McKinley Web site for further guidance.

http://www.mckinley.com

Happy Internet touring to you all!

Internet Highlights

APPENDIX A

Attention CyberSpace cadets! If you want to explore Saturn's rings, or discover what makes your heart beat (romantically as well as biologically), your access is right here in the directory.

Throughout the The McKinley Internet Directory you will find a wide variety of short written descriptions of cyberspace sites that we call Internet Highlights. These Internet sites are places you can explore for fun and to get useful information on a wide variety of subjects. The highlights give you only a sample of the types of places you can "visit" to laugh, learn, or pass the time on the world's largest platter of information resources — the Internet.

More than 150 highlights scattered throughout the directory can be found via the Category and Subcategory fields in the directory. A full index of Internet Highlights with accompanying page numbers can be found below.

Arts & Music

Art Galleries	Arts Wire	19
Art Museums	Museums	25
Art Resources	Leonardo (Online)	29
Artists	Hot Pictures	32
Arts Funding	The Smithsonian	35
Electronic Arts	The X-Files	37
Film & Video	Movie Studios	49
Music Genres	Rock Groups	53
Music Genres	Music Soundtracks	55
Musical Groups	Music Listening	75
Performing Arts	TV Soap Operas	93
Visual Arts	Photography Exhibits	97

Business & Economics

Banking	Cash on the Internet	105
Business Schools	London School of Business	107
Career & Employment	JobServe	111
Commerce	Worldwide Yellow Pages	115
Economics	Personal Finance	117
Home Office	Home Office Resources	121
International Business	The World Bank	127
Investment	Trading Cards	129
Non Profits	Charities	135
Publishing	Macmillan Publications	137
Publishing	Magazines	139
Real Estate	World Real Estate	141
Reference	Home Repair	143
Retail	Starting A Business	147
Services	Women and Credit Histories	149

Communications

Communications	800 Numbers	155
Mass Communications	Address/Zip Codes	157
Networking	World Wide Pen Pals	159
Telecommunications	Telephone Numbers/ Zip Codes	167

Computing & Mathematics

Mathematics	Mathematics Software	197
Mathematics	Geometry	199
Organizations	Dictionary of Online Computing Terms	207
Programming	Supercomputers	211
Resouces	Computer Resources	219
Software	System Software Resources	223
Software	Shareware	231

Education

Educational Projects	George Lucas Foundation	245
Government Libraries	World History	251
Language Acquisition	Learning Another Language	253
Primary & Secondary Education	Foreign Language Dictionaries	259
Resources	People of the Past	263
Universities - Canada	Self Defense	269
Universities - U.S.	Dictionaries & Reference Guides	281

Engineering & Technology

Aeronautical Engineering	Aeronautical Engineering	293

Category	Subcategory	Page
Electrical Engineering	Electrical Engineering	295
Engineering	Engineering Companies	297
Environmental Engineering	Environmental Issues	301
Standards	Computer Standards	307
Transportation Engineering	Starship Design	311

Government & Politics

Category	Subcategory	Page
Agencies	CIA's World Fact Book	317
Countries	Library of Congress	333
Countries	Russia	343
Military	Military Resources	349
Policies	Endangered Species	351
Reference	Maps	357
Reference	Weather Services	359
Regions	World Subway Systems	361

Health & Medicine

Category	Subcategory	Page
Alternative Medicine	Alternative Treatments for Cancer	369
Dental Health	Dental FAQs	373
Disabilities	Disabilities Resources	375
Diseases	AIDS Resources	377
Diseases	Your Heart	379
Family Health	Naming Your Newborn	383
Health Conditions	Chiropractic Services	387
Medical Specialties	Medicine and Health	389
Medical Specialties	Emergency Services	391
Medicine	Parenting	393
Organizations	Self Help Guides	395
Personal Care	Nutrition	397
Public Health	Ergonomics	397
Reference	Nutrients and Drugs	403
Resources	Poison Control	407
Sexuality	Sexuality	409

Humanities & Social Sciences

Category	Subcategory	Page
Anthropology	Birthdays	415
Area & Cultural Studies	Islam	417
Area & Cultural Studies	CLNet	419
Area & Cultural Studies	Judaism	421
Classics	Rare Books	423
History	Black/African Resources	425
Library & Information Studies	Madagascar	429
Library & Information Studies	The Holocaust	431
Literature	Books on Tape	437
Literature	Men's Issues	443
Sociology	TV Talk Shows	447
Women's Studies	Women's Issues	449

Internet

Category	Subcategory	Page
Career & Employment	Careers	455
Internet Access	Wish Lists	457
Internet Issues	Etiquette	459
Internet Protocols	Internet Business Center	463
Internet Resources	The McKinley	467
Internet Security	Child Safety on I-Way	469
Internet Services	The Personals	471
Internet Services	Acronyms	473
Internet Services	Shopping	475
Internet Tools	HotJava	479
Online Games	Internet Games	485

Law & Criminal Justice

Category	Subcategory	Page
Business Law	Business Law	491
Family Law	Family Law	493
Intellectual Property	Intellectual Property Rights	495
Law Schools	Law Schools	497
Legal Resources	Legal Resources	499
Litigation & Procedures	Adoptions	501
Reference	Legal References	503
Reference	Finding Your Family	505

Popular Culture & Entertainment

Category	Subcategory	Page
Automobiles	Buying Classic Automobiles	511
Books	Nostradamus	513
Books	Golf Resources	515
Family & Community	Au Pairs & Child Care Providers	519
Family & Community	Planning Your Wedding	521
Fashion	Fashions	523
Genealogy	Horoscopes	525
General Reference	Generation X	527
Humor	Jokes	529
Lifestyles	Anarchy Online	531
Lifestyles	Confession Booths	535
Magazines & Newspapers	Withcraft & the Occult	537
Magazines & Newspapers	Channeling/Astrology	539
Shopping	Flea Markets	547
Television	Television Game Shows	549
Television	Sports	551
Unexplained Phenomena	Ghosts	553
Unexplained Phenomena	UFOs	555

Religion & Philosophy

Category	Subcategory	Page
Doctrines	Religions	559
Mythology	Mythology	561
Philosophy	Philosophy	563
Religions	Christian Resources	564

Science

Category	Subcategory	Page
Agriculture	Flora and Fauna	567
Aquatic Science	The Arctic	569
Astronomy	The Hubble Space Telescope	573
Biology	Women and Science	577
Botony	Antarctic	583
Chemistry	Chemistry on the Internet	585
Earth Sciences	Ecology	591
Environmental Sciences	Recycling	595
Geosciences	Elements Tables	599
Physics	Physics	605
Physics	Physics Education	609
Space Science	Outer Space	613
Zoology	Zoology	615

Sports & Recreation

Category	Subcategory	Page
Aquatic Sports	Scuba Diving	621
Crafts & Hobbies	Finding a Hobby	623
Food & Dining	Recipes	629
Food & Dining	Restaurants Around the World	631
Gardening	Gardening	637
Motor Sports	Car Clubs	639
Outdoor Recreation	Rock Climbing Resources	641
Outdoor Recreation	English Soccer	643
Pets & Animals	Pets	645
Recreation	Adventure Vacations	649
Sports	Caving (Spelunking)	653
Travel & Tourism	Cruise Lines	657
Travel & Tourism	Travel	661
Travel & Tourism	Shopping Abroad	665
Travel & Tourism	Wines and Wineries	669

International Internet Providers

APPENDIX B

The following is an updated and expanded list of commercial Internet service providers. The entries listed below run businesses that provide electronic accounts through which you can access the Internet. The list also includes non-profit community computing services known as "Free-Nets" which are civic computer operations organized under the National Public Telecomputing Network's principles and standards.

This list provides materials about the services that each company provides as well as contact numbers and access information. While some Internet service providers offer full access to all of the resources on the Internet, others offer only limited access or connections. For example, some providers offer only high speed connections, which can be accessed through either leased or dedicated lines and allow for faster data transfer. Similarly, some Internet service providers include access to the World Wide Web only through SLIP, PPP, or TCP/IP connections, while others provide only email, FTP, or basic UNIX Shell accounts. Commercial accounts, such as UUCP, may also differ from individual accounts.

Listings outside of the US are arranged alphabetically by country. Since some companies allow for guest access to their services, we have included access information for dial-in guest logins. Further information and guest access is also often found on company Web sites and these URLs are also provided. Since service prices change often and vary greatly depending on the type of connection, we have not included this information. However, you can receive updated price listings by calling, sending email, or visiting the internet site of these companies using the information in the table.

Below we have also listed several sites on the Internet that provide up to date listings of Internet providers online.

The most comprehensive of these sites is simply called "The List". The URL for the site is provided below.

The List

http://thelist.com

Other lists of international Internet providers can also be found online.

POCIA (Providers of Commercial Internet Access)

http://www.celestin.com/pocia/other.html

Cyberspace Today

http://www.cybertoday.com/cybertoday/ISPs/ispinfo.html

(Listings start on the next page)

Algeria – Austria

COUNTRY	PROVIDER	SERVICES	PHONE NO.	EMAIL ADDRESS	ACCESS/MORE INFORMATION
Algeria	CERIST	TCP/IP	+213 2 792 136	cerist2@cnuce.cnr.it	
	EUnet Algery	Dialup TCP/IP, Mail	+213 2 369 791	Algeria@EU.net	
Argentina	ARNET		+54 1 313 8082	noc-arnet@atina.ar postmaster@atina.ar	
	RECyT		+54 1 312-8917	ebarone@secyt.gov.ar	
	REDUBA		+54 1 783 0729	postmaster@ccc.uba.edu.ar julian@dcfcen.edu.ar	
	RETINA		+54 1 961 1824	rtperez@arcriba.edu.ar	
	SiON Online Services	UUCP, Email, SLIP/PPP	+541 656 9195	info@sion.com.ar	
	Universidad Nacional de la Plata		+54 21 35102	jdiaz@unlp.edu.ar jdiaz@cespivm2.bitnet	
Aruba	Jacobo Oduber	UUCP Email only	+97 297 8 22699	postmaster@arubanet.com	
Australia	Access One	PPP, V.FC/ V.34/ISDN, Virtual Private Networks, Home Pages	+61 1 008 818 391	info@aone.net.au	http://www.aone.net.au/
	AccServ	Shell, UUCP	+61 03 747 9823	info@ppit.com.au	
	APANA (ACT Region)	UUCP, UNIX Shell, Dialup IP, Permanent IP	+61 06 281 4328	act@apana.org.au	http://www.act.apana.org.au/
	Artsnet Australis	SLIP, PPP via Pegasus Networks	+61 18 376 1831	suephil@peg.apc.org	http://www.peg.apc.org/~artsnet
	AUSNet Services Pty Ltd	SLIP, CSLIP, PPP, ISDN, Frame Relay	+61 2 241 5888	sales@world.net	http://www.world.net/
	AUUG	UNIX, UUCP	+61 06 249 2930		
	Australia Online	SLIP, UUCP	+61 03 888 2622	info@ozonline.com.au	
	Ballarat NetConnect Pty Ltd	Gopher, WWW, FTP, Telnet, Usenet, SLIP/PPP, ISDN	+61 53 332 2140	info@netconnect.com.au	http://www.netconnect.com.au/
	Brisnet	USENET, UUCP, Dial-in IP, Permanent IP	+61 015 576 698		
	connect.com.au.pty ltd	UUCP, SLIP/PPP, Virtual Web Service, PSTN, ISDN	+61 3 528 2239 1 800 818 262	connect@connect.com.au	http://www.connect.com.au/
	DIALix	Shell, UUCP, SLIP/PPP	+61 190 229 2004	info@dialix.com	http://www.DIALix.COM/
	Geko	Shell, SLIP/PPP, Dedicated Lines	+61 2 439 1999	info@geko.com.au	http://www.geko.com.au/
	iiNet Technologies Pty Ltd	Shell, SLIP/PPP, UUCP, Leased Lines	+61 9 307 1183 +61 9 332 7770	iinet@iinet.net.au	http://www.iinet.net.au/
	Informed Technology	SLIP, Shell, WWW	+61 9 245 2279	info@it.com.au	http://www.it.com.au/
	Internet Access Australia	Dial-up SLIP, PPP	+61 03 576 4222		
	InterConnect Australia Pty Ltd	SLIP, PPP, WWW	+61 13 528 2239	info@interconnect.com.au	http://www.interconnect.com.au/
	Kralizec Dialup Internet System	Intermittent, Permanent, Volume-charged, Flat Rate	+61 2 837 1397	info@zeta.org.au	
	Magnadata Public Access Internet Services	Commercial SLIP, PPP	+61 02 264 7308		http://magna.com.au
	The Message eXchange TMXP	SLIP, PPP, ISDN	+61 2 550 4448	info@tmx.com.au	http://www.tmx.com.au/
	Microplex Pty Ltd	SLIP, PPP, Leased Lines	+61 2 438 1234	info@mpx.com.au	http://www.mpx.com.au/
	Pegasus	UUCP, Public Access to Pegasus Networks	1 800 812 812 +61 07 257 1111		
	Pro-Net	Dial up Services, Computer News Services	+61 03 349 2266		
	World Reach Pty Ltd	SLIP/PPP, Web Design, UUCP, Permanent Connections, Installations and Consulting	+61 2 436 3588	info@wr.com.au	http://www.wr.com.au/
	Zip Australia Pty. Ltd	SLIP/PPP, Shell	+61 2 482 7015	info@zip.com.au	http://www.zip.com.au/
Austria	ALPIN, Austrian Link to Progressive International Networking	Mail, Telnet, Hytelnet, WWW (Lynx), Gopher, FTP	+43 0662 45 94 54	support@alpin.or.at	http://alpin.or.at/home.html
	ARGE DATEN	Full Internet Access, Mail, FTP, WWW, Dial-in access	+43 1 489 78 93	info@email.ad.or.at	http://www.ad.or.at
	EUnet EDV DienstleistungsGmbH	UUCP, SLIP, PPP, WWW, Leased Line IP, Frame Relay,	+43 1 317 4969	info@Austria.EU.net	http://www.Austria.EU.net/
	LINK-ATU / Medienzentrum der Hochschuelerschaft an der TU Wien	Shell Access, Zerberus Shell (German and English)	+43 1 586 1868	sysop@link-atu.comlink.apc.org	

Austria – Canada **765**

COUNTRY	PROVIDER	SERVICES	PHONE NO.	EMAIL ADDRESS	ACCESS/MORE INFORMATION
Austria (cont.)	PING - Personal InterNet Gate Austria	SLIP, CSLIP, PPP, ISDN, UUCP	+43 1 319 4336	info@ping.at (German)	http://www.ping.at/
	Vianet Austria Ltd	UUCP,WWW, ISDN, SLIP/CSLIP/PPP, Frame Relay,	+43 1 589 2920	info@via.at	http://www.via.at/
Bahamas	CUNET		+1 809 322 2145	KBETHEL@UBAHAMAS.ORG.BS	
Barbados	CUNET		+1 809 425 1310	WILLIAMS@UWICHILL.EDU.BB	
Belarus	BrcMinsk	SLIP	+717 220 6143	admin@brc.minsk.by	
	Byelorussian Academic and Research Network UNIBEL	IP	+717 220 6134	kritsky@ok.minsk.by	http://unibel.by/ gopher://unibel.by/
Belgium	Arcadis	Full Internet PPP, SLIP	+32 02 534 00 11	info@arcadis.be	
	European LookData Network	Internet Access, MCI Mail Access, Minitel, Videotex	+32 2 468 05 47		
	EUnet Belgium	SLIP, CSLIP, PPP, ISDN, Leased Lines	+32 1 623 60 99	sales@Belgium.EU.net	http://www.Belgium.EU.net/
	I-COM	Access in most of Europe, Direct Access in Belgium	+32 2 215 71 30		
	Infoboard Telematics	SLIP, PPP, ISDN Leased Lines, Web Design	+32 2 475 22 99	info@infoboard.be	http://www.ib.be/
	INnet	ISDN	+32 3 281 49 83	info@inbe.net	
	Interpac	Shell, SLIP/PPP, ISDN, Leased Lines	+32 2 646 60 00	info@interpac.be	http://www.interpac.be/
	KnoopPunt Informatie	SLIP, Mail, APC News	+32 233 8155	info@knooppunt.be	http://kikk.knooppunt.be/
	NFE	News, Email, FTP	+32 15 520279	acl@cormy.nfe.be	
	United Callers	TCP/IP based services, Email, Usenet News	+32 50 45 45 70	info@unicall.be best.of@unicall.be	
	SkyNet	Full IP, PPP to 28.8	+32 02 375 86 26	info@skynet.be	http://www.skynet.be
Belize	CUNET		+501 23 27 32	OLDA@UCB.EDU.BZ	
Bermuda	BERMUDANET	X.25, SDLC, X780, 300-1200 bps, 2400-9600 bps	+1 809 296 1800	info@ibl.bm	http://www.ibl.bm
	Internet (Bermuda) Limited	Full Internet Aaccess, SLIP/PPP, Leased Lines	+1 809 296 1800		
Bolivia	Academic and Research Network		+591 1 31 49 90	clifford@unbol.bo	
Brazil	NGO		+55 021 286 4467/ 286-0348	saff@ibase.br	
	Fapesp		+ 55 011 869 1041	demi@fpsp.fapesp.br	
	RNP :Red Nacional de Pesquisa		+55 21 275 9945 (Rio) +55 11 837 0311 (São Paulo)	algold@lncc.br gomide@fpsp.fapesp.br	
Bulgaria	EUnet Bulgaria	SLIP, PPP	+359 52 259135	postmaster@Bulgaria.EU.net	
Burkina Faso	ORSTOM		+228 30 67 37		
Cameroon	ORSTOM		+237 20 15 08		
Canada	Accent Internet	SLIP, PPP, ISDN	+1 514 737 6077	admin@accent.net	http://www.accent.net/
	Achilles Internet Ltd.	Shell, SLIP, PPP, Dedicated Lines	+1 613 723 6624	info@achilles.net	http://www.achilles.net/
	Alberta Research Council	IP, Domain Names	+1 403 450 5179	ARnet@arc.ab.ca	http://titan.arc.ab.ca/~arnet/ index.html
	Alberta SuperNet Inc.	SLIP, Training, Web Pages	+1 403 441 3663	info@supernet.ab.ca	http://www.supernet.ab.ca/
	The Almanac Users Group		+1 604 245 3214	kmcvay@oneb.almanac. bc.ca (Ken McVay)	telnet to io.org or grin.io.org; Login as 'new'
	Astra Network Inc	SLIP/PPP,	+1 204 987 7050	sales@man.net	http://www.man.net
	Atlantic Connect Inc.	SLIP, PPP	+1 902 429 0222 +1 800 661 0222	sales@warp.atcon.com	http://www.atcon.com/
	auroraNET, Inc.	SLIP, PPP, Leased Lines 56K through T1, UUCP, LAN	+1 604 294 4357 x101	sales@aurora.net	http://www.aurora.net/
	A&W Internet Inc.	SLIP, PPP, Leased Lines 56K through T1, ISDN	+1 604 763 1176	info@awinc.com	http://www.awinc.com/
	Barrie Connex Inc.	Shell, SLIP, CSLIP, PPP, ISDN, UUCP, FTP, WWW	+1 705 725 0819	info@bconnex.net	http://www.bconnex.net/
	BCnet	FTP access	+1 604 822 1348	Mke@BC.net (Mike Patterson)	ftp://ftp.bc.net
	CCI Networks	SLIP/PPP, UUCP, ISDN	+1 403 450 6787	info@ccnet.ab.ca	http://www.ccinet.ab.ca/

COUNTRY	PROVIDER	SERVICES	PHONE NO.	EMAIL ADDRESS	ACCESS/MORE INFORMATION
Canada (cont.)	Channel One Internet Services	SLIP, PPP, ISDN, T1, WWW, Consulting Services	+1 613 236 8601	admin@sonetis.com	http://www.sonetis.com/
	Ciao! Free-Net		+1 604 368-6434	kmcclean@first.etc.bc.ca	
	ClicNet Télécommunications Inc.	Dial-Up Shell, PPP, Permanent Connections, WWW	+1 418 686 2542	info@qbc.clic.net	http://www.qbc.clic.net
	Communications Accessibles Montreal	Shell, SLIP/PPP	+1 514 288 2581	info@CAM.ORG	http://www.cam.org/
	Connection MMIC inc.	SLIP, PPP, Leased lines 56K through T1	+1 514 331 6642	michel@connectmmic.net	http://www.connectmmic.net/homemmic.html
	Cyberstore Systems, Inc.	SLIP, PPP, dedicated lines 56K through T1	+1 604 482 3400	info@cyberstore.net	http://www.cyberstore.net/
	Cyberus Online Inc.	Shell, SLIP, PPP, dedicated lines, Consulting	+1 613 233 1215	info@cyberus.ca	http://www.cyberus.ca/
	DataBridge Internet Services	PPP, Email	+1 905 940 1885	info@databridge.com	http://www.databridge.com/
	DataFlux Systems Limited; Pacific Interconnect	SLIP/PPP, Dedicated Lines	+1 604 479 5748	info@pinc.com	http://www.dataflux.bc.ca/home.html
	Debug Computer Services	BBS, UUCP, Shell	+1 403 248 5798	root@debug.cuc.ab.ca	http://198.53.165.200/
	Fairview Technology Centre Ltd.	Dial-up: 300 - 28.8 K, ISDN: 56K, 128K, Shell, PPP	+1 604 498 4316	bwklatt@ftcnet.com	http://www.ftcnet.com/
	GANet	SLIP/PPP, Shell, 28.8k, IDSN, Leased Lines	+1 614 799 3720	info@ganet.net	http://www.ganet.net/
	Helix Internet	SLIP/PPP, Dedicated Lines, Domain Name services	+1 604 689 8544 +1 800 403 1983	info@helix.net	http://www.helix.net/
	HookUp Communications	Shell, SLIP, PPP, UUCP, ISDN	+1 905 847 8000	info@hookup.net	http://www.hookup.net/
	ICE Online	Shell	+1 604 298 4346	info@iceonline.com	
	IGS Information Gateway Services (Cornwall)	Shell, SLIP, PPP, FTP, WWW, Leased Lines 56k through T1	+1 613 930 9942	info@cnwl.igs.net	http://www.cnwl.igs.net/
	IGS Oshawa (Information Gateway Services)	Shell, SLIP, PPP, FTP, WWW, Leased Lines 56k through T1	+1 905 723 2750	ike@osha.igs.net	http://www.osha.igs.net/
	InfoRamp	IP, PPP, UNIX, Shell, Dedicated 28.8/ISDN Dial-in Access	+1 416 363 9100	staff@inforamp.net	
	Info.web	SLIP, PPP, Leased Lines 56K through T1, UUCP, ISDN	+1 613 225 3354	info@magi.com	http://www.infoweb.magi.com/
	Interactive Telecom Inc.	SLIP, PPP, Dedicated Lines, Consulting, Training	+1 613 727 5258	info@intertel.net	http://www.intertel.net/
	Interlog Internet Services	SLIP, PPP and UNIX Shell	+1 416 975 2655	info@interlog.com	http://www.interlog.com/
	Internet Connect Niagara, Inc.	Shell, SLIP, PPP, T1, Dedicated Lines, WWW	+1 905 988 9909	sales@niagara.com	http://www.niagara.com/
	Internet Direct	SLIP, PPP, Leased Lines 56K through ISDN-128K	+1 604 465 2691	info@direct.ca	http://www.direct.ca/
	Internet North	SLIP, PPP, UUCP, Leased Lines, WWW Pages	+1 403 873 5975	info@internorth.com	http://www.internorth.com/
	Internet services and Information systems (isis) Inc	Shell, SLIP, PPP, Dedicated connections	+1 902 429 4747	info@isisnet.com	http://www.isisnet.com/
	Internex Online, Inc.	Shell, WWW, Web Authoring	+1 416 363 8676	info@io.org	http://www.io.org/
	Island Net	SLIP/PPP, UUCP, Dial Up	+1 604 721 6030	info@islandnet.com	http://www.islandnet.com/
	Island Internet Inc.	Shell, CSLIP, SLIP/PPP, Leased Lines 28.8K through T1	+1 604 753 1139	admin@island.net	http://www.island.net/
	Magic Online Services Winnipeg Inc.	SLIP, PPP, UNIX Shell, Leased Lines 56K through T1	+1 204 949 7777	info.magic.mb.ca	http://www.magic.mb.ca/
	Maritime Internet Services	SLIP, PPP, Shell, UUCP, Web Authoring	+1 506 652 3624	info@mi.net	http://www.mi.net/
	Mature Internet	Shell, SLIP/PPP, 28.8K V.34, ISDN, T1		info@mature.com	http://mature.com/
	MCD*Net	Shell, SLIP, PPP	+1 705 523 0243	info@mcd.on.ca	http://www.mcd.on.ca/
	MegaMedia, Inc.	SLIP, PPP, Web Publishing,	+1 913 532 9055	info@mmedia.com	http://www.mmedia.com/
	MGL Systems Internet	SLIP, 56K, T1	+1 519 822 2922	info@mgl.ca	http://www.mgl.ca/
	Mind Link! Communications Corporation	SLIP/PPP, UUCP	+1 604 668 5000	info@mindlink.bc.ca	access.mbnet.mb.ca; Login as 'guest' http://www.mindlink.net/
	National Capital free-Net		+1 613 788 4448	ncf@freenet.carleton.ca	
	NetAxis Inc. of Montreal	PPP, Web Servers/Pages	+1 514 482 8989	info@NetAxis.qc.ca	http://www.NetAxis.qc.ca

COUNTRY	PROVIDER	SERVICES	PHONE NO.	EMAIL ADDRESS	ACCESS/MORE INFORMATION
Canada (cont.)	Net Access Systems		+1 905 524 3010	info@netaccess.on.ca	
	NETinterior ComputerLinks, Ltd.	Shell, UUCP, SLIP, PPP, Leased Lines	+1 604 851 9700 +1 604 851 9704	info@netinterior.com	http://www.netinterior.com
	NetSet Internet Services	Dial-up, Shell, SLIP, PPP, ISDN, Leased Lines	+1 614 527 9111	info@netset.com	http://www.netset.com/
	Networx	Internet Business Solutions/Full Access	+1 905 528 4638	admin@networx.on.ca	http://www.networx.on.ca/
	9 To 5 Communications	Dial Up SLIP/ ISDN	+1 416 363 9100	staff@inforamp.net	http://www.inforamp.net/
	NLnet	SLIP/PPP, Leased Lines 56K-T1	+1 709 737 4555	admin@nlnet.nf.ca	http://www.nlnet.nf.ca
	Nova Scotia Technology Network Inc. (NSTN		+1 902 4686786	info@nstn.ns.ca	http://www.nstn.ca/
	NSTN Incorporated	SLIP, PPP, UUCP, Leased Lines 9600 - T1, WWW	+1 800 848 6786 +1 902 481 6786	info@nstn.ca	http://www.nstn.ca/
	Nucleus Information Service	SLIP, Leased Lines	+1 403 541 9470	markm@nucleus.com	http://www.nucleus.com/
	OA Internet Inc.	Shell, SLIP, PPP, Dial-Up, ISDN, T1 1.544Mbps, Frame Relay, Web Pages	+1 403 430 0811	info@oanet.com	http://www.oanet.com/
	Okanagan Internet Junction	SLIP/PPP, 56K, T1	+1 604 549 1036	info@junction.net	http://www.junction.net/
	ONet Networking	SLIP, PPP, Leased Lines 19.2K to T1	+1 416 978 4589 +1 416 978 0188	info@onet.on.ca	http://www.onet.on.ca/onet
	Resudox Online Services, Inc.	SLIP, PPP	+1 613 567 6925	admin@2resudox.net	http://resudox.net/resudox/mainpage.html
	ServiceTech, Inc.	Shell, Dial-up PPP and SLIP Access, Leased Lines 56K to T1, ISDN	+1 716 263 3360	sales@servtech.com	http://www.servtech.com/
	Spots InterConnect, Inc.	Shell, PPP, ISDN, WWW	+1 403 571 7768	jason@spots.ab.ca	http://www.spots.ab.ca
	Sunshine Net, Inc.	PPP, WWW	+1 604 886 4120	admin@sunshine.net	http://www.sunshine.net/sunshine.html
	Times.net	Shell, SLIP, PPP, Dedicated Lines, Web Publishing	+1 905 775 4471	rfonger@times.net	http://www.times.net/
	Trytel Internet Inc.	Virtual Web Servers, Dial-up Services	+1 613 722 6321	virtual@trytel.com	http://www.trytel.com/
	Unibase Telecom Ltd.	SLIP/PPP, Leased Lines, WWW Services	+1 306 789 9007	milton@unibase.unibase.com	http://www.unibase.com/
	UUNET-Canada, Inc.	Dial Up, Dedicated Lines, ISDN, WWW	+1 416 368 6621 1 800 463 8123	info@uunet.ca	http://www.uunet.ca/
	WEB	Email, Direct Dial, Conferences, Internet Access	+1 416 596 0212	outreach@web.apc.org	http://www.web.apc.org/webhome.html
	Whistler Networks	PPP, Leased Lines up to T1, DNS, WWW, LAN	+1 604 932 0606	webmaster@whistler.net	http://www.whistler.net/
	Wimsey Information Services	SLIP, PPP, Leased Lines 56K through T1, UUCP, WWW	+1 604 936 8649 +1 604 257 1111	admin@wimsey.com	http://www.wimsey.com/
Caribbean	Caribbean Internet Service, Corp.	Shell, SLIP, PPP	+1 809 728 3992	kmarazzi@caribe.net	http://www.caribo.not/
Chile	Infotrade		+56 2 204 4903		
	RdC S.A. - CHILE, Latin America	SLIP, PPP	+56 2 000 2404	info@mailnet.rdc.cl	http://mailnet.rdc.cl/
	Reuna, Chilean Internet Provider	SLIP, Leased Lines	+56 2 2740403	info@reuna.cl	http://www.reuna.cl
	UNIRED		+56 2 552 2375 (A4908)	ffuentes@tolten.puc.cl	
China	IHEP/CINET (China InterNETworking discussion group)	UUCP, Dedicated Lines		xurs@bepc2.ihep.ac.cn	http://solar.rtd.utk.edu/~china/network/china_network.html
Colombia	Telecom		+57 1 281 9041		
	SAITEL	Full Internet Access	+57 1 334 8149	hcaballe@itecs3.telecom-co.net	
Congo	ORSTOM		+242 83 26 80		
Costa Rica	Red Nacional de Investigacion CRNet		+506 25 59 11	gdeter@ns.cr	
	Fundacion Nahual		+506 22 17 30	hope@huracan.cr	
	Radiografica Costarricense	Shell, TIA, SLIP Leased Line up to 64 Kbps, Dial up	+506 287 0087	mercadeo@sol.racsa.co.cr	http://www.racsa.co.cr
Croatia	CARNet	Shell, SLIP, CSLIP, PPP	+385 146 1431	helpdesk@CARNet.hr	http://www.CARNet.hr/

COUNTRY	PROVIDER	SERVICES	PHONE NO.	EMAIL ADDRESS	ACCESS/MORE INFORMATION
Cuba	CENIAI		+537 62 65 65	jemar@ceniai.cu	
Czech Republic	EUnet Slovakia	UUCP, SLIP, PPP, IP/X.25, Leased Line, WWW	+42 7 725 306	info@Slovakia.EU.net	http://www.eunet.sk/
	ECONNECT		+42 02 66710 366	sysop@ecn.gn.apc.org	
Denmark	Danadata	PPP, ISDN	+45 70 10 80 80	info@danadata.dk	http://www.danadata.dk/
	DKnet	UUCP, SLIP/PPP, WWW	+45 39 17 99 00	info@dknet.dk	http://www.dknet.dk/DKnet/
	Internet Consult	UUCP, Personal IP	+45 32 47 33 55	info@ic.dk	
Dominican Republic	REHRED			sjb@acn.miami.com	
	REDID Red Dominicana de Intercambio para el Dessarrollo		+1 809 535 2422 +1 809 535-6614	pimienta!daniel@redid.org.do	
Ecuador	Ecuanex	UUCP, Fax Info-Servers	+593 2 227 014	intercom@ecuanex.ec	
Egypt	RitseCom	SLIP, Terminal Emulation	+20 2 340 3538	tkamel@ritsec.com.eg	http://ritsec_www.com.eg/
	EUnet Egypt	Dialup TCP/IP, Mail	+20 2 355 7253	ow@estinet.uucp	
	Egyptian National STI Network		+20 2 355 7253	mb@estinet.uucp	
Estonia	Ants Work		+372 007 0142	ants@ioc.ee	
	EENet	UUCP, SLIP, PPP, Leased Lines	+372 743 3635	eenet@eenet.ee	http://www.eenet.ee/
	Esdata Ltd	SLIP, CSLIP, PPP, UUCP, Dial Up, Leased Lines	+372 639 7025	esdata@estnet.ee	http://www.estnet.ee/
Ethiopia	PADIS, Pan African Development Information System	Terminal, UUCP	+251 1 511 167	sysop@padis.gn.apc.org	
Finland	Clinet Ltd.	PPP, Leased Lines	+358 437 5209	clinet@clinet.fi	http://www.clinet.fi/
	ComPart	SLIP, Frame Relay	+358 506 3329	uffe@pcb.compart.fi	http://www.compart.fi/
	EUnet Finland		+358 0 400 2060		
France	CalvaNet	Dial up, Full IP	+33 1 34 63 19 19	rcil@Calvacom.fr	
	DataStar Dialog Europe		+33 1 46 67 78 78	dialog-info@ans.net	
	ECHO		+33 1 41 25 12 12		telnet echo.lu
	EUnet France	UUCP, PPP, ISDN, LAN LL, WWW	+33 1 53 81 60 60	info@EUnet.fr	http://www.EUnet.fr/
	FRANCENET	Shell, Dial Up SLIP, PPP, Full Access	+33 1 40 61 01 76	info@francenet.fr	http://www.Francenet.fr
	Internet-Way	PPP V34, ISDN, LAN, LL, WWW	+33 1 41 43 21 10	info@iway.fr	http://www.iway.fr/
	OLEANE	PPP. ISDN, LAN, LL	+33 1 43 28 32 32	info@oleane.net	http://www.oleane.net/
	Questel		+33 1 46 15 55 55	p.buffet@dm.rs.ch	
	TEASER	Email, Usenet	+33 1 46261510	jcmichot@teaser.com	
	WorldNet	SLIP, PPP, CSLIP	+33 1 40 37 90 90	info@worldnet.net	http://www.worldnet.net/
Georgia	SASKO		+7 8832 955 399	kisho@sanet.ge	
Germany	ARANEA Internet Partner GmbH	Netsurf - Single PPP, Dial up full IP	+49 61 015 35 50	info@ARANEA.net	http://www.ARANEA.net/
	bbTT Electronic Networks GmbH	SLIP, IP, ISDN	+49 30 817 50 99	info@b-2.de.contrib.net	http://www.bbtt.com/
	CUBENet	Dial Up, Full Access, ISDN Leased Lines, Shell, UUCP, PPP, WWW	+49 89 140 16 35	info@cube.net	
	Erlangen Free-Net	Free-Net Telnet Services	+ 49 09 131 85 47 35	gast@freenet-a.fim.uni-erlangen.de	(604) 689-8577, V.32bis; Login as 'gast'
	DFN-Verein		+49 30 88 42 99 22	dfn-verein@dfn.d400.de	http://www.dfn.de/dfn/dfn-gs.html
	ECRC GmbH	ISDN Dial UP, Leased lines	+49 89 92 69 90	internet@ecrc.de	
	EUNet Germany	Dial Up, ISDN, Frame Relay, Leased line	+49 231 972 00	info@Germany.EU.net	
	Individual Network-Rhein-Main	TCP/IP, UUCP	+49 69 390 484 13, +49 69 631 20 83	ip-admins@rhein-main.de	telnet to mindlink.bc.ca; Login as 'guest' http://www.rhein.de/IN/index.html
	INTERACTIVE NETWORK INFORMATIONSSYSTEME	Dial Up, ISDN, WWW, UUCP, PPP, SLIP, WWW	+49 69 59 74 099	johnny@interactive.nacamar.de	
	iMNet	UUCP,IP over ISDN, SLIP/CSLIP/ PPP, WWW Advertising	+49 931 6191 191	info@iM.Net	http://www.iM.Net/
	Netzwerk und Telematic GmbH, Geschaeftsbereich Xlink	IP, ISDN, UUCP	+49 721 96 520	info@xlink.net	http://www.xlink.net/

COUNTRY	PROVIDER	SERVICES	PHONE NO.	EMAIL ADDRESS	ACCESS/MORE INFORMATION
Germany (cont.)	Onlineservice Nuernberg	Mail/News/IP with SLIP or PPP by Modem or ISDN	+49 911 3781 100	info@osn.de	http://www.osn.de/
	PING e.V.	SLIP, CSLIP, PPP, UUCP, Webspace	+49 231 9791 0	info@ping.de	http://www.ping.de/
Ghana	Chonia Informatica		+233 21 669420	info@osagyefo.ghana.net	http://rzunextbet1.unizh.ch/
Greece	FORTHnet	Dial-Up IP, UUCP, Leased Lines	+30 81 391200	pr@forthnet.gr	http://www.forthnet.gr/
	Ariadne	Dial Up service	+30 1 65 13 392		http://www.ariadne-t.gr
Guatemala	MayaNet (Research and Academic Network)		+502 2 69 07 91 al 95	furlan@uvg.gt	
Honduras	CAD Sistemas		+504 57 55 59		
Hong Kong	HKIGS	SLIP, CSLIP, PPP	+852 2527 4888	draw@hk.net	http://www.hk.net/
	Hong Kong Supernet	SLIP/PPP	+852 2358 7924	info@HK.Super.NET	http://www.hk.super.net/
	Internet Online Hong Kong		+852 768 8008	info@iohk.com	
Hungary	EUnet Hungary	UUCP, Shell, SLIP/PPP	+36 1 2698281	info@Hungary.EU.net	http://www.eunet.hu/
Iceland	Centrum.is	PPP, Leased Lines	+354 562 4111	info@centrum.is	http://www.centrum.is
	EUNet Iceland	Dial Up, EMail, TCP/IP	+354 1 694747	postmaster@Iceland.EU.net	
India	aXcess Online Services	Value-Added Online Services: Email etc.	+91 22 493 7676	sharad@axcess.net.in	
	Live Wire! BBS	FidoNet, UUCP	+91 22 577 1111	support@f1.n606.z6.fidonet.org	
	Software Technology Parks of India	High Speed Data Communication Facilities, Full Internet Connectivity		webmaster@stph.net	http://www.stph.net/index.html
	Videsh Sanchar Nigam Limited	Full Internet Connectivity, Email, 2400 bps Dialup - 128K Leased Lines	+91 22 262 4020		
	ERNET	Full Internet Services, 64K Lease lines	+91 22 436 1329	usis@doe.ernet.in	http://shakti.ncst.ernet.in/ernet
	INDIALINK BOMBAY	Full Internet Services	+91 22 262 2388	mki@inbb.gn.apc.org	
	INDIALINK DELHI	Full Internet Services	+91 11 463 5096	leo@unv.ernet.in	
Indonesia	PT IndoInternet		+62 21 727 0162	postmaster@UI.AC.ID	
	Information via Telecom and Satellites	UUCP, SLIP/PPP	+25 519 744-5553	jman@infosat.com	
Ireland	Cork Internet Services, Ltd.	Shell, UUCP, SLIP, PPP, ISDN	+353 21 277 124	info@cis.ie	http://www.cis.ie
	Ireland OnLine	Shell, UUCP, ISDN SLIP/CSLIP/PPP, Leased Lines, WWW	+353 1 855 1739	sales@iol.ie	http://www.iol.ie
	IEunet Ltd	Dial Up IP, WWW, FTP, SLIP, PPP	+353 1 679 0832	info@ieunet.ie info@Ireland.eu.net	
Israel	DataServe Internet services	Shell, SLIP, PPP	+972 3 647 4448	info@datasrv.co.il	
	elroNet	SLIP/PPP, WWW	+1 212 935 3110, +972 4 545 042	info@elron.net	http://www.elron.net/
	NetVision Ltd.	PPP, Dial Up, WWW, Gopher, FTP, Usenet	+972 4 550 330	info@netvision.net.il	http://www.netvision.net.il/
Italy	Abacom s.a.s	SLIP, PPP, ISDN, Dedicated Lines	+39 434 660 911	glatzm@system.abacom.it	http://www.abacom.it.
	D3 Net	Email, WWW, SLIP, ISDN, Full Access	+39 51 521 285	dsnet@dsnet.it	
	I.NET S.p.A.	UUCP, SLIP, CSLIP, PPP, ISDN, Frame Relay, Leased Lines	+39 2 2616 2261	info@inet.it	http://www.inet.it/
	ITnet	SLIP,PPP,ISDN,Frame Relay, X.25	+39 10 6503 641	info@IT.net	http://www.IT.net/
	ItalNet	SLIP, PPP, Access Provider, Consulting, Publishing	+39 142 456 566	info@italnet.it	http://www.italnet.it/italweb
	NETTuno service	SLIP, CSLIP, PPP, ISDN , Frame Relay, Hardwired Lines	+39 51 65 99423 +39 51 65 99411	staff@nettuno.it	http://www.nettuno.it/
	TELNET	Email, WWW, SLIP/PPP, Full Access	+39 382 529 751	info@telnetwork.it	
Ivory Coast	Orstom		+225 24 37 79		
Jamaica	CUNET		+1 809 927 2781	manison@uwimona.edu.jm	
Japan	APICNET		+81 3 3204 8104	kaneko@apic.or.jp richard@apic.or.jp	http://www.apic.or.jp

COUNTRY	PROVIDER	SERVICES	PHONE NO.	EMAIL ADDRESS	ACCESS/MORE INFORMATION
Japan (cont.)	Global OnLine Japan	Shell, PPP, ISDN, Leased Lines, WWW	+81 3 5330 9380	info@gol.com	http://www.gol.com/
	InfoWeb		+81 3 3437 5256	info-staff@web.ad.jp	http://www.web.jp
	Internet Initiative Japan, Inc. (IIJ)	UUCP, PPP	+81 3 5276 6241	info@iij.ad.jp	http://www.iij.ad.jp/
	RIMNET	PPP, Dedicated Line, Dial-up, UUCP	+81 3 5489 5655	ppp-info@st.rim.or.jp	http://www.st.rim.or.jp/
	Twics	Shell, PPP, UUCP, ISDN	+81 3 3351 5977	info@twics.com	http://www.twics.com
Kazakhstan	RelcomSL Stock Co.	SLIP, CSLIP, UUCP	+7 322 262 4990	mailserv@relcom.kz	http://www.relcom.kz/
Kenya	ELCI		+254 2 562 015	sysop@elci.gn.apc.org	
Korea	Dacom	Shell, SLIP/PPP, Dedicated Lines	+82 2 220 5203	help@bora.dacom.co.kr	http://www.dacom.co.kr/
	KORNET (Korea Telecom)	Shell, SLIP/PPP	+82 2 766 5900-2	info@kornet.nm.kr	http://www.kornet.nm.kr/
	NuriNet		+82 2 538 6941	info@inet.co.kr	
Kuwait	Gulfnet Kuwait	Shell, TIA, SLIP/PPP	+965 242 6728	info@kuwait.net	http://www.kuwait.net/
Latin America	ITINET	Basic Internet Connection, Email	+1 305 674 1001	iti@itinet.net	http://itinet.net
Latvia	Balcom	Email, News, UUCP, Shell	+371 342 5200	info@kurz.lv	
	Elcom	Email, News, UUCP, Shell	+371 54 35425	postmaster@latg.lv	
	LvNet-Teleport	UUCP, Shell, SLIP/PPP, Fax-Gate	+371 2 551133	info@lvnet.lv	Login as "guest" http://www.lvnet.lv
	VERSIA Ltd.	Email, News, Shell, UUCP, SLIP, PPP	+371 2 417000	postmaster@vernet.lv	http://www.vernet.lv
Liechtenstein	Ping Net	PPP, Leased Lines, WWW Page Rental, UUCP	+41 768 5316	admin@ping.ch	http://www.ping.li/
Lithuania	AIVA SYSTEM		+370 0122 227905 +370 0122 227825	all@aiva.lt	
	JSV "ELNETA"		+370 0122 22 7905	root@elnet.lt	
	State Enterprise InfoCentras	UUCP, Shell, SLIP, CSLIP, PPP	+370 7 706 952	postmaster@lira.lt	
Luxembourg	Europe Online S.A.	SLIP, PPP, Leased Lines	+352 40 101 226	inet-sales@eo.net	http://www.eo.net/
	EUnet Luxembourg	Dial Up IP, Mail	+352 470261 361	postmaster@Luxembourg.EU.net	
Madagascar	Orstom		+261 23 30 98		
Malaysia	Jaring Net-Malaysia	General Internet	+603 254 9601	noc@jaring.my	http://www.jaring.my/
Mali	Orstom		+223 22 43 05		
Mexico	Giga-Com S.A. de C.V.	WWW, FTP, Telnet, Gopher, SLIP, PPP	+52 8 336 6260	info@mail.giga.com	http://www.giga.com/
	Internet de Mexico	SLIP Connections up to 14,400 bps	+52 5 360 2931	info@mail.internet.com.mx	http://www.internet.com.mx
	Mundo Internet	SLIP	+52 99 81 29 60 Ext. 227, 228	webmaster@kin.cieamer.conacyt.mx	http://w3mint.cieamer.conacyt.mx/
	REPCOM DE MEXICO	Full Internet Access, SLIP/PPP	+52 5 211 2282	silviav@ci.seinet.net.mx	
	SPIN	Full Internet Connectivity, Shell, SLIP, PPP, Dialup and Dedicated Access	+52 5 628 6220	info@spin.com.mx	
Nepal	Mercantile Office Systems		+977 1 220773	kgautam@mosnepal.ernet.in	
The Netherlands	bART	Full Access, SLIP/PPP	+31 70 345 5349	info@bart.nl	http://www.bart.nl
	De Digitale Stad	Freenet, Mail	+31 20 620 0294	helpdesk@dds.hacktic.nl	
	EUnet	Internet services in 38 countries	+31 20 592 5124	info@eu.net	http://www.eu.net/
	GDS	UUCP, Email, Usenet	+31 36 536 1683	henk@hgatenl.hobby.nl	
	Hobbynet	SLIP, CSLIP	+31 36 536 1683	info@hobby.nl	http://www.hobby.nl/
	Internet Access Foundation - The Netherlands	SLIP, ISDN (64 Kbit), UUCP, WWW	+31 15 566 108	info@iaf.nl	http://www.iaf.nl/
	NetLand Internet Services	Shell, SLIP, PPP, WWW	+31 20 694 3664	info@netland.nl	http://www.netland.nl/
	Openworld Foundation	IP, SLIP/PPP, Mail, News, UUCP, UNIX	+31 17 204 0005	info@ow.org staff@ow.org	
	Stichting DataWeb	SLIP, CSLIP, PPP, ISDN	+31 70 381 9218	info@dataweb.nl	http://www.dataweb.nl/
New Zealand	Actrix	PPP, Usenet, BBS	+64 4 4991122	john@actrix.gen.nz actrix.gen.nz guest	http://www.actrix.gen.nz/
	Internet Company of New Zealand	SLIP, UUCP	+64 9 358 1186	info@iconz.co.nz	http://www.es.co.nz/
	Lynx Internet	PPP, Shell, UUCP	+64 3 3790 568	info@lynx.co.nz	http://www.lynx.co.nz/
Nicaragua	UniComp	SLIP, PPP, UUCP	+505 2 783142	computo@uni.ni	
	Nicarao		+505 2 621312	ayuda@nicarao.apc.org	

COUNTRY	PROVIDER	SERVICES	PHONE NO.	EMAIL ADDRESS	ACCESS/MORE INFORMATION
Nicaragua (cont.)	RAIN		+505 2 670274	yadira@uni.ni	
Niger	Orstom		+227 73 20 54		
Norway	DAXNET	ISDN, SLIP, UUCP	+47 22 74 06 20	daxnet@datametrix.no	http://www.datametrix.no/
	HIB-INFONET	Shell, SLIP, Leased Lines	+47 55 54 37 86	info@vestnett.no	http://www.vestnett.no/vestnett/
	NORDnett		+47 75 02 33 98	info@nordnett.no	http://www.nordnett.no/
	Oslonett	Shell, SLIP, PPP, UUCP, ISDN	+47 22 46 10 99	info@oslonett.no	http://www.oslonett.no/
	PowerTech Information Systems Inc.	All types of connections	+47 22 20 33 30	info@powertech.no	http://www.powertech.no/
	Telepost Communications	X.400, Internet Connections	+47 22 73 37 00	firmapost@telepost.telemax.no	http://www.telepost.no
Pakistan	Brain Computer Services	UUCP, PPP	+92 42 541 4444	info@brain.com.pk	http://singnet.com.sg/~brains/
	IMRAN-NET / IMRAN GROUP	Email, WWW, FTP, Domain Name Service	+92 42 583 0847	imran@nargis.imran.com	
Panama	COMMNET Co.		+507 263 4513		
	Universidad de Panama		+507 644242	barragan@huracan.cr	
	Universidad Tecnologica de Panama		+507 641771	vLopez@Huracan.cr	
Paraguay	Digital Electronics Laboratory (L.E.D.)	UUCP	+595 21 334 650	info@ledip.py	
	TELNET, S.A.		+595 21 20 0913		
Peru	Red Cientifica Peruana	Full Service Internet Provider	+511 445 5168	operador@rcp.net.pe	http://www.rcp.net.pe/
Philippines	Email Centre		+632 921 9976	sysop@phil.gn.apc.org	
Portugal	EUnet Portugal	UUCP, SLIP, CSLIP, PPP, ISDN, Leased Lines	+351 1 294 2844	info@puug.pt info@Portugal.EU.net	http://www.Portugal.EU.net/ http://www.puug.pt/
	Telepac Servicos de Telecomunicacoes		+351 1 790 7000	henrique@telepac.pt	
Puerto Rico	Caribbean Internet Service	Dial-in Access, Shell Accounts, SLIP, PPP, Dedicated Lines up to T1	+1 809 728 3992	webmaster@caribe.net	
	CRACIN		+1 809 759 6891	ERivera@mxruc.clu.net	
	CUNET		+1 809 798 2040	jmelen@uamer.clu.net	
Romania	EUnet Romania SRL	Email, UUCP/POP3, TCP/IP	+40 1 312 6886	info@Romania.EU.net	http://www.Romania.EU.net/
	LOGIC	X.25 Protocol	+40 1 617 6333 +40 92 44 6652	Tudor.Panaitescu @alliance-partners.sprint.com	
	PUB net		+40 1 631 4010 ext 387	nini@pub.ro	
	ROEARN net		+40 1 665 2585	estaicut@roearn.ici.ro	
Russia	Demos Plus	Email, UUCP, Usenet, TCP/IP Services, Terminal Access	+7 095 233 0512 +7 095 231 21229	info@demos.su	
	EUnet URSS	Dialup Internet Access (TCP/IP Based Services), Mail	+7 095 198 3796	postmaster@USSR.EU.net	
	GlasNet Computer Network Users Association	SLIP, CSLIP, PPP, UUCP, Terminal Access	+07 095 262 7079	infobooth@glas.apc.org	http://www.glas.apc.org/
	Inforis Co., Ltd	UUCP, Email, Host Dial-up, SLIP, PPP	+7 8312 397562	support@inforis.nnov.su	http://www.inforis.nnov.su/
	InterCommunications, LTD	Dial-up SLIP, LL-19.2k, UUCP	+7 8632 620562	postmaster@icomm.rnd.su	http://www.icomm.ru/
	Relcom/EUnet	UUCP, EMail, SLIP, CSLIP	+7 095 9434735	postmaster@ussr.EU.net	http://www.relcom.EU.net/
	Tambov Center of New Information Technologies	SLIP, CSLIP, PPP	+7 0752 220735	postmaster@tixm.tambov.su	http://www.tixm.tambov.su/
Saint Lucia	CUNET		+1 809 452 3702 +1 809 452 1802	adaniel@isis.org.lc	
Senegal	Orstom		+221 32 34 76		
	MMET Projet RINAF		+221 23 70 68		
Seychelles	Orstom		+248 247 42		
Singapore	Singapore Telecom	Personal IP, Full Access, Terminal, UUCP, WWW	+65 730 8079	sales@singnet.com.sg	http://www.singnet.com.sg/
	National University of Singapore		+65 772 2073	ccethio%nusvm.bitnet @CUNYVM.CUNY.EDU	
Slovakia	EUnet Slovakia	Dialup, Leased line, X.25 (TCP/IP), Mail, News, Shell, FTP, gopher, WWW, UUCP, SLIP, PPP	+42 7 725306 +42 7 377434	info@Slovakia.EU.net	http://www.eunet.sk
Slovenia	K2.net, ABM Ltd.	Shell, SLIP, CSLIP, IP, UUCP, WWW	+386 61 125 0325	info@k2.net	http://www.abm.si/, http://www.k2.net/

COUNTRY	PROVIDER	SERVICES	PHONE NO.	EMAIL ADDRESS	ACCESS/MORE INFORMATION
Slovenia (cont.)	SInet, EUnet/Slovenia, NIL Ltd.	Shell, SLIP/PPP, Leased IP	+386 61 1405 183	info@eunet.si	http://www.eunet.si/
	YUNAC		+386 61 159 199	jerman-blazic@ijs.ac.mail.yu	
South Africa	Aztec Information Management	Shell, SLIP, PPP, UUCP, WWW	+27 21 419 2690	info@aztec.co.za	http://www.aztec.co.za/
	Commercial Internet Services	SLIP, CSLIP, PPP Leased Lines, Consulting	+27 12 841 2892	info@cis.co.za	http://www.cis.co.za/
	Internet Africa	SLIP, PPP, Leased Lines, Frame Relay	0800 020003 (Local); +27 21 683 4370 (international)	info@iafrica.com	http://www.iafrica.com/iafrica/home.html
	Internet Access	UNIX Shell, SLIP, PPP, UUCP, Leased Lines, WWW	+27 21 683 4370	info@iaccess.za	http://www.netline.co.za
	Netline	UNIX Shell, Full Internet Access, Dial-Up SLIP/PPP	+27 011 886 0586	faheem@netlunx.netline.co.za	
	SANGONeT: South Africa's Nonprofit Information and Communications Network	Shell	+27 11 838 6943	sn-info@wn.apc.org	
Spain	bitMailer Online	PPP, Web Creation, Leased Lines, ISDN, Internet Security	+34 1 402 15 51	info@bitmailer.com	http://www.bitmailer.com/
	ENCOMIX	Email, News, UUCP, Full Access, Shell, SLIP, PPP, ISDN	+34 76 556714	sysadmin@encomix.com	
	Goya Servicios Telematicos - EUnet Spain	SLIP, CSLIP, PPP, ISDN, Web Consulting, Leased Lines	+34 1 413 4856	tarifas@eunet.es	http://www.eunett.es/
	SERVICOM	SLIP, PPP, Leased Lines	+34 3 580 9396	jhendler@servicom.es	http://www.servicom.es
Sri Lanka	Lanka Internet Services, Ltd.	SLIP, PPP, Leased Lines	+94 71 30469	info@lanka.net	http://www.lanka.net
Sweden	AlgoNet Sweden	Email, News, DIal Up, IP, SLIP	+46 8 799 30 11	info@algonet.se	
	Bahnhof Internet Access	Full Access, Unix shell, POP (SLIP, CSLIP), WWW pages	+46 18 100899	info@bahnhof.se	http://www.bahnhof.se/
	NetG/ TerraTel	PPP, UUCP, Web pages, Full Access	+46 031 280373	info@netg.se	http://www.netg.se/
Switzerland	EUnet	Leased lines, SLIP/PPP, WWW	+41 1 291 45 80 (German) +41 22 348 80 45 (French)	info@eunet.cj	http://www.eunet.ch//
	Fastnet Sarl	PPP, Leased Lines	+41 21 324 06 76	info@fastnet.ch	http://www.fastnet.ch/
	Internet ProLink	PPP, Leased Lines, Web Page	+41 22 788 8555	info@iprolink.ch	http://www.iprolink.ch/
	Ping Net	PPP, Leased Lines, WWW Pages, UUCP	+41 1 768 5316 +41 21 641 13 39	admin@ping.ch	http://www.ping.ch/
	SWITCH - Swiss Academic & Research Network	SLIP, PPP, Leased Lines	+41 1 268 1515	info@switch.ch	http://www.switch.ch/
Taiwan	Institute for Information industry	SLIP, PPP, Leased Lines, Terminal mode	+886 02 733 6454	service@tpts1.seed.net.tw	http://www.seed.net.tw/
	Pristine	Shell, PPP	+886 2 368 9023	tammy@pristine.com.tw	http://www.pristine.com.tw/
	SeedNet	Full Internet Access	+886 02 733 8779 +886 035 773311 ext512 +886 07 339 4105	service@tpts1.seed.net.tw service@shts.seed.net.tw service@ksts.seed.net.tw	
Thailand	CCAN	Computer Communication Access for NGOs	+66 2 255 5552, +66 2 251 0704		
	Thaisarn Internet Service at NECTEC		+66 2 248 8007	sysadmin@nwg.nectec.or.th	http://www.nectec.or.th/
Togo	Orstom		+228 21 43 44		
Trinidad	CUNET		+1 809 628 8523	LARS_J@NIHERST.GOV.TT	
Tunisia	IRSIT/EUnet Tunisia	SLIP, CSLIP, PPP, IP	+216 1 800 122	info@Tunisia.EU.net	http://gopher.rnrt.tn/
Turkey	TUVAKA		+90 51 887228	Esra@ege.edu.tr	
Uganda	MUKLA	Terminal, Email, UUCP	+256 41 532 479	sysop@mukla.gn.apc.org	
Ukraine	Apex Network Centre	Email and Usenet News via UUCP Dial-up, Shell	+7 0562 476995	vaget@apex.dnepropetrovsk.ua	
	Communication Company Lucky Net Ltd.	Shell, UUCP, SLIP/PPP, Leased Lines	+7 44 290 04 38	info@lucky.net	http://www.lucky.net/
	Crimean Communication Centre	SLIP, T1 Lines	+7 652 257214	sem@snail.crimea.ua	http://www.elis.crimea.ua/
	CS/MONOLIT Network Centre	Email and Usenet News via UUCP Dial-up, Shell	+7 044 2959080	info@UA.NET	

Ukraine – Zimbabwe

COUNTRY	PROVIDER	SERVICES	PHONE NO.	E MAIL ADDRESS	ACCESS/MORE INFORMATION
Ukraine (cont.)	GlasNet-Ukraine Ltd	Email and Conferencing	+7 044 266 9481	support@gluk.apc.org	
	Small Venture DKT Ltd	SLIP, PPP, Dial Up	+7 380 572 445 708	postmaster@rocket.kharkov.ua	
	UkrCom-Plus	Email	+7 380 55 22 6 40 98	mailserv@ukrcom.kherson.ua	
United Kingdom	Absolute Communications Ltd.	Mail, News, SLIP, Leased lines	+44 116 233 0033	sales@foobar.co.uk	
	AirTime Internet Resources Ltd UK	SLIP, PPP, BBS	+44 1254 676921	sales@airtime.co.uk	http://www.airtime.co.uk/
	Aladdin	SLIP, PPP, WWW, ISDN, PSTN, Leased Lines	+44 1489 782221	info@aladdin.co.uk	http://www.aladdin.co.uk/
	CityScape	Shell, SLIP, PPP	+44 1223 566950	sales@ns.cityscape.co.uk	
	CONNECT — PC User GROUP	Email, News, WWW, FTP, Telnet, Gopher, UUCP	+44 181 863 1191	info@ibmpcug.co.uk	http://www.ibmpcug.co.uk
	CIX (Compulink Information eXchange)	Conferencing, Email, Full Access	+44 181 390 8446	cixadmin@cix.compulink.co.uk	http://www.compulink.co.uk/ (719) 632-4111; Login as 'newuser'
	Delphi Internet	Dial Up, FTP, Gopher, Usenet, Email, IRC, Telnet, WWW	+44 171 757 7080	UKSERVICE@DELPHI.COM	
	Demon Internet	Dial Up SLIP/PPP, WWW	+44 181 371 1234	internet@demon.co.uk	http://www.demon.co.uk/
	Direct Connection	TCP/IP, UUCP, Email, Usenet News, Telnet, FTP, WWW	+44 181 317 0100	helpdesk@dircon.co.uk	
	Easynet	SLIP, PPP, WWW, Leased Lines	+44 171 209 0990	admin@easynet.co.uk	http://www.easynet.co.uk/
	EUnet GB Ltd	SLIP, PPP, UUCP	+44 1227 266466	sales@Britain.EU.net	http://www.britain.eu.net/
	Foobar Internet	SLIP, ISDN, Web Design	+44 116 233 0033	sales@foobar.co.uk	http://www.foobar.co.uk/
	Frontier Internet Services	SLIP, PPP, Web Design	+44 171 242 3383	info@ftech.net	http://www.ftech.net/
	GreenNet	SLIP, Email, Conferencing	+44 171 713 1941	support@gn.apc.org	http://www.gn.apc.org/
	Hiway	SLIP, PPP, Dial In	+44 1635 550660	info@inform.hiway.co.uk	http://www.hiway.co.uk/
	MatriX Publishing Network	Full Access to 128 ISDN	+44 171 316 9291	info@mpn.com	http://www.mpn.com
	Mistral Internet	SLIP, PPP	+44 1273 708866	info@mistral.co.uk	http://www.mistral.co.uk
	NETHEAD	Email, TCP/IP PPP Dial-up, Web Design	+44 171 207 1100	info@nethead.co.uk	http://www.nethead.co.uk/
	On-line Entertainment Ltd	SLIP, WWW, Air Warrior, Armoured Assault, Mud, Federation, TV-Net, Forum, Britnet	+44 181 558 6114	mike@mail.on-line.co.uk	http://on-line.co.uk/
	ONYX Internet Service	Email, WWW, FTP, News	+44 1642 210 087	Support@octacon.co.uk	http://www.octacon.co.uk
	PC User Group/WinNET Communications	SLIP, PPP, CSLIP, UUCP, WWW, BBS	+44 181 863 1191	request@win-uk.net	http://www.ibmpcug.co.uk/
	PIPEX (Public IP Exchange Limited)	Shell, SLIP, PPP, WWW, UUCP, ISDN	+44 1223 250 120	sales@pixet.net	http://worldserver.pipex.com/
	Sound & Vision BBS (Worldspan Communications)	BBS, Email, Usenet	+44 181 288 8555	world@span.com	http://span.com/
	Total Connectivity Providers Ltd	SLIP, PPP, CSLIP, WWW,	+44 1703 393392	sales@tcp.co.uk	http://www.tcp.co.uk/
	U-NET Limited	SLIP, PPP, ISDN, WWW	+44 1925 633144	hi@u-net.com	http://www.u-net.com/
	WinNet	Dial Up	+44 181 863 1191	info@win-uk.net	http://www.win-uk.net.uk
	Wintermute Ltd.	SLIP, PPP, BBS, ISDN, Leased Lines	+44 1224 622477	info@wintermute.co.uk	http://www.wintermute.co.uk/
	ZETNET Services	SLIP, WWW	+44 1595 696667	info@zetnet.co.uk	http://www.zetnet.co.uk/
Uruguay	R.A.U.		+598 2 41 3901	holz@seciu.uy, teccom@seciu.uy	
	Chasque (NGO)		+598 2 496 192	apoyo@chasque.apc.org	
Uzbekistan	Firma Kompyuternye kommunikacii		+7 3712 687956	postmaster@ccc.tashkent.su	
Venezuela	ITI DE VENEZUELA, C.A.		+58 2 959 6212		
	NetPoint Communications, Inc.	SLIP, PPP, ISDN, Leased Lines	+1 305 891 1955	info@netpoint.net	http://www.netpoint.net/
	USBnet		+58 2 906 3241	poc@usb.ve postmaster@usb.ve	http://www.usb.ve
Vietnam	NetNam Telematic Services	UUCP	+84 4 346 907	admin@netnam.org.vn	
Zambia	ZAMNET Communication Systems Ltd	SLIP, PPP, Email	+260 1 290358	sales@zamnet.zm	http://www.zamnet.zm/
Zimbabwe	MANGO!			Rob_Borland@mango.apc.org johnux@zimbix.uz.zw	

Commercial Online Data Vendors

It is important to know about the existence of the major online systems like Dialog, Nexis/Lexis, Orbit, and CD Plus, which are accessible over the Internet. These private online worlds are very complementary to the information available over the Internet. Many are quite costly to access, however, and require specially learned research skills to handle their specific search protocols.

These online systems have been building extraordinary archives of information going back decades in many cases—information that allows researchers to gather vast bodies of data literally in minutes from millions of disparate bits of information.

Following is a chart of the major online system providers. You will need to contact them directly to set up a password to their systems and to find out about the availability of online training.

PROVIDER	PHONE	INTERNET ADDRESS
Knight-Ridder Information	+44 171 930 7646	http://ww.rs.ch/www/rs/datastar.html
Dow Jones News Retrieval	(609) 520-4000	http://bis.dowjones.com/djnr.html
Nexis and Lexis	(800) 843-6476	http://www.lexis-nexis.com/lncc/general/telnet.html
BRS (CD Plus)	(800) 950-2371	http://www.ovid.com
Orbit Questel, Inc.	(703) 442-0900	http://www.uestel.orbit.com/patents/telnet.html

Private Network Providers with their own worlds of information

In addition to actual Internet Access Providers, private network providers in the United States and other countries offer a variety of services, including their own worlds of information and proprietary user "environments." Some maintain and make available elaborate and specialized databases for access by their subscribers. They are frequently closed systems, with only Email access to the Internet. However, technologies are being developed by which the private and the public Internet can be made seamless.

Below is a chart giving basic contact information for the major providers that belong to this category.

America Online provides access to a wide variety of media and reference sources, popular newspapers, email, magazines, and vendor support. Chat lines are also a major offering. It offers its own service-based Internet access features. *2.3 million subscribers*

Compuserve has over 2,000 separate resources with many of the largest forums available online. In addition to an array of financial and professional services, Compuserve provides a wide diversity of entertainment services, and a growing shopping service that also offers graphics. *2.7 million subscribers*

Delphi offers a comprehensive selection of news, reference and resources, and computer information, as well as full gateway access to the Internet. Special-interest groups, conferences, email, and online games are major features. It provides access to the Internet. *200,000 subscribers*

GEnie provides a large menu of news and information services, special-interest groups, games, email, and databases. GEnie's RoundTables (RTs) provide discussion areas devoted to specific topics; file libraries, bulletin boards, and real-time chat (RTC) are special features. It provides Internet access. *150,000+ subscribers*

Prodigy is a "family-oriented" service providing shopping, travel, email, and personal finance, and specializes in up-to-the-minute information such as news, sports, and weather. Prodigy also offers a large collection of shareware programs and Internet access. *2 million subscribers*

ZiffNet is an online service with information on buying, using, supporting, and understanding personal computer products. ZiffNet is a major resource for technical support.

PROVIDER	PHONE NO.	EMAIL
America Online	1 (800) 827-6364	
CompuServe	1 (800) 848-8199	
Delphi	1 (800) 544-4005	INFO@delphi.com
E World (Apple)	1 (800) 775-4556	
GEnie	1 (800) 638-9636	
Prodigy	1 (800) 776-3449	
ZiffNet	1 (800) 635-6225	

Glossary of Terms & Acronyms

APPENDIX C

A

Absolute Address An address that indicates, in machine language code, the exact storage location where data or machine instructions are to be found.

Access To find or store information in memory or on a peripheral device such as a magnetic tape or disk drive. To communicate in some way with a device.

Access Method Any of the data management techniques available to the user for transferring data from memory to an input/output device, or vice versa.

Access Time The time interval between the instant at which data is requested to be retrieved or stored, and the instant at which the operation is carried out.

Address A location on a disk or in memory at which a specific piece of information can be stored, or the number assigned to that location. See also absolute address, indirect address.

ADJ The Boolean ADJACENT operator used by WAIS to indicate that the two words on either side of the ADJ tag should sit next to each other in found markets.

ADMD Administrative Management Domain.

.aiff format This is a sound file that is used by Macintosh computers

Anonymous FTP An access command which allows Internet users to retrieve files from various servers without actually having accounts on those servers. A copy of the "anonymous FTP list" enables users to determine the location of files available on the Internet.

Appletalk A local area network protocol developed by Apple to connect peripherals and computers along multiple wiring systems.

Application A computer program designed to perform a specific task.

Archie A method of searching databases on the Internet. It finds relevant files and FTP sites according to the subject, title, or keyword that you enter

Archive
1. The storage of files (often in archived and compressed form) for future use, or the storage area that holds those files.
2. To create an archive, to move a file into an archive, or to bundle multiple files together into a larger archive or library file.

ARPA Advanced Research Projects Agency of the United States Department of Defense.

Artificial Intelligence
1. Computer programs that perform functions, often by imitation, that are normally associated with human reasoning and knowledge.
2. The ability of a device to make computational and evaluative decisions under the control of a program.

ASCII (American Standard Code for Information Interchange) A code used to store files in clear text. It is easily recognized by a multitude of computers which allows file transfer.

ASR Automatic Send and Receive. Having the ability to receive data and produce it on a printer or to send it through a keyboard.

Asynchronous Having a variable time interval between characters, bits, or events.

ATM Asynchronous Transfer Mode. A process that allocates bandwidth using a fixed-size packet (called a cell).

Atob (Pronounced "a to b.") A UNIX program that transfers ASCII files into binary files. The btoa file does the reverse.

AU A filename extension for audio data.

.au format This is a sound file that is used by UNIX computers

Automation The implementation of several processes by automatic means.

B

Backbone A single-protocol connection among different systems. Each system has a gateway to the common backbone protocol.

Bandwidth A measure of network capacity.

baud A measurement of the speed at which data travels. It is another term for bps (bits per second) that is commonly used in telecommunications to describe the speed of a modem, for example a 14.4 modem (14,400 bits per second).

BBS (Bulletin Board System) A computer that gives outside computers with modems dial-up or telnet access privileges. A BBS usually has archives, email, a special topic (local news, witchcraft, games, etc.) and frequently has Internet access.

Binary A number representation comprised of 0's and 1's used by most computers due to its ease of implementation through the use of digital electronics and Boolean algebra.

BinHex This Macintosh program converts binary files to ASCII to send by Email.

Bit Contraction of binary and digit. A bit is the smallest unit of information with which a computer can operate. Each bit is either a one or a zero. Often computers work with chunks of bits rather than one bit at a time; the smallest chunk of bits a computer usually works with consists of 8 bits, or a byte.

Bitmapping A digital representation of an image in which all dots or pixels making up the image correspond to specifically assigned bits in memory.

BITNET Because It's Time Network A low cost, low speed network which was developed to satisfy a need for providing distributed network access beyond the limits of the original ARPAnet network.

Bit rate A measure of audio/video capabilities and associated quality in real time.

Block Physical data consisting of a fixed number of characters or records, and moved as a unit during data transmission.

Body/Subject The body of an Email message is the actual text of a message. The subject is a special field which gives the content of a message. Many SMTP programs take advantage of the Subject line to provide sorting capabilities. Through the clever use of Subject lines, an E-mail handling facility can perform as a small but useful database.

Boolean A system of logic devised by George Boole using a series of symbolic terms such as "and," "or," and "not" to express the relationship of data elements to one another.

Bounced Message An E-mail message that does not reach its destination for several reasons: the address may have been typed incorrectly, the Domain Name Server might not recognize an alias, the recipients computer might be down for maintenance, etc. In such cases, a message is sent back to the sender to inform them that their message has not been delivered. Sometimes, the information provided in the header reveals why the message was undeliverable.

bps (bits per second) A measurement of the speed at which data travels.

Browser An online application that allows a user to read hypertext. The browser permits viewing the contents of nodes and the ability to navigate from one node to another. Mosaic, Lynx and W3 are browsers for the World Wide Web. Browsers act as clients to remote servers.

Btoa (Pronounced "b to a.") A UNIX program that transfers binary files into ASCII files. The atob file does the reverse.

Byte Eight bits. A byte is simply a chunk of 8 ones and zeros. For example 01000001 is a byte. A byte is equal to one column in a file written in character format. (See also Character Encoding Scheme)

C

CCA

1. Common Cryptographic Architecture: IBM encryption software for MVS and DOS applications.
2. Compatible Communications Architecture: network equipment technology protocol for transmitting asynchronous data over X.25 networks. (See X.25.)
3. Communications Control Architecture: a US Navy network that includes an ISDN backbone called bits.

CCITT Consultative Committee Of International Telephone And Telegraph, Part of the International Telecommunications Union, a UN treaty organization that sets international standards for worldwide telecommunication, e.g. X.25. (See X.25.)

CD-ROM Compact Disc Read Only Memory.

Cache A small, fast memory that holds recently-accessed data, designed to speed up subsequent access to already-viewed data. Often applied to processor-memory access and also used for a local copy of data accessible over a network.

Cello A WWW browser that works under Microsoft Windows and allows Internet users to follow Hypertext (or Hypermedia) links to files and information services all over the world. It displays both regular text files and files that are written in HTML format, and will translate different Internet services such as Gopher, News and FTP into a format that appears to the user as if it were a hypertext document. Cello was written by Thomas Bruce of the Legal Information Institute at Cornell Law School.

CERN The European Laboratory for Particle Physics (Conseil Europeen pour la Recherche Nucleaire) where the World Wide Web was created.

Chains In Hypertext, linking randomly located material by means of address information included within the stored item, which cites the location of the succeeding and/or preceding item in the sequence. Chains permit users to traverse the Internet via links within documents to their origin, or cited materials. The "links" of the chain provide navigation information, and the user merely needs to click on a link to be moved to a (possibly remote) document whose address is contained in the link.

Channel Any communications pathway between two computers or between a terminal and a computer. It may refer to the physical medium, such as coaxial cable, or to a specific carrier frequency (subchannel) within a larger channel or wireless medium.

Character Encoding Scheme A method of encoding characters including alphabetic characters (a-z, uppercase and lowercase), numbers 0-9, punctuation and other marks (e.g. comma, period, space, &, *), and various "control characters" (e.g. tab, carriage return, linefeed) using binary numbers. For a computer, for instance, to print a capital A or a number 7 on the computer screen, we must have a way of telling the computer that a particular group of bits represents an A or a 7. There are standards, commonly called "character sets," that establish that a particular byte stands for an A and a different byte stands for a 7. A common standard for representing characters in bytes is known as ASCII.

Character Format Any file format in which information is encoded as characters using only a standard character encoding scheme. A file written in "character format" contains only those bytes that are prescribed in the encoding scheme as corresponding to the characters in the scheme (e.g. alphabetic and numeric characters, punctuation marks, and spaces. A file written in the ASCII character format, for instance, would store the number "7" in eight bits (i.e. one byte) 00010111. A file written in EBCDIC would store the number "7" in eight bits as 11110111.

Checksum A transmitted signature that allows a receiving modem to ascertain the quality of a transferred file. A value is transmitted or stored along with data that is sent. The receiving system recomputes the checksum based upon the received data and compares this value with the one sent with the data. If the two values are the same, the receiver has confidence that the data was received correctly.

Client The user of a network service; also used to describe a computer that relies upon another computer for some or all of its resources.

Client Server

1. Architecture in which the client is the requesting machine (PC or workstation) and the server is the supplying machine (LAN file server, mini or mainframe). The client provides the user interface and performs some or most of the application processing. The server maintains the databases and processes requests from the client to extract data from or update the database. The server also controls the application's integrity and security.
2. Request/supply relationship between programs. Applications can be designed, whether running within the same computer or in multiple computers, in which one program (the client) requests data from another program (the server). For example, in X-window, the server is software that manages the display screen, and the client is the application that asks the server to display something.

Column In a data file, a single vertical column that is one byte in length. Fixed-format data files are traditionally described as being arranged in lines and columns. In a fixed-format file, column locations describe the locations of variables.

Compatibility The ability of one device to interconnect or share programs or data with another by means of sharing the same code, speed, and signal level.

Compress Reduce the size of a file considerably by removing redundant information. Compressed files are more economical to transmit via the Internet or to store. In order to use the file, it must be "exploded", i. e. reconstituted.

Connect Time The time during which an operator is in contact with a computer online. This is different from compute time, in which the operator is actually utilizing the computer's resources.

CREN Corporation for Research and Educational Networking. A merger of BITNET and CSNET networks. See BITNET.

Cross-post The preferred method of posting of a single article simultaneously to several newsgroups, as opposed to posting an article repeatedly, once to each newsgroup, causing users to view it multiple times.

Cyberspace Term coined by William Gibson in his novel *Neuromancer,* to refer to a futuristic computer network that people use by plugging in their brains.

D

Daemon A program not invoked explicitly, but one which runs in the background on a UNIX system. Deamons perform a single function.

DASD Direct Access Storage Device

Data

1. A general term for any collection of information, facts, numbers, letters, or symbols that refer to or describe an object, idea, condition, situation, or other factors.
2. Name of an android in *Star Trek - The Next Generation.*

Database A set of organized data, stored in, or available to, a computer, that can be used by the computer or its operator to perform various tasks. The database is not the program; rather it is the information with which the program will operate.

Datagram The basic unit of information passed across the Internet. It consists of a source and destination address along with data. Large messages are broken into a sequence of IP datagrams.

Data Network A telecommunications network built specifically for data transmission, rather than for voice transmission.

Decryption Decoding a message to its original meaningful form by means of a key.

DES Data Encryption Standard (DES). A popular, standard encryption algorithm. A product cipher that operates on 64-bit blocks of data, using a 56-bit key.

Dial up The process of calling another computer via modem.

Document Delivery A service providing printed copies (full-text) of articles, reports, and publications, usually by subscription to a service, some of which are connected to the Internet.

Domain Name A part of the address naming hierarchy. Syntactically, a domain name consists of a sequence of names or other words separated by periods e.g. @prep.ai.mit.edu

Domain Name Server A computer table which lists the IP numeric addresses of computers on the Internet, and their given common name. It is frequently easier to remember a computer site by name, but the network stores the numerical address. Domain Name Servers keep track of which name belongs to which numerical address.

Domain Name System (DNS) A global naming system for use in UNIX networking for general-purpose, name-to-resource mapping. While in the Internet the network information center manages the higher-echelon domain names and the bulk of the management is decentralized to the lower-echelon sub-domains. Each name server in an Internet community is responsible for a personal piece of the global name hierarchy over which it has authority.

DOS Disk Operating System: any of a number of widely used operating systems, so-called because a primary function they provide is the control of auxiliary storage in the form of disks.

Download To transmit data from one central computer to another device or to a remote terminal.

Driver A program that controls (drives) the operation of a device or interface. The driver program interprets the computer data, providing the commands and signals required by the device or interface. The driver can output directly to the device or interface, or can provide paper output.

DTD Document Type Definition is a type of markup language written using SGML. See also SGML.

Duplex Pertaining to a transmission system where data can be received and transmitted. Half duplex—can only transmit or receive. Full duplex—can transmit and receive simultaneously.

E

E-cash Electronic funds transfer via the Internet. E-cash software stores digital money, signed by a bank, on the user's local computer. Security is provided by a public key digital signature.

EFF Electronic Frontier Foundation. A non-profit civil liberties public interest organization working to protect privacy, freedom of expression, and access to online resources and information.

Electronic Mail A message service using electronics and telecommunications to deliver hard or soft-copy information. These can take the form of text-only messages or of images that include text in font form and graphic material.

Electronic Magazine Electronically published magazines on the Internet. E-zines are distributed via the WWW combining graphics, sounds, and other multimedia, or by way of mailing lists, or downloadable by anonymous FTP.

E-mail See Electronic Mail

Emotives A term coined by Chet Grycz to describe any of a series of typographic symbols (usually made up of colons, dashes, periods, and other diacritics) by which "emotional signals" can be transmitted over the Internet. Such abbreviations are sometimes called "smileys" because they resemble smiling faces, tilted on their side. i.e.: (:-)) Emotives can convey happiness, sadness, pouting, tongue-in-cheek, and a variety of other nuances that are usually conveyed by tone of voice and body language.

Encryption An algorithm designed to protect the interpretation and use of intellectual property in electronic files against unauthorized use.

End User The person or organization who will directly use particular information or devices.

Error Any discrepancy between the theoretically correct behavior or values in a computer and the actual behavior or values. Most computers are specifically designed to detect the presence of errors.

Error Correction Methods of error detection that are used to monitor transmitted or stored data and to correct them. Error detection and correction schemes are often used to correct errors in data stored in RAM.

Escape (esc) A control code that indicates that the following code or codes have a different meaning than they would usually have.

Ethernet A communications protocol developed by Xerox Corporation, widely used for local area networks.

Eudora E-mail program written by Steve Dorner. See Electronic Mail.

E-Zine See Electronic magazine

F

FAQs (Frequently Asked Questions) This term is usually associated with Usenet news. It refers to a list of frequently asked questions by novice internet users about Usenet, software, Web sites and more. A FAQ provides the answers to these questions and it is a good idea to read the FAQs before jumping into a newsgroup conversation.

File A physical unit of storage on a computer disk or tape.

File Server A computer that stores files on the Internet, and makes such files available for access by one of the various Internet access tools.

File Transfer Protocol (FTP) A reliable method of transferring files over the Internet.

Filter (Originally Unix, now also MS-DOS). A program that processes an input data stream into an output data stream in a well-defined way, and does not I/O to anywhere else except in error conditions.

Finger A software application whose purpose it is to query information files about individual Internet users. The user places information regarding a phone number, address, or affiliation in a file, and the finger software is designed to retrieve such files upon request.

Firewall A computer that is used to prevent unauthorized access to a computer system from other computers. It is comparable to having a 24 hour guard at the door of your company's computer system which screens incoming calls and visitors. It keeps your system free from tampering.

Firmware Software that is stored in read-only memory (ROM). Firmware functions are not programmable by the user.

Fixed Format A file structure consisting of physical records of a constant size within which the precise location of each variable is based on the column location and width of the variable.

Flame This is equivalent to "losing one's temper" online, signifying a breach of netiquette. Flaming can mean calling into question a user's opinions or observation. Typing E-mail in all capital letters often signifies flaming.

Flame War An acrimonious dispute conducted on a public electronic forum.

Flash ROM A type of non-volatile storage device similar to EEPROM, but in which erasing can only be done in blocks or the entire chip.

FreeNet An organization whose purpose is to provide access to the Internet to as large a public as possible. The first such effort was established by the highly-successful Cleveland Free Net. Such networks make Internet resources available to the public by providing access at affordable charges. They also frequently provide support and aid in connecting to and navigating across the Internet.

FTP See File Transfer Protocol.

Full-Text Referring to a database that contains entire documents as opposed to citations or abstracts.

G

Gate-Keeping System A method of facilitating as well as controlling the process of gathering, organizing, filtering, distributing, and exchanging information in various formats between sources and users.

Gateway The electronic communications node that connects the individual user with specific mainframes or networks.

Glitch A sudden temporary mishap, error, or malfunction in mechanical, electrical, or electronic equipment.

Gopher This is a search program that allows users to burrow into gopher database servers throughout the internet in search of subjects and text that are of interest to them and then retrieve these files.

GUI Graphical User Interface (GUI). The use of pictures rather than only words to represent the input and output of a program. A program with a GUI runs under some windowing system (e.g. The X Window System, Microsoft Windows, Acorn RISC OS).

H

Handshake A protocol wherein a transmitting device sends a signal, then the receiving device sends a "ready" signal before the transmission continues.

Hard-Wired Pertaining to the direct wiring of a terminal to a computer system (or any device to any device), as opposed to devices that communicate via telephone lines or wireless media.

Header Part of an E-mail message generated by the transmission protocols that provide information about who originated a message, when it was posted, its pathway of travel across the Internet, and certain machine identifications along the way.

Hierarchical File A file containing information that is organized in subordinate levels or with a relational structure.

Home page On the World Wide Web, the top-level document relating to an individual or institution. This often has a URL consisting of just a host name, e.g.. http://www.ncsa.uiuc.edu/. All other pages on a server are usually accessible by following links from the home page.

HOP

1. One file transmission in a series necessary to get a file from point A to point B on a store-and-forward network.

2. To log in to a remote machine, especially via login or telnet. i.e.. "I'll hop over to foovax to FTP that."

Host A system or subsystem in a network that performs actual processing operations against a database, and with which other network devices communicate.

Host Computer The computer and associated database that run as a separate entity, but can be accessed through the network.

Host Site The location (station) that receives communications from the other points in the network, performs operations on them via a host computer, and sends communications back to other points.

HTML Hypertext Mark-up Language. In practical terms, HTML is a collection of styles used to define the various components of a World Wide Web document. Used in WWW documents to embed style information (fonts, font sizes and layout), graphics and hypertext links (URLs) to other Internet files and resources.

http (HyperText Transfer Protocol) This is the standard computer protocol used as a prefix in a URL. It tells the computer that the address that follows is accessible as a WWW site.

Hypertext A term coined by Ted Nelson (Xanadu) to describe a form of relationships that is non-linear. Most text is intended to be read one paragraph at a time in a serial fashion. Given electronic capabilities, it is possible to link one paragraph with another in a different location, perhaps even on an entirely different computer. Hypertext describes these more fluid relationships.

HYTELNET Stands for HyperTelnet. HYTELNET is a database of Telnet sites and other Internet resources that can access other programs when a site has been identified.

I

IAB Internet Architecture Board.

IF Interactive Facsimiles, a computer function that merges voice with facsimile transmissions to be carried over the Internet.

IETF Internet Engineering Task Force. The IETF is an international community of network designers, operators, vendors and researchers whose purpose is to coordinate the operation, management and evolution of the Internet and to resolve short and mid-range protocol and architectural issues. The IETF Secretariat is run by The Corporation for National Research Initiatives with funding from the US Government.

IMAP New protocol retrieving and storing Email, similar to POP (Post Office Protocol). See also POP.

IMHO In My Humble Opinion. Also seen in other forms such as IMO, IMNSHO (In My Not-So-Humble Opinion) and IMAO (In My Arrogant Opinion).

Indirect Address An instruction that references an address specified in the content of another address.

Information Agent A software application whose purpose it is to act on behalf of a database, updating it from information it retrieves from other databases. Archie and Veronica are examples of Information Agents.

Input
1. The process of entering data via a keyboard or terminal or other device.
2. The material that is entered via a keyboard or other device.

Interactive
1. Relating to the ability of a device or procedure that allows an operator to make decisions that influence the outcome of a procedure in process.
2. Pertaining to a device that allows an operator to input data or commands and that then responds in some way to the operator.

Interface The point and manner in which two separate systems or devices connect and interact with one another.

internet (Not capitalized.) Any set of networks interconnected with routers. Different than the Internet.

Internet A concatenation of many individual TCP/IP campus, state, regional, and national networks (such as NSFnet, ARPAnet, and MILnet) into one single logical network all sharing a common addressing scheme.

IP Internet Protocol. See also Protocol.

IP Address The Internet protocol numerical address assigned to each computer on the network, so that its location and activities can be distinguished from other computers.

IRC (Internet Relay Chat) A real-time conversation protocol that allows people to chat with each other on the Internet in 'virtual' rooms. Usually, each room has a designated topic and can be either publicly accessible or by invitation only.

ISDN (Integrated Services Digital Network) A type of dedicated, digital phone line that allows for the simultaneous sending and receiving of data. This creates faster connection time and transfer rates.

J

Jughead Jonzy's Universal Gopher Hierarchy Excavation And Display. Jughead is a tool used by gopher administrators to get menu information from various gopher servers. Jughead was written in ANSI C.

K

Kermit A file transfer protocol named after the puppet Kermit the Frog.

Kernel The level of an operating system or networking system that contains the system-level commands or all of the functions hidden from the user. In a UNIX system, the kernel is a program that contains the device drivers, the memory management routines, the scheduler, and system calls. This program is always running while the system is operating.

Keyword This is a word that points to a topic and can be used to search for articles and information on that topic.

Kill-file A per-user file used by some Usenet reading programs to discard summarily those articles matching some particularly uninteresting patterns of subject, author, or other header lines. To add a person (or subject) to one's kill file is to arrange for that person to be ignored by one's news reader in the future. By extension, it may be used for a decision to ignore the person or subject in other media.

L

LAN See Local Area Network.

Linux An implementation of Unix written from scratch with no proprietary code, for IBM PC compatibles by Linus Torvalds and distributed under the GNU General Public License.

LISTSERV A mailing list program that allows a single email message to be delivered to many addresses simultaneously. In order to receive a listserv message, you must be on the distribution list.

Local Area Network (LAN) A collection of devices and communication channels that connects a group of computers and peripheral devices together so that they may communicate with each other. Typically, local area networks occupy a single building or office area.

Log
1. A record of operations on a file indicating actions such as file creation, modification, errors, and other data.
2. To sign on (log on) or off (log off) a computer system or area. Log on procedures may require operator passwords, or may be accomplished simply by designating the desired area.

Lurkers Term for users who peruse online discussions without contributing.

Lycos Taken from the Latin name for the wolf spider, Lycos is a search engine that accesses a database of over 3.5 million Web sites. It allows users to customize their search with words that act as signifiers which limit or link together a string of keywords.

M

MacTCP Users can configure a TCP/IP connection (including setting IP address, getaways, and Domain Name Servers) when this Apple Computer TCP/IP is placed in the System Folder.

Majordomo A set of programs written in Perl that automate operation of multiple mailing lists. Majordomo automatically handles routine requests to subscribe or unsubscribe; it also has "closed lists" that route all subscription requests to a "list owner" for approval. It also supports "moderated lists" that send all messages to the list owner for approval before they're sent to subscribers.

MAPI Message Application Programming Interface

Mbps Megabits per second. A form of measurement used to determine the amount of data transmitted per time over a network or a modem. One megabit is equal to about one million bits.

Mainframe Large central computers that have vast memory and storage capabilities and high-speed microprocessors allowing them to perform information processing and storage for dumb terminals consisting of keyboards and monitor units.

Maximum Transmission Unit (MTU) The maximum amount of information (in bytes) stored in the packet that transfers requests via the Internet.

MELVYL® A centralized information system for all nine campuses of the University of California. It includes a library catalog database, a periodicals database, article citation databases, and other files and can be accessed via UC lines or the Internet.

Memory The internal storage capacity of a computer system. Memory is generally located on some magnetic device such as disk, drum or core. Data is stored in digitally encoded bytes, and manipulated as needed during calculation processes. The amount of memory a computer has directly affects its ability to perform complex functions.

MHS Message Handling System

MILNET Military network

MIME (Multipurpose Internet Mail Extension) An add-on (extension) mail program that allows users to transmit sound, graphics and video by email.

Mirror site An FTP site containing the same contents as another site.

Mode A particular condition or state under which a computer or other device may operate, such as an insert mode, a communications mode, or a binary mode. Operations or commands may take on different meanings in different modes.

Modem Modulator/demodulator, connects computers at remote sites to the telephone system by converting data from the host computer into electronic signals which are transmitted via the network to the target computer where another modem converts them back into machine-readable data. Modems can send as well as receive data, enabling computers to "converse" with one another.

Mosaic
1. A free Macintosh client browser for World Wide Web servers. The program can access linked data on Internet servers via many protocols: Archie, gopher, wide area information servers, ftp (file transfer protocol), telnet and network news transfer protocol. The program requires system 7 and MacTCP 2.0.2. Mosaic is available via anonymous ftp from ftp.ncsa.uiuc.edu in the directory /MAC/mosaic.
2. Netware for Mac developed by Novell Inc. Allows users to share non-PostScript printers connected to the PC portion of a Netware network. The software intercepts the PostScript print job and translates it into PCL (printer control language) before sending it to the Netware server's print services.
3. A program containing a Trojan horse strain that destroys the directories of all available unlocked hard and floppy disks, including the one it resides on. Even unmounted but available SCSI hard disks are mounted and destroyed by the Trojan.

Mouse A hand-held input device, similar to a keyboard, but limited to such interactions with graphic images on the screen as pointing, clicking, and dragging.

MTU Maximum Transmission Unit. A number that must be provided to a user by a system administrator so the user can configure SLIP.

MUD (Multi-User Dungeon) This is a program that allows multiple users to access the same virtual dungeon simultaneously. It was originally used as an online version of the role-playing game Dungeons and Dragons. Now however, MUDs are being used to hold computer conferences and as educational aids.

Multiplex To transmit simultaneously two or more messages over the same communications channel to different receivers.

MX Record Mail Exchange Record. One of the components through which E-mail that is addressed to you, actually gets to you, the MX Record tells domain name servers about routing and location instructions.

N

Network Two or more computers linked together physically or via telecommunications for the purpose of electronically sharing resources such as computer files, programs, and peripheral devices.

Network Control Program (NCP) A program within the software of a data processing system which controls the performance of a telecommunications network.

Network File System (NFS) A process for mounting magnetic disks on a network so that disks not physically attached to a computer appear as if they were physically attached.

Newsgroup A discussion group on Usenet devoted to a specific topic.

NFS See Network File System.

Node A branching or exchange point in a network.

Noise Unwanted signal or signals on an electrical circuit.

Noise Immunity The ability of a device to accept valid signals while rejecting invalid signals.

Non-Switched Line A communications link permanently installed between two points.

NREN National Research and Education Network. Fiber-optic (improved capacity and transmission speed) network to link all education facilities, including grade schools and libraries, higher education institutions, and government organizations.

NSFNET The National Science Foundation Network. The national backbone network, funded by the National Science Foundation.

NTP Network Time Protocol. A protocol built on top of TCP/IP that assures accurate local timekeeping with reference to radio, atomic, or other clocks located on the Internet. This protocol is capable of synchronizing distributed clocks within milliseconds over long time periods. It is defined in STD 12, RFC 1119.

Null Modem A cable, especially an RS-232 cable used to connect serial ports on two computers directly, rather than via modems.

Numeric Database A database primarily containing numbers.

O

OCR See Optical Character Recognition.

Octet The grouping of eight numbers in a pair and two triplets as used in the domain name system; e.g. 35.222.222.

Offline Pertaining to a device or function that is not electronically connected to the main device. Media transmission from an offline device must be by means of manually carried material (disk or tape) or via telephone lines.

Online Pertaining to devices that are electronically connected to the computer. Generally, an online device is treated as if it were an integral part of the computer system.

Online Public Access Catalog (OPAC) A database of bibliographic records to which the public has access, reflecting the material owned by a library or a consortium of libraries.

OPAC See Online Public Access Catalog.

Operating System The program or set of programs which control a computer's operations and monitor the functions of the other programs.

Optical Character Recognition (OCR) A method of converting graphic symbols (particularly alphanumeric) to electronic signals by means of a reading device that recognizes character shapes. Until recently, material prepared for optical character recognition had to be typed in a specific format, and with a specific type element.

Optical Disk A rigid, plastic disk, 4 ¾" in diameter, with an embedded metallic underside on which data are recorded permanently by laser (ROM - read-only-memory). Also known as compact disk, CD or CD-ROM. Digital information is recorded on a master disk with a strong laser beam. Copies are made by "stamping" 4 ¾ inch disks. They are read by a weaker laser beam. It is a high-density storage medium, with a capacity of 600 megabytes.

Optical Scanner A device that uses light to scan and convert text, graphics, or other visual images into digitized data that can be read by a computer.

OSI Open System Interconnection

P

Packet An addressed data unit of convenient size for transmission through a network.

Parallel Interface A data transmission technique in which a group of binary digits (bits) are transferred simultaneously over multiple lines. Usually, eight bits that correspond to a character are transferred as a single operation.

Parameter

1. A designation for the format of type, as requested by command codes or system defaults. Line length, page depth, typeface, and leading are examples of parameters. Commands which take place as they are entered and do not maintain their effect (such as extra leading, cancel escapement, etc.) are not parameters.

2. Program parameter: A constant or variable which remains unchanged in a subroutine, and fully or partly specifies a process to be performed during the subroutine.

3. Hardware parameter: A parameter characteristic of a machine which establishes certain limitations or capabilities of the machine. For instance, a parameter of a typesetter might be its ability to process 160 lines per minute.

Parity The transmission of data so that all codes have either an even or an odd number of one-bits. Even parity means that one bit has been added to the codes with an odd number of one-bits so the total is even; odd parity means that all the even codes have one bit added to make them have an odd number of one-bits.

Parity Check A method of verifying the accuracy of a transmitted bit pattern by examining the code to determine whether its value is odd or even.

Password An identification number keyed by the operator and checked by the computer before a database can be accessed.

Pay-By-The-Drink A method of charging the user every time a file is accessed, based on the number of connect-time units elapsed and/or records inspected. This is in contrast to paying a subscription or license fee which permits repeated and unlimited access to the file(s) and records for the duration of a stipulated time period.

Peer-To-Peer Network A network in which all connected computers, designated as peers, are treated as equals and the interconnected system does not require a server to process information.

Peripheral A device that is external to the system processor, but operates under the processor's control, such as a line printer or a communications signal.

PGP A high security RSA public-key encryption application for MS-DOS, Unix, VAX/VMS,and other computers. PGP uses a public-key encryption algorithm claimed by US patent #4,405,829. The exclusive rights to this patent are held by the California company, Public Key Partners, and its use may infringe on this patent if used in the USA.

Platform A manufacturer's operating system for functions that have not been standardized in the industry and require intermediary programs to interpret the commands across different systems.

Port A communications channel between a computer and another device, such as a terminal, modem, or printer.

POP Post Office Protocol. A software application that enables individual Email users (POP clients) to retrieve mail from a central mail depository (POP server).

PostScript Software produced by Adobe Systems for desktop publishing that creates a page description language which many laser printers understand.

PPP Point-to-Point Protocol. Like SLIP, PPP is a software application that allows a computer to use Internet protocols to become a terminal node on the Internet. PPP requires a high-speed modem and standard telephone line.

Printer Peripheral device, connected to a computer to render images on paper in black/white or color. Pigments can be transferred from a ribbon pressed against the print surface by an array of wires (matrix or impact printer), heated to sputtering and directed through tiny holes (ink jet) or electrostatically attached to a metal drum and transferred to paper by the xerographic method (laser).

Printout Display of file contents in text or graphic form on paper.

Program Series of instructions to direct the computer to perform specific tasks in a certain order.

Prompt An on-screen processing technique that questions or "prompts" the user of a computer system for responses.

Protocol The proper procedure and sequence of events for data transmission of a particular input device, with regard to code structure, code recognition, and identification of the text stream.

Public Access Provider An online entity that provides Internet access for individuals and organizations.

Q

Query A data message structured so as to elicit a response from a computer.

R

RAM See Random Access Memory.

Random Access Access to data, information, or files without observing any particular order.

Random Access Memory (RAM) A form of volatile memory which allows data (such as documents) to be stored randomly and retrieved directly by an address location. The system accesses the addressed material, with no need to read through intervening data. Information may be retrieved faster using random access memory than from serial media such as tape.

Raw Data Data that has not been processed, reorganized, or manipulated.

Read Only Memory (ROM) Memory that is programmed at the time of manufacture; it may be accessed only and cannot be erased. Being nonvolatile, read-only memory holds its contents after the power is shut off. It can be used to contain an operating system, language translators, and other "permanent" software.

Real Time Pertaining to the performance of a computer in such a way that the operator receives responses quickly enough so that there is no effective delay in the operator's activity.

Remote Pertaining to communication with a device located at some distance from the central device, but connected in some way, with cables, wires, or telephone hookup.

Rich Text Format (RTF) A text exchange standard proposed by Apple to provide an application independent file format including fonts, tab positions, rulers, line breaks, hyphenation, paragraph spacing, embedded objects such as pictures and sounds, and special text styles.

ROM See Read Only Memory.

Router A dedicated computer that sends packets from one place to another, paying attention to the current state of the network.

RS-232 Port A standard plug with 25 pins, used to connect computers and I/O devices.

RSA Encryption A public-key cryptosystem for both encryption and authentication. The entire security of RSA is predicated on the assumption that factoring is difficult; an easy method for factoring large prime numbers would break RSA.

RTF See Rich Text Format

S

Screen The display surface of a video terminal or cathode ray tube.

Scroll A function available on most video terminals where the display image seems to move up and down (or left and right) on the screen to provide incremental viewing of material earlier or later in the file.

Search The electronic comparison of character strings entered by the operator with those contained in files or databases, arranged in Boolean logic expressions.

Server A network computer which shares its resources, such as files and printer, with other computers. e.g. Network file system (NFS).

SFQL See Structured Query Language.

SGML See Standard Generalized Markup Language.

Shareware A method of software distribution in which software is freely distributed and the user can use it before actual purchase.

Sign On To connect with a remote computer by providing identification details and performing appropriate procedures.

Signal The electrical quantity that conveys data from one point to another.

Signature
1. One of the requirements for a fully-functional Internet is to provide unique signatures with which to identify individuals (for example for the purpose of verifying authorization to move funds). A number of cryptographic solutions to individual signatures have been proposed, most of which depend on a unique encoding pattern that is known only to a single individual.
2. In E-mail, a piece of text which identifies the sender of an E-mail message. Some people develop elaborate and attractive signatures by which their messages are personalized.

Simplex A modem that either sends or receives information but cannot do both during one transmission.

Simultaneous Transmission The transmission of data in two directions at once, both sending and receiving, by the same device.

Site License Authorization (usually subject to a fee) to have multiple copies for simultaneous use within a specified organization or location.

SLIP Serial Line Internet Protocol. A software application that allows a computer to use Internet protocols and to become a terminal node on the Internet. SLIP requires a high-speed modem and standard telephone line.

SlipKnot A graphical World-Wide Web browser specifically designed for Microsoft Windows users who have UNIX shell accounts with their service providers. Its primary feature is that SLIP, PPP or TCP/IP services are not required. SlipKnot is distributed as restricted shareware.

Smiley One of the things Internet users have learned is that the written language lacks "emotive" symbols, by which one can tell the emotional timbre of a given E-Mail message. A series of "smileys" have emerged, by which these emotive qualities are sought to be reintroduced in a shorthand fashion. (See also Emotives)

SMTP Simple Mail Transport Protocol. The protocol by which E-Mail messages are managed by computers on the Internet. It provides the possibility of designing E-mail servers and E-mail clients. Many of the popular E-mail handling programs such as Eudora take advantage of the SMTP protocol to make E-mailing easy and efficient.

Snail Mail A name for traditional paper mail that reflects its slow speed in comparison to E-mail.

Socket The Berkeley UNIX mechanism used to create a virtual connection between processes. Sockets form the interface between Unix standard I/O and network communication facilities and are of two types, stream (bi-directional) or datagram (fixed length destination-addressed messages).

Software A term coined to contrast computer programs with the hardware of a computer system. Software is a stored set of instructions that governs the operation of a computer system and makes the hardware run.

Stand-Alone Refers to a device which is capable of performing the functions for which it is designed without the aid of or connection to another, smarter device. The stand-alone device may receive media from another device for processing.

Standard Generalized Markup Language (SGML) Enables data to move between media by describing documents by their structural elements rather than their visual format and thus permitting further analysis or reuse by various application programs.

Star A network configuration in which a central controller communicates directly with each device or station. A diagram of this configuration looks like a star.

Station One of the input or output points of a communications system or of a multi-user computer.

Stop Bit In asynchronous communication, a marker following each character.

String A sequence of entities, such as characters or commands.

Structured Query Language (SQL) [Pronounced 'sequel'] A data access language designed to work with relational databases. First used on IBM's dB2, SQL became a de facto standard in the mid-1980's.

Surfing The enjoyable act of "browsing" for files and interesting gems of information on the Internet. This should be contrasted with the more goal-oriented activity of finding a particular piece of information. The aim of The New Riders' Official Internet Yellow Pages is to facilitate the latter without limiting any of the pleasure of the former.

Synchronous Occurring concurrently, and with a regular or predictable time relationship. In transmission, referring to the ability of the sending and the receiving devices to run continuously at the same frequency.

SYSOP (Systems Operator) This is the person who maintains the daily operation of a BBS.

System A machine or device using various hardware and software to accomplish certain tasks. Commonly composed of a central processor, with one or more input or output devices, and capable of making decisions about the material which is being processed. Various fields of computer technology tend to define "system" in slightly different ways.

T

T1 A high-speed network link used on the Internet (1.54 Megabits/second).

T3 A higher speed network link than T1, used on the Internet (45 Megabits/second).

Tag The HTML coding that allows WWW pages to appear and perform in a certain manner.

TCP/IP (Transmission Control Protocol/Internet Protocol) This is the standard protocol used on the Internet that allows different computers and programs like FTP, Telnet and email to communicate despite not belonging to the same computer network.

Telecommunication The transmission of signals by telegraph, radio, satellite, or some other means that does not involve physical connection between the sending and receiving devices.

Teleprocessing Computer operations carried out via long-distance communications network.

Teletext A generic term for one-way information retrieval systems that broadcast digitally encoded text and graphics to remote users. Teletext users request pages of transmitted data by means of a keyboard.

Telnet An application that allows you to login to other computers throughout the world. It mimics being directly connected to the remote computer.

Terminal A device (usually with a video display) on which an operator may communicate with or receive communication from a computer.

Terminal Emulation A software capability in which a computer or terminal can be made to simulate the characteristics of another terminal for communications compatibility.

Terminal Server A small, specialized networked computer that connects many terminals to a LAN through one network connection. Any user on the network can then connect to various network hosts.

Text A series of words or characters having some meaning to the reader, as opposed to command codes or instructions.

TFTP Trivial File Transfer Protocol. A simple file transfer protocol used for downloading boot code to diskless workstations.

Throughput The net speed of a device or system, including input, output, and processing speeds together. The throughput speed may be slower than the inherent input or output speeds, since input may be slowed by simultaneous output, or vice versa, or input and output may have to take place serially.

TIA The Internet Adapter. A program from Cyberspace Development which runs on a Unix shell account and acts as a SLIP emulator. The user does not maintain an individual Internet address as with a real SLIP account. TIA uses the IP number of the machine it runs on and "redirects" traffic back to the user. Machines do not act as FTP servers, for instance, since there's no IP number for an FTP client elsewhere to connect to.

Timesharing The use of a computer for two or more purposes during the same time interval. The computer shares its attention among the devices by means of some monitoring program.

TLAs (Three Letter Acronyms) - The computer acronyms that frustrate the average person and stand for terms on the Internet.

Token Ring Network A communications network designed so that all computer devices (stations) on the network are connected to a common channel, called a bus. A group of bits (a token) is passed from station to station to give each station in turn the opportunity to transmit data.

Transmission Control Protocol (TCP) A set of protocols, resulting from ARPA efforts, used by the Internet to support services such as remote login (TELNET), file transfer (FTP) and mail (SMTP).

Transparent Pertaining to a process that is thoroughly compatible with another process, so that a user is not necessarily aware that there is more than one process or function involved. A computer program that can be added to an existing program without retraining or re-educating its users is transparent to the original program.

Tree
1. An arrangement of data in a hierarchical form, with each group of data containing subgroups that present more detail.
2. A network configuration in which a central controller communicates to a number of other devices or stations, each of which in turn communicates to another group of devices or stations, in an hierarchy.

Trumpet WinSock A news reader for Microsoft Windows and MS-DOS using the WinSock library. Trumpet is shareware created in Australia.

U

UNIX A computer operating system developed by Bell Laboratories, written in the C programming language, and distinguished by its portability to different computers. It is widely used in graphics workstations.

Upload The function of sending a file from one computer and transferring it to another. The opposite of this term is to "download" or transfer a file from another computer onto one's own.

URL (Uniform Resource Locater) This provides the Internet address and access description for sites on the Internet. If it is on the Internet, it has a URL.

Usenet This is an independent and separate network of newsgroups that operates on the Internet but is not to be confused with the Internet. There are thousands of different newsgroups on different topics. In order to access these groups, you need to be connected to a Usenet server and have a newsreader program. (See part 4 of this directory)

User Friendly A characterization of computer products that are easy to learn or to use.

Uuencode A UNIX program that transfers binary files into ASCII files for transmission via E-mail and newsgroups.

V

Value-Added Enhancement of documents or data to increase their usefulness, such as gate-keeping and validation (i. e. by peer review), or substantive and copy editing by publishers. Libraries add value by selection, cataloging, archiving, and providing access. Electronic publishing adds value by providing full-text searching, audio, video, and animation, also by providing large data sets, reducing the time required for publication, and further by facilitating ease of access from workstations.

Veronica This is similar to Archie as it is a search agent used for searching Internet gopher sites for information by keywords or subjects.

Video Display Terminal (VDT) an operator station that includes a display screen as part of its hardware. VDTs at one time were called CRTs (cathode ray tubes).

Virtual Library Extends resources through access to bibliographic databases, full text files, images, and other information in electronic format.

Voice Grade Referring to the capability of a data transmission circuit to permit a transfer rate of up to 2400 bits per second (BAUD). A voice-grade circuit uses analog phone lines identical to standard telephone equipment, and encodes digital data into tones for transmission.

VRML A draft specification for the design and implementation of a platform-independent language for virtual reality scene description.

W

WAIS (Wide Area Information Server) A method of searching indexed text. It allows users to search multiple databases from one interface.

WAN (Wide Area Network) The larger cousin of LAN. It is a term that applies to a computer network over a large geographic area.

.wav Format This is the sound file format for Window operating system.

Wide Area Information Server (WAIS) A method of searching indexed text. It allows a user to take a hundred files on the topic of numerical analysis and index them into one .SRC file. New resources are announced in a special indexed database called "directory-of-servers."

Winsock The Windows Sockets Specification provides a uniform API to which application developers can program and multiple network software vendors can conform. In terms of a particular version of Microsoft Windows, Winsock defines a binary interface (ABI) such that an application written to the Windows Sockets API can work with a conformant protocol implementation from any network software vendor.

World Wide Web (WWW) A graphical system that enables a user to access Internet documents with hyperlinks to text, sound files, images and movie clips via the Hypertext Markup Language created at CERN in Switzerland.

X

X.25 CCITT standard (1976) for the protocols and message formats that define the interface between a terminal and a packet switching network.

X.400 Global electronic messaging architecture.

XModem Using 128-byte blocks and CRC error checking, XModem is a File Transfer Protocol (FTP).

X Windows System A specification for device-independent windowing operations on bitmap display devices, developed initially by MIT's Project Athena and now a de facto standard. X was named after an earlier window system called "W." (It is a window system called "X", not a system called "X Windows.") Users run on the same computer as the server or on a different computer, communicating over Ethernet via TCP/IP protocols. X users often run on what people usually think of as their server (e.g. a file server), but in X it is the screen and keyboard, etc. which is being "served out" to the applications.

Y

YModem Faster than XModem because it uses 1024-byte blocks as a File Transfer Protocol (FTP).

Z

Z39.50 Application-layer protocol standard developed by the American national standards institute in 1992 for computer-to-computer information retrieval. A number of companies and universities are using it to develop interoperable search-and-retrieval software products for accessing the Internet. The open systems interconnection (OSI) model defines z39.50, but because OSI is not built into the UNIX operating system like TCP/IP, z39.50 was adapted to run over TCP/IP for the Internet.

ZModem The fastest File Transfer Protocol. ZModem operates in batch mode, meaning a user can download or upload several files at a time, and recovers from transmission errors more effectively than other protocols.

Keyword Index

APPENDIX D

3-D *(Computing & Mathematics)* 227
3-D *(Internet)* 487
3-D Graphics *(Arts & Music)* 34
3-D Graphics *(Computing & Mathematics)* 169
3-D Images *(Arts & Music)* 30
3-D Webs *(Arts & Music)* 34, 39

Aboriginal Art *(Arts & Music)* 17, 20
Aboriginal Studies *(Humanities & Social Sciences)* 415, 418, 420
Aborigines *(Humanities & Social Sciences)* 416
Aborigines *(Arts & Music)* 47
Abortion *(Government & Politics)* 344-345
Abortion *(Health & Medicine)* 409-410
Abuse *(Popular Culture & Entertainment)* 524
Abused Children *(Popular Culture & Entertainment)* 518
Academia *(Science)* 584
Academic Jobs *(Education)* 238
Academics *(Engineering & Technology)* 307
Accomodations *(Sports & Recreation)* 659
Accounting *(Business & Economics)* 101, 120, 135, 709
Accounting *(Computing & Mathematics)* 224
Accounting *(Internet)* 455
Acoustics *(Arts & Music)* 66
Acoustics *(Engineering & Technology)* 297
Acronyms *(Popular Culture & Entertainment)* 525
Acting *(Arts & Music)* 33, 47, 94-96
Activism *(Arts & Music)* 27
Activism *(Business & Economics)* 117, 136
Activism *(Communications)* 156, 161
Activism *(Computing & Mathematics)* 206
Activism *(Education)* 253, 255
Activism *(Government & Politics)* 341, 345-346, 349-351, 354, 356
Activism *(Health & Medicine)* 398
Activism *(Internet)* 468
Activism *(Popular Culture & Entertainment)* 520, 530, 538
Activism *(Science)* 566, 592, 602, 612
Actors *(Arts & Music)* 47-48
Adaptive Control *(Engineering & Technology)* 294, 296, 299-300
Addictions *(Health & Medicine)* 688, 720
Admissions *(Education)* 270
Adolescence *(Popular Culture & Entertainment)* 552
Adolescents *(Health & Medicine)* 381
Adoption *(Health & Medicine)* 381, 404
Adoption *(Law & Criminal Justice)* 489
Adoption *(Popular Culture & Entertainment)* 517
Adult Education *(Education)* 239
Adult Videos *(Popular Culture & Entertainment)* 532
Advanced Technology Management *(Business & Economics)* 123
Adventure Games *(Internet)* 483
Adventure Travel *(Sports & Recreation)* 620, 641, 654
Advertisements *(Communications)* 159

Advertising & Marketing *(Business & Economics)* 678, 709
Advertising Agencies *(Business & Economics)* 102-104
Advertising *(Business & Economics)* 102-104, 113, 115, 142
Advertising *(Communications)* 158, 167
Advertising *(Internet)* 455-456
Advertising *(Law & Criminal Justice)* 489
Advertising *(Popular Culture & Entertainment)* 514, 525, 546, 549
Advertising *(Sports & Recreation)* 651, 665
Advice *(Health & Medicine)* 404
Advocacy *(Communications)* 155
Aerodynamics *(Computing & Mathematics)* 174
Aerodynamics *(Engineering & Technology)* 291
Aerodynamics *(Science)* 610, 612
Aeronautical Research *(Science)* 610
Aeronautics *(Engineering & Technology)* 291, 312
Aeronautics *(Government & Politics)* 348
Aeronautics *(Popular Culture & Entertainment)* 523
Aeronautics *(Science)* 609-613
Aeronautics *(Sports & Recreation)* 620, 664
Aerospace Engineering *(Communications)* 167
Aerospace Engineering *(Science)* 609-611
Aesthetics *(Religion & Philosophy)* 558
Affirmative Action *(Government & Politics)* 350
Affirmative Action *(Humanities & Social Sciences)* 448
Africa *(Arts & Music)* 21
Africa *(Education)* 261
Africa *(Government & Politics)* 338, 360
Africa *(Humanities & Social Sciences)* 415
Africa *(Internet)* 481
Africa *(Sports & Recreation)* 643, 658
African Amercians *(Humanities & Social Sciences)* 425
African American Authors *(Humanities & Social Sciences)* 444
African American Studies *(Arts & Music)* 58
African American Studies *(Humanities & Social Sciences)* 417
African American Studies *(Popular Culture & Entertainment)* 517
African Americans *(Arts & Music)* 99
African Americans *(Popular Culture & Entertainment)* 530
African Art *(Arts & Music)* 21-23
African Studies *(Arts & Music)* 22
African Studies *(Government & Politics)* 333, 344, 360
Agencies *(Business & Economics)* 116
Agencies *(Government & Politics)* 719
Aging *(Health & Medicine)* 368, 370, 372, 393, 688, 720
Agriculture *(Education)* 240, 289
Agriculture *(Engineering & Technology)* 292
Agriculture *(Government & Politics)* 314, 316
Agriculture *(Health & Medicine)* 370

Agriculture *(Popular Culture & Entertainment)* 555
Agriculture *(Science)* 565-568, 579, 583, 699, 734
AIDS (Acquired Immune Deficiency Syndrome) *(Education)* 255
AIDS (Acquired Immune Deficiency Syndrome) *(Health & Medicine)* 375, 378, 396-398, 402, 408
Air Force *(Engineering & Technology)* 312
Air Force *(Government & Politics)* 346
Air Mosaic *(Internet)* 476
Air Transportation *(Sports & Recreation)* 620, 661, 663-666, 670
Airlines *(Business & Economics)* 148
Airlines *(Sports & Recreation)* 620, 656-657, 663-664, 666, 670
Airplane Repair *(Business & Economics)* 148
Airplanes *(Sports & Recreation)* 620
Airports *(Sports & Recreation)* 661, 665
Alabama *(Business & Economics)* 113
Alabama *(Government & Politics)* 323
Alaska *(Communications)* 163
Alaska *(Education)* 283
Alaska *(Government & Politics)* 321, 344
Alaska *(Popular Culture & Entertainment)* 521
Alaska *(Science)* 583
Alaska *(Sports & Recreation)* 654, 663
Albums *(Business & Economics)* 148
Alcohol *(Sports & Recreation)* 624-625, 627-628, 630, 633
Alcoholic Beverages *(Business & Economics)* 630
Alcoholic Beverages *(Sports & Recreation)* 632-633
Alcoholism *(Health & Medicine)* 367
Ales *(Business & Economics)* 630
Ales *(Sports & Recreation)* 627
Algebra *(Computing & Mathematics)* 200
Algorithms *(Computing & Mathematics)* 173, 185-186, 189-190, 192, 194, 196, 198-199, 201, 232
Aliens *(Popular Culture & Entertainment)* 553
Allergies *(Health & Medicine)* 383-384, 392, 398
Allergies *(Popular Culture & Entertainment)* 521
Alternative Education *(Communications)* 157
Alternative Education *(Education)* 242, 244, 684, 718
Alternative Education *(Health & Medicine)* 374
Alternative Education *(Science)* 601
Alternative Energy *(Science)* 592
Alternative Medicine *(Health & Medicine)* 368-369, 688, 720
Alternative Music *(Arts & Music)* 52-53, 58, 62, 66, 68-72, 74-82, 84, 86, 88-89
Alternative Music *(Popular Culture & Entertainment)* 540, 554
Alternative Rock *(Arts & Music)* 57
Alumni *(Business & Economics)* 107
Alzheimer's Disease *(Government & Politics)* 365
Alzheimer's Disease *(Health & Medicine)* 375
American Architecture *(Arts & Music)* 17

783

Keyword Index

American Art – Automobile Care

American Art *(Arts & Music)* 22, 25-27
American Culture *(Humanities & Social Sciences)* 415
American History *(Humanities & Social Sciences)* 425
American Literature *(Humanities & Social Sciences)* 436, 438, 444
American Studies *(Humanities & Social Sciences)* 416, 424, 426
Amoeba *(Computing & Mathematics)* 204
Amphibians *(Sports & Recreation)* 644, 646-647
Anagrams *(Humanities & Social Sciences)* 431
Analysis *(Computing & Mathematics)* 679, 711
Analytical Philosophy *(Religion & Philosophy)* 558
Anasazi Architecture *(Arts & Music)* 17
Anatomy *(Science)* 579
Ancient Art *(Arts & Music)* 22, 24
Ancient Art *(Government & Politics)* 339
Ancient Egypt *(Humanities & Social Sciences)* 414
Ancient Greece *(Humanities & Social Sciences)* 422
Ancient History *(Government & Politics)* 339
Anesthesiology *(Health & Medicine)* 389-390
Animal Breeding *(Sports & Recreation)* 645
Animal Husbandry *(Science)* 614-615
Animal Protection *(Sports & Recreation)* 646
Animal Rights *(Science)* 593, 614, 616
Animal Rights *(Sports & Recreation)* 625, 629-630, 632, 643
Animal Science *(Government & Politics)* 319
Animal Science *(Health & Medicine)* 409
Animal Science *(Popular Culture & Entertainment)* 545
Animal Science *(Science)* 601, 614, 616-617
Animal Welfare *(Sports & Recreation)* 647
Animals *(Health & Medicine)* 409
Animals *(Popular Culture & Entertainment)* 544
Animals *(Science)* 601, 614-617
Animals *(Sports & Recreation)* 643-647
Animation *(Arts & Music)* 36, 38, 40, 43-44, 47-48
Animation *(Computing & Mathematics)* 227
Animation *(Health & Medicine)* 404
Animation *(Popular Culture & Entertainment)* 551
Animation *(Science)* 603
Annual Reports *(Business & Economics)* 101, 105, 132, 143
Antarctica *(Science)* 594
Anthropology *(Arts & Music)* 17, 25
Anthropology *(Humanities & Social Sciences)* 413-414, 422, 690, 722
Anthropology *(Popular Culture & Entertainment)* 544
Antiquarian Books *(Popular Culture & Entertainment)* 511
Antiquarian Books *(Sports & Recreation)* 621
Antique Auctions *(Popular Culture & Entertainment)* 546
Antiques Galleries *(Popular Culture & Entertainment)* 546
Antiques *(Business & Economics)* 145-146, 148, 150-151
Antiques *(Popular Culture & Entertainment)* 510, 546
Antiques *(Sports & Recreation)* 621-624
Antiquities *(Arts & Music)* 24
Antisemitism *(Government & Politics)* 358
Apartheid *(Government & Politics)* 340
Apartments *(Business & Economics)* 104
Appalachia *(Arts & Music)* 31
Appeals *(Law & Criminal Justice)* 498
Appliances *(Business & Economics)* 123
Applications *(Computing & Mathematics)* 183, 679
Applications *(Engineering & Technology)* 309
Applied Mathematics *(Science)* 606

Applied Sciences *(Engineering & Technology)* 310
Appraisals *(Business & Economics)* 140
April Fools Day *(Popular Culture & Entertainment)* 526
Aquaculture *(Science)* 568
Aquariums *(Science)* 568, 615
Aquariums *(Sports & Recreation)* 619, 643
Aquatic Science *(Government & Politics)* 317
Aquatic Science *(Science)* 568, 699, 734
Aquatic Science *(Sports & Recreation)* 647
Aquatic Sports *(Sports & Recreation)* 701, 735
Arabic Language *(Education)* 252
Arabic *(Humanities & Social Sciences)* 420
Arbitration *(Law & Criminal Justice)* 500
Arboretums *(Sports & Recreation)* 638
Archaeology *(Arts & Music)* 22, 24, 26, 37
Archaeology *(Humanities & Social Sciences)* 414, 422, 690, 722
Archaeology *(Popular Culture & Entertainment)* 544
Archeology *(Religion & Philosophy)* 562
Archie (Internet Tool) *(Education)* 237
Archie *(Internet)* 476-477
Architects *(Arts & Music)* 16
Architectural Design *(Business & Economics)* 123
Architectural History *(Arts & Music)* 15-16, 21-22
Architectural Images *(Arts & Music)* 15-16
Architectural Visualization *(Arts & Music)* 16
Architecture Education *(Arts & Music)* 16-17
Architecture *(Arts & Music)* 15-17, 24, 26, 28, 33-34, 675, 708
Architecture *(Business & Economics)* 122
Architecture *(Computing & Mathematics)* 172
Architecture *(Engineering & Technology)* 308
Architecture *(Science)* 607
Architecture *(Sports & Recreation)* 662
Archives *(Arts & Music)* 30, 39, 57, 93
Archives *(Business & Economics)* 141
Archives *(Computing & Mathematics)* 177, 200, 213
Archives *(Education)* 261, 272
Archives *(Health & Medicine)* 389-390
Archives *(Humanities & Social Sciences)* 425-426, 431
Archives *(Internet)* 466, 478
Archives *(Popular Culture & Entertainment)* 534, 552
Archives *(Religion & Philosophy)* 563
Archives *(Science)* 574, 590, 592, 599, 603, 612
Archives *(Sports & Recreation)* 624, 629-630, 632, 641, 649
Area & Cultural Studies *(Humanities & Social Sciences)* 690, 722
Argentina *(Communications)* 168
Argentina *(Government & Politics)* 313, 316, 331-332
Argentina *(Internet)* 465
Arizona *(Business & Economics)* 113
Arizona *(Education)* 283
Arizona *(Government & Politics)* 326-329
Arizona *(Health & Medicine)* 407
Arizona *(Popular Culture & Entertainment)* 520
Arkansas *(Education)* 283
Armadillos *(Sports & Recreation)* 644, 646
Army *(Government & Politics)* 346-347, 349
Art Auctions *(Arts & Music)* 31
Art Collections *(Humanities & Social Sciences)* 424
Art Collections *(Popular Culture & Entertainment)* 544-545
Art Competitions *(Arts & Music)* 33
Art Conservation *(Arts & Music)* 22
Art Criticism *(Arts & Music)* 17, 29-30
Art Criticism *(Popular Culture & Entertainment)* 534, 541
Art Education *(Arts & Music)* 17, 19, 27-28
Art Exhibitions *(Arts & Music)* 17-24, 26-27, 29-46, 91, 98-99

Art Exhibitions *(Sports & Recreation)* 624, 667
Art Galleries *(Arts & Music)* 18-19, 22-23, 28, 30, 32, 42, 99
Art History *(Arts & Music)* 17-18, 20, 32, 675
Art Museums *(Arts & Music)* 19, 21-24, 26-27, 30-31
Art Museums *(Popular Culture & Entertainment)* 545
Art Organizations *(Arts & Music)* 27, 32
Art Projects *(Arts & Music)* 18
Art Research *(Arts & Music)* 27
Art Resources *(Arts & Music)* 33, 675
Art Schools *(Arts & Music)* 27-28, 36
Art Theory *(Arts & Music)* 43
Art *(Arts & Music)* 34, 91, 98
Art *(Education)* 244
Art *(Government & Politics)* 328, 331, 338
Art *(Humanities & Social Sciences)* 414-415, 436-437, 439
Art *(Internet)* 461
Art *(Popular Culture & Entertainment)* 524, 543
Art *(Religion & Philosophy)* 562
Art *(Sports & Recreation)* 622, 667
Artifacts *(Humanities & Social Sciences)* 414
Artifacts *(Popular Culture & Entertainment)* 544
Artificial Intelligence *(Communications)* 160, 164
Artificial Intelligence *(Computing & Mathematics)* 170, 175-179, 187-190, 192-193, 212, 230, 680, 711
Artificial Intelligence *(Engineering & Technology)* 303, 306, 310
Artificial Intelligence *(Popular Culture & Entertainment)* 533
Artificial Intelligence *(Science)* 601
Artificial Life *(Computing & Mathematics)* 170, 175, 177
Artists *(Arts & Music)* 17-20, 22, 27, 29-30, 32, 43
Arts Advocacy *(Arts & Music)* 32
Arts Agencies *(Arts & Music)* 32
Arts Education *(Arts & Music)* 28-29, 47
Arts Festivals *(Arts & Music)* 27, 90
Arts Funding *(Arts & Music)* 32-33
Arts *(Arts & Music)* 20, 38
Arts *(Business & Economics)* 113, 115
ASCII Art *(Arts & Music)* 35, 40, 45
Asia *(Arts & Music)* 23
Asia *(Business & Economics)* 125-128, 136
Asia *(Education)* 236, 266, 288
Asia *(Government & Politics)* 316, 331-332, 334, 360, 668
Asia *(Humanities & Social Sciences)* 415, 451
Asia *(Sports & Recreation)* 655
Asian American Issues *(Law & Criminal Justice)* 494
Asian Americans *(Arts & Music)* 47
Asian Americans *(Humanities & Social Sciences)* 416
Asian Arts *(Arts & Music)* 20, 23, 26-27, 29
Asian Literature *(Humanities & Social Sciences)* 439
Asian Studies *(Government & Politics)* 337
Asian Studies *(Humanities & Social Sciences)* 414, 416
Associations *(Business & Economics)* 119
Associations *(Communications)* 153
Associations *(Computing & Mathematics)* 206, 208, 228
Associations *(Education)* 246
Associations *(Internet)* 459
Associations *(Religion & Philosophy)* 560
Associations *(Sports & Recreation)* 621, 626
Asthma *(Health & Medicine)* 383-384
Asthma *(Popular Culture & Entertainment)* 521
Astrology *(Popular Culture & Entertainment)* 524, 554
Astronomy *(Humanities & Social Sciences)* 414
Astronomy *(Popular Culture & Entertainment)* 525

Astronomy *(Science)* 571-574, 584, 607-608, 610-613, 699, 734
Astrophysics *(Science)* 611
Atheism *(Religion & Philosophy)* 557
Athletics *(Sports & Recreation)* 643
ATM (Asynchronous Transfer Mode) *(Communications)* 159
ATM (Asynchronous Transfer Mode) *(Computing & Mathematics)* 182, 201, 228
ATM (Asynchronous Transfer Mode) *(Engineering & Technology)* 296
Atmospheric Sciences *(Popular Culture & Entertainment)* 555
Atmospheric Sciences *(Science)* 587-594, 610
Atomic Energy *(Engineering & Technology)* 304
Attention Deficit Disorder *(Health & Medicine)* 384
Auctioneers *(Business & Economics)* 150
Auctions *(Business & Economics)* 150
Auctions *(Popular Culture & Entertainment)* 510, 546
Auctions *(Sports & Recreation)* 622-623
Audio Books *(Popular Culture & Entertainment)* 512
Audio Recording *(Arts & Music)* 65
Audio Technology *(Arts & Music)* 63, 65-66, 70
Audio Technology *(Engineering & Technology)* 308
Audio Technology *(Health & Medicine)* 405
Audio *(Arts & Music)* 63, 65-66, 70
Audio *(Computing & Mathematics)* 175
Audio *(Engineering & Technology)* 297, 310
Audio-Visual Communications *(Communications)* 166
Audio-Visual Communications *(Computing & Mathematics)* 174
Auditing *(Business & Economics)* 101
Australia *(Arts & Music)* 16, 19-20, 23, 50, 56, 61-63, 73-74, 76, 97
Australia *(Business & Economics)* 107, 125, 148
Australia *(Computing & Mathematics)* 185, 206, 213
Australia *(Education)* 234, 245, 250, 266-267, 288
Australia *(Engineering & Technology)* 301-302, 306
Australia *(Government & Politics)* 320-322, 327, 330-331, 334, 336, 350
Australia *(Humanities & Social Sciences)* 414-416, 444
Australia *(Internet)* 462
Australia *(Law & Criminal Justice)* 499
Australia *(Popular Culture & Entertainment)* 533, 535
Australia *(Science)* 568, 570, 585, 587, 592-594, 597, 601
Australia *(Sports & Recreation)* 621, 638, 640, 644-645, 656, 658-659, 666-667
Austria *(Arts & Music)* 91-92
Austria *(Computing & Mathematics)* 188
Austria *(Education)* 251
Austria *(Humanities & Social Sciences)* 438
Austria *(Sports & Recreation)* 625, 654
Authors *(Humanities & Social Sciences)* 422, 426, 437-438, 440-443
Authors *(Popular Culture & Entertainment)* 512
Autism *(Health & Medicine)* 374, 384
Auto Audio Installation *(Popular Culture & Entertainment)* 509
Auto Audio *(Popular Culture & Entertainment)* 509
Auto Manufacturers *(Popular Culture & Entertainment)* 510
Auto Racing *(Sports & Recreation)* 639
Auto Rental *(Popular Culture & Entertainment)* 510
Auto Showrooms *(Popular Culture & Entertainment)* 509-511
Automation Research *(Computing & Mathematics)* 186
Automobile Care *(Business & Economics)* 122, 125
Automobile Care *(Education)* 256

Automobile Care – Business Communications

Automobile Care *(Popular Culture & Entertainment)* 509-511
Automobile Emergencies *(Business & Economics)* 121
Automobile Equipment *(Popular Culture & Entertainment)* 510
Automobile Financing *(Popular Culture & Entertainment)* 509-510
Automobile Insurance *(Business & Economics)* 121
Automobile Maintenance *(Sports & Recreation)* 638
Automobile Repair *(Business & Economics)* 122, 125
Automobile Repair *(Popular Culture & Entertainment)* 509
Automobiles *(Business & Economics)* 121-122, 124
Automobiles *(Government & Politics)* 362
Automobiles *(Popular Culture & Entertainment)* 509-511, 546, 696
Automobiles *(Sports & Recreation)* 638
Aviation *(Business & Economics)* 148
Aviation *(Engineering & Technology)* 312
Aviation *(Science)* 610
Aviation *(Sports & Recreation)* 620, 642, 654, 665, 701, 735
Awards *(Popular Culture & Entertainment)* 514
Aztec History *(Humanities & Social Sciences)* 425

Baby Products *(Popular Culture & Entertainment)* 547
Backpacking *(Sports & Recreation)* 660
Bagels *(Business & Economics)* 148
Ballet *(Arts & Music)* 54, 91-92, 94-97
Banking *(Business & Economics)* 104-106, 116, 128, 130, 149, 678, 709
Banking *(Government & Politics)* 314
Bargains *(Popular Culture & Entertainment)* 545
Bartending *(Sports & Recreation)* 624, 633
Bartering *(Business & Economics)* 150
Baseball *(Popular Culture & Entertainment)* 540
Baseball *(Sports & Recreation)* 648, 651-652
Basketball *(Popular Culture & Entertainment)* 540
Basketball *(Sports & Recreation)* 640, 649-653
Bath Accessories *(Popular Culture & Entertainment)* 548
Batman *(Business & Economics)* 136
Bats *(Science)* 614
Bauhaus *(Arts & Music)* 15
BBSs (Bulletin Board Systems) *(Internet)* 474
BBSs (Bulletin Board Systems) *(Business & Economics)* 104
BBSs (Bulletin Board Systems) *(Computing & Mathematics)* 226
BBSs (Bulletin Board Systems) *(Internet)* 484
Beat Generation *(Humanities & Social Sciences)* 444
Beatles (The) *(Arts & Music)* 71-73, 75, 77, 79, 81
Beauty *(Popular Culture & Entertainment)* 541
Beds *(Business & Economics)* 146
Beekeeping *(Science)* 565-566
Beer Brewing *(Business & Economics)* 630
Beer *(Popular Culture & Entertainment)* 532
Beer *(Sports & Recreation)* 625, 627, 630, 632-633
Bees *(Science)* 565-566
Beethoven *(Arts & Music)* 51
Behavioral Science *(Humanities & Social Sciences)* 447
Behavioral Science *(Science)* 601
Bel Canto Singing *(Arts & Music)* 94
Belgium *(Arts & Music)* 91
Belgium *(Business & Economics)* 112, 125-126
Belgium *(Communications)* 157-158
Belgium *(Computing & Mathematics)* 189, 209

Belgium *(Education)* 263, 271, 273-274
Belgium *(Government & Politics)* 323, 325, 331, 340, 348
Belgium *(Humanities & Social Sciences)* 433
Belgium *(Popular Culture & Entertainment)* 541
Belgium *(Sports & Recreation)* 625, 649, 660, 663, 668
Belize *(Sports & Recreation)* 655
Benefits *(Business & Economics)* 106
Bermuda *(Business & Economics)* 133
Bermuda *(Sports & Recreation)* 619
Better Business Bureau (BBB) *(Business & Economics)* 116
Beverages *(Business & Economics)* 148
Beverages *(Sports & Recreation)* 625
Bible *(Computing & Mathematics)* 226
Bible *(Humanities & Social Sciences)* 440
Bible *(Religion & Philosophy)* 559-562, 564
Biblical History *(Humanities & Social Sciences)* 414
Biblical Texts *(Religion & Philosophy)* 562
Bibliographies *(Business & Economics)* 138
Bibliographies *(Computing & Mathematics)* 184, 187, 192, 215
Bibliographies *(Education)* 234, 261
Bibliographies *(Humanities & Social Sciences)* 429, 433
Bibliographies *(Internet)* 470
Bibliographies *(Popular Culture & Entertainment)* 515
Bibliographies *(Religion & Philosophy)* 558
Bibliographies *(Science)* 582
Bicycle Racing *(Sports & Recreation)* 640, 642
Bicycling *(Sports & Recreation)* 640-642, 653
Bilingual Education *(Computing & Mathematics)* 228
Bill of Rights *(Government & Politics)* 341, 354
Biochemistry *(Engineering & Technology)* 293
Biochemistry *(Health & Medicine)* 370, 388
Biochemistry *(Science)* 578, 581, 585-586
Biodegradable Products *(Business & Economics)* 148
Biodiversity *(Science)* 565, 569, 579-580, 582, 592-593, 595-596, 602, 615
Bioengineering *(Engineering & Technology)* 292, 719
Biographies *(Arts & Music)* 51, 57, 86
Biographies *(Computing & Mathematics)* 198
Biographies *(Science)* 600
Bioinformatics *(Health & Medicine)* 370-371, 406
Bioinformatics *(Science)* 574, 582, 585, 601, 615
Biological Research *(Engineering & Technology)* 292
Biological Research *(Health & Medicine)* 394
Biological Research *(Science)* 565, 570, 574-580, 586
Biological Resources *(Science)* 581
Biological Sciences *(Computing & Mathematics)* 216
Biological Sciences *(Education)* 256, 260
Biology Journals *(Science)* 577
Biology Research *(Science)* 581, 594
Biology *(Engineering & Technology)* 292
Biology *(Health & Medicine)* 385, 387-388
Biology *(Law & Criminal Justice)* 493
Biology *(Science)* 566, 574-576, 578-579, 582, 584, 586, 588, 592, 602, 613-616, 699, 734
Biomechanics *(Science)* 575
Biomedical Computing *(Science)* 576
Biomedical Conferences *(Science)* 575
Biomedical Engineering *(Health & Medicine)* 370
Biomedical Research *(Computing & Mathematics)* 170
Biomedical Research *(Government & Politics)* 316
Biomedical Research *(Health & Medicine)* 370-372, 392, 398, 403

Biomedical Research *(Science)* 575-581, 584
Biomedical Science *(Computing & Mathematics)* 224
Biomedical Science *(Engineering & Technology)* 296
Biomedical Science *(Science)* 581, 584
Biomedicine *(Computing & Mathematics)* 170
Biomedicine *(Health & Medicine)* 370-371, 385-386, 388, 392, 394, 688, 720
Biomedicine *(Science)* 575, 581, 602
Biophysics *(Science)* 575, 581, 602
Biosciences *(Computing & Mathematics)* 170
Biosciences *(Education)* 241, 274
Biosciences *(Engineering & Technology)* 305
Biosciences *(Health & Medicine)* 388, 392, 402
Biosciences *(Science)* 545, 570, 575-576, 578-579, 604, 607, 700
Biotechnology Law *(Science)* 575
Biotechnology *(Business & Economics)* 125
Biotechnology *(Computing & Mathematics)* 170
Biotechnology *(Engineering & Technology)* 292, 306, 308
Biotechnology *(Government & Politics)* 335
Biotechnology *(Health & Medicine)* 368, 370, 401
Biotechnology *(Science)* 565-567, 574-579, 581, 584
Birds *(Science)* 613-614, 616
Birds *(Sports & Recreation)* 639, 643-648
Birdwatching *(Sports & Recreation)* 644, 646, 648
Birth Records *(Popular Culture & Entertainment)* 522-523
Birthdays *(Popular Culture & Entertainment)* 516
Bisexuality *(Health & Medicine)* 408
Bisexuality *(Popular Culture & Entertainment)* 531-532
Bisexuals *(Popular Culture & Entertainment)* 532
Bitnet *(Internet)* 466
Blues *(Arts & Music)* 51, 57, 68, 73, 78, 82-83, 89
Board Games *(Sports & Recreation)* 635
Boat Construction *(Sports & Recreation)* 620
Boating *(Sports & Recreation)* 620
Bolivia *(Sports & Recreation)* 655
Bonds *(Business & Economics)* 132
Bonsai Trees *(Popular Culture & Entertainment)* 546
Bonsai Trees *(Sports & Recreation)* 636
Booch Method *(Computing & Mathematics)* 212
Book Clubs *(Popular Culture & Entertainment)* 512
Book Collecting *(Popular Culture & Entertainment)* 513
Book News *(Popular Culture & Entertainment)* 512
Book Reviews *(Arts & Music)* 16
Book Reviews *(Sports & Recreation)* 624
Books *(Arts & Music)* 30, 71
Books *(Business & Economics)* 113-114, 124, 136-139
Books *(Communications)* 153
Books *(Education)* 261
Books *(Humanities & Social Sciences)* 422, 426, 429, 434-437, 439-445
Books *(Internet)* 458
Books *(Law & Criminal Justice)* 502
Books *(Popular Culture & Entertainment)* 511-516, 523, 538
Books *(PopularCulture & Entertainment)* 696
Books *(Science)* 585
Books *(Sports & Recreation)* 621, 623
Bookstores *(Business & Economics)* 136, 138-139
Bookstores *(Humanities & Social Sciences)* 443
Bookstores *(Popular Culture & Entertainment)* 512, 514-516

Bosnia *(Humanities & Social Sciences)* 434
Boston *(Arts & Music)* 47, 60, 62
Boston *(Business & Economics)* 108
Boston *(Computing & Mathematics)* 206
Boston *(Sports & Recreation)* 625
Botanical Gardens *(Science)* 583-584
Botanical Gardens *(Sports & Recreation)* 636, 638
Botanical Taxonomy *(Science)* 583
Botany *(Science)* 567, 577, 583-584, 592, 700, 734
Botany *(Sports & Recreation)* 636-637
Bouillabaisse *(Sports & Recreation)* 628
Boutiques *(Popular Culture & Entertainment)* 522
Bowling *(Sports & Recreation)* 644
Boycott *(Health & Medicine)* 398
Brain Research *(Health & Medicine)* 371, 375, 405
Brain Research *(Science)* 601
Brazil *(Computing & Mathematics)* 201
Brazil *(Education)* 275
Brazil *(Engineering & Technology)* 306
Brazil *(Government & Politics)* 324, 331, 335
Brazil *(Popular Culture & Entertainment)* 541, 543
Brazil *(Science)* 579, 587
Breast Cancer *(Health & Medicine)* 376-378, 410
Brewing *(Sports & Recreation)* 633
Bridal Apparel *(Popular Culture & Entertainment)* 522
Bridge *(Sports & Recreation)* 634-635
Bridges *(Arts & Music)* 15
Bridges *(Sports & Recreation)* 654
Britain *(Arts & Music)* 69, 71-72, 76
Britain *(Communications)* 154
Britain *(Law & Criminal Justice)* 506
Britain *(Sports & Recreation)* 638, 670
British Art *(Arts & Music)* 26
British Comedy *(Popular Culture & Entertainment)* 552
British Companies *(Business & Economics)* 127
British Literature *(Humanities & Social Sciences)* 434, 439
Broadband Technology *(Communications)* 161, 164-165
Broadband Technology *(Computing & Mathematics)* 202
Broadband Technology *(Government & Politics)* 364
Broadband Technology *(Internet)* 474
Broadcasting *(Business & Economics)* 122
Broadcasting *(Communications)* 156-158, 162, 167
Broadcasting *(Popular Culture & Entertainment)* 552
Broadway *(Arts & Music)* 91, 95
Brokerage Services *(Business & Economics)* 129, 142
Bronze Age *(Humanities & Social Sciences)* 414
BSDI *(Computing & Mathematics)* 180
Buddhism *(Humanities & Social Sciences)* 435
Buddhism *(Religion & Philosophy)* 564
Budget (US) *(Government & Politics)* 313, 350
Budget Deficit *(Business & Economics)* 117
Budget Travel *(Sports & Recreation)* 654
Bulgaria *(Arts & Music)* 67
Bulgaria *(Government & Politics)* 331, 335
Bulgaria *(Popular Culture & Entertainment)* 530
Bulgaria *(Sports & Recreation)* 666
Bullfighting *(Humanities & Social Sciences)* 418
Bureau of Labor Statistics (US) *(Government & Politics)* 355
Bureau of Mines (US) *(Government & Politics)* 318
Bushwalking *(Humanities & Social Sciences)* 416
Business Communications *(Business & Economics)* 124
Business Communications *(Computing & Mathematics)* 225

Business Conferences – China

Business Conferences *(Business & Economics)* 127
Business Consulting *(Business & Economics)* 120
Business Development *(Business & Economics)* 113, 125
Business Development *(Government & Politics)* 364
Business Development *(Sports & Recreation)* 658
Business Directory *(Business & Economics)* 126
Business Education *(Business & Economics)* 149
Business Education *(Education)* 239
Business Ethics *(Business & Economics)* 134
Business Law *(Government & Politics)* 352
Business Law *(Law & Criminal Justice)* 495, 503
Business Management *(Business & Economics)* 103, 106-107, 133
Business News *(Business & Economics)* 125
Business Planning *(Business & Economics)* 103, 120
Business Research *(Business & Economics)* 149
Business Schools *(Business & Economics)* 107, 109, 678
Business Schools *(Education)* 271
Business Services *(Business & Economics)* 103-104, 119-120, 135-136, 140, 149-150
Business Services *(Engineering & Technology)* 311
Business Strategy *(Business & Economics)* 133-134
Business *(Business & Economics)* 101, 107-108, 112-114, 116, 118-119, 124, 126-128, 130-134, 142, 150
Business *(Education)* 264, 272
Business *(Engineering & Technology)* 307
Business *(Government & Politics)* 315, 322-325, 327-328, 330-331, 337, 347, 351, 357, 362, 364
Business *(Health & Medicine)* 367
Business *(Humanities & Social Sciences)* 419
Business *(Law & Criminal Justice)* 502
Business *(Popular Culture & Entertainment)* 530, 538, 547-548
Business *(Sports & Recreation)* 659-660
Buyers Guides *(Business & Economics)* 146
Buyers Guides *(Popular Culture & Entertainment)* 546

Cable Industry *(Business & Economics)* 117
Cable Industry *(Communications)* 155
Cable Industry *(Popular Culture & Entertainment)* 536
Cable Regulation *(Communications)* 155
Cable Television *(Business & Economics)* 122
Cable Television *(Communications)* 155
Cable Television *(Government & Politics)* 355
Cable Television *(Popular Culture & Entertainment)* 550
Cafes *(Sports & Recreation)* 627, 630
Caffeine *(Sports & Recreation)* 627, 629-630
Cajun Cuisine *(Sports & Recreation)* 626
Cajun Culture *(Internet)* 483
Cajun Food *(Sports & Recreation)* 660
Cajun Music *(Arts & Music)* 51, 91
Calendars *(Science)* 612
California News *(Popular Culture & Entertainment)* 550
California *(Arts & Music)* 23, 26, 30, 38, 62, 90, 94
California *(Business & Economics)* 109-112, 117, 120, 136, 140-141, 151
California *(Communications)* 160, 168
California *(Computing & Mathematics)* 206
California *(Education)* 243, 247, 258, 260, 277, 279-280, 283-284, 286
California *(Engineering & Technology)* 294-295, 297, 300, 305

California *(Government & Politics)* 319, 322-328, 352-353, 355, 361-363, 365
California *(Health & Medicine)* 387, 389, 410
California *(Humanities & Social Sciences)* 424, 447
California *(Internet)* 462
California *(Law & Criminal Justice)* 492-496, 500, 504-505
California *(Popular Culture & Entertainment)* 512, 531, 535, 544, 550, 555
California *(Science)* 583, 592, 599, 612
California *(Sports & Recreation)* 624, 629, 640, 642, 654, 656, 671
Calvin And Hobbes *(Popular Culture & Entertainment)* 526
Camcorders *(Arts & Music)* 50
Cameras *(Business & Economics)* 122
Camping *(Government & Politics)* 324
Camping *(Sports & Recreation)* 631, 641, 654, 659, 671
Campus Information *(Education)* 268-269, 274, 277-280, 283-284, 286-288
Campus Information *(Engineering & Technology)* 310
Campus Information *(Religion & Philosophy)* 563
Campus Networks *(Education)* 243, 246, 280
Campus Wide Information Systems *(Education)* 277-278, 280
Canada *(Arts & Music)* 27, 47-48, 53, 56, 59-62, 72, 76, 82, 91, 94
Canada *(Business & Economics)* 107, 111, 116, 127-128, 142
Canada *(Computing & Mathematics)* 188, 196, 206
Canada *(Education)* 233-234, 236, 238-239, 242, 255-256, 258, 267-269
Canada *(Engineering & Technology)* 294, 300, 307
Canada *(Government & Politics)* 318, 320, 324, 326, 328, 331, 336, 345, 350, 361
Canada *(Health & Medicine)* 371, 374, 393, 405
Canada *(Humanities & Social Sciences)* 413, 424, 429
Canada *(Internet)* 453-455, 462
Canada *(Law & Criminal Justice)* 498
Canada *(Popular Culture & Entertainment)* 535, 540
Canada *(Science)* 571, 588, 607
Canada *(Sports & Recreation)* 619, 632, 656, 658, 663-664, 667, 669-670
Canadian Brass *(Arts & Music)* 73
Canadian Culture *(Arts & Music)* 27
Canadian Heritage *(Popular Culture & Entertainment)* 544
Cancer Research *(Health & Medicine)* 374, 376-378, 406
Cancer *(Health & Medicine)* 370, 374-381, 396, 402, 408
Candy *(Popular Culture & Entertainment)* 629
Canoeing *(Sports & Recreation)* 619, 631
Card Collecting *(Sports & Recreation)* 623
Card Games *(Sports & Recreation)* 634-635
Cardiopulmonary Medicine *(Health & Medicine)* 386
Career & Employment *(Business & Economics)* 678, 709
Career & Employment *(Computing & Mathematics)* 680, 711
Career & Employment *(Government & Politics)* 687, 719
Career & Employment *(Health & Medicine)* 720
Career & Employment *(Humanities & Social Sciences)* 691
Career & Employment *(Science)* 700, 734
Career & Employment *(Sports & Recreation)* 735
Career Services *(Business & Economics)* 109
Career *(Business & Economics)* 109-112
Career *(Communications)* 153-154
Career *(Computing & Mathematics)* 179
Career *(Engineering & Technology)* 293
Career *(Science)* 584
Career *(Sports & Recreation)* 621

Career *(Engineering & Technology)* 292
Caribbean Music *(Arts & Music)* 85
Caribbean *(Education)* 254
Caribbean *(Humanities & Social Sciences)* 419
Caribbean *(Sports & Recreation)* 655
Carnivorous Plants *(Science)* 583
Carpal Tunnel Syndrome *(Health & Medicine)* 384-385
Carpentry *(Sports & Recreation)* 624
Cartoons *(Arts & Music)* 38
Cartoons *(Popular Culture & Entertainment)* 526, 529
Cartoons *(Sports & Recreation)* 623
Cassettes *(Business & Economics)* 147
Cassettes *(Popular Culture & Entertainment)* 513
Catalan *(Humanities & Social Sciences)* 427
Catalogs *(Business & Economics)* 114, 138, 146
Catalogs *(Computing & Mathematics)* 218
Catalogs *(Popular Culture & Entertainment)* 547
Catalogs *(Sports & Recreation)* 632
Catering *(Sports & Recreation)* 632
Catholicism *(Education)* 275
Catholicism *(Religion & Philosophy)* 559
Cats *(Business & Economics)* 114
Cats *(Popular Culture & Entertainment)* 528
Cats *(Sports & Recreation)* 645, 647
Cave Paintings *(Humanities & Social Sciences)* 414
Caving *(Sports & Recreation)* 642
CD ROMs *(Popular Culture & Entertainment)* 543
CD-ROMs *(Arts & Music)* 42, 44
CD-ROMs *(Computing & Mathematics)* 193, 201
CD-ROMs *(Humanities & Social Sciences)* 426
CD-ROMs *(Sports & Recreation)* 654
Celebrities & Personalities *(PopularCulture & Entertainment)* 697
Celebrities *(Arts & Music)* 39
Celebrities *(Popular Culture & Entertainment)* 516, 536, 539
Celebrities *(Sports & Recreation)* 627
Cell Biology *(Health & Medicine)* 370, 387
Cell Biology *(Science)* 576, 578, 580-581
Cellular Communications *(Communications)* 163
Cellular Phones *(Communications)* 161, 164-165
Celtic Culture *(Humanities & Social Sciences)* 419
Celtic Culture *(Religion & Philosophy)* 557
Celtic Music *(Arts & Music)* 63, 74
Censorship *(Communications)* 156
Censorship *(Government & Politics)* 334
Censorship *(Humanities & Social Sciences)* 434, 436
Censorship *(Law & Criminal Justice)* 491
Census (The) *(Government & Politics)* 318, 343, 352, 357-358
Census (The) *(Humanities & Social Sciences)* 448
Census Bureau (US) *(Government & Politics)* 358
Centers For Disease Control *(Health & Medicine)* 396
Central America *(Popular Culture & Entertainment)* 540
Central America *(Sports & Recreation)* 655, 658
Central Europe *(Government & Politics)* 341
Central Europe *(Science)* 568
Central Processing Units (CPUs) *(Computing & Mathematics)* 193
Ceramics *(Arts & Music)* 33
Ceramics *(Sports & Recreation)* 622
Certificates Of Deposit *(Business & Economics)* 132
Chamber Music *(Arts & Music)* 55, 57-59, 61, 78
Chameleons *(Arts & Music)* 74
Chaos Theory *(Computing & Mathematics)* 171, 177, 195, 232
Chaos Theory *(Religion & Philosophy)* 558

Chaos Theory *(Science)* 606
Charities *(Religion & Philosophy)* 562
Charter Services *(Sports & Recreation)* 667
Chat Groups *(Government & Politics)* 329
Chat Groups *(Humanities & Social Sciences)* 432
Chat Groups *(Internet)* 455, 486
Chefs *(Sports & Recreation)* 626, 629
Chemical Analysis *(Science)* 586
Chemical Engineering *(Engineering & Technology)* 293-294, 299-300, 686, 719
Chemical Engineering *(Science)* 586
Chemicals *(Business & Economics)* 125
Chemistry *(Computing & Mathematics)* 221
Chemistry *(Education)* 247
Chemistry *(Engineering & Technology)* 293-294, 303
Chemistry *(Government & Politics)* 350
Chemistry *(Health & Medicine)* 398
Chemistry *(Science)* 574, 584-586, 589, 602-603, 607, 700, 734
Chemotherapy *(Health & Medicine)* 376, 378
Chernobyl *(Government & Politics)* 335
Chess *(Sports & Recreation)* 634-635
Chicago *(Arts & Music)* 16, 49, 74
Chicago *(Business & Economics)* 147
Chicago *(Education)* 284
Chicago *(Government & Politics)* 324, 353
Chicago *(Sports & Recreation)* 658
Chicano Culture *(Business & Economics)* 110
Chicano Culture *(Humanities & Social Sciences)* 416, 419
Child Abuse *(Government & Politics)* 345
Child Care *(Business & Economics)* 520
Child Care *(Government & Politics)* 343
Child Care *(Health & Medicine)* 381-383
Child Care *(Popular Culture & Entertainment)* 517-518, 520, 547
Child Custody *(Law & Criminal Justice)* 494
Child Psychology *(Health & Medicine)* 381
Child Support *(Law & Criminal Justice)* 494-495
Children *(Business & Economics)* 139, 146
Children *(Education)* 255-257, 259, 261
Children *(Government & Politics)* 343
Children *(Health & Medicine)* 381-383, 394
Children *(Popular Culture & Entertainment)* 517-519, 521-522
Children *(Religion & Philosophy)* 562
Children *(Sports & Recreation)* 635
Children's Activities *(Popular Culture & Entertainment)* 519, 521
Children's Fiction *(Popular Culture & Entertainment)* 516
Children's Health *(Health & Medicine)* 384, 393
Children's Literature *(Business & Economics)* 137, 139
Children's Literature *(Humanities & Social Sciences)* 422, 435-439
Children's Literature *(Popular Culture & Entertainment)* 512-513, 519
Children's Online Directory *(Popular Culture & Entertainment)* 521
Children's Programs *(Education)* 257
Children's Programs *(Health & Medicine)* 374
Children's Programs *(Popular Culture & Entertainment)* 518
Children's Rights *(Law & Criminal Justice)* 494
Children's Toys *(Popular Culture & Entertainment)* 524
Chile *(Business & Economics)* 118
Chile *(Computing & Mathematics)* 189
Chile *(Education)* 247, 275-276
Chile *(Engineering & Technology)* 298
Chile *(Government & Politics)* 316
Chile *(Science)* 571
Chile *(Sports & Recreation)* 658
Chili Peppers *(Sports & Recreation)* 626
China *(Business & Economics)* 126
China *(Education)* 255, 260, 265
China *(Government & Politics)* 329, 331-332
China *(Humanities & Social Sciences)* 416-417, 421-422, 435, 437-438, 444

China – Computer-Aided Design (CAD)   787

China *(Popular Culture & Entertainment)* 533
China *(Sports & Recreation)* 623
Chinese Art *(Arts & Music)* 18
Chinese Language *(Computing & Mathematics)* 225
Chinese Language *(Humanities & Social Sciences)* 433
Chinese Language *(Popular Culture & Entertainment)* 533
Chinese Literature *(Government & Politics)* 332
Chinese Literature *(Humanities & Social Sciences)* 422, 435, 437-438, 444
Chinese Studies *(Government & Politics)* 331
Chinese Studies *(Popular Culture & Entertainment)* 533
Chocolate *(Business & Economics)* 113
Chocolate *(Sports & Recreation)* 626-627
Choral Music *(Arts & Music)* 55
Choral Singing *(Arts & Music)* 62, 73
Christian Music *(Arts & Music)* 50, 52, 57-58, 73, 89
Christian Music *(Religion & Philosophy)* 559-560
Christianity *(Humanities & Social Sciences)* 427, 434
Christianity *(Religion & Philosophy)* 559-564
Chromosomes *(Science)* 575
Chronic Fatigue Syndrome *(Health & Medicine)* 384
Churches *(Religion & Philosophy)* 561
CIA (Central Intelligence Agency) *(Government & Politics)* 344
Cigars *(Popular Culture & Entertainment)* 546
Cinema *(Arts & Music)* 48-49
Cinema *(Popular Culture & Entertainment)* 542
Circuit Design *(Engineering & Technology)* 295
Circumcision *(Health & Medicine)* 407
Cities *(Government & Politics)* 327, 687
Cities *(Sports & Recreation)* 658
Civil Engineering *(Computing & Mathematics)* 175
Civil Engineering *(Engineering & Technology)* 294, 298-299, 686, 719
Civil Engineering *(Popular Culture & Entertainment)* 555
Civil Law *(Law & Criminal Justice)* 507
Civil Liberties *(Communications)* 164
Civil Liberties *(Government & Politics)* 345, 357, 361
Civil Liberties *(Internet)* 461
Civil Liberties *(Law & Criminal Justice)* 490-491
Civil Rights *(Computing & Mathematics)* 215
Civil Rights *(Government & Politics)* 354, 362
Civil Rights *(Law & Criminal Justice)* 491-492, 505
Civil Service *(Business & Economics)* 112
Civil War *(Humanities & Social Sciences)* 426
Class Action Suits *(Law & Criminal Justice)* 503
Classic Cars *(Popular Culture & Entertainment)* 510
Classical Music *(Arts & Music)* 51-52, 54-55, 57-70, 72-73, 78, 83-88, 90-92, 94-95, 97
Classical Music *(Popular Culture & Entertainment)* 514
Classical Studies *(Humanities & Social Sciences)* 427, 439
Classics *(Arts & Music)* 22
Classics *(Government & Politics)* 339
Classics *(Humanities & Social Sciences)* 422-424, 434, 440, 444, 691, 723
Classified Ads *(Business & Economics)* 104, 110, 150
Classified Ads *(Popular Culture & Entertainment)* 525
Classified Ads *(Sports & Recreation)* 622
Client Server Technology *(Computing & Mathematics)* 183, 203, 210
Client Server Technology *(Education)* 264

Climatology *(Engineering & Technology)* 301
Climatology *(Government & Politics)* 344
Climatology *(Popular Culture & Entertainment)* 555
Climatology *(Science)* 554, 569-570, 587-590, 592-593, 597, 600
Climbing *(Education)* 275
Clip Art *(Internet)* 463
Clocks *(Sports & Recreation)* 623
Clothing *(Business & Economics)* 103, 112, 115, 148
Clothing *(Popular Culture & Entertainment)* 522, 546
Club Memberships *(Sports & Recreation)* 636
Clubs *(Sports & Recreation)* 638
Co-ops *(Business & Economics)* 142
Coastal Marine Biology *(Science)* 568
Codes *(Law & Criminal Justice)* 489, 492, 495, 505-506
Coffee *(Business & Economics)* 148
Coffee *(Popular Culture & Entertainment)* 626
Coffee *(Sports & Recreation)* 625, 627, 629-630
Cognitive Sciences *(Computing & Mathematics)* 176-178, 186
Cognitive Sciences *(Education)* 252
Cognitive Sciences *(Humanities & Social Sciences)* 432, 445-446
Cognitive Sciences *(Religion & Philosophy)* 558
Cognitive Sciences *(Science)* 600
Coin Collecting *(Popular Culture & Entertainment)* 548
Cold War *(Government & Politics)* 337
Collectibles *(Business & Economics)* 145-146, 148, 150-151
Collectibles *(Education)* 279
Collectibles *(Sports & Recreation)* 621-625, 638
Collectors *(Government & Politics)* 330
Collectors *(Popular Culture & Entertainment)* 510
College Placement *(Education)* 282
College Radio *(Arts & Music)* 61
College Sports *(Sports & Recreation)* 649
Colleges & Universities *(Computing & Mathematics)* 187-188
Colleges & Universities *(Education)* 270, 276, 284, 685
Colleges & Universities *(Engineering & Technology)* 294
Colleges & Universities *(Health & Medicine)* 385
Colleges & Universities *(Education)* 272
Colleges & Universities *(Humanities & Social Sciences)* 418
Colombia *(Government & Politics)* 332
Colombia *(Internet)* 474
Colorado *(Arts & Music)* 59, 64, 66
Colorado *(Education)* 260, 284
Colorado *(Government & Politics)* 326-328, 363-364
Colorado *(Popular Culture & Entertainment)* 554
Colorado *(Science)* 597, 600
Comedy *(Arts & Music)* 31, 46, 81
Comedy *(Communications)* 156
Comedy *(Humanities & Social Sciences)* 444
Comedy *(Popular Culture & Entertainment)* 516, 526, 528, 530, 551-552
Comics *(Arts & Music)* 31, 38, 46
Comics *(Business & Economics)* 138
Comics *(Computing & Mathematics)* 227
Comics *(Popular Culture & Entertainment)* 511, 514, 526-527
Commemorative Coins *(Popular Culture & Entertainment)* 548
Commerce *(Business & Economics)* 106, 120, 126, 142, 678, 709
Commerce *(Engineering & Technology)* 307
Commerce *(Government & Politics)* 313-314, 317, 365
Commerce *(Internet)* 455

Commerce *(Law & Criminal Justice)* 490, 496
Commercial Art Studios *(Arts & Music)* 18
Commercial Databases *(Business & Economics)* 142
Commercial Online Services *(Internet)* 453, 455, 463
Commercial Real Estate *(Business & Economics)* 140, 142
Commercial Vendors *(Computing & Mathematics)* 184
Commodities *(Business & Economics)* 131-132
Commonwealth *(Education)* 251
Commonwealth *(Government & Politics)* 320
Communications Programs *(Communications)* 156
Communications Research *(Communications)* 153, 165-166
Communications Research *(Computing & Mathematics)* 230
Communications Software *(Computing & Mathematics)* 222, 225
Communications Systems *(Business & Economics)* 118
Communications Systems *(Government & Politics)* 359
Communications Technology *(Communications)* 159-161, 165, 168
Communications Technology *(Computing & Mathematics)* 201-202
Communications Technology *(Engineering & Technology)* 291
Communications Technology *(Government & Politics)* 342, 344
Communications Technology *(Internet)* 460
Communications Technology *(Popular Culture & Entertainment)* 543
Communications *(Business & Economics)* 121-122, 139, 150
Communications *(Communications)* 153-155, 157-158, 160-161, 163-164, 166
Communications *(Computing & Mathematics)* 172, 176, 214, 218
Communications *(Education)* 244, 246, 252, 260
Communications *(Engineering & Technology)* 307
Communications *(Government & Politics)* 364
Communications *(Internet)* 461, 474
Communications *(Law & Criminal Justice)* 490-491
Communications *(Popular Culture & Entertainment)* 533, 538, 545, 548, 552
Communism *(Religion & Philosophy)* 557
Community Development *(Government & Politics)* 319
Community Development *(Popular Culture & Entertainment)* 518
Community Information *(Government & Politics)* 321, 364
Community Information *(Health & Medicine)* 373, 405
Community Information *(Humanities & Social Sciences)* 448
Community Information *(Popular Culture & Entertainment)* 537
Community Information *(Sports & Recreation)* 654-655, 663
Community Networking *(Business & Economics)* 113, 118
Community Networking *(Education)* 239, 253
Community Networking *(Government & Politics)* 324, 328, 350, 359-361
Community Networking *(Health & Medicine)* 387
Community Networking *(Internet)* 468, 472-473, 475
Community Networking *(Popular Culture & Entertainment)* 517, 520, 537
Community Networks *(Government & Politics)* 322-323, 325, 327, 329, 359
Community Networks *(Internet)* 454, 473, 485
Community Networks *(Popular Culture & Entertainment)* 532

Community Organizing *(Internet)* 465, 475
Community Services *(Business & Economics)* 107
Community Services *(Computing & Mathematics)* 208, 229
Community Services *(Education)* 235, 238-239, 242, 249, 265, 270, 280, 282
Community Services *(Government & Politics)* 330, 347
Community Services *(Health & Medicine)* 382, 388, 401
Community Services *(Humanities & Social Sciences)* 431
Community Services *(Popular Culture & Entertainment)* 517-518, 520
Community Services *(Religion & Philosophy)* 562
Community Services *(Sports & Recreation)* 669
Community *(Business & Economics)* 136, 520
Community *(Government & Politics)* 321-322, 324-329, 350, 359-360, 362
Community *(Popular Culture & Entertainment)* 518
Compact Discs (CDs) *(Arts & Music)* 55, 58, 64, 67, 69, 73, 84-88, 90-91, 94
Compact Discs (CDs) *(Business & Economics)* 147-148
Companies *(Arts & Music)* 48, 59, 93
Companies *(Business & Economics)* 102, 104-106, 109, 111, 114, 119, 121, 123-125, 128, 138-139, 142-143, 146, 150
Companies *(Communications)* 159, 163
Companies *(Computing & Mathematics)* 170, 172, 174-175, 180-184, 193-194, 202-203, 205-206, 209-210, 220-224, 227, 229
Companies *(Engineering & Technology)* 292, 302-303, 305, 309
Companies *(Government & Politics)* 317
Companies *(Internet)* 472, 481
Companies *(Popular Culture & Entertainment)* 510, 547-548
Companies *(Science)* 574-576, 578, 611
Company Performance *(Business & Economics)* 132
Company Profiles *(Business & Economics)* 126
Comparative Law *(Law & Criminal Justice)* 496
Competitions *(Arts & Music)* 94
Complex Systems *(Computing & Mathematics)* 177
Complex Systems *(Engineering & Technology)* 297, 302, 304
Composers *(Arts & Music)* 51-52, 54-55, 57-58, 63-64, 83-84, 86, 88
Composing *(Arts & Music)* 54, 69
Computation *(Computing & Mathematics)* 187, 195, 200
Computational Chemistry *(Science)* 586
Computational Linguistics *(Computing & Mathematics)* 176-177
Computational Linguistics *(Humanities & Social Sciences)* 432
Computational Neuroscience *(Computing & Mathematics)* 170-175
Computational Neuroscience *(Engineering & Technology)* 304
Computational Sciences *(Communications)* 160
Computational Sciences *(Computing & Mathematics)* 187
Computational Vision *(Computing & Mathematics)* 186
Computer Acronyms *(Computing & Mathematics)* 213
Computer Administration *(Business & Economics)* 149
Computer Administration *(Computing & Mathematics)* 171
Computer Administration *(Education)* 238, 285
Computer Aided Design (CAD) *(Computing & Mathematics)* 172, 175, 181-182, 185
Computer Aided Design (CAD) *(Engineering & Technology)* 299

Keyword Index

Computer Aided Design (CAD) *(Science)* 581
Computer Aided Instruction *(Arts & Music)* 15, 47
Computer Aided Instruction *(Computing & Mathematics)* 195, 224
Computer Aided Instruction *(Education)* 244-247, 249, 254, 257, 262-263, 272
Computer Animation *(Arts & Music)* 44
Computer Animation *(Computing & Mathematics)* 171
Computer Applications *(Communications)* 162
Computer Applications *(Computing & Mathematics)* 170-176, 178, 183, 187, 191, 201, 204, 206-209, 214-215, 217-218, 220-221, 223, 226, 230, 232
Computer Applications *(Education)* 243, 246-247, 253, 261, 275
Computer Applications *(Engineering & Technology)* 309
Computer Applications *(Health & Medicine)* 374
Computer Applications *(Internet)* 476
Computer Applications *(Popular Culture & Entertainment)* 555
Computer Applications *(Science)* 576, 581, 602
Computer Art *(Arts & Music)* 19, 28, 32, 34-47
Computer Art *(Internet)* 463
Computer Art *(Popular Culture & Entertainment)* 536
Computer Books *(Popular Culture & Entertainment)* 515
Computer Conferencing *(Business & Economics)* 151
Computer Conferencing *(Communications)* 159
Computer Conferencing *(Computing & Mathematics)* 202-203
Computer Consulting *(Business & Economics)* 114
Computer Consulting *(Popular Culture & Entertainment)* 550
Computer Databases *(Business & Economics)* 149
Computer Databases *(Education)* 236, 250, 261
Computer Databases *(Engineering & Technology)* 306
Computer Databases *(Government & Politics)* 331
Computer Design *(Arts & Music)* 45
Computer Education *(Computing & Mathematics)* 180, 188
Computer Education *(Education)* 246
Computer Equipment *(Computing & Mathematics)* 222
Computer Ethics *(Computing & Mathematics)* 206
Computer Ethics *(Government & Politics)* 354
Computer Ethics *(Internet)* 470
Computer Ethics *(Law & Criminal Justice)* 491
Computer Games *(Computing & Mathematics)* 224
Computer Games *(Education)* 247
Computer Games *(Internet)* 482, 484
Computer Games *(Sports & Recreation)* 634-636
Computer Graphics *(Arts & Music)* 19, 30, 34-35, 41, 43, 45
Computer Graphics *(Business & Economics)* 148
Computer Graphics *(Computing & Mathematics)* 169, 172-173, 175, 180, 182, 220, 227
Computer Graphics *(Internet)* 478
Computer Graphics *(Science)* 613
Computer Graphics *(Sports & Recreation)* 634
Computer Hardware *(Arts & Music)* 46
Computer Hardware *(Communications)* 159-160, 163

Computer Hardware *(Computing & Mathematics)* 180-184, 193-194, 201-205, 207, 214-215, 217, 219-220, 229-232
Computer Hardware *(Internet)* 466, 481
Computer Humor *(Popular Culture & Entertainment)* 527
Computer Integrated Manufacturing *(Engineering & Technology)* 300
Computer Interface Issues *(Computing & Mathematics)* 186
Computer Magazines *(Computing & Mathematics)* 215
Computer Magazines *(Popular Culture & Entertainment)* 535
Computer Mediated Communication *(Communications)* 153-154
Computer Modeling *(Science)* 598
Computer Music *(Arts & Music)* 43, 64, 67
Computer Networking *(Business & Economics)* 108, 118
Computer Networking *(Communications)* 166
Computer Networking *(Computing & Mathematics)* 182-183, 185-186, 190, 202-204, 206, 215, 222
Computer Networking *(Education)* 244, 246-248, 254, 265, 285
Computer Networking *(Internet)* 473-474, 481-482
Computer Networking *(Popular Culture & Entertainment)* 517, 543
Computer Networking *(Science)* 586
Computer Networks *(Communications)* 159-161, 167
Computer Networks *(Computing & Mathematics)* 194, 222
Computer Networks *(Education)* 248, 255, 275-276, 285, 287
Computer Networks *(Government & Politics)* 314, 316, 327, 360, 364
Computer Networks *(Internet)* 453-454, 465-466, 472, 474, 481-482
Computer News *(Computing & Mathematics)* 175, 227
Computer Organizations *(Government & Politics)* 362
Computer Peripherals *(Business & Economics)* 123
Computer Peripherals *(Computing & Mathematics)* 194, 207
Computer Policy *(Internet)* 461
Computer Products *(Business & Economics)* 114-115, 122
Computer Products *(Communications)* 159-160
Computer Products *(Computing & Mathematics)* 173, 180-184, 214, 217-218, 226
Computer Products *(Popular Culture & Entertainment)* 548
Computer Professionals *(Computing & Mathematics)* 208, 218
Computer Programming *(Computing & Mathematics)* 171-172, 174, 178, 199, 204, 215, 229-230, 232
Computer Programming *(Engineering & Technology)* 298
Computer Programming *(Government & Politics)* 345
Computer Science *(Communications)* 155, 164
Computer Science *(Computing & Mathematics)* 170, 172-173, 176-179, 187-191, 196, 198-199, 201, 204-209, 213-214, 217, 219, 227, 232, 680, 711
Computer Science *(Education)* 248, 258, 264-265, 268, 270-271, 276, 285, 287-288
Computer Science *(Engineering & Technology)* 295-296, 298, 300, 306, 308-311
Computer Science *(Government & Politics)* 347
Computer Science *(Health & Medicine)* 391, 398
Computer Science *(Internet)* 467, 478, 481
Computer Science *(Popular Culture & Entertainment)* 543
Computer Science *(Science)* 603-604

Computer Security *(Computing & Mathematics)* 170-171, 176, 215-217
Computer Security *(Engineering & Technology)* 309
Computer Security *(Internet)* 470-471
Computer Security *(Law & Criminal Justice)* 489
Computer Simulation *(Computing & Mathematics)* 173-174, 183
Computer Simulation *(Science)* 600
Computer Software *(Arts & Music)* 67
Computer Software *(Business & Economics)* 101, 114-115, 119, 128, 132
Computer Software *(Communications)* 165
Computer Software *(Computing & Mathematics)* 172, 184, 190, 196, 220-221, 226-227
Computer Software *(Government & Politics)* 345
Computer Software *(Health & Medicine)* 372
Computer Speech Interfaces *(Computing & Mathematics)* 175
Computer Supplies *(Business & Economics)* 114, 128
Computer Supplies *(Computing & Mathematics)* 185
Computer Systems Architecture *(Computing & Mathematics)* 189, 193, 201, 231
Computer Systems *(Communications)* 168
Computer Systems *(Computing & Mathematics)* 174, 180-184, 186, 194, 207-208, 221-224, 226-227, 229-230
Computer Systems *(Engineering & Technology)* 299
Computer Systems *(Science)* 606
Computer Technology *(Communications)* 163, 166
Computer Technology *(Computing & Mathematics)* 185, 193, 205-209, 229
Computer Technology *(Education)* 272-273
Computer Technology *(Engineering & Technology)* 296, 305-306, 309
Computer Technology *(Health & Medicine)* 374
Computer Technology *(Internet)* 482
Computer Technology *(Popular Culture & Entertainment)* 550
Computer Technology *(Science)* 611
Computer Terminology *(Computing & Mathematics)* 213
Computer User Groups *(Computing & Mathematics)* 208
Computer Viruses *(Computing & Mathematics)* 215-217
Computer Viruses *(Internet)* 470
Computer Visualization *(Computing & Mathematics)* 173, 183
Computer Workgroups *(Computing & Mathematics)* 231
Computers *(Business & Economics)* 114-115, 118, 148
Computers *(Computing & Mathematics)* 182, 194
Computers *(Education)* 245, 256, 273, 279
Computers *(Government & Politics)* 347
Computers *(Health & Medicine)* 409
Computers *(Internet)* 453
Computers *(Law & Criminal Justice)* 503
Computers *(Popular Culture & Entertainment)* 525, 528-529, 535, 548
Computers *(Science)* 572
Computing Services *(Computing & Mathematics)* 228
Computing Services *(Education)* 277
Computing *(Business & Economics)* 101, 124, 138, 149
Computing *(Communications)* 166
Computing *(Computing & Mathematics)* 169, 179, 181-182, 187-189, 191-192
Computing *(Education)* 239, 248, 271-272, 279, 282-283, 285
Computing *(Engineering & Technology)* 295, 299, 305-306, 309
Computing *(Health & Medicine)* 374, 388
Computing *(Humanities & Social Sciences)* 413, 431, 448, 450

Computing *(Popular Culture & Entertainment)* 528
Computing *(Science)* 576, 610
Concerts *(Arts & Music)* 54, 63-64, 70
Concurrent Logic *(Computing & Mathematics)* 171, 188, 191, 210, 229, 232
Concurrent Systems *(Computing & Mathematics)* 174, 215, 232
Condiments *(Sports & Recreation)* 626
Condominiums *(Business & Economics)* 142
Conductors *(Arts & Music)* 54, 64, 90
Conference *(Health & Medicine)* 389
Conferences & Events *(Health & Medicine)* 688
Conferences *(Arts & Music)* 99
Conferences *(Business & Economics)* 122, 145
Conferences *(Computing & Mathematics)* 173, 177, 198, 206, 208-209
Conferences *(Education)* 246
Conferences *(Engineering & Technology)* 304, 312
Conferences *(Government & Politics)* 345-346
Conferences *(Health & Medicine)* 369
Conferences *(Humanities & Social Sciences)* 427
Conferences *(Internet)* 482
Conferences *(Science)* 581, 593, 606
Conferencing *(Internet)* 460
Confession *(Popular Culture & Entertainment)* 527
Configuration Tools *(Computing & Mathematics)* 222
Conflict Resolution *(Business & Economics)* 134
Conflict Resolution *(Law & Criminal Justice)* 500
Conflict Resolution *(Popular Culture & Entertainment)* 517-518
Congress *(Government & Politics)* 340
Connecticut *(Education)* 239, 278, 284, 288
Connecticut *(Popular Culture & Entertainment)* 541
Conservation *(Education)* 255
Conservation *(Engineering & Technology)* 300-301
Conservation *(Government & Politics)* 317, 344-346, 350
Conservation *(Humanities & Social Sciences)* 433
Conservation *(Science)* 582, 584, 592-593, 595-596
Conservation *(Sports & Recreation)* 643, 645
Conservatives *(Government & Politics)* 350, 355
Consignment *(Popular Culture & Entertainment)* 545
Conspiracy *(Popular Culture & Entertainment)* 553
Constitutional Law *(Law & Criminal Justice)* 503, 505, 695, 726
Constitutions *(Government & Politics)* 339, 341, 351-352, 354-355, 358
Constitutions *(Law & Criminal Justice)* 496-497, 505
Constraint Programming *(Computing & Mathematics)* 209
Construction Industry *(Business & Economics)* 140
Construction *(Business & Economics)* 122-123, 146
Construction *(Engineering & Technology)* 298
Consulates *(Government & Politics)* 319
Consultants *(Business & Economics)* 103
Consultants *(Communications)* 159
Consulting Services *(Business & Economics)* 102, 110, 120, 127, 131, 133-134, 148-149
Consulting Services *(Communications)* 156
Consulting Services *(Computing & Mathematics)* 203, 221, 229
Consulting Services *(Internet)* 458
Consulting *(Business & Economics)* 476
Consulting *(Internet)* 456-457, 472-474

Consumer Affairs – Design 789

Consumer Affairs *(Business & Economics)* 116
Consumer Affairs *(Government & Politics)* 315
Consumer Affairs *(Popular Culture & Entertainment)* 509
Consumer Audio *(Arts & Music)* 63, 66
Consumer Credit *(Business & Economics)* 118
Consumer Education *(Business & Economics)* 116
Consumer Education *(Education)* 260
Consumer Electronics *(Arts & Music)* 66
Consumer Electronics *(Engineering & Technology)* 308
Consumer Electronics *(Popular Culture & Entertainment)* 543
Consumer Goods *(Business & Economics)* 102, 114, 116
Consumer Goods *(Popular Culture & Entertainment)* 546
Consumer Guides *(Computing & Mathematics)* 214
Consumer Guides *(Internet)* 454
Consumer Information *(Business & Economics)* 116, 124
Consumer Issues *(Business & Economics)* 678, 709
Consumer Issues *(Health & Medicine)* 396
Consumer Law *(Law & Criminal Justice)* 489
Consumer Protection *(Business & Economics)* 116
Consumer Protection *(Government & Politics)* 350
Consumer Protection *(Health & Medicine)* 374
Consumer Protection *(Popular Culture & Entertainment)* 552
Consumer Rights *(Business & Economics)* 116-117, 119
Consumer Rights *(Law & Criminal Justice)* 489, 507
Consumer Safety *(Government & Politics)* 318
Consumer Watchdog Groups *(Business & Economics)* 117
Contemporary Art *(Arts & Music)* 18, 21-23, 25-26, 30, 98-99
Contemporary Literature *(Business & Economics)* 138
Contemporary Literature *(Humanities & Social Sciences)* 434-435, 440
Contemporary Literature *(Popular Culture & Entertainment)* 533, 537, 541
Contemporary Music *(Arts & Music)* 52, 54, 56, 59, 62, 64, 67-68, 71-75, 77, 80-84, 87, 89
Contemporary Music *(Education)* 236
Continuing Education *(Education)* 239-240, 242-243, 254, 267, 718
Continuing Education *(Engineering & Technology)* 307
Control Engineering *(Engineering & Technology)* 296-297, 303
Conventions *(Arts & Music)* 78
Conventions *(Business & Economics)* 151
Conventions *(Computing & Mathematics)* 207
Conventions *(Humanities & Social Sciences)* 444
Cookbooks *(Popular Culture & Entertainment)* 528
Cookbooks *(Sports & Recreation)* 627, 632
Cooking *(Popular Culture & Entertainment)* 528
Cooking *(Sports & Recreation)* 624-633
Cooperative Networks *(Education)* 236
Copiers *(Business & Economics)* 121
Copyright Law *(Arts & Music)* 66
Copyright Law *(Law & Criminal Justice)* 495-496
Copyright *(Arts & Music)* 38
Corporate Giving *(Popular Culture & Entertainment)* 519
Corporate Law *(Law & Criminal Justice)* 489
Corporate Real Estate *(Business & Economics)* 142

Corporation Guides *(Business & Economics)* 144
Corporations *(Business & Economics)* 132, 144
Corporations *(Communications)* 163
Corporations *(Law & Criminal Justice)* 489, 496
Cosmetics *(Business & Economics)* 145
Cosmology *(Science)* 606, 611
Costa Rica *(Business & Economics)* 142
Costa Rica *(Popular Culture & Entertainment)* 537, 540
Costa Rica *(Science)* 584
Costa Rica *(Sports & Recreation)* 658
Counseling *(Education)* 237
Counseling *(Popular Culture & Entertainment)* 532
Countries *(Government & Politics)* 687, 719
Countries *(Humanities & Social Sciences)* 417
Country Music *(Arts & Music)* 51, 53-55, 62-63
Covered Bridges *(Arts & Music)* 15
Cows *(Sports & Recreation)* 644
Crafts & Hobbies *(Sports & Recreation)* 701, 735
Crafts *(Arts & Music)* 27, 30, 33
Crafts *(Education)* 272, 289
Crafts *(Popular Culture & Entertainment)* 546
Crafts *(Sports & Recreation)* 622-623
Creative Writing *(Education)* 260
Credit Bureaus *(Business & Economics)* 119
Credit Cards *(Business & Economics)* 104-105
Credit Reports *(Business & Economics)* 119
Credit *(Business & Economics)* 116
Creole Cooking *(Sports & Recreation)* 626
Crete *(Sports & Recreation)* 662
Cricket *(Sports & Recreation)* 649
Crime Prevention *(Government & Politics)* 361
Crime *(Government & Politics)* 315
Crime *(Law & Criminal Justice)* 489, 492, 494, 502, 506
Crime *(Popular Culture & Entertainment)* 518, 524
Criminal Justice *(Government & Politics)* 352
Criminal Justice *(Law & Criminal Justice)* 492, 497, 695
Criminals *(Law & Criminal Justice)* 506
Criminology *(Law & Criminal Justice)* 493
Critical Care *(Health & Medicine)* 392
Critical Theory *(Humanities & Social Sciences)* 429
Croatia *(Government & Politics)* 330, 342
Croatia *(Humanities & Social Sciences)* 416
Croatia *(Sports & Recreation)* 626, 666-667
Croquet *(Sports & Recreation)* 651
Cross Cultural Studies *(Humanities & Social Sciences)* 413
Cross Platform Applications *(Computing & Mathematics)* 181, 223
Cruises *(Sports & Recreation)* 667
Cryptography *(Computing & Mathematics)* 171
Cryptography *(Internet)* 471-472
Crystallography *(Science)* 577, 579, 585, 602, 607
CSCW Systems *(Computing & Mathematics)* 186
Cuba *(Education)* 236
Cuba *(Government & Politics)* 334
Cuisine *(Sports & Recreation)* 625, 632
Cultural Art *(Arts & Music)* 20
Cultural Exchange *(Business & Economics)* 126
Cultural Exchange *(Government & Politics)* 341
Cultural Exchange *(Health & Medicine)* 381
Cultural Exchange *(Popular Culture & Entertainment)* 536
Cultural Organizations *(Arts & Music)* 27
Cultural Studies *(Education)* 242, 279
Cultural Studies *(Government & Politics)* 328, 335-338

Cultural Studies *(Humanities & Social Sciences)* 415-420, 424-425, 429, 432, 440
Cultural Studies *(Popular Culture & Entertainment)* 538, 544
Culture *(Government & Politics)* 326, 331, 333-335, 339, 345
Culture *(Popular Culture & Entertainment)* 530, 536, 541
Culture *(Sports & Recreation)* 657-658, 662-664, 667
Curling *(Sports & Recreation)* 649
Currency Converter *(Business & Economics)* 130
Currency *(Business & Economics)* 129, 149
Current Events *(Communications)* 154, 157, 162
Current Events *(Computing & Mathematics)* 217
Current Events *(Education)* 261
Current Events *(Government & Politics)* 319, 333
Current Events *(Humanities & Social Sciences)* 439
Current Events *(Popular Culture & Entertainment)* 523
Curriculum & Instruction *(Education)* 684, 718
Curriculum *(Education)* 241, 247, 256, 258, 260, 265-266, 272, 279, 282-284
Curriculum *(Engineering & Technology)* 300, 302-303
Curriculum *(Humanities & Social Sciences)* 436
CUSeeMe *(Internet)* 460
Customer Support *(Communications)* 164
Cyberbusiness *(Popular Culture & Entertainment)* 543
Cyberculture *(Internet)* 466, 484-485, 487
Cyberculture *(Law & Criminal Justice)* 491
Cyberculture *(Popular Culture & Entertainment)* 525, 543, 551
Cybermalls *(Popular Culture & Entertainment)* 546, 549
Cyberpunk Games *(Internet)* 484
Cyberspace *(Humanities & Social Sciences)* 446, 449
Cyberspace *(Internet)* 458, 482, 484
Cycling *(Sports & Recreation)* 641-642
Czech Republic *(Education)* 270
Czech Republic *(Internet)* 472
Czechoslovakia *(Computing & Mathematics)* 196, 198

Dance Music *(Arts & Music)* 57, 85, 89
Dance *(Arts & Music)* 28, 65, 69, 91-97
Dance *(Sports & Recreation)* 660
Dancing *(Arts & Music)* 91-93
Dancing *(Popular Culture & Entertainment)* 531
Danish Law *(Law & Criminal Justice)* 496
Data Communications *(Business & Economics)* 122
Data Communications *(Communications)* 160-161
Data Communications *(Computing & Mathematics)* 179
Data Communications *(Internet)* 472
Data Management *(Computing & Mathematics)* 181, 228
Data Representation *(Computing & Mathematics)* 183
Data Storage *(Popular Culture & Entertainment)* 523
Data Systems *(Engineering & Technology)* 305
Database Applications *(Computing & Mathematics)* 171, 175, 184-185, 220, 224
Database Management *(Business & Economics)* 149
Database Management *(Communications)* 154
Database Management *(Computing & Mathematics)* 184-185
Database Management *(Humanities & Social Sciences)* 430
Databases *(Arts & Music)* 65
Databases *(Business & Economics)* 123, 144

Databases *(Computing & Mathematics)* 170, 174-175, 184, 187, 192, 196, 200, 212, 215-216
Databases *(Education)* 235-236, 240, 244, 250, 260, 264, 274
Databases *(Government & Politics)* 318, 338
Databases *(Health & Medicine)* 370, 386, 396, 402
Databases *(Humanities & Social Sciences)* 439, 448, 451
Databases *(Internet)* 462, 464, 466, 470, 480
Databases *(Popular Culture & Entertainment)* 524
Databases *(Science)* 566, 568, 570, 572, 574-576, 578-580, 586, 592, 595, 605
Databases *(Sports & Recreation)* 627-628, 630
Dating *(Internet)* 487
Dating *(Popular Culture & Entertainment)* 530, 533
Dead Sea Scrolls *(Religion & Philosophy)* 562
Deafness *(Health & Medicine)* 373, 385
Dealerships *(Business & Economics)* 122
Death Penalty *(Law & Criminal Justice)* 492-493
Death *(Health & Medicine)* 368, 402
Death *(Popular Culture & Entertainment)* 528, 552
Debt Consolidation *(Business & Economics)* 118
Debugging *(Computing & Mathematics)* 214, 225
Declaration of Independence *(Government & Politics)* 355
Decorative Arts *(Arts & Music)* 708
Decorative Lights *(Sports & Recreation)* 623
Deep Ocean Technology *(Science)* 568
Defense *(Education)* 288
Defense *(Government & Politics)* 314, 346-348, 362
Delaware *(Education)* 284
Delaware *(Government & Politics)* 363
Delaware *(Sports & Recreation)* 619
Democracy *(Government & Politics)* 341, 353
Democracy *(Law & Criminal Justice)* 506
Demographics *(Government & Politics)* 332-333, 357-358, 363
Demographics *(Humanities & Social Sciences)* 448
Demographics *(Science)* 601
Demography *(Humanities & Social Sciences)* 416
Denmark *(Communications)* 156
Denmark *(Education)* 270
Denmark *(Government & Politics)* 315, 334
Denmark *(Humanities & Social Sciences)* 430
Denmark *(Law & Criminal Justice)* 496
Denmark *(Sports & Recreation)* 659
Dental Health *(Health & Medicine)* 688, 720
Dentistry *(Health & Medicine)* 372, 388, 406
Department of Commerce (US) *(Government & Politics)* 314
Department of Defense (US) *(Government & Politics)* 347
Department Of Education (US) *(Education)* 245, 249
Department of Energy (US) *(Government & Politics)* 313, 315
Department Of Energy (US) *(Science)* 592
Department of Housing and Urban Development (HUD) (US) *(Government & Politics)* 315
Department of Transportation (US) *(Government & Politics)* 314
Depression *(Health & Medicine)* 392
Dermatology *(Health & Medicine)* 385
Design Arts *(Arts & Music)* 34
Design Firms *(Business & Economics)* 102
Design Industry *(Arts & Music)* 33-34
Design *(Arts & Music)* 15, 27, 34, 40, 675
Design *(Computing & Mathematics)* 195, 213, 231
Design *(Engineering & Technology)* 297-298, 301, 304

Design *(Popular Culture & Entertainment)* 522
Designer Apparel *(Popular Culture & Entertainment)* 522
Desktop Publishing *(Arts & Music)* 44
Desktop Publishing *(Computing & Mathematics)* 171, 226
Detectives *(Popular Culture & Entertainment)* 551
Developing Countries *(Government & Politics)* 346, 350
Development *(Business & Economics)* 120, 122
Development *(Government & Politics)* 360
Developmental Disabilities *(Health & Medicine)* 384
Diabetes *(Health & Medicine)* 377-378, 384
Diaries *(Government & Politics)* 327
Disaster Response *(Engineering & Technology)* 294
Dictionaries *(Arts & Music)* 65, 91
Dictionaries *(Computing & Mathematics)* 214
Dictionaries *(Humanities & Social Sciences)* 428, 432, 438, 440
Dictionaries *(Internet)* 460
Dictionaries *(Popular Culture & Entertainment)* 525
Diet *(Health & Medicine)* 368, 378, 384
Diet *(Sports & Recreation)* 642
Dietary Deficiency *(Health & Medicine)* 401
Diets *(Sports & Recreation)* 630
Differential Equations *(Computing & Mathematics)* 196
Digestive Diseases *(Health & Medicine)* 378
Digital Audio *(Arts & Music)* 63, 65-66, 70
Digital Electronics *(Computing & Mathematics)* 181
Digital Imaging *(Arts & Music)* 18, 36
Digital Media *(Arts & Music)* 34
Digital Photography *(Arts & Music)* 28, 39, 42, 98
Digital Photography *(Computing & Mathematics)* 172
Digital Radiography *(Health & Medicine)* 405
Digital Revolution *(Internet)* 460
Digital Signal Processing *(Engineering & Technology)* 295, 309
Digital Transactions *(Internet)* 456-458
Digital Video *(Arts & Music)* 46
Dining Out *(Sports & Recreation)* 625, 633
Dinosaurs *(Humanities & Social Sciences)* 414
Dinosaurs *(Popular Culture & Entertainment)* 518
Dinosaurs *(Science)* 603
Direct Marketing *(Business & Economics)* 104
Directories *(Arts & Music)* 47, 53
Directories *(Business & Economics)* 134, 145, 149
Directories *(Communications)* 156
Directories *(Internet)* 195, 464, 478
Directories *(Law & Criminal Justice)* 503
Directories *(Popular Culture & Entertainment)* 517, 536
Directories *(Science)* 600
Directories *(Sports & Recreation)* 636
Disabilities *(Health & Medicine)* 372-374, 378, 381-382, 688, 720
Disability Resources *(Business & Economics)* 112
Disability Resources *(Education)* 237
Disability Resources *(Health & Medicine)* 372-374
Disaster Relief *(Government & Politics)* 315, 350, 352-354
Discographies *(Arts & Music)* 63, 71, 82, 90, 95
Discount Shopping *(Popular Culture & Entertainment)* 548
Discussion Lists *(Humanities & Social Sciences)* 440
Diseases *(Health & Medicine)* 368, 376-378, 384-385, 396-397, 400, 688, 720
Disney *(Popular Culture & Entertainment)* 519

Distance Education *(Arts & Music)* 21
Distance Education *(Computing & Mathematics)* 174
Distance Education *(Education)* 239, 241-242, 244, 249, 684, 718
Distance Education *(Health & Medicine)* 397, 404
Distance Education *(Humanities & Social Sciences)* 427
Distance Learning *(Science)* 576
Distributed Applications *(Computing & Mathematics)* 210
Distributed Computing *(Computing & Mathematics)* 215, 229-230, 232
Distributed Intelligence Systems *(Popular Culture & Entertainment)* 520
Distributed Object Management (DOM) *(Computing & Mathematics)* 189
Distributed Systems *(Computing & Mathematics)* 189, 193
Distributed Systems *(Engineering & Technology)* 306
Distributors *(Computing & Mathematics)* 182
Divorce Law *(Law & Criminal Justice)* 494-495, 502
Divorce *(Popular Culture & Entertainment)* 531
DNS (Domain Name Server) *(Internet)* 457, 461
Doctrines *(Government & Politics)* 687, 719
Doctrines *(Religion & Philosophy)* 698
Document Analysis *(Engineering & Technology)* 296
Document Distribution *(Law & Criminal Justice)* 504
Document Management *(Business & Economics)* 138, 150
Document Management *(Computing & Mathematics)* 221
Document Technology *(Engineering & Technology)* 296
Documentaries *(Humanities & Social Sciences)* 413
Documentary Photography *(Arts & Music)* 98
Documents *(Computing & Mathematics)* 212
Documents *(Engineering & Technology)* 305
Documents *(Government & Politics)* 314, 355, 358
Dogs *(Law & Criminal Justice)* 492
Dogs *(Popular Culture & Entertainment)* 528
Dogs *(Sports & Recreation)* 644, 647
Domestic Violence *(Popular Culture & Entertainment)* 518
Dr. Seuss *(Popular Culture & Entertainment)* 513
Drama *(Arts & Music)* 33, 54, 91-92, 94-96
Drama *(Education)* 235
Drama *(Humanities & Social Sciences)* 435-437, 442
Drama *(Popular Culture & Entertainment)* 552
Dramatists *(Humanities & Social Sciences)* 422-423
Dream Interpretation *(Popular Culture & Entertainment)* 553
Dreams *(Health & Medicine)* 385
Dreams *(Popular Culture & Entertainment)* 553
Drinks *(Sports & Recreation)* 633
Drosophila *(Science)* 615-616
Drug Abuse *(Health & Medicine)* 367
Drug Use *(Health & Medicine)* 402
Drugs *(Health & Medicine)* 367, 371, 402, 406-407
Drugs *(Science)* 584
Drums *(Arts & Music)* 65

E-Zines *(Arts & Music)* 30, 39, 54, 62-63, 69-70
E-Zines *(Business & Economics)* 119, 138
E-Zines *(Computing & Mathematics)* 187, 228
E-Zines *(Education)* 251
E-Zines *(Government & Politics)* 354

E-Zines *(Humanities & Social Sciences)* 434, 436, 439-440
E-Zines *(Popular Culture & Entertainment)* 526, 533-534, 536, 541, 550
Early Music *(Arts & Music)* 52, 57-58, 65, 68-69
Earth Observing System *(Science)* 588-589
Earth Sciences *(Education)* 245
Earth Sciences *(Engineering & Technology)* 294, 303
Earth Sciences *(Government & Politics)* 317, 320, 361
Earth Sciences *(Popular Culture & Entertainment)* 524, 545
Earth Sciences *(Science)* 589, 592, 594, 597-600, 700
Earth Sciences *(Sports & Recreation)* 623
Earthquakes *(Government & Politics)* 327
Earthquakes *(Science)* 588-589, 599
East Timor *(Government & Politics)* 338
Eastern Europe *(Computing & Mathematics)* 207, 216
Eastern Europe *(Education)* 238, 252
Eastern Europe *(Government & Politics)* 335, 337
Eastern Europe *(Humanities & Social Sciences)* 416
Eastern Europe *(Law & Criminal Justice)* 497
Eating Disorders *(Health & Medicine)* 409-410
Ecology *(Business & Economics)* 103
Ecology *(Education)* 256, 260
Ecology *(Government & Politics)* 351, 356
Ecology *(Health & Medicine)* 396
Ecology *(Popular Culture & Entertainment)* 545
Ecology *(Science)* 545, 566-568, 570, 581-582, 590, 592-594, 596, 599
Economic Development *(Business & Economics)* 106, 113, 117-118, 126
Economic Development *(Communications)* 167
Economic Development *(Engineering & Technology)* 298
Economic Development *(Government & Politics)* 365
Economic Indicators *(Business & Economics)* 132, 138
Economic Indicators *(Government & Politics)* 364
Economic Justice *(Government & Politics)* 351
Economic Policy *(Business & Economics)* 117-118, 143, 678
Economic Theory *(Business & Economics)* 117
Economics *(Business & Economics)* 106, 108-109, 111, 114, 118, 142, 710
Economics *(Education)* 267, 273
Economics *(Government & Politics)* 313, 316, 318, 341, 344, 346-347, 352, 355, 357, 362, 364
Economics *(Internet)* 456
Economics *(Law & Criminal Justice)* 490
Economics *(Science)* 566, 568
Ecuador *(Communications)* 160
Ecuador *(Education)* 275
Ecuador *(Government & Politics)* 334
Education (College/University) *(Arts & Music)* 33-34
Education (College/University) *(Business & Economics)* 101, 106, 108-110, 118, 129
Education (College/University) *(Communications)* 154, 163, 165
Education (College/University) *(Computing & Mathematics)* 169, 171, 174, 187-190, 192-193, 195-196, 198-200, 205-206, 209, 215-219, 226-227
Education (College/University) *(Education)* 233-244, 247-251, 253-255, 257, 264-265, 267-276, 278-288
Education (College/University) *(Engineering & Technology)* 294-298, 300, 303, 306-310, 312
Education (College/University) *(Government & Politics)* 330, 363

Education (College/University) *(Health & Medicine)* 370, 374, 380-382, 385-394, 398, 400-401, 403-404, 406
Education (College/University) *(Humanities & Social Sciences)* 413, 430-431, 445, 447-448
Education (College/University) *(Law & Criminal Justice)* 498-499
Education (College/University) *(Popular Culture & Entertainment)* 518, 530, 543-544
Education (College/University) *(Religion & Philosophy)* 558, 561, 563
Education (College/University) *(Science)* 565, 568, 574, 586, 588-591, 593-594, 597, 600, 603-604, 607-608, 613, 617
Education *(Arts & Music)* 38
Education *(Business & Economics)* 108, 111
Education *(Communications)* 155-156, 158, 163
Education *(Computing & Mathematics)* 187, 192, 197, 200, 203, 206, 214, 230
Education *(Education)* 239, 241-242, 245-249, 252, 255-256, 258, 262, 264, 268, 272, 284
Education *(Engineering & Technology)* 297-298, 301, 304
Education *(Government & Politics)* 338, 341-342, 353-354
Education *(Health & Medicine)* 400, 406, 408
Education *(Humanities & Social Sciences)* 424, 426-427, 430, 436, 446
Education *(Law & Criminal Justice)* 495
Education *(Popular Culture & Entertainment)* 511, 518-519, 543-544
Education *(Religion & Philosophy)* 559-560
Education *(Science)* 571-572, 581, 584, 586-587, 597, 604, 610-611
Education *(Sports & Recreation)* 666
Educational Institutions *(Communications)* 166
Educational Issues *(Education)* 684, 718
Educational Networks *(Education)* 242, 245, 253, 258, 262
Educational Opportunities *(Education)* 237
Educational Opportunities *(Popular Culture & Entertainment)* 517
Educational Organizations *(Education)* 244, 253
Educational Policy *(Education)* 239, 242-245, 253, 255, 258, 288, 684, 718
Educational Policy *(Government & Politics)* 337
Educational Policy *(Internet)* 461
Educational Programs *(Computing & Mathematics)* 187-188, 192, 200, 206
Educational Programs *(Education)* 246, 257, 259, 266-267, 274, 276-277, 281-286
Educational Programs *(Engineering & Technology)* 310
Educational Programs *(Government & Politics)* 334
Educational Programs *(Health & Medicine)* 389
Educational Programs *(Humanities & Social Sciences)* 445
Educational Programs *(Law & Criminal Justice)* 492
Educational Programs *(Popular Culture & Entertainment)* 517
Educational Programs *(Religion & Philosophy)* 558
Educational Programs *(Science)* 604, 615
Educational Projects *(Education)* 684
Educational Resources *(Arts & Music)* 91
Educational Resources *(Business & Economics)* 118
Educational Resources *(Computing & Mathematics)* 174, 196
Educational Resources *(Education)* 236-237, 242, 247-248, 253, 255-260, 262, 264-265, 268, 271-274, 276-277, 281-288
Educational Resources *(Engineering & Technology)* 309
Educational Resources *(Government & Politics)* 337

Educational Resources – Ethnocentrism

Educational Resources *(Health & Medicine)* 387, 390
Educational Resources *(Humanities & Social Sciences)* 413, 420
Educational Resources *(Popular Culture & Entertainment)* 520-521, 544
Educational Resources *(Religion & Philosophy)* 563
Educational Resources *(Science)* 600, 606, 608
Educational Software *(Computing & Mathematics)* 195, 198, 224
Educational Software *(Education)* 252
Educational Software *(Engineering & Technology)* 302
Educational Software *(Humanities & Social Sciences)* 428-429
Educational Technology *(Computing & Mathematics)* 173, 185
Educational Technology *(Education)* 238, 241, 246, 254, 257-258, 262, 278, 684, 718
Educational Technology *(Engineering & Technology)* 310
Educational Technology *(Internet)* 464
Educational Theory *(Education)* 246, 254
Egypt *(Government & Politics)* 321
Egypt *(Humanities & Social Sciences)* 414
Egypt *(Sports & Recreation)* 658
Egyptian Archaeology *(Humanities & Social Sciences)* 414
Egyptian Art *(Arts & Music)* 27
Egyptian Artifacts *(Humanities & Social Sciences)* 414
El Salvador *(Government & Politics)* 334
Elections *(Government & Politics)* 355, 362
Electrical Engineering *(Engineering & Technology)* 294-296, 298-300, 304-305, 307, 310, 719
Electrical Engineering *(Science)* 600
Electricity *(Business & Economics)* 122-123
Electro-Acoustics *(Engineering & Technology)* 298
Electronic Arts *(Arts & Music)* 16-18, 20, 31-32, 34-47, 97-99, 675, 708
Electronic Arts *(Computing & Mathematics)* 171, 196
Electronic Arts *(Education)* 236
Electronic Books *(Business & Economics)* 139
Electronic Books *(Communications)* 158
Electronic Books *(Humanities & Social Sciences)* 437
Electronic Catalog *(Popular Culture & Entertainment)* 543
Electronic Commerce *(Business & Economics)* 105, 119
Electronic Journals *(Business & Economics)* 139
Electronic Journals *(Engineering & Technology)* 292
Electronic Journals *(Humanities & Social Sciences)* 446
Electronic Journals *(Popular Culture & Entertainment)* 524
Electronic Journals *(Science)* 579-581
Electronic Literacy *(Internet)* 466
Electronic Magazines *(Arts & Music)* 42
Electronic Magazines *(Computing & Mathematics)* 215
Electronic Magazines *(Internet)* 459
Electronic Magazines *(Sports & Recreation)* 666
Electronic Media *(Arts & Music)* 42
Electronic Media *(Business & Economics)* 136-137
Electronic Media *(Communications)* 153
Electronic Media *(Computing & Mathematics)* 173, 176
Electronic Media *(Education)* 261, 264, 277
Electronic Media *(Engineering & Technology)* 310
Electronic Media *(Internet)* 460
Electronic Media *(Popular Culture & Entertainment)* 534, 538
Electronic Money Transfers *(Internet)* 456, 458
Electronic Music *(Arts & Music)* 54, 57, 59, 62-71, 81, 86-89

Electronic Products *(Computing & Mathematics)* 182
Electronic Publishing *(Business & Economics)* 136-138
Electronic Publishing *(Communications)* 166
Electronic Publishing *(Computing & Mathematics)* 175, 198, 215, 228
Electronic Publishing *(Education)* 261
Electronic Publishing *(Humanities & Social Sciences)* 437, 442
Electronic Publishing *(Internet)* 456
Electronic Publishing *(Popular Culture & Entertainment)* 533, 537
Electronic Storefronts *(Internet)* 472
Electronic Texts *(Education)* 234
Electronic Texts *(Humanities & Social Sciences)* 433-434, 436, 438, 440-442
Electronics *(Arts & Music)* 63, 70
Electronics *(Business & Economics)* 124-125, 127
Electronics *(Computing & Mathematics)* 178, 202-203, 230
Electronics *(Engineering & Technology)* 294, 296, 298, 305, 307-308
Electronics *(Popular Culture & Entertainment)* 549
Elephants *(Science)* 593, 615
Elizabethan Drama *(Humanities & Social Sciences)* 423
Emacs *(Computing & Mathematics)* 172, 211, 214
Emacs *(Internet)* 477
Email Addresses *(Engineering & Technology)* 300
Email Directory *(Government & Politics)* 356, 358
Email Software *(Computing & Mathematics)* 225
Email *(Computing & Mathematics)* 183, 225
Email *(Government & Politics)* 327
Email *(Internet)* 459-460, 464-465, 468, 470, 475, 481
Email *(Sports & Recreation)* 635
Embassies *(Government & Politics)* 314, 341
Emergency Medical Services *(Health & Medicine)* 382, 401
Emergency Medical Services *(Sports & Recreation)* 640
Emergency Preparedness *(Government & Politics)* 315, 350, 352
Emerging Markets *(Business & Economics)* 119, 125-126
Employee Benefits *(Business & Economics)* 106
Employment Advertising *(Business & Economics)* 102
Employment Agencies *(Business & Economics)* 110
Employment *(Arts & Music)* 29, 33
Employment *(Business & Economics)* 103, 108, 110-112, 136, 140
Employment *(Communications)* 153-156, 159
Employment *(Computing & Mathematics)* 179, 200, 203, 228
Employment *(Education)* 237-238, 240, 243, 249, 254, 262, 270, 278
Employment *(Engineering & Technology)* 293
Employment *(Government & Politics)* 316, 356, 363
Employment *(Health & Medicine)* 371, 373
Employment *(Humanities & Social Sciences)* 450
Employment *(Internet)* 453
Employment *(Law & Criminal Justice)* 494
Employment *(Popular Culture & Entertainment)* 524, 543
Employment *(Science)* 584-585, 598
Emulators *(Computing & Mathematics)* 172, 203
Encryption *(Computing & Mathematics)* 196, 215
Encryption *(Internet)* 471
Encryption *(Law & Criminal Justice)* 491
Encyclopedias *(Humanities & Social Sciences)* 429
Endangered Species *(Education)* 245, 256, 259

Endangered Species *(Science)* 570, 593, 596, 599, 614
Endangered Species *(Sports & Recreation)* 643-645, 647
Endocrinology *(Health & Medicine)* 380
Energy Conservation *(Business & Economics)* 135
Energy Conservation *(Engineering & Technology)* 304
Energy Conservation *(Popular Culture & Entertainment)* 520
Energy Efficient Products *(Business & Economics)* 145
Energy Sources *(Government & Politics)* 314
Energy *(Business & Economics)* 124, 135
Energy *(Computing & Mathematics)* 190
Energy *(Engineering & Technology)* 300-301, 304, 306, 309, 311
Energy *(Government & Politics)* 314, 318
Energy *(Law & Criminal Justice)* 492
Energy *(Science)* 590, 593, 607
Engineering Design *(Engineering & Technology)* 297-298
Engineering Design *(Science)* 613
Engineering Economics *(Engineering & Technology)* 302
Engineering Education *(Education)* 270
Engineering Journals *(Engineering & Technology)* 298
Engineering *(Business & Economics)* 123, 125
Engineering *(Computing & Mathematics)* 175, 191, 193, 213, 221, 224, 227
Engineering *(Education)* 239-240, 260, 270, 274, 279, 282
Engineering *(Engineering & Technology)* 291-303, 305-306, 308-310, 312, 686
Engineering *(Government & Politics)* 347-349
Engineering *(Science)* 568, 597, 603, 607, 609, 611, 613
England *(Arts & Music)* 26, 99
England *(Education)* 238, 270, 273-274
England *(Health & Medicine)* 371, 387
England *(Popular Culture & Entertainment)* 540
England *(Sports & Recreation)* 651, 655-656, 661, 664, 668
English Literature *(Education)* 240-241, 261
English Literature *(Humanities & Social Sciences)* 433-443
English *(Education)* 260, 262
English *(Humanities & Social Sciences)* 432-433
Entertainment Technology *(Engineering & Technology)* 308
Entertainment *(Arts & Music)* 33, 93
Entertainment *(Business & Economics)* 115, 148, 652
Entertainment *(Popular Culture & Entertainment)* 527, 529
Entertainment *(Sports & Recreation)* 665, 669
Entheogens *(Science)* 584
Entomology *(Popular Culture & Entertainment)* 545
Entomology *(Science)* 565-567, 580, 614-616
Entomology *(Sports & Recreation)* 647
Entrepreneurs *(Business & Economics)* 109
Entrepreneurship *(Business & Economics)* 119-120
Entrepreneurship *(Engineering & Technology)* 311
Environment *(Arts & Music)* 16
Environment *(Business & Economics)* 103, 133, 136
Environment *(Education)* 259-260
Environment *(Engineering & Technology)* 301, 304, 308
Environment *(Government & Politics)* 314, 317-319, 326, 336, 341-342, 345-346, 350-351, 362
Environment *(Humanities & Social Sciences)* 448
Environment *(Popular Culture & Entertainment)* 521, 545

Environment *(Science)* 567-571, 573, 579, 584, 587-588, 592-598
Environment-Safe Products *(Science)* 593
Environmental Activism *(Business & Economics)* 114
Environmental Activism *(Humanities & Social Sciences)* 433
Environmental Awareness *(Popular Culture & Entertainment)* 520
Environmental Awareness *(Science)* 595-596
Environmental Design *(Business & Economics)* 122
Environmental Design *(Engineering & Technology)* 301
Environmental Education *(Education)* 237
Environmental Education *(Science)* 593
Environmental Engineering *(Engineering & Technology)* 300, 686, 719
Environmental Ethics *(Business & Economics)* 134
Environmental Health *(Education)* 245
Environmental Health *(Law & Criminal Justice)* 493
Environmental Health *(Science)* 595
Environmental Issues *(Sports & Recreation)* 637
Environmental Law *(Law & Criminal Justice)* 493
Environmental Monitoring *(Science)* 594
Environmental Organizations *(Government & Politics)* 342, 351
Environmental Organizations *(Science)* 594
Environmental Policy *(Government & Politics)* 341-342, 344
Environmental Policy *(Science)* 591, 596, 601
Environmental Products *(Business & Economics)* 145, 148
Environmental Protection *(Science)* 595-596, 602
Environmental Protection *(Sports & Recreation)* 640
Environmental Reports *(Science)* 596
Environmental Research *(Government & Politics)* 314, 318, 352
Environmental Research *(Science)* 567, 589, 593, 595, 607
Environmental Resources *(Government & Politics)* 342
Environmental Resources *(Science)* 568, 582, 587, 592-593, 595
Environmental Sciences *(Science)* 587-590, 592-596, 599, 700, 735
Environmental Studies *(Education)* 242
Environmental Studies *(Engineering & Technology)* 301
Environmental Studies *(Government & Politics)* 320, 342
Environmental Studies *(Humanities & Social Sciences)* 433
Environmentalism *(Computing & Mathematics)* 208
Environmentalism *(Education)* 266
Environmentalism *(Government & Politics)* 344-346
Epidemiology *(Health & Medicine)* 390, 396-397
Epilepsy *(Computing & Mathematics)* 177
ESL (English As A Second Language) *(Education)* 252, 263
Espresso Machines *(Popular Culture & Entertainment)* 626
Estate Tax *(Business & Economics)* 119
Estonia *(Law & Criminal Justice)* 496
Ethics *(Business & Economics)* 133-134
Ethics *(Computing & Mathematics)* 213, 218
Ethics *(Government & Politics)* 354
Ethics *(Health & Medicine)* 386
Ethics *(Humanities & Social Sciences)* 418
Ethics *(Law & Criminal Justice)* 491, 494, 726
Ethics *(Religion & Philosophy)* 558
Ethnic Music *(Arts & Music)* 51
Ethnic Studies *(Education)* 242
Ethnic Studies *(Humanities & Social Sciences)* 416, 425, 432
Ethnocentrism *(Humanities & Social Sciences)* 415

Ethnography – France

Ethnography *(Humanities & Social Sciences)* 413
Ethnology *(Popular Culture & Entertainment)* 544
Europe *(Arts & Music)* 16, 65, 76, 92, 97
Europe *(Communications)* 166
Europe *(Computing & Mathematics)* 174, 186, 204
Europe *(Education)* 251, 272, 274-275
Europe *(Government & Politics)* 334-335, 342, 360-361
Europe *(Humanities & Social Sciences)* 427, 450
Europe *(Internet)* 473, 481
Europe *(Law & Criminal Justice)* 496
Europe *(Science)* 596, 606, 612
Europe *(Sports & Recreation)* 654, 670
European Businesses *(Business & Economics)* 126
European Community *(Business & Economics)* 117
European Community *(Computing & Mathematics)* 203
European Community *(Government & Politics)* 339, 342, 360
European Community *(Health & Medicine)* 404
European Culture *(Government & Politics)* 323, 339
European Culture *(Humanities & Social Sciences)* 432
European History *(Government & Politics)* 339
European Union *(Business & Economics)* 116-117
European Union *(Government & Politics)* 360
Evangelism *(Religion & Philosophy)* 560
Events *(Arts & Music)* 27, 50-53, 55-56, 59, 61-62, 64-69, 91, 93-94
Events *(Business & Economics)* 122, 148
Events *(Computing & Mathematics)* 209
Events *(Government & Politics)* 319, 363
Events *(Popular Culture & Entertainment)* 510, 512, 545
Events *(Sports & Recreation)* 644, 658, 663, 665
Evidence *(Law & Criminal Justice)* 502
Evolution *(Popular Culture & Entertainment)* 544
Evolution *(Religion & Philosophy)* 558
Evolution *(Science)* 614
Exchange Rates *(Business & Economics)* 129
Exclusive Properties *(Business & Economics)* 140
Executive Branch (US) *(Government & Politics)* 317, 319
Executive Recruiters *(Business & Economics)* 112
Exercise *(Health & Medicine)* 400
Exhibitions *(Arts & Music)* 25
Exhibits *(Arts & Music)* 42
Exotic Animals *(Business & Economics)* 145
Expatriates *(Sports & Recreation)* 659
Expeditions *(Science)* 593
Experimental Medicine *(Health & Medicine)* 402
Experimental Music *(Arts & Music)* 80, 86-87, 89
Expert Systems *(Computing & Mathematics)* 176-178
Express Delivery Services *(Business & Economics)* 150
Extragalactic Phenomena *(Science)* 572

Faculty *(Business & Economics)* 108
Faculty *(Education)* 242, 255
Fair Business Practices *(Business & Economics)* 116
Fairy Tales *(Humanities & Social Sciences)* 437
Family & Community *(Popular Culture & Entertainment)* 697
Family Health *(Health & Medicine)* 720
Family History *(Popular Culture & Entertainment)* 522-523

Family Law *(Law & Criminal Justice)* 494, 696
Family Life *(Popular Culture & Entertainment)* 521
Family *(Health & Medicine)* 381-382, 402
Family *(Popular Culture & Entertainment)* 517, 521-523
Family *(Religion & Philosophy)* 562
Fantasy Literature *(Humanities & Social Sciences)* 433
Fantasy *(Humanities & Social Sciences)* 435-436, 444
Fantasy *(Popular Culture & Entertainment)* 540
FAQs (Frequently Asked Questions) *(Computing & Mathematics)* 176, 205, 210, 212-213, 227
FAQs (Frequently Asked Questions) *(Education)* 262
FAQs (Frequently Asked Questions) *(Health & Medicine)* 378, 396
FAQs (Frequently Asked Questions) *(Internet)* 464, 468-470, 476-477, 480
FAQs (Frequently Asked Questions) *(Sports & Recreation)* 659
Farm Economics *(Science)* 568
Farming *(Science)* 566
Farming *(Sports & Recreation)* 633, 645
Fashion Designers *(Popular Culture & Entertainment)* 522
Fashion *(Business & Economics)* 123
Fashion *(Popular Culture & Entertainment)* 522, 546, 697
Fast Food *(Sports & Recreation)* 626
Fathers *(Popular Culture & Entertainment)* 518
Fauna *(Sports & Recreation)* 648
FAX Software *(Computing & Mathematics)* 223
FBI (Federal Bureau Of Investigation) *(Law & Criminal Justice)* 492
FCC (Federal Communications Commission) *(Business & Economics)* 117
Federal Agencies (US) *(Law & Criminal Justice)* 502
Federal Courts (US) *(Law & Criminal Justice)* 498
Federal Databases (US) *(Business & Economics)* 106
Federal Databases (US) *(Government & Politics)* 316, 356
Federal Databases (US) *(Law & Criminal Justice)* 504
Federal Databases (US) *(Science)* 598
Federal Deposit Insurance Company (FDIC) (US) *(Business & Economics)* 106
Federal Documents (US) *(Government & Politics)* 313, 356
Federal Government (US) *(Business & Economics)* 106, 119
Federal Government (US) *(Government & Politics)* 313-315, 318-320, 346, 350, 356-358, 363
Federal Government (US) *(Science)* 567, 589, 596, 602
Federal Government *(Government & Politics)* 345
Federal Law *(Government & Politics)* 352, 358
Federal Law *(Law & Criminal Justice)* 497, 507
Federal Register (US) *(Government & Politics)* 313, 317
Federal Trade Commission (FTC) *(Business & Economics)* 116
Federal Trade Commission (FTC) *(Law & Criminal Justice)* 489
Felids *(Sports & Recreation)* 647
Fellowships *(Arts & Music)* 32
Fellowships *(Computing & Mathematics)* 200
Fellowships *(Science)* 610
Feminism *(Communications)* 161
Feminism *(Computing & Mathematics)* 218
Feminism *(Government & Politics)* 350
Feminism *(Health & Medicine)* 409
Feminism *(Humanities & Social Sciences)* 429, 450-451

Feminism *(Popular Culture & Entertainment)* 515
Feminist Literature *(Humanities & Social Sciences)* 444
Feminist Music *(Arts & Music)* 77, 82, 85, 88
Ferrets *(Sports & Recreation)* 644
Festivals *(Humanities & Social Sciences)* 443
Fiction *(Arts & Music)* 43
Fiction *(Business & Economics)* 139
Fiction *(Humanities & Social Sciences)* 422, 433-435, 438, 441, 444-445
Fiction *(Popular Culture & Entertainment)* 513-516, 528-529, 535, 538, 540-541
Filings *(Business & Economics)* 144
Film & Video *(Arts & Music)* 99, 675, 708
Film Archives *(Arts & Music)* 47
Film Festivals *(Arts & Music)* 48, 50
Film Festivals *(Popular Culture & Entertainment)* 541
Film History *(Arts & Music)* 47-48, 50
Film Industry *(Arts & Music)* 49
Film Preservation *(Arts & Music)* 50
Film Processing *(Business & Economics)* 122
Film Reviews *(Arts & Music)* 47
Film Technology *(Arts & Music)* 48
Film Technology *(Popular Culture & Entertainment)* 542
Film *(Arts & Music)* 22, 26, 29, 47-50
Film *(Humanities & Social Sciences)* 418
Film *(Popular Culture & Entertainment)* 541-542, 550
Filmmakers *(Arts & Music)* 47-50
Filmmaking *(Arts & Music)* 47-50
Filmmaking *(Communications)* 156
Filmmaking *(Popular Culture & Entertainment)* 543
Films *(Arts & Music)* 61
Finance *(Business & Economics)* 104-106, 119-120, 128, 131, 141-143, 710
Finance *(Education)* 243, 249
Financial Forecasting *(Business & Economics)* 130-131
Financial Information *(Business & Economics)* 136, 140
Financial Planning *(Business & Economics)* 128, 130, 140, 143-144
Financial Research *(Business & Economics)* 117, 119, 130-131, 143
Financial Services *(Business & Economics)* 104-105, 118-119, 128-133
Financial Services *(Internet)* 456
Financial Software *(Computing & Mathematics)* 221
Fine Art *(Arts & Music)* 18, 98
Fine Arts *(Arts & Music)* 21, 28
Finland *(Arts & Music)* 34, 50, 53, 65-66, 92
Finland *(Business & Economics)* 109, 127, 141
Finland *(Communications)* 166
Finland *(Computing & Mathematics)* 190
Finland *(Education)* 254, 270-272, 274-275
Finland *(Engineering & Technology)* 295
Finland *(Government & Politics)* 316, 330
Finland *(Health & Medicine)* 397
Finland *(Internet)* 453-454
Finland *(Popular Culture & Entertainment)* 538
Finland *(Sports & Recreation)* 629-630, 658
Finnish Music *(Arts & Music)* 61
Firearms *(Government & Politics)* 351-352
Firewalls *(Business & Economics)* 122
Firewalls *(Internet)* 470-472
Fireworks *(Engineering & Technology)* 296
First Aid *(Health & Medicine)* 401, 403
Fiscal Policy *(Government & Politics)* 350
Fish *(Science)* 569, 580, 614-615
Fish *(Sports & Recreation)* 642-643
Fishing *(Sports & Recreation)* 642, 654-655
Fitness *(Sports & Recreation)* 641-643
Flags *(Business & Economics)* 145
Flags *(Government & Politics)* 330, 342
Flamenco *(Arts & Music)* 95
Flea Markets *(Sports & Recreation)* 622
Flight Simulation *(Computing & Mathematics)* 176

Flight Simulation *(Sports & Recreation)* 620
Floodlights *(Business & Economics)* 122
Floppy Disks *(Computing & Mathematics)* 193
Flora *(Science)* 582
Florida *(Education)* 278, 284, 286
Florida *(Government & Politics)* 323, 325, 329
Florida *(Internet)* 475
Florida *(Law & Criminal Justice)* 505
Florida *(Science)* 612
Florida *(Sports & Recreation)* 655, 670
Flower Shows *(Sports & Recreation)* 636
Flowers *(Business & Economics)* 145-146, 150
Flowers *(Popular Culture & Entertainment)* 548
Flowers *(Sports & Recreation)* 637
Folk Art *(Arts & Music)* 24, 98
Folk Dance *(Arts & Music)* 92
Folk Music *(Arts & Music)* 50-51, 53-55, 57, 63-67, 70, 72-74, 77-78, 80-83, 85-90
Folklore *(Popular Culture & Entertainment)* 521
Folklore *(Sports & Recreation)* 644
Fonts *(Humanities & Social Sciences)* 429
Food & Dining *(Sports & Recreation)* 702, 736
Food And Drug Administration (FDA) *(Health & Medicine)* 396-397, 402
Food Delivery *(Sports & Recreation)* 627
Food Production *(Business & Economics)* 123
Food Production *(Science)* 566
Food Production *(Sports & Recreation)* 633
Food Sciences *(Health & Medicine)* 395, 397
Food *(Business & Economics)* 146, 148
Food *(Humanities & Social Sciences)* 416
Food *(Popular Culture & Entertainment)* 532, 549, 629
Food *(Sports & Recreation)* 625-633, 671
Football *(Popular Culture & Entertainment)* 540, 549
Football *(Sports & Recreation)* 648-650, 652
Foreign Affairs *(Government & Politics)* 340
Foreign Film *(Arts & Music)* 47-50
Foreign Language Instruction *(Humanities & Social Sciences)* 417
Foreign Language Repositories *(Education)* 275
Foreign Languages *(Humanities & Social Sciences)* 432
Foreign Trade *(Government & Politics)* 340, 343
Forest Management *(Government & Politics)* 344
Forestry *(Government & Politics)* 336
Forestry *(Science)* 566, 588, 598
Format Converters *(Computing & Mathematics)* 220, 225
Former Soviet Union *(Government & Politics)* 337, 341
Fortresses *(Humanities & Social Sciences)* 426
Fossils *(Popular Culture & Entertainment)* 545
Foster Families *(Health & Medicine)* 404
Foster Parenting *(Health & Medicine)* 381
Foxes *(Sports & Recreation)* 643
Fractals *(Arts & Music)* 32, 37-40, 43, 45
Fractals *(Computing & Mathematics)* 177, 186, 195
Frame Relay *(Communications)* 161
Frame Relay *(Internet)* 459
France *(Arts & Music)* 21, 23, 33, 89, 92, 94
France *(Business & Economics)* 107, 127
France *(Communications)* 160, 164-165
France *(Computing & Mathematics)* 173, 191, 198
France *(Education)* 270, 272
France *(Engineering & Technology)* 310
France *(Government & Politics)* 327, 334, 338, 342
France *(Humanities & Social Sciences)* 421, 427, 429, 450
France *(Internet)* 454, 470
France *(Popular Culture & Entertainment)* 528

France – Hang Gliding **793**

France *(Science)* 566, 604-605
France *(Sports & Recreation)* 626, 628, 632, 642, 655, 660, 666
Free Speech *(Communications)* 162
Freedom of Information *(Internet)* 464
Freedom of Speech *(Communications)* 156
Freedom of Speech *(Computing & Mathematics)* 213
Freedom of Speech *(Government & Politics)* 354
Freedom of Speech *(Internet)* 461
Freedom of Speech *(Law & Criminal Justice)* 491
Freenets *(Internet)* 454, 465, 472, 475
Freeware *(Computing & Mathematics)* 205, 216, 222-224, 227-228
Freeware *(Internet)* 480
French Culture *(Government & Politics)* 342
French Literature *(Arts & Music)* 94
French Literature *(Humanities & Social Sciences)* 427, 435, 439-441, 443
French Painting *(Arts & Music)* 32
French *(Education)* 252
French *(Humanities & Social Sciences)* 421, 427, 429
French *(Popular Culture & Entertainment)* 528
Freshwater Fish *(Science)* 568, 614
Frisbee *(Sports & Recreation)* 652
Fruits *(Sports & Recreation)* 632-633
FTP (File Transfer Protocol) *(Computing & Mathematics)* 227
FTP (File Transfer Protocol) *(Internet)* 462, 467
Functional Art *(Arts & Music)* 33
Funding *(Arts & Music)* 28-29
Funding *(Business & Economics)* 101, 149
Funding *(Education)* 685
Funding *(Government & Politics)* 318
Funk Music *(Arts & Music)* 90
Furniture Recycling *(Business & Economics)* 134
Furniture *(Arts & Music)* 33
Furniture *(Business & Economics)* 115, 124, 146
Furniture *(Popular Culture & Entertainment)* 546, 549
Fusion *(Engineering & Technology)* 304
Fusion *(Science)* 607
Future Music *(Arts & Music)* 66
Future Technology *(Science)* 613
Futures *(Business & Economics)* 128, 130-132
Futurism *(Popular Culture & Entertainment)* 527
Fuzzy Logic *(Computing & Mathematics)* 230

Gaelic Poetry *(Humanities & Social Sciences)* 443
Gambling *(Sports & Recreation)* 662, 665, 669
Games *(Computing & Mathematics)* 226
Games *(Humanities & Social Sciences)* 416, 431
Games *(Internet)* 483-484, 486
Games *(Popular Culture & Entertainment)* 519, 524, 543, 554
Games *(Sports & Recreation)* 634-636, 702, 737
Garden Tips *(Sports & Recreation)* 636
Gardening Supplies *(Business & Economics)* 146
Gardening Supplies *(Sports & Recreation)* 636
Gardening *(Business & Economics)* 146-147
Gardening *(Popular Culture & Entertainment)* 539-541
Gardening *(Sports & Recreation)* 636-638, 702, 737
Gardens *(Business & Economics)* 147
Gardens *(Science)* 568, 582-584
Gardens *(Sports & Recreation)* 636-638
Gay Rights *(Health & Medicine)* 408
Gem Dealers *(Sports & Recreation)* 622
Gender Discrimination *(Law & Criminal Justice)* 502
Gender Issues *(Health & Medicine)* 407-408, 537

Gender Issues *(Humanities & Social Sciences)* 415, 439, 450
Gender Studies *(Health & Medicine)* 402
Gene Mapping *(Science)* 580
Genealogy *(Humanities & Social Sciences)* 426
Genealogy *(Popular Culture & Entertainment)* 517, 522-523, 697
Genealogy *(Science)* 581
General Literature *(Humanities & Social Sciences)* 432
General Literature *(Popular Culture & Entertainment)* 553
General Literature *(Religion & Philosophy)* 563
Generation X *(Government & Politics)* 354
Generation X *(Popular Culture & Entertainment)* 533
Genetics *(Engineering & Technology)* 292
Genetics *(Health & Medicine)* 370-371, 378, 387
Genetics *(Science)* 566-567, 574-582, 584, 588, 592, 601-602, 615
Genocide *(Humanities & Social Sciences)* 426
Genomes *(Science)* 565, 576, 579-582
Geodesy *(Science)* 597
Geography *(Engineering & Technology)* 294
Geography *(Government & Politics)* 314, 320, 331, 336
Geography *(Humanities & Social Sciences)* 442, 448, 691, 723
Geography *(Popular Culture & Entertainment)* 536, 554
Geography *(Science)* 571, 588, 590, 594, 597-600
Geological Engineering *(Engineering & Technology)* 294
Geological Landmarks *(Sports & Recreation)* 660
Geology *(Engineering & Technology)* 294, 303
Geology *(Government & Politics)* 318, 347
Geology *(Popular Culture & Entertainment)* 524
Geology *(Science)* 570-571, 586-590, 597-600
Geology *(Sports & Recreation)* 623
Geometry *(Arts & Music)* 35, 42, 44
Geometry *(Computing & Mathematics)* 197
Geophysics *(Science)* 587, 589, 597-599
Georgia *(Education)* 278, 283
Georgia *(Government & Politics)* 321-322
Georgia *(Popular Culture & Entertainment)* 541
Georgia *(Sports & Recreation)* 624, 636, 648, 650, 653, 655, 661
Geosciences *(Science)* 589-590, 595, 597-598, 600-601, 607, 612, 700, 735
Geriatrics *(Health & Medicine)* 368, 370, 403
German Literature *(Humanities & Social Sciences)* 439-440
German Studies *(Humanities & Social Sciences)* 433
German *(Government & Politics)* 332
German *(Humanities & Social Sciences)* 427
Germany *(Arts & Music)* 15, 21, 27, 35, 44, 46, 56
Germany *(Business & Economics)* 106
Germany *(Computing & Mathematics)* 172-173, 184, 186, 188, 192, 196, 201, 204, 217
Germany *(Education)* 233, 251, 271-272, 274, 278
Germany *(Engineering & Technology)* 306
Germany *(Government & Politics)* 320, 323-324, 328, 331-332, 334, 554
Germany *(Health & Medicine)* 377, 389
Germany *(Humanities & Social Sciences)* 422, 425-426, 433, 451
Germany *(Internet)* 454, 460, 466, 468, 473-474
Germany *(Law & Criminal Justice)* 497
Germany *(Popular Culture & Entertainment)* 534, 550
Germany *(Science)* 587, 603, 605, 608, 611
Germany *(Sports & Recreation)* 630, 650-652, 659-660, 662, 664, 667
Gerontology *(Health & Medicine)* 368, 375

Gibraltar *(Arts & Music)* 56
Gifted Students *(Education)* 244
Gifts *(Business & Economics)* 114, 145-146, 150
Gifts *(Popular Culture & Entertainment)* 548-549
Gifts *(Sports & Recreation)* 626, 628
GIS (Geographic Information Systems) *(Science)* 598
GIS (Geographic Information Systems) *(Government & Politics)* 320
GIS (Geographic Information Systems) *(Science)* 589, 595, 598-599
Glass Insulators *(Sports & Recreation)* 622
GNU (GNU's Not Unix) *(Computing & Mathematics)* 170, 172, 205, 212
Go *(Sports & Recreation)* 634-635
God *(Religion & Philosophy)* 561
Golf Courses *(Sports & Recreation)* 650
Golf *(Popular Culture & Entertainment)* 540
Golf *(Sports & Recreation)* 641, 648, 650, 660
Gopher *(Internet)* 464, 477
Gopher *(Humanities & Social Sciences)* 426, 448
Gourmet Food *(Popular Culture & Entertainment)* 549
Gourmet Food *(Sports & Recreation)* 633
Government (US) *(Education)* 243, 249
Government (US) *(Government & Politics)* 314-317, 345, 350
Government Agencies (US) *(Business & Economics)* 120
Government Agencies (US) *(Education)* 255, 262
Government Agencies (US) *(Engineering & Technology)* 300
Government Agencies (US) *(Government & Politics)* 314-315, 320
Government Agencies (US) *(Science)* 611
Government Agencies *(Business & Economics)* 112, 116
Government Agencies *(Computing & Mathematics)* 190
Government Agencies *(Government & Politics)* 348, 356-357
Government Agencies *(Health & Medicine)* 395, 397-399
Government Agencies *(Law & Criminal Justice)* 506
Government Agencies *(Science)* 570, 590
Government Departments *(Government & Politics)* 336, 349
Government Documents (US) *(Government & Politics)* 363
Government Documents (US) *(Law & Criminal Justice)* 497
Government Documents *(Government & Politics)* 314, 331, 355-356, 358
Government Documents *(Health & Medicine)* 399-400
Government Documents *(Popular Culture & Entertainment)* 536
Government Documents *(Science)* 568, 602
Government Policy (US) *(Education)* 244
Government Policy *(Government & Politics)* 320
Government Projects (US) *(Government & Politics)* 315
Government Projects *(Science)* 593
Government Resources (US) *(Education)* 242
Government Resources *(Computing & Mathematics)* 218
Government Securities (US) *(Business & Economics)* 132
Government Securities *(Business & Economics)* 132
Government *(Communications)* 160, 164
Government *(Education)* 242, 250, 279
Government *(Government & Politics)* 316, 320, 322, 324-326, 328-329, 334-339, 342, 346-347, 352-355, 357, 359-361
Government *(Humanities & Social Sciences)* 419
Government *(Law & Criminal Justice)* 493, 496, 504
Government *(Science)* 566, 591, 607
Government *(Sports & Recreation)* 655, 658

Graduate Education *(Education)* 243, 279
Graduate Education *(Engineering & Technology)* 302, 308
Graduate Programs *(Arts & Music)* 15, 17
Graduate Programs *(Business & Economics)* 106, 108-109
Graduate Programs *(Computing & Mathematics)* 192-193
Graduate Programs *(Education)* 239, 261-262, 271, 282
Graduate Programs *(Engineering & Technology)* 294
Graduate Research *(Engineering & Technology)* 299
Graduate Education *(Education)* 267
Graduate Education *(Engineering & Technology)* 309
Graduate Education *(Health & Medicine)* 386, 403
Graduate Education *(Law & Criminal Justice)* 498
Grafitti Art *(Arts & Music)* 18
Grammar *(Humanities & Social Sciences)* 428, 441
Grants (Medical) *(Health & Medicine)* 395
Grants *(Arts & Music)* 28, 32
Grants *(Business & Economics)* 135-136
Grants *(Computing & Mathematics)* 191
Grants *(Education)* 243, 249
Grants *(Government & Politics)* 318
Grants *(Popular Culture & Entertainment)* 519
Grants *(Science)* 594
Graphic Arts *(Arts & Music)* 34
Graphic Design *(Arts & Music)* 20, 35, 98
Graphic Design *(Business & Economics)* 138, 148
Graphic Design *(Computing & Mathematics)* 169
Graphical User Interfaces (GUIs) *(Computing & Mathematics)* 214
Graphics Software *(Computing & Mathematics)* 220, 226
Graphics *(Arts & Music)* 31, 41
Graphics *(Business & Economics)* 138-139, 149
Graphics *(Computing & Mathematics)* 169, 171, 173, 181-182, 193, 212, 215
Graphics *(Health & Medicine)* 370
Graphics *(Internet)* 479
Graphics *(Popular Culture & Entertainment)* 543
Graphics *(Science)* 611
Great Britain *(Religion & Philosophy)* 562
Great Lakes *(Business & Economics)* 118
Greece *(Communications)* 158
Greece *(Sports & Recreation)* 654, 658, 662, 666
Greek Culture *(Humanities & Social Sciences)* 428
Greek Mythology *(Education)* 241
Gregorian Chant *(Arts & Music)* 58
Guatemala *(Government & Politics)* 330, 334
Guides *(Government & Politics)* 338
Guides *(Sports & Recreation)* 642
Guitar *(Arts & Music)* 73, 86, 89-90
Gun Control *(Government & Politics)* 351-352
Guyana *(Government & Politics)* 334
Gynecology *(Health & Medicine)* 404, 409

Habitats *(Science)* 602
Hacking *(Computing & Mathematics)* 214
Hacking *(Internet)* 470
Hacking *(Popular Culture & Entertainment)* 541, 553
Haiku *(Humanities & Social Sciences)* 436-437
Hair Care *(Business & Economics)* 145
Haiti *(Sports & Recreation)* 670
Hallucinogenics *(Science)* 584
Ham Radio *(Communications)* 155
Ham Radio *(Education)* 264
Ham Radio *(Sports & Recreation)* 621, 624
Handheld Computers *(Computing & Mathematics)* 194, 209
Handicaps *(Health & Medicine)* 373-374
Hang Gliding *(Sports & Recreation)* 642

Hard Rock Music – Indian Art

Hard Rock Music *(Arts & Music)* 77-80, 82, 88
Hardcore Music *(Arts & Music)* 72
Hardware Design *(Computing & Mathematics)* 231
Hardware *(Computing & Mathematics)* 218, 222, 680, 711
Hardware *(Engineering & Technology)* 309
Hawaii *(Business & Economics)* 113
Hawaii *(Communications)* 162
Hawaii *(Education)* 236, 239, 284
Hawaii *(Government & Politics)* 363
Hawaii *(Popular Culture & Entertainment)* 517, 544
Hawaii *(Science)* 570, 583
Hawaii *(Sports & Recreation)* 661
Hawaiian Culture *(Sports & Recreation)* 661
Hazardous Materials *(Government & Politics)* 351
Health & Medical Professionals *(Health & Medicine)* 688, 720
Health Care Policy *(Health & Medicine)* 398
Health Care *(Business & Economics)* 106
Health Care *(Health & Medicine)* 368, 377, 379, 381-382, 384-385, 394, 398, 400-401, 408, 410
Health Care *(Law & Criminal Justice)* 494, 500
Health Conditions *(Health & Medicine)* 689, 721
Health Insurance *(Business & Economics)* 106
Health Journals *(Health & Medicine)* 392, 401
Health News *(Health & Medicine)* 379, 397
Health News *(Science)* 595
Health News *(Sports & Recreation)* 642
Health Professions *(Health & Medicine)* 371-372
Health Promotion *(Health & Medicine)* 398
Health Sciences *(Education)* 268
Health Sciences *(Health & Medicine)* 370-371, 386, 388-389, 391, 394, 396, 398, 403-404, 406-407
Health Services *(Health & Medicine)* 407, 537
Health Statistics *(Health & Medicine)* 378, 396
Health *(Business & Economics)* 148, 151
Health *(Government & Politics)* 314, 346
Health *(Health & Medicine)* 376, 382, 385-386, 394-395, 400-401, 405-407
Health *(Popular Culture & Entertainment)* 517, 546, 553
Health *(Science)* 596
Health *(Sports & Recreation)* 625, 632
Hearing Science *(Health & Medicine)* 385
Heart *(Health & Medicine)* 400
Heavy Metal Music *(Arts & Music)* 76, 80-81
Hellenic Culture *(Humanities & Social Sciences)* 422
Hemochromatosis *(Health & Medicine)* 378
Hepatitis *(Health & Medicine)* 398
Herbal Remedies *(Health & Medicine)* 369
Herbarium *(Sports & Recreation)* 638
Herbs *(Health & Medicine)* 369
Herbs *(Sports & Recreation)* 624, 637
Heretic *(Sports & Recreation)* 635
Heritage *(Popular Culture & Entertainment)* 522-523
Herpetology *(Science)* 616
Herpetology *(Sports & Recreation)* 644, 646-647
High Energy Physics *(Science)* 604-608
High Technology *(Business & Economics)* 113, 121, 123-124
Higher Education *(Education)* 238, 240, 248
Hiking *(Government & Politics)* 360
Hiking *(Popular Culture & Entertainment)* 543
Hiking *(Sports & Recreation)* 640, 642, 652, 656, 668
Hindi *(Humanities & Social Sciences)* 428
Hindu Culture *(Humanities & Social Sciences)* 419
Hip-Hop *(Arts & Music)* 54, 65-66
Hip-Hop *(Popular Culture & Entertainment)* 535, 541

Hippocratic Oath *(Health & Medicine)* 400
Hispanic Americans *(Humanities & Social Sciences)* 418
Historic Battles *(Humanities & Social Sciences)* 426
Historic Preservation *(Humanities & Social Sciences)* 414
Historical Documents *(Humanities & Social Sciences)* 426-427
Historical Documents *(Religion & Philosophy)* 562
Historical Sites *(Arts & Music)* 22
History (Ancient) *(Arts & Music)* 21
History (Military) *(Government & Politics)* 339
History (US) *(Humanities & Social Sciences)* 424, 426
History (US) *(Sports & Recreation)* 654, 660
History *(Business & Economics)* 143
History *(Computing & Mathematics)* 197-198, 213
History *(Education)* 235, 256-257
History *(Government & Politics)* 321-327, 329-332, 334, 337, 339
History *(Health & Medicine)* 404
History *(Humanities & Social Sciences)* 414, 417-418, 421, 424-427, 450-451, 691, 723
History *(Popular Culture & Entertainment)* 513, 544
History *(Religion & Philosophy)* 557, 559, 562
History *(Science)* 600
History *(Sports & Recreation)* 654, 656-660, 662-670
Hobbies *(Sports & Recreation)* 622, 650
Hockey *(Sports & Recreation)* 649, 651-652
Holidays *(Popular Culture & Entertainment)* 520
Holistic Health *(Health & Medicine)* 369, 396
Hollywood *(Arts & Music)* 47
Hollywood *(Internet)* 459
Hollywood *(Popular Culture & Entertainment)* 516, 536, 542
Holocaust *(Government & Politics)* 358
Holocaust *(Humanities & Social Sciences)* 424, 426-427
Holocaust *(Religion & Philosophy)* 560
Holography *(Arts & Music)* 98
Holography *(Business & Economics)* 150
Home Automation *(Popular Culture & Entertainment)* 520
Home Improvement *(Business & Economics)* 113, 116
Home Loans *(Business & Economics)* 140
Home Ownership *(Business & Economics)* 116, 140
Home Pages *(Popular Culture & Entertainment)* 509
Home Products *(Business & Economics)* 145
Home Repair *(Popular Culture & Entertainment)* 520
Home Schooling *(Education)* 237
Home Technology *(Business & Economics)* 113
Home *(Arts & Music)* 33
Home *(Business & Economics)* 113, 115-116, 141-142, 146
Home *(Popular Culture & Entertainment)* 521, 546, 549
Homelessness *(Arts & Music)* 98
Homeopathic Medicine *(Health & Medicine)* 369
Homeopathic Medicine *(Popular Culture & Entertainment)* 554
Homosexuality *(Health & Medicine)* 408
Homosexuality *(Popular Culture & Entertainment)* 530-532
Homosexuality *(Sports & Recreation)* 648
Honduras *(Government & Politics)* 335
Hong Kong Movies *(Popular Culture & Entertainment)* 542
Hong Kong *(Arts & Music)* 48
Hong Kong *(Business & Economics)* 126
Hong Kong *(Education)* 254, 260, 265, 288
Hong Kong *(Government & Politics)* 668
Hong Kong *(Internet)* 475, 662

Hong Kong *(Popular Culture & Entertainment)* 542
Hong Kong *(Sports & Recreation)* 657
Horology *(Sports & Recreation)* 623
Horoscopes *(Popular Culture & Entertainment)* 524, 554
Horse Racing *(Sports & Recreation)* 647, 652, 658, 663
Horseback Riding *(Sports & Recreation)* 648
Horses *(Sports & Recreation)* 644, 654
Horticulture *(Popular Culture & Entertainment)* 539-540
Horticulture *(Science)* 565, 582-584
Horticulture *(Sports & Recreation)* 636-638
Hospital Administration *(Health & Medicine)* 380, 394
Hospitals *(Health & Medicine)* 378-379, 388, 390, 392, 394
Hotels *(Sports & Recreation)* 659, 661
House of Representatives (US) *(Government & Politics)* 315, 340, 358
Household Items *(Popular Culture & Entertainment)* 548
Household Products *(Popular Culture & Entertainment)* 521
Housing *(Business & Economics)* 141-142
Housing *(Government & Politics)* 319, 328
How to Guides *(Internet)* 477
HTML (HyperText Markup Language) *(Computing & Mathematics)* 220
HTML (HyperText Markup Language) *(Internet)* 466, 477-480, 482
HTML (HyperText Markup Language) *(Popular Culture & Entertainment)* 525
HTML (HyperText Markup Language) *(Computing & Mathematics)* 175
HTML (HyperText Markup Language) *(Internet)* 464, 476-478
HTTP (HyperText Transport Protocol) *(Internet)* 462
HUD (Housing & Urban Development) *(Government & Politics)* 319
Human Communications *(Communications)* 153-154
Human Communications *(Humanities & Social Sciences)* 439
Human Genome Project *(Engineering & Technology)* 308
Human Genome Project *(Health & Medicine)* 371
Human Genome Project *(Science)* 580-581
Human Languages *(Humanities & Social Sciences)* 428
Human Physiology *(Science)* 578-579, 735
Human Resources *(Business & Economics)* 114, 133
Human Resources *(Engineering & Technology)* 293
Human Resources *(Health & Medicine)* 367
Human Rights *(Business & Economics)* 145
Human Rights *(Government & Politics)* 319, 332-333, 337-338, 340-342, 345-346, 349-351, 353-354, 356, 358
Human Rights *(Health & Medicine)* 394
Human Rights *(Humanities & Social Sciences)* 418
Human Rights *(Popular Culture & Entertainment)* 518
Human Services *(Health & Medicine)* 382
Humanitarianism *(Government & Politics)* 340
Humanities Funding *(Arts & Music)* 32
Humanities *(Computing & Mathematics)* 186
Humanities *(Education)* 244, 248-249, 262, 271
Humanities *(Humanities & Social Sciences)* 416, 436, 447
Humanities *(Popular Culture & Entertainment)* 533
Humor *(Arts & Music)* 31
Humor *(Computing & Mathematics)* 227
Humor *(Government & Politics)* 356
Humor *(Health & Medicine)* 381
Humor *(Humanities & Social Sciences)* 421, 433
Humor *(Law & Criminal Justice)* 498

Humor *(Popular Culture & Entertainment)* 513, 516, 526-530, 539, 543, 553, 697
Humor *(Science)* 616
Humor *(Sports & Recreation)* 646-647
Hungary *(Arts & Music)* 93
Hungary *(Government & Politics)* 335
Hungary *(Sports & Recreation)* 667
Hunger *(Government & Politics)* 354, 356
Hunger *(Health & Medicine)* 394
Hunting *(Sports & Recreation)* 646
Hydrology *(Science)* 590
Hypercard *(Education)* 249
Hyperlexia *(Health & Medicine)* 374
Hypermedia *(Arts & Music)* 41
Hypermedia *(Computing & Mathematics)* 175-176
Hypermedia *(Internet)* 462, 465, 470
Hypertext *(Arts & Music)* 30
Hypertext *(Computing & Mathematics)* 175, 220
Hypertext *(Education)* 241
Hypertext *(Engineering & Technology)* 305
Hypertext *(Humanities & Social Sciences)* 438

Iceland *(Arts & Music)* 83
Iceland *(Government & Politics)* 330
Iceland *(Science)* 590
Iceland *(Sports & Recreation)* 660
Ichthyology *(Science)* 615
ICMA *(Arts & Music)* 67
Icons *(Arts & Music)* 34
Idaho *(Education)* 279, 284
Illinois U.S. Constitution *(Law & Criminal Justice)* 490
Illinois *(Business & Economics)* 108, 128
Illinois *(Computing & Mathematics)* 192
Illinois *(Education)* 280-281, 285
Illinois *(Government & Politics)* 325
Illinois *(Health & Medicine)* 387
Illinois *(Law & Criminal Justice)* 498
Illinois *(Science)* 580
Illinois *(Sports & Recreation)* 636, 657
Illustrations *(Humanities & Social Sciences)* 440
Image Processing *(Communications)* 154
Image Processing *(Computing & Mathematics)* 171, 175, 178, 216
Image Processing *(Engineering & Technology)* 294, 309
Image Processing *(Government & Politics)* 316
Images *(Arts & Music)* 30, 40, 45, 98
Images *(Business & Economics)* 150
Images *(Computing & Mathematics)* 227
Images *(Government & Politics)* 320, 330, 342
Images *(Science)* 572, 574, 582, 611
Images *(Sports & Recreation)* 622
Imaging *(Arts & Music)* 41
Imaging *(Computing & Mathematics)* 171-172, 175
Imaging *(Engineering & Technology)* 294
Imaging *(Health & Medicine)* 387-388
Imaging *(Science)* 579
Immunology *(Health & Medicine)* 370-371, 381, 384, 386, 396-397
Immunology *(Science)* 576
Import-Export *(Business & Economics)* 125-127
Impressionism *(Arts & Music)* 24
In-Line Skating *(Sports & Recreation)* 651
Independent Living Centers *(Health & Medicine)* 373
Independent Music *(Arts & Music)* 58
Indexes *(Government & Politics)* 348
India *(Arts & Music)* 20, 48, 51
India *(Business & Economics)* 126
India *(Computing & Mathematics)* 226
India *(Education)* 253
India *(Engineering & Technology)* 298
India *(Government & Politics)* 322, 335, 338-339
India *(Health & Medicine)* 394
India *(Humanities & Social Sciences)* 439
India *(Religion & Philosophy)* 560
India *(Sports & Recreation)* 628, 664
Indian Art *(Arts & Music)* 18, 20

Indian Art – Internet Business

Indian Art *(Government & Politics)* 339
Indian Music *(Arts & Music)* 51
Indiana *(Arts & Music)* 60
Indiana *(Education)* 248, 280-282
Indiana *(Government & Politics)* 323, 325, 360, 363
Indiana *(Health & Medicine)* 390
Indiana *(Law & Criminal Justice)* 489, 505
Indianapolis 500 *(Sports & Recreation)* 639
Indians *(Humanities & Social Sciences)* 413
Indigenous People *(Government & Politics)* 354
Indigenous People *(Humanities & Social Sciences)* 413, 432
Indigenous Studies *(Arts & Music)* 47
Indigenous Studies *(Humanities & Social Sciences)* 418, 420
Individuals *(Government & Politics)* 687
Individuals *(Law & Criminal Justice)* 726
Individuals *(Religion & Philosophy)* 698
Indonesia *(Government & Politics)* 332, 338
Indonesia *(Humanities & Social Sciences)* 418
Indonesian Art *(Arts & Music)* 27
Industrial Applications *(Computing & Mathematics)* 200
Industrial Automation *(Engineering & Technology)* 301
Industrial Design *(Arts & Music)* 28
Industrial Design *(Engineering & Technology)* 298
Industrial Engineering *(Engineering & Technology)* 299, 302-303, 305, 686
Industrial Music *(Arts & Music)* 54, 80, 82
Industrial Products *(Business & Economics)* 144
Industrial Relations *(Business & Economics)* 133-134
Industrial Research *(Engineering & Technology)* 298, 302
Industries *(Business & Economics)* 678, 710
Industry Mergers *(Business & Economics)* 125
Industry *(Business & Economics)* 114, 118, 126
Industry *(Engineering & Technology)* 306
Industry *(Government & Politics)* 317
Infectious Diseases *(Health & Medicine)* 375, 381, 390, 392, 397-398, 403, 406
Infertility *(Health & Medicine)* 381, 404, 409-410
Informatics *(Computing & Mathematics)* 172, 178, 191, 206, 208, 230
Informatics *(Education)* 270
Informatics *(Science)* 603
Information Resources *(Business & Economics)* 102-103, 132
Information Resources *(Education)* 284
Information Resources *(Health & Medicine)* 370
Information Resources *(Popular Culture & Entertainment)* 510
Information Resources *(Science)* 571, 589, 596-597, 599
Information Retrieval *(Communications)* 162
Information Retrieval *(Computing & Mathematics)* 171-172, 177, 216, 219
Information Retrieval *(Education)* 234-236, 239, 247, 250
Information Retrieval *(Engineering & Technology)* 302, 305
Information Retrieval *(Government & Politics)* 313-314, 357, 361, 365
Information Retrieval *(Health & Medicine)* 388
Information Retrieval *(Humanities & Social Sciences)* 414, 429
Information Retrieval *(Internet)* 470, 476, 481-482
Information Retrieval *(Popular Culture & Entertainment)* 509, 545
Information Retrieval *(Science)* 566, 568
Information Science *(Business & Economics)* 127
Information Science *(Computing & Mathematics)* 176, 178, 190-191, 196, 198, 206

Information Science *(Education)* 233-235, 238, 248, 250, 253, 261-262, 264, 283
Information Science *(Health & Medicine)* 403
Information Science *(Humanities & Social Sciences)* 430
Information Science *(Science)* 601
Information Services *(Business & Economics)* 111, 127, 150
Information Services *(Government & Politics)* 318, 342, 356
Information Services *(Health & Medicine)* 401
Information Services *(Internet)* 454, 473-474, 482
Information Superhighway *(Communications)* 164
Information Superhighway *(Government & Politics)* 345, 352
Information Superhighway *(Internet)* 462, 464
Information Systems *(Business & Economics)* 125
Information Systems *(Communications)* 163-164
Information Systems *(Computing & Mathematics)* 190, 206, 230-232
Information Systems *(Education)* 247, 264, 273, 283
Information Systems *(Government & Politics)* 352
Information Systems *(Internet)* 481-482
Information Systems *(Science)* 588
Information Technology *(Business & Economics)* 122-124, 137, 151
Information Technology *(Communications)* 160-162, 164-166
Information Technology *(Computing & Mathematics)* 175, 191-192, 201, 206, 208, 216, 218, 230
Information Technology *(Education)* 247-249, 251, 253
Information Technology *(Engineering & Technology)* 306-308
Information Technology *(Government & Politics)* 315, 350, 364
Information Technology *(Humanities & Social Sciences)* 429
Information Technology *(Internet)* 454, 474, 482
Information Technology *(Law & Criminal Justice)* 500
Information Technology *(Science)* 596
Information Week *(Computing & Mathematics)* 217
Infrared Processing *(Science)* 611
Infrastructure *(Engineering & Technology)* 298
Injury *(Business & Economics)* 151
Insect Biology *(Science)* 615-616
Insects *(Arts & Music)* 42
Insects *(Science)* 566, 614-616
Insects *(Sports & Recreation)* 628, 647
Insomnia *(Health & Medicine)* 385
Institutions *(Computing & Mathematics)* 191, 201
Instructional Materials *(Arts & Music)* 92, 94, 96
Instructional Materials *(Education)* 245
Instructional Materials *(Science)* 608
Instructional Videos *(Popular Culture & Entertainment)* 548
Instrumental Music *(Arts & Music)* 58, 84, 88
Insults *(Popular Culture & Entertainment)* 530
Insurance Companies *(Business & Economics)* 106
Insurance Industry *(Business & Economics)* 117
Insurance *(Business & Economics)* 106, 119, 121, 123, 140
Insurance *(Law & Criminal Justice)* 500-501
Integrated Circuits *(Computing & Mathematics)* 180
Intellectual History *(Humanities & Social Sciences)* 424
Intellectual Property *(Business & Economics)* 150

Intellectual Property *(Engineering & Technology)* 309
Intellectual Property *(Government & Politics)* 345
Intellectual Property *(Internet)* 461
Intellectual Property *(Law & Criminal Justice)* 491, 726
Intelligent Agents *(Computing & Mathematics)* 179, 206
Intelligent Systems *(Business & Economics)* 123
Interactive Art *(Arts & Music)* 17
Interactive Computing *(Computing & Mathematics)* 178
Interactive Computing *(Engineering & Technology)* 309
Interactive Education *(Education)* 241, 252
Interactive Education *(Health & Medicine)* 396
Interactive Entertainment *(Internet)* 483
Interactive Excercises *(Education)* 245
Interactive Games *(Popular Culture & Entertainment)* 518
Interactive Games *(Sports & Recreation)* 635
Interactive Learning *(Computing & Mathematics)* 198
Interactive Learning *(Education)* 247-248, 258, 263
Interactive Learning *(Humanities & Social Sciences)* 424
Interactive Learning *(Science)* 616
Interactive Media *(Arts & Music)* 28, 32, 42, 90
Interactive Media *(Computing & Mathematics)* 170
Interactive Media *(Popular Culture & Entertainment)* 539, 542
Interactive Media *(Sports & Recreation)* 634
Interactive Technology *(Government & Politics)* 352
Interactive Technology *(Popular Culture & Entertainment)* 543
Interactive Theater *(Arts & Music)* 95
Interactive *(Popular Culture & Entertainment)* 515
Interactivity *(Internet)* 456
Interactivity *(Popular Culture & Entertainment)* 539
Interdisciplinary Studies *(Education)* 241, 259
Interest Rates *(Business & Economics)* 128, 140
Interfaces *(Computing & Mathematics)* 194
Interior Design *(Arts & Music)* 33-34
Interior Design *(Business & Economics)* 122
Internal Revenue Code *(Law & Criminal Justice)* 506
International & Comparative Law *(Law & Criminal Justice)* 696
International Agencies *(Government & Politics)* 343
International Aid *(Education)* 253, 255
International Aid *(Government & Politics)* 343
International Aid *(Health & Medicine)* 394-395, 398
International Art *(Arts & Music)* 27
International Business *(Business & Economics)* 110, 124, 678, 710
International Business *(Education)* 265
International Business *(Engineering & Technology)* 293
International Business *(Government & Politics)* 339
International Communications *(Communications)* 154, 162, 165
International Communications *(Computing & Mathematics)* 225
International Communications *(Popular Culture & Entertainment)* 536
International Cuisine *(Sports & Recreation)* 625, 628
International Development *(Business & Economics)* 106
International Development *(Computing & Mathematics)* 221

International Development *(Education)* 243
International Development *(Government & Politics)* 341-344, 354
International Development *(Internet)* 481
International Documents *(Government & Politics)* 339, 343-344
International Education *(Communications)* 167-168
International Education *(Computing & Mathematics)* 189, 196
International Education *(Education)* 241-243, 251, 253-254, 263, 268, 270-271, 273-274, 288, 685
International Education *(Engineering & Technology)* 298
International Education *(Government & Politics)* 337
International Education *(Health & Medicine)* 383
International Education *(Law & Criminal Justice)* 499
International Education *(Science)* 608
International Finance *(Business & Economics)* 117, 119, 129-131
International Finance *(Government & Politics)* 337
International Law *(Business & Economics)* 142
International Law *(Education)* 279
International Law *(Government & Politics)* 339, 341
International Law *(Law & Criminal Justice)* 493, 496-497, 504-505
International News *(Business & Economics)* 125-126
International News *(Communications)* 158
International News *(Education)* 251, 264
International News *(Government & Politics)* 332-333, 336, 340, 342-343, 353
International News *(Humanities & Social Sciences)* 416
International News *(Popular Culture & Entertainment)* 524, 533-534, 536-541
International Organizations *(Education)* 253
International Organizations *(Government & Politics)* 358
International Politics *(Government & Politics)* 316, 338, 340, 342, 346, 353, 355-356, 360
International Politics *(Internet)* 482
International Politics *(Science)* 602
International Relations *(Education)* 271
International Relations *(Government & Politics)* 313, 339, 341, 343-344
International Relations *(Law & Criminal Justice)* 496
International Research *(Humanities & Social Sciences)* 430, 448
International Soccer *(Sports & Recreation)* 650
International Studies *(Education)* 251
International Trade *(Business & Economics)* 114, 110, 126, 128
International Trade *(Government & Politics)* 351-352
International Travel *(Humanities & Social Sciences)* 421
International Travel *(Sports & Recreation)* 654, 658, 667
International *(Government & Politics)* 687
Internet Access Providers *(Communications)* 164-165
Internet Access Providers *(Computing & Mathematics)* 202
Internet Access Providers *(Internet)* 454-455, 464, 466, 468, 473-474, 482
Internet Access Software *(Computing & Mathematics)* 203
Internet Access *(Communications)* 163, 165
Internet Access *(Computing & Mathematics)* 179, 181
Internet Access *(Education)* 248, 265
Internet Access *(Engineering & Technology)* 297
Internet Access *(Internet)* 461-462, 464, 474, 476, 481, 483, 693, 724
Internet Browsers *(Internet)* 476, 478, 480
Internet Business *(Business & Economics)* 104, 144

Internet Business *(Internet)* 458, 472, 694
Internet Commerce *(Business & Economics)* 114, 149
Internet Commerce *(Internet)* 456-457, 472
Internet Commerce *(Popular Culture & Entertainment)* 548
Internet Communications *(Government & Politics)* 329
Internet Communications *(Humanities & Social Sciences)* 432
Internet Communications *(Internet)* 459-460, 473, 486-487, 694, 725
Internet Communities *(Internet)* 485
Internet Companies *(Internet)* 463-464, 468
Internet Culture *(Arts & Music)* 94
Internet Culture *(Business & Economics)* 102
Internet Culture *(Computing & Mathematics)* 213, 216
Internet Culture *(Humanities & Social Sciences)* 446
Internet Culture *(Internet)* 458, 462-463, 465, 477, 483, 485
Internet Culture *(Popular Culture & Entertainment)* 526
Internet Directories *(Business & Economics)* 130, 143
Internet Directories *(Communications)* 156, 161-162
Internet Directories *(Computing & Mathematics)* 214, 218
Internet Directories *(Education)* 234, 254
Internet Directories *(Government & Politics)* 356, 361
Internet Directories *(Health & Medicine)* 378
Internet Directories *(Humanities & Social Sciences)* 433
Internet Directories *(Internet)* 455, 463-464, 466, 468, 470, 476-477, 480
Internet Directories *(Popular Culture & Entertainment)* 534, 543
Internet Games *(Internet)* 484
Internet Games *(Popular Culture & Entertainment)* 528
Internet Games *(Sports & Recreation)* 634-635
Internet Ghetto Blaster *(Arts & Music)* 65
Internet Guides *(Business & Economics)* 111, 137
Internet Guides *(Education)* 257, 262, 276
Internet Guides *(Engineering & Technology)* 312
Internet Guides *(Health & Medicine)* 376, 378, 400, 405
Internet Guides *(Humanities & Social Sciences)* 421, 430
Internet Guides *(Internet)* 454, 462-469, 477, 479
Internet Guides *(Popular Culture & Entertainment)* 512, 514, 543, 547
Internet Guides *(Science)* 588
Internet History *(Computing & Mathematics)* 191
Internet Host Names *(Popular Culture & Entertainment)* 527
Internet Issues *(Business & Economics)* 144
Internet Issues *(Computing & Mathematics)* 206
Internet Issues *(Government & Politics)* 345
Internet Issues *(Humanities & Social Sciences)* 450
Internet Issues *(Internet)* 454, 458, 461, 467-468, 470, 473, 477, 481-482, 694, 725
Internet Issues *(Law & Criminal Justice)* 491, 494
Internet Magazines *(Communications)* 161
Internet Magazines *(Humanities & Social Sciences)* 417
Internet Magazines *(Popular Culture & Entertainment)* 533, 536-537, 539-540
Internet Marketing *(Business & Economics)* 102-104, 144
Internet Marketing *(Communications)* 154
Internet Marketing *(Internet)* 455-458, 472, 476
Internet Marketing *(Popular Culture & Entertainment)* 514, 547-548

Internet Networking *(Business & Economics)* 126-127, 134-136
Internet Networking *(Communications)* 159-161, 165, 168
Internet Networking *(Computing & Mathematics)* 181, 201-202
Internet Networking *(Education)* 248
Internet Networking *(Government & Politics)* 337, 354
Internet Networking *(Internet)* 461-462, 472, 479, 481-482, 486
Internet Networking *(Science)* 605
Internet Policy *(Internet)* 461-462
Internet Protocols *(Internet)* 457, 460, 462, 468, 475, 481-482, 694, 725
Internet Providers *(Internet)* 464
Internet Publications *(Popular Culture & Entertainment)* 534
Internet Publishing *(Business & Economics)* 138, 144
Internet Publishing *(Computing & Mathematics)* 209, 219
Internet Publishing *(Education)* 235
Internet Publishing *(Health & Medicine)* 382
Internet Publishing *(Internet)* 456, 458, 460, 465-466, 471, 473
Internet Publishing *(Law & Criminal Justice)* 501
Internet Publishing *(Popular Culture & Entertainment)* 519, 536-537, 541
Internet Reference *(Computing & Mathematics)* 214
Internet Reference *(Education)* 258, 285
Internet Reference *(Government & Politics)* 357
Internet Reference *(Internet)* 195, 464, 468-470
Internet Relay Chat *(Internet)* 456, 484, 485, 486
Internet Resources *(Business & Economics)* 110, 137-138, 144
Internet Resources *(Computing & Mathematics)* 170, 182, 191, 219
Internet Resources *(Education)* 233, 241, 244, 247, 255-256, 266
Internet Resources *(Engineering & Technology)* 299
Internet Resources *(Government & Politics)* 331-332, 348, 355, 360
Internet Resources *(Health & Medicine)* 391, 405
Internet Resources *(Humanities & Social Sciences)* 425-426, 440, 448-449
Internet Resources *(Internet)* 465-467, 470, 476-480, 694, 725
Internet Resources *(Popular Culture & Entertainment)* 519, 524, 532, 548
Internet Resources *(Sports & Recreation)* 636-637
Internet Search Tools *(Internet)* 459, 469, 476-478, 480
Internet Security *(Communications)* 159, 165
Internet Security *(Computing & Mathematics)* 176
Internet Security *(Education)* 247
Internet Security *(Internet)* 470-472, 482, 694, 726
Internet Service Providers *(Internet)* 453-454, 458, 466, 481
Internet Services *(Business & Economics)* 140
Internet Services *(Communications)* 166
Internet Services *(Education)* 265, 271
Internet Services *(Government & Politics)* 365
Internet Services *(Internet)* 454, 457, 470, 474, 476, 481, 695, 726
Internet Shopping *(Arts & Music)* 69
Internet Shopping *(Business & Economics)* 103, 113, 146
Internet Shopping *(Computing & Mathematics)* 217
Internet Shopping *(Engineering & Technology)* 311
Internet Shopping *(Popular Culture & Entertainment)* 546-547

Internet Software *(Computing & Mathematics)* 225
Internet Software *(Health & Medicine)* 398
Internet Software *(Internet)* 466
Internet Standards *(Internet)* 457, 460-461, 477, 480-481
Internet Statistics *(Business & Economics)* 104
Internet Statistics *(Internet)* 456, 465
Internet Tools *(Communications)* 161-162
Internet Tools *(Computing & Mathematics)* 216, 225
Internet Tools *(Education)* 288
Internet Tools *(Engineering & Technology)* 310
Internet Tools *(Internet)* 454, 460, 465-466, 468, 470, 476-482, 695
Internet Tools *(Science)* 589
Internet Traffic *(Internet)* 465
Internet Training *(Education)* 248
Internet Training *(Internet)* 457, 465-466, 468
Internet Training *(Popular Culture & Entertainment)* 548
Internet *(Arts & Music)* 68
Internet *(Business & Economics)* 122
Internet *(Computing & Mathematics)* 184
Internet *(Education)* 245
Internet *(Internet)* 453, 480
Internet *(Law & Criminal Justice)* 507
Internet *(Popular Culture & Entertainment)* 534, 550
Internships *(Business & Economics)* 110, 112
Internships *(Computing & Mathematics)* 179
Internships *(Education)* 238
Internships *(Government & Politics)* 316
Internships *(Health & Medicine)* 371
Inventions *(Business & Economics)* 144
Inventions *(Law & Criminal Justice)* 496
Inventors *(Science)* 600
Invertebrates *(Arts & Music)* 37
Invertebrates *(Popular Culture & Entertainment)* 545
Investment Advice *(Business & Economics)* 128-131, 140
Investment Guides *(Business & Economics)* 132
Investment Portfolio *(Business & Economics)* 131
Investment Software *(Business & Economics)* 128, 131
Investment *(Business & Economics)* 105, 118-120, 124, 126, 128-129, 131-132, 138, 678, 710
Investment *(Internet)* 455
Investment *(Popular Culture & Entertainment)* 538
Ionosphere *(Science)* 572
Iowa *(Education)* 234, 280, 285
Iran *(Arts & Music)* 16
Iran *(Humanities & Social Sciences)* 418, 441
Iran *(Sports & Recreation)* 662
Ireland *(Arts & Music)* 39, 64, 89
Ireland *(Communications)* 164
Ireland *(Computing & Mathematics)* 192
Ireland *(Education)* 273
Ireland *(Government & Politics)* 338
Ireland *(Humanities & Social Sciences)* 413, 419
Ireland *(Law & Criminal Justice)* 496
Ireland *(Popular Culture & Entertainment)* 536
Ireland *(Sports & Recreation)* 627, 658, 662, 668-669
Irish Literature *(Humanities & Social Sciences)* 413
Irish Music *(Arts & Music)* 63-64, 80
IRS (Internal Revenue Service) *(Business & Economics)* 133
IRS (Internal Revenue Service) *(Government & Politics)* 314
IRS (Internal Revenue Service) *(Humanities & Social Sciences)* 432
IRS (Internal Revenue Service) *(Internet)* 460

IRS (Internal Revenue Service) *(Law & Criminal Justice)* 506
ISDN *(Communications)* 160, 163, 165
ISDN *(Computing & Mathematics)* 179, 202
Islam *(Arts & Music)* 16
Islam *(Religion & Philosophy)* 560, 563-564
Islamic Architecture *(Arts & Music)* 16
Islamic Art *(Arts & Music)* 23
Islamic Books *(Popular Culture & Entertainment)* 514
Islamic Culture *(Popular Culture & Entertainment)* 514
Islamic Literature *(Religion & Philosophy)* 563
Israel *(Arts & Music)* 17, 26
Israel *(Communications)* 160
Israel *(Computing & Mathematics)* 201-203
Israel *(Education)* 279
Israel *(Humanities & Social Sciences)* 426
Israel *(Law & Criminal Justice)* 493
Israel *(Popular Culture & Entertainment)* 536
Israel *(Religion & Philosophy)* 560
Israel *(Sports & Recreation)* 660, 662-663, 666
Issues *(Government & Politics)* 687, 720
Issues *(Health & Medicine)* 394
Issues *(Internet)* 462
Italian Food *(Sports & Recreation)* 630
Italian Language *(Humanities & Social Sciences)* 428
Italian Literature *(Humanities & Social Sciences)* 428, 438
Italy *(Arts & Music)* 22, 61, 64
Italy *(Computing & Mathematics)* 186-187
Italy *(Education)* 275
Italy *(Engineering & Technology)* 305
Italy *(Government & Politics)* 325, 329, 335, 339
Italy *(Science)* 573, 593, 601, 606, 609
Italy *(Sports & Recreation)* 625, 630, 638, 659-660, 664, 668-670
Ivy League *(Education)* 278

Jade *(Arts & Music)* 18
Jamaica *(Government & Politics)* 335
Jamaica *(Humanities & Social Sciences)* 428
Japan *(Arts & Music)* 29, 60
Japan *(Business & Economics)* 112, 114, 124-125
Japan *(Communications)* 167
Japan *(Education)* 265-266
Japan *(Engineering & Technology)* 293, 299, 311
Japan *(Government & Politics)* 327, 335, 337-338
Japan *(Humanities & Social Sciences)* 415
Japan *(Internet)* 466, 472
Japan *(Popular Culture & Entertainment)* 533
Japan *(Science)* 579
Japan *(Sports & Recreation)* 648, 653, 663, 668
Japanese Art *(Sports & Recreation)* 622
Japanese Business *(Computing & Mathematics)* 181
Japanese Business *(Engineering & Technology)* 300
Japanese Business *(Popular Culture & Entertainment)* 548
Japanese Culture *(Popular Culture & Entertainment)* 539
Japanese Language Software *(Popular Culture & Entertainment)* 524
Japanese Literature *(Humanities & Social Sciences)* 436
Japanese News *(Popular Culture & Entertainment)* 539
Jazz *(Arts & Music)* 51-53, 55-56, 58, 60, 62-63, 68, 70, 77, 80, 84, 87-88, 92, 98
Jeff *(Arts & Music)* 87
Jewelry *(Arts & Music)* 19
Jewelry *(Popular Culture & Entertainment)* 546
Jewish Art *(Arts & Music)* 17, 26
Jewish History *(Government & Politics)* 358
Jewish Politics *(Religion & Philosophy)* 560

Job Listings – Magazines   797

Job Listings *(Business & Economics)* 109-112
Job Listings *(Computing & Mathematics)* 179
Job Listings *(Education)* 237-238
Job Listings *(Health & Medicine)* 371
Job Listings *(Science)* 575, 584, 605
Job Opportunities *(Business & Economics)* 112
Jobs *(Arts & Music)* 29, 91
Jobs *(Business & Economics)* 109-110
Jobs *(Communications)* 154, 165
Jobs *(Computing & Mathematics)* 179
Jobs *(Education)* 237-238
Jobs *(Engineering & Technology)* 292-293
Jobs *(Government & Politics)* 363
Jobs *(Humanities & Social Sciences)* 414, 416
Jobs *(Internet)* 453
Jobs *(Science)* 584-585, 598
Jokes *(Popular Culture & Entertainment)* 525-530
Journalism *(Communications)* 153-154, 156-158, 162
Journalism *(Education)* 245, 260
Journalism *(Government & Politics)* 337
Journalism *(Humanities & Social Sciences)* 434, 445-446
Journalism *(Popular Culture & Entertainment)* 534, 536, 538-539, 541
Journals *(Arts & Music)* 46, 68
Journals *(Business & Economics)* 101, 144
Journals *(Communications)* 154
Journals *(Computing & Mathematics)* 169, 178, 196, 201
Journals *(Education)* 240, 246, 261, 273
Journals *(Health & Medicine)* 374, 402
Journals *(Humanities & Social Sciences)* 417, 423-424, 435, 441-442, 447
Journals *(Popular Culture & Entertainment)* 534
Journals *(Religion & Philosophy)* 557-558
Journals *(Science)* 571, 581, 585, 605, 607
Journals *(Sports & Recreation)* 619
Judaica *(Business & Economics)* 138
Judaism *(Arts & Music)* 62
Judaism *(Humanities & Social Sciences)* 424, 427
Judaism *(Religion & Philosophy)* 559-560, 562-563
Judges *(Law & Criminal Justice)* 490
Judicial Branch *(Law & Criminal Justice)* 490, 500, 502
Juggling *(Sports & Recreation)* 650-651
Jurisprudence *(Law & Criminal Justice)* 500
Juvenile Delinquency *(Law & Criminal Justice)* 492

Kansas *(Government & Politics)* 361
Kansas *(Humanities & Social Sciences)* 426
Kayaking *(Sports & Recreation)* 619
Kentucky *(Arts & Music)* 98
Kentucky *(Education)* 262, 285, 287
Kentucky *(Government & Politics)* 363
Kentucky *(Sports & Recreation)* 658, 663
Kenya *(Sports & Recreation)* 654
Kidney Diseases *(Health & Medicine)* 378, 380, 384
Kids *(Education)* 245, 256
Kids *(Popular Culture & Entertainment)* 518, 521
Knee Boards *(Sports & Recreation)* 619
Knitting *(Sports & Recreation)* 622
Knowledge-Based Systems *(Computing & Mathematics)* 177, 216
Korea *(Arts & Music)* 29
Korea *(Sports & Recreation)* 628
Kosher Foods *(Sports & Recreation)* 628
Kurdish Culture *(Humanities & Social Sciences)* 419

Labor Issues *(Computing & Mathematics)* 208
Labor Issues *(Education)* 255
Labor Unions *(Business & Economics)* 133-134
Labor *(Business & Economics)* 678, 710
Labor *(Government & Politics)* 355

Laboratories *(Computing & Mathematics)* 178
Laboratories *(Science)* 584, 603, 605
Lacrosse *(Sports & Recreation)* 649
Language Acquisition *(Education)* 685
Language Arts *(Education)* 260
Language Instruction *(Education)* 252, 262-263
Language Instruction *(Humanities & Social Sciences)* 427-428, 432
Language Software *(Computing & Mathematics)* 212
Language Software *(Humanities & Social Sciences)* 432
Language *(Computing & Mathematics)* 214
Language *(Humanities & Social Sciences)* 431-433
Language *(Popular Culture & Entertainment)* 551
Languages *(Computing & Mathematics)* 213
Languages *(Education)* 248
Languages *(Government & Politics)* 322
Languages *(Humanities & Social Sciences)* 415, 427-429, 432-433, 436, 444, 691, 723
LANs (Local Area Networks) *(Computing & Mathematics)* 203, 221
Lasers *(Arts & Music)* 98
Lasers *(Engineering & Technology)* 292
Latex *(Computing & Mathematics)* 195
Latin America *(Business & Economics)* 126
Latin America *(Communications)* 160
Latin America *(Education)* 254, 257, 275
Latin America *(Government & Politics)* 316, 334-336, 338, 360
Latin America *(Health & Medicine)* 382
Latin America *(Internet)* 481
Latin America *(Popular Culture & Entertainment)* 537
Latin America *(Sports & Recreation)* 655, 658
Latin American Studies *(Government & Politics)* 332, 334
Latin American Studies *(Humanities & Social Sciences)* 416-419, 421
Latin Americans *(Humanities & Social Sciences)* 419
Latin *(Humanities & Social Sciences)* 427-428
Latino/Chicano Culture *(Humanities & Social Sciences)* 419
Law (International) *(Law & Criminal Justice)* 490, 496-499
Law (Ireland) *(Law & Criminal Justice)* 496
Law (US) *(Government & Politics)* 314-315, 346, 358
Law (US) *(Law & Criminal Justice)* 500, 504-505
Law Enforcement *(Government & Politics)* 362
Law Enforcement *(Law & Criminal Justice)* 492
Law Firms *(Business & Economics)* 119, 144
Law Firms *(Law & Criminal Justice)* 489-490, 495, 498, 500-502
Law Libraries *(Law & Criminal Justice)* 498, 504
Law of Nations *(Law & Criminal Justice)* 496
Law Reviews *(Law & Criminal Justice)* 499, 502
Law Reviews *(Popular Culture & Entertainment)* 524
Law Schools *(Law & Criminal Justice)* 497-499, 504, 696, 726
Law *(Business & Economics)* 118, 139
Law *(Government & Politics)* 337, 341, 351-352, 354
Law *(Law & Criminal Justice)* 490, 492, 494, 496, 498-505
Law *(Popular Culture & Entertainment)* 524
Law *(Science)* 595
Lawyers *(Law & Criminal Justice)* 497, 500, 502, 506
Leadership *(Government & Politics)* 334, 354
Learning Disabilities *(Health & Medicine)* 374, 384

Lebanon *(Government & Politics)* 335
Legal Advice *(Internet)* 461
Legal Advice *(Law & Criminal Justice)* 489-490, 492, 494-495, 501, 504
Legal Ethics *(Law & Criminal Justice)* 494
Legal History & Theory *(Law & Criminal Justice)* 696
Legal History *(Law & Criminal Justice)* 500, 503
Legal Information *(Law & Criminal Justice)* 495, 503-505
Legal Issues *(Internet)* 461
Legal Issues *(Law & Criminal Justice)* 489-491, 495, 500, 503-504, 507, 726
Legal Professions *(Law & Criminal Justice)* 490, 494, 503
Legal Publishers *(Law & Criminal Justice)* 490, 494, 498, 501, 504
Legal Research *(Business & Economics)* 139
Legal Research *(Health & Medicine)* 386
Legal Research *(Law & Criminal Justice)* 497-499, 504
Legal Resources *(Law & Criminal Justice)* 489, 494-497, 500-502, 504, 696
Legal Resources *(Popular Culture & Entertainment)* 517
Legal Services *(Law & Criminal Justice)* 506
Legal Software *(Law & Criminal Justice)* 490
Legal Terminology *(Law & Criminal Justice)* 492
Legends *(Religion & Philosophy)* 557
Legislation *(Business & Economics)* 116
Legislation *(Government & Politics)* 350-351
Legislation *(Health & Medicine)* 379, 399
Legislation *(Law & Criminal Justice)* 492-493, 504, 506
Legislation *(Science)* 591
Legislature *(Law & Criminal Justice)* 505
Lemurs *(Sports & Recreation)* 643
Lens *(Arts & Music)* 88
Lesbian/Gay Literature *(Popular Culture & Entertainment)* 514
Lesbianism *(Health & Medicine)* 408
Lesbianism *(Humanities & Social Sciences)* 450
Lesbianism *(Popular Culture & Entertainment)* 530-532
Lesson Plans *(Education)* 240, 254, 258, 261-262
Liability *(Law & Criminal Justice)* 507
Liberal Arts *(Education)* 277
Libertarian Party *(Government & Politics)* 355
Libertarianism *(Government & Politics)* 339
Libertarianism *(Popular Culture & Entertainment)* 533
Liberty *(Government & Politics)* 354
Libraries *(Arts & Music)* 15, 68
Libraries *(Business & Economics)* 124
Libraries *(Computing & Mathematics)* 215
Libraries *(Education)* 233-236, 248, 250, 260-262, 264-265, 271-272, 277, 280, 285-286, 685
Libraries *(Engineering & Technology)* 298
Libraries *(Government & Politics)* 361
Libraries *(Health & Medicine)* 385-386, 390, 392, 400, 403-404
Libraries *(Humanities & Social Sciences)* 415, 426, 429-431, 438-439, 442, 446, 449
Libraries *(Law & Criminal Justice)* 498, 504
Libraries *(Religion & Philosophy)* 559-560
Libraries *(Science)* 567, 570, 601, 605
Library & Information Studies *(Humanities & Social Sciences)* 691, 723
Library of Congress *(Arts & Music)* 48, 50
Library of Congress *(Education)* 250, 264
Library of Congress *(Government & Politics)* 318, 357
Library of Congress *(Law & Criminal Justice)* 504
Library Science *(Education)* 233-236, 250, 260-262, 264, 280
Library Science *(Health & Medicine)* 404
Library Science *(Humanities & Social Sciences)* 429-431

Library Science *(Science)* 601
Life Sciences *(Science)* 586
Lifestyles *(Popular Culture & Entertainment)* 697
Lighting *(Business & Economics)* 122
Linens *(Popular Culture & Entertainment)* 548
Linguistics *(Computing & Mathematics)* 186, 219, 224
Linguistics *(Education)* 242, 252
Linguistics *(Health & Medicine)* 373
Linguistics *(Humanities & Social Sciences)* 427-428, 431-433, 692, 724
Linguistics *(Popular Culture & Entertainment)* 525, 529, 551
Linguistics *(Science)* 600
Listservs *(Internet)* 466, 468
Literacy *(Communications)* 158
Literacy *(Education)* 243, 262
Literary Awards *(Humanities & Social Sciences)* 426, 434, 441-443
Literary Criticism *(Humanities & Social Sciences)* 422, 429, 432, 434-435, 437-438, 440-441, 444
Literary Criticism *(Popular Culture & Entertainment)* 514
Literary Events *(Popular Culture & Entertainment)* 512
Literary Forums *(Humanities & Social Sciences)* 440
Literary Motifs *(Humanities & Social Sciences)* 444
Literary Studies *(Humanities & Social Sciences)* 430, 444
Literature (English) *(Popular Culture & Entertainment)* 513
Literature (Fantasy) *(Popular Culture & Entertainment)* 516
Literature *(Business & Economics)* 136
Literature *(Education)* 261
Literature *(Humanities & Social Sciences)* 416, 421-423, 426, 430, 433-436, 438-442, 444-445, 451, 692, 724
Literature *(Popular Culture & Entertainment)* 512-514
Literature *(Science)* 601, 617
Litigation & Procedures *(Law & Criminal Justice)* 696
Litigation *(Business & Economics)* 119
Litigation *(Law & Criminal Justice)* 495
Liturgy *(Religion & Philosophy)* 560
Live Music *(Arts & Music)* 64
Loans *(Business & Economics)* 106, 129, 140-141
Local Governments *(Government & Politics)* 363
Locksmiths *(Popular Culture & Entertainment)* 524
Logic *(Computing & Mathematics)* 212, 232
Logic *(Humanities & Social Sciences)* 431
Logic *(Religion & Philosophy)* 558
London *(Arts & Music)* 24, 94
London *(Government & Politics)* 339
London *(Internet)* 484
London *(Popular Culture & Entertainment)* 534
Louisiana *(Arts & Music)* 25, 55
Louisiana *(Education)* 279, 283
Louisiana *(Sports & Recreation)* 628, 660
Love *(Popular Culture & Entertainment)* 532
Lutheranism *(Religion & Philosophy)* 561
Luxembourg *(Arts & Music)* 24
Luxury Condominiums *(Business & Economics)* 140
Lyrics *(Arts & Music)* 71, 75, 79, 82, 85-86, 90

Machinery *(Business & Economics)* 123
Macintosh Tools *(Popular Culture & Entertainment)* 543
Magazines *(Arts & Music)* 28, 31, 40, 50, 53, 66
Magazines *(Business & Economics)* 102, 119, 137, 142, 144
Magazines *(Communications)* 165
Magazines *(Computing & Mathematics)* 215, 217, 230
Magazines *(Education)* 261
Magazines *(Health & Medicine)* 393

Magazines *(Humanities & Social Sciences)* 434
Magazines *(Internet)* 459, 461, 466
Magazines *(Popular Culture & Entertainment)* 526, 533-534, 536-538, 540-541, 556
Magazines *(Religion & Philosophy)* 560
Magazines *(Sports & Recreation)* 621, 623-624, 637
Magic *(Popular Culture & Entertainment)* 554
Magna Carta *(Government & Politics)* 358
Magnesium *(Health & Medicine)* 401
Magnetic Resonance *(Science)* 579
Mail Order Business *(Popular Culture & Entertainment)* 626
Mail Order *(Business & Economics)* 146, 148, 151
Mail Order *(Popular Culture & Entertainment)* 546
Mailing List Management *(Internet)* 477
Mailing Lists *(Education)* 246
Mailing Lists *(Humanities & Social Sciences)* 431, 440
Mailing Lists *(Internet)* 466, 468, 477
Mailing Services *(Business & Economics)* 150
Maine *(Business & Economics)* 127
Maine *(Education)* 236, 276-277, 285, 287
Maine *(Engineering & Technology)* 294, 300
Maine *(Government & Politics)* 363
Maine *(Sports & Recreation)* 664, 667
Mainframe Computers *(Computing & Mathematics)* 184, 194
Malaria *(Health & Medicine)* 398
Malaysia *(Business & Economics)* 128
Malaysia *(Education)* 266
Malaysia *(Government & Politics)* 332, 342
Malaysia *(Humanities & Social Sciences)* 421
Mammals *(Science)* 614
Management of Information Systems (MIS) *(Computing & Mathematics)* 171
Management Science *(Business & Economics)* 109
Management *(Business & Economics)* 108-110, 114, 133-134, 144, 679, 710
Management *(Engineering & Technology)* 306
Management *(Health & Medicine)* 367
Management *(Internet)* 455
Management *(Law & Criminal Justice)* 490
Manufacturers *(Business & Economics)* 122, 136
Manufacturers *(Computing & Mathematics)* 182, 184
Manufacturing Industry *(Engineering & Technology)* 296
Manufacturing *(Business & Economics)* 114, 122, 124-125, 144, 146
Manufacturing *(Computing & Mathematics)* 179, 194, 221
Manufacturing *(Engineering & Technology)* 303, 305
Manuscript Collections *(Humanities & Social Sciences)* 424
Mapmaking *(Government & Politics)* 347
Mapping *(Business & Economics)* 141
Mapping *(Science)* 588, 590, 592, 597-599
Maps *(Government & Politics)* 319, 338, 344, 554
Maps *(Humanities & Social Sciences)* 424
Maps *(Popular Culture & Entertainment)* 523
Maps *(Science)* 589
Maps *(Sports & Recreation)* 630, 659, 668
Marine Biology *(Science)* 568-571, 587
Marine Ecology *(Science)* 570
Marine Geology *(Science)* 571, 589
Marine Life *(Science)* 568
Marine Sciences *(Education)* 236
Marine Sciences *(Engineering & Technology)* 305
Marine Sciences *(Science)* 569-570, 595
Marine World Africa *(Popular Culture & Entertainment)* 544
Market Research *(Business & Economics)* 102, 128

Marketing *(Business & Economics)* 102-104, 107, 114, 120, 134, 137, 142, 149-150
Marketing *(Communications)* 167
Marketing *(Computing & Mathematics)* 202, 215, 222, 224
Marketing *(Health & Medicine)* 370
Marketing *(Internet)* 474
Marketing *(Popular Culture & Entertainment)* 547-548
Marketing *(Sports & Recreation)* 651
Marriage *(Popular Culture & Entertainment)* 520
Maryland *(Education)* 264, 280, 283, 285
Maryland *(Popular Culture & Entertainment)* 533
Mass Communications *(Communications)* 162, 164, 167, 679, 711
Mass Communications *(Internet)* 460
Mass Communications *(Law & Criminal Justice)* 491
Mass Communications *(Popular Culture & Entertainment)* 542, 550, 552
Mass Market *(Popular Culture & Entertainment)* 514
Mass Media *(Communications)* 156-158, 162
Mass Media *(Popular Culture & Entertainment)* 537-539
Massachusetts *(Arts & Music)* 59, 80, 91
Massachusetts *(Business & Economics)* 104, 116
Massachusetts *(Communications)* 154
Massachusetts *(Computing & Mathematics)* 188, 232
Massachusetts *(Education)* 260, 276-277, 279, 283
Massachusetts *(Engineering & Technology)* 308
Massachusetts *(Government & Politics)* 324-325, 329, 340, 363
Massachusetts *(Health & Medicine)* 390
Massachusetts *(Law & Criminal Justice)* 492
Massachusetts *(Religion & Philosophy)* 561
Massachusetts *(Sports & Recreation)* 655-656, 664, 666
Masters of Business Administration *(Business & Economics)* 108
Material Science *(Engineering & Technology)* 303, 686, 719
Material Science *(Science)* 586
Materials Engineering *(Engineering & Technology)* 303
Mathematical Analysis *(Computing & Mathematics)* 169
Mathematical Formulae *(Computing & Mathematics)* 712
Mathematical Philosophy *(Religion & Philosophy)* 558
Mathematical Software *(Computing & Mathematics)* 183, 195-196, 198-199, 201
Mathematics Software *(Computing & Mathematics)* 196, 198-199, 224, 227
Mathematics *(Arts & Music)* 32
Mathematics *(Computing & Mathematics)* 178-179, 186, 191, 194-201, 204, 206-208, 232, 681, 712
Mathematics *(Education)* 240-241, 257
Mathematics *(Engineering & Technology)* 292
Mathematics *(Science)* 597, 603
MATLAB *(Computing & Mathematics)* 198-199
Mayan Culture *(Popular Culture & Entertainment)* 544
MBA Programs *(Business & Economics)* 108-109, 111
MBA Programs *(Education)* 271
MBONE *(Communications)* 159
Mechanical Engineering *(Engineering & Technology)* 291, 298, 308, 686, 719
Mechanical Engineering *(Popular Culture & Entertainment)* 510
Mechanics *(Engineering & Technology)* 299
Mechanics *(Sports & Recreation)* 638-639
Media Arts *(Arts & Music)* 27
Media Research *(Arts & Music)* 27

Media Research *(Business & Economics)* 102
Media *(Business & Economics)* 122, 136
Media *(Communications)* 156, 158, 162
Media *(Computing & Mathematics)* 176
Media *(Education)* 245
Media *(Government & Politics)* 353
Media *(Internet)* 466
Media *(Popular Culture & Entertainment)* 534, 537-540, 543, 550
Media *(Popular Culture & Entertainment)* 697
Mediation *(Business & Economics)* 134
Mediation *(Law & Criminal Justice)* 500
Mediation *(Popular Culture & Entertainment)* 517-518
Medical Administration *(Health & Medicine)* 377, 394
Medical Applications *(Computing & Mathematics)* 226
Medical Assistance *(Health & Medicine)* 374, 382, 404
Medical Education *(Health & Medicine)* 376, 386, 392, 400-401, 405, 407
Medical Ethics *(Health & Medicine)* 400
Medical Images *(Health & Medicine)* 405
Medical Imaging *(Health & Medicine)* 392, 404-405
Medical Informatics *(Health & Medicine)* 372, 386-388, 394, 400, 403-405
Medical Information *(Health & Medicine)* 387, 390, 397, 401
Medical Libraries *(Health & Medicine)* 368, 371, 387
Medical Manufacturing *(Business & Economics)* 114
Medical Photography *(Health & Medicine)* 405
Medical Products *(Communications)* 165
Medical Professionals *(Health & Medicine)* 372, 394, 406
Medical Reference *(Health & Medicine)* 368, 371, 388, 392, 402, 404-405
Medical Research *(Health & Medicine)* 368, 370, 372, 375-377, 379-380, 385-398, 401, 403, 405
Medical Research *(Science)* 602
Medical Resources *(Health & Medicine)* 369, 384, 390, 394, 396, 398, 401-402, 405-406
Medical Schools *(Health & Medicine)* 371, 378, 386-390, 392, 394, 398, 401, 405-406, 689, 721
Medical Software *(Computing & Mathematics)* 173
Medical Software *(Health & Medicine)* 388, 391-392, 404
Medical Supplies *(Business & Economics)* 114
Medical Supplies *(Health & Medicine)* 370
Medical Treatment *(Health & Medicine)* 369, 379-380, 386, 391, 394, 408
Medicare *(Law & Criminal Justice)* 500
Medicine *(Education)* 279, 283
Medicine *(Engineering & Technology)* 292
Medicine *(Government & Politics)* 350
Medicine *(Health & Medicine)* 370, 377, 381, 385-394, 396, 398, 400-406, 689, 721
Medicine *(Science)* 600
Medieval Period *(Humanities & Social Sciences)* 441
Medieval Studies *(Arts & Music)* 21
Medieval Studies *(Humanities & Social Sciences)* 424, 439
Mediterranean Culture *(Education)* 275
Mediterranean Culture *(Humanities & Social Sciences)* 427
Mediterranean Culture *(Sports & Recreation)* 628
Memory *(Humanities & Social Sciences)* 445
Men *(Health & Medicine)* 537
Men *(Popular Culture & Entertainment)* 518
Men's Health *(Health & Medicine)* 380, 400-402, 407-408
Men's Issues *(Health & Medicine)* 400-402, 407, 537
Menopause *(Health & Medicine)* 409-410

Mental Health *(Health & Medicine)* 393-394, 398, 402, 404, 689, 721
Mental Health *(Humanities & Social Sciences)* 445
Mental Health *(Popular Culture & Entertainment)* 533
Mental Imagery *(Humanities & Social Sciences)* 445
Mental Retardation *(Health & Medicine)* 372
Merchandise *(Business & Economics)* 146
Meta-Index (Ambient Music) *(Arts & Music)* 57
Meta-Index (Antiques) *(Sports & Recreation)* 621
Meta-Index (Archaeology) *(Humanities & Social Sciences)* 414
Meta-Index (Architecture) *(Arts & Music)* 15-17
Meta-Index (Art) *(Arts & Music)* 31
Meta-Index (Astronomy) *(Science)* 571
Meta-Index (Authors) *(Popular Culture & Entertainment)* 516
Meta-Index (Beverages) *(Sports & Recreation)* 627, 633
Meta-Index (Business/Economics) *(Internet)* 455
Meta-Index Business *(Business & Economics)* 144
Meta-Index (California) *(Internet)* 462
Meta-Index (Cambodia) *(Government & Politics)* 332
Meta-Index (Cartoons) *(Arts & Music)* 38
Meta-Index (Chemistry) *(Science)* 587
Meta-Index (Chinese) *(Humanities & Social Sciences)* 417
Meta-Index (Communities) *(Internet)* 465
Meta-Index (Computing) *(Computing & Mathematics)* 192
Meta-Index (Cooking) *(Sports & Recreation)* 632
Meta-Index (Disabilities) *(Health & Medicine)* 374
Meta-Index (Education) *(Education)* 261
Meta-Index (Electronic Texts) *(Humanities & Social Sciences)* 445
Meta-Index (Finance) *(Business & Economics)* 143
Meta-Index (Gems) *(Sports & Recreation)* 622
Meta-Index (Germany) *(Government & Politics)* 331
Meta-Index (Germany) *(Internet)* 466, 468
Meta-Index (Humor) *(Popular Culture & Entertainment)* 528, 530
Meta-Index (Indonesia) *(Government & Politics)* 332
Meta-Index (International Cities) *(Sports & Recreation)* 658
Meta-Index (Internet) *(Internet)* 464-465, 467, 470, 480
Meta-Index (Jobs) *(Communications)* 154
Meta-Index (Jokes) *(Popular Culture & Entertainment)* 526
Meta-Index (Laos) *(Government & Politics)* 333
Meta-Index (Law) *(Law & Criminal Justice)* 490
Meta-Index (Macintosh) *(Computing & Mathematics)* 224
Meta-Index (Mathematics) *(Computing & Mathematics)* 201
Meta-Index (Medical) *(Health & Medicine)* 405
Meta-Index (Multimedia) *(Humanities & Social Sciences)* 424
Meta-Index (Music) *(Arts & Music)* 63, 67-68, 70
Meta-Index (Pharmacy) *(Health & Medicine)* 402, 407
Meta-Index (Philosophy) *(Religion & Philosophy)* 558
Meta-Index (Recipes) *(Sports & Recreation)* 624
Meta-Index (Social Science) *(Humanities & Social Sciences)* 449
Meta-Index (Thailand) *(Government & Politics)* 333
Meta-Index (Theater) *(Arts & Music)* 96

Meta-Index (UNIX Security) *(Computing & Mathematics)* 176
Meta-Indexes *(Business & Economics)* 135
Meta-Indexes *(Health & Medicine)* 369, 372, 394
Metallurgy *(Education)* 272
Metallurgy *(Engineering & Technology)* 303
Metalwork *(Arts & Music)* 31
Metaphysics *(Religion & Philosophy)* 558
Meteorology *(Government & Politics)* 344
Meteorology *(Popular Culture & Entertainment)* 554-556
Meteorology *(Science)* 554, 572, 587-592, 594, 597, 600
Mexico *(Engineering & Technology)* 310
Mexico *(Government & Politics)* 336
Mexico *(Humanities & Social Sciences)* 419
Mexico *(Sports & Recreation)* 628
Mice *(Science)* 576
Michigan *(Business & Economics)* 113, 118
Michigan *(Computing & Mathematics)* 232
Michigan *(Education)* 241, 244, 278, 280, 285, 288
Michigan *(Engineering & Technology)* 309
Michigan *(Government & Politics)* 321
Michigan *(Internet)* 472, 474
Michigan *(Popular Culture & Entertainment)* 534, 552, 556
Michigan *(Religion & Philosophy)* 562
Microbiology *(Health & Medicine)* 370-371, 398
Microbiology *(Science)* 576-577
Microelectronics *(Engineering & Technology)* 308
Microsoft Corporation *(Computing & Mathematics)* 224
Microwave Systems *(Communications)* 168
Middle East *(Government & Politics)* 335, 348
Middle East *(Popular Culture & Entertainment)* 536
Middle Eastern Literature *(Humanities & Social Sciences)* 441
Middle Eastern Studies *(Humanities & Social Sciences)* 420
Middle School *(Education)* 257
MIDI (Musical Instrument Digital Interface) *(Arts & Music)* 54, 57, 63, 65, 67, 69, 89
Midwifery *(Health & Medicine)* 368, 372, 410
Migration *(Humanities & Social Sciences)* 448
Military Academies *(Education)* 289
Military Academies *(Government & Politics)* 348
Military Archives (US) *(Humanities & Social Sciences)* 424
Military Music *(Arts & Music)* 62
Military Policy *(Government & Politics)* 347
Military Research *(Government & Politics)* 347-348
Military Science *(Education)* 289
Military Science *(Government & Politics)* 348
Military Technology *(Engineering & Technology)* 298
Military Technology *(Government & Politics)* 347-349
Military *(Education)* 288-289
Military *(Government & Politics)* 314, 319, 342, 346-349, 688
Militias *(Law & Criminal Justice)* 494
Minerals *(Engineering & Technology)* 303
Minerals *(Science)* 586, 597
Minerals *(Sports & Recreation)* 623
Mining *(Education)* 272
Mining *(Engineering & Technology)* 303
Mining *(Government & Politics)* 318
Minnesota *(Arts & Music)* 20
Minnesota *(Education)* 279-280, 282, 286
Minnesota *(Government & Politics)* 340
Minnesota *(Popular Culture & Entertainment)* 551
Minnesota *(Sports & Recreation)* 620, 664
Minority Information *(Government & Politics)* 316
Minority Programs *(Government & Politics)* 316

Minority Programs *(Science)* 584, 594
Minority Resources *(Government & Politics)* 315
Minority Resources *(Science)* 600
Missing Children *(Health & Medicine)* 381-382
Missing Children *(Popular Culture & Entertainment)* 518
Missing Persons *(Business & Economics)* 144
Mississippi *(Education)* 280, 286
Missouri *(Education)* 257, 279, 288
Missouri *(Government & Politics)* 364-365
Mobile Communications *(Communications)* 160-161, 163-166
Mobile Computing *(Communications)* 163
Mobile Computing *(Computing & Mathematics)* 229
Mobile Robotics *(Engineering & Technology)* 305
Mobility Equipment *(Health & Medicine)* 372
Modeling Agencies *(Business & Economics)* 123
Modeling *(Arts & Music)* 38
Modems *(Communications)* 160, 163-164, 167
Modems *(Computing & Mathematics)* 222
Moderates *(Government & Politics)* 316
Modern Art *(Arts & Music)* 20, 32
Modern Art *(Business & Economics)* 145
Molecular Biology *(Engineering & Technology)* 292
Molecular Biology *(Health & Medicine)* 370-371, 387
Molecular Biology *(Science)* 567, 574-582, 586, 601, 615-616
Molecular Imaging *(Science)* 586
Molecular Modeling *(Computing & Mathematics)* 170, 172
Molecular Modeling *(Engineering & Technology)* 294
Molecular Modeling *(Science)* 575, 586
Molecular Physics *(Science)* 601
Monasteries *(Humanities & Social Sciences)* 564
Money Markets *(Business & Economics)* 144
Mongolia *(Humanities & Social Sciences)* 425
Montana *(Business & Economics)* 138
Montana *(Education)* 286
Montana *(Government & Politics)* 364
Montreal *(Education)* 268
Monty Python *(Humanities & Social Sciences)* 433
Monty Python *(Popular Culture & Entertainment)* 530
Mood Disorders *(Health & Medicine)* 393
MOOs (Object Oriented MUDs) *(Internet)* 485
Mormonism *(Religion & Philosophy)* 559
Mortgages *(Business & Economics)* 140, 142
Mosques *(Arts & Music)* 16
Motivational Products *(Business & Economics)* 133
Motor Oils *(Business & Economics)* 121
Motor Racing *(Sports & Recreation)* 638-639
Motor Sports *(Popular Culture & Entertainment)* 509-510
Motor Sports *(Sports & Recreation)* 638-639, 702, 738
Motorcycles *(Popular Culture & Entertainment)* 510
Motorcycles *(Sports & Recreation)* 638-639
Mountain Biking *(Sports & Recreation)* 640, 642
Mountaineering *(Sports & Recreation)* 640
Movie Reviews *(Popular Culture & Entertainment)* 534, 542
Movies *(Arts & Music)* 45, 47-48, 63, 70
Movies *(Engineering & Technology)* 308
Movies *(Popular Culture & Entertainment)* 517, 519, 523, 542-543, 551-552
Movies *(Popular Culture & Entertainment)* 697

MS Windows *(Internet)* 476
MS-DOS *(Health & Medicine)* 390
MUDs (Multi-User Dimensions) *(Internet)* 482-487
Multi-Level Marketing (MLM) *(Business & Economics)* 103
Multichips *(Engineering & Technology)* 296
Multidisciplinary Education *(Engineering & Technology)* 292
Multilingual Resources *(Education)* 252
Multilingual Resources *(Humanities & Social Sciences)* 432
Multimedia Applications *(Law & Criminal Justice)* 502
Multimedia Education *(Arts & Music)* 44
Multimedia Education *(Communications)* 161
Multimedia Education *(Education)* 241
Multimedia Publishing *(Business & Economics)* 138
Multimedia Resources *(Education)* 242
Multimedia Resources *(Government & Politics)* 325
Multimedia Resources *(Health & Medicine)* 371
Multimedia Technologies *(Engineering & Technology)* 310
Multimedia *(Arts & Music)* 17, 19-20, 30, 32, 34, 38-39, 42, 44, 46-48, 63, 90, 94
Multimedia *(Business & Economics)* 102-103, 112, 127, 136-137, 139, 151
Multimedia *(Communications)* 154, 158-159, 162-163, 166
Multimedia *(Computing & Mathematics)* 170, 172, 174, 181, 191, 193, 205, 220
Multimedia *(Education)* 245-246, 249
Multimedia *(Health & Medicine)* 401
Multimedia *(Internet)* 453, 460, 472, 474, 481
Multimedia *(Popular Culture & Entertainment)* 514, 525, 543
Multimedia *(Popular Culture & Entertainment)* 697
Multimedia *(Sports & Recreation)* 654, 665
Multiple Sclerosis *(Health & Medicine)* 378
Municipal Government *(Government & Politics)* 326
Museums & Theme Parks *(Popular Culture & Entertainment)* 697
Museums *(Arts & Music)* 16, 21, 24, 26, 33, 99
Museums *(Communications)* 160
Museums *(Government & Politics)* 313, 321, 339, 342
Museums *(Humanities & Social Sciences)* 414, 420, 424, 427
Museums *(Popular Culture & Entertainment)* 519-520, 544-545
Museums *(Religion & Philosophy)* 560, 563
Museums *(Science)* 602-603, 616
Museums *(Sports & Recreation)* 660, 663
Music Archives *(Arts & Music)* 52, 54, 58, 63, 66-68, 70, 73-75
Music Books *(Popular Culture & Entertainment)* 514
Music Collections *(Arts & Music)* 59
Music Collectors *(Arts & Music)* 52
Music Composition *(Arts & Music)* 67
Music Databases *(Arts & Music)* 52
Music Education *(Arts & Music)* 51, 55-56, 59, 61, 64-65, 68
Music Equipment *(Arts & Music)* 66
Music Festivals *(Arts & Music)* 51, 54, 60, 64, 66
Music Genres *(Arts & Music)* 676, 708
Music History *(Arts & Music)* 51-52, 55-56, 68-69
Music Industry *(Arts & Music)* 52, 57-58, 67, 69
Music Industry *(Business & Economics)* 113
Music Manuscripts *(Arts & Music)* 56, 69
Music Newsletters *(Arts & Music)* 77-78, 92
Music Notation *(Arts & Music)* 67
Music Organizations *(Arts & Music)* 71, 676
Music Publications *(Arts & Music)* 58, 65
Music Publishers *(Arts & Music)* 63
Music Research *(Arts & Music)* 51, 67-68, 70

Music Resources *(Arts & Music)* 57, 59-60, 73, 85, 87, 676
Music Reviews *(Arts & Music)* 52-54, 62, 65, 67-70, 72, 76
Music Schools *(Arts & Music)* 59, 62-64, 66, 81, 97
Music Societies *(Popular Culture & Entertainment)* 514
Music Software *(Arts & Music)* 67-68
Music Software *(Computing & Mathematics)* 222
Music Theory *(Arts & Music)* 59
Music *(Arts & Music)* 27-28, 32, 51-52, 54-55, 57-91, 94-95, 99, 675
Music *(Business & Economics)* 113, 147-148
Music *(Communications)* 158
Music *(Education)* 236
Music *(Government & Politics)* 338
Music *(Humanities & Social Sciences)* 420
Music *(Popular Culture & Entertainment)* 516, 523, 534-535, 543, 546, 551
Music *(Sports & Recreation)* 655
Musical Groups *(Arts & Music)* 71-73, 77-81, 676
Musical Instruments *(Arts & Music)* 52, 58, 63-66, 69, 72
Musical Theater *(Arts & Music)* 91, 93-95
Musicals *(Arts & Music)* 91, 95-96
Musicals *(Humanities & Social Sciences)* 437
Musicians *(Arts & Music)* 51, 57, 83-84, 86-89, 676
Musicology *(Arts & Music)* 58
Muslims *(Religion & Philosophy)* 564
Mutual Funds *(Business & Economics)* 128-131
Mystery Fiction *(Popular Culture & Entertainment)* 551
Mysticism *(Popular Culture & Entertainment)* 554
Mythology Enthusiasts *(Religion & Philosophy)* 557
Mythology *(Humanities & Social Sciences)* 422, 426, 433, 445
Mythology *(Popular Culture & Entertainment)* 553
Mythology *(Religion & Philosophy)* 563, 733
Myths *(Religion & Philosophy)* 557

NAFTA (North American Free Trade Agreement) *(Business & Economics)* 126
NAFTA (North American Free Trade Agreement) *(Government & Politics)* 336, 352
Nanotechnology *(Computing & Mathematics)* 172, 230
Nanotechnology *(Engineering & Technology)* 294, 302
Nanotechnology *(Health & Medicine)* 368, 370
Nanotechnology *(Science)* 601
NASA (National Aeronautics And Space Administration) *(Computing & Mathematics)* 217
NASA (National Aeronautics And Space Administration) *(Education)* 257
NASA (National Aeronautics And Space Administration) *(Engineering & Technology)* 291, 309
NASA (National Aeronautics And Space Administration) *(Government & Politics)* 316
NASA (National Aeronautics And Space Administration) *(Popular Culture & Entertainment)* 523, 525
NASA (National Aeronautics And Space Administration) *(Science)* 571-572, 574, 588, 594, 597-598, 609-613
NASDAQ *(Business & Economics)* 131
National Archives *(Education)* 250
National Center For Atmospheric Research (NCAR) *(Science)* 589
National Institute of Standards and Technology *(Government & Politics)* 316-317

National Institutes Of Health *(Health & Medicine)* 403-404
National Library Of Medicine *(Health & Medicine)* 392
National Park Service (US) *(Government & Politics)* 317
National Parks *(Science)* 593
National Parks *(Sports & Recreation)* 642, 658, 660
National Policy *(Government & Politics)* 319, 331, 348
National Press Club *(Communications)* 156
National Public Radio *(Communications)* 154
National Wildlife System *(Science)* 579
Native American Art *(Arts & Music)* 20-21, 36
Native American Culture *(Popular Culture & Entertainment)* 519
Native Americans *(Education)* 236
Native Americans *(Humanities & Social Sciences)* 418, 420, 424
Native Americans *(Popular Culture & Entertainment)* 519
NATO (North Atlantic Treaty Organization) *(Government & Politics)* 342, 356
Natural Disasters *(Government & Politics)* 327, 363
Natural Foods *(Sports & Recreation)* 636
Natural History Museum *(Popular Culture & Entertainment)* 544
Natural History *(Government & Politics)* 319
Natural History *(Popular Culture & Entertainment)* 544-545
Natural History *(Science)* 580, 602-603, 616
Natural History *(Sports & Recreation)* 645
Natural Language *(Computing & Mathematics)* 224
Natural Language *(Humanities & Social Sciences)* 432
Natural Resources *(Science)* 566, 579, 592, 599
Natural Sciences *(Engineering & Technology)* 299
Natural Sciences *(Popular Culture & Entertainment)* 545
Natural Sciences *(Science)* 545, 588
Nature *(Popular Culture & Entertainment)* 524
Nature *(Science)* 602
Naval Research Laboratory *(Government & Politics)* 348
Navy (US) *(Government & Politics)* 347-348
Navy *(Communications)* 160
Navy *(Popular Culture & Entertainment)* 533
NBA (National Basketball Association) *(Sports & Recreation)* 651
NBC Television *(Popular Culture & Entertainment)* 552
Nebraska *(Education)* 286
Nepal *(Humanities & Social Sciences)* 440
Netherlands *(Arts & Music)* 80
Netherlands *(Computing & Mathematics)* 193
Netherlands *(Education)* 270-273
Netherlands *(Engineering & Technology)* 291
Netherlands *(Internet)* 462, 473
Netherlands *(Popular Culture & Entertainment)* 543
Netherlands *(Sports & Recreation)* 633, 654, 659
Netiquette *(Internet)* 460, 469
Netiquette *(Popular Culture & Entertainment)* 527
Netware *(Computing & Mathematics)* 182
Network Hardware *(Computing & Mathematics)* 202
Network Protocols *(Computing & Mathematics)* 201
Network Providers *(Computing & Mathematics)* 169
Network Security *(Communications)* 160
Network Security *(Computing & Mathematics)* 169
Network Security *(Internet)* 470
Network Servers *(Communications)* 160
Network Servers *(Education)* 242

Network Servers *(Government & Politics)* 328
Network Servers *(Internet)* 454
Networked Information Retrieval *(Internet)* 481
Networking Applications *(Computing & Mathematics)* 174
Networking Software *(Computing & Mathematics)* 205
Networking *(Business & Economics)* 103, 107, 135
Networking *(Communications)* 160-161, 163, 165-167
Networking *(Computing & Mathematics)* 170-171, 173-174, 176, 179-183, 194, 201-203, 205, 207, 221-223, 225, 228-230, 681, 712
Networking *(Education)* 244, 253, 255-256, 258, 260, 264
Networking *(Engineering & Technology)* 296, 308
Networking *(Government & Politics)* 315, 346, 352
Networking *(Health & Medicine)* 387
Networking *(Humanities & Social Sciences)* 430, 446
Networking *(Internet)* 457, 459-460, 470-471, 474, 481, 484, 695
Networking *(Popular Culture & Entertainment)* 544
Networking *(Science)* 606
Networks *(Internet)* 454
Neural Networks *(Computing & Mathematics)* 177, 179, 190
Neural Networks *(Engineering & Technology)* 295
Neurobiology *(Health & Medicine)* 375
Neurobiology *(Science)* 601
Neurology *(Engineering & Technology)* 299
Neurology *(Health & Medicine)* 378, 390, 393, 405-406
Neurology *(Science)* 600-601
Neuromuscular Disorders *(Health & Medicine)* 372
Neurosciences *(Computing & Mathematics)* 177
Neurosciences *(Health & Medicine)* 379
Neurosciences *(Humanities & Social Sciences)* 446
Neurosciences *(Science)* 700, 735
Neurosurgery *(Health & Medicine)* 378-379, 392
Nevada *(Education)* 240, 286
Nevada *(Sports & Recreation)* 662, 669
New Age Philosophy *(Popular Culture & Entertainment)* 531, 534
New Age Philosophy *(Religion & Philosophy)* 557
New England *(Health & Medicine)* 408
New England *(Sports & Recreation)* 633
New Hampshire *(Education)* 278, 282-283
New Hampshire *(Government & Politics)* 365
New Jersey *(Education)* 248, 258, 282
New Jersey *(Government & Politics)* 364
New Media *(Popular Culture & Entertainment)* 539-540
New Mexico *(Arts & Music)* 21
New Mexico *(Computing & Mathematics)* 188
New Mexico *(Education)* 259
New Mexico *(Humanities & Social Sciences)* 418
New York *(Arts & Music)* 24, 28, 30, 36, 56, 64, 68, 74, 93-96
New York *(Business & Economics)* 102, 142
New York *(Computing & Mathematics)* 188
New York *(Education)* 235, 254, 258, 261-262, 278-279, 281-282
New York *(Government & Politics)* 319, 325, 328, 364, 554
New York *(Health & Medicine)* 372, 385-386
New York *(Humanities & Social Sciences)* 420, 446
New York *(Internet)* 474
New York *(Law & Criminal Justice)* 498, 506
New York *(Popular Culture & Entertainment)* 522, 531
New York *(Science)* 587

New York *(Sports & Recreation)* 625, 630, 633, 641, 651, 663, 665
New Zealand *(Arts & Music)* 15-16
New Zealand *(Computing & Mathematics)* 188
New Zealand *(Government & Politics)* 336
New Zealand *(Sports & Recreation)* 638, 640, 654, 662
News Media *(Arts & Music)* 99
News Media *(Business & Economics)* 142
News Media *(Internet)* 469
News Media *(Popular Culture & Entertainment)* 534, 538, 552
News *(Business & Economics)* 133
News *(Communications)* 156
News *(Computing & Mathematics)* 220
News *(Education)* 234, 261
News *(Government & Politics)* 331, 337, 342
News *(Humanities & Social Sciences)* 420, 446
News *(Internet)* 462, 473
News *(Popular Culture & Entertainment)* 519, 524, 533-540, 552, 556
News *(Sports & Recreation)* 635, 640
Newsletters *(Arts & Music)* 62-63, 66, 69
Newsletters *(Business & Economics)* 130, 134, 136, 144
Newsletters *(Engineering & Technology)* 310
Newsletters *(Government & Politics)* 314
Newsletters *(Health & Medicine)* 376, 398, 408
Newsletters *(Humanities & Social Sciences)* 432
Newsletters *(Internet)* 461
Newsletters *(Law & Criminal Justice)* 492
Newspapers *(Internet)* 460
Newspapers *(Popular Culture & Entertainment)* 537-538, 540-541, 556
Newspapers *(Sports & Recreation)* 640
NFS (Network File System) *(Computing & Mathematics)* 203
NGOs (Non Governmental Organizations) *(Business & Economics)* 106
NGOs (Non-Governmental Organizations) *(Government & Politics)* 319
Nicaragua *(Government & Politics)* 336
Non Profit Organizations *(Arts & Music)* 27-28, 32, 38, 91
Non Profit Organizations *(Business & Economics)* 117, 119-120, 128, 134-136, 520, Non Profit Organizations *(Communications)* 161-162
Non Profit Organizations *(Education)* 252-253, 255
Non Profit Organizations *(Engineering & Technology)* 309, 311
Non Profit Organizations *(Government & Politics)* 337, 345, 357
Non Profit Organizations *(Health & Medicine)* 372, 374, 394, 398
Non Profit Organizations *(Humanities & Social Sciences)* 450
Non Profit Organizations *(Law & Criminal Justice)* 506
Nonlinear Science *(Computing & Mathematics)* 186
Nordic Literature *(Humanities & Social Sciences)* 442
North America *(Popular Culture & Entertainment)* 514
North Atlantic Treaty Organization (NATO) *(Government & Politics)* 316
North Carolina *(Arts & Music)* 25
North Carolina *(Communications)* 166
North Carolina *(Education)* 250, 283, 286-287
North Carolina *(Government & Politics)* 326, 364
North Carolina *(Health & Medicine)* 380
North Carolina *(Popular Culture & Entertainment)* 536, 538
North Carolina *(Sports & Recreation)* 657, 665, 670
North Dakota *(Education)* 283
Northern Ireland *(Government & Politics)* 322
Northwest US *(Business & Economics)* 132

Northwest US *(Sports & Recreation)* 671
Norway *(Arts & Music)* 26, 50, 61, 72
Norway *(Education)* 271, 273
Norway *(Humanities & Social Sciences)* 429, 448
Norway *(Popular Culture & Entertainment)* 530
Nova Scotia *(Education)* 237, 267
Nova Scotia *(Government & Politics)* 320-321, 359
Nova Scotia *(Humanities & Social Sciences)* 426
Nova Scotia *(Popular Culture & Entertainment)* 535
Nova Scotia *(Sports & Recreation)* 660, 665
Nuclear Engineering *(Engineering & Technology)* 686
Nuclear Medicine *(Engineering & Technology)* 304
Nuclear Medicine *(Health & Medicine)* 390
Nuclear Physics *(Engineering & Technology)* 304
Nuclear Physics *(Science)* 606-607, 609
Nuclear Power *(Government & Politics)* 335
Nuclear Safety *(Engineering & Technology)* 304
Nuclear Safety *(Government & Politics)* 314, 335
Nuclear Safety *(Science)* 596, 607
Numerical Analysis *(Computing & Mathematics)* 169, 194-196, 198-200, 232
Nurseries *(Business & Economics)* 146-147
Nursing *(Education)* 288
Nursing *(Health & Medicine)* 386, 394, 406
Nutrition *(Business & Economics)* 123
Nutrition *(Health & Medicine)* 368, 379, 382, 395-397, 400-401
Nutrition *(Popular Culture & Entertainment)* 532
Nutrition *(Sports & Recreation)* 642, 671

Obituaries *(Health & Medicine)* 402
Object-Oriented Programming *(Computing & Mathematics)* 170, 186, 209-211, 213
Observatories *(Science)* 571-572, 610
Obstetrics *(Health & Medicine)* 410-411
Occult *(Popular Culture & Entertainment)* 554
Occupational Health & Safety *(Health & Medicine)* 396-397, 399-400
Ocean Ecology *(Science)* 568-570
Ocean *(Popular Culture & Entertainment)* 545
Oceanography *(Computing & Mathematics)* 173, 226
Oceanography *(Science)* 568-571, 581, 587, 590-591, 595
Oceans *(Science)* 569, 571, 590
OCR (Optical Character Recognition) *(Computing & Mathematics)* 171, 216
Office Equipment *(Business & Economics)* 121, 124
Office Equipment *(Popular Culture & Entertainment)* 548
Office Furniture *(Business & Economics)* 134
Office Products *(Business & Economics)* 121
Office Supplies *(Business & Economics)* 146
Ohio *(Business & Economics)* 112
Ohio *(Education)* 244, 260, 276
Ohio *(Government & Politics)* 326, 330
Ohio *(Health & Medicine)* 370
Ohio *(Internet)* 455
Ohio *(Law & Criminal Justice)* 498-499
Oklahoma *(Arts & Music)* 26
Oklahoma *(Education)* 281
Oklahoma *(Government & Politics)* 329
Old English *(Humanities & Social Sciences)* 441
Olympic Games *(Government & Politics)* 321
Olympic Games *(Sports & Recreation)* 648, 650, 653
Oncology *(Health & Medicine)* 374-376, 378-380, 402
Online Advertising *(Popular Culture & Entertainment)* 510

Online Art Galleries – Pharmacology   801

Online Art Galleries *(Arts & Music)* 17-21, 27-28, 31, 44, 59
Online Arts *(Arts & Music)* 20, 23, 29-30
Online Book Catalogue *(Popular Culture & Entertainment)* 516
Online Books *(Business & Economics)* 137-138
Online Books *(Health & Medicine)* 391
Online Books *(Humanities & Social Sciences)* 422-423, 433, 436, 438, 441-442
Online Books *(Popular Culture & Entertainment)* 512
Online Books *(Science)* 585, 606
Online Bookstores *(Business & Economics)* 140
Online Bookstores *(Popular Culture & Entertainment)* 511, 513-516
Online Catalogs *(Business & Economics)* 115, 122, 146
Online Catalogs *(Computing & Mathematics)* 201
Online Catalogs *(Sports & Recreation)* 636-637
Online Chat *(Internet)* 487
Online Directories *(Arts & Music)* 64
Online Directories *(Popular Culture & Entertainment)* 521, 524
Online Games *(Business & Economics)* 131
Online Games *(Internet)* 483-484, 486
Online Games *(Sports & Recreation)* 634-636
Online Guides *(Business & Economics)* 136
Online Guides *(Education)* 254
Online Guides *(Internet)* 466, 468, 662
Online Guides *(Popular Culture & Entertainment)* 525
Online Journals *(Communications)* 157
Online Journals *(Computing & Mathematics)* 177
Online Journals *(Health & Medicine)* 387, 390, 400
Online Learning *(Communications)* 163
Online Learning *(Computing & Mathematics)* 174, 187
Online Learning *(Education)* 256
Online Magazines *(Arts & Music)* 52-54, 62, 65, 99
Online Magazines *(Business & Economics)* 102, 115
Online Magazines *(Computing & Mathematics)* 209, 214-218, 220
Online Magazines *(Health & Medicine)* 368
Online Magazines *(Humanities & Social Sciences)* 435
Online Magazines *(Internet)* 456, 466
Online Magazines *(Popular Culture & Entertainment)* 533, 535, 538, 550
Online Magazines *(Science)* 607
Online Magazines *(Sports & Recreation)* 634
Online Malls *(Business & Economics)* 150
Online Malls *(Popular Culture & Entertainment)* 547
Online Marketing *(Business & Economics)* 102, 140
Online Marketing *(Communications)* 154
Online Marketing *(Popular Culture & Entertainment)* 547-548
Online Music *(Arts & Music)* 50, 54-56, 62, 92
Online Newspapers *(Business & Economics)* 110, 131, 138, 144
Online Newspapers *(Communications)* 158
Online Newspapers *(Education)* 277
Online Newspapers *(Government & Politics)* 330, 356
Online Newspapers *(Popular Culture & Entertainment)* 532-538, 540-541
Online Newspapers *(Sports & Recreation)* 649-650
Online Publications *(Business & Economics)* 102
Online Publications *(Education)* 278
Online Publications *(Engineering & Technology)* 292
Online Publications *(Popular Culture & Entertainment)* 512, 528
Online Publications *(Science)* 578

Online Publications *(Sports & Recreation)* 636-637
Online Publishing *(Communications)* 158
Online Publishing *(Education)* 241
Online Retailers *(Business & Economics)* 146
Online Services *(Business & Economics)* 111, 137
Online Services *(Education)* 234, 285
Online Services *(Government & Politics)* 554
Online Services *(Internet)* 462-464
Online Services *(Popular Culture & Entertainment)* 532, 545
Online Services *(Science)* 570
Online Shopping *(Arts & Music)* 70
Online Shopping *(Business & Economics)* 112, 124, 145-148, 150
Online Shopping *(Computing & Mathematics)* 203, 217-218, 226
Online Shopping *(Education)* 241
Online Shopping *(Health & Medicine)* 383
Online Shopping *(Internet)* 455, 457, 460, 472
Online Shopping *(Popular Culture & Entertainment)* 522, 546-549
Online Shopping *(Sports & Recreation)* 622, 624, 626, 633, 650
Online Stores *(Business & Economics)* 148
OPACs (Online Public Access Catalogs) *(Business & Economics)* 124
OPACs (Online Public Access Catalogs) *(Education)* 233-236
OPACs (Online Public Access Catalogs) *(Humanities & Social Sciences)* 441
Open Systems *(Business & Economics)* 125
Opera Companies *(Arts & Music)* 95
Opera Singers *(Arts & Music)* 85, 92
Opera *(Arts & Music)* 51-52, 54-57, 61-62, 65, 69, 83, 91-92, 94-95
Opera *(Popular Culture & Entertainment)* 514
Operating Systems *(Computing & Mathematics)* 172-174, 180-183, 185, 189, 202-205, 208, 210, 213-214, 216-231, 681, 713
Operations Research *(Computing & Mathematics)* 198
Operations Research *(Engineering & Technology)* 302-303
Optical Character Recognition *(Engineering & Technology)* 296
Optical Engineering *(Engineering & Technology)* 299
Optimization *(Computing & Mathematics)* 232
Optometry *(Health & Medicine)* 389
Oral History *(Education)* 236, 258
Oregon *(Arts & Music)* 17, 60, 95
Oregon *(Education)* 240, 260, 262, 281, 286, 288
Oregon *(Engineering & Technology)* 309
Oregon *(Government & Politics)* 323, 327
Oregon *(Internet)* 474
Oregon *(Sports & Recreation)* 662, 665
Organic Chemistry *(Science)* 586
Organic Foods *(Sports & Recreation)* 633
Organic Gardening *(Sports & Recreation)* 636
Organizational Behavior *(Business & Economics)* 133-134
Organizations *(Arts & Music)* 96
Organizations *(Business & Economics)* 113, 133-134, 145, 149, 710
Organizations *(Communications)* 165, 679
Organizations *(Computing & Mathematics)* 206, 681, 714
Organizations *(Education)* 259, 262, 685
Organizations *(Engineering & Technology)* 293, 305
Organizations *(Government & Politics)* 316, 346, 349-352, 354
Organizations *(Health & Medicine)* 367, 377
Organizations *(Humanities & Social Sciences)* 445
Organizations *(Internet)* 461, 464, 468, 470, 482, 695
Organizations *(Law & Criminal Justice)* 490-494, 696

Organizations *(Religion & Philosophy)* 558-559
Organizations *(Science)* 585, 601, 605, 700, 735
Organizations *(Sports & Recreation)* 638, 640, 651, 702, 738
Oriental Carpets *(Business & Economics)* 146
Orienteering *(Sports & Recreation)* 640
Origami *(Sports & Recreation)* 622
Ornithology *(Science)* 613-614, 616
Ornithology *(Sports & Recreation)* 639, 643-644, 647-648
Orphanages *(Arts & Music)* 80
Outdoor Education *(Education)* 237
Outdoor Education *(Sports & Recreation)* 640
Outdoor Recreation *(Sports & Recreation)* 620, 640, 642, 649, 651, 655, 702, 738
Ozone *(Government & Politics)* 351

Pacific Northwest *(Sports & Recreation)* 642
Pacific Rim *(Sports & Recreation)* 655
Paganism *(Popular Culture & Entertainment)* 552-553
Pagans *(Religion & Philosophy)* 557
Page Description Languages *(Computing & Mathematics)* 212
Paging *(Communications)* 163
Paintball *(Sports & Recreation)* 648
Painting *(Arts & Music)* 18, 31
Paintings *(Arts & Music)* 20, 23, 26, 36
Palaces *(Arts & Music)* 16
Palaeolithic Age *(Humanities & Social Sciences)* 414
Paleontology *(Humanities & Social Sciences)* 414
Paleontology *(Popular Culture & Entertainment)* 545
Paleontology *(Science)* 603, 701, 735
Panama *(Government & Politics)* 336
Paraguay *(Government & Politics)* 336
Parallel Computation Research *(Computing & Mathematics)* 229
Parallel Computing *(Computing & Mathematics)* 178-179, 186, 188, 190, 192-193, 204, 210-211, 215, 230-231
Parallel Computing *(Engineering & Technology)* 299
Paramilitary Groups *(Law & Criminal Justice)* 494
Paranormal *(Popular Culture & Entertainment)* 553
Parasailing *(Sports & Recreation)* 620
Parasitology *(Health & Medicine)* 398
Parenting *(Business & Economics)* 520
Parenting *(Communications)* 155
Parenting *(Education)* 237, 242, 257, 259
Parenting *(Health & Medicine)* 381-383, 404
Parenting *(Popular Culture & Entertainment)* 517-520, 547
Paris *(Arts & Music)* 23-24, 26, 81, 95, 99
Paris *(Sports & Recreation)* 628, 630
Parkinson's Disease *(Health & Medicine)* 378-379
Parliament *(Government & Politics)* 330
Parrots *(Science)* 616
Parrots *(Sports & Recreation)* 645
Particle Accelerators *(Science)* 603-606, 608-609
Particle Physics *(Engineering & Technology)* 304
Particle Physics *(Science)* 603-608
Partnerships *(Business & Economics)* 144
Patent Law *(Business & Economics)* 144
Patent Law *(Law & Criminal Justice)* 491, 496
Patents *(Business & Economics)* 144
Patents *(Science)* 575
Pathology *(Health & Medicine)* 388, 390
Patient Resources *(Health & Medicine)* 376, 378-380
PC Magazine *(Computing & Mathematics)* 218
PC Tools *(Popular Culture & Entertainment)* 543
PC Tools *(Sports & Recreation)* 668

Peace *(Government & Politics)* 342, 353
Peace *(Internet)* 482
Peace *(Popular Culture & Entertainment)* 518, 520
Pedagogy *(Humanities & Social Sciences)* 441
Pediatrics *(Health & Medicine)* 374, 381-382
Penguins *(Sports & Recreation)* 646
Pennsylvania *(Arts & Music)* 15
Pennsylvania *(Business & Economics)* 146
Pennsylvania *(Education)* 277, 282, 286
Pennsylvania *(Humanities & Social Sciences)* 449
Pennsylvania *(Internet)* 454
Pension Plans *(Business & Economics)* 106
Perception *(Health & Medicine)* 404
Perception *(Science)* 578
Perennials *(Sports & Recreation)* 636
Performance Analysis *(Business & Economics)* 118
Performance Art *(Arts & Music)* 28, 32, 49, 94, 98
Performance Art *(Popular Culture & Entertainment)* 521
Performance Schedules *(Arts & Music)* 95
Performing Artists *(Arts & Music)* 85
Performing Arts *(Arts & Music)* 27-29, 33, 91-96, 677, 709
Performing Arts *(Education)* 260
Performing Arts *(Humanities & Social Sciences)* 415
Persia *(Humanities & Social Sciences)* 418
Persian Language *(Humanities & Social Sciences)* 418
Persian Rugs *(Business & Economics)* 145
Personal Ads *(Popular Culture & Entertainment)* 532
Personal Care *(Health & Medicine)* 689, 721
Personal Computers *(Computing & Mathematics)* 214, 216-217, 221, 223, 225
Personal Computers *(Internet)* 466
Personal Development *(Business & Economics)* 133
Personal Digital Assistants *(Computing & Mathematics)* 183, 194
Personal Finance Software *(Computing & Mathematics)* 221
Personal Finance *(Business & Economics)* 118-119, 129
Personal Finance *(Education)* 260
Personal Finance *(Government & Politics)* 314
Personal Finance *(Popular Culture & Entertainment)* 538
Personal Fitness *(Sports & Recreation)* 703, 738
Personal Injury *(Law & Criminal Justice)* 501
Personal Page *(Popular Culture & Entertainment)* 524
Personal Transformation *(Popular Culture & Entertainment)* 533
Personal Wealth *(Business & Economics)* 120
Personalities *(Internet)* 459
Personalities *(Popular Culture & Entertainment)* 516
Personals *(Business & Economics)* 150
Personals *(Popular Culture & Entertainment)* 532-533
Personnel *(Computing & Mathematics)* 218
Peru *(Government & Politics)* 336-337
Peru *(Internet)* 474
Peru *(Sports & Recreation)* 663
Pet Supplies *(Business & Economics)* 145
Petroleum *(Science)* 597
Pets & Animals *(Sports & Recreation)* 703, 738
Pets *(Business & Economics)* 145
Pets *(Health & Medicine)* 409
Pets *(Popular Culture & Entertainment)* 528, 548
Pets *(Sports & Recreation)* 644-647
Pharmaceutical Companies *(Computing & Mathematics)* 170
Pharmaceuticals *(Health & Medicine)* 385
Pharmaceuticals *(Science)* 576
Pharmacology *(Health & Medicine)* 385, 390, 402, 406-407

Pharmacy – Public Television

Pharmacy *(Health & Medicine)* 402
Philanthropy *(Business & Economics)* 134-136
Philippine Literature *(Humanities & Social Sciences)* 441
Philippines *(Business & Economics)* 136
Philippines *(Government & Politics)* 341
Philippines *(Humanities & Social Sciences)* 426
Philology *(Humanities & Social Sciences)* 432
Philosophy *(Humanities & Social Sciences)* 423, 439
Philosophy *(Religion & Philosophy)* 557-558, 562, 564, 698, 733
Phone Books *(Internet)* 481
Phone Companies *(Communications)* 163
Photographers *(Arts & Music)* 97, 99
Photographic Arts *(Arts & Music)* 97, 99
Photography *(Arts & Music)* 17, 19, 28, 30, 38, 44, 97-99
Photography *(Business & Economics)* 122
Photography *(Humanities & Social Sciences)* 446
Photography *(Popular Culture & Entertainment)* 536
Photography *(Science)* 612
Photography *(Sports & Recreation)* 654
Photojournalism *(Arts & Music)* 98-99
Photons *(Science)* 603
Physical Therapy *(Health & Medicine)* 373, 406
Physics Research *(Science)* 603-605
Physics *(Computing & Mathematics)* 190
Physics *(Education)* 279
Physics *(Engineering & Technology)* 291, 295
Physics *(Government & Politics)* 314
Physics *(Science)* 571, 573, 584, 586, 592, 602-609, 701, 735
Pianists *(Arts & Music)* 86
Pictures *(Arts & Music)* 39
Pictures *(Science)* 590
Pinball *(Arts & Music)* 44
Pipe Smoking *(Sports & Recreation)* 622
Pizzas *(Internet)* 458
Planetariums *(Government & Politics)* 322
Planets *(Science)* 573, 611
Plant Clubs *(Sports & Recreation)* 637
Plant Collections *(Sports & Recreation)* 638
Plant Maintenance *(Business & Economics)* 123
Plant Pathology *(Science)* 577
Plant Science *(Science)* 567, 582-584, 594
Planting *(Sports & Recreation)* 636
Plants *(Business & Economics)* 145, 150
Plants *(Popular Culture & Entertainment)* 545
Plants *(Science)* 565, 582-584
Plants *(Sports & Recreation)* 636-637
Plasma Physics *(Science)* 607
Playwrights *(Humanities & Social Sciences)* 435-436, 438, 442-443
Plebiscites *(Government & Politics)* 362
Plumbing *(Popular Culture & Entertainment)* 520
Poetry *(Arts & Music)* 18, 31, 99
Poetry *(Education)* 235-236, 240
Poetry *(Humanities & Social Sciences)* 423, 427, 434-440, 443-444
Poetry *(Popular Culture & Entertainment)* 511, 513, 535
Poetry *(Sports & Recreation)* 625
Poets *(Humanities & Social Sciences)* 438, 441
Poisons *(Health & Medicine)* 403
Poland *(Arts & Music)* 49-50
Poland *(Education)* 252, 270-272, 275
Poland *(Engineering & Technology)* 296, 303, 310
Poland *(Government & Politics)* 336
Poland *(Health & Medicine)* 388
Poland *(Humanities & Social Sciences)* 420, 447
Poland *(Science)* 574, 609
Poland *(Sports & Recreation)* 663
Polar Regions *(Government & Politics)* 361
Polar Regions *(Science)* 587
Police *(Law & Criminal Justice)* 492

Police *(Popular Culture & Entertainment)* 520, 524
Policies *(Government & Politics)* 688
Policy Research *(Government & Politics)* 342, 344, 352, 355
Policy Research *(Science)* 566
Polio *(Health & Medicine)* 406
Political Activism *(Government & Politics)* 353
Political Activism *(Humanities & Social Sciences)* 450
Political Candidates *(Government & Politics)* 362
Political Commentary *(Communications)* 162
Political Commentary *(Popular Culture & Entertainment)* 533-534
Political Freedom *(Government & Politics)* 334
Political Issues *(Government & Politics)* 355
Political Opinions *(Government & Politics)* 354
Political Parties *(Government & Politics)* 339
Political Science *(Business & Economics)* 118
Political Science *(Education)* 249, 254
Political Science *(Government & Politics)* 336, 353-354, 688, 720
Political Science *(Religion & Philosophy)* 557
Politicians *(Government & Politics)* 340, 356
Politicians *(Law & Criminal Justice)* 507
Politics (US) *(Government & Politics)* 355-356, 358
Politics *(Communications)* 155, 158, 162
Politics *(Education)* 254
Politics *(Engineering & Technology)* 304
Politics *(Government & Politics)* 315-316, 331, 337, 341-343, 345, 350-354, 357-358, 362-364
Politics *(Humanities & Social Sciences)* 419-420, 430, 451
Politics *(Popular Culture & Entertainment)* 533
Politics *(Science)* 612
Politics *(Sports & Recreation)* 670
Pollution Prevention *(Science)* 593-594, 596
Pop Music *(Arts & Music)* 52, 70-72, 74-76, 78-79, 83-89, 92
Pop Music *(Popular Culture & Entertainment)* 525
Popular Culture *(Humanities & Social Sciences)* 436, 442
Popular Culture *(Popular Culture & Entertainment)* 537-538, 542, 550, 552
Popular Music *(Arts & Music)* 93
Population Control *(Government & Politics)* 342-343, 358
Population Index *(Government & Politics)* 358
Population Studies *(Government & Politics)* 358
Population Studies *(Health & Medicine)* 368
Population Studies *(Science)* 590
Population *(Humanities & Social Sciences)* 448
Portfolio Management *(Business & Economics)* 129-130
Portfolio Management *(Computing & Mathematics)* 224
Portraits *(Arts & Music)* 99
Portugal *(Computing & Mathematics)* 215
Portugal *(Education)* 273
Portugal *(Government & Politics)* 336
Portugal *(Internet)* 468
Portugal *(Sports & Recreation)* 668
Postal Service (US) *(Government & Politics)* 320
Postcards *(Internet)* 486
Postmodernism *(Arts & Music)* 94
Postmodernism *(Humanities & Social Sciences)* 441
PostScript *(Computing & Mathematics)* 212
Pottery *(Arts & Music)* 33
Power *(Business & Economics)* 123
Pre-Columbian Art *(Arts & Music)* 23
Pre-School Education *(Education)* 256-258

Pre-Teens *(Popular Culture & Entertainment)* 521
Preemption Law *(Law & Criminal Justice)* 503
Pregnancy *(Health & Medicine)* 409-411
Prehistoric Animals *(Science)* 603
Preprints *(Computing & Mathematics)* 185
Presbyopia *(Health & Medicine)* 389
Presidency *(Government & Politics)* 355
Presidents (US) *(Government & Politics)* 340, 354
Press Photography *(Arts & Music)* 98
Previews *(Popular Culture & Entertainment)* 542
Primary & Secondary Education *(Education)* 685, 718
Primary Care *(Health & Medicine)* 403
Primary/Secondary Education *(Business & Economics)* 136, 139
Primary/Secondary Education *(Education)* 237, 241-242, 244-247, 254-263
Primary/Secondary Education *(Health & Medicine)* 400
Primary/Secondary Education *(Popular Culture & Entertainment)* 517-520
Primary/Secondary Education *(Science)* 545, 587, 603, 614
Primatology *(Humanities & Social Sciences)* 447
Primatology *(Sports & Recreation)* 643
Printers *(Business & Economics)* 123
Printers *(Computing & Mathematics)* 175, 194
Printing *(Business & Economics)* 102
Printing *(Computing & Mathematics)* 172
Printmaking *(Arts & Music)* 31
Prints *(Arts & Music)* 22
Privacy *(Government & Politics)* 350
Privacy *(Internet)* 468, 471-472
Privacy *(Law & Criminal Justice)* 504
Pro-Choice *(Government & Politics)* 344
Probability *(Computing & Mathematics)* 177, 228
Process Control *(Engineering & Technology)* 294, 300
Product Information *(Business & Economics)* 116, 124, 145
Product Information *(Communications)* 163-166
Product Information *(Computing & Mathematics)* 183, 194, 202, 229
Product Information *(Education)* 241
Product Information *(Engineering & Technology)* 302
Product Information *(Health & Medicine)* 372, 395
Product Information *(Popular Culture & Entertainment)* 521-522, 546, 549
Product Information *(Science)* 571
Product Information *(Sports & Recreation)* 620
Product Liability *(Government & Politics)* 318
Product Liability *(Law & Criminal Justice)* 489
Production Services *(Business & Economics)* 149
Products *(Business & Economics)* 113
Professional Development *(Science)* 585
Professional Organizations *(Communications)* 162
Professional Organizations *(Humanities & Social Sciences)* 450
Professional Recruitment *(Business & Economics)* 108
Professional Responsibility *(Law & Criminal Justice)* 494
Professional Societies *(Business & Economics)* 145
Professional Societies *(Computing & Mathematics)* 206
Programming Environments *(Computing & Mathematics)* 185, 210
Programming Languages *(Computing & Mathematics)* 171-172, 176, 209-213, 229
Programming Languages *(Internet)* 478
Programming Languages *(Popular Culture & Entertainment)* 525

Programming Theory *(Computing & Mathematics)* 212
Programming *(Computing & Mathematics)* 181-182, 185-187, 189-190, 205, 209-213, 216-217, 221, 225, 227, 230, 232, 682, 715
Programming *(Education)* 241
Programming *(Popular Culture & Entertainment)* 524
Progressive Magazines *(Popular Culture & Entertainment)* 539
Progressive Music *(Arts & Music)* 52, 54, 56, 67, 72-74, 76-80, 82-83, 85, 87
Progressive Politics *(Government & Politics)* 355
Property Law *(Law & Criminal Justice)* 498, 501
Property Listings *(Business & Economics)* 141-142
Property Rights *(Law & Criminal Justice)* 505
Property *(Business & Economics)* 142
Prophecy *(Popular Culture & Entertainment)* 554
Prostate Cancer *(Health & Medicine)* 376, 380, 400
Protected Lands *(Science)* 596
Protein Chemistry *(Science)* 580
Protein *(Health & Medicine)* 370
Proteins *(Science)* 576-578, 586
Protocols *(Computing & Mathematics)* 169, 201, 203, 216, 222-223, 230
Proverbs *(Humanities & Social Sciences)* 440
Prozac *(Health & Medicine)* 392-393
Psychedelics *(Health & Medicine)* 402
Psychiatry *(Health & Medicine)* 393
Psychiatry *(Humanities & Social Sciences)* 445
Psychologists *(Humanities & Social Sciences)* 445
Psychology *(Business & Economics)* 138
Psychology *(Health & Medicine)* 369, 393
Psychology *(Humanities & Social Sciences)* 445-446, 693, 724
Psychology *(Popular Culture & Entertainment)* 517, 553
Psychology *(Science)* 614
Psychopharmacology *(Humanities & Social Sciences)* 445
Psychotherapy *(Business & Economics)* 138
Psychotherapy *(Humanities & Social Sciences)* 446
Public Access Archives *(Health & Medicine)* 398
Public Access Archives *(Internet)* 460
Public Access Archives *(Science)* 595
Public Access Television *(Communications)* 162
Public Broadcasting *(Education)* 242
Public Domain Software *(Computing & Mathematics)* 228
Public Health *(Education)* 245
Public Health *(Health & Medicine)* 386, 390, 392, 396-398, 400, 690, 721
Public Interest Law *(Law & Criminal Justice)* 503
Public Interest *(Arts & Music)* 28
Public Interest *(Communications)* 161
Public Policy *(Engineering & Technology)* 304
Public Policy *(Government & Politics)* 315, 318-319, 340, 352, 354
Public Policy *(Law & Criminal Justice)* 493, 502
Public Records *(Business & Economics)* 144
Public Relations *(Business & Economics)* 102-104
Public Relations *(Communications)* 154, 156
Public Television *(Communications)* 155-156
Public Television *(Education)* 241-242
Public Television *(Government & Politics)* 355
Public Television *(Popular Culture & Entertainment)* 550

Public Transportation – Russia

Public Transportation *(Government & Politics)* 364, 554
Public Transportation *(Popular Culture & Entertainment)* 555
Public Welfare *(Education)* 255
Publications *(Computing & Mathematics)* 187
Publications *(Popular Culture & Entertainment)* 556
Publications *(Science)* 575, 578
Publishers *(Business & Economics)* 139
Publishers *(Computing & Mathematics)* 184, 214-215, 218, 227
Publishers *(Internet)* 461
Publishing *(Business & Economics)* 115, 118, 128, 136-139, 679
Publishing *(Communications)* 153
Publishing *(Computing & Mathematics)* 178, 199, 220, 227
Publishing *(Education)* 246, 255, 261
Publishing *(Government & Politics)* 355, 358
Publishing *(Humanities & Social Sciences)* 443
Publishing *(Popular Culture & Entertainment)* 511-512, 514, 522, 538
Publishing *(Science)* 602
Pubs *(Popular Culture & Entertainment)* 532
Pubs *(Sports & Recreation)* 630
Puerto Rico *(Government & Politics)* 364
Pulmonary System *(Health & Medicine)* 400
Punk Music *(Arts & Music)* 57, 72, 78
Punk Rock *(Arts & Music)* 63, 69, 72-73, 82-83, 85
Punk Rock *(Popular Culture & Entertainment)* 540
Puzzles *(Internet)* 456, 482
Pyramids *(Sports & Recreation)* 658
Pyrotechnics *(Engineering & Technology)* 296

Quality Control *(Engineering & Technology)* 305
Quantum Chemistry *(Science)* 587, 608
Quantum Electronics *(Science)* 606
Quantum Mechanics *(Science)* 603
Quantum Physics *(Science)* 603, 606
Quark *(Science)* 603, 605
Quilting *(Sports & Recreation)* 624
Quotations *(Business & Economics)* 131
Quotations *(Humanities & Social Sciences)* 442
Qur'an *(Religion & Philosophy)* 560

Rabbits *(Sports & Recreation)* 644, 646
Rabies *(Health & Medicine)* 400
Race Relations *(Humanities & Social Sciences)* 448
Racial Equality *(Government & Politics)* 350
Racial Equality *(Popular Culture & Entertainment)* 518
Racing *(Popular Culture & Entertainment)* 540
Racism *(Government & Politics)* 350
Radio Astronomy *(Science)* 572
Radio Broadcasting *(Communications)* 155, 157-158
Radio Communications *(Communications)* 168
Radio Disk Jockeys *(Popular Culture & Entertainment)* 516
Radio Physics *(Science)* 608
Radio Stations *(Arts & Music)* 60
Radio Stations *(Communications)* 156
Radio Telescopes *(Science)* 608
Radio *(Arts & Music)* 60-61, 70
Radio *(Communications)* 154, 156-158, 162
Radio *(Popular Culture & Entertainment)* 524, 550
Radio *(Sports & Recreation)* 621, 624
Radiology *(Health & Medicine)* 372, 388, 390, 392, 400, 404
Ragtime *(Arts & Music)* 56, 66
Railroads *(Engineering & Technology)* 312
Railroads *(Government & Politics)* 554
Rap Music *(Arts & Music)* 54, 62
Rap Music *(Popular Culture & Entertainment)* 535, 541
Rare Books *(Education)* 236

Rare Books *(Humanities & Social Sciences)* 424
Rare Books *(Popular Culture & Entertainment)* 511, 513
Rare Comic Books *(Popular Culture & Entertainment)* 511
Raves *(Arts & Music)* 66
Ray Tracing *(Arts & Music)* 37, 44
Real Estate Agencies *(Business & Economics)* 142
Real Estate Brokers *(Business & Economics)* 141
Real Estate Employment *(Business & Economics)* 141
Real Estate Listings *(Business & Economics)* 140-142
Real Estate *(Business & Economics)* 113, 116, 128, 140-142, 150, 679, 710
Real Estate *(Education)* 288
Real Estate *(Government & Politics)* 325
Real Estate *(Law & Criminal Justice)* 501
Real Estate *(Sports & Recreation)* 656
Real-Time Networking *(Internet)* 462
Recipe Archives *(Sports & Recreation)* 631
Recipes *(Sports & Recreation)* 624-632
Record Labels *(Arts & Music)* 54, 58-59, 61, 66-68, 70, 81, 87
Recording Artists *(Arts & Music)* 83
Recordings *(Arts & Music)* 52, 66-67, 69-70, 72, 77
Recreation *(Internet)* 474, 483
Recreation *(Popular Culture & Entertainment)* 532, 544, 546
Recreation *(Sports & Recreation)* 703, 738
Recycled Products *(Business & Economics)* 146, 148
Recycling Locations *(Popular Culture & Entertainment)* 518
Recycling Resources *(Business & Economics)* 123
Recycling *(Education)* 242
Recycling *(Government & Politics)* 356
Recycling *(Popular Culture & Entertainment)* 518, 520
Recycling *(Science)* 566, 593
Reference *(Arts & Music)* 17, 67
Reference *(Business & Economics)* 101, 135, 139, 710
Reference *(Communications)* 156
Reference *(Computing & Mathematics)* 209, 214
Reference *(Education)* 262
Reference *(Government & Politics)* 331, 344, 360-361, 688
Reference *(Health & Medicine)* 392, 402, 690, 721
Reference *(Humanities & Social Sciences)* 423, 429, 438, 448
Reference *(Internet)* 460, 476, 478
Reference *(Law & Criminal Justice)* 696, 726
Reference *(Popular Culture & Entertainment)* 514
Refugees *(Humanities & Social Sciences)* 421
Reggae Music *(Arts & Music)* 72, 77
Regional Business *(Business & Economics)* 113
Regional Councils *(Government & Politics)* 346
Regions *(Government & Politics)* 688, 720
Regulation *(Business & Economics)* 151
Regulations *(Business & Economics)* 120
Regulations *(Law & Criminal Justice)* 492, 506
Regulatory Agencies *(Government & Politics)* 319
Reinventing Government *(Government & Politics)* 354
Relationships *(Popular Culture & Entertainment)* 531
Relativity (General) *(Computing & Mathematics)* 197
Relativity *(Science)* 607-608
Religion *(Humanities & Social Sciences)* 424, 564
Religion *(Popular Culture & Entertainment)* 526

Religion *(Religion & Philosophy)* 557, 560, 562-563
Religions *(Religion & Philosophy)* 698, 733
Religious History *(Religion & Philosophy)* 699, 734
Religious Leaders *(Religion & Philosophy)* 562
Religious Literature *(Humanities & Social Sciences)* 434
Religious Magazines *(Religion & Philosophy)* 559
Religious Studies *(Religion & Philosophy)* 557, 559, 562, 564
Religious Texts *(Religion & Philosophy)* 559-561, 563
Remote Sensing *(Engineering & Technology)* 292
Remote Sensing *(Science)* 590-591, 597-599
Renaissance Art *(Arts & Music)* 22, 24, 32
Renaissance Art *(Education)* 244
Renaissance Faires *(Popular Culture & Entertainment)* 545
Renaissance Fairs *(Popular Culture & Entertainment)* 531
Renaissance History *(Popular Culture & Entertainment)* 531
Renaissance Studies *(Humanities & Social Sciences)* 424
Renaissance *(Education)* 244
Rental Services *(Popular Culture & Entertainment)* 541
Repetitive Stress Injuries *(Health & Medicine)* 384-385
Reproductive Rights *(Health & Medicine)* 409
Reproductive Rights *(Humanities & Social Sciences)* 450
Reptiles *(Science)* 616
Reptiles *(Sports & Recreation)* 644, 646-647
Republican Party *(Government & Politics)* 350, 352
Research & Development *(Arts & Music)* 33
Research & Development *(Communications)* 159-160
Research & Development *(Computing & Mathematics)* 176-177, 185-186, 195, 199, 203, 205-206, 218, 231
Research & Development *(Education)* 247, 253-255, 258, 273
Research & Development *(Engineering & Technology)* 294, 299
Research & Development *(Health & Medicine)* 385
Research & Development *(Internet)* 472
Research & Development *(Science)* 584, 596, 602, 604, 609
Research Applications *(Computing & Mathematics)* 174
Research Groups *(Engineering & Technology)* 309
Research Institutes *(Business & Economics)* 109
Research Institutes *(Education)* 270
Research Institutes *(Humanities & Social Sciences)* 446
Research Institutes *(Science)* 577-578, 594, 612
Research Institutions *(Computing & Mathematics)* 185, 188, 191-193
Research Laboratories *(Science)* 581
Research Labs *(Computing & Mathematics)* 190
Research Labs *(Engineering & Technology)* 308
Research Labs *(Government & Politics)* 318, 347-348
Research Labs *(Science)* 612
Research Methodology *(Humanities & Social Sciences)* 448
Research Projects *(Education)* 234, 277, 279
Research *(Business & Economics)* 133, 144
Research *(Communications)* 159, 161, 166
Research *(Computing & Mathematics)* 172-174, 183, 185-192, 199-200
Research *(Education)* 253, 261, 276, 286
Research *(Engineering & Technology)* 296, 299-300, 304-305, 309

Research *(Government & Politics)* 315, 318, 334, 338, 343, 347-348, 353, 355, 357, 364
Research *(Health & Medicine)* 378, 384, 390
Research *(Humanities & Social Sciences)* 416, 426, 430, 446, 448
Research *(Internet)* 482
Research *(Law & Criminal Justice)* 504
Research *(Popular Culture & Entertainment)* 520, 524
Research *(Science)* 565-566, 570-573, 577, 579, 581, 583-586, 590, 592-594, 597, 600-601, 607-609, 611-612
Residential Computing *(Education)* 249
Residential Real Estate *(Business & Economics)* 141
Resources *(Education)* 718
Resources *(Health & Medicine)* 690, 721
Resources *(Religion & Philosophy)* 699, 734
Restaurant Guides *(Sports & Recreation)* 624-625, 627, 629-630, 632
Restaurant Reviews *(Sports & Recreation)* 627, 630, 633
Restaurants *(Government & Politics)* 328
Restaurants *(Sports & Recreation)* 624-625, 627-633, 655, 663, 665
Resumes *(Business & Economics)* 109-110, 112
Retail Business *(Business & Economics)* 145
Retail *(Arts & Music)* 55
Retail *(Business & Economics)* 146
Retail *(Popular Culture & Entertainment)* 522, 546
Retailers *(Internet)* 457
Retirement *(Business & Economics)* 106, 130
Retirement *(Health & Medicine)* 368
Reviews *(Arts & Music)* 51
Reviews *(Popular Culture & Entertainment)* 525
Rhine *(Sports & Recreation)* 659
Rhinoceros *(Science)* 593
Rhode Island *(Science)* 600
Risk Management *(Business & Economics)* 123
Rivers *(Science)* 592
Rivers *(Sports & Recreation)* 652
Robotics *(Computing & Mathematics)* 177, 179, 186-188, 190
Robotics *(Education)* 245
Robotics *(Engineering & Technology)* 298, 303, 306, 308
Robots *(Arts & Music)* 43
Rock Climbing *(Sports & Recreation)* 640
Rock Music *(Arts & Music)* 52, 54, 56, 62, 66-90, 93
Rock Music *(Popular Culture & Entertainment)* 540
Rodents *(Sports & Recreation)* 644, 646
Role Models *(Science)* 600
Role-Playing *(Internet)* 482-487
Roman Law *(Law & Criminal Justice)* 500
Romance *(Popular Culture & Entertainment)* 530, 532
Romances *(Popular Culture & Entertainment)* 530
Romantic Poets *(Humanities & Social Sciences)* 434
Rome *(Arts & Music)* 23
Routers *(Computing & Mathematics)* 202
Routing Algorithms *(Internet)* 481
RTF-HTML *(Computing & Mathematics)* 225
Rugby *(Sports & Recreation)* 652
Rural Development *(Health & Medicine)* 398
Russia *(Arts & Music)* 24, 26, 50
Russia *(Business & Economics)* 127-128, 131-132
Russia *(Computing & Mathematics)* 208, 216
Russia *(Education)* 238, 242, 271, 289
Russia *(Government & Politics)* 329, 337, 339, 341, 357
Russia *(Humanities & Social Sciences)* 420
Russia *(Popular Culture & Entertainment)* 540
Russia *(Science)* 606
Russia *(Sports & Recreation)* 620

803

Keyword Index

Russian Documents *(Government & Politics)* 337
Russian Literature *(Humanities & Social Sciences)* 423, 440
Rwanda *(Government & Politics)* 333

Safari *(Sports & Recreation)* 654
Safe Sex *(Health & Medicine)* 408
Sailing *(Sports & Recreation)* 619-620, 653, 655, 658, 664, 666
Sales *(Business & Economics)* 104
Sales *(Education)* 249
Sales *(Popular Culture & Entertainment)* 546, 548
Satellite Communications *(Communications)* 167
Satellite Data *(Science)* 591, 594, 613
Satellite Radio *(Communications)* 154
Satellites *(Communications)* 164
Satellites *(Science)* 571, 588, 591, 598, 610-611
Satire *(Arts & Music)* 73
Satire *(Popular Culture & Entertainment)* 526-527, 534, 552-553
Schedules *(Arts & Music)* 95
Schedules *(Education)* 239
Scholarly Communication *(Government & Politics)* 327
Scholars *(Religion & Philosophy)* 557
Scholarships *(Business & Economics)* 109
Scholarships *(Education)* 249, 254
School Newspapers *(Education)* 257
Schools (Primary/Secondary) *(Education)* 256, 258
Science & Technology *(Government & Politics)* 341
Science Education *(Internet)* 486
Science Fiction *(Arts & Music)* 45, 82
Science Fiction *(Humanities & Social Sciences)* 433, 435-436, 439, 441, 444
Science Fiction *(Internet)* 483-484
Science Fiction *(Popular Culture & Entertainment)* 512-516, 531, 538, 540, 550, 552, 554
Science Fiction/Fantasy *(Humanities & Social Sciences)* 436, 444
Science Museum Of Minnesota *(Popular Culture & Entertainment)* 544
Science Research *(Science)* 604, 614
Science *(Computing & Mathematics)* 206, 227
Science *(Education)* 240-241, 244-246, 260, 268-269, 271, 278-279
Science *(Engineering & Technology)* 305, 308-309
Science *(Government & Politics)* 316-317, 338
Science *(Science)* 601-602
Scientific Applications *(Computing & Mathematics)* 195-196, 199-200
Scientific Communications *(Communications)* 168
Scientific Instruments *(Science)* 602
Scientific Journals *(Humanities & Social Sciences)* 445
Scientific Journals *(Science)* 602, 612
Scientific Publishing *(Business & Economics)* 139
Scientific Publishing *(Science)* 604-605
Scientific Research *(Business & Economics)* 127
Scientific Research *(Computing & Mathematics)* 179, 186, 190-191, 193, 228
Scientific Research *(Education)* 247, 250
Scientific Research *(Engineering & Technology)* 291-292, 299, 302, 308
Scientific Research *(Government & Politics)* 314
Scientific Research *(Humanities & Social Sciences)* 430
Scientific Research *(Popular Culture & Entertainment)* 524
Scientific Research *(Science)* 587, 589, 601-604, 607-612
Scientific Societies *(Education)* 246
Scientific Software *(Science)* 586
Scientific Visualization *(Computing & Mathematics)* 191, 193

Scientists *(Popular Culture & Entertainment)* 544
Scientists *(Science)* 600, 602
Scores *(Business & Economics)* 652
Scores *(Sports & Recreation)* 651
Scotland *(Arts & Music)* 27, 74
Scotland *(Government & Politics)* 326, 337
Scotland *(Humanities & Social Sciences)* 420
Scotland *(Popular Culture & Entertainment)* 511
Scottish Folklore *(Humanities & Social Sciences)* 443
Screenplays *(Arts & Music)* 49
Screenwriting *(Arts & Music)* 33
Scripting Languages *(Computing & Mathematics)* 212
Scuba Diving *(Sports & Recreation)* 619, 656
Sculpture *(Arts & Music)* 21-23, 26-27, 31
Sea Mammals *(Popular Culture & Entertainment)* 544
Sea World *(Popular Culture & Entertainment)* 544
Search And Rescue (SAR) *(Sports & Recreation)* 640
Second Language Acquisition *(Education)* 252
Secretarial Services *(Business & Economics)* 149
Secure Transactions *(Internet)* 456
Securities Exchange Commission (SEC) *(Business & Economics)* 129
Securities Exchange Commission (SEC) *(Law & Criminal Justice)* 489
Securities *(Business & Economics)* 129-132
Securities *(Law & Criminal Justice)* 489
Security Issues *(Computing & Mathematics)* 217, 226
Seismic Data *(Science)* 599
Seismology *(Science)* 587-588, 600, 607
Self-Help Programs *(Popular Culture & Entertainment)* 533
Self-Esteem *(Popular Culture & Entertainment)* 517
Self-Help Programs *(Law & Criminal Justice)* 504
Seminars *(Business & Economics)* 134
Seminars *(Education)* 260
Senate *(Government & Politics)* 362
Senior Services *(Government & Politics)* 365
Servers *(Computing & Mathematics)* 183
Service Providers *(Communications)* 159
Services *(Business & Economics)* 121, 134, 148, 679, 710
Services *(Communications)* 164
Seventh Day Adventists *(Religion & Philosophy)* 560, 562
Sewing *(Sports & Recreation)* 622, 624
Sex Education *(Education)* 255
Sex Education *(Health & Medicine)* 408
Sex *(Popular Culture & Entertainment)* 532
Sexual Abuse *(Health & Medicine)* 381
Sexual Fetishes *(Popular Culture & Entertainment)* 530
Sexual Innuendo *(Popular Culture & Entertainment)* 527
Sexual Orientation *(Health & Medicine)* 408
Sexual Orientation *(Humanities & Social Sciences)* 436
Sexual Orientation *(Popular Culture & Entertainment)* 530-532
Sexuality *(Health & Medicine)* 402, 404, 407-408, 722
Sexually Transmitted Diseases *(Health & Medicine)* 375, 408, 410
Shakespeare Festival *(Sports & Recreation)* 662
Shakespeare *(Popular Culture & Entertainment)* 513
Shareware *(Computing & Mathematics)* 183, 218, 221-222, 224-228
Shareware *(Internet)* 454, 460, 477, 480, 483
Shareware *(Popular Culture & Entertainment)* 543
Shareware *(Sports & Recreation)* 634
Shipping *(Business & Economics)* 150

Shopping Malls *(Business & Economics)* 112-115, 148
Shopping Malls *(Computing & Mathematics)* 185
Shopping Malls *(Popular Culture & Entertainment)* 546, 550
Shopping Malls *(Sports & Recreation)* 655
Shopping *(Business & Economics)* 117, 121
Shopping *(Popular Culture & Entertainment)* 509, 532, 546-549
Shopping *(Sports & Recreation)* 663-665
Short Stories *(Humanities & Social Sciences)* 435, 442, 444
Short Stories *(Popular Culture & Entertainment)* 541
Shortwave Radio *(Communications)* 162
Sikhism *(Religion & Philosophy)* 560
Silent Movies *(Arts & Music)* 50
Silicon Valley *(Business & Economics)* 112
Silicon Valley *(Popular Culture & Entertainment)* 537
Simulation *(Computing & Mathematics)* 182, 185, 220
Simulation *(Internet)* 486
Simulation *(Science)* 616
Simulations *(Computing & Mathematics)* 175
Simulcast *(Communications)* 158
Singapore *(Arts & Music)* 26
Singapore *(Business & Economics)* 108
Singapore *(Computing & Mathematics)* 208
Singapore *(Education)* 265
Singapore *(Engineering & Technology)* 296, 312
Singapore *(Government & Politics)* 331, 333, 338
Singapore *(Law & Criminal Justice)* 505
Singapore *(Science)* 586
Singapore *(Sports & Recreation)* 647, 666
Singles *(Popular Culture & Entertainment)* 518
Ska Music *(Arts & Music)* 81
Skateboarding *(Sports & Recreation)* 652
Ski Conditions *(Popular Culture & Entertainment)* 554
Ski Resorts *(Sports & Recreation)* 640, 642, 651
Skiing *(Government & Politics)* 324, 326
Skiing *(Sports & Recreation)* 619, 640-641, 648, 651-652, 655, 664, 667
Skin Care *(Health & Medicine)* 385
Skydiving *(Sports & Recreation)* 642
Slavic Languages *(Humanities & Social Sciences)* 427
Sleeping *(Popular Culture & Entertainment)* 530
Slovakia *(Communications)* 156
Slovakia *(Education)* 272
Slovakia *(Engineering & Technology)* 310
Slovakia *(Government & Politics)* 337
Slovakia *(Sports & Recreation)* 656
Slovenia *(Government & Politics)* 337
Slovenia *(Sports & Recreation)* 632-633, 663-665
Small Business Administration *(Business & Economics)* 120
Small Business *(Business & Economics)* 120, 144, 149
Small Business *(Internet)* 457
Small Business *(Law & Criminal Justice)* 489
Smithsonian Institution *(Popular Culture & Entertainment)* 545
Smoke-Free Environments *(Health & Medicine)* 398
Smoking *(Health & Medicine)* 367
Smoking *(Popular Culture & Entertainment)* 546
Snakes *(Health & Medicine)* 402
Snakes *(Sports & Recreation)* 646
Snooker *(Sports & Recreation)* 636
Snow Reports *(Popular Culture & Entertainment)* 555
Snowboarding *(Sports & Recreation)* 641, 648, 651-652
Soccer *(Sports & Recreation)* 635, 648-651
Social Events *(Popular Culture & Entertainment)* 532
Social Issues *(Government & Politics)* 318

Social Issues *(Health & Medicine)* 374
Social Law *(Education)* 254
Social Policy *(Government & Politics)* 343-344
Social Responsibility *(Business & Economics)* 145
Social Responsibility *(Computing & Mathematics)* 218
Social Responsibility *(Government & Politics)* 353
Social Responsibility *(Popular Culture & Entertainment)* 534
Social Sciences *(Education)* 254, 264, 268-269, 271, 274, 284
Social Sciences *(Government & Politics)* 352-353
Social Sciences *(Health & Medicine)* 393
Social Sciences *(Humanities & Social Sciences)* 413, 415-416, 430-431, 445-450
Social Security Administration *(Government & Politics)* 318
Social Security Administration *(Health & Medicine)* 395
Social Security *(Government & Politics)* 318
Social Studies *(Government & Politics)* 346
Social Studies *(Humanities & Social Sciences)* 424
Social Theorists *(Government & Politics)* 355
Social Work *(Education)* 255
Social Work *(Humanities & Social Sciences)* 448
Social Work *(Popular Culture & Entertainment)* 517
Social Work *(Science)* 601
Socialism *(Government & Politics)* 355
Societies *(Arts & Music)* 41
Societies *(Computing & Mathematics)* 179, 208
Societies *(Health & Medicine)* 378, 410
Societies *(Sports & Recreation)* 622
Societies *(Communications)* 679
Sociology *(Business & Economics)* 102
Sociology *(Health & Medicine)* 408
Sociology *(Humanities & Social Sciences)* 416, 430-431, 446, 448-450, 564, 693, 724
Software Archives *(Computing & Mathematics)* 174, 218, 221, 224-226
Software Archives *(Education)* 266
Software Defects *(Science)* 590
Software Design *(Computing & Mathematics)* 170, 210
Software Development *(Computing & Mathematics)* 171, 173, 179-181, 183-185, 204, 209-210, 216-217, 219-220, 222, 224, 227, 229
Software Development *(Engineering & Technology)* 305
Software Engineering *(Computing & Mathematics)* 180, 184, 189, 210, 213, 216-217, 232
Software Engineering *(Engineering & Technology)* 303, 311
Software Management Support *(Computing & Mathematics)* 222
Software Publishing *(Business & Economics)* 138
Software Reviews *(Computing & Mathematics)* 220
Software Reviews *(Internet)* 477
Software Utilities *(Computing & Mathematics)* 183
Software Utilities *(Internet)* 463
Software *(Arts & Music)* 16, 30, 40, 64
Software *(Business & Economics)* 123, 134, 138, 146, 149
Software *(Communications)* 160, 164-165
Software *(Computing & Mathematics)* 169-170, 172-176, 180-184, 186-187, 191, 193-195, 197-198, 200-207, 211, 213-228, 682, 716
Software *(Education)* 234, 239, 247-249, 252, 261
Software *(Engineering & Technology)* 291, 298, 304-305
Software *(Health & Medicine)* 374, 405
Software *(Humanities & Social Sciences)* 445

Software – Technological Advances   **805**

Software *(Internet)*   453, 460, 462-463, 470-471, 474-475
Software *(Popular Culture & Entertainment)*   509, 543
Software *(Science)*   586-587, 598, 605, 607, 616
Software *(Sports & Recreation)*   668
Soil Science *(Science)*   567
Solar Cooking *(Sports & Recreation)*   632
Solar Energy *(Engineering & Technology)*   301, 304
Solar Energy *(Science)*   607
Solar Images *(Arts & Music)*   45
Solar System *(Science)*   573
Solid State Physics *(Science)*   607
Songs *(Popular Culture & Entertainment)*   530
Songwriters *(Arts & Music)*   83, 85-86, 88-89
Soul Music *(Arts & Music)*   73
Sound Clips *(Arts & Music)*   79
Sound Clips *(Communications)*   157
Soundblaster *(Computing & Mathematics)*   193
Sourcing Information *(Business & Economics)*   144
South Africa *(Business & Economics)*   124, 128, 132
South Africa *(Education)*   264
South Africa *(Government & Politics)*   338, 340, 360
South Africa *(Internet)*   481
South Africa *(Popular Culture & Entertainment)*   541
South Africa *(Sports & Recreation)*   656
South America *(Government & Politics)*   331-332, 337-338
South America *(Humanities & Social Sciences)*   418, 426
South America *(Popular Culture & Entertainment)*   541
South Carolina *(Education)*   277, 279
South Carolina *(Government & Politics)*   324
South Pacific *(Government & Politics)*   336
South Pacific *(Humanities & Social Sciences)*   421
Southeast Asia *(Arts & Music)*   20
Southeast Asia *(Business & Economics)*   108
Southeast Asia *(Government & Politics)*   331, 338
Southeast Asia *(Humanities & Social Sciences)*   421
Southeast Asia *(Sports & Recreation)*   654
Southern Culture (US) *(Education)*   276
Southern Culture (US) *(Government & Politics)*   359
Southern Culture (US) *(Humanities & Social Sciences)*   416
Southern Culture (US) *(Popular Culture & Entertainment)*   539
Southwestern Art *(Arts & Music)*   98
Southwestern Art *(Arts & Music)*   20-21
Soviet Union *(Government & Politics)*   329
Space Equipment *(Science)*   611
Space Exploration *(Popular Culture & Entertainment)*   526
Space Flight *(Business & Economics)*   121, 123
Space Science *(Business & Economics)*   121, 123-124
Space Science *(Education)*   257
Space Science *(Engineering & Technology)*   291, 309
Space Science *(Internet)*   486
Space Science *(Popular Culture & Entertainment)*   523, 533
Space Science *(Science)*   571-574, 608, 610-611, 701, 735
Space Shuttle Program *(Science)*   612
Space Shuttle *(Science)*   610
Space Systems *(Government & Politics)*   318
Space Systems *(Science)*   611
Space Technology *(Science)*   611
Space *(Arts & Music)*   43
Space *(Engineering & Technology)*   309
Space *(Government & Politics)*   316, 348
Space *(Popular Culture & Entertainment)*   518, 551

Space *(Science)*   571, 573, 612-613
Spacecraft Industry *(Business & Economics)*   121, 123-124
Spain *(Education)*   272
Spain *(Engineering & Technology)*   303
Spain *(Government & Politics)*   314, 323, 329
Spain *(Popular Culture & Entertainment)*   546
Spain *(Sports & Recreation)*   668-669
Spanish Language *(Humanities & Social Sciences)*   435, 440
Spanish *(Education)*   252
Spanish *(Government & Politics)*   330, 341
Spanish *(Humanities & Social Sciences)*   427
Spatial Analysis *(Computing & Mathematics)*   210
Special Education *(Education)*   237
Special Education *(Health & Medicine)*   384
Special Effects *(Arts & Music)*   48
Specialty Foods *(Sports & Recreation)*   632
Spectroscopy *(Science)*   573
Speech Recognition *(Computing & Mathematics)*   210
Speech Recognition *(Science)*   578
Speech Therapy *(Health & Medicine)*   374
Speech *(Health & Medicine)*   404
Spelunking *(Sports & Recreation)*   642
Spices *(Sports & Recreation)*   625-626, 637
Spirits *(Business & Economics)*   148
Spirituality *(Popular Culture & Entertainment)*   531, 534
Spirituality *(Religion & Philosophy)*   560, 564
Spoof *(Popular Culture & Entertainment)*   553
Sports Cars *(Sports & Recreation)*   638
Sports Equipment *(Sports & Recreation)*   619, 651
Sports Events *(Popular Culture & Entertainment)*   548
Sports Magazines *(Popular Culture & Entertainment)*   546
Sports Marketing *(Business & Economics)*   102-103
Sports News *(Sports & Recreation)*   648, 652-653
Sports Physiology *(Sports & Recreation)*   643
Sports Schedules *(Sports & Recreation)*   650-651
Sports Training *(Sports & Recreation)*   652
Sports Visualization *(Humanities & Social Sciences)*   445
Sports *(Health & Medicine)*   382
Sports *(Popular Culture & Entertainment)*   521-522, 538, 549
Sports *(Sports & Recreation)*   621, 641, 643, 649-653, 660, 703, 738
Sportswear *(Business & Economics)*   114
Spreadsheet Applications *(Computing & Mathematics)*   173
Square Dancing *(Arts & Music)*   92, 96
Square Dancing *(Popular Culture & Entertainment)*   531-532
St. Petersburg *(Government & Politics)*   329
St. Petersburg *(Popular Culture & Entertainment)*   540
Stage Design *(Arts & Music)*   37
Stage *(Arts & Music)*   96
Stagecraft *(Arts & Music)*   91-92, 96
Standardized Tests *(Education)*   254, 262-263
Standards *(Computing & Mathematics)*   683, 718
Star Wars *(Arts & Music)*   45
Star Wars *(Sports & Recreation)*   623
States *(Government & Politics)*   688
States *(Law & Criminal Justice)*   489, 505-506
States *(Popular Culture & Entertainment)*   523
Stationary *(Business & Economics)*   146
Statistics *(Business & Economics)*   118
Statistics *(Computing & Mathematics)*   169, 195-196, 198-200, 208, 226, 228, 683, 718
Statistics *(Education)*   240-241, 275
Statistics *(Government & Politics)*   318, 355
Statistics *(Health & Medicine)*   389
Statutes *(Law & Criminal Justice)*   489, 502

Stereograms *(Arts & Music)*   30, 34-35
Stereoscopy *(Arts & Music)*   34
Stock Exchange *(Business & Economics)*   132
Stock Market *(Business & Economics)*   124, 128, 130-132, 138, 143
Stock Photography *(Arts & Music)*   99
Stock Quotes *(Business & Economics)*   128, 130-132
Stocks *(Business & Economics)*   130-132, 143
Stocks *(Popular Culture & Entertainment)*   524
Stonework *(Arts & Music)*   18
Storefronts *(Arts & Music)*   69
Storefronts *(Popular Culture & Entertainment)*   549
Stories *(Humanities & Social Sciences)*   437, 440
Stories *(Popular Culture & Entertainment)*   518
Storytelling *(Popular Culture & Entertainment)*   521
Strategy Games *(Sports & Recreation)*   635
Stretching *(Sports & Recreation)*   643
String Instruments *(Arts & Music)*   63
Structural Engineering *(Engineering & Technology)*   298
Student Associations *(Education)*   253, 279, 288
Student Life *(Education)*   256
Student Life *(Popular Culture & Entertainment)*   519
Student Organizations *(Computing & Mathematics)*   187
Student Projects *(Communications)*   161
Student Projects *(Computing & Mathematics)*   188
Student Projects *(Education)*   240-241, 245-246, 255-256, 258, 270
Students *(Humanities & Social Sciences)*   418
Students *(Religion & Philosophy)*   557
Subscriptions *(Humanities & Social Sciences)*   447
Sustainable Development *(Science)*   568
Subways *(Government & Politics)*   554
Summits *(Government & Politics)*   343
Supercomputers *(Computing & Mathematics)*   174, 181, 184, 186, 189-193, 229-232
Supercomputing *(Computing & Mathematics)*   204, 206, 208, 216, 218, 220
Supercomputing *(Education)*   244
Supercomputing *(Engineering & Technology)*   308
Supercomputing *(Science)*   586, 609
Supermarkets *(Business & Economics)*   146
Support Groups *(Health & Medicine)*   379
Surfing *(Sports & Recreation)*   619, 640, 652
Surgery *(Health & Medicine)*   372, 376, 392, 406
Suriname *(Government & Politics)*   338
Surrealism *(Arts & Music)*   32
Sweatshirts *(Popular Culture & Entertainment)*   548
Sweden *(Arts & Music)*   24, 82, 94
Sweden *(Communications)*   160
Sweden *(Computing & Mathematics)*   186, 189, 191, 208-209, 214
Sweden *(Education)*   234, 270-275
Sweden *(Engineering & Technology)*   294, 299, 303, 306
Sweden *(Government & Politics)*   330, 335
Sweden *(Health & Medicine)*   391, 405
Sweden *(Humanities & Social Sciences)*   432
Sweden *(Internet)*   481
Sweden *(Popular Culture & Entertainment)*   543
Sweden *(Science)*   588
Sweden *(Sports & Recreation)*   631, 664
Switzerland *(Communications)*   161
Switzerland *(Computing & Mathematics)*   186, 189, 198, 205-206
Switzerland *(Education)*   271
Switzerland *(Engineering & Technology)*   295, 307
Switzerland *(Government & Politics)*   353

Switzerland *(Humanities & Social Sciences)*   430
Switzerland *(Internet)*   482
Switzerland *(Science)*   604
Switzerland *(Sports & Recreation)*   654, 666-667
Symbolic Algebra *(Computing & Mathematics)*   191, 194-195, 198
Symbolic Computation *(Computing & Mathematics)*   200
Symmetry *(Arts & Music)*   46
Symphonic Music *(Arts & Music)*   52, 60-61
Symphony Orchestras *(Arts & Music)*   59-63
Synchrotron Radiation *(Science)*   605
Synthesizers *(Arts & Music)*   62, 64, 67, 69
Systems Administration *(Computing & Mathematics)*   203, 205, 229
Systems Analysis *(Computing & Mathematics)*   188
Systems Engineering *(Computing & Mathematics)*   181, 205, 221
Systems Engineering *(Engineering & Technology)*   296, 299, 302
Systems Theory *(Computing & Mathematics)*   178, 186, 212
Systems *(Computing & Mathematics)*   683

Table Games *(Sports & Recreation)*   636
Taiwan *(Communications)*   162
Taiwan *(Computing & Mathematics)*   190
Taiwan *(Education)*   250, 265
Taiwan *(Government & Politics)*   334
Talent Development *(Education)*   244
Tanglewood Music Festival *(Sports & Recreation)*   655
Taoism *(Religion & Philosophy)*   557, 564
Tap Dancing *(Arts & Music)*   96
Tasmania *(Science)*   595
Tasmania *(Sports & Recreation)*   656, 667
Tax Forms *(Law & Criminal Justice)*   506
Tax Law *(Business & Economics)*   133
Tax Law *(Law & Criminal Justice)*   502, 726
Tax Software *(Computing & Mathematics)*   221
Taxation *(Law & Criminal Justice)*   506
Taxes *(Business & Economics)*   106, 132
Taxes *(Government & Politics)*   313-314, 350
Taxes *(Law & Criminal Justice)*   506
TCP/IP *(Internet)*   453, 463, 468
Tea *(Sports & Recreation)*   624-625
Teacher Resources *(Education)*   240
Teacher Resources *(Humanities & Social Sciences)*   436
Technical Books *(Popular Culture & Entertainment)*   516
Technical Communications *(Communications)*   153, 158, 162
Technical Employment *(Business & Economics)*   112
Technical Organizations *(Business & Economics)*   125
Technical Reports *(Business & Economics)*   132
Technical Reports *(Computing & Mathematics)*   185-186, 189, 192, 204, 200
Technical Reports *(Engineering & Technology)*   306, 311
Technical Reports *(Humanities & Social Sciences)*   429
Technical Reports *(Science)*   604, 611
Technical Schools *(Education)*   270
Technical Schools *(Engineering & Technology)*   307, 310
Technical Skills *(Education)*   289
Technical Support *(Communications)*   167
Technical Support *(Computing & Mathematics)*   173, 201-202, 218, 221-223, 228-229
Technical Support *(Government & Politics)*   353
Technical Support *(Health & Medicine)*   388
Technical Training *(Education)*   288
Technical Writing *(Computing & Mathematics)*   189, 199
Techno/Ambient Music *(Arts & Music)*   76, 79, 86-87
Technological Advances *(Education)*   248, 252

Technological Advances *(Engineering & Technology)* 298, 308, 310
Technological Advances *(Government & Politics)* 317
Technology Journals *(Engineering & Technology)* 310
Technology Transfer *(Business & Economics)* 128
Technology Transfer *(Computing & Mathematics)* 175, 190, 193
Technology Transfer *(Engineering & Technology)* 309, 311
Technology Transfer *(Government & Politics)* 314
Technology *(Arts & Music)* 33, 42
Technology *(Business & Economics)* 122, 124-125, 127-128
Technology *(Communications)* 167-168
Technology *(Computing & Mathematics)* 173-174, 176, 178, 180, 189-190, 193, 199-200, 202, 206, 213, 225
Technology *(Education)* 246, 258, 272, 274
Technology *(Engineering & Technology)* 291-292, 298, 300-301, 303, 305-306, 309-310, 312, 686
Technology *(Government & Politics)* 316-317, 319, 347
Technology *(Internet)* 453, 461
Technology *(Popular Culture & Entertainment)* 535-536
Technology *(Science)* 596, 598, 601-603, 607, 610-612
Teenage Issues *(Health & Medicine)* 367
Teenage Issues *(Popular Culture & Entertainment)* 552
Teeth *(Health & Medicine)* 372
Telecommunications Research *(Communications)* 164
Telecommunications *(Business & Economics)* 121-122, 124-127, 135, 151
Telecommunications *(Communications)* 153, 155, 160-161, 163-168, 679, 711
Telecommunications *(Computing & Mathematics)* 174, 180, 201, 203, 209, 228-230
Telecommunications *(Education)* 244
Telecommunications *(Engineering & Technology)* 299, 307, 310
Telecommunications *(Government & Politics)* 317, 338, 352, 359, 363-364
Telecommunications *(Internet)* 460-461, 472-473, 481, 484, 486
Telecommunications *(Law & Criminal Justice)* 490, 502
Telecommunications *(Popular Culture & Entertainment)* 550
Telecomputing *(Communications)* 163
Telephone Directories *(Government & Politics)* 338
Telephones *(Business & Economics)* 124-125
Telephones *(Communications)* 163, 167
Telephones *(Computing & Mathematics)* 180
Telescopes *(Science)* 571-574, 610, 612
Television Networks *(Business & Economics)* 122
Television News *(Popular Culture & Entertainment)* 551
Television Programming *(Education)* 242
Television Programming *(Popular Culture & Entertainment)* 551-552
Television Stations *(Communications)* 156
Television Stations *(Popular Culture & Entertainment)* 550-552
Television *(Arts & Music)* 47-48
Television *(Business & Economics)* 102, 117, 122
Television *(Communications)* 155, 157-158, 167
Television *(Education)* 246
Television *(Government & Politics)* 315
Television *(Popular Culture & Entertainment)* 536, 539, 542, 550-552, 554, 556
Television *(PopularCulture & Entertainment)* 697
Telnet *(Internet)* 455

Tennessee *(Arts & Music)* 55
Tennessee *(Business & Economics)* 109
Tennessee *(Education)* 248, 287
Tennessee *(Government & Politics)* 327, 330
Tennis *(Popular Culture & Entertainment)* 540
Tennis *(Sports & Recreation)* 651
Terminal Emulators *(Computing & Mathematics)* 223
Terminal Illness *(Health & Medicine)* 395
Terminology *(Business & Economics)* 143
Terminology *(Computing & Mathematics)* 214
Testicular Cancer *(Health & Medicine)* 380
TeX *(Computing & Mathematics)* 195-196, 201, 206
TeX *(Science)* 606
Texas *(Arts & Music)* 30, 59
Texas *(Business & Economics)* 145
Texas *(Communications)* 166
Texas *(Computing & Mathematics)* 187
Texas *(Education)* 236, 239, 250, 255-256, 258-259, 282-284, 287
Texas *(Government & Politics)* 320, 322, 324, 326, 330, 365
Texas *(Health & Medicine)* 386, 390, 408
Texas *(Humanities & Social Sciences)* 446
Texas *(Science)* 568
Texas *(Sports & Recreation)* 627, 632, 644, 646, 655, 659
Text Books *(Popular Culture & Entertainment)* 515
Text Processing *(Computing & Mathematics)* 211
Textbooks *(Education)* 241
Textbooks *(Humanities & Social Sciences)* 436
Textbooks *(Popular Culture & Entertainment)* 511
Textiles *(Arts & Music)* 44
Textiles *(Engineering & Technology)* 303
Textiles *(Sports & Recreation)* 622, 624
Thai Culture *(Sports & Recreation)* 632
Thai Food *(Sports & Recreation)* 632
Thai Language *(Humanities & Social Sciences)* 428
Thailand *(Business & Economics)* 126-127
Thailand *(Education)* 265-266
Thailand *(Government & Politics)* 316, 338, 360
Thailand *(Sports & Recreation)* 666
The Times *(Education)* 240
Theater Companies *(Arts & Music)* 94, 96
Theater Reviews *(Popular Culture & Entertainment)* 534
Theater *(Arts & Music)* 33, 37, 91-96
Theater *(Communications)* 156
Theater *(Government & Politics)* 328
Theater *(Humanities & Social Sciences)* 423, 435
Theater *(Sports & Recreation)* 667
Theatrical Lighting *(Arts & Music)* 91
Theology *(Computing & Mathematics)* 226
Theology *(Religion & Philosophy)* 559-560, 564
Theoretical Chemistry *(Science)* 586-587
Theoretical Mathematics *(Computing & Mathematics)* 195, 199
Theoretical Physics *(Science)* 603-606, 608
Theories *(Science)* 604
Theory *(Computing & Mathematics)* 684, 718
Theory *(Health & Medicine)* 368
Thoroughbred Horses *(Sports & Recreation)* 652
Tibet *(Arts & Music)* 23
Tibet *(Government & Politics)* 338
Tibet *(Humanities & Social Sciences)* 418, 420, 422
Tibetans *(Computing & Mathematics)* 219
Tile Puzzles *(Sports & Recreation)* 635
Tires *(Popular Culture & Entertainment)* 510
Tobacco *(Health & Medicine)* 398
Top 40 Radio *(Arts & Music)* 60
Tourism *(Business & Economics)* 103, 115, 126, 128, 130
Tourism *(Communications)* 158
Tourism *(Education)* 265, 274

Tourism *(Government & Politics)* 314, 319-339, 360-365, 554, 668
Tourism *(Humanities & Social Sciences)* 416-417, 421
Tourism *(Popular Culture & Entertainment)* 514, 521, 523, 534, 536, 541, 543, 545
Tourism *(Science)* 593
Tourism *(Sports & Recreation)* 619-620, 630, 648, 650, 654-670
Toxicology *(Health & Medicine)* 388, 398
Toxicology *(Science)* 595-596
Toys *(Business & Economics)* 146
Toys *(Popular Culture & Entertainment)* 518, 547
Toys *(Sports & Recreation)* 624
Trade Agreements *(Government & Politics)* 352
Trade Regulation *(Business & Economics)* 116
Trade Shows *(Arts & Music)* 33-34
Trade Shows *(Business & Economics)* 145
Trade *(Business & Economics)* 118, 123, 125
Trademarks *(Business & Economics)* 150
Trademarks *(Law & Criminal Justice)* 496
Traditional Music *(Arts & Music)* 65, 70
Traffic Reports *(Popular Culture & Entertainment)* 555-556
Training Programs *(Business & Economics)* 133-134
Training *(Communications)* 166
Training *(Internet)* 456, 470
Trampoline *(Sports & Recreation)* 651
Transcription *(Business & Economics)* 149, 151
Transformers *(Popular Culture & Entertainment)* 552
Translation Services *(Business & Economics)* 151
Translation *(Business & Economics)* 114
Transportation Engineering *(Engineering & Technology)* 687
Transportation Law *(Science)* 592, 610
Transportation Research *(Engineering & Technology)* 312
Transportation *(Education)* 235
Transportation *(Engineering & Technology)* 305, 312
Transportation *(Government & Politics)* 314
Transportation *(Popular Culture & Entertainment)* 509-510, 555-556
Transportation *(Science)* 592, 598
Transportation *(Sports & Recreation)* 641, 654, 657, 659, 664-665, 667
Travel & Tourism *(Government & Politics)* 334-336
Travel & Tourism *(Sports & Recreation)* 703, 740
Travel Agencies *(Sports & Recreation)* 670
Travel Information *(Sports & Recreation)* 653, 655, 659, 661-662, 664, 666, 669
Travel Literature *(Humanities & Social Sciences)* 440
Travel Planning *(Sports & Recreation)* 654, 666-668, 670
Travel *(Arts & Music)* 99
Travel *(Business & Economics)* 116
Travel *(Engineering & Technology)* 312
Travel *(Government & Politics)* 328, 339, 360, 363
Travel *(Health & Medicine)* 395
Travel *(Popular Culture & Entertainment)* 510, 523-524, 538, 550, 555
Travel *(Science)* 584
Travel *(Sports & Recreation)* 625, 632, 640, 659, 661-663, 665-666, 670
Treasury Department (US) *(Government & Politics)* 319
Treasury Notes *(Business & Economics)* 132
Treaties *(Business & Economics)* 118
Treaties *(Government & Politics)* 339
Treaties *(Law & Criminal Justice)* 496
Tribal Governments (US) *(Humanities & Social Sciences)* 420
Tropical Databases *(Science)* 579

Tropical Diseases *(Health & Medicine)* 390, 398
Tropical Flowers *(Popular Culture & Entertainment)* 548
Trusts and Estates *(Law & Criminal Justice)* 495
Tunisia *(Sports & Recreation)* 657
Turkey *(Computing & Mathematics)* 226
Turkey *(Education)* 264-265
Turkey *(Engineering & Technology)* 299, 308
Turkey *(Government & Politics)* 321
Turkey *(Humanities & Social Sciences)* 444
Turkey *(Sports & Recreation)* 662
Turnkey Systems *(Computing & Mathematics)* 221
Turtles *(Science)* 570
Tutorials *(Education)* 241
Tutorials *(Internet)* 476
TV Drama *(Popular Culture & Entertainment)* 552

U.S. Constitution *(Law & Criminal Justice)* 491-492
U.S. Geological Survey (USGS) *(Science)* 590
UFO (Unidentified Flying Objects) *(Popular Culture & Entertainment)* 553
Ultrasound *(Health & Medicine)* 405
Undergraduate Education *(Education)* 239, 266-267, 274, 276-278
Undergraduate Programs *(Business & Economics)* 109
Underground Music *(Arts & Music)* 67
Unemployment *(Business & Economics)* 520
Unexplained Phenomena *(PopularCulture & Entertainment)* 698
Unions *(Government & Politics)* 360
United Kingdom *(Arts & Music)* 27, 96, 99
United Kingdom *(Business & Economics)* 104, 108
United Kingdom *(Communications)* 158
United Kingdom *(Computing & Mathematics)* 192
United Kingdom *(Education)* 243, 264, 270, 272, 274-275
United Kingdom *(Engineering & Technology)* 297
United Kingdom *(Government & Politics)* 347, 351, 357, 361
United Kingdom *(Humanities & Social Sciences)* 432, 444, 448
United Kingdom *(Internet)* 466
United Kingdom *(Popular Culture & Entertainment)* 513, 536
United Kingdom *(Science)* 569, 584, 601
United Kingdom *(Sports & Recreation)* 620, 630, 669
United Nations *(Communications)* 168
United Nations *(Engineering & Technology)* 304
United Nations *(Government & Politics)* 343-344, 356, 358
United Nations *(Health & Medicine)* 395
United Nations *(Law & Criminal Justice)* 492, 497
United Nations *(Science)* 566, 596, 613
United States *(Business & Economics)* 134, 140
United States *(Education)* 250
United States *(Government & Politics)* 317, 344-345, 347, 355, 357
United States *(Law & Criminal Justice)* 506
United States *(Popular Culture & Entertainment)* 541
United States *(Sports & Recreation)* 666
Universities (History Of) *(Education)* 243, 267, 270
Universities *(Arts & Music)* 15, 21-23, 25-26, 29, 48, 56, 99
Universities *(Business & Economics)* 103, 106-107, 110
Universities *(Communications)* 156, 160
Universities *(Computing & Mathematics)* 171, 173, 177-178, 185, 186-188, 191-192, 196-202, 211, 221-222, 229-230, 232

Universities – Wine

Universities*(Education)* 233, 235, 237-239, 243, 246, 248, 250, 253-254, 261, 264, 266-274, 276, 279, 286
Universities*(Engineering & Technology)* 299, 304, 310
Universities*(Government & Politics)* 321, 323, 326-329, 363-364
Universities*(Health & Medicine)* 384-386, 388, 395, 405
Universities*(Humanities & Social Sciences)* 413, 415-416, 418, 421, 424, 426-428, 430-431, 438-439, 441-442, 446-447, 449-450
Universities*(Law & Criminal Justice)* 498, 504
Universities*(Science)* 568, 572, 586-588, 590, 596, 600, 602, 608-609, 615-616
Universities*(Sports & Recreation)* 649, 656, 658, 661
University Administration*(Communications)* 165
University Administration*(Computing & Mathematics)* 190
University Administration*(Education)* 234, 237-240, 242-243, 248-249, 255, 265-288
University Administration*(Engineering & Technology)* 306-307, 309-310
University Administration*(Health & Medicine)* 386, 388, 396, 401
University Administration*(Religion & Philosophy)* 562-563
University Bookstores*(Popular Culture & Entertainment)* 516
University Courses*(Humanities & Social Sciences)* 449
University Departments*(Humanities & Social Sciences)* 444
University Of Campus Information*(Education)* 287
University Planning*(Education)* 243, 247
UNIX*(Communications)* 161, 166
UNIX*(Computing & Mathematics)* 181, 204-205, 223, 227, 229
UNIX*(Education)* 248
UNIX*(Internet)* 463-464, 474-475
UNIX*(Popular Culture & Entertainment)* 525
UNIX*(Science)* 606
Urban Agriculture*(Science)* 566
Urban Music*(Arts & Music)* 70, 85, 87
Urban Planning*(Arts & Music)* 16-17
Urban Planning*(Computing & Mathematics)* 172
Urban Planning*(Engineering & Technology)* 312
Urban Planning*(Government & Politics)* 315
Urban Renewal*(Government & Politics)* 353
Urban Studies*(Arts & Music)* 16
Urban Studies*(Humanities & Social Sciences)* 447
URLs (Universal Resource Locators)*(Internet)* 465
Urology*(Health & Medicine)* 380
US Constitution*(Government & Politics)* 339
US Geological Survey*(Science)* 600
US State Department*(Government & Politics)* 319
US Supreme Court*(Law & Criminal Justice)* 497
USA*(Popular Culture & Entertainment)* 544
Used Cars*(Popular Culture & Entertainment)* 509-511
Used Textbooks*(Popular Culture & Entertainment)* 511
Usenet Newsgroups*(Education)* 262
Usenet Newsgroups*(Government & Politics)* 320
Usenet Newsgroups*(Health & Medicine)* 368, 400
Usenet Newsgroups*(Internet)* 465, 467-470, 473, 482
Usenet Newsgroups*(Science)* 575
Usenet Newsgroups*(Sports & Recreation)* 620
Usenet*(Education)* 237
Usenet*(Internet)* 460

Usenet*(Law & Criminal Justice)* 504
User Guides*(Computing & Mathematics)* 217
User Interface Standard*(Computing & Mathematics)* 228
User Interfaces*(Computing & Mathematics)* 209
Utah*(Arts & Music)* 71
Utah*(Education)* 276, 287
Utah*(Law & Criminal Justice)* 499
Utah*(Sports & Recreation)* 640
Utilities*(Business & Economics)* 123, 125
Utility Companies*(Business & Economics)* 117, 122
Utility Software*(Computing & Mathematics)* 173, 183-184, 203, 205, 210, 216, 218, 220-227
Utopia*(Government & Politics)* 361

Vacations*(Sports & Recreation)* 659
Vaccine Research*(Health & Medicine)* 392
Vampires*(Popular Culture & Entertainment)* 552-553
Vancouver*(Government & Politics)* 326
Vancouver*(Internet)* 475
Vancouver*(Sports & Recreation)* 632
Vatican (The)*(Arts & Music)* 22-23
Veganism*(Popular Culture & Entertainment)* 531
Veganism*(Sports & Recreation)* 625
Vegetarianism*(Popular Culture & Entertainment)* 531-533
Vegetarianism*(Sports & Recreation)* 625, 627, 630, 632, 671
Vehicles*(Government & Politics)* 348
Venezuela*(Business & Economics)* 131
Venezuela*(Government & Politics)* 334, 337, 341
Venezuela*(Sports & Recreation)* 668
Vermont*(Education)* 280, 287
Veteran Affairs (US)*(Government & Politics)* 319
Veterinary Care*(Health & Medicine)* 409
Veterinary Care*(Sports & Recreation)* 645-646, 648
Veterinary Medicine*(Health & Medicine)* 409, 690
Veterinary Medicine*(Sports & Recreation)* 644, 646, 648
Veterinary Science*(Health & Medicine)* 409
Veterinary Science*(Science)* 614, 701
Video Games*(Sports & Recreation)* 635
Video Hardware*(Arts & Music)* 40
Video*(Arts & Music)* 23, 28, 34, 39, 47-48, 50, 92, 98
Video*(Business & Economics)* 116, 124, 149
Video*(Communications)* 163
Video*(Computing & Mathematics)* 224
Video*(Humanities & Social Sciences)* 418
Video*(Law & Criminal Justice)* 502
Video*(Popular Culture & Entertainment)* 541-542
Video*(Science)* 571
Videomaking*(Arts & Music)* 50
Videos*(Business & Economics)* 116
Videos*(Education)* 241, 245
Videos*(Popular Culture & Entertainment)* 542, 550
Videos*(Religion & Philosophy)* 562
Videos*(Sports & Recreation)* 637, 650
Vietnam War*(Education)* 233
Vietnamese Americans*(Business & Economics)* 145
Vietnamese Americans*(Humanities & Social Sciences)* 421
Vineyards*(Business & Economics)* 141
Vineyards*(Popular Culture & Entertainment)* 549
Vineyards*(Sports & Recreation)* 633
Violence*(Government & Politics)* 353
Virginia*(Arts & Music)* 31, 95
Virginia*(Business & Economics)* 113
Virginia*(Education)* 240, 250, 287
Virginia*(Government & Politics)* 322-324, 327, 359
Virginia*(Internet)* 472, 483
Virginia*(Sports & Recreation)* 658, 665
Virology*(Health & Medicine)* 370-371

Virtual Art*(Popular Culture & Entertainment)* 544
Virtual Communities*(Internet)* 453, 483-485, 487, 695, 726
Virtual Community*(Government & Politics)* 329
Virtual Community*(Internet)* 460, 468, 482, 486
Virtual Community*(Sports & Recreation)* 635
Virtual Gallery*(Popular Culture & Entertainment)* 544
Virtual Libraries*(Arts & Music)* 33
Virtual Libraries*(Education)* 263
Virtual Libraries*(Humanities & Social Sciences)* 414, 449
Virtual Portfolios*(Arts & Music)* 99
Virtual Reality*(Arts & Music)* 41
Virtual Reality*(Computing & Mathematics)* 170-171, 173, 175, 193
Virtual Reality*(Engineering & Technology)* 310
Virtual Reality*(Internet)* 487
Virtual Reality*(Popular Culture & Entertainment)* 543
Virtual Shopping*(Internet)* 460
Virtual Studios*(Arts & Music)* 46
Virus Detection*(Computing & Mathematics)* 226
Virus Protection*(Computing & Mathematics)* 184
Viruses*(Science)* 577
Visual Arts*(Arts & Music)* 17-18, 20-32, 34-36, 42, 46, 97, 677, 709
Visual Arts*(Humanities & Social Sciences)* 420
Visual Arts*(Sports & Recreation)* 658
Visualization*(Computing & Mathematics)* 172, 175, 185
Vital Statistics*(Government & Politics)* 338
Vitamins*(Health & Medicine)* 379, 395-396
Vocal Music*(Arts & Music)* 95
Vocational Education*(Education)* 245, 288, 686, 719
Volcanos*(Popular Culture & Entertainment)* 524
Volleyball*(Sports & Recreation)* 652
Volunteers*(Business & Economics)* 134-136
Volunteers*(Government & Politics)* 344, 353
Volunteers*(Humanities & Social Sciences)* 414
Volunteers*(Popular Culture & Entertainment)* 517
Voter Guide*(Government & Politics)* 355
Voter Information*(Government & Politics)* 353, 362
Voting*(Government & Politics)* 315, 319, 337, 352, 354, 362, 364
VRML*(Internet)* 458

WAIS (Wide Area Information Service)*(Education)* 244
WAIS (Wide Area Information Service)*(Internet)* 480
Wales*(Government & Politics)* 320
Wales*(Sports & Recreation)* 656
Wall Street*(Business & Economics)* 132
WANs (Wide Area Networks)*(Computing & Mathematics)* 228
WANs (Wide Area Networks)*(Internet)* 459
War Games*(Sports & Recreation)* 648
War*(Government & Politics)* 342, 348
Warsaw*(Humanities & Social Sciences)* 447
Washington (USA)*(Business & Economics)* 142
Washington D.C.*(Arts & Music)* 96
Washington D.C.*(Education)* 278
Washington D.C.*(Government & Politics)* 341
Washington D.C.*(Popular Culture & Entertainment)* 541, 545
Washington State*(Arts & Music)* 52, 81
Washington State*(Government & Politics)* 322, 328
Washington State*(Popular Culture & Entertainment)* 517, 556

Washington State*(Sports & Recreation)* 642
Waste Management*(Science)* 596
Water Quality*(Government & Politics)* 326
Water Quality*(Science)* 571, 590, 594
Water Resources*(Engineering & Technology)* 300
Water Resources*(Science)* 590
Water Skiing*(Sports & Recreation)* 619
Water Sports*(Sports & Recreation)* 620, 652
Water*(Government & Politics)* 362, 365
Wavelets*(Computing & Mathematics)* 201
Weapons*(Government & Politics)* 348-349
Weather & Traffic*(Popular Culture & Entertainment)* 698
Weather Forecasts*(Popular Culture & Entertainment)* 554, 556
Weather GIF Images*(Science)* 598
Weather Reports*(Popular Culture & Entertainment)* 554
Weather Reports*(Sports & Recreation)* 664
Weather Satellites*(Science)* 600
Weather*(Business & Economics)* 122
Weather*(Engineering & Technology)* 305
Weather*(Government & Politics)* 334, 338, 344, 365
Weather*(Popular Culture & Entertainment)* 554-556
Weather*(Science)* 554, 572, 587-591
Weather*(Sports & Recreation)* 640-641, 656, 669
Web Art*(Arts & Music)* 18, 31
Web Authoring*(Internet)* 462, 465, 467, 469, 472, 474, 477-478
Web Browsers*(Internet)* 476
Web Design*(Arts & Music)* 37
Web Development*(Internet)* 458, 465, 469, 480
Web Publishing*(Business & Economics)* 138
Web Servers*(Internet)* 474-475
Web Services*(Internet)* 458
Web Statistics*(Internet)* 456
Weddings*(Business & Economics)* 148
Weddings*(Popular Culture & Entertainment)* 520, 522
Weight Loss*(Health & Medicine)* 400
West Point*(Education)* 289
Wetlands*(Science)* 595
Whale Watching*(Sports & Recreation)* 667
Wheelchairs*(Health & Medicine)* 372
White House*(Government & Politics)* 317, 320, 354
Whois*(Internet)* 476, 479
WICCA*(Religion & Philosophy)* 560
Wilderness*(Sports & Recreation)* 640
Wildlife Conservation*(Science)* 614
Wildlife Conservation*(Sports & Recreation)* 644
Wildlife Rehabilitation*(Science)* 616
Wildlife Rehabilitation*(Sports & Recreation)* 647
Wildlife*(Education)* 255
Wildlife*(Government & Politics)* 317, 319, 345
Wildlife*(Popular Culture & Entertainment)* 544
Wildlife*(Science)* 579, 592
Wildlife*(Sports & Recreation)* 639, 641, 646, 648
Wind Energy*(Science)* 592
Windows*(Business & Economics)* 149
Windows*(Popular Culture & Entertainment)* 535
Windsurfing*(Sports & Recreation)* 620
Wine Bargains*(Sports & Recreation)* 631
Wine History*(Sports & Recreation)* 626, 633
Wine Tasting Organizations*(Sports & Recreation)* 626
Wine Tasting*(Popular Culture & Entertainment)* 549
Wine Tasting*(Sports & Recreation)* 624, 631, 633
Wine*(Business & Economics)* 146
Wine*(Government & Politics)* 322
Wine*(Popular Culture & Entertainment)* 549

Wine *(Sports & Recreation)* 624-625, 632-633
Winemaking *(Sports & Recreation)* 629
Wineries *(Business & Economics)* 124
Wineries *(Sports & Recreation)* 624, 626, 633
Winery Tours *(Sports & Recreation)* 624
Wines *(Business & Economics)* 124, 147-148
Wines *(Sports & Recreation)* 624, 626, 629, 631, 633, 659, 664
Winter Sports *(Sports & Recreation)* 652
Wireless Communications *(Communications)* 160-161
Wireless Communications *(Internet)* 482
Wireless Equipment *(Business & Economics)* 151
Wireless Technology *(Communications)* 163-166
Wireless Technology *(Internet)* 470
Wisconsin *(Business & Economics)* 112
Wisconsin *(Education)* 240, 287-288
Wisconsin *(Engineering & Technology)* 292
Wisconsin *(Government & Politics)* 365
Wisconsin *(Popular Culture & Entertainment)* 556
Witchcraft *(Religion & Philosophy)* 560
Women *(Government & Politics)* 345
Women's Groups *(Humanities & Social Sciences)* 450
Women's Health *(Health & Medicine)* 378, 400, 404, 409-411, 722
Women's Health *(Humanities & Social Sciences)* 450-451
Women's Issues *(Arts & Music)* 28
Women's Issues *(Business & Economics)* 136, 476
Women's Issues *(Computing & Mathematics)* 207, 218
Women's Issues *(Health & Medicine)* 376, 410
Women's Issues *(Humanities & Social Sciences)* 450-451
Women's Issues *(Law & Criminal Justice)* 502
Women's Issues *(Popular Culture & Entertainment)* 541
Women's Sports *(Sports & Recreation)* 642, 650
Women's Studies *(Education)* 276
Women's Studies *(Humanities & Social Sciences)* 433, 435, 450-451, 693, 724
Woodworking *(Sports & Recreation)* 622, 624
Work Environment *(Health & Medicine)* 399-400
Workshops *(Computing & Mathematics)* 185, 189, 192
Workstations *(Computing & Mathematics)* 182-183, 194, 225, 227
World Bank *(Business & Economics)* 106
World Bank *(Government & Politics)* 332-333, 344
World Bank *(Law & Criminal Justice)* 490
World Health *(Health & Medicine)* 401
World History *(Government & Politics)* 339, 341
World Leaders *(Government & Politics)* 343
World Leaders *(Popular Culture & Entertainment)* 516
World Music *(Arts & Music)* 54, 62, 65
World War II *(Arts & Music)* 47
World War II *(Humanities & Social Sciences)* 424
Writers *(Popular Culture & Entertainment)* 512
Writing Resources *(Education)* 257, 262
Writing Resources *(Humanities & Social Sciences)* 437-438
Writing Workshops *(Education)* 262
Writing *(Arts & Music)* 94
Writing *(Education)* 240-241, 243, 246, 252
Writing *(Humanities & Social Sciences)* 434, 436, 441
Writing *(Popular Culture & Entertainment)* 515
WWW (World Wide Web) *(Arts & Music)* 41
WWW (World Wide Web) *(Business & Economics)* 144
WWW (World Wide Web) *(Computing & Mathematics)* 209
WWW (World Wide Web) *(Education)* 241, 267
WWW (World Wide Web) *(Humanities & Social Sciences)* 450
WWW (World Wide Web) *(Internet)* 462-463, 465, 470, 472-480, 482
WWW (World Wide Web) *(Popular Culture & Entertainment)* 528, 537
WWW Servers *(Internet)* 479
Wyoming *(Education)* 250

X Window System *(Computing & Mathematics)* 228
X Windows *(Computing & Mathematics)* 204
X-Ray Astronomy *(Science)* 573
X-Ray Lythography *(Engineering & Technology)* 294
X-Rays *(Health & Medicine)* 404
X-Windows *(Arts & Music)* 47
X.500 *(Internet)* 481

Yellow Pages *(Business & Economics)* 104
Young Artists *(Arts & Music)* 19
Youth *(Government & Politics)* 344
Youth *(Popular Culture & Entertainment)* 521
Yugoslavia *(Arts & Music)* 22
Yugoslavia *(Government & Politics)* 322, 339

Z-Mail *(Internet)* 454
Zen Buddhism *(Health & Medicine)* 395
Zen Buddhism *(Religion & Philosophy)* 557, 562
Zimbabwe *(Arts & Music)* 22
Zines *(Arts & Music)* 30, 57, 62
Zines *(Business & Economics)* 138
Zines *(Communications)* 164
Zines *(Computing & Mathematics)* 213
Zines *(Education)* 257
Zines *(Internet)* 459, 466
Zines *(Popular Culture & Entertainment)* 533, 537, 543, 553
Zines *(Sports & Recreation)* 633
Zookeepers *(Science)* 616
Zookeeping *(Science)* 614-615
Zoological Record *(Science)* 617
Zoology *(Popular Culture & Entertainment)* 545
Zoology *(Science)* 569, 602, 614, 616-617
Zoology *(Sports & Recreation)* 647
Zoos *(Science)* 601, 614
Zoos *(Sports & Recreation)* 646-647

Audience Index

APPENDIX E

3D Designers 487
3D Image Enthusiasts 30
60's Music Enthusiasts 78-79, 87-88

Aboriginal Art Enthusiasts 20
Aboriginal Researchers 415
Aboriginal Studies Students 420
Aborigines 17, 416
Abortion Rights Advocates 350
Abortion-Rights Activists 344
Academic Researchers 190
Academics 33, 118, 137, 153, 156, 169, 176-177, 189-191, 199, 206, 215, 218, 226, 234, 236, 238, 241, 246-250, 253-256, 259-260, 262, 264-265, 270-277, 279-280, 282-288, 296, 306, 308-309, 338, 370, 385-386, 400, 417-418, 422, 429-430, 438, 441, 447, 464, 468, 472, 481, 495, 512-513, 524, 544-545, 568, 574, 576, 586, 588, 594, 603
Accountants 101, 133, 144, 221, 224, 506
Accounting Educators 101
Accounting Students 101, 456
ACLU Members 461
ACLU Supporters 491
ACM Members 175, 195, 200, 218, 228, 231-232
Acoustic Bass Players 69
Acoustic Engineers 297
Acting Students 33, 96
Activists 78, 112, 117, 133-136, 161, 208, 253, 255, 304, 333, 341-342, 345-346, 349-350, 353-356, 361, 408, 420, 426-427, 433, 451, 455, 461, 482, 490-491, 493-494, 496, 504-507, 520, 534, 536, 538, 550, 592-594, 602, 616
Actors 49, 91, 93-96, 423, 437, 443, 450, 542
Actresses 91
Ada Programmers 211
Administrators 237-238, 243, 245, 253, 258, 305, 317, 350, 461
Adobe Users 228
Adolescents 381
Adoptees 381, 404, 517, 522
Adoption Agency Professionals 381-382, 517
Adoptive Parents 381-382, 404, 517
Adults 69, 237, 239, 242, 361, 482, 517, 530-532, 537, 554
Advanced Technology Management Companies 123
Adventure Sport Enthusiasts 642
Adventure Travelers 641
Adventurers 528
Advertisers 102-104, 115, 546, 622
Advertising Agencies 102
Advertising Executives 102
Advertising Professionals 102, 456, 489
Advertisers 546, 549
Aerodynamics Engineers 610
Aerodynamics Researchers 291
Aeronautics Engineers 291, 309, 312, 610, 612-613
Aeronautics Enthusiasts 620
Aerospace Engineers 291-292, 309, 312, 609-612, 620
Aerospace Industry Professionals 127, 167, 609, 611-613, 620
Aerospace Researchers 174, 609
AFL-CIO Members 133
African Americans 99, 128, 415, 417, 425, 448, 517, 530, 600
African Art Enthusiasts 21, 23
African Descendants 425
African Studies Students 128

Africans 333, 360, 417, 481, 643
Agents 123, 522
Agricultural Researchers 555, 566
Agriculturalists 240, 292, 314, 316, 565-568, 579, 582, 584, 594, 636
Agriculture Students 566, 568
Agronomists 568, 594
AIDS Activists 375, 378, 396-397, 408, 532
AIDS Patients 369, 375, 396, 408
AIDS Researchers 375, 378, 397
AIDS Support Groups 408
Aircraft Owners 148
Airplane Enthusiasts 620
Alabama Residents 113, 239, 323
Alaska Residents 163, 283, 321, 344, 362, 521, 654, 663
Alaskan Culture Enthusiasts 283
Alcoholics 367, 410
Allegro Users 204
Allergists 383
Allergy Sufferers 383-384, 528
Alternative Health Care Enthusiasts 445
Alternative Medicine Practitioners 368-369
Alternative Music Enthusiasts 32, 52-53, 58, 63, 66-67, 69-89, 94, 516, 540-541
Alzheimer's Disease Sufferers 375
Amateur Photographers 99
Amateur Radio Enthusiasts 155, 624
Amateur Scientists 240
Ambient Music Enthusiasts 57, 66, 71, 76, 79, 81, 85-89
Ameoba Users 204
American Art Enthusiasts 27
American Business 125
American Indian Culture Enthusiasts 420
American Kennel Club Members 647
American Literature Enthusiasts 436
American Literature Students 438
American Music Enthusiasts 50
American Studies Students 415
Amiga Users 180
Amphibian Enthusiasts 646-647
Anagram Enthusiasts 431
Analysts 264, 593
Anatomists 616
Anorexia Nervosa Sufferers 410
Anesthesiologists 389-390
Anglophiles 26, 74, 483-484, 534, 651
Anglophones 127, 337
Animal Behaviorists 614, 616
Animal Lovers 245, 409, 528, 544-545, 614, 616-617, 643-648
Animal Psychologists 614
Animal Rights Activists 88, 259, 570, 593, 599, 614, 625, 629-630, 632, 646, 671
Animal Trainers 614, 646
Animation Enthusiasts 36, 38, 171
Animators 36, 48, 171, 227
Answering Machine Owners 530
Antarctica Enthusiasts 594
Anthropologists 413-414, 416, 418, 422, 430, 438, 544, 602
Anti-Abortion Activists 345
Anti-Hunting Activists 646
Antique Collectors 145-146, 148, 150-151, 511, 546, 621-624
Antique Dealers 546, 638
Apartment Hunters 104
Apiarists 565-566
Apple Computer Users 220
Apple II Users 220
Applied Physicists 607
Appraisers 140

Aquarium Buyers 643
Aquarium Dealers 643
Aquarium Keepers 615
Aquarium Owners 568, 643
Aquatic Farmers 568
Aquatic Scientists 570
Aquatic Sports Enthusiasts 619
Arabic Students 252
Arabic Writers 479
Archaeologists 21-22, 339, 342, 413-414, 420, 422, 544, 562
Archaeology Educators 414
Archaeology Enthusiasts 414
Archaeology Students 414
Architects 15-17, 28, 33-34, 113, 122-123, 172, 297, 414
Architecture Educators 16-17
Architecture Enthusiasts 15,16-17, 662
Architecture Faculty 16-17
Architecture Historians 15-17, 22
Architecture Scholars 662
Architecture Students 15,16-17, 24
Argentina Residents 313, 316, 324, 465
Argentinians 331
Arizona Residents 113, 326-329, 407, 520
Arizona Tourists 113
Arjuna Users 209
Arkansas Residents 328
Armadillo Enthusiasts 644, 646
Armchair Travelers 24
Art Activists 22, 33
Art Buyers 20, 31, 546
Art Collectors 22, 30, 546
Art Consumers 18-19, 31
Art Critics 29
Art Educators 18-22, 27-28, 31-32, 34, 40-41, 99, 244, 461
Art Enthusiasts 17-24, 27, 29-33, 38-39, 41-42, 91, 95, 98-99, 112-113, 321-326, 329-330, 415-416, 541, 543, 654-655, 657-670
Art Galleries 30
Art Historians 15-18, 20-26, 28, 98, 414, 422, 424, 436, 544
Art History Students 342, 658
Art Organizations 29-30, 416
Art Patrons 17
Art Professionals 18, 26-27, 33, 38, 41
Art Sellers 20, 31
Art Students 18-22, 25-29, 31-32, 34, 40-41, 98-99, 244, 461
Arthururian Enthusiasts 433
Artificial Intelligence Researchers 176-179, 188, 190, 391, 601
Artists 15-17-47, 63, 69, 90, 94, 97-99, 114, 122, 330, 342, 400, 404, 414, 416, 439, 450, 460, 524, 536-537, 543, 562, 654
Arts Advocates 27, 32
Arts Community 17-19, 21-30, 32, 43, 46, 52, 91-92, 98-99, 173, 425, 436, 534, 545
Arts Educators 27, 29, 32, 98
Arts Enthusiasts 27
Arts Students 97
ASCII Art Enthusiasts 45
ASCII Artists 35
ASCII Enthusiasts 35, 45
Asian Americans 47, 350, 415-416
Asian Art Enthusiasts 18, 20, 29
Asian Culture Enthusiasts 539, 655
Asian Literature Enthusiasts 433
Asian Pacific Developers 312
Asian Studies Educators 332-333, 360, 414-415, 429, 441
Asian Studies Students 332-333, 360, 414, 441, 536

Audience Index

809

Asian-Americans – Clergy

Asian-Americans 494
Asians 126-128, 136, 316, 331-334, 360, 536, 657
Asimov Enthusiasts 437
Asthma Sufferers 383
Astrologers 123
Astrology Enthusiasts 462, 530, 554
Astronomers 322, 571-574, 584, 607-608, 610-612, 639
Astronomy Enthusiasts 322, 525, 571, 573-574
Astronomy Students 571-572, 574, 610
Astrophysicists 571-574, 584, 604, 610-612
Atheists 557
Athletes 103, 619, 643, 648-650, 652
ATM (Asynchronous Transfer Mode) Users 159, 164, 202
Atmospheric Researchers 587, 592
Atmospheric Scientists 589, 594, 610
Atomic Physicists 605
Attention Deficit Disorder Sufferers 384
Attorneys 370, 490, 495-496, 503, 505-507
Au Pairs 257, 381, 383, 520
Auction Attenders 546
Audio Enthusiasts 63, 66, 70, 175, 308, 509-510
Audiologists 385
Audiophiles 63, 65, 70, 297, 308
Auditors 101
Australia Residents 61, 97, 267, 321-322, 327, 336, 656, 658-659, 667
Australia Scholars 658
Australian Culture Enthusiasts 20, 50, 62, 331, 462, 582, 587, 659
Australian Music Enthusiasts 63, 533
Australians 19, 23, 56, 73, 76, 107, 200, 206, 213, 235, 245, 250, 266-267, 288, 302, 306, 330-331, 336, 350, 390, 415-416, 444, 462, 476, 493, 535, 568, 570, 582, 592, 594, 597, 601, 638, 640, 644, 666
Austria Residents 654
Austrian Culture Enthusiasts 91
Austrians 92, 188, 438
Authors 139, 169, 434, 444
Automobile Buyers 509-511, 546, 638
Automobile Collectors 638
Automobile Dealers 509-511
Automobile Enthusiasts 124-125, 509-511, 638-639
Automobile Mechanics 125, 509-510
Automobile Owners 121-122, 125, 509-510
Automobile Racers 510, 639
Automobile Racing Enthusiasts 638-639
Automobile Renters 510
Automobile Repair 510
Automobile Sellers 122, 510
Automobile Users 592-593
Aviation Enthusiasts 620, 642
Aviators 610, 620, 665

Backgammon Players 634
Backpacking Enthusiasts 660
Bad Brains Enthusiasts 72
Ballerinas 94
Ballet Dancers 94
Ballet Enthusiasts 91-92, 94-96
Ballistics Engineers 349
Bankers 104-106, 118-119, 141, 149
Banking Industry Analysts 104-106, 456-458
Banking Industry Specialists 344
Banking Professionals 105, 319
Banks 119
Barefoot Skiing Enthusiasts 619
Bargain Hunters 545
Bartenders 628
Baseball Fans 648, 652
Basketball Fans 640, 648-652
Basque Scholars 303
Bassists 63
Bat Conservation International Members 614
Battered Women 518
Bay Area Residents 79
BBC Enthusiasts 158
BBS Users 408, 455, 461, 484
Beatles Fans 71-73, 75, 77, 79, 81, 84, 89, 668
Beekeepers 565-566
Beer Brewers 632
Beer Enthusiasts 532, 625, 632-633

Behavioral Scientists 253, 261
Behaviorists 447, 614
Belgian Business Professionals 126
Belgians 112, 158, 271, 331, 340, 625
Belgium Residents 325, 663
Bermuda Residents 619
Berry Enthusiasts 633
Bible Readers 561
Bible Scholars 559, 561-562
Bibliographers 438
Bicycle Racers 640, 642
Bicycling Enthusiasts 640-642, 671
Bicycling Enthusiasts 641-642
Biochemists 170, 370-371, 376, 567, 575, 578, 585-586, 592
Biodiversity Activists 569
Biodiversity Researchers 615
Bioengineers 292, 580
Biographers 198
Bioinformaticists 370-371, 574-582, 585-586, 601, 615
Biological Researchers 600
Biologists 226, 292, 308, 319, 370, 376, 388, 392, 394, 404, 493, 565-567, 570, 574-582, 584, 587-588, 592, 594, 596, 600-602, 607, 613-616, 647
Biology Educators 577
Biology Researchers 576
Biology Students 576-577
Biomedical Engineers 305
Biomedical Researchers 170, 292, 370-372, 387-388, 392, 394, 403, 574-582, 584-586, 601-602, 614-616
Biomedical Scientists 390, 392
Biomedical Specialists 386, 581
Biophysicists 581
Bioscience Professionals 579
Bioscientists 392, 581
Biotech Researchers 370
Biotechnologists 292, 308, 368, 370-371, 394, 565-566, 574-582, 584, 601-602, 615
Bird Lovers 616, 644-646, 648
Bird Watchers 613-614, 639, 643-648
Bisexual Activists 408
Bisexuals 408, 530-532, 640
Blacksburg Residents 483
Bluegrass Enthusiasts 53
Bluegrass Musicians 54
Blues Enthusiasts 51, 57, 68, 71, 73, 78, 82, 88-89
BMW Motorcycle Riders 638
Board Games Players 635
Boat Builders 620
Boat Owners 620
Boaters 620, 671
Boating Enthusiasts 326, 620
Bodybuilders 643
Bone Marrow Donors 374
Bonsai Enthusiasts 147, 546, 636
Book Buyers 515-516
Book Collectors 511, 513
Book Dealers 71, 138, 435, 511-513, 516
Book Enthusiasts 136, 138, 433, 438, 441, 514
Book Lovers 436, 442
Book Readers 71, 136-139, 416, 422, 434, 437, 441, 443-445, 502, 512, 514, 516, 525, 537, 541, 651
Book Reviewers 236, 512
Booksellers 137-138, 512
Bookworms 511, 513
Bosnians 434
Botanical Garden Enthusiasts 582
Botanical Scholars 321
Botanists 369-370, 565-567, 577, 579, 582-584, 592, 594, 602, 636, 638
Bowlers 644
Brazilian Culture Enthusiasts 331
Brazilians 201, 331, 541, 586-587
Breast Cancer Patients 376, 378
Breeders Enthusiasts 79
Brides 520
Brides-to-Be 522
Bridge Enthusiasts 634-635
Brit-Iron Enthusiasts 638
British 72, 158, 270, 345, 351, 357, 506, 534, 569, 601, 669-670
British Pop Music Enthusiasts 69
British Pop Music Fans 83-84, 90
Broadcasters 162, 550-552
Broadcasting Professionals 46, 158

BSD Users 204
BSD/OS Users 180
Buddhism Scholars 668
Buddhists 420, 557, 562, 564, 671
Budget Travelers 654
Builders 15, 123
Bulgaria Residents 530, 666
Bulgarian Culture Enthusiasts 331
Bulgarian Speakers 530
Bulgarians 67, 331, 335, 530
Bulimia Nervosa Sufferers 410
Business Administrators 317
Business Analysts 102, 106, 118, 126, 128-132, 138, 143, 145, 300, 313, 338, 350, 355, 364, 456
Business Community 312
Business Educators 106-109, 110, 127, 134, 239
Business Educators (University) 106-109
Business Entrepreneurs 113, 120, 303, 321-327, 330, 659-660, 670
Business Leaders 150
Business Owners 101, 114, 120, 133, 144, 315, 351-352, 367, 457, 489
Business Professionals 48, 101-111, 113-121, 123-134, 136, 138, 142-146, 149-150, 159, 160, 163, 165-167, 171, 181-185, 193-194, 202-203, 206, 209, 215, 220, 221, 223-226, 229, 249, 299-300, 302, 306, 309, 311, 314-316, 318-319, 324, 327, 329, 331, 334, 337-339, 341, 355-357, 360-361, 363-365, 374, 399-400, 421, 454-458, 464, 472-474, 481-482, 489-490, 492, 493, 495-496, 500, 505, 518, 519, 524, 527, 530, 538, 540, 545, 547-548, 592-594, 596, 620, 625, 654, 657, 661, 663, 665-668, 670
Business Publishers 140
Business Readers 140, 516
Business Researchers 107, 113, 126, 131-132, 144, 163, 239, 264, 305, 318, 358, 421, 456, 496
Business Students 103, 106-110, 120, 126, 133, 239, 456
Business Students (Graduate) 127
Business Travelers 139, 360, 417, 662
Buyers 140-141, 206, 525
Byzantine Scholars 658

C Programmers 210, 212
C++ Programmers 210, 212
Cable Television Providers 550
CAD Users 172
Cafe Enthusiasts 627
Caffeine Lovers 630
Cajun Food Enthusiasts 660
Cajun Music Enthusiasts 55, 91
Californians 22, 25-26, 29-30, 61, 68, 71, 94, 96, 110-112, 115, 117, 120, 134, 140, 159-160, 206, 277, 287, 300, 319, 322-328, 350, 352, 355, 359, 361-363, 365, 382, 388, 424, 445, 455, 463, 476, 492, 505, 509, 512, 516-518, 532, 534-535, 537, 540, 544, 550, 555, 583, 599, 603, 622, 633, 640, 654-656
Campaign Workers 362
Camping Enthusiasts 360, 402-403, 619, 631, 641, 655-656, 659, 664, 666-667, 671
Canada Residents 59-62, 94, 107, 233, 239, 267-268, 299, 320-321, 324, 328, 359, 370, 372, 405, 424, 430, 454, 534-535, 558, 597, 656, 658, 663-665, 669-670
Canadian Culture Enthusiasts 56, 331, 424
Canadian Scholars 321
Canadians 18, 53, 72-73, 76-77, 91, 103, 116, 142, 186, 188, 215, 221, 233, 239, 256, 267-269, 321, 324, 326, 331, 336, 345, 352, 361, 426, 453, 498, 535, 540, 544, 552, 588, 632, 665, 670
Cancer Patients 368, 374-381, 396, 402
Cancer Specialists 376-378, 406
Cancer Sufferers 376
Candy Lovers 629
Canoers 619, 631
Car Buyers 122
Car Dealers 121
Car Dealerships 122
Card Collectors 112
Card Players 635
Carniverous Plant Enthusiasts 583, 636
Carpenters 116

Cartographers 250, 347, 424
Cartoon Enthusiasts 529
Casting Agents 33
Cat Breeders 645, 647
Cat Lovers 528, 645, 647
Catalan Speakers 427
Catholic Scholars 660
Catholics 559
Caving Enthusiasts 642
CD-I Developers 543
CD-I Users 543
CD-ROM Publishers 42
Celebrity Enthusiasts 39, 516, 536
Cellular Phone Users 161, 164-165
Celtic Enthusiasts 337
Celtic Music Enthusiasts 74, 89
Central Americans 537
Ceramic Artists 622
Ceramic Shoppers 33
Chamber Music Enthusiasts 57, 61
Channel Partners 165
Charities 517
Chatters 329
Cheese Lovers 625
Chefs 123, 625, 627-628, 630-633
Chemical Companies 125
Chemical Engineers 293-294, 300, 584-587
Chemists 221
Chemistry Educators 247, 293, 585-587
Chemistry Engineers 220, 585-586
Chemistry Researchers 586
Chemistry Students 585-586
Chemistry Students (High School/College) 247
Chemistry Students (Secondary) 293, 587
Chemists 293-294, 350, 398, 575, 584-587, 593, 600, 602-603, 607
Chess Enthusiasts 634-635
Chess Players 634-635
Chicanos 110, 416, 418-419
Child Development Professionals 344, 382-383, 518
Childcare Providers 242, 257, 259, 344, 381-383, 410, 494, 517-520, 547
Children 26, 30, 122, 136-137, 139, 146, 161, 242, 246, 256-257, 259, 261, 346, 374, 382-383, 414, 435-439, 442-443, 512-514, 517-519, 521-522, 524, 526, 535, 542, 544-545, 547, 552, 603, 624, 635, 645, 647-648, 653
Children's Rights Activists 161, 246, 344, 382, 517-518
Chile Pepper Enthusiasts 626-627
Chileans 118, 276, 316, 426
China Residents 255
Chinese 126, 255, 329, 331, 334, 416-417, 435, 437, 444, 486, 494, 533, 634-635
Chinese Culture Enthusiasts 475, 542, 662, 666
Chinese Language Students 225
Chinese Linguists 433
Chinese Literature Enthusiasts 421-422, 435, 437-438, 444
Chinese Poetry Enthusiasts 435, 437-438, 444
Chinese Readers 225
Chinese Speakers 190, 250, 265, 417
Chocolate Lovers 549, 626-627
Choral Singers 62
Christian Music Enthusiasts 52, 57
Christians 50, 57, 89, 533, 559-564
Chronic Fatigue Sufferers 384
Cisco Users 202
Civil Engineers 15, 175, 294, 300, 555
Civil Libertarians 490-492
Civil Liberties Activists 162, 352, 461
Civil Rights Activists 156, 350, 434, 473
Civil Servants 255, 317, 345
Classic Car Enthusiasts 510-511
Classical Literature Enthusiasts 432
Classical Music Enthusiasts 51-52, 54-55, 57-65, 67-69, 72-73, 81, 83-88, 90-92, 94, 97, 514
Classical Musicians 63
Classical Philosophers 557
Classical Pop Enthusiasts 56, 92
Classicists 15, 22, 339, 422-423
Classics Researchers 423
Classics Students 422-423, 427-428
Clergy 559

Clients 455
Climatologists 317, 554-556, 569, 587, 589-590, 592-593
Climbing Enthusiasts 275, 631
Clinical Researchers 170
Clinicians 371, 375-376, 378-379, 396, 400
Clock Manufacturers 530
Clowns 651
CMC Researchers 154, 173
Co-op Owners 142
Coaches 382, 621, 640, 653
Codpiece Enthusiasts 522
Coffee Lovers 116, 625-627, 629-630
Coffee Manufacturers 116, 626
Coffee Vendors 116, 626
Coffeehouse Owners 630
Cognitive Scientists 154, 177-178, 186, 252, 445, 578, 600
Coin Collectors 548
Collectors 114, 330, 342, 514, 622-623
College Applicants 283
College Counselors 277
Colombians 474
Colonial History Enthusiasts 329
Colorado Residents 59, 64, 66, 160, 260, 284, 326-328, 360, 363-364
Colorado Springs Residents 554
Comedians 356, 526, 528-530
Comedy Enthusiasts 516
Comedy Fans 50, 156, 516, 526, 530, 551
Comic Book Collectors 511
Comics Enthusiasts 31, 38, 46, 138, 227, 511, 514, 526-527, 552
Commerce Professionals 307
Commerce Specialists 314
Commercial Advertisers 461
Commodities Brokers 132
Communications Engineers 624
Communications Experts 158, 190
Communications Professionals 153-154, 161-164, 166, 168, 202, 218, 299, 315, 474, 538-539
Communications Researchers 153-154, 161, 190, 247, 252, 260, 352, 417, 450, 537
Communications Specialists 117, 122, 153-155, 159-160, 163, 165, 168, 172, 178, 180, 229-230, 315, 536, 550, 602-603
Communications Students 153-154, 156, 158, 161-162, 164, 168, 247, 260, 307, 315
Community Activists 135-136, 321-329, 342, 345, 353, 355-356, 359-362, 454, 465, 468, 472, 475, 522, 539, 654-656, 663
Community Groups 160, 321-326, 328-329, 360, 454, 520, 654-656, 663
Community Leaders 318, 323, 346, 405, 520, 536
Community Networkers 537
Community Networks 365
Community Organizations 361
Compact Disc Users 51-52, 58, 64, 67, 69, 73, 84-88, 90-91, 94
Company Management 151
Complainers 71, 82
Composers 68
Computational Chemists 220
Computational Mathematicians 195, 220
Computational Neuroscientists 178
Computational Scientists 170, 187
Computational Vision Specialists 186
Computer Art Enthusiasts 40
Computer Artists 16-17, 19, 28, 31-32, 34-47, 220, 227, 404-405, 461, 536, 543
Computer Book Readers 515
Computer Dealers 218
Computer Designers 201, 229-230
Computer Educators 172, 246
Computer Engineers 171, 173, 175, 182, 185, 187-188, 191, 193, 204, 207, 210, 212, 216, 218, 221, 229, 294, 305-306
Computer Experts 306
Computer Game Developers 214, 224, 464, 634-635
Computer Game Enthusiasts 225, 453, 483, 634-636
Computer Graphic Artists 41
Computer Graphic Designers 16-17, 30, 34-47, 181, 193, 212, 220, 306, 404-405
Computer Graphics Enthusiasts 34

Computer Hackers 45, 213-214, 489, 524, 541, 553
Computer Hardware Specialists 193-194
Computer Hardware Users 163, 165-166, 193, 201, 231, 466
Computer Industry Professionals 207
Computer Manufacturers 180, 183, 194, 222
Computer Music Researchers 67
Computer Musicians 34, 64-65, 67, 69-71
Computer Network Users 172, 183-184, 186, 203, 206, 222, 454, 473-474
Computer Operators 191, 220, 227
Computer Professionals 114-115, 123-124, 163-164, 166, 169-170, 172-175, 178-183, 185, 187-189, 191-194, 201-210, 213-223, 225-232, 234, 245-247, 267, 270, 275, 295, 305, 316, 319, 332, 345, 370, 374, 450, 455, 459, 470, 472, 478, 482, 504, 524, 541, 576, 588-589, 666
Computer Programmers 34, 45, 119, 122-123, 155, 164, 186, 189, 191, 193-195, 209-213, 215-216, 218, 221, 225, 231-232, 241, 345, 463, 476-479
Computer Researchers 183, 186-187, 189-190, 192, 205, 212, 228-232, 250, 298, 344, 470
Computer Retailers 206
Computer Science Educators 189, 311
Computer Science Students 155, 164, 172, 174, 176-177, 187-189, 192, 209, 214, 217, 219-220, 241, 310
Computer Scientists 154, 160, 166-167, 169-180, 183-196, 198-201, 204-206, 210-213, 215-216, 228-232, 238, 241, 244, 246, 268, 271, 275, 294-296, 300, 306, 308, 311, 347, 361, 429, 431, 462, 470-471, 478, 480, 482, 603, 611
Computer Security Experts 309
Computer Security Specialists 171, 215-217, 470
Computer Software Developers 226
Computer Specialists 155, 164, 174, 176-178, 184, 202, 204, 206-208, 218, 226, 230, 285, 309, 317
Computer System Architects 201, 230
Computer System Designers 162, 175, 180-182, 193, 205, 207-208, 214, 228, 231, 459, 472, 548
Computer System Designers 201
Computer Systems Users 183, 463
Computer Technicians 193
Computer Theorists 185
Computer Users 23, 30, 35, 40, 45, 105, 112-115, 122-124, 126, 128, 135, 138, 148-149, 159-164, 166, 169-170, 172-177, 179-185, 187-188, 191-194, 198, 201, 203-209, 211, 212-230, 234, 244-248, 255, 258, 261, 266-267, 270-272, 274, 277-279, 282-283, 285, 299-300, 306, 309, 318, 348, 354, 360, 364-365, 374, 384-385, 390, 397, 409, 446, 453-455, 457, 463-466, 470, 472, 474-476, 478, 481-483, 489, 491, 504, 514, 524-525, 527, 529, 534-535, 543, 548, 550, 571, 575, 588-589, 610, 668
Computer Visualization Researchers 173
Computer Visualization Specialists 173, 191
Computing Analysts 189, 448
Computing Consultants 163, 166, 457
Computing Experts 388
Computing Professionals 185
Computing Specialists 186
Computing Students 185, 193
Concert Goers 64, 70, 90
Concurrent Logic Programmers 171, 174, 187-188, 191, 204, 210, 215, 229, 232
Condo Owners 142
Conferencing System Users 151, 203
Connecticut Residents 284, 541
Connectivity Hardware Users 159
Conservationists 255, 300-301, 317, 319, 345-346, 350-351, 433, 566-567, 582, 592-593, 595-596, 614, 643-645, 647
Conservatives 162, 340, 350, 352, 354-355, 528, 538
Conspiracy Theory Enthusiasts 553
Constraint Programmers 209
Consultants 120, 151, 156, 365
Consumer Affairs Advocates 117
Consumer Groups 117, 503

Consumers 66, 69, 73, 103-104, 106, 114-118, 121, 123-125, 129, 138, 140, 145-146, 148, 150, 165, 167, 182, 184, 193, 218, 241, 260, 318, 350, 374, 395, 402, 406, 498, 500, 503-504, 510, 521, 545-550, 552, 633, 650-652
Contemporary Music Enthusiasts 54, 58-59, 67, 83-84, 87-89
Continuing Education Students 239
Contractors 123
Control Engineers 303
Convex Computer Users 181
Cooking Enthusiasts 624-630, 632
Cooking Students 628
Cooks 123, 146, 624-633, 671
Copyright Activists 462
Copyright Lawyers 495
Corporations 122, 105
Corporate Lawyers 352, 489
Cosmologists 611
Costa Ricans 537, 540
Counselors 533, 559
Counterculture Enthusiasts 539
Country Music Enthusiasts 51, 53-55, 71, 79, 83, 86-88, 90
Couples 520
CPAs 101
Craft Shoppers 33, 546, 623
Crafts Artists 27
Crafts Enthusiasts 622, 624
Crafts Materials Suppliers 622
Craftspeople 276
Credit Enthusiasts 119
Creditors 106
Crete Residents 662
Cricket Enthusiasts 649
Criminal Lawyers 492, 497
Criminologists 494
Critics 429, 440-441, 542
Croatia Residents 330, 666-667
Croatians 416
Croquet Enthusiasts 651
Cross-Development Programmers 223, 227
Crossword Enthusiasts 540
Cruise Enthusiasts 667
Cryptographers 171, 176, 471-472
Crystallographers 172, 579, 602
Cuban Democaracy Activists 334
Cubans 334
Culinary Professionals 629, 633
Culinary Students 626
Cultural Critics 27, 427
Cultural Studies Enthusiasts 538
Cultural Studies Students 417
Curators 22, 98
Curiosity Seekers 526, 541
Curling Enthusiasts 649
Currency Dealers 129, 149
Cyberculture Enthusiasts 43, 46, 216, 439, 459, 463, 466, 483-487, 522, 526, 553, 652
Cybernauts 44, 213, 439, 459, 484, 553
Cyberpunks 471, 525, 533, 536
Czechs 196

Dallas Business 145
Dance Enthusiasts 57, 69, 91-97, 531-532, 546
Dance Historians 91, 92
Dance Instructors 92
Dance Music Enthusiasts 72, 74, 85, 87
Dance Students 91-93
Dancers 28, 92-96
Danes 156, 195, 315, 334, 659
Data Analysts 183
Data Communicators 472
Database Developers 184, 226
Database Managers 149, 171, 175, 184-185, 189, 210, 216, 219
Database Programmers 216
Database Users 149, 184-185, 261
Deadheads 77, 520
Deaf & Disabled People 374
Deaf People 373
Debtors 118-119
Defendents 492, 494
Defense Analysts 319, 346-347
Defense Contractors 347-349
Defense Industry Followers 314, 319, 346
Delaware Residents 363
Democratic Socialists 353

Democrats 353, 356, 504, 528
Demographers 358
Denmark Residents 156, 496
Dental Patients 372
Dental Students 372
Dentists 372, 388, 392, 396, 406
Depression Sufferers 392
Dermatologists 385
Descent Players 635
Desert Enthusiasts 592
Designers 33-34, 146, 172, 297, 301
Desktop Publishers 47, 171, 212, 220, 226, 228, 543
Desktop Publishers/Designers 44
Dessert Enthusiasts 629
Developers 122, 161, 165, 172, 202
Diabetics 377-378, 380, 384
Dial-Up Internet Users 463, 468
Dietitians 401, 642
Digital Audio Engineers 65
Digital Photographers 28
Digital Photography Enthusiasts 39
Digital Signal Processors 309
Digital Video Engineers 46
Dining Enthusiasts 624-625, 627-628, 630-633
Dinosaur Enthusiasts 414, 544-545, 603
Diplomats 339, 341
Directors 542
Disability Sufferers 378
Disabled People 112, 237, 372-374, 382
Distance Education Teachers 242
Distance Educators 174, 239, 241-242, 252, 427
Distributors 318, 633
Diving Enthusiasts 619
Divorced People 494-495
Doctoral Students 133
Doctors 292, 369, 371, 378-380, 384, 386, 391, 394, 396-398, 400, 405, 407, 601
Document Delivery Professionals 305
Document Management Specialists 221
Document Specialists 296
Documentary Makers 413
Documentation Specialists 226
Documentation Writers 150
Dog Breeders 644
Dog Owners 528, 643-644, 647
Dog Show Personnel 647
Domestic Mediators 518
Doom Enthusiasts 634, 635
Drama Educators 92
Drama Enthusiasts 49, 91-92, 95, 422, 442-443
Drama Students 96
Dreamers 553
Driver's Education Teachers 256
Drivers 362, 510, 638
Drug Educators 402
Drug Users 367, 371, 402, 410, 584
Drummers 65
Dublin Residents 627
Dutch 193, 271-273, 454, 473, 654
Dutch Residents 80
Dutch Speakers 158

Early Music Enthusiasts 52, 57-58, 65, 68-69
Earth Science Educators 245, 608
Earth Scientists 294, 320, 361, 545, 587-590, 597-600, 603
Earthquake Enthusiasts 588
Earthquake Researchers 588
Eastern Europe Residents 303
Eastern Europe Specialists 238
Eastern Europeans 216, 337, 447, 497
Ecologists 301, 346, 356, 361, 396, 524, 565-567, 570, 579, 581, 583, 588, 590, 592-594, 596, 599, 630, 645, 647
Economic Development Experts 106, 118-119, 167, 315, 364
Economic Development Specialists 344
Economics Researchers 117
Economics Students 111, 117, 527
Economics Students (University) 118
Economists 106-109, 111, 113, 117-119, 125, 129, 131-134, 167, 232, 267, 298, 313-316, 318, 344, 346, 350, 355, 360, 364, 456, 490, 527, 568, 588
Edinburgh Residents 27

Editors 99
Education Administrators 198, 206, 237-238, 241-249, 254-255, 257-259, 261-263, 318, 337, 454, 517, 461
Education Administrators (College) 239, 265-266, 270, 272-273, 276-280, 282-284, 293-294, 305, 385, 586
Education Administrators (Primary/Secondary) 244
Education Administrators (University) 248
Education Professionals 241, 244, 265, 269, 279-280, 287-288, 310, 356, 498
Education Reformers 262
Education Researchers 237, 249, 254, 262-263
Education Technologists 245
Education Technology Specialists 173
Educational Professionals 173
Educators 15-18, 21-24, 26-30, 32, 49, 63, 65, 68, 97, 133, 136-137, 146, 154-155, 157-158, 160-162, 165, 174, 176-177, 180, 183, 186, 188, 191-193, 196, 198-201, 206, 208, 214, 230, 232-237, 239-249, 251-259, 261-288, 291-294, 296-302, 305-307, 312, 314, 317, 323, 328, 332, 334, 336-337, 339-341, 345-346, 354, 357-358, 361, 363-364, 376-377, 382, 387, 396, 400-404, 408, 413-416, 418, 420-421, 423, 425-426, 429, 432-433, 436-438, 440, 445-446, 454-455, 464, 468, 472, 474, 482, 494-495, 517-520, 524, 538, 541, 544-545, 557-558, 562-563, 572, 578, 584, 586-587, 589, 592-595, 600, 602-604, 607-608, 610, 614, 616, 624, 648, 658, 662-663, 666
Educators (College) 239, 279, 345, 586, 598
Educators (Primary) 260
Educators (Primary/Secondary) 30, 136, 139, 237-238, 240-242, 244-245, 247, 255-263, 268, 344, 381-383, 400, 422, 424, 426, 435-436, 439, 442-443, 464, 494, 512, 514, 517-521, 523-525, 544, 587, 593, 603, 616
Educators (Secondary) 257
Educators (University) 16, 20, 23, 33, 108-110, 118, 134, 154, 157, 160, 168, 174, 184, 187, 189-192, 195-196, 199, 208, 209, 211, 217, 227-229, 233-243, 247-249, 251, 253-257, 261, 264-279, 278-289, 294-298, 300, 303, 307-310, 318, 319, 327, 334-335, 339, 348, 370, 381, 385-389, 391-392, 395-397, 398, 401, 403, 406, 413, 416, 419-420, 422, 424, 426, 428-436, 438, 440-442, 444, 448, 451, 453, 474, 498-499, 504, 518, 524, 533, 534, 543, 557, 560, 562, 568, 571, 577, 586, 588-589, 597, 600-601, 605, 610, 612, 614, 617, 623
EEC Telecommunications Specialists 166
Egyptian Culture Enthusiasts 414
Egyptians 658
Egyptologists 414
Eiffel Programmers 211
Electric Bass Players 69
Electrical Engineering Educators 296
Electrical Engineering Students 296, 304, 310
Electrical Engineers 167, 178, 181-182, 185, 221, 232, 294-296, 299-300, 305, 307, 600
Electricians 526
Electronic Art Enthusiasts 17-18, 20, 36, 44-45
Electronic Artists 32, 41
Electronic Designers 45
Electronic Engineers 296
Electronic Media Professionals 42
Electronic Money Users 456-458
Electronic Music Enthusiasts 54, 57, 59, 62-67, 69-72, 74, 76, 79, 81, 85-89
Electronic Musicians 64
Electronic Publishers 136-138
Electronic Publishing Enthusiasts 166
Electronics Buyers 104
Electronics Companies 119, 154
Elephant Enthusiasts 615
Elephant Managers 615
Elvis Presley Fans 84
EMACS Users 211
Email Users 161, 164, 183, 225, 285, 358, 454, 459-460, 464, 466, 468, 481
Emergency Medical Technicians 382, 640

Employees 106, 111, 121, 133-134, 317, 367, 373, 397, 494, 503, 642
Employers 102-103, 108-111, 133, 179, 490
Employment Counselors 110-111
Employment Seekers 112
Endocrinologists 380
Energy Researchers 190, 301, 304, 306, 314, 492, 590, 592, 596, 607
Engineering Educators 292, 298, 304, 310
Engineering Job Seekers 108
Engineering Students 292, 296-300, 302-304, 307, 310-311
Engineers 108, 112-113, 121, 123, 153, 175, 180, 183, 185, 193, 198, 213, 221, 227-228, 230, 246, 260, 270-272, 274, 292, 294-311, 335, 347, 349, 364-365, 496, 568, 588-589, 597, 602, 607, 609, 611, 613
Engineers (Biomedical) 296
England Residents 99, 655-656, 661, 668
England Scholars 656
English 540
English Educators 252, 260, 416, 438
English Literature Enthusiasts 241, 261, 419, 430, 432-443, 513
English Students 423, 441
Entertainers 549, 624, 630
Entomologists 545, 565-567, 580, 614-616, 647
Entrepreneurs 93, 109, 113, 114, 119-120, 126, 128, 133, 144, 149-150, 194, 264, 309, 311, 315, 317, 341, 352, 361, 456-457, 489-490, 496
Environmental Activists 568
Environment Economists 341
Environment Policymakers 341
Environmental Activists 134, 342, 356, 590, 592
Environmental Educators 245, 567, 593
Environmental Engineers 300
Environmental Researchers 106, 220, 301, 304, 317, 320, 335-336, 342, 344, 352, 493, 568, 579, 582, 587-599, 607
Environmental Science Students 596
Environmental Scientists 304, 314, 317, 320, 335, 344, 571, 587, 589-592, 594-597, 599-600
Environmental Specialists 595
Environmentalists 103, 114, 122, 127, 134, 161, 208, 242, 245, 255, 260, 301, 304, 314, 317-318, 320, 326, 335, 341-342, 344-346, 350-351, 356, 362, 365, 395, 433, 482, 492-493, 520, 545, 565, 567-571, 579, 582, 584, 587-588, 590-596, 598-599, 602, 632, 637, 640, 646
Environmentally Conscious Home Owners 145
Environmentally Conscious People 145
Environmentally Conscious Shoppers 148
Environmentalists 568
Epidemiologists 396-397
Equestrians 644
ESL Teachers 252
Esoterica Enthusiasts 536
Estonians 496
Ethics Researchers 133
Ethics Students 133
Ethnic Arts Enthusiasts 98
Ethnic Food Enthusiasts 628
Ethnic Music Enthusiasts 70
Ethnic Studies Students 242, 335, 339, 420
Ethnobotanists 583-584
Ethnologists 544
Ethnomusicologists 51
Ethologists 447, 614, 616
Europe Scholars 320, 325
European Business Professionals 126
European Internet Users 334, 342360, 476, 481
Europeans 76, 97, 116, 161, 205, 251-252, 274, 306-307, 334, 342, 344, 360, 473, 534, 596, 612, 667
Event Planners 148, 548, 652
Evolutionists 559
Expatriates 341
Experimental Music Enthusiasts 57, 66, 71, 74, 76, 79-81, 85-89
Expert Witnesses 494, 502
Explorers 659

Facilitators 134
Families 118, 239, 257, 259, 367, 372, 374, 376, 381-382, 402, 404, 420, 494-495, 517, 520, 522-523, 545, 560, 562, 662, 670
Family Physicians 391
Family Planners 517
Family-Owned Businesses 149
Fantasy Enthusiasts 435, 437, 439, 444, 484, 514
Fantasy Literature Enthusiasts 444
Farmers 292, 300, 362, 493, 555, 565-567, 633, 644
Fashion Designers 123, 522
Fashion Enthusiasts 103, 522
Fashion Industry Professionals 522
Fast Food Enthusiasts 626
Fathers 381-382, 409
Fax Users 164, 223, 358
FBI 315
Federal Employees 293, 320
Feminists 82, 99, 161, 350, 409, 430, 433-434, 450-451, 515, 638
Ferret Enthusiasts 644
Festival Enthusiasts 624
Fiction Enthusiasts 94, 156, 321, 413, 416, 421-423, 426, 433-444, 484, 512-516, 523, 528-529, 541
Fiction Writers 516
Filipinos 15, 34, 50, 92, 127, 141, 190, 271-272, 274, 316, 330, 454, 538
Film Buffs 84, 87
Film Directors 48-50
Film Enthusiasts 47-50, 61, 83, 99, 156, 324, 418, 459, 516, 536, 542-543, 550
Film Historians 47-48, 50
Film Professionals 93
Film Researchers 48-50, 99, 542-543
Film Students 47-50
Filmmakers 28, 32, 47-50, 413, 418, 542-543
Financial Advisors 104-106
Financial Analysts 101, 104-105, 119, 128-133, 137-138, 143
Financial Experts 105
Financial Forecasters 130
Financial Institutions 119
Financial Planners 103, 119, 129, 133
Financial Professionals 130, 143
Financial Researchers 106, 132
Financiers 118, 131
Finland Residents 330, 629, 658
Finns 15, 34, 50, 92, 127, 141, 190, 271-272, 274, 316, 330, 454, 538
Fire Fighters 594
Fireworks Enthusiasts 296
First Amendment Activists 491
Fish Enthusiasts 568, 592, 615, 619
Fishery Scientists 569, 615
Fishing Enthusiasts 326-327, 641-642, 654-656
Fitness Enthusiasts 114, 337, 546, 625, 627, 641-643
Flag Enthusiasts 145
Flamenco Enthusiasts 95
Florida Residents 161, 325, 475, 505, 540, 565-566, 655, 670
Florists 145-146, 148, 548, 636
Flower Enthusiasts 146, 150, 582, 636
Folk Dance Enthusiasts 92
Folk Dancers 57, 92, 531-532
Folk Music Enthusiasts 51, 53-55, 57, 63, 65-66, 70-74, 77-78, 80-83, 85-90
Folk Musicians 66
Folk Rock Fans 77, 85, 88
Folklorists 521
Food Enthusiasts 148, 532, 627-628, 630-633
Food Industry Professionals 123
Footbag Enthusiasts 650
Football Fans 522, 548-549, 649-650, 652
Foreign Language Enthusiasts 432
Foresters 588
Fossil Collectors 414
Foster Parents 404
Foundations 134-136, 249
Fox Enthusiasts 643
Foxpro Users 149
Fractal Enthusiasts 196
Framemaker Enthusiasts 261
France Residents 270, 334, 528, 655, 660
Francophiles 24, 94, 99, 334, 342, 427, 440, 528

Free Speech Activists 349
Free-Net Organizers 468, 476
Free-Net Users 465, 472, 593
French 92, 165, 167, 178, 190, 292, 299, 310, 427, 432, 454, 628, 642
French Citizens 421
French Enthusiasts 421
French Food Enthusiasts 630
French Horn Enthusiasts 72
French Language Educators 427
French Language Students 427
French Literature Enthusiasts 439, 441
French Speakers 191, 334, 338, 429, 440, 443, 528
French Students 435, 441, 476, 528
French Studies Students 427
Frida Kahlo Enthusiasts 18
Frisbee Enthusiasts 652
Fundraisers 136, 468
Funk Music Enthusiasts 71, 90
Funkadelic Enthusiasts 90
Furniture Buyers 33, 115, 546, 549
Furniture Dealers 33-34
Furniture Manufacturers 33-34
Futurists 310

Gaelic Language Scholars 413
Gallery Owners 33
Gallery Shoppers 623
Gamblers 132, 548, 647, 652, 662, 665, 669
Game Enthusiasts 43, 416, 483, 550, 554, 634-636, 649
Games Players 224
Gardeners 146-147, 150, 539-541, 582-584, 626, 636-638
Gardening Enthusiasts 146-147, 150, 583-584, 636-638
Gay Rights Activists 408, 530, 532
Gays 378, 397, 407-408, 450, 530-532, 640
Gender Studies Students 408
Genealogists 522-523
Genealogy Enthusiasts 517
General Public 16, 31, 39-40, 43, 50, 102, 104-109, 111, 114, 116-117, 119, 121-126, 129, 134-137, 139, 142, 145-147, 149-150, 154-155, 162, 166-167, 181-182, 204, 218, 233, 235-236, 241-242, 260, 264, 303, 310, 314-316, 318-320, 328, 331, 333, 338, 341-342, 344-345, 347-348, 350, 352-358, 361-362, 368-369, 373, 375, 378, 384, 391-398, 400-402, 404-406, 408, 414-416, 419, 422-424, 427, 431, 434, 436-437, 441, 446, 451, 458, 460-461, 463, 466, 468, 470, 478, 481, 486-487, 489-495, 498, 500-504, 506-507, 509-510, 514, 516-518, 521-524, 526-527, 533-534, 536, 537, 541-542, 544-549, 552, 554-556, 560, 579, 587, 589-595, 610-612, 623, 630, 632, 634, 658, 662, 666
General Relativity Scholars 197
Generation X 70, 82, 354, 533
Genetic Engineers 579
Geneticists 216, 292, 378, 398, 566-567, 575-582, 588, 592
Genome Researchers 579
Geographers 294, 318, 320, 334, 430, 448, 588, 590-591, 597-600
Geography Enthusiasts 424
Geological Engineers 294
Geologists 294, 300, 303, 318, 336, 524, 571, 586-587, 589-590, 597-601
Geophysicists 587, 590, 599
Georgia Residents 283, 655
Geoscientists 597-600
Geriatric Specialists 368, 370
German Enthusiasts 439
German Internet Users 481
German Language Educators 440
German Language Students 439-440
German Speakers 46, 92
German Students 272
German Studies Students 251, 331, 425, 433, 440
German Technicians 324
Germans 21, 172-173, 186, 192-193, 196, 201, 204, 251, 270, 272, 274, 306, 310, 323, 331-332, 334, 389, 426-427, 432, 438-440, 451, 460, 466, 468, 473, 497, 534, 554, 603, 608, 650-651, 659, 664

Germany Residents – Islamic Culture Enthusiasts   813

Germany Residents   320, 323-324, 659-660, 664, 667
Germany Scholars   323
Gerontologists   368
Gift Givers   145-146, 148
Gift Shoppers   548
Gifted Students   262
Gilbert & Sullivan Enthusiasts   92
GIS and IP Professionals   597-598
GIS Professionals   183, 305, 598
GIS Users   598-599
Glasses Makers   389
Glasses Retailers   389
Gluten-Intolerant People   384
GNU Application Developers   170
GNU Programmers   202
GNU Users   170
Golf Club Manufacturers   641
Golf Enthusiasts   326, 648, 650, 655, 660
Golfers   524, 641
Gospel Music Enthusiasts   50-51
Gossips   459, 516, 536
Gothic Rock Enthusiasts   72, 88
Gourmets   624-625, 627-628, 630, 632-633
Government Agencies   119, 162, 309, 315, 318, 348
Government Agency Employees   318, 401, 461
Government Employees   160, 249, 313-317, 326, 347, 350, 355-356, 358, 365, 395, 397-398, 482, 596, 602
Government Officials   218, 250, 313-317, 319-320, 326, 334, 341, 345, 347, 350, 352, 354-358, 361-362, 398-400, 594, 596
Government Researchers   142, 190, 314, 330, 566
Government Students   313-315, 336, 342, 347, 350, 352, 355-357, 360, 504
Government Watchers   155, 162, 356
Graduate Students   544
Graffiti Enthusiasts   18
Grant Writers   32
Grantmakers   135, 149, 249, 374, 519
Grantseekers   32, 136, 149, 249, 318, 374, 519
Graphic Art Enthusiasts   20
Graphic Artists   22, 34, 37, 40-41, 46, 98, 169, 171-173, 182, 220, 227-228, 330, 342, 476-477, 538
Graphic Designers   16, 33-47, 138-139, 148-149, 169, 171, 173, 175, 404-405, 463, 543
Graphic Users   226
Graphics Enthusiasts   611
Graphics Game Players   45
Grass-Roots Organizers   353-354, 520
Greece Residents   422, 654, 658, 666
Greek Culture Enthusiasts   422
Greek Language Speakers   158
Greek Scholars   428, 658, 662
Greek Studies Specialists   422
Greeks   158, 422, 428
Grenoble Residents   327
GUI Enthusiasts   227
Guidance Counselors   156, 288
Guitar Music Enthusiasts   71, 83, 85, 86, 89, 90
Guitarists   87
Gun Control Advocates   494
Gun Enthusiasts   351-352
Gymnasts   651

Hacky-Sack Enthusiasts   650
Haiku Poetry Enthusiasts   436-437
Haiti Residents   670
Ham Radio Enthusiasts   621, 624
Hang Gliding Enthusiasts   642
Hard Rock Fans   72, 77-83, 89
Hard Rock Music Enthusiasts   88
Hardware Designers   183, 210
Hardware Engineers   163, 180
Harley-Davidson Enthusiasts   639
Hartford Residents   284
Hawaii Residents   661
Hawaiian Activists   363
Hawaiians   239, 363, 517, 661
Health Care Consumers   400, 404, 408, 521, 546
Health Care Employees   395, 398
Health Care Officials   372, 400

Health Care Policymakers   350, 394, 396-398, 448
Health Care Professionals   68, 255, 318, 368, 370-381, 384-386, 388-398, 400-407, 409-411, 595
Health Care Providers   255, 354, 369, 371-374, 377-381, 398, 400, 408, 410, 517, 642
Health Care Reformers   398
Health Care Students   398
Health Care Workers   382
Health Educators   376, 380, 395, 398, 400-402, 408
Health Food Supermarkets   148
Health Nuts   134
Health Science Researchers   354, 370-371, 386, 388, 394, 396, 398,594
Health Sciences Students   594
Hearing Impaired   242
Hearing Loss Sufferers   385
Heavy Metal Fans   72-80, 82, 85, 88
Hebrew Scholars   279
Helsinki Residents   454
Herbalists   369
Herpetologists   616, 644, 646-647
High-Energy Physics Researchers   605, 609
Hiking Enthusiasts   321, 327, 360, 543, 640, 655-656, 659-660, 664, 666-667
Hindi Scholars   428
Hindi   419, 428
Hip-Hop Enthusiasts   65-66, 541, 535
Hip-Hop Music Enthusiasts   54
Hispanics   417-419, 448
Historians   21, 197-198, 213, 232, 258, 313, 321, 337, 339-341, 355, 358, 404, 414, 418, 420, 424-427, 434, 436, 451, 522-523, 544-545, 560, 562, 638, 663
History Buffs   26, 197, 228, 320-330, 337, 339, 345, 418, 424-426, 513, 523, 545, 557, 562, 624, 654-670
History Educators   427
History Researchers   557
History Students   16, 424, 427
HIV Positive People   408
Hobbyists   240
Hockey Enthusiasts   648-649, 651-652
Holistic Health Care Practitioners   531
Holistic Health Enthusiasts   369
Holocaust Researchers   427
Holocaust Survivors   424, 426, 444, 560
Holography Enthusiasts   98
Home Buyers   113, 140-142
Home Care Professionals   384
Home Decorators   637
Home Economics Teachers   632
Home Makers   637
Home Owners   113-114, 116, 123, 140, 315, 501, 520, 539-540
Home Page Creators   460, 479-480
Home Page Developers   39, 41, 590
Home Recording Enthusiasts   66
Home Schoolers   237
Homeless Activists   98
Homeopathic Health Care Enthusiasts   368-369
Homeopathic Therapists   369
Hong Kong Natives   254
Hong Kong Residents   48, 662, 668
Horoscope Readers   524, 530, 554
Horse Breeders   647, 652
Horse Lovers   644
Horse Racing Enthusiasts   647, 652, 658
Horseback Riders   648
Horticulturists   539-540, 565, 582-584, 636-638
Hospice Workers   395, 402
House Hunters   141-142
House Plant Enthusiasts   638
HTML Authors   465, 477, 479-480
HTML Enthusiasts   102
HTML Users   220, 225, 458, 476-478
Human Auditory Interface Users   165
Human Resources Departments   110, 112, 371, 456, 525
Human Rights Activists   338, 341, 346, 349, 351, 354, 356, 358, 394, 418, 420-421
Humanists   244, 248-249, 319, 353, 408, 418, 422, 426-427, 494, 518
Humanitarians   340
Humanities Scholars   186, 444

Humor Enthusiasts   17, 31, 38, 46, 99, 156, 356, 425, 462, 469, 512, 525-530, 540, 553
Humorists   73, 513, 528
Hungarian Internet Users   667
Hungarians   335
Hungary Residents   667
Husbands   410, 494-495, 518, 527
Hydrologists   590

IBM Users   208, 541
IC Designers   296
Ice Hockey Fans   653
Ice Skaters   648
Iceland Residents   330, 660
Icelanders   440, 590
Icelandic Literature Enthusiasts   440
Illinois Residents   23, 48-49, 72, 97, 110, 118, 158, 284, 324-325, 353, 580, 614, 657-658
Imaging Specialists   41, 294
Immunologists   370-371, 398
In-Line Skaters   651
Independent Contractors   133
India Culture Enthusiasts   335
India Residents   48, 253, 322, 394, 664
Indian Art Enthusiasts   20
Indian Colleges   249
Indian Literature Enthusiasts   434
Indiana Residents   248, 325, 363, 490, 505
Indianapolis Residents   60
Indians   126, 226, 253, 298, 338-339, 394, 413
Indigenous People   47, 345, 418, 420, 432
Indigo Girls Enthusiasts   77
Individuals   630
Indonesians   418
Industrial Engineers   302-303
Industrial Music Enthusiasts   54, 74, 79, 80-82, 84
Industrial Professionals   305, 399-400
Industry Employees   482
Industry Professionals   347
Industry Researchers   298
Infectious Disease Sufferers   398
Informatics Researchers   178
Information Brokers   162, 208, 477
Information Professionals   125, 151, 163, 172, 218, 244, 248, 278, 345, 430, 464, 468, 480, 534
Information Scientists   161-162, 164-165, 171, 175-176, 196, 198, 208, 230-231, 248, 250, 306, 362, 429, 431, 482
Information Technologists   230, 308, 350
Information Technology Enthusiasts   344
Information Technology Experts   166
Information Technology Professionals   184, 247
Innovators   628
Insect Enthusiasts   566, 615, 647
Institutional Investors   144
Instrumental Music Enthusiasts   52, 58, 84, 87-88
Insurance Professionals   369
Intel Users   208
Intellectuals   121
Interactive Artists   474
Interactive Entertainment Enthusiasts   543
Interactive Game Players   483-484, 634
Interactive Program Developers   170, 539
Interior Decorators   548
Interior Designers   33-34, 113, 115, 546
International Affairs Students   343-344
International Agencies   343
International Aid Agencies   251, 289, 341-344, 353, 566
International Business Educators   342, 481
International Business Professionals   118, 125-128, 134, 323, 331, 336, 340, 342, 351-352, 421, 506, 533, 535-537, 540-541, 655
International Business Students   271
International Business Travelers   332, 335
International Development Professionals   341, 592
International Development Specialists   125, 127, 161, 251, 253, 289, 331, 342-344, 353, 421, 481, 533, 566, 655
International Entrepreneurs   125
International Financiers   106
International Investors   126-127
International Law Students   497

International Lawyers   118, 331, 336, 341, 493, 496-498
International Marketing Professionals   113, 126, 221
International Organizers   465
International Politics Enthusiasts   316
International Relations Scholars   343
International Scientists   606
International Stockbrokers   125-126
International Students   168, 252-253, 263, 265, 275, 279, 288-289, 332, 334-339, 360, 432, 533, 655, 658-659, 668, 670
International Studies Students   251, 343-344
International Trade Executives   114
International Travelers   162, 319-320, 330, 332, 334-335, 338, 340, 344, 421, 536, 584, 620, 640, 654-655, 661, 663-666, 670
Internet Access Providers   127, 159, 164-166, 183, 202, 205, 212, 457, 461-462, 465, 471, 474, 476, 483, 534
Internet Activists   345
Internet Advertisers   547
Internet Business Professionals   461, 470
Internet Consumers   455
Internet Developers   122, 222, 421, 462, 465, 471, 477-478, 480
Internet Engineering Task Force Members   481-482
Internet Entrepreneurs   144
Internet Mailing List Managers   477
Internet Marketers   103-104, 140
Internet Marketing Professionals   456
Internet Newcomers   459, 462-464, 466, 468-469, 476
Internet Newsgroup Subscribers   467
Internet Producers   466
Internet Professionals   144, 209, 456, 458, 461, 464-465, 470, 472, 476-477, 480
Internet Providers   470, 472, 477, 481-482
Internet Publishers   138, 209, 219, 458, 463, 466, 474, 476, 478-480
Internet Researchers   308, 466, 477
Internet Security Managers   472
Internet Security Specialists   470-471
Internet Shoppers   140, 457, 547
Internet Specialists   461-463, 465, 467, 471, 476-481
Internet Trainers   464, 468
Internet Users   23, 30, 35-36, 39, 43-44, 46, 51, 67, 69-70, 103-104, 114, 120, 122, 124, 126, 131, 134, 138, 144, 149-150, 156-157, 159, 161, 164-165, 168, 170-171, 174, 176, 184, 187, 191-192, 194-195, 198-199, 201-205, 207, 213-219, 220-221, 225, 228, 234, 236-237, 241, 245-248, 255-256, 261, 263, 267, 270-272, 274, 276-279, 283, 285, 300, 310, 315, 318-319, 334, 338, 339, 348, 352, 360-361, 365, 376, 382, 390, 397, 400, 402, 406, 414-416, 425, 430, 432-433, 441, 444, 446, 450, 453-487, 491, 494, 504, 519, 521, 524-529, 532-534, 537, 543, 545-550, 552, 554, 558, 560, 568, 571, 589-590, 605, 610, 612, 621, 627, 630, 633-635, 654, 661
Interpreters   151, 432
Inuits   544
Inventors   144, 150, 496
Investigators   315, 502
Investment Bankers   104
Investment Counselors   123
Investors   103-106, 116, 118-125, 128-133, 138, 140-143, 163, 179, 316, 360, 364-365, 456, 465, 494, 502, 524, 538
Iowa Residents   285
Iran Residents   418, 662
Iranian Culture Enthusiasts   418
Iranians   252, 418, 420, 441, 479
IRC Enthusiasts   484
IRC Users   460, 485
Ireland Residents   532, 658, 668
Irish   64, 192, 273, 338, 419, 496, 536, 669
Irish Culture Enthusiasts   662
Irish Literature Enthusiasts   413
Irish Music Enthusiasts   63-64
Irrigation Specialists   362
Irritable Bowel Syndrome Sufferers   384
ISDN Users   160
Islam Religion/Culture Enthusiasts   563
Islamic Book Collectors   514
Islamic Culture Enthusiasts   514

Israel Residents – Motorcycle Enthusiasts

Israel Residents 660, 663
Israelis 160, 202-203, 279, 427, 493, 536, 662
IT Specialists 118
Italian Literature Enthusiasts 438
Italian Students 329
Italians 61, 275, 335, 339, 432, 438, 573, 601, 628, 630, 670
Italy Residents 64, 325, 328-329, 659-660, 664, 668-670

Jamaicans 428
Janet Jackson Enthusiasts 85
Japan Residents 60, 112, 167, 293, 327, 337-338, 648, 663, 668
Japan Scholars 663, 668
Japanese 265, 539
Japanese Americans 265, 415
Japanese Culture Enthusiasts 524, 533, 622
Japanese Literature Enthusiasts 436-437
Japanese Speakers 539
Jazz Enthusiasts 51-53, 55-58, 60, 62, 67, 70, 84, 86-89, 92, 98
Jazz Historians 55
Jazz Improvisation Students 55
Jazz Students 55
Jell-O Enthusiasts 628
Jewelry Enthusiasts 19
Jewelry Shoppers 546
Jewish Mothers 627
Jews 138, 335, 424, 426-427, 444, 493, 536, 559-564, 662, 666
Job Recruiters 110-112, 238, 293, 371, 525, 598
Job Seekers 33, 102-103, 105, 109-112, 114, 140, 154, 156, 179, 200, 237-238, 293, 317, 320, 344, 356, 363, 371, 445, 453, 520, 525, 584, 598
Jockeys 652
John Cage Fans 58
Johns Hopkins University Students 254
Joke Enthusiasts 527
Jokers 156, 526-530, 552
Job Seekers 179
Journalism Educators 156
Journalism Students 310
Journalists 102, 137, 153-154, 156, 158, 162, 244-245, 267, 313-315, 320, 327, 337-339, 340-343, 345-346, 355-358, 362, 365, 396, 416, 434, 436, 441, 446, 504, 524, 526, 528, 534-539, 591, 612, 659
Judaica Scholars 560, 562-563
Judges 119, 490, 494, 497-498, 500, 502, 504-505
Jugglers 650-651
Juggling Enthusiasts 650

Kansas Residents 361
Kayakers 619, 631
Kentucky Residents 262, 287, 363, 658, 663
Kite Flying Enthusiasts 651
Knoxville Residents 19
Koala Enthusiasts 645
Koreans 628
Kurdistan Scholars 419
Kurds 419

Labor Organizers 255
Labor Unions 503
Lacrosse Enthusiasts 649
LAN Specialists 222
LAN Users 202
LAN Administrators 122, 183, 218
LAN Consultants 183, 222
LAN Users 221, 223
Landscape Designers 636
Landscapers 122
Language Arts Educators 252
Language Educators 252, 427, 429, 431
Language Enthusiasts 160
Language Researchers 427, 429, 432
Language Scholars 428, 551
Language Specialists 427-429, 432
Language Students 219, 225, 252, 275, 427-429, 431-432
Laptop Users 666
Large Businesses 123
Large People 522
LaTeX Users 196
Latin America Educators 254

Latin America Residents 254
Latin America Students 254
Latin American Researchers 418, 421
Latin American Studies Students 332, 334-336, 338, 360, 416, 418, 655, 658-659
Latin Americans 118, 126, 131, 142, 313, 316, 324, 330, 337, 417-419, 421, 425, 465, 474
Latin Music Enthusiasts 85
Latin Scholars 248, 263, 427-428
Latin Students 248, 263, 427-428
Latin Studies Students 242
Latinas 419
Latinos 110, 416
Law Educators 498, 502
Law Enforcement Personnel 502
Law Enforcement Professionals 492, 494, 518, 520, 644
Law Professors 491-492, 498-499, 503
Law Students 339, 354, 356-357, 461, 489-492, 494-507, 528
Lawyers 116-117, 119, 139-140, 142, 144, 150, 267, 315, 337, 346, 354, 358, 363-364, 402, 461, 489-507, 517, 524, 528
Learning Disabled People 374, 384
Lebanese Culture Enthusiasts 335
Lecturers 606
Legal Clients 506
Legal Professionals 119, 139, 164, 370, 461, 489-496, 498, 500-505, 524, 528, 595
Legal Publishers 501
Legal Researchers 490, 494, 498, 502-504, 506-507
Legal Scholars 386, 491-492, 497-499, 501, 504-505
Legal Professionals 267
Legislators 243, 318, 491, 496, 504, 506
Lemur Lovers 643
Lenders 141-142
Lesbians 407-408, 450, 530, 532, 640
Liberals 356, 528, 538
Libertarians 340, 350-351, 354-355, 357, 533
Libertarians 339
Librarians 136, 143, 158, 184, 230, 233-236, 238, 244, 248, 250, 255, 260-262, 264, 279, 320, 325, 358, 361, 364, 370, 403, 422, 426, 429-431, 433-434, 436, 440-443, 446, 458, 464-465, 468, 470, 480, 512-514, 523, 558-559, 563, 601
Library Administrators 215, 234-236, 250, 260-262, 264, 285, 430, 601
Library Scientists 264, 431
Library Users 158, 215, 233-236, 250, 260-262, 264, 279, 284-285, 303, 320, 357, 361, 386, 429-430, 446, 601
Light Dealers 623
Lighting Designers 91
Lindy Hop Enthusiasts 94
Linguistics Enthusiasts 433
Linguists 177, 214, 224-225, 243, 252, 263, 322, 337, 415, 417, 427-428, 431-432, 440, 524-525, 529-530, 551, 558, 600
Linux Users 212, 217
LISP Programmers 211
Literary Critics 65, 423, 432-438, 440-442, 444-445, 512, 537, 541
Literary Educators 440
Literary Scholars 240, 250, 413, 421-424, 426, 430, 432-445, 451, 513, 557, 562-563
Literary Theorists 417, 433, 440, 444
Literature 432, 442
Literature Enthusiasts 434
Literature Researchers 440
Literature Students 422, 432, 440-441
Litigants 119, 461, 489-492, 495-496, 500-504
Live Music Enthusiasts 64, 68
Llama Enthusiasts 645
Lobbyists 254, 318, 362
Locksmiths 524
Logicians 232, 431
Loglan Speakers 428
Lojban Speakers 428
Lonely People 532
Loreena McKennitt Enthusiasts 86
Los Angeles Tourists 550
Lotus Users 173
Louisiana Residents 25, 55, 660

MAC Users 158, 172
Macedonia Residents 323

Macintosh Developers 206
Macintosh Programmers 210, 222, 224
Macintosh Users 114, 138, 180, 182-184, 203, 205-206, 209, 214-215, 217, 221-222, 224, 226-227, 252, 291, 390, 420, 453, 466, 476, 478, 529, 543, 666, 668
Magazine Readers 50, 165, 354, 539-541
Magic Enthusiasts 554
Magicians 651
Mail Order Companies 546
Mailing List Users 466
Maine Companies 127
Maine Residents 236, 276-277, 363, 365, 664, 667
Malaysians 266, 421
Management Consultants 224
Management Information Specialists 15, 246, 318, 461, 468
Management Professionals 133-134
Management Students 108
Management Trainers 106, 445, 548
Managers 103, 106-108, 111, 114, 120, 126, 133-135, 144, 153, 163, 179, 301, 305, 364, 367, 456, 621
Manatee Enthusiasts 647
Manitoba Residents 413
Manufacturers 122-123, 165, 305, 316, 318
Manufacturing Engineers 296
Maoris 544
Marin County Residents 361
Marine Biologists 226, 305, 545, 568-571, 589, 595, 616, 667
Marine Enthusiasts 570
Marine Geologists 590
Marine Technologists 570
Mark Twain Enthusiasts 426
Market Analysts 113, 119, 126, 128-132, 138, 143, 181, 224, 313, 330, 502, 538
Market Researchers 114, 224, 502
Marketing Communications 104
Marketing Departments 149
Marketing Executives 102, 104, 113
Marketing Firms 370
Marketing Managers 104, 263
Marketing Professionals 98, 102-103, 120, 131, 139-140, 144, 161, 215, 352, 456-458, 472, 548
Marketing Specialists 102-104, 114, 224, 454
Marsupial Enthusiasts 645
Marxists 557
Maryland Residents 62, 533
Mass Communications Educators 477
Mass Communications Students 117, 155-156, 158, 536, 550
Mass Communications Technicians 536
Massachusetts Residents 28, 47, 59-60, 62, 80, 116, 122, 206, 277, 283, 324-325, 329, 340, 363, 408, 472-473, 561, 656, 664, 666
Material Engineers 303
Material Scientists 303
Math Researchers 196
Math Students 197
Mathematical Biologists 208
Mathematicians 169, 178-179, 183, 185, 191, 194-201, 204, 206-208, 214, 220, 224, 227-228, 232, 241, 246, 257, 271, 277, 308, 597
Mathematics Educators 195-201, 208, 224, 240-241, 245, 257
Mathematics Students 196, 200-201, 224, 240
Mathematics Students (Primary/Secondary) 257
Mayans 414, 544
MBONE Users 462
Mechanical Engineering Students 304
Mechanical Engineers 304, 374
Mechanics 121, 510, 638
Media Analysts 156
Media Critics 102, 156
Media Enthusiasts 27, 47
Media Industry 102
Media Members 98
Media Professionals 27, 102, 151, 156-158, 162, 173, 176, 358, 491, 534, 537-538, 550
Media Researchers 27
Media Specialists 96, 238, 461
Mediators 342, 353, 496, 500, 517-518
Medical Educators 224, 364, 368, 385-390, 392, 394, 398, 401, 403-404, 407, 576

Medical Illustrators 405
Medical Image Specialists 392
Medical Informatics Specialists 226, 394, 404
Medical Patients 369, 374, 394, 402
Medical Practitioners 304, 351, 369, 376, 380-381, 390-392, 394-395, 398, 400-402, 404-405, 407-408, 579
Medical Professionals 114, 151, 173, 226, 275, 369-372, 377, 382, 386-388, 390-392, 394, 401-406
Medical Researchers 178, 367-371, 376-378, 380-381, 385-388, 390-395, 397-398, 400-406, 445, 576, 579, 595, 602
Medical Residents 400
Medical Statisticians 389
Medical Students 224, 371, 377-378, 380-381, 385-392, 394, 396, 400-401, 403-407
Medical Trauma Victims 392
Medieval Literature Enthusiasts 439
Medieval Scholars 424
Medievalists 424, 660
Melbourne Residents 330
Men 70, 376, 380, 400-402, 407-408, 410-411, 450-451, 510, 518, 522, 532, 537, 540
Mental Health Professionals 393-394, 445-446
Mental Health Professionals 398
Mentally Handicapped People 372
Merchants 116, 546, 548
Metallurgists 607
Metalwork Enthusiasts 31
Metaphysics Enthusiasts 558
Meteorologists 317, 344, 362, 554-555, 587-594, 597
Meteorology Students 344, 554, 588, 590
Mexican Americans 417-419
Mexicans 310
Mexico Residents 352
Michigan Residents 113, 118, 240, 321, 472, 474, 481, 534, 552, 556
Microarchitects 190, 210
Microbiologists 398, 577
Microsoft Customers 224
Microsoft Windows Users 174, 182, 219, 476
Microwave System Users 168
Middle East Residents 252, 420, 479
Middle East Scholars 321, 420, 441
MIDI Enthusiasts 54, 65, 67, 69-71, 89
Midwives 410-411
Military Enthusiasts 347-348, 648
Military Historians 339, 342, 346, 348
Military Personnel 161, 288-289, 312, 319, 342, 346-349
Military Researchers 347-348
Military Scientists 347
Military Students 348
Military Enthusiasts 348
Mineral Enthusiasts 303, 586, 623
Mining Professionals 303
Minnesota Residents 20, 251, 340, 398, 542, 551, 664
MIS Managers 184, 203
MIS Professionals 171
Missouri Residents 257, 286, 364-365
Mobile Communicators 161, 164-165
Models 123, 522
Modem Users 163-164, 167, 172, 222, 464
Molecule Structure Analyzers 586
Molecular Biologists 170, 172, 294, 370, 387, 390, 392, 566-567, 574-579, 581-582, 586, 592
Molecular Biotechnologists 567, 574, 578
Molecular Chemists 581
Molecular Ecologists 581
Monks 564
Montana Residents 138, 364, 599
Monty Python Enthusiasts 81
Mormons 559
Mortgage Brokers 140-141
Mortgage Lenders 141, 319
Mosaic Users 606
Mothers 409-410
Motivational Speakers 133
Motor Sports Enthusiasts 639
Motorbike Enthusiasts 639
Motorcycle Enthusiasts 510, 638-639
Motorcycle Racing Enthusiasts 639
Motorcycle Enthusiasts 638

Mountain Biking Enthusiasts – Politicians

Mountain Biking Enthusiasts   640, 642
Mountain Climbing Enthusiasts   51, 667
Mountaineers   640
Movers   142
Movie Buffs   542
Movie Directors   47, 542-543
Movie Enthusiasts   47-48, 63, 517, 525, 539, 541-542, 552
MS-DOS Users   183
MUD Enthusiasts   482-487
Multimedia Artists   453
Multimedia Designers   39, 244
Multimedia Developers   220, 227, 474
Multimedia Enthusiasts   17, 19, 28, 30, 32, 39, 42, 44, 47-48, 69, 94, 124, 158, 162-163, 166, 170, 174, 310, 322, 325, 462, 537, 539, 543
Multimedia Professionals   172, 174
Multiple Sclerosis Sufferers   378
Municipal Staff   356
Museum Enthusiasts   21, 23-24, 26, 30, 321-322, 324-325, 342, 420, 657-658, 660, 662, 666, 668
Museums   30
MUSH Enthusiasts   484
Mushroom Enthusiasts   528
Music Distributors   68
Music Educators   53, 56, 58-59, 65, 67, 73, 222
Music Enthusiasts   29-30, 42, 50-52, 54-95, 147-148, 158, 222, 276, 322, 420, 459, 516, 525, 533, 543, 551, 554, 655, 659, 667-668
Music Historians   51-52, 54-56, 59, 61-64, 66, 68, 78, 98
Music Industry Professionals   53-54, 57, 63, 66
Music Instructors   65
Music Librarians   51-52, 58, 63, 66-70, 322
Music Listeners   64
Music Professionals   52, 62, 78
Music Publishers   63
Music Researchers   52, 54, 58-59, 62-70, 83
Music Students   56, 58, 60-64, 66-69, 91, 97, 222
Music Teachers   61, 68
Musical Theater Enthusiasts   91, 93, 95
Musicals Enthusiasts   94
Musicians   28-30, 32, 43, 50-70, 73, 76-79, 86-87, 89-90, 92, 94, 113, 158, 514, 535, 539-540, 560
Musicologists   55, 58, 68
Muslims   16, 560, 564
Mystery Fiction Enthusiasts   515
Mystery Novel Enthusiasts   241
Mythology Enthusiasts   422, 426, 433, 445, 557, 563
Mythology Students   557

Nanotechnology Enthusiasts   302, 576
Napa Valley Residents   141
NASA Managers   611
NASA Researchers   292, 609, 611-612
Native American Art Enthusiasts   20-21, 36
Native Americans   20, 24, 249, 418, 420, 438, 519, 544
Native Australians   334
Native Canadians   345
NATO Employees   570
NATO Officials   316
Natural Foods Enthusiasts   636
Natural Historians   580
Natural History Enthusiasts   544, 580
Natural History Museum Curators   414
Natural History Scientists   602
Natural Scientists   294, 318, 545, 588, 602
Naturalists   314, 320, 644-645
Nature Buffs   44
Nature Enthusiasts   614
Nature Fans   524
Nature Lovers   314, 544, 546, 601, 616, 637, 640, 644-645, 660
Naval Personnel   348
Naval Researchers   348
Navy Officers   348
NBA Enthusiasts   649
Nepal Residents   440
Nepali Culture Enthusiasts   440
Netherlands Residents   662
Netherlands Residents   273, 659-660
Netscape Users   478

Network Administrators   170, 179-180, 183, 185, 201-203, 205, 207, 213, 216, 220, 222-223, 228, 230, 246, 253, 431, 459, 461-462, 465, 467, 470-471, 477-478, 481, 491
Network Communications Specialists   201, 205, 222, 460
Network Designers   163, 202
Network Developers   159-161, 165, 169, 180, 185, 201-203, 205, 214, 223, 228-229, 275, 306, 308, 322, 324-326, 454, 465, 467-468, 477, 481, 654-656, 663
Network Researchers   161, 222
Network Security Professionals   470
Network Service Providers   169, 180, 185, 205, 364, 462, 468, 474
Network Specialists   179
Network Systems Administrators   184
Network Time Protocols   214
Network Users   126-127, 135-136, 159-161, 165-166, 168, 181, 194, 201-203, 205, 207, 222-223, 228, 322, 324-329, 359-360, 362, 364, 454, 468, 481, 548, 654, 656, 663
Networking Specialists   202
Neural Network Researchers   179, 190
Neurobiologists   371, 375, 601
Neurologists   371-372, 406
Neuroscientists   177, 179, 375, 390, 393, 445, 600-601
Neurosurgeons   390
Neurosurgery Patients   392
Nevada Residents   286, 662, 669
New Age Enthusiasts   531, 534, 557
New Age Music Enthusiasts   534
New Brunswick Companies   127
New England Residents   60, 408
New Hampshire Residents   278, 282-283, 365, 537
New Jersey Residents   96, 258, 364
New Media Artists   32, 539
New Mexico Residents   113, 188, 259
New Mothers   382
New York City Vegetarians   533, 625
New York Culture Enthusiasts   665
New York In-Line Skaters   651
New York Residents   28, 30, 56, 58, 91, 93-95, 105, 140, 142, 261-262, 282, 319, 328, 340, 364, 474, 506, 522, 531-533, 536, 554, 625, 633, 641, 663, 665
New Zealand Culture Enthusiasts   544, 654
New Zealand Residents   188, 336, 638, 662
News Buffs   122, 137, 154-155, 157-158, 261, 327, 337, 363, 446, 460, 462, 473, 524, 526, 534, 539, 552, 554, 560
News Readers   156, 533-535, 538-540
Newspaper Publishers   538
NeXT Developers   227
NeXT Programmers   194
NeXT Users   194, 227
Nightlife Enthusiasts   532
Nintendo Enthusiasts   635
NN Newsreader Users   468
Non-Fiction Enthusiasts   442
Non-governmental Organizations   357
Nonfiction Readers   515
Nonprofit Organizations   38, 117, 119-120, 128, 134-136, 161, 309, 311, 342, 345, 353, 355, 356, 454, 506, 516, 519, 522, 539
Nonprofit Professionals   398
Nordic Literature Enthusiasts   442
North Carolina Residents   25, 326, 364, 536, 538, 657-658, 665, 670
Northern Ireland Residents   322
Norwegian Politicians   356
Norwegian Speakers   26
Norwegians   26, 50, 273, 356, 429, 474, 530
Nose and Throat Specialists   385
Nuclear Engineers   304
Nuclear Physicists   304, 606-607
Nuclear Researchers   604
Nuclear Scientists   304
Numerical Analysts   169, 191, 194-196, 198-201, 206, 232
Nurse Practitioners   372, 392, 396, 406
Nurses   371-372, 377, 380-381, 384, 391-392, 394, 396, 400, 405-406
Nutritionists   123, 372, 395-397, 401-402, 532, 614, 642

Object Oriented Programmers   187, 209, 211-213
Obstetricians   409-411
Occult Enthusiasts   552, 554
Ocean Researchers   570
Oceanographers   173, 226, 568-571, 581, 588-591, 595, 615
Oceanography Students   570
OCR Enthusiasts   216
Office Furniture Buyers   124
Office Suppliers   146
Ohio Residents   25, 112, 326, 330, 498
Oklahoma Residents   26, 281, 288, 329
Olympics Enthusiasts   321, 648, 650, 653
Omaha Residents   454
Oncologists   375-381, 402
Online Businesses   473
Online Marketing Seekers   148
Online Publishers   537
Online Service Users   462-464
Online Shoppers   217-218, 383, 522, 627, 633
Ontario Residents   472
Opera Enthusiasts   52, 54-57, 61-62, 65, 83, 85, 92, 94-95
Opera Fans   514
Opera Music Enthusiasts   51-52
Operating Systems Developers   205
Options Traders   128
Optometrists   389
Oral Surgeons   372
Oregon Residents   26, 60, 72, 95, 262, 281, 323, 327, 474, 555, 662, 665
Organic Businesses   134
Orgone Energy Enthusiasts   445
Orienteering Enthusiasts   640
Ornithologists   613, 616, 639, 643-644, 647-648
OS/2 Programmers   225
Oslo Residents   61
Outdoor Sports Enthusiasts   651
Outdoors Enthusiasts   237, 320, 326, 543, 640-642, 654-656, 662, 664, 667
Owl Enthusiasts   653

Packaging Engineers   296
Paintball Enthusiasts   648
Paleolithic Age Scholars   414
Paleontologists   545, 603
Palindrome Enthusiasts   529
Paragliders   620, 662
Paralegals   496, 503
Parallel Computing Experts   204
Parallel Computing Programmers   171
Parallel Computing Researchers   189, 229-232
Parallel Programmers   187-188, 191, 204, 210, 229
Parasailors   620
Parents   26, 30, 136, 139, 146, 148, 155, 161, 166, 237, 242-243, 245-247, 254, 256-250, 260, 262, 288, 345, 361, 374, 376, 378-379, 381-384, 396, 400, 402, 410, 435-436, 438, 442-443, 512-513, 517-521, 523-524, 543-544, 547, 552, 593, 603, 635, 648, 653
Parents of Autistic Children   384
Parkinson's Disease Patients   378-380
Particle Physicists   604-606
Patent Lawyers   144, 496, 500
Patent Researchers   144, 496
Pathologists   388, 390
Patients   378, 380, 382, 400, 403, 407
PC Developers   174
PC Engineers   174, 214, 218, 538
PC MAC Users   139
PC Owners   204
PC Programmers   203, 213-214, 218, 227, 538
PC Users   115, 158, 173-174, 181-184, 194, 202-205, 208, 210, 212, 214, 216-218, 220-228, 291, 390, 466, 476, 480, 538, 543, 666
PDA Users   183
PDF Users   228
Peace Activists   520
Pediatricians   494
Pen and Ink Art Enthusiasts   18
Penguin Lovers   646
Pennsylvania Residents   60, 72, 120, 128, 135, 282, 309, 311, 520
Percussionists   65
Performance Artists   32

Performers   73, 84, 86-87, 90-91, 94-96
Performing Artists   29, 94-95, 260
Performing Arts Enthusiasts   92, 96
Performing Arts Students   91-92
Period Actors   545
Perl Programmers   212
Persian Culture Enthusiasts   662
Persian Writers   418
Persians   479
Personal Ad Readers   532
Personnel Managers   112, 293
Peru Residents   663
Peruvian Literature Enthusiasts   440
Peruvians   337, 474
Pet Buyers   145
Pet Lovers   548, 644, 646
Pet Owners   114, 145, 409, 528, 616, 644-647
Pet Stores   145
Petroleum Industry Professionals   300
Pharmaceutical Companies   406-407
Pharmaceutical Designers   586
Pharmacists   372, 385, 392, 396, 402, 406
Pharmacologists   376, 402
Phoenix Residents   113
Philadelphia Residents   654
Philanthropists   117, 135-136, 345, 506
Philippine Residents   136
Philosophers   354, 358, 361, 371, 439, 441, 460, 557-559, 562, 564
Philosophy Educators   558
Philosophy Enthusiasts   558
Philosophy Students   558, 564
Photographers   18-19, 28, 30, 37-39, 42, 97-99, 122, 348, 446, 536, 654, 658
Photography Consumers   99
Photography Enthusiasts   17, 24, 44, 97-99, 654
Photojournalism Enthusiasts   99
Photojournalists   98
Physical Therapists   373-374, 406
Physician Assistants   392
Physicians   114, 368-369, 371-372, 374, 376-381, 387-388, 390-392, 394-396, 400-406
Physicists   197, 203, 234, 246, 271, 291, 304, 314, 575, 584, 586, 593, 602-609, 612
Physics Educators   608-609
Physics Students   607-609
Pilots   291, 620
Pittsburgh Residents   454
Pizza Enthusiasts   458
Plant Scientists   584
Plasma Physicists   607
Playwrights   33, 92, 94, 423, 437
Plumbers   520
Poetry Enthusiasts   18, 240, 434-438, 440, 443-444, 511
Poetry Scholars   435
Poets   31, 434-435, 439-440, 535, 625
Poland Residents   270
Police   524
Police Personnel   381-382
Policy Analysts   118, 316, 339, 344, 352, 462
Policymakers   117, 207, 242, 318, 341-342, 345, 350, 351, 462, 493, 555-556, 579, 596
Polio Survivors   406
Polish   49-50, 252, 310, 336, 388, 447, 663
Polish Culture Enthusiasts   420
Polish Speakers   420
Political Activists   136, 155-156, 215, 320, 333-334, 338-340, 342, 345, 349-351, 353-356, 362, 410, 450, 482, 522, 533, 539
Political Advisors   354
Political Advocates   32
Political Analysts   117, 162, 207, 298, 343, 352-353, 357, 362, 364
Political Enthusiasts   360
Political Reformers   507
Political Researchers   162, 244, 313-315, 335-337, 340, 342-343, 347-348, 352-354, 358, 360, 362, 365, 433, 463, 502, 528
Political Science Students   354, 490
Political Scientists   118, 156, 254, 272, 313, 316, 320, 331-333, 336-341, 344, 346, 350, 352-356, 358, 360, 362, 364, 418, 421, 426, 504, 506, 536, 557
Political Theorists   427
Politicians   73, 118, 331, 339, 342, 345-346, 350, 352, 354-355, 360, 362, 364-365, 426, 483, 490, 496, 520, 602

Politics Enthusiasts 316, 350, 355-357, 563
Pollsters 104
Polynesians 583
Pop Culture Enthusiasts 89
Pop Music Enthusiasts 52, 69, 71-89, 276
Pop Music Listeners 79, 87-88
Popular Culture Enthusiasts 30, 63, 84, 147-148, 436, 522, 533-534, 536, 539, 540, 542, 550, 552-553, 560
Popular Music Enthusiasts 60, 68, 71, 74-75, 79-80, 83, 85-87, 93
Population Experts 343
Population Studies Scholars 358, 368, 448
Population Studies Students 448
Portugal Residents 336, 668
Portuguese Speakers 273, 468
Potters 33
Power Plant Operators 304
Practical Jokers 526, 529, 553
Pregnant Women 409-411
Press Photographers 98
Priests 560
Primatologists 447, 617, 643
Princeton Alumni 96
Prisoners 349, 492
Privacy Activists 171, 176, 215, 462, 471, 491
Pro-Choice Activists 409-410
Probation Counselors 492
Producers 92
Professional Audio Engineers 63, 65-66, 70, 297, 308, 310
Professional Cooks 626
Professional Educators 219
Professional Sports Players 621
Professional Women 450, 502
Professionals 399-400, 596
Professors 107-109, 111, 133-134, 241, 243, 249, 254, 257, 270-276, 280, 283-284, 287, 292-293, 296, 299, 306, 430, 446, 496, 511, 558
Programmers 170-172, 174-177, 180, 183, 185-186, 195-196, 199, 203-205, 209-214, 216, 220, 225, 228-230, 458, 474, 527
Programming Language Designers 213
Progressive Music Enthusiasts 52, 54, 56, 73, 75-80, 82-83, 87
Progressives 136, 342, 345, 353, 355-356, 494, 522, 539
Promoters 545
Propulsion Experts 613
Propulsion Scientists 291
Prosecutors 506
Prostate Cancer Sufferers 380
Psychiatrists 381, 393, 445-446, 553
Psychologists 68, 138, 386, 393, 430, 445-446, 518, 532, 553, 614
Psychology Educators 393, 445
Psychology Students 393, 445-446
Psychology Students (Graduate) 446
Psychopharmacologists 445
Public Broadcasters 155
Public Broadcasting Activists 155-157, 242
Public Broadcasting Enthusiasts 154
Public Officials 361, 364
Public Relations Agencies 476
Public Relations Experts 103-104
Public Relations Professionals 156
Public Servants 320
Public Television Enthusiasts 242, 550
Public Transportation Users 554
Publishers 99, 136-139, 228, 456, 472, 512, 535, 538
Publishing Educators 136, 139
Publishing Professionals 136, 138, 162, 445, 511, 537, 541
Publishing Students 136
Pueblo Indians 418
Puerto Ricans 364
Puerto Rico Residents 572
Punk Rock Enthusiasts 71-73, 76, 78, 81-82, 85
Punks 57, 540
Purchasing Agents 125
Purchasing Offices 159
Python Programmers 213

Quilting Enthusiasts 624

Rabbit Lovers 646

Raccoon Enthusiasts 648
Race Car Drivers 510
Radio Astronomers 608
Radio Broadcasters 157-158, 162
Radio Communicators 168
Radio Enthusiasts 60, 62, 154-158, 162, 460, 550, 624
Radio Enthusiasts 156-157, 516
Radio Pirates 158, 460
Radio Professionals 154
Radiologists 374, 376, 378-381, 388, 390, 392, 396, 404
Ragtime Music Enthusiasts 56, 66
Railroad Enthusiasts 312, 656
Rainbow Family Members 520
Rainforest Action Activists 346
Rap Music Enthusiasts 54, 62, 83, 535, 541
Rap Music Enthusiasts 70
Rare Book Dealers 511
Rastafarians 428
Ravers 66
Reading Enthusiasts 31, 137, 156, 158, 241, 261, 419, 422-423, 426, 428, 430, 433-435, 437-445, 511-516, 523, 525, 529-530, 535-536, 540-541, 553
Real Estate Agencies 142
Real Estate Agents 140
Real Estate Brokers 116, 140-142, 160, 315, 319, 525
Real Estate Entrepreneurs 113, 322, 325
Real Estate Lawyers 498
Real Estate Professionals 138, 140-142, 364
Recording Industry Professionals 63, 65, 70
Recreational Companies 474
Recyclers 566
Recycling Enthusiasts 518
Recycling Proponents 520
Reggae Enthusiasts 72, 77, 81, 428
Regulatory Agencies 144
Religious Music Enthusiasts 58
Religious Studies Educators 226, 434, 559-564
Religious Studies Enthusiasts 564
Religious Studies Scholars 427, 560, 562, 663
Religious Studies Students 226, 361, 434, 557, 559-561, 563-564
Renaissance Faire Organizers 545
Renaissance Fantasy Buffs 531
Renaissance Historians 531
Renaissance Scholars 32, 669
Renaissance Students 244
Reptile Enthusiasts 616, 644, 646-647
Republicans 340, 350, 352-354, 504, 528
Research Scientists
Researchers 21-24, 28, 30, 51, 56, 102, 127, 134, 137, 143-144, 151, 154, 160, 166, 168, 170, 173-174, 176, 178-179, 181, 183-187, 189, 191-193, 199-200, 203-206, 208, 212, 221, 226, 228, 233-236, 246, 249-250, 254, 261, 263-265, 267, 270-275, 277-279, 281, 284, 286, 288, 291-292, 294, 296-300, 304, 306, 308-309, 311, 314-318, 328, 331, 335-339, 342, 344, 348-349, 352, 354-355, 357-358, 363, 377, 388, 390, 392, 397, 401, 404, 406, 414-415, 418-421, 424, 427, 429-430, 436, 448, 451, 453-454, 464, 466, 468-470, 472, 474, 480-482, 490-493, 496, 500, 505, 516, 520, 522-525, 532, 534, 543, 552, 562, 565, 568, 570-572, 577-578, 581, 584, 586-589, 592, 594, 598-599, 601-608, 610-612, 615-616, 625
Restaurant Enthusiasts 328, 624, 628, 633
Restauranteurs 116, 549, 630, 633
Retail Businesses 145
Retail Professionals 145
Retailers 116, 318, 546
Retirees 130
Rhinoceros Enthusiasts 644
Rhode Island Residents 122
Rhythm & Blues Enthusiasts 87
RIT Students 187
Road Trip Planners 121
Robot Designers 303
Robot Enthusiasts 298, 303, 437
Robotics Engineers 188, 298, 303
Robotics Enthusiasts 187, 306
Robotics Researchers 186
Rock Climbers 540

Rock Collectors 303, 623
Rock Fans 52, 54, 56-57, 62, 66-67, 69-90, 98, 540
Rock Musicians 54, 82
Rockford Files Fans 551
Rodent Lovers 646
Role Playing Games Enthusiasts 482-487
Romania Residents 668
Romantics 150, 530, 532
Rugby Fans 652
Russia Residents 341
Russian Culture Enthusiasts 24
Russian Literature Enthusiasts 423, 440
Russians 24, 50, 127, 131, 164, 271, 329, 337, 341, 420, 540
Ryuichi Sakamoto Enthusiasts 88

Safari Enthusiasts 654
Sailing Enthusiasts 654-656, 658, 664, 666
Sailors 588, 620
Saints 564
Sales Managers 133
Sales Professionals 104
Satire Enthusiasts 553
Scholars 23, 32, 45, 153, 168, 243, 246, 416, 422, 424, 431-432, 441, 446, 448-450, 544, 557, 562, 571
School Teachers 245
Schools 261, 519, 547
Science Educators 139, 241, 245, 247, 314, 317, 361, 380, 486, 545, 581, 600, 602, 614-616
Science Enthusiasts 241, 600
Science Fiction Enthusiasts 45, 82, 433, 437, 439, 441, 443-444, 483-484, 512-516, 531, 538, 540, 543, 551-552, 554, 623
Science Historians 573
Science Hobbyists 544, 602
Science Researchers 139, 206, 222, 247, 250, 301-302, 304, 309, 314, 317, 544-545, 584, 586-587, 590-591, 597-598, 602, 606, 608, 612
Science Students 486, 588
Scientists 32, 42-43, 68, 126-127, 139, 160, 169, 178, 182-183, 185-186, 190-191, 195, 206, 208, 218, 227-229, 246, 250, 260, 265, 272-274, 279, 284, 287, 292, 296, 298-299, 302, 304, 308-309, 311, 317-318, 331, 350, 370, 388, 474, 544-545, 557, 566, 568-570, 572-576, 578, 580-581, 584-585, 587-591, 593-594, 597, 600-608, 610-611, 616
Scotland Residents 326
Scots 337, 420, 432, 669
Scottish Book Collectors 511
Scottish Culture Enthusiasts 420
Screenwriters 32, 33, 542
Scuba Divers 619
Sculptors 26
Sculpture Enthusiasts 27
Search and Rescue Professionals 381-382
Security Workers 124, 471
SEED Users 175
Seismologists 587-588, 599
Seniors 116, 363, 365, 368, 372-373, 495
Serbians 339
Server Technicians 181
Service Dog Trainers 492
Set Designers 91
Seventh Day Adventists 560
Sewing Enthusiasts 622, 624
Sex Counselors 532
Sex Educators 177, 402
Sex Enthusiasts 407-408, 530, 532, 616
Sex Industry Workers 407
Shakespeare Enthusiasts 310, 422-423, 443, 530, 662
Shakespeare Scholars 423
Shanghai Residents 329
Shareware Users 227
Sherlock Holmes Enthusiasts 241
Shoppers 112-116, 122-123, 145-146, 148, 164, 318, 328, 545-546, 548-549, 622, 626
Shortwave Radio Users 158
Show Dog Owners 644, 647
Sierra Club Members 346
Sikhs 560
Silent Movie Enthusiasts 50
Singapore Residents 26, 265, 385, 505, 647
Singers 95

Single People 114, 487, 518, 530-531, 533
Singles 146, 150
Skateboarders 652
Skaters 653
Ski Enthusiasts 326, 667
Skiing Enthusiasts 337, 554, 619, 640-642, 648, 651, 653, 655
Skydiving Enthusiasts 642
Slavic Linguists 427
Slovakia Residents 310, 337, 656
Slovaks 337, 632
Slovenia Residents 337, 663-665
Slug Enthusiasts 528
Small Business Owners 120, 309, 416, 457, 473, 504
Small Business Professionals 149
Smokers 367, 398, 546, 622
Smoking Researchers 367
Snooker Players 636
Snow Enthusiasts 652
Snowboarders 641, 648
Snowboarding Enthusiasts 651-652
Soccer Fans 332, 540, 635, 649-651
Social Scientists 166, 168, 207, 218, 242, 254-255, 274, 318, 331, 352, 413, 415-416, 418, 430-431, 446-450, 564, 592
Social Studies Educators 258
Social Workers 98, 161, 246, 255, 365, 381, 448, 517
Socialists 355, 557
Sociologists 102, 168, 218, 245, 413, 416, 418, 421, 424, 430-431, 445-451, 520, 537, 553, 564, 592
Software Dealers 138
Software Designers 160, 181, 183-184, 209, 216, 262
Software Developers 35, 170, 173-175, 180-185, 204, 209-210, 213, 216-217, 221-222, 224-225, 228, 262, 305, 404, 477
Software Engineers 170-171, 177, 180-185, 189, 209-210, 213-214, 216, 221, 232, 296, 311, 305, 478
Software Professionals 182-183
Software Programmers 223, 227
Software Shoppers 223
Software Users 114, 159, 161, 163, 190, 193, 198, 460, 464, 477
Solid State Physicists 607
Songwriters 54
Soul Music Enthusiasts 87
Sound Artists 42, 68
Sound Engineers 66
South Africa Researchers 541
South Africa Residents 132, 360
South Africans 128, 158, 264, 338, 340, 481, 541
South America Residents 338
South Americans 668
South Carolina Residents 286, 324
Southeast Asians 338, 421
Southwest Residents 555
Southwestern Art Enthusiasts 20-21
Spa Enthusiasts 656
Space Enthusiasts 291, 523, 551, 571-574, 610-613
Space Flight Enthusiasts 121, 612
Space Professionals 611-612
Space Scientists 121, 123, 190, 291-292, 316, 486, 571-574, 610-613
Space Simulation Enthusiasts 486
Space Students 316, 572, 608, 610, 613
Spacecraft Distributors 124
Spacecraft Manufacturers 124
Spain Residents 303, 323, 329, 669
Spanish 427, 432
Spanish Culture Enthusiasts 435
Spanish Speakers 168, 332, 417, 419, 435
Special Education Educators 237
Special Education Teachers 374, 384
Speech Therapists 384, 578
Speechwriters 426
Spelunkers 658
Spicy Food Enthusiasts 626-627
Spirituality Enthusiasts 564
Spokespersons 156
Sponsors 165
Sports Fans 103, 326, 382, 529, 540-541, 619, 635, 639-642, 648-653, 661
Spring Water Dealers 148

Spring Water Drinkers – Women Business Owners

Spring Water Drinkers 148
Square Dance Enthusiasts 96
Stamp Collectors 320
Stanford University Professors 511
Star Trek Enthusiasts 443, 551-552
Star Wars Enthusiasts 45
State Officials 362-363
Stationary Shoppers 146
Stationary Supply Stores 146
Statisticians 195-196, 198-201, 226, 228, 257, 318, 358
Stock Market Investors 130, 132
Stock Market Players 128
Stockbrokers 103, 119, 128, 130-132, 143, 494, 502
Storytellers 437, 440, 443, 521
Structural Engineers 607
Students 15-16, 18, 21, 23-24, 26-30, 32-33, 35, 38, 48, 51, 56-57, 60-62, 65, 86, 109-111, 134, 146, 156, 160, 168, 170, 173-174, 176-179, 183-184, 186-193, 195-196, 198-201, 204, 206, 208, 212-213, 215, 225-226, 230, 232-236, 238-246, 248-250, 254, 256, 258-260, 262, 264-288, 291-294, 296-301, 305-306, 308-310, 312, 314, 328, 330, 336-337, 346, 348, 351-352, 358, 362-363, 385-387, 389, 392-393, 401, 403, 409, 413-414, 416, 418-419, 421, 424-425, 427, 429-431, 433, 436-437, 440-446, 448-450, 453-455, 462, 468, 470, 474-475, 480-481, 494, 499, 504, 506-507, 511, 519, 533, 538-539, 541, 544-545, 554-555, 557-558, 562-565, 572-574, 576, 581, 586-587, 589, 593-595, 598, 600, 602-604, 606-608, 610-612, 615-616, 625, 650, 662-663, 666, 669
Students (College/University) 118, 188, 233, 235, 273-274, 288, 385, 404, 593
Students (Graduate) 98, 133-134, 179, 195, 197, 238-239 260, 288, 573, 584-585
Students (Primary/Secondary) 26, 30, 156, 241-242, 244-247, 256-259, 261-262, 303, 308, 323, 330, 342, 344, 361, 381, 383, 387, 400, 422, 424, 426, 435, 442-443, 465, 512-514, 518-519, 521, 523-525, 544-545, 584, 603, 610, 616, 623, 626, 635, 650-651
Students (Secondary/University) 21, 28, 107, 187, 191, 208, 217-218, 221, 227, 233, 238, 243-244, 248-249, 229, 253-256, 261-262, 265, 267, 268, 270, 272, 275-280, 282-283, 285, 287-289, 295, 299, 307, 315, 327, 334, 338, 341, 372, 385-386, 388, 395, 398, 400, 403-406, 422, 424, 426, 429, 450-451, 465, 533, 553, 557, 558, 567-568, 617
Students (University) 16, 22-23, 33, 101, 107-111, 113, 118, 134, 143, 156-158, 160, 161, 165, 168, 170, 174, 184, 186-188, 191-192, 199, 211, 217, 228, 233-243, 247-249, 251, 253-257, 260-262, 264, 267-288, 294-295, 297-299, 303, 308-310, 316, 318, 321, 324, 327-330, 332, 334, 335, 337, 339, 345, 348, 352, 358, 360, 362, 364, 370, 372-374, 386, 388, 389, 393, 396-398, 400, 401, 403-406, 408, 413-417, 419-422, 424, 426-429, 430, 436, 438-442, 444-447, 451, 453, 463, 465, 474, 482, 498, 504, 511, 516, 518, 524, 530-532, 534, 543-544, 558-559, 568, 571-573, 576, 585-586, 588-589, 593-594, 597, 600-601, 604-606, 608, 610, 612, 623, 626, 649-652, 654-655, 656-666-668
Sun Microsystems Users 204
Sunbathers 655
Supercomputer Users 191, 208
Supercomputing Experts 190
Supporters of Parkinson's Sufferers 379
Surfing Coaches 619
Surfing Enthusiasts 619-620, 640, 652
Surgeons 292, 380
Suriname Residents 338
Surveyors 104, 141, 294
Suspense Enthusiasts 517
Sweden Residents 94, 330, 335, 664
Swedes 24, 82, 160, 208, 234, 271-274, 294, 299, 308, 335, 428, 432
Swedish Culture Enthusiasts 275
Swing Dance Enthusiasts 93
Swiss 170, 482, 654
Swiss Culture Enthusiasts 654
Switzerland Residents 161, 295, 307, 353, 430, 666

Symphony Conductors 64, 85
Symphony Enthusiasts 59-62, 64
Synth-pop Enthusiasts 74
Synthesizer Users 62, 64, 67, 69
System Designers 306
Systems Administrators 171, 179-183, 189, 198-199, 202-203, 205, 220-221, 228-230, 459, 491, 559
Systems Analysts 175, 202, 205, 470
Systems Architects 229
Systems Designers 201, 598
Systems Engineers 186, 232, 296, 299, 302
Systems Operators 309, 429, 475, 527
Systems Scientists 300

T-Shirt Collectors 548
Taiwan Residents 265
Taiwanese Culture Enthusiasts 162
Taiwanese People 162
Tall People 532
Tallahassee Residents 475
Tap Dancers 96
Tasmanians 595
Tax Accountants 506
Tax Payers 506
Tax Preparers 133
Tax Reformers 350
Tax Specialists 106
Taxonomists 314, 616
Taxpayers 116, 506
Tea Enthusiasts 624-625
Teachers 243
Teachers Aides 258
Technical Associations 125
Technical Companies 125
Technical Educators 309
Technical Laboratories 119
Technical Professionals 183, 208
Technical Readers 516
Technical Researchers 299
Technical Staff 112
Technical Writers 214, 220, 225-226, 306, 311
Technicians 309
Techno Music Enthusiasts 57, 71, 76, 79, 81, 85-86
Techno Music Fans 59
Techno/Ambient Music Enthusiasts 54, 80, 87
Technocrats 56, 72, 77
Technological Businesses 108
Technologists 305, 309, 601
Technology Assessment Professionals 125
Technology Business Professionals 596
Technology Enthusiasts 16, 165, 206, 258, 308, 310, 535-536
Technology Professionals 453
Technology Specialists 16, 172-173, 180, 190, 225, 272, 303, 312
Teddy Bear Enthusiasts 146
Teenagers 73, 408, 518, 542, 551-552
Tel Aviv Residents 26
Telecommunications Engineers 167, 201, 310
Telecommunications Enthusiasts 167
Telecommunications Experts 122, 125, 163-168, 201-202, 209, 310, 317, 352, 363, 502
Telecommunications Industry 163
Telecommunications Professionals 160, 163-164, 166-167, 201, 310, 473
Telecommunications Researchers 164, 229
Television Enthusiasts 47, 122, 157, 167, 464, 525, 528, 539, 541-542, 550-552
Television Industry Professionals 46
Television News Enthusiasts 552
Television Professionals 155, 550
Television Enthusiasts 156
Tennessee Residents 238, 287, 327, 330
Tennis Enthusiasts 651
Tex And Latex Users 195, 201
TeX Users 196
Texas Residents 30, 59, 72, 74, 239, 250, 255-256, 320, 322, 324, 326, 330, 365, 381, 408, 568, 644, 646, 655, 659
Textbook Buyers 511
Thai Culture Enthusiasts 428
Thailand Residents 266, 338, 428, 632
Thais 428
Theater 423

Theater Enthusiasts 29, 91, 94-96, 328, 437, 658-660, 663, 667
Theater Professionals 33, 91, 93-96, 437
Theologians 226, 559-564
Theology Students 560
Theoretical Physicists 304, 606
Theoretical Scientists 581
Therapists 374, 376, 378-379, 385, 396, 518
Thesis Writers 261
Thrill Seekers 620
Tibet Enthusiasts 219, 338
Tibetans 219, 338, 418, 420, 422
TIN Newsreader Users 460
Tinnitus Sufferers 385
Top 40 Music Enthusiasts 60
Tourists 16, 23-26, 33, 51, 66, 91, 93-96, 99, 103, 113-117, 126, 128, 142, 160, 203, 270, 273, 303, 312-313, 316, 320-332, 334-339, 342, 360, 362-365, 414, 417, 420-421, 450, 465, 510, 524, 532, 534-537, 540-541, 543-545, 550, 554-556, 619-620, 624-625, 627-628, 630-632, 642, 646, 648, 650, 654-671
Toxicologists 304, 388, 398
Toy Collectors 624
Trade Regulators 116
Trade Show Attendees 145
Trade Show Exhibitors 150
Trade Specialists 118, 314, 339, 352
Trademark Attorneys 496
Traders 132
Traffic School Instructors 362
Trampoline Enthusiasts 651
Transfer Students 279
Translators 224, 417
Transportation Engineers 312, 556
Transportation Professionals 314, 364, 664
Travel Agents 334-338, 654-655, 658-659, 662, 666-668, 670
Travelers 99, 265, 274, 312, 314, 319, 327-329, 331, 334-337, 339, 360, 364-365, 417, 421, 454, 457, 505, 514, 524, 538, 554, 556, 620, 632, 647, 654-656, 658-663, 665-666, 669-670
Trekkies 551-552
Trial Lawyers 524
Tribal Governments 354
Tropical Disease Specialists 398
Tunisia Residents 657
Turkey Residents 321
Turkish Literature Enthusiasts 264-265, 662, 444
Turks 299, 308
Turtle Enthusiasts 570
TV Enthusiasts 79, 87-88
Twin Cities Residents 551
Typists 384-385

U.S. Army Officials 347
U.S. Citizens 313-315, 319-320, 339, 350, 352, 355-358, 490
U.S. Congress 339, 358
UC Berkeley Alumni 300
Unemployed Workers 363
Union Members 355, 503
United Kingdom Residents 24, 60, 94, 146, 154, 192, 240, 271, 274, 361, 387, 460, 504
United Nations Personnel 343-344
United States Residents 116, 154, 254, 415, 419, 506, 518-519, 532, 556, 593
Universities 119, 121
University Administrators 222, 243, 249-250, 257, 275-276, 280-281, 283-284
University Faculty 255
University of California Alumni 97
UNIX Administrators 176
UNIX Application Developers 223, 227
UNIX Systems Administrators 170, 205, 222, 525, 527
UNIX Users 114, 128, 138, 158, 161, 166, 170, 172, 176, 180-181, 204-205, 208, 211-212, 216, 219, 222-223, 229, 248, 464, 475, 525, 606
Urban Developers 312
Urban Farming Activists 566
Urban Planners 16, 172, 301, 361, 598, 667
Urologists 402, 408
Ascent News Readers 361, 400, 460, 468-469, 473-474, 482
Utah Residents 71, 640

Vampire Enthusiasts 553
Vancouver Residents 475
Vegans 531, 614, 625, 627, 629
Vegetarians 531-533, 593, 614, 625, 627-632, 671
Venezuelans 334, 341
Vermeer Enthusiasts 20
Vermont Residents 280
Veterans 319, 348
Veterinarians 372, 392, 396, 406, 409, 574, 614, 644-646, 648
Victoria Residents 475
Video Amateurs 50
Video Artists 34, 40, 43, 47, 175, 220, 543
Video Enthusiasts 49, 99, 162, 541-542
Video Games Players 635
Video Professionals 50
Vietnamese 145, 421
Vietnamese Americans 145
Violinists 84
Virginia Residents 95, 113, 250, 322, 324, 327, 360, 472, 483, 520, 647,665
Virologists 370-371
Virtual Reality Enthusiasts 16, 41, 163, 170, 215, 227, 310
Virtual Reality Systems Operators 173
Virtual Shoppers 460
Volcano Enthusiasts 600
Volcanologists 524
Volleyball Enthusiasts 652
Volunteers 134-136, 344, 374, 395, 519
Voters 315, 319, 340, 352, 354-355, 362-363, 591
Voyeurs 461

Wales Residents 320-321, 656
Wales Scholars 321, 656
War Historians 348
War Veterans 426
Washington D.C. Residents 96, 115, 340, 142, 322-323, 327-328, 365, 541, 545, 626, 640, 646
Washington State Residents 556
Water Conservationists 590
Water District Professionals 365
Water Skiers 619
Water Sports Enthusiasts 620, 652
Weather Enthusiasts 556
Weather Forecasters 556, 588
Web Designers 148, 537
Web Developers 122, 165, 209, 220, 225, 330, 342, 360, 453, 456, 460, 463, 465, 467, 469-470, 472, 476-480, 526, 562, 635
Web Managers 456
Web Providers 122, 472, 474-475
Web Users 90, 465, 462, 467, 469, 470, 472, 477-480, 537, 635-636
Wedding Planners 148, 522
Weight Trainers 643
Whale Enthusiasts 444, 667
White Water Rafting Enthusiasts 652, 667
Wholesalers 122
Wilderness Enthusiasts 344, 346, 592, 639-641, 643, 648
Wildlife Biologists 255, 319, 345, 592
Wildlife Enthusiasts 255, 345, 614, 645
Wildlife Rehabilitators 610, 617
Windows Application Developers 175, 182, 185, 202-204, 210, 217, 223, 225, 227
Windows NT Administrators 230
Windows NT Developers 220
Windows Programmers 174, 182, 204, 216
Windows System Administrators 222
Windows Users 115, 149, 172-174, 181-183, 185, 194, 202-203, 205, 208, 214-218, 220-228, 252, 453, 463, 476-478, 480, 538, 668
Windsurfing Enthusiasts 620
Wine Drinkers 624
Wine Enthusiasts 124, 147-148, 322, 549, 624, 626, 629, 631, 633, 659, 664
Winter Sports Enthusiasts 653
Wireless Communicators 165, 482
Wisconsin Residents 112, 365, 556
Wives 494-495, 518, 527
Women 28, 47, 70, 77, 99, 150, 207, 218, 350, 354, 376, 378, 400-401, 404, 407-411, 433, 444, 450-451, 476, 494, 502, 517, 522, 532, 537, 540-541, 559, 642, 650
Women Business Owners 450

Women Employees 502
Women Entrepreneurs 476
Women Writers 444
Women's Rights Activists 351, 450
Women's Sports Enthusiasts 650
Women's Studies Educators 218, 240, 439, 451
Women's Studies Students 218, 240, 404, 408, 450-451
Woodworkers 622, 624
Workshop Organizers 134
Workstation Users 204, 219
World Music Enthusiasts 54
World Wide Web Publishers 464
Writers 29-33, 92, 94, 136, 139, 144, 241, 245, 262, 433-436, 438-443, 460, 495, 512-515, 533, 535-536, 538, 541
Wyoming Residents 250

X Windows Users 181, 204

Yachting Enthusiasts 658
Youth 450, 522
Yugoslavia Residents 322
Yugoslavs 339

Zoo Enthusiasts 601, 615, 646-647
Zookeepers 601, 614-615
Zoologists 245, 319, 567, 579, 602, 614, 616-617
Zydeco Music Enthusiasts 660

Add or Update a Resource

APPENDIX F

Let us know about your exciting, informative, or easy-to-use Internet site!

To add or update an Internet resource in the McKinley Internet Directory follow the instructions below.

Here are three easy ways to get your information to us:

1. Go to the McKinley web site and add/update your resource online.
    a. Use your Internet browser to reach us at:

    http://www.mckinley.com

    b. Choose the **Add a Resource** button (hotlink) and fill out the template. Click the **Submit** button to send it to us right away.

2. Use the form on this page to snail mail us at The McKinley Group, Inc., 85 Liberty Ship Way, Suite 201, Sausalito, CA 94965, USA

3. Fax the form to +1 (415) 331-8609.

Disclaimer: Submissions are subject to an editorial review process. Resources accepted into the database are subject to the editorial discretion of the McKinley Group.

Title _____

Umbrella Field
Please select the most appropriate category:
- ☐ Arts & Music
- ☐ Business & Economics
- ☐ Communications
- ☐ Computing & Mathematics
- ☐ Education
- ☐ Engineering & Technology
- ☐ Government & Politics
- ☐ Health & Medicine
- ☐ Humanities & Social Sciences
- ☐ Internet
- ☐ Law & Criminal Justice
- ☐ Popular Culture & Entertainment
- ☐ Religion & Philosophy
- ☐ Science
- ☐ Sports & Recreation

Keywords
Please list up to four keywords that best describe the contents of your resource:
_____   _____
_____   _____

Audience
Please list up to four audiences that best describe the people who could use your resource:
_____   _____
_____   _____

URL
- http **http://** _____
- gopher **gopher://** _____
- ftp **ftp://** _____
- telnet **telnet://** _____
- mailing list **mailto:** _____
- newsgroup **news:** _____

Description
Please print or type a paragraph of 100 words or less to describe your resource:
_____
_____
_____
_____
_____
_____

Is your site ☐ **Commercial** or ☐ **Non-Commercial**?
Please select 'commercial' if you are a business entity. Please select 'non-commercial' if you are an individual, or a government, educational, or non-profit institution.

Is there a ☐ **Cost** to use your internet resource or is it ☐ **Free**?

Is your resource ☐ **Moderated** or ☐ **Not Moderated**?
(You need only check this if your resource is a mailing list or a newsgroup.)

Please enter the Language(s) of resource if other than English _____

Producer Information
Producer: _____
Producer Address: _____
_____
_____

Telephone: _____
Contact Name: _____
Contact Email: _____

Credits for Screen Shots

1995 Year of the Sea Turtle Home Page, reprinted with permission of the Environmental Resources Information Network.
A Clean Well-Lighted Place For Books Home Page. Reprinted with permission.
Above All Travel Home Page, reprinted with permission of Dickerson, Dickerson, Lieberman & Consul.
AccuWeather Home Page ©1995 by AccuWeather, Inc. Reprinted with permission.
ACSN Web Page, reprinted with permission of the AIDS Caregivers Support Network.
Adoptees Mailing List Home Page, reprinted with permission of UC-San Diego.
African-American Mosaic Home Page. Reprinted with permission.
American Childcare Solutions Web Page, reprinted with permission of Bruce Scherzinger, Webmaster.
American Military Catalog Web Page, reprinted with permission of Tachyon Communications Corp.
American Philosophical Association Home Page, reprinted with permission of Occidental College.
Americom Long Distance Area Decoder Home Page. Reprinted with permission.
Anarchy-Online Home Page, reprinted with permission of Andrew Henry, Webmaster.
Arts Wire Home Page. Reprinted with permission.
Attention Deficit Disorder Web Page, reprinted with permission of David Dawson, Webmaster.
Babylon 5 Suite Soundtrack CD Cover ©1995 by Sonic Images. Reprinted with permission.
Bartlett's Familiar Quotations photo and logo, reprinted with permission of Academic Information Systems, Columbia University.
Beastie Boys photograph ©1995 by FISTFULAYEN. Reprinted with permission of The Big Gun Project.
Birth Father Rights and Responsibilities Web Page, reprinted with permission of Judith L. Hengeveld, Webmaster.
Blackbird Caye Resort photos, reprinted with permission of Primus Consulting.
Books That Work Products Home Page. Reprinted with permission.
Briskin's Internet Career Finder Home Page. Reprinted with permission.
Business Plans logo and name ©1995 by Palo Alto Software, Inc. Reprinted with permission.
Canine Activities Web Page, reprinted with permission of Cindy Tittle Moore, Webmaster.
Cedar National Address Server Web Page. Reprinted with permission.
Central Imagery Office Home Page, reprinted with permission of Rick Hough, Webmaster.
Child Safety on the Information Highway Web Page, reprinted with permission of the National Center for Missing and Exploited Children.
Chiropractic Web Page, reprinted with permission of Elwood Chiropractic Center.
CLNET Home Page. Reprinted with permission.
Contemporary Physics Education Project Home Page, reprinted with permission of Lawrence Berkeley Laboratory.
CyberCars Web Page, reprinted with permission of Dan Campbell, Webmaster.
CyberCash logo ©1995 by CyberCash, Inc. Reprinted with permission.
Department of Descriptive Geometry Web Page, reprinted with permission of the Department of Descriptive Geometry, University of Miskolc.
DG XXIV-Consumer Policy Web Page, reprinted with permission of Lewis Rose, Webmaster.
Dining Out on the Web Home Page, reprinted with permission of Sunnyside Computing, Inc.
Distinctive Church Home Page. Reprinted with permission.
Division of Automatic Control Web Page, reprinted with permission of Linkoping University.
Emergency Services World Wide Web Page, reprinted with permission of EMERGENCY.
Environmental Recycling Hotline Web Page, reprinted with permission of J. Lippard, Webmaster.
Environmental Sites on the Internet Home Page, reprinted with permission of the Royal Institute of Technology Library, Stockholm, Sweden.
ESPNET SportsZone Web Page ©1995 ESPN. Reprinted with permission.
European Space Information System Home Page, reprinted with permission of the European Space Agency.
Facets of Religion Web Page, reprinted with permission of the University of Freiburg.
Family Law, An Overview Web Page, reprinted with permission of Mark Ressa, Webmaster.
Family World Web Page. Reprinted with permission.
Famous Birthdays Home Page. Reprinted with permission.
Generation X Home Page, reprinted with permission of Ron Davis, Webmaster.
Heart and EKG Lifeline sketches, reprinted with permission of The Franklin Institute Science Museum.
Herbs and Spices Web Page, reprinted with permission of Ron Lunde, Webmaster.
HighwayOne Home Page. Reprinted with permission.
Himalayan Travel Web Page, reprinted with permission of World Adventures/Himalayan Travel.
Holy Scroll of Sins Web Page, reprinted with permission of Ken Lang, Webmaster.
Hot Java logo, reprinted with permission of Hot Java/Cool Applets.
Hubble Space Telescope's Greatest Hits Home Page, reprinted with permission of the Space Telescope Science Institute.
ICEnet-Women's Issues Web Page. Reprinted with permission.
Images for Art History, reprinted with permission of the Australian National University Art History Department.
Intellectual Property Home Page, reprinted with permission of Mark Ressa, Webmaster.
Internet Adoption Photolisting Home Page, reprinted with permission of Precious in HIS Sight-Internet Adoption Photolisting.
Internet Business Center/Imaginarium. Reprinted with permission.
JobServe Logo, 1995 trademark of JobServe Ltd. Reprinted with permission.
Jokes Web Page, reprinted with permission of Karl Blum, Webmaster.
Law School Admission Info Web Page, reprinted with permission of the University of Virginia.
Law School Web Page, reprinted with permission of The Princeton Review.
Leonardo Online Home Page. Reprinted with permission.
Library of Congress Home Page. Reprinted with permission.
Life Extension Foundation Web Page ©1995 by Life Extension Foundation. Reprinted with permission.
Live From Anarctica Home Page, reprinted with permission of Steven Hodas, Webmaster.
London Business School Home Page created by Adam Nealis. Reprinted with permission.
Marquis Alfieri Host Winery graphic ©1995 by Wines on the Internet. Reprinted with permission.
Mathematics Software, Tools, and Projects Web Page, reprinted with permission of Simon Fraser University.
Mosque of the Internet Home Page. Reprinted with permission.
Mythopoeia on The Net Home Page, reprinted with permission of Anerson Perrault Inc.
Netiquette Home Page, reprinted with permission of Florida Atlantic University.
Netrek Home Page. Reprinted with permission.
No Dogs (or Philosophers) Allowed Home Page. Reprinted with permission.
Nolo Press Web Page, reprinted with permission of Dayna Macey and Nolo Press.
P-Law Home Page. Reprinted with permission.
Parents Helping Parents Web Page reprinted with permission of American Childcare Solutions.
PCs Compleat Home Page ©1995 by PCs Compleat Inc. Reprinted with permission.
Royal Insurance Daily Zodiac Forecast Web Page, reprinted with permission of Jon, Webmaster.
SafeSkills TWMA Homepage, trademark by SafeSkills, Inc. Reprinted with permission.
Shoppers Web Home Page. Reprinted with permission.
Smithsonian Home Page created by Peter House. Reprinted with permission.
Society for Human Sexuality Library Web Page. Reprinted with permission.
Spirit-WWW Web Page, reprinted with permission of Rene Mueller, Webmaster.
Stanford University Zoroastrian Group Web Page. Reprinted with permission.
Subway Navigator Home Page, reprinted with permission of Universite Louis Pasteur.
Supercomputer and Parallel Computer Vendors Web Page, reprinted with permission of Carnegie Mellon University.
Symantec Corporation Web Page. Reprinted with permission.
Taped Editions Web Page. Reprinted with permission.
The 19th Hole Home Page. Reprinted with permission.
The Book of Mutual Funds logo, reprinted with permission of The Cambrex Group.
The Climbing Archive Home Page. Reprinted with permission.
The Covenant of the Goddess Home Page. Reprinted with permission.
The Free On-line Dictionary of Computing Web Page. Reprinted with permission.
The Small Business Resource Center Home Page. Reprinted with permission.
The Stock Solution logo ©1995 by Stock Solution. Reprinted with permission.
Tir na nOg Web Page created by H. Morriszki. Reprinted with permission.
Toyo Engineering Corp. Home Page ©1995 by Toyo Engineering Corporation. Reprinted with permission.
UFO Sightings Web Page, reprinted with permission of Bowling Green State University.
Archive X Web Page, reprinted with permission of Crown Engineering, Inc.
University of Trieste Home Page, reprinted with permission.
VDT Ergonomics Web Page, reprinted with permission of Environmental Health and Safety, University of Virginia.
Virtual Library's Language Web Page, reprinted with permission of Tyler Jones, Webmaster.
WebElements Home Page, reprinted with permission of the College of Chemistry, UC-Berkeley.
What Do You Expect for Free, Vogue? Web Page, reprinted with permission of Chris Powell, Webmaster.
Wines on the Internet Home Page ©1995 by Wines on the Internet. Reprinted with permission.
Women and Credit Histories Web Page created by Lewis Rose. Reprinted with permission.
World History Archives Web Page, reprinted with permission of Haines Brown, Webmaster.
World Wide Yellow Pages Home Page ©1994 by World Wide Yellow Pages. Reprinted with permission.
WWW Acronym and Abbreviation Server Home Page, reprinted with permission of Peter Flynn, Webmaster.

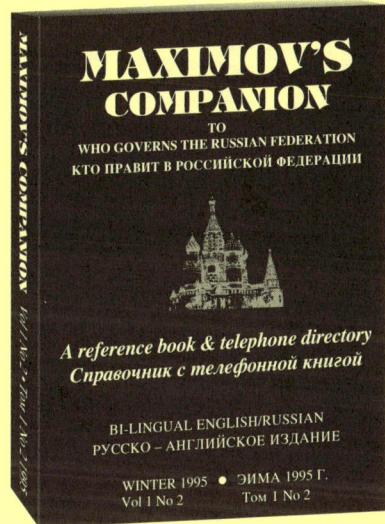

New edition includes details of 5,000 officials and more than 8,000 contact numbers

Discover a new source of political reference for the Russian Federation

Visit our site at http://www.maximov.com and pick up the latest news:

- "Hot Stuff from Maximov's" provides English Language 'Hot News' from leading Russian political and economic commentators and 'Hot Numbers' to follow up

- Full text Introductory Section, Table of Contents, Subject Index and Sample Pages from Maximov's Companion, the leading source of political contact information for Russia

MIKHAIL GORBACHEV praises Maximov's

"An indispensable Companion - authoritative and up to date - I use it every day."

Call, Fax, Mail or E-Mail us today for your FREE brochure & Ad. Rate Card

Maximov Publications

Suite 201, 85 Liberty Ship Way, Sausalito, CA 94965, USA Tel: +1415 331 6785 Fax: +1415 331 8609 E-Mail: maximov@mckinley.com
12 Rozhdestvenka Street, Moscow 103031, Russian Tel: +7 095 925 5696 Fax: +7 095 925 8523 E-Mail: maximov@glas.apc.org
54 Grosvenor St., London W1X 0EU, UK Tel: +44 171 3545 Fax: +44 171 3577 E-Mail: maximov@westcomm.demon.co.uk